THE GOOD, THE BAD—
AND THE AWFUL

This is the newly updated insider's guide to TV movies. It tells you what not to miss—and what to miss. It describes films so bad they're good, and so good they're bad. It identifies the all-time Greats and Classics—and the unforgettable Duds.

They're all listed here in alphabetical order, complete with all the essential information: director, stars, plot, date, color or black-and-white, original length (so you'll know how much they've been cut), key songs (for musicals)—and a concise capsule summary and review of each film.

TV MOVIES

named "Best Reference Book"
of the Decade by *Film Comment*

TV Movies Available in SIGNET and SIGNET CLASSIC Editions

TV MOVIES

1981-82 Edition

EDITED BY

Leonard Maltin

ASSOCIATE EDITORS

Mike Clark
John Cocchi
Alice Tlusty Maltin
Alvin H. Marill

A SIGNET BOOK
NEW AMERICAN LIBRARY
TIMES MIRROR

NAL BOOKS ARE AVAILABLE AT QUANTITY DISCOUNTS
WHEN USED TO PROMOTE PRODUCTS OR SERVICES. FOR
INFORMATION PLEASE WRITE TO PREMIUM MARKETING DIVISION,
THE NEW AMERICAN LIBRARY, INC., 1633 BROADWAY,
NEW YORK, NEW YORK 10019.

SIGNET TRADEMARK REG. U.S. PAT. OFF. AND FOREIGN COUNTRIES
REGISTERED TRADEMARK—MARCA REGISTRADA
HECHO EN CHICAGO, U.S.A.

SIGNET, SIGNET CLASSICS, MENTOR, PLUME, MERIDIAN AND NAL
BOOKS are published by The New American Library, Inc.,
1633 Broadway, New York, New York 10019

First Printing, October, 1980

1 2 3 4 5 6 7 8 9

PRINTED IN THE UNITED STATES OF AMERICA

About the Editor

LEONARD MALTIN was eighteen when the first edition of *TV Movies* was published. Since that time he has written and edited numerous books on film history. For nine years he edited and published *Film Fan Monthly* magazine; his articles have appeared in such publications as *The New York Times, Saturday Review, TV Guide, Variety, Esquire, Film Comment,* and *American Film.* His books include *Of Mice and Magic: A History of American Animated Cartoons, The Great Movie Comedians, The Disney Films, The Art of the Cinematographer, Movie Comedy Teams, The Great Movie Shorts,* and (coauthor) *Our Gang: The Life and Times of the Little Rascals.* He lectures on animated cartoon history around the country, and teaches a course in the subject at The New School for Social Research in New York City. In 1976 he served as guest programmer for the Museum of Modern Art's Bicentennial Salute to American Film Comedy. He lives with his wife, Alice, in Manhattan.

The Associate Editors

MIKE CLARK earned the nickname "Movie Mike" when at age 10 he appeared on the television quiz show *The $64,000 Question* as a film expert. Since then he has attended NYU's Graduate School of Cinema, been the film critic for the *Detroit Free Press*, and is currently Director of the American Film Institute Theater in Washington, D.C.

JOHN COCCHI has lent his research talents to many books on film, and compiled *The Western: A Picture Quiz Book*. For ten years he was the New York correspondent and film reviewer for *Boxoffice* magazine.

ALICE TLUSTY MALTIN is a lifelong film buff who has recently turned her hobby into a professsion. She attended New York University, and spent several years in the publishing industry. In 1975 she married Leonard Maltin and is living happily ever after.

ALVIN H. MARILL has written books on such screen personalities as Katharine Hepburn, Errol Flynn, and Tyrone Power, as well as *Samuel Goldwyn Presents, The Films of Sidney Poitier,* and *Robert Mitchum on the Screen*. His monthly column on films and television appears in *Films in Review* magazine.

Introduction to 1981–82 Edition

This is the fourth edition of *TV Movies*, and I am proud that it is the most complete, up-to-date, and accurate one we've ever compiled.

Our goal remains the same: to provide you with the kind of information you need to make intelligent choices in movie viewing at home . . . and to enhance your enjoyment of those films by providing interesting facts and opinions. We have added some 1,000 new titles to this edition of the book, without dropping older ones, and we'll keep it up as long as the binding will hold!

With every new edition of *TV Movies*, however, there seem to be new challenges—or obstacles—to confront in the pursuit of accuracy and thoroughness. Consider some examples of TV/movie chicanery:

*NBC purchased the 1973 movie *Two-minute Warning* and filmed an additional hour of footage (at a reported cost of $500,000), adding entirely new characters—and a new subplot—to the original, and deleting considerable footage from the theatrical print. The results came to three hours on the network, including commercials. But for the rerun showing, the network *cut its own version* down to two hours.

*Home Box Office, the pay-television network, premiered a "new" movie called *Sparrow* starring Randy Herman; no further information was available on this film. Our research revealed that *Sparrow* was originally two separate one-hour pilot episodes broadcast on CBS-TV—with two entirely different plots, two directors, and two sets of casts except for Herman.

*Universal kicked off its expensive science fiction TV series *Battlestar Galactica* with a three-hour premiere episode in the fall of 1978. Then in 1979 this episode was edited to 125 minutes and shown in theaters, with the straight-faced advertising line, "The original theatrical version of the spectacular television film."

*The producers of the super-hit movie *Saturday Night Fever* took no chances on losing a television sale—plus a substantial adolescent audience—by releasing an R-rated movie full of sex, violence, and four-letter words. They actually filmed an alternate version of the film, with both action and language considerably muted, and won a PG rating for theatrical rerelease. The version which ultimately plays on commercial television will undoubtedly undergo further surgery for mass-audience consumption.

Since these are daily occurrences in the entertainment industry, and not isolated examples, one can readily see that chronicling the television broadcast of movies is becoming more and more difficult. Networks continue to change movie titles at will, distributors offer incorrect years of release in order to make films look newer than they really are, and censors transform theatrical releases like *Taxi Driver* into sanitized products bearing little resemblance to the films people paid money to see.

Fortunately, with the growth of cable TV, pay television, & videocassettes and discs, it is now possible to see uncut, uncensored theatrical films at home. This reaffirms our decision to describe and rate the movies in this book based on their original versions, and not on subsequent mutilations.

As for specific aspects of the new 1981–82 edition of *TV Movies,* it is best to itemize them as follows:

Alphabetization: We remind users of this book that an understanding of proper alphabetization is necessary to find "tricky" titles. *I Wanted Wings* is followed by *I'd Climb the Highest Mountain, I'll Get By,* and *I'm All Right Jack.* You will not find *Idiots Delight* after *I'd Climb the Highest Mountain,* or *Illegal* after *I'll Get By.* All contractions are grouped together, followed by unapostrophied words with the same letters. Similarly, *B.F.'s Daughter* and *J.D.'s Revenge* come at the beginning of those letters' listings, not under Bf and Jd.

Year of Release: We list the original year of theatrical release for all movies (which is not necessarily the same as the year of production). In the past, we had listed foreign films with the year of their U.S. release, but it seems more useful and accurate to give the year the film was first shown in its own country; this can vary from one to five years with its American debut. For obscure movies which have never been released theatrically, we list the year the film was completed.

Running Times: This is the Excedrin headache of *TV Movies,* but our current edition is the most accurate and exhaustively researched to date. More than one hundred older entries have been changed to correct their running times; these figures may disagree with other printed sources, but we can assure you that those sources are merely perpetrating hard-to-kill mistakes. The distributor of the 1936 *Things to Come* claims it is 108 minutes long. We had listed 113 minutes, which was the original British running time, but no such prints exist any more. The *actual* running time is 92 minutes, clocked from a complete release negative. Other films for which we had listed original running times now exist only in edited reissue prints (*Captain Blood, The Lost Patrol, Love Me Tonight, For Whom the Bell Tolls, Mr. Skeffington,* to name a few) and accordingly, we have made note of their new running times.

Two oddities worth noting: films like *Around the World in 80 Days* and *It's a Mad, Mad, Mad, Mad World* have always included overture music (and sometimes intermissions) in their "official" running times; we have changed such films to reflect their actual screen time only. And on silent films, we are listing the running times of the prints most widely available to television, through such distributors as Killiam Shows and Janus Films. We cannot vouch for the length of those same films shown at different speeds, or in different versions.

Finally, on newer films—where running-time discrepancies can be just as sticky—we have taken the official clocked footage length of 35mm prints from a major cable television firm, and believe these figures to be correct.

Whew!

Ratings: We regard this book as an information guide, and make no pretense that our subjective ratings are the final judgment on any movie. They reflect the opinion of our staff, in trying to reach a middle-ground view. Obviously, people who thrive on nothing but car-chase action films will rate *Eat My Dust* higher than *Annie Hall,* but the same thing applies in reverse. Serious film students and buffs derive a different kind of satisfaction from many "cult" directors' work than an average audience could, and this too must be taken into consideration. Subjecting thousands of films to a limited and highly arbitrary BOMB-to-Four-Star rating system is, to say the least, an inexact science, so please use the ratings as a guide, not as the gospel, based on your own point of view and personal preferences.

Movies Made for Television: As before, we do not rate these films on the same scale as theatricals, because we believe them to be a breed apart. Each telefilm is noted **TVM** and given a key-word evaluation: Below Average, Average, or Above Average. While distributors and TV stations insist on calling pilot shows, series episodes, and miniseries entries "movies," we do not, and you will find none of those products listed here. If you try to find a so-called TV movie (made before January 1980) in our book and cannot, chances are it's an old series episode, or several episodes strung together.

Title Changes: Distributors and programmers keep trying to fool us by changing titles of movies—usually unsuccessful movies—for television, and we're doing our best to keep up with the trend. Lately, the networks have been changing the titles of some made-for-TV movies every time they air! We have cross-indexed all title changes noted up to our press time, but of course we cannot predict what other changes may be hatched later on.

Obscure Movies: Remember when you paid $3 to see that Charles Bronson movie *Chino?* How about that Ray Milland favorite *Blackout?* Remember Peter Sellers in *The Blockhouse?* NO? These are just three films which—to our knowledge—never played in any American theaters. But they are among the hundreds of esoteric titles now being shown on pay and commercial television. Frankly, there are far too many obscurities to list in this edition—scores of shlock movies from various countries with nothing to recommend them at all. But we have attempted to list the more visible, more nameworthy films, and have succeeded, after considerable detective work, in finding their country of origin, cast, director, and storylines. But these strange little films multiply like rabbits, so don't be surprised if Telly Savalas or Richard Conte turn up on your tube in some title we haven't yet nailed down. (We will pass on one piece of advice about such obscurities: If they didn't get theatrical showings, or major television sales, there's usually a good reason—they're awful).

Addition of Older Films: Many cable and UHF stations are resurrecting films of the 1930s and 40s which have been dormant for many years, and renewed interest in exclusive "product" has unearthed some older titles which have never been shown on TV. We have added a great many titles to this edition, from Eddie Cantor's *Whoopee* (1930) to Bette Davis' *Parachute Jumper* (1933), from the silent *Pandora's Box* (1929) to the World War II extravaganza *This Is the Army* (1943). But it just isn't possible to list every old movie in this book; there are more than 22,000 films now available to television, and until our publisher sanctions a two-volume hand-sewn set of *TV Movies* we must continue to be selective.

Changes and Corrections from the Last Edition: Once again, we are indebted to the many readers who have taken the time to write in with additions, corrections, and comments on *TV Movies.* Nearly *one thousand* existing entries have been changed or completely rewritten, to reflect everything from the addition of cast names to a revision of our opinion on a film. The memory plays tricks on us all; it's not possible to watch 13,000 films in one week and evaluate them at the exact same point in time. What seems wonderful in memory may not look so good today, while films we took for granted years ago may stand out much more.

It is important to remember that films are not made in a vacuum, and every film exists in the context of other films, as well as in a universal time frame. We've improved our rating on *Smokey and the Bandit*, for instance, not only because it's so phenomenally popular, but because it's so much better than the scores of rip-offs which have followed it. We think a *** rating reflects what most of our readers feel about this movie —and to be sure, this is an example of a film that looks better in comparison to other films than it did on its own in 1973.

When it comes to thanks for a book like this, the list is long but each contribution is important. First, I am grateful to my diligent colleagues, whose knowledge of movies is matched only by the good humor it takes to work on this project. To Mike Clark, John Cocchi, Al Marill, and especially my wife Alice Tlusty Maltin, thank you.

To Jerry Vermilye, Jeanine Basinger, Jerry Beck, Kit Parker, Frank Rowley, Chris Steinbrunner, Herb Graff, William K. Everson, Al Kilgore, Katrine Ames, Corinne and David Chertoka, Louis Black, Michael Schnipper, Peta and Eddie Smith, Don Koll, Larry Casey, Alan Barbour, Allan Greenfield, John Donaldson, Gary Stark, Mrs. Judith Tlusty, Charles Silver and Ron Magliosi of The Museum of Modern

Art Film Study Center, Gary Bordzuk of Universal 16, Douglas Lemza of Films Incorporated, Bill Kenly of Paramount Pictures, Irwin Danels of Columbia Pictures, Dave Wollos of Kino International, John Hall of RKO General Pictures, and Elyse Eisenberg of Showtime, another vote of thanks.

Patrick O'Connor is the editor who gave birth to this book, and Robert Haynie is the man who has kept it alive, so they have earned a permanent thank-you.

And finally, to the countless readers who have sent in their thoughts, their corrections, and their compliments, I am especially indebted. Your response and encouragement has made this project a labor of love—for me, and for everyone who loves movies.

LEONARD MALTIN

Aaron Loves Angela (1975) **C-98m.**
*** D: Gordon Parks Jr. Kevin
Hooks, Moses Gunn, Irene Cara,
Robert Hooks, Ernestine Jackson,
Jose Feliciano. New York-made
variation on Romeo and Juliet, with
black boy (Kevin) in love with
Puerto Rican girl (Cara). OK com-
bination of comedy, drama, violence,
and Feliciano's music.

Aaron Slick From Punkin Crick
(1952) **C-95m.** ** D: Claude Binyon.
Alan Young, Dinah Shore, Adele
Jergens, Robert Merrill, Veda Ann
Borg. Innocuous musical satire of
city slicker trying to fleece innocent
widow Shore. Unmemorable score.

Abandon Ship! (1957-British) **100m.**
D: Richard Sale. Tyrone Power, Mai
Zetterling, Lloyd Nolan, Stephen
Boyd, Moira Lister, James Hayter.
Tyrone is officer suddenly in command of lifeboat holding survivors
from sunken luxury liner. Tense and
exciting study of people fighting to
stay alive while exposed to savage
seas and each other. British title:
SEVEN WAVES AWAY.

Abandoned (1949) **79m.** *½ D:
Joe Newman. Gale Storm, Dennis
O'Keefe, Raymond Burr, Marjorie
Rambeau, Jeff Chandler. Lukewarm
tale of newspaperman O'Keefe helping Storm find her sister's illegitimate baby, and becoming involved
with adoption racket.

Abbott and Costello Go to Mars
(1953) **77m.** *½ D: Charles Lamont.
Robert Paige, Mari Blanchard,
Martha Hyer, Horace McMahon,
Jack Tebler, Hal Forrest, Harold
Goodwin. Unimaginative vehicle has
Bud and Lou sailing through space
with escaped gangster, landing on
most earthlike planet.

Abbott and Costello In Hollywood
(1945) **83m.** ** D: S. Sylvan Simon.
Frances Rafferty, Robert Stanton,
Jean Porter, Warner Anderson. Uneven comedy with A&C as barber
and porter in cinemaland.

**Abbott and Costello In the Foreign
Legion** (1950) **80m.** ** D: Charles
Lamont. Patricia Medina, Walter
Slezak, Douglass Dumbrille. Unex-

ceptional A&C vehicle pitting them
against nasty sergeant Slezak. Best
scene involves mirages in the desert.

Abbott and Costello In the Navy
SEE: **In the Navy**

**Abbott and Costello Meet Captain
Kidd** (1952) **C-70m.** ** D: Charles
Lamont. Charles Laughton, Hillary
Brooke, Fran Warren, Bill Shirley,
Leif Erickson. OK A&C, but poor
Charles Laughton!

**Abbott and Costello Meet Dr. Jekyll
and Mr. Hyde** (1953) **77m.** ** D.
Charles Lamont. Boris Karloff, Craig
Stevens, Reginald Denny, Helen
Westcott, John Dierkes. Disappointing attempt to mix A&C with Jekyll
and Hyde (Karloff), with too few
funny scenes. Special effects are
film's main asset.

**Abbott and Costello Meet Franken-
stein** (1948) **83m.** *** D: Charles
Barton. Lon Chaney, Bela Lugosi,
Glenn Strange, Lenore Aubert, Jane
Randolph, Frank Ferguson. And
Dracula and the Wolf Man too, in
this superb blend of comedy and
horror, never duplicated by A&C or
anyone else. Lugosi is in especially
fine form as the Count.

**Abbott and Costello Meet the Invis-
ible Man** (1951) **82m.** *** D: Charles
Lamont. Nancy Guild, Arthur Franz,
Adele Jergens, Sheldon Leonard. One
of the team's best vehicles, with
Bud and Lou as detectives helping
boxer (Franz) who's been framed to
trap mobster Leonard, with aid of
invisibility formula. Special effects
are top-notch.

**Abbott and Costello Meet the Key-
stone Kops** (1955) **79m.** ** D: Charles
Lamont. Fred Clark, Lynn Bari,
Mack Sennett, Maxie Rosenbloom,
Frank Wilcox, Henry Kulky, Sam
Flint. Low-budget comedy could have
been better. Clark is fine as conniving producer in this synthetic period-
piece of silent-movie days.

**Abbott and Costello Meet the Killer,
Boris Karloff** (1949) **94m.** **½ D:
Charles Barton. Lenore Aubert, Gar
Moore, Donna Martell, Alan Mow-
bray, James Flavin. Pleasant blend
of comedy and whodunit with bodies

hanging in closets and phony mystic Karloff trying to do away with Costello.

Abbott and Costello Meet the Mummy (1955) 79m. **½ D: Charles Lamont. Marie Windsor, Michael Ansara, Dan Seymour, Kurt Katch, Richard Deacon. Amusing adventure with A&C getting mixed up with villainess Windsor, a valuable tomb, and a mummy who's still alive.

Abby (1974) C-92m. **½ D: William Girdler. Carol Speed, William Marshall, Terry Carter, Austin Stoker, Juanita Moore. Not-bad black variation on THE EXORCIST. Speed, wife of minister Carter and daughter-in-law of minister Marshall, is the possessed Abby.

Abdication, The (1974-British) C-103m. ** D: Anthony Harvey. Peter Finch, Liv Ullmann, Cyril Cusack, Paul Rogers, Michael Dunn. Plodding historical drama of what happened to Sweden's Queen Christina when she abdicated to convert to Catholicism. Finch is the Cardinal who must test her sincerity and with whom she falls in love.

Abduction of Saint Anne, The (1975) C-78m. TVM D: Harry Falk. Robert Wagner, E. G. Marshall, Kathleen Quinlan, Lloyd Nolan, William Windom, Martha Scott, James Gregory. Cynical detective (Wagner) and Vatican bishop (Marshall) check reports that a mobster's daughter has miraculous powers and, if so, should be kidnapped by the church. Intriguing combination of religious drama and detective story, compromised by pedestrian telling. Also called THEY'VE KIDNAPPED ANNE BENEDICT. Average.

Abductors, The (1957) 80m. *½ D: Andrew McLaglen. Victor McLaglen, George Macready, Fay Spain, Gavin Muir. Boring account of men attempting to rob Lincoln's grave.

Abe Lincoln In Illinois (1940) 110m. **** D: John Cromwell. Raymond Massey, Gene Lockhart, Ruth Gordon, Mary Howard, Dorothy Tree. First-rate Americana; sincere story of Lincoln's life and career is beautifully acted by Massey, with top support by Gordon as Mary Todd.

Able's Irish Rose (1946) 96m. BOMB D: A. Edward Sutherland. Joanne Dru, Richard Norris, Michael Chekhov, Eric Blore, Art Baker. Outdated when written in 1920s and even worse now. Irish girl marries Jewish boy and families clash.

Abilene Town (1946) 89m. *** D: Edwin L. Marin. Randolph Scott, Ann Dvorak, Edgar Buchanan, Rhonda Fleming, Lloyd Bridges. Above-average Scott vehicle as patient sheriff tries to straighten out homesteader conflict out West after the Civil War.

Abominable Dr. Phibes, The (1971-British) C-90m. *** D: Robert Fuest. Vincent Price, Joseph Cotten, Hugh Griffith, Terry-Thomas, Virginia North. Above-average camp horror film in which Price, disfigured in a car wreck, seeks revenge on those he believes responsible for the death of his wife.

Abominable Snowman of the Himalayas, The (1957-British) 85m. **½ D: Val Guest. Forrest Tucker, Peter Cushing, Richard Wattis, Maureen Connell, Robert Brown. Low-budget but exciting tale of expedition searching for the elusive monster. Strong cast lends credibility. Also known as ABOMINABLE SNOWMAN.

Abominable Snowman SEE: **Abominable Snowman of the Himalayas, The.**

About Face (1952) C-94m. *½ D: Roy Del Ruth. Gordon MacRae, Eddie Bracken, Dick Wesson, Phyllis Kirk, Joel Grey. Dull comedy-musical remake of BROTHER RAT, about three friends in military academy, one of them secretly married.

About Mrs. Leslie (1954) 104m. *** D: Daniel Mann. Shirley Booth, Robert Ryan, Marjie Millar, Alex Nicol. Flashbacks reveal romance between rooming-house owner (Booth) and business magnate (Ryan). Finely acted soaper; forgivable illogical coupling of stars.

Above and Beyond (1952) 122m. *** D: Melvin Frank, Norman Panama. Robert Taylor, Eleanor Parker, James Whitmore, Jim Backus. Meaningful account of U.S. pilot who flew over Hiroshima with first atomic bomb; film focuses on his training and its effect on his personal life.

Above Suspicion (1943) 90m. *** D: Richard Thorpe. Joan Crawford, Fred MacMurray, Conrad Veidt, Basil Rathbone, Reginald Owen, Richard Ainley. Crawford and MacMurray asked to do spy mission during European honeymoon in midst of WW2. Pure escapism, with Joan more than a match for the Nazis.

Above Us the Waves (1956-British) 92m. *** D: Ralph Thomas. John Mills, John Gregson, Donald Sinden,

James Robertson Justice. Utilizing documentary style, film relates account of unrelenting British attempt to destroy Nazi warship. Fine cast in exciting submarine drama.

Abraham Lincoln (1930) 97m. **½ D: D. W. Griffith. Walter Huston, Una Merkel, Edgar Dearing, Russell Simpson, Cameron Prud'homme, Oscar Apfel, Henry B. Walthall. Huston is excellent in this sincere but static biography of Lincoln; cannot match Griffith's silent masterpieces.

Abroad With Two Yanks (1944) 80m. **½ D: Allan Dwan. William Bendix, Helen Walker, Dennis O'Keefe, John Loder, John Abbott. Bendix and O'Keefe are marines on the loose in Australia, both chasing Walker; breezy comedy.

Absent Minded Professor, The (1961) 97m. *** D: Robert Stevenson. Fred MacMurray, Nancy Olson, Keenan Wynn, Tommy Kirk, Ed Wynn, Leon Ames, Elliott Reid. MacMurray discovers flubber (flying rubber) in this Disney audience-pleaser, but no one will believe him except Keenan Wynn, who tries to steal the substance. Broad comedy and bright special effects make this a lot of fun. Followed by sequel SON OF FLUBBER.

Acapulco Gold (1978) C-105m. * D: Burt Brinckerhoff. Marjoe Gortner, Robert Lansing, Ed Nelson, John Harkins, Randi Oakes. Unexceptional drug-smuggling tale benefits from attractive location shooting on Hawaiian island of Kauai.

Accent on Youth (1935) 77m. ** D: Wesley Ruggles. Sylvia Sidney, Herbert Marshall, Phillip Reed, Holmes Herbert, Catharine Doucet. Dated, talky adaptation of Samson Raphaelson's play about a May-December love affair. Remade as *Mr. Music* and *But Not For Me.*

Accident (1967-British) C-105m. ***½ D: Joseph Losey. Dirk Bogarde, Stanley Baker, Jacqueline Sassard, Delphine Seyrig, Alexander Knox, Michael York, Vivien Merchant, Harold Pinter. Complex, thought-provoking script by Harold Pinter uses story (about Oxford professor who falls in love with a student) as just a foundation for examination of characters' thoughts and actions. A challenging film that operates on many levels; entire cast superb, including York in his first major film role.

Accidental Death (1963-British) 57m.

**½ D: Geoffrey Nethercott. John Carson, Jacqueline Ellis, Derrick Sherwin, Richard Vernon. Edgar Wallace suspenser with gimmick of letting the viewer guess the identity of the murderer in question.

Accomplices, The (1959-Italian) 93m. *½ D: Gianni Vernuccio. Sandro Luporini, Sandro Fizzotro, Annabella Incontrera, Jeannie. Lurid, minor film of love triangle, with resulting murder; unconvincing and pat.

Accursed, The (1958-British) 78m. *½ D: Michael McCarthy. Donald Wolfit, Robert Bray, Jane Griffiths, Anton Diffring. Tepid whodunit involving the extinction of veterans of British military unit, and survivors' attempt to find killer.

Accused SEE: Mark of the Hawk

Accused, The (1948) 101m. *** D: William Dieterle. Loretta Young, Robert Cummings, Wendell Corey, Sam Jaffe. Loretta accidentally becomes a murderess in this taut thriller of a woman on the run; good support from Cummings.

Accused of Murder (1956) C-74m. ** D: Joseph Kane. David Brian, Vera Ralston, Sidney Blackmer, Virginia Grey. Bland handling of police detective Brian, entranced with singer Ralston, involved in underworld killing.

Ace Eli and Rodger of the Skies (1973) C-92m. ** D: Bill Sampson (John Erman). Cliff Robertson, Pamela Franklin, Eric Shea, Rosemary Murphy, Bernadette Peters, Alice Ghostley. Tepid tale of 1920s stunt flyer and son who tags along. Muddled film sat on studio shelf a long time; redoctoring didn't help. Story by Steven Spielberg.

Ace High (1969) C-123m. ** D: Giuseppe Colizzi. Eli Wallach, Terence Hill, Bud Spencer, Brock Peters, Kevin McCarthy, Steffen Zacharias. Awkwardly dubbed spaghetti Western tries to imitate Clint Eastwood-Sergio Leone epics, but director Golizzi lacks Leone's style. Hill plays a character named Cat Stevens, but there are no rock songs here.

Ace in the Hole SEE: Big Carnival, The

Aces High (1977-British) C-104m. *** D: Jack Gold. Malcolm McDowell, Christopher Plummer, Simon Ward, Peter Firth. Strong antiwar statement focusing on indoctrination of WW1 pilot Firth and his disillusioned squadron leader (McDowell). Solid British cast (with cameos by John Gielgud, Ray Milland, Trevor Howard, and Richard Johnson) and exciting aerial dogfight sequences highlight this remake of R. C. Sherriff's JOURNEY'S END.

Across 110th Street (1972) C-102m. *** D: Barry Shear. Anthony Quinn, Yaphet Kotto, Anthony Franciosa, Paul Benjamin. Ultraviolent drama of blacks against whites, Mafia against black organized crime, and police against everybody. Exciting and well-paced, but certain to be edited for TV.

Across the Bridge (1957-British) 103m. **½ D: Ken Annakin. Rod Steiger, David Knight, Bernard Lee, Eric Pohlmann. Agreeable study of panicky businessman Steiger on the run from authorities for stealing a fortune; taut performances.

Across the Pacific (1942) 97m. **½ D: John Huston. Humphrey Bogart, Mary Astor, Sydney Greenstreet, Keye Luke, Richard Loo, Monte Blue. Three MALTESE FALCON leads reteamed for enjoyable WW2 adventure. Bogart trails spies in Panama, has running-battle of wits with Greenstreet, all the while romancing enticing Astor.

Across the Wide Missouri (1951) C-78m. **½ D: William Wellman. Clark Gable, Ricardo Montalban, John Hodiak, Adolphe Menjou. On-location filming helps pedestrian Western about pathfinders moving westward in 19th century.

Act of Love (1953) 108m. *** D: Anatole Litvak. Kirk Douglas, Dany Robin, Barbara Laage, Robert Strauss. Sharply portrayed story of U.S. soldier (Douglas) romancing girl (Robin) in WW2 Paris, eventually deserting her, despite good intentions.

Act of Murder, An (1948) 91m. *** D: Michael Gordon. Fredric March, Florence Eldridge, Edmond O'Brien, Geraldine Brooks. March is excellent as strict judge who must judge himself for saving his wife the anguish of illness by killing her; absorbing drama.

Act of the Heart (1970-Canadian) C-103m. *** D: Paul Almond. Genevieve Bujold, Donald Sutherland, Bill Mitchell, Monique Leyrac. Fascinating study of religious fanaticism manifesting itself in one young woman and her love for a Catholic priest. Beautifully atmospheric but ending deeply hurts film.

Act of Violence (1948) 82m. *** D: Fred Zinnemann. Van Heflin, Robert Ryan, Janet Leigh, Mary Astor. Stark melodrama of disturbed man (Ryan) trying to kill old army nemesis (Heflin). Fine vignette by Astor as sympathetic call-girl.

Act of Violence (1979) C-100m. TVM D: Paul Wendkos. Elizabeth Montgomery, James Sloyan, Sean Frye, Roy Poole, Biff McGuire, Linden Chiles. Plucky Ms. M in another of her traditional victim roles, showing true grit as a divorced career woman who's gang mugged. Graphic and, thanks to its leading lady, remarkably arresting. Above average.

Act One (1963) 110m. **½ D: Dore Schary. George Hamilton, Jason Robards, George Segal, Eli Wallach, Sam Levene, Ruth Ford, Jack Klugman. Interesting for oddball cast, this fabrication of writer Moss Hart's autobiography lacks finesse or any sense of reality.

Action in Arabia (1944) 72m. **½ D: Leonide Moguy. George Sanders, Virginia Bruce, Gene Lockhart, Robert Armstrong, Michael Ansara. OK low-budgeter, with reporter Sanders uncovering Nazi plot to gain Arab support in WW2.

Action in the North Atlantic (1943) 127m. *** D: Lloyd Bacon. Humphrey Bogart, Raymond Massey, Alan Hale, Julie Bishop, Ruth Gordon, Sam Levene, Dane Clark. Rousing tribute to WW2 merchant marine, with officers Bogart and Massey, seamen Hale and Levene, usual hothead Clark, and Gordon as Massey's wife.

Action of the Tiger (1957-British) C-94m. **½ D: Terence Young. Van Johnson, Martine Carol, Herbert Lom, Anna Gerber, Sean Connery. Action packed, cliched adventure story with Johnson as the virile American rescuing pro-Western refugees from Albania.

Actors and Sin (1952) 82m. **½ D: Ben Hecht. Edward G. Robinson, Marsha Hunt, Dan O'Herlihy, Eddie Albert, John Crawford. Interesting two-part film: "Actor's Blood," hasbeen actor is overconcerned about daughter's stage career; "Woman of Sin," literary agent's hottest client is a child of 9.

Actress, The (1953) 91m. **½ D: George Cukor. Spencer Tracy, Jean Simmons, Teresa Wright, Anthony Perkins, Mary Wickes. Flavorful account based on Ruth Gordon's experiences as a teen-ager in early 20th-century Massachusetts, determined to

[4]

become an acting star; Tracy is the irascible father.

Ada (1961) **C-109m.** ******* D: Daniel Mann. Susan Hayward, Dean Martin, Wilfrid Hyde-White, Martin Balsam. Rags-to-riches soaper of poor gal (Hayward) maneuvering easygoing Martin to governor's mansion, using hellbent stamina to overcome political corruption. Hayward vs. Hyde-White in state senate is film's highlight.

Adam and Evalyn (1949-British) **92m.** ****½** D: Harold French. Jean Simmons, Stewart Granger, Wilfrid Hyde-White, Helen Cherry, Raymond Young. Pleasant but ordinary tale of gambler Granger and the daughter he adopts when a friend dies. British title: ADAM AND EVELYNE.

Adam and Evelyne See: Adam and Evalyn.

Adam at 6 A.M. (1970) **C-100m.** ******* D: Robert Scheerer. Michael Douglas, Lee Purcell, Joe Don Baker, Grayson Hall, Charles Aidman. Underrated film about young college professor from California who spends summer in Missouri working as a laborer. Authentic location footage and good performances by Purcell and Baker give rare, genuine feeling for the Midwest.

Adam Had Four Sons (1941) **81m.** ******* D: Gregory Ratoff. Ingrid Bergman, Warner Baxter, Susan Hayward, Fay Wray, Richard Denning. Good cast in story of governess Bergman watching over Baxter's family when his wife dies. Hayward is a bit extravagant in this one.

Adam's Rib (1949) **101m.** ******** D: George Cukor. Spencer Tracy, Katharine Hepburn, Judy Holliday, Tom Ewell, Jean Hagen, Polly Moran, David Wayne. Top comedy of husband-wife lawyers on opposing sides of same case. Star duet ably supported by newcomers Holliday, Ewell, Hagen, Wayne. Script by Ruth Gordon and Garson Kanin.

Adam's Woman (1972-British) **C-101m.** ****½** D: Philip Leacock. Beau Bridges, John Mills, Jane Merrow, James Booth, Andrew Keir, Tracy Reed. Interesting if not altogether successful story of innocent Bridges suffering in 19th-century Australian penal colony. Although put on probation, he's still determined to escape.

Adding Machine, The (1969-USA-British) **C-100m.** ****½** D: Jerome Epstein. Milo O'Shea, Phyllis Diller,

Billie Whitelaw, Sydney Chaplin, Julian Glover. Accountant becomes desperate upon learning he's to be replaced by a computer. This Elmer Rice comedy-fantasy is flawed but interesting. Diller has unusual straight role as harridan.

Address Unknown (1944) **72m.** ******* D: William Cameron Menzies. Paul Lukas, Peter Van Eyck, Mady Christians, Emory Parnell. Allies vs. Nazis boiled down to focus on American-German business partners on opposite sides of fence.

Adios Amigo (1975) **C-87m.** ****** D: Fred Williamson. Fred Williamson, Richard Pryor, Thalmus Rasulala, James Brown, Robert Phillips, Mike Henry. Offbeat Western comedy, written, produced, and directed by Williamson, who plays perennial patsy to con-man Pryor. No sex or violence in this innocuous film; too bad it doesn't pull together better.

Admirable Crichton, The (1957-British) **C-94m.** ****** D: Lewis Gilbert. Kenneth More, Diane Cilento, Cecil Parker, Sally Ann Howes, Martita Hunt. Oft-filmed James Barrie classic wears thin: impeccable servant proves to be most resourceful when he and his aristocratic employers are shipwrecked on an island. Retitled: PARADISE LAGOON.

Admiral Was a Lady, The (1950) **87m.** ****** D: Albert Rogell. Edmond O'Brien, Wanda Hendrix, Rudy Vallee, Steve Brodie. Ex-Wave Hendrix encounters quartet of fun-loving, work-hating men, all interested in courting her; weak.

Adorable Creatures (1956-French) **108m.** ****** D: Christian-Jaque. Daniel Gelin, Martine Carol, Edwige Feuillère, Danielle Darrieux, Marilyn Buferd, Louis Seigner. Saucy, inconsequential study of life and love in Gallic country, focusing on bedroom romances.

Adorable Julia (1964-French) **94m.** ******* D: Alfred Weidenmann. Lilli Palmer, Charles Boyer, Jean Sorel, Thomas Fritsch. Charming rendering of Somerset Maugham's novel THEATRE. Middle-aged actress dabbles in romances but allows nothing to interfere with career. Palmer and Boyer are admirable as wife-husband acting team.

Advance to the Rear (1964) **97m.** ****½** D: George Marshall. Glenn Ford, Stella Stevens, Melvyn Douglas, Joan Blondell, Jim Backus, Andrew Prine. During Civil War, Northern soldier rejects are sent to Western territory. Stevens as Reb spy and Blondell as saucy worldly woman add only spice to predictable happenings.

Adventure (1945) 125m. ** D: Victor Fleming. Clark Gable, Greer Garson, Joan Blondell, Thomas Mitchell, Tom Tully, John Qualen, Richard Haydn. Gable's back, Garson's got him; they both sink in cumbersome comedy of seagoing roustabout and meek librarian. Not even breezy Blondell can save it.

Adventure in Baltimore (1949) 89m. ** D: Richard Wallace. Shirley Temple, John Agar, Robert Young, Josephine Hutchinson. Mild romancer of 1900s with Temple full of new-fangled notions, yet seeking old-fashioned romance.

Adventure in Diamonds (1940) 76m. ** D: George Fitzmaurice. George Brent, Isa Miranda, John Loder, Nigel Bruce. Tepid formula programmer dealing with jewel robberies in Africa.

Adventure in Manhattan (1936) 73m. **½ D: Edward Ludwig. Jean Arthur, Joel McCrea, Reginald Owen, Thomas Mitchell, Herman Bing. Bizarre blend of comedy and melodrama with the stars foiling planned bank robbery. Doesn't always work, but interesting.

Adventure in Washington (1941) 84m. ** D: Alfred E. Green. Herbert Marshall, Virginia Bruce, Gene Reynolds, Samuel S. Hinds, Ralph Morgan. Misleading title for tame account of Senator Marshall and his attempts to reform a delinquent youth who is working as a Senate page boy.

Adventure Island (1947) C-66m. ** D: Peter Stewart. Rory Calhoun, Rhonda Fleming, Paul Kelly, John Abbott. Weak remake of EBB TIDE with innocents marooned on island with self-made ruler, who is a maniac. Colorful scenery can't save this.

Adventure of Sherlock Holmes' Smarter Brother, The (1975) C-91m. **½ D: Gene Wilder. Gene Wilder, Madeline Kahn, Marty Feldman, Dom DeLuise, Leo McKern, Roy Kinnear, John LeMesurier. Wilder's first film as writer-director-star is mild spoof of Sherlockian adventures, as Sigerson Holmes becomes involved with music-hall songstress Kahn, a damsel in distress. DeLuise, as hammy opera star, adds film's liveliest moments. Made in England.

Adventurers, The (1952) SEE: Fortune in Diamonds

Adventurers, The (1970) C-171m. BOMB D: Lewis Gilbert. Bekim Fehmiu, Candice Bergen, Ernest Borgnine, Olivia de Havilland, Leigh Taylor-Young, Thommy Berggren, Rossano Brazzi. Three-hour challenge to the kidneys based on Harold Robbins' best-seller about fictional South American republic that has a new revolution every two minutes. Incredible bomb wastes attractive cast and nice photography; some scenes will undoubtedly be cut for TV.

Adventures at Rugby SEE: Tom Brown's School Days

Adventures of Bullwhip Griffin, The (1967) C-110m. *** D: James Neilson. Roddy McDowall, Suzanne Pleshette, Karl Malden, Harry Guardino, Richard Haydn, Hermione Baddeley, Bryan Russell. Bright Disney spoof of gold-rush sagas, with McDowall as Bostonian butler who learns to fend for himself in the wild and woolly West. Clever comic ideas and visual gimmickry make this fun.

Adventures of Captain Fabian (1951) 100m. *½ D: William Marshall. Errol Flynn, Micheline Presle, Agnes Moorehead, Vincent Price. Soggy sea yarn has Flynn involved with gal accused of murder; lackluster costumer.

Adventures of Casanova (1948) 83m. ** D: Roberto Gavaldon. Arturo de Cordova, Lucille Bremer, Turhan Bey, John Sutton. Very ordinary swashbuckler of Casanova de Cordova leading the oppressed people of Sicily against tyrannical rule; this one cries for color.

Adventures of Don Juan (1948) C-110m. *** D: Vincent Sherman. Errol Flynn, Viveca Lindfors, Robert Douglas, Alan Hale, Ann Rutherford, Raymond Burr. Handsome tongue-in-cheek swashbuckler has Errol stringing along countless maidens and even enticing the Queen (Lindfors).

Adventures of Gallant Bess (1948) C-73m. ** D: Lew Landers. Cameron Mitchell, Audrey Long, Fuzzy Knight, James Millican. Mitchell is torn between his girl and his horse in this colorful but routine equestrian drama.

Adventures of Gerard, The (1970-British-Italian-Swiss) C-91m. BOMB D: Jerzy Skolimowski. Peter McEnery, Claudia Cardinale, Eli Wallach, Jack Hawkins, John Neville. Clumsy farce from Arthur Conan

Dyle story about cocky but stupid officer who becomes fall guy for Napoleon's (Wallach) wartime strategy. Filmed in Italy.

Adventures of Hajji Baba, The (1954) C-94m. **½ D: Don Weis. John Derek, Elaine Stewart, Thomas Gomez, Amanda Blake. Derek gives spark to title role, in OK desert tale of his romancing sheik's daughter, who's out to marry heir of rival kingdom.

Adventures of Huckleberry Finn, The (1939) 90m. *** D: Richard Thorpe. Mickey Rooney, Walter Connolly, William Frawley, Rex Ingram, Lynne Carver. Subdued Rooney fine, Ingram excellent as Huck and Jim in classic Mark Twain tale of early 19th-century America; Connolly and Frawley are amusing as riverboat con-artists.

Adventures of Huckleberry Finn, The (1960) C-107m. *** D: Michael Curtiz. Tony Randall, Eddie Hodges, Archie Moore, Patty McCormack, Neville Brand. Good version of Twain's story with an appealing Hodges (Huck) and excellent Archie Moore (Jim). Assorted characters played by veterans Buster Keaton, Andy Devine, Judy Canova, John Carradine, Mickey Shaughnessy, and Sterling Holloway.

Adventures of Marco Polo, The (1938) 100m. **½ D: Archie Mayo. Gary Cooper, Sigrid Gurie, Basil Rathbone, George Barbier, Binnie Barnes, Ernest Truex, Alan Hale. Lighthearted approach to famed explorer's life doesn't always work, but Cooper is pleasant and Rathbone's a good villain; sumptuous production. Look for Lana Turner as one of the handmaidens.

Adventures of Mark Twain, The (1944) 130m. *** D: Irving Rapper. Fredric March, Alexis Smith, Donald Crisp, Alan Hale, C. Aubrey Smith, John Carradine, Percy Kilbride. Life story of great writer-humorist is well-acted and interesting but not in the same league with PASTEUR, ZOLA, etc.

Adventures of Martin Eden, The (1942) 87m. *** D: Sidney Salkow. Glenn Ford, Claire Trevor, Evelyn Keyes, Stuart Erwin, Dickie Moore. Sturdy Jack London tale of seaman aboard terror of a ship, writing account of sailing, fighting for literary recognition.

Adventures of Nick Carter (1972) C-72m. TVM D: Paul Krasny. Robert Conrad, Shelley Winters, Brooke Bundy, Broderick Crawford, Dean Stockwell, Pat O'Brien, Neville Brand, Pernell Roberts. Legendary private-eye Carter (Conrad) sets out to find out who bumped off good friend. Usual assortment of corrupt police types, millionaire robber baron, glamorous nightclub owner, etc.; emphasis on action, not mystery. Average.

Adventures of Robin Hood, The (1938) C-105m. ***½ D: Michael Curtiz, William Keighley. Errol Flynn, Olivia de Havilland, Basil Rathbone, Claude Rains, Patric Knowles, Eugene Pallette, Alan Hale. Dashing Flynn in the definitive swashbuckler, winning hand of de Havilland, foiling evil prince Rains, dueling wicked Rathbone. Beautiful color, production, Oscar-winning music score (by Erich Wolfgang Korngold).

Adventures of Robinson Crusoe (1954) C-90m. *** D: Luis Buñuel. Dan O'Herlihy, James Fernandez, Felipe De Alba, Chel Lopez. Faithful enactment of Defoe book with fine work by O'Herlihy, well-directed and photographed in color.

Adventures of Sadie, The (1955-British) C-88m. **½ D: Noel Langley. Joan Collins, Kenneth More, Hermione Gingold, Robertson Hare. Obvious sex satire relying on premise of Collins stuck on desert isle with love-hungry men.

Adventures of Scaramouche, The (1964-French) C-98m. ** D: Antonio Isamendi. Gerard Barray, Gianna Maria Canale, Michele Girardon, Yvette Lebon. Gallic rendering of Sabatini cloak-and-sword tale has action and wit, but not on grand scale.

Adventures of Sherlock Holmes (1939) 85m. D: Alfred L. Werker. Basil Rathbone, Nigel Bruce, Ida Lupino, Alan Marshal, Terry Kilburn, George Zucco, E. E. Clive, Mary Gordon. SEE: Sherlock Holmes series.

Adventures of Tartu (1943-British) 103m. **½ D: Harold S. Bucquet. Robert Donat, Valerie Hobson, Walter Rilla, Phyllis Morris, Glynis Johns. Improbable but well-acted account of British spy (Donat) trying to help Czech partisans destroy a poison gas factory manned by Nazis. Retitled: TARTU

Adventures of the Queen (1975) C-100m. TVM D: David Lowell Rich. Robert Stack, David Hedison, Ralph Bellamy, Bradford Dillman, Sorrell Booke, Burr de Benning, John Randolph. Stack captains luxury cruise ship threatened with destruction as part of deadly vendetta against eccentric millionaire Bellamy. Predictable Irwin Allen disaster drama, filmed aboard the *Queen Mary.* Below average.

Adventures of the Wilderness Family, The (1975) **C-100m.** *** D: Stewart Raffill. Robert F. Logan, Susan Damante Shaw, Hollye Holmes, Ham Larsen, Buck Flower, William Cornford. Good human interest drama. Modern couple with two children forsake big city for life in magnificent but sometimes dangerous Rocky Mountain region.

Adventures of Tom Sawyer, The (1938) **C-93m.** ***½ D: Norman Taurog. Tommy Kelly, Jackie Moran, Ann Gillis, May Robson, Walter Brennan, Victor Jory. Excellent children's story from Mark Twain is excitingly filmed, with Injun Joe (Jory) sequences the highlights.

Adventuress, The (1947-British) **98m.** ***½ D: Frank Launder. Deborah Kerr, Trevor Howard, Raymond Huntley, Norman Shelley. Kerr is a joy in this change-of-pace espionage tale of young Irish girl who unwittingly aids the Nazis during WW2. Splendid British gem.

Advice to the Lovelorn (1933) **62m.** **½ D: Alfred Werker. Lee Tracy, Sally Blane, Sterling Holloway, Jean Adair, Paul Harvey. Engaging comedy-drama capitalizing on Tracy's success in BLESSED EVENT; here he parlays a lonelyhearts column into business enterprise, with unexpected results. Loosely based on Nathanael West's MISS LONELYHEARTS. Holloway excellent in key supporting role.

Advise and Consent (1962) **139m.** *** D: Otto Preminger. Henry Fonda, Don Murray, Charles Laughton, Walter Pidgeon, Peter Lawford, Gene Tierney, Franchot Tone, Lew Ayres, Burgess Meredith, Paul Ford, George Grizzard. Long but engrossing drama of Washington wheeling and dealing, from Allen Drury novel. Cast is fine, with effective underplaying by Ayres and Tone standing out among more flamboyant performances by Laughton (his last film) and Grizzard.

Affair, The (1973) **C-74m. TVM** D: Gilbert Cates. Natalie Wood, Robert Wagner, Bruce Davison, Jamie Smith Jackson, Kent Smith, Frances Reid, Pat Harrington. Sensitive, careful handling of 30-ish female songwriter

with polio (Wood) experiencing first love affair with lawyer (Wagner). Excellent cast, expert script. Above average.

Affair in Havana (1957) **77m.** *½ D: Laslo Benedek. John Cassavetes, Raymond Burr, Sara Shane, Lila Lazo. Unexciting tale of songwriter in love with crippled man's wife. Filmed in Cuba.

Affair in Monte Carlo (1953-British) **C-75m.** ** D: Victor Saville. Merle Oberon, Richard Todd, Leo Genn, Peter Illing. Rich widow tries to convince gambler that romance is more rewarding than roulette. Monte Carlo backgrounds don't spark this trifle.

Affair in Reno (1957) **75m.** *½ D: R. G. Springsteen. John Lund, John Archer, Doris Singleton, Alan Hale. Inoffensive little film about detective Singleton falling in love with p.r.-man Lund while in Arizona.

Affair in Trinidad (1952) **98m.** **½ D: Vincent Sherman. Rita Hayworth, Glenn Ford, Alexander Scourby, Torin Thatcher, Juanita Moore, Steven Geray. Hayworth and Ford sparkle as cafe singer and brother-in-law seeking her husband's murderer. Hayworth is most enticing.

Affair to Remember, An (1957) **C-115m.** **½ D: Leo McCarey. Cary Grant, Deborah Kerr, Cathleen Nesbitt, Neva Patterson, Richard Denning. Middling remake of McCarey's LOVE AFFAIR (Charles Boyer-Irene Dunne). Bubbling shipboard comedy in first half, overshadowed by draggy soap-opera clichés and unnecessary musical numbers in N.Y. finale.

Affair With a Stranger (1953) **89m.** **½ D: Roy Rowland. Victor Mature, Jean Simmons, Jane Darwell, Dabbs Greer, Olive Carey. Title figure is child adopted by couple on brink of divorce. Formula plot of marital seesaw; stars work well together.

Affairs in Versailles SEE: **Royal Affairs in Versailles**

Affairs of Cellini (1934) **80m.** *** D: Gregory La Cava. Constance Bennett, Fredric March, Frank Morgan, Fay Wray, Jessie Ralph. March is excellent as roguish Renaissance artist who falls in love with Duchess. Lavish production, fine cast make this most entertaining.

Affairs of Dobie Gillis, The (1953) **74m.** *** D: Don Weis. Debbie Reynolds, Bobby Van, Hans Conried, Lurene Tuttle, Bob Fosse. Entertaining musicomedy based on Max Shulman's book of college kids. Debbie and Van a cute couple; Conried the dour prof.

Affairs of Susan, The (1945) 110m. **½ D: William A. Seiter. Joan Fontaine, George Brent, Dennis O'Keefe, Don DeFore, Rita Johnson, Walter Abel. Fairly entertaining comedy of actress Fontaine who does more acting for her beaus than she does onstage. **

Affectionately Yours (1941) 90m. ** D: Lloyd Bacon. Merle Oberon, Dennis Morgan, Rita Hayworth, Ralph Bellamy, George Tobias. Attractive triangle flounders in weak comedy of Morgan trying to win back wife Oberon, with interference from Hayworth. Bellamy is the poor sap again.

Africa Addio (1966-Italian) C-122m. *** D: Gualtiero Jacopetti, Franco Prosperi. Intriguing survey of contemporary Africa focusing on racial differences and variant tribal customs on the continent; overly gruesome at times.

Africa Screams (1949) 79m. *** D: Charles Barton. Bud Abbott, Lou Costello, Hillary Brooke, Max Baer, Clyde Beatty, Frank Buck, Shemp Howard. A&C go on safari in this funny outing full of wheezy but often hilarious gags and routines.

Africa—Texas Style! (1967) C-106m. **½ D: Andrew Marton. Hugh O'Brian, John Mills, Nigel Green, Tom Nardini, Adrienne Corri. Feature (which served as TV pilot) doesn't offer much excitement, with O'Brian helping Mills preserve wild game in the dark continent.

African Elephant, The (1972) C-92m. *** D: Simon Trevor. Excellent documentary on African wildlife centering on elephants and their sometimes strange habits. Released theatrically as KING ELEPHANT.

African Lion, The (1955) C-75m. ***½ D: James Algar. Narrated by Winston Hibler. Outstanding True-Life documentary is perhaps Disney's best. Naturalists Alfred and Elma Milotte filmed the African lion in his native habitat through a year's cycle of seasons. Filled with drama, excitement, color, humor. A gem.

African Queen, The (1951) C-105m. **** D: John Huston. Katharine Hepburn, Humphrey Bogart, Robert Morley, Peter Bull, Theodore Bikel. Superb combination of souse Bogart (who won an Oscar) and spinster Hepburn traveling up the Congo during WWI, combating the elements and the Germans.

African Treasure (1952) 70m. D: Ford Beebe. Johnny Sheffield, Laurette Luez, Lyle Talbot, Arthur Space, Smoki Whitfield. SEE: **Bomba, the Jungle Boy** series.

After Midnight With Boston Blackie (1943) D: Lew Landers. Chester Morris, Ann Savage, George E. Stone, Richard Lane, Cy Kendall, George McKay. SEE: **Boston Blackie** series.

After Office Hours (1935) 75m. **½ D: Robert Z. Leonard. Constance Bennett, Clark Gable, Stuart Erwin, Billie Burke, Harvey Stephens. Socialite Bennett takes job as reporter with editor Gable's newspaper and comes in handy when Gable tries to investigate shady society man Stephens. Forgettable fluff.

After the Fox (1966-British-Italian) C-103m. **½ D: Vittorio De Sica. Peter Sellers, Victor Mature, Britt Ekland, Martin Balsam. Not always successful comedy of Italian movie director (Sellers) is a must for Mature's performance as a fading romantic star with tremendous ego. Script by Neil Simon.

After the Thin Man (1936) 113m. D: W. S. Van Dyke II. William Powell, Myrna Loy, James Stewart, Elissa Landi, Joseph Calleia. SEE: **Thin Man** series.

Against a Crooked Sky (1975) C-89m. ** D: Earl Bellamy. Richard Boone, Stewart Peterson, Geoffrey Land, Jewel Blanch, Henry Wilcoxon, Clint Ritchie. A boy searches for his sister, who's been kidnapped by Indians; simplistic, old-fashioned family western.

Against All Flags (1952) C-83m. **½ D: George Sherman. Errol Flynn, Maureen O'Hara, Anthony Quinn, Mildred Natwick. Flynn found his forte again as dashing British soldier who maneuvers way into pirate fortress, while managing to flirt with O'Hara.

Agatha (1979) C-98m. *** D: Michael Apted. Dustin Hoffman, Vanessa Redgrave, Timothy Dalton, Helen Morse, Celia Gregory, Paul Brooke. Fictional speculation on mystery writer Agatha Christie's famous 11-day disappearance in 1926; Redgrave is superb in this absorbing yarn, Hoffman strangely miscast as smooth American reporter who tracks her down.

Agatha Christie's Endless Night SEE: **Endless Night**

Agent 8¾ (1965-British) C-77m. *** D: Ralph Thomas. Dirk Bogarde,

Sylva Koscina, Leo McKern, Robert Morley, Roger Delgado, John Le Mesurier. Released at height of James Bond craze, this spoof features Bogarde as a bumbling secret agent working in Czechoslovakia. Sometimes witty, bright comedy.

Agent for H.A.R.M. (1966) C-84m. *½ D: Gerd Oswald. Mark Richman, Wendell Corey, Carl Esmond, Barbara Bouchet, Martin Kosleck, Rafael Campos, Alizia Gur. Yet another secret agent adventure, definitely a lesser one, about investigation of scientist who is trying to combat spores that turn people into fungi.

Agony and the Ecstasy, The (1965) C-140m. **½ D: Carol Reed. Charlton Heston, Rex Harrison, Diane Cilento, Harry Andrews, Adolfo Celi. Huge spectacle of Michelangelo's artistic conflicts with Pope Julius II has adequate acting overshadowed by meticulous production. Short documentary on artist's work precedes fragmentary drama based on bits of Irving Stone's novel.

A-Haunting We Will Go (1942) 68m. *½ D: Alfred Werker. Stan Laurel, Oliver Hardy, Dante the Magician, Sheila Ryan, John Shelton, Don Costello, Elisha Cook Jr. One of Stan and Ollie's poorest films, involving them with gangsters, a troublesome coffin, and a hokey stage magician. No magic in this turkey.

Ah, Wilderness (1935) 101m. ***½ D: Clarence Brown. Wallace Beery, Lionel Barrymore, Aline MacMahon, Eric Linden, Cecilia Parker, Mickey Rooney. Rich Americana in this adaptation of Eugene O'Neill play about turn-of-the-century small-town life, focusing on boy who tackles problems of adolescence. Rooney, playing younger brother, took the lead in musical remake SUMMER HOLIDAY.

Ain't Misbehavin' (1955) C-82m. **½ D: Edward Buzzell. Rory Calhoun, Piper Laurie, Jack Carson, Mamie Van Doren, Reginald Gardiner. Harmless musical; lively Laurie marries tycoon Calhoun; he tries to refine her personality.

Air Cadet (1951) 94m. ** D: Joseph Pevney. Stephen McNally, Gail Russell, Alex Nicol, Richard Long, Rock Hudson. Standard training-recruit story, with McNally looking bored as head instructor.

Air Force (1943) 124m. *** D: Howard Hawks. John Garfield, John Ridgely, Gig Young, Arthur Kennedy, Charles Drake, Harry Carey, George Tobias, Faye Emerson. Archetypal WW2 movie, focusing on archetypal bomber crew. Tough to stomach at times ("Fried Jap going down," chimes Tobias after scoring a hit), but generally exciting, well-done.

Air Mail (1932) 83m. *** D: John Ford. Pat O'Brien, Ralph Bellamy, Russell Hopton, Slim Summerville, Frank Albertson, Gloria Stuart. Routine story of pioneer airmail pilots supercharged by fine aerial scenes and good cast. First-rate all the way.

Air Raid Wardens (1943) 67m. ** D: Edward Sedgwick. Stan Laurel, Oliver Hardy, Edgar Kennedy, Jacqueline White, Horace (Stephen) McNally, Donald Meek. Weak, later Laurel and Hardy comedy. One potentially good scene with slow-burn Kennedy doesn't meet expectations.

Airport (1970) C-137m. ***½ D: George Seaton. Burt Lancaster, Dean Martin, George Kennedy, Helen Hayes, Jean Seberg, Jacqueline Bisset, Van Heflin, Maureen Stapleton, Barry Nelson, Dana Wynter, Lloyd Nolan, Barbara Hale. GRAND HOTEL plot formula reaches modern-day zenith in ultraslick, old-fashioned movie that entertains in spite of itself, detailing hectic winter night at metropolitan airport. Plastic performances dominate, with down-to-earth Kennedy, touching Stapleton, and nervous Heflin standing out. Helen Hayes won Oscar as impish stowaway.

Airport 1975 (1974) C-106m. *½ D: Jack Smight. Charlton Heston, Karen Black, George Kennedy, Efrem Zimbalist, Jr., Susan Clark, Helen Reddy, Gloria Swanson, Linda Blair, Dana Andrews, Sid Caesar, Myrna Loy, Nancy Olson, Roy Thinnes, Martha Scott. Yet another jetliner disaster epic, not worth your time unless you get your kicks watching a "Hollywood Squares"-type cast that includes Helen Reddy as a (singing) nun.

Airport '77 (1977) C-113m. **½ D: Jerry Jameson. Jack Lemmon, Lee Grant, Brenda Vaccaro, George Kennedy, James Stewart, Joseph Cotten, Olivia de Havilland, Darren McGavin, Christopher Lee, Monte Markham. All the cliches and stock characters are trucked out for another made-to-order disaster epic, not bad as these things go: Stewart's private luxury jet is sabotaged and sinks in the ocean, forcing daring rescue attempt. Lemmon brings conviction to his role as dedicated pilot. New footage added for network showing.

AKA Cassius Clay (1970) **C-85m.** **½ D: William Cayton. Narrated by Richard Kiley. Interesting documentary about the controversial heavyweight champion.

Aku Aku (1961) **C-60m.** **½ Documentary of anthropologist Thor Heyerdahl's trip to Easter Island and his encounters with the natives.

Al Capone (1959) **105m.** **½ D: Richard Wilson. Rod Steiger, Fay Spain, James Gregory, Martin Balsam, Nehemiah Persoff, Murvyn Vye. Good latter-day gangster biography with Steiger tirading as scarfaced Capone: good supporting cast, bringing back memories of Cagney-Robinson-Bogart films of the 30s.

Al Jennings of Oklahoma (1951) **C-79m.** ** D: Ray Nazarro. Dan Duryea, Gale Storm, Dick Foran, Gloria Henry. Modest Western enhanced by Duryea in title role of gangster who serves his time and goes straight; sporadic action.

Aladdin and His Lamp (1952) **C-67m.** *½ D: Lew Landers. Patricia Medina, Richard Erdman, John Sands, Noreen Nash. Poppycock made by adults based on juvenile fable.

Alakazam the Great (1961) **C-84m.** **½ Voices of Jonathan Winters, Frankie Avalon, Arnold Stang, Sterling Holloway. Japanese-made cartoon is good children's entertainment; story centers on magical monkey's ambitious adventures, from bullfight in the pit of a volcano to an epic battle with Hercules of the Universe.

Alamo, The (1960) **C-190m.** *** D: John Wayne. John Wayne, Richard Widmark, Laurence Harvey, Richard Boone, Carlos Arruza, Frankie Avalon, Pat Wayne, Linda Cristal. Long, and long-winded, saga of the Alamo, with plenty of historical name-dropping and speechifying. Worthwhile for final attack, a truly memorable movie spectacle. Fine music score by Dimitri Tiomkin.

Alaska Seas (1954) **78m.** ** D: Jerry Hopper. Robert Ryan, Jan Sterling, Brian Keith, Gene Barry, Ross Bagdasarian. Crooks will be crooks, in insipid tale of north-country salmon canner who regrets rehiring former partner, now an ex-con. Remake of SPAWN OF THE NORTH.

Albuquerque (1948) **C-89m.** ** D:

Ray Enright. Randolph Scott, Barbara Britton, Gabby Hayes, Lon Chaney, Russell Hayden. Good Western for Scott fans, with young man finally rebelling against overly strict uncle.

Alex and the Gypsy (1976) **C-99m.** **½ D: John Korty. Jack Lemmon, Genevieve Bujold, James Woods, Gino Ardito, Robert Emhardt, Titos Vandis. Meandering story of romance between bailbondsman Lemmon and gypsy Bujold who's accused of attempted murder. Some interesting ideas lost in the muddle of an indecisive film.

Alex in Wonderland (1970) **C-109m.** ** D: Paul Mazursky. Donald Sutherland, Ellen Burstyn, Viola Spolin, Federico Fellini, Jeanne Moreau. Camera follows young film director Sutherland through tedium of his everyday life. Self-indulgent imitation of Fellini (who appears briefly) caused some wags to dub this film 1½. Burstyn stands out as Sutherland's wife.

Alexander Hamilton (1931) **73m.** ** D: John Adolfi. George Arliss, Doris Kenyon, Montagu Love, Dudley Digges, June Collyer, Alan Mowbray, Charles Middleton. Episodic American historical drama of country's earliest financial wizard is interesting but quite stagy.

Alexander the Great (1956) **C-141m.** *** D: Robert Rossen. Richard Burton, Fredric March, Claire Bloom, Danielle Darrieux. Remarkable cast, intelligent acting, but a static epic, lacking essential sweep to make tale of Greek conqueror moving.

Alexander: The Other Side of Dawn (1977) **C-100m.** **TVM** D: John Erman. Leigh J. McCloskey, Eve Plumb, Earl Holliman, Juliet Mills, Jean Hagen, Lonnie Chapman. In sequel to DAWN: PORTRAIT OF A TEENAGE RUNAWAY, country-boy-turned-Hollywood-hustler (McCloskey) tries to find legitimate work in order to marry teen-aged prostitute (Plumb) he had hoped to regenerate, but gets involved with a homosexual football pro. Sordid tale, with McCloskey aping Jon Voight's MIDNIGHT COWBOY characterization. Average.

Alexander's Ragtime Band (1938) **105m.** **½ D: Henry King. Tyrone Power, Alice Faye, Don Ameche, Ethel Merman, Jack Haley, Jean Hersholt. Large-scale musical with stale plot but good stars and a flock of Irving Berlin songs: "Now it Can

Be Told," "My Walking Stick," "I'm Marching Along with Time," title tune.

Alfie (1966-British) **C-114m.** ***½ D: Lewis Gilbert. Michael Caine, Shelley Winters, Millicent Martin, Shirley Anne Field, Vivien Merchant, Denholm Elliot. Well-turned version of Bill Naughton play. Caine is superb as philandering Cockney playboy who can't decide if carefree bachelor life is so bloody marvelous.

Alfred the Great (1969-British) **C-122m.** ** D: Clive Donner. David Hemmings, Michael York, Prunella Ransome, Colin Blakely, Julian Glover, Ian McKellen. Story of young leader of 9th-century England can't decide if it's a serious historical chronicle or broad swashbuckler; succeeds in neither department. Only highlight is series of meticulously filmed battle scenes; otherwise, ambitious script is boring.

Algiers (1938) **95m.** *** D: John Cromwell. Charles Boyer, Sigrid Gurie, Hedy Lamarr, Joseph Calleia, Alan Hale, Gene Lockhart, Johnny Downs. Boyer as Pepe Le Moko, falls in love with alluring Lamarr visiting Casbah district of Algiers: Calleia as police official, Lockhart as informer, stand out in well-cast romance. Remake of French PEPE LE MOKO, remade as CASBAH.

Ali Baba and the Forty Thieves (1944) **C-87m.** **½ D: Arthur Lubin. Maria Montez, Jon Hall, Scotty Beckett, Turhan Bey, Kurt Katch, Andy Devine, Frank Puglia. Colorful escapism with rightful-prince Hall battling evil man who put him out of the way years ago; much footage reused in recent SWORD OF ALI BABA.

Ali Baba Goes to Town (1937) **81m.** *** D: David Butler. Eddie Cantor, Tony Martin, Roland Young, June Lang, John Carradine, Louise Hovick (Gypsy Rose Lee). Entertaining musical comedy sends Cantor back in time but retains topical jokes of 1937; nice production with Cantor in top form. Ends with modern-day movie premiere and glimpses of many stars, from Shirley Temple to Tyrone Power.

Alias a Gentleman (1948) **76m.** ** D: Harry Beaumont. Wallace Beery, Tom Drake, Dorothy Patrick, Gladys George, Leon Ames. Minor saga of an aging jailbird (Beery) who doesn't want to see his daughter involved with shady characters like himself.

Alias Boston Blackie (1942) **67m.** D: Lew Landers. Chester Morris, Adele Mara, Richard Lane, George E. Stone, Lloyd Corrigan, Walter Sande, Larry Parks, Lloyd Bridges. SEE: **Boston Blackie** series.

Alias Bulldog Drummond (1935-British) **73m.** D: Walter Forde. Jack Hulbert, Fay Wray, Claude Hulbert, Ralph Richardson, Paul Graetz. British title BULLDOG JACK. See: **Bulldog Drummond** Series.

Alias Jesse James (1959) **C-92m.** *** D: Norman McLeod. Bob Hope, Rhonda Fleming, Wendell Corey, Jim Davis, Gloria Talbott. One of Hope's funniest has him an insurance salesman out West, mistaken for sharpshooter. Miss Fleming is a lovely Western belle; the two do a cute song together. Many guests appear at the climax.

Alias Nick Beal (1949) **93m.** *** D: John Farrow. Ray Milland, Audrey Totter, Thomas Mitchell, George Macready, Fred Clark. Allegory of Devil (Milland) corrupting honest politician Mitchell with help of trollop Totter. Interesting drama with unusually sinister Milland.

Alias Smith and Jones (1970) **C-90m.** TVM D: Gene Levitt. Peter Duel, Ben Murphy, John Russell, Earl Holliman, Forrest Tucker, James Drury, Susan Saint James. Reworking of BUTCH CASSIDY premise. Two adequate bandits in American West find technology creeping up on them, making their job more difficult. Average.

Alibi Ike (1935) **73m.** *** D: Ray Enright. Joe E. Brown, Olivia de Havilland, William Frawley, Ruth Donnelly, Roscoe Karns. Ingratiating baseball comedy by Ring Lardner, with Joe a tale-spinning pitcher who gets involved in various calamities. Young De Havilland is charming heroine in one of Joe's best vehicles.

Alice Adams (1935) **99m.** ***½ D: George Stevens. Katharine Hepburn, Fred MacMurray, Fred Stone, Evelyn Venable, Frank Albertson. Excellent small-town Americana with social-climbing girl finally finding love in person of unpretentious MacMurray. Booth Tarkington book becomes fine film, if not altogether credible.

Alice Doesn't Live Here Any More (1975) **C-113m.** ***½ D: Martin Scorsese. Ellen Burstyn, Kris Kristofferson, Billy Green Bush, Alfred

Lutter, Diane Ladd, Jodie Foster, Harvey Keitel. Excellent look at a woman's odyssey to find herself—and some measure of happiness—after her husband dies, leaving her and a young son penniless. Kristofferson is gentle, well-meaning man who tries to win her love. Burstyn won well-deserved Oscar for Best Actress. Later transformed into TV sitcom.

Alice in Wonderland (1933) 77m. **½ D: Norman Z. McLeod. Charlotte Henry, Richard Arlen, Gary Cooper, W.C. Fields, Edward Everett Horton, Baby LeRoy, Edna May Oliver, Jack Oakie, many others. Top Paramount stars appear, disguised as various Lewis Carroll characters, in this curious adaptation of the classic story.

Alice in Wonderland (1950-British) C-83m. ** D: Dallas Bower. Carol Marsh, Stephen Murray, Pamela Brown, Felix Aylmer, Ernest Milton. Static adaptation of Lewis Carroll classic with gimmick of mixing live action and puppets; most of the wit and charm are missing.

Alice's Adventures in Wonderland (1972) C-96m. *½ D: William Sterling. Fiona Fullerton, Michael Crawford, Ralph Richardson, Flora Robson, Peter Sellers, Dudley Moore, Michael Jayston. Tedious British film version of Lewis Carroll's classic proves Americans don't have a monopoly on making bad children's musicals. Waste of a good cast.

Alice's Restaurant (1969) C-111m. *** D: Arthur Penn. Arlo Guthrie, Pat Quinn, James Broderick, Michael McClanathan, Geoff Outlaw, Tina Chen. Guthrie's popular record inspired this odd blend of satire, whimsy, melodrama, and social commentary. Generally fun, with quizzically downbeat ending, showing freeform lifestyle of group of friends headed by Broderick and Quinn (as Alice).

Alien (1979) C-124m. **½ D: Ridley Scott. Tom Skerritt, Sigourney Weaver, John Hurt, Ian Holm, Harry Dean Stanton, Yaphet Kotto. Commercial spacecraft unwittingly takes on an alien being which wreaks merciless havoc on the crew. Space-age horror film reverts to 1950s formula story, but adds stomach-churning violence, slime, and shocks. Still, this is some people's idea of a good time. Oscar-winning effects.

Alien Thunder (1973-Canadian) C-90m. ** D: Claude Fournier. Donald Sutherland, Kevin McCarthy, Chief Dan George, Jean Duceppe, Jack Creely, Francine Racette. Mountie Sutherland chases Cree Indian accused of a sergeant's murder in this handsome but tedious actioner. Retitled DAN CANDY'S LAW.

All About Eve (1950) 138m. **** D: Joseph L. Mankiewicz. Bette Davis, Anne Baxter, George Sanders, Celeste Holm, Gary Merrill, Thelma Ritter, Marilyn Monroe, Hugh Marlowe. Cynical view of theater life, filled with epigrammatic gems. Davis glows as aging star, Merrill her young beau, Baxter a grasping actress, Sanders a poison-pen critic, Marlowe a playwright, and Holm his sugary wife. Many Oscars include Best Picture, Best Direction, Best Screenplay, Best Supporting Actor (Sanders).

All American, The (1953) 83m. ** D: Jesse Hibbs. Tony Curtis, Lori Nelson, Richard Long, Mamie Van Doren, Gregg Palmer, Stuart Whitman. Football is secondary aspect of typical romance story between two wholesome young people (Curtis-Nelson).

All-American Boy, The (1973) C-118m. ** D: Charles Eastman. Jon Voight, E. J. Peaker, Ned Glass, Anne Archer, Carol Androsky. Muddled drama about Olympic hopeful Voight's attempt to succeed as a boxer; striking locations of northern California, but that's all.

All Ashore (1953) C-80m. *½ D: Richard Quine. Mickey Rooney, Dick Haymes, Peggy Ryan, Ray MacDonald. Musical yarn of three gobs on shore leave finding gals, sinks despite Rooney's sprite spirit.

All at Sea (1958-British) 87m. *** D: Charles Frend. Alec Guinness, Irene Browne, Percy Herbert, Harold Goodwin. Robust comedy that holds its own throughout. Guinness is admirable as seaman who can't bear sight of water but buys rundown house-laden pier, turning it into an amusement palace.

All Creatures Great and Small (1974) C-92m. *** D: Claude Whatham. Simon Ward, Anthony Hopkins, Lisa Harrow, Brian Stirner, Freddie Jones, T. P. McKenna. Gentle drama about rural English life, taken from James Herriot's autobiographical best-sellers (*If Only They Could Talk* and *It Shouldn't Happen to a Vet*). Ward plays the author in his younger days as apprentice to an eccentric veterinarian, wonderfully acted by Hopkins. Rich period piece.

All Fall Down (1962) 110m. *** D: John Frankenheimer. Warren Beatty, Eva Marie Saint, Karl Malden, Angela Lansbury, Brandon de Wilde. Improbable but absorbing William Inge script about narcissistic young man (Beatty), his admiring younger brother (de Wilde), indulgent parents (Lansbury and Malden), and the older woman (Saint) who suffers tragic results from loving him. Fine performances.

All Hands on Deck (1961) C-98m. ** D: Norman Taurog. Pat Boone, Buddy Hackett, Dennis O'Keefe, Barbara Eden. Innocuous musical comedy of free-wheeling sailors, Boone and Hackett, is lightweight entertainment.

All I Desire (1953) 70m. **½ D: Douglas Sirk. Barbara Stanwyck, Richard Carlson, Lyle Bettger, Lori Nelson, Maureen O'Sullivan. Family togetherness and home-town approval is answer to title, in period-piece uplifted by Stanwyck's valiant performance as erring mother of three who returns to her husband.

All in a Night's Work (1961) C-94m. **½ D: Joseph Anthony. Dean Martin, Shirley MacLaine, Charlie Ruggles, Cliff Robertson. MacLaine was seen leaving room of wealthy executive just before he died; nephew Martin fears she will blackmail the company to keep her "liaison" with the old man quiet. Pleasant formula comedy.

All Mine to Give (1957) C-102m. **½ D: Allen Reisner. Cameron Mitchell, Glynis Johns, Patty McCormack, Hope Emerson. Often touching story of pioneer family in Wisconsin determined to overcome all obstacles.

All My Darling Daughters (1972) C-73m. TVM D: David Lowell Rich. Robert Young, Eve Arden, Raymond Massey, Darleen Carr, Judy Strangis, Jerry Fogel, Darrel Larson. Daughters of Judge Charles Raleigh (Young) all decide to get married on same day. Some amusing incidents.

All My Sons (1948) 94m. *** D: Irving Reis. Edward G. Robinson, Burt Lancaster, Mady Christians, Louisa Horton, Howard Duff. Arthur Miller's compelling drama of family discovering their father's unsavory business ethics during WW2 is well-acted, but quite verbose.

All Night Long (1961-British) 95m. ** D: Michael Relph, Basil Dearden.

Patrick McGoohan, Marti Stevens, Betsy Blair, Keith Michell, Richard Attenborough. Bland mixture of jazz music with modern parable on Othello love triangle. Guest appearances by Dave Brubeck, Tubby Hayes, et al.

All of Me (1934) 75m. ** D: James Flood. Fredric March, Miriam Hopkins, George Raft, Helen Mack, Blanche Frederici. Ineffectual melodrama of professor March yearning for open spaces and lover Hopkins learning about true devotion from gun moll Mack.

All Over Town (1937) 62m. **½ D: James W. Horne. Ole Olsen, Chic Johnson, Mary Howard, Harry Stockwell, Franklin Pangborn, James Finlayson. Low-budget shenanigans, with Olsen and Johnson trying to stage a show in a "jinxed" theater. Spotty, but has some very funny moments.

All Quiet on the Western Front (1930) 105m. **** D: Lewis Milestone. Lew Ayres, Louis Wolheim, Russell Gleason, Beryl Mercer, Ben Alexander, Slim Summerville. Brilliant film of Erich Maria Remarque's pacifist WW1 novel; beautifully acted and directed, with many memorable scenes and an unforgettable ending. Originally released at 140m.

All Screwed Up (1976-Italian) C-105m. *** D: Lina Wertmuller. Luigi Diberti, Nino Bignamini, Lina Polito, Sara Rapisarda. Appealing tragicomedy of two farmers trying to make it in the big city. Wertmuller made it between SEDUCTION OF MIMI and SEVEN BEAUTIES.

All That Heaven Allows (1955) C-89m. *** D: Douglas Sirk. Jane Wyman, Rock Hudson, Agnes Moorehead, Virginia Grey, Conrad Nagel. When widow Wyman allows younger man Hudson to romance her, she faces the ire of friends and society. Nicely mounted production.

All That Jazz (1979) C-123m. **½ D: Bob Fosse. Roy Scheider, Jessica Lange, Ann Reinking, Leland Palmer, Cliff Gorman, Ben Vereen, Erzsebet Foldi. Director-choreographer Fosse's own 8½ casts a self-indulgent and largely negative look at his life; great show biz moments and wonderful dancing are eventually buried in pretensions, and an interminable finale which leaves a bad taste for the whole film.

All That Money Can Buy (1941)

[14]

85m. ***½ D: William Dieterle. Edward Arnold, Walter Huston, James Craig, Anne Shirley, Jane Darwell, Simone Simon, Gene Lockhart. Stephen Vincent Benet's THE DEVIL AND DANIEL WEBSTER is a visual delight with Huston's sparkling performance as "Mr. Scratch" (the Devil) matched by Arnold as the loquacious Webster. Even though current print is cut from 112m. original, it's still a must.

All the Brothers Were Valiant (1953) **C-101m. **½ D: Richard Thorpe.** Robert Taylor, Stewart Granger, Ann Blyth, Keenan Wynn, James Whitmore, Lewis Stone. Water-logged adventurer based on Ben Ames Williams' novel. Taylor and Granger lack conviction as New Bedford whalers having career and romantic conflicts.

All the Fine Young Cannibals (1960) **C-112m. *½ D: Michael Anderson.** Robert Wagner, Natalie Wood, Susan Kohner, George Hamilton, Pearl Bailey, Anne Seymour. Trio of young lovers in a soaper with clichés galore; Pearl Bailey is paired with Robert Wagner.

All the Kind Strangers (1974) **C-78m. TVM D: Burt Kennedy.** Stacy Keach, Samantha Eggar, John Savage, Robby Benson, Arlene Farber, Tim Parkison. Seven backwoods orphans turn remote farmhouse into prison for unsuspecting Keach and Eggar. Children want them to be their foster parents, or disappear permanently. Below average.

All the King's Men (1949) **109m. **** D: Robert Rossen.** Broderick Crawford, Joanne Dru, John Ireland, Mercedes McCambridge, John Derek, Shepperd Strudwick, Anne Seymour. Brilliant adaptation of Robert Penn Warren's Pulitzer Prize winning novel about the rise and fall of a Huey Long-like senator, played by Crawford in the performance of his career. He and McCambridge won well-deserved Oscars.

All the President's Men (1976) **C-138m. **** D: Alan J. Pakula.** Robert Redford, Dustin Hoffman, Jason Robards, Jack Warden, Martin Balsam, Hal Holbrook, Jane Alexander. Redford and Hoffman play real-life *Washington Post* reporters Bob Woodward and Carl Bernstein, who persevered in their investigation of Watergate break-in that led to earthshaking scandal. Best elements of newspaper pictures, detective stories, and thrillers rolled into one superb movie. Robards and screenwriter William Goldman won Oscars.

All the Way Home (1963) **103m. ***½ D: Alex Segal.** Jean Simmons, Robert Preston, Aline MacMahon, Pat Hingle, Michael Kearny, John Cullum, Thomas Chalmers. Outstanding film of James Agee's A DEATH IN THE FAMILY. Preston is subdued in pivotal role (set in rural 1910 America) of father who is accidentally killed, leaving family to interpret meaning of their lives before and after his death. Beautifully done.

All the Young Men (1960) **87m. **½ D: Hall Bartlett.** Alan Ladd, Sidney Poitier, James Darren, Glenn Corbett, Mort Sahl. Hackneyed Korean war story with all the stereotypes present, mouthing the same old platitudes.

All These Women (1964-Swedish) **C-80m. **½ D: Ingmar Bergman.** Jarl Kulle, Harriet Andersson, Bibi Andersson, Allan Edwall. Satirical frolic involving woman-chasing cellist. He bargains with music critic to have biography written by agreeing to play writer's composition.

All This and Heaven Too (1940) **143m. *** D: Anatole Litvak.** Bette Davis, Charles Boyer, Jeffrey Lynn, Barbara O'Neil, Virginia Weidler, Helen Westley, Walter Hampden. Nobleman Boyer falls in love with governess Davis, causing scandal and death; stars do very well in elaborate filmization of Rachel Field book set in 19th-century France.

All This and World War II (1976) **C-88m. ** D: Susan Winslow.** Unusual documentary traces chronology of WW2 with Movietone newsreels and 20th Century-Fox feature film footage, all set to Beatles music! Not as bad as it sounds, but not particularly good either, because there is no point—or point of view.

All Together Now (1975) **C-78m. TVM D: Randall Kleiser.** John Rubinstein, Glynnis O'Connor, Brad Savage, Helen Hunt, Dori Brenner, Bill Macy, Jane Withers. Fact-based tale of orphaned college student who has thirty days to prove himself a fit guardian for his younger brothers and sisters. Inspiring drama. Above average.

All Through the Night (1942) **107m. *** D: Vincent Sherman.** Humphrey Bogart, Conrad Veidt, Kaaren Verne, Jane Darwell, Frank McHugh, Peter

Lorre, Judith Anderson, Jackie Gleason, Phil Silvers. Bogart's gang tracks down Fifth Columnists (Veidt, Lorre, Anderson) in WW2 N.Y.C. Interesting blend of spy, gangster, and comedy genres, with memorable double-talk scene.

Allegheny Uprising (1939) 81m. *** D: William Seiter. John Wayne, Claire Trevor, George Sanders, Brian Donlevy, Robert Barrat, Moroni Olsen, Chill Wills. Wayne leads band of brave men against crooked Donlevy, tyrannical British captain Sanders in pre-Revolutionary colonies. Fine, unpretentious film; Trevor appealing as girl who goes after Wayne.

Alligator Named Daisy, An (1957-British) C-88m. **½ D: J. Lee Thompson. Diana Dors, Donald Sinden, Stanley Holloway, Roland Culver, Margaret Rutherford, Stephen Boyd. Dors reveals pleasing comic talent in fabricated account of salesman who mistakenly picks up someone else's alligator suitcase, leading to complications.

Alligator People, The (1959) 74m. **½ D: Roy Del Ruth. Beverly Garland, George Macready, Lon Chaney, Richard Crane, Frieda Inescort, Bruce Bennett. OK horror entry details transformation of a man into part-reptile; makeup artist is star of production.

Allotment Wives (1945) 83m. ** D: William Nigh. Kay Francis, Paul Kelly, Otto Kruger, Gertrude Michael, Teala Loring. Mild sensationalism involving women who marry servicemen to collect their military pay; not one of Francis' better films.

Almost a Bride SEE: **Kiss For Corliss, A**

Almost Angels (1962) C-93m. **½ D: Steve Previn. Peter Weck, Hans Holt, Fritz Eckhardt, Bruni Lobel, Vincent Winter, Sean Scully. Schmaltzy but entertaining Disney film about two youngsters who become friends in the Vienna Boys Choir. Pleasant story, fine music.

Almost Perfect Affair, An (1979) C-93m. **½ D: Michael Ritchie. Keith Carradine, Monica Vitti, Raf Vallone, Christian De Sica, Dick Anthony Williams. Romantic comedy drama about affair between naive American filmmaker and worldly wife of film producer; set against whirring backdrop of Cannes Film Festival, it will appeal mostly to film buffs and insiders.

Almost Summer (1978) C-88m. *½

D: Martin Davidson. Bruno Kirby, Lee Purcell, John Friedrich, Didi Conn, Thomas Carter, Tim Matheson. End-of-term frolics, and a cutthroat school election, are presented here in much the same fashion as BEACH BLANKET BINGO.

Aloha, Bobby and Rose (1975) C-90m. ** D: Floyd Mutrux. Paul Le Mat, Dianne Hull, Tim McIntire, Leigh French, Martine Bartlett, Robert Carradine. OK melodrama follows predictable pattern as auto mechanic Le Mat (the drag-racer from AMERICAN GRAFFITI) and girlfriend Hull are inadvertently drawn into crime, causing them to take it on the lam with the law in pursuit.

Aloha Means Goodbye (1974) C-100m. TVM D: David Lowell Rich. Sally Struthers, James Franciscus, Joanna Miles, Henry Darrow, Larry Gates, Frank Marth. Young woman fights for her life against rare blood disease and an unscrupulous doctor in need of heart-transplant donor, but manages to enjoy location beauty of Hawaii. Ludicrous. Below average.

Aloma of the South Seas (1941) C-77m. ** D: Alfred Santell. Dorothy Lamour, Jon Hall, Lynne Overman, Philip Reed, Katherine DeMille. Still another sarong saga with native Hall sent to U.S. for education, returning when father dies to stop revolution on once peaceful island.

Along Came a Spider (1969) C-75m. TVM D: Lee Katzin. Suzanne Pleshette, Ed Nelson, Andrew Prine, Brooke Bundy, Richard Anderson, Milton Selzer. Entertaining, occasionally moving drama featuring Pleshette as widow of research scientist torn between instincts and need for vengeance as she befriends scientist professor (Nelson) who had worked on same project that brought about deadly accident. Complete with nail-biting finish; note depiction of college campus. Above average.

Along Came Jones (1945) 90m. *** D: Stuart Heisler. Gary Cooper, Loretta Young, William Demarest, Dan Duryea, Frank Sully, Russell Simpson. Cooper, Young, and Demarest are most ingratiating in very low-key, leisurely Western spoof, with Cooper mistaken for notorious outlaw Duryea.

Along the Great Divide (1951) 88m. **½ D: Raoul Walsh. Kirk Douglas, Virginia Mayo, John Agar, Walter

Brennan. Douglas is appropriately tight-lipped as lawman determined to bring in his man, despite desert storm; some spectacular scenery.

Alpha Caper, The (1973) **C-73m.** TVM D: Robert Michael Lewis. Henry Fonda, Leonard Nimoy, James McEachin, Larry Hagman, John Marley, Elena Verdugo, Noah Beery. Parole officer Forbes (Fonda), disenchanted with the System, convinces three paroled criminals to join him in an armored-car robbery scheme. Emphasis on action and suspense in mechanical narrative brightened only by good cast. Average.

Alphabet Murders, The (1966-British) **90m.** **½ D: Frank Tashlin. Tony Randall, Anita Ekberg, Robert Morley, Guy Rolfe. Flat spy spoof with Randall as Hercule Poirot in England, confounding British Intelligence while trying to find missing Ekberg.

Alphaville (1965-French) **100m.** ** D: Jean-Luc Godard. Eddie Constantine, Anna Karina, Akim Tamiroff, Howard Vernon. Constantine, as super private-eye Lemmy Caution, is sent to futuristic city run by electronic brain to rescue scientist trapped there. Jumbled Godard epic, recommended for New Wave disciples only.

Alvarez Kelly (1966) **C-116m.** **½ D: Edward Dmytryk. William Holden, Richard Widmark, Janice Rule, Victoria Shaw, Patrick O'Neal. Slow-moving Civil War tale. Holden is cattle driver who sells herd to Yankees, then is kidnapped by Reb Widmark who wants him to steal cattle for the South; incongruous love scenes thrown in.

Always a Bride (1954-British) **83m.** ** D: Ralph Smart. Peggy Cummins, Terence Morgan, Ronald Squire, James Hayter. Mild comedy of treasury officer romancing girl, aiding her dad to fleece others.

Always Goodbye (1938) **75m.** **½ D: Sidney Lanfield. Barbara Stanwyck, Herbert Marshall, Ian Hunter, Cesar Romero, Lynn Bari, Binnie Barnes. Still another sacrificing mother tale as Stanwyck is forced to give up her illicit child; nicely done, but the same story.

Always in My Heart (1942) **92m.** *½ D: Jo Graham. Kay Francis, Walter Huston, Gloria Warren, Una O'Connor, Sidney Blackmer. Soaper of convict Huston returning to find wife Francis about to marry Blackmer and a daughter (Warren) who doesn't know him.

Always Leave Them Laughing (1949) **116m.** **½ D: Roy Del Ruth. Milton Berle, Virginia Mayo, Ruth Roman, Bert Lahr, Alan Hale. Berle is at home in tale of cocky comedian's ups and downs. Unfortunately, zesty opening leads into soggy drama. Lahr does his classic "stop in the name of the stationhouse" routine.

Always Together (1948) **78m.** **½ D: Frederick de Cordova. Robert Hutton, Joyce Reynolds, Cecil Kellaway, Ernest Truex; guests Humphrey Bogart, Jack Carson, Dennis Morgan, Janis Paige, Alexis Smith. Innocuous fluff of dying millionaire Kellaway giving money to young Reynolds, then discovering he's quite healthy. Worthwhile only for amusing cameos by many Warner Brothers stars throughout film.

Amarcord (1974-Italian) **C-127m.** ***½ D: Federico Fellini. Magali Noel, Bruno Zanin, Pupella Maggio, Armando Brancia, Giuseppe Lanigro, Josiane Tanzilli. Fellini's nostalgia trip to the Italy of his youth in the 1930s; warm, funny, poignant, bawdy episodes about love, sex, politics, family life, and growing up. Academy Award winner as Best Foreign Film.

Amateur Night at the Dixie Bar and Grill (1979) **C-100m.** TVM D: Joel Schumacher. Victor French, Candy Clark, Louise Latham, Sheree North, Jamie Farr, Henry Gibson. Multi-character comedy drama about country-western talent show at a Southern roadhouse. Surprisingly good vignettes in this film reminiscent of Robert Altman's NASH-VILLE. Above average.

Amazing Colossal Man, The (1957) **80m.** **½ D: Bert I. Gordon. Glenn Langan, Cathy Downs, James Seay, Larry Thor. Thought-provoking sci-fi detailing the mental turmoil army officer undergoes when radioactive explosion causes him to grow to mammoth proportions.

Amazing Dobermans, The (1976) **C-94m.** **½ D: David & Byron Chudnow. James Franciscus, Barbara Eden, Fred Astaire, Jack Carter, Billy Barty. Engaging action comedy that has Bible-quoting ex-con-man Astaire's five remarkable Doberman pinschers help treasury agent Franciscus thwart a racketeer and his gang. Higher-budgeted sequel to THE DOBERMAN GANG and THE DARING DOBERMANS, aided by offbeat casting of Astaire.

Amazing Grace (1974) **C-99m.** ** D:

Stan Lathan. Moms Mabley, Slappy White, Moses Gunn, Rosalind Cash, Dolph Sweet. A few laughs in Philadelphia-made comedy about an elderly busybody who disrupts corrupt Baltimore politics. Mabley's only starring film; cameos by Butterfly McQueen, unrecognizable Stepin Fetchit.

Amazing Howard Hughes, The (1977) C-215m. TVM D: William A. Graham. Tommy Lee Jones, Ed Flanders, James Hampton, Tovah Feldshuh, Lee Purcell, Jim Antonio, Sorrell Booke, Arthur Franz. Surprisingly colorless account of the reclusive millionaire's life. Jones' dull performance easily overshadowed by Flanders as associate Noah Dietrich, Feldshuh as Katharine Hepburn. Occasional intrigue in this ambitious production. Average.

Amazing Doctor Clitterhouse, The (1938) 87m. *** D: Anatole Litvak. Edward G. Robinson, Claire Trevor, Humphrey Bogart, Allen Jenkins, Donald Crisp, Gale Page. Amusing film of "method doctor" Robinson trying to discover what makes a crook tick; he joins Bogart's gang and becomes addicted.

Amazing Mr. Blunden, The (1972-British) C-99m. *** D: Lionel Jeffries. Laurence Naismith, Lynne Frederick, Garry Miller, Rosalyn Landor, Marc Granger, Diana Dors, James Villiers. Dickensian fantasy about a genial ghost who takes two children back in time to help two mistreated tots. Colorful family film whose only liability is somewhat muddled storyline.

Amazing Mr. Williams (1939) 80m. **½ D: Alexander Hall. Melvyn Douglas, Joan Blondell, Clarence Kolb, Ruth Donnelly. Douglas holds up his marriage to investigate murder in this satisfying comedy-mystery.

Amazing Mr. X, The (1948) 78m. **½ D: Bernard Vorhaus. Turhan Bey, Lynn Bari, Cathy O'Donnell, Richard Carlson, Donald Curtis. Phony mystic (Bey) teams up with supposedly dead man (Curtis) to dupe his wealthy "widow" (Bari). Modest but intriguing little film.

Amazing Mrs. Holliday, The (1943) 96m. **½ D: Bruce Manning. Deanna Durbin, Edmond O'Brien, Barry Fitzgerald, Arthur Treacher, Frieda Inescort. Lukewarm WW2 comedy-drama about dedicated missionary Durbin trying to sneak Chinese orphans into U.S. Durbin's

song interludes offer respite from silly plot.

Amazing Transparent Man, The (1960) 58m. BOMB. D: Edgar G. Ulmer. Marguerite Chapman, Douglas Kennedy, James Griffith, Ivan Triesault. Tawdry sci-fi of stereotyped mad scientist inventing formula to make an invisible man his accomplice in bank robberies.

Ambassador's Daughter, The (1956) C-102m. **½ D: Norman Krasna. Olivia de Havilland, John Forsythe, Myrna Loy, Adolphe Menjou. Oomph is missing even though stars give all to uplift sagging comedy of De Havilland out for a fling in Paris, romanced by soldier Forsythe.

Ambush (1949) 89m. **½ D: Sam Wood. Robert Taylor, John Hodiak, Arlene Dahl, Jean Hagen, Chief Thundercloud. Pat Western with Apaches vs. Cavalry, salvaged by star cast.

Ambush at Cimarron Pass (1958) 73m. ** D: Jodie Copelan, Scott Brady, Margia Dean, Baynes Barron, William Vaughn. Title tells all. Look for young Clint Eastwood.

Ambush at Tomahawk Gap (1953) C-73m. *½ D: Fred F. Sears. John Hodiak, John Derek, David Brian, Percy Helton, Maria Elena Marques. Standard oater has quartet of ex-convicts caught by Indian attack. One is left alive; he rides into sunset with newly-found squaw.

Ambush Bay (1966) C-109m. **½ D: Ron Winston. Hugh O'Brian, Mickey Rooney, James Mitchum, Harry Lauter. Lackluster adventures of marine group on Jap-held island during WW2 trying to help partisans—good cast wasted.

Ambush in Leopard Street (1961-British) 60m. *½ D: J. Henry Piperno. James Kenney, Michael Brennan, Bruce Seton, Norman Rodway. Listless crime tale involving heist of diamond shipment.

Ambushers, The (1967) C-102m. **½ D: Henry Levin. Dean Martin, Senta Berger, Janice Rule, James Gregory, Albert Salmi, Kurt Kasznar, Beverly Adams. Usual Matt Helm nonsense; if you liked the others in this series, this will probably suit your taste. As usual, there are plenty of gorgeous girls to hold male viewers' attention.

Amelia Earhart (1976) C-150m. TVM D: George Schaefer. Susan Clark, John Forsythe, Stephen Macht, Susan Oliver, Catherine Burns, Jane Wyatt,

Charles Aidman. Intriguing portrait of a unique woman, her private and public careers, her search for fulfillment as a noted aviatrix. Susan Clark brings famed flier vibrantly to life as a pioneer in women's lib as well as aviation. Compliments, too, to Carol Sobieski for her excellent screenplay. Above average.

America (1924) 93m. *** D: D.W. Griffith. Neil Hamilton, Carol Dempster, Erville Alderson, Charles Emmett Mack, Lee Beggs, Frank McGlynn, Lionel Barrymore. Impressive silent-film treatment of Revolutionary War, with fine battle scenes, period flavor, marred somewhat by silly love story; florid villainy by Barrymore. Still quite good.

America, America (1963) 174m. **** D: Elia Kazan. Stathis Giallelis, Frank Wolff, Elena Karam, Lou Antonio, John Marley, Estelle Hemsley. The dream of passage to America—as it unfolded for late 19th-century immigrants—is movingly captured by writer-director Kazan in this long, absorbing film, based on his uncle's experiences. Heartfelt and heart-rending.

American Christmas Carol, An (1979) C-100m. TVM D: Eric Till. Henry Winkler, David Wayne, Dorian Harewood, Chris Wiggins, R. H. Thompson, Susan Hogan. A lot of facial putty turns "The Fonz" into Scrooge for this update of Dickens' classic set in a Depression-era New England town. Average.

American Dream, An (1966) C-103m. **½ D: Robert Gist. Stuart Whitman, Eleanor Parker, Janet Leigh, Barry Sullivan, Lloyd Nolan. Distorted, watered-down Norman Mailer novel, dealing superficially with TV commentator who's wanted by underworld and police for murdering his wife; nightmare sequences are sterile.

American Empire (1942) 82m. **½ D: William McGann. Richard Dix, Leo Carrillo, Preston Foster, Frances Gifford, Guinn Williams. Dix and Foster join forces to develop cattle empire in Texas after Civil War, but not without problems. Pretty good outdoor actioner.

American Gigolo (1980) C-117m. BOMB D: Paul Schrader. Richard Gere, Lauren Hutton, Hector Elizondo, Nina Van Pallandt. Schrader presents his weakest variation yet on his favorite theme, the seamy side of American life. Feeble morality play, posing as a thriller, is

further undermined by neurasthenic acting and some of the unsexiest sex scenes of all time.

American Graffiti (1973) C-110m. ***½ D: George Lucas. Richard Dreyfuss, Ronny Howard, Paul Le-Mat, Charlie Martin Smith, Cindy Williams, Candy Clark, Mackenzie Phillips, Wolfman Jack, Harrison Ford, Bo Hopkins, Kathy Quinlan, Suzanne Somers. Highly entertaining, insightful mosaic about youngsters "coming of age" after high-school graduation in 1962. Often hilarious, always on-target, this film made Dreyfuss a star and boosted many other careers. Reedited to 112m. for 1978 reissue to play up latter-day stars.

American Guerila in the Philippines (1950) C-105m. **½ D: Fritz Lang. Tyrone Power, Micheline Prelle, Tom Ewell, Jack Elam. If one ignores flaws in overpatriotic script, film is agreeable account of naval officer Power left behind enemy lines on WW2 Pacific island, helping natives combat Japanese.

American Hot Wax (1978) C-91m. *** D: Floyd Mutrux. Tim McIntire, Fran Drescher, Jay Leno, Laraine Newman, Jeff Altman, Chuck Berry, Jerry Lee Lewis, Screamin' Jay Hawkins. Fabricated story of controversial 1950s disc jockey Alan Freed. Uneven dramatically, but McIntire is excellent, period flavor is strong, and the original rock 'n' roll acts are fun to see.

American in Paris, An (1951) C-113m. ***½ D: Vincente Minnelli. Gene Kelly, Leslie Caron, Oscar Levant, Georges Guetary, Nina Foch. Joyous, original musical built around Gershwin score; dazzling in color. Plot of artist Kelly torn between gamine Caron and wealthy Foch is creaky, but the songs, dances, production are superb. Oscars include Best Picture.

American Madness (1932) 81m. *** D: Frank Capra. Walter Huston, Pat O'Brien, Kay Johnson, Constance Cummings, Gavin Gordon. Huston is dynamic as a put-upon bank president in the depths of the Great Depression; vivid, upbeat film marred only by idiotic romantic subplot.

American Romance, An (1944) C-122m. **½ D: King Vidor. Brian Donlevy, Ann Richards, Walter Abel, John Qualen, Stephen McNally. Long, flavorful story of immigrant steelworker's rise to wealth and power. Might have been a better film with someone more magnetic than Donlevy in the lead.

American Success Company, The (1979) C-94m. *½ D: William Richert. Jeff Bridges, Belinda Bauer, Ned Beatty, Steven Keats, Bianca Jagger, John Glover. If you liked WINTER KILLS you might enjoy this black-comedy from writer-director Richert; Bridges plays a loser who decides to assert himself and score in business and in sex. Offbeat, to say the least.

American Tragedy, An (1931) 95m. ** D: Josef von Sternberg. Phillips Holmes, Sylvia Sidney, Frances Dee, Irving Pichel, Frederick Burton, Claire McDowell. Straightforward telling of Theodore Dreiser story about weak young man torn between poor girlfriend and beautiful, wealthy girl who falls in love with him. Sidney is ideally cast, but film is cold and uninvolving; certainly not as florid as remake A PLACE IN THE SUN.

Americanization of Emily, The (1964) 117m. ***½ D: Arthur Hiller. James Garner, Julie Andrews, Melvyn Douglas, James Coburn, Joyce Grenfell, Keenan Wynn, Judy Carne. Garner is fall guy for U.S. admiral's master plan to have American naval officer first Normandy invasion victim, with predictable results. Cynical Garner-Andrews romance blends well with realistic view of life among U.S. military brass.

Americano, The (1955) C-85m. **½ D: William Castle. Glenn Ford, Cesar Romero, Frank Lovejoy, Ursula Thiess, Abbe Lane. Good-guy Ford meets Brazilian bad-guys in standard Western, with change of scenery as major asset.

Americathon (1979) C-90m. BOMB D: Neil Israel. Harvey Korman, John Ritter, Nancy Morgan, Peter Riegert, Fred Willard, Zane Buzby. Unfunny comedy about life in 1998, when America must hold a telethon in order to raise money to save itself. Only spark is set by Buzby as Vietnamese punk-rocker.

Amityville Horror, The (1979) C-117m. ** D: Stuart Rosenberg. James Brolin, Margot Kidder, Rod Steiger, Don Stroud, Murray Hamilton, Michael Sacks, Helen Shaver. Even Steiger's hammiest acting can't kill off the unseen power that dominates the "dream home" of a newlywed couple. Trashy adaptation of Jay Anson's equally trashy bestseller will at least make you feel better about the roaches in your own apartment.

Among the Living (1941) 69m. **½ D: Stuart Heisler. Albert Dekker, Susan Hayward, Harry Carey, Frances Farmer, Gordon Jones. Twin brother murderer causes trouble for innocent Dekker in tense drama.

Amorous Adventures of Moll Flanders, The (1965-British) C-126m. **½ D: Terence Young. Kim Novak, Richard Johnson, Angela Lansbury, George Sanders, Vittorio De Sica, Lilli Palmer, Leo McKern, Cecil Parker. Billed as female Tom Jones, Moll is far from thrilling. Fine cast romps through 18th-century England from bedroom to boudoir, but film needs more spice than Novak can muster.

Amorous Mr. Prawn, The (1962-British) 89m. **½ D: Anthony Kimmins. Joan Greenwood, Cecil Parker, Ian Carmichael, Robert Beatty. Diverting fluff finds wife (Greenwood) of general (Parker) devising a scheme to obtain badly needed money so they can retire in style.

Amsterdam Affair (1968-British) C-91m. **½ D: Gerry O'Hara. Wolfgang Kieling, William Marlowe, Catherine von Schell, Pamela Ann Davy, Josef Dubin-Behrman. Inspector believes there's more to young woman's murder than supposed open-and-shut case against her lover would indicate. Passable thriller, pleasing Amsterdam locations.

Amsterdam Kill, The (1977) C-90m. **½ D: Robert Clouse. Robert Mitchum, Bradford Dillman, Richard Egan, Leslie Nielsen, Keye Luke. Tired drug bust movie gets a shot from Mitchum's presence as a retired narc who's lured back by a former colleague suspected of being part of an international dope ring.

Anastasia (1956) C-105m. **** D: Anatole Litvak. Ingrid Bergman, Yul Brynner, Helen Hayes, Akim Tamiroff. Inspired casting makes this film exceptional. Bergman won Oscar as amnesiac refugee selected by Brynner to impersonate surviving daughter of Russia's last czar. Confrontation scene in which Hayes as grand duchess must determine if girl is her relative is grand.

Anatomist, The (1961-British) 73m. ** D: Leonard William. Alastair Sim, George Cole, Jill Bennett, Margaret Gordon. Respected surgeon encourages corpse-stealing for experiments, causing rash of murders. Sim is wry in tame spooker.

Anatomy of a Marriage (1964-French) 193m. **½ D: André Cayatte. Comprised of: "My Days with Jean-Marc" and "My Nights with Françoise." Jacques Charrier, Marie-Jose Nat, Georges Rivière, Macha Meril. Well-intentioned film which through its two parts attempts to analyze problems of young married couple from each one's point of view; becomes repetitious.

Anatomy of a Murder (1959) 160m. **** D: Otto Preminger. James Stewart, Lee Remick, Ben Gazzara, Arthur O'Connell, Eve Arden, Kathryn Grant, George C. Scott, Orson Bean, Murray Hamilton. Long, exciting courtroom drama; daring when released, tamer now. Large cast is fine: O'Connell as drunken lawyer aroused by Stewart, Joseph Welch as judge, Scott as prosecuting attorney. But Stewart towers over all as witty, easygoing, but cagy defense lawyer. Duke Ellington score.

Anatomy of a Seduction (1979) C-100m. TVM D: Steven Hilliard Stern. Susan Flannery, Jameson Parker, Rita Moreno, Ed Nelson, Michael LeClair. Romantic soaper about frosty divorcee's affair with bosom buddy's college-age son—who is also her own son's best friend. Average.

Anatomy of a Syndicate SEE: **Big Operator, The**

Anchors Aweigh (1945) C-140m. **½ D: George Sidney. Frank Sinatra, Kathryn Grayson, Gene Kelly, Jose Iturbi, Dean Stockwell, Pamela Britton. Popular 40s musical of sailors on leave doesn't hold up storywise, but musical numbers still good: Sinatra's "I Fall in Love Too Easily." Kelly's irresistible dance with Jerry the cartoon mouse.

And Baby Makes Six (1979) C-100m. TVM D: Waris Hussein. Colleen Dewhurst, Warren Oates, Maggie Cooper, Mildred Dunnock, Timothy Hutton, Allyn Ann McLerie. Middle-aged couple with three grown children face parenthood again. Dewhurst pulls this one up by its bootstraps. Above average.

And Baby Makes Three (1949) 84m. ** D: Henry Levin. Robert Young, Barbara Hale, Robert Hutton, Billie Burke, Melville Cooper. OK comedy has Hale about to marry for second time, only to discover she's pregnant, and she really does want to stay married to Hubby #1 (Young).

And God Created Woman (1957-French) C-92m. **½ D: Roger Vadim. Brigitte Bardot, Curt Jurgens, Jean-Louis Trintignant, Christian Marquand, Georges Poujouly, Jean Tissier. Location shooting (at St. Tropez) and famous Bardot figure on display in simple tale of man-teaser finding it hard to resist temptation. Great cast clicks. Beware cuts.

And Hope to Die (1972-French) C-99m. *** D: René Clement. Robert Ryan, Tisa Farrow, Jean-Louis Trintignant, Lea Massari, Aldo Ray. Above-average caper with offbeat touches; gang hired to kidnap girl goes through with scheme even though she's already dead.

And I Alone Survived (1978) C-100m. TVM D: William A. Graham. Blair Brown, David Ackroyd, Vera Miles, G. D. Spradlin, James G. Richardson. Middling dramatization of Lauren Elder's account of her ordeal following a plane crash in the Sierra Nevadas in the spring of 1976. Underdeveloped and overdramatic. Average.

. . . And Justice for All (1979) C-120m. **½ D: Norman Jewison. Al Pacino, Jack Warden, John Forsythe, Lee Strasberg, Jeffrey Tambor, Christine Lahti, Sam Levene. Lawyer Pacino single-handedly battles Maryland's judicial system. Outrageous satire mixes uncomfortably with painfully sad moments, in attempt to make biting statement on buying and selling of justice. Strong performances and good location photography cannot overcome weak script.

And Millions Will Die (1973) C-96m. ** D: Leslie Martinson. Richard Basehart, Susan Strasberg, Leslie Nielsen, Tony Wager, Peter Sumner. Environmental crisis expert Basehart is called in when it's discovered that a madman has buried a time bomb filled with deadly nerve gas beneath the streets of Hong Kong. Lackluster suspense story.

And No One Could Save Her (1973) C-73m. TVM D: Kevin Billington. Lee Remick, Milo O'Shea, Jennie Linden, Frank Grimes, Liam Redmond, Paul Maxwell. Fern O'Neil, young American newlywed, almost goes crazy when immigrant husband disappears mysteriously in Ireland, leaving no traces. Above average.

And Now For Something Completely Different (1972-British) C-89m. *** D: Ian McNaughton. Graham Chap-

[21]

man, John Cleese, Eric Idle, Terry Jones, Michael Palin, Carol Cleveland, Connie Booth. Stars of England's "Monty Python's Flying Circus" show provide rocky but often sidesplitting series of irreverent blackouts, plus some ingenious animated sequences. Fragmented nature makes film wear out its welcome after a half-hour; more tasteless segments will be cut for TV.

. . . And Now Miguel (1966) **C-95m.** *** D: James Clark. Pat Cardi, Michael Ansara, Guy Stockwell, Joe De Santis. Flavorful, leisurely paced account of young boy who wants to join his father on their summer mountain trip to graze sheep; set in Southwest.

And Now My Love (1975-French) **C-121m.** ***½ D: Claude Lelouch. Marthe Keller, Andre Dussollier, Charles Denner, Carla Gravina, Gilbert Becaud, Charles Gerard. A what'll-he-do-next kind of extravaganza, in which Lelouch salutes life, love and the 20th century, using comedy, drama, and music to bring wealthy Keller and ne'er do well Dussollier together for the final fadeout. Film opens in b&w.

And Now the Screaming Starts! (1973-British) **C-87m.** ** D: Roy Ward Baker. Peter Cushing, Stephanie Beacham, Herbert Lom, Patrick Magee, Ian Ogilvy. Beacham weds Ogilvy and finds that she's living in a house that has been under a curse for years; OK horror drama with a good cast.

And Now Tomorrow (1944) **85m.** **½ D: Irving Pichel. Alan Ladd, Loretta Young, Susan Hayward, Barry Sullivan, Beulah Bondi, Cecil Kellaway. Poor doctor Ladd falls in love with deaf socialite patient Young in this Rachel Field romance; sticky going at times.

And Quiet Flows the Don (1960-Russian) **C-107m.** *** D: Sergi Gerasimov. Ellina Bystritskaya, Pyotr Glebov, Zinaida Kirienko, Danilo Ilchenko. Faithful realization of Mikhail Sholokhov novel revolving around life of small village family during WW1 and postwar period. Absorbing study of social upheavals caused by revolution and war.

And So They Were Married (1936) **74m.** **½ D: Elliott Nugent. Melvyn Douglas, Mary Astor, Edith Fellows, Dorothy Stickney, Jackie Moran, Donald Meek. Predictable but amusing little comedy with good co-stars.

And So They Were Married (1944) SEE: **Johnny Doesn't Live Here Any More**

And Soon the Darkness (1970-British) **C-98m.** ** D: Robert Fuest. Pamela Franklin, Michele Dotrice, Sandor Eles, John Nettleton, Clare Kelly. Overly moody thriller with sexual undertones. Franklin is one of two vacationing British nurses bicycling thru rural France, menaced by mysterious sex murderer. Beware cuts.

And Suddenly It's Murder! (1964-Italian) **90m.** **½ D: Mario Camerini. Alberto Sordi, Vittorio Gassman, Silvana Mangano. Frail but frantic minor comedy satire revolving around trip of couples on the Riviera, each suspected of murder.

And the Angels Sing (1944) **96m.** **½ D: George Marshall. Dorothy Lamour, Fred MacMurray, Betty Hutton, Diana Lynn, Raymond Walburn, Eddie Foy Jr. Agreeable musical of singing sister act trying to make it big; MacMurray gives them their break. Brassy Hutton tries to steal the show.

And Then There Were None (1945) **98m.** **** D: Rene Clair. Barry Fitzgerald, Walter Huston, Louis Hayward, Roland Young, June Duprez, C. Aubrey Smith, Judith Anderson, Mischa Auer, Richard Haydn. Highly suspenseful Agatha Christie yarn of ten people invited to lonely island where one by one they're murdered. Great script complemented by superb visual ideas. Remade as TEN LITTLE INDIANS.

And Your Name Is Jonah (1979) **C-100m. TVM** D: Richard Michaels. Sally Struthers, James Woods, Randee Heller, Penny Stanton, Titos Vandis. Earnest drama about couple trying to cope with young son discovered to be deaf after being wrongly institutionalized as retarded. Average.

Anderson Tapes, The (1972) **C-98m.** *** D: Sidney Lumet. Sean Connery, Dyan Cannon, Martin Balsam, Ralph Meeker, Alan King, Margaret Hamilton. Fast-paced thriller of ex-con's master holdup plan, and strange electronic surveillances that have tracked him since he left prison. Climax is particularly exciting.

Androcles and the Lion (1952) **98m.** *** D: Chester Erskine. Jean Simmons, Alan Young, Victor Mature, Maurice Evans, Elsa Lanchester. Shaw's amusing satire of ancient Rome can't be dampened by dull production retelling fable of Christian and the lion he has befriended.

Andromeda Strain, The (1971) C-137m. **½ D: Robert Wise. Arthur Hill, David Wayne, James Olson, Kate Reid, Paula Kelly. Overlong sci-fi thriller in which small team of superscientists tries to isolate deadly strain of virus, racing against time and nuclear detonation. From Michael Crichton's book.

Andy (1965) 86m. *** D: Richard C. Sarafian. Norman Alden, Tamara Daykarhonova, Zvee Scooler, Murvyn Vye. Touching insight into existence of retarded middle-aged man and his unique problems in N.Y.C. slum life.

Andy Hardy One of the most popular series of all time, the Hardy family first appeared in A FAMILY AFFAIR (1937) with Lionel Barrymore and Mickey Rooney as father and son. In 1938 YOU'RE ONLY YOUNG ONCE began the official series in the town of Carvel, with Rooney as Andy Hardy, typical American teen-ager, interested in cars and girls, Lewis Stone as Judge James Hardy, a stern but understanding father, Fay Holden as his "swell" mother, Cecilia Parker as Marian, his older sister striving to be a young lady, Sara Haden as Aunt Millie, and Ann Rutherford as Polly, the girlfriend who was often neglected for other prospects but to whom Andy always returned; George B. Seitz directed most entries in the series. MGM used the films to springboard young starlets such as Judy Garland, Lana Turner, Esther Williams, Kathryn Grayson, and Donna Reed. The Andy Hardy films do not always wear well, with typical Rooney mugging and a plethora of 1940's slang dating them rather badly. In one film Andy tells his dad "You can say that again!" and the Judge replies, "Why should I say it again? Didn't you understand me the first time?" The sentimental nature of much of the series also doesn't fit into today's way of thinking, and in general the Hardy films serve mainly as reminders of an era in Hollywood and in America that is long gone. Indeed, when the cast, except Stone, was reunited, in 1958 for ANDY HARDY COMES HOME, the formula just didn't jell. What survives in the Hardy films is the very real talent that went into them.

Andy Hardy Comes Home (1958)

81m. D: Howard W. Koch. Mickey Rooney, Patricia Breslin, Fay Holden, Cecilia Parker, Sara Haden, Joey Forman, Jerry Colonna, Vaughn Taylor, Frank Ferguson.

Andy Hardy Gets Spring Fever (1939) 85m. D: W. S. Van Dyke II. Lewis Stone, Mickey Rooney, Cecilia Parker, Fay Holden, Ann Rutherford, Sara Haden, Addison Richards.

Andy Hardy Meets Debutante (1940) 86m. D: George B. Seitz. Mickey Rooney, Lewis Stone, Judy Garland, Cecilia Parker, Ann Rutherford, Fay Holden, Diana Lewis, Sara Haden.

Andy Hardy's Blonde Trouble (1944) 107m. D: George B. Seitz. Lewis Stone, Mickey Rooney, Fay Holden, Sara Haden, Herbert Marshall, Bonita Granville, Jean Porter, Keye Luke.

Andy Hardy's Double Life (1942) 92m. D: George B. Seitz. Mickey Rooney, Lewis Stone, Cecilia Parker, Fay Holden, Ann Rutherford, Sara Haden, Bobby Blake, William Lundigan, Susan Peters.

Andy Hardy's Private Secretary (1941) 101m. D: George B. Seitz. Mickey Rooney, Lewis Stone, Fay Holden, Ann Rutherford, Sara Haden, Kathryn Grayson, Ian Hunter, Gene Reynolds.

Angel (1937) 98m. ** D: Ernst Lubitsch. Marlene Dietrich, Herbert Marshall, Melvyn Douglas, Edward Everett Horton, Laura Hope Crews. Disappointing film for Dietrich-Lubitsch team about Marlene leaving husband Marshall for vacation, falling in love with Douglas. Not worthy of star trio.

Angel and the Badman (1947) 100m. *** D: James Edward Grant. John Wayne, Gail Russell, Harry Carey, Irene Rich, Bruce Cabot. First-rate Western with Russell humanizing gunfighter Wayne; predictable plot is extremely well handled.

Angel, Angel, Down We Go SEE: Cult of the Damned

Angel Baby (1961) 97m. *** D: Paul Wendkos, Hubert Cornfield. George Hamilton, Salome Jens, Mercedes McCambridge, Joan Blondell, Henry Jones, Burt Reynolds. Penetrating exposé of evangelistic circuit plying backwood country; Jens in title role, Hamilton the promoter, McCambridge his shrewish wife—marvelous cameos by Blondell and Jones.

Angel Face (1953) 90m. **½ D: Otto Preminger. Robert Mitchum, Jean

Simmons, Herbert Marshall, Mona Freeman, Leon Ames, Barbara O'Neil, Jim Backus. Title figure (Simmons) in slowly-paced film revealed as angel of death causing demise of those who love her.

Angel in My Pocket (1969) C-105m. ** D: Alan Rafkin. Andy Griffith, Lee Meriwether, Jerry Van Dyke, Kay Medford, Edgar Buchanan, Gary Collins. Fans of Griffith's TV series may enjoy homespun story of young minister trying to win confidence of new small-town parish. Predictable situations, cliché dialogue, with Van Dyke intolerable as obnoxious brother-in-law.

Angel Levine, The (1970) C-104m. ***½ D: Jan Kadar. Zero Mostel, Harry Belafonte, Ida Kaminska, Milo O'Shea, Eli Wallach, Anne Jackson, Gloria Foster. Touching, humorous, and sad. Black angel named Levine is on the outs with Heaven, so he tries to help poor old Morris Mishkin. A story many times told, but seldom this well.

Angel on My Shoulder (1946) 101m. *** D: Archie Mayo. Paul Muni, Anne Baxter, Claude Rains, George Cleveland, Onslow Stevens. Entertaining fantasy of murdered convict Muni sent to earth by Devil as respected judge, and his efforts to outwit Satan while still in mortal form.

Angel on the Amazon (1948) 86m. *½ D: John H. Auer. George Brent, Vera Ralston, Constance Bennett, Brian Aherne, Fortunio Bonanova. Ludicrous "romance" with Vera in a state of eternal youth; good cast can't rescue clumsy story.

Angel Wore Red, The (1960) 99m. **½ D: Nunnally Johnson. Ava Gardner, Dirk Bogarde, Joseph Cotten, Vittorio De Sica. Sometimes engrossing tale of clergyman who joins the Spanish loyalist cause and his romance with a good-natured entertainer.

Angela (1955) 81m. ** D: Dennis O'Keefe. Dennis O'Keefe, Mara Lane, Rossano Brazzi, Arnold Foa, Nino Crisman. Poor man's DOUBLE INDEMNITY has O'Keefe drawn into murder and double-dealing by seductive Lane. Standard programmer, filmed in Italy.

Angel's Alley (1948) 67m. D: William Beaudine. Leo Gorcey, Huntz Hall, Billy Benedict, David Gorcey. SEE: Bowery Boys series.

Angels in Disguise (1949) 63m. D: Jean Yarbrough. Leo Gorcey, Huntz

Hall, Gabriel Dell, Mickey Knox, Jean Dean, Bernard Gorcey. SEE Bowery Boys series.

Angels in the Outfield (1951) 102m. *** D: Clarence Brown. Paul Douglas, Janet Leigh, Keenan Wynn, Donna Corcoran. Engaging fantasy as heavenly forces help Pittsburgh Pirates go on a winning streak.

Angels of Darkness (1956-Italian) 84m. ** D: Giuseppe Amato. Linda Darnell, Anthony Quinn, Valentina Cortese, Lea Padovani. Aimless account of life and love among unhappy inhabitants of Rome—waste of stars' abilities.

Angels One Five (1954-British) 98m. ** D: George O'Ferrall. Jack Hawkins, Michael Denison, Dulcie Gray, John Gregson. Grounded for accidental plane mishap, British war pilot (Hawkins) rebels against officers and friends, seeking to fly again.

Angels Over Broadway (1940) 80m. **½ D: Ben Hecht, Lee Garmes. Douglas Fairbanks Jr, Rita Hayworth, Thomas Mitchell, John Qualen, George Watts. Strange Hecht script of sharpster Fairbanks enlisting hard-luck Hayworth in embezzling plot; fine support from Mitchell and Qualen, but film doesn't quite add up.

Angels Wash Their Faces (1939) 76m. **½ D: Ray Enright. Ann Sheridan, Dead End Kids, Frankie Thomas, Bonita Granville, Ronald Reagan, Margaret Hamilton, Marjorie Main. Protective sister Sheridan tries to clear brother Thomas' police record, but he joins Dead End Kids for more trouble. OK juvenile-delinquent drama.

Angels With Dirty Faces (1938) 97m. *** D: Michael Curtiz. James Cagney, Pat O'Brien, Humphrey Bogart, Ann Sheridan, George Bancroft, Billy Halop. Superior cast in tale of two playmates; one (Cagney) becomes a gangster, the other (O'Brien) a priest. The Dead End Kids come to idolize Cagney, much to O'Brien's chagrin.

Angry Breed, The (1969) C-89m. BOMB D: David Commons. Jan Sterling, James MacArthur, William Windom, Jan Murray, Murray McLeod, Lori Martin, Melody Patterson. Vietnam veteran comes to Hollywood after discharge, gets mixed up with a group of motorcyclists. Twelfth-rate in all departments.

Angry Hills, The (1959) 105m. **½ D: Robert Aldrich. Robert Mitchum,

Elisabeth Mueller, Stanley Baker, Gia Scala, Theodore Bikel, Sebastian Cabot. Mitchum shows vim in WW2 actioner as war correspondent plotting escape from Greece with valuable data for Allies.

Angry Red Planet, The (1959) C-83m. ** D: Ib Melchior. Gerald Mohr, Nora Hayden, Les Tremayne, Jack Kruschen, Paul Hahn. Routine Martian travel saga with OK special effects; filmed in "Cinemagic" process.

Angry Silence, The (1960-British) 95m. *** D: Guy Green. Richard Attenborough, Pier Angeli, Michael Craig, Bernard Lee. Rewarding, unheralded film about courageous stand by a simple Britisher who refuses to join a wildcat strike, the repercussions he endures.

Animal Crackers (1930) 98m. *** D: Victor Heerman. Groucho, Harpo, Chico, and Zeppo Marx, Margaret Dumont, Lillian Roth, Louis Sorin, Hal Thompson. Marx Brothers' second movie, adapted from Broadway success, suffers from staginess and musical comedy plotting, but gives the zany foursome plenty of comic elbow-room. "Story" has to do with stolen painting, but never mind: Groucho performs "Hooray for Captain Spaulding," Chico and Harpo play bridge, etc.

Animal Farm (1955-British) C-75m. *** D: John Halas, Joy Batchelor. Good straightforward animated-feature version of George Orwell's satire. Ending changed from original to make it more upbeat, but trenchant views of government still hold fast. Not a kiddie film.

Animal House: SEE National Lampoon's Animal House

Animals, The (1970) C-86m. *½ D: Ron Joy. Henry Silva, Keenan Wynn, Michele Carey, John Anderson, Joseph Turkel. Sadistic Western with routine performances and stereotyped plot. Pretty schoolteacher vows revenge on five brutes who raped and humiliated her after holding up her stagecoach. Similar to the later HANNIE CAULDER.

Anna (1951-Italian) 95m. **½ D: Alberto Lattuada. Silvana Mangano, Raf Vallone, Vittorio Gassman, Gaby Morlay. Thoughtful study of confused young woman who enters convent to avoid deciding which man she really loves, with fates forcing decision upon her.

Anna and the King of Siam (1946)

128m. ***½ D: John Cromwell. Irene Dunne, Rex Harrison, Linda Darnell, Lee J. Cobb, Gale Sondergaard, Mikhail Rasumny. Sumptuous production of 19th-century British governess who journeys to Thailand, engaging in battle of wits with strong-willed ruler. Dunne and Harrison are superb. Remade as musical THE KING AND I.

Anna Christie (1930) 90m. *** D: Clarence Brown. Greta Garbo, Charles Bickford, Marie Dressler, Lee Phelps, George Marion. Garbo is effective in her first talkie as girl with shady past finding love with seaman Bickford, from O'Neill play. Film itself is rather static.

Anna Karenina (1935) 95m. **** D: Clarence Brown. Greta Garbo, Fredric March, Freddie Bartholomew, Maureen O'Sullivan, May Robson, Basil Rathbone. Tolstoy's tragic love chronicle makes excellent Garbo vehicle, with fine support from March as her lover, Rathbone her husband, and Bartholomew, her adoring son. Filmed before with Garbo as LOVE.

Anna Karenina (1948-British) 110m. **½ D: Julien Duvivier. Vivien Leigh, Ralph Richardson, Kieron Moore, Hugh Dempster. Despite excellent cast, strictly turgid adaptation of Tolstoy classic about a woman blindly in love with officer.

Anna Lucasta (1958) 97m. ** D: Arnold Laven. Eartha Kitt, Sammy Davis, Jr., Frederick O'Neal, Henry Scott, Rex Ingram. Tepid melodrama about promiscuous Kitt who leaves home when boyfriend learns her true morality. This all-black remake of 1949 film with Paulette Goddard is based on the play by Philip Yordan.

Annapolis Story, An (1955) C-81m. ** D: Don Siegel. John Derek, Diana Lynn, Kevin McCarthy, Pat Conway. Uninspired reuse of old service-school formula with Derek and McCarthy undergoing rigid training, both romancing Lynn.

Anne of Green Gables (1934) 79m. *** D: George Nicholls, Jr. Anne Shirley, Tom Brown, O. P. Heggie, Helen Westley. Well-handled story of orphan accepted in household, trying to forget past experiences.

Anne of the Indies (1951) C-81m. **½ D: Jacques Tourneur. Jean Peters, Louis Jourdan, Debra Paget, Herbert Marshall. Peters isn't always believable as swaggering pirate, but surrounded by professionals and good production, actioner moves along.

Anne of the Thousand Days (1969) C-145m. *** D: Charles Jarrott. Richard Burton, Genevieve Bujold, Irene Papas, Anthony Quayle, Peter Jeffrey. Often inaccurate but totally engrossing, well-acted historical drama centering on Anne Boleyn and King Henry VIII. Lovely scenery, brilliant performance by Bujold.

Anne of Windy Poplars (1940) 88m. ** D: Jack Hively. Anne Shirley, James Ellison, Henry Travers, Patric Knowles. Fair acting in tired story of teacher overcoming small-town prejudices. Follow-up of ANNE OF GREEN GABLES.

Annie Get Your Gun (1950) C-107m. *** D: George Sidney. Betty Hutton, Howard Keel, Louis Calhern, Edward Arnold, Keenan Wynn, J. Carrol Naish. Lively filming of Irving Berlin's Wild West show musical of Annie Oakley getting her man. Songs include "Anything You Can Do," "Doin' What Comes Naturally."

Annie Hall (1977) C-94m. **** D: Woody Allen. Woody Allen, Diane Keaton, Tony Roberts, Paul Simon, Shelley Duvall, Carol Kane, Colleen Dewhurst. Woody's best film to date, an autobiographical love story with incisive Allenisms on romance, relationships, fame, New York vs. L.A., and sundry other topics. Warm, witty, intelligent Oscar winner for Best Picture, Best Actress, Best Direction, Best Screenplay (Allen and Marshall Brickman).

Annie Oakley (1935) 88m. *** D: George Stevens. Barbara Stanwyck, Preston Foster, Melvyn Douglas, Pert Kelton, Andy Clyde. Lively biography of female sharpshooter Stanwyck and her on-again off-again romance with fellow-performer Foster. Tight direction within episodic scenes, gives believable flavor of late 19th-century America.

Anniversary, The (1968-British) C-95m. **½ D: Roy Ward Baker. Bette Davis, Sheila Hancock, Jack Hedley, James Cossins, Christian Roberts, Elaine Taylor. Human monster Davis uses date of wedding anniversary as excuse to reunite family, continue her stranglehold on them. Adapted from MacIlwraith stage play, film emerges as vehicle for Davis' hammy performance.

Another Dawn (1937) 73m. **½ D: William Dieterle. Kay Francis, Errol Flynn, Ian Hunter, Frieda Inescort, Mary Forbes. Francis is torn between devotion to husband Hunter and officer Flynn in well-paced adventure story set at British army post in African desert.

Another Man, Another Chance (1977-French-U.S.) C-128m. **½ D: Claude Lelouch. James Caan, Genevieve Bujold, Francis Huster, Jennifer Warren, Susan Tyrrell, Rossie Harris. Virtual remake of Lelouch's A MAN AND A WOMAN, with late-1800s Western setting; Bujold and Caan are widow and widower who fall in love after losing their spouses. Mild-mannered to the point of distraction, and much too long.

Another Man's Poison (1952-British) 89m. ** D: Irving Rapper. Bette Davis, Gary Merrill, Emlyn Williams, Anthony Steel. Hazy melodrama with a tame Davis performance as authoress who kills her escaped convict husband and is blackmailed by another con (Merrill) on the loose.

Another Part of the Forest (1948) 107m. *** D: Michael Gordon. Fredric March, Dan Duryea, Edmond O'Brien, Ann Blyth, Florence Eldridge, John Dall. Lillian Hellman's story predates THE LITTLE FOXES by tracing the Hubbard family's ruthlessness; unpleasant but well-acted movie.

Another Thin Man (1939) 105m. D: W. S. Van Dyke II. William Powell, Myrna Loy, Virginia Grey, Otto Kruger, C. Aubrey Smith, Ruth Hussey, Nat Pendleton, Tom Neal, Sheldon Leonard, Marjorie Main. SEE: Thin Man series.

Another Time, Another Place (1958) 98m. **½ D: Lewis Allen. Lana Turner, Barry Sullivan, Glynis Johns, Sean Connery. Unconvincing melodrama; Turner suffers nervous breakdown when her lover is killed during WW2. Filmed in England.

Anthony Adverse (1936) 136m. ***½ D: Mervyn LeRoy. Fredric March, Olivia de Havilland, Donald Woods, Anita Louise, Edmund Gwenn, Claude Rains, Louis Hayward. Blockbuster filmization of Hervey Allen book of young man gaining maturity through adventures in various parts of early 19th-century America, Mexico, et al. Gale Sondergaard won Oscar as Best Supporting Actress; rousing musical score by Erich Wolfgang Korngold.

Antonia: A Portrait of the Woman (1974) C-58m. ***½ D: Judy Collins, Jill Godmilow. Heartfelt documentary about conductor Antonia Brico and her struggle to triumph professionally over sexual prejudice within the symphonic community. Inspiring.

Antony and Cleopatra (1973) **C.160m.** *½ D: Charlton Heston. Charlton Heston, Hildegard Neil, Eric Porter, John Castle, Fernando Rey. Labor-of-love undertaking by Heston results in sluggish treatment of Shakespearean play, hampered by severe budgetary limitations.

Any Number Can Play (1949) **112m.** ** D: Mervyn LeRoy. Clark Gable, Alexis Smith, Wendell Corey, Audrey Totter, Mary Astor, Lewis Stone, Marjorie Rambeau. Low-key drama of gambling-house owner Gable, estranged from wife Smith and son Darryl Hickman. Good character roles breathe life into film.

Any Number Can Win (1963-French) **½ D: Henri Verneuil. Jean Gabin, Alain Delon, Viviane Romance, Carla Marlier. Gabin leads bank robbery in Riviera resort. Comedy and suspense blend in "perfect crime" attempt.

Any Second Now (1969) **C-97m. TVM** D: Gene Levitt. Stewart Granger, Lois Nettleton, Joseph Campanella, Dana Wynter, Katy Jurado, Tom Tully. Professional photographer Dennison (Granger) attempts murder of wife when he realizes she's aware of his infidelity. Better than average.

Any Wednesday (1966) **C-109m.** *** D: Robert Miller. Jane Fonda, Jason Robards, Dean Jones, Rosemary Murphy. Bedroom farce of N.Y.C. executive using his mistress' apartment for business deductions. Fonda is appropriately addled in unstagy sex comedy.

Anyone Can Play (1968-Italian) **C-88m.** ** D: Luigi Zampa. Ursula Andress, Virna Lisi, Claudine Auger, Marisa Mell, Brett Halsey, Jean-Pierre Cassel. Aside from obvious good looks of four leading actresses, tale of adultery in Italy is not one of that country's better farces.

Anything Can Happen (1952) **107m.** ** D: George Seaton. Jose Ferrer, Kim Hunter, Kurt Kasznar, Eugenie Leontovich. Ferrer is overly flavorful as immigrant Russian adapting to American life and courting pert Hunter.

Anything for Love: SEE 11 Harrowhouse.

Anything Goes (1936) 92m. **½ D: Lewis Milestone. Bing Crosby, Ethel Merman, Charlie Ruggles, Ida Lupino, Grace Bradley, Arthur Treacher. Pleasant Crosby shipboard musical with stunning Cole Porter songs: title

tune, "You're The Top," "I Get A Kick Out of You." Mild distortion of Broadway original. Retitled: TOPS IS THE LIMIT.

Anything Goes (1956) **C-106m.** ** D: Robert Lewis. Bing Crosby, Jean-maire, Donald O'Connor, Mitzi Gaynor, Phil Harris. Flat musical involving show business partners Crosby and O'Connor each signing a performer for the leading role in their next show. Some Cole Porter songs remain, but resemblance to original Broadway show is nil.

Anzio (1968-Italian) **C-117m.** ** D: Edward Dmytryk. Robert Mitchum, Peter Falk, Robert Ryan, Earl Holliman, Mark Damon, Arthur Kennedy, Reni Santoni, Patrick Magee. Undistinguished retelling of Allied invasion of Anzio; all-star cast, large-scale action, but nothing memorable.

Apache (1954) **C-91m.** ** D: Robert Aldrich. Burt Lancaster, Jean Peters, John McIntire, Charles (Bronson) Buchinsky. Pacifist Indian (Lancaster) learns might makes right from U.S. cavalry; turns to fighting one man crusade for his tribe's rights. Overacted and improbable.

Apache Ambush (1955) 68m. ** D: Fred F. Sears. Bill Williams, Richard Jaeckel, Movita, Tex Ritter. So what else is new?

Apache Drums (1951) **C-75m.** *½ D: Hugo Fregonese. Stephen McNally, Coleen Gray, Willard Parker, Arthur Shields. Humdrum Western with gambler McNally coming to town's rescue when attacked by Indians.

Apache Gold (1965-German) **C-91m.** **½ D: Harald Reinl. Lex Barker, Mario Adorf, Pierre Brice, Marie Versini. A sort of Eastern-Western has good Indian atmosphere, plenty of action.

Apache Rifles (1964) **C-92m.** **½ D: William Witney. Audie Murphy, Michael Dante, Linda Lawson, John Archer, J. Pat O'Malley. Audie is stalwart cavalry captain assigned to corral renegading Apaches. Stock footage and plot mar potentials of actioner.

Apache Territory (1958) **C-75m.** *½ D: Ray Nazarro. Rory Calhoun, Barbara Bates, John Dehner, Carolyn Craig. Calhoun almost single-handedly routs rampaging Apaches and rescues defenseless Bates.

Apache Uprising (1966) **C-90m.** *½ D: R. G. Springsteen. Rory Calhoun, Corinne Calvet, John Russell, Lon Chaney, Gene Evans, Richard Arlen,

Arthur Hunnicutt, Johnny Mack Brown, Jean Parker. No production values, but cast of familiar names may make it possible for some to sit through standard Western where Rory fights both Indians and outlaws.

Apache War Smoke (1952) 67m. *½ D: Harold F. Kress. Gilbert Roland, Robert Horton, Glenda Farrell, Gene Lockhart, Bobby Blake. Pat Western involving stagecoach robbery and Indian attack on stage-line station. Good supporting cast wasted.

Apache Warrior (1957) 74m. ** D: Elmo Williams. Keith Larsen, Jim Davis, Michael Carr, Eddie Little. When an Indian leader's brother is killed, redskins go on the warpath. Nothing new.

Apartment, The (1960) 125m. **** D: Billy Wilder. Jack Lemmon, Shirley MacLaine, Fred MacMurray, Ray Walston, Jack Kruschen, Edie Adams. Superb comedy-drama which won Best Picture Oscar. Wilder is in top form with a great cast. Lemmon loans his apartment key to boss (MacMurray) in order to further his career, but complications arise when he finds himself emotionally involved with MacMurray's latest girlfriend (MacLaine).

Apartment For Peggy (1948) C-99m. *** D: George Seaton. Jeanne Crain, William Holden, Edmund Gwenn, Gene Lockhart. Breezy story of newlyweds trying to live on college campus; old pros Gwenn and Lockhart steal film from young lovers.

Ape, The (1940) 62m. ** D: William Nigh. Boris Karloff, Gertrude W. Hoffman, Henry Hall, Maris Wrixon. Low-budget shocker with mad doctor Karloff killing and experimenting with title character in order to save girl's life.

Ape Man, The (1943) 64m. ** D: William Beaudine. Bela Lugosi, Louise Currie, Wallace Ford, Henry Hall, Minerva Urecal. Minor horror effort with Lugosi and cast overacting in story of scientist injecting himself to attain power of simian relatives.

Apocalypse Now (1979) C-139m. ***½ D: Francis Coppola. Marlon Brando, Martin Sheen, Robert Duvall, Frederic Forrest, Albert Hall, Sam Bottoms, Larry Fishburne, Dennis Hopper, G. D. Spradlin, Harrison Ford. Coppola's controversial Vietnam war epic, based on Joseph Conrad's *Heart of Darkness*. Special agent Sheen journeys upriver into Vietnam with orders to find and kill errant officer Brando, leading him (and viewer) on a mesmerizing odyssey of turbulent often surreal encounters. Unfortunately film's conclusion—when he does find Brando—is cerebral and murky. Still, a great movie experience most of the way.

Appaloosa, The (1966) C-98m. **½ D: Sidney J. Furie. Marlon Brando, Anjanette Comer, John Saxon, Alex Montoya, Frank Silvera. Brooding Western set in 1870s with Brando trying to recover horse stolen from him by Mexican bandit; slowly paced, well photographed.

Applause (1929) 78m. **½ D: Rouben Mamoulian. Helen Morgan, Joan Peers, Henry Wadsworth, Dorothy Cummins. Revolutionary early talkie with many advanced techniques dates badly because of trite dialogue, but Morgan is fine in seedy N.Y.C. burlesque atmosphere.

Apple Dumpling Gang, The (1975) C-100m. ** D: Norman Tokar. Bill Bixby, Susan Clark, Don Knotts, Tim Conway, David Wayne, Slim Pickens, Harry Morgan. Disney Western comedy with gambler Bixby inheriting three children. Predictable doings sparked by Knotts and Conway as bumbling crooks.

Apple Dumpling Gang Rides Again, The (1979) C-88m. ** D: Vincent McEveety. Tim Conway, Don Knotts, Tim Matheson, Kenneth Mars, Elyssa Davalos, Jack Elam, Robert Pine, Harry Morgan, Ruth Buzzi. More of the same, with Knotts and Conway as bumbling outlaws in the Old West; usual Disney slapstick, without much zip or originality.

Appointment, The (1969) C-100m. **½ D: Sidney Lumet. Omar Sharif, Anouk Aimee, Lotte Lenya. Brilliant attorney falls in love with a girl who eventually ruins him. Soapy and long.

Appointment For Love (1941) 89m. **½ D: William Seiter. Charles Boyer, Margaret Sullavan, Rita Johnson, Reginald Denny, Ruth Terry, Eugene Pallette. Frothy comedy showcasing delightful stars: husband and wife with careers find happy marriage almost impossible.

Appointment In Berlin (1943) 77m. **½ D: Alfred E. Green. George Sanders, Marguerite Chapman, Onslow Stevens, Gale Sondergaard, Alan Napier. Another WW2 intrigue film, better than most, with Sanders joining Nazi radio staff to learn secret plans.

Appointment in Honduras (1953) C-79m. **½ D: Jacques Tourneur. Ann Sheridan, Glenn Ford, Zachary Scott, Jack Elam. Idealistic American (Ford) out to save Latin-American country, corrals villainous companions into helping crusade. Sheridan is not focal point, and a pity.

Appointment in London (1953-British) 96m. *** D: Philip Leacock. Dirk Bogarde, Ian Hunter, Dinah Sheridan, William Sylvester, Walter Fitzgerald, Bryan Forbes. Engrossing story of British bomber squadron in WW2, and high-pressured officer Bogarde who insists on flying dangerous mission in spite of orders to the contrary.

Appointment with a Shadow (1958) 73m. ** D: Richard Carlson. George Nader, Joanna Moore, Brian Keith, Virginia Field, Frank De Kova. Former ace reporter swears off alcohol and scoops big story.

Appointment With Danger (1951) 89m. *** D: Lewis Allen. Alan Ladd, Phyllis Calvert, Paul Stewart, Jan Sterling, Jack Webb. Ladd's rugged performance as crusading postal aviator combatting robbery scheme is aided by good aerial shots.

Appointment With Murder (1948) 67m. D: Jack Bernhard. John Calvert, Catherine Craig, Lyle Talbot, Jack Reitzen, Peter Brocco. SEE: The Falcon series.

Apprenticeship of Duddy Kravitz, The (1974-Canadian) C-121m. ***½ D: Ted Kotcheff. Richard Dreyfuss, Micheline Lanctot, Jack Warden, Randy Quaid, Joseph Wiseman, Denholm Elliott, Joe Silver. Mordecai Richler's vivid comedy-drama of an ambitious kid from Montreal's Jewish ghetto in the 1940s, determined to make good no matter how many toes he steps on. Pretentious bar mitzvah movie made by Duddy's "client," artsy director Elliott, is just one comic highlight.

April Fools, The (1969) C-95m. ** D: Stuart Rosenberg. Jack Lemmon, Catherine Deneuve, Peter Lawford, Harvey Korman, Sally Kellerman, Myrna Loy, Charles Boyer. Attempt at old-fashioned romantic comedy is forced, unbelievable, unfunny. Lemmon is married businessman who decides to chuck it all to run away with Deneuve, who's wasted, along with Loy and Boyer.

April in Paris (1952) C-101m. **½

D: David Butler. Doris Day, Ray Bolger, Claude Dauphin, Eve Miller, George Givot. Drab musical pegged on diplomat Bolger and showgirl Day having uninspired shipboard problems before reaching Paris.

April Love (1957) C-97m. **½ D: Henry Levin. Pat Boone, Shirley Jones, Dolores Michaels, Arthur O'Connell, Matt Crowley. Engaging musical with wholesome Boone visiting relatives' Kentucky farm, falling in love with neighbor Jones.

April Showers (1948) 94m. ** D: James V. Kern. Jack Carson, Ann Sothern, Robert Alda, S. Z. Sakall, Robert Ellis. Hackneyed backstage vaudeville yarn with Carson-Sothern teaming, splitting, reteaming, etc.

Aquarians, The (1970) C-100m. TVM D: Don McDougall. Ricardo Montalban, Jose Ferrer, Leslie Nielsen, Kate Woodville, Curt Lowens, Chris Robinson. Fair Ivan Tors production features Montalban as Dr. Luis Delgado, head of scientist/explorer operation using vessel capable of working at 15,000 feet below sea level. Above average.

Arabella (1969-Italian) C-91m. *½ D: Adriano Barocco. Virna Lisi, James Fox, Margaret Rutherford, Terry-Thomas. Silly drawing-room black comedy in which Thomas plays four different roles, as various victims of Lisi's larceny.

Arabesque (1966) C-105m. *** D: Stanley Donen, Gregory Peck, Alan Badel, Kieron Moore, George Coulouris. Modern secret-agent escapism as Peck is drawn into espionage with Sophia, who was never more beautiful. Exciting, beautifully photographed, minus any message or deep thought.

Arabian Adventure (1979-British) C-98m. **½ D: Kevin Connor. Christopher Lee, Milo O'Shea, Puneet Sira, Oliver Tobias, Emma Samms, Peter Cushing, Mickey Rooney, Capucine. Just what the title says; colorful enough to entertain kids, with enough effects gimmicks and cameo performances to intrigue older viewers as well.

Arabian Nights (1942) C-86m. ** D: John Rawlins. Jon Hall, Maria Montez, Sabu, Leif Erickson, Turhan Bey, Billy Gilbert, Shemp Howard, John Qualen, Thomas Gomez. Good production values evident in average desert meller. Hall again leads movement to depose evil caliph. Corny dialogue.

Arch of Triumph (1948) 120m. **½ D: Lewis Milestone. Ingrid Bergman, Charles Boyer, Charles Laughton, Louis Calhern. Sluggish drama of refugee Boyer falling in love with Bergman in WW2 France, based on Erich Maria Remarque's novel.

Are Husbands Necessary? (1942) 79m. ** D: Norman Taurog. Ray Milland, Betty Field, Patricia Morison, Eugene Pallette, Cecil Kellaway.—And what about this film?

Are Parents People? (1925) 60m. **½ D: Malcolm St. Clair. Betty Bronson, Adolphe Menjou, Florence Vidor, Lawrence Gray. Enjoyable vintage silent with good cast; innocuous story of young Bronson bringing her estranged parents together. No great shakes, but fun.

Are You in the House Alone? (1978) C-100m. TVM D: Walter Grauman. Kathleen Beller, Blythe Danner, Tony Bill, Robin Mattson, Tricia O'Neil, Dennis Quaid. Predictable thriller about high school coed who is target of terror campaign. Unsatisfactory adaptation of Richard Peck's Edgar Mystery Award-winning novel. Average.

Are You With It? (1948) 90m. **½ D: Jack Hively. Donald O'Connor, Olga San Juan, Martha Stewart, Lew Parker. Bright little musical of mathwhiz O'Connor joining a carnival.

Arena (1953) C-83m. ** D: Richard Fleischer. Gig Young, Jean Hagen, Polly Bergen, Henry (Harry) Morgan, Barbara Lawrence, Lee Aaker. Sappy, soapy story of rodeo star (Young) whose marriage is on the skids; film's only value is in realistic rodeo scenes, filmed on location in Arizona. Originally shown in 3-D.

Argentine Nights (1940) 74m. **½ D: Albert S. Rogell. Ritz Brothers, Andrews Sisters, Constance Moore, George Reeves, Peggy Moran, Anne Nagel. Boisterous musical comedy with the Ritzes fleeing the U.S., hooking up with troupe of entertainers in Argentina. Incoherent plotwise, but diverting.

Arise, My Love (1940) 113m. *** D: Mitchell Leisen. Claudette Colbert, Ray Milland, Walter Abel, Dennis O'Keefe, Dick Purcell. News correspondent Colbert loves flyer-offortune Milland, who is working in war-torn Spain. Bright stars make script seem better than it is.

Arizona (1940) 127m. **½ D: Wesley Ruggles. Jean Arthur, William Holden, Warren William, Porter Hall, Paul Harvey. Lively story of determined woman battling corruption and plundering while trying to settle in new Arizona territory. Well done, but seems to go on forever.

Arizona Bushwhackers (1968) C-86m. *½ D: Lesley Selander. Howard Keel, Yvonne De Carlo, John Ireland, Marilyn Maxwell, Scott Brady, Brian Donlevy, Roy Rogers, Jr., James Craig. Confederate spy Keel takes job as sheriff in Arizona and routs Brady, who has been selling weapons to Apaches. Routine Western.

Arizona Mission SEE: **Gun the Man Down**

Arizona Raiders (1965) C-88m. **½ D: William Witney. Audie Murphy, Michael Dante, Ben Cooper, Buster Crabbe, Gloria Talbott. Murphy is confederate army officer heading Arizona rangers after Civil War, involved in battling Quantrill's raiders.

Arizona to Broadway (1933) 66m. ** D: James Tinling. James Dunn, Joan Bennett, Herbert Mundin, Sammy Cohen, Theodore von Eltz, J. Carrol Naish. Joan enlists carnival con-man Dunn's help in reclaiming money lost to gang of swindlers; predictable tale, remade as JITTERBUGS.

Armored Attack SEE: **North Star**

Armored Car Robbery (1950) 68m. *½ D: Richard Fleischer. Charles McGraw, Adele Jergens, William Talman, Steve Brodie. Inoffensive study of attempted large theft and the repercussions on those involved.

Armored Command (1961) 99m. ** D: Byron Haskin. Howard Keel, Tina Louise, Warner Anderson, Burt Reynolds. Bland war film with stars merely going through their paces.

Arnelo Affair, The (1947) 86m. ** D: Arch Oboler. John Hodiak, George Murphy, Frances Gifford, Dean Stockwell, Eve Arden. Neglected wife drawn hypnotically to client of husband finally learns of his involvement in girl's murder.

Arnold (1973) C-100m. **½ D: Georg Fenady. Stella Stevens, Roddy McDowall, Elsa Lanchester, Shani Wallis, Farley Granger, Victor Buono, John McGiver, Patric Knowles. Bizarre horror comedy features novel deaths and offbeat humor, centering around luscious Stevens' marriage to corpse Norman Stuart.

Around the World in 80 Days (1956) C-167m. *** D: Michael Anderson.

David Niven, Cantinflas, Shirley MacLaine, Robert Newton, Marlene Dietrich, all-star cast. Fifties Oscar-winning favorite has lost much of its charm over the years, but even so, Mike Todd's version of the Jules Verne tale offers plenty of entertainment, and more than forty cameo appearances offer plenty of star-gazing for buffs. Great Victor Young score was also an Oscar-winner.

Around the World Under the Sea (1966) C-117m. ** D: Andrew Marton. Lloyd Bridges, Shirley Eaton, David McCallum, Brian Kelly, Keenan Wynn, Marshall Thompson. Several TV personalities appear together in this undistinguished underwater tour about testing earthquake warnings. Eaton adds femininity to otherwise all-male cast.

Arrangement, The (1969) C-120m. BOMB D: Elia Kazan. Kirk Douglas, Faye Dunaway, Deborah Kerr, Richard Boone, Hume Cronyn. Muddled, unpleasant film from Kazan's own novel about man fed up with Madison Avenue rat-race who suddenly goes berserk, reevaluates his life, family, surroundings. Good cast down the drain; Kerr's role is particularly demeaning.

Arrest Bulldog Drummond (1939) 57m. D: James Hogan. John Howard, Heather Angel, H. B. Warner, George Zucco, E. E. Clive, Reginald Denny, John Sutton. SEE: **Bulldog Drummond** series.

Arrividerci, Baby (1966) C-105m. *½ D: Ken Hughes. Tony Curtis, Rosanna Schiaffino, Lionel Jeffries, Zsa Zsa Gabor, Nancy Kwan. Comic theme about Bluebeard type who murders his wives for their money has been handled more successfully by others. Not very funny.

Arrow In the Dust (1954) 80m. ** D: Lesley Selander. Sterling Hayden, Coleen Gray, Keith Larsen, Tom Tully. Deserting horse soldier (Hayden) learns sterling virtues when he assumes identity of dead commanding officer, warding off Indian attack on passing wagon train.

Arrowhead (1953) 105m. **½ D: Charles Marquis Warren. Charlton Heston, Jack Palance, Katy Jurado, Brian Keith, Milburn Stone. Apaches prefer war to peace, with many Indian vs. cavalry skirmishes; Heston and Palance are intense.

Arruza (1972) C-75m. **½ D: Budd Boetticher. Interesting documentary, many years in production, about bull-

fighter Carlos Arruza. Ably photographed and edited, but the impact is nowhere near that of Boetticher's own fictional THE BULLFIGHTER AND THE LADY.

Arsene Lupin (1932) 84m. *** D: Jack Conway. John Barrymore, Lionel Barrymore, Karen Morley, John Miljan, Henry Armetta, Tully Marshall. Ripe detective yarn set in Paris: John is dapper jewel thief—Lionel the harried detective. They make a marvelous team.

Arsenic and Old Lace (1944) 116m. *** D: Frank Capra. Cary Grant, Priscilla Lane, Raymond Massey, Peter Lorre, Jack Carson, Josephine Hull, Jean Adair, James Gleason, Grant Mitchell, John Alexander, Edward Everett Horton. Hilarious adaptation of play about two seemingly harmless old ladies who murder gentlemen callers. Frantic cast is excellent, especially Lorre and Massey as unsuspecting murderers holed up in Brooklyn household. Made in 1941, held back for release.

Art of Crime, The (1975) C-78m. TVM D: Richard Irving. Ron Leibman, Jose Ferrer, David Hedison, Jill Clayburgh, Eugene Roche, Diane Kagan, Cliff Osmond, Mike Kellin. Gypsy antique dealer (Leibman) turns sleuth to clear friend accused of murder. Adapted from Martin Smith's *Gypsy in Amber*, this comedy-drama is long on gypsy folklore and short on suspense. Average.

Art of Love, The (1965) C-99m. ** D: Norman Jewison. James Garner, Dick Van Dyke, Elke Sommer, Angie Dickinson, Ethel Merman, Carl Reiner. Ordinary comedy set in France with a bemused cast headed by Van Dyke as a struggling artist and Sommer as his virtuous girl. Boisterous Merman is a local madam with a yen for singing.

Artists & Models (1937) 97m. **½ D: Raoul Walsh. Jack Benny, Ida Lupino, Judy Canova, Gail Patrick, Richard Arlen, Martha Raye, Connee Boswell, Ethel Clayton. Lupino pretends to be a socialite in flimsy plot with uncharacteristic Benny and songs "Stop You're Breaking My Heart," "Whispers in the Dark." Vintage fun.

Artists and Models (1955) C-109m. *** D: Frank Tashlin. Dean Martin, Jerry Lewis, Shirley MacLaine, Dorothy Malone, Eva Gabor, Anita Ekberg. Overblown daffy-duo shenanigans spiced by feminine beauty and a few wacky sequences, with cartoonist Martin utilizing Lewis' far-out dreams for his strips.

Artists and Models Abroad (1938) 90m. ***** D: Mitchell Leisen. Jack Benny, Joan Bennett, Mary Boland, Charley Grapewin, Yacht Club Boys, Joyce Compton. Breezy, entertaining froth of musical troupe stranded in Paris, perennially saved by conniving boss Benny. Yacht Club Boys sing incredible song, "You're Broke, You Dope."

As If It Were Raining (1963-French) 85m. ****** D: Jose Monter. Eddie Constantine, Henri Cogan, Elisa Montes, Jose Nieto, Sylvia Solar. Constantine is at liberty in Spain, enmeshed in an embezzlement scheme; wooden yarn.

As Long As They're Happy (1957-British) C-76m. ***½** D: J. Lee Thompson. Janette Scott, Jean Carson, Diana Dors, Hugh McDermott, Jack Buchanan. Mini-musical involving daughter of staid British stockholder who falls for visiting song-and-dance man.

As the Sea Rages (1960) 74m. ****** D: Horst Haechler. Maria Schell, Cliff Robertson, Cameron Mitchell. Seaman Robertson arrives in Greece planning a sponge-diving business and meets resistance from townfolk and the elements; muddled script. Filmed in Yugoslavia.

As You Desire Me (1932) 71m. ****½** D: George Fitzmaurice. Greta Garbo, Melvyn Douglas, Erich von Stroheim, Hedda Hopper, Owen Moore. OK adaptation of Pirandello play about amnesiac (Garbo) who returns to husband she doesn't really remember. Never as compelling as it should be.

As Young As You Feel (1951) 77m. ******* D: Harmon Jones. Monty Woolley, Thelma Ritter, David Wayne, Jean Peters, Constance Bennett, Marilyn Monroe. Marvelous cast enhances timely story of Woolley resenting retirement at age 65 and determined to alter corporate policy.

Ash Wednesday (1973) C-99m. BOMB D: Larry Peerce. Elizabeth Taylor, Henry Fonda, Helmut Berger, Keith Baxter, Margaret Blye. Liz undergoes a facelift to regain her youth, but she still looks older than Fonda. Sit through this one and you'll need surgery on your posterior.

Ashanti (1979) C-117m. ****** D: Richard Fleischer. Michael Caine, Peter Ustinov, Beverly Johnson, Kabir Bedi, Omar Sharif, Rex Harrison, William Holden. Beautiful wife (Johnson) of missionary-doctor Caine is kidnapped by slave trader Ustinov, prompting hot pursuit through the mideast. Tepid adventure yarn, despite great cast and promising story elements.

Ashes and Diamonds (1958-Polish) 104m. ******* D: Andrzej Wajda. Zbigniew Cybulski, Ewa Krzyzanowska, Adam Pawlikowski, Bogumil Kobiela, Waclaw Zastrzezynski. Intelligent, penetrating account of resistance movement during closing days of WW2 with anti-Communist partisans engaged in ambushing the new Communist commandant; slowly paced.

Ask Any Girl (1959) C-101m. ******* D: Charles Walters. David Niven, Shirley MacLaine, Gig Young, Rod Taylor, Jim Backus, Elisabeth Fraser. Effervescent gloss of naive MacLaine coming to New York, discovering most men have lecherous designs on girls; she wants a husband, however.

Asphalt Jungle, The (1950) 112m. *****½** D: John Huston. Sterling Hayden, Louis Calhern, Jean Hagen, Marilyn Monroe, Sam Jaffe, James Whitmore, Marc Lawrence. Powerful crime drama, realistically done. Monroe shines in brief bit, with sturdy work by Hayden as thief and Hagen his devoted girl. Remade (and plagiarized) several times.

Assassin (1973-British) C-83m. ****** D: Peter Crane. Ian Hendry, Edward Judd, Frank Windsor, Ray Brooks. Routine cold war espionage film, or, the loneliness of the long-distance assassin.

Assassin, The (1953-British) 90m. ****** D: Ralph Thomas. Richard Todd, Eva Bartok, George Coulouris, Margot Grahame. Todd is detective on manhunt in postwar Venice; usual murders and romance result.

Assassin, The (1961-Italian) 105m. ****½** D: Elio Petri. Marcello Mastroianni, Salvo Randone, Micheline Presle, Cristina Gajoni. Engaging study of scoundrel Mastroianni implicated in a murder, broken by the police, proven innocent, with a wry ending.

Assassination Bureau, The (1969-British) C-110m. ******* D: Basil Dearden. Oliver Reed, Diana Rigg, Telly Savalas, Curt Jurgens, Clive Revill. Fun tale based on Jack London story of secret club that eliminates unworthy people, until greed more than dedication begins to cloud the operation.

Assassination of Trotsky, The (1972-French-Italian-British) **C-103m.** **½ D: Joseph Losey. Richard Burton, Alain Delon, Romy Schneider, Valentina Cortese. Last days of Russian rebel make for uneven melodrama of hunters and hunted. Burton's performance is strong but unconvincing.

Assault on Agathon (1975—British/Greek) **C-96m.** **½ D: Laslo Benedek. Nico Minardos, Nina van Pallandt, Marianne Faithfull, John Woodvine. Tepid drug-dealing thriller with spectacular Greek scenery overshadowing CIA man Minardos' efforts to nab Mr. Big.

Assault on Precinct 13 (1976) **C-90m.** ***½ D: John Carpenter. Austin Stoker, Darwin Joston, Laurie Zimmer, Martin West, Tony Burton, Nancy Loomis. A nearly deserted L.A. police station finds itself under a state of siege by a youth gang in this riveting film, a modern-day paraphrase of Howard Hawks' RIO BRAVO. Writer-director Carpenter also did the music score for this sleeper.

Assault on a Queen (1966) **C-106m.** **½ D: Jack Donohue. Frank Sinatra, Virna Lisi, Tony Franciosa, Richard Conte, Reginald Denny. Sloppy Sinatra vehicle about big heist of H.M.S. *Queen Elizabeth's* vault.

Assault on the Wayne (1970) **C-90m.** TVM D: Marvin Chomsky. Joseph Cotten, Leonard Nimoy, Lloyd Haynes, Dewey Martin, William Windom, Keenan Wynn, Malachi Throne. Commander Philip Kettering handed control of U.S. submarine *Anthony Wayne*, unaware of presence of enemy agents out to seize top-secret device. Good cast. Average.

Assignment, The (1977-Swedish) **C-94m.** **½ D: George Bisset. Christopher Plummer, Thomas Hellberg, Carolyn Seymour, Fernando Rey, Per Oscarsson, Walter Gotell. Modest drama of Swedish diplomat sent to mediate turbulent political situation in Latin American country.

Assignment In Brittany (1943) **96m.** ** D: Jack Conway. Jean-Pierre Aumont, Susan Peters, Richard Whorf, Margaret Wycherly, Signe Hasso, Reginald Owen. Aumont is lookalike for Nazi leader, uses this to his advantage working for French underground; patriotic WW2 melodrama.

Assignment K (1968-British) **97m.** *½ D: Val Guest. Stephen Boyd, Camilla Sparv, Michael Redgrave, Leo McKern, Jeremy Kemp, Robert Hoffman. Still another spy drama—this one a dull story about secret agent Boyd's disillusionment when he discovers that his girl and seemingly everyone he knows is a double agent.

Assignment: Munich (1972) **C-100m.** TVM D: David Lowell Rich. Richard Basehart, Roy Scheider, Lesley Warren, Werner Klemperer. Shady saloon owner in Germany helps U.S. government find gold stolen during WW2. Average.

Assignment—Paris (1952) **85m.** ** D: Robert Parrish. Dana Andrews, Marta Toren, George Sanders, Audrey Totter. Fitfully entertaining drama of reporter Andrews trying to link together threads of plot between Communist countries against the West. Filmed in Paris.

Assignment to Kill (1968) **C-102m.** ** D: Sheldon Reynolds. Patrick O'Neal, Joan Hackett, John Gielgud, Herbert Lom, Eric Portman, Peter Van Eyck, Oscar Homolka. Private eye checks out shady corporation in Switzerland in this unrewarding thriller from the writer-director of TV's "Foreign Intrigue" series.

Astonished Heart, The (1950-British) **92m.** **½ D: Terence Fisher, Anthony Darnborough. Noel Coward, Celia Johnson, Margaret Leighton, Joyce Carey. Drawing-room melodrama about a married psychiatrist who succumbs to the wiles of another woman—an old schoolmate of his wife's—with unhappy results. One of Coward's lesser stories.

Astronauts, The (1971) **C-73m.** TVM D: Robert Michael Lewis. Monte Markham, Jackie Cooper, Susan Clark, Robert Lansing, Wally Shira. Space officials ask civilian to pose as disabled pilot. Average.

Asylum (1972-British) **C-100m.** *** D: Roy Ward Baker. Barbara Parkins, Sylvia Syms, Richard Todd, Peter Cushing, Barry Morse, Britt Ekland, Herbert Lom, Patrick Magee. Four fun chillers woven into puzzle that is solved at the conclusion of the fourth tale. Reissued in 1980 as HOUSE OF CRAZIES.

At Gunpoint (1955) **C-81m.** **½ D: Alfred L. Werker. Fred MacMurray, Dorothy Malone, Walter Brennan, Tommy Rettig, Jack Lambert. MacMurray is well suited to role of peace-loving man drawn into gunplay by taunting outlaws.

At Long Last Love (1975) C-118m. *½ D: Peter Bogdanovich. Burt Reynolds, Cybill Shepherd, Madeline Kahn, Duilio Del Prete, Eileen Brennan, John Hillerman, Mildred Natwick. Burt and Cybill are no Fred and Ginger. Bogdanovich's homage to 1930s Hollywood musicals has everything money can buy—including lavish sets and a Cole Porter score —but lacks the stars to put it over. Reedited for TV by the director.

At Sword's Point (1952) C-81m. **½ D: Lewis Allen. Cornel Wilde, Maureen O'Hara, Robert Douglas, Dan O'Herlihy, Alan Hale Jr., Blanche Yurka. Silly but likable variation on THE THREE MUSKETEERS with energetic cast, vivid technicolor settings.

At the Circus (1939) 87m. **½ D: Edward Buzzell. Groucho, Chico and Harpo Marx, Margaret Dumont, Eve Arden, Nat Pendleton, Kenny Baker, Fritz Feld, Florence Rice. Not top-grade Marx Brothers, but some good scenes as they save circus from bankruptcy; highlight, Groucho singing "Lydia the Tattooed Lady."

At the Earth's Core (1976-British) C-90m. **½ D: Kevin Connor. Doug McClure, Peter Cushing, Caroline Munro, Cy Grant, Godfrey James, Sean Lynch. Colorful fantasy-adventure based on Edgar Rice Burroughs' novel. Inventor Cushing and protégé McClure bore their way from Victorian England to the center of the earth and encounter a lost world of prehistoric beasts and sub-human warriors. Competent special effects make this yarn palatable.

At War with the Army (1950) 93m. **½ D: Hal Walker. Dean Martin, Jerry Lewis, Polly Bergen, Angela Greene, Mike Kellin. In their first starring feature, Dean and Jerry are in the service, with some funny sequences, including memorable soda machine gag.

Athena (1954) C-96m. **½ D: Richard Thorpe. Jane Powell, Debbie Reynolds, Edmund Purdom, Vic Damone, Louis Calhern, Evelyn Varden, Linda Christian. Back Bay lawyer (Purdom) and singer (Damone) romance two sisters living with eccentric grandparents. Wispy plot, average tunes.

Atlantis, the Lost Continent (1961) C-90m. *½ D: George Pal. Anthony Hall, Joyce Taylor, John Dall, Frank de Kova. Unintentionally funny fantasy, occasionally diverting. Good special effects, but basically corny.

Atoll K SEE: **Utopia**

Atomic Brain, The SEE: **Monstrosity**

Atomic City, The (1952) 85m. **½ D: Jerry Hopper. Gene Barry, Nancy Gates, Lydia Clarke, Lee Aaker. Tightly knit caper involving kidnapping of atomic scientist's son, well played by young Aaker.

Atomic Kid, The (1954) 86m. *½ D: Leslie Martinson. Mickey Rooney, Robert Strauss, Elaine Davis, Bill Goodwin. Rooney survives desert atomic blast, discovering he's radioactive. Slight spy comedy.

Atomic Man, The (1956-British) 78m. ** D: Ken Hughes. Gene Nelson, Faith Domergue, Joseph Tomelty, Peter Arne. Bland narrative of reporter and girlfriend encountering scientists who have experimented with nuclear materials and suffered dire consequences.

Atomic Submarine, The (1959) 72m. ** D: Spencer Bennet. Arthur Franz, Dick Foran, Brett Halsey, Tom Conway, Bob Steele, Victor Varconi, Joi Lansing. Programmer sci-fi involving flying saucer lodged in underwater headquarters.

Attack! (1956) 107m. *** D: Robert Aldrich. Jack Palance, Eddie Albert, Lee Marvin, Robert Strauss. Reenactment of the Battle of the Bulge, emphasizing a group of American soldiers; tightly directed, avoids war-flick clichés.

Atragon (1963-Japanese) 96m. ** D: Inoshiro Honda. Tadao Takashima, Yoko Fujiyama, Yu Fujiki, Horisho Koizumi. World is threatened by undersea kingdom in this juvenile sci-fi adventure, with enjoyable (if not believable) special effects.

Attack and Retreat SEE: **Italiano Brava Gente**

Attack of the Crab Monsters (1957) 64m. *½ D: Roger Corman. Richard Garland, Pamela Duncan, Russell Johnson, Leslie Bradley. Poor fools trapped on remote island with ferocious giant crabs. Few thrills.

Attack of the 50 Ft. Woman (1958) 66m. BOMB D: Nathan Juran. Allison Hayes, William Hudson, Yvette Vickers, Roy Gordon. Visitor from outer space creates title monster and predictable results occur.

Attack of the Killer Tomatoes (1978) C-87m. *½ D: John DeBello. David Miller, George Wilson, Sharon Taylor, Jack Riley, Rock Peace. The funniest thing about this horror-movie spoof is the title; too many unfunny stretches otherwise, too few clever ideas.

Attack of the Mayan Mummy (1963) 77m. BOMB D: Jerry Warren. Richard Webb, Nina Knight, John Burton, Steve Conte. Scientist gets patient to revert to former life and reveal site of ancient tomb in this grade-Z outing, comprised largely of Mexican horror-film footage.

Attack of the Puppet People (1958) 78m. *½ D: Bert I. Gordon. John Agar, John Hoyt, June Kenney, Scott Peters. Low-class shocker involving transformation of people into robot dolls; predictable and amateurish.

Attack on Terror: The FBI vs. the Ku Klux Klan (1975) C-215m. TVM D: Marvin Chomsky. Ned Beatty, John Beck, Billy Green Bush, Dabney Coleman, Andrew Duggan, Ed Flanders, George Grizzard, L.Q. Jones, Geoffrey Lewis, Maryln Mason, Wayne Rogers, Peter Strauss, Rip Torn. Docu-drama from FBI files, tying the murder of three civil rights workers in Mississippi in 1964 to the Klan after four-year investigation. Good cast and intelligent approach to basically formula plot. Above average.

Attack on the Iron Coast (1968) C-89m. **½ D: Paul Wendkos. Lloyd Bridges, Andrew Keir, Sue Lloyd, Mark Eden, Maurice Denham. Canadian officer Bridges leads commando attack on German naval base in France during WW2. Capable if unsurprising action film, made in England.

Attempt to Kill (1961-British) 57m. ** D: Royston Morley. Derek Farr, Tony Wright, Richard Pearson, Freda Jackson. Mild Edgar Wallace entry, salvaged by superior cast in predictable Scotland Yard manhunt caper.

Attila (1958-Italian) C-83m. *½ D: Pietro Francisci. Anthony Quinn, Sophia Loren, Henri Vidal, Irene Papas. Inept spectacle with ridiculous script of Attila readying to conquer Rome.

Audrey Rose (1977) C-113m. **½ D: Robert Wise. Marsha Mason, John Beck, Anthony Hopkins, Susan Swift, Norman Lloyd, John Hillerman. Overlong, underplayed reincarnation thriller. Mason and Beck are happily married couple until a stranger (Hopkins) tells them that their 12-year-old girl is his dead daughter returned to life.

Aunt Mary (1979) C-100m. TVM D: Peter Werner. Jean Stapleton, Martin Balsam, Harold Gould, Dolph Sweet, Robbie Rist, Anthony Cafiso, K. C. Martel. Inspirational true-life drama about Mary Dobkin, a physically handicapped Baltimore spinster who became a legend as a sandlot baseball coach. Stapleton sparkles. Above average.

Auntie Mame (1958) C-143m. ***½ D: Morton DaCosta. Rosalind Russell, Forrest Tucker, Coral Browne, Fred Clark, Roger Smith, Patric Knowles, Peggy Cass, Joanna Barnes, Pippa Scott. Colorful film version of Patrick Dennis' novel about his eccentric aunt, who believes that "life is a banquet, and most poor suckers are starving to death." Episodic but highly entertaining, sparked by Russell's tour-de-force performance. Remade as musical MAME.

Autobiography of Miss Jane Pittman, The (1974) C-110m. TVM D: John Korty. Cicely Tyson, Barbara Chaney, Richard Dysart, Katherine Helmond, Michael Murphy, Odetta, Thalmus Rasulala. Acclaimed drama from Ernest J. Gaines' epic novel covering, through the memories of a fictional 110-year-old slave (Tyson), the black experience from the Civil War to the start of civil rights movement. Tyson's tour-de-force performance, Korty's subtle direction, and Tracy Keenan Wynn's intelligent script accounted for three of the nine Emmy Awards given to the film, one of the most ambitious ever made for television.

Autumn Leaves (1956) 108m. **½ D: Robert Aldrich. Joan Crawford, Cliff Robertson, Vera Miles, Lorne Greene. Middle-aged typist marries younger man (Robertson), only to discover he is mentally disturbed and already married. Stalwart performance by Crawford as troubled woman.

Autumn Sonata (1978-Swedish) C-97m. *** D: Ingmar Bergman. Ingrid Bergman, Liv Ullmann, Lena Nyman, Halvar Bjork, Gunnar Bjornstrand. Ingrid, a famed concert pianist, locks horns with daughter Ullmann when they visit for the first time in seven years. Director Bergman's drama is full of déjà vu, but Ingrid's performance keeps it on the track most of the time. Sven Nykvist's photography is peerless.

Avalanche (1946) 70m. *½ D: Irving Allen. Bruce Cabot, Roscoe Karns, Helen Mowery, Veda Ann Borg. Programmer tale of murder and suspense at an isolated ski lodge; shoddy production.

Avalanche (1978) C-91m. ** D. Corey Allen. Rock Hudson, Mia Farrow, Robert Forster, Jeanette Nolan, Rick Moses, Barry Primus. Disaster at the newly opened ski resort where hard-driving tycoon Hudson is determined to double his not insubstantial investment while his ex-wife Mia is making whoopee with one of the locals championing ecology. Stodgy performances almost outweighed by special effects.

Avalanche Express (1979) C-88m. BOMB D: Mark Robson. Lee Marvin, Robert Shaw, Linda Evans, Maximilian Schell, Joe Namath, Mike Connors, Horst Buchholz. KGB head Shaw tries to defect on a Dutch train that's threatened by lots and lots of falling snow. Cast has enough stiffs in it to resemble audition time at the Hollywood Wax Museum. Sadly, final film for both Shaw and director Robson.

Avanti (1972) C-144m. ***½ D: Billy Wilder. Jack Lemmon, Juliet Mills, Clive Revill, Edward Andrews, Gianfranco Barra, Franco Angrisano. Sadly underrated comedy about stuffy Baltimore millionaire who falls in love with daughter of his late father's mistress when he comes to Italy to claim the old man's body. Closer to LOVE IN THE AFTERNOON than Wilder's satirical comedies; lovely scenery, wonderful performances by all.

Avenger, The (1960-German) 102m. **½ D: Karl Anton. Ingrid Van Bergen, Heinz Drache, Ina Duscha, Maria Litto. Above-par shocker based on Edgar Wallace tale of bestial villain beheading several people, mailing them to appropriate recipients.

Away All Boats (1956) C-114m. **½ D: Joseph Pevney. Jeff Chandler, George Nader, Julie Adams, Lex Barker. Improbably heroic and over-partial slanting of America's participation in naval engagements during WW2 mar the movie's total effect.

Awful Dr. Orloff, The (1961-Spanish) 95m. ** D: Jess Franco. Howard Vernon, Conrado Sanmartin, Diana Lorys, Ricardo Valle, Perla Cristal. Medium spooker about deranged surgeon operating on a series of women, trying to find spare parts to revitalize his disfigured daughter.

Awful Truth, The (1937) 92m. ***½ D: Leo McCarey. Irene Dunne, Cary Grant, Ralph Bellamy, Cecil Cunningham, Mary Forbes, Alex D'Arcy. Smash-bang social comedy as Cary and Irene divorce, she to marry hayseed Bellamy, he to wed aristocratic Molly Lamont. Each does his best to spoil the other's plans. Remade as musical: LET'S DO IT AGAIN.

B. F.'s Daughter (1948) 108m. *½ D: Robert Z. Leonard. Barbara Stanwyck, Van Heflin, Charles Coburn, Richard Hart, Keenan Wynn, Margaret Lindsay. Disastrous film of J. P. Marquand novel, with Stanwyck the domineering girl ruining marriage to professor Heflin.

BJ and the Bear (1978) C-100m. TVM D: John Peyser. Greg Evigan, Claude Akins, Mills Watson, Penny Peyser, Julius Harris. Pilot to the hit series (that later spun off SHERIFF LOBO) puts an independent trucker and his traveling buddy, a fun-loving chimp, at odds with a slightly corrupt sheriff who is involved with white slavery. Average.

B.S. I Love You (1971) C-99m. *½ D: Steven Hillard Stern. Peter Kastner, Joanna Cameron, Louise Sorel, Gary Burghoff, Richard B. Shull, Joanna Barnes. Stale "youth" comedy about young ad-man who makes it with both mother and daughter is only for those who haven't seen THE GRADUATE or YOU'RE A BIG BOY NOW. Nude scenes will be missing on TV.

Babbitt (1934) 74m. *** D: William Keighley. Guy Kibbee, Aline MacMahon, Claire Dodd, Nan Grey, Mary Treen. Fine Sinclair Lewis Americana of pettiness, ambition, and social life in small Midwestern town; Kibbee is fine in lead role.

Babe (1975) C-100m. TVM D: Buzz Kulik. Susan Clark, Alex Karras, Slim Pickens, Jeanette Nolan, Ellen Geer, Ford Rainey. Rich, absorbing film biography of Babe Didrickson Zaharias, America's foremost woman athlete, beautifully played by Clark (who won an Emmy for her performance). Ex-football star Karras offers a sensitive portrayal of her wrestler husband George, under Kulik's imaginative direction. The courageous

Babe's tragic story leaves not a dry eye in the house, but secret ingredient here is taste. Above average.

Babe Ruth Story, The (1948) 106m. ** D: Roy Del Ruth. William Bendix, Claire Trevor, Charles Bickford, Sam Levene, William Frawley. "Biography" is insult to famed baseball star; inept.

Babes in Arms (1939) 96m. **½ D: Busby Berkeley. Mickey Rooney, Judy Garland, Charles Winninger, Guy Kibbee, June Preisser, Douglas McPhail. Rodgers and Hart's musical, minus most of their songs, and one that's left, "Where or When," is trammeled to death. What's left is energetic but standard putting-on-a-show vehicle for Mickey and Judy. Dated fun.

Babes in Bagdad (1952) C-79m. BOMB D: Edgar G. Ulmer. Paulette Goddard, Gypsy Rose Lee, Richard Ney, John Boles, Sebastian Cabot. Embarrassing, hokey costumer made even seedier by miscast veteran performers.

Babes in Toyland (1934) 73m. ***½ D: Gus Meins, Charles R. Rogers. Stan Laurel, Oliver Hardy, Charlotte Henry, Henry Brandon, Felix Knight, Jean Darling, Johnny Downs. L&H version of Victor Herbert operetta looks better all the time, compared to lumbering "family musicals" of recent years. Stan and Ollie are in fine form, and fantasy element of Toyland—especially attack by Bogeymen—is excellent. Retitled MARCH OF THE WOODEN SOLDIERS.

Babes in Toyland (1961) C-105m. **½ D: Jack Donohue. Ray Bolger, Tommy Sands, Annette Funicello, Henry Calvin, Gene Sheldon, Tommy Kirk, Ed Wynn. Colorful but contrived Disneyfication of Victor Herbert operetta has no substance or heart; classic songs, visual gimmicks, clowning of Calvin and Sheldon keep it afloat.

Babes on Broadway (1941) 118m. **½ D: Busby Berkeley. Mickey Rooney, Judy Garland, Fay Bainter, Virginia Weidler, Richard Quine. Showcase vehicle for Mickey and Judy's talents, with duo doing everything from imitations of Carmen Miranda and Bernhardt to minstrel numbers. Standout is Judy's "F.D.R. Jones."

Babette Goes to War (1960-French) C-103m. **½ D: Christian-Jaque. Brigitte Bardot, Jacques Charrier, Francis Blanche, Ronald Howard. Bardot is not at her forte playing lighthearted comedy. Flimsy WW2 account of French agent Bardot working for British, being sent back to France to help underground.

Baby, The (1973) C-102m. ** D: Ted Post. Anjanette Comer, Ruth Roman, Mariana Hill. Social worker who gets in too deep with a man-child case, has to kill to keep "baby" at home with her.

Baby and the Battleship, The (1957-British) C-96m. **½ D: Jay Lewis. John Mills, Richard Attenborough, Bryan Forbes, Michael Hordern. Diverting if not hilarious account of gobs who smuggle infant aboard ship, and their antics to keep the child hidden from top brass.

Baby Blue Marine (1976) C-90m. **½ D: John Hancock. Jan-Michael Vincent, Glynnis O'Connor, Katherine Helmond, Dana Elcar, Bert Remsen, Richard Gere, Art Lund. Norman Rockwell's America come to life, in bucolic tale of Marine dropout during WW2 who's mistaken for hero by residents of small town. Too bland to add up.

Baby Doll (1956) 114m. ***½ D: Elia Kazan. Karl Malden, Carroll Baker, Eli Wallach, Mildred Dunnock, Lonny Chapman, Rip Torn. Starkly photographed on location in Mississippi, story revolves around a child bride, her witless and blustery husband, and a smarmy business rival, bent on using both of them. Condemned by Legion of Decency when released, this Tennessee Williams story, although tame by today's standards, still sizzles.

Baby Face Nelson (1957) 85m. ** D: Don Siegel. Mickey Rooney, Carolyn Jones, Cedric Hardwicke, Jack Elam, Ted De Corsia. Rooney gives flavorful performance in title role of gun-happy gangster in Prohibition-Depression days; low-budget product, but action-filled.

Baby Maker, The (1970) C-109m. ** D: James Bridges. Barbara Hershey, Colin Wilcox-Horne, Sam Groom, Scott Glenn, Jeannie Berlin. Childless couple hires young semi-hippie to have a baby by the husband when wife discovers she is sterile. Not a good way to make a living and not a very interesting film; some scenes may be cut for TV.

Baby, the Rain Must Fall (1965) 100m. *** D: Robert Mulligan. Steve McQueen, Lee Remick, Don Murray, Paul Fix, Josephine Hutchinson, Ruth

White. Much underrated account of ex-convict McQueen returning to his wife and daughter, but unable to change his restless ways. Murray is sincere sheriff who tries to help.

Bachelor and the Bobby-Soxer, The (1947) 95m. *** D: Irving Reis. Cary Grant, Myrna Loy, Shirley Temple, Rudy Vallee, Ray Collins, Harry Davenport. Judge Loy orders playboy Grant to wine and dine her sister Temple, so the teen-ager will forget her infatuation for him. Breezy entertainment.

Bachelor Apartment (1931) 83m. **½ D: Lowell Sherman. Lowell Sherman, Irene Dunne, Mae Murray, Claudia Dell, Noel Francis, Bess Flowers. Sophisticated comedy about gay-blade Sherman shuffling his various girls back and forth; ancestor of COME BLOW YOUR HORN, etc.

Bachelor Father (1931) 90m. **½ D: Robert Z. Leonard. Marion Davies, Ralph Forbes, C. Aubrey Smith, Doris Lloyd, Halliwell Hobbes, Ray Milland. Once dashing bachelor Smith, now old and lonely, wants to know his three grown children. Staid but enjoyable adaptation of stage play.

Bachelor Flat (1961) C-91m. ** D: Frank Tashlin. Tuesday Weld, Richard Beymer, Celeste Holm, Terry-Thomas. Weld visits her mother's beach house and finds scientist Thomas at work; she moves in anyway and creates eventual havoc. Thomas has had better material; film's entertainment is all in his lap.

Bachelor in Paradise (1961) C-109m. ** D: Jack Arnold. Bob Hope, Lana Turner, Janis Paige, Jim Hutton, Paula Prentiss, Don Porter, Agnes Moorehead. Hope vehicle about the only bachelor in a community of married couples. Amusing, but not great. Hope has done better; Paige is fun as always.

Bachelor Mother (1939) 81m. ***½ D: Garson Kanin. Ginger Rogers, David Niven, Charles Coburn, Frank Albertson, Ernest Truex. Rogers unwittingly becomes guardian for abandoned baby in this delightful comedy; remade as BUNDLE OF JOY.

Bachelor Party, The (1957) 93m. *** D: Delbert Mann. Don Murray, E. G. Marshall, Jack Warden, Patricia Smith, Carolyn Jones, Larry Blyden, Philip Abbott. Perceptive Paddy Chayefsky drama (originally a TV play) about bachelor party for groom-to-be Abbott, and its emo-

tional effect on other married participants. Jones is exceptional in supporting role.

Back at the Front (1952) 87m. **½ D: George Sherman. Tom Ewell, Harvey Lembeck, Mari Blanchard, Richard Long. Follow-up adventures of Bill Mauldin's army goof-offs Willie and Joe scampering around post-WW2 Tokyo. Retitled: WILLIE AND JOE BACK AT THE FRONT.

Back Door to Heaven (1939) 85m. *** D: William K. Howard. Wallace Ford, Aline MacMahon, Stuart Erwin, Patricia Ellis, Ken Smith, Van Heflin, Jimmy Lydon. Grim social drama focusing on hard life of poor boy and his reasons for choosing life of crime. Much talked about in its day; strong performances by all.

Back From Eternity (1956) 97m. **½ D: John Farrow. Robert Ryan, Anita Ekberg, Rod Steiger, Phyllis Kirk. Moderately engrossing account of victims of plane crash, stranded in South American jungle, and their various reactions to the situation. OK remake of FIVE CAME BACK.

Back From the Dead (1957) 79m. BOMB D: Charles Marquis Warren. Peggie Castle, Arthur Franz, Marsha Hunt, Evelyn Scott, James Bell. Castle is earnest as wife possessed by will of husband's dead first spouse, but cliché-ridden production makes everything ridiculous.

Back Street (1941) 89m. *** D. Robert Stevenson. Charles Boyer, Margaret Sullavan, Richard Carlson, Frank McHugh, Tim Holt. Fine team of Boyer and Sullavan breathes life into Fannie Hurst perennial soaper of woman whose love for man doesn't die when he marries another. First filmed in 1932 with Irene Dunne and John Boles.

Back Street (1961) C-107m. **½ D: David Miller. Susan Hayward, John Gavin, Vera Miles, Virginia Grey. Updated, lavish, unbelievable third version of Fannie Hurst's story of a woman's love for married man. Doesn't play as well as Irene Dunne or Margaret Sullavan versions.

Back to Bataan (1945) 95m. *** D: Edward Dmytryk. John Wayne, Anthony Quinn, Beulah Bondi, Fely Franquelli, Richard Loo, Philip Ahn, Lawrence Tierney. Good sturdy WW2 action film with officer Wayne leading Yank soldiers to victory in the Philippines.

Back to God's Country (1953) C-78m. **½ D: Joseph Pevney. Rock Hudson, Marcia Henderson, Steve Cochran, Hugh O'Brian. Sea captain Hudson and wife Henderson undergo rigors of nature and villainy of Cochran et al before settling, moving onward in the north country for their dream existence.

Back to the Wall (1959-French) 94m. ** D: Edouard Molinaro. Gerard Oury, Jeanne Moreau, Philippe Nicaud, Claire Maurier, Jean Lefebvre. As the adulterous wife, Moreau spins entertaining web of extortion and murder; satisfactory suspenser.

Backfire (1950) 91m. ** D: Vincent Sherman. Virginia Mayo, Gordon MacRae, Edmond O'Brien, Viveca Lindfors, Dane Clark, Ed Begley. OK mystery tale has MacRae search for missing friend through maze of murder and romance.

Backfire (1961-British) 59m. ** D: Paul Almond. Alfred Burke, Zena Marshall, Oliver Johnston. Noel Trevarthen is insurance investigator solving arson and murder at a cosmetics firm; adequate programmer based on Edgar Wallace yarn.

Background to Danger (1943) 80m. *** D: Raoul Walsh. George Raft, Brenda Marshall, Sydney Greenstreet, Peter Lorre, Osa Massen, Kurt Katch. Slam-bang WW2 story with Raft swept into Nazi intrigue in Turkey; terrific car chase highlights fast-moving tale.

Backlash (1947) 66m. ** D: Eugene Forde. Jean Rogers, Richard Travis, Larry Blake, John Eldredge, Leonard Strong, Robert Shayne, Louise Currie, Douglas Fowley. Standard programmer of man trying to frame his wife for murder he committed.

Backlash (1956) C-84m. **½ D: John Sturges. Richard Widmark, Donna Reed, William Campbell, John McIntire, Barton MacLane. Widmark is only survivor of Indian massacre; knowing the whereabouts of buried treasure, he is object of outlaw manhunt.

Backtrack (1969) C-95m. ** D: Earl Bellamy. Neville Brand, James Drury, Doug McClure, Peter Brown, Ida Lupino, Rhonda Fleming, Fernando Lamas. Maverick cowboy on the range. No more than an elongated combination of "The Virginian" and "Laredo" TV segments.

Bad and the Beautiful, The (1952) 118m. ***½ D: Vincente Minnelli. Kirk Douglas, Lana Turner, Dick Powell, Gloria Grahame, Barry Sullivan, Walter Pidgeon, Gilbert Roland. Captivating Hollywood story of ambitious producer (Douglas) told via relationships with actress Turner, writer Powell, director Sullivan. Solid, insightful, witty, with Lana's best performance to date.

Bad Bascomb (1946) 110m. *½ D: S. Sylvan Simon. Wallace Beery, Margaret O'Brien, Marjorie Main, J. Carrol Naish, Marshall Thompson. Overlong Western with fine action scenes, overshadowed by incredibly syrupy scenes with Beery and O'Brien.

Bad Boy (1949) 86m. **½ D: Kurt Neumann. Lloyd Nolan, Jane Wyatt, Audie Murphy, James Gleason, Martha Vickers. Juvenile delinquent rehabilitated by being sent to boys' ranch, where Nolan befriends him. Young Murphy is belligerently effective.

Bad Company (1972) C-93m. ***½ D: Robert Benton. Jeff Bridges, Barry Brown, Jim Davis, David Huddleston, John Savage, Jerry Houser. Highly entertaining "sleeper" about two young drifters of wildly differing temperaments who rob their way West during the Civil War; aided immeasurably by subdued photography and superb musical score.

Bad Day at Black Rock (1954) C-81m. ***½ D: John Sturges. Spencer Tracy, Robert Ryan, Anne Francis, Dean Jagger, Walter Brennan, John Ericson, Ernest Borgnine, Lee Marvin. Powerhouse cast in yarn of one-armed man (Tracy) uncovering skeleton in Western town's closet. Borgnine memorable as slimy heavy.

Bad For Each Other (1953) 83m. **½ D: Irving Rapper. Charlton Heston, Lizabeth Scott, Dianne Foster, Mildred Dunnock, Marjorie Rambeau. Idealistic doctor Heston finds Pennsylvania mining town has more worthy patients than idle social set. Pouty Scott and wise Rambeau are good cast assets.

Bad Girl (1959-British) 100m. *½ D: Herbert Wilcox. Anna Neagle, Sylvia Syms, Norman Wooland, Wilfrid Hyde-White, Kenneth Haigh, Julia Lockwood. Modest trivia enhanced by good cast involving teenager who becomes involved with sordid side of life. Retitled: TEEN-AGE BAD GIRL.

Bad Lord Byron (1951-British) 85m. **½ D: David Macdonald. Dennis Price, Joan Greenwood, Mai Zetterling, Sonia Holm. Potentially exciting but static retelling of the life of 19th-century poet and lover, focusing on his many romances.

Bad Man, The (1941) 70m. **½ D: Richard Thorpe. Wallace Beery, Lionel Barrymore, Laraine Day, Ronald Reagan, Henry Travers. Fairly good co-starring vehicle for Beery, as Western outlaw, and Barrymore, as former friend who depends on the bad man's loyalty.

Bad Man of Brimstone (1938) 90m. ** D: J. Walter Ruben. Wallace Beery, Virginia Bruce, Dennis O'-Keefe, Joseph Calleia, Lewis Stone, Guy Kibbee, Bruce Cabot. Low-grade Western vehicle is for Beery fans, with star as outlaw who is reformed by family revelation.

Bad Man's River (1972) C-89m. ** D: Gene Martin. Lee Van Cleef, James Mason, Gina Lollobrigida, Simon Andreu, Diana Lorys. Van Cleef is head of an outlaw gang repeatedly outsmarted by devilish Lollobrigida in this pallid comedy-western filmed in Spain.

Bad Men of Missouri (1941) 74m. *** D: Ray Enright. Dennis Morgan, Jane Wyman, Wayne Morris, Arthur Kennedy, Victor Jory, Alan Baxter. Younger brothers, enraged by Southern carpetbaggers, turn to lawless life in fictional Western, with good cast.

Bad News Bears, The (1976) C-102m. *** D: Michael Ritchie. Walter Matthau, Tatum O'Neal, Vic Morrow, Joyce Van Patten, Jackie Earle Haley, Alfred Lutter. Bright comedy about hopeless Little League baseball team that scores with an unlikely combination: a beer-guzzling coach (Matthau) and a female star pitcher (O'Neal). Some of film's major appeal—young kids spouting four-letter words—will be lost on TV.

Bad News Bears Go To Japan, The (1978) C-91m. ** D: John Berry. Tony Curtis, Jackie Earle Haley, Tomisaburo Wakayama, George Wyner, Lonny Chapman. Curtis is good as a small-time hustler who sees money-making opportunity in the now-familiar baseball team. Third film was the kids' last, and it's easy to see why.

Bad News Bears in Breaking Training, The (1977) C-100m. **½ D: Michael Pressman. William Devane, Jackie Earle Haley, Jimmy Baio, Clifton James, Chris Barnes. Sentimental sequel to 1976 hit, with dirty talk largely absent. Star of the kids' baseball team, Haley heads for the Houston Astrodome and enlists the aid of estranged father Devane in coaching the misfits. Sporadically funny.

Bad Ronald (1974) C-78m. TVM D: Buzz Kulik. Scott Jacoby, Pippa Scott, John Larch, Dabney Coleman, Kim Hunter, John Fiedler. Family with three daughters moves into an old house unaware that it has a secret room occupied by psychopathic teen-ager who has murdered a taunting peer. Intriguing little thriller; above average.

Bad Seed, The (1956) 129m. *** D: Mervyn LeRoy. Nancy Kelly, Patty McCormack, Henry Jones, Eileen Heckart, Evelyn Varden. Stagy but spellbinding account of malicious child McCormack whose inherited evil causes death of several people.

Badge of Marshal Brennan, The (1957) 76m. *½ D: Albert C. Gannaway. Jim Davis, Arleen Whelan, Lee Van Cleef, Louis Jean Heydt. Uninspired account of criminal Davis mistaken as law enforcer, who redeems himself by corraling rustling gang.

Badge 373 (1973) C-116m. *½ D: Howard W. Koch. Robert Duvall, Verna Bloom, Henry Darrow, Eddie Egan, Felipe Luciano, Tina Christiana. Very minor follow-up to THE FRENCH CONNECTION. Policeman Duvall tries to fight crime syndicate singlehandedly in N.Y.C. Dull.

Badlanders, The (1958) C-83m. *** D: Delmer Daves. Alan Ladd, Ernest Borgnine, Katy Jurado, Claire Kelly. Turn-of-the-century Western set in Arizona with Ladd and Borgnine planning gold robbery, each trying to outsmart the other; nicely handled by all. Remake of THE ASPHALT JUNGLE.

Badlands (1973) C-95m. **½ D: Terrence Malick. Martin Sheen, Sissy Spacek, Warren Oates, Ramon Bieri, Alan Vint. Stark, moody, moderately successful takeoff on the Starkweather-Fugate killing spree in the 50s. Well-cast film has cult following.

Badlands of Dakota (1941) 74m. **½ D: Alfred E. Green. Robert Stack, Ann Rutherford, Richard Dix, Frances Farmer, Broderick Crawford, Hugh Herbert. Brothers Crawford and Stack fight over Rutherford, while Wild Bill Hickok (Dix) does fighting of another kind.

Badlands of Montana (1957) 75m. *½

D: Daniel B. Ullman. Rex Reason, Beverly Garland, Keith Larsen, Jack Kruschen. Unimaginative oater leading up to inevitable climax of former buddies, sheriff and gunslinger, having shoot-out.

Badman's Country (1958) 68m. **½ D: Fred F. Sears. George Montgomery, Buster Crabbe, Neville Brand, Malcolm Atterbury. Fictionalized Western history with name-dropping cast of characters. Sheriff Pat Garrett (Montgomery) joins with Wyatt Earp (Crabbe) and Buffalo Bill (Atterbury) for showdown with outlaw Butch Cassidy (Brand).

Badman's Territory (1946) 97m. *** D: Tim Whelan. Randolph Scott, Ann Richards, Gabby Hayes, Ray Collins, Chief Thundercloud. Sheriff Scott is helpless when bandits flee across border into territory uncontrolled by government; good Western.

Baffled (1972) C-90m. TVM D: Phillip Leacock. Leonard Nimoy, Susan Hampshire, Vera Miles, Rachel Roberts, Jewel Branch, Christopher Benjamin. Contrived but enjoyable race-against-time thriller with Nimoy an American race driver whose visions convince an ESP expert (Hampshire) that people in vision are in danger. Above average.

Bagdad (1949) C-82m. ** D: Charles Lamont. Maureen O'Hara, Paul Christian, Vincent Price, John Sutton. Costume hijinks with O'Hara fetching if not believable as native chieftain's daughter seeking revenge for father's death in old Turkey.

Bahama Passage (1941) C-83m. **½ D: Edward Griffith. Madeleine Carroll, Sterling Hayden, Flora Robson, Leo G. Carroll, Mary Anderson. Scenery is chief asset of routine tale of lovely Madeleine meeting handsome Sterling in beautiful Bahama, with much hamming by Carroll and Robson.

Bailout at 43,000 (1957) 78m. ** D: Francis D. Lyon. John Payne, Karen Steele, Paul Kelly, Richard Eyer, Constance Ford. Dilemma of air force pilot Payne whose relief at not having to test new safety device is outweighed by coward-guilt complex. Routine material is not enhanced by flight sequences or romantic relief.

Bait (1954) 79m. *½ D: Hugo Haas. Cleo Moore, Hugo Haas, John Agar, Emmett Lynn. Plodding melodrama; old geezer Haas connives to get rid of his prospector partner.

Bait, The (1973) C-73m. TVM D: Leonard Horn. Donna Mills, Michael Constantine, Bill Devane, June Lockhart, Thalmus Rasulala. Policewoman-widow (Mills) puts herself on line, demands assignment to rape-murder case. Film has distasteful point of view, occasional suspense, unconvincing characters. Average.

Baker's Hawk (1976) C-98m. *** D: Lyman D. Dayton. Clint Walker, Burl Ives, Diane Baker, Lee H. Montgomery, Alan Young, Taylor Lacher. Fine family drama about young boy (Montgomery) who befriends hermitlike Ives, and comes of age as he participates in parents' struggle against vigilante forces. Beautifully filmed in Utah.

Balalaika (1939) 102m. ** D: Reinhold Schunzel. Nelson Eddy, Ilona Massey, Charles Ruggles, Frank Morgan, Lionel Atwill, George Tobias. Plodding operetta of Russian revolution with little to recommend it.

Balcony, The (1963) 84m. ** D: Joseph Strick. Shelley Winters, Peter Falk, Lee Grant, Ruby Dee, Peter Brocco, Kent Smith, Jeff Corey, Leonard Nimoy. Low-budget, none-too-successful attempt to adapt Jean Genet play to the screen, with Winters as madame who maintains her brothel during a revolution. Grant stands out as Winters' lesbian confidante.

Ball of Fire (1941) 111m. ***½ D: Howard Hawks. Gary Cooper, Barbara Stanwyck, Oscar Homolka, Dana Andrews, Dan Duryea, S. Z. Sakall, Richard Haydn, Gene Krupa. Burlesque dancer moves in with seven prissy professors (led by Cooper) to explain "slang" for their new encyclopedia; delightful twist on Snow White and the Seven Dwarfs by screenwriters Billy Wilder & Charles Brackett. Remade as A SONG IS BORN.

Ballad of a Soldier (1960-Russian) 89m. *** D: Grigori Chukhrai. Vladimir Ivashov, Shanna Prokhorenko, Antonina Maximova, Nikolai Kruchkov. Effectively simple love story of Russian soldier on leave during WW2, who meets and falls in love with unaffected country girl.

Ballad of Andy Crocker, The (1969) C-73m. TVM D: George McCowan. Lee Majors, Joey Heatherton, Jimmy Dean, Agnes Moorehead, Marvin Gaye, Jill Haworth, Lisa Todd. Name in title refers to Vietnam veteran (Majors) returning to home town

and reacting to major changes: former sweetheart now married, former business partner now crooked. Not quite a "ballad" but above average.
Ballad of Josie, The (1967) C-102m. **½ D: Andrew McLaglen. Doris Day, Peter Graves, George Kennedy, Andy Devine, William Talman. Uninspired Western spoof with widow Day running a ranch and trying to lead the good life.

Ballad of Cable Hogue, The (1970) C-121m. *** D: Sam Peckinpah. Jason Robards, Stella Stevens, David Warner, Strother Martin, Slim Pickens, L. Q. Jones. Peckinpah's lyrical, wholly enjoyable fable of loner who builds a life for himself in remote part of the Old West. Stevens has one of her best roles as woman who joins Cable Hogue in quest for the good life. Overlong.

Bambole! (1965-Italian) 111m. ** D: Dino Risi, Luigi Comencini, Franco Rossi, Mauro Bolognini. Virna Lisi, Nino Manfredi, Elke Sommer, Monica Vitti, Gina Lollobrigida, Akim Tamiroff, Jean Sorel. Quartet of stories on Italian life that never sparkles. "The Phone Call," "Treatise on Eugenics," "The Soup," "Monsignor Cupid." Retitled: FOUR KINDS OF LOVE.

Bamboo Prison, The (1954) 80m. ** D: Lewis Seiler. Robert Francis, Dianne Foster, Brian Keith, Jerome Courtland, E. G. Marshall, Earle Hyman. Superficial handling of loyal American soldier Francis posing as informer in North Korean P.O.W. camp to outwit enemy.

Banacek (1972) C-100m. TVM D: Jack Smight. George Peppard, Christine Belford, Don Dubbins, Ed Nelson, Ralph Manza. Boston-based insurance investigator T. Banacek (Peppard) assigned to unusual case of Brinks truck vanishing in middle of Texas highway. Some interesting situations, good direction. Above average; pilot for TV series. Now titled DETOUR TO NOWHERE.

Banana Peel (1965-French) 97m. *** D: Marcel Ophuls. Jeanne Moreau, Jean-Paul Belmondo, Gert Frobe. Rogues cheat millionaire out of a small fortune in this engaging comedy.

Bananas (1971) C-82m. **** D: Woody Allen. Woody Allen, Louise Lasser, Carlos Montalban, Howard Cosell. Hilarious; the usual assortment of good jokes, bad jokes, bizarre ideas built around unlikely premise of Woody becoming involved in revolution South of the border. Look for Sylvester Stallone as hoodlum.

Band of Angels (1957) C-127m. **½ D: Raoul Walsh. Clark Gable, Yvonne De Carlo, Sidney Poitier, Efrem Zimbalist, Jr., Patric Knowles. Flat attempt to make costume epic of Robert Penn Warren's Civil War novel; Gable is Southern gentleman with shady past, in love with high-toned De Carlo who discovers she has Negro ancestors. Poitier is resolute educated slave.

Band Wagon, The (1953) C-112m. **** D: Vincente Minnelli. Fred Astaire, Cyd Charisse, Oscar Levant, Nanette Fabray, Jack Buchanan. Sophisticated backstage musical improves with each viewing. Astaire plays a "washed-up" movie star who tries his luck on Broadway, under the direction of maniacal genius Buchanan. Musical highlights include "Dancing in the Dark," "Shine on Your Shoes," and "That's Entertainment" (all by Howard Dietz and Arthur Schwartz) and Astaire's Mickey Spillane spoof "The Girl Hunt."

Bandido (1956) C-92m. *** D: Richard Fleischer. Robert Mitchum, Zachary Scott, Ursula Thiess, Gilbert Roland, Rodolfo Acosta. Mitchum is gun supplier who tries to play both sides during 1916 Mexican rebellion; constant action, endless cat-and-mouse twists with rival Scott keep this one humming.

Bandit of Sherwood Forest, The (1946) C-86m. **½ D: George Sherman, Henry Levin. Cornel Wilde, Anita Louise, Jill Esmond, Edgar Buchanan. Colorful but standard swashbuckler with Wilde as son of Robin Hood carrying on in faithful tradition with the Merry Men.

Bandit of Zhobe, The (1959-British) C-80m. **½ D: John Gilling. Victor Mature, Anthony Newley, Norman Wooland, Anne Aubrey, Walter Gotell, Sean Kelly. Moderate actioner set in 19th-century India with Mature as native chief turned outlaw combatting the British.

Bandits of Corsica, The (1953) 81m. ** D: Ray Nazarro. Richard Greene, Paula Raymond, Raymond Burr, Lee Van Cleef. Pat costumer with Greene championing cause of the righteous.

Bandolero! (1968) C-106m. **½ D: Andrew V. McLaglen. James Stewart,

Dean Martin, Raquel Welch, George Kennedy, Andrew Prine, Will Geer. Jimmy and Dino play brothers/outlaws whose gang flees across Mexican border with Raquel as hostage. Not exactly like real life, but nice outdoor photography makes it passable escapism.

Bang-Bang Kid, The (1968-Spanish) C-90m. **½ D: Stanley Prager. Guy Madison, Tom Bosley, Sandra Milo, Riccardo Garrone, Jose Caffaral. Offbeat lighthearted turn-of-the-century Western that pits an iron-handed sheriff against an unassuming bumbler and a gun-toting robot called The Bang-Bang Kid.

Bang, Bang, You're Dead! (1966-British) C-92m. **½ D: Don Sharp. Tony Randall, Senta Berger, Terry-Thomas, Herbert Lom, Wilfrid Hyde-White. Unsuspecting Randall gets involved with Moroccan gangsters in OK spoof; good location shooting. Shown on TV as BANG BANG!

Bang the Drum Slowly (1973) C-97m. ***½ D: John Hancock. Robert DeNiro, Michael Moriarty, Vincent Gardenia, Heather MacRae, Barbara Babcock, Phil Foster. Touching study of two professional baseball players on fictional New York team drawn to each other under unusual circumstance. Outstanding performances by two leads, Moriarty as hustling star pitcher, DeNiro as simpleton catcher, in slightly longish episodic script.

Bang You're Dead SEE: **Game of Danger**

Banjo Hackett: Roamin' Free (1976) C-100m. TVM D: Andrew V. McLaglen. Don Meredith, Ike Eisenmann, Jennifer Warren, Chuck Connors, Dan O'Herlihy, Gloria DeHaven, Anne Francis, L. Q. Jones, Jeff Corey, Jan Murray. Itinerant horse trader travels Old West with orphaned 9-year-old nephew in quest of the youngster's stolen Arabian mare. Episodic film benefits from Meredith's easygoing style, fine supporting cast. Average.

Banjo on My Knee (1936) 80m. *** D: John Cromwell. Barbara Stanwyck, Joel McCrea, Walter Brennan, Buddy Ebsen, Helen Westley, Walter Catlett, Tony Martin. Stanwyck's the whole show in riverboat saga, singing with Martin, dancing with Ebsen, scrapping with Katherine DeMille.

Bank Dick, The (1940) 74m. **** D: Eddie Cline. W. C. Fields, Cora Witherspoon, Una Merkel, Evelyn Del Rio, Jessie Ralph, Grady Sutton,

Franklin Pangborn. Classic of insane humor loosely wound about a no-account who becomes a bank guard; Sutton as nitwit prospective son-in-law, Pangborn as bank examiner match the shenanigans of Fields.

Bank Shot (1974) C-83m. *** D. Gower Champion. George C. Scott, Joanna Cassidy, Sorrell Booke, G. Wood, Clifton James, Robert Balaban, Bibi Osterwald. Engaging comedy about Scott heading a gang of bumblers who plan a most unusual bank heist.

Bannerline (1951) 88m. ** D: Don Weis. Keefe Brasselle, Sally Forrest, Lionel Barrymore, Lewis Stone. Brasselle is optimistic fledgling reporter who sparks civic pride into town fighting corruption; film marred by typecasting and clichéd plotline.

Banning (1967) C-102m. *** D: Ron Winston. Robert Wagner, Anjanette Comer, Jill St. John, Guy Stockwell, James Farentino. Pleasing study of corruption in and about a swank L.A. golf club. Wagner, the pro with a past; St. John, the love-hungry gal.

Banyon (1971) C-97m. TVM D: Robert Day. Robert Forster, Darren McGavin, Jose Ferrer, Herb Edelman. Private-eye (and one-time cop) in hot water with police when girl is discovered murdered in his office with his gun. Standard, formula plot made interesting by 1930s-era atmosphere, unusually effective use of color. Above average; pilot for TV series.

Bar Sinister SEE: **It's a Dog's Life**

Barabbas (1962) C-134m. *** D: Richard Fleischer. Anthony Quinn, Silvana Mangano, Arthur Kennedy, Jack Palance, Ernest Borgnine, Katy Jurado. Lavish production, coupled with good script (based on Lagerkvist's novel) and generally fine acting by large cast make for engrossing, literate experience. Overly long.

Barbados Quest SEE: **Murder on Approval**

Barbarella (1968-French-Italian) C-98m. **½ D: Roger Vadim. Jane Fonda, John Phillip Law, Anita Pallenberg, Milo O'Shea, David Hemmings, Marcel Marceau, Claude Dauphin. Unfunny takeoff on the French comic strip about a sexy 41st-century astronaut seems more interesting today, given recent history of both Fonda and Pallenberg. For the midnight-movie crowd.

Barbarian and the Geisha, The (1958) C-105m. **½ D: John Huston. John

Wayne, Eiko Ando, Sam Jaffe, So Yamamura. Twisting of 19th-century history allows Wayne as Ambassador Harris to romance Japanese beauty (Ando). Miscasting of Wayne is ludicrous, throwing costumer amuck.

Barbary Coast (1935) 97m. ***½ D: Howard Hawks. Miriam Hopkins, Edward G. Robinson, Joel McCrea, Walter Brennan, Frank Craven, Brian Donlevy. Lusty tale of San Francisco in the late 19th century with dance-hall queen Hopkins running head-on into big-shot Robinson.

Barbary Coast, The (1974) C-100m. TVM D: Bill Bixby. William Shatner, Dennis Cole, Lynda Day George, John Vernon, Charles Aidman, Michael Ansara, Neville Brand, Bill Bixby. Undercover agent Shatner and casino owner Cole comb boomtown San Francisco for an extortionist. Light-hearted adventure tale attempted to recapture the flair of TV's popular "Wild, Wild West," later became short-lived series under same title. Average.

Barbary Coast Gent (1944) 87m. ** D: Roy Del Ruth. Wallace Beery, Binnie Barnes, John Carradine, Noah Beery, Sr., Frances Rafferty, Chill Wills, Donald Meek. Typical Beery vehicle, with good supporting cast, about smooth-talking bandit who goes straight.

Barefoot Contessa, The (1954) C-128m. *** D: Joseph L. Mankiewicz. Humphrey Bogart, Ava Gardner, Edmond O'Brien, Marius Goring, Rossano Brazzi. Cynical tale of beautiful Ava promoted into Hollywood star by mentor-director Bogart. O'Brien won an Oscar as press agent.

Barefoot Executive, The (1971) C-96m. ** D: Robert Butler. Kurt Russell, Joe Flynn, Harry Morgan, Wally Cox, Heather North, Alan Hewitt, John Ritter. Russell discovers chimp with ability to pick top-rated TV shows, and becomes vice-president of a network. Routine Disney slapstick.

Barefoot in the Park (1967) C-105m. *** D: Gene Saks. Robert Redford, Jane Fonda, Charles Boyer, Mildred Natwick, Herb Edelman. Plotless, entertaining Neil Simon comedy finds Fonda and Redford as newlyweds in four-story walkup apartment. Running gag about climbing stairs grows thin, but film doesn't.

Barefoot Mailman, The (1951) C-83m. ** D: Earl McEvoy. Robert Cummings, Terry Moore, Jerome Courtland, Will Geer. Potentially engaging story of a first postal route in Florida bogs down in tale of former con-man (Cummings) tempted to fleece citizens of Miami with phony railroad stock; Moore is pert leading lady.

Barefoot Savage SEE: **Sensualita**

Barkleys of Broadway, The (1949) C-109m. *** D: Charles Walters. Fred Astaire, Ginger Rogers, Oscar Levant, Billie Burke, Gale Robbins. Astaire and Rogers reteamed after ten years in this witty Comden-Green script about show biz couple who split, then make up. Songs include "You'd Be Hard to Replace," "They Can't Take That Away from Me." Ginger reading "La Marseillaise" is a definite low point.

Barnaby and Me (1977-Australian) C-90m. **½ D: Norman Panama. Sid Caesar, Juliet Mills, Sally Boyden, John Newcombe. Harmless family comedy about American con man who gets involved with a girl and her pet koala bear.

Barnacle Bill (1941) 98m. ** D: Richard Thorpe. Wallace Beery, Marjorie Main, Leo Carrillo, Virginia Weidler, Donald Meek, Barton MacLane. Beery and Main support basically run-of-the-mill material as old salt and woman trying to snare him into marriage.

Baron Blood (1972-Italian) C-90m. **½ D: Mario Bava. Joseph Cotten, Elke Sommer, Massimo Girotti, Rada Rassimov, Antonio Cantafora, Alan Collins. Descendant of evil nobleman attempts "novel" rejuvenation principles. Standard plot livened by unusual settings and lighting.

Baron of Arizona, The (1950) 90m. **½ D: Samuel Fuller. Vincent Price, Ellen Drew, Beulah Bondi, Reed Hadley. Price has field day as landgrabbing scoundrel who almost gains control of Arizona in the 19th century.

Baroness and the Butler, The (1938) 75m. ** D: Walter Lang. William Powell, Annabella, Helen Westley, Henry Stephenson, Joseph Schildkraut, J. Edward Bromberg. Powell leads double life as Annabella's butler and member of parliament. He's fine as usual but script is rather thin.

Baron's African War, The (1943) 100m. **½ D: Spencer Bennet. Rod Cameron, Joan Marsh, Duncan Renaldo, Lionel Royce. Flavorful Republic serial set in WW2 Africa, with Cameron tackling sinister Nazis and

Arabs with equal relish; quite well paced. Reedited movie serial: SECRET SERVICE IN DARKEST AFRICA.

Barquero (1970) C-115m. *½ D: Gordon Douglas. Lee Van Cleef, Warren Oates, Forrest Tucker, Kerwin Mathews, Mariette Hartley. Van Cleef goes after gang of mercenaries who wiped out town. Usual blood and guts, short on sense, long on deaths and mayhem.

Barretts of Wimpole Street, The (1934) 110m. *** D: Sidney Franklin. Norma Shearer, Fredric March, Charles Laughton, Maureen O'Sullivan, Katherine Alexander, Una O'Connor, Ian Wolfe. Handsome, well-acted (if somewhat stodgy) MGM production of classic romance between Elizabeth Barrett and Robert Browning in 19th century England. Retitled for TV: THE FORBIDDEN ALLIANCE.

Barretts of Wimpole Street, The (1957-U.S.-British) C-105m. **½ D: Sidney Franklin. Jennifer Jones, John Gielgud, Bill Travers, Virginia McKenna. Tame interpretation of the lilting romance between poets Browning, Barrett, with actors bogged down in prettified fluff.

Barricade (1939) 71m. ** D: Gregory Ratoff. Alice Faye, Warner Baxter, Charles Winninger, Arthur Treacher, Keye Luke, Moroni Olsen. Faye and Baxter are trapped in Chinese embassy and fall in love; rather tame.

Barricade (1950) C-75m. ** D: Peter Godfrey. Dane Clark, Ruth Roman, Raymond Massey, Robert Douglas. Clark pitted against Massey in gold-mining-camp Western lends a spark to usual battle of good vs. evil. Mild rehash of THE SEA WOLF.

Barrier (1966-Polish) 84m. **½ D: Jerzy Skolimowski. Joanna Szczerbic, Jan Nowicki, Tadeusz Lomnicki, Maria Malicka. Interesting view of youthful attitudes in Poland, combining reportage with fantasy elements. Not a total success, but still intriguing.

Barry Lyndon (1975-British) C-183m. ***½ D: Stanley Kubrick. Ryan O'Neal, Marisa Berenson, Patrick Magee, Hardy Kruger, Steven Berkoff, Gay Hamilton, narrated by Michael Hordern. Exquisite, meticulously detailed period piece stars O'Neal as Thackeray's 18-century rogue-hero who covets success but lets it go to his head. Long, deliberately paced but never boring. Exquisite photography by John Alcott; period music equally fine.

Bartleby (1972-British) C-78m. **½ D: Anthony Friedman. Paul Scofield, John McEnery, Thorley Walters, Colin Jeavons, Raymond Mason. Herman Melville's great short story about 19th-century auditing clerk who refuses to leave job after he is fired is admirably attempted in modern-day update, even though story doesn't really lend itself to filming; Scofield is fine as bewildered but sympathetic boss.

Bashful Elephant, The (1962-German) 82m. BOMB D: Dorrell McGowan, Stuart E. McGowan. Molly Mack, Helmut Schmid, Kai Fischer, Buddy Baer. Supposedly a family film, this import spends more time on an elephant trainer's divorce than anything else. Not worth your time.

Bat, The (1959) 80m. **½ D: Crane Wilbur. Vincent Price, Agnes Moorehead, Gavin Gordon, John Sutton, Lenita Lane, Darla Hood. Faithful adaptation of Mary Roberts Rinehart novel, (filmed before in 1915, 1926 and—as *The Bat Whispers*—in 1930), set in old gothic mansion. Fairly exciting yarn.

Bataan (1943) 114m. *** D: Tay Garnett. Robert Taylor, George Murphy, Thomas Mitchell, Lloyd Nolan, Lee Bowman, Robert Walker, Desi Arnaz, Barry Nelson. Realistically made drama of famous WW2 incident on Pacific Island; good combat scenes.

Bathing Beauty (1944) C-101m. **½ D: George Sidney. Red Skelton, Esther Williams, Basil Rathbone, Ethel Smith, Xavier Cugat, Bill Goodwin. Attractive cast in lavish MGM musical bogged down with silly comedy interludes. One of Rathbone's most thankless roles.

Batman (1966) C-105m. ** D: Leslie Martinson. Adam West, Burt Ward, Burgess Meredith, Cesar Romero, Lee Meriwether, Neil Hamilton, Madge Blake, Reginald Denny. Quickly made feature to cash in on then-hot TV series pulls out all stops, features the Joker, Riddler, Penguin, and Catwoman trying to undo the caped crusader. Unfortunately they don't. For younger minds only.

Batmen of Africa (1936) 100m. ** D: B. Reeves Eason, Joseph Kane. Clyde Beatty, Manuel King, Elaine Shepard, Lucien Prival. Diverting cliffhanger (Republic Pictures' first serial) of Beatty leading expedition to jungle city to rescue captured white girl; good special effects, primitive acting. Reedited movie serial: DARKEST AFRICA.

Battered (1978) C-100m. TVM D: Peter Werner. Karen Grassle, LeVar Burton, Mike Farrell, Joan Blondell, Howard Duff, Chip Fields. Absorbing and disturbing drama interweaves three stories of wife-beating victims; actress Grassle also cowrote this teleplay. Average.

Battle at Apache Pass, The (1952) C-85m. **½ D: George Sherman. Jeff Chandler, John Lund, Beverly Tyler, Richard Egan, Hugh O'Brian, Jay Silverheels. Chandler is Cochise (again) trying to prevent further Indian warring, but for sake of action-hungry viewers he doesn't succeed.

Battle at Bloody Beach (1961) 83m. **½ D: Herbert Coleman. Audie Murphy, Gary Crosby, Dolores Michaels, Alejandro Rey. Sporadically exciting WW2 action with soldier Murphy locating his wife on a Pacific Island, involved with partisan cause and its leader.

Battle Beneath the Earth (1967-British) C-91m. **½ D: Montgomery Tully. Kerwin Mathews, Viviane Ventura, Robert Ayres, Peter Arne, Al Mulock, Martin Benson. Silly but enjoyable pulp fantasy about Chinese plan to invade U.S. through network of tunnels.

Battle Beyond the Sun (1963) C-75m. ** D: Thomas Colchart. Edd Perry, Arla Powell, Andy Stewart, Bruce Hunter. Russian film NEBO ZOWET (1959) refashioned into American product by producer Roger Corman; story deals with rival space missions to Mars. Trivia fans: this dubbed version was supervised by then unknown Francis Ford Coppola.

Battle Circus (1953) 90m. ** D: Richard Brooks. Humphrey Bogart, June Allyson, Keenan Wynn, Robert Keith, Philip Ahn. Soaper of doctor under fire during Korean war; Bogie saddled with bad script and syrupy June.

Battle Cry (1955) C-149m. *** D: Raoul Walsh. Van Heflin, Tab Hunter, Dorothy Malone, Anne Francis, Raymond Massey, Mona Freeman, Aldo Ray. Watered-down version of Leon Uris WW2 marine novel, focusing on servicemen in training, action, and in love. Hunter as wholesome soldier and Malone a love-hungry dame stand out in episodic actioner,

which now seems less than daring.

Battle Flame (1959) 78m. *½ D: R. G. Springsteen. Scott Brady, Elaine Edwards, Robert Blake, Gordon Jones, Wayne Heffley, Richard Harrison. Programmer about Korean War and soldier Brady's romance with nurse Edwards.

Battle for the Planet of the Apes (1973) C-92m. ** D: J. Lee Thompson. Roddy McDowall, Natalie Trundy, Severn Darden, Paul Williams, Claude Akins, John Huston. Substandard; fifth (and last) apes installment attempts to bring entire series full-cycle. Good footage from earlier films helps, but not much.

Battle Hymn (1956) C-108m. *** D: Douglas Sirk. Rock Hudson, Martha Hyer, Anna Kashfi, Dan Duryea, Don DeFore. Hudson turns in convincing performance as clergyman who returns to military duty in Korean War to train fighter pilots; expansive production values.

Battle in Outer Space (1960-Japanese) C-74m. *½ D: Inoshiro Honda. Ryo Ikebe, Kyoko Anzai, Leonard Stanford, Harold Conway. Unexciting sci-fi as Earth prepares for attack from outer space. Plenty of special effects.

Battle of Algiers, The (1966-Italian-Algerian) 123m. *** D: Gilo Pontecorvo. Yacef Saadi, Jean Martin, Brahim Haggiag, Tommaso Neri, Samia Kerbash. Straightforward drama about revolt against the French by Algerians from 1954-1962. Winner of many awards, but the objective, pseudo-documentary fashion in which it was filmed somewhat limits its dramatic power. Nonetheless, a good film.

Battle of Austerlitz, The (1960-French/Italian) C-123m. *½ D: Abel Gance. Claudia Cardinale, Martine Carol, Leslie Caron, Vittorio DeSica, Jean Marais, Ettore Manni, Jack Palance, Orson Welles. International cast reenacts the epic of Napoleon's greatest battle in stultifying fashion. Drastic cutting from original length (166m.) and terrible dubbing job doom it. Originally titled AUSTERLITZ.

Battle of Britain (1969-British) C-132m. ** D: Guy Hamilton. Harry Andrews, Michael Caine, Trevor Howard, Curt Jurgens, Kenneth More, Laurence Olivier, Christopher Plummer, Michael Redgrave, Ralph Richardson, Robert Shaw, Susannah York. Superb aerial sequences, which will suffer on TV anyway, hardly redeem yet another "spot-the-star" WW2 epic, this time about British airmen who prevented threatened Nazi invasion.

Battle of Neretva, The (1971-Yugoslavian-U.S.-Italian-German) C-102m. ** D: Veljko Bulajic. Yul Brynner, Sergei Bondarchuk, Curt Jurgens, Sylva Koscina, Hardy Kruger, Franco Nero, Orson Welles. Originally an Oscar nominee for Best Foreign Film, but when this $12 million spectacle about Nazi invasion of Yugoslavia was cut down from a nearly three-hour running time, it lost most of its coherency. Too bad.

Battle of Rogue River (1954) C-71m. ** D: William Castle. George Montgomery, Richard Denning, Martha Hyer, John Crawford. Much needed action sequence never comes in lopsided Western of Montgomery negotiating Indian truce as settlers seek statehood for Oregon in 1850s.

Battle of the Bulge (1965) C-163m. ** D: Ken Annakin. Henry Fonda, Robert Shaw, Robert Ryan, Dana Andrews, George Montgomery, Ty Hardin, Pier Angeli. Originally produced in Cinerama, this overinflated war drama about an important event cannot triumph over banal script. Read a good book on the subject instead.

Battle of the Coral Sea (1959) 80m. **½ D: Paul Wendkos. Cliff Robertson, Gia Scala, Teru Shimada, Patricia Cutts, Gene Blakely, Gordon Jones. Staunch Robertson is submarine captain on Jap-held island during WW2, seeking to send vital data to U.S. fleet.

Battle of the River Plate SEE: Pursuit of the Graf Spee

Battle of the Sexes, The (1960-British) 88m. *** D: Charles Crichton. Peter Sellers, Robert Morley, Constance Cummings, Jameson Clark. Sparkling British comedy with macabre overtones; Sellers is elderly Scotsman contemplating murder. Supporting cast keeps this moving.

Battle of the Villa Florita, The (1965-British) C-111m. **½ D: Delmer Daves. Maureen O'Hara, Rossano Brazzi, Richard Todd, Phyllis Calvert, Martin Stephens. Unconvincing soaper with O'Hara running off to Italy to carry on with widower Brazzi; predictable interference from each's children.

Battle of the Worlds (1961-Italian) C-84m. *½ D: Anthony Dawson.

Claude Rains, Maya Brent, Bill Carter, Umberto Orsini, Jacqueline Derval. Rains adds some weight to this English-dubbed cheapie about scientists' frantic efforts to stop alien planet from colliding with earth.

Battle Stations (1956) 81m. *½ D: Lewis Seiler. John Lund, William Bendix, Keefe Brasselle, Richard Boone. Rehash about crew in WW2 Pacific and their preparation for fighting the Japs.

Battle Stripe SEE: Men, The

Battle Taxi (1955) 82m. ** D: Herbert L. Strock. Sterling Hayden, Arthur Franz, Marshall Thompson, Joel Marston, Leo Needham. Ordinary tale of Korean War missions; strictly pedestrian.

Battle Zone (1952) 82m. ** D: Lesley Selander. John Hodiak, Linda Christian, Stephen McNally, Philip Ahn. Hodiak vies with McNally for Christian, with brief time out to fight Commies in static Korean War film.

Battleaxe, The (1962-British) 66m. ** D: Godfrey Grayson. Jill Ireland, Francis Matthews, Joan Haythorne, Michael Beint. Obvious sex farce with Matthews suing Ireland for breach of promise, Haythorne in title role supplying expected gags.

Battleground (1949) 118m. *** D: William Wellman. Van Johnson, John Hodiak, Ricardo Montalban, George Murphy, Marshall Thompson. Star-studded replay of Battle of the Bulge: division of American troops, their problems and reactions to war. Slick script, which was awarded Oscar, lacks genuine insight into characterization.

Battleship Potemkin: SEE Potemkin

Battlestar Galactica (1979) C-125m. **½ D: Richard A. Colla. Richard Hatch, Dirk Benedict, Lorne Greene, Ray Milland, Lew Ayres, Jane Seymour, Laurette Spang, Terry Carter. Feature based on premiere episode of short-lived TV series; Greene is commander of airship taking survivors of doomed planet in search of new home. Belongs on small screen, where it's moderately interesting and John Dykstra's special effects come off best.

Battling Bellhop SEE: Kid Galahad

Bay of Saint Michel, The (1963-British) 73m. ** D: John Ainsworth. Keenan Wynn, Mai Zetterling, Ronald Howard, Rona Anderson. Adequate actioner concerning trio of ex-commandos hunting for Nazi buried treasure, with expected conflicts and murders. Retitled: OPERATION MERMAID.

Battling Hoofer SEE: Something to Sing About

Bawdy Adventures of Tom Jones, The (1976-British) C-94m. ** D: Cliff Owen. Nicky Henson, Trevor Howard, Joan Collins, Terry-Thomas, Arthur Lowe, Georgia Brown. Mild doings, based on London stage musical, can't hold a candle to 1963 classic. This time, Tom's (Henson) amorous adventures are pat and predictable, with Collins, as highwaywoman Black Bess, adding only zing.

Baxter (1973) C-100m. *** D: Lionel Jeffries. Patricia Neal, Scott Jacoby, Jean-Pierre Cassel, Lynn Carlin, Britt Ekland, Sally Thomsett, Paul Eddington. Well acted drama about young Jacoby's emotional problems and his relationship with speech therapist Neal, who tries to correct his lisp.

Be Beautiful But Shut Up (1957-French) 94m. ** D: Henri Verneuil. Mylene Demongeot, Henri Vidal, Isabelle Miranda. Unremarkable study of young hoods involved with smuggling and carefree living.

Be Yourself (1930) 77m. ** D: Thornton Freeland, Fanny Brice, Robert Armstrong, Harry Green, Gertrude Astor, Pat Collins. Contrived vehicle for Fanny as nightclub entertainer who falls in love with punchy prizefighter (Armstrong); silly story, overdose of sentiment leave too few moments for star to be herself.

Beach Ball (1965) C-83m. ** D: Lennie Weinrib. Edd Byrnes, Chris Noel, Robert Logan, Gale Gilmore, Aron Kincaid. Different group tries a beach picture, but it's essentially the same. Pretty girls, rock groups, surfing, pretty girls.

Beach Blanket Bingo (1965) C-98m. ** D: William Asher. Frankie Avalon, Annette Funicello, Deborah Walley, Harvey Lembeck, John Ashley, Jody McCrea, Donna Loren, Don Rickles, Paul Lynde, Buster Keaton. Sole attraction is the guest cast of Keaton, Rickles, and Lynde. Otherwise, same surfing and bikini routine. If you've seen one . . .

Beach Party (1963) C-101m. ** D: William Asher. Dorothy Malone, Bob Cummings, Frankie Avalon, Annette Funicello, Morey Amsterdam. First in long line of beach epics, this boasts a good adult cast, mostly wasting their time. Moves swiftly to pie-throwing climax with little rhyme or reason.

Beach Patrol (1979) C-100m. TVM D: Bob Kelljan. Robin Strand, Jonathon Frames, Christine DeLisle, Richard Hill, Paul Burke, Michael V. Gazzo. A "Rookies"-in-dune-buggies series pilot for action freaks and bikini watchers. Below average.

Beach Red (1967) C-105m. *** D: Cornel Wilde. Cornel Wilde, Rip Torn, Burr De Benning, Patrick Wolfe, Jean Wallace. Hard look at military life in South Pacific attempts to show ugly side of war. Likely to be watered down for TV.

Beachcomber, The (1938-British) 80m. *** D: Erich Pommer. Charles Laughton, Elsa Lanchester, Tyrone Guthrie, Robert Newton, Dolly Mollinger. Disheveled bum Laughton, living on island paradise, reformed by missionary Lanchester. Two stars delightful in filmization of Maugham story originally titled VESSEL OF WRATH.

Beachcomber, The (1955-British) C-82m. *** D: Muriel Box. Glynis Johns, Robert Newton, Donald Sinden, Michael Hordern, Donald Pleasence. Remake of Somerset Maugham tale of South Sea island bum entangled with strait-laced sister of missionary is still flavorful.

Beachhead (1954) C-89m. *** D: Stuart Heisler. Tony Curtis, Frank Lovejoy, Mary Murphy, Eduard Franz, Skip Homeier. Nicely handled action of marine quartet on dangerous mission in WW2.

Bears and I, The (1974) C-89m. *½ D: Bernard McEveety. Patrick Wayne, Chief Dan George, Andrew Duggan, Michael Ansara. Vietnam vet Wayne tries to soothe relations in North Woods between Indians and white bigots. Mild Disney film.

Beast From 20,000 Fathoms, The (1953) 80m. ** D: Eugene Lourie. Paul Christian, Paula Raymond, Cecil Kellaway, Donald Woods, Lee Van Cleef, Ross Elliott. Rampaging monster tale with good special effects.

Beast in the Cellar, The (1971-British) C-87m. ** D: James Kelly. Beryl Reid, Flora Robson, John Hamill, T. P. McKenna, Tessa Wyatt. Two sisters hide their maniac brother in the cellar; performance of Reid and Robson brings movie to average level. British running time was 101m.

Beast Must Die, The (1974-British) C-93m. *** D: Paul Annett. Calvin

Lockhart, Peter Cushing, Charles Gray, Marlene Clark, Anton Diffring. New twists on the old were-wolf theme make the difference. Millionaire sportsman Lockhart invites guests to his electronically bugged mansion, knowing one of them is a werewolf. Lockhart is overly mannered, while Cushing gains sympathy in his usual quiet but effective way.

Beast of Budapest, The (1958) 72m. *½ D: Harmon Jones. Gerald Milton, John Hoyt, Greta Thyssen, Michael Mills. Trite rendering of father vs. son conflict over politics, resolved when elder's death awakens son to truth about life in Communist Hungary.

Beast of Hollow Mountain, The (1956) C-80m. **½ D: Edward Nassour, Ismael Rodriguez. Guy Madison, Patricia Medina, Eduardo Noriega, Carlos Rivas. Unusual combination of Western and monster-on-the-loose formula works well, with clever ending. Filmed in Mexico.

Beast with Five Fingers, The (1946) 88m. **½ D: Robert Florey. Robert Alda, Andrea King, Peter Lorre, Victor Francen, J. Carrol Naish. Intriguing if not entirely successful mood-piece about aging pianist and strange doings in his household. Lorre's confrontation with disembodied hand a horror highlight.

Beasts Are on the Streets, The (1978) C-100m. TVM D: Peter Hunt. Carol Lynley, Dale Robinette, Billy Green Bush, Philip Michael Thomas, Anna Lee. Dangerous beasts are accidentally set loose from wild animal park and thousands panic in nearby community. Intelligent story suffers from mediocre script. Average.

Beat Generation, The (1959) 95m. *½ D: Charles Haas. Steve Cochran, Mamie Van Doren, Ray Danton, Fay Spain, Louis Armstrong, Maggie Hayes, Jackie Coogan, Ray Anthony, Maxie Rosenbloom. Exploitation-type story of detective Cochran tracking down insane sexual assaulter; vivid sequences marred by hokey script. Retitled THIS REBEL AGE.

Beat Girl SEE: **Wild For Kicks**

Beat the Devil (1954) 89m. *** D: John Huston. Humphrey Bogart, Jennifer Jones, Gina Lollobrigida, Robert Morley, Peter Lorre, Edward Underdown. Huston and Truman Capote concocted this offbeat, very funny satire of MALTESE FAL-

CON-ish movies on location in Italy. Low-key nature of comedy eluded many people in 1954 and it immediately became a "cult" favorite, which it remains today.

Beau Brummel (1954-U.S.-British) C-113m. **½ D: Curtis Bernhardt. Stewart Granger, Elizabeth Taylor, Peter Ustinov, Robert Morley. Handsome cast in lavish production from Granger's rash of costume epics. Here, he's the famous 19th-century British Casanova-fop.

Beau Geste (1939) 120m. ***½ D: William Wellman. Gary Cooper, Ray Milland, Robert Preston, Brian Donlevy, Susan Hayward, J. Carrol Naish, Albert Dekker, Broderick Crawford, Donald O'Connor. Exciting actioner with Geste brothers (Cooper, Milland, Preston) pitted against tyrannical officer Donlevy in noble tale of Foreign Legion fighting desert hordes. Elaborate remake of Ronald Colman silent is fine entertainment.

Beau Geste (1966) C-103m. **½ D: Douglas Heyes. Telly Savalas, Guy Stockwell, Doug McClure, Leslie Nielsen. Programmer-like version of Christopher Wren adventure tale dealing with honor among brothers in French Foreign Legion, their battle with sadistic commander and rampaging Arabs.

Beau James (1957) C-105m. *** D: Melville Shavelson. Bob Hope, Vera Miles, Paul Douglas, Alexis Smith, Darren McGavin; narrated by Walter Winchell. Flavorful recreation of the political career of Mayor Jimmy Walker in 1920s N.Y.C., based on Gene Fowler's book. Hope is fine in basically noncomic performance. Guest appearances by Jimmy Durante, Jack Benny, George Jessel.

Beauties of the Night (1954-French) 84m. **½ D: René Clair. Gerard Philippe, Martine Carol, Gina Lollobrigida, Magali Vendeuil. Diverting fantasy involving aspiring composer Philippe with a penchant for dreaming and wandering through various eras of history.

Beautiful Blonde from Bashful Bend, The (1949) C-77m. **½ D: Preston Sturges. Betty Grable, Cesar Romero, Rudy Vallee, Olga San Juan, Porter Hall, Sterling Holloway, El Brendel. Film was major flop in 1949, looks somewhat better today; broad Western farce has Grable a gun-toting saloon girl mistaken for schoolmarm in hick town. Hugh Herbert hilarious as nearsighted doctor.

Beautiful but Deadly: SEE Don Is Dead, The

Beautiful Stranger SEE: Twist of Fate

Beauty and the Beast (1946-French) 90m. **** D: Jean Cocteau. Jean Marais, Josette Day, Marcel André. Cocteau's hauntingly beautiful rendition of this classic fable is great fantasy, great filmmaking—beguiling on any level.

Bebo's Girl (1964-Italian) 106m. **½ D: Luigi Comencini. Claudia Cardinale, George Chakiris, Mario Lupi, Dany Paris. At times memorable love story spotlighting Cardinale's decision to leave her new lover in order to reaffirm her attachment with first love, now serving a prison term.

Because He's My Friend (1978-Australian) C-93m. TVM D: Ralph Nelson. Karen Black, Keir Dullea, Jack Thompson, Tom Oliver, Don Reid, Barbara Stephens. Sensitive drama about the plight of parents with a retarded child and the effect on their marriage. The youngster is especially well-played by Australian actor Warwick Poulsen. Above average.

Because of Him (1946) 88m. *** D: Richard Wallace. Deanna Durbin, Franchot Tone, Charles Laughton, Helen Broderick, Donald Meek. Entertaining Durbin vehicle with Deanna becoming protegee of outrageous ham Laughton, convincing playwright Tone that she's star material.

Because of You (1952) 95m. *** D: Joseph Pevney. Loretta Young, Jeff Chandler, Alex Nicol, Frances Dee, Mae Clarke. Nifty tear-jerker has Young a parolee whose marriage is threatened by her past.

Because They're Young (1960) 102m. **½ D: Paul Wendkos. Dick Clark, Michael Callan, Tuesday Weld, Victoria Shaw, Doug McClure. Screen version of John Farris' HARRISON HIGH becomes predictable account of do-gooder teacher Clark trying to help his wayward students.

Becket (1964) C-148m. **** D: Peter Glenville. Richard Burton, Peter O'Toole, John Gielgud, Donald Wolfit, Martita Hunt, Pamela Brown, Felix Aylmer. Stunning film, adapted from Jean Anouilh play, centers on stormy friendship between Archbishop of Canterbury Thomas à Becket and his English King, Henry II. Superbly acted and magnificently photographed on location in England.

Becky Sharp (1935) C-83m. *** D: Rouben Mamoulian. Miriam Hopkins, Frances Dee, Cedric Hardwicke, Billie Burke, Alison Skipworth, Nigel Bruce. Witty, delightfully played adaptation of Thackeray's *Vanity Fair*, with Hopkins as girl whose sole concern is herself. Historically important as first full-technicolor (3-color) feature, though officially available to TV only in b&w at 67m.

Bed Sitting Room, The (British-1969) C-90m. **½ D: Richard Lester. Rita Tushingham, Ralph Richardson, Peter Cook, Dudley Moore, Spike Milligan, Michael Hordern. Moderately successful black-comedy look at distorted, devastated England three years after nuclear war. A few funny bits, great cast, but film doesn't click.

Bedazzled (1967-British) C-107m. *** D: Stanley Donen. Peter Cook, Dudley Moore, Eleanor Bron, Raquel Welch, Alba. Cult film updating Faust legend is as sacrilegious as THE SINGING NUN and usually funnier. The laughs aren't always consistent, but the Cook-Moore team is terrific and Donen's direction stylish.

Bedevilled (1955) C-85m. ** D: Mitchell Leisen. Anne Baxter, Steve Forrest, Simone Renant, Victor Francen. Bizarre yarn of chanteuse Baxter fleeing from murder scene, protected by Forrest, who's studying for priesthood; filmed in Paris.

Bedford Incident, The (1965) 102m. *** D: James B. Harris. Richard Widmark, Sidney Poitier, James MacArthur, Martin Balsam, Wally Cox, Eric Portman, Donald Sutherland. Strong Cold War story of authoritarian Navy captain (Widmark) scouting Russian subs near Greenland and the mental conflicts that develop on his ship. Poitier is reporter too good to be true, Balsam is disliked doctor. Cast excels in intriguing battle of wits.

Bedknobs and Broomsticks (1971) C-117m. *** D: Robert Stevenson. Angela Lansbury, David Tomlinson, Roddy McDowall, Sam Jaffe, Roy Snart, Cindy O'Callaghan, Ian Weighill. Elaborate Disney musical fantasy about amateur witch who helps British cause in WW2; no MARY POPPINS, but quite enjoyable, with Oscar-winning special effects and delightful animated cartoon sequences directed by Ward Kimball.

Bedlam (1946) 79m. *** D: Mark Robson. Boris Karloff, Anna Lee, Ian Wolfe, Richard Fraser, Billy House, Jason Robards, Sr. Atmospheric Val Lewton chiller of courageous Lee trying to expose inadequate conditions at insane asylum, committed to one by institution head Karloff.

Bedtime for Bonzo (1951) 82m. ** D: Frederick de Cordova. Ronald Reagan, Diana Lynn, Walter Slezak, Lucille Barkley. Reagan plays professor who treats a chimp as his child for an heredity experiment, allowing for monkey-shenanigans. Sequel: BONZO GOES TO COLLEGE.

Bedtime Story, A (1933) 87m. **½ D: Norman Taurog. Maurice Chevalier, Helen Twelvetrees, Baby LeRoy, Adrienne Ames, Edward Everett Horton. Breezy Chevalier musical vehicle with Parisian playboy playing father to abandoned baby who interferes with his romancing.

Bedtime Story (1941) 85m. *** D: Alexander Hall. Fredric March, Loretta Young, Robert Benchley, Allyn Joslyn, Eve Arden. Fine cast in sparkling comedy of playwright March trying to stop wife Young from retiring so she can star in his next play.

Bedtime Story (1964) C-99m. **½ D: Ralph Levy. Marlon Brando, David Niven, Shirley Jones, Dody Goodman, Marie Windsor. Offbeat casting of stars provides chief interest in luckluster comedy of Brando and Niven competing for Jones' affection.

Been Down So Long It Looks Like Up to Me (1971) C-90m. *½ D: Jeffrey Young. Barry Primus, Linda DeCoff, David Browning, Susan Tyrell, Philip Shafer, Bruce Davison. Bland, already dated film version of Richard Fariña's novel about hip 1960s-type trying to endure life on a 1958 campus.

Bees, The (1979) C-83m. *½ D: Alfredo Zacharias. John Saxon, Angel Tompkins, John Carradine, Claudio Brook, Alicia Encinias. After THE SWARM, if you sincerely want to see this low-budget disaster film about killer bees, you get what you deserve.

Before and After (1979) C-100m. TVM D: Kim Friedman. Patty Duke Astin, Bradford Dillman, Barbara Feldon, Art Hindle, Rosemary Murphy, Kenneth Mars, Betty White.

So-so comedy/drama about a housewife's battle with a weight problem that threatens her marriage. Average.

Before I Hang (1940) 71m. **½ D: Nick Grinde. Boris Karloff, Evelyn Keyes, Bruce Bennett, Pedro de Cordoba, Edward Van Sloan. Contrived but intriguing tale of madscientist Karloff having unusual serum backfire on him.

Before I Wake SEE: **Shadow of Fear**

Before Winter Comes (1969-British) C-102m. **½ D: J. Lee Thompson. David Niven, Topol, Anna Karina, John Hurt, Anthony Quayle, Ori Levy. Topol is interpreter for British officer Niven in displaced persons' camp following WW2. Uneven comedy-drama with many touching moments, capturing plight of refugees. Topol's warmth shines in winning performance.

Beg, Borrow, or Steal (1973) C-73m. TVM D: David Lowell Rich. Mike Connors, Michael Cole, Kent McCord, Leonard Stone, Henry Beckman, Joel Fabiani. Three unemployed, handicapped men, failing to start own business, eventually devise plan to rob museum of priceless statue, unaware that second party has ideas of his own. Dismal miscasting of leads, forgettable action. Below average.

Beggarman, Thief (1979) C-200m. TVM D: Lawrence Doheny. Jean Simmons, Glenn Ford, Lynn Redgrave, Tovah Feldshuh, Andrew Stevens, Bo Hopkins, Jean-Pierre Aumont, Anne Francis, Anne Jeffreys, Robert Sterling, Susan Strasberg. Further travails of the Jordache family during the late '60s, set against tinselly Cannes Film Festival. High-grade soap opera in the tradition of its multipart predecessor, Irwin Shaw's RICH MAN, POOR MAN. Above average.

Beginning of the End (1957) 73m. ** D: Bert I. Gordon. Peggie Castle, Peter Graves, Morris Ankrum, Richard Benedict. Oversized grasshoppers are true stars of this passable sci-fi with giant insects destroying anything in their path.

Beginning or the End, The (1947) 112m. *** D: Norman Taurog. Brian Donlevy, Robert Walker, Beverly Tyler, Audrey Totter, Hume Cronyn. Engrossing account of atomic bomb development, depicting both human and spectacular aspects.

Beguiled, The (1971) C-109m. ***

D: Don Siegel. Clint Eastwood, Geraldine Page, Elizabeth Hartman, Jo Ann Harris, Darleen Carr, Pamelyn Ferdin. Offbeat, methodically paced story set in Civil War South. Wounded Eastwood brought to girls' school to recuperate; he becomes catalyst for flurry of jealousy and hatred. Unusual Eastwood fare, but for patient viewers, a rich, rewarding film.

Behave Yourself! (1951) 81m. ** D: George Beck. Farley Granger, Shelley Winters, William Demarest, Francis L. Sullivan. Strange casting of Granger-Winters as couple with dog wanted by criminal gang detracts from comic potential of this comedy.

Behind Locked Doors (1948) 62m. ** D: Budd Boetticher. Lucille Bremer, Richard Carlson, Douglas Fowley, Tom Browne Henry. Mishmash of judge on the lam seeking refuge in an insane asylum, and the reporter who tracks him down for the story.

Behind the Badge SEE: **Killing Affair, A**

Behind the Door SEE: **Man with Nine Lives, The**

Behind the Eight Ball (1942) 60m. ** D: Edward F. Cline. Ritz Brothers, Carol Bruce, Grace McDonald, Dick Foran, William Demarest, Johnny Downs. Entertainers get tangled in murder whodunit, with Demarest as determined detective. Typical nonsense plot squeezed in between musical numbers.

Behind the Front (1926) 60m. **½ D: A. Edward Sutherland. Wallace Beery, Mary Brian, Raymond Hatton, Richard Arlen, Tom Kennedy, Chester Conklin, Gertrude Astor. Entertaining silent army comedy, broadly played by buddies Beery and Hatton, supported by fine cast. Many devices have been reused countless times, but they're handled smoothly here.

Behind the High Wall (1956) 85m. ** D: Abner Biberman. Tom Tully, Sylvia Sidney, Betty Lynn, John Gavin. Intertwining yarn of grasping prison warden, his crippled wife (nicely played by Sidney), hidden money, and convict escape plan. Remake of THE BIG GUY.

Behind the Iron Curtain SEE: **Iron Curtain, The**

Behind the Mask (1932) 70m. ** D: John Francis Dillon. Jack Holt, Constance Cummings, Boris Karloff, Edward Van Sloan, Claude King. Secret-service man Holt tries to expose mysterious head of dope ring by getting to know henchman Karloff in this bland thriller.

Behind the Rising Sun (1943) 89m. **½ D: Edward Dmytryk. Margo, Tom Neal, J. Carrol Naish, Robert Ryan, Gloria Holden, Don Douglas, George Givot. Japanese man (Naish) urges his Americanized son (Neal) to become involved in Sino-Japanese war during 1930s, but doesn't like what happens as a result. Interesting for WW2-era point of view.

Behold a Pale Horse (1964) 118m. **½ D: Fred Zinnemann. Gregory Peck, Anthony Quinn, Omar Sharif, Mildred Dunnock, Christian Marquand, Raymond Pellegrin. Peck and Quinn wage an ideological battle in post-Spanish Civil War story of politics and violence that loses its focus and becomes confused talky film. Valiant try by all.

Behold My Wife (1935) 78m. ** D: Mitchell Leisen. Sylvia Sidney, Gene Raymond, Juliette Compton, Laura Hope Crews, Ann Sheridan. Raymond's snobbish family objects to his love for Indian maiden Sidney. Predictable wrong-side-of-the-reservation romance.

Being There (1979) C-130m. **½ D: Hal Ashby. Peter Sellers, Shirley MacLaine, Melvyn Douglas, Jack Warden, Richard Dysart, Richard Basehart. A childlike man (Sellers) chances to meet important, powerful people who interpret his bewildered silence as brilliance. Low-keyed black humor, full of savagely witty comments on American life in the television age, but film is fatally overlong. Adapted by Jerzy Kosinski from his own story. Douglas won Best Supporting Actor Oscar for performance as political kingmaker.

Believe in Me (1971) C-90m. ** D: Stuart Hagmann. Michael Sarrazin, Jacqueline Bisset, Jon Cypher, Allen Garfield, Kurt Dodenhoff. Still another 70s film about drug addiction, and none too good; clean-cut career girl Bisset becomes addicted to speed in the East Village. Performers do their best.

Bell' Antonio (1962-Italian) 101m. **½ D: Mauro Bolognini. Marcello Mastroianni, Claudia Cardinale, Pierre Brasseur, Rina Morelli. OK Italian import of man ridiculed for his sexual impotence, saved by village girl who names him her lover.

Bell, Book and Candle (1958) C-103m. **½ D: Richard Quine. James Stewart, Kim Novak, Jack

Lemmon, Ernie Kovacs, Hermione Gingold. John Van Druten play becomes so-so vehicle to showcase Novak as fetching witch who charms about-to-be-married publisher Stewart. Kovacs and Gingold supply their brand of humor.

Bell for Adano, A (1945) 103m. ***½ D: Henry King. John Hodiak, Gene Tierney, William Bendix, Glenn Langan, Richard Conte, Stanley Prager, Henry (Harry) Morgan. John Hersey's moving narrative of American WW2 occupation of small Italian village; Hodiak is sincere commander, Bendix his aide, blonde Tierney the local girl he is attracted to.

Bell Jar, The (1979) C-107m. **½ D: Larry Peerce. Marilyn Hassett, Julie Harris, Anne Jackson, Barbara Barrie, Robert Klein, Donna Mitchell. Sylvia Plath's virtually unfilmable novel about the crack-up of an overachiever in the 50s has a few powerful scenes and a good supporting performance by Barrie, but doesn't really come off. Hassett is well cast but fails to deliver the truly bravura performance this film needs.

Bellboy, The (1960) 72m. *** D: Jerry Lewis. Jerry Lewis, Alex Gerry, Bob Clayton, Sonny Sands. Amusing series of blackouts with Jerry as a bellboy at Fontainebleau in Miami Beach. No plot but a lot of funny gags. Milton Berle and Walter Winchell have guest appearances.

Belle Le Grand (1951) 90m. *½ D: Allan Dwan. Vera Ralston, John Carroll, William Ching, Muriel Lawrence. Weak Ralston vehicle has her a Western lady gambler willing to play any stakes to win back rambunctious Carroll.

Belle of New York, The (1952) C-82m. **½ D: Charles Walters. Fred Astaire, Vera-Ellen, Marjorie Main, Keenan Wynn, Alice Pearce. Uninspired musical set in Gay 90s N.Y.C. with Astaire a rich playboy chasing mission gal Vera-Ellen; Pearce adds comic touches. Songs include "Let A Little Love Come In."

Belle of the Nineties (1934) 73m. *** D: Leo McCarey. Mae West, Roger Pryor, Johnny Mack Brown, Warren Hymer, Duke Ellington orchestra. Mae struts and sings "My Old Flame" and heats up a gallery of admirers in amusing example of Western humor.

Belle of the Yukon (1944) C-84m. **½ D: William Seiter. Randolph Scott, Gypsy Rose Lee, Dinah Shore, Charles Winninger, William Marshall, Florence Bates. Minor musical of saloon-owner Scott going straight at insistence of his girl (Lee); fast-moving, forgettable.

Belle Starr (1941) C-87m. **½ D: Irving Cummings. Randolph Scott, Gene Tierney, Dana Andrews, John Sheppard (Shepperd Strudwick), Elizabeth Patterson. Sophisticated Tierney miscast as notorious female outlaw in slowly paced account of her criminal career.

Belle Starr's Daughter (1948) 86m. ** D: Lesley Selander. George Montgomery, Rod Cameron, Ruth Roman, Wallace Ford, Isabel Jewell. Roman is title character, coming to rough Western town to avenge her mother's murder; fair Western.

Belles of St. Trinians, The (1955-British) 90m. ***½ D: Frank Launder. Alastair Sim, Joyce Grenfell, George Cole, Hermione Baddeley, Beryl Reid. Hilarious filmization of Ronald Searle's cartoons about completely crazy school for girls, run by dotty headmistress whose brother, a bookie, wants to use school to his advantage. Sim plays dual role in delightful madcap farce which spawned several sequels.

Belles on Their Toes (1952) C-89m. *** D: Henry Levin. Myrna Loy, Jeanne Crain, Debra Paget, Jeffrey Hunter, Edward Arnold, Hoagy Carmichael. Pleasing sequel to CHEAPER BY THE DOZEN focuses on Loy's lecture career and her ability to find romance while tending to her maturing brood. Twentieth Century-Fox backlot seen at its best recapturing 1900s America.

Bellissima (1951-Italian) 95m. **½ D: Luchino Visconti. Anna Magnani, Walter Chiari, Tina Apicella, Gastone Renzelli, Alessandro Blasetti. Lackluster tale of ambitious mother entering her child in talent contest, focusing on repercussion of her pushing child into the limelight.

Bells Are Ringing (1960) C-127m. *** D: Vincente Minnelli. Judy Holliday, Dean Martin, Fred Clark, Eddie Foy, Jr. Sprightly musical comedy by Jule Styne, Betty Comden, and Adolph Green. Holliday, in her last film, is fine as answering-service operator; Martin makes a good leading man. Songs include "Just in Time," "The Party's Over."

Bells of St. Mary's, The (1945) 126m. *** D: Leo McCarey. Bing Crosby, Ingrid Bergman, Henry Travers, William Gargan, Ruth Donnelly, John Carroll, Martha Sleeper. Not the total success of GOING MY WAY, but highly entertaining story of priest Crosby and nun Bergman raising money for new church school.

Beloved Enemy (1936) 90m. *** D: H. C. Potter. Merle Oberon, Brian Aherne, Karen Morley, Henry Stephenson, Jerome Cowan, David Niven, Donald Crisp. High-class love story set during Irish Rebellion with Britisher Oberon in love with rebel leader Aherne.

Beloved Infidel (1959) C-123m. ** D: Henry King. Gregory Peck, Deborah Kerr, Eddie Albert, Philip Ober, Herbert Rudley, John Sutton, Karin Booth, Ken Scott. Ill-conceived casting of Peck as F. Scott Fitzgerald makes romance with Hollywood columnist Sheilah Graham (Kerr) in late 1930 more ludicrous than real; lush photography is only virtue of blunt look at cinema capital.

Beloved Rogue, The (1927) 99m. ***½ D: Alan Crosland. John Barrymore, Conrad Veidt, Marceline Day, Henry Victor, Lawson Butt, Mack Swain, Slim Summerville. Rousing, stunningly filmed story of poet-adventurer François Villon, his battle of wits with Louis XI (Veidt) and his swashbuckling romance with a damsel in distress. Has nothing to do with history; instead, an eye-filling, spirited, tongue-in-cheek costume tale with Barrymore in great form.

Ben (1972) C-95m. *½ D: Phil Karlson. Lee Harcourt Montgomery, Joseph Campanella, Arthur O'Connell, Rosemary Murphy, Meredith Baxter. WILLARD sequel finds sick youth befriended by Ben the rat. Title song summed up situation but spared gory visuals that make this film so bad.

Ben Hur (1959) C-212m. **** D: William Wyler. Charlton Heston, Jack Hawkins, Stephen Boyd, Haya Harareet, Hugh Griffith, Martha Scott, Sam Jaffe. Gargantuan adaptation of Lew Wallace classic combines historical look at Palestine during the time of Christ with melodrama pitting two ex-friends, Judah Ben Hur and Messala, against each other. Heston and Griffith each received Oscars for performances; film garnered nine others, including best director and cinematography. Sea

battle and chariot race among all-time great action scenes, inspired by 1926 silent.

Bend of the River (1952) C-91m. *** D: Anthony Mann. James Stewart, Julia Adams, Arthur Kennedy, Rock Hudson, Lori Nelson, Jay C. Flippen, Harry Morgan. Compelling Western of 1840s Oregon, with bristling conflict between Stewart, outlaw-turned-wagon-train-scout, and Kennedy, his one-time comrade who hijacks settlers' supplies to turn a fast profit.

Beneath the Planet of the Apes (1970) C-95m. **½ D: Ted Post. Charlton Heston, James Franciscus, Kim Hunter, Maurice Evans, Linda Harrison, Victor Buono, Paul Richards, Thomas Gomez. Second APES film still has great sets, makeup and ideas, but somebody let it get away as Apes battle human mutants who survived a nuclear blast many years before.

Beneath the 12 Mile Reef (1953) C-102m. **½ D: Robert Webb. Robert Wagner, Terry Moore, Gilbert Roland, J. Carrol Naish, Richard Boone, Peter Graves. Romeo-Juliet-ish tale of sponge-diving families on Key West, Florida. Scenery outshines all.

Benefit of the Doubt, The (1967-British) C-70m. **½ D: Peter Whitehead. Eric Allan, Mary Allen, Jeremy Anthony, Noel Collins. Documentary shows British view of Vietnam War, featuring scenes from Peter Brook play US (Royal Shakespeare Company); thought-provoking at times. Retitled: US.

Bengal Brigade (1954) C-87m. ** D: Laslo Benedek. Rock Hudson, Arlene Dahl, Ursula Thiess, Torin Thatcher. Stilted costumer with process shots and stock footage, as Hudson stands off natives in 1850s India.

Bengazi (1955) 78m. *½ D: John Brahm. Victor McLaglen, Richard Carlson, Mala Powers. Lackluster adventure of Powers and trio of men entrapped in desert shrine by marauding natives.

Benji (1974) C-86m. ***½ D: Joe Camp. Peter Breck, Deborah Walley, Edgar Buchanan, Frances Bavier, Patsy Garrett. Instant classic of a remarkable dog (played by Higgins) who thwarts the kidnappers of two small children. Texas-made feature is ideal for family viewing.

Benny Goodman Story, The (1955) C-116m. **½ D: Valentine Davies. Steve Allen, Donna Reed, Sammy Davis, Sr., Gene Krupa, Harry James,

[54]

Martha Tilton. Cinematic fiction about life of swing bandleader, focusing on his romance with Reed and rise in musical world. Guest performers spice up Allen's clarinet-playing (dubbed by Goodman).

Berkeley Square (1933) 84m. ******* D: Frank Lloyd. Leslie Howard, Heather Angel, Irene Browne, Beryl Mercer, Samuel S. Hinds. Intriguing fantasy of young American Howard finding himself in 18th-century London, living completely different life. Remade as I'LL NEVER FORGET YOU.

Berlin Affair (1970) C-97m. TVM. D: David Lowell Rich. Darren McGavin, Fritz Weaver, Claude Dauphin, Brian Kelly. Spotty foreign intrigue thriller has OK performances in story of murder-for-hire organization. Music by Francis Lai. Situations implausible, forgettable. Below average.

Berlin Correspondent (1942) 70m. ****½** D: Eugene Forde. Virginia Gilmore, Dana Andrews, Mona Maris, Martin Kosleck, Sig Ruman. Reporter Andrews flees Germany with professor and young girl, amid much patriotic talk.

Berlin Express (1948) 86m. ******* D: Jacques Tourneur. Merle Oberon, Robert Ryan, Charles Korvin, Paul Lukas, Robert Coote. Taut, suspenseful spy story set in post WW2 Europe. Members of several nations combine efforts to save German statesman kidnapped by Nazi underground.

Bermuda Mystery (1944) 65m. ****** D: Benjamin Stoloff. Preston Foster, Ann Rutherford, Charles Butterworth, Helene Reynolds. Mild account of strange murder and dead man's heirs' search to track down criminal.

Bermuda Depths, The (1978) C-100m. TVM D: Tom Kotani. Burl Ives, Leigh McCloskey, Julie Woodson, Carl Weathers, Connie Sellecca. A mysterious beauty and a prehistoric monster puzzle some scientists but offer no challenge to the viewer; crummy sci-fi. Below average.

Bernadette of Lourdes (1961-French) 90m. ****½** D: Robert Darene. Daniele Ajoret, Nadine Alari, Robert Arnoux, Blanchette Brunoy. Straightforward account of the peasant girl who saw a vision and was elevated to sainthood; unpretentious.

Bernardine (1957) C-95m. ****** D: Henry Levin. Pat Boone, Terry Moore, Janet Gaynor, Dean Jagger,

Walter Abel. Very weak look at teen-age life (all different now) marked return of Janet Gaynor to films after twenty years. Wholesome Pat Boone sings and sings and sings. Eh!

Berserk (1967-British) C-96m. ****** D: Jim O'Connolly. Joan Crawford, Ty Hardin, Diana Dors, Michael Gough, Judy Geeson. Sadistic shocker with Crawford the shapely owner of a British circus, haunted by series of brutal murders. Supporting cast lacks verve.

Best Foot Forward (1943) C-95m. ******* D: Edward Buzzell. Lucille Ball, William Gaxton, Virginia Weidler, Tommy Dix, Nancy Walker, Gloria DeHaven, June Allyson. Entertaining film of Broadway musical about movie-star Ball visiting small-town school for a lark; score includes "Buckle Down Winsockie." Harry James and his band do definitive "Two O'Clock Jump," Walker is dynamic plain Jane.

Best House in London, The (1969-British) C-105m. BOMB D: Philip Saville. David Hemmings, Joanna Pettet, George Sanders, Dany Robin, Warren Mitchell. Boring comedy about group of government officials in London who sponsor official bawdy house. Although film didn't deserve "X" rating it got at the time, some of it will probably be trimmed for TV, if anyone cares.

Best Man, The (1964) 102m. ******* D: Franklin Schaffner. Henry Fonda, Cliff Robertson, Edie Adams, Margaret Leighton, Shelley Berman, Lee Tracy, Ann Sothern, Gene Raymond, Richard Arlen, Mahalia Jackson. Sharp filmization of Gore Vidal's play about political conventioning with several determined presidential candidates seeking important endorsement; brittle, engrossing drama.

Best of Enemies, The (1962-British) C-104m. ******* D: Guy Hamilton. David Niven, Michael Wilding, Harry Andrews, Alberto Sordi, Noel Harrison. Nice counterplay between Niven and Sordi, who point out the futility of warfare in this study of WW2.

Best of Everything, The (1959) C-121m. ******* D: Jean Negulesco. Hope Lange, Stephen Boyd, Suzy Parker, Martha Hyer, Joan Crawford, Brian Aherne, Robert Evans, Louis Jourdan. Multifaceted fabrication about women seeking success and love in the publishing jungles of N.Y.C., highlighted by Crawford's performance as tough executive with empty heart of gold; from superficial Rona Jaffe novel.

Best of the Badmen (1951) C-84m. **½ D: William D. Russell. Robert Ryan, Claire Trevor, Robert Preston, Jack Buetel, Walter Brennan, Bruce Cabot. Band of outlaws (including James and Younger brothers) help former Union colonel Ryan in vendetta against detective Preston. Offbeat western has more talk than action.

Best Place to Be, The (1979) C-200m. TVM D: David Miller. Donna Reed, Efrem Zimbalist Jr., Stephanie Zimbalist, Mildred Dunnock, John Phillip Law, Betty White, Leon Ames, Coleen Gray. Lavish "woman's" drama with enough plot threads to keep six soap operas running for months, taken Ross Hunter-style from Helen Van Slyke's longtime best seller and featuring Donna Reed in her widely heralded TV comeback following a 12-year absence. Elegant, but tiresome and average.

Best Things in Life Are Free, The (1956) C-104m. **½ D: Michael Curtiz. Gordon MacRae, Dan Dailey, Ernest Borgnine, Sheree North. Typical of the antiseptic 1950s musicals, this film "recreates" the careers of Tin Pan Alley writers DeSylva, Brown, and Henderson.

Best Years of Our Lives, The (1946) 172m. **** D: William Wyler. Fredric March, Myrna Loy, Teresa Wright, Dana Andrews, Virginia Mayo, Harold Russell, Hoagy Carmichael, Gladys George, Steve Cochran. American classic of three veterans returning home after WW2, readjusting to civilian life. Robert Sherwood's script from MacKinlay Kantor's book perfectly captured mood of postwar U.S., still powerful today. Remade as TVM RETURNING HOME.

Betrayal (1974) C-78m. TVM D: Gordon Hessler. Amanda Blake, Tisha Sterling, Dick Haymes, Sam Groom, Britt Leach, Edward Marshall, Ted Gehring. Lonely widow Blake hires a young woman companion, unaware that the girl and her boyfriend are killer-extortionists who plan to make her their next victim. Standard suspense drama. Average.

Betrayal from the East (1945) 82m.
** D: William Berke. Lee Tracy, Nancy Kelly, Richard Loo, Abner Biberman, Regis Toomey, Philip Ahn. Americans vs. Japanese in usual flag-waving espionage film, no better or worse than most.

Betrayed (1954) C-108m. ** D: Gottfried Reinhardt. Clark Gable, Lana Turner, Victor Mature, Louis Calhern. Unconvincing WW2 espionage melodrama of Dutch underground. Filmed in Holland.

Betrayed Women (1955) 70m. *½ D: Edward L. Cahn. Carole Mathews, Beverly Michaels, Peggy Knudsen, Tom Drake, Sara Haden. Low-key filming of potentially volatile subject, sadistic treatment of inmates in women's prison.

Betsy, The (1978) C-125m. **½ D: Daniel Petrie. Laurence Olivier, Robert Duvall, Katharine Ross, Tommy Lee Jones, Jane Alexander, Lesley-Anne Down, Kathleen Beller. Moderately enjoyable trash, adapted from Harold Robbins' novel about the multigenerational wheelings and dealings between an auto company patriarch and his family. Olivier's hamminess and Down's loveliness are the pluses here.

Better a Widow (1969-Italian) C-105m. *½ D: Duccio Tessari. Virna Lisi, Peter McEnery, Gabriele Ferzetti, Jean Servais, Agnes Spaak. Italian underworld "comedy" is better forgotten.

Better Late Than Never (1979) C-100m. TVM D: Richard Crenna. Harold Gould, Tyne Daly, Strother Martin, Harry Morgan, Victor Buono, George Gobel, Lou Jacobi, Donald Pleasance, Larry Storch. The revolt of a bunch of senior citizens in a retirement home against house rules that limit their freedom is less funny than it could have been. And, yes, the fellow who sings the title song without credit is just who you think it is. Average.

Between Heaven and Hell (1956) C-94m. *** D: Richard Fleischer. Robert Wagner, Terry Moore, Broderick Crawford, Buddy Ebsen. Lightweight cast does extremely well by conventional story of thoughtless Southern boy who matures during army experience.

Between Midnight and Dawn (1950) 89m. ** D: Gordon Douglas. Edmond O'Brien, Gale Storm, Mark Stevens, Roland Winters, Madge Blake. Passable crimeland caper with cops battling escaped crooks.

Between the Lines (1977) **C-101m.**
***½ D: Joan Micklin Silver. John
Heard, Lindsay Crouse, Jeff Goldblum, Jill Eikenberry, Bruno Kirby,
Gwen Welles, Stephen Collins,
Michael J. Pollard. Thoroughly enjoyable sleeper about the emotional
problems of an underground newspaper staff in Boston whose weekly
is about to be purchased by a print
tycoon. The performances by an un-
known cast are first-rate all the way.
Between Time and Eternity (1960-
German) **C-98m.** ****½** D: Arthur
Maria Rabenalt. Lilli Palmer, Willy
Birgel, Ellen Schwiers, Carlos Thomp-
son. Palmer makes tear-jerker believ-
able in story of middle-aged woman
dying of rare disease, seeking romance and fun while she can.
Between Two Women (1944) **83m.**
D: Willis Goldbeck. Van Johnson,
Lionel Barrymore, Gloria DeHaven,
Keenan Wynn, Marilyn Maxwell,
Keye Luke, Alma Kruger. SEE **Dr.
Kildare series.**
Between Two Worlds (1944) **112m.**
**½ D: Edward A. Blatt. John Gar-
field, Eleanor Parker, Sydney Green-
street, Faye Emerson, Paul Henreid,
Sara Allgood, Isobel Elsom, George
Tobias, Edmund Gwenn. Updated re-
make of OUTWARD BOUND has
flaws, but good acting by Warner
Bros. star stock company makes it
worthwhile.
Between Us Girls (1942) **89m.** ****** D:
Henry Koster. Kay Francis, Diana
Barrymore, Robert Cummings, Andy
Devine, John Boles, Scotty Beckett,
Ethel Griffies. Chic Francis and
daughter Barrymore both have ro-
mances at the same time in this OK
comedy. Boles and Cummings are
respective leads.
Beware, My Lovely (1952) **77m.** ****½**
D: Harry Horner. Ida Lupino, Rob-
ert Ryan, Taylor Holmes, O. Z.
Whitehead, Barbara Whiting. Widow
Lupino hires Ryan as handyman, dis-
covers he is psychopath; brooding
and atmospheric.
Beware of Blondie (1950) **66m.** D:
Edward Bernds. Penny Singleton,
Arthur Lake, Larry Simms, Adele
Jergens, Dick Wessel. SEE: **Blondie**
series.
Beware of Children (1961-British)
80m. ***½** D: Gerald Thomas. Leslie
Phillips, Geraldine McEwen, Julia
Lockwood, Noel Purcell. Tedious at-
tempt at lighthearted romp; young
married couple transforms an in-

heritance of land into summer camp
for all sorts of children, focusing
on predictable pranks of youngsters.
Beware of Pity (1946-British) **102m.**
**½ D: Maurice Elvey. Lilli Palmer,
Albert Lieven, Cedric Hardwicke,
Gladys Cooper. Maudlin but effective
yarn of crippled young woman who
finds romance and meaning to life.
Beware, Spooks! (1939) **68m.** ****** D:
Edward Sedgwick. Joe E. Brown,
Mary Carlisle, Clarence Kolb, Marc
Lawrence. Good fun as Brown solves
mystery and becomes hero in Coney
Island fun house.
Beware! The Blob (1972) **C-88m.** ***½**
D: Larry Hagman. Robert Walker,
Richard Stahl, Godfrey Cambridge,
Carol Lynley, Larry Hagman, Shelley
Berman, Marlene Clark. They should
have left it frozen in the arctic.
Weak sequel to famous original
BLOB finds the gooey mess doing
its thing once again. Also known as
SON OF BLOB.
Bewitched (1945) **65m.** ****½** D: Arch
Oboler. Edmund Gwenn, Phyllis
Thaxter, Henry Daniels, Jr., Addison
Richards, Kathleen Lockhart. Inter-
esting story of schizophrenic Thaxter
who commits murder as one girl,
doesn't recall it as the other.
Beyond a Reasonable Doubt (1956)
80m. ****½** D: Fritz Lang. Dana Andrews, Joan Fontaine, Sidney Blackmer, Philip Bourneuf, Barbara Nichols. Far-fetched tale of man who
pretends to be guilty of murder to
get first-hand view of justice system,
unable to prove himself innocent
later on. Pale production values. Intriguing idea doesn't hold up.
Beyond Glory (1948) **82m.** ****½** D:
John Farrow. Alan Ladd, Donna
Reed, George Macready, George
Coulouris. Predictable account of
West Point captain Ladd, a WW2
veteran, on trial for misconduct;
nicely done trivia. Also Audie Murphy's first film.
Beyond Mombasa (1957-U.S.-British)
C-90m. ****** D: George Marshall. Cor-
nel Wilde, Donna Reed, Leo Genn,
Ron Randell, Christopher Lee. Tame
African adventure tale with Wilde
seeking mysterious killers of his
brother and clues to hidden uranium
mine.
Beyond the Bermuda Triangle (1975)
C-78m. TVM D: William A. Graham.
Fred MacMurray, Sam Groom,
Donna Mills, Suzanne Reed, Dana
Plato, Woody Woodbury. Retired

businessman MacMurray probes into mysterious ship and plane disappearances off Florida coast after his friends and fiancee become involved. Foolish, two-dimensional mystery drama; below average.

Beyond the Blue Horizon (1942) C-76m. ** D: Alfred Santell. Dorothy Lamour, Richard Denning, Jack Haley, Walter Abel, Elizabeth Patterson, Abner Biberman, Patricia Morison. Sarong queen Lamour turns out to be heiress to great fortune; witless film wastes more talent than usual.

Beyond the Forest (1949) 96m. ** D: King Vidor. Bette Davis, Joseph Cotten, David Brian, Ruth Roman, Dona Drake, Regis Toomey. Muddled murder story of grasping Davis, her small-town doctor husband (Cotten), and wealthy neighbor (Brian). Davis' overly mannered performance doesn't help.

Beyond the Law (1968-Italian) C-91m. ** D: Giorgio Stegani. Lee Van Cleef, Antonio Sabato, Lionel Stander, Bud Spencer, Gordon Mitchell, Ann Smyrner. Formula Western with a whole lot of Van Cleef and almost as much humor. Bad guy turns good guy, becomes sheriff long enough to get his hands on a shipment of silver, and then splits.

Beyond the Poseidon Adventure (1979) C-122m. *½ D: Irwin Allen. Michael Caine, Sally Field, Telly Savalas, Peter Boyle, Jack Warden, Shirley Knight, Slim Pickens, Shirley Jones, Karl Malden. Following THE SWARM, Caine teamed up with Irwin Allen for their second career killer in a row—a needless Poseidon sequel about attempts to loot the vessel before it sinks into the sea.

Beyond the Time Barrier (1960) 75m. ** D: Edgar G. Ulmer. Robert Clarke, Darlene Tompkins, Arianne Arden, Vladimir Sokoloff. Military plot is thrust into 21st century, seeing tragic results of worldwide epidemic of 1970.

Beyond the Valley of the Dolls (1970) C-109m. **½ D: Russ Meyer. Dolly Read, Cynthia Myers, Marcia McBroom, Michael Blodgett, Edy Williams, Erica Gavin. More a matter of taste than a question of quality, this in-name-only sequel is at least much more enjoyable than the original. Due to its racy nature, however, your TV station will need about 15 car-

toons to fill up a two-hour time slot after the credits are over. "Plot" concerns sexual adventures of three female rock stars.

Beyond Tomorrow (1940) 84m. **½ D: A. Edward Sutherland. Richard Carlson, Jean Parker, Harry Carey, C. Aubrey Smith, Charles Winninger, Maria Ouspenskaya, Rod LaRocque. Sensitive little drama of three wealthy men sharing Christmas with down-and-out Carlson and Parker, who fall in love.

Bhowani Junction (1956-U.S.-British) C-110m. **½ D: George Cukor. Ava Gardner, Stewart Granger, Bill Travers, Abraham Sofaer. Set in post WW2 Pakistan; Gardner is half-caste torn between love of country and love for a British colonel. Based on John Masters novel, film was strikingly photographed on location.

Bible, The (1966-Italian) C-174m. BOMB D: John Huston. Michael Parks, Ulla Bergryd, Richard Harris, John Huston, Stephen Boyd, George C. Scott, Ava Gardner, Peter O'Toole, Franco Nero. Unsuccessful epic dealing with Adam and Eve, Cain and Abel, Noah and the Flood, etc. (first 22 chapters of Genesis). Only Huston himself as Noah escapes heavy-handedness. Definitely one time you should read the book instead.

Bicycle Thief, The (1949-Italian) 90m. **** D: Vittorio De Sica. Lamberto Maggiorani, Lianella Carell, Enzo Staiola, Elena Altieri. Simple, realistic tale of workingman whose job depends on his bicycle, and the shattering week he spends with his young son after it is stolen. An honest, beautiful film; one of the all-time classics.

Big Bad Mama (1974) C-83m. ** D: Steve Carver. Angie Dickinson, William Shatner, Tom Skerritt, Susan Sennett, Robbie Lee, Royal Dano. BONNIE AND CLYDE rehash, distinguished only by offbeat casting of Angie in title role. Frequent nudity may be cut for TV.

Big Bluff, The (1955) 70m. ** D: W. Lee Wilder. John Bromfield, Martha Vickers, Robert Hutton, Rosemarie Bowe. Interesting premise poorly executed. Vickers is fatally ill girl married to fortune-hunter who seeks to murder her when she recovers from illness.

Big Bob Johnson and His Fantastic Speed Circus (1978) C-100m. TVM D: Jack Starrett. Charles Napier,

Maud Adams, Constance Forslund, Robert Stoneman, William Daniels. Rambunctious comedy pitting a rag-tag auto racing team against a blackguard in a Rolls Royce for a run across Louisiana with a fortune at stake. Average.

Big Boodle, The (1957) 83m. *½ D: Richard Wilson. Errol Flynn, Pedro Armendariz, Rossana Rory, Jacques Aubuchon. Seedy programmer emphasizing Flynn's career decline. Tame caper of gangsters and counterfeit money, set in Havana.

Big Bounce, The (1969) C-102m. ** D: Alex March. Ryan O'Neal, Leigh Taylor-Young, James Daly, Robert Webber, Lee Grant, Van Heflin. Muddle-headed tale of drifter O'Neal becoming involved with vixenish Taylor-Young, who has strange ideas of what to do for kicks.

Big Broadcast, The (1932) 78m. *** D: Frank Tuttle. Bing Crosby, Kate Smith, George Burns, Gracie Allen, Stuart Erwin, Leila Hyams, Cab Calloway, Mills Brothers, Boswell Sisters. Failing radio station owned by Burns is saved by all-star show featuring Bing and many radio stars. Many offbeat, bizarre touches in standard love-triangle story make this a delight. Bing sings "Please," "Here Lies Love."

Big Broadcast of 1936, The (1935) 97m. **½ D: Norman Taurog. Jack Oakie, George Burns, Gracie Allen, Lyda Roberti, Henry Wadsworth, Wendy Barrie, C. Henry Gordon, Ethel Merman, Charlie Ruggles, Mary Boland, Bill "Bojangles" Robinson. Curious muddle of specialty acts and nonsensical "plot" involving radio station owner Oakie. Vignettes feature everyone from Amos 'n' Andy to the Vienna Boys Choir. Bing Crosby sings lovely "I Wished on the Moon."

Big Broadcast of 1937, The (1936) 102m. *** D: Mitchell Leisen. Jack Benny, George Burns, Gracie Allen, Bob Burns, Martha Raye, Shirley Ross, Ray Milland. Another plotless but enjoyable variety romp with many stars, plus guests Benny Goodman, Leopold Stokowski, Larry Adler, etc. Songs such as: "Here's Love In Your Eye," "La Bomba," "Night In Manhattan."

Big Broadcast of 1938, The (1938) 90m. ** D: Mitchell Leisen. W. C. Fields, Martha Raye, Dorothy Lamour, Shirley Ross, Lynne Overman, Bob Hope, Ben Blue, Leif Erickson.

Hodgepodge of bad musical numbers from Tito Guizar to Kirsten Flagstad, notable only for Fields' few scenes, Hope and Ross' "Thanks For The Memory."

Big Brown Eyes (1936) 77m. **½ D: Raoul Walsh. Joan Bennett, Cary Grant, Walter Pidgeon, Isabel Jewell, Lloyd Nolan. Bennett helps detective Grant trap a gang of notorious thieves in pleasing romantic mystery.

Big Bus, The (1976) C-85m. **½ D: James Frawley. Joseph Bologna, Stockard Channing, John Beck, Lynn Redgrave, Jose Ferrer, Ruth Gordon, Richard B. Shull, Sally Kellerman, Ned Beatty, Stuart Margolin. Funny spoof of disaster films; using a super-duper Trailways bus; all expected cliches come in for ribbing, but film doesn't sustain its promising idea. Murphy Dunne hilarious as inane cocktail pianist.

Big Cage, The (1933) 76m. **½ D: Kurt Neumann. Clyde Beatty, Anita Page, Wallace Ford, Andy Devine, Raymond Hatton, Mickey Rooney. Good actioner with animal-trainer Beatty and young sidekick Rooney; designed for family-juvenile audiences.

Big Caper, The (1957) 84m. **½ D: Robert Stevens. Rory Calhoun, Mary Costa, James Gregory, Robert Harris. Well-done account of Calhoun and Costa posing as married couple in small town in order to set up gang caper; realities of life reform them.

Big Carnival, The (1951) 112m. *** D: Billy Wilder. Kirk Douglas, Jan Sterling, Bob Arthur, Porter Hall. Unrelenting cynicism is theme of hard-hitting Wilder drama of reporter Douglas, who capitalizes on Albuquerque tragedy. Not for all tastes, but biting and extremely well-acted. Retitled: ACE IN THE HOLE.

Big Circus, The (1959) C-108m. **½ D: Joseph M. Newman. Victor Mature, Red Buttons, Rhonda Fleming, Kathryn Grant, Vincent Price, Peter Lorre, David Nelson, Gilbert Roland, Howard McNear, Steve Allen. Familiar but well-done circus story with exceptional cast (Lorre as a clown is worth the price of admission). Big-top action and intrigue is entertaining.

Big City, The (1937) 80m. **½ D: Frank Borzage. Spencer Tracy, Luise Rainer, Eddie Quillan, William

Demarest, Regis Toomey, Charley Grapewin, Victor Varconi. Cabdriver Tracy and wife Rainer are pitted against crooked taxi bosses in well-acted but average film. Retitled: SKYSCRAPER WILDERNESS.

Big City, The (1948) 103m. **½ D: Norman Taurog. Margaret O'Brien, Robert Preston, Danny Thomas, George Murphy, Betty Garrett. Priest Preston, cantor Thomas, and cop Murphy "adopt" little O'Brien in this maudlin drama.

Big City Blues (1932) 65m. **½ D: Mervyn LeRoy. Joan Blondell, Eric Linden, Inez Courtney, Evalyn Knapp, Guy Kibbee, Humphrey Bogart, Ned Sparks. Polished Warner Bros. programmer of hayseed Linden encountering disillusionment and love in N.Y.C.

Big Clock, The (1948) 95m. *** D: John Farrow. Ray Milland, Charles Laughton, Maureen O'Sullivan, Rita Johnson. Tyrannical editor of crime magazine (Laughton) commits murder; his ace reporter (Milland) tries to solve case. Vibrant melodrama; Elsa Lanchester has hilarious vignette as eccentric artist.

Big Combo, The (1955) 89m. *** D: Joseph H. Lewis. Cornel Wilde, Jean Wallace, Brian Donlevy, Richard Conte, Lee Van Cleef. Raw, violent "film noir" drama of cop (Wilde) tracking down racketeer with help of ex-moll Wallace. Stylishly directed.

Big Country, The (1958) C-166m. *** D: William Wyler. Gregory Peck, Burl Ives, Jean Simmons, Carroll Baker, Charlton Heston, Chuck Connors. Overblown Western has ex-sea captain Peck arrive to marry Baker, but forced to take sides in battle against Ives and sons over water rights. Heston as quick-tempered ranch foreman and Ives (who won an Oscar) as burly patriarch stand out in energetic cast. Jerome Moross' score has become a classic.

Big Cube, The (1969) C-98m. *½ D: Tito Davison. Lana Turner, George Chakiris, Richard Egan, Dan O'Herlihy, Karin Mossberg. Absurd drama about relationship between beautiful young girl, her gigolo boyfriend, and her actress-mother at least offers some unintentional laughs. Several of the actors in this haven't made a movie since, which should tell you something.

Big Deal on Madonna Street (1956-Italian) 91m. ***½ D: Mario Moni-

celli. Vittorio Gassman, Marcello Mastroianni, Renato Salvatori, Rossana Rory, Carla Gravina, Toto. Classic account of misadventures of amateurish crooks attempting to rob a store; hilarious satire on all burglary capers. Retitled: BIG DEAL.

Big Fisherman, The (1959) C-180m. **½ D: Frank Borzage. Howard Keel, John Saxon, Susan Kohner, Herbert Lom, Martha Hyer, Ray Stricklyn, Alexander Scourby. Sprawling religious epic, from Lloyd Douglas' book about the life of St. Peter; seldom dull, but not terribly inspiring.

Big Fix, The (1978) C-108m. *** D: Jeremy Paul Kagan. Richard Dreyfuss, Susan Anspach, Bonnie Bedelia, John Lithgow, Ofelia Medina, Fritz Weaver. Good vehicle for now-familiar Dreyfuss personality as he plays 1960s-campus-radical-turned-private-eye Moses Wine, and becomes involved in tangled whodunit in which a former hippie cult leader figures prominently. Screenplay by Roger L. Simon from his novel.

Big Gamble, The (1961) C-100m. **½ D: Richard Fleischer. Stephen Boyd, Juliette Greco, David Wayne, Sybil Thorndike. Not-too-convincing account of Irish adventurer and bride Greco who dally on the African Ivory Coast seeking to build their future the easy way.

Big Guns SEE: No Way Out

Big Gusher, The (1951) 68m. *½ D: Lew Landers. Wayne Morris, Preston Foster, Dorothy Patrick, Paul Burns. Unshiny account of oil workers involved in hackneyed deadline to strike oil or lose all their savings.

Big Guy, The (1939) 78m. **½ D: Arthur Lubin. Jackie Cooper, Victor McLaglen, Ona Munson, Peggy Moran, Edward Brophy. Fairly interesting story of warden McLaglen given choice between wealth and saving innocent man from death penalty. Remade as BEHIND THE HIGH WALL.

Big Hand for the Little Lady, A (1966) C-95m. *** D: Fielder Cook. Henry Fonda, Joanne Woodward, Jason Robards, Charles Bickford, Burgess Meredith. Excellent comedy centering on poker game in old West. Outstanding cast also includes John Qualen, Paul Ford, and Robert Middleton. There's a neat surprise ending, too.

Big Hangover, The (1950) 82m. **½ D: Norman Krasna. Van Johnson,

Elizabeth Taylor, Leon Ames, Edgar Buchanan, Rosemary DeCamp. Goofy premise of Johnson allergic to liquor but wanting to get ahead in social swing and romance Taylor.

Big Heat, The (1953) 90m. *** D: Fritz Lang. Glenn Ford, Gloria Grahame, Jocelyn Brando, Lee Marvin, Carolyn Jones, Jeanette Nolan. Time has taken the edge off once-searing story of cop determined to bust city crime ring; famous coffee-hurling scene still jolts, and Grahame is excellent as bad-girl who helps Ford.

Big House, The (1930) 80m. *** D: George Hill. Wallace Beery, Chester Morris, Robert Montgomery, Lewis Stone, Karl Dane, Leila Hyams. The original prison drama, this set the pattern for all later copies; it's still good, hard-bitten stuff with one of Beery's best tough-guy roles.

Big House, U.S.A. (1955) 82m. **½ D: Howard W. Koch. Broderick Crawford, Ralph Meeker, Reed Hadley, Charles Bronson, Lon Chaney, Jr. Brutal account of kidnappers and extortion, and the FBI agents sent to track them down.

Big Jack (1949) 85m. ** D: Richard Thorpe. Wallace Beery, Marjorie Main, Edward Arnold, Richard Conte, Vanessa Brown. Beery's last film, rather flat; he and Main are vagabond thieves in colonial America, Conte a moralistic doctor they meet on the road.

Big Jake (1971) C-110m. ** D: George Sherman. John Wayne, Richard Boone, Maureen O'Hara, Patrick Wayne, Chris Mitchum, Bobby Vinton, Bruce Cabot. Uneasy combination of traditional Wayne Western and BUTCH CASSIDY-type spoof has Duke going after baddies who have kidnapped his grandson. Sounds as if it can't miss, but it does; some excessive violence will probably be cut for TV.

Big Jim McLain (1952) 90m. **½ D: Edward Ludwig. John Wayne, James Arness, Nancy Olson, Veda Ann Borg, Hans Conried. One of the few small Wayne films: story filmed in Hawaii tells of zealous government agent Wayne tracking down Communist spy ring.

Big Knife, The (1955) 111m. *** D: Robert Aldrich. Jack Palance, Ida Lupino, Shelley Winters, Rod Steiger, Ilka Chase, Wendell Corey. Clifford Odets' cynical view of Hollywood comes across well in hard-punching film, with fine portrayals that almost overcome stereotypes.

Big Land, The (1957) C-92m. **½ D: Gordon Douglas. Alan Ladd, Virginia Mayo, Edmond O'Brien, Julie Bishop. Cattle owners and grain farmers join together to bring railroad link to Texas; easygoing, familiar.

Big Leaguer, The (1953) 70m. ** D: Robert Aldrich. Edward G. Robinson, Vera-Ellen, Jeff Richards, Richard Jaeckel. Baseball programmer of college-bound boy being scouted for the big diamond. Robinson wasted.

Big Lift, The (1950) 120m. **½ D: George Seaton. Montgomery Clift, Paul Douglas, Cornell Borchers. O. E. Hasse. GI pilots involved in post-WW2 Berlin airlift and romance with German women. More interesting for on location photography than uneven story line.

Big Mo SEE: Maurie

Big Mouth, The (1967) C-107m. **½ D: Jerry Lewis. Jerry Lewis, Harold Stone, Susan Bay, Buddy Lester, Del Moore, Paul Lambert. Typical Lewis effort, with Jerry involved in murder and search for missing treasure; set in Southern California.

Big Night, The (1951) 75m. **½ D: Joseph Losey. John Barrymore, Jr., Preston Foster, Howland Chamberlain, Joan Lorring, Dorothy Comingore, Howard St. John. Brooding account of rebellious teen-ager Barrymore's emotional flare-up with humanity at large; well done.

Big Noise, The (1944) 74m. BOMB D: Malcolm St. Clair. Stan Laurel, Oliver Hardy, Arthur Space, Veda Ann Borg, Bobby Blake, Jack Norton. L&H's worst film, about them delivering a bomb . . . and they do.

Big Operator, The (1959) 91m. ** D: Charles Haas. Mickey Rooney, Steve Cochran, Mamie Van Doren, Mel Torme, Ray Danton, Jim Backus. Ray Anthony, Jackie Coogan. Rooney tries to add vim and vigor to title role as tough hood who goes on violent rampage when federal agents investigate his business activities. Paul Gallico story filmed before as JOE SMITH, AMERICAN. Retitled: ANATOMY OF A SYNDICATE.

Big Parade, The (1925) 126m. **** D: King Vidor. John Gilbert, Renee Adoree, Hobart Bosworth, Claire McDowell, Claire Adams, Karl Dane. One of the best WW1 films ever; clean-shaven Gilbert a wonderful hero, Adoree an unforgettable heroine. Filled with memorable vignettes, and some of the most harrowingly realistic battle scenes ever filmed. A gem.

Big Parade of Comedy SEE: MGM'S Big Parade of Comedy

Big Pond, The (1930) 75m. **½ D: Hobart Henley. Maurice Chevalier, Claudette Colbert, George Barbier, Nat Pendleton. Claudette brings Maurice to America, where to make good he works in chewing gum factory. Chevalier charm overcomes trivia; song: "You Brought A New Kind Of Love To Me."

Big Red (1962) C-89m. *** D: Norman Tokar. Walter Pidgeon, Gilles Payant, Emile Genest, Janette Bertrand, Doris Lussier. Charming, understated Disney drama of young boy who goes to work for wealthy dog fancier (Pidgeon) and becomes devoted to prize Irish setter. Filmed in Canada.

Big Rip-Off, The (1975) C-78m. TVM D: Dean Hargrove. Tony Curtis, Brenda Vaccaro, Roscoe Lee Browne, Larry Hagman, John Dehner, Morgan Woodward. Conman Curtis plots elaborate swindle to recover ransom money from kidnappers of millionaire's wife. Reporter Vaccaro and night club performer Browne are his cohorts in this big rip-off of THE STING that evolved into Curtis' short-lived TV series "McCoy." Average.

Big Risk, The (1960-French) 111m. ** D: Claude Sautet. Jean-Paul Belmondo, Lino Venturi, Marcel Dalio, Sandra Milo. Too-leisurely-paced account of criminal on the lam, who for sake of his family gives himself up to police.

Big Rose: Double Trouble (1974) C-78m. TVM D: Paul Krasny. Shelley Winters, Barry Primus, Lonny Chapman, Michael Constantine, Joan Van Ark, Peggy Walton. Detectives Winters and Primus are hired to expose team of con-artists blackmailing a wealthy contractor. It's fun watching Winters in unlikely role of private investigator; everything else is strictly formula. Below average.

Big Shakedown, The (1934) 64m. ** D: John Francis Dillon. Bette Davis, Ricardo Cortez, Glenda Farrell, Charles Farrell, Adrian Morris. Inconsequential tale. Davis rejects husband Farrell when he joins forces with mobster Cortez in cosmetic fraud.

Big Shot, The (1942) 82m. **½ D: Lewis Seiler. Humphrey Bogart, Irene Manning, Susan Peters, Minor Watson, Chick Chandler, Richard Travis. OK grade-B gangster yarn with Bogey a three-time loser involved in robbery frameup and subsequent prison break.

Big Show, The (1961) C-113m. **½ D: James B. Clark. Esther Williams, Cliff Robertson, Nehemiah Persoff, Robert Vaughn. Drama of family conflict, similar to 1949's HOUSE OF STRANGERS, somehow set in a circus with swimmer Williams in a dramatic role. Glug!

Big Sky, The (1952) 140m. *** D: Howard Hawks. Kirk Douglas, Dewey Martin, Elizabeth Threatt, Arthur Hunnicutt, Buddy Baer, Steven Geray, Hank Worden, Jim Davis. Camaraderie and conflict as furtrapper Douglas leads expedition up the Missouri River. Eventful, evocative film adapted from A. B. Guthrie Jr., book by Dudley Nichols; well-directed by Hawks.

Big Sleep, The (1946) 114m. ***½ D: Howard Hawks. Humphrey Bogart, Lauren Bacall, Dorothy Malone, Martha Vickers, Elisha Cook Jr., Peggy Knudsen, Bob Steele. Bogey is Raymond Chandler's detective Philip Marlowe in exciting, often confusing mystery. Bogart and Bacall bristle, especially with this film's saucy dialogue. Remade in 1978.

Big Sleep, The (1978-British) C-100m. BOMB D: Michael Winner. Robert Mitchum, Sarah Miles, Candy Clark, Richard Boone, James Stewart, Joan Collins, Edward Fox, John Mills, Oliver Reed. Raymond Chandler's classic has its locale switched from L.A. to England, which makes about as much sense as trying to improve on Howard Hawks' 1946 film version.

Big Steal, The (1949) 71m. *** D: Don Siegel. Robert Mitchum, Jane Greer, William Bendix, Patric Knowles, Ramon Novarro. Well-made robbery caper set in Southwest and Mexico with Mitchum hustling after heisters, getting involved with enticing Greer. Full of terrific plot twists.

Big Store, The (1941) 80m. ** D: Charles Riesner. Groucho, Chico and Harpo Marx, Tony Martin, Virginia Grey, Margaret Dumont, Douglass Dumbrille. Big comedown for Marxes in weak film of detective Groucho investigating crooked Dumbrille's department store. Low spot is Martin's crooning "Tenement Symphony."

Big Street, The (1942) 88m. **½ D: Irving Reis. Henry Fonda, Lucille Ball, Barton MacLane, Eugene Pallette, Agnes Moorehead. Damon Runyon fable of timid busboy Fonda who devotes himself to disinterested nightclub singer Ball; wavers from good to too-sticky.

Big T.N.T. Show, The (1966) 93m. ** D: Larry Peerce. David McCallum, Roger Miller, Ray Charles, Joan Baez, The Lovin' Spoonful. Unexciting taping of a "live" youth show, with guest musical artists doing routine numbers; poorly photographed.

Big Town (1947) 60m. ** D: William C. Thomas. Philip Reed, Hillary Brooke, Robert Lowery, Byron Barr. Standard story of newspaper reporter working with police to rid town of dangerous mob.

Big Town After Dark (1947) 69m. ** D: William C. Thomas. Philip Reed, Hillary Brooke, Richard Travis, Anne Gillis. OK drama of daring reporters walking into danger while trying to get lowdown on criminal gang. Retitled: UNDERWORLD AFTER DARK.

Big Trail, The (1930) 110m. *** D: Raoul Walsh. John Wayne, Marguerite Churchill, El Brendel, Tully Marshall, Tyrone Power Sr., David Rollins, Ian Keith. Epic Western may seem creaky to some viewers, but remains one of the most impressive early talkies, with its grand sweep and naturalistic use of sound (originally had wide-screen segments, too). John Wayne was "discovered" for starring role, and already shows easygoing charm.

Big Trees, The (1952) C-89m. **½ D: Felix Feist. Kirk Douglas, Eve Miller, Patrice Wymore, Edgar Buchanan. Douglas is staunch in so-so logging saga of lumbermen vs. homesteaders. Remake of VALLEY OF THE GIANTS.

Big Wave, The (1960-Japanese) 60m. *½ D: Tad Danielewski. Sessue Hayakawa, Ichizo Itami, Mickey Curtis, Koji Shitara. Slowly paced account from Pearl Buck novel involving two boys who are childhood friends but later in life clash over their love for a local girl.

Big Wednesday (1978) C-120m. **½ D: John Milius. Jan-Michael Vincent, William Katt, Gary Busey, Lee Purcell, Patti D'Arbanville, Barbara Hale. Half of a good flick on surfing,

Pacific Coast-style, early Sixties. Up to midway point, a ridiculous comedy about macho Vincent and his fun-loving, destructive ways. As he and buddies Katt and Busey get older and action is brought up to the 70s dramatic content improves and you're made to sympathize with the characters. Katt's real-life mother, Hale, is typecast here.

Big Wheel, The (1949) 92m. **½ D: Edward Ludwig. Mickey Rooney, Thomas Mitchell, Spring Byington, Mary Hatcher, Allen Jenkins, Michael O'Shea. Rooney is determined race-car driver following in father's footsteps despite dad's death on track; familiar plot well done.

Bigamist, The (1953) 80m. **½ D: Ida Lupino. Edmond O'Brien, Joan Fontaine, Ida Lupino, Edmund Gwenn. Mildly sensational account of O'Brien married to two women, torn between his love for both of them.

Bigger Than Life (1956) C-95m. *** D: Nicholas Ray. James Mason, Barbara Rush, Walter Matthau, Robert Simon. Compelling drama of teacher Mason who becomes hooked on drugs, and its devastating effects on him and his family.

Biggest Bundle of Them All, The (1968) C-110m. *½ D: Ken Annakin. Robert Wagner, Raquel Welch, Vittorio De Sica, Edward G. Robinson, Godfrey Cambridge. Supposedly a comedy, film is slapdash tale of amateur criminals who try to kidnap American gangster. Filmed in France and Italy.

Bikini Beach (1964) C-100m. ** D: William Asher. Frankie Avalon, Annette Funicello, Martha Hyer, Harvey Lembeck, Don Rickles. Frankie and Annette are at it again; you know all about it. Same formula casts yet another surfing spectacle.

Bill and Coo (1947) C-61m. *** D: Dean Riesner. Produced and narrated by Ken Murray. Charming, unique live-action film using trained birds in a story situation. A 1947 Oscar winner, recently reedited with new introductory material by Murray.

Bill of Divorcement, A (1932) 69m. *** D: George Cukor. John Barrymore, Katharine Hepburn, Billie Burke, David Manners, Henry Stephenson. Barrymore gives sensitive performance as man released from mental institution who returns to wife Burke and gets to know his daughter for the first time. Dated but worth seeing; notable as Hepburn's screen debut. Originally released at 75m.

Bill of Divorcement, A (1940) 74m. **½ D: John Farrow. Maureen O'Hara, Adolphe Menjou, Fay Bainter, Herbert Marshall, Dame May Whitty. Refilming of '32 drama follows it closely, but cast can't match the original's class. Retitled: NEVER TO LOVE.

Billie (1965) C-87m. **½ D: Don Weis. Patty Duke, Warren Berlinger, Jim Backus, Jane Greer, Billy DeWolfe, Charles Lane, Dick Sargent. Airy comedy of tomboyish Billie (Duke) and her athletic aspirations. Backus and Greer are her perplexed parents, Berlinger her boyfriend. Duke sings, runs, prances.

Billion Dollar Brain (1967-British) C-111m. *** D: Ken Russell. Michael Caine, Karl Malden, Ed Begley, Oscar Homolka, Françoise Dorleac. Third in series which began with IPCRESS FILE finds Harry Palmer (Caine) again up to his neck in exciting espionage, this time in Scandinavia.

Billion Dollar Hobo, The (1978) C-96m. *½ D: Stuart E. McGowan. Tim Conway, Will Geer, Eric Weston, Sydney Lassick, John Myhers, Frank Sivero. Dreary G-rated comedy about bumbling Conway becoming a hobo in order to qualify for inheritance.

Billion Dollar Threat, The (1979) C-100m. TVM D: Barry Shear. Dale Robinette, Ralph Bellamy, Keenan Wynn, Patrick Macnee, Ronnie Carol. Light-hearted pilot to proposed series involving a James Bondish superspy assigned to thwart the plans of a master agent threatening to destroy the planet. Average.

Billy Budd (1962-U.S.-British) 112m. ***½ D: Peter Ustinov. Robert Ryan, Peter Ustinov, Melvyn Douglas, Terence Stamp, Paul Rogers, David McCallum. Melville's classic good vs. evil novella set in British Navy, 1797. Naive, incorruptible seaman is court-martialed for murder of sadistic master-of-arms. ● Film deals simply with heavier issues of morality. Sterling performances by all.

Billy Jack (1972) C-112m. ***½ D: T.C. Frank (Tom Laughlin). Tom Laughlin, Delores Taylor, Clark Howat, Bert Freed, Julie Webb. Uneven in spots, but tremendously powerful tale of prejudices, fears and the spirit of youth. Free school imperiled by reactionary townspeople.

Billy Jack Goes to Washington (1977) C-155m. ** D: Tom Laughlin. Tom Laughlin, Delores Taylor, Sam Wanamaker, Lucie Arnaz. Contrived update of MR. SMITH GOES TO WASHINGTON, with writer-director-star Laughlin, a supposed "everyman," fighting big-time corruption in the Senate. Basic story is still good, but this version goes on forever.

Billy Liar (1963-British) 96m. ***½ D: John Schlesinger. Tom Courtenay, Julie Christie, Mona Washbourne, Ethel Griffies, Finlay Currie. Cast excels in story of ambitious but lazy young man caught in dull job routine who escapes into fantasy world, offering some poignant vignettes of middleclass life. Based on Keith Waterhouse novel and play.

Billy: Portrait of a Street Kid (1977) C-100m. TVM D: Steve Gethers. LeVar Burton, Ossie Davis, Dolph Sweet, Michael Constantine, Tina Andrews. Well-acted but predictable drama of a ghetto youth's dreams of escaping from his dismal existence. Especially good performance from Burton, the UCLA acting student who skyrocketed to fame as Kunta Kinte in ROOTS. Average.

Billy Rose's Diamond Horseshoe SEE: Diamond Horseshoe

Billy Rose's Jumbo (1962) C-125m. *** D: Charles Walters. Doris Day, Stephen Boyd, Jimmy Durante, Martha Raye, Dean Jagger. OK circus picture, at best during Rodgers and Hart songs, well-staged by Busby Berkeley. Durante and Raye are marvelous. Songs include "The Most Beautiful Girl in the World," "My Romance," "This Can't Be Love." Also known as JUMBO.

Billy the Kid (1930) 90m. **½ D: King Vidor. Johnny Mack Brown, Wallace Beery, Kay Johnson, Karl Dane, Roscoe Ates. Realistic early talkie Western with marshal Beery trying to capture outlaw Brown; some performances seem badly dated today. Title changed for TV to: THE HIGHWAYMAN RIDES.

Billy the Kid (1941) C-95m. **½ D: David Miller. Robert Taylor, Brian Donlevy, Ian Hunter, Mary Howard, Gene Lockhart, Lon Chaney Jr. Cast looks uncomfortable in remake of 1930 Western, but plot is sturdy enough for OK viewing, with Taylor in title role and Donlevy as marshal.

Billy the Kid vs. Dracula (1966)

C-95m. *½ D: William Beaudine. Chuck Courtney, John Carradine, Melinda Plowman, Virginia Christine, Walter Janovitz, Bing Russell, Harry Carey Jr. Famed outlaw decides it's time to get married—but doesn't realize that his bride's uncle is a vampire. Campy nonsense.

Billy Two Hats (1974) **C-99m. **½ D:** Ted Kotcheff. Gregory Peck, Desi Arnaz Jr., Jack Warden, Sian Barbara Allen, David Huddleston. Offbeat Western filmed in Israel, about a middle-aged Scot and a young half-Indian pursued by the law for bank robbery. Peck is appealing in unusual character role. Retitled THE LADY AND THE OUTLAW.

Bimbo the Great (1961-German) **C-96m. *½ D:** Harold Philipp, Claus Holm, Germaine Damar, Elma Karlowa, Marina Orschel. Hackneyed circus yarn of high-wire performer discovering wife's death was caused by his step-brother, with inevitable confession scene slightly spiced by potential big-top blaze.

Bingo Long Traveling All-Star and Motor Kings, The (1976) **C-110m. *** D:** John Badham. Billy Dee Williams, James Earl Jones, Richard Pryor, Ted Ross, DeWayne Jessie. Bright, original comedy about baseball player Williams trying to buck owners of Negro National League in 1939 by starting his own razzle-dazzle team.

Biography of a Bachelor Girl (1935) 82m. **½ D:** Edward Griffith. Ann Harding, Robert Montgomery, Edward Everett Horton, Edward Arnold, Una Merkel. Actress Harding publishes autobiography, unwittingly causing trouble for many people involved. Intriguing story, well acted.

Birch Interval (1977) **C-104m. *** D:** Delbert Mann. Eddie Albert, Rip Torn, Ann Wedgeworth, Susan McClung, Brian Part. Eleven-year-old girl, sent to live with relatives in Amish country, finds out about life, love, suffering and compassion. Beautiful, sensitive film.

Bird of Paradise (1932) 80m. ** D:** King Vidor. Joel McCrea, Dolores Del Rio, John Halliday, Skeets Gallegher, Lon Chaney Jr. Exotic but empty South Seas romance with McCrea as adventurer who falls in love with native-girl Del Rio. Handsome but unmoving; remade in 1951.

Bird of Paradise (1951) **C-100m. ** D:** Delmer Daves. Louis Jourdan, Debra Paget, Jeff Chandler, Everett Sloane. Jourdan's marriage to South Sea isle chief's daughter causes native uprising in grandly filmed but vapid tale. Remake of 1932 film.

Bird with the Crystal Plumage, The (1969-Italian-West German) **C-98m. **½ D:** Dario Argento. Tony Musante, Suzy Kendall, Eva Renzi, Enrico Maria Salerno, Mario Adorf, Renato Romano, Umberto Rano, Werner Peters. American writer living in Rome witnesses attempted murder in gallery; he and his mistress become involved in case. Uneven; best viewed on large screen. Beware cuts.

Birdman of Alcatraz (1962) 143m. *** D:** John Frankenheimer. Burt Lancaster, Karl Malden, Thelma Ritter, Betty Field, Neville Brand, Edmond O'Brien, Hugh Marlowe. Pensive study of prisoner Robert Stroud who during his many years in jail became a world-renowned bird authority. Film becomes static despite imaginative sidelights to enlarge scope of action.

Birdmen (1971) **C-73m. TVM D:** Philip Leacock. Doug McClure, Chuck Connors, Richard Basehart, Rene Auberjonois, Max Baer, Don Knight, Tom Skerritt. Uninteresting rehash of POW breakout plot. Captured Allies in German castle build glider to fly to freedom in Switzerland ten miles away. Average. Retitled ESCAPE OF THE BIRDMEN.

Birds, The (1963) **C-120m. ***½ D:** Alfred Hitchcock. Rod Taylor, Tippi Hedren, Suzanne Pleshette, Jessica Tandy, Ethel Griffies, Charles McGraw. Hitchcock's story of a girl (Hedren) and mass bird attacks that follow her around in isolated California community. Not for the squeamish; a delight for those who are game. Hold on to something and watch.

Birds and the Bees, The (1956) **C-94m. ** D:** Norman Taurog. George Gobel, Mitzi Gaynor, David Niven, Reginald Gardiner. Bland remake of THE LADY EVE about rich playboy who breaks off romance with cardshark girlfriend, but later decides he still loves her.

Birds, Bees, and the Italians, The (1967-Italian) 115m. *** D:** Pietro Germi. Virna Lisi, Gastone Moschin, Nora Ricci, Alberto Lionello. Very funny sex farce in which bed partners revolve as if on a merry-go-round.

Birds Do It (1966) **C-95m. ** D:** Andrew Marton. Soupy Sales, Tab

Hunter, Arthur O'Connell, Edward Andrews. Soupy's first starring vehicle has him under the spell of serum that enables him to fly. Fairly entertaining for kids.

Birds of Prey (1973) C-81m. TVM D: William Graham. David Janssen, Ralph Meeker, Elayne Heilveil, Harry Klekas, Sam Dawson. Good suspenser as Salt Lake City traffic-helicopter pilot Janssen witnesses bank robbery in progress, becomes inexorably involved. Above average.

Birth of a Nation, The (1915) 159m. **** D: D. W. Griffith. Lillian Gish, Mae Marsh, Henry B. Walthall, Miriam Cooper, Robert Harron, Wallace Reid, Joseph Henabery. The landmark of American motion pictures. Griffith's epic story of two families during Civil War and Reconstruction is still fascinating. Sometimes the drama survives intact; other times, one must watch in a more historical perspective. Griffith's attitude toward Ku Klux Klan has kept this film a center of controversy for sixty years.

Birth of the Beatles (1979) C-100m. TVM D: Richard Marquand. Stephen Mackenna, Rod Culbertson, John Altman, Ray Ashcroft, Ryan Mitchell, David Wilkinson, Brian Jameson. Dramatization of the early days of John, Paul, George, and Ringo, and the fifth Beatle, Pete Best. Unfamiliar cast of lookalikes pretend to be the Fab Four, and the group Rain sings Beatles songs—but why accept substitutes? Average.

Birth of the Blues (1941) 85m. *** D: Victor Schertzinger. Bing Crosby, Brian Donlevy, Carolyn Lee, Eddie (Rochester) Anderson, Mary Martin. Fiction about Crosby organizing jazz band in New Orleans has great music like "St. Louis Blues," "St. James Infirmary," "Melancholy Baby" and title tune to uplift fair story.

Birthday Party, The (1968-British) C-127m. *** D: William Friedkin. Robert Shaw, Patrick Magee, Dandy Nichols, Sydney Tafler, Moultrie Kelsall, Helen Fraser. Uncinematic film version of Harold Pinter's play about boarding house and its mysterious tenant (Shaw) is helped by good acting and playwright's usual superior dialogue.

Biscuit Eater, The (1940) 83m. *** D: Stuart Heisler. Billy Lee, Cordell Hickman, Helene Millard, Richard Lane, Lester Matthews. Warm, winning adaptation of James Street story

about two boys—one white, one black—who take unwanted dog from litter and try to turn him into champion bird dog. A B picture that was regarded as the "sleeper" of the year.

Biscuit Eater, The (1972) C-90m. **½ D: Vincent McEveety. Earl Holliman, Lew Ayres, Godfrey Cambridge, Patricia Crowley, Beah Richards, Johnny Whitaker, George Spell. Wholesome but uninspired Disney remake of 1940 film with Whitaker and Spell as the young friends who devote themselves to training a champion bird-dog.

Bishop's Wife, The (1947) 108m. *** D: Henry Koster. Cary Grant, Loretta Young, David Niven, Monty Woolley, James Gleason, Gladys Cooper, Elsa Lanchester. Christmas fantasy of suave angel (Grant) coming to earth to help Bishop Niven and wife Young raise money for new church. Engaging performances by all.

Bite the Bullet (1975) C-131m. **** D: Richard Brooks. Gene Hackman, Candice Bergen, James Coburn, Ben Johnson, Ian Bannen, Jan-Michael Vincent. Grand Western in the classic tradition. Disparate types compete in a grueling, 600-mile horse race at the turn of the century; the finalists develop a grudging—and growing—respect for each other. Filmed on magnificent locations.

Bitter Creek (1954) 74m. *½ D: Thomas Carr. Bill Elliott, Carleton Young, Beverly Garland, Claude Akins, Jim Hayward. Tame happenings as Elliott seeks revenge for his brother's untimely death in the old West.

Bitter Rice (1950-Italian) 107m. *** D: Giuseppe De Santis. Silvana Mangano, Vittorio Gassman, Raf Vallone, Doris Dowling, Lia Corelli. Somber account of dank existence of women working the rice fields of Po Valley.

Bitter Sweet (1940) C-92m. ** D: W.S. Van Dyke II. Jeanette MacDonald, Nelson Eddy, George Sanders, Felix Bressart, Lynne Carver, Ian Hunter, Sig Ruman. Ignore plot, enjoy Noel Coward's songs in lavishly filmed operetta. Wonderful Herman Bing provides funniest scene as shopkeeper who hires Nelson and Jeanette to give his daughter music lessons. An earlier British version was filmed in 1933.

Bitter Tea of General Yen, The (1933) 89m. ***½ D: Frank Capra.

Barbara Stanwyck, Nils Asther, Gavin Gordon, Toshia Mori, Richard Loo, Lucien Littlefield, Clara Blandick, Walter Connolly. May seem antiquated to modern audiences, but Capra's sensuous story of American woman's strange fascination with a Chinese warlord is still dazzling. A moody, beautifully atmospheric, sensitively performed film.

Bitter Victory (1958-French) 82m. *** D: Nicholas Ray. Richard Burton, Curt Jurgens, Ruth Roman, Raymond Pellegrin, Anthony Bushnell, Christopher Lee. Strong WW2 story with Jurgens as unfit commander who receives undeserved citation for mission against Rommel's desert headquarters; Roman is his wife who's had prior affair with officer Burton. 103m. versions now in circulation are from British release of this film.

Bittersweet Love (1977) C-92m. *½ D: David Miller. Lana Turner, Robert Lansing, Celeste Holm, Robert Alda, Scott Hylands, Meredith Baxter Birney. Excellent cast wasted on improbable story of young married couple (expecting a baby) suddenly discovering they are half-brother and sister. Termination of pregnancy and marriage are then talked to death.

Black Abbot, The (1963-German) 95m. ** D: Franz Gottlieb. Joachim Fuchsberger, Dieter Borsche, Grit Bottcher, Eva Scholtz. Unearthly "Abbot" is on a killing rampage warding off those who approach country house with buried treasure underneath.

Black and White in Color (1977-French-African) C-90m. ***½ D: Jean-Jacques Annaud. Jean Carmet, Jacques Dufilho, Catherine Rouvel, Jacques Spiesser, Dora Doll. Unusual and witty story of self-satisfied Frenchmen at remote African trading post who are fired by sudden patriotism at outbreak of WW1, and decide to attack nearby German fort. Oscar winner as Best Foreign Film.

Black Angel (1946) 80m. *** D: Roy William Neill. Dan Duryea, June Vincent, Peter Lorre, Broderick Crawford, Wallace Ford. First-rate whodunit (by Cornell Woolrich) of Vincent trying to clear husband of charge that he murdered Duryea's wife. Imaginative film will have you glued to the screen all the way.

Black Arrow, The (1948) 76m. *** D: Gordon Douglas. Louis Hayward,

Janet Blair, George Macready, Edgar Buchanan, Paul Cavanagh. Superior swashbuckler with dashing knight Hayward, lovely heroine Blair, and villain Macready. Truly exciting finale with hero vs. villain in jousting tournament.

Black Bart (1948) C-80m. **½ D: George Sherman. Yvonne De Carlo, Dan Duryea, Jeffrey Lynn, Percy Kilbride. Enticing De Carlo steps between outlaws Duryea and Lynn, foiling their attempt to overthrow Wells Fargo company.

Black Beauty (1946) 74m. **½ D: Max Nosseck. Mona Freeman, Richard Denning, Evelyn Ankers, Terry Kilburn, Arthur Space. Another animal film from famous story of girl's love for her horse; as good as most of others but not in color.

Black Beauty (1971-British) C-106m. **½ D: James Hill. Mark Lester, Walter Slezak, Peter Lee Lawrence, Ursula Glas. Classic story of king of wild horses who couldn't be tamed, remade here as average horse opera.

Black Belly of the Tarantula (1972-Italian) C-88m. *½ D: Paolo Cavara. Giancarlo Giannini, Stefania Sandrelli, Barbara Bouchet. Folks are being murdered in mysterious ways at health and beauty salon; none too exciting.

Black Belt Jones (1974) C-87m. **½ D: Robert Clouse. Jim Kelly, Gloria Hendry, Scatman Crothers, Alan Weeks, Nate Esformes. Black-oriented kung-fu mayhem from the team that made Bruce Lee's ENTER THE DRAGON. Kelly battles the Mafia to save his school of self-defense in Watts area of L.A. No gore; lots of action and comedy.

Black Bird, The (1975) C-98m. BOMB D: David Giler. George Segal, Stephane Audran, Lionel Stander, Lee Patrick, Elisha Cook Jr., Felix Silla, Signe Hasso. Horrendously bad, unfunny takeoff on THE MALTESE FALCON, with Segal as Sam Spade, Jr., not saved by the presence of Patrick and Cook from the '41 cast.

Black Book SEE: **Reign of Terror**

Black Caesar (1973) C-96m. **½ D: Larry Cohen. Fred Williamson, Art Lund, Julius W. Harris, Gloria Hendry, D'Urville Martin. Better-than-average gangster film follows rise to the top of shrewd, bloodthirsty black baddie.

Black Camel (1931) 71m. D: Hamilton MacFadden. Warner Oland, Sally Eilers, Bela Lugosi, Victor Varconi,

Robert Young, Dwight Frye, Mary Gordon. SEE: **Charlie Chan** series.

Black Castle, The (1952) 81m. ** D: Nathan Juran. Richard Greene, Boris Karloff, Stephen McNally, Paula Corday, Lon Chaney Jr., John Hoyt. Uninspired gothic melodrama has Greene investigating disappearance of two friends who were guests of sinister Austrian count (McNally). Karloff reduced to colorless supporting role.

Black Cat, The (1934) 65m. *** D: Edgar G. Ulmer. Boris Karloff, Bela Lugosi, David Manners, Jacqueline Wells (Julie Bishop), Lucille Lund. Polished horror film with bizarre sets, even more bizarre plot, loses a lot on TV, although confrontation of architect and devil-worshiper Karloff and doctor Lugosi is still fascinating.

Black Cat, The (1941) 70m. **½ D: Albert S. Rogell. Basil Rathbone, Hugh Herbert, Broderick Crawford, Bela Lugosi, Gale Sondergaard. Herbert and Crawford provide laughs, the others provide chills, in lively comedy-mystery not to be confused with earlier horror film. Look for Alan Ladd in a small role.

Black Christmas (1975-Canadian) C-100m. **½ D: Bob Clark. Olivia Hussey, Keir Dullea, Margot Kidder, John Saxon, Douglas McGrath. Bizarre horror thriller about warped murderer in sorority house on Christmas Eve and two days following. Not bad; Kidder steals it as a nasty, foul-mouthed sorority sister. Also called SILENT NIGHT, EVIL NIGHT and STRANGER IN THE HOUSE.

Black Cross (1960-Polish) C-175m. ** D: Aleksander Ford. Urszula Modrzynska, Grazyna Staniszewska, Andrzej Szalawski, Henryk Borowski. Unremarkable account of Teutonic knights raiding Poland; notable only for detailed medieval settings; sterile presentation.

Black Dakotas, The (1954) C-65m. ** D: Ray Nazarro. Gary Merrill, Wanda Hendrix, John Bromfield, Noah Beery, Jr. Bland oater of greedy men who try to outwit the redskins and incite a war.

Black Devils of Kali, The: SEE: **Mystery of the Black Jungle**

Black Dragon of Manzanar (1943) 100m. **½ D: William Witney. Rod Cameron, Roland Got, Constance Worth, Nino Pipitone, Noel Cravat. Sufficiently action-packed Republic cliff-hanger with Cameron the dynamic federal agent outdoing Oriental Axis agents during WW2. Re-edited movie serial: G-MEN VS. THE BLACK DRAGON.

Black Eye (1974) C-98m. ** D: Jack Arnold. Fred Williamson, Rosemary Forsyth, Richard Anderson, Teresa Graves, Cyril Delevanti. Involved action-mystery has black private detective Williamson investigating murders connected with a dope ring in Venice, Cal. Bret Morrison, radio's "The Shadow," is a porno moviemaker. Average.

Black Fox, The (1962) 89m. ***½ D: Louis Clyde Stoumen. Narrated by Marlene Dietrich. Exceedingly taut, grim documentary tracing the rise and fall of Adolph Hitler, focusing on his use of power during Third Reich. Academy Award winner as best documentary feature of the year.

Black Friday (1940) 70m. **½ D: Arthur Lubin. Boris Karloff, Bela Lugosi, Stanley Ridges, Anne Nagel, Anne Gwynne, Virginia Brissac. Wellmade little chiller with Karloff putting gangster's brain into a professor's body. Jekyll-Hyde results are fascinating; Ridges excellent as victim. Lugosi has small, thankless role as gangster.

Black Fury (1935) 92m. ***½ D: Michael Curtiz. Paul Muni, Karen Morley, William Gargan, Barton MacLane, Mae Marsh. Tough social drama of coal miners plagued by unsafe conditions, labor strikes, and corruption. Muni memorable as usual in lead role.

Black Girl (1972) C-97m. *** D: Ossie Davis. Brock Peters, Leslie Uggams, Claudia McNeil, Louise Stubbs, Gloria Edwards, Ruby Dee. One of the best black-oriented films concerns an aspiring dancer who joins with her two half-sisters in giving Uggams, who has been raised with them, a difficult time. Generally fine performances.

Black Gold (1963) 98m. ** D: Leslie Martinson. Philip Carey, Diane McBain, James Best, Claude Akins, Iron Eyes Cody. Predictable search for oil set in Oklahoma, with standard villain and supposedly ironic outcome.

Black Gunn (1972) C-98m. ** D: Robert Hartford-Davis. Jim Brown, Martin Landau, Brenda Sykes, Luciana Paluzzi. Black nightclub owner goes after the Man when his brother is killed. Routine black actioner.

Black Hand, The (1950) 93m. *** D: Richard Thorpe. Gene Kelly, J. Carrol Naish, Teresa Celli, Marc Lawrence, Frank Puglia. Kelly avenges his father's murder by the Black Hand society in turn-of-the-century N. Y. Atmospheric, well-made film with Kelly in a rare (and effective) dramatic performance.

Black Hole, The (1979) C-97m. **½ D: Gary Nelson. Maximilian Schell, Anthony Perkins, Robert Forster, Joseph Bottoms, Yvette Mimieux, Ernest Borgnine. U.S. expedition finds long-lost madman in space about to explore a "black hole." Disney studios' ambitious sci-fi effort is a throwback to 1957 Saturday matinee fodder, with thin story, cardboard characters. OK on that level—with great special effects—but should have been much better.

Black Horse Canyon (1954) C-81m. **½ D: Jesse Hibbs. Joel McCrea, Mari Blanchard, Race Gentry, Murvyn Vye. Diverting, gentle Western about rebellious black stallion and those who recapture him.

Black Jack SEE: **Wild in the Sky**

Black Knight, The (1954-U.S.-British) C-85m. **½ D: Tay Garnett. Alan Ladd, Patricia Medina, Andre Morell, Harry Andrews, Peter Cushing. Ladd lends some bounce to small budgeter about mysterious horseman championing King Arthur's cause in merry old England.

Black Legion (1936) 83m. *** D: Archie Mayo. Humphrey Bogart, Erin O'Brien-Moore, Dick Foran, Ann Sheridan. Factory worker Bogart becomes involved with Ku Klux Klan-ish group in powerful social drama, compactly told.

Black Like Me (1964) 107m. **½ D: Carl Lerner. James Whitmore, Roscoe Lee Browne, Sorrell Booke, Will Geer, Al Freeman, Jr., Dan Priest. Exploitation feature pegged on premise of reporter taking medication that allows him to pass for Negro, thus experiencing racial problems firsthand.

Black Magic (1944) 67m. D: Phil Rosen. Sidney Toler, Mantan Moreland, Frances Chan, Jacqueline de Wit, Claudia Dell, Edward Earle, Joseph Crehan. Retitled MEETING AT MIDNIGHT. See **Charlie Chan** series.

Black Magic (1949) 105m. **½ D: Gregory Ratoff. Orson Welles, Akim Tamiroff, Nancy Guild, Raymond Burr, Frank Latimore. Welles is predictably florid in chronicle of famous charlatan Cagliostro who seeks to rise to power in 18th century Italy. (He co-directed this handsome film, uncredited.)

Black Market Baby (1977) C-100m. TVM D: Robert Day. Linda Purl, Desi Arnaz Jr., Bill Bixby, Jessica Walter, David Doyle, Tom Bosley. Unmarried couple struggle with a black market adoption ring out to take their baby. Unpleasantly exploitive social drama done better as a sleazy "B" movie of yore. Below average.

Black Narcissus (1947-British) C-99m. ***½ D: Michael Powell, Emeric Pressburger. Deborah Kerr, Flora Robson, Kathleen Byron, Sabu, Jean Simmons, David Farrar, Jenny Laird, Judith Furse. Excellent filmization of Rumer Godden novel of nuns starting a mission in Himalayas; Kerr is Sister Superior who faces sundry problems. Breathtaking use of color. Only problem: scenes in which Kerr recalls her former life, a key plot element, were censored from American prints of this film.

Black Noon (1971) C-73m. TVM D: Bernard Kowalski. Roy Thinnes, Yvette Mimieux, Gloria Grahame, Lynn Loring, Ray Milland, Henry Silva. Traveling preacher and young wife stumble upon odd religious sect in American West. Last shot of film explains all. Average.

Black Oak Conspiracy (1977) C-92m. **½ D: Bob Kelljan. Jesse Vint, Karen Carlson, Albert Salmi, Seymour Cassel, Robert L. Lyons. Predictable action drama pitting an "average Joe" (Vint) against a crooked sheriff and unscrupulous land grabbers. Situations and dialogue are written to formula.

Black Orchid, The (1959) 96m. **½ D: Martin Ritt. Sophia Loren, Anthony Quinn, Ina Balin, Jimmie Baird, Mark Richman, Naomi Stevens, Frank Puglia. Fabricated soaper of bumbling businessman (Quinn) romancing criminal's widow (Loren) and the problem of convincing their children that marriage will make all their lives better.

Black Orpheus (1960-Brazil) C-98m. ***½ D: Marcel Camus. Breno Mello, Marpessa Dawn, Lourdes De Oliveira, Lea Garcia. Lyrical Brazilian film has achieved near-classic status for its acting, a memorable score, excellent carnival scenes. Worth watching.

Black Patch (1957) 83m. BOMB D: Allen H. Miner. George Montgomery, Diane Brewster, Leo Gordon, Sebastian Cabot. Inconsequential trivia with Montgomery as gun-toting sheriff out to clear his name.

.**Black Pirate, The** (1926) C-85m. *** D: Albert Parker. Douglas Fairbanks Sr., Billie Dove, Andres Randolf, Donald Crisp, Tempe Piggott, Sam De Grasse. Robust silent swashbuckler with Fairbanks a nobleman who turns pirate after being victimized by cutthroats. Originally filmed in early Technicolor process.

Black Pirates, The (1954-Mexican) C-72m. **½ D: Allen H. Miner. Anthony Dexter, Martha Roth, Lon Chaney, Robert Clarke. Uninspired account of pirates searching for gold.

Black Rodeo (1972) C-87m. **½ D: Jeff Kanew. Archie Wycoff, Clarence Gonzalez, Pete Knight, Marval Rogers, Reuben Heura. Offbeat, frequently interesting documentary about a rodeo that takes place largely in Harlem; background music is performed by such stars as B.B. King, Ray Charles, Dee Dee Sharpe.

Black Room, The (1935) 67m. *** D: Roy William Neill. Boris Karloff, Marian Marsh, Robert Allen, Katherine DeMille, John Buckler, Thurston Hall. Excellent, understated thriller of twin brothers (Karloff) and the ancient curse that dominates their lives. One of Karloff's best performances.

Black Rose, The (1950) C-120m. **½ D: Henry Hathaway. Tyrone Power, Orson Welles, Jack Hawkins, Michael Rennie, Herbert Lom, Laurence Harvey, Cecile Aubry. Sweeping pageantry follows Saxon Power on Oriental adventures during 1200s; dynamic action scenes. Filmed in England and North Africa.

Black Sabbath (1964-Italian) C-99m. **½ D: Mario Bava. Boris Karloff, Mark Damon, Suzy Anderson, Jacqueline Pierreux. Italian three-part film hosted by Karloff, who appears in final episode about a vampire controlling an entire family. Other sequences are good, atmospheric.

Black Scorpion, The (1957) 88m. *½ D: Edward Ludwig. Richard Denning, Carlos Rivas, Mara Corday, Mario Navarro. Giant-size title insects run rampant in Mexico; lower-case thriller.

Black Shield of Falworth, The (1954) C-99m. **½ D: Rudolph Maté. Tony Curtis, Janet Leigh, David Farrar,

Barbara Rush, Herbert Marshall. Juvenile version of Howard Pyle novel, MEN OF IRON; Curtis unconvincing as nobility rising through ranks to knighthood in medieval England. Settings, supporting cast bolster production.

Black Sleep, The (1956) 81m. *½ D: Reginald LeBorg. Basil Rathbone, Akim Tamiroff, Lon Chaney, John Carradine, Bela Lugosi. Big horror cast cannot save dull, unatmospheric tale of doctor performing brain transplants in remote castle. Laughable.

Black Spurs (1965) C-81m. *½ D: R. G. Springsteen. Rory Calhoun, Terry Moore, Linda Darnell, Scott Brady, Lon Chaney, Bruce Cabot, Richard Arlen. Ordinary Western with attraction of one-time movie stars including Darnell (her last film). Standard horse opera.

Black Stallion, The (1979) C-103m. *** D: Carroll Ballard. Kelly Reno, Mickey Rooney, Teri Garr, Clarence Muse, Hoyt Axton, Michael Higgins. Exquisitely filmed story of a young boy's adventures with a magnificent black stallion—from a dramatic shipwreck to a racing championship. Too slow at times, but still worthwhile, with many precious moments, and a lovely performance by Rooney as veteran horse trainer.

Black Sunday (1961-Italian) 83m. **½ D: Mario Bava. Barbara Steele, John Richardson, Ivo Garrani, Andrea Checchi. Intriguing story of the one day each century when Satan roams the earth. Steele is a witch who swears vengeance on the descendants of those who killed her hundreds of years ago. Beautifully atmospheric.

Black Sunday (1977) C-143m. *** D: John Frankenheimer. Robert Shaw, Bruce Dern, Marthe Keller, Fritz Weaver, Steven Keats, Bekim Fehmiu, Michael V. Gazzo, William Daniels. International terrorist organization plots to blow up the Super Bowl, enlists the aid of former Vietnam POW Dern, who pilots the TV blimp at football games. Generally compelling adaptation of the best-seller, with Dern at his best.

Black Swan, The (1942) C-85m. *** D: Henry King. Tyrone Power, Maureen O'Hara, Laird Cregar, Thomas Mitchell, George Sanders, Anthony Quinn. Power makes a dashing pirate in this colorful swashbuckler, fighting Sanders and Quinn, rescuing O'Hara from their clutches.

Black Tent, The (1957-British) **C-93m.** ** D: Brian Hurst. Anthony Steel, Donald Sinden, Anna Maria Sandri, Donald Pleasence. Passable mixture of romance and action in the African desert as British soldier Steel romances native chief's daughters and helps tribe fight off Nazi attack.

Black Tuesday (1954) **80m.** *** D: Hugo Fregonese. Edward G. Robinson, Peter Graves, Jean Parker, Milburn Stone. Throwback to 1930-ish gangster films, with Robinson and Graves as escaped convicts being hunted by cops—nice gunplay, with Parker good as the moll.

Black Water Gold (1969) **C-75m.** TVM D: Alan Landsburg. Keir Dullea, Lana Wood, Ricardo Montalban, Bradford Dillman, France Nuyen, Aron Kincaid. Fairly intense (for TV) story of various forces vying for sunken Spanish galleon treasure of Panama Eagles. Above average.

Black Whip, The (1956) **77m.** *½ D: Charles Marquis Warren. Hugh Marlowe, Coleen Gray, Angie Dickenson, Sheb Wooley. Only spice to this oater is bevy of beautiful girls who are rescued by Marlowe.

Black Widow, The SEE: **Somba, The Spider Woman**

Black Widow (1954) **C-95m.** **½ D: Nunnally Johnson. Ginger Rogers, Van Heflin, Gene Tierney, George Raft, Peggy Ann Garner, Reginald Gardiner, Otto Kruger. Detective Raft investigates murder among show biz folk. Slick whodunit, twist finis.

Black Windmill, The (1974-British) **C-106m.** **½ D: Don Siegel. Michael Caine, Joseph O'Conor, Donald Pleasence, John Vernon, Janet Suzman, Delphine Seyrig. Slick, craftsmanlike but generally undistinguished thriller, as espionage agent Caine tries to locate his son's kidnappers. Siegel has done better.

Black Zoo (1963) **88m.** BOMB D: Robert Gordon. Michael Gough, Virginia Grey, Jerome Cowan, Elisha Cook, Jeanne Cooper. Good cast flounders in silly story of killer loose in zoo; from the man who gave you I WAS A TEEN-AGE WERE-WOLF.

Blackbeard, The Pirate (1952) **C-99m.** ** D: Raoul Walsh. Robert Newton, Linda Darnell, William Bendix, Keith Andes, Richard Egan, Irene Ryan. Newton is rambunctious as 17th-century buccaneer, with lovely Darnell his captive; fun for a while,

but Newton's hamming soon grows tiresome.

Blackbeard's Ghost (1968) **C-107m.** *** D: Robert Stevenson. Peter Ustinov, Dean Jones, Suzanne Pleshette, Elsa Lanchester, Joby Baker, Elliott Reid, Richard Deacon. Jones conjures up title character (Ustinov) who helps protect his descendants' home from being taken over by racketeers who want to make it a casino. Engaging slapstick comedy from Disney.

Blackboard Jungle, The (1955) **101m.** ***½ D: Richard Brooks. Glenn Ford, Anne Francis, Louis Calhern, Sidney Poitier, Richard Kiley, Warner Anderson, Vic Morrow. Excellent adaptation of Evan Hunter's novel of a teacher's (Ford) harrowing experiences in N.Y. school system. Poitier memorable as a troubled youth. Hard-hitting entertainment. Look for a young Jamie Farr.

Blackjack Ketchum, Desperado (1956) **76m.** *½ D: Earl Bellamy. Howard Duff, Victor Jory, Maggie Mahoney, Angela Stevens. Former gunslinger must endure another shoot-out before returning to a peaceful way of life.

Blackmail (1929-British) **86m.** *** D: Alfred Hitchcock. Anny Ondra, Sara Allgood, John Longden, Charles Paton, Donald Calthrop, Cyril Ritchard. Young woman kills man who tries to rape her, then finds herself caught between investigating detective (who happens to be her boyfriend) and a blackmailer. Hitchcock's first talking picture is still exciting, especially for fans and students of the director's work.

Blackmail (1939) **81m.** **½ D: H. C. Potter. Edward G. Robinson, Gene Lockhart, Guinn Williams, Ruth Hussey, Esther Dale. Robinson is freed after serving stretch for crime he didn't commit; guilty Lockhart blackmails him in taut drama.

Blackout (1954-British) **87m.** ** D: Terence Fisher. Dane Clark, Belinda Lee, Betty Ann Davies, Eleanor Summerfield. Programmer: down-and-out Clark accepts good-paying job, which leads him into life of crime.

Blackout (1978-Canadian-French) **C-89m.** ** D: Eddy Matalon. Jim Mitchum, Robert Carradine, Belinda Montgomery, June Allyson, Jean-Pierre Aumont, Ray Milland. Violent story of criminals who terrorize apartment dwellers during N.Y.'s 1977 power blackout. Balanced with black comedy for so-so results.

Blackwell's Island (1939) 71m. **½
D: William McGann. John Garfield,
Rosemary Lane, Dick Purcell, Victor
Jory, Stanley Fields, Peggy Shannon.
Peppy little gangster comedy with
Garfield a crusading reporter getting
the rap on thick-witted thug Fields.

Blacula (1972) C-92m. *** D: William Crain. William Marshall, Denise
Nicholas, Vonetta McGee, Thalmus
Rasulala. Dracula bit a Black Prince
and now black vampire is stalking
the streets of modern L.A. Some
terrific shocks, and some very lively
dialogue.

Blade (1973) C-90m. **½ D: Ernest
Pintoff. John Marley, Jon Cypher,
Kathryn Walker, William Prince,
John Schuck, Rue McClanahan. New
York-made actioner about female-
hating Cypher, who indulges in violent
killings, and tough police Lt. Marley,
who tracks him down. A bit pretentious and involved; fairly absorbing.

Blanche Fury (1948-British) C-95m.
*** D: Marc Allegret. Stewart
Granger, Valerie Hobson, Walter
Fitzgerald, Michael Gough, Maurice
Denham. Beautifully mounted gothic
melodrama about a governess who
marries into wealthy family, and the
headstrong steward (Granger) who
aspires to run the estate.

Blast-Off SEE: Those Fantastic Flying Fools

Blaze of Noon (1947) 91m. **½ D:
John Farrow. Anne Baxter, William
Holden, Sonny Tufts, William Bendix, Sterling Hayden. Hokey story of
Holden torn between his wife (Baxter) and true love, flying.

Blazing Forest, The (1952) C-90m.
*½ D: Edward Ludwig. John Payne,
Agnes Moorehead, Richard Arlen,
William Demarest, Susan Morrow.
Felling trees and romancing Moore-
head's niece (Morrow) occupies
Payne till big fire diverts him, but
not the bored viewer.

Blazing Saddles (1974) C-93m. ***½
D: Mel Brooks. Cleavon Little, Gene
Wilder, Slim Pickens, David Hud-
dleston, Madeline Kahn, Harvey
Korman, Alex Karras, Dom DeLuise.
Brooks' first hit movie is a riotous
Western spoof, with Little an un-
likely sheriff, Korman as villainous
Hedley Lamarr, and Kahn as a
Dietrich-like chanteuse. None of
Brooks' later films have topped this
one for sheer belly-laughs. Richard
Pryor was one of the screenwriters.

Bless the Beasts and Children (1972)

C-109m. *** D: Stanley Kramer.
Billy Mumy, Barry Robins, Miles
Chapin, Jesse White. Exciting story
of group of boys and their grim defense of an environmental objective.

Blessed Event (1932) 83m. *** D:
Roy Del Ruth. Lee Tracy, Mary
Brian, Dick Powell, Emma Dunn,
Frank McHugh, Allen Jenkins, Ned
Sparks, Ruth Donnelly. Tracy's most
famous role has him a Walter Winchell prototype whose spicy column
makes him famous but also gets him
in hot water; Powell makes film debut as crooner. Fast-moving, delightful.

Blind Alley (1939) 71m. **½ D:
Charles Vidor. Chester Morris, Ralph
Bellamy, Ann Dvorak, Joan Perry,
Melville Cooper, Rose Stradner,
John Eldredge. One of Hollywood's
first attempts to illustrate psycho-
logical ideas. Morris is troubled
gangster who holds psychiatrist
Bellamy prisoner, and allows him-
self to be analyzed. Dated but in-
teresting. Remade as THE DARK
PAST.

Blind Date SEE: Chance Meeting

Blind Man's Bluff SEE: Cauldron of
Blood

Blind Spot (1947) 73m. *** D: Robert Gordon. Chester Morris, Constance Dowling, Steven Geray, Sid
Tomack. Mystery writer Morris has
to extricate himself from charge of
murdering his publisher in this tight
little mystery.

Blindfold (1966) C-102m. **½ D:
Philip Dunne. Rock Hudson, Claudia
Cardinale, Jack Warden, Guy Stockwell, Anne Seymour. Attractive cast
falters in film that wavers from comedy to mystery. Slapstick scenes seem
incongruous as Hudson engages in
international espionage with a noted
scientist. Shot partly in N.Y.C.

Blindman (1972-Italian) C-105m. **
D: Ferdinando Baldi. Tony Anthony,
Ringo Starr, Agneta Eckemyr, Lloyd
Batista. Blindman (Anthony) seeks
revenge on man who stole fifty mail-
order brides. Mindless entertainment.

Bliss of Mrs. Blossom, The (1968-
U.S.A.-British) C-93m. *** D: Joe
McGrath. Shirley MacLaine, Richard
Attenborough, James Booth, Freddie
Jones, Bob Monkhouse. Oddball,
original comedy with delicious performances. Wife of brassiere manufacturer keeps a lover in their attic
for five years. Bogs down toward
the end, but for the most part a
delight.

Blithe Spirit (1945-British) C-96m. ***½ D: David Lean. Rex Harrison, Constance Cummings, Kay Hammond, Margaret Rutherford, Hugh Wakefield, Joyce Carey. Delicious adaptation of Noel Coward's comedy-fantasy about a man whose long-dead first wife appears to haunt—and taunt—him in his newly married life. Rutherford is wonderful as Madame Arcati, the medium.

Blob, The (1958) C-86m. ** D: Irvin S. Yeaworth, Jr. Steve McQueen, Aneta Corseaut, Earl Rowe, Olin Howlin. OK sci-fi has McQueen accidentally involved in trying to rid humanity of insatiable formless creature from outer space.

Block Busters (1944) 60m. D: Wallace Fox. Leo Gorcey, Huntz Hall, Gabriel Dell, Minerva Urecal, Noah Beery, Sr., Billy Benedict, Harry Langdon. SEE: **Bowery Boys** series.

Block-Heads (1938) 55m. *** D: John G. Blystone. Stan Laurel, Oliver Hardy, Patricia Ellis, Minna Gombell, Billy Gilbert, James Finlayson. Stan's been marching in a trench for twenty years—nobody told him WW1 was over! Ollie brings him home to find he hasn't changed. Top L&H.

Blockade (1938) 85m. *** D: William Dieterle. Madeleine Carroll, Henry Fonda, Leo Carrillo, John Halliday, Vladimir Sokoloff, Reginald Denny. Vivid romance drama of Spanish Civil War with globe-trotting Carroll falling in love with fighting Fonda.

Blockhouse, The (1973-British) C-90m. *½ D: Clive Rees. Peter Sellers, Charles Aznavour, Per Oscarsson, Peter Vaughan, Jeremy Kemp, Alfred Lynch. Dismal, downbeat story of laborers trapped in underground bunker when the Allies land at Normandie on D-Day.

Blonde Blackmailer (1958-British) 58m. BOMB D: Charles Deane. Richard Arlen, Susan Shaw, Constance Leigh, Vincent Ball. Hackneyed plot of innocent ex-con (Arlen) determined to prove innocence and find real killers.

Blonde Bombshell SEE: **Bombshell**

Blonde Crazy (1931) 73m. **½ D: Roy Del Ruth. James Cagney, Joan Blondell, Louis Calhern, Ray Milland, Polly Walters, Nat Pendleton. Dated fun with Cagney as small-time con-man who plays cat-and-mouse with big-time sharpie Calhern. Young Milland appears as lawyer who marries Jimmy's girlfriend, Blondell.

Blonde Dynamite (1950) 66m. D: William Beaudine. Leo Gorcey, Huntz Hall, Gabriel Dell, Adele Jergens, Jody Gilbert. SEE: **Bowery Boys**.

Blonde Fever (1944) 69m. ** D: Richard Whorf. Philip Dorn, Mary Astor, Felix Bressart, Gloria Grahame, Marshall Thompson. Astor lends class to this mild account of widow on the loose in Europe finding love with Dorn, with Grahame as sultry competition.

Blonde In a White Car SEE: **Nude In a White Car**

Blonde Venus (1932) 80m. *** D: Josef von Sternberg. Marlene Dietrich, Herbert Marshall, Cary Grant, Dickie Moore, Sidney Toler. Episodic story of notorious Dietrich leading unsavory life to support herself and child. This is the film where Marlene appears in an ape suit to sing "Hot Voodoo"! Unfortunately, TV prints are missing opening sequence of Dietrich and friends skinny-dipping when Marshall happens along.

Blondie With a vast audience already familiar with the Chic Young comic strip, a Blondie series seemed like a shoo-in in 1938—and it was. The series, with Arthur Lake as Dagwood, Penny Singleton as Blondie, Larry Simms as Baby Dumpling (later Alexander), Marjorie Kent as Cookie, Jonathan Hale as Mr. Dithers (later Jerome Cowan as Mr. Radcliffe), and Daisy as Daisy, prospered for 13 years, spanning 28 episodes. As with most series, the first ones were the best—fresh, and original, with many clever touches belying the fact that they were low-budget films. By the mid-1940s, however, with less capable directors and a fairly standard formula, the films became even more predictable, and the humor more contrived. Nevertheless, Blondie carried on with the same cast until 1951. Unlike some series, the Blondie films actually continued from one to the next, with Baby Dumpling growing up, starting school in the fourth film, taking the name of Alexander in the eleventh. Cookie is also born in the eleventh film, and Daisy has pups in the following one. Many interesting people pop up in the Blondie casts, such as Rita Hayworth in BLONDIE ON A BUDGET, Glenn Ford in BLONDIE PLAYS CUPID, Larry Parks and Janet Blair in BLONDIE GOES TO

COLLEGE, Anita Louise in BLONDIE'S BIG MOMENT, and Adele Jergens in BLONDIE'S ANNIVERSARY. Many character actors appeared as well, with Irving Bacon usually playing the harried Bumstead mailman, Mr. Beasley. After twenty years of TV situation comedies, Blondie has lost some of its punch, but generally still stands out as an enjoyable, smoothly made series of comedies.

Blondie (1938) 69m. D: Frank Strayer. Penny Singleton, Arthur Lake, Larry Simms, Gene Lockhart, Ann Doran, Jonathan Hale, Gordon Oliver, Stanley Andrews.

Blondie Brings Up Baby (1939) 67m. D: Frank Strayer. Penny Singleton, Arthur Lake, Larry Simms, Danny Mummert, Jonathan Hale, Fay Helm, Peggy Ann Garner, Helen Jerome Eddy, Irving Bacon.

Blondie for Victory (1942) 70m. D: Frank Strayer. Penny Singleton, Arthur Lake, Larry Simms, Majelle White, Stuart Erwin, Jonathan Hale, Danny Mummert.

Blondie Goes Latin (1941) 69m. D: Frank Strayer. Penny Singleton, Arthur Lake, Larry Simms, Tito Guizar, Ruth Terry, Danny Mummert, Irving Bacon, Janet Burston.

Blondie Goes to College (1942) 74m. D: Frank Strayer. Penny Singleton, Arthur Lake, Larry Simms, Jonathan Hale, Larry Parks, Janet Blair, Lloyd Bridges, Esther Dale, Adele Mara.

Blondie Has Servant Trouble (1940) 70m. D: Frank Strayer. Penny Singleton, Arthur Lake, Larry Simms, Daisy, Danny Mummert, Jonathan Hale, Arthur Hohl, Esther Dale, Irving Bacon.

Blondie Hits the Jackpot (1949) 66m. D: Edward Bernds. Penny Singleton, Arthur Lake, Larry Simms, Jerome Cowan, Lloyd Corrigan.

Blondie In Society (1941) 75m. D: Frank Strayer. Penny Singleton, Arthur Lake, Larry Simms, Jonathan Hale, Danny Mummert, William Frawley, Edgar Kennedy, Chick Chandler.

Blondie In the Dough (1947) 69m. D: Abby Berlin. Penny Singleton, Arthur Lake, Larry Simms, Marjorie Kent, Jerome Cowan, Hugh Herbert, Clarence Kolb, Danny Mummert.

Blondie Knows Best (1946) 69m. D: Abby Berlin. Penny Singleton, Arthur Lake, Larry Simms, Marjorie Kent, Shemp Howard, Ludwig Donath, Jerome Cowan.

Blondie Meets the Boss (1939) 58m. D: Frank Strayer. Penny Singleton, Arthur Lake, Larry Simms, Dorothy Moore, Jonathan Hale, Stanley Brown, Inez Courtney, Don Beddoe.

Blondie on a Budget (1940) 73m. D: Frank Strayer. Penny Singleton, Arthur Lake, Larry Simms, Danny Mummert, Rita Hayworth, Don Beddoe, John Qualen, Fay Helm.

Blondie Plays Cupid (1940) 68m. D: Frank Strayer. Penny Singleton, Arthur Lake, Larry Simms, Daisy, Jonathan Hale, Danny Mummert, Irving Bacon, Glenn Ford.

Blondie Takes a Vacation (1939) 61m. D: Frank Strayer. Penny Singleton, Arthur Lake, Larry Simms, Danny Mummert, Donald Meek, Elizabeth Dunne, Robert Wilcox, Irving Bacon.

Blondie's Anniversary (1947) 75m. D: Abby Berlin. Penny Singleton, Arthur Lake, Larry Simms, Marjorie Kent, Adele Jergens, Jerome Cowan, Grant Mitchell, William Frawley.

Blondie's Big Deal (1949) 66m. D: Edward Bernds. Penny Singleton, Arthur Lake, Larry Simms, Jerome Cowan, Marjorie Kent, Collette Lyons, Ray Walker, Stanley Andrews, Alan Dinehart III.

Blondie's Big Moment (1947) 69m. D: Abby Berlin. Penny Singleton, Arthur Lake, Larry Simms, Marjorie Kent, Jerome Cowan, Anita Louise, Danny Mummert, Jack Rice, Jack Davis.

Blondie's Blessed Event (1942) 69m. D: Frank Strayer. Penny Singleton, Arthur Lake, Larry Simms, Norma Jean Wayne, Jonathan Hale, Danny Mummert, Hans Conried, Mary Wickes.

Blondie's Hero (1950) 67m. D: Edward Bernds. Penny Singleton, Arthur Lake, Larry Simms, William Frawley, Iris Adrian, Edward Earle.

Blondie's Holiday (1947) 67m. D: Abby Berlin. Arthur Lake, Penny Singleton, Larry Simms, Marjorie Kent, Jerome Cowan, Grant Mitchell, Sid Tomack, Jeff York, Mary Young.

Blondie's Lucky Day (1946) 75m. D: Abby Berlin. Penny Singleton, Arthur Lake, Larry Simms, Marjorie Kent, Frank Jenks, Paul Harvey, Charles Arnt.

Blondie's Reward (1948) 67m. D: Abby Berlin. Penny Singleton, Arthur Lake, Larry Simms, Marjorie Kent, Jerome Cowan, Gay Nelson, Danny Mummert, Paul Harvey, Frank Jenks.

Blondie's Secret (1948) 68m. D: Edward Bernds. Penny Singleton, Arthur Lake, Larry Simms, Marjorie Kent, Jerome Cowan, Thurston Hall, Jack Rice, Danny Mummert, Frank Orth.

Blondie of the Follies (1932) 90m. **½ D: Edmund Goulding. Marion Davies, Robert Montgomery, Billie Dove, Jimmy Durante, ZaSu Pitts, Sidney Toler, Louise Carter. Rival girls in love with Montgomery both become Follies stars—better as musical than as drama. James Gleason fine as Marion's father. Best scene has Davies and Durante spoofing Garbo and Barrymore in GRAND HOTEL.

Blood Alley (1955) C-115m. **½ D: William Wellman. John Wayne, Lauren Bacall, Paul Fix, Mike Mazurki, Anita Ekberg. Enjoyable escapism with Wayne, Bacall, and assorted Chinese escaping down river to Hong Kong pursued by Communists.

Blood and Black Lace (1965-Italian) C-88m. *½ D: Mario Bava. Cameron Mitchell, Eva Bartok, Mary Arden. Sex-killer stalking the streets isn't enough to enliven this film with wooden performances and script.

Blood and Lace (1971) C-87m. BOMB D: Philip Gilbert. Gloria Grahame, Melody Patterson, Milton Selzer, Len Lesser. Rock-bottom cheapie about murders tied in to corrupt orphanage. Don't bother.

Blood and Roses (1961-Italian) C-74m. **½ D: Roger Vadim. Mel Ferrer, Elsa Martinelli, Annette Vadim, Marc Allegret. This story of a jealous girl's obsession with her family's history of vampirism was based on Sheridan Le Fanu's *Carmilla*. Despite some effective moments, film does not succeed.

Blood and Sand (1922) 80m. **½ D: Fred Niblo. Rudolph Valentino, Lila Lee, Nita Naldi, George Field, Walter Long, Leo White. Dated but still absorbing story of bullfighter Valentino torn between good-girl Lee and vampish Naldi. Scenes of hero being seduced are laughable, but bullfight material holds up well. Remade in 1941.

Blood and Sand (1941) C-123m. *** D: Rouben Mamoulian. Tyrone Power, Linda Darnell, Rita Hayworth, Nazimova, Anthony Quinn, J. Carrol Naish, John Carradine, George Reeves. Pastel remake of Valentino's silent film about naive bullfighter who ignores true-love Darnell for temptress Hayworth. Slow-paced romance, uplifted by Nazimova's knowing performance as Power's mother, beautiful color production.

Blood and Steel (1959) 63m. *½ D: Bernard Kowalski. John Lupton, James Edwards, Brett Halsey, John Brinkley. Routine study of U.S. navy men landing on Jap-held island, and their assistance of the partisan cause to free the villagers from bondage.

Blood Arrow (1958) 75m. *½ D: Charles Marquis Warren. Scott Brady, Paul Richards, Phyllis Coates, Don Haggerty. Uninspired tale of Mormon girl Coates trudging through Indian territory to obtain needed medicine, with usual Indian attacks.

Blood Creature SEE: **Terror Is a Man**

Blood Demon, The SEE: **Torture Chamber of Dr. Sadism**

Blood from the Mummy's Tomb (1972-British) C-94m. *** D: Seth Holt, Michael Carreras. Andrew Keir, Valerie Leon, James Villiers, Hugh Burden. Surprisingly satisfying chiller dealing with attempt at reincarnating ancient Egyptian high priestess.

Blood of Dracula (1957) 68m. *½ D: Herbert L. Strock. Sandra Harrison, Gail Ganley, Jerry Blaine, Louise Lewis. Inoffensive programmer about girl being hypnotized into a life of vampirism.

Blood of Dracula's Castle (1967) C-84m. BOMB D: Al Adamson. John Carradine, Paula Raymond, Alex D'Arcy, Robert Dix, Barbara Bishop. Tacky low-budget mixture of vampirism and kinky sex, with Dracula and his bride "collecting" girls and chaining them up.

Blood of Fu Manchu, The (1968) 91m. ** D: Jesus Franco. Christopher Lee, Richard Greene, Gotz George, Howard Marion Crawford, Shirley Eaton, Maria Rohm. Fourth in Lee's international FU MANCHU series, several pegs below its predecessors, finds him in the heart of the Amazon, injecting ten beautiful girls with a deadly potion and dispatching them to give the kiss of death to his enemies in various capitals. Also known as KISS AND KILL.

Blood of the Vampire (1958-British) C-87m. ** D: Henry Cass. Donald Wolfit, Barbara Shelley, Vincent Ball, Victor Maddern. Potentially vivid horror film weakened by slack production: doctor sent to prison becomes involved with inmate vampire in blood-seeking experiments.

Blood Money (1933) 65m.* *** D:

[75]

Rowland Brown. George Bancroft, Frances Dee, Judith Anderson, Chick Chandler, Blossom Seeley. Lively, implausible story of underworld bail-bondsman Bancroft falling for thrill-a-minute socialite Dee, causing friction with Bancroft's female cohort (played by Anderson in incongruously gutsy, glamorous role). Dee's closing scene is a knockout.

Blood on the Arrow (1964) C-91m. *½ D: Sidney Salkow. Dale Robertson, Martha Hyer, Wendell Corey, Elisha Cook, Ted de Corsia. Humdrum Western dealing with Apache massacre and survivors' attempt to rescue their son held captive by redskins.

Blood on the Moon (1948) 88m. *** D: Robert Wise. Robert Mitchum, Barbara Bel Geddes, Robert Preston, Walter Brennan. Tough Western with rivals Mitchum and Preston becoming bitter enemies because of scheme to undo ranchers Bel Geddes-Brennan.

Blood on the Sun (1945) 98m. *** D: Frank Lloyd. James Cagney, Sylvia Sidney, Wallace Ford, Rosemary DeCamp, Robert Armstrong. Cagney, in Japan during the 1930s, smells trouble coming but is virtually helpless; good melodrama.

Blood Rose (1969-French) C-87m. *½ D: Claude Mulot. Philippe Lemaire, Annie Duperey, Howard Vernon, Elisabeth Tessier, Michele Perello. An artist schemes to restore his wife's face, which was disfigured by fire; badly dubbed, low-grade French import.

Blood-Spattered Bride, The (1969-Spanish) C-83m. *½ D: Vincent Aranda. Maribel Martin, Simon Andreu, Alexandra Bastedo, Dean Selmier, Montserrat Julio. Newlyweds in secluded mansion are terrorized by a strange guest, the reincarnation of a murderess dead 200 years. Derivative of Le Fanu's *Carmilla*, but poorly done.

Blood Suckers, The SEE: Return from the Past

Blood, Sweat and Fear (1975-Italian) C-90m. *½ D: Stevio Massi. Lee J. Cobb, Franco Gasparri, Giorgia Albertazzi, Sora Sperati. Plodding action drama involving a cat-and-mouse game between Cobb, as the brains behind a grand-scale drug operation, and Gasparri, as an ambitious young narcotics agent.

Bloodbrothers (1978) C-116m. **½ D: Robert Mulligan. Richard Gere,

Paul Sorvino, Tony Lo Bianco. Interesting if somewhat overblown drama of construction workers in the big city. A bit much at times, best when the actors have a chance to underplay, e.g., Sorvino's touching story of his baby son's death; Gere's interplay with young hospital patients. Gere takes top honors as the son who wants to break away from family tradition.

Bloodhounds of Broadway (1952) C-90m. **½ D: Harmon Jones. Mitzi Gaynor, Scott Brady, Mitzi Green, Michael O'Shea, Marguerite Chapman. Hick Gaynor becomes slick gal in N.Y.C., involved with pseudo-Damon Runyon folk; funny Green has too small a role. Songs include "I Wish I Knew."

Bloodline (1979) C-116m. BOMB D: Terence Young. Audrey Hepburn, Ben Gazzara, James Mason, Michelle Phillips, Omar Sharif, Romy Schneider. Hepburn finds her life endangered after inheriting a Zurich-based pharmaceutical company. Unbearable adaptation of Sidney Sheldon's novel, which was one of those best-sellers California blondes read on the beach when no one wants to play volleyball.

Bloodsport (1973) C-73m. TVM D: Jerrold Freedman. Ben Johnson, Larry Hagman, Gary Busey. Young boy (Busey) groomed by father to become pro football player in exceptional combination character study and drama. Above average.

Bloody Mama (1970) C-90m. *½ D: Roger Corman. Shelley Winters, Don Stroud, Pat Hingle, Robert De Niro, Clint Klimbrough, Robert Walden, Diane Varsi, Bruce Dern, Pamela Dunlop. Excellent performances cannot save sordid story of Ma Barker and her ugly brood. Film unsuccessfully mixes action narrative with psychological study.

Blossoms In the Dust (1941) C-100m. *** D: Mervyn LeRoy. Greer Garson, Walter Pidgeon, Felix Bressart, Marsha Hunt, Fay Holden, Samuel S. Hinds. Slick tear-jerker of Texas orphanage founded by Garson when she loses her own child; tastefully acted.

Blowing Wild (1953) 90m. ** D: Hugo Fregonese. Gary Cooper, Barbara Stanwyck, Ruth Roman, Anthony Quinn, Ward Bond. Tempestuous Stanwyck is married to oil tycoon Quinn, but sets her sights on wildcatter Cooper, who's fully recovered from their one-time affair. Heated emotions can't warm up this plodding story, filmed in Mexico.

Blow-Up (1966-British-Italian) C-108m. ***½ D: Michelangelo Antonioni. Vanessa Redgrave, David Hemmings, Sarah Miles, Jill Kennington, Verushka. Antonioni's hypnotic pop-culture parable of photographer caught in passive lifestyle. Arresting, provocative film, rich in color symbolism, many-layered meanings. Unfortunately, cut for TV.

Blue (1968) C-113m. *½ D: Silvio Narizzano. Terence Stamp, Joanna Pettet, Karl Malden, Ricardo Montalban, Joe DeSantis. Undistinguished, poorly written Western abut American-born, Mexican-raised boy who trusts no one until bullet wounds force him to trust a woman.

Blue Angel, The (1930-German) 90m. ***½ D: Josef von Sternberg. Marlene Dietrich, Emil Jannings, Kurt Gerron, Rosa Valenti, Hans Albers. Ever-fascinating film classic with Jannings as stuffy professor who falls blindly in love with cabaret entertainer Lola-Lola (Dietrich), who ruins his life. Dietrich introduces "Falling in Love Again," in German; shown with subtitles.

Blue Angel, The (1959) C-107m. *½ D: Edward Dmytryk. Curt Jurgens, May Britt, Theodore Bikel, John Banner, Ludwig Stossel, Fabrizio Mioni. Disastrous remake of Josef von Sternberg-Marlene Dietrich classic, from Heinrich Mann's novel of precise professor won over by tawdry nightclub singer.

Blue Bird, The (1940). C-88m. **½ D: Walter Lang. Shirley Temple, Spring Byington, Nigel Bruce, Gale Sondergaard, Eddie Collins, Sybil Jason. Overblown Temple vehicle based on classic story of girl seeking true happiness; slowly paced, but beautifully filmed. Forest-fire sequence is highlight.

Blue Bird, The (1976-Soviet-American) C-99m. ** D: George Cukor. Elizabeth Taylor, Jane Fonda, Ava Gardner, Cicely Tyson, Will Geer, Robert Morley, Harry Andrews. Posh, star-studded but heavy-handed fantasy based on Maeterlinck's play about children seeking the bluebird of happiness. First co-production between U.S. and Russia is unbelievably draggy.

Blue Blood (1951) C-72m. *½ D: Lew Landers. Bill Williams, Jane Nigh, Arthur Shields, Audrey Long. Lackluster racehorse story with a few good moments by Shields as elderly trainer seeking comeback.

Blue Collar (1978) C-114m. ***½ D: Paul Schrader. Richard Pryor, Harvey Keitel, Yaphet Kotto, Ed Begley, Jr., Harry Bellaver, George Memmoli. Punchy, muckraking expose melodrama with Pryor, Keitel, and Kotto delivering strong performances as auto workers who find that it isn't just management ripping them off—it's their own union.

Blue Dahlia, The (1946) 96m. *** D: George Marshall. Alan Ladd, Veronica Lake, William Bendix, Howard da Silva, Hugh Beaumont, Doris Dowling. Exciting Raymond Chandler melodrama has Ladd returning from military service to find wife unfaithful. She's murdered, he's suspected in well-turned film.

Blue Denim (1959) 89m. *** D: Philip Dunne. Carol Lynley, Brandon de Wilde, Macdonald Carey, Marsha Hunt, Warren Berlinger, Roberta Shore. De Wilde and Lynley are striking as teen-agers faced with Carol's pregnancy. Generation gap problem and youths' naiveté date story, but believable performances make it worthwhile.

Blue Gardenia, The (1953) 90m. *** D: Fritz Lang. Anne Baxter, Richard Conte, Ann Sothern, Raymond Burr, Jeff Donnell, George Reeves, Nat King Cole. Engaging murder caper with 1940s flavor. Baxter is accused of murdering wolfish Burr, decides to take columnist Conte's offer of help. Solid film with twist ending.

Blue Grass of Kentucky (1950) C-71m. ** D: William Beaudine. Bill Williams, Jane Nigh, Ralph Morgan. Routine account of horse-breeding families, their rivalry and eventual healing of old wounds when romance blooms between the younger generations.

Blue Hawaii (1961) C-101m. **½ D: Norman Taurog. Elvis Presley, Joan Blackman, Angela Lansbury, Iris Adrian. Agreeable Presley vehicle bolstered by Lansbury's presence as mother of soldier (Presley) returning to islands and working with tourist agency.

Blue Knight, The (1973) C-103m. TVM D: Robert Butler. William Holden, Lee Remick, Joe Santos, Sam Elliott, David Moody, Jamie Farr, Vic Tayback. Holden gives gritty, Emmy-winning performance as

Bumper Morgan, the hero of Joseph Wambaugh's best-selling novel about an aging L.A. street cop. Morgan's last four days on the job find him obsessed with finding a prostitute's killer, while his girlfriend (Remick) anxiously awaits the hour of his retirement. Well-done, authentic police story, superbly performed. Cut down from original four-part, 200-minute presentation. Above average.

Blue Knight, The (1975) C–78m. TVM. D: J. Lee Thompson. George Kennedy, Alex Rocco, Glynn Turman, Verna Bloom, Michael Margotta, Seth Allen. Kennedy assumes role of Bumper Morgan (which he later played in weekly series) as he searches for killer of an aging fellow officer. Kennedy puts his own stamp on the role, but story and approach are definitely formula. Average.

Blue Lagoon, The (1949-British) C–101m. *** D: Frank Launder. Jean Simmons, Donald Houston, Noel Purcell, Cyril Cusack, Maurice Denham. Idyllic romance of Simmons and Houston, shipwrecked on tropic isle, falling in love as they grow to maturity; slowly paced but refreshing.

Blue Lamp, The (1950-British) 84m. *** D: Basil Dearden. Jack Warner, Peggy Evans, Dirk Bogarde, Tessie O'Shea, Jimmy Hanley. Dandy manhunt thriller about Scotland Yard's search for murderer of policeman. Unpretentious and exciting.

Blue Max, The (1966) C–156m. **½ D: John Guillermin. George Peppard, James Mason, Ursula Andress, Jeremy Kemp, Carl Schell. Fantastic aerial photography and memorable Jerry Goldsmith score are the assets of this silly drama, taken from German point of view, about dogfighting in WW1. Steamy Peppard-Andress love scenes aren't bad either, but they may not make it to TV.

Blue Murder at St. Trinian's (1958-British) 86m. *** D: Frank Launder. Joyce Grenfell, Terry-Thomas, George Cole, Alastair Sim. Uncontrollable pupils at madcap school make a robber on the lam wish he'd never hidden out there; deft comedy.

Blue Skies (1946) C–104m. *** D: Stuart Heisler. Fred Astaire, Bing Crosby, Joan Caulfield, Billy DeWolfe, Olga San Juan. Sticky plot salvaged by DeWolfe specialties, dancing by Astaire, songs: title tune, "Puttin' On The Ritz," "A Couple of Song and Dance Men."

Blue Sunshine (1976) C–97m. **½

D: Jeff Lieberman. Zalman King, Deborah Winters, Mark Goddard, Robert Walden, Charles Siebert. Young man accused of murders eludes cops, discovers that apparently "random" killings derive from delayed drug reactions of ten-year-old college class. Offbeat psychological thriller, quite violent at times.

Blue Veil, The (1951) 113m. *** D: Curtis Bernhardt. Jane Wyman, Charles Laughton, Joan Blondell, Richard Carlson, Agnes Moorehead. Wyman is self-sacrificing nursemaid whose life story is chronicled with intertwined episodes of her charges and their families.

Blue Water, White Death (1971) C–99m. *** D: Peter Gimbel. Absorbing study of one of the sea's most colossal beasts, the great white shark.

Bluebeard (1944) 73m. *** D: Edgar G. Ulmer. Jean Parker, John Carradine, Nils Asther, Ludwig Stossel, Iris Adrian, Emmett Lynn. Surprisingly effective story of incurable strangler Carradine, who falls for smart-girl Parker who senses that something is wrong.

Bluebeard (1963-French) C–114m. **½ D: Claude Chabrol. Charles Denner, Michele Morgan, Danielle Darrieux, Hildegarde Neff, Francoise Lugagne. Retelling of life of French wife-killer, far less witty than Chaplin's MONSIEUR VERDOUX. Retitled: LANDRU.

Bluebeard (1972) C–125m. ** D: Edward Dmytryk. Richard Burton, Raquel Welch, Virna Lisi, Joey Heatherton, Nathalie Delon, Karin Schubert. Burton doesn't make much of an impression as world's most famous ladykiller. Women are all beautiful, but script gives them little to do. International production.

Bluebeard's Ten Honeymoons (1960-British) 93m. ** D: W. Lee Wilder. George Sanders, Corinne Calvet, Jean Kent, Patricia Roc. Sanders enlivens OK chronicle of fortune hunter who decides that marrying and murdering a series of women is the key to financial success.

Blueprint for Murder, A (1953) 76m. **½ D: Andrew L. Stone. Joseph Cotten, Jean Peters, Gary Merrill, Jack Kruschen, Mae Marsh. Whodunit has Peters as prime suspect of poison killings, with Cotten seeking the truth.

Blueprint for Robbery (1961) 87m.

**½ D: Jerry Hopper. J. Pat O'-Malley, Robert Wilkie, Robert Gist, Romo Vincent, Tom Duggan. Deliberately offbeat, low-key film of heist engineered by old-timer O'Malley; good moments put this above average, but overall result is unmemorable.

Blues Busters (1950) 67m. D: William Beaudine. Leo Gorcey, Huntz Hall, Adele Jergens, Gabriel Dell, Craig Stevens, William Benedict. SEE: **Bowery Boys** series.

Blues for Lovers (1966-British) 89m. ** D: Paul Henreid. Ray Charles, Tom Bell, Mary Peach, Dawn Addams, Piers Bishop, Betty McDowall. Story of Charles (playing himself) and blind child is maudlin, but fans will like generous footage devoted to Ray's song hits, including "I Got a Woman" and "What'd I Say?"

Blues in the Night (1941) 88m. **½ D: Anatole Litvak. Priscilla Lane, Richard Whorf, Betty Field, Lloyd Nolan, Jack Carson, Elia Kazan, Wallace Ford, Billy Halop, Peter Whitney. Intriguing musical drama abandons early promise for soapy, silly melodramatics, in story of self-destructive musician (Whorf) and his band. Good moments, wonderful Warner Bros. montages, but the great title song is never played once in its entirety!

Blume in Love (1973) C-117m. **½ D: Paul Mazursky. George Segal, Susan Anspach, Kris Kristofferson, Marsha Mason, Shelley Winters, Paul Mazursky. Self-indulgent film about divorce-lawyer Segal refusing to accept fact that his wife (Anspach) has walked out on him, determining to win her back. Good look at modern marriages, but overlong, rambling; Kristofferson delightful as man who moves in with Anspach.

Boardwalk (1979) C-98m. **½ D: Stephen Verona. Ruth Gordon, Lee Strasberg, Janet Leigh, Joe Silver, Eli Mintz, Eddie Barth. Poignant view of elderly couple struggling to survive in decaying neighborhood missteps into DEATH WISH melodramatics for its finale. Fine performances, including Leigh as duty-bound daughter.

Bob & Carol & Ted & Alice (1969) C-104m. *** D: Paul Mazursky. Natalie Wood, Robert Culp, Elliott Gould, Dyan Cannon, Horst Ebersberg, Lee Bergere. Glossy look at modern lifestyles; ultrasophisticated couple (Wood & Culp) try to mod-

ernize thinking of their best friends (Gould & Cannon) about sexual freedom. Sharp observations, fine performances, marred by silly, pretentious finale.

Bob Mathias Story, The (1954) 80m. *** D: Francis D. Lyon. Bob Mathias, Ward Bond, Melba Mathias, Paul Bryar, Ann Doran. Agreeable biography of star track athlete, his sports career, military duty, family life. Mathias turns in an engaging portrayal of himself.

Bobbie Jo and the Outlaw (1976) C-89m. BOMB D: Mark L. Lester. Marjoe Gortner, Lynda Carter, Jesse Vint, Merrie Lynn Ross, Gerrit Graham. Mindless crime-and-car-chase outing has virtually nothing to offer, even for devotees of this "genre."

Bobbikins (1960-British) 89m. ** D: Robert Day. Max Bygraves, Shirley Jones, Steven Stocker, Billie Whitelaw. Gimmicky comedy with British singer Bygraves and Jones the parents of an infant who talks like an adult. Not bad . . . but that awful title!

Bobby Deerfield (1977) C-124m. BOMB D: Sydney Pollack. Al Pacino, Marthe Keller, Anny Duperey, Walter McGinn, Romolo Valli, Stephen Meldegg. Grand Prix race car driver Pacino romances Florentine aristocrat Keller, who is dying of the same unnamed disease that seems to disproportionately afflict movie heroines. Her suffering is nothing compared to the audience's; even Pacino is deadening.

Bobby Ware Is Missing (1955) 67m. *½ D: Thomas Carr. Neville Brand, Arthur Franz, Jean Willes, Walter Reed. Tedious boy-hunt as his parents and sheriff track down kidnappers.

Bobo, The (1967-British) C-105m. ** D: Robert Parrish. Peter Sellers, Britt Ekland, Rossano Brazzi, Adolfo Celi, Fery Mayne, Hattie Jacques. Misfire comedy casts Sellers as aspiring singing matador who's promised a booking if he can seduce Ekland, the most desirable woman in Barcelona, within three days. Filmed in Spain and Rome.

Boccaccio '70 (1962-Italian) C-165m. *** D: Federico Fellini, Luchino Visconti, Vittorio De Sica. Anita Ekberg, Sophia Loren, Romy Schneider, Peppino De Filippo, Dante Maggio, Thomas Milian. Trio of episodes: "The Raffle"—timid soul wins a liaison with a girl as prize; "The Bet"—aristocrat's wife takes a job as her husband's mistress; "The Temptation of Dr. Antonio"—fantasy of puritanical fanatic and a voluptuous poster picture which comes alive.

Body and Soul (1947) 104m. **** D: Robert Rossen. John Garfield, Lilli Palmer, Hazel Brooks, Anne Revere, William Conrad, Joseph Pevney, Canada Lee. Most boxing films pale next to this classic of Garfield working his way up by devious means, becoming famous champ. Superb photography by James Wong Howe.

Body Disappears, The (1941) 72m. ** D: Ross Lederman. Jeffrey Lynn, Jane Wyman, Edward Everett Horton, Marguerite Chapman. Not a very inspired mixture of comedy, suspense, and sci-fi, as Lynn is involved in invisible-making formula causing havoc with the police.

Body Snatcher, The (1945) 77m. ***½ D: Robert Wise. Boris Karloff, Bela Lugosi, Henry Daniell, Edith Atwater, Russell Wade, Rita Corday. Fine, atmospheric tale from Robert Louis Stevenson story of doctor (Daniell) who is forced to deal with scurrilous character (Karloff) in order to get bodies for experiments. One of the classic Val Lewton thrillers.

Body Stealers SEE: **Thin Air**

Bodyguard (1948) 62m. ** D: Richard Fleischer. Lawrence Tierney, Priscilla Lane, Philip Reed, June Clayworth. Routine story of man accused of murder trying to clear himself.

Bodyhold (1949) 63m. *½ D: Seymour Friedman. Willard Parker, Lola Albright, Hillary Brooke, Allen Jenkins, Gordon Jones. Programmer of wrestler and girlfriend seeking to clean up corruption in the fight game.

Boeing Boeing (1965) C-102m. *** D: John Rich. Jerry Lewis, Tony Curtis, Dany Saval, Christiane Schmidtmer, Suzanna Leigh, Thelma Ritter. A surprisingly subdued Lewis is paired with Curtis in story of American newspaperman who runs swinging pad in Paris, constantly stocked with stewardesses, to the chagrin of housekeeper Ritter. Amusing.

Bofors Gun, The (1968) C-106m. *** D: Jack Gold. Nicol Williamson, Ian Holm, David Warner, Richard O'Callaghan, Barry Jackson, Donald Gee. British soldier, on the eve of his return home in 1950s, comes tragically face-to-face with a rebellious Irish gunner. Engrossing drama, well acted.

Bohemian Girl, The (1936) 70m. *** D: James Horne, Charles R. Rogers. Stan Laurel, Oliver Hardy, Thelma Todd, Antonio Moreno, Darla Hood, Jacqueline Wells (Julie Bishop), Mae Busch. Nifty comic opera with Stan and Ollie part of gypsy caravan. They adopt abandoned girl who turns out to be princess.

Bold and the Brave, The (1956) 87m. *** D: Lewis R. Foster. Wendell Corey, Mickey Rooney, Don Taylor, Nicole Maurey. Routine WW2 study of soldiers fighting in Italy, greatly uplifted by unstereotyped performances; Rooney is outstanding.

Bolero (1934) 83m. **½ D: Wesley Ruggles. George Raft, Carole Lombard, Sally Rand, Gertrude Michael, William Frawley, Ray Milland. Silly, protracted story of cocky dancer's rise to fame is made fun by good stars and production values; dance sequences are first-rate, although much of Raft and Lombard's footwork is "doubled" by professionals.

Bomb at 10:10 (1966-Yugoslavian) C-86m. ** D: Charles Damic. George Montgomery, Rada Popovic, Peter Banicevic, Branko Plesa. Thrown-together mishmash with Montgomery escaping from Nazi P.O.W. camp, plotting to help partisans and destroy prison leaders.

Bomb in the High Street (1964-British) 60m. **½ D: Terence Bishop. Ronald Howard, Terry Palmer, Suzanna Leigh. Unpretentious robbery caper involving phony bomb scare to divert authorities from site of crime.

Bomba the Jungle Boy In 1949 producer Walter Mirisch, who has gone on to far greater things, decided to produce a series of low-budget adventure films based on a series of popular juvenile books about a boy who has grown up in the jungle. For this road-company Tarzan series he got Johnny Sheffield, who had played Boy in the Tarzan films, and director Ford Beebe, an expert at making something out of nothing. With a small studio backlot and plenty of footage of wild animals, BOMBA THE JUNGLE BOY emerged, a notbad little adventure. The subsequent eleven films in the series, however, worked their way into a standard formula that by the last episodes was all too familiar. Bomba was made for younger audiences, and the films will probably still please the kids. As for adults, well, there have been worse films than the Bomba series.

Bomba and the Elephant Stampede SEE: **Elephant Stampede**

Bomba and the Hidden City (1950) 71m. D: Ford Beebe. Johnny Sheffield, Sue England, Paul Guilfoyle, Leon Belasco, Smoki Whitfield.

Bomba and the Jungle Girl (1952) 70m. D: Ford Beebe. Johnny Sheffield, Karen Sharpe, Walter Sande, Martin Wilkins.

Bomba on Panther Island (1949) 76m. D: Ford Beebe. Johnny Sheffield, Allene Roberts, Lita Baron, Smoki Whitfield.

Bomba, The Jungle Boy (1949) 70m. D: Ford Beebe. Johnny Sheffield, Peggy Ann Garner, Smoki Whitfield, Onslow Stevens.

Bombardier (1943) 99m. *** D: Richard Wallace. Pat O'Brien, Randolph Scott, Anne Shirley, Eddie Albert, Walter Reed, Robert Ryan, Barton MacLane. Familiar framework of fliers being trained during WW2 comes off well with fast-moving script.

Bombers B-52 (1957) C-106m. **½ D: Gordon Douglas. Natalie Wood, Karl Malden, Marsha Hunt, Efrem Zimbalist, Jr., Dean Jagger. Ordinary love story between army pilot Zimbalist and Wood, with latter's sergeant father objecting, intertwined with good aerial footage of jet plane maneuvers.

Bombs Over Burma (1942) 62m. ** D: Joseph H. Lewis. Anna May Wong, Noel Madison, Dan Seymour, Richard Loo, Nedrick Young, Dennis Moore. Grade-B wartime saga of devoted Wong risking life for sake of China on espionage mission.

Bombshell (1933) 91m. ***½ D: Victor Fleming. Jean Harlow, Lee Tracy, Frank Morgan, Franchot Tone, Una Merkel, Pat O'Brien, C. Aubrey Smith. Devastating satire of 1930s Hollywood, with Harlow a much-used star, Tracy an incredibly unscrupulous publicity director making her life hell. No holds barred. Retitled BLONDE BOMBSHELL.

Bon Voyage (1962) C-130m. *½ D: James Neilson. Fred MacMurray, Jane Wyman, Michael Callan, Deborah Walley, Tommy Kirk, Kevin Corcoran. Slow, drawn-out Disney comedy about "typical" American family's misadventures on trip to Europe. Aimed more at adults than kids, but too draggy and simple-minded for anyone.

Bonjour Tristesse (1958) C-94m. *** D: Otto Preminger. Deborah Kerr, David Niven, Jean Seberg, Mylene Demongeot. Teen-ager does her best to break up romance between playboy widowed father and his mistress, with tragic results. Francoise Sagan's philosophy seeps through glossy production; Kerr exceptionally fine in soaper set on French Riviera.

Bonnie and Clyde (1967) C-111m. **** D: Arthur Penn. Warren Beatty, Faye Dunaway, Michael J. Pollard, Gene Hackman, Estelle Parsons, Denver Pyle, Gene Wilder, Dub Taylor. Trend-setting film about unlikely heroes of 1930s, bank-robbing team, has spawned many imitators but still leads the pack. Plunging from comedy to melodrama and social commentary, it remains vivid, stylish throughout. Impact of final shoot-out is lost through cutting on TV, however.

Bonnie Parker Story, The (1958) 81m. **½ D: William Witney. Dorothy Provine, Jack Hogan, Richard Bakalyan, Joseph Turkel. With the success of BONNIE AND CLYDE, this film takes on added luster, recounting the lurid criminal life of the female crook (Provine); low-budget production.

Bonnie Scotland (1935) 80m. **½ D: James Horne. Stan Laurel, Oliver Hardy, June Lang, William Janney, Anne Grey, Vernon Steele, James Finlayson. Plot sometimes gets in the way of L&H, but their material is well up to par; Stan and Ollie inadvertently join a Scottish military regiment stationed in the desert.

Bonzo Goes to College (1952) 80m. ** D: Frederick de Cordova. Maureen O'Sullivan, Edmund Gwenn, Gigi Perreau, Gene Lockhart, Irene Ryan, David Janssen. Follow-up to BEDTIME FOR BONZO has brainy chimp lead college football team to victory; good cast takes back seat to monkey-shines.

Boogie Man Will Get You, The (1942) 66m. *½ D: Lew Landers. Boris Karloff, Peter Lorre, Jeff Donnell, Larry Parks, Maxie Rosenbloom. Silly, contrived rip-off of ARSENIC AND OLD LACE with Karloff as mad scientist operating in cellar of home that Donnell is trying to turn into hotel.

Book of Numbers (1973) C-80m. **½ D: Raymond St. Jacques. Raymond

[81]

St. Jacques, Phillip Thomas, Freda Payne, Hope Clarke, D'Urville Martin, Gilbert Green. Uneven but sometimes enjoyable story of a black numbers-racket operation in a rural town during the Depression; some nudity may be cut from TV.

Boom (1968-U.S.-British) C-113m. ** D: Joseph Losey. Elizabeth Taylor, Richard Burton, Noel Coward, Joanna Shimkus, Michael Dunn. Thud: Only film buffs who admire Losey's very original directorial style are likely to appreciate fuzzy adaptation of Tennessee Williams' THE MILK TRAIN DOESN'T STOP HERE ANYMORE. Fine on location photography in Sardinia and Rome; good performance by Shimkus can't save this one.

Boom Town (1940) 116m. *** D: Jack Conway. Clark Gable, Spencer Tracy, Claudette Colbert, Hedy Lamarr, Frank Morgan, Lionel Atwill, Chill Wills. No surprises in tale of get-rich-quick drilling for oil, but star-studded cast gives it life.

Boomerang (1947) 88m. **** D: Elia Kazan. Dana Andrews, Jane Wyatt, Lee J. Cobb, Arthur Kennedy, Sam Levene. Priest's murder brings rapid arrest of an innocent man; prosecuting attorney determines to hunt out real facts. Brilliant drama in all respects.

Boot Hill (1969-Italian) C-87m. ** D: Giuseppe Colizzi. Terence Hill, Bud Spencer, Woody Strode, Victor Buono, Lionel Stander, Eduardo Ciannelli. Western ravioli representing another of the traditional teamings of blue-eyed, rock-jawed Hill and his bear of a sidekick Spencer. Uneven pasta of violence and comedy.

Bootleggers (1974) C-101m. ** D: Charles B. Pierce. Paul Koslo, Dennis Fimple, Slim Pickens, Jaclyn Smith, Chuck Pierce, Jr. Typical yahoo action comedy set in 1930s Arkansas with Koslo and Fimple trying to outsmart and outdo rival moonshining family while running their supplies to Memphis.

Boots Malone (1952) 103m. *** D: William Dieterle. William Holden, Johnny Stewart, Ed Begley, Harry Morgan, Whit Bissell. Holden comes alive in role of shady character who reforms when he trains Stewart to become a jockey.

Border Incident (1949) 92m. *** D: Anthony Mann. Ricardo Montalban, George Murphy, Howard da Silva, Teresa Celli, Charles McGraw. Tension-packed story of U.S. agents cracking down on wetback smuggling on Texas-Mexico border. Well directed, and uncompromisingly violent.

Border River (1954) C-80m. ** D: George Sherman. Joel McCrea, Yvonne De Carlo, Pedro Armendariz, Howard Petrie. Mildly intriguing Western about Rebel officer McCrea's mission to buy much-needed weapons from Mexicans to continue fight against Yankees.

Borderline (1950) 88m. **½ D: William Seiter. Fred MacMurray, Claire Trevor, Raymond Burr, Roy Roberts. Trevor and MacMurray work well together as law enforcers each tracking down dope smugglers on Mexican border, neither knowing the other isn't a crook.

Bordertown (1935) 90m. *** D: Archie Mayo. Paul Muni, Bette Davis, Eugene Pallette, Margaret Lindsay. Fine drama of unusual triangle in bordertown cafe, with Davis as flirtatious wife of Pallette with designs on lawyer Muni. Used as basis for later THEY DRIVE BY NIGHT, but more serious in tone.

Borgia Stick, The (1967) C-100m. TVM D: David Lowell Rich. Don Murray, Fritz Weaver, Inger Stevens, Barry Nelson. Fairly grim suspense thriller exposing organized crime involvement in U.S. economy. Fine cast, particularly Weaver, works very well. Above average.

Born Again (1978) C-110m. *½ D: Irving Rapper. Dean Jones, Anne Francis, Jay Robinson, Dana Andrews, Raymond St. Jacques, George Brent. If one is inspired by the religious rebirth of Pres. Nixon's Special Counsel (Charles Colson) after his Washington skullduggery, one might be absorbed by this one-dimensional film account. Others beware!

Born Free (1966-British) .C-96m. ***½ D: James Hill. Virginia McKenna, Bill Travers, Geoffrey Keen, Peter Lukoye. Exceptional adaptation of the late Joy Adamson's book about Elsa the lioness, who was raised as a pet by two Kenya game wardens. Sincere, engrossing film, a must for family viewing. Oscar for best song.

Born Innocent (1974) C-100m. TVM D: Donald Wrye. Linda Blair, Joanna Miles, Kim Hunter, Richard Jaeckel, Mary Murphy, Allyn Ann McLerie, Mitch Vogel. Graphic story of teen-

aged girl's struggle to adjust to rigors of tough juvenile detention home. Uncompromising film, distinguished in its original showing by a realistic rape of Blair by her fellow inmates (now cut from film). Otherwise, played for the sensational; average.
Born Losers (1967) C-112m. **½ D: T. C. Frank (Tom Laughlin). Tom Laughlin, Elizabeth James, Jane Russell, Jeremy Slate, William Wellman Jr., Robert Tessier. Young halfbreed gets involved with motorcycle gang; point of film seems to be qualified indictment of violence, but some gory scenes are gratuitous. Russell has small role as mother of victimized young girl. From the folks who later brought you BILLY JACK.
Born Restless (1959) 79m. ** D: Howard W. Koch. Mamie Van Doren, Jeff Richards, Arthur Hunnicutt, Carol Ohmart, Tom Duggan. Fitfully promising romp with Van Doren-Richards romancing while seeking success as rodeo performers.
Born To Be Bad (1934) 61m. **½ D: Lowell Sherman. Loretta Young, Cary Grant, Henry Travers, Howard Lang, Matt Briggs. Spicy soaper with loose-living Loretta forced to give up son after clash with wealthy Grant.
Born To Be Bad (1950) 94m. **½ D: Nicholas Ray. Joan Fontaine, Robert Ryan, Joan Leslie, Mel Ferrer, Zachary Scott. Fontaine is a ruthless woman who gets her way by manipulating everyone around her. Good cast in somewhat overwrought drama.
Born To Be Loved (1959) 82m. ** D: Hugo Haas. Carol Morris, Vera Vague, Hugo Haas, Dick Kallman, Jacqueline Fontaine. Low-key yarn of poor-but-honest Morris and rich widow Vague seeking romance, helped by elderly music instructor Haas.
Born To Dance (1936) 105m. *** D: Roy Del Ruth. Eleanor Powell, James Stewart, Virginia Bruce, Una Merkel, Sid Silvers, Frances Langford, Raymond Walburn, Buddy Ebsen. Powell bears out title in good Cole Porter musical with sensational footwork and fine songs: "Easy To Love," "I've Got You Under My Skin."
Born to Kill (1947) 92m. ** D: Robert Wise. Claire Trevor, Lawrence Tierney, Walter Slezak, Philip Terry, Elisha Cook Jr., Audrey Long. Unattractive melodrama of psychotic murderer Tierney marrying Long but continuing his philandering with her sister (Trevor).

Born to Kill (1974) SEE: **Cockfighter**
Born to Win (1971) C-90m. **½ D: Ivan Passer. George Segal, Karen Black, Paula Prentiss, Jay Fletcher, Hector Elizondo. Unjustly neglected, but not altogether successful comedy-drama about ex-hairdresser in New York and his $100-a-day heroin habit. Very well acted, particularly by Segal.
Born Yesterday (1950) 103m. ***½ D: George Cukor. Judy Holliday, William Holden, Broderick Crawford, Howard St. John. Junk-dealer-made-good Crawford wants his gal (Holliday) culturfied, hires Holden to teach her in hilarious Garson Kanin comedy set in Washington, D.C. Priceless Judy won Oscar for her Pygmalion performance.
Borsalino (1970-French) C-125m. *** D: Jacques Deray. Jean-Paul Belmondo, Alain Delon, Michel Bouquet, Catherine Rouvel, Francoise Christophe. PUBLIC ENEMY, French-style; delightful seriocomic film of two likable hoods who become gangland chieftains in 1930s Marseilles. Stars in top form; Claude Bolling's infectious music helps, too.
Boss, The (1956) 89m. *** D: Byron Haskin. John Payne, William Bishop, Gloria McGhee, Doe Avedon, Joe Flynn. Effective study of WW1 veteran returning to St. Louis and combatting corruption and crime; one of Payne's best performances as the city's underworld boss.
Boston Blackie Over a span of nine years, Chester Morris starred in fourteen films as Boston Blackie, a former thief now on the right side of the law but preferring to work for himself than for the police. He brought to the role a delightful offhand manner and sense of humor that kept the films fresh even when the scripts weren't. From MEET BOSTON BLACKIE (1941) to BOSTON BLACKIE'S CHINESE VENTURE (1949), Morris was Blackie. Regulars included Richard Lane as a frustrated police detective convinced that Blackie was up to no good, but always one step behind him; George E. Stone as Blackie's talkative dim-witted buddy; and Lloyd Corrigan as a dizzy millionaire pal who'd do anything for a lark. Top-flight directors Robert Florey and Edward Dmytryk got the series started, and when the films fell into less capable hands, Morris and company came to the rescue with consistently ingratiating performances. While no classics, the

Boston Blackie films offer a great deal of fun.

Boston Blackie and the Law (1946) 69m. D: D. Ross Lederman. Chester Morris, Trudy Marshall, Constance Dowling, Richard Lane.

Boston Blackie Booked on Suspicion (1945) 66m. D: Arthur Dreifuss. Chester Morris, Lynn Merrick, Richard Lane, Frank Sully, Steve Cochran.

Boston Blackie Goes Hollywood (1942) 68m. D: Michael Gordon. Chester Morris, George E. Stone, Richard Lane, Forrest Tucker, Constance Worth, Lloyd Corrigan, William Wright.

Boston Blackie's Chinese Venture (1949) 59m. D: Seymour Friedman. Chester Morris, Joan Woodbury, Philip Ahn, Benson Fong.

Boston Blackie's Rendezvous (1945) 64m. D: Arthur Dreifuss. Chester Morris, Nina Foch, Steve Cochran, Richard Lane, George E. Stone, Frank Sully.

Boston Strangler, The (1968) C-120m. *** D: Richard Fleischer. Tony Curtis, Henry Fonda, George Kennedy, Mike Kellin, Hurd Hatfield, Murray Hamilton, Jeff Corey, Sally Kellerman, William Marshall. Absorbing drama, semidocumentary-style, detailing rise, manhunt, capture, prosecution of notorious criminal. Curtis gives startling performance as killer. Complex multi-image technique may be lost on TV, along with several potent scenes.

Botany Bay (1953) C-94m. **½ D: John Farrow. Alan Ladd, James Mason, Patricia Medina, Cedric Hardwicke. Based on Charles Nordhoff novel set in 1790s, picturesque yarn tells of convict ship bound for Australia, focusing on conflict between prisoner Ladd and sadistic skipper Mason, with Medina as Ladd's love interest.

Both Sides of the Law (1954-British) 94m. *** D: Muriel Box. Peggy Cummins, Terence Morgan, Anne Crawford, Rosamund John. Documentary-style account of London policewomen and their daily activity. Unpretentious production allows for good natural performances.

Bottom of the Bottle, The (1956) C-88m. **½ D: Henry Hathaway. Van Johnson, Joseph Cotten, Ruth Roman, Jack Carson. Overblown melodramatics south of the border, involving a seemingly respectable attorney, his alcoholic younger brother, and assorted seedy townfolk.

Boucher, Le (1971-French) C-93m. *** D: Claude Chabrol. Stephane Audran, Jean Yanne, Antonio Passallia, Mario Beccaria, Pasquale Ferone. Another good psychological thriller from Chabrol, focusing on sympathetic murderer and his relationship with beautiful schoolteacher in small French village.

Boulevard Nights (1979) C-102m. ** D: Michael Pressman. Richard Yniguez, Marta Du Bois, Danny De La Paz, Betty Carvalho, Carmen Zapata, James Victor, Victor Millan. Sincere but uninspiring story of Chicano youth who yearns to move away from street-gang life, but drawn back because of hot-blooded young brother. Filmed in the barrios of L.A.

Bound for Glory (1976) C-147m. ***½ D: Hal Ashby. David Carradine, Ronny Cox, Melinda Dillon, Gail Strickland, John Lehne, Ji-Tu Cumbuka. Life of composer-folk singer Woody Guthrie, superbly played by Carradine, with great feel for 1936-40 period as Guthrie travels the country fighting—and singing—for the underdogs, victims of the Great Depression. Haskell Wexler's Oscar-winning photography is tops throughout.

Bounty Hunter, The (1954) C-79m. **½ D: Andre de Toth. Randolph Scott, Dolores Dorn, Marie Windsor, Howard Petrie. Scott is on his horse again, this time tracking down three murderers.

Bounty Killer, The (1965) C-92m. **½ D: Spencer G. Bennet. Dan Duryea, Rod Cameron, Audrey Dalton, Richard Arlen, Buster Crabbe, Fuzzy Knight, Johnny Mack Brown, Bob Steele, Bronco Billy Anderson. Western's chief interest is cast of old-timers from Hollywood oaters of years gone by. Unlike their previous vehicles, this is an adult, low-key Western minus happy ending. Interesting on both counts.

Bounty Man, The (1972) C-73m. TVM D: John Llewellyn Moxey. Clint Walker, Richard Basehart, John Ericson, Margot Kidder, Arthur Hunnicutt, Gene Evans. Surprisingly somber Western with nihilistic point of view. Man-hunter Kincaid (Walker) chases young killer to isolated valley town, in turn chased by gang of cutthroats. Script provides good complications. Above average.

Bowery, The (1933) 90m. ******* D: Raoul Walsh. Wallace Beery, George Raft, Jackie Cooper, Fay Wray, Pert Kelton, Herman Bing. Raft is Steve Brodie, Beery a notorious saloon owner, Cooper his young nemesis in rowdy story of N.Y.C.'s Bowery during the Gay 90s. Pert Kelton is marvelous as Beery's saloon soubrette.

Bowery at Midnight (1942) 63m. ****** D: Wallace Fox. Bela Lugosi, John Archer, Wanda McKay, Tom Neal, Dave O'Brien. Cheap melodrama of mad killer terrorizing Bowery neighborhood.

Bowery Boys, The Sidney Kingsley's serious, dramatic indictment of tenement slums, DEAD END, came to the screen in 1937; unfortunately, it did little to change the slum problem of our cities. What it did do was introduce the Dead End Kids, a group of fun-loving hoodlums headed by Leo Gorcey and Huntz Hall; Warner Bros. used various members of the gang in seven subsequent films of high caliber with such co-stars as Humphrey Bogart and John Garfield. Between 1939 and 1943 various studios used different Dead End Kids in films like LITTLE TOUGH GUYS and serials such as JUNIOR G-MEN. Finally in 1940 most of the separate factions joined at Monogram Studios to begin a low-budget series called THE EAST SIDE KIDS. In 1946 the name changed to the BOWERY BOYS, which remained until 1957. With the exception of early titles like ANGELS WITH DIRTY FACES, not part of the actual series, the Bowery Boys comedies were very-low-budget action comedies with an abundance of silly jokes and primitive sight gags that got worse as the series progressed. Even guests like Bela Lugosi couldn't save them, and one Lugosi effort, SPOOKS RUN WILD, is embarrassing. Budgets on some films were so low one could see actors' shadows on the process-screen sequences. Nevertheless, the films were popular, and are shown constantly on TV. Some offer lightweight entertainment, such as JALOPY, MASTER MINDS, NO HOLDS BARRED, and BOWERY BOYS MEET THE MONSTER. Most of the others are juvenile comedies meant for a juvenile audience. Longest-lasting players in the series were Huntz Hall, Leo Gorcey, Billy Benedict, Bennie Bartlett, David Gorcey, and Bernard Gorcey as the so-called adult Louie Dumbrowski. Others who floated in and out include Gabriel Dell, Bernard Punsley, Billy Halop, Bobby Jordan, and Stanley Clements.

Bowery Battalion (1951) 69m. D: William Beaudine. Leo Gorcey, Huntz Hall, Donald MacBride, Virginia Hewitt, Russell Hicks.

Bowery Blitzkrieg (1941) 62m. D: Wallace Fox. Leo Gorcey, Bobby Jordan, Huntz Hall, Warren Hull, Charlotte Henry, Keye Luke, Bobby Stone.

Bowery Bombshell (1946) 65m. D: Phil Karlson. Leo Gorcey, Huntz Hall, Bobby Jordan, Billy Benedict, Sheldon Leonard, Emmett Vogan.

Bowery Boys Meet the Monsters, The (1954) 65m. D: Edward Bernds. Leo Gorcey, Huntz Hall, Bernard Gorcey, Lloyd Corrigan, Ellen Corby.

Bowery Buckaroos (1947) 66m. D: William Beaudine. Leo Gorcey, Huntz Hall, Bobby Jordan, Gabriel Dell, Billy Benedict.

Bowery Champs (1944) 62m. D: William Beaudine. Leo Gorcey, Huntz Hall, Billy Benedict, Bobby Jordan, Gabriel Dell, Anne Sterling, Evelyn Brent, Ian Keith.

Bowery to Bagdad (1955) 64m. D: Edward Bernds. Huntz Hall, Leo Gorcey, Joan Shawlee, Eric Blore.

Bowery to Broadway (1944) 94m. ****½** D: Charles Lamont. Jack Oakie, Donald Cook, Maria Montez, Louise Allbritton, Susanna Foster, Turhan Bey, Andy Devine, Rosemary DeCamp, Frank McHugh, Ann Blyth, Leo Carrillo, Evelyn Ankers, Peggy Ryan, Donald O'Connor. Film depends solely on its many guest stars for what entertainment it has; limp story of Montez becoming Hollywood star doesn't make it.

Boxer, The SEE: **Ripped Off**

Boxcar Bertha (1972) C-97m. ****** D: Martin Scorsese. Barbara Hershey, David Carradine, Barry Primus, Bernie Casey, John Carradine. Unconvincing railyard Depression drama of unions, riots, and murder. Performances lack substance as does story line.

Boy and His Dog, A (1975) C-87m. ***½** D: L. Q. Jones. Don Johnson, Susanne Benton, Jason Robards, Tiger, Tim McIntire, Charles McGraw. Unpleasant, poorly structured adaptation of Harlan Ellison's novella about a misogynistic society in the post-World War IV civilization 2024. Film has cult following, based mainly on Ellison's original story.

Boy and the Pirates, The (1960) C-82m. **½ D: Bert I. Gordon. Charles Herbert, Susan Gordon, Murvyn Vye, Paul Guilfoyle. Good fantasy-adventure for kids moves along well, has Murvyn Vye giving his all as a pirate.

Boy Cried Murder, The (1966-British) C-86m. **½ D: George Breakston. Veronica Hurst, Phil Brown, Beba Loncar, Frazer MacIntosh, Tim Barrett. A reworking of THE WINDOW set in Adriatic resort town. Youngster noted for his fabrications witnesses a murder; no one but the killer believes him.

Boy, Did I Get a Wrong Number! (1966) C-99m. BOMB D: George Marshall. Bob Hope, Elke Sommer, Phyllis Diller, Cesare Danova, Marjorie Lord. They sure did; result is worthless film that should be avoided. Absolutely painful.

Boy Friend, The (1971-British) C-110m. *** D: Ken Russell. Twiggy, Christopher Gable, Moyra Fraser, Max Adrian, Georgina Hale, Tommy Tune; cameo by Glenda Jackson. Director Russell's homage to Hollywood musicals works on several levels, from tacky matinee performance of a show to fantasy-world conception of same material, all loosely tied to Sandy Wilson's cunning spoof of 1920s musical shows. Busby Berkeley-ish numbers come amazingly close to spirit and execution of the Master himself.

Boy From Indiana (1950) 66m ** D: John Rawlins. Lon McCallister, Lois Butler, Billie Burke, George Cleveland. Modest horseracing yarn, with McCallister grooming his beloved horse while romancing Butler.

Boy From Oklahoma, The (1954) C-88m. **½ D: Michael Curtiz. Will Rogers, Jr., Nancy Olson, Lon Chaney, Anthony Caruso, Wallace Ford, Merv Griffin. Quiet Western film with Rogers as pacifist sheriff who manages to keep the town intact and romance Olson; good production values.

Boy in the Plastic Bubble, The (1976) C-100m. TVM D: Randall Kleiser. John Travolta, Glynnis O'Connor, Robert Reed, Diana Hyland, Ralph Bellamy, Karen Morrow, John Friedrich, Buzz Aldrin. Teen-ager is forced to live in physical and emotional isolation, having been born with an immunity deficiency, and is faced with a life or death situation when he falls in love with girl next door. Hinges on Travolta's earnest performance, but touches of bathos and certain sci-fi attitude in story's approach mar it. Average.

Boy Meets Girl (1938) 80m. **½ D: Lloyd Bacon. James Cagney, Pat O'Brien, Marie Wilson, Ralph Bellamy, Frank McHugh, Dick Foran, Penny Singleton, Ronald Reagan. Screwball spoof of Hollywood sometimes pushes too hard, but has enough sharp dialogue, good satire in tale of two sharpster screenwriters to make it worthwhile.

Boy Named Charlie Brown, A (1969) C-85m. *** D: Bill Melendez. Voices of Peter Robbins, Pamelyn Ferdin, Glenn Gilger, Andy Pforsich. Peanuts gang makes surprisingly successful feature-film debut, with ingenious visual ideas adding to usual fun. Only debit: Rod McKuen's absurd songs.

Boy on a Dolphin (1957) C-111m. **½ D: Jean Negulesco. Alan Ladd, Clifton Webb, Sophia Loren, Laurence Naismith. Grecian isles are backdrop to pedestrian sunken-treasure yarn. Loren, in U.S. film debut, cast as skindiver helping Ladd.

Boy Ten Feet Tall, A (1963-British) C-118m. *** D: Alexander Mackendrick. Edward G. Robinson, Fergus McClelland, Constance Cummings, Harry H. Corbett. Colorful, charming film about orphaned boy traveling through Africa alone to reach his aunt, who lives in Durban. Cut to 88m. for American release, footage was restored for TV print. Originally titled SAMMY GOING SOUTH.

Boy Who Caught a Crook (1961) 72m. ** D: Edward L. Cahn. Wanda Hendrix, Roger Mobley, Don Beddoe, Richard Crane. Title is self-explanatory for this passable programmer.

Boy Who Cried Werewolf, The (1973) C-93m. ** D: Nathan Juran. Kerwin Mathews, Elaine Devry, Scott Sealey, Robert J. Wilke, Susan Foster. Lycanthropy returns in watered-down form: werewolves loose and claiming victims by the score.

Boy Who Stole a Million, The (1960-British) 64m. ** D: Charles Crichton. Maurice Reyna, Virgilio Texera, Marianne Benet, Harold Kasket. Family-type film of youth who gets involved in bank theft to help father with oppressive debts.

Boy With Green Hair, The (1948) C-82m. *** D: Joseph Losey. Dean Stockwell, Pat O'Brien, Robert Ryan, Barbara Hale. Thought-provoking fable of war orphan who becomes social outcast when hair changes color. Competent acting.

Boys, The (1961-British) 123m. *** D: Sidney J. Furie. Richard Todd, Robert Morley, Felix Aylmer, Wilfred Brambell. Engrossing study of attorney (Todd) who trys to uncover motives for crimes allegedly committed by four teenagers.

Boys From Brazil, The (1978) C-123m. **½ D: Franklin Schaffner. Gregory Peck, Laurence Olivier, James Mason, Lilli Palmer, Uta Hagen, Steven Guttenberg, Denholm Elliott, Rosemary Harris, John Dehner, John Rubinstein, Anne Meara. Former Nazi chieftain Dr. Josef Mengele (Peck) has insidious plan to breed new race of Hitlers. Ira Levin's story is interesting but ultimately silly and unbelievable; definitely worth watching, though, for Olivier's brilliant, credible performance as aging Jewish Nazi-hunter.

Boys From Syracuse, The (1940) 73m. *** D: A. Edward Sutherland. Allan Jones, Joe Penner, Martha Raye, Rosemary Lane, Irene Hervey, Eric Blore. Pleasing film of Rodgers-Hart musical based on Shakespeare's "Comedy of Errors," but set in ancient Greece. Songs: "This Can't Be Love," "Falling In Love With Love."

Boys in Company C, The (1978) C-127m. *** D: Sidney J. Furie. Stan Shaw, Andrew Stevens, James Canning, Michael Lembeck, Craig Wasson, Scott Hylands. Shaw (in a standout performance) whips a bunch of green Marine recruits into shape for combat in Vietnam; good, tough film focuses on stupidity of military brass and demoralization of the soldiers.

Boys in the Band, The (1970) C-120m. *** D: William Friedkin. Frederick Combs, Leonard Frey, Cliff Gorman, Reuben Greene, Laurence Luckinbill, Kenneth Nelson. Excellent filmization of Mart Crowley's play about homosexual's birthday party where hidden thoughts and feelings are suddenly and sadly brought into the open. Although a one-set play, it's never static, thanks to Friedkin, fine performances.

Boys' Night Out (1962) C-115m. *** D: Michael Gordon. Kim Novak, James Garner, Tony Randall, Howard Duff, Janet Blair, Patti Page, Zsa Zsa Gabor, Howard Morris. Trio of married men and bachelor Garner decide to set up an apartment equipped with Novak. Script manages some interesting innuendos, with comic relief coming from Blair, Page, and Gabor.

Boys of Paul Street, The (1969-Hungarian-U.S.) C-108m. *** D: Zoltan Fabri. Anthony Kemp, Robert Efford, Gary O'Brien, Mark Colleano. Allegory of children's battle for control of vacant lot in Budapest, from Ferenc Molnar's novel; eloquent statement on war in effective film.

Boys of the City (1940) 65m. D: Joseph H. Lewis. Bobby Jordan, Leo Gorcey, Dave O'Brien, Vince Barnett, George Humbert, Hally Chester. SEE: *Bowery Boys* series.

Boys Town (1938) 96m. *** D: Norman Taurog. Spencer Tracy, Mickey Rooney, Henry Hull, Leslie Fenton, Addison Richards, Edward Norris, Gene Reynolds. Tracy won Oscar as Father Flanagan, who develops school for juvenile delinquents; Rooney is his toughest enrolee. On the syrupy side, but well done. Sequel: MEN OF BOYS TOWN.

Brain, The (1965-German-British) 85m. *** D: Freddie Francis. Peter Van Eyck, Anne Heywood, Cecil Parker, Bernard Lee, Frank Forsyth, Jack MacGowran. Good remake of DONOVAN'S BRAIN, about scientist overtaken by dead man's brain kept "alive" in his laboratory.

Brain, The (1969-French) C-100m. ** D: Gerard Oury. David Niven, Jean-Paul Belmondo, Bourvil, Eli Wallach, Silvia Monti, Fernand Valois. Fine international cast in OK caper comedy about a train heist masterminded by Niven.

Brain from Planet Arous (1958) 70m. ** D: Nathan Juran. John Agar, Joyce Meadows, Robert Fuller, Henry Travis. Lack of imagination in production mars tale of alien force which takes possession of scientist's mind, trying to conquer the world.

Brain Machine, The (1956-British) 72m. ** D: Ken Hughes. Patrick Barr, Elizabeth Allan, Maxwell Reed, Vanda Godsell. Average yarn about drug smuggling and those involved, one of them as the result of mind-shattering machine.

Brain That Wouldn't Die, The (1963)

81m. *½ D: Joseph Green. Herb (Jason) Evers, Virginia Leith, Adele Lamont, Leslie Daniel, Paula Maurice. Poorly produced tale of surgeon trying to find body to attach to fiancee's head (she was decapitated but still lives).

Brainstorm (1965) 114m. ** D: William Conrad. Jeff Hunter, Anne Francis, Dana Andrews, Viveca Lindfors, Stacy Harris, Kathie Brown. Fair thriller about a determined man (Hunter) who attempts the perfect crime in order to eliminate Andrews and marry Francis. Contrived.

Brainwashed (1961-French) 102m. ** D: Gerd Oswald. Curt Jurgens, Claire Bloom, Hansjorg Felmy, Albert Lieven. Austrian Jurgens' struggle to retain sanity while undergoing intense Nazi interrogation is basis of this psychological drama. Strong performances but weak story mars film.

Bramble Bush, The (1960) C-105m. **½ D: Daniel Petrie. Richard Burton, Barbara Rush, Jack Carson, Angie Dickinson. Charles Mergendahl's potboiler becomes superficial gloss with Burton totally ill at ease playing New England doctor returning to Cape Cod, where he falls in love with his dying friend's wife.

Brand New Life, A (1972) C-74m. TVM D: Sam O'Steen. Cloris Leachman, Martin Balsam, Marge Redmond, Gene Nelson, Mildred Dunnock, Wilfrid Hyde-White. Believable melodrama centering on middle-aged couple reacting to unexpected prospect of having first child. Remarkable scripts, performances. Above average.

Branded (1950) C-95m. **½ D: Rudolph Maté. Alan Ladd, Mona Freeman, Charles Bickford, Joseph Calleia, Milburn Stone. Outlaws use carefree Ladd to impersonate rancher Bickford's long-missing son, leading to much different outcome than anticipated; action and love scenes balanced OK.

Brannigan (1975-British) C-111m. **½ D: Douglas Hickox. John Wayne, Richard Attenborough, Judy Geeson, John Vernon, Mel Ferrer, Ralph Meeker. A criminal flees to London to avoid extradition, and Chicago cop Wayne pursues him. Overlong, but change of locale serves Duke well.

Brasher Doubloon, The (1947) 72m. ** D: John Brahm. George Montgomery, Nancy Guild, Conrad Janis, Roy Roberts, Fritz Kortner. Rare coin seems to be object of several murders in very uneven Philip Marlowe detective mystery. Filmed before as TIME TO KILL.

Brass Bottle, The (1964) C-89m. *½ D: Harry Keller. Tony Randall, Burl Ives, Barbara Eden, Edward Andrews, Ann Doran. Juvenile comedy-fantasy about genie Ives coming out of magic bottle to serve Randall. Leading lady Eden fared better when she went into a lamp herself on TV.

Brass Legend, The (1956) 79m. *½ D: Gerd Oswald. Hugh O'Brian, Nancy Gates, Raymond Burr, Reba Tassell. Routine Western uplifted by Burr's villain role.

Brass Target (1978) C-111m. ** D: John Hough. John Cassavetes, Sophia Loren, George Kennedy, Max von Sydow, Robert Vaughn, Bruce Davison, Patrick McGoohan. Rambling thriller speculates that Gen. Patton (Kennedy) was assassinated just after WW2 because of major gold heist perpetrated by his subordinates. Unfocused storyline is major liability; von Sydow is major asset as the killer.

Bravados, The (1958) C-98m. *** D: Henry King. Gregory Peck, Joan Collins, Stephen Boyd, Albert Salmi. Compelling Western starring Peck, seeking four men who raped and killed his wife, discovering that he has become no better than those he hunts.

Brave Bulls, The (1951) 108m. *** D: Robert Rossen. Mel Ferrer, Miroslava, Anthony Quinn, Eugene Iglesias. Flavorful account of public and private life of a matador, based on Tom Lea book. Film admirably captures atmosphere of bullfighting.

Brave Warrior (1952) C-73m. *½ D: Spencer G. Bennet. Jon Hall, Jay Silverheels, Michael Ansara, Christine Larson. Inept yarn, set in 1800s Indiana, has Hall preventing Indian hostilities.

Bravos, The (1971) C-100m. TVM D: Ted Post. George Peppard, Peter Duel, Pernell Roberts, Belinda J. Montgomery, L. Q. Jones, Barry Brown, Vincent Van Patten. Standard Western centering around regular officer assigned to command small fort following end of Civil War. Average.

Bread, Love and Dreams (1954-Italian) 90m. *** D: Luigi Comencini. Vittorio De Sica, Gina Lollobrigida, Marisa Merlini, Roberto Risso. Pep-

pery comedy with spicy Gina vying for attention of town official De Sica.
Break in the Circle (1957-British) C-69m. *½ D: Val Guest. Forrest Tucker, Eva Bartok, Marius Goring, Guy Middleton. Unexciting chase tale has Tucker a boat owner thrust into helping to get scientist out of Communist Germany.
Break of Hearts (1935) 80m. **½ D: Philip Moeller. Katharine Hepburn, Charles Boyer, John Beal, Jean Hersholt, Sam Hardy. Struggling composer Hepburn marries renowned conductor Boyer in this stale but well-acted romantic drama.
Break to Freedom (1955-British) 88m. ** D: Lewis Gilbert. Anthony Steel, Jack Warner, Robert Beatty, William Sylvester, Michael Balfour. Typical P.O.W.s escape-from-German-camp, uplifted by restrained acting.
Breaker! Breaker! (1977) C-86m. BOMB D: Don Hulette. Chuck Norris, George Murdock, Terry O'Connor, Don Gentry. Cheap, stupid actioner with some unintentional comedy. Little made of the CB craze as trucker Norris (real-life Karate champ) searches for kid brother Michael Augenstein in corrupt Judge Murdock's speedtrap town.
Breakfast at Tiffany's (1961) C-115m. ***½ D: Blake Edwards. Audrey Hepburn, George Peppard, Patricia Neal, Buddy Ebsen, Mickey Rooney. Charming film from Truman Capote's story, with Hepburn as Holly Golightly, small-town girl who goes mod in N.Y. Dated trappings don't detract from high comedy and winning romance. Henry Mancini score includes Oscar-winning "Moon River."
Breakfast for Two (1937) 65m. **½ D: Alfred Santell. Barbara Stanwyck, Herbert Marshall, Glenda Farrell, Eric Blore, Frank Thomas, Donald Meek. Energetic Stanwyck helps Marshall's business career and falls in love with him; pleasant.
Breakfast in Hollywood (1946) 100m. *½ D: Harold Schuster. Tom Breneman, Bonita Granville, Beulah Bondi, Edward Ryan, Spike Jones and band. Uninspired film derived from radio series, focusing on romance of G.I. and his sweetheart, with predictable quarrels and eventual happy ending.
Breakheart Pass (1976) C-95m. *** D: Tom Gries. Charles Bronson, Ben Johnson, Richard Crenna, Jill Ireland, Charles Durning, Ed Lauter. Slambang action Western, with second

unit work by Yakima Canutt. Based on Alistair MacLean book and set mainly on a train, it has Bronson as an undercover agent seeking gun runners and confronting a false epidemic.
Breaking Away (1979) C-100m. ***½ D: Peter Yates. Dennis Christopher, Dennis Quaid, Daniel Stern, Jackie Earle Haley, Barbara Barrie, Paul Dooley. Winning, unpretentious film about four college-age friends in Bloomington, Indiana who don't know what to do with their lives; Dooley stands out in first-rate cast as Christopher's bewildered father. This sleeper hit really comes to life with an audience, may not play as well on TV. Steve Tesich's original screenplay won well-deserved Oscar.
Breaking Point, The (1950) 97m. ***½ D: Michael Curtiz. John Garfield, Patricia Neal, Phyllis Thaxter, Wallace Ford, Sherry Jackson. Highvoltage refilming of Hemingway's TO HAVE AND HAVE NOT, with Garfield as skipper so desperate for money he takes on illegal cargo. Garfield and mate Juano Hernandez give superb interpretations.
Breaking Point (1976-Canadian) C-92m. BOMB D: Bob Clark. Bo Svenson, Robert Culp, John Colicos, Belinda J. Montgomery, Stephen Young, Linda Sorenson. Svenson is pursued by Mafiosos after he testifies against them in court. Nothing new here.
Breaking the Sound Barrier (1952-British) 109m. ***½ D: David Lean. Ralph Richardson, Ann Todd, Nigel Patrick, John Austin. Grade-A documentary-style story of early days of jet planes, and men who tested them; Richardson particularly good.
Breaking Up (1978) C-100m. TVM D: Delbert Mann. Lee Remick, Granville Van Dusen, Vicki Dawson, David Stambaugh, Meg Mundy, Frank Latimore. Effective drama about a sophisticated suburbanite forced to drastically change her life when her husband walks out on her and the kids. Remick superior as ever; director Mann and writer Loring Mandel each Emmy Award-nominated. Above average.
Breaking Up Is Hard to Do (1979) C-150m. TVM D: Lou Antonio. Robert Conrad, Ted Bessell, Jeff Conaway, Billy Crystal, Tony Musante, David Ogden Stiers, Bonnie Franklin, Susan Sullivan. Arresting if overlong drama dealing with separation and divorce from

[89]

the man's point of view. The title comes from Neil Sedaka and Howard Greenfield's hit song, which Sedaka sings obligatorily over the credits. Above average.

Breakout (1959-British) **99m.** ****½** D: Don Chaffey. Richard Todd, Richard Attenborough, Michael Wilding, Dennis Price, Bernard Lee. Although format is now familiar, this remains an exciting story of British P.O.W.s attempting escapes from Axis prison camp during WW2. Fine performances all around. Retitled: DANGER WITHIN.

Breakout (1970) **C-100m. TVM** D: Richard Irving. James Drury, Kathryn Hays, Woody Strode, Sean Garrison, Red Buttons, Bert Freed. Prisoner Baker (Drury) creates two "foolproof" plans for escaping maximum security state pen so he can be reunited with wife (Hays) and $50,000 from bank robbery for which he was convicted. Good situations, adequate suspense. Above average.

Breakout (1975) **C-96m.** ******* D: Tom Gries. Charles Bronson, Robert Duvall, Jill Ireland, John Huston, Sheree North, Randy Quaid. Crisp action film generously laced with comedy touches has devil-may-care bush pilot Bronson taking on the job of spiriting Duvall, framed for murder, from a seedy Mexican prison.

Breakthrough (1950) **91m.** ****½** D: Lewis Seiler. David Brian, John Agar, Frank Lovejoy, Paul Picerni, William Self. Saga of men training for combat, their days of fighting and romancing; stark and satisfactory.

Breath of Scandal, A (1960) **C-98m.** ****** D: Michael Curtiz. Sophia Loren, John Gavin, Maurice Chevalier, Isabel Jeans, Angela Lansbury. Molnar's play OLYMPIA is limp costume vehicle for Loren, playing a princess romanced by American Gavin. Chevalier and Lansbury vainly try to pump some life into proceedings.

Breathless (1961-French) **89m.** ******* D: Jean-Luc Godard. Jean Seberg, Jean-Paul Belmondo, Daniel Boulanger, Liliane David. Belmondo is ideally suited to the carefree crook who has an affair with American Seberg, with tragic result. Good candid shots of Paris life.

Breezy (1973) **C-108m.** ****** D: Clint Eastwood. William Holden, Kay Lenz, Roger C. Carmel, Marj Dusay, Shelley Morrison, Joan Hotchkis. Jaded middle-ager finds Truth with a teen-aged hippie in sappy romance.

Fine performances by the leads only help up to a point.

Brenda Starr (1976) **C-78m. TVM** D: Mel Stuart. Jill St. John, Jed Allan, Sorrell Booke, Tabi Cooper, Victor Buono, Barbara Luna, Torin Thatcher. Intrepid comic strip newspaperwoman—played floridly by curvaceous St. John—becomes involved in voodoo, extortion, and strange doings in jungles of Brazil. Played too straight to be fun. Below average.

Brewster McCloud (1970) **C-101m.** ******* D: Robert Altman. Bud Cort, Sally Kellerman, Michael Murphy, William Windom, Shelley Duvall, Rene Auberjonois, Stacy Keach, John Schuck, Margaret Hamilton. Patently indescribable movie following exploits of owlish boy (Cort) whose ambition is to take wing and fly inside Houston Astrodome. Extremely bizarre; for certain tastes, extremely funny. Fans of director Altman have head start.

Brewster's Millions (1945) **79m.** ****½** D: Allan Dwan. Dennis O'Keefe, Helen Walker, Eddie "Rochester" Anderson, June Havoc, Gail Patrick, Mischa Auer. Bright comedy with fine cast; O'Keefe has to spend a million dollars quickly if he is to receive major inheritance.

Brian's Song (1970) **C-73m. TVM** D: Buzz Kulik. Billy Dee Williams, James Caan, Jack Warden, Judy Pace, Shelley Fabares. Exceptional film relating real-life relationship between Chicago Bears football players Brian Piccolo and Gayle Sayers, and tragedy which affects entire team when Piccolo develops cancer. A milestone of excellence in made-for-TV movies. Beautiful score by Michel Legrand.

Bribe, The (1949) **98m.** ****** D: Robert Z. Leonard. Robert Taylor, Ava Gardner, Charles Laughton, Vincent Price, John Hodiak. Taylor looks uncomfortable playing federal man who almost sacrifices all for sultry singer Gardner.

Bridal Path, The (1959-Scottish) **C-95m.** *****½** D: Frank Launder. Bill Travers, Bernadette O'Farrell, Alex MacKenzie, Eric Woodburn, Jack Lambert, John Rae. Charming, flavorful film of young islander who goes to Scottish mainland in search of a wife. Enhanced by beautiful scenery in color.

Bride and the Beast, The (1958) **78m.** BOMB D: Adrian Weiss. Charlotte

Austin, Lance Fuller, Johnny Roth, Steve Calvert. Set in the African jungle, title tells all about explorer's wife and the gorilla who fancies her.

Bride Came C.O.D., The (1941) 92m. ****½** D: William Keighley. James Cagney, Bette Davis, Stuart Erwin, Eugene Pallette, Jack Carson, George Tobias. Unlikely comedy team in vehicle made enjoyable only by their terrific personalities; he's a flier, she's a runaway bride.

Bride Comes Home, The (1935) 82m. ****½** D: Wesley Ruggles. Claudette Colbert, Fred MacMurray, Robert Young, William Collier, Sr., Edgar Kennedy. Breezy fluff with wealthy Young competing against roughneck MacMurray for Claudette's affections in vintage comedy.

Bride for Sale (1949) 87m. ****½** D: William D. Russell. Claudette Colbert, Robert Young, George Brent, Max Baer. Veteran star trio carries on despite thin story of female tax expert (Colbert) seeking wealthy spouse.

Bride Goes Wild, The (1948) 98m. ****½** D: Norman Taurog. Van Johnson, June Allyson, Butch Jenkins, Hume Cronyn, Una Merkel, Arlene Dahl. Silly, sometimes funny tale of Johnson pretending to be Jenkins' father in order to woo Allyson; nice cast does its best.

Bride Is Much Too Beautiful, The (1958-French) 90m. ****½** D: Fred Surin. Brigitte Bardot, Micheline Presle, Louis Jourdan, Marcel Amont. Gallic sex romp with BB a farm girl who becomes famous magazine model.

Bride of Frankenstein (1935) 75m. *****½** D: James Whale. Boris Karloff, Colin Clive, Valerie Hobson, Elsa Lanchester, Ernest Thesiger, Una O'Connor, O. P. Heggie, Dwight Frye. Even better than FRANKENSTEIN, this witty, eye-filling sequel is a superb film any way you slice it. O'Connor's comedy relief is annoying, but monster's visit with blind man, mad-doctor Thesiger's dialogue, and creation of monster's mate more than compensate.

Bride of Vengeance (1949) 91m. ****** D: Mitchell Leisen. Paulette Goddard, John Lund, Macdonald Carey, Raymond Burr, Albert Dekker, Rose Hobart. Medium-warm costumer of medieval Italy with Goddard as the Borgia sent to do mischief but instead falling in love.

Bride Walks Out, The (1936) 75m.

** D: Leigh Jason. Barbara Stanwyck, Gene Raymond, Robert Young, Ned Sparks, Helen Broderick. Flimsy comedy; stars do their best with Stanwyck and Raymond trying to survive on his meager salary.

Bride Wore Black, The (1968-French-Italian) C-107m. ******* D: Francois Truffaut. Jeanne Moreau, Jean Claude Brialy, Michel Bouquet, Charles Denner, Michel Lonsdale, Alexandra Stewart. Moreau takes revenge on the man who shot down her husband on their wedding day; reasonably involving psychological thriller with Hitchcock overtones, right down to Bernard Herrmann's quirky score.

Bride Wore Boots, The (1946) 86m. ****** D: Irving Pichel. Barbara Stanwyck, Robert Cummings, Diana Lynn, Peggy Wood, Robert Benchley, Natalie Wood, Willie Best. Witless comedy of horse-loving Stanwyck saddled by Cummings, who does his best to win her total affection; they all try but script is weak.

Bride Wore Red, The (1937) 103m. ****** D: Dorothy Arzner. Joan Crawford, Franchot Tone, Robert Young, Billie Burke, Reginald Owen. More fashion show than plot in this typical glossy Crawford soaper of girl who works her way up society ladder.

Brides of Dracula, The (1960-British) C-85m. ****½** D: Terence Fisher. Peter Cushing, Martita Hunt, Yvonne Monlaur, Freda Jackson. Above-average entry in Hammer horror series, with the famed vampire's disciple seeking female victims.

Brides of Fu Manchu, The (1966-British) C-94m. ****½** D: Don Sharp. Christopher Lee, Douglas Wilmer, Marie Versini, Tsai Chin. Fu doesn't give up easily, still bent on conquering the world by forcing scientists to develop powerful ray gun. Sequel to FACE OF FU MANCHU, not as good, still diverting.

Bridge, The (1960-German) 100m. ******* D: Bernhard Wicki. Folker Bohnet, Fritz Wepper, Michael Hinz, Frank Glaubrecht. Unrelenting account of teen-age boys drafted into the German army in 1945, as last resort effort to stem Allied invasion.

Bridge at Remagen, The (1969) C-115m. ****½** D: John Guillermin. George Segal, Robert Vaughn, Ben Gazzara, Bradford Dillman, E.G. Marshall, Peter Van Eyck. Well-acted film about group of Allies defending bridge toward the end of

WW2 can't quite overcome familiar plot line; lots of good explosions for those who care.

Bridge of San Luis Rey, The (1944) 85m. ** D: Rowland V. Lee. Lynn Bari, Nazimova, Louis Calhern, Akim Tamiroff, Francis Lederer, Blanche Yurka, Donald Woods. Thornton Wilder's moody, unusual story of five people meeting doom on a rickety bridge makes a slow-moving film.

Bridge on the River Kwai, The (1957-British) C-161m. **** D: David Lean. William Holden, Alec Guinness, Jack Hawkins, Sessue Hayakawa, Geoffrey Horne, James Donald. British soldiers in Japanese prison camp build bridge as futile exercise while Holden plots to destroy it. Psychological battles of will combined with high-powered action sequences make this Oscar-winning film a blockbuster.

Bridge to the Sun (1961) 113m. *** D: Etienne Perier. Carroll Baker, James Shigeta, James Yagi. Well-intentioned telling of Southern girl Baker who marries Japanese diplomat Shigeta and moves to Japan at outbreak of WW2.

Bridge Too Far, A (1977-British) C-175m. ** D: Richard Attenborough. Dirk Bogarde, James Caan, Michael Caine, Sean Connery, Edward Fox, Elliott Gould, Gene Hackman, Anthony Hopkins, Hardy Kruger, Laurence Olivier, Ryan O'Neal, Maximilian Schell, Liv Ullmann, Arthur Hill. Lifeless, overproduced version of the fine Cornelius Ryan book about disastrous 1944 Allied airdrop behind German lines in Holland.

Bridger (1976) C-100m. TVM D: David Lowell Rich. James Wainwright, Ben Murphy, Dirk Blocker, Sally Field, John Anderson, William Windom. Predictable western about legendary mountain man Jim Bridger (Wainwright) who blazes a trail through the Rockies to California in 1830. Cliches and stereotypes bury the action element; subsequently cut to 78m. Average.

Bridges at Toko-Ri, The (1954) C-103m. ***½ D: Mark Robson. William Holden, Grace Kelly, Fredric March, Mickey Rooney, Robert Strauss. Top-flight adventure based on James Michener's book of American flier and family in Korean conflict.

Brief Encounter (1946-British) 85m. **** D: David Lean. Celia Johnson, Trevor Howard, Stanley Holloway, Cyril Raymond, Joyce Carey. Touching interlude of two married people meeting in a train station cafe and their short but poignant romance; effective use of Rachmaninoff's piano concerto highlights believable love affair.

Brief Vacation, A (1975-Italian) C-106m. *** D: Vittorio De Sica. Florinda Bolkan, Renato Salvatori, Daniel Quenaud, Jose Maria Prada, Teresa Gimpera. Poorly educated woman leaves terrible job, despicable in-laws, and callous husband for a comparatively pleasant stay in a TB sanitorium. De Sica's last film benefits from Bolkan's knowing performance.

Brigadoon (1954) C-108m. *** D: Vincente Minnelli. Gene Kelly, Van Johnson, Cyd Charisse, Elaine Stewart, Barry Jones, Hugh Laing. Americans Kelly and Johnson discover magical Scottish village in this entertaining filmization of Lerner & Loewe Broadway hit. Overlooked among 1950s musicals, it may lack innovations but has its own quiet charm, and lovely score.

Brigand, The (1952) C-94m. ** D: Phil Karlson. Anthony Dexter, Anthony Quinn, Gale Robbins, Jody Lawrance. Dexter is lookalike for king and becomes involved with court intrigue; flat costumer.

Brigand of Kandahar, The (1965-British) C-81m. **½ D: John Gilling. Ronald Lewis, Oliver Reed, Duncan Lamont, Yvonne Romain, Catherine Woodville. Mostly nonsense set on British outpost in 1850s India with rampaging natives; good cast tries hard.

Brigham Young—Frontiersman (1940) 114m. ** D: Henry Hathaway. Tyrone Power, Linda Darnell, Dean Jagger, Brian Donlevy, John Carradine, Jane Darwell, Jean Rogers, Mary Astor, Vincent Price. Well-intentioned but ludicrous depiction of Mormon leader with Jagger nominally in the lead, focus shifting to tepid romance between Power and Darnell; Astor all wrong as homespun wife.

Bright Eyes (1934) 83m. **½ D: David Butler. Shirley Temple, James Dunn, Judith Allen, Jane Withers, Lois Wilson, Charles Sellon. Early Shirley, and pretty good, with juvenile villainy from Withers in tale of custody battle over recently orphaned Temple. Includes "On the Good Ship Lollipop."

Bright Leaf (1950) 110m. **½ D: Michael Curtiz. Gary Cooper, Lauren Bacall, Patricia Neal, Jack Carson, Donald Crisp. Loose chronicle of 19th-century tobacco farmer (Cooper) building successful cigarette empire, seeking revenge on old enemies and finding romance.

Bright Lights (1935) 83m. ** D: Busby Berkeley. Joe E. Brown, Ann Dvorak, Patricia Ellis, William Gargan, Joseph Cawthorn, Arthur Treacher. Rags-to-riches show business tale of husband and wife separating while trying to hit it big. Entertaining, but full of clichés.

Bright Road (1953) 69m. ** D: Gerald Mayer. Dorothy Dandridge, Harry Belafonte, Robert Horton, Philip Hepburn. Well-intentioned but labored tale of Negro teacher in small Southern town who tries to solve her young pupils' problems.

Bright Victory (1951) 97m. *** D: Mark Robson. Arthur Kennedy, Peggy Dow, Julia Adams, James Edwards. Touching account of blinded ex-soldier who slowly readjusts to civilian life, even finding love. Potentially sticky subject handled well, with Kennedy excellent in lead role.

Brighton Strangler, The (1945) 67m. ** D: Max Nosseck. John Loder, June Duprez, Michael St. Angel, Miles Mander, Rose Hobart, Gilbert Emery. Strained thriller of demented stage actor Loder with a strangling complex, set in England.

Brimstone (1949) C-90m. ** D: Joseph Kane. Rod Cameron, Walter Brennan, Adrian Booth, Forrest Tucker, Jack Holt. Usual account of cattle-rustling and law enforcer who brings outlaws to justice.

Bring Me the Head of Alfredo Garcia (1974) C-112m. ** D: Sam Peckinpah. Warren Oates, Isela Vega, Gig Young, Robert Webber, Helmut Dantine, Emilio Fernandez, Kris Kristofferson. American piano player in Mexico gets involved with a smorgasbord of psychos; sub-par bloodbath doesn't even have the usual Peckinpah fast pace. Beware of cuts.

Bringing Up Baby (1938) 102m. *** D: Howard Hawks. Katharine Hepburn, Cary Grant, Charlie Ruggles, Barry Fitzgerald, May Robson. Anthropologist Grant gets mixed up with dizzy Hepburn and pet leopard. Fast-moving screwball comedy shows stars in peak form.

Brink's Job, The (1978) C-103m. *** D: William Friedkin. Peter Falk, Peter Boyle, Allen Goorwitz, Warren Oates, Gena Rowlands, Paul Sorvino, Sheldon Leonard. Entertaining, comically oriented account of the infamous 1950 Boston heist, masterminded by Falk and motley gang of accomplices. Excellent period and location flavor.

Brinks: The Great Robbery (1976) C-100m. TVM D: Marvin Chomsky. Carl Betz, Stephen Collins, Burr DeBenning, Michael Gazzo, Cliff Gorman, Darren McGavin, Art Metrano, Leslie Nielsen, Jenny O'Hara. Legendary Boston Brinks' holdup of January 17, 1950, is meticulously restaged, masterminded by McGavin and Gorman, and judged the perfect crime until solved by the FBI. Average.

Britannia Mews SEE: **Forbidden Street, The**

British Agent (1934) 81m. **½ D: Michael Curtiz. Kay Francis, Leslie Howard, William Gargan, Philip Reed. Howard is lead character in peril while in 1910 Russia, falling in love with slinky spy Francis. Good stars in plush blend of spying and romance.

British Intelligence (1940) 62m. ** D: Terry Morse. Boris Karloff, Margaret Lindsay, Maris Wrixon, Holmes Herbert, Leonard Mudie, Bruce Lester. American nonsense about double-agent Lindsay encountering butler-spy Karloff in British official's home; far-fetched story. Remake of THREE FACES EAST (1930).

Broad-Minded (1931) 72m. **½ D: Mervyn LeRoy. Joe E. Brown, William Collier, Jr., Margaret Livingston, Thelma Todd, Bela Lugosi, Ona Munson, Holmes Herbert. Pleasant Brown comedy with added spice of lovely Todd and hilarious cameo by Lugosi as man whose hot dog was stolen.

Broadway (1942) 91m. *** D: William A. Seiter. George Raft, Pat O'Brien, Janet Blair, Broderick Crawford, Marjorie Rambeau, S. Z. Sakall. Raft recalls his days as a nightclub hoofer in this Prohibition era yarn (remake of 1929 film), full of colorful characters and incidents but not made with an eye toward believability. O'Brien is tough copper, Crawford a ruthless gangster.

Broadway Bad (1933) 61m. **½ D: Sidney Lanfield. Joan Blondell, Ricardo Cortez, Ginger Rogers, Adrienne Ames. Chorus girl Blondell is unjustly maligned by husband, decides to milk bad publicity for all it's worth. A 1930s soap given first-class treatment.

Broadway Gondolier (1935) 98m. **½ D: Lloyd Bacon. Dick Powell, Joan Blondell, Adolphe Menjou, Louise Fazenda, William Gargan, Grant Mitchell. Powell goes globetrotting so he'll be discovered by famous producer. Songs include: "Lulu's Back in Town."

Broadway Limited (1941) 74m. **⁻ D: Gordon Douglas. Dennis O'Keefe, Victor McLaglen, Marjorie Woodworth, ZaSu Pitts, Patsy Kelly, George E. Stone, Leonid Kinsky. Considering cast, a big disappointment, though innocuous entertainment: florid director Kinsky makes his new star (Woodworth) the center of publicity stunt that backfires.

Broadway Melody (1929) 104m. **½ D: Harry Beaumont. Bessie Love, Anita Page, Charles King, Jed Prouty, Kenneth Thomson, Edward Dillon, Mary Doran. Early talkie musical of putting-on-the-show is basis of curio with good score by Arthur Freed and Nacio Herb Brown: "You Were Meant For Me," "Wedding of the Painted Doll," etc., and Cohan's "Give My Regards To Broadway." Some sequences originally in color.

Broadway Melody of 1936 (1935) 110m. *** D: Roy Del Ruth. Jack Benny, Eleanor Powell, Robert Taylor, Una Merkel, Sid Silvers, Buddy Ebsen. Pleasant musicomedy with Winchell-like columnist Benny trying to frame producer Taylor via dancer Powell, whose solo spots are pure delight. Arthur Freed-Nacio Herb Brown songs: "You Are My Lucky Star," "Broadway Rhythm," "I've Got A Feelin' You're Foolin'."

Broadway Melody of 1938 (1937) 110m. **½ D: Roy Del Ruth. Robert Taylor, Eleanor Powell, Judy Garland, Sophie Tucker, Binnie Barnes, Buddy Ebsen, Billy Gilbert, Raymond Walburn. Not up to 1936 MELODY, with tuneful but forgettable songs, overbearing Tucker, and elephantine finale. Powell's dancing is great and Garland sings "Dear Mr. Gable."

Broadway Melody of 1940 (1940) 102m. *** D: Norman Taurog. Fred Astaire, George Murphy, Eleanor Powell, Frank Morgan, Ian Hunter, Florence Rice. Friendship and rivalry between dance partners Astaire and

Murphy sparks this delightful, underrated MGM musical, with hilarious vignettes, fine performance from Astaire, outstanding Cole Porter songs, and matchless Astaire-Powell numbers like "Begin the Beguine." If only they'd tie up the plot a bit sooner.

Broadway Rhythm (1944) C-114m. ** D: Roy Del Ruth. George Murphy, Ginny Simms, Charles Winninger, Gloria De Haven, Nancy Walker, Ben Blue, Tommy Dorsey and Orch. Tedious, overlong MGM musical with plot (ex-vaudevillian Winninger at odds with producer-son Murphy) getting in the way of some good songs like "Amor," "All the Things You Are."

Broadway Serenade (1939) 114m. ** D: Robert Z. Leonard. Jeanette MacDonald, Lew Ayres, Ian Hunter, Frank Morgan, Rita Johnson, Virginia Grey, William Gargan, Katharine Alexander. Mediocre musical of songwriter Ayres and wife, singer MacDonald, having careers split up their marriage.

Brock's Last Case (1972) C-100m. TVM D: David Lowell Rich. Richard Widmark, Henry Darrow, Beth Brickell, David Huddleston, Will Geer, John Anderson, Michael Burns. N.Y.C. policeman disenchanted with big city life relocates in small town looking for peace and quiet but finds himself in same predicament. Decent premise doesn't work out. Average.

Broken Arrow (1950) C-93m. *** D: Delmer Daves. James Stewart, Jeff Chandler, Debra Paget, Will Geer, Jay Silverheels. Authentic study of 1870s Apache Chief Cochise (Chandler) and ex-Army man (Stewart) trying to seek accord between feuding redskins and whites. Flavorful and effective; good action sequences.

Broken Blossoms (1919) 68m. **½ D: D. W. Griffith. Lillian Gish, Richard Barthelmess, Donald Crisp, Arthur Howard, Edward Piel. Dated but lovely film of Chinaman Barthelmess protecting frail Gish from clutches of evil Crisp; still creates a mood sustained by sensitive performances. One of Griffith's more modest, and more successful, films.

Broken Lance (1954) C-96m. ***½ D: Edward Dmytryk. Spencer Tracy, Robert Wagner, Jean Peters, Richard Widmark. Tracy is superlative in tight-knit script about patriarchal rancher who finds he's losing control of his cattle empire and his family is fragmenting into warring factions; sharply photographed. Remake of HOUSE OF STRANGERS with Tracy in the Edward G. Robinson role.

Broken Lullaby (1932) **77m.** ******* D: Ernst Lubitsch. Lionel Barrymore, Nancy Carroll, Phillips Holmes, ZaSu Pitts, Lucien Littlefield, Emma Dunn. Retitled: THE MAN I KILLED. Excellent drama of French soldier who feels guilty for killing German during war, then falls in love with dead man's sweetheart.

Bronco Buster (1952) **C-81m.** ****½** D: Budd Boetticher. John Lund, Scott Brady, Joyce Holden, Chill Wills, Casey Tibbs. Minor story of rodeo star Lund helping Brady learn the ropes, but forced to fight him for Holden's love. Good rodeo action.

Brood, The (1979-Canadian) **C-90m.** BOMB D: David Cronenberg. Oliver Reed, Samantha Eggar, Art Hindle, Cindy Hinds, Nuala Fitzgerald, Susan Hogan. Eggar eats her own afterbirth while midget clones beat grandparents and lovely young schoolteachers to death with mallets. It's a big, wide, wonderful world we live in, isn't it?

Broth of a Boy (1959-Irish) **77m.** ****½** D: George Pollock. Barry Fitzgerald, Harry Brogan, Tony Wright, June Thorburn, Eddie Golden. British TV producer hits upon scheme of filming birthday celebration of oldest man in the world, Irish villager Fitzgerald. The latter's battle to get cut of the pie is vehicle for study of human nature; quietly effective.

Brother, Can You Spare a Dime? (1975) **103m.** ****½** D: Philippe Mora. Documentary on 1930s has fuzzy point of view, and no narration to tie footage together; it also mixes newsreels and Hollywood clips. If you know and like the period, the footage will speak for itself and provide a certain measure of entertainment.

Brother John (1972) **C-94m.** ******* D: James Goldstone. Sidney Poitier, Will Geer, Bradford Dillman, Beverly Todd, Paul Winfield. Highly entertaining tale of the Messiah's return —only no one knows that he's come, and that he's black.

Brother Orchid (1940) **91m.** ******* D: Lloyd Bacon. Edward G. Robinson, Ann Sothern, Humphrey Bogart, Ralph Bellamy, Donald Crisp, Allen Jenkins. Farfetched but entertaining yarn of racketeer Robinson who

seeks "the real class" in life. Sothern delightful as his ever-faithful girlfriend.

Brother Rat (1938) **90m.** ******* D: William Keighley. Priscilla Lane, Wayne Morris, Johnnie Davis, Jane Bryan, Eddie Albert, Ronald Reagan, Jane Wyman, William Tracy. Comedy of three pals at Virginia Military Institute isn't as fresh as it was thirty years ago, but still remains entertaining, with enthusiastic performances by all. Remade as ABOUT FACE.

Brother Rat and a Baby (1940) **87m.** ****½** D: Ray Enright. Priscilla Lane, Wayne Morris, Eddie Albert, Jane Bryan, Ronald Reagan, Jane Wyman. Sassy follow-up to BROTHER RAT is not the same success, but still fun with three comrades graduating military school.

Brother Sun, Sister Moon (1973) **C-121m.** ****½** D: Franco Zeffirelli. Graham Faulkner, Judi Bowker, Leigh Lawson, Alec Guinness, Valentina Cortese, Kenneth Carnham. Zeffirelli's wide-eyed youth-oriented slant on Francis of Assisi story runs hot and cold; some delicate, lovely scenes, but other ideas don't always come across. Songs by Donovan.

Brotherhood, The (1968) **C-98m.** ******* D: Martin Ritt. Kirk Douglas, Alex Cord, Irene Papas, Luther Adler, Susan Strasberg, Murray Hamilton. Excellent story of Mafia in changing times; tradition-bound Douglas clashes with younger brother Cord who feels no ties to old-fashioned dictates. Pre-GODFATHER, but in the same league.

Brotherhood of Satan (1971) **C-92m.** ****½** D: Bernard McEveety. Strother Martin, L. Q. Jones, Charles Bateman, Ahna Capri, Charles Robinson. Witches' coven takes over town in this horrifying little terror tale.

Brotherhood of the Bell (1970) **100m.** TVM D: Paul Wendkos. Glenn Ford, Rosemary Forsyth, Dean Jagger, Maurice Evans, William Conrad. Ambitious but hollow story of Ford determined to investigate strange secret fraternity which is bigger and more powerful than he'd imagined.

Brotherhood of the Yakuza: SEE Yakuza, The

Brotherly Love (1970-British) **C-112m.** ******* D: J. Lee Thompson. Peter O'Toole, Susannah York, Michael Craig, Harry Andrews, Cyril Cusack. Very funny study of strange relationships in an upper-class British household. O'Toole and York are delightful.

Brothers (1977) C-104m. **½ D: Arthur Barron. Bernie Casey, Vonetta McGee, Ron O'Neal, Renny Roker, Stu Gilliam, John Lehne. Well-intentioned story based on relationship between militant professor Angela Davis and literate black convict George Jackson during 1960s. Sloppy filmmaking and awkward scripting diminish impact of film's better moments.

Brothers in Law, The (1957-British) 94m. **½ D: Roy Boulting. Richard Attenborough, Ian Carmichael, Terry-Thomas, Jill Adams, Miles Malleson, Raymond Huntley. Misadventures of a young lawyer (Carmichael) fill this amiable British comedy.

Brothers Karamazov, The (1958) C-146m. *** D: Richard Brooks. Yul Brynner, Maria Schell, Claire Bloom, Lee J. Cobb, Richard Basehart, William Shatner, Albert Salmi. Set in 19th-century Russia, film version of Dostoyevsky's tragedy revolving about death of a dominating father (Cobb) and effect on his sons: fun-seeking Brynner, scholarly Basehart, religious Shatner, and epileptic Salmi. Exceptionally well-scripted by Brooks.

Brothers O'Toole, The (1973) C-90m. ** D: Richard Erdman. John Astin, Steve Carlson, Pat Carroll, Hans Conried, Lee Meriwether, Allyn Joslyn, Jesse White. Strictly for the kids is this comedy Western. Actor turned director Erdman has a bit.

Brothers Rico, The (1957) 92m. **½ D: Phil Karlson. Richard Conte, Dianne Foster, Kathryn Grant, Larry Gates, James Darren. Incisive gangster yarn; Conte comes to N.Y.C. to counteract nationwide criminal gang's plot to eliminate his two brothers. Based on Georges Simenon novel, remade for TV as FAMILY RICO.

Browning Version, The (1951-British) 90m. ***½ D: Anthony Asquith. Michael Redgrave, Jean Kent, Nigel Patrick, Wilfrid Hyde-White. Ronald Howard, Bill Travers. Redgrave superb as middle-aged boarding school teacher who realizes he's a failure, with an unfaithful wife and a new teaching position he doesn't want. Cast does full justice to Rattigan's play.

Brute Force (1947) 98m. ***½ D: Jules Dassin. Burt Lancaster, Hume Cronyn, Charles Bickford, Yvonne De Carlo, Ann Blyth, Ella Raines, Howard Duff, Whit Bissell, Jeff Corey, Sam Levene. Tingling, hardbitten prison film with its few cliches punched across solidly. Brutal captain Cronyn is utterly despicable, but you *know* he's going to get it in the end.

Brute Man (1946) 60m. *½ D: Jean Yarbrough. Tom Neal, Rondo Hatton, Jane Adams, Peter Whitney, Jan Wiley. Programmer trivia about manhunt to capture an insane man running rampant.

Buccaneer, The (1938) 124m. *** D: Cecil B. DeMille. Fredric March, Franciska Gaal, Margot Grahame, Akim Tamiroff, Walter Brennan, Anthony Quinn. Typically entertaining epic-scale saga from DeMille, with florid performance by March as pirate-hero Jean Lafitte, who aids American cause during War of 1812. Good storytelling, and good fun.

Buccaneer, The (1958) C-121m. *** D: Anthony Quinn. Yul Brynner, Charlton Heston, Claire Bloom, Charles Boyer. Starchy swashbuckler retelling events during War of 1812 when Andrew Jackson (Heston) is forced to rely on buccaneer Lafitte (Brynner) to stem the British invasion; action is spotty but splashy.

Buccaneer's Girl (1950) C-77m. ** D: Frederick de Cordova. Yvonne De Carlo, Philip Friend, Elsa Lanchester, Andrea King, Henry Daniell. Pure escapism with De Carlo cavorting as New Orleans singer and later leading forces to free pirate-friend from prison.

Buchanan Rides Alone (1958) C-78m. *** D: Budd Boetticher. Randolph Scott, Craig Stevens, Barry Kelley, Tol Avery, Peter Whitney, Manuel Rojas. Scott runs afoul of corrupt family in control of border town; taut B Western never runs out of plot twists.

Buck and the Preacher (1972) C-102m. **½ D: Sidney Poitier. Sidney Poitier, Harry Belafonte, Ruby Dee, Cameron Mitchell, Nita Talbot. Black-oriented Western of "hustler" preacher is long on getting to the action and short on staying with it. Good characterizations are major point of interest.

Buck Benny Rides Again (1940) 82m. *** D: Mark Sandrich. Jack Benny, Ellen Drew, Andy Devine, Phil Harris, Virginia Dale, Dennis Day, Eddie "Rochester" Anderson. Amusing

Western spoof with Jack trying to convince Drew that he's a 100% cowboy. Radio colleagues help out, with Rochester supplying steady flow of funny dialogue.

Buck Privates (1941) 84m. **½ D: Arthur Lubin. Bud Abbott, Lou Costello, Lee Bowman, Alan Curtis, Andrews Sisters, Jane Frazee, Nat Pendleton. Dated but engaging Army opus with Bud and Lou accidentally enlisting. Brassy songs and subplots get in the way, but A&C's routines are among their best; their first starring film.

Buck Privates Come Home (1947) 77m. *** D: Charles Barton. Bud Abbott, Lou Costello, Tom Brown, Joan Fulton (Shawlee), Nat Pendleton, Beverly Simmons, Don Beddoe. One of A&C's most enjoyable romps has boys returning to civilian life and trying to smuggle a young European orphan into this country. Climactic chase a highlight.

Buck Rogers SEE: **Destination Saturn**

Buck Rogers in the 25th Century (1979) C-89m. ** D: Daniel Haller. Gil Gerard, Pamela Hensley, Erin Gray, Tim O'Connor, Henry Silva, Joseph Wiseman. The legendary space hero returns, decked out in contemporary glibness, trying to prove he's not in league with intergalactic pirates. Much of the hardware and gadgetry (along with some footage) is from TV's expensive dud, BATTLESTAR GALACTICA, turned out by the same producers.

Bucket of Blood, A (1959) 66m. **½ D: Roger Corman. Dick Miller, Barboura Morris, Antony Carbone, Ed Nelson. Oddball period-piece from beatnik era with slow-witted character impressing coffeehouse friends with "sculptures" which are a little *too* lifelike.

Buckskin (1968) C-97m. *½ D: Michael Moore. Barry Sullivan, Joan Caulfield, Wendell Corey, Lon Chaney, John Russell, Barbara Hale, Barton MacLane, Leo Gordon. Landbaron Corey tries to force homesteaders out of territory, but Marshal Sullivan is there to stop him in typical Western.

Bucktown (1975) C-94m. *½ D: Arthur Marks. Fred Williamson, Pam Grier, Thalmus Rasulala, Tony King, Bernie Hamilton, Art Lund. Repellent blaxploitation picture about war between whites and blacks in corruption-filled Southern town,

which intensifies when blacks get into office and make things even worse.

Bud and Lou (1978) C-100m. TVM D: Robert C. Thompson. Harvey Korman, Buddy Hackett, Michele Lee, Arte Johnson, Robert Reed. Major intent of this hackneyed biopic on Abbott and Costello is portraying Lou as an s.o.b., but its fatal flaw is Hackett and Korman's painfully unfunny renderings of classic A&C routines. Below average.

Buddy Holly Story, The (1978) C-114m. *** D: Steve Rash. Gary Busey, Don Stroud, Charles Martin Smith, Bill Jordan, Maria Richwine, Conrad Janis. Standard Hollywood bio electrified by Busey's performance as 1950s rock 'n' roll performer who created influential new sound. Busey, Stroud, and Smith actually sing and play their instruments, live-on-film, which gives this movie a uniquely vibrant soundtrack.

Buffalo Bill (1944) C-90m. **½ D: William Wellman. Joel McCrea, Maureen O'Hara, Linda Darnell, Thomas Mitchell, Anthony Quinn, Edgar Buchanan, Chief Thundercloud, Sidney Blackmer. Colorful biography of legendary Westerner should have been much better, but still provides some fun and has good cast.

Buffalo Bill and the Indians, or Sitting Bull's History Lesson (1976) C-120m. ** D: Robert Altman. Paul Newman, Joel Grey, Kevin McCarthy, Burt Lancaster, Geraldine Chaplin, Harvey Keitel, Frank Kaquitts, Will Sampson. Altman makes the point that Buffalo Bill was a flamboyant fraud, then belabors it for two hours. Not without interest, but definitely the director's dullest movie.

Bug (1975) C-100m. ** D: Jeannot Szwarc. Bradford Dillman, Joanna Miles, Richard Gilliland, Jamie Smith Jackson, Alan Fudge, Jesse Vint. Earthquake releases a disgusting variety of beetles from the earth, capable of setting people, animals, and objects on fire. Spray your set with Raid after watching this one.

Bugle Sounds, The (1941) 110m. ** D: S. Sylvan Simon. Wallace Beery, Marjorie Main, Lewis Stone, George Bancroft, Henry O'Neill, Donna Reed. Old-time officer Beery objects to progress in the army, bails cavalry out of trouble in finale. The usual.

Bugles in the Afternoon (1952) C-85m. **½ D: Roy Rowland. Ray Milland, Forrest Tucker, George Reeves, Helena Carter, Gertrude Michael. Standard tale of man branded coward (Milland) during Civil War, with Little Big Horn finale.

Bugs Bunny/Road Runner Movie, The (1979) C-92m. **½ D: Chuck Jones, Phil Monroe. Bugs Bunny, Daffy Duck, Road Runner, Wile E. Coyote, Elmer Fudd, Porky Pig. New footage of Bugs Bunny surrounds this compilation of Chuck Jones' best Warner Bros. cartoon shorts. Not the best way to see these wonderful films, as the repetition grows tiresome, but still worthwhile.

Bugsy Malone (1976-British) C-93m. **½ D: Alan Parker. Scott Baio, Florrie Dugger, Jodie Foster, John Cassisi, Martin Lev. Unique musical spoof of Prohibition-era gangster films with all-kiddie cast; script cliches are intact, but the machine-guns shoot marshmallows instead of bullets. Beautiful production cannot escape coyness and doesn't hold up; plastic rendition of Paul Williams' score doesn't help.

Bull Fighters, The (1945) 61m. ** D: Mal St. Clair. Stan Laurel, Oliver Hardy, Margo Woode, Richard Lane, Carol Andrews, Diosa Costello. One of better L&H later works, involving mistaken identity (Stan is lookalike for famous matador), subsequent nonsense in bull ring.

Bulldog Drummond Hugh "Bulldog" Drummond, an ex-British army officer who yearned for adventure, was created in 1919 by "Sapper" (Herman Cyril McNeile); the character's film possibilities were realized and Drummond was the subject of several silent films. The definitive BULLDOG DRUMMOND was made in 1929 with dashing Ronald Colman in the lead and Claud Allister as his constant companion Algy; Colman also starred in a delightful sequel, BULLDOG DRUMMOND STRIKES BACK, but unfortunately neither of these is on TV. The major series was made in the late 1930s by Paramount, with John Howard as Drummond, John Barrymore as Inspector Neilson of Scotland Yard, Reginald Denny as Algy, E. E. Clive as the butler Tenny, and a variety of girls as love interest for Howard. These were brief (around one hour), entertaining mysteries with such formidable villains as J. Carrol Naish, Anthony Quinn, George Zucco, and Eduardo Ciannelli. In the late 1940s Ron Randell and Tom Conway did two Drummonds each, which weren't bad but didn't catch on. The last one was CALLING BULLDOG DRUMMOND, a 1951 film with Walter Pidgeon in the lead and David Tomlinson as Algy; it was an enjoyable, slickly made film; it was only unfortunate that no one saw fit to continue the series beyond this point. (One attempt to revive the character was a flop: DEADLIER THAN THE MALE, made in 1967, with Richard Johnson.) Other older films that still pop up include such Drummonds as John Lodge and Ray Milland doing their bit in unremarkable but entertaining vehicles.

Bulldog Drummond at Bay (1937-British) 62m. D: Norman Lee. John Lodge, Dorothy Mackaill, Victor Jory, Claud Allister, Hugh Miller, Marie O'Neill, Brian Buchel.

Bulldog Drummond at Bay (1947) 70m. D: Sidney Salkow. Ron Randell, Anita Louise, Pat O'Moore, Terry Kilburn, Holmes Herbert.

Bulldog Drummond Comes Back (1937) 64m. D: Louis King. John Barrymore, John Howard, Louise Campbell, Reginald Denny, E. E. Clive, J. Carrol Naish, John Sutton.

Bulldog Drummond Escapes (1937) 65m. D: James Hogan. Ray Milland, Guy Standing, Heather Angel, Porter Hall, Reginald Denny, E. E. Clive, Fay Holden, Clyde Cook, Walter Kingsford.

Bulldog Drummond in Africa (1938) 60m. D: Louis King. John Howard, Heather Angel, H. B. Warner, J. Carrol Naish, Reginald Denny, Anthony Quinn, Michael Brooke.

Bulldog Drummond Strikes Back (1947) 65m. D: Frank McDonald. Ron Randell, Gloria Henry, Pat O'Moore, Anabel Shaw, Terry Kilburn.

Bulldog Drummond's Bride (1939) 55m. D: James Hogan. John Howard, Heather Angel, H. B. Warner, Reginald Denny, Elizabeth Patterson, Eduardo Ciannelli.

Bulldog Drummond's Peril (1938) 66m. D: James Hogan. John Barrymore, John Howard, Louise Campbell, Reginald Denny, E. E. Clive,

Porter Hall, Elizabeth Patterson, Nydia Westman.

Bulldog Drummond's Revenge (1937) 60m. D: Louis King. John Barrymore, John Howard, Louise Campbell, Reginald Denny, E. E. Clive, Nydia Westman, Lucien Littlefield, John Sutton.

Bulldog Drummond's Secret Police (1939) 56m. D: James Hogan. John Howard, Heather Angel, H. B. Warner, Reginald Denny, Leo G. Carroll, Elizabeth Patterson.

Bulldog Jack SEE: Alias Bulldog Drummond.

Bullet for a Badman (1964) C-80m. **½ D: R. G. Springsteen. Audie Murphy, Darren McGavin, Ruta Lee, Skip Homeier, George Tobias, Bob Steele. Another revenge tale involving outlaw, his ex-wife, and a friend who married her.

Bullet for Joey, A (1955) 85m. **½ D: Lewis Allen. Edward G. Robinson, George Raft, Audrey Totter, Peter Van Eyck. Veteran cast improves caper about Communist agent attempting to kidnap U.S. nuclear scientist.

Bullet for Pretty Boy, A (1970) C-91m. *½ D: Larry Buchanan. Fabian Forte, Jocelyn Lane, Astrid Warner, Michael Haynes. Tough punk (Pretty Boy Floyd) goes on violent rampage. Cheap and bloody, likely to be edited.

Bullet for Stefano (1950-Italian) 96m. ** D: Duilio Coletti. Rossano Brazzi, Valentina Cortese, Carlo Campanini, Lillian Laine. Carefree young man (Brazzi) falls into life of crime and finds it pleasant; cast is engaging.

Bullet for the General, A (1967-Italian) C-115m. ** D: Damiano Damiani. Gian-Maria Volonte, Lou Castel, Klaus Kinski, Martine Beswick. Blond gringo joins marauding guerrillas and contributes to gory bloodletting. Not bad for the genre.

Bullet Is Waiting, A (1954) C-82m. **½ D: John Farrow. Jean Simmons, Rory Calhoun, Stephen McNally, Brian Aherne. Interesting human nature study hinging on sheriff's discovery that his prisoner is really innocent; nice desert locale.

Bullets or Ballots (1936) 77m. *** D: William Keighley. Edward G. Robinson, Joan Blondell, Barton MacLane, Humphrey Bogart, Frank McHugh. Cop Robinson pretends to leave police force to crack citywide mob ring

run by MacLane. Good, tough gangster film.

Bullfighter and the Lady, The (1951) 87m. *** D: Budd Boetticher. Robert Stack, Joy Page, Gilbert Roland, Virginia Grey. Atmospheric account of American Stack coming to Mexico where he learns the true art of bullfighting.

Bullitt (1968) C-113m. ***½ D: Peter Yates. Steve McQueen, Robert Vaughn, Jacqueline Bisset, Don Gordon, Robert Duvall, Simon Oakland, Norman Fell. Definitive McQueen antihero: police detective who senses something fishy behind assignment to guard criminal witness. Taut action-film makes great use of San Francisco locations, especially in now-classic car chase, one of the screen's all-time best.

Bullwhip (1958) C-80m. ** D: Harmon Jones. Guy Madison, Rhonda Fleming, James Griffith, Don Beddoe. Madison is offered the choice of marrying Fleming or being hanged on phony murder charge; expected results.

Bundle of Joy (1956) C-98m. ** D: Norman Taurog. Eddie Fisher, Debbie Reynolds, Adolphe Menjou, Tommy Noonan. Labored musical remake of BACHELOR MOTHER has Reynolds as salesgirl who takes custody of a baby, causing scandal that boyfriend Fisher is child's father.

Bunny Lake Is Missing (1965) 107m. ** D: Otto Preminger. Laurence Olivier, Carol Lynley, Keir Dullea, Noel Coward, Martita Hunt, The Zombies. Aimless story of Lynley's child being kidnapped, subsequent investigation among several homosexual characters and assorted oddballs. Pretty dreary going.

Bunny O'Hare (1972) C-91m. *½ D: Gerd Oswald. Bette Davis, Ernest Borgnine, Jack Cassidy, Joan Delaney, Reva Rose, John Astin. Bizarre, totally inept tale of bank robbers who look like hippies but are actually Davis and Borgnine. Don't bother watching.

Buona Sera, Mrs. Campbell (1968) C-111m. *** D: Melvin Frank. Gina Lollobrigida, Peter Lawford, Shelley Winters, Phil Silvers, Telly Savalas, Lee Grant, Janet Margolin. Bright comedy about Italian woman who's accepted money from three American men who all think they fathered her child during WW2. Now they're all coming back to Italy for Army reunion and "Mrs. Campbell" is in a state of panic. Good fun with top cast.

Bureau of Missing Persons (1933) 79m. **½ D: Roy Del Ruth. Bette Davis, Lewis Stone, Pat O'Brien, Glenda Farrell. Snappy drama with O'Brien aiding Davis to find missing hubby, falling in love with her himself.

Burglar, The (1956) 90m. **½ D: Paul Wendkos. Dan Duryea, Jayne Mansfield, Martha Vickers, Peter Capell, Mickey Shaughnessy, Phoebe Mackay. Odd little film noir about burglars Duryea and Mansfield, who've grown up together, and their unpredictable accomplices in a bizarre burglary.

Burglars, The (1972-French) C-117m. **½ D: Henri Verneuil. Jean-Paul Belmondo, Omar Sharif, Dyan Cannon, Robert Hossein. Routine crime film set against lush Greek backdrop, with good cast. One good chase and it's all over. Remake of THE BURGLAR.

Burma Convoy (1941) 72m. **½ D: Noel Smith. Charles Bickford, Evelyn Ankers, Frank Albertson, Cecil Kellaway, Keye Luke, Turhan Bey. Neat little actioner of conflicting trucking interests involved in carrying needed supplies over the Burma Road during hectic days of WW2.

Burn Witch Burn (1962-British) 90m. *** D: Sidney Hayers. Janet Blair, Peter Wyngarde, Margaret Johnston, Anthony Nicholls. Story of witchcraft entering lives of schoolteacher and his wife builds to shattering suspense, genuinely frightening climax. Filmed before as WEIRD WOMAN, this version scripted by Charles Beaumont and Richard Matheson.

Burning Hills, The (1956) C-94m. ** D: Stuart Heisler. Tab Hunter, Natalie Wood, Skip Homeier, Eduard Franz. Passive Hunter can't spark life into tired script. Man on run from cattle thieves is sheltered by miscast Wood (half-breed Mexican girl).

Burnt Offerings (1976) C-115m. ** D: Dan Curtis. Karen Black, Oliver Reed, Burgess Meredith, Eileen Heckart, Lee Montgomery, Dub Taylor, Bette Davis. Ordinary couple, with young son and aunt in tow, rent an old mansion as summer home, unaware that it's haunted. Strange occurrences lead to totally predictable "surprise" ending. A big buildup to nothing.

Bus Riley's Back in Town (1965) C-93m. **½ D: Harvey Hart. Ann-Margret, Michael Parks, Janet Margolin, Brad Dexter, Kim Darby, Jocelyn Brando, Larry Storch. Muddled William Inge script of folksy people in the Midwest. Parks, ex-sailor, returns home, torn by faltering ambitions and taunted by wealthy ex-girlfriend Ann-Margret. Character cameos make the film worthwhile.

Bus Stop (1956) C-96m. ***½ D: Joshua Logan. Marilyn Monroe, Don Murray, Arthur O'Connell, Betty Field, Eileen Heckart. Excellent comedy-drama proves Monroe knows about acting, playing a chanteuse sensitively. Murray is rowdy cowboy who tries to rope her; Field fine as cafe waitress.

Bushwackers, The (1952) 70m. *½ D: Rod Amateau. Dorothy Malone, John Ireland, Wayne Morris, Lawrence Tierney, Lon Chaney. Confederate army veteran forced into becoming gunman again; Malone wasted here.

Busman's Honeymoon SEE: **Haunted Honeymoon**

Buster and Billie (1974) C-100m. *½ D: Daniel Petrie. Jan-Michael Vincent, Joan Goodfellow, Pamela Sue Martin, Clifton James, Robert Englund. Blubbery account of high school romance in 1948 rural Georgia (the loosest girl in class is redeemed by love) can't overcome a cliched premise.

Buster Keaton Story, The (1957) 91m. *½ D: Sidney Sheldon. Donald O'Connor, Ann Blyth, Rhonda Fleming, Peter Lorre. Weak fiction ignores the facts about silent-star Keaton, making up its own. More private life than on-screen moments are detailed with Blyth as his true love and Fleming as a siren. Little comedy in this tale of a great comedian.

Busting (1974) C-92m. **½ D: Peter Hyams. Elliott Gould, Robert Blake, Allen Garfield, Cornelia Sharpe. Realistic if empty comedy-action-drama with Gould and Blake as unorthodox L.A. vice cops. Gay activists complained about film's few minutes of homosexual caricatures. Hyams, once a CBS-TV newsman, also did script.

Busy Body, The (1967) C-90m. **½ D: William Castle. Sid Caesar, Robert Ryan, Anne Baxter, Kay Medford, Jan Murray, Richard Pryor, Dom DeLuise, Godfrey Cambridge, Marty Ingels, Bill Dana, George Jessel. Broad, forced comedy involving gangsters and corpses, with Caesar as the patsy for Ryan's underworld gang. Supporting comics give film its funniest moments.

But I Don't Want to Get Married (1970) C-72m. TVM D: Jerry Paris. Herschel Bernardi, Shirley Jones, Kay Medford, June Lockhart, Brandon Cruz, Sue Lyon, Nanette Fabray, Jerry Paris. Fair comedy features Bernardi as average-type father recently widowed finding himself irresistible to all sorts of women. Good cast works well with adequate material. Average.

But Not For Me (1959) 105m. *** D: Walter Lang. Clark Gable, Carroll Baker, Lilli Palmer, Barry Coe, Lee J. Cobb, Thomas Gomez, Chic remake of ACCENT ON YOUTH dealing with theatrical producer Gable thwarting advances of young secretary Baker, deciding sophisticated Palmer is more logically suitable.

Butch and Sundance: The Early Days (1979) C-110m. **½ D: Richard Lester. William Katt, Tom Berenger, Jeff Corey, John Schuck, Michael C. Gwynne, Brian Dennehy, Jill Eikenberry. This "prequel" to BUTCH CASSIDY AND THE SUNDANCE KID has everything going for it—engaging performances, beautiful atmosphere and location photography—except a story. Pleasant enough but ultimately disappointing.

Butch Cassidy and the Sundance Kid (1969) C-112m. **** D: George Roy Hill. Paul Newman, Robert Redford, Katharine Ross, Strother Martin, Henry Jones, Jeff Corey, George Furth, Cloris Leachman. Delightful seriocomic character study masquerading as a Western; outlaws Newman and Redford are pursued by relentless but remote sheriff's posse. Many memorable vignettes; Oscar-winning Burt Bacharach score includes "Raindrops Keep Fallin' on My Head." Sharp dialogue by William Goldman.

Butley (1974-British) C-127m. **** D: Harold Pinter. Alan Bates, Jessica Tandy, Richard O'Callaghan, Susan Engel, Georgina Hale. Bates is superb in American Film Theatre presentation, recreating his 1971 London stage role as a disdainful teacher with sexual and other problems. Playwright Pinter made his film directing debut with this outrageous comedy.

Buttercup Chain, The (1971) C-95m.

BOMB D: Robert Ellis Miller. Hywel Bennett, Leigh Taylor-Young, Jane Asher, Sven-Bertil Taube, Clive Revill, Michael Elphnick. Cousins are raised together and find they needn't stop at kissing. Beautifully photographed in Spain, Sweden, and London; otherwise, an atrocity.

Butterfield 8 (1960) C-109m. **½ D: Daniel Mann. Elizabeth Taylor, Laurence Harvey, Eddie Fisher, Dina Merrill, Mildred Dunnock, Susan Oliver, Betty Field. Adaptation of O'Hara novel substitutes clichéd ending in tale of high-class prostitute wanting to go straight, convincing herself she's found Mr. Right. Film's major assets: great supporting cast and old-style performance by Taylor, who won Oscar for it.

Butterflies Are Free (1972) C-109m. *** D: Milton Katselas. Goldie Hawn, Edward Albert, Eileen Heckart, Mike Warren. Filmization of Leonard Gershe's Broadway play detailing blind boy's romance with kookie next-door neighbor (Hawn) and inevitable showdown with his overpossessive mother. Good light entertainment; Heckart won Best Supporting Actress Oscar.

Bwana Devil (1952) C-79m. *½ D: Arch Oboler. Robert Stack, Barbara Britton, Nigel Bruce, Paul McVey. Dud actioner was sparked theatrically as first commercial 3-D feature: man-eating lions set their teeth on railway workers in Africa.

By Love Possessed (1961) C-115m. *** D: John Sturges. Lana Turner, Efrem Zimbalist, Jr., Jason Robards, Jr., George Hamilton, Thomas Mitchell. Not true to James Gould Cozzens novel; ultraglossy romantic vehicle for Turner, whose lover is prominent New England attorney Zimbalist—personable cast.

By the Light of the Silvery Moon (1953) C-102m. **½ D: David Butler. Doris Day, Gordon MacRae, Leon Ames, Rosemary DeCamp, Mary Wickes. Set in post WW1, this Booth Tarkington story finds returning soldier MacRae and fiancée Day readjusting to life. Ames wonderful as father thought to be romancing French actress, and Wickes delightful as family maid. This old-fashioned musical was a sequel to ON MOONLIGHT BAY.

Bye Bye Birdie (1963) C-112m. **½ D: George Sidney. Janet Leigh, Dick Van Dyke, Ann-Margret, Maureen Stapleton, Paul Lynde, Ed Sullivan.

Entertaining version of Broadway musical about rock 'n' roll idol and his adoring fans. Lynde stands out as Ann-Margret's father. Songs include "Put on a Happy Face."

Bye Bye Braverman (1968) C-109m. **½ D: Sidney Lumet. George Segal, Jack Warden, Joseph Wiseman, Sorrell Booke, Jessica Walter, Phyllis Newman, Zohra Lampert, Godfrey Cambridge, Alan King. To paraphrase one of the characters, this film, in the sum of its many parts, yields pleasure of a kind; but fuzzy, unresolved story of four Jewish intellectuals on their way to a friend's funeral is ultimately disappointing. Filmed in New York.

C.C. and Company (1970) C-88m. *½ D: Seymour Robbie. Joe Namath, Ann-Margret, William Smith, Jennifer Billingsley. Joe Namath as a renegade motorcyclist, and Ann-Margret as the girl who tries to tame him. Namath much better on football field than in film.

C-Man (1949) 75m. ** D: Joseph Lerner. Dean Jagger, John Carradine, Harry Landers, Rene Paul. Acceptable programmer with Jagger as customs agent involved in murder and theft case.

Cabaret (1972) C-124m. ***½ D: Bob Fosse. Liza Minnelli, Michael York, Helmut Griem, Joel Grey, Fritz Wepper, Marisa Berenson. Stylish film based on Fred Ebb-John Kander Broadway musical, from John Van Druten's I AM A CAMERA, now more a vehicle for Minnelli in her Oscar-winning performance as Sally Bowles, American girl caught up in phony glitter of prewar Berlin. Song numbers counterpoint dramatic narrative, including newly written "The Money Song," great duet for Minnelli and Oscar-winner Grey. Director Fosse also won Academy Award.

Cabin in the Cotton (1932) 77m. **½ D: Michael Curtiz. Bette Davis, Richard Barthelmess, Dorothy Jordan, Henry B. Walthall, Tully Marshall, Dorothy Peterson. Dated melodrama of sharecroppers with earnest Barthelmess almost led to ruin by Southern belle Davis; exaggerated, but interesting.

Cabin in the Sky (1943) 100m. *** D: Vincente Minnelli. Eddie "Rochester" Anderson, Lena Horne, Ethel Waters, Louis Armstrong, Rex Ingram, Duke Ellington and his Orchestra, The Hall Johnson Choir. Stellar black cast in winning (if somewhat racist) musical fable about forces of good and evil vying for the soul of Little Joe (Anderson). John Bubbles' dancing, Waters singing "Happiness Is Just a Thing Called Joe" among musical highlights.

Cabinet of Dr. Caligari, The (1919-German) 69m. ***½ D: Robert Wiene. Werner Krauss, Conrad Veidt, Lil Dagover. Somewhat stiff but still fascinating German Expressionist film about "magician" Caligari and hypnotic victim who carries out his evil bidding. Landmark film still impresses audiences today.

Cabinet of Caligari (1962) 104m. **½ D: Roger Kay. Dan O'Herlihy, Glynis Johns, Richard Davalos, Lawrence Dobkin, Estelle Winwood, J. Pat O'Malley. Unimaginative remake of the 1919 German classic, removing all the mystery-exotic appeal; Johns tries hard as lady with bizarre nightmares in a mental institution.

Cable Car Murder SEE: Crosscurrent

Cactus Flower (1969) C-103m. **½ D: Gene Saks. Walter Matthau, Ingrid Bergman, Goldie Hawn, Jack Weston, Rick Lenz, Vito Scotti, Irene Hervey. Glossy comedy was pretty thin for Broadway, even thinner on film, with Bergman as prim nurse to dentist Matthau who blossoms when she realizes she's in love with him. Best moments belong to Goldie Hawn, who won Oscar for her supporting role.

Caddy, The (1953) 95m. *½ D: Norman Taurog. Dean Martin, Jerry Lewis, Donna Reed, Fred Clark, Barbara Bates, Joseph Calleia. Weak Martin & Lewis vehicle about golfnut Jerry coaching Dean to be a champion player. Dean sings "That's Amore."

Caesar and Cleopatra (1946-British) C-134m. ** D: Gabriel Pascal. Claude Rains, Vivien Leigh, Stewart Granger, Flora Robson, Francis L. Sullivan, Cecil Parker. Two fine stars suffer through static, boring rendition of George Bernard Shaw's play, which seems to go on forever. Occasional wit and intrigue can't keep this afloat.

Cafe Society (1939) 83m. **½ D: Edward H. Griffith. Madeleine Carroll, Fred MacMurray, Shirley Ross, Jessie Ralph, Claude Gillingwater. This time around Carroll chases Mac-

Murray to win husband on a bet; chic fluff.

Cage Without a Key (1975) C-100m. TVM D: Buzz Kulik. Susan Dey, Jonelle Allen, Sam Bottoms, Michael Brandon, Anne Bloom, Karen Carlson. Prison drama about a teen-aged girl (Susan Dey) who innocently finds herself accomplice to robbery and murder when she accepts a ride with a stranger, and then is wrongly sentenced to jail. Tedious, run-of-the-cell-block tale, resembles 1940s B-movie. Below average.

Caged (1950) 96m. *** D: John Cromwell. Eleanor Parker, Agnes Moorehead, Ellen Corby, Hope Emerson, Jan Sterling, Jane Darwell, Gertrude Michael. Remarkable performances by entire cast in stark record of Parker going to prison and becoming hardened criminal after exposure to brutal jail life. Both Parker and Emerson were nominated for Academy Awards.

Caged Fury (1948) 60m. ** D: William Berke. Richard Denning, Sheila Ryan, Mary Beth Hughes, Buster Crabbe. Not bad low-budgeter about mad killer on the loose in a circus.

Cahill—U.S. Marshal (1973) C-103m. ** D: Andrew V. McLaglen. John Wayne, George Kennedy, Gary Grimes, Neville Brand, Marie Windsor, Harry Carey, Jr. Marshal Wayne's law enforcement duties are complicated as one of his sons threatens to enter a life of crime; routine, violent Western suffers from the same kind of sermonizing that has plagued most of the Duke's recent films.

Cain and Mabel (1936) 90m. ** D: Lloyd Bacon. Marion Davies, Clark Gable, Allen Jenkins, Roscoe Karns, Walter Catlett. Musical romance of prizefighter and showgirl has gargantuan production numbers to overcome stale plot.

Caine Mutiny, The (1954) C-125m. **** D: Edward Dmytryk. Humphrey Bogart, Jose Ferrer, Van Johnson, Robert Francis, May Wynn, Fred MacMurray, E. G. Marshall, Lee Marvin. Naval officers Johnson and Francis mutiny against Capt. Queeg (Bogart) and are court-martialed in this exciting adaptation of Herman Wouk's Pulitzer Prize novel.

Cairo (1942) 101m. ** D: W. S. Van Dyke II. Jeanette MacDonald, Robert Young, Ethel Waters, Reginald Owen, Lionel Atwill, Dooley Wilson. Musi-comedy spoof of WW2

spy films is strained, although stars are pleasant and production is well-mounted.

Calamity Jane (1953) C-101m. *** D: David Butler. Doris Day, Howard Keel, Allyn McLerie, Philip Carey, Gale Robbins. Musical Western with Doris at her bounciest as tomboyish Calamity Jane who changes her ways for Keel. Includes Oscar-winning song: "Secret Love."

Calamity Jane and Sam Bass (1949) C-85m. *½ D: George Sherman. Yvonne De Carlo, Howard Duff, Dorothy Hart, Lloyd Bridges, Milburn Stone. Tattered retelling of 19th-century cowgirl and Texas outlaw, with De Carlo and Duff a disinterested duo.

Calcutta (1947) 83m. **½ D: John Farrow. Alan Ladd, Gail Russell, William Bendix, June Duprez, Lowell Gilmore. Standard actioner with pilot Ladd avenging friend's murder.

California (1946) C-97m. **½ D: John Farrow. Barbara Stanwyck, Ray Milland, Barry Fitzgerald, Albert Dekker, Anthony Quinn, Julia Faye, George Coulouris. Ray is a wagonmaster with a past, Stanwyck a shady gal who makes good in this elaborately ordinary Western.

California Conquest (1952) C-79m. **½ D: Lew Landers. Cornel Wilde, Teresa Wright, John Dehner, Hank Patterson. Film deals with sidelight of American history. Californian Wilde et al under Spanish control help their ally against Russian attempt to confiscate the territory.

California Dreaming (1979) C-92m. *½ D: John Hancock. Glynnis O'Connor, Seymour Cassel, Dennis Christopher, Dorothy Tristan, John Calvin, Jimmy Van Patten. Brainless time-filler about midwestern hick (Christopher) who tries to adapt to California surf-and-sand lifestyle. Film's scenarist, Ned Wynn, adds insult to injury by appearing on-screen as well . . . and overacting.

California Kid, The (1974) C-78m. TVM D: Richard Heffron. Martin Sheen, Vic Morrow, Michelle Phillips, Stuart Margolin, Nick Nolte, Janit Baldwin. Taut, well-made thriller in which psychotic small town sheriff Morrow, who delights in punishing speeders by running them off hairpin mountain curves, is forced into a high-speed auto duel with Sheen, the hot-rodding brother of one of the victims. Above average.

California Split (1974) C-108m. **½

D: Robert Altman. George Segal, Elliott Gould, Ann Prentiss, Gwen Welles, Joseph Walsh, Bert Remsen. Realistic but rambling look at two compulsive gamblers, their strange lifestyles, and the emptiness of winning. Altman's multi-channel soundtrack at its worst only adds to the muddle.

California Straight Ahead (1937) 67m. ** **D:** Arthur Lubin. John Wayne, Louise Latimer, Robert McQade, Theodore Von Eltz, Tully Marshall. Good little actioner with Wayne competing in cross-country race between trucks and train.

California Suite (1978) C-103m. *** **D:** Herbert Ross. Jane Fonda, Alan Alda, Maggie Smith, Michael Caine, Walter Matthau, Elaine May, Richard Pryor, Bill Cosby. Four Neil Simon skits set at the Beverly Hills hotel (and adapted from his Broadway hit). Oscar-winning Smith and husband Caine as gently bickering Britishers in town for Academy Awards come off best; Pryor and Cosby as unfunnily combative "friends" are the worst. Pleasant time-filler.

Call a Messenger (1939) 65m. **D:** Arthur Lubin. Billy Halop, Huntz Hall, William Benedict, David Gorcey, Robert Armstrong, Buster Crabbe, Victor Jory, El Brendel, Mary Carlisle. SEE: Bowery Boys series.

Call Her Mom (1971) C-73m. TVM **D:** Jerry Paris. Connie Stevens, Van Johnson, Charles Nelson Reilly, Jim Hutton, Cyd Charisse, Corbett Monica. Fraternity house takes on waitress as housemother and finds itself (and entire college) center of intense Women's Lib controversy. Needs better script. Average.

Call Her Savage (1932) 88m. **½ **D:** John Francis Dillon. Clara Bow, Monroe Owsley, Gilbert Roland, Thelma Todd, Estelle Taylor. Vehicle for indefatigable Clara Bow ranges from sharp comedy to teary-eyed soap opera, but it's never dull. Bow is amazingly sensual throughout, matched in brief confrontations with Todd; great fun for 1930s film buffs.

Call Him Mr. Shatter (1975-British) C-90m. *½ **D:** Michael Carreras. Stuart Whitman, Peter Cushing, Anton Diffring, Ti Lung, Lily Li. Kung-fu mishmash involving a world-weary international contract killer (Whitman) and hordes of athletic Oriental villains, all involved in an assassination plot against head of East African state. American director Monte Hellman began shooting this one but departed early on.

Call It a Day (1937) 89m. ** **D:** Archie Mayo. Olivia de Havilland, Ian Hunter, Alice Brady, Anita Louise, Peggy Wood, Frieda Inescort, Roland Young, Bonita Granville. Mild fluff of wacky British family's various problems during a normal day.

Call Me Bwana (1963) C-103m. ** **D:** Gordon Douglas. Bob Hope, Anita Ekberg, Edie Adams, Lionel Jeffries, Arnold Palmer. Hope and Adams on an African jungle safari encounter Ekberg and Jeffries—nothing much happens—the ladies are lovely.

Call Me Madam (1953) C-117m. *** **D:** Walter Lang. Ethel Merman, Donald O'Connor, George Sanders, Vera-Ellen, Billy DeWolfe, Walter Slezak, Lilia Skala. Often stagy musical from Irving Berlin tuner based on Perle Mesta's life as Washington, D. C. hostess and Lichtenburg ambassadress. Merman is blowsy delight.

Call Me Mister (1951) C-95m. **½ **D:** Lloyd Bacon. Betty Grable, Dan Dailey, Danny Thomas, Dale Robertson. Acceptable plot line helps buoy this musical. Soldier Dailey, based in Japan, goes AWOL to patch up marriage with Grable traveling with USO troupe.

Call Northside 777 (1948) 111m. ***½ **D:** Henry Hathaway. James Stewart, Richard Conte, Lee J. Cobb, Helen Walker, Moroni Olsen, E. G. Marshall. Absorbing drama of reporter Stewart convinced that convicted killer is innocent, trying to prove it; handled in semi-documentary style. Retitled: CALLING NORTHSIDE 777.

Call of the Wild (1935) 95m. *** **D:** William Wellman. Clark Gable, Loretta Young, Jack Oakie, Reginald Owen. Not really Jack London, but good Northern romp with Gable, Young, and Oakie prospecting in Klondike country, at odds with villain Owen.

Call of the Wild (1972) C-100m. **½ **D:** Ken Annakin. Charlton Heston, Michele Mercier, Maria Rohm, Rik Battaglia. Lackluster version of the Jack London adventure classic, produced by a multinational film combine and wasting the talents of a diverse cast. One redeeming quality: the striking Finnish scenery.

Call of the Wild, The (1976) C-100m. TVM **D:** Jerry Jameson. John Beck,

Bernard Fresson, John McLiam, Donald Moffat, Michael Pataki, Billy Green Bush, Penelope Windust, Johnny Tillotson. Stark but quite graphic remake of Jack London's 1903 tale of gold fever and adventure in the Klondike. In this version, John Beck is eager greenhorn and Fresson is veteran prospector, but the star is sled dog named Buck, who faces the hazards of man as well as nature. Above average.

Call to Danger (1973) C-74m. TVM D: Tom Gries. Peter Graves, Stephen McNally, Diana Muldaur, Ina Balin, Michael Ansara, Clu Gulager, Tina Louise. Undercover investigator for Justice Department must rescue important witness kidnapped by the Mob. Grows increasingly implausible as plot unwinds. Average.

Callaway Went Thataway (1951) 81m. **½ D: Norman Panama, Melvin Frank. Fred MacMurray, Dorothy McGuire, Howard Keel, Jesse White, Fay Roope, Natalie Schafer. Gentle spoof of early-TV "Hopalong Cassidy" craze, with Keel as lookalike who impersonates veteran cowboy star for promotional purposes; good fun until it starts getting serious. Several MGM stars make cameo appearances.

Calling Bulldog Drummond (1951-U.S.A.-British) 80m. D: Victor Saville. Walter Pidgeon, Margaret Leighton, Robert Beatty, David Tomlinson. SEE: *Bulldog Drummond* series.

Calling Dr. Death (1943) 63m. **½ D: Reginald LeBorg. Lon Chaney, Ramsay Ames, Patricia Morison, J. Carrol Naish, David Bruce, Fay Helm. Tight "B" melodrama with doctor Chaney's unfaithful wife found murdered.

Calling Dr. Gillespie (1942) 82m. D: Harold S. Bucquet. Lionel Barrymore, Donna Reed, Phil Brown, Nat Pendleton, Alma Kruger, Mary Nash, Charles Dingle. SEE: **Dr. Kildare** series.

Calling Dr. Kildare (1939) 86m. D: Harold S. Bucquet. Lew Ayres, Lionel Barrymore, Laraine Day, Nat Pendleton, Lana Turner, Samuel S. Hinds, Emma Dunn, Alma Kruger, Marie Blake, Phillip Terry, Donald Barry. SEE: **Dr. Kildare** series.

Calling Homicide (1956) 61m. *½ D: Edward Bernds. Bill Elliott, Don Haggerty, Kathleen Case, Myron Healey. Low-key detective yarn following detective Elliott's search for cop-killer.

Calling Northside 777 SEE: **Call Northside 777**

Calling Philo Vance (1940) 62m. D: William Clemens. James Stephenson, Margot Stevenson, Henry O'Neill, Edward Brophy, Ralph Forbes. SEE: **Philo Vance** series.

Caltiki, the Immortal Monster (1959-Italian) 76m. ** D: Robert Hampton. John Merivale, Didi Sullivan, Gerard Herter, Daniela Rocca. Set in Mexico, sci-fi has blob-ish fiend pursuing members of scientific expedition; poorly conceived but amusing.

Camelot (1967) C-178m. *½ D: Joshua Logan. Richard Harris, Vanessa Redgrave, Franco Nero, David Hemmings, Lionel Jeffries. Appalling film version of Lerner-Loewe musical has only good orchestrations and sporadically good acting to recommend it; no one can sing and production looks cheap, in spite of big budget. Film's nonstop use of close-ups may help it on TV.

Camille (1936) 85m. ***½ D: George Cukor. Greta Garbo, Robert Taylor, Lionel Barrymore, Elizabeth Allen, Laura Hope Crews, Henry Daniell. Garbo is most alluring as Dumas' tragic heroine in 19th-century Paris, but the film lacks punch. Large burden falls on Taylor as Armand, but he's unconvincing. Daniell steals film in a superbly subtle villainous role.

Camp on Blood Island, The (1958-British) 81m. ** D: Val Guest. Andre Morell, Carl Mohner, Walter Fitzgerald, Edward Underdown. So-so gore as inhabitants rebel against brutal commander of prison compound.

Campbell's Kingdom (1958-British) C-102m. ** D: Ralph Thomas. Dirk Bogarde, Stanley Baker, Michael Craig, Barbara Murray. Set in Canadian Rockies, big-budget adventure film focuses on landowner Bogarde's conflict with Baker et al, when latter seeks to build large dam near his property.

Can Ellen Be Saved? (1974) C-78m. TVM D: Harvey Hart. Leslie Nielsen, John Saxon, Michael Parks, Louise Fletcher, Kathy Cannon, Rutanya Alda, Bill Katt, Kathleen Quinlan. Exorcism movie in which Saxon is hired by parents of Cannon to save her from a fanatical religious commune. Unspectacular deprogramming drama that unfolds in totally predictable fashion. Below average.

Can Hieronymus Merkin Ever Forget Mercy Humppe and Find True Happiness? (1969-British) C-106m. *½ D: Anthony Newley. Anthony Newley, Joan Collins, Milton Berle, Connie Kreski, George Jessel, Stubby Kaye. Fellini-influenced mess about song-and-dance man who reviews his debauched past. Lowgrade in all departments; Connie revealed why she was "Playmate of the Year" in original "X"-rated version, but much of her footage will be gone on TV.

Can You Hear the Laughter? The Story of Freddie Prinze (1979) C-100m. TVM D: Burt Brinckerhoff. Ira Angustain, Kevin Hooks, Randée Heller, Devon Ericson, Julie Carmen, Stephen Elliott. Affectionate account of the meteoric rise of the young comedian and his death by suicide in 1977. Angustain (as Prinze) and Hooks (as his closest friend, Nat Blake) are familiar as two of the basketball players on THE WHITE SHADOW. Average.

Canadian Mounties vs. Atomic Invaders SEE: Missile Base at Taniak

Canadian Pacific (1949) C-95m. **½ D: Edwin L. Marin. Randolph Scott, Jane Wyatt, J. Carrol Naish, Victor Jory, Nancy Olson. Scott is railroad surveyor helping with construction of train link, fighting Indians while romancing Wyatt and Olson.

Canadians, The (1961) C-85m. ** D: Burt Kennedy. Robert Ryan, John Dehner, Torin Thatcher, John Sutton, Teresa Stratas. Cornball nonsense about Mounties who pacify war-happy Sioux. Film features Metropolitan Opera singer Stratas to no advantage. Filmed in Canada.

Canaris Master Spy (1954-German) 92m. ** D: Alfred Weidenmann. O. E. Hasse, Martin Held, Barbara Rutting, Adrian Hoven. Potentially interesting account of German Intelligence leader during 1930s who tried to depose Hitler; meandering film.

Canary Murder Case (1929) 81m. D: Malcolm St. Clair. William Powell, Louise Brooks, James Hall, Jean Arthur, Charles Lane. SEE: Philo Vance series.

Can-Can (1960) C-131m. **½ D: Walter Lang. Frank Sinatra, Shirley MacLaine, Maurice Chevalier, Louis Jourdan, Juliet Prowse. Lackluster version of Cole Porter musical of 1890s Paris involving lawyer Sinatra defending MacLaine's right to perform "daring" dance in her nightclub. Chevalier and Jourdan try to inject charm, but Sinatra is blasé and MacLaine shrill. Songs: "C'est Magnifique," "I Love Paris," "Let's Do It," "Just One of Those Things."

Cancel My Reservation (1972) C-99m. BOMB D: Paul Bogart. Bob Hope, Eva Marie Saint, Ralph Bellamy, Forrest Tucker, Anne Archer, Keenan Wynn. Hope should have canceled this movie, a time-wasting turkey about a troubled talk-show host who gets involved in a murder case in Arizona.

Candidate, The (1972) C-109m. *** D: Michael Ritchie. Robert Redford, Peter Boyle, Don Porter, Allen Garfield, Karen Carlson, Melvyn Douglas. Keen-eyed political satire doesn't stray far from reality, which is its problem. Redford is idealist talked into running for Senate with promise of absolute integrity in campaign, since he's bound to lose—or is he?

Candidate for Murder (1962-British) 60m. **½ D: David Villiers. Michael Gough, Erika Remberg, Hans Barsody, John Justin. Gough is deranged husband of actress Remberg, out to kill her; nicely told Edgar Wallace suspenser.

Candleshoe (1977) C-101m. *** D: Norman Tokar. David Niven, Jodie Foster, Helen Hayes, Leo McKern, Veronica Quilligan, Ian Sharrock, Vivian Pickles. Con man McKern tries to pass off orphan Foster as Hayes' heiress in order to locate hidden family treasure. Entertaining Disney comedy filmed in England, with Niven in fine form as disguise-laden butler.

Candy (1968) C-115m. ** D: Christian Marquand. Ewa Aulin, Richard Burton, Marlon Brando, Charles Aznavour, James Coburn, John Huston, Walter Matthau, Ringo Starr, John Astin. Strained sexual satire about a nubile blonde who is attacked by every man she meets. Fair share of funny moments and bright performances (particularly by Burton and Astin), but not enough to sustain 115m. Adapted from Terry Southern and Mason Hoffenberg's book by Buck Henry.

Candy Man, The (1969) 98m. ** D: Herbert J. Leder. George Sanders, Leslie Parrish, Gina Ronan, Menolo Fabregas, Carlos Cortez. Routine kidnap drama filmed in Mexico City involving world-weary British drug pusher and American film star.

Cannibal Attack (1954) 69m. D: Lee

Sholem. Johnny Weissmuller, Judy Walsh, David Bruce, Bruce Cowling. SEE: **Jungle Jim** series.

Cannon (1970) **C-100m. TVM** D: George McCowan. William Conrad, Vera Miles, J. D. Cannon, Lynda Day, Earl Holliman. Overweight private-eye hired by wife of old friend to investigate husband's murder; case becomes linked to small-town corruption. Too many subplots makes for confusion after halfway mark. Above average; pilot for TV series.

Cannon for Cordoba (1970) **C-104m. **½** D: Paul Wendkos. George Peppard, Giovanna Ralli, Raf Vallone, Peter Duel, Don Gordon, John Russell. Peppard leads a band of soldiers against Mexican bandits on the Texas border ca. 1912, and tries to destroy stolen cannons. Standard action fare with a familiar ring.

Cannonball (1976) **C-93m. *** D: Paul Bartel. David Carradine, Bill McKinney, Veronica Hamel, Robert Carradine, Judy Canova. Exuberant fun in this tongue-in-cheek movie about a cross-country race. Cast is filled with director's friends and colleagues, including producer Roger Corman, directors Martin Scorsese, Jonathan Kaplan, and Joe Dante, and a pre-ROCKY Sylvester Stallone. Similar to THE GUMBALL RALLY, released the same year.

Can't Help Singing (1944) **C-89m. **½** D: Frank Ryan. Deanna Durbin, Robert Paige, Akim Tamiroff, Ray Collins, Thomas Gomez. Durbin goes West to find her roaming lover; despite good cast and Jerome Kern songs, it's nothing much.

Canterville Ghost, The (1944) **96m. *** D: Jules Dassin. Charles Laughton, Margaret O'Brien, William Gargan, Rags Ragland, Una O'Connor, Robert Young, Peter Lawford, Mike Mazurki. Enjoyable fantasy of 17th-century ghost Laughton, spellbound until descendant Young performs heroic deed.

Canyon Crossroads (1955) **83m. **½** D: Alfred L. Werker. Richard Basehart, Russell Collins, Phyllis Kirk, Stephen Elliott. On-location filming in Colorado highlights this tale of uranium hunt, with Basehart quite convincing.

Canyon Passage (1946) **C-99m. *** D: Jacques Tourneur. Dana Andrews, Brian Donlevy, Susan Hayward, Ward Bond, Andy Devine, Lloyd Bridges. Plotty, colorful Western mixing action, beautiful scenery, heated love relationships, and Hoagy Carmichael singing "Ole Buttermilk Sky." Well-made and entertaining.

Canyon River (1956) **C-80m. *½** D: Harmon Jones. George Montgomery, Marcia Henderson, Peter Graves, Richard Eyer. Trite Western of Indian and rustler attacks on cattle drive.

Cape Fear (1962) **105m. *** D: J. Lee Thompson. Gregory Peck, Polly Bergen, Robert Mitchum, Martin Balsam, Lori Martin, Jack Kruschen, Telly Savalas. Well-paced suspenser as sadistic Mitchum seeks revenge on Peck and wife Bergen, highlighted by cat-and-mouse chase in Southern bayous.

Cape Town Affair, The (1967) **C-103m. ** D: Robert D. Webb. Claire Trevor, James Brolin, Jacqueline Bisset, Bob Courtney, John Whiteley, Gordon Milholland. Pedestrian remake of PICKUP ON SOUTH STREET, made in South Africa. Interest here is seeing Bisset and Brolin at the beginnings of their careers and Trevor making something different of the old Thelma Ritter role. Story deals with a Commie spy ring in Cape Town and an elusive envelope containing top secret microfilm.

Caper of the Golden Bulls, The (1967) **C-104m. BOMB** D: Russell Rouse. Stephen Boyd, Yvette Mimieux, Giovanna Ralli, Walter Slezak, Vito Scotti. Lots of bull but not much gold in this unendurable "thriller" about bank heist in Pamplona.

Capone (1975) **C-101m. BOMB** D: Steve Carver. Ben Gazzara, Susan Blakely, Harry Guardino, John Cassavetes, Sylvester Stallone, Frank Campanella. Gazzara has cotton in his jowls and a cigar in his mouth, making most of the dialogue in this gangster saga incomprehensible—but that's OK, you've heard it all before. One big shoot-out is stock footage from THE ST. VALENTINE'S DAY MASSACRE.

Caprice (1967) **C-98m. BOMB** D: Frank Tashlin. Doris Day, Richard Harris, Ray Walston, Jack Kruschen, Edward Mulhare, Lilia Skala, Irene Tsu. Terrible vehicle for Doris as industrial spy plunged into international intrigue with fellow-agent Harris. Muddled, unfunny, straining to be "mod."

Capricorn One (1978) **C-124m. **½** D: Peter Hyams. Elliott Gould,

Karen Black, Telly Savalas, James Brolin, Brenda Vaccaro, Sam Waterston, O. J. Simpson, Hal Holbrook, David Huddleston, David Doyle, Denise Nicholas, Robert Walden. Film starts with good premise —about the faking of a NASA space flight—but goes off in too many directions before retrenching for exciting chase finale.

Captain America (1979) C-100m. TVM D: Rod Holcomb. Reb Brown, Len Birman, Heather Menzies, Steve Forrest, Robin Mattson, Joseph Ruskin. Routine attempt to bring legendary comic strip crimefighter to TV, this pilot has his ex-Marine son continuing the family tradition of righting wrongs by pursuing an archcriminal who's aiming a neutron bomb at Phoenix. Below average.

Captain Apache (1971) C-94m. ** D: Alexander Singer. Lee Van Cleef, Carroll Baker, Stuart Whitman, Percy Herbert. Violence in Old West laid on with a trowel. Filled with Western stereotypes.

Captain Blood (1935) 99m. ***½ D: Michael Curtiz. Errol Flynn, Olivia de Havilland, Lionel Atwill, Basil Rathbone, Ross Alexander, Guy Kibbee. Flynn's first swashbuckler hits bullseye; he plays doctor forced to become a pirate, teaming for short spell with French cutthroat Rathbone, but paying more attention to proper young lady De Havilland. Original release print ran 119m.

Captain Blood (1960-French) C-95m. ** D: Andre Hunebelle. Jean Marais, Elsa Martinelli, Arnold Foa, Bourvil, Pierrette Bruno. Set in 17th-century France, this juvenile costumer deals with plot to overthrow throne of Louis XIII.

Captain Boycott (1947-British) 92m. ***½ D: Frank Launder. Stewart Granger, Kathleen Ryan, Cecil Parker, Mervyn Johns, Alastair Sim, Robert Donat. Excellent historical drama of Irish farmers going on strike to protest mistreatment by landowners; Donat appears briefly as Charles Parnell.

Captain Carey, U.S.A. (1950) 83m. *** D: Mitchell Leisen. Alan Ladd, Wanda Hendrix, Francis Lederer, Russ Tamblyn. Nicely turned account of ex-military officer Ladd returning to Italy to uncover informer who cost lives of villagers. Theme song "Mona Lisa" won an Oscar.

Captain Caution (1940) 85m. ** D: Richard Wallace. Victor Mature,

Louise Platt, Leo Carrillo, Bruce Cabot, Vivienne Osborne, Robert Barrat. OK action film of spunky Platt commandeering her father's ship into war; no messages, just fast-moving narrative.

Captain China (1949) 97m. ** D: Lewis R. Foster. John Payne, Gail Russell, Jeffrey Lynn, Lon Chaney, Edgar Bergen. Often listless sea yarn of Payne, seeking out persons responsible for his losing his ship's command.

Captain Eddie (1945) 107m. **½ D: Lloyd Bacon. Fred MacMurray, Lynn Bari, Charles Bickford, Thomas Mitchell, Lloyd Nolan, James Gleason. Routine aviation film doesn't do justice to exciting life of Eddie Rickenbacker; it's standard stuff.

Captain Falcon (1958-Italian) C-97m. *½ D: Carlo Campogalliani. Lex Barker, Rossana Rory, Anna Maria Ferrero, Carla Calo, Massimo Serato. Juvenile account of Barker (Captain Falcon) saving Rory and her principality from clutches of Serato.

Captain From Castile (1947) C-140m. *** D: Henry King. Tyrone Power, Jean Peters, Cesar Romero, Lee J. Cobb, John Sutton. Power is driven to avenge the shabby treatment of his family by Sutton, eventually serves with Cortez (Romero) during the latter's conquest of Mexico. Color and romance for the sake of color and romance; magnificently photographed, with an Alfred Newman score ranking with Hollywood's very best.

Captain Fury (1939) 91m. *** D: Hal Roach. Brian Aherne, Victor McLaglen, Paul Lukas, June Lang, John Carradine. Australia serves as background in story of illustrious adventurer fighting evil head of penal colony.

Captain Hates the Sea (1934) 92m. ** D: Lewis Milestone. Victor McLaglen, John Gilbert, Walter Connolly, Alison Skipworth, Wynne Gibson. Leon Errol, 3 Stooges. Disparate types interact on ocean voyage in this muddled, dimly interesting film.

Captain Horatio Hornblower (1951) C-117m. *** D: Raoul Walsh. Gregory Peck, Virginia Mayo, Robert Beatty, Denis O'Dea. Exciting, well-produced sea epic based on C. M. Forester's British naval hero of the Napoleonic wars.

Captain Is a Lady, The (1940) 63m. ** D: Robert B. Sinclair. Charles

Coburn, Beulah Bondi, Virginia Grey, Helen Broderick, Billie Burke, Dan Dailey. Thin little comedy of Coburn pretending to be a woman to accompany wife Bondi to old ladies' home.

Captain January (1936) 75m. **½ D: David Butler. Shirley Temple, Guy Kibbee, Slim Summerville, Buddy Ebsen. Sentimental family film with Shirley at her best, attaching herself to lighthouse-keeper Kibbee.

Captain John Smith and Pocahontas (1953) C-75m. *½ D: Lew Landers. Anthony Dexter, Jody Lawrence, Alan Hale, Jr., Douglass Dumbrille. Title tells all in pedestrian tale set in colonial America.

Captain Kidd (1945) 89m. ** D: Rowland V. Lee. Charles Laughton, Randolph Scott, Barbara Britton, Reginald Owen, John Carradine, Gilbert Roland, Sheldon Leonard. Even with Laughton, this is slow-going low-budget stuff.

Captain Kidd and the Slave Girl (1954) C-83m. ** D: Lew Landers. Anthony Dexter, Eva Gabor, Alan Hale, Jr., James Seay. Modest costumer has Dexter and Gabor in title roles romping the seas to find treasure for their benefactor.

Captain Kronos—Vampire Hunter (1972-British) C-91m. **½ D: Brian Clemens. Horst Janson, John Carson, Caroline Munro, Ian Hendry, Shane Bryant. Live-action comic strip romp involving a stalwart vampire hunter, his hunchback aide, several damsels in distress and various ruffians falls distressingly flat. Younger viewers might take to it. Originally titled KRONOS.

Captain Lightfoot (1955) C-91m. *** D: Douglas Sirk. Rock Hudson, Barbara Rush, Jeff Morrow, Finlay Currie, Kathleen Ryan. Fine, flavorful costume adventure about 19th-century Irish rebellion and one of its dashing heroes. Beautifully filmed on location in Ireland.

Captain Mephisto and the Transformation Machine (1945) 100m. **½ D: Spencer Bennet, Wallace Grissell, Yakima Canutt. Richard Bailey, Linda Stirling, Roy Barcroft, Kenne Duncan. Diverting Republic cliffhanger with villain Barcroft in rare form as Mephisto, seeking ore deposits from underground hideout. Re-edited movie serial: MANHUNT OF MYSTERY ISLAND.

Captain Nemo and the Underwater City (1970) C-105. **½ D: James Hill. Robert Ryan, Chuck Connors, Nanette Newman, Luciana Paluzzi. Average undersea fantasy centering around Captain Nemo who lives in an underwater fortress.

Captain Newman, M.D. (1963) C-126m. *** D: David Miller. Gregory Peck, Angie Dickinson, Tony Curtis, Eddie Albert, Jane Withers, Bobby Darin, Larry Storch. Alternately dramatic and comic film of Army psychiatrist doesn't always work but is generally entertaining. Darin is surprising in a melodramatic role, but the whole cast is good.

Captain Pirate (1952) C-85m. **½ D: Ralph Murphy. Louis Hayward, Patricia Medina, John Sutton, Charles Irwin, George Givot, Ted de Corsia. Reformed pirate must return to his renegade ways in order to expose the imposter who is using his name; good-enough programmer based on Sabatini's *Captain Blood Returns*.

Captain Scarlett (1953) C-75m. *½ D: Thomas Carr. Richard Greene, Leonora Amar, Nedrick Young, Edourado Noriega. Acceptable costumer with Greene properly dashing.

Captain Sindbad (1963) C-85m. **½ D: Byron Haskin. Guy Williams, Heidi Bruhl, Pedro Armendariz, Abraham Sofaer, Bernie Hamilton. Above average costumer involving Williams capering about as Sindbad.

Captain Sirocco SEE: **Pirates of Capri, The**

Captain Tugboat Annie (1945) 60m. ** D: Phil Rosen. Jane Darwell, Edgar Kennedy, Charles Gordon, Mantan Moreland, Pamela Blake, Hardie Albright, H. B. Warner. Annie sails again in low-budget epic which depends entirely on its stars, Darwell and Kennedy, for its flavor.

Captains Courageous (1937) 116m. **** D: Victor Fleming. Spencer Tracy, Freddie Bartholomew, Melvyn Douglas, Lionel Barrymore, Mickey Rooney, John Carradine, Walter Kingsford. Spoiled rich-boy Bartholomew falls off cruise ship, rescued by Portuguese fisherman Tracy (who won Oscar for role). Boy learns to love seafaring on crusty Barrymore's fishing ship. Enthusiastic cast; topnotch production of Kipling's story.

Captains Courageous (1977) C-110m. TVM D: Harvey Hart. Karl Malden, Jonathan Kahn, Ricardo Montalban, Fritz Weaver, Neville Brand, Fred Gwynne, Johnny Doran. OK redo of the Kipling classic, with the focus back on Captain Disko Troop (Malden) where it belongs. Young Kahn makes the rich kid an obnoxious snip. Montalban takes the old Spencer Tracy role which, without Tracy's overpowering presence, is cut down to size. Average.

Captains of the Clouds (1942) C-113m. *** D: Michael Curtiz. James Cagney, Dennis Morgan, Alan Hale, Brenda Marshall, George Tobias. Cagney and company join Canadian air force as a lark, but prove their worth under fire. Colorful wartime drama.

Captain's Paradise, The (1953-British) 80m. *** D: Anthony Kimmins. Alec Guinness, Yvonne De Carlo, Celia Johnson, Bill Fraser. Guinness has field day as carefree skipper who shuttles back and forth between wives in opposite ports. De Carlo and Johnson make good contrasts as the two women.

Captain's Table, The (1960-British) C-90m. ** D: Jack Lee. John Gregson, Peggy Cummins, Donald Sinden, Nadia Gray. Satisfactory comedy involving skipper of cargo vessel (Gregson) who is given trial command of luxury liner, and the chaos ensuing trying to keep order among crew and passengers.

Captive City, The (1952) 90m. **½ D: Robert Wise. John Forsythe, Joan Camden, Harold J. Kennedy, Marjorie Crosland, Victor Sutherland, Ray Teal, Martin Milner. Small-town newspaper editor investigates local corruption when the law ignores situation. Earnest but undistinguished melodrama.

Captive Girl (1950) 73m. D: William Berke. Johnny Weissmuller, Buster Crabbe, Anita Lhoest, Rick Vallin, John Dehner. SEE: **Jungle Jim** series

Captive Heart, The (1948-British) 86m. ***½ D: Basil Dearden. Michael Redgrave, Rachel Kempson. Basil Radford, Mervyn Johns, Jack Warner, Jimmy Hanley. Compelling examination of British P.O.W.s during WW2 and their German captors with controlled, flawless performance by Redgrave and excellent supporting cast.

Captive Wild Woman (1943) 61m. **½ D: Edward Dmytryk. John Carradine, Evelyn Ankers, Milburn Stone, Acquanetta, Martha MacVicar (Vickers), Lloyd Corrigan. Carradine turns an orangutan into beautiful woman (Acquanetta), who goes berserk with unrequited love. Good fun; Stone's animal-training scenes are stock footage of Clyde Beatty from THE BIG CAGE. Sequels: JUNGLE WOMAN, JUNGLE CAPTIVE.

Capture, The (1950) 81m. **½ D: John Sturges. Lew Ayres, Teresa Wright, Victor Jory, Duncan Renaldo. Straightforward account climaxing in Mexico: detective reinvestigates robbery to learn if he might have shot an innocent man.

Captured (1933) 72m. **½ D: Roy Del Ruth. Leslie Howard, Douglas Fairbanks, Jr., Paul Lukas, Margaret Lindsay. Fair story of honor and love, switching WW1 story from German prison camp, to warfront, to society England. Good cast major asset of production.

Car, The (1977) C-95m. *½ D: Elliot Silverstein. James Brolin, Kathleen Lloyd, John Marley, Ronny Cox, R. G. Armstrong, John Rubinstein. Hokey thriller about a killer car demonically running down most of the cast. Unfortunately it takes over 90 minutes, while "Twilight Zone" once did a tidier, quite similar job in one third the time.

Car Wash (1976) C-97m. **½ D: Michael Schultz. Richard Pryor, Franklin Ajaye, Sully Boyar, Ivan Dixon, George Carlin, Irwin Corey, Melanie Mayron, The Pointer Sisters, Garrett Morris. Boisterous look at L.A. car-wash is light excuse for barely connected comedy set-pieces, involving various and sundry characters, and pulsating soul music performed by Rose Royce. Often very funny, but no awards for good taste.

Caravan (1934) 101m. **½ D: Erik Charrell. Loretta Young, Charles Boyer, Jean Parker, Phillips Holmes, Louise Fazenda. Offbeat musical of royal Loretta forced to marry vagabond Boyer; main interest is curiosity in this not altogether successful film.

Caravans (1978) C-123m. **½ D: James Fargo. Anthony Quinn, Jennifer O'Neill, Michael Sarrazin, Christopher Lee, Joseph Cotten, Barry Sullivan. Expensive-looking version of James Michener's contemporary desert epic; won't fool those who recognize it as an updated horse opera in which the cowboys set out to rescue pretty white girl from Indian tribe where she has become the gun-running chief's squaw.

Carbine Williams (1952) 91m. *** D: Richard Thorpe. James Stewart, Jean Hagen, Wendell Corey, Paul Stewart, James Arness. Sturdy history of the inventor of famed gun, his problems with the law, and his simple family life. Stewart is most convincing in title role.

Cardinal, The (1963) C-175m. **½ D: Otto Preminger. Tom Tryon, Romy Schneider, Carol Lynley, Maggie McNamara, John Saxon, John Huston, Robert Morse, Cecil Kellaway, Dorothy Gish, Burgess Meredith. Long, long story of an Irish-American's rise from priesthood to the college of Cardinals. Has some outstanding vignettes by old pros like Meredith, but emerges as an uneven, occasionally worthwhile film.

Cardinal Richelieu (1935) 83m. **½ D: Rowland V. Lee. George Arliss, Maureen O'Sullivan, Edward Arnold, Cesar Romero. Arliss etches another historical portrayal of France's unscrupulous cardinal who controlled Louis XIII (Arnold). Good cast supports star.

Career (1959) 105m. *** D: Joseph Anthony. Dean Martin, Anthony Franciosa, Shirley MacLaine, Carolyn Jones, Joan Blackman, Robert Middleton, Donna Douglas. Occasionally shrill, generally forceful presentation of an actor's (Franciosa's), tribulations in seeking Broadway fame; Jones is excellent as lonely talent agent.

Career Girl (1959) C-61m. *½ D: Harold David. June Wilkinson, Charles Robert Keane, Lisa Barrie, Joe Sullivan. Sloppy account of Wilkinson going to Hollywood, seeking screen career; sleazy production values.

Carefree (1938) 80m. *** D: Mark Sandrich. Fred Astaire, Ginger Rogers, Ralph Bellamy, Luella Gear, Jack Carson. Madcap Rogers goes to psychiatrist Fred in wacky musicomedy with outstanding Irving Berlin numbers: "Change Partners," "I Used To Be Color Blind."

Caretakers, The (1963) 97m. *** D: Hall Bartlett. Robert Stack, Joan Crawford, Polly Bergen, Susan Oliver, Janis Paige, Constance Ford, Barbara Barrie, Herbert Marshall. At times incisive view of a West Coast mental hospital, marred by flimsy script and poor editing. Good characterizations by Crawford and Ford as nurses, Bergen and Paige as patients.

Carey Treatment, The (1972) C-101m. *** D: Blake Edwards. James Coburn, Jennifer O'Neill, Pat Hingle, Skye Aubrey, Elizabeth Allen, Alex Dreier. Good solid whodunit set in hospital, where doctor Coburn is determined to clear colleague of murder charge. O'Neill provides love interest in complicated but satisfying mystery, shot in Boston.

Cargo to Capetown (1950) 80m. *½ D: Earl McEvoy. Broderick Crawford, John Ireland, Ellen Drew, Edgar Buchanan. Tramp steamer is setting for mild love triangle as Crawford and Ireland vie for Drew.

Caribbean (1952) C-97m. ** D: Edward Ludwig. John Payne, Arlene Dahl, Cedric Hardwicke, Francis L. Sullivan, Woody Strode. Costume vehicle set in 18th century allows Payne to battle pirates and flirt with Dahl.

Cariboo Trail (1950) C-81m. **½ D: Edwin L. Marin. Randolph Scott, George "Gabby" Hayes. Bill Williams, Karin Booth, Victor Jory. Standard telling of conflict between cattlemen and settlers bringing civilization obliterating the grazing lands.

Carleton-Browne of the F.O.: SEE Man in a Cocked Hat

Carmen Jones (1954) C-105m. ***½ D: Otto Preminger. Dorothy Dandridge, Harry Belafonte, Pearl Bailey, Roy Glenn, Diahann Carroll, Brock Peters. Powerful melodrama adapted from Bizet's opera by Oscar Hammerstein II, with exciting music and equally exciting Dandridge as the ultimate femme fatale. Stars' singing voices are all dubbed—Dandridge's by opera star Marilyn Horne.

Carnal Knowledge (1971) C-96m. *** D: Mike Nichols. Jack Nicholson, Candice Bergen, Arthur Garfunkel, Ann-Margret, Rita Moreno, Cynthia O'Neal, Carol Kane. Not a likely candidate for early TV showing. Jules Feiffer's script details sexual attitudes and obsessions of two men from college through middle-age. Thought-provoking but depressing. Ann-Margret won acclaim for performance as Nicholson's kittenish mistress.

Carnival in Costa Rica (1947) C-95m. ** D: Gregory Ratoff. Dick Haymes, Vera-Ellen, Cesar Romero, Celeste Holm, Anne Revere, J. Carrol Naish. Despite fair cast, boring musical of trip to Costa Rica and the shenanigans of newlyweds and their quarreling parents.

Carnival Story (1954) C-95m. ** D: Kurt Neumann. Anne Baxter, Steve Cochran, Lyle Bettger, George Nader, Jay C. Flippen. Sluggish romantic triangle set in Germany, involving high-wire star and two of the circus men in love with her; Baxter sparks some life into show with her performance.

Carolina Cannonball (1955) 74m. *½ D: Charles Lamont. Judy Canova, Andy Clyde, Jack Kruschen, Ross Elliott. Hicksville hokum with Canova involved with enemy agents and a missile that lands in her backyard.

Carousel (1956) C-128m. ***½ D: Henry King. Gordon MacRae, Shirley Jones, Cameron Mitchell, Barbara Ruick, Claramae Turner, Robert Rounseville, Gene Lockhart. Excellent filmization of Rodgers & Hammerstein's memorable adaptation of LILIOM, with MacRae as rowdy carousel barker Billy Bigelow, who tries to change for the better when he falls in love with Jones. Excitement of wide-screen location filming will be minimized on TV, but moving characters, timeless songs ("If I Loved You," "Soliloquoy," "You'll Never Walk Alone," etc.) remain.

Carpetbaggers, The (1964) C-150m. **½ D: Edward Dmytryk. George Peppard, Alan Ladd, Carroll Baker, Bob Cummings, Martha Hyer, Lew Ayres, Martin Balsam, Audrey Totter, Archie Moore. Blowsy claptrap based on Harold Robbins novel of millionaire plane manufacturer (Peppard) dabbling in movies and lovemaking. Set in 1920s-30s; sexploitational values are tame.

Carrie (1952) 118m. **½ D: William Wyler. Jennifer Jones, Laurence Olivier, Miriam Hopkins, Eddie Albert, Mary Murphy. Jones passively plays title role in this turn-of-the-century story of farm girl who becomes famed actress. Olivier is excellent as her married lover. Based on Theodore Dreiser novel.

Carrie (1976) C-97m. **½ D: Brian DePalma. Sissy Spacek, Piper Laurie, William Katt, John Travolta, Amy Irving, Nancy Allen, Betty Buckley. Evocative story of high school misfit degenerates into cheap, gory melodrama when Spacek's telekinetic powers are unleashed in revenge against those who have mocked her. DePalma borrows a great deal from Hitchcock, but has none of the Master's wit or subtlety.

Carrington, V. C. SEE: **Court Martial**

Carry on Admiral SEE: **Ship Was Loaded, The**

Carry on Camping (1972-British) C-89m. ** D: Gerald Thomas. Sidney James, Kenneth Williams, Joan Sims, Barbara Windsor, Bernard Bresslaw, Terry Scott. The gang encounters hippie types at weekend campsite; usual double-entendre jokes in entry from never-ending series.

Carry on Cleo (1965-British) C-92m. **½ D: Gerald Thomas. Amanda Barrie, Sidney James, Kenneth Williams, Joan Sims, Kenneth Connor, Charles Hawtrey. Diverting reworking of ancient history to serve as amusing satire on CLEOPATRA epic, sufficiently laced with hijinks by perennial misfits.

Carry on Doctor (1972-British) C-95m. ** D: Gerald Thomas. Frankie Howerd, Kenneth Williams, Jim Dale, Barbara Windsor. Madcap group takes on medical profession. As usual, interest wanes after an hour and the amount of laughter varies quite a bit.

Carry on Henry VIII (1972-British) C-90m. ** D: Gerald Thomas. Sidney James, Kenneth Williams, Joan Sims, Charles Hawtrey, Barbara Windsor. Lecherous king, ribald times perfect milieu for "Carry On" gang's brand of farce; for fans only. Likely to be trimmed for TV.

Carry on Nurse (1960-British) 90m. *** D: Gerald Thomas. Kenneth Connor, Kenneth Williams, Charles Hawtrey, Terence Longdon. Quite hilarious madcaps with series stock company involved in patients-vs.-hospital-staff battle of authority.

Carry on Sergeant (1959-British) 88m. ** D: Gerald Thomas. William Hartnell, Bob Monkhouse, Shirley Eaton, Eric Barker, Dora Bryan, Bill Owen, Kenneth Connor. This time around prankish misfits are the bane of Army officer's existence, who swears he'll make these recruits spiffy soldiers or bust.

Carry on Spying (1965-British) 88m. **½ D: Gerald Thomas. Kenneth Williams, Barbara Windsor, Bernard Cribbins, Charles Hawtrey, Eric Barker, Victor Maddern. Acceptable James Bond spoof with daffy novice spy-catchers on the hunt for enemy agents who stole secret formula.

Carson City (1952) C-87m. ** D: Andre de Toth. Randolph Scott, Raymond Massey, Lucille Norman, George Cleveland. OK railroad story in 1870s West as construction engineer Scott battles to get the track down.

Carter's Army (1969) C-72m. TVM D: George McCowan. Stephen Boyd,

Robert Hooks, Susan Oliver, Roosevelt Grier, Paul Stewart, Moses Gunn, Richard Pryor. Southern Army captain handed company of all blacks with no prior combat experience to defend dam during WW2. Clichéd, despite good cast. Below average.

Carthage in Flames (1959-Italian) C-96m. ** D: Carmine Gallone. Jose Suarez, Pierre Brasseur, Anne Heywood, Illaria Occhini. Unremarkable mixture of love and intrigue set against backdrop of Rome-Carthage war of 2nd century B.C.; spirited action scenes.

Cartouche (1964 - French - Italian) C-115m. ***½ D: Philippe De Broca. Jean-Paul Belmondo, Claudia Cardinale, Odile Versois, Philippe Lemaire, Marcel Dalio, Noel Roquevert. Colorful, exciting exploits of 18th-century Frenchman and friends who take over crime syndicate in Paris, eventually dedicating their lives to avenging death of co-leader Venus (Cardinale). Rousing action comedy; Cardinale and Belmondo never better.

Casa Ricordi SEE: House of Ricordi
Casablanca (1942) 102m. **** D: Michael Curtiz. Humphrey Bogart, Ingrid Bergman, Paul Henreid, Claude Rains, Peter Lorre, Sydney Greenstreet, Conrad Veidt, Dooley Wilson, S. Z. Sakall, Joy Page. Everything is right in this WW2 classic of war-torn Casablanca with elusive nightclub owner Rick (Bogart) finding old flame (Bergman) and her husband, underground leader Henreid, among skeletons in his closet. Rains is marvelous as dapper police chief, and nobody sings "As Time Goes By" like Dooley Wilson.

Casanova Brown (1944) 94m. **½ D: Sam Wood. Gary Cooper, Teresa Wright, Frank Morgan, Anita Louise, Isabel Elsom. Cooper has divorced Wright, but now she's pregnant; entertaining little comedy with stars outshining material.

Casanova in Burlesque (1944) 74m. **½ D: Leslie Goodwins. Joe E. Brown, June Havoc, Dale Evans, Lucien Littlefield, Ian Keith. Shakespearean professor leads double life as burlesque clown; spirited little comedy with Brown in good form.

Casanova's Big Night (1954) C-86m. *** D: Norman Z. McLeod. Bob Hope, Joan Fontaine, Audrey Dalton, Basil Rathbone, Raymond Burr, Vincent Price. Lavish costumed fun with

Bob masquerading as Casanova (Price) in Venice and wooing lovely Fontaine.

Casbah (1948) 94m. **½ D: John Berry. Yvonne de Carlo, Tony Martin, Peter Lorre, Marta Toren, Hugo Haas. Musical remake of ALGIERS isn't bad, with Martin coming off surprisingly well amid good Harold Arlen-Leo Robin tunes and colorful production; Lorre fine as determined police detective after Martin in the Casbah.

Case Against Brooklyn, The (1958) 82m. *½ D: Paul Wendkos. Darren McGavin, Maggie Hayes, Warren Stevens, Peggy McCay. Unexciting little exposé yarn involves fledgling cop McGavin combatting gambling syndicate in title borough.

Case Against Mrs. Ames, The (1936) 85m. **½ D: William Seiter. Madeleine Carroll, George Brent, Arthur Treacher, Alan Baxter, Beulah Bondi. D. A. Brent finds himself falling in love with beautiful Carroll, suspected of murdering her husband.

Case of Dr. Laurent, The (1958-French) 91m. ** D: Jean-Paul le Chanois. Jean Gabin, Nicole Courcel, Sylvia Monfort, Michel Barbey. Film was exploited theatrically for its frank birth sequence, only small logical sequence in recounting life of country doctor Gabin who advocates natural childbirth.

Case of Mrs. Loring, The SEE: Question of Adultery, A

Case of Rape, A (1974) C-100m. TVM D: Boris Sagal. Elizabeth Montgomery, William Daniels, Cliff Potts, Rosemary Murphy, Ronny Cox, Patricia Smith. Middle-class housewife (Montgomery) reports being raped and finds that her ordeal has only begun, as the personal humiliations from the police, medical personnel, and the courts, and the waning trust from her husband (Cox) make her feel that she is the guilty one. Sensitively handled by Montgomery and director Sagal, but story keeps veering toward the melodramatic. Above average.

Case of the Curious Bride, The (1935) 80m. ** D: Michael Curtiz. Warren William, Margaret Lindsay, Donald Woods, Claire Dodd, Allen Jenkins, Wini Shaw. Shrill Perry Mason film takes offhanded approach to murder mystery with large doses of humor; Perry (William) is more interested in gourmet food than he is in the case! Errol Flynn has small role in his second Hollywood film.

Case of the Red Monkey (1955-British) 73m. ** D: Ken Hughes. Richard Conte, Rona Anderson, Colin Gordon, Russell Napier. Acceptable police-on-the-case fare, tracking down murderers of atomic scientists.

Casey's Shadow (1978) C-117m. **½ D: Martin Ritt. Walter Matthau, Alexis Smith, Robert Webber, Murray Hamilton, Andrew A. Rubin, Stephen Burns. Lackadaisical family film about a ne'er-do-well horse trainer who has to raise three sons after his wife leaves him. Generally satisfactory, but should have been better.

Cash McCall (1959) C-102m. **½ D: Joseph Pevney. James Garner, Natalie Wood, Nina Foch, Dean Jagger, E. G. Marshall, Henry Jones, Otto Kruger, Roland Winters. Garner is just right as business tycoon who adopts new set of values as he romances daughter (Wood) of failing businessman Jagger. Superficial film from Cameron Hawley novel.

Cash on Delivery (1956-British) 82m. ** D: Muriel Box. Shelley Winters, John Gregson, Peggy Cummins, Wilfrid Hyde-White. Story with a twist suffers from sloppy execution. Winters seeks to earn inheritance by preventing ex-husband's wife from having a child. Original title: TO DOROTHY A SON.

Casino Murder Case (1935) 85m. D: Edwin L. Marin. Paul Lukas, Alison Skipworth, Donald Cook, Rosalind Russell, Arthur Byron. SEE: **Philo Vance** series.

Casino Royale (1967-British) C-130m. **½ D: John Huston, Ken Hughes, Robert Parrish, Joe McGrath, Val Guest. Peter Sellers, Ursula Andress, David Niven, Orson Welles, Joanna Pettet, Woody Allen, Deborah Kerr, William Holden, Charles Boyer, John Huston, George Raft, Jean-Paul Belmondo. Gigantic, overdone spoof of James Bond films with Niven as the aging secret agent who relinquishes his position to nephew Allen and host of others. Money, money everywhere, but film is terribly uneven—sometimes funny, often not.

Cass Timberlane (1947) 119m. **½ D: George Sidney. Spencer Tracy, Lana Turner, Zachary Scott, Tom Drake, Mary Astor, Albert Dekker. Overblown adaptation of Sinclair Lewis novel of esteemed judge trying to keep pace with new young wife; not Tracy's cup of tea.

Cassandra Crossing, The (1977-British) C-127m. *** D: George Pan Cosmatos. Richard Harris, Sophia Loren, Burt Lancaster, Ava Gardner, Martin Sheen, O. J. Simpson, John Philip Law, Ingrid Thulin, Alida Valli, Lionel Stander. Entertaining disaster epic as train carrying plague approaches a weakened bridge. Filmed in France, Italy.

Cast a Dark Shadow (1957-British) 84m. *** D: Lewis Gilbert. Dirk Bogarde, Margaret Lockwood, Kay Walsh, Mona Washbourne. Bogarde is well cast as money-grasping wife-killer who is out to do in his latest wife, Lockwood; exciting throughout.

Cast a Giant Shadow (1966) C-142m. ** D: Melville Shavelson. Kirk Douglas, John Wayne, Frank Sinatra, Yul Brynner, Senta Berger, Angie Dickinson, James Donald, Luther Adler, Haym Topol. Hokey bio of Arab-Israeli war hero Mickey Marcus has Kirk leaving Angie's bed to join Senta and several other less sexy freedom fighters. Guest roles by big names make film seem even more silly.

Cast a Long Shadow (1959) C-82m. *½ D: Thomas Carr. Audie Murphy, Terry Moore, John Dehner, James Best, Rita Lynn, Denver Pyle, Ann Doran. Murphy, troubled by shady past, is reformed by being given a ranch and building a new future; plodding oater.

Castaway Cowboy, The (1974) C-91m. ** D: Vincent McEveety. James Garner, Vera Miles, Robert Culp, Eric Shea, Elizabeth Smith, Gregory Sierra. Cowboy Garner is shipwrecked on Hawaiian island, runs into pretty widow and bad-guy Culp who wants her land. Old B-Western plot, Disney-fied on Hawaiian locations.

Castilian, The (1963-Spanish, dubbed) C-129m. **½ D: Javier Seto. Cesar Romero, Alida Valli, Frankie Avalon, Broderick Crawford. Strange grouping of actors are given little support by sticky script in costumer of nobleman Avalon leading his people against invaders.

Castle in the Desert (1942) 62m. D: Harry Lachman. Sidney Toler, Arleen Whelan, Richard Derr, Douglass Dumbrille, Henry Daniell, Victor Sen Yung. See: **Charlie Chan** series.

Castle Keep (1969) C-105m. *½ D: Sydney Pollack. Burt Lancaster, Peter Falk, Patrick O'Neal, Jean-

Pierre Aumont, Scott Wilson, Al Freeman. Pretentious adaptation of William Eastlake's novel about eight soldiers on French border in WW2. Good cast, but film has no coherency.

Castle of Blood SEE: Castle of Terror, The

Castle of Evil (1966) C-81m. BOMB D: Francis D. Lyon. Scott Brady, Virginia Mayo, David Brian, Lisa Gaye, Hugh Marlowe. Electronic man belonging to dead chemist becomes unprogrammed at the reading of his master's will and starts killing the survivors. Producers should have taken the film's production costs and bought a candy bar instead.

Castle of Fu Manchu, The (1968) 92m. BOMB D: Jesus Franco. Christopher Lee, Richard Greene, Maria Perschy, Gunther Stoll, Howard Marion Crawford. Lee buries Fu Manchu with this one—the pits—experimenting with more deadly potions in his castle near Istanbul and parrying with his perennial adversary, Nayland Smith (Greene) of Britain's Home Office. Another international production.

Castle of Terror, The (1964-Italian-French) 85m. ** D: Anthony Dawson. Barbara Steele, George Riviere, Margrete Robsahm, Henry Kruger, Montgomery Glenn, Sylvia Sorente. On a wager, poet spends the night in haunted castle. Atmospheric chiller. Also known as CASTLE OF BLOOD.

Castle of the Living Dead (1964-Italian-French) 90m. ** D: Herbert Wise (Luciano Ricci). Christopher Lee, Gaia Germani, Philippe Leroy, Jacques Stanislawski, Donald Sutherland. Lee is suitably cast as sinister Count Drago, who mummifies visitors to his gothic castle. Unexceptional horror fare.

Castle on the Hudson (1940) 77m. *** D: Anatole Litvak. John Garfield, Pat O'Brien, Ann Sheridan, Burgess Meredith, Jerome Cowan, Henry O'Neill. Faithful remake of 20,000 YEARS IN SING SING is by-now-familiar prisoner vs. warden battle, but an outstanding cast helps elevate it.

Cat, The (1966) C-87m. BOMB D: Ellis Kadison. Peggy Ann Garner, Barry Coe, Roger Perry, Dwayne Redlin. Humdrum account of boy separated from parents on camping trip, saved from rustler's wrath by wildcat he befriended.

Cat and Mouse (1975-French) C-107m. ***½ D: Claude Lelouch.

Michele Morgan, Serge Reggiani, Philippe Leotard, Jean-Pierre Aumont, Valerie Lagrange. Anyone could've killed wealthy Aumont, philandering husband of Morgan, and Inspector Reggiani finds out who and why. Denouement is only letdown in this delightful comedy mystery, written, directed, and produced by master Lelouch. Dazzling views of Paris and the countryside. Released here in 1978.

Cat and the Canary, The (1927) 60m. *** D: Paul Leni. Laura LaPlante, Tully Marshall, Flora Finch, Creighton Hale, Gertrude Astor, Lucien Littlefield. Delightful silent classic, the forerunner of all "old dark house" mysteries, with nice touch of humor throughout as heiress LaPlante and nervous group spend night in haunted house.

Cat and the Canary, The (1978-British) C-90m. **½ D: Radley Metzger. Honor Blackman, Michael Callan, Edward Fox, Wendy Hiller, Olivia Hussey, Carol Lynley, Peter McEnery, Wilfrid Hyde-White. Kinky update of classic John Willard play, filmed before in 1927, 1930, and 1939, about family collecting inheritance by spending night in old dark house. Good cast in uneven blend of melodrama, spoofery, and sex.

Cat and the Fiddle, The (1934) 90m. *** D: William K. Howard. Jeanette MacDonald, Ramon Novarro, Frank Morgan, Charles Butterworth, Jean Hersholt. Delightful Jerome Kern-Oscar Hammerstein operetta, filled with sly comedy and clever ideas. Novarro is a struggling composer who forces his attentions on MacDonald; Morgan is "benefactor" who comes between them. Songs include "The Night Was Made for Love," "She Didn't Say Yes." Final sequence originally filmed in color.

Cat Ballou (1965) C-96m. ***½ D: Elliott Silverstein. Jane Fonda, Lee Marvin, Michael Callan, Dwayne Hickman, Reginald Denny, Jay C. Flippen. Funny Western spoof with Fonda as Cat Ballou, notorious female outlaw, Marvin in an Oscar performance as a drunken gunman. Nat King Cole and Stubby Kaye add to film as strolling minstrels.

Cat Creature, The (1973) C-72m. TVM D: Curtis Harrington. Meredith Baxter, David Hedison, Gale Sondergaard, Stuart Whitman, Keye Luke, John Carradine. Script by Robert

(PSYCHO) Bloch and good direction combine in unusual horror tale of cat goddess possessing victims to gain access to gold amulet. Good suspense, above average.

Cat Creeps, The (1946) 58m. BOMB D: Erle C. Kenton. Noah Beery, Jr., Lois Collier, Paul Kelly, Douglass Dumbrille, Rose Hobart. Lowest of low-grade horrors, with cat possessing dead girl's soul.

Cat from Outer Space, The (1978) C-104m. **½ D: Norman Tokar. Ken Berry, Sandy Duncan, McLean Stevenson, Harry Morgan, Roddy McDowall, Ronnie Schell. Kids will probably like this Disney fantasy-comedy, though it holds few surprises: cat from another world seeks help from U.S. scientists to repair his spaceship, but military protocol and enemy spying get in the way.

Cat Girl (1957-British) 69m. *½ D: Alfred Shaughnessy. Barbara Shelley, Robert Ayres, Kay Callard, Paddy Webster. Shelley is possessed by family curse which transforms her into blood-seeking animal, with rash of murders; pacing and low production values spoil total effect.

Cat o' Nine Tails, The (1971-Italian-German-French) C-112m. BOMB D: Dario Argento. Karl Malden, James Franciscus, Catherine Spaak, Cinzia De Carolis, Carlo Alighiero. Former newsman Malden, now blind, teams with reporter Franciscus to track down psycho killer in this gruesome murder mystery; graphic gore and sex will be cut for TV, but it's no loss. Badly dubbed, to boot.

Cat on a Hot Tin Roof (1958) C-108m. ***½ D: Richard Brooks. Elizabeth Taylor, Paul Newman, Burl Ives, Jack Carson, Judith Anderson. Entire cast is excellent in this tour de force Tennessee Williams story of mendacity uprooting a patriarchal Southern family.

Cat People (1942) 73m. *** D: Jacques Tourneur. Simone Simon, Kent Smith, Tom Conway, Jack Holt, Jane Randolph. Storyline and plot elements don't hold up, but moments of shock and terror are undiminished in the first of producer Val Lewton's famous horror films. Smith falls in love with strange, shy woman (Simon) who fears ancient curse of the panther inside her. Followed by CURSE OF THE CAT PEOPLE.

Cat Women of the Moon (1954) 64m. *½ D: Arthur Hilton. Sonny

Tufts, Victor Jory, Marie Windsor, Bill Phipps, Douglas Fowley, Susan Morrow. All-star cast in tacky sci-fi entry about a moon expedition that discovers female civilization and its underground empire. Originally shown in 3D; also known as ROCKET TO THE MOON. Remade as MISSILE TO THE MOON.

Cat's Paw, The (1934) 90m. **½ D: Sam Taylor. Harold Lloyd, Una Merkel, George Barbier, Alan Dinehart, Grace Bradley, Nat Pendleton. Harold is a missionary's son, raised in China; he comes to U.S. a babe in the woods, is duped into running for Mayor in big city by corrupt politicos who regard him as perfect patsy. Odd Capraesque comedy ends with strange denouement where Lloyd takes law into his own hands. A real curio. Edited for TV.

Catch My Soul (1974) C-95m. *½ D: Patrick McGoohan. Richie Havens, Lance Le Gault, Season Hubley, Tony Joe White, Susan Tyrrell, Delaney and Bonnie Bramlett. Jack Good's rock-opera adaptation of Shakespeare's "Othello," with Havens as sanctimonious preacher and LeGault as his Iago is uninvolving, heavy-handed stuff. Some good music, but if the play's the thing, this one doesn't make it.

Catch-22 (1970) C-121m. **½ D: Mike Nichols. Alan Arkin, Martin Balsam, Richard Benjamin, Art Garfunkel, Jack Gilford, Bob Newhart, Anthony Perkins, Paula Prentiss, Martin Sheen, Jon Voight, Orson Welles. Long, labored, expensive film of Joseph Heller's book halfway succeeds in capturing surrealist insanity of Army life during WW2. Heavy-handedness spoils potential, with good cast trying its best.

Catch Us If You Can SEE: Having a Wild Weekend

Catcher, The (1971) C-100m. TVM D: Allen H. Miner. Michael Witney, Jan-Michael Vincent, Tony Franciosa, Catherine Burns, David Wayne, Mike Kellin, Anne Baxter. Seattle policeman and Harvard grad join forces in locating fugitives, runaway husbands, missing children throughout U.S. Good locations main asset in otherwise unmemorable drama. Average.

Catered Affair, The (1956) 93m. *** D: Richard Brooks. Bette Davis, Ernest Borgnine, Debbie Reynolds, Barry Fitzgerald, Rod Taylor. Davis sheds all glamour as Bronx taxi driver's wife wanting to give daughter ritzy wedding. Based on Paddy Chayefsky TV play.

Catherine the Great (1934-British) 92m. **½ D: Paul Czinner. Douglas Fairbanks, Jr., Elisabeth Bergner, Flora Robson, Joan Gardner, Gerald Du Maurier. Lavish historical drama of Russian czarina whose life is spoiled by rigidly planned marriage. Slow-moving but interesting. Also known as THE RISE OF CATHERINE THE GREAT.

Catlow (1971) C-103m. **½ D: Sam Wanamaker. Yul Brynner, Richard Crenna, Leonard Nimoy, Daliah Lavi, Jo Ann Pflug, Jeff Corey. Outlaw tries to avoid interference on his way to $2 million gold robbery.

Cattle Drive (1951) C-77m. **½ D: Kurt Neumann. Joel McCrea, Dean Stockwell, Leon Ames, Chill Wills. Stockwell does well in role of bratty teen-ager who learns a sense of values from veteran cowhand McCrea on arduous cow drive.

Cattle Empire (1958) C-83m. ** D: Charles Marquis Warren. Joel McCrea, Gloria Talbott, Don Haggerty, Phyllis Coates. McCrea agrees to lead cattle drive, planning revenge on cattle owners who sent him to jail; OK Western.

Cattle King (1963) C-88m. ** D: Tay Garnett. Robert Taylor, Joan Caulfield, Robert Loggia, Robert Middleton, Larry Gates, Malcolm Atterbury. Control of grazing land subject of standard Western confrontation saga, Taylor and Middleton squaring off in forgettable drama.

Cattle Queen of Montana (1954) C-88m. **½ D: Allan Dwan. Barbara Stanwyck, Ronald Reagan, Gene Evans, Lance Fuller. Staunch Stanwyck is determined to keep lands her father left her, despite townfolk and Indians. More talk than real action.

Cattle Town (1952) 71m. ** D: Noel Smith. Dennis Morgan, Philip Carey, Amanda Blake, Rita Moreno, Sheb Wooley, Merv Griffin. Both Warner Bros. and Morgan were at low points when this sad echo of a slick Western was churned out.

Caught (1949) 88m. *** D: Max Ophuls. James Mason, Barbara Bel Geddes, Robert Ryan, Frank Ferguson, Curt Bois, Natalie Schafer. Compelling, intelligent story of young girl who marries powerful millionaire, tries to escape her shallow existence with him. Fine performances, skilled direction by Ophuls.

Caught in the Draft (1941) 82m. *** D: David Butler. Bob Hope, Dorothy Lamour, Lynne Overman, Eddie Bracken. The last thing movie-star Hope wants is to get drafted, but he accidentally enlists himself. Very funny service comedy.

Cauldron of Blood (1967-Spanish-American) C-95m. *½ D: Edward Mann (Santos Alcocer). Boris Karloff, Viveca Lindfors, Jean-Pierre Aumont, Jacqui Speed, Rosenda Monteros. Sordid, sleep-inducing tale of blind sculptor (Karloff) whose skeletal models are actually victims of his murdering wife. Also known as BLIND MAN'S BLUFF.

Cause for Alarm (1951) 74m. **½ D: Tay Garnett. Loretta Young, Barry Sullivan, Bruce Cowling, Margalo Gillmore. Young registers most convincingly as panic-stricken woman being framed for murder by her insane husband Sullivan.

Cavalcade (1933) 110m. *** D: Frank Lloyd. Diana Wynyard, Herbert Mundin, Ursula Jeans, Margaret Lindsay, Clive Brook, Beryl Mercer, Una O'Connor, Billy Bevan. Lavish adaptation of Noel Coward episodic play of British family surviving through war, scandal, depression, etc. Witty Coward songs included.

Cavalry Scout (1951) C-78m. ** D: Lesley Selander. Rod Cameron, Audrey Long, Jim Davis, James Millican. Routine Western of scout Cameron tracking down stolen army goods and romancing Long.

Cave of Outlaws (1951) C-75m. ** D: William Castle. Macdonald Carey, Alexis Smith, Edgar Buchanan, Victor Jory. Search for stolen gold leads ex-con, lawman, miner, et al to title situation; Smith is wasted.

Cavern, The (1966) 83m. **½ D: Edgar G. Ulmer. Rosanna Schiaffino, John Saxon, Brian Aherne, Peter L. Marshall, Larry Hagman, Hans Von Borsody. Six soldiers are trapped for five months in cavern with luscious Schiaffino, but plot contrivance isn't handled badly in above-average programmer.

Ceiling Zero (1935) 95m. *** D: Howard Hawks. James Cagney, Pat O'Brien, June Travis, Stuart Erwin, Barton MacLane. Rival fliers working for same company risk lives, also risk friendship when woman comes between them. Better than most Cagney-O'Brien films. Good aerial photography.

Celebration at Big Sur (1971) C-82m.

** D: Baird Bryant, Johanna Demetrakas. Joan Baez, Crosby, Stills, Nash and Young, Joni Mitchell, John Sebastian, Mimi Fariña. Lesser rock documentary has a few great musical moments, but is poorly pasted together. Rare opportunity to see Joni Mitchell.

Cell 2455, Death Row (1955) 77m. ** D: Fred F. Sears. William Campbell, Kathryn Grant, Vince Edwards, Marian Carr. Unsensational retracing of life of sex-offender Caryl Chessman and his bouts, while in prison, for retrials.

Centennial Summer (1946) C-102m. **½ D: Otto Preminger. Jeanne Crain, Cornel Wilde, Linda Darnell, Dorothy Gish, William Eythe, Constance Bennett, Walter Brennan. Leisurely, plush musical of Philadelphia Exposition of 1876, with sisters Crain and Darnell both after handsome Wilde; nice Jerome Kern score helps.

Ceremony, The (1963) 105m. **½ D: Laurence Harvey. Laurence Harvey, Sarah Miles, Robert Walker, Jr., John Ireland, Ross Martin, Lee Patterson, Noel Purcell. Mishmash about convicted killer rescued by brother who demands liaison with sister-in-law as reward.

Certain Smile, A (1958) C-106m. **½ D: Jean Negulesco. Rossano Brazzi, Joan Fontaine, Bradford Dillman, Christine Carere. Françoise Sagan's novella becomes overblown soap opera in romantic trivia between Parisian students Carere and Dillman, interrupted when she is beguiled by roué Brazzi; chic Fontaine is wasted.

Cervantes SEE: Young Rebels

Cesar and Rosalie (1972-French-Italian-German) C-104m. *** D: Claude Sautet. Yves Montand, Romy Schneider, Sami Frey, Umberto Orsini, Eva Marie Meineke. Appealing stars in typically French story of a menage à trois relationship (a woman and her two lovers) and how it changes over the years.

Chad Hanna (1940) C-86m. ** D: Henry King. Henry Fonda, Dorothy Lamour, Linda Darnell, Guy Kibbee, Jane Darwell, John Carradine. Rather flat circus drama set in 19th-century New York; colorful but empty.

Chadwick Family, The (1974) C-78m. TVM D: David Lowell Rich. Fred MacMurray, Kathleen Maguire, Darleen Carr, Jane Actman, Stephen Nathan, Lara Parker. Undistinguished soap opera, with MacMurray moving from the dad of "My Three Sons" to patriarch of a clan consisting of wife Maguire, three daughters, one son, two sons-in-law, and the Chinese boyfriend of his youngest girl. Average.

Chain Lightning (1950) 94m. ** D: Stuart Heisler. Humphrey Bogart, Eleanor Parker, Raymond Massey, Richard Whorf. Static account of jet pilot Bogart who reforms in an effort to win back Parker; flight scenes uninspired.

Chain of Evidence (1957) 64m. *½ D: Paul Landres. Bill Elliott, Don Haggerty, James Lydon, Claudia Barrett. Programmer has dedicated cop Elliott track down real killer of businessman.

Chained (1934) 71m. **½ D: Clarence Brown. Joan Crawford, Clark Gable, Otto Kruger, Stuart Erwin, Una O'Connor, Akim Tamiroff. Chic formula MGM love triangle with Crawford torn between love for Gable and honorable husband Kruger.

Chairman, The (1969) C-102m. **½ D: J. Lee Thompson. Gregory Peck, Anne Heywood, Arthur Hill, Alan Dobie, Conrad Yama. Lots of talk but little action in story of American scientist sent to Communist China on super-secret espionage mission.

Chalk Garden, The (1964-British) C-106m. *** D: Ronald Neame. Deborah Kerr, Hayley Mills, John Mills, Edith Evans, Felix Aylmer, Elizabeth Sellars. Very-high-class soap opera with good cast supporting story of teenager set on right path by governess Kerr; colorful production, quite entertaining.

Challenge, The (1960) SEE: It Takes a Thief

Challenge, The (1970) C-73m. TVM D: Allen Smithee. Darren McGavin, Broderick Crawford, Mako, James Whitmore, Skip Homeier, Paul Lukas, Sam Elliott. Odd sequence of events —returning orbital missile satellite crash-lands far from designated splashdown area; small Communist country's ship reaches it first and claims right of salvage—brings two nations to brink of nuclear war. Average.

Challenge To Be Free (1976) C-88m. **½ D: Tay Garnett. Mike Mazurki, Vic Christy, Jimmy Kane, Fritz Ford. Fur trapper is pursued by the law in Arctic surroundings; simple and simple-minded, best for younger viewers. Made in 1972 as MAD TRAPPER OF THE YUKON, this marked last film for veteran director Garnett, who appears briefly as Marshal McGee.

Challenge to Lassie (1949) C-76m. ** D: Richard Thorpe. Edmund Gwenn. Geraldine Brooks, Reginald Owen, Sara Allgood, Arthur Shields. Pleasant trivia, with Lassie's ownership in dispute; solid performances by character-actor cast.

Challengers, The (1969) C-100m. TVM D: Leslie Martinson. Darren McGavin, Sean Garrison, Nico Minardos, Anne Baxter, Richard Conte, Farley Granger. Top professional racing drivers competing for Grand Prix; off track, for same girl. Embarrassing script. Below average.

Chamber of Horrors (1940-British) 80m. **½ D: Norman Lee. Leslie Banks, Lilli Palmer, Romilly Lunge, Gina Malo, Richard Bird, Cathleen Nesbitt. Low-budget horror comes over fairly well, with dastardly Banks making his house a mass morgue, menacing lovely Palmer. Based on Edgar Wallace story. Original title: THE DOOR WITH SEVEN LOCKS.

Chamber of Horrors (1966) C-99m. *½ D: Hy Averback. Patrick O'Neal, Cesare Danova, Wilfrid Hyde-White, Patrice Wymore, Suzy Parker, Marie Windsor, Tony Curtis. Wax museum provides setting for uneven mystery about mad killer on the loose. Intended for TV, it has mark of low-budget film. Uses gimmick of horn sounding before each murder.

Champ, The (1931) 87m. **½ D: King Vidor. Wallace Beery, Jackie Cooper, Irene Rich, Roscoe Ates, Edward Brophy, Hale Hamilton. Slow-moving story of young boy's faith in his father, a washed-up prizefighter; worth seeing for fine performances by Cooper and Beery (who won an Oscar). Remade in 1953 (as THE CLOWN) and 1979.

Champ, The (1979) C-121m. *½ D: Franco Zeffirelli. Jon Voight, Faye Dunaway, Ricky Shroder, Jack Warden, Arthur Hill, Strother Martin, Joan Blondell, Elisha Cook. Voight is too intelligent to convince as a dumb pug, and Dunaway, as a loving mother, looks as if she wants to bed down with her kid in hopeless remake of the 1931 sudser. Young Shroder cries (and cries) convincingly.

Champ for a Day (1953) 90m. ** D: William Seiter. Alex Nicol, Audrey Totter, Charles Winninger, Hope

Emerson, Henry Morgan. Brooklyn boxer tracks down friend's murderers; average.

Champagne for Caesar (1950) 99m. *** D: Richard Whorf. Ronald Colman, Celeste Holm, Vincent Price, Barbara Britton, Art Linkletter. Genius Colman becomes national celebrity on TV quiz show; sponsor Price sends temptress Holm to distract big winner. Enjoyable spoof, with Price hilarious as neurotic soap manufacturer.

Champagne Murders, The (1967-French) C-98m. *** D: Claude Chabrol. Anthony Perkins, Maurice Ronet, Stephane Audran, Yvonne Furneaux, Suzanne Lloyd, Catherine Sola. Sale of champagne company to U.S. conglomerate manipulated by various weird, competing types, complicated by murders which point to playboy (Ronet). Murder-mystery narrative backdrop for odd psychological drama; one-of-a-kind film.

Champagne Waltz (1937) 87m. ** D: A. Edward Sutherland. Gladys Swarthout, Fred MacMurray, Jack Oakie, Herman Bing, Vivienne Osborne. Flyweight musical about rivalry between Vienna waltz palace and American jazz band next door gets sillier as it goes along; operatic Swarthout is saddled with mediocre songs, as well. Oakie's comedy relief most welcome.

Champion (1949) 90m. ***½ D: Mark Robson. Kirk Douglas, Marilyn Maxwell, Arthur Kennedy, Ruth Roman, Lola Albright. Unscrupulous boxer punches his way to the top, thrusting aside everybody and everything. Douglas perfectly cast in title role; gripping film.

Champions: A Love Story (1979) C-100m. TVM D: John A. Alonzo. Shirley Knight, Tony Lo Bianco, James Vincent McNichol, Joy Le-Duc, Jennifer Warren, Richard Jaeckel. Teenagers, trying out for the national figure skating championships, fall in love; not unlike ICE CASTLES. Well acted—and skated. Above average.

Chance Meeting (1959-British) 96m. **½ D: Joseph Losey. Hardy Kruger, Stanley Baker, Micheline Presle, Robert Flemyng, Gordon Jackson. Kafkaesque story of painter framed for girlfriend's murder. Intriguing little mystery becomes talky, loses initial momentum. British title: *Blind Date.*

Chance of a Lifetime, The (1943)

65m. D: William Castle. Chester Morris, Eric Rolf, Jeanne Bates, Richard Lane, George E. Stone, Lloyd Corrigan. SEE: **Boston Blackie Series.**

Chandler (1972) C-88m. *½ D: Paul Magwood. Warren Oates, Leslie Caron, Alex Dreier, Gloria Grahame, Mitchell Ryan. Private-eye falls in love with ex-mistress of racketeer. Substandard yarn.

Chandu the Magician (1932) 70m. *½ D: William Cameron Menzies, Marcel Varnel. Edmund Lowe, Bela Lugosi, Irene Ware, Henry B. Walthall, Herbert Mundin. Spiritualist Chandu battles madman whose death ray threatens to destroy world; not as good as most serials of this genre, and even sillier. Disappointing.

Change of Habit (1969) C-93m. ** D: William Graham. Elvis Presley, Mary Tyler Moore, Barbara McNair, Jane Elliot, Leora Dana, Edward Asner, Doro Merande, Regis Toomey. Moore, a nun, is forced to choose between Dr. Presley and the church in substandard drama that at least represents slight change from typical Elvis fare.

Change of Heart (1934) 75m. BOMB D: John G. Blystone. Janet Gaynor, Charles Farrell, Ginger Rogers, James Dunn, Shirley Temple. Two happy young couples come to New York to seek their fortune, only to find disharmony. Likable cast lost in plodding script.

Changeling, The (1979-Canadian) C-109m. *** D: Peter Medak. George C. Scott, Trish Van Devere, Melvyn Douglas, John Colicos, Jean Marsh, Madeleine Thornton-Sherwood. Good, scary ghost story with Scott as recently widowed musician who moves into an old house inhabited by spirit of a child who lived there 70 years ago.

Chaplin Revue, The (1958) 119m. ***½ D: Charles Chaplin. Charlie Chaplin, Edna Purviance, Sydney Chaplin, Mack Swain. Three of Chaplin's best shorts strung together with his own music, narration, and behind-the-scenes footage: A DOG'S LIFE (1918), one of his loveliest films; SHOULDER ARMS (1918), a classic WW1 comedy; and THE PILGRIM (1923), his underrated gem about a convict who disguises as a minister.

Chapman Report, The (1962) C-125m. **½ D: George Cukor. Efrem Zimbalist, Jr., Jane Fonda, Shelley Winters, Claire Bloom, Glynis Johns, Ray Danton, Ty Hardin. Slick, empty yarn about Kinsey-like sex researchers coming to suburban community to get statistical survey, with repercussions on assorted females. Potboiler material elevated by good performances and direction.

Chapter Two (1979) C-124m. ** D: Robert Moore. James Caan, Marsha Mason, Valerie Harper, Joseph Bologna. Neil Simon's autobiographical comedy drama—one of his best Broadway plays—gets lost in screen translation. Caan is miscast as sharp-minded writer who's drawn into new romance (with Mason) before he's really recovered from death of his wife. Long, plastic, and unmoving.

Charade (1963) C-114m. ***½ D: Stanley Donen. Cary Grant, Audrey Hepburn, Walter Matthau, James Coburn, George Kennedy. Suave mystery with Grant aiding widow Hepburn to recover fortune secreted by husband, being sought by trio of sinister crooks; set in chic Paris.

Charge at Feather River, The (1953) C-96m. **½ D: Gordon Douglas. Guy Madison, Vera Miles, Frank Lovejoy, Helen Westcott, Ron Hagerthy. One of many Westerns which literally threw action at viewers to utilize 3-D used for original release; now, just standard.

Charge of the Black Lancers (1961-Italian) C-97m. **½ D: Giacomo Gentilomo. Mel Ferrer, Yvonne Furneaux, Jean Claudio, Leticia Roman. Effective costumer,. wellmounted and fast-paced. Claudio is traitor to country with his brother (Ferrer) leading patriots in defense of homeland.

Charge of the Lancers (1954) C-74m. ** D: William Castle. Paulette Goddard, Jean-Pierre Aumont, Richard Stapley. Stilted affair of gypsy Goddard and British officer Aumont finding romance in midst of Crimean War.

Charge of the Light Brigade, The (1936) 116m. *** D: Michael Curtiz. Errol Flynn, Olivia de Havilland, Patric Knowles, Henry Stephenson, Nigel Bruce, Donald Crisp, David Niven. Thundering action based on Tennyson's poem, with climactic charge into certain death by British army. Lavish production values accent romantic tale of Flynn and De Havilland at army post in India.

Charge of the Light Brigade, The (1968-British) C-130m. **½ D: Tony Richardson. David Hemmings, Vanessa Redgrave, John Gielgud, Harry Andrews, Trevor Howard, Jill Bennett, Mark Burns. Exquisitely made, but ultimately disappointing drama of events leading up to British involvement in Crimean War. Stunning battle sequence cannot make up for dramatic loopholes in this story of military minds gone mad. Clever animated segments by Richard Williams.

Chariots of the Gods? (1974) C-98m. *** D: Harald Reinl. First of too many documentaries about ancient visitors from outer space who helped advance mankind's knowledge centuries ago. Well-made and filled with many natural beauties. Based on Erich Von Daniken's book.

Charleston (1979) C-100m. TVM D: Karen Arthur. Delta Burke, Jordan Clarke, Richard Lawson, Lynne Moody, Patricia Pearcy, Martha Scott. Unfortunate clone of *Gone with the Wind* even has a pouty, self-centered Southern belle who looks like Vivien Leigh. Produced, directed, and written by women, but offers no insights—feminist or otherwise—on familiar material. Below average.

Charley and the Angel (1973) C-93m. **½ D: Vincent McEveety. Fred MacMurray, Cloris Leachman, Harry Morgan, Kurt Russell, Vincent Van Patten, Kathleen Cody. MacMurray learns he has only a short time left on earth from helpful angel (Morgan) and changes his hard ways with family. Lightly amusing Disney film, but the warmth and nostalgia seem artificial this time around.

Charley One-Eye (1973) C-107m. ** D: Don Chaffey. Richard Roundtree, Roy Thinnes, Nigel Davenport, Jill Pearson. Basically two-man show. Black Union Army deserter (Roundtree) and outcast Indian (Thinnes) thrown together in desert wasteland; gradual tragic relationship develops when outside forces interfere. Far too long; should've been a TV movie.

Charley Varrick (1973) C-111m. **½ D: Don Siegel. Walter Matthau, John Vernon, Andy Robinson, Jacqueline Scott, Joe Don Baker, Woodrow Parfrey. Grim chase thriller features Matthau in title role as bank robber discovering too late that small-town take actually is laundered Mafia money. Plausible until halfway mark;

afterwards, despite two offbeat sequences, deteriorates.

Charley's Aunt (1941) 81m. **½ D: Archie Mayo. Jack Benny, Kay Francis, James Ellison, Anne Baxter, Edmund Gwenn, Reginald Owen. Broad but surefire refilming of Brandon Thomas play about Oxford student posing as maiden aunt, joke getting out of hand. Remade as musical WHERE'S CHARLEY?

Charlie Bubbles (1968) C-91m. **½ D: Albert Finney. Albert Finney, Colin Blakeley, Billie Whitelaw, Liza Minnelli. Finney's first directing attempt concerns itself with married writer who begins affair with his secretary. Not especially moving, but Minnelli's debut adds quite a bit of sparkle to film.

Charlie Chan Earl Derr Biggers' character of an Oriental detective on the Honolulu police force first appeared on the screen in 1926, but did not make an impression upon moviegoers until Warner Oland took over the role in 1931 with CHARLIE CHAN CARRIES ON. He essayed the part until his death in 1937, when he was replaced by Sidney Toler. Toler carried on for nine years, and upon his death was replaced in turn by Roland Winters, who starred for the last two years of the fading series. The early entries with Oland are the best, with CHARLIE CHAN AT THE OPERA and ON BROADWAY standing out; Toler's first attempts are quite good, especially CHARLIE CHAN AT TREASURE ISLAND (one of the best in the whole series) and IN PANAMA. But in the 1940s, with less interest and a change of studios, the series declined, and so did Toler. His last efforts, like DANGEROUS MONEY, were pretty bad, and Mr. Toler had aged considerably. The series gave out a dying gasp with Roland Winters, who was totally unsuited for the role. The last Chan film, SKY DRAGON, is unbearable. Despite their age, the early efforts remain fresh and entertaining today, with Charlie constantly at odds with his #1 or #2 son (Keye Luke and Sen Yung, respectively) and mouthing his famous words of wisdom: "Insignificant molehill sometimes more important than conspicuous mountain," etc. Today the Charlie Chan films offer a delightful change of pace and for the most part are highly recommended.

Charlie Chan at Monte Carlo (1937) 71m. D: Eugene Forde. Warner Oland, Keye Luke, Virginia Field, Sidney Blackmer, Harold Huber, Louis Mercier, Robert Kent.

Charlie Chan at the Circus (1936) 72m. D: Harry Lachman. Warner Oland, Keye Luke, George and Olive Brasno, Francis Ford, Maxine Reiner, John McGuire, Shirley Deane, J. Carrol Naish.

Charlie Chan at the Olympics (1937) 71m. D: H. Bruce Humberstone. Warner Oland, Keye Luke, Katherine DeMille, Pauline Moore, C. Henry Gordon, Jonathan Hale, Allan Lane, John Eldredge.

Charlie Chan at the Opera (1936) 66m. D: H. Bruce Humberstone. Warner Oland, Boris Karloff, Keye Luke, Charlotte Henry, Thomas Beck, Gregory Gaye, Nedda Harrigan, William Demarest.

Charlie Chan at the Race Track (1936) 70m. D: H. Bruce Humberstone. Warner Oland, Keye Luke, Helen Wood, Thomas Beck, Alan Dinehart, Gavin Muir, Gloria Roy, Jonathan Hale.

Charlie Chan at the Wax Museum (1940) 63m. D: Lynn Shores. Sidney Toler, Sen Yung, C. Henry Gordon, Marc Lawrence, Joan Valerie, Marguerite Chapman, Ted Osborne, Michael Visaroff.

Charlie Chan at Treasure Island (1939) 75m. D: Norman Foster. Sidney Toler, Cesar Romero, Pauline Moore, Douglass Dumbrille, Billie Seward, Louis Jean Heydt, Charles Halton.

Charlie Chan in Black Magic: SEE: Black Magic

Charlie Chan in City of Darkness (1939) 75m. D: Herbert I. Leeds, Sidney Toler, Lynn Bari, Richard Clarke, Pedro de Cordoba, Douglass Dumbrille, Lon Chaney, Jr., Leo G. Carroll.

Charlie Chan in Egypt (1935) 65m. D: Louis King. Warner Oland, "Pat" Paterson, Thomas Beck, Rita Hayworth, Jameson Thomas, Frank Conroy, Nigel de Brulier, Paul Porcasi, Stepin Fetchit.

Charlie Chan in Honolulu (1938) 65m. D: H. Bruce Humberstone. Sidney Toler, Phyllis Brooks, Sen Yung, Eddie Collins, John King, Claire Dodd, George Zucco, Robert Barrat.

Charlie Chan in London (1934) 79m. D: Eugene Forde. Warner Oland, Ray Milland, Mona Barrie, Drue Leyton, Alan Mowbray, David Torrence, Madge Bellamy.

Charlie Chan in Panama (1940) 67m. D: Norman Foster. Sidney Toler, Jean Rogers, Kane Richmond, Lionel Atwill, Mary Nash, Sen Yung, Chris-Pin Martin.

Charlie Chan in Reno (1939) 70m. D: Norman Foster. Sidney Toler, Ricardo Cortez, Phyllis Brooks, Slim Summerville, Kane Richmond, Robert Lowery, Morgan Conway, Sen Yung.

Charlie Chan in Rio (1941) 60m. D: Harry Lachman. Sidney Toler, Mary Beth Hughes, Cobina Wright, Jr., Ted (Michael) North, Victor Jory, Harold Huber, Sen Yung.

Charlie Chan in Shanghai (1935) 70m. D: James Tinling. Warner Oland, Irene Hervey, Russell Hicks, Keye Luke, Halliwell Hobbes, Charles Locher (Jon Hall).

Charlie Chan in the Secret Service (1944) 63m. D: Phil Rosen. Sidney Toler, Mantan Moreland, Gwen Kenyon, Benson Fong, Eddy Chandler.

Charlie Chan on Broadway (1937) 68m. D: Eugene Forde. Warner Oland, Keye Luke, Joan Marsh, J. Edward Bromberg, Leon Ames, Joan Woodbury, Douglas Fowley, Louise Henry, Donald Woods, Harold Huber.

Charlie Chan's Murder Cruise (1940) 75m. D: Eugene Forde. Sidney Toler, Sen Yung, Marjorie Weaver, Lionel Atwill, Robert Lowery, Don Beddoe, Leo G. Carroll.

Charlie Chan's Secret (1936) 71m. D: Gordon Wiles. Warner Oland, Rosina Lawrence, Charley Quigley, Henrietta Crosman, Edward Trevor, Astrid Allwyn.

Charlie Chaplin Carnival (1938) 75m. **** Four vintage comedies from Chaplin's 1916-17 peak period: "Behind the Screen," "The Count," "The Fireman," "The Vagabond." First one is best, with leading lady Edna Purviance and oversized villain Eric Campbell.

Charlie Chaplin Cavalcade (1938) 75m. **** More priceless gems from 1916-17 period: "One A.M." (Chaplin's famous solo film), "The Rink," "The Pawnshop," "The Floorwalker." All great.

Charlie Chaplin Festival (1938) 75m. **** Best of the Chaplin compilations, which all suffer from obtrusive sound effects and music: "The Adventurer," "The Cure," "Easy Street," "The Immigrant." Four of the greatest comedies ever made—don't miss them.

Charlie Cobb: Nice Night for a Hanging (1977) C-100m. TVM D: Richard Michaels. Clu Gulager, Ralph Bellamy, Stella Stevens, Blair Brown, Pernell Roberts, Christopher Connelly, Tricia O'Neil. Light-hearted Western has Gulager, a resourceful private eye of the 1870s, battling those with evil plans for Ms. Brown, believed to be long-missing daughter of wealthy rancher Bellamy. Average.

Charlie McCarthy, Detective (1939) 65m. **½ D: Frank Tuttle. Edgar Bergen, Charlie McCarthy, Constance Moore, Robert Cummings, Louis Calhern, John Sutton, Harold Huber, Edgar Kennedy. Good murder-mystery with Bergen & McCarthy rivaling Inspector Kennedy's investigation. Good cast, good wrap-up to who-dunit.

Charlie, the Lonesome Cougar (1968) C-75m. **½ No director. Narrated by Rex Allen. Ron Brown, Brian Russell, Linda Wallace, Jim Wilson. Average Disney animal adventure-comedy about a friendly cougar who lives in a lumber camp.

Charlie's Angels (1976) C-78m. TVM D: John Llewellyn Moxey. Kate Jackson, Farrah Fawcett-Majors, Jaclyn Smith, David Doyle, Diana Muldaur, Bo Hopkins, David Ogden Stiers, John Lehne, Tommy Lee Jones. Three attractive female detectives use their wiles to con the killer of a wealthy wine grower into revealing whereabouts of the body. Featherweight cop-show-with-a-twist that snowballed into one of the most popular TV series of the mid-70s and began the Farrah Fawcett-Majors phenomenon. Average.

Charlotte's Web (1973) C-85m. *** D: Charles A. Nichols, Iwao Takamoto. Voices of Debbie Reynolds, Henry Gibson, Paul Lynde, Charles Nelson Reilly. Charming animated feature based on E. B. White classic of barnyard spider who befriends shy piglet. Above average for Hanna-Barbera cartoon studio.

Charlton-Brown of the F.O. SEE: **Man in a Cocked Hat**

Charly (1968) C-103m. ***½ D: Ralph Nelson. Cliff Robertson, Claire Bloom, Lilia Skala, Leon Janney, Dick Van Patten. Robertson won Oscar for fine work as retarded man turned into super-brain in scientific experiment. Bloom is sympathetic case-worker who becomes attached to Charley. Based on Daniel Keyes'

"Flowers for Algernon." First-rate.

Charro! (1969) C-98m. BOMB D: Charles Marquis Warren. Elvis Presley, Ina Balin, Victor French, Lynn Kellogg, Barbara Werle, Paul Brinegar. Attempt to change Presley's image by casting him in straight Western is total failure. Elvis sings only one song.

Chartroose Caboose (1960) C-75m. ** D: William "Red" Reynolds. Molly Bee, Ben Cooper, Edgar Buchanan, Mike McGreevey. Buchanan, an eccentric retired train conductor, shelters a young couple in his strange house, a converted caboose.

Chase, The (1946) 86m. ** D: Arthur Ripley. Robert Cummings, Michele Morgan, Steve Cochran, Peter Lorre. Slow-moving second-rate story set in Cuba with Morgan running off from her husband.

Chase, The (1966) C-135m. **½ D: Arthur Penn. Marlon Brando, Jane Fonda, Robert Redford, Angie Dickinson, Janice Rule, James Fox, Robert Duvall, E. G. Marshall. Intriguing, unsubtle drama of how prison escape by local boy (Redford) affects worthless Texas town and its sheriff (Brando). Notorious for behind-the-scenes conflicts with director Penn, screenwriter Lillian Hellman, and producer Sam Spiegel, it's not surprising that finished product misses the mark.

Chase a Crooked Shadow (1958-British) 87m. *** D: Michael Anderson. Richard Todd, Anne Baxter, Herbert Lom, Alexander Knox. Rich heiress Baxter doubts her sanity when allegedly dead brother Todd appears to claim inheritance; exciting, Hitchcock-like melodrama.

Chase for the Golden Needles SEE: **Golden Needles**

Chase Me Charlie (1932) 61m. ** Narrated by Teddy Bergman. Edna Purviance, Ben Turpin. Inept attempt to string early Chaplin shorts into story line—1914 material used is often weak.

Chastity (1969) C-98m. ** D: Alessio de Paola. Cher, Barbara London, Tom Nolan, Stephen Whittaker. Interesting story of girl who takes to the highway to find life of her own. Cher in solo acting debut is surprisingly good.

Chato's Land (1972-Spanish-British) C-110m. **½ D: Michael Winner. Charles Bronson, Jack Palance, Richard Basehart, Jill Ireland. Posse seeks Indian Bronson in connection with marshal's murder; usual quota of blood in lengthy film.

Chatterbox (1943) 76m. **½ D: Joseph Santley. Joe E. Brown, Judy Canova, Rosemary Lane, John Hubbard, Gus Schilling, Chester Clute, Anne Jeffreys. Entertaining comedy of radio-cowboy Brown (not much of a hero in real life) visiting dude ranch for publicity purposes.

Che! (1969) C-96m. BOMB D: Richard Fleischer. Omar Sharif, Jack Palance, Cesare Danova, Robert Loggia, Woody Strode. Comic-book treatment of famed revolutionary became one of the biggest film jokes of 1960s. However, you haven't lived until you see Palance play Fidel Castro.

Cheap Detective, The (1978) C-92m. *** D: Robert Moore. Peter Falk, Ann-Margret, Eileen Brennan, Sid Caesar, Stockard Channing, James Coco, Dom DeLuise, Louise Fletcher, John Houseman, Madeline Kahn, Fernando Lamas, Marsha Mason, Phil Silvers, Abe Vigoda, Paul Williams, Nicol Williamson. For Neil Simon and Peter Falk to parody Bogart movies like MALTESE FALCON is an easy mark, but it's still pretty funny when not resorting to the obvious.

Cheaper by the Dozen (1950) C-85m. *** D: Walter Lang. Clifton Webb, Myrna Loy, Jeanne Crain, Mildred Natwick, Edgar Buchanan. Charming turn-of-the-century story of the Gilbreth children, twelve strong, their exacting father (well-played by Webb) and mother (Loy). Followed by sequel BELLES ON THEIR TOES.

Cheaters, The (1945) 87m. *** D: Joseph Kane. Joseph Schildkraut, Billie Burke, Eugene Pallette, Ona Munson, Raymond Walburn, Ruth Terry. Excellent cast in enjoyable tale of wealthy family of snobs humanized by downtrodden actor they invite for Christmas dinner. Also known as THE CASTAWAY.

Check and Double Check (1930) 80m. BOMB D: Melville Brown. Freeman Gosden, Charles Correll, Sue Carol, Charles Norton, Ralf Harolde, Duke Ellington and his band. Movie debut for radio's Amos 'n' Andy is a leaden-paced early talkie with stale script and precious little comedy; not nearly as good as a sample radio (or later TV) episode of the show.

Checkered Flag or Crash (1977) C-95m. ** D: Alan Gibson. Joe Don Baker, Susan Sarandon, Larry Hagman, Alan Vint, Parnelli Jones, Logan Clark. A 1,000 mile "off the road" race in the Philippines is the focal point of this unmemorable programmer; for car-action fans only.

Cheers for Miss Bishop (1941) 95m. *** D: Tay Garnett. Martha Scott, William Gargan, Edmund Gwenn, Sterling Holloway, Sidney Blackmer, Mary Anderson, Dorothy Peterson. Sentimental story of schoolteacher Scott, devoting her life to teaching in small Midwestern town. Nicely done.

Cherokee Strip (1940) 86m. **½ D: Lesley Selander. Richard Dix, Florence Rice, Victor Jory, William Henry, Andy Clyde, George E. Stone. Solid if unsurprising little Western with quiet but determined Dix becoming marshal of small town, hoping to get the goods on crooked Jory and his gang.

Cheyenne (1947) 100m. ** D: Raoul Walsh. Dennis Morgan, Jane Wyman, Janis Paige, Bruce Bennett, Alan Hale, Arthur Kennedy, Barton MacLane. Standard Western as gambler attempts to capture outlaw—instead spends time with outlaw's wife.

Cheyenne Autumn (1964) C-160m. *** D: John Ford. Carroll Baker, Richard Widmark, Edward G. Robinson, Dolores Del Rio, Ricardo Montalban, Gilbert Roland, Sal Mineo, Victor Jory. Sprawling account of American Indians' ill treatment at hands of whites; strong story capably filmed by an old master, John Ford.

Cheyenne Social Club, The (1970) C-103m. **½ D: Gene Kelly. Henry Fonda, James Stewart, Shirley Jones, Sue Ane Langdon, Elaine Devry. Jimmy Stewart runs a bawdy house in the Old West. Lots of laughs, but clichés run throughout.

Chicago Calling (1951) 74m. ** D: John Reinhardt. Dan Duryea, Mary Anderson, Gordon Gebert, Ross Elliot. Slim premise has Duryea sitting by telephone awaiting news of estranged family injured in car accident; mild tour de force.

Chicago Confidential (1957) 73m. **½ D: Sidney Salkow. Brian Keith, Beverly Garland, Dick Foran, Beverly Tyler, Elisha Cook. Keith and Garland make good protagonists in their crusade to clean up corruption and crime amid the labor unions of the Windy City.

Chicago Deadline (1949) 87m. **½ D: Lewis Allen. Alan Ladd, Donna

Reed, June Havoc, Irene Hervey, Arthur Kennedy, Shepperd Strudwick. Potentially top-notch actioner bogs down in clichés, with Ladd as crusading reporter in corruption-filled city. Remade as FAME IS THE NAME OF THE GAME.

Chicago Syndicate (1955) 83m. ** D: Fred F. Sears. Dennis O'Keefe, Abbe Lane, Paul Stewart, Xavier Cugat. Passable exposé film involving cleanup of Windy City rackets.

Chicken Chronicles, The (1978) C-95m. *½ D: Francis Simon. Steven Guttenberg, Ed Lauter, Lisa Reeves, Meridith Baer, Branscombe Richmond, Gino Baffa, Phil Silvers. Lowjinks of a high school senior, circa 1969, whose principal preoccupation is bedding the girl of his dreams.

Chicken Every Sunday (1948) 91m. **½ D: George Seaton. Dan Dailey, Celeste Holm, Colleen Townsend, Alan Young, Natalie Wood. Easygoing turn-of-the-century Americana about get-rich-quick schemer Dailey and understanding wife Holm.

Chief Crazy Horse (1955) C-86m. **½ D: George Sherman. Victor Mature, Suzan Ball, John Lund, Ray Danton, Keith Larsen. Clichéd nonsense focusing on Mature in title role as idealistic tough redskin.

Child Is Born, A (1940) 79m. *** D: Lloyd Bacon. Geraldine Fitzgerald, Jeffrey Lynn, Gladys George, Gale Page, Spring Byington, Eve Arden. Smooth, touching remake of LIFE BEGINS about everyday life in maternity ward, involving prisoner Fitzgerald sent to hospital to have her child.

Child Is Waiting, A (1963) 102m. *** D: John Cassavetes. Burt Lancaster, Judy Garland, Gena Rowlands, Steven Hill, Bruce Ritchey. Poignant story of Lancaster's attempts to treat retarded children with the help of overly sympathetic Garland. Sensitive subject handled with honesty and candor.

Child Stealer, The (1979) C-100m. TVM D: Mel Damski. Beau Bridges, Blair Brown, Cristina Raines, David Groh, Eugene Roche, Marj Dusay. Well-acted drama about a young mother who battles to get her children back after her former husband kidnaps them. Above average.

Children of Paradise (1945-French) 188m. **** D: Marcel Carne. Jean-Louis Barrault, Arletty, Pierre Brasseur, Albert Remay, Maria Cesarles, Leon Larive. Story of love affair between pantomimist and beautiful woman is a classic film to see again and again.

Children of the Damned (1964-British) 81m. **½ D: Antone Leader. Ian Hendry, Alan Badel, Barbara Ferris, Patrick White, Bessie Love. Follow-up to VILLAGE OF THE DAMNED suffers from unimaginative account of precocious deadly children and their quest for power.

Children of the Lotus Eater: SEE Psychiatrist: God Bless the Children

Children Shouldn't Play With Dead Things (1972) C-85m. *½ D: Benjamin Clark. Alan Ormsby, Anya Ormsby, Valerie Mauches, Jane Daly, Jeffrey Gillen. Young, kinky moviemakers take over a rural graveyard and unwittingly resurrect the evil dead. Weird.

Children's Hour, The (1962) 107m. **½ D: William Wyler. Audrey Hepburn, Shirley MacLaine, James Garner, Miriam Hopkins, Fay Bainter, Veronica Cartwright. Updated version of Lillian Hellman's play is more explicit in its various themes, including lesbianism, than original THESE THREE, but not half as good. Impact is missing, despite MacLaine and Hepburn as two teachers, Hopkins as meddling aunt, Bainter as questioning grandmother.

Chimes at Midnight (1967-Spanish-Swiss) 115m. *** D: Orson Welles. Orson Welles, Jeanne Moreau, Margaret Rutherford, John Gielgud, Marina Vlady. Welles combined parts of five Shakespeare plays with mixed results, with his own portrayal of Falstaff the most interesting aspect. Well cast, but limited budget hurt the effort; Ralph Richardson narrates. Also known as FALSTAFF.

China (1943) 79m. ** D: John Farrow. Loretta Young, Alan Ladd, William Bendix, Philip Ahn, Iris Wong, Sen Yung. Pat wartime tale of mercenary Ladd who suddenly realizes his true allegiance while helping enemy.

China Clipper (1936) 85m. **½ D: Ray Enright. Pat O'Brien, Beverly Roberts, Ross Alexander, Humphrey Bogart, Marie Wilson, Henry B. Walthall. O'Brien stars as man determined to develop trans-Pacific flights; usual plot of initial failure, grim determination, and neglected wife; fairly well done.

China Corsair (1951) 67m. *½ D: Ray Nazzaro. Jon Hall, Lisa Ferraday, Ron Randell, Douglas Kennedy, Ernest Borgnine. Tinsel-like adventure of Hall's romancing, combatting crooks aboard title ship.

China Doll (1958) 88m. *½ D: Frank Borzage. Victor Mature, Li Li Hua, Bob Mathias, Stuart Whitman. Bizarre story line can't boost dull film of Mature accidentally buying Oriental wife whom he grows to love. When they are killed, daughter comes to U.S.A.

China Gate (1957) 97m. *** D: Samuel Fuller. Gene Barry, Angie Dickinson, Nat "King" Cole, Paul Dubov, Lee Van Cleef, George Givot, Marcel Dalio. International soldiers under French command attack Communist munitions dumps in Indochina. Interesting subplots flesh out Fuller's dynamic action story, with early political view of Vietnam's internal strife.

China Girl (1942) 95m. ** D: Henry Hathaway. Gene Tierney, George Montgomery, Lynn Bari, Victor McLaglen, Sig Ruman, Bobby Blake, Ann Pennington, Philip Ahn. American photographer in mysterious Orient during WW2 is background for unbelievable adventure yarn; Bari best item in film.

China Seas (1935) 90m. *** D: Tay Garnett. Clark Gable, Jean Harlow, Wallace Beery, Lewis Stone, Rosalind Russell, Dudley Digges, Robert Benchley, C. Aubrey Smith. Impossible to dislike film with that cast, even if the story—about mysterious goings-on and relationships on Gable's Hong Kong-bound ship—is ludicrous.

China Sky (1945) 78m. ** D: Ray Enright. Randolph Scott, Ruth Warrick, Ellen Drew, Anthony Quinn, Carol Thurston, Richard Loo. Slow-moving Pearl Buck story of dedicated doctor Scott fighting Japanese with Chinese comrades during WW2.

China Syndrome, The (1979) C-123m. **** D: James Bridges. Jane Fonda, Jack Lemmon, Michael Douglas, Scott Brady, James Hampton, Peter Donat, Wilford Brimley. Heart-pounding drama about attempted cover-up of accident at California nuclear plant is as much a probe of television news as it is a story of nuclear power—and it scores bullseye on both fronts. There is no music score; story tension propels film by itself, along with solid performances by Fonda as TV reporter, Douglas (who also produced film) as

radical cameraman, and especially Lemmon as dedicated plant exec.

China Venture (1953) 83m. **½ D: Don Siegel. Edmond O'Brien, Barry Sullivan, Jocelyn Brando, Richard Loo, Philip Ahn. Exciting WW2 adventure film of marine group on mission to capture Japanese naval commander wanted by U. S. interrogation department.

China's Little Devils (1945) 74m. ** D: Monta Bell. Harry Carey, Paul Kelly, Ducky Louie, Hayward Soo Hoo, Gloria Ann Chew. Patriotic yarn of Chinese waifs helping downed American pilots get going again.

Chinatown (1974) C-131m. **** D: Roman Polanski. Jack Nicholson, Faye Dunaway, John Huston, Perry Lopez, John Hillerman, Darrell Zwerling, Diane Ladd. Bizarre, fascinating mystery in the Hammett-Chandler tradition (and set in the 1930s) with Nicholson as private eye led into a complex, volatile case by femme fatale Dunaway. Director Polanski appears briefly as the hood who knifes Nicholson. Oscar winner for Best Story and Screenplay (Robert Towne).

Chinese Cat, The (1944) 65m. D: Phil Rosen. Sidney Toler, Benson Fong, Joan Woodbury, Mantan Moreland, Sam Flint, John Davidson, Betty Blythe, Jack Norton, Ian Keith. SEE: Charlie Chan series.

Chinese Ring, The (1947) 67m. D: William Beaudine. Roland Winters, Warren Douglas, Victor Sen Yung, Mantan Moreland, Philip Ahn. SEE: Charlie Chan series.

Chino (1973-Italian) C-98m. **½ D: John Sturges. Charles Bronson, Jill Ireland, Vincent Van Patten, Marcel Bozuffi, Fausto Tozzi, Melissa Chimenti. Offbeat Western that barely received theatrical release here in 1976; Bronson plays halfbreed whose attempts to maintain his horse ranch in peace are short-lived.

Chip Off the Old Block (1944) 82m. ** D: Charles Lamont. Donald O'-Connor, Peggy Ryan, Ann Blyth, Helen Vinson, Helen Broderick, Arthur Treacher, Patric Knowles, Ernest Truex. Innocuous wartime musical of misunderstandings, climaxing in teenage romance and musical show, of course.

Chisum (1970) C-111m. **½ D: Andrew V. McLaglen. John Wayne, Forrest Tucker, Christopher George, Ben Johnson, Glenn Corbett, Bruce Cabot, Patric Knowles, Lynda Day, Richard Jaeckel. Cattle-baron Wayne more catalyst than hero in handsomely produced, forgettable Western outing. Corrupt officials threaten to disrupt peaceful territory.

Chitty Chitty Bang Bang (1968) C-142m. *½ D: Ken Hughes. Dick Van Dyke, Sally Ann Howes, Lionel Jeffries, Gert Frobe, Anna Quayle. Children's musical about flying car is one big Edsel itself, with totally forgettable score and some of the shoddiest special effects ever. Based on book by Ian Fleming.

Chloe in the Afternoon (1972-French) C-97m. ***½ D: Eric Rohmer. Bernard Verley, Zouzou, Francoise Verley, Daniel Ceccaldi. No. 6 of Rohmer's "Six Moral Tales" depicts married man's fascination with kooky girl during daylight hours. As Chloe, Zouzou becomes more alluring, as film unwinds.

Chocolate Soldier, The (1941) 102m. ** D: Roy Del Ruth. Nelson Eddy, Rise Stevens, Nigel Bruce, Florence Bates, Dorothy Gilmore, Nydia Westman. Don't expect Oscar Straus' operetta—this is from play THE GUARDSMAN, about married couple performing operettas; too talky, not enough music.

Choirboys, The (1977) C-119m. BOMB D: Robert Aldrich. Charles Durning, Lou Gossett, Perry King, Clyde Kusatsu, Tim McIntire, Randy Quaid, Don Stroud, Burt Young, Robert Webber, Barbara Rhoades. Supposedly comic escapades of L.A. cops who relieve work pressures by raunchy doings. Foul-mouthed, foulminded, heavy-handed film from book by Joseph Wambaugh, who disavowed this turkey.

Chomps (1979) C-89m. *½ D: Don Chaffey. Wesley Eure, Valerie Bertinelli, Conrad Bain, Chuck McCann, Red Buttons, Larry Bishop, Hermione Baddeley, Jim Backus. Cartoonmakers Hanna & Barbera struck out with this Disneyesque comedy about a young inventor (Eure) and his mechanical dog. Originally rated PG for mild profanities voiced by *another* dog in the film—then redubbed for kids' sake.

Chosen, The (1978-Italian-British) C-105m. BOMB D: Alberto De Martino. Kirk Douglas, Agostina Belli, Simon Ward, Anthony Quayle, Virginia McKenna, Alexander Knox. Nuclear power exec Douglas slowly realizes that his son (Ward) is the Antichrist, who plans to use nuclear

power to bring on world destruction. There! We just saved you 105 minutes.

Chosen Survivors (1974) C-99m. ** D: Sutton Roley. Jackie Cooper, Alex Cord, Richard Jaeckel, Bradford Dillman, Pedro Armendariz Jr., Diana Muldaur, Barbara Babcock. Good cast in formula nonsense about group of people "selected" to survive future holocaust in underground shelter. Just one hitch: the shelter is invaded by vampire bats. Dialogue and characterizations from grade-Z movies of the past.

Christina (1974) C-98m. ** D: Paul Krasny. Barbara Parkins, Peter Haskell, James McEachin, Marlyn Mason, Barbara Gordon. Beautiful woman offers unemployed man $25,000 to marry her—in name only —but just as he's falling in love with her, she disappears. Murky suspenser filmed in Canada.

Christine Jorgensen Story, The (1970) 89m. BOMB D: Irving Rapper. John Hansen, Joan Tompkins, Quinn Redeker, John W. Hines, Ellen Clark. Ludicrous biography of famed 50s phenomenon is not exactly an indepth study; one problem is that actor Hansen looks more masculine as female Christine and vice versa.

Christmas Carol, A (1938) 69m. *** D: Edwin L. Marin. Reginald Owen, Gene Lockhart, Kathleen Lockhart, Terry Kilburn, Barry McKay, Lynne Carver, Leo G. Carroll. Nicely done adaptation of Dickens' classic with Owen a well-modulated Scrooge, surrounded by good MGM players and period settings.

Christmas Carol, A (1951-British) 86m. **** D: Brian Desmond Hurst. Alistair Sim, Kathleen Harrison, Jack Warner, Michael Hordern, Mervyn Johns, Hermione Baddeley, George Cole. Superb film is too good to be shown only at Christmastime; always delightful Sim makes Scrooge a three-dimensional character in this faithful, heartwarming rendition of Dickens classic. Patrick Macnee plays young Marley.

Christmas Eve (1947) 90m. *½ D: Edwin L. Marin. George Brent, George Raft, Randolph Scott, Joan Blondell, Virginia Field, Ann Harding, Reginald Denny. Slow-moving mixture of comedy and drama as foster sons discover evil intentions of relations to victimize Harding. Retitled: SINNER'S HOLIDAY.

Christmas Holiday (1944) 92m. **★★★**
D: Robert Siodmak. Deanna Durbin,
Gene Kelly, Gale Sondergaard,
Gladys George, Richard Whorf.
Somerset Maugham novel reset in
America. Crime story with Durbin
gone wrong to help killer-hubby
Kelly; songs include "Spring Will Be
A Little Late this Year."

Christmas In Connecticut (1945)
101m. **★★½** D: Peter Godfrey. Barbara Stanwyck, Dennis Morgan, Sydney Greenstreet, Reginald Gardiner,
S. Z. Sakall, Robert Shayne, Una
O'Connor. Airy fluff of recipe-writer
(Stanwyck) having soldier Morgan
for dinner to impress boss Greenstreet.

Christmas in July (1940) 70m. **★★★½**
D: Preston Sturges. Dick Powell,
Ellen Drew, Raymond Walburn, William Demarest, Ernest Truex, Franklin Pangborn. Top Sturges film of
hopeful contest-winner Powell going
on shopping spree on anticipated winnings. Walburn and Demarest are at
their best.

Christmas Kid, The (1968-Spanish)
C-89m. **★★** D: Sidney Pink. Jeffrey
Hunter, Louis Hayward, Gustavo
Rojo, Perla Cristal, Luis Prendes.
Average frijole western about a
saddletramp's search for his true
identity.

Christmas Lilies of the Field (1979)
C-100m. TVM D: Ralph Nelson.
Billy Dee Williams, Maria Schell,
Fay Hauser, Judith Piquet, Hanna
Hertelendy, Lisa Mann. Joyous followup to Nelson's Oscar-winning
original of 15 years earlier, with
Homer Smith turning up at the
chapel he built in the Arizona desert
and being. conned once again by
Mother Maria—this time to put up
an orphanage and kindergarten.
Above average.

**Christmas Miracle in Caufield,
U.S.A.** (1977) **C**-100m. TVM D:
Jud Taylor. Mitchell Ryan, Kurt
Russell, Andrew Prine, John Carradine, Karen Lamm, Melissa Gilbert.
Coal miners trapped by an underground explosion on Christmas Eve.
Mild drama taken from real life,
but plays in standard TV fashion
like a roadshow "Waltons"—right
down to the off-camera narration by
a younger member of the family
and the final shot of home with the
lights going out. Average.

Christmas That Almost Wasn't, The
(1966-Italian-U.S.) **C**-95m. **★½** D:
Rossano Brazzi. Rossano Brazzi, Paul

Tripp, Lidia Brazzi, Sonny Fox,
Mischa Auer. Santa Claus hijack
makes for weak kiddie fare, none
too thrilling for grownups either.

Christmas to Remember, A (1978)
C-100m. TVM D: George Englund.
Jason Robards, Eva Marie Saint,
Joanne Woodward, George Perry,
Bryan Englund. Sentimental Depression era tale about an elderly farm
couple who take in their city-bred
adolescent grandson for the holidays. High-powered star cast elevates
this already satisfying adaptation of
Glendon Swarthout's novel, *The
Melodeon*. Above average.

Christmas Tree, The (1969) 110m.
★½ D: Terence Young. William
Holden, Virna Lisi, Bourvil, Brook
Fuller, Madeleine Damien. Sappy
tear-jerker about relationship between
young boy and his wealthy father
when the latter learns his son's death
is imminent. Cast is divided between
those who overact and those who
don't seem to care one way or the
other.

Christopher Columbus (1949-British)
C-104m. **★★★** D: David Macdonald.
Fredric March, Florence Eldridge,
Francis L. Sullivan, Nora Swinburne,
James Robertson Justice. Stark, slowly paced biography of 15th-century
explorer, with earnest portrayal by
March in title role; good period setting.

Christopher Strong (1933) 77m. **★★½**
D: Dorothy Arzner. Katharine Hepburn, Colin Clive, Billie Burke, Helen
Chandler, Jack LaRue. Hepburn's an
aviatrix in love with married Clive.
Dated film intriguing for star's performance as headstrong, individualistic woman—and dig that silver lamé
costume.

Chubasco (1968) **C**-100m. **★★½** D: Allen H. Miner. Richard Egan, Christopher Jones, Susan Strasberg, Ann
Sothern, Simon Oakland, Audrey Totter, Preston Foster. Young man working on tuna boat gets along with his
skipper until he learns the boy has
married his daughter; overlong but
likable programmer filmed when
Jones and Strasberg were married in
real life.

Chuka (1967) **C**-105m. **★★** D: Gordon
Douglas. Rod Taylor, John Mills, Ernest Borgnine, Luciana Paluzzi, James
Whitmore, Angela Dorian, Louis
Hayward. Good cast is wasted in
routine Western about grizzled gunfighter who tries to promote peace
between Indians and some undisci-

plined soldiers guarding nearby fort.

Chump at Oxford, A (1940) 63m. **½ D: Alfred Goulding. Stan Laurel, Oliver Hardy, James Finlayson, Forrester Harvey, Wilfred Lucas, Anita Garvin, Peter Cushing. Concussion changes Stan from usual self to aristocratic genius at Oxford; lots of fun.

Cimarron (1960) C-140m. **½ D: Anthony Mann. Glenn Ford, Maria Schell, Anne Baxter, Arthur O'Connell. Edna Ferber's chronicle of frontier life in Oklahoma between 1890-1915 becomes an indifferent sprawling soap opera unsalvaged by a few spectacular scenes. What's worse, this remake keeps the 1930 original off TV.

Cimarron Kid, The (1951) C-84m. ** D: Budd Boetticher. Audie Murphy, Beverly Tyler, James Best, Yvette Dugay. Uninspired formula Western with Murphy in title role, persuaded to give up his criminal life by his sweetheart.

Cincinnati Kid, The (1965) C-113m. **½ D: Norman Jewison. Steve McQueen, Ann-Margret, Edward G. Robinson, Karl Malden, Tuesday Weld, Joan Blondell, Rip Torn, Jack Weston, Cab Calloway. Focus of film is on roving card-sharks who get together for big game; side episodes of meaningless romance. Robinson, Blondell, and Malden come off best as vivid members of the playing profession.

Cinderella Jones (1946) 88m. ** D: Busby Berkeley. Joan Leslie, Robert Alda, S. Z. Sakall, Edward Everett Horton, Ruth Donnelly, Elisha Cook. Silly comedy of girl who must marry brainy husband to collect inheritance; good cast defeated by trivial script.

Cinderella Liberty (1973) C-117m. ***½ D: Mark Rydell. James Caan, Marsha Mason, Eli Wallach, Kirk Calloway, Burt Young, Bruce Kirby Jr., Allyn Ann McLerie, Dabney Coleman. Sensitive, original story about romance between simple, good-hearted sailor and a hooker with an illegitimate black son. Artfully mixes romance and realism, with sterling performances by Caan and Mason.

Cinderfella (1960) C-91m. **½ D: Frank Tashlin. Jerry Lewis, Ed Wynn, Judith Anderson, Anna Maria Alberghetti, Count Basie. Fairy tale classic revamped as a Lewis romp; talky interludes and ineffectual musical sequences featuring Alberghetti.

Cindy (1978) C-100m. TVM. D: William A. Graham. Clifton Davis, Charlaine Woodward, Scoey Mitchell, Mae Mercer, Nell-Ruth Carter, Alaina Reed. Original musical updates Cinderella story to Harlem during WW2; delightful concoction from MTM team with multi-talented black cast. Above average.

Circle, The (1959-British) 84m. **½ D: Gerald Thomas. John Mills, Derek Farr, Roland Culver, Wilfrid Hyde-White. Well-acted, neatly paced murder yarn involving London medico. Retitled: THE VICIOUS CIRCLE.

Circle of Children, A (1977) C-100m. TVM D: Don Taylor. Jane Alexander, Rachel Roberts, David Ogden Stiers, Nan Martin, Matthew Laborteaux. Beautifully acted drama about affluent suburbanite (Alexander) whose volunteer work with emotionally disturbed children fills the void in her life. Mary MacCracken's autobiographical novel served as the basis for this sensitive, intelligent, surprisingly unsentimental film. Jane Alexander's superb performance is matched by that of Rachel Roberts as a gifted, demanding teacher who regards the volunteer merely a hostess out of place. Above average.

Circle of Danger (1951-British) 86m. **½ D: Jacques Tourneur. Ray Milland, Patricia Roc, Marius Goring, Hugh Sinclair. Straightforward account of Milland returning to England to ferret out brother's killers.

Circle of Deception (1961-British) 100m. **½ D: Jack Lee. Bradford Dillman, Suzy Parker, Harry Andrews, Paul Rogers. At times engaging psychological yarn of WW2 espionage agent Dillman who breaks under Axis torture; ironic climax.

Circle of Iron (1979) C-102m. **½ D: Richard Moore. David Carradine, Jeff Cooper, Roddy McDowall, Eli Wallach, Erica Creer, Christopher Lee. Bruce Lee's idea to blend martial arts action and zen philosophy results in strange, sometimes silly, but watchable film. Cooper (looking like California surfer) must pass rites of trial to find secret book of knowledge. Filmed in Israel as THE SILENT FLUTE.

Circumstantial Evidence (1945) 68m. **½ D: John Larkin. Michael O'Shea, Lloyd Nolan, Trudy Marshall, Billy Cummings. Engaging programmer about efforts to save an innocent man from going to the electric chair.

Circus, The (1928) 72m. ***½ D: Charles Chaplin. Charlie Chaplin, Merna Kennedy, Allan Garcia, Betty Morrissey, Harry Crocker. Not the "masterpiece" of THE GOLD RUSH or CITY LIGHTS, Chaplin's last silent film is an unpretentious little gem; story has Charlie accidentally joining traveling circus, falling in love with bareback rider. Hilarious comedy, with memorable finale.

Circus Clown (1934) 63m. ** D: Ray Enright. Joe E. Brown, Dorothy Burgess, Patricia Ellis, Lee Moran, Tom Dugan, William Demarest. Brown mixes comedy and drama in account of circus star whose father objects to his work.

Circus of Fear SEE: Psycho-Circus

Circus of Horrors (1960-British) C-89m. **½ D: Sidney Hayers. Anton Diffring, Erika Remberg, Yvonne Monlaur, Donald Pleasence. A most unethical plastic surgeon and nurse join bizarre circus to escape deformed patient threatening their lives; rousing horror film.

Circus World (1964) C-135m. **½ D: Henry Hathaway. John Wayne, Rita Hayworth, Claudia Cardinale, Lloyd Nolan, Richard Conte. Made in Spain, film has nothing new to offer, but rehashes usual circus formula quite nicely. Climactic fire sequence is truly spectacular.

Cisco Pike (1972) C-94m. *** D: B. L. Norton. Kris Kristofferson, Karen Black, Gene Hackman, Viva!, Roscoe Lee Browne. Surprisingly good drama about crooked cop who gets mixed up with drug dealing; film benefits from good script and fine performances, including singer Kristofferson's (in film debut).

Citadel, The (1938-British) 110m. ***½ D: King Vidor. Robert Donat, Rosalind Russell, Ralph Richardson, Rex Harrison, Emlyn Williams, Penelope Dudley-Ward, Francis L. Sullivan. Superb adaptation of A. J. Cronin novel of impoverished doctor Donat eschewing ideals for wealthy life of treating rich hypochondriacs, neglecting wife and friends in the process; tragedy opens his eyes. Weak ending, but fine acting makes up for it.

Citizen Kane (1941) 119m. **** D: Orson Welles. Orson Welles, Joseph Cotten, Everett Sloane, Agnes Moorehead, Dorothy Comingore, Ray Collins, George Coulouris, Ruth Warrick. Welles' first and best, a film that broke all the rules and invented some new ones, with fascinating story of Hearst-like publisher's rise to power. Music by Bernard Herrmann.

Citizens Band SEE: Handle with Care

City, The (1971) C-100m. TVM D: Daniel Petrie. Anthony Quinn, Skye Aubrey, E. G. Marshall, Robert Reed, Pat Hingle, John Larch, Kaz Garas, Peggy McCay. Unengrossing drama of veteran Albuquerque mayor solving urban problems. Unconvincing situations, some pale performances; pilot for short-lived TV series. Below average.

City, The (1977) C-78m. TVM D: Harvey Hart. Robert Forster, Don Johnson, Ward Costello, Jimmy Dean, Mark Hamill, Susan Sullivan. Police drama with cops Forster and Johnson searching for a psychotic with a deadly grudge against a country singer. Below average.

City Across the River (1949) 90m. **½ D: Maxwell Shane. Stephen McNally, Thelma Ritter, Luis Van Rooten, Jeff Corey, Tony Curtis, Richard Jaeckel. Watered-down version of Irving Shulman's novel THE AMBOY DUKES, involving tough life in Brooklyn slums, with predictable hoods et al.

City After Midnight (1957-British) 84m. *½ D: Compton Bennett. Phyllis Kirk, Dan O'Herlihy, Petula Clark, Wilfrid Hyde-White, Jack Watling. Tame detective film of private eye O'Herlihy investigating death of antique dealer. British title: THAT WOMAN OPPOSITE.

City Beneath the Sea (1953) C-87m. **½ D: Budd Boetticher. Robert Ryan, Mala Powers, Anthony Quinn, Suzan Ball. Inconsequential underwater yarn invigorated by Ryan and Quinn as deep-sea divers hunting treasure off Jamaican coast.

City Beneath the Sea (1970) C-98m. TVM D: Irwin Allen. Robert Wagner, Stuart Whitman, Rosemary Forsyth, Joseph Cotten, Richard Basehart, James Darren. It is 2053 A.D.: Colonists in first underwater city struggle through first year of attempted invasions, ocean horrors, and interpersonal squabbles. Better than average production values thanks to Irwin Allen. Above average.

City for Conquest (1940) 101m. *** D: Anatole Litvak. James Cagney,

Ann Sheridan, Frank Craven, Arthur Kennedy, Donald Crisp, Frank Mc-Hugh, George Tobias, Elia Kazan, Anthony Quinn. Cagney makes this a must as boxer devoted to younger brother Kennedy (his film debut). Beautiful production overshadows film's pretentious faults.

City in Darkness SEE: Charlie Chan in City of Darkness

City Lights (1931) 81m. **** D: Charles Chaplin. Charlie Chaplin, Virginia Cherrill, Harry Myers, Hank Mann. Chaplin's masterpiece tells story of his love for blind flower girl, and his hot-and-cold friendship with a drunken millionaire. Eloquent, moving, and funny.

City of Bad Men (1953) C-82m. ** D: Harmon Jones. Jeanne Crain, Dale Robertson, Richard Boone, Lloyd Bridges, Carl Betz. Robbers attempt to steal prizefight proceeds in 1890s Nevada; film combines Western with recreation of Jim Corbett-Bob Fitzsimmons fight bout.

City of Fear (1959) 81m. *½ D: Irving Lerner. Vince Edwards, Lyle Talbot, John Archer, Steven Ritch, Patricia Blair. Programmer involving escaped convict Edwards sought by police and health officials; container he stole is filled with radioactive material, not money.

City of Fear (1966-British) 90m. *½ D: Peter Bezencenet. Paul Maxwell, Terry Moore, Marisa Mell, Albert Lieven, Pinkas Braun. Tedious caper involving news reporter and refugee going to Hungary to smuggle out pro-Westerners.

City of Shadows (1955) 70m. *½ D: William Witney. Victor McLaglen, John Baer, Kathleen Crowley, Anthony Caruso. Mild happenings about crafty newsboys involved with derelict racketeer McLaglen.

City on a Hunt SEE: No Escape

City on Fire (1979-Canadian) C-101m. *½ D: Alvin Rakoff. Barry Newman, Henry Fonda, Ava Gardner, Shelley Winters, Susan Clark, Leslie Nielsen, James Franciscus, Jonathan Welsh. Dull, fill-in-the-blanks disaster film about citywide fire torched by a disgruntled ex-employee of local oil refinery. For pyromaniacs only.

City Streets (1931) 70m. *** D: Rouben Mamoulian. Gary Cooper, Sylvia Sidney, Paul Lukas, Wynne Gibson, Guy Kibbee, Stanley Fields. Cooper joins prohibition gang as means of springing his girlfriend

(Sidney) from jail; stylish drama from Dashiell Hammett script, more interesting for innovative presentation than predictable story. Sidney's starring debut.

City That Never Sleeps, The (1953) 90m. ** D: John H. Auer. Gig Young, Mala Powers, Edward Arnold, Marie Windsor. Average melodrama of married patrolman Young who almost gives up all for sake of Windsor, tawdry cafe singer; set in Chicago.

City Under the Sea SEE: War Gods of the Deep

Claire's Knee (1971-French) C-103m. **** D: Eric Rohmer. Jean-Claude Brialy, Aurora Cornu, Beatrice Romand, Laurence De Monaghan, Michele Montel. No. 5 of Rohmer's "Six Moral Tales" has widest appeal. Young man about to be married is obsessed with a girl he doesn't even like, his attention focusing on her knee. Full of delicious relationships, but too talky for some viewers.

Clambake (1967) C-97m. *½ D: Arthur Nadel. Elvis Presley, Shelley Fabares, Will Hutchins, Bill Bixby, Gary Merrill, James Gregory. Elvis is a millionaire's son who wants to make it on his own, so he trades places with water-skiing instructor Hutchins in Miami. One of Presley's weakest musical comedies.

Clancy Street Boys (1943) 66m. D: William Beaudine. Leo Gorcey, Huntz Hall, Bobby Jordan, Noah Beery, Sr., Lita Ward, Bennie Bartlett, Ric Vallin, Billy Benedict. SEE: Bowery Boys series

Clarence, The Cross-Eyed Lion (1965) C-98m. **½ D: Andrew Marton. Marshall Thompson, Betsy Drake, Cheryl Miller, Richard Haydn, Alan Caillou. Basis for DAKTARI TV show is good family entertainment set in Africa with adventure and wholesome comedy well blended.

Clash By Night (1952) 105m. *** D: Fritz Lang. Barbara Stanwyck, Paul Douglas, Robert Ryan, Marilyn Monroe, Keith Andes, J. Carrol Naish. Moody, well-acted Clifford Odets story of drifter Stanwyck settling down, marrying good-natured fisherman Douglas. Cynical friend Ryan senses that she's not happy, tries to take advantage. Andes and Monroe provide secondary love interest.

Clash of Steel (1962-French) C-79m. **½ D: Bernard Borderie. Gerard Barray, Gianna Maria Canale, Michele Grellier, Jean Topart. Thin plot involving overthrow of French king,

Henry of Navarre, boosted by lively production and zesty swordplay.

Class of '44 (1973) **C-95m. **½** D: Paul Bogart. Gary Grimes, Jerry Houser, Oliver Conant, Deborah Winters, William Atherton, Sam Bottoms. Sequel to SUMMER OF '42 is less ambitious, a lightly entertaining story centering on Grimes going to college, falling in love, growing up. Good period atmosphere.

Class of Miss MacMichael, The (1978-British) **C-99m. **½** D: Silvio Narizzano. Glenda Jackson, Oliver Reed, Michael Murphy, Rosalind Cash, John Standing, Riba Akabusi, Phil Daniels. Echoes of TO SIR, WITH LOVE don't flatter this shrill tale of a dedicated teacher with a class full of social misfits.

Class of '63 (1973) **C-74m. TVM** D: John Korty. Cliff Gorman, Joan Hackett; James Brolin, Woodrow Chambliss, Ed Lauter, Colby Chester, Graham Beckel. College reunion provides subtle setting for sad tale of dissolving marriage, bittersweet romance; unresolved ending. Full-blooded characters in absorbing, realistic melodrama. Above average.

Claudelle Inglish (1961) 99m. **½** D: Gordon Douglas. Diane McBain, Arthur Kennedy, Constance Ford, Chad Everett. Trite soaper derived from Erskine Caldwell tale of Southern farm gal who gives all to find excitement, with predictable tragedy to all.

Claudia (1943) 91m. *** D: Edmund Goulding. Dorothy McGuire, Robert Young, Ina Claire, Reginald Gardiner, Olga Baclanova, Jean Howard. Warm comedy of young Claudia (McGuire) suddenly marrying, facing adult problems, learning a lot about life in short period; beautifully acted.

Claudia and David (1946) 78m. *** D: Walter Lang. Dorothy McGuire, Robert Young, Mary Astor, John Sutton, Gail Patrick, Florence Bates. Enjoyable follow-up to CLAUDIA with McGuire and Young having a baby, adjusting to suburban life; engaging, well-acted.

Claudine (1974) **C-92m. **½** D: John Berry. Diahann Carroll, James Earl Jones, Lawrence Hilton-Jacobs, Tamu, David Kruger, Adam Wade. Slice-of-life comedy with a serious edge: Romance between garbageman Jones and young ghetto mother Carroll is charming and credible, but the problems of dealing with her

six kids, and their collective poverty, can't be treated so lightly. "Upbeat" finale just doesn't ring true.

Claw Monsters, The (1955) 100m. *½ D: Franklin Adreon. Phyllis Coates, Myron Healey, Arthur Space, John Day, Mike Ragan. Latter-day Republic cliff-hanger is short on action, long on stock footage, in account of out-of-whack scientist guarding his diamond mines via superstitions and animal-skin-covered henchmen. Reedited movie serial: PANTHER GIRL OF THE KONGO

Clay Pigeon (1971) **C-97m. **½** D: Tom Stern, Lane Slate. Tom Stern, Telly Savalas, Robert Vaughn, John Marley, Burgess Meredith, Ivan Dixon. Good cast in dull crime melodrama of Vietnam vet settling into drug scene, eventually experiencing change of heart and going after big-league pusher.

Clear and Present Danger, A (1970) **C-100m. TVM** D: James Goldstone. Hal Holbrook, E. G. Marshall, Joseph Campanella, Jack Albertson, Pat Hingle, Mike Kellin, Jeff Corey. Son of retiring U.S. Senator risks political career in forthright determination to influence public opinion on air pollution. Some good dialogue, acting. Above average.

Cleo from 5 to 7 (1962-French) 90m. *** D: Agnès Varda. Corinne Marchand, Antoine Bourseiller, Dorothée Blanck, Michel Legrand, Anna Karina, Eddie Constantine, Jean-Luc Godard. Intelligent, fluid account of Parisian songstress forced to reevaluate her life while awaiting vital medical report on her physical condition.

Cleopatra (1934) 95m. ***½ D: Cecil B. DeMille. Claudette Colbert, Warren William, Henry Wilcoxon, Gertrude Michael, Joseph Schildkraut, C. Aubrey Smith, Claudia Dell, Robert Warwick. Opulent DeMille version of Cleopatra doesn't date badly, stands out as one of his most intelligent films, thanks in large part to fine performances by all. Top entertainment.

Cleopatra (1963) **C-243m. ** D: Joseph L. Mankiewicz. Elizabeth Taylor, Richard Burton, Rex Harrison, Roddy McDowall, Pamela Brown, Martin Landau, Michael Hordern, Kenneth Haigh, Andrew Keir, Hume Cronyn. Saga of the Nile goes on and on and on; definitely a curiosity item, but you'll be satisfied after an hour. Good acting, especially by Harrison and McDowall, but they are lost in this flat, four-hour misfire.

Cleopatra Jones (1973) C-89m. ** D: Jack Starrett. Tamara Dobson, Bernie Casey, Shelley Winters, Brenda Sykes, Antonio Fargas, Bill McKinney, Esther Rolle. Black bubble-gum stuff with Dobson as karate-chopping government agent who goes after drug kingpins. Lots of action—and violence.

Cleopatra Jones and the Casino of Gold (1975) C-96m. *½ D: Chuck Bail. Tamara Dobson, Stella Stevens, Tanny, Norman Fell, Albert Popwell, Caro Kenyatta, Christopher Hunt. Wild, woolly, sexy, violent sequel to CLEOPATRA JONES. Stevens plays "The Dragon Lady," a tip-off on what to expect.

Cleopatra's Daughter (1960-Italian) C-102m. ** D: Richard McNamara. Debra Paget, Ettore Manni, Erno Crisa, Robert Alda, Corrado Panni. American actors are lost in this costumer, more intent on playing up sadistic sequences; intrigue at Egyptian court the highlight.

Climax, The (1944) C-86m. *** D: George Waggner. Boris Karloff, Gale Sondergaard, Susanna Foster, Turhan Bey, Thomas Gomez, Scotty Beckett. Tense Karloff vehicle of seemingly polished opera physician who is really a murderer; Foster gets to sing, too.

Climb an Angry Mountain (1972) C-97m. TVM D: Leonard Horn. Fess Parker, Barry Nelson, Joe Kapp, Stella Stevens, Marj Dusay, Clay O'Brien. Great location shooting (Northern California) enhances likable drama pitting tough sheriff (Parker) and N.Y. cop against fugitive Indian holding sheriff's son hostage. Above average.

Clinging Vine, The (1926) 71m. **½ D: Paul Sloane. Leatrice Joy, Tom Moore, Toby Claude, Robert Edeson, Dell Henderson. Handsome fluff about unfeminine executive (Joy) who becomes involved in business swindle, and falls in love.

Clipped Wings (1953) 65m. D: Edward Bernds. Leo Gorcey, Huntz Hall, Bernard Gorcey, Mary Treen, Philip Van Zandt, Lyle Talbot. SEE: **Bowery Boys** series.

Clive of India (1935) 90m. **½ D: Richard Boleslawski. Ronald Colman, Loretta Young, Colin Clive, Francis Lister, C. Aubrey Smith, Cesar Romero. Average adventure of British-in-India variety. Colman plays man of destiny, puts down Indian rebellions, defeats tyrant.

Cloak and Dagger (1946) 106m. **½ D: Fritz Lang. Gary Cooper, Lilli Palmer, Robert Alda, Vladimir Sokoloff, Ludwig Stossel. Professor Cooper becomes a secret agent on his trip to Germany; Lang intrigue is not among his best, but still slick.

Cloak Without Dagger SEE: **Operation Conspiracy**

Clock, The (1945) 90m. ***½ D: Vincente Minnelli. Judy Garland, Robert Walker, James Gleason, Keenan Wynn, Marshall Thompson, Lucile Gleason. Soldier Walker has one-day leave in N.Y.C., meets office worker Judy; they spend the day falling in love, encountering friendly milkman Gleason, drunk Wynn; charming little love story with beguiling Garland.

Clockwork Orange, A (1971) C-137m. ***½ D: Stanley Kubrick. Malcolm McDowell, Patrick Magee, Adrienne Corri, Aubrey Morris, James Marcus. Probably the 1970s' most controversial film so far, this vivid adaptation of Anthony Burgess' novel will lose a lot on TV when nudity and violence are cut. In its original form, film is scathing satire on future society, with an excellent performance by McDowell as prime misfit. One of Kubrick's best.

Close Call for Boston Blackie, A (1946) 60m. D: Lew Landers. Chester Morris, Lynn Merrick, Richard Lane, Frank Sully, George E. Stone, Russell Hicks. SEE: **Boston Blackie** series.

Close Call for Ellery Queen (1942) 67m. D: James Hogan. William Gargan, Margaret Lindsay, Ralph Morgan, Edward Norris. SEE: **Ellery Queen** series.

Close Encounters of the Third Kind (1977) C-135m. **** D: Steven Spielberg. Richard Dreyfuss, Francois Truffaut, Teri Garr, Melinda Dillon, Cary Guffey, Bob Balaban. Superb, intelligent sci-fi film about UFO mystery that leads to first contact with alien beings. Dreyfuss is perfect "everyman" swallowed up in frustrating enigma which finally becomes clear. Powerhouse special effects throughout.

Close to My Heart (1951) 90m. *** D: William Keighley. Ray Milland, Gene Tierney, Fay Bainter, Howard St. John. Superior soaper; Tierney attaches herself to waif in Bainter's orphanage, but husband Milland won't allow adoption until child's background is traced.

Cloudburst (1951-British) 83m. **½ D: Francis Searle. Robert Preston, Elizabeth Sellars, Harold Lang, Noel Howlett. Impressive little film of Preston, WW2 veteran working in British Foreign Office, seeking his wife's murderers.

Clouded Yellow, The (1951-British) 85m. *** D: Ralph Thomas. Jean Simmons, Trevor Howard, Barry Jones, Maxwell Reed, Kenneth More. Cast is exceptional in unpretentious murder-hunt film with Simmons seeking to prove her innocence.

Clouds Over Europe (1939-British) 78m. *** D: Tim Whelan. Laurence Olivier, Ralph Richardson, Valerie Hobson, George Curzon, David Tree, George Merritt, Gus McNaughton. Delightful tongue-in-cheek espionage tale, with masterminds stealing British aircraft secrets. Richardson is a joy as lighthearted inspector who cracks the case. Retitled: Q PLANES.

Clown, The (1953) 92m. **½ D: Robert Z. Leonard. Red Skelton, Jane Greer, Tim Considine, Steve Forrest. Sentimental remake of Wallace Beery-Jackie Cooper THE CHAMP about down-and-out comic. Skelton OK in rare dramatic role.

Clowns, The (1971-Italian) ©-90m. ***½ D: Federico Fellini. Fellini's homage to circus clowns is itself a clownish spoof of documentary films, a funny, fully entertaining piece of fluff from this great director, who even makes fun of himself.

Club Havana (1945) 62m. ** D: Edgar G. Ulmer. Tom Neal, Margaret Lindsay, Don Douglas, Gertrude Michael, Isabelita (Lita Baron), Dorothy Morris, Ernest Truex. Roadshow GRAND HOTEL is very cheap production with little of interest.

Clue of the New Pin (1960-British) 58m. *½ D: Allan Davis. Paul Daneman, Bernard Archard, James Villiers, Catherine Woodville, Clive Morton. Old-fashioned Edgar Wallace yarn about "perfect crime," with Villiers a TV interviewer who tangles with murderer; ponderous.

Clue of the Silver Key (1961-British) 59m. **½ D: Gerald Glaister. Bernard Lee, Lyndon Brook, Finlay Currie, Jennifer Danie. Above-par Edgar Wallace yarn, highlighted by Lee's performance as determined Scotland Yard inspector unraveling series of murders.

Cluny Brown (1946) 100m. ***½ D: Ernst Lubitsch. Charles Boyer, Jennifer Jones, Peter Lawford, Helen Walker, Reginald Gardiner, C. Aubrey Smith, Reginald Owen, Richard Haydn. Delightful Lubitsch comedy of romance between plumber Jones and refugee Boyer in pre-WW2 England. Beautiful character performances help out.

Coast of Skeletons (1964) ©-84m. **½ D: Robert Lynn. Richard Todd, Marianne Koch, Vivi Bach, Albert Lieven. Edgar Wallace's "Sanders of the River" is basis for largely rewritten tale of diamond-smuggling doctor now on deathbed; set in Africa.

Cobra, The (1968) ©-93m. BOMB D: Mario Sequi. Dana Andrews, Anita Ekberg, Peter Martell, Elisa Montes, Jesus Puente, Peter Dane. Awful melodrama has tough all-American secret service man Andrews fighting opium smuggling in the middle East; Ekberg still can't act.

Cobra Strikes, The (1948) 62m. ** D: Charles F. Reisner. Sheila Ryan, Richard Fraser, Leslie Brooks, Herbert Heyes. Weak low-budgeter about thief who meddles in inventor's workshop, complications that ensue.

Cobra Woman (1944) C-70m. *** D: Robert Siodmak. Maria Montez, Jon Hall, Sabu, Edgar Barrier, Lois Collier, Lon Chaney Jr., Mary Nash. Camp classic with Montez as twin sisters—one good, one evil. Technicolor fantasy-escape of the 1940s at its zenith.

Cobweb, The (1955) ©-124m. **½ D: Vincente Minnelli. Richard Widmark, Lauren Bacall, Gloria Grahame, Charles Boyer, Lillian Gish, John Kerr, Susan Strasberg, Oscar Levant. Plot-heavy drama involving patients and staff of mental clinic, boosted by varied casting.

Cocaine Cowboys (1979) ©-87m. BOMB D: Ulli Lommel. Jack Palance, Tom Sullivan, Andy Warhol, Suzanna Love, Pete Huckabee. Dreadful film about rock group that supports itself "between engagements" by dope smuggling; filmed at Warhol's Montauk home, where this film should remain.

Cockeyed Cavaliers (1934) 72m. *** D: Mark Sandrich. Bert Wheeler, Robert Woolsey, Thelma Todd, Dorothy Lee, Noah Beery, Franklin Pangborn. Colorful costume comedy with Wheeler & Woolsey trying to crash into society by posing as the King's physicians; lively mix of slapstick, puns, and music.

Cockeyed Cowboys of Calico County (1970) C-99m. ** D: Ranald MacDougall. Dan Blocker, Nanette Fabray, Jim Backus, Wally Cox, Jack Elam, Stubby Kaye, Mickey Rooney, Noah Beery, Marge Champion, Jack Cassidy. Great cast and waste of a movie. Turn-of-the-century progress in the Old West, but villains, varmints and saloons still remain. Originally made for TV, but released to theaters instead.

Cockeyed Miracle, The (1946) 81m. ** D: S. Sylvan Simon. Frank Morgan, Keenan Wynn, Cecil Kellaway, Audrey Totter, Marshall Thompson. Good cast carries weak material. Morgan returns from heaven to make up for financial error he made involving family.

Cockeyed World, The (1929) 118m. *½ D: Raoul Walsh. Victor McLaglen, Edmund Lowe, Lily Damita, El Brendel, Lelia Karnelly, Stuart Erwin. Sequel to WHAT PRICE GLORY? with McLaglen and Lowe as battling Marines Flagg and Quirt sent to South Sea island where fiery Damita captures their attention. Smash hit in 1929, it moves like molasses today, and is no match for GLORY.

Cockfighter (1974) C-83m. *** D: Monte Hellman. Warren Oates, Richard B. Shull, Harry Dean Stanton, Troy Donahue, Millie Perkins. Offbeat, violent but interesting drama of a man who trains fighting cocks in Georgia. Oates is silent until the very end, his thoughts serving as narration. Filmed in Georgia. Also called BORN TO KILL, WILD DRIFTER, GAMBLIN' MAN.

Cockleshell Heroes, The (1956-British) C-97m. ** D: Jose Ferrer. Jose Ferrer, Trevor Howard, Dora Bryan, Anthony Newley, Victor Maddern. Training of special task force troops during WW2 never jells into excitement.

Cocoanut Grove (1938) 85m. ** D: Alfred Santell. Fred MacMurray, Harriet Hilliard, Yacht Club Boys, Ben Blue, Rufe Davis, Billy Lee, Eve Arden. MacMurray's band just has to make good at the Cocoanut Grove audition in this flimsy musical, with nine songs you'll never hear again.

Cocoanuts (1929) 96m. *** D: Joseph Santley, Robert Florey. Groucho, Harpo, Chico, Zeppo Marx, Kay Francis, Oscar Shaw, Mary Eaton, Margaret Dumont. The Marxes' first film suffers from stagy filming

and stale musical subplot, but when the brothers have scenes to themselves it's a riot; best scene comes when Groucho tries to tell Chico about a viaduct.

Code Name: Diamond Head (1977) C-78m. TVM D: Jeannot Szwarc. Roy Thinnes, France Nuyen, Ward Costello, Zulu, Don Knight, Ian McShane, Eric Braeden, Dennis Patrick. Undercover agent Thinnes scours Honolulu to find master spy McShane, hired by a foreign power to steal the formula for a deadly toxic gas. Assembly-line spy thriller hidden in exotic locales. Below average.

Code Name: Heraclitus (1967) C-100m. TVM D: James Goldstone. Stanley Baker, Leslie Nielsen, Jack Weston, Sheree North, Signe Hasso, Kurt Kasznar, Ricardo Montalban. Dead man is "rebuilt" to become a Cold War agent. Slick thriller crawling with spies, counterspies and a gum-chewer named Gannon (Baker) who may or may not have come in from the cold. Stitched together from two "Chrysler Theatre" shows. Above average.

Code Name: Minus One: SEE Gemini Man

Code Name, Red Roses (1969-Italian) C-97m. **½ D: Fernando diLeo. James Daly, Pier Angeli, Michael Wilding, Peter Van Eyck. The old "American saboteur behind enemy lines" plot reenacted by a pretty fair cast. Also called RED ROSES FOR THE FUEHRER.

Code Name: Trixie (1973) C-103m. ** D: George Romero. Lane Carroll, W. G. McMillan, Harold Wayne Jones, Lloyd Hollar, Lynn Lowry. Biological plague hits small Pennsylvania town. The Army is called in to contain it, but townspeople rebel and defy the soldiers. Gory but exciting. Originally titled THE CRAZIES.

Code of Scotland Yard (1948-British) 90m. ** D: George King. Oscar Homolka, Muriel Pavlow, Derek Farr, Kenneth Griffith. Man escaped from Devil's Island runs seemingly innocent antique shop. Nothing special.

Code 7 Victim 5 (1964-British) C-88m. **½ D: Robert Lynn. Lex Barker, Ronald Fraser, Walter Rilla, Dietmar Schonherr. Moderate actioner with Barker investigating murder in South Africa; nicely paced.

Code 645 (1948) 100m. ** D: Fred Brannon, Yakima Canutt. Clayton

Moore, Roy Barcroft, Ramsay Ames, Drew Allen, Tom Steele. Tame Republic cliff-hanger relying on too much stock footage and pat situations in contest between federal agents and escaped arch-criminal with his own master plan of destruction and success. Reedited movie serial: G-MEN NEVER FORGET.

Code Two (1953) 69m. ** D: Fred Wilcox. Ralph Meeker, Sally Forrest, Keenan Wynn, Robert Horton, Jeff Richards. Three recruits on L.A. motorcycle police force face occupational hazards; when Richards is killed, Meeker et al seek to capture those responsible.

Coffee, Tea or Me? (1973) C-73m. TVM D: Norman Panama. Karen Valentine, John Davidson, Michael Anderson Jr., Louise Lasser, Lou Jacobi, Erica Hagen. Decent comedy features Valentine as busy airline stewardess who, thru odd circumstance, has two husbands in separate continents. Weak resolution only liability. Above average.

Coffy (1973) C-91m. **½ D: Jack Hill. Pam Grier, Booker Bradshaw, Robert DoQui, William Elliott, Allan Arbus, Sid Haig. Fast-moving, generally agreeable trash about nurse who goes after junkies who turned her young sister into an addict; lots of nudity will be cut for TV.

Cold Night's Death, A (1973) C-73m. TVM D: Jerrold Freedman. Robert Culp, Eli Wallach, Michael C. Gwynne. Exceptional, offbeat mixture of psychological and physical terror in story of two scientists replacing dead predecessor in wasteland research laboratory. Watch out for that ending. Above average.

Cold Sweat (1970-British) C-94m. ** D: Terence Young. Charles Bronson, Liv Ullmann, James Mason, Jill Ireland, Gabriele Ferzetti, Michel Constantin. Richard Matheson's thriller *Ride the Nightmare* has been converted into a predictable Bronson action movie that has him as an American expatriate in France forced into the drug trade by crime czar Mason.

Cold Turkey (1971) C-106m. *** D: Norman Lear. Dick Van Dyke, Pippa Scott, Tom Poston, Edward Everett Horton, Bob & Ray, Bob Newhart, Vincent Gardenia, Jean Stapleton. Bittersweet satire of contemporary America; minister Van Dyke leads township crusade to stop smoking, in order to win mammoth contest.

Trenchant finale doesn't gibe with rest of film: still worthwhile, with Bob & Ray hilarious as newscasters.

Cold Wind in August, A (1961) 80m. **½ D: Alexander Singer. Lola Albright, Scott Marlowe, Herschel Bernardi, Joe De Santis. Offbeat account of tenement boy Marlowe having affair with stripper Albright; frank, flavorful tale.

Colditz Story, The (1957-British) 97m. ***½ D: Guy Hamilton. John Mills, Eric Portman, Christopher Rhodes, Lionel Jeffries, Bryan Forbes, Ian Carmichael, Richard Wattis, Anton Diffring, Theodore Bikel. Super-solid P.O.W. saga set in Germany's Colditz Castle, supposedly "escape-proof" but challenged by various European prisoners, and a hardy British group in particular.

Cole Younger, Gunfighter (1958) C-78m. ** D: R. G. Springsteen. Frank Lovejoy, James Best, Abby Dalton, Jan Merlin. Modest actioner has gunfights to perk up trite account of 1870s Texas.

Collectioneuse, La (1971-French) C-88m. *** D: Eric Rohmer. Patrick Bauchau, Haydee Politoff, Daniel Pommerulle, Alain Jouffroy, Mijanou Bardot. No. 3 of Rohmer's "Six Moral Tales" is less compelling than later films, still intriguing for fans of contemplative stories in this series, focusing on young man's gradual attraction to aloof young girl sharing summer villa on the Mediterranean. Made in 1967.

Collector, The (1965) C-119m. *** D: William Wyler. Terence Stamp, Samantha Eggar, Maurice Dallimore, Mona Washbourne. Disturbing story of man who collects more than just butterflies, which is where Miss Eggar fits in. Chilling, if not altogether believable.

Colleen (1936) 89m. *** D: Alfred E. Green. Dick Powell, Ruby Keeler, Joan Blondell, Hugh Herbert, Jack Oakie, Louise Fazenda, Paul Draper. Neglected Warner Bros. musical is quite good, with usual boy-meets-girl plot framing tasteful musical numbers: title tune, "An Evening With You," "Boulevardier from the Bronx." Includes perhaps-definitive Hugh Herbert performance.

College (1927) 65m. *** D: James W. Horne. Buster Keaton, Anne Cornwall, Flora Bramley, Harold Goodwin, Grant Withers, Snitz Edwards. Highbrow student Buster has to become an all-star athlete to please his girlfriend; episodic gag structure makes this less impressive than other Keaton features, but it's awfully funny.

College Coach (1933) 75m. **½ D: William Wellman. Dick Powell, Ann Dvorak, Pat O'Brien, Hugh Herbert, Lyle Talbot. Well-paced tale of ruthless football coach O'Brien, neglected wife Dvorak, star player Powell who also likes chemistry. Look for John Wayne in a bit part.

College Confidential (1960) 91m. *½ D: Albert Zugsmith. Steve Allen, Jayne Meadows, Mamie Van Doren, Walter Winchell. Hanky-panky involving college professor (Allen) and the shenanigans of his sexually precocious brood of students; a few violent scenes thrown in for good measure.

College Holiday (1936) 88m. **½ D: Frank Tuttle. Jack Benny, George Burns, Gracie Allen, Mary Boland, Martha Raye, Marsha Hunt, Eleanore Whitney. Benny's hotel needs business, so he induces the college crowd to come; spiffy musical with first-rate cast.

College Humor (1933) 80m. *** D: Wesley Ruggles. Bing Crosby, Jack Oakie, Burns and Allen, Richard Arlen, Mary Carlisle, Mary Kornman, Joseph Sauers (Sawyer). College was never like this. Hokey, entertaining rah-rah musical with Bing a professor (!), Arlen and Oakie football stars, Carlisle and Kornman provide love interest. Songs: "Learn to Croon," "Down the Old Ox Road," among others.

College Swing (1938) 86m. *** D: Raoul Walsh. George Burns, Gracie Allen, Martha Raye, Bob Hope, Edward Everett Horton, Florence George, Ben Blue, Betty Grable, John Payne. Gracie hasn't been able to graduate from school in this entertaining collegiate musicomedy with top cast, forgettable songs like "What Did Romeo Say to Juliet?"

Collision Course (1975) C-100m. TVM D: Anthony Page. Henry Fonda, E. G. Marshall, Lucille Benson, Lloyd Bochner, Ward Costello, Andrew Duggan, Russell Johnson, John Larch, John Randolph, Barry Sullivan, Richard Loo. Fonda is General Douglas MacArthur and Marshall is President Harry Truman in Ernest Kinoy's dramatic reconstruction of events surrounding their

clash over methods to end the Korean War. Talky, static blend of fact and speculation. Average.

Colonel Blimp: SEE Life and Death of Colonel Blimp

Colonel Effingham's Raid (1945) 70m. **½ D: Irving Pichel. Charles Coburn, Joan Bennett, William Eythe, Allyn Joslyn, Elizabeth Patterson, Donald Meek. Entertaining little comedy of ex-officer Coburn fighting to save town's historical landmark; cast supports fair material.

Color Me Dead (1969) C-97m. ** D: Eddie Davis. Tom Tryon, Carolyn Jones, Rick Jason, Patricia Connolly, Tony Ward, Penny Sugg. Story of a slowly poisoned man spending his last days tracking down his own murderer was done better as D.O.A. twenty years before.

Colorado Territory (1949) 94m. *** D: Raoul Walsh. Joel McCrea, Virginia Mayo, Dorothy Malone, Henry Hull, John Archer, Frank Puglia. Strong, fast-moving Western with McCrea an outlaw on the lam; remake of director Walsh's HIGH SIERRA, later remade as I DIED A THOUSAND TIMES.

Colossus of New York, The (1958) 70m. ** D: Eugene Lourie. John Baragrey, Mala Powers, Otto Kruger, Robert Hutton. Doctor implants dead son's brain into oversized robot with predictable chaos.

Colossus: The Forbin Project SEE: Forbin Project, The

Colt .45 (1950) C-74m. **½ D: Edwin L. Marin. Randolph Scott, Zachary Scott, Ruth Roman, Lloyd Bridges, Chief Thundercloud. The renowned title gun is star of this sometimes actionful Western. Retitled: THUNDERCLOUD.

Column South (1953) C-85m. ** D: Frederick de Cordova. Audie Murphy, Joan Evans, Robert Sterling, Ray Collins. OK mixture of Civil War and Indian fighting, as Union officer Murphy champions underdog redskins to prevent hostilities.

Coma (1978) C-113m. *** D: Michael Crichton. Genevieve Bujold, Michael Douglas, Elizabeth Ashley, Rip Torn, Richard Widmark, Lois Chiles. Someone is killing and stealing patients from a big-city hospital, and a woman doctor bucks male superiors to pursue her suspicions. Bujold and Widmark are well-matched adversaries in original suspenser that combines best of hospital pictures and mystery thrillers; scripted by director Crichton from his own novel.

Comanche (1956) C-87m. **** D: George Sherman. Dana Andrews, Kent Smith, Linda Cristal, Nestor Paiva, Henry Brandon. Andrews is staunch as Indian scout seeking to patch redskin-cavalry hostilities. Film is pat Western.

Comanche Station (1960) C-74m. *** D: Budd Boetticher. Randolph Scott, Nancy Gates, Claude Akins, Skip Homeier. Better-than-usual actioner with Scott leading a group through Indian lands, hoping to find his wife who has been kidnapped by redskins.

Comanche Territory (1950) C-76m. **½ D: George Sherman. Maureen O'Hara, Macdonald Carey, Will Geer, James Best, Edmund Cobb. Fictional bio of Western scout Jim Bowie (Carey) who helps Comanches save their lands from whiteskins.

Comancheros, The (1961) C-107m. *** D: Michael Curtiz. John Wayne, Stuart Whitman, Lee Marvin, Ina Balin, Bruce Cabot, Nehemiah Persoff. Well-paced Wayne actioner with Big John a Texas Ranger out to bring in gang supplying firearms and liquor to the Comanches.

Combat Squad (1953) 72m. *½ D: Cy Roth. John Ireland, Lon McCallister, Hal March, Tris Coffin. Weak study of men in war; this time Korea.

Come and Get It (1936) 105m. ***½ D: Howard Hawks, William Wyler. Edward Arnold, Joel McCrea, Frances Farmer, Walter Brennan, Andrea Leeds, Frank Shields. Elaborate filming of Edna Ferber book about life in the lumber country of Wisconsin, with Arnold playing the great American capitalist and Brennan winning Best Supporting Actor Oscar for his fine work.

Come Back, Charleston Blue (1972) C-100m. **½ D: Mark Warren. Raymond St. Jacques, Godfrey Cambridge, Jonelle Allen, Adam Wade, Peter DeAnda. Further adventures of Gravedigger and Coffin on their Harlem police beat. Not nearly as good as original, COTTON COMES TO HARLEM, but diverting, with fine Donny Hathaway score.

Come Back, Little Sheba (1952) 99m. ***½ D: Daniel Mann. Burt Lancaster, Shirley Booth, Terry Moore, Richard Jaeckel. William Inge play is emotional tour de force for Booth (who won an Oscar) as slovenly housewife coping with drunken ex-

chiropractor husband (Lancaster) and boarder Moore, whose curiosity about her landlords sets drama in motion.

Come Blow Your Horn (1963) C-112m. *** D: Bud Yorkin. Frank Sinatra, Lee J. Cobb, Molly Picon, Barbara Rush, Jill St. John, Tony Bill. Sinatra is good as a free-swinging bachelor with wall-to-wall girls and a nagging father (Cobb). He also sings the title song, and teaches kid brother (Bill) the ropes. From Neil Simon play.

Come Dance with Me! (1960-French) C-91m. **½ D: Michel Boisrond. Brigitte Bardot, Henri Vidal, Dawn Addams, Noel Roquevert. Fairly well blended mixture of mystery-comedy involving dentist accused of murdering a barroom pickup and his wife Bardot finding the real killer.

Come Fill the Cup (1951) 113m. **½ D: Gordon Douglas. James Cagney, Phyllis Thaxter, Raymond Massey, James Gleason, Gig Young. Cagney is quite restrained as ex-newspaperman seeking to conquer alcoholism. Fine performance by Gleason as helpful ex-drunk and by Young as drunken playboy.

Come Fly with Me (1963) C-109m. **½ D: Henry Levin. Hugh O'Brian, Pamela Tiffin, Dolores Hart, Karl Boehm, Lois Nettleton, Karl Malden. Flighty fluff of three stewardesses trying to catch husbands, becoming involved with three men on a trans-Atlantic flight. Glossy, easy to take.

Come Live with Me (1941) 86m. *** D: Clarence Brown. James Stewart, Hedy Lamarr, Ian Hunter, Verree Teasdale, Donald Meek, Barton MacLane, Adeline de Walt Reynolds. Charming romantic comedy, with starving writer Stewart marrying Lamarr so she won't be deported. Strong supporting cast, with Reynolds fine as Stewart's mother.

Come Next Spring (1956) C-92m. *** D: R. G. Springsteen. Ann Sheridan, Steve Cochran, Walter Brennan, Sherry Jackson. Arkansas Americana beautifully interpreted by intelligent acting, with Sheridan and Cochran overcoming nature and townfolks to make their farm go.

Come-On, The (1956) 83m. ** D: Russell Birdwell. Anne Baxter, Sterling Hayden, John Hoyt, Jesse White. Baxter is dramatically fine as unscrupulous con-gal involved with murder, but the story is hackneyed.

C'mon, Let's Live a Little (1967) C-85m. ** D: David Butler. Bobby

Vee, Jackie DeShannon, Eddie Hodges, Suzie Kaye, Patsy Kelly, John Ireland Jr. Scatterbrained "comedy"-musical centering on humorous chain of events in country singer's first weeks at college.

Come Out Fighting (1945) 62m. D: William Beaudine. Leo Gorcey, Huntz Hall, Billy Benedict, Gabriel Dell, June Carlson. SEE: **Bowery Boys** series

Come September (1961) C-112m. *** D: Robert Mulligan. Rock Hudson, Gina Lollobrigida, Sandra Dee, Bobby Darin, Walter Slezak. Frothy comedy about the younger generation (Darin and Dee) vs. the "older" folks (Hudson and Lollobrigida) at an Italian villa. Good fun, with some dated Darin vocals.

Come Spy with Me (1967) C-85m. *½ D: Marshall Stone. Troy Donahue, Andrea Dromm, Albert Dekker, Mart Hulswit, Valerie Allen, Dan Ferrone. Except for those who want to tell their friends they actually saw a film called COME SPY WITH ME starring Troy Donahue, this secret-agent flick about blond Dromm's attempts to solve murders of two Americans in the Caribbean isn't worth anyone's time.

Come to the Stable (1949) 94m. *** D: Henry Koster. Loretta Young, Celeste Holm, Hugh Marlowe, Elsa Lanchester, Regis Toomey, Mike Mazurki. Young and Holm register well as French nuns living in New England, seeking aid from a variety of local characters in building a children's dispensary.

Comeback, The (1978-British) C-100m. BOMB D: Pete Walker. Jack Jones, Pamela Stephenson, David Doyle, Bill Owen, Sheila Keith, Richard Johnson. Gruesome story of American singer trying for show-biz comeback in England, drawn instead into chain of gory murders.

Comedians, The (1967) C-160m. **½ D: Peter Glenville. Elizabeth Taylor, Richard Burton, Alec Guinness, Peter Ustinov, Paul Ford, Lillian Gish, Raymond St. Jacques. Excellent cast only partially salvages uninspired adaptation of Graham Greene's novel about political intrigue in Haiti.

Comedy Company, The (1978) C-100m. TVM D: Lee Philips. Jack Albertson, George Burns, Lawrence Hilton-Jacobs, Herbert Edelman, Joyce Van Patten, Susan Sullivan, Michael Brandon, Abe Vigoda. Drama about the efforts of an ex-vaudevillian to keep his failing nightclub alive as a showcase for aspiring comics. Average.

Comedy of Terrors (1963) C-88m. **½ D: Jacques Tourneur. Vincent Price, Peter Lorre, Boris Karloff, Basil Rathbone, Joe E. Brown, Joyce Jameson. Weak horror spoof with undertaker Price trying to hasten customers' demise, "helped" by bumbling assistant Lorre. Great cast saddled with grade-B material.

Comic, The (1969) C-94m. *** D: Carl Reiner. Dick Van Dyke, Michele Lee, Mickey Rooney, Cornel Wilde, Nina Wayne, Pert Kelton, Jeannine Riley. Tragicomic look at life of silent-screen comic with destructive ego; more truth than fiction in absorbing portrait based on composite of several stars. Bittersweet finale beautifully handled; recreations of silent films first-rate. Not a total success, but well-done.

Comes a Horseman (1978) C-118m. **½ D: Alan J. Pakula. Jane Fonda, James Caan, Jason Robards, George Grizzard, Robert Farnsworth, Jim Davis. Starkly simple Western story (set in 1940s) about rival ranch owners whose roots are in the land. Low-key to the point of catatonia, but offers some beautiful tableaux and moving scenes.

Coming Apart (1969) 110m. *½ D: Milton Moses Ginsberg. Rip Torn, Viveca Lindfors, Megan McCormick, Lois Markle, Lynn Swann. Fascinatingly bad drama about psychiatrist who sets up concealed movie camera in his apartment to record the messed-up lives of himself and women who visit him; film will undoubtedly be heavily edited for TV.

Coming Home (1978) C-127m. ***½ D: Hal Ashby. Jane Fonda, Jon Voight, Bruce Dern, Robert Carradine, Robert Ginty, Penelope Milford. Powerful look at the effect of Vietnam war on people at home. Fonda falls in love with paraplegic Voight while her husband (Dern) is overseas. Mature, gripping film, marred only by lapses into melodrama.

Coming-Out Party (1934) 79m. *½ D: John G. Blystone. Frances Dee, Gene Raymond, Alison Skipworth, Nigel Bruce, Harry Green. Tired tale of young socialite Dee in love with jazz musician, fighting her mother's ambitions for her to marry within social class.

Coming-Out Party, A (1962-British)

90m. **½ D: Ken Annakin. James Robertson Justice, Leslie Phillips, Stanley Baxter, Eric Sykes, Richard Wattis. P.O.W. comedy with prisoner Baxter impersonating lookalike Nazi commandant to help peevish scientist Justice escape camp. Original title: A VERY IMPORTANT PERSON.

Comin' Round the Mountain (1951) 77m. ** D: Charles Lamont. Bud Abbott, Lou Costello, Dorothy Shay, Kirby Grant, Joe Sawyer, Glenn Strange. Bud and Lou invade hillbilly country and soon tame the feuding townsfolk with their pranks; standard A&C.

Command, The (1954) C-88m. ** D: David Butler. Guy Madison, Joan Weldon, James Whitmore, Carl Benton Reid. Madison unflinchingly copes with smallpox epidemic and rampaging redskins as he leads troops and civilians through Wyoming Indian lands.

Command Decision (1948) 112m. ***½ D: Sam Wood. Clark Gable, Walter Pidgeon, Van Johnson, Brian Donlevy, Charles Bickford, John Hodiak, Edward Arnold. All-star cast in taut WW2 drama. Commander Gable faced with dilemma of doing what is right or what looks good to public.

Commando (1964-Italian) 90m. **½ D: Frank Wisbar. Stewart Granger, Dorian Gray, Fausto Tozzi, Carlos Casaravilla. Granger leads mission to rescue Algerian rebel leader, later learning ironic political significance. Satisfactory actioner.

Commandos (1968-Italian-German) C-89m. ** D: Armando Crispino. Lee Van Cleef, Jack Kelly, Giampiero Albertini, Marino Masé, Pierre Paulo Capponi, Dulio Del Prete. Cliche-filled war drama with familiar plot: Italian commandos, led by a couple of stalwart Americans, must secure an important oasis in North African desert in advance of Allied landings.

Commandos Strike at Dawn, The (1942) 96m. **½ D: John Farrow. Paul Muni, Anne Lee, Lillian Gish, Cedric Hardwicke, Robert Coote, Ray Collins, Rosemary DeCamp, Alexander Knox. Well-intentioned drama of Norwegian Muni aiding British commandos in attack on Nazis who have invaded Norway. Dated propaganda angle lessens impact today.

Companeros! (1971-Italian-Spanish-German) C-105m. ** D: Sergio Corbucci. Franco Nero, Tomas Milian, Jack Palance, Fernando Rey, Iris Berben, Karin Schubert. Swedish mercenary (Nero) seeks his fortune by running guns in revolution-racked Mexico at the turn of the century. Violent western fare.

Companions In Nightmare (1968) C-99m. TVM D: Norman Lloyd. Melvyn Douglas, Gig Young, Anne Baxter, Patrick O'Neal, Dana Wynter, Leslie Nielsen, William Redfield. Renowned psychiatrist (Douglas) invites hand-picked group of professionals to participate in group therapy experiment, unaware group includes dangerous psychotic. Performances can't hide film's contrived posturing. Average.

Company of Killers (1970) C-88m. ** D: Jerry Thorpe. Van Johnson, Ray Milland, John Saxon, Brian Kelly, Fritz Weaver, Clu Gulager, Susan Oliver, Diana Lynn, Robert Middleton. Gunman (Saxon) working for Murder, Inc. becomes target for his employers and big city police department after patrolman is shot down. Bites off more than it can chew.

Company She Keeps, The (1950) 81m. **½ D: John Cromwell. Lizabeth Scott, Jane Greer, Dennis O'Keefe, Fay Baker, John Hoyt, Don Beddoe. Actors and unique love triangle spice this story of parole officer Greer and ex-con Scott both in love with O'Keefe.

Compulsion (1959) 103m. ***½ D: Richard Fleischer. Orson Welles, Diane Varsi, Dean Stockwell, Bradford Dillman, E. G. Marshall, Martin Milner. Hard-hitting version of Leopold-Loeb thrill murder case of 1920s Chicago. Good characterizations, period decor, and well-edited courtroom scenes highlight picture.

Computer Wore Tennis Shoes, The (1970) C-91m. ** D: Robert Butler. Kurt Russell, Cesar Romero, Joe Flynn, William Schallert, Alan Hewitt, Richard Bakalyan. The first of Disney's carbon-copy-comedies with young Russell has the college whiz injected with a computer-brain, which poses threat to local gangster Romero. Standard slapstick.

Comrade X (1940) 90m. **½ D: King Vidor. Clark Gable, Hedy Lamarr, Felix Bressart, Oscar Homolka, Eve Arden, Sig Ruman. NINOTCHKA-esque plot with American Gable warming up icy Russian Lamarr (a streetcar conductor). Synthetic romance tale never convinces.

Concorde, The—Airport '79 (1979)

C-113m. BOMB D: David Lowell Rich. Alain Delon, Susan Blakely, Robert Wagner, Sylvia Kristel, George Kennedy, Eddie Albert, Bibi Andersson, John Davidson, Andrea Marcovicci, Martha Raye, Cicely Tyson, Jimmie Walker, David Warner, Mercedes McCambridge. Wagner is a brilliant scientist, Kennedy and Andersson make love by the fire, Davidson's hair stays in place when the plane turns upside down, and McCambridge is a Russian gymnastics coach. Thank goodness Charo is around for credibility.

Concrete Cowboys, The (1979) C-100m. TVM D: Burt Kennedy. Jerry Reed, Tom Selleck, Morgan Fairchild, Claude Akins, Gene Evans, Roy Acuff, Barbara Mandrell. Lighthearted mystery adventure about a couple of yahoos in Nashville who find themselves embroiled in an intricate blackmail scheme. Leisurely pace and amiable acting nearly cancel each other out. Average.

Concrete Jungle, The (1962-British) 86m. **½ D: Joseph Losey. Stanley Baker, Margit Saad, Sam Wanamaker, Gregoire Aslan, Jill Bennett, Laurence Naismith, Edward Judd. Thoughtful filming of prison life focusing on convict who escapes and doublecrosses pal. Baker is exceptionally able.

Condemned (1929) 86m. ** D: Wesley Ruggles. Ronald Colman, Ann Harding, Louis Wolheim, Dudley Digges, William Elmer. Attempt to depict social evils of Devil's Island with interspersed romantic plot, in stiff early talkie.

Condemned of Altona, The (1963) 114m. **½ D: Vittorio De Sica. Sophia Loren, Fredric March, Robert Wagner, Maximilian Schell. Sluggish pseudo-intellectual version of Jean-Paul Sartre play about post-WW2 Germany involving dying magnate (March), his two sons—one a playboy (Wagner) with an actress wife (Loren); the other an insane Nazi war criminal (Schell).

Conduct Unbecoming (1975-British) C-107m. **½ D: Michael Anderson. Michael York, Richard Attenborough, Trevor Howard, Stacy Keach, Susannah York, Christopher Plummer. Quaintly old-fashioned drama of honor and outrage among the Bengal Lancers, where an officer's widow (York) is sexually attacked. Too stuffy to be fun, yet too modern

in other ways to be an antique; star performances are saving grace.

Coney Island (1943) C-96m. *** D: Walter Lang. Betty Grable, George Montgomery, Cesar Romero, Charles Winninger, Phil Silvers, Matt Briggs. Breezy, enjoyable turn-of-the-century musical of saloon entertainer Grable turned into famous musical star by hustling Montgomery. Remade as WABASH AVENUE.

Confess, Dr. Corda (1958-German) 81m. ** D: Josef von Baky. Hardy Kruger, Elisabeth Mueller, Lucie Mannheim, Hans Nielsen. Tedious handling of story of Kruger circumstantially involved in death of his mistress, with his attempt to prove innocence at trial.

Confession (1937) 86m. **½ D: Joe May. Kay Francis, Basil Rathbone, Jane Bryan, Ian Hunter, Donald Crisp, Laura Hope Crews, Veda Ann Borg, Robert Barrat. Well-mounted, MADAME X-ish soaper. Francis on trial, details her murder of pianist Rathbone. Francis registers good range of emotions; Crews is fine as empty-headed partygoer.

Confession, The (1970) C-138m. **½ D: Costa-Gavras. Yves Montand, Simone Signoret, Gabriele Ferzetti, Michel Vitold, Jean Bouise. True story of Czechoslovakian Communist Arthur London and his unjustified 1951 purge trial for treason; interesting tale well-acted by Montand, but film is as talky and overrated as Costa-Gavras' other efforts.

Confessions of a Nazi Spy (1939) 102m. *** D: Anatole Litvak. Edward G. Robinson, Francis Lederer, George Sanders, Paul Lukas, Henry O'Neill, James Stephenson, Sig Ruman. Bristling drama of G-man Robinson investigating Nazi underground in U.S. Patriotic zest is forgivable.

Confessions of a Police Captain (1971-Italian) C-102m. **½ D: Damiano Damiani. Martin Balsam, Franco Nero, Marilu Tolo, Claudio Gora. Interesting, sometimes ponderous drama of dedicated cop Balsam caught up in suffocating big-city corruption, as he tries to bring in an elusive criminal.

Confessions of a Window Cleaner (1974-British) C-90m. ** D: Val Guest. Robin Askwith, Anthony Booth, Linda Hayden, Bill Maynard, Dandy Nichols. British sex farce about voyeuristic window-cleaner was dated when it came out; too obvious to be terribly funny. Followed by other CONFESSIONS films which weren't released here.

Confessions of an Opium Eater (1962) 85m. *½ D: Albert Zugsmith. Vincent Price, Linda Ho, Richard Loo, June Kim, Philip Ahn, Victor Sen Yung. Bizarre low-budgeter. Price is hammy in weak tale of slave girls brought to San Francisco and the adventurer who aids them.

Confessions of Boston Blackie (1941) 65m. D: Edward Dmytryk. Chester Morris, Harriet Hilliard, Richard Lane, George E. Stone, Lloyd Corrigan, Joan Woodbury. SEE: Boston Blackie series.

Confessions of Felix Krull, The (1958-German) 107m. **½ D: Kurt Hoffman. Horst Buchholz, Lilo Pulver, Ingrid Andree, Susi Nicoletti. Waggish chronicle of charming rascal Buchholz rising in rank as Parisian hotel employee; based on Thomas Mann novel.

Confessions of Tom Harris (1972) C-98m. ** D: John Derek and David Nelson. Don Murray, Linda Evans, David Brian, Gary Clarke, Logan Ramsey. Offbeat, gritty study of a corrupt, amoral prizefighter, played by Murray who also produced and wrote the story. Co-director (and ex-actor) Derek photographed it.

Confidential Agent (1945) 118m. *** D: Herman Shumlin. Charles Boyer, Lauren Bacall, Peter Lorre, Katina Paxinou, Victor Francen, Wanda Hendrix. Boyer is Graham Greene's hero in engrossing spy yarn of Spanish Civil War; he meets Bacall along the way; they battle enemy agents Lorre and Paxinou.

Confidential Report SEE: Mr. Arkadin

Confidentially Connie (1953) 74m. **½ D: Edward Buzzell. Van Johnson, Janet Leigh, Louis Calhern, Walter Slezak, Gene Lockhart. Mild chuckles as pregnant wife Leigh schemes to get underpaid professor hubby (Johnson) to leave academic circles. Calhern as Van's rich Texan father is amusing.

Confirm or Deny (1941) 73m. **½ D: Archie Mayo. Don Ameche, Joan Bennett, Roddy McDowall, John Loder, Raymond Walburn, Arthur Shields. Love in an air-raid shelter with Ameche and Bennett as reporter and wireless operator; pleasant romance.

Conflict (1945) 86m. **½ D: Curtis Bernhardt. Humphrey Bogart, Alexis Smith, Sydney Greenstreet, Rose Hobart, Charles Drake, Grant Mitchell. Far-fetched story of husband (Bogart) plotting to murder wife (Hobart) to marry her sister (Smith). Unconvincing plot not salvaged by good cast.

Conformist, The (1971-Italian-French-West German) C-115m. ***½ D: Bernardo Bertolucci. Jean-Louis Trintignant, Stefania Sandrelli, Dominique Sanda, Pierre Clementi, Pasquale Fortunato, Gastone Moschin. Disturbing blend of character study and historical context of 1930s. Repressing homosexual drives, Marcello Clerici strives for "acceptable" life as member of Italian Fascist secret service, and middle-class would-be wife chaser, until odd series of events make him a willing murderer. Film's overall mood uniquely tense.

Congo Crossing (1956) C-87m. ** D: Joseph Pevney. Virginia Mayo, George Nader, Peter Lorre, Michael Pate, Rex Ingram. OK adventure yarn set in Africa, involving wanted criminals and construction engineer's attempt to civilize the Congo territory.

Congo Maisie (1940) 70m. D: H. C. Potter. Ann Sothern, John Carroll, Rita Johnson, Shepperd Strudwick, J. M. Kerrigan, E. E. Clive, Everett Brown. SEE: Maisie series

Congratulations, It's a Boy (1971) C-73m. TVM D: William Graham. Bill Bixby, Diane Baker, Jack Albertson, Ann Sothern, Karen Jensen. Fairly entertaining vehicle for Bixby as swinging bachelor confronted by young man who claims to be his son. Average.

Conjugal Bed, The (1963-Italian) 90m. *** D: Marco Ferreri. Ugo Tognazzi, Marina Vlady, Walter Giller, Linda Sini. Tognazzi is admirably suited to role of roué whose marriage to young beauty results in ironic twist of events.

Connecticut Yankee in King Arthur's Court (1949) C-107m. **½ D: Tay Garnett. Bing Crosby, Rhonda Fleming, William Bendix, Cedric Hardwicke, Henry Wilcoxon. Mark Twain's story becomes carefree Crosby musical, with Bing transported into past, branded a wizard. No great songs, but colorful production.

Connecting Rooms (1971-British) C-103m. ** D: Franklin Gollings. Bette Davis, Michael Redgrave, Alexis Kanner, Kay Walsh, Olga Georges-Picot, Leo Genn. Muddled melodrama of relationships in a rooming house. Davis is a street musician, Redgrave a former schoolmaster, and Kanner the rebellious youth who disrupts their equilibrium. Made in 1969, never released here.

Connection (1973) **C-73m.** TVM D: Tom Gries. Charles Durning, Ronny Cox, Zohra Lampert, Dennis Cole, Heather MacRae, Dana Wynter. Deliberately intricate tale of go-between (Durning) arranging meeting of jewel thief and insurance company representatives, capped by mad car chase on Manhattan's West Side. Flawless pacing, great performances. Above average.

Conquered City, The (1962-Italian) **C-87m.** **½ D: Joseph Anthony. David Niven, Ben Gazzara, Michael Craig, Martin Balsam, Lea Massari, Daniela Rocca. Niven and disparate international group are holed up in Athens hotel under siege in waning days of WW2; not-bad programmer released overseas as THE CAPTIVE CITY at 108m.

Conqueror, The (1956) **C-111m.** ** D: Dick Powell. John Wayne, Susan Hayward, Pedro Armendariz, Agnes Moorehead, Thomas Gomez, John Hoyt, William Conrad. Mongols vs. Tartars, and John Wayne vs. the silliest role of his career, Genghis Khan. Expensive epic marked Powell's directorial debut, but neither he nor an earnest Duke could survive the sublime silliness of the whole idea. Camp dialogue to spare.

Conqueror Worm, The (1968-British) **C-98m.** *** D: Michael Reeves. Vincent Price, Ian Ogilvy, Hilary Dwyer, Rupert Davies, Robert Russell, Patrick Wymark, Wilfrid Brambell. As Matthew Hopkins, self-styled witch-hunter during era of Cromwell, Price gives excellent nonhammy performance in underrated low-budget period thriller. Literate, balanced script pits him against young sympathetic lovers Ogilvy and Dwyer. Beware cuts.

Conquerors, The (1932) **80m.** ** D: William Wellman. Richard Dix, Ann Harding, Edna May Oliver, Guy Kibbee, Julie Haydon, Donald Cook. Unabashed rip-off of CIMARRON with Dix and Harding as newlyweds who go West to make their fortune, and build a banking empire that spans fifty years of ups and downs. Some good scenes lost in clichés of this epic saga. Retitled PIONEER BUILDERS.

Conquest (1937) **112m.** *** D: Clarence Brown. Greta Garbo, Charles Boyer, Reginald Owen, Alan Marshal, Henry Stephenson, Leif Erikson, Dame May Whitty. Boyer as Napoleon and Garbo as Polish countess Walewska in fairly interesting costumer with fine performances making up for not-always-thrilling script.

Conquest of Cochise (1953) **C-70m.** ** D: William Castle. John Hodiak, Robert Stack, Joy Page, John Crawford. Unspectacular Indian vs. cavalry, set in 1850s Southwest, as Stack and troops try to calm Cochise's (Hodiak) rampaging braves.

Conquest of Space (1955) **C-80m.** **½ D: Byron Haskin. Eric Fleming, William Hopper, Ross Martin, Walter Brooke, Joan Shawlee. George Pal's special effects bolster this account of space satellite and men who man it.

Conquest of the Planet of the Apes (1972) **C-87m.** **½ D: J. Lee Thompson. Roddy McDowall, Don Murray, Ricardo Montalban, Natalie Trundy, Severn Darden. Fourth APES feature shows how apes came to rebel and subsequently vanquish man. Loosely acted and often trite, but still interesting.

Conrack (1974) **C-107m.** *** D: Martin Ritt. Jon Voight, Paul Winfield, Hume Cronyn, Madge Sinclair, Tina Andrews, Antonio Fargas. Pleasant film based on Pat Conroy's *The Water Is Wide*, about his attempts to bring common-sense education to backward black school on island off South Carolina. Subplot with hermit-like Winfield doesn't work, unfortunately.

Conspiracy of Hearts (1960-British) **116m.** *** D: Ralph Thomas. Lilli Palmer, Sylvia Syms, Yvonne Mitchell, Ronald Lewis. Despite familiar situation of nuns sheltering refugee Jewish youths in Northern Italy, this film manages to be suspenseful and moving.

Conspiracy of Terror (1975) **C-78m.** TVM. D: John Llewellyn Moxey. Michael Constantine, Barbara Rhoades, Mariclare Costello, Roger Perry, David Opatoshu, Logan Ramsey. Husband-wife detective team investigates the case of a man who literally was scared to death and is confronted with satanism in suburbia. Comedy-drama, with "cute" touch of having the ethnically mixed pair working different shifts. Average.

Conspiracy to Kill: SEE **D.A.: Conspiracy to Kill**

Conspirator (1949-British) 85m. **½ D: Victor Saville. Robert Taylor, Elizabeth Taylor, Honor Blackman, Wilfrid Hyde-White. Elizabeth is confronted by the fact that British husband Taylor is a Communist agent; story often better than stars.

Conspirators, The (1944) 101m. **½ D: Jean Negulesco. Hedy Lamarr, Paul Henreid, Sydney Greenstreet, Peter Lorre, Victor Francen, Vladimir Sokoloff, George Macready, Monte Blue, Joseph Calleia. WW2 intrigue in Lisbon, with echoes of CASABLANCA. Opulently done, with fine cast headed by gorgeous Lamarr.

Constant Nymph, The (1943) 112m. ***½ D: Edmund Goulding. Charles Boyer, Joan Fontaine, Alexis Smith, Brenda Marshall, Charles Coburn, Dame May Whitty, Peter Lorre. Impeccable performances in story of young girl (Fontaine) infatuated with suave musician Boyer. Fontaine has never been better.

Constantine and the Cross (1962-Italian) C-120m. *** D: Lionello de Felice. Cornel Wilde, Christine Kaufman, Belinda Lee, Elisa Cegani, Massimo Serato. Intelligent interpretation of 4th century B.C. Emperor (Wilde) battling Romans for Christianity. Good action.

Contempt (1964-Italian) C-103m. **½ D: Jean-Luc Godard. Brigitte Bardot, Jack Palance, Fritz Lang, Giorgia Moll. Pretentious slop about moviemaking set in Rome with veteran director Lang taking role.

Contest Girl (1966-British) C-82m. **½ D: Val Guest. Ian Hendry, Janette Scott, Ronald Fraser, Edmund Purdom, Linda Christian. Film well conveys glamorous and seamy sides of beauty-contest world. Purdom gives effective performance.

Contract on Cherry Street (1977) C-150m. TVM. D: William A. Graham. Frank Sinatra, Harry Guardino, Martin Balsam, Henry Silva, Verna Bloom. Sinatra's first post-retirement movie (first in seven years) has him well cast as a N.Y.C. police inspector tackling organized crime. Aces to this police story. Above average.

Conversation, The (1974) C-113m. **** D: Francis Ford Coppola. Gene Hackman, John Cazale, Allen Garfield, Frederick Forrest, Cindy Williams, Teri Garr, Harrison Ford. Brilliant film about obsessive surveillance expert (Hackman) who makes professional mistake of becoming involved in a case, and finds himself involved with murder and high-level power plays. Coppola's brilliant, disturbing script makes larger statements about privacy and personal responsibility. One of the best films of the 1970s.

Conversation Piece (1977-Italian) C-122m. ** D: Luchino Visconti. Burt Lancaster, Silvana Mangano, Helmut Berger, Claudia Marsani, Claudia Cardinale. Ponderous story of aging, aloof professor Lancaster who becomes involved with matron Mangano's hedonistic children and her young lover, Berger. All talk.

Convicted (1950) 91m. **½ D: Henry Levin. Glenn Ford, Broderick Crawford, Dorothy Malone, Roland Winters, Ed Begley. Sincere account of prison warden's efforts to help unjustly convicted man, and those on the outside seeking actual killer.

Convicts Four (1962) 105m. *** D: Millard Kaufman. Ben Gazzara, Stuart Whitman, Ray Walston, Vincent Price, Rod Steiger, Broderick Crawford, Sammy Davis, Jr., Jack Kruschen. Gazzara gives sincere portrayal as long-term prisoner who becomes professional artist. Oddball supporting cast. Retitled: REPRIEVE

Convoy (1978) C-110m. ** D: Sam Peckinpah. Kris Kristofferson, Ali MacGraw, Ernest Borgnine, Burt Young, Madge Sinclair, Franklyn Ajaye. Amiable comic-book movie about an independent trucker who leads protesting colleagues on a trek through the Southwest. Stupid script and blah acting redeemed somewhat by Peckinpah's punchy directorial style.

Coogan's Bluff (1968) C-100m. *** D: Don Siegel. Clint Eastwood, Lee J. Cobb, Susan Clark, Tisha Sterling, Don Stroud, Betty Field, Tom Tully. Arizona lawman Eastwood comes to New York to show city cops a thing or two about tracking down a wanted man. Stylish action film, good location work. Sterling enjoyable as hippie type.

Cool and the Crazy, The (1958) 78m. *½ D: William Witney. Scott Marlowe, Gigi Perreau, Dick Bakalyan, Dick Jones. Exploitation value of this low-budgeter has lost novelty; dope addict becomes high school gang leader in order to push dope.

Cool Breeze (1972) C-101m. *½ D: Barry Pollack. Thalmus Rasulala,

Judy Pace, Jim Watkins, Lincoln Kilpatrick, Sam Laws, Raymond St. Jacques. Routine remake of THE ASPHALT JUNGLE with plot line updated so that diamond robbery proceeds will go to set up a black people's bank.

Cool Hand Luke (1967) **C-126m.** ***½ D: Stuart Rosenberg. Paul Newman, George Kennedy, J. D. Cannon, Lou Antonio, Robert Drivas, Strother Martin, Jo Van Fleet. Modern slant on prison camps shows little change since Paul Muni; more irreverent, however, with memorably funny egg-eating contest. Top-notch film with Kennedy's Oscar-winning performance as prisoner.

Cool Million (1972) **C-100m. TVM** D. Gene Leavitt. James Farentino, John Vernon, Barbara Bouchet, Jackie Coogan, Christine Belford, Lila Kedrova, Patrick O'Neal. International troubleshooter must locate genuine heiress of $50 million fortune when father dies under mysterious circumstances. Fantasy-world entertainment, not very good. Below average. Retitled MASK OF MARCELLA.

Cool Ones, The (1967) **C-95m.** BOMB. D: Gene Nelson. Roddy McDowall, Debbie Watson, Gil Peterson, Phil Harris, Robert Coote, Glen Campbell, Mrs. Miller. Inane "musical" comedy spoofing trendy music business. Embarrassing on all counts, with broad performances. If you turn up your volume, you might hear a faint laugh track.

Cooley High (1975) **C-107m.** *** D: Michael Schultz. Glynn Turman, Lawrence-Hilton Jacobs, Garrett Morris, Cynthia Davis, Corin Rogers, Maurice Leon Havis. Inner-city ripoff of AMERICAN GRAFFITI (set in Chicago, 1964) is nonetheless pleasing on its own terms, though only on the level of a good TV show. Lots of laughs.

Cop on the Beat (1975) **C-78m.** TVM D: Virgil W. Vogel. Lloyd Bridges, Pat Crowley, Dane Clark, Jim Backus, Dean Stockwell, Della Reese, Janis Paige, Tom Drake, Edie Adams, Don Stroud, Hari Rhodes. Bridges is Joe Forrester, veteran plainclothes cop who voluntarily returns to uniform duty on his old beat to help solve a series of robbery-rapes in the rundown neighborhood. This evolved from TV's "Police Story" and served as a brief

series for always reliable Bridges. Average.

Copacabana (1947) **92m.** ** D: Alfred E. Green. Groucho Marx, Carmen Miranda, Andy Russell, Steve Cochran, Gloria Jean, Louis Sobol, Abel Green, Earl Wilson. Unengrossing musical comedy about wild complications when same girl applies for two jobs at nightclub; cast can't save it.

Cop-Out (1968-British) **C-95m.** **½ D: Pierre Rouve. James Mason, Geraldine Chaplin, Bobby Darin, Paul Bertoya, Ian Ogilvy, Bryan Stanton. OK murder mystery with dated generation-gap overtones. Reclusive lawyer Mason comes out of retirement to defend his daughter's boyfriend on trumped-up murder charge. Remake of 1942 French film STRANGER IN THE HOUSE.

Copper Canyon (1950) **C-83m.** **½ D: John Farrow. Ray Milland, Hedy Lamarr, Macdonald Carey, Mona Freeman. Milland-Lamarr occasionally sparkle in this Western of post-Civil War days and movement West to find riches.

Cops and Robbers (1973) **C-89m.** *** D: Aram Avakian. Cliff Gorman, Joseph Bologna, Dick Ward, Shepperd Strudwick, John Ryan, Ellen Holly. Enjoyable tale about two policemen who pull a million-dollar caper on Wall Street. Funny and exciting, with good location photography.

Cops and Robin, The (1978) **C-100m.** TVM D: Allen Reisner. Ernest Borgnine, Michael Shannon, John Amos, Carol Lynley, Natasha Ryan, Philip Abbott, Terry Kiser. The premise that began with FUTURE COP (with the same stars) and continued in the brief series that followed was given another shot here, with an aging street cop and his partner, a robot programmed to be the perfect policeman, assigned to protect the young daughter of a woman stalked by mobsters. Average.

Corky (1972) **C-88m.** **½ D: Leonard Horn. Robert Blake, Charlotte Rampling, Patrick O'Neal, Christopher Connelly, Ben Johnson, Laurence Luckinbill. Blake's obsession for stock-car racing shuts out everything else in his life, including wife and friends. Good racing sequences, fairly absorbing character study. Originally titled LOOKIN' GOOD.

Corn Is Green, The (1945) **114-m.** ***½ D: Irving Rapper. Bette Davis,

Nigel Bruce, John Dall, Joan Lorring, Rhys Williams, Rosalind Ivan, Mildred Dunnock. Thoughtful acting in this story of devoted middle-aged teacher Davis in Welsh mining town, coming to terms with her prize pupil; from Emlyn Williams play.

Corn is Green, The (1979) C-100m. TVM D: George Cukor. Katharine Hepburn, Ian Saynor, Bill Fraser, Patricia Hayes, Anna Massey. Classy remake of the 1945 movie about a spinster teacher bringing education to North Wales mining community. Story is beginning to wear a bit, but glistens with Hepburn's tour-de-force performance (in her tenth teaming with director Cukor) and on-location filming. Above average.

Cornbread, Earl and Me (1975) C-95m. **½ D: Joe Manduke. Moses Gunn, Bernie Casey, Rosalind Cash, Madge Sinclair, Keith Wilkes, Tierre Turner. Well-intentioned but overly melodramatic account of a black youth, on his way out of the ghetto on a basketball scholarship, who is innocently gunned down by police bullets. Fine performances and warm sense of black life evaporate in TV series cliches.

Cornered (1945) 102m. *** D: Edward Dmytryk. Dick Powell, Walter Slezak, Micheline Cheirel, Nina Vale, Morris Carnovsky. High-tension drama with tough-guy Powell in Buenos Aires tracking down the man who killed his wife during WW2; Powell in peak form.

Coroner Creek (1948) C-93m. ** D: Ray Enright. Randolph Scott, Marguerite Chapman, George Macready, Sally Eilers, Edgar Buchanan. Good little Western: Scott seeks revenge on his fiancee's killer.

Corrupt Ones, The (1966-French-Italian-West German) C-92m. **½ D: James Hill. Robert Stack, Elke Sommer, Nancy Kwan, Christian Marquand, Werner Peters. Knockabout photographer Stack is befriended by stranger who gives him key (literally!) to ancient Chinese emperor's treasure. With better dialogue for its many grotesque characters, film could've been a knockout.

Corruption (1968-British) C-91m. ** D: Robert Hartford-Davis. Peter Cushing, Sue Lloyd, David Lodge, Kate O'Mara. Another film of famed surgeon who will stop at nothing to restore his love's destroyed beauty.

Corpse Came C.O.D., The (1947) 87m. ** D: Henry Levin. George Brent, Joan Blondell, Adele Jergens, Jim Bannon, Leslie Brooks, Grant Mitchell, Una O'Connor. Two rival reporters attempt to solve mystery of dead body showing up at actress' residence. Strictly "B" material.

Corpse Vanishes, The (1942) 64m. *½ D: Wallace Fox. Bela Lugosi, Luana Walters, Tristram Coffin, Minerva Urecal, Vince Barnett. Grade-B horror movie with poor-to-adequate cast; has Lugosi performing experiments to restore wife's youth. Hardly scary.

Corregidor (1943) 73m. ** D: William Nigh. Otto Kruger, Elissa Landi, Donald Woods, Frank Jenks, Rick Vallin, Wanda McKay, Ian Keith. Not a battle-action film but a routine love triangle set against wartime background, rather cheaply done.

Corridors of Blood (1963-British) 87m. **½ D: Robert Day. Boris Karloff, Betta St. John, Christopher Lee, Finlay Currie. At times engaging account of 19th-century British doctor experimenting with anesthetics, creating havoc when he accidentally becomes a dope addict.

Corsican Brothers, The (1941) 112m. *** D: Gregory Ratoff. Douglas Fairbanks Jr., Ruth Warrick, Akim Tamiroff, J. Carrol Naish, H. B. Warner, Henry Wilcoxon. Entertaining swashbuckler from Dumas story of twins who are separated, but remain spiritually tied. Fairbanks excellent in the lead, with strong support, elaborate production values.

Corvette K-225 (1943) 99m. *** D: Richard Rossen. Randolph Scott, James Brown, Ella Raines, Barry Fitzgerald, Andy Devine, Walter Sande, Richard Lane. First-rate war film with Canadian officer Scott fighting to save prominent navy destroyer from enemy attack; realistic film.

Corvette Summer (1978) C-105m. ** D: Matthew Robbins. Mark Hamill, Annie Potts, Eugene Roche, Kim Milford, Richard McKenzie, William Bryant. High schooler Hamill falls for aspiring hooker Potts while in Vegas tracking down the person who stole the sports car restored by his shop class. Bland comedy drama offers Potts' disarmingly off-the-wall performance to keep your attention.

Cosmic Man, The (1959) 72m. *½ D: Herbert Greene. Bruce Bennett, John Carradine, Angela Greene, Paul Langton, Scotty Morrow. Mediocre sci-fi with now-you-see-me, now-you-don't title figure on a mission to earth.

Cossacks, The (1959-Italian) **C-113m.** ** D: Giorgio Rivalta. Edmund Purdom, John Drew Barrymore, Giorgia Moll, Massimo Girotti. Heavy-handed historical tale set in 1850s Russia; Cossack Purdom and son Barrymore clash in loyalties to Czar Alexander II.

Cotter (1973) **C-94m.** **½ D: Paul Stanley. Don Murray, Carol Lynley, Rip Torn, Sherry Jackson. After tragic rodeo incident, unhappy Indian clown (Murray) struggles to re-establish himself in home town. Great cast in fair script that fares best in creating small-town atmosphere.

Cotton Candy (1978) **C-100m. TVM** D: Ron Howard. Charles Martin Smith, Clint Howard, Rance Howard, Leslie King, Kevin Lee Miller. Ron Howard directed (and co-wrote) this featherweight story about high school students who form a rock 'n' roll band in the 1950s. Average.

Cotton Comes to Harlem (1970) **C-97m.** *** D: Ossie Davis. Godfrey Cambridge, Raymond St. Jacques, Calvin Lockhart, Judy Pace, Redd Foxx, Emily Yancy. St. Jacques is Coffin Ed Johnson, Cambridge is Digger Ed Jones, black cops who suspect preacher Lockhart's back-to-Africa campaign is a swindle. Neatly combines action and comedy, with fine use of N.Y.C., Harlem locales; from Chester Himes' novel.

Couch, The (1962) **100m.** **½ D: Owen Crump. Shirley Knight, Grant Williams, Onslow Stevens, William Leslie. Bizarre yarn of psychopathic killer on the prowl while under analysis.

Counsellor-at-Law (1933) **82m.** **** D: William Wyler. John Barrymore, Bebe Daniels, Doris Kenyon, Onslow Stevens, Isabel Jewell, Melvyn Douglas, Thelma Todd, John Qualen. Vivid adaptation of Elmer Rice play about unscrupulous rags-to-riches lawyer who cannot escape his background—and who begins to question his success when he learns his wife has been unfaithful. Barrymore gives one of his greatest performances in meaty, colorful role; Wyler keeps film moving at breakneck pace.

Count Dracula (1970-Italian-Spanish-German) **C-98m.** **½ D: Jess Franco. Christopher Lee, Herbert Lom, Klaus Kinski, Frederick Williams, Maria Rohm, Soledad Miranda. Flawed but interesting low-budget adaptation of Bram Stoker novel which sticks close to its source; Lee turns in remarkably low-key performance. TV prints run 90m.

Count Five and Die (1958-British) **92m.** **½ D: Victor Vicas. Jeffrey Hunter, Nigel Patrick, Ann-Marie Duringer, David Kossoff. WW2 espionage flick has Hunter an American agent working with British to mislead Nazis about Allied landing site.

Count of Bragelonne, The SEE: **Last Musketeer, The**

Count of Monte Cristo, The (1934) **119m.** ***½ D: Rowland V. Lee. Robert Donat, Elissa Landi, Louis Calhern, Sidney Blackmer, Raymond Walburn, O. P. Heggie, Luis Alberni, Irene Hervey. Superb filmization of classic story of Edmond Dantes, who spends years in prison unjustly but escapes to seek revenge on enemies who framed him. Donat leads excellent cast in rousing classic from Dumas' story.

Count of Monte Cristo, The (1954-French) **C-97m.** **½ D: Robert Vernay. Jean Marais, Lia Amanda, Roger Piquat. Seviceable rendition of Alexandre Dumas costume classic.

Count of Monte Cristo, The (1961-French) **C-90m.** **½ D: Claude Autant-Lara. Louis Jourdan, Yvonne Furneaux, Pierre Mondy, Bernard Dheran. Faithful adaptation of Dumas novel, but Jourdan hasn't the zest that Robert Donat gave the role in 1934. Originally 120m.

Count of Monte Cristo, The (1975) **C-100m. TVM** D: David Greene. Richard Chamberlain, Tony Curtis, Trevor Howard, Louis Jourdan, Donald Pleasence, Taryn Power. Lavish costume drama with Chamberlain quite all right as a swashbuckling Edmond Dantes and Curtis as the villainous Mondego. Holds its own against its many predecessors. Average.

Count the Hours (1953) **76m.** ** D: Don Siegel. Teresa Wright, Macdonald Carey, Dolores Moran, Adele Mara. Trim but implausible story of ranch hand and pregnant wife. When police accuse them of murdering their employers, he takes blame so she can have their child.

Count Three and Pray (1955) **C-102m.** **½ D: George Sherman. Van Heflin, Joanne Woodward, Raymond Burr, Nancy Kulp. Atmospheric rural Americana in post-Civil War days, with Heflin exerting influence on townfolk as new pastor with reckless past. Woodward as strong-willed orphan lass and Burr the perennial villain are fine.

Count Yorga, Vampire (1970) C-91m. *** D: Bob Kelljan. Robert Quarry, Roger Perry, Donna Anders, Michael Murphy. Sophisticated, clever(!) vampire (Quarry) establishes coven in modern-day Southern California. Fast-paced and convincing. Beware cuts.

Count Your Blessings (1959) C-102m. ** D: Jean Negulesco. Deborah Kerr, Rossano Brazzi, Maurice Chevalier, Martin Stephens, Tom Helmore, Patricia Medina. Unfunny comedy that even Chevalier's smile can't help. Kerr marries French playboy Brazzi during WW2; he goes off philandering for years. Their child conspires to bring them together again.

Countdown (1968) C-101m. ***½ D: Robert Altman. Robert Duvall, James Caan, Charles Aidman, Joanna Moore, Steve Ihnat, Barbara Baxley, Ted Knight, Michael Murphy. Near-flawless depiction of real-life trials and concerns of American astronauts, their wives, co-workers. Excellent ensemble performances, intelligent script, great use of mood. Dated technology only liability.

Countdown at Kusini (1976-Nigerian) C-101m. ** D: Ossie Davis. Ruby Dee, Ossie Davis, Greg Morris, Tom Aldredge, Michael Ebert, Thomas Baptiste. Well-meaning treatment of liberation of fictional African country, "Fahari" (actually Lagos). Action and ideas are constantly swallowed up by romantic subplot. Film financed by DST Telecommunications, subsidiary of Delta Sigma Theta, world's largest black sorority.

Counter-Attack (1945) 90m. **½ D: Zoltan Korda. Paul Muni, Marguerite Chapman, Larry Parks, Philip Van Zandt, George Macready, Roman Bohnen. Satisfactory WW2 movie of Allied fighters going behind enemy lines to sabotage German positions; no classic, but good.

Counter Tenors, The SEE: White Voices, The

Counterfeit Killer, The (1968) C-95m. ** D: Josef Leytes. Jack Lord, Shirley Knight, Jack Weston, Charles Drake, Joseph Wiseman, Don Hanmer. Adapted from TV film THE FACELESS MAN, meandering actioner has Lord a secret service man

infiltrating a counterfeit syndicate, with predictable results.

Counterfeit Plan, The (1957-British) 80m. ** D: Montgomery Tully. Zachary Scott, Peggie Castle, Mervyn Johns, Sydney Tafler. Scott is appropriately nasty as escaped murderer who sets up international counterfeit syndicate.

Counterfeit Traitor, The (1962) C-140m. ***½ D: George Seaton. William Holden, Lilli Palmer, Hugh Griffith, Erica Beer, Werner Peters, Eva Dahlbeck. Holden runs around Europe as a double agent during WW2, falls in love with Palmer between various dangerous missions. Authentic backgrounds and fine cast. Based on true story.

Counterplot (1959) 76m. ** D: Kurt Neumann. Forrest Tucker, Allison Hayes, Gerald Milton, Edmundo Rivera Alvarez, Jackie Wayne. Mundane hide-and-seeker set in Puerto Rico where Tucker is hiding out from police and his double-dealing attorney.

Counterpoint (1968) C-107m. *½ D: Ralph Nelson. Charlton Heston, Maximilian Schell, Kathryn Hays, Leslie Nielsen, Anton Diffring. Absurd WW2 melodrama about symphony conductor captured by Nazi general, forced to put on private concert; Heston looks comfortable because he doesn't have to change facial expressions while conducting.

Countess Dracula (1972-British) C-94m. ** D: Peter Sasdy. Ingrid Pitt, Nigel Green, Peter Jeffrey, Lesley-Anne Down. Countess masquerades as her own daughter, needs blood to maintain facade of youth. OK shocker.

Countess From Hong Kong, A (1967-British) C-108m. *½ D: Charles Chaplin. Marlon Brando, Sophia Loren, Sydney Chaplin, Tippi Hedren, Patrick Cargill, Margaret Rutherford. Director-writer-composer (and bit-part actor) Chaplin's attempt to make old-fashioned romantic comedy sinks fast, though everybody tries hard. Sophia stows away in shipboard stateroom of diplomat Brando. Badly shot, badly timed, badly scored; a pity.

Countess of Monte Cristo, The (1948) 77m. ** D: Frederick de Cordova. Sonja Henie, Olga San Juan, Dorothy Hart, Michael Kirby, Arthur Treacher. Sonja and Olga pretend to be royal visitors in this limp costume comedy.

Country Girl, The (1954) 104m. ***½ D: George Seaton. Bing Crosby, Grace Kelly, William Holden, Anthony Ross. Kelly won an Oscar as wife of alcoholic singer (Crosby) trying for comeback via help of director (Holden). Crosby excels in one of his finest roles.

Couple Takes a Wife, The (1972) C-73m. TVM D: Jerry Paris. Bill Bixby, Paula Prentiss, Valerie Perrine, Nanette Fabray, Robert Goulet, Myrna Loy, Larry Storch. Good cast works wonders with old-style situation: the Hamiltons (Bixby and Prentiss) decide to take on "second wife," enabling Mrs. Hamilton continue professional career. Above average.

Courage and the Passion, The (1978) C-100m. TVM D: John Llewellyn Moxey. Vince Edwards, Desi Arnaz, Jr., Don Meredith, Trisha Noble, Linda Foster, Robert Hooks, Monty Hall. Pilot about pilots who test jets and bring their personal problems to C.O. Edwards, who put this one together in hopes of having another hit series. Average.

Courage of Black Beauty (1957) C-77m. ** D: Harold Schuster. John Crawford, Diane Brewster, J. Pat O'Malley, John Bryant. Wholesome programmer of Crawford and colt he is given.

Courage of Kavik, The Wolf Dog, The (1980) C-100m. TVM D: Peter Carter. Ronny Cox, John Ireland, Linda Sorenson, Andrew Ian McMillan, Chris Wiggins. Uninspired, Canadian-made boy-and-his-sled-dog tale that won't do preteen viewers any harm. Average.

Courage of Lassie (1946) C-92m. **½ D: Fred Wilcox. Elizabeth Taylor, Frank Morgan, Tom Drake, Selena Royle, George Cleveland. Tasteful, folksy tale of Lassie used in WW2 as a killer dog, Taylor his mistress who reforms him into kindly animal once again.

Courageous Dr. Christian, The (1940) 67m. ** D: Bernard Vorhaus. Jean Hersholt, Dorothy Lovett, Robert Baldwin, Tom Neal, Maude Eburne, Vera Lewis. If you can sit through this you're pretty brave yourself; this time the good doctor is battling a local epidemic.

Court Jester, The (1956) C-101m. **** D: Norman Panama, Melvin Frank. Danny Kaye, Glynis Johns, Basil Rathbone, Angela Lansbury, Cecil Parker, Mildred Natwick, Robert Middleton. One of the best comedies ever made, has Danny as jester who finds himself involved in romance, court intrigue, and a deadly joust. Delightfully complicated comic situations, superbly performed. And remember: the pellet with the poison's in the vessel with the pestle . . .

Court Martial (1955-British) 105m. *** D: Anthony Asquith. David Niven, Margaret Leighton, Victor Maddern, Maurice Denham. Tense courtroom story of officer Niven accused of stealing military funds. The trial reveals provocations of grasping wife. A solid drama. Originally released as CARRINGTON, V. C.

Court-Martial of Billy Mitchell, The (1955) C-100m. *** D: Otto Preminger. Gary Cooper, Charles Bickford, Ralph Bellamy, Rod Steiger, Elizabeth Montgomery. Low-key drama about trial of military pioneer who in 1925 predicted Japanese attack on U.S. Steiger adds spark to slowly-paced film as wily attorney; Montgomery made her movie debut here.

Courtney Affair, The (1947-British) 112m. **½ D: Herbert Wilcox. Anna Neagle, Michael Wilding, Gladys Young, Coral Browne, Michael Medwin. Wealthy young man marries housemaid in this family saga that traces the years 1900-1945; amiable but soapy, this was a big hit in England. Original running time, 120m. Original title: THE COURTNEYS OF CURZON STREET.

Courtneys of Curzon Street, The: SEE Courtney Affair, The

Courtship of Andy Hardy, The (1942) 93m. D: George B. Seitz. Lewis Stone, Mickey Rooney, Cecilia Parker, Fay Holden, Ann Rutherford, Sara Haden, Donna Reed, William Lundigan, Frieda Inescort. SEE: Andy Hardy series.

Courtship of Eddie's Father, The (1963) C-117m. *** D: Vincente Minnelli. Glenn Ford, Shirley Jones, Stella Stevens, Dina Merrill, Roberta Sherwood. Cute family comedy with Ronny Howard trying to find wife for widower father Ford.

Cousin, Cousine (1975-French) C-95m. *** D: Jean-Charles Tacchella. Marie-Christine Barrault, Victor Lanoux, Marie-France Pisier, Guy Marchand, Ginette Garcin, Sybil Maas. Barrault and Lanoux, married to others, become cousins by marriage and decide to go way beyond the kissing stage. Mild, easy-to-take comedy that became a surprise box-office sensation in U.S.

Cousins, The (1959-French) 112m. ** D: Claude Chabrol. Jean-Claude Brialy, Gerard Blain, Juliette Mayniel. Uneven drama concerning competition between cousins Brialy, Blain for affection of Mayniel.

Covenant with Death, A (1967) C-97m. ** D: Lamont Johnson. George Maharis, Laura Devon, Katy Jurado, Earl Holliman, Sidney Blackmer, Gene Hackman. Unjustly convicted murderer kills his hangman and is then found to be innocent of the first offense; what now? Interesting idea is handled too melodramatically to be effective.

Cover Girl (1944) C-107m. *** D: Charles Vidor. Rita Hayworth, Gene Kelly, Lee Bowman, Phil Silvers, Jinx Falkenburg, Eve Arden, Otto Kruger, Anita Colby. Incredibly clichéd plot is overcome by loveliness of Rita, fine musical score including "Long Ago And Far Away," and especially Kelly's solo numbers. Silvers adds some laughs, but Eve Arden steals the film as Kruger's wisecracking assistant.

Cover Girls (1977) C-78m. TVM D: Jerry London. Jayne Kennedy, Cornelia Sharpe, Don Galloway, Vince Edwards, Sean Garrison, George Lazenby. Two fashion models combine photo assignments with work as espionage agents. It's "Charlie's Angels" minus one, a rock-bottom rip-off that proves, as Red Skelton once said, "Imitation isn't the sincerest form of flattery, it's plagiarism." Below average.

Cover Me Babe (1970) C-89m. BOMB D: Noel Black. Robert Forster, Sondra Locke, Susanne Benton, Robert S. Fields, Ken Kercheval, Sam Waterston, Regis Toomey. Depressingly bad movie about student filmmaker who lets nothing stand in the way of gaining a contract. It'll be cut for TV, but it won't matter.

Covered Wagon, The (1923) 60m. **½ D: James Cruze. J. Warren Kerrigan, Lois Wilson, Alan Hale, Ernest Torrence. Slow-paced silent forerunner of Western epics, following a wagon train as it combats Indians and the elements; beautifully photographed, but rather tame today.

Covert Action (1978-Italian) C-95m. *½ D: Romolo Guerrieri. David Janssen, Arthur Kennedy, Corinne Clery, Maurizio Merli, Stefano Satta

Flores. Janssen is former CIA man whose life is imperiled after he writes a book about his experiences. Filmed in Greece.

Cow and I (1961-French) 98m. *** D: Henri Verneuil. Fernandel, Rene Havard, Albert Remy, Bernard Musson. Country-style humor bolstered by Fernandel as peasant escaped from German farm prison, assisted by loyal cow.

Cow Country (1953) 82m. ** D: Lesley Selander, Curtis Bishop. Edmond O'Brien, Helen Westcott, Peggie Castle, Raymond Hatton. Earnest Western of 1880s Texas, with debt-ridden ranchers overcoming all.

Cowboy (1958) C-92m. *** D: Delmer Daves. Glenn Ford, Jack Lemmon, Anna Kashfi, Brian Donlevy, Dick York. Intelligent, atmospheric Western based on Frank Harris' reminiscences as a tenderfoot. Lemmon is Harris, with Ford as his stern boss on eventful cattle roundup.

Cowboy and the Lady, The (1938) 91m. **½ D: H. C. Potter. Gary Cooper, Merle Oberon, Patsy Kelly, Walter Brennan, Fuzzy Knight, Harry Davenport. Aristocratic Oberon falls in love with rodeo star Cooper in mild comedy uplifted by stars.

Cowboy From Brooklyn, The (1938) 80m. **½ D: Lloyd Bacon. Dick Powell, Pat O'Brien, Priscilla Lane, Dick Foran, Ann Sheridan, Johnnie Davis, Ronald Reagan, Emma Dunn. Powell can only get radio job if he proves he's an authentic cowhand. Silly musicomedy includes songs "Ride Tenderfoot Ride," title tune.

Cowboys, The (1972) C-128m. ** D: Mark Rydell. John Wayne, Roscoe Lee Browne, Bruce Dern, Colleen Dewhurst, Slim Pickens. Well-produced but sluggish Western about aging rancher forced to take 11 youngsters with him on cattle drive; some violent scenes may be cut for TV. Disappointing film.

Crack in the Mirror (1960) 97m. *** D: Richard Fleischer. Orson Welles, Juliette Greco, Bradford Dillman, Alexander Knox. Welles, Greco, and Dillman enact contrasting dual roles in intertwining love triangles set in contemporary Paris, involving murder, courtroom trial, and illicit love; novelty eventually wears thin, marring Grade-A effort.

Crack in the World (1965) C-96m. **½ D: Andrew Marton. Dana Andrews, Janette Scott, Kieron Moore, Alexander Knox, Peter Damon. Believable sci-fi about scientists trying to harness earth's inner energy but almost causing destruction of the world; realistic special effects.

Cracker Factory, The (1979) C-100m. TVM D: Burt Brinckerhoff. Natalie Wood, Perry King, Peter Haskell, Vivian Blaine, Juliet Mills, Marian Mercer. Wood shines as a suicidal suburban housewife who's in and out of the asylum throughout this adaptation of Joyce Rebeta-Burditt's novel. Above average.

Crack-Up (1946) 93m. *** D: Irving Reis. Pat O'Brien, Claire Trevor, Herbert Marshall, Wallace Ford. Swindler takes advantage of O'Brien's amnesia to further his art-forging racket. Fine cast in suspenseful mystery.

Craig's Wife (1936) 75m. *** D: Dorothy Arzner. Rosalind Russell, John Boles, Billie Burke, Jane Darwell, Dorothy Wilson, Alma Kruger, Thomas Mitchell. Russell scored first big success as domineering wife who thinks more of material objects than of her husband. Based on George Kelly play, remade as HARRIET CRAIG.

Cranes Are Flying, The (1959-Russian) 94m. ***½ D: Mikhail Kalatozov. Tatyana Samoilova, Alexei Batalov, Vasily Merkuryev, A. Shvorin. Lilting love story set in WW2 Russia. Doctor's son (Batalov) leaves his sweetheart (Samoilova) to join the army. She is seduced by his cousin, marries him, and from subsequent tragedies tries to rebuild her life.

Crash! (1977) C-85m. *½ D: Charles Band. Jose Ferrer, Sue Lyon, John Ericson, Leslie Parrish, John Carradine. Strange, unbelievable mixture of occult and car chase. Jealous invalid-husband Ferrer tries to kill wife Lyon, who uses demonic device to cause mayhem on her own.

Crash (1978) C-100m. TVM D: Barry Shear. William Shatner, Adrienne Barbeau, Eddie Albert, Brooke Bundy, Christopher Connelly, Lorraine Gray, George Maharis, Artie Shaw. Another plane goes down with a flight manifesto of TV familiars. This time the tale is based on fact (and covered similarly in the TV movie THE GHOST OF FLIGHT 401): dramatizing the jetliner disaster in the Florida Everglades in Dec. '72 and the rescue of 73 passengers. Average.

Crash Dive (1943) C-105m. **½ D:

Archie Mayo. Tyrone Power, Anne Baxter, Dana Andrews, James Gleason, Dame May Whitty, Henry (Harry) Morgan. Submarine battleground just backdrop for love story; Power and Andrews both love young Baxter. Oscar-winner for special effects, film's main asset.

Crash Landing (1958) 76m. *½ D: Fred F. Sears. Gary Merrill, Nancy Davis, Irene Hervey, Roger Smith. Insipid revelations of passengers aboard plane facing possible crash landing into the ocean.

Crash of Silence (1953-British) 93m. *** D: Alexander Mackendrick. Phyllis Calvert, Jack Hawkins, Terence Morgan, Mandy Miller. Honest drama of young deaf girl (Miller) and her mother's dilemma: keep her at home or send her to a special school. Sensibly acted. Retitled MANDY.

Crashing Las Vegas (1956) 62m. D: Jean Yarbrough. Leo Gorcey, Huntz Hall, Jimmy Murphy, David Condon. SEE: Bowery Boys series.

Crashout (1955) 90m. **½ D: Lewis R. Foster. William Bendix, Arthur Kennedy, Luther Adler, William Talman. Low-budget but interesting story of prison break headed by Bendix. Kennedy as humane gang member is fine.

Crater Lake Monster, The (1977) C-89m. BOMB D: William R. Stromberg. Richard Cardella, Glenn Roberts, Mark Siegel, Kacey Cobb. A dinosaur egg is hatched at the bottom of Crater Lake, and guess what happens next? Not worth your time.

Crawling Eye, The (1958-British) 85m. **½ D: Quentin Lawrence. Forrest Tucker, Laurence Payne, Janet Munro, Jennifer Jayne, Warren Mitchell. OK, if predictable, tale (adapted by Jimmy Sangster from British TV series "The Trollenberg Terror") about cosmic cloud unleashing title creature on mountaintop. Hampered by low-grade special effects.

Crawling Hand, The (1963) 89m. *½ D: Herbert L. Strock. Peter Breck, Kent Taylor, Rod Lauren, Arline Judge, Alan Hale, Allison Hayes, Alan Hale. Astronaut's disembodied hand instigates rash of stranglings in this amateurish rehash of HANDS OF ORLAC theme. Good for a few (unintended) laughs, anyway.

Crawlspace (1971) C-74m. TVM D: John Newland. Arthur Kennedy, Teresa Wright, Tom Harper, Gene

Roche, Dan Morgan. Retired couple living in New England take in odd young man to fill need for son; he takes up residence in house's cellar. Definitely offbeat combination of character study and psychological thriller. Above average.

Craze (1974-British) **C-96m.** *½ D: Freddie Francis. Jack Palance, Diana Dors, Julie Ege, Trevor Howard, Suzy Kendall, Michael Jayston, Dame Edith Evans. More laughs than horror as antique dealer Palance makes human sacrifices to African idol. Hugh Griffith and Howard wisely kid the material.

Crazies, The SEE: **Code Name: Trixie**

Crazy Desire (1964-Italian) **108m.** ***½ D: Luciano Salce. Ugo Tognazzi, Catherine Spaak, Gianni Garko, Beatrice Altariba. Disarming fluff of Tognazzi enamoured of young funseekers, and Spaak in particular.

Crazy House (1943) **80m.** *** D: Edward F. Cline. Ole Olsen, Chic Johnson, Martha O'Driscoll, Patric Knowles, Cass Daley, Percy Kilbride, Leighton Noble. Olsen & Johnson take over film studio to make epic in frantic musicomedy with guests galore: Basil Rathbone, Count Basie, Allan Jones, Edgar Kennedy, Billy Gilbert, Andy Devine, etc.

Crazy Jack and the Boy SEE: **Silence**

Crazy Joe (1974-Italo-American) **C-100m.** **½ D: Carlo Lizzani. Peter Boyle, Rip Torn, Fred Williamson, Eli Wallach, Paula Prentiss, Luther Adler. Crime drama based on the bloody career of New York racketeer Crazy Joe Gallo is tolerable, due to its cast. Henry Winkler can be seen as a mustached hoodlum.

Crazy Over Horses (1951) **65m.** D: William Beaudine. Huntz Hall, Leo Gorcey, David Gorcey, William Benedict, Bernard Gorcey. SEE: **Bowery Boys** series.

Crazy World of Julius Vrooder, The (1974) **C-89m.** **½ D: Arthur Hiller. Timothy Bottoms, Barbara Hershey, George Marshall, Albert Salmi, Lawrence Pressman. Nobody likes this offbeat comedy of a confused Vietnam vet who acts insane to cope with a crazy world, but it has a certain charm. Veteran director Marshall returned to acting here shortly before his death.

Crazy World of Laurel and Hardy, The (1967) **83m.** **½ Narrated by Garry Moore. Unlike most L&H compilations, this one uses talkie

material as well as silent footage; some good routines are fragmented, with too much lumped together, but Stan and Ollie survive nicely.

Crazylegs (1953) **87m.** *½ D: Francis D. Lyon. Elroy Hirsch, Lloyd Nolan, Joan Vohs, Louise Lorimer. Inconclusive fiction based on the football escapades of Elroy Crazylegs Hirsch with gridiron star playing himself.

Creation of the Humanoids (1962) **C-75m.** BOMB D: Wesley E. Barry. Don Megowan, Frances McCann, Erica Elliott, Don Doolittle. Survivors of atomic war fight for survival against man-made robots which thrive on human blood. A movie only a humanoid could love.

Creature from Black Lake (1976) **C-97m.** ** D: Joy Houck Jr. Jack Elam, Dub Taylor, Dennis Fimple, John David Carson, Bill Thurman. Two young men venture into Louisiana swamps, only to run smack into Bigfoot; not-bad low-budgeter follows familiar formula.

Creature from the Black Lagoon (1954) **79m.** **½ D: Jack Arnold. Richard Carlson, Julia Adams, Richard Denning, Antonio Moreno, Nestor Paiva. Cliches combine with genuine chills in story of expedition which discovers prehistoric gill-man living in inlet off Amazon River. Originally filmed in 3D, loses something on TV.

Creature from the Haunted Sea (1961) **63m.** *½ D: Roger Corman. Antony Carbone, Betsy Jones-Moreland, Edward Wain, E. R. Alvarez, Robert Bean. Gangster tries to cover crime wave by creating panic with story of sea monster . . . then real sea monster shows up. Roger Corman quickie offers some minimal camp value.

Creature of the Walking Dead (1965) **74m.** *½ D: Frederic Corte. Rock Madison, Ann Wells, George Todd, Willard Gross, Bruno Ve Sota. Mad scientist brings his equally mad grandfather back to life, with Frankenstein-ish results, in this impoverished horror quickie.

Creature Walks Among Us, The (1956) **78m.** ** D: John Sherwood. Jeff Morrow, Rex Reason, Leigh Snowden, Gregg Palmer. Follow-up to CREATURE FROM THE BLACK LAGOON has Gill-man caged by humans, returning to ocean after few mild tantrums.

Creature with the Atom Brain (1955) **70m.** ** D: Edward L. Cahn. Richard Denning, Angela Stevens, Gregory Gaye, Tristram Coffin. Passable hokum: scientist revives the dead via high-charged brain tissue, and these robots are used by gangster seeking revenge.

Creature with the Blue Hand (1970-German) C-74m. ** D: Alfred Vohrer. Klaus Kinski, Diana Kerner, Carl Lang, Ilse Page, Harold Leopold. OK Edgar Wallace story has innocent man accused of murders perpetrated by title creature.

Creatures of the Prehistoric Planet: SEE **Vampire Men of the Lost Planet.**

Creatures the World Forgot (1971-British) C-94m. *½ D: Don Chaffey. Julie Ege, Tony Bonner, Robert John, Sue Wilson, Rosalie Crutchley. Hammer Films gives us another prehistoric movie with no dinosaurs and little credibility.

Creeper, The (1948) 64m. ** D: Jean Yarbrough. Onslow Stevens, Eduardo Ciannelli, June Vincent, Ralph Morgan, Janis Wilson. Stevens is mad doctor whose serum turns man into catlike killer.

Creeping Flesh, The (1973-British) C-94m. *** D: Freddie Francis. Peter Cushing, Christopher Lee, Lorna Heilbron, George Benson. Well-intentioned, old-fashioned monster film on reincarnation of ancient evil spirit. Numerous subplots add to the fun.

Creeping Unknown, The (1956- British) 78m. ** D: Val Guest. Brian Donlevy, Margia Dean, Jack Warner, Richard Wordsworth. Ordinary sci-fi with space craft returning to earth with title beast seeking to wreak havoc on all.

Crescendo (1972-British) C-83m. *½ D: Alan Gibson, Stefanie Powers, James Olson, Margaretta Scott, Jane Lapotaire, Joss Ackland. Tiresome chiller has grad student Powers traveling to France for some research on a dead composer, becoming involved with his crazy family.

Crest of the Wave (1954-British) 90m. **½ D: John Boulting, Roy Boulting. Gene Kelly, John Justin, Bernard Lee, Jeff Richards. Static account of navy officer Kelly joining British research group to supervise demolition experiments.

Cries and Whispers (1972-Swedish) C-106m. *** D: Ingmar Bergman. Harriet Andersson, Liv Ullmann, Ingrid Thulin, Kari Sylwan, Erland Josephson, George Arlin, Henning Moritzen. Beautifully photographed and acted drama about lives of a dying woman, her sisters and a servant girl was tremendous critical success, but cutting for TV may hurt it. Film may be too talky for some.

Crime and Passion (1976) C-92m. *½ D: Ivan Passer. Omar Sharif, Karen Black, Joseph Bottoms, Bernhard Wicki. Bizarre comedy-thriller set in Austrian Alps. Sharif is international financier who persuades secretary-mistress Black to wed industrialist Wicki for his money, then finds that they are both marked for death by the husband.

Crime and Punishment (1935) 88m. **½ D: Josef von Sternberg. Edward Arnold, Peter Lorre, Marian Marsh, Tala Birell, Elisabeth Risdon. Fascinating Hollywoodization of Dostoyevsky's novel about man haunted by murder he committed. Low-budget but full of inventive ideas by von Sternberg.

Crime and Punishment (1958-French), 108m. *** D: Georges Lampin. Jean Gabin, Marina Vlady, Ulla Jacobsson, Bernard Blier. Perceptive updating of Dostoyevsky novel set in Paris. Retitled: THE MOST DANGEROUS SIN.

Crime & Punishment, USA (1959) 78m. **½ D: Denis Sanders. George Hamilton, Mary Murphy, Frank Silvera, Marian Seldes, John Harding, Wayne Heffley. Trim, updated version of Dostoyevsky novel has Hamilton (film debut) a law student who becomes involved in robbery and murder.

Crime Against Joe (1956) 69m. ** D: Lee Sholem. John Bromfield, Julie London, Henry Calvin, Patricia Blake. Standard find-the-actual-murderer fare.

Crime Boss (1972-Italian) C-93m. *½ D: Albert DeMartino. Telly Savalas, Antonio Sabato, Paola Tedesca. Crime czar Savalas takes on a young protege and lives to regret it. One of Telly's numerous Mafioso roles before sticking a lollipop in his mouth and a gold badge of the NYPD on his chest. Plodding and written to formula.

Crime by Night (1944) 72m. **½ D: Geoffrey Homes. Jane Wyman, Jerome Cowan, Faye Emerson, Eleanor Parker, Creighton Hale. Good little murder mystery with detective Cowan unwittingly walking into murder case.

Crime Club (1973) C-73m. TVM D:

David Lowell Rich. Lloyd Bridges, Paul Burke, Cloris Leachman, Victor Buono, Barbara Rush, David Hedison, William Devane. Forgettable mystery with Bridges using resources of government-related super-crime-organization to determine cause of the death of a friend's son.

Crime Club (1975) C-78m. TVM D: Jeannot Szwarc. Scott Thomas, Eugene Roche, Robert Lansing, Biff McGuire, Barbara Rhoades, Michael Cristofer. Association of professionals who solve murders are faced with a loser who craves public recognition by confessing to series of icepick murders of young women. This one has "busted pilot" plastered all over it. Average.

Crime Doctor In 1943 Columbia Pictures took Max Marcin's successful radio show CRIME DOCTOR and initiated a film series of that name with Warner Baxter in the lead. The first film set the premise of an amnesia victim named Dr. Ordway becoming the country's leading criminal psychologist, later discovering that he was a gang leader himself before a blow clouded his memory. This idea served as the basis for ten fairly respectable, enjoyable mysteries, all starring Baxter as Ordway. Most of the films followed a standard whodunit formula, but were well acted and directed (by such people as William Castle and George Archainbaud), with competent players rounded up from Columbia's contract list. The films moved along briskly, most of them running barely over an hour. CRIME DOCTOR (1943) is interesting for its depiction of the origin of the character; CRIME DOCTOR'S GAMBLE takes him to Europe for an above-average murder hunt; and SHADOWS IN THE NIGHT has the distinction of refined George Zucco as an arch-fiend. Unremarkable but interesting, the Crime Doctor films held their own among the many mystery series of the day.

Crime Doctor (1943) 66m D: Michael Gordon. Warner Baxter, Margaret Lindsay, John Litel, Ray Collins, Harold Huber, Don Costello, Leon Ames.

Crime Doctor's Courage, The (1945) 70m. D: George Sherman. Warner Baxter, Hillary Brooke, Jerome Cowan, Robert Scott, Lloyd Corrigan, Emory Parnell, Stephen Crane.

Crime Doctor's Diary (1949) 61m. D: Seymour Friedman. Warner Baxter Lois Maxwell, Adele Jergens, Robert Armstrong.

Crime Doctor's Gamble, The (1947) 66m. D: William Castle. Warner Baxter, Micheline Cheirel, Roger Dann, Steven Geray, Marcel Journet.

Crime Doctor's Manhunt (1946) 61m. D: William Castle. Warner Baxter, Ellen Drew, William Frawley, Frank Sully, Claire Carleton, Bernard Nedell.

Crime Doctor's Strangest Case (1943) 68m. D: Eugene J. Forde. Warner Baxter, Lynn Merrick, Reginald Denny, Barton MacLane, Jerome Cowan, Rose Hobart, Gloria Dickson.

Crime Doctor's Warning, The (1945) 69m. D: William Castle. Warner Baxter, John Litel, Dusty Anderson, Coulter Irwin, Miles Mander, John Abbott.

Crime Does Not Pay (1962-French), 159m. **½ D: Gerard Oury. Pierre Brasseur, Gino Cervi, Danielle Darrieux, Gabriele Ferzetti, Annie Girardot, Michele Morgan, Richard Todd. Interesting gimmick for three-part film—would-be-wife-killer goes to cinema showing trio of stories on murder: "The Spider's Web," "The Fenyrou Case," and "The Mask." Retitled: GENTLE ART OF MURDER.

Crime in the Streets (1956) 91m. ** D: Don Siegel. James Whitmore, John Cassavetes, Sal Mineo, Mark Rydell. Cassavetes and Mineo do justice by script as juvenile delinquents planning gang murder, conflicting with social worker Whitmore.

Crime of Dr. Crespi, The (1935) 63m. ** D: John H. Auer. Erich von Stroheim, Dwight Frye, Paul Guilfoyle, Harriett Russell, John Bohn. Von Stroheim gets even with man who loves his girl by planning unspeakable torture for him. Low-grade chiller.

Crime of Dr. Hallet, The (1938) 68m. *½ D: S. Sylvan Simon. Ralph Bellamy, William Gargan, Josephine Hutchinson, Barbara Read, John King. Tedious story of jungle doctor working on fever cure who assumes assistant's identity when the latter dies in experiment. Remade as STRANGE CONQUEST.

Crime of Passion (1957) 84m. **½ D: Gerd Oswald. Barbara Stanwyck, Sterling Hayden, Raymond Burr, Fay Wray, Virginia Grey. Stanwyck is rough and tough as grasping wife who'll do anything to forward hubby's career.

Crime School (1938) 86m. ** D: Lewis Seiler. Humphrey Bogart, Billy Halop, Bobby Jordan, Huntz Hall, Leo Gorcey, Gale Page. If you can see Bogart as a reform school warden, you're already one up on the writers; not bad, but predictable.

Crime Wave (1954) 74m. ** D: Andre de Toth. Sterling Hayden, Gene Nelson, Phyllis Kirk, Charles Bronson, Ted de Corsia. Low-keyed telling of ex-con Nelson's attempt to go straight, despite insistence of crooks that he help on bank robbery; Hayden is toothpick-chewing cop.

Crime Without Passion (1934) 72m. *** D: Ben Hecht, Charles MacArthur. Claude Rains, Margo, Whitney Bourne, Stanley Ridges, Esther Dale, Leslie Adams. Bizarre, fascinating melodrama of callous lawyer Rains, jealous of Margo's escorts. Helen Hayes and Fanny Brice have brief cameos in hotel lobby scene.

Criminal Lawyer (1951) 74m. *½ D: Seymour Friedman. Pat O'Brien, Jane Wyatt, Carl Benton Reid, Mary Castle. Alcoholic attorney O'Brien sobers up to defend friend saddled with homicide charge.

Crimson Blade, The (1963-British) C-82m. **½ D: John Gilling. Lionel Jeffries, Oliver Reed, Jack Hedley, June Thorburn, Duncan Lamont. OK swashbuckler features romance between two young people on opposite side of Cromwell's struggle for power in 17th century; good-looking Hammer production. Originally titled THE SCARLET BLADE.

Crimson Canary, The (1945) 64m. **½ D: John Hoffman. Noah Beery Jr., Lois Collier, Danny Morton, John Litel, Claudia Drake, Steven Geray. Offbeat murder mystery with nightclub musicians the suspects, nicely done.

Crimson Cult, The (1970-British) C-87m. ** D: Vernon Sewell. Mark Eden, Virginia Wetherell, Christopher Lee, Boris Karloff, Michael Gough, Barbara Steele. Lackluster script and pacing major flaws in standard witchcraft thriller featuring aging Karloff as expert on black magic, Steele (in green makeup) as 300-year-old witch.

Crimson Ghost, The SEE: **Cyclotrode "X"**

Crimson Kimono, The (1959) 82m. ** D: Samuel Fuller. Victoria Shaw, Glenn Corbett, James Shigeta, Anna Lee, Paul Dubov, Jaclynne Greene. Two L.A. detectives investigate a stripper's murder in this offbeat little film; more interesting for Sam Fuller buffs than general viewers, who may find story and treatment too low-key and meandering.

Crimson Pirate, The (1952) C-104m. ***½ D: Robert Siodmak. Burt Lancaster, Nick Cravat, Eva Bartok, Torin Thatcher, Christopher Lee. Lancaster and Cravat swashbuckle their way across the Mediterranean in one of the great genre spoofs of all time. Cult film offers loads of laughs to both children and adults.

Cripple Creek (1952) C-78m. **½ D: Ray Nazarro. George Montgomery, Karin Booth, Jerome Courtland, Richard Egan. Government agents Montgomery and Courtland track down mining crooks by joining gang in this average oater.

Crisis (1950) 95m. **½ D: Richard Brooks. Cary Grant, Jose Ferrer, Paula Raymond, Signe Hasso, Ramon Novarro, Antonio Moreno, Leon Ames, Gilbert Roland. Melodrama of American doctor (Grant) held in South American country to treat ailing dictator (Ferrer); intriguing but slow.

Crisis in Mid-air (1979) C-100m. TVM D: Walter Grauman. George Peppard, Karen Grassle, Desi Arnaz, Jr., Don Murray, Martin Milner, Fabian Forte, Michael Constantine, Greg Morris. Overage air traffic controller is accused of responsibility for a midair collision. Timely topic unfortunately run off the TV disaster drama assembly line. Average.

Crisis in Sun Valley (1978) C-100m. TVM D: Paul Stanley. Dale Robinette, Taylor Lacher, Bo Hopkins, Tracy Brooks Swope, John McIntyre, Deborah Winters. Predictable adventure tale dealing with a stalwart sheriff and his deputy in a sleepy ski resort who first emerged in THE DEADLY TRIANGLE. Middling action feature actually combines two individual pilot films strung together in hopes of sparking some interest in a series to have been called STEDMAN. Average.

Criss Cross (1949) 87m. *** D: Robert Siodmak. Burt Lancaster, Yvonne De Carlo, Dan Duryea, Stephen McNally. Low-key robbery yarn sparked by Lancaster and Duryea each trying to do the other in.

Critical List, The (1978) C-200m.

TVM D: Lou Antonio. Lloyd Bridges, Melinda Dillon, Buddy Ebsen, Barbara Parkins, Robert Wagner, Ken Howard, Louis Gossett, Jr., Richard Basehart. Two pilot films combined in search of a series for Bridges as a hospital director whose tribulations appeared to have been recycled from Dr. Gillespie's files of yore. Bridges is earnest and properly concerned, but movie is average and overlong.

Critic's Choice (1963) C-100m. **½ D: Don Weis. Bob Hope, Lucille Ball, Marilyn Maxwell, Rip Torn, Jessie Royce Landis, Marie Windsor, John Dehner. An in-joke Broadway play diluted for movie audience consumption. Lucy as a novice playwright outshines Hope who plays her drama critic hubby. Film emerges as tired, predictable comedy, with best moments contributed by supporting players.

Cromwell (1970-British) C-145m. ** D: Ken Hughes. Richard Harris, Alec Guinness, Robert Morley, Dorothy Tutin, Frank Finlay, Timothy Dalton, Patrick Wymark, Patrick Magee. Turgid historical epic has everything money can buy, but no human feeling underneath. Harris is coldly unsympathetic as 17th-century Briton determined to rid England of tyrannical rule; one feels more sympathy for King Charles I (Guinness), which is not the idea. Great battle scenes, great cinematography, hampered by Harris and amateurish music score.

Crook, The (1971-French) C-120m. *** D: Claude Lelouch. Jean-Louis Trintignant, Daniele Delorme, Charles Denner, Christine Lelouch. Very funny pop-art caper film of incurable thief, his successes and failures.

Crooked Hearts, The (1972) C-74m. TVM D: Jay Sandrich. Rosalind Russell, Douglas Fairbanks Jr., Ross Martin, Maureen O'Sullivan, Kent Smith, Michael Murphy. Members of lonely hearts club stalked by mysterious con-artist supposedly involved with disappearances of wealthy widows. Good cast, good comedy. Above average.

Crooked Road, The (1965-British) 86m. **½ D: Don Chaffey. Robert Ryan, Stewart Granger, Nadia Gray, Marius Goring, George Coulouris. OK battle of wits between dictator Granger and newspaperman Ryan, who's got the goods on him.

Crooked Way, The (1949) 90m. ** D: Robert Florey. John Payne, Sonny Tufts, Ellen Drew, Rhys Williams. Military hero Payne recovers from shellshock to be confronted by criminal past and his old gang seeking to eliminate him.

Crooked Web, The (1955) 77m. *½ D: Nathan Juran. Frank Lovejoy, Mari Blanchard, Richard Denning, Richard Emory. Ponderous unspinning of government officer's ensnaring prime suspect to return to Germany, scene of the crime.

Crooks and Coronets (1970-British) C-106m. ** D: Jim O'Connolly. Telly Savalas, Edith Evans, Warren Oates, Cesar Romero, Harry H. Corbett. Crooks Savalas and Oates are hired to rob Evans' estate, but can't bring themselves to do it once they get to know her. Amiable but ordinary heist comedy.

Crosby Case, The (1934) 60m. **½ D: Edwin L. Marin. Wynne Gibson, Alan Dinehart, Onslow Stevens, Warren Hymer, Skeets Gallagher. Amateur sleuths conduct their own investigation when doctor is murdered; good whodunit, with interesting plot point—a hint of abortion.

Cross and the Switchblade, The (1972) C-106m. *½ D: Don Murray. Pat Boone, Erik Estrada, Jackie Giroux, Jo-Ann Robinson. Crusading minister Boone winds up in New York street-gang rumbles. Uneven, uninteresting, though sincere attempt at uplifting, moralistic filmmaking.

Cross of Iron (1977-British-West German) C-120m. *** D: Sam Peckinpah. James Coburn, Maximilian Schell, James Mason, David Warner, Senta Berger, Klaus Lowitsch. Peckinpah's first war film, told from the viewpoint of Germans on the Russian front in 1943, is compelling without being particularly distinguished. The standard Peckinpah action scenes, excitingly done, will be cut for TV.

Cross of Lorraine, The (1943) 90m. ***½ D: Tay Garnett. Jean-Pierre Aumont, Gene Kelly, Cedric Hardwicke, Richard Whorf, Joseph Calleia, Peter Lorre, Hume Cronyn. High-grade propaganda of WW2 POW camp with hero Aumont rousing defeated Kelly to battle; Whorf is dedicated doctor, Lorre a despicable Nazi, Cronyn a fickle informer.

Crosscurrent (1971) C-73m. TVM D: Jerry Thorpe. Robert Hooks, Jeremy

Slate, Robert Wagner, Carol Lynley, Simon Oakland, Jose Ferrer, John Randolph. Two cops in San Francisco go after the murderer of a cable car passenger. Good cast helps OK thriller; also known as CABLE CAR MURDER.

Crossed Swords (1954-Italian) C-86m. *½ D: Nato de Angelis, Arthur Villiesid, Milton Krims. Errol Flynn, Gina Lollobrigida, Cesare Danova, Nadia Grey. Unsuccessful attempt to recapture flavor of swashbucklers of 1930s; set in 16th-century Italy with Flynn out to save Gina and her father's kingdom.

Crossed Swords (1978) C-113m. ** D: Richard Fleischer. Mark Lester, Oliver Reed, Raquel Welch, Ernest Borgnine, George C. Scott, Rex Harrison, Charlton Heston. Lester is too old for his dual role in flat version of Mark Twain's The Prince and the Pauper. Lavish sets, costumes, and Jack Cardiff's photography will suffer on TV.

Crossfire (1947) 86m. ***½ D: Edward Dmytryk. Robert Young, Robert Mitchum, Robert Ryan, Gloria Grahame, Paul Kelly, Richard Benedict, Sam Levene. Engrossing film of insane ex-soldier leading city police in murderous chase. Anti-Semitic question handled with taste, intelligence.

Crossfire (1975) C-78m. TVM D: William Hale. James Farentino, John Saxon, John O'Neal, Pamela Franklin, Ramon Bieri, Herb Edelman, Lou Frizzell. Undercover cop Farentino infiltrates underworld to learn source of laundered money being used to corrupt city officials. Fairly conventional and muscular. Average.

Crossroads (1942) 84m. *** D: Jack Conway. William Powell, Hedy Lamarr, Claire Trevor, Basil Rathbone, Margaret Wycherly, Felix Bressart, Sig Ruman. Smooth tale of French diplomat Powell victimized by heartless Rathbone, who capitalizes on Powell's having been an amnesiac.

Crosstrap (1961-British) 62m. *½ D: Robert Hartford-Davis. Laurence Payne, Jill Adams, Gary Cockrell, Zena Marshall. Juvenile thriller involving rival gangs of jewel thieves and murder.

Crosswinds (1951) C-93m. ** D: Lewis R. Foster. John Payne, Rhonda Fleming, Forrest Tucker, Robert Lowery. Payne tries to retrieve cargo of gold from plane that crashed in New Guinea, encountering head-hunters, crooks, and gorgeous Fleming.

Crowd, The (1928) 90m. **** D: King Vidor. Eleanor Boardman, James Murray, Bert Roach, Daniel G. Tomlinson, Dell Henderson, Lucy Beaumont. Classic drama about a few happy and many not-so-happy days in the marriage of hard-luck couple. One of the greatest silent films; holds up beautifully.

Crowd Roars, The (1932) 85m. **½ D: Howard Hawks. James Cagney, Joan Blondell, Ann Dvorak, Eric Linden, Guy Kibbee, Frank McHugh. Exciting racing-driver tale with Cagney in typically cocky role, familiar plot devices, but well done by Warner Bros. stock company. Remade as INDIANAPOLIS SPEEDWAY.

Crowd Roars, The (1938) 92m. **½ D: Richard Thorpe. Robert Taylor, Edward Arnold, Frank Morgan, Maureen O'Sullivan, William Gargan, Lionel Stander, Jane Wyman. Tippling Morgan gets son Taylor into fighting game, and involved with underworld chief Arnold in well-handled yarn. Remade as KILLER McCOY.

Crowded Sky, The (1960) C-105m. **½ D: Joseph Pevney. Dana Andrews, Rhonda Fleming, Efrem Zimbalist, Jr., John Kerr, Troy Donahue, Patsy Kelly. Slick film focusing on emotional problems aboard jet liner and navy plane bound for fateful collision; superficial but diverting.

Crowhaven Farm (1970) C-72m. TVM D: Walter Grauman. Hope Lange, Paul Burke, Lloyd Bochner, John Carradine, Cindy Eilbacher. Middle-aged couple (Lange and Burke) inherit farm, move in to patch up strained marriage, eventually adopt child who becomes focal point in supernatural flashback story. Surprise ending in generally well-handled thriller. Above average.

Crucible, The (1958-French) 120m. *** D: Raymond Rouleau. Simone Signoret, Yves Montand, Mylene Demongeot, Raymond Rouleau. If anything, Jean-Paul Sartre's version improves upon Arthur Miller parable of Salem witch trials in 17th-century New England; Signoret is outstanding.

Crucible of Horror (1971-British) C-91m. ** D: Viktors Ritelis. Michael Gough, Sharon Gurney, Yvonne Mitchell. Murdered man returns to haunt the living. Nothing new here.

Cruel Sea, The (1953-British) 121m. ***½ D: Charles Frend. Jack Hawkins, Donald Sinden, Stanley Baker, Virginia McKenna. Well-conceived documentary-style account of British warship during WW2 and its crew.

Cruel Swamp SEE: **Swamp Women**.

Cruel Tower, The (1956) 79m. **½ D: Lew Landers. John Ericson, Mari Blanchard, Charles McGraw, Steve Brodie, Peter Whitney, Alan Hale Jr. Friendship, loyalty, jealousy, and fighting among a crew of high-riggers; standard stuff, pretty well done.

Cruise into Terror (1978) C-100m. TVM D: Bruce Kessler. Dirk Benedict, Frank Converse, John Forsythe, Lynda Day George, Christopher George, Ray Milland, Hugh O'Brian, Stella Stevens. Shipboard terror involving an ancient sarcophagus and some evildoers among the all-star roster. Below average.

Cruising (1980) C-106m. *½ D: William Friedkin. Al Pacino, Paul Sorvino, Karen Allen, Richard Cox, Don Scardino, voice of James Sutorius. Cop Pacino goes underground to ferret out bloody killer of homosexuals in this distasteful, badly scripted film. Gay world presented as sick, degrading, and ritualistic. Filmed on authentic NYC locations. Much will be cut for TV.

Crusades, The (1935) 123m. *** D: Cecil B. DeMille. Loretta Young, Henry Wilcoxon, Ian Keith, Katherine DeMille, C. Aubrey Smith. Love, action, and orgies galore in typical DeMille medieval spectacle that's good for fun, with Young a glamorous heroine.

Cry Baby Killer, The (1958) 62m. *½ D: Jus Addiss. Harry Lauter, Jack Nicholson, Carolyn Mitchell, Brett Halsey, Lynn Cartwright, Ed Nelson. Nicholson's film debut is a Roger Corman quickie about juvenile delinquent who panics when he thinks he's committed murder. A curio at best, with co-scripter Leo Gordon and Corman himself in bit parts. TV print runs 60m.

Cry Danger (1951) 79m. *** D: Richard Parrish. Dick Powell, Rhonda Fleming, Richard Erdman, Regis Toomey. Effective revenge yarn as ex-con Powell hunts down those responsible for his prison term.

Cry for Happy (1961) C-110m. **½ D: George Marshall. Glenn Ford, Donald O'Connor, Miiko Taka, Myoshi Umeki. Poor man's TEAHOUSE OF THE AUGUST MOON, involving Navy photography team in Tokyo using a geisha house for their home.

Cry for Help, A (1975) C-78m. TVM D: Daryl Duke. Robert Culp, Elaine Heilveil, Ken Swofford, Julius Harris, Chuck McCann, Michael Lerner. Cynical radio talk-show host Culp rebuffs a phone-caller threatening suicide, then suspects she may have been serious and frantically tries to locate her with the help of his listeners. Neat initial concept is frittered away in standard rescue drama. Average.

Cry from the Streets, A (1959-British) 99m. *** D: Lewis Gilbert. Max Bygraves, Barbara Murray, Colin Peterson, Dana Wilson, Kathleen Harrison. Poignant handling of story about homeless London children and social workers who attempt to rehabilitate them; plot is forgivably diffuse and episodic.

Cry Havoc (1943) 97m. **½ D: Richard Thorpe. Margaret Sullavan, Ann Sothern, Joan Blondell, Fay Bainter, Marsha Hunt, Ella Raines, Frances Gifford. Sincere story of nurses in Philippines. Like similar SO PROUDLY WE HAIL, it doesn't have impact it had when first released but performances are still good.

Cry in the Night (1956) 75m. **½ D: Frank Tuttle. Edmond O'Brien, Brian Donlevy, Natalie Wood, Raymond Burr. Capable cast enhances this tale of deranged man kidnapping girl from lover, with suspenseful police hunt ensuing.

Cry in the Wilderness, A (1974) C-78m. TVM D: Gordon Hessler. George Kennedy, Joanna Pettet, Lee H. Montgomery, Collin Wilcox-Horne, Roy Poole, Liam Dunn. Bitten by a rabid skunk, farmer Kennedy has himself chained inside his barn to protect his family from his future madness, and then discovers that a flood is coming. Kennedy manipulates audience's terror quotient, while Pettet, as his young, helpless wife, handles hysteria factor. Average.

Cry of Battle (1963) 99m. **½ D: Irving Lerner. Van Heflin, Rita Moreno, James MacArthur, Leopoldo Salcedo. Uneven actioner set in Philippines with MacArthur as son of wealthy businessman who joins partisan cause, finding romance and sense of maturity.

[158]

Cry of the Banshee (1970-British) C-87m. **½ D: Gordon Hessler. Vincent Price, Elisabeth Bergner, Essy Persson, Hugh Griffith, Hilary Dwyer, Sally Geeson, Patrick Mower. Witch Oona (Bergner) summons servant of Satan to avenge nobleman (Price)'s bloody reign of witch-hunting. Confusion sets in midway.

Cry of the City (1948) 95m. **½ D: Robert Siodmak. Victor Mature, Richard Conte, Fred Clark, Shelley Winters, Betty Garde, Debra Paget, Rehash of MANHATTAN MELODRAMA about childhood pals, one who becomes a cop, the other a criminal—slick but predictable.

Cry of the Hunted (1953) 80m. ** D: Joseph H. Lewis. Vittorio Gassman, Barry Sullivan, Polly Bergen, William Conrad. Unnoteworthy chase film involving escaped convict Gassman being sought by lawman Sullivan, with a few atmospheric sequences set in Louisiana marshland.

Cry of the Penguins (1972-British) C-101m. ** D: Al Viola. John Hurt, Hayley Mills, Dudley Sutton, Tony Britton, Thorley Walters, Judy Campbell. Limp yarn that addresses the question: Can a womanizing young biologist find true happiness and redemption among a colony of penguins in the Antarctic? Also called MR. FORBUSH AND THE PENGUINS.

Cry of the Werewolf (1944) 63m. ** D: Henry Levin. Nina Foch, Stephen Crane, Osa Massen, Blanche Yurka, Fritz Lieber. Gypsy girl hears the cry when it's proved her mother was a werewolf; OK low-grade thriller.

Cry Panic (1974) C-78m. TVM D: James Goldstone. John Forsythe, Earl Holliman, Ralph Meeker, Anne Francis, Claudia McNeil, Norman Alden. Forsythe plays a salesman caught in a personal nightmare after he accidentally kills a drunk with his car, and the body has disappeared. Modest little suspense drama. Average.

Cry Rape (1972) C-73m. TVM D: Corey Allen. Andrea Marcovicci, Peter Coffield, Greg Mullavey, Joseph Sirolay, James Luisi, Anthony Costello, Lesley Woods. Two stories in one: first, the problems, indignities, frustrations in reporting rape to authorities; then, standard cops-chasing-suspects fare. Uneven but well done. Average.

Cry Terror (1958) 96m. *** D: Andrew L. Stone. James Mason, Rod Steiger, Inger Stevens, Neville Brand, Angie Dickinson, Jack Klugman. Tight pacing conceals implausibilities in caper of psychopath Steiger forcing Mason to aid him in master extortion plot, filmed on N.Y.C. locations. Stevens good as Mason's frightened but resourceful wife.

Cry the Beloved Country (1951-British) 111m. ***½ D: Zoltan Korda. Canada Lee, Charles Carson, Sidney Poitier, Geoffrey Keen, Reginald Ngeabo. Back country Black minister goes to city in search of his son, now a criminal. First film to deal with Apartheid Policy and wretched living conditions of blacks in South Africa. Alan Paton's book was basis for stage and film musical *Lost in the Stars*. Some TV prints run 96m.

Cry Tough (1959) 83m. ** D: Paul Stanley. John Saxon, Linda Cristal, Joseph Calleia, Arthur Batanides, Joe De Santis, Barbara Luna, Frank Puglia. Saxon emotes well as Puerto Rican ex-con tempted back into criminal life by environment and his old gang. Torrid Saxon-Cristal love scenes shot for foreign markets gave film initial publicity.

Cry Uncle (1971) C-87m. **½ D: John G. Avildsen. Allen Garfield, Madeleine le Roux, Devin Goldenberg, David Kirk, Sean Walsh, Nancy Salmon. Private detective gets involved with murder, sex and blackmail in film of questionable taste; frequently hilarious, however, though quite a few minutes will be cut for TV, if the film makes it at all.

Cry Vengeance (1954) 83m. **½ D: Mark Stevens. Mark Stevens, Martha Hyer, Skip Homeier, Joan Vohs. Stevens lives up to title as innocent ex-con seeking gangsters who sent him to prison.

Cry Wolf (1947) 83m. ** D: Peter Godfrey. Barbara Stanwyck, Errol Flynn, Geraldine Brooks, Richard Basehart, Jerome Cowan. Static adventure-mystery of Stanwyck attempting to untangle family secrets at late husband's estate.

Crystal Ball, The (1943) 81m. ** D: Elliott Nugent. Paulette Goddard, Ray Milland, Virginia Field, Gladys George, William Bendix, Ernest Truex. Weak comedy of beauty-contest loser who becomes fortune-teller; good players left stranded by stale material.

Cuba (1979) C-121m. *** D: Richard Lester. Sean Connery, Brooke Adams, Jack Weston, Hector Elizondo, Denholm Elliott, Chris Sarandon, Lonette McKee. Entertaining adventure film/love story has mercenary Connery renewing an old affair with factory manager Adams against the fall of Battista in late '59. Director Lester is in pretty good form here, with most scenes punctuated by memorable throwaway bits.

Cul-De-Sac (1966-British) 110m. ***½ D: Roman Polanski. Donald Pleasence, Francoise Dorleac, Lionel Stander, Jack MacGowran, Iain Quarrier, Jacqueline Bisset. Macabre comedy about two wounded gangsters who terrorize middle-aged milquetoast and his beautiful young wife. Not a total success, but good cast and stylish direction make it a winner.

Culpepper Cattle Company, The (1972) C-92m. **½ D: Dick Richards. Gary Grimes, Billy "Green" Bush, Luke Askew, Bo Hopkins, Geoffrey Lewis, Wayne Sutherlin. A 16-year-old persuades trail boss to take him along on cattle drive, becomes a man in the process. Fair Western may have some violence cut for TV.

Cult of the Cobra (1955) 82m. **½ D: Francis D. Lyon. Faith Domergue, Richard Long, Marshall Thompson, Jack Kelly, David Janssen. Minor camp masterpiece involves exservicemen being killed by exotic serpent lady Domergue.

Cult of the Damned (1970) C-103m. *½ D: Robert Thom. Jennifer Jones, Jordan Christopher, Holly Near, Roddy McDowall, Lou Rawls, Charles Aidman. Senseless story of lovers, and dozens of other things brewed into one wasteful vat. Also known as ANGEL, ANGEL, DOWN WE GO.

Curley (1947) C-53m. ** D: Bernard Carr. Larry Olsen, Frances Rafferty, Eilene Janssen, Walter Abel. Inconsequential juvenile nonsense about youngsters playing pranks on their schoolteacher. Originally part of HAL ROACH COMEDY CARNIVAL.

Curly Top (1935) 75m. **½ D: Irving Cummings. Shirley Temple, John Boles, Rochelle Hudson, Jane Darwell, Rafaela Ottiano, Arthur Treacher. Shirley sings "Animal Crackers In My Soup" as she plays Cupid again, this time for sister Hudson and handsome Boles.

Curse of Frankenstein, The (1957-British) C-83m. **½ D: Terence Fisher. Peter Cushing, Christopher Lee, Hazel Court, Robert Urquhart, Valerie Gaunt, Noel Hood. OK retelling of original Shelley tale, with Cushing as Baron von Frankenstein, whose experimentation with creation of life becomes an obsession. First of Hammer Films' long-running horror series.

Curse of the Black Widow (1977) C-100m. TVM D: Dan Curtis. Tony Franciosa, Donna Mills, Patty Duke Astin, June Lockhart, June Allyson, Sid Caesar, Vic Morrow, Roz Kelly, Jeff Corey. Chiller about the search for an elusive killer whose victims are wrapped in a spider-like web. Looks like Curtis had this script left over when his "Kolchak: The Night Stalker" series was cancelled. Average.

Curse of the Cat People, The (1944) 70m. *** D: Gunther von Fristch, Robert Wise. Simone Simon, Kent Smith, Jane Randolph, Elizabeth Russell, Ann Carter, Julia Dean. Sequel to CAT PEOPLE creates wonderful atmosphere in story of lonely little girl who conjures up vision of Simon, her father's mysterious first wife. Despite title, not a horror film but a fine, moody fantasy. Produced by Val Lewton.

Curse of the Demon (1958-British) 83m. ***½ D: Jacques Tourneur. Dana Andrews, Peggy Cummins, Niall MacGinnis, Maurice Denham, Athene Seyler. Andrews is a stuffily cynical psychologist who doesn't believe that series of deaths have been caused by ancient curse, but film convinces audience right off the bat and never lets up. Exceptional shocker, originally called NIGHT OF THE DEMON, and running 95m. in British form.

Curse of the Faceless Man (1958) 66m. BOMB D: Edward L. Cahn. Richard Anderson, Elaine Edwards, Adele Mara, Luis Van Rooten. Laughable attempt at horror yarn, with ridiculous title monster aroused from sleep by excavation on site of ancient Pompeii.

Curse of the Fly, The (1965-British) 86m. *½ D: Don Sharp. Brian Donlevy, Carole Gray, George Baker, Michael Graham, Jeremy Wilkins, Charles Carson. Third film based on THE FLY with scores of mutants and a mad doctor who mixes up scientific hodgepodge. Best forgotten.

Curse of the Living Corpse (1964) 84m. ** D: Del Tenney. Helen Warren, Roy R. Sheider (Scheider),

Margo Hartman, Hugh Franklin, Candace Hilligoss. Tepid old-darkhouse murder mystery with dead man supposedly returning to "life" and committing series of killings.

Curse of the Mummy's Tomb, The (1965-British) C-81m. ** D: Michael Carreras. Terence Morgan, Ronald Howard, Fred Clark, Jeanne Roland, George Pastell. Programmer horror attempt involving mummy seeking revenge on people who unearthed him.

Curse of the Stone Hand (1965) 72m. BOMB D: Jerry Warren and Carl Schleppe. John Carradine, Sheila Bon, Ernest Walch, Katherine Victor, Lloyd Nelson. Americanized version of 1959 Mexican film tries to interweave two separate story elements with incoherent results.

Curse of the Swamp Creature (1966) C-80m. BOMB D: Larry Buchanan. John Agar, Francine York, Shirley McLine, Bill Thurman, Jeff Alexander. A geological expedition stumbles onto a mad doctor who's trying to evolve a man-monster. Low-budget junk.

Curse of the Undead (1959) 79m. ** D: Edward Dein. Eric Fleming, Michael Pate, Kathleen Crowley, John Hoyt, Bruce Gordon, Edward Binns. Once-novel mixture of horror-Western tale hasn't much zing. Mysterious stranger has vampirish designs on Crowley.

Curse of the Voodoo (1965-British) 77m. *½ D: Lindsay Shonteff. Bryant Halliday, Dennis Price, Lisa Daniely, Mary Kerridge. Modest film promises some exotic native black magic hi-jinks, but nothing worthwhile occurs.

Curse of the Werewolf, The (1961-British) C-91m. **½ D: Terence Fisher. Clifford Evans, Oliver Reed, Yvonne Romain, Anthony Dawson. Reed has wolf's blood and struggles to control the monster within him; it finally erupts when he is denied his girl's love. Eerie atmosphere pervades this good chiller.

Curse of the Yellow Snake, The (1963-German) 98m. **½ D: Franz Gottlieb. Joachim Fuchsberger, Eddi Arent, Brigitte Grothum, Charles Regnier, Werner Peters, Claus Holm. Edgar Wallace yarn dealing with anti-Western uprising by fanatic Oriental cult; eerie and atmospheric.

Curtain Call at Cactus Creek (1950) C-86m. **½ D: Charles Lamont. Donald O'Connor, Gale Storm, Vincent Price, Walter Brennan, Eve Arden. Sometimes foolish slapstick as O'Connor, touring with road show, gets involved with bank robbers and irate citizens of Arizona.

Curtain Up (1953-British) 81m. **½ D: Ralph Smart. Robert Morley, Margaret Rutherford, Kay Kendall, Joan Rice. Droll little film of rural repertory company battling among themselves as they prepare for their dramatic season.

Curucu, Beast of the Amazon (1956) C-76m. *½ D: Curt Siodmak. John Bromfield, Beverly Garland, Tom Payne, Harvey Chalk. Bromfield and Garland set out on hunt to find title monster. Pure cornball.

Custer of the West (1968-U.S.-Spanish) C-140m. **½ D: Robert Siodmak. Robert Shaw, Mary Ure, Jeffrey Hunter, Robert Ryan, Ty Hardin, Charles Stalnaker, Robert Hall, Lawrence Tierney. Fairly ambitious bio of famed general, originally in Cinerama, suffers from script that doesn't quite know how to characterize its subject. Some prints of this were cut to 120 minutes, so TV running time may not be consistent.

Cutter (1972) C-73m. TVM D: Richard Irving. Peter DeAnda, Cameron Mitchell, Robert Webber, Barbara Rush, Janet MacLachlan. Location shooting (in Chicago) can't help laughable black detective story with DeAnda starring as private eye searching for missing pro football quarterback. Average.

Cutter's Trail (1969) C-100m. TVM D: Vincent McEveety. John Gavin, Marisa Pavan, Joseph Cotten, Beverly Garland. Respectable formula Western has Gavin returning to Santa Fe as marshal only to discover town intimidated by gang; only people who'll help are mother and small boy. Above average.

Cyborg 2087 (1966) C-86m. ** D: Franklin Adreon. Michael Rennie, Wendell Corey, Eduard Franz, Karen Steele, Warren Stevens. Future Earth civilization sends cyborg—part machine, part human—back in time to 1960s so future can be changed. Good idea all but ruined due to unconvincing script and TV-style production.

Cyclops, The (1957) 75m. ** D: Bert I. Gordon. James Craig, Gloria Talbott, Lon Chaney Jr., Tom Drake. Expedition scours Mexico in search of Talbott's lost brother, discovers that radiation has transformed him into an enormous monster. Nothing much in this cheapie.

Cyclotrode "X" (1946) 100m. **½ D: William Witney, Fred Brannon. Charles Quigley, Linda Stirling, Clayton Moore, I. Stanford Jolley. Well-paced Republic cliff-hanger, with bouncy action as sinister Crimson Ghost tries to gain control of super-nuclear device. Reedited movie serial: THE CRIMSON GHOST.

Cynara (1932) 78m. ** D: King Vidor. Ronald Colman, Kay Francis, Henry Stephenson, Phyllis Barry, Paul Porcasi. Badly dated film about British lawyer who has interlude with working girl while wife is away; Colman is good as usual.

Cynthia (1947) 98m. *½ D: Robert Z. Leonard. Elizabeth Taylor, George Murphy, S. Z. Sakall, Mary Astor, Gene Lockhart, Spring Byington, Jimmy Lydon. Sugary film of sickly girl Taylor finding outlet in music; good cast wasted.

Cyrano de Bergerac (1950) 112m. **** D: Michael Gordon. Jose Ferrer, Mala Powers, William Prince, Morris Carnovsky, Elena Verdugo. Ferrer received an Oscar for portraying the tragic wit, renowned for his nose but longing for love of a beautiful lady. Based on Edmond Rostand play of 17th-century Paris.

D.A.: Conspiracy to Kill (1970) C-100m. TVM D: Jack Webb. Robert Conrad, Belinda Montgomery, William Conrad, Don Stroud, Steve Ihnat. Standard crime drama has energetic district attorney proving drugstore owner is robbery mastermind involved in murder. Unconvincing characters but fair action. Average.

D.A.: Murder One (1969) C-100m. TVM D: Jack Webb. Robert Conrad, Howard Duff, Diane Baker, J. D. Cannon, Alfred Ryder, Scott Brady, Gerald S. O'Loughlin. Good cast struggles through Jack Webb production featuring Conrad as stereotyped deputy D.A. showing up his superiors in case involving insulin overdose. Average. Retitled MURDER ONE.

D-Day on Mars (1945) 100m. ** D: Spencer Bennet, Fred Brannon. Dennis Moore, Linda Stirling, Roy Barcroft, James Craven, Bud Geary, Mary Moore. Average Republic nonsense keyed on action of dynamic Purple Monster fighting against alien forces bent on taking over earth; Stirling

is the fetching heroine. Reedited movie serial: THE PURPLE MONSTER STRIKES.

D-Day the Sixth of June (1956) C-106m. *** D: Henry Koster. Robert Taylor, Richard Todd, Dana Wynter, Edmond O'Brien. Well executed study of the Normandy invasion during WW2, with massive action shots; film focuses on American officer Taylor and British leader Todd, their professional and personal problems.

D. I., The (1957) 106m. ** D: Jack Webb. Jack Webb, Don Dubbins, Lin McCarthy, Barbara Pepper. Potentially intriguing narrative of marine drill instructor pushing his men to breaking point, becomes typical bootcamp account of life at Parris Island.

D.O.A. (1949) 83m. *** D: Rudolph Mate. Edmond O'Brien, Pamela Britton, Luther Adler, Neville Brand, Henry Hart, Virginia Lee, Beverly (Garland) Campbell. Surprisingly well-done suspenser involving O'Brien trying to find out who has given him a slow-acting poison and why. Remade as COLOR ME DEAD.

Daddy, I Don't Like It Like This (1978) C-100m. TVM D: Adell Aldrich. Talia Shire, Burt Young, Doug McKeon, Melanie Griffith, Erica Yohn. Youngster withdraws into his own world unable to cope with the bickering of his parents because of their unfulfilled dreams. Veteran director Robert Aldrich's daughter Adell made her own directing debut here, working with a somewhat pallid script by star Burt Young. Average.

Daddy Long Legs (1955) C-126m. **½ D: Jean Negulesco. Fred Astaire, Leslie Caron, Terry Moore, Thelma Ritter, Fred Clark. Overly long adaptation of Jean Webster novel about playboy (Astaire) anonymously sponsoring waif's (Caron) school education, falling in love; some imaginative dance numbers.

Daddy's Gone A-Hunting (1969) C-108m. *** D: Mark Robson. Carol White, Paul Burke, Scott Hylands, Rachel Ames, Mala Powers. Psycho stalks innocent young girl through streets of San Francisco. Some of the shocks may be lessened on TV screen, but still exciting thriller.

Daffodil Killer SEE: **Devil's Daffodil**
Daggers of Blood SEE: **With Fire and Sword**

Daisy Kenyon (1947) 99m. **½ D: Otto Preminger. Joan Crawford, Dana

Andrews, Henry Fonda, Ruth Warrick, Martha Stewart, Peggy Ann Garner. Love triangle starts intelligently, bogs down halfway into typical soapy histrionics. Good performances; handsomely filmed.

Daisy Miller (1974) C-91m. **½ D: Peter Bogdanovich. Cybill Shepherd, Barry Brown, Cloris Leachman, Mildred Natwick, Eileen Brennan, Duilio Del Prete. Handsome, intelligent adaptation of Henry James' story misses the mark; the tone is cold, and Shepherd's hollow performance as a naive American courting European society in the late 1800s nearly sinks the film.

Dakota (1945) 82m. ** D: Joseph Kane. John Wayne, Vera Ralston, Walter Brennan, Ward Bond, Ona Munson, Hugo Haas. Sprawling Wayne vehicle with Duke involved in pioneer railroad territory dispute; Vera is his lovely wife!

Dakota Incident (1956) C-88m. **½ D: Lewis R. Foster. Linda Darnell, Dale Robertson, John Lund, Ward Bond. Indians attack stagecoach, leading to fight to the finish.

Dakota Lil (1950) C-88m. ** D: Lesley Selander. George Montgomery, Marie Windsor, Rod Cameron, Marion Martin, Wallace Ford. Pedestrian Western saved by Windsor's vitality in title role as crook who helps lawmen trap railroad thieves.

Daleks—Invasion Earth 2150 A.D. (1966-British) C-84m. **½ D: Gordon Flemyng. Peter Cushing, Bernard Cribbins, Andrew Keir, Ray Brooks. Futuristic sci-fi deals with Daleks' conquest of earth, turning people into robots; moves along at nice clip. Retitled: INVASION EARTH 2150 A.D. Sequel to DR. WHO AND THE DALEKS.

Dallas (1950) C-94m. **½ D: Stuart Heisler. Gary Cooper, Ruth Roman, Steve Cochran, Raymond Massey, Antonio Moreno. Cooper returns to Big D of post-Civil War days seeking revenge; finds love with Roman and gunplay from Cochran and other intended victims.

Dallas Cowboys Cheerleaders (1979) C-100m. TVM D: Bruce Bilson. Jane Seymour, Laraine Stephens, Bert Convy, Laura Tewes, Pamela Susan Shoop, Katherine Baumann, Bucky Dent. Featherweight "inside story" about the famed cheerleading squad whose suggestive attire and movements spice many Sunday afternoon football halftime shows. Below average.

Dallas Cowboys Cheerleaders II (1980) C-100m. TVM D: Michael O'Herlihy. John Davidson, Laraine Stephens, Roxanne Gregory, Duane Thomas, Julie Hill, Texie Waterman. Witless sequel to one of the highest-rated and most jiggly made-for-TV movies. For those deeply concerned, it focuses on the concocted conflicts the famed cheerleader squad faces while preparing dance routines for Super Bowl Sunday! Below average.

Dalton Girls, The (1957) 71m. *½ D: Reginald LeBorg. Merry Anders, Penny Edwards, Sue George, John Russell, Lisa Davis. Gimmick of female bandits wears thin in mild Western of Dalton Brothers' relatives carrying on in family tradition.

Dam Busters, The (1954-British) 102m. ***½ D: Michael Anderson. Richard Todd, Michael Redgrave, Ursula Jeans, Basil Sydney. During WW2, British devise an ingenious plan to blow up Germans' Ruhr dam. Exciting and intelligent film.

Dames (1934) 90m. *** D: Ray Enright. Joan Blondell, Dick Powell, Ruby Keeler, ZaSu Pitts, Hugh Herbert, Guy Kibbee, Phil Regan. Short on plot (let's-back-a-Broadway-musical) but top Busby Berkeley production ensembles like "I Only Have Eyes For You" and incredible "When You Were A Smile On Your Mother's Lips And A Twinkle In Your Daddy's Eye."

Damien-Omen II (1978) C-107m. **½ D: Don Taylor. William Holden, Lee Grant, Lew Ayres, Sylvia Sidney, Robert Foxworth, Jonathan Scott-Taylor. Sequel to huge hit of 1976 is less effective, still has shock value with grisly murders (some of which may not survive TV cutting) and good work from Holden. Best scene is Ayres' death under an icy lake. Scott-Taylor is the demon child, Holden and Grant his stupidly unsuspecting kin. Taylor took over directing from Michael Hodges, who worked on screenplay.

Damn Citizen (1958) 88m. **½ D: Robert Gordon. Keith Andes, Maggie Hayes, Gene Evans, Lynn Bari. Realistically told account of WW2 veteran (Andes) hired to wipe out corruption in state police.

Damn the Defiant! (1962-British) C-101m. *** D: Lewis Gilbert. Alec Guinness, Dirk Bogarde, Maurice Denham, Nigel Stock, Richard Carpenter, Anthony Quayle. Bogarde vs. Guinness in stalwart tale of British warship during Napoleonic campaign. Production shows great attention to historic detail.

Damn Yankees (1958) **C-110m.** *** D: George Abbott, Stanley Donen. Tab Hunter, Gwen Verdon, Ray Walston, Russ Brown. The Devil (Walston) and his temptress Lola (Verdon) rejuvenate baseball fan as star player Hunter; lively adaptation of Broadway show, with Bob Fosse choreography. Songs include "Whatever Lola Wants," "(You Gotta Have) Heart."

Damnation Alley (1977) **C-91m.** *½ D: Jack Smight. Jan-Michael Vincent, George Peppard, Dominique Sanda, Paul Winfield, Jackie Earle Haley. Five survivors of nuclear wipeout travel cross-country in search of civilization. Futuristic van in which they travel is more interesting than story or characters in this uninspiring sci-fi saga.

Damned, The (1962) SEE: These Are the Damned

Damned, The (1969-Italian-West German) **C-155m.** *** D: Luchino Visconti. Dirk Bogarde, Ingrid Thulin, Helmut Griem, Helmut Berger, Charlotte Rampling, Florinda Bolkan. Slow, grim drama depicting Nazi machinations and takeover of German industrialist family with few sympathetic characters. Beware cuts in controversial X-rated film.

Damned Don't Cry, The (1950) **103m.** **½ D: Vincent Sherman. Joan Crawford, David Brian, Steve Cochran, Kent Smith, Richard Egan. Follow-up to FLAMINGO ROAD formula; Crawford is well cast as lower-class gal rising to wealth via wit and looks, discovering too late that a gangster's moll has no right to love and happiness.

Damon and Pythias (1962-Italian) **C-99m.** ** D: Curtis Bernhardt. Guy Williams, Don Burnett, Ilaria Occhini, Liana Orfei, Arnoldo Foa. Title reveals all in this routine costumer making legendary figures juvenile cardboard heroes.

Damsel in Distress, A (1937) **98m.** *** D: George Stevens. Fred Astaire, George Burns, Gracie Allen, Joan Fontaine, Constance Collier, Reginald Gardiner, Montagu Love. Bright Gershwin musical set in London; Fontaine is heiress whom Astaire thinks is a chorus girl. Burns & Allen have never been better, even get to

sing and dance. Songs include "Foggy Day in London Town," "Nice Work if You Can Get It."

Dan Candy's Law SEE: **Alien Thunder**

Dance, Fools, Dance (1931) **81m.** **½ D: Harry Beaumont. Joan Crawford, Cliff Edwards, Clark Gable, Earl Foxe, Lester Vail, Natalie Moorhead. Crawford, alone in the world, becomes reporter out to expose mobster Gable by winning him over. Interesting for early Gable-Crawford teaming; brisk drama.

Dance, Girl, Dance (1940) **90m.** **½ D: Dorothy Arzner. Maureen O'Hara, Louis Hayward, Lucille Ball, Virginia Field, Ralph Bellamy, Maria Ouspenskaya, Mary Carlisle. Innocent young girl (O'Hara) aspires to be a ballerina, but protective Ball steers her toward burlesque instead. Film has won latter-day acclaim for feminist angles, especially O'Hara's closing speech; unfortunately, it's not as good as one would like it to be. Lucy is terrific as Bubbles.

Dance Hall (1941) **74m.** *½ D: Irving Pichel. Carole Landis, Cesar Romero, William Henry, June Storey. Mild romantic musical with Romero, who runs a dance hall, falling in love with worker Landis.

Dance of Death (1968-British) **C-138m.** *** D: Daniel Giles. Laurence Olivier, Geraldine McEwan, Robert Lang, Malcolm Reynolds, Janina Faye, Carolyn Jones. Film version of National Theatre production of August Strindberg's angst-laden play about an aging sea captain, notable chiefly for Olivier's fiery performance. Unreleased in U.S. until 1979.

Dance with Me Henry (1956) **79m.** *½ D: Charles Barton. Lou Costello, Bud Abbott, Gigi Perreau, Rusty Hamer. Low-grade Abbott and Costello involving the duo's ownership of run-down amusement park and two kids they've adopted; their last film together.

Dancers in the Dark (1932) **60m.** **½ D: David Burton. Miriam Hopkins, Jack Oakie, George Raft, William Collier Jr., Eugene Pallette, Lyda Roberti. Bandleader Oakie tries to kindle romance with taxi-dancer Hopkins, by sending her boyfriend (Collier) out of town, but doesn't reckon with gangster Raft falling for her too. Good stars help murky drama.

Dancing in the Dark (1949) **C-92m.**

**½ D: Irving Reis. William Powell, Betsy Drake, Mark Stevens, Adolphe Menjou, Walter Catlett. Occasionally bubbly musical comedy with Powell hoping to cement good relations with film company by signing Broadway star; he becomes intrigued with talents of unknown girl, who turns out to be his daughter.

Dancing Lady (1933) 94m. **½ D: Robert Z. Leonard. Joan Crawford, Clark Gable, Franchot Tone, May Robson, Nelson Eddy, Fred Astaire, Robert Benchley, Ted Healy, Three Stooges. Crawford sings and dances in glossy musicomedy of her romance with stage manager Gable and playboy Tone. Astaire's first film. Songs: "Everything I Have Is Yours," title tune.

Dancing Masters, The (1943) 63m. *½ D: Mal St. Clair. Oliver Hardy, Stan Laurel, Trudy Marshall, Robert Bailey, Matt Briggs, Margaret Dumont. L&H overcome by routine material, special effects that look phony. Robert Mitchum has bit as a hood.

Dancing Mothers (1926) 60m. **½ D: Herbert Brenon. Clara Bow, Alice Joyce, Dorothy Cumming, Norman Trevor. Sprightly account of Flapper Bow defying conventions as prototype of the Jazz Age. Silent film has simple plot but enthusiastic performances.

Dancing on a Dime (1940) 74m. **½ D: Joseph Santley. Grace McDonald, Robert Paige, Virginia Dale, Peter Lind Hayes. Programmer musical with wispy plot allowing for McDonald et al to do some dancing and vocalizing, such as "I Hear Music." Not bad.

Dandy in Aspic, A (1968-British) C-107m. ** D: Anthony Mann. Laurence Harvey, Tom Courtenay, Mia Farrow, Lionel Stander, Harry Andrews, Peter Cook. Wooden spy melodrama in which principals keep switching sides so rapidly it becomes impossible to follow. Mann died during filming; Harvey completed director's chores.

Danger by My Side (1962-British) 63m. ** D: Charles Saunders. Anthony Oliver, Maureen Connell, Alan Tilvern, Bill Nagy. Connell hunts her brother's murderer by taking a job in a strip club; standard detective caper.

Danger in Paradise (1977) C-100m. TVM D: Marvin Chomsky. Cliff Potts, John Dehner, Ina Balin, Bill Lucking, Jean-Marie Hon, Michael Mullins. Dreary action drama with stock characters—all unsympathetic.

Prodigal son Potts battles wicked stepmother Balin, in cahoots with land developers, for control of ailing father's huge Hawaiian ranch estate. Below average.

Danger—Love at Work (1937) 81m. **½ D: Otto Preminger. Ann Sothern, Jack Haley, Mary Boland, John Carradine, Edward Everett Horton, E. E. Clive, Stanley Fields. Wacky comedy of family headed by nutty Boland involved in shotgun wedding of Sothern and Haley.

Danger Route (1968-British) C-90m. ** D: Seth Holt. Richard Johnson, Carol Lynley, Barbara Bouchet, Sylvia Sims, Diana Dors, Harry Andrews, Gordon Jackson, Sam Wanamaker. Appearance (in both senses of the word) of Lynley and Bouchet give a little boost to typical secret-agent tale with several plot twists.

Danger Signal (1945) 78m. ** D: Robert Florey. Faye Emerson, Zachary Scott, Rosemary DeCamp, Bruce Bennett, Mona Freeman. No-account Scott comes between Emerson and her family in this routine drama; Scott is a most convincing heel.

Danger Within SEE: Breakout

Dangerous (1935) 72m. **½ D: Alfred E. Green. Bette Davis, Franchot Tone, Margaret Lindsay, Alison Skipworth, John Eldredge. Former star Davis, on the skids, rehabilitated by Tone in good but syrupy tale, with Oscar-winning performance by Davis.

Dangerous Crossing (1953) 75m. **½ D: Joseph M. Newman. Jeanne Crain, Michael Rennie, Carl Betz, Casey Adams. Well-acted suspenser has Crain a new bride on ocean liner whose husband mysteriously disappears.

Dangerous Days of Kiowa Jones, The (1966) C-83m. TVM D: Alex March. Robert Horton, Diane Baker, Sal Mineo, Nehemiah Persoff, Gary Merrill. Fair Western adventure features Horton in good performance as drifter agreeing to transport criminal to jail. Average.

Dangerous Exile (1958-British) C-90m. ** D: Brian Desmond Hurst. Louis Jourdan, Belinda Lee, Keith Michell, Richard O'Sullivan. Jourdan is properly dashing in OK adventurer in which he saves royalty from execution during French revolution, aided by English lass (Lee).

Dangerous Female (1931) 80m. *** D: Roy Del Ruth. Bebe Daniels, Ricardo Cortez, Dudley Digges, Robert Elliott, Thelma Todd, Una Merkel. First film version of Dashiell Hammett's THE MALTESE FALCON quite good, with Cortez more of a ladies' man than Bogart; otherwise quite similar, in scramble for priceless artifact involving private-eye Sam Spade. Remade as SATAN MET A LADY, then MALTESE FALCON. This version retitled for TV.

Dangerous Friend, A: SEE Todd Killings, The

Dangerous Mission (1954) C-75m. ** D: Louis King. Victor Mature, Piper Laurie, Vincent Price, William Bendix, Betta St. John. Laurie, witness to gang murder, flees N.Y.C. to Glacier National Park, where girlhunt climaxes.

Dangerous Money (1946) 64m. D: Terry Morse. Sidney Toler, Gloria Warren, Victor Sen Yung, Rick Vallin, Joseph Crehan. SEE: Charlie Chan series.

Dangerous Moonlight (1941-British) 83m. *** D: Brian Desmond Hurst. Anton Walbrook, Sally Gray, Derrick de Marney, Keneth Kent. Intelligently presented account of concert pianist who becomes a member of the British bomber squadron during WW2; musical interludes well handled. Retitled: SUICIDE SQUADRON.

Dangerous Partners (1945) 74m. **½ D: Edward L. Cahn. James Craig, Signe Hasso, Edmund Gwenn, Audrey Totter, Mabel Paige. Craig and Hasso stumble into fortune in airplane accident; ensuing complications and chase are exciting.

Dangerous Profession, A (1949) 79m. ** D: Ted Tetzlaff. George Raft, Pat O'Brien, Ella Raines, Jim Backus, Roland Winters, Robert Gist. Mystery yarn involving ex-bondsman, blackmail, and murder; not bad but standard.

Dangerous to Know (1938) 70m. **½ D: Robert Florey. Akim Tamiroff, Anna May Wong, Gail Patrick, Lloyd Nolan, Harvey Stephens, Anthony Quinn. Neat little "B" about mobster Tamiroff fixing things so he can marry high-class Patrick; everything backfires.

Dangerous When Wet (1953) C-95m. ** D: Charles Walters. Esther Williams, Fernando Lamas, Jack Carson, Charlotte Greenwood, Denise Darcel. Williams is Midwestern lass hankering to win fame and fortune by swimming English Channel; Lamas romances her in between laps, Greenwood supplies brief comic moments.

Dangerously They Live (1941) 71m. **½ D: Robert Florey. John Garfield, Nancy Coleman, Raymond Massey, Moroni Olsen, Lee Patrick. When spy Coleman is captured by Nazis, doctor Garfield comes to her aid. Tried-and-true WW2 spy melodrama.

Dangers of the Canadian Mounted SEE: R.C.M.P. and the Treasure of Genghis Khan

Daniel Boone, Trail Blazer (1956) C-76m. **½ D: Albert C. Gannaway, Ismael Rodriguez. Bruce Bennett, Lon Chaney, Faron Young, Kem Dibbs. Generally well-acted low-budget version of life of famous frontier scout and his skirmishes with redskins. Filmed in Mexico.

Dante's Inferno (1935) 88m. **½ D: Harry Lachman. Spencer Tracy, Claire Trevor, Henry B. Walthall, Alan Dinehart, Scotty Beckett. No Dante in this yarn of carnival owner who gets too big for his own good; just one scene showing Satan's paradise in good Tracy vehicle. Young Rita Hayworth dances in one scene.

Darby O'Gill and the Little People (1959) C-93m. ***½ D: Robert Stevenson. Albert Sharpe, Janet Munro, Sean Connery, Jimmy O'Dea, Kieron Moore, Estelle Winwood. Outstanding Disney fantasy about an Irish caretaker (Sharpe) who spins so many tales that no one believes him when he says he's befriended the King of Leprechauns. An utter delight, with dazzling special effects —and some truly terrifying moments along with the whimsy.

Darby's Rangers (1958) 121m. **½ D: William Wellman. James Garner, Etchika Choureau, Jack Warden, Edward Byrnes, David Janssen. Garner does well in WW2 actioner as leader of assault troops in North Africa and Italy, focusing on relationship among his command and their shore romances.

Daring Dobermans, The (1973) C-90m. **½ D: Byron Chudnow. Charles Knox Robinson, Tim Considine, David Moses, Claudio Martinez, Joan Caulfield. Sequel to THE DOBERMAN GANG provides amiable family viewing as the canines are trained for another daring heist by a new gang of crooks.

Daring Game (1968) C-100m. **½ D: Laslo Benedek. Lloyd Bridges, Nico Minardos, Michael Ansara, Joan Blackman. Not bad adventure tale of underwater expert (guess who?) in search of husband and daughter of his former girlfriend.

Daring Young Man (1942) 73m. ** D: Frank Strayer. Joe E. Brown, Marguerite Chapman, William Wright, Roger Clark. Brown is able to make this formula Nazi spy chase comedy of passable interest; set in N.Y.C.

Dark, The (1979) C-92m. ** D: John (Bud) Cardos. William Devane, Cathy Lee Crosby, Richard Jaeckel, Keenan Wynn, Jacquelyn Hyde, Biff Elliott, Vivian Blaine. Fairly well made but predictable entry in the alien rampage cycle, with writer Devane and TV reporter Crosby cracking mysterious crime wave in California town.

Dark Alibi (1946) 61m. D: Phil Karlson. Sidney Toler, Mantan Moreland, Ben Carter, Benson Fong, Russell Hicks, Joyce Compton, Edward Earle. SEE: **Charlie Chan** series.

Dark Angel, The (1935) 110m. *** D: Sidney Franklin. Fredric March, Merle Oberon, Herbert Marshall, Janet Beecher, John Halliday. Well-acted soaper of two men in love with same woman; fighting in WW1, one of them going blind.

Dark at the Top of the Stairs, The (1960) C-123m. *** D: Delbert Mann. Robert Preston, Dorothy McGuire, Eve Arden, Angela Lansbury, Shirley Knight. Superficial handling of William Inge play set in 1920s Oklahoma, revolving around Preston's family and neighbors, their problems and frustrations; still good. Arden and Lansbury come off best.

Dark Avenger, The SEE: **Warriors, The**

Dark City (1950) 88m. **½ D: William Dieterle. Charlton Heston, Lizabeth Scott, Viveca Lindfors, Dean Jagger, Jack Webb. In first major film role, Heston portrays jilted WW2 veteran-turned-gambler who becomes object of gangster manhunt. Scott and Webb uplift predictable casino-club-naked-city proceedings.

Dark Command (1940) 94m. *** D: Raoul Walsh. John Wayne, Claire Trevor, Walter Pidgeon, Roy Rogers, George "Gabby" Hayes, Marjorie Main. Pidgeon plays character patterned after 1860s renegade Quantrill, small-town despot who (in this story) launches his terror raids after clashing with newly elected marshal Wayne. Dramatically uneven, but entertaining.

Dark Corner, The (1946) 99m. *** D: Henry Hathaway. Lucille Ball, Clifton Webb, William Bendix, Mark Stevens, Reed Hadley, Constance Collier. Top-notch mystery with secretary Ball helping boss Stevens escape from phony murder charge. Well-acted, exciting film.

Dark Delusion (1947) 90m. D: Willis Goldbeck. Lionel Barrymore, James Craig, Lucille Bremer, Jayne Meadows, Warner Anderson. SEE: **Dr. Kildare** series.

Dark Eyes of London SEE: **Human Monster, The**

Dark Hazard (1934) 72m. ** D: Alfred E. Green. Edward G. Robinson, Genevieve Tobin, Glenda Farrell, Henry B. Walthall, Sidney Toler. Robinson is bright spot of programmer about his precarious married life to Tobin, endangered by girlfriend Farrell and urge to gamble.

Dark Horse (1932) 75m. **½ D: Alfred E. Green. Warren William, Bette Davis, Guy Kibbee, Vivienne Osborne, Frank McHugh. Lively political spoof with nitwit Kibbee running for governor with help from campaign manager William and co-worker Davis.

Dark Intruder (1965) 59m. *** D: Harvey Hart. Leslie Nielsen, Judi Meredith, Mark Richman, Werner Klemperer, Gilbert Green, Charles Bolender. Uneven performances major liability in near-flawless supernatural thriller. Occult expert called in by San Francisco police in connection with series of weird murders. Intricate plot and exceptional use of time period blending with suspense make this a one-of-a-kind movie. Made as TV pilot for unsold series.

Dark Journey (1937-British) 82m. *** D: Victor Saville. Conrad Veidt, Vivien Leigh, Joan Gardner, Anthony Bushell, Ursula Jeans. Handsome, engrossing love story between British and German spies in WW1 Stockholm. Young Leigh is radiant.

Dark Mirror, The (1946) 85m. *** D: Robert Siodmak. Olivia de Havilland, Lew Ayres, Thomas Mitchell, Richard Long, Charles Evans, Garry Owen. De Havilland plays twin sisters—one good, one disturbed—who are implicated in murder. One of Hollywood's post-WW2 forays into psychological drama; no longer fresh, but still entertaining.

Dark of the Sun (1968-British) C-101m. *** D: Jack Cardiff. Rod Taylor, Yvette Mimieux, Jim Brown, Kenneth More, Peter Carsten, Andre Morell, Calvin Lockhart. Excellent cast in nerve-wracking actioner with Taylor the leader of mercenary expedition to retrieve uncut diamonds and beseiged refugees in Congo. One of Taylor's best pictures. Beware cuts in violent scenes.

Dark Passage (1947) 106m. *** D: Delmer Daves. Humphrey Bogart, Lauren Bacall, Bruce Bennett, Agnes Moorehead. Engrossing caper of escaped convict (Bogart) undergoing plastic surgery, hiding out at Bacall's apartment till his face heals. Stars outshine far-fetched happenings.

Dark Past, The (1948) 75m. *** D: Rudolph Mate. William Holden, Nina Foch, Lee J. Cobb, Adele Jergens, Stephen Dunne. Absorbing narrative of mad killer holding psychologist prisoner and latter's attempts to talk sense into the maniac. Remake of BLIND ALLEY.

Dark Places (1974-British) C-91m. *½ D: Don Sharp. Christopher Lee, Joan Collins, Robert Hardy, Herbert Lom, Jane Birkin, Jean Marsh. Mild horror thriller. Hardy, heir to an insane murderer's estate, is possessed by his spirit, kills those who try to do him out of it.

Dark Sands (1937-British) 77m. ** D: Thornton Freeland. Paul Robeson, Henry Wilcoxon, Wallace Ford, Princess Kouka, John Laurie. Weak drama with American deserter Robeson joining African desert tribe to avoid corporal punishment. Robeson again defeated by his material. Originally titled JERICHO.

Dark Secret of Harvest Home (1978) C-200m. TVM D: Leo Penn. Bette Davis, David Ackroyd, Rosanna Arquette, Rene Auberjonois, Norman Lloyd. Leisurely gothic horror tale set in New England village where Bette and other weirdos maintain ritualistic life-style, to the dismay of commercial artist who has moved his family there from Manhattan. Adapted from Thomas Tryon's novel *Harvest Home;* narrated in eerie fashion by Donald Pleasence. Above average.

Dark Side of Innocence, The (1976) C-78m. TVM D: Jerry Thorpe. Joanna Pettet, Ann Archer, John Anderson, Kim Hunter, Lawrence Casey, Claudette Nevins. Contemporary soap opera focusing primarily on Pettet, an affluent housewife oppressed by her domesticity who walks out on her husband and two kids, and Archer, her sister embittered by a recent divorce. Average.

Dark Star (1974) C-83m. **½ D: John Carpenter. Dan O'Bannon, Dre Pahich, Brian Narelle. Satiric, spaced-out version of 2001 with three desperate astronauts whose mission is to bomb unstable planets. Enjoyable for sci-fi fans and surfers; stretches its shoestring budget pretty well.

Dark Victory (1939) 106m. ***½ D: Edmund Goulding. Bette Davis, George Brent, Humphrey Bogart, Geraldine Fitzgerald, Ronald Reagan, Cora Witherspoon, Henry Travers. Definitive Davis performance as spoiled socialite whose life is ending; Brent as brain surgeon husband, Fitzgerald as devoted friend register in good soaper. Bogart as Irish stable master seems out of place. Remade as STOLEN HOURS.

Dark Victory (1976) C-150m. TVM D: Robert Butler. Elizabeth Montgomery, Anthony Hopkins, Michele Lee, Janet McLachlan, Michael Lerner, John Elerick, Vic Tayback, Herbert Berghof. Updated version of Bette Davis classic has Montgomery as TV producer who falls in love with the doctor who tells her she has a brain tumor. Former four-hankie weeper now is curiously unaffecting, despite the professionalism of its cast. Updating failed to help the old chestnut, nor did the subsequent slicing of an hour of running time. Average.

Dark Waters (1944) 90m. ** D: Andre de Toth. Merle Oberon, Franchot Tone, Thomas Mitchell, Fay Bainter, Rex Ingram, John Qualen, Elisha Cook, Jr. Cast sinks into the bog (some literally) in confused film of innocent girl staying with peculiar family.

Darker Side of Terror, The (1979) C-100m. TVM D: Gus Trikonis. Robert Forster, Adrienne Barbeau, Ray Milland, David Sheiner, John Lehne. Inept psychological thriller about a researcher who agrees to have himself cloned and then must fight his look-alike for his wife's affections. Below average.

Darker Than Amber (1970) C-97m. **½ D: Robert Clouse. Rod Taylor, Suzy Kendall, Theodore Bikel, Jane Russell, James Booth, Janet MacLachlan. OK action melodrama casts Taylor as famous paperback detective, Travis McGee; he's after thugs who beat up Kendall. Good location photography in Miami and Caribbean.

Darkest Africa SEE: **Batmen of Africa**

Darling (1965-British) 122m. ***½ D: John Schlesinger. Julie Christie, Dirk Bogarde, Laurence Harvey, Roland Curram, Jose Luis de Villalonga, Alex Scott, Basil Henson. Christie won Oscar as girl who rises from commonplace life to marry an Italian noble, with several unsatisfactory love affairs in between. Film's cynical approach and flowing style improve the proceedings.

Darling, How Could You (1951) 96m. **½ D: Mitchell Leisen. Joan Fontaine, John Lund, Mona Freeman, Peter Hanson. Chic stars brighten old-fashioned James Barrie play about teen-ager who thinks her mother (Fontaine) is having an affair.

Darling Lili (1970) C-136m. *** D: Blake Edwards. Julie Andrews, Rock Hudson, Jeremy Kemp, Lance Percival, Jacques Marin, Michael Witney. Largely overlooked when released, very entertaining spoof has Andrews and Hudson at their best, along with writer/director Edwards, keeping tongue-in-cheek but not becoming coy in telling story of German spy Julie posing as London entertainer during WW1, falling in love with squadron commander Hudson. Great fun, good music.

Darwin Adventure, The (1972) C-91m. **½ D: Jack Couffer. Nicholas Clay, Susan Macready, Ian Richardson, Christopher Martin. Curious tale focusing on career of Charles Darwin and his theories on evolution of man.

Date With Judy, A (1948) C-113m. **½ D: Richard Thorpe. Wallace Beery, Jane Powell, Elizabeth Taylor, Carmen Miranda, Xavier Cugat, Robert Stack. Weak musicomedy of two teen-agers involved in family shenanigans; highlight is Beery dancing with Miranda.

Date with the Falcon, A (1941) 63m. D: Irving Reis. George Sanders, Wendy Barrie, Allen Jenkins, James Gleason, Mona Maris, Frank Moran. SEE: **Falcon series**

Daughter of Dr. Jekyll (1957) 71m. *½ D: Edgar G. Ulmer. John Agar, Gloria Talbott, Arthur Shields, John Dierkes. Silly spinoff on Robert Louis Stevenson's novel. Talbott thinks she is cursed with inheritance of part human, part monster.

Daughter of Mata Hari SEE: **Mata Hari's Daughter**

Daughter of Rosie O'Grady, The (1950) C-104m. **½ D: David Butler. June Haver, Gordon MacRae, Debbie Reynolds, Gene Nelson, James Barton, S. Z. Sakall, Jane Darwell. Formula period musical with Haver in title role singing turn-of-the-century favorites. Talented MacRae is her love interest, and Sakall is forced to give another cuddly stereotype.

Daughter of Shanghai (1937) 63m. ** D: Robert Florey. Anna May Wong, Charles Bickford, Buster Crabbe, Cecil Cunningham, J. Carrol Naish, Anthony Quinn, Philip Ahn. Good-girl Wong seeks to expose illegal alien racket in tight-knit "B" actioner.

Daughter of the Mind (1969) C-73m. TVM D: Walter Grauman. Ray Milland, Gene Tierney, Don Murray, George Macready. Professor Constable (Milland), convinced daughter trying to communicate from beyond grave, hires parapsychologist; FBI steps in due to scientists's previous work with government. Wide-eyed and inconsequential. Average, from Paul Gallico story.

Daughters Courageous (1939) 107m. *** D: Michael Curtiz. John Garfield, Claude Rains, Fay Bainter, Priscilla Lane, Rosemary Lane, Lola Lane, Gale Page, May Robson, Donald Crisp, Frank McHugh. Rehash of FOUR DAUGHTERS with same cast, made enjoyable by natural performances of Lane sisters, fine work by Garfield.

Daughters of Destiny (1954-French) 94m. ** D: Marcel Pagliero. Claudette Colbert, Michele Morgan, André Clement, Daniel Ivernel. Overblown, sluggish trio of tales telling of three famous women of history: Elizabeth I, Lysistrata, Joan of Arc.

Daughters of Joshua Cabe, The (1972) C-73m. TVM D: Philip Leacock. Buddy Ebsen, Karen Valentine, Lesley Warren, Sandra Dee, Jack Elam, Leif Erickson, Don Stroud. New homesteading law and refusal of daughters to return West forces trapper Cabe (Ebsen) to hire three women to pose as his children. Typical unbelievable Western. Average.

Daughters of Joshua Cabe Return, The (1975) C-78m. TVM D: David Lowell Rich. Dan Dailey, Ronne Troup, Christina Hart, Brooke Adams, Dub Taylor, Carl Betz, Arthur Hunnicutt, Terry Wilson, Kathleen Freeman. Sequel to 1972 movie with Dailey taking over as the rascally rancher, who, with the three shady ladies he has hired to pose as his daughters, is outwitted by the real dad of one of them, who holds her for a ransom Cabe cannot pay. Average.

Daughters of Satan (1972) C-96m. ** D: Hollingsworth Morse. Tom Selleck, Barra Grant, Tani Phelps Guthrie, Paraluman. Witches' curses, mumbo jumbo, and a lot of hokum as young girl is lured into witches' coven.

David and Bathsheba (1951) C-116m. ** D: Henry King. Gregory Peck, Susan Hayward, Raymond Massey, Kieron Moore, James Robertson Justice. Biblical epic with good production values but generally boring script; only fair performances.

David and Goliath (1961-Italian) C-95m. ** D: Richard Pottier, Ferdinando Baldi. Orson Welles, Ivo Payer, Edward Hilton, Eleonora Rossi-Drago, Massimo Serato. Juvenile spectacle based on biblical tale, with wooden script, bad acting, Welles as hefty King Saul.

David and Lisa (1963) 94m. *** D: Frank Perry. Keir Dullea, Janet Margolin, Howard da Silva, Neva Patterson, Clifton James. Independently made film about two disturbed teen-agers is excellent, sensitively played by newcomers Dullea and Margolin. Da Silva is fine as an understanding doctor.

David Copperfield (1935) 133m. **** D: George Cukor. W. C. Fields, Lionel Barrymore, Madge Evans, Maureen O'Sullivan, Edna May Oliver, Lewis Stone, Basil Rathbone, Roland Young. Another expensive MGM Dickens classic well mounted with unforgettable characterizations by Fields (Micawber), Rathbone (Murdstone), Young (Uriah Heep), Oliver (Aunt Betsy), helping to bring story of British youth in old England to life. A must. Freddie Bartholomew is David as a boy, Frank Lawton plays him as an adult.

David Copperfield (1970) C-110m. TVM D: Delbert Mann. Robin Phillips, Susan Hampshire, Edith Evans, Michael Redgrave, Ralph Richardson, Laurence Olivier, Wendy Hiller, Emlyn Williams, Richard Attenborough. Top-drawer cast in moody new version of the classic. The giants of the English theater give what support they can to a rather limp script and an unanimated lead. Average.

David Harum (1934) 83m. **½ D: James Cruze. Will Rogers, Louise Dresser, Evelyn Venable, Kent Taylor, Stepin Fetchit, Noah Beery, Charles Middleton. Foxy rancher Rogers plays matchmaker for Venable and Taylor, while spinning his own brand of folksy humor.

Davy Crockett and the River Pirates (1956) C-81m. **½ D: Norman Foster. Fess Parker, Buddy Ebsen, Jeff York, Kenneth Tobey, Clem Bevans, Irvin Ashkenazy. Second CROCKETT feature strung together from two Disney TV shows; first half is comic riverboat race with Mike Fink (York), second half is more serious confrontation with Indians. Lightweight fun.

Davy Crockett, Indian Scout (1950) 71m. ** D: Lew Landers. George Montgomery, Ellen Drew, Philip Reed, Chief Thundercloud. Montgomery in title role is contrast to Fess Parker's portrayal of historical figure in minor Western dealing with Indian attacks on wagon trains.

Davy Crockett, King of the Wild Frontier (1955) C-93m. *** D: Norman Foster. Fess Parker, Buddy Ebsen, Basil Ruysdael, Hans Conried, William Bakewell, Kenneth Tobey. Originally filmed as three segments for Disney's TV show, this created a nationwide phenomenon in 1955; it's still fun today with Parker as famous Indian scout and Ebsen as his pal George Russel, whose adventures take them from Washington, D.C. to the Alamo.

Dawn at Socorro (1954) C-80m. **½ D: George Sherman. Rory Calhoun, Piper Laurie, David Brian, Kathleen Hughes, Edgar Buchanan, Alex Nicol. Calhoun is gunslinger wishing to reform, but fate forces inevitable shootout.

Dawn Patrol, The (1938) 103m. ***½ D: Edmund Goulding. Errol Flynn, Basil Rathbone, David Niven, Donald Crisp, Melville Cooper, Barry Fitzgerald. Remake of 1930 classic is fine actioner of WW1 flyers in France; Rathbone as stern officer forced to send up green recruits, Flynn and Niven as pilot buddies, all excellent.

Dawn: Portrait of a Teenage Runaway (1976) C-100m. TVM D: Randall Kleiser. Eve Plumb, Leigh J. McCloskey, Bo Hopkins, Georg Stanford Brown, Lynn Carlin, Marg DeLain, Joan Prather, Anne Seymour, William Schallert. Fifteen-year-old Plumb turns to prostitution when she cannot find legitimate work after running away from her cocktail waitress mom Carlin. Serious social issue exploited for cheap sensationalism. Below average.

Day at the Races, A (1937) 111m. ***½ D: Sam Wood. Groucho, Harpo and Chico Marx, Allan Jones, Maureen O'Sullivan, Margaret Dumont, Douglass Dumbrille. Groucho is Dr. Hackenbush, treating hypochondriac Dumont; many classic scenes (Chico selling Groucho race tips, etc.) but not the success A NIGHT AT THE OPERA was, due to less exciting music and subplot.

Day for Night (1973-French) C-120m. ***½ D: François Truffaut. Jacqueline Bisset, Jean-Pierre Leaud, François Truffaut, Jean-Pierre Aumont, Valentina Cortese, Alexandra Stewart. Enjoyable fluff about a motion picture director (Truffaut) and his problems in trying to film a silly love story; bright performances and a loving look into the intricacies of filmmaking. Oscar winner as Best Foreign Film.

Day in the Death of Joe Egg, A (1972-British) C-106m. ***½ D: Peter Medak. Alan Bates, Janet Suzman, Peter Bowles, Sheila Gish. Excellent black comedy by Peter Nichols; couple with spastic child contemplate mercy-killing. Not a crowdpleaser, but extremely well done.

Day of Anger (1969-Italian) C-109m. *½ D: Tonino Valerii. Lee Van Cleef, Giuliano Gemma, Walter Rilla, Christa Linder, Ennio Balbo, Lukas Ammann. Story of callous gunman and his relationship with young protege is below par, even for an Italian Western; only for the Van Cleef cult.

Day of Fury, A (1956) C-78m. *** D: Harmon Jones. Dale Robertson, Mara Corday, Jock Mahoney, Carl Benton Reid. Offbeat study of rebellious Robertson who can't cope with conventions of Western town he lives in.

Day of the Animals (1977) C-98m. **½ D: William Girdler. Christopher George, Lynda Day George, Leslie Nielsen, Richard Jaeckel, Michael Ansara, Ruth Roman. Fair action thriller in the nature-on-the-rampage mold, with a cast of back packers in the High Sierras at the mercy of hostile creatures crazed by the sun's radiation after the earth's ozone layer has been ecologically destroyed. Final score: beasts 7, cast 0 (in acting as well as survival).

Day of the Bad Man (1958) C-81m. ** D: Harry Keller. Fred MacMurray, Joan Weldon, John Ericson, Robert Middleton. MacMurray is appropriately stiff in tame account of country judge holding off condemned man's brothers so scheduled hanging can occur.

Day of the Dolphin, The (1973) C-104m. ** D: Mike Nichols. George C. Scott, Trish Van Devere, Paul Sorvino, Fritz Weaver, John Korkes, Edward Herrmann. Big-budget misfire about scientist Scott, his trained dolphins, and an assassination plot. A waste of many talents.

Day of the Evil Gun (1968) C-93m. ** D: Jerry Thorpe. Glenn Ford, Arthur Kennedy, Dean Jagger, John Anderson, Paul Fix, Nino Minardos, Royal Dano. Very routine Western with Ford and Kennedy going after Indians who abducted the former's wife; Kennedy is smooth in likable-villain role he's played many times.

Day of the Jackal, The (1973-British-French) C-141m. ***½ D: Fred Zinnemann. Edward Fox, Alan Badel, Tony Britton, Cyril Cusack, Michel Lonsdale, Eric Porter, Delphine Seyrig. Exciting adaptation of Frederick Forsyth's best-seller about plot to assassinate De Gaulle and the painstaking preparations of the assassin. Beautifully filmed throughout Europe with a first-rate cast.

Day of the Locust, The (1975) C-144m. ***½ D: John Schlesinger. Donald Sutherland, Karen Black, Burgess Meredith, William Atherton, Geraldine Page, Richard A. Dysart, Bo Hopkins. Excellent adaptation of Nathanael West's sweeping novel about Hollywood's nether world in 1930s, seen mostly through eyes of a young artist (Atherton) who finds little glamor and a lot of broken-down people in tinseltown. Disturbing, depressing . . . and absolutely fascinating.

Day of the Outlaw (1959) 91m. ** D: Andre de Toth. Robert Ryan, Burl Ives, Tina Louise, Alan Marshal, Nehemiah Persoff, Venetia Stevenson. Stark, gripping Western melodrama of outlaw Ives and gang taking over isolated Western town.

Day of the Triffids, The (1963-British) C-95m. **½ D: Steve Sekely. Howard Keel, Nicole Maurey, Janette Scott, Kieron Moore, Mervyn Johns. Meteor showers blind local populace and drop dandelion-like fluff which grow into man-eating plants. Good special effects.

Day of the Wolves (1973) C-95m. **½ D: Ferde Grofe Jr. Richard Egan, Martha Hyer, Rick Jason, Jan Murray. Ex-sheriff Egan tries to thwart bizarre attempt by strange group of men to isolate his town for three days, in order to pull off "perfect crime."

Day That Shook the World, The (1977) C-111m. ** D: Veljko Bulajic. Christopher Plummer, Florinda Balkan, Maximillian Schell. Plodding historical drama surrounding the events leading up to WW1 with the death of Archduke Ferdinand (Plummer) at Sarajevo. Yugoslavian-made with a humorless international cast, resulting in tedious though epic-sized chronicle.

Day the Earth Caught Fire, The (1962-British) 99m. *** D: Val Guest. Edward Judd, Janet Munro, Leo McKern, Michael Goodliffe, Bernard Braden. Intelligent, absorbing sci-fi drama of gradual chaos resulting from atomic explosion, focusing on drifter-reporter (Judd) who is more involved than most.

Day the Earth Moved, The (1974) C-78m. TVM D: Robert Michael Lewis. Jackie Cooper, Stella Stevens, Cleavon Little, William Windom, Beverly Garland, Lucille Benson, Kelly Thordsen. Aerial photographers Cooper and Little have less trouble predicting an iminent earthquake than in convincing some townspeople to get out before the walls come tumbling down on them. Modest thriller with competent performances and special effects. Average.

Day the Earth Stood Still, The (1951) 92m. ***½ D: Robert Wise. Michael Rennie, Patricia Neal, Hugh Marlowe, Sam Jaffe. Superior sci-fi with Rennie as a visitor from another planet on an exploratory mission to earth. Klaatu barada nikto!

Day the Fish Came Out, The (1967-Greek-British) C-109m. BOMB D: Michael Cacoyannis. Tom Courtenay, Candice Bergen, Colin Blakely, Sam Wanamaker, Ian Ogilvy. Plot about the loss of two atom bombs over the Aegean Sea provides framework for disastrous comedy about homosexuals; combo of Candy Bergen plus whips, chains, and leather doesn't work.

Day the Hot Line Got Hot, The (1969) C-92m. *½ D: Etienne Perier. Robert Taylor, Charles Boyer, George Chakiris, Dominique Fabre, Gerard Tichy. Hollow attempt at topicality as secret agents mess up Moscow-Washington hot line, causing international crisis.

Day the Sky Exploded, The (1958-Italian) 80m. ** D: Paolo Heusch. Paul Hubschmid, Madeleine Fischer, Fiorella Mari, Ivo Garrani. Film doesn't live up to potential excitement as exploding missile in outer space sends debris to earth, causing chaos.

Day the World Ended, The (1956) 82m. ** D: Roger Corman. Richard Denning, Lori Nelson, Adele Jergens, Touch (Mike) Connors. Modest sci-fi involving survivors of radiation blast and interplay of human nature that causes friction among the group.

Day They Robbed the Bank of England, The (1960-British) 85m. *** D: John Guillermin. Aldo Ray, Elizabeth Sellars, Peter OToole, Hugh Griffith, Kieron Moore, Albert Sharpe. IRA members plan to rob the Bank of England in this meticulous caper film.

Day-Time Wife (1939) 71m. ** D: Gregory Ratoff. Tyrone Power, Linda Darnell, Warren William, Binnie Barnes, Wendy Barrie. Power and Darnell make an engaging couple, even in lightweight fare such as this: wife gets office job to see if work is really all play.

Daybreak (1946-British) 88m. ** D: Compton Bennett. Eric Portman, Ann Todd, Maxwell Reed, Bill Owen, Jane Hylton. Murky tale of young couple living on houseboat, with infidelity causing traumatic repercussion to all.

Daydreamer, The (1966) C-98m. *** D: Jules Bass. Ray Bolger, Jack Gilford, Margaret Hamilton, Paul O'Keefe, voices of Tallulah Bankhead, Boris Karloff, Burl Ives, Victor Borge, Terry-Thomas, Patty Duke. Partly animated story of Hans Christian Andersen as a 13-year-old who meets many of the fairy tale characters he later writes about. Surprisingly pleasant.

Days of Glory (1944) 86m. **½ D: Jacques Tourneur. Gregory Peck, Alan Reed, Maria Palmer, Lowell Gilmore, Tamara Toumanova. Sincere but plodding WW2 action drama with the Russians combatting Nazi enemies.

Days of Heaven (1978) C-95m. ***½ D: Terrence Malick. Richard Gere, Brooke Adams, Sam Shepard, Linda Manz, Robert Wilke, Jackie Shultis, Stuart Margolin. Exquisite mood-piece about a turbulent love triangle set against midwestern wheat harvests at the turn of the century. Shot in 70mm, its visual beauty will be diminished on TV, leaving only the story—which is second priority here. Nestor Alemandros won well-deserved Oscar for his cinematography.

Days of Thrills and Laughter (1961) 93m. **** Compiled by Robert Youngson. The third Youngson compilation of old movie clips is as funny and exciting as his first two. Scenes with Laurel and Hardy, Chaplin, the Keystone Kops, and others are hilarious, and action scenes with Doug Fairbanks and Pearl White are still fun. Nostalgic and thoroughly enjoyable.

Days of Wine and Roses (1962) 117m. ***½ D: Blake Edwards. Jack Lemmon, Lee Remick, Charles Bickford, Jack Klugman, Alan Hewitt, Tom Palmer, Jack Albertson. Modern LOST WEEKEND set in San Francisco, with Lemmon marrying Remick and pulling her into state of alcoholism. Realistic direction and uncompromising writing combine for excellent results; poignant score by Henry Mancini.

Dayton's Devils (1968) C-107m. ** D: Jack Shea. Rory Calhoun, Leslie Nielson, Lainie Kazan, Hans Gudegast (Eric Braeden), Barry Sadler. Another heist film, this time about plot to rob an Air Force base of $2¼ million; Lainie's rendition of "Sunny" provides film's only special moment.

De Sade (1969-British) C-92m. ** D: Cy Endfield. Keir Dullea, Senta Berger, Lilli Palmer, Anna Massey, John Huston. Fictionalized biography of world's most celebrated sexual and physical pervert. If you're expecting something raunchy, forget it. Pretty tepid stuff.

Dead Are Alive, The (1972-Yugoslavian-German-Italian) C-98m. *½ D: Armando Crispino. Alex Cord, Samantha Eggar, John Marley, Nadja Tiller, Horst Frank, Enzo Tarascio. Confused, uninteresting suspenser dealing with series of murders that take place while archeologists are studying ancient tombs; Eggar is wasted. Some scenes may be cut for TV.

Dead Don't Die, The (1975) C-78m. TVM D: Curtis Harrington. George Hamilton, Ray Milland, Linda Cristal, Ralph Meeker, Joan Blondell,

James McEachin. Creaky 1930s thriller has Hamilton, out to clear his executed brother's name, clashing with a crazed zombie master who has hatched a plot to rule the world with his army of living dead. Below average.

Dead End (1937) 93m. ***½ D: William Wyler. Sylvia Sidney, Joel McCrea, Humphrey Bogart, Wendy Barrie, Claire Trevor, Marjorie Main, Huntz Hall, Leo Gorcey, Gabriel Dell, Ward Bond, Billy Halop, Bernard Punsley, Allen Jenkins. Grim Sidney Kingsley play of slum life shows vignettes of humanity at breaking point in N.Y.C. tenement slums; extremely well directed, engrossing. Film introduced Dead End Kids.

Dead Heat on a Merry-Go-Round (1966) C-104m. *** D: Bernard Girard. James Coburn, Camilla Sparv, Aldo Ray, Ross Martin, Severn Darden, Robert Webber. Involved crime movie about intricate plan to rob airport bank (with surprise ending). All-round very good film with excellent cast.

Dead Man's Eyes (1944) 64m. ** D: Reginald LeBorg. Lon Chaney Jr., Jean Parker, Paul Kelly, Thomas Gomez, Acquanetta. Interesting yarn of blind man (Chaney) accused of murdering girlfriend's father, whose announced intention was to bequeath his eyes to Chaney for transplant operation.

Dead Men Tell (1941) 60m. D: Harry Lachman. Sidney Toler, Sheila Ryan, Robert Weldon, Victor Sen Yung, Don Douglas, Kay Aldridge. SEE: Charlie Chan series.

Dead Men Tell No Tales (1971) C-73m. TVM D: Walter Grauman. Christopher George, Judy Carne, Patricia Barry, Richard Anderson. Engaging chase-thriller with sense of humor. Paid assassins mistake travel photographer (George) for real quarry. Carne stars as former girlfriend who decides to help hero. Above average.

Dead of Night (1946-British) 102m. **** D: Cavalcanti, Basil Dearden, Robert Hamer, Charles Crichton. Mervyn Johns, Roland Culver, Antony Baird, Judy Kelly, Miles Malleson, Sally Ann Howes, Googie Withers, Ralph Michael, Michael Redgrave, Basil Radford, Naunton Wayne. Classic chiller involving gathering of people who have experienced dreams which seem to repeat themselves in reality; final sequence with Redgrave as a ventriloquist is a knockout. American version ran 77m., but fuller edition has been restored for TV.

Dead Reckoning (1947) 100m. ******* D: John Cromwell. Humphrey Bogart, Lizabeth Scott, Morris Carnovsky, William Prince, Wallace Ford, Charles Cane. Bogart's fine as tough WW2 veteran solving soldier-buddy's murder. Well-acted drama.

Dead Ringer (1964) 115m. ****½** D: Paul Henreid. Bette Davis, Karl Malden, Peter Lawford, Jean Hagen, George Macready, Estelle Winwood. A double dose of Davis, playing twin sisters bearing a long-time grudge over a man, the sinister one trying to get even. Far-fetched but fun; Bette's vehicle all the way.

Dead Run (1969) C-92m. ****** D: Christian-Jacque. Peter Lawford, Countess Ira Furstenberg, George Geret. Stolen defense plans in Berlin and Rome. Dull, but Lawford and beautiful on-location filming help a bit.

Deadfall (1968-British) C-120m. ****** D: Bryan Forbes. Michael Caine, Giovanna Ralli, Eric Portman, Nanette Newman, David Buck. Jewel thief falls in love with beautiful woman who is married to her homosexual father. And you think you have problems? Overdirected film is not as interesting as it sounds.

Deadlier Than the Male (1957-French) 104m. ****** D: Julien Duvivier. Jean Gabin, Daniele Delorme, Lucienne Bogaert, Gerard Blain. Delorme encamps in ex-stepfather's home, planning to marry and then murder him; Gabin is stodgy as girl's intended victim.

Deadlier Than the Male (1967-British) C-101m. ****½** D: Ralph Thomas. Richard Johnson, Elke Sommer, Sylva Koscina, Nigel Green, Suzanna Leigh. Standard fare which half-heartedly resurrects Bulldog Drummond, trying to solve whodunit centering around two shapely suspects.

Deadliest Season, The (1977) C-100m. TVM D: Robert Markowitz. Michael Moriarty, Kevin Conway, Meryl Streep, Sully Boyar, Jill Eikenberry, Walter McGinn, Andrew Duggan, Patrick O'Neal, Mason Adams. Hard-hitting pro hockey drama about a defenseman (Moriarty) whose aggressiveness endears him to the fans and his bosses until he critically injures another player and is tried

for manslaughter. Thought-provoking but violent Ernest Kinoy screenplay marred only by Moriarty's curiously mannered performance in leading role. Above average.

Deadliest Sin, The (1956-British) 77m. ***½** D: Ken Hughes. Sydney Chaplin, Audrey Dalton, John Bentley, Peter Hammond. Good triumphing over evil is moral of this slight story of thief involved in murder.

Deadline at Dawn (1946) 83m. ****½** D: Harold Clurman. Susan Hayward, Paul Lukas, Bill Williams, Osa Massen, Lola Lane. Fairly interesting murder mystery by Clifford Odets with suspected sailor Williams and singer Hayward helping to clear him.

Deadline U.S.A. (1952) 87m. ******* D: Richard Brooks. Humphrey Bogart, Ethel Barrymore, Kim Hunter, Ed Begley, Paul Stewart, Jim Backus. Biting account of newspaper's struggle to survive and maintain civic duty. Bogey is editor, Begley his assistant, Stewart a sports reporter who brings in wanted man; most enjoyable.

Deadlock (1969) C-99m. TVM D: Lamont Johnson. Leslie Nielsen, Hari Rhodes, Dana Elcar, Max Julien, Melvin Stuart, Ruby Dee, Aldo Ray. Intelligent study of election-year politics and ghetto turmoil. D. A. Washburn (Rhodes) accepts mayor's assignment to head special investigatory panel in death of newspaperman who had covered touchy racial issue. Excellent performances, realistic tension. Above average.

Deadly Affair, The (1967) C-107m. ******* D: Sidney Lumet. James Mason, Simone Signoret, Maximilian Schell, Harriet Andersson, Harry Andrews, Lynn Redgrave. Top-notch suspense tale with British agent Mason trying to unravel complicated mystery behind an agency official's suicide. Filmed in England and based on John Le Carre's novel "Call For The Dead."

Deadly Bees, The (1967-British) C-85m. ****** D: Freddie Francis. Suzanna Leigh, Guy Doleman, Catherine Finn, Katy Wild, Frank Finlay. High-powered shock scenes involving swarming bees are only worthwhile attraction in horror film marred by dull script.

Deadly Companions, The (1961) C-90m. ****½** D: Sam Peckinpah. Maureen O'Hara, Brian Keith, Steve Cochran, Chill Wills. Ex-army officer accidentally kills O'Hara's son and he makes amends by escorting the funeral procession through Indian country.

Deadly Dream (1971) C-73m. TVM D: Alf Kjellin. Lloyd Bridges, Janet Leigh, Leif Erickson, Carl Betz, Don Stroud, Richard Jaeckel, Phillip Pine. Poor examination of dream-vs.-reality issue. Man has recurring and episodic dream that strange men belonging to "tribunal" chase after him. Adequate performances, but script and direction are real nightmare. Average.

Deadly Game (1977) C-100m. TVM D: Lane Slate. Andy Griffith, Mitzi Hoag, Claude Earl Jones, Sharon Spellman, Dan O'Herlihy, Morgan Woodward. Sequel to WINTER KILL offers Griffith in further adventures of small town sheriff Abel Marsh. Here he investigates the destruction and scandal caused by chemical spillage from an army tanker truck. Average.

Deadly Harvest (1972) C-73m. TVM D: Michael O'Herlihy. Richard Boone, Patty Duke, Michael Constantine, Murray Hamilton, Jack Kruschen. Semi-idyllic existence of ex-spy-turned-grape-grower shattered when bomb shows up in his pickup truck. Frustratingly uneven; some good performances, some bad; occasional good mood, often too rushed. Average.

Deadly Hero (1976) C-102m. ** D: Ivan Nagy. Don Murray, Diahn Williams, James Earl Jones, Lilia Skala, George S. Irving, Cochata Ferrell. Interesting premise: righteous cop (Murray) saves woman's life by killing her attacker (Jones) . . . but then woman begins to question the cop's actions and motives. Performances outshine violent presentation.

Deadly Hunt, The (1971) C-74m. TVM D: John Newland. Jim Hutton, Anjanette Comer, Tony Franciosa, Peter Lawford, Tim McIntire. Young businessman and wife (Hutton & Comer) on hunting trip discover themselves targets of paid assassins, caught in forest fire. Good location and stunt work major distinctions of acceptable chase-thriller. Above average.

Deadly Is the Female: SEE **Gun Crazy**

Deadly Mantis, The (1957) 78m. ** D: Nathan Juran. Craig Stevens, William Hopper, Alix Talton, Donald Randolph. N.Y.C. is threatened again, here by giant insect heading south

after Arctic tour de force; obligatory love story interrupts special effects.

Deadly Ray from Mars, The (1938) 99m. **½ D: Ford Beebe, Robert Hill. Buster Crabbe, Jean Rogers, Charles Middleton, Frank Shannon, Donald Kerr, Beatrice Roberts. Newly edited version of FLASH GORDON'S TRIP TO MARS serial. Flash, Dale Arden, and Dr. Zarkov seek mysterious force which drains nitrogen from earth's atmosphere, eventually discover Ming's behind it all. Uninspired handling of original footage.

Deadly Strangers (1974-British) C-93m. *** D: Sidney Hayers. Hayley Mills, Simon Ward, Sterling Hayden, Ken Hutchison, Peter Jeffrey. Lurid, exciting thriller about Mills offering a ride to young man, unaware that a violent patient has escaped from a nearby mental hospital. Beware of cuts.

Deadly Tower, The (1975) C-100m. TVM D: Jerry Jameson. Kurt Russell, Richard Yniguez, John Forsythe, Ned Beatty, Pernell Roberts, Clifton James, Paul Carr, Alan Vint, Pepe Serena, Maria Elena Cordero. Fact-based drama about Charles Whitman (Russell), who holed up in University of Texas tower in August, 1966, and fired at all in sight, killing 13 and wounding 33. Authentic, well-made recreation of the fateful event, with acting honors going to Yniguez as Mexican-American police officer and Beatty as passerby who reluctantly agrees to help him. Above average.

Deadly Trackers, The (1973) C-110m. BOMB. D: Barry Shear. Richard Harris, Rod Taylor, Al Lettieri, Neville Brand, William Smith, Isela Vega. Deadly oater dwells on violence. Harris, Irish sheriff of a small Texas town, trails bank robber Taylor and gang to Mexico to avenge the deaths of wife and son. Sam Fuller wrote the story and was the original director.

Deadly Trap, The (1971-French-Italian) C-96m. BOMB D: Rene Clement. Faye Dunaway, Frank Langella, Barbara Parkins, Karen Glanguernon, Maurice Ronet. A deadly bore, about an industrious espionage organization that goes after one-time member Langella by harrassing his emotionally fragile wife (Dunaway).

Deadly Triangle, The (1977) C-78m. TVM D: Charles Dubin. Dale Robinette, Taylor Larcher, Geoffrey

Lewis, Robert Lansing, Diana Muldaur, Linda Scruggs Bogart. Ex-Olympic downhill racer turned sheriff investigates a murder in his ski-resort town. Run-of-the-mill series pilot.

Deadman's Curve (1978) C-100m. TVM D: Richard Compton. Richard Hatch, Bruce Davison, Pamela Bellwood, Susan Sullivan, Dick Clark, Wolfman Jack. Passable biography based on the meteoric tragedy-marred careers of Jan Berry and Dean Torrence, late '50s rock idols who popularized the Surfing Sound. Average.

Dealing: Or the Berkeley-to-Boston Forty-Brick Lost-Bag Blues (1972) C-99m. ***½ D: Paul Williams. Barbara Hershey, Robert F. Lyons, Charles Durning, Joy Bang, John Lithgow. If this supremely enjoyable comedy-thriller about marijuana dealing makes it to TV at all, many of the nude (and also the best) scenes will be cut. Well-acted and directed film is much better than original novel with same title.

Dear Brat (1951) 82m. **½ D: William A. Seiter. Mona Freeman, Billy DeWolfe, Edward Arnold, Lyle Bettger. Another follow-up to DEAR RUTH has Freeman in title role involved with a crook trying to reform.

Dear Brigitte (1965) C-100m. **½ D: Henry Koster. James Stewart, Glynis Johns, Fabian, Billy Mumy, John Williams, Jack Kruschen, Ed Wynn. Guest: Brigitte Bardot. Good cast in OK family farce about an 8-year-old genius (Stewart's son, Mumy) with a crush on Brigitte Bardot. Bardot makes a brief appearance at the end. Film tries hard to be whimsical but is contrived instead.

Dear, Dead Delilah (1972) C-90m. *½ D: John Farris. Agnes Moorehead, Will Geer, Michael Ansara, Patricia Carmichael, Dennis Patrick. Low-budgeter about grisly competition for $600,000 buried somewhere around home of dying Moorehead. Filmed in Nashville, originally 95m. For axe-murder aficionados only.

Dear Heart (1964) 114m. *** D: Delbert Mann. Glenn Ford, Geraldine Page, Michael Anderson, Jr., Barbara Nichols, Angela Lansbury, Alice Pearce, Mary Wickes. Winning romance story with Ford and Page visiting N.Y.C. for conventions, falling in love; excellent characterizations with fine comedy supporting players.

Dear Inspector (1978-French) C-

105m. *** D: Philippe De Broca. Annie Girardot, Philippe Noiret, Catherine Aric, Hubert Deschamps, Paulette Dubost. Pleasant, if ephemeral and ultimately silly comedy about the offbeat romance between a lady sleuth and a droll musician. Girardot and Noiret click together, and Aric is a real looker. Originally called DEAR DETECTIVE.

Dear Ruth (1947) 95m. **½ D: William D. Russell. Joan Caulfield, William Holden, Mona Freeman, Edward Arnold, Billy DeWolfe. Bouncy, naive comedy of errors with young girl pretending to be her older sister to impress soldier she corresponds with.

Dear Wife (1949) 88m. **½ D: Richard Haydn. Joan Caulfield, William Holden, Edward Arnold, Billy DeWolfe, Mona Freeman. Follow-up to DEAR RUTH focuses on Freeman's antics to get Holden elected to the state senate, although her politician father Arnold is seeking same position.

Death Among Friends (1975) C-78m. TVM D: Paul Wendkos. Kate Reid, John Anderson, A. Martinez, Martin Balsam, Jack Cassidy, Paul Henreid, Pamela Hemsley, William Smith, Lynda Day George, Denver Pyle. Affable lady police lieutenant tries to solve the murder of an international financier. Reid nearly succeeds in pulling this police story up from the predictable. Average.

Death and the Maiden: SEE Hawkins on Murder

Death at Love House (1976) C-78m. TVM D: E. W. Swackhamer. Robert Wagner, Kate Jackson, Sylvia Sidney, Joan Blondell, Dorothy Lamour, John Carradine, Bill Macy, Marianna Hill. "Nostalgia thriller" about obsession of young writer (Wagner) for long-dead movie queen who was supposed to have had an affair with his father and whose spirit reaches out from her glass tomb to destroy him. Creepy and unbelievable, but it's fun to see screen veterans and magnificent Harold Lloyd estate where this was filmed. Average.

Death Be Not Proud (1975) C-100m. TVM D: Donald Wrye. Arthur Hill, Jane Alexander, Robby Benson, Linden Chiles, Ralph Clanton, Wendy Phillips. Sterling version of John Gunther's 1949 account of his son's courageous battle against the brain tumor that killed him at 17. Perceptive portrayals by Hill as famed author and Benson as young

Johnny, with a glowing one by Jane Alexander. Memorable true-life drama. Above average.

Death Cruise (1974) C-78m. TVM D: Ralph Senesky. Richard Long, Polly Bergen, Edward Albert, Kate Jackson, Celeste Holm, Tom Bosley, Michael Constantine, Cesare Danova. Three couples win all-expenses-paid vacations, then realize on board ship that they are marked for death. Disaster drama sails along familiar seas. Below average.

Death in Canaan, A (1978) C-120m. TVM D: Tony Richardson. Stefanie Powers, Paul Clemens, Tom Atkins, Brian Dennehy, Jacqueline Brooks, James Sutorius. Dramatization of the sensational Connecticut murder case involving a local teenager suspected of the mutilation murder of his mother. Tony Richardson made his American TV directing debut here, and Paul Clemens, son of actress Eleanor Parker, made his acting debut as Peter Reilly, the accused. Above average.

Death in Small Doses (1957) 79m. *½ D: Joseph M. Newman. Peter Graves, Mala Powers, Chuck Connors, Merry Anders. Low-budget drama of narcotics use among truck drivers; dull presentation.

Death in Venice (1971-Italian) C-130m. ***½ D: Luchino Visconti. Dirk Bogarde, Mark Burns, Marisa Berenson, Bjorn Andresen, Silvana Mangano, Luigi Battaglia. Study of an artist, his loves, his homosexuality, and continuous search for beauty. Thomas Mann's slow-moving classic is splendidly brought to the screen.

Death Kiss, The (1933) 75m. *** D: Edwin L. Marin. Bela Lugosi, David Manners, Adrienne Ames, John Wray, Vince Barnett, Edward Van Sloan. Minor but entertaining whodunit set inside a movie studio, where an actor is killed while filming a scene. Nice atmosphere of a studio at work.

Death Moon (1978) C-89m. TVM D: Bruce Kessler. France Nuyen, Robert Foxworth, Joe Penny, Barbara Trentham, Debralee Scott. Beautiful Hawaii, vacationing executive, local witch with supernatural powers. Below average.

Death of a Gunfighter (1969) C-100m. **½ D: Allen Smithee. Richard Widmark, Lena Horne, John Saxon, Michael McGreevey, Darleen Carr, Carroll O'Connor, Kent Smith. Down-

beat but interesting Western drama of unwanted sheriff who refuses to be fired. Horne wasted as Widmark's occasional love interest. Directed by Robert Totten and Don Siegel, credited to fictitious Smithee.

Death of a Salesman (1951) 115m. ***½ D: Laslo Benedek. Fredric March, Mildred Dunnock, Kevin McCarthy, Cameron Mitchell. Arthur Miller social drama of middle-aged man at end of emotional rope is transformed to the screen intact, with stagy flashbacks. March in title role can't fathom why business and family life failed; Dunnock is patient wife; McCarthy and Mitchell are disillusioned sons. Superb.

Death of a Scoundrel (1956) 119m. **½ D: Charles Martin. George Sanders, Yvonne de Carlo, Zsa Zsa Gabor, Victor Jory. Episodic chronicle of foreigner coming to U.S., ingratiating himself with an assortment of women whom he cons into helping him get ahead. Low-budget but fascinating.

Death of Her Innocence SEE: Our Time

Death of Innocence, A (1971) C-73m. TVM D: Paul Wendkos. Shelley Winters, Arthur Kennedy, Tisha Sterling, Ann Sothern, John Randolph. Parents from Idaho (Winters & Randolph) journey to New York to attend daughter's murder trial; visit becomes major emotional experience for mother. Better than average script, overblown performances, good direction. Above average.

Death of Me Yet, The (1971) C-73m. TVM D: John Llewellyn Moxey. Doug McClure, Darren McGavin, Richard Basehart, Rosemary Forsyth, Meg Foster, Dana Elcar. Happily married newspaper editor in small town, actually ex-spy for U.S. in Russia, suddenly questioned by government agent (McGavin) and sought by another agent. Good suspense, adequate performances. Above average.

Death of Ocean View Park, The (1979) C-100m. TVM D: E. W. Swackhamer. Mike Connors, Martin Landau, Diana Canova, Perry Lang, James Stephens, Caroline McWilliams, Mare Winningham. Hurricane levels a seaside amusement park on a holiday weekend, and lots of familiar TV personalities panic with conviction. Special effects are surprisingly mediocre, considering that an actual park was destroyed for the film. Average.

Death of Richie, The (1977) C-100m. TVM D: Paul Wendkos. Ben Gazzara, Robby Benson, Lance Kerwin, Eileen Brennan, Charles Fleischer, Clint Howard. A family is torn apart by teen-aged son's drug addiction. Gazzara is splendid as straight-arrow father who brings himself to kill the boy; intelligent script from Thomas Thompson's nonfiction book *Richie* occasionally becomes maudlin. Average.

Death on the Freeway (1979) C-100m. TVM D: Hal Needham. Shelley Hack, George Hamilton, Frank Gorshin, Peter Graves, Harriet Nelson, Barbara Rush, Dinah Shore, Abe Vigoda, Hal Needham. Comely TV reporter goes after the maniac methodically terrorizing lone women drivers with his van on the L.A. freeways. Stunt work (supervised by Needham) more than compensates for nonacting of the leading lady. Average.

Death on the Nile (1978-British) C-140m. **½ D: John Guillermin. Peter Ustinov, Bette Davis, David Niven, Mia Farrow, Angela Lansbury, George Kennedy, Maggie Smith, Jack Warden, Lois Chiles, Olivia Hussey. Visually sumptuous but only marginally engrossing Agatha Christie mystery has Hercule Poiret (Ustinov) playing detective games with a dozen or so suspects after the murder of Chiles. A deserving Oscar winner for costume design.

Death Penalty (1980) C-100m. TVM D: Waris Hussein. Colleen Dewhurst, Dana Elcar, Joe Morton, David Labiosa, Dan Hedaya, Ted Ross. Slow-moving drama about a strong-willed psychologist's struggle to save a street-gang teenager from going to the electric chair for a double murder. Average.

Death Race (1973) C-73m. TVM D: David Lowell Rich, Lloyd Bridges, Doug McClure, Roy Thinnes, Eric Braeden, Dennis Rucker. Two Americans in wounded fighter plane vs. German tank separated from its squad; drawn-out, boring WW2 adventure. Below average.

Death Race 2000 (1975) C-80m. **½ D: Paul Bartel. David Carradine, Simone Griffith, Sylvester Stallone, Louisa Moritz, Mary Woronov. Outrageous tongue-in-cheek action film about futuristic society where no-holds-barred auto race is the national sport, and violence is cheered. Fast-paced fun.

Death Rage (1976-Italian) C-98m. *½ D: Anthony M. Dawson. Yul Brynner, Barbara Bouchet, Martin Balsam, Massimo Ranieri. Brynner plays American hit man who's duped into agreeing to kill underworld kingpin in Naples. All this picture kills is time. TV print runs 90m.

Death Rides a Horse (1969-Italian) C-114m. ** D: Giulio Petroni. Lee Van Cleef, John Phillip Law. Luigi Pistilli, Anthony Dawson (Antonio Margheretti). Long, drawn-out Italian revenge Western with Law seeking murderers of his family, unaware that his companion (Van Cleef) is one of them.

Death Scream (1975) C-100m. TVM D: Richard T. Heffron. Raul Julia, John Ryan, Phillip Clark, Lucie Arnaz, Edward Asner, Art Carney, Diahann Carroll, Kate Jackson, Cloris Leachman, Tina Louise, Nancy Walker, Eric Braeden, Allyn Ann McLerie, Todd Sussman. Thriller, based on Kitty Genovese murder in New York, involves fifteen neighbors who witnessed killing, did nothing to help, and refused to co-operate with police. Provocative theme deteriorates into formula cop story. Subsequently retitled THE WOMAN WHO CRIED MURDER. Average.

Death Sentence (1974) C-78m. TVM D: E. W. Swackhamer. Cloris Leachman, Laurence Luckinbill, Nick Nolte, William Schallert, Alan Oppenheimer, Yvonne Wilder. Juror Leachman discovers that the wrong man is on trial for murder and finds her own life threatened by the real one—her husband. If you can accept a sequestered juror slipping away at night to play sleuth, you'll accept anything. Below average.

Death Squad, The (1974) C-78m. TVM D: Harry Falk. Robert Forster, Michelle Phillips, Claude Akins, Mark Goddard, Melvyn Douglas, Ken Tobey, Dennis Patrick. Tough ex-cop is recruited to root out rotten apples on police roster, a self-styled assassination squad that methodically executes criminals released on legal technicalities. If it all sounds familiar, refer to MAGNUM FORCE. Below average.

Death Stalk (1974) C-78m. TVM D: Robert Day. Vince Edwards, Anjanette Comer, Robert 'Webber, Carol Lynley, Vic Morrow, Neville

Brand, Norman Fell. Two men desperately try to save their wives, abducted by four convicts fleeing in rubber rafts down treacherous river. Hokey suspense tale wastes good cast and splendid scenery, including the expected rapids-run. Below average.

Death Takes a Holiday (1934) 78m. ***½ D: Mitchell Leisen. Fredric March, Evelyn Venable, Guy Standing, Gail Patrick, Helen Westley. Fascinating allegory about Death (March) entering the human world to discover what makes us tick, and falling in love.

Death Takes a Holiday (1971) C-73m. TVM D: Robert Butler. Melvyn Douglas, Myrna Loy, Yvette Mimieux, Monte Markham, Maureen Reagan. Silly update of 1934 version with Death on Earth trying to understand why people cling to existence, falling in love with beautiful woman. Unbearable script, sloppy direction. Below average.

Death Weekend SEE: House by the Lake

Death Wish (1974) C-93m. ***½ D: Michael Winner. Charles Bronson, Hope Lange, Vincent Gardenia, Steven Keats, William Redfield, Stuart Margolin. Audience manipulation at its zenith: businessman Bronson's wife and daughter are savagely raped, and the wife dies, turning mild-mannered Bronson into a vigilante on N.Y.C. streets. Chilling but irresistible.

Deathdream (1972) C-90m. *½ D: Bob Clark. John Marley, Richard Backus, Lynn Carlin, Henderson Forsythe. Backus is Vietnam vet, thought dead, who returns to his family a virtual stranger with a murderous lust for blood. Grim, fairly shocking.

Deathmaster, The (1972) C-88m. ** D: Ray Danton. Robert Quarry, Bill Ewing, Brenda Dickson, John Fiedler, Betty Ann Rees, William Jordan. Spellbinding stranger (Quarry) leads on a group of unsuspecting hippies; their "guru" turns out to be a vampire in this bloody, run-of-the-mill outing.

Deathsport (1978) C-90m. ** D: Henry Suso, Allan Arkush. David Carradine, Claudia Jennings, Richard Lynch, David McLean, Jesse Vint. Follow-up to DEATH RACE 2000 again puts Carradine into future world where he and Jennings battle destructo-cycles to survive. Not as

campy or enjoyable as earlier film, though Claudia unclothed is a visual asset.

Decameron Nights (1953-British) C-87m. ** D: Hugo Fregonese. Joan Fontaine, Louis Jourdan, Binnie Barnes, Joan Collins, Marjorie Rhodes. Distillation of robust medieval tales with Jourdan the storyspinning Boccaccio seeking fair Fontaine's love.

Deception (1946) 112m. ***½ D: Irving Rapper. Bette Davis, Claude Rains, Paul Henreid, John Abbott, Benson Fong. Acting duel de force by Davis and Rains as pianist and her jealous benefactor, with Henreid overshadowed by star duo.

Decision Against Time (1957-British) 87m. **½ D: Charles Crichton. Jack Hawkins, Elizabeth Sellars, Eddie Byrne, Lionel Jeffries, Donald Pleasence. Hawkins is effective as test pilot giving all to save troubled craft for boss and to protect job future.

Decision at Sundown (1957) C-95m. **½ D: Budd Boetticher. Randolph Scott, John Carroll, Karen Steele, Noah Beery, John Litel. Scott tracks down man supposedly responsible for his wife's suicide in this odd but interesting Western.

Decision Before Dawn (1951) 119m. *** D: Anatole Litvak. Richard Basehart, Gary Merrill, Oskar Werner, Hildegarde Neff. Werner is exceptional in realistic WW2 thriller of Nazi P.O.W. returning to Germany as American spy.

Decision of Christopher Blake, The (1948) 75m. **½ D: Peter Godfrey. Alexis Smith, Robert Douglas, Cecil Kellaway, Ted Donaldson, John Hoyt. Insipid drama of child suffering from his parents' divorce. Not slickly done, with sugary ending.

Decks Ran Red, The (1958) 84m. **½ D: Andrew L. Stone. James Mason, Dorothy Dandridge, Broderick Crawford, Stuart Whitman. Bizarre sea yarn with strange casting, involves sailors' attempt to murder freighter captain and use vessel for salvage.

Decline and Fall of a Bird Watcher (1969-British) C-86m. ** D: John Krish. Robin Phillips, Colin Blakely, Leo McKern, Genevieve Page, Felix Aylmer, Robert Harris, Donald Wolfit, Patrick Magee. Uneven, often labored satirical farce about a young man who joins faculty of strange boys' school and becomes involved with manipulative older woman

(Page). Adapted from Evelyn Waugh's novel.

Deep, The (1977) C-123m. ** D: Peter Yates. Robert Shaw, Jacqueline Bisset, Nick Nolte, Louis Gossett, Eli Wallach, Robert Tessier. Endless film of Peter Benchley's novel about innocent couple who hit on treasure and drugs while scuba-diving off Bermuda coast. Gratuitous violence and titillation—not to mention unbelievable plot—sink this handsome production. NBC added 53m. for its first network showing.

Deep Blue Sea, The (1955-British) C-99m. **½ D: Anatole Litvak. Vivien Leigh, Kenneth More, Eric Portman, Emlyn Williams. Terence Rattigan play of marital infidelity and the repercussions on Leigh, frustrated well-married woman; slow-moving, but thoughtfully presented.

Deep in My Heart (1954) C-132m. **½ D: Stanley Donen. Jose Ferrer, Merle Oberon, Helen Traubel, Doe Avedon, Walter Pidgeon, Paul Henreid. Sigmund Romberg's life bad excuse for horde of guest stars, but musical numbers are satisfying. Guests include Ann Miller, Gene Kelly, Tony Martin, Rosemary Clooney.

Deep Six, The (1958) C-105m. **½ D: Rudolph Mate. Alan Ladd, Dianne Foster, William Bendix, Keenan Wynn, James Whitmore, Joey Bishop. Ladd is Quaker naval officer during WW2 who compensates for past inaction by heading dangerous shore mission; Bendix gives able support.

Deep Valley (1947) 104m. *** D: Jean Negulesco. Ida Lupino, Dane Clark, Wayne Morris, Fay Bainter, Henry Hull. Into Lupino's humdrum farm life comes a gangster from nearby prison camp; first rate cast in excellent drama.

Deep Waters (1948) 85m. ** D: Henry King. Dana Andrews, Jean Peters, Cesar Romero, Dean Stockwell, Anne Revere, Ed Begley. Slick empty tale of fisherman Andrews and landlubber Peters brought together by cute little Stockwell.

Deer Hunter, The (1978) C-183m. **** D: Michael Cimino. Robert DeNiro, John Cazale, John Savage, Meryl Streep, Christopher Walken, George Dzunda, Chuck Aspegren. Stunning film about young Pennsylvania steelworkers, their lives before, during, and after wartime duty in Vietnam. Long but not overlong, this sensitive, painful, evocative work packs an emotional wallop. 5 Academy Awards include Best Picture, Best Director, Best Supporting Actor (Walken).

Deerslayer, The (1957) C-78m. *½ D: Kurt Neumann. Lex Barker, Forrest Tucker, Rita Moreno, Jay C. Flippen. James Fenimore Cooper's Leatherstocking novel of white man (Barker) raised by Indians is given pedestrian treatment, virtually all indoor sets and rear-screen projection.

Deerslayer, The (1978) C-74m. TVM D: Dick Friedenberg. Steve Forrest, Ned Romero, John Anderson, Victor Mohica, Joan Prather, Charles Dierkop. Trim "Classics Illustrated" treatment of the James Fenimore Cooper tale, a follow-up to a companion version of LAST OF THE MOHICANS also with Forrest and Romero as Hawkeye and Chingachgook. Average.

Defection of Simas Kudirka, The (1978) C-100m. TVM D: David Lowell Rich. Alan Arkin, Richard Jordan, Donald Pleasence, John McMartin, Shirley Knight. Absorbing drama, based on the Lithuanian seaman's abortive 1970 attempt at freedom by jumping ship in Portsmouth, New Hampshire. Arkin added another intriguing portrait to his personal acting gallery; and director Rich won an Emmy Award. Above average.

Defector, The (1966) C-106m. **½ D: Raoul Levy. Montgomery Clift, Hardy Kruger, Roddy McDowall, David Opatoshu. Hackneyed Cold War spy trivia filmed in Europe, interesting only as Clift's last film; good cameo by McDowall.

Defiant Ones, The (1958) 97m. **** D: Stanley Kramer. Tony Curtis, Sidney Poitier, Theodore Bikel, Charles McGraw, Cara Williams, Lon Chaney, Jr. Engrossing story of two escaped convicts (Curtis and Poitier) shackled together as they flee from police in the South. Fine performances by Williams and Chaney as people they meet along the way.

Delancey Street: The Crisis Within (1975) C-78m. TVM D: James Frawley. Walter McGinn, Carmine Caridi, Michael Conrad, Lou Gossett, Mark Hamill, Barbara Babcock. Fact-based drama of San Francisco halfway house helping ex-cons and former junkies to get back on their feet.

Earnest performance, admirable story. Above average.

Delicate Balance, A (1973) **C-132m. ** D:** Tony Richardson. Katharine Hepburn, Paul Scofield, Lee Remick, Kate Reid, Joseph Cotten, Betsy Blair. Edward Albee's Pulitzer Prize-winning play about a neurotic Connecticut family and the old friends who decide to move in with them indefinitely makes for stagy, uninvolving film, extraordinary cast notwithstanding. An American Film Theater Production.

Delicate Delinquent, The (1957) **100m. *** D:** Don McGuire. Jerry Lewis, Martha Hyer, Darren McGavin, Horace McMahon. Jerry's first solo effort after Dean Martin split-up has him as delinquent who becomes a cop with McGavin's help. Not as wacky as later vehicles, this one hits the right note.

Delicious (1931) **106m. *½ D:** David Butler. Janet Gaynor, Charles Farrell, El Brendel, Raoul Roulien, Virginia Cherrill. Insipid romance; Janet as Irish colleen emigrating to N.Y.C. who falls in love with wealthy Farrell. Brief highlights in Gershwin score are bizarre dream sequence of Janet's welcome to America, and "New York Rhapsody."

Delightfully Dangerous (1945) **93m. **½ D:** Arthur Lubin. Jane Powell, Ralph Bellamy, Constance Moore, Morton Gould Orchestra, Arthur Treacher, Louise Beavers. Pleasant froth of sisters Powell (sedate) and Moore (stripper) competing for Bellamy's love.

Deliver Us From Evil (1973) **C-78m. TVM** D: Boris Sagal. George Kennedy, Jan-Michael Vincent, Bradford Dillman, Jack Weston, Jim Davis, Charles Aidman, Allen Pinson. Five "honest" men catch and kill a skyjacker during a camping trip and then get greedy about his $600,000 loot. So-so variation on THE TREASURE OF SIERRA MADRE. Average.

Deliverance (1972) **C-109m. **** D:** John Boorman. Jon Voight, Burt Reynolds, Ned Beatty, Ronny Cox, Billy McKinney, Herbert "Cowboy" Coward, James Dickey. Superlative recreation of Dickey novel of four Atlanta businessmen who get more than they bargained for during a weekend canoe trip. McKinney and Coward are two of the most terrifying film villains in history.

Delphi Bureau, The (1972) **C-99m. TVM** D: Paul Wendkos. Laurence Luckinbill, Joanna Pettet, Celeste Holm, Bob Crane, Cameron Mitchell, Dean Jagger, Bradford Dillman. Fast-paced, sometimes effective cold-war thriller with U.S. in balance-of-power struggle. Shallow characterizations in this pilot for TV series; average.

Delta County, U.S.A. (1977) **C-100m. TVM** D: Glenn Jordan. Jim Antonio, Doney Oatman, Peter Donat, Joanna Miles, Jeff Conaway, Robert Hays, Lola Albright, Michele Carey. Contemporary multi-story drama dissecting life in rural Southern community, involving old-line families, traditional values and restless youth. PEYTON PLACE with a different accent. Average.

Delta Factor, The (1970) **C-91m. ** D:** Tay Garnett. Christopher George, Yvette Mimieux, Diane McBain, Ralph Taeger. OK Mickey Spillane tale about a private eye on a CIA mission to rescue a scientist imprisoned on an island.

Dementia 13 (1963) **81m. ** D:** Francis Ford Coppola. William Campbell, Luana Anders, Bart Patton, Mary Mitchel, Patrick Magee. Gory horror film, set in Ireland, about an axe-murder that takes place during reading of a will. Coppola's screen debut, filmed for about 29¢ for producer Roger Corman, may be worth a look for curiosity's sake.

Demetrius and the Gladiators (1954) **C-101m. **½ D:** Delmer Daves. Victor Mature, Susan Hayward, Michael Rennie, Debra Paget, Anne Bancroft, Richard Egan, Ernest Borgnine. Hokey sequel to THE ROBE has Emperor Caligula (Jay Robinson) searching for magic robe of Christ; Mature dallies with royal Hayward.

Demon (1977) **C-95m. **½ D:** Larry Cohen. Tony Lo Bianco, Sandy Dennis, Sylvia Sidney, Deborah Raffin, Sam Levene, Richard Lynch, Mike Kellin. Weird, confused shocker by the maker of IT'S ALIVE. New York cop Lo Bianco investigates motiveless killings by ordinary people possessed by demons. Some good scenes. Formerly titled GOD TOLD ME TO.

Demon Planet, The SEE: Planet of the Vampires

Demon Seed (1977) **C-94m. ***½ D:** Donald Cammell. Julie Christie, Fritz Weaver, Gerrit Graham, Berry Kroeger, Lisa Lu. Intelligent futuristic thriller, provocatively written, stylishly directed, and well-acted, especially by Christie, the beauty terrorized by an ultra-sophisticated computer (voice of Robert Vaughn) that has decided to take over the world. As riveting as it is bizarre.

Demoniaque (1958-French) **97m.** **½ D: Luis Saslavsky. Francois Perier, Micheline Presle, Jeanne Moreau, Madeleine Robinson. Perky yarn of French P.O.W. escaping and seeking refuge with girl his dead buddy romanced via the mails; girl believes him to be the letter-writer.

Den of Doom SEE: **Glass Cage**

Dentist in the Chair (1961-British) **84m.** ** D: Don Chaffey. Peggy Cummins, Bob Monkhouse, Kenneth Connor, Eric Barker. Occasionally amusing shenanigans of dentists involved in crooked dealings, trying to undo their mischievious thefts.

Denver and Rio Grande, The (1952) **C-89m.** **½ D: Byron Haskin. Edmond O'Brien, Sterling Hayden, Dean Jagger, ZaSu Pitts, J. Carrol Naish. Another railroad rivalry Western as two competing companies battle elements and each other to complete tie-line through title area.

Deported (1950) **80m.** **½ D: Robert Siodmak, Marta Toren, Jeff Chandler, Claude Dauphin, Carlo Rizzo. Engaging gangster yarn with Chandler deported to Italy, involved in the black market, but going straight to win Toren's love.

Deputies, The (1976) **C-100m. TVM** D: Virgil W. Vogel. Jim Davis, Don Johnson, Charles Martin Smith, Nicholas Hammond, Barbara Parkins, Glenn Corbett, Andrew Prine, Moses Gunn, Darleen Carr. Frontier Lawman Davis and young deputies seek psychopath with vendetta against prostitutes. Old West melodrama best described as "The Rookies" on horseback. Average.

Derby (1971) **C-96m.** **½ D: Robert Kaylor. Charlie O'Connell, Eddie Krebs, Mike Snell, Christina Snell, Butch Snell. Documentary about roller derby stars and hopefuls is uneven; some scenes are vivid, others talky and dull. Provides a good look at one segment of Middle America.

Derby Day (1952-British) **84m.** **½ D: Herbert Wilcox. Anna Neagle, Michael Wilding, John McCallum, Googie Withers. Diverting study of human nature, as an assortment of people intermingle at Epsom Downs

race track. Retitled: **FOUR AGAINST FATE.**

Desert Attack (1960-British) **132m.** *** D: J. Lee Thompson. John Mills, Sylvia Syms, Anthony Quayle, Harry Andrews, Diane Clare. Well-handled psychological drama of British ambulance officer, two nurses, and a German soldier brought together in African desert. Original title: ICE COLD IN ALEX.

Desert Desperados (1959) **81m.** *½ D: Steve Sekely. Ruth Roman, Akim Tamiroff, Otello Toso, Gianni Glori. Unsuccessful mishmash of romance and unconvincing intrigue set in Egyptian desert; wasting Roman's most capable talents. Retitled: THE SINNER.

Desert Fox, The (1951) **88m.** *** D: Henry Hathaway. James Mason, Cedric Hardwicke, Jessica Tandy, Luther Adler. Mason standout as Field Marshal Rommel in sensitive account of his military defeat in WW2 Africa and disillusioned return to Hitler Germany. Mason repeated role in later DESERT RATS.

Desert Fury (1947) **C-95m.** **½ D: Lewis Allen. John Hodiak, Lizabeth Scott, Burt Lancaster, Mary Astor, Wendell Corey. Mild drama of love and mystery among gamblers, stolen by Astor in bristling character portrayal.

Desert Hawk, The (1950) **C-77m.** ** D: Frederick de Cordova. Yvonne De Carlo, Richard Greene, Jackie Gleason, Rock Hudson, George Macready. Pat Arabian desert tale, interesting for Gleason and Hudson in secondary roles.

Desert Hell (1958) **82m.** ** D: Charles Marquis Warren. Brian Keith, Barbara Hale, Richard Denning, Johnny Desmond. French Foreign Legion battles warring Arabs to save peace; very little of promised action given to viewer.

Desert Legion (1953) **C-86m.** ** D: Joseph Pevney. Alan Ladd, Richard Conte, Arlene Dahl, Akim Tamiroff. Mild Ladd entry of battling French Foreign Legion.

Desert Patrol (1958-British) **78m.** **½ D: Guy Green. Richard Attenborough, John Gregson, Michael Craig, Vincent Ball. Staunch account of British patrol attempting to blow up Axis fuel dump before pending WW2 battle of El Alamein. Originally titled SEA OF SAND.

Desert Rats, The (1953) **88m.** *** D: Robert Wise. Richard Burton, James

Mason, Robert Newton, Chips Rafferty. Fine WW2 actioner with Mason convincing as Field Marshal Rommel (played same role in earlier DESERT FOX); Burton is British commando trying to ward off Germans in North Africa.

Desert Song, The (1953) C-110m. **½ D: H. Bruce Humberstone. Kathryn Grayson, Gordon MacRae, Steve Cochran, Raymond Massey. Third filming of Sigmund Romberg operetta set in Africa creaks along on thin plot. American MacRae is secret leader of good natives (Riffs) in battle against evil Arabs. Songs: "The Riff Song," "One Alone."

Deserter, The (1971) C-99m. *½ D: Burt Kennedy. Bekim Fehmiu, John Huston, Richard Crenna, Chuck Connors, Ricardo Montalban, Ian Bannen, Brandon de Wilde, Slim Pickens, Woody Strode, Patrick Wayne. Dull Cavalry pic about Indian fighting on Mexican border. Cast is capable, except for Fehmiu, who didn't improve after THE ADVENTURERS.

Design for Living (1933) 90m. ***½ D: Ernst Lubitsch. Gary Cooper, Fredric March, Miriam Hopkins, Edward Everett Horton, Franklin Pangborn. Hopkins leaves starving suitors Cooper and March to marry wealthy Horton in chic fluff by Noel Coward, with most of the witty innuendos left intact. Delightful.

Design for Scandal (1941) 85m. **½ D: Norman Taurog. Rosalind Russell, Walter Pidgeon, Edward Arnold, Lee Bowman, Jane Rogers, Mary Beth Hughes, Guy Kibbee. Deft performances by stars in comedy of reporter Pidgeon doing sensational story involving prominent female judge Russell.

Designing Woman (1957) C-118m. *** D: Vincente Minnelli. Gregory Peck, Lauren Bacall, Dolores Gray, Sam Levene, Chuck Connors. Sportswriter and fashion designer run head-on in this chic comedy reminiscent of the great Hepburn-Tracy comedies. Bacall and Peck do their best.

Desire (1936) 89m. *** D: Frank Borzage. Marlene Dietrich, Gary Cooper, John Halliday, William Frawley, Ernest Cossart, Akim Tamiroff. American car-designer Cooper falls in love with jewel thief Dietrich. Sophisticated romancer set in Spain; Marlene sings "Awake In A Dream."

Desire in the Dust (1960) 102m. **½

D: William F. Claxton. Raymond Burr, Martha Hyer, Joan Bennett, Ken Scott. Good casting carries this turgid soaper of a Southern aristocrat with a yen for politics, who tries to hide the shady past of some family members.

Desire Me (1947) 91m. ** D: George Cukor, Mervyn LeRoy. Greer Garson, Robert Mitchum, Richard Hart, George Zucco, Morris Ankrum. Weak melodramatic romance with poor Garson caught between new love and old husband, presumed dead, who returns to make problems. Familiar story not helped by limp script.

Desire Under the Elms (1958) 114m. **½ D: Delbert Mann. Sophia Loren, Anthony Perkins, Burl Ives, Frank Overton. Eugene O'Neill stage piece about family hatred and greed for land. Loren miscast as Ives' young wife in love with stepson Perkins, but she sparks some life into brooding account of 19th-century New England farm story.

Desiree (1954) C-110m. **½ D: Henry Koster. Marlon Brando, Jean Simmons, Merle Oberon, Michael Rennie, Cameron Mitchell, Elizabeth Sellars. Tepid, elaborate costumer: Brando plays a confused Napoleon, Simmons his seamstress love who marries another man; Oberon, Empress Josephine (quite lovely). Fiction and fact are muddled backdrop for rise and fall of the Emperor; few action scenes.

Desk Set (1957) C-103m. ***½ D: Walter Lang. Spencer Tracy, Katharine Hepburn, Joan Blondell, Gig Young, Dina Merrill. Broadway play becomes a vehicle for Hepburn and Tracy, a guarantee for top entertainment. He's an efficiency expert automating her research department at a TV network; they clash, argue, and fall in love. Great fun.

Despair (1979-West German) C-119m. *** D: Rainer Werner Fassbinder. Dirk Bogarde, Andrea Ferreol, Volker Spengler, Klaus Lowitsch. Playwright Tom Stoppard's script for the Nabokov novel concentrates too many of its wittiest lines in the first third, but the film still has its moments. Bogarde is brilliant as the Russian emigre who runs a German chocolate factory as the Nazis start to take power.

Desperadoes, The (1943) C-85m. *** D: Charles Vidor. Randolph Scott, Glenn Ford, Claire Trevor, Evelyn

Keyes, Edgar Buchanan, Raymond Walburn, Guinn Williams. Pretty good Western; bandit Ford goes straight, joins forces with marshal Scott to clean up town.

Desperados, The (1969) C-91m. **½ D: Henry Levin. Vince Edwards, Jack Palance, George Maharis, Neville Brand, Sylvia Sims. Civil War deserters ravage the West. Not bad.

Desperados Are in Town, The (1956) 73m. *½ D: Kurt Neumann. Robert Arthur, Kathy Nolan, Rhys Williams, Rhodes Reason. Bland oater of young man proving his worth by killing outlaws who murdered his friend.

Desperate Chance for Ellery Queen (1942) 70m. D: James Hogan. William Gargan, Margaret Lindsay, Charley Grapewin, John Litel, Lilian Bond, James Burke, Jack LaRue. SEE: Ellery Queen series.

Desperate Characters (1971) C-88m. *** D: Frank D. Gilroy. Shirley MacLaine, Kenneth Mars, Gerald O'Loughlin, Sada Thompson, Jack Somack. Story of the horrors of day-to-day living in New York City is a bit too theatrical in origin, but benefits from excellent acting; possibly MacLaine's best performance.

Desperate Hours, The (1955) 112m. ***½ D: William Wyler. Humphrey Bogart, Fredric March, Arthur Kennedy, Martha Scott, Dewey Martin, Gig Young, Robert Middleton, Richard Eyer. Excellently acted account of escaped convicts terrorizing family household, allowing for interplay of emotional clashes. Based on Broadway play and actual events.

Desperate Journey (1942) 107m. *** D: Raoul Walsh. Errol Flynn, Raymond Massey, Ronald Reagan, Nancy Coleman, Alan Hale, Arthur Kennedy, Albert Basserman. Spirited WW2 drama of American pilots stranded in Germany, struggling to cross border; propaganda interludes are forgivable.

Desperate Man, The (1959-British) 57m. *½ D: Peter Maxwell. Jill Ireland, Conrad Phillips, William Hartnell, Charles Gray. Dull yarn of reporter Phillips and gal (Ireland) involved in tracking down a Sussex crook; photography only virtue.

Desperate Miles, The (1975) C-78m. TVM D: Daniel Haller. Tony Musante, Joanna Pettet, Jeanette Nolan, Lynn Loring, John Larch. Fact-based drama of disabled Vietnam vet who makes grueling 130-mile trip in wheelchair to prove his independence. Sunk by maudlin, cliché-ridden script and Musante's monotonous performance. Below average.

Desperate Mission (1971) C-100m. TVM D: Earl Bellamy. Ricardo Montalban, Slim Pickens, Earl Holliman, Ina Balin, Roosevelt Grier. Newcomer to wandering band in Spanish California helps out in escorting wife of wealthy landowner to San Francisco. Forgettable resolution, adequate performances. Average.

Desperate Moment (1953-British) 88m. **½ D: Compton Bennett. Dirk Bogarde, Mai Zetterling, Philip Friend, Gerard Heinz. Taut melodrama involving displaced person in post-WW2 Berlin falsely accused of homicide; sensibly acted.

Desperate Ones, The (1968-Italian) C-104m. **½ D: Alexander Ramati. Maximilian Schell, Raf Vallone, Irene Papas, Theodore Bikel. Siberian labor camp escapees join Polish army. Okay if nothing else is on.

Desperate Search (1952) 73m. **½ D: Joseph H. Lewis. Howard Keel, Jane Greer, Patricia Medina, Keenan Wynn. Trim film of two kids stranded in Canadian wastelands after plane crash, and their father's efforts to find them.

Desperate Siege SEE: Rawhide

Desperate Women (1978) C-100m. TVM D: Earl Bellamy. Susan St. James, Dan Haggerty, Ronee Blakely, Ann Dusenberry, Max Gail. Three scrappy female prisoners, abandoned in the desert, team up with laconic ex-gunslinger to outsmart a ratty gang of desperadoes in this ragtag western comedy. Average.

Destination Fury (1961-French) 85m. ** D: Giorgio Bianchi. Eddie Constantine, Renato Rascel, Dorian Gray, Pierre Grasset. Silly spy spoof with Constantine a double-agent involved with Interpol.

Destination Gobi (1953) C-89m. **½ D: Robert Wise. Richard Widmark, Don Taylor, Darryl Hickman, Martin Milner. Unusual WW2 actioner involving U.S. naval men joining forces with natives against Japanese assaults; nice action sequences.

Destination Inner Space (1966) C-92m. ** D: Francis D. Lyon. Sheree North, Scott Brady, Gary Merrill, John Howard. Programmer sci-fi set on ocean's bottom with a most unterrifying monster on the prowl.

Destination Moon (1950) C-91m. **½ D: Irving Pichel. John Archer, Warner Anderson, Tom Powers, Dick Wesson, Erin O'Brien-Moore. One of the pioneer sci-fi films, modestly produced but still effective. Produced by George Pal.

Destination Saturn (1939) 91m. **½ D: Ford Beebe, Saul Goodkind. Buster Crabbe, Constance Moore, Jackie Moran, Jack Mulhall, Anthony Warde, C. Montague Shaw. Newly edited version of BUCK ROGERS serial. Buck and Buddy Wade, revived from suspended animation by future Earth scientists, fight Killer Kane and his supergangsters. Uninspired handling of original footage.

Destination 60,000 (1957) 65m. BOMB D: George Waggner. Preston Foster, Pat Conway, Jeff Donnell, Coleen Gray. Worn-out premise of test pilots zooming through space, families waiting nervously on the ground.

Destination Tokyo (1943) 135m. *** D: Delmer Daves. Cary Grant, John Garfield, Alan Hale, John Ridgely, Dane Clark, Warner Anderson, William Prince. Suspenseful WW2 account of U.S. submarine sent into Japanese waters and interaction among crew. Commander Grant, seamen Garfield and Clark ring true.

Destiny (1944) 65m. ** D: Reginald LeBorg. Gloria Jean, Alan Curtis, Frank Craven, Grace McDonald. Routine study of man sent to prison on homicide charge, and snowballing effects on his life. Expanded from sequence originally shot for FLESH AND FANTASY.

Destiny of a Spy (1969) C-99m. TVM D: Boris Sagal. Lorne Greene, Rachel Roberts, Anthony Quayle, James Donald, Patrick Magee, Patrick Newell. Dissatisfied Russian spy (Greene) reluctantly comes out of retirement, accepts assignment in London investigating death of British scientist. Effective subplot involving budding love affair with British double agent (Roberts). Good production. Above average.

Destroy All Monsters (1968-Japanese) C-88m. ** D: Ishiro Honda. Akira Kubo, Jun Tazaki, Yoshio Tsuchiya, Kyoko Ai, All-star monster cast (from Toho Studios) teams up to combat alien forces bent on destruction. Godzilla, Mothra, Ro-

dan, and other favorites are on hand in this juvenile epic.

Destroyer (1943) 99m. **½ D: William Seiter. Edward G. Robinson, Glenn Ford, Marguerite Chapman, Edgar Buchanan, Leo Gorcey, Regis Toomey, Ed Brophy. Predictable wartime drama of aging seaman Robinson shown up by novice Ford; of course Eddie comes through in the end.

Destructors, The (1968) C-97m. ** D: Francis D. Lyon. Richard Egan, Patricia Owens, John Ericson, Michael Ansara, Joan Blackman. Programmer nonsense with Egan a federal agent hunting international thieves who stole laser rubies.

Destructors, The (1974-British) C-89m. *** D: Robert Parrish. Anthony Quinn, Michael Caine, James Mason, Maureen Kerwin, Marcel Bozzufi. Good French-made crime meller with Quinn a U.S. drug agent out to stop kingpin Mason. An animated Caine is fine as a likeable assassin. Original title: THE MARSEILLE CONTRACT.

Destry (1954) C-95m. **½ D: George Marshall. Audie Murphy, Mari Blanchard, Lyle Bettger, Lori Nelson, Thomas Mitchell, Edgar Buchanan, Wallace Ford. Audie is gunshy sheriff who tames town and dance-hall girl without violence. Earlier version still unsurpassed.

Destry Rides Again (1939) 94m. ***½ D: George Marshall. James Stewart, Marlene Dietrich, Charles Winninger, Brian Donlevy, Una Merkel, Irene Hervey, Jack Carson, Billy Gilbert, Samuel S. Hinds. Slambang, action-filled Western satire, with Stewart taming rowdy town without violence and tangling with boisterous dance-hall girl Dietrich. Marlene sings "See What the Boys in the Back Room Will Have" in this oft-filmed Max Brand story.

Detective, The (1954-British) 91m. *** D: Robert Hamer. Alec Guinness, Joan Greenwood, Peter Finch, Cecil Parker, Bernard Lee, Sidney James. Guinness in rare form as G. K. Chesterton's sleuth after stolen art treasures. Remake of Walter Connolly's 1935 FATHER BROWN, DETECTIVE.

Detective, The (1968) C-114m. *** D: Gordon Douglas. Frank Sinatra, Lee Remick, Ralph Meeker, Jacqueline Bisset, William Windom, Al Freeman, Tony Musante, Jack Klugman. Trashy script, based on best-selling novel, is more than redeemed by fast, no-nonsense direction and good acting, particularly by Sinatra and Freeman; tale of cops vs. homosexuals is cut for TV.

Detective Kitty O'Day (1944) 63m. ** D: William Beaudine. Jean Parker, Peter Cookson, Tim Ryan, Veda Ann Borg. Parker adds bubbly zest as amateur sleuth who sets out to solve a crime; pleasant fluff on low-budget scale.

Detective Story (1951) 103m. ***½ D: William Wyler. Kirk Douglas, Eleanor Parker, William Bendix, Lee Grant. Sidney Kingsley's once-forceful play of life at N.Y.C. police precinct has lost much of its punch but is still fine film; Douglas is hardhitting detective, Parker his ignored wife, Bendix in one of his best roles as sympathetic sergeant.

Detour (1945) 69m. **½ D: Edgar G. Ulmer. Tom Neal, Ann Savage, Claudia Drake, Edmund MacDonald, Tim Ryan, Esther Howard. Intriguing film about hitchhiker who gets involved with femme fatale Savage, and murder. Ultracheap movie has cult following among film buffs.

Detour to Nowhere SEE: **Banacek**

Devil, The SEE: **To Bed . . . Or Not To Bed**

Devil and Daniel Webster, The SEE: **All That Money Can Buy.**

Devil and Miss Jones, The (1941) 92m. ***½ D: Sam Wood. Jean Arthur, Robert Cummings, Charles Coburn, Spring Byington, S. Z. Sakall, William Demarest. Delightful social comedy by Norman Krasna; millionaire Coburn masquerades as clerk in his own department store to investigate employee complaints. A must.

Devil and Miss Sarah, The (1971) C-73m. TVM D: Michael Caffey. Gene Barry, James Drury, Janice Rule, Donald Moffat, Logan Ramsey, Charles McGraw, Slim Pickens. Thoroughly predictable minor Western featuring battle for possession of sanity by young bride: will Satanist outlaw Rankin win out over husband? Below average.

Devil and the Deep (1932) 78m. **½ D: Marion Gering. Tallulah Bankhead, Gary Cooper, Charles Laughton, Cary Grant, Paul Porcasi. Overplayed but lush melodrama of Bankhead, her suitors Grant and Cooper, and jealous husband, submarine commander Laughton.

Devil and the Ten Commandments,

The (1962-French) 143m. **½ D: Julien Duvivier. Michel Simon, Lucien Baroux, Claude Nollier, Dany Saval, Charles Aznavour. Episodic film in ten parts illustrating each of the commandments—too often superficial instead of cynical.

Devil at 4 O'Clock, The (1961) C-126m. **½ D: Mervyn LeRoy. Spencer Tracy, Frank Sinatra, Jean-Pierre Aumont, Kerwin Mathews, Barbara Luna. Static production, not saved by volcanic eruption climax, involving priest Tracy helping to evacuate children's hospital in midst of lava flow. Stars are lost in weak film.

Devil Bat (1941) 69m. ** D: Jean Yarbrough. Bela Lugosi, Suzanne Kaaren, Dave O'Brien, Guy Usher, Yolande Mallot, Donald Kerr. Lugosi raises bats and trains them to suck victim's blood on cue.

Devil Bat's Daughter (1946) 66m. ** D: Frank Wisbar. Rosemary La Planche, Molly Lamont, John James, Ed Cassidy. OK mystery with La Planche going crazy while her strange father fools around with killer bats.

Devil Commands, The (1941) 65m. **½ D: Edward Dmytryk. Boris Karloff, Amanda Duff, Richard Fiske, Anne Revere, Ralph Penny, Dorothy Adams, Kenneth MacDonald. Improbable but intriguing chiller of scientist Karloff obsessed with idea of communicating with dead wife. Predictable but fun. Only debit: the absurd narration.

Devil Dog: The Hound of Hell (1978) C-100m. TVM D: Curtis Harrington. Richard Crenna, Yvette Mimieux, Kim Richards, Ike Eisenmann, Victor Jory, Martine Beswick. Chiller about a family falling under the spell of a dog imbued with the spirit of the devil. Average.

Devil Dogs of the Air (1935) 86m. ** D: Lloyd Bacon. James Cagney, Pat O'Brien, Margaret Lindsay, Frank McHugh. Tiresome potboiler with Marine Air Corps rivalry between Cagney and O'Brien. Their personalities, and good stunt-flying scenes, are only saving grace.

Devil Doll, The (1936) 79m. *** D: Tod Browning. Lionel Barrymore, Maureen O'Sullivan, Frank Lawton, Robert Grieg, Lucy Beaumont, Henry B. Walthall, Grace Ford, Rafaela Ottiano. Very entertaining yarn of Devil's Island escapee Barrymore shrinking humans to doll-size to carry out nefarious schemes.

Devil Doll (1964-British) 80m. *** D: Lindsay Shonteff, Bryant Halliday, William Sylvester, Yvonne Romain, Philip Ray. Underrated British macabre mystery features very good Halliday performance as hypnotist-ventriloquist trying to transfer soul into dummy. Atmospheric, with countless subplots.

Devil Goddess (1955) 70m. D: Spencer Bennet. Johnny Weissmuller, Angela Stevens, Selmer Jackson, William Tannen, Ed Hilton, William M. Griffith. SEE: Jungle Jim series.

Devil in Love, The (1968-Italian) 97m. *½ D: Ettore Scola. Vittorio Gassman, Mickey Rooney, Claudine Auger, Ettore Manni, Annabella Incontrera. Gassman comes up from Hell during the French Renaissance to botch up an impending peace between Rome and Florence, but loses his powers when he falls for Auger. Comedy is both heavy-handed and unfunny, a bad combination.

Devil in the Flesh (1946-French) 110m. ***½ D: Claude Autant-Lara. Gerard Philippe, Micheline Presle, Denise Grey. Exquisitely filmed, compassionate story of love affair between married woman and sensitive high school student during WWI. Controversial in its day because of sensual love scenes and cuckolding of soldier husband.

Devil Is a Sissy, The (1936) 92m. **½ D: W. S. Van Dyke. Freddie Bartholomew, Mickey Rooney, Jackie Cooper, Ian Hunter, Peggy Conklin, Katherine Alexander. Three top juvenile stars outclass their material in this rambling, episodic tale of tenement-district pals and British newcomer (Bartholomew) who tries to join their gang.

Devil Is a Woman, The (1935) 83m. *** D: Josef von Sternberg. Marlene Dietrich, Lionel Atwill, Cesar Romero, Edward Everett Horton, Alison Skipworth. Sumptuous-looking film about alluring but heartless woman and the men who all but ruin their lives for her, set against backdrop of 19th century Spanish revolution. Hypnotic, if dramatically shaky; Luis Bunuel used same source material for THAT OBSCURE OBJECT OF DESIRE.

Devil Makes Three, The (1952) 96m. ** D: Andrew Marton. Gene Kelly, Pier Angeli, Richard Egan, Claus Clausen. Kelly always seems pretentious in straight roles: here he's a soldier returning to Munich to thank family who helped him during WW2;

he becomes involved with daughter Angeli and black market gangs.

Devil Pays Off (1941) 56m. ** D: John H. Auer. J. Edward Bromberg, Osa Massen, William Wright, Margaret Tallichet. Meager account of one-time navy man trying to redeem his honor by tracking down espionage agents within the naval service.

Devil Rides Out, The (1968-British) C-95m. *** D: Terence Fisher. Christopher Lee, Charles Gray, Nike Arrighi, Patrick Mower, Sarah Lawson, Paul Eddington. Taut filmization of Dennis Wheatley's novel. Duc de Richleau (Lee) assists young friend under spell of Mocate, ultra-evil Satanist. Watch out for that climax! Also titled THE DEVIL'S BRIDE.

Devil-Ship Pirates (1964-British) C-89m. **½ D: Don Sharp. Christopher Lee, Andrew Kier, Michael Ripper, John Cairney. Good little movie of stray Spanish ships conquering English countryside, unaware that the Armada has been defeated.

Devil Times Five (1974) 90m. **½ D: Sean McGregor. Gene Evans, Sorrell Booke, Shelley Morrison, Dawn Lyn, Leif Garrett, Taylor Lacher. Five children who escape from state mental institution take refuge in Evans' winter retreat and terrorize its inhabitants. Not bad. Originally released as PEOPLE TOYS.

Devil to Pay, The (1931) 74m. **½ D: George Fitzmaurice. Ronald Colman, Loretta Young, David Torrence, Myrna Loy, Mary Forbes, Paul Cavanagh. Early talkie shows its age, but Colman is fine in this drawing room comedy.

Devils, The (1971-British) C-109m. **½ D: Ken Russell. Oliver Reed, Vanessa Redgrave, Dudley Sutton, Max Adrian, Gemma Jones, Murray Melvin, Michael Gothard. Fine performances save confused mixture of history, comedy, and surrealism in wide-eyed adaptation of Whiting play and Huxley book dealing with witchcraft and politics in 17th-century France. A mad movie, with fiery finale not for the squeamish. Beware cuts.

Devil's Angels (1967) C-84m. *½ D: Daniel Haller. John Cassavetes, Beverly Adams, Mimsy Farmer, Leo Gordon. Killer cyclists head for outlaw sanctuary breaking everything in their way. Lurid and cheap.

Devil's Bait (1959-British) 58m. *½
D: Peter Graham Scott. Geoffrey
Keen, Jane Hylton, Gordon Jackson,
Dermot Kelly. Intriguing if leisurely
paced "B" film, about baker and his
wife who accidentally put poison in
their wares, trying to find purchasers.

**Devil's Bride, The SEE: The Devil
Rides Out**

Devil's Brigade, The (1968) C-130m.
** D: Andrew V. McLaglen. William Holden, Cliff Robertson, Vince
Edwards, Michael Rennie, Dana Andrews, Carroll O'Connor. Standard
WW2 fare about reckless recruits
fashioned into creditable fighting unit
is rehashed here for more than two
hours. Holden is wasted once again.

Devil's Brother, The (1933) 88m. ***
D: Hal Roach, Charles R. Rogers.
Stan Laurel, Oliver Hardy, Dennis
King, Thelma Todd, James Finlayson, Henry Armetta. L&H adaptation of operetta with King as romantic lead, a famous bandit, the
boys as would-be assistants. One of
their best. Originally titled: FRA
DIAVOLO.

Devil's Canyon (1953) C-92m. ** D:
Alfred L. Werker. Virginia Mayo,
Dale Robertson, Stephen McNally,
Arthur Hunnicutt. Former marshal
put in prison for shoot-outs, where
he's entangled in prison riot.

Devil's Cargo (1948) 61m. D: John
F. Link. John Calvert, Rochelle Hud-
son, Roscoe Karns, Lyle Talbot,
Tom Kennedy, Theodore Von Eltz.
SEE: The Falcon series.

Devil's Daffodil, The (1961-British)
86m. ** D: Akos Rathony. William
Lucas, Penelope Horner, Christopher
Lee, Ingrid van Bergen, Albert
Lieven. Flabby entry in Edgar Wallace series, involving rash of murders linked with dope smuggling
into England. Retitled: DAFFODIL
KILLER.

Devil's Daughter, The (1972) C-74m.
TVM D: Jeannot Szwarc. Belinda
Montgomery, Shelley Winters, Robert
Foxworth, Joseph Cotten, Jonathan
Frid, Robert Cornthwaite. At funeral
of mother, Montgomery is befriended
by Winters who claims long friendship with deceased; actually Montgomery is needed to fulfill pact
in Devil-worshipping group. Great
ROSEMARY'S BABY-ish premise
rendered inconsequential by indifferent dialogue, acting, direction. Average.

Devil's Disciple, The (1959-British)
82m. ***½ D: Guy Hamilton. Burt
Lancaster, Kirk Douglas, Laurence
Olivier, Janette Scott, Eva LeGal-
lienne, Harry Andrews, Basil Sydney. Sparkling adaptation of George
Bernard Shaw's satire, set during
American Revolution, with standout
performances by Lancaster, Douglas,
and Olivier.

Devil's Doorway (1950) 84m. *** D:
Anthony Mann. Robert Taylor, Louis
Calhern, Paula Raymond, Marshall
Thompson. Well-turned Western with
offbeat casting of Taylor as Indian
who served in Civil War, returning
home to find that he must fight to
right the injustices done against his
people.

Devil's Eight, The (1969) C-97m. **
D: Burt Topper. Christopher George,
Fabian, Ralph Meeker, Leslie Parrish. Federal agent helps six convicts escape from road gang to train
them to smash moonshine rings. Undistinguished.

Devil's Eye, The (1960-Swedish) 90m.
**½ D: Ingmar Bergman. Jarl Kulle,
Bibi Andersson, Nils Poppe, Sture
Lagerwall. Confused account of the
demon sending envoy Kulle to rob
Andersson of her virginity; long
morality dialogue uplifted by cast.

Devil's Hairpin, The (1957) C-82m.
**½ D: Cornel Wilde. Cornel Wilde,
Jean Wallace, Mary Astor, Arthur
Franz. Wilde is reckless sports car
champion who learns fair play on
the track; obligatory racing scenes
above average.

Devil's Henchman, The (1949) 69m.
** D: Seymour Friedman. Warner
Baxter, Mary Beth Hughes, Mike
Mazurki, Harry Shannon. In this
programmer, Baxter sets out to capture waterfront gang and becomes
involved in murder.

**Devil's Imposter, The SEE: Pope
Joan**

Devil's in Love, The (1933) 71m.
**½ D: William Dieterle. Loretta
Young, Victor Jory, Vivienne Osborne, C. Henry Gordon, David
Manners, J. Carrol Naish. Very odd,
well-made film about doctor falsely
accused of murder, efforts to clear
his name. Bela Lugosi has good,
small role as prosecuting attorney.

Devil's Island (1940) 62m. **½ D:
William Clemens. Boris Karloff,
Nedda Harrigan, James Stephenson,
Adia Kuznetzoff, Will Stanton, Ed-
ward Keane. Above-average Karloff
vehicle of innocent doctor exiled

to Devil's Island, mistreated by supervisor Stephenson, saved in twist finish.

Devil's Mask, The (1946) 66m. ** D: Henry Levin. Jim Bannon, Anita Louise, Michael Duane, Mona Barrie, Ludwig Donath, Barton Yarborough. OK entry in short-lived I LOVE A MYSTERY series with Bannon as Jack Packard, Yarborough as Doc Young. Intriguing if far-fetched story involving shrunken heads and murder, spoiled by obvious identity of killer.

Devil's Messenger (1961-Swedish) 72m. *½ D: Curt Siodmak. Lon Chaney, Karen Kadler, John Crawford. Sultry girl is sent to earth to help Satan carry out master plan that will envelop the world; hazy plot, poor production values. Originally three episodes of unsold TV series "#13 Demon Street."

Devil's Own, The (1966-British) C-90m. *** D: Cyril Frankel. Joan Fontaine, Kay Walsh, Alec McCowen, Ann Bell, Ingrid Brett, Gwen Ffrangcon-Davies. Good British chiller with Fontaine as headmistress of private school who learns that a student is to be sacrificed by a local voodoo cult. British title: THE WITCHES.

Devil's Playground (1937) 74m. **½ D: Erle C. Kenton. Richard Dix, Dolores Del Rio, Chester Morris, Pierre Watkin, Ward Bond. Good combination of action and romance with diver Dix discovering wife Del Rio in love with Morris; exciting underwater climax. Remake of 1928 Frank Capra film SUBMARINE.

Devil's Rain, The (1975) C-85m. **½ D: Robert Fuest. Ernest Borgnine, Ida Lupino, William Shatner, Tom Skerritt, Eddie Albert, Keenan Wynn, Joan Prather. Offbeat approach to story of devil worshippers provides some effective horror and also some unintentional humor. Most of the cast melts in a memorable finale. Look for John Travolta in a bit part.

Devil's Wanton, The (1962-Swedish) 72m. **½ D: Ingmar Bergman. Doris Svenlund, Birger Malmsten, Eva Henning, Hasse Ekman. Sober account of desperate girl finding romance with another equally unhappy soul, reaffirming their faith in humanity.

Devil's Widow, The (1972) C-107m. ** D: Roddy McDowall. Ava Gardner, Ian McShane, Stephanie Beacham,

Cyril Cusack, Richard Wattis, David Whitman, Madeline Smith. McDowall's directorial debut is a too-arty drama about aging Ava's attempts to keep her young lovers from straying too much. Formerly called TAMLIN.

Devotion (1946) 107m. **½ D: Curtis Bernhardt. Olivia de Havilland, Ida Lupino, Paul Henreid, Sydney Greenstreet, Nancy Coleman, Arthur Kennedy, Dame May Whitty. Powerful real-life story of Brontë sisters becomes routine love triangle with Henreid in the middle; intense, dramatic performances make it worthwhile. Made in 1943.

Diabolical Dr. Mabuse, The SEE: Secret of Dr. Mabuse, The

Diabolique (1955-French) 107m. ***½ D: Henri-Georges Clouzot. Simone Signoret, Vera Clouzot, Paul Meurisse, Charles Vanel. Classic thriller of murder plot gone awry; builds slowly, deliberately to chilling climax.

Diagnosis: Murder (1976-British) C-95m. *** D: Sidney Hayers. Christopher Lee, Judy Geeson, Jon Finch, Tony Beckley, Dilys Hamlett, Jane Merrow. Psychiatrist is drawn into bizarre sequence of events when his wife disappears and he is accused of murdering her. Solid little suspenser.

Dial Hot Line (1969) C-100m. TVM D: Jerry Thorpe. Vince Edwards, Chelsea Brown, Kim Hunter, Lane Bradbury, June Harding. Unconvincing lead performance by Edwards as head of psychiatric telephone service with story centering around three different young subjects. Average.

Dial M for Murder (1954) C-105m. *** D: Alfred Hitchcock. Ray Milland, Grace Kelly, Robert Cummings, John Williams, Anthony Dawson. Frederick Knott's suspense play of man plotting wife's murder and subsequent police investigation; intriguing but not top Hitchcock.

Dial 1119 (1950) 75m. ** D: Gerald Mayer. Marshall Thompson, Virginia Field, Andrea King, Sam Levene, Keefe Brasselle. Modest suspenser hinged on plot of killer holding a group of bar patrons hostages.

Diamond Earrings SEE: Earrings of Madame de . . .

Diamond Head (1962) C-107m. **½ D: Guy Green. Charlton Heston, Yvette Mimieux, George Chakiris, France Nuyen, James Darren, Aline MacMahon, Elizabeth Allen. Soap opera set in Hawaii with Heston the domineering head of his family, whose dictates almost ruin their lives.

Diamond Horseshoe (1945) C-104m. *** D: George Seaton. Betty Grable, Dick Haymes, Phil Silvers, William Gaxton, Beatrice Kay, Carmen Cavallaro. Colorful musical set in Billy Rose's famous cabaret, with Grable giving up luxury for medical student Haymes. Song "The More I See You." Original title: BILLY ROSE'S DIAMOND HORSESHOE.

Diamond Jim (1935) 93m. *** D: A. Edward Sutherland. Edward Arnold, Jean Arthur, Binnie Barnes, Cesar Romero, Eric Blore. Big-budget biography of eccentric millionaire of 19th century whose appetite for money only matched by love of food and Lillian Russell; Arthur has dual role in recreation of Gay 90s era. Most entertaining.

Diamond Queen, The (1953) C-80m. ** D: John Brahm. Fernando Lamas, Arlene Dahl, Gilbert Roland, Michael Ansara. Dahl is dazzling title figure over whom Lamas and Roland fight in costumer set in India.

Diamond Wizard, The (1954-British) 83m. ** D: Dennis O'Keefe. Dennis O'Keefe, Margaret Sheridan, Philip Friend, Allan Wheatley. OK caper of U.S. and British agents tracking down diamond counterfeiters.

Diamonds (1975-Israeli) C-101m. ** D: Menahem Golan. Robert Shaw, Richard Roundtree, Shelley Winters, Barbara (Hershey) Seagull, Shai K. Ophir. OK heist movie with Shaw in dual role, as diamond merchant who masterminds break-in at Tel Aviv diamond vault, and twin brother who designed the security system there. Good location work in Tel Aviv and Jerusalem.

Diamonds and Crime SEE: **Hi Diddle Diddle**

Diamonds Are Forever (1971-British) C-119m. ***½ D: Guy Hamilton. Sean Connery, Jill St. John, Charles Gray, Lana Wood, Jimmy Dean, Bruce Cabot. After a two-picture hiatus, Connery returned as James Bond in this colorful comic-book adventure set in Las Vegas; closer in spirit to Republic serials than Ian Fleming, but great fun.

Diamonds for Breakfast (1968-British) C-102m. ** D: Christopher Morahan. Marcello Mastroianni, Rita Tushingham, Warren Mitchell, Elaine Taylor, Francisca Tu, Maggie Blye. Son of Russian nobleman tries to steal royal diamonds his father gambled away on the night of his birth. Offbeat comedy caper with fantasy elements just doesn't work, relies heavily on Mastroianni charm.

Diane (1956) C-110m. **½ D: David Miller. Lana Turner, Pedro Armendariz, Roger Moore, Marisa Pavan, Sir Cedric Hardwicke, Henry Daniell. Although predictable, medieval romance has good cast, gorgeous sets and costumes, and comes off surprisingly well. Lana looks lovely, and Miklos Rosza's score helps set the mood.

Diary of a Bachelor (1964) 88m. *½ D: Sandy Howard. William Traylor, Dagne Crane, Joe Silver, Chris Noel, Paula Stewart. Meager pickings. Fiancee reads boyfriend's daily ledger and decides he'd better mend his ways; time passes and he has, but she's changed her way of life.

Diary of a Chambermaid, The (1946) 86m. **½ D: Jean Renoir. Paulette Goddard, Burgess Meredith, Hurd Hatfield, Florence Bates, Irene Ryan, Francis Lederer, Judith Anderson, Almira Sessions. Attempt to make foreign-style film in Hollywood doesn't work. Nineteenth-century chambermaid Goddard is hired by Hatfield's mother.

Diary of a Chambermaid (1965-French) 79m. ***½ D: Luis Buñuel. Jeanne Moreau, Michel Piccoli, Georges Geret, Francoise Lugagne, Daniel Ivernel, Jean Ozenne. Remake of Jean Renoir's 1946 film concerns fascism in France in 1939 and how the bourgeoisie are viewed by maid Moreau. Sharp, unrelenting film from one of the great directors.

Diary of a Mad Housewife (1970) C-94m. **½ D: Frank Perry. Richard Benjamin, Frank Langella, Carrie Snodgress, Lorraine Cullen, Frannie Michel, Katherine Meskill. Interesting but pointless story of harried New York wife finding much needed release via affair with self-centered Langella. Asinine husband Benjamin would drive anyone mad. Peter Boyle has prominent bit in final scene.

Diary of a Madman (1963) C-96m. **½ D: Reginald Le Borg. Vincent Price, Nancy Kovack, Chris Warfield, Ian Wolfe, Nelson Olmstead. Bizarre yarn with Price in title role of law official possessed with homicidal urge; incredible yet entertaining.

Diary of Anne Frank, The (1959) 180m. ***½ D: George Stevens,

Millie Perkins, Joseph Schildkraut, Shelley Winters, Richard Beymer, Lou Jacobi, Diane Baker, Ed Wynn. Meticulously produced version of Broadway drama dealing with Jewish refugees hiding in WW2 Amsterdam. Perkins never captures pivotal charm of title character; Winters won Supporting Actress Oscar as shrill Mrs. Van Daan, ever fearful of Nazi arrest; Schildkraut fine as Father Frank, the lone survivor. Moving Alfred Newman score.

Diary of a Teenage Hitchhiker (1979) C-100m. TVM D: Ted Post. Dick Van Patten, Katherine Helmond, James Carroll Jordan, Charlene Tilton, Katy Kurtzman, Christopher Knight. Tawdry drama dramatizing the risk of soliciting rides from strangers. Below average.

Dick Tracy, Detective (1945) 62m. ** D: William Berke. Morgan Conway, Anne Jeffreys, Mike Mazurki, Jane Greer. Programmer entry about Chester Gould's square-jawed detective combatting crime; needed production values are lacking. Originally titled DICK TRACY.

Dick Tracy Meets Gruesome (1947) 65m. ** D: John Rawlins. Boris Karloff, Ralph Byrd, Anne Gwynne, Edward Ashley, June Clayworth. Karloff as the nemesis of Tracy adds some spice to this series' entry; predictable but enjoyable.

Dick Tracy Versus Cueball (1946) 62m. ** D: Gordon Douglas. Morgan Conway, Anne Jeffreys, Lyle Latell, Rita Corday, Dick Wessel. Ralph Byrd is definitive screen Tracy, but he isn't in this one; Conway does his best in OK entry in the Tracy series.

Dick Tracy's Dilemma (1947) 60m. ** D: John Rawlins. Ralph Byrd, Lyle Latell, Kay Christopher, Jack Lambert, Ian Keith. RKO contract players abound in this Tracy series entry; fast pacing makes predictable crime-solving satisfactory.

Dick Turpin (1925) 73m. *** D. John G. Blystone. Tom Mix, Kathleen Myers, Philo McCullough, Alan Hale, Bull Montana. Mix abandoned cowboy clothes to play famous English highwayman, but retained surefire formula of action and comedy in this enjoyable vehicle.

Did You Hear the One About the Traveling Saleslady? (1968) C-97m. BOMB D: Don Weis. Phyllis Diller, Bob Denver, Joe Flynn, Eileen Wesson, Jeanette Nolan, Bob Hastings.

You've all heard it, so why bother watching this dud. For only the most fervent fans of Miss Diller.

Die! Die! My Darling! (1965-British) C-97m. **½ D: Silvio Narizzano. Tallulah Bankhead, Stefanie Powers, Peter Vaughan, Donald Sutherland, Tootha Joyce. Tallulah, in her last film, has field day as weirdo who keeps Powers under lock and key for personal vengeance against the death of her son. Engaging fun, especially for Bankhead devotees.

Die, Monster, Die! (1965) C-80m. ** D: Daniel Haller. Boris Karloff, Nick Adams, Freda Jackson, Suzan Farmer, Terence de Marney, Patrick Magee. Based on H. P. Lovecraft story, this thriller has Karloff a recluse who discovers a meteor which gives him strange powers. Good premise is not carried out well.

Different Story, A (1978) C-108m. **½ D: Paul Aaron. Perry King, Meg Foster, Valerie Curtin, Peter Donat, Richard Bull, Barbara Collentine. Gays King and Foster get married to prevent his deportation, then fall in love. Sounds terrible, but first half is surprisingly good until film succumbs to conventionality in later scenes. Foster is terrific.

Dig That Uranium (1956) 61m. D: Edward Bernds. Leo Gorcey, Huntz Hall, Bernard Gorcey, Mary Beth Hughes. SEE: Bowery Boys series

Digby—The Biggest Dog in the World (1974-British) C-88m. BOMB. D: Joseph McGrath. Jim Dale, Spike Milligan, Milo O'Shea, Angela Douglas, Norman Rossington. Poor comedy-fantasy concerning liquid Project X, which causes sheepdog Digby to grow to huge proportions. Bad special effects, too. Written by Ted Key, creator of "Hazel," strictly for kids.

Dillinger (1945) 89m. *** D: Max Nosseck. Edmund Lowe, Anne Jeffreys, Lawrence Tierney, Eduardo Ciannelli, Elisha Cook, Jr., Marc Lawrence. Tierney is well cast as famed criminal Dillinger; the film zips along retracing his gunslinging career. Quite good.

Dillinger (1973) C-96m. *** D: John Milius. Warren Oates, Ben Johnson, Cloris Leachman, Michelle Phillips, Richard Dreyfuss. Heavily romanticized gangster movie is aided by some of the roughest, most violent gun battles ever staged on screen. Story follows Dillinger midway through his bank-robbing career up until his death outside the Biograph Theatre.

Dime With a Halo (1963) 97m. **½ D: Boris Sagal. Barbara Luna, Roger Mobley, Paul Langton, Rafael Lopez, Manuel Padilla. Five poor Mexican kids steal ten cents from church collection plate and bet on a race-horse. Minor but winning little film.

Dimples (1936) 78m. **½ D: William Seiter. Shirley Temple, Frank Morgan, Helen Westley, Robert Kent, Stepin Fetchit, Astrid Allwyn. Prime Shirley Temple, with our heroine doing her best to save her destitute father, played by marvelous Morgan. Songs: "Oh Mister Man Up In The Moon," "What Did The Bluebird Say."

Dingaka (1965-South Africa) C-98m. **½ D: Jamie Uys. Stanley Baker, Juliet Prowse, Ken Gampu, Siegfried Mynhardt, Bob Courtney. Film focuses on contrasting white-Negro ways of life and the clashes of the two cultures; production bogs down in stereotypes.

Dinky (1935) 65m. ** D: D. Ross Lederman, Howard Bretherton. Jackie Cooper, Mary Astor, Roger Pryor, Henry Armetta. Astor is framed, accused of fraud. She tries to keep it from hurting son Cooper in military school. Fairly interesting tale offers nothing special.

Dinner at Eight (1933) 113m. **** D: George Cukor. Marie Dressler, John Barrymore, Wallace Beery, Jean Harlow, Lionel Barrymore, Lee Tracy, Billie Burke, Jean Hersholt, May Robson, Madge Evans, Phillips Holmes, Edmund Lowe. Vintage MGM constellation of stars portray various strata of society in N.Y.C., invited to dine and shine; Harlow in fine comedy form, but Dressler as dowager steals focus in filmization of George Kaufman-Edna Ferber play. Don't miss this one.

Dinner at the Ritz (1937-British) 77m. **½ D: Harold Schuster. Annabella, Paul Lukas, David Niven, Romney Brent. Diverting murder whodunit with Annabella seeking the killer of her father; classy settings spice film.

Dino (1957) 94m. **½ D: Thomas Carr. Sal Mineo, Brian Keith, Susan Kohner, Joe De Santis. Mineo at his rebellious best playing juvenile delinquent befriended by social worker Keith and gal Kohner.

Dinosaurus! (1960) C-85m. **½ D: Irvin S. Yeaworth, Jr. Ward Ram-

sey, Paul Lukather, Kristina Hanson, Alan Roberts. Interesting and unintentionally amusing story of hazards faced by caveman and two prehistoric monsters who are accidently unearthed on an isolated tropical island.

Dion Brothers, The SEE: **Gravy Train**

Diplomaniacs (1933) 76m. *** D: William A. Seiter. Bert Wheeler, Robert Woolsey, Marjorie White, Louis Calhern, Edgar Kennedy, Hugh Herbert. Genuinely odd but endearing nonsense musical comedy about barbers from Indian reservation sent to Geneva peace conference. Reminiscent of MILLION DOLLAR LEGS and DUCK SOUP, with memorable comic performances by Herbert—as wise-saying Chinaman—and Calhern.

Diplomatic Courier (1952) 97m. *** D: Henry Hathaway. Tyrone Power, Patricia Neal, Hildegarde Neff, Karl Malden. Power seeks to avenge friend's death in Trieste, becomes involved in international espionage. Cold War film is exciting, well acted.

Dirigible (1931) 93m. **½ D: Frank Capra. Jack Holt, Ralph Graves, Fay Wray, Hobart Bosworth, Roscoe Karns. Frank Wead story about Navy pilots' experimental use of dirigibles in the Antarctic has plenty of action and guts, but a sappy romantic story to weigh it down. On the whole, an interesting antique.

Dirt Gang, The (1972) C-89m. *½ D: Jerry Jameson. Paul Carr, Michael Pataki, Lee DeBroux, Jon Shank, Nancy Harris, T.J. Escott. Dirt is right; unremarkable motorcycle gang film.

Dirty Dingus Magee (1970) C-91m. **½ D: Burt Kennedy. Frank Sinatra, George Kennedy, Anne Jackson, Lois Nettleton, Jack Elam, Harry Carey, Jr. Saddletramp Sinatra is friend to all, and that gets him after him. Dull.

in trouble when his friends come
Dirty Dozen, The (1967) C-150m. ***½ D: Robert Aldrich. Lee Marvin, Ernest Borgnine, Jim Brown, John Cassavetes, Robert Ryan, Charles Bronson, Donald Sutherland. Big boxoffice hit about 12 murderers, rapists and other assorted prisoners who get a chance to redeem themselves in WW2. Exciting, funny and well acted, especially by Marvin and Cassavetes. Some violent scenes may be cut on TV.

Dirty Game, The (1966-Italian) 91m. **✶✶½** D: Terence Young, Christian-Jaque, Carlo Lizzani. Henry Fonda, Vittorio Gassman, Annie Girardot, Robert Ryan, Peter Van Eyck. Hodgepodge of stories dealing with espionage in post-WW2 era; none of episodes is convincing, stars don't help much.

Dirty Harry (1971) C-102m. **✶✶✶** D: Don Siegel. Clint Eastwood, Harry Guardino, Reni Santoni, John Vernon, John Larch, Andy Robinson. Riveting action film with Eastwood as iconoclastic cop determined to bring in psychotic killer Robinson, even if he has to break some rules. Brilliantly filmed and edited for maximum impact.

Dirty Heroes (1969-Italian) C-105m. **✶✶½** D: Alberto DeMartino. Frederick Stafford, Daniela Bianchi, Curt Jurgens, John Ireland, Adolfo Celi, Michael Constantine. Wartime escape and revenge action drama—a poor man's DIRTY DOZEN—with a gang of ex-cons turned G.I.'s working behind enemy lines in Holland.

Dirty Knight's Work (1976-British) C-88m. **✶✶½** D: Kevin Connor. John Mills, Donald Pleasence, Barbara Hershey, David Birney, Margaret Leighton, Peter Cushing. Anglo-American Birney enlists Mills' help in solving his father's murder, zeroes in on strange society of latter-day knights with vigilante tendencies. Offbeat and mildly diverting. Original title: TRIAL BY COMBAT.

Dirty Little Billy (1972) C-100m. **✶✶✶** D: Stan Dragoti. Michael J. Pollard, Lee Purcell, Charles Aidman, Richard Evans. Offbeat story based on early life of one of the West's most notorious outlaws. Grimy, muddy, adventurous; not a normal Western by any stretch of the imagination.

Dirty Mary, Crazy Larry (1974) C-93m. **✶✶✶** D: John Hough. Peter Fonda, Susan George, Adam Roarke, Vic Morrow, Roddy McDowall. Very fast action as racing driver Fonda, pickup George and mechanic Roarke demolish every car in sight while escaping with supermarket loot. Hardly a letup, and good of its type.

Dirty Money (1972-French) C-98m. **✶✶½** D: Jean-Pierre Melville. Alain Delon, Richard Crenna, Catherine Deneuve, Ricardo Cucciolla, Michael Conrad. Pedestrian melodrama of bank robbery and drug trafficking. Delon and Crenna are muscular, Deneuve and the scenery gorgeous.

Disappearance of Aimee, The (1976) C-110m. TVM D: Anthony Harvey. Faye Dunaway, Bette Davis, James Sloyan, James Woods, John Lehne, Lelia Goldoni, Barry Brown, Severn Darden. Period drama covering, through a courtroom hearing, the sensational disappearance and reappearance of the famed preacher, Aimee Semple McPherson, in 1926. Dunaway is fascinating as Aimee, Davis feisty as her mother in this absorbing, richly atmospheric dramatization. Above average.

Disappearance of Flight 412, The (1974) C-78m. TVM D: Jud Taylor. Glenn Ford, Bradford Dillman, Guy Stockwell, David Soul, Robert F. Lyons, Kent Smith, Jack Ging, Greg Mullavey. After two jets from commander Ford's unit mysteriously vanish while pursuing UFOs, he rips through military red tape to find out why the Air Force officially will not recognize the incident and stumbles onto a right-wing conspiracy. Average.

Disaster on the Coastliner (1979) C-100m. TVM D: Richard Sarafian. Lloyd Bridges, Raymond Burr, Robert Fuller, Pat Hingle, E. G. Marshall, Yvette Mimieux, William Shatner, Paul L. Smith. Vengeful computer genius sets two passenger trains on a collision course in this fairly intelligent suspense thriller with lots of unplugged holes. Average.

Discreet Charm of the Bourgeoisie, The (1972-French) C-100m. **✶✶✶✶** D: Luis Buñuel. Fernando Rey, Delphine Seyrig, Stephane Audran, Bulle Ogier, Jean-Pierre Cassel, Michel Piccoli. A Buñuel joke on his audience, using friends' attempts to have dinner party as excuse for series of surrealistic sequences. Reality and illusion soon blur into one, with delicious comic results. Oscar-winner as Best Foreign Film.

Disembodied, The (1957) 65m. **✶½** D: Walter Grauman. Paul Burke, Allison Hayes, Eugenia Paul, Robert Christopher. Standard voodoo chiller situated in dark jungle; usual results.

Dishonorable Discharge (1958-French) 105m. **✶✶** D: Bernard Borderie. Eddie Constantine, Pascale Roberts, Lino Ventura, Lise Bourdin. Variation on Hemingway's TO HAVE AND HAVE NOT, with Constantine skippering luxury ship loaded with hidden dope; flabby film.

Dishonored (1931) 91m. **✶✶½** D:

[193]

Josef von Sternberg. Marlene Dietrich, Victor McLaglen, Lew Cody, Warner Oland, Gustav von Seyffertitz. Alluring Dietrich makes the most of a creaky script with Marlene as a secret agent X-27 during WW1. Worth seeing for Dietrich's masquerade as peasant girl.

Dishonored Lady (1947) 85m. *½ D: Robert Stevenson. Hedy Lamarr, Dennis O'Keefe, John Loder, William Lundigan, Natalie Schafer, Paul Cavanagh. Limp Lamarr vehicle of glamorous magazine art director accused of murder; ponderous.

Disorderly Orderly, The (1964) C-90m. *** D: Frank Tashlin. Jerry Lewis, Glenda Farrell, Susan Oliver, Everett Sloane, Jack E. Leonard, Alice Pearce, Kathleen Freeman, Barbara Nichols, Milton Frome. First-rate slapstick and sight gags (including a wild chase finale) mix with cloying sentiment as Jerry runs amuck in a nursing home. Best scene: Jerry's suffering of "sympathy pains" as patient Pearce complains of her ills.

Dispatch From Reuters, A (1940) 89m. **½ D: William Dieterle. Edward G. Robinson, Edna Best, Eddie Albert, Albert Basserman, Gene Lockhart, Nigel Bruce, Otto Kruger. Warner Bros. biography series slipped a notch in this retelling of first news service in Europe. Good production values but emotional impact needed to tag episodes is missing.

Disputed Passage (1939) 87m. **½ D: Frank Borzage. Dorothy Lamour, Akim Tamiroff, John Howard, Victor Varconi, Keye Luke, Elisabeth Risdon, Philip Ahn. Average drama of conflict between scientists in their ideals. One believes that there's no place for marriage in science field.

Disraeli (1929) 89m. *** D: Alfred E. Green. George Arliss, Joan Bennett, Florence Arliss, Anthony Bushell, David Torrence, Ivan Simpson. Somewhat stagy but effective vehicle for Arliss, who won Oscar as cunning British prime minister: great statesman, devoted husband, and matchmaker (for Bennett and Bushell). Very much a one-man show.

Distant Drums (1951) C-101m. ** D: Raoul Walsh. Gary Cooper, Mari Aldon, Richard Webb, Ray Teal. Tame actioner of Seminole Indians on warpath in early 19th-century Florida, with Cooper as stalwart swamp fighter.

Distant Trumpet, A (1964) C-117m.

**½ D: Raoul Walsh. Troy Donahue, Suzanne Pleshette, Kent Smith, Claude Akins, James Gregory. Paul Horgan's novel gets short-circuited in stock presentation of army men in the Old West combatting warring Indians while romancing women on the post; good supporting cast.

Dive Bomber (1941) C-133m. *** D: Michael Curtiz. Errol Flynn, Fred MacMurray, Ralph Bellamy, Alexis Smith, Robert Armstrong, Regis Toomey, Craig Stevens. Exciting, well-paced aviation film of experiments to eliminate pilot-blackout. Flynn, MacMurray, and Smith perform well in formula war story.

Divided Heart (1953-British) 89m. *** D: Charles Crichton. Cornell Borchers, Yvonne Mitchell, Armin Dahlen, Alexander Knox. Intelligent study of dilemma parents face when their adopted child's real mother shows up, demanding her son back.

Divorce (1945) 71m. ** D: William Nigh. Kay Francis, Bruce Cabot, Helen Mack, Craig Reynolds, Larry Olsen, Mary Gordon. Francis is city girl who returns to home town, enticing Cabot away from Mack and family; satisfactory programmer.

Divorce, American Style (1967) C-109m. *** D: Bud Yorkin. Dick Van Dyke, Debbie Reynolds, Jason Robards, Jean Simmons, Van Johnson, Joe Flynn, Shelley Berman, Martin Gabel, Lee Grant, Pat Collins, Tom Bosley. Highly entertaining comedy of Van Dyke and Reynolds finding more problems than they expected when they get divorced. Stars are unusually good in offbeat roles.

Divorce His—Divorce Hers (1973) C-148m. TVM D: Waris Hussein. Elizabeth Taylor, Richard Burton, Carrie Nye, Barry Foster, Gabriele Ferzetti. Adequate examination of husband-wife relationship in limbo, in two sections: first, through eyes of husband arriving in Rome, then through eyes of wife who has new lover. Uneven script has embarrassing moments, good performances. Average.

Divorce—Italian Style (1962-Italian) 104m. ***½ D: Pietro Germi. Marcello Mastroianni, Daniela Rocca, Stefania Sandrelli, Leopoldo Trieste. Marcello can't stomach his wife and schemes to marry another girl. Flavorful Italian film provides hilarious comedy with ironic ending.

Divorce of Lady X, The (1938-British) C-90m. *** D: Tim Whelan.

Merle Oberon, Laurence Olivier, Binnie Barnes, Ralph Richardson, Morton Selten, J. H. Roberts. Frothy British comedy with fine cast; Olivier is innocently implicated in Oberon's divorce.

Dixie (1943) C-89m. ******* D: A. Edward Sutherland. Bing Crosby, Dorothy Lamour, Billy DeWolfe, Marjorie Reynolds, Lynne Overman, Raymond Walburn, Eddie Foy, Jr., Grant Mitchell. Atmosphere overshadows plot in this biography of pioneer minstrel Dan Emmett, who wrote title song; Bing also sings "Sunday, Monday and Always."

Do Not Disturb (1965) C-102m. ****½** D: Ralph Levy. Doris Day, Rod Taylor, Hermione Baddeley, Sergio Fantoni, Reginald Gardiner, Mike Romanoff, Leon Askin. Mild Day vehicle with Taylor as executive husband who brings her to suburban England. She meets suave Fantoni, enraging jealous hubby. Not up to her earlier fashion romps.

Do Not Fold, Spindle or Mutilate (1971) C-71m. TVM D: Ted Post. Helen Hayes, Myrna Loy, Mildred Natwick, Sylvia Sidney, Vince Edwards, John Beradino. Four elderly ladies, practical-joke enthusiasts, create mythical girl for computer dating questionnaire, thirst for even more bizarre thrills. Way in which prank turns frightening could've been handled far, far better; otherwise, good performances. Average.

Do You Love Me? (1946) C-91m. ****½** D: Gregory Ratoff. Maureen O'Hara, Dick Haymes, Harry James, Reginald Gardiner, Alma Kruger. Lightweight musical of band-singer Haymes romancing college dean O'Hara.

Do You Take This Stranger (1970) C-100m. TVM D: Richard Heffron. Gene Barry, Lloyd Bridges, Diane Baker, Joseph Cotten, Susan Oliver, Sidney Blackmer. OK drama featuring Barry as man who has million dollars within grasp if he can persuade another to assume his identity; terminal disease victim is likely candidate. Good complications, fair performances. Average.

Doberman Gang, The (1972) C-87m. ****½** D: Byron Chudnow. Byron Mabe, Julie Parrish, Hal Reed, Simmy Bow, Jojo D'Amore. Trim low-budget heist movie about a crook's ingenious plan to use six dobermans to pull off bank job. Dogs steal not only the loot but the

picture, and starred in two sequels.

Doc Savage, The Man of Bronze (1975) C-100m. ***½** D: Michael Anderson. Ron Ely, Paul Gleason, Bill Lucking, Michael Miller, Paul Wexler. The pulp magazine hero gets camp treatment in a poor spoof with very few laughs, as Doc (Ely) and his Fabulous Five battle gold-greedy Capt. Seas (Wexler). Produced, not wisely, by George Pal, with Sousa marches on the soundtrack.

Dock Brief, The (1962-British) 88m. ****½** D: James Hill. Peter Sellers, Richard Attenborough, Beryl Reid, David Lodge. Sellers is aging barrister who incompetently represents accused killer Attenborough with strange results; pleasant comic satire.

Docks of New Orleans (1948) 64m. D: Derwin Abrahams. Roland Winters, Victor Sen Yung, Mantan Moreland, John Gallaudet, Virginia Dale. SEE: **Charlie Chan** series.

Docks of New York (1945) 61m. D: Wallace Fox. Leo Gorcey, Huntz Hall, Billy Benedict, Gloria Pope, Carlyle Blackwell, Jr., Bud Gorman, George Meeker. SEE: **Bowery Boys** series.

Doctor and the Girl, The (1949) 98m. ****½** D: Curtis Bernhardt. Glenn Ford, Charles Coburn, Gloria DeHaven, Janet Leigh, Warner Anderson. Ford is appropriately sterile as idealistic young doctor who married poor girl and practices medicine in slum area of N.Y.C.

Doctor at Large (1957-British) C-98m. ****½** D: Ralph Thomas. Dirk Bogarde, James Robertson Justice, Shirley Eaton, George Coulouris, Anne Heywood, Lionel Jeffries. Another entry in pleasing series, with novice doctor Bogarde seeking staff position in wealthy hospital.

Doctor at Sea (1956-British) C-92m. ****½** D: Ralph Thomas. Dirk Bogarde, Brigitte Bardot, Brenda De Banzie, James Robertson Justice. Bogarde prefers bachelor life and signs on a freight boat as ship's doctor, becoming involved with BB.

Dr. Black Mr. Hyde (1976) C-87m. ****½** D: William Crain. Bernie Casey, Rosalind Cash, Marie O'Henry, Ji-Tu Cumbuka, Milt Kogan, Stu Gilliam. Lab scientist Casey tests experimental serum on himself and turns into monster. No surprises, but not bad, either, with Casey doing first-rate job as Jekyll-Hyde character.

Doctor Blood's Coffin (1961-British) C-92m. **½ D: Sidney Furie. Kieron Moore, Hazel Court, Ian Hunter, Fred Johnson. Capable cast in well-paced chiller set in lonely village where people are being used for mysterious scientific experiments.

Dr. Bull (1933) 75m. *** D: John Ford. Will Rogers, Marion Nixon, Ralph Morgan, Rochelle Hudson, Berton Churchill, Louise Dresser. Rogers in fine form as country doctor battling small-town pettiness as much as fighting illness. Stereotyped characters are perfect foils for Rogers' common-sense pronouncements; director Ford provides ideal atmosphere.

Dr. Christian Meets the Women (1940) 68m. ** D: William McGann. Jean Hersholt, Dorothy Lovett, Edgar Kennedy, Rod LaRocque, Frank Albertson, Marilyn (later Lynn) Merrick. Film deals with crooked medico who comes into contact with the good doctor. Typical series entry.

Dr. Cook's Garden (1970) C-73m. TVM D: Ted Post. Bing Crosby, Frank Converse, Blythe Danner, Abby Lewis, Barney Hughes, Bethel Leslie. Converse's return to Greenfield, Vermont, and the kindly doctor who raised him degenerates into cheap horror by halfway mark. Even Crosby as central character can't cut it. Adapted from play by Ira Levin. Below average.

Dr. Cyclops (1940) C-75m. **½ D: Ernest Schoedsack. Albert Dekker, Thomas Coley, Janice Logan, Victor Kilian, Charles Halton. Title character (Dekker) shrinks humans to doll-size; plot is average, but special effects always intrigue.

Doctor Death, Seeker of Souls (1973) C-93m. *½ D: Eddie Saeta. John Considine, Barry Coe, Cheryl Miller, Florence Marly, Jo Morrow. Cheap horror item about the transferring of souls by 1,000-year-old Considine. Few effective moments include Moe (Three Stooges) Howard in a gag bit.

Doctor Dolittle (1967) C-152m. *½ D: Richard Fleischer. Rex Harrison, Samantha Eggar, Anthony Newley, Richard Attenborough, Peter Bull. Robert Surtees' photography is great, and that's it for this colossal musical dud that almost ruined its studio. The charm of Hugh Lofting's stories is gone. One merit: if you have unruly children, it may put them to sleep.

Dr. Ehrlich's Magic Bullet (1940) 103m. **** D: William Dieterle. Edward G. Robinson, Ruth Gordon, Otto Kruger, Donald Crisp, Maria Ouspenskaya, Montagu Love, Sig Ruman, Donald Meek. Outstanding chronicle of 19th-century German scientist who developed cure for venereal disease. Robinson earnest in interpreting superior script; surprisingly compelling.

Dr. Faustus (1968-British) C-93m. ** D: Richard Burton. Nevill Coghill, Richard Burton, Andreas Teuber, Ian Marter, Elizabeth Taylor. Burton's retelling of Faustus legend lacks everything but a buxom Mrs. Burton in brief sequence as Helen of Troy. Strictly for their fans.

Doctor Franken (1980) C-100m. TVM D: Marvin J. Chomsky. Robert Vaughn, Robert Perrault, David Selby, Terri Garr, Joseph Sommer, Cynthia Harris. Contemporary rehash of Mary Shelley's Frankenstein saga tells, in this prospective series pilot, how a single-minded New York surgeon rebuilds a shattered body from spare parts he acquires at work. And it's acted perfectly straight! Average.

Dr. Gillespie's Criminal Case (1943) 89m. D: Willis Goldbeck. Lionel Barrymore, Van Johnson, Donna Reed, Keye Luke, John Craven, Nat Pendleton, Marilyn Maxwell. SEE: **Dr. Kildare** series.

Dr. Gillespie's New Assistant (1942) 87m. D: Willis Goldbeck. Lionel Barrymore, Van Johnson, Susan Peters, Keye Luke, Richard Quine, Alma Kruger, Rose Hobart, Nat Pendleton, Stephen McNally, Marie Blake, Ann Richards. SEE: **Dr. Kildare** series.

Dr. Goldfoot and the Bikini Machine (1966) C-90m. *½ D: Norman Taurog. Vincent Price, Frankie Avalon, Dwayne Hickman, Susan Hart, Fred Clark. Mad scientist tries to make a fortune manufacturing lifelike lady robots to marry wealthy men. Just bad.

Dr. Goldfoot and the Girl Bombs (1966-Italian) C-85m. *½ D: Mario Bava. Vincent Price, Fabian, Franco Franchi, Moana Tahi. Dumb sequel to DR. GOLDFOOT AND THE BIKINI MACHINE finds Price now backed by Red China, dropping actual girl bombs into the laps of unsuspecting generals.

Doctor In Love (1962-British) C-93m. ** D: Ralph Thomas. Michael Craig, Virginia Maskell, Leslie Phillips,

Carole Lesley, James Robertson Justice. Craig inherited Bogarde's role in DOCTOR series. This entry centers on young medic's inability to avoid romantic attachments.

Doctor in the House (1953-British) C-92m. ***½ D: Ralph Thomas. Dirk Bogarde, Muriel Pavlow, Kenneth More, Donald Sinden, Kay Kendall. Hilarious British comedy beginning series of humorous accounts of young doctors intent on love and adventure as well as becoming wealthy physicians.

Doctor in Trouble (1970-British) C-90m. ** D: Ralph Thomas. Leslie Phillips, Harry Secombe, James Robertson Justice, Angela Scoular, Irene Handl, Robert Morley. Fair entry in the on-and-off British comedy series concerns Dr. Phillips' problems when he stows away on ocean liner; good supporting cast help a bit.

Dr. Jekyll and Mr. Hyde (1920) 63m. *** D: John S. Robertson. John Barrymore, Martha Mansfield, Brandon Hurst, Nita Naldi, Charles Lane, Louis Wolheim. One of several silent versions of famous tale, this one can hold its own next to the later March and Tracy filmings; Barrymore is superb as curious doctor who ventures into the unknown, emerging as evil Mr. Hyde. Bravura performance sparks well-made production.

Dr. Jekyll and Mr. Hyde (1931) 90m. *** D: Rouben Mamoulian. Fredric March, Miriam Hopkins, Rose Hobart, Holmes Herbert, Halliwell Hobbes. Exciting, floridly cinematic version of famous story with March in Oscar-winning portrayal of tormented doctor, Hopkins superb as tantalizing Ivy.

Dr. Jekyll and Mr. Hyde (1941) 127m. *** D: Victor Fleming. Spencer Tracy, Ingrid Bergman, Lana Turner, Donald Crisp, Barton MacLane, C. Aubrey Smith, Sara Allgood. Tracy and Bergman are excellent in thoughtful, lush remake of Robert Louis Stevenson's classic, which stresses Hyde's emotion rather than physical horror.

Dr. Jekyll and Sister Hyde (1972-British) C-95m. **½ D: Roy Ward Baker. Ralph Bates, Martine Beswick, Gerald Sim, Lewis Fiander, Susan Broderick. Interesting twist to classic tale finds the good doctor discovering that his evil life is brought out in the form of a beautiful but dangerous woman. No thrills but fun.

Dr. Kildare From 1938 to 1947, this series, set in Blair General Hospital, was one of the most successful and entertaining of all. INTERNES CAN'T TAKE MONEY (1937, Paramount) was the first film based on Max Brand's characters, with Joel McCrea as Kildare, but it was not part of the series and did not use any of the later familiar roles. The first official entry, YOUNG DR. KILDARE, starred Lew Ayres as Kildare, Lionel Barrymore as Dr. Gillespie, Laraine Day (Mary Lamont), Alma Kruger (Nurse Molly Byrd), Walter Kingsford (Dr. Carewe, head of the hospital), Nat Pendleton (Joe Wayman, ambulance driver), Emma Dunn and Samuel S. Hinds (Dr. Kildare's benevolent parents), Nell Craig (Nurse Parker), Marie Blake (Sally, switchboard operator), Frank Orth (Mike), and George Reed (Conover). Indeed, the Kildare series had more running characters than most others. Laraine Day left the series after DR. KILDARE'S WEDDING DAY, and the parents left along with Lew Ayres after DR. KILDARE'S VICTORY. Van Johnson and Keye Luke spent several films trying to become Dr. Gillespie's assistant, with Marilyn Maxwell as love interest for Van. Philip Dorn tried out in CALLING DR. GILLESPIE, and James Craig finished the series with DARK DELUSION. Lionel Barrymore appeared in all of them as the crusty Dr. Gillespie, and supported those entries with lesser plots and casts, often by himself. Each film had at least three plots going at once, with a stress on comedy as well as non-gory hospital drama. None of the Kildare films is bad; a few are mediocre, but most of the films are quite enjoyable, with such interesting names as Lana Turner, Ava Gardner, Robert Young, and Red Skelton turning up from time to time.

Dr. Kildare Goes Home (1940) 78m. D: Harold S. Bucquet. Lew Ayres, Lionel Barrymore, Laraine Day, Samuel S. Hinds, Gene Lockhart, Nat Pendleton.

Dr. Kildare's Crisis (1940) 75m. D: Harold S. Bucquet. Lew Ayres, Lionel Barrymore, Laraine Day, Robert Young, Nat Pendleton, Walter Kingsford, Alma Kruger.

Dr. Kildare's Strange Case (1940) 76m. D: Harold S. Bucquet. Lew Ayres, Lionel Barrymore, Laraine Day, Shepperd Strudwick, Samuel S. Hinds, Emma Dunn, Nat Pendleton.

Dr. Kildare's Victory (1941) 92m. D: W. S. Van Dyke, II. Lew Ayres, Lionel Barrymore, Ann Ayars, Robert Sterling, Jean Rogers, Alma Kruger.

Dr. Kildare's Wedding Day (1941) 82m. D: Harold S. Bucquet. Lew Ayres, Lionel Barrymore, Laraine Day, Red Skelton, Alma Kruger, Samuel S. Hinds, Nils Asther.

Dr. Max (1974) C-78m. TVM D: James Goldstone. Lee J. Cobb, Janet Ward, Robert Lipton, David Sheiner, Katherine Helmond, Sorrell Booke. Irascible old G.P. remains dedicated to his less affluent patients in a run-down Baltimore neighborhood, tending to their personal and medical problems and those of his own family. Cobb is his usual larger-than-life self as the curmudgeonly medic. Average.

Dr. No (1963) C-111m. ***½ D: Terence Young. Sean Connery, Ursula Andress, Joseph Wiseman, Jack Lord, Bernard Lee, Lois Maxwell. First James Bond film is least pretentious, with meatier story, better all-round production of Ian Fleming caper. Bond investigates strange occurrences in Jamaica; encounters master-fiend Dr. No (Wiseman).

Dr. Phibes Rises Again (1972) C-89m. **½ D: Robert Fuest. Vincent Price, Robert Quarry, Valli Kemp, Fiona Lewis, Peter Cushing, Beryl Reid, Terry-Thomas, Hugh Griffith. Campy sequel to THE ABOMINABLE DR. PHIBES finds Price still looking for elixir to revive his dead wife, with Quarry hot on his trail throughout Egypt.

Dr. Rhythm (1938) 80m. **½ D: Frank Tuttle. Bing Crosby, Mary Carlisle, Beatrice Lillie, Andy Devine, Laura Hope Crews, Rufe Davis. Bing battles another silly script playing bodyguard for Carlisle in Lillie's house. Bea isn't allowed to let go, which might have perked up film.

Doctor Satan's Robot (1940) 100m. **½ D: William Witney, John English. Eduardo Ciannelli, Robert Wilcox, William Newell, Ella Neal, C. Montague Shaw. Ciannelli as mad Dr. Satan gives this Republic cliffhanger a zingy flair, with Wilcox et al battling the seemingly invincible robot who can even do a double-take. Reedited movie serial: MYSTERIOUS DR. SATAN.

Dr. Scorpion (1978) C-100m. TVM D: Richard Lang. Nick Mancuso, Christine Lehti, Richard T. Herd, Roscoe Lee Brown, Denny Miller, Sandra Kerns. Another of the fondly remembered comic book heroes comes to TV to thwart a power-mad genius' plot to rule the world. The popcorn brigade might go for the silliness. Below average.

Dr. Socrates (1935) 70m. **½ D: William Dieterle. Paul Muni, Ann Dvorak, Barton MacLane, Raymond Brown, Mayo Methot. Enjoyable, offbeat film about small-town doctor Muni who unwillingly becomes official doctor for wounded mobsters. Fine performances by all. Remade as KING OF THE UNDERWORLD with Kay Francis in the Muni role!

Dr. Strange (1978) C-100m. TVM D: Philip DeGuere. Peter Hooten, Clyde Kusatsu, Jessica Walter, John Mills, Philip Sterling. Marvel Comics Group hero gets a shot at a series in this pilot dealing in the occult, with tongue firmly in cheek. Plot has him joining forces with a world-weary sorcerer (played con brio by Sir John Mills) to stop a beautiful witch from adding to her collection of men's souls. Above average.

Dr. Strangelove or: How I Learned to Stop Worrying and Love the Bomb (1964-British) 93m. **** D: Stanley Kubrick. Peter Sellers, George C. Scott, Sterling Hayden, Slim Pickens, Keenan Wynn, Peter Bull. U.S. President must contend with the Russians and his own political and military leaders when a fanatical general launches A-bomb attack on U.S.S.R. Sellers plays the President, British captain, and mad inventor of the Bomb in this brilliant black comedy, which seems better with each passing year. Sellers' phone conversation with Soviet Premier is classic. Outstanding cast.

Doctor Takes a Wife, The (1940) 89m. *** D: Alexander Hall. Ray Milland, Loretta Young, Reginald Gardiner, Gail Patrick, Edmund Gwenn, Frank Sully, Gordon Jones. Milland is mistaken for Young's husband, then forced to pretend he is. Stars and material spark each other at a lively pace.

Dr. Terror's Gallery of Horrors SEE: **Return from the Past**

Dr. Terror's House of Horrors (1965-British) C-98m. **½ D: Freddie

Francis. Peter Cushing, Christopher Lee, Roy Castle, Donald Sutherland, Neil McCallum, Max Adrian, Edward Underdown. Don't let title steer you from this intelligent episodic thriller about a strange doctor (Cushing) who tells five men's fortunes on a train. Enjoyable horror-fantasy.

Dr. Who and the Daleks (1965-British) C-85m. **½ D: Gordon Flemyng. Peter Cushing, Roy Castle, Jennie Linden, Geoffrey Toone. U.S. release of BBC serial has good acting, nice suspense in imaginative story of future society. Followed by DA-LEKS—INVASION EARTH.

Doctor X (1932) 80m. *** D: Michael Curtiz. Lionel Atwill, Fay Wray, Lee Tracy, Preston Foster, Robert Warwick, Mae Busch. Beautifully handled old-style thriller of full moon strangler traced by police to laboratory. Comedy relief is only weakness. Filmed in early Technicolor process but shown today in b&w only.

Doctor, You've Got to Be Kidding (1967) C-94m. BOMB D: Peter Tewksbury. Sandra Dee, George Hamilton, Celeste Holm, Bill Bixby, Dick Kallman, Mort Sahl, Dwayne Hickman, Allen Jenkins. Dee would rather marry the boss than pursue singing career. Even *her* singing might have helped this alleged comedy.

Doctor Zhivago (1965) C-197m. *** D: David Lean. Omar Sharif, Julie Christie, Geraldine Chaplin, Rod Steiger, Alec Guinness, Ralph Richardson, Tom Courtenay, Rita Tushingham. Overlong and overeverything film version of Boris Pasternak novel is nevertheless one of the most popular movies ever; most of the cast seems non-Russian, but there are some stirring scenes, great exodus sequence on train, and unforgettable performance by Christie.

Doctor's Dilemma (1958-British) C-99m. *** D: Anthony Asquith. Leslie Caron, Dirk Bogarde, Alastair Sim, Robert Morley. Bubbly Shaw period play of young wife Caron conniving to convince medical specialists that her scoundrel husband is worth saving.

Doctors' Private Lives (1978) C-100m. TVM D: Steven Hilliard Stern. John Gavin, Donna Mills, Ed Nelson, Barbara Anderson, Bettye Ackerman, John Randolph. Sudsy drama about the medical profession which spanned the mercifully brief

(four-show) hospital-based series in the spring of 1979. Average.

Doctors' Wives (1971) C-100m. *½ D: George Schaefer. Dyan Cannon, Richard Crenna, Gene Hackman, Rachel Roberts, Carroll O'Connor, Janice Rule, Diana Sands, Cara Williams, Ralph Bellamy. Super-sudsy soaper sparked by mysterious murder of cheating wife; glossy garbage.

Dodge City (1939) C-105m. *** D: Michael Curtiz. Errol Flynn, Olivia de Havilland, Ann Sheridan, Bruce Cabot, Frank McHugh, Alan Hale, John Litel, Victor Jory, Ward Bond, Cora Witherspoon. Errol tames the West and De Havilland, in entertaining large-scale Western, with Warner Bros. stock company giving good vignettes. As dance-hall gal, Sheridan sings one number, has even less dialogue.

Dodsworth (1936) 101m. **** D: William Wyler. Walter Huston, Ruth Chatterton, Paul Lukas, Mary Astor, David Niven, Maria Ouspenskaya. Superb adaptation of Sinclair Lewis novel about middle-aged American industrialist who retires, goes to Europe, where he and his wife find new set of values and new relationships. Intelligently written, beautifully filmed, extremely well acted. John Payne makes screen debut in small role.

Dog, a Mouse and a Sputnik, A SEE: **Sputnik**

Dog and Cat (1977) C-78m. TVM D: Bob Kelljan. Lou Antonio, Kim Bassinger, Matt Clark, Charles Cioffi, Richard Lynch, Dale Robinette, Dick Wesson. Flip streetwise detective and hip country girl he inherits as partner delve into porno business to nail kingpin. Offbeat characters and glib dialogue try to lift formula cop show out of the ordinary. Average.

Dog Day Afternoon (1975) C-130m. ***½ D: Sidney Lumet. Al Pacino, John Cazale, Charles Durning, James Broderick, Chris Sarandon, Carol Kane. Incredible-but-true story of a loser (Pacino) who holds up a Brooklyn bank to raise money for his lover's sex-change operation, and sees simple heist snowball into a citywide incident. Pacino's performance, and Lumet's flavorful N.Y. atmosphere, obscure the fact that this is much ado about nothing.

Dog of Flanders, A (1959) C-96m. ** D: James B. Clark. David Ladd, Donald Crisp, Theodore Bikel, Max

Croiset, Monique Ahrens. Tear-jerker for children about a boy, his dog, and friends they make. Crisp and Bikel have good character roles.

Dogs (1976) **C-90m. BOMB D:** Burt Brinckerhoff. David McCallum, George Wyner, Eric Server, Sandra McCabe, Sterling Swanson. Low-budget yawner about a pack of dogs on the prowl. Get out the flea powder.

Doll Face (1945) **80m. **½ D:** Lewis Seiler. Vivian Blaine, Dennis O'Keefe, Perry Como, Carmen Miranda, Martha Stewart, Michael Dunne. Burlesque dancer Blaine makes good in the big time; pleasant musical with Como's hit "Hubba Hubba Hubba."

Dollars($) (1972) **C-119m. ***½ D:** Richard Brooks. Warren Beatty, Goldie Hawn, Gert Frobe, Robert Webber, Scott Brady. Top-notch caper thriller set in Germany with unusual chase that goes on for more than a fifth of the film.

Doll's House, A (1973-British) **C-95m. **½ D:** Patrick Garland. Claire Bloom, Anthony Hopkins, Ralph Richardson, Denholm Elliott, Anna Massey, Edith Evans. Bloom and Hopkins give thoughtful performances in this rather stagy filmization of Ibsen's play. Still, the words are there and the play is a strong statement about women's (and all people's) rights to be human beings.

Doll's House, A (1973-British) **C-103m. **½ D:** Joseph Losey. Jane Fonda, David Warner, Trevor Howard, Delphine Seyrig, Edward Fox. Moderately successful, cinematic version of Ibsen play, worth a look for Fonda's controversial interpretation of a 19th-century liberated woman. Howard shines as the dying Dr. Rank.

Dolly Sisters, The (1945) **C-114m. **½ D:** Irving Cummings. Betty Grable, John Payne, June Haver, S. Z. Sakall, Reginald Gardiner. Sassy hokum with two lovely stars and a bevy of old song favorites from vaudeville's golden age.

Dolwyn (1949-British) **90m. **½ D:** Emlyn Williams. Dame Edith Evans, Richard Burton, Anthony James, Emlyn Williams. Well-acted study of Evans, who, out of desire for revenge, comes to aid of her town; good character delineation. Retitled: LAST DAYS OF DOLWYN, THE; WOMAN OF DOLWYN.

Domino Kid, The (1957) **73m. *½ D:** Ray Nazarro. Rory Calhoun, Kristine Miller, Andrew Duggan, Roy Barcroft. Revenge-oater with Calhoun returning to Lone Star State to seek killers of his family.

Domino Principle, The (1977) **C-97m. BOMB D:** Stanley Kramer. Gene Hackman, Candice Bergen, Richard Widmark, Mickey Rooney, Edward Albert, Eli Wallach. Muddled thriller about lunkhead Hackman's recruitment by a mysterious organization bent on political assassination. Bergen fails to convince as a lower-middle-class housewife.

Don Is Dead, The (1973) **C-115m. *½ D:** Richard Fleischer. Anthony Quinn, Frederic Forrest, Robert Forster, Al Lettieri, Angel Tompkins, Ina Balin. Wars among Mafia families and heirs apparent to Mr. Big form the convoluted plot of this trashy, derivative gangster saga. Retitled BEAUTIFUL BUT DEADLY.

Don Quixote (1973) **C-107m. *** D:** Rudolf Nureyev, Robert Helpmann. Nureyev, Helpmann, Lucette Aldous, Australian Ballet. Fine ballet version of Cervantes' classic, choreographed by Nureyev, who plays barber Basilio; Helpmann is the wandering knight. Not just for ballet buffs.

Dona Flor and Her Two Husbands (1978-Brazilian) **C-106m. ***½ D:** Bruno Barretto. Sonia Braga, Jose Wilker, Mauro Mendoca, Dinorah Brillanti. Braga is torn between giving body and soul to the dead, irresponsible husband who keeps returning to earth, or to the considerate dullard who's become her new mate. Original fantasy is extremely sexy, with some of Braga's best scenes likely to be trimmed for noncable showings.

Don't Be Afraid of the Dark (1973) **C-74m. TVM D:** John Newland. Kim Darby, Jim Hutton, Pedro Armendariz Jr., Barbara Anderson, William Demarest, Lesley Woods, Robert Cleaves. Young couple (Darby & Hutton) inherit strange house occupied by small creatures out to possess wife. Decent premise ruined by indifferent script, situations. Average.

Don't Bother to Knock (1952) **76m. **½ D:** Roy Baker. Richard Widmark, Marilyn Monroe, Anne Bancroft, Jeanne Cagney, Elisha Cook, Jr., Gloria Blondell. Title has more punch than improbable yarn of mentally disturbed Monroe hired as babysitter in large hotel, saved from killing herself and charge by tough-but-good Widmark.

Don't Drink the Water (1969) C-100m. ** D: Howard Morris. Jackie Gleason, Estelle Parsons, Ted Bessell, Joan Delaney, Michael Constantine, Howard St. John, Avery Schreiber. Uninspired adaptation of Woody Allen play about American family held prisoner in Iron Curtain country of Vulgaria, and their desperate attempts to escape. Cast works hard, with sporadic results.

Don't Give Up the Ship (1959) 89m. *** D: Norman Taurog. Jerry Lewis, Dina Merrill, Diana Spencer, Mickey Shaughnessy, Robert Middleton, Gale Gordon, Claude Akins. Top comedy with Jerry as an ensign who lost a battleship during war and doesn't remember how. Shaughnessy is pal who helps look for it underwater. One of Lewis' all-time best.

Don't Go Near the Water (1957) C-102m. *½ D: Charles Walters. Glenn Ford, Gia Scala, Anne Francis, Fred Clark, Eva Gabor. Submerged comedy of sailors in the South Pacific of WW2 building a recreation hall. Clark, as a frustrated officer, is best thing in slow film.

Don't Just Stand There (1968) C-100m. **½ D: Ron Winston. Robert Wagner, Mary Tyler Moore, Harvey Korman, Glynis Johns, Barbara Rhoades. Frantic comedy with perky stars; Wagner and Moore try to unravel mystery of disappearance of authoress Johns after writing the first half of a new book. Players' vivacity makes script seem better than it is.

Don't Look in the Basement (1972) C-95m. *½ D: S. F. Brownrigg. William McGee, Annie MacAdams, Rosie Holotik, Gene Ross, Jessie Lee Fulton, Camilla Carr. Amateurish horror thriller about inmates of secluded Florida insane asylum who contrive a bloody takeover.

Don't Look Now (1973-British) C-110m. *** D: Nicolas Roeg. Julie Christie, Donald Sutherland, Hilary Mason, Clelia Matania, Massimo Serato. Arty, over-indulgent but gripping Daphne Du Maurier occult thriller about parents of drowned child and their horror-laden visit to Venice. A memorably steamy love scene and violent climax may be cut for TV.

Don't Make Waves (1967) C-97m. *** D: Alexander Mackendrick. Tony Curtis, Claudia Cardinale, Sharon Tate, Robert Webber, Mort Sahl, Jim Backus, Edgar Bergen. The one gem out of nine million bad Tony Curtis comedy vehicles; satire on Southern California has good direction, funny performance by Sharon Tate, catchy title song sung by the Byrds. Good fun.

Don't Push, I'll Charge When I'm Ready (1969) C-100m. TVM D: Nathaniel Lande. Enzo Cerusico, Sue Lyon, Cesar Romero, Soupy Sales. Acceptable WW2 comedy has Italian P.O.W. in America drafted into Army. Average.

Don't Raise the Bridge, Lower the River (1968) C-99m. ** D: Jerry Paris. Jerry Lewis, Terry-Thomas, Jacqueline Pearce, Bernard Cribbins, Patricia Routledge. Jerry plays American in England whose get-rich-quick schemes have put him on verge of divorce; mild Lewis comedy, not as offensive as some.

Don't Take It to Heart (1945-British) 89m. *** D: Jeffrey Dell. Richard Greene, Patricia Medina, Richard Bird, Wylie Watson, Ernest Thesiger, Ronald Squire. Pleasant romantic comedy of ghost-ridden castle; Greene helps Medina and her townfolk overcome avaricious landowner.

Don't Touch the Loot SEE: **Grisbi**

Don't Trust Your Husband SEE: **Innocent Affair, An**

Don't Turn the Other Cheek (1973-Italian) C-93m. **½ D: Duccio Tessari. Franco Nero, Lynn Redgrave, Eli Wallach, Marilu Tolo, Horst Janson. Slapstick spaghetti Western detailing exploits of unlikely trio; a fiery, revolution-fomenting Irish journalist (Redgrave), a bogus Russian prince (Nero), and a seedy Mexican bandit (Wallach) with proverbial heart of gold.

Don't Worry, We'll Think of a Title (1966) 83m. BOMB D: Harmon Jones. Morey Amsterdam, Rose Marie, Joey Adams, Danny Thomas, Milton Berle, Nick Adams. Grade-Z shambles, despite many guest cameos by big TV and movie stars. Start worrying when you turn it on.

Don Juan Quilligan (1945) 75m. **½ D: Frank Tuttle. William Bendix, Joan Blondell, Phil Silvers, Anne Revere, B. S. Pully, Mary Treen. Through mishap Bendix is married to two girls at same time; lightweight comedy.

Dondi (1961) 100m. BOMB D: Albert Zugsmith. David Janssen, Patti Page, David Kory, Walter Winchell, Gale Gordon. Watch this film and you'll know why Janssen became a fugitive!

Donkey Skin (1971-French) **C-90m.** *** D: Jacques Demy. Catherine Deneuve, Jacques Perrin, Jean Marais, Delphine Seyrig. Charming adaptation of Charles Perrault's fairy tale about widowed King who vows that his new Queen must be as beautiful as his first. Sumptuous color production, witty script by director Demy.

Donner Pass: The Road to Survival (1978) **C-100m. TVM** D: James L. Conway. Robert Fuller, Andrew Prine, Michael Callan, Diane McBain, John Anderson, John Doucette. "Classics Illustrated" version of the true-life travails of a wagon train of pioneers who were snowbound on their westward trek and forced to turn to cannibalism. Family adventure despite the grim underlying theme. Average.

Doomsday Machine, The (1972) **C-88m.** *½ D: Lee Sholem, Harry Hope. Denny Miller, Mala Powers, Bobby Van, Ruta Lee, Grant Williams, Henry Wilcoxon. Saga of outer-space mission in the future looks more like something out of the 1950s.

Donovan's Brain (1953) **83m.** *** D: Felix Feist. Lew Ayres, Gene Evans, Nancy Davis, Steve Brodie. Scientist Ayres is overtaken by brain of dead industrialist which he has kept alive in his laboratory; intriguing story, modest but capable production. Story by Curt Siodmak filmed before as THE LADY AND THE MONSTER, and again as THE BRAIN.

Donovan's Reef (1963) **C-109m.** *** D: John Ford. John Wayne, Lee Marvin, Elizabeth Allen, Jack Warden, Cesar Romero, Dorothy Lamour. Action-comedy bounces along with a good cast. Wayne and his freewheeling friends on a Pacific island are disrupted by Warden's grown daughter (Allen) who comes to visit. Lots of fun.

Doolins of Oklahoma, The (1949) **90m.** **½ D: Gordon Douglas. Randolph Scott, George Macready, Louise Allbritton, John Ireland. Action-packed western with Scott as head of the Doolin gang, who decides to give up his life of crime.

Doomsday Flight, The (1966) **C-100m. TVM** D: William Graham, Jack Lord, Edmond O'Brien, Van Johnson, Katherine Crawford, John Saxon, Michael Sarrazin. Occasional suspense in Rod Serling-scripted story of madman (O'Brien) blackmailing airline, planting altitude activated bomb. As a thriller, pretty good; otherwise, characterizations and dialogue clichéd.

Door With Seven Locks, The (1962-German) **96m.** **½ D: Alfred Vohrer. Eddie Arent, Heinz Drache, Klaus Kinski, Adi Berber, Sabina Sesselman. Bizarre account of man who leaves in his will seven keys to treasure vault, with expected friction and murder; from Edgar Wallace story made before as CHAMBER OF HORRORS.

Double, The (1963-British) **56m.** ** D: Lionel Harris. Jeannette Sterke, Alan MacNaughton, Robert Brown, Jane Griffiths. Meandering Edgar Wallace yarn. MacNaughton, suffering from amnesia, seeks to unravel his life, revealing espionage plot.

Double Bunk (1960-British) **92m.** *½ D: C. M. Pennington-Richards. Ian Carmichael, Janette Scott, Sidney James, Liz Fraser. Slapstick account of Carmichael-Scott navigating their houseboat down the Thames, with predictable sight gags.

Double Confession (1951-British) **86m.** ** D: Harry Reynolds. Derek Farr, Joan Hopkins, Peter Lorre. Potentially exciting study of human nature given pedestrian treatment: film centers on various people who happen to be at seaside resort beach.

Double Cross (1941) **66m.** *½ D: Albert Kelley. Kane Richmond, Pauline Moore, Wynne Gibson. Mild account of cop seeking to get the goods on criminal gang; nothing unusual.

Double Cross (1949-Italian) **77m.** **½ D: Riccardo Freda. Vittorio Gassman, Amedeo Nazzari, Gianna Maria Canale. Acceptable account of two crooks who doublecross each other, with the victim seeking revenge years later.

Double Cross (1956-British) **71m.** ** D: Anthony Squire. Donald Houston, Fay Compton, Anton Diffring, Delphi Lawrence. Mild account of foreign agents involved in typical espionage plot to steal government secrets.

Double Crossbones (1951) **C-75m.** ** D: Charles Barton. Donald O'Connor, Helena Carter, Will Geer, Hope Emerson, Glenn Strange. O'Connor is would-be buccaneer who seeks to win his sweetheart and expose crooked city official. Light satire which doesn't quite come off.

Double Dynamite (1951) 80m. ** D: Irving Cummings, Jr. Frank Sinatra, Jane Russell, Groucho Marx, Don McGuire. Star trio were at career low points when flat comedy was made; Sinatra is bank clerk accused of theft.

Double Exposure (1944) 63m. ** D: William Berke. Chester Morris, Nancy Kelly, Jane Farrar, Richard Gaines. Fairly entertaining saga of girl who unwittingly takes photograph of murder.

Double Indemnity (1944) 106m. **** D: Billy Wilder. Barbara Stanwyck, Fred MacMurray, Edward G. Robinson, Porter Hall, Fortunio Bonanova, Jean Heather. Raymond Chandler-James Cain script packs fireworks in account of insurance salesman MacMurray coerced into murder plot by alluring Stanwyck and subsequent investigation by Fred's boss Robinson.

Double Indemnity (1973) C-73m. TVM D: Jack Smight. Richard Crenna, Lee J. Cobb, Samantha Eggar, Kathleen Cody, Arch Johnson, John Fiedler, Robert Webber. Remake of 1944 version with Eggar seducing insurance investigator Crenna into husband-murdering scheme. Follows original almost shot-for-shot, but overall effect is lifeless, unconvincing. Average.

Double Life, A (1947) 104m. **** D: George Cukor. Ronald Colman, Signe Hasso, Edmond O'Brien, Shelley Winters, Ray Collins. Colman gives a bravura Oscar-winning performance as actor whose stage roles affect his real-life actions; brilliant melodrama by Ruth Gordon-Garson Kanin.

Double Man, The (1967-British) C-105m. **½ D: Franklin Schaffner. Yul Brynner, Britt Ekland, Clive Revill, Anton Diffring, Moira Lister, Lloyd Nolan. Unconvincing spy thriller with Brynner playing both unemotional C.I.A. agent *and* East German lookalike. Excellent photography will suffer on TV.

Double McGuffin, The (1979) C-89m. **½ D: Joe Camp. Ernest Borgnine, George Kennedy, Elke Sommer, Rod Browning, Dion Pride, Lisa Whelchel, Jeff Nicholson, Michael Gerard. Teenagers stumble onto clues leading to assassination plot, but no one will believe them. Family-oriented thriller from creator of BENJI. Orson Welles explains film's title at the outset, for non-Hitchcock devotees.

Double or Nothing (1937) 95m. **½ D: Theodore Reed. Bing Crosby, Martha Raye, Andy Devine, Mary Carlisle, William Frawley, Fay Holden, Frances Faye. Entertaining musical about four people given 30 days to double gifts of $5000. Several good specialty acts thrown in for good measure, and Bing sings "The Moon Got in My Eyes."

Double Trouble (1967) C-90m. ** D: Norman Taurog. Elvis Presley, Annette Day, John Williams, Yvonne Romain, The Wiere Brothers, Chips Rafferty. Teen-age heiress falls for pop singer Presley when he's performing in England; usual Elvis fare, but he does sing "Long Legged Girl," one of his best post-Army tunes.

Double Wedding (1937) 87m. *** D: Richard Thorpe. William Powell, Myrna Loy, Florence Rice, Edgar Kennedy, Sidney Toler, Mary Gordon. Wackier than usual for Powell and Loy, as avant-garde painter and dress designer who want Loy's sister Rice to marry, but do it themselves.

Dough Boys (1930) 65m. *½ D: Edward Sedgwick. Buster Keaton, Sally Eilers, Cliff Edwards, Edward Brophy, Victor Potel. One of Buster's worst films, with obnoxious sergeant Brophy overriding few comic moments, some bright spots with "Ukulele Ike" Edwards in tiresome Army comedy.

Doughgirls, The (1944) 102m. **½ D: James V. Kern. Ann Sheridan, Alexis Smith, Jane Wyman, Eve Arden, Jack Carson, Charlie Ruggles, Alan Mowbray, Craig Stevens, Regis Toomey. Brittle comedy, still another variation on crowded-situation-in-wartime-Washington, with newlyweds Carson and Wyman on hectic honeymoon. Arden standout as Russian army officer.

Dove, The (1974) C-105m. **½ D: Charles Jarrott. Joseph Bottoms, Deborah Raffin, John McLiam, Dabney Coleman. Pleasant round-the-world adventure based on true story of 16-year-old who sails to every imaginable port. Filmed on location; produced by Gregory Peck.

Down Among the Sheltering Palms (1953) C-87m. ** D: Edmund Goulding. William Lundigan, Jane Greer, Mitzi Gaynor, David Wayne, Gloria DeHaven, Billy Gilbert, Jack Paar. Poor man's SOUTH PACIFIC recounts love problems of two U.S.

army officers stationed in Pacific after WW2.

Down Argentine Way (1940) C-94m. **½ D: Irving Cummings. Don Ameche, Betty Grable, Carmen Miranda, Charlotte Greenwood, J. Carrol Naish, Henry Stephenson. Flimsy, entertaining musical; Grable's first solo film hit as wealthy American in love with horsebreeder Ameche.

Down Memory Lane (1949) 72m. *** D: Phil Karlson (new footage). Steve Allen, Franklin Pangborn, Frank Nelson, Mack Sennett; scenes of W. C. Fields, Bing Crosby, others. Allen decides to show old Sennett comedies on his TV show. OK framework for silent clips of Ben Turpin, Gloria Swanson, etc. Fields' classic THE DENTIST and Crosby's BLUE OF THE NIGHT both shown almost in toto, making silly Allen footage worth watching.

Down Three Dark Streets (1954) 85m. **½ D: Arnold Laven. Broderick Crawford, Ruth Roman, Martha Hyer, Marisa Pavan. Smoothly done interweaving episodes, pegged on FBI agent following through on trio of dead buddy's cases; Roman quite effective.

Down to Earth (1932) 73m. **½ D: David Butler. Will Rogers, Irene Rich, Dorothy Jordan, Mary Carlisle, Matty Kemp. Homer Croy's sequel to THEY HAD TO SEE PARIS has nouveau riche Midwesterner Rogers putting an end to his family's foolish spending by declaring that he's broke. OK Rogers vehicle, but not up to his best film efforts.

Down to Earth (1947) C-101m. ** D: Alexander Hall. Rita Hayworth, Larry Parks, Marc Platt, Roland Culver, James Gleason, Edward Everett Horton. Terpsichore, the Goddess of Dance (Hayworth), comes to earth to help Parks with his mythological musical play. Rita's beauty is only asset of this hack musical, which appropriates Gleason, Horton and Culver characters from HERE COMES MR. JORDAN.

Down to the Sea in Ships (1922) 83m. **½ D: Elmer Clifton. William Walcott, Marguerite Courtot, Clara Bow, Raymond McKee, J. Thornton Baston. Archaic plot line of romantic conflict in a whaling family enhanced by vivid atmosphere of on-location shooting in New England, striking photography on board actual whaling ships at sea. Also notable as Clara Bow's film debut.

Down to the Sea in Ships (1949) 120m. *** D: Henry Hathaway. Richard Widmark, Lionel Barrymore, Dean Stockwell, Cecil Kellaway, Gene Lockhart. Young Stockwell fulfills seafaring goal on crusty Barrymore's whaling ship, under guidance of sailor Widmark. Good atmospheric yarn.

Downhill Racer (1969) C-102m. *** D: Michael Ritchie. Robert Redford, Gene Hackman, Camilla Sparv, Karl Michael Vogler, Jim McMullan, Christian Doermer. Vivid study of an empty life, with Redford as small-town egotist who joins U.S. Olympic ski team. Basically a character study; problem is an unappealing character. Dazzling ski scenes make lulls worth enduring.

Dracula (1931) 75m. ***½ D: Tod Browning. Bela Lugosi, David Manners, Helen Chandler, Dwight Frye, Edward Van Sloan, Herbert Bunston, Frances Dade. Classic horror film of Transylvanian vampire working his evil spell on perplexed group of Londoners. Lugosi's most famous role with his definitive interpretation of the Count.

Dracula (1973) C-100m. TVM D: Dan Curtis. Jack Palance, Simon Ward, Nigel Davenport, Pamela Brown, Fiona Lewis, Penelope Horner, Murray Brown. The indomitable count of Transylvania lives in the person of Palance, who plays Bram Stoker's vampire king as a slightly pathetic figure, a victim of twisted fate. Sterling cast, Richard Matheson's faithful adaptation, and Oswald Morris' exceptional photography, rich in gothic touches, add to this classy new version of the old chestnut. Above average.

Dracula (1979) C-109m. *½ D: John Badham. Frank Langella, Laurence Olivier, Donald Pleasence, Kate Nelligan, Trevor Eve, Janine Duvitski, Tony Haygarth. Murky retelling of Bram Stoker classic, with Langella's acclaimed Broadway characterization lost amid trendy horror gimmicks and ill-conceived changes in original story. Filmed in England.

Dracula A.D. 1972 (1972-British) C-100m. ** D: Alan Gibson. Peter Cushing, Christopher Lee, Stephanie Beacham, Michael Coles, Christopher Neame. Far-fetched, confusing tale of modern-day descendant of Dr. Van Helsing (Cushing) battling recently revived vampire (Lee). Somewhat jarring to see Dracula amid 1970s youth setting.

Dracula Has Risen From The Grave (1968-British) **C-92m.** **½ D: Freddie Francis. Christopher Lee, Rupert Davies, Veronica Carlson, Barbara Ewing, Barry Andrews, Michael Ripper. Dracula runs afoul of small-town monsignor when he pursues the churchman's beautiful blonde niece. Pretty good Hammer horror.

Dracula—Prince of Darkness (1966-British) **C-90m.** ** D: Terence Fisher. Christopher Lee, Barbara Shelley, Andrew Keir, Suzan Farmer. Sequel to HORROR OF DRACULA doesn't measure up. Lee is reincarnated as the evil Count who wreaks terror on a group of tourists in a secluded castle.

Dracula vs. Frankenstein (1971) C-90m. BOMB D: Al Adamson. J. Carrol Naish, Lon Chaney, Zandor Vorkov, Russ Tamblyn, Jim Davis, Anthony Eisley. Self-conscious comedy masquerading as horror film wasting talents of old-timers Naish and Chaney; Dracula makes deal with aging Dr. Frankenstein so as to have steady supply of blood.

Dracula's Daughter (1936) 72m. *** D: Lambert Hillyer. Otto Kruger, Marguerite Churchill, Gloria Holden, Irving Pichel, Edward Van Sloan, Nan Grey. Daughter is quite a match for poor boy she falls in love with. Holden is fine in title role, making the vampirish proceedings believable.

Dracula's Dog (1978) C-90m. ** D: Albert Band. Jose Ferrer, Michael Pataki, Reggie Nalder, Jan Shutan, Libbie Chase, John Levin. Transylvanian vampire and bloodthirsty dog, endowed with vampirish traits by the original Count, go to L.A. to find Dracula's last living descendant. Horror cheapie with admittedly novel twist.

Dragnet (1954) C-89m. *** D: Jack Webb. Jack Webb, Ben Alexander, Richard Boone, Ann Robinson, Stacy Harris, Virginia Gregg. While investigating brutal murder, Sgt. Friday and Officer Frank Smith ignore 57 varieties of civil liberties; feature film version of classic TV show evokes its era better than almost anything. Highly recommended on a nonesthetic level.

Dragnet (1969) C-97m. TVM D: Jack Webb. Jack Webb, Harry Morgan, Vic Perrin, Virginia Gregg, Gene Evans, John Rosenboro. Friday and

Gannon investigate series of murders of pretty models with vaguely identified male only suspect. Slightly better production than series; direction and dialogue same as show. Average.

Dragon Murder Case (1934) 68m. D: H. Bruce Humberstone. Warren William, Margaret Lindsay, Lyle Talbot, Eugene Pallette, Dorothy Tree. SEE: Philo Vance series.

Dragon Seed (1944) 145m. **½ D: Jack Conway, Harold S. Bucquet. Katharine Hepburn, Walter Huston, Aline MacMahon, Turhan Bey, Hurd Hatfield, Agnes Moorehead, Frances Rafferty, J. Carrol Naish, Akim Tamiroff, Henry Travers. Well-meant but overlong film of Pearl Buck's tale of Chinese town torn asunder by Japanese occupation; fascinating attempts at Oriental characterization.

Dragonfly Squadron (1954) 82m. ** D: Lesley Selander. John Hodiak, Barbara Britton, Bruce Bennett, Jess Barker. Usual Korean War story, alternating between pilots in the air and their romantic problems on ground.

Dragonwyck (1946) 103m. **½ D: Joseph L. Mankiewicz. Gene Tierney, Walter Huston, Vincent Price, Anne Revere, Spring Byington, Harry Morgan, Jessica Tandy, Trudy Marshall. Period chiller set at a gloomy mansion on the Hudson, with good cast but episodic presentation.

Dragoon Wells Massacre (1957) C-88m. ** D: Harold Schuster. Barry Sullivan, Dennis O'Keefe, Mona Freeman, Katy Jurado, Sebastian Cabot. Marauding Apaches force lawmen and renegades to join forces for self-protection; some action-packed scenes.

Dramatic School (1938) 80m. **½ D: Robert B. Sinclair. Luise Rainer, Paulette Goddard, Alan Marshal, Lana Turner, Anthony Allan (John Hubbard), Henry Stephenson, Genevieve Tobin. Carbon-copy STAGE DOOR with Rainer the center of attraction as fanciful girl who makes good in both marriage and career; look for Ann Rutherford, Dick Haymes, Hans Conried in early bit roles.

Drango (1957) 92m. ** D: Hall Bartlett, Jules Bricken. Jeff Chandler, Joanne Dru, Julie London, Donald Crisp. Chandler is Yankee Civil War veteran assigned to restore order to Southern town his command plundered. OK Western.

Dream for Christmas, A (1973) C-100m. TVM D: Ralph Senesky. Hari Rhodes, Beah Richards, Lynn Hamilton, George Spell, Juanita Moore, Joel Fluellen, Marlin Adams, Robert DoQui, Ta Ronce Allen, Clarence Muse. Inspirational story (by Earl "The Waltons" Hamner, Jr.) about black minister who takes his family from Arkansas to L.A. for his new assignment: a poor congregation in a church earmarked for demolition. Above average.

Dream Girl (1948) 85m. ** D: Mitchell Leisen. Betty Hutton, Macdonald Carey, Virginia Field, Patric Knowles, Walter Abel, Peggy Wood. Hutton stars as female Walter Mitty with constant daydreams; low-brow version of Elmer Rice play.

Dream Makers, The (1975) C-78m. TVM D: Boris Sagal. James Franciscus, Diane Baker, John Astin, Kenny Rogers, Mickey Jones, Jamie Donnelly, Devon Ericson, Steven Keats. College professor Franciscus leaves security of the campus to become recording company executive, only to be enmeshed in payola scandal. Muddled attempt at expose of the recording industry. Below average.

Dream of Kings, A (1969) C-107m. *** D: Daniel Mann. Anthony Quinn, Irene Papas, Inger Stevens, Sam Levene, Radames Pera, Val Avery. Emotional study of robust Quinn trying to find money to take ailing son to Greece. Vivid look at Greek community in Chicago; heartrending story by Harry Alan Petrakis. Stevens exceptional as young widow attracted to Quinn.

Dream of Passion, A (1978-Greek) C-106m. BOMB D: Jules Dassin. Melina Mercouri, Ellen Burstyn, Andreas Voutsinas, Despo Diamantidou, Dimitris Papamichael. Aside from Burstyn's powerhouse performance as an American jailed in Greece for killing her three children, this attempt to parallel her story with Medea's is the kind of idea that should never have left the story conference. Mercouri is typically hammy as the actress who takes up her cause.

Dream Wife (1953) 101m. *½ D: Sidney Sheldon. Cary Grant, Deborah Kerr, Walter Pidgeon, Buddy Baer, Movita, Steve Forrest. Silly bedroom comedy about Grant "marrying" an Eastern princess for goodwill reasons. Cast is wasted.

Dreamboat (1952) 83m. *** D: Claude Binyon. Ginger Rogers, Clifton Webb, Jeffrey Hunter, Anne Francis, Elsa Lanchester. Clever romp: silent-star Rogers cashes in on old movies now on TV, to chagrin to co-star Webb, now a distinguished professor. Scenes showing their old silent films are most enjoyable.

Dreamer (1979) C-86m. ** D: Noel Nosseck. Tim Matheson, Susan Blakely, Jack Warden, Richard B. Shull, Barbara Stuart, Pedro Gonzalez-Gonzalez. Bowling, a sport only slightly more cinematic than isometric exercises, gets the "Rocky" treatment in this bland rags-to-riches story. Having Matheson's bowling ball made of Flubber might have helped pick up the pace.

Dressed to Kill (1946) 72m. D: Roy William Neill. Basil Rathbone, Nigel Bruce, Patricia Morison, Edmond Breon, Carl Harbord, Patricia Cameron, Tom Dillon. SEE: **Sherlock Holmes** series.

Drive a Crooked Road (1954) 82m. ** D: Richard Quine. Mickey Rooney, Dianne Foster, Kevin McCarthy, Jack Kelly, Harry Landers. Quietly paced film of auto mechanic Rooney dreaming of being racing-car champ; instead becomes chump for gangsters, due to girlfriend.

Drive Hard, Drive Fast (1969) C-73m. TVM D: Douglas Heyes. Brian Kelly, Joan Collins, Henry Silva, Joseph Campanella, Karen Huston, Todd Martin. Odd murder drama with professional racing backdrop. Scheming wife (Collins) involves innocent man in husband's plan. Typical complications and doublecrosses in hohum script which cast can't save. Below average.

Drive, He Said (1972) C-90m. **½ D: Jack Nicholson. William Tepper, Karen Black, Michael Margotta, Bruce Dern, Robert Towne, Henry Jaglom. Confusing tale of youth alienation contains fine performances but loses itself in its attempt to cover all the bases.

Drive-In (1976) C-96m. ** D: Rod Amateau. Lisa Lemole, Glen Morshower, Gary Cavagnaro, Billy Milliken, Lee Newsom, Regan Kee. Amiable low-budget trash about a night in the life of teenaged yahoos at a Texas drive-in during the unreeling of a campy disaster film (which takes up much of the screen time). Gets better after 20 beers.

Driver, The (1978) C-90m. *** D:

Walter Hill. Ryan O'Neal, Bruce Dern, Ronee Blakely, Matt Clark, Felice Orlandi. Tense throwback to the Hollywood film noir era pits getaway driver O'Neal against creepy cop Dern. Oddball melodrama doesn't seem like much at the time, but has a way of staying with you afterwards. Great car chase sequences.

Driver's Seat, The (1973-Italian) C-101m. *½ D: Giuseppe Patroni Griffi. Elizabeth Taylor, Ian Bannen, Mona Washbourne, Andy Warhol. Slow, tedious, complex melodrama with Taylor in one of her worst roles as psychotic spinster undergoing series of adventures as she seeks to keep date with lover-murderer.

Drowning Pool, The (1976) C-108m. **½ D: Stuart Rosenberg. Paul Newman, Joanne Woodward, Tony Francoisa, Murray Hamilton, Melanie Griffith, Richard Jaeckel. Newman returns as Ross McDonald's private eye Harper in slickly made but murky whodunit filmed in New Orleans.

Drum (1976) C-110m. BOMB D: Steve Carver. Warren Oates, Ken Norton, Isela Vega, Pam Grier, Yaphet Kotto, John Colicos. Continuation of MANDINGO—a new and dreadful low in lurid characters and incidents. Ken Norton in title role generates neither interest nor sympathy.

Drum, The SEE: **Drums**

Drum Beat (1954) C-111m. ** D: Delmer Daves. Alan Ladd, Audrey Dalton, Marisa Pavan, Robert Keith. Post-Civil War tale has Ladd as Indian fighter assigned to negotiate peacefully with warring Indian group.

Drums (1938-British) C-99m. *** D: Zoltan Korda. Sabu, Raymond Massey, Valerie Hobson, Roger Livesey, David Tree. Fine, colorful adventure with precocious Sabu rescuing British cavalry in 19th-century India; atmospheric and actionful. Originally titled THE DRUM.

Drums Across the River (1954) C-78m. ** D: Nathan Juran. Audie Murphy, Lisa Gaye, Walter Brennan, Lyle Bettger. Murphy ties in with gold-jumpers overrunning Indian land, redeems himself by joining forces against these men to achieve peace.

Drums Along the Mohawk (1939) C-103m. ***½ D: John Ford. Claudette Colbert, Henry Fonda, Edna May Oliver, John Carradine, Jessie Ralph, Arthur Shields, Robert Lowery, Ward Bond. John Ford richly captures flavor of Colonial life in this vigorous, appealing story of settlers in upstate N.Y. during Revolutionary War. Action, drama, sentiment, and humor are deftly interwoven in beautiful Technicolor production.

Drums In the Deep South (1951) C-87m. ** D: William Cameron Menzies. James Craig, Barbara Payton, Guy Madison, Barton MacLane, Craig Stevens. Stagnant Civil War yarn of West Pointers who find themselves fighting for opposite causes.

Drums of Tahiti (1954) C-73m. BOMB D: William Castle. Dennis O'Keefe, Patricia Medina, Francis L. Sullivan, George Keymas. Three-D process only redeeming virtue of trite costumer (lost to viewer of course). O'-Keefe is footloose American who aids revolt against French annexation attempt of Tahiti.

DuBarry Was a Lady (1943) C-101m. *** D: Roy Del Ruth. Red Skelton, Lucille Ball, Gene Kelly, Virginia O'Brien, Zero Mostel, Donald Meek, George Givot, Louise Beavers, Tommy Dorsey and Orchestra. Minus most of Cole Porter's score (except "Friendship") this changed DU-BARRY is still fun with Skelton imagining himself in Madame DuBarry's French court; slow moving in spots.

Duchess and the Dirtwater Fox, The (1976) C-103m. *½ D: Melvin Frank. George Segal, Goldie Hawn, Conrad Janis, Thayer David, Roy Jenson, Bob Hoy. Dumb comedy about cardsharp Segal and dance-hall cutie Hawn teaming up in the Old West. Occasional laughs, inappropriate song interludes.

Duchess of Idaho (1950) C-98m. **½ D: Robert Z. Leonard. Esther Williams, Van Johnson, John Lund, Paula Raymond, Amanda Blake, Eleanor Powell, Lena Horne. Williams' vehicle takes her to Sun Valley, where she's trying to help patch up roommate's romance but falls in love herself. MGM guest stars pep up the formula production.

Duck Soup (1933) 70m. **** D: Leo McCarey. Groucho, Harpo, Chico, Zeppo Marx, Margaret Dumont, Louis Calhern, Raquel Torres, Edmund Breese, Edgar Kennedy. Groucho is Rufus T. Firefly, King of Freedonia, in matchless comedy satire on toy kingdoms, with more zany routines than a circus. Don't miss it. **Duck, You Sucker** (1972-Italian) C-139m. *** D: Sergio Leone. Rod Steiger, James Coburn, Romolo Valli, Maria Monti. Big, sprawling story of Mexican-type revolution, and how peasant thief Steiger gets talked into taking sides by foreigner Coburn. Tremendous action sequences; Leone's wry touches make it worthwhile diversion. Also known as A FIST-FUL OF DYNAMITE.

Dude Goes West, The (1948) 87m. ** D: Kurt Neumann. Eddie Albert, Gale Storm, James Gleason, Binnie Barnes, Gilbert Roland, Barton MacLane. Innocuous little comedy of Easterner Albert becoming a Western hero.

Duel (1971) C-90m. TVM D: Steven Spielberg. Dennis Weaver, Tim Herbert, Charles Peel, Eddie Firestone. Businessman driving rented car on lonely stretch of road begins to realize that the driver of a diesel truck (whom he cannot see) is out to get him. This TV movie put director Spielberg (JAWS, CLOSE ENCOUNTERS) on the map, and rightly so; superb suspense film, from Richard Matheson's script. Originally telecast at 73m.

Duel at Apache Wells (1957) 70m. *½ D: Joe Kane. Anna Maria Alberghetti, Ben Cooper, Jim Davis, Bob Steele, Frank Puglia. Title tells more than all in standard oater.

Duel at Diablo (1966) C-103m. *** D: Ralph Nelson. James Garner, Sidney Poitier, Bibi Andersson, Dennis Weaver, Bill Travers. Aging Indians vs. cavalry formula comes alive in this exciting Western; offbeat casting with tight direction. Some may find it too violent, but a must for action and Western fans.

Duel at Silver Creek, The (1952) C-77m. *½ D: Don Siegel. Audie Murphy, Stephen McNally, Faith Domergue, Susan Cabot, Gerald Mohr. Ponderous oater has Murphy as the "Silver Kid" helping marshal fight town criminals.

Duel at the Rio Grande (1962-Italian) C-93m. ** D: Mario Caiano. Sean Flynn, Danielle de Metz, Folco Lulli, Armando Calvo. Bland reworking of THE MARK OF ZORRO, with Flynn uneasy in lead role.

Duel In Durango SEE: **Gun Duel In Durango**

Duel in the Jungle (1954-British) C-102m. **½ D: George Marshall. Dana Andrews, Jeanne Crain, David Farrar, George Coulouris, Wilfred Hyde-White. Action-paced adventure of insurance investigator tracking allegedly dead man to Africa. Strong cast.

Duel in the Sun (1946) C-130m. *** D: King Vidor. Jennifer Jones, Joseph Cotten, Gregory Peck, Lionel Barrymore, Lillian Gish, Herbert Marshall, Walter Huston, Butterfly McQueen, Charles Bickford, Harry Carey. Producer-writer David O. Selznick's ambitious attempt to duplicate success of GONE WITH THE WIND: big, brawling, engrossing, often stupid sex-Western, with half-breed Jones caught between brothers Peck and Cotten. Great in color, with some memorable scenes and an unexpectedly bizarre finale.

Duel of Champions (1961-Italian) C-105m. ** D: Ferdinando Baldi. Alan Ladd, Franca Bettoja, Franco Fabrizi, Robert Keith, Luciano Marin. Stodgy epic set in ancient Rome with bored-looking Ladd the Roman leader who challenges forces of Alba.

Duel of the Titans (1961-Italian) C-88m. ** D: Sergio Corbucci. Steve Reeves, Gordon Scott, Virna Lisi, Massimo Girotti. Reeves is Romulus and Scott is Remus in this fictional account of justice overcoming tyranny in ancient Rome.

Duellists, The (1978-British) C-101m. *** D: Ridley Scott. Keith Carradine, Harvey Keitel, Albert Finney, Edward Fox, Cristina Raines, Robert Stephens, Diana Quick. Competent screen version of Joseph Conrad's *The Duel*, concerns long-running feud between French officers Carradine and Keitel during the Napoleonic wars. Supporting players are more convincing than two leads, but film is among most staggeringly beautiful of recent years.

Duffy (1968-U.S.A.-British) C-101m. *½ D: Robert Parrish. James Coburn, James Mason, James Fox, Susannah York, John Alderton. Scummy crime comedy about two half-brothers who decide to rob their father of bank notes he is transporting by ship. A waste of everyone's talents and lovely on location photography.

Duffy of San Quentin (1954) 78m. **½ D: Walter Doniger. Louis Hayward, Joanne Dru, Paul Kelly, Maureen O'Sullivan, George Macready. Low-keyed account of Warden Duffy's reforms within the famed prison. Followed by THE STEEL CAGE.

Duffy's Tavern (1945) 97m. BOMB D: Hal Walker. Barry Sullivan, Marjorie Reynolds, Bing Crosby, Dorothy Lamour, Alan Ladd, Betty Hutton, Eddie Bracken, Veronica Lake, Robert Benchley, Paulette Goddard, Brian Donlevy. Disastrous "comedy" of radio character Ed Gardner trying to save Duffy's Tavern, Victor Moore trying to save his record company. No redeeming values despite guest appearances by several dozen Paramount stars.

Duke of West Point, The (1938) 109m. **½ D: Alfred E. Green. Louis Hayward, Joan Fontaine, Tom Brown, Richard Carlson, Alan Curtis, Donald Barry. Predictable West Point saga of honor and love at the Academy is trite but entertaining, with Fontaine winning as the ingenue.

Dulcimer Street (1948-British) 112m. **½ D: Sidney Gilliat. Richard Attenborough, Alastair Sim, Stephen Murray, Fay Compton. Atmospheric account of a slum area of London and its inhabitants who champion one of their own accused of murder. Retitled: LONDON BELONGS TO ME.

Dulcy (1940) 64m. *½ D: S. Sylvan Simon. Ann Sothern, Ian Hunter, Roland Young Reginald Gardiner, Billie Burke, Lynne Carver, Dan Dailey, Jr. Pretty bad comedy of Chinese orphan mending new family's problems. Good cast with inferior material.

Dumbo (1941) C-64m. **** D: Ben Sharpsteen. Voices of Sterling Holloway, Edward Brophy, Verna Felton, Herman Bing, Cliff Edwards. One of Walt Disney's most charming animated films, about pint-sized elephant with giant-sized ears, and how his friend Timothy the Mouse helps build his confidence. Never a dull moment, but pink-elephants dream sequence is special treat.

Dummy (1979) C-100m. TVM D: Frank Perry. Paul Sorvino, LeVar Burton, Brian Dennehy, Rose Gregorio, Gregg Henry. Real-life account of the relationship between a deaf and dumb black youth accused of murder and the deaf court-appointed attorney who defended him in the precedent-setting Chicago trial. Tour-de-force roles for Sorvino, exceptionally good as the lawyer, and Burton. Above average.

Dunkirk (1958-British) 113m. **½ D: Leslie Norman. John Mills, Robert Urquhart, Ray Jackson, Meredith Edwards. Documentary-style drama recounting 1940 evacuation of Allied troops, relying too much on newsreel footage.

Dunwich Horror, The (1970) C-90m. **½ D: Daniel Haller. Sandra Dee, Dean Stockwell, Ed Begley, Sam Jaffe. Chiller of strange terror that lurks in the village of Dunwich. Often effective, but ending ruins the whole film.

Durant Affair, The (1962-British) 73m. *½ D: Godfrey Grayson. Jane Griffiths, Conrad Phillips, Nigel Green, Simon Lack. Flabby courtroom melodrama.

Dust Be My Destiny (1939) 88m. **½ D: Lewis Seiler. John Garfield, Priscilla Lane, Alan Hale, Frank McHugh, John Litel, Billy Halop, Henry Armetta, Stanley Ridges. Garfield ideally cast as young misfit trying to find himself, with Lane a good partner in his search.

Dusty and Sweets McGee (1971) C-95m. ***½ D: Floyd Mutrux. Unconventional, no-holds-barred documentary detailing day-to-day life of various heroin addicts in Los Angeles area. Beware cuts. Among real-life addicts and pushers shown is Billy Gray of T.V.'s FATHER KNOWS BEST.

Dying Room Only (1973) C-74m. TVM D: Phillip Leacock. Cloris Leachman, Ross Martin, Ned Beatty, Louise Latham, Dana Elcar, Dabney Coleman. Couple traveling back to L.A. via desert by car stop off at roadside diner; husband mysteriously disappears. Excellent mood thanks to Richard Matheson's surprise-ending script, thoughtful direction, and small ensemble cast. Above average.

Dynamite (1929) 129m. *** D: Cecil B. DeMille. Conrad Nagel, Kay Johnson, Charles Bickford, Julia Faye, Joel McCrea. Enough plot for seven films in this silly but fascinating early talkie: aristocratic Johnson marries miner Bickford, who's about to be executed, to gain inheritance . . . then Bickford is cleared. Typical DeMille entertainment.

Dynamite (1949) 69m. *½ D: William H. Pine. William Gargan, Virginia Welles, Richard Crane, Irving Bacon, Frank Ferguson, Mary Newton. Young commercial dynamiter Crane clashes with older colleague Gargan over affections of Welles in standard B-opus.

Each Dawn I Die (1939) 92m. **★★★** D: William Keighley. James Cagney, George Raft, George Bancroft, Jane Bryan, Maxie Rosenbloom, Thurston Hall. Reporter Cagney is framed, sent to prison, where he meets tough-guy Raft. Good performances all around, but last half of film becomes outrageously improbable.

Eagle, The (1925) 72m. **★★★** D: Clarence Brown. Rudolph Valentino, Vilma Banky, Louise Dresser, Albert Conti, James Marcus, George Nichols. Valentino plays a sort of Russian Robin Hood in this entertaining costume picture, winning the hand of Vilma Banky while trying to outwit Czarina Dresser, angry because he snubbed her advances.

Eagle and the Hawk (1933) 68m. **★★★½** D: Stuart Walker. Fredric March, Cary Grant, Jack Oakie, Carole Lombard, Guy Standing, Douglas Scott. Well-produced antiwar film with reluctant hero March, copilot Grant, everyone's friend Oakie, society girl Lombard. Still timely.

Eagle and the Hawk (1950) C-104m. **★★½** D: Lewis R. Foster. John Payne, Rhonda Fleming, Dennis O'Keefe, Thomas Gomez, Fred Clark. Contrived actioner set in 1860s Mexico-Texas with O'Keefe and Payne U.S. law enforcers stifling coup to make Maximilian ruler of Mexico; Fleming is fetching love interest.

Eagle Has Landed, The (1977) C-123m. **★★★** D: John Sturges. Michael Caine, Donald Sutherland, Robert Duvall, Jenny Agutter, Donald Pleasence, Anthony Quayle. Action-packed wartime adventure taken from fanciful best-seller about Nazi plot to kidnap Winston Churchill. Hardly a dull moment, thanks to solid cast and lively, twist-laden story.

Eagles Over London (1970-Italian) C-97m. **★★½** D: Enzo Castellari. Frederick Stafford, Van Johnson, Francisco Rabal, Evelyn Stewart, Christian Hay. German intelligence group infiltrates British High Command on the eve of Battle of Britain. Shopworn war drama that shows what's become of ex-MGM teen-age heartthrob Johnson.

Eagle Squadron (1942) 109m. **★★½** D: Arthur Lubin. Robert Stack, Eddie Albert, Diana Barrymore, Nigel Bruce, Jon Hall, Evelyn Ankers, Gladys Cooper, Mary Carr. Usual WW2 action and romance as young American fliers fought the war in the RAF. Good action scenes help average script.

Earl Carroll Vanities (1945) 91m. **★★½** D: Joseph Santley. Dennis O'Keefe, Constance Moore, Eve Arden, Otto Kruger. Republic Pictures tried hard to give this musical class, but zest and production values are lacking; Arden adds her usual quips.

Earl of Chicago, The (1940) 85m. **★★½** D: Richard Thorpe. Robert Montgomery, Edward Arnold, Reginald Owen, Edmund Gwenn. Montgomery can't put over far-fetched tale of Chicago mobster inheriting English title. His awkward performance strains film's credibility.

Early to Bed (1936) 75m. **★★½** D: Norman Z. McLeod. Mary Boland, Charlie Ruggles, George Barbier, Gail Patrick, Robert McWade, Lucien Littlefield. Ruggles' sleepwalking involves him in shady adventure with gangsters. Boland-Ruggles make sparkling team.

Earrings of Madame de, The (1954-French) 105m. **★★★½** D: Max Ophuls. Charles Boyer, Danielle Darrieux, Vittorio De Sica. Captivating story of fickle woman's regard for significant pair of earrings; masterfully filmed and acted.

Earth II (1971) C-100m. TVM D: Tom Gries. Hari Rhodes, Gary Lockwood, Tony Franciosa, Gary Merrill, Lew Ayres, Scott Hylands. Workable premise that doesn't lead anywhere; depiction of day-to-day operations of space station, with good performances battling forgettable dialogue. Average.

Earth Dies Screaming, The (1964-British) 62m. **★★½** D: Terence Fisher. Willard Parker, Virginia Field, Dennis Price, Vanda Godsell. Grim British thriller with invaders taking over remote village; packs great initial suspense but labors.

Earth vs. the Flying Saucers (1956) 83m. **★★** D: Fred F. Sears. Hugh Marlowe, Joan Taylor, Donald Curtis, Morris Ankrum. Ray Harryhausen's superb special effects are the only thing worth watching in this sci-fi that records efforts of scientists on Earth to combat inhabitants from outer space.

Earthquake (1974) C-129m. BOMB D: Mark Robson. Charlton Heston, Ava Gardner, George Kennedy, Genevieve Bujold, Richard Roundtree, Lorne Greene, Barry Sullivan, Marjoe Gortner, Lloyd Nolan, Victoria Principal. Title tells the story in hackneyed disaster epic originally released in Sensurround. Marjoe as a sex deviate and Gardner as Lorne Greene's *daughter* tie for film's top casting honors. Additional footage was included in first network showing.

Earthworm Tractors (1936) 63m. **½ D: Ray Enright. Joe E. Brown, June Travis, Guy Kibbee, Dick Foran, Carol Hughes, Gene Lockhart, Olin Howland. Fair cast with Brown as *Saturday Evening Post* character Alexander Botts, salesman extraordinaire.

East End Chant SEE: Limehouse Blues

East of Eden (1955) C-115m. **** D: Elia Kazan. James Dean, Julie Harris, Raymond Massey, Jo Van Fleet, Burl Ives, Richard Davalos, Albert Dekker. Emotionally overwhelming adaptation of the Steinbeck novel about two brothers' rivalry for the love of their father; affects today's generation as much as those who witnessed Dean's starring debut a quarter century ago. Van Fleet won Oscar as boys' mother.

East of Sudan (1966-British) C-84m. ** D: Nathan Juran. Anthony Quayle, Sylvia Sims, Derek Fowlds, Jenny Agutter, Johnny Sekka, British trooper falls for English governess when he leads her and several others to safety from Arabs in 1880s; OK juvenile adventure.

East of Sumatra (1953) C-82m. **½ D: Budd Boetticher. Jeff Chandler, Marilyn Maxwell, Anthony Quinn, Suzan Ball, Peter Graves. Satisfactory actioner set on Pacific island. Chandler is mining engineer trying to prevent native uprising while romancing Maxwell; Quinn effective as villain.

East of the River (1940) 73m. **½ D: Alfred E. Green. John Garfield, Brenda Marshall, Marjorie Rambeau, William Lundigan. Another variation of MANHATTAN MELODRAMA, with two childhood pals growing up on opposite sides of the law. Rambeau gives a fine performance.

East Side of Heaven (1939) 90m. **½ D: David Butler. Bing Crosby, Joan Blondell, Mischa Auer, Irene Hervey, C. Aubrey Smith, Baby Sandy. Cute Crosby comedy with songs; Bing becomes guardian of abandoned baby, croons title tune, "Sing A Song Of Sunbeams."

East Side, West Side (1949) 108m. **½ D: Mervyn LeRoy. Barbara Stanwyck, James Mason, Ava Gardner, Van Heflin, Cyd Charisse, Gale Sondergaard, William Frawley. Stanwyck-Mason have pivotal roles as chic N.Y.C. society couple with abundant marital woes, stirred up by alluring Gardner and understanding Heflin. Static MGM version of Marcia Davenport's superficial novel.

Easter Parade (1948) C-103m. ***½ D: Charles Walters. Judy Garland, Fred Astaire, Peter Lawford, Ann Miller, Jules Munshin. Delightful Irving Berlin musical with Astaire trying to forget ex-dance partner Miller as he rises to stardom with Judy. One good song after another, Astaire and Garland in top form.

Easy Come, Easy Go (1947) 77m. **½ D: John Farrow. Barry Fitzgerald, Diana Lynn, Sonny Tufts, Dick Foran, Frank McHugh, Allen Jenkins. Fitzgerald is his usual self as a horseplayer who refuses to let daughter Lynn get married.

Easy Come, Easy Go (1967) C-95m. *½ D: John Rich. Elvis Presley, Dodie Marshal, Pat Priest, Elsa Lanchester, Frank McHugh. Presley's a frogman diving for buried treasure in this hackneyed excuse to get him to sing underwater.

Easy Go SEE: Free and Easy.

Easy Life, The (1963-Italian) 105m. *** D: Dino Risi. Vittorio Gassman, Catherine Spaak, Jean-Louis Trintignant, Luciana Angiolillo. Gassman has proper joie de vivre for playing middle-aged playboy who introduces student Trintignant to life of frolic with tragic results; well-played and haunting.

Easy Living (1937) 86m. *** D: Mitchell Leisen. Jean Arthur, Edward Arnold, Ray Milland, Franklin Pangborn, William Demarest, Mary Nash, Luis Alberni. Millionaire Arnold throws spoiled-wife's mink out the window; it drops on unsuspecting working girl Arthur. Arnold's son Milland, off making his career, falls in love. The girl: Arthur. Delightful comedy written by Preston Sturges.

Easy Living (1949) 77m. *** D: Jacques Tourneur. Victor Mature, Lizabeth Scott, Lucille Ball, Sonny Tufts, Lloyd Nolan, Paul Stewart, Jeff Donnell, Jack Paar, Art Baker. Mature is aging football star who can't adjust to impending retirement —especially under constant pressure from grasping wife Scott. Intelligent film from Irwin Shaw story, with good performance from Lucy as team secretary in love with Mature.

Easy Rider (1969) C-94m. ***½ D: Dennis Hopper. Peter Fonda, Dennis Hopper, Jack Nicholson, Luana Anders, Robert Walker, Karen Black. The film that nearly ruined Hollywood when every studio tried to duplicate its success. Script, direction, photography, music are fine, Nicholson's performance great, but this tale of two motorcyclists "searching for America" may not survive the TV editors' scissors.

Easy to Love (1953) C-96m. **½ D: Charles Walters. Esther Williams, Van Johnson, Tony Martin, Carroll Baker. Pleasant Williams aquatic vehicle set at Cypress Gardens, with Johnson and Martin vying for her love. Spectacular production numbers by Busby Berkeley.

Easy to Wed (1946) C-110m. **½ D: Edward Buzzell. Van Johnson, Esther Williams, Lucille Ball, Keenan Wynn, Cecil Kellaway. Remake of LIBELED LADY can't hold a candle to original, but remains passable comedy, with Lucy in one of her first major comedy showcases.

Easy Way, The SEE: **Room For One More**

Eat My Dust! (1976) C-90m. *½ D: Charles Griffith. Ron Howard, Christopher Norris, Warren Kemmerling, Dave Madden, Rance Howard, Clint Howard. Nerve-wracking yarn about two young drivers unable to satisfy passion for speed. Hang on!

Ebb Tide (1937) C-94m. **½ D: James Hogan. Frances Farmer, Ray Milland, Oscar Homolka, Lloyd Nolan, Barry Fitzgerald, David Torrence. Hokey but entertaining outdoors picture in color with Homolka a madman on strange island. Remade as ADVENTURE ISLAND.

Ebony, Ivory and Jade (1979) C-78m. TVM D: John Llewellyn Moxey. Bert Convy, Debbie Allen, Martha Smith, Claude Akins, Nina Foch, Ji-Tu Cumbuka. Las Vegas performer and two comely showgirls double as undercover agents to protect "guest" scientist Foch from terrorists in this routine series pilot that never made it to series. Below average.

Echoes of a Summer (1976) C-99m.

** D: Don Taylor. Richard Harris, Lois Nettleton, Jodie Foster, Geraldine Fitzgerald, William Windom, Brad Savage. Another film in the "disease" genre, as 12-year-old Foster's stolid reaction to impending death inspires those around her. Overwritten tearjerker, but Jodie is always worth a look.

Eddie Cantor Story, The (1953) C-116m. *½ D: Alfred E. Green. Keefe Brasselle, Marilyn Erskine, Aline MacMahon, Marie Windsor. If Brasselle doesn't turn you off as Cantor, MacMahon's Grandma Esther or a putty-nosed young actor (Jackie Barnett) playing Jimmy Durante certainly will.

Eddy Duchin Story, The (1956) C-123m. ** D: George Sidney. Tyrone Power, Kim Novak, Victoria Shaw, James Whitmore. Glossy Hollywood biography of pianist-bandleader of 30s-40s; Power tries hard (Carmen Cavallaro dubs at keyboard). Tearjerker ending and theme song memorable.

Edge of Darkness (1943) 120m. ***½ D: Lewis Milestone. Errol Flynn, Ann Sheridan, Walter Huston, Nancy Coleman, Helmut Dantine, Judith Anderson, Ruth Gordon, John Beal, Roman Bohnen. Intense, compelling drama of underground movement in Norway during Nazi takeover in WW2. Eye-popping camera work complements fine performances.

Edge of Doom (1950) 99m. ** D: Mark Robson. Dana Andrews, Farley Granger, Joan Evans, Mala Powers, Adele Jergens. Granger reaches peak of histrionic despair in moody piece about young man baffled by poverty, religion, murder, and assorted other problems.

Edge of Eternity (1959) C-80m. ** D: Don Siegel. Cornel Wilde, Victoria Shaw, Mickey Shaughnessy, Edgar Buchanan, Rian Garrick, Jack Elam. Deputy sheriff Wilde tracks killers to Grand Canyon, leading to shoot-out on mining buckets suspended on cables way above canyon.

Edge of Hell (1956) 76m. *½ D: Hugo Haas. Hugo Haas, Francesca de Scaffa, Ken Carlton, June Hammerstein. Offbeat, minor film of pauper Haas, his beloved dog, and small boy who enters on the scene.

Edge of the City (1957) 85m. **** D: Martin Ritt. John Cassavetes, Sidney Poitier, Jack Warden, Ruby Dee, Kathleen Maguire, Ruth White. Somber, realistic account of N.Y.C.

waterfront life and corruption. Friendship of army deserter Cassavetes and dock worker Poitier, both conflicting with union racketeer Warden, provides focus for reflections on integration and integrity in lower-class society. Masterfully acted by all.

Edison, The Man (1940) 107m. *** D: Clarence Brown. Spencer Tracy, Rita Johnson, Lynne Overman, Charles Coburn, Gene Lockhart, Henry Travers, Felix Bressart. Sequel to YOUNG TOM EDISON perfectly casts Tracy as earnest inventor with passion for mechanical ingenuity. Facts and MGM fantasy combine well in sentimental treatment.

Education of Sonny Carson, The (1974) C-105m. **½ D: Michael Campus. Rony Clanton, Don Gordon, Joyce Walker, Paul Benjamin, Ram John Holder. Interesting if overemotional drama of rebellious black youth in Brooklyn of the 50s and 60s, based on his autobiography.

Edward, My Son (1949-British) 112m. *** D: George Cukor. Spencer Tracy, Deborah Kerr, Ian Hunter, James Donald, Mervyn Johns, Felix Aylmer, Leueen McGarth. Film recounts rocky marriage of British couple Tracy and Kerr who discover they drove their son to suicide. Gimmicks of Tracy talking to viewer, title character never being shown, come off as forced.

Effect of Gamma Rays on Man-in-the-Moon Marigolds, The (1972) C-100m. *** D: Paul Newman. Joanne Woodward, Nell Potts, Roberta Wallach, Judith Lowry. Woodward gives superb performance in tale of secluded boor of a mother and her two strange daughters. Screenplay by Paul Zindel from his Pulitzer Prize-winning play.

Egg and I, The (1947) 108m. *** D: Chester Erskine. Claudette Colbert, Fred MacMurray, Marjorie Main, Louise Allbritton, Percy Kilbride. Colbert is delightful as city girl who marries chicken farmer MacMurray and struggles to survive on his farm; first appearance of Ma and Pa Kettle.

Egyptian, The (1954) C-140m. **½ D: Michael Curtiz. Edmund Purdom, Jean Simmons, Victor Mature, Gene Tierney, Michael Wilding, Peter Ustinov. Beautiful scenery and sets make for great atmosphere in otherwise uneven biblical spectacle. Some good acting by Purdom, others wasted.

8½ (1963-Italian) 135m. **** D: Federico Fellini. Marcello Mastroiani, Claudia Cardinale, Anouk Aimee, Sandra Milo, Barbara Steele. Fellini's unique self-analytical movie casts Mastroiani as a filmmaker trying to develop a new project, amid frequent visions and countless subplots. A long, difficult, but fascinating film, overflowing with creative and technical wizardry. Certainly one of the most intensely personal statements ever made on film.

Eiger Sanction, The (1975) C-128m. *½ D: Clint Eastwood. Clint Eastwood, George Kennedy, Vonetta McGee, Jack Cassidy, Thayer David, Heidi Bruhl, Reiner Schoene. Misfire of pseudo-James Bond material, often unintentionally funny. Thrilling mountain-climbing climax does not make up for film's many faults and unending length. Jack Cassidy as gay, treacherous spy contributes the only creative acting.

Eight Iron Men (1952) 80m. **½ D: Edward Dmytryk. Lee Marvin, Richard Kiley, Nick Dennis, Arthur Franz, Mary Castle. WW2 actioner focusing on a group of soldiers, strain they undergo during continued enemy attack.

Eight O'clock Walk (1952-British) 87m. **½ D: Lance Comfort. Richard Attenborough, Cathy O'Donnell, Derek Farr, Ian Hunter. Courtroom drama manages to create pace and tension, involving murder trial; nicely played by Attenborough.

Eight on the Lam (1967) C-106m. BOMB D: George Marshall. Bob Hope, Phyllis Diller, Jonathan Winters, Jill St. John, Shirley Eaton. Another of Hope's horrible recent comedies casts him as a widower with seven children who finds $10,-000; even Winters can't help this dud.

Eighteen and Anxious (1957) 93m. ** D: Joe Parker. Martha Scott, Jim Backus, Mary Webster, William Campbell, Jackie Coogan. Oddball cast atones for amateurish muck about pregnant teen-ager forced to face life's realities.

80 Steps to Jonah (1969) C-107m. ** D: Gerd Oswald. Wayne Newton, Jo Van Fleet, Keenan Wynn, Diana Ewing, Slim Pickens, Sal Mineo. Loner through rotten circumstances must escape police clutches for good, stumbles upon camp for blind children; new world changes his outlook on life. Major liability: casting of Newton in leading role.

80,000 Suspects (1963-British) 113m. ** D: Val Guest. Claire Bloom, Richard Johnson, Yolande Donlan, Cyril Cusack. Capable cast saddled with yarn of doctor (Johnson) and wife (Bloom) finding new love together while combating local smallpox outbreak.

El Alamein (1953) 67m. ** D: Fred F. Sears. Scott Brady, Edward Ashley, Rita Moreno, Michael Pate. No surprises in WW2 desert actioner with Brady heading group being attacked by Germans.

El Cid (1961) C-184m. *** D: Anthony Mann. Charlton Heston, Sophia Loren, Raf Vallone, Genevieve Page, Hurd Hatfield. Mammoth spectacle with above-average script and acting in film of legandary Cid (Heston) who drove Moors from Spain.

El Condor (1970) C-102m. ** D: John Guillermin. Jim Brown, Lee Van Cleef, Patrick O'Neal, Marianna Hill, Iron Eyes Cody, Elisha Cook, Jr. Unless your TV editor digs frontal nudity, the key scene may be missing from otherwise slow Western about two drifters in search of some gold supposedly buried in Mexican fortress; Marianna Hill looks good even with her clothes on.

El Dorado (1967) C-127m. *** D: Howard Hawks. John Wayne, Robert Mitchum, James Caan, Charlene Holt, Michele Carey, Arthur Hunnicutt. Loose remake of Hawks' own RIO BRAVO is not as good as the original, but not many Westerns are; tale of a gunfighter who helps out his drunken sheriff pal is smooth mix of comedy and action. Good performance by Caan.

El Greco (1966-Italian-French) C-95m. ** D: Luciano Salce. Mel Ferrer, Rosanna Schiaffino, Franco Giacobini, Renzo Giovampietro, Adolfo Celi. Despite lavish trappings, story of painter reduced to soap-opera terms falls flat. Beautiful color, but no plot of any distinction.

El Paso (1949) C-92m. ** D: Lewis R. Foster. John Payne, Gail Russell, Sterling Hayden, Gabby Hayes. Routine Western of post-Civil War Texas, with Payne an attorney who discovers gunplay more than words will rid town of crooks.

Eleanor Roosevelt Story, The (1965) 91m. ***½ D: Richard Kaplan. Narrated by Archibald Macleish, Eric Sevareid, Francis Cole. Intelligently handled account of a great American citizen, who overcomes personal obstacles to become a beacon of human kindness. Music score by Ezra Laderman.

Electra Glide in Blue (1973) C-106m. *** D: James William Guercio. Robert Blake, Billy Green Bush, Mitchell Ryan, Jeannine Riley, Elisha Cook, Jr., Royal Dano. Violent film about highway cop Blake making up in brains what he lacks in height. Striking action sequences and good characterizations.

Electric Horseman, The (1979) C-120m. **½ D: Sydney Pollack. Robert Redford, Jane Fonda, Valerie Perrine, Willie Nelson, John Saxon, Nicolas Coster. Innocuous rip-off of LONELY ARE THE BRAVE tries to palm off Redford as a near-derelict who steals a $12 million thoroughbred from a Vegas hotel and heads for some grazing land. Pleasant, to be sure, but considering the people involved, a disappointment.

Electronic Monster, The (1960-British) 72m. *½ D: Montgomery Tully. Rod Cameron, Mary Murphy, Meredith Edwards, Peter Illing. Cameron investigates actress' death, revealing strange experiments at a clinic; scientific gadgetry has its moments.

Elephant Boy (1937-British) 80m. *** D: Robert Flaherty. Sabu, W. E. Holloway, Walter Hudd, Allan Jeayes, Bruce Gordon, D. J. Williams. Successful adaptation of Rudyard Kipling story. Native boy Sabu (in film debut) claims he knows location of elephant burying ground. Atmospheric direction.

Elephant Gun (1959-British) C-84m. ** D: Ken Annakin. Belinda Lee, Michael Craig, Patrick McGoohan, Anna Gaylor, Eric Pohlmann, Pamela Stirling. Jungle love triangle has virtue of on-location shooting in Africa.

Elephant Stampede (1951) 71m. D: Ford Beebe. Johnny Sheffield, Donna Martell, Edith Evanson, Martin Wilkins, Myron Healey, Leonard Mudie, Guy Kingsford. SEE: **Bomba the Jungle Boy** series.

Elephant Walk (1954) C-103m. ** D: William Dieterle. Elizabeth Taylor, Dana Andrews, Peter Finch, Abraham Sofaer. Overblown melodrama set on Ceylon tea plantation, with

Taylor as Finch's new bride who must cope with environment and his father complex. Pachyderm stampede climax comes none too soon. Vivien Leigh, replaced by Taylor, can be seen in long shots.

Elevator, The (1974) C-78m. TVM D: Jerry Jameson. James Farentino, Roddy McDowall, Craig Stevens, Myrna Loy, Teresa Wright, Carol Lynley, Don Stroud, Barry Livingston. Standard amount of all-star thrills when a group of people are stuck between floors in high-rise building with claustrophobic thief (Farentino) trying to flee from his latest heist. Average.

11 Harrowhouse (1974-British) C-98m. *** D: Aram Avakian. Charles Grodin, Candice Bergen, James Mason, Trevor Howard, John Gielgud, Helen Cherry. Funny action spoof of heist films, as diamond merchant Grodin robs the world clearinghouse for gems. Grodin also adapted Gerald A. Browne's best-selling novel. Retitled: ANYTHING FOR LOVE.

11th Victim (1979) C-100m. TVM D: Jonathan Kaplan. Bess Armstrong, Max Gail, Harold Gould, Pamela Ludwig, Eric Burdon, Annazette Chase. Standard exploitation drama involving small town newswoman who goes to Hollywood looking for the killer of her prostitute sister. Average.

Elizabeth the Queen SEE: Private Lives of Elizabeth and Essex, The

Ella Cinders (1926) 60m. *** D: Alfred E. Green. Colleen Moore, Lloyd Hughes, Jed Prouty, Harry Langdon. Excellent Colleen Moore silent vehicle about small-town girl going to Hollywood to make good; bright and peppy, with amusing guest appearance by Langdon.

Ellery Queen Perhaps the most successful series of detective stories ever written, the Ellery Queen mysteries rank as one of the least successful film series. A few scattered attempts to film Queen stories in the 1930s with Donald Cook and Eddie Quillan never aroused much interest. Then in 1940, Columbia began a series starring Ralph Bellamy as Ellery Queen, Charley Grapewin as his Inspector father, Margaret Lindsay as his Girl Friday Nikki, and James Burke as Inspector Queen's dim-witted aide. The very first entry, ELLERY QUEEN, MASTER DETECTIVE, belied its title by making Bellamy an incredible "comic" bumbler, an inexplicable characterization that lasted through all of Bellamy's films in the series. Heavy doses of comedy relief in entries like ELLERY QUEEN AND THE MURDER RING were not offset by solid mystery angles, and the films, though only one hour long, moved like molasses. A switch in casting making William Gargan the lead character in 1942 did not help matters, with the actual suspects becoming more obvious than ever. Gargan's three efforts as Queen were undistinguished, and his last episode, ENEMY AGENTS MEET ELLERY QUEEN, was also the last in the short-lived series. Consistent top-quality casting with character actors like Eduardo Ciannelli, Blanche Yurka, George Zucco, Leon Ames, and former director Fred Niblo could do nothing to offset the lifeless scripts and turgid direction. None of the films in the series is really worthwhile, a distinct disappointment to the mystery fans who came to regard the Ellery Queen stories as top-grade in the mystery genre.

Ellery Queen (1975) C-78m. TVM D: David Greene. Jim Hutton, David Wayne, Ray Milland, Kim Hunter, Monte Markham, John Hillerman, John Larch, Tim O'Connor. Preoccupied sleuth Ellery helps his police inspector dad in solving a fashion designer's murder. The Ellery Queen mystery *The Fourth Side of the Triangle* served as the source for this entertaining, light-hearted period detective movie that preceded the popular TV series. Above average.

Ellery Queen and the Murder Ring (1941) 65m. D: James Hogan. Ralph Bellamy, Margaret Lindsay, Charley Grapewin, Mona Barrie, Paul Hurst, James Burke, Blanche Yurka.

Ellery Queen and the Perfect Crime (1941) 68m. D: James Hogan. Ralph Bellamy, Margaret Lindsay, Charley Grapewin, Spring Byington, H. B. Warner, James Burke.

Ellery Queen: Don't Look Behind You (1971) C-100m. TVM D: Barry Shear. Peter Lawford, Harry Morgan, Stefanie Powers, E. G. Marshall, Coleen Gray, Morgan Sterne, Skye Aubrey. Entertaining, easily forgettable murder mystery has famed detective taking over police-baffling Hydra case. Relationship between Lawford and Morgan starts out well but disappears as film progresses. Average.

Ellery Queen, Master Detective (1940) 66m. D: Kurt Neumann. Ralph Bellamy, Margaret Lindsay, Charley Grapewin, James Burke, Michael Whalen, Marsha Hunt.

Ellery Queen's Penthouse Mystery (1941) 69m. D: James Hogan. Ralph Bellamy, Charley Grapewin, Margaret Lindsay, James Burke, Anna May Wong, Eduardo Ciannelli, Frank Albertson.

Elmer Gantry (1960) C-145m. ***½ D: Richard Brooks. Burt Lancaster, Jean Simmons, Dean Jagger, Arthur Kennedy, Shirley Jones. Charlatan Lancaster joins evangelist Simmons, exploiting her touring show; newspaperman Kennedy tries to expose their hypocrisy. Lancaster won Oscar in title role, as did Jones, playing jilted-girlfriend-turned-prostitute. Vibrant handling of Sinclair Lewis story of 1920s Midwest is a must-see film.

Elmer the Great (1933) 74m. *** D: Mervyn LeRoy. Joe E. Brown, Patricia Ellis, Claire Dodd, Sterling Holloway, Jessie Ralph. Excellent Ring Lardner baseball comedy, filmed before as FAST COMPANY, of naive country boy who becomes ball star, gets involved with crooks at the same time.

Elopement (1951) 82m. ** D: Henry Koster. Clifton Webb, Anne Francis, Charles Bickford, William Lundigan, Reginald Gardiner. Tame proceedings despite Webb's arch performance as Francis' father, who disapproves of her marriage to Lundigan.

Elusive Corporal, The (1963-French, dubbed) 108m. **½ D: Jean Renoir. Jean-Pierre Cassel, Claude Brasseur, Claude Rich, O. E. Hasse. Flavorful if predictable account of Frenchmen in German prison camp during WW2, determined to escape.

Elusive Pimpernel, The (1950-British) C-109m. *** D: Michael Powell, Emeric Pressburger. David Niven, Margaret Leighton, Cyril Cusack, Jack Hawkins, Arlette Marchal, Robert Coote, Patrick Macnee. Colorful remake of THE SCARLET PIMPERNEL with Niven as British fop who secretly aids victims of Reign of Terror; lively fun.

Elvira Madigan (1967-Swedish) C-89m. *** D: Bo Widerberg. Pia Degermark, Thommy Berggren, Lennart Malmen, Nina Widerberg, Cleo Jensen. Combination of attractive stars, lovers-on-the-run theme, and lovely soft-focus photography made this click with public. Stylistically a bit too much like a shampoo commercial, but film has undeniable appeal.

Elvis (1979) C-150m. TVM D: John Carpenter. Kurt Russell, Shelley Winters, Pat Hingle, Season Hubley, Bing Russell. The Presley saga affectionately and believably retold, from his youth to his career as a club entertainer in 1969. Russell surprisingly effective as Elvis, whose songs were dubbed by country singer Ronnie McDowell. One of the highest rated TV movies ever—even outdrawing GONE WITH THE WIND, shown opposite at its premiere. Above average.

Elvis on Tour (1972) C-93m. ** D: Pierre Adidge, Robert Abel. Static study of rock 'n' roll's biggest superstar going through his paces at a series of concerts around the country. Even the music is not up to standard.

Elvis: That's the Way It Is (1970) C-97m. *** D: Denis Sanders. Engaging look at Elvis Presley offstage, preparing major nightclub act, culminating in opening-night performance in Las Vegas. Well-filmed if one-sided documentary paints vivid picture of Elvis as master showman.

Embassy (1972-British) C-90m. **½ D: Gordon Hessler. Richard Roundtree, Chuck Connors, Max von Sydow, Ray Milland, Broderick Crawford, Marie-Jose Nat. Spotty spy thriller about Russian defector Von Sydow seeking asylum and the State Department's efforts to have agent Roundtree smuggle him out of the mideast under KGB man Connors' nose. Good cast works valiantly with contrived plot, talky script.

Embraceable You (1948) 80m. ** D: Felix Jacoves. Dane Clark, Geraldine Brooks, S. Z. Sakall, Wallace Ford. Tough-guy Clark injures young girl, then falls in love with her, in this sentimental romance.

Embryo (1976) C-104m. ** D: Ralph Nelson. Rock Hudson, Diane Ladd, Barbara Carrera, Roddy McDowall, Anne Schedeen. Sometimes interesting, sometimes repulsive horror sci-fi about woman and dog grown from fetuses outside the womb—with terrifying results.

Emergency (1962-British) 63m. ** D:

Francis Searle. Glyn Houston, Zena Walker, Dermot Walsh, Colin Tapley. Adequate programmer dealing with Walker-Walsh reaffirming their marriage while waiting for blood donor to save their daughter's life.

Emergency (1971) C-100m. D: Christian Nyby. Robert Fuller, Julie London, Bobby Troup, Randolph Mantooth, Kevin Tighe. Daily adventures, foibles of L.A. county paramedics unit and backup hospital personnel. Only difference between this and TV series is the running time. Average; pilot for later TV series produced by Jack Webb.

Emergency Wedding (1950) 78m. ** D: Edward Buzzell. Barbara Hale, Larry Parks, Una Merkel, Jim Backus, Queenie Smith. Sterile remake of YOU BELONG TO ME detailing jealous Parks who thinks new wife, doctor Hale, spends too much time with her male patients.

Emigrants, The (1972-Swedish) C-148m. *** D: Jan Troell. Max Von Sydow, Liv Ullmann, Eddie Axberg, Svenolof Bern, Aina Alfredsson, Allan Edwall. Rambling but generally good saga about several Swedes who emigrate to America in 19th century. Sequel, THE NEW LAND, is even better.

Emil and the Detectives (1964) C-99m. *½ D: Peter Tewksbury. Walter Slezak, Bryan Russell, Roger Mobley, Heinz Schubert, Peter Erlich, Cindy Cassell. Turgid Disney version of Erich Kastner's children's book, about a young boy who is robbed and determines to nail the thief, with the help of young detective friends. Filmed in Germany.

Emma (1932) 73m. ***½ D: Clarence Brown. Marie Dressler, Richard Cromwell, Jean Hersholt, Myrna Loy, John Miljan, Leila Bennett. Beautiful film with Dressler at her best, as down-to-earth woman who works as housemaid-nanny for family and eventually marries widowed father (Hersholt). Sentimental movie never cloys, thanks to wonderful Marie.

Emperor Jones, The (1933) 72m. **½ D: Dudley Murphy. Paul Robeson, Dudley Digges, Frank Wilson, Fredi Washington, Ruby Elzy. Robeson plays Pullman porter who escapes from chain gang and improbably becomes King of a Caribbean island. Pretentious adaptation of Eugene O'Neill play derives its chief interest

and value from Robeson himself. Look for Moms Mabley in bit part.

Emperor of the North Pole (1973) C-118m. **½ D: Robert Aldrich. Lee Marvin, Ernest Borgnine, Keith Carradine, Charles Tyner, Malcolm Atterbury. Disappointing saga of evil trainsman who kills hoboes if he catches them trying to steal a free ride. Extremely violent. Retitled: EMPEROR OF THE NORTH.

Emperor Waltz, The (1948) C-106m. **½ D: Billy Wilder. Bing Crosby, Joan Fontaine, Roland Culver, Lucile Watson, Richard Haydn, Sig Ruman. Lavish but standard Crosby musical set in Franz Joseph Austria (on Hollywood's backlots) with Bing selling record-players to royalty. Awfully schmaltzy material for writer-director Wilder.

Emperor's Candlesticks, The (1937) 89m. **½ D: George Fitzmaurice. William Powell, Luise Rainer, Robert Young, Maureen O'Sullivan, Frank Morgan, Emma Dunn, Douglass Dumbrille. Romance and intrigue in Russia between Powell and Rainer, spies on opposite sides of the fence; lavish frou-frou.

Empire of the Ants (1977) C-90m. ** D: Bert I. Gordon. Joan Collins, Robert Lansing, Albert Salmi, John David Carson, Robert Pine, Jacqueline Scott. Laughable man-vs.-giant insects chiller from H. G. Wells' story. Vacationers on an isolated island find themselves at the mercy of voracious ants that have become monsters after feasting on a leaking barrel of radioactive waste.

Enchanted April (1935) 66m. ** D: Harry Beaumont. Ann Harding, Frank Morgan, Katharine Alexander, Reginald Owen, Jane Baxter. Slightly overworn drama of four different women spending their vacation at same Italian villa; Harding is staunch.

Enchanted Cottage, The (1945) 91m. **½ D: John Cromwell. Dorothy McGuire, Robert Young, Herbert Marshall, Mildred Natwick, Spring Byington, Hillary Brooke. Fantasy set in New England cottage where two misfits find love; sensitively handled, from Arthur Pinero play.

Enchanted Forest (1945) C-78m. **½ D: Lew Landers. Edmund Lowe, Brenda Joyce, Billy Severn, Harry Davenport, John Litel. Nicely done story of young boy who learns about life from old man who lives amid nature in the forest.

Enchanted Island (1958) **C-94m.** *½ D: Allan Dwan. Dana Andrews, Jane Powell, Don Dubbins, Arthur Shields. Miscast, low-budget version of Herman Melville's TYPEE. Andrews is deserter from American whaling ship who finds love with native girl Powell on South Sea island; some minor uprisings by local cannibals for good measure.

Enchantment (1948) **102m.** *** D: Irving Reis. David Niven, Teresa Wright, Evelyn Keyes, Farley Granger, Jayne Meadows, Leo G. Carroll. Weepy romancer with elderly Niven recalling his tragic love as he watches grandson Granger embark upon his own love life.

Encore (1952-British) **89m.** *** D: Pat Jackson, Anthony Pelissier, Harold French. Nigel Patrick, Roland Culver, Kay Walsh, Glynis Johns, Terence Morgan. Entertaining trilogy of Somerset Maugham stories: brothers try to outdo one another over money; grouchy matron almost ruins ship cruise; apprehensive circus performer faces a crisis.

End, The (1978) **C-100m.** *** D: Burt Reynolds. Burt Reynolds, Sally Field, Dom DeLuise, Joanne Woodward, Kristy McNichol, Robby Benson, David Steinberg, Norman Fell, Carl Reiner, Pat O'Brien, Myrna Loy. Uneven but original black comedy about man who learns he's dying, and decides to commit suicide. DeLuise is achingly funny as Burt's schizophrenic sanitarium pal, and Reynold's final soliloquy is great.

End of Desire (1962-French) **C-86m.** ** D: Alexandre Astruc. Maria Schell, Christian Marquand, Pascale Petit, Ivan Desny. Schell is only bright light in De Maupassant tale of wife who discovers her husband loves her money and prefers to romance servant (Antonella Lualdi).

End of the Affair, The (1955-British) **106m.** **½ D: Edward Dmytryk. Deborah Kerr, Van Johnson, John Mills, Peter Cushing, Michael Goodliffe. Graham Greene's mystic-religious novel about a wartime love affair in London loses much in screen version, especially from bad Johnson portrayal; Kerr is earnest.

End of the River, The (1947-British) **80m.** ** D: Derek Twist. Sabu, Bibi Ferreira, Esmond Knight, Torin Thatcher, Robert Douglas. Native boy Sabu fights for acceptance in white world; ambitious drama suffers from mediocre casting.

End of the Road (1970) **C-110m.** ***½ D: Aram Avakian. Stacy Keach, Harris Yulin, Dorothy Tristan, James Earl Jones, Grayson Hall, Ray Brock, James Coco. Keach and Jones give stinging performances in solid filmization of bizarre John Barth novel about unstable college instructor who becomes involved with the wife of a professor. Tristan is superb in crucial and difficult role. TV cuts are likely.

End of the World (1977) **C-87m.** ** D: John Hayes. Christopher Lee, Sue Lyon, Kirk Scott, Lew Ayres, Macdonald Carey, Dean Jagger, Liz Ross. Lee plays a priest and his sinister "double" in this strange sci-fi tale about imminent world destruction by alien invaders. Opens strong but drifts into dullness.

Endless Night (1971-British) **C-99m.** *** D: Sidney Gilliat. Hayley Mills, Hywel Bennett, Britt Ekland, George Sanders, Per Oscarsson, Peter Bowles, Lois Maxwell. Gripping Agatha Christie thriller about chauffeur (Bennett) who marries rich American girl (Mills) and moves into "dream house" which turns out to be more a nightmare. Also known as *Agatha Christie's Endless Night*.

Endless Summer, The (1966) **C-95m.** *** D: Bruce Brown. Mike Hynson, Robert August. Superior documentary on surfing, filmed on location around the world, with a most diverting tongue-in-cheek narrative.

Enemy Agents Meet Ellery Queen (1942) **65m.** D: James Hogan. William Gargan, Gale Sondergaard, Margaret Lindsay, Charley Grapewin, Gilbert Roland. SEE Ellery Queen series.

Enemy Below, The (1957) **C-98m.** *** D: Dick Powell. Robert Mitchum, Curt Jurgens, Theodore Bikel, Doug McClure, Russell Collins, David Hedison. Select WW2 submarine chase tale, which manages to garner interest from usual crew interaction of U.S. vs. Germany in underwater action; special effects notable.

Enemy From Space (1957-British) **84m.** ** D: Val Guest. Brian Donlevy, Michael Ripper, Sidney James, Bryan Forbes. Undistinguished sci-fi which leaves mandatory monster from outer space to one's imagination but spells out dreary plot in detail.

Enemy General, The (1960) 74m.
**½ D: George Sherman. Van
Johnson, Jean-Pierre Aumont, Dany
Carrel, John Van Dreelen. OSS
officer (Johnson) and French resistance leader Aumont join forces
to rescue Nazi general (Van Dreelen) who wants to defect to Allies;
satisfactory handling of middling
material.

Enforcer, The (1951) 87m. *** D:
Bretaigne Windust, Humphrey Bogart, Zero Mostel, Ted de Corsia,
Everett Sloane, Roy Roberts. Bogey
is D.A. cracking down on crime
ring led by Sloane in this raw drama,
realistically done.

Enforcer, The (1976) C-96m. *** D:
James Fargo, Clint Eastwood, Tyne
Daly, Harry Guardino, Bradford
Dillman, John Mitchum, DeVeren
Bookwalter, John Crawford. Dirty
Harry Callahan (Eastwood) has to
contend with a female partner (Daly)
as he goes after an underground
terrorist group in San Francisco.
Violent, bubble-gum-mentality script,
but part of a formula that just seems
to work. The third Dirty Harry picture.

England Made Me (1973-British)
C-100m. *** D: Peter Duffell. Peter
Finch, Michael York, Hildegard
Neil, Michael Hordern, Joss Ackland. Unappreciated in its initial release, drama of a powerful financier
in Nazi Germany of 1935 is absorbing, thoughtful fare. Made in Yugoslavia.

Ensign Pulver (1964) C-104m. ** D:
Joshua Logan. Robert Walker, Jr.,
Burl Ives, Walter Matthau, Tommy
Sands, James Farentino, Diana
Sands, Kay Medford, Millie Perkins.
Flat sequel to MR. ROBERTS has
Walker sinking in Jack Lemmon role
amid synthetic seaboard and coral
isle shenanigans.

Enter Arsene Lupin (1944) 72m. **
D: Ford Beebe. Charles Korvin, Ella
Raines, J. Carrol Naish, George Dolenz, Gale Sondergaard. Good supporting cast of villains gives zest to
tame tale of naive heroine possessing
a wealth of jewels.

Enter Laughing (1967) C-112m. **
D: Carl Reiner. Jose Ferrer, Shelley
Winters, Elaine May, Jack Gilford,
Reni Santoni, Janet Margolin, David
Opatoshu, Michael J. Pollard, Don
Rickles, Nancy Kovack, Rob Reiner.
Reiner's funny semi-autobiographical
Broadway play becomes bland screen
comedy as youngster struggles to

make it as an actor, despite all
manner of problems in his way.

Enter Madame (1935) 83m. **½ D:
Elliott Nugent. Elissa Landi, Cary
Grant, Lynne Overman, Sharon
Lynne, Frank Albertson. Grant marries opera star Landi and winds up
taking back seat to her career; pleasant romantic comedy.

Enter the Dragon (1973) C-97m.
***½ D: Robert Clouse. Bruce Lee,
John Saxon, Jim Kelly. Almost perfect action film that forgets about
plot and concentrates on mind-
boggling action. Martial arts expert
Lee (in last complete film role) infiltrates strange tournament on island
fortress.

Entertainer, The (1960-British) 97m.
***½ D: Tony Richardson. Lau-
rence Olivier, Brenda De Banzie, Albert Finney, Alan Bates, Joan Plowright, Roger Livesey, Shirley Ann
Field. Seedy vaudevillian (Olivier)
ruins everyone's life and won't catch
on. Film captures flavor of chintzy
seaside resort, complementing Olivier's brilliance as egotistical song-and-
dance man.

Entertainer, The (1975) C-100m.
TVM D: Donald Wrye. Jack Lemmon, Ray Bolger, Sada Thompson,
Tyne Daly, Allyn Ann McLerie,
Michael Cristofer, Annette O'Toole,
Mitch Ryan. Third-rate vaudevillian
Archie Rice plays out his life in a
seedy California burlesque house in
the 1940s, vainly trying to emulate
his once-famous father (Bolger) now
living on faded memories. Lemmon
is good, but no Olivier; Bolger is
excellent as the father. Unrelenting
drama punctuated by eight Marvin
Hamlisch songs. Average.

Entertaining Mr. Sloane (1970-Brit-
ish) C-94m. **½ D: Douglas Hickox.
Beryl Reid, Harry Andrews, Peter
McEnery, Alan Webb. Acting by
McEnery, Reid, and Andrews is extraordinary in story of young man
who becomes involved with both
brother and sister. Handling and
script are uneven, but film is worthwhile for performances alone.

Equinox (1971) C-80m. ** D: Jack
Woods. Edward Connell, Barbara
Hewitt, Frank Boers Jr., Robin
Christopher, Jack Woods, Fritz Lieber. Archaeology students confront
Satanism—and mutant-like monsters
—while searching for vanished professor. Late-1960s amateur film was
expanded for theatrical release, mix-

ing B-movie clichés with good special effects.

Equus (1977) C-138m. ** D: Sidney Lumet. Richard Burton, Peter Firth, Colin Blakeley, Joan Plowright, Harry Andrews, Eileen Atkins, Jenny Agutter. Peter Shaffer's shattering play makes bumpy screen adaptation, its vivid theatricality lost on film; Burton plays troubled psychiatrist trying to unlock deep-rooted problems of stable boy Firth.

Eric (1975) C-100m. TVM D: James Goldstone. Patricia Neal, John Savage, Claude Akins, Sian Barbara Allen, Mark Hamill, Nehemiah Persoff, Tom Clancy. Sensitive weeper about athletic youth who, aware of his terminal illness, refuses to give up. Based on Doris Lund's book about her own teen-aged son, given dignity by the steady performances of Savage in title role and Neal as his valiant mother. Above average.

Erik the Conqueror (1963-Italian) C-81m. ** D: Mario Bava. Cameron Mitchell, Alice Kessler, Ellen Kessler, Françoise Christophe. Unexceptional account of 10th-century Viking life, with Mitchell fighting for virtue and love.

Errand Boy, The (1961) 92m. **½ D: Jerry Lewis. Jerry Lewis, Brian Donlevy, Howard McNear, Sig Ruman, Fritz Feld, Iris Adrian, Kathleen Freeman, Doodles Weaver. Jerry on the loose in a movie studio has its moments. Long string of gags provide the laughter; veteran character actors produce the sparkle.

Escapade (1957-British) 87m. *** D: Philip Leacock. John Mills, Yvonne Michell, Alastair Sim, Jeremy Spenser, Andrew Ray. Theme of pacifism adds substance to film about problems and pranks of boys at English private school. Earnest and well done.

Escapade in Japan (1957) C-92m. ** D: Arthur Lubin. Teresa Wright, Cameron Mitchell, Jon Provost, Philip Ober. Premise of American boy and Japanese friend seeking former's parents is acceptable excuse for nice scenic tour of Japan.

Escape (1940) 104m. *** D: Mervyn LeRoy. Norma Shearer, Robert Taylor, Conrad Veidt, Nazimova, Felix Bressart. Countess Shearer helps Taylor get his mother (Nazimova) out of German concentration camp before WW2; polished, with sterling cast.

Escape (1948-British) 78m. *** D: Joseph L. Mankiewicz. Rex Harrison, Peggy Cummins, William Hartnell, Norman Wooland, Jill Esmond. Compelling account of man sent to prison, unjustly in his opinion; his attempted escape climaxes narrative.

Escape (1970) C-73m. TVM D: John Llewellyn Moxey. Christopher George, Avery Schreiber, Marlyn Mason, William Windom, Gloria Grahame, John Vernon. After almost losing his life trying to prevent kidnapping of scientist, magician-adventurer, with help of sidekick and scientist's daughter (Mason), battles with mysterious mad scientist over plot to destroy earth. Dumb characterizations, silly dialogue, passable action.

Escape from Alcatraz (1979) C-112m. *** D: Donald Siegel. Clint Eastwood, Patrick McGoohan, Roberts Blossom, Jack Thibeau, Fred Ward, Paul Benjamin. Straightforward, methodical telling of true story about 1962 breakout from supposedly impregnable prison. Vivid and credible throughout.

Escape from Bogen County (1977) C-100m. TVM D: Steven Stern. Jaclyn Smith, Mitchell Ryan, Michael Parks, Henry Gibson, Pat Hingle, Philip Abbott. Tawdry drama about a vicious political czar who strips his wife of her civil rights and imprisons her in their mansion when she threatens to expose his ruthlessness. Below average.

Escape From East Berlin (1962) 94m. ** D: Robert Siodmak. Don Murray, Christine Kaufmann, Werner Klemperer, Ingrid van Bergen, Karl Schell. At least Murray is earnest.

Escape From Fort Bravo (1953) C-98m. *** D: John Sturges. William Holden, Eleanor Parker, John Forsythe, Polly Bergen, William Demarest. Well-executed Western set in 1860s Arizona, balancing North-South conflict with whites vs. Indians, climaxed by tense redskin ambush.

Escape From Red Rock (1958) 75m. *½ D: Edward Bernds. Brian Donlevy, Jay C. Flippen, Eilene Janssen, Gary Murray. Modest oater of rancher and gal involved in theft, being chased into Indian country by pursuing posse; film has virtue of Donlevy's presence.

Escape From San Quentin (1957) 81m. BOMB D: Fred F. Sears.

Johnny Desmond, Merry Anders, Richard Devon, Roy Engel. Drab film has Desmond as runaway convict who decides to give himself and buddy up to police.

Escape From the Planet of the Apes (1971) C-98m. *** D: Don Taylor. Roddy McDowall, Kim Hunter, Bradford Dillman, Natalie Trundy, Eric Braeden, William Windom, Sal Mineo, Ricardo Montalban. Third in series is best of the sequels, with the Apes in modern-day Los Angeles; ingeniously paves the way for 4th and 5th entries in series.

Escape From Zahrain (1962) C-93m. *½ D: Ronald Neame. Yul Brynner, Sal Mineo, Madlyn Rhue, Jack Warden, James Mason, Jay Novello. Plodding film of five prisoners escaping from jail in Mideastern country, being chased across desert. Nice photography at least.

Escape in the Desert (1945) 81m. ** D: Edward A. Blatt. Philip Dorn, Helmut Dantine, Jean Sullivan, Alan Hale. Tame remake of THE PETRIFIED FOREST involving American flyer encountering Nazi at desert hotel.

Escape in the Fog (1945) 65m. ** D: Budd Boetticher. Nina Foch, William Wright, Otto Kruger, Konstantin Shayne. Eerie programmer of girl who has strange dream of murder being committed and encounters the dream victim in real life.

Escape Me Never (1947) 104m. *½ D: Peter Godfrey. Errol Flynn, Ida Lupino, Eleanor Parker, Gig Young, Reginald Denny, Isobel Elsom. Sappy remake of 1935 Elisabeth Bergner vehicle, with Lupino as an itinerant waif (!) and Flynn as struggling composer who marries her but takes up with his brother's aristocratic fiancée (Parker). Forget it.

Escape of the Birdmen: SEE Birdmen

Escape to Athena (1979-British) C-101m. **½ D: George Pan Cosmatos. Roger Moore, Telly Savalas, David Niven, Claudia Cardinale, Richard Roundtree, Stefanie Powers, Sonny Bono, Elliott Gould, William Holden. Agreeable time-filler, with all-star cast in outlandish adventure yarn about WW2 POWs planning escape and art heist at the same time. Released in England at 125m.

Escape to Glory (1940) 74m. *** D: John Brahm. Constance Bennett, Pat O'Brien, John Halliday, Alan Baxter,

Melville Cooper. British ship is attacked by German sub at outbreak of WW2, giving pause to various passengers on-board—including a German doctor. Thoughtful, atmospheric B-picture with minimal amount of cliches.

Escape to Mindnao (1968) C-95m. TVM D: Don McDougall. George Maharis, Ronald Remy, Nehemiah Persoff, James Shigeta, Willi Coopman. Two American P.O.W.s break out of Japanese prison, must make it back to U.S. forces via Dutch black market freighter with valuable enemy decoder. Contrived, unbelievable resolutions; film should have been made for longer running time. Below average.

Escape to the Sun (1972-British-Israeli) 105m. *½ D: Menahem Golan. Laurence Harvey, Josephine Chaplin, John Ireland, Lila Kedrova, Jack Hawkins, Clive Revill. Suspense tale about aftermath of unsuccessful attempt by Soviet Jews to hijack a plane wastes a capable cast.

Escape to Witch Mountain (1975) C-97m. ***½ D: John Hough. Eddie Albert, Ray Milland, Kim Richards, Ike Eisenmann, Donald Pleasence. Excellent Disney mystery-fantasy: two children with mysterious powers try to discover their origins, while being pursued by evil Milland, who wants to use their powers for his own purposes. Followed by sequel RETURN FROM WITCH MOUNTAIN.

Escort for Hire (1960-British) C-66m. ** D: Godfrey Grayson. June Thorburn, Noel Trevarthan, Peter Murray, Jill Melford, Guy Middleton. Clichéd murder yarn, enhanced by Technicolor, with Trevarthan an out-of-work actor joining escort service, becoming involved in murder.

Escort West (1959) 75m. **½ D: Francis D. Lyon. Victor Mature, Elaine Stewart, Faith Domergue, Reba Waters, Noah Beery, Leo Gordon, Rex Ingram. Fairly good Western with Confederate soldier and 10-year-old daughter heading West, encountering two women who survived renegade attack and saved Army payroll.

Espionage Agent (1939) 83m. ** D: Lloyd Bacon. Joel McCrea, Brenda Marshall, George Bancroft, Jeffrey Lynn, James Stephenson, Martin Kosleck. Formula spy caper with

McCrea and Marshall tracking down the head of notorious spy ring.

Esther and the King (1960-U.S.A.-Italian) C-109m. ** D: Raoul Walsh. Joan Collins, Richard Egan, Denis O'Dea, Sergio Fantoni. Cardboard biblical costumer pretends to recreate 4th-century B.C. Persia, with stony performances by Collins and Egan as the king and the Jewish maiden he wants to replace murdered queen. Filmed in Italy.

Esther Waters (1948-British) 108m. **½ D: Peter Proud. Dirk Bogarde, Fay Compton, Kathleen Ryan, Cyril Cusack, Mary Clare. Well-appointed account of rogue Bogarde involved with lovely damsels frequenting the racetracks; set in 19th-century England. Film bogs down into soaper of gloomy married life, marring initial zest.

Eternal Sea, The (1955) 103m. **½ D: John H. Auer. Sterling Hayden, Alexis Smith, Dean Jagger, Virginia Grey. Well-played biography of Admiral John Hoskins' efforts to retain active command despite WW2 injury. Hayden is restrained in lead role; modest production values.

Eternally Yours (1939) 95m. **½ D: Tay Garnett. Loretta Young, David Niven, Hugh Herbert, C. Aubrey Smith, Billie Burke, Broderick Crawford, ZaSu Pitts, Eve Arden. Wayout idea comes off fairly well; Young is married to magician Niven, thinks his tricks are taking precedence to their married life.

Europa '51 SEE: Greatest Love, The

Eva (1965-British) 115m. *** D: Joseph Losey. Jeanne Moreau, Stanley Baker, Virna Lisi, Nona Medici, Francesco Rissone, James Villiers. Brooding account of writer Baker whose continued attraction for Eva (Moreau) causes wife (Lisi) to have tragic death. Premise isn't always workable, but Moreau is well cast as personification of evil.

Europeans, The (1979) C-90m. *** D: James Ivory. Lee Remick, Robin Ellis, Wesley Addy, Tim Choate, Lisa Eichhorn, Tim Woodward, Kristin Griffith. Meticulous film of Henry James novel vividly recreates 19th-century life in New England, as the arrival of two foreign cousins disrupts the stern-faced calm of a plain American family. Deliberately paced, but richly rewarding.

Eve (1968-British-Spanish) C-94m. BOMB. D: Jeremy Summers. Robert Walker, Jr., Celeste Yarnall, Herbert Lom, Christopher Lee, Fred Clark, Maria Rohm. Pilot is saved from Amazon savages by white jungle goddess who wields strange power over her subjects. Save yourself and don't watch.

Eve Knew Her Apples (1945) 64m. **½ D: Will Jason. Ann Miller, William Wright, Robert Williams, Ray Walker. Sprightly musical variation of IT HAPPENED ONE NIGHT, with Miller on the lam from her marriage-minded fiancé.

Eve of St. Mark, The (1944) 96m. *** D: John M. Stahl. Anne Baxter, William Eythe, Michael O'Shea, Vincent Price, Dickie Moore. Human focus on WW2 in tale of soldier Eythe and girl friend Baxter at outset of war; not always successful Maxwell Anderson story.

Evel Knievel (1972) C-90m. **½ D: Marvin Chomsky. George Hamilton, Sue Lyon, Bert Freed, Rod Cameron. Biography of daredevil motorcyclist contains some great action footage; modest but effective film.

Evelyn Prentice (1934) 80m. **½ D: William K. Howard. William Powell, Myrna Loy, Una Merkel, Rosalind Russell, Isabel Jewell, Harvey Stephens. Story of successful attorney who doesn't know his own wife is in trouble is too drawn-out, ultimately too implausible. Cast rises above material, but Cora Sue Collins is an obnoxious brat. Remade as STRONGER THAN DESIRE.

Ever Since Eve (1937) 79m. *½ D: Lloyd Bacon. Marion Davies, Robert Montgomery, Frank McHugh, Patsy Kelly, Allen Jenkins, Louise Fazenda, Barton MacLane. Davies makes herself homely in order to avoid being harrassed on the job; dreary comedy tests the mettle of Warner Bros. stock cast. This was Marion's last film.

Evergreen (1934-British) 90m. *** D: Victor Saville. Jessie Matthews, Sonnie Hale, Betty Balfour, Barry Mackay, Ivor MacLaren. British musical-comedy star's best known film is enjoyable fluff about young girl who becomes a stage sensation masquerading as her long-retired mother. Rodgers and Hart score includes "Dancing on the Ceiling."

Every Bastard a King (1970-Israeli) C-93m. BOMB D: Uri Zohar. Pier Angeli, William Berger, Oded Kotler, Yehoram Gaon, Ori Levy. Story of journalist and his mistress, set against the 6-day Israeli-Egyptian War, is a slapdash effort with nothing to recommend it. Retitled EVERY MAN A KING for TV purposes.

Every Day's A Holiday (1937) 80m. *** D: A. Edward Sutherland. Mae West, Edmund Lowe, Charles Butterworth, Charles Winninger, Walter Catlett, Lloyd Nolan, Louis Armstrong. Mae sells Herman Bing the Brooklyn Bridge, so police detective Lowe orders her to leave New York. She returns to help expose crooked police chief Nolan. Gay 90s setting for fast-moving West vehicle.

Every Girl Should Be Married (1948) 85m. **½ D: Don Hartman. Cary Grant, Franchot Tone, Diana Lynn, Betsy Drake, Alan Mowbray. Airy comedy of girl (Drake) setting out to trap bachelor (Grant) into marriage; Tone has thankless "other man" role.

Every Little Crook and Nanny (1972) C-91m. ** D: Cy Howard. Lynn Redgrave, Victor Mature, Paul Sand, Austin Pendelton, John Astin, Dom DeLuise, Pat Harrington, Severn Darden. Good idea gets away in this comic crime-and-caper film. One bright spot: Mature's gangster portrayal.

Every Man A King SEE: **Every Bastard A King**

Every Man Is My Enemy (1967-Italian) C-93m. *½ D: Francesco Prosperi. Robert Webber, Elsa Martinelli, Jean Servais, Martina Berti, Pierre Zimmer. Mafia hit-man Webber tries to pull off major diamond heist in Marseilles, with predictable complications.

Every Man Needs One (1972) C-74m. TVM D: Jerry Paris. Connie Stevens, Ken Berry, Gail Fisher, Steve Franken, Henry Gibson, Louise Sorel, Carol Wayne, Jerry Paris. Bachelor architect forced to eat words, hire "know it all" woman (Stevens) as assistant. Typical TV-style comedy complete with accommodating Women's Lib slant. Average.

Every Which Way But Loose (1978) C-119m. BOMB D: James Fargo. Clint Eastwood, Sondra Locke, Geoffrey Lewis, Beverly D'Angelo, Ruth Gordon. Clint takes the first pickup truck to Stupidsville, with an orangutan as his best friend, in this bizarre change of pace for the ac-

tion star. The clumsiest comedy of the year.

Everybody Does It (1949) 98m. ***½ D: Edmund Goulding. Paul Douglas, Linda Darnell, Celeste Holm, Charles Coburn, Millard Mitchell. Exceptionally amusing yarn of aspiring singer Holm, harried husband Douglas, and prima donna Darnell. Celeste wants vocal career, Douglas gets one instead. Remake of WIFE, HUSBAND, AND FRIEND.

Everybody Sing (1938) 80m. ** D: Edwin L. Marin. Allan Jones, Judy Garland, Fanny Brice, Reginald Owen, Billie Burke, Reginald Gardiner. Shrill musical with stupid plot, unmemorable songs; good cast fighting weak material about nutty family involved in putting on a show. After loud finale you'll be waiting for a sequel called EVERYBODY SHUT UP.

Everything But the Truth (1956) C-83m. ** D: Jerry Hopper. Maureen O'Hara, John Forsythe, Tim Hovey, Frank Faylen. When youngster Hovey joins truth pledge crusade at school, repercussions to his family and townfolk grow; cutesy.

Everything Happens at Night (1939) 77m. *** D: Irving Cummings. Sonja Henie, Ray Milland, Robert Cummings, Alan Dinehart, Fritz Feld, Jody Gilbert, Victor Varconi. One of Henie's best romantic skating vehicles, with Milland and Cummings as rival writers vying for girl's attention.

Everything I Have Is Yours (1952) C-92m. ** D: Robert Z. Leonard. Marge and Gower Champion, Dennis O'Keefe, Eduard Franz. Champions play dance team who finally get Broadway break, only to discover she's pregnant. Mild musical helped by stars' multitalents.

Everything You Always Wanted to Know About Sex (But Were Afraid to Ask) (1972) C-87m. *** D: Woody Allen. Woody Allen, John Carradine, Lou Jacobi, Louise Lasser, Anthony Quayle, Lynn Redgrave, Tony Randall, Burt Reynolds, Gene Wilder. Woody's most cinematic comedy, also most uneven, most tasteless. In multi-episode feature based very loosely on Dr. David Reuben's book, only a few segments stand out: final sequence inside male body is a comic gem. Not likely to withstand TV scissors.

Everything's Ducky (1961) 81m. **

D: Don Taylor. Mickey Rooney, Buddy Hackett, Jackie Cooper, Roland Winters. Nonsense of Rooney-Hackett teaming up with talking duck, with trio ending up on navy missile orbiting earth; strictly for kids.

Evictors, The (1979) C-92m. *½ D: Charles B. Pierce. Michael Parks, Jessica Harper, Vic Morrow, Sue Ann Langdon, Dennis Fimple, Bill Thurman. Couple moves into eerie house, unaware of its violent history. Tired rehash of an all too familiar formula.

Evil, The (1978) C-90m. **½ D: Gus Trikonis. Richard Crenna, Joanna Pettet, Andrew Prine, Cassie Yates, Lynne Moody, Victor Buono, George O'Hanlon Jr. Doctor Crenna rents "haunted" house to use as clinic, but he and associates are violently victimized by powers within. Slow-moving film covers familiar ground; some chills, much gore.

Evil Eye, The (1962-Italian) 92m. **½ D: Mario Bava. Leticia Roman, John Saxon, Valentina Cortese, Dante Di Paolo. Incredible but enjoyable chiller set in Rome, with Roman involved in a series of unsolved brutal murders.

Evil of Frankenstein, The (1964-British) C-87m. ** D: Freddie Francis. Peter Cushing, Duncan Lamont, Peter Woodthorpe, James Maxwell. Tepid entry in the famed monster series, with Cushing unfreezing his namesake who inevitably goes on the rampage.

Evil Roy Slade (1971) C-100m. TVM D: Jerry Paris. John Astin, Edie Adams, Milton Berle, Pam Austin, Dom DeLuise, Mickey Rooney, Dick Shawn. Excellent cast tries hard in absurd attempt at bizarre Western comedy à la CAT BALLOU. Life and times of bumbling outlaw Slade and change in attitude after falling in love with beautiful girl (Austin). Script not bad; fault lies in what's done with it. Average.

Ex-Champ (1939) 64m. ** D: Phil Rosen. Victor McLaglen, Tom Brown, Nan Grey, Constance Moore. Routine programmer of old salty boxer trying to do good deed for his son, in dutch with the gambling syndicate.

Ex-Lady (1933) 65m. ** D: Robert Florey. Bette Davis, Gene Raymond, Frank McHugh, Claire Dodd, Ferdinand Gottschalk. Davis is a gorgeous man-trap in this programmer, wanting love, not marriage.

Ex-Mrs. Bradford, The (1936) 80m. *** D: Stephen Roberts. William Powell, Jean Arthur, James Gleason, Eric Blore, Robert Armstrong. Chic à la THIN MAN comedy-mystery, with Powell teaming with ex-wife Arthur to crack a case.

Exclusive (1937) 85m. **½ D: Alexander Hall. Fred MacMurray, Frances Farmer, Charlie Ruggles, Lloyd Nolan, Fay Holden, Ralph Morgan, Horace McMahon. Lively newspaper story has Farmer joining tabloid in direct competition with her father (Ruggles) and boyfriend (MacMurray), who are also reporters.

Exclusive Story (1936) 75m. **½ D: George B. Seitz. Franchot Tone, Madge Evans, Stuart Erwin, Joseph Calleia, Robert Barrat, J. Farrell MacDonald, Louise Henry. Fast-paced B-picture with Tone as newspaper attorney trying to get the goods on Calleia and falling in love with Evans.

Excuse My Dust (1951) C-82m. **½ D: Roy Rowland. Red Skelton, Sally Forrest, Macdonald Carey, Monica Lewis, William Demarest. Amiable Skelton musicomedy. Red invents automobile which almost costs him his sweetheart; her father owns town livery stable.

Execution of Private Slovik, The (1974) C-120m. TVM D: Lamont Johnson. Martin Sheen, Mariclare Costello, Ned Beatty, Gary Busey, Matt Clark, Ben Hammer, Charles Haid. Solid drama enhanced by Sheen's beautiful performance as Eddie Slovik, the only American soldier since the Civil War to be executed for desertion (in 1945). Thoughtful, literate adaptation of William Bradford Huie's controversial book. Above average.

Executive Action (1973) C-91m. BOMB D: David Miller. Burt Lancaster, Robert Ryan, Will Geer, Gilbert Green, John Anderson. Excruciatingly dull thriller promised to clear the air about JFK's assassination but was more successful at clearing theaters. Ryan's last film.

Executive Suite (1954) 104m. *** D: Robert Wise. William Holden, June Allyson, Barbara Stanwyck, Fredric March, Walter Pidgeon, Louis Calhern, Shelley Winters, Paul Douglas, Nina Foch, Dean Jagger. Slick, multifaceted story of company power struggle with top cast, from Cameron

Hawley novel. Similar film PATTERNS is much better.

Exile, The (1947) 95m. **½ D: Max Ophuls. Douglas Fairbanks, Jr., Maria Montez, Paule Croset (Rita Corday), Henry Daniell, Nigel Bruce, Robert Coote. OK swashbuckler with exiled king Fairbanks falling in love with common girl; guest appearance by Montez, fine support by Bruce.

Exo-Man, The (1977) C-100m. TVM D: Richard Irving. David Ackroyd, Anne Schedeen, A. Martinez, Jose Ferrer, Harry Morgan, Kevin McCarthy, Jack Colvin, Donald Moffat. Paralyzed by the syndicate, physics professor Ackroyd creates a special "exo" suit to make him sufficiently mobile to take vengeance on his attackers. Disappointing and dull "superman" story. Below average.

Exodus (1960) C-213m. *** D: Otto Preminger. Paul Newman, Eva Marie Saint, Ralph Richardson, Peter Lawford, Lee J. Cobb, Sal Mineo, Hugh Griffith, Felix Aylmer, John Derek, Jill Haworth, Leon Uris' sprawling history of Palestinian war for liberation becomes sporadic action epic. Newman as Israeli resistance leader, Saint as non-Jewish army nurse aren't a convincing duo; supporting roles offer stereotypes. Best scene shows refugees escaping Cyprus detention center, running British blockade into homeland.

Exorcist, The (1973) C-121m. ***½ D: William Friedkin. Ellen Burstyn, Max von Sydow, Lee J. Cobb, Kitty Winn, Jack MacGowran, Jason Miller, Linda Blair. Intense, well-mounted adaptation of William Peter Blatty's best-seller calculated to keep your stomach in knots from start to finish. Blair is "normal" 12-year-old whose body is possessed by the Devil, Miller a troubled priest who attempts to confront the demon in her—and in himself. Oscar-winner for screenplay.

Exorcist II: The Heretic (1977) C-120m. *½ D: John Boorman. Richard Burton, Linda Blair, Louise Fletcher, Kitty Winn, James Earl Jones, Ned Beatty, Max von Sydow. Preposterous sequel to 1973 hit. Special effects are only virtue in this turkey about priest (Burton) trying to unravel mystery of demon still living inside Blair. Reedited after initial release, but no improvements noticeable.

Experiment in Terror (1962) 123m. *** D: Blake Edwards. Glenn Ford, Lee Remick, Stefanie Powers, Ross Martin, Roy Poole, Ned Glass. Taut suspenser as F.B.I. agent Ford tracks down killer (Martin) who has kidnapped bank teller Remick's sister (Powers). Remick and Martin are extremely convincing.

Experiment Perilous (1944) 91m. *** D: Jacques Tourneur. Hedy Lamarr, George Brent, Paul Lukas, Albert Dekker, Margaret Wycherly, Julia Dean. Good melodrama in the GASLIGHT tradition, with beautiful Lamarr menaced by husband (Lukas), aided by detective Brent.

Explosion (1969-Canadian) C-96m. *½ D: Jules Bricken. Don Stroud, Richard Conte, Gordon Thomson, Michele Chicoine, Cecil Linder, Robin Ward. Teenager haunted by his brother's death in Vietnam goes to Canada to avoid the draft, but drifts into crime instead. Heavy-handed melodrama.

Explosive Generation, The (1961) 89m. ** D: Buzz Kulik. William Shatner, Patty McCormack, Billy Gray, Steve Dunne. Film fails to be exploitational: Shatner is high school teacher expelled for conducting sex talks in class; school board and parent group eventually reach compromise.

Expresso Bongo (1960-British) 108m. *** D: Val Guest. Laurence Harvey, Sylvia Syms, Yolande Donlan, Cliff Richard. Harvey is ideally cast as opportunist talent agent who almost makes the big time with bongo-playing discovery Richard, but bluffs himself back into small time.

Extra Girl, The (1923) 69m. **½ D: F. Richard Jones. Mabel Normand, Ralph Graves, George Nichols, Anna Hernandez, Vernon Dent. Mack Sennett silent feature is far from prime, but still has its moments, thanks to classic comedienne Normand and an obliging lion. Dramatic interludes in Hollywood rags-to-riches saga don't suit the feature as a whole.

Extraordinary Seaman, The (1969) C-80m. BOMB. D: John Frankenheimer. David Niven, Faye Dunaway, Alan Alda, Mickey Rooney, Jack Carter, Juano Hernandez. Extraordinarily muddled "comedy" of eccentric Niven piloting long-lost abandoned ship during WW2; shows signs of tampering from original conception of film, which barely received theatrical release. Best moments are clips from 1940s newsreels.

Extreme Close-Up (1973) C-80m. *½ D: Jeannot Szwarc. James McMullan, James A. Watson, Jr., Kate Woodville, Bara Byrnes, Al Checco. Ludicrous drama about snoopers and snooping equipment has topicality working for it, but that's all; some nudity will be cut for TV.

Eye Creatures, The (1965) 80m. *½ D: Larry Buchanan. John Ashley, Cynthia Hull, Warren Hammack, Chet Davis, Bill Peck. Gory horror film about title creatures and the intrepid band that tries to fight them off.

Eye for an Eye, An (1966) C-92m. ** D: Michael Moore. Robert Lansing, Pat Wayne, Slim Pickens, Gloria Talbott. Oater with twist: two physically disabled men, who can function via teamwork as one sharpshooter, hunt down killers of older man's family.

Eye of the Cat (1969) C-102m. **½ D: David Lowell Rich. Michael Sarrazin, Gayle Hunnicutt, Eleanor Parker, Tim Henry, Laurence Naismith. Glossy but intriguing suspenser with seductive Hunnicutt teaming with Sarrazin to murder his aunt (Parker), who keeps a houseful of felines. Most terrifying scene has wheelchaired Parker tottering atop a San Francisco hill. Important note: new scenes were added to film for network TV showing to make it "less intense." Rating is based on original.

Eye of the Devil (1967-British) 92m. **½ D: J. Lee Thompson. Deborah Kerr, David Niven, Donald Pleasence, Edward Mulhare, Flora Robson, Emlyn Williams, Sharon Tate, David Hemmings, John Le Mesurier. Excellent cast in-odd, low-key thriller set in France. The Marquis de Bellac (Niven) abruptly leaves wife in Paris to "do what he must" at ancestral estate near Bordeaux. Strange continuity due to cuts before initial release. Also titled: 13.

Eye Witness (1950-British) 104m. **½ D: Robert Montgomery. Robert Montgomery, Felix Aylmer, Leslie Banks, Michael Ripper, Patricia Wayne (Cutts). Unpretentious yarn of American attorney Montgomery in London to defend friend accused of homicide, coping with contrasting British legal system while hunting

title figure. Originally titled YOUR WITNESS.

Eyes in the Night (1942) 80m. *** D: Fred Zinnemann. Ann Harding, Edward Arnold, Donna Reed, Stephen McNally, Reginald Denny, Rosemary DeCamp, Mantan Moreland. Above-par mystery with Arnold as blind detective Duncan McClain helping Reed and Harding. Director Zinnemann's feature film debut.

Eyes of Charles Sand, The (1972) C-75m. TVM D: Reza Badiyi. Peter Haskell, Barbara Rush, Sharon Farrell, Bradford Dillman, Joan Bennett, Adam West, Ivor Francis. Despite excellent names connected with script (Henry Farrel & Stanford Whitmore), predictable, largely boring ESP-gimmicked mystery featuring troubled lead character (Haskell) who can flash onto future. Average.

Eyes of Laura Mars (1978) C-103m. **½ D: Irvin Kershner. Faye Dunaway, Tommy Lee Jones, Brad Dourif, Rene Auberjonois, Raul Julia, Frank Adonis. A high-fashion photographer has frightening premonitions of grisly murders; some genuine suspense, lots of red herrings, and a silly resolution add up to an OK thriller . . . but Dunaway's kinky colleagues and their life-styles are a real turnoff.

Eyes of the Underworld (1943) 61m. **½ D: Roy William Neill. Richard Dix, Wendy Barrie, Lon Chaney, Lloyd Corrigan, Don Porter, Billy Lee, Marc Lawrence. Police chief Dix is on the spot/when mobster uncovers his old prison record; good crime story.

Eyewitness SEE: **Sudden Terror**

FBI Girl (1951) 74m. ** D: William Berke. Cesar Romero, George Brent, Audrey Totter, Tom Drake, Raymond Burr. Title tells all in standard fare about federal agency tracking down extortion gang.

FBI 99 (1945) 100m. ** D: Spencer Bennet, Wallace Grissell, Yakima Canutt. Marten Lamont, Helen Talbot, George J. Lewis, Lorna Gray, Hal Taliaferro. Satisfactory Republic cliffhanger involving federal agents' persistent attempts to overcome criminal syndicate planning robbery capers et al. Reedited movie serial: FEDERAL OPERATOR 99.

FBI Story, The (1959) C-149m. *** D: Mervyn LeRoy. James Stewart, Vera Miles, Murray Hamilton, Larry

Pennell, Nick Adams, Diane Jergens, Joyce Taylor. Well-mounted fabrication of history of F.B.I. as seen through career of agent Stewart, allowing for episodic sidelights into action-packed capers and view of his personal life.

F.B.I. Story—The FBI Versus Alvin Karpis, Public Enemy Number One, The (1974) C-100m. TVM D: Marvin Chomsky. Robert Foxworth, David Wayne, Kay Lenz, Gary Lockwood, Anne Francis, Harris Yulin, Chris Robinson, Eileen Heckart. Depression-era desperado Karpis (Foxworth) is hounded by J. Edgar Hoover (Yulin), who made a personal crusade of catching the crook. Authentically recreated dramatization in the old Warner Bros. pseudo-newsreel gangster style. Average.

F.I.S.T. (1978) C-145m. **½ D: Norman Jewison. Sylvester Stallone, Rod Steiger, Peter Boyle, Melinda Dillon, David Huffman, Tony Lo Bianco. Stallone's one-dimensional performance prevents this well-produced epic about a Hoffa-like labor kingpin from sustaining a strong first half. Peter Boyle does well with a role inspired by former Teamster boss Dave Beck.

FM (1978) C-105m. ** D: John A. Alonzo. Michael Brandon, Eileen Brennan, Alex Karras, Cleavon Little, Martin Mull, Cassie Yates, Norman Lloyd. Innocuous film about footloose FM station that refuses to bow to commercial pressures. Agreeable cast sabotaged by brainless script and an ending that's too silly for words. Concert appearances by Linda Ronstadt and Jimmy Buffett.

F. Scott Fitzgerald in Hollywood (1976) C-100m. TVM D: Anthony Page. Jason Miller, Tuesday Weld, Julia Foster, Dolores Sutton, Suzanne Benton, Michael Lerner, Tom Ligon, John Randolph. Fitzgerald's Hollywood career, his marriage to the ill-fated Zelda (Weld is super), his affair with Sheilah Graham (Foster). Brilliant career made fuzzy by Miller's gloomy performance and James Costigan's muddled script, giving the viewer not much more than a broken-spirited and rather abusive alcoholic. A good opportunity passed up. Average.

Fabiola (1951-Italian) 96m. **** D: Alessandro Blasetti. Michele Morgan, Henri Vidal, Michel Simon, Gino Cervi. Excellently produced and acted spectacle. Roman aristocracy plots massive Christian massacre before Constantine reaches Rome. Best of Italian spectacles, although cut quite a bit.

Fabulous Baron Munchausen, The (1961-Czech) C-84m. **½ D: Karel Zeman. Milos Kopecky, Jana Brejchova, Rudolph Jelinek, Jan Werich. Filmmaker Zeman (FABULOUS WORLD OF JULES VERNE) provides another visual delight here, but his episodic fantasy—which takes his hero from the inside of a whale to the surface of the moon—is stilted and uninvolving.

Fabulous Dorseys, The (1947) 88m. ** D: Alfred E. Green. Tommy Dorsey, Jimmy Dorsey, Janet Blair, Paul Whiteman, William Lundigan. Limp "biography" of band-leading brothers, constantly arguing in between "Marie," "Green Eyes," and other hit songs.

Fabulous Joe, The (1947) C-60m. ** D: Bernard Carr, Harve Foster. Marie Wilson, Walter Abel, Margot Grahame, Donald Meek. Abel is typecast in this featurized segment from THE HAL ROACH COMEDY CARNIVAL (1947). He's harassed husband who gains moral support from talking dog.

Fabulous Suzanne, The (1946) 71m. ** D: Steve Sekely. Barbara Britton, Rudy Vallee, Otto Kruger, Richard Denning, Veda Ann Borg. Fair potential of romantic story of woman who has more luck at horses than with men doesn't come across, due to script and indifferent acting.

Fabulous World of Jules Verne, The (1958-Czech) 83m. **½ D: Karel Zeman. Lubor Tokos, Arnost Navratil, Miroslav Holub, Zatloukalova. Zeman's ingenious visual effects, reproducing the look of 19th century engravings, outshine leaden enactment of fanciful sci-fi story by Verne. Released here in 1961 with Americanized names in credits and pointless introduction by Hugh Downs.

Face Behind the Mask, The (1941) 69m. *** D: Robert Florey. Peter Lorre, Evelyn Keyes, Don Beddoe, George E. Stone, John Tyrell. Model "B" film of immigrant Lorre having face disfigured in fire, donning mask, bitterly turning to life of crime. Extremely well done on slim budget.

Face in the Crowd, A (1957) 125m. ***½ D: Elia Kazan. Andy Griffith,

Patricia Neal, Anthony Franciosa, Walter Matthau, Lee Remick, Kay Medford. Perceptive script by Budd Schulberg about homespun hobo (Griffith) discovered by Neal and promoted into successful TV star. Cast gives life to fascinating story.

Face in the Rain, A (1963) 91m. **½ D: Irvin Kershner. Rory Calhoun, Marina Berti, Niall MacGinnis, Massimo Giuliani. At times tense melodrama of Calhoun, U.S. spy, being hidden in Italy by partisan whose wife has been associating with Axis.

Face of a Fugitive (1959) C-81m. ** D: Paul Wendkos. Fred MacMurray, Lin McCarthy, Dorothy Green, James Coburn, Alan Baxter, Myrna Fahey. OK Western about MacMurray forced to start over again in a new town when he's falsely accused of murder; his past still haunts him.

Face of Fear, The (1971) C-72m. TVM D: George McCowan. Elizabeth Ashley, Ricardo Montalban, Jack Warden, Dane Clark, Burr DeBenning, Charles Dierkop. Young schoolteacher raised in Idaho learns she's to die of leukemia, journeys to San Francisco, eventually pays to be killed, then discovers she won't die. Very entertaining suspense film with wry humor, two well-drawn (for TV) characterizations, and believable dialogue. Above average.

Face of Fire (1959) 83m. *** D: Albert Band. Cameron Mitchell, James Whitmore, Bettye Ackerman, Royal Dano, Robert Simon, Richard Erdman. Unique adaptation of Stephen Crane short story "The Monster" about man disfigured while saving child from fire. Uneven cast, good direction.

Face of Fu Manchu, The (1965-British) C-96m. *** D: Don Sharp. Christopher Lee, Nigel Green, James Robertson Justice, Howard Marion-Crawford, Tsai Chin, Walter Rilla. First of wild new series with Emperor Fu bent on conquering West. Great 1920s atmosphere, good international cast.

Face of Marble (1946) 70m. ** D: William Beaudine. John Carradine, Claudia Drake, Robert Shayne, Maris Wrixon. Another mad doctor with new technique for bringing dead back to life. Carradine is good, others less impressive.

Face of the Frog (1959-German) 92m. ** D: Harold Reinl. Joachim Fuchsberger, Fritz Rasp, Siegfied Lowitz, Joachen Brochmann. Lowitz is Inspector Elk tracking down the "Frog" in this routine Edgar Wallace actioner; serial-like techniques utilized. Retitled: FELLOWSHIP OF THE FROG.

Face That Launched a Thousand Ships, The SEE: Loves of Three Queens

Face to Face (1952) 92m. **½ D: John Brahm, Bretaigne Windust. James Mason, Michael Pate, Robert Preston, Marjorie Steele. Quiet two-part film: Joseph Conrad's SECRET SHARER faithfully filmed with Mason as captain, Pate as fugitive; Stephen Crane's BRIDE COMES TO YELLOW SKY bland with Preston bringing bride Steele out West.

Face to Face (Swedish-1976) C-136m. *** D: Ingmar Bergman. Liv Ullmann, Erland Josephson, Gunnar Bjornstrand, Aino Taube-Henrikson, Kari Sylwan, Sif Ruud. Brilliant Ullmann performance and Sven Nykvist photography compensate somewhat for déjà vu feeling one gets from drama about woman psychiatrist who suffers severe nervous breakdown. As harrowing as they come; not for every taste or mood.

Face to the Wind (1972) C-93m. ** D: William A. Graham. Cliff Potts, Xochitl, Harry Dean Stanton, Don Wilbanks. Drifter falls in love with Indian girl, with tragic consequences, in this violent Western. Its title (and alleged year of release) keeps changing but the film doesn't get any better. Also known as COUNT YOUR BULLETS, CRY FOR ME BILLY, and APACHE MASSACRE.

Faces (1968) 130m. ***½ D: John Cassavetes. John Marley, Gena Rowlands, Lynn Carlin, Seymour Cassel, Fred Draper, Val Avery. Highly personal drama about assorted infidelities is one of the few underground films to make it with general public. Very powerful film with great acting, especially by Carlin and Cassel.

Facts of Life, The (1960) 103m. *** D: Melvin Frank. Bob Hope, Lucille Ball, Ruth Hussey, Don DeFore. Sophisticated comedy with Bob and Lucy leaving their spouses for an interlude together. The two stars make a good team worth watching.

Fade-In (1968) C-93m. ** D: Allen Smithee (Jud Taylor). Burt Reynolds, Barbara Loden, Noam Pitlik, Patricia Casey, Jane Hampton, Joseph Perry. Odd little film made concurrently with BLUE, about love affair between film editor Loden and man she meets while working on location. Not very good, but a definite curio; never released theatrically.

Fahrenheit 451 (1967) C-111m. ******* D: Francois Truffaut. Julie Christie, Oskar Werner, Cyril Cusack, Anton Diffring, Jeremy Spenser, Bee Duffell, Alex Scott. Odd but generally slow-going adaptation of Ray Bradbury sci-fi novel depicting future Earth civilization where all printed reading material is banned. Though viewer interest held throughout, film has curiously reserved, unemotional feel to it.

Fail-Safe (1964) 111m. *****½** D: Sidney Lumet. Henry Fonda, Walter Matthau, Fritz Weaver, Dan O'Herlihy, Sorrell Booke, Larry Hagman, Frank Overton. U.S. plane is accidentally charged with mission to bomb U.S.S.R., plunging heads of American and Russian governments into crisis of decisionmaking as time runs out. High-tension drama done with taste and intelligence.

Falling of Raymond, The (1971) C-73m. TVM D: Boris Sagal. Jane Wyman, Dean Stockwell, Dana Andrews, Murray Hamilton, Tim O'Connor, Paul Henreid. Forgettable suspense drama about mental defective threatening high school teacher who flunked him in English. Film looks as if directed by hypnosis. Below average.

Fair Wind to Java (1953) C-92m. ****½** D: Joseph Kane. Fred MacMurray, Vera Ralston, Victor McLaglen, Robert Douglas, Philip Ahn. MacMurray is out of place in period sea yarn of skipper seeking jewels. Ralston is exotic love interest.

Faithful in My Fashion (1946) 81m. ****** D: Sidney Salkow. Donna Reed, Tom Drake, Edward Everett Horton, Spring Byington, Sig Ruman. Stale comedy-romance as soldier on leave discovers his girl engaged to someone else. Good cast in familiar settings.

Faithless (1932) 76m. ****½** D: Harry Beaumont. Tallulah Bankhead, Robert Montgomery, Hugh Herbert, Louise Closser Hale, Henry Kolker. Impoverished Bankhead tries to start life fresh after dismal past; polished soaper.

Fake, The (1953-British) 80m. ****** D: Godfrey Grayson. Dennis O'Keefe, Coleen Gray, Guy Middleton, John Laurie. Famous painting is stolen,

starting a police hunt; OK crime drama.

Fakers, The (1970) C-98m. BOMB D: Al Adamson. Broderick Crawford, Kent Taylor, Scott Brady, John Carradine. Pretty threadbare story about an F.B.I. undercover agent and his beautiful partner who chase Nazi war criminals and counterfeiters. Originally titled HELL'S BLOODY DEVILS.

The Falcon Michael Arlen's debonair trouble-shooter, the Falcon, served as the basis for sixteen above-average mysteries in the 1940s, and while the series cannot be called unusual, one of its entries presented a perhaps-unique situation. George Sanders had played the character in three films when, in 1942, he decided to leave the series. In THE FALCON'S BROTHER it was arranged to put him out of the way so his brother could take over for him. What made the transition unique was that Sanders' real-life brother, Tom Conway, was the replacement; he carried on for nine subsequent films. John Calvert played the character in three final low-budget films which aren't really part of the main series. Various character actors came in and out of the series playing cronies of the Falcon, such as Allen Jenkins, Ed Brophy, Eddie Dunn, and Ed Gargan. James Gleason played a thick-witted inspector in the first few films, and Cliff Clark took over for the rest. In fact, some of the films had so much comedy relief, one yearned for some mystery relief from the comedy! One interesting gimmick in several films had a beautiful girl enter near the end of the picture to alert the Falcon to danger in a new location; this would lead into the next film in which the Falcon and the girl would embark upon the new mystery. One entry, THE FALCON TAKES OVER, was from a Raymond Chandler novel FAREWELL MY LOVELY which was remade as MURDER MY SWEET with Dick Powell as Phillip Marlowe. Such young hopefuls as Wendy Barrie, Barbara Hale, Lynn Bari, Jane Greer, Harriet Hilliard, and Rita Corday (Paule Croset) appeared in the series from time to time; and to the everlasting glory of that great neurotic-character actor Elisha Cook, Jr., THE FALCON'S ALIBI cast him as a homicidal disk jockey!

Falcon and the Co-eds, The (1943) 68m. D: William Clemens. Tom Conway, Jean Brooks, Rita Corday, Amelita Ward, Isabel Jewell, George Givot, Cliff Clark, Dorothy Malone (in a bit).

Falcon in Danger, The (1943) 73m. D: William Clemens. Tom Conway, Jean Brooks, Elaine Shepard, Amelita Ward, Cliff Clark, Ed Gargan.

Falcon in Hollywood, The (1944) 67m. D: Gordon Douglas. Tom Conway, Barbara Hale, Veda Ann Borg, Sheldon Leonard, Frank Jenks, Rita Corday, John Abbott.

Falcon in Mexico, The (1944) 70m. D: William Berke. Tom Conway, Mona Maris, Nestor Paiva, Bryant Washburn, Emory Parnell.

Falcon in San Francisco, The (1945) 66m. D: Joseph H. Lewis. Tom Conway, Rita Corday, Edward Brophy, Sharyn Moffett, Fay Helm, Robert Armstrong.

Falcon Out West, The (1944) 64m. D: William Clemens. Tom Conway, Barbara Hale, Ed Gargan, Lyle Talbot, Chief Thundercloud, Joan Barclay, Minor Watson.

Falcon Strikes Back, The (1943) 66m. D: Edward Dmytryk. Tom Conway, Harriet Hilliard, Jane Randolph, Edgar Kennedy, Cliff Edwards, Rita Corday, Wynne Gibson.

Falcon Takes Over, The (1942) 63m. D: Irving Reis. George Sanders, Lynn Bari, James Gleason, Allen Jenkins, Helen Gilbert, Ward Bond, Anne Revere, Hans Conried.

Falcon's Adventure, The (1946) 61m. D: William Berke. Tom Conway, Madge Meredith, Edward S. Brophy, Robert Warwick, Myrna Dell, Ian Wolfe.

Falcon's Alibi, The (1946) 62m. D: Ray McCarey. Tom Conway, Rita Corday, Vince Barnett, Jane Greer, Elisha Cook, Jr., Al Bridge, Jason Robards, Sr.

Falcon's Brother, The (1942) 63m. D: Stanley Logan. George Sanders, Tom Conway, Jane Randolph, Keye Luke, Charles Arnt.

Fall of the Roman Empire, The (1964) C-149m. ***½ D: Anthony Mann. Sophia Loren, Stephen Boyd, James Mason, Alec Guinness, Christopher Plummer, Anthony Quayle, John Ireland, Mel Ferrer, Omar Sharif, Eric Porter. Intelligent scripting, good direction, and fine acting place this far above the usual emptyheaded spectacle. Mason and Guinness are superb; several action sequences are outstanding. A winner all the way.

Fallen Angel (1945) 97m. **½ D: Otto Preminger. Alice Faye, Dana Andrews, Linda Darnell, Charles Bickford, Anne Revere, Bruce Cabot, John Carradine. Andrews plans to dump wife Faye for Darnell, when latter is murdered; offbeat production.

Fallen Idol, The (1949-British) 94m. ***½ D: Carol Reed. Ralph Richardson, Michele Morgan, Bobby Henrey, Sonia Dresdel. Incisive study of human relations based on Graham Greene story of young boy who idolizes the household servant suspected of murdering his wife. Highly professional production.

Fallen Sparrow, The (1943) 94m. *** D: Richard Wallace. John Garfield, Maureen O'Hara, Walter Slezak, Patricia Morison, Martha O'Driscoll, Bruce Edwards, John Banner. Puzzling WW2 thriller with Garfield returning from Spanish Civil War to find American-based Nazis after him for artifact he's supposed to have.

Fame Is the Name of the Game (1966) C-100m. TVM D: Stuart Rosenberg. Tony Franciosa, Jill St. John, Jack Klugman, George Macready, Lee Bowman, Susan Saint James. Big-time magazine writer Dillon investigates death of call girl; trail leads to various business and criminal types. Remake of CHICAGO DEADLINE (1949) features good cast and performances, uneven direction, pacing, and overall point of view. Later spawned TV series. Average.

Fame is the Spur (1946-British) 116m. **½ D: John and Roy Boulting. Michael Redgrave, Rosamund John, Anthony Wager, Brian Weske. Thoughtful if slow-moving chronicle of Redgrave portraying a noted politician-diplomat who rises from poverty to fame.

Family, The (1970-Italian) C-100m. **½ D: Sergio Sollima. Charles Bronson, Jill Ireland, Telly Savalas, Michel Constantin, Umberto Orsini, George Savalas. Fast pacing fails to hide cliches in this action drama about an ex-con (Bronson) in singleminded hunt for the man who framed him and stole his girl. Lots of chefs involved in writing this brew, among them Lina Wertmuller. Also called VIOLENT CITY.

Family Affair, A (1937) 69m. D: George B. Seitz. Lionel Barrymore, Mickey Rooney, Spring Byington, Cecilia Parker, Eric Linden, Julie Haydon, Sara Haden, Charley Grapewin. SEE: **Andy Hardy** series.

Family Flight (1972) C-73m. TVM D: Marvin Chomsky. Rod Taylor, Kristoffer Tabori, Dina Merrill, Janet Margolin, Gene Nelson, Richard Roat. Family takes flying vacation to help ease failing home life, crashlands, finds they must cooperate to fight for survival. Performances by three leads film's sole asset. Average.

Family Honeymoon (1948) 80m. **½ D: Claude Binyon. Claudette Colbert, Fred MacMurray, Rita Johnson, Gigi Perreau. What could have been fine comedy turns out to be uneven farce as widow takes children on second honeymoon. Very good cast does its best.

Family Jewels, The (1965) C-100m. **½ D: Jerry Lewis. Jerry Lewis, Donna Butterworth, Sebastian Cabot, Robert Strauss, Milton Frome. Depending on your taste for Lewis, you'll either be in ecstasy or writhing on the floor in pain because he plays seven parts—all of them as potential guardians of little girl who is inheriting several million dollars.

Family Kovack, The (1974) C-78m. TVM D: Ralph Senensky. James Sloyan, Sarah Cunningham, Andy Robinson, Tammi Bula, Richard Gilliland, Renne Jarrett, Mary La Roche. Drama concerning the efforts of a closely knit clan to prove oldest son innocent of bribery. Serviceable vehicle with competent cast that might have made a TV series but didn't; should not be confused with "The Family Holvak," which did. Average.

Family Man, The (1979) C-100m. TVM D: Glenn Jordan. Edward Asner, Meredith Baxter Birney, Anne Jackson, Paul Clemens, Mary-Joan Negro. A happily married executive is torn between his infatuation for a beautiful young woman and his love for his wife and family. Daytime soap opera with prime prime-time cast. Average.

Family Nobody Wanted, The (1975) C-78m. TVM D: Ralph Senensky. Shirley Jones, James Olson, Katherine Helmond, Woodrow Parfrey, Claudia Bryar, Ann Doran. Impoverished minister and wife struggle to provide a home for their large brood of racially mixed, adopted children. Winning story tends to get cutesy, but stable performances keep it in line. Average.

Family Plot (1976) C-120m. **½ D: Alfred Hitchcock. Karen Black, Bruce Dern, Barbara Harris, William Devane, Ed Lauter, Cathleen Nesbitt. Hitchcock coasts along in this tongue-in-cheek thriller. Harris is phony psychic who gets involved in a murder plot hatched by sinister Devane. Mildly entertaining but never credible.

Family Rico, The (1972) C-73m. TVM D: Paul Wendkos. Ben Gazzara, Sal Mineo, Jo Van Fleet, James Farentino, Sian Barbara Allen, Dane Clark, Leif Erickson. Solid TV adaptation of Georges Simenon novel concerning torn loyalties of organized crime family leader. Good cast working with fairly realistic material. Above average. Filmed before as THE BROTHERS RICO.

Family Secret, The (1951) 85m. **½ D: Henry Levin. John Derek, Lee J. Cobb, Erin O'Brien-Moore, Jody Lawrance. Good drama involving Cobb who defends man accused for crime which son committed.

Family Upside Down, A (1978) C-100m. TVM D: David Lowell Rich. Helen Hayes, Fred Astaire, Efrem Zimbalist, Jr., Pat Crowley, Patty Duke Astin. Affecting drama about an elderly couple who become dependent on their grown children. Astaire won an Emmy Award and Hayes, Astin, and Zimbalist all received nominations. Above average.

Family Way, The (1966-British) C-115m. *** D: Roy Boulting. Hayley Mills, Hywel Bennett, John Mills, Marjorie Rhodes, Avril Angers, Murray Head. Winning comedy about young newlyweds' problems, including impotence, and difficulty of living in same house as her parents. This warm, gentle film was actually considered controversial in 1967 when released in U.S.!

Fan, The (1949) 89m. ** D: Otto Preminger. Jeanne Crain, Madeleine Carroll, George Sanders, Richard Greene. Oscar Wilde's comedy of manners LADY WINDEMERE'S FAN, involving marital indiscretion and social-climbing in Victorian England, loses much of its wit in film version. Remake of 1925 silent.

Fan's Notes, A (1972-Canadian) C-100m. ** D: Eric Till. Jerry Ohrbach, Burgess Meredith, Patricia Collins, Julia Ann Robinson, Rosemary

Murphy. Confused, football-obsessed writer becomes disillusioned with the Great American Dream of success and conformity, and ends up in mental hospital. Unfortunate misfire of Frederick Exley's highly regarded novel.

Fan-Fan the Tulip (1951-French) **96m.** *** D: Christian-Jaque. Gerard Philippe, Gina Lollobrigida, Noel Roquevert, Olivier Hussenot, Marcel Herrard, Sylvie Pelayo. Most delightful satire of swashbuckling epics, with Philippe ideally cast as the sword-wielding, love-hungry 18th-century Frenchman joining Louis XV's army. Retitled: SOLDIER IN LOVE.

Fanatics, The (1957-French) **85m.** ** D: Alex Joffe. Pierre Fresnay, Michel Auclair, Gregoire Aslan, Betty Schneider. Occasionally taut tale of assassination plot on South American dictator, efforts of one rebel member to stop bomb explosion.

Fancy Pants (1950) **C-92m.** *** D: George Marshall. Mr. Robert Hope (formerly Bob), Lucille Ball, Bruce Cabot, Jack Kirkwood, Lea Penman, Eric Blore. Amusing remake of RUGGLES OF RED GAP with English valet Hope accompanying nouveau riche wildcat Lucy to her Western home.

Fanfare for a Death Scene (1964) **C-73m. TVM** D: Leslie Stevens. Richard Egan, Burgess Meredith, Viveca Lindfors, Telly Savalas, Tina Louise, Edward Asner. Special agent Egan hunts for vanished physicist whose secret formula is sought by the enemy. Atmospheric but standard spy tale spiked by New Orleans jazz with trumpeter Al Hirt. Average.

Fanny (1961) **C-133m.** *** D: Joshua Logan. Leslie Caron, Maurice Chevalier, Charles Boyer, Horst Buchholz, Baccaloni, Lionel Jeffries. Gorgeously photographed and beautifully scored dramatic version of Marcel Pagnol's trilogy involving young girl left with child by adventure-seeking sailor. Chevalier and Boyer give flavorful performances.

Fanny By Gaslight SEE: Man of Evil

Fantastic Planet, The (1973-French) **C-72m.** **½ D: Rene Laloux. Interesting animated feature about futuristic planet where men are dominated by superdeveloped mechanized race. Worthwhile, but misses target by being too static, too aloof.

Fantastic Voyage (1966) **C-100m.** ***½ D: Richard Fleischer. Stephen Boyd, Raquel Welch, Edmond O'-Brien, Donald Pleasence, Arthur O'Connell, William Redfield, Arthur Kennedy. Tremendously entertaining science fiction story of medical team reduced to microscopic size, injected inside human body. Film's great effects will be lost on TV screen, but story and action will keep you glued to your seat nevertheless.

Fantasy Island (1977) **C-100m. TVM** D: Richard Lang. Ricardo Montalban, Bill Bixby, Sandra Dee, Peter Lawford, Carol Lynley, Hugh O'Brian, Eleanor Parker, Victoria Principal, Dick Sargent. Dreams come true on mysterious millionaire Montalban's glamorous island paradise, where for $50,000 each, guests can live out their treasured fantasies. Derivative idea which spawned TV series. Below average.

Fantomas Against Scotland Yard (1966-French) **C-104m.** **½ D: Andre Hunebelle. Jean Marais, Louis De Funes, Mylene Demongeot, Henri Serre. Satirical cliff-hanger-type adventure yarn, with Marais as supercriminal engaged in a number of athletic escapades. Retitled: FANTOMAS.

Far Country, The (1955) **C-97m.** *** D: Anthony Mann. James Stewart, Ruth Roman, Corinne Calvet, Walter Brennan, Jay C. Flippen, John McIntire, Harry Morgan. Cattleman Stewart, a confirmed loner, brings his herd to Alaska and finds nothing but trouble; solid Western saga set against colorful backdrop of mining camp towns.

Far from the Madding Crowd (1967-British) **C-169m.** ***½ D: John Schlesinger. Julie Christie, Peter Finch, Terence Stamp, Alan Bates, Prunella Ransome. Shamefully underrated adaptation of Thomas Hardy novel about beautiful woman and her profound effect on three men. Superb production, with brilliant photography, score, and performances by Finch and Bates.

Far Horizons, The (1955) **C-108m.** **½ D: Rudolph Maté. Fred MacMurray, Charlton Heston, Donna Reed, Barbara Hale, William Demarest. Movie fiction about Lewis and Clark expedition, beautifully photographed; sporadic action; implausible love interest.

Farewell Again (1937-British) **81m.** **½ D: Tim Whelan. Leslie Banks,

Flora Robson, Sebastian Shaw, Patricia Hilliard. Neatly handled minor film detailing events in the lives of British soldiers on short leave before embarking for the front again.

Farewell Friend (1968-French) C-119m. ** D: Jean Herman. Alain Delon, Charles Bronson. Mercenaries return to Marseilles following service in Algeria, team up for robbery but inevitably clash. Ordinary and overlong.

Farewell, My Lovely (1975-British) C-97m. *** D: Dick Richards. Robert Mitchum, Charlotte Rampling, John Ireland, Sylvia Miles, Jack O'Halloran, Anthony Zerbe, Harry Dean Stanton. Third film version of Raymond Chandler novel tries too hard to evoke its period, but gets by anyway; Mitchum is appealing as a tired Philip Marlowe.

Farewell to Arms, A (1932) 78m. *** D: Frank Borzage. Helen Hayes, Gary Cooper, Adolphe Menjou, Mary Philips, Jack LaRue, Blanche Frederici. Lushly romantic adaptation of Hemingway novel about ill-fated WW1 romance between American soldier and British nurse; dated but well done.

Farewell to Arms, A (1957) C-152m. **½ D: Charles Vidor. Rock Hudson, Jennifer Jones, Vittorio De Sica, Alberto Sordi, Mercedes McCambridge, Elaine Stritch, Oscar Homolka. Overblown, padded remake has unconvincing leads, static treatment of WW1 story so romantically told in Hemingway novel. Hudson is American ambulance driver wounded in WW1 Italy who falls in love with nurse Jones.

Farewell to Manzanar (1976) C-105m. TVM D: John Korty. Yuki Shimoda, Nobu McCarthy, Clyde Kasatu, Mako, Akemi Kikimura, Pat Morita, James Saito. Factual story of one Japanese-American family's internment in WW2 detention camp. Sad, often hidden slice of American history, beautifully directed by Korty and captured in the screenplay by Jeanne Wakatuski Houston (who lived it) and her husband James D. Houston, taken from their stirring book. Not to be missed.

Farmer, The (1977) C-98m. BOMB D: David Berlatsky. Gary Conway, Angel Tompkins, Michael Dante, George Memmoli, Ken Renard. Sadistic, amateurish actioner set in Georgia just after WW2. Vet Conway tries to keep his farm going,

gets mixed up with the syndicate. Lots of anachronistic errors, including the whole movie.

Farmer Takes a Wife, The (1935) **½ D: Victor Fleming. Janet Gaynor, Henry Fonda, Charles Bickford, Slim Summerville, Jane Withers. Vintage romance of farmers living by the Erie Canal in 1800s; Fonda's first film, and he's still enjoyable as Gaynor's suitor.

Farmer Takes a Wife, The (1953) 81m. ** D: Henry Levin. Betty Grable, Dale Robertson, Thelma Ritter, John Carroll, Eddie Foy, Jr. Musical remake of 1935 film is slow-paced account of life in 1800s along the Erie Canal.

Farmer's Daughter, The (1940) 60m. ** D: James Hogan. Martha Raye, Charlie Ruggles, Richard Denning, Gertrude Michael, William Frawley. Not to be confused with later film, this one is about show business on the farm circuit, worthwhile only for Raye.

Farmer's Daughter, The (1947) 97m. ***½ D: H. C. Potter. Loretta Young, Joseph Cotten, Ethel Barrymore, Charles Bickford, Rose Hobart, Harry Davenport, Lex Barker, James Aurness (Arness), Keith Andes. Young won Oscar for her performance as headstrong Swedish girl who fights for congressional seat against the man she loves. Delightful comedy with excellent cast. Basis for later TV series.

Fashions (1934) 78m. *** D: William Dieterle. William Powell, Bette Davis, Verree Teasdale, Reginald Owen, Frank McHugh, Phillip Reed, Hugh Herbert. Trivial but enjoyable romp of con-man Powell and designer Davis conquering the Paris fashion world. Fine cast glides along with dapper Powell; Busby Berkeley's "Spin a Little Web of Dreams" number is great fun. Original title: FASHIONS OF 1934.

Fast and Loose (1930) 75m. *½ D: Fred Newmeyer. Miriam Hopkins, Carole Lombard, Frank Morgan, Ilka Chase, Charles Starrett. Attempt at witty comedy doesn't come through; Hopkins' first film; Lombard has small role.

Fast and Loose (1939) 80m. **½ D: Edwin L. Marin. Robert Montgomery, Rosalind Russell, Reginald Owen, Ralph Morgan, Sidney Blackmer. Average mystery about theft of

Shakespearean manuscript during weekend stay at owner's estate.

Fast and Sexy (1960-Italian) **C-98m.** **½ D: Vittorio De Sica. Gina Lollobrigida, Dale Robertson, Vittorio De Sica, Carla Macelloni. Lollobrigida is fun-loving widow who returns to her village seeking new husband.

Fast and the Furious, The (1954) 73m. ** D: Edwards Sampson. John Ireland, Dorothy Malone, Iris Adrian, Bruce Carlisle, Jean Howell, Larry Thor. Ireland is fugitive on the lam from murder frameup who jockeys Malone's sports car, with uninspired romantic interludes and cops-on-the-chase sequences.

Fast Break (1979) **C-107m.** *** D: Jack Smight. Gabriel Kaplan, Howard Sylvester, Mike Warren, Bernard King, Red Brown, Mavis Washington, Bert Remsen, Rhonda Bates, K. Callan. Basketball coach Kaplan accepts post at midwestern college, but brings his N.Y. street players along with him. Perfect, innocuous TV fare, with some good laughs and exciting game climax.

Fast Charlie, The—Moonbeam Rider (1979) **C-99m.** **½ D: Steve Carver. David Carradine, Brenda Vaccaro, L. Q. Jones, R. G. Armstrong, Jesse Vint. Period action comedy-drama about a WW1 deserter who enters the first long-distance motorcycle race. Appealing performance by Vaccaro as an early-day bike groupie and picturesque recreations of post-WW1 America are definite pluses.

Fast Company (1953) 67m. ** D: John Sturges. Polly Bergen, Howard Keel, Marjorie Main, Nina Foch, Iron Eyes Cody. Not very exciting musical comedy about horse who prances to music, owned by racing enthusiast Bergen.

Fast Friends (1979) **C-100m. TVM** D: Steven Hilliard Stern. Carrie Snodgress, Dick Shawn, Edie Adams, Michael Parks, Jed Allan, Mackenzie Phillips, Vivian Blaine. Far from engrossing drama about a divorcee's struggle to make it on her own in the broadcasting game. Average.

Fastest Guitar Alive, The (1968) **C-87m.** ** D: Michael Moore. Roy Orbison, Sammy Jackson, Maggie Pierce, Joan Freeman. Undercover Confederate spies steal a fortune from enemy right before the Civil War ends, then find they have to

return it without anyone knowing; poor action tale.

Fastest Gun Alive, The (1956) 92m. *** D: Russell Rouse. Glenn Ford, Jeanne Crain, Broderick Crawford, Russ Tamblyn. Sincere Western with a moral. Ford is a peace-loving storekeeper trying to live down renown as fast gunslinger, but there's always someone waiting to challenge him.

Fat City (1972) **C-100m.** *** D: John Huston. Stacy Keach, Jeff Bridges, Susan Tyrell, Candy Clark, Nicholas Colasanto. Taut adaptation of Leonard Gardner's novel about tanktown boxer and his young protégé is Huston's best film in 20 years; Keach, Bridges, and Tyrell are all fine.

Fat Man, The (1951) 77m. **½ D: William Castle. J. Scott Smart, Julie London, Rock Hudson, Jayne Meadows. Heavyweight detective investigates dentist's murder, leading him to criminal at the circus; offbeat.

Fatal Desire (1953-Italian) 80m. ** D: Carmine Gallone. Anthony Quinn, Kerima, May Britt, Ettore Manni, Umberto Spadaro, voice of Tito Gobbi. Nonmusical version of Mascagni's opera *Cavalleria Rusticana*, about love, adultery, and revenge in small Sicilian town. Originally filmed in color and 3D, not released in U.S. until 1963 in b&w.

Fatal Witness, The (1945) 59m. *½ D: Lesley Selander. Evelyn Ankers, Richard Fraser, George Leigh, Barbara Everest, Frederick Worlock. Quickie mystery yarn with obvious plot about wealthy matron's murder, capture of culprit.

Fate Is the Hunter (1964) 106m. **½ D: Ralph Nelson. Glenn Ford, Nancy Kwan, Rod Taylor, Suzanne Pleshette, Jane Russell, Wally Cox. One-note drama of investigation into cause of controversial plane crash. Good cast works with routine script.

Fate Takes a Hand (1961-British) 72m. **½ D: Max Varnel. Ronald Howard, Christina Gregg, Basil Dignam, Sheila Whittingham. Agreeable format about bag of mail recovered fifteen years after a robbery; effect of letters on recipients allows for five trim little tales.

Father Brown: SEE Detective, The (1954)

Father Goose (1964) **C-115m.** *** D: Ralph Nelson. Cary Grant, Leslie Caron, Trevor Howard, Jack Good, Nicole Felsette. Grant goes native as shiftless bum on a South Seas island during WW2. Caron is schoolteacher who, with her girls in tow, tames Grant. Lightweight and enjoyable.

Father Is a Bachelor (1950) 84m. ** D: Norman Foster, Abby Berlin. William Holden, Coleen Gray, Mary Jane Saunders, Stuart Erwin, Sig Ruman. Vagabond Holden with five "adopted" kids meets Gray who wants to marry him; "cute" comedy.

Father Makes Good (1950) 61m. *½ D: Jean Yarbrough. Raymond Walburn, Walter Catlett, Barbara Brown, Gertrude Astor. Mild little film in Walburn series of small-town man who purchases a cow to show his contempt for new milk tax.

Father of the Bride (1950) 93m. **** D: Vincente Minnelli. Spencer Tracy, Elizabeth Taylor, Joan Bennett, Billie Burke, Leo G. Carroll, Russ Tamblyn. Liz is marrying Don Taylor, but Dad (Tracy) has all the aggravation. Perceptive view of American life, witty script by Frances Goodrich & Albert Hackett, and peerless Tracy performance.

Father Takes a Wife (1941) 79m. **½ D: Jack Hively. Adolphe Menjou, Gloria Swanson, John Howard, Desi Arnaz, Helen Broderick, Florence Rice, Neil Hamilton. Pleasant little comedy about glamorous stage star (Swanson) who "settles down" and marries Menjou, but takes on opera singer Arnaz as her protege.

Father Takes the Air (1951) 61m. *½ D: Frank McDonald. Raymond Walburn, Walter Catlett, Florence Bates, Gary Gray. Walburn is involved with local flying school, and accidentally captures a crook.

Father Was a Fullback (1949) 84m. **½ D: John M. Stahl. Fred MacMurray, Maureen O'Hara, Betty Lynn, Rudy Vallee, Thelma Ritter, Natalie Wood. Wholesome comedy with most engaging cast. MacMurray is football coach with as many household problems as on the gridiron.

Father's Little Dividend (1951) 82m. *** D: Vincente Minnelli. Spencer Tracy, Joan Bennett, Elizabeth Taylor, Don Taylor, Billie Burke. Delightful sequel to FATHER OF THE BRIDE with same cast. Now Tracy is going to be a grandfather and he doesn't look forward to it.

Father's Wild Game (1950) 61m. *½ D: Herbert I. Leeds. Raymond Walburn, Walter Catlett, Jane Darwell, Roscoe Ates, Ann Tyrrell. In this entry, Walburn is protesting inflation

at the meat market and decides to hunt wild game himself.

Fathom (1967) C-99m. *** D: Leslie H. Martinson. Raquel Welch, Tony Franciosa, Ronald Fraser, Greta Chi, Richard Briers, Clive Revill. Fast-paced, tongue-in-cheek spy caper with sky-diver Welch getting mixed up with dubious good-guy Franciosa. Great fun, with Revill's performance as eccentric millionaire stealing the show.

Fazil (1928) 88m. ** D: Howard Hawks. Charles Farrell, Greta Nissen, Mae Busch, Vadim Uraneff, Tyler Brooke, John Boles. Strange casting of Farrell as desert sheik is just one oddity in this opulent romance. Visually stunning but dramatically far-fetched. Silent film with original 1928 music score.

Fear (1946) 68m. *½ D: Alfred Zeisler. Peter Cookson, Warren William, Anne Gwynne, James Cardwell, Nestor Paiva. Rather tepid remake of Dostoyevsky's CRIME AND PUNISHMENT, suffering from low-budget production values.

Fear in the Night (1947) 72m. *** D: Maxwell Shane. Paul Kelly, Ann Doran, Kay Scott, DeForest Kelley, Robert Emmett Keane. Nifty, exciting chiller involving man who commits murder while under hypnosis. Remade as NIGHTMARE.

Fear Is the Key (1972-British) C-103m. *½ D: Michael Tuchner. Barry Newman, Suzy Kendall, John Vernon, Dolph Sweet, Ben Kingsley. Confused, unsatisfying Alistair MacLean thriller about a man driven to extremes in pursuit of stolen booty —and revenge for the murder of his wife and child.

Fear No Evil (1969) C-98m. TVM D: Paul Wendkos. Louis Jourdan, Bradford Dillman, Lynda Day, Marsha Hunt, Wilfrid Hyde-White, Carroll O'Connor. Antique mirror actually entrance to another supernatural world. Scientist (Dillman) buys it; after he dies in accident, fiancee learns it can bring him back. Good cast in moderately inventive examination of magic. Fairly offbeat, above average.

Fear on Trial (1975) C-100m. TVM D: Lamont Johnson. George C. Scott, William Devane, Dorothy Tristan, John Houseman, Judd Hirsch, Lois Nettleton, Milt Kogan, Ben Piazza. Superb drama about blacklisting and subsequent libel trial of 1950s broadcaster John Henry Faulk.

Scott etches another memorable portrait as attorney Louis Nizer; Devane is equally as fine as Faulk. Writer David Rintels won an Emmy for his teleplay. Above average.

Fear Strikes Out (1957) 100m. ******* D: Robert Mulligan. Anthony Perkins, Karl Malden, Norma Moore, Adam Williams, Perry Wilson. Stark account of baseball star Jimmy Piersall and his bout with mental illness. Perkins properly intense in star role.

Fearless Fagan (1952) 79m. ****** D: Stanley Donen. Carleton Carpenter, Janet Leigh, Keenan Wynn, Richard Anderson, Ellen Corby, Barbara Ruick. Title character is circus lion who accompanies his dimwitted master (Carpenter) into the Army, with predictable results. Inconsequential comedy.

Fearless Vampire Killers or: Pardon Me, But Your Teeth Are in My Neck, The (1967-British) C-98m. *****½** D: Roman Polanski. Jack MacGowran, Sharon Tate, Alfie Bass, Ferdy Mayne, Terry Downes, Roman Polanski. Near-brilliant mixture of humor and horror plus excellent production as Professor Abronsius and assistant Alfred (great bumbling idiot team) attempt to destroy family of Slovonic vampires. Odd continuity due to 20 minutes cut prior to initial release.

Fearmakers, The (1958) 83m. ****½** D: Jacques Tourneur. Dana Andrews, Dick Foran, Mel Torme, Marilee Earle. Well-done Communist witch-hunt theme as returning war veteran Andrews discovers subversives in his Washington, D. C. ad agency.

Feathered Serpent, The (1948) 61m. D: William Beaudine. Roland Winters, Keye Luke, Victor Sen Yung, Mantan Moreland, Carol Forman, Robert Livingston, Nils Asther. SEE: **Charlie Chan** series.

Federal Agents vs. Underworld Inc. SEE: **Golden Hands of Kurigal**

Federal Operator 99 SEE: **FBI 99**

Fedora (1978-German) C-114m. ****½** D: Billy Wilder. William Holden, Marthe Keller, Hildegarde Knef, Jose Ferrer, Frances Sternhagen, Henry Fonda, Michael York, Mario Adorf. Stylish but ponderous filmization of Thomas Tryon's short story about a producer's disastrous attempt to lure a Garbo-esque actress out of seclusion. Wilder's potshots at today's films and filmmakers might

carry more weight if his own film were better.

Feet First (1930) 83m. ****½** D: Clyde Bruckman. Harold Lloyd, Barbara Kent, Robert McWade, Lillianne Leighton, Henry Hall. Lloyd talkie tries to rekindle spirit of his silent comedies with middling results. Episodic film has some very funny moments, but Harold's building-ledge routine doesn't quite come off. Edited for TV.

Fellini Roma (1972-Italian) C-128m. ******* D: Federico Fellini. Peter Gonzales, Britta Barnes, Pia De Doses, Fiona Florence, Marne Maitland, Renato Giovannoli, Federico Fellini. Famed director's impressionistic ode to Eternal City of his youth, his adolescence, and the present—complete with fantasy sequence and usual carnival-of-life point of view.

Fellini Satyricon (1970-Italian) C-120m. ******* D: Federico Fellini. Martin Potter, Hiram Keller, Max Born, Capucine, Salvo Randone. Opinions vary on merits of this visually stunning but overindulgent spectacle on ancient Rome, but TV is no place to arbitrate; if the censors don't ruin it, commercial interruptions will.

Fellini's Casanova (1977-Italian) C-158m. ****½** D: Federico Fellini. Donald Sutherland, Tina Aumont, Cicely Browne, John Karlsen, Daniel Emilfork Berenstein. Uninvolving if opulent version of 18th-century lover's life, made entirely at Rome's Cinecitta Studios. Sutherland is enigmatic, the film stylized to a sometimes absurd degree. Nino Rota's music helps.

Fellowship of the Frog SEE: **Face of the Frog**

Female and the Flesh SEE: **Light Across the Street**

Female Animal, The (1958) 84m. ****½** D: Harry Keller. Hedy Lamarr, Jane Powell, Jan Sterling, George Nader. Sad waste of Lamarr as mature Hollywood star who grapples with adopted daughter Powell over Nader.

Female Artillery (1973) C-73m. TVM D: Marvin Chomsky. Dennis Weaver, Ida Lupino, Sally Ann Howes, Linda Evans, Albert Salmi, Anna Navarro. Boring adventure with comedy undertones features Weaver as man on run from gang, hiding stolen money with female wagon train who, in turn, steal it from him to force him to lead them to nearby fort. Laughable resolution, negligible suspense, adequate performances. Average.

Female Jungle (1956) 56m. ** D: Bruno Ve Sota. Jayne Mansfield, Lawrence Tierney, John Carradine, Kathleen Crowley, Rex Thorsen, Burt Carlisle, Bruno Ve Sota. Attempt at sensationalism in this murder yarn fails to catch on; Tierney is cop seeking killer of cinema lovely.

Female Instinct: SEE **Snoop Sisters, The**

Female on the Beach (1955) 97m. *** D: Joseph Pevney. Joan Crawford, Jeff Chandler, Jan Sterling, Cecil Kellaway, Judith Evelyn, Natalie Schafer. Crawford makes this mystery believable as woman who suspects her lover (Chandler) may want to do her in. Sterling offers contrasting performance and fine support.

Female Trap, The: SEE **Name of the Game is Kill, The**

Feminine Touch, The (1941) 97m. **½ D: W. S. Van Dyke, II. Rosalind Russell, Don Ameche, Kay Francis, Van Heflin, Donald Meek, Gordon Jones. Brittle comedy of author Ameche writing book on jealousy, finding himself a victim when he brings wife Russell to N.Y.C.; she suspects he's carrying on with glamorous Francis.

Feminist and the Fuzz, The (1970) C-73m. TVM D: Jerry Paris. Barbara Eden, David Hartman, Jo Anne Worley, Harry Morgan, Julie Newmar, Roger Perry. Contrived comedy throws two stereotypes—male chauvinist cop and Women's Libber—together as San Francisco apartment roommates with typical TV style resolution of initial differences. Good cast deserves far, far better. Average.

Femme Infidele, La (1969-French) C-98m. ***½ D: Claude Chabrol. Stephane Audran, Michel Bouquet, Maurice Ronet, Stephen Di Napolo, Michel Duchaussoy. Atmospheric drama about wife who earns more respect for her husband when he murders her lover; Audran and Bouquet are fine in yet another memorable film from director Chabrol.

Fer-de-Lance (1974) C-100m. TVM D: Russ Mayberry. David Janssen, Hope Lange, Ivan Dixon, Jason Evers, Ben Piazza, Charles Robinson. Suspense tale about a submarine wedged below the sea, terrorized from within by deadly snakes. Ridiculous story and charac-

ters, with creepy-crawlers for those who like that kind of thing. Below average.

Fernandel the Dressmaker (1957-French) 84m. **½ D: Jean Boyer. Fernandel, Suzy Delair, Françoise Fabian, Georges Chamarat. Undemanding plot has him wanting to be high-fashion designer rather than drab man's tailor.

Ferry Cross the Mersey (1965-British) 88m. ** D: Jeremy Summers. Gerry and the Pacemakers, Cilla Black, The Fourmost, Jimmy Saville. Made to cash in on lead group's popularity, film tells supposed story of their rise to fame.

Ferry to Hong Kong (1961-British) C-103m. **½ D: Lewis Gilbert. Orson Welles, Curt Jurgens, Sylvia Syms, Jeremy Spenser. Welles and Jurgens have field day as straight-faced ferry boat skipper and drunken Austrian on trip to Macao. Film is otherwise just routine.

Feudin' Fools (1952) 63m. D: William Beaudine. Leo Gorcey, Huntz Hall, Dorothy Ford, Lyle Talbot, Benny Baker, Russell Simpson. SEE: **Bowery Boys** series.

Feudin', Fussin' and A-Fightin' (1948) 78m. ** D: George Sherman. Donald O'Connor, Marjorie Main, Percy Kilbride, Penny Edwards. Title and cast names tell all; loud and brassy.

Fever in the Blood, A (1961) 117m. **½ D: Vincent Sherman. Efrem Zimbalist, Jr., Angie Dickinson, Herbert Marshall, Don Ameche, Jack Kelly, Carroll O'Connor. Turgid dramatics focusing on murder trial which various candidates for governorship utilize to further political ambitions; film lacks verve.

Fickle Finger of Fate, The (1967-Spanish) C-91m. *½ D: Richard Rush. Tab Hunter, Luis Prendes, Patty Shepard, Gustavo Rojo, Fernando Hilbeck. Low-budget comedy thriller about an American engineer who finds himself a patsy for smugglers trying to get some art objects out of Madrid.

Fiddler on the Roof (1971) C-181m. *** D: Norman Jewison. Chaim Topol, Norma Crane, Leonard Frey, Molly Picon, Paul Mann, Rosalind Harris, Michele Marsh, Neva Small, Candice Bonstein. Rousing, colorful location-filmed adaptation of Joseph Stein's hit play based on Sholem Aleichem stories of humble village of Anatevka. Topol is hearty as

Tevye, trying to preserve Jewish heritage against growing odds. Sheldon Harnick-Jerry Bock score melodically performed; Isaac Stern's violin featured on soundtrack.

Fiend Who Walked the West, The (1958) 101m. **½ D: Gordon Douglas. Hugh O'Brian, Robert Evans, Dolores Michaels, Linda Cristal, Stephen McNally. Interesting if not altogether successful transposition of KISS OF DEATH to Western setting, with Evans ludicrous in the Widmark psycho role.

Fiend Without a Face (1958-British) 74m. *½ D: Arthur Crabtree. Marshall Thompson, Kim Parker, Terence Kilburn, Michael Balfour, Gil Winfield. Scientist materializes thoughts in form of invisible brain-shaped creatures which kill people for food. Horrific climax; good special effects.

Fiercest Heart, The (1961) C-91m. ** D: George Sherman. Stuart Whitman, Juliet Prowse, Ken Scott, Raymond Massey, Geraldine Fitzgerald. Good cast and action-packed skirmishes with Zulus can't raise this programmer to any heights. Set in Africa.

Fiesta (1947) C-104m. ** D: Richard Thorpe. Esther Williams, Akim Tamiroff, Ricardo Montalban, John Carroll, Mary Astor, Cyd Charisse. Williams trades in her bathing suit for a toreador outfit in this weak musical opus.

15 Malden Lane (1936) 65m. ** D: Allan Dwan. Claire Trevor, Cesar Romero, Douglas Fowley, Lloyd Nolan, Lester Matthews. Trevor lures Romero in order to crack his underworld gang in this satisfactory programmer.

Fifth Avenue Girl (1939) 83m. ** D: Gregory LaCava. Ginger Rogers, Walter Connolly, Verree Teasdale, James Ellison, Tim Holt, Kathryn Adams. Tiresome "social comedy" with Rogers as homeless girl taken in by unhappy millionaire Connolly; even Ginger is lifeless in this film that purports to show that poor is better than rich, if you've got a head on your shoulders.

Fifth Day of Peace, The (1972-Italian) C-100m. ** D: Guilliano Montaldo. Richard Johnson, Franco Nero, Bud Spencer, Michael Goodliffe, Helmut Schneider. Episodic story of several disillusioned WW1 German soldiers aimlessly wandering war-ravaged Italian countryside following the armistice.

Fifth Musketeer, The (1979-Austrian) C-103m. **½ D: Ken Annakin. Beau Bridges, Sylvia Kristel, Ursula Andress, Cornel Wilde, Ian McShane, Lloyd Bridges, Alan Hale Jr., Jose Ferrer, Helmut Dantine, Rex Harrison, Olivia de Havilland. Lavish, well-cast remake of THE MAN IN THE IRON MASK has nothing new to offer, but retells Dumas' story in capable fashion. Major points of interest: Austrian location work and veteran cast.

55 Days at Peking (1963) C-150m. *** D: Nicholas Ray. Charlton Heston, Ava Gardner, David Niven, Flora Robson, John Ireland, Paul Lukas, Jacques Sernas. Stars provide most of the interest in this confusing historical account of Boxer Rebellion in 1900s China.

Fifty Roads to Town (1937) 81m. **½ D: Norman Taurog. Don Ameche, Ann Sothern, Slim Summerville, Jane Darwell, John Qualen, Stepin Fetchit, Oscar Apfel, Russell Hicks. Above-par comedy of Ameche and Sothern, both on the lam for different reasons, snowbound together in small inn.

52nd Street (1937) 80m. ** D: Harold Young. Ian Hunter, Leo Carrillo, Pat Paterson, Kenny Baker, Ella Logan, ZaSu Pitts. Fictionalized story of how 52nd St. became nightclub row in the 1930s; soggy drama punctuated by appearances of some 52nd St. entertainers like Jerry Colonna, Georgie Tapps, Pat Harrington Sr.

52 Miles to Midnight SEE: **Hot Rods to Hell**

Fighter, The (1952) 78m. **½ D: Herbert Kline. Richard Conte, Vanessa Brown, Lee J. Cobb, Roberta Haynes. Absorbing tale set in Mexico with Conte a boxer who uses winnings to buy arms to seek revenge for family's murder.

Fighter Attack (1953) C-80m. ** D: Lesley Selander. Sterling Hayden, J. Carrol Naish, Joy Page, Paul Fierro. Modest film uses flashback to recount Hayden's last important mission in Italy during WW2.

Fighter Squadron (1948) C-96m. ** D: Raoul Walsh. Edmond O'Brien, Robert Stack, John Rodney, Tom D'Andrea, Henry Hull. OK WW2 drama of dedicated flier O'Brien, has abundance of clichés weighing against good action sequences. Rock Hudson's first film.

Fighting Chance, The (1955) 70m. **
D: William Witney. Rod Cameron, Julie London, Ben Cooper, Taylor Holmes, Bob Steele. Standard fare. Horse trainer and jockey friend both fall in love with London and come to odds with each other.

Fighting Coast Guard (1951) 86m. **½ D: Joseph Kane. Brian Donlevy, Forrest Tucker, Ella Raines, John Russell. Better than usual entry in training-for-war film, mixing romance with military action during WW2.

Fighting Devil Dogs SEE: Torpedo of Doom

Fighting Father Dunne (1948) 93m. **½ D: Ted Tetzlaff. Pat O'Brien, Darryl Hickman, Charles Kemper, Una O'Connor. Road company BOYS TOWN with O'Brien doing his usual competent work.

Fighting Fools (1949) 69m. D: Reginald Le Borg. Leo Gorcey, Huntz Hall, Gabriel Dell, Frankie Darro, Lyle Talbot, Evelynne Eaton, Benny Bartlett, Bernard Gorcey. SEE: Bowery Boys series

Fighting Guardsman (1945) 84m. ** D: Henry Levin. Willard Parker, Anita Louise, Janis Carter, John Loder, Edgar Buchanan, George Macready, Lloyd Corrigan. OK costumer of oppressed Frenchmen rising against tyranny in days before French Revolution.

Fighting Kentuckian, The (1949) 100m. **½ D: George Waggner. John Wayne, Vera Ralston, Philip Dorn, Oliver Hardy, Marie Windsor. Frontierland around 1810 is setting for two-fisted saga of Kentuckian (Wayne) combating land-grabbing criminals and courting Ralston, French General's daughter.

Fighting Lawman, The (1953) 71m. *½ D: Thomas Carr. Wayne Morris, Virginia Grey, Harry Lauter, John Kellogg, Myron Healey, Dick Rich. Grey tries to work with flimsy script as gal out to grab loot from robbers, pursued by sheriff.

Fighting Mad (1976) C-90m. **½ D: Jonathan Demme. Peter Fonda, Lynn Lowry, John Doucette, Philip Carey, Scott Glen, Kathleen Miller. Typical revenge picture, with peaceable Fonda driven to violence by ruthless landowner who wants to take over Fonda's farm. On-target for this kind of entertainment.

Fighting Man of the Plains (1949) C-94m. **½ D: Edwin L. Marin.

Randolph Scott, Bill Williams, Jane Nigh, Victor Jory. Scott seeks to avenge brother's murder, but kills the wrong man. OK Western, with Dale Robertson in first prominent role as Jesse James.

Fighting O'Flynn, The (1949) 94m. **½ D: Arthur Pierson. Douglas Fairbanks, Jr., Richard Greene, Helena Carter, Patricia Medina. Enjoyable swashbuckler set in 1800s Ireland with Fairbanks-Greene vying in love and intrigue.

Fighting Prince of Donegal, The (1966) C-112m. *** D: Michael O'Herlihy. Peter McEnery, Susan Hampshire, Tom Adams, Gordon Jackson, Andrew Keir, Donal McCann. Fine Disney swashbuckler made in England, with McEnery as new head of Irish clan who tries to unite his country but runs afoul of villainous Jackson. Vivid, colorful fun.

Fighting Seabees, The (1944) 100m. *** D: Edward Ludwig. John Wayne, Susan Hayward, Dennis O'Keefe, William Frawley, Duncan Renaldo. Spirited WW2 saga of valiant seabees Wayne and O'Keefe stationed in China, fighting for Hayward.

Fighting 69th, The (1940) 90m. **½ D: William Keighley. James Cagney, Pat O'Brien, George Brent, Jeffrey Lynn, Alan Hale, Frank McHugh, Dennis Morgan. Overripe WW1 tale mixes roughneck comedy, exciting battle action, sloppy sentiment, incredible characterizations (especially Cagney's) detailing exploits of famed Irish regiment.

Fighting Trouble (1956) 61m. D: George Blair. Huntz Hall, Stanley Clements, Adele Jergens, Joseph Downing. SEE: Bowery Boys series

Fighting Wildcats, The (1957-British) 74m. ** D: Arthur Crabtree. Keefe Brasselle, Kay Callard, Karel Stepanek, Ursula Howells. Innocuous intrigue set in London and Middle East involving gangsters. Original title: WEST OF SUEZ.

File of the Golden Goose, The (1969-British) C-105m. ** D: Sam Wanamaker. Yul Brynner, Charles Gray, Edward Woodward, John Barrie, Adrienne Corri. Strictly formula effort with American agent and Scotland Yard man going undercover in London to get the goods on murderous counterfeiting gang.

File on Thelma Jordan, The (1949)

100m. **½ D: Robert Siodmak. Barbara Stanwyck, Wendell Corey, Joan Tetzel, Paul Kelly. Murky drama, focusing largely on romance between D.A. Corey and shady lady Stanwyck. Retitled: THELMA JORDAN.

Fillmore (1972) **C-105m. *** D:** Richard T. Hoffner. Bill Graham, The Grateful Dead, It's a Beautiful Day, Santana, Jefferson Airplane, Quicksilver Messenger Service. Good rock documentary about Fillmore West's final days is made even better by extensive footage of its magnetic owner, Bill Graham, on the phone and on stage; one of the better films of its kind.

Final Chapter—Walking Tall (1977) **C-112m. BOMB D:** Jack Starrett. Bo Svenson, Margaret Blye, Forrest Tucker, Lurene Tuttle, Morgan Woodward, Libby Boone. Yet another saga about true-life Tennessee sheriff, Buford Pusser, and inferior to the other two. Since he dies at the end of this one, let us hope that it is indeed the final chapter.

Final Crash, The: SEE Steelyard Blues

Final Test, The (1953-British) **84m. **½ D:** Anthony Asquith. Jack Warner, Robert Morley, George Relph, Adrianne Allen. Droll, minor comedy of father-son rivalry over charming Allen.

Finders Keepers (1951) **74m. **½ D:** Frederick de Cordova. Tom Ewell, Julia Adams, Evelyn Varden, Dusty Henley. Scatterbrained comedy that chugs down at end. Ewell and Varden enliven proceedings about a little boy who comes home with a cartful of money.

Fine Madness, A (1966) **C-104m. *** D:** Irvin Kershner. Sean Connery, Joanne Woodward, Jean Seberg, Patrick O'Neal, Colleen Dewhurst, Renee Taylor. Sturdy adaptation of Elliott Baker novel about individualist, rebellious poet and his capers in N.Y.C.

Fine Pair, A (1969) **C-89m. BOMB D:** Francesco Maselli. Rock Hudson, Claudia Cardinale, Thomas Milian, Leon Askin, Ellen Corby, Walter Giller. New York policeman Hudson falls for Cardinale, daughter of an old pal, and helps her rob some jewels in terrible comedy-thriller minus laughs or suspense.

Finger Man (1955) **82m. ** D:** Harold Schuster. Frank Lovejoy, Forrest Tucker, Peggie Castle, Glenn Gordon, Evelynne Eaton. Convincing performances uplift account of federal agents capturing liquor gang.

Finger of Guilt (1956-British) **84m. **½ D:** Joseph Losey. Richard Basehart, Mary Murphy, Constance Cummings, Roger Livesey, Mervyn Johns, Faith Brook. Film director Basehart is blackmailed by woman claiming to be his mistress, which threatens his career and marriage. Intriguing film with disappointing resolution; good look inside British film studio, however. Directed by blacklistee Losey under pseudonyms Alec Snowden/Joseph Walton. British title: THE INTIMATE STRANGER.

Finger on the Trigger (1965) **C-87m. BOMB D:** Sidney Pink. Rory Calhoun, James Philbrook, Todd Martin, Silvia Solar, Brad Talbot. Reb and Yankee veterans join forces to secure buried treasure while holding off hostile Indians. Made in Spain.

Fingers (1978) **C-91m. ***½ D:** James Toback. Harvey Keitel, Jim Brown, Tisa Farrow, Michael V. Gazzo, Tanya Roberts, Marian Seldes. Crude but powerful melodrama about an aspiring concert pianist who "collects" on debts owed to his domineering father. Though much admired by the genteel François Truffaut, the film is not for viewers repelled by graphic violence or kinky sex.

Fingers at the Window (1942) **80m. **½ D:** Charles Lederer. Lew Ayres, Laraine Day, Basil Rathbone, Walter Kingsford. Miles Mander, James Flavin. Entertaining mystery of Ayres-Day tracking down maniac killer masterminding repeated axe murders.

Finian's Rainbow (1968) **C-145m. **½ D:** Francis Ford Coppola. Fred Astaire, Petula Clark, Tommy Steele, Keenan Wynn, Al Freeman Jr., Don Francks, Barbara Hancock. Burton Lane-E.Y.Harburg musical was ahead of its time in late 1940s, combining subtle social commentary with tuneful Irish musical setting. Film, made 20 years later, has Astaire, those fine songs, colorful scenery, but somehow misses the mark. Still OK entertainment.

Finishing School (1934) **73m. **½ D:** Wanda Tuchock, George Nicholls Jr. Frances Dee, Bruce Cabot, Ginger Rogers, Beulah Bondi, Billie Burke, John Halliday. Interesting look at exclusive girls' school where hypocrisy reigns; wealthy Dee falls in love with struggling hospital intern Cabot.

Finnegan's Wake (1965) 97m. ***½ D: Mary Ellen Bute. Page Johnson, Martin J. Kelly, Jane Reilly, Peter Haskell. James Joyce's classic story of Irish tavern-keeper who dreams of attending his own wake is brought to the screen with great energy and control.

Fire! (1977) C-100m. TVM D: Earl Bellamy. Ernest Borgnihe, Vera Miles, Patty Duke Astin, Alex Cord, Lloyd Nolan, Ty Hardin, Donna Mills, Neville Brand, Gene Evans. Mountain community is threatened by forest fire started by convict to cover escape from road gang. Carefully structured suspense in the familiar Irwin Allen "popular catastrophe" style. Average.

Fire Down Below (1957-British) C-116m. **½ D: Robert Parrish. Rita Hayworth, Robert Mitchum, Jack Lemmon, Herbert Lom, Anthony Newley. Contrived but entertaining melodrama of Mitchum-Lemmon, owners of tramp boat, falling in love with shady Hayworth on voyage between islands.

Fire in the Sky, A (1978) C-150m. TVM D: Jerry Jameson. Richard Crenna, Elizabeth Ashley, David Dukes, Joanna Miles, Lloyd Bochner, Andrew Duggan. Disaster flick about a comet hurtling toward Phœnix, Arizona, is blessed with striking special effects and miniature work to offset the tedium of the multicharacter plot. Average.

Fire Over Africa (1954) C-84m. ** D: Richard Sale. Maureen O'Hara, Macdonald Carey, Binnie Barnes, Guy Middleton, Hugh McDermott. O'Hara makes a pretty law enforcer traveling to Africa to track down dope-smuggling syndicate. Filmed on location.

Fire Over England (1937-British) 89m. *** D: William K. Howard. Laurence Olivier, Flora Robson, Vivien Leigh, Raymond Massey, Leslie Banks, Cecil Mainwaring. Nice historical drama of British-Spanish conflict in 1500s with flawless performance by Robson (Queen Elizabeth), fine villainy by Massey, romantic support by Olivier and Leigh.

Fire Sale (1977) C-88m. BOMB D: Alan Arkin. Alan Arkin, Rob Reiner, Vincent Gardenia, Anjanette Comer, Kay Medford, Sid Caesar, Barbara Dana. Wretched black comedy about a department store owner and his two sons gives bad taste a bad name. Truly unbearable.

Fireball, The (1950) 84m. *** D: Tay Garnett. Mickey Rooney, Pat O'Brien, Beverly Tyler, Marilyn Monroe, Milburn Stone, Glenn Corbett. Rooney's energetic performance carries this film. Orphan boy devotes himself to becoming big-time roller-skating champ.

Fireball Forward (1972) C-100m. TVM D: Marvin Chomsky. Ben Gazzara, Eddie Albert, Ricardo Montalban, Dana Elcar, L. Q. Jones, Anne Francis. Adequate WW2 story has Gazzara assuming command of "hard luck" division in France with usual subplots (traitor in the ranks, female journalist, etc.). Holds its own; could have been theatrical movie. Above average.

Firechasers, The (1970-British) C-101m. ** D: Sidney Hayers. Chad Everett, Anjanette Comer, Keith Barron, Joanne Dainton, Rupert Davies, John Loder. Strong production values in familiar story of insurance investigator hunting for arsonist.

Firecreek (1968) C-104m. **½ D: Vincent McEveety. James Stewart, Henry Fonda, Inger Stevens, Gary Lockwood, Dean Jagger, Ed Begley, Jay C. Flippen, Jack Elam, Barbara Luna. Somber Western has makings of a classic at outset, but goes astray, and goes on too long. Stewart is mild-mannered part-time sheriff in small town terrorized by Fonda and fellow plunderers. Beautifully photographed, but unrelentingly downbeat.

Firefly, The (1937) 131m. **½ D: Robert Z. Leonard. Jeanette MacDonald, Allan Jones, Warren William, Billy Gilbert, Henry Daniell, Douglass Dumbrille, George Zucco. Tried-and-true operetta moves slowly and goes on too long, but Jones' "Donkey Serenade" and Jeanette's vivacity remain enjoyable.

Firehouse (1972) C-73m. TVM D: Alex March. Richard Roundtree, Vince Edwards, Andrew Duggan, Richard Jaeckel, Val Avery, Paul Le Mat. Tense situation develops when, after death of fireman, fire station accepts black rookie (Roundtree) as probational replacement. Resolution barely makes it, thanks to unusually fine combination of stock footage and studio work. Pilot for short-lived TV series. Above average.

Fireman Save My Child (1932) 67m.
** D: Lloyd Bacon. Joe E. Brown,
Evalyn Knapp, Guy Kibbee, Virginia
Sale. Amusing Brown romp with Joe
dividing his time between fire-fight-
ing and baseball.

Fireman Save My Child (1954) 80m.
*½ D: Leslie Goodwins. Spike
Jones, The City Slickers, Buddy
Hackett, Hugh O'Brian, Adele Jergens. Sloppy slapstick with Spike
Jones et al manning fire station in
1900s San Francisco, running amuck
when they receive a new fire engine.

Firemen's Ball, The (1968-Czech)
C-73m. ** D: Milos Forman. Jan
Vostrcil, Josef Sebanek, Josef Val-
noha, Josef Kolb, Vaclav Stockel.
Acclaimed comedy of small-town
firemen's ball which turns into
sprawling disaster apparently has
elusive charm that completely
escaped us.

Firepower (1979-British) C-104m.
**½ D: Michael Winner. Sophia
Loren, James Coburn, O. J. Simpson, Eli Wallach, Anthony Franciosa, George Grizzard, Vincent
Gardenia, Victor Mature. Another
international all-star action thriller,
with beautiful people in beautiful
locations (this time, the Caribbean).
Inane, complicated story has Loren
seeking revenge for murder of her
chemist husband. Passable time-
filler, especially on TV.

First Comes Courage (1943) 88m.
**½ D: Dorothy Arzner. Merle
Oberon, Brian Aherne, Carl Esmond,
Fritz Leiber, Erik Rolf. Fairly good
wartime film of Norwegian Oberon
using her feminine wiles to extract
secrets from Nazi officer.

First Legion, The (1951) 86m. ***
D: Douglas Sirk. Charles Boyer,
William Demarest, Lyle Bettger, Barbara Rush. Engrossing low-key account of Jesuit priest who is dubious
about an alleged miracle occurring in
his town. Boyer gives one of his best
performances.

First Love (1939) 84m. *** D. Henry
Koster. Deanna Durbin, Robert
Stack, Helen Parrish, Eugene Pallette, Leatrice Joy, Marcia Mae
Jones, Frank Jenks. Charming love
story of orphaned girl (Durbin) going to live with uncle and finding
romance with Stack (in his film
debut). Durbin sings: "Amapola"
and other songs.

First Love (1958-Italian) 103m. **
D: Mario Camerini. Carla Gravina,
Raf Mattioli, Lorella De Luca,
Luciano Marin. Simple, unengross-
ing account of the pangs of adoles-
cent love.

First Love (1970-British-French-
Swiss) C-90m. *** D: Maximilian
Schell. John Moulder Brown, Dominique Sanda, Maximilian Schell, John
Osborne. Original, often moving
story of young lovers is total concept of Schell. While his direction
often wanders, his script is extremely
good.

First Love (1977) C-92m. ** D: Joan
Darling. William Katt, Susan Dey,
John Heard, Beverly D'Angelo,
Robert Loggia. Youthful romance
between right-thinking college boy
and girl who's involved with older
man; muddled film with unsatisfying
conclusion.

First Man Into Space (1959-British)
77m. *½ D: Robert Day. Marshall
Thompson, Marla Landi, Robert
Ayres, Bill Nagy, Carl Jaffe, Bill Edwards. Uninspired account of test
pilot who is exposed to radioactivity,
causing severe repercussions to all.

First Men in the Moon (1964-British)
C-103m. *** D: Nathan Juran. Edward Judd, Martha Hyer, Lionel
Jeffries, Erik Chitty. Lavish adaptation of H. G. Wells novel is heavy-
handed at times, overloaded with
comic relief, but still worthwhile;
good Ray Harryhausen special effects.

First Spaceship on Venus (1960-
German) C-78m. *½ D: Kurt Maet-
zig. Yoko Tani, Oldrich Lukes,
Ignacy Machowski, Julius Ongewe.
Few special effects can't salvage this
wooden account of international
group trekking to Venus to save the
world; set in 1980s.

First Texan, The (1956) 82m. **½
D: Byron Haskin. Joel McCrea, Felicia Farr, Jeff Morrow, Wallace
Ford. McCrea is forceful as Sam
Houston, leading Texans in fight
against Mexico for independence;
good action sequences.

First 36 Hours of Dr. Durant, The
(1975) C-78m. TVM D: Alexander
Singer. Scott Hylands, Lawrence
Pressman, Katherine Helmond, Dana
Andrews, Renne Jarrett, Peter Donat,
David Doyle. Idealistic surgical resident Hylands, during his first hectic
36 hours on call, confronts the realities of medical ethics with a life
and a career at stake. Not bad, although the AMA might argue the
point. Average.

First Time, The (1952) 89m. ** D: Frank Tashlin. Robert Cummings, Barbara Hale, Jeff Donnell, Mona Barrie, Cora Witherspoon. Predictable comedy pegged on young couple's many problems with raising a young, baby.

First Time, The (1969) C-90m. *½ D: James Neilson. Jacqueline Bisset, Wes Stern, Rick Kelman, Wink Roberts, Gerald Parkes. Combination of OZZIE AND HARRIET and WALK ON THE WILD SIDE concerns a teen-ager's sexual initiation; Bisset is attractive, but doesn't anyone in Hollywood know how contemporary adolescents really talk and act?

First To Fight (1967) C-97m. **½ D: Christian Nyby. Chad Everett, Marilyn Devin, Dean Jagger, Bobby Troup, Claude Akins, Gene Hackman. Conventional WW2 yarn with Everett the one-time hero who almost loses his courage on the battlefield.

First Traveling Saleslady, The (1956) C-92m. ** D: Arthur Lubin. Ginger Rogers, Barry Nelson, Carol Channing, David Brian, James Arness, Clint Eastwood. Rogers and Channing try to elevate plodding comedy of girdle-sellers in the old West.

First Yank Into Tokyo (1945) 82m. ** D: Gordon Douglas. Tom Neal, Barbara Hale, Marc Cramer, Richard Loo, Keye Luke, Leonard Strong, Benson Fong. Low-budget quickie made to be topical isn't so any more, and it's not too good either; Neal undergoes plastic surgery to obtain Japanese secrets.

First, You Cry (1978) C-100m. TVM D: George Schaefer. Mary Tyler Moore, Anthony Perkins, Richard Crenna, Jennifer Warren, Florence Eldridge, Don Johnson. Well-intentioned and well-received but curiously unenthralling dramatization of news correspondent Betty Rollin's book about her mastectomy, providing perky Moore with an offbeat dramatic role. Average.

Fish that Saved Pittsburgh, The (1979) C-102m. *½ D: Gilbert Moses. Julius Erving, James Bond III, Stockard Channing, Jonathan Winters, Meadowlark Lemon, Nicholas Pryor. Losing basketball team tries astrology to put them in winners' circle; low-grade comedy with disco soundtrack. Basketball hijinks are only saving grace.

Fistful of Dollars, A (1966-Italian-West German-Spanish) C-96m. **½ D: Sergio Leone. Clint Eastwood, Marianne Koch, Gian Maria Volonté, Wolfgang Lukschy, Mario Brega, Carol Brown. Uneven but entertaining spaghetti Western has Eastwood, cynical stranger in San Miguel, manipulating—and manipulated by! —two rival families. This is the film that made Eastwood an international superstar. Made in '64 and based on the Japanese film YOJIMBO.

Fistful of Dynamite, A. SEE: Duck, You Sucker

Fists of Fury (1972-Chinese) C-103m. ** D: Lo Wei. Bruce Lee, Miao Ker Hsiu, James Tien, Robert Baker. Kung Fu actioner finds honorable Bruce Lee defending honor by destroying world. Very violent.

Fitzwilly (1967) C-102m. **½ D: Delbert Mann. Dick Van Dyke, Barbara Feldon, Edith Evans, John McGiver, Harry Townes, John Fiedler, Norman Fell, Cecil Kellaway. Ordinary fluff about butler who has to rob Gimbel's on Christmas Eve to save his employer. Van Dyke's screen career was hurt by too many films like this one.

Five (1951) 93m. *½ D: Arch Oboler. William Phipps, Susan Douglas, James Anderson, Charles Lampkin, Earl Lee. One of writer-director Oboler's periodic film curios, filmed at his own Frank Lloyd Wright home; radio actors star in talky, pretentious drama about survivors of devastating radiation attack.

5 Against the House (1955) 84m. *** D: Phil Karlson. Guy Madison, Kim Novak, Brian Keith, Kerwin Mathews, William Conrad, Alvy Moore. "Perfect crime" caper has five friends set out to rob Reno, Nevada casino. Execution of robbery, along with gorgeous Novak, keep this film rolling along.

Five Angles on Murder SEE: Woman In Question

5 Branded Women (1960) 106m. ** D: Martin Ritt. Van Heflin, Silvana Mangano, Jeanne Moreau, Vera Miles, Barbara Bel Geddes, Carla Gravina. Overambitious production, badly miscast, set in WW2 Middle Europe. Five girls scorned by partisans for consorting with Nazis prove their patriotism.

Five Came Back (1939) 75m. *** D: John Farrow. Chester Morris, Lucille Ball, Wendy Barrie, John Carradine, Allen Jenkins, Joseph Calleia, C.

Aubrey Smith, Patric Knowles. This "sleeper" shows its age a bit, but remains interesting for colorful character studies among passengers on plane downed in Amazon jungle. Remade by director Farrow as BACK FROM ETERNITY in 1956.

Five Card Stud (1968) C-103m. *½ D: Henry Hathaway. Dean Martin, Robert Mitchum, Inger Stevens, Roddy McDowall, Katherine Justice. Dino is a gambler and Mitchum virtually repeats his NIGHT OF THE HUNTER role in surprisingly disappointing Western; Maurice Jarre's Dr. Zhivago-on-the-range musical score doesn't help. Probably director Hathaway's worst Western.

Five Day Lover SEE: **Time Out for Love**

Five Days from Home (1978) C-109m. ** D: George Peppard. George Peppard, Neville Brand, Savannah Smith, Sherry Boucher, Victor Campos, Robert Donner. Peppard breaks out of Louisiana prison, determined to reach L.A. and see his hospitalized son. Well-intentioned but improbable film.

Five Desperate Women (1971) C-73m. TVM D: Ted Post. Robert Conrad, Anjanette Comer, Bradford Dillman, Joan Hackett, Denise Nicholas, Stefanie Powers. Forced character-study thriller has five female graduates of Brindley College reunited on rented island mansion stalked by mental hospital escapee. Which man: caretaker or boatman? Typical new-dangers-every-second approach can't hide formula plot. Average.

Five Easy Pieces (1970) C-96m. **** D: Bob Rafelson. Jack Nicholson, Karen Black, Billy Green Bush, Fannie Flagg, Susan Anspach, Sally Struthers, Ralph Waite. Brilliant character study of musician with great promise who gave up a career to work on an oil rig. Nicholson's performance is best, but Black, Anspach, and Bush all contribute heavily. Helena Kallianiotes hilarious as malcontent hitchhiker.

Five Finger Exercise (1962) 109m. **½ D: Daniel Mann. Rosalind Russell, Jack Hawkins, Maximilian Schell, Richard Beymer, Lana Wood, Annette Gorman. Peter Shaffer's play suffers from change of locale and alteration of original ideas; now it becomes embarrassing soap opera of possessive mother in love with

daughter's tutor. Stars are miscast but try their best.

Five Fingers (1952) 108m. *** D: Joseph L. Mankiewicz. James Mason, Danielle Darrieux, Michael Rennie, Richard Loo. Polished espionage film is endowed with fine Mason performance as unsuspected spy working for Germans during WW2.

Five Fingers of Death (1973-Chinese) C-102m. *½ D: Cheng Chang Ho. Lo Lieh, Wang Ping, Wang Ching-Feng. Only interesting in that it is the Kung Fu film that began the craze. Family honor defended with every part of the body except the mouth, which is horrendously dubbed.

Five Gates to Hell (1959) 98m. *½ D: James Clavell. Neville Brand, Benson Fong, Shirley Knight, Ken Scott, John Morley, Dolores Michaels, Nancy Kulp. Overly melodramatic plot of American nurses captured by Chinese mercenaries and the various ordeals they undergo.

Five Golden Dragons (1967-British) C-93m. ** D: Jeremy Summers. Bob Cummings, Margaret Lee, Maria Perschy, Brian Donlevy, Christopher Lee, George Raft, Dan Duryea. Cummings is naive American caught up in international crime in Hong Kong; a most conventional actioner, not saved by veteran guest stars.

Five Golden Hours (1961-British) 90m. **½ D: Mario Zampi. Ernie Kovacs, Cyd Charisse, George Sanders, Kay Hammond, Dennis Price. Comedy mishmash wavering between satire and slapstick as con man plots to utilize a witch to bedevil rich victims.

Five Graves to Cairo (1943) 96m. ***½ D: Billy Wilder. Franchot Tone, Anne Baxter, Akim Tamiroff, Erich von Stroheim, Peter Van Eyck. WW2 intrigue situated in Sahara oasis hotel run by Tamiroff and Baxter; Tone attempts to obtain secrets from visiting Field Marshal Rommel (Von Stroheim). Fine cast in convincing drama.

Five Guns West (1955) C-78m. ** D: Roger Corman. John Lund, Dorothy Malone, Mike Connors, Jack Ingram. Rebel soldiers, ex-convicts, hold up a Yankee stagecoach to obtain cache of money.

500 Pound Jerk, The (1972) C-73m. TVM D: William Kronick. James Franciscus, Alex Karras, Hope Lange, Howard Cosell, Victor

Spinetti, Claudio Butenuth. Odd mixture of comedy and realism in lumpy tale of Olympic weight-lifter falling in love with Soviet athlete. Average.

Five Man Army, The (1970) C-107m. *½ D: Don Taylor. Peter Graves, James Daly, Bud Spencer, Tetsuro Tamba, Nino Castelnuovo. Ordinary adventure piece about five men who try to rob gold shipment being delivered to Mexican dictator in 1913; film is no WILD BUNCH.

Five Miles To Midnight (1963) 110m. **½ D: Anatole Litvak. Tony Perkins, Sophia Loren, Gig Young, Jean-Pierre Aumont, Pascale Roberts. Jumbled murder mystery with Perkins convincing wife Loren to collect insurance money when it's thought he's been killed, with ironic results.

Five Million Years to Earth (1968-British) C-98m. *** D: Roy Ward Baker. James Donald, Barbara Shelley, Andrew Keir, Julian Glover, Maurice Good. Workers unearth spaceship and remains of alien crew in modern-day London. Good cast, great script complications, and suspense in fine example of what can be done on meager budget. Only subject matter will turn some viewers off. Originally released as QUATERMASS AND THE PIT.

Five on the Black Hand Side (1973) C-96m. **½ D: Oscar Williams. Clarice Taylor, Leonard Jackson, Virginia Capers, D'Urville Martin, Glynn Turman, Godfrey Cambridge. Black family comedy about patriarchal barber was once refreshing amidst many black exploitation films, now seems foolish.

Five Pennies, The (1959) C-117m. **½ D: Melville Shavelson. Danny Kaye, Barbara Bel Geddes, Tuesday Weld, Louis Armstrong, Bob Crosby, Harry Guardino, Ray Anthony, Shelley Manne, Bobby Troup. Danny plays jazz trumpeter Red Nichols in this sentimental biography. Only bright spots are musical numbers, especially duets with Kaye and Armstrong.

Five Star Final (1931) 89m. *** D: Mervyn LeRoy. Edward G. Robinson, H. B. Warner, Marian Marsh, George E. Stone, Ona Munson, Boris Karloff, Aline MacMahon. Powerful drama of sensationalist newspaper sometimes falls apart with bad acting by second leads, but editor Robinson and unscrupulous reporter Karloff make it a must.

Five Steps to Danger (1957) 80m. **

D: Henry S. Kesler. Ruth Roman, Sterling Hayden, Werner Klemperer, Richard Gaines. By-now clichéd spy drama, enhanced by Roman and Hayden.

5,000 Fingers of Dr. T., The (1953) C-88m. *** D: Roy Rowland. Peter Lind Hayes, Mary Healy, Tommy Rettig, Hans Conried. Largely ignored, one of Hollywood's best fantasies, devised by Dr. Seuss. Boy has nightmare about cruel piano teacher (Conried) ruling over land where kidnapped youngsters are forced to play the piano. Song numbers slow action.

$5.20 an Hour Dream, The (1980) C-100m. TVM D: Russ Mayberry. Linda Lavin, Richard Jaeckel, Nicholas Pryor, Pamela McMyler, Mayf Nutter. Feminist blue-collar drama, not dissimilar to NORMA RAE, about a divorced mother determined to get a higher-paying factory job on the traditionally all-male assembly line. Predictable at every turn. Average.

Five Weeks in a Balloon (1962) C-101m. **½ D: Irwin Allen. Red Buttons, Barbara Eden, Fabian, Cedric Hardwicke, Peter Lorre, Richard Haydn, Barbara Luna. Innocuous entertainment with formula script from Jules Verne tale of balloon expedition to Africa. Buoyed by fine cast, including veterans Billy Gilbert, Herbert Marshall, Reginald Owen, Henry Daniell.

Fixed Bayonets (1951) 92m. **½ D: Samuel Fuller. Richard Basehart, Gene Evans, Michael O'Shea, Richard Hylton, Craig Hill. Taut Korean War drama of platoon cut off from the rest of its outfit; typical tough Fuller production.

Fixer, The (1968) C-132m. **½ D: John Frankenheimer. Alan Bates, Dirk Bogarde, Georgia Brown, Hugh Griffith, Elizabeth Hartman, David Warner, Carol White. Good acting helps, but Bernard Malamud's acclaimed novel fails on the screen; story of unjustly imprisoned Jewish handyman in turn-of-the-century Russia concerns itself too much with the thoughts of its main character to be effective as film.

Flame, The (1947) 97m. ** D: John H. Auer. Vera Ralston, John Carroll, Robert Paige, Broderick Crawford, Henry Travers, Constance Dowling. Routine story of woman falling in love with intended victim of blackmail plot.

Flame and the Arrow, The (1950) C-88m. *** D: Jacques Tourneur. Burt Lancaster, Virginia Mayo, Robert Douglas, Aline MacMahon. Bouncy, colorful action with Lancaster romping through his gymnastics as rebel leader in medieval Italy leading his people on to victory. Mayo is gorgeous heroine.

Flame and the Flesh (1954) C-104m. ** D: Richard Thorpe. Lana Turner, Pier Angeli, Carlos Thompson, Bonar Colleano, Charles Goldner, Peter Illing. Pointless Turner romance vehicle filmed in Europe, involving brunette Lana being romanced by continental Thompson, causing a lot of misery.

Flame Barrier, The (1958) 70m. *½ D: Paul Landres. Arthur Franz, Kathleen Crowley, Robert Brown, Vincent Padula. A satellite downed in jungle is discovered embedded in an ultra-hot alien organism. Fair cast tries hard in ineffectual story.

Flame Is Love, The (1979) C-100m. TVM D: Michael O'Herlihy. Linda Purl, Shane Briant, Timothy Dalton, Richard Johnson, Joan Greenwood, Paul Lavers. Florid romantic melodrama about American heiress' encounters with love and intrigue in Paris while traveling to England to marry her sweetheart at the turn of the century. Perfunctory acting mars the filming of Barbara Cartland's popular novel. Average.

Flame of Araby (1951) C-77m. **½ D: Charles Lamont. Maureen O'Hara, Jeff Chandler, Maxwell Reed, Susan Cabot. O'Hara, looking fetching as ever, rides through this costumer of the Far East, involving battle over a prize horse.

Flame of the Barbary Coast (1945) 91m. **½ D: Joseph Kane. John Wayne, Ann Dvorak, Joseph Schildkraut, William Frawley, Virginia Grey. Hick rancher competes with slick Schildkraut for savvy saloon singer Dvorak; undemanding fluff, with Republic Pictures' version of the San Francisco earthquake.

Flame of Calcutta (1953) C-70m. *½ D: Seymour Friedman. Denise Darcel, Patric Knowles, Paul Cavanagh. Darcel champions her people's cause in this costumer set in India in 1750. Low-grade nonsense.

Flame of New Orleans, The (1941) 78m. *** D: René Clair. Marlene Dietrich, Bruce Cabot, Roland Young, Laura Hope Crews, Mischa Auer, Andy Devine. Dietrich turns up in New Orleans and can have her pick of any man in town, can't decide between wealthy Young or hardworking Cabot. Picturesque, entertaining.

Flame of Stamboul (1951) 68m. *½ D: Ray Nazarro. Richard Denning, Lisa Ferraday, Norman Lloyd, Nestor Paiva. Programmer about espionage in ancient title city.

Flame of the Islands (1955) C-90m. ** D: Edward Ludwig. Yvonne De Carlo, Howard Duff, Zachary Scott, Kurt Kasznar, Barbara O'Neil. Caribbean scenery and sultry De Carlo provide most of the spice in this tale of a cafe singer and the men who fall in love with her.

Flame Over India (1959-British) C-130m. *** D: J. Lee Thompson. Lauren Bacall, Kenneth More, Herbert Lom, Wilfrid Hyde-White. Fast-paced actioner set on northern frontier of India as British soldiers accompanied by governess Bacall seek to speed an Indian prince to safety aboard a run-down train. Originally titled NORTH WEST FRONTIER.

Flame Within, The (1935) 71m. ** D: Edmund Goulding. Ann Harding, Herbert Marshall, Maureen O'Sullivan, Louis Hayward. Tired story of unrequited love. Young woman psychiatrist falls in love with patient, despite fact that she knows that it could never succeed.

Flaming Feather (1951) C-77m. *** D: Ray Enright. Sterling Hayden, Forrest Tucker, Barbara Rush, Arleen Whelan. Rousing Western as vigilantes rescue white woman from renegade Indians.

Flaming Frontier (1958-Canadian) 70m. *½ D: Sam Newfeld. Bruce Bennett, Jim Davis, Paisley Maxwell, Cecil Linder, Peter Humphreys. Indian war is averted by half-breed army officer; very cheap Western.

Flaming Star (1960) C-101m. *** D: Don Siegel. Elvis Presley, Barbara Eden, Steve Forrest, Dolores Del Rio, John McIntire. Elvis is excellent as a half-breed Indian who must choose sides when his mother's people go on the warpath. No songs after the first ten minutes but lots of action; along with JAILHOUSE ROCK, Presley's best film.

Flamingo Road (1949) 94m. *** D:

Michael Curtiz. Joan Crawford, Zachary Scott, Sydney Greenstreet, David Brian, Gertrude Michael, Gladys George. Crawford is excellent as tough carnival dancer ditched in small town where she soon is loving Scott and Brian and matching wits with corrupt politician Greenstreet.

Flap (1970) C-106m. ** D: Carol Reed. Anthony Quinn, Claude Akins, Tony Bill, Victor Jory, Shelley Winters. Uneven story of Indian outcast. You're supposed to pity Flapping Eagle, but script is so weak that the chances are you won't. At times funny, but supposedly tragic in its implications.

Flareup (1969) C-100m. **½ D: James Neilson. Raquel Welch, James Stacy, Luke Askew, Don Chastain, Ron Rifkin, Jeane Byron. Go-go-dancer Raquel gets stalked from Las Vegas to L.A. by psycopathic ex-husband of friend who blames her for breakup of the marriage. Fast melodrama is helped by good location footage.

Flash and the Firecat (1975) C-84m. *½ D: Ferd and Beverly Sebastian. Roger Davis, Tricia Sembera, Dub Taylor, Richard Kiel, Joan Shawlee, Philip Burns. Road-company Bonnie and Clyde try for one big heist; film's only novelty is the characters' use of dune buggies for transportation.

Flash Gordon SEE: **Perils from the Planet Mongo**

Flash Gordon SEE: **Spaceship to The Unknown**

Flash Gordon Conquers the Universe SEE: **Purple Death from Outer Space**

Flash Gordon's Trip to Mars SEE: **Deadly Ray From Mars, The**

Flat Top (1952) C-83m. **½ D: Lesley Selander. Sterling Hayden, Richard Carlson, Bill Phipps, Keith Larsen. Well-paced WW2 film of training of aircraft-carrier fighter pilots. Film integrates news footage successfully.

Flatbed Annie & Sweetiepie: Lady Truckers (1979) C-100m. TVM D: Robert Greenwald. Annie Potts, Kim Darby, Harry Dean Stanton, Arthur Godfrey, Rory Calhoun, Billy Carter. Like the title says, with Potts and Darby acting like a pair of good old boys to keep their expensive rig out of the clutches of repossessors as well as hijackers. Average.

Flaxy Martin (1949) 86m. **½ D: Richard Bare. Virginia Mayo, Zachary Scott, Dorothy Malone, Tom D'Andrea, Helen Westcott, Elisha Cook, Jr. Smooth melodrama of lawyer framed by client on a murder charge.

Flea in Her Ear, A (1968-U.S.-French) C-94m. ** D: Jacques Charon. Rex Harrison, Rosemary Harris, Louis Jourdan, Rachel Roberts. Unfunny farce about philandering barrister. Some of the slapstick gags go on interminably.

Fleet's In, The (1942) 93m. *** D: Victor Schertzinger. Dorothy Lamour, William Holden, Betty Hutton, Eddie Bracken, Rod Cameron, Leif Erickson, Jimmy Dorsey Orchestra with Helen O'Connell, Bob Eberle. Bright wartime musical with reputed romeo Holden trying to melt iceberg Lamour. Bracken and Hutton provide laughs. Specialty numbers by Hutton, Gil Lamb, Cass Daley; songs include "Tangerine," "I Remember You," title tune. Remake of 1936 LADY BE CAREFUL.

Flesh (1932) 95m. *** D: John Ford. Wallace Beery, Karen Morley, Ricardo Cortez, Jean Hersholt, Herman Bing, John Miljan. Unusual, melancholy drama with Beery as simple-minded German wrestler in love with Morley—who tries to hide her shady relationship with no-good Cortez.

Flesh and Blood (1949-British) 102m. ** D: Anthony Kimmins. Richard Todd, Glynis Johns, Joan Greenwood. Turbulent study of generations of family life, focusing on clashes and romances of parents and children.

Flesh and Blood (1979) C-200m. TVM D: Jud Taylor. Tom Berenger, Mitchell Ryan, Suzanne Pleshette, John Cassavetes, Kristin Griffith, Denzel Washington. The rise and fall of a young street tough who becomes a heavyweight contender. Based on Pete Hamill's best seller, spiced with incest subplot, stunningly filmed by Vilmos Zsigmond. Above average.

Flesh and Desire (1955-French) 94m. ** D: Jean Josipovici. Rossano Brazzi, Viviane Romance, Peter Van Eyck, Jean-Paul Roussjlon. Turgid farm romance tale of virile Brazzi's appearance setting into motion jealousy and murder.

Flesh and Fantasy (1943) 93m. *** D: Julien Duvivier. Charles Boyer,

Edward G. Robinson, Barbara Stanwyck, Robert Benchley, Betty Field, Robert Cummings, Thomas Mitchell, Charles Winninger. Three-part film of supernatural linked by Benchley; Field is ugly girl turned beauty by Cummings' love; Robinson's life is changed by fortune-teller Mitchell; Boyer is psychic circus star haunted by Stanwyck. Robinson episode most interesting.

Flesh and Flame SEE: **Night of the Quarter Moon**

Flesh and Fury (1952) 82m. **½ D: Joseph Pevney. Tony Curtis, Jan Sterling, Mona Freeman, Wallace Ford, Harry Guardino. Curtis gives presentable performance as deaf prizefighter who seeks to regain hearing and love of decent girl.

Flesh and the Devil (1927) 109m. *** D: Clarence Brown. Greta Garbo, John Gilbert, Lars Hanson, Barbara Kent, William Orlamond, George Fawcett, Eugenie Besserer. Garbo at her most seductive as temptress who comes between old friends Gilbert and Hanson. Pulsatingly romantic, beautifully filmed, probably the best Garbo-Gilbert love match. But talk about surprise endings!

Flesh and the Woman (1958-French) C-102m. ** D: Robert Siodmak. Gina Lollobrigida, Jean-Claude Pascal, Arletty, Raymond Pellegrin. Whole film is Lollobrigida, who plays dual roles; a Parisian whose corrupt ways cause her husband to join the Foreign Legion, and a lookalike prostitute in Algiers.

Flesh Eaters, The (1966) 87m. *½ D: Jack Curtis. Rita Morley, Martin Kosleck, Byron Sanders, Barbara Walken. Crazed marine biologist exploits sea life and eventually creates a monster that destroys him. Too bad it takes so long.

Flight Command (1940) 110m. ** D: Frank Borzage. Robert Taylor, Ruth Hussey, Walter Pidgeon, Paul Kelly, Nat Pendleton, Shepperd Strudwick, Red Skelton, Dick Purcell. Hackneyed story with good cast as upstart Taylor tries to make the grade in naval flight squadron.

Flight for Freedom (1943) 99m. **½ D: Lothar Mendes. Rosalind Russell, Fred MacMurray, Herbert Marshall, Eduardo Ciannelli, Walter Kingsford. Pseudo-biography of Amelia Earhart has dynamic Russell as aviatrix whose devotion to flying alienates her from MacMurray.

Flight from Ashiya (1964) C-100m. ** D: Michael Anderson. Yul Brynner, Richard Widmark, George Chakiris, Suzy Parker, Shirley Knight. Slow movie dealing with three aviators in rescue attempt over Pacific. "Big name" cast will attract; stiff script.

Flight from Destiny (1941) 73m. *** D: Vincent Sherman. Geraldine Fitzgerald, Thomas Mitchell, Jeffrey Lynn, James Stephenson, Mona Maris, Jonathan Hale. Well-acted tale of Mitchell, with short time to live, helping young couple by clearing young Lynn of charges brought against him; Fitzgerald a joy as Lynn's wife.

Flight Lieutenant (1942) 80m. *½ D: Sidney Salkow. Pat O'Brien, Glenn Ford, Evelyn Keyes, Minor Watson, Larry Parks, Lloyd Bridges, Hugh Beaumont. Commander Watson has sore memories of Ford's father (O'Brien), making life difficult; tired programmer.

Flight Nurse (1953) 90m. ** D: Allan Dwan. Joan Leslie, Forrest Tucker, Jeff Donnell, Arthur Franz. Leslie elevates this tame production of Army nurse in Korean War who finds a new romance.

Flight of the Doves (1971-British) C-105m. ** D: Ralph Nelson. Ron Moody, Jack Wild, Dorothy McGuire, Stanley Holloway, Helen Raye, William Rushton. Calculated cuteness mars tale of two Liverpool children who flee to Ireland to visit their grandmother; good cast isn't seen to best advantage.

Flight of the Lost Balloon (1961) C-91m. *½ D: Nathan Juran. Marshall Thompson, Mala Powers, James Lanphier, Douglas Kennedy. Potentially interesting mixture of sci-fi and adventure drowns in low-budget telling of Thompson using balloon transport to travel across African wasteland to find missing explorer.

Flight of the Phoenix (1966) C-147m. ***½ D: Robert Aldrich. James Stewart, Richard Attenborough, Peter Finch, Hardy Kruger, Ernest Borgnine, Ian Bannen, Ronald Fraser, Christian Marquand, Dan Duryea, George Kennedy. A plane crash leaves a group of men stranded in the Arabian desert; film avoids clichés as tension mounts among the men. Stewart as the captain, Attenborough as the navigator stand out in uniformly fine cast.

Flight to Fury (1966) 80m. ** D: Monte Hellman. Dewey Martin, Fay Spain, Jack Nicholson, Jacqueline Hellman, Vic Diaz. Odd group of adventurers headed for Philippines location and hidden diamonds when plane crashes. Low-budgeter has its points, but never really comes across. Initially released as 62 minutes, later reedited.

Flight to Holocaust (1977) C-100m. TVM D: Bernard Kowalski. Patrick Wayne, Christopher Mitchum, Desi Arnaz Jr., Sid Caesar, Rory Calhoun, Lloyd Nolan, Paul Williams, Fawne Harriman. Professional troubleshooters involved in freeing passengers of private plane that crashed and lodged in side of skyscraper. Contrived disaster-rescue tale with several second-generation film personalities competing with ludicrous special effects. Below average.

Flight to Hong Kong (1956) 88m. ** D: Joseph M. Newman. Rory Calhoun, Barbara Rush, Dolores Donlon, Soo Yong. Standard fare of gangster in Far East preferring Rush to his smuggler friends; it almost costs him his life.

Flight to Mars (1951) C-72m. ** D: Lesley Selander. Marguerite Chapman, Cameron Mitchell, Virginia Huston, Arthur Franz. Adequate sci-fi about scientists and newspapermen who land on Mars and discover a lost civilization. Special effects hampered by modest budget.

Flight to Nowhere (1946) 75m. BOMB D: William Rowland. Evelyn Ankers, Alan Curtis, Jack Holt, Jerome Cowan, Micheline Cheirel. Dismal cheapie about international spies maneuvering to grab nuclear secrets.

Flight to Tangier (1953) C-90m. **½ D: Charles Marquis Warren. Joan Fontaine, Jack Palance, Corinne Calvet, Robert Douglas. Fast-paced drama involving a cache of money aboard plane that has crashed, and the assorted people chasing after the loot.

Flim Flam Man, The (1967) C-115m. *** D: Irvin Kershner. George C. Scott, Sue Lyon, Michael Sarrazin, Harry Morgan, Jack Albertson, Alice Ghostley, Albert Salmi, Slim Pickens. Scott is engaging as a veteran Southern con-man who takes on young Sarrazin as apprentice in his travels, but finds the novice a bit too honest. Entertaining comedy.

Flipper (1963) C-90m. **½ D: James Clark. Chuck Connors, Luke Halpin, Kathleen Maguire, Connie Scott. Typical wholesome family fare about a boy who befriends a dolphin; kids will certainly enjoy it. Spun off into later TV series.

Flirtation Walk (1934) 97m. **½ D: Frank Borzage. Dick Powell, Ruby Keeler, Pat O'Brien, Ross Alexander, Guinn Williams, Henry O'Neill. West Point plot is clichéd and trivial as usual as cadet Powell falls in love with officer's daughter Keeler; some fairly good numbers highlighted by "Mr. and Mrs. Is The Name."

Flirting with Fate (1938) 69m. ** D: Frank McDonald. Joe E. Brown, Leo Carrillo, Beverly Roberts, Wynne Gibson, Steffi Duna, Stanley Fields, Charles Judels. Juvenile slapstick with Joe heading a vaudeville troupe stranded in South America. Carrillo fun as influential bandit, Duna's offkey singing good for a few laughs, but basically a weak comedy.

Flood! (1976) C-100m. TVM D: Earl Bellamy. Robert Culp, Martin Milner, Barbara Hershey, Richard Basehart, Carol Lynley, Roddy McDowall, Cameron Mitchell, Eric Olson, Teresa Wright. Cynical helicopter pilot Culp is pressed into reluctant service when a small town is devastated by a flood after a faulty dam bursts. Irwin Allen's first made-for-TV disaster movie, slick and predictable. Average.

Flood Tide (1958) 82m. **½ D: Abner Biberman. George Nader, Cornell Borchers, Michel Ray, Judson Pratt. Soapy mystery of an innocent man being convicted of murder on the say-so of a lame child, reputed to be a first-class liar.

Floods of Fear (1959-British) 82m. ** D: Charles Crichton. Howard Keel, Anne Heywood, Cyril Cusack, Harry H. Corbett, John Crawford. Adequate drama about prisoner Keel on the lam, who performs heroic deeds during flood, later proving innocence and winning girl's love.

Floradora Girl, The (1930) 80m. *** D: Harry Beaumont. Marion Davies, Lawrence Gray, Walter Catlett, Louis John Bartels, Ilka Chase, Vivien Oakland, Jed Prouty, Sam Hardy. Charming piece of nostalgia with Marion only one of famed Floradora Sextette of Gay 90s to spurn wealthy admirers and seek true love. Some scenes originally in color.

Florian (1940) 91m. ****** D: Edwin L. Marin. Robert Young, Helen Gilbert, Charles Coburn, Lee Bowman, Reginald Owen, Lucile Watson. Young and Gilbert, poor man and rich girl, marry, united by their love of horses.

Florida Special (1936) 70m. ****** D: Ralph Murphy. Jack Oakie, Sally Eilers, Kent Taylor, Frances Drake, J. Farrell MacDonald, Sam (Schlepperman) Hearn, Claude Gillingwater, Sidney Blackmer. Romance, mystery, and murder aboard southbound train. Song: "It's You I'm Talking About." Fun, but nothing special.

Flower Drum Song (1961) C-133m. ****** D: Henry Koster. Nancy Kwan, James Shigeta, Miyoshi Umeki, Juanita Hall, Benson Fong. Pleasant enough Rodgers and Hammerstein musical. No great songs, but listenable score and good choreography stringing together story of San Francisco's Chinatown. Major problem: it goes on too long.

Flower in His Month, The (1975-Italian) C-113m. ***½** D: Luigi Zampa. Jennifer O'Neill, James Mason, Franco Nero, Orazio Orlando. O'Neill moves to small Italian town and finds its people paralyzed by fear, but unwilling to tell her why. Murky thriller isn't worth the time it takes to figure out.

Flowing Gold (1940) 82m. ****½** D: Alfred E. Green. John Garfield, Frances Farmer, Pat O'Brien, Raymond Walburn, Cliff Edwards, Tom Kennedy. Dynamic Garfield in story that doesn't flow; standard fare of men trying to succeed with oil well.

Fluffy (1965) C-92m. ****** D: Earl Bellamy. Tony Randall, Shirley Jones, Edward Andrews, Ernest Truex, Howard Morris, Dick Sargent. Silly film dealing with professor Randall experimenting with a lion; he can't shake the beast, causing all sorts of repercussions, even winning Jones' affection.

Fly, The (1958) C-94m. ******* D: Kurt Neumann. David Hedison, Patricia Owens, Vincent Price, Herbert Marshall. Improbable but diverting sci-fi of scientist who experiments with disintegration machine and has his atomic pattern traded with that of a fly.

Flying Deuces, The (1939) 65m. *******
D: A. Edward Sutherland. Stan Laurel, Oliver Hardy, Jean Parker, Reginald Gardiner, Charles Middleton, James Finlayson. Stan and Ollie join the Foreign Legion so Ollie can forget unhappy romance; usual complications result. Faster paced than most L&H films; includes song and dance to "Shine On, Harvest Moon."

Flying Down to Rio (1933) 89m. ******* D: Thornton Freeland. Dolores Del Rio, Gene Raymond, Raul Roulien, Ginger Rogers, Fred Astaire, Blanche Frederici, Eric Blore. Slim vehicle memorable for its scene of dancing girls cavorting on the plane's wing, plus Astaire and Rogers doing "The Carioca" in their first screen teaming.

Flying Fontaines, The (1959) C-84m. ****½** D: George Sherman. Michael Callan, Evy Norlund, Joan Evans, Joe De Santis, Roger Perry, Rian Garrick. Circus yarn involving egocentric high-wire artist Callan who covets one of the showgirls, and the repercussions involved.

Flying High (1931) 80m. ****½** D: Charles F. Riesner. Bert Lahr, Charlotte Greenwood, Pat O'Brien, Kathryn Crawford, Charles Winninger, Hedda Hopper, Guy Kibbee. Dated, oddball comedy about harebrained inventor Lahr concocting an "aerocopter" machine; Lahr (in Hollywood debut) and Greenwood are fun together. Some DeSylva-Brown-Henderson songs carried over from Broadway production.

Flying High (1978) C-97m. TVM D: Peter Hunt. Kathryn Witt, Pat Klous, Connie Sellecca, Marcia Wallace, Jim Hutton. Middling comedy about airline stewardesses aloft and aground that spawned a brief series. Average.

Flying Irishman, The (1939) 72m. ****** D: Leigh Jason. Douglas Corrigan, Paul Kelly, Robert Armstrong, Gene Reynolds. Routine biog, largely fictional, dealing with life of Douglas "Wrong Way" Corrigan.

Flying Leathernecks (1951) C-102m. ******* D: Nicholas Ray. John Wayne, Robert Ryan, Don Taylor, Janis Carter. Rugged WW2 actioner with Wayne stauncher than usual. Good fighting scenes.

Flying Missile, The (1950) 93m. ****** D: Henry Levin. Glenn Ford, Viveca Lindfors, Henry O'Neill, Jerry Paris, Richard Quine. Clichéd WW2 story

[250]

of commander Ford's attempt to modernize his fighting ship, with predictable results.

Flying Saucer, The (1950) 69m. *½ D: Mikel Conrad. Mikel Conrad, Pat Garrison, Russell Hicks, Denver Pyle. Sci-fi set in Alaska will leave you cold.

Flying Serpent, The (1946) 59m. ** D: Sherman Scott (Sam Newfield). George Zucco, Ralph Lewis, Hope Kramer, Eddie Acuff, Milton Kibbee. Zucco sole interest in "B" movie, reminiscent of serials. Doctor protects Aztec treasure with prehistoric bird. Bad script.

Flying Tigers (1942) 102m. **½ D: David Miller. John Wayne, John Carroll, Anna Lee, Paul Kelly, Mae Clarke, Gordon Jones. Good Wayne vehicle of famous Flying Tigers stationed in WW2 China. Exciting dogfight scenes top fair production values.

Flying Wild (1941) 62m. D: William West. Leo Gorcey, Bobby Jordan, Donald Haines, Joan Barclay, David Gorcey, Bobby Stone, Sunshine Sammy Morrison. SEE: **Bowery Boys** series.

Fog Island (1945) 72m. *½ D: Terry Morse. George Zucco, Lionel Atwill, Veda Ann Borg, Jerome Cowan, Sharon Douglas. Grade-B chiller situated at eerie mansion with usual gathering of people suspecting one another of murder and intrigue; Zucco and Atwill are potentially terrific team.

Fog Over Frisco (1934) 68m. ** D: William Dieterle. Bette Davis, Lyle Talbot, Margaret Lindsay, Donald Woods, Henry O'Neill. Quick-paced Warner Bros. programmer enhanced by Davis as reckless young girl who gets involved with mobsters; sister Lindsay tries to help.

Folies Bergère (1935) 84m. ***½ D: Roy Del Ruth. Maurice Chevalier, Ann Sothern, Merle Oberon, Eric Blore, Ferdinand Munier. Entertainer Chevalier is asked to pose as aristocratic businessman, temporarily deserting fiery Sothern for elegant Oberon. Delightful; excellent Busby Berkeley-ish musical numbers won 1935 Oscar. Remade as THAT NIGHT IN RIO and ON THE RIVIERA.

Folies Bergère (1958-French) C-90m. ** D: Henri Decoin. Jeanmaire, Eddie Constantine, Nadia Gray, Ives Robert. Slim plot allows for expansive cafe production numbers in tale of American crooner in Paris who almost loses wife when she becomes more successful in show biz than he.

Folks at the Red Wolf Inn SEE: **Terror House**

Follow a Star (1960-British) 93m. *½ D: Robert Asher. Norman Wisdom, Jerry Desmonde, June Laverick. Flabby slapstick musical involving zany Wisdom as a cleaning store worker who is stagestruck.

Follow Me, Boys! (1966) C-131m. **½ D: Norman Tokar. Fred MacMurray, Vera Miles, Lillian Gish, Charlie Ruggles, Elliott Reid, Kurt Russell. Mile-high Disney corn about simple fellow who settles in small town during 1930s and starts Boy Scout troop, devoting his life to this inspiring pursuit. A little less syrup would have helped, but it's done with great conviction.

Follow That Camel (1967-British) C-95m. **½ D: Gerald Thomas. Phil Silvers, Jim Dale, Peter Butterworth, Charles Hawtrey, Kenneth Williams, Anita Harris, Joan Sims. Silvers as conniving sergeant livens up standard CARRY ON outing with Foreign Legion setting.

Follow That Dream (1962) C-110m. **½ D: Gordon Douglas. Elvis Presley, Arthur O'Connell, Anne Helm, Joanna Moore, Jack Kruschen, Simon Oakland. Presley and family move to southern Florida where they intend to homestead, despite all opposition. Based on Richard Powell's PIONEER GO HOME.

Follow That Woman (1945) 69m. ** D: Lew Landers. Nancy Kelly, William Gargan, Regis Toomey, Ed Gargan, Byron Barr, Pierre Watkin. Predictable murder yarn, heightened by Kelly's sincerity as woman implicated in murder; Gargan her husband trying to solve case.

Follow the Boys (1944) 122m. *** D: A. Edward Sutherland. Marlene Dietrich, George Raft, Orson Welles, Vera Zorina, Dinah Shore, W. C. Fields, Jeanette MacDonald, Maria Montez, Andrews Sisters, Sophie Tucker, Nigel Bruce, Gale Sondergaard. Universal Pictures' entry in all-star WW2 series has Raft organizing USO shows, Welles sawing Dietrich in half, MacDonald singing "Beyond The Blue Horizon," Fields doing classic pool-table routine, etc. Lots of fun.

Follow the Boys (1963) C-95m. ** D: Richard Thorpe. Connie Francis,

Paula Prentiss, Ron Randell, Janis Paige, Russ Tamblyn. Dumb comedy unspiked by Francis' singing or antics as quartet of girls chase around the French Riviera seeking husbands.

Follow the Fleet (1936) 110m. ******** D: Mark Sandrich. Fred Astaire, Ginger Rogers, Randolph Scott, Harriet Hilliard, Astrid Allwyn, Betty Grable. Delightful musical with sailors Astaire and Scott romancing sisters Rogers and Hilliard. Irving Berlin songs include "Let's Face the Music and Dance," "Let Yourself Go," "We Saw the Sea." Look for Lucille Ball in one brief scene.

Follow the Leader (1944) 64m. D: William Beaudine. Leo Gorcey, Huntz Hall, Gabriel Dell, Joan Marsh, Mary Gordon, J. Farrell MacDonald, Billy Benedict. SEE: Bowery Boys series.

Follow the Sun (1951) 93m. ****½** D: Sidney Lanfield. Glenn Ford, Anne Baxter, Dennis O'Keefe, June Havoc. Fictionalized sports biography of golfer Ben Hogan with hokey dramatics to fill in lean spots.

Folly to be Wise (1952-British) 91m. ******* D: Frank Launder. Alastair Sim, Elizabeth Allan, Roland Culver, Martita Hunt. Generally amusing nonsense with Sim an Army chaplain trying to enliven service life with various unique entertainment programs.

Food of the Gods (1976) C-88m. ****** D: Bert I. Gordon. Marjoe Gortner, Pamela Franklin, Ida Lupino, Jon Cypher, Ralph Meeker, Belinda Belaski. Fair-to-middling adaptation of H. G. Wells novel. Strange substance causes giant growth in wasps, worms, chickens and rats. Not for squeamish.

Fool Killer, The (1965) 100m. ******* D: Servando Gonzalez. Anthony Perkins, Edward Albert, Dana Elcar, Henry Hull, Salome Jens, Arnold Moss. Set in post-Civil War South, film relates unusual adventures of runaway orphan (Albert) and his meeting with strange young man (Perkins). Interesting and offbeat.

Fools (1970) C-97m. BOMB D: Tom Gries. Jason Robards, Katharine Ross, Scott Hylands, Roy C. Jenson, Mark Bramhall. Wretchedly acted, written, and directed drama about love affair in San Francisco between horror movie star and beautiful, neglected wife of a lawyer. Story line

is vaguely similar to PETULIA but the execution certainly isn't.

Fools for Scandal (1938) 81m. ****½** D: Mervyn LeRoy. Carole Lombard, Fernand Gravet, Ralph Bellamy, Allen Jenkins, Isabel Jeans, Marie Wilson. Generally a misfire, despite lovely Lombard as movie star who meets impoverished nobleman Gravet in Paris; Bellamy plays the sap again.

Fools' Parade (1971) C-98m. ****** D: Andrew V. McLaglen. James Stewart, George Kennedy, Anne Baxter, Strother Martin, Kurt Russell, William Windom, Kathy Cannon. Another great Stewart performance can't save melodramatic treatment of Davis Grubb novel. Story of three ex-cons stalked by their former prison guard is unintentionally funny too many times to be taken seriously.

Footlight Glamour (1943) 75m. D: Frank Strayer. Penny Singleton, Arthur Lake, Larry Simms, Ann Savage, Jonathan Hale, Thurston Hall. SEE: Blondie series.

Footlight Parade (1933) 105m. *****½** D: Lloyd Bacon. James Cagney, Joan Blondell, Ruby Keeler, Dick Powell, Guy Kibbee, Ruth Donnelly, Hugh Herbert, Frank McHugh. Cagney plays a stage director who tries to outdo himself with spectacular musical numbers. Fast-paced Warner Bros. opus winds up with three incredible Busby Berkeley numbers back-to-back: "Shanghai Lil," "Honeymoon Hotel," and "By a Waterfall."

Footlight Serenade (1942) 80m. ****½** D: Gregory Ratoff. Betty Grable, Victor Mature, John Payne, Jane Wyman, Phil Silvers, James Gleason, Mantan Moreland, Cobina Wright, Jr. Standard backstage musical with boxer Mature turning to Broadway for change, meeting Grable. No memorable songs.

Footsteps (1972) C-73m. TVM D: Paul Wendkos. Richard Crenna, Joanna Pettet, Forrest Tucker, Clu Gulager, Ned Beatty, Allen Garfield. OK study of monstrous Paddy O'Connor (Crenna) arriving at success-starved college as assistant football coach, determined to eliminate all opposition. Good performances by entire cast, interesting point of view. Above average. Also titled: NICE GUYS FINISH LAST.

Footsteps in the Dark (1941) 96m.

**½ D: Lloyd Bacon. Errol Flynn, Brenda Marshall, Ralph Bellamy, Alan Hale, Lee Patrick, Allen Jenkins. Flashy comedy-mystery with Flynn as playboy doubling as independent detective.

Footsteps in the Fog (1955-British) C-90m. *** D: Arthur Lubin. Stewart Granger, Jean Simmons, Finlay Currie, Bill Travers, Ronald Squire. Cat-and-mouse battle involving servant girl who blackmails her employer for having murdered his wife. Fine acting, rich Victorian atmosphere.

Footsteps in the Night (1957) 62m. *½ D: Jean Yarbrough. Bill Elliott, Don Haggerty, Eleanore Tanin, Zena Marshall. Programmer detective tale with Elliott solving the murder of a friend, occurring at a motel.

For A Few Dollars More (1967-Italian-Spanish-West German) C-130m. **½ D: Sergio Leone. Clint Eastwood, Lee Van Cleef, Gian Maria Volonté, Jose Egger, Rosemarie Dexter, Mara Krup, Klaus Kinski, Mario Brega. Two cynical gunmen (Van Cleef & Eastwood) form an uneasy alliance in their quest for outlaw Indio. Slightly draggy. Beware cuts. Sequel to FISTFUL OF DOLLARS.

For Better For Worse (1954-British) C-83m. **½ D: J. Lee Thompson. Dirk Bogarde, Susan Stephen, Cecil Parker, Eileen Herlie. Intelligently handled account of young married couple harrassed by bills, in-laws, and marital adjustment.

For Better, For Worse SEE: Zandy's Bride.

For Heaven's Sake (1926) 86m. (includes excerpt from DR. JACK) **** D: Sam Taylor. Harold Lloyd, Jobyna Ralston, Noah Young, James Mason, Paul Weigel. Screamingly funny silent comedy has Lloyd a blase young millionaire whose crush on Ralston inspires him to help attract "customers" for her father's Bowery Mission. Even THE FRENCH CONNECTION hasn't dimmed the luster of Lloyd's chase climax on L.A. streets. Edited for TV and paired with excerpts from 1922 feature DR. JACK.

For Heaven's Sake (1950) 92m. **½ D: George Seaton. Clifton Webb, Joan Bennett, Robert Cummings, Edmund Gwenn, Joan Blondell. Droll fantasy with Webb and Gwenn two angels sent to earth to speed along the arrival of Bennett and Cumming's heavenly baby.

For Love of Benji (1977) C-84m. *** D: Joe Camp. Benji, Patsy Garrett, Cynthia Smith, Allen Fiuzat, Ed Nelson, Peter Bowles, Bridget Armstrong. Moviedom's smartest pooch since Lassie in his second delightful screen adventure, this time scampering through the streets of Athens with secret agents in pursuit, trying to get the formula tattoed on his paw. Fine family entertainment.

For Love of Ivy (1968) C-102m. ** D: Daniel Mann. Sidney Poitier, Abbey Lincoln, Beau Bridges, Leon Bibb, Nan Martin, Lauri Peters, Carroll O'Connor. Family wants to keep maid, so they find her a beau; ho-hum black romance.

For Love or Money (1963) C-108m. **½ D: Michael Gordon. Kirk Douglas, Mitzi Gaynor, Gig Young, Thelma Ritter, William Bendix, Julie Newmar. Comedy strains to be funnier than it is. Widow Ritter hires lawyer Douglas to find spouses for her three daughters.

For Me and My Gal (1942) 104m. **½ D: Busby Berkeley. Judy Garland, Gene Kelly, George Murphy, Horace (Stephen) McNally, Marta Eggerth, Keenan Wynn, Richard Quine, Ben Blue. Music sustains oldhat plot of vaudeville couple determined to play Palace, circa WW1. Kelly's film debut enhanced by Garland-Kelly singing favorite songs.

For Men Only (1952) 93m. ** D: Paul Henreid. Paul Henreid, Kathleen Hughes, Russell Johnson, James Dobson, Margaret Field, Vera Miles, Douglas Kennedy, O. Z. Whitehead. Sincere if obvious study of fraternity hazing that gets out of hand on a college campus. Retitled: THE TALL LIE.

For Pete's Sake (1974) C-90m. **½ D: Peter Yates. Barbra Streisand, Michael Sarrazin, Estelle Parsons, William Redfield, Molly Picon. Amiable, featherweight comedy about devoted wife who tries to raise money for her ambitious cab-driver husband, and gets involved with assorted nuts and underworld types. Streisand is fine in forgettable film.

For Singles Only (1968) C-91m. BOMB D: Arthur Dreifuss. John Saxon, Mary Ann Mobley, Milton Berle, Lana Wood, Mark Richman, Chris Noel, The Nitty Gritty Dirt Band. Certainly not for those who like good movies. Two girls move into singles apartment where Berle is social director; result is film that features a rape, an attempted suicide, and several songs.

For the First Time (1959) C-97m. **½ D: Rudy Maté. Mario Lanza, Johanna Von Koszian, Kurt Kasznar, Zsa Zsa Gabor, Hans Sohnker. Lanza is typecast as fiery opera singer who falls in love with beautiful deaf girl in Capri. Not bad, with plenty of music to satisfy Lanza fans; this was his last film.

For the Love of Mary (1948) 90m. **½ D: Frederick de Cordova. Deanna Durbin, Edmond O'Brien, Don Taylor, Jeffrey Lynn. Airy fluff with Durbin a White House switchboard operator getting political figures and her own romance tangled up.

For the Love of Mike (1960) C-84m. **½ D: George Sherman. Richard Basehart, Stuart Erwin, Arthur Shields, Armando Silvestre. Mild happenings as Indian boy trains a horse, hoping to use prize money for a village shrine.

For Those Who Think Young (1964) C-96m. ** D: Leslie Martinson. James Darren, Pamela Tiffin, Tina Louise, Paul Lynde, Woody Woodbury. Witless plug for Pepsi is about low-jinks at college, undistinguished by Nancy Sinatra and Claudia Martin's presence, or cameos by George Raft, Robert Armstrong, Allen Jenkins et al.

For Whom the Bell Tolls (1943) C-130m. ***½ D: Sam Wood. Gary Cooper, Ingrid Bergman, Akim Tamiroff, Arturo de Cordova, Joseph Calleia, Katina Paxinou, Vladimir Sokoloff, Mikhail Rasumny, Fortunio Bonanova. Hemingway story of U.S. mercenary Cooper fighting for Spain with motley crew of peasants, including Bergman; tense action, beautiful color, great love scenes, marvelous Victor Young score. Paxinou won Best Supporting Actress Oscar. Originally released at 170m.

Forbidden (1953) 85m. **½ D: Rudolph Maté. Tony Curtis, Joanne Dru, Lyle Bettger, Marvin Miller, Victor Sen Yung. Curtis and Dru are engaging in story of gangland chief seeking the whereabouts of girlfriend (Dru), hiring Curtis to find her.

Forbidden Alliance SEE: **Barretts of Wimpole Street** (1934)

Forbidden Cargo (1956-British) 83m. ** D: Harold French. Nigel Patrick, Elizabeth Sellars, Terence Morgan,

Jack Warner. Modest drama about customs agents clashing with dope-smuggling syndicate.

Forbidden Fruit (1959-French) 97m. **½ D: Henri Verneuil. Fernandel, Francoise Arnoul, Claude Nollier, Sylvie, Jacques Castelot. Unpretentious little film of Fernandel's touching love affair with a young maiden.

Forbidden Games (1951-French) 87m. ***½ D: Rene Clement. Brigitte Fossey, Georges Poujouly, Louis Herbert. During WW2, young Parisian girl is orphaned and taken in by simple peasant family; she develops friendship with their youngest son, and shares with him a private world which the grownups cannot understand. Sad, intensely moving film.

Forbidden Island (1959) C-66m. *½ D: Charles B. Griffith. Jon Hall, Nan Adams, John Farrow, Jonathan Haze, Greigh Phillips. Sleazy film with Hall a skindiver seeking to find sunken treasure before a gang of crooks uncovers the loot.

Forbidden Planet (1956) C-98m. ***½ D: Fred McLeod Wilcox. Walter Pidgeon, Anne Francis, Leslie Nielsen, Warren Stevens, Earl Holliman. Sci-fi version of Shakespeare's "The Tempest" remains one of the most ambitious and intelligent films of its genre; only slow, deliberate pacing works against it, as Nielsen and fellow space travelers visit planet where expatriate Pidgeon has built a one-man empire, with daughter Francis and obedient Robby the Robot.

Forbidden Street, The (1949-British) 91m. ** D: Jean Negulesco. Dana Andrews, Maureen O'Hara, Sybil Thorndike, Wilfrid Hyde-White, Fay Compton. Fanciful melodrama of wealthy O'Hara defying her family by marrying down-and-out artist Andrews. Set in 1870s England. Originally titled BRITANNIA MEWS.

Forbin Project, The (1970) C-100m. *** D: Joseph Sargent. Eric Braeden, Susan Clark, Gordon Pinsent, William Schallert. Well-directed suspense thriller. Computer runs amok and uses its superior intelligence to sabotage man at every turn. Chilling and believable. Also titled COLOSSUS: THE FORBIN PROJECT.

Force Five (1975) C-78m. TVM. D: Walter Graumann. Gerald Gordon, Nick Pryor, James Hampton, Bradford Dillman, David Spielberg, Leif

Erickson. Hard-nosed veteran cop Gordon heads a special undercover squad of ex-cons to fight street crime, using their specialized skills. It's THE DIRTY DOZEN minus seven in mufti. Below average.

Force of Arms (1951) 100m. **½ D: Michael Curtiz. William Holden, Nancy Olson, Frank Lovejoy, Gene Evans. Updating of Hemingway's A FAREWELL TO ARMS to WW2 Italy, with Holden-Olson teaming acceptable.

Force of Evil (1948) 78m. **½ D: Abraham Polonsky. John Garfield, Beatrice Pearson, Thomas Gomez, Roy Roberts, Marie Windsor. Ambitious lawyer abandons his ideals and achieves success working for big-time racketeer. Striking, moody film examines forces of moral corruption; intriguing but not altogether successful.

Force of One, A (1979) C-90m. **½ D: Paul Aaron. Chuck Norris, Jennifer O'Neill, Clu Gulager, Ron O'Neal, James Whitmore Jr., Clint Ritchie, Pepe Serna. Followup to GOOD GUYS WEAR BLACK has karate champ Norris using his expertise to help California town combat drug trafficking. OK action fare.

Force 10 from Navarone (1978-British) C-118m. BOMB D: Guy Hamilton. Robert Shaw, Harrison Ford, Edward Fox, Franco Nero, Barbara Bach, Carl Weathers, Richard Kiel. Awful sequel to classic GUNS OF NAVARONE, poor in all departments, although Shaw, Ford, and Nero try to give it a lift. Mixed group (naturally), hindered by traitor Nero, attempt to blow a bridge vital to Nazis. They blew the film instead.

Foreign Affair, A (1948) 116m. ***½ D: Billy Wilder. Jean Arthur, Marlene Dietrich, John Lund, Millard Mitchell. Staid Arthur is sent to Berlin to investigate post-WW2 conditions, finds romance instead, with hot competition from Dietrich. Marlene sings "Black Market," "Ruins of Berlin," but Jean Arthur's Iowa State Song equally memorable in great Wilder comedy.

Foreign Correspondent (1940) 119m. **** D: Alfred Hitchcock. Joel McCrea, Laraine Day, Herbert Marshall, George Sanders, Albert Basserman, Robert Benchley, Eduardo Ciannelli, Edmund Gwenn. McCrea in title role caught in middle of spy ring with reporters Sanders and

Benchley, innocent Day, suspicious father Marshall. Pace and atmosphere are a tribute to the director in tremendously entertaining film.

Foreign Exchange (1969) C-72m. TVM D: Roy Baker. Robert Horton, Sebastian Cabot, Jill St. John, Eric Pohlmann, Dudley Foster, Clive Graham. So-called cynical exploits of American forced to work for British secret service in devious plan to have himself exchanged for former Russian defector jailed in England. If you miss one minute of plot, you'll probably be lost. Average.

Foreign Intrigue (1956) C-100m. **½ D: Sheldon Reynolds. Robert Mitchum, Genevieve Page, Ingrid Thulin, Frederick O'Brady. Based on TV series, film has virtue of on-location shooting in Europe as unemotional Mitchum checks out the cause of his employer's death.

Foreman Went to France, The (1942-British) 88m. **½ D: Charles Frend. Clifford Evans, Constance Cummings, Robert Morley, Mervyn Johns, Gordon Jackson, Ernest Milton. Documentary-style tale of industrial engineer who journeys to France during WW2 to help save secret machinery from being confiscated by the Axis.

Forest Rangers, The (1942) C-87m. **½ D: George Marshall. Fred MacMurray, Paulette Goddard, Susan Hayward, Albert Dekker, Rod Cameron, Lynne Overman, Eugene Pallette. Hayward tries to show ranger MacMurray that he's made a mistake marrying wealthy Goddard in this OK romance with good action scenes.

Forever (1978) C-100m. TVM D: John Korty. Stephanie Zimbalist, Dean Butler, John Friedrich, Beth Raines, Jordan Clarke. Romantic drama about a teenage girl's first real love, taken from Judy Blume's starry-eyed novel. Average.

Forever Amber (1947) C-140m. **½ D: Otto Preminger. Linda Darnell, Cornel Wilde, Richard Greene, George Sanders, Jessica Tandy, Anne Revere, Leo G. Carroll. Standard costume drama of 17th-century England, with Darnell forfeiting love for success in court of Charles II. Plush production from Kathleen Windsor novel.

Forever and a Day (1943) 104m. **** D: René Clair, Edmund Goulding,

Cedric Hardwicke, Frank Lloyd, Victor Saville, Robert Stevenson, Herbert Wilcox. Brian Aherne, Robert Cummings, Ida Lupino, Charles Laughton, Herbert Marshall, Ray Milland, Anna Neagle, Merle Oberon, Claude Rains, Victor McLaglen, Roland Young, C. Aubrey Smith, Edward Everett Horton, Elsa Lanchester, Edmund Gwenn. Eighty-odd British stars appear in episodic film of British house, its inhabitants over the years. Fine entertainment, once-in-a-lifetime cast.

Forever Darling (1956) C-96m. **½ D: Alexander Hall. Lucille Ball, Desi Arnaz, James Mason, Louis Calhern. Ball's madcap antics nearly drive husband Arnaz to divorce, but guardian angel Mason saves the day. Contrived but enjoyable.

Forever Female (1953) 93m. ***½ D: Irving Rapper. Ginger Rogers, William Holden, Paul Douglas, Pat Crowley, James Gleason. Top-notch show business comedy, with Rogers the star who finally realizes she is too old for the ingenue role, allowing writer Holden to cast Crowley in the part. Film captures flavor of the Broadway, summer stock scene.

Forever My Love (1962-German) C-147m. **½ D: Ernst Marischka. Romy Schneider, Karl Boehm, Magda Schneider, Vilma Degischer. Typical German confection dealing with 19th-century Austrian Emperor Franz Josef and Empress Elizabeth.

Forger of London (1961-German) 91m. ** D: Harald Reinl. Eddi Arent, Viktor de Kowa, Karin Dor, Hellmut Lange, Robert Graf. Scotland Yard investigates counterfeit gang tied in with prime suspect, an amnesiac playboy; from Edgar Wallace tale.

Forgiven Sinner, The (1961-French) 101m. **½ D: Jean-Pierre Melville. Jean Paul Belmondo, Emmanuele Riva, Patricia Gozzi, Irene Tunc. Belmondo gives subdued, offbeat performance as clergyman trying to set shady woman onto the path of righteousness.

Forgotten Man, The (1971) C-73m. TVM D: Walter Grauman. Dennis Weaver, Anne Francis, Lois Nettleton, Andrew Duggan, Pamelyn Ferdin, Percy Rodrigues. North Vietnam escapee returns home and finds wife remarried, business sold, daughter adopted. Location-shot, film softpedals its anger. Good performances. Average.

Forgotten Woman (1939) 63m. **½ D: Harold Young. Sigrid Gurie, William Lundigan, Eve Arden, Elizabeth Risdon, Virginia Brissac. Overnight star (and overnight fadeout) Gurie is helpless woman, framed by influential gangsters, suffering on trial.

Forsaking All Others (1934) 84m. ** D: W. S. Van Dyke II. Clark Gable, Joan Crawford, Robert Montgomery, Charles Butterworth, Billie Burke, Rosalind Russell. MGM superstars do their best with mediocre script. Gable stands by Joan for 20 years, but she never realizes that he loves her, and nearly marries Montgomery. Butterworth's droll humor most welcome in this soggy saga.

Fort Algiers (1953) 78m. ** D: Lesley Selander. Yvonne De Carlo, Carlos Thompson, Raymond Burr, Leif Erickson. De Carlo romps through this adventure set in Algiers, dealing with villainous Arab leader inciting the natives to rebel.

Fort Apache (1948) 127m. *** D: John Ford. John Wayne, Henry Fonda, Shirley Temple, Pedro Armendariz, John Agar, Anna Lee, Victor McLaglen, Ward Bond. Fonda is effectively cast against type, as stubborn martinet who rubs his own men—as well as neighboring Indians —the wrong way. First of Ford's cavalry trilogy tells its story slowly, deliberately, with time for comedy and telling characterizations.

Fort Defiance (1951) C-81m. **½ D: John Rawlins. Dane Clark, Ben Johnson, Peter Graves, Tracey Roberts. Film focuses on human relations in between preparations for threatened Indian attacks.

Fort Dobbs (1958) 90m. ** D: Gordon Douglas. Clint Walker, Virginia Mayo, Brian Keith, Richard Eyer. Rugged Walker is believable as hero who fights all obstacles in the old West to make decent life for himself and Mayo.

Fort Massacre (1958) C-80m. ** D: Joseph M. Newman. Joel McCrea, Forrest Tucker, Susan Cabot, John Russell. McCrea is leader of troop platoon which constantly is entangled with redskin skirmishes.

Fort Osage (1952) C-72m. BOMB D: Lesley Selander. Rod Cameron, Jane Nigh, Douglas Kennedy, Iron Eyes Cody. Inept Grade-D Western involving perennial Indian uprisings.

Fort Ti (1953) C-73m. ** D: William Castle. George Montgomery, Joan

Vohs, Irving Bacon, James Seay. Best facet of this oater set during French-Indian war of 1760s was 3-D effects, lost to TV viewers.

Fort Utah (1968) C-83m. *½ D: Lesley Selander. John Ireland, Virginia Mayo, Scott Brady, John Russell, Robert Strauss, James Craig, Richard Arlen, Jim Davis, Don "Red" Barry. Former gunfighter Ireland fights Brady, who is stirring up Indians around Fort Utah. See it only if you like the cast.

Fort Vengeance (1953) 75m. *½ D: Lesley Selander. James Craig, Rita Moreno, Keith Larsen, Reginald Denny, Emory Parnell. Film lacks much-needed action in its account of Pacific Northwest and mounties chasing fur thieves, quelling Indian uprisings.

Fort Worth (1951) C-80m. ** D: Edwin L. Marin. Randolph Scott, David Brian, Phyllis Thaxter, Helena Carter. Scott learns that pen is not mightier than the sword; he's a gunslinger who becomes newspaper editor but can only rid town of outlaws via six-shooter.

Fort Yuma (1955) C-78m. ** D: Lesley Selander. Peter Graves, Joan Taylor, Addison Richards, Joan Vohs. Indians go on warpath when their chief is killed. Occasionally good combat sequences.

Fortune, The (1975) C-88m. **½ D: Mike Nichols. Jack Nicholson, Warren Beatty, Stockard Channing, Florence Stanley, Richard B. Shull. Nicholson and Beatty play Laurel and Hardy in this uneven 1920s comedy about two bumblers who plan to murder a dizzy heiress to get her money. Worth seeing if only for Nicholson's wonderful comic performance. David Shire's period music is nice, too.

Fortune and Men's Eyes (1971-Canadian) C-102m. **½ D: Harvey Hart. Wendell Burton, Michael Greer, Zooey (David) Hall, Danny Freedman. Homosexuality in prison is the theme; sincere but exploitative, unpleasant. Due for heavy cutting if shown at all on TV.

Fortune Cookie, The (1966) 125m. *** D: Billy Wilder. Jack Lemmon, Walter Matthau, Ron Rich, Cliff Osmond, Judi West, Lurene Tuttle. Biting Wilder comedy about TV cameraman (Lemmon) injured during football game and shyster lawyer (Matthau) who exaggerates damages for insurance purposes. Matthau's Oscar-winning performance hits home.

Fortune in Diamonds (1952-British) 74m. ** D: David MacDonald. Dennis Price, Jack Hawkins, Siobhan McKenna. Good cast of disparate types all thirsting for cache of gems hidden in the heart of African jungle. Retitled: THE ADVENTURERS.

Fortunes of Captain Blood (1950) 91m. ** D: Gordon Douglas. Louis Hayward, Patricia Medina, George Macready, Terry Kilburn. This filming of Sabatini novel lacks flair and scope of the Flynn version. Costumer recounts tale of Irish doctor who becomes notorious pirate to revenge wrongdoings.

Forty Carats (1973) C-110m. **½ D: Milton Katselas. Liv Ullmann, Edward Albert, Gene Kelly, Binnie Barnes, Deborah Raffin, Billy Green Bush, Nancy Walker. Bright Broadway comedy adapted from French farce suffers in transference to screen, mainly from miscasting of Ullmann as 40-ish New York divorcee, pursued by 20-ish Albert. Otherwise, glossy, mildly amusing; pepped up by Barnes and Kelly.

Forty-Eight Hour Mile, The (1970) C-97m. TVM D: Gene Levitt. Darren McGavin, William Windom, Kathy Brown, Carrie Snodgress. Private-eye's unusual assignment leads to tragic resolution involving two women in love with same man. Excellent performances, offbeat point of view. Strung together from two episodes of "The Outsider." Above average.

Forty Guns (1957) 80m. **½ D: Samuel Fuller. Barbara Stanwyck, Barry Sullivan, Dean Jagger, John Ericson, Gene Barry. Florid, wildly dramatic Sam Fuller Western with Stanwyck as self-appointed land baroness of Tombstone Territory—until marshal Sullivan shows up.

40 Guns to Apache Pass (1966) C-95m. ** D: William Witney. Audie Murphy, Michael Burns, Kenneth Tobey, Laraine Stephens, Michael Blodgett, Michael Keep. Standard Murphy Western with every horse-opera cliche intact: plot centers around missing shipment of rifles.

Forty Little Mothers (1940) 90m. **½ D: Busby Berkeley. Eddie Cantor, Judith Anderson, Ralph Morgan, Rita Johnson, Bonita Granville, Diana Lewis. Second-rate Cantor, as reluctant schoolteacher. Veronica Lake is one of the mothers.

Forty Pounds of Trouble (1963) C-106m. **½ D: Norman Jewison. Tony Curtis, Phil Silvers, Suzanne Pleshette, Larry Storch, Howard Morris, Stubby Kaye, Claire Wilcox, Jack La Rue. "Cute" Curtis comedy of casino manager who "adopts" little girl with endless complications occurring. Disneyland locations enhance film and fine character actors pep it up. Carbon copy of LITTLE MISS MARKER.

49th Man, The (1953) 73m. **½ D: Fred F. Sears. John Ireland, Richard Denning, Suzanne Dalbert, Touch (Michael) Connors, Peter Marshall. Suspenseful account of federal agents tracking down foreign spies smuggling parts of atomic bomb into U.S. for later detonation.

Forty-Ninth Parallel (1941-British) 105m. ***½ D: Michael Powell. Anton Walbrook, Eric Portman, Leslie Howard, Raymond Massey, Laurence Olivier, Glynis Johns, Finlay Currie. Taut, exciting WW2 yarn of Nazi servicemen seeking to reach Canadian land when their U-boat is sunk; top-notch cast; rich suspense and characterizations. Retitled: THE INVADERS.

Forty-Second Street (1933) 90m. **** D: Lloyd Bacon. Warner Baxter, Ruby Keeler, George Brent, Bebe Daniels, Dick Powell, Guy Kibbee, Una Merkel, Ginger Rogers, Ned Sparks, George E. Stone. Definitive backstage musical which invented many key clichés; ailing director Baxter puts his all into directing show, then leading lady Daniels twists her ankle! Good thing Ruby Keeler's on hand. Songs include title tune, "Young and Healthy," "You're Getting to Be a Habit with Me," "Shuffle Off to Buffalo." Busby Berkeley's musical numbers still sensational.

Foster and Laurie (1975) C-100m. TVM D: John Llewellyn Moxey. Perry King, Dorian Harewood, Talia Shire, Jonelle Allen, Roger Aaron Brown, Victor Campos. True-life story of two N.Y.C. cops killed in brutal ambush by militant extremist group attempting to terrorize the Police Department. More than a simple cop movie, this concentrates on characterization and the personal relationship between Italian Rocco Laurie (King) and his black partner, Gregory Foster (Harewood). Excellent performances. Above average.

Foul Play (1978) C-116m. **½ D: Colin Higgins. Goldie Hawn, Chevy Chase, Burgess Meredith, Dudley Moore, Rachel Roberts, Eugene Roche, Marilyn Sokol, Billy Barty. Innocent woman gets caught in strange murder plot in San Francisco; no one believes her except detective Chase, who's falling in love with her. Likable stars, good fun, but protracted story, tasteless comedy, and Hitchcock plagiarism detract.

Fountain, The (1934) 83m. **½ D: John Cromwell. Ann Harding, Brian Aherne, Paul Lukas, Jean Hersholt, Ian Wolfe. WW1 romance with Harding torn between former sweetheart Aherne and husband Lukas. Handsome but tedious.

Fountainhead, The (1949) 114m. **½ D: King Vidor. Gary Cooper, Patricia Neal, Raymond Massey, Kent Smith, Robert Douglas, Henry Hull, Ray Collins, Jerome Cowan. Ambitious but confused version of Ayn Rand philosophic novel, spotlighting an idealistic architect's clash with compromises of big business; cast does what it can with the script.

Four Against Fate SEE: Derby Day

Four Bags Full (1956-French) 84m. **½ D: Claude Autant-Lara. Jean Gabin, Bourvil, Jeanette Batti, Louis de Funes. Slender comedy vehicle for two top stars, involving duo who smuggle meat across French border during WW2.

Four Clowns (1970) 97m. **** D: Robert Youngson. Laurel and Hardy, Buster Keaton, Charley Chase. A must for viewers of all ages; some of the best silent comedy ever. Interesting solo footage of Laurel and Hardy; Keaton's classic "Seven Chances"; hilarious sequences with underrated Chase including his best short, "Limousine Love." One of compiler Youngson's very best efforts.

4D Man (1959) C-85m. **½ D: Irvin S. Yeaworth, Jr. Robert Lansing, Lee Meriwether, James Congdon, Guy Raymond, Robert Strauss, Patty Duke. Well-handled sci-fi of scientist who learns art of transposing matter, thus giving him power to pass through any substance.

Four Dark Hours SEE: Green Cockatoo, The

Four Daughters (1938) 90m. ***½ D: Michael Curtiz. Claude Rains, Rosemary Lane, Lola Lane, Priscilla Lane, Gale Page, John Garfield, Jeffrey Lynn, Frank McHugh, May Robson, Dick Foran. Believable, beautifully acted soaper of small-town life; four young women with musical father Rains have lives altered by four young men. Garfield is superb in first film break, matched by fine cast. Remade as YOUNG AT HEART.

Four Days' Leave (1950) 98m. ** D: Leopold Lindtberg. Cornel Wilde, Josette Day, Simone Signoret, Alan Hale, Jr. Rather tame account of GI Wilde finding romance while on leave in Switzerland.

Four Desperate Men (1960-Australian) 104m. **½ D: Harry Watt. Aldo Ray, Heather Sears. Stark study of human nature as quartet of hardened thugs decide whether or not to set off huge bomb that would destroy Sydney harbor. Original title: THE SIEGE OF PINCHGUT.

Four Deuces, The (1975) C-87m. **½ D: William H. Bushnell, Jr. Jack Palance, Carol Lynley, Warren Berlinger, Adam Roarke, E. J. Peaker, Gianni Russo. Action comedy/drama involving Prohibition Era bootleggers. Palance is a gang lord whose mob and casino bear the film's title, Lynley is the moll he loves and fights for.

Four Faces West (1948) 90m. **½ D: Alfred E. Green. Joel McCrea, Frances Dee, Charles Bickford, Joseph Calleia. Quiet Western of fugitive pursued by determined sheriff, with cast giving intelligent interpretation to standard formula.

Four Fast Guns (1959) 72m. *½ D: William J. Hole, Jr. James Craig, Martha Vickers, Edgar Buchanan, Brett Halsey, Paul Richards. Shootout of good vs. bad pits brother against brother.

Four Feathers, The (1939-British) C-115m. ***½ D: Zoltan Korda. Ralph Richardson, C. Aubrey Smith, June Duprez, Clive Baxter, John Clements, Jack Allen, Donald Gray. Grand adventure from A. E. W. Mason story of tradition-bound Britisher who must prove he's not a coward by helping army comrades combat Sudan uprising. Smith is just wonderful as tale-spinning army veteran. Remade as STORM OVER THE NILE.

Four Feathers, The (1977) C-110m. TVM D: Don Sharp. Beau Bridges, Robert Powell, Simon Ward, Richard Johnson, Jane Seymour, Harry Andrews. Robust retelling (fifth time around) of the great adventure classic. Dandy entertainment. Above average.

Four Flies on Grey Velvet (1972-Italian) C-101m. ** D: Dario Argento. Michael Brandon, Mimsy Farmer, Bud Spencer, Francine Racette. Unabsorbing psychological murder-mystery with performers who walk through their rôles in a very disinterested fashion.

Four for Texas (1963) C-124m. *** D: Robert Aldrich. Frank Sinatra, Dean Martin, Anita Ekberg, Ursula Andress, Victor Buono, Charles Bronson, Three Stooges, Mike Mazurki. Nonsensical Sinatra-Martin romp set in the old West, with their antics only outdone by Buono as villainous banker. Ekberg and Andress both outstanding scenery attractions.

Four Frightened People (1934) 78m. **½ D: Cecil B. DeMille. Claudette Colbert, Herbert Marshall, Mary Boland, Leo Carrillo, William Gargan. Unspectacular DeMille vehicle of four disparate types lost in dense jungle. Colbert is plain Jane who gets prettier scene by scene; wry Boland steals the show.

Four Girls in Town (1956) C-85m. *** D: Jack Sher. George Nader, Julie Adams, Gia Scala, Marianne Cook, Elsa Martinelli. Clichéd but absorbing account of four contrasting would-be stars coming to Hollywood seeking fame and romance; excellent musical score by Alex North.

Four Guns to the Border (1954) C-82m. **½ D: Richard Carlson. Rory Calhoun, Colleen Miller, George Nader, Walter Brennan, Nina Foch. Better than usual handling of outlaws vs. Indians, with slight morality lesson for finale.

Four Horsemen of the Apocalypse (1962) C-153m. **½ D: Vincente Minnelli. Glenn Ford, Ingrid Thulin, Charles Boyer, Lee J. Cobb, Paul Henreid, Paul Lukas, Yvette Mimieux, Karl Boehm. Compared to silent version, this is glossy, padded trash, losing all sense of reality in its telling of a family whose members fight on opposite sides during WW2. Allegedly Angela Lansbury dubbed in Thulin's lines.

400 Blows, The (1959-French) 99m.
**** D: François Truffaut. Jean-Pierre Leaud, Patrick Auffray, Claire Maurier, Albert Remy. Captivating study of Parisian youth who turns to life of small-time crime as a reaction to derelict parents. First of Truffaut's autobiographical Antoine Doinel series.

Four in a Jeep (1951-Swiss) 97m.
**½ D: Leopold Lindtberg. Viveca Lindfors, Ralph Meeker, Joseph Yadin, Michael Medwin. On-location shooting in Vienna, Lindfors' creditable performance as refugee seeking international M.P.s help make this a diverting film.

Four Jills in a Jeep (1944) 89m. **
D: William Seiter. Kay Francis, Martha Raye, Carole Landis, Mitzi Mayfair, Phil Silvers, Alice Faye, Betty Grable, Carmen Miranda. Fictionalized account of female entertainers working for USO overseas; pat film despite several guest stars.

Four Kinds of Love SEE: Bambole!

Four Men and A Prayer (1938) 85m.
*** D: John Ford. Loretta Young, Richard Greene, George Sanders, David Niven, C. Aubrey Smith, William Henry, J. Edward Bromberg, Alan Hale, Reginald Denny, John Carradine. Compelling story of four brothers determined to unravel mystery behind their father's murder; handsome, well-paced production.

Four Mothers (1941) 86m. **½ D: William Keighley. Priscilla Lane, Rosemary Lane, Lola Lane, Gale Page, Claude Rains, Jeffrey Lynn, May Robson, Eddie Albert. FOUR DAUGHTERS formula wearing thin in soapy tale of Albert going bankrupt, whole family helping out.

Four Musketeers, The (1975) C-108m.
*** D: Richard Lester. Oliver Reed, Raquel Welch, Richard Chamberlain, Frank Finlay, Michael York, Christopher Lee, Jean-Pierre Cassel, Geraldine Chaplin, Simon Ward, Faye Dunaway, Charlton Heston. Second half of Lester's irreverent but amusing approach to Dumas with less emphasis on slapstick this time around. Rich cast in top form.

Four Poster, The (1952) 103m. ***½
D: Irving Reis. Rex Harrison, Lilli Palmer. Jan de Hartog play is tour de force for stars who enact various phases of married couple's life; warm, witty script; superb performances enhanced by ingenious animated interludes by UPA studio.

Four Skulls of Jonathan Drake, The (1959) 70m. ** D: Edward L. Cahn. Eduard Franz, Valerie French, Henry Daniell, Grant Richards, Paul Cavanagh, Howard Wendell. Acceptable horror fare involving centuries-old voodoo curse upon family and contemporary scientist who puts an end to the weird goings-on.

Four Sons (1928) 100m. **½ D: John Ford. James Hall, Margaret Mann, Earle Foxe, Charles Morton, Francis X. Bushman Jr., George Meeker. Ford's famous tearjerker about a Bavarian woman who sees her sons die in WW1 until only one is left. More interesting for film buffs than general audiences today.

Four Sons (1940) 89m. **½ D: Archie Mayo. Don Ameche, Eugenie Leontovich, Mary Beth Hughes, Alan Curtis, George Ernest, Robert Lowery. Czech family affected by Nazi rise to power; not unlike MORTAL STORM, with sons choosing different allegiances. Remake of 1928 silent.

Four Ways Out (1954-Italian) 77m.
**½ D: Pietro Germi. Gina Lollobrigida, Renato Baldini, Cosetta Greco, Paul Muller, Enzio Maggio. Drama points up futility of a robbery by quartet who individually plan their own escapes, all to no avail.

Four Wives (1939) 110m. **½ D: Michael Curtiz. Claude Rains, Eddie Albert, Priscilla Lane, Rosemary Lane, Lola Lane, Gale Page, John Garfield, May Robson, Frank McHugh, Jeffrey Lynn. Rains' daughters are all married, but life isn't easy for them. Garfield appears briefly in flashback.

Four's a Crowd (1938) 91m. **½ D: Michael Curtiz. Errol Flynn, Olivia de Havilland, Rosalind Russell, Patric Knowles, Hugh Herbert. Light-headed romance in which everyone loves another; straight comedy's a switch for Flynn, who proves he can handle genre well.

14 Hours (1951) 92m. *** D: Henry Hathaway. Paul Douglas, Richard Basehart, Barbara Bel Geddes, Debra Paget. Well-done suspenser of man threatening to throw himself off ledge. Grace Kelly's film debut.

Fox, The (1968) C-110m. *** D: Mark Rydell. Sandy Dennis, Keir Dullea, Anne Heywood, Glyn Morris. Nicely crafted tale of two women who develop intimate relationship only to be split apart by an intruder who happens among them. Lesbian theme may keep this off TV. Filmed in Canada.

Foxes of Harrow, The (1947) 117m. **½ D: John M. Stahl. Rex Harrison, Maureen O'Hara, Richard Haydn, Victor McLaglen, Vanessa Brown, Patricia Medina, Gene Lockhart. Lavish but lumbering tale of philanderer breaking up his marriage to seek affluence and fame in New Orleans in 1820. It's pretty stale despite the trimmings.

Foxfire (1955) C-92m. *** D: Joseph Pevney. Jane Russell, Jeff Chandler, Dan Duryea, Mara Corday, Barton MacLane. Russell and Chandler work well together as married couple who almost divorce because of his obsessive working habits as mining engineer.

Foxhole in Cairo (1961-British) 79m. **½ D: John Moxey. James Robertson Justice, Adrian Hoven, Peter Van Eyck, Neil McCallum. Sensibly told account of counterintelligence at work in Egypt during WW2 with British vs. Rommel's Nazis.

Foxiest Girl in Paris (1956-French) 100m. **½ D: Roger De Broin. Martine Carol, Michel Piccoli, Mischa Auer. Sultry Carol, a fashion model, becomes amateur sleuth to solve a robbery and a murder.

Foxy Brown (1974) C-94m. *½ D: Jack Hill. Pam Grier, Peter Brown, Terry Carter, Kathryn Loder. Violence and little else in tale of nurse Grier and her vendetta against drug ring that killed her lover.

Fra Diavolo SEE: **Devil's Brother**

Fragment of Fear (1971) C-96m. ** D: Richard C. Sarafian. David Hemmings, Gayle Hunnicutt, Flora Robson, Wilfrid Hyde-White, Daniel Massey, Roland Culver, Adolfo Celi, Mona Washbourne. Hemmings is good in disappointing murder mystery that begins well, then falls apart. Photographed by the great Oswald Morris. Made in England.

Framed (1947) 82m. ** D: Richard Wallace. Glenn Ford, Janis Carter, Barry Sullivan, Edgar Buchanan, Karen Morley. Title almost self-explanatory. Innocent man mistaken for robber is brought in, enabling real thief to escape.

Framed (1975) C-106m. **½ D: Phil Karlson. Joe Don Baker, Conny Van Dyke, Gabriel Dell, John Mar-

ley, Brock Peters, Roy Jenson. Railroaded to jail, Baker vows revenge on the corrupt cops who put him there. The writer, director, and star of WALKING TALL, old hands at this kind of action melodrama, make the most of the situation.

Francis (the Talking Mule) Never hailed as an artistic triumph, the Francis series made up for that in box-office receipts from 1950 to 1956. Based on a book by David Stern, each of the seven films dealt with a sincere but stupid young man (at West Point he is 647th in a class of 647) led into and out of trouble by a canny talking mule. The off-screen voice was Chill Wills, the on-screen bumbler was Donald O'Connor in all but the last film, which starred Mickey Rooney. O'Connor recently explained, "When you've made six pictures and the mule still gets more fan mail than you do . . ." Universal worked their contract starlets (Piper Laurie, Martha Hyer, Julia Adams, etc.) into the series as love interests, but the center of attraction was always the mule. The films, except the last one, were all about on a par: silly but amusing. The first six films were directed by Arthur Lubin, who went on to create a similar TV series called MR. ED, about a talking horse.

Francis (1950) 91m. D: Arthur Lubin. Donald O'Connor, Patricia Medina, ZaSu Pitts, Ray Collins.

Francis Covers the Big Town (1953) 86m. D: Arthur Lubin. Donald O'Connor, Gene Lockhart, Nancy Guild, Gale Gordon.

Francis Gary Powers: The True Story of the U-2 Spy Incident (1976) C-100m. TVM D: Delbert Mann. Lee Majors, Nehemiah Persoff, Noah Beery Jr., William Daniels, Lew Ayres, Brooke Bundy, Jim McMullen, Biff McGuire, James Gregory. Docu-drama about the pilot shot down over Russia during a spy mission. Majors does yeoman work as Powers, depicting the anguish he undergoes at the hands of Russian interrogator Persoff, excellent in his role. Despite its familiarity, story should have been more engrossing. Average.

Francis Goes to the Races (1951) 88m. D: Arthur Lubin. Donald O'Connor, Piper Laurie, Cecil Kellaway, Jesse White.

Francis Goes to West Point (1952) 81m. D: Arthur Lubin. Donald O'-

Connor, Lori Nelson, William Reynolds, James Best, Les Tremayne, David Janssen.

Francis in the Haunted House (1956) **80m.** D: Charles Lamont. Mickey Rooney, Virginia Welles, Paul Cavanagh, David Janssen.

Francis in the Navy (1955) **80m.** D: Arthur Lubin. Donald O'Connor, Martha Hyer, Jim Backus, Paul Burke, David Janssen, Clint Eastwood, Martin Milner.

Francis Joins the Wacs (1954) **94m.** D: Arthur Lubin. Donald O'Connor, Julia Adams, Mamie Van Doren, Chill Wills, Lynn Bari, ZaSu Pitts.

Francis of Assisi (1961) **C-111m.** **½ D: Michael Curtiz. Bradford Dillman, Dolores Hart, Stuart Whitman, Cecil Kellaway, Finlay Currie, Pedro Armendariz. Lavish religious epic dealing with story of founder of school of monks with sympathetic performance by Dillman. Good cast and atmosphere. Script tends to sag at wrong moments.

Frankenstein (1931) **71m.** *** D: James Whale. Colin Clive, Mae Clarke, Boris Karloff, John Boles, Edward Van Sloan, Lionel Belmore, Dwight Frye. Definitive monster movie of mad scientist Clive creating being (Karloff), accidentally using criminal brain. Impressive production, although creaky in plot development of Mary Shelley tale.

Frankenstein and the Monster from Hell (1974-British) **C-93m.** ** D: Terence Fisher. Peter Cushing, Shane Briant, Madeline Smith, Dave Prowse, John Stratton. Guess who runs a hospital for the criminally insane? Mild entry in the Frankenstein cycle is amusing if you catch it in the right frame of mind.

Frankenstein Conquers the World (1966-Japanese) **C-87m.** ** D: Inoshiro Honda. Nick Adams, Tadao Takashima, Kumi Mizuno. Grade-C horror film, with Adams a scientist in Tokyo trying to combat overgrown human monster terrorizing the countryside; poor special effects.

Frankenstein Created Woman (1967-British) **C-92m.** ** D: Terence Fisher. Peter Cushing, Susan Denberg, Robert Morris, Barry Warren, Thorley Walters, Duncan Lamont. Dr. Frankenstein (Cushing) tries to put the soul of recently (and wrongly) executed man into body of scarred lover (Denberg). Everything goes wrong, including script.

Frankenstein Meets the Space Monster (1965) **78m.** BOMB D: Robert Gaffney. James Karen, David Kerman, Nancy Marshall, Marilyn Hanold. Low-grade horror entry dealing with interplanetary robot whose mechanism runs amuck as he goes berserk.

Frankenstein Meets the Wolf Man (1943) **72m.** **½ D: Roy William Neill. Lon Chaney, Bela Lugosi, Patric Knowles, Ilona Massey, Dennis Hoey, Maria Ouspenskaya, Lionel Atwill. Impressive duo in atmospheric horror film about determined scientist tampering with unknown.

Frankenstein Must Be Destroyed (1970-British) **C-101m.** **½ D: Terence Fisher. Peter Cushing, Simon Ward, Veronica Carlson, Freddie Jones. Average retelling of Frankenstein story; different passageways, same hokum.

Frankenstein — 1970 (1958) **83m.** BOMB D: Howard W. Koch. Boris Karloff, Tom Duggan, Jana Lund, Donald Barry. Poor sci-fi, almost sacrilegious to the name of Frankenstein; no monster, just talk. Karloff is lost in this jumble.

Frankenstein: The True Story (1973) **C-200m.** TVM D: Jack Smight. James Mason, Leonard Whiting, Michael Sarrazin, David McCallum, Jane Seymour, Michael Wilding, Margaret Leighton, Ralph Richardson, Agnes Moorehead, John Gielgud, Tom Baker. Epic retelling of Mary Shelley's frightmare with brilliant Christopher Isherwood screenplay; not quite the letter of the novel, but competes favorably with the immortal Karloff movies on the theme by sheer spectacle. Creature, played stunningly by Sarrazin, is not the traditional stitched-together ogre, but a dashing Victorian rogue who proceeds to physically degenerate while various psychological avenues are explored. Marvelous cast in this thinking-man's horror movie. Above average.

Frankenstein's Daughter (1959) **85m.** BOMB D: Richard Cunha. John Ashley, Sandra Knight, Donald Murphy, Sally Todd, Harold Lloyd, Jr. Low-grade descendant of famed monster series with a new female horror-robot being created with typical results; tinsel sets.

Frankie and Johnny (1966) **C-87m.** **½ D: Frederick de Cordova. Elvis Presley, Donna Douglas, Harry Morgan, Sue Ane Langdon, Nancy Kovack. Saloon song expanded into feature film story for Elvis. Riverboat setting, cohort Morgan, several pretty starlets, and tuneful songs make this a satisfactory time-filler.

Frantic (1958-French) **90m. **½ D:** Louis Malle. Jeanne Moreau, Maurice Ronet, Georges Poujouly, Yori Bertin, Jean Wall. A man and woman plan to murder her husband, but fall short of committing a "perfect crime." Intriguing, but doesn't hold up.

Fraternity Row (1977) **C-101m. *** D:** Thomas J. Tobin. Peter Fox, Gregory Harrison, Scott Newman (Paul Newman's late son), Nancy Morgan, Robert Emhardt, Wendy Phillips. Well-done drama of campus life at exclusive Eastern college, 1954. Writer-producer Charles Gary Allison used USC students and crew, got professional Hollywood advice for polished look at tragic, fact-based, fraternity hazing. Cliff Robertson narrates, Don McLean did original score.

Fraulein (1958) **C-98m. ** D:** Henry Koster. Dana Wynter, Mel Ferrer, Dolores Michaels, Maggie Hayes. Bizarre tale of German girl in post-WW2 Berlin helping American soldier, then being held by the Communists. Wynter miscast.

Fraulein Doktor (1969-Italian-Yugoslavian) **C-102m. *** D:** Alberto Lattuada. Suzy Kendall, Kenneth More, Capucine, James Booth, Alexander Knox, Nigel Green. Big cast and budget in rarely seen European antiwar film centering on career of double-agent during WW1. Some of the battle sequences impressive.

Freaky Friday (1977) **C-95m. *** D:** Gary Nelson. Barbara Harris, Jodie Foster, John Astin, Patsy Kelly, Dick Van Patten, Sorrell Booke. Harris and Foster shine as mother and daughter who magically switch personalities for a day; their performances make this exceptional Disney fare, even though Mary Rodgers' script winds up with formula slapstick chase.

Freckles (1960) **C-84m. *½ D:** Andrew V. McLaglen. Martin West, Carol Christensen, Jack Lambert, Roy Barcroft, Ken Curtis, Steven Peck. Bland study of crippled youth who manages to be accepted as normal working member of lumber camp.

Free and Easy (1930) **75m. **½ D:** Edward Sedgwick. Buster Keaton,

Anita Page, Robert Montgomery, Edgar Dearing, Lionel Barrymore, Dorothy Sebastian, Trixie Friganza. Interesting early talkie musicomedy of Keaton becoming movie star; many guest appearances by Cecil B. DeMille, William Haines et al to boost uneven film. Retitled: EASY GO.

Free, Blonde and Twenty One (1940) **67m. *½ D:** Ricardo Cortez. Lynn Bari, Mary Beth Hughes, Joan Davis, Henry Wilcoxon. Low-grade hokum about gold-digging gals on the make for wealthy men.

Free for All (1949) **83m. ** D:** Charles Barton. Robert Cummings, Ann Blyth, Percy Kilbride, Ray Collins. Mild froth about Cummings inventing instant gasoline.

Free Soul, A (1931) **91m. *** D:** Clarence Brown. Norma Shearer, Lionel Barrymore, Clark Gable, Leslie Howard, James Gleason, George Irving. Outstanding acting makes dated story worthwhile. Shearer falls for gangster Gable whom her drunken lawyer father Barrymore (in Oscar-winning performance) has defended on murder charge. Film gave big boost to Gable's budding career. Remade as THE GIRL WHO HAD EVERYTHING.

Freebie and the Bean (1974) **C-113m. ** D:** Richard Rush. James Caan, Alan Arkin, Loretta Swit, Jack Kruschen, Mike Kellin. Some good action, but mostly ridiculous humor as San Francisco cops Arkin and Caan nearly wreck the city trying to get the goods on numbers racketeer Kruschen. Valerie (Rhoda) Harper has a nice scene as Arkin's Latin wife.

Freedom Riders, The SEE: Undercover with the KKK

Freedom Road (1979) **C-200m. TVM D:** Jan Kadar. Muhammad Ali, Kris Kristofferson, Ron O'Neal, Barbara-O Jones, Edward Herrmann, John McLiam, Ernest Dixon. Lumbering adaptation of sprawling Howard Fast novel about an ex-slave's rise to U.S. Senator in Reconstruction Days, hampered by nonacting of Ali in the crucial lead. Ossie Davis provides dignified narration to director Kadar's last film. Average.

French Cancan SEE: Only the French Can

French Connection, The (1971) **C-104m. **** D:** William Friedkin. Gene Hackman, Fernando Rey, Roy Scheider, Tony LoBianco, Marcel

Bozzuffi. Fine action film detailing attempted international heroin smuggle into New York, and maverick detective who stops it. Academy Awards include Best Picture, Best Actor, Best Director, Best Screenplay, Best Editing, the latter particularly for one of the most exciting car chases ever put on film.

French Connection II, The (1975) C-119m. **½ D: John Frankenheimer. Gene Hackman, Fernando Rey, Bernard Fresson, Jean-Pierre Castaldi, Charles Milot, Cathleen Nesbitt. Gruff N.Y. cop Popeye Doyle goes to Marseilles, determined to nail narcotics king (Rey) who eluded him in America. Enjoyable opening and riveting chase finale are separated by long, agonizing drug segment that weighs whole film down.

French Conspiracy, The (1973-French) C-124m. ** D: Yves Boisset. Jean Louis Trintignant, Jean Seberg, Gian Maria Volonte, Roy Scheider, Michel Piccoli. Originally in French, this French-Italian-German coproduction is a political drama centering around left-wing reporter Trintignant, pawn in a plot to assassinate Third World leader Volonte. Realistic but unexciting.

French Key, The (1946) 64m. **½ D: Walter Colmes. Albert Dekker, Mike Mazurki, Evelyn Ankers, John Eldredge, Frank Fenton, Richard Arlen, Byron Foulger. Dekker gives mystery drama some class in this murder yarn.

French Line, The (1954) C-102m. ** D: Lloyd Bacon. Jane Russell, Gilbert Roland, Arthur Hunnicutt, Mary McCarty. Russell's bust in 3-D was the gimmick to sell this dull musical. All that's left is flat tale of wealthy girl in Paris being romanced by Parisian. McCarty's wisecracking is a blessing.

French Postcards (1979) C-92m. ** D: Willard Huyck. Miles Chapin, Blanche Baker, David Marshall Grant, Valerie Quennessen, Marie-France Pisier, Jean Rochefort. American college students spend junior year abroad in choppy comedy from screenwriting team that wrote AMERICAN GRAFFITI. Pisier shines as a footloose wife, but some of the leads aren't as appealing.

French They Are a Funny Race, The (1956-French) 83m. ** D: Preston Sturges. Jack Buchanan, Noel-Noel, Martine Carol, Genevieve Brunet.

Director-writer Sturges' last film is pretty much a misfire, with Buchanan as veddy-British major whose marriage to Frenchwoman sparks continuing nationalistic arguments.

Frenchie (1950) C-81m. ** D: Louis King. Joel McCrea, Shelley Winters, John Russell, John Emery, George Cleveland, Elsa Lanchester, Marie Windsor. When her father is murdered, Winters returns home and opens a saloon, planning revenge. Bland Western based on DESTRY RIDES AGAIN.

Frenchman's Creek (1944) C-113m. *** D: Mitchell Leisen. Joan Fontaine, Arturo de Cordova, Basil Rathbone, Nigel Bruce, Cecil Kellaway, Ralph Forbes, George Kirby. Colorful escapism of Fontaine romanced by dashing pirate De Cordova; good supporting cast.

Frenzy (1972-British) C-116m. ***½ D: Alfred Hitchcock. Jon Finch, Barry Foster, Barbara Leigh-Hunt, Anna Massey, Alec McCowen, Vivien Merchant, Billie Whitelaw. Hitchcock in full gear, telling story of suave London strangler (Foster) and innocent man (Finch) suspected of crime wave. All classic Hitchcock elements are here, including delicious black humor, several astounding camera shots. Script by Anthony Shaffer.

Fresh From Paris (1955) C-70m. *½ D: Leslie Goodwins. Forrest Tucker, Margaret Whiting, Martha Hyer. Grade-C musical filmed at Moulin Rouge cafe in Hollywood, with tiresome musical interludes. Original title: PARIS FOLLIES OF 1956.

Freshman, The (1925) 70m. *** D: Sam Taylor and Fred Newmeyer. Harold Lloyd, Jobyna Ralston, Brooks Benedict, James Anderson, Hazel Keener. One of Lloyd's best remembered films casts him as collegiate patsy who'll do anything to be popular on campus, unaware that everyone is making fun of him. Football game finale is one of several comic highlights. Edited for TV.

Freud (1962) 120m. ***½ D: John Huston. Montgomery Clift, Susannah York, Larry Parks, David McCallum, Susan Kohner, Eileen Herlie. Intelligent, unglamorous account of Sigmund Freud as young doctor, focusing on his early psychiatric theories and treatments and his struggle for their acceptance among Viennese medical colleagues. Fascinating dream sequence. Originally released at 139m.

[264]

Friday Foster (1975) C-90m. ** D: Arthur Marks. Pam Grier, Yaphet Kotto, Godfrey Cambridge, Thalmus Rasulala, Eartha Kitt, Jim Backus. Black bubble-gum nonsense based on comic strip about fashion photographer who gets involved in mystery and intrigue; here she tries to foil assassination/conspiracy plot against black politicians.

Frieda (1947-British) 97m. *** D: Basil Dearden. David Farrar, Glynis Johns, Mai Zetterling, Flora Robson, Albert Lieven. Interesting study of Farrar bringing German wife Zetterling back home to England, and bigotry they encounter.

Friendly Enemies (1942) 95m. **½ D: Allan Dwan. Charles Winninger, Charlie Ruggles, James Craig, Nancy Kelly. Thoughtful minor film of conflicts between lifelong friends when WW1 breaks out and their German heritage leads to friction.

Friendly Fire (1979) C-150m. TVM D: David Greene. Carol Burnett, Ned Beatty, Sam Waterston, Dennis Erdman, Timothy Hutton. Gripping if overlong drama about a rural American couple who try to cope with governmental indifference to learn the truth behind their son's death in Vietnam. Burnett seems somewhat sullen in her one-note portrayal of real-life war activist Peg Mullen, but Beatty is outstanding as her husband. Above average.

Friendly Persuasion (1956) C-140m. **** D: William Wyler. Gary Cooper, Dorothy McGuire, Marjorie Main, Anthony Perkins, Richard Eyer, Robert Middleton, Walter Catlett. Charming account of Quaker family struggling to maintain its identity amid confusion and heartbreak of Civil War. Warm, winning performances in this beautifully made film. Music by Dimitri Tiomkin.

Friendly Persuasion (1975) C-100m. TVM D: Joseph Sargent. Richard Kiley, Shirley Knight, Clifton James, Michael O'Keefe, Kevin O'Keefe, Tracie Savage, Sparky Marcus. Picturesque, well-acted drama about a gentle Quaker couple who risk their lives to help a pair of runaway slaves seeking freedom. Kiley and Knight compare admirably to Gary Cooper and Dorothy McGuire, who stared in 1956 film classic. Above average.

Friends of Eddie Coyle, The (1973) C-102m. ***½ D: Peter Yates. Robert Mitchum, Peter Boyle, Richard Jordan, Steven Keats, Alex Rocco, Mitchell Ryan. Ultrarealistic depiction of criminals and police, as hardened con labors to supply guns and make deal with cops. Bleak nightmare picture of underworld enhanced by numerous Boston locations, flawless performances. Only liabilities: film's offbeat low-key narrative approach and finale.

Friendships, Secrets and Lies (1979) C-100m. TVM D: Ann Zane Shanks and Marlena Laird. Cathryn Damon, Shelley Fabares, Sondra Locke, Tina Louise, Paula Prentiss, Stella Stevens, Loretta Swit. Seven college sorority sisters relive the past when a baby's skeleton is discovered as the old house on campus is razed. Uninspired telling of Babs H. Deal's novel, *The Walls Come Tumbling Down*, with an all-female cast (and virtually an all-female production crew). Average.

Fright (1971-British) C-87m. ** D: Peter Collinson. Susan George, Honor Blackman, Ian Bannen, John Gregson, George Cole, Dennis Waterman. Young baby-sitter (George) spends terror-filled evening at country house, menaced by mental hospital escapee. Contrived, mechanical direction and so-so script. Beware cuts.

Frightened Bride, The (1953-British) 75m. ** D: Terence Young. Andre Morell, Flora Robson, Mai Zetterling, Michael Denison, Mervyn Johns. Murder haunts a family when the youngest son becomes involved in homicide.

Frightened City, The (1962-British) 97m. **½ D: John Lemont. Herbert Lom, John Gregson, Sean Connery, Alfred Marks, Yvonne Romain. Interesting inside look at a London racketeer amalgamating various city gangs for master plan syndicate.

Frisco Kid (1935) 77m. ** D: Lloyd Bacon. James Cagney, Margaret Lindsay, Ricardo Cortez, Lili Damita, Fred Kohler, George E. Stone, Donald Woods. Routine drama of Barbary Coast with Cagney fighting his way to the top, almost dethroned by local gangs but saved by blueblood Lindsay.

Frisco Kid, The (1979) C-122m. **½ D: Robert Aldrich. Gene Wilder, Harrison Ford, Ramon Bieri, Val Bisoglio, George Ralph DiCenzo, Leo Fuchs, Penny Peyser. Offbeat story of Polish rabbi crossing U.S. in 1850 and developing friendship with young bank robber. Wilder's performance, and some charming vignettes, make up for many other shortcomings.

Frisco Sal (1945) 63m. ** D: George Waggner. Susanna Foster, Turhan Bey, Alan Curtis, Andy Devine, Thomas Gomez, Samuel S. Hinds. Tepid costume drama of Foster out West in California, determined to find her brother's killer.

Frisky (1955-Italian) 98m. **½ D: Luigi Comencini. Gina Lollobrigida, Vittorio De Sica, Roberto Risso, Marisa Merlini. Lollobrigida provides sufficient sex appeal to carry simple tale of flirtatious village girl who beats out competition in winning heart of police official De Sica.

Fritz The Cat (1972) C-78m. *** D: Ralph Bakshi. X-rated animated feature somewhat based on Robert Crumb's underground comics character. Flawed but engaging, irreverent look at radical-hip lifestyles of the 1960s, geared for people who experienced that era. Imaginatively conceived cartoon.

Frogmen, The (1951) 96m. *** D: Lloyd Bacon. Richard Widmark, Dana Andrews, Gary Merrill, Jeffrey Hunter. Intriguing look at underwater demolition squads in action in the Pacific during WW2.

Frogs (1972) C-91m. **½ D: George McCowan. Ray Milland, Sam Elliott, Joan Van Ark, Adam Roarke, Judy Pace. Patriarchal Milland has been destroying bayou wildlife and now the reptiles are out to destroy his whole family. Dumb but enjoyable thriller.

From Beyond the Grave (1976-British) C-97m. *** D: Kevin Connor. Peter Cushing, Margaret Leighton, Ian Bannen, Donald Pleasence, David Warner, Diana Dors, Angela Pleasence, Nyree Dawn Porter, Lesley-Anne Down. Neat multi-storied horror pic. Visitors to Cushing's little antique shop, Temptations Ltd., meet terrible fates. Leighton excels as a wacky clairvoyant. Made in 1973.

From Hell It Came (1957) 71m. *½ D: Dan Milner. Tod Andrews, Tina Carver, Linda Watkins, John McNamara, Gregg Palmer, Robert Swan. Monstrous limb rises from grave of native chief's son, causing terror in South Seas village.

From Hell to Borneo (1964) C-96m. ** D: George Montgomery. George Montgomery, Julie Gregg, Torin Thatcher, Lisa Moreno. Filmed in the Philippines, tale recounts Montgomery's efforts to maintain sanctity of his private island against aggressive crooks and smugglers.

From Hell to Texas (1958) C-100m. **½ D: Henry Hathaway. Don Murray, Diane Varsi, Chill Wills, Dennis Hopper. Sincere Western with Murray on the run with posse on his trail for accidentally killing a man.

From Here to Eternity (1953) 118m. **** D: Fred Zinnemann. Burt Lancaster, Montgomery Clift, Deborah Kerr, Frank Sinatra, Donna Reed, Ernest Borgnine, George Reeves. Excellent film of Army life in Hawaii at start of WW2. Sinatra and Reed won Oscars in this tight version of James Jones' novel; powerful and engrossing.

From Nashville with Music (1969) C-87m. *½ D: Eddie Crandall. Marilyn Maxwell, Leo G. Carroll, Gonzalez-Gonzalez, Marty Robbins, Merle Haggard, Buck Owens. Some good C&W music, but one is better off buying the performers' albums instead of suffering through this story of N.Y.C. couple who go to the Grand Ole Opry by mistake.

From Russia with Love (1963-British) C-118m. ***½ D: Terence Young. Sean Connery, Daniela Bianchi, Lotte Lenya, Pedro Armendariz, Robert Shaw, Lois Maxwell. Second James Bond film is one of the best; plenty of suspense and action, and one of the longest, most exciting fight scenes ever staged. Lenya makes a very sinister spy.

From the Earth to the Moon (1958) C-100m. **½ D: Byron Haskin. Joseph Cotten, George Sanders, Debra Paget, Don Dubbins. Jules Verne's fiction doesn't float well in contrived sci-fi of early rocket flight to the moon. Veteran cast looks most uncomfortable.

From the Mixed-Up Files of Mrs. Basil E. Frankweiler (1973) C-105m. **½ D: Fielder Cook. Ingrid Bergman, Sally Prager, Johnny Doran, George Rose, Georgann Johnson, Richard Mulligan, Madeline Kahn. Fanciful tale of New Jersey kids Prager and Doran who hide out in New York's Metropolitan Museum, creating a dream world and befriending recluse Bergman, seen too briefly. Best for children. Reissued as THE HIDEAWAYS.

From the Terrace (1960) C-144m. ***

D: Mark Robson. Paul Newman, Joanne Woodward, Myrna Loy, Ina Balin, Leon Ames, Elizabeth Allen, Barbara Eden, George Grizzard. John O'Hara's ironic chronicle of poor boy's rise to financial and social success is superficial film. Woodward is chic and Newman wooden; Loy superb as drunken mother.

From This Day Forward (1946) 95m. *** D: John Berry. Joan Fontaine, Mark Stevens, Rosemary DeCamp, Henry (Harry) Morgan, Arline Judge, Bobby Driscoll, Mary Treen. Agreeable soaper of Fontaine and Stevens readjusting their lives when he returns from war, and their struggle to get on in the world.

Front, The (1976) C-94m. **** D: Martin Ritt. Woody Allen, Zero Mostel, Herschel Bernardi, Michael Murphy, Andrea Marcovicci, Remak Ramsay, Joshua Shelley. Bull's-eye comedy with serious theme; Allen is a shnook enlisted by blacklisted writers to put his name on their scripts, during 1950s "witch-hunt" era, leading to various complications. Allen's casting is perfect, and Mostel is standout as "tainted" comic fighting for survival. Original script by blacklistee Walter Bernstein.

Front Page, The (1931) 103m. ***½ D: Lewis Milestone. Adolphe Menjou, Pat O'Brien, Mary Brian, Edward Everett Horton, Walter Catlett, Mae Clarke, George E. Stone. First filming of Hecht-MacArthur play is forceful, funny, and flamboyantly directed, with Menjou and O'Brien a good pair as battling editor and reporter in Chicago. Stands up quite well alongside remake HIS GIRL FRIDAY.

Front Page, The (1974) C-105m. *** D: Billy Wilder. Jack Lemmon, Walter Matthau, Carol Burnett, Susan Sarandon, Vincent Gardenia, David Wayne, Allen Garfield, Austin Pendleton, Charles Durning. Third filming of the Hecht-MacArthur play about wild and woolly Chicago newspaperman in the 1920s has hardly anything new to offer (except four-letter words) but remains an enjoyable vehicle for this fine cast. Only Burnett misses the boat in an overblown cameo.

Front Page Story (1954-British) 99m. **½ D: Gordon Parry. Jack Hawkins, Elizabeth Allan, Eva Bartok, Martin Miller, Derek Farr. Solid performances enhance story of many problems confronting newspaper editor: pending divorce, murder, lost children, and a rebellious staff.

Front Page Woman (1935) 82m. **½ D: Michael Curtiz. Bette Davis, George Brent, Winifred Shaw, Roscoe Karns, Joseph Crehan. Breezy yarn of rival reporters Davis and Brent trying to outdo each other covering unusual fire story; prime ingenue Davis fare.

Frontier Gal (1945) C-84m. **½ D: Charles Lamont. Yvonne De Carlo, Rod Cameron, Andy Devine, Fuzzy Knight, Andrew Tombes, Sheldon Leonard, Clara Blandick. Sex in the West as saloon queen De Carlo falls in love with outlaw Cameron; no sympathy from villain Leonard in OK Western-comedy.

Frontier Gun (1958) 70m. ** D: Paul Landres. John Agar, Robert Strauss, Barton MacLane, Morris Ankrum. Agar is honest sheriff who discovers that gunplay is only solution to town's crooks.

Frontier Hellcat (1966-German) C-98m. **½ D: Alfred Vohrer. Stewart Granger, Elke Sommer, Pierre Brice, Gotz George. Another Karl May WINNETOU story, which captures flavor of Old West, recounting adventure of pioneers passing through Rockies.

Frontier Uprising (1961) 68m. *½ D: Edward L. Cahn. James Davis, Nancy Hadley, Ken Mayer, Nestor Paiva. Scout leading pioneers to West Coast in 1840s discovers that Mexico and U.S. are at war.

Frozen Dead, The (1967-British) C-95m. **½ D: Herbert J. Leder. Dana Andrews, Anna Palk, Philip Gilbert, Kathleen Breck, Karel Stepanek. Bizarre account of scientist Andrews who froze group of Nazi leaders, now trying to revive them and the Third Reich; sloppy production values mar tale. Released theatrically in b&w.

Frozen Ghost, The (1945) 61m. ** D: Harold Young. Lon Chaney, Evelyn Ankers, Milburn Stone, Douglass Dumbrille, Martin Kosleck, Elena Verdugo. Typical 1940s Chaney nonsense about tormented hypnotist who stumbles into murder plot.

Fugitive, The (1947) 104m. ***½ D: John Ford. Henry Fonda, Dolores Del Rio, Pedro Armendariz, J. Carrol Naish, Leo Carrillo. Brooding drama set in Mexico with revolutionist priest turned in by man who once sheltered him. Good cast works well.

Fugitive Kind, The (1959) 135m. **½ D: Sidney Lumet. Marlon Brando, Anna Magnani, Joanne Woodward, Maureen Stapleton, Victor Jory, R. G. Armstrong. Uneven filming of Tennessee Williams' ORPHEUS DESCENDING, with strange casting. Wandering bum (Brando) arrives in Southern town, sparking romances with middle-aged married woman (Magnani) and spunky Woodward. Movie gets nowhere.

Full Confession (1939) 73m. ** D: John Farrow. Victor McLaglen, Sally Eilers, Joseph Calleia, Barry Fitzgerald. Mild yet effective yarn of clergyman who listens to a criminal's confessions and convinces him that he should go to the police to save innocent man accused of crime.

Full of Life (1956) 91m. *** D: Richard Quine. Judy Holliday, Richard Conte, Salvatore Baccaloni, Esther Minciotti. Holliday's antics as pregnant wife are almost matched by Baccaloni as excitable father-in-law with his own way of running things.

Full Treatment, The SEE: Stop Me Before I Kill!

Fuller Brush Girl, The (1950) 85m. ** D: Lloyd Bacon. Lucille Ball, Eddie Albert, Jeff Donnell, Jerome Cowan, Lee Patrick. Acceptable slapstick with energetic Lucy as door-to-door salesgirl, mixed up with thieves.

Fuller Brush Man, The (1948) 93m. **½ D: S. Sylvan Simon. Red Skelton, Janet Blair, Don McGuire, Adele Jergens, Ross Ford, Hillary Brooke. Usual Skelton slapstick, with Red involved in murder while valiantly trying to succeed as a door-to-door salesman.

Fun In Acapulco (1963) C-97m. **½ D: Richard Thorpe. Elvis Presley, Ursula Andress, Paul Lukas, Alejandro Rey. Scenery outshines story of Presley working as lifeguard and entertainer in Mexican resort city. Lukas is amusing as temperamental chef; lush scenery.

Fun on a Weekend (1947) 93m. ** D: Andrew L. Stone. Eddie Bracken, Priscilla Lane, Tom Conway, Allen Jenkins, Arthur Treacher, Alma Kruger. Scatterbrain fluff as Bracken and Lane maneuver their way from penniless fortune to love and riches, all in the course of a day.

Fun With Dick and Jane (1977) C-95m. **½ D: Ted Kotcheff. Jane Fonda, George Segal, Ed McMahon, Dick Gautier, Allan Miller, John Dehner. Lightly amusing comedy about Segal losing his job, he and wife Fonda trying to cope with no income and finally turning to crime. Falls apart after promising start, becomes fragmented and pointless.

Funeral in Berlin (1966) C-102m. ** D: Guy Hamilton. Michael Caine, Eva Renzi, Paul Hubschmid, Oscar Homolka, Guy Doleman. Second of three Harry Palmer films featuring Caine as the British spy arranging for defection of Russian officer in charge of Berlin war security. Caine and Homolka are good, Renzi attractive, but slow-moving tale just doesn't click.

Funny Face (1957) C-103m. ***½ D: Stanley Donen. Audrey Hepburn, Fred Astaire, Kay Thompson, Michel Auclair, Suzy Parker, Ruta Lee. Chic musical with lilting Gershwin score and gorgeous shots of Paris. Astaire is fashion photographer who makes drab Hepburn into glamorous model. Thompson is wisecracking fashion editor.

Funny Girl (1968) C-155m. *** D: William Wyler. Barbra Streisand, Omar Sharif, Kay Medford, Anne Francis, Walter Pidgeon, Lee Allen, Gerald Mohr. Streisand's Oscar-winning film debut as Fanny Brice, singer-comedienne whose unhappy private life contrasted comic antics onstage. Bad as biography, but first-rate as musical, including fine Bob Merrill-Jule Styne score, memorable tugboat finale to "Don't Rain on My Parade."

Funny Lady (1975) C-137m. **½ D: Herbert Ross. Barbra Streisand, James Caan, Omar Sharif, Roddy McDowall, Ben Vereen, Carole Wells. Sequel to FUNNY GIRL shows Fanny Brice at height of her career, meeting and marrying ambitious showman Billy Rose (Caan). Disjointed film has fine moments of music and comedy, but a cliche-ridden script to contend with.

Funny Thing Happened on the Way to the Forum, A (1966) C-99m. **½ D: Richard Lester. Zero Mostel, Phil Silvers, Buster Keaton, Jack Gilford, Michael Crawford, Annette Andre, Michael Hordern. Frenzied adaptation of Broadway musical about conniving slave (Mostel) in ancient Rome; tries too hard, comes off forced. Still, with great comic cast, there's plenty worth seeing. Self-spoof on song "Lovely" is a highlight; score by Stephen Sondheim.

Funnyman (1971) **C-98m.** *** D: John Korty. Peter Bonerz, Sandra Archer, Carol Androsky, Larry Hankin, Barbara Hiken, Gerald Hiken. Winning little film about improvisational comic (Bonerz) who's nagged by idea that he should be doing something more "important." Features great skits by The Committee, funny animated spoofs by director Korty.

Furies, The (1950) **109m.** *** D: Anthony Mann. Barbara Stanwyck, Walter Huston, Wendell Corey, Gilbert Roland, Judith Anderson, Beulah Bondi. Western centering on the conflict between strong-minded Stanwyck and her dogmatic cattle-rancher father Huston; quite talky.

Further Adventures of the Wilderness Family (1978) **C-105m.** *** D: Frank Zuniga. Robert Logan, Susan D. Shaw, Heather Rattray, Ham Larsen, George (Buck) Flower, Brian Cutler. This clone of 1975's family hit ADVENTURES OF . . . has same cast, same elements, same magnificent Colorado scenery. So who's to argue with success?

Further Perils of Laurel and Hardy, The (1968) **99m.** **½ D: Robert Youngson. Laurel and Hardy, Charley Chase, Max Davidson, James Finlayson. Repetitious format of "episodes" dulls edge of great material, but still fun, with rare L&H silent footage, pleasing interludes by Chase and Davidson.

Fury (1936) **94m.** ***½ D: Fritz Lang. Sylvia Sidney, Spencer Tracy, Walter Abel, Bruce Cabot, Edward Ellis, Walter Brennan, Frank Albertson. Still timely drama of lynch mobs and mob role in small town, making hardened criminal of innocent Tracy, spoiling his love for sweetheart Sidney.

Fury, The (1978) **C-118m.** *** D: Brian De Palma. Kirk Douglas, John Cassavetes, Carrie Snodgress, Amy Irving, Fiona Lewis, Andrew Stevens, Charles Durning. Stylish trash about young woman with psychokinetic powers, and Douglas' desperate attempt to save his similarly gifted son from being used—or destroyed. Bloody and violent—the ultimate litmus test for those who prefer form over content.

Fury at Furnace Creek (1948) **88m.** ** D: H. Bruce Humberstone. Victor Mature, Coleen Gray, Glenn Langan,

Reginald Gardiner, Albert Dekker. Ordinary Western tale of Mature erasing mar on father's career against formidable opposition.

Fury at Gunsight Pass (1956) **68m.** ** D: Fred F. Sears. David Brian, Neville Brand, Richard Long, Lisa Davis. Occasionally actionful Western, in which outlaw gang takes over a town.

Fury at Showdown (1957) **75m.** *½ D: Gerd Oswald. John Derek, John Smith, Carolyn Craig, Nick Adams. Peace-loving man branded a coward, must shoot it out to rescue his girl.

Fury at Smugglers' Bay (1963-British) **92m.** ** D: John Gilling. Peter Cushing, Michele Mercier, Bernard Lee, George Coulouris, Liz Fraser. Sea yarn of pirates scavenging passing ships and reaping rewards off the English coastline.

Fury of Hercules, The (1961-Italian) **C-95m.** ** D: V. Scega. Brad Harris, Brigitte Corey, Mara Berni, Carlo Tamberlani, Serge Gainsbourg. Harris is musclebound hero who helps Corey and her followers overcome evil ruler of their land; standard production.

Fury of the Congo (1951) **69m.** D: William Berke. Johnny Weissmuller, Sherry Moreland, William Henry, Lyle Talbot. SEE: **Jungle Jim** series.

Fury of the Pagans (1963-Italian) **86m.** ** D: Guido Malatesta. Edmund Purdom, Rossana Podesta, Livio Lorenzon, Carlo Calo. Routine adventure set in ancient Rome, with Purdom leading his tribe to victory and rescuing his true love.

Fury of the Wolf Man, The (1970-Spanish) **C-80m.** BOMB D: Jose Maria Zabalza. Paul Naschy, Perla Cristal, Michael Rivers, Veronica Lujan, Mark Stevens. You'd be furious too if you had to appear in a film like this; English-dubbed garbage about scientist who turns into helpless werewolf.

Future Cop (1976) **C-78m.** TVM D: Jud Taylor. Ernest Borgnine, Michael Shannon, John Amos, John Larch, Herbert Nelson, Ronnie Clair Edwards. Boisterous veteran cop and his robot partner, programmed to be the perfect policeman, team up to track a gang of car thieves. Borgnine's blustering and Shannon's affability make the silly premise bearable if not workable—although it subsequently became a series. Average.

Futureworld (1976) **C-104m.** *** D:

Richard T. Heffron. Peter Fonda, Blythe Danner, Arthur Hill, Yul Brynner, Stuart Margolin, John Ryan. Suspenseful sequel to WESTWORLD has overtones of INVASION OF THE BODY SNATCHERS as robot duplicates try to take over. Short on action but intelligently done.

Futz (1969) C-92m. *½ D: Tom O'Horgan. Seth Allen, John Bakos, Mari-Claire Charba, Peter Craig. Director O'Horgan, whose youthful touch made this a mild off-Broadway hit, brings bizarre tale to screen with disastrous results. No plot worth describing, except that there's a man in love with a pig.

Fuzz (1972) C-92m. ** D: Richard A. Colla. Burt Reynolds, Raquel Welch, Yul Brynner, Jack Weston, Tom Skerritt, James McEachin, Steve Ihnat. Oddball film tries to mix laughs and excitement, to be the M*A*S*H of police dramas, but doesn't have the style to pull it off; another disappointment for Reynolds fans.

Fuzzy Pink Nightgown, The (1957) 87m. ** D: Norman Taurog. Jane Russell, Ralph Meeker, Adolphe Menjou, Keenan Wynn, Fred Clark, Una Merkel. Outside of Russell's appearance, film is boring satire. When movie star is kidnapped, everyone thinks it's a publicity gag.

G.I. Blues (1960) C-104m. *** D: Norman Taurog. Elvis Presley, Juliet Prowse, Robert Ivers, Leticia Roman. Prowse's versatile performance uplifts standard Presley fare of G.I. trio in Germany forming a music group.

G-Men (1935) 85m. ***½ D: William Keighley. James Cagney, Ann Dvorak, Margaret Lindsay, Robert Armstrong, Barton MacLane, Lloyd Nolan, William Harrigan. Although raised by an underworld figure, Cagney joins F.B.I. when a pal is killed by gangsters, puts his first-hand knowledge to use. Exciting film, beautifully shot; prologue with David Brian added for 1949 reissue.

G-Men Never Forget SEE: **Code 645**
G-Men vs the Black Dragon SEE: **Black Dragon of Manzanar**
Gable and Lombard (1976) C-131m. BOMB D: Sidney J. Furie. James Brolin, Jill Clayburgh, Allen Garfield, Red Buttons, Joanne Linville,

Melanie Mayron. Pure tripe about offscreen romance of two great stars. Brolin and Clayburgh are game but one-dimensional; script and direction are hopeless.

Gabriel Over the White House (1933) 87m. *** D: Gregory La Cava. Walter Huston, Karen Morley, Franchot Tone, C. Henry Gordon, Samuel S. Hinds, Jean Parker, Dickie Moore. Dizzying Depression fantasy of crooked Huston elected President, experiencing mysterious change that turns him into Superpresident, determined to eliminate racketeers, find world peace. Bizarre, fascinating.

Gaby (1956) C-97m. **½ D: Curtis Bernhardt. Leslie Caron, John Kerr, Sir Cedric Hardwicke, Taina Elg. Remake of WATERLOO BRIDGE, telling of ballerina Caron and her romance with soldier Kerr in WW2 England; not up to original.

Gaily, Gaily (1969) C-107m. ** D: Norman Jewison. Beau Bridges, Melina Mercouri, Brian Keith, George Kennedy, Hume Cronyn, Margot Kidder, Wilfrid Hyde-White, Melodie Johnson. Ben Hecht's colorful memories of apprenticeship on Chicago newspaper are destroyed by silly, hollow script that even changes "Hecht" to "Harvey." Expensive sets, period flavor are only bright spots in contrived comedy.

Gal Who Took the West, The (1949) C-84m. ** D: Frederick de Cordova. Yvonne De Carlo, Charles Coburn, Scott Brady, John Russell. De Carlo is attractive as singer in 1890s Arizona who allows Brady and Russell to court her.

Galileo (1973-British) C-145m. *** D: Joseph Losey. Topol, Edward Fox, Colin Blakely, Georgia Brown, Clive Revill, Margaret Leighton, John Gielgud. Bertolt Brecht's play, whose 1947 U.S. premiere was staged by director Losey, turned into unremarkable but generally satisfactory film. Topol is a little much as the scientist whose theories of the universe confound the church, but supporting actors are excellent. An American Film Theatre Production.

Gallant Bess (1946) C-101m. ** D: Andrew Marton. Marshall Thompson, George Tobias, Jim Davis, Chill Wills. Confusing yarn of horse and its master is acceptably acted but will bore most viewers.

Gallant Blade, The (1948) C-81m. ** D: Henry Levin. Larry Parks,

Marguerite Chapman, Victor Jory, George Macready. Colorful, standard swashbuckler with dashing Parks protecting French general from villainous plot.

Gallant Hours, The (1960) 111m. *** D: Robert Montgomery. James Cagney, Dennis Weaver, Ward Costello, Richard Jaeckel. Sincere, low-key biog of Admiral Halsey played documentary-style. Cagney is reserved and effective, but production needs livening.

Gallant Journey (1946) 85m. **½ D: William Wellman. Glenn Ford, Janet Blair, Charles Ruggles, Henry Travers, Arthur Shields, Selena Royle. Ford pioneers glider plane development in 19th century. OK, but not as stirring as it's meant to be.

Gallant Lady (1934) 86m. ** D: Gregory LaCava. Ann Harding, Clive Brook, Otto Kruger, Tulio Carminati, Dickie Moore, Janet Beecher. Handsome but standard soaper about unwed Harding giving up baby for adoption, later hoping for second chance when adopted mother dies.

Galloping Major (1950-British) 82m. ** D: Henry Cornelius. Basil Radford, Jimmy Hanley, Janette Scott, A. E. Matthews. Uninspired comedy about horseracing, with slow-running nag winning the day.

Gambit (1966) C-109m. *** D: Ronald Neame. Michael Caine, Shirley MacLaine, Herbert Lom, Roger C. Carmel, John Abbott. Gimmicky robbery yarn with scoundrel Caine hiring Eurasian MacLaine to carry out perfect heist of invaluable piece of sculpture; great fun.

Gambler, The (1974) C-111m. ** D: Karel Reisz. James Caan, Paul Sorvino, Lauren Hutton, Morris Carnovsky, Jacqueline Brooks, Burt Young. Misfire about college prof Caan's compulsion to gamble; much inferior to Altman's CALIFORNIA SPLIT.

Gambler and the Lady, The (1952-British) 71m. *½ D: Patrick Jenkins, Sam Newfield. Dane Clark, Kathleen Byron, Naomi Chance, Meredith Edwards, Anthony Forwood, Eric Pohlmann. Tepid little drama of gambling man Clark who falls in love, altering his unorthodox way of life.

Gambler From Natchez, The (1954) C-88m. ** D: Henry Levin. Dale Robertson, Debra Paget, Thomas Gomez, Lisa Daniels. Set in 1840s, film focuses on Robertson's plot to eliminate trio of men who shot his father, a gambler caught cheating.

Gamblers, The (1969) C-93m. **½ D: Ron Winston. Suzy Kendall, Don Gordon, Pierre Olaf, Kenneth Griffith, Stuart Margolin, Faith Domergue. A team of card sharps work a cruise ship for high stakes; interesting international cast, nice views of Dubrovnik, resort town in Yugoslavia.

Gambler's Choice (1944) 66m. ** D: Frank McDonald. Chester Morris, Nancy Kelly, Russell Hayden, Lee Patrick, Lyle Talbot, Sheldon Leonard. Another variation of MANHATTAN MELODRAMA—three kids grow up; one becomes a lawman, another a shady gambler, the third the nice girl they both love.

Gamblin' Man SEE: Cockfighter

Gambling House (1950) 80m. ** D: Ted Tetzlaff. Victor Mature, Terry Moore, William Bendix, Cleo Moore, Ann Doran. At times overly melodramatic account of man acquitted for murder, facing deportation as undesirable alien.

Gambling Lady (1934) 66m. **½ D: Archie Mayo. Barbara Stanwyck, Pat O'Brien, Claire Dodd, Joel McCrea, C. Aubrey Smith, Arthur Treacher. Family disapproves when wealthy McCrea marries gambler's daughter Stanwyck, but she proves her worth when McCrea encounters trouble.

Game of Danger (1954-British) 88m. **½ D: Lance Comfort. Jack Warner, Veronica Hurst, Derek Farr. Offbeat study of two youngsters involved in homicide, with strange effects on their lives. Original title: BANG YOU'RE DEAD.

Game of Death, A (1946) 72m. *½ D: Robert Wise. John Loder, Audrey Long, Edgar Barrier, Russell Wade. Potentially interesting tale about crazed island inhabitant who hunts down shipwrecked victims for amusement; poorly produced film. Rehash of MOST DANGEROUS GAME, refilmed as RUN FOR THE SUN.

Game of Death (1979) C-102m. *½ D: Robert Clouse. Bruce Lee, Gig Young, Dean Jagger, Hugh O'Brian, Colleen Camp, Kareem Abdul-Jabbar, Chuck Norris. Producer Raymond Chow took 10 minutes of Bruce Lee footage—from his last, uncompleted movie—and constructed story of crime and revenge around it, with embarrassing attempts to hide the fact that a stand-in is used throughout. For diehards only.

Games (1967) C-100m. **½ D: Curtis Harrington. Simone Signoret, James Caan, Katharine Ross, Don Stroud, Kent Smith, Estelle Winwood. After arrival of mysterious Signoret at kinky newlywed N.Y.C. apartment, borderline pranks become deadly conspiracy. The trick: guess who's doublecrossing whom. Attempts at deeper meanings unfulfilling, despite good cast.

Games, The (1970-British) C-97m. *½ D: Michael Winner. Michael Crawford, Stanley Baker, Ryan O'Neal, Charles Aznavour, Jeremy Kemp, Elaine Taylor, Kent Smith, Sam Elliott, Mona Washbourne. Dull film on potentially interesting subject: preparation of four runners for grueling 26-mile marathon in the Olympics. Rafer Johnson plays one of the commentators.

Games of Desire (1968) 90m. ** D: Hans Albin. Ingrid Thulin, Claudine Auger, Paul Hubschmid. Thulin is married to Sweden's ambassador to Greece, forced to make love with various men because her husband digs his male secretary. Tepid tale of depravity doesn't have many explicit scenes to cut for TV, which will make the film longer than anyone wants.

Gamma People, The (1956-British) 79m. ** D: John Gilling. Paul Douglas, Eva Bartok, Leslie Phillips, Walter Rilla. Minor horror entry involving Communist scientist with a device to turn people into robot creatures.

Gammera, The Invincible (1966-Japanese-U.S.) 88m. *½ D: Noriaki Yuasi. Brian Donlevy, Albert Dekker, John Baragrey. A giant, jet-propelled fire-breathing space turtle terrorizes the earth following atomic explosion. First in a series of juvenile sci-fi films.

Gang Busters (1955) 78m. ** D: Bill Karan. Myron Healey, Don C. Harvey, Sam Edwards, Frank Gerstle. Standard prison-life drama, focusing on breakout plan.

Gang That Couldn't Shoot Straight, The (1971) C-96m. ** D: James Goldstone. Jerry Orbach, Leigh Taylor-Young, Jo Van Fleet, Lionel Stander, Robert De Niro. Film version of Jimmy Breslin's best-seller about some comical, twelfth-rate New York crooks is well cast, but adapted in slapdash fashion and directed without much feeling for the material.

Gang War (1958) 75m. **½ D: Gene Fowler, Jr. Charles Bronson, Kent Taylor, Jennifer Holden, John Doucette. Grade-B film tracing the savage events resulting from a teacher testifying against gang brutality.

Gang War (1962-British) 65m. ** D: Frank Marshall. Sean Kelly, Eira Heath, David Davies, Sean Sullivan. Tame account of life among London gangsters.

Gang's All Here, The (1943) C-103m. **½ D: Busby Berkeley. Alice Faye, Carmen Miranda, James Ellison, Charlotte Greenwood, Eugene Pallette, Edward Everett Horton, Benny Goodman, Sheila Ryan. Splashy wartime musical is terrible, but fun; Miranda in fine form with "The Lady in the Tutti Frutti Hat," some awkward Berkeley numbers, and Benny Goodman singing (!).

Gangster, The (1947) 84m. *** D: Gordon Wiles. Barry Sullivan, Belita, Joan Lorring, Akim Tamiroff, Harry Morgan, John Ireland, Fifi D'Orsay, Shelley Winters. Sullivan gives strong performance as man who falls victim to his slum environment and ends up a vengeful crook.

Gangster Boss (1959-French) 100m. ** D: Henri Verneuil. Fernandel, Papouf, Gino Cervi. Buffoon Fernandel becomes involved with criminal gang when he accidentally snatches parcel containing stolen loot.

Gangster Story (1960) 65m. **½ D: Walter Matthau. Walter Matthau, Carol Grace, Bruce McFarlan, Garrett Wallberg. Straightforward, tight little gangster chronicle, focusing on the crook's gal who tries to reform him.

Gangway for Tomorrow (1943) 69m. ** D: John H. Auer. Margo, John Carradine, Robert Ryan, Amelita Ward, William Terry, Harry Davenport, James Bell, Charles Arnt, Wally Brown, Alan Carney. Lives of five workers in wartime munitions plant told in flashbacks; badly dated wartime fare with occasional bright moments. Written by Arch Oboler.

Garden Murder Case, The (1936) 62m. D: Edwin L. Marin. Edmund Lowe, Virginia Bruce, Benita Hume, Douglas Walton, Nat Pendleton, Gene Lockhart. See: Philo Vance series.

Garden of Allah, The (1936) C-85m. *** D: Richard Boleslawski. Marlene Dietrich, Charles Boyer, Tilly Losch, Basil Rathbone, Joseph Schildkraut,

Henry (Brandon) Kleinbach, John Carradine. Sensitive, well-played romance in the Algerian desert, with sultry Dietrich meeting her match in ascetic Boyer; Technicolor shares credit for lavish production.

Garden of Evil (1954) C-100m. **½ D: Henry Hathaway. Gary Cooper, Susan Hayward, Richard Widmark, Hugh Marlowe, Cameron Mitchell, Rita Moreno. Meandering adventure story set in 1850s Mexico, with trio escorting Hayward through bandit territory to save her husband.

Garden of the Finzi-Continis, The (1971-Italian) C-95m. **** D: Vittorio De Sica. Dominique Sanda, Lino Capolicchio, Helmut Berger, Fabio Testi, Romolo Valli. Exquisitely photographed, Oscar-winning foreign film about aristocratic Jewish family in Fascist-dominated Italy. Key scene involved nudity which may present a problem on TV.

Garden of the Moon (1938) 94m. **½ D: Busby Berkeley. Pat O'Brien, Margaret Lindsay, John Payne, Johnnie Davis, Melville Cooper, Isabel Jeans, Penny Singleton. Nightclub owner O'Brien and bandleader Payne have running feud; plot is pleasant excuse to work in many Berkeley numbers: "Girlfriend Of The Whirling Dervish," "Love Is Where You Find It," title tune.

Gargoyles (1972) C-74m. TVM D: B. W. L. Norton. Cornel Wilde, Jennifer Salt, Bernie Casey, Grayson Hall, Woodrow Chamblis, Scott Glenn. Anthropologist Wilde and daughter on trip to Mexico, stop off at wilderness curio station, come upon unusual skeleton. A very good beginning but deteriorates halfway through story. Flawless use of locations. Average.

Garment Jungle, The (1957) 88m. **½ D: Vincent Sherman. Lee J. Cobb, Kerwin Mathews, Gia Scala, Richard Boone. Well-handled account of union-gangster corruption in dressmaking industry, with romantic interludes slowing down violent pace.

Gas-s-s-s (1970) C-90m. *** D: Roger Corman. Bud Cort, Cindy Williams, Robert Corff, Ben Vereen, Talia Coppola (Shire), Elaine Giftos. Insane, often uproarious story focusing on reactions of youngsters in crisis: a gas kills everyone on Earth over 30 years of age. Disjointed but stay with it.

Gaslight (1944) 114m. *** D: George Cukor. Ingrid Bergman, Charles Boyer, Dame May Whitty, Angela Lansbury, Terry Moore, Halliwell Hobbes. The bloom has worn off this classic chiller about a man trying to drive his wife insane, but lush production, Victorian flavor, and fine performances remain intact.

Gaslight Follies (1955) 110m. *½ D: Joseph E. Levine. Charlie Chaplin, Douglas Fairbanks, Mary Pickford, Will Rogers. If it's possible to take priceless footage of Chaplin and his silent contemporaries and end up with a horrible hodgepodge, this film has done it. A mess.

Gate of Hell (1954-Japanese) C-89m. ***½ D: Teinosuke Kinugasa. Machiko Kyo, Kazuo Hasegawa, Isao Yamagata, Koreya Senda. Stark historical film set in 12th-century Japan of young woman who prefers death to submitting to conqueror of her homeland. Lavishly produced.

Gates of Paris (1958-French) 103m. **½ D: René Clair. Pierre Brasseur, Georges Brassens, Henri Vidal, Dany Carrel. Offbeat story of souse who gains a sense of importance when a criminal seeks refuge in his home.

Gateway (1938) 73m. **½ D: Alfred L. Werker. Don Ameche, Arleen Whelan, Gregory Ratoff, Binnie Barnes, Gilbert Roland, Raymond Walburn, John Carradine. Irish immigrant Whelan pursued by various men during ocean crossing, becomes involved with gangster Roland. Formula story given interesting flavor by Ellis Island background.

Gathering, The (1977) C-100m. TVM D: Randal Kleiser. Edward Asner, Maureen Stapleton, Lawrence Pressman, Stephanie Zimbalist, Bruce Davison, John Randolph. Sentimental Christmas drama of a man who seeks to reunite his shattered family for one final celebration before he dies. Asner is solid as usual, but Stapleton is simply luminous as the wife who had lost him in his drive for success. Above average.

Gathering, Part II, The (1979) C-100m. TVM D: Charles S. Dubin. Maureen Stapleton, Efrem Zimbalist, Jr., Jameson Parker, Bruce Davison, Lawrence Pressman, Gail Strickland. Soapy sequel in which a widow's Christmas reunion with her grown children is marred by the arrival of a new man in her life. Ed Asner's photograph throughout reminds all how glowing the original was. Average.

Gathering of Eagles, A (1963) C-

115m. ***½ D: Delbert Mann. Rock Hudson, Rod Taylor, Mary Peach, Robert Lansing, Barry Sullivan, Henry Silva. Film uses formula of men in training and their off-duty activities to focus on the Strategic Air Command, with Hudson giving very creditable performance.

Gator (1976) C-116m. ** D: Burt Reynolds. Burt Reynolds, Jack Weston, Lauren Hutton, Jerry Reed, Alice Ghostley, Mike Douglas, Dub Taylor. Not-so-hot sequel to WHITE LIGHTNING, on attempts of Justice Dept. agent Weston and moonshiner ex-con Reynolds, to get the goods on corrupt southern politicians. Some good action shots but film is overlong and poorly constructed.

Gauntlet, The (1977) C-109m. *** D: Clint Eastwood. Clint Eastwood, Sondra Locke, Pat Hingle, William Prince, Bill McKinney, Mara Corday. Eastwood stars as a none-too-clever cop escorting hooker Locke to trial; corrupt officials are determined to stop them, whatever the cost. Exciting at times, though its credibility factor is low.

Gay Adventure, The (1953-British) 87m. *** D: Gordon Parry. Burgess Meredith, Jean-Pierre Aumont, Paul Valenska, Kathleen Harrison. Interestingly done yarn of trio of men on a train theorizing about pretty girl sitting across from them.

Gay Bride, The (1934) 80m. ** D: Jack Conway. Carole Lombard, Chester Morris, ZaSu Pitts, Leo Carrillo, Nat Pendleton. Unsatisfying blend of comedy and melodrama with gold-digging Lombard hitching herself to succession of gangsters.

Gay Desperado, The (1936) 85m. *** D: Rouben Mamoulian. Nino Martini, Ida Lupino, Leo Carrillo, Harold Huber, Mischa Auer, James Blakely, Stanley Fields. Entertaining musical spoof, with Carrillo's cutthroats holding heiress Lupino prisoner. Song: "The World Is Mine Tonight."

Gay Divorcee, The (1934) 107m. ***½ D: Mark Sandrich. Fred Astaire, Ginger Rogers, Alice Brady, Edward Everett Horton, Erik Rhodes, Betty Grable. Top Astaire-Rogers froth with usual needless plot and unusual musical numbers, including Oscar-winning "Continental," "Night and Day." Rhodes is memorable as would-be co-respondent in divorce case.

Gay Falcon, The (1941) 67m. D:

Irving Reis. George Sanders, Wendy Barrie, Allen Jenkins, Anne Hunter, Gladys Cooper. SEE: Falcon series.

Gay Purr-ee (1963) C-86m. **½ D: Abe Levitow. Animated cartoon with the voices of Judy Garland, Robert Goulet, Red Buttons, Hermione Gingold, Paul Frees, Morey Amsterdam. Stylish cartoon from UPA studio, too sophisticated in many ways for kiddies. Adults will enjoy Garland and Goulet singing fairly good songs; broader characters played by others will attract youngsters.

Gay Lady, The (1949-British) C-91m. **½ D: Brian Desmond Hurst. Jean Kent, James Donald, Hugh Sinclair, Bill Owen. Well-produced period drama of theater girl who marries nobility and becomes a celebrity; saucy presentation. Retitled: TROTTIE TRUE.

Gay Sisters, The (1942) 108m. ** D: Irving Rapper. Barbara Stanwyck, George Brent, Geraldine Fitzgerald, Gig Young, Nancy Coleman, Donald Crisp, Gene Lockhart, Anne Revere. Stanwyck secretly marries Brent to gain inheritance money in thin soaper, immensely aided by Fitzgerald and Coleman as her two sisters.

Gazebo, The (1959) 100m. *** D: George Marshall. Glenn Ford, Debbie Reynolds, Carl Reiner, Doro Merande, John McGiver, Mabel Albertson. Off-beat comedy involving murder and a backyard gazebo that covers up crime. Character actors McGiver and Merande wrap this up, but stars are competent.

Geisha Boy, The (1958) C-98m. **½ D: Frank Tashlin. Jerry Lewis, Marie McDonald, Sessue Hayakawa, Nobu McCarthy. Jerry, an inept magician, travels to the Far East, with disastrous consequences. Imaginative visual gags highspot this comedy.

Gemini Man (1976) C-100m. TVM D: Alan Levi. Ben Murphy, Katherine Crawford, Richard Dysart, Dana Elcar, Paul Shenar, Cheryl Miller. H. G. Wells' *The Invisible Man* recycled with Murphy as daredevil secret agent whose transient invisibility (result of technological accident) makes him the bane of various saboteurs. Predictable spy show with fantasy element, later a short-lived TV series. Below average. Retitled CODE NAME: MINUS ONE.

Gene Krupa Story, The (1959) 101m. **½ D: Don Weis. Sal Mineo, Susan

Kohner, James Darren, Susan Oliver, Yvonne Craig, Lawrence Dobkin, Red Nichols, Buddy Lester. Hackneyed version of great drummer's life, his ups and downs, and his siege of dope addiction.

General, The (1927) 74m. ***½ D: Buster Keaton. Buster Keaton, Marion Mack, Glen Cavender, Jim Farley, Joseph Keaton. One of Keaton's best silent features, setting comedy against true Civil War story of stolen train, Union spies. Not as fanciful as other Keaton films, but beautifully done; Disney did same story in 1956 as THE GREAT LOCOMOTIVE CHASE.

General Della Rovere (1960-Italian) 129m. ***½ D: Roberto Rossellini. Vittorio De Sica, Hannes Messemer, Sandra Milo, Giovanna Ralli, Mary Greco, Linda Veras, Anne Vernon. Brilliantly acted account of De Sica forced to impersonate Axis general, with the role and situation going to his head; slowly paced but well-executed study.

General Died at Dawn, The (1936) 97m. ***½ D: Lewis Milestone. Gary Cooper, Madeleine Carroll, Akim Tamiroff, Dudley Digges, Porter Hall, William Frawley. Fine, atmospheric drama of Oriental intrigue, with mercenary Cooper falling in love with spy Carroll while battling evil warlord Tamiroff. Author John O'-Hara has cameo as reporter on train.

Generation (1969) C-104m. ** D: George Schaefer. David Janssen, Kim Darby, Carl Reiner, Peter Duel, Andrew Prine, James Coco, Sam Waterston. Darby helps otherwise dreary comedy based on Broadway play about just-married couple who infuriate the girl's father when husband plans to deliver their soon-to-arrive baby himself; plays like a TV sit-com.

Genesis II (1973) C-97m. TVM D: John Llewellyn Moxey. Alex Cord, Mariette Hartley, Lynn Marta, Percy Rodrigues, Harvey Jason, Ted Cassidy. Disappointing sci-fi adventure. Cord is unique survivor of 20th-century holocaust as earth divides into two rival factions. Created by "Star Trek's" Gene Roddenberry, but owes a great deal to "Flash Gordon." Average.

Genevieve (1954-British) C-86m. ***½ D: Henry Cornelius. John Gregson, Dinah Sheridan, Kenneth More, Kay Kendall. High-grade comedy rising above slapstick in tale of cross-country race between two couples in old-roadster cars.

Genghis Khan (1965) C-124m. **½ D: Henry Levin. Omar Sharif, Stephen Boyd, James Mason, Eli Wallach, Francoise Dorleac, Telly Savalas, Robert Morley, Yvonne Mitchell, Woody Strode. Laughable epic with gross miscasting and juvenile script, loosely based on legend of Chinese leader. No sweep or spectacle, but radiant Dorleac and earnest Sharif.

Gentle Annie (1944) 80m. ** D: Andrew Marton. Donna Reed, Marjorie Main, Harry Morgan, James Craig, Barton MacLane. Main vehicle about female outlaw with heart of gold.

Gentle Art of Murder SEE: **Crime Does Not Pay**

Gentle Giant (1967) C-93m. *** D: James Neilson. Dennis Weaver, Vera Miles, Clint Howard, Ralph Meeker, Huntz Hall. Feature film which hatched TV series GENTLE BEN is appealing children's story of boy and his pet bear.

Gentle Gunman, The (1952-British) 86m. *** D: Basil Dearden. Dirk Bogarde, John Mills, Elizabeth Sellars, Robert Beatty. Unpretentious actioner of Irish revolution and enthusiast whose attempt to prove his pariotism backfires.

Gentle Rain, The (1966) C-110m. **½ D: Burt Balaban. Christopher George, Lynda Day, Fay Spain, Maria Helena Diaz, Lon Clark. Frigid N.Y. woman goes to Rio de Janeiro, falls for draughtsman who has been mute ever since he failed to save life of his former girlfriend in car crash. Fair drama, may have some mild nudity cut for TV.

Gentle Touch, The (1955-British) C-86m. ** D: Pat Jackson. George Baker, Belinda Lee. Delphi Lawrence, Adrienne Corri, Diana Wynyard. Good cast, tame script—narrative of nurses' workday problems.

Gentleman After Dark (1942) 77m. ** D: Edwin L. Marin. Brian Donlevy, Miriam Hopkins, Preston Foster, Harold Huber. Hodgepodge yarn of man escaping prison to redeem honor of his daughter by killing his shady wife; good cast stifled by sloppy script. Remake of FORGOTTEN FACES.

Gentleman at Heart, A (1942) 66m. **½ D: Ray McCarey. Cesar Romero, Carole Landis, Milton Berle, J. Carrol Naish, Richard Derr.

Modest little comedy about bookie Romero discovering there's money in art forgery.

Gentleman Jim (1942) 104m. ***½ D: Raoul Walsh. Errol Flynn, Alexis Smith, Jack Carson, Alan Hale, Minor Watson, Ward Bond, Arthur Shields. Sassy biography of polished boxer Jim Corbett in fight game's early days. Flynn is dynamic in title role, supported by colorful cast.

Gentleman's Agreement (1947) 118m. *** D: Elia Kazan. Gregory Peck, Dorothy McGuire, John Garfield, Celeste Holm, Anne Revere, June Havoc, Albert Dekker, Jane Wyatt, Dean Stockwell. Sincere adaptation of Laura Z. Hobson's novel of writer (Peck) pretending to be Jewish, discovering rampant anti-Semitism. Holm won Supporting Actress Oscar as chic but lonely fashion editor. Then-daring approach to subject matter is tame now.

Gentlemen Marry Brunettes (1955) C-97m. ** D: Richard Sale. Jane Russell, Jeanne Crain, Alan Young, Rudy Vallee, Scott Brady. Anita Loos' follow-up to GENTLEMEN PREFER BLONDES has Russell and Crain, two sisters in show biz in Paris, trying to avoid romances. Not up to original.

Gentlemen Prefer Blondes (1953) C-91m. **½ D: Howard Hawks. Jane Russell, Marilyn Monroe, Charles Coburn, Tommy Noonan, George Winslow. Pleasant musicomedy from Anita Loos' tale of two girls from Little Rock making good in Paris. Gals are knockouts, but plot drags. Song: "Diamonds Are a Girl's Best Friend."

George Raft Story, The (1961) 106m. **½ D: Joseph M. Newman. Ray Danton, Jayne Mansfield, Barbara Nichols, Julie London, Neville Brand, Frank Gorshin. Danton is good in title role of fast-moving account of Raft's rise from Broadway dancer to top Hollywood star. How much is true, who can say?

George Washington Slept Here (1942) 93m. **½ D: William Keighley. Jack Benny, Ann Sheridan, Charles Coburn, Hattie McDaniel, Percy Kilbride, Franklin Pangborn. Brittle but dated comedy of N.Y.C. couple moving to the country and a dilapidated house. Benny plays himself smoothly, Sheridan is good straight-woman to the wacky, predictable turmoil.

George White's Scandals (1934) 80m. **½ D: George White, Thornton Freeland, Harry Lachman. Rudy Vallee, Jimmy Durante, Alice Faye, Adrienne Ames, Gregory Ratoff, Cliff Edwards, Dixie Dunbar, Gertrude Michael, George White. Idiotic backstage romance plot propels entertaining, expensive musical; Faye, in film debut, sings "Oh, You Nasty Man," one of several big production numbers.

George White's Scandals (1935) 83m. ** D: George White. Alice Faye, James Dunn, Ned Sparks, Lyda Roberti, Cliff Edwards, Arline Judge, Eleanor Powell, George White, Benny Rubin. Tired show biz story of producer White seeing talented Alice in small-town show, bringing her (and her pals) to N.Y.C., where success poses problems. Story, songs all routine, but good cast gives it some life; Powell's dancing film debut.

George White's Scandals (1945) 95m. ** D: Felix E. Feist. Joan Davis, Jack Haley, Phillip Terry, Martha Holliday, Jane Greer. Mild musical heightened by Davis' zany antics, involving the usual show biz clichés. Slapstick saves hackneyed plot.

Georgia, Georgia (1972) C-91m. **½ D: Stig Bjorkman. Diana Sands, Dirk Benedict, Minnie Gentry. Black singer's involvement with white photographer and some American defectors. Interesting but uneven.

Georgy Girl (1966-British) 100m. ***½ D: Silvio Narizzano. Lynn Redgrave, James Mason, Alan Bates, Charlotte Rampling, Bill Owen, Claire Kelly. Delightful, adult British comedy of modern-day morals, with Redgrave as ugly-duckling Georgy, Mason as the wealthy, aging married man who wants her for his mistress. Entire cast is excellent, with Rampling scoring as Georgy's bitchy roommate.

Geronimo (1939) 89m. ** D: Paul H. Sloane. Preston Foster, Ellen Drew, Andy Devine, Gene Lockhart, Ralph Morgan, Marjorie Gateson, Chief Thundercloud. Run-of-the-mill Western marred by overuse of stock footage and bad process shots to simulate outdoor scenes. Lockhart getting just desserts is best item in trivial Indian vs. cavalry contest. Remake of LIVES OF A BENGAL LANCER.

Geronimo (1962) C-101m. **½ D: Arnold Laven. Chuck Connors, Kamala Devi, Ross Martin, Adam West, Pat Conway, Larry Dobkin.

Exciting Indians-on-the-warpath, with Connors satisfactory in title role.

Gervaise (1956-French) 116m. *** D: Rene Clement. Maria Schell, Francois Perier, Suzy Delair, Armand Mestral. Splendidly acted version of Emile Zola tale of Schell struggling to keep her family going but finally succumbing to tawdry life of her drunken husband.

Get Carter (1971-British) C-112m. *** D: Mike Hodges. Michael Caine, Ian Hendry, Britt Ekland, John Osborne, Tom Beckley, George Sewell. Lean, tough action melodrama with Caine as small-time gangster investigating his brother's death; good work by Caine, vivid seediness captured by writer-director Hodges. Remade one year later with black cast as HIT MAN.

Get Christie Love! (1974) C-100m. TVM D: William A. Graham. Teresa Graves, Harry Guardino, Louise Sorel, Paul Stevens, Andy Romano, Debbie Dozier. Shapely female cop goes undercover to crack a huge drug empire. Dorothy Uhnak's detective novel was the source, the later police woman series was the result. Lots of action. Average.

Get Hep to Love (1944) 71m. *½ D: Charles Lamont. Gloria Jean, Donald O'Connor, Jane Frazee, Robert Paige. Weak musical with precocious musical personality Jean running away to find happier home and singing career.

Get Out of Town (1962) 62m. ** D: Charles Davis. Douglas Wilson, Jeanne Baird, Marilyn O'Connor, Tony Louis. Contrived account of ex-gangster returned home to locate his brother's killer.

Get Out Your Handkerchiefs (1978-French-Belgian) C-109m. ***½ D: Bertrand Blier. Gerard Depardieu, Patrick Dewaere, Carol Laure, Riton, Michel Serreault, Eleonore Hirt. Disarming film about a man who will do almost anything to keep his sexually frustrated wife happy; highly unconventional. Oscar winner for Best Foreign Film.

Get to Know Your Rabbit (1973) C-91m. **½ D: Brian DePalma. Tom Smothers, John Astin, Suzanne Zenor, Samantha Jones, Allen Garfield, Katharine Ross, Orson Welles. Offbeat comedy was barely released, and heavily tampered with at that; starts with great premise of Smothers dropping out of establishment life to become tap-dancing magician, then loses itself along the way. Still

has some inventive moments, funny ideas.

Get Yourself A College Girl (1964) C-88m. *½ D: Sidney Miller. Chad Everett, Nancy Sinatra, Mary Ann Mobley, Dave Clark Five, The Animals. Songwriter who is undergraduate at a staid girls' school falls in love with a music publisher at resort hotel. Strictly for dropouts.

Getaway, The (1972) C-122m. *** D: Sam Peckinpah. Steve McQueen, Ali MacGraw, Ben Johnson, Sally Struthers, Al Lettieri, Slim Pickens. Exciting, enjoyable film built around a chase. Bank robber McQueen and wife MacGraw take it on the lam when robbery goes haywire. Many fine vignettes, including hair-raising episode on garbage truck.

Getting Away From It All (1971) C-74m. TVM D: Lee Philips. Gary Collins, E. J. Peaker, Barbara Feldon, Larry Hagman, Jim Backus, Burgess Meredith. Two middle-aged, middle-class couples sell houses, quit work to find idyllic "back to nature" existence, decide to return to civilization. Contrived and infuriating, with unconvincing performances. Below average.

Getting Gertie's Garter (1945) 72m. **½ D: Allan Dwan. Dennis O'Keefe, Marie McDonald, Barry Sullivan, Binnie Barnes, Sheila Ryan, J. Carrol Naish, Jerome Cowan. Similar to UP IN MABEL'S ROOM, a funny little comedy of O'Keefe trying to retrieve embarrassing memento without wife's knowledge.

Getting Married (1978) C-100m. TVM D: Steven Hilliard Stern. Richard Thomas, Bess Armstrong, Van Johnson, Katherine Helmond, Mark Harmon, Fabian, Dena Dietrich. Romantic fluff set in a TV newsroom manned by lots of attractive people. Average.

Getting Straight (1970) C-124m. **½ D: Richard Rush. Elliott Gould, Candice Bergen, Jeff Corey, Max Julien, Cecil Kellaway. Already a period piece, but central issue of graduate student Gould choosing between academic double-talk and his beliefs remains relevant. Gould's personality propels glossy film.

Ghidrah, the Three-Headed Monster (1965-Japanese) C-85m. **½ D: Inoshiro Honda. Yosuke Natsuki, Yuriko Hoshi, Hiroshi Koizumi, Emi Ito. Ingenious scripter works three favorites into plot (Mothra, Rodan,

Godzilla). Trio champions people of Tokyo against rampaging title fiend.

Ghost and Mr. Chicken, The (1966) C-90m. **½ D: Alan Rafkin. Don Knotts, Joan Staley, Skip Homeier, Dick Sargent, Reta Shaw. Featherweight comedy with Knotts a would-be reporter seeking the big scoop.

Ghost and Mrs. Muir, The (1947) 104m. ***½ D: Joseph L. Mankiewicz. Gene Tierney, Rex Harrison, George Sanders, Edna Best, Vanessa Brown, Anna Lee, Robert Coote, Natalie Wood. A lonely widow is romanced by the ghost of a sea captain in her "haunted" New England cottage. Charming, beautifully made fantasy, a distant cousin to the later TV sitcom of the same name.

Ghost Breakers (1940) 82m. *** D: George Marshall. Bob Hope, Paulette Goddard, Richard Carlson, Paul Lukas, Anthony Quinn, Willie Best. More plot than usual in a Hope film as Bob and Paulette investigate eerie Cuban mansion which she's inherited. Some real chills as well as laughs in this first-rate film.

Ghost Catchers (1944) 67m. *** D: Edward F. Cline. Ole Olsen, Chic Johnson, Gloria Jean, Martha O'-Driscoll, Leo Carrillo, Andy Devine, Walter Catlett, Lon Chaney Jr. One of Olsen and Johnson's wackiest comedies, with duo as nightclub owners who help Southern colonel Catlett and his daughters, who have just moved into haunted house.

Ghost Chasers (1951) 69m. D: William Beaudine. Leo Gorcey, Huntz Hall, Jan Kayne, Bernard Gorcey, Lloyd Corrigan, Billy Benedict. SEE: Bowery Boys series.

Ghost Comes Home, The (1940) 79m. ** D: William Thiele. Frank Morgan, Billie Burke, Ann Rutherford, John Shelton, Reginald Owen, Donald Meek. Morgan, thought dead, returns to family which has been doing fine without him; cast does its best with fair material.

Ghost Diver (1957) 76m. *½ D: Richard Einfeld, Merrill G. White. James Craig, Audrey Totter, Nico Minardos, Lowell Brown. Programmer of underwater search for treasure city.

Ghost Goes West, The (1936-British) 78m. *** D: René Clair. Robert Donat, Eugene Pallette, Jean Parker, Elsa Lanchester. Pallette purchases castle haunted by ghost of fast-living ancestor of hero Donat in amusing fantasy-comedy penned by Robert Sherwood.

Ghost In the Invisible Bikini (1966) C-82m. ** D: Don Weis. Tommy Kirk, Aron Kincaid, Nancy Sinatra, Harvey Lembeck, Claudia Martin, Francis X. Bushman, Boris Karloff, Patsy Kelly, Basil Rathbone, Benny Rubin. Sluggish blend of macabre and beach boys provides uneven mixture; veteran greats like Rathbone wasting their time.

Ghost of Dragstrip Hollow, The (1959) 65m. BOMB D: William Hole, Jr. Jody Fair, Martin Braddock, Russ Bender, Leon Tyler, Elaine DuPont. Trite mixture of hot rod gangs and haunted house formulas, with most uneven results.

Ghost of Flight 401, The (1978) C-100m. TVM D: Steven Hilliard Stern. Ernest Borgnine, Gary Lockwood, Tina Chen, Kim Basinger, Eugene Roche, Beverly Todd. Supernatural mystery about the ghost (Borgnine) of the pilot of the plane that crashed in Florida Everglades around Christmas of 1972 and the legend of its presence in the cockpit of later flights. Taken from John C. Fuller's intriguing book. Average.

Ghost of Frankenstein, The (1942) 68m. **½ D: Erle C. Kenton. Sir Cedric Hardwicke, Lon Chaney, Lionel Atwill, Ralph Bellamy, Bela Lugosi, Evelyn Ankers. Sequel to SON OF FRANKENSTEIN. Ygor returns to foul professor's plan to replace monster's brain with that of educated man. Good cast manages to save stale plot.

Ghost of the China Sea (1958) 79m. ** D: Fred F. Sears. David Brian, Lynn Bernay, Jonathan Haze, Norman Wright. Brian et al flee Japanese invasion of Philippines; nothing new here.

Ghost of Zorro (1959) 69m. ** D: Fred C. Brannon. Clayton Moore, Pamela Blake, Roy Barcroft, George J. Lewis, Eugene Roth. Feature version of 1949 serial is a confusingly edited account of descendant of Zorro adopting same guise to combat outlaws destroying telegraph lines.

Ghost Ship (1952-British) 69m. ** D: Vernon Sewell. Dermot Walsh, Hazel Court, Hugh Burden, John Robinson, Joss Ambler. Small-budget yarn about young couple purchasing a haunted yacht.

Ghost Ship, The (1943) 69m. *** D: Mark Robson. Richard Dix, Russell Wade, Edith Barrett, Ben Bard,

Lawrence Tierney. Offbeat Val Lewton melodrama about young man who signs on merchant ship run by power-crazy captain (Dix) who's obsessed with "authority." Absorbing mood-piece with unfortunately abrupt conclusion.

Ghosts—Italian Style (1969-Italian) C-92m. ** D: Renato Castellani. Sophia Loren, Vittorio Gassman, Mario Adorf, Margaret Lee, Aldo Guiffre, Francisco Tensi. Newlyweds Loren and Gassman move into haunted house. Weak vehicle for engaging stars.

Ghosts of Rome (1961-Italian) C-105m. **½ D: Antonio Pietrangeli. Marcello Mastroianni, Belinda Lee, Sandra Milo, Vittorio Gassman, Franca Marzi. Scatterbrain antics of oddball characters inhabiting rundown house soon to be demolished, with prospects of finding new quarters frightening them all.

Ghosts on the Loose (1943) 65m. D: William Beaudine. Leo Gorcey, Huntz Hall, Bobby Jordan, Bela Lugosi, Ava Gardner, Rick Vallin, Minerva Urecal. SEE: Bowery Boys series.

Ghoul, The (1933-British) 73m. *** D: T. Hayes Hunter. Boris Karloff, Cedric Hardwicke, Ernest Thesiger, Dorothy Hyson, Anthony Bushell, Ralph Richardson. England's answer to Hollywood's horror films: Karloff is buried with jewel from Egyptian tomb, threatens to come back to life if anyone tries to steal it. Slow going until Karloff's resurrection; then it really hums. Remade as 1962 comedy NO PLACE LIKE HOMICIDE!

Giant (1956) C-201m. **** D: George Stevens. Elizabeth Taylor, Rock Hudson, James Dean, Carroll Baker, Jane Withers, Chill Wills, Mercedes McCambridge, Dennis Hopper, Sal Mineo, Rod Taylor. Near-legendary epic based on Edna Ferber's novel about two generations of Texans holds up beautifully when not broken up into two nights on TV. Hudson's best performance, close to Taylor's best, and Dean's last film. Stevens won an Oscar for his direction.

Giant Behemoth, The (1959-British) 80m. ** D: Eugene Lourie. Gene Evans, Andre Morell, John Turner, Leigh Madison, Jack MacGowran. Title monster on the rampage; OK, no more.

Giant Claw, The (1957) 76m. *½ D: Fred F. Sears. Jeff Morrow, Mara Corday, Morris Ankrum, Edgar Barrier. Lack of decent special effects ruins the running battle between colossal bird and fighter jets. Big bird is laughable.

Giant Gila Monster, The (1959) 74m. ** D: Ray Kellogg. Don Sullivan, Lisa Simone, Shug Fisher, Jerry Cortwright, Beverly Thurman, Don Flourney, Pat Simmons. Typical horror drama of lurking creature causing series of strange murders.

Giant of Metropolis, The (1962-Italian) C-82m. ** D: Umberto Scarpelli. Mitchell Gordon, Roldano Lupi, Bella Cortez, Liana Orfei. Uneven mixture of costumer and sci-fi with a dash of sadism, set in 10,000 B.C.

Giant Spider Invasion, The (1975) C-82m. BOMB D: Bill Rebane. Steve Brodie, Barbara Hale, Leslie Parrish, Alan Hale, Robert Easton, Bill Williams. Veteran cast can't do much for this tacky horror opus filmed in Wisconsin.

Giants of Thessaly, The (1960-Italian) C-86m. ** D: Riccardo Freda. Roland Carey, Ziva Rodann, Massimo Girotti, Alberto Farnese. Episodic sword-and-sandal account of Jason (Carey) and Orpheus (Girotti) seeking golden fleece, with expected clashes with monsters, evil women, etc.

Gideon of Scotland Yard (1958-British) C-91m. *½ D: John Ford. Jack Hawkins, Dianne Foster, Cyril Cusack, Andrew Ray, James Hayter, Ronald Howard, Anna Massey, Anna Lee. A typical day in the life of a Scotland Yard inspector; Hawkins is likable but the film is unbelievably dull. A surprising dud from director Ford. British title: GIDEON'S DAY.

Gideon's Day SEE: **Gideon of Scotland Yard**

Gidget (1959) C-95m. **½ D: Paul Wendkos. Sandra Dee, James Darren, Cliff Robertson, Arthur O'Connell, Joby Baker, Yvonne Craig, Doug McClure. First and best of series has spirited Dee in title role, with Robertson most engaging as beach bum who almost wins her away from surfer Darren.

Gidget Gets Married (1972) C-73m. TVM D: E. W. Swackhamer. Michael Burns, Monie Ellis, Don Ameche, Joan Bennett, Macdonald Carey, Corrine Camacho. Boring situation comedy (minus laugh track) featuring Burns and Ellis as young newlyweds in Glossop, Maryland; he an engineer, she a dissatisfied housewife. Tame humor, unbelievable plot. Below average.

Gidget Goes Hawaiian (1961) C-102m. ** D: Paul Wendkos. James Darren, Michael Callan, Deborah Walley, Carl Reiner, Peggy Cass, Eddie Foy, Jr. Inane follow-up has teenager off to the Islands, with embarrassing results for all.

Gidget Goes to Rome (1963) C-101m. ** D: Paul Wendkos. Cindy Carol, James Darren, Jessie Royce Landis, Cesare Danova, Jeff Donnell. Mild follow-up has fetching teen-ager off to Italy involved in predictable romancing.

Gidget Grows Up (1970) C-75m. TVM D: James Sheldon. Karen Valentine, Edward Mulhare, Paul Petersen, Nina Foch, Paul Lynde, Warner Anderson, Bob Cummings. Moving to New York, after short return to surfing life, Gidget takes job as U.N. guide, becomes involved in "first adult love affair." Romance never more unbelievable, nor dialogue more naive. Only Lynde has good material. Average.

Gift, The (1979) C-100m. TVM D: Don Taylor. Glenn Ford, Gary Frank, Julie Harris, Allison Argo, Maggie Cooper, Tom Clancy. Poignant period piece (the '50s) about a sailor who returns to his old Brooklyn neighborhood on Christmas leave. Ford's eye-opening performance as his hard-drinking, Irish-brogued, peg-legged father makes this one shine. Based on Pete Hamill's novel. Above average.

Gift of Love, The (1958) C-105m. ** D: Jean Negulesco. Lauren Bacall, Robert Stack, Evelyn Rudie, Lorne Greene, Anne Seymour. If you could put up with SENTIMENTAL JOURNEY you might bear this remake, which isn't even as good. Bacall dies but returns to earth as guiding spirit for her husband and daughter.

Gift of Love, The (1978) C-100m. TVM D: Don Chaffey. Marie Osmond, Timothy Bottoms, Bethel Leslie, June Lockhart, Donald Moffat, David Wayne, James Woods. Sticky-sweet adaptation of O. Henry's *The Gift of the Magi* as a costume vehicle for Marie Osmond's acting debut. Veteran David Wayne is on hand to narrate in the guise of O. Henry. Average.

Gigantis, the Fire Monster (1959-Japanese) 78m. ** D: Motoyoshi,

Hugo Grimaldi. Hiroshi Koizumi, Setsuko Makayama, Mindru Chiaki. Two giant monsters battle to destroy each other and the world. First sequel to GODZILLA, renamed.

Gigi (1958) C-116m. **** D: Vincente Minnelli. Leslie Caron, Maurice Chevalier, Louis Jourdan, Hermione Gingold, Jacques Bergerac, Eva Gabor. Charming turn-of-the-century Parisian musical based on Colette's story of a French girl who becomes a lady. Entire cast is fine; Chevalier and Gingold memorable in their duet, "I Remember It Well." Songs include: "Thank Heaven For Little Girls," "Gigi." Winner of many Academy Awards; a must.

Gigot (1962) C-104m. *** D: Gene Kelly. Jackie Gleason, Katherine Kath, Gabrielle Dorziat, Albert Remy, Yvonne Constant. Sentimental, well-acted tale of a deaf mute (Gleason) and a young girl in Paris. Simple film, well done; Gleason is excellent.

Gilda (1946) 110m. *** D: Charles Vidor. Rita Hayworth, Glenn Ford, George Macready, Joseph Calleia, Steven Geray. Highly charged story of emotional triangle—mysterious South American casino owner Macready, his new man-Friday Ford, and Macready's alluring wife (Hayworth)—unfortunately cops out with silly resolution. Rita has never been sexier, especially when singing "Put the Blame on Mame."

Gilded Lily, The (1935) 80m. *** D: Wesley Ruggles. Claudette Colbert, Fred MacMurray, Ray Milland, C. Aubrey Smith, Edward Craven. Colbert has to choose between aristocratic Milland and down-to-earth MacMurray. Fine romantic fluff.

Gildersleeve's Ghost (1944) 64m. ** D: Gordon Douglas. Harold Peary, Marion Martin, Richard LeGrand, Amelita Ward. Programmer entry in the Great Gildersleeve series, involving mixture of spooks and gangsters, with predictable results.

Gimme Shelter (1970) C-91m. **** D: David Maysles. Rolling Stones, Jefferson Airplane, Melvin Belli. Outstanding documentary of the Rolling Stones and the famous Altamont Speedway free concert that resulted in chaos and murder. Chilling, beautifully handled; worth watching.

Ginger in the Morning (1973) C-89m. **½ D: Gordon Wiles. Sissy Spacek, Monte Markham, Mark Miller, Susan Oliver, Slim Pickens.

So-so romantic comedy about a lonely salesman who picks up a comely hitchhiker. He's attracted to her young, fresh independence; she's drawn to his old-fashioned romanticism.

Girl, a Guy, and a Gob, A (1941) 91m. ** D: Richard Jones. George Murphy, Lucille Ball, Edmond O'Brien, Henry Travers, Franklin Pangborn, George Cleveland. Not very original triangle love story, with Ball undecided between Murphy and O'Brien.

Girl Called Hatter Fox, The (1977) C-100m. TVM D: George Schaefer. Ronny Cox, Joanelle Romero, Conchata Ferrell, John Durren, Donald Hotten. Drama pitting medical science against witchcraft in the attempt to salvage a teen-aged Indian girl's life. Average.

Girl Can't Help It, The (1956) C-99m. ** D: Frank Tashlin. Tom Ewell, Jayne Mansfield, Edmond O'Brien, Julie London. One-joke film about press agent Ewell trying to hype gangster's girlfriend (Mansfield) to stardom. Some good Tashlin sight gags, but more rock 'n' roll (with many guest stars) than satire.

Girl Crazy (1943) 99m. ***½ D: Norman Taurog. Mickey Rooney, Judy Garland, Gil Stratton, Robert E. Strickland, "Rags" Ragland, June Allyson, Nancy Walker, Guy Kibbee. Rooney sent to small Southwestern school to forget girls, but he meets Garland and that's that. Great Gershwin score! Remade as WHEN THE BOYS MEET THE GIRLS.

Girl from Jones Beach, The (1949) 78m. ** D: Peter Godfrey. Ronald Reagan, Virginia Mayo, Eddie Bracken, Dona Drake, Henry Travers, Jerome Cowan. Nice little film of Reagan meeting his dream girl at the beach.

Girl from Manhattan, The (1948) 81m. ** D: Alfred E. Green. Dorothy Lamour, George Montgomery, Charles Laughton, Hugh Herbert, Constance Collier, Ernest Truex. Weary tale of big-city gal (Lamour) returning home, finding love there.

Girl from Missouri, The (1934) 75m. *** D: Jack Conway. Jean Harlow, Lionel Barrymore, Franchot Tone, Lewis Stone, Patsy Kelly, Alan Mowbray. Delightful fluff about good-girl Harlow trying to win a millionaire without sacrificing her integrity. Wisecracking Kelly as her girlfriend is a treat.

Girl from Petrovka, The (1974) C-104m. ** D: Robert Ellis Miller. Goldie Hawn, Hal Holbrook, Anthony Hopkins, Gregoire Aslan, Anton Dolin. Old-fashioned comedy-drama about a bittersweet affair between American correspondent Holbrook and Russian Hawn. Filmed in Vienna and Hollywood, doubling for Moscow.

Girl from Scotland Yard, The (1937) 62m. *½ D: Robert Vignola. Karen Morley, Robert Baldwin, Katherine Alexander, Eduardo Ciannelli, Milli Monti. Escapist story of girl trying to track down mysterious madman with destruction ray is poorly handled; not nearly as much fun as it might have been.

Girl from 10th Avenue (1935) 69m. ** D: Alfred E. Green. Bette Davis, Ian Hunter, Colin Clive, Alison Skipworth, John Eldredge. Old soap rehashed nicely with Hunter marrying Davis during drunken spree, regretting it when ex-wife wants him back. Acting saves it.

Girl-Getters, The (1966-British) 79m. *** D: Michael Winner. Oliver Reed, Jane Merrow, Barbara Ferris, Julia Foster. Realistic study of hoodlum youths at British seaside resort, their prankish games and romances; intelligently portrayed. Retitled: THE SYSTEM.

Girl Happy (1965) C-96m. **½ D: Boris Sagal. Elvis Presley, Shelley Fabares, Harold J. Stone, Gary Crosby, Joby Baker, Nita Talbot, Mary Ann Mobley, Chris Noel, Jackie Coogan. Formula Presley musical with tiresome plot of Elvis in Fort Lauderdale chaperoning Fabares, daughter of Chicago mobster.

Girl He Left Behind, The (1956) 103m. **½ D: David Butler. Tab Hunter, Natalie Wood, Jessie Royce Landis, Jim Backus. Reminiscent of SEE HERE PRIVATE HARGROVE, without any of the warmth or humor. Hunter is new recruit in Army.

Girl Hunters, The (1963) 103m. **½ D: Roy Rowland. Mickey Spillane, Lloyd Nolan, Shirley Eaton, Hy Gardner. Spillane plays his own fictional detective Mike Hammer in this rugged murder mystery, filmed in England.

Girl in a Million, A (1946-British) 81m. ** D: Francis Searle. Joan Greenwood, Hugh Williams, Yvonne Owen, Edward Lexy, Jane Hylton, Michael Hordern. Sometimes wacky comedy focusing on deaf mute who uses her charm to reform several cantankerous gentlemen.

Girl in Black Stockings, The (1957) 73m. ** D: Howard W. Koch. Lex Barker, Anne Bancroft, Mamie Van Doren, Ron Randell, Marie Windsor. Minor murder mystery with some nice touches and good performances; set at chic Utah resort.

Girl in Every Port, A (1928) 62m. **½ D: Howard Hawks. Victor McLaglen, Marcia Casajuana, Natalie Joyce, Louise Brooks, Robert Armstrong. Broad, brawling comedy about two swaggering sailors and their amorous rivalries around the world. Dated, to say the least, but enthusiasm still puts it over. Remade as GOLDIE.

Girl in Every Port, A (1952) 86m. ** D: Chester Erskine. Groucho Marx, William Bendix, Marie Wilson, Don DeFore, Gene Lockhart. Nonsense of two gobs who hide a racehorse aboard ship. Great grouping of comedians wasted.

Girl in His Pocket (1957-French) 82m. **½ D: Pierre Kast. Jean Marais, Agnes Laurent, Genevieve Page. Strange tale of scientist who invents shrinking formula, changing his romantic life with unforetold complications.

Girl in Room 13 (1961) C-97m. *½ D: Richard Cunha. Brian Donlevy, Andrea Bayard, Elizabeth Howard, Victor Merinow, John Herbert. Lowgrade private eye story set in Brazil, with Donlevy tracking down a murder and counterfeit gang.

Girl in the Empty Grave, The (1977) C-100m. TVM D: Lou Antonio. Andy Griffith, James Cromwell, Mitzi Hoag, Claude Earl Jones, Jonathan Banks, Robert F. Simon. Small-town sheriff Griffith (again) doggedly pursues a murderer. Below average.

Girl in the Kremlin, The (1957) 81m. ** D: Russell Birdwell. Lex Barker, Zsa Zsa Gabor, Jeffrey Stone, William Schallert. Espionage hokum involving Gabor in dual role as twins, one of whom is Stalin's mistress.

Girl in the Painting (1948-British) 89m. *** D: Terence Fisher. Mai Zetterling, Robert Beatty, Guy Rolfe, Herbert Lom, Patrick Holt. Intriguing drama of serviceman involved in strange case of amnesiac girl seeking her lost past in Germany. Retitled: PORTRAIT FROM LIFE.

Girl in the Park, The SEE: **Sanctuary of Fear.**

Girl in the Red Velvet Swing, The (1955) C-109m. **½ D: Richard Fleischer. Ray Milland, Joan Collins, Farley Granger, Cornelia Otis Skinner, Glenda Farrell, Luther Adler. Glossy, fictionalized account of Evelyn Nesbit-Stanford White-Harry Thaw escapade of early 20th-century N.Y.C. Showgirl falls in love with prominent architect, which upsets mentally disturbed millionaire.

Girl in the Woods (1958) 71m. *½ D: Tom Gries. Forrest Tucker, Maggie Hayes, Barton MacLane, Diana Francis. Lumbering tale of lumbermen's lives.

Girl in White, The (1952) 93m. ** D: John Sturges. June Allyson, Arthur Kennedy, Gary Merrill, Mildred Dunnock, James Arness. Clichéd account of first female doctor in N.Y.C. Allyson tries to perk up lifeless script.

Girl Most Likely, The (1957) C-98m. *** D: Mitchell Leisen. Jane Powell, Cliff Robertson, Keith Andes, Tommy Noonan, Una Merkel. Musical remake of TOM, DICK AND HARRY comes off as bright, cheerful entertainment. A girl must decide which one of trio she'll wed; Kaye Ballard does very well in supporting role. Choreography by Gower Champion.

Girl Most Likely to . . . , The (1973) C-74m. TVM D: Lee Philips. Stockard Channing, Edward Asner, Warren Berlinger, Suzanne Zenor, Larry Wilcox, Jim Backus, Fred Grandy, Carl Ballantine. Clever comedy coscripted by comedienne Joan Rivers has ugly duckling made beautiful by plastic surgery, seeking revenge on men who made life miserable for her. Above average.

Girl Named Sooner, A (1975) C-115m. TVM D: Delbert Mann. Lee Remick, Richard Crenna, Don Murray, Anne Francis, Cloris Leachman, Susan Deer. Eight-year-old girl, raised by eccentric old woman in backwoods of Indiana, becomes the ward of a childless couple whose lives she enriches. Touching family entertainment, adapted from Suzanne Clauser's acclaimed 1972 novel, and well nigh stolen by Cloris Leachman as Old Mam, the feisty crone. Above average.

Girl Named Tamiko, A (1962) C-110m. **½ D: John Sturges. Laurence Harvey, France Nuyen, Martha Hyer, Gary Merrill, Michael Wilding, Miyoshi Umeki, Lee Patrick. Overblown soaper set in Tokyo. Harvey charms Hyer into proposing marriage so he can get U.S. citizenship. Nuyen is sweet Oriental whom Harvey really loves.

Girl Next Door, The (1953) C-92m. **½ D: Richard Sale. Dan Dailey, June Haver, Dennis Day, Cara Williams, Natalie Schafer. Pleasing musical of singing star Haver moving to new home and falling in love with neighbor Dailey, a cartoonist.

Girl of the Golden West, The (1938) 120m. **½ D: Robert Z. Leonard. Jeanette MacDonald, Nelson Eddy, Walter Pidgeon, Leo Carrillo, Buddy Ebsen, Leonard Penn. Oft-produced tale of love affair of good-girl MacDonald and bandit Eddy, with tuneful Gus Kahn-Sigmund Romberg score that didn't produce any hits.

Girl of the Night (1960) 93m. **½ D: Joseph Cates. Anne Francis, Lloyd Nolan, Kay Medford, John Kerr. Francis gives a vivid performance as prostitute undergoing psychoanalysis.

Girl on the Bridge (1951) 77m. BOMB D: Hugo Haas. Hugo Haas, Beverly Michaels, Robert Dane, Johnny Close, Anthony Jochim. Trashy study of Michaels as a so-called femme fatale and her effect on the men in her life.

Girl on the Late, Late Show, The (1974) C-78m. TVM D: Gary Nelson. Don Murray, Laraine Stephens, Bert Convy, Yvonne DeCarlo, Gloria Grahame, Van Johnson, Ralph Meeker, Cameron Mitchell, Mary Ann Mobley, Joe Santos, John Ireland, Walter Pidgeon, Sherry Jackson. Movieland murders follow TV producer Murray in his search for 50s film queen Grahame, who mysteriously vanished at the height of her career. Nostalgia buffs will find this a feast while detective nuts will spot the baddie early on. Average.

Girl Rush, The (1955) C-85m. **½ D: Robert Pirosh. Rosalind Russell, Fernando Lamas, Eddie Albert, Gloria DeHaven, Marion Lorne. Russell inherits a Las Vegas casino and determines to make it go, romanced by Lamas. Minor musical numbers and forced gaiety are all too evident.

Girl Shy (1924) 65m. *** D: Fred Newmeyer, Sam Taylor. Harold Lloyd, Jobyna Ralston, Richard Daniels, Carlton Griffin. Enjoyable Lloyd vehicle mixes comedy and sentiment, with a chase finale.

Harold is a small-town boy who's petrified of women but writes book on lovemaking secrets! Fantasy scenes of his love life mark highlight. Edited for TV.

Girl Trouble (1942) 82m. ** D: Harold Schuster. Don Ameche, Joan Bennett, Billie Burke, Frank Craven, Vivian Blaine. Pleasant frou-frou with Ameche and Bennett involved in business and romancing, with fine support from the adept scatterbrain Burke.

Girl Who Came Gift-Wrapped, The (1974) C-78m. TVM D: Bruce Bilson. Karen Valentine, Richard Long, Tom Bosley, Farrah Fawcett, Dave Madden, Louise Sorel. Country cutie Karen comes to big city looking for husband and setting her sights on bachelor Long, decides to give herself to him as a birthday present. Comic tale with large doses of leering sex and suggestive poses, but Karen looks great bikini clad. Average.

Girl Who Couldn't Say No, The (1970-Italian) C-83m. ** D: Franco Brusati. Virna Lisi, George Segal, Lila Kedrova, Akim Tamiroff, Paola Pitagora, Felicity Mason. Square Segal and childhood friend Lisi fall for each other, but just can't maintain a permanent relationship; mild comedy.

Girl Who Had Everything, The (1953) 69m. **½ D: Richard Thorpe. Elizabeth Taylor, Fernando Lamas, William Powell, Gig Young. Murky melodrama with top cast. Girl falls in love with criminal client of her attorney father. Remake of A FREE SOUL.

Girl Who Knew Too Much (1969) C-96m. ** D: Francis D. Lyon. Adam West, Nancy Kwan, Nehemiah Persoff, Robert Alda. Adventurer who is hired to find the killer of a syndicate boss discovers Communist plot to infiltrate organized crime.

Girl With a Suitcase (1960-Italian) 96m. ***½ D: Valerio Zurlini. Claudia Cardinale, Jacques Perrin, Luciana Angelillo, Corrado Pani. Impressive Italian film of devoted but shady girl Cardinale following her ex-lover to Parma, only to fall in love with his adolescent brother. Confusing at times, but extremely well acted, worth seeing.

Girlfriends (1978) C-88m. *** D: Claudia Weill. Melanie Mayron, Anita Skinner, Eli Wallach, Christopher Guest, Bob Balaban, Viveca

Lindfors, Mike Kellin. A young woman tries to cope with love, a career, and personal independence after her roommate/girlfriend leaves to get married. Mayron's warm, winning performance helps likable but uneven film over its rough spots.

Girls' Dormitory (1936) 66m. **½ D: Irving Cummings. Herbert Marshall, Ruth Chatterton, Simone Simon, Constance Collier, J. Edward Bromberg, Dixie Dunbar, Tyrone Power. Fairly standard tale of girl's infatuation for school head Marshall spotlights newcomer Simon, who does quite well, and young leading man Power in featured role.

Girls! Girls! Girls! (1962) C-106m. **½ D: Norman Taurog. Elvis Presley, Stella Stevens, Laurel Goodwin, Jeremy Slate, Benson Fong, Robert Strauss, Ginny Tiu. Presley is chased by a mass of girls and can't decide which one he prefers.

Girls in Prison (1956) 87m. *½ D: Edward L. Cahn. Richard Denning, Joan Taylor, Adele Jergens, Helen Gilbert, Lance Fuller, Jane Darwell, Raymond Hatton, Mae Marsh. Tawdry study of prison life with usual female stereotype prisoners.

Girls in the Night (1953) 83m. ** D: Jack Arnold. Joyce Holden, Glenda Farrell, Harvey Lembeck, Patricia Hardy, Jaclynne Greene. Compact account of young people seeking to better their lives, blighted by N.Y.C. tenement existence.

Girls in the Office, The (1979) C-100m. TVM D: Ted Post. Susan St. James, Barbara Eden, Tony Roberts, David Wayne, Penny Peyser, Joe Penny. Four women working in a Houston department store must choose between love and success in this standard romantic comedy. Average.

Girls of Huntington House, The (1973) C-73m. TVM D: Alf Kjellin. Shirley Jones, Mercedes McCambridge, Sissy Spacek, William Windom, Pamela Sue Martin, Darrell Larson. Weak melodrama takes place in school for unwed mothers where unmarried teacher finds herself drawn more and more to students' individual problems. Conceived from kids' point of view, but unmemorable dialogue and anticlimax will help film be quickly forgotten. Average.

Girls of Pleasure Island, The (1953) C-95m. **½ D: F. Hugh Herbert, Alvin Ganzer. Leo Genn, Don Taylor, Gene Barry, Elsa Lanchester, Audrey Dalton. Unfunny comedy involving Genn and brood of daughters combating swarm of G.I.s who establish a base on their island.

Girls of the Night (1959-French) 114m. **½ D: Maurice Cloche. Georges Marchal, Nicole Berger, Claus Holm, Kay Fischer, Gil Vidal. Sensible telling of plight of group of prostitutes, and clergyman who tries to help them.

Girls on the Beach, The (1965) C-80m. *½ D: William N. Witney. Martin West, Noreen Corcoran, Peter Brooks, Michael Love, Alan Jardin, Lana Wood, The Beach Boys, Lesley Gore. Three coeds meet three groovy guys when they spend the summer at sorority beach house; Beach Boys sing two tunes in predictable comedy.

Girls on the Loose (1958) 78m. ** D: Paul Henreid. Mara Corday, Lita Milan, Barbara Bostock, Mark Richman. Drama unfolds account of Corday heading robbery gang, and eventual downfall.

Girls Town (1959) 92m. *½ D: Charles Haas. Mamie Van Doren, Mel Torme, Paul Anka, Ray Anthony, Maggie Hayes, Cathy Crosby, Gigi Perreau, Gloria Talbott, Jim Mitchum. Bad girl accused of crime sent to correctional institution, finds real culprit. Fails at being a sensational-type film. Retitled: INNOCENT AND THE DAMNED.

Git (1965) C-90m. *½ D: Ellis Kadison. Jack Chaplain, Heather North, Leslie Bradley, Richard Webb. Young boy and daughter of dog-breeder widower set out to train a renegade setter. Woof woof.

Give a Girl a Break (1953) C-82m. **½ D: Stanley Donen. Marge and Gower Champion, Debbie Reynolds, Kurt Kasznar, Larry Keating. Bland musical of a show producer, his emotional star, and the girl seeking the lead role.

Give 'Em Hell (1954-French) 90m. **½ D: John Berry. Eddie Constantine, Mai Britt, Jean Danet, Jean Carmet. If not taken seriously, amusing gangster yarn of Johnny Jordan (Constantine), with usual amount of fisticuffs and gunplay.

Give 'em Hell, Harry! (1975) C-102m. *** D: Steve Binder. Straight reproduction of James Whitmore's one-man stage triumph as Harry Truman, covering high points in both the political and personal life of our 33rd President.

Give Me a Sailor (1938) 80m. **½ D: Elliott Nugent. Martha Raye, Bob Hope, Betty Grable, Jack Whiting, Clarence Kolb, J. C. Nugent. Fast-moving musicomedy of sailor Hope's complicated love affairs. Raye is always worth watching; undistinguished score.

Give Me Your Heart (1936) 87m. **½ D: Archie Mayo. Kay Francis, George Brent, Roland Young, Patric Knowles, Henry Stephenson, Frieda Inescort, Helen Flint. Involved romance of Francis, the English lord she loves, his crippled wife, Kay's baby, and her protector. All is peg for chic Francis-Brent repartee and glamorous wardrobe changes.

Give My Regards to Broadway (1948) C-89m. ** D: Lloyd Bacon. Dan Dailey, Charles Winninger, Nancy Guild, Charles Ruggles, Fay Bainter. Blah musical of old-time vaudevillian Winninger refusing to admit that the family act should break up.

Give Us Wings (1940) 62m. D: Charles Lamont. Billy Halop, Huntz Hall, Gabriel Dell, Anne Gwynne, Bernard Punsley, Bobby Jordan, Wallace Ford, Victor Jory. SEE: Bowery Boys series.

Gizmo (1977) C/B&W-77m. **½ D: Howard Smith. Entertaining compilation of film clips on 20th-century "inventors" and their often outlandish contraptions. Good fun, though it can't quite sustain feature-length film.

Gladiator, The (1938) 70m. **½ D: Edward Sedgwick. Joe E. Brown, Man Mountain Dean, June Travis, Dickie Moore, Lucien Littlefield. Timid boy (Brown) takes serum, becomes all-star hero at college. Simple, sincere, enjoyable.

Glass Alibi, The (1946) 70m. ** D: W. Lee Wilder. Paul Kelly, Douglas Fowley, Anne Gwynne, Maris Wrixon, Jack Conrad. Satisfactory drama involving con-man who thinks marrying a dying heiress is a sure bet, till he discovers she's recovering.

Glass Bottom Boat, The (1966) C-110m. *** D: Frank Tashlin. Doris Day, Rod Taylor, Arthur Godfrey, Paul Lynde, Eric Fleming, Alice Pearce, Ellen Corby. Better paced than usual Day nonsense, with Doris trying to steal Taylor's business secrets. Godfrey is Day's father, skip-

per of title vehicle. Lots of slapstick in this one.

Glass Cage, The (1964) 78m. *½ D: Antonio Santean. John Hoyt, Elisha Cook, Arline Sax, Robert Keljan. Programmer of burglar shot in self-defense and romance developing between police investigator and suspect. Retitled: DEN OF DOOM.

Glass House, The (1972) C-73m. TVM D: Tom Gries. Vic Morrow, Clu Gulager, Billy Dee Williams, Dean Jagger, Alan Alda. Gripping account of what it's like to be in state prison, adapted from story by Truman Capote. Location-shot, with many real-life prisoners in supporting cast. Above average.

Glass Houses (1972) C-90m. ** D: Alexander Singer. Jennifer O'Neill, Bernard Barrow, Deirdre Lenihan, Ann Summers, Phillip Pine, Lloyd Kino. Downgrade drama about infidelity and incestuous desire is mildly interesting in a lurid kind of way; O'Neill's first film, but released after RIO LOBO and SUMMER OF '42.

Glass Key, The (1935) 80m. *** D: Frank Tuttle. George Raft, Claire Dodd, Edward Arnold, Rosalind Keith, Ray Milland, Guinn Williams. Solid Dashiell Hammett story about politician Arnold getting involved in mysterious murder, Raft trying to dig out the facts. Drags during second half, but still quite good. Remade in 1942.

Glass Key, The (1942) 85m. ***½ D: Stuart Heisler. Veronica Lake, Alan Ladd, Brian Donlevy, William Bendix, Bonita Granville, Richard Denning. Fast-moving remake of 1935 film with wardheeler Donlevy accused of murder, henchman Ladd bailing him out. Lake fine as mysterious love interest, Bendix effective as brutal bodyguard.

Glass Menagerie, The (1950) 107m. *** D: Irving Rapper. Jane Wyman, Kirk Douglas, Gertrude Lawrence, Arthur Kennedy. More notable for its cast and intention than results. Slow-moving version of Tennessee Williams' drama of lame girl, her faded Southern belle mother, and idealistic brother, all living in their own fragile dream worlds.

Glass Mountain, The (1950-British) 94m. *** D: Henry Cass. Valentina Cortese, Michael Denison, Dulcie Gray, Sebastian Shaw. Beautifully-made film of a British composer who writes an opera, inspired by majestic Italian Alps. A treat for music-lovers, with many singers from La Scala appearing in opera sequence.

Glass Slipper, The (1955) C-94m. **½ D: Charles Walters. Leslie Caron, Michael Wilding, Keenan Wynn, Estelle Winwood, Elsa Lanchester, Amanda Blake. Silky musical of Cinderella story with talky plot bogging down lilting fantasy dance and song sequences.

Glass Sphinx, The (1967-Italian-Spanish) C-91m. *½ D: Luigi Scattini. Robert Taylor, Anita Ekberg, Gianna Serra, Jack Stuart, Angel Del Pozo, Jose Truchado. World-famous archeologist Taylor on trail of tomb of glass sphinx containing magic elixir; foreign agents have similar idea. Confusing and forgettable.

Glass Tomb, The (1955-British) 59m. ** D: Montgomery Tully. John Ireland, Honor Blackman, Geoffrey Keen, Eric Pohlmann, Sydney Tafler, Liam Redmond, Sam Kydd. Bizarre carnival backgrounds give this typical murder tale some spice.

Glass Tower, The (1957-German) 92m. **½ D: Harold Braun. Lilli Palmer, O. E. Hasse, Peter Van Eyck, Brigitte Horney, Hannes Messemer. Interesting study of overly jealous husband keeping beautiful wife Palmer a prisoner so she won't be tempted by other men; well acted.

Glass Wall, The (1953) 80m. ** D: Maxwell Shane. Vittorio Gassman, Gloria Grahame, Ann Robinson, Jerry Paris, Kathleen Freeman. Drama of refugee Gassman who illegally came to N.Y.C. and, rather than accept deportation, goes on the lam.

Glass Web, The (1953) 81m. *** D: Jack Arnold. Edward G. Robinson, John Forsythe, Marcia Henderson, Richard Denning. Robinson is fine as criminal research authority for TV mystery show, who commits murder utilized as basis for one of the programs.

Glenn Miller Story, The (1954) C-116m. *** D: Anthony Mann. James Stewart, June Allyson, Charles Drake, George Tobias, Harry Morgan, Frances Langford, Louis Armstrong, Gene Krupa. Marvelous music is most of this film, sentimental story the rest. All of Miller's hits played, many guest performers.

Stewart most convincing as popular bandleader.

Global Affair, A (1964) 84m. **½ D: Jack Arnold. Bob Hope, Yvonne De Carlo, Robert Sterling, John Mc-Giver, Lilo Pulver. Unwitty Hope vehicle has Bob in charge of a baby found at U.N., with female representative from each nation demanding the child.

Glory (1956) C-100m. ** D: David Butler. Margaret O'Brien, Walter Brennan, Charlotte Greenwood, John Lupton. Bland horseracing story, with grown-up O'Brien as gal who owns champion horse.

Glory Alley (1952) 79m. **½ D: Raoul Walsh. Ralph Meeker, Leslie Caron, Gilbert Roland, Louis Armstrong, John McIntire. Just before the championship bout, boxer Meeker quits the fight game. Series of flashbacks tells his intriguing story. New Orleans backgrounds allow for some good musical interludes.

Glory Boy SEE: **My Old Man's Place**

Glory Brigade, The (1953) 82m. ** D: Robert D. Webb. Victor Mature, Alexander Scourby, Lee Marvin, Richard Egan, Alvy Moore. Passable Korean War actioner with good cast.

Glory Guys, The (1965) C-112m. ** D: Arnold Laven. Tom Tryon, Harve Presnell, Michael Anderson, Jr., Senta Berger, James Caan, Slim Pickens. Lumbering Western of life and love in the Old West; cliché-ridden instead of bullet-packing action.

Gnome-Mobile, The (1967) C-90m. *** D: Robert Stevenson. Walter Brennan, Matthew Garber, Karen Dotrice, Richard Deacon, Tom Lowell, Sean McClory, Ed Wynn. Crusty businessman Brennan, his niece and nephew discover gnomes in redwood forest, try to protect them from freak-show entrepreneur, and land-destroyers. Lively Disney fantasy outing with top special effects, broad comedy highlights.

Go Ask Alice (1972) C-73m. TVM D: John Korty. Jamie Smith-Jackson, Andy Griffith, William Shatner, Julie Adams. Strong performances, semi-documentary style combine in study of high school student's battle with drug addiction. Above average.

Go For Broke! (1951) 92m. *** D: Robert Pirosh. Van Johnson, Gianna Maria Canale, Warner Anderson, Lane Nakana, George Miki. WW2 story with a twist. Johnson is commander of special U.S. squad made up of American-Japanese team.

Go Into Your Dance (1935) 89m. **½ D: Archie Mayo. Al Jolson, Ruby Keeler, Glenda Farrell, Helen Morgan, Patsy Kelly, Benny Rubin, Phil Regan, Barton MacLane. Flimsy plot allows Jolson and Keeler to sing and dance through seven listenable tunes in OK musical; highlight: "About A Quarter To Nine."

Go, Man, Go (1954) 82m. **½ D: James Wong Howe. Dane Clark, Pat Breslin, Sidney Poitier, Edmond Ryan. Imaginative telling of the formation of Harlem Globetrotters and their rise as famed basketball team.

Go Naked In the World (1961) C-103m. ** D: Ranald MacDougall. Gina Lollobrigida, Anthony Franciosa, Ernest Borgnine, Luana Patten. Turgid melodrama badly cast. Easy-loving Lollobrigida hooks Franciosa, much to his father's (Borgnine's) dismay.

Go Tell the Spartans (1978) C-114m. **½ D: Ted Post. Burt Lancaster, Craig Wasson, Jonathan Goldsmith, Marc Singer, Joe Unger. OK Vietnam war picture, set in early '64, was underrated by some critics, overrated by others. Burt shines as "advisory group" commander who is already starting to have his doubts about the war.

Go West (1940) 81m. ** D: Edward Buzzell. Groucho, Chico, and Harpo Marx, John Carroll, Diana Lewis, Walter Woolf King, Robert Barrat. Big letdown from Marxes, until hilarious train-ride climax. Occasional bits sparkle through humdrum script.

Go West, Young Girl (1978) C-74m. TVM D: Alan J. Levi. Karen Valentine, Sandra Will, Stuart Whitman, Richard Jaeckel, David Dukes, John Payne. Lighthearted Western pits a peppery gal from back East and a cavalry officer's widow agin gamblers, bounty hunters, and leering lawmen as they go in search of Billy the Kid. Average.

Go West, Young Man (1936) 82m. *** D: Henry Hathaway. Mae West, Randolph Scott, Warren William, Alice Brady, Elizabeth Patterson, Lyle Talbot, Isabel Jewell. Movie queen Mae is stuck in the sticks, but passes time nicely with handsome farm-boy Scott. Not top-notch West, but still fun.

Go-Between, The (1971-British) C-116m. ***½ D: Joseph Losey. Julie Christie, Alan Bates, Dominic Guard, Margaret Leighton, Michael Redgrave. Beguiling film from L. P. Hartley story of boy who becomes messenger for love notes between aristocratic Christie and farmer Bates. Lushly filmed, full of nuances, fine performances. Script by Harold Pinter. A mood piece, not for all tastes.

God Forgives, I Don't (1969-Italian-Spanish) C-101m. *½ D: Giuseppe Colizzi. Terence Hill, Bud Spencer, Frank Wolff, Gina Rovere, Jose Manuel Martin. In spite of colorful title, this spaghetti Western about an attempt to find some buried loot is like a thousand others.

God Is My Co-Pilot (1945) 90m. **½ D: Robert Florey. Dennis Morgan, Raymond Massey, Andrea King, Alan Hale, Dane Clark, John Ridgely, Stanley Ridges, Donald Woods. Well-intentioned drama of WW2 pilots bogs down in clichés, still has many good scenes.

God Is My Partner (1957) 80m. ** D: William F. Claxton. Walter Brennan, John Hoyt, Marion Ross, Jesse White, Nancy Kulp. Sincere but hokey little film of old-timer who feels he owes a spiritual obligation which he can redeem by giving away his money.

God Told Me To SEE: Demon

God's Country (1946) C-62m. ** D: Robert E. Tansey. Buster Keaton, Robert Lowery, Helen Gilbert, William Farnum. Chief virtue of this flabby Western is Keaton prancing around trying to recreate some of his better pantomime skits.

God's Country and the Woman (1936) C-80m. ** D: William Keighley. George Brent, Beverly Roberts, Barton MacLane, Robert Barrat, Alan Hale, Joseph King. Routine tale of Brent and Roberts running rival lumber companies; color is only asset.

God's Little Acre (1958) 110m. *** D: Anthony Mann. Robert Ryan, Tina Louise, Aldo Ray, Buddy Hackett, Jack Lord, Fay Spain, Michael Landon. Effective Americana of Georgia farmers as seen by Erskine Caldwell, focusing on amusing as well as lusty, violent aspects of their existence.

Godchild, The (1974) C-78. TVM D: John Badham. Jack Palance, Jack Warden, Keith Carradine, Ed Lauter, Jose Perez, Fionnuala Flanagan,

Bill McKinney. Seventh version (at least) of THE THREE GODFATHERS, with three Civil War prisoners, fleeing both Confederates and Apaches, risking freedom to become guardians of the baby they deliver for a dying woman in the desert. Peter B. Kyne's Western classic starkly recreated for TV but John Ford's 1948 movie still casts a mighty long shadow. Average.

Goddess, The (1958) 105m. *** D: John Cromwell. Kim Stanley, Lloyd Bridges, Steven Hill, Betty Lou Holland, Patty Duke. Absorbing biography of an ambitious girl seeking Hollywood fame. Author Paddy Chayefsky based his story somewhat on Marilyn Monroe; the film captures tragedy of the real-life Monroe with fine acting by Stanley and Bridges, among others.

Goddess of Love (1960-Italian) C-68m. *½ D: W. Tourjansky. Belinda Lee, Jacques Sernas, Massimo Girotti, Maria Frau. Drivel concerning country girl who becomes prostitute when her lover is killed. Set in ancient times.

Godfather, The (1972) C-175m. ***½ D: Francis Ford Coppola. Marlon Brando, Al Pacino, James Caan, Richard Castellano, Robert Duvall, Sterling Hayden, John Marley, Richard Conte, Diane Keaton, Al Martino. The 1970s answer to GONE WITH THE WIND, from Mario Puzo's novel on life and times of Mafia patriarch Don Corleone (Brando) and family. A film of epic proportions, masterfully done, but based on pulp fiction, its classic status derives from enormous popularity and fine filmmaking, not from any inherent greatness. Brando won, and refused, Oscar.

Godfather, Part II, The (1974) C-200m. **** D: Francis Ford Coppola. Al Pacino, Robert Duvall, Diane Keaton, Robert DeNiro, John Cazale, Talia Shire, Lee Strasberg, Michael V. Gazzo. They said it couldn't be done, but writer-director Coppola made a sequel to THE GODFATHER that's just as compelling. This one contrasts the life of melancholy "don" (Pacino) with early days of his father (DeNiro) as an immigrant in N.Y. Winner of seven Oscars including Best Picture, Best Screenplay, Best Supporting Actor (DeNiro).

Godspell (1973) C-103m. **½ D: David Greene. Victor Garber, David Haskell, Jerry Sroka, Lynne Thigpen, Katie Hanley, Robin Lamont. Sophomoric updating of Jesus' life with young bouncy disciples following their leader around modern-day New York. Energetic; brilliant use of N.Y.C. locations, good score by Stephen Schwartz including "Day by Day," but hollow and unmoving.

Godzilla SEE: **Godzilla, King of the Monsters**

Godzilla, King of the Monsters (1956-Japanese) 80m. **½ D: Terry Morse, Inoshiro Honda. Raymond Burr, Takashi Shimura, Momoko Kochi, Akira Takarada, Akihiko Hirata. Special effects are the star of this film. Retitled: GODZILLA.

Godzilla vs. Megalon (1976-Japanese) C-80m. *½ D: Jun Fukuda. Katsuhiko Sasaki, Hiroyuki Kawase, Yutaka Hayashi, Robert Dunham. Series sinks to new low as Godzilla teams up with robot superhero against Megalon and his pal Gigan. Incredibly cheap, with lots of unintended laughs. A hoho from Toho.

Godzilla vs. the Smog Monster (1972-Japanese) C-87m. *½ D: Yoshimitu Banno. Akira Yamauchi, Hiroyuki Kawase, Toshio Shibaki. Godzilla freelances as do-gooder in ridding Japan of monster born of waste, fed on factory fumes and smog. Dubbed and daffy.

Godzilla vs. the Thing (1964-Japanese) C-90m. **½ D: Inoshiro Honda. Okira Takarada, Yuriko Hiroshi Koisumi, Yu Fujiki. Vivid special effects highlight battle between reptile Godzilla and Mothra, giant moth.

Godzilla's Revenge (1969-Japanese) C-69m. **½ D: Inoshiro Honda. Kenji Sahara, Tomonori Yazaki, Machiko Naka, Sachio Sakai, Chotaro Togin, Yoshibumi Tujima. Fantasy of child daydreaming of adventures with Godzilla's son and other monsters. Good juvenile sci-fi.

Gog (1954) C-85m. ** D: Herbert L. Strock. Richard Egan, Constance Dowling, Herbert Marshall, John Wengraf. Machine-made brain is utilized to sabotage missile station; OK sci-fi.

Goin' Cocoanuts (1978) C-96m. ** D: Howard Morris. Donny and Marie Osmond, Herbert Edelman, Kenneth Mars, Chrystin Sinclaire, Ted Cassidy, Marc Lawrence, Khigh Dhiegh, Harold Sakata. Bad guys go after Marie's necklace in Hawaii, but the villainy, like the story, is strictly kindergarten level. Kids may go for it . . . and of course, Donny and Marie get to sing.

Goin' Down the Road (1970-Canadian) C-90m. ***½ D: Donald Shebib. Doug McGrath, Paul Bradley, Jayne Eastwood, Cayle Chernin, Nicole Morin. Award-winning film made for less than $100,000 puts all but a few Hollywood blockbusters to shame; modest tale of two unlucky Nova Scotians and their near-tragic finish packs a memorable punch. McGrath and Bradley are remarkably good.

Goin' South (1978) C-109m. *** D: Jack Nicholson. Jack Nicholson, Mary Steenburgen, Christopher Lloyd, John Belushi, Veronica Cartwright, Richard Bradford. Amusing Western comedy, not for all tastes, has Nicholson saving himself from lynch mob by marrying a spinster. Steenburgen is refreshingly offbeat and Belushi's disappointingly small role is a real hoot.

Goin' to Town (1935) 74m. *** D: Alexander Hall. Mae West, Paul Cavanagh, Ivan Lebedeff, Marjorie Gateson, Tito Coral. Good West vehicle of dance-hall girl trying to crash society, highlight: Mae doing "Samson and Delilah" scenes.

Going Hollywood (1933) 80m. *** D: Raoul Walsh. Marion Davies, Bing Crosby, Fifi D'Orsay, Stuart Erwin, Ned Sparks, Patsy Kelly. Enjoyable fluff with Davies following crooner Crosby to Hollywood determined to win him away from tempestuous screen star D'Orsay. Patsy Kelly all but steals film from stars. Songs include "Temptation," "We'll Make Hay While the Sun Shines."

Going Home (1971) C-97m. *** D: Herbert B. Leonard. Robert Mitchum, Jan-Michael Vincent, Brenda Vaccaro, Jason Bernard, Sally Kirkland, Josh Mostel. Powerful, if downbeat, study of young man's troubled relationship with his father, who's just been released from prison after serving time for killing his wife.

Going in Style (1979) C-96m. ***½ D: Martin Brest. George Burns, Art Carney, Lee Strasberg, Charles Hallahan, Pamela Payton-Wright. Three retirees in Queens get more than they bargain for when they rob a bank in Manhattan to relieve their boredom. Unexpected gem from a 28-year-old filmmaker is predictably funny but unpredictably moving, with Burns standing out in a terrific cast.

Going My Way (1944) 130m. ***½ D: Leo McCarey. Bing Crosby, Barry Fitzgerald, Rise Stevens, Gene Lockhart, Frank McHugh, James Brown, Jean Heather, Stanley Clements, Carl Switzer, Porter Hall. Multiple-award-winning story of down-to-earth priest (Crosby) winning over aging superior (Fitzgerald) and sidewalk gang of kids. Holds up quite well. Songs: title tune, "Swinging On A Star," "Too-ra-Loo-ra-Loo-ra."

Going Places (1938) 84m. ** D: Ray Enright. Dick Powell, Anita Louise, Allen Jenkins, Ronald Reagan. Nonsensical musical with a variety of songs, steeplechase riding, and obligatory romantic interludes.

Going Steady (1958) 79m. *½ D: Fred F. Sears. Molly Bee, Bill Goodwin, Alan Reed, Jr., Irene Hervey. Uninspired happenings involving secretly married teen-agers and the repercussions when in-laws discover fact.

Gold (1974-British) C-120m. *** D: Peter Hunt. Roger Moore, Susannah York, Ray Milland, Bradford Dillman, John Gielgud. Grand-scale adventure action yarn about plot to control price of gold on world market by destroying South African mine. Moore is stalwart hero. Long but entertaining.

Gold Diggers of 1933 (1933) 96m. ***½ D: Mervyn LeRoy. Joan Blondell, Ruby Keeler, Aline MacMahon, Dick Powell, Guy Kibbee, Warren William, Ned Sparks, Ginger Rogers, Sterling Holloway. Another spectacular Busby Berkeley dance outing in familiar let's produce-a-Broadway-show plot. Highlights: Blondell's "Forgotten Man," Rogers' "We're In The Money," chorus gals' "Shadow Waltz."

Gold Diggers of 1935 (1935) 95m. *** D: Busby Berkeley. Dick Powell, Adolphe Menjou, Gloria Stuart, Alice Brady, Glenda Farrell, Frank McHugh, Winifred Shaw. Big-scale Berkeley musical with stereotypes providing plot line and laughs between fantastic precision production numbers, including "The Words Are In My Heart" and film classic "Lullaby Of Broadway," sung by Wini Shaw.

Gold Diggers of 1937 (1936) 100m. **½ D: Lloyd Bacon. Dick Powell, Joan Blondell, Glenda Farrell, Victor Moore, Lee Dixon, Osgood Perkins. Those gold-diggers won't give up; this time it's a group of insurance salesmen backing a show. Top song: "With Plenty of Money and You."

Gold for the Caesars (1964-French-Italian) C-86m. *½ D: Andre de Toth; Jeffrey Hunter, Mylene Demongeot, Ron Randell, Massimo Giulio Bosetti, Ettore Manni. Still another Roman slave epic starring an American actor who'd look more at home in David and Ricky Nelson's fraternity; this time it's Jeffrey Hunter. Nothing special.

Gold Is Where You Find It (1938) C-90m. **½ D: Michael Curtiz. George Brent, Olivia de Havilland, Claude Rains, Margaret Lindsay, John Litel, Barton MacLane. And gold-rush miners find it on California farmland, starting bitter feud in brisk film, perked by good cast.

Gold of Naples, The (1954-Italian) 107m. *** D: Vittorio De Sica. Sophia Loren, Vittorio De Sica, Toto, Silvana Mangano, Paolo Stoppa. Four vignettes—poignant, perceptive, hilarious in turn: Loren as philandering wife of pizza baker; De Sica as avid card player upstaged by 8-year-old; Toto as Milquetoast family man; Mangano as prostitute involved in unusual marriage.

Gold of the Amazon Women (1979) C-100m. TVM D: Mark L. Lester. Bo Svenson, Anita Ekberg, Donald Pleasence, Richard Romanus, Maggie Jean Smith. Two fortune hunters stumble upon society of modern-day Amazons who follow the pair out of the jungle to downtown Manhattan. Silly B-minus movie stuff that brought '50s screen sex queen Ekberg out of obscurity. Below average.

Gold Raiders (1951) 56m. *½ D: Edward Bernds. George O'Brien, Three Stooges, Sheila Ryan, Clem Bevans, Lyle Talbot. Three Stooges add the only life to this flabby Western, with their usual shenanigans foiling the crooks and saving the day.

Gold Rush, The (1925) 82m. **** D: Charlie Chaplin. Charlie Chaplin, Georgia Hale, Mack Swain, Tom Murray. Immortal Chaplin classic, pitting Little Tramp against Yukon,

affections of dance-hall girl, whims of a burly prospector. Dance of the rolls, eating leather shoe, cabin tottering over cliff—all highlights of wonderful, timeless comedy.

Gold Rush Maisie (1940) 82m. D: Edwin L. Marin. Ann Sothern, Lee Bowman, Slim Summerville, Virginia Weidler, Mary Nash, John F. Hamilton. SEE: Maisie series.

Goldbergs, The (1950) 83m. **½ D: Walter Hart. Gertrude Berg, Philip Loeb, Eli Mintz, Betty Walker, David Opatoshu, Barbara Rush. Warm, human story of famous radio-TV Bronx family and their everyday problems. Retitled: MOLLY

Golden Age of Comedy, The (1957) 78m. **** D: Compiled by Robert Youngson. Laurel and Hardy, Carole Lombard, Ben Turpin, Will Rogers, Harry Langdon. Peerless grouping of some of silent comedy's greatest moments, including Rogers' classic spoofs of silent stars, and ending with Laurel and Hardy's legendary pie fight from BATTLE OF THE CENTURY.

Golden Arrow, The (1936) 68m. **½ D: Alfred E. Green. Bette Davis, George Brent, Eugene Pallette, Dick Foran, Carol Hughes, Catherine Doucet. Pleasant but featherweight comedy of "heiress" Davis and down-to-earth reporter Brent establishing marriage of convenience.

Golden Blade, The (1953) C-81m. **½ D: Nathan Juran. Rock Hudson, Piper Laurie, Gene Evans, Kathleen Hughes. OK swashbuckler with Hudson going through gymnastics in Bagdad to save Laurie and help virtue triumph; strictly formula production.

Golden Boy (1939) 99m. **½ D: Rouben Mamoulian. Barbara Stanwyck, Adolphe Menjou, William Holden, Lee J. Cobb, Joseph Calleia, Sam Levene, Don Beddoe. Clifford Odets' narrative of music-minded boy who becomes prizefighter dates badly; Holden, in starring debut, still good, but Cobb blows the works with his Henry Armetta imitation.

Golden Coach, The (1952-Italian) C-105m. ** D: Jean Renoir. Anna Magnani, Odoardo Spadaro, Nada Fiorelli, Dante, Duncan Lamont. Puzzling yarn set in 18th-century South America, revolving around fiery actress Magnani and her assorted love affairs.

Golden Earrings (1947) 95m. **½

D: Mitchell Leisen. Ray Milland, Marlene Dietrich, Murvyn Vye, Dennis Hoey, Quentin Reynolds. Incredible yet enjoyable escapism set in WW2 Europe has Milland joining gypsy Dietrich for espionage work; Dietrich most convincing. Gypsy Vye sings title song.

Golden Eye, The (1948) 69m. **D:** William Beaudine. Roland Winters, Victor Sen Yung, Tim Ryan, Wanda McKay, Bruce Kellogg, Evelyn Brent. SEE: **Charlie Chan** series.

Golden Gate Murders, The (1979) C-100m. TVM **D:** Walter Grauman. David Janssen, Susannah York, Tim O'Connor, Lloyd Bochner, Kim Hunter, Richard O'Brien. Gruff detective and pretty nun join forces to prove that a priest who fell from the Golden Gate Bridge was murdered and not a suicide. Accept initial premise of the cop/nun relationship, ignore the terrible studio recreation of the San Francisco landmark and you might have some fun. Being shown theatrically as SPECTER ON THE BRIDGE. Average.

Golden Girl (1951) C-108m. **½ **D:** Lloyd Bacon. Mitzi Gaynor, Dale Robertson, Dennis Day, Una Merkel. Undistinguished musical set in California during Civil War, with Gaynor portraying entertainer Lotta Crabtree who's intrigued by Rebel officer Robertson.

Golden Gloves Story, The (1950) 76m. *½ **D:** Felix E. Feist. James Dunn, Dewey Martin, Kay Westfall, Kevin O'Morrison. Ordinary fare dealing with two boxers and the effects of the pending championship bout on their lives.

Golden Hands of Kurigal (1949) 100m. *½ **D:** Fred C. Brannon. Kirk Alyn, Rosemary La Planche, Roy Barcroft, Carol Forman, James Dale, Bruce Edwards. Spotty Republic cliff-hanger of federal agent (Alyn) rescuing missing archaeologist held by arch-criminal. Reedited movie serial: FEDERAL AGENTS VS. UNDERWORLD INC.

Golden Hawk, The (1952) C-83m. ** **D:** Sidney Salkow. Rhonda Fleming, Sterling Hayden, John Sutton, Raymond Hatton. Frank Yerby's novel of Spanish-English fight against France in 17th century, set in Caribbean seas.

Golden Heist, The SEE: **Inside Out**

Golden Horde, The (1951) C-77m. ** **D:** George Sherman. Ann Blyth, David Farrar, George Macready, Henry Brandon, Richard Egan. Typical Arabian adventure set in 13th century, with Blyth using her brains to outwit invaders of her people's city.

Golden Idol, The (1954) 71m. **D:** Ford Beebe. Johnny Sheffield, Anne Kimbell, Paul Guilfoyle, Smoki Whitfield. SEE: **Bomba the Jungle Boy** series.

Golden Madonna, The (1949-British) 88m. **½ **D:** Ladislas Vajda. Phyllis Calvert, Michael Rennie, Tullio Carminati. Lively romantic yarn of Yankee lass inheriting an Italian villa and, aided by Rennie, seeking to retrieve a holy painting.

Golden Mask, The (1954-British) C-88m. **½ **D:** Jack Lee. Van Heflin, Wanda Hendrix, Eric Portman, Charles Goldner. Intelligent adventure yarn of people seeking fabulous treasure mask in Egyptian desert.

Golden Mistress, The (1954) C-82m. ** **D:** Joel Judge (Abner Biberman). John Agar, Rosemarie Bowe, Abner Biberman, Andre Narcisse. Agar comes to Bowe's rescue in hunting out alleged voodoo killers of her father.

Golden Needles (1974) C-92m. ** **D:** Robert Clouse. Joe Don Baker, Elizabeth Ashley, Jim Kelly, Burgess Meredith, Ann Sothern. Everyone seems out of place in this Hong Kong-L.A. filmed action pic about a scramble for golden statue containing youth-restoring acupuncture needles. Silly. Aka THE CHASE FOR THE GOLDEN NEEDLES.

Golden Rendezvous (1977) C-103m. ** **D:** Ashley Lazarus. Richard Harris, Ann Turkel, David Janssen, Burgess Meredith, John Vernon, Gordon Jackson, Keith Baxter, Dorothy Malone, John Carradine. Attractive cast in pointless Alistair MacLean story of gambling ship held hostage by terrorists.

Golden Salamander, The (1951-British) 96m. *** **D:** Ronald Neame. Trevor Howard, Anouk Aimee, Walter Rilla, Herbert Lom, Wilfrid Hyde-White. Courting a Tunisian girl, Howard becomes involved in gun smuggling; taut actioner.

Golden Voyage of Sinbad, The (1974-British) C-105m. *** **D:** Gordon Hessler. John Phillip Law, Caroline Munro, Tom Baker, Douglas Wilmer, Gregoire Aslan, John Garfield Jr. Delightful rehash of earlier Sinbad adventures that evokes Saturday matinee fare of the 1950s, with Ray Harryhausen's finest "Dynamation" effects: a ship's figurehead comes to life, and a six-armed statue does sword-battle with Sinbad in action highlights. Grand entertainment.

Golden West, The (1932) 74m. **½ D: David Howard. George O'Brien, Janet Chandler, Marion Burns, Arthur Pierson, Onslow Stevens. Solid Zane Grey story of O'Brien leaving town after feud killing, encountering Indians; son, raised as an Indian after father killed in massacre. Good "B+" Western.

Goldengirl (1979) C-104m. ** D: Joseph Sargent. Susan Anton, Curt Jurgens, Robert Culp, Leslie Caron, Harry Guardino, Jessica Walter. Statuesque Anton is more or less turned into a robot so she can become a star in the Olympics. So-so.

Goldfinger (1964-British) C-111m. ***½ D: Guy Hamilton. Sean Connery, Gert Frobe, Honor Blackman, Shirley Eaton, Bernard Lee, Lois Maxwell, Harold Sakata. Entertaining, exciting James Bond adventure, third in the series. Full of ingenious gadgets and nefarious villains, with hair-raising climax. Frobe (Goldfinger) and Sakata (Oddjob) are villains in the classic tradition.

Goldie and the Boxer (1979) C-100m. TVM D: David Miller. O. J. Simpson, Melissa Michaelsen, Vincent Gardenia, Phil Silvers, Madlyn Rhue, Anzanette Chase. Pedestrian tale—fodder for countless B movies of yore—about a struggling fighter and an orphan who adopts him. Below average.

Goldwyn Follies, The (1938) C-120m. *½ D: George Marshall. Adolphe Menjou, Andrea Leeds, Kenny Baker, The Ritz Brothers, Zorina, Helen Jepson, Bobby Clark, Edgar Bergen & Charlie McCarthy. Dreadful hodgepodge as producer Menjou hires Leeds as "Miss Humanity," to judge his movies from average person's point of view. She probably would have skipped this one. Ritz Bros. come off best, while Baker sings "Love Walked In" about thirty times. George Balanchine's ballet a matter of taste.

Good Fellows, The (1943) 70m. ** D: Jo Graham. Cecil Kellaway, Mabel Paige, Helen Walker, James Brown. Pleasant fluff about a man who neglects his family in favor of a beloved fraternal lodge.

Goliath Against the Giants (1961-

Italian) C-90m. *½ D: Guido Malatesta. Brad Harris, Gloria Milland, Fernando Rey, Barbara Carrol. Juvenile cartoon characterizations in this sword-and-sandal, with Harris overcoming sea creatures, Amazons, and his people's enemies.

Goliath and the Barbarians (1960-Italian) C-86m. ** D: Carlo Campogalliani. Steve Reeves, Bruce Cabot, Giulia Rubini, Chelo Alonso, Arturo Dominici, Gino Scotti. Muscleman Reeves comes to the rescue of Italy by holding off rampaging hordes pressing down from the Alps.

Goliath and the Dragon (1960-Italian) C-87m. BOMB D: Vittorio Cottafavi. Mark Forest, Broderick Crawford, Gaby Andre, Leonora Ruffo. Baby-style fantasy costumer with embarrassing performances by all; poor special effects, with Forest challenging villainous Crawford.

Goliath and the Vampires (1964-Italian) C-91m. *½ D: Giacomo Gentilomo. Gordon Scott, Jacques Sernas, Gianna Maria Canale. Cloak-and-sandal nonsense; spotty special effects add only color to film.

Gone Are the Days (1963) 97m. *** D: Nicholas Webster. Ossie Davis, Ruby Dee, Sorrell Booke, Godfrey Cambridge, Alan Alda, Beah Richards. Davis' satiric fable "Purlie Victorious" survives cheap film adaptation, thanks to buoyant performances and basic story: self-appointed preacher schemes to undo a despotic plantation owner, as a symbolic freeing of his people from the ways of the Old South. Alda's film debut.

Gone With the Wind (1939) C-222m. **** D: Victor Fleming. Clark Gable, Vivien Leigh, Leslie Howard, Olivia de Havilland, Thomas Mitchell, Hattie McDaniel, Ona Munson, Ann Rutherford, Evelyn Keyes, Butterfly McQueen. If not the greatest movie ever made, certainly one of the greatest examples of storytelling on film, maintaining interest for nearly four hours. Margaret Mitchell's story is, in effect, a Civil War soap opera, focusing on vixenish Southern belle Scarlett O'Hara, brilliantly played by Leigh; she won Oscar, as did the picture, McDaniel, director Fleming, screenwriter Sidney Howard, among many others. Memorable music by Max Steiner in this one-of-a-kind film produced by David O. Selznick.

Good Against Evil (1977) C-78m. TVM D: Paul Wendkos. Dack Rambo, Dan O'Herlihy, Elyssa Davalos, Richard Lynch, John Harkins, Jenny O'Hara, Lelia Goldoni. Itinerant writer falls for woman chosen by satanic cult to bear the devil's child. O'Herlihy has flamboyant role as priest called upon to perform traditional exorcism. Silly supernatural thriller. Below average.

Good Dame (1934) 74m. *½ D: Marion Gering. Fredric March, Sylvia Sidney, Jack LaRue, Helene Chadwick, Noel Francis, Russell Hopton. March and Sidney deserve better than this: tired story of carnival huckster redeemed by the love of a good woman.

Good Day for a Hanging (1958) C-85m. **½ D: Nathan Juran. Fred MacMurray, Maggie Hayes, Robert Vaughn, Denver Pyle. Straightforward account of MacMurray taking over for slain sheriff and bringing in killer, only to find townspeople don't care if murderer is sentenced.

Good Die Young, The (1954-British) 100m. ** D: Lewis Gilbert. Laurence Harvey, Gloria Grahame, Richard Basehart, Stanley Baker, Margaret Leighton. Good cast in standard robbery tale, concentrating on escape attempt.

Good Earth, The (1937) 138m. **** D: Sidney Franklin. Paul Muni, Luise Rainer, Walter Connolly, Charley Grapewin, Jessie Ralph, Tilly Losch, Keye Luke, Harold Huber. Mammoth Pearl Buck Chinese novel recreated in detail, telling story of greed ruining lives of simple farming couple. Rainer won Oscar as the ever-patient wife of Muni; special effects outstanding.

Good Fairy, The (1935) 90m. ***½ D: William Wyler. Margaret Sullavan, Herbert Marshall, Frank Morgan, Reginald Owen, Alan Hale, Beulah Bondi, Cesar Romero. Sparkling romantic comedy, adapted from Molnar play by Preston Sturges, as wide-eyed Sullavan tries to act as "good fairy" to struggling lawyer Marshall, while hotly pursued by wealthy Morgan. Hilarious, charming; movie spoof near beginning is priceless. Remade as I'LL BE YOURS.

Good Girls Go to Paris (1939) 75m. **½ D: Alexander Hall. Melvyn Douglas, Joan Blondell, Walter Connolly, Alan Curtis, Isabel Jeans, Clarence Kolb. Spunky waitress Blondell will do anything to visit France; she sees a good prospect in millionaire Douglas.

Good Guys and the Bad Guys, The (1969) C-91m. **½ D: Burt Kennedy. Robert Mitchum, George Kennedy, David Carradine, Tina Louise, Douglas Fowley, Lois Nettleton, Martin Balsam, John Carradine. Mild Western comedy-drama has aging marshal Mitchum going after lifelong foe Kennedy, who has been abandoned by his outlaw gang for being over the hill.

Good Guys Wear Black (1979) C-96m. ** D: Ted Post. Chuck Norris, Anne Archer, James Franciscus, Lloyd Haines, Dana Andrews, Jim Backus. Norris jumps feet first through a windshield and threatens to rearrange the face of bellman Backus—all in the name of national security. Silly political paranoia thriller kills time easily enough.

Good Humor Man, The (1950) 79m. **½ D: Lloyd Bacon. Jack Carson, Lola Albright, Jean Wallace, George Reeves, Richard Egan. Rambunctious antics with Carson in title role, getting involved in murder plot, aided by gang of "Captain Marvel Kids."

Good Luck, Miss Wyckoff (1979) C-105m. BOMB D: Marvin J. Chomsky. Anne Heywood, Donald Pleasence, Robert Vaughn, Carolyn Jones, Dorothy Malone, Ronee Blakely, John Lafayette, Earl Holliman. Repressed schoolteacher's first taste of sex comes via rape, in awkward adaptation of William Inge novel. Good cast generally wasted.

Good Morning, Miss Dove (1955) C-107m. *** D: Henry Koster. Jennifer Jones, Robert Stack, Marshall Thompson, Chuck Connors, Jerry Paris, Mary Wickes, Robert Douglas. For several generations, small town spinster schoolteacher has touched and helped shape lives of her students. Now hospitalized, her past is revealed through flashbacks. Sentimental, warm, and wonderful.

Good Neighbor Sam (1964) C-130m. *** D: David Swift. Jack Lemmon, Romy Schneider, Edward G. Robinson, Michael Connors, Dorothy Provine, Neil Hamilton, Joyce Jameson. Good comedy of Lemmon's adventures pretending he's not married to his real wife but to luscious neighbor Schneider. Plenty of sight gags and good chase scenes make this a lot of fun.

Good News (1947) C-95m. **½ D: Charles Walters. June Allyson, Peter Lawford, Patricia Marshall, Joan McCracken, Mel Torme. Average 1920s college campus musical with last-minute touchdowns, complicated subplots all neatly coming together at the end. Bright score includes "Varsity Drag," "The French Lesson." Remake of 1930 version of this DeSylva-Brown-Henderson show.

Good Sam (1948) 113m. ** D: Leo McCarey. Gary Cooper, Ann Sheridan, Ray Collins, Edmund Lowe, Joan Lorring, Ruth Roman. Almost complete misfire, despite cast and director. Cooper is incurable good Samaritan in this lifeless comedy.

Good, the Bad, and the Ugly, The (1968-Italian-Spanish) C-161m. *** D: Sergio Leone. Clint Eastwood, Lee Van Cleef, Eli Wallach, Rada Rassimov, Mario Brega, Chelo Alonso. Humor and pathos evenly mixed in effective nihilistic Western detailing three gunmen's hunt for Confederate government treasure chest during Civil War. Will suffer on small screen.

Good Time Girl (1950-British) 81m. *½ D: David MacDonald. Jean Kent, Dennis Price, Herbert Lom, Flora Robson. Inoffensive trivia about young girl prevented from wayward life by a judge's telling of tragic fate of another teen-ager.

Good Times (1967) C-91m. **½ D: William Friedkin. Sonny and Cher, George Sanders, Norman Alden, Larry Duran. Back when the singing duo was considered kooky, they made this enjoyable little film, with Sonny fantasizing their potential movie roles. This was also director Friedkin's first feature.

Goodbye Again (1961) 120m. *** D: Anatole Litvak. Ingrid Bergman, Tony Perkins, Yves Montand, Jessie Royce Landis, Diahann Carroll. Francoise Sagan's chic soaper becomes teary Bergman vehicle of middle-aged woman having affair with Perkins, still craving playboy Montand. Set in Paris.

Goodbye Charlie (1964) C-117m. *½ D: Vicente Minnelli. Tony Curtis, Debbie Reynolds, Pat Boone, Walter Matthau, Martin Gabel. Tasteless, flat version of George Axelrod's play; crude gangster dies and comes back to earth as Reynolds.

Goodbye Columbus (1969) C-105m. *** D: Larry Peerce. Richard Benjamin, Ali MacGraw, Jack Klugman, Nan Martin, Michael Meyers. Philip Roth's stinging portrait of successful suburban family as seen through eyes of young man (Benjamin) who falls in love with daughter (MacGraw). Benjamin's screen debut, MacGraw's first starring role; director's father Jan Peerce has cameo role at wedding. But unknown Meyers steals show as Ali's brother.

Goodbye Girl, The (1977) C-110m. ***½ D: Herbert Ross. Richard Dreyfuss, Marsha Mason, Quinn Cummings, Paul Benedict, Barbara Rhoades. Neil Simon's warmest comedy to date puts young actor Dreyfuss and dumped-on divorcée Mason together as unwilling tenants of the same N.Y. apartment, explores their growing relationship. High-caliber script and performances to match; Dreyfuss won Oscar as Best Actor.

Goodbye, Mr. Chips (1939-British) 114m. ***½ D: Sam Wood. Robert Donat, Greer Garson, Paul von Hernreid (Henreid), Terry Kilburn, John Mills. Donat won well-deserved Oscar for memorable portrayal of shy schoolmaster who devotes his life to "his boys," only coming out of his shell when he meets Garson. Extreme length works against film's honest sentiment, but Donat makes it all worthwhile. Based on James Hilton's novel.

Goodbye, Mr. Chips (1969) C-151m. ** D: Herbert Ross. Peter O'Toole, Petula Clark, Michael Redgrave, George Baker, Sian Phillips, Michael Bryant. Lumbering musical remake of 1939 classic. O'Toole is good as prim schoolteacher, but Clark's role as showgirl is shallow, ludicrous. Mediocre songs don't help; what emotion there is gets lost when film plods on to modern-day anticlimax.

Goodbye, My Fancy (1951) 107m. *** D: Vincent Sherman. Joan Crawford, Robert Young, Frank Lovejoy, Eve Arden. Congresswoman Crawford returns to her old college, more to see former boyfriend Young than to receive honorary degree. Lovejoy is callous newsman.

Good-bye, My Lady (1956) 95m. **½ D: William Wellman. Walter Brennan, Phil Harris, Brandon de Wilde,

Sidney Poitier. James Street novel of small boy (De Wilde), an elderly man (Brennan), and the dog that brings joy into their lives is easy going, poignant film, set in the South.

Goodbye, Norma Jean (1976) C-95m. BOMB D: Larry Buchanan. Misty Rowe, Terence Locke, Patch Mackenzie, Preston Hanson. Sleazy look at adolescent Marilyn Monroe and her rocky road to stardom; what will have to be cut for TV will leave behind even less reason to watch this piece of tripe.

Goodbye, Raggedy Ann (1971) C-73m. TVM D: Fielder Cook. Mia Farrow, Hal Holbrook, John Colicos, Martin Sheen, Paul Warfield. Tear-jerker fluctuates between convincing scenes and unintentional comedy. Overly sensitive Hollywood starlet on brink of suicide must change her notions of success. Average.

Goodnight, My Love (1972) C-73m. TVM D: Peter Hyams. Richard Boone, Barbara Bain, Michael Dunn, Victor Buono, Gianni Russo. Down-and-out detective team have visit from seemingly innocent blonde who wants fiancé found. Not quite MALTESE FALCON takeoff as claimed, film has offbeat point of view with a timeless atmosphere; excellent direction. Above average.

Goose and the Gander, The (1935) 65m. ** D: Alfred E. Green. Kay Francis, George Brent, Genevieve Tobin, John Eldredge, Claire Dodd. Woman's story of high-living Francis keeping an eye on ex-husband Brent.

Gordon's War (1973) C-90m. *** D: Ossie Davis. Paul Winfield, Carl Lee, David Downing, Tony King. When a Vietnam vet comes home to find his wife hooked on drugs, he trains four-man army to destroy the pushers. Good action, but gets lost toward the end.

Gorgeous Hussy, The (1936) 102m. **½ D: Clarence Brown. Lionel Barrymore, Joan Crawford, Robert Taylor, Franchot Tone, Melvyn Douglas, James Stewart. Star-studded cast in strained historical drama of Andrew Jackson's belle, who disgraces herself and those connected with her. Crawford et al are beautifully costumed in well-appointed settings.

Gorgo (1961-British) C-78m. **½ D: Eugene Lourie. Bill Travers, William Sylvester, Vincent Winter,

Bruce Seton, Joseph O'Conor. Good sci-fi story of captured baby sea monster put into London circus and gigantic parent coming to rescue it. Exciting special effects.

Gorgon, The (1964-British) C-83m. **½ D: Terence Fisher. Christopher Lee, Richard Pasco, Barbara Shelley, Michael Goodliffe. A spirit inhabits the body of beautiful girl and gives her gaze that turns others to stone. Atmospheric.

Gorilla SEE: **Nabonga**

Gorilla, The (1939) 66m. ** D: Allan Dwan. The Ritz Brothers, Anita Louise, Patsy Kelly, Lionel Atwill, Bela Lugosi, Joseph Calleia. Disappointing comedy-whodunit with the Ritz Brothers as fumbling detectives prowling around old-dark-house in search of murderer. Lugosi is wasted.

Gorilla at Large (1954) C-84m. *** D: Harmon Jones. Cameron Mitchell, Anne Bancroft, Lee J. Cobb, Raymond Burr. Offbeat murder mystery at amusement park, with exceptionally able cast.

Gorilla Man, The (1942) 64m. ** D: D. Ross Lederman. John Loder, Ruth Ford, Marian Hall, Richard Fraser, Creighton Hale. Title is misleading. Pro-Nazis try to discredit RAF pilot by linking him with series of brutal murders. Grade-B material with adequate acting.

Gospel According to St. Matthew, The (1966-Italian-French) 135m. **** D: Pier Paolo Pasolini. Enrique Irazoqui, Margherita Caruso, Susanna Pasolini, Marcello Morante, Mario Socrate. Unconventional, austere film on life and teachings of Christ, based solely on writings of the Apostle, Matthew. Amateur cast (including director's mother) is expressive and moves with quiet dignity. Ironically, director of this masterpiece is a Marxist.

Gospel Road, The (1973) C-83m. **½ D: Robert Elfstrom. Johnny Cash, June Carter, Robert Elfstrom. Musical journey through Holy Land follows story of Jesus from his birth to his death and resurrection. Sincere but not especially good.

Government Girl (1943) 94m. **½ D: Dudley Nichols. Olivia de Havilland, Sonny Tufts, Anne Shirley, Jess Barker, James Dunn, Paul Stewart, Agnes Moorehead. Tufts has clear field in wartime Washington, but De Havilland gets him;

that's about it for this breezy comedy.

Gracie Allen Murder Case, The (1939) 74m. D: Alfred E. Green. Gracie Allen, Warren William, Ellen Drew, Kent Taylor, Jerome Cowan, Judith Barrett, Donald MacBride, William Demarest, H.B. Warner. SEE: **Philo Vance** series

Graduate, The (1967) C-105m. **** D: Mike Nichols. Anne Bancroft, Dustin Hoffman, Katharine Ross, Murray Hamilton, William Daniels, Elizabeth Wilson. 1967 Best Director Oscar went to Nichols for this landmark American comedy. Postgrad Hoffman (in his first major role) courts both Ross and her seductive mother (Bancroft) which leads to tremendous complications. One of the most beautiful soundtracks ever, provided by Simon and Garfunkel.

Grande Bourgeoise, La (1974-Italian) C-115m. **½ D: Mauro Bolognini. Catherine Deneuve, Giancarlo Giannini, Fernando Rey, Tina Aumont, Paolo Bonicelli. Strong cast adds some punch to true story about Giannini's murder of sister Deneuve's loutish husband and the political storm it generates. Stylish but not terribly compelling.

Grand Central Murder (1942) 73m. **½ D: S. Sylvan Simon. Van Heflin, Patricia Dane, Cecilia Parker, Virginia Grey, Samuel S. Hinds, Sam Levene, Tom Conway. Slick, fast-moving B whodunit, with Heflin investigating actress' murder on private train car at Grand Central Station.

Grand Duel, The (1972-Italian) C-92m. *½ D: Giancarlo Santi. Lee Van Cleef, Peter O'Brien, Marc Mazza, Jess Hahn, Horst Frank. Typically spare spaghetti Western with mysterious gunman Van Cleef becoming guardian angel to a man wrongly accused of murder.

Grand Hotel (1932) 113m. **** D: Edmund Goulding. Greta Garbo, Joan Crawford, John Barrymore, Wallace Beery, Lionel Barrymore, Lewis Stone, Jean Hersholt. Vicki Baum's novel of plush Berlin hotel where "nothing ever happens." Stars prove the contrary: Garbo as lonely ballerina, John B. her jewel-thief lover, Lionel B. a dying man, Crawford an ambitious stenographer, Beery a hardened businessman, Stone the observer. A must.

Grand Illusion (1937-French) 111m.

**** D: Jean Renoir. Jean Gabin, Pierre Fresnay, Erich von Stroheim, Dalio, Dita Parlo, Carette. Renoir's classic treatise on war, focusing on French prisoners during WW1 and their cultured German commandant. Beautiful performances enhance an eloquent script.

Grand Prix (1966) C-175m. ** D: John Frankenheimer. James Garner, Eva Marie Saint, Yves Montand, Toshiro Mifune, Brian Bedford, Jessica Walter, Francoise Hardy. Big cast is saddled with rambling script about personal lives of auto racers and their loves; use of split screen and spectacular racing sequences won't mean much on TV.

Grand Slam (1968-Italian-U.S.) C-120m. *** D: Giuliano Montaldo. Edward G. Robinson, Janet Leigh, Adolfo Celi, Klaus Kinski, Georges Rigaud, Robert Hoffman. International jewel-heist film, with all the trappings. Nothing new, but smoothly done, most enjoyable.

Grand Theft Auto (1977) C-84m. ** D: Ron Howard. Ron Howard, Nancy Morgan, Marion Ross, Pete Isacksen, Barry Cahill. Young Howard's directorial debut (he also co-scripted with his actor-father Rance) is typical unsophisticated car-crash action fare, no better or worse than most.

Grande Bouffe, La (1973-French) C-125m. *** D: Marco Ferreri. Marcello Mastroianni, Philippe Noiret, Michel Piccoli, Ugo Tognazzi, Andrea Ferreol. Deliberately tasteless but often very funny spoof of gluttony, as four friends decide to eat themselves to death.

Grandma's Boy (1922) 81m. (includes excerpt from A SAILOR-MADE MAN) *** D: Fred Newmeyer. Harold Lloyd, Mildred Davis, Anna Townsend, Charles Stevenson, Noah Young, Dick Sutherland. Lloyd's first great success casts him as a mousy small-town type inspired to fight for his girl—and his honor —by his grandma's tales of family heritage. Still entertaining. Edited for TV and paired with excerpt from 1921 feature A SAILOR-MADE MAN.

Grapes of Wrath, The (1940) 129m. **** D: John Ford. Henry Fonda, Jane Darwell, John Carradine, Charley Grapewin, Dorris Bowden, Russell Simpson, John Qualen. Steinbeck Americana of Okies moving from dust bowl to California during

Depression, lovingly brought to screen. Darwell won an Oscar as determined family head; Fonda plays her ex-con son. Don't miss this one.

Grass Is Always Greener Over the Septic Tank, The (1978) C-100m. TVM D: Robert Day. Carol Burnett, Charles Grodin, Alex Rocco, Linda Gray, Robert Sampson, Vicki Belmonte. The Erma Bombeck book lost some of its humor in this still-amiable translation to the screen, telling of a New York couple who decide to swap the hassle of big city living for suburbia. Originally intended to test the waters as a possible Burnett series. Average.

Grass is Greener, The (1960) C-105m. *** D: Stanley Donen. Cary Grant, Deborah Kerr, Robert Mitchum, Jean Simmons. Chic drawing-room fare that suffers from staginess. Grant-Kerr marriage is threatened by Simmons and Mitchum romancing the two, respectively.

Grave Robbers from Outer Space SEE: Plan 9 from Outer Space

Gravy Train, The (1974) C-96m. **½ D: Jack Starrett. Stacy Keach, Frederic Forrest, Margot Kidder, Barry Primus, Richard Romanus, Denny Miller. Okay blend of fast-moving action and comedy as West Virginia brothers Keach and Forrest develop a liking for crime. Also known as THE DION BROTHERS.

Gray Lady Down (1978) C-111m. ** D: David Greene. Charlton Heston, David Carradine, Stacy Keach, Ned Beatty, Ronny Cox, Rosemary Forsyth. Tired drama about rescue of nuclear submarine, captained by Heston. Good special effects, and colorful performance by Carradine as designer of experimental diving craft. Look for Christopher Reeve as one of the officers.

Grayeagle (1978) C-104m. **½ D: Charles B. Pierce. Ben Johnson, Iron Eyes Cody, Lana Wood, Jack Elam, Paul Fix, Alex Cord, Charles B. Pierce. Interesting if flawed rehash of THE SEARCHERS with Johnson tracking the Indian (Cord) who kidnapped his daughter. Good classic Western style an asset, sluggish pacing a drawback. Produced, directed, written by Pierce, who also appears in cast.

Grazie Zia SEE: Thank You, Aunt

Grease (1978) C-110m. *** D: Randal Kleiser. John Travolta, Olivia Newton-John, Stockard Channing, Jeff Conaway, Didi Conn, Eve

Arden, Sid Caesar. Energetic, imaginative filming of long-running Broadway show that fantasizes life in the 1950s; spirited cast, clever ideas, and Patricia Birch's choreography make it fun.

Greased Lightning (1977) C-94m. ** D: Michael Schultz. Richard Pryor, Beau Bridges, Pam Grier, Cleavon Little, Vincent Gardenia, Richie Havens, Julian Bond. Spirited cast does little to enliven plodding, episodic bio of Wendell Scott, the first black racing car driver. A waste of Pryor, both dramatically and comically.

Greaser's Palace (1972) C-91m. *** D: Robert Downey. Albert Henderson, Luana Anders, George Morgan, Larry Moyer, Michael Sullivan, James Antonio, Ron Nealy, John Paul Hudson. Super offbeat Jesus Christ parody with Western setting. Drifter (Henderson) discovers "true identity" and heals "sick" cowboys in crazy, tiny town. Not likely to survive intact on TV.

Great American Beauty Contest, The (1973) C-74m. TVM D: Robert Day. Eleanor Parker, Bob Cummings, Louis Jourdan, Joanna Cameron, Susan Damonte, Tracy Reed. Offbeat, behind-the-scenes look at present-day big-time pageant, complete with sordid intrigues, rumors of rigging, etc., enlivened by social-commentary point of view. Good performances, especially Parker's. Above average.

Great American Broadcast, The (1941) 92m. **½ D: Archie Mayo. Alice Faye, John Payne, Jack Oakie, Cesar Romero, The Four Ink Spots, James Newill, Mary Beth Hughes. Fictional fun of development of radio industry, with such musical guests as zany Wiere Brothers. Entertaining; bright cast.

Great American Cowboy, The (1974) C-90m. *** D: Kieth Merrill. Narrated by Joel McCrea. Exciting documentary on rodeo life focuses on rodeo superstar Larry Mahan and his competition with newcomer Phil Lyne. Oscar-winner as Best Documentary Feature.

Great American Pastime, The (1956) 89m. ** D: Herman Hoffman. Tom Ewell, Anne Francis, Ann Miller, Dean Jones, Ruby Dee. Ewell manages to work some enthusiasm into this programmer about Little League baseball and its effect on suburban families.

Great American Tragedy, A (1972) C-73m. TVM D: J. Lee Thompson. George Kennedy, Vera Miles, William Windom, Hilarie Thompson, Nancy Hadley, Kevin McCarthy. Family experiences economic realities of life when aerospace engineer (Kennedy) gets laid off. Staunch middle-class point of view, OK performances, upbeat ending. Average.

Great Balloon Adventure, The SEE Olly, Olly Oxen Free

Great Bank Hoax, The (1977) C-89m. **½ D: Joseph Jacoby. Richard Basehart, Burgess Meredith, Paul Sand, Ned Beatty, Michael Murphy, Charlene Dallas, Arthur Godfrey. Unremarkable but diverting comedy, a Watergate allegory about bank officials who try to cover up embezzlement by arranging an even bigger theft. Originally titled THE GREAT GEORGIA BANK HOAX.

Great Bank Robbery, The (1969) C-98m. *½ D: Hy Averback. Zero Mostel, Kim Novak, Clint Walker, Claude Akins, Akim Tamiroff, Larry Storch. Bogus preacher and company, Mexican gang led by Tamiroff, and local outlaws all compete for control of the town of Friendly. Spoof of Westerns is a total dud. Be warned.

Great Brain, The (1978) C-82m. *** D: Sidney Levin. Jimmy Osmond, James Jarnigan, Len Birman, Pat Delaney, Fran Ryan, John Fredric Hart. Ambling but enjoyable family film produced by The Osmonds from John D. Fitzgerald's award-winning book. Young Jimmy plays a Tom Sawyer-ish con artist at the turn of the century.

Great British Train Robbery, The (1967-Germany) 104m. *** D: John Olden, Claus Peter Witt. Horst Tappert, Hans Cossy, Gunther Neutze, Isa Miranda. Absorbing true study of mammoth robbery of British mails by an ingenious band of outlaws.

Great Caruso, The (1951) C-109m. *** D: Richard Thorpe. Mario Lanza, Ann Blyth, Jarmila Novotna, Dorothy Kirsten. Outstanding mixture of biographical fiction about the great singer. Fine music, and Lanza's voice, overcome some creaky dialogue.

Great Catherine (1968-British) C-98m. *½ D: Gordon Flemyng. Peter O'Toole, Jeanne Moreau, Zero Mostel, Jack Hawkins, Akim Tamiroff. Terrible adaptation of George Bernard Shaw's comedy about Catherine the Great wastes capable cast; wait for revival of Dietrich's THE SCARLET EMPRESS.

Great Chase, The (1963) 77m. ***½ Narrated by Frank Gallop. Buster Keaton, Douglas Fairbanks, Sr., Pearl White, Richard Barthelmess, Lillian Gish. Entertaining silent-film compilation of great chase scenes from THE MARK OF ZORRO, WAY DOWN EAST, etc., with most of film devoted to Keaton's classic, THE GENERAL.

Great Dan Patch, The (1949) 94m. **½ D: Joseph M. Newman. Dennis O'Keefe, Gail Russell, Ruth Warrick, Charlotte Greenwood. Acceptable horseracing yarn.

Great Day (1946-British) 94m. **½ D: Lance Comfort. Eric Portman, Flora Robson, Sheila Sim, Walter Fitzgerald. Somber, effective study of the courageous women who helped Britain win WW2.

Great Day in the Morning (1956) C-92m. **½ D: Jacques Tourneur. Virginia Mayo, Robert Stack, Ruth Roman, Alex Nicol, Raymond Burr. Good cast, beautiful color scenery help so-so story of pre-Civil War Colorado, when gold rush fever and separationist sentiments clashed.

Great Diamond Robbery, The (1953) 69m. ** D: Robert Z. Leonard. Red Skelton, Cara Williams, James Whitmore, Dorothy Stickney, Steven Geray. Limp vehicle buoyed by Skelton. Red is hoodwinked by jewel thief who wants him to recut huge diamond.

Great Dictator, The (1940) 128m. ***½ D: Charles Chaplin. Charlie Chaplin, Paulette Goddard, Jack Oakie, Reginald Gardiner, Maurice Moscovich, Billy Gilbert, Henry Daniell. Chaplin's unusual comedy combines slapstick, satire, and social commentary, as he plays dual role of Jewish ghetto barber and dictator Adenoid Hynkel of Tomania. Unique, surprisingly effective film also features Oakie in unforgettable portrayal of "Benzino Napaloni" of rival country Bacteria.

Great Escape, The (1963) C-168m. **** D: John Sturges. Steve McQueen, James Garner, Richard Attenborough, Charles Bronson, James Coburn, David McCallum, Donald Pleasence. Allied P.O.W.s plot massive escape from German prison camp. Based on true story, this blockbuster was beautifully photographed on location in Germany. Rip-roaring excitement with marvelous international cast.

Great Expectations (1934) 100m. **½ D: Stuart Walker. Jane Wyatt, Phillips Holmes, George Breakston, Henry Hull, Florence Reed, Alan Hale, Francis L. Sullivan. Acceptable version of Dickens' story about young boy and unknown benefactor, is dwarfed by '46 classic. Sullivan plays Jaggers in both films.

Great Expectations (1946-British) 118m. **** D: David Lean. John Mills, Valerie Hobson, Bernard Miles, Francis L. Sullivan, Martita Hunt, Alec Guinness, Finlay Currie, Anthony Wager, Jean Simmons. Dickens' tale of mysterious benefactor making poor, young orphan a gentleman of means. A faithful adaptation and an exquisite film; superb cast.

Great Flamarion, The (1945) 78m. **½ D: Anthony Mann. Erich von Stroheim, Mary Beth Hughes, Dan Duryea, Stephen Barclay, Lester Allen, Esther Howard. Better than most of Stroheim's cheapies, this one has him doublecrossed by circus star Hughes to make way for Duryea.

Great Gambini, The (1937) 70m. **½ D: Charles Vidor. Akim Tamiroff, Marian Marsh, Genevieve Tobin, William Demarest, Reginald Denny, Roland Drew. Engaging low-budget film, with Tamiroff starring as magico who predicts deaths, becomes his own victim.

Great Garrick, The (1937) 91m. *** D: James Whale. Brian Aherne, Olivia de Havilland, Edward Everett Horton, Melville Cooper, Lionel Atwill, Lana Turner, Marie Wilson. Members of the Comédie Française perpetrate a hoax to deflate the ego of pompous David Garrick (Aherne) in this entertaining, fictitious yarn about real-life British actor.

Great Gatsby, The (1949) 92m. *** D: Elliott Nugent. Alan Ladd, Betty Field, Macdonald Carey, Barry Sullivan, Ruth Hussey, Shelley Winters, Howard DaSilva. Valiant attempt to reproduce 1920s atmosphere of F. Scott Fitzgerald novel, with Ladd the gangster out to recapture his lost love. Made before in 1926, remade in 1974.

Great Gatsby, The (1974) C-144m. **½ D: Jack Clayton. Robert Redford, Mia Farrow, Bruce Dern, Karen Black, Scott Wilson, Sam Waterston, Lois Chiles, Howard Da Silva. Bland adaptation of F. Scott Fitzgerald's jazz-age novel about a golden boy in Long Island society; faithful to the book, and visually opulent, but lacks substance and power. Script by Francis Ford Coppola.

Great Georgia Bank Hoax, The SEE: **Great Bank Hoax, The**

Great Gilbert and Sullivan, The (1953-British) C-105m. ***½ D: Sidney Gilliat. Robert Morley, Maurice Evans, Eileen Herlie, Peter Finch, Martyn Green. Highly flavorful biography of operetta composers with many highlights from their works.

Great Guns (1941) 74m. ** D: Monty Banks. Stan Laurel, Oliver Hardy, Sheila Ryan, Dick Nelson, Edmund MacDonald. Later L&H Army comedy is weak, not as bad as some but far below their classic films.

Great Guy (1936) 75m. ** D: John G. Blystone. James Cagney, Mae Clarke, James Burke, Edward Brophy, Henry Kolker, Bernadene Hayes, Edward McNamara. Secondrate Cagney in low-budget production about inspector crusading against corruption in meat business.

Great Houdinis, The (1976) C-100m. TVM D: Melville Shavelson. Paul Michael Glaser, Sally Struthers, Ruth Gordon, Vivian Vance, Adrienne Barbeau, Peter Cushing, Bill Bixby, Jack Carter, Nina Foch, Maureen O'Sullivan, Wifrid Hyde-White, Clive Revill, Geoffrey Lewis. Drama about life and times of the famed illusionist-escape artist whose career masks obsession with the occult. Brisk direction and literate script (both by Shavelson), wonderful performance by Ruth Gordon as Houdini's possessive mother. Above average.

Great Ice Rip-Off, The (1974) C-78m. TVM D: Dan Curtis. Lee J. Cobb, Gig Young, Grayson Hall, Robert Walden, Matt Clark, Geoffrey Lewis. Grumpy retired cop Cobb matches wits with jewel thief Young and his gang during cross-country bus chase. Light-hearted suspense caper, tossed off by a couple of old pros and, uncharacteristically, occult-horror director Curtis. Above average.

Great Imposter, The (1960) 112m. *** D: Robert Mulligan. Tony Curtis, Edmond O'Brien, Arthur O'Connell, Gary Merrill. Incredible story of Ferdinand Demara, who succeeded in a variety of professional guises. Film is episodic and pat.

Great Jesse James Raid, The (1953)

C-74m. **½ D: Reginald Le Borg. Willard Parker, Barbara Payton, Tom Neal, Wallace Ford. Generally action-packed tale blending fact and legend about the notorious outlaw and his last big robbery caper.

Great Jewel Robber, The (1950) 91m. ** D: Peter Godfrey. David Brian, Marjorie Reynolds, John Archer, Warren Douglas. Brian chomps through title role; film recounts his many criminal capers.

Great John L., The (1945) 96m. **½ D: Frank Tuttle. Greg McClure, Linda Darnell, Barbara Britton, Lee Sullivan, Otto Kruger, Wallace Ford, George Matthews, Rory Calhoun. Not bad little biography of famous boxer's rise and fall, his two loves and unhappy end.

Great K&A Train Robbery, The (1926) 53m. ***½ D: Lewis Seiler. Tom Mix, Dorothy Dwan, William Walling, Harry Grippe, Tony. Silent screen's most popular cowboy star in one of his greatest films: rollicking fun, filmed on magnificent locations in Colorado.

Great Lie, The (1941) 107m. *** D: Edmund Goulding. Bette Davis, Mary Astor, George Brent, Lucile Watson, Hattie McDaniel, Grant Mitchell. Brent marries Davis when alliance with Astor is annulled. He is lost in plane crash, leaving Davis and pregnant Astor to battle each other and the elements. Well-mounted soaper won Astor an Oscar as fiery concert pianist.

Great Locomotive Chase, The (1956) C-85m. *** D: Francis D. Lyon. Fess Parker, Jeffrey Hunter, Jeff York, John Lupton, Eddie Firestone, Kenneth Tobey. True story of Andrews' Raiders (filmed before by Buster Keaton as THE GENERAL) comes to life in colorful Disney film; Parker is famous Union spy who leads a rowdy band in capturing and "kidnapping" a Confederate railroad train during Civil War.

Great Lover, The (1949) 80m. *** D: Alexander Hall. Bob Hope, Rhonda Fleming, Roland Young, Roland Culver, George Reeves, Jim Backus. Vintage Hope; Bob's a boy scout leader on ship filled with his troop, luscious Fleming, and murderer Young.

Great McGinty, The (1940) 81m. **½ D: Preston Sturges. Brian Donlevy, Muriel Angelus, Akim Tamiroff, Allyn Joslyn, William Demarest. Sturges' first film as writer-director

dates badly, no longer the stinging political satire it once was; Donlevy plays a bum who rises to power, then loses it all. Oscar-winning screenplay still has fine moments, and Sturges' stock company of supporting players to give it life.

Great Man, The (1956) 92m. ***½ D: Jose Ferrer. Jose Ferrer, Dean Jagger, Keenan Wynn, Julie London, Jim Backus, Ed Wynn. Well-loved TV star dies and Ferrer prepares memorial show, only to discover star was a despicable phony. Hard-bitten look at TV industry; top performances by senior and junior Wynns.

Great Man Votes, The (1939) 70m. ***½ D: Garson Kanin. John Barrymore, Peter Holden, Virginia Weidler, Donald MacBride, William Demarest. Simple, sincere, delightful film of Barrymore, once a professor, now a souse, fighting for custody of his children, suddenly elevated to new stature when election-time rolls around. MacBride fun as small-time politico, Demarest an energetic campaign promoter.

Great Manhunt, The (1950-British) 97m. *** D: Sidney Gilliat. Douglas Fairbanks, Jr., Glynis Johns, Jack Hawkins, Herbert Lom. Genuine suspenser; American doctor tries to flee Middle European country with valuable information. Retitled STATE SECRET.

Great Man's Lady, The (1942) 90m. **½ D: William Wellman. Barbara Stanwyck, Joel McCrea, Brian Donlevy, Thurston Hall, K. T. Stevens, Lucien Littlefield. Saga of the West is no great shakes as McCrea dreams of oil wells, Donlevy takes his girl. Stanwyck ages to 100 years to frame story.

Great Man's Whiskers, The (1971) C-100m. TVM D: Philip Leacock. Dennis Weaver, Ann Sothern, John McGiver, Harve Presnell, Beth Brickell, Cindy Eilbacher. Weak comedy-drama about President Lincoln rerouting train tour after receiving letter from 10-year-old girl urging him to grow whiskers. Political aspect of plot doesn't work; historically unbelievable, too. Below average.

Great Mike, The (1944) 70m. ** D: Wallace Fox. Stuart Erwin, Robert (Buzz) Henry, Marion Martin, Carl Switzer, Pierre Watkin. Sloppy comedy-drama of horse-racing, with Erwin as lovable rogue who trains unlikely horse to win big race.

Great Missouri Raid, The (1950) C-83m. ** D: Gordon Douglas. Wendell Corey, Macdonald Carey, Ellen Drew, Ward Bond, Anne Revere. Another account of the infamous outlaws, James brothers and Younger brothers.

Great Moment, The (1944) 83m. ** D: Preston Sturges. Joel McCrea, Betty Field, Harry Carey, William Demarest, Franklin Pangborn, Grady Sutton, Louis Jean Heydt, Jimmy Conlin. Confused biography of anasthesia inventor wavers from comedy to drama; ineffectual, filled with frustrating flashbacks. Very offbeat for writer-director Sturges.

Great Niagara, The (1974) C-78m. TVM D: William Hale. Richard Boone, Michael Sacks, Randy Quaid, Jennifer Salt, Burt Young. Offbeat outdoor adventure about a bitter, obsessed old cripple (Boone) who endangers his sons' lives by forcing them to challenge Niagara Falls in a barrel to continue a family tradition. Evocative drama, set in the Depression 30s, with generous supply of thrills. Average.

Great Northfield Minnesota Raid, The (1972) C-91m. **½ D: Philip Kaufman. Cliff Robertson, Robert Duvall, Luke Askew, R. G. Armstrong, Dana Elcar, Donald Moffat, John Pearce, Matt Clark, Wayne Sutherlin. New-style Western showing famous robbery scheme from seamy side. Vivid portraits of Younger brothers, James brothers, but muddled point of view.

Great O'Malley, The (1937) 71m. *½ D: William Dieterle. Pat O'Brien, Humphrey Bogart, Ann Sheridan, Donald Crisp, Mary Gordon, Frieda Inescort, Sybil Jason. Syrupy film of ruthless cop O'Brien and poor man Bogart who has lame daughter and turns to crime to support her. Pretty sticky stuff.

Great Profile, The (1940) 82m. **½ D: Walter Lang. John Barrymore, Mary Beth Hughes, Gregory Ratoff, John Payne, Anne Baxter, Lionel Atwill, Edward Brophy. Barrymore on downslide provides some laughs in self-parodying tale of aging, conceited actor.

Great Race, The (1965) C-150m. **½ D: Blake Edwards. Tony Curtis, Natalie Wood, Jack Lemmon, Peter Falk, Keenan Wynn, Larry Storch, Dorothy Provine, Arthur O'Connell, Vivian Vance, Ross Martin, George Macready. Long, sometimes funny, often labored comedy, not the greatest ever made, as advertised. Duel sequence and barroom brawl are highlights, but pie fight falls flat, other gimmicks don't work. Definitely a mixed bag; one good song, "The Sweetheart Tree."

Great Rupert, The (1950) 86m. **½ D: Irving Pichel. Jimmy Durante, Terry Moore, Tom Drake, Queenie Smith, Chick Chandler. Agreeable comedy of a trained squirrel who discovers a cache of money.

Great St. Louis Bank Robbery, The (1959) 86m. *½ D: Charles Guggenheim, John Stix. Steve McQueen, David Clarke, Crahan Denton, Molly McCarthy, James Dukas. Modest robbery caper with virtue of McQueen in cast.

Great Scout and Cathouse Thursday (1976) C-102m. **½ D: Don Taylor. Lee Marvin, Oliver Reed, Robert Culp, Elizabeth Ashley, Strother Martin, Sylvia Miles, Kay Lenz. Broad, unsubtle comedy set in Colorado of 1908 involves swindles, defanged snake, kidnapped prostitutes, and robbery of proceeds from big boxing match. Could have been funnier.

Great Sinner, The (1949) 110m. **½ D: Robert Siodmak. Gregory Peck, Ava Gardner, Melvyn Douglas, Walter Huston, Ethel Barrymore. Murky romance lavishly produced, meandering along with tale of Peck saving Gardner from drowning in gambling fever—then catching it himself.

Great Sioux Massacre, The (1965) C-91m. **½ D: Sidney Salkow. Joseph Cotten, Darren McGavin, Philip Carey, Julie Sommars, Nancy Kovack, John Matthews, Frank Ferguson. Good acting enhances this version of Custer's last stand.

Great Sioux Uprising, The (1953) C-80m. **½ D: Lloyd Bacon. Jeff Chandler, Faith Domergue, Lyle Bettger, Glenn Strange. Chandler as ex-Yankee officer is adequate in formula Western about threatened Indian war.

Great Smokey Roadblock, The (1976) C-106m. **½ D: John Leone. Henry Fonda, Eileen Brennan, John Byner, Dub Taylor, Susan Sarandon, Melanie Mayron. Innocuous story of aging trucker (Fonda) attempting one perfect cross-country run before his truck is repossessed; some nice vignettes.

Great Spy Mission, The SEE: Operation Crossbow

Great Texas Dynamite Chase, The (1977) C-90m. *½ D: Michael Pressman. Claudia Jennings, Jocelyn Jones, Johnny Crawford, Chris Pennock, Tara Strohmeier. A pair of sexy female bank robbers take to the roads in this all-too-typical low-budgeter.

Great Train Robbery, The (1979) C-111m. *** D: Michael Crichton. Sean Connery, Donald Sutherland, Lesley-Anne Down, Alan Webb, Malcolm Terris, Robert Lang. Stylish fun as an elegant trio conspire to pull off the greatest heist of all time, in the mid-1800s: stealing shipment of gold from a moving train! Crichton based his script on true incident, filmed it against beautiful British countryside. British title: THE FIRST GREAT TRAIN ROBBERY.

Great Victor Herbert, The (1939) 84m. **½ D: Andrew L. Stone. Allan Jones, Mary Martin, Walter Connolly, Lee Bowman, Susanna Foster, Jerome Cowan. Music overshadows plot in this fanciful biography of composer in turn-of-the-century N.Y.C. "March Of The Toys," "Ah Sweet Mystery Of Life," etc. are included.

Great Waldo Pepper, The (1975) C-107m. *** D: George Roy Hill. Robert Redford, Bo Svenson, Bo Brundin, Susan Sarandon, Geoffrey Lewis, Edward Herrmann, Margot Kidder. Boxoffice disappointment from director of BUTCH CASSIDY and THE STING is a much more personal film, even though brilliantly photographed story of aviation pioneers wavers uncomfortably between slapstick and drama. Worth a look.

Great Wallendas, The (1978) C-100m. TVM D: Larry Elikann. Lloyd Bridges, Britt Ekland, Taina Elg, Cathy Rigby, Michael McGuire, John Van Dreelin. Straightforward drama based on the legendary circus family of high-wire artists whose career has been stalked by tragedy. Enthralling when up in the air. Average.

Great Waltz, The (1938) 102m. **½ D: Julien Duvivier. Luise Rainer, Fernand Gravet, Miliza Korjus, Hugh Herbert, Lionel Atwill, Curt Bois. Music outdoes drama in this elaborately produced biography of composer Johann Strauss, with plenty of waltzes covering up a standard triangle tale.

Great Waltz, The (1972) C-135m.

BOMB D: Andrew L. Stone. Horst Bucholz, Mary Costa, Rossano Brazzi, Nigel Patrick, Yvonne Mitchell, James Faulkner. Bio of Johann Strauss is unintentionally funny in the way director Stone's SONG OF NORWAY was, but after 135 minutes, even the laughs begin to subside. Filmed on location in Austria.

Great War, The (1959-Italian-French) 118m. ** D: Mario Monicelli. Vittorio Gassman, Alberto Sordi, Silvana Mangano, Folco Lulli. Uneven, episodic comedy-drama of two goldbricking pals during WW1, somewhat reminiscent of WHAT PRICE GLORY? but not nearly as good. Released here in 1961.

Great White Hope, The (1970) C-101m. *** D: Martin Ritt. James Earl Jones, Jane Alexander, Lou Gilbert, Joel Fluellen, Chester Morris, Robert Webber, R. G. Armstrong, Hal Holbrook, Beah Richards, Moses Gunn. Supercharged adaptation of Broadway success with Jones and Alexander repeating stage roles as Jack Jefferson, famed heavyweight champion, and white mistress. Not a boxing film or social doctrine, but emotional character study. Holds up until final scene, which doesn't ring true.

Great Ziegfeld, The (1936) 180m. ***½ D: Robert Z. Leonard. William Powell, Myrna Loy, Luise Rainer, Frank Morgan, Fannie Brice, Virginia Bruce, Reginald Owen, Ray Bolger, Dennis Morgan. Spectacular biography of great 20th-century showman, with extravagant musical numbers, stunning Oscar-winning performance by Rainer as Anna Held.

Greatest, The (1977) C-101m. *½ D: Tom Gries. Muhammad Ali, Ernest Borgnine, John Marley, Robert Duvall, James Earl Jones, Roger E. Mosley, Ben Johnson, Paul Winfield, Lloyd Haynes, Dina Merrill. Potentially exciting screen bio of the great heavyweight champ becomes an episodic mess suffering from a script devoid of dramatic focus and ham-handed direction. Ironically, Mosley's performance as Sonny Liston has the charisma Ali's lacks.

Great Battle, The (1978-German-Yugoslavian) C-97m. BOMB D: Humphrey Longan. Helmut Berger, Samantha Eggar, Giuliano Gemma, John Huston, Stacy Keach, Henry Fonda, Edwige French. Amateurish muddle about WW2 combines tired vignettes with well-known stars, dubbed sequences with others, and newsreel footage narrated by Orson Welles. A waste of everybody's time.

Greatest Gift, The (1974) **C-100m.** TVM D: Boris Sagal. Glenn Ford, Julie Harris, Lance Kerwin, Harris Yulin, Charles Tyner, Dabbs Greer. Rural, poverty-stricken preacher (Ford) battles ruthless sheriff (Yulin) and restless church deacons in struggle to support family in small Southern town in 1940. Sentimental, homespun, with a violent turn. Subsequently it became "The Family Holvak" as a series. Above average.

Greatest Love, The (1951-Italian) **116m.** *½ D: Roberto Rossellini. Ingrid Bergman, Alexander Knox, Giulietta Masina, Teresa Pellati, Sandro Frachina. Slow-moving, dull account of life and fickle meaning of romance; waste of everyone's efforts. Retitled: EUROPA '51.

Greatest Show on Earth, The (1952) **C-153m.** ***½ D: Cecil B. DeMille. Betty Hutton, Charlton Heston, Cornel Wilde, Dorothy Lamour, Gloria Grahame, James Stewart, Henry Wilcoxon, Lawrence Tierney, Lyle Bettger. Big package of fun from DeMille, complete with hokey performances, clichés, big-top excitement. Stewart well cast as circus clown, tops rest of cast. Some funny surprise guests appear.

Greatest Story Ever Told, The (1965) **C-141m.** **½ D: George Stevens. Max Von Sydow, Charlton Heston, Carroll Baker, Angela Lansbury, Sidney Poitier, Shelley Winters, John Wayne, Ed Wynn, Jose Ferrer, Van Heflin, Claude Rains, Telly Savalas, many others. Some of the most spectacular scenes ever filmed lose all validity because of incessant cameos that run throughout film. Would *you* believe John Wayne as a Roman officer supervising Christ's crucifixion?

Greatest Thing That Almost Happened, The (1977) **C-100m.** TVM D: Gilbert Moses. Jimmie Walker, James Earl Jones, Deborah Allen, Tamu, Kevin Hooks, Sandra Sharp. A teenaged tearjerker involving a high school athlete stricken with leukemia and his insensitive father who never had time for him. Average.

Greek Tycoon, The (1978) **C-106m.** ** D: J. Lee Thompson. Anthony Quinn, Jacqueline Bisset, Raf Vallone, Edward Albert, Charles Durning, Camilla Sparv, James Franciscus.

Pointless fabrication about romance and marriage of Aristotle you-know-who and a certain president's widow. Beautiful settings add only luster to this tepid script that doesn't even rate as good trash.

Greeks Had a Word for Them, The (1932) **79m.** *** D: Lowell Sherman. Joan Blondell, Ina Claire, Madge Evans, David Manners, Lowell Sherman. Retitled: THREE BROADWAY GIRLS. Vintage comedy of three gold-digging girls looking for husbands; still entertaining although redone several times, including HOW TO MARRY A MILLIONAIRE.

Green Archer, The (1961-German) **95m.** **½ D: Jurgen Roland. Gert Frobe, Karin Dor, Klausjurgen Wussow, Edith Teichman. Nicely paced actioner with plenty of excitement as masked archer eliminates his victims, baffles police; from Edgar Wallace novel.

Green Berets, The (1968) **C-141m.** BOMB D: John Wayne, Ray Kellogg. John Wayne, David Janssen, Jim Hutton, Aldo Ray, Raymond St. Jacques, Bruce Cabot, Jack Soo, Patrick Wayne. Politics aside, this overlong, incredibly clichéd salute to the Special Forces has enough absurd situations and unfunny comedy relief to offend anyone; don't miss now-famous final scene, where the sun sinks into the East.

Green Cockatoo, The (1937-British) **65m.** ** D: William Cameron Menzies. John Mills, Rene Ray, Robert Newton, Charles Oliver, Bruce Seton. Considering credentials of this film (story by Graham Greene, director Menzies, etc.) the results are particularly disappointing: song-and-dance man Mills and Ray unravel mystery surrounding murder of his brother (Newton). Originally titled FOUR DARK HOURS.

Green Dolphin Street (1947) **141m.** **½ D: Victor Saville. Lana Turner, Van Heflin, Donna Reed, Richard Hart, Frank Morgan, Edmund Gwenn. If only for its glossy production values, this plodding costumer has merit. Story of two sisters (Turner, Reed) after the same man in New Zealand is tedious; set in 19th century.

Green-Eyed Blonde, The (1957) **76m.** ** D: Bernard Girard. Susan Oliver, Tommie Moore, Juanita Moore, Evelyn Scott, Roy Glenn. Oliver in title role is properly rebellious as teen-

Green Eyes (1976) **C-100m. TVM** D: John Erman. Paul Winfield, Rita Tushingham, Jonathan Lippe, Victoria Racimo, Royce Wallace, Claudia Bryar. Disillusioned ex-GI Winfield returns to Vietnam to search for the son he left behind with his common-law prostitute wife. Poignant drama with a moving performance by Winfield. Above average.

Green Fire (1954) **C-100m. **½** D: Andrew Marton. Grace Kelly, Stewart Granger, Paul Douglas, John Ericson, Murvyn Vye. Hokum of conflict between owners of emerald mines and tobacco fields, set in South America; attractive stars, slimy villian (Vye).

Green for Danger (1947-British) **93m. **** D: Sidney Gilliat. Sally Gray, Trevor Howard, Leo Genn, Rosamund John, Alastair Sim. Arresting whodunit set at provincial English hospital during WW2. Tension neatly counterbalanced by droll wit of Sim as implacable Scotland Yard inspector.

Green Glove, The (1952) **88m. **½** D: Rudolph Maté. Glenn Ford, Geraldine Brooks, Cedric Hardwicke, George Macready. Occasionally interesting tale of Ford returning to France to find cache of gems he hid during WW2, becoming involved in murder.

Green Goddess, The (1930) **80m. **** D: Alfred E. Green. George Arliss, Alice Joyce, H. B. Warner, Ralph Forbes, Reginald Sheffield, Nigel de Brulier, Ivan Simpson. Stagy early talkie, with Arliss a self-righteous potentate who holds innocent Britishers prisoners.

Green Grass of Wyoming (1948) **C-89m. **½** D: Louis King. Peggy Cummins, Robert Arthur, Charles Coburn, Lloyd Nolan. Atmospheric tale of rival horse-breeding families; the usual, but nicely done.

Green Grow the Rushes (1951-British) **80m. *** D: Derek Twist. Richard Burton, Honor Blackman, Roger Livesey, Geoffrey Keen, Archie Duncan. Delightful comedy of villagers trying to hide their whiskey-brewing from interfering government agents.

Green Hell (1940) **87m. **½** D: James Whale. Douglas Fairbanks, Jr., Joan Bennett, Alan Hale, John Howard, George Bancroft, Vincent Price, George Sanders. Standard jungle-expedition film worthwhile for fine cast.

Green Light (1937) **85m. **½** D: Frank Borzage. Errol Flynn, Anita Louise, Margaret Lindsay, Cedric Hardwicke, Erin O'Brien-Moore, Henry Kolker, Spring Byington, Russell Simpson, Pierre Watkin. Dedicated doctor gives up practice when man dies on his operating table; offbeat casting for Flynn, but interesting film. Based on Lloyd C. Douglas novel.

Green Man, The (1957-British) **80m. *** D: Robert Day. Alastair Sim, George Cole, Terry-Thomas, Jill Adams, Avril Angers. Droll comedy of a seemingly timid clockmaker who prefers his part-time job as paid assassin.

Green Mansions (1959) **C-101m. **½** D: Mel Ferrer. Audrey Hepburn, Anthony Perkins, Lee J. Cobb, Sessue Hayakawa, Henry Silva, Nehemiah Persoff. W. H. Hudson's romance set in South America suffers from miscast Hepburn as Rima the Bird Girl, whom fate decrees shall not leave her sanctuary. Perkins properly puzzled as male lead.

Green Pastures, The (1936) **90m. ***½** D: William Keighley, Marc Connelly. Rex Ingram, Oscar Polk, Eddie Anderson, Frank Wilson, George Reed, Abraham Gleaves, Myrtle Anderson. All-Negro cast in Marc Connelly fable of life in heaven, and biblical stories which give more meaning to Adam, Noah, and Moses than many so-called biblical films. Ingram is fine as "de Lawd."

Green Promise, The (1949) **93m. **½** D: William D. Russell. Marguerite Chapman, Walter Brennan, Robert Paige, Natalie Wood. Grim little film of Brennan and his four children trying to eke out a living on their farm; unpretentious and engaging.

Green Scarf, The (1955-British) **96m. *** D: George More O'Ferrall. Michael Redgrave, Ann Todd, Kieron Moore, Leo Genn. Imaginative handling of blind man accused of homicide, defended by aging attorney; set in Paris.

Green Slime, The (1969-Japanese-U.S.) **C-88m. *½** D: Kinji Fukasaku. Robert Horton, Richard Jaeckel, Luciana Paluzzi, Bud Widom. Corny space substance is gonna do in the world if a few intrepid space explorers can't find a way to stop it. Not as much fun as it sounds.

Green Years, The (1946) 127m. ***** D: Victor Saville. Charles Coburn, Tom Drake, Hume Cronyn, Gladys Cooper, Dean Stockwell. Touching story of young boy brought up in Scotland under domineering parentage, loved only by grandfather.

Greene Murder Case, The (1929) 69m. D: Frank Tuttle. William Powell, Florence Eldridge, Ulrich Haupt, Jean Arthur, Eugene Pallette. SEE: **Philo Vance** series.

Greenwich Village (1944) C-82m. ****** D: Walter Lang. Carmen Miranda, Don Ameche, William Bendix, Vivian Blaine, Felix Bressart, Tony and Sally De Marco, Step Brothers. Limp musical with dubious casting, routine score.

Greetings (1968) C-88m. ****½** D: Brian De Palma. Jonathan Warden, Robert De Niro, Gerrit Graham, Richard Hamilton, Megan McCormick, Allen Garfield. Dated but intriguing antiestablishment comedy, made on a shoestring, and capturing in abstract fashion some of the youthful counter-culture attitudes of the 1960s. Interesting, too, for fledgling work of De Niro and director-writer De Palma.

Greyfriars Bobby (1961) C-91m. ****½** D: Don Chaffey. Donald Crisp, Laurence Naismith, Alex MacKenzie, Kay Walsh, Duncan MacRae, Gordon Jackson. British Disney film based on true story of dog who became "neighborhood pet" in Edinburgh during 19th century through unusual circumstances. Great charm, fine performances offset by slow pacing.

Griffin and Phoenix: A Love Story (1976) C-100m. TVM D: Daryl Duke. Peter Falk, Jill Clayburgh, John Lehne, Dorothy Tristan, Ben Hammer, John Harkins. Tearjerker about two doomed people sharing a brief but buoyant affair. The stars do wonders brightening a maudlin tale. Average.

Grip of the Strangler SEE: **Haunted Strangler, The**

Grisbi (1953-French) 94m. ****½** D: Jacques Becker. Jean Gabin, Jeanne Moreau, Rene Dary, Lino Ventura, Dora Doll. Gabin is tough in unorthodox tale of Parisian underground, involving gold heist and its mysterious

disappearence. Retitled: DON'T TOUCH THE LOOT.

Grissly's Millions (1944) 54m. ****½** D: John English. Paul Kelly, Virginia Grey, Don Douglas, Elisabeth Risdon. Programmer involving murder of wealthy man and the typical manhunt for the killer; smoothly done.

Grissom Gang, The (1971) C-127m. ****½** D: Robert Aldrich. Kim Darby, Scott Wilson, Tony Musante, Connie Stevens, Irene Dailey, Robert Lansing. Youthful kidnapper Wilson finds himself falling in love with his victim (Darby) in this strange, violent film . . . an odd mixture of elements from BONNIE AND CLYDE and Faulkner's SANCTUARY. Remake of 1948 British film NO ORCHIDS FOR MISS BLANDISH.

Grizzly (1976) C-92m. ****** D: William Girdler. Christopher George, Andrew Prine, Richard Jaeckel, Joan McCall, Joe Dorsey. OK rip-off of JAWS about an 18-foot, 2000-pound grizzly bear who launches series of attacks on campers in national park. Might be subtitled CLAWS.

Groom Wore Spurs, The (1951) 80m. ****** D: Richard Whorf. Ginger Rogers, Jack Carson, Joan Davis, Stanley Ridges. Occasionally zesty comedy of attorney Rogers marrying cowboy actor Carson, divorcing him, but coming to his defense in criminal case.

Groove Tube, The (1974) C-75m. ****½** D: Ken Shapiro. Ken Shapiro, Lane Sarasohn, Chevy Chase, Richard Belzer, Mary Mendham, Bill Kemmill. Sometimes funny, sometimes stupid R-rated collection of satirical episodes about television. Definitely has its heart in the right place, but a mixed bag.

Grounds for Marriage (1950) 91m. ****½** D: Robert Z. Leonard. Van Johnson, Kathryn Grayson, Paula Raymond, Barry Sullivan, Lewis Stone. Cutesy musicomedy of opera star Grayson and her ex-husband, physician Johnson.

Groundstar Conspiracy, The (1972-Canadian) C-96m. ****½** D: Lamont Johnson. George Peppard, Michael Sarrazin, Christine Belford. When explosion smashes secret space project, espionage work first begins. Tightly made, but poor dialogue.

Group, The (1966) C-150m. ******* D: Sidney Lumet. Candice Bergen, Joan Hackett, Elizabeth Hartman, Shirley Knight, Joanna Pettet, Mary-Robin

Redd, Jessica Walter, Kathleen Widdoes, James Broderick, Larry Hagman, Hal Holbrook. Uneven, but generally good adaptation of Mary McCarthy's high-class soap opera about eight graduates of Vassar-type college. Knight and Hackett stand out in excellent cast.

Guadalcanal Diary (1943) 93m. ***½ D: Lewis Seiler. Preston Foster, Lloyd Nolan, William Bendix, Richard Conte, Anthony Quinn, Richard Jaeckel. Richard Tregaskis' hot-off-the-wire account of Marines fighting for vital Pacific base becomes one of best WW2 actioners; large, competent cast.

Guardsman, The (1931) 89m. *** D: Sidney Franklin. Alfred Lunt, Lynn Fontanne, Roland Young, ZaSu Pitts, Maude Eburne, Herman Bing. The Lunts' only starring film is charming tour de force from Molnar's comedy of jealous husband testing his wife's fidelity. Remade as THE CHOCOLATE SOLDIER.

Guerre est Finie, La (1967-French-Swedish) 121m. **** D: Alain Resnais. Yves Montand, Ingrid Thulin, Genevieve Bujold, Dominique Rozan, Juan-François Remi. Aging, tired Spanish revolutionary Montand has to face the fact that his 25 years of work have achieved virtually nothing. Powerhouse Montand-Thulin-Bujold trio is in peak form, script is intelligent, Resnais direction his best to date.

Guerrillas in Pink Lace (1964) C-96m. *½ D: George Montgomery. George Montgomery, Valerie Varda, Roby Grace, Joan Shawlee. Poorly produced yarn filmed in Philippines about Montgomery and group of showgirls on the lam from Manila and the Japs.

Guess Who's Coming to Dinner? (1967) C-108m. *** D: Stanley Kramer. Spencer Tracy, Katharine Hepburn, Sidney Poitier, Katharine Houghton, Cecil Kellaway, Beah Richards, Roy E. Glenn Sr. Glossy tale of mixed marriage as Houghton brings home fiancé Poitier to meet her perplexed parents. Fluff is given strength by Oscar-winning Hepburn, and Tracy in his last film appearance.

Guess Who's Sleeping in My Bed? (1973) C-74m. TVM D: Theodore Flicker. Barbara Eden, Dean Jones, Kenneth Mars, Susanne Benton, Reta Shaw, Todd Lookinland. Ex-husband too lazy to find work ingratiates his way into former wife's house, stays there with his family and all but ruins her sex life. Entertaining comedy with memorable performances by Eden, Jones, Mars, and Benton. Above average.

Guest in the House (1944) 121m. **½ D: John Brahm. Anne Baxter, Ralph Bellamy, Aline MacMahon, Ruth Warrick, Jerome Cowan, Margaret Hamilton, Marie McDonald. Baxter is disturbed girl who turns a happy household into one of chaos in this grim melodrama.

Guest Wife (1945) 90m. **½ D: Sam Wood. Claudette Colbert, Don Ameche, Dick Foran, Charles Dingle, Grant Mitchell, Wilma Francis. Breezy comedy depends on stars for flair; they do just fine, with Claudette posing as Ameche's wife to husband Foran's chagrin.

Guide for the Married Man, A (1967) C-89m. ***½ D: Gene Kelly. Walter Matthau, Inger Stevens, Robert Morse, Sue Ane Langdon, Claire Kelly, Elaine Devry; guest stars Lucille Ball, Jack Benny, Polly Bergen, Joey Bishop, Sid Caesar, Art Carney, Wally Cox, Jayne Mansfield, Hal March, Louis Nye, Carl Reiner, Phil Silvers, Terry-Thomas, Ben Blue, Ann Morgan Guilbert, Jeffrey Hunter, Marty Ingels, Sam Jaffe. Consistently funny, imaginative adult comedy of Morse trying to teach faithful husband Matthau the ABC's of adultery, with the aid of many guest stars who demonstrate Morse's theories. Joke of it all is that Matthau is married to gorgeous Inger Stevens!

Guide for the Married Woman, A (1978) C-100m. TVM D: Hy Averback. Cybill Shepherd, Charles Frank, Barbara Feldon, Eve Arden, George Gobel, Bill Dana, John Hillerman, Bonnie Franklin, John Byner, John Beradino, Mary Frances Crosby. There's a smile or two to be had as lots of familiar TV faces pop up to help daydreaming housewife Shepherd looking for some innocent romance to spice up her life. A belated, so-so followup by writer Frank Tarloff to his very funny *A Guide for the Married Man* (1967). Average.

Guilt of Janet Ames, The (1947) 83m. *** D: Henry Levin. Rosalind Russell, Melvyn Douglas, Sid Caesar, Betsy Blair, Nina Foch, Charles

Cane, Harry Von Zell. Good casting highlights well-done film of Russell at the end of her rope when husband dies and she seeks the cause.

Guilty, The (1947) 70m. **½ D: John Reinhardt. Bonita Granville, Don Castle, Wally Cassell, Regis Toomey. At times engaging murder yarn; twin sisters clash over their love for Castle.

Guilty Bystander (1950) 92m. **½ D: Joseph Lerner. Zachary Scott, Faye Emerson, Mary Boland, Sam Levene, Kay Medford. Down-and-out ex-house detective finds new zest for life when estranged wife reports their child kidnapped.

Guilty of Treason (1949) 86m. **½ D: Felix E. Feist. Charles Bickford, Paul Kelly, Bonita Granville, Richard Derr. Splendidly acted account of the famed Cardinal Mindszenty trial in Hungary, marred by low production values.

Guilty or Innocent: The Sam Sheppard Murder Case (1975) C-150m. TVM D: Robert Michael Lewis. George Peppard, Barnard Hughes, Walter McGinn, William Windom, Nina Van Pallandt, Paul Fix, William Dozier, George Murdock, Claudette Nevins, Kathleen Crawford, John Crawford. Peppard is famed Cleveland osteopathic surgeon convicted in 1954 of the murder of his wife, then retried twelve years later. Striking performance by McGinn as F. Lee Bailey, the flamboyant lawyer whose defense in retrial of Sheppard made him courtroom superstar. Above average.

Gulliver's Travels (1939) C-74m. **½ D: Dave Fleischer. Singing voices of Lanny Ross, Jessica Dragonette. Max Fleischer's feature-length cartoon version of Jonathan Swift tale suffers from weak scripting, never getting audience involved in story. Town-crier Gabby is obnoxious, but he's got film's most memorable song, "All's Well."

Gulliver's Travels (1977-British/Belgian) C-80m. ** D: Peter Hunt. Richard Harris, Catherine Schell, Norman Shelley, Meredith Edwards, Julian Glover, Murray Melvin, Bessie Love. Unimaginative adult treatment of the Jonathan Swift classic, with songs. Harris is well cast but film falls flat.

Gulliver's Travels Beyond the Moon (1966-Japanese) C-78m. ** D: Yoshio Kuroda. OK animated feature has

Gulliver and companions going into outer space; acceptable kiddie fare.

Gumball Rally, The (1976) C-107m. **½ D: Chuck Bail. Michael Sarrazin, Tim McIntire, Raul Julia, Susan Flannery, Gary Busey, Steven Keats, J. Pat O'Malley. Featherweight entertainment about free-for-all cross-country road rally; lots of good stuntwork, no real violence. Similar to CANNONBALL, made the same year.

Gumshoe (1972-British) C-88m. **½ D: Stephen Frears. Albert Finney, Billie Whitelaw, Frank Finlay, Janice Rule, Caroline Seymour. Whimsical crime-comedy of small-time British vaudevillian who has seen too many Bogart films and decides to play private-eye.

Gun, The (1974) C-78m. TVM D: John Badham. Stephen Elliott, Jean Le Bouvier, Wallace Rooney, David Huffman, Pepe Serna, Edith Diaz. Odyssey of an American handgun—like the legendary overcoat in *Tales of Manhattan*—forms this episodic story sketching the dramatic changes in the lives of its various owners. Absorbing film with no stars, just sterling character actors and taut direction. Above average.

Gun and the Pulpit, The (1974) C-78m. TVM D: Daniel Petrie. Marjoe Gortner, Slim Pickens, David Huddleston, Geoffrey Lewis, Estelle Parsons, Pamela Sue Martin, Jeff Corey. Evangelist-turned-actor Marjoe is a gunslinger who masquerades as a preacher and fights for law and order in both guises. Average.

Gun Battle at Monterey (1957) 67m. *½ D: Carl G. Hittleman, Sidney A. Franklin, Jr. Sterling Hayden, Pamela Duncan, Mary Beth Hughes, Lee Van Cleef, Byron Foulger, Ted de Corsia. Unremarkable oater with stern Hayden the gunslinger out for revenge against former friend.

Gun Belt (1953) C-77m. **½ D: Ray Nazarro. George Montgomery, Tab Hunter, Helen Westcott, Jack Elam. Notorious outlaw trying to go straight is implicated in crime by his old gang.

Gun Brothers (1956) 79m. ** D: Sidney Salkow. Buster Crabbe, Ann Robinson, Neville Brand, Michael Ansara. Innocuous Western of two brothers, one who becomes a rancher, the other an outlaw who wants to go straight.

Gun Crazy (1949) 86m. ***½ D: Joseph H. Lewis. Peggy Cummins,

John Dall, Berry Kroeger, Morris Carnovsky, Annabel Shaw, Harry Lewis, Nedrick Young. Knockout of a "sleeper" in the BONNIE AND CLYDE tradition, stylishly (and sometimes startlingly) directed. Cummins is femme fatale who leads guncrazy Dall into life of crime. Also known as DEADLY IS THE FEMALE.

Gun Duel in Durango (1957) 73m. ** D: Sidney Salkow. George Montgomery, Steve Brodie, Bobby Clark, Mary Treen. Montgomery must wipe out his outlaw gang before he can reform. Retitled: DUEL IN DURANGO.

Gun for a Coward (1957) C-73m. **½ D: Abner Biberman. Fred MacMurray, Jeffrey Hunter, Janice Rule, Chill Wills, Dean Stockwell, Josephine Hutchison. MacMurray is rancher with two younger brothers, each with contrasting personalities, leading to predictable results.

Gun Fury (1953) C-83m. **½ D: Raoul Walsh. Rock Hudson, Donna Reed, Phil Carey, Lee Marvin, Neville Brand, Leo Gordon. Hudson goes after men who have kidnapped his fiancée (Reed); formidable villainy, good Arizona locations. Originally shown in 3-D.

Gun Glory (1957) C-89m. ** D: Roy Rowland. Stewart Granger, Rhonda Fleming, Chill Wills, James Gregory. Granger is reformed gunslinger rejected by his community until outlaw rampage allows him to redeem himself.

Gun Hawk, The (1963) C-92m. **½ D: Edward Ludwig. Rory Calhoun, Rod Cameron, Ruta Lee, John Litel, Lane Bradford. Outlaw Cameron attempts to reform Calhoun, who's heading for criminal life.

Gun Riders (1970) C-98m. BOMB D: Al Adamson. Jim Davis, Scott Brady, Robert Dix, John Carradine. Ruthless gunman terrorizes settlers one more time, but a good gunman is there to stop him. Cast is full of Western veterans, but they're not much help. Released as FIVE BLOODY GRAVES.

Gun Runners, The (1958) 83m. ** D: Don Siegel. Audie Murphy, Eddie Albert, Patricia Owens, Everett Sloane, Jack Elam. Murphy is involved with gun-smuggling to Cuba; standard plot stolen from TO HAVE AND HAVE NOT.

Gun That Won the West, The (1955) C-71m. ** D: William Castle. Dennis Morgan, Paula Raymond, Richard Denning, Robert Bice. Harmless Grade-B Western of cavalry's use of Springfield rifles to put down Indian uprising.

Gun the Man Down (1956) 78m. ** D: Andrew V. McLaglen. James Arness, Angie Dickinson, Robert Wilke, Emile Meyer. Wounded outlaw swears vengeance on cohorts who left him during holdup. Retitled: ARIZONA MISSION.

Gunfight, A (1971) C-90m. **½ D: Lamont Johnson. Kirk Douglas, Johnny Cash, Jane Alexander, Raf Vallone, Karen Black. Two aging gunfighters meet and decide to sell tickets for a winner-take-all final bout.

Gunfight at Dodge City, The (1959) C-81m. ** D: Joseph M. Newman. Joel McCrea, Julie Adams, John McIntire, Nancy Gates, Richard Anderson, James Westerfield. McCrea plays Bat Masterson, who cleans up gangster-ridden town with ironic results.

Gunfight at Indian Gap (1957) 70m. *½ D: Joseph Kane. Vera Ralston, Anthony George, George Macready, Glenn Strange. Exactly what the title implies, with lovely Ralston to boot.

Gunfight at the O.K. Corral (1957) C-122m. *** D: John Sturges. Burt Lancaster, Kirk Douglas, Rhonda Fleming, Jo Van Fleet, John Ireland, Lee Van Cleef. Stimulating Western filled with tense action sequences in recreating the Doc Holliday-Wyatt Earp battle with Clanton gang.

Gunfight in Abilene (1967) C-86m. **½ D: William Hale. Bobby Darin, Emily Banks, Leslie Nielsen, Michael Sarrazin. Undistinguished post-Civil War account of gun-shy Darin, town sheriff, taking up arms against outlaws.

Gunfighter, The (1950) 84m. ***½ D: Henry King. Gregory Peck, Helen Westcott, Jean Parker, Karl Malden, Richard Jaeckel. Peck is most impressive as gunslinger trying to overcome his bloody past. A top-notch Western.

Gunfighters (1947) C-87m. **½ D: George Waggner. Randolph Scott, Barbara Britton, Dorothy Hart, Bruce Cabot, Charles Grapewin, Forrest Tucker. Strictly average story of gunfighter who vows never again to spill blood. Good cast, but there must be fifty like this one.

Gunfire (1950) 60m. *½ D: William

Berke. Don Barry, Robert Lowery, Wally Vernon, Pamela Blake. Flabby Western cashing in on the Jesse James legend, as a man resembling Frank James creates a series of robberies.

Gung Ho! (1943) 88m. **½ D: Ray Enright. Randolph Scott, Grace McDonald, Alan Curtis, Noah Beery Jr., J. Carrol Naish, David Bruce, Robert Mitchum, Sam Levene. Typical WW2 action film is marked by outrageous jingoism, celebrating the bloodthirsty misfits of the "gung ho" squadron as great American patriots. A jaw-dropping experience.

Gunga Din (1939) 117m. **** D: George Stevens. Cary Grant, Victor McLaglen, Douglas Fairbanks, Jr., Joan Fontaine, Sam Jaffe, Eduardo Ciannelli, Montagu Love, Abner Biberman, Robert Coote. THE Hollywood action-adventure yarn, somehow based on Kipling, with three soldiers-comrades in 19th-century India battling savage punjabs: water boy Jaffe saves the day. Splendid work by everyone. Remade as SERGEANTS THREE and SOLDIERS THREE. Most TV prints run 96m.

Gunman's Walk (1958) C-97m. *** D: Phil Karlson. Van Heflin, Tab Hunter, Kathryn Grant, James Darren. Rancher Heflin tries to train sons Hunter and Darren to be respectable citizens, but clashing personalities cause outburst of violence. Tight-knit Western.

Gunmen from Laredo (1959) C-67m. BOMB D: Wallace MacDonald. Robert Knapp, Jana Davi, Walter Coy, Paul Birch, Don C. Harvey. Hackneyed hunt-the-real-killer Western.

Gunmen of the Rio Grande (1965-Italian) C-86m. ** D: Tulio Demicheli. Guy Madison, Madeleine LeBeau, Carolyn Davys, Massimo Serato. Madison portrays Wyatt Earp, who helps heroine ward off schemes of grasping mine owner.

Gunn (1967) C-94m. *½ D: Blake Edwards. Craig Stevens, Laura Devon, Edward Asner, Sherry Jackson, Helen Traubel, Albert Paulsen. Unsuccessful attempt to recapture flavor of PETER GUNN TV series; Herschel Bernardi, Lola Albright sorely missed, along with quiet understatement and wit that made it memorable. New story is tasteless, violent whodunit involving curious madam.

Gunpoint (1966) C-86m. ** D: Earl Bellamy. Audie Murphy, Joan Staley, Warren Stevens, Edgar Buchanan. Murphy as sheriff gathers a posse to catch outlaw gang who have kidnapped saloon girl.

Guns at Batasi (1964-British) 103m. **½ D: John Guillermin. Richard Attenborough, Jack Hakwins, Mia Farrow, Flora Robson, John Leyton. Acting is all in this intelligent if predictable account of British military life in present-day Africa.

Guns for San Sebastian (1968) C-111m. ** D: Henri Verneuil. Anthony Quinn, Anjanette Comer, Charles Bronson, Sam Jaffe, Silvia Pinal. Quinn plays a popular bandit who helps Mexican village defeat some Yaquis Indians after he is mistaken for a priest, but his personal magnetism isn't enough to combat ridiculous script.

Guns of Darkness (1962) 95m. **½ D: Anthony Asquith. David Niven, Leslie Caron, David Opatoshu, James Robertson Justice, Eleanor Summerfield, Ian Hunter. Civilized drama of Niven searching for life's meaning, set in South America.

Guns of Fort Petticoat, The (1957) C-82m. *** D: George Marshall. Audie Murphy, Kathryn Grant, Hope Emerson, Jeff Donnell, Isobel Elsom. Most enjoyable Western, with Army deserter Murphy supervising a group of Texan women in the art of warfare against pending Indian attack.

Guns of Navarone, The (1961) C-157m. ***½ D: J. Lee Thompson. Gregory Peck, David Niven, Anthony Quinn, Stanley Baker, Anthony Quayle, James Darren, Irene Papas, Gia Scala, James Robertson Justice, Richard Harris. Explosive action film of allied commandos during WW2 plotting to destroy German boats and munitions; high-powered adventure throughout in this first-rate production.

Guns of the Black Witch (1961-Italian) C-83m. ** D: Domenico Paolella. Don Megowan, Silvana Pampanini, Emma Danieli, Livio Lorenzon. Tepid account of pirate leader Megowan out to avenge his father's death; Pampanini his love interest. Set in 17th-century Caribbean.

Guns of the Magnificent Seven (1969) C-106m. **½ D: Paul Wendkos. George Kennedy, Monte Markham, James Whitmore, Reni Santoni, Bernie Casey, Joe Don Baker, Scott Thomas, Michael Ansara, Fernando Rey. Third time out, the "Seven" plot to free Mexican revolutionary leader from a well-guarded fortress. Nothing new, but well done, with plenty of action.

Guns of the Timberland (1960) C-91m. **½ D: Robert D. Webb. Alan Ladd, Jeanne Crain, Gilbert Roland, Frankie Avalon. Pat telling of loggers vs. townpeople.

Gunsight Ridge (1957) 85m. ** D: Francis D. Lyon. Joel McCrea, Mark Stevens, Joan Weldon, Addison Richards, Slim Pickens. Townsfolk finally band together to rid themselves of outlaws; OK Western.

Gunslinger, The (1956) C-83m. *½ D: Roger Corman. John Ireland, Beverly Garland, Allison Hayes, Martin Kingsley. Strange little Western of female marshal trying to maintain law and order in outlaw-ridden town.

Gunsmoke (1953) C-79m. **½ D: Nathan Juran. Audie Murphy, Susan Cabot, Paul Kelly, Charles Drake, Jack Kelly. Compact Western with Murphy reforming to run a ranch and marry his employer's daughter.

Gunsmoke in Tucson (1958) C-80m. **½ D: Thomas Carr. Mark Stevens, Forrest Tucker, Gale Robbins, Gail Kobe, Bill Henry. Sheriff vs. outlaw brother in Arizona territory; not bad.

Guru, The (1969) C-112m. ** D: James Ivory. Michael York, Rita Tushingham, Utpal Dutt, Saeed Jaffrey, Madhur Jaffrey. Sincere but uninvolving story of rock star York who goes to India to learn sitar, meditation from guru Dutt. Director Ivory dwells on Indian lifestyle, settings; Tushingham provides welcome lighter moments in slow-moving film.

Gus (1976) C-96m. *** D: Vincent McEveety. Edward Asner, Don Knotts, Gary Grimes, Tim Conway, Liberty Williams, Dick Van Patten. Football-kicking mule catapults a last-place team to victory; crooks try to kidnap Gus with usual results, including slapstick chase through a supermarket. Entertaining Disney comedy.

Guy Called Caesar, A (1962-British) 62m. *½ D: Frank Marshall. Conrad Phillips, George Moon, Phillip O'Flynn, Maureen Toal. Sloppy account of gangsters on the loose in England, with the inevitable showdown with cops.

Guy Named Joe, A (1943) 120m. **½ D: Victor Fleming. Spencer Tracy, Irene Dunne, Van Johnson, Ward Bond, James Gleason, Lionel Barrymore, Barry Nelson, Esther Williams. Good cast flounders in meandering fantasy about heavenly Tracy coming to earth to lend a hand to WW2 serviceman Johnson.

Guy Who Came Back, The (1951) 91m. ** D: Joseph M. Newman. Paul Douglas, Linda Darnell, Joan Bennett, Don DeFore, Zero Mostel. Cast is above such material but does well by it: ex-football star tries to "find himself."

Guyana: Cult of the Damned (1980-Mexican-Spanish-Panamanian) C-90m. *½ D: Rene Cardona Jr. Stuart Whitman, Gene Barry, John Ireland, Joseph Cotten, Bradford Dillman, Jennifer Ashley, Yvonne De Carlo. Not easy to turn the awesomeness of the Jonestown tragedy—where cult followers committed mass suicide—into lackluster drama, but that's what they've done here.

Guys and Dolls (1955) C-150m. *** D: Joseph L. Mankiewicz. Frank Sinatra, Marlon Brando, Jean Simmons, Vivian Blaine, Stubby Kaye, Veda Ann Borg, Sheldon Leonard. Despite widespread criticism of Brando, lavish musical comedy is most enjoyable. Damon Runyon characters sing fine Frank Loesser score in story of New York gamblers and their gals. Songs: "Guys And Dolls," "Luck Be A Lady," and Kaye's unfogettable "Sit Down, You're Rocking The Boat."

Gypsy (1962) C-149m. **½ D: Mervyn LeRoy. Rosalind Russell, Natalie Wood, Karl Malden, Paul Wallace, Betty Bruce, Parley Baer, Harry Shannon. Fair adaptation of Broadway show with a fine score, including "Everything's Coming Up Roses," "Small World," "Let Me Entertain You." Russell is a good stage mother, but Natalie is no Gypsy Rose Lee.

Gypsy and the Gentleman, The (1958-British) C-89m. **½ D: Joseph Losey. Melina Mercouri, Keith Michell, Patrick McGoohan, Flora Robson. Mercouri as fiery gypsy makes a spicy drama of her love affair with a member of the nobility.

Gypsy Colt (1954) C-72m. **½ D: Andrew Marton. Donna Corcoran, Ward Bond, Frances Dee, Larry Keating. Tender little film of faithful horse who returns to mistress after parents have sold it to racing stable. Remake of LASSIE COME HOME.

Gypsy Fury (1951-Swedish-French) 63m. ** D: Christian-Jaque. Viveca Lindfors, Christopher Kent, Romney Brent, Johnny Chabot, Lauritz Falk. Fable about gypsy and the aristocratic lover who gives up all to marry her.

Gypsy Girl (1966-British) C-102m. **½ D: John Mills. Hayley Mills, Ian McShane, Laurence Naismith, Geoffrey Bayldon. Brooding account of backward Hayley Mills finding her first romance with McShane; atmospheric but meandering. Originally titled SKY WEST AND CROOKED.

Gypsy Moths, The (1969) C-110m. *** D: John Frankenheimer. Burt Lancaster, Deborah Kerr, Gene Hackman, Scott Wilson, Bonnie Bedelia, William Windom, Sheree North. Story of three skydivers in Kansas captures the Midwest well; Kerr, Wilson and Bedelia help raise potential soap opera to the level of "personal drama."

Gypsy Wildcat (1944) C-75m. ** D: Roy William Neill. Maria Montez, Jon Hall, Nigel Bruce, Leo Carrillo, Gale Sondergaard, Douglass Dumbrille. Lowbrow saga of princess raised by gypsies; colorful, splashy, but routine.

H. G. Wells' New Invisible Man SEE: New Invisible Man, The

H. M. Pulham, Esq. (1941) 120m. ***½ D: King Vidor. Hedy Lamarr, Robert Young, Ruth Hussey, Charles Coburn, Van Heflin, Fay Holden, Bonita Granville. Upper-class Bostonian Young has fling in N.Y.C. before returning to family duties; Lamarr gives one of her best performances in this John P. Marquand story.

H-Man, The (1958-Japanese) C-79m. ** D: Inoshiro Honda. Kenji Sahara, Yumi Shirakawa, Akihiko Hirata, Koreya Senda. Good special effects marred by dumb script involving radioactive liquid causing havoc in Tokyo, subplot of cops vs. underworld.

Hail, Hero! (1969) C-97m. *½ D: David Miller. Michael Douglas, Arthur Kennedy, Teresa Wright, John Larch, Charles Drake, Peter Strauss. Talky, overblown drama about a well-scrubbed hippie (Douglas) who confronts his family as he sorts out his feelings about Vietnam war. Notable only as screen debuts for Douglas and Strauss. Originally 100m.

Hail, Mafia (1965) 89m. **½ D: Raoul Levy. Henry Silva, Jack Klugman, Eddie Constantine, Elsa Martinelli, Micheline Presle. Fairly interesting melodrama about hired killers going after a witness to gangland mayhem; film has some good European players and nice photography by Raoul Coutard.

Hail the Conquering Hero (1944) 101m. **** D: Preston Sturges. Eddie Bracken, Ella Raines, Raymond Walburn, William Demarest, Elizabeth Patterson, Jimmy Conlin, Franklin Pangborn, Jack Norton, Paul Porcasi. Frail Bracken, rejected by army, is mistaken for war hero by home town. Satirical Sturges at his best, with Demarest and Pangborn stealing much of the proceedings.

Hair (1979) C-121m. **½ D: Milos Forman. John Savage, Treat Williams, Beverly D'Angelo, Annie Golden, Dorsey Wright, Don Dacus, Cheryl Barnes, Nicholas Ray. James Rado-Gerome Ragni-Galt MacDermot's hit musical play celebrated the 60s as the Age of Aquarius; unfortunately, it's now a "period musical" and its impact considerably muffled. Story of straitlaced midwesterner who falls in with N.Y. hippies has exciting musical moments, but doesn't hang together.

Hairy Ape, The (1944) 90m. *** D: Alfred Santell. William Bendix, Susan Hayward, John Loder, Alan Napier, Dorothy Comingore, Eddie Kane. Well-acted film of O'Neill's play of bestial ship stoker in love with socialite passenger Hayward; unpleasant, thought-provoking film.

Hal Roach Comedy Carnival SEE: Curley

Hal Roach Comedy Carnival, The SEE: Fabulous Joe, The

Half a Hero (1953) 71m. ** D: Don Weis. Red Skelton, Jean Hagen, Charles Dingle, Willard Waterman, Mary Wickes, Polly Bergen. Subdued Skelton vehicle written by Max Shulman casts him in situation-comedy mold, as N.Y. magazine writer who tries suburban life for background on story. Pretty bland.

Half A Sixpence (1969) C-148m. *½ D: George Sidney. Tommy Steele,

Julia Foster, Penelope Horner, Cyril Ritchard, Grover Dale. Boisterous but cardboard musical based on show adapted from H. G. Wells' "Kipps," about draper's assistant who inherits fortune, tries to crash society. Colorfully filmed in England, but totally without charm.

Half Angel (1951) C-77m. **½ D: Richard Sale. Loretta Young, Joseph Cotten, Cecil Kellaway, Jim Backus. Pleasant comedy of Young blessed with sleepwalking troubles, leading to romantic complications.

Half-Breed, The (1952) C-81m. ** D: Lewis D. Collins. Robert Young, Janis Carter, Jack Buetel, Barton MacLane, Porter Hall. Unstimulating Western about Indian attacks on the whites.

Half-Human (1955-Japanese) 70m. *½ D: Inoshiro Honda, Kenneth Crane. John Carradine, Morris Ankrum, Russ Thorson, Robert Karnes. Low-budget horror yarn slopped together, involving a most unconvincing prehistoric zombie monster.

Half-Naked Truth, The (1932) 77m. *** D: Gregory LaCava. Lupe Velez, Lee Tracy, Eugene Pallette, Frank Morgan. Delightful comedy about wiseguy carnival pitchman (Tracy) scheming to make Velez an instant celebrity; plenty of laughs, and wonderful performance by Morgan as neurotic Ziegfeld-ish producer.

Halfway House, The (1943-British) 95m. **½ D: Basil Dearden. Mervyn Johns, Glynis Johns, Francoise Rosay, Tom Walls, Alfred Drayton, Sally Ann Howes. Pleasant but low-key fantasy of disparate people brought together at mysterious country inn run by quiet but all-seeing Johns and his daughter.

Hallelujah Trail, The (1965) C-165m. **½ D: John Sturges. Burt Lancaster, Lee Remick, Jim Hutton, Brian Keith, Martin Landau, Donald Pleasence. Remick is rambunctious temperance leader out to reform Lancaster et al in the old West; lumbering satire goes on and on.

Halliday Brand, The (1957) 77m. **½ D: Joseph H. Lewis. Joseph Cotten, Viveca Lindfors, Betsy Blair, Ward Bond. Brooding Western about rancher whose domination of family and workers leads to gunplay and revenge. Weak script; strong performances.

Halloween (1978) C-93m. *** D: John Carpenter. Donald Pleasence, Jamie Lee Curtis, Nancy Loomis, P. J. Soles, Charles Cyphers, Kyle Richards. Low-budget thriller about psychotic murderer who struck on Halloween as a child, and threatens to do so again. Well-made, with lots of scares, plus in-joke references for film buffs.

Halls of Anger (1970) C-96m. **½ D: Paul Bogart. Calvin Lockhart, Janet MacLachlan, James A. Watson, Jr., Rob Reiner. Average violence-in-school story. No better, no worse than a half a dozen predecessors.

Halls of Montezuma (1950) C-113m. **½ D: Lewis Milestone. Richard Widmark, Jack Palance, Robert Wagner, Jack Webb, Reginald Gardiner, Karl Malden, Philip Ahn. Grim WW2 actioner dealing with marine action in the Pacific. Good cast makes stereotypes acceptable.

Hamlet (1948-British) 153m. **** D: Laurence Olivier. Laurence Olivier, Eileen Herlie, Basil Sydney, Felix Aylmer, Jean Simmons. Brilliant adaptation of Shakespeare's play about Danish prince "who just couldn't make up his mind." Hauntingly photographed in Elsinore, Denmark. Won Oscars for Best Picture, Best Actor (Olivier).

Hamlet (1969-British) C-114m. **½ D: Tony Richardson. Nicol Williamson, Gordon Jackson, Anthony Hopkins, Judy Parfitt, Mark Dignam, Marianne Faithfull. Richardson and Williamson moved their boisterous interpretation of the Shakespeare play from stage to screen with only fair results; perhaps the irritating overuse of close-ups will play better on TV. Interesting casting of Faithfull as Ophelia.

Hammer (1972) C-92m. *½ D: Bruce Clark. Fred Williamson, Bernie Hamilton, Vonetta McGee, William Smith, Charles Lampkin. Black boxer takes on the syndicate in fast, but mindless melodrama. Some violence may be cut.

Hammerhead (1968-British) C-99m. *½ D: David Miller. Vince Edwards, Judy Geeson, Diana Dors, Peter Vaughan, Beverly Adams. Weak James Bond carbon copy, tale of supercriminal pursued by soldier of fortune.

Hammersmith Is Out (1972) C-108m. ** D: Peter Ustinov. Elizabeth Taylor, Richard Burton, Peter Ustinov, Beau Bridges, Leon Askin, Leon Ames, John Schuck, George Raft.

Grotesque comedy about mental patient, his male nurse, and a hash slinger proves once again that Liz and Dick will do anything for money; cast has more fun than viewers.

Hand, The (1960-British) 60m. *½ D: Henry Cass. Derek Bond, Ronald Leigh Hunt, Reed De Rouen, Ray Cooney. Slowly paced murder caper, with Scotland Yard tracking down one-armed killer; a few gruesome scenes.

Hand in Hand (1960-British) 75m. **½ D: Philip Leacock. Loretta Parry, Philip Needs, John Gregson, Sybil Thorndike. Good film with a moral for children, about a Jewish girl and a Catholic boy who become friends and learn about each other. Adults may find it hard to take at times.

Hand of the Gallows SEE: Terrible People, The

Handle with Care (1958) 82m. **½ D: David Friedkin. Dean Jones, Joan O'Brien, Thomas Mitchell, John Smith, Walter Abel. Earnest minor film about law student Jones investigating crime within the town where classmates are assigned mock grand-jury work.

Handle With Care (1977) C-98m. *** D: Jonathan Demme. Paul LeMat, Candy Clark, Ann Wedgeworth, Marcia Rodd, Charles Napier, Alix Elias, Roberts Blossom. Fine character studies and vignettes make up for shortcomings in bright, original film. Loosely revolves around LeMat and his obsession with C.B. radio; subplot with bigamist truckdriver is hilarious. Originally released as CITIZENS BAND.

Hands Across the Table (1935) 80m. *** D: Mitchell Leisen. Carole Lombard, Fred MacMurray, Ralph Bellamy, Astrid Allwyn, Marie Prevost. Lombard sparkles as fortune-hunting manicurist who has to choose between MacMurray and Bellamy.

Hands of a Stranger (1962) 86m. **½ D: Newton Arnold. Paul Lukather, Joan Harvey, Irish McCalla, Barry Gordon, Michael Rye. Another version of THE HANDS OF ORLAC, with a pianist receiving a hand-transplant from a criminal, causing him to go berserk.

Hands of the Ripper (1971-British) C-85m. ** D: Peter Sasdy. Eric Porter, Angharad Rees, Jane Merrow, Keith Bell, Derek Godfrey. Early believer in Freud tries to help young daughter of Jack the Ripper. Great atmosphere, solid performances, but after good start, plot dissolves into series of bloody murders. Beware of cuts and don't see it late at night.

Hang 'em High (1968) C-114m. **½ D: Ted Post. Clint Eastwood, Inger Stevens, Ed Begley, Pat Hingle, Arlene Golonka, James MacArthur, Ruth White, Ben Johnson, Charles McGraw, Bruce Dern, Alan Hale Jr., Dennis Hopper. Slick American attempt at spaghetti Western comes off fairly well. Eastwood survives his own hanging, swears vengeance on nine men who lynched him. Fine supporting cast; nice cameo by cowboy veteran Bob Steele as dungeon prisoner.

Hanged Man, The (1964) C-87m. TVM D: Don Siegel. Edmond O'Brien, Vera Miles, Robert Culp, Gene Raymond, J. Carrol Naish, Brenda Scott. Man sets out to avenge murder of friend, winds up in New Orleans Mardi Gras where he meets young woman. Culp and Miles stand out in otherwise OK cast but film over all seems insignificant. Average. Remake of RIDE THE PINK HORSE.

Hanged Man, The (1974) C-78m. TVM D: Michael Caffey. Steve Forrest, Dean Jagger, Cameron Mitchell, Sharon Acker, Will Geer, Brendon Boone. Gunslinger Forrest miraculously survives his own execution and becomes an Old West soldier of fortune. Interesting idea routinely told. Average.

Hanging by a Thread (1979) C-200m. TVM D: Georg Fenady. Sam Groom, Patty Duke Astin, Burt Convy, Burr DeBenning, Donna Mills, Cameron Mitchell. Party of friends dangle above a mountain gorge in a disabled tram reliving the past in this bloated Irwin Allen disaster flick that could have been resolved in 90 minutes or less. Average.

Hanging Tree, The (1959) C-106m. *** D: Delmer Daves. Gary Cooper, Maria Schell, Karl Malden, George C. Scott, Karl Swenson, Ben Piazza, Virginia Gregg. Literate, low-key Western with outstanding performance by Schell as a blind girl nursed by Cooper, a frontier doctor with a past. Not for all tastes.

Hangman, The (1959) 86m. ** D: Michael Curtiz. Robert Taylor, Tina

Louise, Fess Parker, Jack Lord, Mickey Shaughnessy, Shirley Harmer. Rugged Taylor is the lawman who must buck the entire Western town defending a man wanted for murder.

Hangman's House (1928) 72m. *** D: John Ford. June Collyer, Larry Kent, Earle Foxe, Victor McLaglen, Hobart Bosworth. Florid melodrama of frustrated romance and family honor, elevated by sumptuous production and Ford's sure direction. Steeplechase scene predates the one in THE QUIET MAN, and ironically, you can spot young John Wayne as a spectator along the railing!

Hangman's Knot (1952) C-81m. **½ D: Roy Huggins. Randolph Scott, Donna Reed, Claude Jarman, Jr., Richard Denning, Lee Marvin. Above-par Scott Western involving Rebs robbing gold shipment and officer Scott deciding they should return it.

Hangmen Also Die (1943) 131m. **½ D: Fritz Lang. Brian Donlevy, Walter Brennan, Anna Lee, Gene Lockhart, Dennis O'Keefe. OK WW2 drama written by Bertolt Brecht; lethargic Donlevy performance as assassin of notorious Nazi leader; exciting climax including frame-up of Lockhart.

Hangover Square (1945) 77m. *** D: John Brahm. Laird Cregar, Linda Darnell, George Sanders, Glenn Langan, Faye Marlowe, Alan Napier, Frederic Worlock. Unbalanced pianist-composer experiences periods of insanity, goes on murder sprees. Good cast, script, and music.

Hangup (1974) C-94m. ** D: Henry Hathaway. William Elliott, Markl Bey, Cliff Potts, Michael Lerner, Timothy Blake. Disappointing black-oriented actioner about a drug racket; Hathaway has done many fine films, but this isn't one. Bey is good as a doomed prostitute. Also known as SUPER DUDE.

Hannah Lee SEE: **Outlaw Territory**

Hannibal (1960-U.S.A.-Italian) C-103m. ** D: Edgar G. Ulmer. Victor Mature, Rita Gam, Gabriele Ferzetti, Milly Vitale. Lowbrow production makes famed Carthaginian foe of Rome a cardboard figure.

Hannibal Brooks (1969-British) C-101m. **½ D: Michael Winner. Oliver Reed, Michael J. Pollard, Wolfgang Preiss, Helmut Lohner, Karin Baal, Peter Karsten. Pleasant, forgettable film of British P.O.W.

Reed assigned to evacuate valuable elephant from Munich zoo during WW2; forced to go on foot, he turns trip into escape plan. Wavers from comedy to melodrama, with Pollard major comic character; good action climax.

Hannie Caulder (1971-British) C-85m. ** D: Burt Kennedy. Raquel Welch, Robert Culp, Strother Martin, Ernest Borgnine, Jack Elam, Diana Dors, Christopher Lee, Stephen Boyd. Raquel becomes a gunslinger to avenge her rape and her husband's murder by trio of outlaw goons. Only standout: Culp's performance.

Hans Christian Andersen (1952) C-105m. **½ D: Charles Vidor. Danny Kaye, Farley Granger, Jeanmaire, Roland Petit, John Qualen. Melodic Frank Loesser score ("Inchworm," "Ugly Duckling," "Thumbelina," etc.) can't save glossy musical biography of vagabond tale-teller.

Happening, The (1967) 101m. ** D: Elliot Silverstein. Anthony Quinn, Faye Dunaway, George Maharis, Michael Parks, Robert Walker, Milton Berle. Lighthearted and lightheaded caper story centering around kidnapping of a wealthy man (Quinn).

Happiest Days of Your Life, The (1950-British) 81m. *** D: Frank Launder. Alastair Sim, Margaret Rutherford, Richard Wattis, Joyce Grenfell. Unsung comedy involving a boys' school sharing quarters with a displaced girls' academy, frantic resulting situations.

Happiest Millionaire, The (1967) C-164m. **½ D: Norman Tokar. Fred MacMurray, Tommy Steele, Greer Garson, Geraldine Page, Gladys Cooper, Hermione Baddeley, Lesley Ann Warren, John Davidson. Lively but overlong and uninvolving Disney musical, about Philadelphia household of eccentric millionaire Anthony J. Drexel Biddle (MacMurray). Lightly entertaining, but not for nearly three hours.

Happily Ever After (1978) C-100m. TVM D: Robert Scheerer. Suzanne Somers, Bruce Boxleitner, Eric Braeden, John Rubinstein, Ron Hayes. In her first starring role, Suzanne is an aspiring singer torn between hitting it big in Las Vegas or running off with the hick who's smitten with her. Below average.

Happiness Cage, The (1972) C-94m. **½ D: Bernard Girard. Christo-

[314]

pher Walken, Joss Ackland, Ralph Meeker, Ronny Cox, Marco St. John, Tom Aldredge. Uneven but thought-provoking drama about doctor in Germany who utilizes shock treatment on soldiers to stabilize aggressive behavior. Also known as THE MIND SNATCHERS.

Happy Anniversary (1959) 81m. **½ D: David Miller. David Niven, Mitzi Gaynor, Carl Reiner, Loring Smith, Monique Van Vooren, Patty Duke, Elizabeth Wilson. Funny but strained comedy of married couple Niven-Gaynor being embarrassed by daughter Duke telling the nation on TV show that father was indiscreet in his younger days.

Happy Birthday, Wanda June (1971) C-105m. *** D: Mark Robson. Rod Steiger, Susannah York, George Grizzard, Don Murray, William Hickey, Pamelyn Ferdin. Stagy but enjoyable film of Kurt Vonnegut, Jr.'s play about male chauvinist explorer who returns home after seven years, finds his wife matured (and engaged), and his values now obsolete. Fine performances of Vonnegut's funny black-humor situations and dialogue; Hickey hilarious as Steiger's buddy.

Happy Ending, The (1969) C-112m. **½ D: Richard Brooks. Jean Simmons, John Forsythe, Lloyd Bridges, Shirley Jones, Teresa Wright, Dick Shawn, Nanette Fabray, Robert Darin, Tina Louise. Initially intriguing view of modern marriage drones on interminably, as Simmons walks out on husband and family trying to find herself. Michel Legrand score highlighted by "What Are You Doing the Rest of Your Life?"

Happy Go Lovely (1951-British) C-87m. ** D: H. Bruce Humberstone. David Niven, Vera-Ellen, Cesar Romero, Bobby Howes, Diane Hart. Minor musical about producer who hires a chorus girl hoping that her boyfriend has money to invest in the show.

Happy Go Lucky (1943) C-81m. **½ D: Curtis Bernhardt. Mary Martin, Dick Powell, Eddie Bracken, Betty Hutton, Rudy Vallee, Mabel Paige. Happy little musical with flighty plot, no great songs, but spirited cast to keep it moving.

Happy Hooker, The (1975) C-96m. BOMB D: Nicholas Sgarro. Lynn Redgrave, Jean Pierre Aumont, Lovelady Powell, Nicholas Pryor, Eliza-

beth Wilson, Tom Poston. Pointless version of Xaviera Hollander's bestseller about her transformation from secretary to N.Y.'s most prominent madam is so sterilized that it might as well have starred Kate Smith.

Happy Is the Bride (1959-British) 84m. ** D: Roy Boulting. Ian Carmichael, Janette Scott, Cecil Parker, Terry-Thomas, Joyce Grenfell, Eric Barker, Virginia Maskell. Restrained slapstick revolving around couple trying desperately to get through their wedding day.

Happy Land (1943) 73m. **½ D: Irving Pichel. Don Ameche, Frances Dee, Harry Carey, Ann Rutherford, Cara Williams, Richard Crane, Henry (Harry) Morgan, Dickie Moore. Sincere but not always successful Americana of grieving father learning meaning of war as he questions his son's death in WW2.

Happy Landing (1938) 102m. **½ D: Roy Del Ruth. Sonja Henie, Don Ameche, Cesar Romero, Ethel Merman, Jean Hersholt, Billy Gilbert. Predictable Henie vehicle is not up to her other musicals. Pilot Ameche lands near her home; romance blossoms instantly.

Happy Mother's Day, Love George (1973) C-90m. ** D: Darren McGavin. Patricia Neal, Cloris Leachman, Bobby Darin, Ron Howard, Simon Oakland. Unconvincing horror tale, despite some clever attempts by director McGavin to spice it up. Strange doings in seaside house has two great gory murders, but everything else is weak. Retitled: RUN, STRANGER, RUN.

Happy New Year (1973-French) C-112m. *** D: Claude Lelouch. Lino Ventura, Francoise Fabian, Charles Gerard, Andre Falcon. Two thieves plot a robbery, one falls hard for the liberated charmer who runs the antique shop next to the target. Bright romantic caper film is easy to take.

Happy Thieves, The (1962) 88m. **½ D: George Marshall. Rex Harrison, Rita Hayworth, Joseph Wiseman, Gregoire Aslan, Alida Valli. Sad pairing of star duo, out of place in museum theft caper, set in Spain.

Happy Time, The (1952) 94m. **½ D: Richard Fleischer. Charles Boyer, Louis Jourdan, Marsha Hunt, Linda Christian, Bobby Driscoll. Pleasant nostalgia dealing with everyday events in life of a typical family, set in 1920s Canada.

Happy Years, The (1950) C-110m. *** D: William Wellman. Dean Stockwell, Scotty Beckett, Darryl Hickman, Leo G. Carroll, Margalo Gillmore. Owen Johnson's LAWRENCEVILLE STORIES served as basis for this account of high-spirited youth who finds new values at prep school.

Harbor Lights (1963) 68m. BOMB D: Maury Dexter. Kent Taylor, Jeff Morrow, Miriam Colon, Allan Sague. Cheap film of intrigue, with "B" picture perennial Taylor. Congratulations to anyone who can find some relation between title and what goes on in film.

Harbor of Missing Men (1950) 60m. *½ D: R. G. Springsteen. Richard Denning, Barbra Fuller, Steven Geray, George Zucco, Ray Teal, Percy Helton. Unsparkling Republic Picture programmer with Denning innocently involved with jewel smuggling.

Hard Boiled Mahoney (1947) 63m. D: William Beaudine. Leo Gorcey, Huntz Hall, Betty Compson, Bobby Jordan, Gabriel Dell, Billy Benedict, David Gorcey. SEE: **Bowery Boys** series.

Hard Contract (1969) C-107m. **½ D: S. Lee Pogostin. James Coburn, Lee Remick, Lilli Palmer, Burgess Meredith, Patrick Magee, Sterling Hayden. Hired killer Coburn starts to have self-doubts when a woman (Remick) humanizes him. Film is too concerned with making an "important statement" to become particularly entertaining or involving.

Hard Day's Night, A (1964-British) 85m. **** D: Richard Lester. John Lennon, Paul McCartney, George Harrison, Ringo Starr, Wilfred Brambell, Victor Spinetti, Anna Quayle. First Beatles film is director Lester's idea of a typical day in the group's life. He lets his imagination run wild; result is a visual delight, with many Beatles songs on the soundtrack.

Hard Driver SEE: **Last American Hero, The**

Hard, Fast and Beautiful (1951) 79m. ** D: Ida Lupino. Claire Trevor, Sally Forrest, Carleton Young, Robert Clarke. Satisfactory drama: tennis player is driven by social-climbing mother, almost costing the girl her boyfriend.

Hard Man, The (1957) C-80m. ** D: George Sherman. Guy Madison, Lorne Greene, Valerie French, Trevor Bardette. Madison is earnest sheriff who falls in love with murdered rancher's widow.

Hard Times (1975) C-97m. *** D: Walter Hill. Charles Bronson, James Coburn, Jill Ireland, Strother Martin, Maggie Blye, Michael McGuire. Bronson is a tight-lipped streetfighter and Coburn is the sharpster who arranges his bare-knuckled bouts in 1930s New Orleans. Colorful (but violent) entertainment.

Hard to Get (1938) 80m. *** D: Ray Enright. Dick Powell, Olivia de Havilland, Charles Winninger, Allen Jenkins, Bonita Granville, Penny Singleton. Good variation on spoiled-rich-girl-meets-poor-but-hardworking-boy idea. Winninger, as Olivia's wealthy father, and Singleton, as their maid, are hilarious. Film is full of great supporting comics (Grady Sutton, Thurston Hall, Arthur Housman, etc.), and includes "You Must Have Been a Beautiful Baby."

Hard to Handle (1933) 75m. **½ D: Mervyn LeRoy. James Cagney, Mary Brian, Ruth Donnelly, Allen Jenkins, Emma Dunn. It's all Cagney, and he's fine as sharper who arranges marathon dance as publicity stunt; Donnelly helps out as Brian's mother.

Hard Way, The (1942) 109m. *** D: Vincent Sherman. Ida Lupino, Dennis Morgan, Joan Leslie, Jack Carson, Gladys George, Julie Bishop. Intriguing but artificial story of strong-willed Lupino pushing younger sister Leslie into show business career. Holds up until improbable finale, although it seems unlikely that Broadway would cheer Leslie as the greatest discovery of the age. Morgan, Carson match Lupino's fine performance.

Hardcase (1971) C-74m. TVM D: John Llewellyn Moxey. Clint Walker, Stefanie Powers, Pedro Armendariz, Jr., Alex Karras, Luis Mirando. Interesting period Western featuring Walker as soldier of fortune who joins up with Mexican revolutionaries, discovers wife amongst them. Dialogue not bad, situations sometimes believable. Otherwise, pace of film too rushed. Average.

Hardcore (1979) C-108m. **½ D: Paul Schrader. George C. Scott,

Peter Boyle, Season Hubley, Dick Sargent, Leonard Gaines, David Nichols. Calvinist midwesterner Scott (in powerful performance) searches for teenage daughter who's inexplicably dropped out. His journey into nether world of prostitution and porno films is at times fascinating, sad, and repellent. Film marred by unbelievable conclusion.

Harder They Come, The (1973-Jamaican) **C-98m.** *** D: Perry Henzell. Jimmy Cliff, Janet Barkley, Carl Bradshaw, Ras Daniel Hartman, Bobby Charlton. At first glance, a rather crude Jamaican film about aspiring singer Cliff, but before you know it, you're involved and on the edge of your seat. In addition, an excellent, unusual music track.

Harder They Fall, The (1956) **109m.** ***½ D: Mark Robson. Humphrey Bogart, Rod Steiger, Jan Sterling, Mike Lane, Max Baer. Bogart's last feature casts him as cynical sportswriter-turned-press agent who realizes for the first time how badly prizefighters are manipulated by their unfeeling managers. Powerful drama by Budd Schulberg.

Hardys Ride High, The (1939) **80m.** D: George B. Seitz. Lewis Stone, Mickey Rooney, Cecilia Parker, Fay Holden, Ann Rutherford, Sara Haden, Virginia Grey, Marsha Hunt, William T. Orr. SEE: Andy Hardy series.

Harem Girl (1952) **70m.** ** D: Edward Bernds. Joan Davis, Peggie Castle, Arthur Blake, Minerva Urecal. Wacky Davis does her best to enliven slim vehicle about her substituting for a princess.

Harlan County, U.S.A. (1977) **C-103m.** *** D: Barbara Kopple. Gripping, human documentary about the strike of Kentucky mine workers against the Eastover Mining Company, a subsidiary of Duke Power. An Oscar winner as well as a hit at the New York Film Festival.

Harlem Globetrotters, The (1951) **80m.** ** D: Phil Brown. Thomas Gomez, Dorothy Dandridge, Bill Walker, Angela Clarke. Vehicle built around famed basketball team, with a few romantic interludes.

Harlow (1965) **C-125m.** **½ D: Gordon Douglas. Carroll Baker, Peter Lawford, Red Buttons, Michael Connors, Raf Vallone, Angela Lansbury, Martin Balsam, Leslie Nielsen. Slick, colorful garbage will hold your interest, but doesn't ring true. Baker

could never match the real Harlow, but Vallone and Lansbury are good as her stepfather and mother.

Harlow (1965) **109m.** ** D: Alex Segal. Carol Lynley, Efrem Zimbalist, Jr., Barry Sullivan, Hurd Hatfield, Ginger Rogers, Hermione Baddeley, Lloyd Bochner, Audrey Totter, John Williams, Robert Strauss. Amateurish off-the-cuff tedium loosely based on screen star of the 1930s. Rogers as Mama Harlow is best. Shot on videotape.

Harold and Maude (1972) **C-90m.** ***½ D: Hal Ashby. Bud Cort, Ruth Gordon, Vivian Pickles, Cyril Cusack, Charles Tyner, Ellen Geer. Black comedy focuses on loving relationship between 20-year-old Cort, who's obsessed with death, and 79-year-old swinger Gordon. Dismissed at time of release, this has become a cult favorite, and the cornerstone of writer Colin Higgins' reputation. Cort's phony suicides are hilarious.

Harold Lloyd's World of Comedy (1962) **94m.** *** Compiled by Harold Lloyd. Harold Lloyd, Bebe Daniels, Mildred Davis. Delightful comedy scenes show why Lloyd was so popular in the 1920s. Highlights include classic building-climbing episode and other great sight gags. A real gem.

Harold Robbins' The Betsy SEE: Betsy, The

Harold Robbins' The Pirate (1978) **C-200m.** TVM D: Ken Annakin. Franco Nero, Anne Archer, Olivia Hussey, Ian McShane, Christopher Lee, James Franciscus, Eli Wallach, Stuart Whitman. Expensively mounted and deliciously lurid romantic pap in the best Robbins' tradition, set against a backdrop of Arab-Israeli intrigue, with Nero playing a tempestuous Jewish-born Arab-raised oil sheik with a frosty American wife and a daughter who grows up to become a PLO fanatic. Tedious and predictable. Average. (Also known as THE PIRATE.)

Harness, The (1971) **C-100m.** TVM D: Daniel Mann. Lorne Greene, Julie Sommars, Murray Hamilton, Louise Latham, Lee Harcourt Montgomery, Henry Beckman, Joan Tompkins, Robert Karnes. Fairly strong, Steinbeck-based love story: Greene as middle-aged widower, Sommars as young woman. Good location filming, believable script. Above average.

Harper (1966) **C-121m.** ***½ D: Jack Smight. Paul Newman, Lauren

Bacall, Julie Harris, Shelley Winters, Robert Wagner, Janet Leigh, Arthur Hill. High-grade actioner: Newman is private eye hired by Bacall to investigate disappearance of her husband; blowsy Winters, frustrated Harris are involved in fast-paced, sophisticated yarn.

Harper Valley P.T.A. (1978) C-93m. *½ D: Richard Bennett. Barbara Eden, Ronny Cox, Nanette Fabray, Susan Swift, Louis Nye, Pat Paulsen, John Fiedler, Audrey Christie. Long-ago hit song "inspired" this uninspired comedy about a sexy young woman who outsmarts the haughty hypocrites of her local P.T.A. Labored laughs for the yahoo crowd.

Harpy (1970) C-100m. TVM D: Jerald Seth Sindell. Hugh O'Brian, Elizabeth Ashley, Tom Nardini, Marlyn Mason, Mark Miller. Extremely odd (and near brilliant) combination of character study and horror show, most of it occurring at architect's desert home involving ex-wife, ranch assistant, and architect himself. Formula bloody ending, in mysterious tale of passion, actually works. Above average.

Harrad Experiment, The (1973) C-88m. **½ D: Ted Post. Don Johnson, James Whitmore, Tippi Hedren, B. Kirby, Jr., Laurie Walters, Robert Middleton, Victoria Thompson. Fair adaptation of offbeat bestseller by Robert Rimmer in which experimental coed college pushes policy of sexual freedom. Two pairs of relationships singled out as in book, but film actually should've been longer! Beware cuts. Improvisational group Ace Trucking Co., appears as themselves.

Harrad Summer (1974) C-103m. **½ D: Steven H. Stern. Richard Doran, Victoria Thompson, Laurie Walters, Robert Reiser, Bill Dana, Marty Allen, Fair sequel to THE HARRAD EXPERIMENT, about sex-education school for young students. This takes them back to their homes, where they can apply what they've learned.

Harriet Craig (1950) 94m. *** D: Vincent Sherman. Joan Crawford, Wendell Corey, Lucile Watson, Allyn Joslyn, Ellen Corby. Remake of CRAIG'S WIFE is well cast, with Crawford in title role of perfectionist wife who'll stop at nothing to have her house and life run as she wishes.

Harry and Tonto (1974) C-115m. *** D: Paul Mazursky. Art Carney, Ellen Burstyn, Chief Dan George, Geraldine Fitzgerald, Larry Hagman, Arthur Hunnicutt, Barbara Rhoades. An old man takes a cross-country trip with his cat as companion. Art Carney won an Oscar for his performance in this bittersweet, episodic comedy.

Harry and Walter Go to New York (1976) C-123m. ** D: Mark Rydell. James Caan, Elliott Gould, Diane Keaton, Michael Caine, Charles Durning, Lesley Ann Warren, Val Avery, Jack Gilford, Carol Kane. Lavish but lopsided period farce with Caan and Gould as low-grade vaudevillians in the 1890s who wind up trying their luck as safecrackers in N.Y. Spirited but strenuous comedy misses the mark.

Harry Black and the Tiger (1958-British) C-107m. BOMB D: Hugo Fregonese. Stewart Granger, Barbara Rush, Anthony Steel, I. S. Johar. Moldy jungle film tangled in the underbrush, with flashbacks causing confusion. Filmed in India. Sorry, Harry.

Hart to Hart (1979) C-100m. TVM D: Tom Mankiewicz. Robert Wagner, Stefanie Powers, Lionel Stander, Roddy McDowall, Jill St. John, Stella Stevens, Eugene Roche, Clifton James. Wagner and Powers play jet-setters who, in true Nick and Nora Charles fashion, dabble in detective work to solve the mysterious death of a close friend at a glamorous health spa. Pilot for hit series also offers a gag walk-on by Natalie Wood, billed in closing credits as Natasha Gurdin. Average.

Harry in Your Pocket (1973) C-103m. *** D: Bruce Geller. James Coburn, Michael Sarrazin, Trish Van Devere, Walter Pidgeon. Engaging story of group of super-pickpockets and how they prey upon innocent victims. Pidgeon steals the film as sleazy professional crook.

Harum Scarum (1965) C-95m. **½ D: Gene Nelson. Elvis Presley, Mary Ann Mobley, Fran Jeffries, Michael Ansara, Jay Novello, Philip Reed, Theo Marcuse, Billy Barty. Visiting the Middle East gives usual Presley musical formula a change of scenery, albeit back-lot desert locations.

Harvey (1950) 104m. ***½ D: Henry Koster. James Stewart, Josephine Hull, Cecil Kellaway, Peggy Dow, Jesse White, Ida Moore. Stewart gives one of his best performances as tippler Elwood P. Dowd, whose companion is a six-foot rabbit named Harvey. Hull won Oscar as distraught relative. From Mary Chase's play.

Harvey Girls, The (1946) C-101m. *** D: George Sidney. Judy Garland, Ray Bolger, John Hodiak, Angela Lansbury, Preston Foster, Virginia O'Brien, Marjorie Main, Kenny Baker, Cyd Charisse. Westward expansion brings with it Fred Harvey's railroad station restaurants, and proper young waitresses who have civilizing influence on rowdy communities. Silly script made entertaining by good cast and a few musical highlights (like Oscar-winning "Atchison, Topeka, and the Santa Fe").

Harvey Middleman, Fireman (1965) C-75m. ** D: Ernest Pintoff. Gene Troobnick, Hermione Gingold, Patricia Harty, Arlene Golonka, Will MacKenzie, Charles Durning. Lowkey comedy about mild-mannered fireman trying to coordinate fantasy and real life; amiable but unfocused film was animator Pintoff's first live-action feature.

Has Anybody Seen My Gal? (1952) C-89m. ** D: Douglas Sirk. Charles Coburn, Piper Laurie, Rock Hudson, Gigi Perreau, Lynn Bari. Pleasant lightweight musical about family inheriting big sum of money, and wacky repercussions. Set in 1920s.

Hasty Heart, The (1949-British) 99m. ***½ D: Vincent Sherman. Ronald Reagan, Patricia Neal, Richard Todd, Anthony Nicholls, Howard Crawford. Sensitive film version of John Patrick play, focusing on proud Scottish soldier who discovers he has short time to live and friendships he finally makes among his hospital mates.

Hatari! (1962) C-159m. ***½ D: Howard Hawks. John Wayne, Elsa Martinelli, Red Buttons, Hardy Kruger, Gerard Blain, Bruce Cabot. Marvelous lighthearted action film of wild-animal hunters in Africa, with just-right mixture of adventure and comedy. Wayne at his best, rest of the cast fine. Notable Henry Mancini score.

Hatchet Man, The (1932) 74m. **½ D: William Wellman. Edward G. Robinson, Loretta Young, Dudley Digges, Blanche Frederici, J. Carrol Naish, Willie Fung. Interesting contra-type casting about San Francis-

co's Tong wars and Robinson's affair with Young.

Hatfields and the McCoys, The (1975) 74m. TVM D: Clyde Ware. Jack Palance, Steve Forrest, Richard Hatch, Karen Lamm, James Keach, Joan Caulfield. Drama about the petty thievery and the ill-starred love that changed sporadic violence into the legendary feud of the 1880s. Palance and Forrest are the patriarchs of the opposing clans. Average.

Hatful of Rain, A (1957) 109m. *** D: Fred Zinnemann. Eva Marie Saint, Don Murray, Anthony Franciosa, Lloyd Nolan, Henry Silva. Realistic melodrama of the living hell dope addict Murray undergoes, and the effects on those around him; fine performances.

Hatter's Castle (1941-British) 90m. **½ D: Lance Comfort. Deborah Kerr, James Mason, Robert Newton, Emlyn Williams. Fine cast must support fair material in tale of poor man who relentlessly pursues his dream of social acceptance; from A. J. Cronin's novel.

Haunted Honeymoon (1940-British) 83m. **½ D: Arthur B. Woods. Robert Montgomery, Constance Cummings, Leslie Banks, Seymour Hicks, Robert Newton, Googie Withers. Famed amateur criminologist Lord Peter Wimsey (Montgomery) marries mystery writer (Cummings) and settles down to quiet honeymoon—until murder enters the picture and demands their involvement. Montgomery miscast as Dorothy L. Sayers' witty sleuth. Originally titled BUSMAN'S HONEYMOON.

Haunted Strangler, The (1958-British) 81m. **½ D: Robert Day. Boris Karloff, Anthony Dawson, Elizabeth Allan, Derek Birch, Jean Kent. Offbeat yarn of mystery writer investigating case of murderer hung twenty years ago, with dismaying results. Originally titled GRIP OF THE STRANGLER.

Haunting, The (1963) 112m. ***½ D: Robert Wise. Julie Harris, Claire Bloom, Richard Johnson, Russ Tamblyn, Lois Maxwell, Fay Compton. Ninety-year-old New England house is setting for chosen group being introduced to the supernatural, with hair-raising results. See it with a friend! Filmed in England.

Haunts of the Very Rich (1972) C-72m. TVM D: Paul Wendkos. Lloyd Bridges, Cloris Leachman, Edward

Asner, Anne Francis, Tony Bill, Donna Mills, Robert Reed, Moses Gunn. Mixed up reworking of NO EXIT premise. Seven vacationers agree to be flown to tropical paradise, even though they aren't told exactly where they are. Offbeat location work only asset in otherwise plainly acted, unimaginatively scripted allegory. Forget about ending. Average.

Hauser's Memory (1970) **C-100m.** TVM D: Boris Sagal. Robert Webber, Susan Strasberg, David McCallum, Leslie Nielsen, Lilli Palmer. Psychological thriller based on Curt Siodmak story; scientist McCallum injects himself with another man's brain fluid, enabling him to relive man's WW2 experiences. Filmed in Europe. Average.

Have Rocket, Will Travel (1959) **76m. **½** D: David Lowell Rich. The Three Stooges, Jerome Cowan, Anna Lisa, Bob Colbert. Good slapstick with the Stooges accidentally launched into space, where they meet a unicorn and become national heroes.

Having a Wild Weekend (1965-British) **91m. **½** D: John Boorman. Dave Clark, Barbara Ferris, Lenny Davidson, Rick Huxley, Mike Smith, Denis Payton, David Lodge. Just as The Dave Clark Five tried to steal some of the Beatles' thunder, this fast-paced trifle tried to capture success of A HARD DAY'S NIGHT. Director Boorman's first film. Originally titled CATCH US IF YOU CAN.

Having Babies (1976) **C-100m. TVM** D: Robert Day. Desi Arnaz, Jr., Adrienne Barbeau, Ronny Cox, Harry Guardino, Tom Kennedy, Vicki Lawrence, Richard Masur, Greg Mullavey, Linda Purl, Jan Sterling, Karen Valentine, Abe Vigoda, Jessica Walter. Drama interweaving stories of four couples as they experience childbirth by the "natural" Lamaze method. Topical subject, familiar TV faces, dumb dialogue. Followed by sequels and then a weekly series. Average.

Having Babies II (1977) **C-100m. TVM** D: Richard Michaels. Tony Bill, Cliff Gorman, Carol Lynley, Paula Prentiss, Wayne Rogers, Nicholas Pryor, Lee Meriwether. Another dose of emotional crises involving birth, adoption and first love affecting the lives of several couples. The

usual multi-character suds capped by actual birth of twins. Average.

Having Babies III (1978) **C-100m.** TVM D: Jackie Cooper. Susan Sullivan, Dennis Howard, Beverly Todd, Mitchell Ryan, Patty Duke Astin, Jamie Jackson Smith, Phil Foster. Third trip to the delivery room before the series that quickly was retitled JULIE FARR, M.D. (for Sullivan's character) and tried in several formats over subsequent seasons. Movie gave Astin another of her many Emmy nominations. Average.

Having Wonderful Crime (1945) **70m. *** D: A. Edward Sutherland. Pat O'Brien, George Murphy, Carole Landis, Lenore Aubert, George Zucco. Lighthearted mystery of trio of friends investigating magic act which ended in murder; O'Brien a lot of fun.

Having Wonderful Time (1938) **71m. **½** D: Alfred Santell. Ginger Rogers, Douglas Fairbanks, Jr., Peggy Conklin, Lucille Ball, Lee Bowman, Eve Arden, Red Skelton. Big cast in OK film about Catskills resort hotel; Ginger wants culture on summer vacation but gets Doug instead. Skelton does well in feature film debut.

Hawaii (1966) **C-171m. *** D: George Roy Hill. Julie Andrews, Max von Sydow, Richard Harris, Torin Thatcher, Gene Hackman, Carroll O'Connor. Sprawling filmization of James Michener's novel plays well on TV, where cutting actually helps. Story follows growth of Hawaii in 1800s as fierce but well-intentioned missionary tries to bring religion to the undeveloped islands. Uneven but generally entertaining epic. Originally released at 189m.

Hawaii Five-O (1968) **C-100m. TVM** D: Leonard Freeman. Jack Lord, Nancy Kwan, Leslie Nielsen, Andrew Duggan, Lew Ayres, James Gregory. Supposedly realistic depiction of high-tension police force headed by taskmaster McGarrett (Lord) trying to uncover deadly Chinese weapon hidden aboard tramp steamer. Pilot for TV series; average.

Hawaiians, The (1970) **C-134m. *** D: Tom Gries. Charlton Heston, Geraldine Chaplin, John Phillip Law, Tina Chen, Alec McCowen, Mako. Epic narrative of seafaring Heston returning home to a restless, changing Hawaii. Film follows several decades of relationships, conflict, hardship, progress, sex, leprosy—you name it. Compelling, colorful storytelling, with outstanding performance by Chen.

Hawk of the Wilderness SEE: Lost Island of Kioga

Hawkins on Murder (1973) C-74m. TVM D: Jud Taylor. James Stewart, Bonnie Bedelia, Margaret Markov, Strother Martin, Kate Reid, David Huddleston, Antoinette Bower. Pilot for Stewart's TV series surrounds likable star with good cast in OK mystery/courtroom drama about heiress accused in triple murder. Some scenes were shot at lavish Harold Lloyd estate. Above average. Retitled DEATH AND THE MAIDEN.

Hawmps! (1976) C-113m. ** D: Joe Camp. James Hampton, Christopher Connelly, Slim Pickens, Jack Elam, Denver Pyle. Amusing idea based on real life incident: camels trained as Army mounts in Texas desert. Some comedy results, but how far can you stretch one idea? Certainly not 113 minutes!

Hazard (1948) 95m. ** D: George Marshall. Paulette Goddard, Macdonald Carey, Fred Clark, Stanley Clements. Routine comedy of private-eye Carey following Goddard, falling in love in the process.

He Married His Wife (1940) 83m. ** D: Roy Del Ruth. Joel McCrea, Nancy Kelly, Roland Young, Mary Boland, Cesar Romero. McCrea doesn't want to bear the expense of divorce; solution is obvious, and so is most of the film.

He Ran All the Way (1951) 77m. **½ D: John Berry. John Garfield, Shelley Winters, Wallace Ford, Selena Royle, Gladys George. Garfield is criminal on the lam hiding out at Winters' home, with predictable results. Garfield's last film.

He Rides Tall (1964) 84m. **½ D: R. G. Springsteen. Tony Young, Dan Duryea, Madlyn Rhue, George Petrie. Stark Western about the sheriff forced to shoot it out with foster-father's son.

He Stayed for Breakfast (1940) 89m. ** D: Alexander Hall. Loretta Young, Melvyn Douglas, Una O'Connor, Eugene Pallette, Alan Marshal. NINOTCHKA and COMRADE X

in reverse, as Russian Douglas is Americanized by beautiful Young; trivial.

He Walked by Night (1948) 79m. *** D: Alfred L. Werker. Richard Basehart, Scott Brady, Roy Roberts, Whit Bissell, Jack Webb. Grade-A drama of killer hunted by police; told in semi-documentary style. Effective performances by all.

He Was Her Man (1934) 70m. ** D: Lloyd Bacon. James Cagney, Joan Blondell, Victor Jory, Frank Craven, Sarah Padden. Most disappointing for Cagney as con-man who snatches Blondell away from Jory, who tries to get even.

He Who Gets Slapped (1924) 85m. *** D: Victor Seastrom. Lon Chaney, Norma Shearer, John Gilbert, Tully Marshall, Marc McDermott, Ford Sterling. Brilliant scientist tries to bury personal tragedy under mask of circus clown, who falls in love with beautiful bareback rider (Shearer). Famous story becomes Pagliacci-type vehicle for Chaney.

He Who Rides a Tiger (1966-British) 103m. ** D: Charles Crichton. Tom Bell, Judi Dench, Paul Rogers, Kay Walsh, Ray McAnally. Cat burglar is nice to children and is further softened by love, but he still has professional problems; OK programmer.

He's a Cockeyed Wonder (1950) 77m. *½ D: Peter Godfrey. Mickey Rooney, Terry Moore, William Demarest, Ross Ford, Mike Mazurki. Bland Rooney film has him as energetic young man who captures a gang of robbers and gets to marry his boss' daughter.

Head (1968) C-86m. *** D: Bob Rafelson. The Monkees, Victor Mature, Annette Funicello, Timothy Carey, Logan Ramsey, Frank Zappa, Jack Nicholson. Far-out film debut for TV rock group was written (or concocted) by Rafelson and Nicholson before they made big splash with FIVE EASY PIECES, this overlooked item is a delightful explosion of crazy ideas with no coherent plot, using many old film clips, and such unlikely guest stars as Annette and Victor Mature. Well worth seeing.

Head, The (1959-German) 92m. ** D: Victor Trivas. Horst Frank, Karin Kernke, Michel Simon, Helmut Schmid, Dieter Eppler. Old-fashioned chiller involving head-transplants, with obligatory murders and blood-drenched revenge; not very convincing.

Head of a Tyrant (1958-Italian) €-83m. ** D: Fernando Cerchio. Massimo Girotti, Isabelle Corey, Renato Baldini, Yvette Masson. Humdrum spectacle involving seige of Bethulia by Assyrians, with Corey playing the legendary Judith.

Head Over Heels (1979) €-97m. **½ D: Joan Micklin Silver. John Heard, Mary Beth Hurt, Peter Riegert, Kenneth McMillan, Gloria Grahame, Nora Heflin. Low-key story of Heard's obsession with winning back former girlfriend Hurt; the kind of film that engenders strictly personal reactions—it will either charm or annoy you. Based on Ann Beattie's *Chilly Scenes of Winter.*

Heading for Heaven (1947) 71m. *½ D: Lewis D. Collins. Stuart Erwin, Glenda Farrell, Irene Ryan, Milburn Stone, Selmer Jackson, Janis Wilson. Soggy account of well-meaning Erwin trying to build model middle-income-bracket community, but being fleeced by racketeers.

Headless Ghost, The (1958-British) BOMB D: Peter Graham Scott. Richard Lyon, Liliane Sottane, David Rose, Clive Revill, Carl Bernard, Trevor Barnett. Brainless horror flick with students investigating a haunted castle.

Headline Hunters (1955) 70m. ** D: William Witney. Rod Cameron, Julie Bishop, Ben Cooper, Raymond Greenleaf. Uninspired tale of fledgling reporter tracking down big-city racketeers. Remake of 1940 BEHIND THE NEWS.

Headlines of Destruction (1955-French) ** D: John Berry. Eddie Constantine, Bella Darvi, Paul Frankeur, Walter Chiari. Interesting concept poorly executed; Darvi is defense attorney involved with Constantine in trial of man accused of murder.

Healers, The (1974) €-100m. TVM D: Tom Gries. John Forsythe, Kate Woodville, Season Hubley, Pat Harrington, Anthony Zerbe, Beverly Garland, John McIntire. Hospital drama with the harassed director of the medical center (Forsythe) at the core. Performances are adequate, the plot written to formula. Average.

Hear Me Good (1957) 80m. *½ D: Don McGuire. Hal March, Joe E. Ross, Merry Anders, Jean Willes.

Trivia concerning a fixed beauty contest.

Heart Is a Lonely Hunter, The (1968) €-125m. **½ D: Robert Ellis Miller. Alan Arkin, Sondra Locke, Laurinda Barrett, Stacy Keach, Chuck McCann, Cicely Tyson. Good acting by Arkin and entire cast helps this rambling adaptation of Carson McCullers' novel about the way a deaf mute helps those around him; film would have been better as a period-piece.

Heart of the Matter, The (1954-British) 100m. *** D: George More O'Ferrall. Trevor Howard, Elizabeth Allan, Maria Schell, Denholm Elliott. Graham Greene's novel of inner and outward conflict set in South Africa, with Howard as police officer on verge of mental collapse.

Heartbeat (1946) 102m. ** D: Sam Wood. Ginger Rogers, Jean-Pierre Aumont, Adolphe Menjou, Basil Rathbone, Melville Cooper. So-so drama of lady pickpocket and diplomat who eventually fall for each other; benefits from good cast.

Heartbreak Kid, The (1972) €-104m. *** D: Elaine May. Charles Grodin, Cybill Shepherd, Jeannie Berlin, Eddie Albert, Audra Lindley. Neil Simon's supreme comedy of embarrassment, from Bruce Jay Friedman's idea. Jewish boy (Grodin) gets married (to Berlin) but meets beautiful Waspish blonde (Shepherd) on honeymoon, and determines to juggle plans. Either hilarious or horrifying, depending on your point of view; directed for maximum impact by May, whose daughter plays Grodin's bride.

Hearts and Minds (1974) €-110m. ***½ D: Peter Davis. Oscar-winning documentary about our misguided involvement in Vietnam was political hot potato for awhile, but may rate more frequent showings now that the country has caught up with it. Packs a wallop, regardless of one's political persuasion.

Hearts Divided (1936) 87m. ** D: Frank Borzage. Marion Davies, Dick Powell, Charlie Ruggles, Claude Rains, Edward Everett Horton, Arthur Treacher. Davies is French girl and Powell is Napoleon's brother in OK musical romance.

Hearts of the West (1975) €-102m. *** D: Howard Zieff. Jeff Bridges, Andy Griffith, Donald Pleasence, Blythe Danner, Alan Arkin, Richard B. Shull. Offbeat comedy about starry-eyed Bridges who comes to Hollywood in the 1930s hoping to be a Western writer, winds up in cheap cowboy films instead. Enjoyable but low-key.

Hearts of the World (1918) 122m. **½ D: D.W. Griffith. Lillian Gish, Dorothy Gish, Robert Harron, Kate Bruce, Ben Alexander, George Fawcett, George Siegmann. Griffith's epic of WW1, shot in England and France; melodramatic story of a young man gone to war, the sufferings of his family and homeland, was made as propaganda to convince America to enter WW1. Dorothy Gish has fine comedy role, young Noel Coward a small part as man with wheelbarrow and villager, Erich von Stroheim a lusty German. For these highlights, other good moments, worth seeing.

Heat of Anger (1971) C-74m. TVM D: Don Taylor. Susan Hayward, James Stacy, Lee J. Cobb, Fritz Weaver, Bettye Ackerman. Familiar blend of courtroom stereotypes in story of assured lady attorney teaming up with young lawyer in defense of accused murderer (with construction site as crime's setting). Good cast cannot redeem script. Average.

Heat Wave (1954-British) 68m. *½ D: Ken Hughes. Alex Nicol, Hillary Brooke, Paul Carpenter, Sidney James. Tame murder yarn, with Brooke the sultry dame involved in homicide.

Heat Wave! (1974) C-78m. TVM D: Jerry Jameson. Ben Murphy, Bonnie Bedelia, Lew Ayres, David Huddleston, John Anderson, Robert Hogan, Dana Elcar. Young clerk and his pregnant wife struggle to escape from a catastrophic heat wave. The cast sweats this one out in standard style. Average.

Heat's On, The (1943) 80m. ** D: Gregory Ratoff. Mae West, Victor Moore, William Gaxton, Lester Allen, Mary Roche, Xavier Cugat. The heat's off in West's only flat comedy. Mae is submerged by this low-budget nightclub musical, her last starring vehicle.

Heaven Can Wait (1943) C-112m. ***½ D: Ernst Lubitsch. Gene Tierney, Don Ameche, Charles Coburn, Marjorie Main, Laird Cregar, Spring Byington, Allyn Joslyn, Eugene Palette, Signe Hasso, Louis Calhern. Excellent comedy-fantasy with Lubitsch touch, of sinner Ameche, circa 1890, requesting admission to Hades.

Heaven Can Wait (1978) C-100m. *** D: Warren Beatty and Buck Henry. Warren Beatty, Julie Christie, Jack Warden, Dyan Cannon, Charles Grodin, James Mason, Buck Henry, Vincent Gardenia. Gentle, pleasing remake of HERE COMES MR. JORDAN with Beatty as good-natured football player who is taken to heaven ahead of schedule, and has to return to "life" in another man's body. Amiable but never moving, with Christie miscast as the woman who inspires Beatty.

Heaven Knows, Mr. Allison (1957) C-107m. *** D: John Huston. Deborah Kerr, Robert Mitchum. Marvelous duo of nun Kerr stranded on WW2 Jap-infested Pacific island with Marine (Mitchum).

Heaven Only Knows (1947) 95m. **½ D: Albert S. Rogell. Robert Cummings, Brian Donlevy, Jorja Curtwright, Marjorie Reynolds, Bill Goodwin, John Litel, Stuart Erwin. Strictly standard Western with fantasy touches as angel Cummings descends to earth to help soulless gambler. Good cast but nothing new. Retitled: MONTANA MIKE.

Heaven With a Barbed Wire Fence (1939) 62m. **½ D: Ricardo Cortez. Jean Rogers, Glenn Ford, Raymond Walburn, Marjorie Rambeau, Richard Conte. Good little romance with down-and-out Rogers and Ford deciding to marry despite many obstacles.

Heaven with a Gun (1969) C-101m. **½ D: Lee H. Katzin. Glenn Ford, Carolyn Jones, Barbara Hershey, John Anderson, David Carradine. Peace-loving man is forced to return to world of violence in the Old West when danger threatens. Uneven.

Heavenly Body, The (1943) 95m. ** D: Alexander Hall. Hedy Lamarr, William Powell, James Craig, Fay Bainter, Henry O'Neill, Spring Byington. Hedy is heavenly, but script is silly; astrologer Powell suspects neglected wife Lamarr of being unfaithful.

Heavenly Days (1944) 71m. ** D: Howard Estabrook. Fibber McGee and Molly, Barbara Hale, Eugene Pallette, Gordon Oliver. Mild entry in famed radio comedians' series, with the battling married couple off to Washington to help run the Senate.

Heavens Above! (1963-British) 119m. *** D: John and Roy Boulting. Peter Sellers, Cecil Parker, Isabel Jeans,

Eric Sykes. Wry satire on British clergy life, with Sellers top-notch as the reverend who becomes bishop in outer space.

Heavy Traffic (1973) C-76m. ***½ D: Ralph Bakshi. No way this X-rated animated feature could be salvaged for TV. Somewhat pretentious and largely gross in telling story of young New Yorker depressed by sights and sounds around him, finding refuge at drawing-board. Given dazzling cinematic treatment, with often revolutionary combination of live-action and animation. Some brilliant set-pieces within loose story framework.

Hedda (1975-British) C-104m. **½ D: Trevor Nunn. Glenda Jackson, Peter Eyre, Timothy West, Jennie Linden, Patrick Stewart, Royal Shakespeare Company production of Ibsen's "Hedda Gabler" attains a modicum of vitality from Jackson's showy performance in the title role. So-so.

Heidi (1937) 88m. **½ D: Allan Dwan. Shirley Temple, Jean Hersholt, Arthur Treacher, Helen Westley, Mady Christians, Sidney Blackmer, Sig Ruman, Marcia Mae Jones, Mary Nash. Classic children's story set in 19th-century Switzerland is good vehicle for Shirley, playing girl taken from grandfather (Hersholt) to live with cruel Nash. Nice tear-jerker for children.

Heidi (1952-Swiss) *** D: Luigi Comencini. Elsbeth Sigmund, Heinrich Gretler, Thomas Klameth, Elsie Attenoff. Faithful, flavorful retelling of Johanna Spyri's children's classic.

Heidi (1965-Austrian-German) C-95m. *** D: Werner Jacobs. Eva Marie Singhammer, Gertraud Mittermayr, Gustav Knuth, Lotte Ledl. Fine retelling of classic children's story about young girl who leaves her cozy home in Swiss Alps for adventures in the world below.

Heidi (1968) C-110m. TVM D: Delbert Mann. Maximilian Schell, Jean Simmons, Michael Redgrave, Walter Slezak, Jennifer Edwards, Peter Van Eyck. Well-made version of the classic story, with Edwards (daughter of Julie Andrews and Blake Edwards) leading a good cast. Script by Earl Hamner Jr. of "The Waltons" fame. Above average.

Heidi and Peter (1955-Swiss) C-89m. **½ D: Franz Schnyder. Heinrich Gretler, Elsbeth Sigmund, Thomas Klameth, Anita Mey. Further adventures of Johanna Spyri's characters, involving flood threatening Heidi's village.

Heiress, The (1949) 115m. **** D: William Wyler. Olivia de Havilland, Ralph Richardson, Montgomery Clift, Miriam Hopkins, Vanessa Brown. Henry James' novel WASHINGTON SQUARE receives plush screen treatment with Oscar-winning De Havilland as spinster wooed by fortune-hunter Clift in early 20th-century N.Y.C. Music by Aaron Copland.

Heist, The (1972) C-73m. TVM D: Don McDougall. Christopher George, Elizabeth Ashley, Howard Duff, Norman Fell, Michael Bell, Robert Mandan. Tough cop (Duff) is convinced armored car guard Craddock (George) engineered bank robbery via clever alibi, even though film clearly shows man innocent. Predictable resolution, fair performances, and closing sequence that must be seen to be believed. Average.

Helen Morgan Story, The (1957) 118m. **½ D: Michael Curtiz. Ann Blyth, Paul Newman, Richard Carlson, Gene Evans, Cara Williams. Fiction about dynamic 1920-30s torch singer, overfocusing on her romances and alcoholism: Blyth never captures the star's pathos or greatness. She's dubbed by Gogi Grant.

Helen of Troy (1955) C-118m. ** D: Robert Wise. Stanley Baker, Rossana Podesta, Brigitte Bardot, Jacques Sernas, Cedric Hardwicke, Harry Andrews. Sweeping pageantry, but empty script spoils this version of story about the woman who caused the Trojan War. Filmed in Italy.

Hell and High Water (1954) C-103m. **½ D: Samuel Fuller. Richard Widmark, Bella Darvi, Victor Francen, Cameron Mitchell, Gene Evans, David Wayne. Uneven mixture of romance, espionage, and a demolition caper, stemming from U.S. sub's mission to Arctic; originally released in Cinemascope, which gave tame film some novelty.

Hell Below (1933) 105m. **½ D: Jack Conway. Robert Montgomery, Walter Huston, Madge Evans, Jimmy Durante, Robert Young, Sterling Holloway, Eugene Pallette. Vintage submarine drama surpasses many more elaborate efforts; Huston is captain, Montgomery his seaman nemesis.

Hell Below Zero (1954) **C-91m.** **
D: Mark Robson. Alan Ladd, Joan
Tetzel, Basil Sydney, Stanley Baker.
Tepid adventure yarn casting Ladd
as helper of Tetzel, who commands
a whaling vessel while searching for
her dad's killer. Made in England.

Hell Bent for Leather (1960) **C-82m.**
**½ D: George Sherman. Audie
Murphy, Felicia Farr, Stephen Mc-
Nally, Robert Middleton. Western
focuses on battle of power between
reward-hungry sheriff and innocent
man mistaken for killer.

Hell Canyon Outlaws (1957) **72m.** **
D: Paul Landres. Dale Robertson,
Brian Keith, Rossana Rory, Dick
Kallman, Buddy Baer. Triumph
against outlaw forces in the Old
West; that's it.

Hell Divers (1932) **113m.** ** D:
George Hill. Wallace Beery, Clark
Gable, Conrad Nagel, Dorothy Jordan, Marjorie Rambeau, Marie Prevost, Cliff Edwards. Beery and Gable
are boisterous rivals in the Naval
Ail Force in this often lively but
overlong MGM effort, with some
still-exciting aerial action. Watch for
young Robert Young as a sailor.

Hell Drivers (1958-British) **91m.** **½
D: Cy Endfield. Stanley Baker, Herbert Lom, Peggy Cummins, Patrick
McGoohan. Taut account of truck
drivers carrying explosive cargoes
over rugged roads.

Hell in the Pacific (1968) **C-103m.**
*** D: John Boorman. Lee Marvin,
Toshiro Mifune. Two men, one
American, one Japanese, confront
each other on deserted Pacific island
during WW2. Gripping idea well executed, with two dynamic actors;
only the finale disappoints.

Hell Is for Heroes (1962) **90m.** ***
D: Don Siegel. Steve McQueen, Bobby Darin, Fess Parker, Harry Guardino, James Coburn, Mike Kellin,
Nick Adams, Bob Newhart. Action-
packed war film that minimizes clichés; rugged cast put through grueling paces.

Hell on Devil's Island (1957) **74m.**
*½ D: Christian Nyby. Helmut
Dantine, William Talman, Donna
Martell, Rex Ingram, Alan Lee. Un-
lurid exposé of unsavory working
conditions in prison mining operations.

Hell on Frisco Bay (1955) **C-98m.**
**½ D: Frank Tuttle. Alan Ladd,
Edward G. Robinson, Joanne Dru,
William Demarest, Fay Wray. Thir-

ties-style gangster film recounting the
exposure of crime syndicate and its
head; actionful, with good cast.

Hell Ship Mutiny (1957) **66m.** *½
D: Lee Sholem and Elmo Williams.
Jon Hall, John Carradine, Peter
Lorre, Roberta Haynes, Mike Mazurki, Stanley Adams. Hall looks bored
in rehash of South Seas tale of ship
captain overcoming sinister forces exploiting the natives.

Hell to Eternity (1960) **132m.** **½
D: Phil Karlson. Jeffrey Hunter, David Janssen, Vic Damone, Patricia
Owens. Hunter gives credence to role
of American raised in Japanese
household in L.A. who finds his
background valuable when WW2
starts.

Hell Up in Harlem (1973) **C-96m.**
BOMB D: Larry Cohen. Fred Williamson, Julius W. Harris, Gloria
Hendry, Margaret Avery, D'Urville
Martin. Excessively violent, poorly
filmed sequel to "Black Caesar" as
Fred makes New York a decent
place to live by annihilating all who
stand in his way.

Hell with Heroes, The (1968) **C-95m.**
**½ D: Joseph Sargent. Rod Tay-
lor, Claudia Cardinale, Harry Guardino, Kevin McCarthy, Peter Duel,
William Marshall. OK pulp fiction
about WW2 flyers Taylor and Duel
who run air-cargo service, become
involved with notorious smuggler
Guardino and his mistress (Cardinale). Unprofound, but slickly done.

Hell's Angels (1930) **125m.** ***½ D:
Howard Hughes. Ben Lyon, James
Hall, Jean Harlow, John Darrow,
Lucien Prival, Roy Wilson. Hughes'
expensive, indulgent WW1 aviation
film is in a class by itself; slow-
moving and sometimes corny story-
wise, but unmatched for aerial spectacle. Also the film that launched
Harlow ("Do you mind if I change
into something more comfortable?")
to stardom.

Hell's Angels on Wheels (1967) **C-
95m.** **½ D: Richard Rush. Adam
Roarke, Jack Nicholson, Sabrina
Scharf, Jana Taylor, John Garwood.
Excellent photography by then-
unknown Laszlo Kovacs, and Nicholson's characterization as gas station
attendant named Poet make this one
tough to resist on a trash level.
Famed Angel Sonny Barger is credited as technical advisor.

Hell's Crossroads (1957) **73m.** ** D:
Franklin Adreon. Stephen McNally,
Peggie Castle, Robert Vaughn, Bar-

ton MacLane. Oater involving members of the James Brothers outlaw gang.

Hell's Five Hours (1958) 73m. ** D: Jack L. Copeland. Stephen McNally, Coleen Gray, Vic Morrow, Maurice Manson. Several people are held prisoners at missile depot by Morrow, bent on blowing the place sky-high.

Hell's Half Acre (1954) 91m. *½ D: John H. Auer. Wendell Corey, Evelyn Keyes, Elsa Lanchester, Marie Windsor. Strange little film of wife who goes to Hawaii in search of missing husband.

Hell's Horizon (1955) 80m. ** D: Tom Gries. John Ireland, Marla English, Bill Williams, Hugh Beaumont, Jerry Paris, Kenneth Duncan. Interaction among men of bombing squad in the Korean War.

Hell's House (1932) 72m. ** D: Howard Higgins. Junior Durkin, Pat O'Brien, Bette Davis, Junior Coghlan, Charley Grapewin, Emma Dunn. Low-budget quickie about naïve kid who takes rap for bootlegger and goes to poorly run boys' reformatory. Interesting mainly for early appearances of O'Brien and Davis.

Hell's Island (1955) C-84m. *** D: Phil Karlson. John Payne, Mary Murphy, Francis L. Sullivan, Eduardo Noriega, Paul Picerni. Tough, violent melodrama about Payne's pursuit of stolen gem, and relationship with deceitful former girlfriend; hard-bitten, serpentine script has echoes of THE MALTESE FALCON, and even a Sydney Greenstreet figure in the person of Sullivan.

Hell's Kitchen (1939) 81m. **½ D: Lewis Seiler, E. A. Dupont. Ronald Reagan, Stanley Fields, Grant Mitchell, Margaret Lindsay, Dead End Kids. Ex-con Fields goes straight, tries to bail Dead End Kids out of their usual trouble, sets them on the right road.

Hell's Long Road (1963-Italian) C-89m. **½ D: Charles Roberti. Elena Brazzi, Kay Nolandi, Berto Frankis, Bela Kaivi, Marcello Charli. Offbeat costume sudser set in ancient Rome during rule of Nero (Frankis), focusing on personal life of arch senator (Charli) and romance with splendiforous Brazzi; vivid settings.

Hell's Outpost (1954) 90m. ** D: Joseph Kane. Rod Cameron, Joan Leslie, Chill Wills, John Russell. Cameron is ambitious miner in this sturdy little film; Leslie is the fetching love interest.

Hellcats of the Navy (1957) 82m. **½ D: Nathan Juran. Ronald Reagan, Nancy Davis, Arthur Franz, Harry Lauter, Selmer Jackson. Satisfactory actioner of WW2 exploits of U.S. submarine and its crew.

Heller in Pink Tights (1960) C-100m. **½ D: George Cukor. Sophia Loren, Anthony Quinn, Margaret O'-Brien, Steve Forrest, Edmund Lowe. Odd-ball Western involving traveling show troupe and their encounters with belligerent townsfolk and Indians; colorful production.

Hellfighters (1969) C-121m. ** D: Andrew V. McLaglen. John Wayne, Katharine Ross, Jim Hutton, Vera Miles, Bruce Cabot, Jay C. Flippen. Comic-book adventure about men who fight oil fires is made endurable by good cast.

Hellgate (1952) 87m. **½ D: Charles Marquis Warren. Sterling Hayden, Joan Leslie, James Arness, Ward Bond. Offbeat account of Hayden falsely sent to prison, and strange manner in which he redeems himself during prison breakout. Reworking of THE PRISONER OF SHARK ISLAND.

Hellions, The (1962-British) C-87m. **½ D: Ken Annakin. Richard Todd, Anne Aubrey, Lionel Jeffries, Zena Walker, Jamie Uys, Marty Wilde. Western revenge plot transferred to 19th-century South Africa; inevitable shoot-out intact.

Hello, Dolly! (1969) C-118m. **½ D: Gene Kelly. Barbra Streisand, Walter Matthau, Michael Crawford, E.J. Peaker, Louis Armstrong. Splashy cinema treatment of smash Broadway play with Jerry Herman's popular score. Dolly Levi insists on playing matchmaker, even when it's she herself who gets matched. Overblown and unmemorable, but colorful diversion. Based on Thornton Wilder's THE MATCHMAKER.

Hello Down There (1969) C-98m. *½ D: Jack Arnold. Tony Randall, Janet Leigh, Jim Backus, Roddy McDowall, Ken Berry, Merv Griffin, Richard Dreyfuss. So-called comedy about family living in experimental underwater home might entertain children if you pay them to watch it.

Hello Elephant (1952-Italian) 78m. *½ D: Gianni Franciolini. Vittorio De Sica, Sabu, Maria Mercader, Nando Bruno. Misfire of comedy-satire involving royalty who bestows an elephant on one of his subjects as a fitting reward. Retitled: PARDON MY TRUNK.

Hello, Frisco, Hello (1943) C-98m. ** D: H. Bruce Humberstone. Alice Faye, John Payne, Jack Oakie, Lynn Bari, Laird Cregar, June Havoc, Ward Bond. Hackneyed musicomedy of Faye aiming for stardom; period piece, with Oscar-winning song: "You'll Never Know." Big comedown from earlier musicals with star trio.

Hello-Goodbye (1970-British) C-107m. BOMB D: Jean Negulesco. Michael Crawford, Curt Jurgens, Genevieve Gilles, Ira Furstenberg, Lon Satton. Abysmal love triangle which goes nowhere and makes no sense. Awful, loose, and annoying.

Hello Sister (1933) 62m. **½ D: Erich von Stroheim, Alfred Werker. James Dunn, Boots Mallory, ZaSu Pitts, Minna Gombell. Innocuous boy-meets-girl story of special interest to film buffs. Originally filmed by Von Stroheim as WALKING DOWN BROADWAY; later reedited, partially refilmed; enough bizarre touches remain to reveal Von Stroheim's touch, however.

Hello Sucker (1941) 60m. *½ D: Edward Cline. Peggy Moran, Tom Brown, Walter Catlett, Hugh Herbert. Dingy little film of Moran and Brown acquiring vaudeville booking agency, making it a success and finding love with one another.

Hellstrom Chronicle, The (1971) C-90m. **½ D: Walon Green. Documentary about man's impending struggle against insects won at Cannes and somehow beat THE SORROW AND THE PITY for the Oscar, but sappy narration and repetitive structure lessen its effect.

Hellzapoppin (1941) 84m. *** D: H. C. Potter. Ole Olsen, Chic Johnson, Martha Raye, Mischa Auer, Jane Frazee, Hugh Herbert. Can't capture madness of Broadway show, but makes good try with some funny gimmicks and wacky supporting cast.

Help! (1965-British) C-90m. ***½ D: Richard Lester. John Lennon, Paul McCartney, George Harrison, Ringo Starr, Leo McKern, Eleanor Bron, Victor Spinetti, Roy Kinnear, Patrick Cargill. Crazy, funny film, the Beatles' second. Lots of wild gags, many songs, a religious sect attempts to recover a sacrificial ring from Ringo.

Helter Skelter (1976) C-194m. TVM D: Tom Gries. George DiCenzo, Steve Railsback, Nancy Wolfe, Marilyn Burns, Christina Hart, Cathey Paine, Alan Oppenheimer. Electrifying film of prosecutor Vincent Bugliosi's best-seller about the trackdown and trial of Charles Manson and his spaced-out "family" in California. Serious, intense, and frightening, with a vivid performance by Railsback as Manson. Above average.

Hemingway's Adventures of a Young Man (1962) C-145m. ** D: Martin Ritt. Richard Beymer, Diane Baker, Paul Newman, Eli Wallach, Arthur Kennedy, Ricardo Montalban, Dan Dailey, Susan Strasberg, Fred Clark, Corinne Calvet. Overblown, cornball, embarrassing the memory of famed American writer; pretentious in thought and drawn-out plot, loosely based on autobiographical data in author's stories.

Hennessy (1975-British) C-103m. **½ D: Don Sharp. Rod Steiger, Lee Remick, Richard Johnson, Trevor Howard, Peter Egan, Eric Porter. Interesting but unbelievable thriller about Irish man whose wife and child are killed in Belfast violence, stirring him to plan bombing of Parliament on opening day when the Royal Family attends.

Henry Aldrich Teen-aged Henry Aldrich was Paramount's answer to MGM's Andy Hardy series, and while the Aldrich films were less popular, less prestigious, and shorterlived, they were then, and remain today, well-crafted, entertaining little films, without any of the pretentiousness and calculated coyness that marred the Hardy series. Henry and group were the invention of Clifford Goldsmith, whose play WHAT A LIFE opened in 1938 on Broadway, spawning a radio series with Ezra Stone repeating his stage role of Henry. In 1939, Paramount turned the hit play into a pleasant film, retaining Betty Field (as Henry's plain-jane girlfriend) and Vaughan Glaser (as dour principal Mr. Bradley) from the original cast, but bypassing Ezra Stone in favor of Jackie Cooper, and casting Eddie Bracken as Henry's pal Dizzy. Best of all, Paramount assigned their writing team of Billy Wilder and Charles Brackett to provide the script—an unlikely pair for such Middle American doings, but welcome nonetheless. Two years passed before the studio decided to turn the Aldrich movie into a regular series, a decision strengthened no doubt by the continuing popularity of the radio show. In 1941, Jackie Cooper and Eddie Bracken repeated their roles in a second outing, LIFE WITH HENRY, a typically silly but likable effort. Then Paramount cast a newcomer, Jimmy Lydon, in the key role of Henry and surrounded him with a new supporting cast for a string of actual series films: Charles Smith as his laconic but shifty pal Dizzy, John Litel as his stern father, Olive Blakeney as his forgiving mother, and welcome Vaughan Glaser as the forever-pouting principal. A new director, ex-film editor Hugh Bennett, was added to comprise the working unit that turned out nine films over the next four years. The Aldrich films, timed around 70 minutes, fell into a pattern that proved generally successful: putting hopelessly blundering Henry into an increasingly complicated series of mishaps which would alienate him from his parents, sometimes his friends, and often the entire town, before culminating in a major action and/or slapstick climax in which Henry would be vindicated. In HENRY ALDRICH FOR PRESIDENT the finale is a wild airplane ride; in HENRY AND DIZZY it's a runaway motorboat; in HENRY ALDRICH, BOY SCOUT it's a cliff-hanger rescue; and best of all, in HENRY ALDRICH, EDITOR there is a truly exciting fire sequence. The films are consistently well-paced and slickly filmed, never belying their modest budgets, and filled with engaging players: Mary Anderson as Henry's girlfriend in several entries (later replaced by Diana Lynn, and other less notable starlets), Frances Gifford as a movie star who accepts Henry's prom invitation as a publicity stunt in HENRY ALDRICH GETS GLAMOUR, Fritz Feld as a famous musician whose Stradivarius is accidentally "borrowed" by Henry in HENRY ALDRICH SWINGS IT; Lucien Littlefield as an antagonistic teacher in two of the episodes; June Preisser as a vamp in HENRY ALDRICH FOR PRESIDENT; and Vera Vague as a potential wife for Mr. Bradley in HENRY ALDRICH PLAYS

CUPID. Best of all is Francis Pierlot as a character called Nero Smith, a pyromaniac who announces his intentions to Henry, leading to suspicions and troubles galore in perhaps the best series entry, HENRY ALDRICH, EDITOR. HENRY ALDRICH'S LITTLE SECRET is the last and easily the weakest film of the nine Lydon pictures, but the other eight maintain a surprisingly good standard of filmmaking quality and good, lightweight entertainment. The players fill their often silly roles with the kind of conviction that gets an audience involved, but the scripts take sly winks at the same audience every once in a while to reassure us that it's not to be taken too seriously (the name of the resort near Centerville is Lake Wopacotapotalong). Henry Aldrich later went on to a short-lived TV series with Bobby Ellis in the lead, but to most people, Jimmy Lydon is best identified with the role of America's dumbest high-schooler—dumb, yet in an odd way, endearing.

Henry Aldrich, Boy Scout (1944) 66m. D: Hugh Bennett. Jimmy Lydon, Charles Smith, John Litel, Olive Blakeney, Joan Mortimer, Darryl Hickman, Minor Watson, Richard Haydn.

Henry Aldrich, Editor (1942) 71m. D: Hugh Bennett. Jimmy Lydon, Charles Smith, John Litel, Olive Blakeney, Rita Quigley, Vaughan Glaser, Francis Pierlot.

Henry Aldrich for President (1941) 73m. D: Hugh Bennett. Jimmy Lydon, Charles Smith, June Preisser, Mary Anderson, Martha O'Driscoll, Dorothy Peterson, John Litel, Rod Cameron, Lucien Littlefield, Kenneth Howell.

Henry Aldrich Gets Glamour (1943) 75m. D: Hugh Bennett. Jimmy Lydon, Charles Smith, John Litel, Olive Blakeney, Diana Lynn, Frances Gifford, Gail Russell, Bill Goodwin, Vaughan Glaser.

Henry Aldrich Haunts A House (1943) 73m. D: Hugh Bennett. Jimmy Lydon, Charles Smith, John Litel, Olive Blakeney, Joan Mortimer, Vaughan Glaser, Jackie Moran, Lucien Littlefield.

Henry Aldrich Plays Cupid (1944) 65m. D: Hugh Bennett. Jimmy Lydon, Charles Smith, John Litel, Olive Blakeney, Diana Lynn, Vaughan

Glaser, Vera Vague, Paul Harvey, Barbara Pepper.

Henry Aldrich Swings It (1943) 64m. D: Hugh Bennett. Jimmy Lydon, Charles Smith, John Litel, Olive Blakeney, Mimi Chandler, Vaughan Glaser, Marion Hall, Fritz Feld, Beverly Hudson.

Henry Aldrich's Little Secret (1944) 75m. D: Hugh Bennett. Jimmy Lydon, Charles Smith, Joan Mortimer, John Litel, Olive Blakeney, Ann Doran, John David Robb, Tina Thayer, Sarah Edwards.

Henry and Dizzy (1942) 71m. D: Hugh Bennett. Jimmy Lydon, Charles Smith, Mary Anderson, John Litel, Olive Blakeney, Maude Eburne, Vaughan Glaser, Shirley Coates, Olin Howland, Minerva Urecal, Trevor Bardette.

Henry VIII and His Six Wives (1973-British) C-125m. ***½ D: Waris Hussein. Keith Michell, Donald Pleasence, Charlotte Rampling, Jane Asher, Lynne Frederick. Adapted from BBC-TV series, historical pageant divides time evenly among the wives, Rampling and Frederick coming off best. Michell is exceptional as the King.

Henry V (1945-British) C-137m. **** D: Laurence Olivier. Laurence Olivier, Robert Newton, Leslie Banks, Renee Asherson, Esmond Knight, Leo Genn, Ralph Truman. Olivier's masterful rendition of Shakespeare play is a cinematic treat, filmed in rich color and framed by ingenious presentation of a typical performance at the Globe Theater during 1500s.

Henry, the Rainmaker (1949) 64m. *½ D: Jean Yarbrough. Raymond Walburn, Walter Catlett, William Tracy, Mary Stuart. Mild little comedy of homey Walburn who develops a "scientific" way to make rain.

Her Adventurous Night (1946) 76m. **½ D: John Rawlins. Dennis O'Keefe, Helen Walker, Tom Powers, Fuzzy Knight. Youngster with wild imagination fabricates tale of murder and crime, causing parents to go to jail and the youth's life put in peril.

Her Cardboard Lover (1942) 93m. *½ D: George Cukor. Norma Shearer, Robert Taylor, George Sanders, Frank McHugh, Elizabeth Patterson. Tired comedy that chic Shearer couldn't salvage. Her last film to date.

Her Enlisted Man SEE: Red Salute

Her First Romance (1951) 73m. *½ D: Seymour Friedman. Margaret O'Brien, Allen Martin, Jr., Jimmy Hunt, Sharyn Moffett. O'Brien's first grown-up role and her first screen kiss are only assets of this plodding summer camp story.

Her Highness and the Bellboy (1945) 112m. **½ D: Richard Thorpe. Hedy Lamarr, Robert Walker, June Allyson, Carl Esmond, Agnes Moorehead, Rags Ragland. Sentimental fluff of N.Y.C. bellboy Walker, crippled girlfriend Allyson, captivating Princess (Lamarr) he escorts; a bit creaky.

Her Husband's Affairs (1947) 83m. *½ D: S. Sylvan Simon. Lucille Ball, Franchot Tone, Edward Everett Horton, Mikhail Rasumny, Gene Lockhart, Nana Bryant. Pretty sterile comedy about Ball learning not to poke into husband's business affairs.

Her Jungle Love (1938) C-81m. **½ D: George Archainbaud. Dorothy Lamour, Ray Milland, Lynne Overman, J. Carrol Naish, Dorothy Howe (Virginia Vale). Flyers Milland and Overman stranded on tropical isle with Lamour; Ray teaches her how to kiss, Naish tries to destroy everyone in this escapist fare.

Her Kind of Man (1946) 78m. ** D: Frederick de Cordova. Dane Clark, Janis Paige, Zachary Scott, Faye Emerson, George Tobias. Lukewarm drama of young singer with gangster background making good in Big City and falling in love with gossip columnist. Fair cast.

Her Lucky Night (1945) 63m. ** D: Edward Lilley. Andrews Sisters, Martha O'Driscoll, Noah Beery, Jr., George Barbier, Grady Sutton, Ida Moore. Minor comedy with singing trio seeking romance at any cost.

Her Majesty, Love (1931) 75m. *½ D: William Dieterle. Marilyn Miller, W. C. Fields, Leon Errol, Ford Sterling, Chester Conklin, Ben Lyon, Virginia Sale. Unbearable musical with sweet Miller in love with Lyon in old Berlin. Errol as persistent suitor, Fields as juggling father, provide only uplifting moments.

Her Man Gilbey (1948-British) 89m. **½ D: Harold French. Albert Lieven, Margaret Rutherford, Peggy Cummins, Martin Miller. Capable cast nicely handles contrived yarn of quartet of people whose lives intertwine in Geneva.

Her Panelled Door (1951-British)

[329]

84m. * D:** Ladislas Vajda. Phyllis Calvert, Edward Underdown, Helen Cherry, Richard Burton. During an air raid Calvert is shellshocked, forgetting her past, leading to dramatic results. Thoughtful study.

Her Primitive Man (1944) 79m. *½ D: Charles Lamont. Robert Paige, Louise Allbritton, Robert Benchley, Edward Everett Horton. Grade-C flick with Paige pretending to be a savage to win love of anthropologist Allbritton.

Her Sister's Secret (1946) 86m. **½ D: Edgar G. Ulmer. Nancy Coleman, Margaret Lindsay, Felix Bressart, Regis Toomey, Philip Reed, Henry Stephenson. Young woman discovers she's pregnant after brief affair. Fair weeper with competent cast.

Her 12 Men (1954) C-91m. ** D: Robert Z. Leonard. Greer Garson, Robert Ryan, Barry Sullivan, Richard Haydn. Maudlin script has Greer as dedicated teacher in boys' school; tries unsuccessfully to repeat success of MR. CHIPS and MISS DOVE.

Herbie Goes to Monte Carlo (1977) C-91m. ** D: Vincent McEveety. Dean Jones, Don Knotts, Julie Sommers, Roy Kinnear, Jacque Marin. Spy ring hides diamond in Herbie the Volkswagen's gas tank while Jones is racing in Europe. Disney's LOVE BUG formula is starting to run out of gas.

Herbie Rides Again (1974) C-88m. **½ D: Robert Stevenson. Helen Hayes, Ken Berry, Stefanie Powers, Keenan Wynn, John McIntire, Huntz Hall. OK sequel to THE LOVE BUG with similar special effects, as Herbie the Volkswagen tries to help Hayes and Berry steer clear of evil Alonzo Hawk (Wynn). Typical Disney slapstick.

Hercules (1959-Italian) C-107m. **½ D: Pietro Francisci. Steve Reeves, Sylva Koscina, Fabrizio Mioni, Ivo Garrani, Gina Rovere. Prototype of all cloak-and-sandal pictures to come: Reeves as musclebound mythical hero who undergoes myriad of ordeals for woman he loves.

Hercules Against Rome (1960-Italian) C-87m. ** D: Piero Pierott. Alan Steel, Wandisa Guida, Livio Lorenzon, Daniele Vargas. Steel fights a series of unconvincing villains to protect the late emperor's daughter.

Hercules Against the Moon Men (1964-Italian) C-88m. ** D: Giacomo Gentilomo. Alan Steel, Jany Clair, Anna-Maria Polani, Nando Tamberlani. Steel is muscular hero who frees people of Samar from control of magical lunar people holding them in bondage; potential action never occurs.

Hercules Against the Sons of the Sun (1963-Italian) C-91m. ** D: Osvaldo Civirani. Mark Forrest, Anna Pace, Giuliano Gemma, Andrea Rhu. Setting is pre-Columbian America, but the adventure is the same as usual.

Hercules and the Captive Women (1963-Italian) C-87m. ** D: Vittorio Cottafavi. Reg Park, Fay Spain, Ettore Manni, Mario Petri. Cardboard costumer with Park vs. Spain, the despotic ruler of Atlantis.

Hercules in the Haunted World (1961-Italian) C-83m. ** D: Mario Bava. Reg Park, Christopher Lee, Leonora Ruffo, Giorgio Ardisson, Ida Galli. Occasionally sparked by atmospheric settings, this sword-and-sandal epic narrates adventures of Park in the devil's kingdom.

Hercules, Samson and Ulysses (1965-Italian) C-85m. ** D: Pietro Francisci. Kirk Morris, Richard Lloyd, Liana Orfei, Enzo Cerusico. Title alerts one for gymnastics of trio of legendary musclemen.

Hercules Unchained (1960-Italian) C-101m. ** D: Pietro Francisci. Steve Reeves, Sylva Koscina, Primo Carnera, Sylvia Lopez. Par for the muscleman hero entry, dealing with rescue of his bride-to-be.

Here Come the Co-eds (1945) 87m. **½ D: Jean Yarbrough. Bud Abbott, Lou Costello, Peggy Ryan, Martha O'Driscoll, June Vincent, Lon Chaney, Donald Cook. Pretty zany Abbott and Costello comedy of two wacky caretakers turning formerly staid girls' school on its ear.

Here Come the Girls (1953) C-78m. **½ D: Claude Binyon. Bob Hope, Arlene Dahl, Rosemary Clooney, Tony Martin, Fred Clark. At times amusing romp with Hope a naive show biz-ite who becomes involved with killer on the loose.

Here Come the Marines (1952) 66m. D: William Beaudine. Leo Gorcey, Huntz Hall, Bernard Gorcey, Gil Stratton, Jr., Arthur Space, Tim Ryan. SEE: Bowery Boys series.

Here Come the Nelsons (1952) 76m. ** D: Fredrick de Cordova. Ozzie, Harriet, David, Ricky Nelson, Rock Hudson, Ann Doran, Jim Backus.

Expanded version of typical radio-TV Nelson family fare, dealing with gangsters.

Here Come the Tigers (1978) C-90m. *½ D: Sean S. Cunningham. Richard Lincoln, James Zvanut, Samantha Grey, Manny Lieberman, William Caldwell. Kids will have no trouble pinning this as a shameless ripoff of THE BAD NEWS BEARS—and nowhere near as good.

Here Come the Waves (1944) 99m. *** D: Mark Sandrich. Bing Crosby, Betty Hutton, Sonny Tufts, Ann Doran, Catherine Craig. Zippy wartime musicomedy of singer Crosby joining the navy. Hit song "Accent-u-ate the Positive."

Here Comes Every Body (1973) 110m. *½ D: John Whitmore. Dull documentary about encounter groups in California is only for those with an extraordinary interest in the subject.

Here Comes Mr. Jordan (1941) 93m. **** D: Alexander Hall. Robert Montgomery, Evelyn Keyes, Claude Rains, Rita Johnson, Edward Everett Horton, James Gleason, John Emery. Excellent fantasy-comedy of prizefighter Montgomery accidentally sent to heaven before his time, forced to occupy a new body on earth. Hollywood moviemaking at its best, with firstrate cast and performances. Characters used again in DOWN TO EARTH (1947); film remade as HEAVEN CAN WAIT in 1978.

Here Comes the Groom (1951) 113m. *** D: Frank Capra. Bing Crosby, Jane Wyman, Franchot Tone, Alexis Smith, Anna Maria Alberghetti, Alan Reed, Louis Armstrong, Cass Daley. Crosby is relaxed news reporter in love with Wyman. Tone and Smith secondary love interests. Song "In the Cool, Cool, Cool of the Evening" won an Oscar in this lightweight outing.

Here Comes the Navy (1934) 86m. **½ D: Lloyd Bacon. James Cagney, Pat O'Brien, Gloria Stuart, Dorothy Tree, Frank McHugh. Enjoyable but standard tale of cocky Cagney who becomes navy hero; nothing new, but well done.

Here Is My Heart (1934) 77m. **½ D: Frank Tuttle. Bing Crosby, Kitty Carlisle, Roland Young, Alison Skipworth, Reginald Owen. Bing's a radio star in love with princess Carlisle in this flimsy little musical. Songs include "Love Is Just Around the Corner."

Here We Go Round the Mulberry Bush (1968-British) C-96m. **½ D: Clive Donner. Barry Evans, Judy Geeson, Angela Scoular, Sheila White, Vanessa Howard, Denholm Elliott. British teen-ager Evans is hung up on girls, but finds his pursuits a constant dead-end. Amusing, often clever adolescent romp; music by Stevie Winwood & Traffic, Spencer Davis Group.

Hero, The (1972) C-97m. **½ D: Richard Harris. Richard Harris, Romy Schneider, Kim Burfield, Maurice Kaufman, Yossi Yadin. Old-fashioned film about a soccer star and the young boy who idolizes him; partly filmed in Israel.

Hero Ain't Nothin' But a Sandwich, A (1978) C-105m. **½ D: Ralph Nelson. Cicely Tyson, Paul Winfield, Larry B. Scott, Helen Martin, Glynn Turman, David Groh. Well-meaning drama (from Alice Childress' book) about intelligent but alienated black ghetto youth who takes up drugs. Moralistic film may get PTA recommendations, but doesn't really deliver: young Scott's performance is major asset.

Herod the Great (1960-Italian) C-93m. *½ D: Arnaldo Genoino. Edmund Purdom, Sylvia Lopez, Sandra Milo, Alberto Lupo. Juvenile account of ruler of ancient Judea, his warring and his jealousy of wife's admirers.

Heroes (1977) C-113m. **½ D: Jeremy Paul Kagan. Henry Winkler, Sally Field, Harrison Ford, Val Avery, Olivia Cole, Hector Elias. Innocuous film marked Winkler's first starring role, as crazy Vietnam vet who chases a dream of wealth and success cross-country; Field is appealing as the girl he meets and wins along the way.

Heroes, The (1972) C-99m. ** D: Duccio Tessari. Rod Steiger, Rod Taylor, Rossana Schiaffino, Claude Brasseur, Terry-Thomas. International multi-star production is saddled with middling script about motley crew banding together for major heist of "lost" military money.

Heroes for Sale (1933) 73m. **½ D: William Wellman. Loretta Young, Aline MacMahon, Richard Barthelmess, Grant Mitchell, Ward Bond, Douglass Dumbrille. Low-key Depression story of ex-soldier Barthelmess trying to make something of himself, thwarted at every turn.

Heroes of Telemark, The (1965-

British) C-131m. **½ D: Anthony Mann. Kirk Douglas, Richard Harris, Michael Redgrave, Mervyn Johns, Eric Porter. Douglas and Harris spend more time battling each other than the Nazis overrunning Norway in this pictorially gorgeous (filmed on location), predictable blow-up-the-German-factory yarn.

Hero's Island (1962) C-94m. **½ D: Leslie Stevens. James Mason, Kate Manx, Neville Brand, Rip Torn, Warren Oates, Brendan Dillon. Peculiar mixture of adventure and soap opera set on 18th-century island near North Carolina, involving pirates and homesteaders.

Hers to Hold (1943) 94m. ** D: Frank Ryan. Deanna Durbin, Joseph Cotten, Charles Winninger, Nella Walker, Gus Schilling, Ludwig Stossel, Irving Bacon. Grown-up Durbin is in love with serviceman Cotten in undistinguished romance, brightened by Deanna's singing. Songs: "Begin The Beguine," etc.

Hester Street (1975) 92m. ***½ D: Joan Micklin Silver. Steven Keats, Carol Kane, Mel Howard, Dorrie Kavanaugh, Doris Roberts, Stephen Strimpell. Young Jewish immigrant (Kane) joins her husband in New York at turn of the century, only to find that he has forsaken his Old World ways and expects her to do the same. Disarmingly simple story, outstanding period flavor.

Hex (1973) C-92m. *½ D: Leo Garen. Keith Carradine, Tina Herazo, Hilarie Thompson, Gary Busey, Robert Walker, Dan Haggerty, John Carradine. Off-the-wall bike movie that involves a motorcycle gang with occultism in post-WW1 Nebraska. You've got to be high to go for this one.

Hey Boy! Hey Girl! (1959) 81m. *½ D: David Lowell Rich. Louis Prima, Keely Smith, James Gregory, Henry Slate, Asa Maynor, Sam Butera and the Witnesses. Low-budget film helped only by music of Prima, Keely Smith, and their musicians.

Hey, I'm Alive! (1975) C-78m. TVM D: Lawrence Schiller. Edward Asner, Sally Struthers, Milton Selzer, Hagan Beggs, Maria Hernandez, Claudine Melgrave. Fact-based drama about two plane crash survivors who spent 49 days in the Yukon wilderness subsisting on melted snow while awaiting rescue. Good work by Asner and Struthers. Average.

Hey, Let's Twist! (1961) 80m. BOMB D: Greg Garrison. Joey Dee, The Starliters, Peppermint Loungers, Jo Ann Campbell. Let's not. This minor film came out at the height of the Twist dance rage and wasn't very good then . . . now it's just a bad way to kill 80 minutes.

Hey, Rookie (1944) 77m. **½ D: Charles Barton. Larry Parks, Ann Miller, Condos Brothers, Joe Sawyer, Jack Gilford, Selmer Jackson. Typical let's-put-on-a-show-for-the-servicemen, allowing for Miller's versatility to shine through.

Hey There It's Yogi Bear (1964) C-89m. ** D: William Hanna, Joseph Barbera. Voices of: Mel Blanc, J. Pat O'Malley, Julie Bennett, Daws Butler, Don Messick. First full-length cartoon from Hanna-Barbera studio stars Yogi Bear in amusing musical tale for younger folk.

Hi Diddle Diddle (1943) 72m. **½ D: Andrew L. Stone. Adolphe Menjou, Martha Scott, Pola Negri, Dennis O'Keefe, Billie Burke, June Havoc, Walter Kingsford. OK screwball comedy of young lovers and wacky con-artist parents, notable for appearance of silent-screen vamp Negri. Also known as DIAMONDS AND CRIME.

Hi, Nellie (1934) 75m. **½ D: Mervyn LeRoy. Paul Muni, Glenda Farrell, Berton Churchill, Donald Meek, Marjorie Gateson. Minor but enjoyable Muni as ex-editor who now writes advice to lovelorn, gets involved in citywide racket as well.

Hiawatha (1952) C-80m. *½ D: Kurt Neumann. Vincent Edwards, Keith Larsen, Michael Tolan, Yvette Dugay. Juvenile low-budget version of the Longfellow classic.

Hickey and Boggs (1972) C-111m. **½ D: Robert Culp. Bill Cosby, Robert Culp, Rosalind Cash, Sheila Sullivan, Isabel Sanford, Ta-Ronce Allen, Lou Frizzell. Unexceptional but tolerable action pic about two down-and-out private-eyes will appeal to those who liked Cosby and Culp on TV's I SPY.

Hidden Eye, The (1945) 69m. **½ D: Richard Whorf. Edward Arnold, Frances Rafferty, Ray Collins, Paul Langton, Raymond Largay, William Phillips. Follow-up to EYES IN THE NIGHT, with blind detective Arnold making good use of other senses to solve murder mystery; fast-moving, entertaining mystery.

Hidden Fear (1957) 83m. *½ D: Andre de Toth. John Payne, Alexander Knox, Conrad Nagel, Natalie Norwick. On-location filming in Copenhagen is chief virtue of mild huntdown-the-murderer plot.

Hidden Homicide (1959-British) 70m. *½ D: Tony Young. Griffith Jones, James Kenney, Patricia Laffan, Bruce Seton, Charles Farrell. Circumstantial evidence makes writer think he's a murderer.

Hidden Room, The (1949-British) 98m. *** D: Edward Dmytryk. Robert Newton, Sally Gray, Naunton Wayne, Phil Brown, Michael Balfour, Olga Lindo. Very effective suspenser involving Newton's plan to eliminate a man threatening his marriage; nifty climax. Retitled: OBSESSION.

Hideaways, The SEE: From the Mixed-Up Files of Mrs. Basil E. Frankweiler

Hiding Place, The (1975) C-145m. **½ D: James F. Collier. Julie Harris, Eileen Heckart, Arthur O'-Connell, Jeanette Clift, Robert Rietty, Pamela Sholto. Well-meaning, sometimes effective, but draggy, predictable story of Dutch Christians aiding Jews in WW2. Produced by Billy Graham's Evangelistic Association.

Hideout, The (1961-French) 80m. **½ D: Raoul Andre. Marcel Mouloudji, Yves Vincent, Francis Blanche, Louise Garletti. Diverting account of Mouloudji seeking refuge in an insane asylum during WW2, kept there as a patient.

High and Dry (1954-British) 93m. **½ D: Alexander Mackendrick. Paul Douglas, Alex Mackenzie, James Copeland, Abe Barker. Satisfactory, minor yarn about U.S. financier Douglas in conflict with the captain of broken-down ship carrying valuable cargo; static at times. Originally titled THE MAGGIE.

High and Low (1962-Japanese) 142m. *** D: Akira Kurosawa. Toshiro Mifune, Kyoko Kagawa. Carefully paced study of Mifune, business executive who is financially ruined when he nobly pays ransom money to kidnappers who mistakenly stole his chauffeur's son.

High and the Mighty, The (1954) C-147m. *** D: William Wellman. John Wayne, Claire Trevor, Laraine Day, Robert Stack, Jan Sterling, Phil Harris. GRAND HOTEL takes wings in lengthy movie of disabled airplane and passengers who meditate about their lives. Big John whistles title tune from Dimitri Tiomkin score.

High Anxiety (1977) C-94m. **½ D: Mel Brooks. Mel Brooks, Madeline Kahn, Cloris Leachman, Harvey Korman, Dick Van Patten, Ron Carey, Howard Morris. Affectionate, well-made but uneven spoof of Hitchcock films with Brooks as psychiatrist who walks into trouble as new head of trouble-ridden sanitarium. Isolated moments of great comedy bolster uneven film.

High Barbaree (1947) 91m. ** D: Jack Conway. Van Johnson, June Allyson, Thomas Mitchell, Marilyn Maxwell, Cameron Mitchell. Navy flier's life story told in flashback as he awaits rescue in plane in ocean. Good cast in inferior story.

High Commissioner, The (1968-British) C-93m. *½ D: Ralph Thomas. Christopher Plummer, Rod Taylor, Lilli Palmer, Camilla Sparv, Daliah Lavi, Clive Revill, Franchot Tone. Wonderful cast is wasted in tired spy thriller about diplomat involved in murder at height of Cold War negotiations. British title: NOBODY RUNS FOREVER.

High Crime (1973-Italian) C-100m. ** D: Enzo G. Castellari. Franco Nero, James Whitmore, Fernando Rey, Della Boccardo. Italian-made action drama pits Genovese narcotics cop Nero against mafioso Rey. Energetic but predictable.

High Flight (1958-British) 89m. *½ D: John Gilling. Ray Milland, Bernard Lee, Kenneth Haigh, Anthony Newley. Stale British drama of recruits in training for the RAF—not as good as I WANTED WINGS. Last reel, in the air, only exciting scene.

High Fury (1948-British) 71m. ** D: Harold French. Madeleine Carroll, Ian Hunter, Michael Rennie, Anne Marie Blanc. Standard film of couple quarreling over adopting war orphan. Nice locations in Switzerland. Originally titled WHITE CRADLE INN.

High Hell (1958-British) 87m. **½ D: Burt Balaban. John Derek, Elaine Stewart, Rodney Burke, Patrick Allen. Mine owner's wife has an affair with husband's partner; trio snowbound for winter fight about it.

High Ice (1980) C-100m. TVM D:

Eugene S. Jones. David Janssen, Tony Musante, Madge Sinclair, Dorian Harewood, Warren Stevens, Gretchen Corbett, Allison Argo, James G. Richardson. Dandy thriller about the rescue of three weekend climbers from a tiny mountainside ledge, pitting gruff veteran ranger Janssen against by-the-book army colonel Musante. Above average.

High Lonesome (1950) C-81m. ** D: Alan LeMay. John Barrymore, Jr., Chill Wills, Lois Butler, Jack Elam. Moody little drama set in the West with Barrymore a brooding youth involved with killers.

High Midnight (1979) C-100m. TVM D: Daniel Haller. Mike Connors, David Birney, Christine Belford, Granville Van Dusen, George DiCenzo. Blue collar worker Birney seeks revenge for the murder of his family in a mistaken no-knock drug raid and stalks Connors, head of the narcotics squad responsible. Average.

High Noon (1952) 85m. **** D: Fred Zinnemann. Gary Cooper, Grace Kelly, Lloyd Bridges, Thomas Mitchell, Katy Jurado, Otto Kruger, Lon Chaney. Retiring sheriff Cooper feels responsibility to ungrateful town when challenged by gunfighter. Oscar-winning Western with Dimitri Tiomkin theme, memorable cameos by character actors. Cooper awarded Oscar for his role.

High Plains Drifter (1973) C-105m. *** D: Clint Eastwood. Clint Eastwood, Verna Bloom, Marianna Hill, Mitchell Ryan, Jack Ging, Stefan Gierasch. Moody, self-conscious but compelling story of drifter hired by townspeople to protect them from vengeful outlaws who have just been released from prison. Half-serious, half tongue-in-cheek, with great role for midget Billy Curtis.

High Risk (1976) C-78m. TVM D: Sam O'Steen. Victor Buono, Joseph Sirola, Don Stroud, JoAnna Kara Cameron, Ronne Troup, Wolf Roth. Comedy adventure with six former circus performers in a caper to carry off priceless artifact from a foreign embassy in broad daylight. Average.

High School Confidential! (1958) 85m. *½ D: Jack Arnold. Russ Tamblyn, Jan Sterling, John Drew Barrymore, Mamie Van Doren. Amateurish mishmash involving young undercover agent infiltrating school dope-pushing gang to get evidence. Retitled: YOUNG HELLIONS.

High Sierra (1941) 100m. *** D: Raoul Walsh. Humphrey Bogart, Ida Lupino, Alan Curtis, Arthur Kennedy, Joan Leslie, Henry Hull, Henry Travers, Cornel Wilde. Bogey is Mad Dog Earle, killer with a soft heart on the lam from police, in rousing gangster caper. Lupino as the moll and Leslie as the lame innocent Bogart befriends offer interesting contrast. Not always convincing. Remade as I DIED A THOUSAND TIMES, and COLORADO TERRITORY.

High Society (1955) 61m. D: William Beaudine. Leo Gorcey, Huntz Hall, Bernard Gorcey, Amanda Blake, David Condon (Gorcey), Addison Richards, Paul Harvey, Bennie Bartlett. SEE: **Bowery Boys** series.

High Society (1956) C-107m. *** D: Charles Walters. Bing Crosby, Grace Kelly, Frank Sinatra, Celeste Holm, Louis Calhern, Louis Armstrong. Fluffy remake of PHILADELPHIA STORY is enjoyable, but has lost all the bite of the original. Kelly is about to marry John Lund when ex-hubby Crosby arrives, along with reporters Sinatra and Holm. Cole Porter songs include "True Love," "Did You Evah?" "You're Sensational."

High Terrace (1956-British) 77m. ** D: Henry Cass. Dale Robertson, Lois Maxwell, Derek Bond, Eric Pohlmann. Fledgling actress is implicated in murder in minor drama.

High Tide (1947) 72m. **½ D: John Reinhardt. Lee Tracy, Don Castle, Julie Bishop, Regis Toomey, Anabel Shaw, Francis Ford. Low-budget gets good mileage from players convincingly relating story of newspaper's attempts to prevent racketeers taking over city.

High Time (1960) C-103m. **½ D: Blake Edwards. Bing Crosby, Fabian, Tuesday Weld, Nicole Maurey. Middling Crosby vehicle has Bing a widower resuming college career and trying to be one of the boys; forced comedy.

High Treason (1952-British) 93m. **½ D: Roy Boulting. Andre Morell, Liam Redmond, Mary Morris. Well-handled drama involving complex caper to instigate chaos in English industrial life via high-explosive bomb.

High Velocity (1977) C-105m. ** D: Remi Kramer. Ben Gazzara, Paul Winfield, Britt Ekland, Keenan Wynn, Alejandro Rey, Victoria

Racimo. Hard-nosed Vietnam vets are hired to spring an international executive who's been kidnapped. Standard action fare, unworthy of good cast.

High Wall (1947) 99m. *** D: Curtis Bernhardt. Robert Taylor, Audrey Totter, Herbert Marshall, Dorothy Patrick, H. B. Warner, Warner Anderson. Well-paced mystery of former air force bomber pilot who attempts to establish innocence in murder case by working with psychiatrist.

High, Wide, and Handsome (1937) 112m. **½ D: Rouben Mamoulian. Irene Dunne, Randolph Scott, Dorothy Lamour, Elizabeth Patterson, Charles Bickford, Raymond Walburn, Alan Hale, Akim Tamiroff, William Frawley. Jerome Kern-Oscar Hammerstein old-time musical of determined Scott drilling for oil in 19th-century Pennsylvania, fighting corrupt Hale. Corny plot put over by energetic cast; result is entertaining. Songs include "The Folks Who Live On The Hill."

High Wind in Jamaica, A (1965-British) C-104m. *** D: Alexander Mackendrick. Anthony Quinn, James Coburn, Dennis Price, Gert Frobe, Lila Kedrova, Nigel Davenport, Kenneth J. Warren. Excellent cast and intelligent script about group of children who reveal their basic natures when left adrift aboard a pirate vessel.

High-Ballin' (1978-U.S.-Canadian) C-100m. **½ D: Peter Carter. Peter Fonda, Jerry Reed, Helen Shaver, Chris Wiggins, David Ferry, Chris Longevin. Good-buddy truckdrivers Fonda and Reed battle a truck kingpin's goons who want to force them off the road for good. Predictable action fare, with added spice from female trucker Shaver.

Higher and Higher (1943) 90m. **½ D: Tim Whelan. Michele Morgan, Jack Haley, Frank Sinatra, Leon Errol, Marcy McGuire, Victor Borge, Mary Wickes, Mel Torme. Bright, breezy, generally witless musical, with good cheer compensating for lack of material, as once-wealthy Errol schemes with his own servants to raise money. Sinatra's songs are fine: "The Music Stopped," "I Couldn't Sleep a Wink Last Night."

Highly Dangerous (1951-British) 88m. **½ D: Roy Baker. Dane Clark, Marius Goring, Margaret Lockwood,

Wilfrid Hyde-White, Olaf Pooley, Eric Pohlmann. Clark is American reporter accompanying scientist (Lockwood) on secret mission; well paced.

Highway Dragnet (1954) 71m. ** D: Nathan Juran. Richard Conte, Joan Bennett, Wanda Hendrix, Reed Hadley, Mary Beth Hughes. Tawdry caper of Conte trying to prove his innocence of a murder rap.

Highway 301 (1950) 83m. ** D: Andrew L. Stone. Steve Cochran, Virginia Grey, Robert Webber, Richard Egan. Good little gangster film relating robbery capers in straightforward manner.

Highway to Battle (1960-British) 71m. ** D: Ernest Morris. Gerard Heinz, Margaret Tyzack, Peter Reynolds, Richard Shaw. Trim little film set in 1935 England involving Nazi diplomats who try to defect, chased by Gestapo agents.

Highwayman, The (1951) C-82m. **½ D: Lesley Selander. Charles Coburn, Wanda Hendrix, Philip Friend, Cecil Kellaway, Victor Jory. Filmization of famous poem, involving innkeeper's daughter in love with nobleman who masquerades as bandit to help the oppressed; set in 1760s England.

Highwayman Rides, The: SEE: Billy the Kid

Hijack (1973) C-73m. TVM D: Leonard Horn. David Janssen, Keenan Wynn, Ronald Feinberg, Lee Purcell, Jeanette Nolan, William Schallert. Two truckdrivers, unaware of nature of cargo, menaced by criminals not afraid of going all the way for possession of government secret material. Janssen and Wynn work well together, but script full of implausible situations and resolution. Average.

Hilda Crane (1956) C-87m. **½ D: Philip Dunne. Jean Simmons, Guy Madison, Jean-Pierre Aumont, Judith Evelyn, Evelyn Varden. Florid melodrama of Simmons, two-time divorcee, who returns home to learn what life means.

Hill, The (1965) 122m. *** D: Sidney Lumet. Sean Connery, Harry Andrews, Ian Bannen, Ossie Davis, Michael Redgrave, Alfred Lynch, Roy Kinnear. Powerful drama of military prison camp, with fine performances by all. One problem: British actors bark at each other and much dialogue is unintelligible to American ears. Good luck.

Hill 24 Doesn't Answer (1955-Israeli) 100m. *** D: Thorold Dickinson. Edward Mulhare, Haya Harareet, Michael Wager, Arieh Lavi. Night before cease fire during Arab-Israeli War 1948, four volunteers set out to hold hill until morning and claim it for Israel. Realistic, swiftly paced film.

Hills of Home (1948) C-97m. *** D: Fred M. Wilcox. Edmund Gwenn, Donald Crisp, Tom Drake, Janet Leigh. Gwenn stars in Lassie movie about doctor convincing Scottish father to urge son to study medicine.

Hills Run Red, The (1966-Italian) C-89m. ** D: Carlo Lizzani. Thomas Hunter, Henry Silva, Dan Duryea, Nando Gazzola. Civil War Western of stolen payrolls; poorly dubbed and loosely acted.

Hindenburg, The (1975) C-125m. ** D: Robert Wise. George C. Scott, Anne Bancroft, William Atherton, Roy Thinnes, Gig Young, Burgess Meredith, Charles Durning, Richard A. Dysart, Robert Clary, Rene Auberjonois. Intriguing premise, that 1937 airship disaster was an act of sabotage, undermined by silly Grand Hotel-type characters and unexciting denouement combining original newsreel footage and newly-shot material. Five minutes were added to film for network showing.

Hippodrome (1961-German) C-96m. **½ D: Herbert Gruber. Gerhard Reidmann, Margit Nunke, Willy Birgel, Mady Rahl, Walter Giller. Atmospheric circus mystery yarn, integrating varied circus acts with tale of murder and lust under big top.

Hips, Hips, Hooray (1934) 68m. *** D: Mark Sandrich. Bert Wheeler, Robert Woolsey, Dorothy Lee, Thelma Todd, Ruth Etting, George Meeker. One of Wheeler & Woolsey's best vehicles is a lavish, risqué musical comedy about their invasion of Todd's ailing beauty business. Wild production numbers, plus a nice song from Etting.

Hired Gun, The (1957) 63m. **½ D: Ray Nazarro. Rory Calhoun, Anne Francis, Vince Edwards, John Litel, Chuck Connors. Francis is fetching as condemned killer Calhoun determines to prove innocent.

Hired Hand, The (1971) C-93m. *** D: Peter Fonda. Peter Fonda, Warren Oates, Verna Bloom, Robert Pratt, Severn Darden. First-rate photography and good performances by Oates and Bloom aid this offbeat, sometimes pretentious Western about cowboy who goes to work for the wife he deserted seven years before.

Hired Wife (1940) 93m. *** D: William A. Seiter. Rosalind Russell, Brian Aherne, Virginia Bruce, Robert Benchley, John Carroll. Secretary Russell marries boss Aherne for business reasons; then the fun begins. Hilarious trifle with cast of comedy experts.

Hireling, The (1973-British) C-108m. ***½ D: Alan Bridges. Robert Shaw, Sarah Miles, Peter Egan, Elizabeth Sellars, Caroline Mortimer, Patricia Lawrence. Artistic adaptation of L. P. Hartley novel of stifling class system of England. Chauffeur Leadbetter (Shaw) helps upperclass woman (Miles) out of mental depression, mistakenly assumes she's interested in him. Ensemble British cast, good direction.

Hiroshima, Mon Amour (1960-French) 88m. ***½ D: Alain Resnais. Emmanuele Riva, Eiji Okada, Stella Dassas, Pierre Barband. Thoughtful study of French movie actress and Japanese architect whose sensual love affair in 1950 Hiroshima evokes strange memories of the past and thoughts of the future.

His Brother's Wife (1936) 90m. ** D: W. S. Van Dyke, II. Barbara Stanwyck, Robert Taylor, Jean Hersholt, Joseph Calleia, John Eldredge, Samuel S. Hinds. Glossy soaper of dedicated scientist Taylor scorning Stanwyck, who marries his brother Eldredge for spite.

His Butler's Sister (1943) 94m. **½ D: Frank Borzage. Deanna Durbin, Pat O'Brien, Franchot Tone, Evelyn Ankers, Else Janssen, Walter Catlett, Iris Adrian, Akim Tamiroff, Alan Mowbray. Entertaining romantic comedy of maid Durbin in love with boss Tone; musical scenes not too exciting, but film is spry.

His Girl Friday (1940) 92m. **** D: Howard Hawks. Cary Grant, Rosalind Russell, Ralph Bellamy, Gene Lockhart, Helen Mack, Porter Hall, Roscoe Karns, John Qualen, Frank Jenks, Billy Gilbert. Fine comedy remake of THE FRONT PAGE with Grant as conniving editor, Russell as star reporter, Bellamy as hayseed she's trying to marry amid hot murder story. Terrific character actors add sparkle to must-see film.

His Kind of Woman (1951) 120m. **½ D: John Farrow. Robert Mitchum, Jane Russell, Vincent Price, Tim Holt. Coy little film involving deported racketeer trying to sneak back into U.S., and Mitchum, who helps prevent it.

His Majesty O'Keefe (1953) C-92m. **½ D: Byron Haskin. Burt Lancaster, Joan Rice, Benson Fong, Philip Ahn, Grant Taylor. Another athletic Lancaster buccaneer romp, set in the South Seas.

His Woman (1931) 80m. ** D: Edward Sloman. Gary Cooper, Claudette Colbert, Douglass Dumbrille, Harry Davenport. Stiff, early-talkie romance between skipper Cooper and passenger, nurse Colbert.

History Is Made at Night (1937) 97m. ***½ D: Frank Borzage. Charles Boyer, Jean Arthur, Leo Carrillo, Colin Clive, Andre St. Maur. Excellent tragicomedy of despicable husband Clive divorcing Arthur, who falls for suave Boyer.

History of Mr. Polly, The (1949-British) 96m. *** D: Anthony Pelissier. John Mills, Sally Ann Howes, Finlay Currie, Megs Jenkins, Diana Churchill. H. G. Wells' yarn of romantic idler who goes on a bicycle tour, hoping to find new values in life; admirably acted.

Hit (1973) C-134m. *** D: Sidney J. Furie. Billy Dee Williams, Paul Hampton, Richard Pryor, Gwen Welles. Detailed and overlong, but exciting story of black U.S. agent who seeks revenge on top drug importers in Marseilles who are indirectly responsible for his daughter's death.

Hit and Run (1957) 84m. BOMB D: Hugo Haas. Hugo Haas, Cleo Moore, Vince Edwards. Trash involving Haas' efforts to rid himself of wife's young boyfriend.

Hit Lady (1974) C-78m. TVM D: Tracy Keenan Wynn. Yvette Mimieux, Joseph Campanella, Clu Gulager, Dack Rambo, Keenan Wynn. Mimieux wrote this one and stars as a successful artist who moonlights (in bikini) as a ruthless syndicate assassin. Middling gangster flick with a twist told in its title. Average.

Hit Man (1972) C-90m. ** D: George Armitage. Bernie Casey, Pamela Grier, Lisa Moore, Don Diamond. Reworking of GET CARTER in

black mold. Big rubout is key to crime story, and it loses steam before long.

Hit the Deck (1955) C-112m. **½ D: Roy Rowland. Jane Powell, Tony Martin, Debbie Reynolds, Ann Miller, Vic Damone, Russ Tamblyn, Walter Pidgeon, Kay Armen, Gene Raymond. Second-string MGM musical of sailors on shore leave is pleasant time-filler, no more, with nice Vincent Youmans songs like "Halleleujah," "Sometimes I'm Happy," "More Than You Know."

Hit the Ice (1943) 82m. ** D: Charles Lamont. Bud Abbott, Lou Costello, Ginny Simms, Patric Knowles, Elyse Knox, Sheldon Leonard, Marc Lawrence, Joseph Sawyer. Bud and Lou are newspaper photographers involved with gang of thugs in zany comedy with good gags on skating rink.

Hitch-Hiker, The (1953) 71m. *** D: Ida Lupino. Edmond O'Brien, Frank Lovejoy, William Talman, Jose Torvay. Tense account of two vacationing businessmen held captive by a psychopath.

Hitchhike! (1974) C-78m. TVM D: Gordon Hessler. Cloris Leachman, Michael Brandon, Henry Darrow, Cameron Mitchell, John Elerick, Linden Chiles. Lonely middle-aged vacationer is unaware that the young hitchhiker she has picked up killed his stepmother moments ago. Below average.

Hitched (1971) C-73m. TVM D: Boris Sagal. Tim Matheson, Sally Field, Neville Brand, Kathleen Freeman, Don Knight. Lame, predictable Western with comedy undertones featuring two newlyweds thwarting half-hearted crooked deal. Below average.

Hitler (1962) 107m. **½ D: Stuart Heisler. Richard Basehart, Cordula Trantow, Maria Emo, Martin Kosleck, John Banner, Carl Esmond. Basehart gives a cerebral interpretation to the career of the leader of the Third Reich.

Hitler—Dead or Alive (1943) 70m. ** D: Nick Grinde. Ward Bond, Dorothy Tree, Warren Hymer, Paul Fix, Russell Hicks, Felix Basch, Bobs Watson. Low-budget epic of con-men shooting for high stakes by attempting to kill the Fuehrer.

Hitler Gang, The (1944) 101m. **½ D: John Farrow. Robert Watson, Martin Kosleck, Victor Varconi,

Luis Van Rooten, Sig Ruman, Tonio Selwart, Ludwig Donath. Historical drama of Hitler's rise to power had greatest impact on WW2 audiences but is still fairly interesting, though dwarfed by recent documentaries.

Hitler: The Last Ten Days (1973-British-Italian) C-108m. ** D: Ennio de Concini. Alec Guinness, Simon Ward, Adolfo Celi, Diane Cilento, Gabriele Ferzetti, Eric Porter, Doris Kunstmann. Strange treatment of Hitler's final tyrannies is grimly amusing at times; muddled film doesn't really work.

Hitler's Children (1942) 83m. *** D: Edward Dmytryk, Irving Reis. Tim Holt, Bonita Granville, Kent Smith, Otto Kruger, H. B. Warner, Lloyd Corrigan. Engrossing exploitation film of young people forced to live life of horror in Nazi Germany.

Hitler's Gold SEE: **Inside Out**

Hitler's Madman (1943) 84m. **½ D: Douglas Sirk. Patricia Morison, John Carradine, Alan Curtis, Ralph Morgan, Howard Freeman, Ludwig Stossel, Edgar Kennedy. Exciting saga based on true story of small Czech village destroyed by Nazis, and commander Heydrich, assassinated by determined Czechs. Look for Ava Gardner in a small part.

Hitting a New High (1937) 85m. **½ D: Raoul Walsh. Lily Pons, Jack Oakie, Edward Everett Horton, Lucille Ball, Eric Blore, Eduardo Ciannelli. Title refers to Pons' voice, not the film per se; fluffy musical romance relies on supporting cast for entertainment.

Hiya, Chum (1943) 61m. *½ D: Harold Young. Ritz Brothers, Jane Frazee, Robert Paige, June Clyde, Edmund MacDonald. Entertainers find themselves in small boom-town, and open a restaurant there. Weak musical comedy, if that's what you want to call it.

Hobson's Choice (1954-British) 107m. *** D: David Lean. Charles Laughton, John Mills, Brenda De Banzie, Daphne Anderson. Laughton is delightful as bootshop owner in the 1890s who has decided whom his two daughters will marry despite their complaints.

Hoffman (1970-British) C-116m. *** D: Alvin Rakoff. Peter Sellers, Sinead Cusack, Jeremy Bulloch, Ruth Dunning. Very odd, low-key dual character study with Sellers blackmailing attractive young bride-to-be

to spend weekend with him. Slightly overlong; great performance.

Hold Back the Dawn (1941) 115m. ***½ D: Mitchell Leisen. Charles Boyer, Olivia de Havilland, Paulette Goddard, Victor Francen, Walter Abel, Rosemary DeCamp. First-rate soaper with Billy Wilder-Charles Brackett script of gigolo Boyer marrying spinsterish Olivia to get into U.S.

Hold Back the Night (1956) 80m. **½ D: Allan Dwan. John Payne, Mona Freeman, Peter Graves, Chuck Connors. Korean War officer Payne recounts facts about bottle of liquor he always has with him.

Hold Back Tomorrow (1955) 75m. *½ D: Hugo Haas. Cleo Moore, John Agar, Frank de Kova, Harry Guardino, Jan Englund. Strange B-film concerning condemned murderer who marries a girl on the night before his execution.

Hold 'Em Jail (1932) 74m. **½ D: Norman Taurog. Bert Wheeler, Robert Woolsey, Betty Grable, Edgar Kennedy, Edna May Oliver, Roscoe Ates. Silly comedy about privileged prisoners (Wheeler & Woolsey) at Kennedy's Bidemore Prison who start competitive football team. Some good laughs.

Hold On! (1966) C-85m. **½ D: Arthur Lubin. Peter Noone, Herman's Hermits, Sue Ane Langdon, Karl Green, Shelley Fabares. U.S. tour by rock 'n' roll group is thin plot on which to hinge a display of Herman's Hermits musical talents, with pretty girls thrown into story for diversion.

Hold That Baby (1949) 64m. D: Reginald Le Borg. Leo Gorcey, Huntz Hall, Gabriel Dell, Frankie Darro, Billy Benedict, John Kellogg, Anabel Shaw, Bernard Gorcey. SEE: **Bowery Boys** series.

Hold That Blonde (1945) 76m. ** D: George Marshall. Eddie Bracken, Veronica Lake, Albert Dekker, Frank Fenton, George Zucco, Donald MacBride. OK comedy, sometimes strained, of kleptomaniac Bracken tangling with sultry thief Lake.

Hold That Co-ed (1938) 80m. *** D: George Marshall. John Barrymore, George Murphy, Marjorie Weaver, Joan Davis, Jack Haley, George Barbier. Good musicomedy supercharged by Barrymore as windy politician; he makes the whole film.

Hold That Ghost (1941) 86m. ***

D: Arthur Lubin. Bud Abbott, Lou Costello, Richard Carlson, Joan Davis, Mischa Auer, Evelyn Ankers. Prime A&C, with the boys loose in haunted house. Fine cast includes hilarious Davis as professional radio screamer.

Hold That Hypnotist (1957) 61m. **D:** Austin Jewell. Huntz Hall, Stanley Clements, Jane Nigh, David Condon. SEE: **Bowery Boys** series.

Hold That Line (1952) 64m. **D:** William Beaudine. Leo Gorcey, Huntz Hall, John Bromfield, Veda Ann Borg, Pierre Watkin. SEE: **Bowery Boys** series.

Hold Your Man (1933) 89m. ******* D: Sam Wood. Jean Harlow, Clark Gable, Stuart Erwin, Elizabeth Patterson, Blanche Frederici. Gable and Harlow are flawless lovers in this delightful comedy-drama; the two stars really sparkle here.

Hole In the Head, A (1959) C-120m. ****** D: Frank Capra. Frank Sinatra, Edward G. Robinson, Eleanor Parker, Carolyn Jones, Thelma Ritter, Eddie Hodges, Keenan Wynn, Joi Lansing. Sticky story of Sinatra and his son (Hodges) doesn't seem sincere. Only distinction is Oscar-winning song, "High Hopes."

Holiday (1938) 93m. *****½** D: George Cukor. Katharine Hepburn, Cary Grant, Doris Nolan, Lew Ayres, Edward Everett Horton, Binnie Barnes, Henry Daniell. Fine, literate adaptation of Philip Barry's play (filmed before in 1930) about nonconformist Grant confronting stuffy N.Y.C. society family, finding his match in Hepburn. Delightful film.

Holiday Affair (1949) 87m. ******* D: Don Hartman. Robert Mitchum, Janet Leigh, Wendell Corey, Gordon Gebert. Well-done Christmas season story about widow Leigh, her small son, and two contrasting men courting her.

Holiday Camp (1948-British) 97m. ****½** D: Ken Annakin. Dennis Price, Flora Robson, Jack Warner. Pleasantly handled account of life and love at British summer resort; atmospheric, with good characterizations.

Holiday for Lovers (1959) C-103m. ****½** D: Henry Levin. Clifton Webb, Jane Wyman, Jill St. John, Carol Lynley, Paul Henreid, Gary Crosby, Jose Greco. Arch Dr. Webb and Wyman escort attractive daughters on South American vacation, with predictable mating.

Holiday for Sinners (1952) 72m. ****½** D: Gerald Mayer. Gig Young, Janice Rule, Keenan Wynn, William Campbell. Strange goings-on at Mardi Gras as several people try to forget their troublesome lives and have a good time.

Holiday in Mexico (1946) C-127m. ******* D: George Sidney. Walter Pidgeon, Ilona Massey, Roddy McDowall, Jose Iturbi, Xavier Cugat, Jane Powell. Engaging, well-cast musical comedy of daughter of ambassador falling for noted musician.

Holiday Inn (1942) 101m. ******* D: Mark Sandrich. Bing Crosby, Fred Astaire, Marjorie Reynolds, Virginia Dale, Walter Abel, Louise Beavers. Perky musical with great Irving Berlin songs. Bing introduces "White Christmas," Fred dances . . . who needs much of a plot? Better than partial remake, WHITE CHRISTMAS.

Hollow Image (1979) C-100m. TVM D: Marvin J. Chomsky. Robert Hooks, Saundra Sharp, Dick Anthony Williams, Hattie Winston, Morgan Freeman. Black career girl is torn between her chic new life in the world of fashion and her roots in Harlem with an old beau. Occasionally pretentious black awareness movie with standout performances by Williams and Freeman. Above average.

Hollow Triumph (1948) 83m. ******* D: Steve Sekely. Paul Henreid, Joan Bennett, Eduard Franz, Leslie Brooks. Tense melodrama of killer assuming identity of lookalike doctor. Retitled: THE SCAR.

Holly and the Ivy, The (1953-British) 80m. ******* D: George More O'Ferrall. Ralph Richardson, Celia Johnson, Margaret Leighton, Denholm Elliott, Hugh Williams, Roland Culver. Straightforward adaptation of Wynyard Browne play revolving around Christmas holiday with Richardson, the small-town cleric learning about his three grown-up children; nicely acted.

Hollywood Canteen (1944) 124m. ****½** D: Delmer Daves. Joan Crawford, Bette Davis, John Garfield, Sydney Greenstreet, Peter Lorre, Ida Lupino, Eleanor Parker, Alexis Smith, Barbara Stanwyck, S. Z. Sakall, Joan Leslie, Andrews Sisters, Jack Benny, Eddie Cantor, Jack Carson, Faye Emerson, Irene Manning, Janis Paige. A bevy of Warner Bros. stars make token appearances in this all-star movie, which offers some fun. Loosely hinged tale of G.I. (Robert Hutton) wanting to date Leslie; Davis, who founded the Canteen, explains its function.

Hollywood Cavalcade (1939) C-96m. *** D: Irving Cummings. Alice Faye, Don Ameche, Al Jolson, Mack Sennett, Stuart Erwin, Buster Keaton, Mary Forbes, Chester Conklin, Rin-Tin-Tin, Jr. First half a delight, with Don bringing Alice to Hollywood in silent days with flavorful recreation of old-time comedies; remainder of film bogs down in phony dramatics.

Hollywood Party (1934) 68m. **½ No director credited. Jimmy Durante, Laurel and Hardy, Lupe Velez, Polly Moran, Charles Butterworth, Eddie Quillan, June Clyde, George Givot, Jack Pearl, Ted Healy and the Three Stooges, many others. Musical comedy hodgepodge built around screen star Durante throwing a gala party. Romantic subplot is for the birds, but Stan and Ollie battling fiery Velez, Durante as Schnarzan, befuddled Butterworth and opening title tune make it worthwhile. Richard Boleslawski, Allan Dwan, Roy Rowland directed various scenes without credit; TV print is missing appearance by Mickey Mouse and color Disney cartoon "Hot Chocolate Soldiers."

Hollywood Hotel (1937) 109m. **½ D: Busby Berkeley. Dick Powell, Rosemary and Lola Lane, Hugh Herbert, Glenda Farrell, Johnnie Davis, Louella Parsons, Frances Langford, Fritz Feld, Allyn Joslyn, Alan Mowbray. Title sums it up, with plenty of guests, music, and songs like "I'm Like a Fish Out of Water" and "Hooray for Hollywood."

Hollywood or Bust (1956) C-95m. **½ D: Frank Tashlin. Dean Martin, Jerry Lewis, Anita Ekberg, Pat Crowley. Star-struck Lewis teams up with gambler Martin on trek to crash the movie capital; typical comedy by the frantic team.

Hollywood Revue of 1929, The (1929) 130m. ** D: Charles Riesner. Conrad Nagel, Jack Benny, John Gilbert, Norma Shearer, Joan Crawford, Laurel and Hardy, Bessie Love, Lionel Barrymore, Marion Davies, Buster Keaton, Marie Dressler, Polly Moran, many others. MGM's all-star revue introducing its silent-film stars as talkie personalities, co-hosted by Benny and Nagel. Definitely a curio for film buffs, rough sledding for others. TV print at 116 minutes is missing some material; several scenes originally filmed in color.

Hollywood Story (1951) 77m. **½ D: William Castle. Richard Conte, Julia Adams, Richard Egan, Henry Hull. Trying to solve an old murder, producer makes a picture on the subject, hoping to uncover culprit.

Holy Matrimony (1943) 87m. *** D: John M. Stahl. Monty Woolley, Gracie Fields, Laird Cregar, Una O'Connor, Alan Mowbray, Melville Cooper, Franklin Pangborn. Delightful tale of artist Woolley assuming late butler's identity to avoid publicity, finding many complications. Remake of 1933 film HIS DOUBLE LIFE.

Hombre (1967) C-111m. *** D: Martin Ritt. Paul Newman, Fredric March, Richard Boone, Diane Cilento, Cameron Mitchell, Barbara Rush, Martin Balsam. Interesting story of Indian-raised Newman trying to survive in white man's world in Arizona circa 1880. Encounters with various characters on a stagecoach provide basis for film's action and drama; well acted, entertaining.

Home at Seven (1953-British) 85m. *** D: Ralph Richardson. Ralph Richardson, Margaret Leighton, Jack Hawkins, Campbell Singer. Taut thriller involving bank clerk who can't account for a day in his life when a murder and a bank robbery occurred. Retitled: MURDER ON MONDAY.

Home Before Dark (1958) 136m. *** D: Mervyn LeRoy. Jean Simmons, Dan O'Herlihy, Rhonda Fleming, Efrem Zimbalist, Jr. Shiny but poignant telling of Simmons readjustment to life after nervous breakdown; on-location shooting in Massachusetts.

Home for the Holidays (1972) C-74m. TVM D: John Llewellyn Moxey. Eleanor Parker, Sally Field, Jessica Walter, Julie Harris, Jill Haworth, Walter Brennan. Aging and vulnerable Ben Morgan (Brennan) convinces four daughters to stay and protect his life during Christmas reunion. Cause: homicidal maniac. Some good situations and pacing, but you've seen it all before. Average.

Home from the Hill (1960) C-150m. *** D: Vincente Minnelli. Robert Mitchum, Eleanor Parker, George Peppard, George Hamilton. Despite MGM sheen, film glows with fine performances in turgid study of Southern landowner and his relationship with wife, son, and illegitimate offspring.

Home in Indiana (1944) C-103m. *** D: Henry Hathaway. Walter Brennan, Jeanne Crain, June Haver, Charlotte Greenwood, Lon McCallister, Ward Bond, Willie Best, George Cleveland. Typical horseracing saga gets a good rehashing here with colorful production and sincere performances; climactic race is well-handled.

Home Is the Hero (1959-Irish) 83m. **½ D: Fielder Cook. Walter Macken, Eileen Crowe, Arthur Kennedy, Joan O'Hara. Modest yarn with Abbey Theatre group, telling story of ex-con (Macken) trying to pick up pieces of home-life.

Home of the Brave (1949) 85m. *** D: Mark Robson. James Edwards, Douglas Dick, Steve Brodie, Jeff Corey, Lloyd Bridges. More daring when made than now, but still hardhitting WW2 account of Negro soldier who suffers more abuse from fellow-G.I.s than from missions against the enemy. From Arthur Laurents' play.

Home, Sweet Homicide (1946) 90m. ** D: Lloyd Bacon. Peggy Ann Garner, Randolph Scott, Lynn Bari, Dean Stockwell. Nothing-special comedy-mystery, as children of mystery writer solve local murder and find husband for their mother.

Home to Stay (1978) C-74m. TVM D: Delbert Mann. Henry Fonda, Michael McGuire, Frances Hyland, David Stambaugh, Kirsten Vigard. Sentimental tale of a teenager and the trip she takes with her spirited grandfather to keep him from being sent to a home for the aged. Fonda, as usual, is dignity personified in this Canadian-filmed story taken from Janet Majerus' *Grandpa and Frank*. Above average.

Homebodies (1974) C-96m. **½ D: Larry Yust. Frances Fuller, Ian Wolfe, Ruth McDevitt, Paula Trueman, Peter Brocco, William Hansen. Bizarre horror comedy-drama will depend on one's taste for enjoyment. Elderly tenants of condemned building resort to murder to keep their home. Good cast, including Douglas Fowley as the builder. Made in Cincinnati.

Homecoming (1948) 113m. ** D: Mervyn LeRoy. Clark Gable, Lana Turner, Anne Baxter, John Hodiak, Ray Collins, Cameron Mitchell. Gable and Turner have exciting WW2 romance in the trenches, but that can't support 113 minutes of dreary drama; one of Gable's lesser efforts.

Homecoming, The (1973) C-111m. ***½ D: Peter Hall. Cyril Cusack, Ian Holm, Michael Jayston, Vivien Merchant, Terence Rigby, Paul Rogers. Jayston, long separated from his London family, brings wife Merchant home to meet his father and two brothers. Film version of the Harold Pinter play is among the most satisfactory of all stage-to-screen adaptations. An American Film Theater Production.

Homer (1970) C-91m. *½ D: John Trent. Don Scardino, Alex Nicol, Tisa Farrow, Lenka Peterson, Ralph Endersby, Trudy Young. Well-meaning but cliché-ridden drama about small-town teen-ager, generation gap, Vietnam War protests, rock music, sex. You've seen it all before.

Homestretch, The (1947) C-96m. ** D: H. Bruce Humberstone. Cornel Wilde, Maureen O'Hara, Glenn Langan, Helen Walker, James Gleason. Harmless film of romance between young girl and horse-owner suffers from uneven acting and script.

Hometown USA (1979) C-93m. **½ D: Max Baer. Gary Springer, David Wilson, Brian Kerwin, Pat Delaney, Julie Parsons. Yet another nostalgic look at teenagers in the late 1950s; makes up in spirit and period flavor what it may lack in originality.

Homicidal (1961) 87m. **½ D: William Castle. Glenn Corbett, Patricia Breslin, Jean Arless, Eugenie Leontovich. Film almost makes it as genuine shocker, filled with terrifying occurrences; set in spooky old house.

Hondo (1953) C-84m. *** D: John Farrow. John Wayne, Geraldine Page, Ward Bond, James Arness, Lee Aaker. Well-done Western, with Wayne the Army soldier who comes across a widow and her son living in a farmhouse in a deserted area of southwest Texas, unalarmed about pending Indian uprising. Page won an Oscar nomination. Originally shown in 3D.

Honey Pot, The (1967) C-131m. **½ D: Joseph L. Mankiewicz. Rex Harrison, Susan Hayward, Cliff Robertson, Capucine, Edie Adams, Maggie Smith, Adolfo Celi. Director/writer Mankiewicz updates VOLPONE in sly blend of high comedy and whodunit. Harrison pretends to be dying, sends for former mistresses to see their reactions; hoax evolves into elaborate murder scheme. Never as amusing as one would like it to be. Also known as IT COMES UP MURDER.

Honeychile (1951) C-90m. *½ D: R. G. Springsteen. Judy Canova, Eddie Foy, Jr., Alan Hale, Jr., Walter Catlett. Cornball stuff involving Canova in the music-publishing business.

Honeymoon (1947) 74m. ** D: William Keighley. Shirley Temple, Franchot Tone, Guy Madison, Lina Romay, Gene Lockhart, Grant Mitchell. Unmemorable mixture of romance and comedy in story of G.I. who longs for fiancée in Mexico during three-day pass. Good cast fails to make film click.

Honeymoon (1959-Spanish) C-90m. ** D: Michael Powell. Anthony Steel, Ludmilla Tcherina, Antonio, Rosita Segovia. Muddled romancer intertwined with ballet sequences. Steel on wedding trip with Tcherina, encounters Antonio who tries to court the ex-ballerina. Excerpts from ballets LOS AMANTES DE TERUEL and EL AMOR BRUJO.

Honeymoon Ahead (1945) 60m. ** D: Reginald Le Borg. Allan Jones, Raymond Walburn, Grace McDonald, Vivian Austin. Nonsensical trivia involving kindly prisoner (head of convicts' choir) and his involvement with the world outside the big walls.

Honeymoon for Three (1941) 77m. **½ D: Lloyd Bacon. Ann Sheridan, George Brent, Charlie Ruggles, Osa Massen, Walter Catlett, Jane Wyman. Breezy comedy of novelist Brent warding off female admirers by pretending to be married; Sheridan is his witty, amorous secretary.

Honeymoon Hotel (1964) C-89m. *½ D: Henry Levin. Robert Goulet, Jill St. John, Nancy Kwan, Robert Morse, Elsa Lanchester, Keenan Wynn. Asinine shenanigans with bachelors Goulet and Morse arriving at resort for newlyweds. Lanchester is fun despite all.

Honeymoon in Bali (1939) 95m. *** D: Edward H. Griffith. Fred MacMurray, Madeleine Carroll, Allan Jones, Osa Massen, Helen Broderick, Akim Tamiroff. Funny romantic boy-chases-girl film, with MacMurray after beautiful Carroll with interference from aristocratic Jones.

Honeymoon Killers, The (1970) 108m. *** D: Leonard Kastle. Shirley Stoler, Tony LoBianco, Mary Jane Higby, Doris Roberts. True story of couple who murder "lonelyhearts" women after stripping them of their savings. Terse and chilling.

Honeymoon Machine, The (1961) C-87m. **½ D: Richard Thorpe. Steve McQueen, Jim Hutton, Paula Prentiss, Brigid Bazlen, Dean Jagger, Jack Weston. Pleasant comedy with a spirited cast about two sailors who find a way to beat the roulette table in Monte Carlo. Easy to take, easy to forget.

Honeymoon with a Stranger (1969) C-74m. TVM D: John Peyser. Janet Leigh, Rossano Brazzi, Joseph Lenzi, Cesare Danova, Barbara Steele, Eric Braeden. After blissful wedding night, American newlywed discovers husband missing and strange man claiming to be genuine article. Routine story enhanced by location filming in Spain. Average.

Hong Kong (1951) C-92m. ** D: Lewis R. Foster. Ronald Reagan, Rhonda Fleming, Nigel Bruce, Marvin Miller. Mediocre account of Reagan trying to heist a valuable antique from orphaned girl but going straight before finale. Strictly backlot Hong Kong.

Hong Kong Affair (1958) 79m. *½ D: Paul F. Heard. Jack Kelly, May Wynn, Richard Loo, Lo Lita Shek. Kelly is the Yank who comes to the Orient to investigate his property holdings, getting more than he bargained for.

Hong Kong Confidential (1958) 67m. **½ D: Edward L. Cahn. Gene Barry, Beverly Tyler, Allison Hayes, Noel Drayton. Harmless "B" film about Anglo-American agents rescuing a kidnapped Arabian prince.

Honkers, The (1972) C-102m. **½ D: Steve Ihnat. James Coburn, Lois Nettleton, Slim Pickens, Anne Archer, Richard Anderson, Joan Huntington, Jim Davis. Theme about aging rodeo performer was handled better in J. W. COOP and JUNIOR BONNER; actor Ihnat died shortly after directing this film.

Honky (1972) C-89m. *½ D: William A. Graham. Brenda Sykes, John Neilson, William Marshall, Amentah Dymally. White "all-American" boy falls for drug-pushing black swinger. Lurid and mundane.

Honky Tonk (1941) 105m. **½ D: Jack Conway. Clark Gable, Lana Turner, Frank Morgan, Claire Trevor, Marjorie Main, Albert Dekker, Chill Wills. Good-gal Lana loves gambler Gable in romantic Western that's fun for a spell, then drags into talky marathon. Morgan and Wills offer fine character performances.

Honky Tonk (1974) C-90m. TVM D: Don Taylor. Richard Crenna, Stella Stevens, Margot Kidder, Will Geer, John Dehner, Geoffrey Lewis, Gregory Sierra. Pleasant remake of Gable-Turner vehicle with smooth cast enacting con man/respectable lady/dance-hall girl triangle. Average.

Honolulu (1939) 83m. **½ D: Edward Buzzell. Eleanor Powell, Robert Young, George Burns, Gracie Allen, Rita Johnson, Willie Fung, Sig Ruman, Ruth Hussey. Standard musical about mistaken identities. Screen idol changes places with plantation owner.

Honor Thy Father (1971) C-100m. TVM D: Paul Wendkos. Joseph Bologna, Raf Vallone, Brenda Vaccaro, Richard Castellano, Joe De Santis, Gilbert Green, Marc Lawrence. Extraordinary slice-of-life presentation of day-to-day operations of organized crime family, written (primarily) around Bill Bonanno character. Adapted from Gay Talese book. Within TV restrictions, not bad. Above average.

Hoodlum, The (1951) 61m. ** D: Max Nosseck. Lawrence Tierney, Allene Roberts, Marjorie Riordan, Lisa Golm. Once a crook, always a crook is plot of this caper about ex-con planning bank robbery.

Hoodlum Empire (1952) 98m. **½ D: Joseph Kane. Brian Donlevy, Claire Trevor, Forrest Tucker, Vera Ralston, Luther Adler. Cast is sufficiently versed in format to make this exposé of a crime syndicate better than average.

Hoodlum Priest, The (1961) 101m. *** D: Irvin Kershner. Don Murray, Larry Gates, Keir Dullea, Logan Ramsey, Cindi Wood. Based on real-life clergyman who devoted himself to trying to help would-be criminals, focusing on Murray's efforts to rehabilitate delinquent Dullea; splendidly acted.

Hoodlum Saint, The (1946) 91m. **½ D: Norman Taurog. William Powell, Esther Williams, Angela Lansbury, James Gleason, Rags Ragland, Lewis Stone, Emma Dunn. Modest film benefits from good Powell performance as cynic who sees The Light.

Hook, The (1963) 98m. *** D: George Seaton. Kirk Douglas, Robert Walker, Jr., Nick Adams, Nehemiah Persoff. Film examines men at war (Korean) and the taking of one life, face-to-face, as opposed to killing many in battle. Earnest, thought-provoking. Music by harmonica virtuoso Larry Adler.

Hook, Line & Sinker (1969) C-91m. BOMB. D: George Marshall. Jerry Lewis, Peter Lawford, Anne Francis, Pedro Gonzalez, Jimmy Miller, Kathleen Freeman. Potentially funny premise about supposedly dying man who runs up $100,000 in credit card debts, only to discover he's healthy, is totally botched; even Lewis fans will be bored.

Hooked Generation (1969) C-92m. BOMB. D: William Grefe. Jeremy Slate, Willie Pastrano, Steve Alaimo, John David Chandler, Socrates Ballis. Narcotics peddlers slaughter their Cuban contacts, Coast Guard, and kidnap innocent victims; poor excuse for a film.

Hooper (1978) C-100m. *** D: Hal Needham. Burt Reynolds, Jan-Michael Vincent, Sally Field, Brian Keith, John Marley, James Best, Robert Klein. Lighthearted look at ace Hollywood stunt man Reynolds, his freewheeling life-style, and the young tyro who gets him to try the biggest stunt of all.

Hooray for Love (1935) 72m. *** D: Walter Lang. Ann Sothern, Gene Raymond, Bill Robinson, Maria Gambarelli, Pert Kelton, Fats Waller. Modest but very entertaining backstage musical with Sothern and Raymond the pleasing romantic leads, Robinson and Waller contributing fine musical specialties, Kelton adding laughs as aspiring soprano.

Hoppity Goes to Town (1941) C-77m. **½ D: Dave Fleischer. Pleasant animated feature about residents of bug-ville and their various problems —living in a human world, and threatened by villainous C. Bagley Beetle. Good-looking but uncompelling story-wise, with unmemorable Frank Loesser-Hoagy Carmichael score. Originally released as MR. BUG GOES TO TOWN.

Horizons West (1952) C-81m. **½ D: Budd Boetticher. Robert Ryan, Julia Adams, Rock Hudson, Raymond Burr, James Arness. Standard Western of two brothers on the opposite sides of the law.

Horizontal Lieutenant, The (1962) C-90m. **½ D: Richard Thorpe. Jim Hutton, Paula Prentiss, Miyoshi Umeki, Jim Backus, Jack Carter, Marty Ingels, Charles McGraw. Artificial service comedy set on WW2 Pacific island involving army officer Hutton's capture of innocuous supply thief.

Horn Blows at Midnight, The (1945) 78m. **½ D: Raoul Walsh. Jack Benny, Alexis Smith, Dolores Moran, Allyn Joslyn, Reginald Gardiner, Guy Kibbee. Enjoyable fantasy of angel (Benny) sent to destroy earth with Gabriel's horn; Franklin Pangborn standout as flustered hotel detective. Not as bad as Benny pretends it is.

Hornet's Nest (1970) C-110m. **½ D: Phil Karlson. Rock Hudson, Sylva Koscina, Sergio Fantoni, Jacques Sernas, Giacomo Rossi Stuart, Tom Felleghi. Hudson and group of Italian children plot to blow up Nazi-controlled dam. Reasonably well done and exciting.

Horrible Dr. Hichcock, The (1962-Italian) C-76m. **½ D: Robert Hampton. Robert Flemyng, Barbara Steele, Teresa Fitzgerald, Maria Teresa Vianello. Flavorful Gothic horror yarn, with Flemyng the deranged doctor trying to revive his long-dead first wife; Steele is hysterical second bride.

Horror Castle (1963-Italian) C-83m. *½ D: Anthony Dawson. Christopher Lee, Rossana Podesta, George Riviere, Jim Nolan, Anny Belli Uberti. Chiller about a demented WW2 victim running rampant in a Rhine castle, using assorted torture chamber devices on unsuspecting people. The effect is numbing. Also known as THE VIRGIN OF NUREMBURG and TERROR CASTLE. British title THE CASTLE OF TERROR.

Horror Chamber of Dr. Faustus (1960-French) 84m. ** D: Georges Franju. Pierre Brasseur, Alida Valli, Edith Scob. Gory chiller of demented physician seeking facial transplants for his disfigured daughter, with tragic results. Original title: EYES WITHOUT A FACE.

Horror Creatures of the Prehistoric Planet SEE: **Vampire Men of the Lost Planet**

Horror Express (1972-Spanish) C-88m. *** D: Eugenio Martin. Christopher Lee, Peter Cushing, Telly Savalas, Silvia Tortosa, Jorge Rigaud, Helga Line. Crackerjack horror movie, ingeniously staged and well acted by the genre's superstars. Turn-of-the-century chiller has a long-frozen monster coming to life while being transported from Asia to the West. Lee and Cushing are rival anthropologists aboard the train and Savalas is a power-crazed Cossack officer. Also known as PANIC ON THE TRANS-SIBERIAN EXPRESS.

Horror Hotel (1963-British) 76m. **½ D: John Moxey. Dennis Lotis, Christopher Lee, Betta St. John, Patricia Jessel. Seventeenth-century witch burned at the stake maintains an inn to lure victims for blood sacrifice to the devil.

Horror House (1969-British) C-79m. *½ D: Michael Armstrong. Frankie Avalon, Jill Haworth, Dennis Price, George Sewell, Gina Warwick, Richard O'Sullivan. Below-standard thriller using dog-eared "let's-spend-a-night-in-a-haunted-house" script. Frankie should have stayed on the beach with Annette.

Horror Island (1941) 60m. **½ D: George Waggner. Dick Foran, Leo Carrillo, Peggy Moran, Fuzzy Knight, John Eldredge, Lewis Howard, Iris Adrian. Fast-paced, diverting period "B" film has various colorful types converging at isolated manor; one by one, they're stalked and murdered.

Horror at 37,000 Feet (1972) C-73m. TVM D: David Lowell Rich. William Shatner, Roy Thinnes, Buddy Ebsen, Tammy Grimes, Lynn Loring, France Nuyen. OK fantasy premise disintegrates into forgettable suspense drama of ancient evil aboard transatlantic commercial flight. Below average.

Horror of Dracula (1958-British) C-82m. *** D: Terence Fisher. Peter Cushing, Michael Gough, Melissa

Stribling, Christopher Lee. Vivid re-telling of the vampire classic, well handled.

Horror of Frankenstein, The (1970-British) **C-95m.** ** D: Jimmy Sangster. Ralph Bates, Kate O'Mara, Graham Jones, Veronica Carlson, Bernard Archard, Dennis Price, Joan Rice. New kind of Dr. Frankenstein: he arranges murder of father, cheats on his wife, kills his best friend, while creating new, laughable monster. For aficionados only.

Horror of Party Beach, The (1964) **72m.** BOMB D: Del Tenney. John Scott, Alice Lyon, Allen Laurel, Eulabelle Moore, Marilyn Clark. Monsters from the ocean floor go on rampage against harmless teenagers —or is it the other way around? Oh, never mind.

Horror of the Blood Monster SEE: Vampire Men of the Lost Planet

Horror on Snape Island (1972) **C-85m.** BOMB D: Jim O'Connolly. Bryant Halliday, Jill Haworth, Anna Paok, Jack Watson, Mark Edwards, Derek Fowlds. One of the horrors is a series of brutal murders masterminded by lunatic; another one is the film itself. Retitled TOWER OF EVIL.

Horrors of the Black Museum (1959-British) **C-95m.** **½ D: Arthur Crabtree. Michael Gough, June Cunningham, Graham Curnow, Shirley Ann Field, Geoffrey Keen. Gruesome sequences highlight chiller about writer who uses his hypnotized helper to commit a series of killings.

Horse Feathers (1932) **70m.** ***½ D: Norman Z. McLeod. Groucho, Harpo, Chico, and Zeppo Marx, Thelma Todd, Nat Pendleton. Groucho is head of Huxley College, building up football team to play rival Darwin U. in crazy Marx nonsense. The password is "swordfish."

Horse in the Gray Flannel Suit, The (1968) **C-113m.** *** D: Norman Tokar. Dean Jones, Diane Baker, Lloyd Bochner, Fred Clark, Ellen Janov, Kurt Russell. Cheerful Disney comedy about advertising man (Jones) who finds a way to link his daughter's devotion to horses with an ad campaign.

Horse Soldiers, The (1959) **C-119m.** *** D: John Ford. John Wayne, William Holden, Constance Towers, Althea Gibson, Hoot Gibson, Anna Lee, Russell Simpson. Large-scale oater about Yankees' drive through the South to help speed Civil War victory. Typical Wayne actioner.

Horsemen, The (1971) **C-109m.** **½ D: John Frankenheimer. Omar Sharif, Leigh Taylor-Young, Jack Palance, David De, Peter Jeffrey. Shariff enters grueling buzkashi tournament to please his demanding father (Palance) and prove his machismo. Old-fashioned action-adventure mixes uncomfortably with soul-searching in Dalton Trumbo's script. Filmed in Afghanistan and Spain.

Horse's Mouth, The (1958-British) **C-93m.** ***½ D: Ronald Neame. Alec Guinness, Kay Walsh, Renee Houston, Mike Morgan. Joyce Cary's wry novel is admirably handled, with Guinness as the eccentric painter living on the cuff, seeking oddball surfaces to use for his more ambitious paintings.

Hospital, The (1971) **C-103m.** ***½ D: Arthur Hiller. George C. Scott, Diana Rigg, Barnard Hughes, Nancy Marchand, Richard Dysart. Sardonically funny view of modern city hospital where bitterly discouraged doctor (Scott) is drawn into chaos by crazy girl (Rigg) and her scheming father. Paddy Chayefsky's Oscar winning script makes fun of serious situation by turning it into Marx Brothers-ish lunacy; ultimate truth in what's being said leaves viewer somewhat sad.

Hostage, The (1967) **C-84m.** **½ D: Russell S. Doughton, Jr. Don O'-Kelly, Dean Stanton, John Carradine, Ron Hagerthy, Ann Doran. Well-done low-budget film about a six-year-old who stows away on moving van driven by two murderers. Shot entirely on location in Iowa.

Hostage Heart, The (1977) **C-100m.** TVM D: Bernard McEveety. Bradford Dillman, Loretta Swit, Vic Morrow, Cameron Mitchell, Belinda J. Montgomery, Sharon Acker, Stephen Davies. Terrorists break into a hospital operating room and hold a billionaire, undergoing a heart operation, for millions in ransom. Familiar premise given interesting twist, but the characters are stereotyped. Average.

Hostages (1943) **88m.** ** D: Frank Tuttle. Luise Rainer, William Bendix, Roland Varno, Oscar Homolka, Katina Paxinou, Paul Lukas. Routine tale of underground movement in WW2; Bendix outshines Rainer acting-wise.

[345]

Hostile Guns (1967) C-91m. **½ D: R. G. Springsteen. George Montgomery, Yvonne De Carlo, Tab Hunter, Brian Donlevy, John Russell. U.S. marshal, transporting prisoners to penitentiary, discovers that female prisoner is a woman he once loved. Typical.

Hot Blood (1956) C-85m. **½ D: Nicholas Ray. Jane Russell, Cornel Wilde, Luther Adler, Joseph Calleia. Jane Russell shakes her tambourines and drives Cornel Wilde, in this strange gypsy yarn.

Hot Lead and Cold Feet (1978) C-90m. *** D: Robert Butler. Jim Dale, Darren McGavin, Karen Valentine, Jack Elam, Don Knotts, John Williams. Amiable Disney Western spoof with lots of slapstick features British comic Dale in three roles: tough patriarch, tougher gunfighter son, and meek twin, a Salvation Army lad. The brothers participate in a wild obstacle race to gain possession of the town, then to defeat villainous Mayor McGavin. Good Oregon location filming.

Hot Millions (1968-British) C-105m. *** D: Eric Till. Peter Ustinov, Maggie Smith, Karl Malden, Bob Newhart, Robert Morley, Cesar Romero. Wry piece of fluff about group of off-beat crooks who use a computer to pull off bank heist. Good performers aid pleasant romp, which became one of the biggest sleepers of its year.

Hot News (1953) 68m. *½ D: Edward Bernds. Stanley Clements, Gloria Henry, Ted de Corsia, Veda Ann Borg. Programmer tale of dedicated newspaperman cleaning up crime syndicate involved in sporting events.

Hot Pepper (1933) 76m. **½ D: John G. Blystone. Victor McLaglen, Edmund Lowe, Lupe Velez, El Brendel. Another reprise of feud between Flagg (McLaglen) and Quirt (Lowe), now civilians involved in nightclub, with spitfire Velez the woman they fight over. Constant wisecracks are a bit forced, but stars milk script for all it's worth.

Hot Potato (1976) C-87m. *½ D: Oscar Williams. Jim Kelly, George Memmoli, Geoffrey Binney, Irene Tsu, Judith Brown. Idiotic action film in which karate expert Kelly and two cohorts try to rescue kidnapped Senator's daughter from Oriental villain. Comic-book stuff. Filmed in Thailand.

Hot Rock, The (1972) C-105m. *** D: Peter Yates. Robert Redford, George Segal, Ron Leibman, Paul Sand, Zero Mostel, Moses Gunn. Light, funny caper comedy where inept robbers blunder every step of carefully planned jewel heist. Best bit: the raid on the police station.

Hot Rod (1979) C-100m. TVM D: George Armitage. Gregg Henry, Robert Culp, Pernell Roberts, Robin Mattson, Grant Goodeve. Local dragstrip championship pits a freewheeling outsider against the son of the town boss who has the race fixed. Lots of revving engines and screeching tires drown out the dumb dialogue. Average.

Hot Rod Gang (1958) 72m. *½ D: Lew Landers. John Ashley, Gene Vincent, Jody Fair, Steve Drexel. Cheap little flick about hot-rod-happy youth with yearning to enter the big race, using his singing talents to get the cash.

Hot Rod Girl (1956) 75m. BOMB D: Leslie Martinson. Lori Nelson, Chuck Connors, John Smith, Frank Gorshin, Roxanne Arlen, Dabbs Greer. Tedious trash, with Nelson in title role as "hip" gal who helps crack down on city hot-car racing.

Hot Rod Rumble (1957) 79m. *½ D: Leslie Martinson. Brett Halsey, Richard Hartunian, Joey Forman, Leigh Snowden. Title tells all in this formula programmer of juvenile delinquents.

Hot Rods to Hell (1967) C-92m. **½ D: John Brahm. Dana Andrews, Jeanne Crain, Mimsy Farmer, Laurie Mock. Sluggish yarn of Andrews and family tormented by hot-rod-happy juvenile delinquents. Original title: 52 MILES TO MIDNIGHT.

Hot Shots (1956) 61m. D: Jean Yarbrough. Huntz Hall, Stanley Clements, Joi Lansing, Phil Phillips. SEE: Bowery Boys series.

Hot Spell (1958) 86m. *** D: Daniel Mann. Shirley Booth, Anthony Quinn, Shirley MacLaine, Earl Holliman. Booth makes soaper worthwhile; she's middle-aged housewife trying to conceal misery at husband Quinn's philandering while seeking to solve her children's problems.

Hot Stuff (1979) C-87m. **½ D: Dom DeLuise. Dom DeLuise, Suzanne Pleshette, Jerry Reed, Luis Avalos, Ossie Davis. Four Miami cops set up a "Sting"-like operation to fence stolen goods. Unexceptional but pleasant trifle that surprises by treating its characters as real human beings instead of cartoon stereotypes.

Hot Summer Night (1957) 86m. **½ D: David Friedkin. Leslie Nielsen, Colleen Miller, Edward Andrews, Claude Akins, Paul Richards. Offbeat story about reporter seeking an interview with leader of robbery gang.

Hotel (1967) C-124m. ** D: Richard Quine. Rod Taylor, Catherine Spaak, Karl Malden, Melvyn Douglas, Richard Conte, Michael Rennie, Merle Oberon, Kevin McCarthy. Adaptation of still another Arthur Hailey multicharactered novel is not all that inferior to AIRPORT, but that's faint praise; Douglas has some good scenes.

Hotel Berlin (1945) 98m. **½ D: Peter Godfrey. Helmut Dantine, Andrea King, Raymond Massey, Faye Emerson, Peter Lorre, Alan Hale. GRAND HOTEL author Baum tries again with sundry characters based in hotel during decline of Nazi Germany; good cast makes it generally interesting.

Hotel for Women (1939) 83m. ** D: Gregory Ratoff. Linda Darnell, Ann Sothern, Elsa Maxwell, Lynn Bari, Sidney Blackmer, Alan Dinehart. Weak film about group of manhunting girls, noteworthy only as Darnell's film debut. Originally titled ELSA MAXWELL'S HOTEL FOR WOMEN.

Hotel Imperial (1939) 67m. ** D: Robert Florey. Isa Miranda, Ray Milland, Reginald Owen, Gene Lockhart, Albert Dekker. Miranda encounters intrigue while searching for man responsible for her sister's death; fairly entertaining drama. Remake of 1927 silent film.

Hotel Paradiso (1966-British) C-96m. **½ D: Peter Glenville. Alec Guinness, Gina Lollobrigida, Peter Morley, Akim Tamiroff. Pretentious farce of manners is only fitfully amusing; meek Guinness tries to carry on his rendezvous with gorgeous neighbor Gina, but everything interferes.

Hotel Reserve (1944-British) 79m. *** D: Lance Comfort, Max Greene. James Mason, Lucie Mannheim, Herbert Lom, Patricia Medina, Anthony Shaw, David Ward. Suspenseful, moody film about visitor at French resort during WW2 accused of being Nazi spy, trying to prove innocence. Based on Eric Ambler novel.

Hotel Sahara (1951-British) 96m.

**½ D: Ken Annakin. Yvonne De Carlo, Peter Ustinov, David Tomlinson, Roland Culver. Pleasant fluff about North African hotel owner and beautiful fiancée who must shift "loyalties" every time new army marches into town during WW2.

Houdini (1953) C-106m. **½ D: George Marshall. Tony Curtis, Janet Leigh, Torin Thatcher, Ian Wolfe, Sig Ruman. Fanciful biography of famed escape artist; more fiction than fact, perhaps better this way.

Hound of the Baskervilles, The (1939) 80m. D: Sidney Lanfield. Basil Rathbone, Nigel Bruce, Richard Greene, Wendy Barrie, Lionel Atwill, John Carradine, Beryl Mercer, Mary Gordon, E. E. Clive, Ralph Forbes, Ivan Simpson. SEE: Sherlock Holmes series.

Hound of the Baskervilles, The (1959-British) C-84m. *** D: Terence Fisher. Peter Cushing, Christopher Lee, Andre Morell, Marla Landi, Miles Malleson, John LeMesurier. Cushing is well cast as Sherlock Holmes in this atmospheric Hammer Films adaptation of the Conan Doyle classic.

Hound of the Baskervilles, The (1972) C-73m. TVM D: Barry Crane. Stewart Granger, William Shatner, Bernard Fox, John Williams, Anthony Zerbe, Jane Merrow. Ludicrous remake of Conan Doyle spellbinder with casting least of its problems. Nuance, tension, situation all made lurid by script, pacing, production values. For masochists only. Below average.

Hour Before the Dawn, The (1944) 75m. ** D: Frank Tuttle. Franchot Tone, Veronica Lake, John Sutton, Binnie Barnes, Henry Stephenson, Mary Gordon, Nils Asther. Polished, empty WW2 romance-espionage, with Tone falling for Nazi spy Lake; unlikely casting doesn't help.

Hour of Decision (1955-British) 74m. ** D: Pennington Richards. Jeff Morrow, Hazel Court, Anthony Dawson, Lionel Jeffries, Carl Bernard, Robert Sansom. Morrow is newspaperman who tracks down murderer of fellow columnist, discovering his wife was involved with the man.

Hour of Glory SEE: **Small Back Room, The**

Hour of the Gun (1967) C-100m. ** D: John Sturges. James Garner, Jason Robards, Robert Ryan, Albert

Salmi, Charles Aidman, Steve Ihnat, Jon Voight. Western about Ike Clanton and the Earp Brothers after O.K. Corral shoot-up begins well, becomes increasingly tedious. Robards has a good time as Doc Holliday.

Hour of the Wolf (1968-Swedish) 88m. *** D: Ingmar Bergman. Liv Ullmann, Max von Sydow, Erland Josephson, Gertrud Fridh, Gudrun Brost. Lesser Bergman about painter Von Sydow, wife Ullmann, and apparitions he sees when they retreat to deserted island. The acting, as usual, is first-rate.

Hour of 13, The (1952) 79m. **½ D: Harold French. Peter Lawford, Dawn Addams, Roland Culver, Colin Gordon. Mystery yarn set in 1890s London, with Lawford a ritzy thief who develops a heart of gold in order to do a good deed for society. Remake of 1934 film THE MYSTERY OF MR. X.

Hours of Love, The (1965-Italian) 89m. **½ D: Luciano Salce. Ugo Tognazzi, Emmanuele Riva, Barbara Steele, Umberto D'Orsi, Mara Berni. Pleasant little sex farce proving the adage that illicit love is sweeter than blessed marriage.

House Across the Bay, The (1940) 86m. **½ D: Archie Mayo. George Raft, Joan Bennett, Lloyd Nolan, Gladys George, Walter Pidgeon, June Knight. Raft's out to get Pidgeon, who has taken wife Bennett from him while he's been in jail. Familiar but exciting film.

House Across the Street, The (1949) 69m. ** D: Richard Bare. Wayne Morris, Janis Paige, James Mitchell, Alan Hale, Bruce Bennett. Pleasant little comedy of newspaperman who hunts down murderer. Paige is peppery as always.

House by the Lake, The (1977-Canadian) C-89m. *½ D: William Fruet. Brenda Vaccaro, Don Stroud, Chuck Shamata, Richard Ayres, Kyle Edwards. Violent thriller of four morons led by Stroud who invade weekend retreat of lovers Vaccaro and Shamata. Stroud and Vaccaro are good. Originally titled DEATH WEEKEND.

House by the River, The (1950) 88m. *** D: Fritz Lang. Louis Hayward, Jane Wyatt, Lee Bowman, Ann Shoemaker, Kathleen Freeman. Strange, moody tale of larcenous husband (Hayward) who spins web of evil that involves his wife (Wyatt) and brother (Bowman). Overwrought

at times—particularly near the end—but full of fascinating touches, striking atmosphere.

House Calls (1978) C-98m. ***½ D: Howard Zieff. Walter Matthau, Glenda Jackson, Art Carney, Richard Benjamin, Candice Azzara, Dick O'Neill, Thayer David. Matthau plays recently widowed doctor who tries to woo feisty Jackson without sacrificing his independence, in this laughing-out-loud contemporary comedy. Carney hilarious as addlebrained head of surgery at Matthau's hospital. Later a TV series.

House of Bamboo (1955) C-102m. **½ D: Samuel Fuller. Robert Ryan, Robert Stack, Shirley Yamaguchi, Cameron Mitchell, Sessue Hayakawa. Picturesque if not credible story of army officers and Japanese police tracking down a gang of former soldiers working for a well-organized syndicate.

House of Cards (1969) C-105m. ** D: John Guillermin. George Peppard, Inger Stevens, Orson Welles, Keith Michell, Ralph Michael, Maxine Audley. Down-and-out boxer/adventurer (Peppard) hired by rich widow (Stevens) to tutor her young son becomes pawn of Fascist millionaires and generals intent on retaking Europe. Sound familiar? One good chase, though.

House of Crazies SEE: Asylum
House of Dark Shadows (1970) C-96m. **½ D: Dan Curtis. Jonathan Frid, Joan Bennett, Grayson Hall, Kathryn Leigh Scott, Roger Davis, Thayer David. Adapted from popular TV serial, vampire comes to ancient estate, launching series of mysterious attacks. Comic-book level script enhanced by florid performances, and several good scares. Followed by sequel NIGHT OF DARK SHADOWS.

House of Dracula (1945) 67m. ** D: Erle C. Kenton. Lon Chaney, John Carradine, Martha O'Driscoll, Lionel Atwill, Jane Adams, Onslow Stevens. Scientist Stevens treats Dracula, Wolfman, and Frankenstein; eventually turns into vampire. Good cast but script fluctuates.

House of Exorcism, The SEE: Lisa and the Devil
House of Fear (1939) 67m. **½ D: Joe May. William Gargan, Irene Hervey, Alan Dinehart, Walter Woolf King, Dorothy Arnold, El Brendel, Harvey Stephens, Robert Coote. Murderer stalks New York

theater; offbeat show business character in pretty good whodunit. Remake of 1928 film THE LAST WARNING.

House of Fear, The (1945) 69m. D: Roy William Neill. Basil Rathbone, Nigel Bruce, Dennis Hoey, Aubrey Mather, Paul Cavanagh, Holmes Herbert, Gavin Muir. SEE: **Sherlock Holmes** series.

House of Frankenstein (1945) 71m. **½ D: Erle C. Kenton. Boris Karloff, Lon Chaney, J. Carrol Naish, John Carradine, Anne Gwynne, Peter Coe, Lionel Atwill, George Zucco. Traveling freak show exhibitor sidelines as mad scientist seeking revenge from past enemies. Good cast makes script bearable.

House of Fright SEE: **Two Faces of Dr. Jekyll, The**

House of Horrors (1946) 65m. ** D: Jean Yarbrough. Bill Goodwin, Robert Lowery, Virginia Grey, Rondo Hatton, Martin Kosleck. Slightly below average horror meller. Frustrated artist uses fiend The Creeper to knock off critics. Laughable script, adequate acting.

House of Intrigue, The (1959-Italian) C-94m. **½ D: Duilio Coletti. Curt Jurgens, Dawn Addams, Folco Lulli, Dario Michaelis, Philippe Hersent. WW2 espionage caper with pleasing on-location European backgrounds.

House of Mystery (1961-British) 56m. **½ D: Vernon Sewell. Jane Hylton, Peter Dyneley, Nanette Newman, Maurice Kaufman, John Merivale. Nifty little story of haunted house, with its new owners learning the mysterious history of the premises; supernatural played up well.

House of Numbers (1957) 92m. **½ D: Russell Rouse. Jack Palance, Barbara Lang, Harold J. Stone, Edward Platt. Palance plays dual role as man seeking to spring gangster brother from prison and take his place.

House of 1,000 Dolls (1967-British-Spanish) C-83m. *½ D: Jeremy Summers. Vincent Price, Martha Hyer, George Nader, Anne Smyrner, Wolfgang Kieling, Sancho Garcia, Maria Rohm. Vacationing couple in Tangiers befriended by young man convinced that his fiancée has been abducted into white slavery ring. Incredible dialogue, with Price walking through film in a daze.

House of Ricordi (1956-Italian)

C-117m. ** D: Carmine Gallone. Paolo Stoppa, Roland Alexandre, Marta Toren, Roldano Lupi. Passable biography of well-known music-publishing house, set in the 18th century, with many musical interludes. Retitled: CASA RICORDI.

House of Rothschild (1934) 88m. *** D: Alfred L. Werker. George Arliss, Boris Karloff, Loretta Young, Robert Young, Florence Arliss, C. Aubrey Smith. Elaborate, entertaining chronicle of famed banking family, with Arliss as Nathan Rothschild at time of Napoleonic Wars, Loretta his daughter, R. Young her suitor, Karloff as civilized villain. Finale originally shot in color.

House of Seven Corpses, The (1973) C-90m. ** D: Paul Harrison. John Ireland, Faith Domergue, John Carradine, Carol Wells, Charles McCauley, Jerry Stricklen. A film crew uses a supposedly haunted house for location work on a horror film, and learns to regret it; low-budget, but not bad.

House of Seven Gables, The (1940) 89m. *** D: Joe May. George Sanders, Margaret Lindsay, Vincent Price, Nan Grey, Alan Napier. Good adaptation of Hawthorne's classic novel. Set in 17th-century New England, jealous brother sends sister's fiancée to prison. Fine performances.

House of Strangers (1949) 101m. ***\ D: Joseph L. Mankiewicz. Edward G. Robinson, Susan Hayward, Richard Conte, Luther Adler. Dynamic drama of ruthless financier Robinson who uses his four sons to suit his own schemes. Unique plot line has been utilized for many subsequent films in various disguises.

House of the Black Death (1965) 80m. *½ D: Harold Daniels. Lon Chaney Jr., John Carradine, Andrea King, Tom Drake, Dolores Faith, Sabrina. Warlock holds people captive in a creepy old house; terribly dragged out, grade-Z stuff.

House of the Seven Hawks, The (1959) 92m. **½ D: Richard Thorpe. Robert Taylor, Nicole Maurey, Linda Christian, Donald Wolfit, David Kossoff, Eric Pohlmann. Diverting account of skipper Taylor involved in shipboard murder and hunt for long-lost Nazi loot. Made in England.

House of Usher (1960) C-85m. ***½ D: Roger Corman. Vincent Price, Mark Damon, Myrna Fahey, Harry Ellerbe. First-rate horror film based on classic tale by Edgar Allan Poe.

When beautiful young girl's suitor arrives to ask her hand in marriage, the doors of the house of Usher fling open, and terror begins.

House of Wax (1953) C-88m. ***** D: Andre de Toth. Vincent Price, Frank Lovejoy, Phyllis Kirk, Carolyn Jones, Paul Cavanagh, Charles Buchinski (Bronson). Remake of MYSTERY OF THE WAX MUSEUM has Price as vengeful fiend who rebuilds his fire-destroyed showplace by using human victims as wax figures. Jones excellent as innocent girl. Originally filmed in 3-D with many sequences designed to show off that process.

House of Women (1962) 85m. ****½** D: Walter Doniger. Shirley Knight, Andrew Duggan, Constance Ford, Barbara Nichols, Margaret Hayes, Virginia Gregg. Trite rendition of conditions in a women's prison elevated by good cast and fast pacing. Remake of CAGED.

House on Garibaldi Street, The (1979) C-100m. TVM D: Peter Collinson. Topol, Martin Balsam, Janet Suzman, Nick Mancuso, Leo McKern. Textbook spy thriller about the capture of Adolph Eichmann by Israeli agents in Argentina in 1960; good, but nearly drowns itself in polemics. Filmed in Spain with international cast. Average.

House on Greenapple Road, The (1970) C-113m. TVM D: Robert Day. Christopher George, Janet Leigh, Julie Harris, Tim O'Connor, Walter Pidgeon, Barry Sullivan. Entertaining police mystery set in suburban California town, supposedly illustrating average town police practices and state government politics. Mild-mannered husband (O'Connor) fears for life of promiscuous wife (Leigh). Too confused for own good by halfway mark. Average.

House on Haunted Hill (1958) 75m. ****** D: William Castle. Vincent Price, Carol Ohmart, Richard Long, Alan Marshal, Elisha Cook, Jr. Updating of the old dark house theme isn't bad; Price as the spooky proprietor and the others his wary guests. Cook has a great closing line.

House on Marsh Road, The SEE: Invisible Creature, The

House on 92nd St., The (1945) 88m. ******* D: Henry Hathaway. William Eythe, Lloyd Nolan, Signe Hasso, Gene Lockhart, Leo G. Carroll, Lydia St. Clair. Trend-setting documentary-style spy film of WW2 ac-

tivity in N.Y.C., with realism the true star.

House on Telegraph Hill (1951) 93m. ****½** D: Robert Wise. Richard Basehart, Valentina Cortese, William Lundigan, Fay Baker. Good cast in intriguing tale of WW2 refugee assuming dead woman's identity so that she can come to San Francisco where wealthy relatives reside.

House That Dripped Blood, The (1971-British) C-101m. ****½** D: Peter Duffell. John Bennett, John Bryans, Denholm Elliott, Joanna Dunham, Tom Adams, Peter Cushing, Christopher Lee, Nyree Dawn Porter, Ingrid Pitt. Entertaining four-part horror film with a bit too much tongue in cheek, revolving around suitably creepy-looking mansion purchased by new, hesitant owner. Best segments: first and last.

House That Screamed, The (1970-Spanish) C-94m. ***½** D: Narcisco Ibanez Serrador. Lilli Palmer, Christina Galbo, John Moulder Brown, Mary Maude, Candida Losada. Grisly horror at a home for troubled girls, where disciplinarian Palmer and her sex-starved son (Brown) make life difficult—to say the least—for the young ladies.

House That Would Not Die, The (1970) C-72m. TVM D: John Llewellyn Moxey. Barbara Stanwyck, Michael Anderson, Jr., Doreen Lang, Richard Egan, Katherine Winn, Mabel Albertson. Thriller built around Revolutionary Era haunted house. With longer running time, Henry Farrell-scripted story could've been great. One or two unusual situations, otherwise average.

Houseboat (1958) C-110m. *****½** D: Melville Shavelson. Cary Grant, Sophia Loren, Martha Hyer, Harry Guardino, Eduardo Ciannelli, Murray Hamilton. Loren becomes Grant's housekeeper and takes his three motherless kids in hand. Predictable romance ensues, in this delightful comedy. Guardino hilarious as houseboat handyman.

Housekeeper's Daughter, The (1939) 79m. ****** D: Hal Roach. Joan Bennett, Victor Mature, Adolphe Menjou, William Gargan. Pleasant murder mystery enhanced by chic Bennett, who helps crack a homicide case. Mature's film debut.

Housewife (1934) 69m. ****** D: Alfred E. Green. Bette Davis, George Brent, Ann Dvorak, John Halliday, Ruth Donnelly. Little punch in story of struggling copywriter Brent deserting wife Dvorak for old-flame Davis (playing unsubtle vamp).

Houston Story, The (1956) 79m. **½ D: William Castle. Gene Barry, Barbara Hale, Edward Arnold, Paul Richards, Jeanne Cooper. Barry portrays greedy oil worker who plans to take over crime syndicate involved in stealing oil.

Houston, We've Got a Problem (1974) C-78m. TVM D: Lawrence Doheny. Robert Culp, Clu Gulager, Sandra Dee, Gary Collins, Ed Nelson, Sheila Sullivan, Steve Franken. Fictionalized account of the flight of ill-fated Apollo 13 and the traumatic effect the spacecraft explosion has on the flight controllers. Nononsense performances mesh with real-life tragedy. Average.

How Awful About Allan (1970) C-72m. TVM D: Curtis Harrington. Anthony Perkins, Julie Harris, Joan Hackett, Kent Smith, Robert H. Harris. Guilt-ridden blind mental patient Perkins thinks release from hospital and closeness to sister Katherine (Harris) will cure him. Considering talent connected with script, direction, and cast, film is major disappointment. Below average.

How Do I Love Thee? (1970) C-110m. *½ D: Michael Gordon. Jackie Gleason, Maureen O'Hara, Shelley Winters, Rosemary Forsyth, Rick Lenz, Clinton Robinson. Pleasant cast can't do much for sloppily sentimental film about Gleason's inability to relate to his son, a philosophy professor. Plays like a TV show, and a bad one at that.

How Funny Can Sex Be? (1976-Italian) C-97m. **½ D: Dino Risi. Giancarlo Giannini, Laura Antonelli, Alberto Lionelli, Duilio Del Prete, Paola Barbone, Carla Mancini. Eight bawdy episodes on love, sex, and marriage. More misses than hits, but buoyed by Giannini's comic prowess and Antonelli's tantalizing beauty. Released here after Giannini's success in Wertmuller films.

How Green Was My Valley (1941) 118m. **** D: John Ford. Walter Pidgeon, Maureen O'Hara, Donald Crisp, Anna Lee, Roddy McDowall, John Loder, Sara Allgood, Barry Fitzgerald. Warm drama of Welsh coal miners, centering on Crisp's large, close-knit family. Beautifully filmed, lovingly directed, winner of many Academy Awards.

How I Spent My Summer Vacation (1967) C-100m. TVM D: William Hale. Robert Wagner, Lola Albright, Peter Lawford, Walter Pidgeon, Jill St. John. Odd suspenser follows disenchanted drifter Wagner as he becomes unaccountably interested in events leading up to death of millionaire Lawford. Good performances and locations suffer from muddy script. Below average.

How I Won the War (1967-British) C-109m. *** D: Richard Lester. Michael Crawford, John Lennon, Roy Kinnear, Jack MacGowran. Often hilarious study of one man's military career and strange way he has of reminiscing by distorting the truth.

How Sweet It Is (1968) C-99m. *½ D: Jerry Paris. James Garner, Debbie Reynolds, Maurice Ronet, Paul Lynde, Marcel Dalio, Terry-Thomas. Married couple with teen-age son goes to Europe to revitalize themselves, but Mom starts to dally with sexy Frenchman. Bland comedy looks like a TV show and is about as memorable.

How the West Was Won (1963) C-155m. ***½ D: John Ford, Henry Hathaway, George Marshall. George Peppard, Debbie Reynolds, Carroll Baker, James Stewart, Henry Fonda, John Wayne, Gregory Peck, All-Star Cast. Blockbuster epic about three generations of Western pioneers isn't same experience on TV it was on Cinerama screen, but good cast, first-rate photography and lovely Alfred Newman score still make it top entertainment. Peppard stands out with excellent portrayal.

How to Be Very, Very Popular (1955) C-89m. **½ D: Nunnally Johnson. Betty Grable, Robert Cummings, Charles Coburn, Sheree North, Fred Clark, Alice Pearce, Orson Bean. Grable and North on the lam hide in a college fraternity in this semi-remake of SHE LOVES ME NOT. Sheree does wild "Shake, Rattle and Roll" number, stealing Grable's spotlight.

How to Break Up a Happy Divorce (1976) C-78m. TVM D: Jerry Paris. Barbara Eden, Hal Linden, Peter Bonerz, Marcia Rodd, Harold Gould, Liberty Williams. Madcap comedy involving a pretty divorcee trying to win back her ex-husband by playing on his jealousy and dating a slick man-about-town. Sight-gag-happy farce loaded with quickie comic bits. Average.

How to Commit Marriage (1969) C-95m. ** D: Norman Panama. Bob Hope, Jackie Gleason, Jane Wyman, Maureen Arthur, Leslie Nielsen, Tina Louise, Irwin Corey. Above average for recent Hope movies, but still a far cry from great comedy. Hope and Wyman are about to divorce when their daughter announces plans to marry Gleason's son. "Mod" elements of script were already dated when film came out.

How to Frame a Figg (1971) C-103m. ** D: Alan Rafkin. Don Knotts, Joe Flynn, Elaine Joyce, Edward Andrews, Yvonne Craig. Simplistic chap (Knotts) finds trouble behind every doorway as he is made patsy for crooked politicians. Usual unsubtle Knotts comedy.

How to Make a Monster (1958) 74m. BOMB D: Herbert L. Strock. Robert Harris, Walter Reed, Gary Clarke, Paul Brinegar. Dismal chiller involving studio makeup artist who goes berserk and turns his creations into zombie-like killers. Color sequences.

How to Marry a Millionaire (1953) C-95m. *** D: Jean Negulesco. Marilyn Monroe, Betty Grable, Lauren Bacall, William Powell, Rory Calhoun, David Wayne, Fred Clark. Terrific ensemble work in dandy comedy of three man-hunting females pooling their resources to trap eligible bachelors. Remake of THE GREEKS HAD A WORD FOR THEM.

How to Murder a Rich Uncle (1957-British) 80m. ** D: Nigel Patrick. Charles Coburn, Nigel Patrick, Wendy Hiller, Anthony Newley, Michael Caine. Coburn is wry as American returning home to England only to find his relatives want to kill him for his money.

How to Murder Your Wife (1965) C-118m. *** D: Richard Quine. Jack Lemmon, Virna Lisi, Terry-Thomas, Eddie Mayehoff, Claire Trevor, Sidney Blackmer, Max Showalter, Jack Albertson, Mary Wickes. Engaging comedy that almost holds up to finale. Cartoonist Lemmon marries Lisi while drunk and spends rest of picture devising ways to get rid of her. Mayehoff is standout as Lemmon's lawyer friend.

How to Pick Up Girls! (1978) C-100m. TVM D: Bill Persky. Desi Arnaz, Jr., Bess Armstrong, Fred McCarren, Polly Bergen, Richard Dawson, Alan King, Abe Vigoda, Deborah Raffin. Naive small towner (McCarren) comes to the Big Apple and stumbles onto the secret of successful girl-chasing to the dismay of his sophisticated buddy (Arnaz) from back home, now a full-time swinger. Amiable sitcom treatment of Eric Weber's funny book. Average.

How to Save a Marriage (And Ruin Your Life) (1968) C-108m. *½ D: Fielder Cook. Dean Martin, Stella Stevens, Eli Wallach, Anne Jackson, Betty Field, Jack Albertson. Typical 1960s sex farce has swinging bachelor Dino mistaking Stella for his best friend's mistress, with predictable complications. Stevens is wasted once again.

How to Steal a Million (1966) C-127m. *** D: William Wyler. Audrey Hepburn, Peter O'Toole, Charles Boyer, Eli Wallach, Hugh Griffith. Hepburn and O'Toole are a delightful match in this sophisticated comedy about a million-dollar theft in a Paris art museum. Boyer, O'Toole's boss, and Griffith, Hepburn's father, are equally good.

How to Steal an Airplane (1971) C-100m. TVM D: Leslie Martinson. Peter Duel, Clinton Greyn, Sal Mineo, Katherine Crawford, Claudine Longet. Deceptive title hides good combination of action and laughs as American and Welshman plan to get back at playboy son of Latin dictator. Offbeat casting, script. Above average.

How to Stuff a Wild Bikini (1965) C-90m. ** D: William Asher. Annette Funicello, Dwayne Hickman, Brian Donlevy, Harvey Lembeck, Beverly Adams, Jody McCrea, John Ashley, Buster Keaton, Mickey Rooney. Beach party romp time. Training manual one can do without, although Keaton and Rooney appear.

How to Succeed in Business Without Really Trying (1967) C-119m. ***½ D: David Swift. Robert Morse, Michele Lee, Rudy Vallee, Anthony Teague, Maureen Arthur, Sammy Smith. Delightful, original musical from Broadway hit about ambitious window-washer (Morse) who uses wiles, and a handbook, to rise to prominence in Vallee's Worldwide Wicket Co. Superb farce, good Frank Loesser songs, imaginative staging of musical numbers. Screen debuts for Lee and Arthur.

Howards of Virginia, The (1940) 122m. **½ D: Frank Lloyd. Cary Grant, Martha Scott, Cedric Hardwicke, Alan Marshal, Richard Carlson, Paul Kelly, Irving Bacon. Historical account of Revolutionary War is OK, but too long for such standard retelling.

Howling in the Woods, A (1971) C-100m. TVM D: Daniel Petrie. Barbara Eden, John Rubinstein, Vera Miles, Larry Hagman, Tyne Daly, Ford Rainey, Ruta Lee. Complicated double conspiracy only revelation in thriller involving disillusioned wife vacationing wth relatives at Lake Tahoe lodge, and husband not far behind. Average.

Huckleberry Finn (1974) C-118m. ** D: J. Lee Thompson. Jeff East, Paul Winfield, Harvey Korman, David Wayne, Arthur O'Connell, Gary Merrill. Little of Mark Twain is left in this handsome but empty-headed musical version of his classic story. Score by Richard and Robert Sherman is as forgettable as their script.

Huckleberry Finn (1975) C-78m. TVM D: Robert Totten. Ron Howard, Donny Most, Antonio Fargas, Jack Elam, Merle Haggard, Royal Dano, Rance Howard, Clint Howard. Folksy treatment of the classic by Twain (played by Dano), minus the social criticism and sinister aspects of the literary adventure favorite. Above average.

Hucksters, The (1947) 115m. *** D: Jack Conway. Clark Gable, Deborah Kerr, Sydney Greenstreet, Adolphe Menjou, Ava Gardner, Keenan Wynn, Edward Arnold. Glossy dig at advertising and radio industries, with Gable battling for integrity among yes-men. Greenstreet memorable as despotic head of soap company; Kerr's first American movie.

Hud (1963) 112m. **** D: Martin Ritt. Paul Newman, Patricia Neal, Melvyn Douglas, Brandon de Wilde, John Ashley. Excellent story of moral degradation set in modern West, with impeccable performances by all. Miss Neal won Best Actress Oscar as family housekeeper who doesn't want to get involved with no-account Newman. Douglas received Best Supporting Oscar as Newman's ethical, uncompromising father.

Hudson's Bay (1940) 95m. **½ D: Irving Pichel. Paul Muni, Gene Tierney, Laird Cregar, John Sutton, Virginia Field, Vincent Price, Nigel Bruce. Muni's good, but life of founder of Hudson Bay fur-trading company lacks punch. Expansive production.

Hue and Cry (1950-British) 82m. *** D: Charles Crichton. Alastair Sim, Jack Warner, Frederick Piper, Jack Lambert, Joan Dowling. Outrageous romp with wry Sim having field-day involved with youngsters and rambunctious youths.

Hugo the Hippo (1976) C-90m. **½ D: William Feigenbaum. Voices of Burl Ives, Marie and Jimmy Osmond, Robert Morley, Paul Lynde. OK children's cartoon musical about a youngster's attempt to save a hippo from extinction in ancient Zanzibar.

Huk (1956) C-84m. *½ D: John Barnwell. George Montgomery, Mona Freeman, John Baer, James Bell. Philippine-made hokum about Montgomery returning to the Islands to revenge his dad's murder.

Human Comedy, The (1943) 118m. ***½ D: Clarence Brown. Mickey Rooney, Frank Morgan, James Craig, Marsha Hunt, Fay Bainter, Ray Collins. Filmization of Saroyan novel is long but generally excellent tale of Rooney supporting family during WW2; memorable Americana.

Human Desire (1954) 90m. *** D: Fritz Lang. Glenn Ford, Gloria Grahame, Broderick Crawford, Edgar Buchanan, Kathleen Case. Sultry Grahame as Crawford's man-hungry wife hopes to get Ford to do away with her undesirable spouse; a minor classic.

Human Duplicators, The (1965) C-82m. ** D: Hugo Grimaldi. George Nader, Barbara Nichols, George Macready, Dolores Faith, Hugh Beaumont, Richard Arlen. Quickie production mars gimmick of outer-space aliens coming to earth to establish human-like agents.

Human Factor, The (1975-Anglo-Italian) C-96m. *½ D: Edward Dmytryk. George Kennedy, John Mills, Raf Vallone, Rita Tushingham, Barry Sullivan, Arthur Franz. Amoral murder rampage when Kennedy tracks down Berkeley-graduate killers of his family through computer and bloodily dispatches same. Every one dehumanized.

Human Factor, The (1979) C-115m. ** D: Otto Preminger. Nicol Williamson, Iman, Derek Jacobi, Richard Attenborough, Robert Morley, Ann Todd, John Gielgud. Dry, un-

[353]

exciting filmization of Graham Greene's spy novel about a British double agent (Williamson) who's forced to defect to Russia. Top cast, script by Tom Stoppard, but results are mediocre.

Human Feelings (1978) C-100m. TVM D: Ernest Pintoff. Nancy Walker, Billy Crystal, Pamela Sue Martin, Squire Fridell, Jack Carter, Donna Pescow, Armand Assante. Inspired by OH, GOD!, this series pilot casts Walker as God and Crystal as an eager young angel who has six days to clean up Las Vegas. Good performers do their best with middling material. Average.

Human Jungle, The (1954) 82m. **½ D: Joseph M. Newman. Gary Merrill, Jan Sterling, Paula Raymond, Emile Meyer, Regis Toomey, Chuck Connors. Documentary-style account of a typical day at a busy police precinct house; nicely done.

Human Monster, The (1939-British) 73m. ** D: Walter Summers. Bela Lugosi, Hugh Williams, Greta Gynt, Edmon Ryan, Wilfred Walter. Absurd, sometimes engaging Edgar Wallace tale of evil Lugosi using blind men as pawns in elaborate murder scheme. Original title: DARK EYES OF LONDON.

Humoresque (1946) 125m. ***½ D: Jean Negulesco. Joan Crawford, John Garfield, Oscar Levant, J. Carrol Naish, Craig Stevens, Tom D'Andrea, Peggy Knudsen, Paul Cavanagh. Ambitious violinist Garfield gets involved with wealthy, unstable patroness Crawford. No cardboard soap opera this; superb performances, handsome production, hilarious support from Levant, and a knockout finale. Perhaps Crawford's finest hour.

Hunchback of Notre Dame, The (1923) 93m. *** D: Wallace Worsley. Lon Chaney, Patsy Ruth Miller, Ernest Torrence, Tully Marshall, Norman Kerry. Lavish filming of Hugo classic, capturing flair of medieval Paris and strange attraction of outcast Chaney for dancing girl (Miller). Silent classic holds up well, with Chaney's makeup still incredible.

Hunchback of Notre Dame, The (1939) 117m. *** D: William Dieterle. Charles Laughton, Maureen O'Hara, Cedric Hardwicke, Thomas Mitchell, Edmond O'Brien, Walter Hampden, George Zucco. Fine remake of Lon Chaney silent with

Laughton as hunchback bell-ringer in Paris of the Middle Ages.

Hunchback of Notre Dame, The (1957-French) C-104m. **½ D: Jean Delannoy. Gina Lollobrigida, Anthony Quinn, Jean Danet, Alain Cuny. Quinn makes a valiant try in lead role, but film misses scope and flavor of Victor Hugo novel.

Hungry Hill (1947-British) 92m. ** D: Brian Desmond Hurst. Margaret Lockwood, Dennis Price, Cecil Parker, Jean Simmons, Eileen Herlie, Siobhan McKenna. Based on Daphne DuMaurier's book focusing on 19th-century Irish family with their vices and virtues highlighted; capable cast.

Hunt the Man Down (1950) 68m. ** D: George Archainbaud. Gig Young, Lynne Roberts, Willard Parker, Gerald Mohr. Adequate courtroomer involving public defender whose key witness is presently in a mental institution.

Hunted SEE: Stranger In Between, The

Hunted, The (1948) 67m. **½ D: Jack Bernhard. Preston Foster, Belita, Pierre Watkin, Edna Holland. Trim minor film with Foster a cop out to reform girlfriend Belita; efficiently produced.

Hunted Lady, The (1977) C-100m. TVM D: Richard Lang. Donna Mills, Robert Reed, Lawrence Casey, Andrew Duggan, Will Sampson, Alan Feinstein. Undercover police woman flees for her life after being framed by mobsters. Predictable pilot movie melding elements from "The Fugitive" and "Police Woman." Average.

Hunter (1971) C-73m. TVM D: Leonard Horn. John Vernon, Steve Ihnat, Fritz Weaver, Edward Binns, Sabrina Scharf, Barbara Rhoades. Enemy brainwash scheme uncovered when government agent survives racetrack crackup. But for what purpose? Sloppy, mechanical pace ruins good premise. Average.

Hunters, The (1958) C-108m. **½ D: Dick Powell. Robert Mitchum, Robert Wagner, Richard Egan, Mai Britt. Story of Korean War pilots with their assorted personal and career problems.

Hunters Are for Killing (1970) C-100m. TVM D: Bernard Kowalski. Burt Reynolds, Melvyn Douglas, Suzanne Pleshette, Martin Balsam, Larry Storch, Peter Brown. Ex-con (Reynolds), after drifting around for

3 years, decides it's time to return to home town, tyrannical father who refused to come to his aid during murder trial, woman he loves, etc. Uneven film fluctuates from scene to scene. Not bad, in all. Above average.

Hunters of the Reef (1978) C-100m. TVM D: Alex Singer. Michael Parks, Mary Louise Weller, William Windom, Felton Perry, Steve Macht, Katy Kurtzman. Rival salvage crews vie for sunken treasure in shark infested waters. Pilot to a proposed TV series using concept and characters created by Peter (JAWS) Benchley. Predictable action adventure. Average.

Hunting Party, The (1971) C-108m. BOMB D: Don Medford. Oliver Reed, Candice Bergen, Gene Hackman, Simon Oakland, Ronald Howard, G. D. Spradlin. When this terrible Western about rape, adultery, and a bordello-equipped train is cut by censors because of its incredible violence, it will make even less sense than it did originally; film wastes good cast.

Hurricane (1974) C-78m. TVM D: Jerry Jameson. Larry Hagman, Martin Milner, Jessica Walter, Barry Sullivan, Will Geer, Frank Sutton, Michael Learned, Lonny Chapman. Vivid hurricane footage easily outshines a GRAND HOTEL-like collection of stereotyped characters trapped in disaster area. Below average.

Hurricane (1979) C-119m. BOMB D: Jan Troell. Jason Robards, Mia Farrow, Max Von Sydow, Trevor Howard, Dayton Ka'ne, Timothy Bottoms, James Keach. Look what just blew in: a $22 million remake of the 1937 picture that may well put you to sleep!

Hurricane, The (1937) 102m. ***½ D: John Ford. Jon Hall, Dorothy Lamour, Mary Astor, C. Aubrey Smith, Raymond Massey, Thomas Mitchell, John Carradine, Jerome Cowan. First-rate escapism on isle of Manikoora, where idyllic native life of Hall and Lamour is disrupted by vindictive governor Massey. Climactic hurricane effects have never been equaled. Disastrously remade in 1979.

Hurricane Island (1951) C-70m. *½ D: Lew Landers. Jon Hall, Marie Windsor, Marc Lawrence, Edgar Barrier. Low-budget nonsense involv-

ing the fountain of youth and female buccaneer.

Hurricane Smith (1952) C-90m. ** D: Jerry Hopper. Yvonne De Carlo, John Ireland, James Craig, Forrest Tucker. Romance and a search for gold are the substance of this tale involving a ship beached on a South Sea island.

Hurry Sundown (1967) C-142m. ** D: Otto Preminger. Michael Caine, Jane Fonda, John Phillip Law, Diahann Carroll, Faye Dunaway, Robert Hooks, Robert Reed, Burgess Meredith, George Kennedy. Often ludicrous, overripe melodrama with ruthless Southerner determined to buy up cousin's land, stopping at nothing to achieve goal. A curio for Fonda and Caine's offbeat casting. Some sexual innuendoes cut for TV.

Hurry Up, or I'll Be 30 (1973) C-88m. ** D: Joseph Jacoby. John Lefkowitz, Linda De Coff, Ronald Anton, Maureen Byrnes, Danny DeVito. Mild low-budget comedy about efforts of schnook (Lefkowitz) to get his life in order before he hits 30. Made in New York.

Husbands (1970) C-138m. **½ D: John Cassavetes. Ben Gazzara, Peter Falk, John Cassavetes, Jenny Runacre, Jenny Lee Wright, Noelle Kao. Cassavetes' follow-up to FACES is not nearly as good; story about trio of middle-aged buddies who take off for Europe when their best friend dies is far too overindulgent. Film has a few very good scenes.

Hush . . . Hush, Sweet Charlotte (1965) 133m. *** D: Robert Aldrich. Bette Davis, Olivia de Havilland, Joseph Cotten, Agnes Moorehead, Cecil Kellaway, Victor Buono, Mary Astor. Macabre story of a family with a skeleton in its closet, confusing at times but worth watching for its cast. Bette is Olivia's victimized cousin; Cotten is Olivia's boyfriend.

Hustle (1975) C-120m. BOMB D: Robert Aldrich. Burt Reynolds, Catherine Deneuve, Ben Johnson, Paul Winfield, Eileen Brennan, Eddie Albert, Ernest Borgnine, Jack Carter. Pretentious, foul-mouthed and foul-minded story about an L.A. cop and a high-class call-girl who dream of escaping from their gritty life but never quite make it. This one's the pits.

Hustler, The (1961) 135m. **** D: Robert Rossen. Paul Newman, Jackie Gleason, Piper Laurie, George C. Scott, Myron McCormick. Realistic study of pool hustler Newman, outstanding as disenchanted drifter. Memorable performances by Scott and Gleason (Minnesota Fats). Dingy N.Y.C. pool-hall atmosphere vividly realized.

Hustling (1975) C-100m. TVM D: Joseph Sargent. Lee Remick, Jill Clayburgh, Monte Markham, Alex Rocco, Dick O'Neill, Burt Young, Melanie Mayron. Searing drama about prostitution racket, well-acted by Remick as an investigative reporter (à la Gail Sheehy, who wrote the book on which this was based) and Clayburgh, giving a gritty portrait of a hooker. Played for the sensational. Above average.

Hypnotic Eye, The (1960) 79m. ** D: George Blair. Jacques Bergerac, Merry Anders, Marcia Henderson, Allison Hayes. Partially successful chiller of theatrical mesmerizer with penchant for having female victims disfigure themselves.

I Accuse! (1958-British) 99m. **½ D: Jose Ferrer. Jose Ferrer, Anton Walbrook, Viveca Lindfors, Leo Genn. Sincere but pretentious narrative of the trial of French officer Alfred Dreyfus; he is sent to Devil's Island, causing great repercussions.

I Aim at the Stars (1960) 107m. *** D: J. Lee Thompson. Curt Jurgens, Victoria Shaw, Herbert Lom, Gia Scala. Low-key fictional history of Nazi missile scientist Werner Von Braun and his problems adjusting to life in America.

I Am a Camera (1955-British) 98m. ***½ D: Henry Cornelius. Julie Harris, Laurence Harvey, Shelley Winters, Ron Randell, Patrick McGoohan, Peter Prowse. John Van Druten's play of prewar Berlin is recaptured, with Harris most vivid as fun-loving gal who'll accept anything from anyone. Made into Broadway musical and film CABARET.

I Am a Dancer (1973) C-93m. *** D: Pierre Jourdan, Bryan Forbes. Documentary on Rudolf Nureyev is handled a little better than many dance films and may interest a larger audience than usual; includes shots of rehearsals and lots of footage with Margot Fonteyn.

I Am a Fugitive from a Chain Gang (1932) 90m. **** D: Mervyn LeRoy. Paul Muni, Glenda Farrell, Helen Vinson, Preston Foster, Edward Ellis, Allen Jenkins. Still packs a wallop after all these years, with Muni as innocent man brutally victimized by criminal justice system. Haunting finale is justly famous. Shown on TV as I AM A FUGITIVE.

I Am a Thief (1935) 64m. ** D: Robert Florey. Mary Astor, Ricardo Cortez, Dudley Digges, Robert Barrat, Irving Pichel. Stilted adventure of jewel thieves and insurance fraud set on Orient Express. Good cast can't save indifferent script.

I Am the Law (1938) 83m. **½ D: Alexander Hall. Edward G. Robinson, Otto Kruger, Wendy Barrie, John Beal, Louis Jean Heydt, Fay Helm, Barbara O'Neil. No surprises in this story of D.A. Robinson fighting corrupt city government, but it's done so smoothly you forget you've seen it before. Don't miss E.G. dancing the Big Apple at the beginning.

I Became a Criminal (1948-British) 80m. **½ D: Alberto Cavalcanti. Trevor Howard, Sally Gray, Rene Ray, Griffith Jones, Mary Merrall, Vida Hope, Eve Ashley. Often entertaining study of black market syndicate and its operations; sturdy cast. Retitled: THEY MADE ME A CRIMINAL.

I Believe In You (1952-British) 93m. **½ D: Michael Relph, Basil Dearden. Cecil Parker, Celia Johnson, Harry Fowler, Godfrey Tearle, Laurence Harvey. Intelligent study of methods used by probation officers to reform their charges; tight editing.

I Bury the Living (1958) 76m. ** D: Albert Band. Richard Boone, Theodore Bikel, Peggy Maurer, Herbert Anderson. Lugubrious goings-on involving a cemetery caretaker who plots victims' deaths.

I Can Get It for You Wholesale (1951) 90m. *** D :Michael Gordon. Susan Hayward, Dan Dailey, Sam Jaffe, George Sanders. Jerome Weidman's flavorful novel about New York garment industry, with Hayward the fiery designer who'll cheat anybody to get ahead. Retitled: ONLY THE BEST.

I Confess (1953) 95m. **½ D: Alfred Hitchcock. Montgomery Clift, Anne Baxter, Karl Malden, Brian Aherne, Dolly Haas, O. E. Hasse. A priest (Clift) hears a murderer's confession and is himself accused of the crime. Lesser Hitchcock film, made in Canada, is nevertheless intriguing for its stark photography and unspoken symbolism.

I Could Go on Singing (1963-British) C-99m. **½ D: Ronald Neame. Judy Garland, Dirk Bogarde, Jack Klugman, Aline MacMahon, Gregory Phillips. Garland is famed singer returning to England to claim illegitimate son living with real father (Bogarde). Garland is exceptional in singing sequences revealing the true Judy. Sadly, this was her last film.

I Cover Big Town (1947) 63m. ** D: William C. Thomas. Philip Reed, Hillary Brooke, Robert Lowery, Robert Shayne, Louis Jean Heydt. Uninspired mystery has female reporter solving complicated murder case. Uneven cast. Retitled: I COVER THE UNDERWORLD.

I Cover the Underworld (1955) 70m. *½ D: R. G. Springsteen. Sean McClory, Ray Middleton, Lee Van Cleef, Joanne Jordan. Republic programmer of clergyman whose twin brother is an about-to-be-released gangster.

I Cover the Underworld (1947) SEE: I Cover Big Town

I Cover the War (1937) 68m. ** D: Arthur Lubin. John Wayne, Gwen Gaze, Major Sam Harris, James Bush, Don Barclay. Second-rate pulp fiction about correspondent Wayne tangling with Arab rebel leader.

I Cover the Waterfront (1933) 70m. *** D: James Cruze. Claudette Colbert, Ernest Torrence, Ben Lyon, Wilfred Lucas, George Humbert. Hard-hitting account of dockside reporter falling in love with daughter (Colbert) of seafaring smuggler Torrence.

I Deal in Danger (1966) C-89m. **½ D: Walter Grauman. Robert Goulet, Christine Carere, Donald Harron, Werner Peters. Feature version of TV series BLUE LIGHT involves adventures of Goulet pretending to be Nazi convert in order to help Allies.

I Died a Thousand Times (1955) C-109m. ** D: Stuart Heisler. Jack Palance, Shelley Winters, Lori Nelson, Lee Marvin, Lon Chaney. Overblown remake of Bogart's HIGH SIERRA with Palance as mad killer with soft spot for crippled girl (Nelson). Winters is his moll in this gangster runthrough.

I Don't Care Girl, The (1953) C-78m. **½ D: Lloyd Bacon. Mitzi Gaynor, David Wayne, Oscar Levant, Warren Stevens. Premise of George Jessel preparing film biography of Eva Tanguay is vehicle to recreate facets in life of the vaudeville star.

I Dood It (1943) 102m. ** D: Vincente Minnelli. Red Skelton, Eleanor Powell, Richard Ainley, Patricia Dane, Lena Horne, Hazel Scott, Jimmy Dorsey and orchestra. Strained, overlong musicomedy about a tailor and his movie-star sweetheart; good songs include "Star Eyes" and "Taking a Chance on Love," but patchwork film lifts its big finale from Powell's earlier BORN TO DANCE!

I Dream of Jeannie (1952) C-90m. ** D: Allan Dwan. Ray Middleton, Bill Shirley, Muriel Lawrence, Lynn Bari, Louise Beavers, James Kirkwood. Fictional biog of Stephen Foster, 19th-century American composer, suffers from low-budget Republic production.

I Dream Too Much (1935) 95m. **½ D: John Cromwell. Lily Pons, Henry Fonda, Eric Blore, Lucille Ball, Osgood Perkins. One of Pons' typical operatic vehicles; she and Fonda are married couple with career problems.

I Drink Your Blood (1970) C-88m. ** D: David Durston. Bhaskar, Jadine Wong, Ronda Fultz, George Patterson. To get revenge on sadistic band of hippies, young boy gives them meat pies infected with rabies and they go homicidally crazy.

I Eat Your Skin (1964) 82m. BOMB D: Del Tenney. William Joyce, Heather Hewitt, Betty Hyatt Linton, Dan Stapleton, Walter Coy, Robert Stanton. Scientifically-created zombies menace two-fisted hero on Caribbean island. Worthless. First released in 1971.

I Escaped from Devil's Island (1973) C-89m. BOMB. D: William Witney. Jim Brown, Christopher George, Paul Richards, Rick Ely, Richard Rust, Jan Merlin. Produced by the Corman boys (Roger and Gene) in Mexico and the Caribbean, this actioner is an insult to vet director Witney's standing) with buffs who know his earlier work. Violent, vulgar.

I Escaped from the Gestapo (1943) 75m. ** D: Harold Young. Dean Jagger, John Carradine, Mary Brian, William Henry, Sidney Blackmer, Ian Keith. Low-budget WW2 thriller; title tells the story. Retitled: NO ES-CAPE.

I.F. Stone's Weekly (1973) 62m. ***½ D: Jerry Bruck, Jr. Loving, concise documentary of the maverick Washington journalist is often funny and always moving. Narrated by Tom Wicker.

I Found Stella Parish (1935) 84m. ** D: Mervyn LeRoy. Kay Francis, Ian Hunter, Paul Lukas, Sybil Jason, Jessie Ralph, Barton MacLane. Shady actress with a past (Francis) comes to U.S. with her daughter (Jason) hoping for a quiet future; mild soaper.

I Have Seven Daughters SEE: My Seven Little Sins

I, Jane Doe (1948) 85m. *½ D: John H. Auer. Ruth Hussey, John Carroll, Vera Ralston, Gene Lockhart, John Howard, John Litel. Ludicrous courtroom "drama" of murderess Ralston, with the victim's wife (Hussey) defending her.

I Know Where I'm Going (1947-British) 91m. **** D: Michael Powell, Emeric Pressburger. Wendy Hiller, Roger Livesey, Finlay Currie, Pamela Brown, Valentine Dyall, Petula Clark. Simple film of headstrong girl who plans to marry for money, stranded in Scottish seacoast town for a week, where she meets and slowly falls in love with Livesey. Very little plot, but an abundance of charm and wit. A quiet gem.

I Know Why the Caged Bird Sings (1979) C-100m. TVM D: Fielder Cook. Diahann Carroll, Ruby Dee, Paul Benjamin, Roger E. Mosley, Esther Rolle, Madge Sinclair, Constance Good. Black writer Maya Angelou's remembrances of her childhood in the Depression era South. Good is more than good as young Maya and Rolle is a tower of strength as the grandmother who raises her. Above average.

I Like Money (1962-British) C-97m. **½ D: Peter Sellers. Peter Sellers, Nadia Gray, Herbert Lom, Leo McKern, Martita Hunt, John Neville, Michael Gough, Billie Whitelaw. Subdued satirical remake of TOPAZE, with Sellers the timid schoolteacher who becomes an unscrupulous businessman.

I Live My Life (1935) 81m. ** D: W. S. Van Dyke II. Joan Crawford, Brian Aherne, Frank Morgan, Aline MacMahon, Eric Blore. Crawford and Aherne are in love, but she's

flighty and he's an archeologist. Glossy and empty.

I Love a Bandleader (1945) 70m. ** D: Del Lord. Phil Harris, Leslie Brooks, Walter Catlett, Eddie Anderson, Frank Sully, Pierre Watkin. Formula claptrap about meek Harris who becomes swinging bandleader; actors' natural abilities rise above material.

I Love a Mystery (1945) 70m. **½ D: Henry Levin. Jim Bannon, Nina Foch, George Macready, Barton Yarborough, Carole Mathews, Lester Matthews. Bizarre, entertaining whodunit based on popular radio show, with Bannon as Jack Packard, Yarborough as Doc Young. This one involves strange Oriental cult, and a prophecy of doom for bewildered Macready.

I Love a Mystery (1967) C-100m. TVM D: Leslie Stevens. Ida Lupino, David Hartman, Les Crane, Jack Weston, Terry-Thomas, Hagan Beggs, Don Knotts. Depressing attempt at adventure-comedy in spoof of old-time radio series features three detectives representing insurance company in search for missing billionaire; instead they find they've been lured to island. Waste of good cast. Below average.

I Love a Soldier (1944) 106m. ** D: Mark Sandrich. Paulette Goddard, Sonny Tufts, Beulah Bondi, Mary Treen, Barry Fitzgerald. Reteaming of Goddard and Tufts after their hit in SO PROUDLY WE HAIL doesn't match original; story examines problems of wartime marriages.

I Love Melvin (1953) C-76m. **½ D: Don Weis. Donald O'Connor, Debbie Reynolds, Una Merkel, Allyn Joslyn, Jim Backus. Pleasant musicomedy of magazine photographer O'Connor and would-be cinema star Reynolds. Guest appearance by Robert Taylor.

I Love My Wife (1970) C-95m. ** D: Mel Stuart. Elliott Gould, Brenda Vaccaro, Angel Tompkins, Dabney Coleman, Joan Tompkins. The kind of comedy for which the word "vehicle" was invented. Rarely funny chronicle of Gould's lifelong sexual hangups suffers from witless script, bland direction.

I Love Trouble (1948) 94m. *** D: S. Sylvan Simon. Franchot Tone, Janet Blair, Janis Carter, Adele Jergens, Glenda Farrell. Flippant mystery with private-eye Tone romancing

Blair while searching for her missing sister-in-law.

I Love You Again (1940) 99m. ★★★½ D: W. S. Van Dyke II. William Powell, Myrna Loy, Frank McHugh, Edmund Lowe, Donald Douglas, Nella Walker. Hilarious story of amnesiac Powell—solid citizen in a small town—reverting to former life as con-man, but trying to forestall divorce proceedings by "his" wife (Loy). Ingenious script by Charles Lederer, George Oppenheimer and Harry Kurnitz.

I Love You, Alice B. Toklas (1968) C-93m. ★★★½ D: Hy Averback. Peter Sellers, Jo Van Fleet, Leigh Taylor-Young, Joyce Van Patten. Excellent comedy about the freaking out of mild-mannered L.A. lawyer. Sellers never better. Written by Larry Tucker and Paul Mazursky.

I Love You, Goodbye (1974) C-78m. TVM D: Sam O'Steen. Hope Lange, Earl Holliman, Michael Murphy, Patricia Smith, Kerry Shuttleton, Brian Andrews. Frustrated suburban housewife decides to leave her family to make it on her own. Gentle feminist drama, well-acted by Lange. Average.

I Love, You Love (1961-Italian) C-84m. ★★½ D: Alessandro Blasetti. Marny Trio, Fattini and Cairoli, Don Yada's Japanese Dance Troupe, The Benitez Sisters. Documentary-style survey of love in various capitals of the worlds, occasionally spiced by imaginative use of footage.

I Loved a Woman (1933) 91m. BOMB D: Alfred E. Green. Edward G. Robinson, Kay Francis, Genevieve Tobin, J. Farrell MacDonald, Robert Barrat. Robinson plays meatpacking plant owner whose life is destroyed by enticing, ambitious opera singer Francis. Absurd story moves like molasses; dialogue is good only for (unintended) laughs.

I Married a Communist (1949) 73m. ★★½ D: Robert Stevenson. Laraine Day, Robert Ryan, John Agar, Thomas Gomez, Janis Carter. Gomez is murderous Communist who blackmails shipping executive Ryan over past activities in this wildly "patriotic" film. Interestng, if not credible. Retitled WOMAN ON PIER 13.

I Married a Monster from Outer Space (1958) 78m. ★★ D: Gene Fowler, Jr. Tom Tryon, Gloria Talbott, Ken Lynch, John Eldredge. Wife discovers what she thought was her husband is an alien monster with sinister plans; promised action never delivered.

I Married a Witch (1942) 76m. ★★★ D: René Clair. Fredric March, Veronica Lake, Robert Benchley, Susan Hayward, Cecil Kellaway, Elizabeth Patterson. Witch burned in Salem centuries ago (Lake) comes back to haunt descendants of Puritan (March) who sent her to her death. Special effects heighten amusing comedy-fantasy.

I Married a Woman (1958) 84m. ★★ D: Hal Kanter. George Gobel, Diana Dors, Adolphe Menjou, Jessie Royce Landis. Lackluster events concerning harassed ad man Gobel who'd rather spend time with his gorgeous wife than overtime at the office.

I Married an Angel (1942) 84m. ★★ D: W. S. Van Dyke II. Jeanette MacDonald, Nelson Eddy, Edward Everett Horton, Binnie Barnes, Reginald Owen, Douglass Dumbrille. Playboy Eddy dreams that he marries an angel (MacDonald) in this bizarre adaptation of Rodgers and Hart musical. This was MacDonald and Eddy's last film together. Songs include "Spring is Here," title tune.

I Met Him in Paris (1937) 86m. ★★½ D: Wesley Ruggles. Claudette Colbert, Melvyn Douglas, Robert Young, Lee Bowman, Mona Barrie, Fritz Feld. Prolonged romantic comedy dependent entirely on charm of its stars. Vacationing Colbert, in Paris, then Switzerland, has to choose from Bowman, Young, and Douglas (you guess who wins out).

I Met My Love Again (1938) 77m. ★★½ D: Arthur Ripley, Joshua Logan. Joan Bennett, Henry Fonda, Dame May Whitty, Alan Marshal, Louise Platt, Alan Baxter, Tim Holt. Familiar soaper of young girl Bennett running off with amorous author, with tragic consequences; acting surpasses script.

I, Mobster (1958) 80m. ★★½ D: Roger Corman. Steve Cochran, Lita Milan, Robert Strauss, Celia Lovsky. Rugged account of Cochran's life as gangster and events in his crime-filled life.

I, Monster (1972-British) C-74m. ★★ D: Stephen Weeks. Christopher Lee, Peter Cushing, Mike Raven, Richard Hurndall, George Merritt, Kenneth J. Warren. Good, atmospheric production and ensemble performances cannot completely redeem boring adaptation of Stevenson's DR. JEKYLL AND MR. HYDE. This time, early student of Freud develops serum to relieve human inhibitions.

I Never Promised You a Rose Garden (1977) C-96m. *** D: Anthony Page. Bibi Andersson, Kathleen Quinlan, Reni Santoni, Susan Tyrrell, Signe Hasso, Diane Varsi. Intelligent adaptation of Hannah Green's book about her treatment for schizophrenia as a teenager, focusing on relationship between her (Quinlan) and dedicated psychiatrist (Andersson). Graphic, clinical approach is often disturbing.

I Never Sang for My Father (1970) C-93m. ***½ D: Gilbert Cates. Melvyn Douglas, Gene Hackman, Dorothy Stickney, Estelle Parsons, Elizabeth Hubbard, Lovelady Powell. Sensitive adaptation of Robert Anderson play about grown man (Hackman) faced with problem of caring for elderly father (Douglas). Fine job all around, but extremely depressing.

I Passed for White (1960) 93m. ** D: Fred M. Wilcox. Sonya Wilde, James Franciscus, Pat Michon, Elizabeth Council, Griffin Crafts, Isabelle Cooley. Exploitation film handled with slight dignity involving light-skinned Negress and her rich white boyfriend.

I Remember Mama (1948) 134m. ***½ D: George Stevens. Irene Dunne, Barbara Bel Geddes, Oscar Homolka, Philip Dorn. Grade-A sentimental drama with Dunne as Mama raising her Norwegian family in San Francisco; not for the hardboiled, a delight for others. From John Van Druten's play. Supporting actress Ellen Corby was nominated for an Academy Award.

I Sailed to Tahiti with an All Girl Crew (1968) C-95m. *½ D: Richard L. Bare. Gardner McKay, Fred Clark, Diane McBain, Pat Buttram. One of the all-time camp classics, if only for its title. Unfortunately, film doesn't live down to its expectations.

I Saw What You Did (1965) 82m. *** D: William Castle. Joan Crawford, John Ireland, Leif Erickson, Pat Breslin, Andi Garrett. Taut chiller of two youths who accidentally become involved with a vicious murderer.

I Shot Jesse James (1949) 81m. ** D: Samuel Fuller. Preston Foster, Barbara Britton, John Ireland, Reed Hadley, J. Edward Bromberg. Flamboyant directional touches (in Fuller's first film) cannot redeem essential dullness of story about Bob Ford, the man who plugged Jesse in the back.

I Stand Condemned (1935-British) 75m. **½ D: Anthony Asquith. Harry Baur, Laurence Olivier, Penelope Dudley Ward, Robert Cochran, Morton Selten, Athene Seyler. Inconsequential story of jealous Russian framing young officer as a spy, to eliminate him from rivalry over woman. Worth seeing to watch young, dashing Olivier. British title: MOSCOW NIGHTS.

I Take This Woman (1940) 97m. ** D: W. S. Van Dyke II. Spencer Tracy, Hedy Lamarr, Verree Teasdale, Kent Taylor, Laraine Day, Mona Barrie, Jack Carson. Disappointing soaper with dedicated doctor Tracy sacrificing all for Lamarr, who at first isn't grateful. Not up to stars' talents.

I Thank a Fool (1962-British) C-100m. ** D: Robert Stevens. Susan Hayward, Peter Finch, Diane Cilento, Cyril Cusack, Kieron Moore, Athene Seyler. Dreary, far-fetched story about Hayward spending a year and a half in prison for mercy-killing, then becoming involved with lawyer Finch, who prosecuted her case, with bizarre results.

I, the Jury (1953) 87m. ** D: Harry Essex. Biff Elliot, Preston Foster, Peggie Castle, Elisha Cook Jr., John Qualen. Undistinguished Mickey Spillane caper with Mike Hammer seeking the one who killed his friend.

I Wake Up Screaming (1941) 82m. *** D: H. Bruce Humberstone. Betty Grable, Victor Mature, Carole Landis, Laird Cregar, William Gargan, Alan Mowbray. Entertaining whodunit with Grable and Mature implicated in Betty's sister's (Landis') murder, pursued by determined cop Cregar. Twist finish to good mystery. Remade as VICKI.

I Walk Alone (1947) 98m. ** D: Byron Haskin. Burt Lancaster, Lizabeth Scott, Kirk Douglas, Wendell Corey, Kristine Miller, George Rigaud, Marc Lawrence. A prison term changes Lancaster's outlook on life, and return to outside world makes him bitter. Good cast, weak film.

I Walk the Line (1970) C-95m. **½ D: John Frankenheimer. Gregory

Peck, Tuesday Weld, Estelle Parsons, Ralph Meeker, Lonny Chapman. Rural sheriff Peck falls for moonshiner's daughter Weld, thereby destroying both his professional and personal life. Offbeat but aimless drama, helped by excellent Weld performance. Johnny Cash sings five songs.

I Walked with a Zombie (1943) 69m. ***½ D: Jacques Tourneur. Frances Dee, Tom Conway, James Ellison, Edith Barrett, Christine Gordon, Theresa Harris, James Bell. Nurse Dee comes to Caribbean island to treat zombie-like wife of troubled Conway, finds skeletons in family closet, plus local voodoo rituals and legends that cannot be ignored. Exceptional Val Lewton shocker with rich atmosphere, mesmerizing story.

I Wanna Hold Your Hand (1978) C-104m. *** D: Robert Zemeckis. Nancy Allen, Bobby DiCicco, Marc McClure, Susan Kendall Newman, Theresa Saldana, Will Jordan. Teenagers connive to get tickets for the Beatles' first appearance on "The Ed Sullivan Show." If this original comedy seems occasionally silly and overbearing, that's the price it pays for being a generally accurate portrayal of a raucous event. Comedian Jordan is as hilariously Sullivan-like as ever.

I Want a Divorce (1940) 75m. **½ D: Ralph Murphy. Joan Blondell, Dick Powell, Gloria Dickson, Frank Fay, Dorothy Burgess, Jessie Ralph, Harry Davenport, Conrad Nagel. Powell and Blondell have just gotten married but already they're beginning to wonder.

I Want Her Dead SEE: W

I Want to Keep My Baby (1976) C-100m. TVM D: Jerry Thorpe. Mariel Hemingway, Susan Anspach, Jack Rader, Dori Brenner, Vince Bagetta. Pregnant teenager decides to have her child and raise it herself. Social drama written and acted with intelligence and vitality, despite a touch of sensationalism. Above average.

I Want to Live! (1958) 120m. ***½ D: Robert Wise. Susan Hayward, Simon Oakland, Virginia Vincent, Theodore Bikel. Hayward won an Oscar for her gutsy performance as prostitute-crook Barbara Graham who (according to the film) is framed for murder and goes to gas chamber. Smart presentation, fine

acting, memorable jazz score by Johnny Mandel.

I Want What I Want (1972-British) C-91m. **½ D: John Dexter. Anne Heywood, Harry Andrews, Jill Bennett, Nigel Flatley, Paul Rogers. Interesting little piece about sexual crisis in the life of man who wants to be a woman. Some sex-change material may be deleted for TV.

I Want You (1951) 102m. *** D: Mark Robson. Dana Andrews, Dorothy McGuire, Farley Granger, Peggy Dow. Perhaps-pretentious soaper, but emotional account of Korean War's effect on an American family.

I Wanted Wings (1941) 131m. ** D: Mitchell Leisen. Ray Milland, William Holden, Wayne Morris, Brian Donlevy, Constance Moore, Veronica Lake, Hedda Hopper. Stale plot of three men undergoing air force training served to introduce Lake as star material; that remains only real point of interest.

I Was a Communist for the FBI (1951) 83m. **½ D: Gordon Douglas. Frank Lovejoy, Dorothy Hart, Philip Carey, James Millican. Documentary-style counterspy caper, low key and effective.

I Was a Male War Bride (1949) 105m. *** D: Howard Hawks. Cary Grant, Ann Sheridan, Marion Marshall, Randy Stuart, William Neff, Ken Tobey. Delightful comedy of errors has French Army officer Grant trying to accompany WAC wife Sheridan back to U.S. with hilarious results. Grant in drag makes this one worth watching.

I Was a Shoplifter (1950) 82m. **½ D: Charles Lamont. Scott Brady, Mona Freeman, Charles Drake, Andrea King. Interesting study of crime syndicate blackmailing compulsive stealers into joining their gang, and police breakup of crooked dealings. One of Tony Curtis' early films.

I Was a Teen-age Frankenstein (1957) 72m. *½ D: Herbert L. Strock. Whit Bissell, Gary Conway, Phyllis Coates, Robert Burton. Programmer-type horror film aimed at the teen-age market. Pretty bad.

I Was a Teen-age Werewolf (1957) 70m. ** D: Gene Fowler, Jr. Michael Landon, Yvonne Lime, Whit Bissell, Vladimir Sokoloff, Guy Williams. Interesting mixture of juvenile delinquency and horror monster marred by low production values.

I Was an Adventuress (1940) 81m.

**½ D: Gregory Ratoff. Vera Zorina, Erich von Stroheim, Richard Greene, Peter Lorre, Sig Ruman. Jewel-thief Zorina goes straight, marries Greene, but can't shake off former associates Von Stroheim, Lorre, et al. With that cast, it should have been better.

I Was an American Spy (1951) 85m. ****½ D:** Lesley Selander. Ann Dvorak, Gene Evans, Douglas Kennedy, Richard Loo, Philip Ahn, Lisa Ferraday. Dvorak is chanteuse in Manila who helps combat Japanese attack in WW2 spy story, elevated by veteran star. Song: "Because of You."

I Was Monty's Double (1958-British) 100m. *****½ D:** John Guillermin. M. E. Clifton-James, John Mills, Cecil Parker, Marius Goring, Michael Hordern, Leslie Phillips, Bryan Forbes. Exciting, true WW2 story of actor persuaded to pose as Gen. Montgomery in order to divert German intelligence in North Africa. Cast is first-rate.

I Will, I Will . . . For Now (1976) C-96m. **** D:** Norman Panama. Elliott Gould, Diane Keaton, Paul Sorvino, Victoria Principal, Robert Alda, Warren Berlinger. Fair satire on frigidity, infidelity, marriage counselling and a sex clinic. Gould and ex-wife Keaton spend film rediscovering each other.

I Wonder Who's Killing Her Now? (1976) C-87m. ****½ D:** Steven H. Stern. Bob Dishy, Joanna Barnes, Bill Dana, Vito Scotti. Luckless husband (Dishy) hires someone to bump off his wife (Barnes) to collect insurance money, then tries to call it off; uneven but often funny farce, written by Woody Allen's frequent collaborator Mickey Rose.

I Wonder Who's Kissing Her Now (1947) C-104m. ****½ D:** Lloyd Bacon. June Haver, Mark Stevens, Martha Stewart, Reginald Gardiner, Lenore Aubert, William Frawley. Engrossing recreation of life and loves of 1890s songwriter, Joseph E. Howard. As usual, music is better than script.

I'd Climb the Highest Mountain (1951) C-88m. ***** D:** Henry King. Susan Hayward, William Lundigan, Rory Calhoun, Barbara Bates, Gene Lockhart. Touching story of 1900s family life in Georgia, reflecting Americana at its best.

I'd Rather Be Rich (1964) C-96m. ****½ D:** Jack Smight. Sandra Dee, Maurice Chevalier, Andy Williams, Robert Goulet, Gene Raymond, Charles Ruggles, Hermione Gingold. Airy remake of IT STARTED WITH EVE. Dee finds substitute fiancé to please dying grandfather who wants to see her happy. Only Chevalier-Gingold scenes have spice.

I'll Be Seeing You (1944) 85m. ****½ D:** William Dieterle. Ginger Rogers, Joseph Cotten, Shirley Temple, Spring Byington, Tom Tully. Overblown David Selznick schmaltz. Rogers, convict home on leave, meets disturbed soldier Cotten; they fall in love.

I'll Be Yours (1947) 93m. ****½ D:** William A. Seiter. Deanna Durbin, Tom Drake, Adolphe Menjou, William Bendix, Franklin Pangborn. Pleasant but undistinguished remake of THE GOOD FAIRY with Deanna in hot water after telling white lie to wealthy and amorous Menjou.

I'll Cry Tomorrow (1955) 117m. *****½ D:** Daniel Mann. Susan Hayward, Richard Conte, Jo Van Fleet, Ray Danton, Eddie Albert, Margo. Superlative portrayal by Hayward of star Lillian Roth, her assorted marriages and alcoholic problems. Everything a movie biography should be.

I'll Get By (1950) C-83m. ****½ D:** Richard Sale. June Haver, William Lundigan, Gloria DeHaven, Dennis Day, Thelma Ritter. Remake of TIN PAN ALLEY, involving songwriter and his gal; Jeanne Crain, Victor Mature, Dan Dailey make guest appearances.

I'll Get You (1953-British) 79m. **** D:** Seymour Friedman. George Raft, Sally Gray. OK gangster yarn of Raft (FBI man) and Gray (British Intelligence) cracking a kidnapping syndicate. Originally titled ESCAPE ROUTE.

I'll Give a Million (1938) 72m. **** D:** Walter Lang. Warner Baxter, Lynn Bari, Jean Hersholt, John Carradine, Peter Lorre. Amusing little idyll of rumor that an eccentric millionaire is posing as a hobo, causing droll results.

I'll Never Forget What's 'is Name (1967-British) C-99m. *****½ D:** Michael Winner. Orson Welles, Oliver Reed, Carol White, Harry Andrews, Marianne Faithfull, Peter Graves. Excellent comedy-drama in which one man rebels against his good life and tries vainly to go back to simpler days.

I'll Never Forget You (1951) C-90m.

**½ D: Roy Baker. Tyrone Power, Ann Blyth, Michael Rennie, Dennis Price, Beatrice Campbell. American (Power) working in London is transported back to 18th century, where he falls in love with Blyth. Remake of BERKELEY SQUARE (1933, with Leslie Howard). Opens in b&w, switches to color.

I'll Remember April (1945) 63m. *½ D: Harold Young. Gloria Jean, Kirby Grant, Samuel S. Hinds, Milburn Stone, Addison Richards, Mary Forbes. Jean lacks verve as goodie-goodie vocalist out to solve crime for which Dad was blamed.

I'll See You in My Dreams (1951) 110m. **½ D: Michael Curtiz. Doris Day, Danny Thomas, Frank Lovejoy, Patrice Wymore, James Gleason. Warner Bros. formula musical biography at its hokiest: trite telling of Gus Kahn's life and times; Day is bouncy.

I'll Take Romance (1937) 85m. **½ D: Edward H. Griffith. Grace Moore, Melvyn Douglas, Stuart Erwin, Helen Westley, Margaret Hamilton. Silly story of opera star Moore kidnapped by agent Douglas has lovely title tune, operatic arias to keep it moving along.

I'll Take Sweden (1965) C-96m. ** D: Frederick de Cordova. Bob Hope, Dina Merrill, Tuesday Weld, Frankie Avalon, Jeremy Slate. Pseudo-sexy Hope vehicle, with everyone frantic over life and love; witless proceedings, lacking usual Hope humor.

I'll Tell the World (1945) 61m. ** D: Leslie Goodwins. Lee Tracy, Brenda Joyce, Raymond Walburn, June Preisser, Thomas Gomez, Howard Freeman, Lorin Raker. Minor comedy with idea-man Tracy saving Walburn's failing radio station.

I'm All Right, Jack (1960-British) 104m. ***½ D: John and Roy Boulting. Ian Carmichael, Peter Sellers, Terry-Thomas, Richard Attenborough, Dennis Price, Margaret Rutherford. Carmichael works for his uncle and unwittingly upsets an elaborate and crooked business scheme in this memorable comedy. Sellers wonderful as labor leader.

I'm No Angel (1933) 87m. ***½ D: Wesley Ruggles. Mae West, Cary Grant, Edward Arnold, Gertrude Michael, Kent Taylor. West in rare form as star of Arnold's sideshow who chases after playboy Grant; highlight is Mae's courtroom plea.

I've Always Loved You (1946) C-117m. *** D: Frank Borzage. Philip Dorn, Catherine McLeod, William Carter, Maria Ouspenskaya, Felix Bressart. Lavish romancer with classical music background; Ouspenskaya stands out in cast.

I've Lived Before (1956) 82m. **½ D: Richard Bartlett. Jock Mahoney, Leigh Snowden, Ann Harding, John McIntire, Raymond Bailey. Strange small-budget film about pilot who thinks he is an aviator who died in WW1.

Ice Castles (1979) C-109m. *** D: Donald Wrye. Lynn-Holly Johnson, Robby Benson, Colleen Dewhurst, Tom Skerritt, Jennifer Warren, David Huffman. Successful ice skating career of Iowa farm girl is halted after she is blinded in freak accident. Tops for the disease/affliction genre, with well-photographed skating sequences and good performances by all.

Ice Cold in Alex SEE: Desert Attack

Ice Palace (1960) C-143m. **½ D: Vincent Sherman. Richard Burton, Robert Ryan, Carolyn Jones, Martha Hyer, Jim Backus, Ray Danton, Shirley Knight, Diane McBain. Filmization of Edna Ferber novel about development of Alaska's statehood, focusing on incredibly hokey lifelong battle between Burton and Ryan.

Ice Station Zebra (1968) C-148m. **½ D: John Sturges. Rock Hudson, Ernest Borgnine, Patrick McGoohan, Jim Brown, Tony Bill, Lloyd Nolan. Standard Cold War nail-biter with all-male cast has Hudson a sub commander sailing for North Pole to await orders, not knowing that Cold War incident will ensue; McGoohan a British agent out to trap a Russian spy. Big screen impact may lose on TV.

Iceland (1942) 79m. ** D: H. Bruce Humberstone. Sonja Henie, John Payne, Jack Oakie, Felix Bressart, Osa Massen, Joan Merrill. Labored love story defeats this Henie musical, although skating and singing interludes are pleasant; song standard, "There Will Never Be Another You."

Iceman Cometh, The (1973) C-239m. ***½ D: John Frankenheimer. Lee Marvin, Fredric March, Robert Ryan, Jeff Bridges, Martyn Green, Moses Gunn, Bradford Dillman, Evans Evans. Remarkably successful film of Eugene O'Neill's play about assorted barflies in a 1912 saloon; Marvin's Hickey is only adequate, but Ryan dominates an outstanding supporting cast. An American Film Theatre production.

Ideal Husband, An (1948-British) C-96m. **½ D: Alexander Korda. Paulette Goddard, Michael Wilding, Diana Wynyard, C. Aubrey Smith, Glynis Johns, Michael Medwin. Oscar Wilde's drawing room comedy receives classy presentation but is slow-moving.

Identity Unknown (1945) 71m. ** D: Walter Colmes. Richard Arlen, Cheryl Walker, Roger Pryor, Bobby Driscoll, Lola Lane, Ian Keith. Amnesiac soldier Arlen returning from WW2 tries to learn his identity in minor but fairly interesting drama.

Idiot, The (1960-Russian) C-122m. **½ D: Ivan Pyrlev. Julia Borisova, Yuri Yakovlev, N. Podgorny, L. Parkhomenko, R. Maximova, N. Pazhitnov. Faithful if not inspired adaptation of Dostoyevsky novel of tormented soul and his peculiar interactions with others.

Idiot's Delight (1939) 105m. ***½ D: Clarence Brown. Norma Shearer, Clark Gable, Edward Arnold, Charles Coburn, Joseph Schildkraut, Virginia Grey, Burgess Mededith. Gable's a song-and-dance man stranded at frontier hotel near Italian border. There he encounters Shearer, an old romance, in thoughtful adaptation of Robert Sherwood's pre-WW2 pacifist play.

Idol, The (1966) 107m. ** D: Daniel Petrie. Jennifer Jones, Michael Parks, John Leyton, Jennifer Hilary, Guy Doleman. Trash about worthless type who makes it with both mother and girl of his best friend; interesting only as chance to see latter-day Jones and watch Parks try to ape James Dean. Filmed in England.

If (1969-British) C-111m. **** D: Lindsay Anderson. Malcolm McDowall, David Wood, Richard Warwick, Robert Swann. Magnificent, surrealistic study of students at boarding school who plot revolution —or do they? Originally X-rated, later trimmed for wider acceptance.

If a Man Answers (1962) C-102m. **½ D: Henry Levin. Sandra Dee, Bobby Darin, Stefanie Powers, Cesar Romero, Micheline Presle, John Lund. Trite pap of Dee and Darin

trying to outdo each other with jealousy-baiting antics.

If Ever I See You Again (1978) C-105m. *½ D: Joe Brooks. Joe Brooks, Shelley Hack, Jimmy Breslin, Jerry Keller, George Plimpton, Danielle Brisebois. Producer-director-writer - composer - arranger - conductor Brooks' followup to his mediocre YOU LIGHT UP MY LIFE is even worse; this time he stars, as a songwriter trying to rekindle old flame with Hack (in her starring movie debut).

If He Hollers, Let Him Go (1968) C-106m. *½ D: Charles Martin. Raymond St. Jacques, Kevin McCarthy, Barbara McNair, Dana Wynter, Arthur O'Connell, John Russell, Ann Prentiss, Royal Dano. Prison escapee St. Jacques tries to clear himself of false rape-murder charge. Lots of clichés, and McNair's celebrated *Playboy* Magazine footage will never make it to TV.

If I Had a Million (1932) 88m. ***½ D: James Cruze, H. Bruce Humberstone, Stephen Roberts, William A. Seiter, Ernst Lubitsch, Norman Taurog. Gary Cooper, George Raft, Mary Boland, Charles Laughton, W. C. Fields, Wynne Gibson, Gene Raymond, Charlie Ruggles, Alison Skipworth, Jack Oakie, Frances Dee. Wealthy Richard Bennett gives that sum to various people to see their reactions; all of them interesting in star-studded episodes.

If I Had My Way (1940) 94m. **½ D: David Butler. Bing Crosby, Gloria Jean, Charles Winninger, El Brendel, Allyn Joslyn, Claire Dodd. Title tune is chief asset of pleasant but standard Crosby vehicle in which he helps little Gloria find her guardian, vaudevillian Winninger.

If I Were King (1938) 100m. *** D: Frank Lloyd. Ronald Colman, Frances Dee, Basil Rathbone, Ellen Drew, C. V. France, Henry Wilcoxon, Heather Thatcher, Sidney Toler. Preston Sturges script of roguish poet Francois Villon (Colman) in battle of wits with King Louis XI (Rathbone) plays with facts but makes good entertainment.

If I'm Lucky (1946) 79m. ** D: Lewis Seiler. Perry Como, Carmen Miranda, Phil Silvers, Vivian Blaine. Lukewarm musical with Harry James' band involved in political campaign; Miranda is good as always. Remake of THANKS A MILLION.

If It's Tuesday, This Must Be Belgium (1969) C-99m. *** D: Mel Stuart. Suzanne Pleshette, Ian McShane, Mildred Natwick, Murray Hamilton, Sandy Baron, Michael Constantine, Norman Fell, Peggy Cass. Funny study of Americans abroad on quickie tour; filmed throughout Europe. Host of cameos sprinkled throughout.

If Things Were Different (1980) C-100m. TVM D: Robert Lewis. Suzanne Pleshette, Tony Roberts, Don Murray, Arte Johnson, Chuck McCann, Dan Shor. Slick drama about a suburban housewife who's at wits end trying to hold her family together when hubby has a nervous breakdown. Suzanne's valiant but the lady as written is just too perfect. Average.

If This Be Sin (1950-British) 72m. ** D: Gregory Ratoff. Myrna Loy, Peggy Cummins, Richard Greene, Elizabeth Allan. Maudlin multi-love-affair story set on isle of Capri. Originally titled THAT DANGEROUS AGE.

If Tomorrow Comes (1971) C-73m. TVM D: George McCowan. Patty Duke, Frank Liu, James Whitmore, Anne Baxter, Pat Hingle. California, 1941: young girl falls in love with Japanese-American; due to prejudices and tense atmosphere, they keep marriage secret. Enter Pearl Harbor. Typically stereotyped, one-sided; film's point of view and overall feel designed not to offend anyone. Average.

If Winter Comes (1947) 97m. ** D: Victor Saville. Walter Pidgeon, Deborah Kerr, Angela Lansbury, Binnie Barnes, Janet Leigh, Dame May Whitty, Reginald Owen. Good cast fails to enliven wooden drama of young man who finds happiness by following code of honor; set in England.

If You Could Only Cook (1935) 70m. *** D: William A. Seiter. Herbert Marshall, Jean Arthur, Leo Carrillo, Lionel Stander, Alan Edwards. Arthur and Marshall are superb team in comedy of wealthy couple pretending to be mobster Carrillo's maid and butler.

If You Knew Susie (1948) 90m. **½ D: Gordon Douglas. Eddie Cantor, Joan Davis, Allyn Joslyn, Charles Dingle. Weak film of show biz couple is a delight for Cantor-Davis fans but pointless for others.

Ill Met By Moonlight SEE: Night Ambush

Illegal (1955) 88m. **½ D: Lewis Allen. Edward G. Robinson, Nina Foch, Hugh Marlowe, Jayne Mansfield, Albert Dekker, Ellen Corby, De Forest Kelley, Howard St. John. Former D.A. Robinson becomes criminal attorney with gangster client, but lays reputation—and life —on the line to defend former assistant Foch for homicide. Valiant attempt to recapture spark of earlier Robinson vehicles; remake of THE MOUTHPIECE.

Illegal Entry (1949) 84m. **½ D: Frederick de Cordova. Howard Duff, Marta Toren, George Brent, Gar Moore. Harsh narrative of federal agent assigned to uncover smuggling racket.

Illicit (1931) 81m. ** D: Archie Mayo. Barbara Stanwyck, James Rennie, Ricardo Cortez, Joan Blondell, Charles Butterworth. Stanwyck fears that marriage with Rennie will destroy their love, and is proven correct, in this silly film.

Illicit Interlude (1951-Swedish) 90m. **½ D: Ingmar Bergman. Maj-Britt Nilsson, Alf Kjellin, Birger Malmsten, Georg Funkquist. Moody film using flashback retells Britt-Nilsson's romance with now-dead lover, and its relationship to her present frame of mind. Original title: SUMMERPLAY; also known as SUMMER INTERLUDE.

Illustrated Man, The (1969) C-103m. *** D: Jack Smight. Rod Steiger, Claire Bloom, Robert Drivas, Don Dubbins, Jason Evers, Tom Weldon. Offbeat, fragment story of "chance" meeting of young wanderer (Drivas) and strange, tattooed man (Steiger) with flashbacks and flash-forwards, derived from Ray Bradbury stories. Moody, tough to digest, will suffer via interruptions.

Imitation General (1958) 88m. **½ D: George Marshall. Glenn Ford, Red Buttons, Taina Elg, Dean Jones. Travesty of what WW2 was all about has Ford taking place of killed superior officer, saving day and winning Elg.

Imitation of Life (1934) 106m. **½ D: John M. Stahl. Claudette Colbert, Warren William, Rochelle Hudson, Louise Beavers, Fredi Washington, Ned Sparks, Alan Hale, Henry Armetta. Believable but dated first version of Fannie Hurst's soaper of working-girl Colbert who makes good with Beavers' pancake recipe; Washington is fine as latter's daughter who passes for white. Ultra-sentimental.

Imitation of Life (1959) C-124m. ***½ D: Douglas Sirk. Lana Turner, John Gavin, Sandra Dee, Dan O'Herlihy, Susan Kohner, Robert Alda, Juanita Moore, Mahalia Jackson, Troy Donahue. Plush remake of Fannie Hurst story, with Turner as career-driven actress; Moore is the good-hearted black woman who shares her life, and whose troubled daughter (Kohner) passes for white. Fine performances and direction overcome possible soapiness to make this quite credible and moving.

Immortal, The (1969) C-75m. TVM D: Joseph Sargent. Christopher George, Jessica Walter, Barry Sullivan, Carol Lynley, Ralph Bellamy. Uneven mixture of sci-fi (from James Gunn novel) and drama. Racetrack driver discovers blood contains freak antibodies making him immune to aging process. Complications and subplots need far more running time. Average.

Immortal Battalion, The (1944-British) 91m. *** D: Carol Reed. David Niven, Raymond Huntley, Stanley Holloway, Leo Genn, Hugh Burden. Rugged WW2 actioner set during North African campaign. Retitled: THE WAY AHEAD.

Immortal Monster, The SEE: Caltiki, The Immortal Monster.

Immortal Sergeant, The (1943) 91m. **½ D: John M. Stahl. Henry Fonda, Maureen O'Hara, Thomas Mitchell, Allyn Joslyn, Reginald Gardiner, Melville Cooper. OK wartime drama of inexperienced corporal (Fonda) who is forced to take command of patrol in Africa after sergeant dies.

Immortal Story, The (1969) 63m. *** D: Orson Welles. Orson Welles, Jeanne Moreau, Roger Coggio, Norman Ashley. Interesting tale of merchant who contrives to make sailor's myth of seducing a wealthy man's wife come true. Generally well done and, at times, dazzling; originally made for French television.

Impact (1949) 111m. **½ D: Arthur Lubin. Brian Donlevy, Ella Raines, Helen Walker, Charles Coburn, Anna May Wong. Deftly told yarn of woman and boyfriend planning to murder her husband, with ironic results.

Impasse (1970) C-100m. *** D: Richard Benedict. Burt Reynolds, Anne Francis, Vic Diaz, Jeff Corey. Romantic mystery goes nowhere fast, but you may have fun guessing who will do what to whom.

Impatient Years, The (1944) 91m. **½ D: Irving Cummings. Jean Arthur, Lee Bowman, Charles Coburn, Edgar Buchanan, Harry Davenport, Grant Mitchell, Jane Darwell. Thin comedy of soldier Bowman returning to civilian life with wife Arthur, finding trouble readjusting.

Impatient Heart, The (1971) C-100m. TVM D: John Badham. Carrie Snodgress, Michael Brandon, Michael Constantine, Marian Hailey, Hector Elizondo. Young social worker seems to be able to solve everyone's personal problems except her own. Fair melodrama with strong lead performances. Above average.

Imperfect Lady, The (1947) 97m. ** D: Lewis Allen. Teresa Wright, Ray Milland, Cedric Hardwicke, Virginia Field, Anthony Quinn, Reginald Owen. Undistinguished drama of Parliament member falling in love with ballerina in London during 1890s.

Impersonator, The (1961-British) 64m. ** D: Alfred Shaughnessy. John Crawford, Jane Griffiths, Patricia Burke, John Salew, Yvonne Ball. Satisfactory chiller programmer of murder in a small village, with Crawford trying to clear himself; offbeat climax.

Importance of Being Earnest, The (1952-British) C-95m. *** D: Anthony Asquith. Michael Redgrave, Michael Dennison, Richard Wattis, Edith Evans, Margaret Rutherford, Joan Greenwood, Dorothy Tutin. Oscar Wilde's peerless comedy of manners set in Victorian England is given admirable treatment by most able cast.

Impossible Years, The (1968) C-92m. BOMB D: Michael Gordon. David Niven, Lola Albright, Chad Everett, Ozzie Nelson, Cristina Ferrare. Stupid, leering sex farce based on the hit Broadway play about psychiatrist who has problems of his own with nubile young daughter; the most obscene G-rated film of all.

Imposter, The (1944) 95m. **½ D: Julien Duvivier. Jean Gabin, Richard Whorf, Allyn Joslyn, Ellen Drew, Peter Van Eyck, Ralph Morgan. Well-acted but ordinary story of patriotic Frenchman who escapes prison, assumes new identity to join WW2 fight again. Retitled: STRANGE CONFESSION.

Imposter, The (1975) C-78m. TVM D: Edward M. Abroms. Paul Hecht, Nancy Kelly, Meredith Baxter, Jack Ging, Barbara Baxley, John Vernon, Edward Asner. Ex-Army intelligence officer Hecht accepts $5000 to impersonate a man targeted for assassination. Routine movie and projected series pilot. Average.

In a Lonely Place (1950) 91m. *** D: Nicholas Ray. Humphrey Bogart, Gloria Grahame, Frank Lovejoy, Robert Warwick, Jeff Donnell, Martha Stewart. Offbeat drama of screenwriter Bogart falling for Grahame, who helps clear him when he's accused of murder.

In Broad Daylight (1971) C-73m. TVM D: Robert Day. Richard Boone, Suzanne Pleshette, Stella Stevens, Fred Beir, John Marley, Whit Bissell. Recently blinded movie star (Boone) discovers wife's infidelity, plots double murder. Excellent cast in straightforward, no-nonsense suspense film. Above average.

In Caliente (1935) 84m. **½ D: Lloyd Bacon. Dolores Del Rio, Pat O'Brien, Leo Carrillo, Glenda Farrell, Wini Shaw, Judy Canova, Edward Everett Horton. Enjoyable nonsense, spiced by Busby Berkeley geometric dance numbers, including "The Lady in Red."

In Cold Blood (1967) 134m. **** D: Richard Brooks. Robert Blake, Scott Wilson, John Forsythe, Paul Stewart, Gerald S. O'Loughlin, Jeff Corey. Excellent semidocumentary adaptation of Truman Capote's book, tracing stories of two young killers (Blake, Wilson), their motives and eventual arrest after slaughtering innocent family. Incisive, engrossing, unsensational; masterful script, direction by Brooks; fine black-and-white photography by Conrad Hall.

In Enemy Country (1968) C-107m. ** D: Harry Keller. Tony Franciosa, Anjanette Comer, Guy Stockwell, Paul Hubschmid, Tom Bell, Emile Genest. So-so programmer of WW2 intrigue, set in France and England, filmed on Universal Pictures' backlot. Not very convincing.

In Fast Company (1946) 61m. D: Del Lord. Leo Gorcey, Huntz Hall, Jane Randolph, Judy Clark, Bobby Jordan. SEE: Bowery Boys series.

In Harm's Way (1965) 165m. **½ D: Otto Preminger. John Wayne, Kirk Douglas, Patricia Neal, Tom Tryon, Paula Prentiss, Henry Fonda, Dana Andrews, Brandon de Wilde. Overlong, overacted, and overly pretentious story of Navy man who goes out to capture strategic islands held by Japanese during WW2.

In Like Flint (1967) C-114m. **½ D: Gordon Douglas. James Coburn, Lee J. Cobb, Jean Hale, Andrew Duggan. Weak sequel to OUR MAN FLINT finds our hero going against secret society of women plotting to take over the world.

In Love and War (1958) C-111m. **½ D: Philip Dunne. Robert Wagner, Dana Wynter, Jeffrey Hunter, Hope Lange. WW2 film in 1940s style, tracing the effects of war on three soldiers; handsome cast uplifts soaper.

In Name Only (1939) 102m. *** D: John Cromwell. Carole Lombard, Cary Grant, Kay Francis, Charles Coburn, Helen Vinson, Peggy Ann Garner. High-grade soaper of married Grant in love with Lombard, trying desperately to obtain a divorce. Francis gives good performance as selfish socialite wife.

In Name Only (1969) C-75m. TVM D: E. W. Swackhamer. Michael Callan, Ann Prentiss, Paul Ford, Eve Arden, Elsa Lanchester, Ruth Buzzi, Chris Connelly. Several marriages set up by young Callan and Prentiss discovered illegal; couples must be found and remarried. Pleasant comedy, if not taken too seriously, thanks to good cast, dialogue. Above average.

In Old California (1942) 88m. ** D: William McGann. John Wayne, Binnie Barnes, Albert Dekker, Helen Parrish, Patsy Kelly, Edgar Kennedy, Dick Purcell, Harry Shannon. Wayne moves into Western town controlled by shifty Dekker, with inevitable confrontation.

In Old Chicago (1938) 115m. ***½ D: Henry King. Tyrone Power, Alice Faye, Don Ameche, Alice Brady, Andy Devine, Brian Donlevy, Phyllis Brooks, Tom Brown. Lavish periodpiece building up to Chicago fire of 1871; Oscar-winning Brady is Mrs. O'Leary, whose sons Power, Ameche, and Brown find their own adventures in the Windy City.

In Old Kentucky (1935) 86m. **½ D: George Marshall. Will Rogers, Dorothy Wilson, Bill "Bojangles"

Robinson, Russell Hardie, Louise Henry, Charles Sellon. Story is as old as the hills—a family feud—but Rogers' natural charm and Bojangles' fantastic footwork make it most enjoyable. Rogers' last film.

In Old Oklahoma SEE: **War of the Wildcats, The**

In Our Time (1944) 110m. **½ D: Vincent Sherman. Ida Lupino, Paul Henreid, Nazimova, Nancy Coleman, Mary Boland, Victor Francen, Michael Chekhov. Lupino and Henreid try to save Poland from Nazi takeover in plush soaper that seeks to be meaningful propaganda; Nazimova is touching as Henreid's aristocratic mother. Never quite hits the mark.

In Praise of Older Women (1978-Canadian) C-108m. BOMB D: George Kaczender. Tom Berenger, Karen Black, Susan Strasberg, Helen Shaver, Alexandra Stewart, Marilyn Lightstone. Hungarian stud recalls nearly two decades' worth of conquests, all of whom are paraded across the screen in various stages of undress. Strasberg and Stewart are particularly praiseworthy, but nothing else is in this tease of a movie.

In Search of America (1970) C-72m. TVM D: Paul Bogart. Carl Betz, Vera Miles, Ruth McDevitt, Jeff Bridges, Renne Jarrett, Howard Duff, Kim Hunter. Mike Olsen (Bridges) stuns family when he refuses to go to college, eventually convinces entire family to reexamine their goals. Game attempt at relevance can't cut it, despite efforts by large, distinguished cast. Average.

In Search of Gregory (1970-British) C-90m. ** D: Peter Wood. Julie Christie, Michael Sarrazin, John Hurt, Adolfo Celi, Paola Pitagora. Muddled film set in Geneva, about two potential lovers who fantasize about, but never meet, each other.

In Search of Noah's Ark (1976) C-95m. *½ D: James L. Conway. Narrated by Brad Crandall. Cheaply made documentary reveals "new evidence" that Noah's ark really existed. Premise may hold your attention.

In Search of the Castaways (1962) C-100m. **½ D: Robert Stevenson. Hayley Mills, Maurice Chevalier, George Sanders, Wilfrid Hyde-White, Michael Anderson Jr., Keith Hamshire. Expedition tries to locate missing sea captain, in journey that encounters fire, flood, earthquake and other disasters. Disney adaptation of Jules Verne suffers from muddled continuity; good cast does its best.

In Society (1944) 75m. ** D: Jean Yarbrough. Bud Abbott, Lou Costello, Marion Hutton, Arthur Treacher, Thomas Gomez, Thurston Hall, Kirby Grant. Minor A&C, with the boys as plumbers mistaken for members of society; hectic slapstick finale.

In Tandem (1974) C-78m. TVM D: Bernard Kowalski. Claude Akins, Frank Converse, Sondra Blake, Richard Angarola, Ann Coleman, Janis Hansen, Titos Vandis. Tough veteran and young college-educated partner, gypsy truckers, get involved in a labor dispute in citrus country. Rugged performances led to subsequent MOVIN' ON series; retitled MOVIN' ON. Average.

In the Cool of the Day (1963-British) C-89m. **½ D: Robert Stevens. Jane Fonda, Peter Finch, Angela Lansbury, Arthur Hill, Constance Cummings. Finch loves Fonda although he's married to Lansbury. Turgid soaper filmed largely in Greece.

In the French Style (1963) 105m. **½ D: Robert Parrish. Jean Seberg, Stanley Baker, Addison Powell, James Leo Herlihy, Philippe Forquet, Claudine Auger. Two short stories by Irwin Shaw are basis for this overlong account of American girl who discovers transient affairs are marring her life.

In the Glitter Palace (1977) C-100m. TVM D: Robert Butler. Chad Everett, Barbara Hershey, Anthony Zerbe, Howard Duff, David Wayne, Tisha Sterling. Sleazy murder melodrama in which lawyer/detective Everett is dragged into the case of a lesbian charged with killing her blackmailer. Below average.

In the Good Old Summertime (1949) C-102m. *** D: Robert Z. Leonard. Judy Garland, Van Johnson, S. Z. Sakall, Spring Byington, Buster Keaton. Musical remake of THE SHOP AROUND THE CORNER, with Garland and Johnson the pen pals who fall in love. Not up to most MGM Garland vehicles, but pleasant. That's young Liza Minnelli with Judy in the finale.

In the Heat of the Night (1967) C-109m. ***½ D: Norman Jewison. Sidney Poitier, Rod Steiger, Warren Oates, Lee Grant, Scott Wilson, Quentin Dean, James Patterson. Redneck police chief and visiting black cop join forces to solve Mississippi murder case in taut, atmospheric film that won Best Picture, Best Screenplay, Best Actor (Steiger) Academy Awards. Excellent supporting work from Grant and Oates. Poitier did two sequels as Virgil Tibbs, neither as good as this one.

In the Matter of Karen Ann Quinlan (1977) C-100m. TVM D: Hal Jordan, Brian Keith, Piper Laurie, David Huffman, Biff McGuire, David Spielberg, Stephanie Zimbalist, Louise Latham. Docu-drama exploring legal, moral and ethical aspects of the case of New Jersey woman whose parents (Keith and Laurie) argued her right to die with dignity and wanted life-saving machines turned off after she lapsed into a coma and suffered brain damage. Good performances, talky script, tiresome movie. Average.

In the Meantime, Darling (1944) 72m. ** D: Otto Preminger. Jeanne Crain, Eugene Pallette, Mary Nash, Cara Williams, Reed Hadley, Frank Latimore, Blake Edwards. Whimsical comedy of rich-girl Crain "roughing it" when she marries soldier Latimore.

In the Money (1958) 61m. D: William Beaudine. Huntz Hall, Stanley Clements, Patricia Donahue, Paul Cavanagh. SEE: Bowery Boys series.

In the Navy (1941) 85m. **½ D: Arthur Lubin. Bud Abbott, Lou Costello, Dick Powell, The Andrews Sisters, Claire Dodd, Dick Foran. Bud and Lou are somehow in the Navy; Lou has hallucinations and nearly wrecks the entire fleet by playing captain. Powell and Andrews Sisters provide songs.

In the Wake of a Stranger (1958-British) 69m. ** D: David Eady. Tony Wright, Shirley Eaton, Danny Green, Harry H. Corbett, Willoughby Goddard, Barbara Archer. Sailor implicated in murder tries to clear himself; just fair.

In This Our Life (1942) 97m. *** D: John Huston. Bette Davis, Olivia de Havilland, George Brent, Dennis Morgan, Charles Coburn, Frank Craven, Billie Burke. Fine drama of neurotic family with husband-stealing Davis ruining sister's (De Havilland's) life, and eventually her own; Davis at histrionic height. Based on Ellen Glasgow novel. Walter Huston has cameo role as bartender in one scene.

In Which We Serve (1942-British) 115m. **** D. Noel Coward, David Lean. Noel Coward, John Mills, Bernard Miles, Celia Johnson, Kay Walsh, Michael Wilding. Unlike many WW2 films, this masterpiece doesn't date one bit; superb film about men on a British fighting ship, told through flashback. Written, co-directed, and scored by co-star Coward.

Inadmissible Evidence (1968-British) 96m. **½ D: Anthony Page. Nicol Williamson, Eleanor Fazan, Jill Bennett, Peter Sallis, David Valia, Eileen Atkins. John Osborne's play about barrister who has reached saturation point with everyone and everything preserves Williamson's fine stage performance, but result is still photographed play, not a film.

Incendiary Blonde (1945) C-113m. *** D: George Marshall. Betty Hutton, Arturo de Cordova, Charlie Ruggles, Albert Dekker, Barry Fitzgerald, Mary Phillips, Bill Goodwin. Hollywoodized biography of 1920s nightclub queen Texas Guinan is Hutton all over. Plenty of old-time songs.

Incident, The (1967) 107m. *** D: Larry Peerce. Tony Musante, Martin Sheen, Beau Bridges, Jack Gilford, Thelma Ritter, Brock Peters, Ruby Dee, Ed McMahon. Tough, brutal story of two drunken hoods who terrorize subway car's passengers. Well-made but unpleasant.

Incident at Midnight (1963-British) 58m. ** D: Norman Harrison. Anton Diffring. William Sylvester, Tony Garnett, Martin Miller. Based on Edgar Wallace short story, film deals with drugstore hangout of dope addicts and gangsters who ply their trade there; trim yarn.

Incident at Phantom Hill (1966) C-88m. **½ D: Earl Bellamy. Robert Fuller, Dan Duryea, Jocelyn Lane, Claude Akins. Solid little Western about greedy trio chasing after horde of gold, combating Indians, the elements, and each other.

Incident in San Francisco (1970) C-98m. TVM D: Don Medford. Richard Kiley, Chris Connelly, Leslie Nielsen, Phyllis Thaxter, John Marley. Middle-aged businessman (Kiley) cannot prove innocence in assault-case-turned-murder, but young newspaperman (Connelly) attempts single-handed crusade. Well executed, but script unconvincing at wrong moments. Forget about ending. Above average.

Incident on a Dark Street (1972) C-73m. TVM D: Buzz Kulik. James Olson, Richard Castellano, William Shatner, David Canary, Robert Pine. Uneven but interesting crime-actioner detailing typical day-in-the-life of a big city D.A. office, centering on murder of man as he left nightclub. OK performances, fair resolution. Average.

Incredible Hulk, The (1977) C-100m. TVM D: Kenneth Johnson. Bill Bixby, Susan Sullivan, Jack Colvin, Lou Ferrigno, Susan Batson, Charles Siebert. Sci-Fi adventure drama in the Jekyll and Hyde mold, taken from Marvel Comics. Bixby plays the hapless scientist whose radiation experiments turn him into a homeless wanderer and powerful seven-foot monster (played by Ferrigno) when enraged. Good for some laughs, some thrills. Pilot for the series. Average.

Incredible Journey, The (1963) C-80m. *** D: Fletcher Markle. Emile Genest, John Drainie, Tommy Tweed, Sandra Scott. Entertaining, well-made Disney story of three pets—two dogs and a cat—who make 250 mile journey across Canada on their own to be with their family of humans.

Incredible Journey of Doctor Meg Laurel, The (1979) C-150m. TVM D: Guy Green. Lindsay Wagner, Jane Wyman, Dorothy McGuire, Gary Lockwood, Brock Peters, Andrew Duggan, James Woods. Lady doctor returns from the big city to bring modern medicine to her kinfolk in Appalachia of the '30s and runs afoul of the local medicine woman (Miss Jane Wyman, as she is billed). Average.

Incredible Melting Man, The (1978) C-86m. *½ D: William Sachs. Alex Rebar, Burr DeBenning, Myron Healey, Michael Aldredge, Ann Sweeney, Lisle Wilson. Rebar is only survivor of outer space mission which has turned his body into a melting muck. Cheap, old-fashioned B horror film whose only saving grace is Rick Baker's excellent makeup effects.

Incredible Mr. Limpet, The (1964) C-102m. ** D: Arthur Lubin. Don Knotts, Jack Weston, Elizabeth MacRae, Andrew Duggan. Cornball, preposterous vehicle for Knotts as timid soul who becomes dolphin (via animation) aiding U.S. navy during WW2 and finding true love with a fish. Strictly for fans, and for kids.

Incredible Petrified World, The (1958) 78m. BOMB D: Jerry Warren. John Carradine, Allen Windsor, Phyllis Coates, Lloyd Nelson, George Skaff. Four people explore the ocean in diving bell and are plunged into land of catacombed tunnels. Don't get trapped into watching it.

Incredible Rocky Mountain Race (1977) C-100m. TVM D: James L. Conway. Christopher Connelly, Forrest Tucker, Larry Storch, Whit Bissell, Bill Zuckert, Mike Mazurki, Jack Kruschen. Madcap western involving a cross-country grudge race between young Mark Twain (Connelly) and his longtime rival, Mike Fink (Tucker). Average.

Incredible Sarah, The (1976) C-106m. ** D: Richard Fleischer. Glenda Jackson, Daniel Massey, Yvonne Mitchell, Douglas Wilmer, David Langton, Simon Williams. Broadly sketched portrait of legendary French actress Sarah Bernhardt; Jackson chews the scenery in a flamboyant performance, but someone should have chewed up the script instead. Filmed in England.

Incredible Shrinking Man, The (1957) 81m. *** D: Jack Arnold. Grant Williams, Randy Stuart, April Kent, Paul Langton, William Schallert. Outstanding special effects highlight intelligent story. Williams' mysterious shrinkage forces him to view the world—and himself—in a different light than ever before. Existential script by Richard Matheson.

Incredible Two-Headed Transplant, The (1971) C-88m. *½ D: Anthony M. Lanza. Bruce Dern, Pat Priest, Casey Kasem, Albert Cole, John Bloom, Berry Kroeger. The head of an insane murderer is attached to the head of a mental retardate. Which head made this film?

Indestructible Man, The (1956) 70m. ** D: Jack Pollexfen. Lon Chaney, Jr., Marian Carr, Casey Adams, Ross Elliott, Stuart Randall. Man returns from the dead seeking revenge on robbery cohorts who betrayed him; OK science-fiction.

Indian Fighter, The (1955) C-88m. *** D: Andre de Toth. Kirk Douglas, Walter Matthau, Elsa Martinelli, Walter Abel, Lon Chaney. Exciting account of Douglas leading wagon train through rampaging Indian country.

Indian Love Call SEE: Rose Marie

Indian Scarf, The (1963-German) 85m. ** D: Alfred Vohrer. Heinz Drache, Gisela Uhlen, Corny Collins, Klaus Kinski. Edgar Wallace suspenser, with heirs to an estate being strangled one by one during sojourn at benefactor's country home.

Indian Uprising (1952) C-75m. ** D: Ray Nazarro. George Montgomery, Audrey Long, Carl Benton Reid, Robert Shayne. Geronimo on the warpath again.

Indict and Convict (1973) C-100m. TVM D: Boris Sagal. George Grizzard, Reni Santoni, Susan Howard, Ed Flanders, Eli Wallach, William Shatner, Harry Guardino. Drama traces investigation of deputy DA Shatner, accused of murdering his wife and her lover, although he was 150 miles away at the time. Good cast sparks courtroom action under Judge Myrna Loy. Above average.

Indiscreet (1958) C-100m. *** D: Stanley Donen. Cary Grant, Ingrid Bergman, Cecil Parker, Phyllis Calvert. Bergman is renowned actress whom American playboy Grant romances and can't forget. Delightful social comedy based on Norman Krasna play KIND SIR. Made in England.

Indiscretion of an American Wife (1954) 63m. **½ D: Vittorio De Sica. Jennifer Jones, Montgomery Clift, Gino Cervi, Richard Beymer. Turgid melodrama set in Rome's railway station, with Jones the adulterous wife meeting lover Clift for one more clinch.

Inferno (1953) C-83m. **½ D: Roy Baker. Robert Ryan, Rhonda Fleming, William Lundigan, Henry Hull, Carl Betz. Fleming plots rich husband's (Ryan's) demise, with surprising results. Good desert sequences.

Information Received (1962-British) 77m. ** D: Robert Lynn. Sabina Sesselman, William Sylvester, Hermione Baddeley, Edward Underdown. Potentially effective seesaw cat-and-mouse account of criminals Sesselman and Sylvester each trying to kill the other.

Informer, The (1935) 91m. **** D: John Ford. Victor McLaglen, Heather Angel, Preston Foster, Margot Grahame, Wallace Ford, Una O'Connor, Joseph Sawyer. Masterpiece study of human nature tells of harddrinking McLaglen, who informs on buddy to collect reward during Irish Rebellion. Powerful drama, memorable Max Steiner score.

Informers, The SEE: **Underworld Informers**

Infra-Man (1976-Japanese) C-92m. *½ D: Hua-Shan. Li Hsiu-Hsien,

Wang Hsieh, Terry Liu. A bionic superhero vs. a dragon lady and her monsters; awful dubbing and story, though some of the action is good. Good for laughs, at least.

Inglorious Bastards, The (1978-Italian) C-100m. ** D: Enzo G. Castellari. Ian Bannen, Bo Svenson, Fred Williamson, Peter Hooten, Michael Pergolani. Five soldiers about to be court martialled during WW2 take off through France, hoping to make the Swiss border. Farfetched story with a few good action scenes.

Inherit the Wind (1960) 127m. ***½ D: Stanley Kramer. Spencer Tracy, Fredric March, Gene Kelly, Florence Eldridge, Dick York, Donna Anderson. Jerome Lawrence and Robert E. Lee's play brought to movies with two pros in leads: March and Tracy as the prototypes of blustery William Jennings Bryan and Clarence Darrow, battling theory of evolution in famous Monkey Trial. Kelly not perfectly suited for his role, but York as the teacher, Elliott Reid as lawyer, and Harry Morgan as judge are all fine.

Inheritance, The (1947-British) 90m. *** D: Charles Frank. Jean Simmons, Derrick DeMarney, Derek Bond, Katina Paxinou. Well-appointed chiller, with Simmons as innocent preyed upon by corrupt uncle; situated in Victorian London and Paris. Retitled: UNCLE SILAS.

Initiation of Sarah, The (1978) C-100m. TVM D: Robert Day. Kay Lenz, Shelley Winters, Kathryn Crosby, Tony Bill, Elizabeth Stack, Morgan Brittany, Tisa Farrow. Occult tale surrounding a college sorority initiation; one of the coeds falls under the spell of witch Winters. Average.

In-Laws, The (1979) C-103m. *** D: Arthur Hiller. Peter Falk, Alan Arkin, Richard Libertini, Nancy Dussault, Penny Peyser, Arlene Golonka, Michael Lembeck. Wacky comedy about a dentist (Arkin) who becomes involved in the bizarre intrigues of his daughter's father-in-law-to-be (Falk), who claims to be a CIA agent. Commendably unpredictable from start to finish.

Inn of the Sixth Happiness, The (1958) C-158m. *** D: Mark Robson. Ingrid Bergman, Curt Jurgens, Robert Donat, Ronald Squire, Athene Seyler, Richard Wattis. True story of English missionary and how she leads children on dangerous journey through enemy territory in pre-WW2 China. Bergman is wonderful and Donat memorable in final screen performance. Simple and effective music score.

Inn on the River, The (1962-German) 95m. **½ D: Alfred Vohrer. Joachim Fuchsberger, Klaus Kinski, Brigitte Grothum, Richard Much. Remake of THE RETURN OF THE FROG (1939), this Edgar Wallace yarn involves series of brutal murders on the waterfront by the "Shark's" gang.

Inner Sanctum (1948) 62m. ** D: Lew Landers. Charles Russell, Mary Beth Hughes, Lee Patrick, Nana Bryant. Satisfactory low-budgeter based on famous radio show, with fortune-teller predicting tragedy for a young girl on a train.

Innocent, The (1979-Italian) C-115m. **** D: Luchino Visconti. Giancarlo Giannini, Laura Antonelli, Jennifer O'Neill. Director Visconti's final film is among his greatest, a lavishly mounted tragedy about a Sicilian aristocrat who has the tables turned on him by the luscious wife he has chosen to ignore. Antonelli's nude scenes may be cut.

Innocent Affair, An (1948) 90m. ** D: Lloyd Bacon. Fred MacMurray, Madeleine Carroll, Buddy Rogers, Rita Johnson, Alan Mowbray, Louise Allbritton, Anne Nagel. Outmoded marital sex comedy of love and jealousy, bolstered by pros MacMurray-Carroll. Retitled: DON'T TRUST YOUR HUSBAND.

Innocent and the Damned SEE: Girls Town

Innocent Bystanders (1973-British) C-111m. **½ D: Peter Collinson. Stanley Baker, Geraldine Chaplin, Donald Pleasence, Dana Andrews, Sue Lloyd, Derren Nesbitt. Baker plays James Bond-like character involved in international manhunt for Russian scientist who has escaped from Siberia. Well-made but standard fare, with heavy doses of sadism and violence.

Innocents, The (1961-British) 100m. ***½ D: Jack Clayton. Deborah Kerr, Michael Redgrave, Peter Wyngarde, Megs Jenkins, Pamela Franklin, Martin Stephens. First-rate thriller based on Henry James' "The Turn of the Screw," with Kerr as governess haunted by specters that may or may not be real. Script by William Archibald and Truman Capote, brilliantly realized on film.

Innocents in Paris (1955-British) 93m. *** D: Gordon Parry. Alastair Sim, Claude Dauphin, Claire Bloom, Laurence Harvey, Margaret Rutherford. Most engaging comedy about seven diverse types crossing the channel to France, each having wacky adventures.

Inserts (1976-British) C-117m. BOMB D: John Byrum. Richard Dreyfuss, Jessica Harper, Veronica Cartwright, Bob Hoskins, Stephen Davies. Pretentious, unending nonsense played out by five characters on one set: decaying Hollywood mansion in early thirties where once-famous director now makes "porno" films. Dreadful.

Inside Daisy Clover (1965) C-128m. **½ D: Robert Mulligan. Natalie Wood, Robert Redford, Christopher Plummer, Roddy McDowall, Ruth Gordon, Katherine Bard. Potentially biting account of Wood's rise as Hollywood star in 1930s misfires; pat situations with caricatures instead of people.

Inside Detroit (1955) 82m. ** D: Fred F. Sears. Dennis O'Keefe, Pat O'Brien, Margaret Field, Mark Damon. Ordinary exposé-style narrative of corruption in automobile industry.

Inside Job (1946) 65m. ** D: Jean Yarbrough. Preston Foster, Ann Rutherford, Alan Curtis, Jimmy Moss. Sensible minor film of struggling young marrieds tempted to enter life of crime to solve their financial problems.

Inside Out (1975-British) C-97m. **½ D: Peter Duffell. Telly Savalas, James Mason, Robert Culp, Aldo Ray, Charles Korvin. Savalas engineers break-in at maximum security prison in East Germany to free notorious war criminal who knows whereabouts of a secret cache of gold. Not bad international caper. Retitled HITLER'S GOLD and THE GOLDEN HEIST.

Inside Story, The (1948) 87m. ** D: Allan Dwan. Marsha Hunt, William Lundigan, Charles Winninger, Gail Patrick. Warm, minor film set in Depression days in Vermont, involving sudden circulation of large amount of money.

Inside Straight (1951) 89m. **½ D: Gerald Mayer. David Brian, Arlene Dahl, Barry Sullivan, Mercedes McCambridge. Study of greed and corruption as ambitious man rises to fortune in 1870s San Francisco only to find life empty.

Inside the Mafia (1959) 72m. **½ D: Edward L. Cahn. Cameron Mitchell, Elaine Edwards, Robert Strauss, Jim L. Brown, Ted de Corsia, Grant Richards. Gun-blasting account of the Black Hand organization, with cast having field-day.

Inside the Walls of Folsom Prison (1951) 87m. ** D: Crane Wilbur. Steve Cochran, David Brian, Philip Carey, Ted de Corsia. Moderately successful account of crusade to improve harsh penitentiary conditions.

Inspector Calls, An (1954-British) 80m. *** D: Guy Hamilton. Alastair Sim, Arthur Young, Olga Lindo, Eileen Moore. J. B. Priestley's play detailing British police detective's (Sim's) investigation of girl's murder. Via flashbacks he learns a family's responsibility for her fate. Clever plot finale.

Inspector Clouseau (1968) C-94m. ** D: Bud Yorkin. Alan Arkin, Delia Boccardo, Frank Finlay, Patrick Cargill, Beryl Reid, Barry Foster. Scotland Yard calls on inept French detective to crack potential robbery; in spite of Arkin's talents, Peter Sellers is too well identified with the role (THE PINK PANTHER, A SHOT IN THE DARK) for one to fully accept his characterization. Besides, film isn't particularly funny. Made in England.

Inspector General, The (1949) C-102m. *** D: Henry Koster. Danny Kaye, Walter Slezak, Barbara Bates, Elsa Lanchester, Gene Lockhart, Alan Hale, Walter Catlett. Kaye has nice vehicle as town buffoon who pretends to be visiting bureaucrat; set in 1800s Russia.

Inspector Maigret (1958-French) 110m. **½ D: Jean Delannoy. Jean Gabin, Annie Girardot, Oliver Hussenot, Jeanne Boitel. Famed French detective must track down notorious woman-killer. Retitled: WOMAN-BAIT.

Inspiration (1931) 74m. **½ D: Clarence Brown. Greta Garbo, Robert Montgomery, Lewis Stone, Marjorie Rambeau, Beryl Mercer, Oscar Apfel. Lesser Garbo about beautiful Parisian woman whose past makes her decide to leave Montgomery, even though she still loves him. Garbo has had much better material than this modern version of Alphonse Daudet's SAPPHO.

Institute for Revenge (1979) C-78m.

TVM D: Ken Annakin. Sam Groom, Lauren Hutton, Lane Binkley, Leslie Nielsen, Ray Walston, George Hamilton, Robert Coote. Tongue-in-cheek sci-fi about a sophisticated computer that assigns human operatives to correct wrongs against the defenseless and non-violently bring in the evildoers. Pilot to a prospective series. Average.

Intent to Kill (1958-British) 89m. **½ D: Jack Cardiff. Richard Todd, Betsy Drake, Herbert Lom, Warren Stevens. Potboiler about attempted assassination of Latin American dictator who has gone north for brain surgery.

Interiors (1978) C-99m. ***½ D: Woody Allen. Diane Keaton, Geraldine Page, E. G. Marshall, Maureen Stapleton, Kristin Griffith, Marybeth Hurt, Richard Jordan, Sam Waterston. Woody Allen's first screen drama as writer-director is an Ingmar Bergmanesque study of a family full of unhappy, frustrated men and women; this drama of anguished lives is not for all tastes, but extremely well done.

Interlude (1957) C-90m. **½ D: Douglas Sirk. June Allyson, Rossano Brazzi, Marianne Cook, Jane Wyatt, Francoise Rosay. Adequate tearjerker of Allyson falling in love with Continental composer Brazzi, whose wife refuses to accept the situation. Remade in 1968 under same title.

Interlude (1968-British) C-113m. *** D: Kevin Billington. Oskar Werner, Barbara Ferris, Virginia Maskell, Donald Sutherland, Nora Swinbourne, Alan Webb. Charming, sentimental tale of symphony conductor and reporter who have an affair; told in flashback.

Intermezzo (1939) 70m. ***½ D: Gregory Ratoff. Leslie Howard, Ingrid Bergman, Edna Best, Cecil Kellaway, John Halliday. One of the best love stories ever filmed, as married Howard, renowned violinist, has an affair with musical protegee Bergman (in her first English-speaking film). Short and sweet, highlighted by Robert Henning-Heinz Provost love theme.

International House (1933) 70m. ***½ D: A. Edward Sutherland. W. C. Fields, Peggy Hopkins Joyce, Stuart Erwin, George Burns, Gracie Allen, Bela Lugosi, Franklin Pangborn, Rudy Vallee, Sterling Holloway, Cab Calloway. Offbeat, delightful film with early television experiment bringing people from all over the world to large Oriental hotel. Spotlight alternates between Fields and Burns and Allen, all in rare form, with guest spots by various radio entertainers. Short and sweet, a must-see film.

International Lady (1941) 102m. **½ D: Tim Whelan. Ilona Massey, George Brent, Basil Rathbone, Gene Lockhart. Really fun flick: Massey a femme fatale spy, Brent the U.S. government agent involved in cracking espionage ring. Superficial but entertaining.

International Settlement (1938) 75m. ** D: Eugene Forde. George Sanders, Dolores Del Rio, June Lang, Dick Baldwin, Leon Ames, John Carradine, Harold Huber. Mediocre tale of Shanghai intrigue with Sanders masquerading as notorious smuggler, pursued by various crooks and sultry Del Rio.

International Squadron (1941) 87m. **½ D: Lothar Mendes. Ronald Reagan, James Stephenson, Julie Bishop, Cliff Edwards, Reginald Denny. Air force straightens out no-account Reagan and turns him into fighting ace. Standard war story.

International Velvet (1978-British) C-127m. *** D: Bryan Forbes. Tatum O'Neal, Christopher Plummer, Anthony Hopkins, Nanette Newman, Dinsdale Landen. Long overdue sequel to NATIONAL VELVET (1944) has Velvet (Newman) a grown woman with a live-in lover (Plummer) and a niece (O'Neal) primed to follow in her footsteps as an Olympic horsewoman. Too lengthy and shunned by the critics, but deftly played by Hopkins and Plummer; exquisitely filmed, entertaining.

Internecine Project, The (1974-British) C-89m. ** D: Ken Hughes. James Coburn, Lee Grant, Harry Andrews, Ian Hendry, Michael Jayston, Keenan Wynn. Lackluster espionage drama with Coburn as opportunist who tries to eliminate skeletons in his closet by having a handful of industrial spies kill each other off.

Internes Can't Take Money (1937) 77m. D: Alfred Santell. Barbara Stanwyck, Joel McCrea, Lloyd Nolan, Stanley Ridges, Lee Bowman, Irving Bacon, Pierre Watkin, Charles Lane, Fay Holden. SEE: **Dr. Kildare series.**

Interns, The (1962) 120m. *** D: David Swift. Michael Callan, Cliff Robertson, James MacArthur, Nick Adams, Suzy Parker, Haya Harareet, Stefanie Powers, Buddy Ebsen, Telly Savalas. Glossy, renovated DR. KILDARE soap opera, kept afloat by an interesting young cast. Followed by sequel NEW INTERNS, THE.

Interrupted Journey (1949-British) 80m. **½ D: Daniel Birt. Richard Todd, Valerie Hobson. Eerie film about Todd involved in bizarre dream concerning his marital life and its present complexities.

Interrupted Melody (1955) C-106m. *** D: Curtis Bernhardt. Eleanor Parker, Glenn Ford, Roger Moore, Cecil Kellaway. Fine biography of Marjorie Lawrence, Australian opera star, who made a comeback after being crippled by polio. Eileen Farrell sings for Parker.

Intimacy (1966) 87m. *½ D: Victor Stoloff. Jack Ging, Nancy Malone, Joan Blackman, Barry Sullivan, Jackie de Shannon. Grade-C drama may get more interesting response on TV than it deserves, since plot involves the spying on a Washington official by hidden cameras.

Intimate Lighting (1966-Czech) 72m. *** D: Ivan Passer. Vera Kresadlova, Zdenek Brezusek, Karel Blazek, Jaroslava Stedra, Jan Vostrcil, Vlastmila Vlkova, Karel Uhlik. Unpretentious, day-in-the-life story of two old friends, professional musicians, reuniting after long absence at country home. Excellent performances.

Intimate Stranger, The SEE: **Finger of Guilt**

Intimate Strangers (1977) C-100m. TVM D: John Llewellyn Moxey. Dennis Weaver, Sally Struthers, Tyne Daly, Larry Hagman, Melvyn Douglas, Quinn Cummings. Overlong drama about a battered wife and the destruction of a marriage. Offbeat roles for its two stars plus a sparkling cameo by Douglas as Weaver's mean old buzzard of a father. Average.

Intolerance (1916) 123m. **** D: D. W. Griffith. Lillian Gish, Robert Harron, Mae Marsh, Constance Talmadge, Bessie Love, Seena Owen, Alfred Paget, many others. Surely one of the all-time great movies, although be prepared for melodrama, preaching, and some hokey title cards. Man's inhumanity to man and his sins are examined in series of four interlocking tales from Babylonian times to modern day.

Intrigue (1947) 90m. ** D: Edwin L.

Marin. George Raft, June Havoc, Helena Carter, Tom Tully, Marvin Miller, Dan Seymour, Philip Ahn. Predictable Raft vehicle of ex-military man with mar on his record turning Shanghai crime ring over to cops to clear himself.

Intruder, The (1955-British) 84m. **½ D: Guy Hamilton. Jack Hawkins, Hugh Williams, Michael Medwin, Dennis Price, Dora Bryan. Hawkins is resolute army veteran who digs into past to discover why one of his old military group went astray.

Intruder in the Dust (1949) 87m. *** D: Clarence Brown. David Brian, Claude Jarman, Jr., Juano Hernandez, Porter Hall, Elizabeth Patterson. William Faulkner novel holds up well in screen version. Negro in Southern town is accused of murder, and gathering mob wants to lynch him.

Intruders, The (1967) C-95m. TVM D: William Graham. Don Murray, Edmond O'Brien, John Saxon, Anne Francis, Gene Evans, Edward Andrews. Half breed ex-con Billy Pye (Saxon) returns to Medelia to become lawman, vindicate himself from frame-up. Many subplots and characters to get into, but nothing comes together, thanks to script. Average.

Invaders, The SEE: **Forty-Ninth Parallel**

Invaders from Mars (1953) C-78m. *** D: William Cameron Menzies. Helena Carter, Arthur Franz, Jimmy Hunt, Leif Erickson, Hillary Brooke, Bert Freed. Stylish sci-fi told from little boy's point of view, as he alone witnesses invasion of aliens who capture and brainwash residents of small average town.

Invasion (1966-British) 82m. **½ D: Alan Bridges. Edward Judd, Yoko Tani, Lyndon Brook, Eric Young, Anthony Shark, Stephanie Bidmead. Entertaining little sci-fi flick involving interplanetary travelers forced to land on earth, and their conflict with humans.

Invasion Earth 2150 A.D. SEE: **Daleks—Invasion Earth 2150 A.D.**

Invasion of Johnson County, The (1976) C-100m. TVM D: Jerry Jameson. Bill Bixby, Bo Hopkins, John Hillerman, Billy Green Bush, Stephen Elliott, Luke Askew. City slicker and country bumpkin versus land barons and their gunslingers to foil a land-grab scheme in the Old West. Offbeat hoss-opera with a witty script and enough action to please every western fan. Above average.

Invasion of the Animal People (1962) 73m. *½ D: Virgil Vogel, Jerry Warren. Robert Burton, Barbara Wilson, Sten Gester, Bengt Bomgren. John Carradine is narrator and American link for Swedish-made 1960 production about rampaging monster who escapes from spaceship and terrorizes Lapland. Low-grade nonsense.

Invasion of the Body Snatchers (1956) 80m. ***½ D: Don Siegel. Kevin McCarthy, Dana Wynter, Larry Gates, King Donovan, Carolyn Jones. Classic 1950s sci-fi retains all its chills, telling story of small town where inhabitants are taken over by alien "pods." Director Siegel's original ending has recently been restored to theatrical prints . . . perhaps this more frightening version will be on TV as well. Remade in 1978.

Invasion of the Body Snatchers (1978) C-115m. *** D: Philip Kaufman. Donald Sutherland, Brooke Adams, Leonard Nimoy, Jeff Goldblum, Veronica Cartwright. Chilling remake of 1956 classic with many new twists and turns; unfortunately, it runs out of steam and offers one climax too many. Kevin McCarthy and Don Siegel, star and director of original film, have significant cameo roles . . . but look fast for Robert Duvall.

Invasion of the Saucer-Men (1957) 69m. *½ D: Edward L. Cahn. Steve Terrell, Gloria Castillo, Frank Gorshin, Raymond Hatton, Ed Nelson. Minor sci-fi of title monsters being outdone by the ingenuity of teenagers.

Invasion, U.S.A. (1952) 74m. *½ D: Alfred E. Green. Gerald Mohr, Peggie Castle, Dan O'Herlihy, Phyllis Coates. Oddball but unsuccessful sci-fi with Red enemies invading Alaska.

Investigation of a Citizen Above Suspicion (1970-Italian) C-115m. *** D: Elio Petri. Gian Maria Volonte, Florinda Bolkan, Salvo Randone, Gianni Santuccio, Arturo Dominici. Oscar-winning foreign film about powerful police chief who slashes the throat of his mistress, then waits entire movie to see if he'll be caught. Interesting, but not overly gripping.

Invincible Gladiator (1962-Italian) C-96m. **½ D: Anthony Momplet. Richard Harrison, Isabelle Corey,

Joseph Marco. Above-average spectacle with good battle sequences, set typically in ancient Rome, with Harrison as Rezius, who helps the oppressed peasants.

Invincible Six, The (1968) C-96m. **½ D: Jean Negulesco. Stuart Whitman, Elke Sommer, Curt Jurgens, James Mitchum, Ian Ogilvy. Energetic action film about a motley crew on the lam who come to the aid of isolated villagers under the thumb of a bandit gang. It's THE MAGNIFICENT SEVEN transplanted to the present day mid-East in this Iranian-made production.

Invisible Agent (1942) 81m. ** D: Edwin L. Marin. Ilona Massey, Jon Hall, Peter Lorre, Cedric Hardwicke, J. Edward Bromberg, John Litel. Hall plays agent fighting Nazis with invisibility. Fun for the kids; dialogue is witless.

Invisible Boy, The (1957) 85m. **½ D: Herman Hoffman. Richard Eyer, Diane Brewster, Philip Abbot, Harold J. Stone. One of the earlier sci-fi flicks to deal with the unwieldy computers gone berserk and powerhappy; not bad. Also features Robby the Robot (from FORBIDDEN PLANET).

Invisible Creature, The (1959-British) 70m. ** D: Montgomery Tully. Sandra Dorne, Patricia Dainton, Tony Wright. Oddball little film of ghost that interferes with homicide plot in eerie English mansion. Retitled: THE HOUSE ON MARSH ROAD.

Invisible Dr. Mabuse, The (1961-German) 89m. **½ D: Harald Reinl. Lex Barker, Karin Dor, Siegfried Lowitz, Wolfgang Preiss, Rudolf Fernau. Well-paced entry in archvillain series, with U. S. detective Barker in Germany to track down killer, involved with Mabuse (Preiss); offbeat setting enhances film.

Invisible Ghost, The (1941) 64m. ** D: Joseph H. Lewis. Bela Lugosi, Polly Ann Young, John McGuire, Clarence Muse, Terry Walker, Betty Compson. Low-grade horror about domineering wife who hypnotizes her husband into murder plot.

Invisible Invaders (1959) 67m. *½ D: Edward L. Cahn. John Agar, Jean Byron, Robert Hutton, Philip Tonge, John Carradine, Hal Torey. Low-grade thriller with few surprises.

Invisible Man, The (1933) 71m. ***½ D: James Whale. Claude Rains, Gloria Stuart, Una O'Connor, William Harrigan, E. E. Clive, Dudley Digges. H. G. Wells' fantasy brilliantly materializes on screen in thriller of mad scientist who makes himself invisible, wreaking havoc on British country village. Rains' starring debut. Dated but still enjoyable.

Invisible Man, The (1975) C-78m. TVM D: Robert Michael Lewis. David McCallum, Melinda Fee, Jackie Cooper, Henry Darrow, Alex Henteloff, Arch Johnson. Contemporized version of the H. G. Wells classic about a scientist who learns the secret of invisibility but later runs into complications. Should have disappeared before becoming a subsequent series. Below average.

Invisible Man Returns, The (1940) 81m. *** D: Joe May. Cedric Hardwicke, Vincent Price, John Sutton, Nan Grey, Cecil Kellaway, Alan Napier. Fine follow-up to exciting original, with Price going invisible to clear himself of murder charge.

Invisible Man's Revenge, The (1944) 77m. **½ D: Ford Beebe. Jon Hall, Alan Curtis, Evelyn Ankers, Leon Errol, John Carradine, Gale Sondergaard, Ian Wolfe, Billy Bevan. Hall made invisible by doctor to obtain estate; he then kills doctor after being refused visibility. Better-than-average cast saves rather innocuous script.

Invisible Monster, The SEE: **Slaves of the Invisible Monster**

Invisible Ray, The (1936) 81m. **½ D: Lambert Hillyer. Boris Karloff, Bela Lugosi, Frances Drake, Frank Lawton, Walter Kingsford, Beulah Bondi. Scientist Karloff contracts radiation that gives him touch of death, and slowly deteriorates his mind. Interesting yarn, but a notch below other Karloff-Lugosi vehicles.

Invisible Stripes (1939) 82m. *** D: Lloyd Bacon. George Raft, Jane Bryan, William Holden, Flora Robson, Humphrey Bogart, Paul Kelly, Moroni Olsen, Tully Marshall. Earnest account of parolee Raft trying to go straight, protecting brother Holden from gangster Bogart; subdued acting is effective.

Invisible Woman, The (1941) 72m. **½ D: A. Edward Sutherland. Virginia Bruce, John Barrymore, John Howard, Charlie Ruggles, Oscar Homolka, Edward Brophy. Gimmick film about screwy professor Barrymore making model Bruce invisible; hardly a classic, but enjoyable.

Invitation (1952) 84m. **½ D: Gottfried Reinhardt. Van Johnson, Dorothy McGuire, Louis Calhern, Ray Collins, Ruth Roman. Society tearjerker decked out in MGM gloss about invalid McGuire; her father (Calhern) tries to buy Johnson to romance dying daughter.

Invitation to a Gunfighter (1964) C-92m. **½ D: Richard Wilson. Yul Brynner, George Segal, Janice Rule, Pat Hingle, Brad Dexter. Cast surpasses turgid script about town that hires gunslinger to kill an outcast, with surprising results; overly talky.

Invitation to Happiness (1939) 95m. **½ D: Wesley Ruggles. Irene Dunne, Fred MacMurray, Charles Ruggles, William Collier, Sr., Eddie Hogan. Ordinary story, well acted: society girl marries fighter, but marriage can't survive because of his driving ambition in boxing ring.

Invitation to the Dance (1956) C-93m. **½ D: Gene Kelly. Gene Kelly, Igor Youskevitch, Claire Sombert, David Paltenghi, Daphne Dale, Claude Bessy, Tommy Rall, Carol Haney. Kelly's ambitious film tells three stories entirely in dance. Earnest but uninspired, until final "Sinbad" segment with Kelly in Hanna-Barbera cartoon world.

Ipcress File, The (1965-British) C-108m. ***½ D: Sidney J. Furie. Michael Caine, Nigel Green, Guy Doleman, Sue Lloyd, Gordon Jackson. First and best of Len Deighton's Harry Palmer series, with Caine unemotional Cockney crook turned secret agent, involved in grueling mental torture caper.

Irene (1940) 104m. **½ D: Herbert Wilcox. Anna Neagle, Ray Milland, Roland Young, Alan Marshal, May Robson, Billie Burke, Arthur Treacher. Pleasant remake of venerable musical (done as a silent film with Colleen Moore) minus most of the songs. Wealthy playboy Milland romances working-girl Neagle; some offbeat touches make it pleasing. "Alice Blue Gown" sequence filmed in color.

Irish Eyes Are Smiling (1944) C-90m. **½ D: Gregory Ratoff. June Haver, Monty Woolley, Dick Haymes, Anthony Quinn, Maxie Rosenbloom, Veda Ann Borg. Colorful corn about composer of famous Irish songs, with pleasant cast and familiar tunes.

Irish in Us, The (1935) 84m. ** D: Lloyd Bacon. James Cagney, Pat O'Brien, Olivia de Havilland, Frank McHugh, Allen Jenkins. Pretty stale comedy about rivalry between policemen and prizefighters, with good cast to hold one's interest.

Irish Whiskey Rebellion (1972) C-93m. ** D: J. C. Works (Chester Erskine). William Devane, Anne Meara, Richard Mulligan, David Groh, Judie Rolin, William Challee, Stephen Joyce. Pedestrian action tale of Irish rum-running during America's Prohibition era hoping to raise money for IRA struggles back home. Strong performances by all.

Irma la Douce (1963) C-142m. **½ D: Billy Wilder. Shirley MacLaine, Jack Lemmon, Lou Jacobi, Herschel Bernardi, Hope Holiday. Wilder's straight-comedy adaptation of Broadway musical is quite raw, definitely not for the tiny tots, as gendarme Lemmon becomes involved with prostitute MacLaine. Reteaming of stars and director can't equal THE APARTMENT.

Iron Curtain, The (1948) 87m. *** D: William Wellman. Dana Andrews, Gene Tierney, June Havoc, Berry Kroeger, Edna Best. Excellent cast and intelligent direction make this Cold War espionage story set in Canada of superior caliber. Retitled: BEHIND THE IRON CURTAIN.

Iron Glove, The (1954) C-77m. **½ D: William Castle. Robert Stack, Ursula Thiess, Richard Stapley, Charles Irwin, Alan Hale, Jr. Typical swashbuckler about 18th-century England and Prince James, pretender to the throne.

Iron Horse, The (1924) 119m. *** D: John Ford. George O'Brien, Madge Bellamy, Cyril Chadwick, Fred Kohler, Gladys Hulette, J. Farrell MacDonald. Epic-scale silent film about building of transcontinental railroad, intertwined with predictable human-interest subplots involving surveyor O'Brien, sweetheart Bellamy, traitor Kohler, etc. Storywise, film may seem hackneyed today, but it's important to note that this movie *invented* what later became clichés.

Iron Major, The (1943) 85m. **½ D: Ray Enright. Pat O'Brien, Ruth Warrick, Robert Ryan, Leon Ames, Russell Wade, Bruce Edwards. Good biography of Frank Cavanaugh, who in civilian life was famous football coach, in WW1 became a military hero; O'Brien is convincing in lead.

Iron Man (1931) 73m. ** D: Tod Browning. Lew Ayres, Jean Harlow,

Robert Armstrong, John Miljan, Eddie Dillon. Routine early talkie of prizefighter Ayres and gold-digging wife Harlow (who hadn't clicked yet in films). Manager-pal Armstrong is only one who sees through her. Filmed in 1937 as SOME BLONDES ARE DANGEROUS.

Iron Man (1951) 82m. **½ D: Joseph Pevney. Jeff Chandler, Evelyn Keyes, Stephen McNally, Joyce Holden, Rock Hudson. Remake of Harlow film focuses more on boxer (Chandler) and his unhappy rise in the boxing world.

Iron Mask, The (1929) 87m. *** D: Allan Dwan. Douglas Fairbanks, Belle Bennett, Marguerite De La Motte, Dorothy Revier, Vera Lewis, William Bakewell, Nigel De Brulier, Ullrich Haupt. Dumas tale later filmed as THE MAN IN THE IRON MASK told from point of view of D'Artagnan (Fairbanks), who becomes Louis XIV's protector from birth to later time when scheming Rochefort (Haupt) tries to pass off twin brother as heir to throne. Lavish swashbuckler originally had talkie sequences; current print all silent.

Iron Mistress, The (1952) C-110m. **½ D: Gordon Douglas. Alan Ladd, Virginia Mayo, Joseph Calleia, Phyllis Kirk. Spotty Western adventure of Jim Bowie (Ladd), who invented the famed two-edged knife.

Iron Petticoat, The (1956) C-87m. **½ D: Ralph Thomas. Bob Hope, Katharine Hepburn, James Robertson Justice, Robert Helpmann, David Kossoff. Curious comedy made in England tries to update NINOTCHKA theme with Hepburn as humorless Russian and Hope as American military man who tries to win her over. Stars' surprising rapport is film's chief value; mediocre script and direction kill the rest.

Iron Sheriff, The (1957) 73m. *½ D: Sidney Salkow. Sterling Hayden, Constance Ford, John Dehner, Kent Taylor, Darryl Hickman. Marshal Hayden sets out to prove son is not guilty of murder.

Ironside (1967) C-98m. TVM D: James Goldstone. Raymond Burr, Geraldine Brooks, Gene Lyons, Don Galloway, Don Mitchell, Barbara Anderson. Excellent performance by Burr and tight direction highlight sympathetic, suspenseful story of San Francisco police inspector shot and paralyzed by sniper, reacting to public pressure and friends who rally 'round him. Above average. Pilot for TV series.

Iroquois Trail, The (1950) 85m. ** D: Phil Karlson. George Montgomery, Brenda Marshall, Dan O'Herlihy, Glenn Langan. Too often flabby account of French and Indian War, lacking sufficient plot motivation and action sequences.

Is My Face Red? (1932) 66m. **½ D: William A. Seiter. Ricardo Cortez, Helen Twelvetrees, Jill Esmond, Robert Armstrong, Sidney Toler, ZaSu Pitts. Cortez plays Walter Winchell-like columnist in this pleasant, topical picture—but he's such a total heel that our sympathies aren't with him when script demands they should be.

Is Paris Burning? (1966) 173m. ** D: René Clement. Jean-Paul Belmondo, Charles Boyer, Leslie Caron, Alain Delon, Kirk Douglas, Glenn Ford, Gert Frobe, Simone Signoret, Orson Welles, Claude Dauphin. Rambling pseudo-documentary-style re-creation of WW2 France, showing liberation of Paris and Nazis' attempt to burn the city. Cameos by international players confuse blotchy film made in Europe.

Isadora (1969-British) C-168m. ***½ D: Karel Reisz. Vanessa Redgrave, James Fox, Jason Robards, Ivan Tchenko, John Fraser. Extremely long but gripping study of Isadora Duncan, first of modern dancers and most prominent free-thinker of her time. Interesting technique and carefully studied performances combine together in this offbeat biography. Also titled: THE LOVES OF ISADORA.

Ishi: The Last of His Tribe (1978) C-150m. TVM D: Robert Ellis Miller. Dennis Weaver, Elroy Phil Casados, Devon Ericson, Joseph Running Fox, Lois Red Elk, Michael Medina. Absorbing drama traces the life of the last Yahi Indian from childhood to his early death, and his friendship with an anthropologist (Weaver). Interesting adaptation of Theodora Kroeber's book was started by Dalton Trumbo (who died while writing it) and completed by his son Christopher. Above average.

Island, The (1962-Japanese) 96m. *** D: Kaneto Shindo. Nobuko Otowa, Taiji Tonoyama, Shinji Tanaka, Masanori Horimoto. Engrossing documentary-style study of peasant family living on rocky island near Japan, struggling to survive.

Island at the Top of the World, The (1974) C-93m. **½ D: Robert Stevenson. David Hartman, Donald Sinden, Jacques Marin, Mako, David Gwillim, Agneta Eckemyr. Disney's attempt to score again in Jules Verne territory misses bullseye; simplistic, derivative story of Arctic expedition which stumbles across "lost" Viking civilization is mainly for kids.

Island in the Sky (1953) 109m. **½ D: William Wellman. John Wayne, Lloyd Nolan, James Arness, Andy Devine. Sometimes actionful search for downed troop plane set in WW2 off Greenland coast.

Island in the Sun (1957) C-119m. ** D: Robert Rossen. James Mason, Joan Fontaine, Dorothy Dandridge, Joan Collins, Michael Rennie, Diana Wynyard, John Williams, Stephen Boyd, Harry Belafonte. Misfire adaptation of Alec Waugh's book about idyllic West Indies island torn by racial struggle. Good cast can't do much with unconvincing script.

Island of Desire (1952-British) C-103m. *½ D: Gordon Douglas. Linda Darnell, Tab Hunter, Donald Gray, Sheila Chong. Sun-drenched, romantic WW2 drama of nurse, marine, and injured pilot all washed ashore on tropical desert island. Parched performances. British title: SATURDAY'S ISLAND.

Island of Dr. Moreau, The (1977) C-104m. *** D: Don Taylor. Burt Lancaster, Michael York, Nigel Davenport, Barbara Carrera, Richard Basehart. Handsomely produced remake of H. G. Wells' ISLAND OF LOST SOULS with Lancaster as demented doctor who has spent years creating half-man, half-beast "humanimals," heading a solid cast. Good horror-fantasy chiller.

Island of Doomed Men (1940) 67m. ** D: Charles Barton. Peter Lorre, Robert Wilcox, Rochelle Hudson, George E. Stone, Don Beddoe, Kenneth MacDonald. Low-grade melodrama even Lorre can't save as man who traps unsuspecting victims on island, turns them into his slaves.

Island of Lost Men (1939) 63m. *½ D: Kurt Neumann. Anna May Wong, J. Carrol Naish, Eric Blore, Ernest Truex, Anthony Quinn, Broderick Crawford. Generally dull mystery of Wong searching for Oriental general along the waterfront. A few

atmospheric scenes, but stilted dialogue throughout.

Island of Lost Souls (1933) 70m. *** D: Erle C. Kenton. Charles Laughton, Bela Lugosi, Richard Arlen, Stanley Fields, Kathleen Burke, Joe Bonomo, Leila Hyams. Renowned horror film of mad scientist Laughton changing jungle beasts into "mansters," human savages. Laughton overplays, but it is worth seeing. Remade as ISLAND OF DR. MOREAU.

Island of Lost Women (1959) 71m. ** D: Frank Tuttle. Jeff Richards, Venetia Stevenson, John Smith, Diane Jergens, Alan Napier, June Blair. Plane forced down on remote island leads to complications with scientist and daughters who inhabit the jungle isle.

Island of Love (1963) C-101m. **½ D: Morton Da Costa. Robert Preston, Tony Randall, Giorgia Moll, Walter Matthau, Betty Bruce. Dud attempt to make bubbly romantic comedy. Filmed in Greece.

Island of Terror (1967-British) C-90m. ** D: Terence Fisher. Peter Cushing, Edward Judd, Carole Gray, Niall MacGinnis. Sci-fi tale about cancer research gone wild and mutations that result is directed and acted by veterans of the field, but result is nothing special.

Island of the Doomed SEE: **Man-Eater of Hydra**

Island Princess, The (1955-Italian) C-98m. ** D: Paolo Moffa. Marcello Mastroianni, Silvana Pampanini, Gustavo Rojo. Rather hackneyed yarn set in 1500s, with Mastroianni a Spanish captain falling in love with princess of the Canary Islands.

Island Rescue (1952-British) 87m. ** D: Ralph Thomas. David Niven, Glynis Johns, George Coulouris, Barry Jones, Noel Purcell. Lukewarm comedy involving rescue of cows from German-occupied island during WW2. Retitled: APPOINTMENT WITH VENUS.

Islander, The (1978) C-100m. TVM D: Paul Krasny. Dennis Weaver, Sharon Gless, Peter Mark Richman, Bernadette Peters, Robert Vaughn, Sheldon Leonard. Lawyer Weaver retires to Hawaii to run a hotel, but soon finds himself involved with a variety of characters in various degrees of trouble with the law. OK series pilot. Average.

Islands in the Stream (1977) C-105m. **½ D: Franklin J. Schaffner.

George C. Scott, David Hemmings, Claire Bloom, Susan Tyrrell, Gilbert Roland, Richard Evans. Film version of Hemingway novel about an island-dwelling sculptor and his three sons begins well but falls apart completely in the final third. Still one of the better adaptations of this author, with one of Scott's best performances.

Isle of Fury (1936) 60m. ** D: Frank McDonald. Humphrey Bogart, Margaret Lindsay, Donald Woods, Paul Graetz, Gordon Hart, E. E. Clive. Mild remake of Somerset Maugham novel NARROW CORNER (1933), involving love triangle on South Sea island; early Bogart.

Isle of Sin (1960-German) 63m. *½ D: Johannes Kai. Christiane Nielsen, Erwin Strahl, Jan Hendriks, Slavo Schwaiger. Trite tale of passengers on plane which crashes on deserted island, with expected friction between types.

Isle of the Dead (1945) 72m. *** D: Mark Robson. Boris Karloff, Ellen Drew, Marc Cramer, Katherine Emery, Helene Thimig, Jason Robards. Eerie horror tale of assorted characters stranded on Greek island during quarantine. Good Val Lewton production.

Isle of the Snake People SEE: **Snake People**

Isn't It Romantic? (1948) 87m. ** D: Norman Z. McLeod. Veronica Lake, Mary Hatcher, Mona Freeman, Billy DeWolfe, Ronald Culver, Pearl Bailey. No.

Isn't It Shocking? (1973) C-73m. TVM D: John Badham. Alan Alda, Louise Lasser, Edmond O'Brien, Ruth Gordon, Will Geer, Dorothy Tristan, Lloyd Nolan. Virtually everything clicks in brilliant, oddball comedy-mystery about series of bizarre murders disrupting usual day-to-day routine of small New England town's police department. Excellent cast, script, direction. A film to remember. Above average.

Istanbul (1957) C-84m. ** D: Joseph Pevney. Errol Flynn, Cornell Borchers, John Bentley, Torin Thatcher, Nat King Cole. Unsatisfying drama of adventurer Flynn returning to title city to find cache of gems, discovering his old girlfriend still alive. Remake of SINGAPORE.

Istanbul Express (1968) C-94m. TVM D: Richard Irving. Gene Barry, John Saxon, Senta Berger, Mary Ann Mobley, Tom Simcox, Trans-Europa Express main scene of action in tired espionage adventure film featuring Barry as one of several spies vying for research notes of deceased scientist. Inconsequential. Average.

It (1927) 72m. **½ D: Clarence Badger. Clara Bow, Antonio Moreno, William Austin, Jacqueline Gadsdon (later Jane Daly), Gary Cooper. Inane plot about gold-digging shopgirl with eyes for her handsome boss serves as showcase for the 1920s' most effervescent screen personality, Clara Bow.

It (1967) 96m. ** D: Herbert J. Leder. Roddy McDowall, Jill Haworth, Ernest Clark, Paul Maxwell, Aubrey Richards. McDowall brings hulking stone statue to life and soon finds it makes a great murderer. Kill it! Filmed in England.

It Ain't Hay (1943) 80m. **½ D: Erle C. Kenton. Bud Abbott, Lou Costello, Patsy O'Connor, Grace McDonald, Leighton Noble, Cecil Kellaway, Eugene Pallette, Eddie Quillan. Pretty good A&C from Damon Runyon story of racehorse Teabiscuit; good supporting cast helps.

It All Came True (1940) 97m. **½ D: Lewis Seiler. Ann Sheridan, Humphrey Bogart, Jeffrey Lynn, ZaSu Pitts, Jessie Busley, Una O'Connor, Grant Mitchell, Felix Bressart. Offbeat story combines comedy, drama, music, and sentiment as gangster Bogart hides out in quaint boarding house. Fine showcase for Sheridan, who sings "Angel in Disguise" and "The Gaucho Serenade."

It Always Rains on Sunday (1948-British) 92m. ***½ D: Robert Hamer. Googie Withers, Edward Chapman, Sydney Tafler, Jane Hylton, Alfie Bass, Hermione Baddeley. Excellent mosaic of characters whose lives intertwine in a drab London neighborhood.

It Came from Beneath the Sea (1955) 80m. *** D: Robert Gordon. Kenneth Tobey, Faith Domergue, Donald Curtis, Ian Keith, Harry Lauter. Breathtaking special effects highlight this sci-fi thriller. Huge monster emerges from Pacific Ocean and wreaks havoc on San Francisco. First film made by Ray Harryhausen-Charles H. Schneer team.

It Came from Outer Space (1953) 81m. **½ D: Jack Arnold. Richard Carlson, Barbara Rush, Charles Drake, Kathleen Hughes. Slow-paced sci-fi promising much but delivering little real suspense as townsfolk react to invasion of unknown monsters from beyond. Originally in 3D.

It Comes Up Murder SEE: **Honey Pot, The**

It Conquered the World (1956) 68m. ** D: Roger Corman. Peter Graves, Beverly Garland, Lee Van Cleef, Sally Fraser. Low-budget sci-fi which intelligently attempts to create atmospheric excitement in yarn of superego power from another world.

It Couldn't Happen to a Nicer Guy (1974) C-78m. TVM D: Cy Howard. Paul Sorvino, Michael Learned, Bob Dishy, Adam Arkin, Ed Barth, Roger Bowen. Farce about a mild-mannered salesman who has trouble convincing anyone he has been raped at gunpoint by a beautiful woman. Silly, but versatile Sorvino manages to pull it off. Average.

It Grows on Trees (1952) 84m. ** D: Arthur Lubin. Irene Dunne, Dean Jagger, Richard Crenna, Les Tremayne. Dunne's last feature to date is slim vehicle of wife who discovers backyard foliage is blossoming crisp money.

It Had To Be You (1947) 98m. **½ D: Don Hartman, Rudolph Maté. Ginger Rogers, Cornel Wilde, Percy Waram, Spring Byington, Ron Randell. Rogers has severe indecision before every scheduled marriage, until dream-lover Wilde appears. Airy, fanciful comedy.

It Had to Happen (1936) 79m. ** D: Roy Del Ruth. George Raft, Leo Carrillo, Rosalind Russell, Alan Dinehart, Arline Judge. Odd story of Raft working his way from Italian immigrant to political power in N.Y., trying to romance upper-class Russell.

It Happened at Lakewood Manor (1977) C-100m. TVM D: Robert Sheerer. Lynda Day George, Robert Foxworth, Myrna Loy, Suzanne Somers. Insects on the rampage, or what happens when the traditional stellar TV cast vacationing at a secluded lodge tampers with Mother Nature. Predictable horrors, and the squeamish are forewarned. Average. Retitled PANIC AT LAKEWOOD MANOR.

It Happened at the World's Fair (1963) C-105m. *** D: Norman Taurog. Elvis Presley, Joan O'Brien, Gary Lockwood, Yvonne Craig. Entertaining Presley vehicle set at Seattle World's Fair, with Elvis and O'Brien brought together by little Ginny Tiu. Listenable tunes help make this most enjoyable.

It Happened in Brooklyn (1947) 105m. ** D: Richard Whorf. Frank Sinatra, Kathryn Grayson, Jimmy Durante, Peter Lawford, Gloria Grahame. Hokey musical of group of Brooklynites trying to make it big in show biz; all coating, no substance. One good song, "Time After Time," and Durante in fine form.

It Happened on 5th Avenue (1947) 115m. ** D: Roy Del Ruth. Don DeFore, Ann Harding, Charlie Ruggles, Victor Moore, Gale Storm, Grant Mitchell. Overlong comedy about elegant N.Y.C. mansion taken over by thoughtful bum, who invites horde of friends and real owner in disguise to be his guests.

It Happened One Christmas (1977) C-112m. TVM D: Donald Wrye. Marlo Thomas, Wayne Rogers, Orson Welles, Cloris Leachman, Barney Martin, Karen Carlson, Doris Roberts. IT'S A WONDERFUL LIFE with change of sex only proves how wonderful the original by Frank Capra was—and is. This one goes on forever, and that's just one of the problems. Anyway, earnestly made. Average.

It Happened One Night (1934) 105m. **** D: Frank Capra. Clark Gable, Claudette Colbert, Walter Connolly, Roscoe Karns, Alan Hale, Ward Bond. Oscar-studded screwball comedy doesn't age a bit. Still as enchanting as ever, with reporter Gable and runaway heiress Colbert falling in love on rural bus trip. Hitch-hiking scene, the Walls of Jericho, other memorable scenes remain fresh and delightful. Remade as musicals EVE KNEW HER APPLES and YOU CAN'T RUN AWAY FROM IT.

It Happened One Summer SEE: **State Fair**

It Happened to Jane (1959) C-98m. **½ D: Richard Quine. Doris Day, Jack Lemmon, Ernie Kovacs, Steve Forrest, Teddy Rooney, Russ Brown, Mary Wickes, Parker Fennelly. Funny little comedy with Doris and Lemmon running Maine lobstery, tangling with villain Kovacs (who hams mercilessly). Breezy and likable. Also known as TWINKLE AND SHINE.

It Happened Tomorrow (1944) 84m. ***½ D: René Clair. Dick Powell, Linda Darnell, Jack Oakie, Edgar

Kennedy, Edward Brophy, George Cleveland, Sig Ruman. Nifty fantasy-comedy of reporter Powell receiving news 24 hours before it occurs; set at turn of the century. Fine cast.

It Happens Every Spring (1949) 80m. ***½ D: Lloyd Bacon. Ray Milland, Jean Peters, Paul Douglas, Ed Begley. Clever little film of chemistry professor (Milland) accidently discovering a chemical mixture which causes baseballs to avoid all wooden surfaces, namely bats. A most enjoyable and unpretentious picture.

It Happens Every Thursday (1953) 80m. *** D: Joseph Pevney. Loretta Young, John Forsythe, Frank McHugh, Edgar Buchanan. Warm comedy about married couple who buy small-town newspaper and try every method conceivable to make it click.

It Lives Again (1978) C-91m. *½ D: Larry Cohen. Frederic Forrest, Kathleen Lloyd, John Ryan, John Marley, Andrew Duggan, Eddie Constantine. Sequel to IT'S ALIVE retains all the qualities of the original, so if you liked the first one . . .

It Only Happens to Others (1971-French-Italian) C-88m. ** D: Nadine Trintignant. Marcello Mastroianni, Catherine Deneuve, Serge Marquard, Dominique Labourier, Catherine Allegret. Loss of young child causes happily married couple to withdraw from society. Heavy on the syrup.

It Should Happen to You (1954) 81m. *** D: George Cukor. Judy Holliday, Peter Lawford, Jack Lemmon, Michael O'Shea, Vaughn Taylor. Raucous comedy about publicity-seeking actress (Holliday) who has her name plastered on billboards in N.Y.C. with deft results.

It Shouldn't Happen to a Dog (1946) 70m. **½ D: Herbert I. Leeds. Carole Landis, Allyn Joslyn, Margo Woode, Henry (Harry) Morgan, Reed Hadley, Jean Wallace. Fluff of fast-talking reporter, policewoman, and a troublesome dog.

It Started in Naples (1960) C-100m. **½ D: Melville Shavelson. Clark Gable, Sophia Loren, Vittorio De Sica, Marietto, Paolo Carlini, Claudio Ermelli. Gable is American lawyer, in Italy to bring nephew back to America; only Aunt Sophia won't agree. Star duo never clicks as love match, but they do their best.

It Started with a Kiss (1959) C-104m. **½ D: George Marshall. Glenn Ford, Debbie Reynolds, Eva Gabor, Fred Clark, Edgar Buchanan, Harry Morgan. Airy comedy about wacky Reynolds and her army officer husband Ford, trying to make a go of marriage, set in Spain.

It Started with Eve (1941) 90m. *** D: Henry Koster. Deanna Durbin, Charles Laughton, Robert Cummings, Guy Kibbee, Margaret Tallichet, Walter Catlett. Delightful romantic comedy; Deanna poses as Cummings' fiancee to please his dying father (Laughton). Trouble starts when Laughton shows signs of recovery. Remade as I'D RATHER BE RICH.

It Takes a Thief (1960-British) 90m. ** D: John Gilling. Jayne Mansfield, Anthony Quayle, Carl Mohner, Edward Judd. Mansfield is gangland leader with big heist in the workings; supporting cast uplifts flick. Original title: THE CHALLENGE.

It Takes All Kinds (1969) C-98m. ** D: Eddie Davis. Robert Lansing, Vera Miles, Barry Sullivan, Sid Melton, Penny Sugg. Fair doublecross drama about Miles' shielding of Lansing when he accidentally kills sailor in a brawl in Australia. Nothing special.

It! The Terror from Beyond Space (1958) 69m. *½ D: Edward L. Cahn. Marshall Thompson, Shawn Smith, Kim Spalding, Ann Doran. Mild scifi of space ship returning to earth with a most unwelcome creature stowed away on it.

It's a Big Country (1951) 89m. *** D: Charles Vidor, Richard Thorpe, John Sturges, Don Hartman, Don Weis, Clarence Brown, William Wellman. Ethel Barrymore, Keefe Brasselle, Gary Cooper, Nancy Davis, Gene Kelly, Keenan Wynn, Fredric March, Van Johnson, James Whitmore. Dore Schary's plug for America uses several pointless episodes about the variety of people and places in U.S. Other segments make up for it in very uneven film.

It's a Bikini World (1967) C-86m. *½ D: Stephanie Rothman. Deborah Walley, Tommy Kirk, Bob Pickett, Suzie Kaye, The Animals, The Gentrys. Superlover Kirk loves bikinied Debbie, but she doesn't dig him until he masquerades as an intellectual. Not among the best of its kind, if there even *is* a best of its kind.

It's a Dog's Life (1955) C-88m. **½ D: Herman Hoffman. Jeff Richards, Edmund Gwenn, Dean Jagger, Sally Fraser. Film uses gimmick of having the canine star tell his life story from slums to luxury. Retitled: BAR SINISTER.

It's A Gift (1934) 73m. **** D: Norman Z. McLeod. W. C. Fields, Baby LeRoy, Kathleen Howard, Tommy Bupp, Morgan Wallace. Fields is a grocery store owner who goes West with his family. Beautiful comedy routines in one of the Great Man's unforgettable films. Charles Sellon as a blind man, T. Roy Barnes as a salesman looking for Carl LaFong, contribute some hilarious moments. A remake of Fields' silent film IT'S THE OLD ARMY GAME.

It's A Great Feeling (1949) C-85m. *** D: David Butler. Dennis Morgan, Doris Day, Jack Carson, Bill Goodwin. Gentle spoof of Hollywood with Carson's ego making filming difficult for himself and partner Morgan; guest appearances by many Warner Bros. players and directors, including Joan Crawford, Gary Cooper, Errol Flynn, Edward G. Robinson.

It's a Great Life (1943) 75m. D: Frank Strayer. Penny Singleton, Arthur Lake, Larry Simms, Hugh Herbert, Jonathan Hale, Danny Mummert, Alan Dinehart. SEE: Blondie series.

It's a Joke, Son (1947) 63m. ** D: Ben Stoloff. Kenny Delmar, Una Merkel, June Lockhart, Kenneth Farrell, Douglass Dumbrille. Folksy comedy featuring further exploits of Senator Claghorn (Delmar) from the Fred Allen radio show.

It's a Mad Mad Mad Mad World (1963) C-154m. **½ D: Stanley Kramer. Spencer Tracy, Edie Adams, Milton Berle, Sid Caesar, Buddy Hackett, Ethel Merman, Mickey Rooney, Dick Shawn, Dorothy Provine, Phil Silvers, Jonathan Winters, many guest stars. Supercomedy cast in attempt at supercomedy, about group of people racing to find hidden treasure under watchful eye of detective Tracy. Big, splashy, generally funny, but bigness doesn't equal greatness. Originally shown in Cinerama process at 192m.

It's a Pleasure! (1945) C-90m. ** D: William A. Seiter. Sonja Henie, Michael O'Shea, Bill Johnson, Marie McDonald, Gus Schilling, Iris Adrian. Skater Henie and hockey player O'Shea get married but can't seem to break the ice; pretty weak.

It's A Wonderful Life (1946) 129m. ***½ D: Frank Capra. James Stewart, Donna Reed, Lionel Barrymore, Henry Travers, Beulah Bondi, Gloria Grahame, Thomas Mitchell, H. B. Warner, Frank Albertson, Ward Bond, Frank Faylen. Sentimental tale of Stewart, who works all his life to make good in small town, thinking he's failed and trying to end his life. Guardian angel Travers comes to show him his mistake. Only Capra and this cast could pull it off so well. Remade for TV as IT HAPPENED ONE CHRISTMAS.

It's a Wonderful World (1939) 86m. *** D: W. S. Van Dyke II. Claudette Colbert, James Stewart, Guy Kibbee, Nat Pendleton, Edgar Kennedy, Sidney Blackmer, Hans Conried. Screwball comedy with Colbert a runaway poetess, Stewart a fugitive chased by cops Pendleton and Kennedy. Very, very funny, with Stewart having a field-day.

It's Alive (1974) C-91m. *½ D: Larry Cohen. John Ryan, Sharon Farrell, Andrew Duggan, Guy Stockwell, James Dixon, Michael Ansara. Shlocky though definitely offbeat trash about a baby who goes on a murderous rampage. Even a Bernard Herrmann musical score doesn't help.

It's Always Fair Weather (1955) C-102m. *** D: Gene Kelly, Stanley Donen. Gene Kelly, Dan Dailey, Michael Kidd, Cyd Charisse, Dolores Gray, David Burns. Three WW2 buddies meet ten years after their discharge and find they have nothing in common. Pungent Comden and Green script falls short of perfection but still has wonderful moments, and some first-rate musical numbers. Best: the ash-can dance, although clever use of wide-screen is lost on TV.

It's in the Air (1935) 80m. ** D: Charles Reisner. Jack Benny, Una Merkel, Ted Healy, Nat Pendleton, Mary Carlisle, Grant Mitchell. Uncharacteristic Benny as con-artist who goes to ex-wife Merkel for help. Fair comedy; mainly a curiosity item.

It's in the Bag (1945) 87m. *** D: Richard Wallace. Fred Allen, Binnie

Barnes, Robert Benchley, Sidney Toler, Jack Benny, Don Ameche, Victor Moore, Rudy Vallee, William Bendix. Story similar to THE TWELVE CHAIRS with flea-circus promoter Allen entitled to inheritance; plot soon goes out the window in favor of unrelated but amusing episodes, including hilarious encounter between Allen and Benny.

It's Love I'm After (1937) 90m. *** D: Archie Mayo. Bette Davis, Leslie Howard, Olivia de Havilland, Patric Knowles, Eric Blore, Bonita Granville, Spring Byington, Veda Ann Borg. Delightful, witty comedy of ego-struck actor Howard and his fiancee/co-star Davis, who explodes when he becomes involved with infatuated admirer De Havilland. Reminiscent in spirit of 20TH CENTURY; Blore is marvelous as Howard's ultradedicated valet.

It's Never Too Late (1956-British) C-95m. **½ D: Michael McCarthy. Phyllis Calvert, Guy Rolfe, Sarah Lawson, Peter Illing, Patrick Barr. Pleasant frou-frou about Calvert becoming famed writer, caught between choice of being good mother or living a celebrity's life.

It's Only Money (1962) 84m. *** D: Frank Tashlin. Jerry Lewis, Zachary Scott, Joan O'Brien, Mae Questel, Jesse White, Jack Weston. Jerry, a TV repairman turned detective, in a wacky comedy, one of his better later films. Slapstick and sight gags blend perfectly.

It's Showtime (1976) C/B&W-86m. *** No director credit. Delightful compilation of animal sequences from movies, reaching back to Rin Tin Tin's silent films. Maximum footage from NATIONAL VELVET and LASSIE COME HOME, but everything—from canine version of "Singin' in the Rain" to Bonzo the Chimp being bottle-fed by Ronald Reagan—is great fun.

Ivan the Terrible, Part One (1943-Russian) 96m. **** D: Sergei Eisenstein. Nikolai Cherkasov, Ludmila Tselivskovskaya, Serafima Birman. Film spectacle of the highest order. Eisenstein's incredibly lavish, detailed chronicle of Czar Ivan IV's life from coronation to defeat to reinstatement, forging fascinating image of the man and his country. Enhanced by Prokofiev's original score. Heavy going, but worthwhile.

Italian Connection, The (1973-Italian) C-92m. ** D: Fernando Di Leo.

Henry Silva, Woody Strode, Mario Adorf, Luciana Paluzzi, Sylva Koscina, Adolfo Celi. Violent gangster meller has Milanese hood Adorf set up by gang boss Celi for the blame in a six million dollar heroin heist. For action fans only.

Italian Job, The (1969-British) C-101m. **½ D: Peter Collinson. Michael Caine, Noel Coward, Maggie Blye, Benny Hill, Tony Beckley, Raf Vallone. $4,000,000 in gold bullion's the object in average caper film about prison-based mastermind Coward's plan to divert authorities in Turin, Italy, cause "history's biggest traffic jam." Wild chases galore, but characterizations pat, forgettable.

Italiano Brava Gente (1965-Italian) 156m. *** D: Giuseppe De Santis. Arthur Kennedy, Peter Falk, Tatyana Samoilova, Rafaelle Pisu, Andrea Checchi. Expansive chronicle of Italian-Russian warfront during WW2, focusing on a variety of strata of soldiers and civilians. Much edited since European opening. Retitled: ATTACK AND RETREAT.

Ivanhoe (1952) C-106m. *** D: Richard Thorpe. Robert Taylor, Elizabeth Taylor, Joan Fontaine, George Sanders, Finlay Currie, Sebastian Cabot. Almost a classic spectacular, marred by draggy scripting of Walter Scott's epic of England in Middle Ages, in days of chivalrous knights; beautifully photographed on location in Great Britain.

It's Your Move (1968-Italian-Spanish) C-93m. ** D: Robert Fiz. Edward G. Robinson, Terry-Thomas, Adolfo Celi. Good cast aids limp tale of Englishman who uses lookalikes for four bank tellers to pull off robbery.

Ivory Hunter (1951-British) C-97m. **½ D: Harry Watt. Anthony Steel, Dinah Sheridan, Harold Warrender, William Simons. Documentary-ish account of establishment of Mount Kilimanjaro Game Preserve Park in Africa. Retitled: WHERE NO VULTURES FLY.

Ivy (1947) 99m. **½ D: Sam Wood. Joan Fontaine, Patric Knowles, Herbert Marshall, Richard Ney, Cedric Hardwicke, Lucile Watson. Average drama of murderess snared in her own seemingly faultless plans. Good cast gives film added boost.

J. D.'s Revenge (1976) C-95m. ** D: Arthur Marks. Glynn Turman,

Joan Pringle, Lou Gossett, Carl Crudup, James Louis Watkins, Alice Jubert. Black horror melodrama: possession of innocent man by vengeful spirit. Fairly well executed.

J. W. Coop (1972) C-112m. ***½ D: Cliff Robertson. Cliff Robertson, Geraldine Page, Cristina Ferrare, R. G. Armstrong, John Crawford. Vivid character study of none-too-bright drifter who sets his sights on becoming No. 1 rodeo star. Tour de force for director/writer/star Robertson, who scores in all departments.

Jabberwocky (1977-British) C-100m. **½ D: Terry Gilliam. Michael Palin, Max Wall, Deborah Fallender, John Le Mesurier, Annette Badland. Director Gilliam of MONTY PYTHON AND THE HOLY GRAIL fame gives us another satire of medieval times, but the humor is even more spotty than its predecessor's. For fans.

Jack and the Beanstalk (1952) C-87m. **½ D: Jean Yarbrough. Bud Abbott, Lou Costello, Dorothy Ford, Barbara Brown, Buddy Baer. A&C version of fairy tale OK for kids, but not as funny as their earlier films. Begins in b&w, switches to color.

Jack Johnson (1971) 90m. *** D: William Cayton. Narrated by Brock Peters. Documentary on world-famous heavyweight champion. Features excellent jazz score by Miles Davis.

Jack London (1943) 94m. *½ D: Alfred Santell. Michael O'Shea, Susan Hayward, Osa Massen, Harry Davenport, Frank Craven, Virginia Mayo. Hokey, episodic "biography" of famed writer spends too much time maligning Japanese—which was supposed to give topical slant to this period drama in 1943.

Jack McCall, Desperado (1953) C-76m. ** D: Sidney Salkow. George Montgomery, Angela Stevens, Jay Silverheels, Douglas Kennedy. Civil War yarn of Southerner Montgomery capturing man who framed him as spy.

Jack of Diamonds (1967-U.S.-German) C-105m. *½ D: Don Taylor. George Hamilton, Joseph Cotten, Marie Laforet, Maurice Evans, Carroll Baker, Zsa Zsa Gabor, Lilli Palmer. Hamilton plays a cat burglar who robs jewels from Baker, Gabor, and Palmer, who are "special guests" in this film. Skip this

one and wait for TO CATCH A THIEF to be shown.

Jack Slade (1953) 90m. ** D: Harold Schuster. Mark Stevens, Dorothy Malone, Barton MacLane, John Litel. Oater programmer of Stevens turning criminal with tragic results; Malone is wasted.

Jack the Giant Killer (1962) C-94m. *** D: Nathan Juran. Kerwin Mathews, Judi Meredith, Torin Thatcher, Walter Burke. Marvelous special effects make this costume adventure yarn (in the SINBAD tradition) a lot of fun.

Jack the Ripper (1960-British) 88m. ** D: Robert Baker, Monty Berman. Lee Patterson, Eddie Byrne, George Rose, Betty McDowall. Middling retelling of notorious knife-wielder, with alternating scenes of Scotland Yard and fiend at work in London. Sometimes hits the mark with gory sensationalism.

Jackals, The (1967) C-105m. ** D: Robert D. Webb. Vincent Price, Diana Ivarson, Robert Gunner, Bob Courtney, Patrick Mynhardt. William Wellman's striking YELLOW SKY reset in the South African Transvaal, with six bandits terrorizing a grizzled old miner (Price) and his granddaughter into surrendering their gold cache.

Jackass Mail (1942) 80m. ** D: Norman Z. McLeod. Wallace Beery, Marjorie Main, J. Carrol Naish, Darryl Hickman, William Haade, Dick Curtis. Easygoing Beery vehicle about fugitive who accidentally becomes a hero. Take it or leave it; no harm done either way.

Jackie Robinson Story, The (1950) 76m. *** D: Alfred E. Green. Jackie Robinson, Ruby Dee, Louise Beavers, Minor Watson, Richard Lane. Straightforward account of baseball star, with effective telling of racial issues involved.

Jackpot, The (1950) 87m. **½ D: Walter Lang. James Stewart, Barbara Hale, James Gleason, Fred Clark, Natalie Wood. Dated, minor comedy, uplifted by stars; Stewart is winner of radio contest but can't pay taxes on winnings.

Jackson County Jail (1976) C-89m. **½ D: Michael Miller. Yvette Mimieux, Tommy Lee Jones, Robert Carradine, Frederic Cook, Severn Darden, Howard Hessemann. Prisoner Yvette, dumped on by everyone she meets, goes on the lam with fellow inmate in yet another chase pic.

Livelier than most, this one has developed a cult reputation. Miller later "remade" it for TV as OUTSIDE CHANCE.

Jacob the Liar (1977-German) C-95m. *** D: Frank Beyer. Vlastimil Brodsky, Erwin Geschonneck, Manuela Simon, Henry Hubchen, Blanche Kommerell. Touching, sometimes comic tale of Polish Jew Brodsky, whose false tales to fellow ghetto dwellers give some hope against their Nazi captors. Brodsky won a Best Actor Award at the Berlin Film Festival, film was an Oscar nominee here.

Jacob Two-Two Meets the Hooded Fang (1977-Canadian) C-80m. **½ D: Theodore J. Flicker. Stephen Rosenberg, Alex Karras, Guy L'Ecuyer, Joy Coghill, Earl Pennington, Claude Gail. Engaging fantasy for kids written by Mordecai Richler, about a boy who dreams he's sent to children's prison. Low-budget production values are unfortunate detriment.

Jacqueline (1956-British) C-92m. *** D: Roy Baker. John Gregson, Kathleen Ryan, Jacqueline Ryan, Noel Purcell, Cyril Cusack. Captivating drama of lovable little Irish girl and how she helps her tippler father find work. Lots of warmth.

Jacqueline Susann's Once Is Not Enough (1975) C-121m. BOMB D: Guy Green. Kirk Douglas, Alexis Smith, David Janssen, Deborah Raffin, George Hamilton, Melina Mercouri, Brenda Vaccaro. Trashy film based on Susann's trashy novel of jet-set intrigue, and a blossoming young woman (Raffin) with a father-fixation. Incurably stupid, and surprisingly dull. Vaccaro offers brightest moments as unabashed man-chaser.

Jacques Brel Is Alive and Well and Living in Paris (1975) C-98m. ** D: Denis Heroux. Elly Stone, Mort Shuman, Joe Masiell, Jacques Brel. Musical revue featuring 26 bittersweet songs on life, love, war and death by Belgian balladeer Jacques Brel. No plot, no dialogue. Based on 1968 stage revue. An American Film Theater Production.

Jade Mask, The (1945) 66m. D: Phil Rosen. Sidney Toler, Mantan Moreland, Edwin Luke, Janet Warren, Edith Evanson, Alan Bridge, Ralph Lewis. SEE: Charlie Chan series.

Jaguar (1956) 66m. *½ D: George Blair. Sabu, Chiquita, Barton Mac-Lane, Jonathan Hale, Mike Connors. Presence of former elephant-boy Sabu is only virtue of ridiculous programmer about mysterious murders on an oilfield.

Jaguar Lives! (1979) C-90m. *½ D: Ernest Pintoff. Joe Lewis, Christopher Lee, Donald Pleasence, Barbara Bach, Capucine, Joseph Wiseman, Woody Strode, John Huston. Karate champ Lewis is featured in this predictable action cheapie as a special agent sent to dispatch narcotics biggies in various world capitals. Top cast, but don't be fooled.

Jail Busters (1955) 61m. D: William Beaudine. Leo Gorcey, Huntz Hall, Percy Helton, Lyle Talbot, Fritz Feld, Barton MacLane. SEE: Bowery Boys series.

Jailhouse Rock (1957) 96m. *** D: Richard Thorpe. Elvis Presley, Judy Tyler, Vaughn Taylor, Dean Jones, Mickey Shaughnessy. Elvis learns to pick a guitar in the Big House, later becomes a surly rock star. Presley's best film captures the legend in all his nostril-flaring, pre-Army glory. Great Leiber-Stoller score.

Jalopy (1953) 62m. D: William Beaudine. Leo Gorcey, Huntz Hall, Bernard Gorcey, Robert Lowery, Murray Alper. SEE: Bowery Boys series.

Jam Session (1944) 77m. ** D: Charles Barton. Ann Miller, Jess Barker, Charles Brown, Eddie Kane, Louis Armstrong, Charlie Barnet Orchestra, Nan Wynn, Pied Pipers. Mild musical of showgirl Miller trying to crash Hollywood; notable for many musical guests doing enjoyable specialty numbers.

Jamaica Inn (1939-British) 98m. ** D: Alfred Hitchcock. Charles Laughton, Maureen O'Hara, Leslie Banks, Robert Newton, Emlyn Williams, Mervyn Johns. Stodgy Victorian costumer of cutthroat band headed by nobleman Laughton; O'Hara is lovely, but plodding Hitchcock film is disappointing.

Jamaica Run (1953) C-92m. ** D: Lewis R. Foster. Ray Milland, Arlene Dahl, Wendell Corey, Patric Knowles. Ray goes salvage-diving in the Caribbean for Dahl's nutty family. Unexciting production.

James at 15 (1977) C-100m. TVM D: Joseph Hardy. Lance Kerwin, Linden Chiles, Lynn Carlin, Melissa Sue Anderson, Kate Jackson, Kim Richards. Comedy-drama about the problems and pain of adolescence, with Kerwin, smitten with a high school cheerleader, faced with moving across the country with his parents. Arch family sitcom with standard plot twists. A series subsequently evolved. Average.

James Dean (1976) C-100m. TVM D: Robert Butler. Stephen McHattie, Michael Brandon, Dane Clark, Meg Foster, Candy Clark, Jayne Meadows. Dramatization of the memoirs of William Bast, Dean's roommate, from their meeting as acting students until Dean's death. McHattie is excellent in title role, Brandon is fine as writer Bast. Bast's script, though, is a bore. Average.

James Dean Story, The (1957) 82m. ** D: George W. George, Robert Altman. Narrated by Martin Gabel. Uninspired use of available material makes this a slow-moving documentary on life of 1950s movie star.

James Michener's Dynasty (1976) C-100m. TVM D: Lee Philips. Sarah Miles, Stacy Keach, Harris Yulin, Granville Van Dusen, Amy Irving, Harrison Ford. Ohio dirt farmers establish a powerful family business in the mid-19th century. Strong performances by Yulin, Miles and Keach as husband, wife and the brother-in-law for whom she abandons her family, but epic qualities are sacrificed to running time and the plot suffers. Average.

Jane Eyre (1944) 96m. *** D: Robert Stevenson. Orson Welles, Joan Fontaine, Margaret O'Brien, Peggy Ann Garner, John Sutton. Artistically successful if slow-moving version of Charlotte Brontë novel about orphan girl who grows up to become a governess in mysterious household. One of Elizabeth Taylor's early films.

Jane Eyre (1971) C-110m. TVM D: Delbert Mann. George C. Scott, Susannah York, Ian Bannen, Jack Hawkins, Rachel Kempson, Jean Marsh, Nyree Dawn Porter. Sumptuous Gothic settings and Scott's great performance highlight this pleasant if somewhat uninspired retelling of the Brontë classic. Above average.

Janie (1944) 106m. **½ D: Michael Curtiz. Joyce Reynolds, Edward Arnold, Ann Harding, Robert Benchley, Robert Hutton, Alan Hale, Hattie McDaniel. Naïve (now) but pleasant comedy about small-town girl falling in love with serviceman despite father's objections to love-hungry soldiers.

Janie Gets Married (1946) 89m. **½ D: Vincent Sherman. Joan Leslie, Robert Hutton, Edward Arnold, Ann Harding, Robert Benchley, Dorothy Malone. Pleasant follow-up to JANIE, with bright-eyed Leslie helping soldier-hubby Hutton readjust to civilian life.

Janis (1975) C-96m. *** D: Howard Alk, Seaton Findlay. Documentary on Janis Joplin was filmed with cooperation of her family, so it ignores the singer's darker side. OK within its limits, with a dozen or so songs performed.

Japanese War Bride (1952) 91m. **½ D: King Vidor. Don Taylor, Shirley Yamaguchi, Cameron Mitchell, Marie Windsor, Philip Ahn. Penetrating study of WW2 veterans who return to life in U.S.A. with Oriental brides.

Jason and the Argonauts (1963-British) C-104m. *** D: Don Chaffey. Todd Armstrong, Gary Raymond, Nancy Kovack, Honor Blackman, Nigel Green. Good special effects (by Ray Harryhausen) and colorful backgrounds in fable about Jason's search for golden fleece.

Jassy (1947-British) C-96m. **½ D: Bernard Knowles. Margaret Lockwood, Patricia Roc, Dennis Price, Dermot Walsh, Basil Sydney, Nora Swinburne. Brooding drama of gypsy girl accused of causing her husband's death; well-mounted 19th century yarn.

Java Head (1934-British) 70m. ** D: J. Walter Ruben. Anna May Wong, Elizabeth Allan, Edmund Gwenn, John Loder, Ralph Richardson, Herbert Lomas. Nothing-special drama about two sons given shipping business by aging father. One, of course, attempts to take over. Good cast in very uneven film.

Jaws (1975) C-124m. **** D: Steven Spielberg. Roy Scheider, Robert Shaw, Richard Dreyfuss, Lorraine Gary, Murray Hamilton, Carl Gottlieb. Smash hit put director Spielberg on the map, and rightly so: a rare case of a bubble-gum story (by Peter Benchley) scoring as a terrific movie. The story: New England shore community is terrorized by shark attacks; local cop (Scheider) icthyologist (Dreyfuss) and salty shark expert (Shaw) determine to kill the attacker. Hold onto your seats! John Williams' atmospheric music score won an Oscar.

Jaws 2 (1978) C-117m. **½ D: Jeannot Szwarc. Roy Scheider, Lorraine Gary, Murray Hamilton, Joseph Mascolo, Jeffrey Kramer, Collin Wilcox. Just when you thought it was safe to turn on your TV set again, here comes another gratuitous sequel. The shark scenes deliver the goods, but Robert Shaw and Richard Dreyfuss are sorely needed when the film is on land.

Jayhawkers, The (1959) C-100m. **½ D: Melvin Frank. Jeff Chandler, Fess Parker, Nicole Maurey, Henry Silva, Herbert Rudley. Turgid Western set in 1850s, with Chandler and Parker battling for power, Maurey the love interest.

Jazz Boat (1960-British) 90m. **½ D: Ken Hughes. Anthony Newley, Anne Aubrey, Lionel Jeffries, David Lodge, Bernie Winters, James Booth. Energetic caper of handyman Newley pretending to be a crook and then having to carry through, with dire results.

Jazz Singer, The (1927) 89m. **½ D: Alan Crosland. Al Jolson, May McAvoy, Warner Oland, Eugenie Besserer, Otto Lederer. Legendary first talkie is actually silent with several sound musical sequences. Story of Cantor Oland's son (Jolson) going into show business is creaky, but this movie milestone should be seen once. Songs: "Mammy," "Toot Toot Tootsie," etc. Look fast for Myrna Loy as a chorus girl.

Jazz Singer, The (1953) C-107m. *** D: Michael Curtiz. Danny Thomas, Peggy Lee, Mildred Dunnock, Eduard Franz. Well-done remake of famous first talkie of young man who dares to make it as singer rather than cantor. Score nominated for Oscar. Some big names in cast may make this one interesting.

Jealousy (1945) 71m. ** D: Gustav Machaty. John Loder, Nils Asther, Jane Randolph, Karen Morley. Obvious plot line of renowned writer being murdered and wrong person accused; well served by capable cast.

Jeanne Eagels (1957) 109m. **½ D: George Sidney. Kim Novak, Jeff Chandler, Agnes Moorehead, Gene Lockhart, Virginia Grey. Novak tries but can't rise to demands of portraying famed actress of 1920s. Chandler is her virile love interest.

Jennie Gerhardt (1933) 85m. *** D: Marion Gering. Sylvia Sidney, Donald Cook, Mary Astor, Edward Arnold, Louise Carver, Cora Sue Collins, H. B. Warner. Meticulously produced version of Theodore Dreiser saga of poor-girl Sidney finding kind benefactor Arnold, losing him, and living as Cook's back-street lover. Actors and elaborate production lend credibility to episodic soaper set at turn of the century.

Jennifer (1953) 73m. **½ D: Joel Newton. Ida Lupino, Howard Duff, Robert Nichols, Mary Shipp. Turgid programmer of Lupino working at eerie old mansion where she discovers a murder.

Jennifer (1978) C-90m. ** D: Brice Mack. Lisa Pelikan, Bert Convy, Nina Foch, Amy Johnston, John Gavin, Jeff Corey, Wesley Eure. Unusually good cast in blatant rip-off of CARRIE, with Pelikan as ostracized high-school girl whose powers include ability to unleash deadly snakes on her victims.

Jennifer: A Woman's Story (1979) C-100m. TVM D: Guy Green. Elizabeth Montgomery, Bradford Dillman, Scott Hylands, James Booth, John Beal, Robin Gammell. Wealthy ship tycoon's widow finds herself locked in battle with boardroom associates who are trying to wrest the business from her. Average.

Jennifer on My Mind (1971) C-90m. BOMB D: Noel Black. Michael Brandon, Tippy Walker, Lou Gilbert, Steve Vinovich, Peter Bonerz, Renee Taylor, Chuck McCann. Probably the worst of many 70's drug films released in the early 70's; rootless American drifter and rich American girl smoke grass in Venice, advance to hard drugs back home. Awful script is by Erich Segal.

Jenny (1970) C-88m. BOMB D: George Bloomfield. Marlo Thomas, Alan Alda, Marian Hailey, Elizabeth Wilson, Vincent Gardenia, Stephen Strimpell. Sappy soaper about filmmaker who marries pregnant girl in order to avoid the draft. Opening scene includes a clip from A PLACE IN THE SUN, which is best thing in film.

Jeopardy (1953) 69m. **½ D: John Sturges. Barbara Stanwyck, Barry Sullivan, Ralph Meeker, Lee Aaker. Taut but superficial account of Stanwyck trying to save husband from drowning.

Jeremiah Johnson (1972) C-107m. *** D: Sydney Pollack. Robert Redford, Will Geer, Stefan Gierasch, Allyn Ann McLerie, Charles Tyner, Josh Albee. Atmospheric chronicle of life of a mountain man, surviving wintry wilderness, Indians, rival trappers. Unfortunately, film doesn't know where to quit, rambling on to inconclusive ending. Geer is delightful as feisty mountain hermit.

Jeremy (1973) C-90m. *** D: Arthur Barron. Robby Benson, Glynnis O'-Connor, Len Bari, Leonard Cimino, Ned Wilson, Chris Bohn. Two shy teen-agers in New York meet, fall in love, then separate. Poignant and real; situations, characters, and atmosphere are memorable. Some scenes cut for TV, others added from cutting-room floor to build running time.

Jericho Mile, The (1979) C-100m. TVM D: Michael Mann. Peter Strauss, Roger E. Mosley, Brian Dennehy, Billy Green Bush, Ed Lauter, Beverly Todd. Folson Prison lifer works at becoming the world's fastest runner and aims for a spot on the Olympic team. Offbeat, gritty, and thoughtful. Above average.

Jerk, The (1979) C-104m. **½ D: Carl Reiner. Steve Martin, Bernadette Peters, Catlin Adams, Mabel King, Richard Ward, Dick Anthony Williams, Bill Macy, Jackie Mason. Martin's first starring feature is a hit-or-miss comedy about the misadventures of a terminally stupid young man. Some very funny moments, but after a while they're spread pretty thin.

Jesse James (1939) C-105m. *** D: Henry King. Tyrone Power, Henry Fonda, Nancy Kelly, Randolph Scott, Henry Hull, Brian Donlevy, Jane Darwell. Sprawling, glamorous Western with Power and Fonda as Jesse and Frank James; movie builds for audience acceptance that Jesse was misguided; sturdy presentation.

Jesse James Meets Frankenstein's Daughter (1966) C-88m. *½ D: William Beaudine. John Lupton, Estelita, Cal Bolder, Steven Geray, Jim Davis. Low-budget nonsense mixture of horror and Western genres, with title monster practicing weird experiments, conflicting with noted outlaw.

Jesse James vs. the Daltons (1954) C-65m. ** D: William Castle. Brett King, Barbara Lawrence, James Griffith, Bill Phipps, John Cliff. Bland shoot-out between alleged son of Jesse James and the other notorious outlaw gang.

Jesse James' Women (1954) C-83m. *½ D: Donald Barry. Don Barry, Jack Buetel, Peggie Castle, Lita

Baron. Romancing a variety of women leaves James little time for outlaw activities; cute premise doesn't work out.

Jessica (1962) C-112m. **½ D: Jean Negulesco. Angie Dickinson, Maurice Chevalier, Noel-Noel, Gabriele Ferzetti, Sylva Koscina, Agnes Moorehead. Dickinson is an Italian midwife who has men in her village lusting for her, with Chevalier as the local priest. Malarkey.

Jesus (1979) C-117m. **½ D: Peter Sykes, John Kirsh. Brian Deacon, Rivka Noiman, Yossef Shiloah, Niko Nitai, Gadi Roi, David Goldberg. Narrated by Alexander Scourby. Straightforward but unmemorable retelling of Jesus' life, produced by The Genesis Project and filmed in Israel.

Jesus Christ, Superstar (1973) C-103m. *** D: Norman Jewison. Ted Neeley, Carl Anderson, Yvonne Elliman, Barry Dennen, Joshua Mostel, Bob Bingham. From record album to Broadway show to motion picture—film retains the heavily influenced score, adds some interesting settings and visual trappings. It's not everyone's cup of religious experience, but certainly innovative.

Jesus Trip, The (1971) C-84m. ** D: Russ Mayberry. Tippy Walker, Robert Porter, Billy "Green" Bush, Frank Orsati, Robert Tessier, Allan Gibbs. Motorcycle gang kidnaps attractive young nun in film that isn't as bad as it sounds; cast is good.

Jet Attack (1958) 68m. BOMB D: Edward L. Cahn. John Agar, Audrey Totter, Gregory Walcott, James Dobson. Sloppy Korean War programmer about rescue of U.S. scientist caught behind North Korean lines.

Jet Over the Atlantic (1960) 95m. ** D: Byron Haskin. Guy Madison, Virginia Mayo, George Raft, Ilona Massey. Capable cast in clichéd situation of plane with engine trouble. Madison's the former air force pilot saving the day; predictable plot line.

Jet Pilot (1957) C-112m. ** D: Josef von Sternberg. John Wayne, Janet Leigh, Jay C. Flippen, Paul Fix, Richard Rober, Roland Winters, Hans Conried. One of Howard Hughes' movie curios, updating his HELLS ANGELS interest in aviation with cold war theme, as American pilot Wayne falls in love with Russian jet ace Leigh. Ridiculous, to say the least, though some of its humor seems to have been intentional. Completed in 1950, unreleased for seven years!

Jewel Robbery (1932) 70m. ******* D: William Dieterle. William Powell, Kay Francis, Hardie Albright, C. Henry Gordon, Helen Vinson, Herman Bing. Lubitsch-like bauble of noblewoman Francis falling in love with debonair burglar Powell during theft. Breathlessly paced, handsome comedy.

Jezebel (1938) 103m. *****½** D: William Wyler. Bette Davis, Henry Fonda, George Brent, Margaret Lindsay, Donald Crisp, Fay Bainter, Spring Byington, Richard Cromwell. Davis won her second Oscar as temptestuous Southern belle who goes too far to make fiancé Fonda jealous; Bainter also received Oscar as Davis' sympathetic aunt. Fine production, entire cast excellent.

Jigsaw (1949) 70m. ****** D: Fletcher Markle. Franchot Tone, Jean Wallace, Myron McCormick, Marc Lawrence, Betty Harper (Doe Avedon). Pedestrian caper of assistant D.A. solving murder, spiked by guest appearances of Marlene Dietrich, Henry Fonda, John Garfield, Burgess Meredith, Marsha Hunt. Retitled: GUN MOLL.

Jigsaw (1968) C-97m. ****½** D: James Goldstone. Harry Guardino, Bradford Dillman, Hope Lange, Pat Hingle, Diana Hyland, Victor Jory. Fast-paced, utterly confusing yarn about amnesiac Dillman trying to figure out his past and unravel murder caper he was involved in. Frantic editing and music don't help viewer; remake of MIRAGE.

Jigsaw (1971) C-100m. TVM D: William Graham. James Wainwright, Vera Miles, Richard Kiley, Andrew Duggan, Edmond O'Brien. Cop specializing in missing-persons cases discovers he's been lured into sophisticated cover-up scheme. Occasional tension, but should have been far better. Pilot to short-lived series; later retitled MAN ON THE MOVE. Average.

Jim Thorpe—All American (1951) 107m. ******* D: Michael Curtiz. Burt Lancaster, Charles Bickford, Steve Cochran, Phyllis Thaxter. Lancaster pushes hard to make clichéd script detailing life of famed athlete rise to some meaning.

Jimi Hendrix (1973) C-102m. ****½** No director credited. Documentary on life of noted black rock guitarist; good segments from various concerts, interviews with those who knew him well. Beware cuts.

Jimmy and Sally (1933) 68m. ****½** D: James Tinling. James Dunn, Claire Trevor, Harvey Stephens, Lya Lys, Jed Prouty. Go-getter Dunn lets his ambition cloud his devotion to Trevor in amiable little film of no consequence whatsoever.

Jimmy the Gent (1934) 67m. ****½** D: Michael Curtiz. James Cagney, Bette Davis, Alice White, Allen Jenkins, Philip Reed, Mayo Methot. Crooked businessman Cagney pretends to refine himself to impress Davis in this bouncy comedy.

Jinx Money (1948) 61m. D: William Beaudine. Leo Gorcey, Huntz Hall, Billy Benedict, David Gorcey, Bennie Bartlett, Sheldon Leonard, Donald MacBride, Wanda McKay, John Eldredge. SEE: Bowery Boys series.

Jitterbugs (1943) 74m. ****** D: Mal St. Clair. Stan Laurel, Oliver Hardy, Vivian Blaine, Robert Bailey, Douglas Fowley, Noel Madison. One of the team's better later efforts, with Blaine sharing the spotlight and doing quite nicely. Ollie's scene with Southern belle Lee Patrick is a gem.

Jivaro (1954) C-91m. ****** D: Edward Ludwig. Fernando Lamas, Rhonda Fleming, Brian Keith, Lon Chaney, Richard Denning. Cornball adventure in wild head-hunting country, with gold-hungry group seeking valuable ore.

Joan of Arc (1948) C-100m. ****½** D: Victor Fleming. Ingrid Bergman, Jose Ferrer, Francis L. Sullivan, J. Carrol Naish, Ward Bond. Bergman is staunchly sincere in this overlong, faithful adaptation of Maxwell Anderson's play. Not enough spectacle to balance talky sequences. Originally released theatrically at 145m.

Joan of Ozark (1942) 80m. ****** D: Joseph Santley. Judy Canova, Joe E. Brown, Eddie Foy, Jr., Jerome Cowan, Alexander Granach, Anne Jeffreys. Hillbilly Canova hunts down Nazi underground ring in U.S.

Joan of Paris (1942) 95m. *****½** D: Robert Stevenson. Michele Morgan, Paul Henreid, Thomas Mitchell, Laird Cregar, May Robson, Alexander Granach, Alan Ladd. Excellent WW2 tale of dedicated Morgan giving herself up so Henreid and fellow-pilots can return to Allied lines.

Joanna (1968-British) C-107m. ****½** D: Michael Sarne. Genevieve Waite, Christian Doermer, Calvin Lockhart, Donald Sutherland, Glenna Forster-

Jones. Flashy story of wide-eyed girl falling in with loose-living London crowd, growing up through heartbreak, conflict. Sutherland steals film in flamboyant role as frail, wealthy young man trying to enjoy life to fullest.

Joe (1970) C-107m. **½ D: John G. Avildsen. Peter Boyle, Dennis Patrick, K. Callan, Audrey Caire, Susan Sarandon, Patrick McDermott. Sleeper film brought Boyle to prominence as hardhat bigot who practices genteel blackmail on executive Patrick, who's murdered his daughter's hippie boyfriend. Overrated film owes much to Boyle's characterization, not to contrived plot. Cut for TV.

Joe Butterfly (1957) C-90m. **½ D: Jesse Hibbs. Audie Murphy, Burgess Meredith, George Nader, Keenan Wynn, Fred Clark. Another variation on TEAHOUSE OF THE AUGUST MOON, set in post-WW2 Japan. American soldiers at mercy of wily Jap Meredith to get needed supplies.

Joe Dakota (1957) C-79m. **½ D: Richard Bartlett, Jock Mahoney, Luana Patten, Charles McGraw, Lee Van Cleef. Folksy oater of Mahoney renewing a town's pride in itself.

Joe Hill (1971-Swedish) C-114m. *** D: Bo Widerberg. Thommy Berggren, Ania Schmidt, Kelvin Malave, Everl Anderson, Cathy Smith. Fabricated story of legendary labor leader has usual Widerberg matter-of-taste glossiness, but also some affecting scenes and pleasant performances. Joan Baez sings title song.

Joe Kidd (1972) C-88m. ** D: John Sturges. Clint Eastwood, Robert Duvall, John Saxon, Don Stroud, Stella Garcia, James Wainwright. Eastwood is hired to hunt down some Mexican-Americans by land baron Duvall in ordinary Western; nice photography and a rousing scene where Eastwood drives a train through a barroom.

Joe Louis Story, The (1953) 88m. ** D: Robert Gordon. Coley Wallace, Paul Stewart, Hilda Simms, James Edwards. Tame biography of famed boxer.

Joe Macbeth (1955-British) 90m. **½ D: Ken Hughes. Paul Douglas, Ruth Roman, Bonar Colleano, Gregoire Aslan, Sidney James. Interesting variation on Shakespeare's MACBETH, adapted to gangland life.

Joe Panther (1976) C-110m. *** D: Paul Krasny. Brian Keith, Ricardo

Montalban, Alan Feinstein, Cliff Osmond, A Martinez, Ray Tracey. Good family film about modern-day Seminole youth (Tracey) striving to make his way in the white man's world.

Joe Smith, American (1942) 63m. ** D: Richard Thorpe. Robert Young, Marsha Hunt, Harvey Stephens, Darryl Hickman. Dated WW2 morale-booster about kidnapped munitions worker Young who refuses to divulge secrets to Nazis. Paul Gallico story remade as THE BIG OPERATOR.

John and Mary (1969) C-92m. **½ D: Peter Yates. Dustin Hoffman, Mia Farrow, Michael Tolan, Sunny Griffin. John and Mary meet, make love, but don't know if the relationship should end right there. Innocuous, uncompelling trifle. Hoffman seems to be sleepwalking; audience may join him.

John F. Kennedy: Years of Lightning, Day of Drums (1966) C-85m. **** D: Bruce Herschensohn. Brilliant documentary, originally commissioned by the United States Intelligence Agency, on the life and times of John Kennedy.

John Goldfarb, Please Come Home (1964) C-96m. *½ D: J. Lee Thompson. Shirley MacLaine, Peter Ustinov, Richard Crenna, Jim Backus, Fred Clark. Trapped in desert kingdom, two Americans (pilot, gal reporter) conspire to help Arabian chief Ustinov's football team beat Notre Dame. Notre Dame University found this spoof so offensive it sued in court; the viewer has an easier alternative.

John Loves Mary (1949) 96m. **½ D: David Butler. Ronald Reagan, Patricia Neal, Jack Carson, Wayne Morris, Edward Arnold. Bright WW2 comedy of Reagan marrying British gal so she can come to U.S.; seems naive now. Neal's film debut.

John Meade's Woman (1937) 87m. ** D: Richard Wallace. Edward Arnold, Gail Patrick, Francine Larrimore, George Bancroft, Aileen Pringle, Sidney Blackmer. Arnold plays another Great American Businessman, marrying one girl to spite another. Idea backfires; so does film.

John O'Hara's Gibbsville SEE: Turning Point of Jim Malloy, The
John Paul Jones (1959) C-126m. **½ D: John Farrow. Robert Stack, Marisa Pavan, Charles Coburn, Erin

O'Brien, Macdonald Carey, Jean-Pierre Aumont, Peter Cushing, Bruce Cabot, Bette Davis. Empty spectacle of 18th-century American hero, with cameo by Davis as Russian empress.

Johnny Allegro (1949) 81m. **½ D: Ted Tetzlaff. Nina Foch, George Raft, George Macready, Will Geer, Seamy gangster melodrama of ex-racketeer Raft helping federal agents capture counterfeiting gang.

Johnny Angel (1945) 79m. *** D: Edwin L. Marin. George Raft, Claire Trevor, Signe Hasso, Lowell Gilmore, Hoagy Carmichael, Marvin Miller. Tough, well-done melodrama, with Raft cleaning up notorious mob, solving mystery of father's murder. Trevor lends good support.

Johnny Apollo (1940) 93m. *** D: Henry Hathaway. Tyrone Power, Lloyd Nolan, Dorothy Lamour, Edward Arnold, Charles Grapewin, Lionel Atwill, Marc Lawrence. Good-natured Power turns crook, resentful of father Arnold, white-collar thief. Good acting, especially by Lamour as girlfriend, improves film.

Johnny Belinda (1948) 103m. ***½ D: Jean Negulesco. Jane Wyman, Lew Ayres, Charles Bickford, Jan Sterling, Agnes Moorehead, Stephen McNally. Sensitively acted, atmospheric drama of young deaf-mute girl (Wyman) and doctor (Ayres) who works with her. Setting of provincial fishing-farming community vividly realized. Wyman won an Oscar for her fine performance.

Johnny Come Lately (1943) 97m. **½ D: William K. Howard. James Cagney, Grace George, Marjorie Main, Marjorie Lord, Hattie McDaniel, Ed McNamara. Tame but amusing Cagney vehicle, with Jimmy as wandering newspaperman who helps elderly editor George in small-town political battle.

Johnny Concho (1956) 84m. **½ D: Don McGuire. Frank Sinatra, Keenan Wynn, William Conrad, Phyllis Kirk, Wallace Ford, Dorothy Adams. Plodding Western with novelty of Sinatra as cowardly soul who must build courage for inevitable shoot-out.

Johnny Cool (1963) 101m. *** D: William Asher. Henry Silva, Elizabeth Montgomery, Sammy Davis, Jr., Wanda Hendrix, Telly Savalas, Jim Backus, Joey Bishop. Sadistic study of vicious gangster seeking revenge. Brutal account, realistically told.

Johnny Dark (1954) C-85m. **½ D: George Sherman. Tony Curtis, Piper Laurie, Don Taylor, Paul Kelly, Ilka Chase, Sidney Blackmer. Curtis is energetic as auto designer who enters big sports-car race.

Johnny Doesn't Live Here Any More (1944) 77m. **½ D: Joe May. Simone Simon, James Ellison, Minna Gombell, Alan Dinehart, Robert Mitchum, Grady Sutton. WW2 ancestor of THE APARTMENT, with Simon's flat becoming a madhouse, all ending happily with marriage. Retitled: AND SO THEY WERE MARRIED.

Johnny Eager (1941) 107m. *** D: Mervyn LeRoy. Robert Taylor, Lana Turner, Edward Arnold, Van Heflin, Robert Sterling, Patricia Dane, Glenda Farrell. Slick MGM melodrama with convoluted plot about sociology student (and daughter of D.A. Arnold) Turner falling in love with unscrupulous racketeer Taylor. Heflin won Best Supporting Actor Oscar for his performance as Taylor's alcoholic friend.

Johnny Got His Gun (1971) C-111m. ** D: Dalton Trumbo. Timothy Bottoms, Kathy Fields, Marsha Hunt, Jason Robards, Donald Sutherland, Diane Varsi. Morbid film version of Trumbo's novel about WW1 basket case has moving opening and climax, but everything in the middle is either talky, pretentious, or amateurish. Opening good-bye sequence includes nudity, and may not make it to TV.

Johnny Guitar (1954) C-110m. ***½ D: Nicholas Ray. Joan Crawford, Sterling Hayden, Scott Brady, Mercedes McCambridge, Ward Bond, Ben Cooper, Ernest Borgnine, John Carradine. The screen's great kinky western, a memorable confrontation between saloonkeeper Crawford and righteous hellion McCambridge, who wants her run out of town and/or hanged. Simply fascinating, with symbolism rampant throughout.

Johnny Hamlet (1972-U.S.-Italian) C-91m. ** D: Enzo G. Castellari. Chip Corman, Gilbert Roland, Horst Frank. Southerner returns home to Texas, gets involved in robbery, murder, and torture in this typical oater.

Johnny Holiday (1949) 92m. *** D: Willis Goldbeck. William Bendix, Allen Martin, Jr., Stanley Clements,

Jack Hagen. Remarkably sincere study of juvenile delinquent torn between friends from dishonest past and those trying to help him at reform farm.

Johnny in the Clouds (1945-British) 87m. ***½ D: Anthony Asquith. Michael Redgrave, John Mills, Rosamund John, Douglass Montgomery, Renee Asherson, Joyce Carey, Stanley Holloway. Excellent British wartime drama of young man who must choose between love and devotion to military service; fine cast, script, production. Original title: THE WAY TO THE STARS.

Johnny Nobody (1961-British) 88m. *** D: Nigel Patrick. Nigel Patrick, Yvonne Mitchell, Aldo Ray, William Bendix, Cyril Cusack. Irish priest suspects murder when drunken author is killed. Unusual plot twists with religious overtones. Neat, well-made little thriller.

Johnny O'Clock (1947) 95m. **½ D: Robert Rossen. Dick Powell, Evelyn Keyes, Lee J. Cobb, Ellen Drew, Nina Foch. Cast and director make script about high-class gambler in trouble with the law seem better than it is; Powell is fine in lead role.

Johnny One Eye (1950) 78m. ** D: Robert Florey. Pat O'Brien, Wayne Morris, Dolores Moran, Gayle Reed. Schmaltzy Damon Runyon yarn of O'Brien, a gangster with proverbial heart of gold on the lam.

Johnny Reno (1966) C-83m. BOMB D: R.G. Springsteen. Dana Andrews, Jane Russell, Lon Chaney, John Agar, Lyle Bettger, Tom Drake, Richard Arlen, Robert Lowery. Laughably clichéd Western has Marshal Andrews trying to save accused killer from lynching. Only for buffs who want to play "spot the star."

Johnny Rocco (1958) 84m. ** D: Paul Landres. Richard Eyer, Stephen McNally, Coleen Gray, Russ Conway. Gangster's son (Eyer) is focal point of gangland hunt because he witnessed a killing; OK drama.

Johnny Stool Pigeon (1949) 76m. **½ D: William Castle. Howard Duff, Shelley Winters, Dan Duryea, Anthony Curtis. Turgid drama of convict being sprung from prison so he can lead federal agents to former gang members.

Johnny Tiger (1966) C-102m. **½ D: Paul Wendkos. Robert Taylor, Geraldine Brooks, Chad Everett,

Brenda Scott. Set in Florida, tame tale of teacher Taylor, doctor Brooks, and half-breed Seminole Everett trying to come to conclusions about Indians' role in modern world.

Johnny Tremain (1957) C-80m. *** D: Robert Stevenson. Hal Stalmaster, Luana Patten, Jeff York, Sebastian Cabot, Dick Beymer, Walter Sande. Excellent Disney film for young people, from Esther Forbes' novel about a young boy who gets involved in the Revolutionary War; sprinkles fiction with fact to bring history to life.

Johnny Trouble (1957) 80m. **½ D: John H. Auer. Ethel Barrymore (her final performance), Cecil Kellaway, Carolyn Jones, Stuart Whitman. Tender story of elderly woman convinced that long-missing son will return and that he wasn't a bad boy. Remake of SOMEONE TO REMEMBER (1943).

Johnny, We Hardly Knew Ye (1977) C-100m. TVM D: Gilbert Cates. Paul Rudd, Kevin Conway, Burgess Meredith, William Prince, Richard Venture, Shirley Rich, Joseph Bova. Well-acted account of John F. Kennedy's first try for public office, based on 1972 best-seller. Rudd tries but lacks JFK's charisma; Meredith's charm makes up for it as "Honey Fitz" Fitzgerald. Average.

Johnny Yuma (1966-Spanish-Italian) C-99m. ** D: Romolo Guerrieri. Mark Damon, Lawrence Dobkin, Rosalba Neri, Louis Vanner. Blood-drenched story of man fighting for his inheritance. Much of the gore is bound to be cut for TV.

Johnstown Flood, The (1926) 70m. **½ D: Irving Cummings. George O'Brien, Florence Gilbert, Janet Gaynor, Anders Randolph. Silent-era "disaster film" and no worse than a lot of newer ones; compactly told, with good special effects for that time.

Joker Is Wild, The (1957) 123m. *** D: Charles Vidor. Frank Sinatra, Mitzi Gaynor, Jeanne Crain, Eddie Albert, Beverly Garland, Jackie Coogan. Sinatra is fine in biography of nightclub performer Joe E. Lewis, with Crain and Gaynor diverting as his two loves. Song "All The Way" won an Oscar.

Jokers, The (1966-British) C-94m. *** D: Michael Winner. Michael Crawford, Oliver Reed, Gabriella Licudi, Harry Andrews, James Donald, Daniel Massey. Droll satire on the

Establishment with Reed and Crawford two brothers from upper classes, putting everyone on and carrying out perfect caper; ironic results.

Jolly Bad Fellow, A (1964-British) 94m. ** D: Don Chaffey. Leo McKern, Janet Munro, Maxine Audley, Duncan MacRae. Peculiar yarn of college professor who plays God by trying to kill those people whom he feels are evil parasites; strange blend of drama-satire. Retitled: THEY ALL DIED LAUGHING.

Jolson Sings Again (1949) C-96m. ** D: Henry Levin. Larry Parks, Barbara Hale, William Demarest, Ludwig Donath. Attempt to continue THE JOLSON STORY is pointless, especially when Parks (playing Jolson) meets Parks (playing Parks). Jolson standards are still good to hear.

Jolson Story, The (1946) C-128m. ***½ D: Alfred E. Green. Larry Parks, Evelyn Keyes, William Demarest, Bill Goodwin, Ludwig Donath. Smooth biography of all-time great Al Jolson, with Parks giving his all in story of brash vaudeville performer's rise in the show biz world. Songs: "Swanee," "April Showers," "Mammy," etc. dubbed by Jolson.

Jonathan Livingston Seagull (1973) C-120m. **½ D: Hall Bartlett. Unique film based on Richard Bach's best-seller about an existential seagull. Superb photography allows us to take bird's point of view as he forsakes his flock to explore wonders of flying. Dialogue doesn't work nearly as well, nor does Neil Diamond's overbearing score.

Jordan Chance, The (1978) C-100m. TVM D: Jules Irving. Raymond Burr, Ted Shackelford, James Canning, Stella Stevens, John McIntire, Peter Haskell. Prominent attorney (and one-time con) heads foundation to help those wrongly accused and unjustly convicted in this pilot to another lawyer series for Burr. Average.

Jory (1972) C-96m. ** D: Jorge Fons. John Marley, B. J. Thomas, Robby Benson, Brad Dexter, Patricia Aspillaga. Familiar Western about 15-year-old who becomes a man when father and close friends are senselessly murdered. Filmed in Mexico.

Joseph and His Brethren (1962) C-103m. ** D: Irving Rapper. Marietto, Geoffrey Horne, Belinda Lee, Finlay Currie, Antonio Segurini,

Charles Borromel, Carlo Giustini. Juvenile biblical tale, lavishly produced but empty-headed.

Joseph Andrews (1977-British) C-103m. ** D: Tony Richardson. Ann Margret, Peter Firth, Michael Hordern, Beryl Reid, Jim Dale, Natalie Ogle, Peter Bull. Director Richardson returns to Henry Fielding but the TOM JONES lightning fails to strike again; well photographed farce based on concealed identities is dull throughout.

Josette (1938) 73m. **½ D: Allan Dwan. Don Ameche, Simone Simon, Robert Young, Bert Lahr, Joan Davis, Tala Birell, Paul Hurst, William Collier, Sr. Above-par musicomedy of mistaken identity, with sturdy cast and such forgettable songs as "May I Drop A Petal In Your Glass of Wine."

Journey, The (1959) C-125m. *** D: Anatole Litvak. Deborah Kerr, Yul Brynner, Jason Robards, Jr., Robert Morley, E. G. Marshall, Anne Jackson, Ronny Howard, Kurt Kasznar, Anouk Aimee. Heady melodrama set in 1956 Budapest, with assorted types seeking to leave. Offbeat romance between Kerr and Communist officer Brynner.

Journey Back to Oz (1974) C-90m. **½ D: Hal Sutherland. Voices of Liza Minnelli, Milton Berle, Margaret Hamilton, Jack E. Leonard, Paul Lynde, Ethel Merman, Mickey Rooney, Rise Stevens, Danny Thomas, Mel Blanc. Long-delayed (made in 1964) animated sequel to classic "Wizard of Oz," without the Wizard. Okay for the kids; main interest for grownups is familiar voices, and Minnelli doing her late mother's role.

Journey for Margaret (1942) 81m. *** D: W. S. Van Dyke II. Robert Young, Laraine Day, Fay Bainter, Nigel Bruce, Margaret O'Brien, William Severn. Stirring WW2 drama of children left homeless by British bombing. O'Brien is very appealing scene-stealer, Young her adopted father.

Journey from Darkness (1975) C-100m. TVM D: James Goldstone. Marc Singer, Kay Lenz, Wendell Burton, William Windom, Joseph Campanella, Jack Warden, Dorothy Tristan. Fact-based drama about blind college student's struggle to get into medical school. Sincere work by the cast keeps this tale of courage on track. Average.

Journey Into Fear (1942) 69m. ***
D: Norman Foster. Orson Welles, Joseph Cotten, Dolores Del Rio, Ruth Warrick, Agnes Moorehead. Often baffling WW2 spy drama started by Welles, taken out of his hands. Much of tale of smuggling munitions into Turkey still exciting.

Journey Into Fear (1975-Canadian) C-103m. ** D: Daniel Mann. Sam Waterston, Zero Mostel, Yvette Mimieux, Scott Marlowe, Ian McShane, Joseph Wiseman, Shelley Winters, Stanley Holloway, Donald Pleasence, Vincent Price. Muddled remake of 1942 film, shot throughout Europe, with Waterston as research geologist who becomes involved in international intrigue.

Journey Into Light (1951) 87m. **½ D: Stuart Heisler. Sterling Hayden, Viveca Lindfors, Thomas Mitchell, H. B. Warner, Ludwig Donath. Thought-provoking theme, poorly paced; Hayden is clergyman who finds his belief in God again with aid of blind Lindfors.

Journey of Robert F. Kennedy SEE: Unfinished Journey of Robert F. Kennedy, The

Journey Through Rosebud (1972) C-93m. **½ D: Tom Gries. Robert Forster, Kristoffer Tabori, Victoria Racimo, Eddie Little Sky, Roy Jenson, Wright King. Sympathetic but dully directed drama about the modern-day Indian's plight. Location footage in South Dakota helps.

Journey to Freedom (1957) 60m. *½ D: Robert C. Dertano. Jacques Scott, Genevieve Aumont, Morgan Lane, Fred Kohler, Don Marlowe. Lukewarm spy hunt, with Communist agents tracking down pro-American refugee now in the U.S.

Journey to Shiloh (1968) C-101m. *½ D: William Hale. James Caan, Michael Sarrazin, Brenda Scott, Don Stroud, Paul Petersen. Limp Civil War programmer about young Texans anxious to engage in battle. Veterans Rex Ingram, John Doucette, and Noah Beery are lost in this jumble.

Journey to the Center of the Earth (1959) C-132m. *** D: Henry Levin. James Mason, Pat Boone, Arlene Dahl, Diane Baker, Thayer David, Alan Napier. Entertaining, old-fashioned fantasy-adventure, from Jules Verne's story of daring expedition headed by Mason; long in telling, with silly digressions, but generally fun.

Journey to the Center of Time (1967) C-82m. *½ D: D. L. Hewitt. Scott Brady, Gigi Perreau, Anthony Eisley, Abraham Sofaer. Time-warp troubles as travelers get stuck in a few tight places.

Journey to the Far Side of the Sun (1969-British) C-99m. *** D: Robert Parrish. Roy Thinnes, Lynn Loring, Herbert Lom, Patrick Wymark. Entertaining exploration of a planet that is hidden behind the sun. The ending makes the movie. Originally titled DOPPELGANGER.

Journey to the Lost City (1960-German) C-94m. **½ D: Fritz Lang. Debra Paget, Paul Christian (a/k/a Hubschmid), Walter Reyer, Claus Holm, Sabina Bettmann. On-location filming in India enhances story of Britisher's romance with native dancing girl, but it's slow moving most of the way.

Journey to the Seventh Planet (1962) C-83m. ** D: Sidney Pink. John Agar, Greta Thyssen, Ann Smyrner, Mimi Heinrich, Carl Ottosen. Passable sci-fi of exploratory trip to foreign planet and attempt to destroy alien forces there.

Journey Together (1946-British) 80m. ** D: John Boulting. Richard Attenborough, Jack Watling, Edward G. Robinson, Bessie Love. More of a documentary than a feature story, this film retraces lives of U.S. fliers in England during WW2.

Joy House (1964-French) 98m. **½ D: René Clement. Jane Fonda, Alain Delon, Lola Albright, Sorrell Booke. Living on his looks, a playboy on the run seeks refuge in gloomy French mansion run by two American women. Fate and quicker wits than his control this brooding tale of irony. Original title: LOVE CAGE.

Joy in the Morning (1965) C-103m. ** D: Alex Segal. Richard Chamberlain, Yvette Mimieux, Arthur Kennedy, Sidney Blackmer. Betty Smith's gentle novel of struggling law student and his marital problems becomes mild vehicle for Chamberlain, who crusades for human dignity amid stereotypes of a college town.

Joy of Living (1938) 90m. *** D: Tay Garnett. Irene Dunne, Douglas Fairbanks, Jr., Alice Brady, Guy Kibbee, Jean Dixon, Eric Blore, Lucille Ball. Delightful screwball musicomedy with gay-blade Fairbanks wooing singing star Dunne.

Joy of Loving SEE: School for Love

Joy Ride (1958) 60m. *½ D: Edward Bernds. Rad Fulton, Ann Doran, Regis Toomey, Nicholas King. Minor account of middle-aged man trying to reform hot-rod gang members; occasionally bristling.

Joyride (1977) C-92m. ** D: Joseph Ruben. Desi Arnaz, Jr., Robert Carradine, Melanie Griffith, Anne Lockhart, Tom Ligon, Cliff Lenz. Meandering tale of two young-and-footloose couples on the road to Alaska looking for adventure but drifting into crime. Four show-biz offspring play the leads: the sons of Desi Arnaz and John Carradine, the daughters of Tippi Hedren and June Lockhart.

Juarez (1939) 132m. *** D: William Dieterle. Paul Muni, Bette Davis, Brian Aherne, Claude Rains, John Garfield, Gale Sondergaard, Donald Crisp, Gilbert Roland, Louis Calhern, Grant Mitchell. Interesting biography of Mexican leader (Muni), with unforgettable performance by Rains as Napoleon III; also notable is Garfield's offbeat casting as Mexican Gen. Diaz. Elaborately done, but never as inspiring as it's intended to be.

Jubal (1956) C-101m. **½ D: Delmer Daves. Glenn Ford, Ernest Borgnine, Rod Steiger, Valerie French, Felicia Farr, Noah Beery, Jr. Smoldering Western involving tense interaction on Borgnine's ranch; cast gives appropriately brooding performances.

Jubilee Trail (1954) C-103m. **½ D: Joseph Kane. Vera Ralston, Joan Leslie, Forrest Tucker, John Russell, Ray Middleton, Pat O'Brien. Expansive Republic Western vehicle for Ralston as heart-of-gold chanteuse sorting out rancher's life in old California.

Judge, The (1949) 69m. *½ D: Elmer Clifton. Milburn Stone, Katherine DeMille, Paul Guilfoyle, Jonathan Hale, Norman Budd. Cheapie flick vaguely detailing man's moral disintegration from respected attorney to fugitive criminal.

Judge and Jake Wyler, The (1972) C-100m. TVM D: David Lowell Rich. Bette Davis, Doug McClure, Eric Braeden, James McEachin, Kent Smith, Joan Van Ark. Tolerable whodunit with sense of humor. Eccentric judge (Davis) takes on parolee as detective partner in new agency investigating suspicious death of businessman. For TV, good banter, convincing situations. Above average.

Judge Dee and the Monastery Murder (1974) C-100m. TVM D: Jeremy Kagan. Khigh Dhiegh, Mako, Soon-Taik Oh, Miiko Taka, Irene Tsu, James Hong, Keye Luke. Murder mystery with a definite twist: the detective is a seventh century Chinese sleuth. Based on Robert Van Gulick's Judge Dee mysteries; decidedly offbeat and lavishly made. Above average.

Judge Hardy & Son (1939) 87m. D: George B. Seitz. Lewis Stone, Mickey Rooney, Cecilia Parker, Fay Holden, Sara Haden, Ann Rutherford, June Preisser, Maria Ouspenskaya, Henry Hull, Martha O'Driscoll. SEE: Andy Hardy series.

Judge Hardy's Children (1938) 78m. D: George B. Seitz. Lewis Stone, Mickey Rooney, Cecilia Parker, Fay Holden, Betty Ross Clark, Ann Rutherford, Robert Whitney, Ruth Hussey. SEE: Andy Hardy series.

Judge Horton and the Scottsboro Boys (1976) C-100m. TVM D: Fielder Cook. Arthur Hill, Vera Miles, Lewis J. Stadlen, Ken Kercheval, Ellen Barber, Susan Lederer, Tom Ligon. Excellent courtroom-based drama detailing 1931 rape trial of nine blacks and the embattled Southern judge who presided over the proceedings. Hill is the backbone of virtue as the courageous judge. Above average.

Judge Priest (1934) 80m. ***½ D: John Ford. Will Rogers, Tom Brown, Anita Louise, Henry B. Walthall, Stepin Fetchit, Hattie McDaniel. Exceptional slice of Americana with Rogers as commonsensical yet controversial judge in small town; full of warm and funny character vignettes. Ford remade it in 1953 as THE SUN SHINES BRIGHT.

Judge Steps Out, The (1949) 91m. **½ D: Boris Ingster. Alexander Knox, Ann Sothern, George Tobias, Sharyn Moffett. Mild froth as prim judge Knox finds refuge in being short-order cook on days off from bench.

Judgment at Nuremberg (1961) 178m. **** D: Stanley Kramer. Spencer Tracy, Burt Lancaster, Richard Widmark, Marlene Dietrich, Judy Garland, Maximilian Schell, Montgomery Clift, William Shatner. Superior production revolving around U.S. judge Tracy presiding over German war-criminal trials. Schell won Oscar as defense attorney. Fine performances by Dietrich as widow of German officer, Garland as hausfrau, Clift as unbalanced war camp victim.

Judith (1966) **C-109m. BOMB** D: Daniel Mann. Sophia Loren, Peter Finch, Jack Hawkins, Hans Verner, Zharira Charifai. Austrian Jewess Loren survives prison camp with makeup intact, comes to Israel in 1948 to locate Nazi husband who betrayed her. Film is both dull and unbelievable, a bad combination.

Juggernaut (1974-British) **C-109m.** *** D: Richard Lester. Richard Harris, Omar Sharif, David Hemmings, Anthony Hopkins, Shirley Knight, Ian Holm, Roy Kinnear. Surprisingly effective thriller about bomb threat on luxury ocean liner, and demolition experts' attempts to avoid disaster. Harris is first-rate and so is Lester's direction of a familiar formula story.

Juggler, The (1953) **86m.** **½ D: Edward Dmytryk. Kirk Douglas, Milly Vitale, Paul Stewart, Alf Kjellin. Sentimental account of Jewish refugee Douglas going to Israel to rebuild his life, overcoming bitterness from life in a concentration camp.

Juke Box Rhythm (1959) **81m.** *½ D: Arthur Driefuss. Jo Morrow, Jack Jones, Brian Donlevy, George Jessel, Hans Conried, Karin Booth, Marjorie Reynolds, Fritz Feld. Minor songfest musical worthwhile only for veteran cast and young Jones on his way up.

Juke Girl (1942) **90m.** **½ D: Curtis Bernhardt. Ann Sheridan, Ronald Reagan, Richard Whorf, Gene Lockhart, Faye Emerson, George Tobias. Saga of fruit-workers' troubles in Florida never really hits the mark, but Sheridan and Reagan are good as laborers who get involved in murder.

Jules and Jim (1961-French) **104m.** **** D: Francois Truffaut. Jeanne Moreau, Oskar Werner, Henri Serre, Marie Dubois, Vanna Urbino. Truffaut's memorable tale of three people in love, and how the years affect their interrelationships. A film of rare beauty and charm.

Julia (1977) **C-118m.** **** D: Fred Zinnemann. Jane Fonda, Vanessa Redgrave, Jason Robards, Maximilian Schell, Hal Holbrook, Rosemary Murphy, Meryl Streep, Lisa Pelikan, Cathleen Nesbitt. Fonda plays Lillian Hellman in adaptation of author's story in *Pentimento* about her exuberant, unusual friend Julia, and how she drew Hellman into involvement with European resistance movement in 1930s. Fine storytelling in beautifully crafted film; Robards, screenwriter Alvin Sargent, and radiant Redgrave won Oscars.

Julia Misbehaves (1948) **99m.** *** D: Jack Conway. Greer Garson, Walter Pidgeon, Peter Lawford, Elizabeth Taylor, Cesar Romero, Mary Boland, Nigel Bruce. Bouncy account of showgal Garson returning to dignified husband Pidgeon when daughter Taylor is about to marry; Romero is fun as bragging acrobat. Stars seem right at home with slapstick situations.

Julie (1956) **99m.** **½ D: Andrew L. Stone. Doris Day, Louis Jourdan, Barry Sullivan, Frank Lovejoy, Mae Marsh. Shrill melodrama of Day being chased by psychopathic husband who murdered his first spouse; tense till preposterous climax.

Juliet of the Spirits (1965-Italian) **C-148m.** *** D: Federico Fellini. Giulietta Masina, Sandra Milo, Mario Pisu, Valentina Cortese, Lou Gilbert, Sylva Koscina. Surrealistic fantasy triggered by wife's fears that her well-to-do husband is cheating on her. A film requiring viewer to delve into woman's psyche via a rash of symbolism; counterbalanced with rich visual delights.

Julietta (1957-French) **96m.** **½ D: Marc Chamarat. Jean Marais, Jeanne Moreau, Dany Robin, Denise Grey. Frilly comedy with sturdy cast. Heroine journeys to marry a prince, misses her train and dallies with handsome lawyer.

Julius Caesar (1953) **120m.** ***½ D: Joseph L. Mankiewicz. Marlon Brando, James Mason, John Gielgud, Louis Calhern, Edmond O'Brien, Greer Garson, Deborah Kerr. Superior adaptation of William Shakespeare's play of political power and honor in ancient Rome, lavishly produced with excellent cast.

Julius Caesar (1971) **C-117m.** **½ D: Stuart Burge. Charlton Heston, Jason Robards, John Gielgud, Richard Johnson, Richard Vaughn, Richard Chamberlain, Diana Rigg, Jill Bennett, Christopher Lee. Technically ragged, but acceptable version of Shakespeare play, negated somewhat by Robards' zombie-like portrayal of

Brutus. The 1953 Mankiewicz version is much better.

Jumbo SEE: **Billy Rose's Jumbo**

Jump Into Hell (1955) 93m. **½ D: David Butler. Jacques Sernas, Kurt Kasznar, Peter Van Eyck, Pat Blake. Neatly paced actioner of paratroopers involved in Indochina war.

Jumping Jacks (1952) 96m. **½ D: Norman Taurog. Dean Martin, Jerry Lewis, Mona Freeman, Don DeFore, Robert Strauss. Daffy duo has good opportunity for plenty of sight gags when they join military paratroop squad.

June Bride (1948) 97m. *** D: Bretaigne Windust. Bette Davis, Robert Montgomery, Fay Bainter, Tom Tully, Barbara Bates, Jerome Cowan. Flippant comedy of magazine writers Davis and Montgomery inspired by feature story they are doing on June brides.

Jungle, The (1952) 74m. *½ D: William Berke. Rod Cameron, Cesar Romero, Marie Windsor, Sulchana. Low-grade chiller with too many backlot sets and stock shots; story centers on journey into India jungle, prehistoric monsters romping about.

Jungle Book, The (1942) C-109m. *** D: Zoltan Korda. Sabu, Joseph Calleia, John Qualen, Frank Puglia, Rosemary DeCamp. Colorful Kipling fantasy of boy (Sabu) raised by wolves. Exciting family fare, showing great imagination.

Jungle Captive (1945) 63m. BOMB D: Harold Young. Otto Kruger, Amelita Ward, Phil Brown, Vicky Lane, Jerome Cowan, Rondo Hatton. Sloppy Universal quickie dealing with mad scientist's attempt to transform "ape woman" into beautiful girl.

Jungle Cat (1960) C-70m. **½ D: James Algar. Narrated by Winston Hibler. One of Disney's weaker True-Life Adventures suffers from script and presentation, not raw material: wildlife footage of the title character, a jaguar, is excellent.

Jungle Drums of Africa SEE: **U-238 and the Witch Doctor**

Jungle Fighters SEE: **Long, the Short and the Tall, The**

Jungle Gents (1954) 64m. D: Edward Bernds, Austen Jewell. Leo Gorcey, Huntz Hall, Laurette Luez, Bernard Gorcey, David Condon. SEE: **Bowery Boys** series.

Jungle Girl SEE: **Bomba and the Jungle Girl**

Jungle Goddess (1948) 65m. *½ D: Lewis D. Collins. Ralph Byrd, George Reeves, Wanda McKay, Armida. Very low-budget swamp saga is good only for laughs.

Jungle Gold (1944) 100m. ** D: Spencer Bennet, Wallace Grissell. Allan Lane, Linda Stirling, Duncan Renaldo, George J. Lewis. Republic cliffhanger vehicle for the Queen of the serials. Stirling (Tiger Woman) romps through innumerable adventures to prevent wrong parties from uncovering gold treasure. Re-edited movie serial: THE TIGER WOMAN, reissued under title PERILS OF THE DARKEST JUNGLE.

Jungle Jim When athletic Johnny Weissmuller left the Tarzan series after sixteen years in the role, enterprising producer Sam Katzman proposed a new series that would enable the more mature but still rugged star to cavort in familiar surroundings. It was Jungle Jim, presold to an anxious audience via a successful comic strip and radio show. One critic accurately summed it up as "Tarzan with clothes on." The series was sure-fire and performed well at the box office for seven years, despite a conspicuous absence of commendation by the critics. From the first film, JUNGLE JIM, to the last, CANNIBAL ATTACK, the series was noted for its incredible plots and rousing action scenes, aimed primarily at juvenile audiences. Most efforts had Jungle Jim helping some Columbia Pictures heroine in distress (a lady scientist seeking a rare drug, a WAC captain lost in the jungle, etc.) and getting tangled up with hostile natives, voodoo curses, and nefarious villains (often all three at once). In the last three films of the series (JUNGLE MOON MEN, DEVIL GODDESS, CANNIBAL ATTACK) the name Jungle Jim was dropped and Weissmuller played himself, but the format remained the same, with Johnny's ever-faithful chimpanzee friend Timba at his side. Perhaps the highlight of the series was CAPTIVE GIRL, an average entry which had the distinction of Buster Crabbe, whose career paralleled Weissmuller's in many ways, as the villain.

Jungle Jim (1948) 73m. D: William Berke. Johnny Weissmuller, Virginia Grey, George Reeves, Lita Baron.

Jungle Jim in the Forbidden Land

(1952) 65m. D: Lew Landers. Johnny Weissmuller, Angela Greene, Jean Willes, William Fawcett.

Jungle Man-Eaters (1954) 68m. D: Lee Sholem. Johnny Weissmuller, Karin Booth, Richard Stapley, Bernard Hamilton. SEE: **Jungle Jim** series.

Jungle Manhunt (1951) 66m. D: Lew Landers. Johnny Weissmuller, Bob Waterfield, Sheila Ryan, Rick Vallin, Lyle Talbot. SEE: **Jungle Jim** series.

Jungle Moon Men (1955) 70m. D: Charles S. Gould. Johnny Weissmuller, Jean Byron, Helene Stanton, Myron Healey. SEE: **Jungle Jim** series.

Jungle Princess, The (1936) 85m. *** D: William Thiele. Dorothy Lamour, Ray Milland, Akim Tamiroff, Lynne Overman, Molly Lamont, Mala, Hugh Buckler. Lamour's first sarong film is quite unpretentious and pleasant; Milland is explorer who brings her back to civilization.

Jungle Woman (1944) 54m. *½ D: Reginald LeBorg. Acquanetta, Evelyn Ankers, J. Carrol Naish, Samuel S. Hinds. Silly horror quickie about transformation of ape into native woman.

Junior Bonner (1972) C-103m. ***½ D: Sam Peckinpah. Steve McQueen, Robert Preston, Ida Lupino, Ben Johnson, Joe Don Baker, Barbara Leigh, Mary Murphy. Totally captivating rodeo comedy-drama as an aging McQueen returns to his home and family to take part in a local contest. Peckinpah's most gentle film is full of natural performances, particularly by Preston and Lupino as McQueen's estranged parents.

Junior Miss (1945) 94m. **½ D: George Seaton. Peggy Ann Garner, Allyn Joslyn, Michael Dunne, Faye Marlowe, Mona Freeman, Sylvia Field, Barbara Whiting. Naive but entertaining comedy of teen-ager Garner and harried father Joslyn, based on Broadway play.

Jupiter's Darling (1955) C-96m. **½ D: George Sidney. Esther Williams, Howard Keel, George Sanders, Marge and Gower Champion, Norma Varden. Lavish musical of Robert Sherwood's ROAD TO ROME, which bogs down in tedium: Williams is temptress who dallies with Hannibal (Keel) to prevent attack on Rome.

Jury of One (1974-French-Italian) C-97m. ** D: Andre Cayatte. Sophia Loren, Jean Gabin, Henri Garcin, Julien Bertheau, Michel Albertini.

Plodding melodrama about a woman who goes to outrageous extremes to protect her son, on trial for murder and rape. Gabin plays the judge. Also known as THE VERDICT.

Just a Little Inconvenience (1977) C-100m. TVM D: Theodore J. Flicker. Lee Majors, James Stacy, Barbara Hershey, Charles Cioffi, Jim Davis. Vietnam veteran Majors attempts to rehabilitate his best friend who lost an arm and a leg during the war. Actor Stacy delivers an inspirational portrayal in film close to the heart of producer Majors. The script, though, is unmoving. Average.

Just Across the Street (1952) 78m. ** D: Joseph Pevney. Ann Sheridan, John Lund, Cecil Kellaway, Natalie Schafer, Harvey Lembeck. Mild shenanigans with working-gal Sheridan being mistaken for wealthy estate owner.

Just an Old Sweet Song (1976) C-78m. TVM D: Robert Ellis Miller. Cicely Tyson, Robert Hooks, Kevin Hooks, Eric Hooks, Beah Richards, Lincoln Kilpatrick, Edward Binns, Minnie Gentry. Melvin Van Peebles' contemporary drama about a black family from Detroit whose two-week vacation in the South changes their lives. Lovingly acted family film. Above average.

Just Around the Corner (1938) 70m. ** D: Irving Cummings. Shirley Temple, Joan Davis, Charles Farrell, Amanda Duff, Bill Robinson, Bert Lahr. A good place to be for most of this film, one of Shirley's lesser efforts. Musical numbers with Robinson still a delight, though.

Just Before Dawn (1946) 65m. D: William Castle. Warner Baxter, Adele Roberts, Charles D. Brown, Martin Kosleck, Mona Barrie, Marvin Miller. SEE: **Crime Doctor** series.

Just for You (1952) C-104m. *** D: Elliott Nugent. Bing Crosby, Jane Wyman, Ethel Barrymore, Natalie Wood, Cora Witherspoon. Zesty musical of producer Crosby who can't be bothered with his growing children, till Wyman shows him the way.

Just Imagine (1930) 102m. *½ D: David Butler. El Brendel, Maureen O'Sullivan, John Garrick, Marjorie White, Frank Albertson, Hobart Bosworth. Famous but utterly disappointing sci-fi musical set in 1980, with Brendel, officially dead since

1930, suddenly revived and unable to get used to phenomenal changes in living. Futuristic sets, gags, costumes made tremendous impression on everyone who saw film in 1930, but alas, it doesn't wear well at all. Songs by DeSylva-Brown-Henderson.

Just Me and You (1978) C-100m. TVM D: John Erman. Louise Lasser, Charles Grodin, Julie Bovasso, Paul Fix, Michael Aldredge. Comedy-drama about a cross country odyssey shared by a dizzy New York dame and a down-to-earth salesman. Louise Lasser (MARY HARTMAN) wrote this one, probably after overdosing on Judy Holliday movies, but it misfires. Average.

Just Off Broadway (1942) 66m. ** D: Herbert I. Leeds. Lloyd Nolan, Marjorie Weaver, Phil Silvers, Janis Carter. Acceptable Michael Shayne caper, with swanky dame on trial for murder; outcome is easy for mystery fans.

Just Tell Me What You Want (1980) C-112m. **½ D: Sidney Lumet. Ali MacGraw, Alan King, Peter Weller, Myrna Loy, Dina Merrill, Keenan Wynn, Tony Roberts. Vicarious interest in life-styles of the rich and powerful gives chief interest to this uneven comedy about a capricious tycoon (King) and his long-time mistress (MacGraw).

Just This Once (1952) 90m. **½ D: Don Weis. Janet Leigh, Peter Lawford, Lewis Stone, Marilyn Erskine, Richard Anderson. Cute little comedy of stern Leigh in charge of playboy Lawford's dwindling fortunes, and their inevitable romance.

Just Tony (1922) 58m. **½ D: Lynn Reynolds. Tom Mix, Claire Adams, J. P. Lockney, Duke Lee, Frank Campeau. Amiable Tom Mix Western sheds spotlight on his beloved horse Tony, tracing his life from mistreated mustang to benevolent protector of cowboy Mix.

Just You and Me, Kid (1979) C-95m. *½ D: Leonard Stern. George Burns, Brooke Shields, Lorraine Gary, Nicolas Coster, Burl Ives, Ray Bolger, Leon Ames, Carl Ballantine, Keye Luke. Burns struggles to keep awful comedy afloat, but it ain't easy. Shields plays a runaway who comes to stay with the ex-vaudevillian. Commercial interruptions might help this one.

Justine (1969) C-116m. *** D: George Cukor. Anouk Aimee, Dirk Bogarde, Robert Forster, Anna Ka-

rina, Phillipe Noiret, Michael York. Stylish film won't please fans of Lawrence Durrell's *Alexandria Quartet*, but works as exotic kitsch; Cukor's great use of wide screen won't mean much on TV. Filmed in Tunis.

Kaleidoscope (1966) C-103m. ** D: Jack Smight. Warren Beatty, Susannah York, Clive Revill, Eric Porter, Murray Melvin. Idea of Beatty-York teaming can't miss, but does, in bland comedy about American playboy/card-shark forced to capture narcotics smuggler or go to jail. Flashy but forgettable. Filmed in England.

Kanal (1956-Polish) 90m. *** D: Andrezej Wajda. Teresa Izewska, Tadeusz Janczar, Wienczylaw Glinski, Wladyslaw Sheybal. Intense, stark study of partisans involved in Warsaw rebellion during 1944 when Nazis occupied country. Retitled: THEY LOVED LIFE.

Kangaroo (1952) C-84m. ** D: Lewis Milestone. Maureen O'Hara, Peter Lawford, Finlay Currie, Richard Boone. Uninspired blend of romance and adventure, salvaged by good on-location Australian landscapes and fetching O'Hara.

Kansan, The (1943) 79m. **½ D: George Archainbaud. Richard Dix, Jane Wyatt, Victor Jory, Albert Dekker, Eugene Pallette, Robert Armstrong. Zippy Western, with Dix becoming town hero, taming gangsters, but facing more trouble with corrupt town official.

Kansas City Bomber (1972) C-99m. ** D: Jerrold Freedman. Raquel Welch, Kevin McCarthy, Helena Kallianiotes, Norman Alden, Jeanne Cooper, Mary Kay Pass, Dick Lane. Once you've seen five minutes, it doesn't pay to stay through the rest. Raquel stars as good-hearted roller derby star who has female colleagues jealous, male employers drooling. Dialogue, situations often unintentionally funny.

Kansas City Confidential (1952) 98m. *** D: Phil Karlson. John Payne, Coleen Gray, Preston Foster, Neville Brand, Lee Van Cleef, Jack Elam. Tough action drama with ex-con Payne nailed for armored robbery he didn't commit, determined to expose cunning mastermind Foster. Silly wrap-up scene is only detraction.

Kansas City Kitty (1944) 63m. ** D: Del Lord. Joan Davis, Bob Crosby, Jane Frazee, Erik Rolf. Programmer sparked by Davis, involved in purchase of song-publishing company on the skids.

Kansas City Massacre, The (1975) C-100m. TVM D: Dan Curtis. Dale Robertson, Bo Hopkins, Robert Walden, Scott Brady, Mills Watson, Harris Yulin, Matt Clark. Action-packed period piece, sequel to MELVIN PURVIS, G-MAN (1974), has indomitable Purvis (cigar-chomping Robertson) vying with Pretty Boy Floyd, Baby Face Nelson, John Dillinger, Alvin Karpis and other public enemies. Snappily directed, with a dandy cast and a sense of humor. Above average.

Kansas Pacific (1953) C-73m. ** D: Ray Nazarro. Sterling Hayden, Eve Miller, Barton MacLane, Reed Hadley, Irving Bacon. Inoffensive account of building of title railway during 1860s, with Reb soldiers trying to prevent its completion.

Kansas Raiders (1950) C-80m. *½ D: Ray Enright. Audie Murphy, Brian Donlevy, Marguerite Chapman, Tony Curtis, Richard Arlen. Formula Western has Jesse James (Murphy) joining Quantrill's Raiders during the Civil War.

Kashmiri Run (1969-Spanish) C-101m. ** D: John Peyser. Pernell Roberts, Alexandra Bastedo, Julian Mateos, Gloria Gamata. Two men and a girl try to stay one step ahead of the Chinese Communists while fleeing Tibet in this plodding actioner.

Kate Bliss and the Ticker Tape Kid (1978) C-100m. TVM D: Burt Kennedy. Suzanne Pleshette, Don Meredith, Tony Randall, Burgess Meredith, Harry Morgan, David Huddleston, Harry Carey, Jr. Western comedy involving a lady detective from back east, a stuffy English rancher with a rustling problem, and a dapper bandit who fashions himself as a western Robin Hood. Good cast plays it well. Above average.

Kate McShane (1975) C-78m. TVM D: Marvin Chomsky. Anne Meara, Sean McClory, Charles Haid, Cal Bellini, Christine Belford, Charles Cioffi. Flamboyant lady lawyer teams up with dad, a retired cop, and brother, a priest/university law professor, to defend society woman accused of murder. Routine drama with Meara miscast here and in series that followed. Average.

Katherine (1975) C-100m. TVM D: Jeremy Kagan. Art Carney, Sissy Spacek, Henry Winkler, Julie Kavner, Jane Wyatt, Hector Elias, Jenny Sullivan. Absorbing drama about one young woman's radical experience, from innocent to activist to terrorist. Spacek is remarkable in title role. Subsequently cut to 78m. Above average.

Kathleen (1941) 88m. ** D: Harold S. Bucquet. Shirley Temple, Herbert Marshall, Laraine Day, Gail Patrick, Felix Bressart. Predictable story of neglected daughter Temple bringing widower father Marshall and Day together.

Kathy O' (1958) C-99m. **½ D: Jack Sher. Dan Duryea, Jan Sterling, Patty McCormack, Mary Fickett. Sluggish frolic of temperamental child star McCormack and her desperate public relations agent Duryea.

Katie Did It (1951) 81m. **½ D: Frederick de Cordova. Ann Blyth, Mark Stevens, Cecil Kellaway, Jesse White. Blyth is perkier than usual as square New England librarian who becomes hep when romanced by swinging New Yorker Stevens.

Katie: Portrait of a Centerfold (1978) C-100m. TVM D: Robert Greenwald. Kim Basinger, Glynn Turman, Vivian Blaine, Dorothy Malone, Fabian, Tab Hunter, Don Johnson, Melanie Mayron. Naive beauty queen from Texas grows up fast after going to Hollywood in search of stardom. Below average.

Kazablan (1974-Israeli) C-114m. *** D: Menahem Golan. Yehoram Gaon, Arie Elias, Efrat Lavie, Joseph Graber. Entertaining musical made in Old Jaffa and Jerusalem, in English, based on a popular show. Gaon repeats his stage role as streetwise war hero out to save his neighborhood from being torn down. Excellent color and location work.

Keefer (1978) C-74m. TVM D: Barry Shear. William Conrad, Kate Woodville, Michael O'Hare, Cathy Lee Crosby, Jeremy Kemp, Brioni Farrell. Crack team of World War II secret agents led by Conrad (in this post-CANNON pilot) face predictable risks and formula action behind enemy lines. Average.

Keegans, The (1976) C-78m. TVM D: John Badham. Adam Roarke, Spencer Mulligan, Heather Menzies, Tom Clancy, Joan Leslie, Paul Shenar, Judd Hirsch, Janit Baldwin, Penelope Windust. Crime drama concerning investigative reporter's attempts to clear his pro-football brother of murdering their sister's attacker. Average.

Keep 'em Flying (1941) 86m. **½ D: Arthur Lubin. Bud Abbott, Lou Costello, Carol Bruce, Martha Raye, William Gargan, Dick Foran. Good A&C mixed in with clichéd plot of stunt-pilot Foran unable to accustom himself to Air Force discipline. Raye is fun playing twins.

Keep 'em Slugging (1943) 60m. D: Christy Cabanne. Bobby Jordan, Huntz Hall, Gabriel Dell, Norman Abbott, Evelyn Ankers. SEE: Bowery Boys series.

Keep Your Powder Dry (1945) 93m. ** D: Edward Buzzell. Lana Turner, Laraine Day, Susan Peters, Agnes Moorehead, Bill Johnson, Natalie Schafer, Lee Patrick. Hackneyed tale of WW2 WACs, glossy on the outside, empty on the inside.

Keeper of the Flame (1942) 100m. *** D: George Cukor. Spencer Tracy, Katharine Hepburn, Richard Whorf, Margaret Wycherly, Forrest Tucker, Frank Craven. Interesting but dated drama of reporter Tracy exposing unsavory background of late American hero; Hepburn is man's widow.

Kelly and Me (1957) C-86m. ** D: Robert Z. Leonard. Van Johnson, Piper Laurie, Martha Hyer, Onslow Stevens. Johnson is unsuccessful hoofer who hits movie big-time with talented dog for partner. Mild musical.

Kelly's Heroes (1970) C-145m. **½ D: Brian G. Hutton. Clint Eastwood, Telly Savalas, Don Rickles, Donald Sutherland, Carroll O'Connor, Gavin MacLeod. Large-scale WW2 film tries for Sergeant Bilko-ish atmosphere with middling results; hippie Sutherland isn't credible in 1940s setting. But actionful aspects of Savalas and Eastwood's far-fetched gold heist behind enemy lines make film worth watching.

Kennel Murder Case, The (1933) 73m. D: Michael Curtiz. William Powell, Mary Astor, Eugene Pallette, Ralph Morgan, Helen Vinson, Jack LaRue, Robert Barrat, Arthur Hohl, Paul Cavanagh. SEE: Philo Vance series.

Kenner (1969) C-92m. ** D: Steve Sekely. Jim Brown, Madlyn Rhue, Robert Coote, Ricky Cordell,

Charles Horvath. Small, bittersweet romance of soldier of fortune in Bombay (filmed on location), whose search for partner's murderer involves young native dancer.

Kenny & Co. (1976) C-90m. **½ D: Don Coscarelli. Dan McCann, Mike Baldwin, Jeff Roth, Ralph Richmond, Reggie Bannister. Sweet-natured, upbeat look at adolescent life, focusing on one boy's growing pains. Virtually a one-man-show behind the camera by young Coscarelli.

Kentuckian, The (1955) C-104m. **½ D: Burt Lancaster. Burt Lancaster, Diana Lynn, Walter Matthau, John Carradine, Una Merkel. Spirited Western set in 1820s has Lancaster battling all odds to reach Texas and begin new life.

Kentucky (1938) C-95m. *** D: David Butler. Loretta Young, Richard Greene, Walter Brennan, Douglass Dumbrille, Karen Morley, Moroni Olsen, Russell Hicks. Lushly filmed story of rival horsebreeding families in blue-grass country, with lovers Young and Greene clinching at finale. Brennan won Best Supporting Actor Oscar.

Kentucky Fried Movie, The (1977) C-90m. *** D: John Landis. Evan Kim, Master Bong Soo Han, Bill Bixby, George Lazenby, Henry Gibson, Donald Sutherland, Boni Enten. Vulgar, often funny skits strung together. Best: a lengthy Bruce Lee takeoff, a black and white spoof of the old courtroom TV shows. Idea originated with Kentucky Fried Theatre, a Madison, Wisconsin satirical group transplanted to L.A.

Kentucky Moonshine (1938) 85m. ** D: David Butler. Tony Martin, Marjorie Weaver, Ritz Brothers, Slim Summerville, John Carradine. Slim little vehicle with Ritz Brothers causing chaos amidst feuding hillbillies in Kentucky; Martin and Weaver are the love/musical interest.

Kentucky Kernels (1934) 75m. *** D: George Stevens. Bert Wheeler, Robert Woolsey, Mary Carlisle, Spanky McFarland, Noah Beery, Lucille LaVerne. Wheeler & Woolsey take little Spanky into the deep South to collect inheritance, but find themselves in the midst of a family feud. Good vehicle for the team with great slapstick finale.

Kettles in the Ozarks, The (1956) 81m. D: Charles Lamont. Marjorie Main, Arthur Hunnicutt, Una Merkel, Ted de Corsia, Olive Sturgess. SEE: **Ma and Pa Kettle** series.

Kettles on Old Macdonald's Farm, The (1957) 80m. D: Virgil Vogel. Marjorie Main, Parker Fennelly, Gloria Talbott, John Smith, Pat Morrow. SEE: **Ma and Pa Kettle** series.

Key, The (1958-British) 125m. **½ D: Carol Reed. William Holden, Sophia Loren, Trevor Howard, Oscar Homolka. Jan de Hartog novel becomes pointless romance tale. Loren is disillusioned woman passing out key to her room to series of naval captains during WW2, hoping to make their dangerous lives a little happier.

Key Largo (1948) 101m. ***½ D: John Huston. Humphrey Bogart, Edward G. Robinson, Lauren Bacall, Lionel Barrymore, Claire Trevor, Thomas Gomez. Dandy cast in adaptation of Maxwell Anderson's play about tough gangster (Robinson) holding people captive in Florida hotel during rough storm. Trevor won Best Supporting Actress Oscar as Robinson's boozy moll.

Key Man (1954-British) 78m. **½ D: Montgomery Tully. Angela Lansbury, Keith Andes, Brian Keith. Competent little picture about illicit love affair leading to mysterious accidents involving Lansbury's architect husband. Retitled: A LIFE AT STAKE.

Key to the City (1950) 99m. **½ D: George Sidney. Clark Gable, Loretta Young, Frank Morgan, Marilyn Maxwell, Raymond Burr, James Gleason. Bland romance between Gable and Young, two mayors who meet at convention in San Francisco.

Key West (1972) C-100m. TVM D: Philip Leacock. Stephen Boyd, Woody Strode, Sheree North, Earl Hindman, Tiffany Bolling, William Prince. Ex-CIA operative and friend, now running boat service in Florida, become involved in chase for incriminating evidence involving U.S. Senator. Good cast, story overcome uninspired direction; above average.

Key Witness (1960) 82m. **½ D: Phil Karlson. Jeffrey Hunter, Pat Crowley, Dennis Hopper, Joby Baker, Susan Harrison, Johnny Nash, Corey Allen. Overlong but effective narrative of pressures from street gang on Hunter's family to prevent his wife from testifying in criminal case.

Keys of the Kingdom (1944) 137m.

*** D: John M. Stahl. Gregory Peck, Thomas Mitchell, Vincent Price, Edmund Gwenn, Roddy McDowall, Cedric Hardwicke, Peggy Ann Garner. Peck is fine in this long but generally good film about missionary's life (played as boy by McDowall); from A. J. Cronin novel.

Khartoum (1966-British) C-134m. ** D: Basil Dearden. Charlton Heston, Laurence Olivier, Richard Johnson, Ralph Richardson, Alexander Knox, Johnny Sekka. Dull historical spectacle about "Chinese" Gordon and his famous defeat by Arab tribesman in 1833. Olivier is good, Heston better than usual, but film is way too talky for a spectacle.

Khyber Patrol (1954) C-71m. ** D: Seymour Friedman. Richard Egan, Dawn Addams, Patric Knowles, Raymond Burr. Cast is above pedestrian film of British officers fighting in India, with usual love conflicts.

Kid, The (1921) 60m. ***½ D: Charles Chaplin. Charlie Chaplin, Jackie Coogan, Edna Purviance, Chuck Reisner, Lita Grey. Chaplin's first real feature mixes slapstick and sentiment in a winning combination, as the Tramp raises a streetwise orphan. Wonderful film launched Coogan as major child star, and it's easy to see why.

Kid Blue (1973) C-100m. *½ D: James Frawley. Dennis Hopper, Warren Oates, Ben Johnson, Peter Boyle, Janice Rule, Lee Purcell. Pseudo-hip Western comedy about misfit Hopper's faltering attempts to exist in small Texas town in early 20th century. Laughs, excitement, and interest are at a minimum here in spite of cast; Hopper is too old for his role.

Kid Brother, The (1927) 82m. **** D: Ted Wilde and J. A. Howe. Harold Lloyd, Jobyna Ralston, Walter James, Leo Willis, Olin Francis. Delightful winning, beautifully filmed silent comedy with Harold as Cinderella-type kid brother in robust all-male family, who gets to prove his mettle in exciting finale where he subdues beefy villain. One of Lloyd's all-time best.

Kid Dynamite (1943) 73m. D: Wallace Fox. Leo Gorcey, Huntz Hall, Bobby Jordan, Gabriel Dell, Pamela Blake, Bennie Bartlett, Sammy Morrison. SEE: **Bowery Boys** series.

Kid for Two Farthings, A (1956-British) C-91m. *** D: Carol Reed. Celia Johnson, Diana Dors, David Kossoff, Brenda De Banzie, Primo

Carnera, Lou Jacobi. Imaginative fable of London youth who buys a little goat thinking him a unicorn, leading to some delightful vignettes on human nature.

Kid from Brooklyn, The (1946) C-113m. *** D: Norman Z. McLeod. Danny Kaye, Virginia Mayo, Vera-Ellen, Steve Cochran, Eve Arden, Walter Abel, Lionel Stander, Fay Bainter. Comedy of milkman accidentally turned into prizefighter is often overdone but still a funny Kaye vehicle; remake of Harold Lloyd's MILKY WAY.

Kid from Cleveland, The (1949) 89m. ** D: Herbert Kline. George Brent, Lynn Bari, Rusty Tamblyn, Tommy Cook, Ann Doran. Brent is a sports reporter involved with a disturbed youth; Cleveland Indians ball team play themselves. A bit sticky at times.

Kid from Kansas, The (1941) 66m. *½ D: William Nigh. Leo Carrillo, Andy Devine, Dick Foran, Ann Doran. When a fruit buyer offers ridiculously low prices for planters' crops, competitors take drastic measures; low budget, low quality.

Kid from Left Field, The (1953) 80m. ** D: Harmon Jones. Dan Dailey, Anne Bancroft, Billy Chapin, Lloyd Bridges, Ray Collins, Richard Egan. Homey little film with Dailey as ex-baseball star turned ballpark vendor who uses his son as cover while trying to turn a losing team around.

Kid from Left Field, The (1979) C-100m. TVM D: Adell Aldrich. Gary Coleman, Robert Guillaume, Tab Hunter, Tricia O'Neil, Gary Collins, Ed McMahon. Appealing remake of 1953 baseball movie about a bat,boy who guides the San Diego Padres from the cellar to the World Series, using the strategy passed on by his father, a big league has-been reduced to hawking hot dogs in the stands. Above average.

Kid from Spain, The (1932) 90m. *** D: Leo McCarey. Eddie Cantor, Lyda Roberti, Robert Young, Ruth Hall, John Miljan, Stanley Fields. Lavish Cantor musical with Eddie mistaken for famed bullfighter; Roberti is his vivacious leading lady. Striking Busby Berkeley musical numbers; look for Paulette Goddard and Betty Grable in the chorus line.

Kid from Texas, The (1950) C-78m. ** D: Kurt Neumann. Audie Mur-

phy, Gale Storm, Albert Dekker, Shepperd Strudwick. Another version of life of Billy the Kid, with Murphy in title role, Storm the romantic interest.

Kid Galahad (1937) 101m. *** D: Michael Curtiz. Edward G. Robinson, Bette Davis, Humphrey Bogart, Wayne Morris, Jane Bryan, Harry Carey, Veda Ann Borg. Well-paced actioner of promoter Robinson making naive Morris boxing star, losing his girl Davis to him at same time. Retitled: BATTLING BELLHOP. Remade as THE WAGONS ROLL AT NIGHT.

Kid Galahad (1962) C-95m. **½ D: Phil Karlson. Elvis Presley, Gig Young, Lola Albright, Joan Blackman, Charles Bronson, Ned Glass. Remake lacks wallop of original. Presley is boxer who wins championship fight but prefers quieter life of garage mechanic.

Kid Millions (1934) 90m. *** D: Roy Del Ruth. Eddie Cantor, Ethel Merman, Ann Sothern, George Murphy, Warren Hymer. Elaborate Cantor musical about Eddie inheriting a fortune. Musical numbers and comedy set-pieces boost a weak script. Color segment in ice-cream factory a delight. Songs include "When My Ship Comes In." Lucille Ball is one of the Goldwyn Girls in this one.

Kid Rodelo (1966) 91m. *½ D: Richard Carlson. Don Murray, Janet Leigh, Broderick Crawford, Richard Carlson. After jail term, cowboys go off to search for hidden $50,000 in gold. You've seen it all before. Filmed in Spain.

Kidnap Syndicate (1975-Italian) C-83m. ** D: Fernando diLeo. James Mason, Valentina Cortesa, Luc Merenda, Irina Maleeva, Vittorio Caprioli. Crime drama about the snatching of two youngsters—the son of a multimillionaire and an auto mechanic's boy—and how the industrialist's rash actions cause all manner of violence and a rampage of vengeance.

Kidnapped (1938) 90m. **½ D: Alfred L. Werker. Warner Baxter, Freddie Bartholomew, Arleen Whelan, C. Aubrey Smith, Reginald Owen, John Carradine, Nigel Bruce. Good adventure yarn of 1750s Scotland and England but not Robert Louis Stevenson; fine cast in generally entertaining script.

Kidnapped (1948) 80m. ** D: William Beaudine. Roddy McDowall, Sue England, Dan O'Herlihy, Roland Winters, Jeff Corey. Disappointing low-budget adaptation of Robert Louis Stevenson novel.

Kidnapped (1960) C-97m. **½ D: Robert Stevenson. Peter Finch, James MacArthur, Bernard Lee, Niall MacGinnis, John Laurie, Finlay Currie, Peter O'Toole. Disney feature filmed in England is faithful to Robert Louis Stevenson's classic novel, but surprisingly dull. Good cast and vivid atmosphere are its major assets.

Kidnapped (1971-British) C-100m. ** D: Delbert Mann. Michael Caine, Trevor Howard, Jack Hawkins, Donald Pleasence, Gordon Jackson, Vivien Heilbron. Disappointing version of Stevenson tale is made endurable by Caine's pleasing performance as Alan Breck.

Kids Are Alright, The (1979) C-97m. *** D: Jeff Stein. Overlong and disjointed, yet frequently exhilarating documentary on The Who that manages to capture the anarchic spirit of the group—and of rock and roll.

Kill A Dragon (1967) C-91m. *½ D: Michael Moore. Jack Palance, Fernando Lamas, Aldo Ray, Alizia Gur. Complicated, far-fetched tale of feudal baron in modern China and his American adversary.

Kill Her Gently (1957-British) 73m. ** D: Charles Saunders. Marc Lawrence, Maureen Connell, George Mikell, Griffith Jones, John Gayford. Brutal "B" film of supposedly cured mental patient hiring two convicts-at-large to kill his wife.

Kill! Kill! Kill! (1972-French-Spanish-German-Italian) C-90m. *½ D: Romain Gary. Jean Seberg, James Mason, Stephen Boyd, Curt Jurgens, Daniel Emilfork. Interpol agent Mason, on the trail of Italian drug kingpins, gets competition from fellow agent Boyd, who believes in playing dirty. Hardened violence clashes with writer-director Gary's purple prose. Original title KILL, at 102m.

Kill Me If You Can (1977) C-100m. TVM D: Buzz Kulik. Alan Alda, Talia Shire, John Hillerman, Walter McGinn, Barnard Hughes, John Randolph, Ben Piazza. Fact-based drama about Caryl Chessman, the "red light bandit" who spent twelve years on San Quentin's death row before being executed in 1960. Alda's superb portrayal of Chessman gives

this one guts. Takes, naturally, the anti-capital-punishment view. Death-penalty advocates should stick with CELL 2455, DEATH ROW (1955), taken from Chessman's best-seller. Above average.

Kill Me Tomorrow (1957-British) 80m. ** D: Terence Fisher. Pat O'Brien, Lois Maxwell, George Coulouris, Robert Brown, Tommy Steele. Adequate "B" film about newspaperman cracking murder case leading to arrest of diamond-smuggling syndicate.

Kill or Be Killed (1950) 67m. *½ D: Max Nosseck. Lawrence Tierney, George Coulouris, Marissa O'Brien, Rudolph Anders. Pedestrian account of man on lam hunted down in jungle by law enforcers.

Kill the Umpire (1950) 78m. **½ D: Lloyd Bacon. William Bendix, Una Merkel, Ray Collins, Gloria Henry, William Frawley, Tom D'Andrea. Lightweight comedy about baseball lover who becomes baseball's most hated man, the umpire. Ends with spectacular slapstick chase. Screenplay by Frank Tashlin.

Killdozer (1974) C-78m. TVM D: Jerry London. Clint Walker, Carl Betz, Neville Brand, James Wainwright, James Watson, Jr., Robert Urich. Alien being turns bulldozer against hard-hat crew bossed by Walker. Man-vs.-machine thriller in the shadow of "Duel." Average.

Killer Ape (1953) 68m. D: Spencer Bennet. Johnny Weissmuller, Carol Thurston, Max Palmer, Nestor Paiva, Nick Stuart. SEE: **Jungle Jim** series.

Killer Bees (1974) C-78m. TVM D: Curtis Harrington. Gloria Swanson, Edward Albert, Kate Jackson, Robert Davis, Don McGovern, Craig Stevens. Symbolic drama with Swanson a winegrowing family matriarch with strange power over a colony of bees thriving in the vineyard. Middling thriller with stagey acting and unexplained mittle-European accents. Below average.

Killer Fish (1979-Italian-Brazilian) C-101m. ** D: Anthony M. Dawson (Antonio Margheriti). Lee Majors, Karen Black, James Franciscus, Margaux Hemingway, Marisa Berenson, Gary Collins. Pursuit of stolen jewels dumped in lake full of deadly piranha fish forms basis for this predictable outing filmed in Brazil. Same fishy predators were used in much more enjoyable film, PIRANHA.

Killer By Night (1971) C-100m. TVM
D: Bernard McEveety. Robert Wagner, Diane Baker, Greg Morris, Theodore Bikel, Robert Lansing, Mercedes McCambridge. Somewhat tame attempt at two-sided approach to mad-killer-on-loose story. Diphtheria outbreak conflicts with police efforts until source for both problems found to be one and same. Only asset good atmosphere. Average.

Killer Elite, The (1975) C-122m. **
D: Sam Peckinpah. James Caan, Robert Duvall, Arthur Hill, Bo Hopkins, Mako, Burt Young, Gig Young. Mercenary Duvall double-crosses partner Caan, leading to characteristic but lesser Peckinpah bloodbath involving the CIA. Trashy script slightly redeemed by director's flair for action sequences.

Killer Force (1975) C-101m. ** D: Val Guest. Peter Fonda, Telly Savalas, Hugh O'Brian, Christopher Lee, Maud Adams, O. J. Simpson, Ian Yule. Dirty doings at diamond syndicate's desert mine in South Africa. Has cast and potential but overly diffuse and complex.

Killer Inside Me, The (1976) C-99m.
*** D: Burt Kennedy. Stacy Keach, Susan Tyrrell, Keenan Wynn, Tisha Sterling, Don Stroud, Charles McGraw. Bizarre opus about a psychotic deputy sheriff (flashbacks accounting for his present state) about to go off the deep end; saved and made believable by strong performance from Keach.

Killer Is Loose, The (1956) 73m.
**½ D: Budd Boetticher. Joseph Cotten, Rhonda Fleming, Wendell Corey, Alan Hale, Michael Pate. Fairly tense vengeance tale of ex-con swearing to get even with detective who nabbed him.

Killer Leopard (1954) 70m. D: Ford Beebe, Edward Morey, Jr. Johnny Sheffield, Beverly Garland, Barry Bernard, Donald Murphy. SEE: Bomba, the Jungle Boy series.

Killer McCoy (1947) 104m. *** D: Roy Rowland. Mickey Rooney, Brian Donlevy, Ann Blyth, James Dunn, Tom Tully, Sam Levene. Good drama of fighter Rooney accidentally involved in murder, with fine supporting cast of promoters and racketeers. Remake of THE CROWD ROARS (1938).

Killer on Board (1977) C-100m.
TVM D: Philip Leacock. Claude Akins, Beatrice Straight, George Hamilton, Patty Duke Astin, Frank Converse, Jane Seymour, William Daniels. So-so drama involving vacationers on a cruise ship who are infected with a deadly virus and must be quarantined. Echoes of "The Cassandra Crossing" with a change of locale. Average.

Killer Shark (1950) 76m. *½ D: Budd Boetticher. Roddy McDowall, Laurette Luez, Roland Winters, Edward Norris, Douglas Fowley, Dick Moore. Back Bay-ite McDowall learns new values as skipper of shark-hunting vessel; cheapie film.

Killer Spy (1958-French) 82m. ** D: Georges Lampin. Jean Marais, Nadja Tiller, Andre Luguet, Bernadette Lafont. Capable cast tries to instill life into this spy-and-murder yarn; scenery outshines script.

Killer that Stalked New York, The (1950) 79m. **½ D: Earl McEvoy. Evelyn Keyes, Charles Korvin, William Bishop, Dorothy Malone. Interesting "B" film of a diamond-smuggling couple sought by police because they contracted contagious disease while abroad.

Killer Who Wouldn't Die, The (1976) C-100m. TVM D: William Hale. Mike Connors, Samantha Eggar, Patrick O'Neal, Clu Gulager, James Shigeta, Robert Colbert, Robert Hooks, Gregoire Aslan, Mariette Hartley. Detective-turned-charter boat operator takes up search for the killer of his undercover agent friend, and becomes entangled in a network of espionage. Busted pilot with Connors back in the "Mannix" mold. Average.

Killer's Carnival (1965) C-95m. **½ D: Albert Cardiff, Robert Lynn, Sheldon Reynolds. Stewart Granger, Lex Barker, Pierre Brice, Karin Dor, Pascal Petit. Three stories of intrigue set in Rome, Vienna, and Brazil; tired cast in OK espionage tales.

Killer's Kiss (1955) 67m. ** D: Stanley Kubrick. Frank Silvera, Jamie Smith, Irene Kane, Jerry Jarret. Meandering account of revenge when boxer's courting of working-girl causes her boss to commit murder. Interesting early Kubrick.

Killers, The (1946) 105m. **** D: Robert Siodmak. Burt Lancaster, Ava Gardner, Edmond O'Brien, Albert Dekker, Sam Levene, Charles D. Brown. Compelling crime story of ex-fighter found murdered, subsequent investigation. Film provides fireworks, early success of Lancaster (in film debut) and Gardner.

Killers, The (1964) **C-95m.** **½ D:** Don Siegel. Lee Marvin, Angie Dickinson, Ronald Reagan, John Cassavetes, Claude Akins. Shot for TV but thought too violent, this was released in theaters—now it's back on TV. Loosely based on Hemingway short story, violent film tells of teacher's involvement in robbery plot, eventual murder.

Killers Are Challenged SEE: Secret Agent Fireball

Killers from Space (1954) **71m.** ** D: W. Lee Wilder. Peter Graves, James Seay, Barbara Bestar, Frank Gerstle, Steve Pendleton. Graves is captured by alien space invaders who want vital information.

Killers of Kilimanjaro (1960-British) **C-91m.** ** D: Richard Thorpe. Robert Taylor, Anne Aubrey, John Dimech, Gregoire Aslan, Anthony Newley, Martin Boddey. Spotty adventure yarn of railroad-building in East Africa.

Killers Three (1968) **C-88m.** BOMB D: Bruce Kessler. Robert Walker, Diane Varsi, Dick Clark, Norman Alden, Maureen Arthur, Merle Haggard. Take-off on BONNIE AND CLYDE doesn't offer much by way of comparison, unless you find the idea of Dick Clark in wirerims a gas.

Killing, The (1956) **83m.** ***½ D: Stanley Kubrick. Sterling Hayden, Coleen Gray, Vince Edwards, Jay C. Flippen, Marie Windsor, Ted de Corsia, Elisha Cook Jr., Timothy Carey. Early Kubrick classic about elaborate racetrack robbery. Carey's cool killer, Cook's doomed marriage to Windsor among highlights. Major flaw: DRAGNET-like narration.

Killing Affair, A (1977) **C-100m.** TVM D: Richard Sarafian. Elizabeth Montgomery, O. J. Simpson, Rosalind Cash, Dean Stockwell, Dolph Sweet. Two detectives working on a homicide case become involved in (interracial) love affair. A cop show is a cop show, even if the leads make a handsome couple. Average. Retitled BEHIND THE BADGE.

Killing Game, The (1967-French) **C-94m.** **½ D: Alain Jessua. Jean-Pierre Cassel, Claudine Auger, Michael Duchaussoy, Eleanore Hirt. Mystery comic strip writer comes up with his ultimate puzzler. Not bad.

Killing of a Chinese Bookie, The (1976) **C-136m.** *½ D: John Cassavetes. Ben Gazzara, Timothy

Agoglia Carey, Seymour Cassel, Azizi Johari, Meade Roberts, Alice Friedland. Strange, self-indulgent (even for Cassavetes) home movie centering around the owner of a strip joint, the mob and what used to be called "B-girls." Small cult may take to this; others beware.

Killing of Sister George, The (1968) **C-138m.** *** D: Robert Aldrich. Beryl Reid, Susannah York, Coral Browne, Ronald Fraser, Patricia Medina. Good, if somewhat sensationalized study of lesbianism from Frank Marcus' play. Contains several fine performances. Possibly too frank for TV. Made in England.

Killing Stone (1978) **C-100m.** TVM D: Michael Landon. Gil Gerard, J. D. Cannon, Jim Davis, Matthew Laborteaux, Corinne Michaels, Nehemiah Persoff. A writer is freed after ten years in prison, determined to find real murderer of U.S. Senator's son. Pilot for a prospective series, believe it or not. Average.

Kilroy Was Here (1947) **68m.** *½ D: Phil Karlson. Jackie Cooper, Jackie Coogan, Wanda McKay, Frank Jenks. Supposedly topical comedy (then) is pretty limp now, with innocent victim of "Kilroy Was Here" joke trying to lead normal life despite his name.

Kim (1950) **C-113m.** ***½ D: Victor Saville. Errol Flynn, Dean Stockwell, Paul Lukas, Thomas Gomez, Cecil Kellaway. Rousing actioner based on Kipling classic, set in 1880s India, with British soldiers combatting rebellious natives. Flavorful production.

Kimberley Jim (1965-South African) **C-82m.** ** D: Emil Nofal. Jim Reeves, Madeleine Usher, Clive Parnell, Arthur Swemmer, Mike Holt. Minor musical of two carefree gamblers who win diamond mine in fixed poker game, and then have a change of heart. Rare screen appearance by late country singer Reeves.

Kind Hearts and Coronets (1949-British) **104m.** ***½ D: Robert Hamer. Dennis Price, Valerie Hobson, Joan Greenwood, Alec Guinness. Peerless black comedy of castoff member of titled family setting out to eliminate them all. Guinness plays eight roles.

Kind Lady (1951) **78m.** *** D: John Sturges. Ethel Barrymore, Maurice Evans, Angela Lansbury, Betsy Blair. Bleak drama, excellently acted, of con-man Evans ingratiating himself into Barrymore's home and fleecing her.

Kind of Loving, A (1962-British) 112m. *** D: John Schlesinger. Alan Bates, June Ritchie, Thora Hird, Bert Palmer, Gwen Nelson, Malcolm Patton. Intelligent account of young couple forced to marry when girl becomes pregnant, detailing their home life; well acted.

King: A Filmed Record . . . Montgomery to Memphis (1970) 153m. ***½ D: Joseph L. Mankiewicz, Sidney Lumet. Superior documentary covering life of Dr. Martin Luther King from 1955 until his death in 1968 is marred only by the pretentious and unnecessary "bridges" featuring such stars as Paul Newman, Joanne Woodward, and James Earl Jones. Otherwise, well-chosen compilation of news footage carries tremendous wallop.

King and Country (1964-British) 90m. ***½ D: Joseph Losey. Dirk Bogarde, Tom Courtenay, Leo McKern, Barry Foster, James Villiers, Peter Copley. Vivid antiwar treatise beautifully acted by strong supporting cast. Bogarde is detached Army captain lawyer assigned to defend deserter private Courtenay during WW1.

King and Four Queens, The (1956) C-86m. **½ D: Raoul Walsh. Clark Gable, Eleanor Parker, Jo Van Fleet, Jean Willes, Barbara Nichols, Sara Shane, Jay C. Flippen. Static misfire with Gable on the search for money hidden by husbands of four women he encounters.

King and I, The (1956) C-133m. ***½ D: Walter Lang. Deborah Kerr, Yul Brynner, Rita Moreno, Martin Benson, Terry Saunders, Rex Thompson, Alan Mowbray. Excellent Rodgers and Hammerstein musicalization of ANNA AND THE KING OF SIAM: Kerr is widowed teacher who runs head-on into the stubborn King (Brynner), gradually falling in love with him; beautifully acted. Songs: "Hello Young Lovers," "Getting to Know You," "Shall We Dance," "Something Wonderful." Kerr's singing voice was dubbed by Marni Nixon.

King and the Chorus Girl, The (1937) 94m. **½ D: Mervyn LeRoy. Joan Blondell, Fernand Gravet, Edward Everett Horton, Jane Wyman. Gravet is nobleman on a lark, finding true love with beautiful chorine Blondell. Lively production.

King Creole (1958) 116m. **½ D: Michael Curtiz. Elvis Presley, Carolyn Jones, Dolores Hart, Dean Jagger. Harold Robbins' seamy book A STONE FOR DANNY FISHER is toned down considerably to make a musical-drama vehicle for Presley.

King in New York, A (1957-British) 105m. **½ D: Charles Chaplin. Charles Chaplin, Dawn Addams, Oliver Johnston, Maxine Audley, Harry Green, Michael Chaplin. Unseen in U.S. until 1973, supposedly anti-American film is rather mild satire of 1950s sensibilities, witch hunts, and technology. Chaplin overindulges himself, and film lacks focus, but there are good moments, and interesting performance by son Michael as young malcontent.

King In Shadow (1956-German) 87m. ** D: Harald Braun. O. W. Fischer, Horst Buchholz, Odile Versois, Gunther Hadank. Buchholz is mentally disturbed young King of Sweden in 1760s; court intrigue encouraged by his domineering mother (Versois) makes only occasionally interesting costume tale.

King Kong (1933) 100m. **** D: Merian C. Cooper, Ernest B. Schoedsack. Fay Wray, Bruce Cabot, Robert Armstrong, Noble Johnson, James Flavin, Victor Wong, Frank Reicher. Classic version of beauty-and-beast theme is a moviegoing must, with special effects and animation of monster Kong still unsurpassed. Final sequence atop Empire State Building is now folklore; Max Steiner music score also memorable.

King Kong (1976) C-134m. *½ D: John Guillermin. Jeff Bridges, Charles Grodin, Jessica Lange, John Randolph, Rene Auberjonois, Julius Harris, Jack O'Halloran, Ed Lauter. Addle-brained remake of 1933 classic has great potential but dispels all the mythic, larger-than-life qualities of the original with idiotic characters and campy approach. Highly-touted special effects run hot-and-cold; real marvel is Rick Baker in a gorilla suit.

King Kong Escapes (1968-Japanese) C-96m. BOMB D: Inoshiro Honda. Rhodes Reason, Mie Hama, Linda Miller, Akira Takarada. Contrived new plot involving girl who wins ape's heart, battle against would-be world conqueror. Kong never had it so bad.

King Kong vs. Godzilla (1963-Japanese) C-90m. **½ D: Thomas

[408]

Montgomery. Michael Keith, James Yagi, Tadao Takashima, Mie Hama. Good special effects make hokey plot worthwhile; two famed monsters clash.

King Lear (1971-British) 137m. ***½ D: Peter Brook. Paul Scofield, Irene Worth, Jack MacGowran, Alan Webb, Cyril Cusack, Patrick Magee. This version of Shakespeare tragedy could be heavy going for the uninitiated, but often a strong and rewarding experience. Starkly photographed in Denmark.

King of Alcatraz (1938) 56m. **½ D: Robert Florey. J. Carrol Naish, Gail Patrick, Lloyd Nolan, Harry Carey, Robert Preston, Anthony Quinn. Alcatraz escapee Naish takes over passenger ship, encountering rough-and-tumble seamen Nolan and Preston. Film moves like lightning, with outstanding cast making you forget this is just a "B" picture.

King of Burlesque (1935) 83m. **½ D: Sidney Lanfield. Warner Baxter, Jack Oakie, Alice Faye, Mona Barrie, Dixie Dunbar. Dumb but enjoyable musical; cliché-ridden story of burlesque producer who risks all on ambitious Broadway show. Faye, Fats Waller (used all too briefly), hit song "I'm Shootin' High" provide highspots.

King of Chinatown (1939) 60m. **½ D: Nick Grinde. Anna May Wong, Sidney Toler, Akim Tamiroff, J. Carrol Naish, Anthony Quinn, Roscoe Karns, Philip Ahn. Interesting little "B" movie with good cast, about underworld racketeers trying to gain power in Chinatown.

King of Hearts (1967-French-British) C-102m. *** D: Philippe De Broca. Alan Bates, Pierre Brasseur, Jean-Claude Brialy, Genevieve Bujold, Francoise Christophe, Adolfo Celi. Scotsman Bates walks into French town in WW1 that has been abandoned by everyone except those in the insane asylum. Stylish film isn't for all tastes, but has become a staple in revival theaters in recent years. Offbeat.

King of Kings, The (1927) 115m. *** D: Cecil B. DeMille. H. B. Warner, Ernest Torrence, Jacqueline Logan, Joseph Schildkraut, Victor Varconi, Robert Edeson, William Boyd. Lavish silent film holds up rather well, benefits from DeMille's superb storytelling skills and reverence for the subject.

King of Kings (1961) C-168m. ***½ D: Nicholas Ray. Jeffrey Hunter, Siobhan McKenna, Robert Ryan, Hurd Hatfield, Viveca Lindfors, Rita Gam, Rip Torn. The life of Christ, intelligently told and beautifully filmed; full of deeply moving moments, such as the Sermon on the mount. Not without flaws, but well worthwhile; grandly filmed in CinemaScope, bound to lose some of its visual impact on TV.

King of Marvin Gardens, The (1972) C-104m. ***½ D: Bob Rafelson. Jack Nicholson, Bruce Dern, Ellen Burstyn, Julia Anne Robinson, Scatman Crothers. Pretentious but genuinely haunting, original drama about Nicholson's failure to discourage brother Dern's outlandish financial schemes. Burstyn's performance as an aging beauty is chilling in its perfection, and Laszlo Kovacs' photography rates with the best of the decade.

King of the Coral Sea (1956-Australian) 74m. **½ D: Lee Robinson. Chips Rafferty, Charles Tingwell, Ilma Adey, Rod Taylor, Lloyd Berrell, Reginald Lye. On-location filming in Australia aids this account of wetback smuggling into the country.

King of the Grizzlies (1970) C-93m. **½ D: Ron Kelly. John Yesno, Chris Wiggins, Hugh Webster, Jack Van Evera; narrated by Winston Hibler. Standard Disney animal-adventure about Indian who was "brother" to bear as a cub, and who now faces the full-grown grizzly in a different light. Filmed in the Canadian Rockies.

King of the Gypsies (1978) C-112m. ** D: Frank Pierson. Sterling Hayden, Shelley Winters, Susan Sarandon, Judd Hirsch, Eric Roberts, Brooke Shields, Annette O'Toole. Story of American gypsy boy (Roberts) born to lead his people; fascinating insights into gypsy life at the outset, but soon descends into ludicrously muddled plot. Standout performance by Hayden.

King of the Jungle (1933) 65m. **½ D: H. Bruce Humberstone, Max Marcin. Buster Crabbe, Frances Dee, Douglass Dumbrille, Sidney Toler, Nydia Westman. Imitation Tarzan comes off well, with Crabbe being dragged into civilization against his will.

King of the Khyber Rifles (1953) C-100m. **½ D: Henry King. Tyrone Power, Terry Moore, Michael Rennie, John Justin. Power is half-caste

British officer involved in native skirmishes, Moore the general's daughter he loves. Film lacks finesse or any sense of Kipling reality-fantasy.

King of the Roaring 20's—The Story of Arnold Rothstein (1961) 106m. **½ D: Joseph M. Newman. David Janssen, Dianne Foster, Jack Carson, Diana Dors, Mickey Rooney. Gunroaring narrative of notorious gangster's life and crimes.

King of the Rocket Men SEE: Lost Planet Airmen

King of the Underworld (1939) 69m. ** D: Lewis Seiler. Humphrey Bogart, Kay Francis, James Stephenson, John Eldredge, Jessie Busley. Farfetched story of doctor Francis becoming involved with Bogart's underworld gang; ludicrous finale. Remake of DR. SOCRATES.

King of the Wild Horses (1947) 79m. *½ D: George Archainbaud. Preston Foster, Gail Patrick, Bill Sheffield, Guinn Williams. Youth's companionship with fierce stallion is focus of this mild Western.

King of the Wild Stallions (1959) C-75m. ** D: R. G. Springsteen. George Montgomery, Diane Brewster, Edgar Buchanan, Emile Meyer, Byron Foulger. Horse is the hero of this oater, protecting a widow and her son.

King of the Zombies (1941) 67m. *½ D: Jean Yarbrough. Dick Purcell, Joan Woodbury, Mantan Moreland, Henry Victor, John Archer. Scientist develops corps of zombies to use in WW2 missions; ridiculous.

King, Queen and Knave (1972) C-92m. BOMB D: Jerzy Skolimowski. David Niven, Gina Loflobrigida, John Moulder-Brown, Mario Adorf. Coarse, heavy-handed adaptation of Vladimir Nabokov story about a klutzy youth who falls in love with his sexy aunt (Lollobrigida).

King Rat (1965-British) 133m. *** D: Bryan Forbes. George Segal, Tom Courtenay, James Fox, Patrick O'Neal, Denholm Elliott, James Donald, John Mills, Alan Webb. James Clavell novel of WW2 Japanese POW camp, focusing on effect of captivity on Allied prisoners. Thoughtful presentation rises above clichés; many exciting scenes.

King Richard and the Crusaders (1954) C-114m. **½ D: David Butler. Rex Harrison, Virginia Mayo, George Sanders, Laurence Harvey, Robert Douglas. Cardboard costumer of Middle Ages, with laughable script.

King Solomon's Mines (1937-British) 80m. *** D: Robert Stevenson. Paul Robeson, Cedric Hardwicke, Roland Young, John Loder, Anna Lee. Robust adventure given full-blooded treatment by fine cast, scouring Africa in search of treasure-filled mines. One of Robeson's best screen roles even allows him to sing. H. Rider Haggard story remade in 1950.

King Solomon's Mines (1950) C-102m. ***½ D: Compton Bennett, Andrew Marton. Deborah Kerr, Stewart Granger, Richard Carlson, Hugo Haas. Remake of H. Rider Haggard story is given polished production, with Granger-Kerr-Carlson trio leading safari in search for famed diamond mines.

King Steps Out, The (1936) 85m. *** D: Josef von Sternberg. Grace Moore, Franchot Tone, Walter Connolly, Raymond Walburn, Elizabeth Risdon, Nana Bryant, Victor Jory. Fanciful musical romance with fine cast supporting Moore's lovely voice; direction big asset to otherwise average musical.

King's Pirate, The (1967) C-100m. **½ D: Don Weis. Doug McClure, Jill St. John, Guy Stockwell, Mary Ann Mobley. Cardboard, juvenile swashbuckler set in 18th century, with McClure the nominal hero. Remake of AGAINST ALL FLAGS.

King's Row (1941) 127m. ***½ D: Sam Wood. Ann Sheridan, Robert Cummings, Ronald Reagan, Betty Field, Charles Coburn, Claude Rains, Judith Anderson, Maria Ouspenskaya. Forerunner of PEYTON PLACE still retains its sweep of life in pre-WW1 Midwestern town, with the fates of many townsfolk intertwined. Erich Wolfgang Korngold music score backs up plush production, fine characterizations.

King's Story, A (1967-British) C-100m. *** D: Harry Booth. With the voices of Orson Welles, Flora Robson, Patrick Wymark, David Warner. Strong documentary focusing on early life of Duke of Windsor and his ultimate abdication from throne of England to marry the woman he loved.

King's Thief, The (1955) C-78m. *** D: Robert Z. Leonard. David Niven, Ann Blyth, George Sanders, Edmund Purdom, Roger Moore, Alan Mowbray. Ornately produced costumer of 17th-century court intrigue involving England's King Charles II.

King's Vacation (1933) 60m. **½ D: John G. Adolfi. George Arliss, Dudley Digges, Dick Powell, Patricia Ellis, Florence Arliss. Refreshing story of monarch's experiences before he realizes that marriage of state holds love and true values.

Kingdom of the Spiders (1977) C-94m. *** D: John (Bud) Cardos. William Shatner, Tiffany Bolling, Woody Strode, Lieux Dressler, Altovise Davis. Unsurprising but well-made chiller about veterinarian Shatner and entomologist Bolling discovering that tarantulas are going on the warpath in Arizona.

Kingfisher Caper, The (1975-South African) C-90m. **½ D: Dirk De-Villiers. Hayley Mills, David McCallum, Jon Cypher. Typical tale of intrigue, love and passion interwoven with a family feud over the running of a South African diamond empire.

Kings Go Forth (1958) 109m. *** D: Delmer Daves. Frank Sinatra, Tony Curtis, Natalie Wood, Leora Dana. Soapy yet telling account of two contrasting G.I.s in WW2 France involved with part-Negro Wood, their three-cornered romance.

Kings of the Sun (1963) C-108m. **½ D: J. Lee Thompson. Yul Brynner, George Chakiris, Shirley Anne Field, Richard Basehart, Brad Dexter. Skin-deep spectacle, badly cast, telling of Mayan leader who comes to America with surviving tribesmen and encounters savage Indians. Filmed in Mexico.

Kingston (1976) C-100m. TVM D: Robert Day. Raymond Burr, Bradford Dillman, James Merrill, James Canning, Biff McGuire, Robert Sampson. Freelance journalist Burr is hired by publishing mogul to investigate strange editorial positions on her papers and uncovers a plot using nuclear power plants to take over the world. Pilot for the series. Average.

Kismet (1944) C-100m. *** D: William Dieterle. Ronald Colman, Marlene Dietrich, Edward Arnold, Florence Bates, James Craig, Joy Ann Page, Harry Davenport. Unremarkable but entertaining color fable of Arabian Nights, hokey but worthwhile if only for Dietrich's dancing scene with her body painted gold. Remade as Broadway musical, filmed in 1955. Retitled: ORIENTAL DREAM.

Kismet (1955) C-113m. **½ D: Vincente Minnelli. Howard Keel, Ann Blyth, Dolores Gray, Monty Woolley, Sebastian Cabot, Vic Damone. Opulent but static filming of Robert Wright-George Forrest musical. Songs: "Stranger In Paradise," "Baubles, Bangles, and Beads."

Kiss and Kill SEE: **Blood of Fu Manchu**

Kiss and Tell (1945) 90m. **½ D: Richard Wallace. Shirley Temple, Jerome Courtland, Walter Abel, Katharine Alexander, Robert Benchley, Porter Hall. Film of successful Broadway play about wacky teenager Corliss Archer is a bit forced but generally funny; one of Temple's better grown-up roles.

Kiss Before Dying, A (1956) C-94m. *** D: Gerd Oswald. Robert Wagner, Jeffrey Hunter, Virginia Leith, Joanne Woodward, Mary Astor, George Macready. Black adventure tale with Wagner superb as psychopathic killer and Astor his devoted mother; well paced.

Kiss for Corliss, A (1949) 88m. ** D: Richard Wallace. Shirley Temple, David Niven, Tom Tully, Virginia Welles. Puffed-up comedy of teenager Temple convincing all that she and playboy Niven are going together; naïve fluff. Limp follow-up to KISS AND TELL with Shirley as Corliss Archer. Retitled: ALMOST A BRIDE.

Kiss In the Dark, A (1949) 87m. ** D: Delmer Daves. David Niven, Jane Wyman, Victor Moore, Wayne Morris, Broderick Crawford. Drab comedy effort involving pianist Niven, who gets more than he bargained for when he inherits an apartment building.

Kiss Kiss-Bang Bang (1966-Spanish) C-90m. **½ D: Duccio Tessari. Giuliano Gemma, George Martin, Antonio Casas, Daniel Vargas. Routine spy yarn of British Secret Service efforts to prevent sale of secret formula to foreign powers.

Kiss Me Deadly (1955) 105m. ***½ D: Robert Aldrich. Ralph Meeker, Albert Dekker, Paul Stewart, Cloris Leachman, Maxine Cooper, Gaby Rodgers. Meeker is a perfect Mike Hammer in moody, fast and violent adaptation of the Mickey Spillane novel. Years ahead of its time, a major influence on the French New Wave directors and one of Aldrich's best films.

Kiss Me Kate (1953) C-109m. *** D: George Sidney. Kathryn Grayson, Howard Keel, Ann Miller, Bobby

Van, Keenan Wynn, James Whitmore, Bob Fosse. Bright filmization of Cole Porter's Broadway musical, adapted from Shakespeare's "Taming of the Shrew." Grayson and Keel are married couple whose off-stage and on-stage lives intertwine. Songs include "So in Love," "Always True to You in my Fashion," "Brush Up Your Shakespeare."

Kiss Me, Kill Me (1976) C-78m. TVM D: Michael O'Herlihy. Stella Stevens, Michael Anderson, Jr., Dabney Coleman, Claude Akins, Pat O'Brien, Robert Vaughn, Tisha Sterling. D.A.'s special investigator Stevens goes on trail of young schoolteacher's killer and allows herself to be bait to trap psycho. Strictly in "Police Woman" rut, but nice bit by veteran Pat O'Brien as morgue attendant. Average.

Kiss Me, Stupid (1964) 124m. *½ D: Billy Wilder. Dean Martin, Kim Novak, Ray Walston, Felicia Farr, Cliff Osmond, Barbara Pepper. Wilder and I.A.L. Diamond's off-center comedy was dismissed as smut in 1964 and hasn't improved much with age: amateur songwriter Walston tries to sell his material to Martin but worries that the entertainer is out to seduce his beautiful wife.

KISS Meets the Phantom of the Park (1978) C-100m. TVM D: Gordon Hessler. KISS (Peter Criss, Ace Frehley, Gene Simmons, Paul Stanley), Anthony Zerbe, Carmine Caridi, Deborah Ryan, Terry Webster. The famed rock group (in their acting debut) try to thwart a mad scientist's plan to clone the foursome for evil purposes. The vast KISS army will go for this, and so will those wanting to see Zerbe at his slimiest. Average.

Kiss of Death (1947) 98m. ***½ D: Henry Hathaway. Victor Mature, Brian Donlevy, Coleen Gray, Richard Widmark, Karl Malden, Taylor Holmes. Grim melodrama of captured thief who informs on his gang. Terrific suspense; one of Mature's best performances. Widmark established his chilling portrait of psychopathic hit man. Remade as THE FIEND WHO WALKED THE WEST.

Kiss of Evil SEE: Kiss of the Vampire

Kiss of Fire (1955) C-87m. **½ D: Joseph M. Newman. Barbara Rush, Jack Palance, Rex Reason, Martha Hyer. Run-of-the-mill costumer. Rush

gives up Spanish throne to remain in America with true love.

Kiss of the Tarantula (1972) C-85m. *½ D: Chris Munger. Suzanne Ling, Eric Mason, Herman Wallner, Patricia Landon, Beverly Eddins. Unstable teenager uses pet tarantulas against her stepfather and other "enemies." Heavy-handed.

Kiss of the Vampire (1963-British) C-88m. **½ D: Don Sharp. Clifford Evans, Edward DeSouza, Noel Willman, Jennifer Daniel. Intelligent treatment of vampire tale, well done in color, with many chilling sequences. Unfortunately, much of film's punch is lost in reedited TV version known as KISS OF EVIL.

Kiss the Blood Off My Hands (1948) 79m. ** D: Norman Foster. Joan Fontaine, Burt Lancaster, Robert Newton, Lewis Russell. Title suggests film's unlikely combination of love and murder, which doesn't mix well.

Kiss the Boys Goodbye (1941) 85m. **½ D: Victor Schertzinger. Mary Martin, Don Ameche, Oscar Levant, Virginia Dale, Barbara Jo Allen (Vera Vague), Raymond Walburn, Elizabeth Patterson, Connee Boswell. Enjoyable backstage musical of aspiring actress and director, with good support from Levant and bright score.

Kiss the Girls and Make Them Die (1966-Italian) C-101m. BOMB D: Henry Levin. Michael Connors, Dorothy Provine, Terry-Thomas, Raf Vallone, Beverly Adams, Oliver McGreevy. Dull spy spoof about power-crazy industrialist who has a satellite capable of sterilizing the world, which is something Bond, Flint, and Matt Helm wouldn't mind. Awful film.

Kiss the Other Sheik (1968-Italian-French) C-85m. BOMB D: Luciano Salce, Eduardo De Filippo. Marcello Mastroianni, Pamela Tiffin, Virna Lisi, Luciano Salce. Off-color and off-base comedy of crazy man and his sexy wife.

Kiss Them for Me (1957) C-105m. **½ D: Stanley Donen. Cary Grant, Jayne Mansfield, Leif Erickson, Suzy Parker, Larry Blyden, Ray Walston. Forced comedy about romantic entanglements of navy officers on shore leave.

Kiss Tomorrow Goodbye (1950) 102m. **½ D: Gordon Douglas. James Cagney, Barbara Payton, Helena Carter, Luther Adler, William Frawley. Turgid gangster caper with Cagney in rare form as convict-at-large who marries but still has itchy trigger finger.

Kisses for My President (1964) 113m. **½ D: Curtis Bernhardt. Fred MacMurray, Polly Bergen, Arlene Dahl, Edward Andrews, Eli Wallach. Thirties-style comedy of Bergen becoming President of the U.S., with MacMurray her husband caught in unprecedented protocol. Sometimes funny, often witless.

Kissin' Cousins (1964) C-96m. **½ D: Gene Nelson. Elvis Presley, Arthur O'Connell, Glenda Farrell, Pamela Austin, Yvonne Craig. Presley is military officer trying to convince yokel relative to allow missile site to be built on homestead; usual amount of singing.

Kissing Bandit, The (1948) C-102m. ** D: Laslo Benedek. Frank Sinatra, Kathryn Grayson, Ann Miller, J. Carrol Naish, Ricardo Montalban, Mildred Natwick, Cyd Charisse, Billy Gilbert. Frail Sinatra vehicle about son of Western kissing bandit who picks up where Dad left off; song "Siesta" sums it up.

Kit Carson (1940) 97m. *** D: George B. Seitz. Jon Hall, Lynn Bari, Dana Andrews, Harold Huber, Ward Bond, Renie Riano, Clayton Moore. Sturdy Western with Hall in title role, Andrews as cavalry officer, Bari the woman they fight over; plenty of action in Indian territory.

Kitten with a Whip (1964) 83m. ** D: Douglas Heyes. Ann-Margret, John Forsythe, Patricia Barry, Peter Brown, Ann Doran. Uninspired account of delinquent (Ann-Margret) and friends forcing businessman Forsythe to drive them to Mexico.

Kitty (1945) 104m. *** D: Mitchell Leisen. Paulette Goddard, Ray Milland, Patric Knowles, Reginald Owen, Cecil Kellaway, Constance Collier. Overlong costumer of girl's rise from guttersnipe to lady in 18th-century England with help of impoverished artist Milland; one of Goddard's best roles.

Kitty Foyle (1940) 107m. ***½ D: Sam Wood. Ginger Rogers, Dennis Morgan, James Craig, Eduardo Ciannelli, Ernest Cossart, Gladys Cooper. Tender love story won Rogers an Oscar as Christopher Morley's working-girl heroine; Ciannelli memorable as speakeasy waiter.

Klansman, The (1974) C-112m. BOMB D: Terence Young. Lee Marvin, Richard Burton, Cameron Mitchell, Lola Falana, Luciana Paluzzi, Linda Evans, O. J. Simpson. Thoroughly trashy racial meller casts Marvin as a Southern sheriff and Burton as a local landowner who get involved in a hotbed (and hot beds) of racial activity. Hopeless.

Klondike Annie (1936) 80m. *** D: Raoul Walsh. Mae West, Victor McLaglen, Philip Reed, Harold Huber, Soo Yong, Lucile Webster Gleason. West and McLaglen are rugged team, with Mae on the lam from police, going to the Yukon and masquerading as Salvation Army worker. West chants: "I'm An Occidental Woman in An Oriental Mood For Love," and other hits.

Klondike Kate (1943) 64m. *½ D: William Castle. Ann Savage, Tom Neal, Glenda Farrell, Constance Worth, Sheldon Leonard, Lester Allen. Low-budget humdrum of innocent Neal accused of murder in Alaska, fighting for his life and his girl.

Klute (1971) C-114m. ***½ D: Alan J. Pakula. Jane Fonda, Donald Sutherland, Charles Cioffi, Roy Scheider, Dorothy Tristan, Rita Gam, Jean Stapleton. Fine combination detective-thriller/character-study, with Sutherland a private-eye searching for suburban husband last seen in N.Y.C. Fonda is call girl who once saw man in question; her performance won Best Actress Oscar.

Knack, and How to Get It, The (1965-British) 84m. ***½ D: Richard Lester. Rita Tushingham, Ray Brooks, Michael Crawford, Donal Donnelly. One of the funniest comedies ever imported from Britain. One man's a whiz with the ladies, and his buddy simply wants to learn his secret. Fast-moving, constantly funny.

Knave of Hearts SEE: **Lovers, Happy Lovers**

Knickerbocker Holiday (1944) 85m. ** D: Harry Brown. Nelson Eddy, Charles Coburn, Constance Dowling, Shelley Winters, Percy Kilbride, Chester Conklin. Plodding film of Kurt Weill-Maxwell Anderson musical of New York's early days, with score including "September Song."

Knife in the Water (1962-Polish) 94m. **** D: Roman Polanski. Leon Niemczyk, Jolanta Umecka, Zygmunt Malanowicz. Absorbing drama grows out of the tensions created when a couple off for a sailing weekend pick up a student hitchhiker. Polanski's first feature film is a brilliant piece of cinematic storytelling, and a must-see movie.

Knight Without Armour (1937-British) 107m. *** D: Jacques Feyder. Marlene Dietrich, Robert Donat, Irene Vanbrugh, Herbert Lomas, Miles Malleson, David Tree. Secret agent Donat helps Czarina Dietrich flee Russian revolutionaries. Sumptuous production merely backdrop for two stars.

Knights of the Round Table (1953) C-115m. **½ D: Richard Thorpe. Robert Taylor, Ava Gardner, Mel Ferrer, Stanley Baker, Felix Aylmer. MGM's first wide-screen film (made in England) was excuse for this pretty but empty mini-spectacle of King Arthur's Court, revealing famous love triangle.

Knock on Any Door (1949) 100m. **½ D: Nicholas Ray. Humphrey Bogart, John Derek, George Macready, Allene Roberts, Susan Perry. More a showcase for young Derek—as a "victim of society" who turns to crime—than a vehicle for Bogart, as the conscience-stricken attorney who defends him. Serious but dated drama.

Knock on Wood (1954) C-103m. *** D: Norman Panama, Melvin Frank. Danny Kaye, Mai Zetterling, Torin Thatcher, David Burns, Leon Askin, Abner Biberman. Superior Kaye vehicle involved with beautiful Zetterling and international spies; good Kaye routines.

Knockout (1941) 73m. **½ D: William Clemens. Arthur Kennedy, Virginia Field, Anthony Quinn, Olympe Bradna. Slick little programmer of a prizefighter seesawing between fame and folly.

Knute Rockne—All American (1940) 98m. *** D: Lloyd Bacon. Pat O'Brien, Gale Page, Donald Crisp, Ronald Reagan, Albert Bassermann, John Qualen. Lots of standard football stuff, but O'Brien as famed Notre Dame coach and Reagan as star player George Gipp make this one memorable. Important note: several scenes, including famous "win it for the Gipper" moment, are cut from all TV prints due to legal complications, so don't blame your local station.

Kojak and the Marcus-Nelson Murders SEE: **Marcus-Nelson Murders, The**

Kon-Tiki (1951) 73m. *** Narrated by Ben Grauer. This documentary won an Oscar in 1951; it traces Thor Heyerdahl's raft trip from Peru to Tahiti, substantiating his theory that sailing boats in ancient times crossed the Pacific Ocean.

Kona Coast (1968) C-93m. **½ D: Lamont Johnson. Richard Boone, Vera Miles, Joan Blondell, Steve Ihnat, Chips Rafferty, Kent Smith. Good cast in routine melodrama of fishing boat skipper's fight to get the guys who murdered his daughter. Fifties rock star Duane Eddy has small part. Filmed in Hawaii.

Konga (1961-British) C-90m. *½ D: John Lemont. Michael Gough, Margo Johns, Jess Conrad, Claire Gordon. Small monkey grows into huge beast threatening the people of London; silly sci-fi.

Kongo (1932) 85m. *** D: William Cowan. Walter Huston, Lupe Velez, Conrad Nagel, Virginia Bruce, C. Henry Gordon. Bizarre, fascinating melodrama of crippled madman Huston ruling African colony, seeking revenge on man who paralyzed him by torturing his daughter (Bruce). Likely to be trimmed by sensitive TV stations; not for the squeamish. Remake of WEST OF ZANZIBAR.

Koroshi (1967) C-93m. TVM D: Peter Yates, Michael Truman. Patrick McGoohan, Yoko Tani, Amanda Barrie, Ronald Howard, George Coulouris. British agent John Drake sent to Japan to combat deadly sect of assassins based on secret offshore island. First half better than second (originally two episodes of SECRET AGENT series); generally uncontrived, exciting. Average.

Kotch (1971) C-113m. ***½ D: Jack Lemmon. Walter Matthau, Deborah Winters, Felicia Farr, Charles Aidman. Heartwarming comedy of elderly man who refuses to be put out to pasture by his children. Matthau superb in Lemmon's first directorial effort.

Kramer vs. Kramer (1979) C-105m. **** D: Robert Benton. Dustin Hoffman, Meryl Streep, Jane Alexander, Justin Henry, Howard Duff, George Coe. Wife walks out on upwardly mobile husband, leaving him to fend for himself and their young son; an intelligent, beautifully crafted, intensely moving film. Adapted from Avery Corman's novel and acted to perfection by entire cast. Oscar winner as Best Picture, Best Actor, Best Screenplay, Best Director, Best Supporting Actress (Streep).

Krakatoa, East of Java (1969) C-

[414]

101m. **½ D: Bernard Kowalski. Maximilian Schell, Diane Baker, Brian Keith, Barbara Werle, John Leyton, Rossano Brazzi, Sal Mineo. Muddled epic-adventure of disparate group sailing for location of treasure-laden sunken ship. Attempt at Jules Verne-ish saga hampered by shallow characterizations, dialogue, but action footage is first-rate, climaxed by volcanic explosion and tidal wave. Shot in Cinerama; heavily cut after premiere, leaving story more jumbled than before. P.S.: Krakatoa is *West* of Java. Retitled VOLCANO.

Kremlin Letter, The (1970) C-113m. *½ D: John Huston. Bibi Andersson, Richard Boone, Max von Sydow, Orson Welles, Patrick O'Neal, Barbara Parkins, Dean Jagger, George Sanders, Raf Vallone. Dull, complicated thriller based on best-seller concerns efforts to retrieve bogus treaty supposedly signed by U.S. and Soviet Union that will pit them against Red China. Good cast is thrown away; film does provide rare opportunity to see Sanders in drag.

Kronos (1957) 78m. ** D: Kurt Neumann. Jeff Morrow, Barbara Lawrence, John Emery, Morris Ankrum. Potentially good sci-fi lacks the imaginative special effects to carry the vehicle of rampaging monster.

Kung Fu (1971) C-75m. TVM D: Jerry Thorpe. David Carradine, Barry Sullivan, Keith Carradine, Philip Ahn, Keye Luke. Half-American/half-Chinese, young Kwai Chang Kane, Bhuddist monk, flees mainland China to American West with Imperial government out to get him. Stylish use of pseudo-karate; offbeat direction to counterpoint script's moods; good performances. Above average; pilot for TV series.

L-Shaped Room, The (1963-British) 125m. *** D: Bryan Forbes. Leslie Caron, Tom Bell, Brock Peters, Avis Bunnage, Emlyn Williams, Cicely Courtneidge. Adult love story sensibly handled. Caron is convincing as unwed pregnant girl jilted by lover, left to face life in her squalid surroundings.

La Dolce Vita (1961-Italian) 175m. ***½ D: Federico Fellini. Marcello Mastroianni, Anita Ekberg, Anouk Aimee, Lex Barker, Nadia Gray, Alain Cuny. Lengthy trend-setting film, not as ambiguous as other Fellini works—much more entertaining, with strong cast. Mastroianni stars as gossip columnist who sees his life in shallow Rome society as worthless but can't change.

La Parisienne (1958-French) C-85m. **½ D: Michel Boisrond. Brigitte Bardot, Charles Boyer, Henri Vidal, Andre Luguet, Nadia Gray. At times spicy account of plucky Bardot involved with visiting royalty, much to her diplomat father's dismay.

La Strada (1954-Italian) 115m. **** D: Federico Fellini. Anthony Quinn, Giulietta Masina, Richard Basehart, Aldo Silvana, Marcella Rovere, Livia Venturini. Deceptively simple tale of brutish strongman Quinn who takes simple-minded waif Masina with him as he tours from town to town, encountering acrobat Basehart, who enjoys teasing Quinn. Vivid performances help bring sensitive story to life; should be seen more than once.

La Viaccia (1962-Italian) 103m. **½ D: Mauro Bolognini. Jean-Paul Belmondo, Claudia Cardinale, Pietro Germi, Romolo Valli, Gabriella Pallotta, Gina Sammarco. Zesty yarn of country youth finding romance in the city with prostitute. Retitled: THE LOVEMAKERS.

La Vie de Chateau SEE: **Matter of Resistance, A**

Lacy and the Mississippi Queen (1978) C-74m. TVM D: Robert Butler. Kathleen Lloyd, Debra Feuer, Edward Andrews, Jack Elam, James Keach, Matt Clark, David Comfort. Gun-toting tomboy joins forces with her long lost sister, a bubble-headed beauty, to avenge their father's killing—with the help of a drunken Indian. Lighthearted western pilot. Average.

Lad: A Dog (1962) C-98m. **½ D: Aram Avakian, Leslie H. Martinson. Peter Breck, Peggy McCay, Carroll O'Connor, Angela Cartwright, Maurice Dallimore. Genuine if schmaltzy version of Albert Payson Terhune novel of dog who brings new zest for life to lame child.

Ladies and Gentlemen, the Rolling Stones (1975) C-90m. **½ D: Rollin Binzer. Disappointing documentary on the rock group's 1972 U.S. tour is unworthy of subject, but fans should take a look. Loss of quadrophonic sound on TV screens will hurt.

Ladies Courageous (1944) 88m. ** D: John Rawlins. Loretta Young, Geraldine Fitzgerald, Diana Barry-

[415]

more, Evelyn Ankers, Frank Jenks, Ruth Roman, Anne Gwynne, Philip Terry, Lois Collier, Kane Richmond. Well-meant idea fails because of hackneyed script and situations; saga of the WAFs during WW2 who played a vital part in air warfare.

Ladies in Love (1936) 97m. **½ D: Edward Griffith. Janet Gaynor, Loretta Young, Constance Bennett, Simone Simon, Don Ameche, Paul Lukas, Tyrone Power. Man-hunting girls in Budapest stick together to find likely victims; large cast makes it entertaining; young Power seen to good advantage.

Ladies in Retirement (1941) 92m. *** D: Charles Vidor. Ida Lupino, Louis Hayward, Evelyn Keyes, Elsa Lanchester, Edith Barrett, Isobel Elsom, Emma Dunn. Static but well-made gothic melodrama about housekeeper Lupino's attempt to cover up murder in eccentric British household. Not as potent—or as shocking —as it must have been in 1941, but still good. Remade as THE MAD ROOM.

Ladies' Man (1931) 70m. *½ D: Lothar Mendes. William Powell, Kay Francis, Carole Lombard, Gilbert Emery, John Holland. Lifeless story of gigolo Powell becoming involved with society mother (Olive Tell) and daughter (Lombard), trying to find true happiness with Francis. Strange, downbeat film.

Ladies' Man (1947) 91m. ** D: William D. Russell. Eddie Bracken, Cass Daley, Virginia Welles, Spike Jones and His City Slickers. Brassy comedy of hayseed inheriting a fortune, coming to New York to paint the town.

Ladies' Man, The (1961) C-106m. *** D: Jerry Lewis. Jerry Lewis, Helen Traubel, Jack Kruschen, Doodles Weaver. Pretty funny comedy with Jerry the handyman in a girls' school run by Helen Traubel (Mrs. Wellenmelon). Jerry Lester and George Raft have amusing cameo appearances.

Ladies of Leisure (1930) 98m. **½ D: Frank Capra. Barbara Stanwyck, Ralph Graves, Lowell Sherman, Marie Prevost, Nance O'Neill, George Fawcett. Stanwyck falls in love with playboy-artist Graves, but cannot shake her reputation as golddigger. Creaky story made worthwhile by Stanwyck's believable performance and Capra's fluent filmmaking technique.

Ladies of the Big House (1931) 76m. **½ D: Marion Gering. Sylvia Sidney, Gene Raymond, Wynne Gibson, Purnell Pratt, Louise Beavers, Jane Darwell, Noel Francis. Sidney is framed and imprisoned; a tearful, well-acted prison drama.

Ladies of the Chorus (1949) 61m. ** D: Phil Karlson. Adele Jergens, Rand Brooks, Marilyn Monroe, Nana Bryant. Cheapie about burlesque chorines and their offstage romances. Primary interest is young, beautiful Monroe as one of the ladies.

Ladies Should Listen (1934) 62m. ** D: Frank Tuttle. Cary Grant, Frances Drake, Edward Everett Horton, Nydia Westman, Ann Sheridan. Grant's life is manipulated by telephone operator Drake in flimsy comedy, no great shakes.

Ladies Who Do (1963-British) 85m. **½ D: C. M. Pennington-Richards. Peggy Mount, Robert Morley, Harry H. Corbett, Nigel Davenport, Carol White, Miriam Karlin. When a charwoman discovers that waste paper scraps contain valuable stock market tips, a mild satire on British financial world unfolds.

Lady and the Bandit, The (1951) 79m. ** D: Ralph Murphy. Louis Hayward, Patricia Medina, Suzanne Dalbert, Tom Tully. Harmless costumer about career and love of highwayman Dick Turpin.

Lady and the Mob, The (1939) 66m. **½ D: Ben Stoloff. Fay Bainter, Lee Bowman, Ida Lupino, Henry Armetta. Bainter gives dignity to this mini-tale of eccentric rich lady involved with gangster mob.

Lady and the Monster, The (1944) 86m. **½ D: George Sherman. Vera Ralston, Erich von Stroheim, Richard Arlen, Sidney Blackmer. Pretty good chiller of mysterious brain taking over man's life. Remade as DONOVAN'S BRAIN.

Lady and the Outlaw, The SEE: Billy Two Hats

Lady Be Good (1941) 111m. *** D: Norman Z. McLeod. Eleanor Powell, Ann Sothern, Robert Young, Lionel Barrymore, John Carroll, Red Skelton, Virginia O'Brien. Spunky musical of married songwriters Sothern and Young, with dancer Powell and comic Skelton for good measure. Fine score: title tune, "Fascinating

Rhythm," "You'll Never Know," "Last Time I Saw Paris."

Lady by Choice (1934) 78m. **½ D: David Burton. Carole Lombard, May Robson, Roger Pryor, Walter Connolly, Arthur Hohl. Enjoyable follow-up to LADY FOR A DAY; dancer Lombard takes in scraggly Robson, makes her proper lady.

Lady Caroline Lamb (1972-British) C-118m. BOMB D: Robert Bolt. Sarah Miles, Jon Finch, Richard Chamberlain, John Mills, Margaret Leighton, Ralph Richardson, Laurence Olivier. Wretched filmization of famous story; wife of English politician scandalizes everyone by her open affair with Lord Byron. Banal script is often unintentionally funny.

Lady Confesses, The (1945) 66m. *½ D: Sam Newfield. Mary Beth Hughes, Hugh Beaumont, Edmund McDonald, Claudia Drake, Emmett Vogan. Quickie independent flick enhanced by Hughes in title role as gal willing to take murder rap to protect boyfriend.

Lady Consents, The (1936) 75m. **½ D: Stephen Roberts. Ann Harding, Herbert Marshall, Margaret Lindsay, Walter Abel. Pat triangle with married Marshall discovering that he still loves his ex-wife.

Lady Dances, The SEE: **Merry Widow, The** (1934)

Lady Doctor (1956-Italian) 90m. **½ D: Camillo Mastrocinque. Abbe Lane, Vittorio De Sica, Toto, Titina De Filippo, German Cobos, Teddy Reno. Pungent nonsense as Toto and De Sica try to con doctor Lane out of a fortune hidden in her house.

Lady Dracula (1973) C-80m. BOMB D: Richard Blackburn. Cheryl Smith, Lesley Gilb, William Whitton, Richard Blackburn. Perfectly awful lowbudgeter about a lady vampire with lesbian tendencies. Bring back Gloria Holden! Also known as LEGENDARY CURSE OF LEMORA and LEMORA, THE LADY DRACULA.

Lady Eve, The (1941) 97m. *** D: Preston Sturges. Barbara Stanwyck, Henry Fonda, Charles Coburn, Eugene Pallette, William Demarest. Classic Sturges comedy doesn't wear as well as others, but remains fast-moving spoof of boy-meets-girl theme, with Stanwyck a sharpster and Fonda the clod to end all clods. Remade as THE BIRDS AND THE BEES.

Lady for a Day (1933) 88m. *** D: Frank Capra. Warren William, May Robson, Guy Kibbee; Glenda Farrell, Jean Parker, Nat Pendleton. Sentimental Damon Runyon fable of seedy apple vendor Robson transformed into perfect lady by producer William. Remade as POCKETFUL OF MIRACLES.

Lady for a Night (1941) 87m. ** D: Leigh Jason. Joan Blondell, John Wayne, Ray Middleton, Philip Merivale, Blanche Yurka, Edith Barrett. Plodding costume drama of woman gambling-boat owner marrying wealthy man for position, then implicated in murder. Good cast out of place.

Lady from Cheyenne (1941) 87m. **½ D: Frank Lloyd. Loretta Young, Robert Preston, Edward Arnold, Frank Craven, Gladys George. Average fare of Young et al conspiring to get themselves on jury, with both political parties becoming involved.

Lady from Chungking (1942) 66m. ** D: William Nigh. Anna May Wong, Harold Huber, Mae Clarke, Rick Vallin, Paul Bryar. Middling account of Wong heading band of Chinese partisans against Japs during WW2.

Lady from Louisiana (1941) 82m. **½ D: Bernard Vorhaus. John Wayne, Osa Massen, Ray Middleton, Henry Stephenson, Helen Westley, Jack Pennick. Wayne and Massen fall in love, then discover they're on opposite sides of gambling controversy; so-so period-piece.

Lady from Shanghai, The (1948) 87m. *** D: Orson Welles. Rita Hayworth, Orson Welles, Everett Sloane, Glenn Anders, Ted de Corsia, Gus Schilling. The camera's the star of this Welles thriller, with the cast incidental in bizarre murder-mystery plot; hall of mirrors scene is fascinating.

Lady from Texas, The (1951) C-77m. ** D: Joseph Pevney. Howard Duff, Mona Freeman, Josephine Hull, Gene Lockhart, Craig Stevens. Strange minor film of eccentric old lady Hull; Duff and Freeman come to her rescue.

Lady Gambles, The (1949) 99m. *** D: Michael Gordon. Barbara Stanwyck, Robert Preston, Stephen McNally, Edith Barrett. Dynamic acting by Stanwyck as compulsive gambler buoys this bland tale of a woman who almost wrecks her marriage.

Lady Godiva (1955) C-89m. **½ D: Arthur Lubin. Maureen O'Hara, George Nader, Victor McLaglen, Torin Thatcher, Robert Warwick. Cardboard costumer involving famed lady and her horseback ride set in Middle Ages England . . . and what a dull ride!

Lady Hamilton SEE: That Hamilton Woman

Lady Has Plans, The (1942) 77m. ** D: Sidney Lanfield. Paulette Goddard, Ray Milland, Roland Young, Albert Dekker, Margaret Hayes, Cecil Kellaway. Jumbled spy comedy with innocent Goddard suspected of being agent and Milland tailing her in Lisbon.

Lady Ice (1973) C-93m. ** D: Tom Gries. Donald Sutherland, Jennifer O'Neill, Robert Duvall, Patrick Magee, Eric Braeden, Jon Cypher. Dull caper film pairs insurance investigator Sutherland and wealthy O'Neill, whose father is a major "fence" for stolen jewels. Good cast wasted.

Lady in a Cage (1964) 93m. **½ D: Walter Grauman. Olivia de Havilland, Ann Sothern, Jeff Corey, James Caan, Rafael Campos. What seems like another imitation of PSYCHO is actually a serious and well-acted thriller that can stand on its own merits.

Lady in a Jam (1942) 78m. **½ D: Gregory La Cava. Irene Dunne, Patric Knowles, Ralph Bellamy, Eugene Pallette, Queenie Vassar, Jane Garland. Thirties-type screwball comedy doesn't really hit bull's-eye, with wacky Dunne convincing psychiatrist Knowles to marry her to cure her ills.

Lady in Cement (1968) C-93m. ** D: Gordon Douglas. Frank Sinatra, Raquel Welch, Dan Blocker, Richard Conte, Martin Gabel, Lainie Kazan, Richard Deacon, Joe E. Lewis. Sequel to TONY ROME finds Sinatra discovering nude corpse with feet encased in cement. Typical private-eye hokum, with heavy doses of violence, leering sex.

Lady in Distress (1939-British) 76m. *** D: Herbert Mason. Paul Lukas, Sally Gray, Michael Redgrave, Patricia Roc, Hartley Power. Redgrave falls for wife of jealous magician after witnessing what looked like her murder. Originally titled A WINDOW IN LONDON.

Lady in Question, The (1940) 81m. **½ D: Charles Vidor. Brian Aherne, Rita Hayworth, Glenn Ford, Irene Rich, George Coulouris, Lloyd Corrigan. Aherne plays a juror interested in defendant Hayworth. He manages to save her, but later falls prey to jealousy. Varies awkwardly from comedy to drama.

Lady in Red, The (1979) C-93m. ** D: Lewis Teague. Pamela Sue Martin, Robert Conrad, Louise Fletcher, Robert Hogan, Laurie Heineman, Glenn Withrow. Martin suffers a life on the lam, before and after her period of notoriety as girlfriend of John Dillinger (Conrad). Lurid, low-budget retread of familiar story elements.

Lady in the Car with Glasses and a Gun, The (1970-British) C-105m. **½ D: Anatole Litvak. Samantha Eggar, Oliver Reed, John McEnery, Stephane Audran, Billie Dixon. Eggar is best thing about otherwise unexceptional film. Psychological thriller about attempt to drive young woman crazy is only occasionally interesting.

Lady in the Dark (1944) C-100m. **½ D: Mitchell Leisen. Ginger Rogers, Ray Milland, Jon Hall, Warner Baxter, Barry Sullivan, Gail Russell, Billy Daniel. Unremarkable, lavish version of Kurt Weill musical minus most of the songs. Then-novel subject of psychoanalysis is now mundane, undoing effect of story about fashion magazine editor in mental turmoil.

Lady in the Iron Mask (1952) C-78m. ** D: Ralph Murphy. Louis Hayward, Patricia Medina, Alan Hale, John Sutton. Variation of Dumas tale, with Three Musketeers still about; moderate costumer.

Lady in the Lake (1946) 103m. **½ D: Robert Montgomery. Robert Montgomery, Audrey Totter, Lloyd Nolan, Tom Tully, Leon Ames, Jayne Meadows. Raymond Chandler whodunit has novelty of camera taking first-person point of view of detective Philip Marlowe (Montgomery); unfortunately, confusing plot is presented in more prosaic (and dated) manner.

Lady in the Morgue (1938) 67m. ** D: Otis Garrett. Preston Foster, Patricia Ellis, Frank Jenks, Barbara Pepper. When a girl's body is stolen from city morgue, law enforcers set out to solve snowballing mystery; acceptable programmer.

Lady Is Willing, The (1942) 92m. *** D: Mitchell Leisen. Marlene

Dietrich, Fred MacMurray, Aline MacMahon, Arline Judge, Stanley Ridges, Roger Clark. Agreeable comedy; glamorous Dietrich wants to adopt a baby, so she marries pediatrician MacMurray. Dramatic segment near the end spoils lively mood.

Lady Killer (1933) 76m. ******* D: Roy Del Ruth. James Cagney, Mae Clarke, Leslie Fenton, Margaret Lindsay, Henry O'Neill, Raymond Hatton, George Chandler. Vintage Cagney, with tangy tale of mobster becoming Hollywood actor, torn between two professions; Cagney repeats his Clarke slapfest.

Lady L (1966-British) C-107m. ****½** D: Peter Ustinov. Sophia Loren, Paul Newman, David Niven, Claude Dauphin, Philippe Noiret, Michel Piccoli. Stars and sets are elegant, but this wacky comedy set in early 20-century London and Paris fizzles, despite Ustinov's writing, directing, and cameo appearance.

Lady Liberty (1972-Italian) C-95m. ***½** D: Mario Monicelli. Sophia Loren, William Devane, Luigi Proietti, Beeson Carroll. Dull comedy of bride-to-be immigrant and her problems with American bureaucracy. Watch for Warhol's Candy Darling in transvestite cameo.

Lady Luck (1946) 97m. ******* D: Edwin L. Marin. Robert Young, Barbara Hale, Frank Morgan, James Gleason. Hale marries gambler Young with hopes of reforming him but meets more problems than she bargained for.

Lady of Burlesque (1943) 91m. ******* D: William Wellman. Barbara Stanwyck, Michael O'Shea, J. Edward Bromberg, Iris Adrian, Marion Martin, Pinky Lee, Frank Conroy, Gloria Dickson. Gypsy Rose Lee's G-STRING MURDERS makes amusing film. Series of murders of burlesque dolls sets Stanwyck's mind working to solve mystery.

Lady of Secrets (1936) 73m. ****½** D: Marion Gering. Ruth Chatterton, Otto Kruger, Lionel Atwill, Marian Marsh, Lloyd Nolan, Robert Allen. Smooth but soapy story of woman whose one unhappy love affair has made her live a life of seclusion. Good cast makes standard film worth seeing.

Lady of the House (1978) C-100m. TVM D: Ralph Nelson and Vincent Sherman. Dyan Cannon, Armand Assante, Zohra Lampert, Susan Ty-

rell, Melvin Belli. Cannon gives a colorful performance as flamboyant San Francisco madam of the late '30s who rose to power and respectability and became mayor of Sausalito, California in '76. Above average.

Lady of the Tropics (1939) 92m. ****** D: Jack Conway. Hedy Lamarr, Robert Taylor, Joseph Schildkraut, Frederick Worlock, Natalie Moorhead. Sad love affair between playboy Taylor and halfbreed Lamarr in exotic setting; slow-moving.

Lady of Vengeance (1957-British) 73m. ****** D: Burt Balaban. Dennis O'Keefe, Ann Sears, Patrick Barr, Vernon Greeves. Tedious account of man hiring killer to avenge a girl's death, becoming embroiled in further murder.

Lady on a Train (1945) 93m. ******* D: Charles David. Deanna Durbin, Ralph Bellamy, Edward Everett Horton, George Coulouris, Allen Jenkins, David Bruce, Patricia Morison, Dan Duryea. Excellent comedy/murder-mystery with Deanna witnessing a murder, then getting involved with nutty family of the deceased tycoon. You'll never guess killer's identity in neatly plotted yarn which even allows Deanna to sing a few tunes.

Lady Pays Off, The (1951) 80m. ****½** D: Douglas Sirk. Linda Darnell, Stephen McNally, Gigi Perreau, Virginia Field. Fanciful drama of schoolteacher Darnell who must pay off gambling debts in Rèno by tutoring casino owner's daughter.

Lady Possessed (1952-British) 87m. ****** D: William Spier, Roy Kellino. James Mason, June Havoc, Pamela Kellino, Fay Compton, Odette Myrtil. Bizarre film of ill woman thinking she is controlled by will of Mason's dead wife.

Lady Says No, The (1951) 80m. ****** D: Frank Ross. David Niven, Joan Caulfield, Lenore Lonergan, James Robertson Justice. Lightweight comedy of fickle Caulfield, who won't decide if marriage is for her.

Lady Scarface (1941) 69m. ****** D: Frank Woodruff. Dennis O'Keefe, Judith Anderson, Frances Neal, Mildred Coles, Eric Blore, Marc Lawrence. Anderson tries to elevate this episodic yarn of police hunting for dangerous gunwoman and her gang.

Lady Sings the Blues (1972) C-144m. ****½** D: Sidney J. Furie. Diana Ross, Billy Dee Williams, Richard

Pryor, James Callahan, Paul Hampton, Sid Melton. Black version of Hollywood cliché-biography, sparked by superb performance by Ross as Billie Holiday, legendary jazz singer whose life was ruined by drug addiction. Valueless as biography, but OK as soap opera, with delightful support from Pryor as "Piano Man."

Lady Surrenders, A SEE: Love Story (1944)

Lady Takes a Chance, A (1943) 86m. *** D: William A. Seiter. Jean Arthur, John Wayne, Charles Winninger, Phil Silvers, Mary Field, Don Costello. Wayne and Arthur make fine comedy team as burly rodeo star and wide-eyed city girl who falls for him; Silvers adds zip as bus-tour guide.

Lady Takes a Flyer, The (1958) C-94m. **½ D: Jack Arnold. Lana Turner, Jeff Chandler, Richard Denning, Andra Martin. Different-type Turner fare. Lana is lady flier who marries pilot Chandler, each finds it hard to settle down to married life.

Lady Takes a Sailor, The (1949) 99m. ** D: Michael Curtiz. Jane Wyman, Dennis Morgan, Eve Arden, Robert Douglas, Allyn Joslyn. Featherweight comedy fully described by title tag.

Lady Vanishes, The (1938-British) 97m. ***½ D: Alfred Hitchcock. Margaret Lockwood, Michael Redgrave, Paul Lukas, Dame May Whitty, Cecil Parker. Vintage mystery, with Lockwood and Redgrave looking for kidnapped Whitty on train ride through Europe; taut suspense laced with delicious humor.

Lady Vanishes, The (1979-British) C-99m. **½ D: Anthony Page. Elliott Gould, Cybill Shepherd, Angela Lansbury, Herbert Lom, Arthur Lowe, Ian Carmichael. Remake of Hitchcock classic changes lead characters—none too successfully—but retains some of the suspense, and rich supporting characters, of the original. Script by George Axelrod.

Lady Wants Mink, The (1953) C-92m. *** D: William A. Seiter. Eve Arden, Ruth Hussey, Dennis O'Keefe, William Demarest, Gene Lockhart. Most diverting little film of wife Hussey breeding mink to get the coat she's always wanted.

Lady with a Dog (1959-Russian) 90m. **½ D: Josif Heifits. Iya Savvina, Alexei Batalov, Ala Chostakova, N. Alisova. Intelligent tale of

adulterous love, sensibly handled, with no contrived ending.

Lady with a Lamp, The (1951-British) 112m. *** D: Herbert Wilcox. Anna Neagle, Michael Wilding, Felix Aylmer, Maureen Pryor, Gladys Young, Julian D'Albie. Methodical recreation of 19th Century nurse-crusader Florence Nightingale, tastefully enacted by Neagle.

Lady with Red Hair, The (1940) 81m. **½ D: Curtis Bernhardt. Miriam Hopkins, Claude Rains, Richard Ainley, Laura Hope Crews, Helen Westley, John Litel, Victor Jory. Breathless pace, likable cast make up for silliness in story of actress Mrs. Leslie Carter and her colorful mentor David Belasco. Look fast for young Cornel Wilde at boarding house.

Lady Without Passport, A (1950) 72m. **½ D: Joseph H. Lewis. Hedy Lamarr, John Hodiak, James Craig, George Macready. Turgid melodrama as Lamarr seeks to leave Havana, former romantic and business associations behind her.

Ladykillers, The (1955-British) C-94m. ***½ D: Alexander Mackendrick. Alec Guinness, Cecil Parker, Herbert Lom, Peter Sellers, Danny Green, Katie Johnson, Frankie Howerd. Droll comedy of not-so-bright crooks involved with seemingly harmless old lady. Guinness scores again, with top-notch supporting cast in this little English gem.

Lady's from Kentucky, The (1939) 67m. **½ D: Alexander Hall. George Raft, Ellen Drew, Hugh Herbert, ZaSu Pitts, Louise Beavers, Stanley Andrews. Regardless of title, Raft's horse takes precedence over his lady in this usual but well-done horseracing saga.

Lady's Morals, A (1930) 75m. ** D: Sidney Franklin. Grace Moore, Reginald Denny, Wallace Beery, Jobyna Howland. First attempt to make star of opera singer Moore doesn't click. She plays Jenny Lind, who learns value of love from devoted Denny.

Lafayette (1963-French) C-110m. ** D: Jean Dreville. Jack Hawkins, Orson Welles, Howard St. John, Edmund Purdom, Vittorio De Sica, Michel Le Royer. Overblown, badly scripted costumer of famed 18th-century Frenchman, resulting in episodic minor spectacle film.

Lafayette Escadrille (1958) 93m. **½ D: William Wellman. Tab Hunter, Etchika Choureau, Marcel Dalio,

David Janssen. Attempted epic of famous French flying legion of WW1 becomes pat actioner with typical romantic interlude, featuring wholesome Hunter.

Lake Placid Serenade (1944) 85m. ** D: Steve Sekely. Vera Ralston, Robert Livingston, Vera Vague, Eugene Pallette, Stephanie Bachelor, Walter Catlett, John Litel, Roy Rogers, Twinkle Watts. Ice-skater's rise to fame, featuring lovely Ralston . . . ugh!

Lancer Spy (1937) 84m. *** D: Gregory Ratoff. Dolores Del Rio, George Sanders, Peter Lorre, Joseph Schildkraut, Virginia Field, Sig Ruman, Fritz Feld. Sanders disguises himself as Nazi officer to get information in this taut thriller; Del Rio has to choose between love and loyalty to her country.

Land of the Pharaohs (1955) C-106m. ** D: Howard Hawks. Jack Hawkins, Joan Collins, Dewey Martin, Alexis Minotis. Well-intentioned, literate spectacle that bogs down for lack of action: set in ancient Egypt.

Land Raiders (1970) C-100m. ** D: Nathan Juran. Telly Savalas, George Maharis, Arlene Dahl, Janet Landgard, Jocelyn Lane, George Coulouris, Guy Rolfe. Even if you can accept Savalas and Maharis as brothers, this Western about family feuds amidst Indian attacks has little to offer.

Land That Time Forgot, The (1975-British) C-90m. **½ D: Kevin Connor. Doug McClure, John McEnery, Susan Penhaligon, Keith Barron, Anthony Ainley. Edgar Rice Burroughs' 1918 fantasy novel about Germans and Americans in WW1 submarine discovering unknown land in South America. Not bad as adventure yarn but special effects (dinosaurs, volcanic eruption) are not convincing. Followed by sequel THE PEOPLE THAT TIME FORGOT.

Land Unknown, The (1957) 78m. ** D: Virgil Vogel. Jock Mahoney, Shawn Smith, Henry Brandon, Douglas Kennedy. Mahoney leads expedition in search of missing husband and stumbles upon prehistoric monsters. Adequate special effects.

Landlord, The (1970) C-113m. ***½ D: Hal Ashby. Beau Bridges, Pearl Bailey, Diana Sands, Louis Gossett, Lee Grant, Susan Anspach. Vibrant comedy-drama with Bridges as aimless rich-kid who buys Harlem tenement planning to renovate it for

himself, changing plans when he meets tenants. Delightful comic touches combined with perceptive sidelights on black experience; Ashby's first film as director.

Landru SEE: Bluebeard

Lanigan's Rabbi (1976) C-100m. TVM D: Lou Antonio. Art Carney, Stuart Margolin, Janet Margolin, Janis Paige, Lorraine Gary, Robert Reed. Mystery-comedy teams small town police chief with local rabbi to solve killing of woman whose body was found on front steps of synagogue. Carney at his best. Based on Harry Kemelman's best-selling *Friday the Rabbi Slept Late.* Above average.

Larceny (1948) 89m. **½ D: George Sherman. John Payne, Joan Caulfield, Dan Duryea, Shelley Winters, Dorothy Hart. Slick but ordinary underworld tale, with roguish Payne deciding to help lovely Caulfield; Duryea is slimy villain.

Larceny, Inc. (1942) 95m. ***½ D: Lloyd Bacon. Edward G. Robinson, Jane Wyman, Broderick Crawford, Jack Carson, Anthony Quinn, Edward Brophy. Hilarious little comedy of ex-cons Robinson, Crawford, and Brophy using luggage store as front for shady activities; villain Quinn tries to horn in. Look for Jackie Gleason in a small role as a soda jerk.

Las Vegas Lady (1976) C-87m. BOMB D: Noel Nosseck. Stella Stevens, Stuart Whitman, George DiCenzo, Lynne Moody, Linda Scruggs, Joseph Della Sorte, Jesse White. Less than routine heist pic about a security guard who flips for title femme. Even "Las Vegas Hillbillies" is better.

Las Vegas Shakedown (1955) 79m. ** D: Sidney Salkow. Dennis O'Keefe, Coleen Gray, Charles Winninger, Thomas Gomez, Elizabeth Patterson, Robert Armstrong. Improbable yet diverting account of O'Keefe's effort to run an honest gambling house, with on-location filming in Las Vegas.

Las Vegas Story, The (1952) 88m. ** D: Robert Stevenson. Jane Russell, Victor Mature, Vincent Price, Hoagy Carmichael, Brad Dexter. Synthetic murder yarn supposedly set in gambling capital, sparked by Russell's vitality.

Laserblast (1978) C-90m. **½ D: Michael Raye. Kim Milford, Cheryl

Smith, Roddy McDowall, Ron Masock, Keenan Wynn, Dennis Burkley. Low-budget sci-fi with teenage Milford finding alien ray gun which enables him to become a creature who can destroy his enemies. David Allen's stop-motion effects are a highlight.

Lassie Come Home (1943) C-88m. *** D: Fred M. Wilcox. Roddy McDowall, Donald Crisp, Dame May Whitty, Edmund Gwenn, Nigel Bruce, Elsa Lanchester, Elizabeth Taylor. Winning, wonderful film of poor family forced to sell their beloved dog, who undertakes tortuous journey to return to them. Remade as GYPSY COLT.

Last Adventure, The (1967-French) C-102m. **½ D: Robert Enrico. Alain Delon, Lino Venturi, Joanna Shimkus, Hans Meyer. Two adventurers and a beautiful young woman go on very engaging treasure hunt.

Last American Hero, The (1973) C-100m. *** D: Lamont Johnson. Jeff Bridges, Valerie Perrine, Geraldine Fitzgerald, Art Lund, Gary Busey, Ed Lauter, Ned Beatty. Unusual, engrossing saga of Junior Jackson, North Carolinian backwoods moonshiner and racing fanatic, pitting his ability against the System. Three-dimensional, believable characters enhance somewhat cynical point of view. Retitled HARD DRIVER.

Last Angry Man, The (1959) 100m. *** D: Daniel Mann. Paul Muni, David Wayne, Betsy Palmer, Luther Adler, Joby Baker, Joanna Moore, Godfrey Cambridge. Sentimental story of an old, dedicated family doctor in Brooklyn whose life is going to be portrayed on TV. Muni (in his last film) makes it worth seeing. Adapted from Gerald Green's book.

Last Angry Man, The (1974) C-78m. TVM D: Jerrold Freedman. Pat Hingle, Lynn Carlin, Paul Jabara, Tracy Bogart, Sorrell Booke, Penny Stanton, Ann Doran, Andrew Duggan. Hingle is irascible and concerned Jewish doctor in Brooklyn of 1936, the role played by Paul Muni in 1959. OK remake. Average.

Last Blitzkrieg, The (1958) 84m. ** D: Arthur Dreifuss. Van Johnson, Kerwin Mathews, Dick York, Larry Storch. WW2 actioner trying to focus on German point of view.

Last Bridge, The (1957-Austrian) 90m. ***½ D: Helmut Kautner. Maria Schell, Bernhard Wicki, Barbara Rutting, Carl Mohner. Schell gives well-modulated performance as German doctor captured by Yugoslavian partisans during WW2, first administering medical aid reluctantly, then realizing all people deserve equal attention.

Last Challenge, The (1967) C-105m. ** D: Richard Thorpe. Glenn Ford, Angie Dickinson, Chad Everett, Gary Merrill, Jack Elam, Delphi Lawrence, Royal Dano. Punk Everett is out to get Marshal Ford in well-cast but routine Western; Angie plays saloon-keeper, which makes one wonder why the two men don't just settle their problems over a drink.

Last Chance, The (1968-Italian) C-91m. ** D: Niny Rosati. Tab Hunter, Michael Rennie, Daniela Bianchi, Liz Barrett. American journalist Hunter is given valuable documents about an international crime syndicate and finds himself a hunted man. Listless thriller.

Last Child, The (1971) C-73m. TVM D: John Llewellyn Moxey. Michael Cole, Janet Margolin, Van Heflin, Harry Guardino, Edward Asner, Barbara Babcock. 1994: U.S. government forbids more than one child per family. The Millers (Cole & Margolin) seek escape from prison by running to Canada, pursued by authorities, finally aided by retired U.S. Senator (Heflin). Accent on drama, soft-pedaling aspects of totalitarianism, but action and performances (including Heflin's last) more than adequate. Above average.

Last Circus Show, The (1974-Italian) C-91m. ** D: Mario Garriazzo. James Whitmore, Lee J. Cobb, Cyril Cusack, Renato Cestie. Family-style tearjerker about a young boy who tries to reunite his parents, then falls deathly ill and begs to see a circus performance. Also known as THE BALLOON VENDOR.

Last Command, The (1955) C-110m. **½ D: Frank Lloyd. Sterling Hayden, Anna Maria Alberghetti, Richard Carlson, Ernest Borgnine, J. Carrol Naish, Virginia Grey, Ben Cooper. Elaborate, sweeping account of the battle of the Alamo, hampered by tedious script.

Last Cry for Help, A (1979) C-100m. TVM D: Hal Sitowitz. Linda Purl, Shirley Jones, Tony LoBianco, Murray Hamilton, Grant Goodeve. High school coed withdraws into world of her own, fearing she is not living up to parents' expectations, and attempts suicide. Average.

Last Day, The (1975) **C-100m. TVM** D: Vincent McEveety. Richard Widmark, Christopher Connelly, Robert Conrad, Gene Evans, Richard Jaeckel, Tim Matheson, Barbara Rush, Tom Skerritt, Loretta Swit. Western about retired gunman (Widmark) forced to defend his town when the Dalton gang rides in for its final bank heist. Straightforward hoss-opera gussied up with pseudo-documentary touch and narration by Harry Morgan. Above average.

Last Day of the War, The (1969) **C-96m. **** D: J. A. Bardew. George Maharis, Maria Perschy, James Philbrook, Gerard Herter. Germans and Americans race to find noted German scientist during waning days of WW2. Low-grade drama filmed in Spain.

Last Days of Dolwyn, The SEE: **Dolwyn**

Last Days of Man on Earth, The (1973-British) **C-78m. *½** D: Robert Fuest. Jon Finch, Jenny Runacre, Sterling Hayden, Patrick Magee, Hugh Griffith, Harry Andrews. Muddled sci-fi comedy set in Lapland, London and Turkey as world nears its end. A few scattered laughs. Longer, original British version (called **THE LAST PROGRAMME**) had more substance.

Last Days of Pompeii, The (1935) **96m. ***** D: Ernest B. Schoedsack. Preston Foster, Basil Rathbone, Dorothy Wilson, David Holt, Alan Hale, John Wood, Louis Calhern. Blacksmith Foster aspires to wealth and power as gladiator; climactic spectacle scenes are thrilling and expertly done.

Last Days of Pompeii, The (1960-Italian) **C-105m. **½** D: Mario Bonnard. Steve Reeves, Christine Kaufmann, Barbara Carroll, Anne Marie Baumann, Mimmo Palmara. New version of venerable tale focuses on muscleman Reeves and synthetic account of Christian martyrs. Very little spectacle.

Last Detail, The (1973) **C-105m. ***½** D: Hal Ashby. Jack Nicholson, Otis Young, Randy Quaid, Clifton James, Carol Kane, Michael Moriarty. Superior comedy-drama about two career sailors ordered to transport a kleptomaniac prisoner to the brig. Robert Towne's brilliant off-color dialogue (certain to be cut

for TV) contributes to a quintessential Nicholson performance.

Last Dinosaur, The (1977) **C-100m. TVM** D: Alex Grasshoff and Tom Kotani. Richard Boone, Joan Van Ark, Steven Keats, Luther Rackley, Tatsu Nakamura. Fantasy tale, made in Japan, about the world's richest man who invades a newly-discovered prehistoric world to stalk a Tyrannosaurus Rex. Entertaining foolishness out of the "Godzilla" school, originally intended for theaters. Average.

Last Embrace (1979) **C-102m. ***** D: Jonathan Demme. Roy Scheider, Janet Margolin, John Glover, Sam Levene, Christopher Walken, Charles Napier. Government undercover agent Scheider sees wife ambushed, spends rest of the picture in various stages of mental disorder. One of the better Hitchcock-influenced suspense thrillers offers good performances and a punchy climax.

Last Escape, The (1970) **C-90m. *½** D: Walter Grauman. Stuart Whitman, John Collin, Pinkas Braun, Martin Jarvis, Gunther Neutze, Margit Saad. O.S.S Captain Whitman is ordered to sneak rocket expert out of Germany near the end of WW2 with predictable results.

Last Frontier, The (1955) **C-98m. **½** D: Anthony Mann. Victor Mature, Guy Madison, Robert Preston, James Whitmore, Anne Bancroft. Three wilderness scouts see their lives change with coming of cavalry outpost and military martinet (Preston). Offbeat characterizations in this cavalry drama.

Last Gangster, The (1937) **81m. ***** D: Edward Ludwig. Edward G. Robinson, Rosa Stradner, James Stewart, John Carradine, Sidney Blackmer, Louise Beavers, Edward Brophy. Thoughtful gangster film has Robinson released from jail, trying to reinstate himself as powerful mobster; side action involves ex-wife, now remarried and not wanting anything to do with him.

Last Gentleman, The (1934) **80m. ***** D: Sidney Lanfield. George Arliss, Edna May Oliver, Charlotte Henry, Janet Beecher, Ralph Morgan, Edward Ellis, Donald Meek. Delightful comedy with Arliss as dying millionaire whose family descends on him in hopes of carting away a piece of his fortune. Ingenious denouements gives Arliss last laugh.

Last Giraffe, The (1979) **C-100m.**

TVM D: Jack Couffer. Susan Anspach, Simon Ward, Gordon Jackson, Don Warrington, Saeed Jaffrey. American wild-life photographer and safari-guide husband fight to save the endangered Rothschild giraffe of Kenya from poachers in this entertaining adaptation of the book *Raising Daisy Rothschild*. Above average.

Last Grenade, The (1970-British) C-94m. **½ D: Gordon Flemyng. Stanley Baker, Alex Cord, Honor Blackman, Richard Attenborough, Rafer Johnson, Andrew Keir. Solid cast in grim, unevenly plotted tale of duel to death between two British mercenaries. Good location shooting can't hide lack of character development, motivation.

Last Hard Men, The (1976) C-98m. ** D: Andrew V. McLaglen. Charlton Heston, James Coburn, Barbara Hershey, Michael Parks, Christopher Mitchum, Jorge Rivero. Violent oater, familiar plot: escaped killer Coburn and men kidnap Hershey, daughter of aging lawman Heston, who had sent him up. Good character work by Parks.

Last Holiday (1950-British) 89m. *** D: Henry Cass. Alec Guinness, Kay Walsh, Bernard Lee, Beatrice Campbell, Wilfrid Hyde-White. Droll, biting account of Guinness thinking he is dying, living it up at ritzy resort; twist ending adds strength to film.

Last Hours Before Morning (1975) C-78m. TVM D: Joseph Hardy. Ed Lauter, Thalmus Rasulala, George Murdock, Sheila Sullivan, Rhonda Fleming, Robert Alda, Kaz Garas, Victoria Principal, Don Porter, Art Lund. Period detective movie about a hot-shot house detective who moonlights by chasing deadbeats and stumbles onto a jewel robbery/homicide. Interesting performance by Lauter in a rare starring role. Average.

Last Hunt, The (1956) C-108m. **½ D: Richard Brooks. Robert Taylor, Stewart Granger, Lloyd Nolan, Debra Paget, Russ Tamblyn, Constance Ford. Rampaging buffalo herd is primary excitement of Taylor-Granger feuding partnership in 1880s West.

Last Hurrah, The (1958) 121m. ***½ D: John Ford. Spencer Tracy, Jeffrey Hunter, Dianne Foster, Basil Rathbone, Pat O'Brien, Donald Crisp, James Gleason, Ed Brophy, John Carradine, Ricardo Cortez, Frank McHugh, Jane Darwell. Flavorful version of Edwin O'Connor novel of politics, loosely based on life of Boston's Mayor Curley. Top-notch veteran cast makes film sparkle.

Last Hurrah, The (1977) C-110m. TVM D: Vincent Sherman. Carroll O'Connor, John Anderson, Dana Andrews, Jack Carter, Mariette Hartley, Burgess Meredith, Patrick O'Neal, Patrick Wayne, Kitty Winn. O'Connor not only plays Mayor Frank Skeffington but also wrote this adaptation of the Edwin O'Connor best seller. Doesn't hold a candle to John Ford's 1958 movie. Average.

Last Laugh, The (1924-German) 77m. ***½ D: F. W. Murnau. Emil Jannings. Silent-film classic told entirely by camera, without title cards. Jannings plays proud doorman at posh hotel who is suddenly and summarily demoted; film details his utter and grievous humiliation. Brilliantly filmed by pioneer cameraman Karl Freund, with towering performance by Jannings.

Last Man on Earth, The (1964-U.S.-Italian) 86m. ** D: Sidney Salkow. Vincent Price, Franca Bettoia, Emma Danieli, Giacomo Rossi-Stuart, Tony Cerevi. Often crude chiller with Price the sole survivor of plague, besieged by victims who arise at night thirsting for his blood; erratic production. Based on Richard Matheson's "I Am Legend"; remade as THE OMEGA MAN.

Last Man to Hang, The (1956-British) 75m. ** D: Terence Fisher. Tom Conway, Elizabeth Sellars, Eunice Gayson, Freda Jackson, Raymond Huntley, Anthony Newley. Forthright courtroom film of man on trial for alleged murder of wife.

Last Married Couple in America, The (1980) C-103m. *½ D: Gilbert Cates. George Segal, Natalie Wood, Richard Benjamin, Valerie Harper, Bob Dishy, Dom DeLuise. Likable cast in stupid sex comedy about happily married couple so upset by breakup of married friends that they begin to question their own relationship. Smutty and ridiculous.

Last Mile, The (1959) 81m. **½ D: Howard W. Koch. Mickey Rooney, Clifford David, Harry Millard, Don "Red" Barry, Ford Rainey, Leon Janney. Above-par account of attempted breakout from big house by those on death row. Rooney is excellent. Adapted from play by John Wexley and filmed before in 1932.

Last Movie, The (1971) C-108m. *½ D: Dennis Hopper. Dennis Hopper, Julie Adams, Peter Fonda, Kris Kristofferson, Sylvia Miles, John Phillip Law, Rod Cameron, Sam Fuller. Hopper's fatally pretentious follow-up to EASY RIDER is interesting only as curio; incomprehensible story of small Peruvian village after a movie company pulls out has lovely photography, good acting by Adams. Otherwise, you've been warned.

Last Musketeer, The (1954-French) C-95m. ** D: Fernando Cerchio. Georges Marchal, Dawn Addams, Jacques Dumesnil. Another variation on the THREE MUSKETEERS, with Marchal as D'Artagnan combating corruption in Louis XIV's court; adequate swashbuckler. Retitled: THE COUNT OF BRAGELONNE.

Last of Mrs. Cheyney, The (1937) 98m. *** D: Richard Boleslawski. Joan Crawford, William Powell, Robert Montgomery, Frank Morgan, Jessie Ralph, Nigel Bruce. Glossy remake of Norma Shearer's 1929 success, from Frederick Lonsdale's play about a chic American jewel thief in England. Great fun for star watchers (especially since it's been out of circulation for many years), though it was considered a dated dud in 1937. Remade in 1951 as THE LAW AND THE LADY.

Last of Sheila, The (1973) C-120m. ***½ D: Herbert Ross. James Coburn, James Mason, Dyan Cannon, Ian McShane, Joan Hackett, Raquel Welch, Richard Benjamin. Super murder-puzzler about jet-set gamester who devises what turns into a deadly game of whodunit. Many red herrings make it all the more fun. Script by Anthony Perkins and Stephen Sondheim.

Last of the Badmen (1957) C-79m. ** D: Paul Landres. George Montgomery, Meg Randall, James Best, Michael Ansara, Keith Larsen. Western about Chicago detectives in 1880s chasing after killers of their fellow-worker.

Last of the Buccaneers (1950) C-79m. *½ D: Lew Landers. Paul Henreid, Jack Oakie, Mary Anderson, John Dehner. Quickie costumer tainting the legendary name of Jean Lafitte with plodding account of his post-War of 1812 exploits.

Last of the Comanches (1952) C-85m.

** D: Andre de Toth. Broderick Crawford, Barbara Hale, Lloyd Bridges, Martin Milner, John War Eagle. Trite rehash of cavalrymen fighting off Indian attack. Western remake of SAHARA.

Last of the Fast Guns, The (1958) C-82m. ** D: George Sherman. Jock Mahoney, Gilbert Roland, Linda Cristal, Eduard Franz. Adequately told Western of search for missing man, and obstacles the hired gunslinger must overcome.

Last of the Good Guys (1978) C-100m. TVM D: Theodore J. Flicker. Robert Culp, Dennis Dugan, Richard Narita, Ji-Tu Cumbuka, Larry Hagman, Marlyn Mason. Comedy-drama pitting a hard-nosed by-the-book police sergeant against a bunch of rookies trying to help a dying veteran cop protect his pension. Average.

Last of the Mobile Hot-Shots (1970) C-108m. ** D: Sidney Lumet. James Coburn, Lynn Redgrave, Robert Hooks, Perry Hayes, Reggie King. Ambitious flop from Tennessee Williams' "Seven Descents of Myrtle" about volatile triangle set in Deep South.

Last of the Mohicans, The (1936) 91m. *** D: George B. Seitz. Randolph Scott, Binnie Barnes, Heather Angel, Hugh Buckler, Henry Wilcoxon, Bruce Cabot. Big-scale action based on James Fenimore Cooper tale of the French-Indian War in colonial America. Cabot makes good villainous Indian.

Last of the Mohicans (1977) C-100m. TVM D: James L. Conway. Steve Forrest, Ned Romero, Andrew Prine, Robert Tessier, Don Shanks, Jane Actman. Sturdy new version of the adventure classic, with Forrest fine as the stalwart Hawkeye. Above average.

Last of the Redmen (1947) C-77m. **½ D: George Sherman. Jon Hall, Michael O'Shea, Evelyn Ankers, Julie Bishop, Buster Crabbe. OK color Western with thoughtful Indian (Hall) facing decision involving group of ambushed white men; loosely based on James Fenimore Cooper's LAST OF THE MOHICANS.

Last of the Red Hot Lovers (1972) C-98m. BOMB D: Gene Saks. Alan Arkin, Sally Kellerman, Paula Prentiss, Renee Taylor. Appalling film version of typical Neil Simon play concerns Arkin's unsuccessful attempts to carry on sneaky love affair with three different women (not all at once). Actors scream at each other for more than an hour and a half in shoddy production for which the term "photographed stage play" must have been invented.

Last of the Secret Agents?, The (1966) C-90m. *½ D: Norman Abbott. Marty Allen, Steve Rossi, John Williams, Nancy Sinatra, Lou Jacobi. Tiring spoof on spy movies ends up unintentional self-mockery. Strictly for Allen and Rossi fans.

Last of the Ski Bums (1969) C-86m. *** D: Dick Barrymore. Ron Funk, Mike Zuetell, Ed Ricks. Made by same team that produced THE ENDLESS SUMMER, film details exploits of three men who win large sum of money, spend it on long ski holiday. Not only will effect diminish on small screen, film includes weak narrative whose point of view conflicts with beauty of visuals.

Last of the Vikings, The (1960-Italian) C-102m. ** D: Giacomo Gentilomo. Cameron Mitchell, Edmund Purdom, Isabelle Corey, Helene Remy. Filmed with gusto, elaborate epic deals with Mitchell out to punish the Norse for devastating his homelands; poorly acted.

Last Outpost, The (1935) 70m. *** D: Louis Gasnier, Charles Barton. Cary Grant, Claude Rains, Gertrude Michael, Kathleen Burke, Colin Tapley, Akim Tamiroff. Exciting action-adventure with British troops in Africa, along lines of LOST PATROL, BENGAL LANCERS, etc.

Last Outpost, The (1951) C-88m. **½ D: Lewis R. Foster. Ronald Reagan, Rhonda Fleming, Bruce Bennett, Bill Williams. Burst of action saves worn-out yarn of two brothers on opposite sides of Civil War, teaming up to fight off Indian attack.

Last Picture Show, The (1971) 114m. **** D: Peter Bogdanovich. Timothy Bottoms, Jeff Bridges, Ben Johnson, Cloris Leachman, Ellen Burstyn, Cybill Shepherd, Eileen Brennan. Brilliant study of life in small Texas town during 1950s, and how characters' lives intertwine, from Larry McMurtry's book. Oscars went to Johnson and Leachman for sensitive performances, but entire cast works at same level.

Last Posse, The (1953) 73m. ** D: Alfred L. Werker. Broderick Crawford, John Derek, Charles Bickford, Wanda Hendrix, Warner Anderson.

Sheriff's men track down robbers, not without surprising results.

Last Programme, The SEE: **Last Days of Man on Earth**

Last Rebel, The (1971) C-89m. BOMB D: Denys McCoy. Joe Namath, Jack Elam, Woody Strode, Ty Hardin, Victoria George. Namath plays Confederate soldier who raises havoc in small Missouri town after the Civil War. Film has obvious camp value, but it's not enough; Joe makes Ty Hardin look like John Gielgud.

Last Remake of Beau Geste, The (1977) C-83m. **½ D: Marty Feldman. Marty Feldman, Ann-Margret, Michael York, Peter Ustinov, James Earl Jones, Trevor Howard, Henry Gibson, Terry-Thomas, Spike Milligan, Roy Kinnear. After uproarious first half, Feldman's Foreign Legion spoof falters and gropes its way to weak conclusion. Enough belly-laughs to make it worthwhile, and sidesplitting performance by butler Milligan.

Last Ride, The (1944) 56m. ** D: D. Ross Lederman. Richard Travis, Eleanor Parker, Charles Lang, Jack LaRue. Smooth programmer involving a series of "accidental" deaths and the detective who tracks down the "murderer."

Last Ride of the Dalton Gang, The (1979) C-150m. TVM D: Dan Curtis. Cliff Potts, Randy Quaid, Larry Wilcox, Jack Palance, Dale Robertson, Bo Hopkins, Sharon Farrell, Harris Yulin. Old-fashioned shoot-em-up recounting (with huge doses of humor) the adventures of the Old West's infamous gang—here intimating that the Dalton's were inept boobs. The opening and closing, in 1930s Hollywood, is gratuitous. Average.

Last Roman, The (1968-German/Rumanian) 92m. ** D: Robert Siodmak. Laurence Harvey, Orson Welles, Sylva Koscina, Honor Blackman, Michael Dunn, Harriet Andersson, Lang Jeffries, Robert Hoffman. Big cast in spears and togas look baffled at what has become of Felix Dann's German bestseller *Kamf um Rom* about the decline of the Roman Empire. Telescoped from a two-part spectacular.

Last Run, The (1971) C-99m. **½ D: Richard Fleischer. George C. Scott, Tony Musante, Trish Van Devere, Colleen Dewhurst. Mediocre tale of aging gangland driver who has to make one more run for his ego. Great photography by Sven Nykvist. Started by John Huston, majority of film directed by Fleischer.

Last Safari, The (1967-British) C-110m. ** D: Henry Hathaway. Kaz Garas, Stewart Granger, Gabriella Licudi, Johnny Sekka, Liam Redmond. Uninteresting action tale with depressed professional hunter (Stewart) coming to terms with himself and rich young couple who hire him. Good cast can't handle script.

Last Shot You Hear, The (1969-British) 87m. *½ D: Gordon Hessler. Hugh Marlowe, Zena Walker, Patricia Haines, William Dysart, Thorley Walters. Complicated, dull story of marriage counselor Marlowe's understandable problem when his wife takes a lover.

Last Stagecoach West (1957) 67m. *½ D: Joseph Kane. Jim Davis, Victor Jory, Mary Castle, Lee Van Cleef. Fair cast cannot save bland Western about stage-driver who loses government contracts and goes out of business.

Last Summer (1969) C-97m. ***½ D: Frank Perry. Richard Thomas, Barbara Hershey, Bruce Davison, Cathy Burns. Powerful story based on Evan Hunter novel of teenagers playing on the beach in a summer resort. The film follows their games, their sexual awakenings, and how evil manifests itself with calculated determination. Cathy Burns is a standout.

Last Sunset, The (1961) C-112m. **½ D: Robert Aldrich. Rock Hudson, Kirk Douglas, Dorothy Malone, Joseph Cotten, Carol Lynley. Curious film of three men pursuing the same woman (Malone). Amid a cattle roundup, there is much meditation by all.

Last Survivors, The (1975) C-78m. TVM D: Lee H. Katzin. Martin Sheen, Diane Baker, Tom Bosley, Christopher George, Bruce Davison, Anne Francis, Percy Rodriguez, Anne Seymour, Bethel Leslie. Sea drama with Sheen deciding who stays in the overcrowded lifeboat and who goes overboard. Twice (or more) told harrowing tale done better by Tyrone Power in ABANDON SHIP. Average.

Last Tango in Paris (1973-French-Italian) C-129m. *** D: Bernardo Bertolucci. Marlon Brando, Maria Schneider, Jean-Pierre Leaud, Darling Legitimus, Catherine Sola, Mauro Marchetti, Dan Diament. Already legendary drama about widower Brando's degradation of Schneider may never make it to TV, but who would have guessed in 1969 that the Mets would win the World Series and John Wayne would win an Oscar within six months of each other? Alternately gripping and boring story was overrated by some critics and underrated by others; Schneider is almost good enough to triumph over her miscasting; and Brando's performance is in a class with his job in ON THE WATERFRONT.

Last Ten Days, The (1956-German) 113m. *** D: G. W. Pabst. Albin Skoda, Oskar Werner, Lotte Tobisch, Willy Krause, Helga Kennedy-Dohrn. Finely etched study of downfall of leader of Third Reich. Retitled: LAST TEN DAYS OF ADOLPH HITLER.

Last Tenant, The (1978) C-100m. TVM D: Jud Taylor. Tony LoBianco, Lee Strasberg, Christine Lehti, Danny Aiello, Julie Bovasso. Acclaimed drama about the effects on a middle-aged bachelor's pending marriage when the family decides he must care for their aging father. George Rubino won an Emmy Award for his original teleplay, lovingly acted by LoBianco and Strasberg. Above average.

Last Time I Saw Archie, The (1961) 98m. *½ D: Jack Webb. Robert Mitchum, Jack Webb, Martha Hyer, France Nuyen. Off-duty from DRAGNET, Webb directed and co-starred in this dull Army comedy about conman Mitchum.

Last Time I Saw Paris, The (1954) C-116m. *** D: Richard Brooks. Elizabeth Taylor, Van Johnson, Donna Reed, Walter Pidgeon, Eva Gabor. Updated version of F. Scott Fitzgerald story, set in post-WW2 Paris, of ruined marriages and disillusioned people. MGM gloss helps.

Last Train from Bombay (1952) 72m. *½ D: Fred F. Sears. Jon Hall, Christine Larson, Lisa Ferraday, Douglas Kennedy. Hall single-handedly attempts to prevent a train wreck; set in India.

Last Train from Gun Hill (1959) C-94m. *** D: John Sturges. Kirk Douglas, Anthony Quinn, Carolyn Jones, Earl Holliman, Brad Dexter, Brian Hutton, Ziva Rodann. Superior Western of staunch sheriff determined to leave Gun Hill with murder suspect, despite necessity for shoot-out.

Last Train from Madrid, The (1937) 77m. *** D: James Hogan. Lew Ayres, Dorothy Lamour, Gilbert Roland, Anthony Quinn, Lee Bowman, Karen Morley, Helen Mack, Evelyn Brent, Robert Cummings, Lionel Atwill, Olympe Bradna. Imitation GRAND HOTEL works out quite well, linking vignettes of various people escaping from wartorn Spain during 1930s. Modest but well-made film, with impressive cast.

Last Tycoon, The (1976) C-125m. ***½ D: Elia Kazan. Robert De-Niro, Tony Curtis, Robert Mitchum, Jeanne Moreau, Jack Nicholson, Donald Pleasence, Ingrid Boulting, Ray Milland, Dana Andrews, Theresa Russell, John Carradine. Lowkeyed but effective Harold Pinter adaptation of F. Scott Fitzgerald's final novel benefits immeasurably from DeNiro's great, uncharacteristic performance as 1930s movie producer who is slowly working himself to death. Along with Joan Micklin Silver's BERNICE BOBS HER HAIR, the best Fitzgerald yet put on the screen.

Last Valley, The (1971-British) C-128m. ** D: James Clavell. Michael Caine, Omar Sharif, Florinda Bolkan, Nigel Davenport, Per Oscarsson, Arthur O'Connell. Thinking man's adventure epic is an unfortunate misfire; 17th-century story brings warrior Caine and his soldiers to peaceful valley which has remained untouched by the Thirty Years War.

Last Voyage, The (1960) C-91m. *** D: Andrew L. Stone. Robert Stack, Dorothy Malone, George Sanders, Edmond O'Brien, Woody Strode. Engrossing drama of luxury ship that goes down at sea, and the ways the crew and passengers are affected. Sanders is ill-fated captain, Stack and Malone a married couple in jeopardy.

Last Wagon, The (1956) C-99m. *** D: Delmer Daves. Richard Widmark, Felicia Farr, Susan Kohner, Tommy Rettig, Stephanie Griffin, Ray Stricklyn, Nick Adams. Widmark is condemned killer who saves remnants of wagon train after Indian attack, leading them to safety. Clichéd plot well handled.

Last Waltz, The (1978) C-117m. **** D: Martin Scorsese. The Band, Bob Dylan, Neil Young, Joni Mitch-

ell, Van Morrison, Eric Clapton, Neil Diamond, The Staples, Muddy Waters, Emmylou Harris. Truly wonderful documentary about The Band's Thanksgiving, 1976 farewell concert, filmed by state-of-the-art Hollywood talent. A pair of studio-shot numbers involving The Staples and Harris are as exciting to watch as listen to, but the whole film is beautifully done.

Last Wave, The (1977-Australian) C-106m. *** D: Peter Weir. Richard Chamberlain, Olivia Hammett, Gulpilil, Frederick Parslow, Vivean Gray, Nanjiwarra Amagula. Fascinating chiller about Australian lawyer (Chamberlain) defending aborigine accused of murder. Modern symbolism and ancient tribal rituals make for unusual and absorbing film.

Last Woman on Earth, The (1961) C-71m. BOMB D: Roger Corman. Antony Carbone, Edward Wain, Betsy Jones-Moreland. Dull three-cornered romance involving last survivors on earth after radioactive blast.

Last Year at Marienbad (1962-French) 93m. *** D: Alain Resnais. Delphine Seyrig, Giorgio Albertazzi, Sacha Pitoeff, Francoise Bertin, Luce Garcia-Ville. Beautifully photographed but murky, bewildering story of young man attempting to lure a woman to run away with him.

Late George Apley, The (1947) 98m. *** D: Joseph L. Mankiewicz. Ronald Colman, Peggy Cummins, Vanessa Brown, Richard Haydn, Charles Russell. Film of J. P. Marquand's satire on blue-blooded Boston families lacks punch of Mankiewicz's other films, but is still entertaining.

Late Liz, The (1971) C-119m. BOMB D: Dick Ross. Anne Baxter, Steve Forrest, James Gregory, Coleen Gray, Joan Hotchkis, Jack Albertson. Campy drama about Baxter's rejection of alcohol due to religion is well-intentioned, but hardly convincing as presented here; viewers may need a good stiff drink by the time it's over.

Late Show, The (1977) C-94m. ***½ D: Robert Benton. Art Carney, Lily Tomlin, Bill Macy, Eugene Roche, Joanna Cassidy, John Considine, Howard Duff. Carney is an aging private eye who tries to solve murder of his ex-partner (Duff), "helped" by flaky, aimless young woman (Tomlin). Echoes of Chandler and Hammett resound in Benton's complex but likable script;

chemistry between Carney and Tomlin is perfect.

Latin Lovers (1953) C-104m. **½ D: Mervyn LeRoy. Lana Turner, Ricardo Montalban, John Lund, Jean Hagen, Louis Calhern. Hokey romance yarn set in South America, with Turner ambling about seeking true love; pointless script.

Latin Lovers (1961-Italian) 80m. ** D: Lorenza Mazzetti, et al. Maria di Giuseppe, Mariella Zanetti, Jose Creci, Renza Volpi. Eight episodes dealing with love in Italy; most tales superficial and strained.

Latitude Zero (1970-Japanese) C-99m. ** D: Ishiro Hondo. Joseph Cotten, Cesar Romero, Richard Jaeckel, Patricia Medina, Linda Haynes, Akira Takarada. Better than average imported cast helps usual wide-eyed sci-fi adventure of underwater civilization of benevolent geniuses fighting legions of Malic (Romero), out to control world. Some good sets, but action and suspense poorly handled.

Laughing Policeman, The (1974) C-111m. **½ D: Stuart Rosenberg. Walter Matthau, Bruce Dern, Lou Gossett, Albert Paulsen, Anthony Zerbe, Anthony Costello. Reasonably engrossing San Francisco cop drama about search for mass slayer of some bus passengers. Matthau and Dern are good as cops with contrasting styles.

Laughter (1930) 81m. **½ D: Harry D'Arrast. Nancy Carroll, Fredric March, Frank Morgan, Leonard Carey. Lumpy film with a few bright sequences about Follies girl Carroll marrying millionaire but finding life empty, unhappy.

Laughter In Paradise (1951-British) 95m. **½ D: Mario Zampi. Alastair Sim, Fay Compton, Audrey Hepburn, Beatrice Campbell. Witty study of human nature, as four recipients of large bequests must carry out peculiar tasks to get inheritance.

Laughter in the Dark (1969-British) C-101m. ** D: Tony Richardson. Nicol Williamson, Anna Karina, Jean-Claude Drouot, Peter Bowles, Sian Phillips. Excruciating film from Nabokov novel about wealthy married man (Williamson) whose fascination with young girl (Karina) backfires at every turn, eventually ruining his life. Exceedingly unpleasant, and seemingly interminable.

Laura (1944) 88m. **** D: Otto Prem-

inger. Gene Tierney, Dana Andrews, Clifton Webb, Vincent Price, Judith Anderson, Grant Mitchell, Lane Chandler, Dorothy Adams. Classic mystery with lovely Tierney supposedly killed, detective Andrews trying to assemble murder puzzle. Fascinating, witty, a classic, with Webb standout as cynical columnist. Also features David Raksin's theme. Rouben Mamoulian started directing film, Preminger took over.

Laurel and Hardy's Laughing 20's (1965) 90m. ***½ Compiled by Robert Youngson. Stan Laurel, Oliver Hardy, Charley Chase, Edgar Kennedy, James Finlayson, Anita Garvin. Some of L&H's best moments on film are included, with everything from pie-throwing to pants-ripping. Also some excellent sequences of Charley Chase, adding to the fun.

Lavender Hill Mob, The (1950-British) 82m. ***½ D: Charles Crichton. Alec Guinness, Stanley Holloway, Sidney James, Alfie Bass. Excellent comedy with droll Guinness a timid bank clerk who has perfect scheme for robbing the safe, with a madcap chase climax. Look for Audrey Hepburn.

L'Avventura (1960-Italian) 145m. ***½ D: Michelangelo Antonioni. Monica Vitti, Gabriele Ferzetti, Lea Massari, Dominique Blanchar, James Addams. Woman's disappearance prompts examinations of relationships among weekend yachting group. Incisive filmmaking, but not for all tastes.

Law, The SEE: **Where the Hot Wind Blows**

Law, The (1974) C-120m. TVM D: John Badham. Judd Hirsch, John Beck, Bonnie Franklin, Barbara Baxley, Sam Wanamaker, Allan Arbus, John Hillerman, Gary Busey. Outstanding drama depicting criminal-justice system of a large city as public defender Hirsch pursues case surrounding a football superstar's torture-killing. Brisk and biting, first-rate performances. Above average.

Law and Disorder (1958-British) 76m. **½ D: Charles Crichton. Michael Redgrave, Robert Morley, Ronald Squire, Elizabeth Sellars. Brisk comedy of con-man who gives up life of crime to avoid embarrassing situation of making up stories to tell prim son.

Law and Disorder (1974) C-103m. *** D: Ivan Passer. Carroll O'Connor, Ernest Borgnine, Ann Wedgeworth, Anita Dangler, Leslie Ackerman, Karen Black, Jack Kehoe. Intelligent, original comedy-drama of two middle-aged New Yorkers incensed at rising crime who become auxiliary cops. At first they treat it as a lark, but soon it becomes deadly serious. Full of fine perceptions, interesting vignettes.

Law and Jake Wade, The (1958) C-86m. ******* D: John Sturges. Robert Taylor, Richard Widmark, Patricia Owens, Robert Middleton. Robust Western of outlaw forcing his cohort-turned-good to lead him to buried loot. Taylor and Widmark make good adversaries.

Law and Order (1932) 70m. *****½** D: Edward L. Cahn. Walter Huston, Harry Carey, Raymond Hatton, Russell Hopton, Ralph Ince, Andy Devine. Exceptional western that takes familiar story (Wyatt Earp and Doc Holliday vs. the Clantons) and tells it with style but no flourishes: stark, realistic, and the finale is a knockout. Co-scripted by John Huston.

Law and Order (1976) C-150m. TVM D: Marvin Chomsky. Darren McGavin, Keir Dullea, Robert Reed, Suzanne Pleshette, James Olson, Teri Garr, Scott Brady, Will Geer, Jeanette Nolan, Whitney Blake, Biff McGuire. Sprawling TV movie from Dorothy Uhnak's best-seller tells of three generations of Irish-American New York cops. Strong performances all around. Above average.

Law and the Lady, The (1951) 104m. ****½** D: Edwin H. Knopf. Greer Garson, Michael Wilding, Fernando Lamas, Marjorie Main, Hayden Rorke, Margalo Gillmore. Stylish if standard remake of THE LAST OF MRS. CHEYNEY with Garson (gowned by Cecil Beaton) teaming up with Wilding for slick society jewel robberies.

Law Is the Law, The (1959-French) 103m. ****½** D: Christian-Jaque. Fernandel, Toto, Mario Besozzi, René Genin. Two top Continental comedians work well together in yarn of French customs official and his crooked pal smuggling items over the border.

Law of the Lawless (1964) C-88m. ****½** D: William F. Claxton. Dale Robertson, Yvonne De Carlo, William Bendix, Bruce Cabot, Richard Arlen, John Agar, Lon Chaney, Kent Taylor. Veteran cast is chief interest of this programmer, with Robertson an

ex-gunman turned judge, saving the town from outlaws.

Law of the Tropics (1941) 76m. ****** D: Ray Enright. Constance Bennett, Jeffrey Lynn, Regis Toomey, Mona Maris, Hobart Bosworth. Fair cast in routine drama of man discovering his wife is accused murderess. Remake of OIL FOR THE LAMPS OF CHINA.

Law vs. Billy the Kid, The (1954) C-73m. ****** D: William Castle. Scott Brady, Betta St. John, James Griffith, Alan Hale, Jr., Paul Cavanagh. Title gives away plot line of unmemorable Western.

Lawless, The (1950) 83m. ****** D: Joseph Losey. Gail Russell, Macdonald Carey, Lalo Rios, Lee Patrick, John Sands, Martha Hyer. Vaguely interesting study of Mexican-American fruit-pickers in Southern California, with facets of racial discrimination pointed out.

Lawless Breed, The (1952) C-83m. ******* D: Raoul Walsh. Rock Hudson, Julia Adams, Hugh O'Brian, Michael Ansara, Dennis Weaver. Moving western story of John Wesley Hardin (Hudson), who tries to steer his son from outlaw path by recounting story of his life. Well done.

Lawless Eighties, The (1957) 70m. ****** D: Joseph Kane. Buster Crabbe, John Smith, Ted de Corsia, Marilyn Saris. Crabbe and solid backup cast provide average story of gunfighter who protects circuit rider beaten up by thugs.

Lawless Street, A (1955) C-78m. ****½** D: Joseph H. Lewis. Randolph Scott, Angela Lansbury, Warner Anderson, Jean Parker, Wallace Ford, Ruth Donnelly, Michael Pate. Hard-bitten marshal Scott tries to eliminate evil forces from western town, then confronts his bittersweet past when musical star Lansbury comes to town. Above average western with disappointing resolution.

Lawman (1970) C-98m. ******* D: Michael Winner. Burt Lancaster, Robert Ryan, Lee J. Cobb, Sheree North, Joseph Wiseman, Robert Duvall, Albert Salmi. Intriguing thought-Western about stoic marshal (Lancaster) who comes into unfamiliar town to bring back wanted men, refusing to sway from duty although entire town turns against him. Unsatisfactory resolution mars otherwise compelling story.

Lawrence of Arabia (1962) C-222m. ******* D: David Lean. Peter O'Toole, Alec Guinness, Anthony Quinn, Jack

Hawkins, Claude Rains, Anthony Quayle, Arthur Kennedy, Omar Sharif, Jose Ferrer. Slow-moving blockbuster biography of enigmatic adventurer T. E. Lawrence has fine performances, breathtaking photography (by Freddie Young) which stands to lose on TV screen. Ambling script, general overlength mar total effectiveness; won Best Picture, Best Director, Best Cinematography Oscars, among others, and made O'Toole a star.

Lawyer, The (1970) C-117m. **½ D: Sidney J. Furie. Barry Newman, Harold Gould, Diana Muldaur, Robert Colbert, Kathleen Crowley. Lively story loosely based on famous Dr. Sam Sheppard murder case; Newman is stubborn young lawyer defending doctor accused of murdering his wife, battling legal protocol and uncooperative client. Unexceptional but diverting. Newman later revived role in TV series "Petrocelli."

Lawyer Man (1932) 72m. **½ D: William Dieterle. William Powell, Joan Blondell, Claire Dodd, Sheila Terry, Alan Dinehart. Lawyer working his way up gets involved with gangsters; Powell and Blondell bring this one up to par.

Lay That Rifle Down (1955) 71m. *½ D: Charles Lamont. Judy Canova, Robert Lowery, Jacqueline de Wit, Richard Deacon, Tweeny Canova. Mild Canova musicomedy, with Judy an overworked drudge in Southern town with hopes of being chic.

Lazybones (1925) 79m. *** D: Frank Borzage. Charles "Buck" Jones, Madge Bellamy, Virginia Marshall, Edythe Chapman, Leslie Fenton, ZaSu Pitts. Poignant evocation of small-town life at turn of the century, focusing on aimless titlecharacter (Jones) and his on-again, off-again romance with a local girl. Unusual role for Jones, better known as cowboy hero.

Le Mans (1971) C-106m. *** D: Lee H. Katzin. Steve McQueen, Siegfried Rauch, Elga Andersen, Ronald Leigh-Hunt. Exciting study of Grand Prix auto racing with exceptionally fine camera work on the track.

League of Gentlemen, The (1960-British) 114m. *** D: Basil Dearden. Jack Hawkins, Nigel Patrick, Bryan Forbes, Kieron Moore, Patrick Wymark, Richard Attenborough. Engrossing study of former service officer utilizing ex-Army demolition

specialists to aid him in big bank heist.

Learning Tree, The (1969) C-107m. **½ D: Gordon Parks. Kyle Johnson, Alex Clarke, Estelle Evans, Dana Elcar, Mita Waters. Parks called virtually every shot in brilliantly photographed but surprisingly mild film version of his autobiographical novel about young black growing up in Kansas. Film's appeal lies more in its intentions than in what it actually accomplishes.

Lease of Life (1955-British) C-93m. **½ D: Charles French. Robert Donat, Kay Walsh, Denholm Elliott, Adrienne Corri, Cyril Raymond. Donat makes anything worth watching, even this mild tale of poor-but-honest country vicar with one year to live, struggling to make ends meet, and maintain his integrity.

Leather Boys, The (1966-British) 105m. *** D: Sidney J. Furie. Rita Tushingham, Colin Campbell, Dudley Sutton, Gladys Henson. Uncompromising study of impulsive Tushingham's incompatible marriage to motorcycle-loving mechanic, focusing on their opposing viewpoints and sleazy environment.

Leather Gloves (1948) 75m. ** D: Richard Quine, William Asher. Cameron Mitchell, Virginia Grey, Sam Levene, Jane Nigh, Henry O'Neill, Blake Edwards. Fight flick about on-the-skids boxer Mitchell lacks sufficient punch to push over clichés.

Leather Saint, The (1956) 86m. **½ D: Alvin Ganzer. Paul Douglas, John Derek, Jody Lawrance, Cesar Romero, Ernest Truex. Forthright account of clergyman who becomes a boxer to earn money to help congregation.

Leave Her to Heaven (1945) C-110m. *** D: John M. Stahl. Gene Tierney, Cornel Wilde, Jeanne Crain, Vincent Price, Mary Philips, Ray Collins, Darryl Hickman, Gene Lockhart. Tierney is fiery as wife possessive of husband's attention, willing to commit murder to have her way; handsomely mounted production.

Leave It To Blondie (1945) 75m. D: Abby Berlin. Penny Singleton, Arthur Lake, Larry Simms, Marjorie Kent, Jonathan Hale, Chick Chandler, Danny Mummert, Arthur Space. SEE: **Blondie** series.

Leave It to Henry (1949) 57m. *½ D: Jean Yarbrough. Raymond Walburn, Walter Catlett, Gary Gray, Mary Stuart. Quickie film has Walburn destroying the town bridge when son is fired as toll-booth collector.

Leave Yesterday Behind (1978) **C-100m. TVM** D: Richard Michaels. John Ritter, Carrie Fisher, Buddy Ebsen, Ed Nelson, Robert Urich, Carmine Zapata. Paralyzed in college polo match, veterinary student falls for young woman who dumps her fiancé for him. Soapy. Average.

Leda SEE: Web of Passion

Leech Woman, The (1960) 77m. *½ D: Edward Dein. Coleen Gray, Grant Williams, Philip Terry, Gloria Talbott, John Van Dreelen. Sloppy production about woman who finds youth-giving formula with unspectacular results.

Left Hand of God, The (1955) **C-87m.** *** D: Edward Dmytryk. Humphrey Bogart, Gene Tierney, Lee J. Cobb, Agnes Moorehead, E. G. Marshall, Benson Fong. Bogart manages to be convincing as American caught in post-WW2 China, posing as clergyman with diverting results.

Left-Handed Gun, The (1958) 102m. **½ D: Arthur Penn. Paul Newman, Lita Milan, John Dehner, Hurd Hatfield. Faltering psychological Western dealing with Billy the Kid's career, method-acted by Newman.

Left Right and Center (1961-British) 95m. **½ D: Sidney Gilliat. Ian Carmichael, Patricia Bredin, Alastair Sim, Eric Barker. Simple, entertaining comedy about opponents in political campaign falling in love. Sim is hilarious, as always, as Carmichael's conniving uncle.

Legacy, The (1979) **C-100m.** **½ D: Richard Marquand. Katharine Ross, Sam Elliott, John Standing, Ian Hogg, Margaret Tyzack, Charles Gray, Lee Montague, Roger Daltrey. Two Americans find themselves among group of people shanghaied to British mansion where strange deaths and an occult ceremony await. Acceptable fare for fans of this genre. Filmed in England.

Legend of Frenchie King, The (1971-French-Spanish-Italian-British) **C-97m.** *½ D: Christian Jaque, Guy Casaril. Brigitte Bardot, Claudia Cardinale, Michael J. Pollard, Patty Shepard, Micheline Presle. Clumsy attempt at bawdy western in the style of VIVA MARIA, with Bardot and her sisters as female outlaws at a French settlement in New Mexico, circa 1880. Badly dubbed.

Legend of Hell House, The (1973-British) **C-95m.** *** D: John Hough.

Roddy McDowall, Pamela Franklin, Clive Revill, Gayle Hunnicutt. Harrowing story of occult phenomena as four researchers agree to spend one week in house known to be inhabited by spirits. Not the usual ghost story, but certain to curl a few hairs. Written by Richard Matheson.

Legend of Lizzie Borden, The (1975) **C-100m. TVM** D: Paul Wendkos. Elizabeth Montgomery, Ed Flanders, Fionnuala Flanagan, Katherine Helmond, Fritz Weaver, Don Porter, John Beal. Realistic drama blending fact and speculation about New England spinster accused of the axe murders of her father and stepmother. Atmospheric as well as graphic with a thoughtful performance by Montgomery. Above average.

Legend of Lobo, The (1962) **C-67m.** **½ No director credited. Narrated by Rex Allen, with songs by Sons of the Pioneers. Disney film follows a wolf named Lobo from birth to adulthood, as he learns the ways of life in the West. Well-done, if unmemorable, with bright soundtrack.

Legend of Lylah Clare, The (1968) **C-130m.** ** D: Robert Aldrich. Kim Novak, Peter Finch, Ernest Borgnine, Milton Selzer, Valentina Cortese. Has-been Hollywood director fashions young woman into the image of his late wife for screen biography; flamboyantly awful, but some think it's so bad it's good. Judge for yourself.

Legend of Nigger Charley, The (1972) **C-98m.** **½ D: Martin Goldman. Fred Williamson, D'Urville Martin, Don Pedro Colley, Gertrude Jeanette, Marcia McBroom, Alan Gifford. Some violence may be cut in this routine black Western about Virginia slave who becomes a fugitive after killing treacherous overseer; Lloyd Price sings title tune.

Legend of the Golden Gun, The (1979) **C-100m. TVM** D: Alan J. Levi. Jeff Osterhage, Hal Holbrook, Keir Dullea, Carl Franklin, Michelle Carey. Offbeat western fantasy about a sagebrush golden boy who becomes the protégé of a legendary gunslinger. Not bad, despite Dullea's interpretation of Custer as a send-up of Douglas MacArthur. Pilot to a proposed series. Average.

Legend of the Lost (1957) **C-109m.** ** D: Henry Hathaway. John Wayne, Sophia Loren, Rossano Brazzi, Kurt Kasznar, Sonia Moser. Incredibly insipid hodgepodge interesting as curio: Wayne and Brazzi on treasure hunt in Sahara battle over rights to Loren.

Legend of the Sea Wolf SEE: **Wolf Larsen** (1975)

Legend of Tom Dooley, The (1959) 79m. ** D: Ted Post. Michael Landon, Jo Morrow, Jack Hogan, Richard Rust, Dee Pollock, Ken Lynch. Landon is pleasing in title role of Rebel soldier who robs a stage for the cause, only to discover war is over and he's now an outlaw.

Legend of Valentino, The (1975) C-100m. TVM D: Melville Shavelson. Franco Nero, Suzanne Pleshette, Judd Hirsch, Lesley Warren, Milton Berle, Yvette Mimieux, Harold Stone. Romantic fiction (as it was labeled) based on life and myth of 1920s star. Nero and Pleshette are just fair as Valentino and June Mathis, the screenwriter who discovered him. Place this one about equidistant between Nureyev's Valentino and Anthony Dexter's. Average.

Legendary Champions, The (1968) 77m. *** D: Harry Chapin. Narrated by Norman Rose. Excellent documentary on boxing's heavyweight champions from 1882 to 1929.

Legendary Curse of Lemora SEE: **Lady Dracula**

Legion of the Doomed (1958) 75m. *½ D: Thor Brooks. Bill Williams, Dawn Richard, Anthony Caruso, Kurt Kreuger. Minor actioner about French Foreign Legion and its perennial battle with the natives.

Lemon Drop Kid, The (1951) 91m. *** D: Sidney Lanfield. Bob Hope, Marilyn Maxwell, Lloyd Nolan, Jane Darwell. Hope is hilarious as racetrack tout who owes big money to gangster and must pay or else. Adapted from Damon Runyon story, filmed before in 1934.

Lemonade Joe (1967-Czech) 84m. *** D: Oldrich Lipsky. Carl Fiala, Olga Schoberova, Veta Fialova, Miles Kopeck, Rudy Dale, Joseph Nomaz. Sometimes repetitious but often quite funny spoof of the American Western; title refers to hero, who drinks Kola Loca lemonade instead of booze.

Lemora, The Lady Dracula SEE: **Lady Dracula.**

Lenny (1974) 112m. **** D: Bob Fosse. Dustin Hoffman, Valerie Perrine, Jan Miner, Stanley Beck, Gary Morton. Powerful biography of troubled nightclub comic Lenny Bruce, whose hip humor and scatological dialogue made him a controversial figure in the 1950s. Fine direction, evocative b&w camerawork showcase excellent performances by Hoffman and Perrine (as Lenny's wife, stripper Honey Harlowe).

Leo the Last (1970-British) C-103m. ** D: John Boorman. Marcello Mastroianni, Billie Whitelaw, Calvin Lockhart, Glenna Forster-Jones, Graham Crowden. Oddball film about reticent Mastroianni, last in a line of princes, who gradually emerges from decaying London mansion to become involved with people living on his black ghetto block. Enigmatic, unsatisfying film, with occasional bright touches.

Leopard, The (1963-Italian) C-165m. *** D: Luchino Visconti. Burt Lancaster, Alain Delon, Claudia Cardinale, Rina Morelli, Paolo Stoppa. Meticulously produced version of famed novel of 19th-century life in Sicily, with revolution crumbling social structure. Slow pacing and dubbing make atmospheric account tough going.

Leopard in the Snow (1978-Canadian-British) C-90m. **½ D: Gerry O'Hara. Keir Dullea, Susan Penhaligon, Kenneth More, Billie Whitelaw, Jeremy Kemp, Yvonne Manners. First movie produced by publishers of Harlequin Romance paperbacks is predictably tearful love story about English girl who falls for a testy, reclusive American who's afraid to admit his feelings.

Leopard Man, The (1943) 66m. ***½ D: Jacques Tourneur. Dennis O'Keefe, Margo, Jean Brooks, Isabel Jewell, James Bell, Margaret Landry, Abner Biberman. Superb Val Lewton suspense tale of series of murders in small New Mexico town blamed on leopard which escaped from traveling show.

Lepke (1975) C-110m. **½ D: Menahem Golan. Tony Curtis, Anjanette Comer, Michael Callan, Warren Berlinger, Milton Berle, Vic Tayback. Cut above usual gangster film with Curtis surprisingly convincing as title character, head of Thirties' Murder Inc. Berle has serious cameo as Comer's father.

Les Biches (1968-French-Italian) C-104m. ***½ D: Claude Chabrol. Jean-Louis Trintignant, Jacqueline Sassard, Stephane Audran, Nane Germon. Excellent film of rich, aging lesbian who picks up unformed waif who earns her living drawing on the sidewalks of Paris.

Les Girls (1957) C-114m. ***½ D: George Cukor. Gene Kelly, Kay Kendall, Mitzi Gaynor, Taina Elg, Jacques Bergerac. Charming, sprightly musical involving three show girls who (via flashback) reveal their relationship to hoofer Kelly; chicly handled in all departments, with Cole Porter tunes.

Les Miserables (1935) 108m. ***½ D: Richard Boleslawski. Fredric March, Charles Laughton, Cedric Hardwicke, Rochelle Hudson, Frances Drake, John Beal, Florence Eldridge. Meticulous production of Victor Hugo's classic tale. Minor thief March tries to bury past and become respectable town mayor, but police inspector Javert (Laughton) won't let him. John Carradine has intriguing bit part as student radical.

Les Miserables (1952) 104m. *** D: Lewis Milestone. Michael Rennie, Robert Newton, Sylvia Sidney, Edmund Gwenn, Cameron Mitchell, Elsa Lanchester, Florence Bates. Glossy but thoughtful remake of the venerable Victor Hugo classic.

Les Miserables (1978) C-150m. TVM D: Glenn Jordan. Richard Jordan, Anthony Perkins, Cyril Cusack, Claude Dauphin, John Gielgud, Flora Robson, Celia Johnson, Joyce Redman. Lavish remake of the perennial with a cerebral interpretation of Valjean by Jordan and a determined one of Javert by Perkins. Sparkling cameos by Dauphin (in his last role) and some British stalwarts. Above average.

Let Freedom Ring (1939) 100m. **½ D: Jack Conway. Nelson Eddy, Virginia Bruce, Victor McLaglen, Lionel Barrymore, Edward Arnold, Guy Kibbee, Raymond Walburn. Hokey but enjoyable pap of crusading Eddy righting wrongs in home town, combating crooked bosses.

Let It Be (1970-British) C-80m. *** D: Michael Lindsay-Hogg. John Lennon, Paul McCartney, Ringo Starr, George Harrison. Uneven, draggy documentary is rescued and abetted by brilliant score by the Beatles. When they perform it becomes magical; when the extras are thrown in it becomes a bore.

Let No Man Write My Epitaph (1960) 106m. *** D: Philip Leacock. Burl Ives, Shelley Winters, James Darren, Jean Seberg, Ricardo Montalban, Ella Fitzgerald. Bizarre account of slum life, focusing on Darren and his dope-addicted mother involved with a variety of corrupt individuals. Sequel to KNOCK ON ANY DOOR.

Let the Good Times Roll (1973) C-98m. *** D: Sid Levin, Bob Abel. Chuck Berry, Chubby Checker, Bo Diddley, Little Richard, Five Satins, Shirelles, Coasters, Bill Haley and the Comets. Rockumentary with flavor and wit. Study of 1950s told through incredible compilation of film footage, and some fine performances by leading rock 'n' rollers from the period in revival concerts. Unfortunately, imaginative multi-image widescreen effects are lost on TV.

Let Us Live (1939) 68m. **½ D: John Brahm. Maureen O'Sullivan, Henry Fonda, Ralph Bellamy, Alan Baxter, Stanley Ridges. Weepy melodrama about innocent man Fonda convicted of murder and his girl O'Sullivan trying to clear him.

Let's Be Happy (1957-British) C-93m. **½ D: Henry Levin. Tony Martin, Vera-Ellen, Zena Marshall, Guy Middleton. Featherweight musical of girl going to Scotland to claim a castle she's inherited.

Let's Dance (1950) C-112m. **½ D: Norman Z. McLeod. Betty Hutton, Fred Astaire, Roland Young, Ruth Warrick, Shepperd Strudwick. Slim plot line of Hutton's efforts to win her son back from Back Bay in-laws. Astaire's dancing is film's highlight.

Let's Do It Again (1953) C-95m. *** D: Alexander Hall. Jane Wyman, Ray Milland, Aldo Ray, Leon Ames. Musical remake of AWFUL TRUTH with Milland in Cary Grant's role, Wyman in Irene Dunne's, and Ray in Ralph Bellamy's. Songs add to spicy plot, but no classic like original '37 film.

Let's Do It Again (1975) C-112m. *** D: Melville Tucker. Sidney Poitier, Bill Cosby, Jimmie Walker, Calvin Lockhart, John Amos, Denise Nicholas, Lee Chamberlain. Hilarious sequel to "Uptown Saturday Night;" slick mixture of lodge brothers, boxing, gambling and hypnotism.

Let's Face It (1943) 76m. ** D: Sidney Lanfield. Bob Hope, Betty Hutton, ZaSu Pitts, Phyllis Povah, Dave Willock, Eve Arden. Brassy comedy with loud Hutton competing with Hope for laughs in forced wartime comedy of soldiers hired as male companions.

Let's Get Tough! (1942) 62m. D: Wallace Fox. Leo Gorcey, Bobby Jordan, Huntz Hall, Gabriel Dell, Tom Brown, Florence Rice. SEE: **Bowery Boys** series.

Let's Go Navy (1951) 68m. D: William Beaudine. Leo Gorcey, Huntz Hall, Allen Jenkins, Charlita, Dorothy Ford, Tom Neal. SEE: **Bowery Boys** series.

Let's Kill Uncle (1966-British) C-92m. **½ D: William Castle. Nigel Green, Mary Badham, Pat Cardi, Robert Pickering, Linda Lawson, Reff Sanchez, Nestor Paiva. Green's ham is just right for this outrageous tale of 12-year-old who tries to kill his uncle because his uncle is trying to kill him, thanks to a $5 million inheritance. Lots of hokey thrills involving sharks, tarantulas and the like.

Let's Live a Little (1948) 85m. **½ D: Richard Wallace. Hedy Lamarr, Robert Cummings, Anna Sten, Robert Shayne, Mary Treen. Amusing but unspectacular romantic comedy, with Lamarr and Cummings falling in love.

Let's Make It Legal (1951) 77m. **½ D: Richard Sale. Claudette Colbert, Macdonald Carey, Zachary Scott, Robert Wagner, Marilyn Monroe. OK comedy of couple planning divorce but parting as friends. Good cast is main asset.

Let's Make Love (1960) C-118m. *** D: George Cukor. Marilyn Monroe, Yves Montand, Tony Randall, Frankie Vaughan, Wilfrid Hyde-White, David Burns. Millionaire Montand hears of show spoofing him, wants to stop it, then meets cast member Monroe. To join cast, he hires Bing Crosby to teach him to sing, Milton Berle to coach on comedy, Gene Kelly to make him dance. Bubbly cast.

Let's Make Music (1940) 85m. **½ D: Leslie Goodwins. Bob Crosby, Jean Rogers, Elisabeth Risdon, Joseph Buloff. Nathanael West wrote this entertaining B musical about bandleader Crosby turning prim schoolteacher's football victory song into a hit. Good fun; other songs include "Big Noise from Winnetka."

Let's Make Up (1955-British) C-94m. ** D: Herbert Wilcox. Errol Flynn, Anna Neagle, David Farrar, Kathleen Harrison, Peter Graves. Froth about overimaginative Neagle trying to decide between suitors Flynn and Farrar. Original title: LILACS IN THE SPRING.

Let's Scare Jessica to Death (1971) C-89m. **½ D: John Hancock. Zohra Lampert, Barton Heyman, Kevin O'Connor, Mari-Claire Costello, Gretchen Corbet. Creepy little tale of murder and deception as unstable girl gets full fright-treatment at country home.

Let's Switch! (1975) C-78m. TVM D: Alan Rafkin. Barbara Eden, Barbara Feldon, George Furth, Richard Schaal, Pat Harrington, Barra Grant, Penny Marshall, Joyce Van Patten, Kaye Stevens, Barbara Cason. Fluff concerning a woman's magazine editor and her homemaker chum swapping life styles. Loaded with familiar sitcom performers, who provide no surprises. Average.

Let's Talk About Men (1976-Italian) 93m. *** D: Lina Wertmuller. Nino Manfredi, Luciana Paluzzi, Margaret Lee, Milena Vukotic, Patrizia De-Clara, Alfredo Baranchini. Amusing episodic film (four stories tied to a fifth): Manfredi competently and comically plays five different men involved with different women and situations. Made in '65, right after Wertmuller's similar LET'S TALK ABOUT WOMEN, this took 11 years to cross the ocean but was worth the wait.

Letter, The (1940) 95m. ***½ D: William Wyler. Bette Davis, Herbert Marshall, James Stephenson, Frieda Inescort, Gale Sondergaard. Lushly photographed Somerset Maugham drama set in Malaya, tells of murderess (Davis) who tries to cover up her deed by pleading self-defense. Davis quite appealing in her unsympathetic role. Previously filmed in 1929 (also with Herbert Marshall in cast).

Letter for Evie, A (1945) 89m. ** D: Jules Dassin. Marsha Hunt, John Carroll, Spring Byington, Hume Cronyn, Pamela Britton, Norman Lloyd. Inconsequential romancer; Hunt is torn between pen-pal Cronyn and his buddy Carroll.

Letter from an Unknown Woman (1948) 90m. *** D: Max Ophuls. Joan Fontaine, Louis Jourdan, Mady Christians, Marcel Journet, Art Smith. Lush romantic flavor of direction and performances obscures clichés and improbabilities in story of Fontaine's lifelong infatuation with musician Jourdan.

Letter of Introduction (1938) 104m. **½ D: John M. Stahl. Adolphe

·Menjou, Andrea Leeds, Edgar Bergen (and Charlie McCarthy), George Murphy, Rita Johnson, Eve Arden, Ann Sheridan. Smoothly done account of aspiring actress Leeds trying to make it without famous father's (Menjou's) help; personality-plus cast.

Letter to Three Wives, A (1948) 103m. ******** D: Joseph L. Mankiewicz. Jeanne Crain, Linda Darnell, Ann Sothern, Kirk Douglas, Paul Douglas, Jeffrey Lynn, Thelma Ritter. Delicious Americana showing reactions of three women who receive a letter from town flirt who has run off with one of their husbands. Celeste Holm does the voice of the letter's authoress.

Letters, The (1973) C-74m. TVM D: Gene Nelson, Paul Krasny. John Forsythe, Pamela Franklin, Ida Lupino, Dina Merrill, Ben Murphy, Leslie Nielsen, Jane Powell. Clever three-part drama that uses letter-writing as unifying element in tales of souring and unrequited love. Standard situations milked for all possible melodrama, good performances by excellent cast notwithstanding. Average.

Letters from Frank (1979) C-100m. TVM D: Edward Parone. Art Carney, Maureen Stapleton, Mike Farrell, Lew Ayres, Margaret Hamilton, Gail Strickland. Affecting drama about enforced retirement, with Carney tops as a newspaper man done out of a job by a computer. Above average.

Letters from Three Lovers (1973) C-73m. TVM D: John Erman. Martin Sheen, Belinda J. Montgomery, Ken Berry, Juliet Mills, June Allyson, Robert Sterling, Barry Sullivan, Henry Jones. Three-part drama zeroes in on couples in situations somehow incomplete without letters delivered. Corny linking device (Jones as mailman) spoils a lot of intended effect. Average.

Libel (1959-British) 100m. ****½** D: Anthony Asquith. Dirk Bogarde, Olivia de Havilland, Robert Morley, Paul Massie, Wilfrid Hyde-White. Good cast sidetracked by muddled script about upper-class man suing for claim that he is an impostor, with his wife not so sure he isn't.

Libeled Lady (1936) 98m. ******** D: Jack Conway. Jean Harlow, William Powell, Myrna Loy, Spencer Tracy, Walter Connolly, Charley Grapewin,

Cora Witherspoon. Wonderful comedy with the four stars working at full steam: conniving newspaper editor Tracy uses his fiancee (Harlow) and ex-employee (Powell) to get the goods on hot-headed heiress Loy—but everything goes wrong. Sit back and enjoy. Remade as EASY TO WED.

Liberation of L. B. Jones, The (1970) C-102m. ****½** D: William Wyler. Lee J. Cobb, Anthony Zerbe, Roscoe Lee Browne, Lola Falana, Lee Majors, Barbara Hershey, Yaphet Kotto, Chill Wills. Militant tale of racism in the South. Some good performances, especially Falana's, but slow pace and many subplots hurt.

License to Kill (1964-French) 95m. ****** D: Henri Decoin. Eddie Constantine, Yvonne Monlaur, Daphne Dayle, Paul Frankeur, Vladimir Inkijinoff, Charles Belmont. Constantine is modern-day Nick Carter involved with Oriental spies and superduper guided missile weapon wanted by Allies; elaborate nonsense.

Lies My Father Told Me (1975-Canadian) C-102m. *****½** D: Jan Kadar. Yossi Yadin, Len Birman, Marilyn Lightstone, Jeffrey Lynas, Ted Allan. Tender film about young boy in Canadian-Jewish ghetto of the 1920s who idolizes his grandfather, a simple, old-fashioned junk collector. Author Ted Allan plays Mr. Baumgarten. Simple and moving drama.

Lt. Robin Crusoe, U.S.N. (1966) C-110m. BOMB D: Byron Paul. Dick Van Dyke, Nancy Kwan, Akim Tamiroff, Arthur Malet, Tyler McVey. Labored Disney comedy is unworthy of Van Dyke, who plays modern-day Robinson Crusoe, a navy pilot who drifts onto deserted island, becomes involved with pretty native girl. Film has virtually nothing of merit to recommend.

Lieutenant Schuster's Wife (1972) C-73m. TVM D: David Lowell Rich. Lee Grant, Jack Warden, Paul Burke, Don Galloway, Eartha Kitt, Nehemiah Persoff. Solid performance by Lee Grant in title role as typical N.Y.C. cop's wife trying to vindicate husband's memory and to put herself back together after his murder. Short running time and commercial imposition give film hard time to speak its mind, some subordinate roles seem stereotyped, and film's resolution guessed after first third over. Average.

Lieutenant Wore Skirts, The (1956) **C-99m.** **½ D: Frank Tashlin. Tom Ewell, Sheree North, Rita Moreno, Rick Jason, Les Tremayne, Jean Willes, Alice Reinhart. Ewell makes nonsense acceptable as he chases after wife who reenlisted in service thinking he'd been drafted again.

Life and Assassination of the Kingfish, The (1977) **C-100m. TVM** D: Robert Collins. Edward Asner, Nicholas Pryor, Diane Kagan, Fred Cook, Dorrie Kavanaugh, Gary Allen. Asner stands out in this docudrama of controversial Huey Long, and overcomes a cliched script with his tour-de-force performance. Above average.

Life and Death of Colonel Blimp (1943-British) **C-163m.** ***½ D: Michael Powell, Emeric Pressburger. Roger Livesey, Deborah Kerr, Anton Walbrook, James McKechnie, Neville Mapp. Fine satire set during early 20th century, digging at stolid British soldiers involved in Boer War and WW1. Caused some controversy when released in England during WW2, was badly edited there, even worse for U.S. release. Complete print is finally available—but only in b&w.

Life and Times of Grizzly Adams, The (1976) **C-93m.** *½ D: Richard Friedenberg. Dan Haggerty, Don Shanks, Lisa Jones, Marjorie Harper, Bozo. Poorly made, clumsily scripted family/wilderness saga, about fur trapper innocently pursued for crime, who finds peace in the mountains where he befriends a massive bear. Led to subsequent TV series.

Life and Times of Judge Roy Bean, The (1972) **C-120m.** *** D: John Huston. Paul Newman, Ava Gardner, Victoria Principal, Jacqueline Bisset, Anthony Perkins, Tab Hunter, John Huston, Stacy Keach, Roddy McDowall, Ned Beatty. Tongue-in-cheek Western saga with surrealistic touches. Newman plays self-appointed "Judge" who rules over barren territory, encountering various colorful characters as town grows and matures. Engaging cameos by Keach, Huston, McDowall, and Gardner as Lily Langtry.

Life at Stake, A SEE: Key Man
Life at the Top (1965-British) **117m.** **½ D: Ted Kotcheff. Laurence Harvey, Jean Simmons, Honor Blackman, Michael Craig, Donald Wolfit,

Robert Morley, Margaret Johnston, Nigel Davenport. Follow-up to ROOM AT THE TOP picks up the account a decade later; film lacks flavor or life—best moments are flashbacks to Signoret-Harvey romance.

Life Begins (1932) **71m.** *** D: James Flood, Elliott Nugent. Loretta Young, Aline MacMahon, Glenda Farrell, Vivienne Osborne, Eric Linden, Preston Foster, Elizabeth Patterson, Dorothy Tree. Offbeat film of maternity ward, with fine Warner Bros. cast depicting nurses, mothers, and others involved in life-giving process. Remade as A CHILD IS BORN.

Life Begins at College SEE: Life Begins in College

Life Begins at Eight-Thirty (1942) **85m.** *** D: Irving Pichel. Monty Woolley, Ida Lupino, Cornel Wilde, Sara Allgood, Melville Cooper, J. Edward Bromberg. Drunken washed-up actor Woolley disrupts daughter Lupino's life. Highlight is scene of Woolley as intoxicated Santa Claus.

Life Begins at Forty (1935) **85m.** *** D: George Marshall. Will Rogers, Rochelle Hudson, Richard Cromwell, Jane Darwell, Slim Summerville, George Barbier, Thomas Beck, Sterling Holloway. Delightful Americana, with newspaper editor Rogers trying to clear name of Cromwell, who was framed for bank robbery years ago. Rogers' comments on American life are surprisingly contemporary.

Life Begins for Andy Hardy (1941) **100m.** D: George B. Seitz. Lewis Stone, Mickey Rooney, Judy Garland, Fay Holden, Ann Rutherford, Sara Haden. SEE: **Andy Hardy** series.

Life Begins in College (1937) **94m.** **½ D: William A. Seiter. Joan Davis, Tony Martin, Ritz Brothers, Gloria Stuart, Nat Pendleton, Fred Stone. Sis-boom-bah college nonsense with zany Ritz trio helping the school team win the big game. Pendleton is fun as an Indian who comes to college.

Life in the Balance, A (1955) **74m.** ** D: Harry Horner. Ricardo Montalban, Anne Bancroft, Lee Marvin, Jose Perez. Lukewarm narrative set in a Latin American city, about a series of woman-killings; the police hunt for guilty person.

Life of Brian, The (1979) **C-93m.** *** D: Terry Jones. Graham Chapman, John Cleese, Terry Gilliam,

[437]

Eric Idle, Terry Jones, Michael Palin. This Monty Python religious parable will probably offend every denomination equally, but it shouldn't. Story of a man whose life parallels Christ is the funniest and most sustained feature yet from Britain's bad boys.

Life of Emile Zola, The (1937) 116m. **** D: William Dieterle. Paul Muni, Gale Sondergaard, Joseph Schildkraut, Gloria Holden, Donald Crisp, Erin O'Brien-Moore, Morris Carnovsky, Louis Calhern, Harry Davenport, Marcia Mae Jones, Dickie Moore, Ralph Morgan. Sincere biography of famed 19th-century French writer who rose to cause of wrongly accused Captain Dreyfus (Schildkraut); detailed production filled with fine vignettes.

Life of Her Own, A (1950) 108m. **½ D: George Cukor. Lana Turner, Ray Milland, Tom Ewell, Louis Calhern, Ann Dvorak, Margaret Phillips, Jean Hagen, Barry Sullivan, Phyllis Kirk. Turner is at the center of three-cornered romance leading to heartbreak for all. MGM fluff; Dvorak wraps it up with her expert portrayal of an aging model.

Life of Vergie Winters, The (1934) 82m. **½ D: Alfred Santell. Ann Harding, John Boles, Helen Vinson, Betty Furness, Lon Chaney, Jr., Bonita Granville. Successful adaption of Louis Bromfield weeper chronicling life of Harding, who defies small-town gossip, following her own instincts.

Life Upside Down (1965-French) 93m. **½ D: Alain Jessua. Charles Denner, Anna Gaylor, Guy Saint-Jean, Nicole Gueden, Jean Yanne. Somber account of Denner, whose retreat from reality becomes so absorbing that he no longer cares about everyday life.

Life with Blondie (1946) 64m. D: Abby Berlin. Jonathan Hale, Ernest Truex, Marc Lawrence, Veda Ann Borg, Jack Rice, Penny Singleton, Arthur Lake, Larry Simms, Marjorie Kent. SEE: Blondie series.

Life with Father (1947) C-118m. **** D: Michael Curtiz. Irene Dunne, William Powell, Edmund Gwenn, ZaSu Pitts, Elizabeth Taylor, Jimmy Lydon, Martin Milner. Rich adaptation of long-running Broadway play by Howard Lindsay and Russel Crouse based on Clarence Day's story of growing up in turn-of-the-century New York with

his loving but eccentric father. Utterly delightful, and a handsome production as well.

Life with Henry (1941) 80m. D: Ted Reed. Jackie Cooper, Leila Ernst, Eddie Bracken, Fred Niblo, Hedda Hopper, Kay Stewart, Moroni Olsen, Rod Cameron, Pierre Watkin, Lucien Littlefield, Frank M. Thomas. SEE: Henry Aldrich series.

Lifeboat (1944) 96m. ***½ D: Alfred Hitchcock. Tallulah Bankhead, William Bendix, John Hodiak, Mary Anderson, Walter Slezak, Canada Lee, Hume Cronyn, Heather Angel, Henry Hull. Penetrating revelations about shipwreck survivors adrift in lonely lifeboat during WW2. Bankhead remarkable as spoiled rich girl, Slezak fine as Nazi taken aboard.

Lifeguard (1976) C-96m. **½ D: Daniel Petrie. Sam Elliott, Anne Archer, Kathleen Quinlan, Stephen Young, Parker Stevenson, Steve Burns, Sharon Weber. After his 15-year high school reunion, Elliott can't decide whether to chuck the title job to become a salesman. Slight drama resembles made-for-TV movie, but attractive cast and locations make it pleasant enough.

Light Across the Street, The (1957-French) 76m. **½ D: George Lacombe. Brigitte Bardot, Raymond Pellegrin, Berval, Roger Pigaut. Above-par Bardot fare, involving three-cornered romance leading to murder. Retitled: FEMALE AND THE FLESH.

Light at the Edge of the World, The (1971-Spanish-Liechtensteinian) C-119m. *½ D: Kevin Billington. Kirk Douglas, Yul Brynner, Samantha Eggar, Jean Claude Druout, Fernando Rey. Amidst their fight for possession of an island, lighthouse keeper Douglas and sea pirate Brynner battle it out for affections of shipwreck victim Eggar. Jules Verne tale has some excitement, but is more often unintentionally funny.

Light Fingers (1957-British) 90m. ** D: Terry Bishop. Guy Rolfe, Eunice Gayson, Roland Culver, Lonnie Donegan, Hy Hazell, Ronald Howard. Miserly husband (Culver) thinks wife is kleptomaniac; hires bodyguard butler who is really a thief. Adequate production.

Light in the Forest, The (1958) C-93m. *** D: Herschel Daugherty. James MacArthur, Carol Lynley, Fess Parker, Wendell Corey, Joanne

Dru, Jessica Tandy, Joseph Calleia, John McIntire. Absorbing Disney film for young people, based on Conrad Richter's story of a white boy raised by Indians, who has difficulty readjusting to life with his real parents. MacArthur's second film, Lynley's film debut.

Light in the Piazza (1962) C-101m. ***½ D: Guy Green. Olivia de Havilland, Rossano Brazzi, Yvette Mimieux, George Hamilton, Barry Sullivan. Splendid soaper that moves smoothly. Mother is anxious to marry off retarded daughter but isn't sure she's being fair to suitor. Beautifully filmed on location in Italy.

Light That Failed, The (1939) 97m. *** D: William Wellman. Ronald Colman, Walter Huston, Ida Lupino, Dudley Digges, Muriel Angelus, Fay Helm, Francis McDonald. Fine cast in Kipling melodrama of London artist Colman going blind, determined to finish portrait of Lupino, whose florid cockney performance steals film.

Light Touch, The (1951) 110m. **½ D: Richard Brooks. Stewart Granger, Pier Angeli, George Sanders, Kurt Kasznar. On-location shooting in Europe perks up lukewarm drama of art thief Granger and his innocent girlfriend Angeli.

Lightning Strikes Twice (1951) 91m. **½ D: King Vidor. Richard Todd, Ruth Roman, Mercedes McCambridge, Zachary Scott. Muddled yet engaging yarn of ex-con returning home to start new life, finding actual killer of his wife.

Like Mom, Like Me (1978) C-100m. TVM. D: Michael Pressman. Linda Lavin, Kristy McNichol, Patrick O'Neal, Max Gail, Lawrence Pressman. Mother and daughter face new life when dad deserts them, and mom's new relationships with men are mirrored by her teenager. Well acted, thoughtful drama. Above average.

Like Normal People (1979) C-100m. TVM D: Harvey Hart. Shaun Cassidy, Linda Purl, Zalman King, Hope Lange, Michael McGuire, Maureen Arthur. Rock idol Shaun Cassidy's dramatic acting debut was in this drama of mentally retarded young adults who decide to marry despite angry resistance from their families. Virtually identical to NO OTHER LOVE. Average.

Likely Story, A (1947) 88m. **½ D:

H. C. Potter. Bill Williams, Barbara Hale, Sam Levene, Lanny Rees. OK comedy about veterinarian mistakenly thinking he's about to die, taking a last fling, finding romance with Hale and misadventures with crooks.

Li'l Abner (1959) C-113m. **½ D: Melvin Frank. Leslie Parrish, Peter Palmer, Stubby Kaye, Howard St. John, Julie Newmar, Stella Stevens, Billie Hayes, Robert Strauss. Lively Gene DePaul-Johnny Mercer musical is loud and brassy, with corny comedy, some good songs. Stubby Kaye is fine as Marryin' Sam; other Dogpatch characters vividly enacted.

Lilacs in the Spring SEE: **Let's Make Up**

Lili (1953) C-81m. **** D: Charles Walters. Leslie Caron, Mel Ferrer, Zsa Zsa Gabor, Jean-Pierre Aumont, Amanda Blake, Kurt Kasznar. Enchanting musical with Leslie as French orphan who attaches herself to carnival and self-pitying puppeteer Ferrer. Includes the song "Hi Lili, Hi Lo."

Lili Marlene (1950-British) 75m. ** D: Arthur Crabtree. Hugh McDermott, Lisa Daniely, John Blythe, Stanley Baker. Potentially exciting film is middling fare, with Daniely the girl used by the Nazis to broadcast pessimistic news to British army.

Lilies of the Field (1963) 93m. *** D: Ralph Nelson. Sidney Poitier, Lilia Skala, Lisa Mann, Isa Crino, Stanley Adams. A "little" film that made good, won Poitier an Oscar as handyman who helps build chapel for Skala and her German-speaking nuns. Quiet, well-acted, enjoyable.

Lilith (1964) 114m. **½ D: Robert Rossen. Warren Beatty, Jean Seberg, Peter Fonda, Kim Hunter, Jessica Walter, Anne Meacham, Gene Hackman. Fairly faithful version of controversial novel is generally underrated. Benefits from performances of now well-known actors.

Lillian Russell (1940) 127m. ** D: Irving Cummings. Alice Faye, Don Ameche, Henry Fonda, Edward Arnold, Warren William, Leo Carrillo, Nigel Bruce. Strained biog of early 20th-century star; lavish backgrounds and weak plot line diminish Faye's vehicle; Arnold repeats his Diamond Jim Brady role with gusto.

Limehouse Blues (1934) 65m. ** D: Alexander Hall. George Raft, Jean Parker, Anna May Wong, Kent Taylor, Billy Bevan. Good atmosphere but no script to match. Parker has shady past, tries to start fresh with roustabout Oriental Raft who has jealous mistress Wong. Retitled: EAST END CHANT.

Limelight (1952) **145m.** *** D: Charles Chaplin. Charles Chaplin, Claire Bloom, Sydney Chaplin, Nigel Bruce, Buster Keaton. Sentimental story of aging, washed-up music hall clown (Chaplin) who saves ballerina Bloom from suicide and regains his own confidence while building her up. Overlong, indulgent Chaplin effort still has many moving scenes, historic teaming of Chaplin and Keaton in comedy skit.

Limping Man, The (1953-British) **76m.** ** D: Charles De Latour. Lloyd Bridges, Moira Lister, Leslie Phillips, Helene Cordet, Alan Wheatley. Bridges is ex-G.I. returning to England to renew romance with Lister, discovering she's involved with racketeers. Nothing special.

Linda (1973) **C-73m. TVM** D: Jack Smight. Stella Stevens, Ed Nelson, John Saxon, John McIntire, Ford Rainey, Mary Robin-Redd. Stevens has field-day as title character, scheming wife who murders wife of her lover, makes it look as if her husband (Nelson) was responsible. Only problem is film's hurried pace; otherwise pretty good.

Lindbergh Kidnapping Case, The (1976) **C-150m. TVM** D: Buzz Kulik. Cliff DeYoung, Anthony Hopkins, Joseph Cotten, Denise Alexander, Sian Barbara Allen, Martin Balsam, Peter Donat, John Fink, Dean Jagger, Laurence Luckinbill, Tony Roberts, Kate Woodville, Keenan Wynn, Walter Pidgeon. Quality dramatization of 1932 kidnapping of infant Jon Lindbergh, and the apprehension, trial and execution of Bruno Hauptmann. Lindbergh lookalike DeYoung is rather bland, but Hopkins is terrific as Hauptmann and JP Miller's incisive screenplay gives it a firm thumbs-up. Above average.

Lineup, The (1958) **86m.** **½ D: Don Siegel. Warner Anderson, Emile Meyer, Eli Wallach, Richard Jaeckel, Robert Keith. Expanded version of TV series set in San Francisco, focusing on gun-happy hoodlum after a cache of dope. Cult favorite with fans of director Siegel,

but on the whole, pretty ordinary except for final car-chase stunt.

Lion, The (1962) **C-96m.** ** D: Jack Cardiff. William Holden, Trevor Howard, Capucine, Pamela Franklin, Samuel Romboh, Christopher Agunda. Beautiful scenery of Kenya is far better than melodrama about young girl attached to pet lion, with family concerned it is turning her into a savage.

Lion and the Horse, The (1952) **C-83m.** ** D: Louis King. Steve Cochran, Bob Steele, Sherry Jackson, Ray Teal. Warm "B" film of valiant horse who combats a fierce mountain lion; geared for children.

Lion Hunters, The (1951) **75m.** D: Ford Beebe. Johnny Sheffield, Morris Ankrum, Ann B. Todd, Douglas Kennedy. SEE: **Bomba, the Jungle Boy** series.

Lion in Winter, The (1968-British) **C-135m.** **** D: Anthony Harvey. Peter O'Toole, Katharine Hepburn, Jane Merrow, Timothy Dalton, Anthony Hopkins, Nigel Stock. Brilliant, fierce, and personal drama of Henry II deliberating over a successor on fateful Christmas eve. Hepburn co-won Best Actress Oscar for her strong performance as Eleanor of Aquitaine.

Lion Is in the Streets, A (1953) **C-88m.** **½ D: Raoul Walsh. James Cagney, Barbara Hale, Anne Francis, Warner Anderson, John McIntire, Jeanne Cagney, Lon Chaney Jr., Frank McHugh. Cagney, in a Huey Long take-off, is lively as a swamp peddler turned politician, but rambling screenplay prevents film from having much impact. Well photographed by Harry Stradling.

Lion of St. Mark, The (1963-Italian) **C-87m.** ** D: Luigi Capuano. Gordon Scott, Gianna Maria Canale, Rik Battaglia, Alberto Farnese. Canale is pirate girl who wins the love of Scott, heir to the throne of Venice, in this routine period yarn.

Lipstick (1976) **C-89m.** BOMB D: Lamont Johnson. Margaux Hemingway, Chris Sarandon, Perry King, Anne Bancroft, Robin Gammell, Mariel Hemingway. Gorgeous model is brutally raped, must ultimately take justice into her own hands. Totally wretched film gives new dimension to term, "exploitation picture."

Liquidator, The (1966-British) **C-105m.** **½ D: Jack Cardiff. Rod Taylor, Trevor Howard, Jill St.

John, Wilfrid Hyde-White. Nice location photography and adequate acting add up to a rather limp Bondian imitation. Even Taylor can't save this one.

Lisa (1962) C-112m. **½ D: Philip Dunne. Stephen Boyd, Dolores Hart, Hugh Griffith, Donald Pleasence, Harry Andrews. Jan de Hartog's suspenseful novel of young Jewish girl being pursued by ex-Nazi in post WW2 Europe, is an exciting film despite gaps in story logic. Stylishly photographed on location.

Lisa and the Devil (1975-Italian) C-93m. BOMB D: Mario Bava. Telly Savalas, Elke Sommer, Sylva Koscina, Alida Valli, Robert Alda, Gabriele Tinti. Incoherent witch's brew of devil worshipping, exorcism, and perfectly awful acting that has Savalas as a lollipop-popping M.C. in a house of horrors where one of the wax dummies may or may not be a girl possessed by satan. Also called THE HOUSE OF EXORCISM.

Lisbon (1956) C-90m. **½ D: R. Milland. Ray Milland, Maureen O'Hara, Claude Rains, Yvonne Furneaux, Francis Lederer, Percy Marmont, Jay Novello. On-location tale of international thief Rains hiring skipper Milland to rescue Maureen's husband from Communist imprisonment. Nice scenery, nothing special.

List of Adrian Messenger, The (1963) 98m. *** D: John Huston. George C. Scott, Clive Brook, Dana Wynter, Herbert Marshall, Tony Curtis, Kirk Douglas, Burt Lancaster, Robert Mitchum, Frank Sinatra. Good murder mystery has a gimmick: Curtis, Douglas, Lancaster, Mitchum, and Sinatra are disguised in character roles. All that trouble wasn't necessary; the mystery is good on its own.

Listen, Darling (1938) 70m. **½ D: Edwin L. Marin. Judy Garland, Freddie Bartholomew, Mary Astor, Walter Pidgeon, Alan Hale, Scotty Beckett. Judy and Freddie try to land mother (Astor) a husband; Garland sings "Zing Went The Strings Of My Heart."

Lisztomania (1975-British) C-105m. *½ D: Ken Russell. Roger Daltrey, Sara Kestelman, Paul Nicholas, Fiona Lewis, Ringo Starr. So-called biography of Franz Liszt is, in truth, one of Ken Russell's most outlandish extravaganzas; director's devotees may enjoy this visual, aural

(and sexual) assault. Others beware!

Little Accident (1939) 65m. *½ D: Charles Lamont. Hugh Herbert, Baby Sandy, Florence Rice, Richard Carlson, Ernest Truex, Joy Hodges, Edgar Kennedy. Advice-columnist Herbert finds abandoned baby, decides to raise it himself. Forgettable comedy with OK cast.

Little Annie Rooney (1925) 97m. ** D: William Beaudine. Mary Pickford, William Haines, Walter James, Gordon Griffith, Carlo Schippa. One of Mary's weaker starring vehicles mixes comedy, sentiment, melodrama, and blarney in uneven doses, as ragamuffin girl and her brother set out to avenge their policeman-father's murder.

Little Ark, The (1972) C-100m. *** D: James B. Clark. Theodore Bikel, Philip Frame, Genevieve Ambas, Max Croiset, Johan De Slaa, Lo Van Hensbergen. Another good children's film from producer Robert Radnitz; this one concerns two Dutch youngsters who try to find their father after being separated from him during a flood.

Little Big Horn (1951) 86m. **½ D: Charles Marquis Warren. Lloyd Bridges, John Ireland, Marie Windsor, Reed Hadley. Small-budget film manages to generate excitement in its account of Custer's last stand.

Little Big Man (1970) C-150m. **** D: Arthur Penn. Dustin Hoffman, Faye Dunaway, Martin Balsam, Richard Mulligan, Chief Dan George, Jeff Corey, Amy Eccles. Sprawling, superb filmization of Thomas Berger's novel about Jack Crabb, 121-year-old man who reminisces about his life and times as young pioneer, adopted Indian, drinking pal of Wild Bill Hickok, medicine-show hustler, and survivor of Custer's Last Stand. Rich humor, colorful characterizations, moving tragedy are among ingredients, and they all click.

Little Bit of Heaven, A (1940) 87m. ** D: Andrew Marton. Gloria Jean, Robert Stack, Hugh Herbert, C. Aubrey Smith, Stuart Erwin, Nan Grey. Jean has vocal outing as 12-year-old singer supporting family; OK vehicle.

Little Boy Lost (1953) 95m. *** D: George Seaton. Bing Crosby, Claude Dauphin, Nicole Maurey, Gabrielle Dorziat. Synthetic tear-jerker set in post-WW2 France, where newspaperman Crosby is trying to locate his son, not knowing which boy at orphanage is his.

Little Caesar (1930) 80m. ***½ D: Mervyn LeRoy. Edward G. Robinson, Douglas Fairbanks, Jr., Glenda Farrell, Stanley Fields, Sidney Blackmer, Ralph Ince, George E. Stone. Small-time hood becomes underworld big-shot; Robinson as Caesar Enrico Bandello gives memorable performance in classic gangster film, still exciting.

Little Colonel, The (1935) 80m. *** D: David Butler. Shirley Temple, Lionel Barrymore, Evelyn Venable, John Lodge, Sidney Blackmer, Bill Robinson. Even non-fans should like this, one of Shirley's best films, as she mends broken ties between Grandpa Barrymore and Mama Venable in the Reconstruction South . . . and does that famous step dance with Robinson.

Little Egypt (1951) C-82m. **½ D: Frederick de Cordova. Mark Stevens, Rhonda Fleming, Nancy Guild, Charles Drake. Chicago Fair in the 1890s is setting for tale of entrepreneurs who popularized the later-famous belly dancer.

Little Fauss and Big Halsy (1970) C-97m. **½ D: Sidney J. Furie. Robert Redford, Michael J. Pollard, Lauren Hutton, Noah Beery, Lucille Benson. So-so character study of two motorcycle racers, one timid and gullible (Pollard), the other a self-centered braggart (Redford) who takes advantage of cohort. Beery outstanding in rich character role as Pollard's father.

Little Foxes, The (1941) 116m. ***½ D: William Wyler. Bette Davis, Herbert Marshall, Teresa Wright, Richard Carlson, Patricia Collinge, Dan Duryea, Charles Dingle. Outstanding filmization of Lillian Hellman's play of greed and corruption within a Southern family on the financial outs, headed by majestic Davis as ruthless Regina. Sequel: ANOTHER PART OF THE FOREST.

Little Fugitive, The (1953) 75m. *** D: Ray Ashley. Richie Andrusco, Rickie Brewster, Winifred Cushing, Will Lee. Minor classic based on adventures of little boy wandering around Coney Island who thinks he killed his brother.

Little Game, A (1971) C-73m. TVM D: Paul Wendkos. Ed Nelson, Diane Baker, Katy Jurado, Howard Duff. Eleven-year old son may be responsible for murder; father thinks he might be next victim. Unusual premise rendered ridiculous by wide-eyed script, lackluster direction. Average.

Little Giant (1946) 91m. ** D: William A. Seiter. Bud Abbott, Lou Costello, Brenda Joyce, Jacqueline de Wit, George Cleveland, Elena Verdugo, Mary Gordon. Fair A&C with Lou becoming a vacuum cleaner salesman in series of familiar but amusing routines. Bud and Lou work separately in this one.

Little Girl Who Lives Down the Lane, The (1976) C-94m. *½ D: Nicolas Gessner. Jodie Foster, Martin Sheen, Alexis Smith, Mort Shuman, Scott Jacoby. Foster is once again the best thing about an otherwise sorry film; this time she's normal-acting adolescent who murders people on the side.

Little House on the Prairie (1974) C-100m. TVM D: Michael Landon. Michael Landon, Karen Grassle, Melissa Gilbert, Melissa Sue Anderson, Lindsay Sidney Green Bush, Victor French. Family drama taken from Laura Ingalls Wilder's novel of her ancestors' adventure-filled life on Kansas frontier. Heartwarming, pilot to the high-rated series. Above average.

Little Hut, The (1957-British) C-78m. **½ D: Mark Robson. Ava Gardner, Stewart Granger, David Niven, Finlay Currie. Smutty Andre Roussin play becomes static comedy of innuendoes, with Gardner stranded on desert isle with husband and boyfriend.

Little Kidnappers, The (1953-British) 95m. ***½ D: Philip Leacock. Jon Whiteley, Vincent Winter, Adrienne Corri, Duncan Macrae, Jean Anderson, Theodore Bikel. Splendid children's story set in Nova Scotia, 1900. Two orphan youngsters "adopt" abandoned baby when strict grandfather forbids them having a dog. British title: THE KIDNAPPERS.

Little Ladies of the Night (1977) C-100m. TVM D: Marvin Chomsky. David Soul, Lou Gossett, Linda Purl, Clifton James, Carolyn Jones, Paul Burke, Lana Wood, Kathleen Quinlan, Vic Tayback, Dorothy Malone. Drama about teenaged runaway Purl being drawn into world of pimps and prostitutes. Exploitation masquerading as socially significant drama. Below average.

Little Lord Fauntleroy (1936) 98m. *** D: John Cromwell. Freddie Bartholomew, C. Aubrey Smith, Guy Kibbee, Dolores Costello, Mickey Rooney, Jessie Ralph. Young New Yorker Bartholomew suddenly finds himself a British lord in this charming film from classic story. Story and acting are often dated, but high production values make one forget dull spots.

Little Men (1940) 84m. ** D: Norman Z. McLeod. Kay Francis, Jack Oakie, George Bancroft, Jimmy Lydon, Ann Gillis. Louisa May Alcott tale is updated and revised, becoming routine adolescent tale.

Little Minister, The (1934) 110m. ***½ D: Richard Wallace. Katharine Hepburn, John Beal, Donald Crisp, Andy Clyde, Beryl Mercer. Charming film of James M. Barrie story of Scottish pastor falling in love, with Hepburn radiant in period romance tale.

Little Miss Broadway (1938) 70m. ** D: Irving Cummings. Shirley Temple, George Murphy, Jimmy Durante, Phyllis Brooks, Edna May Oliver, George Barbier. Not bad Temple, with Shirley bringing Oliver's theatrical boarding house to life; Shirley and Durante are good together. Songs: "Be Optimistic," "If All the World Were Paper," "Hop Skip and Jump."

Little Miss Marker (1934) 80m. *** D: Alexander Hall. Adolphe Menjou, Shirley Temple, Dorothy Dell, Charles Bickford, Lynne Overman. Winning Damon Runyon tale of bookie Menjou and N.Y.C. gambling colony reformed by adorable little Shirley when she is left as IOU for a debt. Remade as SORROWFUL JONES and FORTY POUNDS OF TROUBLE, and again in 1980.

Little Mo (1978) C-150m TVM D: Daniel Haller. Glynnis O'Connor, Michael Learned, Anne Baxter, Claude Akins, Martin Milner, Anne Francis, Leslie Nielsen. Inspired if slow-moving drama about teenage tennis great Maureen Connolly and her battle with cancer. Average.

Little Murders (1971) C-110m. *** D: Alan Arkin. Elliott Gould, Marcia Rodd, Vincent Gardenia, Elizabeth Wilson, Jon Korkes, Donald Sutherland, Lou Jacobi, Alan Arkin. Jules Feiffer's ultrablack comedy about life in nightmarish N.Y.C. focuses on aggressive urbanite (Rodd) who lassoes passive

photographer Gould into marriage. Superb performance by Gardenia as Rodd's father, hilarious cameo by Arkin as mind-blown detective, but even funniest moments are overshadowed by frighteningly depressing atmosphere.

Little Nellie Kelly (1940) 100m. **½ D: Norman Taurog. Judy Garland, George Murphy, Charles Winninger, Douglas McPhail. Lightweight musical based on George M. Cohan play about Judy patching up differences between father Murphy and grandfather Winninger. Garland sings "It's A Great Day For The Irish," "Singin' In The Rain," others.

Little Night Music, A (1978) G-124m. *½ D: Harold Prince. Elizabeth Taylor, Diana Rigg, Len Cariou, Lesley-Anne Down, Hermione Gingold, Lawrence Guittard. Laughably stilted film version of the Stephen Sondheim stage musical, which in turn was based on Ingmar Bergman's sex-at-a-country-estate comedy, SMILES OF A SUMMER NIGHT. Liz's rendition of "Send in the Clowns" is no chart buster.

Little Nuns, The (1965-Italian) 101m. **½ D: Luciano Salce. Catherine Spaak, Sylva Koscina, Amedeo Nazzari, Didi Perego, Umberto D'Orsi. Innocent little film of nuns trying to persuade airline to re-route their jets, which disturb the convent.

Little Old New York (1940) 100m. **½ D: Henry King. Alice Faye, Brenda Joyce, Fred MacMurray, Richard Greene, Henry Stephenson. Claims to be story of Fulton and his steamboat; merely serves as framework for standard romance.

Little Prince, The (1974-British) C-88m. **½ D: Stanley Donen. Richard Kiley, Steven Warner, Bob Fosse, Gene Wilder, Joss Ackland, Clive Revill. Antoine de St. Exupery's children's book is considered a classic, but this film doesn't do it justice. Kiley plays aviator who counsels and guides a young boy who wants to learn about life. Unmemorable score by Lerner and Loewe is just one of this fable's major letdowns.

Little Princess, The (1939) C-91m. *** D: Walter Lang. Shirley Temple, Richard Greene, Anita Louise, Ian Hunter, Cesar Romero, Arthur Treacher, Marcia Mae Jones. Shirley stars as a Victorian waif who makes good in this lavishly mounted, colorful production.

Little Romance, A (1979) C-108m. *** D: George Roy Hill. Laurence Olivier, Arthur Hill, Sally Kellerman, Thelonious Bernard, Broderick Crawford, Diane Lane. Engaging film about relationship of young American girl (Lane) living in Paris and a charming French Boy (Bernard). A throwback to director Hill's WORLD OF HENRY ORIENT in its winning treatment of adolescence, but not quite as good. Crawford has amusing cameo as himself.

Little Shepherd of Kingdom Come, The (1961) C-108m. **½ D: Andrew V. McLaglen. Jimmie Rodgers, Luana Patten, Chill Wills, Neil Hamilton. Bland family-type film of boy who fought for the North during Civil War and his return to rural life.

Little Shop of Horrors, The (1960) 70m. *** D: Roger Corman. Jonathan Haze, Jackie Joseph, Mel Welles, Dick Miller, Jack Nicholson. Cult "classic" of black comedy about strange young shnook who murders people to feed a bloodthirsty plant. Nicholson has hilarious role as masochist who thrives on dental pain. Corman claims this was shot in two days, and it looks that way.

Little Women (1933) 115m. **** D: George Cukor. Katharine Hepburn, Joan Bennett, Paul Lukas, Frances Dee, Jean Parker, Edna May Oliver, Douglass Montgomery, Spring Byington. Film offers endless pleasure no matter how many times you've seen it; a faithful, beautiful adaptation of Alcott's book, with uniformly superb cast.

Little Women (1949) C-121m. **½ D: Mervyn LeRoy. June Allyson, Peter Lawford, Margaret O'Brien, Elizabeth Taylor, Janet Leigh, Mary Astor. Glossy remake of Louisa May Alcott's gentle account of teenage girls finding maturity and romance—patly cast.

Little Women (1978) C-200m. TVM D: David Lowell Rich. Meredith Baxter Birney, Susan Dey, Ann Dusenberry, Eve Plumb, Dorothy McGuire, Robert Young, Greer Garson, Cliff Potts, William Shatner. Sugarplum refilming of the classic, sparked by McGuire's Marmee and Garson's Aunt March (her TV movie debut). The pallid short-lived series spun off from this. Above average.

Little World of Don Camillo (1951-Franco-Italian) 96m. **½ D: Julien Duvivier. Fernandel, Sylvie, Gino Cervi. Fernandel romps through role of small-town priest who can't keep out of mischief; here he combats Communist threat to his village.

Littlest Hobo, The (1958) 77m. **½ D: Charles Rondeau. Buddy Hart, Wendy Stuart, Carlyle Mitchell, Howard Hoffman. Aimed at child audience, film recounts tale of dog who saves his master's pet lamb from being killed.

Littlest Horse Thieves, The (1977) C-104m. *** D: Charles Jarrott. Alastair Sim, Peter Barkworth, Maurice Colbourne, Susan Tebbs, Andrew Harrison, Chloe Franks. Well-made Disney period piece, filmed in England, about three children's efforts to save pit-ponies who work the mines from abuse and death. Set at the turn of the century. Good location photography.

Littlest Outlaw, The (1955) C-75m. *** D: Roberto Gavaldon. Pedro Armendariz, Joseph Calleia, Rodolfo Acosta, Andres Velasquez, Pepe Ortiz. Unpretentious little Disney film about Mexican boy (Velasquez) who runs away with a horse rather than see it killed for its misdeeds; filmed on location.

Littlest Rebel, The (1935) 70m. *** D: David Butler. Shirley Temple, John Boles, Jack Holt, Karen Morley, Bill Robinson. Top-notch Temple as Shirley saves soldier-daddy Boles from Civil War imprisonment by seeing President Lincoln; dances with Robinson are always a treat.

Live a Little, Love a Little (1968) C-90m. ** D: Norman Taurog. Elvis Presley, Michele Carey, Don Porter, Rudy Vallee, Dick Sargent, Sterling Holloway, Eddie Hodges. Elvis manages to land two well-paying photographer's jobs and work them both by hopping back and forth from office to office. Pleasant, if standard, Presley fare.

Live a Little, Steal a Lot (1975) C-101m. **½ D: Marvin Chomsky. Robert Conrad, Don Stroud, Donna Mills, Robyn Millan, Luther Adler, Paul Stewart. Unremarkable but engrossing yarn based on real-life story of two Florida beach bums who engineered "impossible" heist of 564-carat "Star of India." Fine TOPKAPI-like caper scenes, plus good speedboat chase. Originally titled MURPH THE SURF. Retitled YOU CAN'T STEAL LOVE.

Live Again, Die Again (1974) **C-78m. TVM** D: Richard A. Colla. Cliff Potts, Walter Pidgeon, Donna Mills, Geraldine Page, Vera Miles, Mike Farrell, Lurene Tuttle. Cryogenics thriller of a beautiful woman (Mills), brought back to her family after 34 years in suspended animation, who discovers somebody is trying to kill her. Average.

Live and Let Die (1973-British) **C-121m. **½** D: Guy Hamilton. Roger Moore, Yaphet Kotto, Jane Seymour, Clifton James, Geoffrey Holder, Bernard Lee, Lois Maxwell. Barely memorable, overlong James Bond movie seems merely an excuse to film wild chase sequences; superagent goes after master criminal subverting U.S. economy via drugs. Works on level of old-time serial.

Live Fast, Die Young (1958) **82m. ** D: Paul Henreid. Mary Murphy, Norma Eberhardt, Michael Connors. Turgid "B" film of runaway girl and her sister who prevents her from starting a life of crime.

Live for Life (1967-French-Italian) **C-130m. **½** D: Claude Lelouch. Yves Montand, Annie Girardot, Candice Bergen, Irene Tunc, Anouck Ferjac. TV documentary producer Montand leaves wife Girardot for fashion model Bergen in glossy film helped by some good acting; picture was follow-up to Lelouch's A MAN AND A WOMAN.

Live It Up SEE: Sing and Swing

Live, Love and Learn (1937) **78m. **½** D: George Fitzmaurice. Robert Montgomery, Rosalind Russell, Mickey Rooney, Helen Vinson, Monty Woolley, E. E. Clive, Al Shean, Billy Gilbert. Contract stars glide through this formula MGM fluff, with ritzy Russell marrying nonconformist artist Montgomery.

Live Wires (1946) **64m.** D: Phil Karlson. Leo Gorcey, Huntz Hall, Bobby Jordan, Billy Benedict, William Frambes, Pamela Blake. SEE: Bowery Boys series.

Lively Set, The (1964) **C-95m. **½** D: Jack Arnold. James Darren, Pamela Tiffin, Doug McClure, Marilyn Maxwell, Charles Drake, Greg Morris. Empty-headed account of the swinging crowd at college, especially those involved in sportscar racing.

Lives of a Bengal Lancer (1935)

109m. **** D: Henry Hathaway. Gary Cooper, Franchot Tone, Richard Cromwell, Sir Guy Standing, C. Aubrey Smith, Monte Blue, Kathleen Burke. Delightful Hollywood foray into British Empire; Cooper and Tone are pals in famed British regiment, Cromwell the callow son of commander Standing whom they take under their wing. Top story, action, repartee—and wonderful snake-charming scene.

Lives of Jenny Dolan, The (1975) **C-100m. TVM** D: Jerry Jameson. Shirley Jones, Lynn Carlin, James Darren, Farley Granger, George Grizzard, David Hedison, Stephen McNally, Ian McShane, Pernell Roberts, Percy Rodriguez, Collin Wilcox, Dana Wynter, Stephen Boyd, Charles Drake, Virginia Grey. Glamorous newspaper reporter, investigating assassination of political figure, finds her own life in danger. Producer Ross Hunter's first TV movie has Jones sleuthing in mink and changing eye-popping wardrobe in every scene. The plot's familiar, too, if you've caught THE PARALLAX VIEW. Below average.

Living Desert, The (1953) **C-73m. *** D: James Algar. Narrated by Winston Hibler. Disney's first True-Life Adventure feature has dazzling footage of the American desert and its inhabitants, but attracted justifiable criticism for its gimmicky treatment of some material like the famous "scorpion dance." Still worthwhile. Academy Award winner.

Living Free (1972-British) **C-91m. **½** D: Jack Couffer. Susan Hampshire, Nigel Davenport, Geoffrey Keen. Sequel to BORN FREE detailing further adventures of Lioness Elsa and her three cubs. Nice photography but far too leisurely in pace.

Living in a Big Way (1947) **103m. ** D: Gregory La Cava. Gene Kelly, Marie McDonald, Charles Winninger, Phyllis Thaxter, Spring Byington. Soldier Kelly finds his wartime marriage a disappointment.

Living It Up (1954) **C-95m. *** D: Norman Taurog. Dean Martin, Jerry Lewis, Janet Leigh, Edward Arnold, Fred Clark, Sheree North. Bright remake of NOTHING SACRED. Jerry has Lombard's role as supposed radiation victim brought to N.Y.C. as publicity stunt by reporter Leigh. Martin is Jerry's doctor.

Living on Velvet (1935) 80m. ** D: Frank Borzage. Kay Francis, George Brent, Warren William, Russell Hicks, Maude Turner Gordon, Samuel S. Hinds. Romance between Brent, in state of shock, and upper-class Francis, who vanishes when he gains senses. Chic fluff.

Lizzie (1957) 81m. **½ D: Hugo Haas. Eleanor Parker, Richard Boone, Joan Blondell, Hugo Haas, Ric Roman. Shirley Jackson's THE BIRD'S NEST is basis for sensibly acted melodrama of Parker discovering she has split personality.

Lloyds of London (1936) 115m. ***½ D: Henry King. Freddie Bartholomew, Madeleine Carroll, Sir Guy Standing, Tyrone Power, C. Aubrey Smith, Virginia Field, George Sanders. Handsomely mounted fiction of rise of British insurance company; young messenger boy Bartholomew grows up to be Power, who competes with Sanders for affection of Carroll.

Loan Shark (1952) 74m. ** D: Seymour Friedman. George Raft, Dorothy Hart, Paul Stewart, John Hoyt. Raft tries hard to instill life into flabby yarn about ex-convict smashing a loan-shark racket.

Local Boy Makes Good (1931) 67m. **½ D: Mervyn LeRoy. Joe E. Brown, Dorothy Lee, Ruth Hall, Robert Bennett, Edward Woods. Entertaining Brown vehicle, with mousy Joe turning into a track-and-field star.

Lock, Stock and Barrel (1970) C-100m. TVM D: Jerry Thorpe. Tim Matheson, Belinda Montgomery, Claude Akins, Jack Albertson, Neville Brand, Burgess Meredith. Displeased father chases after eloping couple (Matheson & Montgomery) in episodic journey towards Oregon. Old West adventure story with supposedly nostalgic, tongue-in-cheek attitude lumbers along, due to so-so script, sloppy direction. Average.

Lock Up Your Daughters! (1969-British) C-102m. BOMB D: Peter Coe. Christopher Plummer, Susannah York, Glynis Johns, Ian Bannen, Tom Bell, Elaine Taylor. Film version of Henry Fielding play tries to be another TOM JONES, but tale of mistaken identities in 18th-century England couldn't be more forced.

Locker Sixty-Nine (1962-British) 56m. ** D: Norman Harrison. Eddie Byrne, Paul Daneman, Walter Brown, Penelope Horner. Byrne is the private-eye framed for his boss' murder in this typically gimmicky Edgar Wallace mystery tale.

Locket, The (1946) 86m. ** D: John Brahm. Laraine Day, Brian Aherne, Robert Mitchum, Gene Raymond, Sharyn Moffet, Ricardo Cortez. Weak drama of psychopathic Day has confusing construction in unconvincing tale of girl who destroys men. Film has distinction of the most flashbacks within flashbacks of any picture we've seen.

Locusts (1974) C-78m. TVM D: Richard Heffron. Ben Johnson, Ron Howard, Katherine Helmond, Lisa Gerritsen, Belinda Balaski, Rance Howard. Thriller about a swarm of grasshoppers threatening to destroy an entire town's harvest and a local lad, discharged from the Air Force as unfit to fly, trying to conquer his personal terror. Formula. Average.

Lodger, The (1944) 84m. *** D: John Brahm. Merle Oberon, George Sanders, Laird Cregar, Cedric Hardwicke, Sara Allgood, Doris Lloyd, Olaf Hytten, Billy Bevan. That new lodger at a turn-of-the-century London boarding house is Jack the Ripper. Good, atmospheric chiller with fine performances.

Log of the Black Pearl, The (1975) C-100m. TVM D: Andrew McLaglen. Ralph Bellamy, Kiel Martin, Jack Kruschen, Glenn Corbett, Anne Archer, Henry Wilcoxon. Modern-day adventure about search for sunken treasure. Average.

Logan's Run (1976) C-120m. ** D: Michael Anderson. Michael York, Jenny Agutter, Richard Jordan, Peter Ustinov, Farrah Fawcett-Majors, Roscoe Lee Browne. Dazzling first half—showing life of unending pleasure and extinction at age 30 in the year 2274—is canceled out by dreary second half, rehash of BENEATH THE PLANET OF THE APES. Later a brief TV series.

Lola (1970-British-Italian) C-88m. ** D: Richard Donner. Charles Bronson, Susan George, Trevor Howard, Kay Medford, Jack Hawkins, Lionel Jeffries, Robert Morley. Young school-girl is seduced by 38-year-old porno book writer; falls flat.

Lola Montes (1955-French) C-110m. *** D: Max Ophuls. Martine Carol, Peter Ustinov, Anton Walbrook, Oskar Werner, Ivan Desny. Legendary film about beautiful circus performer and her effect on various men nonetheless suffers from Carol's lack of magnetism in title role. Ophuls' superb use of wide screen won't mean much on TV.

Lolita (1962-British) **152m.** ******* D: Stanley Kubrick. James Mason, Shelley Winters, Peter Sellers, Sue Lyon, Marianne Stone, Diana Decker. Strange film from Vladimir Nabokov's provocative novel. Sexually precocious Lyon becomes involved with stolid professor Mason, and bizarre Sellers provides peculiar romance leading to murder and lust. Winters outstanding as Lyon's sex-starved mother.

Lolly Madonna XXX (1973) **C-103m.** ****** D: Richard C. Sarafian. Rod Steiger, Robert Ryan, Jeff Bridges, Scott Wilson, Season Hubley, Katherine Squire, Ed Lauter. Modern-day Hatfields-Coys feud erupts between two backwoods families, prompted by mistaken identity situation involving innocent girl (Hubley). Histrionics galore, but no point to it all.

London Belongs to Me SEE: Dulcimer Street

Lone Gun, The (1954) **C-78m.** ****** D: Ray Nazarro. George Montgomery, Dorothy Malone, Frank Faylen, Neville Brand. Standard Western of valiant hero shooting it out with outlaws, winning hand of rancher's daughter, nicely played by Malone.

Lone Hand (1953) **C-80m.** ****½** D: George Sherman. Joel McCrea, Barbara Hale, James Arness, Charles Drake. Sturdy McCrea is undercover agent posing as outlaw to get the goods on a gang.

Lone Ranger, The (1956) **C-86m.** ****½** D: Stuart Heisler. Clayton Moore, Jay Silverheels, Lyle Bettger, Bonita Granville, Perry Lopez, Robert Wilke. Based on radio and TV series, film focuses on Masked Man and Tonto trying to pacify warminded Indians.

Lone Ranger and the Lost City of Gold, The (1958) **C-80m.** ****** D: Lesley Selander. Clayton Moore, Jay Silverheels, Douglas Kennedy, Charles Watts. Typical Lone Ranger fiction for younger audiences, involving hooded killers and mysterious clues to a hidden treasure city.

Lone Star (1952) **94m.** ****½** D: Vincent Sherman. Clark Gable, Ava Gardner, Lionel Barrymore, Beulah Bondi, Broderick Crawford, Ed Begley. Texas fights for independence, with good guy Gable vs. badman Crawford, Ava the woman in between. OK oater.

Lone Texan (1959) **70m.** ***½** D: Paul Landres. Willard Parker, Grant Williams, Audrey Dalton, Douglas Kennedy, June Blair. Oater's potential never realized. Civil War veteran returns home to find brother a corrupt sheriff.

Lone Wolf, The Michael Lanyard, better known as the Lone Wolf, figured as the leading character in fourteen films from 1935 to 1949. Louis Joseph Vance's character was a jewel thief who would always sacrifice his own ambitions to help a lady in distress; after the first two films he turned to the right side of the law. Melvyn Douglas played the dapper character in 1935's stylish, delightful LONE WOLF RETURNS, with Gail Patrick as leading lady, and Francis Lederer essayed the role in 1938's LONE WOLF IN PARIS with Frances Drake as a rival thief. In 1939 Warren William took over the role and played Lanyard in eight low-budget, fast-moving, enjoyable films which lacked the class of the first two entries but had a certain charm of their own. There was a heavy accent on comedy, and Eric Blore was added to the cast as Lanyard's valet Jamison, who not only served as comic relief but usually got tangled up in the plot as well. William's best effort by far was his first, THE LONE WOLF SPY HUNT, in which he was aided by a delightfully screwball Ida Lupino as his girlfriend, an alluring Rita Hayworth as a slinky spy, Ralph Morgan as the spy leader, and Virginia Weidler as his curious daughter. Unfortunately the other films in the series lacked the same impressive casts, but William carried them quite well, and the plots, were harmless enough. After a respite of a few years, Gerald Mohr took up the role for several fairly good efforts like LONE WOLF IN LONDON, which brought back valet Eric Blore. Ron Randell played Lanyard in the final entry, THE LONE WOLF AND HIS LADY. An enjoyable if not compelling series was the LONE WOLF, with THE LONE WOLF SPY HUNT measuring up as an excellent, chic, entertaining film by any standards.

Lone Wolf and His Lady, The (1949) 60m. D: John Hoffman. Ron Randell, June Vincent, Alan Mowbray, William Frawley.

Lone Wolf in London, The (1947) 68m. D: Leslie Goodwins. Gerald Mohr, Nancy Saunders, Eric Blore, Evelyn Ankers.

Lone Wolf in Mexico, The (1947) 69m. D: D. Ross Lederman. Gerald Mohr, Sheila Ryan, Jacqueline de Wit, Eric Blore, Nestor Paiva, John Gallaudet.

Lone Wolf in Paris, The (1938) 66m. D: Albert S. Rogell. Francis Lederer, Frances Drake, Walter Kingsford, Leona Maricle, Olaf Hytten, Albert Van Dekker.

Lone Wolf Keeps a Date, The (1941) 65m. D: Sidney Salkow. Warren William, Frances Robinson, Bruce Bennett, Eric Blore, Thurston Hall, Jed Prouty.

Lone Wolf Meets a Lady, The (1940) 71m. D: Sidney Salkow. Warren William, Eric Blore, Jean Muir, Warren Hull, Thurston Hall, Victor Jory, Roger Pryor.

Lone Wolf Returns, The (1935) 69m. D: Roy William Neill. Melvyn Douglas, Gail Patrick, Tala Birell, Arthur Hohl, Thurston Hall.

Lone Wolf Spy Hunt, The (1939) 67m. D: Peter Godfrey. Warren William, Ida Lupino, Rita Hayworth, Virginia Weidler, Ralph Morgan, Don Beddoe.

Lone Wolf Strikes, The (1940) 57m. D: Sidney Salkow. Warren William, Joan Perry, Alan Baxter, Astrid Allwyn, Eric Blore, Montagu Love, Robert Wilcox.

Lone Wolf Takes a Chance, The (1941) 76m. D: Sidney Salkow. Warren William, June Storey, Henry Wilcoxon, Eric Blore, Thurston Hall, Don Beddoe, Evalyn Knapp.

Loneliness of the Long Distance Runner, The (1962-British) 103m. **** D: Tony Richardson. Michael Redgrave, Tom Courtenay, Avis Bunnage, Peter Madden, Alec McCowen, James Fox, Julia Foster. Engrossing story of rebellious young man chosen to represent reform school in track race. Superbly acted film confronts society, its mores and institutions. Key British film of 1960s.

Loneliest Runner, The (1976) C-78m. TVM D: Michael Landon. Lance Kerwin, Michael Landon, Brian Keith, DeAnn Mears, Melissa Sue Anderson, Walter Edminson, Rafer Johnson. Sensitive drama about the misery and humiliation suffered by a teenaged bed-wetter, a talented athlete who subsequently becomes an Olympic star. Producer-director Landon wrote this from personal experience and turns up briefly to play the title character as an adult. Average.

Lonely Are the Brave (1962) 107m. *** D: David Miller. Kirk Douglas, Gena Rowlands, Walter Matthau, Michael Kane, Carroll O'Connor, William Schallert. Penetrating study of rebellious cowboy Douglas escaping from jail, pursued by posse utilizing modern means of communications and transportation.

Lonely Man, The (1957) 87m. *** D: Henry Levin. Anthony Perkins, Jack Palance, Elaine Aiken, Neville Brand, Claude Akins. Solid acting and taut direction remove sting of hackneyed gunslinger-trying-to-reform plot.

Lonely Profession, The (1969) C-96m. TVM D: Douglas Heyes. Harry Guardino, Dean Jagger, Barbara McNair, Joseph Cotten, Ina Balin, Dina Merrill, Fernando Lamas. Brave attempt at painting complete, no-nonsense view of realistic private-eye with rounded, big-name cast as gumshoe Gordon (Guardino) must establish own innocence and figure out murder of shipping tycoon's mistress. Good results by any medium's standards. Above average.

Loners, The (1972) C-79m. ** D: Sutton Roley. Dean Stockwell, Tod Sussman, Scott Brady, Gloria Grahame, Pat Stitch, Alex Dreier, Tim Rooney. Standard bike movie with several screen veterans and a plot involving three drop-out cyclists who turn their backs on society and take it on the lam across the Southwest. All too familiar.

Lonesome Trail, The (1955) 73m. ** D: Richard Bartlett. John Agar, Wayne Morris, Edgar Buchanan, Adele Jergens. Offbeat oater with ranch owner fighting off land-grabbers, using bow and arrow instead of conventional six-shooter.

Lonelyhearts (1958) 108m. **½ D: Vincent J. Donehue. Montgomery Clift, Robert Ryan, Myrna Loy, Dolores Hart, Maureen Stapleton. Unsuccessful attempt to make meaningful film about assorted emotionally unhappy people, tied together by gimmick of Clift being assigned the lonely-hearts column on his newspaper.

Long Ago Tomorrow (1971-British) 100m. ** D: Bryan Forbes. Malcolm McDowell, Nanette Newman, Georgia Brown, Bernard Lee, Gerald Sim, Michael Flanders. Rather wrong-headed drama of love between paraplegics. Could have been sensitive if script and direction weren't so porous and obvious. Original title: THE RAGING MOON.

Long and the Short and the Tall, The (1961-British) 105m. *** D: Leslie Norman. Richard Todd, Laurence Harvey, Richard Harris, Ronald Fraser. Well-delineated account of British patrol unit during WW2, focusing on their conflicting personalities and raids on Japs. Retitled: JUNGLE FIGHTERS.

Long Arm SEE: Third Key, The

Long Dark Hall, The (1951-British) 86m. **½ D: Anthony Bushell, Reginald Beck. Rex Harrison, Lilli Palmer, Tania Held, Henrietta Barry. Sturdy melodrama of man accused of killing girlfriend, with wife remaining loyal to him.

Long Day's Dying, The (1968-British) C-93m. *½ D: Peter Collinson. David Hemmings, Tom Bell, Tony Beckley, Alan Dobie. Dull story traces the stops of three British soldiers and their German captive during weary trek through European countryside.

Long Day's Journey Into Night (1962) 136m. **** D: Sidney Lumet. Katharine Hepburn, Ralph Richardson, Jason Robards, Jr., Dean Stockwell, Jeanne Barr. Faithful, stagy adaptation of Eugene O'Neill's detailed study of family in the 1910s. Hepburn is dope-addicted wife, Richardson her pompous actor husband, Stockwell the son dying of TB, and Robards the alcoholic son. Originally 174m.

Long Duel, The (1967-British) C-115m. **½ D: Ken Annakin. Yul Brynner, Trevor Howard, Harry Andrews, Andrew Keir. Brynner leads peasant revolt against British raj in 1920s India; routine adventure saga.

Long Goodbye, The (1973) C-112m. **½ D: Robert Altman. Elliott Gould, Nina Van Pallandt, Sterling Hayden, Mark Rydell, Henry Gibson, Jim Bouton. Somewhat unrewarding muddle based on Raymond Chandler's book, with Gould a laconic Philip Marlowe mixed up with missing money, an alcoholic Hollywood writer, his worried wife, other assorted loonies. Some nice offbeat touches from director Altman, good performances, but doesn't add up.

Long Gray Line, The (1955) C-138m. *** D: John Ford. Tyrone Power, Maureen O'Hara, Robert Francis, Ward Bond, Donald Crisp, Betsy Palmer. Lengthy sentimental melodrama of West Point athletic trainer Power and his many years at the Academy. O'Hara is radiant as his wife.

Long Haul, The (1957-British) 88m. ** D: Ken Hughes. Victor Mature, Diana Dors, Patrick Allen, Gene Anderson. Mature is truck driver whose turbulent marriage paves way for his becoming involved with crooks. Minor fare.

Long, Hot Summer, The (1958) C-117m. *** D: Martin Ritt. Paul Newman, Joanne Woodward, Anthony Franciosa, Orson Welles, Lee Remick, Angela Lansbury. Well-blended William Faulkner short stories make a flavorful, brooding drama of domineering Southerner (Welles) and a wandering handyman (Newman), who decides to stick around and marry Woodward. Excellent Alex North score, weak finish to strong film.

Long John Silver (1954-Australian) C-109m. **½ D: Byron Haskin. Robert Newton, Connie Gilchrist, Kit Taylor, Grant Taylor. Newton reprises title role from TREASURE ISLAND (with same director as the Disney film) and chews the scenery in this loose adaptation of Robert Louis Stevenson. One of Rod Taylor's earliest films.

Long Journey Back (1978) C-100m. TVM D: Mel Damski. Mike Connors, Cloris Leachman, Stephanie Zimbalist, Katy Kurtzman. Fact-based drama about a high school teenager's courageous fight after a school bus accident leaves her emotionally and physically handicapped. Average.

Long, Long Trailer, The (1954) C-103m. **½ D: Vincente Minnelli. Lucille Ball, Desi Arnaz, Marjorie Main, Keenan Wynn, Gladys Hurlbut. Pleasant vehicle for Lucy and Desi, on honeymoon with cumbersome trailer that creates havoc for the duo.

Long Lost Father (1934) 63m. **½ D: Ernest B. Schoedsack. John Barrymore, Helen Chandler, Donald Cook, Alan Mowbray, Claude King. Minor Barrymore vehicle casts him as man who deserted daughter Chandler years ago, tries to make up for it when she gets in a jam.

Long Memory, The (1952-British) 91m. *** D: Robert Hamer. John Mills, John McCallum, Elizabeth Sellars, Geoffrey Keen, John Chandos, Vida Hope. Mills is framed for murder by girlfriend Sellars. When released from prison twelve years later, he sets out to prove his innocence. Well done drama.

Long Night, The (1947) 101m. ** D: Anatole Litvak. Henry Fonda, Barbara Bel Geddes, Vincent Price, Ann Dvorak, Queenie Smith. Plodding drama of killer hiding out overnight with girl who tries to get him to confess; pretty tired drama. Remake of Jean Gabin film DAYBREAK.

Long Ride from Hell, A (1970-Italian) C-94m. *½ D: Alex Burks. Steve Reeves, Wayde Preston, Dick Palmer, Silvana Venturelli, Lee Burton, Ted Carter. Title is another instance of truth-in-advertising; dreary Western co-authored by Reeves has to do with rancher who tries to clear himself of phony train-robbery charge.

Long Ride Home, The SEE: Time for Killing, A

Long Rope, The (1961) 61m. ** D: William Witney. Hugh Marlowe, Robert Wilke, Alan Hale, John Alonzo. Lumbering minor oater about circuit judge seeking aid of gunslinger to prevent injustice done to Mexican youth on trial for murder.

Long Shadow, The (1961-British) 64m. *½ D: Peter Maxwell. John Crawford, Susan Hampshire, Bill Nagy, Humphrey Lestocq. Flabby espionage caper set in 1950s Vienna, with Crawford an American foreign correspondent caught up in it all.

Long Ships, The (1964-British-Yugoslav) C-125m. ** D: Jack Cardiff. Richard Widmark, Sidney Poitier, Rosanna Schiaffino, Russ Tamblyn, Oscar Homolka, Colin Blakely. Fairly elaborate but comic-book-level costume adventure of Vikings battling Moors for fabled treasure. Good cast deserves better.

Long Voyage Home, The (1940) 105m. **** D: John Ford. John Wayne, Thomas Mitchell, Ian Hunter, Barry Fitzgerald, Wilfrid Lawson, Mildred Natwick, John Qualen. Beautiful Ford film of Eugene O'Neill short plays about seafaring friends who share same thoughts, ambitions. One of Wayne's outstanding performances.

Long Wait, The (1954) 93m. ** D: Victor Saville. Anthony Quinn, Charles Coburn, Gene Evans, Peggie Castle, Dolores Donlan, Mary Ellen Kay. Meandering, actionless account of man with loss of memory discovering he's been framed for several crimes.

Longest Day, The (1962) 180m. **** D: Ken Annakin, Andrew Marton, Bernhard Wicki. John Wayne, Rod Steiger, Robert Ryan, Peter Lawford, Henry Fonda, Red Buttons, Mel Ferrer, many others. One of the last great WW2 films on this kind of scale. Brilliant retelling of the Allied invasion of Normandy, complete with all-star international cast, recreation of events on a grand scale.

Longest Hundred Miles, The (1967) C-93m. TVM D: Don Weis. Doug McClure, Katharine Ross, Ricardo Montalban. Philippine locations refreshing change of pace from backlot tedium in WW2 actioner involving G.I., Army nurse, native children, and priest fleeing from Japanese invasion. Fair performances, some good situations. Average. Also titled: ESCAPE FROM BATAAN.

Longest Night, The (1972) C-74m. TVM D: Jack Smight. David Janssen, James Farentino, Phyllis Thaxter, Sallie Shockley, Skye Aubrey, Mike Farrell. Upper-middle-class daughter (Shockley) abducted by clever duo and hidden in compartment below ground level. Not the slice-of-life documentary it should've been; stuffy, slick, only moderately tense. Even so, above average.

Longest Yard, The (1974) C-123m. *** D: Robert Aldrich. Burt Reynolds, Eddie Albert, Ed Lauter, Michael Conrad, Jim Hampton, Bernadette Peters. Convict Reynolds, a former football pro, quarterbacks a squad of dirty players against warden Albert's hand-picked team.

An audience picture if there ever was one; good fun.

Longstreet (1970) **C-93m. TVM** D: Joseph Sargent. James Franciscus, Bradford Dillman, John McIntire, Jeannette Nolan, Martine Beswick. New Orleans-based insurance investigator blinded in explosion which kills wife, must regain self-respect, dignity in new world, solve mystery of assailant's identities. OK juggling of suspense and character study. Above average; pilot for TV series.

Look Back in Anger (1958-British) **99m.** ***½ D: Tony Richardson. Richard Burton, Claire Bloom, Edith Evans, Mary Ure, Gary Raymond, Glen Byam Shaw, Donald Pleasence. John Osborne's trend-setting angry-young-man play, with Burton rebelling against life and wife, realistically filmed and acted; dialogue bristles.

Look for the Silver Lining (1949) **C-100m.** **½ D: David Butler. June Haver, Ray Bolger, Gordon MacRae, Charles Ruggles, Rosemary DeCamp. Superficial biography of Marilyn Miller's career in show business, with vintage vaudeville numbers bolstering trivial plot line.

Look in Any Window (1961) **87m.** ** D: William Alland. Paul Anka, Ruth Roman, Alex Nicol, Gigi Perreau, Jack Cassidy. Attempted lurid account of young man turned to crime by unhappy home life; tame film.

Look What's Happened to Rosemary's Baby (1976) **C-100m. TVM** D: Sam O'Steen. Stephen McHattie, Patty Duke Astin, Broderick Crawford, Ruth Gordon, Lloyd Haynes, David Huffman, Tina Louise, George Maharis, Ray Milland, Donna Mills. Sequel to the 1968 occult blockbuster traces growth to adulthood of the demon child (McHattie). Patty Duke Astin is his distraught mommy; Milland and Gordon (recreating her original role) head the coven of devil worshippers. Uninspired successor to the Polanski classic. Below average.

Looking for Danger (1957) **62m.** D: Austen Jewell. Huntz Hall, Stanley Clements, Eddie LeRoy, Otto Reichow. SEE: Bowery Boys series.

Looking for Love (1964) **C-83m.** BOMB D: Don Weis. Connie Francis, Susan Oliver, Jim Hutton, Barbara Nichols, Danny Thomas, Johnny Carson, George Hamilton,

Paula Prentiss. They should have looked for a script instead. Very weak, with "guest stars" thrown in. Susan Oliver tries, as Connie's best friend.

Looking for Mr. Goodbar (1977) **C-135m.** *½ D: Richard Brooks. Diane Keaton, Richard Gere, William Atherton, Tuesday Weld, Richard Kiley, LeVar Burton. Sordid rewrite of Judith Rossner's novel begins as intelligent study of repressed young girl, then wallows endlessly in her new "liberated" lifestyle. Keaton's performance outclasses this pointless movie. Seems much too gamy for TV.

Looking Glass War, The (1970-British) **C-108m.** *½ D: Frank R. Pierson. Christopher Jones, Pia Degermark, Ralph Richardson, Anthony Hopkins, Paul Rogers, Susan George. Dull film version of John Le Carré's best-seller has Jones risking his life to photograph a rocket in East Berlin. Good opportunity to study the leads' bone structure, since they never change facial expressions.

Loophole (1954) **80m.** **½ D: Harold D. Schuster. Barry Sullivan, Charles McGraw, Dorothy Malone, Don Haggerty, Mary Beth Hughes, Don Beddoe. Imaginative handling of oft-told tale of bank employee accused of theft, catching actual crooks.

Loose in London (1953) **63m.** D: Edward Bernds. Leo Gorcey, Huntz Hall, Bernard Gorcey, Norma Varden, Angela Greene. SEE: Bowery Boys series.

Loot (1972-British) **C-96m.** ** D: Silvio Narizzano. Richard Attenborough, Lee Remick, Milo O'Shea, Joe Lynch. Redundant crime-caper movie finds Attenborough going after small fortune in loot with help from assorted entourage. Black comedy by Joe Orton.

Looters, The (1955) **87m.** **½ D: Abner Biberman. Rory Calhoun, Julie Adams, Ray Danton, Thomas Gomez. OK drama of survivors of plane crash fighting amongst themselves for money aboard wreckage.

Lord Jeff (1938) **78m.** ** D: Sam Wood. Freddie Bartholomew, Mickey Rooney, Charles Coburn, Herbert Mundin, Terry Kilburn, Gale Sondergaard, Peter Lawford. Acceptable family film about good-boy Bartholomew led astray, sent to straighten out at naval school.

Lord Jim (1965) **C-154m.** **½ D:

Richard Brooks. Peter O'Toole, James Mason, Curt Jurgens, Eli Wallach, Jack Hawkins, Paul Lukas, Daliah Lavi, Akim Tamiroff. Overlong, uneven adaptation of Joseph Conrad's story about idealistic young man in British Merchant Marine in the 19th-century who is discredited as a coward and lives with that scar for the rest of his life. Film's great moments provided by outstanding supporting cast.

Lord Love a Duck (1966) 104m. *** D: George Axelrod. Tuesday Weld, Roddy McDowall, Lola Albright, Martin West, Ruth Gordon, Harvey Korman, Martin Gabel, Sarah Marshall, Lynn Carey. Madcap black comedy about progressive Southern California high school where botany is called "plant skills." Film wavers uncomfortably between comedy and drama at times, but really delivers some belly laughs. Terrific performances in movie that was ahead of its time.

Lord of the Flies (1963-British) 90m. *** D: Peter Brook. James Aubrey, Tom Chapin, Hugh Edwards, Roger Elwin, Tom Gaman. Unique story of a group of British schoolboys stranded on remote island. Their gradual degeneration into a savage horde is compelling. Adapted from William Golding's novel.

Lord of the Jungle (1955) 69m. D: Ford Beebe. Johnny Sheffield, Wayne Morris, Nancy Hale, Smoki Whitfield, Paul Picerni. SEE: **Bomba, The Jungle Boy** series.

Lord of the Rings, The (1978) C-133m. **½ D: Ralph Bakshi. Voices of Christopher Guard, William Squire, John Hurt, Michael Sholes, Dominic Guard. Ambitious animated version of J. R. R. Tolkien's fantasy saga covers 1½ books of his trilogy (ending rather abruptly). Story of different races in Middle Earth competing for ownership of all-powerful Rings is inspired and exciting, but begins to drag—and confuse—during last hour. Bakshi's technique awkwardly combines animation and live-action tracings.

Lords of Flatbush, The (1974) C-88m. *** D: Stephen F. Verona, Martin Davidson. Perry King, Sylvester Stallone, Henry Winkler, Paul Mace, Susan Blakely. Fun story of a Flatbush gang, circa 1957, with original music score. Training ground for two major talents, Stallone writing some of the dialogue

and Winkler trying out his Fonzie character.

Lorna Doone (1951) C-88m. **½ D: Phil Karlson. Barbara Hale, Richard Greene, Carl Benton Reid, William Bishop. Middling screen version of Richard D. Blackmore's novel of 1860s England, with farmers rebelling against oppressive landlords. Done on small budget, but not bad.

Los Tarantos (1964-Spanish) C-81m. *** D: Rovira-Beleta. Carmen Amaya, Sara Lezana, Daniel Martin, Antonio Prieto. Sentimental yet touching account of two young people from rival gypsy families falling in love, with tragic results.

Loser Takes All (1956-British) C-88m. ** D: Ken Annakin. Rossano Brazzi, Glynis Johns, Robert Morley, Tony Britton, Geoffrey Keen, Peter Illing. Brazzi and Johns celebrate their honeymoon in Monte Carlo and try out their "perfect system" for winning at roulette, with unusual effect on their marriage. On-location filming helps.

Los Olvidados (1950-Mexican) 88m. ***½ D: Luis Buñuel. Alfonso Mejia, Roberto Cobo, Estela Inda, Miguel Inclan. Gripping story of juvenile delinquency among slums of Mexico, with surreal dream sequences interspersed. An offbeat winner from Buñuel, also known as THE YOUNG AND THE DAMNED.

Loss of Innocence (1961-British) C-99m. **½ D: Lewis Gilbert. Kenneth More, Danielle Darrieux, Susannah York, Maurice Denham. York gives poignant performance as teenager who, through love affair, becomes a woman; events leave her and younger sisters and brother stranded on the Continent. Original title: THE GREENGAGE SUMMER.

Lost (1955-British) C-89m. **½ D: Guy Green. David Farrar, David Knight, Julia Arnall, Anthony Oliver, Marjorie Rhodes. Offbeat account of effects of a child kidnapping on parents, police, press, and crooks.

Lost and Found (1979) C-112m. ** D: Melvin Frank. George Segal, Glenda Jackson, Maureen Stapleton, Hollis McLaren, John Cunningham, Paul Sorvino. Widowed college prof and British divorcee meet in a French ski resort and quickly cool their romance by marrying. Attempt to recapture the success of the overrated A TOUCH OF CLASS is just more old fashioned nonsense posing as hip comedy.

Lost Angel (1943) 91m. **½ D: Roy Rowland. Margaret O'Brien, James Craig, Marsha Hunt, Philip Merivale, Henry O'Neill, Donald Meek, Keenan Wynn. O'Brien is winning as precocious child—trained as a genius by scientists—who learns life's simple pleasures when she moves in with reporter Craig.

Lost Boundaries (1949) 99m. *** D: Alfred L. Werker. Beatrice Pearson, Mel Ferrer, Richard Hylton, Carleton Carpenter, Susan Douglas, Canada Lee. Negro family passes for white in New England town, till their heritage is discovered. One of the first racially conscious films; not bad.

Lost Command (1966) C-130m. *** D: Mark Robson. Anthony Quinn, Alain Delon, George Segal, Michele Morgan, Maurice Ronet, Claudia Cardinale, Gregoire Aslan, Jean Servais. Taut, well-made story of French-Algerian guerrilla warfare in North Africa, with Quinn as the peasant who has risen to a position of command. Fine international cast, good direction, and some top-notch action sequences blend very well.

Lost Continent, The (1951) 86m. ** D: Samuel Newfield. Cesar Romero, Hillary Brooke, John Hoyt, Acquanetta. Lavish production values are obviously lacking as Romero leads expedition to prehistoric mountaintop to recover missing rocket.

Lost Continent, The (1968-British) C-89m. **½ D: Michael Carreras. Eric Porter, Hildegard Knef, Suzanna Leigh, Tony Beckley, Nigel Stock, Neil McCallum. Tramp steamer wanders into uncharted seas, finds isolated freak civilization derived from Spanish monarchy. Good cast handles lopsided script straightfaced; occasional good action.

Lost Flight (1969) C-105m. TVM D: Leonard Horn. Lloyd Bridges, Anne Francis, Ralph Meeker, Bobby Van, Billy Dee Williams. Commercial jet crash-lands on Pacific island; survivors must exist by their wits, learn to work together. Foolish subplots, OK performances, much location work, but direction and script totally mismatched. Average.

Lost Honeymoon (1947) 71m. ** D: Leigh Jason. Franchot Tone, Ann Richards, Frances Rafferty, Una O'Connor, Winston Severn. Trivial comedy of amnesiac Tone discovering he's the father of two children.

Lost Horizon (1937) 116½m. **** D: Frank Capra. Ronald Colman, Jane Wyatt, John Howard, Edward Everett Horton, Margo, Sam Jaffe, H. B. Warner, Isabel Jewell, Thomas Mitchell. James Hilton's classic story about five people kidnapped to strange Tibetan land where health, peace, and longevity reign. A rare movie experience, with haunting finale. TV prints recently lengthened from 108m; more "lost" footage from original 130m. version recently found may yet be added.

Lost Horizon (1973) C-143m. *½ D: Charles Jarrott. Peter Finch, Liv Ullmann, Sally Kellerman, George Kennedy, Michael York, Olivia Hussey, Bobby Van, James Shigeta, Charles Boyer, John Gielgud. First half-hour copies 1937 film scene-for-scene, and everything's fine; then we get to Shangri-La and awful Burt Bacharach-Hal David songs, and it falls apart. "Lost" is right.

Lost in a Harem (1944) 89m. **½ D: Charles Riesner. Bud Abbott, Lou Costello, Marilyn Maxwell, John Conte, Douglass Dumbrille, Lottie Harrison, Jimmy Dorsey Orchestra. Slicker-than-usual A&C (made on infrequent trip to MGM), but strictly routine. Some good scenes here and there with sultan Dumbrille; Maxwell is perfect harem girl.

Lost in Alaska (1952) 76m. *½ D: Jean Yarbrough. Bud Abbott, Lou Costello, Mitzi Green, Tom Ewell, Bruce Cabot. Unremarkable slapstick set in 1890s, with A&C off to the wilds to help a friend but doing more hindering.

Lost in the Stars (1974) C-114m. *** D: Daniel Mann. Brock Peters, Melba Moore, Raymond St. Jacques, Clifton Davis, Paula Kelly. Good American Film Theatre version of the Kurt Weill-Maxwell Anderson musical, based on Alan Paton's *Cry, the Beloved Country.* Owes much of its power to Peters' portrayal of the South African minister. Filmed in Jamaica, B. W. I., and Hollywood.

Lost Island of Kioga (1938) 100m. ** D: William Witney, John English. Bruce Bennett, Mala, Monte Blue, Jill Martin, Noble Johnson. Acceptable Republic cliff-hanger with white native muscleman (Bennett) saving shipwrecked survivors from a variety of near-disasters; better than usual settings. Reedited movie serial: HAWK OF THE WILDERNESS.

Lost Lagoon (1958) 79m. *½ D: John Rawlins. Jeffrey Lynn, Peter Donat, Leila Barry, Don Gibson. Bland account of Lynn starting life anew on South Sea island. His sense of responsibility to family spoils idyll.

Lost Man, The (1969) C-122m. **½ D: Robert Alan Aurthur. Sidney Poitier, Joanna Shimkus, Al Freeman, Jr., Michael Tolan, Leon Bibb, Richard Dysart, David Steinberg, Paul Winfield. Uncomfortable updating of ODD MAN OUT from an Irish setting to present-day black underground has some tension, but doesn't really work. Poitier, Shimkus, and Freeman are good.

Lost Missile, The (1958) 70m. ** D: Lester Berke. Robert Loggia, Ellen Parker, Larry Kerr, Philip Pine. Unexciting narrative of race-against-time to destroy a rocket before it explodes in N.Y.C.

Lost Moment, The (1947) 88m. *** D: Martin Gabel. Robert Cummings, Susan Hayward, Agnes Moorehead, Joan Lorring, Eduardo Ciannelli. Henry James' ASPERN PAPERS becomes offbeat drama. Publisher Cummings in Italy seeking lost love letters of famous writer, comes across neurotic Hayward who claims to have access to them.

Lost Patrol, The (1934) 65m. **** D: John Ford. Victor McLaglen, Boris Karloff, Wallace Ford, Reginald Denny, Alan Hale, J. M. Kerrigan, Billy Bevan. McLaglen's small British military group lost in Mesopotamian desert, as Arabs repeatedly attack the dwindling unit. Classic actioner filled with slice-of life stereotypes, headed by religious fanatic Karloff. Fast-moving, great fun, great Max Steiner score. Original release print ran 74m.

Lost Planet Airmen (1949) 65m. *½ D: Fred Brannon. Tristram Coffin, Mae Clarke, Dale Van Sickel, Tom Steele, Buddy Roosevelt, House Peters, Jr. Feature version of Republic Pictures' twelve-chapter serial KING OF THE ROCKET MEN. This condensation poorly highlights the scheme of mad scientist trying to rule the world. Special effects are main virtue.

Lost Squadron, The (1932) 72m. **½ D: George Archainbaud. Richard Dix, Mary Astor, Erich von Stroheim, Joel McCrea, Dorothy Jordan, Robert Armstrong. WW1 pilots forced to find work as stunt flyers for movies; interesting idea boosted by Von Stroheim's overacting as director "Erich von Furst."

Lost Tribe, The (1949) 72m. D: William Berke. Johnny Weissmuller, Myrna Dell, Elena Verdugo, Joseph Vitale. SEE: Jungle Jim series.

Lost Volcano, The (1950) 67m. D: Ford Beebe. Johnny Sheffield, Donald Woods, Marjorie Lord, John Ridgely, Elena Verdugo. SEE: Bomba, The Jungle Boy series.

Lost Weekend, The (1945) 101m. **** D: Billy Wilder. Ray Milland, Jane Wyman, Philip Terry, Howard da Silva, Doris Dowling, Frank Faylen, Mary Young. Unrelenting drama of alcoholism with superb Wilder script, powerhouse performance by Milland which won him an Oscar. Fine support from bartender Da Silva, sanitarium worker Faylen.

Lost World, The (1925) 60m. **½ D: Harry Hoyt. Bessie Love, Wallace Beery, Lewis Stone, Lloyd Hughes. Silent film version of A. Conan Doyle adventure yarn is remarkable for special effects recreating prehistoric beasts encountered on scientific trip to deserted island. Monsters make film worthwhile.

Lost World, The (1960) C-98m. ** D: Irwin Allen. Michael Rennie, Jill St. John, David Hedison, Claude Rains, Fernando Lamas, Richard Haydn. Despite cinematic advances, this remake of the 1925 film doesn't match original's special effects. OK juvenile entry of an expedition into remote territory hopefully inhabited by prehistoric monsters.

Lottery Bride, The (1930) 80m. **½ D: Paul Stein. Jeanette MacDonald, John Garrick, Joe E. Brown, ZaSu Pitts, Robert Chisholm. Delightfully creaky musical with Yukon setting; Jeanette must deny her true love when she becomes lottery-bride for his older brother. Impressive sets, forgettable music, enjoyable comic relief from Brown and Pitts.

Louis Armstrong—Chicago Style (1976) C-78m. TVM D: Lee Philips. Ben Vereen, Margaret Avery, Red Buttons, Janet MacLachlan, Ketty Lester, Albert Paulsen. Dramatization of an incident in Satchmo's life when a death threat from Chicago gangsters unexpectedly made him an international figure. Vereen makes valiant stab at playing Louis, but the script is undeserving of the musical giant. Below average.

Louisa (1950) 90m. *** D: Alexander Hall. Spring Byington, Charles Coburn, Edmund Gwenn, Ronald Reagan, Piper Laurie, Ruth Hussey. Delightful romantic yarn of Byington seeking to become a December bride, undecided between Coburn and Gwenn; most disarming.

Louisiana Hayride (1944) 67m. ** D: Charles Barton. Judy Canova, Ross Hunter, Minerva Urecal, Lloyd Bridges, Russell Hicks. Hillbilly Canova goes Hollywood in this typical cornball vehicle.

Louisiana Purchase (1941) C-98m. **½ D: Irving Cummings. Bob Hope, Vera Zorina, Victor Moore, Irene Bordoni, Dona Drake. Brassy Irving Berlin musicomedy, with Hope's comedy very funny, especially famous filibuster scene in Congress. Opening scene of chorus girls singing lines about characters being fictitious is probably a movie first . . . and last.

Love (1927) 96m. **½ D: Edmund Goulding. Greta Garbo, John Gilbert, George Fawcett, Emily Fitzroy, Brandon Hurst, Philippe De Lacy. Silent version of ANNA KARENINA in modern setting, as married Garbo falls in love with dashing military guard Gilbert, an affair doomed from start. Weak entry for famed screen lovers, with Gilbert's eyebrow-raising gestures at their worst. Much better when remade as ANNA KARENINA. This print has incongruous happy ending tacked on in 1927 to please audiences.

Love Affair (1939) 87m. ***½ D: Leo McCarey. Irene Dunne, Charles Boyer, Maria Ouspenskaya, Lee Bowman, Astrid Allwyn, Maurice Moscovich. Superior comedy-drama about shipboard romance whose continuation on-shore is interrupted by unforseen circumstances. Dunne and Boyer are a marvelous match. Remade by the same director as AN AFFAIR TO REMEMBER.

Love Affair, A: The Eleanor and Lou Gehrig Story (1978) C-96m. TVM D: Fielder Cook. Blythe Danner, Edward Herrmann, Patricia Neal, Jane Wyatt, Gerald S. O'Loughlin, Ramon Bieri, Georgia Engel. Danner & Herrmann shine as Eleanor & Lou in this loving re-

telling of the saga—unlike PRIDE OF THE YANKEES, told from her point of view. Above average.

Love Among the Ruins (1975) C-100m. TVM D: George Cukor. Katharine Hepburn, Laurence Olivier, Colin Blakeley, Joan Sims, Richard Pearson, ~Leigh Lawson. Grand romantic comedy teaming two acting legends for the first time. Aging actress being sued by a young gigolo for breach of promise is defended by a prominent barrister who had been her long-ago lover. Rich and lustrous with Emmy Awards for its two stars, to director Cukor (his TV movie debut) and to writer James Costigan. Bouquets all around. Above average.

Love and Anarchy (1973-Italian) C-108m. *** D: Lina Wertmuller. Giancarlo Giannini, Mariangela Melato, Lina Polito, Eros Pagni, Pina Cel, Elena Fiore. Italian bumpkin Giannini tries to assassinate Mussolini in 1932, falls for a prostitute in the brothel serving as his base of operation. Uneven but stylish drama helped establish Wertmuller's considerable reputation.

Love and Bullets (1979-British) C-103m. ** D: Stuart Rosenberg. Charles Bronson, Rod Steiger, Jill Ireland, Strother Martin, Bradford Dillman, Henry Silva. Bronson is supposed to nab gangster's moll Ireland for the FBI, but falls in love with her during his pursuit in Switzerland. Routine action yarn for Bronson fans only.

Love and Death (1975) C-82m. *** D: Woody Allen. Woody Allen, Diane Keaton, Harold Gould, Alfred Lutter, Olga Georges-Picot, Zvee Scooler. Woody's most pretentious film won applause for its spoofs of Russian literature and foreign films, but this tale of a devout coward in the Napoleonic wars is more like a remake of Bob Hope's MONSIEUR BEAUCAIRE. Funny but uneven.

Love and Kisses (1965) C-87m. **½ D: Ozzie Nelson. Rick Nelson, Kristin Nelson, Jack Kelly, Jerry Van Dyke, Pert Kelton, Madelyn Hines. Harmless fare; Rick gets married, disrupting his family's life.

Love and Larceny (1963-Italian) 94m. **½ D: Dino Risi. Vittorio Gassman, Anna Maria Ferrero, Dorian Gray, Peppino De Filippo. Saucy comedy of exuberant con-man Gassman making no pretense about his carefree life and pleasures.

Love and Learn (1947) 83m. ** D: Frederick de Cordova. Jack Carson, Robert Hutton, Martha Vickers, Janis Paige, Otto Kruger. Overdone idea of songwriters Carson and Hutton waiting for their big break; young girl comes to their aid, but she doesn't save film.

Love and Marriage (1964-Italian) 106m. **½ D: Gianni Puccini and Nino Guerrini. Sylva Koscina, Philippe Leroy, Amadeo Girard, April Hennessy. Funny film in four segments relating to male-female relationships of an amorous variety.

Love and Pain (and the Whole Damn Thing) (1972) C-110m. *** D: Alan J. Pakula. Maggie Smith, Timothy Bottoms. Charming story of two introverts who miraculously and humorously find each other, fall in love while touring Spain.

Love and the Frenchwoman (1961-French) 143m. *** D: Jean Delannoy, Michel Boisrond, René Clair, Christian-Jaque, Jean-Paul Lechannois. Martine Lambert, Claude Rich, Dany Robin, Jean-Paul Belmondo, Annie Girardot, Martine Carol. Savory account of the seven ages of love in a woman's life, sensitively acted.

Love and the Midnight Auto Supply (1978) C-93m. *½ D: James Polakoff. Michael Parks, Linda Cristal, Scott Jacoby, Colleen Camp, John Ireland, Rory Calhoun, Rod Cameron. Yahoo action-comedy has ringleader of stolen auto-parts gang turning Robin Hood to help farm workers combat corrupt politicians.

Love at First Bite (1979) C-96m. *** D: Stan Dragoti. George Hamilton, Susan St. James, Richard Benjamin, Dick Shawn, Arte Johnson, Sherman Hemsley, Isabel Sanford. Silly but likable comedy about Count Dracula's adventures in New York City, and love affair with fashion model St. James. Hamilton's comic performance is bloody good.

Love at Twenty (1963-International) 113m. **½ D: Francois Truffaut, Renzo Rossellini, Shintaro Ishihara, Max Ophuls, Andrzej Wajda. Jean-Pierre Leaud, Eleonora Rossi-Drago, Zbigniew Cybulski, Nami Tamara. Quintet of middling stories produced in France, Germany, Italy, Japan, Poland; variations on theme of love among younger generation.

Love Before Breakfast (1936) 70m. **½ D: Walter Lang. Carole Lombard, Preston Foster, Cesar Romero,

Janet Beecher, Betty Lawford, Douglas Blackley (Robert Kent). Fast-starting comedy slows down to obvious ending, but Lombard as object of Foster's and Romero's attention is worth viewing.

Love Boat, The (1976) C-100m. TVM D: Richard Kinon and Alan Meyerson. Don Adams, Tom Bosley, Florence Henderson, Gabriel Kaplan, Harvey Korman, Cloris Leachman, Hal Linden, Karen Valentine, Ted Hamilton, Dick Van Patten. Four interrelated comedy tales involving misadventures of passengers and crew aboard cruise ship. Guest star passengers do wonders with threadbare material in this movie that puts TV's popular "Love, American Style" asea. Later a series itself. Average.

Love Boat II, The (1977) C-100m. TVM D: Hy Averback. Ken Berry, Bert Convy, Celeste Holm, Hope Lange, Kristy McNichol, Robert Reed, Craig Stevens, Marcia Strassman, Tracy Brooks Swope, Lyle Waggoner. The popularity of its predecessor prompted another quartet of stories, enacted by a similarly familiar roster of TV names, and this one led to a weekly series. Average.

Love Bug, The (1969) C-107m. ***½ D: Robert Stevenson. Dean Jones, Michele Lee, Buddy Hackett, David Tomlinson, Joe Flynn, Benson Fong, Iris Adrian. Delightful Disney comedy about a Volkswagen with a mind of its own; subtle it ain't, but the slapstick and stunts are great fun to watch. Followed by two HERBIE sequels.

Love Crazy (1941) 99m. **½ D: Jack Conway. William Powell, Myrna Loy, Gail Patrick, Jack Carson, Florence Bates, Sidney Blackmer, Sig Ruman. One misunderstanding leads to another in this energetic marital farce that loses steam halfway through. Highlighted by Powell's attempts to prove himself insane, and Carson's hilarious characterization as Ward Willoughby.

Love Finds Andy Hardy (1938) 90m. D: George B. Seitz. Mickey Rooney, Lewis Stone, Judy Garland, Cecilia Parker, Fay Holden, Lana Turner, Ann Rutherford, Betty Ross Clark, Marie Blake. SEE: **Andy Hardy** series.

Love for Ransom SEE: **Roger & Harry: The Mitera Target.**

Love for Rent (1979) C-100m. TVM D: David Miller. Annette O'Toole,

Lisa Eilbacher, Rhonda Fleming, Darren McGavin, Eugene Roche, David Selby. Innocuous TV programmer about two sisters who become seduced by big city glamour and wind up as high-priced call girls in an escort service. Below average.

Love from a Stranger (1947) 81m. **½ D: Richard Whorf. Sylvia Sidney, John Hodiak, John Howard, Isobel Elsom, Ernest Cossart. Capable cast goes through familiar paces in SUSPICION-like story of woman who learns she's married a killer. Filmed before in 1937; from an Agatha Christie story.

Love God?, The (1969) C-101m. ** D: Nat Hiken. Don Knotts, Anne Francis, Edmond O'Brien, James Gregory, Maureen Arthur, Maggie Peterson, Jesslyn Fax. Comedy for those who are amused by Knotts playing Hugh Hefner type; film is final work of Nat Hiken, who created Sergeant Bilko in better days.

Love Goddesses, The (1965) 87m. *** Compiled by Saul J. Turell and Graeme Ferguson. Marilyn Monroe, Mae West, Jean Harlow, Theda Bara, Rita Hayworth, Claudette Colbert, Dorothy Lamour, many others. Compilation covers a lot of ground, featuring many major female stars from silent days to the present. Not always the ideal clips, but well done, with many welcome classic scenes. Some color sequences. Revised for theatrical reissue in 1972.

Love Happy (1949) 91m. **½ D: David Miller. Harpo, Chico, and Groucho Marx, Ilona Massey, Vera-Ellen, Marion Hutton, Raymond Burr. No NIGHT AT THE OPERA, but even diluted Marx Brothers are better than none. Putting on a musical forms background for Harpo's antics, with Chico in support, Groucho in a few unrelated scenes. Marilyn Monroe has a brief bit.

Love Has Many Faces (1965) C-105m. **½ D: Alexander Singer. Lana Turner, Cliff Robertson, Hugh O'Brian, Ruth Roman, Stefanie Powers, Virginia Grey. Timid attempt at lurid soaper; playgirl Turner's costume changes are the highlights. O'Brian and Robertson are gigolos. Filmed in Acapulco.

Love Hate Love (1970) C-72m. TVM D: George McCowan. Ryan O'Neal, Lesley Warren, Peter Haskell, Henry Jones, Jeff Donnell, Jack Mullaney. Fair twist of triangle drama. Fashion model engaged to engineer (O'Neal) falls in love with jet setter (Haskell) who turns out to be psychotic. Competent performances, fair situations, one genuine moment of suspense. Average.

Love, Honor and Goodbye (1945) 87m. ** D: Albert S. Rogell. Virginia Bruce, Nils Asther, Victor McLaglen, Helen Broderick, Veda Ann Borg, Edward Ashley. Bruce is actress in Broadway show, spending more time at rehearsals than with hubby. Mild frou-frou.

Love in a Goldfish Bowl (1961) C-88m. BOMB D: Jack Sher. Tommy Sands, Fabian, Jan Sterling, Edward Andrews. Film is as bad as its title, a worthless, boring trifle about teenagers taking over a beach house. Forget it.

Love in Bloom (1935) 75m. ** D: Elliott Nugent. George Burns, Gracie Allen, Joe Morrison, Dixie Lee, J. C. Nugent, Lee Kohlmar. Burns and Allen are forced to take back seat to sappy romantic story about struggling songwriter and his girlfriend; George and Gracie give this minor film its only value.

Love in the Afternoon (1957) 130m. ***½ D: Billy Wilder. Gary Cooper, Audrey Hepburn, Maurice Chevalier, John McGiver. Forget age difference between Cooper and Hepburn and enjoy sparkling romantic comedy, with Chevalier as Audrey's private-eye dad. McGiver lends good support in witty Wilder comedy set in Paris.

Love in the City (1953-Italian) 90m. ** D: Michelangelo Antonioni, Federico Fellini, Dino Risi, Carlo Lizzani, Alberto Lattuada, Maselli Zavattini. Ugo Tognazzi, Maresa Gallo, Caterina Rigoglioso, Silvio Lillo, Angela Pierro. Six-part film using a hidden-camera technique to give production seeming reality as it relates various aspects of romance in Rome.

Love Is a Ball (1963) C-111m. **½ D: David Swift. Glenn Ford, Hope Lange, Charles Boyer, Ricardo Montalban, Telly Savalas. Forced froth trying hard to be chic; gold-digging and romance on the Riviera.

Love Is a Many Splendored Thing (1955) C-102m. *** D: Henry King. Jennifer Jones, William Holden, Isobel Elsom, Jorja Curtright, Virginia Gregg, Torin Thatcher, Richard Loo. Well-mounted soaper set in Hong Kong at time of Korean

War. Eurasian doctor Jones falls in love with war correspondent Holden. Trite plot, beautifully executed.

Love Is Better than Ever (1952) 81m. **½ D: Stanley Donen. Elizabeth Taylor, Larry Parks, Josephine Hutchinson, Tom Tully, Ann Doran. Froth involving talent agent Parks' decision to marry Taylor. Mild music, luscious Liz.

Love Is News (1937) 78m. ** D: Tay Garnett. Tyrone Power, Loretta Young, Don Ameche, Slim Summerville, George Sanders, Jane Darwell, Stepin Fetchit, Pauline Moore, Elisha Cook, Jr., Dudley Digges, Walter Catlett. Comedy misfire of heiress Young marrying reporter Power to get even for his stories about her. Better in remake THAT WONDERFUL URGE.

Love Is Not Enough (1978) C-100m. TVM D: Ivan Dixon. Bernie Casey, Stuart K. Robinson, Renee Brown, Dain Turner, Stu Gilliam, Eddie Singleton. Warm but predictable comedy-drama about a Detroit black family's search for the better life in California. A very brief series called HARRIS AND COMPANY spun off from this pilot. Average.

Love Laughs at Andy Hardy (1946) 93m. D: Willis Goldbeck. Mickey Rooney, Lewis Stone, Sara Haden, Bonita Granville, Lina Romay, Fay Holden, Dorothy Ford. SEE: Andy Hardy series.

Love Letters (1945) 101m. ** D: William Dieterle. Jennifer Jones, Joseph Cotten, Ann Richards, Anita Louise, Cecil Kellaway, Gladys Cooper. Artificial soaper of amnesiac Jones cured by Cotten's love; only real asset is Victor Young's lovely title song.

Love Lottery, The (1953-British) C-89m. ** D: Charles Crichton. David Niven, Peggy Cummins, Anne Vernon, Herbert Lom, Hugh McDermott. Niven is famed movie star involved in international lottery; the winner gets him! Vernon is the girl he really loves. Potential satire never comes off. Humphrey Bogart has guest bit at finale.

Love Machine, The (1971) C-108m. *½ D: Jack Haley, Jr. John Phillip Law, Dyan Cannon, Robert Ryan, Jackie Cooper, David Hemmings, Shecky Greene. Ridiculous screen version of Jacqueline Susann story of Robin Stone, ruthless man at the top in show biz who uses others for self-gain.

Love Me Forever (1935) 90m. **½ D: Victor Schertzinger. Grace Moore, Leo Carrillo, Robert Allen, Spring Byington, Douglass Dumbrille. Entertaining musical of down-and-out singer who miraculously rises to top and becomes star. Good cast helped make Moore become star in real life too.

Love Me or Leave Me (1955) C-122m. ***½ D: Charles Vidor. Doris Day, James Cagney, Cameron Mitchell, Robert Keith, Tom Tully. Doris is singer Ruth Etting, Cagney her gangster boyfriend, the Gimp. Fine musical biography has great songs of 1920s: "Ten Cents A Dance," "Never Look Back," title tune, etc.

Love Me Tender (1956) 89m. **½ D: Robert D. Webb. Richard Egan, Debra Paget, Elvis Presley, Robert Middleton, William Campbell, Neville Brand, Mildred Dunnock. Presley's film debut is Civil War yarn of conflicting politics among sons in a Southern family, and their mutual love for Paget.

Love Me Tonight (1932) 96m. **** D: Rouben Mamoulian. Maurice Chevalier, Jeanette MacDonald, Charlie Ruggles, Myrna Loy, C. Aubrey Smith, Charles Butterworth. One of the best musicals ever made; Chevalier plays a tailor who falls in love with a princess (MacDonald). Along the way they get to sing Rodgers and Hart's "Lover," "Mimi," "Isn't It Romantic?" among others. Mamoulian's ingenious ideas keep this fresh and alive. Originally released at 104m.

Love Nest (1951) 84m. ** D: Joseph M. Newman. June Haver, William Lundigan, Frank Fay, Marilyn Monroe, Jack Paar, Leatrice Joy. Tepid comedy based on premise that wacky goings-on in apartment building can carry a film.

Love on a Pillow (1963-French) C-102m. ** D: Roger Vadim. Brigitte Bardot, Robert Hossein, James Robertson Justice, Jean-Marc Bory. Charitable Bardot bestows her pleasures on young man, hoping to divert his intended suicide; saucy little comedy.

Love on the Dole (1941-British) 89m. *** D: John Baxter. Deborah Kerr, Clifford Evans, Mary Merrall, George Carney, Geoffrey Hibbert, Joyce O'Neill. Serious, well-acted study of struggling London family during Depression. From Walter Greenwood novel.

Love on the Run (1936) 80m. **½ D: W. S. Van Dyke II. Joan Crawford, Clark Gable, Franchot Tone, Reginald Owen, Mona Barrie, Ivan Lebedeff, Charles Judels. Another film that's all stars and no plot to support them. If you like Gable or Crawford, you'll enjoy this globe-trotting romance involving foreign correspondents and Continental spies.

Love Parade, The (1929) 110m. *** D: Ernst Lubitsch. Maurice Chevalier, Jeanette MacDonald, Lillian Roth, Lionel Belmore, Lupino Lane, Ben Turpin. Initial teaming of Chevalier and MacDonald is enjoyable operetta with chic Lubitsch touch, about love among French royalty. Virginia Bruce is one of Jeanette's ladies-in-waiting. "Dream Lover" is film's best song.

Love Slaves of the Amazon (1957) C-81m. ** D: Curt Siodmak. Don Taylor, Eduardo Ciannelli, Gianna Segale, Harvey Chalk. Title tag removes all surprises about this programmer.

Love Story (1944-British) 108m. *** D: Leslie Arliss. Margaret Lockwood, Stewart Granger, Patricia Roc, Tom Walls, Reginald Purdell, Moira Lister. No relation to later hit film, this one has dying pianist Lockwood finding true love at summer resort with pilot Granger, whose eyesight is failing. Originally released here as A LADY SURRENDERS.

Love Story (1970) C-99m. *** D: Arthur Hiller. Ali MacGraw, Ryan O'Neal, Ray Milland, John Marley, Katharine Balfour. Just what it says: simple, modern boy-meets-girl story, set against modern New England college backdrop, tinged with tragedy of girl's sudden illness. Straightforward filming of Erich Segal's book can't hold a candle to older Hollywood schmaltz, but on its own terms, pretty good. Followed by sequel OLIVER'S STORY.

Love That Brute (1950) 85m. **½ D: Alexander Hall. Paul Douglas, Jean Peters, Cesar Romero, Joan Davis, Arthur Treacher. Douglas comes off well as loud-talking, good-natured prohibition racketeer with a yen for innocent Peters. Remake of TALL, DARK AND HANDSOME.

Love Thy Neighbor (1940) 82m. ** D: Mark Sandrich. Jack Benny, Fred Allen, Mary Martin, Verree Teasdale, Eddie "Rochester" Anderson, Virginia Dale, Theresa Harris. Contrived attempt to capitalize on Benny-Allen radio feud. Martin still good, though, and Rochester has some sprightly scenes, but disappointment for fans of both Benny and Allen.

Love Under Fire (1937) 75m. **½ D: George Marshall. Loretta Young, Don Ameche, Frances Drake, Walter Catlett, Sig Ruman, John Carradine, Holmes Herbert. Romance and adventure as detective Ameche has to arrest alleged thief Young in Madrid amid Spanish Civil War. Disjointed but enjoyable.

Love War, The (1970) C-74m. TVM D: George McCowan. Lloyd Bridges, Angie Dickinson, Harry Basch, Dan Travanty, Byron Foulger, Judy Jordan. Two planets decide to end quarrel over Earth by arranging contest to the death in small town. Victor gets total control. Typical TV resolution. Subplot has "romance" between Argon Kyle and Zynan Sandy. Foolish drama must be seen to be believed. Below average.

Love with the Proper Stranger (1963) 100m. *** D: Robert Mulligan. Natalie Wood, Steve McQueen, Edie Adams, Herschel Bernardi, Tom Bosley. Nifty, cynical romance tale of working-girl Wood and trumpet-player McQueen. Much N.Y.C. on-location filming, good support from Adams.

Love's Dark Ride (1978) C-100m. TVM D: Delbert Mann. Cliff Potts, Carrie Snodgress, Jane Seymour, Granville Van Dusen, Shelly Novack, Tom Sullivan. Tepid fact-based drama about an ad executive who is blinded in a gun accident and falls in love with a nightclub entertainer he has befriended. Average.

Love's Savage Fury (1979) C-100m. TVM D: Joseph Hardy. Jennifer O'Neill, Perry King, Raymond Burr, Connie Stevens, Robert Reed, Ed Lauter. Petulant southern belle fights to hold onto the family mansion when the Union boys march through in this blatant ripoff of GONE WITH THE WIND—and even the letters of the title sweep across the screen in the opening credits! Below average (and contempt).

Loved One, The (1965) 116m. ***½ D: Tony Richardson. Robert Morse, Jonathan Winters, Anjanette Comer, Rod Steiger, Dana Andrews, Milton

Berle, James Coburn, John Gielgud, Tab Hunter, Margaret Leighton, Liberace, Roddy McDowall, Robert Morley, Lionel Stander. Correctly advertised as the picture with something to offend everyone. Britisher Morse attends to uncle's burial in California, encountering bizarre aspects of funeral business. Often howlingly funny, and equally gross. Once seen, Mrs. Joyboy can never be forgotten.

Lovely Way to Die, A (1968) C-103m. **½ D: David Lowell Rich. Kirk Douglas, Sylva Koscina, Eli Wallach, Kenneth Haigh, Sharon Farrell, Gordon Peter, Martyn Green. Odd detective suspenser. Douglas is likable cop turned private-eye assigned by D.A. (Wallach) to protect Koscina, awaiting murder trial. Pacing and script offbeat at right moments, otherwise standard. Look for Ali MacGraw in screen debut.

Lovemakers, The SEE: La Viaccia.
Lover Boy SEE: Lovers, Happy Lovers!

Lover Come Back (1946) 90m. **½ D: William A. Seiter. Lucille Ball, George Brent, Vera Zorina, Carl Esmond, William Wright, Charles Winninger. Bright little comedy of Lucy suing Brent for divorce when she sees his companion during war, photographer Zorina. Retitled WHEN LOVERS MEET.

Lover Come Back (1961) C-107m. ***½ D: Delbert Mann. Rock Hudson, Doris Day, Tony Randall, Edie Adams, Jack Oakie. Early Day-Hudson vehicle is one of the best. Funny, fast-moving comedy, with Doris' honor at stake until the last reel. Edie Adams stands out in a supporting role.

Lovers, The (1959-French) 90m. *** D: Louis Malle. Jeanne Moreau, Alain Cuny, Jose-Luis de Villalonga, Jean-Marc Bory. Sensational, chic love tale of Moreau bored with husband and home, having a most sensual romance with an overnight guest.

Lovers and Lollipops (1956) 80m. **½ D: Morris Engel, Ruth Orkin. Lori March, Gerald O'Loughlin, Cathy Dunn, William Ward. Pleasing minor film of romance between widow and professional man, disrupted by her daughter's jealousy of their happiness.

Lovers and Other Strangers (1970) C-106m. ***½ D: Cy Howard. Gig

Young, Bea Arthur, Bonnie Bedelia, Anne Jackson, Harry Guardino, Michael Brandon, Richard Castellano, Bob Dishy, Marian Hailey, Cloris Leachman, Anne Meara. Vividly real, genuinely funny movie about side-effects, reverberations when young couple gets married. Film won fame for Castellano, with catch-line "So what's the story?" just one of many memorable vignettes. Gig Young delightful as perennially cheerful father of the bride.

Lovers, Happy Lovers! (1954-British) 105m. **½ D: René Clement. Gerard Philippe, Valerie Hobson, Joan Greenwood, Margaret Johnston, Natasha Parry. Philippe is footloose playboy in London who finally meets his match and is marriage-bound. Original title: KNAVE OF HEARTS. Retitled: LOVER BOY.

Lovers Like Us (1975-French) C-103m. **½ D: Jean-Paul Rappeneau. Catherine Deneuve, Yves Montand, Luigi Vanucchi, Tony Roberts, Dana Wynter. Globetrotting screwball comedy has Deneuve and Montand running away from their respective spouses, meeting and falling in love with each other. Nothing special, but easy to take.

Lovers of Montparnasse, The (1957-French) 103m. **½ D: Jacques Becker. Gerard Philippe, Lilli Palmer, Anouk Aimee, Lea Padovani, Lino Ventura, Gerald Sety. Fictionalized biog of 1900s painter Modigliani, his romances and escapades; cast is forced into stereotyped performances. Original title: MONTPARNASSE 19.

Lovers of Paris (1957-French) 115m. **½ D: Julien Duvivier. Gerard Philippe, Danielle Darrieux, Dany Carrel. Spirited drama of Philippe coming to Paris bent on success and marriage; Darrieux is his perfect choice. Original title: POT-BOUILLE.

Loves and Times of Scaramouche, The (1975-Italian) C-95m. *½ D: Enzo G. Castellari. Michael Sarrazin, Ursula Andress, Aldo Maccione, Giancarlo Prete, Michael Forest. Scaramouche has his way with women, and runs afoul of an oafish Napoleon in this energetic but empty-headed farce. Maccione adds some laughs as Bonaparte. Poorly dubbed. Filmed in Rome and Zagreb.

Loves of a Blonde (1965-Czech) 88m. ***½ D: Milos Forman. Hana

Brejchova, Josef Sebanek, Vladimir Pucholt, Jan Vostreil. Thoroughly engaging boy-meets-girl comedy, directed with sensitivity and a remarkable feel for original cinema.

Loves of Carmen, The (1948) **C-99m. **½ D: Charles Vidor. Rita Hayworth, Glenn Ford, Ron Randell, Victor Jory, Luther Adler. Hayworth's beauty is all there is in this colorful but routine retelling of the story of a gypsy man-killer, minus Bizet's music.

Loves of Edgar Allan Poe, The (1942) 67m. ** D: Harry Lachman. Linda Darnell, John (Shepperd Strudwick) Shepperd, Virginia Gilmore, Jane Darwell, Mary Howard. Plodding biography of 19th-century writer and women who influenced him.

Loves of Isadora, The SEE: Isadora

Loves of Salammbo, The (1962-Italian) C-72m. ** D: Sergio Grieco. Jeanne Valerie, Jacques Sernas, Edmund Purdom, Arnold Foa, Riccardo Garrone. Spectacle features Purdom in an uneven tale of Carthaginians battling the Mercenaries. Filmed on location.

Loves of Sunya, The (1927) 80m. *** D: Albert Parker. Gloria Swanson, John Boles, Anders Randolph, Andres de Segurola, Hugh Miller, Pauline Garon. Lavish vehicle for silent-star Swanson has Eastern yogi enabling her to envision her life with each of three suitors. Soap opera deluxe, remake of earlier EYES OF YOUTH.

Loves of Three Queens (1953-Italian) 90m. ** D: Marc Allegret. Hedy Lamarr, Massimo Serato, Cathy O'Donnell, Luigi Tosi, Guido Celano, Robert Beatty. Three-part film involving lives and loves of Genevieve of Brabant, Empress Josephine, and Helen of Troy (Lamarr). Originally three-hour meandering epic, now chopped down; still lacks continuity or interest. Retitled: THE FACE THAT LAUNCHED A THOUSAND SHIPS.

Lovey: A Circle of Children, Part II (1978) C-100m. TVM D: Jud Taylor. Jane Alexander, Ronny Cox, Kris McKeon, Jeff Lynas, Danny Aiello. Alexander reprises her role from A CIRCLE OF CHILDREN as a teacher of disturbed youngsters —and again is top-notch. Above average.

Lovin' Molly (1974) C-98. ** D: Sidney Lumet. Anthony Perkins,

Beau Bridges, Blythe Danner, Edward Binns, Susan Sarandon, Conrad Fowkes. Danner is just right in otherwise indifferent filmization of Larry McMurtry's novel *Leaving Cheyenne*, about two friends in Texas and their lifelong love for the same woman.

Loving (1970) C-90m. ***½ D: Irvin Kershner. George Segal, Eva Marie Saint, Sterling Hayden, Keenan Wynn, Nancie Phillips, Janis Young. Extremely good drama chronicles Segal's marital and occupational problems. Director Kershner has great feeling for day-to-day detail, but film's superb climax involves public lovemaking, so may not fare well on TV.

Loving You (1957) C-101m. **½ D: Hal Kanter. Elvis Presley, Lizabeth Scott, Wendell Corey, Dolores Hart, James Gleason. Scott discovers Presley and he becomes singing idol; formula musical.

Love-Ins, The (1967) C-91m. BOMB D: Arthur Dreifuss. Richard Todd, James MacArthur, Susan Oliver, Mark Goddard, Carol Booth, Joe Pyne. Todd does Timothy Leary takeoff in laughable film about West Coast professor who uses LSD for religious meditation.

Lucan (1977) C-78m. TVM D: David Greene. Kevin Brophy, Stockard Channing, Ned Beatty, William Jordan, Lou Frizzell, George Wyner. Youth who spent his first ten years running wild and raised by wolves strikes out in search of his identity. Of its type, pretty good, and it bred a series. Average.

Lucas Tanner (1974) C-78m. TVM D: Richard Donner. David Hartman, Rosemary Murphy, Kathleen Quinlan, Nancy Malone, Ramon Bieri, Michael Baselson. High school teacher's career is threatened after a student's death when rumor spreads that his negligence killed the boy. Hartman's ingratiating style made this and the later series winners. Above average.

Luck of Ginger Coffey, The (1964-Canadian) 100m. ***½ D: Irvin Kershner. Robert Shaw, Mary Ure, Liam Redmond, Tom Harvey, Libby McClintock. Shaw is superb as Irishborn dreamer moved to Montreal with wife and child, unwilling to face realities of workaday life.

Luck of the Irish, The (1948) 99m. **½ D: Henry Koster. Tyrone Power, Anne Baxter, Cecil Kellaway, Lee

J. Cobb, Jayne Meadows. Leprechaun Kellaway becomes reporter Power's conscience in this "cute" but unremarkable romance.

Lucky Jim (1957-British) 95m. **½ D: John Boulting. Ian Carmichael, Terry-Thomas, Hugh Griffith, Sharon Acker, Jean Anderson. Comic misadventures of puckish history professor at provincial British university; amusing adaptation of Kingsley Amis book, though not up to Boulting Brothers standard.

Lucky Jordan (1942) 84m. **½ D: Frank Tuttle. Alan Ladd, Helen Walker, Marie McDonald, Mabel Paige, Sheldon Leonard, Lloyd Corrigan. Far-fetched story of army conman Ladd involved with Nazi agents with USO worker Walker (her feature-film debut).

Lucky Lady (1975) C-118m. ** D: Stanley Donen. Gene Hackman, Liza Minnelli, Burt Reynolds, Geoffrey Lewis, John Hillerman, Robby Benson, Michael Hordern. Star trio make an engaging team, as amateur rum-runners in the 1930s who practice a menage-a-trois after business hours . . . but the script goes astray and drags along to a limp conclusion. Unfortunate waste of talent.

Lucky Losers (1950) 69m. D: William Beaudine. Leo Gorcey, Huntz Hall, Hillary Brooke, Gabriel Dell, Lyle Talbot, Bernard Gorcey, William Benedict, Joseph Turkel, Frank Jenks. SEE: Bowery Boys series.

Lucky Luciano (1974-Italian) C-110m. ** D: Francesco Rosi. Gian-Maria Volonte, Rod Steiger, Edmond O'Brien, Vincent Gardenia, Charles Cioffi. Fair Italian-French-American co-production about the deported crime kingpin, given a good interpretation by Volonte. Former federal narcotics agent Charles Siragusa, Luciano's real-life nemesis, plays himself.

Lucky Me (1954) C-100m. ** D: Jack Donohue. Doris Day, Robert Cummings, Phil Silvers, Eddie Foy, Nancy Walker, Martha Hyer. Unemployed chorus girl in Florida finds love instead of work. Lackluster musical with then-widescreen-novelty lost to viewers. Angie Dickinson's first film.

Lucky Nick Cain (1951) 87m. **½ D: Joseph M. Newman. George Raft, Coleen Gray, Charles Goldner, Walter Rilla. Acceptable gangster yarn of Raft involved with

counterfeiting gang, accused of murder; filmed in Italy.

Lucky Night (1939) 90m. *½ D: Norman Taurog. Myrna Loy, Robert Taylor, Henry O'Neill, Marjorie Main, Irving Bacon. Fizzle with Loy and Taylor as struggling young marrieds.

Lucky Partners (1940) 99m. **½ D: Lewis Milestone. Ronald Colman, Ginger Rogers, Jack Carson, Spring Byington, Cecilia Loftus, Harry Davenport. Far-fetched comedy about Colman and Rogers winning sweepstakes together, then taking "imaginary" honeymoon. Stars buoy so-so script.

Lucky Stiff, The (1949) 99m. ** D: Lewis R. Foster. Dorothy Lamour, Brian Donlevy, Claire Trevor, Irene Hervey, Marjorie Rambeau. Sturdy cast in slim vehicle of lawyer setting trap for actual killer after girl suspect has death sentence reprieved.

Lucky to Be a Woman (1958-Italian) 95m. **½ D: Alessandro Blasetti. Charles Boyer, Sophia Loren, Marcello Mastroianni, Nino Besozzi, Titina De Filippo. Boyer is lecherous count who helps make peasant gal Loren a cultured movie star; Mastroianni is her photographer boyfriend; charmingly acted.

Lucy Gallant (1955) C-104m. **½ D: Robert Parrish. Charlton Heston, Jane Wyman, Thelma Ritter, Claire Trevor, William Demarest, Wallace Ford. Spiritless soaper of successbent Wyman rejecting suitors Heston et al, wanting to get ahead instead; set in Western oil town.

Ludwig (1973-Italian-French-German) C-173m. ** D: Luchino Visconti. Helmut Berger, Romy Schneider, Trevor Howard, Silvana Mangano, Helmut Griem, Gert Frobe. Lavish film about Mad King of Bavaria keeps main character so cold, aloof that one feels no sympathy; after nearly three hours, effect is deadening. Authentic locations are breathtaking, Schneider and Howard excellent, but slow-moving film doesn't work.

Lullaby of Broadway, The (1951) C-92m. **½ D: David Butler. Doris Day, Gene Nelson, S. Z. Sakall, Billy DeWolfe, Gladys George. Another Doris Day-Warner Bros. vehicle, with Doris a singer returning to N.Y.C. to discover mother (George) is down-and-out chanteuse.

Lulu Belle (1948) 87m. ** D: Leslie Fenton. Dorothy Lamour, George Montgomery, Albert Dekker, Otto Kruger, Glenda Farrell. Hackneyed drama of singer Lamour stepping on anyone and everyone to achieve fame.

Lumiere (1976-French) C-95m. **½ D: Jeanne Moreau. Jeanne Moreau, Francine Racette, Lucia Bose, Caroline Cartier, Marie Henriau, Keith Carradine, Bruno Ganz, Francois Simon. Elaborate but not very involving drama about four actresses of different ages and status and their relationships with careers, men, each other. Curio is worth seeing for Moreau's directorial debut.

Luna (1979) C-137m. *** D: Bernardo Bertolucci. Jill Clayburgh, Matthew Barry, Veronica Lazar, Renato Salvatori, Fred Gwynne, Alida Valli. Initially dazzling tale of a male adolescent's identity crisis becomes ponderous when it turns into a mother-son soap opera with incestuous implications. Cinematically exciting, nonetheless, with a bravura finale.

Lure of the Swamp (1957) 74m. *½ D: Hubert Cornfield. Marshall Thompson, Willard Parker, Joan Vohs, Jack Elam. Tawdry "B" film of man's lust for wealth, leading to destruction of group hunting loot in murky swamp.

Lure of the Wilderness (1952) C-92m. **½ D: Jean Negulesco. Jeffrey Hunter, Jean Peters, Constance Smith, Walter Brennan, Jack Elam. Remake of SWAMP WATER doesn't match earlier version's atmosphere of Southern swamps where murderer holds young man hostage to keep his whereabouts secret.

Lured (1947) 102m. **½ D: Douglas Sirk. George Sanders, Lucille Ball, Charles Coburn, Alan Mowbray, Cedric Hardwicke, Boris Karloff. Ball turns detective in this melodrama, encounters strange characters and harrowing experiences while tracking murderer; pretty good, with top cast.

Lust for Evil SEE: **Purple Noon**

Lust for Gold (1949) 90m. **½ D: S. Sylvan Simon. Ida Lupino, Glenn Ford, Gig Young, Jay Silverheels, Eddy Waller. Lupino gets overly dramatic as grasping woman stopping at nothing to obtain riches of gold-laden mine.

Lust for Life (1956) C-122m. **** D: Vincente Minnelli. Kirk Douglas, Anthony Quinn, James Donald, Pamela Brown, Everett Sloane. Brilliant adaptation of Irving Stone's biography of painter Van Gogh, vividly portraying his anguished life. Quinn won well-deserved Oscar for performance as painter-friend Gaugin, in this exquisite color production.

Lusty Men, The (1952) 113m. *** D: Nicholas Ray. Susan Hayward, Robert Mitchum, Arthur Kennedy, Arthur Hunnicutt. Atmospheric rodeo tale, solidly acted by all.

Luther (1974-British) C-112m. **½ D: Guy Green. Stacy Keach, Patrick Magee, Hugh Griffith, Robert Stephens, Alan Badel. Sincere but placid American Film Theatre recreation of John Osborne's play about Martin Luther (Keach), founder of a new religion.

Luv (1967) C-95m. *½ D: Clive Donner. Jack Lemmon, Peter Falk, Elaine May, Eddie Mayehoff, Paul Hartman, Severn Darden. Murray Schisgal's three-character hit play about pseudo-intellectuals was not a natural for the screen anyway, but this version is truly an abomination. The cast tries.

Luxury Liner (1948) C-98m. ** D: Richard Whorf. George Brent, Jane Powell, Lauritz Melchior, Frances Gifford, Xavier Cugat. MGM fluff aboard a cruise ship, with Powell singing her heart out.

Lydia (1941) 104m. *** D: Julien Duvivier. Merle Oberon, Edna May Oliver, Alan Marshal, Joseph Cotten, Hans Yaray, George Reeves. Sentimental tale of elderly woman (Oberon) meeting her former beaus and recalling their courtship. Adapted from famous French film CARNET DU BAL.

Lydia Bailey (1952) C-89m. **½ D: Jean Negulesco. Dale Robertson, Anne Francis, Luis Van Rooten, Juanita Moore, William Marshall. Handsome but empty version of Kenneth Roberts actioner of 1800s Haiti and revolt against French rulers.

M (1931-German) 99m. **** D: Fritz Lang. Peter Lorre, Ellen Widmann, Inge Landgut, Gustav Grundgens. Harrowing melodrama about psychotic child-murderer brought to justice by Berlin underworld. One of the all-time greats, with Lorre's performance a masterpiece.

M (1951) 88m. **½ D: Joseph

Losey. David Wayne, Howard da Silva, Luther Adler, Karen Morley, Jorja Curtright, Martin Gabel. Tepid remake of famed Peter Lorre German classic, concerning child-killer hunted down by fellow-criminals not wanting police investigation of underworld.

Ma and Pa Kettle Betty MacDonald's best-selling book THE EGG AND I told of the hardships a city girl faced moving with her husband to a rural chicken farm. Among the problems were the incredible local characters, two of whom, Ma and Pa Kettle, were given prime footage in the screen version of THE EGG AND I. Played by veterans Marjorie Main and Percy Kilbride, the hillbilly duo created a hit and became the stars of their own series, which was extremely popular through the 1950s. Rambunctious Ma and hesitant Pa's adventures were not exactly out of Noel Coward, but they scored a hit and the two stars were naturals for the roles. In fact, the role of Ma was not so different from the stereotyped character Marjorie Main had become associated with in scores of other films. Meg Randall and Lori Nelson took turns playing the eldest daughter in the Kettle's tremendous brood (at least a dozen kids), as the Kettles battled with neighbors and local authorities, visiting Paris, Hawaii, and New York, and engaged in predictable but amusing situations for eight years. In 1955 Percy Kilbride left the series; Arthur Hunnicutt played a "cousin" in THE KETTLES IN THE OZARKS and Parker Fennelly took his turn in THE KETTLES ON OLD MACDONALD'S FARM, but neither one caught on and the series came to an end in 1957. Intellectuals liked to assume that the cornball humor had lost its audience, but then several years later a TV show called THE BEVERLY HILLBILLIES came along to prove them wrong.

Ma and Pa Kettle (1949) **75m.** D: Charles Lamont. Marjorie Main, Percy Kilbride, Richard Long, Meg Randall, Patricia Alphin, Esther Dale.

Ma and Pa Kettle at Home (1954) **81m.** D: Charles Lamont. Marjorie Main, Percy Kilbride, Alice Kelley, Brett Halsey, Alan Mowbray, Oliver Blake, Stan Ross.

Ma and Pa Kettle at the Fair (1952) **78m.** D: Charles Barton. Marjorie Main, Percy Kilbride, Lori Nelson, James Best, Esther Dale.

Ma and Pa Kettle at Waikiki (1955) **79m.** D: Lee Sholem. Marjorie Main, Percy Kilbride, Lori Nelson, Lowell Gilmore, Mabel Albertson, Ida Moore.

Ma and Pa Kettle Back on the Farm (1951) **80m.** D: Edward Sedgwick. Marjorie Main, Percy Kilbride, Richard Long, Barbara Brown, Meg Randall.

Ma and Pa Kettle Go to Town (1950) **79m.** D: Charles Lamont. Percy Kilbride, Marjorie Main, Richard Long, Jim Backus, Hal March, Meg Randall.

Ma and Pa Kettle on Vacation (1953) **75m.** D: Charles Lamont. Percy Kilbride, Marjorie Main, Ray Collins, Sig Ruman, Jack Kruschen, Teddy Hart.

Ma Barker's Killer Brood (1960) **82m. **** D: Bill Karn. Lurene Tuttle, Tris Coffin, Paul Dubov, Nelson Leigh. Energetic performance by Tuttle in lead role and occasional bursts of gunplay hoist this programmer gangster yarn above tedium.

Macabre (1958) **73m. **** D: William Castle. William Prince, Jim Backus, Christine White, Jacqueline Scott. Weird goings-on in small town when doctor's wife and her sister are murdered. Film promises much, delivers little.

Macahans, The (1976) **C-125m. TVM** D: Bernard McEveety. James Arness, Eva Marie Saint, Bruce Boxleitner, Richard Kiley, Gene Evans, John Crawford. Arness' first post-"Gunsmoke" role as a buckskin-clad mountain scout guiding his brother's family on its westward trek from pre-Civil War Virginia. William Conrad narrates this lusty outdoor drama based in part on "How the West was Won"; later it became a mini-series using that title. Above average.

Macao (1952) **80m. **** D: Josef von Sternberg. Robert Mitchum, Jane Russell, William Bendix, Gloria Grahame, Thomas Gomez, Philip Ahn. Flat yarn supposedly set in murky title port, with Russell a singer and Mitchum the action-seeking man she loves.

MacArthur (1977) **C-144m. ***** D: Joseph Sargent. Gregory Peck, Dan

O'Herlihy, Ed Flanders, Sandy Kenyon, Dick O'Neill, Marj Dusay, Art Fleming. Solid, absorbing saga of flamboyant military chief during WW2 and Korean War. Peck is excellent but film doesn't pack the punch of PATTON.

Macbeth (1948) 89m. *** D: Orson Welles. Orson Welles, Jeanette Nolan, Dan O'Herlihy, Edgar Barrier, Roddy McDowall, Robert Coote. Strange Welles version of Shakespeare, made quickly on old Western sets; worth seeing once, for sure. Original 105m. version has recently been discovered, but not yet released to TV.

Macbeth (1971-British) C-140m. ***½ D: Roman Polanski. Jon Finch, Francesca Annis, Martin Shaw, Nicholas Selby, John Stride, Stephan Chase. Gripping, atmospheric recreation of Shakespeare tragedy of young Scots nobleman lusting for power, driven onward by crazed wife and prophecies. Great example of film storytelling, thanks to excellent direction. Extreme violence may be cut for TV.

McCabe and Mrs. Miller (1971) C-121m. ***½ D: Robert Altman. Warren Beatty, Julie Christie, Rene Auberjonois, Hugh Millais, Shelley Duvall, Michael Murphy, John Schuck, Keith Carradine. Richly textured mood piece about an ambitious small-timer who opens a bordello in turn-of-the-century boom town. Altman deglamorizes Hollywood image of the period with his realistic visions, and Beatty is first-rate as the two-bit braggart McCabe.

McCloud: Who Killed Miss U.S.A.? (1969) C-100m. TVM D: Richard Colla. Dennis Weaver, Craig Stevens, Diana Muldaur, Mark Richman, Terry Carter, Raul Julia, Shelly Novack, Julie Newmar. U.S. deputy marshal assigned to transport valuable witness from New Mexico to N.Y.C. must prove worth to Eastern superiors when he loses witness soon after he disembarks from plane. Good location work in pilot for long-running series, inspired by movie COOGAN'S BLUFF. Above average. Retitled PORTRAIT OF A DEAD GIRL.

McConnell Story, The (1955) C-107m. *** D: Gordon Douglas. Alan Ladd, June Allyson, James Whitmore, Frank Faylen. Weepy yet effective fictional biography of jet test

pilot, with Allyson as his understanding wife.

McGuire, Go Home! (1966-British) C-101m. **½ D: Ralph Thomas. Dirk Bogarde, George Chakiris, Susan Strasberg, Denholm Elliott. Set in 1954 Cyprus; peppy account of terrorist campaign against British occupation, with side-plot of officer Bogarde in love with American girl Strasberg.

McHale's Navy (1964) C-93m. ** D: Edward J. Montagne. Ernest Borgnine, Joe Flynn, Tim Conway, Claudine Longet, Jean Willes, George Kennedy. Usual shenanigans from PT 73 in the Pacific during WW2, expanded from TV series, of same title. Show was half hour, so feature comes off weak.

McHale's Navy Joins the Air Force (1965) C-90m. ** D: Edward J. Montagne. Joe Flynn, Tim Conway, Bob Hastings, Gary Vinson, Billy Sands, Jean Hale, Susan Silo, Edson Stroll, John Wright, Cliff Norton. Generally uninspired comedy with familiar crew from TV series, unimpressive due to television look.

Machine Gun Kelly (1958) 80m. **½ D: Roger Corman. Charles Bronson, Susan Cabot, Barboura Morris, Morey Amsterdam, Wally Campo, Jack Lambert, Connie Gilchrist. With typical efficiency, Corman gives this gangster chronicle pacing and more than passing interest. Bronson is fine in title role.

Machine Gun McCain (1970-Italian) C-94m. ** D: Giuliano Montaldo. John Cassavetes, Britt Ekland, Peter Falk, Gabriele Ferzetti, Salvo Randone, Gena Rowlands. Junk about just-released gangster who tries to rob Mafia-controlled casino in Las Vegas.

Macho Callahan (1970) C-99m. **½ D: Bernard Kowalski. David Janssen, Lee J. Cobb, Jean Seberg, David Carradine, Pedro Armendariz, Jr., James Booth, Richard Anderson. Janssen miscast as Civil War P.O.W.-escapee, out to kill man who got him arrested in first place; will recognize latter by his yellow shoes. Interesting view of West, but dialogue often unbelievable.

Maciste—The Mighty (1960-Italian) C-87m. ** D: Carlo Campogalliani. Mark Forrest, Chelo Alonso, Angelo Zanolli, Federica Ranchi. Forrest in title role tries to instill some animation in wooden tale of old Egypt and the barbaric Persians.

Mack, The (1973) **C-110m.** ** D: Michael Campus. Max Julien, Don Gordon, Richard Pryor, Carol Speed, Roger E. Mosley, William C. Watson. Extremely violent melodrama about a black pimp in Oakland will have some footage cut for TV; otherwise, film is standard fare.

McKenna's Gold (1969) **C-128m.** **½ D: J. Lee Thompson. Gregory Peck, Omar Sharif, Telly Savalas, Camilla Sparv, Keenan Wynn, Julie Newmar, Lee J. Cobb, Raymond Massey, Burgess Meredith, Anthony Quayle, Edward G. Robinson, Eli Wallach, Ted Cassidy, Eduardo Ciannelli. Overblown adventure saga about search for lost canyon of gold, with doublecrosses, conflicts, mysterious clues, etc. Fine cast saddled with ludicrous script, made worse by pre-release tampering that cut extremely long film, leaving abrupt denouement, several loose ends.

McKenzie Break, The (1970) **C-106m.** *** D: Lamont Johnson. Brian Keith, Helmut Griem, Ian Hendry, Jack Watson, Patrick O'Connell. Daring escape from a P.O.W. camp for Germans in Scotland makes for engrossing movie fare.

Mackintosh and T.J. (1975) **C-96m.** ** D: Marvin J. Chomsky. Roy Rogers, Clay O'Brien, Billy Green Bush, Andrew Robinson, Joan Hackett. Old-fashioned modern-day Western about an aging ranch hand and a young boy. Those charmed by the idea of a Roy Rogers comeback will want to see it; others beware. Music by Waylon Jennings.

Mackintosh Man, The (1973) **C-105m.** **½ D: John Huston. Paul Newman, Dominique Sanda, James Mason, Harry Andrews, Ian Bannen, Nigel Patrick, Michael Hordern. Well-made espionage thriller has only one problem: it's all been done before. Filmed in Ireland, England, and Malta.

McLintock! (1963) **C-127m.** *** D: Andrew V. McLaglen. John Wayne, Maureen O'Hara, Patrick Wayne, Stefanie Powers, Yvonne De Carlo, Chill Wills, Bruce Cabot, Jack Kruschen, Jerry Van Dyke. Rowdy, lively Western-comedy with Wayne encountering his refined wife O'Hara, who wants a divorce, and his grown-up daughter Powers, caught between father and mother. Plenty of slapstick to keep things moving; entertaining.

McMasters, The (1970) **C-89/97m.** **½ D: Alf Kjellin. Burl Ives, Brock Peters, David Carradine, Nancy Kwan, Jack Palance, John Carradine. Pretty grim drama of bigotry and violence gone crazy as black Union soldier (Peters) returns to ranch of former master (Ives), eventually made co-owner of land. Dual running times indicates two different endings: bad guys (led by Palance) win out or good guys emerge victorious. Both versions were released to theaters.

McNaughton's Daughter (1976) **C-100m. TVM** D: Jerry London. Susan Clark, Ricardo Montalban, James Callahan, John Elerick, Vera Miles, Ralph Bellamy, Mike Farrell. Deputy D.A. (Clark) prosecutes saint-like missionary Miles on homicide charges. Projected for a TV series but busted. Average.

Macomber Affair, The (1947) **89m.** ***½ D: Zoltan Korda. Gregory Peck, Joan Bennett, Robert Preston, Reginald Denny, Carl Harbord. Penetrating, intelligent filmization of Hemingway story about conflicts that develop when hunter Peck takes married couple (Preston, Bennett) on safari. Bristling performances help make this one of the most vivid screen adaptations of a Hemingway work.

Macon County Line (1974) **C-89m.** **½ D: Richard Compton. Alan Vint, Cheryl Waters, Max Baer Jr., Jesse Vint, Joan Blackman, Geoffrey Lewis. Bloody thriller based on fact, set in 1954 Georgia; three outsiders are pursued for a murder they didn't commit. Baer produced and wrote it. Bobbie Gentry sings her own theme song.

McQ (1974) **C-116m.** ** D: John Sturges. John Wayne, Eddie Albert, Diana Muldaur, Colleen Dewhurst, Clu Gulager, David Huddleston, Al Lettieri, Julie Adams. One of Duke's all-time worst has the aging star trying to be Clint Eastwood in a violent, modern-day cops-and-robbers story.

Macumba Love (1960) **C-86m.** *½ D: Douglas Fowley. Walter Reed, Ziva Rodann, William Wellman, Jr., June Wilkinson. Trivia of author delving into voodoo practices in South America.

Mad About Men (1954-British) **C-90m.** ** D: Ralph Thomas. Glynis

Johns, Donald Sinden, Anne Crawford, Margaret Rutherford, Dora Bryan, Noel Purcell. Mermaid and young woman look-alike change places in this pleasant fantasy, and love takes its course. Sequel to MIRANDA.

Mad About Music (1938) 98m. *** D: Norman Taurog. Deanna Durbin, Herbert Marshall, Gail Patrick, Arthur Treacher, Helen Parrish, Marcia Mae Jones, William Frawley. Excellent Durbin vehicle; busy mother Patrick leaves Deanna in Swiss girls' school, where she pretends Marshall is her father. Holds up better than remake TOY TIGER.

Mad Adventures of Rabbi Jacob, The (1974-French) C-96m. *** D: Gerard Oury. Louis De Funes, Suzy Delair, Marcel Dalio, Claude Giraud, Claude Pieplu. Broad slapstick comedy about hotheaded businessman who—for complicated reasons—is forced to disguise himself as a rabbi. Uneven but often quite funny, with echoes of silent-screen humor.

Mad at the World (1955) 72m. *½ D: Harry Essex. Frank Lovejoy, Keefe Brasselle, Cathy O'Donnell, Karen Sharpe. Pointless study of Brasselle seeking vengeance on teenage slum gang who harmed his baby; Lovejoy the detective in the case.

Mad Bomber, The (1972) C-95m. ** D: Bert I. Gordon. Vince Edwards, Chuck Connors, Neville Brand, Hank Brandt, Cristina Hart. Hard-nosed cop Edwards relentlessly dogs paranoid villain Connors who's out to waste those he imagines have wronged him.

Mad Bull (1977) C-100m. TVM D: Walter Doniger and Len Steckler. Alex Karras, Susan Anspach, Nicholas Colosanto, Elisha Cook, Jr., Mike Mazurki, Christopher DeRose. Hulking wrestler becomes involved with warm, sensitive woman. Off-the-beaten path drama involving ex-football pro Karras in the bizarre world of wrestling. Average.

Mad Doctor, The (1941) 90m. ** D: Tim Whelan. Basil Rathbone, Ellen Drew, John Howard, Barbara Jo Allen (Vera Vague), Ralph Morgan. Standard B film has Rathbone as doctor who marries pretty women and then does away with them.

Mad Doctor of Market Street, The (1942) 61m. *½ D: Joseph H. Lewis. Una Merkel, Claire Dodd, Lionel At-

will. Mini-chiller from Universal Pictures about insane scientist on Pacific Isle using natives for strange experiments.

Mad Dog Coll (1961) 86m. *½ D: Burt Balaban. John Davis Chandler, Brooke Hayward, Kay Doubleday, Jerry Orbach, Telly Savalas. Minor account of gangster who rises to top of heap and gets just desserts.

Mad Dog Morgan (1976-Australian) C-102m. *** D: Philippe Mora. Dennis Hopper, Jack Thompson, David Gulpilil, Frank Thring, Michael Pate. Hopper gives lively performance as legendary Australian outlaw of the 1800s in this moody, well-made film; TV print runs 93m.

Mad Executioners, The (1963-German) 94m. ** D: Edwin Zbonek. Wolfgang Preiss, Harry Riebauer, Rudolph Fernau, Chris Howland. Muddled Edgar Wallace-ish suspenser about Scotland Yard inspector setting up his own court of justice to execute criminals.

Mad Genius, The (1931) 81m. *** D: Michael Curtiz. John Barrymore, Marian Marsh, Donald Cook, Carmel Myers, Charles Butterworth, Mae Madison, Frankie Darro, Luis Alberni, Boris Karloff. Followup to SVENGALI has Barrymore a deranged entrepreneur who lives vicariously through Cook's dancing career. Bizarre, entertaining film with hilarious Butterworth as Barrymore's crony, Alberni as a dope-fiend. Karloff has small role near the beginning.

Mad Ghoul, The (1943) 65m. **½ D: James Hogan. David Bruce, Evelyn Ankers, George Zucco, Turhan Bey, Charles McGraw, Robert Armstrong, Milburn Stone, Rose Hobart. Strong cast buoys grim story of scientist and his strange life-preserving methods.

Mad Little Island (1957-British) C-94m. ** D: Michael Relph. Jeannie Carson, Donald Sinden, Roland Culver, Catherine Lacey. Tame goings-on as island dwellers join together to prevent their land becoming missile base.

Mad Love (1935) 83m. *** D: Karl Freund. Peter Lorre, Frances Drake, Colin Clive, Isabel Jewell, Ted Healy, Sara Haden, Edward Brophy, Keye Luke. Famous Hands-of-Orlac story refitted for Lorre as mad doctor in love with married Drake. He agrees to operate on her husband's hands with disastrous results. Lavishly done, good chiller.

Mad Magician, The (1954) 72m. **½
D: John Brahm. Vincent Price, Mary Murphy, Eva Gabor, Patrick O'Neal, John Emery. Far-fetched hokum of demented magico whose gimmicks eventually backfire and destroy him. Shot in 3-D; most effects retain excitement on small screen.

Mad Miss Manton, The (1938) 80m. **½ D: Leigh Jason. Barbara Stanwyck, Henry Fonda, Sam Levene, Frances Mercer, Stanley Ridges, Vicki Lester, Whitney Bourne, Hattie McDaniel, Penny Singleton, Grady Sutton. Socialite Stanwyck involves her friends in murder mystery; trivial but very enjoyable film, with sleuthing and slapstick combined.

Mad Monster, The (1942) 72m. *½ D: Sam Newfield. Johnny Downs, George Zucco, Anne Nagel, Sarah Padden, Glenn Strange, Gordon DeMain. Dull, low-budget mad-scientist thriller drags heavy feet for unintended laughs. Zucco effortlessly steals show as crazed doctor changing man into beast.

Mad Monster Party (1967) C-94m. ** D: Jules Báss. Voices of Phyllis Diller, Boris Karloff, Gale Garnett, Ethel Ennis. Famous monsters, animated, all brought together for reunion. Dracula and Frankenstein are two of the party-givers in this silly Saturday kiddie feature.

Mad Room, The (1969) C-92m. ** D: Bernard Girard. Stella Stevens, Shelley Winters, James Ward, Carol Cole, Severn Darden, Beverly Garland, Michael Burns. Mild but unexceptional remake of LADIES IN RETIREMENT concerns the skeletons in Stella's closet. Grisly tale has a few shocking scenes.

Mad Wednesday SEE: **Sin of Harold Diddlebock, The**

Madam Satan (1930) 105m. *** D: Cecil B. DeMille. Kay Johnson, Reginald Denny, Roland Young, Lillian Roth, Elsa Peterson, Tyler Brooke. Bizarre semimusical extravaganza with placid Johnson posing as wicked Madam Satan to win back errant husband Denny. Mad party scene on Zeppelin is certainly an eye-popper.

Madame (1962-French) C-104m. **½ D: Christian-Jaque. Sophia Loren, Robert Hossein, Julien Bertheau, Marina Berti. Uninspired remake of MADAME SANS-GENE with Lo-

ren, who uses looks and wits to rise from laundress to nobility in Napoleonic France.

Madame Bovary (1949) 115m. **½ D: Vincente Minnelli. Jennifer Jones, James Mason, Van Heflin, Louis Jourdan, Gene Lockhart, Gladys Cooper, George Zucco. Static rendition of Gustave Flaubert's 19th-century novel of sensual French woman who sacrifices everyone for her love whims. Jones is too sedate in lead role.

Madame Butterfly (1932) 86m. **½ D: Marion Gering. Sylvia Sidney, Cary Grant, Charlie Ruggles, Irving Pichel, Helen Jerome Eddy. Puccini opera (minus music) of Oriental woman in love with American (Grant) is sensitive, tragic romance, dated but well handled.

Madame Curie (1943) 124m. *** D: Mervyn LeRoy. Greer Garson, Walter Pidgeon, Henry Travers, Albert Basserman, Robert Walker, C. Aubrey Smith. Despite stretches of plodding footage, biography of famed female scientist is generally excellent. Garson and Pidgeon team well, as usual.

Madame Rosa (1977-French) C-105m. **½ D: Moshe Mizrahi. Simone Signoret, Samy Ben Youb, Claude Dauphin, Gabriel Jabbour, Michal Bat Adam, Costa Gavras. Signoret's magnetic performance gives substance to this interesting but aimless film about an aging madam who earns her keep by sheltering prostitutes' children. Oscar winner as Best Foreign Film.

Madame Sin (1971) C-73m. TVM D: David Greene. Robert Wagner, Bette Davis, Roy Kinnear, Paul Maxwell, Denholm Elliott. Evil genius (Davis) uses former C.I.A. agent as pawn for control of Polaris submarine. Elaborate production has Bad beating out Good at end; with Bette in charge, well worth seeing. Above average.

Madame X (1966) C-100m. **½ D: David Lowell Rich. Lana Turner, John Forsythe, Constance Bennett, Ricardo Montalban, Burgess Meredith, Keir Dullea, Virginia Grey. Plush remake of perennial soaper of attorney defending a woman accused of murder, not knowing it's his mother. Fine cast and varied backgrounds bolster Turner's pivotal performance. Constance Bennett's last film.

Made For Each Other (1939) 85m. *** D: John Cromwell. Carole Lombard, James Stewart, Charles Coburn, Lucile Watson, Alma Kruger, Esther Dale, Ward Bond, Louise Beavers. First-rate soaper of struggling young marrieds Stewart and Lombard, battling meddling in-laws, poverty, illness, etc. Fine acting makes this all work.

Made For Each Other (1971) C-107m. *** D: Robert B. Bean. Renee Taylor, Joseph Bologna, Paul Sorvino, Olympia Dukakis. Exceptionally funny tale of two oddball types who meet at encounter session and fall in love. Original screenplay by Taylor and Bologna.

Made in Italy (1967-Italian-French) 101m. **½ D: Nanni Loy. Virna Lisi, Anna Magnani, Sylva Koscina, Walter Chiari, Lea Massari, Alberto Sordi, Jean Sorel, Catherine Spaak. Enjoyable collage of short vignettes about natives, tourists, sophisticates, laborers and all others in Italy. Episodic, of course, but well done.

Made in Paris (1966) C-101m. **½ D: Boris Sagal. Ann-Margret, Louis Jourdan, Richard Crenna, Edie Adams, Chad Everett. Witless, unpolished shenanigans of Ann-Margret, fashion designer in France, falling for Jourdan.

Madeleine (1949-British) 101m. **½ D: David Lean. Ann Todd, Leslie Banks, Elizabeth Sellars, Ivor Barnard. Superior cast improves oft-told drama of woman accused of murdering her lover. Retitled: STRANGE CASE OF MADELEINE.

Madeleine (1958-German) 86m. *½ D: Kurt Meisel. Eva Bartok, Sabina Sesselmann, Ilse Steppat, Alexander Kerst. Unsensational study of prostitutes, with a witless plot of Bartok trying to shed her shady past.

Mademoiselle Fifi (1944) 69m. **½ D: Robert Wise. Simone Simon, John Emery, Kurt Kreuger, Alan Napier, Jason Robards Sr., Helen Freeman, Norma Varden. A laundress reveals more integrity and patriotic spirit than her condescending fellow passengers on an eventful coach ride during the Franco-Prussian war. Uneven Val Lewton production (with allegorical implications about WW2), adapted from two Guy de Maupassant stories.

Mademoiselle Striptease SEE: Please! Mr. Balzac

Madhouse (1974-British) C-89m. ***
D: Jim Clark. Vincent Price, Peter Cushing, Robert Quarry, Adrienne Corri, Natasha Payne, Linda Hayden. Diverting little horror item with Price a demented actor taking delicious revenge on those responsible for grisly death of his fiancée. Good if somewhat unimaginative adaptation of Angus Hall's novel *Devilday*.

Madigan (1968) C-101m. ***½ D: Donald Siegel. Richard Widmark, Henry Fonda, Harry Guardino, Inger Stevens, James Whitmore, Michael Dunn, Steve Inhat, Sheree North. Excellent, unpretentious film blends day-to-day problems of detective Madigan (Widmark) with endless dilemmas facing police commissioner Fonda. Shot largely on location in N.Y.C., with fine work by Guardino, Whitmore, and supporting cast. Later adapted as TV series.

Madigan's Millions (1970) C-94m. BOMB D: Stanley Prager. Dustin Hoffman, Elsa Martinelli, Cesar Romero. Pre-GRADUATE Hoffman is caught in amateurish movie released to capitalize on later success; he plays bumbling treasury agent sent to Italy to recover money stolen by recently murdered gangster Romero. Inept.

Madison Avenue (1962) 94m. **½ D: H. Bruce Humberstone. Dana Andrews, Eleanor Parker, Jeanne Crain, Eddie Albert, Howard St. John, Henry Daniell, Kathleen Freeman. Tightly produced programmer centering on machinations in N.Y.C.'s advertising jungle.

Madmen of Mandoras (1964) 74m. ** D: David Bradley. Carlos Rivas, Marshall Reed, Nestor Paiva, Scott Peters. Weird minor chiller of bloblike monster seeking to destroy the world.

Madonna of the Seven Moons (1946-British) 88m. *** D: Arthur Crabtree. Phyllis Calvert, Stewart Granger, Patricia Roc, Jean Kent, John Stuart, Peter Glenville. Calvert is pushed in two directions because of strange gypsy curse; she is wife, mother, and mistress at same time. Taut melodrama, may be considered "camp" in some circles.

Madonna's Secret, The (1946) 79m. ** D: William Thiele. Francis Lederer, Gail Patrick, Ann Rutherford, Linda Stirling, John Litel, Pierre Watkin. OK whodunit involving hunt for killer of murdered artist's model.

Madron (1970) C-93m. ** D: Jerry

[469]

Hopper, Richard Boone, Leslie Caron, Paul Smith, Gabi Amrani, Chaim Banai, Avraham Telya. A nun who survived wagon-train massacre and a scowling gunslinger try to elude Apaches on the warpath in this ho-hum Western shot in Israel's Negev desert.

Madwoman of Chaillot, The (1969) C-132m. ** D: Bryan Forbes. Katharine Hepburn, Charles Boyer, Claude Dauphin, Edith Evans, John Gavin, Paul Henreid, Oscar Homolka, Margaret Leighton, Giulietta Masina, Nanette Newman, Richard Chamberlain, Yul Brynner, Donald Pleasence, Danny Kaye. Unfortunate misfire, with Hepburn as eccentric woman who refuses to believe the world no longer beautiful. Stellar cast wasted in heavy-handed allegory that just doesn't work; adapted from Jean Giradoux' play.

Maedchen in Uniform (1965-German) C-91m. **½ D: Geza Radvanyi. Lilli Palmer, Romy Schneider, Christine Kaufmann, Therese Giehse. Rather talky story of girls' school and one particularly sensitive youngster (Schneider) who is attracted to her teacher (Palmer). Remake of famous early German sound movie is shade above average.

Magee and the Lady (1978-Australian) C-92m. TVM D: Gene Levitt. Tony Lo Bianco, Sally Kellerman, Anne Semler, Rod Mulligan, Kevin Leslie. Elements of THE AFRICAN QUEEN and SWEPT AWAY combine in story of skipper's attempt to stall repossession of his freighter by kidnapping the feisty daughter of the man who's threatening to foreclose on him. Average. Originally titled SHE'LL BE SWEET.

Magic (1978) C-106m. ** D: Richard Attenborough. Anthony Hopkins, Ann-Margret, Burgess Meredith, Ed Lauter, Jerry Houser, David Ogden Stiers. Ludicrous thriller about demented ventriloquist Hopkins who's tormented by his dummy—even as he tries to rekindle romance with high-school sweetie Ann-Margret. Wait for a rerun of DEAD OF NIGHT instead.

Maggie, The SEE: High and Dry

Magic Bow, The (1947-British) 105m. **½ D: Bernard Knowles. Stewart Granger, Phyllis Calvert, Jean Kent, Dennis Price, Cecil Parker. As usual, music overshadows weak plot in biography of violinist Paganini.

Magic Box, The (1951-British) C-

103m. **** D: John Boulting. Robert Donat, Maria Schell, Margaret Johnston, Robert Beatty; guests Laurence Olivier, Michael Redgrave, Eric Portman, Glynis Johns, Emlyn Williams, Richard Attenborough, Stanley Holloway, Margaret Rutherford, Peter Ustinov, Bessie Love, Cecil Parker, etc. Practically every British star appears in this superb biography of William Friese-Greene, the forgotten inventor of movies. Beautifully done; one scene where Donat perfects the invention, pulling in a cop off the street (Olivier) to see it, is superb.

Magic Carpet, The (1951) C-84m. ** D: Lew Landers. Lucille Ball, John Agar, Patricia Medina, Raymond Burr, George Tobias. Mild costumer that has virtue of Ball as heroine, and little else.

Magic Carpet (1971) C-100m. TVM D: William Graham. Susan St. James, Robert Pratt, Cliff Potts, Enzo Cerusico, Jim Backus, Wally Cox, Abby Dalton. Easygoing comedy with mystery overtones has fill-in tour guide (St. James) earning her way through college in Rome, experiencing various problems in connection with odd assortment of bus passengers. Enjoyable, unpretentious dialogue, clever situations. Above average.

Magic Christian, The (1970-British) C-93m. *** D: Joseph McGrath. Peter Sellers, Ringo Starr, Richard Attenborough, Christopher Lee, Raquel Welch. Terry Southern's insane black comedy: world's wealthiest man and his protege wreak havoc on society by demonstrating how vulnerable man really is in series of wacky schemes. Beware cuts for TV.

Magic Face, The (1951) 89m. ** D: Frank Tuttle. Luther Adler, Patricia Knight, William L. Shirer, Ilka Windish. Low-key study of impersonator who murders Hitler and assumes his place; Adler rises above material.

Magic Fire (1956) C-95m. ** D: William Dieterle. Yvonne De Carlo, Carlos Thompson, Rita Gam, Valentina Cortese, Alan Badel. Low-budget musical biography of 19th-century German composer Richard Wagner.

Magic Garden of Stanley Sweetheart, The (1970) C-117m. *½ D: Leonard Horn. Don Johnson, Linda Gillin, Michael Greer, Dianne Hull, Holly

Near, Victoria Racimo. Vapid film from Robert Westerbrook's novel about sexual and drug-oriented experiences of aimless college student trying to put his head together. A yawn, except for Greer, and Stanley's underground film "Headless." Sure to be cut if accepted at all by TV.

Magic of Lassie, The (1978) C-100m. **½ D: Don Chaffey. James Stewart, Lassie, Mickey Rooney, Alice Faye, Stephanie Zimbalist, Pernell Roberts, Michael Sharrett, Mike Mazurki. Stewart is worth watching in this bland family film, as grandfather of Zimbalist and Sharrett, who are forced to turn over their beloved Lassie to mean owner Roberts. Songs performed by Pat and Debby Boone, plus Faye and even Stewart.

Magic Sword, The (1962) C-80m. **½ D: Bert I. Gordon. Basil Rathbone, Estelle Winwood, Gary Lockwood, Anne Helm, Liam Sullivan, Jacques Gallo. Fanciful juvenile costumer with fine special effects, pleasing cast.

Magic Town (1947) 103m. *** D: William Wellman. James Stewart, Jane Wyman, Kent Smith, Regis Toomey, Donald Meek. Intriguing satire of pollster Stewart finding perfect average American town, which ruins itself when people are told his discovery. Doesn't always hit bull's-eye, but remains engrossing throughout; written by Frank Capra's frequent scripter, Robert Riskin.

Magic World of Topo Gigio, The (1965-Italian) C-75m. *½ D: Luca de Rico. Ermanno Roveri, Ignazio Colnaghi, Frederica Milani, Topo Gigio. Cash-in on the popular puppet act from Ed Sullivan show. Poorly done animation, but children might enjoy it.

Magician, The (1959-Swedish) 102m. *** D: Ingmar Bergman. Max von Sydow, Ingrid Thulin, Gunnar Bjornstrand, Naima Wifstrand, Bibi Andersson. Brooding, complex account set in 19th-century Sweden involving mesmerizer and magician who becomes involved in murder and afterlife; revealing parable of life's realities.

Magician of Lublin, The (1979) C-105. *½ D: Menachem Golan. Alan Arkin, Louise Fletcher, Valerie Perrine, Shelley Winters, Lou Jacobi, Maia Danziger. Turn-of-the-century Jewish magician tries for the big time in stilted, poorly acted version of Issac Bashevis Singer's Polish-based novel. However, you do get to see Winters destroy a jailhouse even more impressively than Sam Jaffe's elephant did in GUNGA DIN.

Magnet, The (1951-British) 78m. *** D: Charles Frend. William Fox, Kay Walsh, Stephen Murray, Meredith Edwards. Disarming study of fun-loving children at play, told intelligently from their own point of view; no phony psychology thrown in. Young William Fox is known today as James Fox.

Magnetic Monster, The (1953) 76m. **½ D: Curt Siodmak. Richard Carlson, King Donovan, Jean Byron, Byron Foulger. Magnetic isotope is stolen, grows in size and creates havoc; stunning climax features special effects lifted from 1930s German film, GOLD.

Magnificent Ambersons, The (1942) 88m. **** D: Orson Welles. Joseph Cotten, Dolores Costello, Anne Baxter, Tim Holt, Agnes Moorehead, Ray Collins. Brilliant drama from Booth Tarkington novel of family unwilling to change its way of life with the times; mother and son conflict over her lover. Welles' follow-up to CITIZEN KANE is equally exciting in its own way.

Magnificent Brute, The (1936) 80m. ** D: John G. Blystone. Victor McLaglen, Binnie Barnes, William Hall, Jean Dixon. Pertly acted love triangle, with McLaglen the roughneck blast furnace boss, involved in romance and stolen money.

Magnificent Cuckold, The (1966-Italian) 111m. **½ D: Antonio Pietrangeli. Claudia Cardinale, Ugo Tognazzi, Michele Girardon, Bernard Blier. Saucy sex comedy of marital infidelity, with Tognazzi, the businessman husband of Cardinale, outwitted by his curvaceous wife.

Magnificent Doll (1946) 95m. ** D: Frank Borzage. Ginger Rogers, Burgess Meredith, David Niven, Horace (Stephen) McNally, Peggy Wood. Rogers just isn't right as Dolly Madison, and historical drama with Meredith as President Madison and Niven as Aaron Burr falls flat.

Magnificent Dope, The (1942) 83m. *** D: Walter Lang. Henry Fonda, Lynn Bari, Don Ameche, Edward Everett Horton, Hobart Cavanaugh, Pierre Watkin. Entertaining comedy of hopeless hayseed Fonda who shows up sharper Ameche in big city; Bari is the girl between them.

Magnificent Fraud, The (1939) 78m. ** D: Robert Florey. Akim Tamiroff, Lloyd Nolan, Mary Boland, Patricia Morison. Spry Paramount "B" film involving South American republic and its phony dictator.

Magnificent Magnet of Santa Mesa, The (1977) C-78m. TVM D: Hy Averback. Michael Burns, Dick Blasucci, Jane Connell, Keene Curtis, Susan Blanchard, Harry Morgan, Tom Poston, Susan M. Sullivan, Conrad Janis. Disney-esque farce with young scientist (Burns) inventing an energy disk that can solve the world's problems, then trying to protect it from his altruistic bosses. The performances: stereotyped and frantic; the special effects: rock bottom. Below average.

Magnificent Matador, The (1955) C-94m. **½ D: Budd Boetticher. Anthony Quinn, Maureen O'Hara, Manuel Rojas, Thomas Gomez, Richard Denning, Lola Albright. Another of director Boetticher's bullfighting films has Quinn an aging matador who reexamines his commitment to bullfighting, while protecting his young "protege" (Rojas) and being romanced by American O'Hara.

Magnificent Obsession (1935) 90m. *** D: John M. Stahl. Irene Dunne, Robert Taylor, Betty Furness, Charles Butterworth, Sara Haden, Ralph Morgan. Dated but sincere adaptation of Lloyd Douglas' story about drunken playboy who mends his ways, becomes respected surgeon in order to restore the eyesight of a woman (Dunne) he blinded in an auto accident. Original running time was 112m.

Magnificent Obsession (1954) C-108m. *** D: Douglas Sirk. Jane Wyman, Rock Hudson, Barbara Rush, Otto Kruger, Agnes Moorehead. Director Sirk pulls out all the stops in this baroque, melodramatic remake of 1935 film which remains faithful to original story.

Magnificent Roughnecks (1956) 73m. BOMB D: Sherman A. Rose. Jack Carson, Mickey Rooney, Nancy Gates, Jeff Donnell. Allied Artists disaster with two "comics" as partners trying to wildcat oilfields.

Magnificent Seven, The (1960) C-126m. *** D: John Sturges. Yul Brynner, Eli Wallach, Steve McQueen, Horst Buchholz, James Coburn, Charles Bronson, Robert Vaughn. Rousing Western actioner derived from Japanese film SEVEN SAMURAI. Paid gunslingers blast away at bandits, devastating small Mexican town.

Magnificent Seven Ride!, The (1972) C-100m. **½ D: George McGowan. Lee Van Cleef, Stefanie Powers, Mariette Hartley, Michael Callan, Luke Askew, Pedro Armendariz, Jr. Newly married gunfighter decides to help his buddy fight bandits after they kidnap his wife. Third "ride" for the Seven isn't bad.

Magnificent Sinner (1963-French) C-91m. ** D: Robert Siodmak. Romy Schneider, Curt Jurgens, Pierre Blanchar, Monique Melinand. Lackluster proceedings of Schneider as mistress to Russian Czar, involved in court intrigue.

Magnificent Yankee, The (1950) 80m. *** D: John Sturges. Louis Calhern, Ann Harding, Eduard Franz, James Lydon, Philip Ober. Calhern as Oliver Wendell Holmes, Supreme Court Justice, and Harding his patient wife, give poignancy to this sensitive biographical study.

Magnum Force (1973) C-124m **½ D: Ted Post. Clint Eastwood, Hal Holbrook, Mitchell Ryan, David Soul, Felton Perry, Robert Urich, Kip Niven, Tim Matheson. Eastwood's second go-round as individualistic San Francisco cop Dirty Harry Callahan. This time he traces a series of mysterious slayings to the police department itself, and finds himself in extra-hot water. Some brutal scenes; not nearly as stylish as the original DIRTY HARRY.

Magus, The (1968-British) C-117m. BOMB D: Guy Green. Anthony Quinn, Michael Caine, Candice Bergen, Anna Karina, Paul Stassino, Julian Glover. Pretentious, hopelessly confusing story from John Fowles' novel about a magus, or magician (Quinn), who tries to control destiny of Caine, new arrival on his Greek island. At first mazelike story is fun, but with no relief it grows tiresome.

Mahogany (1975) C-109m. *½ D: Berry Gordy. Diana Ross, Billy Dee Williams, Anthony Perkins, Jean-Pierre Aumont, Beah Richards, Nina Foch. Silly, contrived affair about fashion designer who becomes world famous, then finds happiness only in arms of unsuccessful boy friend. Wooden performances except for Perkins' extension of PSYCHO role.

Maid in Paris (1957-French) 84m. ** D: Gaspard-Hult. Dany Robin, Daniel Gelin, Marie Daems, Tilda Thamar. Bland story of girl going to the big city seeking romance.

Maid of Salem (1937) 86m. *** D: Frank Lloyd. Claudette Colbert, Fred MacMurray, Louise Dresser, Gale Sondergaard, Beulah Bondi, Bonita Granville, Virginia Weidler, Donald Meek, Harvey Stephens, Edward Ellis, Mme. Sul-te-wan. Colonial witch-burning era is backdrop for fine drama with many similarities to Arthur Miller's CRUCIBLE (minus the philosophy).

Maid's Night Out (1938) 64m. ** D: Ben Holmes. Joan Fontaine, Allan Lane, Hedda Hopper, George Irving, William Brisbane, Billy Gilbert, Cecil Kellaway. Fontaine is one of those heiresses of the 1930s, mistaken for housemaid, in mild low-budget comedy.

Maids, The (1975-British) C-95m. ** D: Christopher Miles. Glenda Jackson, Susannah York, Vivien Merchant, Mark Burns. Jean Genet's windy, pointless, exasperating play about two maids who hate their mistress. Excellent acting wasted on tripe. An American Film Theater Production.

Mail Order Bride (1964) C-83m. **½ D: Burt Kennedy. Buddy Ebsen, Keir Dullea, Lois Nettleton, Warren Oates, Marie Windsor. Young man gets supervised by his father's old friend until he is finally ready to settle down. The old friend figures marrying might help some.

Mailbag Robbery (1958-British) 70m. ** D: Compton Bennett. Lee Patterson, Kay Callard, Alan Gifford, Kerry Jordan. Title explains full contents of programmer.

Main Chance, The (1966-British) 60m. **½ D: John Knight. Gregoire Aslan, Tracy Reed, Edward De-Souza, Stanley Meadows. Offbeat account of diamond robbery.

Main Event, The (1979) C-112m. *½ D: Howard Zieff. Barbra Streisand, Ryan O'Neal, Paul Sand, Whitman Mayo, Patti D'Arbanville, Richard Lawson, James Gregory. Torturous farce about a bankrupt executive who inherits a hapless boxer and goads him into resuming his career. O'Neal comes off slightly better than Streisand, but only because his yell-ing and screaming isn't as abrasive as hers.

Main Street After Dark (1944) 57m. **½ D: Edward L. Cahn. Edward Arnold, Audrey Totter, Dan Duryea, Hume Cronyn, Selena Royle. Offbeat drama of family pickpocket gang put out of business by civic clean-up campaign.

Main Street to Broadway (1953) 102m. **½ D: Tay Garnett. Tom Morton, Mary Murphy; guest stars Tallulah Bankhead, Ethel and Lionel Barrymore, Gertrude Berg, Rex Harrison, Lilli Palmer, Mary Martin, Agnes Moorehead, Herb Shriner. Thin tale of girl deciding between would-be playwright and successful N.Y.C. businessman. Vehicle allows for interesting cameos by host of theatrical luminaries.

Maisie Maisie was a middling series of ten MGM features made between 1939 and 1947, starring lively Ann Sothern as a brassy showgirl involved in a progression of topical if trivial situations encompassing the changing role of American women during WW2 America. The series never rose above the "B" category; all were filmed in black and white and ran about 85 minutes. Production values were too often static, utilizing rear projection and indoor sets to establish the varied locales of the episodes. The Maisie series relied almost exclusively on Miss Sothern's vivacious personality to carry the slight tales of the conventional tough-girl-with-a-heart-of-gold. Her co-stars were competent contract players such as Lew Ayres, John Hodiak, Robert Sterling, and George Murphy. Unlike the Andy Hardy series, few fledgling starlets appeared in these features, although guests like Red Skelton helped out from time to time. In general the series lacked a basic continuity and flavor; the earlier entries such as MAISIE and CONGO MAISIE (a remake of the Gable-Harlow RED DUST), while no classics, had more punch than later efforts such as UNDERCOVER MAISIE.

Maisie (1939) 74m. D: Edwin L. Marin. Ann Sothern, Robert Young, Ruth Hussey, Ian Hunter, George Tobias.

Maisie Gets Her Man (1942) 85m. D: Roy Del Ruth. Ann Sothern, Red Skelton, Leo Gorcey, Pamela Blake, Allen Jenkins, Donald Meek, Walter

Catlett, Fritz Feld, Rags Ragland, Frank Jenks.

Maisie Goes to Reno (1944) 90m. D: Harry Beaumont. Ann Sothern, John Hodiak, Tom Drake, Ava Gardner, Donald Meek.

Maisie Was a Lady (1941) 79m. D: Edwin L. Marin. Ann Sothern, Lew Ayres, Maureen O'Sullivan, C. Aubrey Smith, Joan Perry, Paul Cavanagh.

Major and the Minor, The (1942) 100m. ***½ D: Billy Wilder. Ginger Rogers, Ray Milland, Rita Johnson, Robert Benchley, Diana Lynn, Norma Varden. Memorable comedy of working-girl Rogers disguised as 12-year-old to save train fare, becoming involved with Milland's military school. Wilder's first directorial effort is still amusing. Remade as YOU'RE NEVER TOO YOUNG.

Major Barbara (1941-British) 115m. **** D: Gabriel Pascal. Wendy Hiller, Rex Harrison, Robert Morley, Robert Newton, Emlyn Williams, Sybil Thorndike, Deborah Kerr. Topnotch adaptation of Shaw play about wealthy girl who joins Salvation Army. Excellent cast in intelligent comedy.

Major Dundee (1965) C-134m. **½ D: Sam Peckinpah. Charlton Heston, Richard Harris, Jim Hutton, James Coburn, Michael Anderson, Jr., Senta Berger, Warren Oates, Slim Pickens. Very fine cast and lavish production make up for overlong, confused story of cavalry officer (Heston) who leads assorted misfits against Apaches.

Majority of One, A (1961) C-153m. **½ D: Mervyn LeRoy. Rosalind Russell, Alec Guinness, Ray Danton, Madlyn Rhue, Mae Questel. Compared to Broadway play, this is overblown, overacted account of Jewish matron Russell falling in love with Japanese widower Guinness.

Make Haste to Live (1954) 90m. **½ D: William A. Seiter. Dorothy McGuire, Stephen McNally, Mary Murphy, Edgar Buchanan, John Howard. McGuire gives believable performance as woman faced with criminal husband returned to seek vengeance.

Make Me an Offer (1955-British) C-88m. **½ D: Cyril Frankel. Peter Finch, Adrienne Corri, Rosalie Crutchley, Finlay Currie. Satisfactory highbrow shenanigans in the antique-buying field, with Finch after priceless vase.

Make Me an Offer (1980) C-100m.

TVM D: Jerry Paris. Susan Blakely, Patrick O'Neal, John Rubinstein, Edie Adams, Stella Stevens, Kathleen Lloyd. Sitcom-style romantic pap set against the real estate game in Southern California. Average.

Make Mine Laughs (1949) 64m. *½ D: Richard Fleischer. Frances Langford, Joan Davis, Leon Errol, Ray Bolger, Gil Lamb. RKO mini-musical, no more than uninspired footage lumped together à la vaudeville.

Make Mine Mink (1960-British) 100m. *** D: Robert Asher. Terry-Thomas, Athene Seyler, Hattie Jacques, Billie Whitelaw, Elspeth Duxbury, Raymond Huntley. Former military man Terry-Thomas organizes unlikely band of fur thieves in this delightful British farce.

Make Way For a Lady (1936) 65m. ** D: David Burton. Herbert Marshall, Anne Shirley, Gertrude Michael, Margot Grahame, Clara Blandick, Frank Coghlan, Jr. Routine comedy of Shirley playing matchmaker for her widowed father Marshall; pleasant enough, but just average.

Make Way For Tomorrow (1937) 92m. ***½ D: Leo McCarey. Victor Moore, Beulah Bondi, Fay Bainter, Thomas Mitchell, Porter Hall, Barbara Reed, Louise Beavers. Sensitive film of elderly couple in financial difficulty, shunted by their children, unwanted and unloved; shatteringly true, beautifully done.

Make Your Own Bed (1944) 82m. *½ D: Peter Godfrey. Jack Carson, Jane Wyman, Alan Hale, Irene Manning, George Tobias, Ricardo Cortez. Forced comedy of detective Carson disguised as butler, Wyman as maid, to get lowdown on racketeer.

Mako: The Jaws of Death (1976) C-93m. **½ D: William Grefe. Richard Jaeckel, Jennifer Bishop, Harold Sakata, John Chandler, Buffy Dee. Good horror premise has Jaeckel a friend and protector of sharks who goes berserk when both he and his "friends" are exploited. Shown theatrically as THE JAWS OF DEATH.

Malaga (1960-British) 97m. **½ D: Laslo Benedek. Trevor Howard, Dorothy Dandridge, Edmund Purdom, Michael Hordern. Bizarre casting in routine robbery tale is primary diversion. Originally titled MOMENT OF DANGER.

Malaya (1949) 98m. **½ D: Richard

Thorpe. Spencer Tracy, James Stewart, Valentina Cortese, Sydney Greenstreet. Routine WW2 melodrama set in the Pacific, about Allies' efforts to smuggle out rubber. Good cast let down by so-so script.

Male Animal, The (1942) 101m. ***½ D: Elliott Nugent. Henry Fonda, Olivia de Havilland, Jack Carson, Joan Leslie, Herbert Anderson, Don DeFore, Hattie MacDaniel, Eugene Pallette. Intelligent, entertaining Elliott Nugent-James Thurber comedy of college professor Fonda defending his rights, while losing wife De Havilland to old-flame Carson. Fine performances in this fine, contemporary film, with spoof on typical football rallies a highlight. Remade as SHE'S WORKING HER WAY THROUGH COLLEGE.

Male Hunt (1965-French) 92m. *** D: Edouard Molinaro. Jean-Paul Belmondo, Jean-Claude Brialy, Catherine Deneuve, Francoise Dorleac, Marie Laforet. Spicy romp about trio of Frenchmen avoiding the clutches of marriage-minded women.

Mallory: Circumstantial Evidence (1976) C-100m. TVM D: Boris Sagal. Raymond Burr, Robert Loggia, Roger Robinson, Mark Hamill, Peter Mark Richman, A Martinez. Burr is celebrated lawyer with a tarnished reputation whose client, a car thief, is charged with committing homicide in jail. A pilot that got Burr out of the wheelchair. Average.

Malta Story, The (1953-British) 98m. **½ D: Brian Desmond Hurst. Alec Guinness, Jack Hawkins, Anthony Steele, Muriel Pavlow. On-location filming of this WW2 British-air-force-in-action yarn is sparked by underplayed acting.

Maltese Bippy, The (1969) C-88m. ** D: Norman Panama. Dan Rowan, Dick Martin, Carol Lynley, Julie Newmar, Mildred Natwick, Fritz Weaver, Robert Reed. Werewolves, haunted houses, good cast, but few true laughs in tired horror-movie spoof.

Maltese Falcon, The (1941) 100m. **** D: John Huston. Humphrey Bogart, Mary Astor, Peter Lorre, Sydney Greenstreet, Gladys George, Barton MacLane, Elisha Cook, Jr., Lee Patrick, Jerome Cowan. Outstanding detective drama improves with each viewing; Bogey is Dashiell Hammett's "hero" Sam Spade, Astor his client, Lorre the evasive Joel Cairo, Greenstreet the Fat Man, and Cook the neurotic gunsel Wilmer. Huston's first directorial attempt moves at lightning pace, with cameo by his father Walter Huston as Captain Jacoby. Previously filmed in 1931 and in 1936 as SATAN MET A LADY.

Maltese Falcon (1931) SEE: **Dangerous Female**

Mambo (1955-Italian) 94m. **½ D: Robert Rossen. Shelley Winters, Silvana Mangano, Michael Rennie, Katherine Dunham, Vittorio Gassman, Eduardo Ciannelli. Muddled yet unusual account of working gal becoming famed dancer; offbeat entertainment.

Mame (1974) C-131m. BOMB D: Gene Saks. Lucille Ball, Beatrice Arthur, Robert Preston, Jane Connell, Bruce Davison, Kirby Furlong. Hopelessly out-of-date musical taken from the Broadway hit and based on "Auntie Mame" will embarrass even those who love Lucy. Calling Fred and Ethel Mertz.

Mammy (1930) 84m. ** D: Michael Curtiz. Al Jolson, Lois Moran, Louise Dresser, Lowell Sherman, Hobart Bosworth. Story of backstage murder is only tolerable during musical numbers; Jolson sings "Let me Sing and I'm Happy." Some sequences originally filmed in color.

Mam'zelle Pigalle (1958-French) C-77m. **½ D: Michel Boisrond. Brigitte Bardot, Jean Bretonniere, Francoise Fabian, Bernard Lancret. Not as saucy as most BB flicks; here she's a songstress mixed up with counterfeiters. Retitled: NAUGHTY GIRL.

Man, The (1972) C-93m. ** D: Joseph Sargent. James Earl Jones, Martin Balsam, Burgess Meredith, Lew Ayres, William Windom, Barbara Rush, Janet MacLachlan. Black Senator Jones becomes President of U.S. after freak disaster kills chief executive in Europe. Originally made for TV but released theatrically; marginally interesting Rod Serling adaptation of Irving Wallace bestseller plus acceptable performances add up to forgettable experience. Cameo appearance by Jack Benny.

Man About the House, A (1947-British) 83m. **½ D: Leslie Arliss. Kieron Moore, Margaret Johnston, Dulcie Gray, Guy Middleton. Murky drama of British girls almost outmaneuvered by Italian con-artist.

Man About Town (1939) 85m. **½

[475]

D: Mark Sandrich. Jack Benny, Dorothy Lamour, Edward Arnold, Binnie Barnes, Phil Harris, Betty Grable, Monty Woolley, Eddie "Rochester" Anderson. Jack tries to crash London society while there with his troupe; lively but undistinguished musical.

Man, a Woman and a Bank, A (1979-Canadian) C-100m. **½ D: Noel Black. Donald Sutherland, Brooke Adams, Paul Mazursky, Allen Magicovsky, Leigh Hamilton. Needless but inoffensive caper movie about a $4 million bank heist, with pleasing performances by the three leads. Magicovsky isn't too appealing as a suicidal whipped cream freak, but how many suicidal whipped cream freaks do you know that ARE?

Man About Town (1947-French) 89m. *** D: René Clair. Maurice Chevalier, Francois Perier, Marcelle Derrien, Dany Robin. Chevalier in a quaint musical, doing what he knows best: a boulevardier with an eye for les femmes.

Man Afraid (1957) 84m. **½ D: Harry Keller. George Nader, Phyllis Thaxter, Tim Hovey, Reta Shaw, Martin Milner. Well-acted story of clergyman Nader protecting family against father of boy he killed in self-defense.

Man Alive (1945) 70m. **½ D: Ray Enright. Pat O'Brien, Adolphe Menjou, Ellen Drew, Rudy Vallee, Fortunio Bonanova, Joseph Crehan, Jonathan Hale, Minna Gombell, Jason Robards, Sr. Amusing comedy of O'Brien, supposedly dead, playing ghost to scare away wife's new love interest; not overdone, moves along at brisk pace.

Man Alone, A (1955) C-96m. **½ D: Ray Milland. Ray Milland, Mary Murphy, Ward Bond, Raymond Burr, Lee Van Cleef. Intelligent oater of fugitive from lynch mob (Milland) hiding with sheriff's daughter (Murphy) in small town. Milland's first directorial attempt isn't bad.

Man and a Woman, A (1966-French) C-102m. ***½ D: Claude Lelouch. Anouk Aimee, Jean-Louis Trintignant, Pierre Barouh, Valerie Lagrange. Moving romantic drama about young widow and widower who fall in love; one of the 1960s' most popular love stories, thanks to intelligent script, winning performances, innovative direction and camerawork, Francis Lai's music score. Oscar winner for Best Foreign Film, Best Original Screenplay. Remade by writer-director Lelouch in 1977 as ANOTHER MAN, ANOTHER CHANCE.

Man and Boy (1972) C-98m. **½ D: E. W. Swackhamer. Bill Cosby, Gloria Foster, Leif Erickson, George Spell, Douglas Turner Ward, John Anderson, Yaphet Kotto, Henry Silva, Dub Taylor. Civil War veteran and young son take after the thief who has stolen their horse in a kind of black BICYCLE THIEF. Decent enough family film.

Man at the Carlton Tower (1961-British) 57m. ** D: Robert Tronson. Maxine Audley, Lee Montague, Allan Cuthbertson, Terence Alexander. Routine Edgar Wallace thriller churned out against backdrop of plush London hotel involving jewel robbery and murder.

Man at the Top (1975-British) C-92m. *** D: Mike Vardy. Kenneth Haigh, Nanette Newman, Harry Andrews, John Quentin, Mary Maude. Feature spin-off of British TV show which in turn is a spin-off of ROOM AT THE TOP, with Haigh as Joe Compton, now caught in EXECUTIVE SUITE-type business conflicts.

Man Bait (1952-U.S.-British) 78m. **½ D: Terence Fisher. George Brent, Marguerite Chapman, Diana Dors, Raymond Huntley, Peter Reynolds. British made suspense programmer has Brent a book dealer entangled in blackmail and murder. British title: THE LAST PAGE.

Man Beast (1955) 72m. BOMB D: Jerry Warren. Rock Madison, Virginia Maynor, George Skaff, Lloyd Nelson, Tom Maruzzi. An expedition goes in search of the abominable snowman but comes up with a turkey instead.

Man Behind the Gun, The (1952) C-82m. ** D: Felix E. Feist. Randolph Scott, Patrice Wymore, Philip Carey, Dick Wesson, Lina Romay. Army man Scott goes undercover to investigate southern California secessionist movement in 1850s. Formula stuff.

Man Betrayed, A (1941) 83m. ** D: John H. Auer. John Wayne, Frances Dee, Edward Ellis, Wallace Ford, Ward Bond, Harold Huber, Alexander Granach. Country lawyer crusades against father of girlfriend to prove that he's crooked politician.

Minor melodrama. Retitled: WHEEL OF FORTUNE.

Man Between, The (1953-British) 100m. *** D: Carol Reed. James Mason, Claire Bloom, Hildegarde Neff, Geoffrey Toone. Well-handled suspenser set in post-WW2 Berlin, with Mason pulled by conflicting political loyalties.

Man Called Adam, A (1966) 102m. ** D: Leo Penn. Sammy Davis, Jr., Ossie Davis, Cicely Tyson, Louis Armstrong, Frank Sinatra, Jr., Peter Lawford, Mel Torme. Pretentious melodrama of trumpet-player Davis trying to find some purpose in life; amateurishly produced.

Man Called Dagger, A (1967) C-86m. BOMB D: Richard Rush. Terry Moore, Jan Murray, Sue Ane Langdon, Paul Mantee, Eileen O'Neill, Maureen Arthur. Ex-Nazi scientist journeys to L.A. followed by secret agent Richard Dagger to assist former S.S. colonel (Murray) in world-conquering plan. Embarrassing script, acting.

Man Called Flintstone, The (1966) C-87m. **½ D: Joseph Barbera, William Hanna. Voices of Alan Reed, Mel Blanc, Jean Vander Pyl, June Foray. Feature-length cartoon based on TV series of Stone Age characters; satirizes superspy films. Mainly for kids.

Man Called Gannon, A (1969) C-105m. *½ D: James Goldstone. Tony Franciosa, Michael Sarrazin, Judi West, Susan Oliver. Remade version of MAN WITHOUT A STAR is poor substitute. It's ranchwar time again . . .

Man Called Horse, A (1970) C-114m. **½ D: Elliott Silverstein. Richard Harris, Judith Anderson, Jean Gascon, Manu Tupou, Corinna Tsopei, Dub Taylor. English aristocrat gets captured by Sioux Indians in the Dakotas, undergoes torture to prove his worth. Sometimes gripping, sometimes gory film has lots of violence that may be cut for TV. Followed by RETURN OF A MAN CALLED HORSE.

Man Called Peter, A (1955) C-119m. *** D: Henry Koster. Richard Todd, Jean Peters, Marjorie Rambeau, Doris Lloyd, Emmett Lynn. Moving account of Scotsman Peter Marshall who became clergyman and U.S. Senate chaplain; sensitively played by Todd, with fine supporting cast.

Man Called Sledge, A (1970-Italian)

C-93m. ** D: Vic Morrow. James Garner, Dennis Weaver, Claude Akins, John Marley, Laura Antonelli, Wade Preston. Violent Western about a gunman whose gang goes after a cache of gold stored in a prison, and then fights over the loot. Notable mainly for Garner's atypical role as brutal outlaw.

Man Could Get Killed, A (1966) C-99m. **½ D: Ronald Neame, Cliff Owen. James Garner, Melina Mercouri, Sandra Dee, Tony Franciosa, Robert Coote, Roland Culver. Businessman Garner is mistaken for international spy in this so-so secret agent spoof with beautiful Rome and Lisbon locations.

Man Detained (1961-British) 59m. **½ D: Robert Tronson. Bernard Archard, Elvi Hale, Paul Stassino, Michael Coles. Trim Edgar Wallace yarn, enhanced by Hale's performance as secretary involved with counterfeiting gang and murder.

Man for All Seasons, A (1966-British) C-120m. **** D: Fred Zinnemann. Paul Scofield, Wendy Hiller, Leo McKern, Robert Shaw, Orson Welles, Susannah York, Nigel Davenport, Vanessa Redgrave. Splendid film about Sir Thomas More's personal conflict when King Henry VIII asks his support in break with Pope and formation of Church of England. Scofield's rich characterization matched by superb cast, vivid atmosphere. Oscars include Best Actor, Best Director, Best Picture.

Man Friday (1976-British) C-115m. *½ D: Jack Gold. Peter O'Toole, Richard Roundtree, Peter Cellier, Christopher Cabot, Joel Fluellen. Defoe classic rewritten to conform to today's racial standards. Amid gore and confusing flashbacks "Friday" revolts against bondage, outwits master "Crusoe," and also drives him mad (as shown in Cannes, Crusoe, having failed to "educate" Friday to British standards, and himself refused admission to Friday's tribe, blows his brains out!).

Man from Atlantis (1977) C-100m. TVM D: Lee H. Katzin. Patrick Duffy, Belinda Montgomery, Art Lund, Dean Santoro, Victor Buono, Lawrence Pressman. Sci-fier about last surviving citizen of underwater kingdom who teams up with a pretty marine biologist to fight evil on Earth. Duffy is quite good as underwater romantic lead with webbed hands who outswims and outleaps dolphins, and made an unlikely hero for subsequent TV series. Above average.

Man from Atlantis: The Death Scouts (1977) **C-**100m. TVM D: Marc Daniels, Patrick Duffy, Belinda Montgomery, Kenneth Tigar, Alan Fudge, Tiffany Bolling, Burr De-Benning, Russell Arms, Annette Cardona. Sci-fi drama in which title humanoid tries to thwart an invasion of earth by water-breathing aliens of another planet. Enjoyable nonsense. Average.

Man from Bitter Ridge, The (1955) **C-**80m. **½ D: Jack Arnold. Lex Barker, Mara Corday, Stephen McNally, Trevor Bardette. Peppy oater of Barker tracking down outlaws by tying in with local banker.

Man from Button Willow, The (1965) **C-**84m. ** D: David Detiege. Cartoon Western featuring the voices of Dale Robertson, Edgar Buchanan, Howard Keel, Herschel Bernardi, Ross Martin and others is only for small kiddies; story deals with America's first undercover agent in 1869 who prevents crooks from forcing settlers to get rid of their land.

Man from Cairo (1953-Italian) 81m. ** D: Edoardo Anton. George Raft, Gianna Maria Canale, Massimo Serato. Disappointing mishmash of intrigue set in Africa, with everyone scurrying about for gold.

Man from Colorado, The (1948) **C-**99m. *** D: Henry Levin. Glenn Ford, William Holden, Ellen Drew, Ray Collins, Edgar Buchanan. Unusual Western of brutal Ford appointed Federal judge, taking tyrannical hold of the territory.

Man from Dakota, The (1940) 75m. **½ D: Leslie Fenton. Wallace Beery, John Howard, Dolores Del Rio, Donald Meek, Robert Barrat. Above-average Beery vehicle set in Civil War times, with glamorous Del Rio helping him and Howard, Union spies, cross Confederate lines.

Man from Del Rio (1956) 82m. ** D: Harry Horner. Anthony Quinn, Katy Jurado, Peter Whitney, Douglas Fowley, John Larch, Whit Bissell. Dank Western of Mexican gunslinger Quinn saving a town from outlaws.

Man from Down Under, The (1943) 103m. **½ D: Robert Z. Leonard. Charles Laughton, Binnie Barnes, Richard Carlson, Donna Reed, Christopher Severn, Clyde Cook. Well-meaning Laughton claims two

orphan waifs as his own children, raising them in Australia. Entertaining, trivial little comedy.

Man from God's Country (1958) **C-**72m. ** D: Paul Landres. George Montgomery, Randy Stuart, Gregg Barton, Kim Charney, Susan Cummings. Quiet oater involving landhungry ranchers trying to outfox the railroad.

Man from Hong Kong, The (1975-Australian-Chinese) **C-**103m. ** D: Brian Trenchard Smith. Jimmy Wang Yu, George Lazenby, Ros Spiers, Hugh Keays-Byrne, Rebecca Gilling. Undemanding action fans should get their fill in this stunt-crazy story of Hong Kong emissary called to Sydney to help nail drug kingpin.

Man from Laramie, The (1955) **C-**104m. *** D: Anthony Mann. James Stewart, Arthur Kennedy, Donald Crisp, Cathy O'Donnell, Alex Nicol, Aline MacMahon, Wallace Ford. Taut action tale of revenge, with Stewart seeking those who killed his brother.

Man from O.R.G.Y. (1970) **C-**92m. *½ D: James A. Hill. Robert Walker, Steve Rossi, Slappy White, Louisa Moritz. Banal counterespionage comedy-drama. Who's got the secrets?

Man from Planet X, The (1951) 70m. *½ D: Edgar G. Ulmer. Robert Clarke, Margaret Field, Raymond Bond, William Schallert. Scottish Highlands are visited by alien from wandering planet; at first he is benign, but evil designs of Schallert turn him against human race.

Man from the Alamo, The (1953) **C-**79m. **½ D: Budd Boetticher. Glenn Ford, Julia Adams, Victor Jory, Hugh O'Brian. Fictional historical sidelight with Ford surviving Alamo massacre and helping General Houston fight the Mexicans. More action sequences would have helped.

Man from the Diner's Club, The (1963) 96m. **½ D: Frank Tashlin. Danny Kaye, Martha Hyer, Cara Williams, Telly Savalas, Everett Sloane, George Kennedy. Silly shenanigans of Diner's Club employee Kaye involved with Damon Runyonish gangsters. Danny has certainly had more inspired antics than these.

Man from Yesterday, The (1932) 71m. *** D: Berthold Viertel. Claudette Colbert, Clive Brook, Charles Boyer, Andy Devine, Alan Mowbray. Story of Colbert marrying

Boyer thinking husband Brook has died is surprisingly well done, thanks mainly to top performances.

Man Hunt (1941) 105m. ***½ D: Fritz Lang. Walter Pidgeon, Joan Bennett, George Sanders, John Carradine, Roddy McDowall. Farfetched yet absorbing drama of man attempting to kill Hitler, getting into more trouble than he bargained for. Tense, well-done.

Man Hunter, The (1969) C-98m. TVM D: Don Taylor. Sandra Dee, Roy Thinnes, William Smith, Al Hirt. Safari hunter hired by American banker to avenge death of son during small-town bank robbery. Typical premise-gone-awry situation, due to contrived plotting. Average.

Man I Killed, The SEE: **Broken Lullaby.**

Man I Love, The (1946) 96m. *** D: Raoul Walsh. Ida Lupino, Robert Alda, Bruce Bennett, Andrea King, Dolores Moran, Martha Vickers, Alan Hale. Slick, well-acted melodrama casts Ida as nightclub singer who falls in love with no-good mobster Alda. Forget logic and just enjoy. This film inspired Scorsese's NEW YORK, NEW YORK.

Man I Married, The (1940) 77m. *** D: Irving Pichel. Joan Bennett, Francis Lederer, Lloyd Nolan, Anna Sten, Otto Kruger. Strong story of German Lederer taken in by Nazi propaganda while American wife Bennett tries to stop him. Taut, exciting script.

Man in a Cocked Hat (1959-British) 88m. *** D: Jeffrey Dell, Roy Boulting. Terry-Thomas, Peter Sellers, Luciana Paluzzi, Thorley Walters, Ian Bannen, John Le Mesurier, Miles Malleson. Screwball farce about Island of Gallardia, a British protectorate forgotten for 50 years; when rediscovered, bumbling Terry-Thomas of the Foreign Office is left in charge. British title: CARLETON-BROWNE OF THE F.O.

Man in Grey, The (1945-British) 116m. *** D: Leslie Arliss. Margaret Lockwood, James Mason, Phyllis Calvert, Stewart Granger, Martita Hunt. Elaborate costumer with good performances but trite script of crisscross love affair among royalty.

Man in Half Moon Street, The (1944) 92m. **½ D: Ralph Murphy. Nils Asther, Helen Walker, Brandon Hurst, Reginald Sheffield. Not-bad horror tale of scientist Asther experimenting with rejuvenation; done on better scale than many of these tired epics. Remade as THE MAN WHO COULD CHEAT DEATH.

Man in Hiding (1953-British) 79m. *½ D: Terence Fisher. Paul Henreid, Lois Maxwell, Kieron Moore, Hugh Sinclair. Tame detective-capturing-elusive-killer plot.

Man in the Attic (1954) 82m. **½ D: Hugo Fregonese. Jack Palance, Constance Smith, Byron Palmer, Frances Bavier, Rhys Williams, Sean McClory, Isabel Jewell, Leslie Bradley. Flavorful account of notorious Jack the Ripper, with Palance going full-blast.

Man Killer (1933) 67m. **½ D: Michael Curtiz. William Powell, Margaret Lindsay, Ruth Donnelly, Arthur Hohl, Natalie Moorehead, Arthur Byron. Powell accepts job with shady private-detective Hohl and agrees to dupe wealthy Lindsay, but falls in love with her instead. Warner Bros. programmer picks up after a slow start. Originally released as PRIVATE DETECTIVE 62.

Man in the Dark (1953) 70m. **½ D: Lew Landers. Edmond O'Brien, Audrey Totter, Ruth Warren, Ted de Corsia, Horace McMahon. Convict O'Brien undergoes brain surgery to eliminate criminal bent, and loses memory in the process; his old cohorts only care that he remember where he stashed their stolen loot. Routine remake of THE MAN WHO LIVED TWICE was originally shown in 3-D.

Man in the Glass Booth, The (1975) C-117m. **½ D: Arthur Hiller. Maximilian Schell, Lois Nettleton, Luther Adler, Lawrence Pressman, Henry Brown, Richard Rasof. American Film Theatre version of Robert Shaw's play about a glib industrialist brought to trial for Nazi war crimes. Schell is good, but overall effect is contrived. Shaw had his name removed from credits of film.

Man in the Gray Flannel Suit, The (1956) C-153m. ***½ D: Nunnally Johnson. Gregory Peck, Jennifer Jones, Fredric March, Marisa Pavan, Lee J. Cobb, Ann Harding, Keenan Wynn. Sloan Wilson's slick novel of Madison Avenue executive struggling to get ahead and to find meaning to his home life. Nice cameo by Harding as March's wife.

Man in the Iron Mask, The (1939) 110m. *** D: James Whale. Louis

Hayward, Joan Bennett, Warren William, Joseph Schildkraut, Alan Hale, Walter Kingsford, Marion Martin. Rousing adventure of twin brothers: one becomes King of France, the other a carefree gay blade raised by D'Artagnan (William) and the 3 Musketeers. Fine swashbuckler.

Man in the Iron Mask, The (1977) C-100m. TVM D: Mike Newell. Richard Chamberlain, Patrick Mc-Goohan, Louis Jourdan, Jenny Agutter, Vivien Merchant, Ian Holm, Ralph Richardson. Stylish romantic adventure in this version of the Dumas classic acted with panache by a sterling cast. Chamberlain can swashbuckle with the best of them. Grand entertainment. Above average.

Man in the Middle (1964-British) 94m. ** D: Guy Hamilton. Robert Mitchum, France Nuyen, Barry Sullivan, Keenan Wynn, Alexander Knox, Trevor Howard. Unconvincing, confusing film of Howard Fast novel THE WINSTON AFFAIR, about American military officer accused of homicide; static courtroom sequences.

Man in the Moon (1961-British) 98m. *** D: Basil Dearden. Kenneth More, Shirley Anne Field, Norman Bird, Michael Hordern, John Phillips. Top comedy satirizing space race. Government recruits man unaffected by cold, heat, speed, etc., to be perfect astronaut.

Man in the Net, The (1959) 97m. **½ D: Michael Curtiz. Alan Ladd, Carolyn Jones, Diane Brewster, Charles McGraw, John Lupton, Tom Helmore. Fair drama of Ladd trying to clear himself of murder charge for wife's death.

Man in the Road, The (1957-British) 83m. *½ D: Lance Comfort. Derek Farr, Ella Raines, Donald Wolfit, Karel Stepanek. Despite sturdy cast, humdrum telling of Communists trying to get scientist to divulge secret formula.

Man in the Saddle (1951) C-87m. ** D: Andre de Toth. Randolph Scott, Joan Leslie, Ellen Drew, Alexander Knox. Scott is involved in romantic triangle causing death on the range; justice triumphs.

Man in the Santa Claus Suit, The (1978) C-100m. TVM D: Corey Allen. Fred Astaire, Gary Burghoff, John Byner, Bert Convy, Nanette Fabray, Harold Gould. Yuletide fantasy of

how Astaire (playing seven different characters) affects the lives of a variety of familiar TV faces. He also sings the title song—delightfully. Average.

Man in the Shadow (1957) 80m. **½ D: Jack Arnold. Orson Welles, Jeff Chandler, Colleen Miller, James Gleason. Welles chomps his way through role of rancher responsible for helper's death. Chandler is the earnest sheriff.

Man in the Vault (1956) 73m. *½ D: Andrew V. McLaglen. William Campbell, Karen Sharpe, Anita Ekberg, Berry Kroeger, Paul Fix. Programmer of drab locksmith involved in robbery; nothing special.

Man in the White Suit, The (1952-British) 84m. ***½ D: Alexander Mackendrick. Alec Guinness, Joan Greenwood, Cecil Parker, Michael Gough, Ernest Thesiger. Guinness is inventor who discovers a fabric that can't wear out or soil; dismayed garment manufacturers set out to buy his formula. Most engaging comedy.

Man in the Wilderness (1971) C-105m. *** D: Richard C. Sarafian. Richard Harris, John Huston, John Bindon, Ben Carruthers, Prunella Ransome, Henry Wilcoxon. Trapper Harris abandoned in wasteland, must fight for survival, and revenge as well. Well-made, engrossing, but bloody film.

Man Inside, The (1958-British) 90m. *½ D: John Gilling. Jack Palance, Anita Ekberg, Nigel Patrick, Anthony Newley. Shoddy robbery caper with private investigator hunting jewel thieves throughout Europe.

Man is Armed, The (1956) 70m. *½ D: Franklin Adreon. Dane Clark, William Talman, May Wynn, Robert Horton, Barton MacLane. Lowjinks about robbery; competent cast stifled by incompetent production.

Man Named John, A (1968-Italian) C-94m. *** D: Ermano Olmi. Rod Steiger. Excellent documentary on Pope John XXIII, encompassing many facets of his life, work, and beliefs on mankind.

Man of Aran (1934-British) 77m. **** D: Robert Flaherty. Colman (Tiger) King, Maggie Dillane. Superb, classic documentary about day-to-day existence, and constant fight for survival, of fisherman in remote Irish coastal community. Scenes at sea are breathtaking.

Man of a Thousand Faces (1957)

122m. ***½ D: Joseph Pevney. James Cagney, Dorothy Malone, Jane Greer, Marjorie Rambeau, Jim Backus, Snub Pollard, Jeanne Cagney. Surprisingly dedicated, well-acted biography of silent star Lon Chaney. Cagney as Chaney, Malone as disturbed first wife, Greer as wife who brings him happiness, are all fine. Chaney's life and screen career are recreated with taste (if not accuracy). Touching portrayal of movie extra by Rambeau.

Man of Conflict (1953) 72m. ** D: Hal Makelim. Edward Arnold, John Agar, Susan Morrow, Russell Hicks. Lukewarm drama of generation clash between father Arnold and son Agar over business and philosophy of life.

Man of Conquest (1939) 105m. **½ D: George Nicholls, Jr. Richard Dix, Gail Patrick, Edward Ellis, Joan Fontaine. Republic Pictures tried to give this biography of Texas' Sam Houston good production values, but script slows down action.

Man of Evil (1944-British) 90m. ** D: Anthony Asquith. Phyllis Calvert, James Mason, Stewart Granger, Wilfrid Lawson, Jean Kent. Elaborate but ponderous costumer of maniac who tries to run people's lives to suit his fancy; overdone and not effective. Original title: FANNY BY GASLIGHT.

Man of Iron (1956-Italian) 116m. *** D: Pietro Germi. Pietro Germi, Luisa Della Noce, Sylva Koscina, Carlo Giuffre. Somber account of Germi, railroad engineer, whose life takes a tragic turn, affecting his whole family; realistically presented. Original title: THE RAILROAD MAN.

Man of La Mancha (1972) C-130m. BOMB D: Arthur Hiller. Peter O'Toole, Sophia Loren, James Coco, Harry Andrews, John Castle. Plodding, abysmal adaptation of Dale Wasserman's popular musical based on DON QUIXOTE, with Joe Darion-Mitch Leigh score. Beautiful source material has been raped, murdered, and buried.

Man of Legend (1971-Italian-Spanish) 97m. **½ D: Sergio Grieco. Peter Strauss, Tina Aumont, Luciana Paluzzi, Massimo Serato. WWI German soldier, mistaken for spy and condemned to death, flees to Africa, joins French Foreign Legion, falls in with Moroccan rebels and steals the heart of the chief's daughter. Uninspired sex-and-sand saga.

Man of the West (1958) C-100m. *** D: Anthony Mann. Gary Cooper, Julie London, Lee J. Cobb, Arthur O'Connell, Jack Lord, John Dehner, Royal Dano. Dismissed in 1958, this powerful story deserves another look. Cooper plays a reformed outlaw who is forced to rejoin his ex-boss (Cobb) to save himself and other innocent people from the gang's mistreatment. Strong, epic-scale Western, with script by Reginald Rose.

Man of the World (1931) 71m. ** D: Richard Wallace. William Powell, Carole Lombard, Wynne Gibson, Guy Kibbee, George Chandler. Routine tale of good-girl Lombard in love with con-man Powell.

Man on a String (1960) 92m. *** D: Andre de Toth. Ernest Borgnine, Kerwin Mathews, Colleen Dewhurst, Alexander Scourby, Glenn Corbett. Fictionalized account of counterspy Boris Morros, involved in Russian-U.S. Cold War conflict. Taut action sequences.

Man on a String (1971) C-73m. TVM D: Joseph Sargent. Christopher George, William Schallert, Joel Grey, Jack Warden, Kitty Winn, Michael Baseleon. Undercover government agent maneuvers two Mafia families into confrontation, almost dies when identity is discovered. Predictable. Average.

Man on a Swing (1974) C-110m. **½ D: Frank Perry. Cliff Robertson, Joel Grey, Dorothy Tristan, Elizabeth Wilson, George Voskovec. Mysterious clairvoyant (Grey) offers to help a cop (Robertson) solve sex-slaying that's been troubling him, but generates more questions than answers. Intriguing idea sadly misses the mark by building up to an unsatisfying conclusion.

Man on a Tightrope (1953) 105m. *** D: Elia Kazan. Fredric March, Gloria Grahame, Terry Moore, Cameron Mitchell, Adolphe Menjou. Atmospheric circus drama of troupe planning to escape from behind the Iron Curtain; sturdy cast.

Man on Fire (1957) 95m. **½ D: Ranald MacDougall. Bing Crosby, Mary Fickett, Inger Stevens, E.G. Marshall, Malcolm Broderick, Anne Seymour, Richard Eastham. Divorced father (Crosby) refuses to grant his remarried ex-wife partial custody of their son in this modest domestic drama.

Man on the Eiffel Tower, The (1949) C-97m. *** D: Burgess Meredith. Charles Laughton, Franchot Tone, Burgess Meredith, Robert Hutton, Jean Wallace, Patricia Roc, Wilfrid Hyde-White, Belita. Taut psychological drama filmed in Paris involving cat-and-mouse game between police investigator and suspected murderer. Meredith's first try at directing a feature film.

Man on the Flying Trapeze, The (1935) 65m. ***½ D: Clyde Bruckman. W. C. Fields, Mary Brian, Kathleen Howard, Grady Sutton, Vera Lewis. Hilarious Fieldsian study in frustration, with able assistance from hardboiled wife Howard, good-for-nothing Sutton. Best sequence has W. C. receiving four traffic tickets in a row!

Man on the Move SEE: **Jigsaw** (1971)

Man on the Outside (1975) C-100m. TVM D: Boris Sagal. Lorne Greene, James Olson, Lee H. Montgomery, Lorraine Gary, Brooke Bundy. Retired police captain's son is shot down before his eyes and his grandson is kidnapped by a syndicate hit man. Greene is properly strong in the lead, leading to a short-lived series called "Griff." Average.

Man on the Roof (1977–Swedish) C-110m. ***½ D: Bo Widerberg. Gustav Lindstedt, Hakan Serner, Sven Wallter, Thomas Hellberg. A cop killer is the subject of a Stockholm manhunt in this police film with substance and style. Absorbing for its look at police methodology as well as its suspense and action.

Man or Gun (1958) 79m. ** D: Albert Gannaway. Macdonald Carey, Audrey Totter, James Craig, James Gleason. Bland Western with Carey cleaning up the town.

Man Outside, The (1968–British) C-98m. **½ D: Samuel Gallu. Van Heflin, Heidelinde Weis, Pinkas Braun, Peter Vaughan, Charles Gray, Ronnie Barker. Heflin is fired from CIA job but cannot extricate himself from international tug-of-war over Russian defector; unpretentious spy stuff.

Man-Proof (1938) 74m. ** D: Richard Thorpe. Myrna Loy, Franchot Tone, Rosalind Russell, Walter Pidgeon, Nana Bryant, Rita Johnson, Ruth Hussey. Flimsy plot with bright stars: Loy and Russell both love Pidgeon, but Tone is ready to step in any time.

Man They Could Not Hang, The (1939) 72m. **½ D: Nick Grinde. Boris Karloff, Lorna Gray, Robert Wilcox, Roger Pryor, Ann Doran. Karloff's done the same plot before, but it's still good; hanged man brought back to life seeks revenge on his killers.

Man to Man Talk (1958–French) 89m. ** D: Luis Saslavski. Yves Montand, Nicole Berger, Yves Noel. Trite little tale of father forced to explain facts of life to youngster when mother is having a baby. Retitled: PREMIER MAY.

Man-Trap (1961) 93m. **½ D: Edmond O'Brien. Jeffrey Hunter, David Janssen, Stella Stevens, Hugh Sanders. Capable cast involved in adultery, robbery and disaster; unusual fling at directing by O'Brien.

Man Upstairs, The (1958–British) 88m. *** D: Don Chaffey. Richard Attenborough, Bernard Lee, Donald Houston, Virginia Maskell. Compact study, excellently acted, of Attenborough, a man gone berserk much to everyone's amazement.

Man Who Broke the Bank at Monte Carlo, The (1935) 66m. **½ D: Stephen Roberts. Ronald Colman, Joan Bennett, Colin Clive, Nigel Bruce, Montagu Love, Ferdinand Gottschalk. Flimsy film carried by Colman charm, translating famous title song into story of man who calculates to clean out treasury of Riviera gambling establishment.

Man Who Came to Dinner, The (1941) 112m. ***½ D: William Keighley. Monty Woolley, Bette Davis, Ann Sheridan, Billie Burke, Richard Travis, Grant Mitchell, Mary Wickes, Elizabeth Fraser, Reginald Gardiner. Pompous author Woolley is forced to stay with Burke's family for the winter, driving them crazy with assorted wacky friends passing through. Davis has thankless role, but oomph-girl Sheridan is in peak form.

Man Who Changed His Mind SEE: **Man Who Lived Again, The**

Man Who Cheated Himself, The (1950) 81m. **½ D: Felix E. Feist. Lee J. Cobb, Jane Wyatt, John Dall, Terry Frost. Good cast uplifts typical murder film.

Man Who Could Cheat Death, The (1959–British) C-83m. ** D: Terence Fisher. Anton Diffring, Hazel Court, Christopher Lee, Arnold Marle, Delphi Lawrence. Turgid remake of THE MAN IN HALF

MOON STREET, about man trying to rekindle romance with former girlfriend; typical Hammer production.

Man Who Could Talk to Kids, The (1973) C-74m. TVM D: Donald Wrye. Peter Boyle, Scott Jacoby, Robert Reed, Collin Wilcox-Horne, Tyne Daly, Denise Nickerson, Jack Wade. Parents upset by their withdrawn, rebellious teen-age son, must resort to social worker (Boyle) to reunite family. Documentary approach to direction enhances effect. Above average.

Man Who Could Work Miracles, The (1937-British) 82m. ***½ D: Lothar Mendes. Roland Young, Ralph Richardson, Joan Gardner, Ernest Thesiger, Wallace Lupino, George Zucco, Bernard Nedell, H. G. Wells' fantasy of timid British department store clerk (Young) endowed with power to do anything he wants. Special effects are marvelous, supported by good cast, in charming film.

Man Who Cried Wolf, The (1937) 66m. **½ D: Lewis R. Foster. Lewis Stone, Tom Brown, Barbara Read, Robert Gleckler, Forrester Harvey. Hammy actor Stone confesses to various murders, convinces cops he's crazy, planning perfect alibi for real killing. Cheaply filmed, Stone is mainstay of film, with Marjorie Main in good supporting role as society woman.

Man Who Dared, The (1933) 75m. **½ D: Hamilton McFadden. Preston Foster, Zita Johann, Joan Marsh, Frank Sheridan. Modest but engrossing film based on life of Anton Cermak, Polish immigrant who became Chicago mayor and died when hit by bullet intended for FDR. Foster is excellent.

Man Who Died Twice, The (1958) 70m. ** D: Joseph Kane. Rod Cameron, Vera Ralston, Mike Mazurki, Gerald Milton. Ralston's last film to date is mild account of chanteuse involved in murder.

Man Who Died Twice, The (1970) C-100m. TVM D: Joseph Sargent. Stuart Whitman, Brigitte Fossey, Jeremy Slate, Bernard Lee, Severn Darden, Peter Damon. Odd plot features Whitman as aimless drifter and painter in Spain, attracted to depressed French girl, unaware of her love's shady background. Various well-conceived supporting characters make lead character's pre-

vious life interesting, but film as whole fails to jell. Above average.

Man Who Fell to Earth, The (1976-British) C-125m. ***½ D: Nicolas Roeg. David Bowie, Rip Torn, Candy Clark, Buck Henry, Bernie Casey, Jackson D. Kane. Title character ostensibly heads world conglomerate, but is actually here to find water for his planet. Highly original, fabulously photographed sci-fi drama is riveting for the first two-thirds, goes downhill toward the end. Still tops of its kind. Released in England at 140m.

Man Who Finally Died, The (1962-British) 100m. ** D: Quentin Lawrence. Stanley Baker, Peter Cushing, Mai Zetterling, Eric Portman, Niall MacGinnis, Nigel Green, Barbara Everest. Tepid attempt at Hitchcocklike thriller: Baker returns to German home town and tries to discover what happened to his father during WW2.

Man Who Haunted Himself, The (1970-British) C-94m. ** D: Basil Dearden. Roger Moore, Hildegard Neil, Alastair Mackenzie, Hugh Mackenzie, Kevork Malikyan. Strange psychological drama about aftermath of a car crash involving Moore. Mildly interesting; good location footage of London.

Man Who Knew Too Much, The (1934-British) 84m. *** D: Alfred Hitchcock. Leslie Banks, Edna Best, Peter Lorre, Nova Pilbeam, Frank Vosper, Pierre Fresnay. Film buffs argue which version of exciting story is better. We vote for this one, with Hitchcock in fine form weaving dry British humor into a story of heartpounding suspense: young girl is kidnapped to prevent her parents from revealing what they've learned about assassination plot.

Man Who Knew Too Much, The (1956) C-120m. **½ D: Alfred Hitchcock. James Stewart, Doris Day, Brenda De Banzie, Bernard Miles, Ralph Truman, Alan Mowbray, Carolyn Jones, Hillary Brooke. Hitchcock's remake of his 1934 film is disappointing. Even famous Albert Hall murder sequence rings flat in tale of American couple accidentally involved in international intrigue. Doris' song "Que Sera, Sera" grows tiresome after several performances.

Man Who Lived Again, The (1936-British) 61m. ** D: Robert Stevenson. Boris Karloff, Anna Lee, John Loder, Frank Cellier, Lyn Harding,

Cecil Parker. Mad-doctor plot X-22 again, with Karloff transplanting brains from one human to another; not bad. Retitled: MAN WHO CHANGED HIS MIND.

Man Who Lived Twice, The (1936) 73m. **½ D: Harry Lachman. Ralph Bellamy, Marian Marsh, Thurston Hall, Isabel Jewell, Nana Bryant, Ward Bond. Killer (Bellamy) ditches his cohorts, undergoes brain surgery which literally changes him into a new man. Interesting premise should have made for better film. Remade as MAN IN THE DARK (1953).

Man Who Loved Cat Dancing, The (1973) C-114m. *** D: Richard C. Sarafian. Burt Reynolds, Sarah Miles, George Hamilton, Lee J. Cobb, Jack Warden, Jay Silverheels. Western tale of defiant woman who leaves her husband and takes up riding along with a band of outlaws. Sluggish in spots, but enjoyable, nonetheless.

Man Who Loved Redheads, The (1955-British) C-103m. *** D: Harold French. John Justin, Moira Shearer, Roland Culver, Denholm Elliott, Harry Andrews, Patricia Cutts. Delightful British comedy written by Terence Rattigan about a man with lifelong crush on redheads, dating back to boyhood meeting with beautiful Shearer. American print runs 89m.

Man Who Never Was, The (1956-British) C-103m. *** D: Ronald Neame. Clifton Webb, Gloria Grahame, Robert Flemyng, Josephine Griffin, Stephen Boyd. Good WW2 spy yarn based on true story of Allies planting elaborate red herring to divert attention from invasion of Sicily.

Man Who Played God, The (1932) 81m. **½ D: John G. Adolfi. George Arliss, Bette Davis, Violet Heming, Louise Closser Hale, Donald Cook, Ray Milland. Well-acted tale of musician Arliss going deaf, infatuated student Davis sticking by him. Not as stagy as other Arliss films, with Bette getting her first break and young Milland in a small role. Remade as SINCERELY YOURS.

Man Who Reclaimed His Head, The (1934) 80m. *** D: Edward Ludwig. Claude Rains, Lionel Atwill, Joan Bennett, Baby Jane, Henry O'Neill, Wallace Ford. Odd drama adapted from Jean Bart stage play, told in flashback. Struggling writer and advocate of world peace used by capitalists (led by Atwill) to their own, selfish ends. Unusual story well acted, especially by Rains, but too slowly paced.

Man Who Skied Down Everest, The (1976-Japanese) C-86m. **½ Irresistible idea for a documentary (Japanese sports figure Yuichiro Miura's 1970 expedition) sabotaged by inane narration on soundtrack of English language version. Oscar winner for Best Documentary.

Man Who Shot Liberty Valance, The (1962) 122m. **½ D: John Ford. James Stewart, John Wayne, Vera Miles, Lee Marvin, Edmond O'Brien, Andy Devine, Woody Strode, Ken Murray, John Qualen. Fine cast, directed by Western master Ford, produces a passable film. Marvin stands out as a despicable villain; Wayne and Stewart fight over Miles. O'Brien doesn't bother with subtlety in role of boozing newspaperman.

Man Who Talked Too Much, The (1940) 75m. **½ D: Vincent Sherman. George Brent, Virginia Bruce, Brenda Marshall, Richard Barthelmess, William Lundigan, George Tobias. Good courtroom drama with D.A. Brent and lawyer Lundigan, brothers fighting same case. Remake of THE MOUTHPIECE, made again as ILLEGAL.

Man Who Turned to Stone, The (1957) 80m. BOMB D: Leslie Kardos. Victor Jory, Ann Doran, Charlotte Austin, William Hudson, Paul Cavanagh, Jean Willes, Victor Varconi. Weirdos find life-restoring formula. Hokum!

Man Who Understood Women, The (1959) C-105m. **½ D: Nunnally Johnson. Leslie Caron, Henry Fonda, Cesare Danova, Myron McCormick, Marcel Dalio, Conrad Nagel. Unsatisfactory narrative of moviemaker genius Fonda who hasn't slightest notion of how to treat wife Caron.

Man Who Wanted to Live Forever, The (1970) C-100m. TVM D: John Trent. Stuart Whitman, Sandy Dennis, Burl Ives. New head of heart research center in Canadian wilderness slowly realizes diabolical purpose of current project. Poor climax, script, and dialogue. Average: Jumbled due to cutting from original length used for foreign release. Alternate title: ONLY WAY OUT IS DEAD.

Man Who Would Be King, The
(1975) C-129m. *** D: John Huston.
Sean Connery, Michael Caine, Christopher Plummer, Saeed Jaffrey, Shakira Caine. Old-fashioned adventure and derring-do from Kipling via Huston: two British soldier-pals try to bamboozle high priests of remote Kafiristan into turning over their riches by convincing them that Connery is a God. Caine and Connery are ideal, and film is entertaining, but lacks the buoyancy to make it another GUNGA DIN.

Man Who Wouldn't Die, The (1942) 65m. ** D: Herbert I. Leeds. Lloyd Nolan, Marjorie Weaver, Helene Reynolds, Henry Wilcoxon. Nolan is efficient as wisecracking detective Mike Shayne with a tougher caper than usual.

Man Who Wouldn't Talk, The (1940) 72m. ** D: David Burton. Lloyd Nolan, Jean Rogers, Onslow Stevens, Eric Blore, Mae Marsh. Routine drama with Nolan refusing to defend himself on murder charge; silly ending. Based on one-act play THE VALIANT filmed in 1929 with Paul Muni.

Man Who Wouldn't Talk, The (1958-British) 97m. *½ D: Herbert Wilcox. Anna Neagle, Anthony Quayle, Zsa Zsa Gabor, Katherine Kath, Dora Bryan. Britain's foremost female lawyer (Neagle) defends Quayle on murder charge, even though he cannot speak, for fear of revealing top-secret information. Dreadful.

Man With a Cloak, The (1951) 81m. **½ D: Fletcher Markle. Joseph Cotten, Barbara Stanwyck, Louis Calhern, Leslie Caron. Period melodrama of Stanwyck's love for Cotten, revealed in climax to be famous American writer.

Man with a Million (1954-British) C-90m. **½ D: Ronald Neame. Gregory Peck, Jane Griffith, Ronald Squire, A. E. Matthews, Wilfrid Hyde-White, Reginald Beckwith. Often tedious telling of Mark Twain story of American Peck given million-pound note, and the havoc it causes. Original title: THE MILLION POUND NOTE.

Man with Connections, The (1970-French) C-93m. **½ D: Claude Berri. Guy Bedos, Yves Robert, Rosy Varte, Georges Geret, Zorica Lozic. Good-natured comedy about young Frenchman who tries to use "pull" to make Army hitch as pleasant as possible. Berri's autobiographical film is, like his others, amiable, quietly entertaining.

Man With My Face, The (1951) 86m. ** D: Edward Montagne. Barry Nelson, Lynn Ainley, John Harvey, Carole Mathews. Good plot idea not handled too well: predicament of businessman who discovers lookalike has taken over his life completely.

Man with Nine Lives, The (1940) 73m. **½ D: Nick Grinde. Boris Karloff, Roger Pryor, Jo Ann Sayers, Stanley Brown, John Dilson, Hal Taliaferro. Scientist Karloff seeks cure for cancer by freezing bodies in suspended animation. Hokey, but fun when Karloff dethaws. Also known as BEHIND THE DOOR.

Man with the Balloons, The (1968-Italian-French) 85m. ** D: Marco Ferreri. Marcello Mastroianni, Catherine Spaak. Mastroianni plays successful businessman who loses his girl, eventually goes mad because he becomes obsessed with finding out how much air a balloon needs before it bursts. Offbeat idea, to be sure, but result is just plain silly.

Man With the Golden Arm, The (1955) 119m. *** D: Otto Preminger. Frank Sinatra, Eleanor Parker, Kim Novak, Darren McGavin, Arnold Stang, Doro Merande. Then-daring film of drug addiction is now dated, but still powerful; Sinatra as addict, Parker the crippled wife. Memorable Elmer Bernstein jazz score.

Man With the Golden Gun, The (1974-British) C-125m. *** D: Guy Hamilton. Roger Moore, Christopher Lee, Britt Ekland, Maud Adams, Herve Villechaize. Moore's second time as super agent James Bond is good, gimmicky fun but the actor had one more film to go (THE SPY WHO LOVED ME) before actually growing into the character. Great car stunts, worldwide locales.

Man With the Gun (1955) 83m. **½ D: Richard Wilson. Robert Mitchum, Jan Sterling, Angie Dickinson, Barbara Lawrence, Karen Sharpe, Henry Hull. Mitchum as lawman who brings peace to a Western town is the whole show.

Man With the Power, The (1977) C-100m. TVM D: Nicholas Sgarro. Bob Neill, Persis Khambatta, Tim O'Connor, Vic Morrow, Roger Perry. High school teacher discovers he has inherited superhuman powers from his dad, a native of another planet, and is made an operative of a secret government agency. Entertaining "Six Million Dollar Man" stuff but this fellow does it, literally, with the blink of an eye. Average.

Man With Two Faces, The (1934) 72m. ** D: Archie Mayo. Edward G. Robinson, Mary Astor, Ricardo Cortez, Mae Clarke, Louis Calhern. So-so murder yarn of death of cruel husband investigated by police.

Man Without a Country, The (1973) C-78m. TVM D: Delbert Mann. Cliff Robertson, Beau Bridges, Peter Strauss, Robert Ryan, Walter Abel, John Cullum, Geoffrey Holder, Sheppard Strudwick, Patricia Elliott. Tour-de-force performance by Robertson as Philip Nolan makes this filming of the Edward Everett Hale classic shine. Not much action but a magnificent character study. Above average.

Man Without a Star (1955) C-89m. *** D: King Vidor. Kirk Douglas, Jeanne Crain, Claire Trevor, Richard Boone, Jay C. Flippen, William Campbell. Rugged western with individualist Douglas helping Crain keep her ranch land, dallying with saloon gal Trevor. Remade as A MAN CALLED GANNON.

Mandrake (1979) C-100m. TVM D: Harry Falk. Anthony Herrera, Simone Griffeth, Ji-Tu Cumbuka, Gretchen Corbett, Peter Haskell, Robert Reed. The long-time comic-strip favorite's TV debut in this pilot had him using his legendary legerdermain to fight an extortionist trying to take a business tycoon for $10-million. Average.

Man-Eater of Hydra (1967-West German-Spanish) C-88m. ** D: Mel Welles, Cameron Mitchell, Elisa Montes, George Martin, Kay Fischer, Ralph Naukoff. Remote island with meat-eating plants is setting for predictable, mildly entertaining horror pic. Interesting special effects and atmosphere obscure silly script. Alternate title: ISLAND OF THE DOOMED.

Man-Eater of Kumaon (1948) 79m. **½ D: Byron Haskin. Sabu, Wendell Corey, Joy Ann Page, Morris Carnovsky, Argentina Brunetti. Good adventure tale of hunter determined to kill deadly tiger on the loose.

Maneaters Are Loose! (1978) C-100m. TVM D: Timothy Galfas. Tom Skerritt, Steve Forrest, G. D. Spradlin, Harry Morgan, Diana Muldaur, Dabney Coleman. Down-and-out animal trainer abandons his tigers near a small California community and lets them fend for themselves. Average.

Man-Made Monster (1941) 59m. ** D: George Waggner. Lionel Atwill, Lon Chaney, Jr., Anne Nagel, Frank Albertson, Samuel S. Hinds, William B. Davidson, Ben Taggart, Connie Bergen. Sci-fi yarn of scientist Atwill making Chaney invulnerable to electricity; fairly well done. Mainly for fans of the genre.

Man's Castle (1933) 75m. ***½ D: Frank Borzage. Spencer Tracy, Loretta Young, Glenda Farrell, Arthur Hohl, Walter Connolly, Marjorie Rambeau. Lovely little Depression film of young couple struggling for happiness despite poverty.

Man's Favorite Sport? (1964) C-120m. **½ D: Howard Hawks. Rock Hudson, Paula Prentiss, John McGiver, Maria Perschy, Roscoe Karns. Labored comedy of author Hudson trying to live up to his book on outdoor life, with predictable sight gags about fishing.

Manchu Eagle Murder Caper Mystery (1973) C-80m. **½ D: Dean Hargrove. Gabriel Dell, Will Geer, Joyce Van Patten, Anjanette Comer, Jackie Coogan, Huntz Hall, Barbara Harris. Fairly successful satire of tough private eye melodramas of 1940s. Cast and director on top of their material help make up for cheapness of production.

Manchurian Candidate, The (1962) 126m. ***½ D: John Frankenheimer. Frank Sinatra, Laurence Harvey, Janet Leigh, Angela Lansbury, Henry Silva, James Gregory. Topical drama of political assassination, brilliantly directed, with cast filling their roles admirably; set in Korea and U.S. Lansbury stands out in fine cast.

Mandalay (1934) 65m. **½ D: Michael Curtiz. Kay Francis, Lyle Talbot, Warner Oland, Rafaela Ottiano, Ruth Donnelly, Shirley Temple. Exotic Rangoon is setting for yarn about shady girl Francis in love with alcoholic medico Talbot.

Mandy SEE: **Crash of Silence**

Maneater (1973) C-78m. TVM D: Vince Edwards. Ben Gazzara, Sheree North, Kip Niven, Laurette Spang, Richard Basehart, Claire Brennan. Four city-bred vacationers vs. two hungry tigers set on them by mad animal trainer Basehart. Interesting thriller written by director Edwards and acted with verve by good cast. Above average.

Manfish (1956) C-76m. ** D: W. Lee Wilder. John Bromfield, Lon Chaney, Victor Jory, Barbara Nichols. Variation of Edgar Allan Poe's GOLD BUG story. Film is timid account of treasure hunt in Jamaica.

Manhandled (1949) 97m. ** D: Lewis R. Foster. Dan Duryea, Dorothy Lamour, Sterling Hayden, Irene Hervey. Turgid murder drama that reliable cast can't salvage; incredibly slow.

Manhattan (1979) 96m. ***½ D: Woody Allen. Woody Allen, Diane Keaton, Michael Murphy, Mariel Hemingway, Anne Byrne, Meryl Streep. Bittersweet slice-of-life about a New York comedy writer and his cerebral friends; blisteringly accurate and ultimately poignant, a worthy followup to Woody's ANNIE HALL.

Manhattan Melodrama (1934) 93m. *** D: W. S. Van Dyke, II. Clark Gable, William Powell, Myrna Loy, Leo Carrillo, Isabel Jewell, Mickey Rooney, Nat Pendleton. Boyhood chums Gable and Powell become gangster and D. A., respectively; friendship and love for Loy conflict in interesting drama. Story reused many times, seldom topped this version.

Manhunt in the Jungle (1958) C-79m. BOMB D: Tom McGowan. Robin Hughes, Luis Alvarez, James Wilson, Jorge Montoro, John B. Symmes. Hackneyed safari set in Brazil.

Manhunter (1974) C-78m TVM D: Walter Grauman. Ken Howard, Gary Lockwood, Tim O'Connor, James Olson, Stefanie Powers, John Anderson, L. Q. Jones. Period action drama pitting ex-marine (WWI) Howard against Bonnie-and-Clyde style bank robbers. Later became a series. Average.

Maniac (1962-British) 86m. **½ D: Michael Carreras. Kerwin Mathews, Nadia Gray, Donald Houston, Justine Lord. One of the better British thrillers made in wake of PSYCHO, with Mathews as vacationing artist in France arousing hatred of girlfriend's sick father. Good plot twists.

Manila Calling (1942) 81m. ** D: Herbert I. Leeds. Lloyd Nolan, Carole Landis, Cornel Wilde, James Gleason, Martin Kosleck, Ralph Byrd, Elisha Cook, Jr., Louis Jean Heydt. Pat WW2 film of one guy taking 'em all on with his small but dedicated outfit.

Manitou, The (1978) C-104m. BOMB D: William Girdler. Tony Curtis, Susan Strasberg, Michal Ansara, Ann Sothern, Burgess Meredith, Stella Stevens. Long-dead Indian medicine man gets himself resurrected through a fetus on Susan Strasberg's neck. Veterans Curtis, Sothern, and Meredith look properly embarrassed.

Mannequin (1937) 95m. **½ D: Frank Borzage. Joan Crawford, Spencer Tracy, Alan Curtis, Ralph Morgan, Leo Gorcey, Elisabeth Risdon. Prototype rags-to-riches soaper, with working-girl Crawford getting ahead via wealthy Tracy. Predictable script, but nice job by stars, usual MGM gloss (even in the tenements!).

Manpower (1941) 105m. *** D: Raoul Walsh. Edward G. Robinson, Marlene Dietrich, George Raft, Alan Hale, Walter Catlett, Frank McHugh, Eve Arden. Lively, typical Warner Bros. film, with nightclub "hostess" Dietrich coming between Robinson and Raft. One scene in a diner is worth the price of admission.

Mansion of the Doomed (1977) C-85m. *½ D: Michael Pataki. Richard Basehart, Gloria Grahame, Trish Stewart, Lance Henrikson, Al Ferrara. Eye surgeon Basehart seeks eyeballs for blinded daughter from hapless victims who pile up in basement. Cheap horror opus.

Manuela SEE: **Stowaway Girl**

Many Rivers to Cross (1955) C-92m. **½ D: Roy Rowland. Robert Taylor, Eleanor Parker, Victor McLaglen, James Arness, Josephine Hutchinson, Rosemary DeCamp. Parker shows more vim and vigor than Taylor in this 1800s Western, centering on her yen for him.

Mara Maru (1952) 98m. **½ D: Gordon Douglas, Errol Flynn, Ruth Roman, Raymond Burr, Richard Webb, Nestor Paiva. Turgid flick of Flynn vs. Burr for sunken treasure, with Roman the love interest.

Mara of the Wilderness (1965) C-90m. **½ D: Frank McDonald. Adam West, Linda Saunders, Theo Marcuse, Denver Pyle, Sean McClory. Sometimes diverting account of Saunders, who grew up in the wild north country, with West trying to rehabilitate her.

Maracaibo (1958) C-88m. **½ D: Cornel Wilde. Cornel Wilde, Jean Wallace, Abbe Lane, Francis Lederer, Michael Landon. Wilde is expert firefighter who goes to Venezuela to combat oil blaze, romancing ex-girlfriend between action scenes.

Marat Sade (Persecution and Assassination of Jean-Paul Marat as Performed by the Inmates of the Asylum of Charenton Under the Direction of the Marquis de Sade) (1967-British) C-115m. **** D: Peter Brook. Patrick Magee, Clifford Rose, Glenda Jackson, Ian Richardson, Brenda Kempner, Ruth Baker, Michael Williams, Freddie Jones. Chilling adaptation of Peter Weiss play about "performance" staged by inmates of French insane asylum, under direction of Marquis de Sade. Lurid atmosphere is so vivid that it seems actors are breathing down your neck; brilliantly directed by Brook. Not for weak stomachs.

Marathon (1980) C-100m. TVM D: Jackie Cooper. Bob Newhart, Leigh Taylor-Young, Herb Edelman, Dick Gautier, Anita Gillette, John Hillerman. Flat comedy dealing with a happily married middle-aged stockbroker whose head is turned by a pretty young thing and is encouraged to move from casual jogging to marathon running. Average.

Marathon Man (1976) C-125m. **½ D: John Schlesinger. Dustin Hoffman, Laurence Olivier, Roy Scheider, William Devane, Marthe Keller, Fritz Weaver. Glossy thriller adapted by William Goldman from his book. Basic premise of graduate student Hoffman propelled into dizzying world of international intrigue spoiled by repellent violence and some gaping story holes. Hoffman and arch-villain Olivier are superb but the film doesn't do them justice.

Marauders, The (1955) C-81m. ** D: Gerald Mayer. Dan Duryea, Jeff Richards, Keenan Wynn, Jarma Lewis. OK story of rancher fighting against greedy cattle ranchers.

March of the Wooden Soldiers SEE: **Babes in Toyland**

March or Die (1977) C-104m. ** D: Dick Richards. Gene Hackman, Terence Hill, Max Von Sydow, Catherine Deneuve, Ian Holm. Homage to French Foreign Legion adventures of filmdom's past. Good cast wages losing battle with static script and walks downheartedly through action scenes. Disappointing epic-that-might-have-been.

Marciano (1979) C-100m. TVM D: Bernard L. Kowalski. Tony Lo Bianco, Belinda J. Montgomery, Vincent Gardenia, Richard Herd, Dolph Sweet. The story of heavyweight champ Rocky Marciano—the only fighter to retire from the ring undefeated with a perfect record. The focus here is on his less-than-enthralling private life, and the romantic slush sends Rocky down for the long count. Average.

Marco (1973) C-109m. ** D: Seymour Robbie. Desi Arnaz Jr., Jack Weston, Zero Mostel. Lavish but lumbering musical, filmed on Oriental locations, with Arnaz as young Marco Polo and Mostel as Kublai Khan. Disappointing.

Marco Polo (1962-Italian) C-90m. **½ D: Hugo Fregonese. Rory Calhoun, Yoko Tani, Robert Hundar, Camillo Pilotto, Pierre Cressoy, Michael Chow. Unspectacular epic about medieval adventurer and his journey to China. Calhoun and film lack needed vigor.

Marco the Magnificent (1966) C-100m. **½ D: Denys De La Patelliere, Noel Howard. Horst Buchholz, Anthony Quinn, Omar Sharif, Elsa Martinelli, Akim Tamiroff, Orson Welles. Laughable mini-epic, extremely choppy, with episodic sequences pretending to recount events in life of medieval adventurer.

Marcus-Nelson Murders, The (1973) 148m. TVM D: Joseph Sargent. Telly Savalas, Marjoe Gortner, Jose Ferrer, Ned Beatty, Allen Garfield, Lorraine Gary, Gene Woodbury, Chita Rivera. Top-notch thriller about hard-boiled detective's efforts to keep a ghetto teenager from being wrongly convicted of murder. Based on real life Wylie-Hoffert murders in N.Y. in 1963, it became pilot for long-running Kojak series, won Emmys for director Sargent and writer Abby Mann, and stardom for Savalas. Also known as KOJAK AND THE MARCUS-NELSON MURDERS. Above average.

Marcus Welby, M.D. (1968) C-100m. TVM D: David Lowell Rich. Robert Young, James Brolin, Anne Baxter, Peter Duel, Susan Strasberg, Lew Ayres. When neighborhood doctor, after suffering mild coronary, finally hires assistant to lighten work load, help turns out to be as irascible and stubborn as himself. No different from subsequent TV series. Average. Retitled A MATTER OF HUMANITIES.

Mardi Gras (1958) C-107m. **½ D:

Edmund Goulding. Pat Boone, Christine Carere, Tommy Sands, Sheree North, Gary Crosby. Perky, unpretentious musical with energetic cast. Boone wins military school raffle date with movie star Carere.

Margie (1946) C-94m. *** D: Henry King. Jeanne Crain, Glenn Langan, Lynn Bari, Esther Dale, Hobart Cavanaugh, Ann B. Todd. Occasionally cloying but entertaining tale of teenagers during the roaring 20s; good song "3:00 in the Morning," title tune.

Margin for Error (1943) 74m. ** D: Otto Preminger. Joan Bennett, Milton Berle, Otto Preminger, Carl Esmond, Howard Freeman, Ed McNamara. Dated, awkward "comedy" of Jewish cop Berle assigned to guard German consul in N.Y.C. during WW2. Director Preminger should have told actor Preminger to stop overacting.

Marianne (1929) 112m. *** D: Robert Z. Leonard. Marion Davies, George Baxter, Lawrence Gray, Cliff Edwards, Benny Rubin. Davies' first talkie also one of her best; fine vehicle for her charm and comic talent as French girl pursued by two American soldiers during WW1.

Marie Antoinette (1938) 160m. **½ D: W. S. Van Dyke II. Norma Shearer, Tyrone Power, John Barrymore, Robert Morley, Gladys George, Anita Louise, Joseph Schildkraut. Opulent MGM production of life of 18th-century French queen lacks pace but has good acting, with great performance by Morley as Louis XVI. Shearer captures essence of title role as costumer retells her life from Austrian princess to doomed queen of crumbling empire.

Marie Antoinette (1955-French) C-108m. **½ D: Jean Delannoy. Michele Morgan, Richard Todd, Jean Morel. Epic on life of famed 18th-century French queen has marvelous Morgan in title role but lacks perspective and scope.

Marilyn (1963) 83m. **½ Narrated by Rock Hudson. Standard, often patronizing documentary on Marilyn Monroe built around clips from most of her movies, including the unfinished SOMETHING'S GOT TO GIVE.

Marine Raiders (1944) 91m. ** D: Harold D. Schuster. Pat O'Brien, Robert Ryan, Ruth Hussey, Frank McHugh, Barton MacLane. Typical RKO WW2 film, this time focusing on marines training for warfare.

Marines, Let's Go (1961) C-104m. *½ D: Raoul Walsh. Tom Tryon, David Hedison, Barbara Stuart, William Tyler. Tedium of four G.I.s on leave in Tokyo.

Marjoe (1972) C-88m. **½ D: Howard Smith, Sarah Kernochan. Oscar-winning documentary about life of fake evangelist Marjoe Gortner is certainly interesting, but is a little too pleased with itself, a little too pat to be totally convincing. Marjoe himself is likable enough.

Marjorie Morningstar (1958) C-123m. **½ D: Irving Rapper. Gene Kelly, Natalie Wood, Claire Trevor, Ed Wynn, Everett Sloane, Carolyn Jones, Martin Milner. Wood is only adequate as Herman Wouk's heroine in tale of N.Y.C. gal aspiring to greatness but ending up a suburban housewife, with Kelly her summer romance.

Mark, The (1961-British) 127m. **** D: Guy Green. Stuart Whitman, Maria Schell, Rod Steiger, Brenda De Banzie. Whitman received Oscar nomination for portrayal of emotionally broken sex criminal who has served time, now wants to make new start. Excellent cast and direction.

Mark of the Gorilla (1950) 68m. D: William Berke. Johnny Weissmuller, Trudy Marshall, Onslow Stevens, Selmer Jackson. SEE: Jungle Jim series.

Mark of the Hawk, The (1957-British) C-83m. *** D: Michael Audley. Eartha Kitt, Sidney Poitier, Juano Hernandez, John McIntire. Unusual tale intelligently acted, set in contemporary Africa, with peaceful vs. violent means for Negro equality the main theme. Originally titled ACCUSED.

Mark of the Renegade (1951) C-81m. **½ D: Hugo Fregonese. Ricardo Montalban, Cyd Charisse, J. Carrol Naish, Gilbert Roland. Peculiar Western tale of 1820s, with Montalban an outlaw who romances Charisse.

Mark of the Vampire (1935) 61m. *** D: Tod Browning. Lionel Barrymore, Elizabeth Allan, Bela Lugosi, Lionel Atwill, Carol Borland, Jean Hersholt, Donald Meek. Delightful, intriguing tale of vampires terrorizing rural village; inspector Atwill, vampire-expert Barrymore investigate. Beautifully done, with an incredible ending.

Mark of the Vampire (1957) SEE: Vampire, The

Mark of the Whistler, The (1944) 61m. D: William Castle. Richard Dix, Janis Carter, Porter Hall, Paul Guilfoyle, John Calvert. SEE: The Whistler series.

Mark of Zorro, The (1920) 90m. *** D: Fred Niblo. Douglas Fairbanks Sr., Marguerite De La Motte, Noah Beery, Robert McKim, Charles Mailes. Silent classic with Fairbanks as the hero of old California, perhaps Doug's best film. Nonstop fun.

Mark of Zorro, The (1940) 93m. ***½ D: Rouben Mamoulian. Tyrone Power, Linda Darnell, Basil Rathbone, Gale Sondergaard, Eugene Pallette, J. Edward Bromberg. Lavish swashbuckler with Power as foppish son of California aristocrat in 1800s, masquerading as dashing avenger of evil: climactic duel with Rathbone a cinematic gem.

Mark of Zorro, The (1974) C-78m. TVM D: Don McDougall. Frank Langella, Ricardo Montalban, Gilbert Roland, Yvonne de Carlo, Louise Sorel, Anne Archer, Robert Middleton. Langella buckles and swashes in this tepid remake. Montalban is properly villainous, Roland surprisingly spry at wall-scaling. Best of all: unforgettable Alfred Newman musical score from the 1940 film, interpolated here. Average.

Marked Woman (1937) 99m. *** D: Lloyd Bacon. Bette Davis, Humphrey Bogart, Lola Lane, Isabel Jewell, Jane Bryan, Eduardo Ciannelli, Allen Jenkins, Mayo Methot. Bristling gangster drama of D.A. Bogart convincing Bette and four girlfriends to testify against their boss, underworld king Ciannelli.

Marksman, The (1953) 62m. *½ D: Lewis D. Collins. Wayne Morris, Elena Verdugo, Frank Ferguson, Rick Vallin. Flabby little tale of Morris, a law enforcer with a telescopic gun, chasing after outlaws.

Marlowe (1969) C-95m. *** D: Paul Bogart, James Garner, Gayle Hunnicutt, Carroll O'Connor, Rita Moreno, Sharon Farrell, William Daniels, Jackie Coogan. Slick updating of Raymond Chandler's THE LITTLE SISTER with Garner as Philip Marlowe, hired by girl to find missing brother. Really belongs in 1940s, but works fairly well; Moreno memorable as stripper who helps solve case in exciting finale (which may be trimmed for TV).

Marnie (1964) C-129m. *** D: Alfred Hitchcock. Sean Connery, Tippi Hedren, Diane Baker, Martin Gabel, Louise Latham, Alan Napier. This story of a habitual thief (Hedren) whose employer (Connery) is determined to understand her illness was considered a misfire in 1964 . . . but there's more than meets the eye, especially for Hitchcock buffs.

Maroc 7 (1967-British) C-91m. ** D: Gerry O'Hara. Gene Barry, Elsa Martinelli, Cyd Charisse, Leslie Phillips. Slow robbery-murder tale of secret agent out to catch split-personality thief.

Marooned (1969) C-134m. ** D: John Sturges. Gregory Peck, Richard Crenna, James Franciscus, David Janssen, Gene Hackman, Lee Grant, Nancy Kovack, Mariette Hartley. Glossy but disappointing story of astronauts unable to return to earth, while space agency head Peck tries to keep lid from blowing off. Alternately boring and excruciating; climactic scenes in space produce agony, not excitement. Oscar-winning special effects are chief asset.

Marquise of O, The (1976-French-German) C-102m. *** D: Eric Rohmer. Edith Clever, Bruno Ganz, Peter Luhr, Edda Seippel, Otto Sander. Delicate, disarmingly simple story set in 18th century Italy; a young widow saved from rape by a Russian soldier during Franco-Prussian war finds herself pregnant some months later, and doesn't understand how. Beautiful period flavor, but film's charm is very low-key.

Marriage-Go-Round, The (1960) C-98m. **½ D: Walter Lang. Susan Hayward, James Mason, Julie Newmar, Robert Paige, June Clayworth. Film version of Leslie Stevens' saucy play about marriage: Mason is professor attracted to free-love-oriented Newmar. Amusing, but lacks real bite.

Marriage is a Private Affair (1944) 116m. ** D: Robert Z. Leonard. Lana Turner, James Craig, John Hodiak, Frances Gifford, Hugh Marlowe, Keenan Wynn. Somewhat dated, glossy MGM yarn of man-chasing Turner, not about to be stopped just because she's married.

Marriage Is Alive and Well (1980) C-100m. TVM D: Russ Mayberry. Joe Namath, Jack Albertson, Melinda Dillon, Judd Hirsch, Susan Sullivan, Fred McCarren, Nicholas Pryor. Standard sitcom view of marriage with Namath playing a free-lance wedding photographer tying together several occasionally humorous vignettes. Average.

Marriage Italian-Style (1964-Italian) C-102m. *** D: Vittorio De Sica. Sophia Loren, Marcello Mastroianni, Aldo Puglisi, Pia Lindstrom, Vito Moriconi. Spicy account of Loren's efforts to get long-time lover Mastroianni to marry her and stay her husband.

Marriage of a Young Stockbroker, The (1971) C-95m. **½ D: Lawrence Turman. Richard Benjamin, Joanna Shimkus, Elizabeth Ashley, Adam West, Patricia Barry, Tiffany Bolling. Humorous and sad depiction of marital breakdown; husband indulges in voyeurism, wife has own problems. Good cast working with script that seems uncertain as to what point it wants to drive across. Beware cuts.

Marriage on the Rocks (1965) C-109m. **½ D: Jack Donohue. Frank Sinatra, Deborah Kerr, Dean Martin, Cesar Romero, Hermione Baddeley, Tony Bill, Nancy Sinatra, John McGiver, Trini Lopez. Frank and Deborah have marital spat, get quickie Mexican divorce, she ends up married to his best pal, Dino. Good cast helps typical comedy.

Marriage: Year One (1971) C-100m. TVM D: William Graham. Sally Field, Robert Pratt, Cicely Tyson, William Windom, Agnes Moorehead, Neville Brand. Tedious love story, with modern city important backdrop as two newlyweds try to make it through first tough year. Great supporting cast only asset. Average.

Married Woman, The (1965-French) 94m. **½ D: Jean-Luc Godard. Macha Meril, Philippe Leroy, Bernard Noel. Turgid three-cornered romance, with Meril involved with husband and lover; often pretentious film.

Marry Me Again (1953) 73m. ** D: Frank Tashlin. Robert Cummings, Marie Wilson, Mary Costa, Jess Barker. Mild shenanigans of aviator Cummings and beauty contest winner Wilson's on-again, off-again romance.

Marry Me, Marry Me (1969-French) C-87m. *** D: Claude Berri. Elizabeth Wiener, Regine, Claude Berri, Luisa Colpeyn. Delightful story of love and (what else?) marriage, Berri-style.

Marrying Kind, The (1952) 93m. *** D: George Cukor. Judy Holliday, Aldo Ray, Madge Kennedy, Mickey Shaughnessy, Griff Barnett. Bitter-sweet drama of young couple on verge of divorce recalling their life together via flashbacks; sensitive performers outshine soapy script.

Marseilles Contract, The SEE: Destructors, The

Marshal's Daughter, The (1953) 71m. *½ D: William Berke. Ken Murray, Laurie Anders, Preston Foster, Hoot Gibson. Cornpone oater with Murray and Anders ridding their town of outlaws: Tex Ritter even sings a song, with veteran Gibson in supporting role.

Marty (1955) 91m. ***½ D: Delbert Mann. Ernest Borgnine, Betsy Blair, Joe De Santis, Esther Minciotti, Jerry Paris, Karen Steele. Oscar for Borgnine as Bronx butcher who doesn't hope to find love, but does, in this incisive Paddy Chayefsky script, originally a TV play.

Marx Brothers at the Circus SEE: At the Circus

Marx Brothers Go West SEE: Go West

Mary and Joseph: A Story of Faith (1979) C-100m. TVM D: Eric Till. Blanche Baker, Jeff East, Colleen Dewhurst, Stephen McHattie, Lloyd Bochner, Paul Hecht. Pedestrian what-might-have-been depiction of Biblical events focusing on Christ's parents as a struggling young couple and the early days of their marriage. The leads play it as a pair of American youngsters plunked down in Biblical Nazareth. Below average.

Mary Burns, Fugitive (1935) 84m. *** D: William K. Howard. Sylvia Sidney, Melvyn Douglas, Pert Kelton, Alan Baxter, Wallace Ford, Brian Donlevy. Fine gangster melodrama. Sidney is dragged into underworld, valiantly tries to escape her gangster lover (Baxter).

Mary Jane Harper Cried Last Night (1977) C-100m. TVM D: Allen Reisner. Susan Dey, Bernie Casey, Tricia O'Neil, John Vernon, Kevin McCarthy. Drama about child abuse benefits from a sensitive script and sincere performances by all involved. Average.

Mary, Mary (1963) C-126m. **½ D: Mervyn LeRoy. Debbie Reynolds, Barry Nelson, Michael Rennie, Diane McBain. Unremarkable, stagy adaptation of Jean Kerr's sex comedy.

Mary of Scotland (1936) 123m. ***½ D: John Ford. Katharine Hepburn, Fredric March, Florence Eldridge, Douglas Walton, John Carradine, Robert Barrat. Lavish, excellent historical drama, with Hepburn playing Scottish queen sentenced to death by jealous English rival Elizabeth.

Mary, Queen of Scots (1971) C-128m. *** D: Charles Jarrott. Vanessa Redgrave, Glenda Jackson, Patrick McGoohan, Timothy Dalton, Nigel Davenport, Trevor Howard, Daniel Massey, Ian Holm. Inaccurate history lesson but good costume drama, with strong performances from Redgrave as Mary, Jackson as Queen Elizabeth, rivals for power in Tudor England.

Mary White (1977) C-100m. TVM D: Jud Taylor. Ed Flanders, Kathleen Beller, Fionnula Flanagan, Tim Matheson, Donald Moffat. Moving drama, told poetically, based on the writings of Pulitzer Prize-winning newsman William Allen White after the tragic death of his teenaged daughter in 1921. Leisurely-paced, not for every taste, but class tells and so does Ed Flanders, who is superb. Above average.

Maryjane (1968) C-104m. *½ D: Maury Dexter. Fabian, Diane McBain, Michael Margotta, Kevin Coughlin, Patty McCormack. 1960s version of REEFER MADNESS casts Fabian as high school art teacher who tries to keep his students from smoking grass; film is terrible, but may play better if you're stoned.

Maryland (1940) C-92m. **½ D: Henry King. Walter Brennan, Fay Bainter, Brenda Joyce, John Payne, Charles Ruggles, Marjorie Weaver. Predictable story given elaborate treatment. Bainter refuses to let son Payne ride horses since his father was killed that way. Beautiful color scenery.

Masculine-Feminine (1966-French-Swedish) 103m. *** D: Jean-Luc Godard. Jean-Pierre Leaud, Chantal Goya, Marlene Jobert, Michel Debord, Catherine-Isabelle Duport, Eva-Britt Strandberg, Brigitte Bardot. Engaging, original concoction mixes politics, sex, comedy, nostalgia with standard boy-meets-girl theme. Interviewer journalist Leaud has affair with would-be rock star Madeleine in 1960s Paris.

M*A*S*H (1970) C-113m. **** D: Robert Altman. Donald Sutherland, Elliott Gould, Tom Skerritt, Sally Kellerman, Robert Duvall, Jo Ann Pflug, Rene Auberjonois, Roger Bowen, Gary Burghoff, Fred Williamson, John Schuck. Altman's first major success gave new meaning to the word "irreverence," set new style for contemporary filmmaking; follows black-comedy exploits of wild and woolly medical unit during Korean War in hilarious, episodic fashion.

Mask of Dijon, The (1946) 73m. ** D: Lewis Landers. Erich von Stroheim, Jeanne Bates, Denise Vernac, William Wright, Edward Van Sloan. Stroheim is hypnotist who has delusions of grandeur, and schemes in murder attempts; exciting finish.

Mask of Dimitrios, The (1944) 95m. *** D: Jean Negulesco. Peter Lorre, Sydney Greenstreet, Zachary Scott, Faye Emerson, Victor Francen, Eduardo Ciannelli, Florence Bates. Fine, offbeat mystery-melodrama with mild-mannered mystery writer Lorre reviewing life of notorious scoundrel Scott. As always, Lorre and Greenstreet make a marvelous team.

Mask of Fu Manchu, The (1932) 72m. **½ D: Charles Brabin. Boris Karloff, Lewis Stone, Karen Morley, Myrna Loy, Charles Starrett, Jean Hersholt. Elaborate chiller of Chinese madman Karloff menacing expedition in tomb of Ghengis Khan; ornate and hokey, but fun. Loy has exotic role in one of her pre-Thin Man ventures.

Mask of Marcella SEE: Cool Million

Mask of Sheba, The (1969) C-100m. TVM D: David Lowell Rich. Walter Pidgeon, Inger Stevens, Eric Braeden, William Marshall, Stephen Young. Typical jungle drama mixes search for missing safari members, gold statue coveted by natives, treacherous territory, angry tribesmen, intrigue within rescue party. Cast tries hard but script stacked against them. Below average.

Mask of the Avenger (1951) C-83m. ** D: Phil Karlson. John Derek, Anthony Quinn, Jody Lawrance, Arnold Moss. Not up to snuff; man posing as count of Monte Cristo is involved in swordplay.

Masked Marvel, The SEE: Sakima and the Masked Marvel

Masque of the Red Death, The (1964) C-86m. *** D: Roger Corman.

Vincent Price, Hazel Court, Jane Asher, David Weston, Patrick Magee, Skip Martin, Nigel Green. Stylish distillation of two Poe stories features Price as Prince Prospero in eerie, timeless castle stalked by hooded death figures. Made in England.

Masquerade (1965-British) **C-101m.** **½ D: Basil Dearden. Cliff Robertson, Jack Hawkins, Marisa Mell, Michel Piccoli, Bill Fraser, John Le-Mesurier. Above-average spy satire highlighted by Robertson's portrayal of recruited agent. Good support casting with good location shooting to give Arabic atmosphere.

Masquerade in Mexico (1945) **96m.** ** D: Mitchell Leisen. Dorothy Lamour, Arturo de Cordova, Patric Knowles, Ann Dvorak, George Rigaud, Natalie Schafer, Billy Daniels. Frivolous plot, forgettable songs combine in this limp musicomedy of bullfighters, romance, and Mexican intrigue. Remake of MIDNIGHT (1939).

Masquerader, The (1933) **78m.** **½ D: Richard Wallace. Ronald Colman, Elissa Landi, Halliwell Hobbes, Helen Jerome Eddy. Dated but enjoyable film goes on theory that two Colmans are better than one; journalist pretends he is member of Parliament; both roles played by Colman.

Massacre (1956) **C-76m.** ** D: Louis King. Dane Clark, James Craig, Marta Roth, Miguel Torruco, Jaime Fernandez. Uninspired account of greedy Indian gun-sellers.

Massacre at Fort Holman SEE: A Reason to Live, A Reason to Die
Massacre in Rome (1973-Italian) **C-103m.** *** D: George Pan Cosmatos. Richard Burton, Marcello Mastroianni, Leo McKern, John Steiner, Anthony Steel. Good drama has priest Mastroianni opposed to idealistic German Colonel Burton, who must execute 330 Roman hostages in retaliation for the deaths of 33 Nazi soldiers.

Massacre River (1949) **75m.** *½ D: John Rawlins. Guy Madison, Rory Calhoun, Johnny Sands, Carole Mathews, Cathy Downs. Minor Western of trio of soldiers fighting over gals.

Master Gunfighter, The (1975) **C-121m.** BOMB D: Frank Laughlin. Tom Laughlin, Ron O'Neal, Lincoln Kilpatrick, GeoAnn Sosa, Barbara Carrera, Victor Campos. Billy Jack's creator-star is an intense gunfighter who hates to kill but does it just the same. Lots of rhetoric.

Master Minds (1949) **64m.** D: Jean Yarbrough. Leo Gorcey, Huntz Hall, Glenn Strange, Gabriel Dell, Alan Napier, Jane Adams, Billy Benedict, Bernard Gorcey, Bennie Bartlett, David Gorcey. SEE: **Bowery Boys** series.

Master of Ballantrae, The (1953) **C-89m.** **½ D: William Keighley. Errol Flynn, Roger Livesey, Anthony Steel, Yvonne Furneaux. Robert Louis Stevenson's historical yarn. Flynn involved in plot to make Bonnie Prince Charles king of England; on-location filming in Great Britain adds scope to costumer.

Master of the World (1961) **C-104m.** *** D: William Witney. Vincent Price, Charles Bronson, Mary Webster, Henry Hull, Richard Harrison. Good science-fiction based on Jules Verne's stories about a man (Price) who sees himself as the world's ruler, operating from a futuristic zeppelin. Very well done.

Master Race, The (1944) **96m.** *** D: Herbert J. Biberman. George Coulouris, Stanley Ridges, Osa Massen, Nancy Gates, Lloyd Bridges. Engrossing account of German officer who escapes when Nazi empire is destroyed, continuing to plot even afterward.

Master Spy (1964-British) **71m.** **½ D: Montgomery Tully. Stephen Murray, June Thorburn, Alan Wheatley, John Carson. OK drama of Allied counteragent escaping from Communist prison.

Master Touch, The (1974) **C-96m.** ** D: Michele Lupo. Kirk Douglas, Florinda Bolkan, Giuliano Gemma, Rene Koldehoff. Waste of talent Italian-West German co-production. Safecracker Douglas, just out of jail, attempts to rob an insurance company.

Mastermind (1976) **C-131m.** *** D: Alex March. Zero Mostel, Bradford Dillman, Keiko Kishi, Gawn Grainger, Herbert Berghoff, Jules Munshin, Sorrell Booke. Enjoyable spoof of Charlie Chan films with Mostel as Inspector Hoku, who tries to protect robot-like invention sought by international interests. Some good slapstick, rousing car chase. Received limited release after sitting on shelf since 1969.

Masterson of Kansas (1954) **C-73m.** ** D: William Castle. George Montgomery, Nancy Gates, James Griffith, Jean Willes, Benny Rubin. Despite presence of trio of famed gunmen, Doc Holliday, Wyatt Earp and Bat Masterson, film is still standard oater.

Mata Hari (1932) 90m. *** D: George Fitzmaurice. Greta Garbo, Ramon Novarro, Lionel Barrymore, Lewis Stone, C. Henry Gordon, Karen Morley. Garbo is the alluring spy of WW1, beguiling everyone from Novarro to Barrymore. Highlights: Garbo's exotic dance sequence, Morley stalked by gang executioner.

Mata Hari's Daughter (1954-Italian) C-102m. ** D: Renzo Meruis. Frank Latimore, Ludmilla Tcherina, Erno Crisa. Humdrum account of alleged daughter of famed WW1 spy in 1940 Java involved in espionage; sterile dubbing. Retitled: DAUGHTER OF MATA HARI.

Matchless (1967-Italian) C-104m. ** D: Alberto Lattuada. Patrick O'Neal, Ira Furstenberg, Donald Pleasence, Henry Silva. American journalist is tortured in order to obtain information about a lethal chemical substance.

Matchmaker, The (1958) 101m. *** D: Joseph Anthony. Shirley Booth, Anthony Perkins, Shirley MacLaine, Paul Ford, Robert Morse. Thornton Wilder's comedy (Pre-HELLO DOLLY) of turn-of-the century Yonkers matchmaker (Booth) seeking a wife for cantankerous shopowner. Good period-piece; Booth is bright.

Matilda (1978) C-103m. BOMB D: Daniel Mann. Elliott Gould, Robert Mitchum, Harry Guardino, Clive Revill, Karen Carlson, Lionel Stander, Larry Pennell. Good cast wasted in awful kiddie pic about a boxing kangaroo, played by a man in a suit (Gary Morgan).

Mating Game, The (1959) C-96m. *** D: George Marshall. Debbie Reynolds, Tony Randall, Paul Douglas, Fred Clark, Una Merkel, Philip Ober, Charles Lane. Zippy comedy romp of tax agent Randall falling in love with farm girl Reynolds, with Douglas rambunctious as Debbie's father.

Mating of Millie, The (1948) 87m. **½ D: Henry Levin. Glenn Ford, Evelyn Keyes, Ron Randell, Willard Parker, Virginia Hunter. Ford tries to help Keyes trap a husband so she can adopt a child, but falls in love with her himself.

Mating Season, The (1951) 101m.

***½ D: Mitchell Leisen. Gene Tierney, John Lund, Miriam Hopkins, Thelma Ritter, Jan Sterling, Larry Keating, James Lorimer. Excellent, underrated comedy with cynical undertones about the American dream. Hardworking Lund marries socialite Tierney, suffers embarrassment when his plain-talking mother (Ritter) comes to town and is mistaken for servant. Ritter is simply superb.

Matt Helm (1975) C-78m. TVM D: Buzz Kulik. Tony Franciosa, Ann Turkel, Gene Evans, Patrick MacNee, Hari Rhodes, James Shigeta, Laraine Stephens, John Vernon. Private eye Helm finds himself neck deep in international black market arms operation while trying to protect a movie star whose life is threatened. When ol' Dino played Helm in four movies, he was a crack secret agent and more entertaining. Series pilot. Average.

Mattei Affair, The (1973-Italian) C-118m. **½ D: Francesco Rosi. Gian Maria Volonte, Luigi Squarizina, Peter Baldwin. Semi-documentary study of rise of Italian industrialist and his mysterious death.

Matter of Humanities, A: SEE Marcus Welby, M.D.

Matter of Innocence, A (1968-British) C-102m. **½ D: Guy Green. Hayley Mills, Trevor Howard, Sashi Kapoor, Brenda De Banzie. Plain Jane (Mills) travels to Singapore with aunt, has an affair with Eurasian Kapoor and becomes woman. Trite soaper with unusual role for suave Howard; from Noel Coward story "Pretty Polly."

Matter of Resistance, A (1966-French) 92m. **½ D: Jean-Paul Rappeneau. Catherine Deneuve, Philippe Noiret, Pierre Brasseur, Mary Marquet, Henri Garcin, Carlos Thompson. Pleasant French comedy of bored housewife (Deneuve) who welcomes arrival of soldiers to her village prior to Normandy invasion. Originally titled LA VIE DE CHATEAU.

Matter of Time, A (1976) C-99m. BOMB D: Vincente Minnelli. Liza Minnelli, Ingrid Bergman, Charles Boyer, Spiros Andros, Tina Aumont, Anna Proclemer. Depressing schmaltz about a chambermaid in pre-WW1 Europe taught to love life by a batty contessa. Director Minnelli's worst film, though, for his part, he denounced this version as edited.

Matter of Who, A (1962-British) 90m. *** D: Don Chaffey. Terry-Thomas, Alex Nicol, Sonja Ziemann, Guy Deghy, Richard Briers, Carol White, Honor Blackman. Thomas goes through madcap antics involving World Health Organization's tracking down of disease-carrier.

Matter of Wife . . . and Death, A (1975) C-78m. TVM D: Marvin Chomsky. Rod Taylor, Joe Santos, Luke Askew, Tom Drake, John Colicos, Anita Gillette, Ann Archer, Lynda Carter, Cesare Danova. Freewheeling private eye Taylor goes after the killers of friend, a small-time hood, and gets involved in big-time gambling operation. Taylor plays Shamus, the unorthodox detective done on the big screen by Burt Reynolds. Average.

Maurie (1973) C-113m. ** D: Daniel Mann. Bernie Casey, Bo Svenson, Janet MacLachlan, Stephanie Edwards, Paulene Myers, Bill Walker. Well-meaning but downbeat tear-jerker based on true story of basketball star Maurice Stokes (Casey). His sudden paralysis spurs teammate Jack Twyman (Svenson) to devote himself to Maurie's rehabilitation. Too similar to other sports-tragedy films to stand out. Shown on TV as BIG MO.

Maverick Queen, The (1956) C-92m. **½ D: Joseph Kane. Barbara Stanwyck, Barry Sullivan, Scott Brady, Mary Murphy, Wallace Ford. Stanwyck is peppy as outlaw who's willing to go straight for lawman Sullivan.

Maxime (1958-French) 93m. **½ D: Henri Verneuil. Michele Morgan, Charles Boyer, Arletty, Felix Marten. Morgan is good match for Parisian scoundrel Boyer in this love tale set in 1910s.

Maya (1966) C-91m. ** D: John Berry. Clint Walker, Jay North, I. S. Johar, Sajid Kahn, Jairaj, Sonia Sahni. Silly juvenile jungle tale has young North temporarily losing respect for his big-game hunter father Walker, who has lost his nerve.

Maybe I'll Come Home in the Spring (1970) C-74m. TVM D: Joseph Sargent. Sally Field, Jackie Cooper, Eleanor Parker, Lane Bradbury, David Carradine, Ed Lauter. Year in the life of Miller family: Denise (Field) can't take home life, splits for commune existence, returns

after disillusionment and drug experiences take toll. Experiences after she returns make film worthwhile, refusing to pull punches. Game attempt at scripting without set lines of dialogue. Above average.

Mayday at 40,000 Feet! (1976) C-100m. TVM D: Robert Butler. David Janssen, Don Meredith, Christopher George, Ray Milland, Lynda Day George, Marjoe Gortner, Broderick Crawford, Jane Powell. All-star cast aloft with Janssen at the controls, a ruthless killer in first-class, the 747 disabled and the airport snowed in. Just what you'd expect from the title. Average.

Mayerling (1969-British) C-140m. **½ D: Terence Young. Omar Sharif, Catherine Deneuve, James Mason, Ava Gardner, James Robertson Justice, Genevieve Page. Remake of 1937 classic casts Sharif as Austrian prince who defies convention, and his father (Mason), by falling in love with commoner Deneuve. Old-fashioned tragic romance is pleasant but uncompelling. Justice steals film as spirited Prince of Wales.

Mayflower: The Pilgrims' Adventure (1979) C-100m. TVM D: George Schaeffer. Anthony Hopkins, Richard Crenna, Jenny Agutter, Trish Van Devere, John Heffernan, David Dukes, Michael Beck. Lavish production, earnest performances, period costumes—but it's reduced to soap opera circa 1620. Stick with Spencer Tracy & friends in PLYMOUTH ADVENTURE. Average.

Maytime (1937) 132m. *** D: Robert Z. Leonard. Jeanette MacDonald, Nelson Eddy, John Barrymore, Herman Bing, Rafaela Ottiano, Paul Porcasi, Sig Ruman. One of singing duo's best films, despite occasional heavy-handedness and piercing operatic sequence near the end. Exquisite filming of simple story: opera star and penniless singer fall in love in Paris, but her husband/mentor (Barrymore) interferes. Songs include "Will You Remember," "Sweetheart."

Maytime in Mayfair (1952-British) 94m. **½ D: Herbert Wilcox. Anna Neagle, Michael Wilding, Peter Graves, Nicholas Phipps. Guided tour through chic London with its society folks, enhanced by Neagle and Wilding.

Maze, The (1953) 81m. ** D: William Cameron Menzies. Richard

Carlson, Veronica Hurst, Hillary Brooke, Michael Pate. Spotty chiller, with eerie British castle inherited by Carlson the focal point.

Me and the Colonel (1958) 109m. **½ D: Peter Glenville. Danny Kaye, Curt Jurgens, Nicole Maurey, Francoise Rosay. Franz Werfel's JACOBOWSKY AND THE COLONEL is source for spotty satire; Jacobowsky is played by Kaye, and Jurgens is the anti-Semitic military officer, both brought together during crisis in WW2. Filmed in France.

Me and My Gal (1932) 78m. *** D: Raoul Walsh. Spencer Tracy, Joan Bennett, Marion Burns, George Walsh, J. Farrell MacDonald, Noel Madison. Wholly entertaining film blending comedy, romance, melodrama in one neat package; cop Tracy falls in love with waitress Bennett, whose sister and father become involved with a gangster. Stars at their most charming, with bottomless reserve of snappy dialogue.

Me, Natalie (1969) C-111m. **½ D: Fred Coe. Patty Duke, James Farentino, Martin Balsam, Elsa Lanchester, Salome Jens, Nancy Marchand, Deborah Winters, Al Pacino. Soap opera-ish tale about unattractive New York girl struggling to find herself gets tremendous boost by Duke's great performance; otherwise, film wavers uncomfortably between comedy and drama.

Meal, The (1975) C-90m. ** D: R. John Hugh. Dina Merrill, Carl Betz, Leon Ames, Susan Logan, Vicki Powers, Steve Potter. Symbolic but brutal film, toned down for TV, about a wealthy woman who invites a group of the rich and powerful to a banquet, lets them devour the feast as they expose and devour each other's lives.

Mean Dog Blues (1978) C-108m. **½ D: Mel Stuart. George Kennedy, Gregg Henry, Kay Lenz, Scatman Crothers, Tina Louise, Felton Perry, Gregory Sierra, James Wainwright, William Windom. Henry is railroaded onto prison farm run by Kennedy and a team of bloodthirsty Dobermans, in this unsurprising but well-made action film.

Mean Johnny Barrows (1976) C-85m. ** D: Fred Williamson. Fred Williamson, Jenny Sherman, Aaron Banks, Anthony Caruso, Luther Adler, Stuart Whitman, Roddy McDowall, Elliott Gould. Mean but dull; Vietnam vet gets involved with the Mafia. Williamson made directorial debut with this slow-paced film, notable for unlikely cast, and Gould's incongruous comedy relief.

Mean Streets (1973) C-110m. **** D: Martin Scorsese. Robert DeNiro, Harvey Keitel, David Proval, Amy Robinson, Richard Romanus, Cesare Danova. Masterpiece about smalltime hood Keitel, irresponsible friend De Niro and their knockabout cronies in New York's Little Italy. Technically dazzling film put director Scorsese on the map and deservedly so. Beware of cuts.

Meanest Man in the World, The (1943) 57m. *** D: Sidney Lanfield. Jack Benny, Priscilla Lane, Eddie "Rochester" Anderson, Edmund Gwenn, Matt Briggs, Anne Revere. Snappy yarn of good-natured lawyer Benny discovering that he can only succeed in business by being nasty. Benny-Rochester repartee is hilarious; film is a must for Benny devotees.

Meatballs (1979-Canadian) C-92m. ** D: Ivan Reitman. Bill Murray, Harvey Atkin, Kate Lynch, Russ Banham, Kristine DeBell, Sarah Torgov. Alternately cruel and sloppily sentimental comedy about summer camp will no doubt wow fifth graders of all ages, though myopic screen characters named "Spaz" aren't really all that funny. Pretty desperate.

Mechanic, The (1972) C-100m. **½ D: Michael Winner. Charles Bronson, Keenan Wynn, Jan-Michael Vincent, Jill Ireland. Detailed study of James Bond-type assassin and youth he trains to take his place. Worth watching for the double-twist ending.

Medal for Benny, A (1945) 77m. ***½ D: Irving Pichel. Dorothy Lamour, Arturo de Cordova, J. Carrol Naish, Mikhail Rasumny, Fernando Alvarado, Charles Dingle, Frank McHugh. Small town hypocritically honoring one of its war dead; Steinbeck script is sharp, excellent comedy-drama.

Medical Story (1975) C-100m. TVM D: Gary Nelson. Beau Bridges, Jose Ferrer, Claude Akins, Wendell Burton, Shirley Knight, Carl Reiner, Martha Scott, Sidney Chaplin. Idealistic intern Bridges clashes with noted gynecologist Ferrer over unnecessary surgery. Intelligent drama by Abby Mann that led the way to the subsequent hospital anthology series. Average.

Medium, The (1951) 84m. **½ D: Gian-Carlo Menotti. Marie Powers, Anna Maria Alberghetti, Leo Coleman, Belva Kibler. Murky filmization of Gian-Carlo Menotti opera about eccentric spiritualist, the girl living in her seedy apartment, the outcast mute boy in love with girl.

Medium Cool (1969) C-110m. **** D: Haskell Wexler. Robert Forster, Verna Bloom, Peter Bonerz, Marianna Hill, Harold Blankenship. Arresting, unique film of TV cameraman (Forster) who remains detached though surrounded by events that demand his involvement. Director/writer/cameraman Wexler used real footage of his actors at 1968 Democratic convention in Chicago, and subsequent riots, as basis for ultra-realistic film.

Medusa Touch, The (1978-British) C-110m. ** D: Jack Gold. Richard Burton, Lino Ventura, Lee Remick, Harry Andrews, Alan Badel, Marie-Christine Barrault, Jeremy Brett, Michael Hordern, Gordon Jackson, Derek Jacobi. Burton has spent his whole life willing people's deaths, and now he's completely out of control; Remick is his psychiatrist in this derivative, unappealing film.

Meet Boston Blackie (1941) 61m. D: Robert Florey. Chester Morris, Rochelle Hudson, Richard Lane, Charles Wagenheim, Constance Worth. SEE: **Boston Blackie** series.

Meet Danny Wilson (1952) 86m. **½ D: Joseph Pevney. Frank Sinatra, Shelley Winters, Alex Nicol, Raymond Burr. Sinatra gives solid performance as entertainer involved with racketeers; script wavers.

Meet Dr. Christian (1939) 63m. ** D: Bernard Vorhaus. Jean Hersholt, Dorothy Lovett, Robert Baldwin, Enid Bennett, Paul Harvey, Marcia Mae Jones, Jackie Moran. Overly folksy entry in film series of small-town doctor who solves everyone's difficulties.

Meet John Doe (1941) 132m. *** D: Frank Capra. Gary Cooper, Barbara Stanwyck, Edward Arnold, Walter Brennan, Spring Byington, James Gleason, Gene Lockhart. Overlong but interesting social commentary, with naive Cooper hired to spearhead national goodwill drive benefitting corrupt politician Arnold. Wordy idealism can't bury good characterizations, usual Capra touches. Many existing prints (from reissue) run 123m.

Meet Me After the Show (1951) C-86m. **½ D: Richard Sale. Betty Grable, Macdonald Carey, Rory Calhoun, Eddie Albert, Lois Andrews, Irene Ryan. Undistinguished Grable musical lacking bounce of her other vehicles, with usual show biz storyline.

Meet Me at the Fair (1952) C-87m. **½ D: Douglas Sirk. Dan Dailey, Diana Lynn, Hugh O'Brian, Carole Mathews, Rhys Williams. Dailey is good as a sideshow medicine man who helps a young orphan and courts Lynn; pleasant musical.

Meet Me in Las Vegas (1956) C-112m. **½ D: Roy Rowland. Dan Dailey, Cyd Charisse, Agnes Moorehead, Lili Darvas, Jim Backus. Charisse's dancing is highlight of mild musical involving rancher Dailey and ballet star Cyd in gambling capital.

Meet Me in St. Louis (1944) C-113m. **** D: Vincente Minnelli. Judy Garland, Margaret O'Brien, Mary Astor, Lucille Bremer, Marjorie Main, June Lockhart, Harry Davenport, Leon Ames, Tom Drake. Captivating musical of St. Louis during 1903 World's Fair. Judy lilts "The Boy Next Door" (Drake), "Trolley Song," title tune, "Have Yourself a Merry Little Christmas" in beautiful pastel settings. Ames and Astor are heads of a wholesome American family, O'Brien an appealing little sister.

Meet Me Tonight SEE: **Tonight at 8:30**

Meet Mr. Lucifer (1953-British) 83m. ** D: Anthony Pelissier. Stanley Holloway, Peggy Cummins, Jack Watling, Barbara Murray. Meek little satire on the evils of television, with Holloway in dual role as Devil and his earthly helper.

Meet the Chump (1941) 60m. ** D: Edward Cline. Hugh Herbert, Lewis Howard, Jeanne Kelly (Brooks), Anne Nagel, Kathryn Adams, Shemp Howard, Richard Lane. Wacky Hugh plays inept trustee of estate due young Howard, desperate to find a way to cover the fact that he's dissipated $10 million. Mildly amusing, but generally routine.

Meet the People (1944) 100m. **½ D: Charles Riesner. Lucille Ball, Dick Powell, Virginia O'Brien, Bert Lahr, Rags Ragland, June Allyson, Mata and Hari. OK musicomedy of ex-stage star Ball trying to revive career; so-so score, many guests (Spike Jones, Vaughn Monroe, etc.).

Meet the Stewarts (1942) 73m. **½ D: Alfred E. Green. William Holden, Frances Dee, Grant Mitchell, Anne Revere, Mary Gordon, Marjorie Gateson, Margaret Hamilton, Don Beddoe. Wealthy girl marries hardworking Holden, can't adjust to new financial arrangement; not earthshaking, but enjoyable.

Mein Kampf (1961-Swedish) 121m. *** Narrated by Claude Stephenson. Technically smooth documentary on horrors of Nazi Germany. Restrained narration lets the visual speak for itself.

Melba (1953-British) C-113m. **½ D: Lewis Milestone. Patrice Munsel, Robert Morley, Sybil Thorndike, Martita Hunt, John McCallum. Occasionally interesting biography of Australian opera star Nellie Melba.

Melinda (1972) C-109m. *½ D: Hugh A. Robertson. Calvin Lockhart, Rosalind Cash, Vonetta McGee, Paul Stevens, Rockne Tarkington. Black disc jockey goes after his girlfriend's killers in violent melodrama; some scenes may be cut.

Melody (1971-British) C-103m. *** D: Waris Hussein. Jack Wild, Mark Lester, Tracy Hyde, Sheila Steafel, Kate Williams, Roy Kinnear. Adolescent view of life, disarmingly played by Lester and Wild (from OLIVER!) as friends who rebel against adult establishment, particularly when Lester and girlfriend Hyde decide they want to get married. Music by The Bee Gees.

Melody for Three (1941) 67m. ** D: Erle C. Kenton. Jean Hersholt, Fay Wray, Walter Woolf King, Astrid Allwyn, Schuyler Standish. Another Dr. Christian saga, enhanced only by presence of lovely Wray, stuck with sagging script.

Melvin Purvis—G-Man (1974) C-78m. TVM D: Dan Curtis. Dale Robertson, Harris Yulin, Margaret Blye, Matt Clark, Elliott Street, John Karlen, David Canary, Dick Sargent. Robertson flamboyantly portrays lawman Purvis in this breezy fictional account (by John Milius) of his pursuit of Machine Gun Kelly (Yulin) through the midwest of the early '30s. A wonderful send-up of the type of gangster movie they don't make anymore. Above average.

Member of the Wedding, The (1952) 91m. *** D: Fred Zinnemann. Ethel Waters, Julie Harris, Brandon de Wilde, Arthur Franz, Nancy Gates, James Edwards. Carson McCullers' sensitive account of child Harris prodded into growing up by her brother's forthcoming marriage. Cast makes slow-moving film worthwhile.

Memory of Justice, The (1976) C-278m. **** D: Marcel Ophuls. Outstanding documentary from the director of THE SORROW AND THE PITY questions how one country can pass judgment on the atrocities of others by examining the Nuremberg trials and their aftermath, the French performance in Algeria and the American intervention in Vietnam. Always riveting in spite of its mammoth length.

Memory of Us (1974) C-93m. **½ D: H. Kaye Dyal. Ellen Geer, Jon Cypher, Barbara Colby, Peter Brown, Robert Hogan, Rose Marie, Will Geer. Modest, interesting contemporary drama about a happily married woman who begins to question her role as wife and mother; script by star Ellen Geer, whose father Will makes brief appearance.

Men, The (1950) 85m. ***½ D: Fred Zinnemann. Marlon Brando, Teresa Wright, Jack Webb, Everett Sloane, Howard St. John. Brando excels in film debut as ex-GI trying to readjust to life after wartime injury; low-keyed acting is most effective. Retitled: BATTLE STRIPE.

Men Against the Sky (1940) 75m. *½ D: Leslie Goodwins. Richard Dix, Wendy Barrie, Kent Taylor, Edmund Lowe, Granville Bates, Grant Withers. Veteran cast in RKO programmer about personnel at aircraft-building plant.

Men Are Not Gods (1937-British) 82m. **½ D: Walter Reisch. Miriam Hopkins, Gertrude Lawrence, Sebastian Shaw, Rex Harrison, A. E. Matthews. Talky predecessor to A DOUBLE LIFE, with Harrison et al almost making their play-acting OTHELLO come true.

Men in Her Diary (1945) 73m. **½ D: Charles Barton. Peggy Ryan, Jon Hall, Louise Allbritton, Ernest Truex, Virginia Grey, William Terry, Alan Mowbray, Eric Blore, Maxie Rosenbloom. Zesty comedy of jealous wife, helpless husband, and knockout secretary; vivacious Allbritton never really got her due in films, is seen to good advantage here.

Men in Her Life, The (1941) 90m.

**½ D: Gregory Ratoff. Loretta Young, Conrad Veidt, Dean Jagger, Eugenie Leontovich, John Shepperd, (Shepperd Strudwick), Otto Kruger. Ballerina Young marries her dancing teacher but recalls many suitors she's known in the past. Fairly interesting love-life saga.

Men in War (1957) 104m. **½ D: Anthony Mann. Robert Ryan, Aldo Ray, Robert Keith, Vic Morrow, James Edwards, Scott Marlowe, Victor Sen Yung. Standard war film set in Korea in 1950s, with good action scenes distinguishing usual story.

Men in White (1934) 80m. **½ D: Richard Boleslawski. Clark Gable, Myrna Loy, Jean Hersholt, Elizabeth Allan, Otto Kruger, Wallace Ford, Henry B. Walthall, Samuel S. Hinds. Sterling cast in sterile filming of Sidney Kingsley's play; Gable is doctor torn between study with Hersholt and marriage to society girl Loy.

Men of Boys Town (1941) 106m. **½ D: Norman Taurog. Spencer Tracy, Mickey Rooney, Bobs Watson, Larry Nunn, Darryl Hickman, Henry O'Neill, Lee J. Cobb. If you liked BOYS TOWN . . .

Men of Brazil (1960-Brazil) C-68m. ** D: Nelson Marcellino de Carvalho, Otto Lopes Barbosa, Carlos Anselmo. Damasio Cardoso, Nair Cardoso, Nelson Marcellino de Carvalho, Odette de Carvalho. Strained diatribe on labor unions, mixed with farfetched human-interest dramatics.

Men of Sherwood Forest (1954-British) C-77m. ** D: Val Guest. Don Taylor, Reginald Beckwith, Eileen Moore, David King Wood. Yet another Robin Hood yarn, with Taylor properly sword-wielding and cavalier.

Men of the Dragon (1974) C-78m. TVM D: Harry Falk. Jared Martin, Kati Saylor, Robert Ito, Lee Tit War, David Chow, Joseph Wiseman. Chopsocky action, a TV-movie rarity, with a team of kung fu experts thwarting a gang of modern-day white slavers. The pits. Below average.

Men of the Fighting Lady (1954) C-80m. *** D: Andrew Marton. Van Johnson, Walter Pidgeon, Louis Calhern, Dewey Martin, Keenan Wynn, Frank Lovejoy, Robert Horton, Bert Freed. Above-par Korean War actioner, focusing on lives of men on U. S. aircraft carrier.

Men of Two Worlds (1946-British) C-107m. ** D: Thorold Dickinson. Phyllis Calvert, Eric Portman, Robert Adams, Cathleen Nesbitt, Orlando Martins, Cyril Raymond. Unhappy conglomeration of clichés about well-meaning British officials trying to protect natives in Africa. Retitled WITCH DOCTOR.

Men With Wings (1938) C-105m. **½ D: William Wellman. Fred MacMurray, Louise Campbell, Ray Milland, Andy Devine, Walter Abel, Virginia Weidler. Fictional tale of the epic of flight, with usual love triangle. After good start, it drags on. Donald O'Connor is one of the kids in the opening scenes.

Men Without Souls (1940) 62m. ** D: Nick Grinde. Barton MacLane, John Litel, Rochelle Hudson, Glenn Ford, Don Beddoe, Cy Kendall. Strictly standard prison film, with young Ford caught up in prison scandal. MacLane repeats role from dozens of other bighouse epics.

Menace in the Night (1958-British) 78m. *½ D: Lance Comfort. Griffith Jones, Lisa Gastoni, Vincent Ball, Eddie Byrne. Tired tale of witness to murder being pressured by gang not to testify.

Mephisto Waltz, The (1971) C-108m. *** D: Paul Wendkos. Alan Alda, Jacqueline Bisset, Barbara Parkins, Curt Jurgens, Bradford Dillman, William Windom. Chiller about young journalist who falls prey to Satanic cult after meeting dying concert pianist Jurgens; good occult story with some truly frightening moments.

Mercenary, The (1970-Italian) C-105m. **½ D: Sergio Corbucci. Franco Nero, Tony Musante, Jack Palance, Giovanna Ralli. Better-than-average Italian pasta western with loads of action and violence and a welcome serving of humor. At odds with one another: a stalwart mercenary (Nero), his sadistic rival (Palance), a patriotic revolutionary (Musante), a lusty peasant girl and a greedy mineowner.

Merrill's Marauders (1962) C-98m. **½ D: Samuel Fuller. Jeff Chandler, Ty Hardin, Peter Brown, Andrew Duggan, Will Hutchins. Rugged action scenes spark this typical WW2 actioner set in Burma.

Merrily We Go to Hell (1932) 78m. *½ D: Dorothy Arzner. Fredric March, Sylvia Sidney, Adrienne Allen, Skeets Gallagher, Kent Taylor, Cary Grant. Plodding story (despite intriguing title) of heiress Sidney marrying reporter March on whim, discovering that he's a problem-drinker. Starts well but sinks fast.

Merrily We Live (1938) 90m. *** D: Norman Z. McLeod. Constance Bennett, Brian Aherne, Alan Mowbray, Billie Burke, Bonita Granville, Tom Brown, Ann Dvorak, Patsy Kelly. It's all been done before, but fluttery Burke hiring suave Aherne as butler who tames spoiled Bennett is still engaging fun.

Merry Andrew (1958) C-103m. **½ D: Michael Kidd. Danny Kaye, Pier Angeli, Baccaloni, Robert Coote. Danny is a British teacher-archeologist with a yen for the circus and one of its performers (Angeli) in this bright musicomedy. Not as wacky as earlier Kaye efforts, but good.

Merry Go Round of 1938 (1937) 87m. **½ D: Irving Cummings. Bert Lahr, Jimmy Savo, Billy House, Mischa Auer, Alice Brady, Joy Hodges, Louise Fazenda. Disappointing backstage story with sentimental overtones as comedy foursome adopts little girl. Good specialty acts, great cast make tired tale endurable.

Merry Monahans, The (1944) 91m. *** D: Charles Lamont. Donald O'Connor, Peggy Ryan, Jack Oakie, Ann Blyth, Rosemary DeCamp, Isabel Jewell, Marion Martin, John Miljan. Spirited cast breathes life into bland vaudeville tale, doing old song favorites like "When You Wore A Tulip."

Merry Widow, The (1934) 99m. *** D: Ernst Lubitsch. Maurice Chevalier, Jeanette MacDonald, Una Merkel, Edward Everett Horton, George Barbier, Herman Bing. Lavish, delightful filming of Lehar operetta, with usual Lubitsch charm and hand-picked cast. Infectious score is still first-rate. Retitled: THE LADY DANCES.

Merry Widow, The (1952) C-105m. **½ D: Curtis Bernhardt. Lana Turner, Fernando Lamas, Una Merkel, Richard Haydn. Franz Lehar's operetta seems dated and trite in plush but unenthusiastic remake.

Message from Space (1978-Japanese) C-105m. **½ D: Kinji Fukasaku. Vic Morrow, Sonny Chiba, Philip Casnoff, Peggy Lee Brennan, Sue Shiomi, Tetsuro Tamba. Embattled planet sends SOS, and intergalactic team comes to its rescue. Cardboard performances take back seat to special effects and "cute" robot, both obviously patterned after STAR WARS.

Message to Garcia, A (1936) 77m. *** D: George Marshall. Wallace Beery, Barbara Stanwyck, John Boles, Alan Hale, Mona Barrie, Herbert Mundin. Historical fiction about agent Boles trying to reach General Garcia during Spanish-American war, with dubious help of roguish Beery and well-bred Stanwyck. Very entertaining.

Message to My Daughter (1973) C-78m. TVM. D: Robert Michael Lewis. Martin Sheen, Bonnie Bedelia, Kitty Winn, Neva Paterson, Mark Slade, Lucille Benson. Poignant melodrama about confused teenager (Winn) who finds emotional strength from tapes recorded years earlier by her long-deceased mother (Bedelia). Quality casting makes the difference on this weeper, not unlike SUNSHINE. Average.

Meteor (1979) C-103m. BOMB D: Ronald Neame. Sean Connery, Natalie Wood, Karl Malden, Brian Keith, Henry Fonda, Martin Landau, Trevor Howard, Richard Dysart. Switzerland, Hong Kong, and Manhattan all get a big piece of the rock when a giant meteor comes crashing to earth. American International's entry in the sci-fi blockbuster sweepstakes is as shoddy as a $17 million movie can be.

Metropolis (1926-German) 120m. **** D: Fritz Lang. Brigitte Helm, Alfred Abel, Gustav Froelich, Rudolf Klein-Rogge, Fritz Rasp. Classic silent-film fantasy of futuristic city and its mechanized society, with upper-class young man abandoning his life of luxury to join oppressed workers in a revolt. Heavy going at times, but startling set design and special effects command attention throughout.

Mexican Hayride (1948) 77m. ** D: Charles Barton. Bud Abbott, Lou Costello, Virginia Grey, Luba Malina, John Hubbard, Pedro de Cordoba, Fritz Feld. Typical A&C nonsense, with the boys on a wild goose chase with a mine deed in Mexico.

Mexican Manhunt (1953) 71m. *½ D: Rex Bailey. George Brent, Hillary Brooke, Morris Ankrum, Karen Sharpe. Actors walk through thin script about solving of old crime.

MGM's Big Parade of Comedy (1964)

100m. **½ Compiled by Robert Youngson, Fifty of the greatest stars of all time appear in this compilation, but too briefly. Harlow's scenes are seconds long; you can miss others if you blink. Still worthwhile for many priceless sequences with Garbo, Laurel and Hardy, Keaton, Gable, Robert Benchley, Marion Davies, Marx Brothers, et al.

Miami Expose (1956) **73m.** *½ D: Fred F. Sears. Lee J. Cobb, Patricia Medina, Edward Arnold, Michael Granger. Boring round-up of criminal syndicate in Sunshine State.

Miami Story, The (1954) **75m.** ** D: Fred F. Sears. Barry Sullivan, Luther Adler, John Baer, Adele Jergens, Beverly Garland. Stern ex-con Sullivan redeems himself in Florida resort city.

Michael Shayne, Private Detective (1940) **77m.** **½ D: Eugene Forde. Lloyd Nolan, Marjorie Weaver, Joan Valerie, Walter Abel, Elizabeth Patterson, Donald MacBride. Nolan gives vivid portrayal of detective Shayne, keeping an eye on heavy gambler Weaver in average private-eye thriller.

Michigan Kid (1947) **C-69m.** ** D: Ray Taylor. Jon Hall, Victor McLaglen, Rita Johnson, Andy Devine, Byron Foulger. Colorful but routine refilming of Rex Beach story of female ranch-owner Johnson falling victim to corrupt town government.

Mickey (1948) **C-87m.** ** D: Ralph Murphy. Lois Butler, Bill Goodwin, Irene Hervey, Hattie McDaniel, John Sutton, Rose Hobart. Naive yarn about rambunctious teen-ager (Butler) who turns matchmaker for father (Goodwin).

Mickey One (1965) **93m.** *** D: Arthur Penn. Warren Beatty, Hurd Hatfield, Alexandra Stewart, Teddy Hart, Jeff Corey, Franchot Tone. Beatty stars as confused nightclub comedian looking for new life and some worthwhile values. Will disturb some because of hero's offbeat character. Highly underrated, quite good.

Midas Run (1969) **C-106m.** **½ D: Alf Kjellin. Fred Astaire, Richard Crenna, Anne Heywood, Ralph Richardson, Roddy McDowall, Cesar Romero. British secret serviceman plots a daring gold heist in this routine caper film, enlivened by Astaire's peerless presence in the lead. Fred Astaire Jr. appears briefly as copilot of plane.

Middle of the Night (1959) **118m.** **½ D: Delbert Mann. Kim Novak, Fredric March, Glenda Farrell, Jan Norris, Lee Grant, Effie Afton, Martin Balsam, Joan Copeland. Slow-moving screen version of Paddy Chayefsky play, with March a middle-aged man about to marry much younger Novak.

Midnight (1934) **80m.** **½ D: Chester Erskine. Sidney Fox, O. P. Heggie, Henry Hull, Margaret Wycherly, Lynne Overman, Richard Whorf, Humphrey Bogart. Jury foreman is persecuted by the press—and even his family—after sending woman to the electric chair. Dated but interesting theatrical piece, reissued as CALL IT MURDER to capitalize on Bogart's later stardom.

Midnight (1939) **94m.** ***½ D: Mitchell Leisen. Claudette Colbert, Don Ameche, John Barrymore, Francis Lederer, Mary Astor, Hedda Hopper. Stars glide through chic Parisian marital mixup in near-classic comedy with Billy Wilder-Charles Brackett script. A gem, with Barrymore's comedics memorable. Remade as MASQUERADE IN MEXICO.

Midnight Cowboy (1969) **C-113m.** *** D: John Schlesinger. Dustin Hoffman, Jon Voight, Sylvia Miles, John McGiver, Brenda Vaccaro, Barnard Hughes, Ruth White, Jennifer Salt. Oscar-winning X-rated film is essentially old-fashioned movie with perverse modern twists: hayseed Voight comes to New York, becomes a stud, develops friendship with seedy Ratso Rizzo (Hoffman). Seamiest side of N.Y.C. life is backdrop for compelling character study.

Midnight Express (1978) **C-121m.** ***½ D: Alan Parker. Brad Davis, Irene Miracle, Bo Hopkins, Randy Quaid, John Hurt, Mike Kellin, Paul Smith. Riveting, harshly violent story of young American Billy Hayes (Davis), who faces physical and emotional brutalization in Turkish prison after being caught drug-smuggling. Great moviemaking, though not as faithful to Hayes' true story as filmmakers would have us believe. Oscar winner for Oliver Stone's script and Giorgio Moroder's score.

Midnight Lace (1960) **C-108m.** *** D: David Miller. Doris Day, Rex Harrison, John Gavin, Myrna Loy, Roddy McDowall, Herbert Marshall, Natasha Parry. Shrill murder mystery; unbelievable plot line, but star cast and decor smooth over rough spots. Set in London.

Midnight Man, The (1974) C-117m. **½ D: Roland Kibbee, Burt Lancaster. Burt Lancaster, Susan Clark, Cameron Mitchell, Morgan Woodward, Joan Lorring. Involved, overlong mystery with Lancaster as college security officer looking into a coed's murder. Lancaster also cowrote and co-produced.

Midnight Story, The (1957) 89m. **½ D: Joseph Pevney. Tony Curtis, Marisa Pavan, Gilbert Roland, Ted de Corsia, Kathleen Freeman. Atmospheric murder yarn with Curtis an ex-cop seeking the culprit who killed neighborhood priest.

Midsummer Night's Dream, A (1935) 132m. *** D: Max Reinhardt, William Dieterle. James Cagney, Dick Powell, Olivia de Havilland, Joe E. Brown, Jean Muir, Mickey Rooney, Verree Teasdale, Ian Hunter, Hugh Herbert, Victor Jory, Ross Alexander. Hollywood-Shakespeare has good and bad points; Cagney as Bottom and the Mendelssohn music are among good parts; Hugh Herbert and other incongruous cast members make up the latter. After a while Rooney (as Puck) gets to be a bit too much.

Midsummer Night's Dream, A (1966) C-93m. **½ D: Dan Eriksen. Suzanne Farrell, Edward Villella, Arthur Mitchell, Mimi Paul, Nicholas Magallanes. Filmed record of New York City Ballet's presentation of Shakespeare's comedy is mostly for dance buffs; film makes some attempt to be cinematic, but not enough.

Midsummer Night's Dream, A (1968-British) C-124m. **½ D: Peter Hall. Diana Rigg, David Warner, Michael Jayston, Ian Richardson, Judi Dench, Ian Holm, Bill Travers. Fine cast of England's Royal Shakespeare Co. in middling performance of the Shakespeare classic.

Midway (1976) C-132m. ** D: Jack Smight. Charlton Heston, Henry Fonda, James Coburn, Glenn Ford, Hal Holbrook, Robert Mitchum, Cliff Robertson. Close to being a "rip-off" as prominent cast acts to cans of stock shots from THIRTY SECONDS OVER TOKYO, antique Japanese war films, and actual wartime footage. Silly soap opera (Heston's ensign son in love with Japanese girl) doesn't help. The wonder is that some of the drama and impact of the great naval battle still comes through.

Mighty Barnum, The (1934) 87m. *** D: Walter Lang. Wallace Beery, Adolphe Menjou, Virginia Bruce, Rochelle Hudson, Janet Beecher, Herman Bing. Fanciful biography of world-famous showman, with Menjou as his reluctant partner Bailey. More Beery than Barnum.

Mighty Crusaders, The (1957-Italian) C-87m. ** D: Carlo Ludovico Bragaglia. Francisco Rabal, Sylva Koscina, Gianna Maria Canale, Rik Battaglia. Sloppy picturization of Tasso's epic poem, with contrived love tale between Saracen and Christian backdrop to siege of Jerusalem; amateurish production values.

Mighty Joe Young (1949) 94m. *** D: Ernest B. Schoedsack. Terry Moore, Ben Johnson, Robert Armstrong, Mr. Joseph Young, Frank McHugh. Updating of KING KONG theme has comparable special effects, but no matching story line, and Moore is no Fay Wray. Mr. Young is good, though.

Mighty McGurk, The (1946) 85m. *½ D: John Waters. Wallace Beery, Dean Stockwell, Dorothy Patrick, Edward Arnold, Aline McMahon, Cameron Mitchell. Formula Beery vehicle with the star a punchy prize-fighter and Stockwell as adorable boy he adopts.

Mighty Ursus, The (1962-Italian) C-92m. ** D: Carlo Campogalliani. Ed Fury, Christina Gajoni, Maria Orfei, Mario Scaccia, Mary Marlon, Luis Prendez. In title role Fury goes through expected gymnastics, rescuing his woman from marauding natives.

Mikado, The (1939) C-90m. *** D: Victor Schertzinger. Kenny Baker, John Barclay, Martyn Green, Jean Colin, Constance Wills. Baker may not be the ideal Nanki-Poo, but this color film of Gilbert and Sullivan's operetta is still worthwhile, with the marvelous G&S songs intact.

Mikey and Nicky (1976) C-119m. **½ D: Elaine May. Peter Falk, John Cassavetes, Ned Beatty, Rose Arrick, Carol Grace, Joyce Van Patten. Ragged film (in the editing room for several years) improves as it goes along, examining relationship between small-time hoods who were childhood pals. Superb performances by Falk and Cassavetes.

Mildred Pierce (1945) 109m. ***½ D: Michael Curtiz. Joan Crawford,

Jack Carson, Zachary Scott, Eve Arden, Bruce Bennett, Ann Blyth. Crawford won an Oscar as housewife-turned-waitress who finds success in business but loses control of ungrateful daughter Blyth—especially when she finds they're competing for the love of the same man. Solid adaptation of James M. Cain's novel with top supporting cast.

Milkman, The (1950) 87m. ****** D: Charles Barton. Donald O'Connor, Jimmy Durante, Joyce Holden, Piper Laurie, Henry O'Neill. Trivia of O'Connor working for dairy company, with Durante doing his best to liven up the proceedings.

Milky Way, The (1970-French) C-102m. ******** D: Luis Buñuel. Paul Frankeur, Laurent Terzieff, Alain Cuny, Bernard Verley, Michel Piccoli, Pierre Clementi, Georges Marchal, Delphine Seyrig. Two men making religious pilgrimage through France form basis for string of Buñuel "jokes," parables, surrealistic visions. Heretic, funny, haunting, thoroughly enjoyable.

Millerson Case, The (1947) 72m. D: George Archainbaud. Warner Baxter, Nancy Saunders, Barbara Pepper, Clem Bevans, Griff Barnett, Paul Guilfoyle. SEE: **Crime Doctor** series.

Million Dollar Baby (1941) 100m. ****** D: Curtis Bernhardt. Priscilla Lane, Ronald Reagan, Jeffrey Lynn, May Robson, Lee Patrick, Helen Westley, John Qualen. Timeworn Warner Bros. entry of spankingly naive Lane who inherits lots of money, getting lots of headaches.

Million Dollar Kid (1944) 65m. D: Wallace Fox. Leo Gorcey, Huntz Hall, Gabriel Dell, Louise Currie, Noah Beery, Sr., Iris Adrian, Mary Gordon. SEE: **Bowery Boys** series.

Million Dollar Legs (1932) 64m. *****½** D: Edward Cline. W. C. Fields, Jack Oakie, Andy Clyde, Ben Turpin, Dickie Moore, Billy Gilbert, Lyda Roberti. Wacky nonsense with Fields as President of Klopstokia, a nutty country entering the Olympics. Oakie is a young American pursuing W. C.'s daughter, Susan Fleming. Many fine comics appear in cameos.

Million Dollar Legs (1939) 65m. ****½** D: Nick Grinde. Betty Grable, Jackie Coogan, Donald O'Connor, Buster Crabbe, Peter Lind Hayes, Richard Denning. Title supposedly refers to winning horse, but Grable is star so draw your own assump-

tions. Pleasant college comedy of school trying to keep on its feet has nothing to do with W. C. Fields film of same name.

Million Dollar Mermaid (1952) C-115m. ****½** D: Mervyn LeRoy. Esther Williams, Victor Mature, Walter Pidgeon, David Brian, Jesse White. Williams does OK as aquatic star Annette Kellerman, alternating her swimming with romancing Mature. Some typically elaborate production numbers by Busby Berkeley

Million Dollar Rip-Off, The (1976) C-78m. TVM D: Alexander Singer. Freddie Prinze, Allen Garfield, Linda Scruggs Bogart, Joanna de Varona, Christine Belford, Brooke Mills. Heist movie; ex-con electronics wizard Prinze and four female accomplices knock over Chicago subway system, to the annoyance of ulcer-ridden detective Garfield. Below average.

Million Dollar Weekend (1948) 72m. ****** D: Gene Raymond. Gene Raymond, Francis Lederer, Stephanie Pauli (Osa Massen), Robert Warwick, James Craven. Average mystery yarn with veteran cast. Stockbroker steals firm's money and heads for Hawaii, where complications snowball. Star Raymond also directed.

Million Eyes of Su-Muru, The (1967) C-95m. ****** D: Lindsay Shonteff. Frankie Avalon, George Nader, Shirley Eaton, Wilfrid Hyde-White. Tongue-in-cheek tale of murder and women's organization bent on enslaving all of mankind. From a Sax Rohmer story.

Million Pound Note, The SEE: **Man with a Million**

Millionaire, The (1978) C-100m. TVM. D: Don Weis. Martin Balsam, Edward Albert, The Hudson Bros., Pat Crowley, Ralph Bellamy, Jane Wyatt, John Ireland, William Demarest, Robert Quarry. Updated version of 1950s TV series with eccentric (and never seen) John Beresford Tipton doling out million-dollar cashier checks through his discreet right-hand man, Michael Anthony (played here by Quarry). Familiar faces, familiar situations. Average.

Millionaire for Christy, A (1951) 91m. ******* D: George Marshall. Fred MacMurray, Eleanor Parker, Richard Carlson, Una Merkel. 1930s-type screwball comedy; fast, unpretentious, very funny, with winning performances by Parker and MacMurray in tale of gold-digging girl out to snare rich husband.

Millionairess, The (1960-British) C-90m. **½ D: Anthony Asquith. Sophia Loren, Peter Sellers, Alastair Sim, Vittorio De Sica, Dennis Price. Loren is an heiress who thinks money can buy anything, until she meets Indian doctor Sellers, who won't sell his principles, or his love. Sophia was never more stunning, but this adaptation of G. B. Shaw's play is heavy-handed comedy.

Min and Bill (1930) 70m. **½ D: George Hill. Marie Dressler, Wallace Beery, Dorothy Jordan, Marjorie Rambeau, Frank McGlynn. Sentimental early talkie with unforgettable team of Beery and Dressler as waterfront characters trying to protect Marie's daughter (Jordan) from being taken to "proper" home. Dressler won an Academy Award for her performance.

Mind Benders, The (1963-British) 101m. *** D: Basil Dearden. Dirk Bogarde, Mary Ure, John Clements, Michael Bryant, Wendy Craig. Top cast in slow-moving but compelling account of experiments testing man's will power and senses, with espionage theme weaved into plot.

Mind of Mr. Soames, The (1970-British) C-95m. ***½ D: Alan Cooke. Terence Stamp, Robert Vaughn, Nigel Davenport, Christian Roberts. Exceptionally fine sci-fi tale of man who has been in a coma since birth; finally revived, he must be taught thirty years' worth of knowledge in brief span of time.

Mind Over Murder (1979) C-100m. TVM D: Ivan Nagy. Deborah Raffin, David Ackroyd, Bruce Davison, Andrew Prine, Christopher Carey. Model with precognition senses she's being stalked by a killer in this tepid thriller. Average.

Mind Snatchers, The SEE: Happiness Cage, The

Mine Own Executioner (1948) 103m. *** D: Anthony Kimmins. Burgess Meredith, Dulcie Gray, Kieron Moore, Christine Norden, Michael Shepley. Realistic drama of quack psychiatrist Meredith encountering trouble of his own; some fine suspenseful sequences.

Miniskirt Mob, The (1968) C-82m. *½ D: Maury Dexter. Jeremy Slate, Diane McBain, Sherry Jackson, Patty McCormack, Ross Hagen, Harry Dean Stanton, Ronnie Rondell. McBain plays leader of female motorcycle gang, even though she looks as if she'd be more comfortable on a Tournament of Roses float. Those who like the title will probably like the film.

Ministry of Fear (1944) 85m. ***½ D: Fritz Lang. Ray Milland, Marjorie Reynolds, Carl Esmond, Dan Duryea, Hillary Brooke, Alan Napier, Percy Waram. Beautifully atmospheric thriller of wartime London, with Milland framed in complicated espionage plot; good cast, fine touches by director Lang.

Miniver Story, The (1950) 104m. **½ D: H. C. Potter. Greer Garson, Walter Pidgeon, John Hodiak, Leo Genn, Cathy O'Donnell, Henry Wilcoxon, Reginald Owen, Peter Finch. Sequel to MRS. MINIVER (filmed this time in England) doesn't work as well, but Garson and Pidgeon have some poignant scenes as family reunited in post-WW2 England.

Minnie and Moskowitz (1971) C-114m. *** D: John Cassavetes. Gena Rowlands, Seymour Cassel, Val Avery, Tim Carey, Katherine Cassavetes, Elsie Ames. Cassavetes' most likable film chronicles manic romance between lonely museum curator (Rowlands) and crazy parking-lot attendant (Cassel). Touching, amusing, and most enjoyable.

Minotaur, The (1961-Italian) C-92m. *½ D: Silvio Amadio. Bob Mathias, Rosanna Schiaffino, Alberto Lupo, Rik Battaglia. Occasional atmosphere and Schiaffino's appearance still cannot elevate story of mythological hero thwarting attempt of evil queen to subjugate city-dwellers with hideous monster.

Minstrel Man (1977) C-100m. TVM D: William A. Graham. Glynn Turman, Ted Ross, Stanley Clay, Saundra Sharp, Art Evans, Gene Bell. Engrossing drama tracing the era of black minstrelsy and the evolution of ragtime at the turn of the century. Rich performances by Turman as ambitious song-and-dance man, Clay as a dedicated musician racked by racial consciousness, Ross as rascally impresario. Outstanding.

Minute to Pray, a Second to Die, A (1967-Italian) C-97m. *** D: Franco Giraldi. Alex Cord, Arthur Kennedy, Robert Ryan, Nicoletta Machiavelli, Mario Brega. Outlaw seeks refuge in Escondido from outlaws, bounty hunters, territorial lawmen, and anyone out to take advantage of his occasional paralytic seizures. Outstanding color photography adds to great atmosphere.

Miracle, The (1959) C-121m. **½ D: Irving Rapper. Carroll Baker, Roger Moore, Walter Slezak, Vittorio Gassman, Katina Paxinou, Dennis King, Isobel Elsom. Claptrap vehicle resurrected as glossy, empty spectacle of 1810s Spain, with Baker the would-be nun unsure of her decision, Moore the soldier she romances.

Miracle in the Rain (1956) 107m. **½ D: Rudolph Maté. Jane Wyman, Van Johnson, Peggie Castle, Fred Clark, Eileen Heckart, Josephine Hutchinson, Barbara Nichols, William Gargan. Above-par soaper of two lost souls, Wyman and Johnson, falling in love in N.Y.C. LAUGH-IN's Arte Johnson has a featured role.

Miracle of Fatima SEE: **Miracle of Our Lady of Fatima, The.**

Miracle of Morgan's Creek, The (1944) 99m. **** D: Preston Sturges. Eddie Bracken, Betty Hutton, Diana Lynn, Brian Donlevy, William Demarest, Porter Hall, Almira Sessions, Jimmy Conlin. Frantic, hilarious comedy of Betty attending all-night party, forgetting who's the father of her offspring nine months later. Bracken and Demarest have never been better than in this gem.

Miracle of Our Lady of Fatima, The (1952) C-102m. *** D: John Brahm. Gilbert Roland, Angela Clarke, Frank Silvera, Jay Novello, Sherry Jackson. Tastefully handled account of religious miracle witnessed by farm children in 1910s; intelligent script. Retitled: MIRACLE OF FATIMA.

Miracle of the Bells, The (1948) 120m. *½ D: Irving Pichel. Fred MacMurray, Valli, Frank Sinatra, Lee J. Cobb, Charles Meredith. Contrived story of miracle occurring when movie star is laid to rest in coal-mining home town; often ludicrous, despite sincere cast.

Miracle of the Hills (1959) 73m. *½ D: Paul Landres. Rex Reason, Theona Bryant, Jay North, Gilbert Smith, Tracy Stratford, Gene Roth. Timid little Western of town-running gal who bucks new clergyman.

Miracle of the White Stallions (1963) C-117m. *½ D: Arthur Hiller. Robert Taylor, Lilli Palmer, Curt Jurgens, Eddie Albert, James Franciscus, John Larch. Long, talky, confusing drama about evacuation of prized Lippizan horses from Vienna during WW2. A most un-Disneylike Disney film.

Miracle on 34th Street (1947) 96m. ***½ D: George Seaton. Maureen O'Hara, John Payne, Edmund Gwenn, Gene Lockhart, Natalie Wood, Porter Hall, William Frawley, Thelma Ritter. Classic Valentine Davies fable of "Kris Kringle" (Gwenn) working in Macy's, encountering unbelieving child (Wood), going on trial to prove he's Santa. Delightful comedy-fantasy.

Miracle on 34th Street (1973) C-100m. TVM D: Fielder Cook. Jane Alexander, David Hartman, Roddy McDowall, Sebastian Cabot, Suzanne Davidson, Jim Backus, Tom Bosley, David Doyle, James Gregory, Roland Winters. Heartwarming humor and old-fashioned whimsey in this TV adaptation of the 1947 Christmas classic. Good cast, but the plot's awfully dated now. Average.

Miracle Woman, The (1931) 87m. *** D: Frank Capra. Barbara Stanwyck, David Manners, Sam Hardy, Beryl Mercer, Russell Hopton. Stanwyck plays an evangelist (patterned after Aimee Semple McPherson) whose splashy sermons become big business. Manners is a blind man who falls in love with her. Story contrivances overcome by fine performances, direction, and camerawork (by Joseph Walker).

Miracle Worker, The (1962) 107m. ***½ D: Arthur Penn. Anne Bancroft, Patty Duke, Victor Jory, Inga Swenson, Andrew Prine, Kathleen Comegys. Broadway play is filmized with few changes. Duke and Bancroft unforgettable as Helen Keller and her devoted teacher (both won Oscars for their performances). Worthwhile; the fight-for-authority sequence especially memorable.

Miracle Worker, The (1979) C-100m. TVM D: Paul Aaron. Patty Duke Astin, Melissa Gilbert, Diana Muldaur, Charles Siebert, Anne Seymour, Stanley Wells. Powerful refilming of the William Gibson classic about young Helen Keller's first encounters with Anne Sullivan, who would be her teacher and life-long companion. Having Patty Duke Astin—who won an Oscar as Keller in 1962—play Sullivan was more a novelty than an inspired piece of casting, making this one just a notch below its predecessor. Still above average.

Miraculous Journey (1948) **C-83m.** *½ D: Peter Stewart (Sam Newfield). Rory Calhoun, Andrew Long, Virginia Grey, George Cleveland. Substandard psychological study of victims of plane crash in jungle.

Mirage (1965) **109m.** *** D: Edward Dmytryk. Gregory Peck, Diane Baker, Walter Matthau, Kevin McCarthy, Jack Weston, Leif Erickson, Walter Abel, George Kennedy. Fine Hitchcock-like thriller, with Peck the victim of amnesia, and everyone else out to get him. Matthau steals film as easygoing private-eye; interesting on-location footage in N.Y.C. Remade as JIGSAW.

Miranda (1948-British) **80m.** **½ D: Ken Annakin. Glynis Johns, Griffith Jones, Googie Withers, John McCallum, Margaret Rutherford. Droll frou-frou of mermaid preferring sophisticated land-life to the sea; capably played by all. Johns is a very fetching mermaid.

Mirror Has Two Faces, The (1959-French) **98m.** **½ D: Andre Cayatte. Michele Morgan, Bourvil, Gerald Oury, Ivan Desny, Elizabeth Manet, Sylvie, Sandra Milo. Morgan is quite good as woman who begins life anew after plastic surgery.

Mirror, Mirror (1979) **C-100m. TVM** D: Joanna Lee. Janet Leigh, Lee Meriwether, Loretta Swit, Robert Vaughn, Peter Bonerz, Christopher Lemmon, Robin Mattson. Three women's efforts to reshape their lives through cosmetic surgery. Earnest but less than uplifting. Average.

Misadventures of Merlin Jones, The (1964) **C-88m.** *½ D: Robert Stevenson. Tommy Kirk, Annette Funicello, Leon Ames, Stuart Erwin, Alan Hewitt, Connie Gilchrist. Skimpy Disney comedy about college brain (Kirk) and his misadventures with mind-reading and hypnotism.

Misfits, The (1961) **124m.** *** D: John Huston. Clark Gable, Marilyn Monroe, Montgomery Clift, Thelma Ritter, Eli Wallach, James Barton, Estelle Winwood. Unsatisfying but engrossing parable authored by Arthur Miller, involving disillusioned divorcee Monroe and her brooding cowboy friends. Both Monroe's and Gable's last film.

Miss Annie Rooney (1942) **84m.** **D: Edwin L. Marin. Shirley Temple, William Gargan, Guy Kibbee, Dickie Moore, Peggy Ryan, Gloria Holden,

Selmer Jackson, June Lockhart, Virginia Sale. Moore gives Shirley her first screen kiss in slight tale of girl from wrong side of tracks in love with rich boy.

Miss Grant Takes Richmond (1949) **87m.** **½ D: Lloyd Bacon. Lucille Ball, William Holden, Janis Carter, James Gleason, Frank McHugh. Ball is wacky secretary innocently involved with crooks; she's the whole show.

Miss Pinkerton (1932) **66m.** ** D: Lloyd Bacon. Joan Blondell, George Brent, John Wray, Ruth Hall, C. Henry Gordon, Elizabeth Patterson, Holmes Herbert. Nurse Blondell has sixth sense for mysteries, decides to go after one in easy-to-take story.

Miss Robin Crusoe (1954) **C-75m.** *½ D: Eugene Frenke. Amanda Blake, George Nader, Rosalind Hayes. Female version of Robinson Crusoe; nothing added, a lot to be desired.

Miss Robin Hood (1952-British) **78m.** ** D: John Guillermin. Margaret Rutherford, Richard Hearne, Edward Lexy, Frances Rowe. OK mixture of fantasy and farce, with Rutherford an elderly nut seeking retrieval of family whiskey formula; Hearne is meek girl's-magazine writer who aids her.

Miss Sadie Thompson (1953) **C-91m.** *** D: Curtis Bernhardt. Rita Hayworth, Jose Ferrer, Aldo Ray, Russell Collins, Charles Bronson. Rita Hayworth gives a provocative performance in remake of Somerset Maugham's RAIN.

Miss Susie Slagle's (1945) **88m.** **½ D: John Berry. Veronica Lake, Sonny Tufts, Joan Caulfield, Lillian Gish, Ray Collins, Billy DeWolfe, Lloyd Bridges. Mild tale of turn-of-the-century boarding house for aspiring doctors and nurses.

Miss Tatlock's Millions (1948) **101m.** **½ D: Richard Haydn. John Lund, Wanda Hendrix, Monty Woolley, Robert Stack, Ilka Chase, Dorothy Stickney. Original comedy of Hollywood stunt man who must masquerade as a nitwit to help young heiress; offbeat, to say the least.

Missile Base at Taniak (1953) **100m.** *½ D: Franklin Adreon. William Henry, Susan Morrow, Arthur Space, Dale Van Sickel. Uninspired Republic cliff-hanger concerning Canadian mounties' efforts to track down foreign agents setting up rocket centers to launch projectiles and destroy key American cities. Reedited movie serial: CANADIAN MOUNTIES VS. ATOMIC INVADERS.

Missile Monsters (1958) 75m. *½ D: Fred C. Brannon. Walter Reed, Lois Collier, Gregory Gay, James Craven. Tedious sci-fi about Martian attempt to take over the earth via guided missiles. Adapted from 1951 serial FLYING DISC MAN FROM MARS.

Missile to the Moon (1959) 78m. *½ D: Richard Cunha. Richard Travis, Cathy Downs, K. T. Stevens, Tommy Cook. Preposterous low-budget sci-fi about lunar expedition finding sinister female presiding over race of moon-women. Lots of laughs, for all the wrong reasons. Remake of CAT-WOMEN OF THE MOON (ROCKET TO THE MOON).

Missiles From Hell (1958-British) 72m. ** D: Vernon Sewell. Michael Rennie, Patricia Medina, Milly Vitale, David Knight. British work with Polish partisans during WW2 to obtain projectile weapon held by Nazis; choppy editing.

Missing Are Deadly, The (1974) C-78m. TVM D: Don McDougall. Ed Nelson, Jose Ferrer, Leonard Nimoy, George O'Hanlon, Jr., Marjorie Lord, Kathleen Quinlan. Suspense tale about the panic caused when disturbed teenager takes a rat infected with a deadly virus from his father's lab. Average.

Missing Corpse, The (1945) 62m. *½ D: Albert Herman. J. Edward Bromberg, Eric Sinclair, Frank Jenks, Isabel Randolph, Paul Guilfoyle, John Shay, Lorell Sheldon. Cheaply made chiller of harried newspaperman Bromberg involved in murder mystery.

Missing Guest, The (1938) 68m. *½ D: John Rawlins. Paul Kelly, Constance Moore, William Lundigan, Edwin Stanley, Selmer Jackson, Billy Wayne. As in many 1930s "B" melodramas, a newspaper reporter (named "Scoop," no less) is on hand when murders are being committed, this time in a haunted house. Routine. Filmed before as SECRET OF THE BLUE ROOM and again as MURDER IN THE BLUE ROOM.

Missing Juror, The (1944) 66m. *** D: Budd Boetticher. Jim Bannon, Janis Carter, George Macready, Jean Stevens, Joseph Crehan, Carole Mathews. Brisk, engrossing drama of unknown killer taking revenge on jury that sent innocent man to his death; low budget, but quite good.

Mission Batangas (1969) C-100m. *½ D: Keith Larsen. Dennis Weaver, Vera Miles, Keith Larsen, Vic Diaz. Callous American flyer in early WW2 eventually becomes a hero; poor excuse for a war movie.

Mission Mars (1968) C-95m. *½ D: Nick Webster. Darren McGavin, Nick Adams, George DeVries, Heather Hewitt, Michael DeBeausset, Shirley Parker. Typical astronaut drama has three U.S. space men battling unseen forces while on a mission.

Mission Over Korea (1953) 85m. *½ D: Fred F. Sears. John Hodiak, John Derek, Maureen O'Sullivan, Audrey Totter. Substandard Korean War tale.

Mission Stardust (1968-Italian) C-95m. *½ D: Primo Zeglio. Essy Persson, Lang Jeffries, John Karelsen, Pinkas Braun, Luis Davila. Space expedition from Earth lands on Moon and encounters alien space ship whose beings are suffering from a mysterious disease. Based on first of internationally popular "Perry Rhodan" series of novels, but worthless nonetheless.

Mission to Moscow (1943) 123m. ***½ D: Michael Curtiz. Walter Huston, Ann Harding, Oscar Homolka, George Tobias, Gene Lockhart, Frieda Inescort, Eleanor Parker, Richard Travis. Excellent, important film of real-life ambassador Joseph Davies in then-peaceful Russia. Well-done, giving interesting insights to American concepts of USSR at the time.

Mississippi (1935) 73m. ***½ D: A. Edward Sutherland. Bing Crosby, W. C. Fields, Joan Bennett, Queenie Smith, Gail Patrick, Claude Gillingwater. Fine cast in musicomedy of riverboat captain Fields and singer Crosby, with Rodgers-Hart score including "It's Easy To Remember But So Hard to Forget." Unforgettable poker game with W. C. Look quickly for Ann Sheridan.

Mississippi Gambler (1953) C-98m. **½ D: Rudolph Maté. Tyrone Power, Piper Laurie, Julia Adams, John McIntire, Dennis Weaver. Power is title figure with ambitions of establishing a gambling business in New Orleans.

Mississippi Mermaid (1970-French) C-110m. *** D: Francois Truffaut. Jean-Paul Belmondo, Catherine Deneuve, Michel Bouquet, Nelly Borgeaud. One of the director's few flops,

but any film with Belmondo-Deneuve-Truffaut combo is of interest; story concerns tobacco planter whose mailorder bride turns out to be Deneuve. Always buy brand names.
Missouri Breaks, The (1976) C-126m. BOMB D: Arthur Penn. Marlon Brando, Jack Nicholson, Kathleen Lloyd, Randy Quaid, Frederick Forrest, Harry Dean Stanton. Dynamite star combo in hired gun vs. horse thief confrontation—all for naught. Jumbled, excessively violent pseudo-event; a great director's worst film and one of the worst "big" movies ever made.
Missouri Traveler, The (1958) C-104m. **½ D: Jerry Hopper. Brandon de Wilde, Lee Marvin, Gary Merrill, Mary Hosford, Paul Ford. Folksy, minor account of orphaned youth (De Wilde) finding new roots in Southern country town in 1910s; earnest but predictable.
Mr. Ace (1946) 84m. **½ D: Edwin L. Marin. George Raft, Sylvia Sidney, Stanley Ridges, Sara Haden, Jerome Cowan. Ordinary dirty-politics drama of office-seeking Sidney using Raft to achieve her goals.
Mr. and Mrs. Bo Jo Jones (1971) C-73m. TVM D: Robert Day. Desi Arnaz Jr., Chris Norris, Dan Dailey, Dina Merrill, Susan Strasberg. Young couple in 50s small town undergoing parental and neighborhood pressures. Despite OK performances, mediocre script makes film forgettable. Average.
Mr. and Mrs. North (1941) 67m. **½ D: Robert B. Sinclair. Gracie Allen, William Post, Jr., Paul Kelly, Rose Hobart, Virginia Grey, Tom Conway. Radio characters come to screen in comedy involving dead bodies being discovered; sometimes funny, sometimes forced.
Mr. and Mrs. Smith (1941) 95m. *** D: Alfred Hitchcock. Carole Lombard, Robert Montgomery, Gene Raymond, Jack Carson, Philip Merivale, Betty Compson, Lucile Watson. Madcap comedy of Lombard and Montgomery discovering their marriage wasn't legal. Not many Hitchcock touches, but bouncy.
Mr. Arkadin (1955-British) 99m. **½ D: Orson Welles. Orson Welles, Michael Redgrave, Patricia Medina, Akim Tamiroff, Mischa Auer. Brooding, rambling drama about oddball financier. Retitled: CONFIDENTIAL REPORT.

Mr. Belvedere Goes to College (1949) 83m. ** D: Elliott Nugent. Clifton Webb, Shirley Temple, Tom Drake, Alan Young, Jessie Royce Landis. The sharp-tongued character from SITTING PRETTY enrolls in college, with predictable results. Nothing special.
Mr. Belvedere Rings the Bell (1951) 87m. **½ D: Henry Koster. Clifton Webb, Joanne Dru, Hugh Marlowe, Zero Mostel, Doro Merande, Billy Lynn. Another follow-up to SITTING PRETTY isn't as witty. Webb enters old folks' home to prove his theory that age has nothing to do with leading a full life.
Mr. Billion (1977) C-93m. ** D: Jonathan Kaplan. Terence Hill, Valerie Perrine, Jackie Gleason, Slim Pickens, Chill Wills, William Redfield. Uninspired comedy about a lowly Italian mechanic on a mad, cross-country scramble to claim a billion dollar legacy, and the attempts of scoundrels to swindle him out of it.
Mr. Blandings Builds His Dream House (1948) 94m. *** D: H. C. Potter. Cary Grant, Myrna Loy, Melvyn Douglas, Sharyn Moffet, Connie Marshall, Louise Beavers. Slick comedy of city couple attempting to build a house in the country; expertly handled.
Mister Buddwing (1966) 100m. **½ D: Delbert Mann. James Garner, Jean Simmons, Suzanne Pleshette, Angela Lansbury, Katharine Ross, Raymond St. Jacques, Nichelle Nichols. Misfire; over-familiar amnesia plot with Garner trying to fill in his past, meeting assorted women who might have been part of his prior life.
Mr. Bug Goes to Town SEE: Hoppity Goes to Town
Mister Cory (1957) C-92m. **½ D: Blake Edwards. Tony Curtis, Charles Bickford, Martha Hyer, Kathryn Grant. Curtis does OK as poor-boy-turned-rich-gambler who returns to home town to show off his wealth.
Mr. Deeds Goes to Town (1936) 115m. **** D: Frank Capra. Gary Cooper, Jean Arthur, George Bancroft, Lionel Stander, Douglass Dumbrille, Mayo Methot, Raymond Walburn. Cooper is Longfellow Deeds, who inherits 20 million dollars and wants to spend it on people during Depression; Arthur is appealing as city reporter captivated by the naive Deeds.
Mr. Denning Drives North (1953-

British) 93m. **½ D: Anthony Kimmins. John Mills, Phyllis Calvert, Eileen Moore, Sam Wanamaker. Cast's sincerity makes this murder yarn palatable, the biggest hunt being for the corpus delicti.

Mister Drake's Duck (1950-British) 76m. *** D: Val Guest. Douglas Fairbanks, Jr., Yolande Donlan, Howard Marion-Crawford, Reginald Beckwith. Droll comedy of Fairbanks on honeymoon getting more publicity than he bargained for when pet duck lays radioactive eggs.

Mister 880 (1950) 90m. *** D: Edmund Goulding. Dorothy McGuire, Burt Lancaster, Edmund Gwenn, Millard Mitchell. Easygoing comedy, with Gwenn an elderly counterfeiter tracked down by federal agent Lancaster.

Mr. Hex (1946) 63m. D: William Beaudine. Leo Gorcey, Huntz Hall, Bobby Jordan, Gabriel Dell, Gale Robbins, Billy Benedict, David Gorcey, Ian Keith. SEE: **Bowery Boys** series.

Mr. Hobbs Takes a Vacation (1962) C-116m. **½ D: Henry Koster. James Stewart, Maureen O'Hara, Fabian, John Saxon, Marie Wilson, Reginald Gardiner, Laurie Peters. Ultra-wholesome family fare. Stewart and O'Hara, taking brood to seaside summer house, try to meet family problems.

Mr. Horn (1979) C-200m. TVM D: Jack Starrett. David Carradine, Richard Widmark, Karen Black, Jeremy Slate, Enrique Lucero, Jack Starrett. Rambling, episodic western about legendary frontier folk hero Tom Horn. Average.

Mr. Hulot's Holiday (1954-French) 114m. *** D: Jacques Tati. Jacques Tati, Nathalie Pascaud, Michelle Rolla, Valentine Camax, Louis Perrault. Tati introduced his delightful Hulot character in this amusing excursion to a French resort town; a fond throwback to the days of silent-screen comedy.

Mr. Imperium (1951) C-87m. **½ D: Don Hartman. Lana Turner, Ezio Pinza, Marjorie Main, Barry Sullivan, Cedric Hardwicke, Debbie Reynolds. Threadbare romance between Turner and Pinza, now a monarch; colorful but paper-thin.

Mr. Inside/Mr. Outside (1973) C-74m. TVM D: William Graham. Hal Linden, Tony Lo Bianco, Phil Bruns, Paul Benjamin, Stefan Schnabel, Arnold Soboloff. Tough, atmospheric crime drama with two N.Y.C. cops working to foil diamond smugglers. Excellent action compensates for OK scripting. Average.

Mr. Jerico (1969) C-85m. TVM D: Sidney Hayers. Patrick Macnee, Marty Allen, Connie Stevens, Herbert Lom, Leonardo Pieroni, Peter Yapp. Con-man Jerico (Macnee) and assistant not only party after famed Gemini diamond owned by corrupt millionaire (Lom) on Malta, but who has real one? Good dialogue, but plot twists lack punch. One good chase involving great location work. Above average.

Mr. Kingstreet's War (1973) C-92m. **½ D: Percival Rubens. John Saxon, Tippi Hedren, Rossano Brazzi, Brian O'Shaughnessy. Loner and his wife find idyllic life at African game preserve disrupted by WW2 and set out to do something about it. Interesting and unusual.

Mr. Lucky (1943) 100m. *** D: H. C. Potter. Cary Grant, Laraine Day, Charles Bickford, Gladys Cooper, Alan Carney, Henry Stephenson, Paul Stewart, Kay Johnson, Florence Bates. Gambling-ship-owner Grant intends to fleece virtuous Day, instead falls in love and goes straight. Basis for later TV series has spirited cast, engaging script.

Mr. Majestyk (1974) C-103m. ** D: Richard Fleischer. Charles Bronson, Al Lettieri, Linda Cristal, Lee Purcell, Paul Koslo, Alejandro Rey. About average Bronson thriller, casting him as Colorado watermelon farmer (!) marked for destruction by syndicate hit man Lettieri.

Mister Moses (1965-British) C-113m. **½ D: Ronald Neame. Robert Mitchum, Carroll Baker, Ian Bannen, Alexander Knox, Raymond St. Jacques, Reginald Beckwith. Malarkey of rugged Mitchum and virtuous Baker leading African native tribe to their new homeland.

Mr. Moto With the Charlie Chan films going strong, John P. Marquand's character of a seemingly timid but cunning and intelligent sleuth named Mr. Moto seemed a natural for the movies. Twentieth Century-Fox, the same studio that was making the Chans, inaugurated the series in 1937 with THINK FAST, MR. MOTO, with the offbeat casting of Peter Lorre in the lead. Lorre fell into the role of the crafty, lighthearted Moto quite well, and played the character in all eight Moto films, through 1939. The series was entertaining, but somehow lacked the heart of the Chan films. Fortunately, they were endowed with slick productions and fine casts of character actors, which tended to overshadow the films' shortcomings. Moto globetrotted from country to country, solving various mysteries with and without the help of police authorities, and confronted such formidable villains as Sig Ruman, Sidney Blackmer, John Carradine, Leon Ames, Ricardo Cortez, Jean Hersholt and Lionel Atwill. Needless to say, the diminutive Lorre was victorious in every encounter, with the negligible help of such "assistants" as dimwitted Warren Hymer in MR. MOTO IN DANGER ISLAND. Many consider THANK YOU MR. MOTO (1938) the best of the series, with our hero hunting for a valuable map leading to an ancient treasure. In 1965 Fox decided to revive the long-dormant Moto character in a very low-budget second feature called appropriately enough, THE RETURN OF MR. MOTO. Movie villain Henry Silva starred as Moto, but the film was cheaply done and completely unfaithful to the original conception of the character. Hopefully, future movie historians will ignore the recent failure and realize that for everyone Peter Lorre was *the* Mr. Moto.

Mr. Moto in Danger Island (1939) 63m. D: Herbert I. Leeds. Peter Lorre, Jean Hersholt, Amanda Duff, Warren Hymer, Richard Lane, Leon Ames, Douglass Dumbrille, Robert Lowery.

Mr. Moto Takes a Chance (1938) 63m. D: Norman Foster. Peter Lorre, Rochelle Hudson, Robert Kent, J. Edward Bromberg, Chick Chandler, George Regas, Fredrik Vogeding.

Mr. Moto Takes a Vacation (1939) 61m. D: Norman Foster. Peter Lorre, Joseph Schildkraut, Lionel Atwill, Virginia Field, Iva Stewart, Victor Varconi, John Davidson.

Mr. Moto's Gamble (1938) 71m. D: James Tinling. Peter Lorre, Keye Luke, Dick Baldwin, Lynn Bari, Douglas Fowley, Jayne Regan, Harold Huber, Maxie Rosenbloom.

Mr. Moto's Last Warning (1939) 71m. D: Norman Foster. Peter Lorre, Ricardo Cortez, Virginia Field, John Carradine, George Sanders, Robert Coote, John Davidson.

Mr. Muggs Rides Again (1945) 63m. D: Wallace Fox. Leo Gorcey, Huntz Hall, Billy Benedict, Nancy Brinckman, George Meeker, Pierre Watkin, Bernard Thomas. SEE: **Bowery Boys** series.

Mr. Music (1950) 113m. **½ D: Richard Haydn. Bing Crosby, Nancy Olson, Charles Coburn, Ruth Hussey, Marge and Gower Champion, Peggy Lee, Groucho Marx. Easygoing vehicle for crooner Crosby as Broadway producer who wants to live the easy life.

Mr. Peabody and the Mermaid (1948) 89m. **½ D: Irving Pichel. William Powell, Ann Blyth, Irene Hervey, Andrea King, Clinton Sundberg. Comedy-fantasy has its moments, with unsuspecting Powell coming across a lovely mermaid while fishing. Powell makes anything look good.

Mr. Perrin and Mr. Traill (1948-British) 90m. ** D: Lawrence Huntington. Marius Goring, David Farrar, Greta Gynt, Raymond Huntley. Lukewarm study of progressive vs. conservative schoolteaching.

Mr. Quilp (1975-British) C-118m. *** D: Michael Tuchner. Anthony Newley, David Hemmings, David Warner, Michael Hordern, Jill Bennett, Sarah Jane Varley. Entertaining musical version of Dickens' "Old Curiosity Shop" with songs by Newley and musical score by Elmer Bernstein. Light-hearted until last reel when it goes serious in the Dickens vein.

Mr. Ricco (1975) C-98m. ** D: Paul Bogart. Dean Martin, Eugene Roche, Thalmus Rasulala, Geraldine Brooks, Denise Nicholas, Cindy Williams. Martin in offbeat casting as criminal lawyer involved with racist killings, sex and assorted violence, but looks too tired to care. Good mystery angle.

Mister Roberts (1955) C-123m. **** D: John Ford, Mervyn LeRoy. Henry Fonda, James Cagney, William Powell, Jack Lemmon, Betsy Palmer, Ward Bond, Nick Adams. Superb comedy-drama of WW2 cargo ship and its restless officer (Fonda) yearning for combat. Cagney as eccentric captain, Powell as philosophical doctor, Lemmon in Academy Award-winning performance as Ensign Pulver, all great.

Mr. Robinson Crusoe (1932) 76m. *** D: Edward Sutherland. Douglas Fairbanks Sr., William Farnum,

Earle Browne, Maria Alba. An aging but agile Doug is up to his old tricks, betting that he can survive on a South Sea island à la Robinson Crusoe. Great fun; lovely score by Alfred Newman.

Mr. Sardonicus (1961) 89m. ** D: William Castle. Oscar Homolka, Ronald Lewis, Audrey Dalton, Guy Rolfe. Recluse count with hideous grin pasted on face lures wife's boyfriend/doctor to castle to cure him. Minor fare despite good ending.

Mister Scoutmaster (1953) 87m. *** D: Henry Levin. Clifton Webb, Edmund Gwenn, George Winslow, Frances Dee, Veda Ann Borg. Childhater Webb becomes scoutmaster in this airy film which will appeal mainly to kids.

Mr. Sebastian SEE: Sebastian

Mr. Skeffington (1944) 127m. *** D: Vincent Sherman. Bette Davis, Claude Rains, Walter Abel, Richard Waring, Jerome Cowan, Charles Drake, Gigi Perreau. Grand soap opera spanning several decades of N.Y.C. life from 1900s onward. Davis is vain society woman who marries stockbroker Rains for convenience, discovering his true love for her only after many years. Lavish settings, bravura Davis performance. Cut from original 146m. release.

Mr. Skitch (1933) 70m. **½ D: James Cruze. Will Rogers, ZaSu Pitts, Rochelle Hudson, Charles Starrett, Eugene Pallette, Harry Green. Airy Rogers vehicle following family's adventures traveling by car to California. Pure fluff, highlighted by British entertainer Florence Desmond's comic impressions of costar Pitts, and Greta Garbo.

Mr. Smith Goes to Washington (1939) 129m. **** D: Frank Capra. James Stewart, Jean Arthur, Claude Rains, Edward Arnold, Guy Kibbee, Thomas Mitchell, Eugene Pallette, Beulah Bondi, Harry Carey, Jack Carson. Stewart is young idealist who finds nothing but corruption in U.S. Senate; fine Capra Americana, with Stewart's top performance bolstered by Arthur as hard-boiled dame won over by earnest Mr. Smith, and a stellar supporting cast. Remade as BILLY JACK GOES TO WASHINGTON.

Mr. Soft Touch (1949) 93m. ** D: Henry Levin, Gordon Douglas. Glenn Ford, Evelyn Keyes, John Ireland, Beulah Bondi, Percy Kilbride, Ted de Corsia. Ford and Keyes are mild romantic duo in unimportant story of ex-G.I. involved with social worker and gangster-run nightclub.

Mister Superinvisible (1973) C-91m. **½ D: Anthony M. Dawson (Antonio Margheriti). Dean Jones, Ingeborg Schoener, Gastone Moschin, Peter Carsten. Engaging Italian-German-Spanish comedy made in Geneva has American researcher Jones becoming invisible as he seeks a cure for the common cold. Good for kids, okay for grownups.

Mr. Sycamore (1974) C-88m. *½ D: Pancho Kohner. Jason Robards, Sandy Dennis, Jean Simmons, Robert Easton, Mark Miller. A milquetoasty mailman with a nagging wife (and a crush on local librarian) decides to escape rat race by turning into a tree! A definite curio, sadly defeated by heavy-handed treatment of material.

Mr. Universe (1951) 79m. *½ D: Joseph Lerner. Jack Carson, Janis Paige, Vincent Edwards, Bert Lahr, Robert Alda. Quickie comedy with good cast wasted on bad material; young Edwards plays wrestler promoted by Carson.

Mister V SEE: Pimpernel Smith

Mr. Winkle Goes to War (1944) 80m. **½ D: Alfred E. Green. Edward G. Robinson, Ruth Warrick, Ted Donaldson, Robert Armstrong, Ann Shoemaker. Minor yarn of aging henpecked man accidentally drafted during WW2, who becomes military hero. Spirited Robinson is enjoyable.

Mr. Wise Guy (1942) 70m. D: William Nigh. Leo Gorcey, Huntz Hall, Bobby Jordan, Guinn Williams, Billy Gilbert, Benny Rubin, Douglas Fowley, Ann Doran, Jack Mulhall, Warren Hymer, David Gorcey. SEE: Bowery Boys series.

Misty (1961) C-92m. *** D: James B. Clark. David Ladd, Pam Smith, Arthur O'Connell, Anne Seymour. Marguerite Henry's popular children's book is nicely realized, with Ladd and Smith as children on island off Virginia coast who fall in love with a wild horse.

Mrs. Brown, You've Got a Lovely Daughter (1968-British) C-110m. ** D: Saul Swimmer. Herman's Hermits, Stanley Holloway, Mona Washbourne, Sarah Caldwell. Silly story about racing greyhound named Mrs. Brown.

Mrs. Mike (1949) 99m. **½ D: Louis King. Dick Powell, Evelyn Keyes, J.

M. Kerrigan, Angela Clarke. Powell and Keyes are pleasing duo, as Canadian mountie indoctrinates his urban wife to rural life.

Mrs. Miniver (1942) 134m. ***½ D: William Wyler. Greer Garson, Walter Pidgeon, Dame May Whitty, Teresa Wright, Reginald Owen, Henry Travers, Richard Ney, Tom Conway, Henry Wilcoxon. Garson, Wright and director Wyler were among Oscar-winners in emotional story of family struggling through German Blitz of England. Still good.

Mrs. O'Malley and Mr. Malone (1950) 69m. ** D: Norman Taurog. Marjorie Main, James Whitmore, Ann Dvorak, Fred Clark, Dorothy Malone, Phyllis Kirk. Main is rambunctious but can't elevate film about small-towner winning prize contest, involved with murder on a New York-bound train. Whitmore is most enjoyable.

Mrs. Parkington (1944) 124m. *** D: Tay Garnett. Greer Garson, Walter Pidgeon, Edward Arnold, Gladys Cooper, Agnes Moorehead, Peter Lawford, Dan Duryea, Selena Royle, Lee Patrick. Determined Garson has lofty ambitions, marries wealthy but homespun Pidgeon, and pushes her way into society; overlong, well-mounted soaper.

Mrs. Pollifax—Spy (1971) C-110m. *½ D: Leslie Martinson. Rosalind Russell, Darren McGavin, Nehemiah Persoff, Harold Gould, Albert Paulsen, John Beck. A bored widow volunteers as a CIA agent—and gets accepted—in this lame comedy spy caper. Russell's last film (for which she did the screenplay, under pseudonym) is also, sad to say, one of her worst.

Mrs. R's Daughter (1979) C-100m. TVM D: Dan Curtis. Cloris Leachman, Season Hubley, Donald Moffat, John McIntire, Stephen Elliott, Ron Rifkin. The frustrating battle of a determined mother to bring her daughter's rapist to trial. Hell hath no fury like an angry Leachman, and it's proved in this none-too-encouraging glimpse at our contemporary court system. Average.

Mrs. Sundance (1974) C-78m. TVM D: Marvin Chomsky. Elizabeth Montgomery, Robert Foxworth, L. Q. Jones, Arthur Hunnicutt, Lurene Tuttle, Claudette Nevins. Further adventures of Etta Pace, widow of The Sundance Kid (of "Butch Cassidy and—" fame), who leads a fugitive's existence brightened by the memory of her late husband. Light-hearted western tries vainly to recapture the charm of its blockbuster predecessor. Average.

Mrs. Sundance Rides Again SEE: **Wanted: The Sundance Woman**

Mrs. Wiggs of the Cabbage Patch (1934) 80m. *** D: Norman Taurog. W. C. Fields, Pauline Lord, ZaSu Pitts, Evelyn Venable, Kent Taylor, Donald Meek, Virginia Weidler. More story than Fields in this one, a melodrama of poor woman about to be evicted; the domestic scenes with W. C. and Pitts are priceless.

Mrs. Wiggs of the Cabbage Patch (1942) 80m. **½ D: Ralph Murphy. Fay Bainter, Hugh Herbert, Vera Vague, Barbara Britton, Carolyn Lee, Billy Lee, Carl Switzer, Moroni Olsen. Abandoned wife with large family waits patiently for husband to return. A notch above average.

Mitchell (1975) C-96m. **½ D: Andrew V. McLaglen. Joe Don Baker, Martin Balsam, Linda Evans, John Saxon, Merlin Olsen, Morgan Paull. Baker plays tough cop whose singleminded pursuit of drug ring leads to expected action and violence; slick handling of typical action fodder.

Mixed Company (1974) C-109m. **½ D: Melville Shavelson. Barbara Harris, Joseph Bologna, Tom Bosley, Lisa Gerritsen, Dorothy Shay. Less than heartwarming but still entertaining comedy of losing basketball coach Bologna coping with wife Harris' adopting orphans of mixed ethnic backgrounds.

Mob, The (1951) 87m. ** D: Robert Parrish. Broderick Crawford, Betty Buehler, Richard Kiley, Otto Hulett, Neville Brand, Ernest Borgnine, Charles Bronson. Study of lawman cracking waterfront gang syndicate; Crawford is good but script is second-rate. Interesting cast, however.

Mob Town (1941) 70m. D: William Nigh. Billy Halop, Huntz Hall, Gabriel Dell, Bernard Punsley, Dick Foran, Anne Gwynne, Samuel S. Hinds. SEE: **Bowery Boys** series.

Mobile Two (1975) C-78m. TVM D: David Moessinger. Jackie Cooper, Julie Gregg, Mark Wheeler, Edd Byrnes, Jack Hogan, Joe E. Tata. Jack Webb-produced story about investigative TV reporter's various assignments (in proven tradition of Webb's "Adam-12" and "Emergency"). Standard TV fodder that led to a brief series, "Mobile One" (accounting, presumably, for a lower budget). Average.

Moby Dick (1930) 75m. **½ D: Lloyd Bacon. John Barrymore, Joan Bennett, Walter Long, Nigel De Brulier, Noble Johnson, Virginia Sale. Not Melville, but good, with Barrymore vivid as Captain Ahab; good special effects, too. Pointless love story added to original narrative, as in Barrymore's earlier silent-film version, THE SEA BEAST.

Moby Dick (1956) C-116m. *** D: John Huston. Gregory Peck, Richard Basehart, Leo Genn, Orson Welles, James Robertson Justice. Moody, spotty version of Herman Melville sea classic, with Peck miscast as Captain Ahab. Some fine scenes scattered about.

Model and the Marriage Broker, The (1951) 103m. *** D: George Cukor. Jeanne Crain, Scott Brady, Thelma Ritter, Zero Mostel, Michael O'Shea, Frank Fontaine, Nancy Kulp. The title tells all as fast-talking Ritter pairs up Crain and Brady.

Model For Murder (1958-British) 75m. ** D: Terry Bishop. Keith Andes, Hazel Court, Jean Aubrey, Michael Gough. Andes is American in England seeking late brother's girlfriend, becoming involved in jewel robbery. Adequate yarn.

Model Shop, The (1969-French) C-95m. *** D: Jacques Demy. Anouk Aimee, Gary Lockwood, Alexandra Hay, Carole Cole, Severn Darden, Tom Fielding. Twenty-four hours in life of disenchanted young architect (Lockwood), his affair with recently abandoned fashion model (Aimee). Director Demy's eye for L.A. (film's setting) is striking, but overall feel to story is ambiguous.

Model Wife (1941) 78m. **½ D: Leigh Jason. Joan Blondell, Dick Powell, Lee Bowman, Charlie Ruggles, Lucile Watson, Ruth Donnelly, Billy Gilbert. Joan's boss won't let her get married, but she does, to Powell, and has to keep it a secret. Fairly amusing comedy.

Modern Times (1936) 89m. **** D: Charles Chaplin. Charlie Chaplin, Paulette Goddard, Henry Bergman, Chester Conklin, Stanley "Tiny" Sandford. Charlie attacks the machine age in unforgettable fashion, with sharp pokes at other social ills and the struggle of modern-day survival. Goddard is the gamin who becomes his partner in life. Chaplin's last silent film (with his own music—including "Smile"—sound effects, and gibberish song) is consistently hilarious.

Modesty Blaise (1966-British) C-119m. ** D: Joseph Losey. Monica Vitti, Dirk Bogarde, Terence Stamp, Harry Andrews, Michael Craig, Scilla Gabel, Tina Marquand, Clive Revill, Alexander Knox. Director Losey ate watermelon, pickles, and ice cream, went to sleep, woke up, and made this film. Made at the height of the pop-art craze, it tries to be a spoof at times, doesn't know what it's supposed to be at other moments.

Mogambo (1953) C-115m. ***½ D: John Ford. Clark Gable, Ava Gardner, Grace Kelly, Laurence Naismith, Donald Sinden. Lusty remake of RED DUST. Gable repeats his role, Ava replaces Harlow, Kelly has Mary Astor's part. Romantic triangle in Africa combines love and action; beautifully filmed in color.

Mohammad, Messenger of God (1977-Arabic) C-180m. *** D: Moustapha Akkad. Anthony Quinn, Irene Papas, Michael Ansara, Johnny Sekka, Michael Forest, Neville Jason. Spectacle of the beginnings of Moslem religion is sincere effort, more impressive with action than religious angles. In accordance with the religion, Mohammad is never shown.

Mohawk (1956) C-79m. **½ D: Kurt Neumann. Scott Brady, Rita Gam, Neville Brand, Lori Nelson, Allison Hayes. Bouncy Western of Indian uprising thwarted by peace-loving Brady and squaw Gam.

Mokey (1942) 88m. ** D: Wells Root. Dan Dailey, Donna Reed, Bobby Blake, William "Buckwheat" Thomas, Cordell Hickman, Matt Moore, Etta McDaniel. Reed has problems with her stepson, who almost winds up in reform school. Typical of genre.

Mole People, The (1956) 78m. ** D: Virgil Vogel. John Agar, Cynthia Patrick, Hugh Beaumont, Alan Napier. Dank horror tale set in Asia involving underground people with warped thoughts.

Molly SEE: **Goldbergs, The**

Molly and Lawless John (1972) C-97m. ** D: Gary Nelson. Vera Miles, Clu Gulager, Sam Elliott, John Anderson. Young criminal dupes sheriff's wife into running away with him; OK Western with Miles' capable performance.

Molly and Me (1945) 76m. *** D: Lewis Seiler. Gracie Fields, Monty

Woolley, Roddy McDowall, Reginald Gardiner, Natalie Schafer, Edith Barrett, Clifford Brooke. Entertaining little comedy of Fields becoming Woolley's housekeeper, taking over his life as well. Well played by fine cast.

Molly Maguires, The (1970) C-123m. ****½** D: Martin Ritt. Sean Connery, Richard Harris, Samantha Eggar, Frank Finlay, Art Lund, Anthony Costello. Well-crafted film about secret society of Irish mine-workers in Pennsylvania, circa 1876, led by Connery; newcomer Harris is working as informer. Vivid atmosphere, good performances, but downbeat film lacks appeal, and is hurt by inconclusive ending.

Moment by Moment (1978) C-102m. BOMB D: Jane Wagner. Lilly Tomlin, John Travolta, Andra Akers, Bert Kramer, Shelley R. Bonus. A role-reversal romance with Travolta as the sex object that gives new dimension to the word "boring."

Moment of Danger SEE: **Malaga**

Moment of Truth, The (1952-French) 90m. ** D: Jean Delannoy. Michele Morgan, Jean Gabin, Daniel Gelin, Simone Paris. Effective playing of trite yarn of married couple realizing how little they know each other.

Moment to Moment (1966) C-108m. ****½** D: Mervyn LeRoy. Jean Seberg, Honor Blackman, Sean Garrison, Arthur Hill. Unconvincing, confused murder mystery set on the Riviera, but filmed largely on Universal's sound stage.

Mondo Cane (1963-Italian) C-105m. ****½** Producer: Gualtiero Jacopetti. First and best of Italian shockumentaries, with dubbed American narration; focuses on peculiarities of man in various parts of the world. Features song "More."

Money From Home (1953) C-100m. ****½** D: George Marshall. Dean Martin, Jerry Lewis, Pat Crowley, Robert Strauss, Jack Kruschen. Average hijinks of duo involved with gangsters, steeplechase racing, Arab ruler and his harem.

Money Jungle, The (1968) C-95m. ** D: Francis D. Lyon. John Ericson, Lola Albright, Leslie Parrish, Nehemiah Persoff, Charles Drake, Kent Smith, Don Rickles. Geologists involved in oil-rights bidding are being knocked off, but Ericson is there to stop them; good cast wasted.

Money Money Money (1973-French) C-113 m. ******* D: Claude Lelouch.

Lino Ventura, Jacques Brel, Charles Denner, Aldo Maccione, Charles Gerard. Gang of successful thieves decide that changing times demand their switch to political crimes, which pay more handsomely. Clever, funny spoof of our heated political era as seen through eyes of men whose only belief is in money.

Money to Burn (1973) C-73m. TVM D: Robert Michael Lewis. E. G. Marshall, Mildred Natwick, Alejandro Rey, Cleavon Little, David Doyle, Charles McGraw, Ronald Feinberg, Lou Frizzell. Marshall's the standout in tale of fairly clever scheme to make use of counterfeit currency printed up in federal penitentiary. Average.

Money Trap, The (1966) 92m. ****½** D: Burt Kennedy. Glenn Ford, Rita Hayworth, Elke Sommer, Joseph Cotten, Ricardo Montalban. Ford is detective turned crook in pedestrian murder yarn. Hayworth most convincing as middle-aged woman no longer self-sufficient.

Money, Women and Guns (1958) C-80m. ** D: Richard Bartlett. Jock Mahoney, Kim Hunter, Tim Hovey, Gene Evans. Modest Western about lawman sent to track down killers and to find heirs to victim's will.

Mongo's Back in Town (1971) C-73m. TVM D: Marvin Chomsky. Joe Don Baker, Telly Savalas, Sally Field, Anne Francis, Charles Cioffi, Martin Sheen. Ultragrim, deliberately slow-moving crime drama has recently released con (Baker) returning to home town, hired by brother to kill rival. Adaptation of story by actual convict strong on atmosphere but uncertain about point of view. Above average.

Mongols, The (1960-Italian) C-102m. ** D: Andre de Toth, Leopoldo Savona. Jack Palance, Anita Ekberg, Antonella Lualdi, Franco Silva. Unimaginative spectacle set in 19th century, with Palance the son of Genghis Khan on the rampage in Europe, Ekberg his girl.

Monitors, The (1969) C-89m. *½ D: Jack Shea. Guy Stockwell, Susan Oliver, Avery Schreiber, Sherry Jackson, Shepperd Strudwick, Keenan Wynn, Ed Begley, Larry Storch. Crazy story about right-wing fanatics plotting to overthrow robot-like monitors that try to regiment human emotions in a positive way; includes cameos by Alan Arkin and Everett Dirksen.

Monk, The (1969) C-73m. TVM. D: George McCowan. George Maharis, Janet Leigh, Jack Albertson, Carl Betz, Edward G. Robinson, Jr., Linda Marsh. Stereotyped modern-day private-eye Gus Monk (Maharis) framed into embarrassing situation when man who gave him envelope for safekeeping is found murdered. Embarrassing dialogue, predictable resolution, unbelievable villains. Below average.

Monkey Business (1931) 77m. ***½ D: Norman Z. McLeod. Groucho, Harpo, Chico, Zeppo Marx, Thelma Todd, Ruth Hall, Harry Woods. Four brothers stow away on luxury liner; Groucho goes after Thelma, all four pretend to be Maurice Chevalier to get off ship. Full quota of sight gags and puns in typically wacky comedy.

Monkey Business (1952) 97m. *** D: Howard Hawks. Ginger Rogers, Cary Grant, Charles Coburn, Marilyn Monroe, Hugh Marlowe. Grant discovers rejuvenation serum which affects him, his wife Rogers, boss Coburn, and secretary Monroe in this wacky comedy. Coburn's classic line to MM: "Get someone to type this."

Monkey Hustle (1977) C-90m. *½ D: Arthur Marks. Yaphet Kotto, Rosalind Cash, Rudy Ray Moore, Kirk Calloway, Randy Brooks. Appealing cast is only saving grace of dumb comedy actioner designed for black audiences, shot in Chicago. Kotto is a black Fagin; ghetto neighborhood's demise for an expressway forms a bit of plot.

Monkey on My Back (1957) 93m. **½ D: Andre de Toth. Cameron Mitchell, Paul Richards, Dianne Foster, Jack Albertson, Kathy Garver. Mitchell as fighter Barney Ross, who became a dope addict, turns in sincere performance. Well-meant, engrossing little film.

Monkeys, Go Home! (1967) C-101m. ** D: Andrew V. McLaglen. Maurice Chevalier, Dean Jones, Yvette Mimieux, Bernard Woringer, Clement Harari, Yvonne Constant. Disney trivia about a man who inherits French olive farm and trains monkeys to pick his crop. Gossamerthin, for kids only.

Monkey's Uncle, The (1965) C-87m. ** D: Robert Stevenson. Tommy Kirk, Annette Funicello, Leon Ames, Frank Faylen, Arthur O'Connell, Norman Grabowski. Juvenile Disney comedy has Kirk again as Merlin Jones, college whiz-kid who first tries sleep-learning method on monkey, then sets himself up in makeshift flying machine. Flight sequences provide brightest moments.

Monolith Monsters, The (1957) 77m. ** D: John Sherwood. Lola Albright, Grant Williams, Les Tremayne, Trevor Bardette. For a change of pace, the title villains are slabs of rocks sucking out human energy.

Monsieur Beaucaire (1946) 93m. *** D: George Marshall. Bob Hope, Joan Caulfield, Patric Knowles, Marjorie Reynolds, Cecil Kellaway, Joseph Schildkraut, Reginald Owen, Constance Collier. Pleasing Hope vehicle with Bob in costume as barber sent on mission as dead duck sure to be murdered. Plush settings, funny gags.

Monsieur Verdoux (1947) 123m. ***½ D: Charles Chaplin. Charles Chaplin, Martha Raye, Isobel Elsom, Marilyn Nash, Irving Bacon, William Frawley. Chaplin's controversial black comedy about a Parisian Bluebeard who murders wives for their money was twenty years ahead of its time; its wry humor and pacifist sentiments make it quite contemporary when seen today. Broad comic sequence with Raye is particular highlight.

Monsoon (1953) C-79m. *½ D: Rodney Amateau. Ursula Thiess, Diana Douglas, George Nader, Ellen Corby. Trite drama of several people destroyed by their passions; set in India.

Monster, The (1925) 86m. ** D: Roland West. Lon Chaney, Gertrude Olmstead, Hallam Cooley, Johnny Arthur, Charles Sellon. Overdose of comedy relief hampers moody Chaney mad-doctor doings; still OK, though, as whole film has tongue-in-cheek. From Crane Wilbur's play.

Monster and the Girl, The (1941) 65m. **½ D: Stuart Heisler. Ellen Drew, Robert Paige, Paul Lukas, Joseph Calleia, George Zucco, Rod Cameron. Unusual B-film starts off with story of gangsters dragging Drew into life of prostitution, then veers off into horror as Zucco transfers her dead brother's brain into body of a gorilla! White slavery angle more original than the mad-scientist stuff.

Monster from the Ocean Floor, The (1954) 64m. BOMB D: Wyott Ordung. Anne Kimball, Stuart Wade, Wyott Ordung. One of producer Roger Corman's earliest efforts is a dreadful film about a squid-like creature pursued by a minisubmarine; 20,000 yawns under the sea.

Monster of Piedras Blancas, The (1958) 71m. *½ D: Irvin Berwick. Les Tremayne, Forrest Lewis, John Harmon, Frank Arvidson, Wayne Berwick. Sluggish chiller with crustacean terror thirsting for blood on a deserted seacoast; obvious and amateurish.

Monster Maker, The (1944) 62m. ** D: Sam Newfield. J. Carrol Naish, Ralph Morgan, Wanda McKay, Terry Frost. For horror buffs, a low-budget yarn of mad-scientist Naish transplanting something-or-other to create his strange beings.

Monster on the Campus (1958) 76m. **½ D: Jack Arnold. Arthur Franz, Joanna Moore, Judson Pratt, Nancy Walters, Troy Donahue. Above-par chiller involving blood formula that turns a college professor into rampaging beast.

Monster That Challenged the World, The (1957) 83m. **½ D: Arnold Laven. Tim Holt, Audrey Dalton, Hans Conried, Casey Adams. Imaginative special effects improve this chiller about oversized water monster.

Monster Zero (1966-Japanese) C-90m. *½ D: Inoshiro Honda. Nick Adams, Akira Takarada. Monster Zero captures Godzilla and Rodan and threatens to destroy earth with his two enslaved cohorts. Laughable.

Monstrosity (1964) 72m. *½ D: Joseph Mascelli. Frank Gerstle, Erika Peters, Judy Bamber, Frank Fowler, Marjorie Eaton. Eaton is wealthy matron who hires doctor (Gerstle) to perform brain transplant on her; lumbering mess. Retitled: ATOMIC BRAIN, THE.

Montana (1950) C-76m. **½ D: Ray Enright. Errol Flynn, Alexis Smith, S. Z. Sakall, Monte Blue, Douglas Kennedy. Slick yet unexciting Western with formula Warner Bros. plot line and type casting; minor Flynn vehicle.

Montana Belle (1952) C-81m. ** D: Allan Dwan. Jane Russell, George Brent, Scott Brady, Andy Devine, Forrest Tucker. Mildly interesting Western with Russell as Belle Starr, involved with fellow-outlaws, the Dalton brothers.

Montana Mike SEE: **Heaven Only Knows**

Montana Territory (1952) C-64m. **

D: Ray Nazarro. Lon McCallister, Wanda Hendrix, Preston Foster, Jack Elam, Clayton Moore. McCallister is deputized cowboy who's out to bring in the outlaws.

Monte Carlo (1930) 90m. **½ D: Ernst Lubitsch. Jeanette MacDonald, Jack Buchanan, ZaSu Pitts, Claude Allister, Tyler Brooke. Dated but enjoyable musical froth with Jeanette an impoverished countess wooed by royal Buchanan, who's incognito of course. Lubitsch's methods of integrating songs into the film were innovations in 1930; most memorable is "Beyond the Blue Horizon."

Monte Carlo Story, The (1957-Italian) C-99m. ** D: Samuel Taylor. Marlene Dietrich, Vittorio De Sica, Arthur O'Connell, Natalie Trundy, Mischa Auer. Charming stars try to support thin story of troubled romance between two compulsive gamblers; filmed on location.

Monte Walsh (1970) C-106m. *** D: William Fraker. Lee Marvin, Jeanne Moreau, Jack Palance, Mitch Ryan, Jim Davis, Allyn Ann McLerie. Melancholy Western with Marvin a veteran cowboy who finds himself part of a dying West. Sensitive filming of novel by Jack Schaefer (who wrote SHANE). Fine performance by Palance in atypical good-guy role.

Monterey Pop (1969) C-88m. ***½ D: James Desmond, Barry Feinstein, D. A. Pennebaker, Albert Maysles, Roger Murphy, Richard Leacock and Nick Proferes. Otis Redding, Mamas and Papas, Jimi Hendrix, The Who, Janis Joplin, Animals, Jefferson Airplane. First major rock concert film, and certainly one of the best ever.

Monty Python and the Holy Grail (1974-British) C-90m. **½ D: Terry Gilliam, Terry Jones. Graham Chapman, John Cleese, Terry Gilliam, Eric Idle, Terry Jones, Michael Palin. The Python troupe's second feature is wildly uneven, starting out well and then getting lost—in the "story" of a medieval crusade. Some inspired lunacy, and a lot of dry stretches. Recommended for fans only.

Monty Python's Life of Brian SEE: **Life of Brian**

Moon and Sixpence, The (1942) 89m. *** D: Albert Lewin. George Sanders, Herbert Marshall, Doris Dudley, Eric Blore, Elena Verdugo, Florence Bates, Albert Basserman, Heather Thatcher. Faithful film of

Maugham's tale of man who decides to fulfill lifelong ambition to paint, moving to Tahitian island. Superb acting by Sanders in lead, Marshall as the author.

Moon Is Blue, The (1953) 95m. **½ D: Otto Preminger. William Holden, David Niven, Maggie McNamara, Tom Tully. Once-saucy sex comedy now seems tame, too much a filmed stage play, with most innuendoes lacking punch.

Moon Is Down, The (1943) 90m. *** D: Irving Pichel. Cedric Hardwicke, Henry Travers, Lee J. Cobb, Dorris Bowden, Margaret Wycherly, Peter Van Eyck, William Post, Jr. Fine drama from Steinbeck novel of Norway's invasion by Nazis, tracing local effect and reactions.

Moon of the Wolf (1972) C-73m. TVM D: Daniel Petrie. David Janssen, Barbara Rush, Bradford Dillman, John Beradino, Geoffrey Lewis, Royal Dano. Muddy motivation major liability in somewhat likeable modern day thriller involving werewolf in Louisiana. Resolution is offbeat but forgettable. Average.

Moon Over Burma (1940) 76m. ** D: Louis King. Dorothy Lamour, Preston Foster, Robert Preston, Doris Nolan, Albert Basserman, Frederick Worlock. Island setting tries to cover up for same old triangle with Foster and Preston fighting over Lamour.

Moon Over Miami (1941) C-91m. *** D: Walter Lang. Don Ameche, Betty Grable, Robert Cummings, Carole Landis, Charlotte Greenwood, Jack Haley. Grable, sister Landis, and Greenwood go fortune-hunting in Miami, come up with more than they bargained for in smoothly entertaining musical romance, especially nice in color. Tuneful songs include title tune, "You Started Something." Remake of THREE BLIND MICE, also remade as THREE LITTLE GIRLS IN BLUE.

Moon Pilot (1962) C-98m. *** D: James Neilson. Tom Tryon, Brian Keith, Edmond O'Brien, Dany Saval, Tommy Kirk, Bob Sweeney, Kent Smith. Dated but enjoyable Disney comedy about astronaut Tryon who meets mysterious girl from another planet (Saval) just before his mission.

Moon-Spinners, The (1964) C-118m. **½ D: James Neilson. Hayley Mills, Eli Wallach, Pola Negri, Peter McEnery, Joan Greenwood, Irene

Papas. Disney's attempt at Hitchcock-like intrigue with a light touch has Hayley a vacationer in Crete who becomes involved with jewelry-smuggling ring. Too long and muddled to hit bullseye, but still entertaining, with Negri (off-screen since 1943) an enjoyable villainess.

Moon Zero Two (1970-British) C-100m. *½ D: Roy Ward Baker. James Olson, Catherina Von Schell, Warren Mitchell, Adrienne Corri, Ori Levy, Dudley Foster. Sci-fi adventure is almost like a Western, with people making mining claims on the moon and having to fight for their rights. You've seen it before without the craters.

Moon's Our Home, The (1936) 76m. ** D: William A. Seiter. Margaret Sullavan, Henry Fonda, Charles Butterworth, Beulah Bondi, Walter Brennan. Flyweight comedy about turbulent courtship and marriage of movie star and N.Y. novelist; too silly to matter, though stars do their best. (Footnote: Fonda and Sullavan had already been married and divorced when this film was made).

Moonfleet (1955) C-89m. **½ D: Fritz Lang. Stewart Granger, Jon Whiteley, George Sanders, Viveca Lindfors, Joan Greenwood, Ian Wolfe. Tepid 18th-century story of Britisher Granger becoming a buccaneer.

Moonlight and Cactus (1944) 60m. *½ D: Edward Cline. Andrews Sisters, Elyse Knox, Leo Carrillo, Eddie Quillan, Shemp Howard, Minerva Urecal. Singing trio find themselves out West running a ranch and chasing romance. Lightweight production.

Moonlight Sonata (1938-British) 80m. **½ D: Lothar Mendes. Ignace Jan Paderewski, Charles Farrell, Marie Tempest, Barbara Greene, Eric Portman. Well-made but stodgy romance, set in household of Swedish baroness, is excuse for screen appearance by famous concert pianist.

Moonlighter, The (1953) 75m. ** D: Roy Rowland. Barbara Stanwyck, Fred MacMurray, Ward Bond, William Ching, John Dierkes, Jack Elam. Dull Western with its 3-D virtue lost to TV viewers; MacMurray is a rustler and Stanwyck his ex-girlfriend.

Moonraker (1979) C-126m. ** D: Lewis Gilbert. Roger Moore, Lois Chiles, Michael Lonsdale, Richard Kiel, Corinne Clery, Bernard Lee, Desmond Llewelyn, Lois Maxwell. James Bond no longer resembles Ian

[517]

Fleming's creation; now he's a tired punster pursuing an intergalactic madman. Overblown comic-strip adventure is strictly for the bubble-gum set . . . but tune in for eye-popping free-fall opening, the best part of this movie.

Moonraker, The (1958-British) C-82m. *** D: David MacDonald. George Baker, Sylvia Syms, Peter Arne, Marius Goring. Well-mounted costumer set in 1650s England, involving followers of Charles Stuart.

Moonrise (1948) 90m. **½ D: Frank Borzage. Dane Clark, Gail Russell, Ethel Barrymore, Allyn Joslyn, Harry Morgan, Lloyd Bridges, Selena Royle, Rex Ingram. Low-key drama of man unwittingly murdering someone, on the run from the law with his devoted girl; good cast helps so-so material.

Moonrunners (1974) C-102m. ** D: Gy Waldron. James Mitchum, Kiel Martin, Arthur Hunnicutt, Joan Blackman, Waylon Jennings, Chris Forbes. Action-comedy about modern day bootleggers sputters because of Mitchum's lethargic acting and the script's lack of credibility.

Moonshine County Express (1977) C-95m. **½ D: Gus Trikonis. John Saxon, Susan Howard, William Conrad, Morgan Woodward, Claudia Jennings, Jeff Corey, Dub Taylor, Maureen McCormack. Murdered moonshiner's three sexy daughters decide to compete with local biggie (Conrad) whom they believe caused their father's death. Pretty good action programmer.

Moonshine War, The (1970) C-100m. ** D: Richard Quine. Richard Widmark, Alan Alda, Patrick McGoohan, Melodie Johnson, Will Geer, Joe Williams, Lee Hazlewood. Tediously plotted mixture of comedy and drama during late Prohibition era enlivened by unusual cast and honest attempt to evoke country atmosphere.

Moontide (1942) 94m. **½ D: Archie Mayo. Jean Gabin, Ida Lupino, Thomas Mitchell, Claude Rains, Jerome Cowan, Helene Reynolds, Ralph Byrd, Sen Yung, Tully Marshall. Jean Gabin's portrayal of rough seaman who cares for potential suicide (Lupino) saves an otherwise average "realistic" movie.

More American Graffiti (1979) C-111m. *½ D: B. W. L. Norton. Candy Clark, Bo Hopkins, Ron Howard, Paul Le Mat, Mackenzie Phillips, Charles Martin Smith, Cindy Williams, Anna Bjorn. More is less, in this sequel to 1973 hit, placing that film's likable characters in a quartet of pointless vignettes which are pointlessly intercut.

More Dead Than Alive (1969) C-101m. ** D: Robert Sparr. Clint Walker, Vincent Price, Anne Francis, Paul Hampton. Modest Western about a gunslinger traveling in a side show as sharpshooter.

More Than a Miracle (1967-Italian-French) C-105m. ** D: Francesco Rosi. Sophia Loren, Omar Sharif, Dolores Del Rio, George Wilson, Leslie French, Marina Malfatti. Sophia has never looked better but this absurd fairy tale about a prince and a peasant girl is just a waste of time.

More Than a Secretary (1936) 77m. ** D: Alfred E. Green. Jean Arthur, George Brent, Lionel Stander, Ruth Donnelly, Reginald Denny, Dorothea Kent. Arthur's charm gives distinction to routine comedy of secretary in love with handsome boss Brent.

More Than Friends (1979) C-100m. TVM D: Jim Burrows. Penny Marshall, Rob Reiner, Kay Medford, Claudette Nevins, Dabney Coleman. Occasionally hilarious romantic comedy by Reiner loosely based on his early courtship with his wife Penny Marshall (of LAVERNE AND SHIRLEY). Above average.

More the Merrier, The (1943) 104m. *** D: George Stevens. Jean Arthur, Joel McCrea, Charles Coburn, Richard Gaines, Bruce Bennett, Ann Savage, Ann Doran, Frank Sully, Grady Sutton. Working-girl Arthur finds herself sharing small apartment in WW2 Washington with McCrea and Coburn (who won an Oscar for this). Later remade as WALK DON'T RUN, but peerless Arthur can't be beat.

Morgan! (1966-British) 97m. ***½ D: Karel Reisz. Vanessa Redgrave, David Warner, Robert Stephens, Irene Handl. Decidedly offbeat gem. Artist Warner verges on insanity, keyed off by wife Redgrave's divorcing him, and goes on eccentric escapades.

Morgan the Pirate (1961-Italian) C-95m. ** D: Andre de Toth. Steve Reeves, Valerie Lagrange, Lydia Alfonsi, Chelo Alonso. Considering cast and Reeves' career, fairly likely and interesting swashbuckler based on life of illustrious pirate.

Morituri SEE: **Saboteur: Code Name Morituri**

Morning After, The (1974) C-78m. TVM D: Richard T. Heffron. Dick Van Dyke, Lynn Carlin, Don Porter, Linda Lavin, Richard Derr, Robert Hover. Forceful movie with Van Dyke making an auspicious dramatic debut in his portrait of a corporate executive turned alcoholic. Above average.

Morning Departure SEE: **Operation Disaster**

Morning Glory (1933) 74m. *** D: Lowell Sherman. Katharine Hepburn, Adolphe Menjou, Douglas Fairbanks Jr., C. Aubrey Smith, Mary Duncan. Dated but lovely film from Zoe Akins' play about stagestruck young girl called Eva Lovelace who tries to succeed in N.Y.C. Good cast, sharp script, but it's magically compelling Hepburn who makes this memorable; she won first Oscar for her work. Remade as STAGE STRUCK.

Morocco (1930) 92m. *** D: Josef von Sternberg. Gary Cooper, Marlene Dietrich, Adolphe Menjou, Francis McDonald, Eve Southern, Paul Porcasi. Dietrich is alluring cafe performer who gives up wealthy Menjou to follow legionnaire lover Cooper across the desert. Marlene sings "What Am I Bid?" in her first American film.

Mortal Storm, The (1940) 100m. ***½ D: Frank Borzage. Margaret Sullavan, James Stewart, Robert Young, Frank Morgan, Robert Stack, Bonita Granville, Irene Rich, Maria Ouspenskaya. Nazi takeover in Germany splits family, ruins life of father, professor Morgan; Stewart tries to leave country with professor's daughter (Sullavan). Sincere filming of Phyllis Bottome's novel is beautifully acted, with one of Morgan's finest performances.

Moscow Nights SEE: **I Stand Condemned**

Mosquito Squadron (1969-British) C-90m. **½ D: Boris Sagal. David McCallum, Suzanne Neve, David Buck, David Dundas, Dinsdale Landen, Charles Gray. Good ensemble performances in tired story of Canadian-born RAF pilot (McCallum)'s crucial behind-the-lines mission to destroy Germany's ultimate weapon project.

Moss Rose (1947) 82m. **½ D:

Gregory Ratoff. Peggy Cummins, Victor Mature, Ethel Barrymore, Vincent Price, Margo Woode. OK period-piece of ambitious chorus girl who blackmails her way into high society; scheme nearly backfires on her.

Most Dangerous Game, The (1932) 63m. *** D: Ernest B. Shoedsack and Irving Pichel. Joel McCrea, Fay Wray, Leslie Banks, Robert Armstrong, Noble Johnson. Vivid telling of Richard Connell's famous, oft-filmed story about a megalomaniac named Count Zaroff who hunts human beings on his remote island. Banks is a florid, sometimes campy villain. Made at the same time as KING KONG by many of the same people. Remade as GAME OF DEATH and RUN FOR THE SUN.

Most Dangerous Man Alive (1961) 82m. ** D: Allan Dwan. Ron Randell, Debra Paget, Elaine Stewart, Anthony Caruso, Gregg Palmer. Inventive premise adequately handled; escaped convict involved in chemical explosion is transformed into "iron man" and seeks revenge on enemies.

Most Dangerous Sin, The SEE: **Crime and Punishment** (1958)

Most Wanted (1976) C-78m. TVM D: Walter Grauman. Robert Stack, Shelly Novack, Leslie Charleson, Tom Selleck, Kitty Winn, Sheree North, Stephen McNally. Stack heads special police unit in search of a nun killer and winds up with another TV series. Average.

Most Wanted Man SEE: **Most Wanted Man in the World, The**

Most Wanted Man in the World, The (1953-French) 85m. ** D: Henri Verneuil, Fernandel, Zsa Zsa Gabor, Nicole Maurey, Alfred Adam. Fernandel vehicle is heavy-handed buffoonery, with bucolic comic mistaken for arch-criminal. Retitled: MOST WANTED MAN, THE.

Most Wonderful Moment, The (1959-Italian) 94m. ** D: Luciano Emmer. Marcello Mastroianni, Giovanna Ralli, Marisa Merlini, Ernesto Calindri. Lackluster account of doctor Mastroianni and nurse Ralli, involved in new method of childbirth.

Mother and Daughter—The Loving War (1980) C-100m. TVM. D: Burt Brinckerhoff. Tuesday Weld, Frances Sternhagen, Kathleen Beller, Jeanne Lang, Ed Winter. A young woman turns to her mother for help when her teenage daughter begins to rebel

—just as *she* did twenty years ago. Above average.

Mother Carey's Chickens (1938) 82m. ** D: Rowland V. Lee. Fay Bainter, Anne Shirley, Ruby Keeler, James Ellison, Walter Brennan, Frank Albertson, Virginia Weidler, Ralph Morgan. Bainter is mother, Keeler and Shirley her "chickens" in ordinary tear-jerker romance based on Kate Douglas Wiggin's novel.

Mother Didn't Tell Me (1950) 88m. **½ D: Claude Binyon. Dorothy McGuire, William Lundigan, June Havoc, Gary Merrill, Jessie Royce Landis. McGuire brightens this lightweight comedy. Naive young woman marries a doctor, not contemplating demands of being a professional man's wife.

Mother Is a Freshman (1949) C-81m. **½ D: Lloyd Bacon. Loretta Young, Van Johnson, Rudy Vallee, Barbara Lawrence, Robert Arthur, Betty Lynn. Refreshing, wholesome confection; Young and daughter Lynn both attend college, vying for Van's affection.

Mother, Jugs & Speed (1976) C-95m. *** D: Peter Yates. Bill Cosby, Raquel Welch, Harvey Keitel, Allen Garfield, Larry Hagman, Bruce Davison. Hilarious black comedy about a rundown ambulance service more interested in number of patients serviced than their welfare. Hagman especially good as oversexed driver.

Mother Wore Tights (1947) C-107m. *** D: Walter Lang. Betty Grable, Dan Dailey, Mona Freeman, Connie Marshall, Vanessa Brown, Veda Ann Borg. One of Grable's most popular films. About a vaudeville couple, with colorful production, costumes, and nostalgic songs, plus specialty act by Señor Wences.

Mothra (1962-Japanese) C-100m. ** D: Inoshiro Honda, Lee Kresel. Franky Sakai, Hiroshi Koizumi, Kyoko Kagawa, Emi Itoh, Yumi Itoh, Jelly Itoh, Ken Uehara. Satisfactory Japanese science-fiction of flying monster who disrupts Tokyo, submitting only to the control of twin girls with supernatural powers.

Motorcycle Gang (1957) 78m. *½ D: Edward L. Cahn. Anne Neyland. John Ashley, Carl Switzer, Raymond Hatton, Edmund Cobb. Cheap production dealing with crackdown on rampaging cycle gang.

Moulin Rouge (1952) C-123m. **** D: John Huston. Jose Ferrer, Zsa Gabor, Suzanne Flon, Eric Pohlmann, Colette Marchand, Christopher Lee, Michael Balfour. Oscar winning masterpiece based on life of Toulouse-Lautrec, the 19th Century Parisian artist whose growth was stunted by childhood accident. Huston brilliantly captures the flavor of Montmartre, its characters, and Lautrec's sadly distorted view of life. Excellent cast; memorable theme song.

Mountain, The (1956) C-105m. **½ D: Edward Dmytryk. Spencer Tracy, Robert Wagner, Claire Trevor, William Demarest, Richard Arlen, E. G. Marshall. Turgid tale of brothers Tracy and Wagner climbing peak to reach wreckage, for different reasons.

Mountain Family Robinson (1979) C-100m. **½ D: John Cotter. Robert F. Logan, Susan Damante Shaw, William Bryant, Heather Rattray, Ham Larsen, George (Buck) Flower. Kids may not understand "déjà vu," but they'll feel it if they watch this clone of earlier Wilderness Family pictures. Not bad, but so similar to others it hardly seems worth the effort.

Mountain Road, The (1960) 102m. **½ D: Daniel Mann. James Stewart, Lisa Lu, Glenn Corbett, Henry (Harry) Morgan, Frank Silvera, James Best. Stewart is always worth watching, but this saga of American squadron working in China during waning days of WW2 is pretty flat.

Mourning Becomes Electra (1947) 173m. **½ D: Dudley Nichols. Rosalind Russell, Michael Redgrave, Raymond Massey, Katina Paxinou, Nancy Coleman, Leo Genn, Kirk Douglas. Eugene O'Neill's play set in New England and adapted from the Greek tragedy *Oresteia*. Civil War general is killed by wife and their children seek revenge. Heavy, talky drama, even in 105m. version shown on TV.

Mouse and his Child, The (1977) C-83m. BOMB D: Fred Wolf, Chuck Swenson. Voices of Peter Ustinov, Alan Barzman, Marcy Swenson, Cloris Leachman, Andy Devine, Sally Kellerman. Boring animated film about a toy mouse and his child, and their adventures in the real world. Talk, talk, talk and no action.

Mouse on the Moon, The (1963-British) C-82m. ***½ D: Richard Lester. Margaret Rutherford, Bernard Cribbins, Ron Moody, Terry-Thomas,

Michael Crawford. Hilarious sequel to THE MOUSE THAT ROARED, about Duchy of Grand Fenwick. Tiny country enters space race, with little help from its befuddled Grand Duchess, Margaret Rutherford.

Mouse That Roared, The (1959-British) C-83m. ***½ D: Jack Arnold. Peter Sellers, Jean Seberg, David Kossoff, William Hartnell, Monty Landis, Leo McKern. Hilarious satire about the Duchy of Grand Fenwick declaring war on the U. S. Sellers stars in three roles, equally amusing. Gag before opening titles is a masterpiece.

Mousey (1974) C-78m. TVM D: Daniel Petrie. Kirk Douglas, Jean Seberg, John Vernon, Bessie Love, Suzanne Lloyd, Sam Wanamaker, James Bradford. Thriller about a milquetoast teacher (Douglas) who stops at nothing to take vengeance on his ex-wife. Tightly made, and Kirk's wonderfully sinister. Above average.

Mouthpiece, The (1932) 90m. ***½ D: Elliott Nugent, James Flood. Warren William, Sidney Fox, Mae Madison, Aline MacMahon, John Wray. Solid story based on life of flamboyant attorney William Fallon; up-and-coming prosecutor in D.A.'s office turns to defending people instead, becomes slick and successful, leaving morals behind. First-rate all the way. Remade as THE MAN WHO TALKED TOO MUCH and ILLEGAL.

Move (1970) C-90m. BOMB D: Stuart Rosenberg. Elliott Gould, Paula Prentiss, Genevieve Waite, John Larch, Joe Silver, Ron O'Neal. One of those comedies that helped to kill Gould's career within a year; porn-writer/dog-walker has problems when he moves from one apartment to another, but not as many as viewers will have trying to make sense out of the film.

Move Over, Darling (1963) C-103m. **½ D: Michael Gordon. Doris Day, James Garner, Polly Bergen, Thelma Ritter, Fred Clark, Chuck Connors. Day, Garner, and Bergen redo the Irene Dunne, Cary Grant, and Gail Patrick roles from MY FAVORITE WIFE in this amusing film. Edgar Buchanan stands out as a judge confused by the wife-brought-back-to-life situation.

Movie Crazy (1932) 84m. *** D: Clyde Bruckman. Harold Lloyd, Constance Cummings, Kenneth

Thomson, Sydney Jarvis, Eddie Fetherstone. Lloyd's best talkie recaptures the spirit of his silent-comedy hits, telling story of small-town boy who goes to Hollywood with stars in his eyes, gets rude awakening but finally makes good. Includes his famous magician's coat scene. Cummings is a charming leading lady.

Movie Maker, The (1967) C-91m. TVM D: Josef Leytes. Rod Steiger, Robert Culp, Anna Lee, James Dunn, Sally Kellerman. Strong performances, by Steiger and Culp in drama detailing rivalry for control of movie studio. Stagy enactment of Rod Serling script. Originally a two-part "Chrysler Theatre" of 1965. Above average.

Movie Movie (1978) C/B&W-107m. *** D: Stanley Donen. George C. Scott, Trish Van Devere, Eli Wallach, Red Buttons, Barbara Harris, Barry Bostwick, Harry Hamlin, Art Carney, Rebecca York, Ann Reinking. Affectionate parody of 1930s double feature: "Dynamite Hands" is b&w boxing saga with Hamlin in the John Garfield-ish role; "Baxter's Beauties of 1933" is Busby Berkeley-type musical, with numbers staged by Michael Kidd (who plays Hamlin's father in first story). There's even a Coming Attractions prevue!

Movie Murderer, The (1970) C-99m. TVM D: Boris Sagal. Arthur Kennedy, Robert Webber, Warren Oates. Arsonist specializing in destroying jet liners inadvertently filmed, searches for negatives, becomes quarry of insurance investigator and detective. Passable hunter-versus-hunted story with good performances, novelty value of many vintage film clips. Average.

Movin' On SEE: In Tandem

Moving Target (1967-Italian) C-92m. *½ D: Sergio Corbucci. Ty Hardin, Michael Rennie, Grazielle Granata, Paola Pitagora, Vittorio Caprioli. Incredibly plotted spy/counterspy stuff set in Athens, marred even further by sadistic, explicitly violent action.

Moving Violation (1976) C-91m. ** D: Charles S. Dubin. Stephen McHattie, Kay Lenz, Eddie Albert, Lonny Chapman, Will Geer, Jack Murdock, John S. Ragin. Redneck sheriff goes after young couple, leading to usual car-chase action. So what else is new?

Mudlark, The (1950) 99m. *** D:

Jean Negulesco. Irene Dunne, Alec Guinness, Finlay Currie, Anthony Steele, Andrew Ray, Beatrice Campbell, Wilfrid Hyde-White. Offbeat drama of Queen Victoria (Dunne), a recluse since her husband's death, coming back to reality after meeting waif who stole into her castle. Dunne does quite well as Queen, with Guinness a joy as Disraeli. Filmed in England.

Mug Town (1943) 60m. D: Ray Taylor. Billy Halop, Huntz Hall, Bernard Punsley, Gabriel Dell, Tommy Kelly, Grace McDonald, Edward Norris. SEE: **Bowery Boys** series.

Mulligan's Stew (1977) C-78m. TVM D: Noel Black. Lawrence Pressman, Elinor Donahue, Johnny Whitaker, Alex Karras, K. C. Martel, Julie Haddock. Sentimental comedy about high school coach with wife and three kids who takes four orphans into his house. The innumerable complications have been similarly explored in "Mixed Company" as well as TV's "Fish" but they developed a series from this one regardless. Average.

Mummy, The (1932) 72m. ***½ D: Karl Freund. Boris Karloff, Zita Johann, David Manners, Bramwell Fletcher, Noble Johnson. Horror classic. Egyptian mummy, revived after thousands of years, believes Johann is reincarnation of ancient mate. Remarkable makeup and atmosphere make it chills ahead of many sequels.

Mummy, The (1959-British) C-88m. **½ D: Terence Fisher. Peter Cushing, Christopher Lee, Yvonne Furneaux, Eddie Byrne, Felix Aylmer, Raymond Huntley. Against warnings of severe consequences, archaeologists desecrate ancient tomb of Egyptian Princess Ananka. They return to England and those consequences. Stylish Hammer horror film.

Mummy's Curse, The (1944) 62m. ** D: Leslie Goodwins. Lon Chaney Jr., Peter Coe, Virginia Christine, Kay Harding, Dennis Moore, Martin Kosleck, Kurt Katch. When the mummy of Princess Ananka (Christine) is dug up in a swamp and she is restored to womanhood, can Kharis (Chaney) be far behind? All-too-predictable rehash of mummy theme.

Mummy's Ghost, The (1944) 60m. ** D: Reginald LeBorg. John Carradine, Lon Chaney, Robert Lowery,

Ramsay Ames, George Zucco. Above-average cast can't do much with far-fetched tale of mummy searching America for ancient heartthrob, reborn as American girl.

Mummy's Hand, The (1940) 67m. ** D: Christy Cabanne. Dick Foran, Peggy Moran, Wallace Ford, Eduardo Ciannelli, George Zucco, Cecil Kellaway, Tom Tyler. Absurd story of ancient mummy coming to life to protect lover's tomb from scientist's interference. Cowboy star Tyler is a listless mummy.

Mummy's Shroud, The (1967-British) C-90m. BOMB D: John Gilling. Andre Morell, John Phillips, David Buck, Elizabeth Sellars, Maggie Kimberley, Michael Ripper. Archeologists hunt for tomb of Egyptian pharaoh nearly 4000 years old, which is about the same age as the script.

Mummy's Tomb, The (1942) 61m. *½ D: Harold Young. Lon Chaney, Dick Foran, John Hubbard, Elyse Knox, George Zucco, Wallace Ford, Turhan Bey, Mary Gordon. One of the weakest in Mummy series. Colorful cast struggles through "B" plot of Egyptian finding remains of mummy and reviving it.

Mumsy, Nanny, Sonny and Girly (1970-British) C-101m. BOMB D: Freddie Francis. Vanessa Howard, Michael Bryant, Ursula Howells, Pat Heywood, Howard Trevor. Rockbottom murder tale of eccentric family where children's "game-playing" has lethal overtones. Stupid. Also known as GIRLY.

Munster, Go Home (1966) C-96m. **½ D: Earl Bellamy. Fred Gwynne, Yvonne De Carlo, Terry-Thomas, Hermione Gingold, John Carradine, Debby Watson, Butch Patrick. Based on TV series. Monster family goes to England to claim a castle they've inherited; juvenile production.

Muppet Movie, The (1979) C-94m. *** D: James Frawley. Kermit the Frog, Miss Piggy, Fozzie Bear, and the Muppets (Jim Henson, Frank Oz, Jerry Nelson, Richard Hunt, Dave Goelz), Charles Durning, Austin Pendleton. Enjoyable showcase for Jim Henson's irresistible characters, charting Kermit's odyssey from a Georgia swamp to Hollywood. Unnecessary movie-star cameos and pedestrian music score can't dim Muppets' appeal. Trimmed from 97m. after initial release.

Murder (1930-British) 92m. *** D: Alfred Hitchcock. Herbert Marshall,

Norah Baring, Phyllis Konstam, Edward Chapman. Good early Hitchcock casts Marshall as actor who serves on jury at murder trial and believes accused woman innocent.

Murder Ahoy (1964-British) 93m. ***½ D: George Pollock. Margaret Rutherford, Lionel Jeffries, Charles Tingwell. Miss Marple goes after murderers and solves the case before the bobbies. Delightful mystery based on Agatha Christie novel.

Murder at 45 R.P.M. (1960-French) 105m. **½ D: Etienne Perier. Danielle Darrieux, Michel Auclair, Jean Servais, Henri Guisol. Darrieux is an engaging songstress, whose husband seemingly returns from the grave to haunt her and lover (Auclair); neat plot twists, but slow-moving.

Murder at the Gallop (1963-British) 81m. ***½ D: George Pollock. Margaret Rutherford, Robert Morley, Flora Robson, Charles Tingwell. Amateur sleuth Miss Marple suspects foul play when wealthy old recluse dies. Based on Agatha Christie's book, "After the Funeral."

Murder at the Mardi Gras (1978) C-100m. TVM D: Ken Annakin. Didi Conn, Bill Daily, David Groh, David Wayne, Harry Morgan, Joyce Van Patten, Barbi Benton. Featherbrained thriller about a bubble-headed girl (Conn) who witnesses title crime, then is stalked by the killer. How did a director like Annakin get involved with this? Below average.

Murder at the Vanities (1934) 89m. **½ D: Mitchell Leisen. Jack Oakie, Kitty Carlisle, Carl Brisson, Victor McLaglen, Donald Meek, Gail Patrick, Toby Wing, Jessie Ralph, Dorothy Stickney. Offbeat murder mystery set backstage at Earl Carroll's Vanities, with detective McLaglen holding everyone under suspicion, including show's stars (Carlisle, Brisson). Songs include "Cocktails for Two," bizarre "Sweet Marijuana" number; look for Ann Sheridan as chorus girl.

Murder at the World Series (1977) C-100m. TVM D: Andrew McLaglen. Lynda Day George, Murray Hamilton, Karen Valentine, Michael Parks, Janet Leigh, Hugh O'Brian, Nancy Kelly, Joseph Wiseman, Tamara Dobson, Gerald S. O'Loughlin. Psycho plots bizarre kidnapping during the World Series at Houston Astrodome. Predictable, second-rate

thriller with the usual all-star cast of stereotypes. Below average.

Murder by Contract (1958) 81m. ** D: Irving Lerner. Vince Edwards, Philip Pine, Herschel Bernardi, Caprice Toriel. Intriguing little film about a hired killer and what makes him tick; ultimately sabotaged by pretentious dialogue and posturing.

Murder by Death (1976) C-94m. *** D: Robert Moore. Peter Sellers, Peter Falk, David Niven, Maggie Smith, James Coco, Alec Guinness, Elsa Lanchester, Eileen Brennan, Nancy Walker, Estelle Winwood, Truman Capote. Capote invites world's greatest detectives to his home and involves them in a baffling whodunit. Neil Simon spoofs such characters as Charlie Chan, Miss Marple, and Sam Spade in this enjoyable comedy.

Murder by Decree (1979-Canadian-British) C-121m. *** D: Bob Clark. Christopher Plummer, James Mason, Donald Sutherland, Genevieve Bujold, Susan Clark, David Hemmings, Frank Finlay, John Gielgud. Sherlock Holmes investigates slayings of prostitutes by Jack the Ripper, with surprising results. Involved, often lurid story doesn't sustain through conclusion, but flaws overshadowed by warm interpretations of Holmes and Watson by Plummer and Mason.

Murder by Natural Causes (1979) C-100m. TVM D: Robert Day. Hal Holbrook, Katharine Ross, Richard Anderson, Barry Bostwick, Bill Fiore, Jeff Donnell. Oustanding thinking man's thriller that has the unfaithful wife of a famed mentalist trying to do him in by literally scaring him to death. Well-acted and written—and don't blink for the last reel or you'll miss countless clever twists. Above average.

Murder Clinic (1966-Italian-French) C-87m. *½ D: William Hamilton (Elio Scardamaglia). William Berger, Francoise Prevost, Mary Young, Barbara Wilson, Delphia Maurin. Period thriller of isolated clinic peopled with eccentric patients, terrorized by monster which roams in corridors and woods outside. Slow going.

Murder, Czech Style (1968-Czech) 90m. **½ D: Jiri Weiss. Rudolf Hrusinsky, Kyeta Fialova, Vaclav Voska, Vladimir Mensik. Clever, gentle spoof of romantic triangle melodramas, with pudgy middle-aged clerk (Hrusinsky) marrying beautiful woman, realizing she's been cheating on him, planning revenge, via dream sequences.

Murder Game, The (1966-British) 75m. *½ D: Sidney Salkow. Ken Scott, Marla Landi, Trader Faulkner, Conrad Phillips, Gerald Sim, Duncan Lamont. Routine murder-blackmail drama about woman who skips out on her husband, changes her name, then marries again.

Murder, He Says (1945) 91m. *** D: George Marshall. Fred MacMurray, Helen Walker, Marjorie Main, Jean Heather, Porter Hall, Peter Whitney, Barbara Pepper, Mabel Paige. Zany slapstick of insurance salesman MacMurray encountering Main's family of hayseed murderers. Too strong at times, but generally funny.

Murder in Greenwich Village (1937) 68m. ** D: Albert S. Rogell. Richard Arlen, Fay Wray, Raymond Walburn, Wyn Cahoon, Scott Colton, Thurston Hall. Dated romantic mystery comedy with heiress Wray using photographer Arlen as alibi for whereabouts when murder took place. Mystery is secondary, solved only as an afterthought.

Murder in Music City (1979) C-100m. TVM D: Leo Penn. Sonny Bono, Lee Purcell, Claude Akins, Belinda Montgomery, Harry Bellaver. The cherished memory of Nick and Nora Charles is tarnished with this tacky (rather than wacky) whodunit pilot that sends a brash songwriter-turned-detective and his photographer's model bride on the trail of a killer in Nashville. Below average.

Murder in Peyton Place (1977) C-100m. TVM D: Bruce Kessler. Christopher Connelly, Dorothy Malone, Ed Nelson, Stella Stevens, Janet Margolin, David Hedison, Tim O'Connor. Mystery-drama reuniting members of the old TV series following strange deaths of Allison MacKenzie and Rodney Harrington (whom everyone remembers as Mia Farrow and Ryan O'Neal before they became stars). Everything's the same in town—with ten years of gossip and intrigue added. Average.

Murder in the Air (1940) 55m. *½ D: Lewis Seiler. Ronald Reagan, John Litel, Lya Lys, James Stephenson, Eddie Foy, Jr., Robert Warwick. Juvenile secret agent yarn, with Reagan assigned to stop enemy agents from stealing secret plans.

Murder in the Blue Room (1944) 61m. ** D: Leslie Goodwins. Anne Gwynne, Donald Cook, John Litel, Grace McDonald, Betty Kean, June Preisser, Regis Toomey. Film has distinction of being an Old Dark House musical, but otherwise has nothing to recommend it. Typical brassy songs against OK whodunit background; filmed before as THE MISSING GUEST and SECRET OF THE BLUE ROOM.

Murder in the Music Hall (1946) 84m. ** D: John English. Vera Hruba Ralston, William Marshall, Helen Walker, Nancy Kelly, William Gargan, Ann Rutherford, Julie Bishop. Not-bad whodunit, a backstage murder with above-average cast for low-grade Republic Pictures.

Murder, Inc. (1960) 103m. *** D: Burt Balaban, Stuart Rosenberg. Stuart Whitman, May Britt, Henry Morgan, Peter Falk, David J. Stewart, Simon Oakland. Blasting gun action, taut direction, and fierce performances make this gangster saga well above par.

Murder is My Beat (1955) 77m. ** D: Edgar G. Ulmer. Paul Langton, Barbara Payton, Robert Shayne, Selena Royle. Standard "B" treatment of alleged killer Payton discovering actual criminal.

Murder is My Business (1946) 64m. ** D: Sam Newfield. Hugh Beaumont, Cheryl Walker, Lyle Talbot, George Meeker, Pierre Watkin. Programmer Mike Shayne caper, with Beaumont a tame shamus on prowl for killer.

Murder Man, The (1935) 70m. **½ D: Tim Whelan. Spencer Tracy, Virginia Bruce, Lionel Atwill, Harvey Stephens, Robert Barrat, James Stewart. Reporter Tracy convinces cops someone else is guilty of murder he actually committed. Good melodrama is also Stewart's first film.

Murder Most Foul (1965-British) 90m. *** D: George Pollock. Margaret Rutherford, Ron Moody, Charles Tingwell, Andrew Cruickshank. When Miss Marple is lone jury member who believes defendant is innocent, she sets out to prove it. Based on Agatha Christie's MRS. McGINTY'S DEAD.

Murder My Sweet (1944) 95m. *** D: Edward Dmytryk. Dick Powell, Claire Trevor, Anne Shirley, Otto Kruger, Mike Mazurki. Based on Raymond Chandler's book FARE-

WELL MY LOVELY, this remake of THE FALCON TAKES OVER gave Powell new image as hardboiled detective Philip Marlowe, involved in homicide and blackmail. Remade as FAREWELL, MY LOVELY in 1975.

Murder on Approval (1956-British) 90m. ** D: Bernard Knowles. Tom Conway, Delphi Lawrence, Brian Worth, Michael Balfour. Veteran detective-player Conway can't save humdrum treasure-hunt caper. Retitled: BARBADOS QUEST.

Murder on Flight 502 (1975) C-100m. TVM D: George McCowan. Ralph Bellamy, Polly Bergen, Theodore Bikel, Sonny Bono, Dane Clark, Laraine Day, Fernando Lamas, George Maharis, Farrah Fawcett-Majors, Hugh O'Brian, Molly Picon, Walter Pidgeon, Robert Stack, Rosemarie Stack. All-star cast is terrorized by a maniac on a transatlantic jumbo jet piloted by Stack. Seems we've heard that story before. Average.

Murder on Monday SEE: **Home at Seven**

Murder on the Orient Express (1974-British) C-127m. *** D: Sidney Lumet. Albert Finney, Lauren Bacall, Martin Balsam, Ingrid Bergman, Jacqueline Bisset, Jean-Pierre Cassel, Sean Connery, John Gielgud, Wendy Hiller, Anthony Perkins, Vanessa Redgrave, Rachel Roberts, Richard Widmark, Michael York. Elegant all-star production of Agatha Christie's whodunit set in the 1930s, with unrecognizable Finney as super-sleuth Hercule Poirot, and all his suspects on the same railroad train. Colorful entertainment, but awfully sluggish; sharp viewers will be able to guess the denouement, as well. Bergman won Best Supporting Actress Oscar.

Murder Once Removed (1971) C-74m. TVM D: Charles Dubin. John Forsythe, Richard Kiley, Barbara Bain, Joseph Campanella, Wendell Burton. "Perfect crime" attempted by respectable doctor. Cast provides ensemble quality to plot, atmosphere convincing, but film is carbon copy of 100 you've seen before. Average.

Murder One SEE: **D.A.: Murder One**

Murder or Mercy (1974) C-78m. TVM D: Harvey Hart. Bradford Dillman, Melvyn Douglas, David Birney, Mildred Dunnock, Denver Pyle, Robert Webber, Kent Smith. Courtroom drama about mercy killing, with noted doctor Douglas on trial for the death of his terminally ill wife. Douglas and Dunnock are wonderful as always, but the plot too closely resembles AN ACT OF MURDER. Average.

Murder Over New York (1940) 65m. D: Harry Lachman. Sidney Toler, Marjorie Weaver, Robert Lowery, Ricardo Cortez, Donald MacBride, Melville Cooper, Sen Yung. SEE: **Charlie Chan** series.

Murder, She Said (1962-British) 87m. *** D: George Pollock. Margaret Rutherford, Arthur Kennedy, Muriel Pavlow, James Robertson Jusice. Miss Marple takes a job as a domestic in order to solve a murder she witnessed.

Murder Will Out (1952-British) 83m. *** D: John Gilling. Valerie Hobson, Edward Underdown, James Robertson Justice, Henry Kendall. Underplayed suspenser with creditable red herrings to engage the viewer. Retitled: THE VOICE OF MERRILL.

Murderer's Row (1966) C-108m. *½ D: Henry Levin. Dean Martin, Ann-Margret, Karl Malden, Camilla Sparv, James Gregory, Beverly Adams. Nice Riviera scenery can't help another stupid Matt Helm secret-agent farce; villain Malden kidnaps Ann-Margret's father in this one.

Murders in the Rue Morgue (1932) 75m. ** D: Robert Florey. Bela Lugosi, Sidney Fox, Leon Ames, Brandon Hurst, Arlene Francis. Very mild horror film based on Poe story, with Lugosi as fiendish Dr. Mirakle, with eyes on lovely Fox as the bride of his pet ape. Remade as PHANTOM OF THE RUE MORGUE.

Murders in the Rue Morgue (1971) C-87m. *½ D: Gordon Hessler. Jason Robards, Herbert Lom, Christine Kaufman, Lilli Palmer, Adolfo Celi, Maria Perschy, Michael Dunn. Sensationalistic reworking of Poe story; players at Grand Guignol-type theater suddenly become victims of real-life murders, gory goings-on.

Murdock's Gang (1973) C-74m. TVM D: Charles S. Dubin. Alex Dreier, Janet Leigh, Murray Hamilton, William Daniels, Harold Gould, Don Knight. Embezzling bookkeeper is object of search by disbarred attorney (Dreier) and group of ex-cons. Colorful cast and amusing situations in inconsequential but diverting tale. Average.

Muriel (1963-French) **C**-115m. **½
D: Alain Resnais. Delphine Seyrig, Jean-Pierre Kerien, Nita Klein, Claude Sainval. Confusing/depressing/brilliant film (take your choice). Not for all tastes, this French film of people who lead empty lives isn't an evening of fun. Cinema students may find interest in Resnais' direction.

Murphy's War (1971-British) **C**-108m. *** D: Peter Yates. Peter O'Toole, Sian Phillips, Phillipe Noiret, Horst Janson, John Hallam, Ingo Morgendorf. Well-staged, gripping action sequences combine with psychological study of British seaman (O'Toole) only survivor of German massacre, out to get revenge. Good idea, but nonaction sequences tend to bog film down.

Muscle Beach Party (1964) **C**-94m. ** D: William Asher. Frankie Avalon, Annette Funicello, Morey Amsterdam, Buddy Hackett, Luciana Paluzzi. Here they are again, dancing on the shores of sunny California. Hackett and Amsterdam try to liven it up.

Music for Millions (1944) 120m. **½ D: Henry Koster. Margaret O'Brien, Jimmy Durante, June Allyson, Marsha Hunt, Hugh Herbert, Jose Iturbi, Connie Gilchrist, Harry Davenport. Teary tale of sisters joining the great Iturbi's orchestra is overly long; Durante steals film with "Umbriago."

Music in My Heart (1940) 70m. ** D: Joseph Santley. Tony Martin, Rita Hayworth, Edith Fellows, Alan Mowbray, Eric Blore, George Tobias. Routine musical of Continental Martin cast in show where he meets lovely Hayworth. One good song, "It's a Blue World."

Music in the Air (1934) 85m. *** D: Joe May. Gloria Swanson, John Boles, Douglass Montgomery, June Lang, Reginald Owen, Al Shean. Predictable plot given chic treatment; leading-lady Swanson and lyricist Boles constantly quarreling, trying jealousy ploy when naïve young couple come on the scene. Good Jerome Kern-Oscar Hammerstein score enhances bright production.

Music is Magic (1935) 65m. ** D: George Marshall. Alice Faye, Ray Walker, Bebe Daniels, Frank Mitchell, Jack Durant. Limp musical of fading star Daniels and rising Faye,

with no great songs and not much else either.

Music Man, The (1962) **C**-151m. ***½ D: Morton Da Costa. Robert Preston, Shirley Jones, Buddy Hackett, Hermione Gingold, Paul Ford, Pert Kelton. Exuberant musical with Preston dynamic as Professor Harold Hill, the traveling music man stranded in turn-of-the-century River City. Jones is Marian the librarian, Gingold the mayor's wife. Score includes "76 Trombones," "Till There Was You."

Musketeers of the Sea (1960-Italian) **C**-116m. ** D: Massimo Patrizi. Robert Alda, Pier Angeli, Aldo Ray. Anonymous sea yarn, standard in all departments, involving search for gold in Maracaibo.

Mustang Country (1976) **C**-79m. *** D: John Champion. Joel McCrea, Robert Fuller, Patrick Wayne, Nika Mina. Excellent western set along Montana-Canadian border in 1925. 70 year old McCrea most convincing as ex-rancher and rodeo star who shares adventures with runaway Indian boy while hunting a wild stallion.

Mutations, The (1973-British) **C**-92m. ** D: Jack Cardiff. Donald Pleasence, Tom Baker, Brad Harris, Julie Edge, Michael Dunn, Jill Haworth. Scientist Pleasence is crossbreeding humans with plants—and his unsuspecting university students are being abducted as guinea pigs. Predictable story with truly grotesque elements—and characters. Not recommended for dinnertime viewing.

Mutineers, The (1949) 60m. *½ D: Jean Yarbrough. Jon Hall, Adele Jergens, George Reeves, Noel Cravat. Hastily-thrown-together flick of Hall and mates combating rebellion aboard ship. Retitled: PIRATE SHIP.

Mutiny (1952) 77m. *½ D: Edward Dmytryk. Mark Stevens, Angela Lansbury, Patric Knowles, Gene Evans. Sloppy flick of Stevens et al trying to capture gold to help cause against British during War of 1812.

Mutiny in Outer Space (1965) 81m. *½ D: Hugo Grimaldi. William Leslie, Dolores Faith, Pamela Curran, Richard Garland, Harold Lloyd, Jr., James Dobson, Glenn Langan. Creeping fungus starts killing astronauts on the way back from trip to the moon in OK sci-fi meller.

Mutiny on the Bounty (1935) 132m. **** D: Frank Lloyd. Charles

Laughton, Clark Gable, Franchot Tone, Herbert Mundin, Eddie Quillan, Dudley Digges, Donald Crisp, Movita. Vivid Nordhoff-Hall account of mutiny against tyrannical Captain Bligh (Laughton) on worldwide sea voyage, with all the horrors of 18th-century British sea life portrayed. Won Oscar as Best Picture; knots ahead of recent remake.

Mutiny on the Bounty (1962) C-179m. **½ D: Lewis Milestone. Marlon Brando, Trevor Howard, Richard Harris, Hugh Griffith, Richard Haydn, Tim Seely, Percy Herbert, Tarita. Lavish remake of the 1935 classic can't come near it, although it's visually beautiful; Howard is good as Captain Bligh, but Brando is all wrong as Fletcher Christian. Where are you, Clark Gable?

My Bill (1938) 64m. **½ D: John Farrow. Kay Francis, Bonita Granville, Anita Louise, Bobby Jordan, Dickie Moore. Francis is poverty-stricken widow with four children, involved in scandal; OK soaper.

My Blood Runs Cold (1965) 104m. **½ D: William Conrad. Troy Donahue, Joey Heatherton, Barry Sullivan, Jeanette Nolan. Young man thinks girl is long-dead ancestor, and recalls love affair from generations before. Not all that bad, but not worth missing I LOVE LUCY for either.

My Blue Heaven (1950) C-96m. **½ D: Henry Koster. Betty Grable, Dan Dailey, David Wayne, Jane Wyatt, Mitzi Gaynor, Una Merkel. Pleasing musicomedy with Grable and Dailey as radio stars who try to adopt a child.

My Boys are Good Boys (1978) C-90m. *½ D: Bethel Buckalew. Ralph Meeker, Ida Lupino, Lloyd Nolan, David F. Doyle, Sean T. Roche. Odd little film mixes 1940s approach to juvenile delinquency with far-fetched story of teenagers robbing armored car. Produced by Meeker and his wife.

My Brother Talks to Horses (1946) 93m. ** D: Fred Zinnemann. "Butch" Jenkins, Peter Lawford, Beverly Tyler, Edward Arnold, Charlie Ruggles, Spring Byington. Gimmick comedy that's fun at the start but drags to slow finish.

My Brother's Keeper (1949-British) 96m. ** D: Alfred Roome. Jack Warner, Jane Hylton, George Cole, Bill Owen, David Tomlinson. Hunt-the-escaped-convicts film has gimmick of the two escaped prisoners being handcuffed together.

My Cousin Rachel (1952) 98m. *** D: Henry Koster. Olivia de Havilland, Richard Burton, Audrey Dalton, John Sutton, Ronald Squire. Successful filmization of Daphne du Maurier mystery, with Burton trying to discover if De Havilland is guilty or innocent of murder and intrigue.

My Darling Clementine (1946) 97m. **** D: John Ford. Henry Fonda, Linda Darnell, Victor Mature, Walter Brennan, Tim Holt, Ward Bond, Alan Mowbray, John Ireland. Beautifully directed, low-key western about Wyatt Earp (Fonda) and Doc Holliday (Mature), leading to inevitable gunfight at O.K. Corral. One of director Ford's finest films, and an American classic.

My Darling Daughters' Anniversary (1973) C-74m. TVM D: Joseph Pevney. Robert Young, Ruth Hussey, Darleen Carr, Darrell Larson, Judy Strangis, Jerry Fogel, Sharon Gless, Colby Chester. Now that Judge Raleigh has married off his daughters, what's to become of his widower status? Amusing sequel to ALL MY DARLING DAUGHTERS has a couple of decent situations, adequate performances. Average.

My Daughter Joy SEE: **Operation X**

My Dear Secretary (1948) 94m. **½ D: Charles Martin. Laraine Day, Kirk Douglas, Keenan Wynn, Helen Walker, Rudy Vallee, Florence Bates, Alan Mowbray. Bright, trivial comedy of writer Douglas and best-seller authoress Day; Wynn steals the show. Douglas is a bit too earnest at times.

My Dream Is Yours (1949) C-101m. **½ D: Michael Curtiz. Jack Carson, Doris Day, Lee Bowman, Adolphe Menjou, Eve Arden. Carson makes Doris a radio star in standard musicomedy; highlights are Bugs Bunny dream sequence, Edgar Kennedy's role as Day's uncle.

My Fair Lady (1964) C-170m. ***½ D: George Cukor. Rex Harrison, Audrey Hepburn, Stanley Holloway, Wilfrid Hyde-White, Gladys Cooper, Jeremy Brett, Theodore Bikel. Ultra-smooth filmization of Lerner and Loewe's enchanting musical from Shaw's PYGMALION, with Prof. Henry Higgins (Harrison) transforming guttersnipe Hepburn into regal lady, to win a bet. Sumptuously filmed, a must in color, with

"The Rain in Spain," fantasy "Just You Wait," Harrison's soliloquys among highlights.

My Father's House (1975) C-100m. TVM. D: Alex Segal. Cliff Robertson, Robert Preston, Eileen Brennan, Rosemary Forsyth, Michael-James Wixted, Brad Savage, Ruth McDevitt. Contemporary drama, slowed by repetitious flashbacks, about heart-attack patient (Robertson) whose fond memories of his father (Preston) and his childhood in simpler times make him question the life he has created for his own family. Good cast does its best. Average.

My Favorite Blonde (1942) 78m. *** D: Sidney Lanfield. Bob Hope, Madeleine Carroll, Gale Sondergaard, George Zucco, Victor Varconi. Bob and his trained penguin become sitting ducks when spy Madeleine uses them to help deliver secret orders; very funny Hope vehicle.

My Favorite Brunette (1947) 87m. *** D: Elliott Nugent. Bob Hope, Dorothy Lamour, Peter Lorre, Lon Chaney, John Hoyt. Better-than-usual Hope nonsense with Bob as a photographer mixed up with mobsters; Lorre and Chaney add authenticity.

My Favorite Spy (1942) 86m. ** D: Tay Garnett. Kay Kyser, Ellen Drew, Jane Wyman, Robert Armstrong, William Demarest, Una O'Connor, Helen Westley, George Cleveland, Ish Kabibble. How did we win WW2 with bandleader Kyser as spy? Nonsensical musicomedy tries to explain.

My Favorite Spy (1951) 93m. *** D: Norman Z. McLeod. Bob Hope, Hedy Lamarr, Francis L. Sullivan, John Archer, Iris Adrian, Arnold Moss. Bob resembles murdered spy, finds himself thrust into international intrigue. Fast-moving fun, with glamorous Hedy aiding Bob on all counts.

My Favorite Wife (1940) 88m. *** D: Garson Kanin. Cary Grant, Irene Dunne, Gail Patrick, Randolph Scott, Ann Shoemaker, Scotty Beckett, Donald MacBride. Dunne, supposedly dead, returns to U.S. to find hubby Grant remarried to Patrick, in familiar but witty marital mixup, remade as MOVE OVER, DARLING.

My Foolish Heart (1949) 98m. *** D: Mark Robson. Dana Andrews, Susan Hayward, Kent Smith, Lois Wheeler, Jessie Royce Landis, Robert Keith, Gigi Perreau. Deftly handled sentimental WW2 romance tale between soldier Andrews and Hayward; Victor Young's lovely theme helps, too.

My Forbidden Past (1951) 81m. **½ D: Robert Stevenson. Robert Mitchum, Ava Gardner, Melvyn Douglas, Janis Carter. Period drama of shady girl Gardner coming into money, but unable to buy affection of doctor Mitchum.

My Friend Flicka (1943) C-89m. *** D: Harold Schuster. Roddy McDowall, Preston Foster, Rita Johnson, Jeff Corey, James Bell. Sentimental story of boy who loves rebellious horse; nicely done, beautifully filmed in color. Followed by sequel THUNDERHEAD, SON OF FLICKA.

My Friend Irma (1949) 103m. ** D: George Marshall. John Lund, Diana Lynn, Don DeFore, Marie Wilson, Dean Martin, Jerry Lewis. Based on radio series, movie concerns Wilson in title role as dumb blonde, encountering wacky Martin and Lewis in their film debut.

My Friend Irma Goes West (1950) 90m. **½ D: Hal Walker. Marie Wilson, Diana Lynn, Dean Martin, Jerry Lewis, Corinne Calvet, John Lund. Daffy Irma (Wilson) and pals join Martin and Lewis on their trek to Hollywood.

My Gal Sal (1942) C-103m. *** D: Irving Cummings. Rita Hayworth, Victor Mature, John Sutton, Carole Landis, James Gleason, Phil Silvers, Mona Maris, Hermes Pan, Walter Catlett. Nostalgic Gay 90s musical about songwriter Paul Dresser (Mature) in love with beautiful singer Hayworth. Includes Dresser's songs, such as title tune and other old-time numbers.

My Geisha (1962) C-120m. **½ D: Jack Cardiff. Shirley MacLaine, Yves Montand, Edward G. Robinson, Robert Cummings, Yoko Tani. Occasionally amusing comedy. MacLaine is movie star who tries the hard way to convince husband-director Montand that she's right for his movie. Filmed in Japan.

My Girl Tisa (1948) 95m. **½ D: Elliott Nugent. Lilli Palmer, Sam Wanamaker, Akim Tamiroff, Gale Robbins, Stella Adler. Sincere but uninspiring tale of devoted immigrant girl Palmer working to bring her father to the U. S. Palmer is fine as usual in lead.

My Gun is Quick (1957) 88m. *½ D: George White, Phil Victor. Robert Bray, Whitney Blake, Pamela Duncan, Donald Randolph. Drab Mickey Spillane yarn about detective Mike Hammer tracking down a murderer.

My Husband Is Missing (1978) C-100m TVM D: Richard Michaels. Sally Struthers, Tony Musante, Martine Beswicke, James Hong, Jeff David, Nam Loc. Sincere but somber odyssey of a Vietnam war widow who goes to Hanoi seeking word of her MIA husband. Average.

My Life With Caroline (1941) 81m. **½ D: Lewis Milestone. Ronald Colman, Anna Lee, Charles Winninger, Reginald Gardiner, Gilbert Roland. Colman's charm sustains this frothy comedy of man suspecting his wife of having a lover.

My Little Chickadee (1940) 83m. **½ D: Edward Cline. Mae West, W. C. Fields, Joseph Calleia, Dick Foran, Ruth Donnelly, Margaret Hamilton, Donald Meek. Team of West and Fields out West is good, but should have been funnier; W. C.'s saloon scenes are notable.

My Love Came Back (1940) 81m. **½ D: Curtis Bernhardt. Olivia de Havilland, Jeffrey Lynn, Eddie Albert, Jane Wyman, Charles Winninger, Spring Byington, Grant Mitchell. Entertaining little romance of violinist De Havilland looking for husband.

My Love for Yours SEE: **Innocent Affair, An**

My Lucky Star (1938) 84m. **½ D: Roy Del Ruth. Sonja Henie, Richard Greene, Cesar Romero, Buddy Ebsen, Joan Davis, Arthur Treacher. Henie as attractive coed; an excuse for her ice-skating and such songs as "This May Be The Night," "The All-American Swing," "I've Got A Date With A Dream."

My Man and I (1952) 99m. **½ D: William Wellman. Shelley Winters, Ricardo Montalban, Wendell Corey, Claire Trevor. Trials and tribulations of kindly Mexican worker Montalban; good cast helps OK script.

My Man Godfrey (1936) 95m. ***½ D: Gregory La Cava. William Powell, Carole Lombard, Gail Patrick, Alice Brady, Eugene Pallette, Alan Mowbray, Mischa Auer. Delightful romp with Lombard and crazy household hiring Powell as butler. Mischa Auer is impressive as starv-

ing artist, sheltered by patroness Brady. Less dated comedy of manners than 1957 remake.

My Man Godfrey (1957) C-92m. **½ D: Henry Koster. June Allyson, David Niven, Martha Hyer, Eva Gabor, Jeff Donnell. Shallow compared to original, but on its own a harmless comedy of rich gal Allyson finding life's truths from butler Niven.

My Name is Ivan (1963-Russian) 94m. *** D: Andrei Tarkovsky. Kolya Burlaiev, Valentin Zubkov, Ye Zharikov. Taut account of Russian youth sent as spy into Nazi territory. Retitled: THE YOUNGEST SPY.

My Name is Julia Ross (1945) 65m. ***½ D: Joseph H. Lewis. Nina Foch, Dame May Whitty, George Macready, Roland Varno, Anita Bolster, Doris Lloyd. Little gem of unsuspecting girl given new identity by madman Macready. First-rate thriller.

My Name Is Nobody (1974-Italian) C-115m. *** D: Tonino Valerii. Henry Fonda, Terence Hill, Leo Gordon, Geoffrey Lewis, R. G. Armstrong. Underrated, enjoyable if overlong Western spoof with Hill as an easygoing gunman who worships aging Fonda, a gunfighter who wants to retire. Italo-French-German co-production, filmed in the U. S. and Spain.

My Night at Maud's (1970-French) 105m. *** D: Eric Rohmer. Jean-Louis Trintignant, Francoise Fabian, Marie-Christine Barrault, Antoine Vitez. No. 3 of Rohmer's "Six Moral Tales" is most intellectual, with Trintignant as moral Catholic man infatuated with woman completely unlike himself. Talky, fascinating, more specialized in appeal than later entries in series.

My Old Man (1979) C-100m. TVM D: John Erman. Kristy McNichol, Warren Oates, Eileen Brennan, Mark Arnold, David Margulies. The saga of a spunky teenage girl and her down-and-out horse trainer dad, from a Hemingway short story. Sound familiar? Try Wallace Beery and Jackie Cooper four decades removed. Average.

My Old Man's Place (1972) C-93m. **½ D: Edwin Sherin. Mitchell Ryan, Arthur Kennedy, William Devane, Michael Moriarty, Topo Swope. Returned soldiers eventually show psychotic tendencies and begin a spree of rape and murder. Not profound, but interesting. Original title: GLORY BOY.

My Outlaw Brother (1951) 82m. ** D: Elliott Nugent. Mickey Rooney, Wanda Hendrix, Robert Preston, Robert Stack. Dude Rooney discovers brother is outlaw, joins with Texas Rangers to fight crime.

My Own True Love (1948) 84m. ** D: Compton Bennett. Melvyn Douglas, Phyllis Calvert, Wanda Hendrix, Philip Friend, Binnie Barnes. Calvert is placed in the awkward position of choosing between two suitors, a father and son; drama lacks ring of truth.

My Pal Gus (1952) 83m. **½ D: Robert Parrish. Richard Widmark, Joanne Dru, Audrey Totter, George Winslow, Regis Toomey. Wholesome film of Widmark coming to realize importance of son Winslow, finding romance with teacher Dru.

My Reputation (1946) 94m. *** D: Curtis Bernhardt. Barbara Stanwyck, George Brent, Warner Anderson, Lucile Watson, John Ridgely, Eve Arden. Well-mounted Warner Bros. soaper; widow Stanwyck is center of scandal when she dates Brent soon after her husband's death.

My Seven Little Sins (1954-French) C-98m. ** D: Jean Boyer. Maurice Chevalier, Collette Ripert, Paolo Stoppa, Delia Scala. Pleasant, inconsequential musicomedy, with Chevalier an old roué "adopting" group of Riviera chorines. Retitled: I HAVE SEVEN DAUGHTERS.

My Side of the Mountain (1969) C-100m. **½ D: James B. Clark. Ted Eccles, Theodore Bikel, Tudi Wiggins, Frank Perry, Peggi Loder. Children should enjoy this tale about 13-year-old Canadian boy who runs away from home to get closer to nature. Dialogue is a little banal for adults, but the premise is so attractive, they may enjoy it, too.

My Sister Eileen (1942) 96m. **½ D: Alexander Hall. Rosalind Russell, Brian Aherne, Janet Blair, George Tobias, Allyn Joslyn, Elizabeth Patterson, June Havoc. Amusing tale of two Ohio girls trying to survive in Greenwich Village apartment; strained at times. Belongs mainly to Russell as older sister of knockout Blair.

My Sister Eileen (1955) C-108m. ***½ D: Richard Quine. Betty Garrett, Janet Leigh, Jack Lemmon,

Kurt Kasznar, Dick York, Horace McMahon, Bob Fosse, Tommy Rall. Delightful, unpretentious musical version of 1942 comedy of Ohio girls seeking success while living in nutty Greenwich Village apartment. Lemmon even sings in this one.

My Six Convicts (1952) 104m. *** D: Hugo Fregonese. Millard Mitchell, Gilbert Roland, John Beal, Marshall Thompson, Regis Toomey. Unusual comedy of prison life centering on title group who manage to make jail routine tolerable, egged on by prison psychiatrist.

My Six Loves (1963) C-101m. **½ D: Gower Champion. Debbie Reynolds, Cliff Robertson, David Janssen, Eileen Heckart, Hans Conried, Alice Pearce, Jim Backus. Syrupy fluff of theater star Reynolds "adopting" six waifs; courted by clergyman Robertson among others.

My Son John (1952) 122m. **½ D: Leo McCarey. Helen Hayes, Robert Walker, Dean Jagger, Van Heflin, Frank McHugh, Richard Jaeckel. Archetypal apple-pie parents (Hayes, Jagger) suspect their son (Walker) of being a Communist in this reactionary period piece. Dramatically overwrought, but fascinating as social history. Walker (who's superb) died before film was finished; most shots of him in final reel are cribbed from STRANGERS ON A TRAIN.

My Son, My Son (1940) 115m. ** D: Charles Vidor. Madeleine Carroll, Brian Aherne, Louis Hayward, Laraine Day, Henry Hull, Josephine Hutchinson, Scotty Beckett. Drawnout, unconvincing tale of rags-to-riches Aherne who spoils his son, lives to regret. Some good performances wasted on banal script.

My Son, The Hero (1963-Italian) C-111m. ** D: Duccio Tessari. Pedro Armendariz, Jacqueline Sassard, Antonella Lualdi, Tanya Lopert. Italian spectacle with good twist. Instead of typical, ludicrous dialogue, U. S. firm dubbed Jewish accents onto the track.

My Sweet Charlie (1970) C-97m. TVM D: Lamont Johnson. Patty Duke, Al Freeman Jr., Ford Rainey, William Hardy, Chris Wilson, Noble Willingham. White unwed mother and black New York lawyer thrown together in abandoned house in rural Texas. Good adaptation of Westheimer novel, excellent performances, total effect believable and moving. Above average; this earned theatrical showings after debut on TV.

My Uncle (1958-French) C-110m. **** D: Jacques Tati. Jacques Tati, Jean-Pierre Zola, Adrienne Servantie, Alain Bécourt. Tati revives silent comedy in this French gem reminiscent of Keaton's pantomime films of yore. Refreshing change of pace, wonderful fun.

My Wife's Best Friend (1952) 87m. ** D: Richard Sale. Anne Baxter, Macdonald Carey, Cecil Kellaway, Leif Erickson, Frances Bavier. Unexceptional film of married couple Baxter-Carey confessing their past indiscretions when their plane seems about to crash.

My Wild Irish Rose (1947) C-101m. ** D: David Butler. Dennis Morgan, Andrea King, Arlene Dahl, Alan Hale, George Tobias. Irish songs galore support limp biography of songwriter Chauncey Olcott.

Myra Breckinridge (1970) C-94m. BOMB D: Michael Sarne. Mae West, John Huston, Raquel Welch, Rex Reed, Farrah Fawcett, Jim Backus, John Carradine, Andy Devine, Grady Sutton. Gore Vidal's loosely structured comic novel about sex-change operation was probably unfilmable, but this version doesn't even give book a chance; as bad as any movie ever made, it tastelessly exploits many old Hollywood favorites through film clips.

Mysterians, The (1959-Japanese) C-85m. **½ D: Inoshiro Honda. Kenji Sahara, Yumi Shirakawa, Momoko Kochi, Akihiko Hirata. When their planet is destroyed, highly intellectual aliens try to invade earth to carry on their civilization; above average.

Mysterious Doctor, The (1943) 57m. **½ D: Ben Stoloff. John Loder, Eleanor Parker, Bruce Lester, Lester Matthews, Forrester Harvey. Average story of a doctor who murders people to keep secret of his being Nazi. Moor locations interesting; cast adequate.

Mysterious Dr. Satan SEE: **Doctor Satan's Robot**

Mysterious Intruder, The (1946) 61m. D: William Castle. Richard Dix, Nina Vale, Regis Toomey, Pamela Blake, Charles Lane, Helen Mowery, Mike Mazurki. SEE: **The Whistler** series.

Mysterious Island (1961-British) C-101m. *** D: Cy Endfield. Michael Craig, Joan Greenwood, Michael Callan, Gary Merrill, Herbert Lom. De-

liberately paced fantasy adventure based on two-part Jules Verne novel. Confederate prison escapees, blown off course, find uncharted island with gigantic animals. Great special effects by Ray Harryhausen.

Mysterious Island of Beautiful Women (1979) C-100m. TVM D: Joseph Pevney. Steven Keats, Peter Lawford, Clint Walker, Jaime Lyn Bauer, Jayne Kennedy, Kathryn Davis, Rosalind Chao. Six men fight for survival on a South Sea island populated by a tribe of hostile, bikini-clad lovelies. Unfortunately, nobody plays this one for laughs. Below average.

Mysterious Island of Captain Nemo, The (1974-French-Italian) C-96m. ** D: Juan Antonio Bardem, Henri Colpi. Omar Sharif, Philippe Nicaud, Gerard Tichy, Jess Hahn, Rafael Bardem, Ambrose M'Bia. Jules Verne's Nemo (Sharif) again sees service in juvenile-level action piece, a bit less acceptable than others in this vein.

Mysterious Lady (1928) 96m. **½ D: Fred Niblo. Greta Garbo, Conrad Nagel, Gustav von Seyffertitz, Albert Pollet, Edward Connelly. Austrian military officer (Nagel) falls in love with Garbo, unaware that she's a Russian spy. Another contrived plot made worthwhile by Garbo herself.

Mysterious Magician, The (1965-German) 95m. **½ D: Alfred Vohrer. Joachim Fuchsberger, Eddi Arent, Sophie Hardy, Karl John, Heinz Drache. Mysterious murderwave in London causes Scotland Yard to suspect that the "Wizard," archfiend, is still alive; enjoyable suspenser from Edgar Wallace story.

Mysterious Mr. Moto (1938) 62m. D: Norman Foster. Peter Lorre, Henry Wilcoxon, Mary Maguire, Erik Rhodes, Harold Huber, Leon Ames, Forrester Harvey. SEE: **Mr. Moto** series.

Mystery of Edwin Drood, The (1935) 86m. *** D: Stuart Walker. Claude Rains, Douglass Montgomery, Heather Angel, David Manners, E. E. Clive, Valerie Hobson. Seemingly respectable Rains is responsible for series of horrible murders. Fine thriller adapted from Dickens' unfinished novel.

Mystery of Marie Roget, The (1942) 91m. **½ D: Phil Rosen. Maria Montez, Maria Ouspenskaya, John Litel, Patric Knowles, Charles Middleton. Poe story provides basis for fairly good murder mystery. Detective tries to unravel mystery of actress' strange disappearance.

Mystery of the Black Jungle (1955-German) 72m. *½ D: Ralph Murphy. Lex Barker, Jane Maxwell, Luigi Tosi, Paul Muller. Embarrassing lowjinks set in India involving idol-worshiping natives. Retitled: THE BLACK DEVILS OF KALI.

Mystery of the Golden Eye (1948) 68m. D: William Beaudine. Roland Winters, Wanda McKay, Mantan Moreland, Victor Sen Yung, Bruce Kellogg, Tim Ryan, Evelyn Brent. See: **Charlie Chan** series.

Mystery of the Wax Museum (1933) C-77m. **½ D: Michael Curtiz. Lionel Atwill, Fay Wray, Glenda Farrell, Allen Vincent, Frank McHugh. Long-unseen horror film disappoints somewhat in overabundant "comic relief" and contrivances, but basic plot line of madman Atwill encasing victims in wax, with Wray next on his list, is still exciting. Filmed in early two-color Technicolor. Remade as HOUSE OF WAX.

Mystery of the White Room (1939) 58m. *** D: Otis Garrett. Bruce Cabot, Helen Mack, Constance Worth, Joan Woodbury, Mabel Todd, Tom Dugan. Very good "Crime Club" mystery of murders in an operating room; modest, nicely done.

Mystery of Thug Island, The (1964-Italian-West German) C-96m. D: Luigi Capuano. *½ Guy Madison, Peter Van Eyck, Giacomo Rossi Stuart, Ivan Desny, Inge Schoener. Below-average execution of formula plot: daughter of British army captain is captured by Thuggee sect in India, becomes member of tribe. Bulk of film takes place 15 years after abduction with usual complications.

Mystery Street (1950) 93m. **½ D: John Sturges. Ricardo Montalban, Sally Forrest, Bruce Bennett, Elsa Lanchester, Marshall Thompson, Jan Sterling. Trim murder caper set in Boston, nicely done, with fine cast.

Mystery Submarine (1950) 78m. **½ D: Douglas Sirk. Macdonald Carey, Marta Toren, Carl Esmond, Ludwig Donath. Involved plot of military officer Carey being instrumental in destruction of Nazi sub in South America.

Mystery Submarine (1963-British) 90m. *½ D: C. M. Pennington-Richards. Edward Judd, James Robertson Justice, Laurence Payne, Arthur O'Sullivan, Albert Lieven. A tame WW2 espionage tale of German submarine manned by British crew, only to be recaptured by English fleet. Alternate title: DECOY.

Nabonga (1944) 75m. *½ D: Sam Newfield. Buster Crabbe, Julie London, Fifi D'Orsay, Barton MacLane, Bryant Washburn. Incredible cheapie of plane-crash survivor (London) making friends with local gorilla. Good for laughs, anyway. Retitled: GORILLA.

Naked Alibi (1954) 86m. **½ D: Jerry Hopper. Sterling Hayden, Gloria Grahame, Gene Barry, Marcia Henderson, Casey Adams. Hayden is persistent ex-cop hunting down actual killer to prove his innocence.

Naked and the Dead, The (1958) C-131m. *** D: Raoul Walsh. Aldo Ray, Cliff Robertson, Raymond Massey, Lili St. Cyr, Barbara Nichols. Norman Mailer's intensive novel of WW2 soldiers in action gets a superficial but rugged filmization.

Naked Brigade, The (1965) 99m. ** D: Maury Dexter. Shirley Eaton, Ken Scott, Mary Chronopoulou, John Holland, Sonia Zoidou. Mild WW2 actioner of Eaton hiding from Nazi invasion of Crete.

Naked City, The (1948) 96m. ***½ D: Jules Dassin. Barry Fitzgerald, Howard Duff, Dorothy Hart, Don Taylor, Ted de Corsia. Realistic police drama shot on location with N.Y.C. settings overshadowing actual story of young girl brutally murdered, subsequent manhunt.

Naked Dawn, The (1955) C-82m. **½ D: Edgar G. Ulmer. Arthur Kennedy, Betta St. John, Roy Engel, Eugene Iglesias, Charita. Acceptable robbery caper of initial act snowballing into series of crimes.

Naked Earth (1958-British) 96m. *½ D: Vincent Sherman. Juliette Greco, Richard Todd, John Kitzmiller, Finlay Currie. Misguided soap opera set in 1890s Africa, trying to build up aspiring star Greco.

Naked Edge, The (1961) 99m. **½ D: Michael Anderson. Gary Cooper, Deborah Kerr, Eric Portman, Diane Cilento, Hermione Gingold, Michael Wilding. Uneven suspenser of Kerr thinking husband Cooper is guilty of murder. Cooper's last film, made in London.

Naked Heart, The (1949-Canadian) 96m. ** D: Marc Allegret. Michele Morgan, Kieron Moore, Francoise Rosay, Jack Watling. Little of consequence happens in this sad story based on book MARIA CHAPDE-LAINE by Louis Herman.

Naked Hills, The (1956) C-73m. *½ D: Josef Shaftel. David Wayne, Keenan Wynn, James Barton, Marcia Henderson, Jim Backus. Raggedy account of Wayne who has gold fever and spends life searching for ore, ignoring wife and family.

Naked in the Sun (1957) C-79m. ** D: R. John Hugh. James Craig, Lita Milan, Barton MacLane, Tony Hunter. Somewhat sluggish account of Indian tribes involved with slave traders.

Naked Jungle, The (1954) C-95m. *** D: Byron Haskin. Eleanor Parker, Charlton Heston, Abraham Sofaer, William Conrad. High-class South American jungle adventure, with Heston and wife Parker surrounded on their plantation by advancing army of red ants.

Naked Kiss, The (1964) 93m. **½ D: Samuel Fuller. Constance Towers, Anthony Eisley, Virginia Grey, Betty Bronson, Patsy Kelly, Michael Dante. Girl arrested for murder reveals her shady past; lurid but provocative melodrama.

Naked Maja, The (1959) C-111m. ** D: Henry Koster. Ava Gardner, Anthony Franciosa, Amedeo Nazzari, Gino Cervi, Massimo Serato, Lea Padovani, Carlo Rizzo. Mishmash involving 18th-century Spanish painter Goya and famed model for title painting.

Naked Night, The SEE: Sawdust and Tinsel

Naked Paradise (1957) C-68m. BOMB D: Roger Corman. Richard Denning, Beverly Garland, Lisa Montell, Richard Miller, Leslie Bradley. On-location filming in Hawaii can't salvage this balderdash about crooks using cruise boat to rob local plantations. Retitled: THUNDER OVER HAWAII.

Naked Prey, The (1966) C-94m. *** D: Cornel Wilde. Cornel Wilde, Gert Van Den Bergh, Ken Gampu. Harrowing, well-done safari movie. African natives give prisoner Wilde headstart before they close in on him for kill, forcing Wilde to combat them with savage tactics; memorable brutal sequences.

Naked Runner, The (1967-British) C-104m. *½ D: Sidney J. Furie. Frank Sinatra, Peter Vaughan, Toby Robins, Edward Fox. Dull spy melodrama focusing on American (Sinatra) who is pawn in bizarre plot to get him to assassinate enemy agent. Farfetched, too heavily plotted.

Naked Spur, The (1953) C-91m. ***½ D: Anthony Mann. James Stewart, Janet Leigh, Ralph Meeker, Robert Ryan, Millard Mitchell. One of the best Westerns ever made: a tough, hard litle film about self-styled bounty hunter Stewart trying to capture Ryan, who stirs tension among Stewart's newly-acquired "partners." Strikingly directed and photographed on location in the Rockies.

Naked Street, The (1955) 84m. ** D: Maxwell Shane. Farley Granger, Anthony Quinn, Anne Bancroft, Peter Graves, Jerry Paris, Jeanne Cooper. Capable cast wasted in bland yarn of reporter exposing crime syndicate.

Naked Truth, The SEE: Your Past Is Showing

Nakia (1974) C-78m. TVM D: Leonard Horn. Robert Forster, Arthur Kennedy, Linda Evans, Chief George Clutesi, Stephen McNally, Christopher Stone. American Indian deputy sheriff torn between his heritage and his job, with strong overtones of "Billy Jack." Forster is granite-like and no-nonsense in the lead, Kennedy provides the nuances as his boss. Both were in TV series which later spun off. Average.

Name of the Game is Kill, The (1968) C-88m. ** D: Gunnar Hellstrom. Jack Lord, Susan Strasberg, Collin Wilcox, Tisha Sterling, T. C. Jones. Crazy melodrama concerns refugee Lord's problems in Arizona when he gets mixed up with a trio of sisters and their mother. Retitled THE FEMALE TRAP.

Namu the Killer Whale (1966) C-88m. **½ D: Laslo Benedek. Robert Lansing, John Anderson, Lee Meriwether, Richard Erdman, Robin Mattson. Intriguing tale, based on true story of naturalist Lansing capturing and training a killer whale. Nicely done, good family fare.

Nana (1934) 89m. **½ D: Dorothy Arzner. Anna Sten, Phillips Holmes, Lionel Atwill, Muriel Kirkland, Richard Bennett, Mae Clarke. Initially interesting adaptation of Emile Zola story of luxury-loving woman in tragic love affair runs out of steam towards the middle. Producer Samuel Goldwyn's attempt to make a new Garbo out of exotic Sten.

Nancy Drew and the Hidden Staircase (1939) 60m. *½ D: William Clemens. Bonita Granville, Frankie Thomas, John Litel, Frank Orth, Vera Lewis. Formula happenings as Granville et al aid elderly spinsters being victimized by crooks.

Nancy Drew, Detective (1938) 60m. *½ D: William Clemens. Bonita Granville, John Litel, James Stephenson, Frankie Thomas. Timid entry in girl-detective series, as amateur sleuth tries to help rich woman involved with gangsters.

Nancy Drew—Reporter (1939) 68m. *½ D: William Clemens. Bonita Granville, John Litel, Frankie Thomas. Granville comes to rescue of another elderly victim of crooked schemes.

Nancy Drew—Trouble Shooter (1939) 69m. *½ D: William Clemens. Bonita Granville, John Litel, Frankie Thomas, Aldrich Bowker, Renie Riano. Warner Bros. mystery programmer loosely based on famed girls' story heroine, with Granville tracking down crooks.

Nancy Goes to Rio (1950) C-99m. **½ D: Robert Z. Leonard. Ann Sothern, Jane Powell, Barry Sullivan, Carmen Miranda, Louis Calhern, Fortunio Bonanova, Hans Conried. Snappy MGM musical with Powell and mother (Sothern) both actresses in South American resort, competing for juicy stage roles and rich men.

Nancy Steel is Missing (1937) 85m. **½ D: George Marshall. Victor McLaglen, Walter Connolly, Peter Lorre, June Lang, Jane Darwell, John Carradine. Story of ex-con McLaglen passing off Lang as long-ago kidnapped child is pat but smooth-going.

Nanny, The (1965-British) 93m. *** D: Seth Holt. Bette Davis, Wendy Craig, Jill Bennett, James Villiers, Pamela Franklin, William Dix, Maurice Denham. Twisting, scary plot plus fine direction reap results. Suspects of child murder narrowed to governess Davis and disturbed youngster Dix.

Nanook of the North (1922) 55m. *** D: Robert Flaherty. Pioneer documentary of Eskimos' daily life with-

stands the test of time quite well, remains an absorbing saga, well filmed. Set the standard for many documentaries to follow. Soundtrack added in 1939.

Napoleon and Samantha (1972) C-92m. **½ D: Bernard McEveety. Michael Douglas, Jodie Foster, Johnny Whitaker, Will Geer, Arch Johnson, Henry Jones. Disney tale of two kids who run away with pet lion is OK family fare.

Narrow Corner, The (1933) 71m. ** D: Alfred E. Green. Douglas Fairbanks, Jr., Patricia Ellis, Ralph Bellamy, Dudley Digges, Sidney Toler, Willie Fung. Fairbanks is kidnapped by crooks to avoid his talking; he is taken to East Indies where romance and intrigue blossom. OK drama of Somerset Maugham novel. Remade as ISLE OF FURY.

Narrow Margin, The (1952) 70m. **½ D: Richard Fleischer. Charles McGraw, Marie Windsor, Jacqueline White, Queenie Leonard. Effective yarn of jury witness on train, suspect for variety of happenings. One of Windsor's best roles.

Nashville (1975) C-159m. **** D: Robert Altman. Henry Gibson, Karen Black, Ronee Blakley, Keith Carradine, Geraldine Chaplin, Lily Tomlin, Michael Murphy, Barbara Harris, Allen Garfield, Ned Beatty, Barbara Baxley, Shelley Duvall. Altman's brilliant mosaic of American life as seen through 24 characters involved in Nashville political rally. Full of cogent character studies, comic and poignant vignettes, done in seemingly free-form style. Carradine's song "I'm Easy" won an Oscar.

Nasty Habits (1977) C-96m. *½ D: Michael Lindsay-Hogg. Glenda Jackson, Melina Mercouri, Geraldine Page, Sandy Dennis, Anne Jackson, Anne Meara, Susan Penhaligon, Edith Evans. Labored comedy sets allegory of Nixon and Watergate scandal in Philadelphia convent, with Jackson as conniving Mother Superior. A one-joke film. Shot mostly in England.

Nasty Rabbit, The (1964) C-85m. ** D: James Landis. Arch Hall, Jr., Micha Terr, Melissa Morgan, John Akana. Weak spoof with serious overtones involving Russian attempt to set loose a disease-infected rabbit in the U. S. Retitled: SPIES A GO GO.

National Lampoon's Animal House

(1978) C-109m. ** D: John Landis. John Belushi, Tim Matheson, John Vernon, Verna Bloom, Thomas Hulce, Cesare Danova, Peter Riegert, Stephen Furst, Donald Sutherland. Spoof of early-1960s college life is only sporadically funny, depends largely on Belushi's mugging as frat-house animal. Not nearly as roisterous or amusing as any issue of the Lampoon.

National Velvet (1944) C-125m. ***½ D: Clarence Brown. Mickey Rooney, Elizabeth Taylor, Donald Crisp, Anne Revere, Angela Lansbury, Reginald Owen, Norma Varden. Excellent family film of determined kids training horse to win famed Grand National Race; Revere won Best Supporting Actress Oscar. Followed years later by sequel INTERNATIONAL VELVET.

Nativity, The (1978) C-100m. TVM D: Bernard L. Kowalski. Madeline Stowe, John Shea, Jane Wyatt, Paul Stewart, Audrey Totter, Leo McKern. Reverent Biblical retelling of the Joseph and Mary story hampered by pedestrian performances by the two leads and so-so direction by Kowalski. Average.

Natural Enemies (1979) C-100m. *½ D: Jeff Kanew. Hal Holbrook, Louise Fletcher, Peter Armstrong, Beth Berridge, Steve Austin, Jose Ferrer, Viveca Lindfors. Successful publisher Holbrook wakes up one day with the urge to kill his family. Cold, uninvolving, and (needless to say) strange little film, feature debut for director-writer-editor Kanew.

Naughty But Nice (1939) 90m. **½ D: Ray Enright. Dick Powell, Ann Sheridan, Gale Page, Helen Broderick, Ronald Reagan, Allen Jenkins, ZaSu Pitts, Jerry Colonna. Stuffy music professor Powell unwittingly writes popular song hit, leading to various complications and gradual personality change. Silly but fun; songs adapted from Wagner, Liszt, Mozart, Bach.

Naughty Girl SEE: Mam'zelle Pigalle

Naughty Marietta (1935) 80m. **½ D: W. S. Van Dyke II. Jeanette MacDonald, Nelson Eddy, Frank Morgan, Elsa Lanchester, Douglass Dumbrille, Cecilia Parker. First teaming of Eddy and MacDonald has her a French princess running off to America, falling in love with Indian scout Eddy. Victor Herbert songs:

"Tramp, Tramp, Tramp," and "Ah Sweet Mystery of Life."

Naughty Nineties, The (1945) 76m. ** D: Jean Yarbrough. Bud Abbott, Lou Costello, Alan Curtis, Rita Johnson, Henry Travers, Lois Collier, Joe Sawyer, Joe Kirk. Ordinary A&C comedy of riverboat gamblers, sparked by duo's verbal exchanges (including "Who's on First?") and slapstick finale.

Navajo Joe (1966-Italian) C-89m. *½ D: Sergio Corbucci. Burt Reynolds, Aldo San Brell, Tanya Lopert, Fernando Rey. Sole survivor of massacre swears revenge on his enemies in tepid Italian Western.

Navy Blue and Gold (1937) 94m. **½ D: Sam Wood. Robert Young, James Stewart, Tom Brown, Florence Rice, Billie Burke, Lionel Barrymore, Paul Kelly, Samuel S. Hinds. Hackneyed but entertaining saga of three pals (one rich and innocent, one a cynic, and one mysterious "with a past") going to Annapolis. Predictable football game climax is fun.

Navy Blues (1941) 108m. *** D: Lloyd Bacon. Ann Sheridan, Jack Oakle, Martha Raye, Jack Haley, Herbert Anderson, Jack Carson. Brassy musical with fine cast (including young Jackie Gleason), with Raye stealing most of the film.

Navy Comes Through, The (1942) 82m. ** D: A. Edward Sutherland. Pat O'Brien, George Murphy, Jane Wyatt, Jackie Cooper, Carl Esmond, Max Baer, Desi Arnaz. RKO programmer dealing with merchant marines in action during WW2.

Navy vs. the Night Monsters, The (1966) C-90m. BOMB D: Michael Hoey. Mamie Van Doren, Anthony Eisley, Pamela Mason, Bill Gray, Bobby Van, Walter Sande, Edward Faulkner, Phillip Terry. 1) Look at the title. 2) Examine the cast. 3) Be aware that the plot involves omniverous trees. 4) Don't say you weren't warned.

Navy Wife (1956) 83m. *½ D: Edward Bernds. Joan Bennett, Gary Merrill, Shirley Yamaguchi, Maurice Manson, Judy Nugent. Trivial tale of Japanese women revolting to obtain equal treatment from their men as they observe American military and their wives.

Neanderthal Man, The (1953) 78m. *½ D: E. A. Dupont. Robert Shayne, Richard Crane, Robert Long,

Doris Merrick. Typical horror film from fifties. Scientist Shayne experiments with animals and himself, with new serum. Cast fails to save film.

Nearly a Nasty Accident (1962-British) 86m. ** D: Don Chaffey. Jimmy Edwards, Kenneth Connor, Shirley Eaton, Richard Wattis, Ronnie Stevens, Jon Pertwee, Eric Barker. Minor comedy of mechanic who innocently puts the touch of disaster on everyone.

'Neath Brooklyn Bridge (1942) 61m. D: Wallace Fox. Leo Gorcey, Huntz Hall, Bobby Jordan, Gabriel Dell, Noah Beery, Jr., Sunshine Sammy Morrison, Jack Mulhall, Dave O'Brien, Anne Gillis. SEE: **Bowery Boys** series.

Nebraskan, The (1953) C-68m. ** D: Fred F. Sears. Phil Carey, Roberta Haynes, Wallace Ford, Richard Webb, Lee Van Cleef, Jay Silverheels. Tame Western of white man justice preventing Indian uprising.

Necromancy (1972) C-83m. *½ D: Bert I. Gordon. Orson Welles, Pamela Franklin, Michael Ontkean, Lee Purcell, Harvey Jason. Occult forces are at work, but unfortunately so are the poor craftsmen in this thriller of small-town witchery.

Ned Kelly (1970-British) C-100m. **½ D: Tony Richardson. Mick Jagger, Clarissa Kaye, Mark McManus, Frank Thring. Rambling film of Australian cowboy. Worth watching if you like Jagger; otherwise, stay away.

Negatives (1968-British) C-90m. ** D: Peter Medak. Peter McEnery, Diane Cilento, Glenda Jackson, Maurice Denham, Steven Lewis, Norman Rossington. Strange movie about unmarried couple who dress up like famed Dr. Crippen and his wife for kicks; he later switches his characterization to Baron von Richtofen. Jackson is good, but direction is too mannered.

Nelson Affair, The (1973-British) C-118m. **½ D: James Cellan Jones. Glenda Jackson, Peter Finch, Michael Jayston, Anthony Quayle, Margaret Leighton, Dominic Guard, Nigel Stock, Barbara Leigh-Hunt. Handsome retelling of Lord Nelson-Lady Hamilton affair, making the "Lady" a slut; interesting but claustrophobic—even climactic sea battle was shot indoors!

Neon Ceiling, The (1970) C-100m. TVM D: Frank R. Pierson. Lee Grant, Gig Young, Denise Nickerson, Herb Edelman, William Smithers. Woman and daughter, finding refuge from bad marriage in desert cafe-gas station, meet up with stranger who eventually becomes part of new start. Good cast deserves far better material. Average.

Neptune Disaster, The SEE: **Neptune Factor, The**

Neptune Factor, The (1973-Canadian) C-98m. ** D: Daniel Petrie. Ben Gazzara, Yvette Mimieux, Walter Pidgeon, Ernest Borgnine. Deep-sea-diving sub races to save three men trapped by an earthquake in ocean floor laboratory. Soggy underwater yarn. Also known as AN UNDERWATER ODYSSEY and THE NEPTUNE DISASTER.

Neptune's Daughter (1949) C-93m. *** D: Edward Buzzell. Esther Williams, Red Skelton, Keenan Wynn, Betty Garrett, Ricardo Montalban, Mel Blanc. Musical romance with Esther a bathing-suit designer, Skelton a no-account mistaken for polo star by Garrett. Bubbly fun, with Academy Award-winning song: "Baby It's Cold Outside."

Nero Wolfe (1977) C-100m. TVM D: Frank D. Gilroy. Thayer David, Anne Baxter, Tom Mason, Brooke Adams, John Randolph, Biff McGuire. Director Gilroy adapted Rex Stout's "The Doorbell Rings" as pilot for projected Nero Wolfe series, and did a fine job, but ideally cast David's untimely death ended those plans. Worth watching, especially for mystery fans. Above average.

Network (1976) C-120m. ***½ D: Sidney Lumet. Faye Dunaway, William Holden, Peter Finch, Robert Duvall, Wesley Addy, Ned Beatty, Beatrice Straight. Paddy Chayefsky's potent (if pretentious) putdown of television non-ethics is actually a larger comment on our manipulated society. Sizzling performances by newscaster-turned-oracle Finch, his Edward R. Murrow-like colleague Holden, abandoned wife Straight, ruthless programming executive Dunaway, and evangelistical board chairman Beatty. Chayefsky, Dunaway, Straight, and Finch all won Oscars—Finch's posthumously.

Nevada (1944) 62m. ** D: Edward Killy. Robert Mitchum, Anne Jeffreys, Guinn "Big Boy" Williams, Nancy Gates, Harry Woods. Standard Zane Grey Western of good-guy Mitchum mopping up gang of outlaws. Filmed before in 1935.

Nevada Smith (1966) C-135m. *** D: Henry Hathaway. Steve McQueen, Karl Malden, Brian Keith, Arthur Kennedy, Suzanne Pleshette, Raf Vallone, Pat Hingle, Howard da Silva, Martin Landau. Good Western story. Smith swears revenge for senseless murder of his parents at the hands of outlaw gang. Based on character from THE CARPETBAGGERS.

Nevada Smith (1975) C-78m. TVM D: Gordon Douglas. Cliff Potts, Lorne Greene, Adam West, Warren Vanders, Jorge Luke, Jerry Gatlin. Western drama inspired by Steve McQueen movie and characters from Harold Robbins' "The Carpetbaggers," with half-breed (Potts) joining his former mentor (Greene) to escort a shipment of explosives across Utah Territory. Standard fare. Average.

Nevadan, The (1950) C-81m. ** D: Gordon Douglas. Randolph Scott, Dorothy Malone, Forrest Tucker, George Macready, Jock Mahoney. Stern Scott is the lawman who tracks down crooks, still finding time to court Malone.

Never a Dull Moment (1943) 60m. **½ D: Edward Lilley. Ritz Brothers, Frances Langford, Stuart Crawford, Elisabeth Risdon, Mary Beth Hughes, George Zucco, Jack LaRue, Franklin Pangborn. Pretty good comedy with the Ritzes getting involved with gang of hoods; fast-paced, with LaRue enjoyable as semicomic heavy.

Never a Dull Moment (1950) 89m. **½ D: George Marshall. Irene Dunne, Fred MacMurray, William Demarest, Natalie Wood, Andy Devine, Ann Doran, Gigi Perreau. Middling froth of chic Dunne marrying rancher MacMurray, adjusting to country life and his two daughters.

Never a Dull Moment (1968) C-100m. ** D: Jerry Paris. Dick Van Dyke, Edward G. Robinson, Dorothy Provine, Henry Silva, Joanna Moore, Tony Bill. Tired Disney comedy belies title, as TV performer Van Dyke gets involved with gangsters; even Robinson's performance is lifeless.

Never Fear (1950) 82m. ** D: Ida Lupino. Sally Forrest, Keefe Brasselle, Hugh O'Brian, Eve Miller, Larry Dobkin. Low-budget flick; Forrest is gal who overcomes polio and

its disastrous effect on her dancing career.

Never Give a Sucker an Even Break (1941) 71m. ***½ D: Edward Cline. W. C. Fields, Gloria Jean, Leon Errol, Susan Miller, Franklin Pangborn, Margaret Dumont. Completely insane comedy with Fields playing himself; no coherent plot, many loose ends, and a lot of funny scenes. Dumont plays "Mrs. Hemoglobin." Climactic chase is a classic, reused by Abbott and Costello in IN SOCIETY.

Never Give an Inch SEE: **Sometimes a Great Notion**

Never Let Go (1963-British) 90m. ** D: John Guillermin. Richard Todd, Peter Sellers, Elizabeth Sellars, Carol White, Mervyn Johns. Sellers gives heavy-handed performance as ruthless and sadistic racketeer in weak story about car thievery. Billed as his first dramatic role, it was a poor choice.

Never Let Me Go (1953) 94m. **½ D: Delmer Daves. Clark Gable, Gene Tierney, Bernard Miles, Richard Haydn, Kenneth More, Belita, Theodore Bikel. Unconvincing yet smooth account of Gable trying to smuggle ballerina-wife Tierney out of Russia.

Never Love a Stranger (1958) 91m. ** D: Robert Stevens. John Drew Barrymore, Lita Milan, Peg Murray, Robert Bray, Steve McQueen. Chronicle of a racketeer, from Harold Robbins' novel; predictable all the way.

Never on Sunday (1960-Greek) 91m. ***½ D: Jules Dassin. Melina Mercouri, Jules Dassin, Georges Foundas, Titos Vandis, Mitsos Liguisos, Despo Diamantidou. Charming idyll of intellectual boob coming to Greece, trying to make earthy prostitute Mercouri cultured. Grand entertainment, with memorable title song.

Never Put It in Writing (1964) 93m. *½ D: Andrew Stone. Pat Boone, Milo O'Shea, Fidelma Murphy, Reginald Beckwith, Harry Brogan. Grade-B comedy, set in London, with Pat trying to retrieve a letter that will get him fired from his job if the boss sees it. Not much.

Never Say Die (1939) 80m. *** D: Elliott Nugent. Martha Raye, Bob Hope, Andy Devine, Gale Sondergaard, Sig Ruman, Alan Mowbray, Monty Woolley. Bob marries Martha at Swiss spa of Bad Gaswasser, thinking he has only two weeks to live. Good cast in lively, trivial romp.

Never Say Goodbye (1946) **97m.** ****½** D: James V. Kern. Errol Flynn, Eleanor Parker, Lucile Watson, S. Z. Sakall, Hattie McDaniel, Forrest Tucker, Donald Woods. Flynn tries hard in routine comedy of husband rewinning his divorce-bound wife.

Never Say Goodbye (1956) **C-96m.** ****½** D: Jerry Hopper. Rock Hudson, Cornell Borchers, George Sanders, Ray Collins, David Janssen, Shelley Fabares. Spotty tear-jerker of Hudson and Borchers, long separated, discovering one another again and creating fit home for their child. Remake of THIS LOVE OF OURS.

Never So Few (1959) **C-124m.** ****½** D: John Sturges. Frank Sinatra, Gina Lollobrigida, Peter Lawford, Steve McQueen, Richard Johnson, Paul Henreid, Brian Donlevy, Dean Jones, Charles Bronson. WW2 action and romance tale filled with salty performances which make one forget the clichés and improbabilities.

Never Steal Anything Small (1959) **C-94m.** ****½** D: Charles Lederer. James Cagney, Shirley Jones, Roger Smith, Cara Williams, Nehemiah Persoff, Royal Dano, Horace McMahon. Odd musical comedy-drama, with Cagney a waterfront union racketeer who'll do anything to win union election. From Maxwell Anderson-Rouben Mamoulian play THE DEVIL'S HORNPIPE.

Never to Love SEE: Bill of Divorcement, A (1940)

Never Too Late (1965) **C-105m.** ****½** D: Bud Yorkin. Paul Ford, Connie Stevens, Maureen O'Sullivan, Jim Hutton, Jane Wyatt, Henry Jones, Lloyd Nolan. Occasionally amusing film version of hit Broadway play about impending parenthood of middle-agers Ford and O'Sullivan. Older performers are funny; Hutton, Stevens, script, and direction are not.

Never Trust a Gambler (1951) **79m.** ***½** D: Ralph Murphy. Dane Clark, Cathy O'Donnell, Tom Drake, Jeff Corey, Myrna Dell. Hackneyed account of man on the run, seeking shelter from ex-wife who has fallen in love with detective seeking him.

Never Wave at a WAC (1952) **87m.** ****½** D: Norman Z. McLeod. Rosalind Russell, Marie Wilson, Paul Douglas, Arleen Whelan, Hillary Brooke, Louise Beavers, Frieda Inescort. Expanded from a TV play,

this farce involves socialite Russell joining the WACs, forced to buckle down to hard work; Wilson as dumb comrade-at-arms is most diverting.

New Adventures of Heidi, The (1978) **C-100m. TVM** D: Ralph Senensky. Katy Kurtzman, Burl Ives, John Gavin Marlyn Mason, Sean Marshall. The Johanna Spyri perennial given an unfortunate contemporary setting (The Big Apple!) and an unmemorable musicalization. Heidi go home. Average.

New Adventures of Tarzan (1935) **75m.** ***** D: Edward Kull. Herman Brix (Bruce Bennett), Ula Holt, Don Costello, Frank Baker, Lewis Sargent, Dale Walsh. SEE: **Tarzan** series.

New Centurions, The (1972) **C-103m.** ******* D: Richard Fleischer. George C. Scott, Stacy Keach, Jane Alexander, Rosalind Cash, Scott Wilson, Erik Estrada, Clifton James. Fine, episodic adaptation of Joseph Wambaugh novel of rookie cops on modern-day L.A. police force, ultimately pessimistic in outlook. Great casting, performances: good storytelling.

New Daughters of Joshua Cabe (1976) **C-78m. TVM** D: Bruce Bilson. John McIntire, Jeanette Nolan, Liberty Williams, Renne Jarrett, Lezlie Dalton, Jack Elam, John Dehner, Geoffrey Lewis. Third time around for rascally Joshua with the three gals he's passed off as his daughters coming to his rescue after he's framed for murder. Cabe and the girls have been different in all three films, which is more than can be said of the plot. Below average.

New Faces (1954) **C-99m.** ****½** D: Harry Horner. Ronny Graham, Robert Clary, Eartha Kitt, Alice Ghostley, Paul Lynde. Vaudeville hodgepodge of variety numbers, without enhancement of wide screen. Based on Leonard Sillman's popular Broadway revue, which was springboard for much new talent. One of the writers was Mel Brooks.

New Faces of 1937 (1937) **100m.** ****** D: Leigh Jason. Joe Penner, Milton Berle, Parkyakarkus, Harriet Hilliard, Jerome Cowan. Silly movie with same initial premise as THE PRODUCERS, as Berle is patsy left as owner of unwatchable Broadway show. Comic highlight is Berle's stockbroker skit with Richard Lane; Ann Miller featured in finale as one of the New Faces.

New Interns, The (1964) 123m. **½ D: John Rich. Michael Callan, Dean Jones, Telly Savalas, Inger Stevens, George Segal, Greg Morris, Stefanie Powers, Lee Patrick, Barbara Eden. Follow-up to THE INTERNS contains usual hospital soap opera with better than average cast and a nifty party sequence.

New Invisible Man, The (1957-Mexican) 89m. ** D: Alfredo Crevena. Arturo de Cordova, Ana Luisa Peluffo, Augusto Benedico, Raul Meraz. OK Mexican update of the classic H. G. Wells story. Also known as H. G. WELLS' NEW INVISIBLE MAN.

New Kind of Love, A (1963) C-110m. **½ D: Melville Shavelson. Paul Newman, Joanne Woodward, Thelma Ritter, Eva Gabor, Maurice Chevalier, George Tobias. Newman as reporter and Woodward as fashion buyer on the loose in Paris fall in love; lacks oomph to make fluff worthwhile.

New Land, The (1973-Swedish) C-161m. ***½ D: Jan Troell. Max von Sydow, Liv Ullmann, Eddie Axberg, Hans Alfredson, Monica Zetterlund, Per Oscarsson. Sequel to THE EMIGRANTS follows same characters as they settle in Minnesota, up to the ends of their lives. Fine epic contains superior performances, photography, many stirring scenes. A real winner.

New Leaf, A (1971) C-102m. **½ D: Elaine May. Walter Matthau, Elaine May, Jack Weston, George Rose, William Redfield, James Coco. Amusing comedy of destitute playboy Matthau planning to marry and murder klutzy May in order to inherit her fortune. Many funny moments, highlighted by May's performance, but topped by curious resolution, lack of strong overall impact. Director/writer/star May disavowed finished film, which was reedited by others.

New Maverick, The (1978) C-100m. TVM D: Hy Averback. Charles Frank, Susan Blanchard, James Garner, Jack Kelly, Susan Sullivan, Eugene Roche, George Loros. Stars of well-remembered MAVERICK show (Garner and Kelly) appear in this new series pilot to introduce their equally crafty Harvard-dropout nephew (Frank), who pursues his own freewheeling western adventures. Good fun. Above average.

New Mexico (1951) C-76m. **½ D: Irving Reis. Lew Ayres, Marilyn Maxwell, Robert Hutton, Andy Devine, Raymond Burr. Moderately exciting Western of cavalry vs. Indians.

New Moon (1940) 105m. **½ D: Robert Z. Leonard. Jeanette MacDonald, Nelson Eddy, Mary Boland, George Zucco, H. B. Warner, Grant Mitchell, Stanley Fields. Nelson and Jeanette in old Louisiana, falling in love, singing "One Kiss," "Softly as in a Morning Sunrise," "Lover Come Back to Me," "Stout-Hearted Men." Oscar Hammerstein-Sigmund Romberg score sung before in 1930 filming with Lawrence Tibbett, Grace Moore, retitled PARISIAN BELLE for TV.

New, Original Wonder Woman, The (1975) C-78m. TVM D: Leonard Horn. Lynda Carter, Lyle Waggoner, John Randolph, Red Buttons, Stella Stevens, Cloris Leachman, Eric Braeden, Henry Gibson, Fannie Flagg. The 1940s comic book heroine performs proverbial incredible exploits anew. The campiest movie this side of "Batman"—and a subsequent series. Silly but tolerable. Average.

New Orleans (1947) 89m. **½ D: Arthur Lubin. Arturo de Cordova, Dorothy Patrick, Billie Holiday, Louis Armstrong, Woody Herman & Band, Meade Lux Lewis, other jazz stars. Hackneyed fictionalization of the birth of jazz, spanning 40 years, but there's plenty of good music. Holliday (cast as a maid!) does "Do You Know What it Means to Miss New Orleans" with Armstrong and all-star band, and it's sublime. Shelley Winters appears briefly as De Cordova's secretary.

New Orleans After Dark (1958) 69m. *½ D: John Sledge. Stacy Harris, Louis Sirgo, Ellen Moore, Tommy Pelle. Programmer about capture of dope smugglers.

New Orleans Uncensored (1955) 76m. *½ D: William Castle. Arthur Franz, Beverly Garland, Helene Stanton, Michael Ansara. Weak exposé account of racketeer-busting in Louisiana, with competent cast trying to overcome script.

New York Confidential (1955) 87m. **½ D: Russell Rouse. Broderick Crawford, Richard Conte, Marilyn Maxwell, Anne Bancroft, J. Carrol Naish. Energetic cast perks up formula exposé of racketeer narrative.

New York, New York (1977) **C-137m.** BOMB D: Martin Scorsese. Liza Minnelli, Robert DeNiro, Lionel Stander, Barry Primus, Mary Kay Place. Scorsese creates a milestone: the first sick Hollywood musical. DeNiro plays a totally repellent musician who falls in love with singer Minnelli during the 1940s. Overlong, meandering, this has nothing to do with "nostalgia" despite its elaborate trappings. Originally released at 153m.

New York Town (1941) **94m.** **½ D: Charles Vidor. Fred MacMurray, Mary Martin, Robert Preston, Akim Tamiroff, Lynne Overman, Eric Blore, Fuzzy Knight. Bright little comedy of wide-eyed Martin manhunting in N.Y.C., assisted by photographer MacMurray. Songs include "Love In Bloom."

Newman's Law (1974) **C-98m.** *½ D: Richard Heffron. George Peppard, Roger Robinson, Eugene Roche, Gordon Pinsent, Louis Zorich. Honest cop Peppard, bounced from the force for alleged corruption, investigates the case on his own. Dreary and predictable.

News Hounds (1947) **68m.** D: William Beaudine. Leo Gorcey, Huntz Hall, Bobby Jordan, Christine McIntyre, Gabriel Dell, Billy Benedict. SEE: Bowery Boys series.

Next Man, The (1976) **C-108m.** *** D: Richard C. Sarafian. Sean Connery, Cornelia Sharpe, Albert Paulsen, Adolfo Celi, Charles Cioffi. Good melodrama in which scenics (New York, Bavaria, Germany, London, Morocco etc.) and violence are blended to tell of international hitlady Sharpe falling in love with Saudi Arabian ambassador (Connery) as he tries to arrange peace with Palestine.

Next Stop, Greenwich Village (1976) **C-109m.** *** D: Paul Mazursky. Lenny Baker, Shelley Winters, Ellen Greene, Christopher Walken, Lou Jacobi, Mike Kellin. Comic and poignant film about Brooklyn boy Baker who moves to Greenwich Village in 1953 hoping to become an actor. Wonderful period atmosphere and characterizations; Winters is excellent as Baker's domineering mother.

Next Time We Love (1936) **87m.** *** D: Edward H. Griffith. Margaret Sullavan, James Stewart, Ray Milland, Grant Mitchell, Robert McWade, Anna Demetrio. Trim romantic

soaper with Milland in love with actress Sullavan, who is married to struggling reporter Stewart.

Next to No Time (1960-British) **C-93m.** *** D: Henry Cornelius. Kenneth More, Betsy Drake, Bessie Love, Harry Green, Patrick Barr, Roland Culver. Whimsical comedy from Paul Gallico story, about mild-mannered engineer (More) who loses inhibitions on ocean voyage where he's trying to put over important business deal.

Next Voice You Hear, The (1950) **82m.** **½ D: William Wellman. James Whitmore, Nancy Davis, Lillian Bronson, Jeff Corey. Cast manages to keep story of hearing the voice of God on radio somewhat believable. Not as convincing as intended.

Niagara (1953) **C-89m.** *** D: Henry Hathaway. Marilyn Monroe, Joseph Cotten, Jean Peters, Don Wilson, Richard Allan, Casey Adams. Black murder tale of honeymoon couple staying at Niagara Falls, the wife planning to kill husband.

Nice Girl? (1941) **95m.** *** D: William A. Seiter. Deanna Durbin, Franchot Tone, Walter Brennan, Robert Stack, Robert Benchley. Little Deanna grows up in this cute comedy, with Tone and Stack developing amorous ideas about her. Songs: "Love At Last," "Thank You America."

Nice Girl Like Me, A (1969-British) **C-91m.** **½ D: Desmond Davis. Barbara Ferris, Harry Andrews, Gladys Cooper, Bill Hinnant, James Villiers, Joyce Carey. Misadventures of a naive young girl who is perpetually pregnant; innocuous British comedy.

Nice Little Bank That Should be Robbed, A (1958) **87m.** ** D: Henry Levin. Tom Ewell, Mickey Rooney, Mickey Shaughnessy, Dina Merrill. Cast is game, but story is pure cornball about goofy crooks using their gains to buy a racehorse.

Nicholas and Alexandra (1971-British) **C-183m.** **½ D: Franklin Schaffner. Michael Jayston, Janet Suzman, Tom Baker, Harry Andrews, Jack Hawkins, Laurence Olivier, Michael Redgrave, Alexander Knox, Curt Jurgens. Lavishly filmed, well-acted chronicle of Russian leaders, and revolution that turned their world upside down. Sure and steady, but eventually tedious, despite cameos by Olivier et al.

Nicholas Nickleby (1947-British) 95m. *** D: Alberto Cavalcanti. Derek Bond, Cedric Hardwicke, Mary Merrall, Sally Ann Howes, Bernard Miles. Dandy British film of Dickens' story of young boy's attempts to shield family from cruel uncle; worthwhile viewing.

Nick and Nora (1975) C-78m. TVM D: Seymour Burns. Craig Stevens, Jo Ann Pflug, Jack Kruschen, Charles Macaulay, Denny Miller, Whit Bissell. The two leads desecrate the memories of William Powell and Myrna Loy in this dreadful "update" of THE THIN MAN. Perfectly awful.

Nick Carter—Master Detective (1939) 60m. **½ D: Jacques Tourneur. Walter Pidgeon, Rita Johnson, Henry Hull, Donald Meek, Milburn Stone, Addison Richards, Sterling Holloway. Pidgeon is good, tracking down industrial spy in slickly done detective film.

Nickel Ride, The (1975) C-99m. ** D: Robert Mulligan. Jason Miller, Linda Haynes, Victor French, John Hillerman, Bo Hopkins. Uneven and generally obscure little drama about a syndicate contact man (Miller) who keeps keys to L.A. warehouses used by dealers in stolen goods.

Nickelodeon (1976) C-121m. *** D: Peter Bogdanovich. Ryan O'Neal, Burt Reynolds, Tatum O'Neal, Brian Keith, Stella Stevens, John Ritter, Jane Hitchcock, Harry Carey Jr. Heartfelt valentine to early days of moviemaking, with O'Neal literally stumbling into his job as director, Reynolds an overnight screen hero. Based on actual reminiscences of such veterans as Raoul Walsh and Allan Dwan, film unfortunately loses steam halfway through . . . remains entertaining on the whole, sparked by fine cast.

Nicky's World (1974) C-78m. TVM D: Paul Stanley. Mark Shera, Charles Cioffi, George Voskovec, Despo, Olympia Dukakis, Emily Bindiger. Teenager in close-knit Greek-American family searches for the culprit who put the torch to his parents' bakery. Family drama in "The Waltons" tradition. Average.

Night After Night (1932) 70m. ** D: Archie Mayo. George Raft, Mae West, Constance Cummings, Wynne Gibson, Roscoe Karns, Louis Calhern, Alison Skipworth. Story of nightclub owner Raft's infatuation with "classy" Cummings is a crashing bore, but when Mae West comes on the screen lights up. It's her film debut, and she's in rare form.

Night Ambush (1957-British) 93m. *** D: Michael Powell, Emeric Pressburger. Dirk Bogarde, Marius Goring, David Oxley, Cyril Cusack. Taut WW2 actioner set in Crete, with fine British cast. Originally titled: ILL MET BY MOONLIGHT.

Night and Day (1946) C-128m. ** D: Michael Curtiz. Cary Grant, Alexis Smith, Monty Woolley, Ginny Simms, Jane Wyman, Eve Arden, Mary Martin, Victor Francen, Alan Hale, Dorothy Malone. Music only worthy aspect of fabricated biography of songwriter Cole Porter, stiffly played by Grant, who even sings "You're The Top." Martin recreates "My Heart Belongs To Daddy" in film's highlight.

Night and the City (1950) 95m. **½ D: Jules Dassin. Richard Widmark, Gene Tierney, Googie Withers, Hugh Marlowe, Herbert Lom. Slowly paced yet effective account of Widmark on the lam from gangland reprisal; filmed in England.

Night at the Opera, A (1935) 90m. **** D: Sam Wood. Groucho, Chico, Harpo Marx, Kitty Carlisle, Allan Jones, Walter King, Margaret Dumont, Sig Ruman. Captivating lunacy of comedy trio blends perfectly with nice score sung by Jones and Carlisle, as the brothers destroy Ruman's opera with the greatest of ease.

Night Caller (1975-French-Italian) C-91m. ** D: Henri Verneuil. Jean-Paul Belmondo, Charles Denner, Adalberto-Maria Meril, Lea Massari, Rosy Varte. Detective Belmondo tackles both a bank robbery case and an obscene phone caller who murders women at the end of the line. Action but little else.

Night Caller from Outer Space (1965-British) 84m. **½ D: John Gilling. John Saxon, Maurice Denham, Patricia Haines, Alfred Burke, Jack Watson. Well done, sci-fi thriller of alien mutant kidnapping humans to take back to his troubled planet.

Night Chase (1970) C-100m. TVM D: Jack Starrett. David Janssen, Yaphet Kotto, Victoria Vetri, Elisha Cook Jr., Joe De Santis. Wealthy businessman, fleeing wife-murder, forced to hire out cab to drive to Mexico. Great on-the-road drama; suspense falls apart at resolution. Above average.

Night Club Scandal (1937) 70m. **½ D: Ralph Murphy. John Barrymore, Lynne Overman, Louise Campbell, Charles Bickford, Evelyn Brent, Elizabeth Patterson, J. Carrol Naish. Enjoyable "B" mystery with detectives seeking murderer who tried to frame innocent man. Barrymore is the guilty party. Remake of 1932 film GUILTY AS HELL.

Night Creature (1978) C-83m. BOMB D: Lee Madden. Donald Pleasence, Nancy Kwan, Ross Hagen, Lesly Fine, Jennifer Rhodes. Macho writer Pleasence lives on Xanadu-like island retreat near Thailand, but a prowling leopard is giving him the jitters. A low-grade thriller, minus the thrills. Also known as OUT OF THE DARKNESS.

Night Creatures (1962-British) C-81m. **½ D: Peter Graham Scott. Peter Cushing, Yvonne Romain, Patrick Allen, Oliver Reed, Michael Ripper, Martin Benson, David Lodge. In 18th Century England, country parson is also the notorious "dead" pirate leader of smugglers who pose as ghosts. Remake of DR. SYN. Good fun with some scary moments.

Night Cries (1978) C-100m. TVM D: Richard Lang. Susan St. James, Michael Parks, Jamie Smith Jackson, William Conrad, Delores Dorn, Cathleen Nesbitt. Young mother is haunted by dreams that her dead child is alive and in danger. Middling suspense tale. Average.

Night Digger, The (1971-British) C-100m. *** D: Alastair Reid. Patricia Neal, Pamela Brown, Nicholas Clay, Jean Anderson, Graham Crowden, Yootha Joyce. Odd, usually effective psychological thriller adapted from Joy Cowley novel by Roald Dahl. With the unexpected arrival of young handyman, sad relationship between two country women takes turn for the better, until they discover what he does on off-hours. Excellent performances, fine Bernard Herrmann score.

Night Editor (1946) 68m. ** D: Henry Levin. William Gargan, Janis Carter, Jeff Donnell, Coulter Irwin. Minor yarn about Gargan, a law enforcer gone wrong, trying to redeem himself.

Night Evelyn Came Out of the Grave, The (1971-Italian) C-90m. *½ D: Emilio Miraglia. Anthony Steffen, Marina Malfatti, Rod Murdock, Giacomo Rossi-Stuart, Umberto Raho. Dreadful horror whodunit about British lord, released from psychiatric clinic following his wife's death, who begins to suspect that she is still alive when her crypt is discovered empty.

Night Fighters (1960-British) 85m. **½ D: Tay Garnett. Robert Mitchum, Anne Heywood, Dan O'Herlihy, Cyril Cusack, Richard Harris, Marianne Benet. Sporadically actionful tale of Irish Revolution, with Mitchum joining the cause against his will. Original title: A TERRIBLE BEAUTY.

Night Freight (1955) 79m. **½ D: Jean Yarbrough. Forrest Tucker, Barbara Britton, Keith Larsen, Thomas Gomez. Straightforward tale about railroad competing with trucking line for survival.

Night Full of Rain (1978) C-104m. ** D: Lina Wertmuller. Giancarlo Giannini, Candice Bergen, Allison Tucker, Jill Eikenberry, Anne Byrne. Wertmuller's first English language effort (shot in Rome and San Francisco) is unsatisfying fantasy drama about relationship between journalist Giannini and feminist wife Bergen, who's quite good. Full title: THE END OF THE WORLD IN OUR USUAL BED IN A NIGHT FULL OF RAIN.

Night Gallery (1969) C-98m. TVM D: Boris Sagal, Steven Spielberg, Barry Shear, Roddy McDowall, Ossie Davis, Barry Sullivan, Tom Bosley, George Macready, Joan Crawford, Richard Kiley, Sam Jaffe. Three-story anthology, each part revolving around lessons learned (via Rod Serling) from paintings: despicable nephew speeds up death of wealthy old man, art collector arranges for eye transplant, death camp fugitive in South American country. Effective mixture of melodrama, morality, and supernatural. Spawned TV series. Above average.

Night Games (1974) C-78m. TVM D: Don Taylor. Barry Newman, Susan Howard, Albert Salmi, Luke Askew, JoAnna Cameron, Anjanette Comer, Ralph Meeker, Stefanie Powers. Newman reprises the role he first did in "The Lawyer" in 1970, this time establishing himself in a small Arizona town and defending socialite Powers accused of murdering her husabnd. "Petrocelli" TV series spun off from this film. Average.

Night Has a Thousand Eyes (1948) 80m. **½ D: John Farrow. Edward G. Robinson, Gail Russell, John Lund, Virginia Bruce, William Demarest. Intriguing story of magician who has uncanny power to predict the future; script is corny at times.

Night Heaven Fell, The (1958-French) C-90m. **½ D: Roger Vadim. Brigitte Bardot, Alida Valli, Stephen Boyd, Pepe Nieto. Turgid drama of Bardot dallying with Boyd, who's planning to kill her uncle.

Night Holds Terror, The (1955) 86m. ** D: Andrew L. Stone. Jack Kelly, Hildy Parks, Vince Edwards, John Cassavetes, Jack Kruschen, Joel Marston, Jonathan Hale. Somber little film of family being held captive for ransom.

Night in Casablanca, A (1946) 85m. *** D: Archie Mayo. Groucho, Harpo, Chico Marx, Lisette Verea, Charles Drake, Lois Collier, Dan Seymour, Sig Ruman. No classic, but many funny sequences in latter-day Marx outing, ferreting out spies in Casablanca hotel.

Night in New Orleans, A (1942) 75m. *½ D: William Clemens. Preston Foster, Patricia Morison, Albert Dekker, Charles Butterworth, Dooley Wilson, Cecil Kellaway. Thin yarn of Morison trying to clear husband Foster of murder charge.

Night in Paradise, A (1946) C-84m. **½ D: Arthur Lubin. Merle Oberon, Turhan Bey, Thomas Gomez, Gale Sondergaard, Ray Collins, Ernest Truex. Tongue-in-cheek costumer of Aesop wooing lovely princess Oberon in ancient times; colorful, pleasant at best.

Night Into Morning (1951) 86m. *** D: Fletcher Markle. Ray Milland, John Hodiak, Nancy Davis, Lewis Stone, Jean Hagen, Rosemary De-Camp. Small-town professor loses family in fire, almost ruins own life through drink and self-pity. Realistic settings in modest production, with fine performance by Milland.

Night Is My Future (1947-Swedish) 87m. **½ D: Ingmar Bergman. Mai Zetterling, Birger Malmsten, Olof Winnerstrand, Naima Wifstrand, Hilda Borgstrom. Somber, brooding tale of blind young man finding happiness with Zetterling.

Night Key (1937) 67m. *½ D: Lloyd Corrigan. Boris Karloff, Warren Hull, Jean Rogers, Hobart Cavanaugh. Unimaginative yarn about crooks forcing inventor to help them with their crimes.

Night Monster (1942) 80m. **½ D: Ford Beebe. Irene Hervey, Don Porter, Nils Asther, Lionel Atwill, Leif Erickson, Bela Lugosi, Ralph Morgan. Intriguing grade-B thriller about creepy figure stalking country estate, murdering doctors who are treating crippled Morgan.

Night Moves (1975) C-95m. ***½ D: Arthur Penn. Gene Hackman, Jennifer Warren, Susan Clark, Edward Binns, Harris Yulin, Melanie Griffith. L.A. detective Hackman puts aside his marital woes to track nymphet Griffith to Florida Keys. Complicated but underrated psychological suspenser leads to stunning climax.

Night Must Fall (1937) 117m. ***½ D: Richard Thorpe. Robert Montgomery, Rosalind Russell, Dame May Whitty, Alan Marshal, Kathleen Harrison, E. E. Clive, Merle Tottenham. Famous film of Emlyn Williams' suspenseful play of girl (Russell) slowly learning identity of mysterious brutal killer terrorizing the countryside. Montgomery has showy role in sometimes stagy but generally effective film, with outstanding aid from Russell and Whitty.

Night Must Fall (1964-British) 105m. **½ D: Karel Reisz. Albert Finney, Susan Hampshire, Mona Washbourne, Sheila Hancock. Cerebral attempt to match flair of original, this remake is too obvious and theatrical for any credibility.

Night My Number Came Up, The (1955-British) 94m. **** D: Leslie Norman. Michael Redgrave, Sheila Sim, Alexander Knox, Denholm Elliott. First-rate suspense film will have you holding your breath as it recounts tale of routine military flight, the fate of which may or may not depend on a prophetic dream.

Night Nurse (1931) 72m. *** D: William Wellman. Barbara Stanwyck, Ben Lyon, Joan Blondell, Clark Gable, Charlotte Merriam, Charles Winninger. Excellent, hard-bitten tale of nurse (Stanwyck) who can't ignore strange goings-on in home where she works. Blondell adds zingy support; one of Gable's most impressive early appearances. Still potent today.

Night of Dark Shadows (1971) C-97m. BOMB D: Dan Curtis. David Selby, Lara Parker, Kate Jackson, Grayson Hall, John Karlen, Nancy

Barrett. Ripoff exploitation film taken from once popular TV show concerns ghosts and reincarnation in New England. Yecch! Sequel to HOUSE OF DARK SHADOWS.

Night of January 16th, The (1941) 79m. *½ D: William Clemens. Robert Preston, Ellen Drew, Nils Asther, Donald Douglas, Rod Cameron, Alice White, Cecil Kellaway. Hit Broadway play receives lackluster screen treatment; a talky and uninspired whodunit.

Night of Terror (1972) C-73m. TVM D: Jeannot Szwarc. Donna Mills, Martin Balsam, Chuck Connors, Catherine Burns, Eddie Egan, Agnes Moorehead. Violent, paranoid thriller hinging on unremembered clues, vulnerable woman, syndicate runner with nothing to lose. OK performances but plot built around pileup of crazy situations. Average.

Night of the Blood Beast (1958) 65m. *½ D: Bernard Kowalski. Michael Emmet, Angela Greene, John Baer, Ed Nelson, Tyler McVey. Silly Roger Corman production about astronaut who returns from space with alien cells inside his body.

Night of the Blood Monster (1972-British) C-84m. ** D: Jess Franco. Christopher Lee, Maria Schell, Leo Genn, Maria Rohm, Margaret Lee. Witch-hunts and mayhem in the time of King Henry V.

Night of the Following Day, The (1969) C-93m. **½ D: Hubert Cornfield. Marlon Brando, Richard Boone, Rita Moreno, Pamela Franklin, Jess Hahn, Gerard Buhr. Good cast makes this sordid tale of young girl's kidnapping somewhat more interesting than it should be; film is pretty rough in spots and may be edited for TV. Filmed in France.

Night of the Generals (1967-British) C-148m. ** D: Anatole Litvak. Peter O'Toole, Omar Sharif, Tom Courtenay, Donald Pleasence, Joanna Pettet, Christopher Plummer, John Gregson, Philippe Noiret. Essentially a WW2 whodunit, film has potential but gets lost in murky script, lifeless performances. A dud.

Night of the Grizzly, The (1966) C-102m. **½ D: Joseph Pevney. Clint Walker, Martha Hyer, Keenan Wynn, Nancy Kulp, Ron Ely, Regis Toomey, Jack Elam. Acceptable Western of rancher Walker overcoming all obstacles, even a persistent vicious bear, to Western life.

Night of the Hunter, The (1955) 93m. *** D: Charles Laughton. Robert Mitchum, Shelley Winters, Lillian Gish, Evelyn Varden, Peter Graves, James Gleason. Brooding tale of psychopathic killer Mitchum hunting for cache of stolen money, menacing everyone who stands in his way. Laughton's only fling at directing is quite good.

Night of the Iguana, The (1964) 125m. *** D: John Huston. Richard Burton, Deborah Kerr, Ava Gardner, Sue Lyon, Skip Ward, Grayson Hall, Cyril Delevanti. More interesting for its cast than for plodding tale based on Tennessee Williams play; former clergyman Burton, a bus-tour guide in Mexico, is involved with Kerr, Gardner, and Lyon.

Night of the Lepus (1972) C-88m. *½ D: William F. Claxton. Stuart Whitman, Janet Leigh, Rory Calhoun, DeForest Kelley, Paul Fix, Melanie Fullerton. Rabbits weighing 150 pounds and standing four feet high terrorize the countryside; National Guard, not Elmer Fudd, comes to the rescue.

Night of the Living Dead (1968) 90m. *** D: George A. Romero. Judith O'Dea, Russell Streiner, Duane Jones, Karl Hardman. The most horrifying, stomach-churning charnel in the history of horror. The dead come alive and eat the flesh of the living. May be heavily watered down for TV.

Night of the Quarter Moon (1959) 96m. *½ D: Hugo Haas. Julie London, John Drew Barrymore, Nat King Cole, Dean Jones, James Edwards, Anna Kashfi, Agnes Moorehead, Jackie Coogan. Trite handling of miscegenation theme; good cast wasted. Retitled: FLESH AND FLAME.

Night Passage (1957) C-90m. *** D: James Neilson. James Stewart, Audie Murphy, Dan Duryea, Brandon de Wilde, Dianne Foster. Soundly handled Western of Stewart working for railroad and brother Murphy belonging to gang planning to rob train payroll; exciting climactic shoot-out.

Night People (1954) C-93m. *** D: Nunnally Johnson. Gregory Peck, Broderick Crawford, Anita Bjork, Rita Gam, Walter Abel, Buddy Ebsen. Sensibly told, intertwining plots of Cold War espionage; filmed on location in Berlin.

Night Porter, The (1974-Italian) C-115m. ** D: Liliana Cavani. Dirk

Bogarde, Charlotte Rampling, Philippe Leroy, Gabrielle Ferzetti, Isa Miranda. Bizarre drama, set in 1957, about a sado-masochistic relationship between an ex-Nazi and the woman he used to abuse sexually in a concentration camp. Only for students of the sleazy, and they should beware of cuts.

Night Rider, The (1979) C-78m. TVM D: Hy Averback. David Selby, Percy Rodrigues, Kim Cattrall, George Grizzard, Anthony Herrera, Pernell Roberts, Anna Lee, Harris Yulin. So-So *Zorro* variant with a New Orleans dandy-by-day donning mask and cape after dark to right assorted wrongs and to avenge his family's murder. Swashbuckler pilot without panache. Average.

Night Runner, The (1957) 79m. ** D: Abner Biberman. Ray Danton, Colleen Miller, Merry Anders, Eddy Waller. Violent "B" film of insane Danton on killing spree, about to gun down his girlfriend.

Night Slaves (1970) C-73m. TVM D: Ted Post. James Franciscus, Lee Grant, Scott Marlowe, Andrew Prine, Tisha Sterling, Leslie Nielsen. Aliens hypnotize town residents into helping repair spacecraft. Story built up as mystery, from point of view of vacationing couple (Franciscus & Grant). Good story hurt by indifferent script and direction. Average.

Night Song (1947) 101m. ** D: John Cromwell. Dana Andrews, Merle Oberon, Ethel Barrymore, Hoagy Carmichael, Jacqueline White. Overlong, soapy drama of socialite Oberon falling in love with blind pianist Andrews.

Night Stalker, The (1971) C-73m. TVM D: John Llewellyn Moxey. Darren McGavin, Carol Lynley, Simon Oakland, Ralph Meeker, Claude Akins, Kent Smith, Barry Atwater. Wise-guy reporter assigned to series of strange murders in Las Vegas. Near-brilliant mixture of double-edged horror, comedy; well-constructed script. Kudos to flawless cast. Above average. (Later a TV series.)

Night Strangler, The (1972) C-74m. TVM D: Dan Curtis. Darren McGavin, Simon Oakland, Jo Ann Pflug, Richard Anderson, John Carradine, Margaret Hamilton, Wally Cox. Sequel to THE NIGHT STALKER. Reporter, eking out living in Seattle, latches onto series of murders involving blood drainage by

syringe, discovers secret underground city and lone "resident." Great cast, but script has problems, mixing good laughs with horror. Above average.

Night Terror (1977) C-78m. TVM D: E. W. Swackhamer. Valerie Harper, Richard Romanus, Nicholas Pryor, John Quade, Michael Tolan, Beatrice Manley, Quinn Cummings. Housewife Harper vs. psychopath Romanus whom she had seen shooting a highway patrolman. Another relentless pursuit suspense story that's resolved predictably by the fade-out. Average.

Night That Panicked America, The (1975) C-100m. TVM D: Joseph Sargent. Vic Morrow, Cliff De Young, Michael Constantine, Walter McGinn, Eileen Brennan, Meredith Baxter, Tom Bosley, Will Geer, Paul Shenar. Intriguing recreation of Orson Welles' famed "War of the Worlds" broadcast on Hallowe'en night, 1938, intermixed with various real-life mini-dramas. Shenar offers an interesting Welles, but author Nicholas Meyer could have side-stepped the soap opera stuff. Later cut to 78m. Above average.

Night the World Exploded, The (1957) 94m. ** D: Fred F. Sears. Kathryn Grant, William Leslie, Tris Coffin, Raymond Greenleaf, Marshall Reed. Lack of visual excitement weakens this sci-fi of scientists fighting to prevent the title catastrophe.

Night They Raided Minsky's, The (1968) C-99m. *** D: William Friedkin. Jason Robards, Britt Ekland, Norman Wisdom, Forrest Tucker, Harry Andrews, Joseph Wiseman, Denholm Elliott, Elliott Gould, Jack Burns, Bert Lahr. Flavorful period-piece about Quaker girl who comes to New York, gets involved with burlesque comic Robards. Many nice backstage and on-stage moments. Abruptness of Lahr's role due to his death during filming.

Night They Took Miss Beautiful, The (1977) C-100m. TVM D: Robert Michael Lewis. Chuck Connors, Gary Collins, Henry Gibson, Peter Haskell, Sheree North, Phil Silvers, Stella Stevens. Skyjack drama involving a terrorist group headed by North, five beauty pageant finalists who are abducted, and deadly mutant germs for conducting bacterial warfare. Routine thriller with a planeload of familiar TV personalities. Average.

Night to Remember, A (1943) 91m. ***½ D: Richard Wallace. Loretta Young, Brian Aherne, Jeff Donnell, William Wright, Sidney Toler, Gale Sondergaard, Donald MacBride, Blanche Yurka. Sparkling comedy-mystery of whodunit author Aherne and wife Young trying to solve murder.

Night to Remember, A (1958-British) 123m. **** D: Roy Baker. Kenneth More, David McCallum, Jill Dixon, Laurence Naismith, Frank Lawton, Honor Blackman, Alec McCowen, George Rose. Meticulously produced documentary-style account of sinking of the passenger liner Titanic. Vivid enacting of Walter Lord's book.

Night Train (1959-Polish) 90m. ** D: Jerzy Kawalerowicz. Lucyna Winnicka, Leon Niemczyk, Teresa Szmigielowna, Zbigniew Cybulski. Murky account of young woman on a train, forced to share compartment with a doctor; their lack of communication and presence of killer on train are film's focal points.

Night unto Night (1949) 92m. **½ D: Don Siegel. Ronald Reagan, Viveca Lindfors, Broderick Crawford, Osa Massen, Craig Stevens, Rosemary DeCamp. Somber romance story of dying scientist and mentally ill widow who find love together.

Night Visitor, The (1970) C-106m. **½ D: Laslo Benedek. Max von Sydow, Liv Ullmann, Trevor Howard, Per Oscarsson, Rupert Davies, Andrew Keir. An inmate plots to escape from an asylum for the criminally insane for one night, to avenge himself on people who put him away. Ponderous, heavy in detail, but interesting. Filmed in Denmark and Sweden.

Night Walker, The (1964) 86m. *** D: William Castle. Barbara Stanwyck, Robert Taylor, Lloyd Bochner, Rochelle Hudson, Judi Meredith, Hayden Rorke. One of better Castle horror films has Stanwyck as wealthy widow discovering cause of recurring dreams about lost husband. Effective psychological thriller with good cast.

Night Watch (1973-British) C-105m. **½ D: Brian G. Hutton. Elizabeth Taylor, Laurence Harvey, Billie Whitelaw, Robert Lang, Tony Britton. Woman (Taylor) believes she has witnessed a murder, but cannot prove it. Tired plot based on Lucille Fletcher play.

Night Without Sleep (1952) 77m. ** D: Roy Baker. Linda Darnell, Gary Merrill, Hildegarde Neff, Hugh Beaumont, Mae Marsh. Pat treatment of man thinking he's committed murder.

Nightcomers, The (1972-British) C-96m. ** D: Michael Winner. Marlon Brando, Stephanie Beacham, Thora Hird, Harry Andrews, Verna Harvey, Christopher Ellis, Anna Palk. Poor direction hurts attempt to chronicle what happened to the children in Henry James' TURN OF THE SCREW before original story began; considerable footage should be missing on TV.

Nightfall (1956) 78m. *** D: Jacques Tourneur. Aldo Ray, Brian Keith, Anne Bancroft, Jocelyn Brando, James Gregory, Frank Albertson. Fast-moving, well-made story of innocent man wanted by police for killing of friend, chased by actual killers for stolen money he found.

Nightmare (1956) 89m. **½ D: Maxwell Shane. Edward G. Robinson, Kevin McCarthy, Connie Russell, Virginia Christine. McCarthy is musician involved in bizarre murder set in New Orleans; OK mystery, with Robinson sparking proceedings. Remake of FEAR IN THE NIGHT.

Nightmare (1964-British) 82m. *** D: Freddie Francis. David Knight, Moira Redmond, Brenda Bruce, John Welsh. Well-directed thriller with enough subplots to keep any viewer busy. Girl is blackmailed into committing murder by scheming gardener.

Nightmare (1974) C-78m. TVM D: William Hale. Richard Crenna, Patty Duke Astin, Vic Morrow, Peter Bromilow, Arch Johnson, Richard Schaal. Witness to a killing realizes he may be the sniper's next target. Bread and butter TV thriller. Average.

Nightmare Alley (1947) 111m. ***½ D: Edmund Goulding. Tyrone Power, Joan Blondell, Coleen Gray, Helen Walker, Mike Mazurki. Morbid story of carnival heel Power entangled with mind-reading Blondell, blackmailing psychiatrist Walker, other assorted weirdos in original, fascinating melodrama.

Nightmare Castle (1966-Italian) 90m. ** D: Allan Grunewald. Barbara Steele, Paul Mueller, Helga Line, Lawrence Clift. Typically atmospheric European horror film about doctor experimenting in regeneration of human blood through electrical impulses. Good photography.

Nightmare Hotel (1970-Spanish) C-95m. ** D: Eugenio Martin. Judy Geeson, Aurora Bautista, Esperanza Roy, Victor Alcazar, Lone Fleming. Geeson goes to small Spanish inn looking for relative who has disappeared, and confronts two mad sisters who run establishment; several murders follow. Passable thriller.

Nightmare in Badham County (1976) C-100m. TVM D: John Llewellyn Moxey. Deborah Raffin, Lynne Moody, Ralph Bellamy, Chuck Connors, Tina Louise, Robert Reed, Della Reese, Lana Wood, Fionnuala Flanagan. Exploitation drama about two comely hitchhikers tossed into a rural prison farm after spurning the advances of leacherous sheriff Connors. Stereotype acting; ditto for dialogue. Below average.

Nightmare in Blood (1976) C-89m. **½ D: John Stanley. Jerry Walter, Dan Caldwell, Barrie Youngfellow, Kathleen Quinlan, Kerwin Mathews. Horror film actor visiting fan convention turns out to be a real vampire after all; low-budget film made in San Francisco will appeal particularly to horror buffs for its many in-jokes.

Nightmare in Chicago (1964) C-80m. TVM D: Robert Altman. Philip Abbott, Robert Ridgley, Ted Knight, Charles McGraw, John Alonzo, Barbara Turner. Psychotic killer, known to tri-State police via newspapers as Georgie Porgie, terrorizes Chicago area for 72 hours in mad murder spree. Totally location-shot, film does resemble nightmare. (Originally a two-part "Kraft Mystery Theater.") Above average.

Nightmare in the Sun (1965) C-80m. *½ D: Marc Lawrence. John Derek, Aldo Ray, Arthur O'Connell, Ursula Andress. Lackluster account of innocent man hunted for crime by people who know he was framed; contrived production.

Nightmare in Wax (1969) C-91m. ** D: Bud Townsend. Cameron Mitchell, Anne Helm, Scott Brady, Berry Kroeger, Victoria Carroll. Paraphrase of HOUSE OF WAX has Mitchell as former movie make-up man whose wax museum is full of actors "missing" from the studio.

Nights of Cabiria (1957-Italian) 110m. **** D: Federico Fellini. Giulietta Masina, Francois Perier, Amedeo Nazzari, Franca Marzi, Dorian Gray. Masina is a joy as waifish prostitute dreaming of rich, wonderful life but always finding sorrow. Basis for Broadway musical and film SWEET CHARITY. One of Fellini's best; a must-see film.

Nights of Rasputin (1960-Italian) C-95m. ** D: Pierre Chenal. Edmund Purdom, Gianna Maria Canale, John Drew Barrymore, Jany Clair. Purdom is miscast as Rasputin in this plodding retelling of the conniving quack who gained power in Czarina Alexandra's court.

Nightwing (1979) C-105m. *½ D: Arthur Hiller. Nick Mancuso, David Warner, Kathryn Harrold, Stephen Macht, Strother Martin. Warner is an oddball who comes to Arizona to kill vampire bats in their caves. Well, it's a living—and we wish filmmakers who make shlock like this would start earning theirs.

Nikki, Wild Dog of the North (1961) C-74m. *** D: Jack Couffer, Don Haldane. Jean Coutu, Emile Genest, Uriel Luft, Robert Rivard. Wolfdog Nikki is separated from his master, a Canadian trapper, and fends for himself in a variety of adventures. Exciting Disney film.

Nine Girls (1944) 78m. **½ D: Leigh Jason. Ann Harding, Evelyn Keyes, Jinx Falkenburg, Anita Louise, Jeff Donnell, Nina Foch, Marcia Mae Jones, Leslie Brooks, Lynn Merrick, Shirley Mills, William Demarest. Wisecrack-laden comedy mystery about murder at a sorority house.

Nine Hours to Rama (1963) C-125m. **½ D: Mark Robson. Horst Buchholz, Jose Ferrer, Robert Morley, Diane Baker, Harry Andrews. Ambitious attempt to make meaningful story of events leading up to assassination of Mahatma Gandhi; bogs down in trite script. Filmed on location in India.

1984 (1956-British) 91m. *** D: Michael Anderson. Edmond O'Brien, Michael Redgrave, Jan Sterling, David Kossoff, Mervyn Johns, Donald Pleasence. Thought-provoking version of George Orwell's futuristic novel. Lovers O'Brien and Sterling are trapped in all-powerful state, try valiantly to rebel against "Big Brother."

1941 (1979) C-118m. **½ D: Steven Spielberg. Dan Aykroyd, Ned Beatty, John Belushi, Treat Williams, Nancy Allen, Robert Stack, Tim Matheson,

Toshiro Mifune, Christopher Lee, Bobby DiCicco, Dianne Kay, Murray Hamilton, Lorraine Gary, Slim Pickens. Gargantuan comedy from the bigger-is-funner school of filmmaking. Some excellent vignettes and dazzling special effects in freewheeling story of war panic in California following Pearl Harbor attack, but on the whole film suffers from overkill.

1900 (1977-Italian-French-German) C-243m. ***½ D: Bernardo Bertolucci. Robert De Niro, Gerard Depardieu, Donald Sutherland, Burt Lancaster, Dominique Sanda, Stephania Sandrelli, Sterling Hayden. Sweeping chronicle of 20th-century Italy focusing on two contrasting families; ambitious, powerful film full of potent, beautiful images. Continuity problems caused, no doubt, by trimming from 6-hour original; beware further cutting.

Ninety Degrees in the Shade (1964-Czech) 90m. **½ D: Jiri Weiss. Anne Heywood, James Booth, Donald Wolfit, Ann Todd. Turgid account of Heywood, who works in food store, accused of theft; intertwined with passionate love episodes. Czech-made, with British stars.

99 and 44/100% Dead (1974) C-98m. BOMB. D: John Frankenheimer. Richard Harris, Chuck Connors, Edmond O'Brien, Bradford Dillman, Ann Turkel. Terrible takeoff on gangster movies, shot in Seattle, L.A. and Silver Springs, Fla. Only positive note is that it brought Harris and co-star Turkel together in real-life wedlock.

99 River Street (1953) 83m. *** D: Phil Karlson. John Payne, Evelyn Keyes, Brad Dexter, Peggie Castle, Ian Wolfe, Frank Faylen. Rugged crime caper with Payne caught up in tawdry surroundings, trying to prove himself innocent of murder charge. Unpretentious film really packs a punch.

99 Women (1969-Spanish-German-British-Italian) C-90m. *½ D: Jess Franco. Maria Schell, Luciana Paluzzi, Mercedes McCambridge, Herbert Lom. Absurd drama about lesbianism in women's prison may have some scenes cut for TV, unless film puts the censors to sleep.

92 in the Shade (1975) C-93m. *** D: Thomas McGuane. Peter Fonda, Warren Oates, Margot Kidder, Burgess Meredith, Harry Dean Stanton, Sylvia Miles, Elizabeth Ashley. National Book Award-nominated novel about rival fishing boat captains in Florida Keys; directed by the author. Wildly uneven but well cast and frequently hilarious.

Ninotchka (1939) 110m. ***½ D: Ernst Lubitsch. Greta Garbo, Melvyn Douglas, Ina Claire, Bela Lugosi, Sig Ruman, Felix Bressart, Richard Carle. Amid much outdated sociological banter, a lighthearted Garbo still shines. Lubitsch's comedy pegged on tale of cold Russian agent Garbo coming to Paris, falling in love with gay-blade Douglas. Supporting cast shows fine comedy flair. Basis for Broadway musical and film SILK STOCKINGS.

Nitwits, The (1935) 81m. *** D: George Stevens. Bert Wheeler, Robert Woolsey, Betty Grable, Hale Hamilton, Evelyn Brent, Erik Rhodes. Enjoyable Wheeler & Woolsey vehicle mixes their nonsense comedy with murder mystery in an office building; smashing slapstick climax.

No Blade of Grass (1970) C-97m. *½ D: Cornel Wilde. Nigel Davenport, Jean Wallace, John Hamill, Lynne Frederick, Patrick Holt, Anthony May. Sober-sided film trying to drive home ecology message is just an update of films like PANIC IN YEAR ZERO, with family fleeing virus-stricken London for Scottish countryside, facing panic and attack along the way.

No Deposit, No Return (1976) C-112m. **½ D: Norman Tokar. David Niven, Darren McGavin, Don Knotts, Herschel Bernardi, Barbara Feldon, Brad Savage, Kim Richards. Two neglected kids stage their own bogus kidnapping to stir up attention and enable them to join their mother in Hong Kong. OK Disney comedy with so-so material enlivened by good cast.

No Down Payment (1957) 105m. *** D: Martin Ritt. Joanne Woodward, Jeffrey Hunter, Sheree North, Tony Randall, Cameron Mitchell, Patricia Owens, Barbara Rush, Pat Hingle. Turgid suburban soaper of intertwining problems of several young married couples; very capable cast.

No Drums, No Bugles (1971) C-85m. **½ D: Clyde Ware. Martin Sheen. Nicely done drama, based on West Virginia legend about conscientious objector during Civil War who spends three years in a cave rather than fight. Good acting by Sheen, the only one on screen for most of film.

No Escape (1953) 76m. *½ D: Charles Bennett. Lew Ayres, Marjorie Steele, Sonny Tufts, Gertrude Michael. Modest narrative about couple seeking actual killer to clear themselves of homicide charge. Retitled: CITY ON A HUNT.

No Escape (1943) SEE: I Escaped From the Gestapo

No Highway in the Sky (1951-British) 98m. *** D: Henry Koster. James Stewart, Marlene Dietrich, Glynis Johns, Jack Hawkins, Elizabeth Allan, Kenneth More. Excellent drama of Stewart's discovery of metal fatigue causing plane crashes; Dietrich a glamorous passenger on crash-bound plane; Johns a girl in love with Stewart.

No Holds Barred (1952) 65m. D: William Beaudine. Leo Gorcey, Huntz Hall, Marjorie Reynolds, Bernard Gorcey, Tim Ryan, Leonard Penn. SEE: Bowery Boys series.

No Leave, No Love (1946) 119m. ** D: Charles Martin. Van Johnson, Keenan Wynn, Pat Kirkwood, Guy Lombardo, Edward Arnold, Marie Wilson. No script, no laughs; Johnson and Wynn are sailors on the town in this overlong romantic comedy.

No Love for Johnnie (1961-British) 110m. *** D: Ralph Thomas. Peter Finch, Stanley Holloway, Mary Peach, Mervyn Johns, Donald Pleasence, Dennis Price. Civilized study of politician who cares only about winning the election.

No Man Is an Island (1962) C-114m. **½ D: John Monks, Jr., Richard Goldstone. Jeffrey Hunter, Marshall Thompson, Barbara Perez, Ronald Remy, Paul Edwards, Jr., Rolf Bayer, Vicente Liwanag. Spotty production values mar true story of serviceman Hunter trapped on Guam during the three years Japanese controlled area.

No Man of Her Own (1932) 85m. **½ D: Wesley Ruggles. Clark Gable, Carole Lombard, Dorothy Mackaill, Grant Mitchell, Elizabeth Patterson, Lillian Harmer. Snappy story of heel reformed by good girl, noteworthy for only co-starring of Gable-Lombard.

No Man of Her Own (1950) 98m. **½ D: Mitchell Leisen. Barbara Stanwyck, John Lund, Jane Cowl, Phyllis Thaxter, Richard Denning, Milburn Stone. Turgid drama based

on Cornell Woolrich tale of Stanwyck assuming another's identity, later being blackmailed by ex-boyfriend.

No Man's Woman (1955) 70m. ** D: Franklin Adreon. Marie Windsor, John Archer, Patric Knowles, Nancy Gates, Louis Jean Heydt. OK whodunit about finding murderer of strong-willed woman.

No Mercy Man, The SEE: Trained to Kill

No Minor Vices (1948) 96m. ** D: Lewis Milestone. Dana Andrews, Lilli Palmer, Louis Jourdan, Jane Wyatt, Norman Lloyd. Comedy of mooching house guest Jourdan winning over Andrews' wife Palmer; starts out well but bogs down.

No More Ladies (1935) 81m. **½ D: Edward H. Griffith. Joan Crawford, Robert Montgomery, Charlie Ruggles, Franchot Tone, Edna May Oliver, Gail Patrick. Crawford marries playboy Montgomery, tries to settle him down by making him jealous over her attention to Tone. Airy comedy. Joan Burfield (Fontaine) makes film debut here.

No My Darling Daughter (1964-British) 97m. **½ D: Betty Box. Michael Redgrave, Michael Craig, Juliet Mills, Roger Livesey. Generally funny film with Mills, rich industrialist's daughter, torn between two suitors, playboy and hard-working businessman.

No Name on the Bullet (1959) C-77m. **½ D: Jack Arnold. Audie Murphy, Charles Drake, Joan Evans, Virginia Grey, Warren Stevens, R. G. Armstrong. Different-type Western; psychological study of townfolk's reaction when hired gunslinger arrives.

No One Man (1932) 73m. ** D: Lloyd Corrigan. Carole Lombard, Ricardo Cortez, Paul Lukas, George Barbier. Another tired love triangle, with spoiled rich-girl Lombard caught between suave but heartless Cortez and earnest doctor Lukas. Becomes laughable before long.

No Other Love (1979) C-100m. TVM D: Richard Pearce. Richard Thomas, Julie Kavner, Elizabeth Allen, Rogert Loggia, Scott Jacoby, Frances Lee McCain. Sensitive drama focusing on love affair of two mentally retarded young people. Thomas and Kavner's acting gives this one the edge over the similar LIKE NORMAL PEOPLE. Above average.

No Place for Jennifer (1951-British)

89m. ** D: Henry Cass. Leo Genn, Rosamund John, Beatrice Campbell, Guy Middleton. Low-key sob story of little girl with bleak future when parents divorce.

No Place Like Homicide! (1962-British) 87m. ** D: Pat Jackson. Kenneth Connor, Sidney James, Shirley Eaton, Donald Pleasence, Dennis Price, Michael Gough. At times strained satire about group of people gathered at haunted house for the reading of a will. Remake of THE GHOUL. Original title: WHAT A CARVE UP!

No Place to Hide (1956) C-71m. **½ D: Josef Shaftel. David Brian, Marsha Hunt, Hugh Corcoran, Ike Jariega, Jr., Celia Flor. Tense account of search for two children who accidentally have disease-spreading pellets in their possession; filmed in Philippines.

No Place to Land (1958) 78m. *½ D: Albert Gannaway. John Ireland, Mari Blanchard, Gail Russell, Jackie Coogan. Sleazy little film of three-cornered romance, leading nowhere.

No Place to Run (1972) C-73m. TVM D: Delbert Mann. Herschel Bernardi, Stefanie Powers, Larry Hagman, Scott Jacoby, Neville Brand, Tom Bosley. Old shopkeeper Malsh (Bernardi) decides to take adopted son and flee to Canada when authorities decide failing health and retirement not right for boy (Jacoby). Fair dialogue and performances, but script's point of view questionable. Above average.

No Questions Asked (1951) 81m. **½ D: Harold F. Kress. Barry Sullivan, Arlene Dahl, Jean Hagen, George Murphy, William Reynolds, Mari Blanchard. Snappy little film of Sullivan seeking easy road to success via crime rackets.

No Road Back (1957-British) 83m. ** D: Montgomery Tully. Sean Connery, Skip Homeier, Paul Carpenter, Patricia Dainton, Norman Wooland, Margaret Rawlings. Blind and deaf woman sacrifices everything for her son, and becomes involved with criminals—who then try to pin robbery on the innocent son. Plodding melodrama.

No Room for the Groom (1952) 82m. **½ D: Douglas Sirk. Tony Curtis, Piper Laurie, Spring Byington, Don DeFore, Jack Kelly. Harmless shenanigans of ex-G.I. Curtis returning home to find it filled with in-laws.

No Room to Run (1978-Australian)

C-97m. TVM D: Robert Michael Lewis. Richard Benjamin, Paula Prentiss, Barry Sullivan, Noel Ferrier, Ray Barrett. Boring tale of intrigue with lawyer Benjamin swallowed up by high-level intrigue on business trip to Australia. Below average.

No Sad Songs for Me (1950) 89m. *** D: Rudolph Maté. Margaret Sullavan, Wendell Corey, Viveca Lindfors, Natalie Wood, Ann Doran. Moving account of dying mother Sullavan preparing her family to go on without her. Ironically, Sullavan's last film.

No Time for Comedy (1940) 98m. **½ D: William Keighley. James Stewart, Rosalind Russell, Genevieve Tobin, Charles Ruggles, Allyn Joslyn, Louise Beavers. Slick but dated adaptation of S. N. Behrman play about actress who tries to keep her playwright-husband from taking himself too seriously. Smoothly done but artificial.

No Time for Flowers (1952) 83m. ** D: Don Siegel. Viveca Lindfors, Paul Christian, Ludwig Stossel, Manfred Ingor. Low-grade version of Ninotchka theme set in Prague; a pale shadow of its ancestor.

No Time for Love (1943) 83m. *** D: Mitchell Leisen. Claudette Colbert, Fred MacMurray, Ilka Chase, Richard Haydn, Paul McGrath, June Havoc. Sophisticated romance between photographer Colbert and illiterate MacMurray, who becomes her un-chic assistant, in good form here.

No Time for Sergeants (1958) 111m. ***½ D: Mervyn LeRoy. Andy Griffith, Myron McCormick, Nick Adams, Murray Hamilton, Don Knotts. Funny army comedy based on Broadway play. Griffith and McCormick repeat roles as hayseed inducted into service and his harried sergeant. Griffith's best film, with good support from Adams, and in a small role, Don Knotts.

No Time to Be Young (1957) 82m. ** D: David Lowell Rich. Robert Vaughn, Roger Smith, Merry Anders, Kathy Nolan. Programmer of supermarket robbery and repercussions thereafter to those involved. Early effort of four cast members who fared better on TV.

No Trees in the Street (1958-British) 108m. ** D: J. Lee Thompson. Sylvia Syms, Stanley Holloway, Herbert Lom, Ronald Howard, Joan Miller. Lower-class British life examined for its strengths and weaknesses; too sterile a human document.

No Way Out (1950) 106m. ***½ D: Joseph L. Mankiewicz. Richard Widmark, Linda Darnell, Stephen McNally, Sidney Poitier, Ruby Dee, Ossie Davis, Bill Walker. Violent tale of racial hatred involving bigot Widmark, who has gangster pals avenge his brother's death by creating race riots. Film was far ahead of its time; still engrossing today. Poitier's first film.

No Way Out (1972-Italian) C-100m. *½ D: Duccio Tessari. Alain Delon, Richard Conte, Carla Gravina, Roger Hanin, Nicoletta Machiavelli. Boring Mafia movie about a hit-man (Delon) who turns on his bosses, four crime kingpins, when they kill his wife and child to dissuade him from hanging up his guns. Also called BIG GUNS.

No Way to Treat a Lady (1968) C-108m. ***½ D: Jack Smight. Rod Steiger, Lee Remick, George Segal, Eileen Heckart, Murray Hamilton, Michael Dunn, Barbara Baxley, Ruth White. Delicious blend of romantic comedy and murder, with Steiger as flamboyant ladykiller, Segal as "Mo Brummel," cop on his trail, Remick as Segal's new lady-friend who could be next victim.

Noah's Ark (1929) 75m. **½ D: Michael Curtiz. Dolores Costello, George O'Brien, Noah Beery, Louise Fazenda, Guinn Williams, Paul McAllister, Myrna Loy. Silent film revamped in 1957 by Robert Youngson, eliminating subtitles (and a few talkie sequences), replacing them with narration detracts somewhat from film's impact, but climactic flood sequence still impressive. Modern-day allegory of biblical story is interesting, but ineffective.

Nob Hill (1945) C-95m. *½ D: Henry Hathaway. George Raft, Joan Bennett, Vivian Blaine, Peggy Ann Garner, Alan Reed, B. S. Pully, Emil Coleman. Glossy trash of saloonowner Raft stepping up in society to win high-class Bennett.

Nobody Lives Forever (1946) 100m. *** D: Jean Negulesco. John Garfield, Geraldine Fitzgerald, Walter Brennan, Faye Emerson, George Coulouris, George Tobias. Well-done but familiar yarn of con-man Garfield fleecing rich widow Fitzgerald, then falling in love for real.

Nobody Runs Forever SEE: High Commissioner, The.

Nobody Waved Goodbye (1965-Canadian) 80m. *** D: Don Owen. Peter Kastner, Julie Biggs, Claude Rae, Toby Tarnow, Charmion King, Ron Taylor. Straightforward account of teen-ager fed up with the generation gap, leaving home for anywhere or nowhere.

Nobody's Perfect (1968) C-103m. **½ D: Alan Rafkin. Doug McClure, Nancy Kwan, James Whitmore, David Hartman, Gary Vinson. Witless military service comedy involving pat shenanigans of U.S. submarine based in Japan, with every predictable gimmick thrown in.

Nocturne (1946) 88m. *** D: Edwin L. Marin. George Raft, Lynn Bari, Virginia Huston, Joseph Pevney, Myrna Dell. Detective Raft is convinced supposed suicide was murder; police force suspends him, but he continues investigations on his own; taut private-eye thriller.

None But the Brave (1965) C-105m. **½ D: Frank Sinatra. Frank Sinatra, Clint Walker, Tommy Sands, Tony Bill, Brad Dexter. Taut war drama focusing on crew of cracked-up plane and Japanese army patrol who make peace on a remote island during WW2.

None But the Lonely Heart (1944) 113m. **½ D: Clifford Odets. Cary Grant, Ethel Barrymore, Barry Fitzgerald, Jane Wyatt, Dan Duryea, George Coulouris, June Duprez. Odets' moody drama of a Cockney drifter features one of Grant's most ambitious performances, and some fine moments, but suffers from censorship restrictions of the time, and misplaced WW2 rhetoric. Barrymore won Supporting Actress Oscar as Grant's dying mother.

None Shall Escape (1944) 85m. *** D: Andre de Toth. Marsha Hunt, Alexander Knox, Henry Travers, Richard Crane, Dorothy Morris, Trevor Bardette. Trial of Nazi officer reviews his savage career, in taut drama that retains quite a punch.

Non-Stop New York (1937-British) 71m. *** D: Robert Stevenson. John Loder, Anna Lee, Francis L. Sullivan, Frank Cellier, Desmond Tester. Fast-paced, tongue-in-cheek Hitchcock-like yarn about a woman who can provide alibi for innocent man accused of murder—but no one will believe her. Love that luxury airplane!

Noose Hangs High, The (1948) 77m. **½ D: Charles Barton. Bud Abbott, Lou Costello, Joseph Calleia, Leon Errol, Cathy Downs, Mike Mazurki, Fritz Feld. Mistaken identity leads to complications with the boys robbed of a large sum of money; typical A&C, bolstered by presence of Errol.

Nora Prentiss (1947) 111m. **½ D: Vincent Sherman. Ann Sheridan, Kent Smith, Robert Alda, Bruce Bennett, Rosemary DeCamp. Chanteuse Sheridan ruins doctor Smith's life; contrived but glossy melodrama.

Norliss Tapes, The (1973) C-98m. TVM D: Dan Curtis. Roy Thinnes, Angie Dickinson, Claude Akins, Michele Carey, Vonetta McGee, Hurd Hatfield, Don Porter. Unsuccessful pilot about writer who investigates the supernatural, here on the trail of a vampire killer loose in Monterey, California. Above average.

Norma Rae (1979) C-113m. *** D: Martin Ritt. Sally Field, Ron Leibman, Beau Bridges, Pat Hingle, Barbara Baxley, Gail Strickland, Lonnie Chapman. Field is excellent in Oscar-winning performance as poor Southern textile worker gradually won over toward unionization by N.Y. labor organizer. Entertaining, though not entirely believable; haunting theme "It Goes Like it Goes" sung by Jennifer Warnes, won an Oscar.

Norman . . . Is That You? (1976) C-91m. ** D: George Schlatter. Redd Foxx, Pearl Bailey, Dennis Dugan, Michael Warren, Tamara Dobson, Vernee Watson, Jayne Meadows. Leering comedy based on flop Broadway show and revamped with Black stars: Foxx is distraught when he discovers his son is gay, and determines to "straighten him out."

Norseman, The (1978) C-90m. *½ D: Charles B. Pierce. Lee Majors, Cornel Wilde, Mel Ferrer, Jack Elam, Chris Connelly, Kathleen Freeman, Susie Coelho, Denny Miller. Stodgy period adventure casts Majors as 11th-century Viking prince who sails to North America in search of his father, a norse King abducted by Indians. Majors' first starring movie is definitely minor league.

North Avenue Irregulars, The (1979) C-99m. **½ D: Bruce Bilson. Edward Herrmann, Barbara Harris, Susan Clark, Karen Valentine, Michael Constantine, Cloris Leachman, Patsy Kelly, Virginia Capers.

Young priest (Herrmann) enlists churchgoing ladies for crime-fighting brigade; innocuous Disney comedy starts well but reverts to formula, including obligatory car pile-up finale. Fine actresses like Harris, Clark, and Leachman utterly wasted.

North Dallas Forty (1979) C-119m. ***½ D: Ted Kotcheff. Nick Nolte, Mac Davis, Charles Durning, Dayle Haddon, G. D. Spradlin, Bo Svenson, Steve Forrest. Seriocomic version of Peter Gent's best-seller about labor abuse in the National Football League is the best gridiron film ever made and one of the best on any sport, Super Bowl-level performances for the most part.

North By Northwest (1959) C-136m. ***½ D: Alfred Hitchcock. Cary Grant, Eva Marie Saint, James Mason, Jessie Royce Landis, Martin Landau, Leo G. Carroll, Philip Ober. Lively Hitchcock thriller with Grant mistaken for a spy by secret agent Mason and accomplice Saint. Good cast helps maintain excitement. Mount Rushmore climax and cropdusting scenes are now classics.

North Star, The (1943) 105m. **½ D: Lewis Milestone. Anne Baxter, Dana Andrews, Walter Huston, Ann Harding, Erich von Stroheim, Jane Withers, Farley Granger, Walter Brennan. Dramatic battle sequences in WW2 Russia marred by uninteresting stretches until German Von Stroheim matches wits with village leader Huston. Harding a joy as his gentle peasant wife, who undergoes torture stoically; Withers unusually good in her scenes. Later edited to 82m. to deemphasize the good Russians, and retitled ARMORED ATTACK.

North to Alaska (1960) C-122m. *** D: Henry Hathaway. John Wayne, Stewart Granger, Ernie Kovacs, Fabian, Capucine, Mickey Shaughnessy. Fast-moving actioner with delightful tongue-in-cheek approach; set in the north country. Two-fisted Wayne is the whole show.

Northern Pursuit (1943) 94m. **½ D: Raoul Walsh. Errol Flynn, Julie Bishop, Helmut Dantine, John Ridgely, Gene Lockhart, Tom Tully. Mountie Flynn tracks his man, a downed Nazi pilot, throughout Canada in this standard but slickly done drama, aided by Warner Bros. stock cast.

Northwest Mounted Police (1940) C-125m. **½ D: Cecil B. DeMille.

Gary Cooper, Madeleine Carroll, Preston Foster, Paulette Goddard, Robert Preston, George Bancroft, Akim Tamiroff, Lon Chaney, Jr. DeMille at his most ridiculous, with Cooper as Dusty Rivers, Goddard a fiery half-breed in love with Preston, Lynne Overman as Scottish philosopher in superficial tale of Texas Ranger searching for fugitive in Canada. Much of outdoor action filmed on obviously indoor sets.

Northwest Outpost (1947) 91m. *½ D: Allan Dwan. Nelson Eddy, Ilona Massey, Hugo Haas, Elsa Lanchester, Lenore Ulric. Rudolf Friml operetta of California cavalrymen lumbers along pretty lamely.

Northwest Passage (1940) C-125m. ***½ D: King Vidor. Spencer Tracy, Robert Young, Walter Brennan, Ruth Hussey, Nat Pendleton, Robert Barrat, Addison Richards. Gritty, evocative filming of Kenneth Roberts' book about Rogers' Rangers and their stoic leader (Tracy), enduring hardships and frustrations while opening up new territory in Colonial America. Young and Brennan are greenhorns who learn hard knocks under taskmaster Tracy.

Northwest Stampede (1948) C-79m. **½ D: Albert S. Rogell. Joan Leslie, James Craig, Jack Oakie, Chill Wills, Victor Kilian, Stanley Andrews. Lightweight oater about lady rancher Leslie competing with cowboy Craig for prize horses.

Norwood (1970) C-96m. ** D: Jack Haley, Jr. Glen Campbell, Kim Darby, Joe Namath, Carol Lynley, Pat Hingle, Tisha Sterling, Dom DeLuise. Ex-Marine Campbell hits the road for series of unrelated adventures with service buddy Namath, a midget (Billy Curtis), a Greenwich Village girl (Sterling), a shiftless brother-in-law (DeLuise), a dancing chicken, and a young girl (Darby) with whom he falls in love. Easy to take, but pointless.

Nosferatu (1922-German) 63m. ***½ D: F. W. Murnau. Max Schreck, Alexander Granach, Gustav von Wangenheim, Greta Schroeder. First film version of Bram Stoker's Dracula is brilliantly eerie, full of imaginative touches that none of the later films quite recaptured. Schreck's vampire is also the ugliest in film history.

Nosferatu (1979-West German) C-105m. ***½ D: Werner Herzog. Klaus Kinski, Isabelle Adjani, Bruno Ganz, Roland Topor. Spooky, funny, reverent remake of F. W. Murnau's vampire masterpiece should please Dracula fans of all persuasions. Kinski is magnificent as the good Count, and Adjani's classic beauty is utilized to the hilt.

Not as a Stranger (1955) 125m. *** D: Stanley Kramer. Olivia de Havilland, Frank Sinatra, Robert Mitchum, Charles Bickford, Gloria Grahame, Broderick Crawford, Lee Marvin, Lon Chaney. Morton Thompson novel of Mitchum marrying nurse De Havilland who supports him through medical school despite oft-strained relationship. Glossy tribute to medical profession contains excellent performances by all.

Not of This Earth (1957) 67m. ** D: Roger Corman. Paul Birch, Beverly Garland, Morgan Jones, William Roerick. Low-budget Corman film of advance scout for interplanetary force. Fair cast enables one to bear defects.

Not Wanted (1949) 94m. **½ D: Elmer Clifton. Sally Forrest, Keefe Brasselle, Leo Penn, Dorothy Adams. Well-intentioned account of unwed mother seeking affection and understanding; produced and co-scripted by Ida Lupino.

Not With My Wife You Don't! (1966) C-118m. **½ D: Norman Panama. Tony Curtis, Virna Lisi, George C. Scott, Carroll O'Connor, Richard Eastham. Trivial fluff about air force officer Curtis and bored wife Lisi; pointless and aimless, but attractive to the eye.

Nothing but a Man (1964) 92m. *** D: Michael Roemer. Ivan Dixon, Abbey Lincoln, Gloria Foster, Julius Harris, Martin Priest. Sincere study of Negro worker Dixon deciding that his family should not suffer from his frustrations over racial inequality.

Nothing but the Best (1964-British) 99m. ***½ D: Clive Donner. Alan Bates, Denholm Elliott, Harry Andrews, Millicent Martin, Pauline Delany. Biting look at social-climbing playboy Bates who commits murder to get ahead in the world.

Nothing But Trouble (1944) 69m. ** D: Sam Taylor. Stan Laurel, Oliver Hardy, Mary Boland, David Leland, Henry O'Neill. Lesser L&H vehicle with duo hired as servants, meeting young boy king whose life is in danger. Boland is amusing as usual.

Nothing Sacred (1937) C-75m. ***½

D: William Wellman. Carole Lombard, Fredric March, Walter Connolly, Charles Winninger, Sig Ruman, Frank Fay. Classic comedy about hotshot reporter (March) who exploits Vermont girl's "imminent" death for headline value in N.Y.C. Ben Hecht's cynical script vividly enacted by March and Lombard (at her best). Gershwinesque music score by Oscar Levant. Remade as LIVING IT UP.

Notorious (1946) 101m. ***½ D: Alfred Hitchcock. Cary Grant, Ingrid Bergman, Claude Rains, Louis Calhern, Reinhold Schunzel, Moroni Olsen. Top-notch espionage tale set in WW2 South America, with Ingrid marrying spy Rains to aid U.S. and agent Grant. Frank, tense, well acted, with amazingly suspenseful climax.

Notorious Gentleman (1945-British) 108m. *** D: Frank Launder, Sidney Gilliat. Rex Harrison, Lilli Palmer, Godfrey Tearle, Griffith Jones, Margaret Johnston. Well-mounted telling of playboy Harrison's moral disintegration, leading dissolute life. Original title: THE RAKE'S PROGRESS.

Notorious Landlady, The (1962) 123m. **½ D: Richard Quine. Kim Novak, Jack Lemmon, Fred Astaire, Lionel Jeffries, Estelle Winwood, Maxwell Reed. Lemmon entranced by houseowner Novak, decides to find out if she really did kill her husband; set in London. Offbeat comedy-mystery.

Notorious Lone Wolf, The (1946) 64m. D: D. Ross Lederman. Gerald Mohr, Janis Carter, Eric Blore, John Abbott, William B. Davidson, Don Beddoe, Adele Roberts. SEE: Lone Wolf series.

Notorious Mr. Monks, The (1958) 70m. ** D: Joseph Kane. Vera Ralston, Don Kelly, Paul Fix, Leo Gordon. Tame Ralston vehicle involving a hitchhiker and murder.

Notorious Sophie Lang (1934) 64m. **½ D: Ralph Murphy. Gertrude Michael, Paul Cavanagh, Alison Skipworth, Leon Errol, Arthur Hoyt. Tightly knit yarn of police using title character (Michael) to lead them to international crime ring.

Novel Affair, A (1958-British) C-83m. *** D: Muriel Box. Ralph Richardson, Margaret Leighton, Patricia Dainton, Carlo Justini. Amusing tale of Leighton who writes a sexy novel, finding the fantasy come true.

Now and Forever (1934) 81m. **½ D: Henry Hathaway. Gary Cooper, Carole Lombard, Shirley Temple, Sir Guy Standing, Charlotte Granville, Harry Stubbs. Standard jewel-thief-going-straight yarn; Lombard overshadowed by Cooper and Temple.

Now, Voyager (1942) 117m. ***½ D: Irving Rapper. Bette Davis, Claude Rains, Paul Henreid, Gladys Cooper, Bonita Granville, Janis Wilson, Ilka Chase, John Loder, Lee Patrick. Vintage, first-class soaper with Bette as sheltered spinster brought out of her shell by psychiatrist Rains, falling in love with suave Henreid, helping shy girl Wilson. All this set to beautiful Max Steiner music makes top entertainment of this kind.

Now You See Him, Now You Don't (1972) C-88m. **½ D: Robert Butler. Kurt Russell, Cesar Romero, Joe Flynn, Jim Backus, William Windom, Michael McGreevy. Student Russell invents invisible spray and tries to stay one step ahead of crooks who want it. Some good Disney effects in this so-so comedy.

Now You See It, Now You Don't (1967) C-100m TVM D: Don Weis. Jonathan Winters, Luciana Paluzzi, Jack Weston, Steve Allen, Jayne Meadows. Mild-mannered, bumbling art expert hired by insurance company, responsible for security of Rembrandt painting on loan from Louvre. Couple of good gags in middling comedy with laughable stereotypes out to steal painting. Average.

Nowhere to Hide (1977) C-78m. TVM D: Jack Starrett. Lee Van Cleef, Tony Musante, Charles Robinson, Lelia Goldoni, Noel Fournier, Russell Johnson, Edward Anhalt. U.S. Marshal (Van Cleef) protects former syndicate hit man (Musante) who is to testify against his ex-boss. The stuff B-movies did so well. Below average.

Nowhere to Run (1978) C-100m. TVM D: Richard Lang. David Janssen, Stefanie Powers, Allen Garfield, Linda Evans, Neva Patterson, John Randolph. Good yarn of Janssen's elaborate scheme to get his money-grabbing wife and the gumshoe she's hired off his back. Above average.

Nude In a White Car (1960-French) 87m. **½ D: Robert Hossein. Marina Vlady, Robert Hossein, Odile Versois, Helena Manson, Henri Cremieux. Hossein's only clue to a crime is title person; suspenser set on French Riviera. Retitled: BLONDE IN A WHITE CAR.

Number One (1969) C-105m. *½ D: Tom Gries. Charlton Heston, Jessica Walter, Bruce Dern, John Randolph, Diana Muldaur. Heston turns in his loincloth for a jockstrap in this ludicrous drama about a New Orleans Saints quarterback who's fighting advancing age; interesting subject matter deserves better treatment.

Number Six (1962-British) 59m. ** D: Robert Tronson. Nadja Regin, Ivan Desny, Brian Bedford, Michael Goodliffe. Regin is heiress mixed up in espionage and murder; OK Edgar Wallace suspenser.

Nun and the Sergeant, The (1962) 73m. ** D: Franklin Adreon. Robert Webber, Anna Sten, Leo Gordon, Hari Rhodes, Robert Easton, Dale Ishimoto, Linda Wong. Set in Korea during the war; title tells rest.

Nun's Story, The (1959) C-149m. ***½ D: Fred Zinnemann. Audrey Hepburn, Peter Finch, Edith Evans, Peggy Ashcroft, Dean Jagger, Mildred Dunnock. Tasteful filming of Kathryn Hulme book, with Hepburn the nun who serves in Belgian Congo and later leaves convent. Colleen Dewhurst, as a homicidal patient, is electrifying.

Nunzio (1978) C-87m. **½ D: Paul Williams. David Proval, James Andronica, Tovah Feldshuh, Morgana King, Vincent Russo, Theresa Saldana, Monica Lewis. Retarded Brooklyn grocery delivery boy Proval imagines he's Superman, falls in love with bakery assistant Feldshuh. Mild story enhanced by Proval's fine performance; script by Andronica, who plays his tough but loving brother.

Nurse Edith Cavell (1939) 95m. *** D: Herbert Wilcox. Anna Neagle, Edna May Oliver, George Sanders, ZaSu Pitts, May Robson, H. B. Warner, Robert Coote. Neagle is fine as dedicated WW1 nurse who worked on battlefield to aid wounded soldiers. Sturdy production.

Nutty, Naughty Chateau (1964-French) C-100m. **½ D: Roger Vadim. Monica Vitti, Curt Jurgens, Jean-Claude Brialy, Sylvie, Jean-Louis Trintignant, Francoise Hardy. Bizarre minor comedy involving the strange inhabitants of a castle romping about in 1750s styles; most diverting cast. Based on a Francoise Sagan play.

Nutty Professor, The (1963) C-107m. *** D: Jerry Lewis. Jerry Lewis, Stella Stevens, Del Moore, Kathleen Freeman, Med Flory, Howard Morris. Lewis' wildest (and most narcicisstic) comedy casts him as chipmunk-faced college professor who does Jekyll-and-Hyde transformation into Mr. Cool. More interesting than funny. Lewis buffs regard this as his masterpiece.

Nyoka and the Lost Secrets of Hippocrates (1942) 100m. **½ D: William Witney. Kay Aldridge, Clayton Moore, William Benedict, Lorna Gray, Charles Middleton. Enjoyable, campy cliff-hanger set in Africa with Kay Aldridge (Nyoka) pitted against Lorna Gray (Vultura) in search for mystical tablets. Reedited movie serial: PERILS OF NYOKA. Reissued under title: NYOKA AND THE TIGERMEN.

Nyoka and the Tigermen SEE: Nyoka and the Lost Secrets of Hippocrates

O. Henry's Full House (1952) 117m. **½ D: Henry Hathaway, Howard Hawks, Henry King, Henry Koster, Jean Negulesco. Fred Allen, Anne Baxter, Charles Laughton, Marilyn Monroe, Gregory Ratoff, Jeanne Crain, Oscar Levant, Jean Peters, Richard Widmark, Farley Granger. Five varying stories by O'Henry; cast better than script. "The Clarion Call," "Last Leaf," "Ransom of Red Chief," "Gift of the Magi," and "Cop and the Anthem."

O Lucky Man (1973-British) C-148m. **** D: Lindsay Anderson. Malcolm McDowell, Rachel Roberts, Ralph Richardson, Alan Price, Lindsay Anderson. Mammoth allegory with surrealistic flavor about young coffee salesman who pushes his way to the top only to fall and rise again. Brilliant performances throughout, incredible score by Alan Price, make this a memorable screen experience.

O.S.S. (1946) 107m. *** D: Irving Pichel. Alan Ladd, Geraldine Fitzgerald, Patric Knowles, Richard Benedict, Richard Webb, Don Beddoe, Onslow Stevens. Brisk WW2 espionage film with Ladd and company on important mission in France unaware that D-Day is rapidly approaching.

O. S. S. 117—Mission for a Killer (1966-French) C-84m. **½ D: Andre

Hunebelle. Frederick Stafford, Mylene Demongeot, Raymond Pellegrin. At times interesting malarkey about super spy trying to combat a world-hungry political organization.

Oasis (1955-French) C-84m. ** D: Yves Allegret. Michele Morgan, Pierre Brasseur, Cornell Borchers, Carl Raddatz. Morgan's radiance brightens this oft-told story of gold-smuggling in Africa.

Objective, Burma! (1945) 142m. ***½ D: Raoul Walsh. Errol Flynn, William Prince, James Brown, George Tobias, Henry Hull, Warner Anderson. Zestful WW2 action film with Flynn and company as paratroopers invading Burma to wipe out important Japanese post; top excitement.

Obliging Young Lady (1941) 80m. **½ D: Richard Wallace. Eve Arden, Edmond O'Brien, Ruth Warrick, Joan Carroll, Franklin Pangborn, George Cleveland. Agreeable comedy about youngster, center of custody fight, finding herself the focal point at a country resort.

Oblong Box, The (1969-British) C-91m. ** D: Gordon Hessler. Vincent Price, Christopher Lee, Alastair Williamson, Hillary Dwyer, Peter Arne, Maxwell Shaw, Sally Geeson. Boring treatment of halfway interesting situation: Price plays British aristocrat tormented by disfigured brother who's kept in tower room, periodically, he escapes and goes on the town. Hammy performances, long drawn-out narrative, lackluster direction (some of it by Michael Reeves).

Obsessed, The (1951-British) 77m. ** D: Maurice Elvey. David Farrar, Geraldine Fitzgerald, Roland Culver, Jean Cadell. Lackluster story of Farrar suspected of homicide.

Obsession (1976) C-98m. **½ D: Brian DePalma. Cliff Robertson, Genevieve Bujold, John Lithgow, Sylvia Kuumba Williams, Wanda Blackman. Viewers who don't remember Hitchcock's VERTIGO might enjoy this rehash by DePalma and writer Paul Schrader. Robertson loses his wife and child to kidnappers, then miraculously finds wife "reborn" in another woman. Holds up until denouement.

Obsession SEE: Hidden Room, The

Ocean's Eleven (1960) C-127m. **½ D: Lewis Milestone. Frank Sinatra, Dean Martin, Sammy Davis, Jr., Peter Lawford, Angie Dickinson, Richard Conte, Cesar Romero, Pa-

trice Wymore, Joey Bishop, Akim Tamiroff. Fanciful crime comedy about eleven-man team headed by Danny Ocean (Sinatra) attempting a "caper" in Las Vegas. Everyone's in it, but no one does much, including some surprise guests. There is a clever twist ending, though.

October Man, The (1947-British) 89m. *** D: Roy Baker. John Mills, Kay Walsh, Joan Greenwood, Felix Aylmer, John Boxer. Intelligently presented study of Mills trying to prove he's innocent of homicide, not always sure of it himself.

October Moth (1959-British) 54m. *½ D: John Kruse. Lee Patterson, Lana Morris, Peter Dyneley, Robert Crawdon. Turgid melodrama set on lonely farm, with Morris trying to cope with dim-witted brother (Patterson) who has injured a passerby.

Odd Couple, The (1968) C-105m. *** D: Gene Saks. Jack Lemmon, Walter Matthau, John Fiedler, Herb Edelman, Monica Evans, Carole Shelley. Film version of Neil Simon stage hit about two divorced men living together, sloppy Oscar (Matthau) and fussy Felix (Lemmon). Lemmon's realistic performance makes character melancholy instead of funny; other surefire comic sequences remain intact. Later developed into TV series.

Odd Man Out (1947-British) 113m. **** D: Carol Reed. James Mason, Kathleen Ryan, Robert Newton, Dan O'Herlihy, Robert Beatty, Fay Compson, Cyril Cusack. Incredibly suspenseful tale of Irish rebel leader hunted by police after daring robbery. Watch this one! Remade as THE LOST MAN.

Odds Against Tomorrow (1959) 95m. *** D: Robert Wise. Harry Belafonte, Robert Ryan, Shelley Winters, Ed Begley, Gloria Grahame. Brutal robbery story with entire cast pulling out all stops; taut, exciting drama.

Ode to Billy Joe (1976) C-108m. ** D: Max Baer. Robby Benson, Glynis O'Connor, Joan Hotchkiss, Sandy McPeak, James Best, Terence Goodman. Bobbie Gentry's 1967 song hit provides basis for standard rural romance that grows progressively ridiculous. Benson and O'Connor, reunited after JEREMY, still have appeal.

Odessa File, The (1974-British) C-128m. **½ D: Ronald Neame. Jon Voight, Maximilian Schell, Maria Schell, Mary Tamm, Derek Jacobi,

Klaus Lowitsch. Voight carries this plodding adaptation of the Frederick Forsyth best-seller, set in 1963, about a German journalist who tracks down former Nazis. OK time killer, nothing more.

Odette (1951-British) 100m. ******* D: Herbert Wilcox. Anna Neagle, Trevor Howard, Marius Goring, Peter Ustinov, Bernard Lee. Neagle is excellent in true story of Odette Churchill, undercover British agent imprisoned by Nazis during WW2.

Odongo (1956-British) C-85m. BOMB D: John Gilling. Rhonda Fleming, Macdonald Carey, Juma, Eleanor Summerfield, Francis De Wolff. Juvenile jungle flick about search for missing native boy.

Oedipus Rex (1957-Canadian) C-87m. ****½** D: Tyrone Guthrie. Douglas Rain, Douglas Campbell, Eric House, Eleanor Stuart. Restrained, professional rendering of Sophocles' Greek tragedy.

Oedipus the King (1967-British) C-97m. ****½** D: Philip Saville. Christopher Plummer, Orson Welles, Lilli Palmer, Richard Johnson, Cyril Cusack, Roger Livesey, Donald Sutherland. Film version of Sophocles play is OK for students who have a test on it the next day, but others won't appreciate this version. Pretty static.

Of Flesh and Blood (1962-French) C-92m. ****½** D: Christian Marquand. Robert Hossein, Renato Salvatori, Anouk Aimee, André Bervil, Jean Lefebvre. Murky account of passerby Salvatori having an affair with Aimee, involved with card-cheatturned-murderer Hossein.

Of Human Bondage (1934) 83m. ******* D: John Cromwell. Leslie Howard, Bette Davis, Frances Dee, Kay Johnson, Reginald Denny, Alan Hale, Reginald Owen. Smoothly filmed, well-acted version of W. Somerset Maugham's story of doctor Howard's strange infatuation with a vulgar waitress (Davis). Many find Davis' performance overdone, but by any standards it's powerfully impressive, and put her on the map in Hollywood. Howard, lovely Johnson, others are superb.

Of Human Bondage (1964-British) 98m. ****½** D: Ken Hughes. Kim Novak, Laurence Harvey, Siobhan McKenna, Robert Morley, Roger Livesey, Nanette Newman. Third and least successful filming of Maugham novel of doctor's passion for lowbrow waitress, marred by miscasting and general superficiality.

Of Human Hearts (1938) 100m. ****½** D: Clarence Brown. Walter Huston, James Stewart, Gene Reynolds, Beulah Bondi, Guy Kibbee, Charles Coburn, John Carradine, Ann Rutherford. Odd blend of potent 19th-century Americana and mile-high corn, in tale of dedicated preacher Huston who never established rapport with his son. When Abraham Lincoln (Carradine) lectures Stewart about neglecting his mother, it gets to be a bit much.

Of Life and Love (1957-Italian) 103m. ****½** D: Aldo Fabrizi, Luchino Visconti, Mario Soldati, Giorgio Pastina. Anna Magnani, Walter Chiari, Natale Cirino, Turi Pandolfini, Myriam Bru, Lucia Bose. Four satisfactory episodes, three of which are based on Pirandello tales; fourth is actual event in Magnani's life (THE LAPDOG).

Of Love and Desire (1963) C-97m. ***½** D: Richard Rush. Merle Oberon, Steve Cochran, Curt Jurgens, John Agar, Steve Brodie. Beautiful settings (including Oberon's lavish Mexican home) offset overwrought sexual drama of neurotic woman who plays with the affection of several men—including her own stepbrother.

Of Mice and Men (1939) 107m. ******** D: Lewis Milestone. Lon Chaney, Jr., Burgess Meredith, Betty Field, Charles Bickford, Bob Steele, Noah Beery, Jr. Chaney gives best performance of his career as feeble-brained Lenny who, with migrant-worker Meredith, tries to live peacefully on ranch. Steinbeck's morality tale remains intact in sensitive screen version. Music by Aaron Copland.

Off Limits (1953) 89m. ******* D: George Marshall. Bob Hope, Mickey Rooney, Marilyn Maxwell, Marvin Miller. Peppy shenanigans with Hope and Rooney in the Army, Maxwell a nightclub singer.

Offence, The (1973-British) C-112m. ******* D: Sidney Lumet. Sean Connery, Trevor Howard, Vivien Merchant, Ian Bannen, Derek Newark. Good drama about how London detective Connery's frustrations cause him to beat a suspect to death; a fine performance by Connery.

Oh Dad, Poor Dad, Mama's Hung You in the Closet and I'm Feeling So Sad (1967) C-86m. ****½** D: Richard Quine. Rosalind Russell, Robert Morse, Barbara Harris, Hugh Griffith, Jonathan Winters, Lionel Jeffries, Cyril Delavanti. Impressive cast tries to sustain black comedy about overpossessive widow (Russell) and weirdo son (Morse) taking vacation on tropical island accompanied by coffin of late husband.

Oh, God! (1977) C-104m. *** D: Carl Reiner. George Burns, John Denver, Teri Garr, Paul Sorvino, George Furth, Ralph Bellamy, Barnard Hughes. God appears in person of Burns to summon Denver as his messenger, to tell the world that he's alive and well. Film eschews cheap jokes to build a credible story with warm performances and upbeat message.

Oh, Men! Oh, Women! (1957) C-90m. **½ D: Nunnally Johnson. Ginger Rogers, David Niven, Dan Dailey, Barbara Rush, Tony Randall. Often bouncy sex farce revolving around psychiatrist and his assorted patients. Randall's film debut.

Oh, Susanna (1951) C-90m. ** D: Joseph Kane. Rod Cameron, Forrest Tucker, Adrian Booth, Chill Wills. Too much feuding between cavalry officers and too little real action mar this Western.

Oh! Those Most Secret Agents (1966-Italian) C-83m. *½ D: Lucio Fulci. Franco Franchi, Ciccio Ingrassia, Ingrid Schoeller, Arnoldo Tieri. Pathetic superspy spoof. Retitled: WORST SECRET AGENTS.

Oh! What a Lovely War (1969-British) C-139m. **½ D: Richard Attenborough. Laurence Olivier, John Gielgud, Ralph Richardson, Michael Redgrave, John Mills, Vanessa Redgrave, Dirk Bogarde, Susannah York, Maggie Smith, Jack Hawkins, Kenneth More, Corin Redgrave. Actor Attenborough's directing debut; impressive but cumbersome series of vignettes on WW1, ranging from colorful musical numbers to poignant human sidelights. Beautifully designed, wildly cinematic, but too drawn-out to make maximum antiwar impact.

Oh, You Beautiful Doll (1949) C-93m. **½ D: John M. Stahl. June Haver, Mark Stevens, S. Z. Sakall, Charlotte Greenwood, Gale Robbins, Jay C. Flippen. Chipper period musical, with wispy career biog of serious composer whose works become popular hits.

O'Hara: U.S. Treasury (1971) C-100m. TVM D: Jack Webb. David Janssen, William Conrad, Lana Wood, Jerome Thor, Gary Crosby, Charles McGraw. Standard, unimaginative Jack Webb production portraying efficiency of government agents cracking down on narcotics smuggling ring. Adequate performances, fair action every second. Average; pilot for TV series.

OHMS (1980) C-100m. TVM D: Dick Lowry. Ralph Waite, David Birney, Talia Balsam, Dixie Carter, Cameron Mitchell, Leslie Nielsen, Paul Hecht. Farmer Waite and activist Birney battle a power company planning to run a million volt line across local farmlands. Sincere ecology awareness drama becomes too pat and cops out at the end. Average.

Oil for the Lamps of China (1935) 110m. *** D: Mervyn LeRoy. Pat O'Brien, Josephine Hutchinson, Jean Muir, Lyle Talbot, Arthur Byron, John Eldredge, Henry O'Neill, Donald Crisp. Tear-jerker drama of American oil-company representative in China, dedicating his life to his work, finding sympathetic wife, beset by myriad problems. Well-produced drama. Remade as LAW OF THE TROPICS.

Okinawa (1952) 67m. ** D: George Brooks. Pat O'Brien, Cameron Mitchell, James Dobson, Richard Denning, Richard Benedict, Alvy Moore. Adequate programmer about the men on a warship during the Pacific campaign of WW2.

Oklahoma! (1955) C-145m. *** D: Fred Zinnemann. Gordon MacRae, Shirley Jones, Charlotte Greenwood, Rod Steiger, Gloria Grahame, Eddie Albert, James Whitmore, Gene Nelson. Rodgers and Hammerstein's trend-setting 1943 musical comes to screen in tremendous, generally entertaining form. Too long, but songs like "People Will Say We're in Love" and the many other hits, plus Greenwood's comedy and Grahame's offbeat casting, keep film alive.

Oklahoma Annie (1952) C-90m. *½ D: R. G. Springsteen. Judy Canova, John Russell, Grant Withers, Allen Jenkins, Almira Sessions, Minerva Urecal. Rambunctious Canova is involved with mopping up corruption in her Western town.

Oklahoma Crude (1973) C-108m. *** D: Stanley Kramer. George C. Scott, Faye Dunaway, John Mills, Jack Palance, Harvey Jason, Woodrow Parfrey. Old-fashioned, nonthink entertainment. Strong-willed, man-hating Dunaway determined to defend lone oil well from pressures of Palance, who represents big oil trust, hires drifter Scott to help her. Scott gives brilliant comic performance in mildly enjoyable film.

Oklahoma Kid, The (1939) 85m. *** D: Lloyd Bacon. James Cagney, Humphrey Bogart, Rosemary Lane, Donald Crisp, Ward Bond. Cagney's the hero, Bogey's the villain in this sturdy Western. Classic scene has Cagney singing "I Don't Want to Play in Your Yard."

Oklahoma Territory (1960) 67m. ** D: Edward L. Cahn. Bill Williams, Gloria Talbott, Ted de Corsia, Grant Richards, Walter Sande. Western concentrating on Williams' effort to find actual killer of local Indian agent.

Oklahoma Woman, The (1956) 72m. BOMB D: Roger Corman. Richard Denning, Peggie Castle, Cathy Downs, Mike Connors, Tudor Owen. Denning is ex-con trying to go right back on the farm, but fate intervenes. A nothing film.

Oklahoman, The (1957) C-80m. ** D: Francis D. Lyon. Joel McCrea, Barbara Hale, Brad Dexter, Gloria Talbott, Verna Felton, Douglas Dick. Restrained Western with McCrea helping an outcast Indian protect his rights.

Old Acquaintance (1943) 100m. *** D: Vincent Sherman. Bette Davis, Miriam Hopkins, Gig Young, John Loder, Dolores Moran, Phillip Reed, Roscoe Karns. Well-matched stars of THE OLD MAID who are reunited as childhood friends who evolve personal and professional rivalry that lasts twenty years. Davis is noble and Hopkins is bitchy in this entertaining film.

Old Boyfriends (1979) C-103m. BOMB D: Joan Tewkesbury. Talia Shire, Richard Jordan, Keith Carradine, John Belushi, John Houseman, Buck Henry. Distressing botch of an intriguing idea about woman who seeks out her former lovers in an attempt to analyze her past. Shire is too lightweight to carry the acting load, and Belushi is totally wasted.

Old Curiosity Shop, The SEE: Mr. Quilp

Old Dark House, The (1932) 71m. ***½ D: James Whale. Boris Karloff, Melvyn Douglas, Charles Laughton, Gloria Stuart, Lilian Bond, Ernest Thesiger, Raymond Massey. Outstanding melodrama (with tongue-in-cheek) gathers stranded travelers in mysterious household, where brutish butler Karloff is just one of many strange characters. A real gem.

Old Dark House, The (1963-British) C-86m. **½ D: William Castle. Tom Poston, Robert Morley, Peter Bull, Joyce Grenfell, Janette Scott. Uneven blend of comedy and chiller, with Poston at loose ends in eerie mansion. Released theatrically in b&w.

Old Dracula (1974-British) C-89m. *½ D: Clive Donner. David Niven, Teresa Graves, Peter Bayliss, Jennie Linden, Linda Hayden, Bernard Bresslaw. Niven somehow maintains his dignity in this one-joke Dracula spoof that has him extracting samples from the necks of various Playboy Bunnies in search of correct blood type to resurrect his departed wife.

Old-Fashioned Way, The (1934) 66m. ***½ D: William Beaudine. W. C. Fields, Judith Allen, Joe Morrison, Baby LeRoy, Jack Mulhall, Oscar Apfel. Fields is in fine form managing troupe of old-time melodrama THE DRUNKARD, encountering various troubles as they travel from town to town. Baby LeRoy has memorable scene throwing W.C.'s watch into a jar of molasses.

Old Hutch (1936) 80m. ** D: J. Walter Ruben. Wallace Beery, Eric Linden, Cecilia Parker, Elizabeth Patterson, Robert McWade. Cute story of shiftless bum discovering $1000, trying to use it without arousing suspicion.

Old Maid, The (1939) 95m. ***½ D: Edmund Goulding. Bette Davis, Miriam Hopkins, George Brent, Jane Bryan, Donald Crisp, Louise Fazenda, Jerome Cowan. Soap opera par excellence based on Zoë Akins play about unwed mother (Davis), whose unsuspecting daughter Bryan grows up ignoring her, loving Bette's scheming cousin Hopkins. The two female stars create fireworks as they enact this chronicle of love and hate in the 1860s.

Old Man and the Sea, The (1958) C-86m. *** D: John Sturges. Spencer Tracy, Felipe Pazos, Harry Bellaver. Well-intentioned but uneven parable of aging fisherman's daily battle with the elements. Tracy is the whole film, making the most of Hemingway's un-filmic story.

Old Man Rhythm (1935) 75m. **½

D: Edward Ludwig. Charles "Buddy" Rogers, George Barbier, Barbara Kent, Grace Bradley, Betty Grable, Eric Blore. Business tycoon Barbier goes back to college to keep an eye on his playboy son (Rogers) in this light, fluffy musical; songwriter Johnny Mercer appears as one of the students.

Old Man Who Cried Wolf, The (1970) C-73m. TVM D: Walter Grauman. Edward G. Robinson, Martin Balsam, Diane Baker, Percy Rodrigues, Ruth Roman, Sam Jaffe. Emile Pulska (Robinson) can't even convince own family that good friend Stillman (Jaffe) died of wounds from assault, not from natural causes. Unconvincing drama, despite good performances. Average.

Old Yeller (1957) C-83m. *** D: Robert Stevenson. Dorothy McGuire, Fess Parker, Tommy Kirk, Kevin Corcoran, Jeff York, Beverly Washburn, Chuck Connors. Disney's first film about a boy and his dog, from Fred Gipson's popular novel, is still one of the best. Atmospheric recreation of farm life in 1859 Texas, where Kirk becomes attached to a yellow hunting dog.

Oldest Profession, The (1967-French-German-Italian) C-97m. *½ D: Franco Indovina, Mauro Bolognini, Philippe De Broca, Michel Pfleghar, Claude Autant-Lara, Jean-Luc Godard. Elsa Martinelli, Jeanne Moreau, Raquel Welch, Anna Karina, France Anglade. Totally unfunny six-part story of prostitution through the ages.

Oliver! (1968-British) C-153m. **** D: Carol Reed. Ron Moody, Oliver Reed, Shani Wallis, Mark Lester, Jack Wild, Harry Secombe, Hugh Griffith, Sheila White. Superb Oscar-winning musical by Lionel Bart from Dickens' OLIVER TWIST about young boy (Lester) swept into gang of youthful thieves led by scurrilous Fagin (Moody). Fine settings, atmosphere complement rousing score including "Consider Yourself," "As Long as He Needs Me"; spirited choreography by Onna White. Many Oscars include Best Picture and Best Director.

Oliver Twist (1948-British) 105m. **** D: David Lean. Alec Guinness, Robert Newton, John Howard Davies, Kay Walsh, Francis L. Sullivan, Anthony Newley, Henry Stephenson. Superlative realization of Dickens tale of ill-treated London waif involved with arch-fiend Fagin (Guinness) and his youthful gang, headed by the Artful Dodger (Newley). Later musicalized as OLIVER.

Oliver's Story (1978) C-92m. *½ D: John Korty. Ryan O'Neal, Candice Bergen, Nicola Pagett, Edward Binns, Ray Milland. Sequel to LOVE STORY pits money against money this time around, as O'Neal romances heiress to Bonwit Teller fortune. Tough to see how anyone could care by now, and judging from the film's box office performance, not many did.

Olly, Olly, Oxen Free (1978) C-83m. ** D: Richard A. Colla. Katharine Hepburn, Kevin McKenzie, Dennis Dimster, Peter Kilman. Hepburn plays a colorful junk dealer who befriends two young boys and helps them realize their dream of hot-air ballooning. Kate's always worth watching, but except for airborne scenes, this film is nothing special. Also known as THE GREAT BALLOON ADVENTURE.

Omar Khayyam (1957) C-101m. **½ D: William Dieterle. Cornel Wilde, Debra Paget, John Derek, Raymond Massey, Michael Rennie, Yma Sumac, Sebastian Cabot. Childish but spirited costumer set in medieval Persia; cast defeated by juvenile script.

Omega Man, The (1971) C-98m. **½ D: Boris Sagal. Charlton Heston, Rosalind Cash, Anthony Zerbe, Paul Koslo, Lincoln Kilpatrick, Eric Laneuville. Visually striking but unsatisfying second filming of Richard Matheson's sci-fi thriller "I am Legend" involving frenzy of a man immune to germs that are decimating earth's population after the ultimate war. Heston is superior to Vincent Price (who had role in THE LAST MAN ON EARTH).

Omen, The (1976) C-111m. **½ D: Richard Donner. Gregory Peck, Lee Remick, Billie Whitelaw, David Warner, Harvey Stephens, Patrick Troughton. Effective but sensationalistic horror piece on the coming of the "antiChrist," personified in young son of Peck and Remick, Americans living in England. Plenty of gore and a now-famous decapitation, for those who like that kind of thing.

On a Clear Day You Can See Forever (1970) C-129m. **½ D: Vincente Minnelli. Barbra Streisand, Yves Montand, Bob Newhart, Larry

Blyden, Simon Oakland, Jack Nicholson. Colorful entertainment from Alan Jay Lerner-Burton Lane show about girl (Streisand) whose psychiatrist (Montand) discovers that she lived a former life, in 19th-century England. Sumptuous flashback scenes outclass fragmented modernday plot, much of it apparently left on cutting-room floor. Glossy but never involving.

On an Island With You (1948) C-107m. **½ D: Richard Thorpe. Esther Williams, Peter Lawford, Ricardo Montalban, Jimmy Durante, Cyd Charisse, Xavier Cugat, Leon Ames. Splashy, colorful Williams vehicle of movie star who finds offscreen romance on location in Hawaii.

On Any Sunday (1971) C-91m. *** D: Bruce Brown. Steve McQueen, Mert Lawwill, Malcolm Smith. Fine documentary on many aspects of motorcycling by Bruce Brown of ENDLESS SUMMER fame.

On Approval (1944-British) 80m. *** D: Clive Brook. Beatrice Lillie, Clive Brook, Googie Withers, Roland Culver. Minor British gem showcasting the hilarious Bea Lillie as woman who exchanges boyfriends with her companion. Drawing-room comedy par excellence.

On Borrowed Time (1939) 99m. *** D: Harold S. Bucquet. Lionel Barrymore, Cedric Hardwicke, Beulah Bondi, Una Merkel, Ian Wolfe, Philip Terry, Eily Malyon. Engrossing fable of Death, Mr. Brink (Hardwicke), coming for grandpa Barrymore, finding himself trapped in tree by Lionel and grandson Bobs Watson.

On Dangerous Ground (1951) 82m. *** D: Nicholas Ray. Robert Ryan, Ida Lupino, Ward Bond, Ed Begley, Cleo Moore, Charles Kemper. Effective mood-piece with hardened city cop Ryan softened by blind-girl Lupino, whose brother is involved in rural manhunt.

On Dress Parade (1939) 62m. D: William Clemens. Billy Halop, Bobby Jordan, Huntz Hall, Gabriel Dell, Leo Gorcey, Selmer Jackson, John Litel, Bernard Punsley. SEE: Bowery Boys series.

On Her Majesty's Secret Service (1969-British) C-140m. ***½ D: Peter Hunt. George Lazenby, Diana Rigg, Gabrielle Ferzetti, Telly Savalas, Bernard Lee, Lois Maxwell. Usual globe-hopping Bond vs. Blofeld plot with novel twist: agent Bond has legitimate affair with Spanish contessa (Rigg)! Lazenby, first non-Connery Bond, ok, but incredible action sequences take first chair.

On Moonlight Bay (1951) C-95m. **½ D: Roy Del Ruth. Doris Day, Gordon MacRae, Billy Gray, Mary Wickes, Leon Ames, Rosemary DeCamp. Turn-of-the-century, folksy musical based on Booth Tarkington story with tomboy (Day) and next door neighbor (MacRae) the wholesome young lovers. Followed by sequel BY THE LIGHT OF THE SILVERY MOON.

On My Way to the Crusades, I Met a Girl Who . . . (1969-Italian) C-93m. BOMB D: Pasquale Festa Campanile. Tony Curtis, Monica Vitti, Hugh Griffith, John Richardson, Ivo Garrani, Nino Castelnuovo. Weak comedy, if that's the word, about Vitti's chastity belt was held back from release for a long time, and no wonder.

On Our Merry Way (1948) 107m. **½ D: King Vidor, Leslie Fenton. Burgess Meredith, Paulette Goddard, Fred MacMurray, Hugh Herbert, James Stewart, Henry Fonda, Dorothy Lamour, Victor Moore. Episodic film has good Stewart-Fonda segment, but flock of stars can't overcome mediocre stretches as reporter Meredith asks various people about their relationship to children. Fonda-Stewart story written by John O'Hara, directed by George Stevens.

On Stage Everybody (1945) 65m. ** D: Jean Yarbrough. Jack Oakie, Peggy Ryan, Otto Kruger, Julie London, Wallace Ford, King Sisters. Run-of-the-mill Universal musical, with frantic Oakie helping to put on the big radio variety program.

On the Avenue (1937) 89m. *** D: Roy Del Ruth. Dick Powell, Madeleine Carroll, Alice Faye, Ritz Brothers, Alan Mowbray, Billy Gilbert, Cora Witherspoon, Joan Davis, Sig Ruman. Tasteful, intelligent musical of socialite Carroll getting involved with stage star Powell. One good Irving Berlin song after another: "I've Got My Love To Keep Me Warm," "This Year's Kisses," "Let's Go Slumming," "The Girl on the Police Gazette."

On the Beach (1959) 133m. **** D: Stanley Kramer. Gregory Peck, Ava Gardner, Fred Astaire, Anthony Perkins, Donna Anderson, John Tate, Guy Doleman. Thoughtful

[561]

version of Nevil Shute's novel about Australians awaiting effects of explosion that has destroyed the rest of the world. Good performances by all, including Astaire in a straight role.

On the Beat (1962-British) 105m. **½ D: Robert Asher. Norman Wisdom, Jennifer Jayne, Raymond Huntley, David Lodge. Overly cute comedy with Wisdom a dumb-bunny helping Scotland Yard round up a criminal gang; too many pat routines and stereotyped performances.

On The Double (1961) C-92m. *** D: Melville Shavelson. Danny Kaye, Dana Wynter, Wilfrid Hyde-White, Margaret Rutherford, Diana Dors. Danny's resemblance to English general makes him valuable as a WW2 spy. At one point he does a Dietrich imitation! Similar to early Kaye vehicle ON THE RIVIERA, but just as enjoyable.

On the Isle of Samoa (1950) 65m. *½ D: William Berke. Jon Hall, Susan Cabot, Raymond Greenleaf, Henry Marco. Sloppy little story of Hall finding love with native girl, inspiring him to clear up his shady past.

On the Loose (1951) 78m. *½ D: Charles Lederer. Joan Evans, Melvyn Douglas, Lynn Bari, Robert Arthur, Hugh O'Brian. Lukewarm drama of overindulgent parents and their wayward daughter.

On the Riviera (1951) C-90m. *** D: Walter Lang. Danny Kaye, Gene Tierney, Corinne Calvet, Marcel Dalio, Jean Murat. Bouncy musicomedy with Danny in dual role as entertainer and French military hero. "Ballin' the Jack," other songs in lively film. Gwen Verdon is one of chorus girls. Remake of Maurice Chevalier's FOLIES BERGERE.

On the Threshold of Space (1956) C-98m. **½ D: Robert D. Webb. Guy Madison, Virginia Leith, John Hodiak, Dean Jagger, Warren Stevens. Capable cast merely bridges the span between sequences of astronaut endurance tests and other space-flight maneuvers.

On the Town (1949) C-98m. **** D: Gene Kelly, Stanley Donen. Gene Kelly, Frank Sinatra, Vera-Ellen, Betty Garrett, Ann Miller, Jules Munshin, Alice Pearce. Sparkling Comden-Green musical of three sailors and their gals in N.Y.C. for a day. "New York, New York" heads good score. Fluid choreography, with dandy comedy relief by Garrett and Pearce.

On the Waterfront (1954) 108m. **** D: Elia Kazan. Marlon Brando, Eva Marie Saint, Karl Malden, Lee J. Cobb, Rod Steiger, Pat Henning, Leif Erickson. Budd Schulberg's unflinching account of N.Y. harbor unions, with Brando unforgettable as misfit, Steiger his crafty brother, Cobb his waterfront boss, and Saint the girl he loves. Winner of 8 Oscars including Best Picture, Best Actor (Brando), Supporting Actress (Saint), Director, Original Screenplay.

On the Yard (1979) C-102m. ** D: Raphael D. Silver. John Heard, Thomas D. Waites, Mike Kellin, Richard Bright, Joe Grifasi, Lane Smith. Convict Heard makes a fatal mistake by mixing it up with jailhouse kingpin Waites. So-so prison picture seems hardly worth the effort, though Kellin is memorable as an aging loser trying to get paroled.

On Trial (1953-French) 70m. ** D: Julien Duvivier. Madeleine Robinson, Daniel Gelin, Eleonora Rossi-Drago, Charles Vanel, Anton Walbrook, Jacques Chabassol. Chabassol, son of D.A. Vanel, investigates conviction of Gelin, discovering disparity between justice and truth; well-intentioned film gone astray.

On Your Toes (1939) 94m. **½ D: Ray Enright. Vera Zorina, Eddie Albert, Frank McHugh, Alan Hale, James Gleason. Long-winded account of backstage jealousy and attempted murder, highlighted by Zorina's footwork in ballet (including "Slaughter on Tenth Avenue").

Once a Thief (1950) 88m. ** D: W. Lee Wilder. June Havoc, Cesar Romero, Marie McDonald, Lon Chaney, Iris Adrian. Solid little film of shoplifter Havoc and her tawdry romance with Romero.

Once a Thief (1965) 107m. ** D: Ralph Nelson. Ann-Margret, Alain Delon, Van Heflin, Jack Palance. When young ex-con tries to go straight, he finds himself the pawn in another crime. Not at all interesting.

Once Before I Die (1965) C-97m. **½ D: John Derek. Ursula Andress, John Derek, Rod Lauren, Richard Jaeckel, Ron Ely. Brutal, offbeat story of band of American soldiers in Philippines during WW2, trying to survive Japanese attack.

Andress is only woman in group, and you can guess the rest.

Once In a Lifetime (1932) 90m. *** D: Russell Mack. Jack Oakie, Sidney Fox, Aline MacMahon, Russell Hopton, ZaSu Pitts, Gregory Ratoff. Stagebound but still hilarious adaptation of Kaufman-Hart play about a trio of connivers who take advantage of Hollywood's state of panic when talkies arrive.

Once in Paris . . . (1978) C-100m. *** D: Frank D. Gilroy. Wayne Rogers, Gayle Hunnicutt, Jack Lenoir, Clement Harari, Tanya Lopert, Doris Roberts. Gilroy produced, directed, and wrote this charming tale of Hollywood screenwriter who goes to Paris to work on script, falls in love instead. Lovely location filming.

Once Is Not Enough SEE: Jacqueline Susann's Once Is Not Enough

Once More My Darling (1949) 94m. **½ D: Robert Montgomery. Robert Montgomery, Ann Blyth, Jane Cowl, Taylor Holmes, Charles McGraw. Satisfying comedy of young girl infatuated with middle-aged movie star.

Once More, With Feeling (1960-British) C-92m. **½ D: Stanley Donen, Yul Brynner, Kay Kendall, Maxwell Shaw, Mervyn Johns. Despite sparkling Kendall (her last film) as musical conductor Brynner's dissatisfied wife, this marital sex comedy fizzles.

Once Upon a Dead Man (1971) C-100m. TVM D: Leonard Stern. Rock Hudson, Susan St. James, Jack Albertson, Rene Auberjonois, Kurt Kasznar, Jonathan Harris. Stolen sarcophagus precipitates San Francisco police commissioner's involvement in case. Standard, homespun police drama. Average; pilot for McMILLAN AND WIFE TV series.

Once Upon a Family (1980) C-100m. TVM D: Richard Michaels. Barry Bostwick, Maureen Anderman, Lee Chamberlin, Nancy Marchand, Lara Parker, John Pleshette, Marcia Strassman, Elizabeth Wilson. When mommy walks, daddy struggles to succeed as a single parent in this TV carbon of KRAMER VS. KRAMER, plagued by pedestrian acting and writing. Average.

Once Upon a Honeymoon (1942) 117m. **½ D: Leo McCarey. Ginger Rogers, Cary Grant, Walter Slezak, Albert Dekker, Albert Basserman. Slightly dated adventure comedy of innocent Ginger marrying Nazi officer, with Cary rescuing her. Slezak is perfect as Rogers' Hitlerite spouse.

Once Upon a Horse (1958) 85m. **½ D: Hal Kanter. Dan Rowan, Dick Martin, Martha Hyer, Leif Erickson, John McGiver, David Burns, James Gleason. Oddball Western spoof runs hot and cold, with some nutty gags and enough spark to make it worth watching. Old-time Western stars Bob Steele, Kermit Maynard, Tom Keene, Bob Livingston appear briefly as themselves.

Once Upon a Time (1944) 89m. **½ D: Alexander Hall. Cary Grant, Janet Blair, James Gleason, Ted Donaldson, Art Baker. Amusing comedy-fantasy of entrepreneur Grant promoting a dancing caterpillar; trivial fun.

Once Upon a Time in the West (1969-Italian) C-165m. ***½ D: Sergio Leone. Henry Fonda, Claudia Cardinale, Jason Robards, Charles Bronson, Frank Wolff, Keenan Wynn, Lionel Stander, Jack Elam, Woody Strode. Director Leone's follow-up to his Clint Eastwood Westerns is already regarded as minor classic by film cultists; exciting tale is helped by successful offbeat casting of Fonda as meanest of all possible villains.

Once You Kiss a Stranger (1969) C-106m. BOMB D: Robert Sparr. Paul Burke, Carol Lynley, Martha Hyer, Peter Lind Hayes, Philip Carey, Stephen McNally, Whit Bissell. Thinly disguised remake of STRANGERS ON A TRAIN, with Lynley as nut who pulls golfer Burke into bizarre "reciprocal murder" scheme. Slick but empty-headed, laughable.

One and Only, The (1978) C-98m. **½ D: Carl Reiner. Henry Winkler, Kim Darby, Gene Saks, Herve Villechaize, William Daniels, Polly Holliday. Winkler is a brash college kid determined to make it in show biz, who winds up a flamboyant wrestler. Some truly funny moments build to gradual disenchantment with his basically obnoxious character.

One and Only Genuine Original Family Band, The (1968) C-117m. **½ D: Michael O'Herlihy. Walter Brennan, Buddy Ebsen, Lesley Ann Warren, John Davidson, Janet Blair, Kurt Russell. Musical family becomes involved in 1888 Presidential campaign; innocuous Disney entertainment with forgettable songs by the Sherman Brothers. Goldie Hawn has tiny part as giggling dancer.

One Big Affair (1952) 80m. ** D: Peter Godfrey. Evelyn Keyes, Dennis O'Keefe, Mary Anderson, Connie Gilchrist. On-location filming in Mexico highlights this lightweight romance yarn of Keyes and O'Keefe.

One Body Too Many (1944) 75m. ** D: Frank McDonald. Bela Lugosi, Jack Haley, Jean Parker, Blanche Yurka, Lyle Talbot, Douglas Fowley. Detective comedy-spoof with Lugosi tossed in for good measure; Haley is carefree salesman mistaken for private eye, forced to solve caper.

One Dangerous Night (1943) 77m. D: Michael Gordon. Warren William, Marguerite Chapman, Eric Blore, Mona Barrie, Tala Birell, Margaret Hayes, Ann Savage. SEE: Lone Wolf series.

One Day in the Life of Ivan Denisovich (1971-British-Norwegian) C-100m. **½ D: Casper Wrede. Tom Courtenay, Espen Skjonberg, James Maxwell, Alfred Burke, Eric Thompson. Another instance where a novel was just too difficult to film; Alexander Solzhenitsyn's story of a prisoner in Siberian labor camp only occasionally works on the screen. Good photography.

One Desire (1955) C-94m. **½ D: Jerry Hopper. Anne Baxter, Rock Hudson, Julie Adams, Natalie Wood, Betty Garde. Baxter's strong performance as woman in love with gambler Hudson elevates standard soaper.

One-Eyed Jacks (1961) C-141m. *** D: Marlon Brando. Marlon Brando, Karl Malden, Pina Pellicer, Katy Jurado, Ben Johnson, Slim Pickens. Fascinating but flawed psychological western with outlaw Brando seeking revenge on former friend Malden, now a sheriff. Visually striking, and a rich character study, but overlong.

One Eyed Soldiers (1966-U.S.-British-Yugoslavian) C-80m. *½ D: Jean Christophe. Dale Robertson, Luciana Paluzzi, Guy Deghy, Andrew Faulds, Mila Avramovic. Dying man leaves his daughter a clue to whereabouts of money in Swiss bank, leading to international scramble for the loot. You've seen it all before.

One Fatal Hour SEE: **Two Against the World**

One Flew Over the Cuckoo's Nest (1975) C-129m. **** D: Milos Forman. Jack Nicholson, Louise Fletcher, William Redfield, Michael Beryman, Brad Dourif, Peter Brocco, Will Sampson. Ken Kesey's story is a triumph of the human spirit; a feisty misfit (Nicholson) enters an insane asylum and inspires his fellow patients to assert themselves, to the chagrin of strong-willed head nurse (Fletcher). The first film since IT HAPPENED ONE NIGHT to win all five top Oscars: Best Picture, Best Actor, Best Actress, Best Director, Best Screenplay (Lawrence Hauben, Bo Goldman).

One Foot in Heaven (1941) 108m. ***½ D: Irving Rapper. Fredric March, Martha Scott, Beulah Bondi, Gene Lockhart, Elisabeth Fraser, Harry Davenport, Laura Hope Crews, Grant Mitchell. Superior acting in honest, appealing story of minister and wife facing various problems as church life and 20th-century America clash. Very entertaining, with memorable scene of minister March going to his first movie (a William S. Hart silent).

One Foot in Hell (1960) C-90m. **½ D: James B. Clark. Alan Ladd, Don Murray, Dan O'Herlihy, Dolores Michaels, Barry Coe, Larry Gates, Karl Swenson. Ambitious in intent but peculiar production of sheriff seeking retribution for death of his wife.

One for the Book SEE: **Voice of the Turtle**

One Girl's Confession (1953) 74m. BOMB D: Hugo Haas. Cleo Moore, Hugo Haas, Glenn Langan, Russ Conway. Moore is gal gone wrong, serving her time and starting new life. Another gem from Hugo Haas.

One Good Turn (1954-British) 78m. ** D: John Paddy Carstairs. Norman Wisdom, Joan Rice, Shirley Abicair, William Russell, Thora Hird. Minor musical vehicle for man-on-the-street comedian Wisdom, putting forth such homey tunes as "Take a Step In The Right Direction."

One Horse Town SEE: **Small Town Girl**

One Hour with You (1932) 80m. ***½ D: Ernst Lubitsch, George Cukor. Maurice Chevalier, Jeanette MacDonald, Genevieve Tobin, Roland Young, Charlie Ruggles. Chic romance of happily married couple upset by arrival of flirtatious Tobin. Remake of Lubitsch's 1924 THE MARRIAGE CIRCLE; started by Cukor, completed by Lubitsch with Cukor as his assistant. Songs include title tune, "What Would You Do?"

One Hundred Men and a Girl (1937) 84m. ***½ D: Henry Koster. Deanna Durbin, Leopold Stokowski, Adolphe Menjou, Alice Brady, Eugene Pallette, Mischa Auer, Frank Jenks, Billy Gilbert. Superior blend of music and comedy as Deanne pesters conductor Stokowski to give work to her unemployed father and musician friends. Brimming with charm—and beautiful music.

100 Rifles (1969) C-110m. ** D: Tom Gries. Jim Brown, Raquel Welch, Burt Reynolds, Fernando Lamas, Dan O'Herlihy. Overripe Western saga has deputy Brown going after Reynolds, fleeing with shipment of guns into Mexico, but meeting and falling for guerrilla leader Welch. Reynolds easily steals film.

One in a Million (1936) 95m. *** D: Sidney Lanfield. Sonja Henie, Adolphe Menjou, Don Ameche, Ned Sparks, Jean Hersholt, The Ritz Brothers, Arline Judge. Henie in film debut is surrounded by fine cast. Skating scenes are most enjoyable, lively music helping, too. The Ritz Brothers are in fine form, with amusing horror-film spoof.

One in a Million: The Ron LeFlore Story (1978) C-100m. TVM D: William A. Graham. LeVar Burton, Madge Sinclair, Paul Benjamin, James Luisi, Billy Martin, Zakes Mokae. Well-acted story of the Detroit Tigers' baseball great from his days as a streetcorner punk to his conviction for armed robbery and his one-in-a-million chance to make good on the outside. Inspiring and above average.

One Is a Lonely Number (1972) C-97m. *** D: Mel Stuart. Trish Van Devere, Monte Markham, Janet Leigh, Melvyn Douglas, Jane Elliott, Jonathan Lippe. Sympathetic performance by Van Devere helps this better-than-usual soaper about life of an attractive divorcee; good supporting work by Douglas and Leigh.

One Last Fling (1949) 74m. ** D: Peter Godfrey. Alexis Smith, Zachary Scott, Douglas Kennedy, Ann Doran, Veda Ann Borg, Helen Westcott. Limp tale of overly suspicious wife

checking up on her husband by going to work for him.

One Little Indian (1973) C-90m. **½ D: Bernard McEveety. James Garner, Vera Miles, Clay O'Brien, Pat Hingle, Andrew Prine, Jodie Foster. Garner is AWOL cavalry corporal escaping through desert with young Indian boy. Unusual Disney comedy-drama.

One Man Jury (1978) C-104m. *½ D: Charles Martin. Jack Palance, Christopher Mitchum, Pamela Shoop, Angel Tompkins, Joe Spinell, Cara Williams. DIRTY HARRY rip-off with Palance as vigilante cop who administers his own brand of violent justice on some particularly repulsive felons.

One Man's Way (1964) 105m. *** D: Denis Sanders. Don Murray, Diana Hyland, Veronica Cartwright, Ian Wolfe, Virginia Christine, Carol Ohmart, William Windom. Tasteful fictionalized biography of Norman Vincent Peale, his religious convictions and preaching; Murray is earnest in lead role.

One Million B.C. (1940) 80m. **½ D: Hal Roach, Hal Roach Jr. Victor Mature, Carole Landis, Lon Chaney, Jr., John Hubbard, Mamo Clark, Jean Porter. Bizarre caveman saga told in flashback is real curio, part of it directed by silent-film pioneer D. W. Griffith. Excellent special effects.

$1,000,000 Duck (1971) C-92m. **½ D: Vincent McEveety. Dean Jones, Sandy Duncan, Joe Flynn, Tony Roberts, James Gregory, Lee H. Montgomery. A duck who lays golden eggs spurs predictable twists and turns in this standard Disney comedy.

One Million Years B. C. (1966-British) C-100m. ** D: Don Chaffey. John Richardson, Raquel Welch, Percy Herbert, Robert Brown, Martine Beswick, Jean Wladon, Lisa Thomas. Silly prehistoric saga which capitalized on Miss Welch's anatomy in its advertising; that remains its only real virtue.

One Minute to Zero (1952) 105m. **½ D: Tay Garnett. Robert Mitchum, Ann Blyth, William Talman, Richard Egan, Charles McGraw. Mitchum adds guts to generally bloodless tale about Korean War.

One More Time (1970) C-93m. *½ D: Jerry Lewis. Peter Lawford, Sammy Davis, Jr., Esther Anderson, Maggie Wright. Sequel to SALT

AND PEPPER is far worse. They still own nightclub, still can't keep their noses out of trouble.

One More Tomorrow (1946) 88m. ** D: Peter Godfrey. Ann Sheridan, Dennis Morgan, Alexis Smith, John Loder, Jane Wyman, Reginald Gardiner. Light-comedy players flounder in overambitious reworking of Philip Barry's THE ANIMAL KINGDOM.

One More Train to Rob (1971) C-108m. **½ D: Andrew V. McLaglen. George Peppard, Diana Muldaur, John Vernon, France Nuyen, Steve Sandor. Peppard seeks revenge on former robbery partner who sent him to jail. Unremarkable Western has some flavor, nice supporting cast of familiar faces.

One Mysterious Night (1944) 61m. D: Budd Boetticher. Chester Morris, Janis Carter, Richard Lane, William Wright, George E. Stone, Dorothy Malone, Joseph Crehan. SEE: **Boston Blackie** series.

One Night in Lisbon (1941) 97m. **½ D: Edward H. Griffith. Fred MacMurray, Madeleine Carroll, Patricia Morison, Billie Burke, John Loder. Mild screwball comedy with gorgeous Carroll falling in love with flier MacMurray despite interference from his ex (Morison).

One Night in the Tropics (1940) 82m. **½ D: A. Edward Sutherland. Allan Jones, Nancy Kelly, Bud Abbott, Lou Costello, Robert Cummings, Leo Carrillo, Mary Boland. Ambitious but unmemorable musical with songs by Jerome Kern, Oscar Hammerstein, and Dorothy Fields, from Earl Derr Biggers' gimmicky story "Love Insurance" (filmed before in 1929 and 1924). Abbott and Costello, in film debut, have secondary roles to Jones-Kelly-Cummings love triangle.

One Night of Love (1934) 80m. ***½ D: Victor Schertzinger. Grace Moore, Tullio Carminati, Lyle Talbot, Mona Barrie, Luis Alberni, Jessie Ralph. Classic musical of aspiring opera star Moore and her demanding teacher Carminati, a delight from start to finish with Miss Moore performing several operatic excerpts. A must for music-lovers, film remains remarkably fresh.

One Night With You (1948-British) 90m. ** D: Terence Young. Nino Martini, Patricia Roc, Bonar Colleano, Guy Middleton, Stanley Holloway, Miles Malleson. Diluted musical with socialite Roc intrigued by singer Martini.

One of My Wives Is Missing (1976) C-100m. TVM D: Glenn Jordan. Jack Klugman, Elizabeth Ashley, James Franciscus, Joel Fabiani, Ruth McDevitt, Milton Seltzer. Small-town cop faces baffling case when rich vacationer's wife disappears and later turns up, only to be claimed an imposter. Good suspense drama and good Klugman, as usual. Above average.

One of Our Aircraft Is Missing (1941-British) 106m. ***½ D: Michael Powell and Emeric Pressburger. Godfrey Tearle, Eric Portman, Hugh Williams, Pamela Brown, Googie Withers, Peter Ustinov, Roland Culver. Thoughtful study of RAF pilots who crash-land in Netherlands, seek to return to England.

One of Our Dinosaurs Is Missing (1976) C-93m. BOMB D: Robert Stevenson. Peter Ustinov, Helen Hayes, Clive Revill, Derek Nimmo, Joan Sims. The Disney studio's answer to insomnia, a boring film about spy with secret formula hidden in dinosaur bone, and a group of nannies determined to retrieve stolen skeleton. Filmed in England.

One of Our Own (1975) C-100m. TVM D: Richard Sarafian. George Peppard, William Daniels, Louise Sorel, Strother Martin, Oscar Homolka, Zohra Lampert. Chief neurosurgeon Peppard faces a familiar series of crises as hospital administrator and predictably resolves all outstanding situations. He later continued his character in the brief "Doctors' Hospital" series. Average.

One on One (1977) C-98m. *** D: Lamont Johnson. Robby Benson, Annette O'Toole, G. D. Spradlin, Gail Strickland, Melanie Griffith. Benson co-wrote this sincere, upbeat film about naive basketball player who tries to buck corrupt world of college athletics, and sadistic coach Spradlin. Director Johnson plays Benson's alumni big-brother.

One Potato, Two Potato (1964) 92m. ***½ D: Larry Peerce. Barbara Barrie, Bernie Hamilton, Richard Mulligan, Robert Earl Jones, Harry Bellaver, Faith Burwell, Tom Ligon. Frank study of interracial marriage, beautifully acted, with intelligent script.

One Spy Too Many (1966) C-102m. ** D: Joseph Sargent. Robert

Vaughn, David McCallum, Rip Torn, Dorothy Provine, Leo G. Carroll. Feature edited from MAN FROM UNCLE TV-er, has Torn trying to take over the world, while putting wife Provine out of the way.

One Step to Eternity (1955-French) 94m. ** D: Henri Decoin. Danielle Darrieux, Michel Auclair, Corinne Calvet, Gil Delamare. Capable cast led astray by meandering production about unknown persons trying to kill four women.

One Step to Hell (1967) C-90m. ** D: Sandy Howard. Ty Hardin, Pier Angeli, George Sanders, Rossano Brazzi, Helga Line, Jorge Rigaud. Crude period melodrama in turn-of-the-century African bush. Lawman Hardin pursues gang of vicious killers.

One Sunday Afternoon (1948) C-90m. **½ D: Raoul Walsh. Dennis Morgan, Janis Paige, Don DeFore, Dorothy Malone, Ben Blue. Musical remake of STRAWBERRY BLONDE is pleasant but nothing more, with attractive cast and unmemorable songs.

One That Got Away, The (1958-British) 106m. *** D: Roy Baker. Hardy Kruger, Colin Gordon, Michael Goodliffe, Terence Alexander. Kruger gives sincere performance as Nazi prisoner in England who believes it is his duty to escape and get back to Germany. Many exciting moments.

One Third of a Nation (1939) 79m. **½ D: Dudley Murphy. Sylvia Sidney, Leif Erickson, Myron McCormick, Hiram Sherman, Sidney Lumet, Iris Adrian, Byron Russell. Sidney is poor girl yearning for escape from tenements, meeting man who could make the change for her. Still timely social document.

1001 Arabian Nights (1959) C-75m. **½ D: Jack Kinney. Voices of Jim Backus, Kathryn Grant, Dwayne Hickman, Hans Conried, Herschel Bernardi, Alan Reed. Elaborate updating of Arabian Nights tales featuring nearsighted Mr. Magoo has a nice score, pleasing animation, especially in color.

One Touch of Venus (1948) 81m. **½ D: William A. Seiter. Ava Gardner, Robert Walker, Dick Haymes, Eve Arden, Olga San Juan, Tom Conway. Broadway success of young man in love with store-window statue of Venus which suddenly comes to life; not great, but amusing, with good cast. Lovely Kurt Weill-Ogden Nash score includes "Speak Low."

One, Two, Three (1961) 108m. **** D: Billy Wilder. James Cagney, Arlene Francis, Horst Buchholz, Pamela Tiffin, Lilo Pulver, Red Buttons. Hilarious Wilder comedy about Coke executive (Cagney) in contemporary West Berlin. Cagney is a marvel to watch in this fast-paced comedy; brisk Andre Previn score helps.

One Way Passage (1932) 69m. ***½ D: Tay Garnett. Kay Francis, William Powell, Aline MacMahon, Warren Hymer, Frank McHugh, Herbert Mundin. Tender shipboard romance of con-man Powell and fatally ill Francis, splendidly acted, with good support by MacMahon and McHugh as two other con-artists playing Cupid. Remade as TILL WE MEET AGAIN.

One-Way Street (1950) 79m. **½ D: Hugo Fregonese. James Mason, Marta Toren, Dan Duryea, William Conrad, Jack Elam. Turgid crime story of doctor (Mason) involved with gangland robberies, trying to reform.

One Way to Love (1945) 83m. ** D: Ray Enright. Chester Morris, Janis Carter, Marguerite Chapman, Willard Parker. Pleasant programmer about two radio writers finding romance and new program ideas on cross-country train trip.

One Woman's Story (1949-British) 86m. ***½ D: David Lean. Ann Todd, Claude Rains, Trevor Howard, Isabel Dean, Arthur Howard, Wilfrid Hyde-White. Intelligent romancer of married woman encountering former lover, finding herself involved with him again.

Onion Field, The (1979) C-122m. ‡** D: Harold Becker. John Savage, James Woods, Franklyn Seales, Ted Danson, Ronny Cox, Diane Hull. Heart-wrenching true story about a cop who cracks up after his partner is murdered was adapted by author Joseph Wambaugh without any studio interference. Well acted and impassioned, but never quite peaks.

Onionhead (1958) 110m. **½ D: Norman Taurog. Andy Griffith, Felicia Farr, Walter Matthau, Erin O'Brien, Joey Bishop. Film tries to capture flavor of NO TIME FOR

SERGEANTS but is pat imitation of life in the Coast Guard.

Only Angels Have Wings (1939) 121m. ***½ D: Howard Hawks. Cary Grant, Jean Arthur, Richard Barthelmess, Rita Hayworth, Thomas Mitchell, Sig Ruman, John Carroll, Allyn Joslyn. Mail fliers in South America provide background for interesting story: showgirl Arthur falls in love with Grant; Rita is bored with husband Barthelmess.

Only Game in Town, The (1970) C-113m. *** D: George Stevens. Elizabeth Taylor, Warren Beatty, Charles Braswell, Hank Henry, Olga Valery. Romance of chorus girl and gambler takes place in Las Vegas, but was shot in Paris and suffers for it; restriction of action to indoor scenes slows pace of this pleasant adaptation of Frank D. Gilroy's play. Beatty is excellent.

Only the Best SEE: **I Can Get It for You Wholesale**

Only the French Can (1955-French) C-93m. **½ D: Jean Renoir. Jean Gabin, Francoise Arnoul, Maria Felix, Edith Piaf. Pictorially flattering but static musical about nightclub owner Gabin discovering the cancan dance. Retitled: FRENCH CANCAN.

Only the Valiant (1951) 105m. ** D: Gordon Douglas. Gregory Peck, Barbara Payton, Ward Bond, Gig Young, Lon Chaney, Neville Brand, Jeff Corey. Unmemorable oater of army officer Peck showing his courage by holding off the rampaging Indians.

Only Two Can Play (1962-British) 106m. *** D: Sidney Gilliat. Peter Sellers, Mai Zetterling, Virginia Maskell, Richard Attenborough, Kenneth Griffith. Well-intentioned filming of Kingsley Amis novel, striving for quick laughs rather than satire. Sellers is librarian flirting with society woman Zetterling.

Only Way Out Is Dead SEE: **Man Who Wanted to Live Forever, The**

Only When I Larf (1968-British) C-104m. **½ D: Basil Dearden. Richard Attenborough, David Hemmings, Alexandra Stewart, Nicholas Pennell. Fun con-game film finds three confidence men scheming to sell militant African diplomat scrap metal in ammunition cases.

Only with Married Men (1974) C-78m. TVM D: Jerry Paris. David Birney, Michele Lee, John Astin, Judy Carne, Dom DeLuise, Gavin MacLeod. Romantic fluff involving a sexy girl who avoids commitment by dating only married men and a bachelor who pretends he's wed to woo and win her. Consider the possibilities and guess the outcome. Average.

Open City (1946-Italian) 105m. **** D: Roberto Rossellini. Aldo Fabrizi, Anna Magnani, Marcello Pagliero, Maria Michi, Vito Annicchiarico, Nando Bruno, Harry Feist. Classic Rossellini account of Italian underground movement during Nazi occupation of Rome; powerful moviemaking gem.

Open Season (1974-Spanish) C-103m. BOMB D: Peter Collinson. Peter Fonda, John Philip Law, Richard Lynch, William Holden, Cornelia Sharpe. Sordid mixture of violence and sex as three Vietnam War buddies hunt humans.

Open the Door and See All the People (1964) 82m. **½ D: Jerome Hill. Maybelle Nash, Alec Wilder, Charles Rydell, Ellen Martin. Weird little comedy of elderly twin sisters, their contrasting personalities and rivalry.

Operation Amsterdam (1960-British) 105m. **½ D: Michael McCarthy. Peter Finch, Eva Bartok, Tony Britton, Alexander Knox, Malcolm Keen. Standard wartime suspense fare as British expedition tries to sneak a cache of diamonds out of Holland before Nazis can get to them.

Operation Bikini (1963) 83m. ** D: Anthony Carras. Tab Hunter, Frankie Avalon, Eva Six, Scott Brady, Gary Crosby, Jim Backus. Occasionally perky cast livens tame WW2 narrative of attempt to destroy sunken treasure before enemy grabs it. Some color sequences.

Operation Bottleneck (1961) 78m. *½ D: Edward L. Cahn. Ron Foster, Miiko Taka, Norman Alden, John Clarke. Mini-actioner of WW2 Burma; not much to offer.

Operation CIA (1965) 90m. **½ D: Christian Nyby. Burt Reynolds, Kieu Chinh, Danielle Aubry, John Hoyt, Cyril Collack. Diverting drama set in Saigon; federal agent Reynolds uncovers a misplaced secret message meant for Allies.

Operation Conspiracy (1957-British) 69m. *½ D: Joseph Sterling. Philip Friend, Mary Mackenzie, Leslie Dwyer, Allan Cuthbertson. Timid little espionage film. Retitled: CLOAK WITHOUT DAGGER.

Operation Cross Eagles (1969) C-90m. *½ D: Richard Conte. Richard Conte, Rory Calhoun, Aili King, Phil Brown. Undistinguished war film about a WW2 mission in Yugoslavia to rescue captured American officer.

Operation Crossbow (1965) C-116m. ***½ D: Michael Anderson. George Peppard, Sophia Loren, Trevor Howard, Tom Courtenay, Anthony Quayle, John Mills, Sylvia Syms, Richard Todd. Fine "impossible mission" tale of small band of commandos out to destroy Nazi secret missile stronghold during WW2. Sensational ending, and the pyrotechnics are dazzling. Also known as THE GREAT SPY MISSION.

Operation Daybreak (1976) C-102m. **½ D: Lewis Gilbert. Timothy Bottoms, Martin Shaw, Joss Ackland, Nicola Pagett, Anthony Andrews, Anton Diffring. Well-made but uninspiring account of Czech underground's attempt to assassinate Reinhard "Hangman" Heydrich, Hitler's right-hand man, during WW2. Retitled PRICE OF FREEDOM.

Operation Disaster (1951-British) 102m. *** D: Roy Baker. John Mills, Helen Cherry, Richard Attenborough, Lana Morris, Nigel Patrick. Vivid actioner of submarine warfare during WW2, tautly presented. Originally titled MORNING DEPARTURE.

Operation Eichmann (1961) 93m. **½ D: R. G. Springsteen. Werner Klemperer, Ruta Lee, Donald Buka, Barbara Turner, John Banner. Fairly intriguing account of the Nazi leader's postwar life and his capture by Israelis.

Operation Haylift (1950) 75m. ** D: William Berke. Bill Williams, Ann Rutherford, Jane Nigh, Tom Brown. Minor account of air force assisting farmers to save stranded cattle during snowstorm.

Operation Heartbeat SEE: U.M.C.

Operation Kid Brother (1967-Italian) C-104m. *½ D: Alberto De Martino. Neil Connery, Daniela Bianchi, Adolfo Celi, Bernard Lee, Anthony Dawson, Lois Maxwell. Screen debut of Sean Connery's brother in James Bond spinoff a disaster, in tale of master criminal (Celi)'s plan to blackmail Allied governments into controlling half of world's gold supply. Negligible suspense, confusing

dialogue, occasional good use of locations.

Operation Mad Ball (1957) 105m. ** D: Richard Quine. Jack Lemmon, Kathryn Grant, Mickey Rooney, Ernie Kovacs, Arthur O'Connell, James Darren, Roger Smith. Weak service comedy about crafty soldiers planning wild party off base. Dull stretches, few gags. O'Connell comes off better than supposed comedians in film.

Operation Mermaid SEE: Bay of Saint Michel

Operation Pacific (1951) 111m. *** D: George Waggner. John Wayne, Patricia Neal, Ward Bond, Scott Forbes. Overzealous Wayne is ultra-dedicated to his navy command; the few WW2 action scenes are taut, and Neal makes a believable love interest.

Operation Petticoat (1959) C-124m. ***½ D: Blake Edwards. Cary Grant, Tony Curtis, Dina Merrill, Gene Evans, Arthur O'Connell, Richard Sargent, Virginia Gregg. Hilarious comedy about submarine captain Grant who's determined to make his injured ship seaworthy again, and con-artist Curtis who wheels and deals to reach that goal. Some truly memorable gags; Grant and Curtis are a dynamite team in this happy film.

Operation Petticoat (1977) C-100m. TVM D: John Astin. John Astin, Richard Gilliland, Jackie Cooper, Yvonne Wilder, Richard Bresthoff, Jamie Lee Curtis. Here's that pink sub and the WW2 nurses reluctantly aboard in a silly rehash of the fondly remembered Cary Grant-Tony Curtis movie. Of single interest: one of the friendly nurses is Curtis' pretty daughter. Pilot for the TV series. Average.

Operation St. Peter's (1968-Italian) C-100m. ** D: Lucio Fulci. Edward G. Robinson, Lando Buzzanca, Jean-Claude Brialy. Heist film with a twist: attempt to steal Michelangelo's Pietà from Vatican, which is tough to fence. Average.

Operation Secret (1952) 108m. ** D: Lewis Seiler. Cornel Wilde, Steve Cochran, Phyllis Thaxter, Karl Malden, Dan O'Herlihy. Tame WW2 actioner involving a traitor in midst of Allied division.

Operation Snafu (1965-British) 97m. **½ D: Cyril Frankel. Alfred Lynch, Sean Connery, Cecil Parker, Stanley Holloway, Alan King, Wilfrid Hyde-White, Eric Barker, Kathleen Harrison. Sluggish WW2 account of two buddies becoming heroes unintentionally; most capable cast. Retitled: OPERATION WARHEAD. Originally titled ON THE FIDDLE.

Operation Snatch (1962-British) 83m. ** D: Robert Day. Terry-Thomas, George Sanders, Lionel Jeffries, Jackie Lane, Lee Montague, Michael Trubshawe. Fitfully funny satire involving British attempt to keep "their flag flying" on Gibraltar during WW2.

Operation Thunderbolt (1977) C-125m. ** D: Menahem Golan. Yehoram Gaon, Klaus Kinski, Assaf Dayan, Shai K. Ophir, Sybil Danning. Stunning retelling of the famed raid by Israeli commandos on July 4, 1976 to rescue 104 hijacked passengers from a plane at Entebbe in Uganda. The stamp of official Israeli approval given this film, along with government cooperation, and dedicated performances by a basically Israeli cast make this one outshine both star-laden American-made dramatizations, RAID ON ENTEBBE and VICTORY AT ENTEBBE.

Operation Warhead SEE: **Operation Snafu**

Operation X (1951-British) 79m. ** D: Gregory Ratoff. Edward G. Robinson, Peggy Cummins, Richard Greene, Nora Swinburne. Heady yarn with Robinson overly ambitious businessman forgetting his scruples. Original title: MY DAUGHTER JOY.

Opposite Sex, The (1956) C-117m. *** D: David Miller. June Allyson, Joan Collins, Dolores Gray, Ann Sheridan, Joan Blondell, Ann Miller, Agnes Moorehead, Carolyn Jones, Charlotte Greenwood. Well-heeled musical remake of Clare Boothe Luce's THE WOMEN has stellar cast, but still pales next to brittle original (Shearer, Crawford, Russell, etc.). Major difference: music and men appear in this expanded version.

Optimists, The (1973-British) C-110m. *** D: Anthony Simmons. Peter Sellers, Donna Mullane, John Chaffey, David Daker. Entertaining comedy-drama of London busker (street entertainer) Sellers and the two tough little kids he takes in hand. Songs by Lionel Bart include effective "Sometimes."

Orca (1977) C-92m. ** D: Michael Anderson. Richard Harris, Charlotte Rampling, Will Sampson, Bo Derek, Keenan Wynn, Robert Carradine. Killer whale revenges himself on bounty hunter Harris and crew for killing pregnant mate. For undiscriminating action fans.

Orchestra Wives (1942) 98m. **½ D: Archie Mayo. George Montgomery, Glenn Miller, Lynn Bari, Carole Landis, Cesar Romero, Ann Rutherford, Virginia Gilmore, Mary Beth Hughes, Jackie Gleason. Story woven around Glenn Miller's band and the musicians' neglected wives. Not bad, with vintage music. "I've Got a Gal in Kalamazoo," "At Last," "Serenade in Blue."

Ordeal (1973) C-74m. TVM D: Lee H. Katzin. Arthur Hill, Diana Muldaur, James Stacy, Macdonald Carey, Michael Ansara. Mojave Desert location shooting enhances morality tale of scheming wife (Muldaur) abandoning broken-legged husband (Hill) in wilderness. Film suggests profound themes but refuses to admit so. Average.

Ordeal of Patty Hearst, The (1979) C-150m. TVM D: Paul Wendkos. Dennis Weaver, Lisa Eilbacher, David Haskell, Stephen Elliott, Felton Perry. Self-named headline story is recreated through the eyes of an FBI agent who turned this bizarre kidnap case into his eve-of-retirement crusade. Average.

Ordered to Love (1960-German) 82m. **½ D: Werner Klinger. Maria Perschy, Marisa Mell, Rosemarie Kirstein, Birgitt Bergen. Potentially explosive film gets tame treatment; account of Nazi "breeding" camps for new generation of master race soldiers.

Orders are Orders (1954-British) ** D: David Paltenghi. Margot Grahame, Maureen Swanson, Peter Sellers, Tony Hancock, Sidney James. Hancock as befuddled lieutenant is best item in this slapstick yarn of movie company using an Army barracks for headquarters. Based on a 1932 play, filmed once before.

Orders to Kill (1958-British) 93m. **½ D: Anthony Asquith. Eddie Albert, Paul Massie, Lillian Gish, James Robertson Justice. Low-key account of American agent sent into France to kill a traitor.

Oregon Passage (1957) C-82m. *½ D: Paul Landres. John Ericson, Lola Albright, Edward Platt, Jon Shepodd. Bland fare about army officer trying to do good, but interfering with Indian way of life.

Oregon Trail, The (1959) C-86m. ** D: Gene Fowler, Jr. Fred MacMurray, William Bishop, Nina Shipman, Gloria Talbott, Henry Hull, John Carradine. Uneventful Western with MacMurray a reporter investigating Indian attacks on settlers; set in 19th-century Oregon.

Oregon Trail, The (1976) C-110m. TVM D: Boris Sagal. Rod Taylor, Blair Brown, David Huddleston, Linda Purl, G. D. Spradlin, Douglas V. Fowley. Pioneer family pulls up stakes and heads West for a new life. Solid outdoor drama blessed with the usual strong performance by Taylor, who also starred in the subsequent series. Average.

Organization, The (1971) C-107m. *** D: Don Medford. Sidney Poitier, Barbara McNair, Sheree North, Gerald S. O'Loughlin, Raul Julia, Fred Beir. Poitier, again as San Francisco Police Lieutenant Virgil Tibbs, joins forces (and risks career) with addict-related activists out to nail major dope-smuggling operation. Realistic ending, well-thought-out chases.

Organizer, The (1964-Italian) 126m. *** D: Mario Monicelli. Marcello Mastroianni, Annie Girardot, Renato Salvatori, Bernard Blier. Serious look at labor union efforts in Italy, with Mastroianni giving low-keyed performance in title role.

Oriental Dream SEE: **Kismet**

Orphan Train (1979) C-150m. TVM D: William A. Graham. Jill Eikenberry, Kevin Dobson, Linda Manz, Graham Fletcher-Cook, Melissa Michaelsen. Historical drama taken from Dorothea G. Petrie's novel dealing with a dedicated young social worker, a newspaper photographer, and a group of slum kids on their mid-19th century railroad odyssey from Manhattan to new lives out West. Above average.

Orphans of the Storm (1922) 125m. *** D: D. W. Griffith. Lillian Gish, Dorothy Gish, Joseph Schildkraut, Morgan Wallace, Lucille LaVerne, Sheldon Lewis, Frank Puglia, Creighton Hale, Monte Blue. Griffith's epic film about sisters cruelly separated, one blind and raised by thieves, one innocent and plundered by lecherous aristocrats. Implausible plot segues into French Revolution, with lavish settings and race-to-the-rescue climax. For all its creaky situations, and extreme length, still a dazzling film.

Orpheus (1949-French) 86m. *** D: Jean Cocteau. Jean Marais, Francois Perier, Maria Casares, Marie Dea. Compelling, cinematic allegory set in modern times with poet Marais encountering Princess of Death, exploring their mutual fascination. Heavy-handed at times but still fascinating.

Oscar, The (1966) C-119m. **½ D: Russell Rouse. Stephen Boyd, Elke Sommer, Eleanor Parker, Milton Berle, Joseph Cotten, Jill St. John, Ernest Borgnine, Edie Adams, Tony Bennett, Jean Hale. Shiny tinsel view of Hollywood and those competing for Academy Awards; Parker as love-hungry talent agent comes off best. Loosely based on Richard Sale novel, with many guest stars thrown in. Some of the dialogue is so bad it's laughable.

Oscar Wilde (1960-British) 96m. *** D: Gregory Ratoff. Robert Morley, Phyllis Calvert, John Neville, Ralph Richardson, Dennis Price, Alexander Knox. Morley is ideally cast as famed 19th century playwright and wit, in film that focuses on his traumatic trials and eventual conviction for sodomy. Released at the same time as THE TRIALS OF OSCAR WILDE with Peter Finch.

O'Shaughnessy's Boy (1935) 88m. **½ D: Richard Boleslawski. Wallace Beery, Jackie Cooper, Spanky McFarland, Henry Stephenson, Leona Maricle, Sara Haden. Sentimental tale of Beery searching for his son, taken from him by cruel wife.

Othello (1955-Italian) 92m. **½ D: Orson Welles. Orson Welles, Suzanne Cloutier, Robert Coote, Michael Lawrence, Fay Compton. Welles gives an intelligent but overdramatic interpretation to Shakespeare's tale of the Moor jealous of his Desdemona.

Othello (1965-British) C-166m. **** D: Stuart Burge. Laurence Olivier, Frank Finlay, Maggie Smith, Joyce Redman. Brilliant transferral to the screen of Shakespeare's immortal story of the Moor of Venice.

Other, The (1972) C-100m. *** D: Robert Mulligan. Uta Hagen, Diana Muldaur, Chris Udvarnoky, Martin Udvarnoky. Eerie tale of supernatural, with twin brothers representing good and evil. Stark, chilling mood tale from Thomas Tryon's novel.

Other Love, The (1947) 95m. **½ D: Andre de Toth. Barbara Stanwyck,

David Niven, Richard Conte, Maria Palmer, Joan Lorring, Gilbert Roland, Richard Hale, Lenore Aubert. Dying Stanwyck decides to live wild life with gambler Conte, unaware that doctor Niven loves her. Not convincing, but enjoyable.

Other Man, The (1970) **C-99m. TVM** D: Richard Colla. Joan Hackett, Roy Thinnes, Tammy Grimes, Arthur Hill, Virginia Gregg, Rodolfo Hoyos. Husband's disinterest propels wife into clandestine affair with stranger, attempted murder the outcome. Fairly tense situation at film's climax, but overindulgent direction and script detract. Average.

Other Men's Women (1931) **70m. **½** D: William A. Wellman. Grant Withers, Mary Astor, Regis Toomey, James Cagney, Joan Blondell. Love triangle set in the world of railroad men; interesting melodrama, dated in some ways, but vivid in its atmosphere, with great action finale. Cagney and Blondell have supporting roles.

Other Side of Hell, The (1978) **C-150m. TVM** D: Jan Kadar. Alan Arkin, Roger E. Mosley, Morgan Woodward, Seamon Glass. Harrowing tale of a man's fight to get out of a mental institution, made even more depressing by Arkin's overly intense acting style. Average.

Other Side of Midnight, The (1977) **C-165m. BOMB** D: Charles Jarrott. Marie-France Pisier, John Beck, Susan Sarandon, Raf Vallone, Clu Gulager, Christian Marquand, Michael Lerner. Trashy novel gets the film treatment it deserves in ponderous story, set from 1939-1947, about a woman who parlays her body into film stardom. Dull, as opposed to lively, drek.

Other Side of the Mountain, The (1975) **C-101m. **½** D: Larry Peerce. Marilyn Hassett, Beau Bridges, Belinda J. Montgomery, Nan Martin, William Bryant, Dabney Coleman. Pleasantly performed but undistinguished true-life tragedy about skier Jill Kinmont, once a shoo-in for the Olympics until a sporting accident left her paralyzed from the shoulders down. Followed by 1978 sequel.

Other Side of the Mountain Part 2, The (1978) **C-100m. **½** D: Larry Peerce. Marilyn Hassett, Timothy Bottoms, Nan Martin, Belinda J. Montgomery, Gretchen Corbett, William Bryant. Smooth continuation of story of crippled skier Jill Kinmont (Hassett), who finds true love with trucker Bottoms. Timothy's real-life father James plays his dad in this film.

Other Woman, The (1954) **81m. BOMB** D: Hugo Haas. Hugo Haas, Cleo Moore, Lance Fuller, Lucille Barkley, Jack Macy, John Qualen. Nonsense involving a girl's plot for revenge on her former boss.

Otley (1969-British) **C-90m. **** D: Dick Clement. Tom Courtenay, Romy Schneider, Alan Badel, James Villiers, Leonard Rossiter, Fiona Lewis. Static spy spoof about petty thief and beautiful secret agent is helped a bit by Courtenay and Schneider, but otherwise has little to recommend it.

Our Betters (1933) **78m. **½** D: George Cukor. Constance Bennett, Gilbert Roland, Charles Starrett, Anita Louise, Alan Mowbray, Minor Watson, Violet Kemble-Cooper. Dated but enjoyable film of Somerset Maugham drawing-room comedy about British lord marrying rich American girl.

Our Blushing Brides (1928) **97m. *** D: Harry Beaumont. Joan Crawford, Johnny Mack Brown, Dorothy Sebastian, Nils Asther, Anita Page. One of the best Jazz Age silents, with absurdly melodramatic story: flapper Joan loses Johnny to Anita, who's been pushed into marriage against her will.

Our Daily Bread (1934) **74m. **½** D: King Vidor. Karen Morley, Tom Keene, John Qualen, Barbara Pepper, Addison Richards, Harry Holman. Hailed as a classic, this Depression drama is intriguing in its communal back-to-the-soil message, but spoiled by terrible performance by leading-man Keene. Final irrigation sequence is memorable, however.

Our Dancing Daughters (1928) **97m. *** D: Harry Beaumont. Joan Crawford, Johnny Mack Brown, Dorothy Sebastian, Nils Asther, Anita Page, Kathlyn Williams, Edward Nugent. One of the best Jazz Age silents, with absurdly melodramatic story: flapper Joan loses Johnny to Anita Page, who's been pushed into marriage against her will. Crystallization of the Roaring 20s.

Our Hearts Were Growing Up (1946) **83m. **½** D: William D. Russell. Gail Russell, Diana Lynn, Brian Donlevy, James Brown, Bill Edwards, William Demarest. Follow-up to OUR HEARTS WERE YOUNG AND GAY doesn't match it, with girls on their own at Princeton.

Our Hearts Were Young and Gay (1944) 81m. *** D: Lewis Allen. Gail Russell, Diana Lynn, Charlie Ruggles, Dorothy Gish, James Brown, Bill Edwards, Beulah Bondi, Alma Kruger. Extremely pleasant bit of fluff from Cornelia Otis Skinner's memory of traveling to Europe during 1920s with her girlfriend Emily Kimbrough. Followed by sequel, OUR HEARTS WERE GROWING UP.

Our Little Girl (1935) 63m. **½ D: John Robertson. Shirley Temple, Rosemary Ames, Joel McCrea, Lyle Talbot, Erin O'Brien-Moore. Usual Temple plot of Shirley bringing separated parents McCrea and Ames together again.

Our Man Flint (1966) C-107m. **½ D: Daniel Mann. James Coburn, Lee J. Cobb, Gila Golan, Edward Mulhare, Benson Fong, Gianna Serra. One of the countless James Bond spoofs, this saga of the man from Z.O.W.I.E. starts briskly, becomes forced after a while. Coburn makes a zesty hero, Golan an attractive decoration.

Our Man Flint: Dead on Target (1976) C-78m. TVM D: Joseph L. Scanlon. Ray Danton, Sharon Acker, Lawrence Dane, Donnelly Rhodes, Linda Sorenson, Susan Sullivan. Tired action film has super agent Derek Flint assigned to the rescue of a kidnapped oil executive. Below average.

Our Man in Havana (1960-British) 107m. **½ D: Carol Reed. Alec Guinness, Burl Ives, Maureen O'Hara, Ernie Kovacs, Noel Coward, Ralph Richardson, Jo Morrow. Weak satirical spy spoof, claiming origin from Graham Greene novel. Guinness is vacuum cleaner salesman who becomes British agent.

Our Men in Bagdad (1967-Italian) C-100m. *½ D: Paolo Bianchini. Rory Calhoun, Roger Hanin, Evi Marandi, Ralph Baldwin, Jean Gaven, Lea Padovani. Unsurprising espionage caper set in the Middle East.

Our Miss Brooks (1956) 85m. **½ D: Al Lewis. Eve Arden, Gale Gordon, Don Porter, Robert Rockwell, Jane Morgan, Richard Crenna. Fea-

ture version of TV series, with Arden as Connie Brooks, Gordon as Principal Osgood Conklin, Rockwell as Mr. Boynton, and young Crenna as student Walter Denton. OK entry for series fans.

Our Mother's House (1967-British) C-105m. *** D: Jack Clayton. Dirk Bogarde, Margaret Brooks, Louis Sheldon-Williams, John Gugolka, Pamela Franklin, Mark Lester. Children's scheme to carry on normally when their mother dies works well until their worthless father shows up. Director Clayton gets fine performances from all in offbeat film.

Our Relations (1936) 65m. **½ D: Harry Lachman. Stan Laurel, Oliver Hardy, Alan Hale, Sidney Toler, Daphne Pollard, Betty Healy, James Finlayson, Arthur Housman, Iris Adrian, Lona Andre. Duo in amusing comedy of errors with their twin brothers; best scenes in Hale's beer garden.

Our Time (1974) C-88m. **½ D: Peter Hyams. Pamela Sue Martin, Parker Stevenson, Betsy Slade, George O'Hanlon, Jr., Karen Balkin. Nice nostalgic tale of young love, set in a Massachusetts girls' school in 1955. Bad color photography mars otherwise effective comedic and dramatic elements. Retitled DEATH OF HER INNOCENCE.

Our Town (1940) 90m. ***½ D: Sam Wood. William Holden, Martha Scott, Fay Bainter, Beulah Bondi, Thomas Mitchell, Guy Kibbee. Sensitive adaptation of Thornton Wilder play about small New England town with human drama and conflict in every family.

Our Very Own (1950) 93m. **½ D: David Miller. Ann Blyth, Farley Granger, Jane Wyatt, Donald Cook, Ann Dvorak, Natalie Wood, Martin Milner. Melodramatic account of Blyth's shock upon discovering she's an adopted child.

Our Vines Have Tender Grapes (1945) 105m. ***½ D: Roy Rowland. Edward G. Robinson, Margaret O'Brien, James Craig, Frances Gifford, Agnes Moorehead, Morris Carnovsky. Excellent view of American life in Wisconsin town with uncharacteristic Robinson as O'Brien's kind, understanding father.

Our Wife (1941) 95m. **½ D: John M. Stahl. Melvyn Douglas, Ruth Hussey, Ellen Drew, Charles Coburn, John Hubbard. Douglas adds dignity to this OK marital comedy involving musician seeking divorce to marry another.

Our Winning Season (1978) **C-92m.** ** D: Joseph Ruben. Scott Jacoby, Deborah Benson, Dennis Quaid, Randy Herman, Joe Penny, Jan Smithers, P. J. Soles. Yet another 1960s high school film focuses mostly on growing pains of aspiring track star Jacoby; not bad, but awfully familiar.

Out All Night (1933) **68m.** ** D: Sam Taylor. ZaSu Pitts, Slim Summerville, Laura Hope Crews, Shirley Grey, Alexander Carr. OK film from long-run teaming of Pitts and Summerville; this time, he's a mother-dominated young man who marries ZaSu against Mama's wishes.

Out of It (1969) **95m.** **½ D: Paul Williams. Barry Gordon, Jon Voight, Lada Edmund, Jr., Gretchen Corbett, Peter Grad. Generally amusing film about high school intellectual (Gordon) bucking high school athlete (Voight). A throwback to the days when life was one big Archie comic book.

Out of Season (1975-British) **C-90m.** ** D: Alan Bridges. Vanessa Redgrave, Cliff Robertson, Susan George. Mood-triangle affair: dark stranger returns to English seaside resort twenty years after affair with woman who now has grown daughter. Hints of incest and unresolved ending. Formerly titled WINTER RATES, played Berlin Festival, had limited release in this country.

Out of Sight (1966) **C-87m.** *½ D: Lennie Weinrib. Jonathan Daly, Karen Jensen, Robert Pine, Carole Shelayne, Gary Lewis and The Playboys. Silly combination of beach and spy formulas doesn't succeed in either department.

Out of the Blue (1947) **84m.** **½ D: Leigh Jason. Virginia Mayo, George Brent, Turhan Bey, Ann Dvorak, Carole Landis, Hadda Brooks. Naive Brent is in trouble when far from innocent young woman is discovered unconscious in his apartment; fluffy fun. Dvorak is a delight in an offbeat role.

Out of the Clouds (1957-British) **C-80m.** ** D: Michael Relph, Basil Dearden. Anthony Steel, James Robertson Justice, Gordon Harker, Bernard Lee, Megs Jenkins. Work and play among commercial pilots; nothing special.

Out of the Darkness SEE: **Night Creature**

Out of the Fog (1941) **93m.** *** D: Anatole Litvak. Ida Lupino, John Garfield, Thomas Mitchell, Eddie Albert, George Tobias, Leo Gorcey. Fine filmization of Irwin Shaw's THE GENTLE PEOPLE, about gangster terrorizing innocent Brooklyn family.

Out of the Frying Pan SEE: **Young and Willing**

Out of the Past (1947) **97m.** ***½ D: Jacques Tourneur. Robert Mitchum, Jane Greer, Kirk Douglas, Richard Webb, Rhonda Fleming, Dickie Moore, Steve Brodie. Mitchum finds he can't escape former life when one-time employer (gangster Douglas) and lover (Greer) entangle him in web of murder and double-dealings. Classic example of 1940s "film noir," with dialogue a particular standout. Script by Geoffrey Homes from his novel *Build my Gallows High.*

Out of this World (1945) **96m.** **½ D: Hal Walker. Eddie Bracken, Veronica Lake, Diana Lynn, Cass Daley, Parkyakarkus, Donald MacBride, Florence Bates, Gary, Philip, Dennis and Lindsay Crosby. Bracken becomes pop crooner; a cute idea mercilessly padded with loud musical specialities by Daley, Lynn, and guest stars.

Out of Towners, The (1970) **C-97m.** **½ D: Arthur Hiller. Jack Lemmon, Sandy Dennis, Sandy Baron, Anne Meara, Carlos Montalban, Billy Dee Williams. Excruciating Neil Simon script about stupidly stubborn Lemmon and wife Dennis having everything imaginable go wrong on trip to N.Y.C. More harrowing than funny, with curiously unsympathetic leading characters. Final gag (a hijacking) was cut on network TV, killing film's punch line.

Out West with the Hardys (1938) **90m.** D: George B. Seitz. Lewis Stone, Mickey Rooney, Cecilia Parker, Fay Holden, Ann Rutherford, Sara Haden, Don Castle, Virginia Weidler, Gordon Jones, Ralph Morgan. SEE: **Andy Hardy** series.

Outback (1971-Australian) **C-99m.** *** D: Ted Kotcheff. Gary Bond, Donald Pleasence, Chips Rafferty, Sylvia Kay, Jack Thompson. Intriguing film about sensitive schoolteacher whose personality disintegrates after interaction with rough, primitive men in Australian outback. Toned down for TV from original 114m. version; still unlikely to be endorsed by Australian tourist commission.

Outcast, The (1954) C-90m. **½ D: William Witney. John Derek, Joan Evans, Jim Davis, Catherine McLeod, Ben Cooper. Simply told Western of Derek battling to win his rightful inheritance.

Outcast of the Islands (1951-British) 102m. ***½ D: Carol Reed. Ralph Richardson, Wendy Hiller, Trevor Howard, Robert Morley, Kerima, George Coulouris, Wilfrid Hyde-White. Compelling adaptation of Joseph Conrad story set on Malayan island, where a desperate, misguided man turns to crime and soon becomes the object of massive man-hunt. Excellent job all around. Some TV prints run 94m.

Outcasts of the City (1958) 61m. *½ D: Boris Petroff. Osa Massen, Robert Hutton, Maria Palmer, Nestor Paiva, George Neise. Junky flick of pilot Hutton involved with German doll Palmer.

Outcasts of Poker Flat, The (1952) 81m. **½ D: Joseph M. Newman. Anne Baxter, Miriam Hopkins, Dale Robertson, Cameron Mitchell, John Ridgely. Obvious, uninspired version of Bret Harte tale of social rejects trapped together in cabin during snowstorm. Filmed before in 1937.

Outcry, The (1957-Italian) 115m. **½ D: Michelangelo Antonioni. Steve Cochran, Alida Valli, Dorian Gray, Betsy Blair, Lyn Shaw. Leisurely paced yet compelling study of Cochran's mental disintegration due to lack of communication with those he loves; Cochran is quite good. Original title: IL GRIDO.

Outfit, The (1974) C-103m. **½ D: John Flynn. Robert Duvall, Karen Black, Joe Don Baker, Robert Ryan, Timothy Carey, Richard Jaeckel, Sheree North, Jane Greer, Elisha Cook, Jr., Marie Windsor. Engagingly trashy mob melodrama, with ex-con Duvall tackling the syndicate responsible for his brother's death. Solid supporting cast helps.

Outlaw, The (1943) 117m. *** D: Howard Hughes. Jane Russell, Jack Buetel, Walter Huston, Thomas Mitchell, Mimi Aguglia, Joe Sawyer. Notorious "sex western" (and Russell's ballyhooed screen debut) is actually compelling—if offbeat—story of Billy the Kid, with principal honors going to Huston as Doc Holliday. Filmed in 1941 and directed mostly by Howard Hawks,

though Hughes' interest in Russell's bosom is more than evident.

Outlaw Blues (1977) C-100m. *** D: Richard T. Heffron. Peter Fonda, Susan Saint James, John Crawford, James Callahan, Michael Lerner. Ex-convict Fonda is promoted into a country star by back-up singer Saint James, to the consternation of star Callahan, who had stolen Fonda's song. Saint James is good in her first major movie role; the picture is fun when it isn't too silly.

Outlaw Josey Wales, The (1976) C-135m. *** D: Clint Eastwood. Clint Eastwood, Chief Dan George, Sondra Locke, Bill McKinney, John Vernon, Paula Trueman, Sam Bottoms. Long, large-scale Western set in post-Civil War era; Eastwood is a peaceful farmer who turns vigilante when Union soldiers murder his family. He in turn has a price on his head, propelling cat-and-mouse chase odyssey that's the foundation of this film.

Outlaw Stallion, The (1954) C-64m. *½ D: Fred F. Sears. Phil Carey, Dorothy Patrick, Billy Gray, Roy Roberts, Gordon Jones. Programmer of horse thieves conning ranch woman and her son to get their herd.

Outlaw Territory (1953) C-79m. **½ D: John Ireland, Lee Garmes. Macdonald Carey, Joanne Dru, John Ireland, Don Haggerty, Peter Ireland, Frank Ferguson. Carey is hired killer who runs afoul of marshal Ireland, and arouses the interest of cafe-owner Dru, against her better judgment. Routine Western shot in 3-D; original title: HANNAH LEE.

Outlaw's Daughter, The (1954) C-75m. *½ D: Wesley Barry. Bill Williams, Kelly Ryan, Jim Davis, George Cleveland, Elisha Cook. Weak oater of stagecoach robbery and girl implicated because her elderly father used to be an outlaw.

Outlaw's Son (1957) 89m. ** D: Lesley Selander. Dane Clark, Ben Cooper, Lori Nelson, Ellen Drew, Eddie Foy III. Clark is most earnest in modest Western about outlaw and the son he deserted years before.

Outlaws is Coming, The (1965) 89m. **½ D: Norman Maurer. The 3 Stooges, Adam West, Nancy Kovack, Mort Mills, Don Lamond, Emil Sitka, Joe Bolton, Henry Gibson. One of the Stooges' best features, with some sharp satire and good Western atmosphere as the boys, their cowardly friend (West), and

Annie Oakley (Kovack) combat an army of gunslingers and a genteel crook. Local TV kiddie-show hosts cast as outlaws, Gibson as a hip Indian.

Outpost in Malaya (1952-British) 88m. **½ D: Ken Annakin. Claudette Colbert, Jack Hawkins, Anthony Steel, Jeremy Spencer. Mostly about marital disharmony on a rubber plantation. Original title: PLANTER'S WIFE.

Outpost in Morocco (1949) 92m. ** D: Robert Florey. George Raft, Marie Windsor, Akim Tamiroff, John Litel, Eduard Franz. Cardboard adventure saga of good-guy Raft battling desert foes while romancing enemy-girl Windsor.

Outrage (1973) C-78m. TVM D: Richard T. Heffron. Robert Culp, Marlyn Mason, Beah Richards, Jacqueline Scott, Ramon Bieri, Thomas Leopold. Local doctor (Culp) turns vigilante to deal with teen gang terrorizing his upper-middle class neighbors. Or your-average-outraged-citizen plot. Average.

Outrage, The (1964) 97m. **½ D: Martin Ritt. Paul Newman, Edward G. Robinson, Claire Bloom, Laurence Harvey, William Shatner, Albert Salmi. Pretentious fizzle, based on Japanese film RASHOMON, with Newman hamming it as Mexican bandit who allegedly rapes Bloom while husband Harvey stands by. Robinson as philosophical narrator is best thing about film.

Outrageous! (1977-Canadian) C-100m. *** D: Richard Benner. Craig Russell, Hollis McLaren, Richert Easley, Allan Moyle, Helen Shaver. Excellent comedy-drama about a very odd couple: gay hairdresser and a pregnant mental patient. McLaren's effective emoting is outshone by female impersonator Russell's flamboyant playing and imitations of Garland, Davis, Bankhead, etc.

Outriders, The (1950) C-93m. ** D: Roy Rowland. Joel McCrea, Arlene Dahl, Barry Sullivan, Claude Jarman, Jr., Ramon Novarro. Standard account of Reb soldiers trying to capture gold shipment for Confederate cause.

Outside Chance (1978) C-100m. TVM D: Michael Miller. Yvette Mimieux, Royce D. Applegate, Dick Armstrong, Beverly Atkinson, Susan Batson. Unusual misfire begins as a precis-rehash of same director's

1976 JACKSON COUNTY JAIL (also starring Mimieux)—then goes off in new directions, getting as "lurid" as TV standards will allow. Below average.

Outside In (1972) C-90m. ** D: Allen Baron. Darrel Larson, Heather Menzies, Dennis Olivieri, Peggy Feury, Logan Ramsey, John Bill. Long-haired draft-dodger returns home for father's funeral, immediately splits when Feds show up. Unintentionally funny "youth" movie filmed mostly on location in and around L.A. area. Beware cuts.

Outside Man, The (1973) C-104m. *** D: Jacques Deray. Jean-Louis Trintignant, Ann-Margret, Angie Dickinson, Roy Scheider, Michel Constantin, Georgia Engel. Okay French-American actioner, made in L.A., as interesting for its cast as its offbeat quality. Hired killer Trintignant kills gang boss Ted de Corsia, then must elude Scheider, who's out to eliminate him. Ann-Margret's plunging neckline and a shootout around de Corsia's bier (he's embalmed in a sitting position) are worth looking at, also Engel's dumb housewife.

Outside the Law (1956) 81m. *½ D: Jack Arnold. Ray Danton, Leigh Snowden, Grant Williams, Onslow Stevens. Half-baked yarn of Danton proving his worth by snaring counterfeiters.

Outside the Wall (1950) 80m. **½ D: Crane Wilbur. Richard Basehart, Dorothy Hart, Marilyn Maxwell, Signe Hasso, Harry Morgan. Excellent cast carries off this tale of former convict snafuing a robbery syndicate.

Outsider, The (1961) 108m. **½ D: Delbert Mann. Tony Curtis, James Franciscus, Bruce Bennett, Gregory Walcott, Vivian Nathan. Potentially gutsy account of American Indian Ira Hayes who was one of the marines to raise U.S. flag at Iwo Jima, becomes timid formula biography.

Outsider, The (1967) C-98m. TVM D: William Graham. Darren McGavin, Anna Hagan, Edmond O'Brien, Sean Garrison, Shirley Knight, Nancy Malone, Ann Sothern. Unusual private-eye whodunit with McGavin featured as David Ross, excon, hired by theatrical manager who suspects one of his employees of embezzlement. Good performances, fair mood. Average; pilot for TV series.

Over-Exposed (1956) 80m. *½ D: Lewis Seiler. Cleo Moore, Richard Crenna, Isobel Elsom, Raymond Greenleaf, Shirley Thomas. Flabby study of blackmail, with Cleo Moore vacationing from Hugo Haas spectacles . . . some vacation!

Over My Dead Body (1942) 68m. **½ D: Malcolm St. Clair. Milton Berle, Mary Beth Hughes, Reginald Denny, Frank Orth, William Davidson. Berle gives peppery performance in farfetched yarn about amateur sleuth who accidentally frames himself for murder.

Over the Edge (1979) C-95m. **½ D: Jonathan Kaplan. Michael Kramer, Pamela Ludwig, Matt Dillon, Vincent Spano, Tom Fergus, Andy Romano, Ellen Geer. Restless kids run toward violence in the affluent suburbs, in this well-made B picture. Barely released theatrically, but already developing a cult following.

Over the Hill Gang, The (1969) C-73m. TVM D: Jean Yarbrough. Edgar Buchanan, Andy Devine, Jack Elam, Gypsy Rose Lee, Kris Nelson, Rick Nelson, Pat O'Brien. Fair Western comedy detailing attempts by retired Texas Rangers to clean up corrupt town, first by using old skills, then "strategy." Good cast, adequate script, some clever situations. Average.

Over the Hill Gang Rides Again, The (1970) C-73m. TVM D: George McCowan. Walter Brennan, Fred Astaire, Edgar Buchanan, Andy Devine, Chill Wills, Lana Wood. Coming to aid old-time friend-turned-drunk, retired Texas Rangers find they've been made deputies of Waco. Standout performance by Astaire in otherwise mediocre comedy-Western. Average.

Over the Moon (1937-British) C-78m. *½ D: Thornton Freeland, William K. Howard. Merle Oberon, Rex Harrison, Robert Douglas, Louis Borell. Disappointingly bad comedy of country girl squandering inherited fortune. Interesting cast cannot save clinker.

Over 21 (1945) 102m. *** D: Charles Vidor. Irene Dunne, Alexander Knox, Charles Coburn, Jeff Donnell, Lee Patrick, Phil Brown, Cora Witherspoon. Zesty comedy of middle-aged Knox trying to survive in officer's training for WW2 service,

with help of wife Dunne; from Ruth Gordon's play.

Overboard (1978) C-100m. TVM D: John Newland. Angie Dickinson, Cliff Robertson, Andrew Duggan, Stephen Elliott, Skip Homeier, Lewis VanBergen, Michael Strong. Bored wife falls overboard while sailboating off Tahiti with disinterested husband, and bobs around for nearly two hours reliving their marriage in flashback. Average.

Overcoat, The (1959-Russian) 73m. **** D: Alexei Batalov. Roland Bykov, Y. Tolubeyev. Charming, fully realized rendition of Gogol's oft-filmed story about lowly clerk and the effect a new overcoat has on his life. Runs full gamut of emotions in simple, moving style; not shown here until 1965.

Overland Pacific (1954) C-73m. ** D: Fred F. Sears. Jock Mahoney, Peggie Castle, Adele Jergens, William Bishop. Mahoney is staunch railroad investigator trying to get at crux of Indian attacks on the trains.

Owen Marshall, Counsellor at Law (1971) C-100m. TVM D: Buzz Kulik. Arthur Hill, Vera Miles, Joseph Campanella, Dana Wynter, William Shatner, Bruce Davison. Hippie accused of murdering socialite wife; case becomes crucial to recently widowed lawyer (Hill) as hate campaign simmers in background. One-dimensional characters fill this boring pilot for TV series. Below average. Retitled A PATTERN OF MORALITY.

Owl and the Pussycat, The (1970) C-95m. *** D: Herbert Ross. Barbra Streisand, George Segal, Robert Klein, Allen Garfield, Roz Kelly. Broadway comedy about semi-illiterate prostitute and stuffy intellectual sometimes substitutes bombast for wit, but the laughs are there. The Streisand-Segal pairing really works, but some of their dialogue may not make it to TV.

Ox-Bow Incident, The (1943) 75m. **** D: William Wellman. Henry Fonda, Dana Andrews, Mary Beth Hughes, Anthony Quinn, William Blythe, Henry (Harry) Morgan, Jane Darwell, Frank Conroy, Harry Davenport. The irony and terror of mob rule are vividly depicted in this unforgettable drama about a lynch mob taking the law into its own hands, despite protests of some levelheaded onlookers. Based on Walter

Van Tilburg Clark's book; superb script by Dudley Nichols.

P.J. (1968) C-109m. ** D: John Guillermin. George Peppard, Raymond Burr, Gayle Hunnicutt, Brock Peters, Wilfrid Hyde-White, Coleen Gray, Susan St. James. Private-eye takes job bodyguarding the mistress of a tycoon. OK for those who'll sit through any film of this genre, but no big deal; TV print runs 101m, and cuts out much violence—including memorable subway death.

PT 109 (1963) C-140m. ** D: Leslie Martinson. Cliff Robertson, Robert Culp, Ty Hardin, James Gregory, Robert Blake. Standard action film based on true story of PT-boat and commander John F. Kennedy, neither here nor there; for younger audiences.

PT Raiders SEE: Ship That Died of Shame, The

Pacific Destiny (1956-British) C-97m. ** D: Wolf Rilla. Denholm Elliott, Susan Stephen, Michael Hordern, Gordon Jackson, Inia Te Wiata. Boring (but true) story of Arthur Grimble, who serves in South Seas for British Colonial service circa 1912, and tries to quell native disputes.

Pacific Liner (1939) 75m. ** D: Lew Landers. Chester Morris, Wendy Barrie, Victor McLaglen, Barry Fitzgerald. Formula programmer focusing on breakout of epidemic and mutiny aboard a ship; cast is better than the material.

Pacific Vibrations (1971) C-92m. **½ D. John Severson. Jock Sutherland, Rolf Aurness, Corky Carroll, Tom Stone, Mike Tabeling. Colorful surfing documentary.

Pack, The (1977) C-99m. **½ D: Robert Clouse. Joe Don Baker, Hope Alexander-Willis, Richard B. Shull, R. G. Armstrong, Ned Wertimer, Bibi Besch. Predictable but well-made story of resort islanders terrorized by abandoned dogs who have become a bloodthirsty pack.

Pack Up Your Troubles (1932) 68m. **½ D: George Marshall, Ray McCarey. Stan Laurel, Oliver Hardy, Mary Carr, James Finlayson, Charles Middleton, Grady Sutton, Billy Gilbert. Daffy duo are drafted during WW1; after some Army shenanigans they try to locate relatives of late pal's daughter. Good fun.

Pack Up Your Troubles (1939) 75m.

** D: H. Bruce Humberstone. Ritz Brothers, Jane Withers, Lynn Bari, Joseph Schildkraut, Stanley Fields, Leon Ames. Watch the Ritz Brothers' opening routine, then forget the rest of this WW1 hodgepodge, especially when Jane is focus of the film.

Pad and How to Use It, The (1966) C-86m. **½ D: Brian Hutton. Brian Bedford, Julie Sommars, James Farentino, Edy Williams. Peter Shaffer play THE PRIVATE EAR is basis for sex romp involving Bedford's attempt to become Sommars' lover.

Paddy (1970-Irish) C-97m. ** D: Daniel Haller. Milo O'Shea, Des Cave, Dearbhla Molloy, Judy Cornwell, Donal LeBlanc. Irish lover Cave tries to juggle varied sexual encounters with uninspired home life in ordinary comedy-drama.

Pagan Love Song (1950) C-76m. ** D: Robert Alton. Esther Williams, Howard Keel, Minna Gombell, Rita Moreno. Stale MGM musical; Keel goes to Tahiti, romances Williams.

Pagans, The (1958-Italian) 80m. *½ D: Ferrucio Cereo. Pierre Cressoy, Helen Remy, Vittorio Sanipoli, Luigi Tosi, Franco Fabrizi. Uninspired costumer set in Rome, with the Spanish invaders ramming the city walls.

Page Miss Glory (1935) 90m. **½ D: Mervyn LeRoy. Marion Davies, Pat O'Brien, Dick Powell, Mary Astor, Frank McHugh, Lyle Talbot, Patsy Kelly, Allen Jenkins, Barton MacLane. Fine cast overshadows Davies in this amiable spoof of publicity stunts, with con-man O'Brien winning beauty contest with composite photograph of nonexistent girl.

Paid (1931) 80m. **½ D: Sam Wood. Joan Crawford, Kent Douglass (Douglass Montgomery), Robert Armstrong, Marie Prevost, John Miljan, Polly Moran. Not-bad early Crawford. Innocent girl sent to prison; she hardens and seeks revenge. Remade as WITHIN THE LAW.

Paid in Full (1950) 105m. **½ D: William Dieterle. Robert Cummings, Lizabeth Scott, Diana Lynn, Eve Arden. Turgid soaper involving sisters Scott and Lynn both in love with Cummings.

Paid to Kill (1954-British) 70m. ** D: Montgomery Tully. Dane Clark, Paul Carpenter, Thea Gregory, Anthony Forwood. Oft-told premise of man who hires hood to kill him for insurance and changes his mind.

Paint Your Wagon (1969) C-166m. *** D: Joshua Logan. Lee Marvin, Clint Eastwood, Jean Seberg, Harve Presnell, Ray Walston, Tom Ligon, Alan Dexter. Splashy, expensive musical from Lerner-Loewe play about gold-rush days in No-Name City, California, where prospectors Marvin and Eastwood share one wife (Seberg) whom they bought at auction. Pure entertainment; witty, often risque script liable to be cut for TV. Presnell outshines cast of nonsingers with "They Call the Wind Maria."

Painted Hills, The (1951) C-65m. **½ D: Howard F. Kress. Paul Kelly, Bruce Cowling, Gary Gray, Art Smith. Nicely photographed Lassie tale set in 1870s West.

Painted Veil, The (1934) 83m. **½ D: Richard Boleslawsky. Greta Garbo, Herbert Marshall, George Brent, Warner Oland, Jean Hersholt. Set in mysterious Orient, film tells Maugham's story of unfaithful wife mending her ways. Mundane script uplifted by Garbo's personality, supported by Marshall as her husband, Brent as her lover. Remade as THE SEVENTH SIN.

Painting the Clouds with Sunshine (1951) C-87m. ** D: David Butler. Dennis Morgan, Virginia Mayo, Gene Nelson, Lucille Norman, Virginia Gibson, Tom Conway. Lukewarm musical of trio of gold-diggers in Las Vegas searching for rich husbands, a mild reworking of an old musical formula.

Paisan (1947-Italian) 90m. ***½ D: Roberto Rossellini. Carmela Sazio, Gar Moore, Robert van Loon, Maria Michi, Bill Tubbs, Carla Pisacane, Harriet White. Stark realism via six vignettes of effect of Allied soldiers in WW2 Italy; largely unprofessional cast.

Pajama Game, The (1957) C-101m. *** D: George Abbott and Stanley Donen. Doris Day, John Raitt, Carol Haney, Eddie Foy, Jr., Barbara Nichols, Reta Shaw. Rousing movie version of Broadway musical, with Day a joy as the head of factory grievance's committee and Raitt the foreman. Songs by Richard Adler and Jerry Ross.

Pajama Party (1964) C-85m. **½ D: Don Weis. Tommy Kirk, Annette Funicello, Elsa Lanchester, Buster Keaton, Dorothy Lamour, Harvey Lembeck. Mild mixture of sci-fi and beach party shenanigans; notable only for supporting veteran cast.

Pal Joey (1957) C-111m. *** D: George Sidney. Rita Hayworth, Frank Sinatra, Kim Novak, Barbara Nichols, Elizabeth Patterson, Bobby Sherwood. Heel-hero of Rodgers and Hart's musical becomes a flippant nice guy who seeks to build a sleek nightclub in Frisco. Hayworth and Novak battle over Frank with diverting results. Songs: "Bewitched, Bothered, and Bewildered," "Small Hotel," "My Funny Valentine," "The Lady Is a Tramp," etc.

Paleface, The (1948) C-91m. *** D: Norman Z. McLeod. Bob Hope, Jane Russell, Robert Armstrong, Iris Adrian, Robert Watson, Jack Searle. Enjoyable Western-comedy with timid Bob backed up by sharpshooting Russell in gunfighting encounters; Oscar-winning song "Buttons and Bows." Remade as THE SHAKIEST GUN IN THE WEST.

Palm Beach Story, The (1942) 90m. ***½ D: Preston Sturges. Claudette Colbert, Joel McCrea, Mary Astor, Rudy Vallee, William Demarest, Jack Norton, Franklin Pangborn, Jimmy Conlin. Hilarious screwball comedy with Claudette running away from hubby McCrea, landing in Palm Beach with nutty millionairess Astor and her bumbling brother Vallee, who steals the film from everyone.

Palm Springs Weekend (1963) C-100m. **½ D: Norman Taurog. Troy Donahue, Connie Stevens, Stefanie Powers, Robert Conrad, Ty Hardin, Jack Weston, Andrew Duggan. Cast tries to play teen-agers; yarn of group on a spree in resort town is mostly predictable.

Palmy Days (1931) 77m. **½ D: A. Edward. Sutherland. Eddie Cantor, Charlotte Greenwood, Charles Middleton, George Raft, Walter Catlett. Elaborate early musical. Cantor romps through story of patsy for shady fortune-telling gang.

Palooka (1934) 86m. *** D: Benjamin Stoloff. Jimmy Durante, Stu Erwin, Lupe Velez, Marjorie Rambeau, Robert Armstrong, Mary Carlisle, William Cagney, Thelma Todd. Not much relation to Ham Fisher's comic strip, but delightful entertainment with Erwin as naive young man brought into fight game by flashy promoter Knobby Walsh (Durante).

Fine cast includes James Cagney's lookalike brother William, and has Schnozzola in top form.

Pan Americana (1945) 84m. ** D: John H. Auer. Philip Terry, Eve Arden, Robert Benchley, Audrey Long, Jane Greer. Another 40s gesture toward Latin-American goodwill. Romantic trivia of magazine writers visiting South American country.

Panache (1976) C-78m. TVM D: Gary Nelson. Rene Auberjonois, David Healy, Charles Frank, Charles Seibert, Amy Irving, John Doucette, Joseph Ruskin. Lavishly-produced swashbuckler send-up, mixing romance, swordplay, political treachery and pratfalls in 17th century France. The title serves as the name of the hero and the spirit of the movie. An unheralded dandy. Above average.

Panama Hattie (1942) 79m. **½ D: Norman Z. McLeod. Ann Sothern, Red Skelton, Rags Ragland, Ben Blue, Marsha Hunt, Virginia O'Brien, Alan Mowbray, Lena Horne, Dan Dailey, Carl Esmond. Successful Cole Porter musical (starring Ethel Merman) about nightclub owner in Panama, falls flat on screen. Porter's score mostly absent.

Panama Sal (1957) 70m. BOMB D: William Witney. Elena Verdugo, Carlos Rivas, Joe Flynn, Edward Kemmer. Lowjinks blend of poor comedy and flat songs.

Pancho Villa (1972-Spanish) C-92m. ** D: Eugenio Martin. Telly Savalas, Clint Walker, Anne Francis, Chuck Connors, Angel del Pozo, Luis Davila. Noisy but dull period piece has Savalas chewing up scenery in title role, Walker playing gun-runner on his payroll, and Connors as polo-playing military martinet. Hang on, though, for smashing climax as two trains collide head-on.

Pandora and the Flying Dutchman (1951-British) C-123m. **½ D: Albert Lewin. James Mason, Ava Gardner, Nigel Patrick, Sheila Sim, Harold Warrender. Slowly paced fantasy romance with Gardner encountering mysterious Mason who seems to have no future, just an endless past.

Pandora's Box (1928) 110m. **** D: G. W. Pabst. Louise Brooks, Fritz Kortner, Franz (Francis) Lederer, Carl Goetz. Hypnotic silent film stars legendary Brooks as flower girl who becomes protégé—then wife—

of newspaper editor, with bizarre and unexpected consequences. Striking sexuality and drama, with Brooks an unforgettable lulu.

Panic at Lakewood Manor SEE: It Happened at Lakewood Manor

Panic Button (1964) 90m. **½ D: George Sherman. Maurice Chevalier, Eleanor Parker, Jayne Mansfield, Michael Connors, Akim Tamiroff. Good cast wasted in amateurish production involving the making of a TV pilot in Italy that's supposed to flop so gangster producers will have legitimate tax loss.

Panic in Echo Park (1977) C-78m. TVM D: John Llewellyn Moxey. Dorian Harewood, Robin Gammell, Catlin Adams, Ramon Bieri, Movita, Tamu. Determined physician Harewood fights hospital authority and city government to trace cause of apparent epidemic. He's street-wise, the film's predictable. Average.

Panic in Needle Park, The (1971) C-110m. ***½ D: Jerry Schatzberg. Al Pacino, Kitty Winn, Alan Vint, Richard Bright, Kiel Martin, Michael McClanathan. Easily the best of many drug-abuse films made in the early 1970s. Spunky small-time crook and decent young girl get hooked on heroin and go straight downhill. Pacino and Winn are tremendous.

Panic in the City (1967) C-97m. ** D: Eddie Davis. Howard Duff, Linda Cristal, Stephen McNally, Nehemiah Persoff. Attempt by subversives to start World War 3 by detonating a bomb in L.A. has the aging Duff in a dizzy attempt to stop it.

Panic in the Parlor (1957-British) 81m. **½ D: Gordon Parry. Peggy Mount, Shirley Eaton, Gordon Jackson, Ronald Lewis. Broad but diverting humor about a sailor coming home to get married, and the chaos it causes all concerned. Originally titled SAILOR BEWARE!

Panic in the Streets (1950) 93m. *** D: Elia Kazan. Richard Widmark, Paul Douglas, Barbara Bel Geddes, Jack Palance, Zero Mostel. Taut drama involving gun-happy gangsters, one of whom is a carrier of disease, and the police-hunt to find him.

Panic in Year Zero (1962) 95m. **½ D: Ray Milland. Ray Milland, Jean Hagen, Frankie Avalon, Mary Mitchel, Joan Freeman, Richard Garland. Intriguing film about family that escapes atomic bomb explosion to find a situation of every-man-for-himself. Milland doubles as actor-director. Good cast, but loud, tinny music spoils much of film's effects.

Panic on the 5:22 (1974) C-78m. TVM D: Harvey Hart. Ina Balin, Bernie Casey, Andrew Duggan, Dana Elcar, Eduard Franz, Lynda Day George, Laurence Luckinbill, Reni Santoni. Passengers on a commuters' club car are terrorized by three toughs. Echoes of THE INCIDENT, done earlier and better. Average.

Pantaloons (1957-French) C-93m. **½ D: John Berry. Fernandel, Carmen Sevilla, Christine Carrere, Fernando Rey. Fernandel stars in this brisk little period-piece as a phony gay-blade intent on female conquests.

Panther Girl of the Kongo SEE: Claw Monsters, The

Panther Island SEE: Bomba on Panther Island

Papa, Mama, the Maid and I (1956-French) 94m. **½ D: Jean-Paul Le Chanois. Fernand Ledoux, Gaby Morlay, Nicole Courcel, Robert Lamoureux. Sometimes saucy sex comedy, fully explained by title tag.

Papa's Delicate Condition (1963) C-98m. **½ D: George Marshall. Jackie Gleason, Glynis Johns, Charlie Ruggles, Laurel Goodwin, Elisha Cook, Juanita Moore, Murray Hamilton. Amusing nostalgia of Corinne Griffith's childhood; Gleason dominates everything as tipsy railroad inspector father; set in 1900s. Oscar-winning song "Call Me Irresponsible."

Paper Chase, The (1973) C-111m. *** D: James Bridges. Timothy Bottoms, Lindsay Wagner, John Houseman, Graham Beckel, Edward Herrmann, Bob Lydiard. The pressures of Bottoms' freshman year in Harvard Law School are intensified when he falls for the daughter of his tyrannical prof. Bottoms is likable as the student, and Oscar-winning Houseman is outstanding as the professor (a role he repeated in the subsequent TV series). Fine Gordon Willis photography.

Paper Lion (1968) C-107m. *** D: Alex March. Alan Alda, Lauren Hutton, Alex Karras, David Doyle, Ann Turkel, John Gordy, Roger Brown. Funny film, loosely based on George Plimpton's book, about that writer's experiences when he becomes honorary member of Detroit Lions football team. Even non-football fans should enjoy this one, especially scenes with Karras. Look for Roy Scheider in small role.

Paper Man (1971) C-73m. TVM D: Walter Grauman. Dean Stockwell, Stefanie Powers, James Stacy, Tina Chen. College computer workers find themselves in eerie situation that began innocuously with credit card scheme. Excellent idea gone awry, thanks to rotten script, indifferent acting. Average.

Paper Moon (1973) 102m. **** D: Peter Bogdanovich. Ryan O'Neal, Tatum O'Neal, Madeline Kahn, John Hillerman, P. J. Johnson. Unbeatable entertainment, harking back to Damon Runyon-esque 1930s, as con man O'Neal unwillingly latches onto young girl (his real-life daughter) who's pretty sharp herself. Tatum made her film debut here, and won an Oscar for her scene-stealing work; Kahn is fun, too, as Trixie Delight.

Paper Tiger (1976-British) C-99m. ** D: Ken Annakin. David Niven, Toshiro Mifune, Hardy Kruger, Ando, Ivan Desny, Ronald Fraser. Lackluster tale of a plucky kidnapped lad (Ando) and his English tutor (Niven). Since the boy is the son of Japanese ambassador Mifune, Niven sees the chance to act out his many tales of heroism that have impressed the youngster. Tepid action involving political terrorism and Disney-style cuteness muck up the proceedings entirely.

Paperback Hero (1973-Canadian) C-94m. **½ D: Peter Pearson. Keir Dullea, Elizabeth Ashley, John Beck, Dayle Haddon. Local hockey hero and womanizer leads fantasy life as town gunslinger. Interesting misfire.

Papillon (1973) C-150m. *** D: Franklin J. Schaffner. Steve McQueen, Dustin Hoffman, Victor Jory, Don Gordon, Anthony Zerbe, Robert Deman. Henri Charriere—"the butterfly"—is determined to escape from Devil's Island, despite the odds, in this exciting adventure yarn. Extreme length and graphic realism work against its total success.

Parachute Battalion (1941) 75m. ** D: Leslie Goodwins. Edmond O'Brien, Nancy Kelly, Robert Preston, Harry Carey, Buddy Ebsen, Paul Kelly. Efficient WW2 programmer which gets a bit sticky with flag-waving.

Parachute Jumper (1933) 65m. **½ D: Alfred E. Green. Douglas Fairbanks Jr., Leo Carrillo, Bette Davis, Frank McHugh, Claire Dodd. Former flyers Fairbanks and McHugh strike up fast friendship with Davis, but all three are victimized by involvement with gangster Carrillo. Fast-moving, enjoyable Warner Bros. programmer.

Paradine Case, The (1948) 125m. **½ D: Alfred Hitchcock. Gregory Peck, Ann Todd, Charles Laughton, Charles Coburn, Ethel Barrymore, Louis Jourdan, Valli. Talk, talk, talk in complicated, stagy courtroom drama, set in England. Below par for Hitchcock.

Paradise Alley (1961) 85m. *½ D: Hugo Haas. Marie Windsor, Hugo Haas, Billy Gilbert, Carol Morris, Chester Conklin, Margaret Hamilton, Corinne Griffith. Grade-D mishmash about elderly moviemaker involved in amateur film production. Interesting only for veteran cast. Original title: STARS IN THE BACK YARD.

Paradise Alley (1978) C-109m. *½ D: Sylvester Stallone. Sylvester Stallone, Lee Canalito, Armand Assante, Frank McRae, Anne Archer, Kevin Conway, Joyce Ignalls. Stallone wrote and directed this Damon Runyonesque story of three none-too-bright brothers from the N.Y. tenements. Some nice moments lost in comic-book-level dramatics. Director Stallone clearly admires his star.

Paradise Connection, The (1979) C-100m. TVM D: Michael Preece. Buddy Ebsen, Bonnie Ebsen, John Colicos, Marj Dusay, Brian Kerwin. In this pilot to a post-BARNABY JONES project, Ebsen (who also produced it) is a Chicago lawyer who goes to Hawaii in search of his estranged son who, he learns, is involved in drug smuggling. Average.

Paradise for Three (1938) 75m. ** D: Edward Buzzell. Frank Morgan, Robert Young,* Mary Astor, Edna May Oliver, Florence Rice, Reginald Owen, Henry Hull. Strange story of American businessman trying to mingle with German people to discover how they live. Good cast helps fair script.

Paradise, Hawaiian Style (1966) C-91m. **½ D: Michael Moore. Elvis Presley, Suzanna Leigh, James Shigeta, Donna Butterworth. Rehash of Presley's earlier BLUE HAWAII, with Elvis a pilot who runs a charter service while romancing local dolls. Attractive fluff.

Paradise Lagoon SEE: **Admirable Crichton, The**

Parallax View, The (1974) C-102m. ***½ D: Alan J. Pakula. Warren Beatty, Paula Prentiss, William Daniels, Walter McGinn, Hume Cronyn, Kenneth Mars. Director-photographer-production designer team of "All the President's Men" gives this political thriller a brilliant "look" as reporter Beatty investigates a senator's assassination. Frightening story unfolds with each piece of evidence he uncovers. Gripping to the very end.

Paramount on Parade (1930) 102m. **½ D: Dorothy Arzner, Otto Brower, Edmund Goulding, Victor Heerman, Edwin Knopf, Rowland V. Lee, Ernst Lubitsch, Lothar Mendes, Victor Schertzinger, A. Edward Sutherland, Frank Tuttle. Jean Arthur, Clara Bow, Maurice Chevalier, Gary Cooper, Nancy Carroll, Leon Errol, Stuart Erwin, Kay Francis, Fredric March, Helen Kane, Jack Oakie, William Powell, Buddy Rogers, many others. Variety revue designed to show off Paramount Pictures' stars of early-talkie era; skits, songs, dance numbers of variable quality, generally fun. TV print runs 75 minutes, missing several sequences originally shot in color.

Paranoia (1969) C-91m. BOMB D: Umberto Lenzi. Carroll Baker, Lou Castel, Collette Descombes, Tino Carraro. Trash about sexy widow involved in various sexual encounters will no doubt be edited for TV.

Paranoiac (1963-British) 80m. **½ D: Freddie Francis. Janette Scott, Oliver Reed, Liliane Brousse, Alexander Davion, Sheila Burrell, Maurice Denham. Murder, impersonation, insanity all part of thriller set in large English country estate.

Paratrooper, The (1954-British) C-87m. ** D: Terence Young. Alan Ladd, Leo Genn, Susan Stephen, Harry Andrews. Minor Ladd vehicle involving special tactical forces and Ladd's guilt-ridden past. Original title: THE RED BERET.

Pardners (1956) C-90m. **½ D: Norman Taurog. Jerry Lewis, Dean Martin, Lori Nelson, Jackie Loughery, John Baragrey, Jeff Morrow, Agnes Moorehead, Lon Chaney, Jr. Vehicle is good excuse for above-par hijinks of Martin and Lewis on Western farm. Remake of RHYTHM ON THE RANGE.

Pardon Mon Affaire (1977-French) C-105m. *** D: Yves Robert. Jean Rochefort, Claude Brasseur, Guy

[582]

Bedos, Victor Lanoux, Daniele Delorme, Anny Duperey. Sprightly comedy about efforts of happily married Rochefort to meet and court a dazzling model he spots in a parking garage. Another enjoyable French farce from director Robert.

Pardon My French (1951-U.S.-French) 81m. **½ D: Bernard Vorhaus. Paul Henreid, Merle Oberon, Paul Bonifas, Maximilliene, Jim Gerald. Fluff of Oberon inheriting a mansion in France occupied by charming composer Henreid.

Pardon My Past (1945) 88m. *** D: Leslie Fenton. Fred MacMurray, Marguerite Chapman, Akim Tamiroff, William Demarest, Rita Johnson, Harry Davenport. Excellent tale of unsuspecting MacMurray, lookalike for famous playboy, incurring his debts and many enemies; fine comedy-drama.

Pardon My Rhythm (1944) 62m. ** D: Felix E. Feist. Gloria Jean, Evelyn Ankers, Patric Knowles, Bob Crosby. Naive minor musical set in ultra-wholesome high school, with Gloria the singing belle of the ball.

Pardon My Sarong (1942) 84m. *** D: Erle C. Kenton. Lou Costello, Bud Abbott, Lionel Atwill, Nan Wynn, Four Ink Spots, Virginia Bruce, Tip, Tap, Toe. A&C in good form as bus drivers who end up on tropical island, getting involved with notorious jewel thieves.

Pardon My Trunk SEE: **Hello Elephant**

Pardon Us (1931) 55m. **½ D: James Parrott. Stan Laurel, Oliver Hardy, Wilfred Lucas, Walter Long, James Finlayson, June Marlowe. L&H's first starring feature film is amusing spoof of THE BIG HOUSE and prison films in general; slow pacing is major debit, but many funny bits make it a must for fans of Stan and Ollie.

Parent Trap, The (1961) C-124m. *** D: David Swift. Hayley Mills, Maureen O'Hara, Brian Keith, Charlie Ruggles, Una Merkel, Leo G. Carroll, Joanna Barnes. Hayley plays twins who've never met until their divorced parents send them to the same summer camp; after initial rivalry they join forces to reunite their mom and dad. Attempt to mix slapstick and sophistication doesn't work, but overall it's fun. Erich Kastner's story filmed before as 1953

British film TWICE UPON A TIME.

Paris After Dark (1943) 85m. ** D: Leonide Moguy. George Sanders, Philip Dorn, Brenda Marshall, Madeleine LeBeau, Marcel Dalio. Tame anti-Nazi film with husband and wife on opposite sides of fence.

Paris Blues (1961) 98m. *** D: Martin Ritt. Paul Newman, Joanne Woodward, Diahann Carroll, Sidney Poitier, Louis Armstrong. Film improves with each viewing; offbeat account of musicians Newman-Poitier in Left Bank Paris, romancing tourists Woodward-Carroll.

Paris Calling (1941) 95m. *** D: Edwin L. Marin. Elisabeth Bergner, Randolph Scott, Basil Rathbone, Gale Sondergaard, Eduardo Ciannelli, Lee J. Cobb. Exciting story of underground movement in Paris to destroy Nazis occupying France, with topnotch cast.

Paris Does Strange Things (1957-French) C-86m. ** D: Jean Renoir. Ingrid Bergman, Mel Ferrer, Jean Marais, Elina Labourdette, Juliette Greco, Magali Noel. Beautifully photographed costume romance, with empty script and lifeless performances.

Paris Express, The (1953-British) C-83m. **½ D: Harold French. Claude Rains, Marta Toren, Marius Goring, Herbert Lom. Sturdy cast intertwined in tales of embezzlement, murder, and adultery aboard train heading for Paris.

Paris Follies of 1956 SEE: **Fresh From Paris**

Paris Holiday (1958) C-100m. **½ D: Gerd Oswald. Bob Hope, Fernandel, Anita Ekberg, Martha Hyer, Preston Sturges. Mixture of French and American farce humor makes for uneven entertainment, with Hope in France to buy a new screenplay.

Paris Honeymoon (1939) 92m. **½ D: Frank Tuttle. Bing Crosby, Shirley Ross, Edward Everett Horton, Akim Tamiroff, Ben Blue, Rafaela Ottiano, Raymond Hatton. Texan Crosby visits France planning to marry Ross, but meets native Franciska Gaal and falls in love with her.

Paris Model (1953) 81m. *½ D: Alfred E. Green. Eva Gabor, Tom Conway, Paulette Goddard, Marilyn Maxwell, Cecil Kellaway, Barbara Lawrence, Florence Bates. Lackluster vehicle for veteran actors, revolving around a dress and four women who purchase copies of same.

Paris Playboys (1954) 62m. D: William Beaudine. Leo Gorcey, Huntz Hall, Bernard Gorcey, Veola Vonn, Steven Geray. SEE: **Bowery Boys** series.

Paris Underground (1945) 97m. **½ D: Gregory Ratoff. Constance Bennett, Gracie Fields, George Rigaud, Kurt Kreuger, Leslie Vincent, Charles Andre. Well-acted story of American Bennett and Britisher Fields working in underground movement even while imprisoned in Nazi POW camp.

Paris Was Made for Lovers SEE: **Time for Loving**

Paris When It Sizzles (1964) C-110m. *½ D: Richard Quine. William Holden, Audrey Hepburn, Noel Coward, Gregoire Aislan. Labored, unfunny comedy defeats a game cast, in story of screenwriter and secretary who act out movie fantasies in order to finish script. Paris locations, cameos by Marlene Dietrich and other stars don't help.

Park Row (1952) 83m. *** D: Samuel Fuller. Gene Evans, Mary Welch, Herbert Heyes, Tina Rome, Forrest Taylor. Good, tough little film with newsman Evans starting his own paper, rivaling newspaper magnate Welch in 1880s New York.

Parole, Inc. (1949) 71m. ** D: Alfred Zeisler. Michael O'Shea, Evelyn Ankers, Turhan Bey, Lyle Talbot. Turgid independent cheapie with low-budget class, about crackdown on gangster infiltration of parole system.

Parrish (1961) C-140m. *½ D: Delmer Daves. Claudette Colbert, Troy Donahue, Karl Malden, Dean Jagger, Connie Stevens, Diane McBain, Sharon Hugueny, Madeleine Sherwood. Slurpy soaper is so bad that at times it's funny; emotionless Donahue lives with his mother (Colbert) on Jagger's tobacco plantation and falls in love with three girls there. Malden overplays tyrannical tobacco czar to the nth degree.

Parson and the Outlaw, The (1957) C-71m. *½ D: Oliver Drake. Anthony Dexter, Sonny Tufts, Marie Windsor, Buddy Rogers, Jean Parker, Bob Steele. Minor version of life and times of Billy the Kid.

Parson of Panamint, The (1941) 84m. **½ D: William McGann. Charlie Ruggles, Ellen Drew, Phillip Terry, Joseph Schildkraut, Porter Hall. Minor, offbeat Western with Terry as preacher in mining town, involved

in murder while reforming the community.

Part-Time Wife (1961-British) 70m. *½ D: Max Varnel. Anton Rodgers, Nyree Dawn Porter, Kenneth J. Warren, Henry McCarthy. Lumbering account of Rodgers loaning wife Porter to scoundrel friend Warren, who wants to make an impression; wooden farce.

Part 2, Sounder (1976) C-98m. ***½ D: William A. Graham. Harold Sylvester, Ebony Wright, Taj Mahal, Annazette Chase, Darryl Young. Excellent follow-up to SOUNDER, retaining the dignity and human values in the continuing tale of a proud family of Depression-era Southern sharecroppers.

Part 2, Walking Tall (1975) C-109m. ** D: Earl Bellamy. Bo Svenson, Luke Askew, Robert DoQui, Bruce Glover, Richard Jaeckel, Noah Beery, Jr. Tepid follow-up to ultra-violent movie about club-swinging Tennessee Sheriff Buford Pusser. Svenson now takes the role of the one-man crusader against organized crime, but makes him come off like a standard TV hero rather than a real-life character.

Party, The (1968) C-99m. *** D: Blake Edwards. Peter Sellers, Claudine Longet, Marge Champion, Denny Miller, Gavin McLeod. Side-splitting gags highlight loosely structured film about chic Hollywood party attended by bumbling Indian actor (Sellers). Doesn't hold up to the very end, but has some memorable set-pieces.

Party Crashers, The (1958) 78m. *½ D: Bernard Girard. Mark Damon, Bobby Driscoll, Connie Stevens, Frances Farmer. Sleazy goings-on of teen-age gangs who become involved in reckless mayhem.

Party Girl (1958) C-99m. *** D: Nicholas Ray. Robert Taylor, Cyd Charisse, Lee J. Cobb, John Ireland, Kent Smith. Crooked lawyer (Taylor) and showgirl (Charisse) try to break free from Chicago mob life. Raw, violent period drama; Ray's stylish treatment has won this film a cult following.

Party's Over, The (1966-British) 94m. ** D: Guy Hamilton. Oliver Reed, Ann Lynn, Clifford David, Louise Sorel, Eddie Albert. Sordid drama of wealthy American girl becoming involved with group of aimless London youths, with tragic results.

Passage, The (1979-British) C-99m.

**½ D: J. Lee Thompson. Anthony Quinn, James Mason, Malcolm McDowell, Patricia Neal, Kay Lenz, Christopher Lee, Paul Clemens, Michael Lonsdale, Marcel Bozzuffi. Trashy WW2 story of Basque guide Quinn helping chemist Mason and his family escape over the Pyrenees with Nazi fanatic McDowell in hot pursuit. McDowell's campy performance must be seen to be disbelieved.

Passage to Marseilles (1944) 110m. **½ D: Michael Curtiz. Humphrey Bogart, Michele Morgan, Claude Rains, Philip Dorn, Sydney Greenstreet, Peter Lorre, George Tobias, Helmut Dantine, John Loder, Eduardo Ciannelli. WW2 Devil's Island escape film marred by flashback-within-flashback confusion. Disappointing for such a fine cast, but still good.

Passage West (1951) C-80m. *½ D: Lewis R. Foster. John Payne, Dennis O'Keefe, Arleen Whelan, Mary Beth Hughes, Frank Faylen, Dooley Wilson. Outlaws join up with wagon train with predictable results.

Passenger, The (1975-Italian) C-119m. **½ D: Michelangelo Antonioni. Jack Nicholson, Maria Schneider, Jenny Runacre, Ian Hendry, Stephen Berkoff, Ambrose Bia. Enigmatic narrative about dissatisfied TV reporter on assignment in Africa who exchanges identities with an Englishman who has died suddenly in a hotel room. Some found this brilliant; judge for yourself.

Passion (1954) C-84m. **½ D: Allan Dwan. Cornel Wilde, Yvonne De Carlo, Raymond Burr, Lon Chaney, John Qualen. Picturesque tale of old California, with Wilde the outlaw seeking revenge for wrongs done to his family.

Passionate Friends, The (1949-British) 95m. **½ D: David Lean. Ann Todd, Trevor Howard, Claude Rains, Betty Ann Davies, Isabel Dean, Wilfrid Hyde White. Predictable love triangle among the upper classes, enhanced by strong cast and Lean's craftsmanship. Based on H. G. Wells novel.

Passionate Plumber, The (1932) 73m. ** D: Edward Sedgwick. Buster Keaton, Jimmy Durante, Irene Purcell, Polly Moran, Gilbert Roland, Mona Maris. Stilted adaptation of HER CARDBOARD LOVER as vehicle for Keaton, hired by Parisienne Purcell to make lover Roland jealous.

Truly funny moments are few and far between.

Passionate Sentry, The (1952-British) 84m. ** D: Anthony Kimmins. Nigel Patrick, Peggy Cummins, Valerie Hobson, George Cole, A. E. Matthews, Anthony Bushell. Wispy romantic comedy about madcap gal who falls in love with a guard at Buckingham Palace. Retitled: WHO GOES THERE?

Passionate Thief, The (1960-Italian) 105m. **½ D: Mario Monicelli. Anna Magnani, Toto, Ben Gazzara, Fred Clark, Edy Vessel. Offbeat serio-comedy with Magnani a film extra, Gazzara a pickpocket, Toto an unemployed actor—all meshed together in a minor tale of love and larceny.

Passport to Adventure SEE: Passport to Destiny

Passport to China (1961-British) C-75m. ** D: Michael Carreras. Richard Basehart, Alan Gifford, Athene Seyler, Burt Kwouk, Eric Pohlmann. Uninspired help-the-refugee-out-of-Red-China caper.

Passport to Destiny (1944) 64m. ** D: Ray McCarey. Elsa Lanchester, Gordon Oliver, Lloyd Corrigan, Gavin Muir, Lenore Aubert, Fritz Feld. Tidy programmer with Elsa a patriotic scrubwoman determined to eliminate the Fuehrer. Retitled: PASSPORT TO ADVENTURE.

Passport to Pimlico (1948-British) 85m. ***½ D: Henry Cornelius. Stanley Holloway, Margaret Rutherford, Betty Warren, Hermione Baddeley, Barbara Murray, Paul Dupuis. Salty farce of ancient treaty enabling small group of people to form their own bounded terrirtory in the middle of London.

Passport to Suez (1943) 71m. D: Andre de Toth. Warren William, Ann Savage, Eric Blore, Robert Stanford, Sheldon Leonard, Lloyd Bridges, Gavin Muir. SEE: Lone Wolf series.

Passport to Treason (1955-British) 70m. *½ D: Robert S. Baker. Rod Cameron, Lois Maxwell, Clifford Evans. Minor drama, with Cameron trying to solve homicide case for sake of friend.

Password is Courage, The (1963-British) 116m. *** D: Andrew L. Stone. Dirk Bogarde, Maria Perschy, Alfred Lynch, Nigel Stock, Reginald Beckwith, Richard Marner. Bogarde tops a fine cast in droll account of

British soldier's plot to escape from WW2 prison camp.

Pat and Mike (1952) 95m. *** D: George Cukor. Spencer Tracy, Katharine Hepburn, Aldo Ray, William Ching, Jim Backus, Carl Switzer, Charles Buchinski (Bronson), William Self. Hepburn is Pat, top female athlete; Tracy is Mike, her manager, in pleasing comedy, not up to duo's other films. Ray is good as thick-witted sports star.

Pat Garrett and Billy the Kid (1973) C-106m. ** D: Sam Peckinpah. James Coburn, Kris Kristofferson, Richard Jaeckel, Katy Jurado, Chill Wills, Jason Robards, Bob Dylan, Rita Coolidge. Boredom reigns supreme in retelling of Western saga of Sheriff Garrett going after his excrony Billy the Kid. Many familiar character actors can't breathe life into inexplicably dull film. Dylan's score equally unmemorable.

Patch of Blue, A (1965) 105m. *** D: Guy Green. Sidney Poitier, Elizabeth Hartman, Shelley Winters, Wallace Ford, Ivan Dixon, John Qualen, Elisabeth Fraser. Sensitive drama of blind girl (Hartman) falling in love with black man (Poitier); well acted, not too sticky. Winters won Oscar for her performance as Hartman's harridan mother.

Pather Panchali (1958-Indian) 112m. *** D: Satyajit Ray. Kanu Banerjii, Karuna Barnerjii, Subir Banerjii, Runki Banerjii. Unrelenting study of life in poverty-stricken Indian village; gripping, realistic. Music by Ravi Shankar.

Pathfinder, The (1952) C-78m. *½ D: Sidney Salkow. George Montgomery, Helena Carter, Jay Silverheels, Elena Verdugo, Chief Yowlachie. Low-budget version of James Fenimore Cooper tale of 1750s Great Lakes area, with Indian and French attacks on Americans.

Paths of Glory (1957) 86m. **** D: Stanley Kubrick. Kirk Douglas, Ralph Meeker, Adolphe Menjou, George Macready, Wayne Morris, Timothy Carey. One of the finest indictments of war ever produced. Superb acting by all. Forceful direction in powerful story of Army politics in WW1 France.

Patrick (1978-Australian) C-96m. *½ D: Richard Franklin. Susan Penhaligon, Robert Helpmann, Robert Thompson, Rod Mullinar, Bruce Barry, Julia Blake. Patrick's in a

comatose state after violently murdering his mum, but his psychokinetic powers are still intact, as the hospital staff soon discovers in this tacky thriller.

Patsy, The (1964) C-101m. ** D: Jerry Lewis. Jerry Lewis, Ina Balin, Everett Sloane, Keenan Wynn, Peter Lorre, John Carradine, Neil Hamilton, Nancy Kulp. Forced, unfunny combination of humor and pathos, much inferior to somewhat similar ERRAND BOY. Even first-rate supporting cast can't bail itself out.

Pattern of Morality, A SEE: Owen Marshall, Counsellor at Law

Patterns (1956) 83m. ***½ D: Fielder Cook. Van Heflin, Everett Sloane, Ed Begley, Beatrice Straight, Elizabeth Wilson. Trenchant Rod Serling drama of company power struggle, with bravura performance by Begley. Executive psychology of mid-50s is dated, but much better than similar EXECUTIVE SUITE.

Patton (1970) C-169m. **** D: Franklin Schaffner. George C. Scott, Karl Malden, Stephen Young, Michael Strong, Frank Latimore, James Edwards, Lawrence Dobkin, Michael Bates, Tim Considine. Milestone in screen biographies; Scott unforgettable as eccentric, brilliant General George Patton, whose temper often interferes with command during WW2. Malden equally impressive as General Omar Bradley in intelligently written, finely wrought biographical war drama. Winner of eight Oscars, including Best Film, Best Director, Best Story and Screenplay, Best Actor.

Paula (1952) 80m. **½ D: Rudolph Mate. Loretta Young, Kent Smith, Alexander Knox, Tommy Rettig. Young gives credibility to role of woman who repents for hit-and-run accident by helping injured child regain his speech.

Pawnbroker, The (1965) 116m. **** D: Sidney Lumet. Rod Steiger, Geraldine Fitzgerald, Brock Peters, Jaime Sanchez, Thelma Oliver, Juano Hernandez. Important, engrossing film shot on location in New York. Steiger is excellent as Sol Nazerman, a Jewish pawnbroker in Harlem who lives in a sheltered world with haunting memories of Nazi prison camps.

Pawnee (1957) C-80m. ** D: George Waggner. George Montgomery, Bill Williams, Lola Albright, Francis J.

McDonald, Raymond Hatton. Pat Western about Indian-raised white man with conflicting loyalties.

Pay or Die (1960) 110m. **½ D: Richard Wilson. Ernest Borgnine, Zohra Lampert, Al Austin, John Duke, Robert Ellenstein, Franco Corsaro, Mario Siletti. Above-par, flavorful account of Mafia activities in 1910s N.Y.C.; sturdy performances.

Payday (1973) C-103m. ***½ D: Daryl Duke. Rip Torn, Ahna Capri, Elayne Heilveil, Cliff Emmich, Michael C. Gwynne. Being on the road with country-singer Torn is truly an experience; very well done. Engrossing film with excellent acting, fine script.

Payment Deferred (1932) 75m. *** D: Lothar Mendes. Charles Laughton, Maureen O'Sullivan, Dorothy Peterson, Verree Teasdale, Ray Milland, Billy Bevan. Laughton is memorable as meek man who inadvertently gets involved in murder. Excellent melodrama with fine supporting cast.

Payment on Demand (1951) 90m. *** D: Curtis Bernhardt. Bette Davis, Barry Sullivan, Peggie Castle, Jane Cowl, Kent Taylor, Betty Lynn, John Sutton, Frances Dee, Otto Kruger. Well-handled chronicle of Davis-Sullivan marriage, highlighting events which lead to divorce.

Payroll (1961-British) 94m. **½ D: Sidney Hayers. Michael Craig, Francoise Prevost, Billie Whitelaw, William Lucas, Kenneth Griffith, Tom Bell. Well-handled account involving widow of payroll guard tracking down culprits.

Peace Killers, The (1971) C-88m. *½ D: Douglas Schwartz. Clint Ritchie, Jesse Walton, Paul Prokop, Darlene Duralia. Motorcycle hoods ravage peaceful commune like Attila the Hun. Sick, Sick, Sick.

Peacemaker, The (1956) 82m. ** D: Ted Post. James Mitchell, Rosemarie Bowe, Robert Armstrong, Jan Merlin, Dorothy Patrick, Jess Barker, Hugh Sanders. Ex-gunslinger, now clergyman, tries to clean up the town.

Pearl, The (1948) 77m. ***½ D: Emilio Fernandez. Pedro Armendariz, Maria Elena Marques. Mexican-filmed John Steinbeck tale of poor fisherman whose life is unhappily altered by finding valuable pearl; subtle and poignant.

Pearl of Death, The (1944) 69m. D: Roy William Neill. Basil Rathbone, Nigel Bruce, Evelyn Ankers, Miles Mander, Dennis Hoey, Rondo Hatton, Richard Nugent, Mary Gordon, Holmes Herbert. SEE: **Sherlock Holmes** series.

Pearl of the South Pacific (1955) C-86m. *½ D: Allan Dwan. Virginia Mayo, Dennis Morgan, David Farrar, Murvyn Vye. Dud of a film trying to be exotic, intriguing; just a boring murder tale.

Peck's Bad Boy (1921) 51m. *** D: Sam Wood. Jackie Coogan, Wheeler Oakman, Doris May, Raymond Hatton, Lillian Leighton. Still-fresh and enjoyable vehicle for child-star Coogan as young mischief-maker; clever card-titles written by humorist Irvin S. Cobb.

Peck's Bad Boy (1934) 70m. **½ D: Edward Cline. Jackie Cooper, Thomas Meighan, Jackie Searle, O. P. Heggie. Cooper is ideally cast in familiar tale of troublesome brat causing his parents endless problems.

Peck's Bad Boy With the Circus (1938) 78m. ** D: Edward Cline. Tommy Kelly, Ann Gillis, Edgar Kennedy, Billy Gilbert, Benita Hume, Spanky MacFarland, Grant Mitchell. Standard circus story slanted for kiddies. Kennedy and Gilbert wrap this one up.

Pedestrian, The (1974-German) C-97m. ***½ D: Maximilian Schell. Gustav Rudolf Sellner, Peter Hall, Maximilian Schell, Gila von Weitershausen, Elisabeth Bergner. Excellent award-winner examines death and guilt, when successful industrialist Sellner is revealed to have been a Nazi officer who participated in the slaughter of a Greek village. Veteran actresses Bergner, Francoise Rosay, Lil Dagover and Peggy Ashcroft are in one scene.

Peeper (1975) C-87m. *½ D: Peter Hyams. Michael Caine, Natalie Wood, Kitty Winn, Thayer David, Liam Dunn, Dorothy Adams. Tepid take-off of 40s detective dramas with Caine becoming involved with a weird family while trying to locate the long-lost daughter of his client.

Peeping Tom (1960-British) 109m. *** D: Michael Powell. Carl Boehm, Moira Shearer, Anna Massey. Maxine Audley, Brenda Bruce, Martin Miller. Sensational film—denounced in 1960—has developed a fervent following in recent years; personal feelings will dictate your reaction to strong, sick story of psychopathic murderer who photographs his victims at the moment of death.

Peggy (1950) C-77m. **½ D: Frederick de Cordova. Diana Lynn, Charles Coburn, Charlotte Greenwood, Rock Hudson, Jerome Cowan, Barbara Lawrence. Lightweight comedy of sisters Lynn and Lawrence entered in Rose Bowl Parade beauty contest.

Peking Express (1951) 95m. **½ D: William Dieterle. Joseph Cotten, Corinne Calvet, Edmund Gwenn, Marvin Miller, Benson Fong. Remake of SHANGHAI EXPRESS lacks flavor or distinction. Cotten is the doctor and Calvet the shady lady he encounters on train.

Penalty, The (1941) 81m. ** D: Harold S. Bucquet. Edward Arnold, Lionel Barrymore, Marsha Hunt, Robert Sterling, Gene Reynolds, Emma Dunn, Veda Ann Borg. Unengrossing mystery-drama of F.B.I. agent's scheme to catch gangster by using his son for bait. Good cast in dull script.

Pendulum (1969) C-106m. **½ D: George Schaefer. George Peppard, Jean Seberg, Richard Kiley, Charles McGraw, Madeleine Sherwood, Robert F. Lyons, Marj Dusay. Half-baked whodunit has intriguing aspects but leaves too many loose ends, as police captain Peppard is suddenly accused of murder. Smoothly done, with flashy role for Sherwood as mother of young criminal, good score by Walter Scharf, but no great shakes.

Penelope (1966) C-97m. *½ D: Arthur Hiller. Natalie Wood, Ian Bannen, Dick Shawn, Peter Falk, Jonathan Winters, Lila Kedrova, Lou Jacobi. Neglected Nat robs her husband's bank of $60,000 in this quite unfunny comedy; Winters' bit lasts only three minutes.

Penguin Pool Murder, The (1932) 70m. *** D: George Archainbaud. Edna May Oliver, James Gleason, Mae Clarke, Robert Armstrong, Donald Cook. Cop Gleason and schoolteacher Oliver team up to solve unusual murder in entertaining film that launched short-lived series.

Pennies from Heaven (1936) 90m. ** D: Norman Z. McLeod. Bing Crosby, Edith Fellows, Madge Evans, Louis Armstrong, Donald Meek. Title tune is chief asset of OK Crosby vehicle about a drifter who befriends or-

phaned girl (Fellows) and her grandfather (Meek).

Penny Princess (1951-British) C-91m. *** D: Val Guest. Dirk Bogarde, Yolande Donlan, Fletcher Lightfoot, Kynaston Reeves. Charming froufrou of American Donlan going to Europe to collect inheritance of small principality, and Bogarde who courts her.

Penny Serenade (1941) 125m. ***½ D: George Stevens. Irene Dunne, Cary Grant, Beulah Bondi, Edgar Buchanan, Ann Doran, Eva Lee Kuney. Couple adopts child after their baby dies in attempt to find happiness. Soapy drama extremely well acted.

Penrod and His Twin Brother (1938) 63m. ** D: William McGann. Billy Mauch, Bobby Mauch, Frank Craven, Spring Byington, Charles Halton, Claudia Coleman. Penrod gets blamed for something he didn't do; answer is his lookalike who's really guilty. Vaguely captures 1900s Midwest America.

Penrod and Sam (1937) 64m. **½ D: William McGann. Billy Mauch, Frank Craven, Spring Byington, Craig Reynolds, Bernice Pilot. Based on Booth Tarkington characters, family-style film relates tale of Mauch getting involved with bank robbers.

Penrod's Double Trouble (1938) 61m. ** D: Lewis Seiler. Billy Mauch, Bobby Mauch, Dick Purcell, Gene Lockhart, Kathleen Lockhart, Hugh O'Connell. There's a reward up for Penrod's return, but a lookalike is turned in instead. Satisfactory for younger audiences; based on Booth Tarkington characters.

Penthouse, The (1967-British) C-96m. *½ D: Peter Collinson. Suzy Kendall, Terence Morgan, Tony Beckley, Martine Beswick. Lurid thriller of adulterous couple whose "love nest" is invaded by two thugs who, by torture, bring out true nature of the pair.

People, The (1971) C-74m. TVM D: John Korty. Kim Darby, Dan O'Herlihy, Diane Varsi, William Shatner. Young teacher taking job in desolate area discovers she's got out-of-the-ordinary kids for students. Adaptation of Zenna Henderson novel leaves lots to be desired, but performances, script's uneven qualities and atmosphere still worthwhile. Above average sci-fi.

People Against O'Hara, The (1951)

102m. **½ D: John Sturges. Spencer Tracy, Pat O'Brien, Diana Lynn, John Hodiak, Eduardo Ciannelli, Jay C. Flippen, James Arness. Middling drama, with Tracy a noted criminal lawyer who repents for unethical behavior during a case.

People Next Door, The (1970) C-93m. *** D: David Greene. Eli Wallach, Julie Harris, Deborah Winters, Stephen McHattie, Hal Holbrook, Cloris Leachman, Nehemiah Persoff. Near excellent drama centering on two average suburban families, the Masons and the Hoffmans, and revelations concerning their children, themselves. Knowledgeable depiction of effects of drug-taking, believable dialogue, but cast doesn't seem just right.

People That Time Forgot, The (1977-British) C-90m. **½ D: Kevin Connor. Patrick Wayne, Doug McClure, Sarah Douglas, Dana Gillespie, Thorley Walters, Shane Rimmer. OK sequel to "The Land That Time Forgot." Wayne leads a party onto a lost island in 1919 to find friend McClure, lost three years before. Based on Edgar Rice Burroughs' book, film has some effective monsters, though special effects are erratic.

People Toys SEE: **Devil Times Five**

People vs. Dr. Kildare, The (1941) 78m. D: Harold S. Bucquet. Lew Ayres, Lionel Barrymore, Laraine Day, Bonita Granville, Alma Kruger, Red Skelton, Paul Stanton. Diana Lewis. SEE: **Dr. Kildare** series.

People Will Talk (1935) 67m. **½ D: Alfred Santell. Mary Boland, Charles Ruggles, Leila Hyams, Dean Jagger, Ruthelma Stevens, Hans Steinke. Slim plot about married couple pretending to fight to teach daughter a lesson. Boland and Ruggles could read a newspaper and make it funny.

People Will Talk (1951) 110m. ***½ D: Joseph L. Mankiewicz. Cary Grant, Jeanne Crain, Finlay Currie, Walter Slezak, Hume Cronyn, Sidney Blackmer. Genuinely offbeat, absorbing comedy-drama of philosophic doctor Grant and patient Crain who becomes his wife. Fine cast in talky but most worthwhile film.

Pepe (1960) C-195m. BOMB D: George Sidney. Cantinflas, Dan Dailey, Shirley Jones, 35 guest stars. Incredibly long, pointless film wastes talents of Cantinflas and many, many others (Edward G. Robinson, Maurice Chevalier, etc.). This one's only if you're desperate.

Pepe Le Moko (1937-French) 86m. **** D: Julien Duvivier. Jean Gabin, Mireille Balin, Gabriel Gabrio, Lucas Gridoux. Gabin is magnetic (in role that brought him international prominence) as gangster who eludes capture in Casbah section of Algiers, until he is lured out of hiding by a beautiful woman. Exquisitely photographed and directed; faithfully remade the following year as ALGIERS, later musicalized as CASBAH.

Percy (1971-British) C-100m. BOMB D: Ralph Thomas. Hywel Bennett, Denholm Elliott, Elke Sommer, Britt Ekland, Cyd Hayman, Janet Key. This comedy is about the world's first penis transplant . . . but not the last.

Perfect Couple, A (1979) C-110m. *** D: Robert Altman. Paul Dooley, Marta Heflin, Titos Vandis, Belita Moreno, Henry Gibson, Dimitra Arliss, Alan Nicholls, Ted Neely. Offbeat but endearing romantic comedy about unlikely matchup (by computer dating) of straitlaced Dooley—under the thumb of his overbearing father —and singer Heflin—whose life is wrapped up with her familial rock group. Enjoyable music by Neely's ad-hoc group Keepin' 'em Off the Streets.

Perfect Friday (1970-British) 94m. *** D: Peter Hall. Stanley Baker, Ursula Andress, David Warner, Patience Collier, T.P. McKenna. Staid bank employee Baker decides to break loose, and plans daring heist, with beautiful Andress and her oddball husband Warner in cahoots. Entertaining caper movie with some delicious twists.

Perfect Furlough, The (1958) C-93m. **½ D: Blake Edwards. Tony Curtis, Janet Leigh, Keenan Wynn, Linda Cristal, Elaine Stritch, Troy Donahue. Diverting comedy of soldier Curtis winning trip to France, romancing military psychiatrist Leigh.

Perfect Gentlemen (1978) C-100m. TVM D: Jackie Cooper. Lauren Bacall, Ruth Gordon, Sandy Dennis, Lisa Pelikan, Robert Alda, Stephen Pearlman. Engaging bank heist tale involving three prison widows and a safe-cracking old lady. Above average.

Perfect Marriage, The (1946) 87m. ** D: Lewis Allen. Loretta Young, David Niven, Eddie Albert, Charles

Ruggles, Virginia Field, Rita Johnson, ZaSu Pitts. Niven's tired of wife Young; Young's tired of husband Niven; tired comedy-drama.

Perfect Strangers (1945) SEE: Vacation From Marriage

Perfect Strangers (1950) 88m. **½ D: Bretaigne Windust. Ginger Rogers, Dennis Morgan, Thelma Ritter, Margalo Gillmore, Paul Ford, Alan Reed. Rogers and Morgan are jury members who fall in love; engaging romance story.

Perfect Woman, The (1949-British) 72m. **½ D: Bernard Knowles. Patricia Roc, Stanley Holloway, Nigel Patrick, Irene Handl, Patti Morgan. Mild satire on well-meaning professor who decides to show up society by creating a woman with no social flaws.

Performance (1970-British) C-105m. *** D: Donald Cammell, Nicolas Roeg. James Fox, Mick Jagger, Anita Pallenberg, Michele Breton, Ann Sidney, John Burdon. Psychological melodrama about criminal on the lam and rock performer, and how their lives intertwine. Not for all tastes, but a bizarre and unique film; Jagger's performance of "Memo from Turner" a highlight.

Perilous Holiday (1946) 89m. *** D: Edward H. Griffith. Pat O'Brien, Ruth Warrick, Alan Hale, Edgar Buchanan, Audrey Long. Another good O'Brien vehicle, with troubleshooter encountering dangerous counterfeiting gang south of the border.

Perilous Journey, A (1953) 90m. ** D: R. G. Springsteen. Vera Ralston, David Brian, Scott Brady, Virginia Grey, Ben Cooper, Hope Emerson, Veda Ann Borg, Leif Erickson. Predictable but diverting Western of a ship manned by women who are heading to California to find husbands.

Perilous Voyage (1969) C-97m. TVM D: William Graham. Michael Parks, William Shatner, Michael Tolan, Louise Sorel. Boat and passengers held hostage by revolutionary. Stereotyped characters, nothing in script to make situation novel. Below average.

Perils from the Planet Mongo (1936) 91m. **½ D: Frederick Stephani. Buster Crabbe, Jean Rogers, Frank Shannon, Charles Middleton, Priscilla Lawson, John Lipson. Newly edited version of FLASH GORDON serial covering second half of original story. On Mongo, Flash, Dale Arden, and Dr. Zarkov contend with various of the planet's civilizations, eventually restore Prince Barin as rightful ruler, return to Earth. Uninspired handling of footage from this great serial.

Perils of Nyoka SEE: Nyoka and the Lost Secrets of Hippocrates

Perils of Pauline, The (1947) C-96m. *** D: George Marshall. Betty Hutton, John Lund, Constance Collier, Billy de Wolfe, William Demarest. Lively, entertaining musical-comedy purports to be biography of silent-screen heroine Pearl White, and isn't; energetic Hutton, good Frank Loesser songs, colorful atmosphere, and presence of silent-film veterans make up for it . . . until sappy denouement.

Perils of Pauline, The (1967) C-99m. ** D: Herbert Leonard, Joshua Shelley. Pat Boone, Terry-Thomas, Pamela Austin, Edward Everett Horton, Hamilton Camp. Cutesy expanded TV pilot, with Boone traveling around the globe seeking childhood sweetheart Austin; overlong, mainly for kids.

Perils of the Darkest Jungle SEE: Jungle Gold

Period of Adjustment (1962) 112m. *** D: George Roy Hill. Tony Franciosa, Jane Fonda, Jim Hutton, Lois Nettleton, John McGiver, Jack Albertson. Newlyweds (Fonda and Hutton) try to help troubled marriage of Nettleton and Franciosa, in this heartwarming comedy by Tennessee Williams. Engaging performers make the most of both comic and tender moments.

Permission to Kill (1975-British) C-96m. *** D: Cyril Frankel. Dirk Bogarde, Ava Gardner, Bekim Fehmiu, Timothy Dalton, Frederic Forrest. Fascinating expose of spying as dirty business. Bogarde, spy chief of "Western Intelligence Liaison," tries to prevent Fehmiu, head of "National Freedom Party" from returning to his dictator-controlled country. Beautiful, exciting production.

Perri (1957) C-75m. *** D: N. Paul Kenworthy Jr., Ralph Wright. Narrated by Winston Hibler. Unusual Disney film combines elements of BAMBI with True-Life nature photography, in a romanticized look at a squirrel through the cycle of four seasons in the forest. Based on Felix Salten's book.

Personal Affair (1954-British) **82m.**
**** D: Anthony Pelissier. Gene Tierney, Leo Genn, Glynis Johns, Walter Fitzgerald, Pamela Brown. Timid murder story involving suspected schoolteacher.

Personal Property (1937) **84m. **½**
D: W. S. Van Dyke, II. Jean Harlow, Robert Taylor, Una O'Connor, Reginald Owen, Cora Witherspoon. Taylor stiffly maneuvers through a series of masquerades, and finally courts Harlow in this MGM fluff. Remake of 1931 film THE MAN IN POSSESSION.

Persuader, The (1957) **72m. **** D:
Dick Ross. William Talman, James Craig, Kristine Miller, Darryl Hickman. Another Western involved with clergyman taking up arms to combat outlaws.

Pete 'n' Tillie (1972) **C-100m. **½**
D: Martin Ritt. Walter Matthau, Carol Burnett, Geraldine Page, Barry Nelson, Rene Auberjonois, Lee H. Montgomery, Henry Jones, Kent Smith. Slick comedy-drama has its moments as wry bachelor Matthau laconically woos and marries Burnett. Later turn to melodrama doesn't work, however, and supporting characters Page and Auberjonois simply don't make sense. Enough good points for innocuous entertainment.

Pete Kelly's Blues (1955) **C-95m.**
½ D: Jack Webb. Jack Webb, Janet Leigh, Edmond O'Brien, Peggy Lee, Andy Devine, Lee Marvin, Jayne Mansfield, Ella Fitzgerald, Martin Milner. Realistic to the point of tedium, this film recreates the jazz age of the 1920s and musicians involved. Cast perks goings-on, despite Webb. Peggy Lee, in a rare dramatic role, was nominated for an Academy Award.

Pete's Dragon (1977) **C-134m. **** D:
Don Chaffey. Helen Reddy, Jim Dale, Mickey Rooney, Red Buttons, Shelley Winters, Sean Marshall, Jane Kean. Heavy-handed Disney musical about orphaned boy and his only friend, a protective dragon. Endearing animated "monster" almost makes up for the live actors' tiresome mugging. Another try for MARY POPPINS magic that doesn't come close.

Peter Ibbetson (1935) **88m. **½** D:
Henry Hathaway. Gary Cooper, Ann Harding, John Halliday, Ida Lupino,

Douglass Dumbrille, Virginia Weidler, Dickie Moore, Doris Lloyd. Elaborate romantic drama of man who kills ex-sweetheart's husband, pays for it for the rest of his life.

Peter Lundy and the Medicine Hat Stallion (1977) **C-100m. TVM** D:
Michael O'Herlihy. Leif Garrett, Milo O'Shea, Mitch Ryan, Bibi Besch, Charles Tyner, John Anderson, John Quade. Teenaged frontier lad bocomes a rider for the Pony Express in the mid-1800s in this Disney-like adventure tale. Good family entertainment. Above average.

Peter Rabbit and Tales of Beatrix Potter (1971-British) **C-90m. ***½**
D: Reginald Mills. Beautiful ballet film with Royal Ballet Company, which tells of the adventures of several creatures by the pond; interesting version of Beatrix Potter tales.

Petrified Forest, The (1936) **83m.**
½ D: Archie Mayo. Leslie Howard, Bette Davis, Dick Foran. Humphrey Bogart, Genevieve Tobin, Charley Grapewin, Porter Hall. Robert Sherwood play, focusing on ironic survival of the physically fit in civilized world. Bogart is Duke Mantee, escaped gangster, who holds writer Howard, dreamer Davis, and others hostage at roadside restaurant in Arizona. Stagy, but extremely well acted and surprisingly fresh.

Petticoat Fever (1936) **81m. **½**
D: George Fitzmaurice. Robert Montgomery, Myrna Loy, Reginald Owen, Irving Bacon. Professionally handled comedy with lonely Montgomery (working for U.S. in northlands) romancing pilot Loy, whose plane crashes nearby.

Petty Girl, The (1950) **C-87m. **½**
D: Henry Levin. Robert Cummings, Joan Caulfield, Elsa Lanchester, Melville Cooper, Mary Wickes, Tippi Hedren. Mild comedy of artist Cummings falling for prudish Caulfield, with Lanchester stealing every scene she's in.

Petulia (1968) **C-105m. **** D:
Richard Lester. Julie Christie, George C. Scott, Richard Chamberlain, Shirley Knight, Arthur Hill, Joseph Cotten, Pippa Scott, Kathleen Widdoes. Brilliant film, set against mid-60s San Francisco scene, about recently divorced doctor and his relationship with unhappily married kook. Terrific acting, especially by Scott and Knight, in one of decade's top films.

Peyton Place (1957) C-162m. ***½ D: Mark Robson. Lana Turner, Hope Lange, Arthur Kennedy, Lloyd Nolan, Lee Philips, Terry Moore, Russ Tamblyn, Betty Field, David Nelson, Mildred Dunnock, Diane Varsi. Grace Metalious' sexsational novel receives Grade-A filming. Soaper story of small New England town life has virtue of strong cast, gorgeous photography, and Franz Waxman's score. Won many Academy Award nominations.

Phantasm (1979) C-87m. *½ D: Don Coscarelli. Michael Baldwin, Bill Thornbury, Reggie Bannister, Kathy Lester, Angus Scrimm. Two not very interesting brothers take on a flying object that punctures skulls, as well as a creepy cemetery worker whose ties are so thin he should be playing "Louie, Louie" at a 1963 prom.

Phantom from Space (1953) 72m. *½ D: W. Lee Wilder. Ted Cooper Rudolph Anders, Noreen Nash, Harry Landers. Dull sci-fi horror opus about invisible alien stranded on Earth.

Phantom Lady (1944) 87m. ***½ D: Robert Siodmak. Ella Raines, Franchot Tone, Alan Curtis, Thomas Gomez, Elisha Cook, Jr., Fay Helm, Andrew Tombes, Regis Toomey. First-rate suspense yarn of innocent man (Curtis) framed for murder of his wife. Secretary Raines seeks real killer with help of Curtis' best friend (Tone) and detective (Gomez).

Phantom of Crestwood, The (1932) 77m. *** D: J. Walter Ruben. Ricardo Cortez, Karen Morley, Anita Louise, Pauline Frederick, H. B. Warner, Sam Hardy, Skeets Gallagher. First-rate whodunit with crafty Morley calling together the men in her life for mass-blackmail scheme, resulting in murder. Eye-riveting flashback technique highlights solid mystery.

Phantom of Hollywood, The (1974) C-78m. TVM D: Gene Levitt. Skye Aubrey, Jack Cassidy, Jackie Coogan, Broderick Crawford, Peter Haskell, John Ireland, Peter Lawford, Kent Taylor, Corinne Calvet, Bill Williams. A movie buff's dream as a masked monster goes on a rampage against those selling his home, the MGM back lot. Silly but watchable. Average.

Phantom of the Opera, The (1925) 79m. ***½ D: Rupert Julian. Lon Chaney, Mary Philbin, Norman Kerry, Snitz Edwards, Gibson Gowland, John Sainpolis, Virginia Pearson, Arthur Edmund Carewe. Not so much a horror film as great melodrama, with Chaney as vengeful composer who lives in catacombs of the Paris Opera, kidnapping young Philbin as new protege. Famed unmasking scene still packs a jolt; several scenes originally filmed in color. One of Chaney's finest hours.

Phantom of the Opera (1943) C-92m. *** D: Arthur Lubin. Nelson Eddy, Susanna Foster, Claude Rains, Edgar Barrier, Jane Farrar, J. Edward Bromberg, Hume Cronyn. Not up to 1925 silent, but far ahead of 1962 remake. Too much emphasis on Eddy, but Rains is fine and film is colorful depiction of crazed inhabitant of Paris Opera catacombs.

Phantom of the Opera, The (1962-British) C-84m. ** D: Terence Fisher. Herbert Lom, Heather Sears, Thorley Walters, Edward DeSouza, Michael Gough, Martin Miller. Third version of horror classic, too slow-moving to be effective. There are occasional moments of terror, but generally it's a plodding film, not up to first two.

Phantom of the Paradise (1974) C-92m. *** D: Brian DePalma. Paul Williams, William Finley, Jessica Harper, George Memmoli, Gerrit Graham. Perennial opera fable is switched to rock setting with mildly amusing results. Graham generates some laughs as "Beef," a cowardly performer.

Phantom of the Rue Morgue (1954) C-84m. ** D: Roy Del Ruth. Karl Malden, Claude Dauphin, Patricia Medina, Steve Forrest, Merv Griffin, Erin O'Brien-Moore. Chiller lacks flavor of Poe story, and Malden hams it up too much. Remake of MURDERS IN THE RUE MORGUE.

Phantom Planet, The (1961) 82m. *½ D: William Marshall. Dean Fredericks, Coleen Gray, Tony Dexter, Dolores Faith, Francis X. Bushman. Dull low-budget sci-fi, distinguished only by Bushman's appearance as alien leader.

Phantom President, The (1932) 80m. ** D: Norman Taurog. George M. Cohan, Claudette Colbert, Jimmy Durante, Sidney Toler. Musical antique about presidential candidate, with lookalike entertainer (Cohan) falling in love with former's girl (Colbert). Interesting only as a curio, with forgettable Rodgers-Hart score.

Phantom Stagecoach, The (1957) 69m. *½ D: Ray Nazarro. William Bishop, Kathleen Crowley, Richard Webb, Frank Ferguson. Programmer Western about clashing stagecoach lines competing for business.

Phantom Thief, The (1946) 65m. D: D. Ross Lederman. Chester Morris, Jeff Donnell, Richard Lane, Dusty Anderson, George E. Stone, Marvin Miller, Murray Alper. SEE: Boston Blackie series.

Phantom Tollbooth, The (1970) C-90m. **½ D: David Monahan, Chuck Jones, Abe Levitow. Butch Patrick, and voices of Hans Conried, Mel Blanc, Candy Candido, Daws Butler, June Foray. Daydreaming youngster (Patrick, in live-action) travels to cartoon world of words, sounds, letters, music. OK adaptation of Norman Juster's book, but a bit heavy-handed.

Pharaoh's Curse (1957) 66m. ** D: Lee Sholem. Mark Dana, Ziva Rodann, Diane Brewster. Standard story of Egyptian expedition finding centuries-old monster guarding tomb.

Pharaoh's Woman, The (1960-Italian) C-87m. ** D: Giorgio Rivalta. Linda Cristal, Pierre Brice, Armando Francioli, John Drew Barrymore. Senseless epic set in Egypt, with Francioli combating Barrymore, pretender to the throne; ornate settings.

Phase IV (1974) C-83m. **½ D: Saul Bass. Nigel Davenport, Lynne Fredericks, Michael Murphy, Alan Gifford, Helen Horton, Robert Henderson. Ants are (again) attacking the world, but striking visual style of Bass, here making his feature debut, makes it easier to take the standard sci-fi characterizations.

Phenix City Story, The (1955) 100m. *** D: Phil Karlson. John McIntire, Richard Kiley, Kathryn Grant, Edward Andrews. Fast-paced exposé film, compactly told, with realistic production, fine performances as lawyer returns to corrupt home town, tries to do something about it. Sometimes shown without 13-minute prologue.

Phffft (1954) 91m. *** D: Mark Robson. Judy Holliday, Jack Lemmon, Jack Carson, Kim Novak, Donald Curtis. Saucy sex romp, with Holliday and Lemmon discovering that they were better off before they divorced.

Philadelphia, Here I Come (1975) C-95m. **½ D: John Quested. Donal McCann, Des Cave, Siobhan McKenna, Eamon Kelly, Fiedlma Murphy, Liam Redmond. Brian Friel adapted his own stage play about a young man and his alter ego who debate whether or not he should leave his dreary Irish home town and join an aunt in Philadelphia, U.S.A. Filmed on location with fine performances. An American Film Theatre Presentation.

Philadelphia Story, The (1940) 112m. **** D: George Cukor. Cary Grant, Katharine Hepburn, James Stewart, Ruth Hussey, John Howard, Roland Young, Henry Daniell, Virginia Weidler. Talky but brilliant adaptation of Philip Barry play about society girl who yearns for down-to-earth romance; Grant is her ex-husband, Stewart a reporter who falls in love with her. Entire cast is excellent, but Stewart really shines in his offbeat, Academy Award–winning role. Remade as HIGH SOCIETY.

Philo Vance Debonair detective Philo Vance, created by master novelist S. S. Van Dine (real name Willard Wright) enjoyed a long and varied screen career, in the guise of many different actors, in films made over a span of some twenty years by several different studios. The man most closely identified with the role was William Powell, who starred in the first three mysteries for Paramount: THE CANARY MURDER CASE, THE GREENE MURDER CASE, and THE BENSON MURDER CASE. While these very early talkies are somewhat stilted (particularly CANARY, which was completed as a silent film, then hastily adapted for sound) the whodunit angles are first-rate, as urbane Powell solves the bizarre N.Y.C.-based murders. Eugene Pallette was a fine foil as skeptical Sergeant Heath of the homicide squad, with E. H. Calvert as the N.Y.C. D.A. MGM interrupted this series with one of its own, THE BISHOP MURDER CASE, casting Basil Rathbone as Vance; though a clever whodunit, with the villain matching his crimes to Mother Goose rhymes, the film was all but done in by a snail-like pacing. Powell's last appearance as Vance was in Warner Brothers' THE KENNEL MURDER CASE, probably the best film in the series, brilliantly directed by Michael Curtiz, and also one of the most complex cases of all. None of the later Vance outings reached this peak of ingenuity and sophisticated filmmaking, although Warren William did well in THE DRAGON MURDER CASE at Warners. MGM's next duo cast Paul Lukas in THE CASINO MURDER CASE, and Edmund Lowe in THE GARDEN MURDER CASE; slickly done, they suffered from formula scripting, acting, and direction. Wilfrid Hyde-White starred in a British production of THE SCARAB MURDER CASE in 1936, but this one never found its way to America. Meanwhile, Paramount remade THE GREENE MURDER CASE as NIGHT OF MYSTERY, a routine "B" with Grant Richards, and Warren William returned for THE GRACIE ALLEN MURDER CASE, with Vance taking back seat to the comedienne, whose stupidity became a bit overpowering in this story written for her by Van Dine. Warners then redid THE KENNEL MURDER CASE as CALLING PHILO VANCE, another forgettable "B" with James Stephenson in the role. Philo Vance went into retirement until 1947, when cheapie company PRC brought him back for three final outings, all surprisingly good little whodunits: William Wright starred in PHILO VANCE RETURNS, and Alan Curtis was a deadpan hero in PHILO VANCE'S GAMBLE, and the best of all, PHILO VANCE'S SECRET MISSION, with perky Sheila Ryan as his sleuthing girlfriend. The character of Philo Vance, sophisticated and aloof, did not really fit the hard-boiled detective image of the 1940s and 1950s, so the character never appeared again onscreen, but his better outings, from the beginning and end of his film career, remain first-rate murder mysteries today.

Philo Vance Returns (1947) 64m. D: William Beaudine. William Wright, Terry Austin, Leon Belasco, Clara Blandick, Iris Adrian, Frank Wilcox.

Philo Vance's Gamble (1947) 62m. D: Basil Wrangell. Alan Curtis, Terry Austin, Frank Jenks, Tala Birell, Gavin Gordon.

Philo Vance's Secret Mission (1947) 58m. D: Reginald Le Borg. Alan Curtis, Sheila Ryan, Tala Birell, Frank Jenks, James Bell.

Phone Call from a Stranger (1952) 96m. *** D: Jean Negulesco. Bette Davis, Shelley Winters, Gary Merrill, Michael Rennie, Keenan Wynn, Evelyn Varden, Warren Stevens. Engrossing narrative of Merrill, survivor of a plane crash, visiting families of various victims.

Phony American, The (1962-German) 72m. **½ D: Akos Rathony. William Bendix, Christine Kaufmann, Michael Hinz, Ron Randell. Strange casting is more interesting than tale of a German WW2 orphan, now grown up, wishing to become an American, and a U.S. air force pilot.

Photo Finish (1957-French) 110m. ** D: Norbert Carbonnaux. Fernand Gravet, Jean Richard, Micheline, Louis de Funes. Strained comedy about con-men at work at the racetrack.

Picasso Summer, The (1969) C-90m. *½ D: Serge Bourguignon. Albert Finney, Yvette Mimieux. Boring, rambling tale of young couple so enamored by paintings that they take European vacation to find Picasso himself, wind up breaking up. Animated sequence midway can stand on its own without surrounding plot. Based on Ray Bradbury story.

Piccadilly Incident (1946-British) 88m. *** D: Herbert Wilcox. Anna Neagle, Michael Wilding, Michael Laurence, Reginald Owen, Frances Mercer. Familiar Enoch Arden theme of supposedly dead wife appearing after husband has remarried. Good British cast gives life to oft-filmed plot.

Piccadilly Jim (1936) 100m. **½ D: Robert Z. Leonard. Robert Montgomery, Madge Evans, Frank Morgan, Eric Blore, Billie Burke. Fine light-comedy players in P. G. Wodehouse story of father and son's romantic pursuits; ultimately defeated by overlength.

Pick a Star (1937) 70m. **½ D: Edward Sedgwick. Jack Haley, Rosina Lawrence, Patsy Kelly, Mischa Auer, Tom Dugan, Stan Laurel, Oliver Hardy. Mistaken as L&H vehicle, actually a Hal Roach production about small-town girl (Lawrence) hoping for stardom in Hollywood. Sappy story, bizarre musical production numbers, but guest stars L&H have two very funny scenes.

Pickup (1951) 78m. *½ D: Hugo Haas. Beverly Michaels, Allan Nixon, Howland Chamberlin, Jo Carroll Dennison, Hugo Haas. Drab little account of older man marrying Michaels, who plans to have him killed.

Pickup Alley (1957-British) 92m. *½ D: John Gilling. Victor Mature, Anita Ekberg, Trevor Howard, Eric Pohlmann. Lackluster account of federal agent's tracking down of dope-smuggling syndicate.

Pickup on 101 (1972) C-93m. ** D: John Florea. Jack Albertson, Lesley Warren, Martin Sheen, Michael Ontkean, Hal Baylor, George Chandler. Coed who wants to be liberated hits the road with rock musician and friendly hobo in this inoffensive melodrama.

Pickup on South Street (1953) 80m. ***½ D: Samuel Fuller. Richard Widmark, Jean Peters, Thelma Ritter, Richard Kiley, Murvyn Vye. Pickpocket Widmark inadvertently acquires top-secret microfilm, and becomes target for espionage agents. Tough, brutal, well-made film, with superb performance by Ritter as street peddler who also sells information. Remade as THE CAPE-TOWN AFFAIR.

Pickwick Papers (1954-British) 109m. *** D: Noel Langley. James Hayter, James Donald, Hermione Baddeley, Kathleen Harrison, Hermione Gingold, Joyce Grenfell, Alexander Gauge, Lionel Murton, Nigel Patrick. Flavorful, episodic version of Dickens' classic of sly actor whose underhanded enterprises pay off.

Picnic (1955) C-115m. ***½ D: Joshua Logan. William Holden, Rosalind Russell, Kim Novak, Betty Field, Cliff Robertson, Arthur O'Connell, Verna Felton, Susan Strasberg, Nick Adams, Phyllis Newman. Excellent film of William Inge play about drifter (Holden) who stops over in Kansas, stealing alluring Novak from his old buddy Robertson. Russell and O'Connell almost steal film in second leads, and supporting roles are expertly filled by Field, Felton, and the others.

Picnic at Hanging Rock (1975-Australian) C-110m. *** D: Peter Weir. Rachel Roberts, Dominic Guard, Helen Morse, Jacki Weaver, Vivean Gray, Anne Lambert. Moody, atmospheric film set in 1900 about three schoolgirls and their teacher who mysteriously disappear during an outing one sunny day. Eerie and richly textured by director Weir (THE LAST WAVE).

Picture Mommy Dead (1966) C-88m. **½ D: Bert I. Gordon. Don Ameche, Martha Hyer, Zsa Zsa Gabor, Signe Hasso, Susan Gordon. Hokey melodrama with Hyer newly married to Ameche, battling stepdaughter Gordon, possessed by late mother's spirit.

Picture of Dorian Gray, The (1945) 110m. ***½ D: Albert Lewin. George Sanders, Hurd Hatfield, Donna Reed, Angela Lansbury, Peter Lawford. Haunting Oscar Wilde story of man whose painting ages while he retains youth; young Lansbury chirps "Little Yellow Bird," Sanders elegant as sophisticated heavy.

Picture Snatcher (1933) 77m. *** D: Lloyd Bacon. James Cagney, Ralph Bellamy, Alice White, Patricia Ellis, Ralf Harolde. Fast, funny, exciting little film based on true story of daring photographer who got taboo photo of woman in electric chair.

Piece of the Action, A (1977) C-135m. **½ D: Sidney Poitier. Sidney Poitier, Bill Cosby, James Earl Jones, Denise Nicholas, Hope Clarke, Tracy Reed, Titos Vandis, Ja'net DuBois. Third Poitier-Cosby teaming casts them as con men obliged to help social worker set ghetto kids on the right track. Typical comic crime material offset by serious, sometimes preachy moments.

Pied Piper, The (1942) 86m. *** D: Irving Pichel. Monty Woolley, Roddy McDowall, Otto Preminger, Anne Baxter, Peggy Ann Garner. Woolley, not very fond of children, finds himself leading a swarm of them on chase from the Nazis. Entertaining wartime film.

Pied Piper, The (1972-British) C-90m. ***½ D: Jacques Demy. Donovan, Donald Pleasence, Jack Wild, Diana Dors, John Hurt. Chilling story of piper who rids evil hamlet of rats. While originally conceived as children's tale, director Demy succeeds in weaving grimy portrait of the Middle Ages.

Pied Piper of Hamelin (1957) C-87m. TVM D: Bretaigne Windust. Van Johnson, Kay Starr, Claude Rains, Jim Backus, Doodles Weaver. TV special of famed children's tale, musicalized, with Johnson in title role; uses haunting Edvard Grieg music for effective results.

Pier 13 (1940) 66m. *½ D: Eugene Forde. Lynn Bari, Lloyd Nolan, Joan Valerie, Douglas Fowley. Nolan is cop trailing waterfront crooks in this 20th Century-Fox programmer.

Pierrot Le Fou (1965-French-Italian) C-110m. ***½ D: Jean-Luc Godard. Jean-Paul Belmondo, Anna Karina, Dirk Sanders, Raymond Devos. Man who resumes love affair with old flame finds himself caught in web of intrigue and murder in this brilliantly directed melodrama.

Pigeon, The (1969) C-74m. TVM D: Earl Bellamy. Sammy Davis, Jr., Dorothy Malone, Pat Boone, Ricardo Montalban, Victoria Vetri. Private-eye driven by events to help old flame and daughter to retrieve diary and protect them from gang of criminals. Despite efforts of cast, singularly uninvolving drama, fair direction. Average.

Pigeons (1971) C-87m. *½ D: John Dexter. Jordan Christopher, Jill O'Hara, Robert Walden, Kate Reid, William Redfield, Lois Nettleton, Elaine Stritch, Melba Moore. Smug film about 24-year-old Princeton graduate who drives a taxi in Manhattan. The character is unattractive and film looks as if it were designed for stage, not screen. Also known as THE SIDELONG GLANCES OF A PIGEON KICKER.

Pigeon That Took Rome, The (1962) 101m. **½ D: Melville Shavelson. Charlton Heston, Elsa Martinelli, Harry Guardino, Baccaloni, Marietto, Gabriella Pallotta, Debbie Price, Brian Donlevy. Sometimes amusing WW2 comedy of Heston, behind enemy lines, using pigeons to send messages to Allies, romancing local girl.

Pigskin Parade (1936) 95m. *** D: David Butler. Stuart Erwin, Judy Garland, Patsy Kelly, Jack Haley, Johnny Downs, Betty Grable. Entertaining football musicomedy with fine cast; songs include: "It's Love I'm After," "You Say the Darndest Things." Garland's first feature film.

Pilgrimage (1933) 95m. **½ D: John Ford. Henrietta Crosman, Heather Angel, Norman Foster, Marian Nixon, Lucille La Verne, Hedda Hopper, Charles Grapewin. Unusual film, beautifully directed by Ford, about old woman who breaks up son's romance by sending him off to war

(WW1), living to regret it, but finding solace on visit to France. Delicately sentimental, it works up to a point, then goes overboard, but still has some memorable sequences.

Pillars of the Sky (1956) C-95m. **½ D: George Marshall. Jeff Chandler, Dorothy Malone, Ward Bond, Keith Andes, Lee Marvin, Sydney Chaplin. Chandler is apt as swaggering army officer fighting Indians, courting Malone.

Pillow of Death (1945) 55m. ** D: Wallace Fox. Lon Chaney, Brenda Joyce, J. Edward Bromberg, Rosalind Ivan, Clara Blandick. Another Chaney murder vehicle with lawyer Lon turning to murder to clear the way for his true love.

Pillow Talk (1959) C-105m. ***½ D: Michael Gordon. Doris Day, Rock Hudson, Tony Randall, Thelma Ritter, Nick Adams, Julia Meade, Allen Jenkins, Lee Patrick. Rock pursues Doris, with interference from Randall and sideline witticisms from Ritter. Imaginative sex comedy has two stars sharing a party line without knowing each other's identity. Fast-moving; plush sets, gorgeous fashions.

Pillow to Post (1945) 92m. ** D: Vincent Sherman. Ida Lupino, Sydney Greenstreet, William Prince, Stuart Erwin, Ruth Donnelly, Barbara Brown. Obvious WW2 comedy of salesgirl Lupino having soldier Prince pose as her husband so she can get a room; good cast saddled with predictable script.

Pilot No. 5 (1943) 70m. ** D: George Sidney. Franchot Tone, Marsha Hunt, Gene Kelly, Van Johnson, Alan Baxter, Dick Simmons. Sad waste of fine cast, as Tone takes on suicide mission and others recall his jumbled life.

Pimpernel Smith (1941-British) 122m. *** D: Leslie Howard. Leslie Howard, Mary Morris, Francis L. Sullivan, Hugh McDermott. Zesty updating of THE SCARLET PIMPERNEL to WW2, with Howard replaying the role of the savior of Nazi-hounded individuals. Retitled: MISTER V.

Pin-Up Girl (1944) C-83m. **½ D: H. Bruce Humberstone. Betty Grable, Martha Raye, John Harvey, Joe E. Brown, Eugene Pallette, Mantan Moreland, Charlie Spivak Orchestra. One of Grable's weaker vehicles, despite support from Raye and Brown; songs are nil, so is plot.

Pine Canyon Is Burning (1977) C-78m. TVM D: Chris Nyby III. Kent McCord, Diana Muldaur, Andrew Duggan, Richard Bakalyan, Megan McCord, Shane Sinutko. Family adventure film has McCord as a widowered fireman raising his two small children while operating a one-man fire-rescue station. Below average.

Pink Jungle, The (1968) C-104m. **½ D: Delbert Mann. James Garner, Eva Renzi, George Kennedy, Nigel Green, Michael Ansara, George Rose. Offbeat blend of comedy and adventure with photographer Garner and model Renzi involved in diamond smuggling while on-location in Africa. Film shifts gears too often, but provides lighthearted entertainment.

Pink Panther, The (1964) C-113m. **½ D: Blake Edwards. Peter Sellers, David Niven, Robert Wagner, Claudia Cardinale, Capucine, Fran Jeffries. Slickly made comedy caper about rival jewel thieves introduced Sellers as bumbling Inspector Clouseau, but like later entries in series, this one is labored and overdone. Beautiful Swiss scenery helps.

Pink Panther Strikes Again, The (1976-British) C-103m. ***½ D: Blake Edwards. Peter Sellers, Herbert Lom, Colin Blakely, Leonard Rossiter, Lesley-Anne Down, Burt Kwouk. Fifth PINK PANTHER may be funniest yet. Sellers' former boss (Lom) goes crazy, threatens to destroy the world with a ray-gun he has commandeered. Sellers' hilarious characterization as Inspector Clouseau is backed up by better-than-usual gags—with the usual number of pain-and-destruction jokes thrown in for good measure.

Pinky (1949) 102m. *** D: Elia Kazan. Jeanne Crain, Ethel Barrymore, Ethel Waters, Nina Mae McKinney, William Lundigan. Pioneer racial drama of Negro girl passing for white, returning to Southern home; still has impact, with fine support from Mmes. Waters and Barrymore.

Pioneer Builders SEE: **Conquerors, The**

Pioneer Woman (1973) C-78m. TVM D: Buzz Kulik. Joanna Pettet, William Shatner, David Janssen, Lance LeGault, Helen Hunt, Russell Baer. Frontier drama about joys and hardships of homesteading in Wyoming circa 1867. The Old West from the woman's viewpoint. Average.

Pipe Dreams (1976) C-89m. **½ D: Stephen Verona. Gladys Knight, Barry Hankerson, Bruce French, Sherry Bain, Wayne Tippit, Altovise Davis. Singing star Knight makes film debut in highly dramatic story set against Alaskan pipeline. Excellent location shooting. Soundtrack filled with songs by Knight and her group, the Pips.

Piranha (1978) C-92m. *** D: Joe Dante. Bradford Dillman, Heather Menzies, Kevin McCarthy, Keenan Wynn, Dick Miller, Barbara Steele, Belinda Belaski, Bruce Gordon. Fast paced, funny spoof of JAWS and countless 1950s sci-fi films; in jokes and campy supporting cast will make it particular fun for film buffs.

Pirate, The (1948) C-102m. *** D: Vincente Minnelli. Judy Garland, Gene Kelly, Walter Slezak, Gladys Cooper, Reginald Owen, George Zucco, The Nicholas Brothers. Judy thinks circus clown Kelly is really Caribbean pirate; lavish costuming, dancing, and Cole Porter songs bolster stagy plot. Kelly's dances are exhilarating, as usual.

Pirate and the Slave Girl (1961-Italian) C-87m. ** D: Piero Pierotti. Lex Barker, Massimo Serato, Chelo Alonso, Michele Malaspina, Enzo Maggio. Formula costumer with Barker the hero who sees the light of the true cause, helping benevolent pirates vs. wicked governor.

Pirate Ship SEE: **Mutineers, The**

Pirates of Blood River, The (1962-British) C-87m. ** D: John Gilling. Kerwin Mathews, Glenn Corbett, Christopher Lee, Marla Landi, Oliver Reed, Andrew Keir, Peter Arne. Earnest but hackneyed account of Huguenots fighting off buccaneers.

Pirates of Capri, The (1949) 94m. ** D: Edgar G. Ulmer. Louis Hayward, Binnie Barnes, Alan Curtis, Rudolph (Massimo) Serato. Below-average adventure film has Neapolitan natives revolting against tyrant. Lots of action but not much else. Filmed in Italy. Retitled: CAPTAIN SIROCCO.

Pirates of Monterey (1947) C-77m. ** D: Alfred L. Werker. Maria Montez, Rod Cameron, Mikhail Rasumny, Philip Reed, Gilbert Roland, Gale Sondergaard. Dull film of exciting period in history, the fight against Mexican control of California in the 1800s.

Pirates of Tortuga (1961) C-97m. ** D: Robert D. Webb. Ken Scott,

John Richardson, Letitia Roman, Dave King, Rafer Johnson. Lumbering costumer involving buccaneer Sir Henry Morgan.

Pirates of Tripoli (1955) C-72m. ** D: Felix E. Feist. Paul Henreid, Patricia Medina, Paul Newland, John Miljan, William Fawcett. Veteran cast tries to be lively in tired costumer, with colorful scenery the only virtue.

Pistol for Ringo, A (1966-Italian) C-97m. **½ D: Duccio Tessari. Montgomery Wood, Fernando Sancho, Hally Hammond, Nieves Navarro. Wood is the gun-shooting hero in Texas where he combats marauding Mexicans hiding out at a ranch.

Pit and the Pendulum, The (1961) C-80m. ***½ D: Roger Corman. Vincent Price, John Kerr, Barbara Steele, Luana Anders, Antony Carbone. Slick horror tale set right after Spanish Inquisition. Price thinks he is his late father, the most vicious torturer during bloody inquisition. Beautifully staged; watch out for that incredible pendulum . . . and bear with weak first half.

Pit Stop (1969) 92m. BOMB D: Jack Hill. Brian Donlevy, Richard Davalos, Ellen McRae (Burstyn), Sid Haig, Beverly Washburn, George Washburn. Donlevy runs racing organization that will stop at nothing to win, in extremely low-budget action pic.

Pitfall, The (1948) 84m. ***½ D: Andre de Toth. Dick Powell, Lizabeth Scott, Jane Wyatt, Raymond Burr, Ann Doran. Taut melodrama of happily married Powell regretting brief fling with shady Scott.

Pittsburgh (1942) 90m. ** D: Lewis Seiler. Marlene Dietrich, John Wayne, Randolph Scott, Louise Allbritton, Thomas Gomez, Shemp Howard. Big John loves the coal and steel business more than he does Marlene, which leaves field open for rival Scott. Slow-moving despite cast.

Place Called Glory, A (1966-German) C-92m. ** D: Ralph Gideon. Lex Barker, Pierre Brice, Marianne Koch, Jorge Rigaud. German-made Western with Karl May's recurring characters Winnetou and Old Satterhand. Plot killed by dubbing.

Place Called Today, A (1972) C-103m. *½ D: Don Schain. J. Herbert Kerr, Cheri Caffaro, Lana Wood. Violent political campaign includes several key murders and a lot of sex. For TV the murders will be in; count on the sex being out.

Place for Lovers, A (1969-Italian) C-90m. BOMB D: Vittorio De Sica. Faye Dunaway, Marcello Mastroianni, Caroline Mortimer, Karin Engh. One well-known critic called this "the most godawful piece of pseudo-romantic slop I've ever seen!" Love story about American fashion designer and Italian engineer marks career low points for Dunaway, Mastroianni, De Sica.

Place in the Sun, A (1951) 122m. *** D: George Stevens. Montgomery Clift, Elizabeth Taylor, Shelley Winters, Keefe Brasselle, Raymond Burr, Anne Revere. Ambitious film seems curiously dated already; remake of Dreiser's AN AMERICAN TRAGEDY derives most of its power from Clift's brilliant performance, almost matched by Winters as plain girl who loses him to alluring Taylor. Depiction of the idle rich, and American morals, seems outdated, and Burr's scenes as fiery D.A. are downright absurd. Everyone gets A for effort; six Oscars included Best Direction, Best Screenplay, Best Scoring, Best Cinematography (b&w).

Place of One's Own, A (1945-British) 92m. **½ D: Bernard Knowles. James Mason, Margaret Lockwood, Barbara Mullen, Dennis Price, Helen Haye, Ernest Thesiger. Well-made film about couple who buy "haunted" house, and young woman who becomes possessed by spirit of former owner. Weakened by low-key presentation, but kept going by good performances. Mason plays unusual role of older, retired man.

Plague of the Zombies, The (1966-British) C-90m. **½ D: John Gilling. Andre Morell, Diane Clare, Brook Williams, Jacqueline Pearce. Beautiful low-key photography and direction in fairly tense story of voodoo cult in Cornish village.

Plainsman, The (1936) 115m. *** D: Cecil B. DeMille. Gary Cooper, Jean Arthur, Charles Bickford, James Ellison, Porter Hall, Victor Varconi, Anthony Quinn. Big Western with Cooper as Wild Bill Hickok, Arthur as Calamity Jane, plenty of well-paced action, with offbeat romance tossed in.

Plainsman, The (1966) C-92m. *½ D: David Lowell Rich. Don Murray, Guy Stockwell, Abby Dalton, Bradford Dillman, Leslie Nielsen. Static remake of the Cooper-Arthur vehicle, that is dull even on its own.

Plainsman and the Lady, The (1946) 87m. ** D: Joseph Kane. William Elliott, Vera Ralston, Gail Patrick, Joseph Schildkraut, Andy Clyde. Wild Bill Elliott is tame in uninspiring saga of pony express pioneer battling slimy villains and winning lovely Ralston.

Plan 9 From Outer Space (1959) 79m. BOMB D: Edward Wood, Jr. Gregory Walcott, Mona McKinnon, Bela Lugosi, Lyle Talbot, Joanna Lee. Wacked-out sci-fi that isn't much of anything. Alien forces seek aid of human zombies. Retitled: GRAVE ROBBERS FROM OUTER SPACE. Lugosi died during production, and it shows.

Planet Earth (1974) C-78m. TVM D: Marc Daniels. John Saxon, Janet Margolin, Ted Cassidy, Diana Muldaur, Johana DeWinter, Christopher Gary. Sci-fi fun as future race of humans finds itself in combat with a sadistic matriarchy. Sequel to GENESIS II (1972), though less elaborate. Average.

Planet of Blood (1966) C-80m. **½ D: Curtis Harrington. John Saxon, Basil Rathbone, Judi Meredith, Dennis Hopper, Florence Marly. Space vampire brought to earth. Only thing that saves this one from the gutter is bizarre climax, if you can wait that long. Also titled QUEEN OF BLOOD.

Planet of the Apes (1968) C-112m. ***½ D: Franklin J. Schaffner. Charlton Heston, Roddy McDowall, Kim Hunter, Maurice Evans, James Whitmore, James Daly, Linda Harrison. Modern near-classic sci-fi. Heston one of group of surviving astronauts in shocking future world where apes are masters, humans slaves. Only liabilities: somewhat familiar plot, self-conscious humor; otherwise, a must-see. Rod Serling scripted from Pierre Boulle's novel, spawning a raft of follow-ups. Makeup created by John Chambers.

Planet of the Vampires (1965-Italian) C-86m. **½ D: Mario Bava. Barry Sullivan, Norma Bengell, Angel Aranda, Evi Marandi, Fernando Villena. Eerily photographed, atmospheric science-fantasy of spaceship looking for missing comrades on misty planet where strange power controls their minds. Also known as THE DEMON PLANET.

Planet on the Prowl SEE: **War Between the Planets**

Planets Against Us (1961-Italian-French) 85m. *½ D: Romano Ferrara. Michel Lemoine, Maria Pia Luzi, Jany Clair, Marco Guglielmi, Otello Toso. Human-like aliens come to earth and destroy everyone they touch. Pretty bad.

Platinum Blonde (1931) 90m. *** D: Frank Capra. Jean Harlow, Loretta Young, Robert Williams, Louise Closser Hale, Donald Dillaway, Walter Catlett. Snappy comedy about wisecracking reporter who marries wealthy girl (Harlow) but can't stand confinement of life among high society. Despite engaging presence of Harlow and Young, it's Williams' show all the way.

Platinum High School (1960) 93m. ** D: Charles Haas. Mickey Rooney, Terry Moore, Dan Duryea, Yvette Mimieux, Conway Twitty, Jimmy Boyd. Limp attempt at sensationalism, with Rooney a father discovering that his son's death at school wasn't accidental. Retitled: TROUBLE AT 16.

Play Dirty (1969-British) C-117m. *** D: Andre de Toth. Michael Caine, Nigel Davenport, Nigel Green, Harry Andrews, Aly Ben Ayed. British army captain leads group of ex-cons into the North African campaign in WW2; film invites comparison with THE DIRTY DOZEN and holds its own quite well.

Play Girl (1940) 75m. **½ D: Frank Woodruff. Kay Francis, Nigel Bruce, James Ellison, Margaret Hamilton, Mildred Coles. Francis is hip golddigger who teaches younger women how to fleece clients; offbeat programmer.

Play It Again, Sam (1972) C-87m. ***½ D: Herbert Ross. Woody Allen, Diane Keaton, Tony Roberts, Jerry Lacy, Susan Anspach, Jennifer Salt, Joy Bang, Viva. Delightful adaptation of Woody's own play about film buff haunted by Bogart in fumbling attempts to meet a girl, after his wife divorces him. More "conventional" than other Allen films, but just as funny.

Play It As It Lays (1972) C-99m. **½ D: Frank Perry. Tuesday Weld, Anthony Perkins, Tammy Grimes, Adam Roarke, Ruth Ford, Eddie Firestone. Film version of Joan Didion's best seller about neglected wife of self-centered film director is helped by Weld-Perkins casting. Story is believable enough, but rambles inconclusively.

Play It Cool (1962-British) 82m. *½ D: Michael Winner. Billy Fury, Michael Anderson, Jr., Dennis Price, Richard Wattis, Anna Palk, Keith Hamshere, Ray Brooks. Mild rock 'n' roll entry, with thin plot line of groovy group preventing a rich girl from going wrong.

Play Misty for Me (1971) C-102m. *** D: Clint Eastwood. Clint Eastwood, Jessica Walter, Donna Mills, John Larch. Well-done story of late night radio D.J. who gets involved in murder. Eastwood's first film as director; his frequent director, Don Siegel, plays Murphy the bartender.

Players (1979) C-120m. BOMB D: Anthony Harvey. Ali MacGraw, Dean-Paul Martin, Maximilian Schell, Pancho Gonzalez, Steve Guttenberg, Melissa Prophet. Aspiring tennis pro has to choose between forehand and foreplay when he falls for a "kept" woman. There's something wrong with any movie where Pancho Gonzalez gives the best performance.

Playgirl (1954) 85m. **½ D: Joseph Pevney. Shelley Winters, Barry Sullivan, Gregg Palmer, Richard Long, Kent Taylor. Winters is most comfortable in drama about girl involved with gangsters.

Playmates (1941) 94m. *½ D: David Butler. Kay Kyser, Lupe Velez, John Barrymore, May Robson, Patsy Kelly, Peter Lind Hayes. Poor musical "comedy" of Shakespearean actor teaming up with bandleader to pay back taxes. Film is unbelievably bad at times, only worth seeing for poor John Barrymore.

Playmates (1972) C-73m. TVM D: Theodore Flicker. Alan Alda, Connie Stevens, Doug McClure, Barbara Feldon, Tiger Williams, Severn Darden. Chance meeting of divorced men (Alda and McClure) slowly precipitates plan to check up on ex-wives. Fairly intelligent complications; cast seems to be enjoying themselves. Above average.

Plaza Suite (1971) C-115m. *** D: Arthur Hiller. Walter Matthau, Maureen Stapleton, Barbara Harris, Lee Grant, Louise Sorel. One of Neil Simon's funniest plays well-adapted to screen. Three separate stories about people staying in certain room at famed New York hotel, with Matthau in all three vignettes. Best

one is the last, with Matthau as flustered father of a reluctant bride.

Please Believe Me (1950) 87m. **½ D: Norman Taurog. Deborah Kerr, Robert Walker, James Whitmore, Peter Lawford, Mark Stevens, Spring Byington. Pleasant fluff of Britisher Kerr aboard liner headed for America, wooed by assorted bachelors aboard, who think she's an heiress.

Please Don't Eat the Daisies (1960) C-111m. *** D: Charles Walters. Doris Day, David Niven, Janis Paige, Spring Byington, Richard Haydn, Patsy Kelly. Bright film based on Jean Kerr's play about a drama critic and his family. Doris sings title song; her kids are very amusing, as are Byington (the mother-in-law), Kelly (housekeeper), and especially Janis Paige as a temperamental star.

Please! Mr. Balzac (1957-French) 99m. *** D: Marc Allegret. Daniel Gelin, Brigitte Bardot, Robert Hirsch, Darry Cowl. Engaging BB romp of girl involved in theft of rare book and her shenanigans to become disinvolved. Retitled: MADEMOISELLE STRIPTEASE.

Please Murder Me (1956) 78m. **½ D: Peter Godfrey. Angela Lansbury, Raymond Burr, Dick Foran, John Dehner, Lamont Johnson. Lansbury and Burr's energetic performances elevate this homicide yarn.

Please Turn Over (1960-British) 86m. **½ D: Gerald Thomas. Ted Ray, Jean Kent, Leslie Phillips, Joan Sims, Julia Lockwood, Tim Seely. OK froth about wife's lurid novel-writing and the repercussions it causes.

Pleasure Cove (1979) C-100m. TVM D: Bruce Bilson. Tom Jones, Constance Forslund, Melody Anderson, Joan Hackett, Harry Guardino, Shelley Fabares, Jerry Lacy. Busted-series pilot taking the LOVE-BOAT multiplot premise and relocating it at a posh resort. Average.

Pleasure Cruise (1933) 72m. **½ D: Frank Tuttle. Charlie Ruggles, Genevieve Tobin, Ralph Forbes, Una O'Connor, Herbert Mundin, Minna Gombell. Husband and wife take "separate vacations," but he jealously follows her on board ocean liner. Chic Lubitsch-like comedy runs out of steam halfway through.

Pleasure of His Company, The (1961) C-115m. ***½ D: George Seaton. Fred Astaire, Lilli Palmer,

Debbie Reynolds, Tab Hunter, Charlie Ruggles. Delightful piece of fluff with Astaire and Palmer at their best. He is her ex-husband who comes to visit and enchant his daughter (Reynolds) and hound Lilli's new spouse (Gary Merrill). Entire cast is in rare form.

Pleasure Seekers, The (1964) C-107m. **½ D: Jean Negulesco. Ann-Margret, Tony Franciosa, Carol Lynley, Gene Tierney, Brian Keith, Gardner McKay, Isobel Elsom. Glossy romance à la THREE COINS IN THE FOUNTAIN of three girls seeking fun in Spain.

Plot Thickens, The (1936) 69m. **½ D: Ben Holmes. James Gleason, ZaSu Pitts, Oscar Apfel, Owen Davis, Jr., Louise Latimer. Entry in Hildegarde Withers mystery-comedy series with Pitts the school-marm who helps solve robbery and murder with inspector Gleason.

Plough and the Stars, The (1936) 78m. ** D: John Ford. Barbara Stanwyck, Preston Foster, Barry Fitzgerald, Una O'Connor, J. M. Kerrigan. Dreary, theatrical filmization of Sean O'Casey's play with Foster as Irish revolutionary leader and Stanwyck as long-suffering wife who fears for his life.

Plunder of the Sun (1953) 81m. **½ D: John Farrow. Glenn Ford, Diana Lynn, Patricia Medina, Francis L. Sullivan. Competent cast in above-average goings-on. Ford is involved with treasure hunt and murder in Mexico.

Plunder Road (1957) 71m. **½ D: Hubert Cornfield. Gene Raymond, Jeanne Cooper, Wayne Morris, Elisha Cook, Jr., Stafford Repp. A little "sleeper" about robbery caper, with competent cast giving life to intriguing story.

Plunderers, The (1948) C-87m. ** D: Joseph Kane. Rod Cameron, Ilona Massey, Adrian Booth, Forrest Tucker. OK Republic Western involving outlaws and Army joining forces against rampaging redskins; clichés are there.

Plunderers, The (1960) 93m. **½ D: Joseph Pevney. Jeff Chandler, John Saxon, Dolores Hart, Marsha Hunt, Jay C. Flippen, Ray Stricklyn, James Westerfield. Above-par study of outlaws interacting with honest townsfolk.

Plunderers of Painted Flats (1959) 77m. *½ D: Albert C. Gannaway. Corinne Calvet, John Carroll, Skip

Homeier, George Macready, Edmund Lowe, Bea Benadaret, Madge Kennedy, Joe Besser. Flabby Western of cowpoke seeking his father's killer.

Plymouth Adventure (1952) C-105m. *** D: Clarence Brown. Spencer Tracy, Gene Tierney, Van Johnson, Leo Genn, Dawn Addams. Superficial soap opera, glossily done, of the 17th-century settlers who came to Massachusetts.

Poacher's Daughter, The (1960-Irish) 74m. **½ D: George Pollock. Julie Harris, Harry Brogan, Tim Seeley, Marie Keen, Brid Lynch, Noel Magee, Paul Farrell. Harris lends authenticity in title role as simple girl who straightens out her philandering boyfriend. Originally titled SALLY'S IRISH ROGUE.

Pocket Money (1972) C-102m. **½ D: Stuart Rosenberg. Paul Newman, Lee Marvin, Strother Martin, Christine Belford, Kelly Jean Peters, Fred Graham, Wayne Rogers. Debt-ridden cowboy and shifty pal get mixed up with crooked cattleman in modern-day Western. Strangely tepid comedy is helped by good Lazlo Kovacs photography, nice bit by Peters. Marvin's car in this is the damndest thing you'll ever see.

Pocketful of Miracles (1961) C-136m. **½ D: Frank Capra. Bette Davis, Glenn Ford, Hope Lange, Thomas Mitchell, Peter Falk, Edward Everett Horton, Ann-Margret, Jack Elam. Capra's remake of his 1933 LADY FOR A DAY is just as sentimental, but doesn't work as well. Bette is Apple Annie, a Damon Runyon character; Ford is the producer who turns her into a lady. Ann-Margret is appealing in her first film.

Point, The (1971) 73m. TVM D: Fred Wolff. Narrated by Dustin Hoffman. Engaging children's cartoon about boy banished from homeland because his head is round, not pointed like everyone else's. Charming score by Harry Nilsson.

Point Blank (1967) C-92m. ***½ D: John Boorman. Lee Marvin, Angie Dickinson, Keenan Wynn, Carroll O'Connor, Lloyd Bochner, Michael Strong, John Vernon. Marvin, shot and left for dead by unfaithful wife and mobster boyfriend, gets revenge two years later. Taut thriller, ignored in 1967, but now regarded as a top film of the mid-60s. Some scenes may be cut.

Poison Ivy (1953-French) 90m. **

D: Bernard Borderie. Eddie Constantine, Dominique Wilms, Howard Vernon, Dario Moreno, Gaston Modot. Constantine is again FBI agent Lemmy Caution, involved in stolen gold shipment in North Africa; grade-B actioner.

Police Story (1973) **C-100m. TVM D:** William Graham. Vic Morrow, Chuck Connors, Diane Baker, Edward Asner, Harry Guardino, Ralph Meeker. Long-sought criminal vows defiance, cop La Frieda (Morrow) vows capture. Joseph Wambaugh-based script includes interesting station atmosphere, department hassles. OK job, with Morrow solid as usual; clever direction. Above average.

Polly of the Circus (1932) **69m. ** D:** Alfred Santell. Clark Gable, Marion Davies, Raymond Hatton, C. Aubrey Smith, Maude Eburne. Unlikely story and casting, with Davies as sexy trapeze performer who's injured, recovers during extended stay at home of Gable, a minister living in splendor. Interesting only as curio; Ray Milland has bit part as usher.

Pollyanna (1960) **C-134m. ***½ D:** David Swift. Hayley Mills, Jane Wyman, Richard Egan, Karl Malden, Nancy Olson, Adolphe Menjou, Donald Crisp, Agnes Moorehead. Disney's treatment of Eleanor Porter story (filmed before with Mary Pickford) is first-rate, as "the glad girl" spreads cheer to misanthropes of a New England town . . . including her own Aunt Polly (Wyman). Fine direction and script by Swift, excellent performances all around.

Polo Joe (1936) **62m. ** D:** William McGann. Joe E. Brown, Carol Hughes, Skeets Gallagher, Joseph King, Gordon (Bill) Elliott, George E. Stone. Typical Brown comedy in which Joe's got to learn polo fast to impress his girl.

Pontius Pilate (1966-Italian-French) **C-100m. ** D:** Irving Rapper. Jean Marais, Jeanne Crain, Basil Rathbone, John Drew Barrymore, Massimo Serato, Leticia Roman. Adequate retelling of events before and after Christ's crucifixion from viewpoint of Roman procurator. Dubbing and confused script hamper good intentions. Barrymore plays Christ and Judas.

Pony Express (1953) **C-101m. *** D:** Jerry Hopper. Charlton Heston, Rhonda Fleming, Jan Sterling, Forrest Tucker. Exuberant action Western (set in 1860s) of the founding of mail routes westward, involving historical figures Buffalo Bill and Wild Bill Hickok.

Pony Express Rider (1976) **C-100m. *** D:** Hal Harrison Jr. Stewart Peterson, Henry Wilcoxon, Buck Taylor, Maureen McCormick, Joan Caulfield, Ken Curtis, Slim Pickens, Dub Taylor, Jack Elam. Good family outing with Peterson joining Pony Express in 1860 to help find the man whom he believes has killed his father.

Pony Soldier (1952) **C-82m. **½ D:** Joseph M. Newman. Tyrone Power, Cameron Mitchell, Robert Horton, Thomas Gomez, Penny Edwards. Power is sturdy in actioner about Canadian mounties and their efforts to stave off Indian war.

Poor Devil (1972) **C-100m. TVM D:** Robert Scheerer. Sammy Davis, Jr., Jack Klugman, Christopher Lee, Gino Conforti, Adam West, Madlyn Rhue. Silly mixture of farce and low-I.Q. drama as lowly assistant in Hell dreams of chance to earn stripes on Earth. Crazy cast, with Lee alternately playing straight and for laughs as Lucifer. Average.

Poor Little Rich Girl, The (1936) **72m. ***½ D:** Irving Cummings. Shirley Temple, Alice Faye, Jack Haley, Gloria Stuart, Michael Whalen, Claude Gillingwater, Henry Armetta. One of Shirley's best films, a top musical on any terms, with Temple running away from home, joining vaudeville team Haley & Faye, winning over crusty Gillingwater, eventually joining her father (Whalen) and lovely Stuart. Best of all is closing "Military Man" number.

Popcorn (1970) **C-85m. *½ D:** Peter Clifton. Mick Jagger, Jimi Hendrix, Rolling Stones, Otis Redding, Bee-Gees, Joe Cocker. Don't be misled by the talent assembled; most of them seem to have been captured during their worst performances for this concert film.

Pope Joan (1972-British) **C-132m. BOMB D:** Michael Anderson. Liv Ullmann, Keir Dullea, Robert Beatty, Jeremy Kemp, Olivia de Havilland, Patrick Magee, Maximilian Schell, Trevor Howard, Franco Nero. Dim story of girl who, disguised as man, works her way up to the papacy, only to be destroyed when revealed. Performers seem to be embarrassed, as well they should.

Rereleased under title THE DEVIL'S IMPOSTER, with much material cut.

Popi (1969) **C-115m.** *****½** D: Arthur Hiller. Alan Arkin, Rita Moreno, Miguel Alejandro, Ruben Figueroa. Charming story of poverty in the ghetto, focusing on one man's often zany antics in securing better life for his children. Odd ending for far-fetched story.

Poppy (1936) **75m.** ****½** D: A. Edward Sutherland. W. C. Fields, Rochelle Hudson, Richard Cromwell, Catherine Doucet, Lynne Overman. Mild Fields, re-creating his stage role as Hudson's ever-conniving dad. Too much romantic subplot, not enough of W. C.'s antics. Filmed before as SALLY OF THE SAWDUST.

Poppy Is Also a Flower, The (1966) **C-100m.** BOMB D: Terence Young. Senta Berger, Stephen Boyd, E. G. Marshall, Trevor Howard, Eli Wallach, Marcello Mastroianni, Angie Dickinson, Rita Hayworth, Yul Brynner, Trini Lopez, Gilbert Roland, Bessie Love. Incredibly bad feature from story by Ian Fleming, originally produced as United Nations project for TV. Acting is downright poor at times.

Porgy and Bess (1959) **C-138m.** ****½** D: Otto Preminger. Sidney Poitier, Dorothy Dandridge, Pearl Bailey, Sammy Davis, Jr., Brock Peters, Diahann Carroll, Ivan Dixon. Classic Gershwin folk opera is a bit stiff, but contains unforgettable melodies: "Summertime," "It Ain't Necessarily So," "I Got Plenty Of Nothin." Davis top-drawer as Sportin' Life.

Pork Chop Hill (1959) **97m.** ******* D: Lewis Milestone. Gregory Peck, Harry Guardino, Rip Torn, George Peppard, James Edwards, Bob Steele, Woody Strode. Grim Korean War actioner with Peck et al rugged and believable.

Port Afrique (1956-British) **C-92m.** ****** D: Rudolph Maté. Pier Angeli, Anthony Newley, Christopher Lee, Dennis Price, Eugene Deckers, Pat O'Mera, Maureen Connell, James Hayter, Phil Carey. Bernard Dryer's picaresque actioner gets middling screen version; adulterous wife's past comes to light when husband investigates her death.

Port of Hell (1954) **80m.** ****** D: Harold Schuster. Wayne Morris, Dane Clark, Carole Mathews, Otto Waldis, Marshall Thompson, Marjorie Lord, Tom Hubbard. Poor production values detract from tense situation of skipper et al trying to take an A-bomb out to sea before it explodes.

Port of New York (1949) **96m.** ****** D: Laslo Benedek. Scott Brady, Richard Rober, K. T. Stevens, Yul Brynner. Gloomy tale of customs agents cracking down on narcotics smuggling; Brynner's film debut.

Port of Seven Seas (1938) **81m.** ****** D: James Whale. Wallace Beery, Frank Morgan, Maureen O'Sullivan, John Beal, Jessie Ralph, Cora Witherspoon. Marcel Pagnol's FANNY isn't quite suitable Beery material, but he and good cast try their best as O'Sullivan falls in love with adventuresome sailor.

Portnoy's Complaint (1972) **C-101m.** BOMB D: Ernest Lehman. Richard Benjamin, Karen Black, Lee Grant, Jack Somack, Jeannie Berlin, Jill Clayburgh. Karen Black's excellent portrayal of "Monkey" is buried in otherwise incredibly inept filmization of Philip Roth's novel about a not exactly warm relationship between Jewish boy and his mother. Terrible direction.

Portrait From Life SEE: **Girl in the Painting.**

Portrait in Black (1960) **C-112m.** ****½** D: Michael Gordon. Lana Turner, Anthony Quinn, Sandra Dee, John Saxon, Richard Basehart, Lloyd Nolan, Ray Walston, Anna May Wong. Average murder mystery filled with gaping holes that producer Ross Hunter tried to hide with glamorous decor and offbeat casting.

Portrait of a Dead Girl SEE: **McCloud: Who Killed Miss U.S.A.?**

Portrait of a Mobster (1961) **108m.** ****½** D: Joseph Pevney. Vic Morrow, Leslie Parrish, Peter Breck, Ray Danton, Norman Alden, Ken Lynch. Better-than-usual chronicle of a gangster's rise in the underworld.

Portrait of a Sinner (1959-British) **96m.** ****½** D: Robert Siodmak. William Bendix, Nadja Tiller, Tony Britton, Donald Wolfit, Adrienne Corri, Joyce Carey. Tiller is effective in leading role as corrupting female who taints all in her path. Based on Robin Maugham story. Alternate title: THE ROUGH AND THE SMOOTH.

Portrait of a Stripper (1979) **C-100m.** TVM D: John A. Alonzo.

Lesley Ann Warren, Edward Herrmann, Vic Tayback, Sheree North, Allan Miller, K. C. Martel. A young widow supports her son by stripping in local nightclub, while fighting custody battle with the boy's grandfather. Pure sleaze. Below average.

Portrait of Clare (1951-British) 94m. ** D: Lance Comfort. Margaret Johnston, Richard Todd, Robin Bailey, Ronald Howard. Unpretentious little film, pegged on gimmick of woman telling granddaughter about her past romances.

Portrait of Jennie (1948) 86m. ***½ D: William Dieterle. Jennifer Jones, Joseph Cotten, Ethel Barrymore, Lillian Gish, David Wayne, Henry Hull. Atmospheric film from Robert Nathan's story of strange other-worldly girl who inspires artist Cotten. Haunting, beautifully acted.

Poseidon Adventure, The (1972) C-117m. *** D: Ronald Neame. Gene Hackman, Ernest Borgnine, Red Buttons, Carol Lynley, Roddy McDowall, Stella Stevens, Shelley Winters, Jack Albertson, Leslie Nielsen, Pamela Sue Martin, Arthur O'Connell, Eric Shea. Mindless but engrossing, highly charged entertainment. Luxury cruise ship capsized by tidal wave, leaving small band of survivors to make way to top (bottom) of ship and hopefully escape. Introductory sequences are laughably bad, but one soon gets caught up in story and ignores script's weaknesses.

Posse (1975) C-94m. *** D: Kirk Douglas. Kirk Douglas, Bruce Dern, Bo Hopkins, James Stacy, Luke Askew, David Canary. Offbeat but solid Western about a cynical lawman who tries to fulfill political ambitions by capturing an escaped robber. Well photographed and performed.

Posse From Hell (1961) C-89m. ** D: Herbert Coleman. Audie Murphy, John Saxon, Zohra Lampert, Vic Morrow, Lee Van Cleef. Murphy is tight-lipped gunslinger hunting outlaws who killed his sheriff pal. The usual.

Possessed (1931) 72m. **½ D: Clarence Brown. Joan Crawford, Clark Gable, Wallace Ford, Skeets Gallagher, John Miljan. Better-than-usual soaper with Crawford sacrificing her happiness for Gable's career. Good performances put this one above most of its kind.

Possessed (1947) 108m. *** D:

Curtis Bernhardt. Joan Crawford, Van Heflin, Raymond Massey, Geraldine Brooks, Stanley Ridges. Crawford gives fine performance in intelligent study of woman whose subtle mental problems ruin her life. Heflin and Massey are the men in her life; Brooks is radiant as Massey's daughter.

Possessed, The (1977) C-78m. TVM D: Jerry Thorpe. James Farentino, Joan Hackett, Claudette Nevins, Eugene Roche, Harrison Ford, Ann Dusenberry. Supernatural drama with Farentino, a defrocked priest, called upon to do an exorcism at Hackett's exclusive girls' school. She keeps it from going off the deep end. Average.

Possession of Joel Delaney, The (1972) C-105m. *** D: Waris Hussein. Shirley MacLaine, Perry King, Lisa Kohane, David Elliott, Michael Hordern, Miriam Colon, Lovelady Powell. Uneven but satisfying mix of horror and social commentary with MacLaine, affluent Manhattanite, unsympathetic central character threatened by mysterious transformations of her brother Joel. Offbeat throughout.

Possessors, The (1958-French) 94m. **½ D: Denys De La Patelliere. Jean Gabin, Jean Desailly, Pierre Brasseur, Emmanuelle Riva, Bernard Blier. Diffuse yet forceful study of patriarch Gabin forcing issues to make his family self-sufficient.

Postman Always Rings Twice, The (1946) 113m. **** D: Tay Garnett. Lana Turner, John Garfield, Cecil Kellaway, Hume Cronyn, Audrey Totter, Leon Ames. Garfield and Turner sparkle in bristling drama of lovers who get her husband (Kellaway) out of the way; A-1 James Cain story. (Filmed twice before, in France and Italy.)

Postman's Knock (1962-British) 87m. ** D: Robert Lynn. Spike Milligan, Barbara Shelley, John Wood, Miles Malleson, Ronald Adam, Wilfrid Lawson. Milligan is an overly efficient postal worker who upsets the equilibrium of the London post office—and some ambitious thieves. Scattered laughs in this generally heavy-handed comedy.

Postmark for Danger (1956-British) 84m. ** D: Guy Green. Terry Moore, Robert Beatty, William Sylvester, Josephine Griffin. Mild Scotland Yard investigation story.

Pot O' Gold (1941) 86m. ** D:

George Marshall. James Stewart, Paulette Goddard, Horace Heidt, Charles Winninger, Mary Gordon, Frank Melton, Jed Prouty. Harmless musical of boy who manages to get Heidt band on uncle's radio program.

Potemkin (1925-Russian) 65m. **** D: Sergi Eisenstein. Alexander Antonov, Vladimir Barsky, Grigori Alexandrov, Mikhail Goronorov. Landmark film about 1905 Revolution goes beyond status of mere classic; unlike many staples of film history classes, this one has the power to grip any audience. Odessa Steps sequence is possibly the most famous movie scene of all time.

Powder River (1953) C-78m. ** D: Louis King. Rory Calhoun, Corinne Calvet, Cameron Mitchell, Carl Betz. Straightforward minor Western, with Calhoun becoming town sheriff and clearing up a friend's murder.

Powderkeg (1970) C-100m. TVM D: Douglas Heyes. Rod Taylor, Dennis Cole, Michael Ansara, Fernando Lamas, Tisha Sterling. 1914: Troubleshooters hired to retrieve hijacked train. Great action ruined by sloppy direction. Average; pilot for TV series THE BEARCATS.

Power (1980) C-200m. TVM. D: Barry Shear and Virgil Vogel. Joe Don Baker, Karen Black, Howard Da Silva, Ralph Bellamy, Red Buttons, Brian Keith, Jo Van Fleet, Victor Jory, Paul Stewart, Scott Brady. An influential labor leader's rise to power from the docks of Chicago during the Depression. Big cast populates this sprawling saga written by Oscar winner Ernest Tidyman (THE FRENCH CONNECTION) that's actually the thinly disguised story of Jimmy Hoffa. Above average.

Power, The (1968) C-109m. *½ D: Byron Haskin. George Hamilton, Suzanne Pleshette, Richard Carlson, Yvonne De Carlo, Earl Holliman, Gary Merrill, Ken Murray, Barbara Nichols, Arthur O'Connell, Nehemiah Persoff, Aldo Ray, Michael Rennie. Powerful force that can change mental and physical makeup of anybody and anything wastes its time trying to kill George Hamilton. Producer George Pal has done much better sci-fi.

Power and the Glory, The (1933) 76m. *** D: William K. Howard. Spencer Tracy, Colleen Moore, Ralph Morgan, Helen Vinson. Considered by many a precursor to CITIZEN KANE, Preston Sturges' script tells rags-to-riches story of callous industrialist (Tracy) in flashback. Silent-star Moore gives sensitive performance as Tracy's wife.

Power and the Prize, The (1956) 98m. **½ D: Henry Koster. Robert Taylor, Elisabeth Mueller, Burl Ives, Charles Coburn, Cedric Hardwicke, Mary Astor. Sporadically effective study of big men in corporation and their private lives.

Power of the Whistler, The (1945) 66m. D: Lew Landers. Richard Dix, Janis Carter, Jeff Donnell, Loren Tindall, Tala Birell, John Abbott. SEE: Whistler series.

Power Within, The (1979) C-78m. TVM D: John Llewellyn Moxey. Art Hindle, Edward Binns, Eric Braeden, Susan Sullivan, David Hedison, Richard Sargent. Barnstorming pilot is struck by ligtning, acquires mysterious powers, and is menaced by enemy agents who want his secret. Silly attempt to grab THE INCREDIBLE HULK'S audience. Below average.

Powers Girl, The (1942) 93m. ** D: Norman Z. McLeod. George Murphy, Anne Shirley, Dennis Day, Benny Goodman, Carole Landis. Trifling plot revolving about Shirley's attempt to become member of famed modeling school, with musical numbers tossed in.

Practically Yours (1944) 90m. ** D: Mitchell Leisen. Claudette Colbert, Fred MacMurray, Gil Lamb, Robert Benchley, Rosemary DeCamp, Cecil Kellaway. Stars' expertise redeems contrived story of girl intercepting pilot's message to his dog.

Pray for the Wildcats (1974) C-100m. TVM D: Robert Michael Lewis. Andy Griffith, William Shatner, Angie Dickinson, Janet Margolin, Robert Reed, Marjoe Gortner, Lorraine Gray. Mildly diverting "macho" flick about three advertising executives who are forced to join their sadistic client (Griffith) on a desert motorcycle trip. Average.

Prehistoric Women (1950) C-74m. BOMB D: Gregg Tallas. Laurette Luez, Allan Nixon, Joan Shawlee, Judy Landon. Ludicrous account of cavewomen hunting for their mates, only good for laughs.

Prehistoric Women (1967-British) C-91m. *½ D: Michael Carreras. Michael Latimer, Martine Beswick, Edina Ronay, Carol White, John

Raglan, Stephanie Randall. Curious white hunter in early 1900s defies jungle taboos, is magically transported to ancient Amazon jungle civilization. Contrived and silly; you may question necessity of returning to 20th century. Beware cuts.

Premature Burial, The (1962) C-81m. ** D: Roger Corman. Ray Milland, Hazel Court, Richard Ney, Heather Angel, Alan Napier, John Dierkes. Title tells the story in another of Corman's Poe adaptations, with a 1962 Milland unconvincingly cast as medical student. Lavish (for this series) but not one of director's best.

Premier May SEE: **Man to Man Talk**

Premonition, The (1976) C-94m. ** D: Robert Allen Schnitzer. Sharon Farrell, Richard Lynch, Jeff Corey, Ellen Barber, Edward Bell. Muddled script works against eerie atmosphere in this supernatural tale that stresses parapsychology as clue to young girl's disappearance. Mediocre results. Filmed in Mississippi.

Prescription: Murder (1967) C-99m. TVM D: Richard Irving. Peter Falk, Gene Barry, Katherine Justice, William Windom, Nina Foch, Anthony James, Virginia Gregg. Doc Fleming (Barry) thinks he's committed foolproof murder of wife, so at first he humors efforts of seemingly slow-witted police lieutenant (Falk) to check alibi. Interesting debut of Columbo-ish character with excellent cast, subplots. Above average.

Presenting Lily Mars (1943) 104m. ** D: Norman Taurog. Judy Garland, Van Heflin, Fay Bainter, Richard Carlson, Spring Byington, Marta Eggerth, Marilyn Maxwell. Well, there she is, and there lies the script. Stale story of determined girl getting big chance on Broadway only comes alive when Judy sings.

President's Analyst, The (1967) C-104m. **** D: Theodore J. Flicker. James Coburn, Godfrey Cambridge, Severn Darden, Joan Delaney, Pat Harrington, Will Geer, William Daniels. Totally nutty, brilliantly maneuvered satire of many sacred cows, as Coburn is pursued by half the government when he quits title job. The ending is a beauty.

President's Lady, The (1953) 96m. *** D: Henry Levin. Charlton Heston, Susan Hayward, John McIntire, Fay Bainter, Carl Betz. Heston as Andrew Jackson and Hayward the lady with a past he marries work well together in this fictional history of 1800s America.

President's Mistress, The (1978) C-100m. TVM D: John Llewellyn Moxey. Beau Bridges, Susan Blanchard, Karen Grassle, Larry Hagman, Joel Fabiani, Don Porter. Government courier is caught in a conspiracy after learning his murdered sister was the President's mistress as well as a Soviet spy. Average.

President's Plane Is Missing, The (1971) C-100m. TVM D: Daryl Duke. Buddy Ebsen, Peter Graves, Arthur Kennedy, Rip Torn, Louise Sorel, Raymond Massey, James Wainwright, Mercedes McCambridge. Adaptation of Robert Serling novel depicts second-by-second crises concerning international plot to overthrow U.S. government. Impressive cast cannot obscure faulty narrative and direction. Average.

Pressure Point (1962) 91m. *** D: Hubert Cornfield. Sidney Poitier, Bobby Darin, Peter Falk, Carl Benton Reid, Mary Munday, Barry Gordon, Howard Caine. Intelligent drama, with Poitier the prison psychiatrist trying to ferret out the problems of his Nazi patient (Darin).

Prestige (1932) 71m. **½ D: Tay Garnett. Ann Harding, Melvyn Douglas, Adolphe Menjou, Clarence Muse, Ian MacLaren. Flamboyant direction and solid performances elevate hackneyed melodrama about life at British Army outpost in the Far East where White Supremacy—and Douglas' sanity—are threatened.

Pretender, The (1947) 69m. **½ D: W. Lee Wilder. Albert Dekker, Catherine Craig, Linda Stirling, Charles Drake, Charles Middleton, Alan Carney. Dekker gives sharply etched performance as N.Y.C. financier trying to do in a competitor, discovering he may be the victim instead.

Pretty Baby (1950) 92m. ** D: Bretaigne Windust. Dennis Morgan, Betsy Drake, Zachary Scott, Edmund Gwenn, Barbara Billingsley. Coy minor comedy involving working-girl Drake, who snowballs a gimmick to a get a subway seat on the morning train into a good job and romance.

Pretty Baby (1978) C-109m. **½ D: Louis Malle. Brooke Shields, Keith Carradine, Susan Sarandon, Frances Faye, Antonio Fargas, Matthew Anton. Beautifully mounted but distressingly low-keyed story of marriage between a 12-year-old New

Orleans prostitute and an older photographer, set around time of WW1. Shields is striking in title role, but Carradine is his lifeless self.

Pretty Boy Floyd (1960) 96m. ** D: Herbert J. Leder. John Ericson, Barry Newman, Joan Harvey, Herb (Jason) Evers, Carl York, Roy Fant, Shirley Smith. Average chronicle of infamous 1930s gangster, played energetically by Ericson.

Pretty Maids All in a Row (1971) C-92m. *** D: Roger Vadim. Rock Hudson, Angie Dickinson, Telly Savalas, John David Carson, Roddy McDowall, Keenan Wynn, Amy Eccles, Barbara Leigh. Silly but enjoyable black comedy; high school guidance-counselor/coach Hudson advises frustrated Carson in sexual matters, while school is plagued with murders of pretty female students. Likely to be cut for TV.

Pretty Poison (1968) C-89m. *** D: Noel Black. Anthony Perkins, Tuesday Weld, Beverly Garland, John Randolph, Dick O'Neill. Oddball arsonist Perkins enlists aid of sexy high-schooler Weld for scheme he's unhatching, but soon discovers that she's got stranger notions than his! Bright, original story sparked by vivid performance by Weld.

Price of Fear, The (1956) 79m. **½ D: Abner Biberman. Merle Oberon, Lex Barker, Charles Drake, Gia Scala, Warren Stevens. Middling account of Oberon involved in hit-and-run accident which snowballs her life into disaster.

Price of Freedom, The SEE: **Operation Daybreak**

Pride and Prejudice (1940) 118m. **** D: Robert Z. Leonard. Greer Garson, Laurence Olivier, Edna May Oliver, Edmund Gwenn, Mary Boland, Maureen O'Sullivan, Karen Morley, Ann Rutherford, Marsha Hunt. Outstanding adaptation of Jane Austen's novel about five husband-hunting sisters in 19th-century England. Excellent cast, fine period flavor in classic comedy of manners.

Pride and the Passion, The (1957) C-132m. **½ D: Stanley Kramer. Cary Grant, Frank Sinatra, Sophia Loren, Theodore Bikel, John Wengraf. Miscast actioner involving capture of huge cannon by French partisans in 19th century Spain. Spectacle scenes—filmed on location —are impressive, but most of the film is ridiculous.

Pride of St. Louis, The (1952) 93m.

**½ D: Harmon Jones. Dan Dailey, Joanne Dru, Richard Crenna, Hugh Sanders. Pleasing if fanciful biography of baseball player Dizzy Dean.

Pride of the Blue Grass (1954) C-71m. ** D: William Beaudine. Lloyd Bridges, Vera Miles, Margaret Sheridan, Arthur Shields. Familiar racetrack story; competent production.

Pride of the Bowery (1940) 63m. D: Joseph H. Lewis. Leo Gorcey, Bobby Jordan, Donald Haines, Carlton Young, Kenneth Howell, David Gorcey. SEE: **Bowery Boys** series.

Pride of the Marines (1945) 119m. ***½ D: Delmer Daves. John Garfield, Eleanor Parker, Dane Clark, John Ridgely, Rosemary DeCamp, Ann Doran, Ann Todd, Warren Douglas. Ensemble acting by Warner Bros. stock company enhances true account of Marine blinded during Japanese attack, with Garfield as injured Al Schmid, Clark as sympathetic buddy.

Pride of the Yankees, The (1942) 127m. **** D: Sam Wood. Gary Cooper, Teresa Wright, Babe Ruth, Walter Brennan, Dan Duryea, Ludwig Stossel, Addison Richards, Hardie Albright. Superb biography of baseball star Lou Gehrig, with Cooper giving excellent performance; fine support from Wright as devoted wife. Truly memorable final sequence.

Priest Killer (1971) C-100m. TVM D: Richard Colla. George Kennedy, Raymond Burr, Don Galloway, Don Mitchell, Louise Latham, Anthony Zerbe, Peter Brocco. Priest and chief of detectives combine forces in search of motive for series of murders of Catholic priests. Standard ordering of events, characters, obstacles in path of hero, all leading to expected resolution. Average.

Priest's Wife, The (1971-Italian-French) C-106m. *½ D: Dino Risi. Sophia Loren, Marcello Mastroianni, Venantino Venantini, Jacques Stany, Pippo Starnazza, Augusto Mastrantoni. Barely entertaining mixture of drama and humor with Loren disillusioned singer who thinks she can convince priest to obtain release from his vow of celibacy and marry her. Weightier handling of subject matter can be heard on radio talk shows; film seems designed merely as vehicle for two stars.

Prime Cut (1972) C-91m. ** D: Michael Ritchie. Lee Marvin, Gene Hackman, Angel Tompkins, Gregory

Walcott, Sissy Spacek. Midwest mobster tries wiping out opposition by every violent means imaginable, including a reaper. Poorly written script, totally unbelievable. Much gore will go for TV version.

Prime of Miss Jean Brodie, The (1969) C-116m. ***½ D: Ronald Neame. Maggie Smith, Robert Stephens, Pamela Franklin, Gordon Jackson, Celia Johnson, Jane Carr. Oscar-winning showcase for Smith as eccentric teacher in Edinburgh school who wields a spellbinding influence on her "girls." Remarkable character study, adapted from stage version of Muriel Spark's novel; filmed on location.

Primrose Path, The (1940) 93m. **½ D: Gregory La Cava. Ginger Rogers, Joel McCrea, Marjorie Rambeau, Miles Mander, Henry Travers. Girl from wrong side of the tracks falls in love with ambitious young McCrea; starts engagingly, drifts into dreary soap opera and melodramatics. Rambeau is excellent as Ginger's prostitute mother.

Prince and the Pauper, The (1937) 120m. ***½ D: William Keighley. Errol Flynn, Billy and Bobby Mauch, Claude Rains, Alan Hale, Montagu Love, Henry Stephenson, Barton MacLane. Rousing filmization of Mark Twain's story of young lookalikes, one a mistreated urchin, the other a prince, exchanging places. Great music score by Erich Wolfgang Korngold.

Prince and the Showgirl, The (1957) C-117m. **½ D: Laurence Olivier. Marilyn Monroe, Laurence Olivier, Sybil Thorndike, Jeremy Spencer, Richard Wattis. Thoughtful but slow-moving comedy of saucy American showgirl Monroe being romanced by Prince Regent of Carpathia (Olivier) during the 1911 coronation of George V. Filmed in England, with delightful performances by Monroe and Olivier.

Prince of Central Park, The (1977) C-76m. TVM D: Harvey Hart. Ruth Gordon, T. J. Hargrave, Lisa Richard, Brooke Shields, Marc Vahanian. Engaging tale of a pair of orphans living in a tree in Central Park and the lonely old lady who befriends them. Adapted from Evan Rhodes' ingratiating novel. Above average.

Prince of Foxes (1949) 107m. **½ D: Henry King. Tyrone Power, Wanda Hendrix, Orson Welles, Marina Berti, Everett Sloane, Katina Paxinou. Lavish, incredibly handsome costume epic of medieval Italy (filmed on location), with adventurer Power defying all-powerful Cesare Borgia. Story elements don't match visual impact of film.

Prince of Pirates (1953) C-80m. **½ D: Sidney Salkow. John Derek, Barbara Rush, Whitfield Connor, Edgar Barrier. Enjoyable little costumer involving French-Spanish wars.

Prince of Players (1955) C-102m. **½ D: Philip Dunne. Richard Burton, Maggie McNamara, Raymond Massey, Charles Bickford, John Derek, Eva Le Gallienne, Mae Marsh, Sarah Padden. Burton is 19th-century actor Edwin Booth, embroiled in more offstage drama than on. Shakespearean excerpts thrown in; well performed by earnest cast.

Prince of Thieves, The (1948) C-72m. ** D: Howard Bretherton. Jon Hall, Patricia Morison, Adele Jergens, Alan Mowbray, Michael Duane. Colorful swashbuckler of Robin Hood and Maid Marian, aimed at juvenile audiences.

Prince Valiant (1954) C-100m. **½ D: Henry Hathaway. James Mason, Janet Leigh, Robert Wagner, Debra Paget, Sterling Hayden. Famed cartoon character becomes cardboard costumer decked out in 20th Century-Fox splendor, battling and loving in Middle Ages England.

Prince Who Was a Thief, The (1951) C-88m. **½ D: Rudolph Maté. Tony Curtis, Piper Laurie, Everett Sloane, Jeff Corey, Betty Garde. Juvenile costumer sparked by enthusiastic performances.

Princess and the Pirate, The (1944) C-94m. *** D: David Butler. Bob Hope, Virginia Mayo, Walter Brennan, Walter Slezak, Victor McLaglen. One of Bob's wackiest; he and glamorous Virginia are on the lam from pirate McLaglen, trapped by potentate Slezak. Brennan is hilarious in truly offbeat pirate role.

Princess Comes Across, The (1936) 76m. *** D: William K. Howard. Carole Lombard, Fred MacMurray, Douglass Dumbrille, Alison Skipworth, William Frawley, Porter Hall. Lombard, posing as royalty on ocean voyage, meets romantic MacMurray; together they are involved in murder mystery. Delightful blend of comedy and mystery.

Princess of the Nile (1954) C-71m. **½ D: Harmon Jones. Debra

Paget, Jeffrey Hunter, Michael Rennie, Dona Drake, Wally Cassell. Hokey script diverts any potential this costumer may have had.

Princess O'Rourke (1943) 94m. **½ D: Norman Krasna. Olivia de Havilland, Robert Cummings, Charles Coburn, Jack Carson, Jane Wyman, Harry Davenport, Gladys Cooper. Very dated comedy starts charmingly with pilot Cummings falling in love with Princess De Havilland, bogs down in no longer timely situations, unbearably coy finale involving (supposedly) F.D.R. himself. Krasna won Best Screenplay Oscar that year.

Prisoner, The (1955-British) 91m. *** D: Peter Glenville. Alec Guinness, Jack Hawkins, Raymond Huntley, Wilfrid Lawson. Grim account of cardinal in iron curtain country undergoing grueling interrogation. Guinness-Hawkins interplay is superb.

Prisoner of Second Avenue, The (1975) C-105m. ***½ D: Melvin Frank. Jack Lemmon, Anne Bancroft, Gene Saks, Elizabeth Wilson, Florence Stanley. Neil Simon walks a tightrope between comedy and melancholia, and never falls, thanks to warm performances by Lemmon, as suddenly unemployed executive who has a nervous breakdown, and Bancroft, as his understanding wife. Look for Sylvester Stallone as a would-be pickpocket.

Prisoner of Shark Island, The (1936) 95m. ***½ D: John Ford. Warner Baxter, Gloria Stuart, Claude Gillingwater, John Carradine, Harry Carey, Arthur Byron, Ernest Whitman. Excellent film based on true story of Dr. Samuel Mudd, who innocently treated John Wilkes Booth's leg after Lincoln assassination, and was sentenced to life imprisonment. Gripping story; Baxter superb, Carradine memorable as villainous sergeant, Whitman fine as Baxter's black comrade. Remade as HELLGATE.

Prisoner of the Iron Mask, The (1962-Italian) C-80m. **½ D: Francesco De Feo. Michel Lemoine, Wandisa Guida, Andrea Bosic, Jany Clair, Giovanni Materassi. Typical costumer; title tells all.

Prisoner of the Volga (1960-Yugoslavian) C-102m. ** D: W. Tourjansky. John Derek, Elsa Martinelli, Dawn Addams, Wolfgang Preiss, Gert Frobe. Well-mounted but ordinary costume drama of soldier who

suffers when he seeks revenge on general who impregnated his wife.

Prisoner of War (1954) 80m. ** D: Andrew Marton. Ronald Reagan, Steve Forrest, Dewey Martin, Stephen Bekassy. Bland account of P.O.W.'s in Korean War.

Prisoner of Zenda, The (1937) 101m. ***½ D: John Cromwell. Ronald Colman, Madeleine Carroll, Mary Astor, Douglas Fairbanks, Jr., C. Aubrey Smith, Raymond Massey, Montagu Love, Alexander D'Arcy. Lavish costumer with excellent casting; Colman is forced to substitute for lookalike cousin, the King of Ruritanian country, but commoner Colman falls in love with regal Carroll. Fairbanks is outstanding as Rupert of Hentzau.

Prisoner of Zenda, The (1952) C-101m. *** D: Richard Thorpe. Stewart Granger, Deborah Kerr, Jane Greer, Louis Calhern, Lewis Stone, James Mason. Plush remake of Colman classic with spirited cast. Traveler who is deadringer for small European country's king becomes involved in plot of murder.

Prisoner of Zenda, The (1979) C-108m. BOMB D: Richard Quine. Peter Sellers, Lynne Frederick, Lionel Jeffries, Elke Sommer, Gregory Sierra, Jeremy Kemp, Catherine Schell. Famous swashbuckler is played for laughs, but there aren't any. The kind of picture that helped to destroy Sellers' career until the second series of Clouseau pictures rescued it.

Prisoners of the Casbah (1953) C-78m. *½ D: Richard Bare. Gloria Grahame, Turhan Bey, Cesar Romero, Nestor Paiva. Low-budget costumer with diverting cast.

Prisonniere, La (1969-French) 104m. ** D: Henri-Georges Clouzot. Laurent Terzieff, Bernard Fresson, Elisabeth Wiener, Dany Carrel, Dario Moreno, Daniel Riviere. From the director of DIABOLIQUE comes this obscure, confused study of woman obsessed with a photographer of sado-masochism. Strikingly photographed, but erotic sequences will probably be cut for TV.

Private Affairs of Bel Ami, The (1947) 112m. ***½ D: Albert Lewin. George Sanders, Angela Lansbury, Ann Dvorak, Frances Dee, Albert Bassermann, Warren William, John Carradine. Delicious, literate adaptation of Guy de Maupassant's "story of a rogue," Sanders, who gets ahead by using his charm on prominent women, denying himself the real love of Lansbury. Fine gallery of performances; beautifully photographed by Russell Metty.

Private Buckaroo (1942) 68m. ** D: Edward Cline. The Andrews Sisters, Dick Foran, Joe E. Lewis, Jennifer Holt. Mini-musical from Universal Pictures is vehicle for 1940s favorite sister trio, accompanied by Harry James et al in Army camp show.

Private Detective 62 SEE: **Man Killer**

Private Eyes (1953) 64m. D: Edward Bernds. Leo Gorcey, Huntz Hall, Bernard Gorcey, Chick Chandler, Myron Healey, Tim Ryan. SEE: **Bowery Boys** series.

Private Files of J. Edgar Hoover, The (1977) C-112m. **½ D: Larry Cohen. Broderick Crawford, Dan Dailey, Jose Ferrer, Rip Torn, Michael Parks, Raymond St. Jacques, Ronee Blakley. Sleazy bio of former FBI chief makes for great camp with its all-star lineup of true-life political personalities. The New-Heights-in-Screen-Surrealism Award goes to the Miklos Rozsa-scored scene in which John Edgar gets drunk listening to sex tapes of a government official.

Private Hell 36 (1954) 81m. **½ D: Don Siegel. Ida Lupino, Steve Cochran, Howard Duff, Dean Jagger, Dorothy Malone. Well-balanced account of greed corrupting supposedly honest people.

Private Life of Don Juan, The (1934-British) 80m. ** D: Alexander Korda. Douglas Fairbanks, Merle Oberon, Binnie Barnes, Joan Gardner, Benita Hume, Athene Seyler, Melville Cooper. Lifeless costumer with aging Fairbanks in title role, pursuing a bevy of beauties. This was his final film.

Private Life of Henry VIII, The (1933-British) 97m. **** D: Alexander Korda. Charles Laughton, Binnie Barnes, Robert Donat, Elsa Lanchester, Merle Oberon, Miles Mander, Wendy Barrie, John Loder. Sweeping historical chronicle of 16th-century British monarch, magnificently captured by Laughton, revealing man and king; Lanchester fine as Anne of Cleves, with top supporting cast.

Private Life of Sherlock Holmes, The (1970) C-125m. ***½ D: Billy Wilder. Robert Stephens, Colin Blakely, Irene Handl, Stanley Holloway,

Christopher Lee, Genevieve Page, Clive Revill. Atypical but extremely personal Wilder film takes melancholy look at famed sleuth. Acting, photography and score are tops in neglected film whose reputation should soar in future years. Made in England.

Private Lives (1931) 84m. *** D: Sidney Franklin. Norma Shearer, Robert Montgomery, Una Merkel, Reginald Denny. Sparkling adaptation of Noel Coward comedy about bickering couple; a stylish treat all the way.

Private Lives of Adam and Eve, The (1960) C-87m. *½ D: Albert Zugsmith, Mickey Rooney. Mickey Rooney, Mamie Van Doren, Fay Spain, Mel Torme, Martin Milner, Tuesday Weld. Bizarre, crude attempt at mixing contemporary soap opera with parallels to the past via dream sequences.

Private Lives of Elizabeth and Essex, The (1939) C-106m. ***½ D: Michael Curtiz. Bette Davis, Errol Flynn, Olivia de Havilland, Donald Crisp, Vincent Price, Nanette Fabray, Henry Daniell, Robert Warwick, Henry Stephenson, Leo G. Carroll. Colorful, elaborate costume drama with outstanding performance by Davis as queen whose love for dashing Flynn is thwarted. Not authentic history, but good drama. Also known as ELIZABETH THE QUEEN.

Private Navy of Sgt. O'Farrell, The (1968) C-92m. BOMB D: Frank Tashlin. Bob Hope, Phyllis Diller, Jeffrey Hunter, Gina Lollobrigida, Mylene Demongeot, John Mhyers, Mako. O'Farrell tries to import some beautiful nurses to improve his men's morale, gets Diller instead. Of the many terrible Hope comedies of the 1960s, this may be the worst. Unfunny and even offensive.

Private Number (1936) 80m. ** D: Roy Rel Ruth. Robert Taylor, Loretta Young, Patsy Kelly, Basil Rathbone, Marjorie Gateson, Paul Harvey, Joe E. Lewis. Not to disgrace family, wealthy Taylor must keep marriage to family housemaid Young a secret. Tearful soaper is OK.

Private War of Major Benson, The (1955) C-100m. **½ D: Jerry Hopper. Charlton Heston, Julie Adams, William Demarest, Tim Hovey, Sal Mineo, David Janssen. Hovey is the little boy at military school who charms rugged commander Heston into sympathetic person; Adams is the love interest.

Private Worlds (1935) 84m. **½ D: Gregory La Cava. Claudette Colbert, Charles Boyer, Joan Bennett, Joel McCrea, Helen Vinson, Esther Dale, Jean Rouverol. Dated but engrossing tale of mental institution, with doctors Boyer and Colbert giving restrained performances; noteworthy support by Bennett.

Private's Affair, A (1959) C-92m. **½ D: Raoul Walsh. Sal Mineo, Christine Carere, Barry Coe, Barbara Eden, Gary Crosby, Terry Moore, Jim Backus, Jessie Royce Landis. Energetic young cast involved in putting on the "big Army show" on TV.

Private's Progress (1956-British) 99m. *** D: John Boulting. Richard Attenborough, Jill Adams, Dennis Price, Terry-Thomas, Ian Carmichael, Peter Jones. Prize collection of funny men, splendidly played by cast, involved in Army shenanigans.

Privilege (1967-British) C-101m. *** D: Peter Watkins. Paul Jones, Jean Shrimpton, Marc London, Max Bacon, Jeremy Child. Overambitious yet effective account of 1970s England where all-powerful welfare state manipulates masses through such media as pop singers. Jones is good as disillusioned teen-age idol.

Prize, The (1963) C-136m. *** D: Mark Robson. Paul Newman, Edward G. Robinson, Elke Sommer, Diane Baker, Micheline Presle, Leo G. Carroll. Irving Wallace novel is mere stepping stone for glossy spy yarn set in Stockholm, involving participants in Nobel Prize ceremony. Newman and Sommer make handsome leads; Robinson has dual role. Fast-moving fun.

Prize of Arms, A (1961-British) 105m. **½ D: Cliff Owen. Stanley Baker, Tom Bell, Helmut Schmid, John Phillips. Effective yarn is hindered by heavy British accents ruining much dialogue. Tale unfolds methodical plan for big heist of Army funds.

Prize of Gold, A (1955-British) C-98m. *** D: Mark Robson. Richard Widmark, Mai Zetterling, Nigel Patrick, Donald Wolfit, Eric Pohlmann. Taut caper in post-WW2 Berlin involving a planned heist of gold from the air lift circuit.

Prize Fighter, The (1979) C-99m. ** D: Michael Preece. Tim Conway,

Don Knotts, David Wayne, Robin Clarke, Cisse Cameron, Mary Ellen O'Neill, Michael LaGuardia. If you like Knotts and Conway, you'll probably get through this lame, kiddie-oriented comedy about a dumb boxer and his smart-aleck manager, set in the 1930s.

Prizefighter and the Lady, The (1933) 102m. *** D: W. S. Van Dyke. Myrna Loy, Max Baer, Otto Kruger, Walter Huston, Jack Dempsey, Jess Willard, James J. Jeffries. Entertaining film breathes life into potential clichés; Baer falls for high-class gangster's moll Loy. Exciting prizefight finale.

Probe (1972) C-97m. TVM D: Russell Mayberry. Hugh O'Brian, Elke Sommer, Sir John Gielgud, Burgess Meredith, Lilia Skala, Kent Smith. Stolen gems assignment for wired-up space-age detective in tame chase-thriller that exploits electronic gimmickry as just prop to hang standard plot onto. Average; pilot for TV series. Retitled SEARCH.

Prodigal, The (1955) C-114m. **½ D: Richard Thorpe. Lana Turner, Edmund Purdom, James Mitchell, Louis Calhern, Audrey Dalton, Neville Brand, Taina Elg, Cecil Kellaway, Henry Daniell, Walter Hampden, Joseph Wiseman. Juvenile biblical semi-spectacle, with Turner the evil goddess of love corrupting Purdom; glossy MGM production.

Producers, The (1968) C-98m. ***½ D: Mel Brooks. Zero Mostel, Gene Wilder, Dick Shawn, Kenneth Mars, Estelle Winwood, Christopher Hewett. Brooks' first feature film is a cult favorite, the kind of film that gets funnier with repeated viewings; outrageous in the truest sense of the word, it tells of huckster Mostel pulling meek accountant Wilder into get-rich-scheme of producing a flop Broadway show—to be called "Springtime for Hitler." Trimmed for TV.

Profane Comedy, The SEE: Set This Town on Fire

Professional Soldier (1935) 75m. **½ D: Tay Garnett. Victor McLaglen, Freddie Bartholomew, Gloria Stuart, Constance Collier, Michael Whalen. McLaglen is hired to kidnap prince Bartholomew, but mutual friendship gets in the way. Good teaming supports average script.

Professional Sweetheart (1933) 68m. ** D: William A. Seiter. Ginger Rogers, ZaSu Pitts, Norman Foster,

Frank McHugh, Edgar Kennedy, Betty Furness, Gregory Ratoff. Good cast can't put over weak radio spoof, with Rogers as airwaves star who becomes engaged to hick Foster in publicity stunt.

Professionals, The (1966) C-117m. *** D: Richard Brooks. Burt Lancaster, Lee Marvin, Robert Ryan, Jack Palance, Claudia Cardinale, Woody Strode, Ralph Bellamy. Bellamy employs four soldiers-of-fortune to rescue his wife (Cardinale) from Mexican varmint Palance. Far-fetched story, but real action and taut excitement throughout.

Professor Beware (1938) 87m. **½ D: Elliott Nugent. Harold Lloyd, Phyllis Welch, William Frawley, Etienne Girardot, Raymond Walburn, Lionel Stander, Thurston Hall, Cora Witherspoon. One of Lloyd's last vehicles has good moments, but tale of archeologist searching for rare tablet is thin.

Project X (1968) C-97m. **½ D: William Castle. Christopher George, Greta Baldwin, Henry Jones, Monte Markham, Phillip Pine. Offbeat but ultimately unconvincing mixture of time travel, biological warfare, and psychology in tale of future Earth civilization searching for secret germ formula. Their amnesiac secret agent has it; how to get it?

Projected Man, The (1967-British) C-77m. *½ D: Ian Curteis. Bryant Haliday, Mary Peach, Norman Wooland, Ronald Allen, Derek Farr. Story of scientist who learns how to change matter into energy, then back to another form of matter, is somewhat reminiscent of THE FLY but not as good.

Projectionist, The (1971) C-85m. **½ D: Harry Hurwitz. Chuck McCann, Ina Balin, Rodney Dangerfield, Jara Kohout, Harry Hurwitz, Robert Staats. Independently made film has ups and downs, but many pearly moments in story of daydreaming projectionist McCann who envisions himself a superhero, Captain Flash. Many film clips imaginatively used; best of all is coming-attractions trailer for the end of the world.

Promise, The (1979) C-98m. BOMB D: Gilbert Cates. Kathleen Quinlan, Stephen Collins, Beatrice Straight, Laurence Luckinbill, William Prince. Boy loves girl. Girl loses face in car accident. Boy thinks girl dead. Girl gets new face from plastic surgeon. Boy falls for old girl's new face.

Viewer runs screaming from TV room.

Promise Her Anything (1966) C-98m. **½ D: Arthur Hiller. Warren Beatty, Leslie Caron, Bob Cummings, Hermione Gingold. Limp premise of blue-moviemaker (Beatty) taking care of neighbor Caron's baby. Filmed in England but supposed to be Greenwich Village.

Promise Him Anything (1974) C-78m. TVM D: Edward Parone. Eddie Albert, Frederic Forrest, Meg Foster, William Schallert, Tom Ewell, Aldo Ray, Steven Keats. Comedy tracing the tangled romantic web of a young man who sues his computer date for breach of promise. Sprightly performed fluff. Average.

Promises in the Dark (1979) C-115m. **½ D: Jerome Hellman. Marsha Mason, Ned Beatty, Susan Clark, Michael Brandon, Kathleen Beller, Paul Clemens, Donald Moffat. Unrelievedly depressing (though well-made) film about young girl (Beller) dying of cancer, and her compassionate doctor (Mason).

Promoter, The (1952-British) 88m. *** D: Ronald Neame. Alec Guinness, Glynis Johns, Valerie Hobson, Petula Clark, Michael Hordern. Amusing vehicle showing Guinness virtuosity with droll comedian in rags-to-riches chronicle of a con-artist.

Prophecy (1979) C-100m. *½ D: John Frankenheimer. Talia Shire, Robert Foxworth, Armand Assante, Richard Dysart, Victoria Racimo. Classical musician and her doctor husband fight off a giant salami in upstate Maine after mercury poisoning turns animals into huge mutants and worse. Ridiculous horror film is good for a few laughs.

Proud and Profane, The (1956) 111m. **½ D: George Seaton. William Holden, Deborah Kerr, Thelma Ritter, Dewey Martin, William Redfield. Spotty WW2 romance story has many parallels to FROM HERE TO ETERNITY, but Kerr-Holden romance is never believable.

Proud and the Beautiful, The (1956-French) 94m. *** D: Yves Allegret. Michele Morgan, Gerard Philippe, Victor Manuel Mendoza, Michele Cordoue. Morgan and Philippe interact beautifully as widow in Mexico whose love for down-and-out doctor helps him regain sense of values.

Proud and the Damned, The (1973) C-94m. ** D: Ferde Grofe Jr.

Chuck Connors, Jose Greco, Cesar Romero, Aron Kincaid, Anita Quinn. Uneven performances and script in formula story of Civil War veterans and mercenaries drifting through Latin America, caught up in local revolution.

Proud Ones, The (1956) C-94m. **½ D: Robert D. Webb. Robert Ryan, Virginia Mayo, Jeffrey Hunter, Robert Middleton, Walter Brennan. Staunch acting involving the inevitable showdown between sheriff and outlaws perks up this Western.

Proud Rebel, The (1958) C-103m. *** D: Michael Curtiz. Alan Ladd, Olivia de Havilland, Dean Jagger, David Ladd, Cecil Kellaway, Henry Hull. Well-presented study of two-fisted Ladd seeking medical help for mute son; De Havilland is the woman who tames him.

Proud Valley (1940-British) 77m. **½ D: Pen Tennyson. Paul Robeson, Edward Chapman, Simon Lach, Rachel Thomas, Edward Rigby. Mild drama of Welsh coal-mining village beset by mine shutdown; uplifted only by Robeson's commanding presence and fine voice.

Providence (1977-British) C-104m. ** D: Alain Resnais. Dirk Bogarde, John Gielgud, Ellen Burstyn, David Warner, Elaine Stritch. Odd fantasy marked director Resnais' English-language debut. Writer Gielgud tries to complete his last novel, juxtaposes imagined thoughts about his family with real-life encounters. Muddled drama.

Prowler, The (1951) 92m. *** D: Joseph Losey. Van Heflin, Evelyn Keyes, John Maxwell, Katharine Warren. Well-handled suspenser of Heflin in love with Keyes, planning to kill her rich husband.

Prudence and the Pill (1968-British) C-98m. **½ D: Fielder Cook, Ronald Neame. Deborah Kerr, David Niven, Robert Coote, Irina Demick, Joyce Redman, Judy Geeson, Keith Michell. Labored comedy treatment of modern sexual mores. Niven thinks he can patch up his in-name-only marriage by substituting aspirin for his wife's birth control pills. Good cast and performances, but weak script.

Psych-Out (1968) C-101m. ** D: Richard Rush. Susan Strasberg, Dean Stockwell, Jack Nicholson, Bruce Dern, Adam Roarke, Max Julien. Strasberg is deaf teenage runaway who becomes involved with Haight-Ashbury hippies and their drug world in late 1960s. The usual.

Psyche '59 (1964-British) 94m. **½ D: Alexander Singer. Patricia Neal, Curt Jurgens, Samantha Eggar, Ian Bannen, Elspeth March. Turgid melodrama involving infidelity, with good cast doing their best.

Psychiatrist: God Bless the Children, The (1970) C-100m. TVM D: Jerrold Friedman. Roy Thinnes, Peter Duel, Luther Adler, John Rubinstein, Joy Bang, Norman Alden, Barry Brown. Entertaining drama showcases new group therapy techniques applied to young patients; stagy dialogue, fiery performances. Above average. Retitled: CHILDREN OF THE LOTUS EATER.

Psychic, The (1978-Italian) C-89m. BOMB D: Lucio Fulci. Jennifer O'Neill, Gabriele Ferzetti, Marc Porel, Gianni Garko, Evelyn Stewart. O'Neill has frightening premonitions of deaths in this low-grade thriller.

Public Enemy's Wife (1936) 69m. **½ D: Nick Grinde. Pat O'Brien, Margaret Lindsay, Robert Armstrong, Cesar Romero, Dick Foran. Romero is good as mobster serving life whose insane jealousy over wife (Lindsay) makes her a perfect pawn for G-Man O'Brien. Not-bad Warner Bros. "B."

Psychic Killer (1975) C-90m. BOMB D: Raymond Danton. Jim Hutton, Julie Adams, Paul Burke, Aldo Ray, Neville Brand, Whit Bissell. Ugly, violent shocker of mental institute patient who acquires psychic powers to revenge himself on those who wronged him. Lots of cameos: Rod Cameron, Nehemiah Persoff, Della Reese, others.

Psycho (1960) 109m. ***½ D: Alfred Hitchcock. Anthony Perkins, Janet Leigh, Vera Miles, John Gavin, Martin Balsam, John McIntire, Patricia Hitchcock. Hitchcock's very black comedy is suspenseful and confusing, with the now-legendary shower scene to keep everyone awake. Beware of cuts in some violent scenes. Chilling Bernard Herrmann score.

Psycho-Circus (1967-British-West German) C-65m. **½ D: John Moxey. Christopher Lee, Heinz Drache, Margaret Lee, Suzy Kendall, Leo Genn. Confused (due to distributor cuts) Edgar Wallace-based story of murderer stalking odd assortment of characters in big top. Is it hooded Gregor the knife thrower? Short running time gives film old-style serial-type pacing. Alternate title: CIRCUS OF FEAR.

Psychomania (1964) 90m. **½ D: Richard Hilliard. Lee Philips, Shepperd Strudwick, Jean Hale, James Farentino, Richard Van Patten. Offbeat chiller of killer on the rampage at a college.

Psychopath, The (1966-British) 83m. *** D: Freddie Francis. Patrick Wymark, Margaret Johnston, John Standing, Judy Huxtable. A demented killer leaves dolls as his calling card at the scene of the murders; well made thriller from Robert Bloch script.

Public Enemy (1931) 84m. ***½ D: William Wellman. James Cagney, Jean Harlow, Eddie Woods, Beryl Mercer, Donald Cook, Joan Blondell, Mae Clarke. Prohibition gangster's rise and fall put Cagney on the map, and deservedly so; he makes up for film's occasional flaws and dated notions. Still pretty powerful, though; this is the one where he smashes a grapefruit in Clarke's face. Originally released at 96m.

Public Eye, The (1972-British) C-95m. **½ D: Carol Reed. Mia Farrow, Topol, Michael Jayston, Margaret Rawlings, Annette Crosbie, Dudley Foster. Stuffy husband hires private-eye to watch his wife, but the sleuth falls for her. Fair expansion of Peter Shaffer's play, THE PUBLIC EYE; Farrow is good, but Topol's grin is flashed once too often.

Public Hero Number One (1935) 81m. *** D: J. Walter Ruben. Lionel Barrymore, Jean Arthur, Chester Morris, Joseph Calleia, Paul Kelly, Lewis Stone, Sam Baker. Fine tale of G-man Morris tracking down mobster Calleia with help of Barrymore and complication of Calleia's sister Jean Arthur. Most enjoyable.

Public Pigeon No. One (1957) C-79m. ** D: Norman Z. McLeod. Red Skelton, Vivian Blaine, Janet Blair, Allyn Joslyn, Jay C. Flippen. Bland Skelton vehicle with Red accidentally exposing gang of crooks; typical slapstick.

Pulp (1972) C-95m. *** D: Michael Hodges. Michael Caine, Mickey Rooney, Lionel Stander, Lizabeth Scott, Nadia Cassini, Al Lettieri, Dennis Price. Rooney, a retired expatriate Hollywood actor, hires paperback writer Caine to ghost his autobiography. Uneven, but good

fun and well acted, especially by Rooney.

Pumping Iron (1977) C-85m. *** D: George Butler, Robert Fiore. Unambitious but frequently funny and offbeat documentary about bodybuilding on a competitive level. Film is aided by the considerable charm of six-time Mr. Olympic winner, Arnold Schwarzenegger.

Pumpkin Eater, The (1964-British) 110m. *** D: Jack Clayton. Anne Bancroft, Peter Finch, James Mason, Cedric Hardwicke, Alan Webb, Richard Johnson, Maggie Smith, Eric Porter. Intelligent soap opera, with top-notch acting by Bancroft as much-married woman who discovers husband has been unfaithful.

Punch and Jody (1974) C-78m. TVM D: Barry Shear. Glenn Ford, Ruth Roman, Pam Griffin, Kathleen Widdoes, Susan Brown, Parley Baer, Donald Barry. Circus drifter Ford suddenly finds himself with custody of teen-aged daughter he never knew. Sawdust, tears and Gilbraltar-like Ford for those who like these ingredients. Average.

Puppet on a Chain (1970-British) C-98m. *½ D: Geoffrey Reeve. Sven-Bertil Taube, Barbara Parkins, Alexander Knox, Patrick Allen. Half-baked version of Alistair MacLean's thriller about international drug trafficking; only an exciting speedboat chase keeps this from total disaster.

Pure Hell of St. Trinian's, The (1961-British) 94m. ** D: Frank Launder. Cecil Parker, Joyce Grenfell, George Cole, Thorley Walters. Absence of Alastair Sim from series lessens glow; outrageous girls' school is visited by sheik seeking harem gals.

Purlie Victorious SEE: Gone Are the Days

Purple Death from Outer Space (1940) 87m. **½ D: Ford Beebe, Ray Taylor. Buster Crabbe, Carol Hughes, Charles Middleton, Frank Shannon, Anne Gwynne, Roland Drew. Newly edited version of FLASH GORDON CONQUERS THE UNIVERSE serial has Flash, Dale Arden, and Dr. Zarkov discovering Ming's new plan to control Earth, join forces with Arboria, Prince Barin, and Aura to counteract threat. Uninspired handling of original footage.

Purple Gang, The (1960) 85m. ** D: Frank McDonald. Barry Sullivan, Robert Blake, Elaine Edwards, Marc Cavell, Jody Lawrance, Suzy Marquette, Joseph Turkel. Capable cast, limp police-vs.-gangster yarn.

Purple Heart, The (1944) 99m. ******* D: Lewis Milestone. Dana Andrews, Farley Granger, Sam Levene, Richard Conte, Tala Birell, Nestor Paiva, Benson Fong, Marshall Thompson. Absorbing tale of U.S. air force crew shot down during Tokyo raid receives strong performances by good cast.

Purple Hills, The (1961) C-60m. *½ D: Maury Dexter. Gene Nelson, Joanna Barnes, Kent Taylor, Russ Bender. Cheapie oater, with ex-dancer Nelson unconvincing as cowpoke on the run from rampaging Indians.

Purple Mask, The (1955) C-82m. **½ D: H. Bruce Humberstone. Tony Curtis, Gene Barry, Angela Lansbury, Colleen Miller, Dan O'-Herlihy. Set in the early 19th-century France; Curtis is sword-wielding nobleman out to champion the cause of justice.

Purple Monster Strikes, The SEE: **D-Day on Mars**

Purple Noon (1961-French) C-115m. *** D: Rene Clement. Alain Delon, Marie Laforet, Maurice Ronet, Frank Latimore, Ave Ninchi. Marvelously photographed, tautly edited study of playboy Delon who commits murder and thinks he has gotten away with it. Retitled LUST FOR EVIL.

Purple Plain, The (1955-British) C-100m. *** D: Robert Parrish. Gregory Peck, Bernard Lee, Win Min Than, Maurice Denham, Brenda De Banzie. Set in WW2 Burma; Peck is neurotic pilot whose plane crashes, forcing him to fight his way to freedom and new sense of values.

Pursued (1947) 101m. *** D: Raoul Walsh. Teresa Wright, Robert Mitchum, Judith Anderson, Dean Jagger, John Rodney. Grim Western of determined Mitchum out to find father's killers; very well acted, suspenseful.

Pursuers, The (1961-British) 63m. ** D: Godfrey Grayson. Cyril Shaps, Francis Matthews, Susan Denny, Sheldon Lawrence. Trim programmer with Matthews tracking down Nazi war criminal Shaps in England; conventionally told.

Pursuit (1972) C-73m. TVM D: Michael Crichton. Ben Gazzara, E. G. Marshall, William Windom, Joseph Wiseman, Jim McMullan, Martin Sheen. Extremist aching for confrontation in convention city threatens mass destruction with deadly government nerve gas. Based on

novel by John Lange (Michael Crichton); fair tension and OK dialog as agent Graves (Gazzara) must outwit adversary at his own game. Above average.

Pursuit of Happiness, The (1971) C-98m. *** D: Robert Mulligan. Michael Sarrazin, Barbara Hershey, Robert Klein, Sada Thompson, Arthur Hill, E. G. Marshall. Director Mulligan has made lots of overrated films, but he never got enough credit for this sympathetic tale of young man sent to jail more for his attitude in court than any particular offense. Good performances.

Pursuit of the Graf Spee (1957-British) C-106m. **½ D: Michael Powell, Emeric Pressburger. John Gregson, Anthony Quayle, Peter Finch, Ian Hunter, Bernard Lee, Patrick Macnee, Christopher Lee. Taut documentary-style account of WW2 chase of German warship by British forces. Original title: THE BATTLE OF THE RIVER PLATE.

Pursuit to Algiers (1945) 65m. D: Roy William Neill. Basil Rathbone, Nigel Bruce, Marjorie Riordan, Rosalind Ivan, Martin Kosleck, John Abbott, Frederick K. Worlock. SEE: **Sherlock Holmes** series.

Pushover (1954) 88m. **½ D: Richard Quine. Fred MacMurray, Kim Novak, Phil Carey, Dorothy Malone, E. G. Marshall. MacMurray is cop who falls in love with gangster moll Novak; supporting cast reduced to stereotypes in moody actioner.

Putney Swope (1969) C-88m. **** D: Robert Downey. Arnold Johnson, Ruth Hermine, Pepi Hermine, Allen Garfield. Hilarious story of blacks taking over Madison Avenue ad agency, instituting considerable changes. Best bit: series of commercial spoofs. Probably too outrageous for TV.

Puzzle (1978-Australian) C-90m. TVM D: Gordon Hessler. James Franciscus, Wendy Hughes, Sir Robert Helpmann, Peter Gwynne, Gerald Kennedy, Kerry McGuire. Muddled melodrama involving a faded tennis ace, his ex-wife who is seeking his help in finding a cache of gold bars her recently departed second husband had embezzled, and a probable murder. Average.

Puzzle of a Downfall Child (1970) C-104m. ** D: Jerry Schatzberg. Faye Dunaway, Barry Primus, Viveca Lindfors, Barry Morse, Roy Scheider.

Puzzling is the word for this confusing story of fashion model trying to put together the pieces of her unhappy life.

Puzzle of the Red Orchid, The (1962-German) 94m. ** D: Helmut Ashley. Christopher Lee, Marisa Mell, Klaus Kinski, Fritz Rasp, Adrian Hoven. Moderate Edgar Wallace entry; Scotland Yard and F.B.I. track down international crime syndicate. Retitled: THE SECRET OF THE RED ORCHID.

Pygmalion (1938-British) 95m. **** D: Anthony Asquith, Leslie Howard. Leslie Howard, Wendy Hiller, Wilfrid Lawson, Marie Lohr, David Tree. Superlative filmization of G. B. Shaw play which became MY FAIR LADY. Howard excels as the professor, with Hiller his Cockney pupil.

Pygmy Island (1950) 69m. D: William Berke. Johnny Weissmuller, Ann Savage, David Bruce, Tristram Coffin, Steven Geray. SEE: **Jungle Jim** series.

Pyro (1964-Spanish) C-99m. **½ D: Julio Coll. Barry Sullivan, Martha Hyer, Sherry Moreland, Soledad Miranda. Strange chiller of man burned in fire seeking revenge on ex-girlfriend who started it.

Pyx, The (1973-Canadian) C-111m. ***½ D: Harvey Hart, Karen Black, Christopher Plummer, Donald Pilon, Lee Broker, Yvette Brind'Amour. Ignored in this country, this Montreal-made suspenser is an excellent blend of horror, science-fiction and detective thriller with a mystical theme. Police sgt. Plummer investigates prostitute Black's death, finds a devil cult, numerous decadent suspects and a new twist on Catholic guilt.

Q Planes SEE: **Clouds Over Europe**

Quackser Fortune Has A Cousin in the Bronx (1970-Irish) C-90m. ***½ D: Waris Hussein. Gene Wilder, Margot Kidder, Eileen Colgen, Seamus Ford. Delightfully offbeat love story. Quackser Fortune follows the horses around Dublin selling their manure for gardening. The day the horses are replaced by cars he falls in love with an American coed. Original in every way.

Quadrophenia (1979) C-115m. ***½ D: Franc Roddam. Phil Daniels, Mark Wingett, Philip Davis, Leslie Ash, Garry Cooper. Superior mixture of early '60s "Angry Young Man" drama and rock movie tells of teenage gang battles between Mods and Rockers on the English seaside. A real sleeper.

Quality Street (1937) 84m. *** D: George Stevens. Katharine Hepburn, Franchot Tone, Fay Bainter, Eric Blore, Cora Witherspoon, Estelle Winwood. Hepburn is radiant in delicate adaptation of James Barrie's whimsical play: "old maid" masquerades as her own niece in order to win back the love of a man who hasn't seen her in ten years.

Quantez (1957) C-80m. **½ D: Harry Keller. Fred MacMurray, Dorothy Malone, Sydney Chaplin, John Gavin. Above-par Western involving robbery gang heading for Mexico border, encountering stiff opposition along the way.

Quantrill's Raiders (1958) C-68m. ** D: Edward Bernds. Steve Cochran, Diane Brewster, Leo Gordon, Gale Robbins. Predictable Civil War account of the outlaw's planned attack on a Kansas arsenal.

Quarantined (1970) C-74m. TVM D: Leo Penn, John Dehner, Gary Collins, Sharon Farrell, Wally Cox, Sam Jaffe, Susan Howard, Dan Ferrone. Daily tribulations of famous country clinic run by Bedford family, complicated by problems of rebellious son, uncooperative movie star, and cholera epidemic. Fast-paced, convincing situations, decent dialogue. Above average.

Quare Fellow, The (1962-Irish) 85m. ***½ D: Arthur Dreifuss. Patrick McGoohan, Sylvia Syms, Walter Macken, Dermot Kelly, Jack Cunningham, Hilton Edwards. Irish-made adaptation of Behan play deals with new prison guard, well-played by McGoohan, who changes mind about views on capital punishment. Finely acted, excellent script.

Quartet (1949-British) 120m. **** D: Ken Annakin, Arthur Crabtree, Harold French, Ralph Smart. Basil Radford, Naunton Wayne, Mai Zetterling, Ian Fleming, Jack Raine, Dirk Bogarde. Superb movie with Somerset Maugham introducing four of his tales, each with different casts and moods.

Quatermass and the Pit See: **Five Million Years to Earth**

Quebec (1951) C-85m. ** D: George Templeton. John Barrymore, Jr., Corinne Calvet, Barbara Rush, Patric Knowles. Historical nonsense set in

1830s Canada during revolt against England. Filmed on location.

Queen Bee (1955) 95m. *** D: Ranald MacDougall. Joan Crawford, Barry Sullivan, Betsy Palmer, John Ireland, Fay Wray, Tim Hovey. Crawford in title role has field-day maneuvering the lives of all in her Southern mansion, with husband Sullivan providing the final ironic twist.

Queen Christina (1933) 97m. **** D: Rouben Mamoulian. Greta Garbo, John Gilbert, Ian Keith, Lewis Stone, C. Aubrey Smith, Gustav von Seyffertitz, Reginald Owen, Elizabeth Young. Probably Garbo's best film, with a haunting performance by the radiant star as 17th-century Swedish queen who relinquishes her throne for her lover, Gilbert. Garbo and Gilbert's love scenes together are truly memorable, as is the famous final shot. Don't miss this one.

Queen of Babylon, The (1956-Italian) C-98m. *½ D: Carlo Bragaglia. Rhonda Fleming, Ricardo Montalban, Roldano Lupi, Carlo Ninchi. American stars can't elevate elephantine study of ancient Babylonia.

Queen of Burlesque (1946) 70m. *½ D: Sam Newfield. Evelyn Ankers, Carleton G. Young, Marion Martin, Rose La Rose, Alice Fleming, Craig Reynolds. Low-budget suspenser unstrung backstage at burlesque theater.

Queen of Outer Space (1958) C-80m. *½ D: Edward Bernds. Zsa Zsa Gabor, Eric Fleming, Laurie Mitchell, Paul Birch. Inane sci-fi about expedition that crash-lands on Venus, where planet is ruled entirely by women. At least some of the laughs are intentional.

Queen of Spades (1960-Russian) C-100m. **½ D: Roman Tikhomirov. Oleg Strizhenov, Zurab Anzhaparidze, Olga Krasina, Tamara Milashkina. Stark version of Tchaikovsky opera PIKOVAYA DAMA, performed by Bolshoi Theater company; deals with young man consumed by gambling urge, leading to his and girlfriend's destruction.

Queen of Spades, The (1949-British) 95m. *** D: Thorold Dickinson. Anton Walbrook, Edith Evans, Ronald Howard, Mary Jerrold, Yvonne Mitchell, Anthony Dawson. Unusual, macabre fantasy from Alexander Pushkin story about Russian officer obsessed with learning the secret

of winning at cards. Well-mounted production, set in 1806.

Queen of the Nile (1961-Italian) C-85m. ** D: Fernando Cerchio. Jeanne Crain, Vincent Price, Edmund Purdom, Amedeo Nazzari. Dull account of court life in 2000 B.C. Egypt. Not even campy.

Queen of the Pirates (1960-Italian) C-79m. ** D: Mario Costa. Gianna Maria Canale, Massimo Serato, Scilla Gabel, Paul Muller. Vivid setting can't salvage wooden account of Canale in title role overcoming tyrannical Duke of Doruzzo (Muller).

Queen of the Stardust Ballroom (1975) C-100m. TVM D: Sam O'Steen. Maureen Stapleton, Charles Durning, Michael Brandon, Michael Strong, Charlotte Rae. Beautifully realized love story between a widowed grandmother and a married mailman who meet at a local dance hall. A filmed song of joy with sensitive performances by the two leads. Above average.

Queen's Guards, The (1960-British) C-110m. ** D: Michael Powell. Daniel Massey, Robert Stephens, Raymond Massey, Ursula Jeans. Tedious, patriotic chronicle of young Massey distinguishing himself in service, saving family name; humdrum film.

Quentin Durward (1955) C-101m. **½ D: Richard Thorpe. Robert Taylor, Kay Kendall, Robert Morley, George Cole, Alec Clunes, Duncan Lamont, Marius Goring. Taylor plays Sir Walter Scott's dashing Scots hero in this handsome but static costumer about Louis XVI's reign in 14th-century France.

Quest, The (1976) C-100m. TVM D: Lee H. Katzin. Tim Matheson, Kurt Russell, Brian Keith, Keenan Wynn, Will Hutchins, Cameron Mitchell, Neville Brand, Morgan Woodward, Art Lund. Two brothers search the Old West for their sister, captured years earlier by Indians. Evokes memories of John Ford's THE SEARCHERS but worth seeing for colorful performances of veteran actors Keith, Wynn and Mitchell, and for refreshing touches like a horse-camel race. Later evolved into a series. Average.

Quest for Love (1971-British) C-90m. *** D: Ralph Thomas. Tom Bell, Joan Collins, Denholm Elliott, Laurence Naismith, Lyn Ashley, Juliet Harmer, Neil McCallum, Simon Ward. Intriguing sci-fi story of man who accidentally passes into another dimension on Earth almost identical to ours, with some strange differences.

Question of Adultery, A (1959-British) 86m. **½ D: Don Chaffey. Julie London, Anthony Steel, Basil Sydney, Donald Houston, Anton Diffring, Andrew Cruickshank. Tepid drama involving pros and cons of artificial insemination. Retitled: THE CASE OF MRS. LORING.

Question of Guilt, A (1978) C-100m. TVM D: Robert Butler. Tuesday Weld, Ron Liebman, Peter Masterson, Alex Rocco, Viveca Lindfors, Lana Wood. Flashy, fun-loving divorcee is accused of murdering her child in this drama obviously inspired by the headline-making Alice Crimmins case in New York. Average.

Question of Love, A (1978) C-100m. TVM D: Jerry Thorpe. Gena Rowlands, Jane Alexander, Ned Beatty, Clu Gulager, Bonnie Bedelia, James Sutorious. Top-notch cast enriches this sensitive fact-based drama about two lesbians and the custody battle one has with her ex-husband over their young son. Above average.

Questor Tapes, The (1974) C-100m. TVM D: Richard A. Colla. Robert Foxworth, Mike Farrell, John Vernon, Lew Ayres, James Shigeta, Robert Douglas, Dana Wynter. Scifier about sophisticated android (Foxworth) looking for his identity, using his computerized brain to locate his missing creator. Despite the twist of having a robot as the lead, only mild diversion. Average.

Quick Before It Melts (1964) C-98m. **½ D: Delbert Mann. George Maharis, Robert Morse, Anjanette Comer, James Gregory, Yvonne Craig, Doodles Weaver. Trivia involving Maharis and Morse in the Antarctic; they have bright idea of bringing in a planeload of girls, with predictable results.

Quick Gun, The (1964) C-87m. ** D: Sidney Salkow. Audie Murphy, Merry Anders, James Best, Ted de Corsia, Frank Ferguson, Raymond Hatton. Formula Murphy Western, with Audie redeeming himself by combating town outlaws.

Quick, Let's Get Married (1964) C-96m. BOMB D: William Dieterle. Ginger Rogers, Ray Milland, Barbara Eden, Michael Ansara, Walter Abel, Elliott Gould. Easy to see why this dud never really got released; bordello madam Rogers and adventurer Milland perpetrate "miracle" hoax on gullible prostitute (Eden). Gould makes inauspicious film debut as deaf mute. Also known as SEVEN DIFFERENT WAYS.

Quick Millions (1931) 72m. **½ D: Rowland Brown. Spencer Tracy, Marguerite Churchill, Sally Eilers, Robert Burns, John Wray, George Raft. OK gangster film with Tracy as ambitious truck driver who climbs to top of the rackets. Nothing special, except to see dynamic early Tracy.

Quicksand (1950) 79m. **½ D: Irving Pichel. Mickey Rooney, Jeanne Cagney, Barbara Bates, Peter Lorre, Minerva Urecal. Earnest little film with Rooney a simple workingman whose first minor criminal act snowballs into tragedy.

Quiet American, The (1958) 120m. **½ D: Joseph L. Mankiewicz. Audie Murphy, Michael Redgrave, Claude Dauphin, Giorgia Moll. At times effective account of Murphy, who comes to Saigon with his own plans for ending the warring there.

Quiet Man, The (1952) C-129m. **** D: John Ford. John Wayne, Maureen O'Hara, Barry Fitzgerald, Victor McLaglen, Mildred Natwick, Arthur Shields, Ward Bond. American boxer Wayne returns to native Ireland, wins over townsfolk, and tames strong-willed O'Hara. Boisterous blarney, with beautiful scenery and equally beautiful music by Victor Young. Oscar winner for director Ford.

Quiet Please, Murder (1942) 70m. **½ D: John Larkin. George Sanders, Gail Patrick, Richard Denning, Sidney Blackmer, Lynne Roberts, Kurt Katch, Minerva Urecal, Theodore von Eltz. Offbeat, intriguing yarn of master forger Sanders stealing priceless Shakespeare volume, passing off his copies as the original. Murder and romance expertly woven into story.

Quincannon, Frontier Scout (1956) C-83m. *½ D: Lesley Selander. Tony Martin, Peggie Castle, John Bromfield, John Smith, Ron Randell. Martin is miscast in title role of programmer.

Quiller Memorandum, The (1966-British) C-105m. *** D: Michael Anderson. George Segal, Alec Guinness, Max von Sydow, Senta Berger, George Sanders, Robert Helpmann. Good Harold Pinter script about

American secret agent who investigates neo-Nazi movement in modern-day Berlin. Film is a relief from most spy films of the 60s.

Quinns, The (1977) C-78m. TVM D: Daniel Petrie. Barry Bostwick, Blair Brown, Susan Browning, Geraldine Fitzgerald, Peter Masterson, Virginia Vestoff. Soap opera focusing on three generations of Irish-American New York City firefighters. Average.

Quintet (1979) C-110m. ** D: Robert Altman. Paul Newman, Bibi Andersson, Fernando Rey, Vittorio Gassman, Nina Van Pallandt, Brigitte Fossey, David Langton. Pretentious, unappealing story about cutthroat game of survival in a frozen city of the future. Not as puzzling as it is ponderous.

Quo Vadis (1951) C-171m. *** D: Mervyn LeRoy. Robert Taylor, Deborah Kerr, Leo Genn, Peter Ustinov, Patricia Laffan, Finlay Currie, Abraham Sofaer. Marathon epic based on Henryk Sienkiewicz novel of the persecution of Christians during reign of Emperor Nero in ancient Rome; lavish in every detail, most serviceable cast.

Ra Expeditions, The (1971-Norwegian) C-93m. *** D: Lennart Ehrenborg. Narrated by Thor Heyerdahl and Roscoe Lee Browne. Exciting documentary about modern adventurer Heyerdahl's determination to cross the Atlantic in a papyrus boat, to prove theory that such a voyage was made thousands of years ago. Fine follow-up to KON-TIKI.

R.C.M.P. and the Treasure of Genghis Khan (1948) 100m. *½ D: Fred Brannon, Yakima Canutt. Jim Bannon, Virginia Belmont, Anthony Warde, Dorothy Granger. Spotty actioner with too few real cliff-hangers, dealing with Canadian mounties' efforts to combat criminal syndicate searching for fabled Oriental buried treasure. Reedited movie serial: DANGERS OF THE CANADIAN MOUNTED.

R.P.M. (1970) C-97m. *½ D: Stanley Kramer. Anthony Quinn, Ann-Margret, Gary Lockwood, Paul Winfield, Graham Jarvis, Alan Hewitt. Old-fashioned liberal Quinn becomes head of university, then authorizes a police bust of radicals to save institution. Ideal match of inept Erich Segal script with equally bad Kramer direction gives film certain camp value, but otherwise, look out.

RX Murder (1958-British) 85m. ** D: Derek Twist. Rick Jason, Marius Goring, Lisa Gastoni, Mary Merrall. Jason stars as American physician settling in British village to find strange murder. Fair mystery.

Rabbit, Run (1970) C-94m. ** D: Jack Smight. James Caan, Anjanette Comer, Jack Albertson, Melodie Johnson, Henry Jones, Carmen Mathews. Brilliant cast, brilliant book (by John Updike) and awful film centering around former high school athlete who suddenly finds that life is tougher than being on the playing field.

Rabbit Test (1978) C-86m. **½ D: Joan Rivers. Billy Crystal, Alex Rocco, Joan Prather, Doris Roberts, George Gobel, Imogene Coca. Rivers' first film is like low-budget Mel Brooks: wacky comedy surrounding slim plot about first pregnant man. Some wild ideas, mostly in bad taste. Many guest-star cameos.

Rabbit Trap, The (1959) 72m. **½ D: Philip Leacock. Ernest Borgnine, David Brian, Bethel Leslie, Kevin Corcoran, June Blair, Jeanette Nolan, Don Rickles. Intelligent if slow-moving study of motivational factors behind Borgnine's compulsive work life and ignoring of his family.

Race for Your Life, Charlie Brown (1977) C-75m. **½ D: Bill Melendez. Voices of Duncan Watson, Greg Felton, Stuart Brotman, Gail Davis, Liam Martin. Third animated feature based on Charles Schulz's *Peanuts* comic strip is set in summer camp, highlighted by treacherous raft race. Mildly entertaining, but lacks punch.

Race Street (1948) 79m. ** D: Edwin L. Marin. George Raft, William Bendix, Marilyn Maxwell, Frank Faylen, Henry (Harry) Morgan, Gale Robbins. San Francisco bookie is up against extortion ring in this well-acted but ordinary crime story.

Race with the Devil (1975) C-88m. BOMB D: Jack Starrett. Peter Fonda, Warren Oates, Loretta Swit, Lara Parker, R. G. Armstrong. Two vacationing couples are pursued by local witches after witnessing a human sacrifice. It takes quite a human sacrifice to sit through this film.

Racers, The (1955) C-112m. **½ D: Henry Hathaway. Kirk Douglas, Bella Darvi, Gilbert Roland, Lee J.

Cobb, Cesar Romero, Katy Jurado. Hackneyed sports-car racing yarn, not salvaged by Douglas' dynamics or European location shooting.

Rachel and the Stranger (1948) 93m. *** D: Norman Foster. Loretta Young, William Holden, Robert Mitchum, Tom Tully, Sara Haden. Star trio are fine in this Western of man whose love for his wife is first aroused when stranger Mitchum visits their home.

Rachel, Rachel (1968) C-101m. ***½ D: Paul Newman. Joanne Woodward, James Olson, Kate Harrington, Estelle Parsons, Donald Moffatt, Terry Kiser. Beautifully sensitive, mature film about spinster schoolteacher trying to come out of her shell; Woodward is superb, directed here by husband Newman.

Racing Fever (1964) C-80m. BOMB D: William Grefe. Joe Morrison, Charles Martin, Maxine Carroll, Barbara Biggart. Torrid trash of speedboat racing, an accidental killing, and revenge.

Rack, The (1956) 100m. *** D: Arnold Laven. Paul Newman, Wendell Corey, Walter Pidgeon, Edmond O'Brien, Anne Francis, Lee Marvin. Newman is pensively convincing as Korean War veteran on trial for treason, with Pidgeon as his father and Francis his friend. Slick production adapted from Rod Serling teleplay.

Racket, The (1951) 88m. *** D: John Cromwell. Robert Mitchum, Lizabeth Scott, Robert Ryan, William Talman. Taut melodrama of rugged police captain fighting corruption in the city; sensibly acted.

Racket Busters (1938) 71m. ** D: Lloyd Bacon. George Brent, Humphrey Bogart, Gloria Dickson, Allen Jenkins, Walter Abel, Henry O'Neill, Penny Singleton. Mobster Bogie's going to take over the trucking business, but Brent doesn't want to cooperate. Standard programmer moves along well.

Racquet (1979) C-89m. *½ D: David Winters. Bert Convy, Edie Adams, Lynda Day George, Phil Silvers, Bobby Riggs, Susan Tyrrell, Bruce Kimmel, Bjorn Borg. Pea-brained comedy with Convy as Beverly Hills tennis pro who uses his sex appeal to raise money for a court of his own.

Radar Men From the Moon SEE: Retik, The Moon Menace

Rafferty and the Gold Dust Twins (1975) C-92m. **½ D: Dick Richards. Alan Arkin, Sally Kellerman, MacKenzie Phillips, Alex Rocco, Charlie Martin Smith, Harry Dean Stanton. Appealing but aimless film about a pair of women who force nebbish Arkin to drive them to New Orleans from L.A. Retitled RAFFERTY AND THE HIGHWAY HUSTLERS for TV.

Raffles (1940) 72m. **½ D: Sam Wood. David Niven, Olivia de Havilland, Dudley Digges, Dame May Whitty, Douglas Walton, Lionel Pape. Mild remake of E. W. Hornung's famous tale of gentleman jewel thief; pleasant but nothing special. John Barrymore filmed it in 1917, Ronald Colman in 1930.

Rage (1966) C-103m. *½ D: Gilberto Gazcon. Glenn Ford, Stella Stevens, David Reynoso, Armando Silvestre, Ariadna Welter. Overstated drama of misanthropic doctor Ford who contracts rabies and races clock across Mexican desert to get help.

Rage (1972) C-104m. ** D: George C. Scott. George C. Scott, Richard Basehart, Martin Sheen, Barnard Hughes, Nicolas Beauvy, Paul Stevens. When peaceful rancher Scott's young son is killed by chemical testing, he takes revenge on those responsible for accident. Good photography, but Scott's transition from nice-guy to killer isn't convincing.

Rage at Dawn (1955) C-87m. ** D: Tim Whelan. Randolph Scott, Forrest Tucker, Mala Powers, J. Carrol Naish, Edgar Buchanan. Routine Scott Western entry, with Randy et al involved in hunting down outlaw gang.

Rage in Heaven (1941) 83m. ** D: W. S. Van Dyke II. Robert Montgomery, Ingrid Bergman, George Sanders, Lucile Watson, Oscar Homolka, Philip Merivale, Matthew Boulton. Disappointing story of mentally disturbed steel mill owner who suggests double suicide scheme; set in England.

Rage of Paris, The (1938) 75m. *** D: Henry Koster. Danielle Darrieux, Douglas Fairbanks, Jr., Mischa Auer, Louis Hayward, Helen Broderick. Fast-talkers team up to use lovely Darrieux to snare rich husband; fast-paced comedy is fun all the way, Darrieux a delight. Same team that Hollywoodized neophyte Deanna Durbin concocted this winsome image for the French actress.

Rage of the Buccaneers, The (1961-Italian) C-88m. ** D: Mario Costa. Ricardo Montalban, Vincent Price, Giulia Rubini, Liana Orfei. Juvenile but bouncy yarn which is set more on land than at sea, with pirate Montalban vs. Price, villainous governor's secretary.

Rage to Live (1965) 101m. ** D: Walter Grauman. Suzanne Pleshette, Bradford Dillman, Ben Gazzara, Peter Graves, Bethel Leslie, James Gregory. Poor version of John O'Hara novel of free-swinging girl who tries marriage only to discover she still needs to have affairs with men.

Raggedy Ann and Andy (1977) C-85m. *½ D: Richard Williams. Slow-moving, uninvolving children's cartoon with endless songs by Joe Raposo that stop action dead in its tracks. Appealing characters with nowhere to go; only highlight is Camel with Wrinkled Knees singing "Song Blue."

Raging Moon SEE: Long Ago, Tomorrow

Raging Tide, The (1951) 93m. **½ D: George Sherman. Richard Conte, Shelley Winters, Stephen McNally, Charles Bickford. Stereotyped script and typecast acting make this murderer-on-the-run yarn tame.

Raid, The (1954) C-83m. *** D: Hugo Fregonese. Van Heflin, Anne Bancroft, Richard Boone, Lee Marvin, Tommy Rettig. Well-handled story of Confederate prisoners escaping from jail in upper New England, with Bancroft and Rettig trying to snafu their marauding.

Raid on Entebbe (1977) C-150m. TVM D: Irvin Kershner. Peter Finch, Charles Bronson, Horst Buchholz, Martin Balsam, John Saxon, Jack Warden, Sylvia Sidney, Yaphet Kotto. Intelligent drama about Israeli commando rescue of hijacked hostages at Entebbe, Uganda, on July 4, 1976. Finch's last work on film garnered him an Emmy nomination. Covers same ground as VICTORY AT ENTEBBE and OPERATION THUNDERBOLT. Above average.

Raid on Rommel (1971) C-99m. *½ D: Henry Hathaway. Richard Burton, John Colicos, Clinton Greyn, Wolfgang Preiss. Poor excuse to utilize old desert footage and new faces in worn-out WW2 format.

Raiders, The (1952) C-80m. **½

D: Lesley Selander. Richard Conte, Viveca Lindfors, Barbara Britton, Hugh O'Brian, Richard Martin, William Reynolds. Sometimes with-it oater about judge during California gold rush days, leading a land-grabbing gang. Retitled: RIDERS OF VENGEANCE.

Raiders, The (1963) C-75m. **½ D: Herschel Daugherty. Robert Culp, Brian Keith, Judi Meredith, James McMullan, Alfred Ryder, Simon Oakland. Enthusiastic cast helps this story of cattle drives and the railroad expansion westward.

Raiders of Leyte Gulf, The (1963) 80m. **½ D: Eddie Romero. Michael Parsons, Leopold Salcedo, Jennings Sturgeon, Liza Moreno, Efren Reyes. Gritty account of WW2 against Japanese forces, filmed in the Philippines.

Raiders of Old California (1957) 72m. BOMB D: Albert Gannaway. Jim Davis, Arleen Whelan, Lee Van Cleef, Louis Jean Heydt. Minor Western set in the 1850s.

Raiders of the Seven Seas (1953) C-88m. **½ D: Sidney Salkow. John Payne, Donna Reed, Gerald Mohr, Lon Chaney. Pirate Barbarossa saves countess from marriage to cutthroat, eventually falls in love.

Railroad Man, The SEE: Man of Iron

Rails Into Laramie (1954) C-81m. ** D: Jesse Hibbs. John Payne, Mari Blanchard, Dan Duryea, Joyce MacKenzie, Barton MacLane. Pat movie of Payne's efforts to clean up title town and keep railroad construction moving westward.

Railway Children, The (1972-British) C-102m. *** D: Lionel Jeffries. Dinah Sheridan, Bernard Cribbins, William Mervyn, Iain Cuthbertson, Jenny Agutter, Gary Warren. Charming story of youthful trio whose one goal is to clear their father of false espionage prison sentence. Lovely Yorkshire locales add to overall effectiveness.

Rain (1932) 93m. **½ D: Lewis Milestone. Joan Crawford, Walter Huston, William Gargan, Guy Kibbee, Walter Catlett, Beulah Bondi. Considered a flop in 1932, this version of Maugham's story looks better today. Crawford is good as South Seas island trollop confronted by fire-and-brimstone preacher Huston. Director Milestone does gymnastics with camera during stagier scenes;

an interesting antique. Filmed again as MISS SADIE THOMPSON.

Rain People, The (1969) C-102m. *** D: Francis Ford Coppola. James Caan, Shirley Knight, Robert Duvall, Marya Zimmet, Tom Aldredge, Lloyd Crews. Pregnant Long Island housewife, unable to take married life, flees husband and picks up simple-minded football player on the road. Strong acting and direction triumph over weak script in film whose subject matter was years ahead of its time.

Rainbow (1978) C-100m. TVM D: Jackie Cooper. Andrea McArdle, Don Murray, Piper Laurie, Martin Balsam, Michael Parks, Jack Carter, Donna Pescow. Young Judy Garland's rise from struggling vaudeville performer to THE WIZARD OF OZ, with the star of Broadway's ANNIE completely miscast in the lead. Story is seemingly accurate and given a touch of authenticity by director Jackie Cooper, one-time Garland beau in his youth. Average.

Rainbow Island (1944) C-97m. **½ D: Ralph Murphy. Dorothy Lamour, Eddie Bracken, Gil Lamb, Barry Sullivan, Anne Revere, Olga San Juan, Elena Verdugo, Yvonne De Carlo. Good cast main asset in musical comedy of merchant marines stranded on island with beautiful natives.

Rainbow Jacket, The (1954-British) C-99m. ** D: Basil Dearden. Kay Walsh, Bill Owen, Fella Edmonds, Robert Morley. Colorful racetrack sequences spark this predictable study of Owen, veteran jockey gone wrong, who teaches Edmonds how to race properly.

Rainbow 'Round My Shoulder (1952) C-78m. *½ D: Richard Quine. Frankie Laine, Billy Daniels, Charlotte Austin, Arthur Franz, Barbara Whiting. Comedown from 1940s all-star musicals. Here Austin is gal thrust into movie career. "Musical" interludes are passé.

Rainbow Trail, The (1925) 58m. *** D: Lynn Reynolds. Tom Mix, Anne Cornwall, George Bancroft, Lucien Littlefield, Mark Hamilton, Vivien Oakland. Sequel to RIDERS OF THE PURPLE SAGE, another robust Zane Grey tale about man who determines to penetrate isolated Paradise Valley, where his uncle trapped himself with a young woman. Handsome production of oft-filmed story.

Rainmaker, The (1956) C-121m. *** D: Joseph Anthony. Burt Lancaster, Katharine Hepburn, Wendell Corey, Lloyd Bridges, Earl Holliman, Cameron Prud'homme, Wallace Ford. Hepburn brings conviction to story of spinster in Southwestern town romanced by glib con-man (Lancaster). N. Richard Nash play was later musicalized as 110 IN THE SHADE.

Rains Came, The (1939) 104m. **½ D: Clarence Brown. Myrna Loy, Tyrone Power, George Brent, Brenda Joyce, Nigel Bruce, Maria Ouspenskaya, Joseph Schildkraut, Laura Hope Crews. Louis Bromfield novel reduced to Hollywood terms. Indian Power loves socialite Loy. Good earthquake scenes. Remade as THE RAINS OF RANCHIPUR.

Rains of Ranchipur, The (1955) C-104m. **½ D: Jean Negulesco. Lana Turner, Richard Burton, Fred MacMurray, Joan Caulfield, Michael Rennie, Eugenie Leontovich. Superficial remake of THE RAINS CAME; story of wife of Englishman having affair with Hindu doctor. Attractive in color.

Raintree County (1957) C-168m. *** D: Edward Dmytryk. Montgomery Clift, Elizabeth Taylor, Eva Marie Saint, Lee Marvin, Nigel Patrick, Rod Taylor, Agnes Moorehead, Walter Abel. Elaborate but confused Civil War romantic epic. Taylor has mild tour de force as Southern belle bent on having everything. Clift as her love interest is erratic.

Raisin in the Sun, A (1961) 128m. **** D: Daniel Petrie. Sidney Poitier, Claudia McNeil, Ruby Dee, Diana Sands, Ivan Dixon. Lorraine Hansberry play receives perceptive handling by outstanding cast in drama of Chicago Negro family and their attempts to find sense in their constrained existence.

Raising a Riot (1957-British) C-90m. ** D: Wendy Toye. Kenneth More, Shelagh Fraser, Ronald Squire, Bill Shine. Predictable situation comedy of More trying to cope with his rambunctious trio of children.

Raising the Wind (1961-British) C-91m. **½ D: Gerald Thomas. James Robertson Justice, Leslie Phillips, Sidney James, Paul Massie, Kenneth Williams. Zany shenanigans of eccentric group of students at a London school of music; well paced.

Rally 'Round the Flag Boys! (1958) C-106m. **½ D: Leo McCarey. Paul Newman, Joanne Woodward, Joan

Collins, Jack Carson. Disappointing film of Max Shulman's book about small community in uproar over projected missile base. Wit is noticeably lacking.

Ramona (1936) C-90m. ** D: Henry King. Loretta Young, Don Ameche, Kent Taylor, Pauline Frederick, Jane Darwell, Katherine DeMille. Ofttold tale doesn't wear well, with Young and Ameche as Indians in love, shunned by American society. Settings are picturesque.

Rampage (1963) C-98m. **½ D: Phil Karlson. Robert Mitchum, Elsa Martinelli, Jack Hawkins, Sabu, Cely Carillo, Emile Genest. German gamehunter (Hawkins), his mistress (Martinelli), and hunting guide (Mitchum) form love triangle, with men battling for Elsa. Elmer Bernstein's score is memorable.

Rampage at Apache Wells (1966-German) C-90m. ** D: Harold Philipps. Stewart Granger, Pierre Brice, Macha Meril, Harold Leipnitz. Granger stars as Old Shatterhand, who fights for rights of Indians taken in by crooked white men. Adequate acting cannot compete with atrocious dubbing.

Ramparts of Clay (1971-French-Algerian) C-85m. *** D: Jean-Louis Bertucelli. Leila Schenna. Intriguing film about Tunisian woman, disillusioned with her way of life, who becomes involved with strike between a wealthy company and poor villagers. Very strong for patient, critical viewers; for others, boredom.

Ramrod (1947) 94m. **½ D: Andre de Toth. Veronica Lake, Joel McCrea, Arleen Whelan, Don DeFore, Preston Foster, Charles Ruggles, Donald Crisp, Lloyd Bridges. Fairly good Western of territorial dispute between ranch-owner Lake and her father (Ruggles). Good supporting cast.

Rancho Deluxe (1975) C-93m. ***½ D: Frank Perry. Jeff Bridges, Sam Waterston, Elizabeth Ashley, Charlene Dallas, Clifton James, Slim Pickens, Harry Dean Stanton. Already a cult favorite, this offbeat comedy centers on two casual cattle rustlers; written by Thomas McGuane (92 IN THE SHADE), with music by Jimmy Buffett.

Rancho Notorious (1952) C-89m. *** D: Fritz Lang. Marlene Dietrich, Arthur Kennedy, Mel Ferrer, Lloyd Gough, Gloria Henry, William Frawley, Jack Elam, George Reeves. Entertaining, offbeat Western with Kennedy looking for murderer of his sweetheart, ending up at Marlene's bandit hideout. Colorful characters spice up routine story.

Random Harvest (1942) 128m. *** D: Mervyn LeRoy. Greer Garson, Ronald Colman, Philip Dorn, Susan Peters, Reginald Owen, Bramwell Fletcher, Margaret Wycherly, Ann Richards. James Hilton story about amnesiac (Colman) who forgets the woman he loves, and her attempt to rekindle their relationship. Garson does memorable kilt-dance in an atypical role. Colman, LeRoy, Peters, film and screenplay all received Oscar nominations.

Rangers of Fortune (1940) 80m. **½ D: Sam Wood. Fred MacMurray, Albert Dekker, Gilbert Roland, Patricia Morison, Dick Foran, Joseph Schildkraut. Smartly-whipped-together yarn of trio fleeing Mexicans, stopping off in Southwestern town to offer assistance.

Ransom (1956) 109m. **½ D: Alex Segal. Glenn Ford, Donna Reed, Leslie Nielsen, Juano Hernandez, Alexander Scourby, Juanita Moore, Robert Keith. Brooding narrative of Ford's efforts to rescue his son who's been kidnapped.

Ransom for a Dead Man (1971) C-100m. TVM D: Richard Irving. Lee Grant, Peter Falk, John Fink, Harold Gould, Patricia Mattick, Paul Carr. Lawyer Williams (Grant) murders husband but is foiled in escape plan by deceptively simple-minded police lieutenant (Falk). Good script, performances by entire cast. Pilot for COLUMBO series.

Ransom for Alice (1977) C-78m. TVM D: David Lowell Rich. Gil Gerard, Yvette Mimieux, Charles Napier, Gene Barry, Harris Yulin, Laurie Prange, Barnard Hughes, Gavin MacLeod. Cop show set in 1890s Seattle with Gerard and Mimieux as deputy marshals turned agile undercover agents to crack a white slavery ring. Average.

Rape of Malaya SEE: **Town Like Alice, A**

Rapture (1965-French) 104m. *** D: John Guillermin. Melvyn Douglas, Dean Stockwell, Patricia Gozzi, Gunnel Lindblom, Leslie Sands. Intensive, sensitive account of Gozzi's tragic romance with Stockwell, a man on the run.

Rare Breed, The (1966) C-108m. **½ D: Andrew V. McLaglen. James

Stewart, Maureen O'Hara, Brian Keith, Juliet Mills. Wholesome oater, with fetching O'Hara as woman who brings Hereford bull to U.S. to be bred, and can't decide whether to marry ranch owner Keith or former associate Stewart.

Rascal (1969) C-85m. **½ D: Norman Tokar. Steve Forrest, Bill Mumy, Pamela Toll, Bettye Ackerman, Elsa Lanchester, Henry Jones. Disney adaptation of Sterling North's well-regarded autobiographical novel about his boyhood friendship with raccoon; reworked to Disney formula, with pleasant but predictable results.

Rashomon (1951-Japanese) 90m. ***½ D: Akira Kurosawa. Toshiro Mifune, Machiko Kyo, Masayuki Mori, Takashi Shimura. Superlative study of truth and human nature as four people involved in a rape-murder tell varying accounts of what happened. Remade as THE OUTRAGE.

Rasputin and the Empress (1932) 123m. *** D: Richard Boleslawsky. John, Ethel and Lionel Barrymore, Ralph Morgan, Diana Wynyard, C. Henry Gordon. Good drama that should have been great, with all three Barrymores in colorful roles, unfolding story of mad monk's plotting against Russia.

Rasputin—the Mad Monk (1966-British) C-92m. ** D: Don Sharp. Christopher Lee, Barbara Shelley, Richard Pasco, Francis Matthews. Confused historical drama of "monk" who actually controlled Russia before Revolution. Script uncommonly bad; Lee's performance manages to redeem film.

Rat Race, The (1960) C-105m. *** D: Robert Mulligan. Tony Curtis, Debbie Reynolds, Jack Oakie, Kay Medford, Don Rickles, Joe Bushkin. Comedy-drama of would-be musician (Curtis) and dancer (Reynolds) coming to N.Y.C., platonically sharing an apartment, and falling in love. Nice comic cameos by Oakie and Medford. Based on Garson Kanin play.

Rationing (1944) 93m. **½ D: Willis Goldbeck. Wallace Beery, Marjorie Main, Donald Meek, Gloria Dickson, Henry O'Neill, Connie Gilchrist. Butcher in small town is main character in story of problems during WW2; typical Beery vehicle.

Raton Pass (1951) 84m. **½ D: Edwin L. Marin. Dennis Morgan, Patricia Neal, Steve Cochran, Scott Forbes, Dorothy Hart. Middling Warner Bros. Western, with Morgan and Neal married couple fighting each other for cattle empire.

Rattle of a Simple Man (1964-British) 96m. *** D: Muriel Box. Harry H. Corbett, Diane Cilento, Thora Hird, Michael Medwin. Pleasant saucy sex comedy of timid soul Corbett spending the night with Cilento to win a bet; set in London.

Ravagers (1979) C-91m. BOMB D: Richard Compton. Richard Harris, Ann Turkel, Ernest Borgnine, Art Carney, Anthony James, Woody Strode, Alana Hamilton. Instant tax loss finds Harris searching for civilization in 1991 after most human life has been wiped out. Instead, he finds Borgnine.

Ravagers, The (1965) 79m. *½ D: Eddie Romero. John Saxon, Fernando Poe, Jr., Bronwyn Fitzsimmons, Mike Parsons, Kristina Scott. Uninspired account of Allied fight against Japanese in WW2 Philippines; filmed on location. Fitzsimmons, incidentally, is Maureen O'Hara's daughter.

Raven, The (1935) 62m. *** D: Louis Friedlander (Lew Landers). Boris Karloff, Bela Lugosi, Irene Ware, Lester Matthews, Samuel S. Hinds. Momentous teaming of horror greats with Lugosi as doctor with Poe-obsession, Karloff a victim of his wicked schemes. Hinds is subjected to torture from PIT AND THE PENDULUM in film's climax. Great fun throughout.

Raven, The (1963) C-86m. *** D: Roger Corman. Vincent Price, Boris Karloff, Peter Lorre, Hazel Court, Jack Nicholson. Funny horror satire by Corman finds sorcerers Price and Lorre challenging power-hungry colleague Karloff. Climactic sorcerer's duel is a highlight.

Ravine, The (1969-Italian-Yugoslavian) C-97m. ** D: Paolo Cavara. David McCallum, Nicoletta Machiavelli, John Crawford, Lars Loch, Demeter Bietnc. Tepid story of German soldier (McCallum) who falls in love with sniper he is supposed to kill during WW2.

Ravishing Idiot (1965-French) 110m. ** D: Edouard Molinaro. Anthony Perkins, Brigitte Bardot. Bungler used to help steal file on NATO ship maneuvers. Supposedly it's funny, but don't you believe it.

Raw Deal (1948) 79m. *** D: Anthony Mann. Dennis O'Keefe, Claire

Trevor, Marsha Hunt, Raymond Burr, John Ireland. Beautifully made, hard-boiled story of O'Keefe escaping from jail to take out revenge on slimy Burr, who framed him; what's more, he gets caught between love of two women. Tough and convincing, with Burr a sadistic heavy.

Raw Edge (1956) **C-76m. **½ D: John Sherwood. Rory Calhoun, Yvonne De Carlo, Mara Corday, Rex Reason, Neville Brand. Bizarre premise routinely told; rancher's workers plan to kill him, with his widow to be the prize stake.

Raw Wind in Eden (1958) **C-89m. **½ D: Richard Wilson. Esther Williams, Jeff Chandler, Rossana Podesta, Carlos Thompson. Melodramatic soaper of clash and romance on small isolated island when yacht is wrecked in a storm.

Rawhide (1951) 86m. **½ D: Henry Hathaway. Tyrone Power, Susan Hayward, Hugh Marlowe, Dean Jagger, Edgar Buchanan, Jack Elam. Climactic shoot-out sparks this Western of outlaws holding group of people captive at stagecoach station. Remake of 1936 gangster film SHOW THEM NO MERCY. Retitled: DESPERATE SIEGE.

Rawhide Trail, The (1958) 67m. *½ D: Robert Gordan. Rex Reason, Nancy Gates, Richard Erdman, Ann Doran. Humdrum tale of duo proving their innocence of helping the Indians attack settlers.

Rawhide Years, The (1956) **C-85m. ** D: Rudolph Maté. Tony Curtis, Colleen Miller, Arthur Kennedy, William Demarest, William Gargan. Youthful Curtis perks this routine fare of gambler trying to clear himself of murder charge.

Raymie (1950) 72m. ** D: Frank McDonald. David Ladd, Julie Adams, John Agar, Charles Winninger, Richard Arlen, Frank Ferguson, Ray Kellogg. Quiet little film about youngster (Ladd) whose greatest ambition is to catch the big fish that always eludes him.

Razor's Edge, The (1946) 146m. ***½ D: Edmund Goulding. Tyrone Power, Gene Tierney, John Payne, Anne Baxter, Clifton Webb, Herbert Marshall. Maugham's philosophical novel, with Marshall as the author, Power as hero seeking goodness in life, Baxter in Oscar-winning role as a dipsomaniac, Elsa Lanchester sparkling in bit as social secretary. Long but engrossing.

Reach for Glory (1963-British) 89m. **½ D: Philip Leacock. Harry Andrews, Kay Walsh, Oliver Grimm, Michael Anderson, Jr., Martin Tomlinson, Alexis Kanner. Sensitive if minor tale about WW2 England, involving youths and their special code of ethics, leading to one member's death.

Reach for the Sky (1956-British) 123m. **½ D: Lewis Gilbert. Kenneth More, Muriel Pavlow, Alexander Knox, Sydney Tafler, Nigel Green. Sensibly told account of British pilot who overcame leg injury to continue his flying career.

Reaching for the Moon (1931) 90m. **½ D: Edmund Goulding. Douglas Fairbanks, Sr., Bebe Daniels, Edward Everett Horton, Jack Mulhall, Helen Jerome Eddy, Bing Crosby. Enjoyable Depression film of financier Fairbanks, with Horton as his valet, Bebe the girl, and Crosby singing one song.

Reaching for the Sun (1941) 90m. **½ D: William Wellman. Joel McCrea, Ellen Drew, Eddie Bracken, Albert Dekker, Billy Gilbert, George Chandler. OK comedy of North Woods clam-digger who journeys to Detroit to earn money for outboard motor.

Real American Story, A (1978) C-100m. TVM D: Lou Antonio. Brian Dennehy, Forrest Tucker, Brian Kerwin, Ken Howard, Sheree North, Lane Bradbury. Folk hero Buford Pusser, the club-wielding law-and-order sheriff of Selmer, Tennessee, whose career inspired three ultraviolent movies beginning with WALKING TALL is the subject of this film, battling a dapper local moonshiner this time. Average.

Real Glory, The (1939) 95m. *** D: Henry Hathaway. Gary Cooper, David Niven, Andrea Leeds, Reginald Owen, Kay Johnson, Broderick Crawford, Vladimir Sokoloff, Henry Kolker. Cooper's fine as Army medic who solves all of Philippines' medical and military problems almost single-handedly after destructive Spanish-American War. Excellent action scenes.

Real Life (1979) C-99m. **½ D: Albert Brooks. Albert Brooks, Charles Grodin, Frances Lee McCain, J. A. Preston, Matthew Tobin. Writer-director-comedian Brooks' first feature doesn't sustain its comic premise as well as his hilarious short subjects, but still presents the world's greatest put-on artist in a compatible vehicle; as a shifty opportunist who sets out to make a filmed record of a typical American family.

Reap the Wild Wind (1942) C-124m. *** D: Cecil B. DeMille. Ray Milland, John Wayne, Paulette Goddard, Raymond Massey, Robert Preston, Susan Hayward, Charles Bickford, Hedda Hopper, Louise Beavers, Martha O'Driscoll, Lynne Overman. Brawling DeMille hokum of 19th-century salvagers in Georgia, with Goddard as fiery Southern belle. Milland and Wayne fighting for her, Massey as odious villain. Exciting underwater scenes; Milland good in offbeat characterization.

Rear Window (1954) C-122m. **** D: Alfred Hitchcock. James Stewart, Grace Kelly, Wendell Corey, Thelma Ritter, Raymond Burr, Judith Evelyn. Grade-A Hitchcock has Stewart confined to wheelchair, using binoculars to spy on courtyard neighbors, discovering murder. Kelly chic as society girlfriend, Ritter wry as housekeeper.

Reason to Live, a Reason to Die, A (1974-Italian) C-92m. ** D: Tonino Valerii. James Coburn, Telly Savalas, Bud Spencer, Robert Burton. Ordinary Western, an Italian-French-West German-Spanish co-production. Union Colonel Coburn and seven condemned men attempt to recapture a Missouri fort from brutal Confederate Major Savalas. Retitled MASSACRE AT FORT HOLMAN.

Rebecca (1940) 130m. **** D: Alfred Hitchcock. Laurence Olivier, Joan Fontaine, George Sanders, Judith Anderson, Nigel Bruce, Reginald Denny. Oscar-winning adaptation of Daphne du Maurier tale of girl who marries British nobleman but lives in shadow of former wife. Stunning performances by Fontaine and Anderson; Academy Award winner as Best Picture.

Rebecca of Sunnybrook Farm (1938) 80m. **½ D: Allan Dwan. Shirley Temple, Randolph Scott, Jack Haley, Gloria Stuart, Phyllis Brooks, Helen Westley, Slim Summerville. Misleading title has nothing to do with famous story; this is story of Shirley becoming radio star while Scott and Stuart romance. Shirley also dances with "Bojangles" Robinson.

Rebel in Town (1956) 78m. ** D: Alfred L. Werker. John Payne, Ruth Roman, J. Carrol Naish, Ben Cooper, John Smith. Sensitive minor Western; renegade is present when his brother accidentally kills a child. Ironic events bring him into contact with boy's father.

Rebel Rousers (1967) C-78m. **½ D: Martin B. Cohen. Cameron Mitchell, Jack Nicholson, Bruce Dern, Diane Ladd, Harry Dean Stanton. Architect Mitchell isn't pleased when Dern holds drag-race to see who will "win" Dern's pregnant girlfriend. Nicholson, decked out in outrageous striped pants, steals the show in this amusing time-capsule.

Rebel Set, The (1959) 72m. *½ D: Gene Fowler, Jr. Gregg Palmer, Kathleen Crowley, Edward Platt, Ned Glass, John Lupton. Minor crime caper involving youths used by gangster to help carry out a robbery.

Rebel Without a Cause (1955) C-111m. ***½ D: Nicholas Ray. James Dean, Natalie Wood, Sal Mineo, Jim Backus, Ann Doran, Dennis Hopper, Nick Adams. Classic study of preconditioned juvenile delinquency, with gutsy telling of why Dean-Wood-Mineo became involved in tragic outcome.

Reckless (1935) 96m. ** D: Victor Fleming. Jean Harlow, William Powell, Franchot Tone, May Robson, Ted Healy, Nat Pendleton, Rosalind Russell. Big cast, big production, musical numbers—all can't save script of chorus girl tangling up several people's lives. Tired and phony.

Reckless Moment, The (1949) 82m. ***½ D: Max Ophuls. James Mason, Joan Bennett, Geraldine Brooks, Henry O'Neill, Shepperd Strudwick, Roy Roberts. Bennett becomes a murderer, pursued by blackmailer Mason. First-rate suspenser.

Reckoning, The (1969-British) C-111m. **½ D: Jack Gold. Nicol Williamson, Rachel Roberts, Paul Rogers, Zena Walker, Ann Bell. Contrived, latter day "angry young man" film, with Williamson (excellent as usual) as brooding businessman incapable of living in harmony with society, and out to avenge long-ago slight to his father.

Red Alert (1977) C-100m. TVM D: William Hale. William Devane, Michael Brandon, Adrienne Barbeau, Ralph Waite, David Hayward, M. Emmet Walsh. Taut suspense thriller about an accident at a nuclear power plant. Interesting science-fact with

Devane and Waite as antagonists. Average.

Red Badge of Courage, The (1951) 69m. ***½ D: John Huston. Audie Murphy, Bill Mauldin, John Dierkes, Royal Dano, Arthur Hunnicutt, Douglas Dick. Stephen Crane's human focus on Civil War, not treated as spectacle, resulting in realistic drama with natural performances.

Red Badge of Courage, The (1974) C-78m. TVM D: Lee Philips. Richard Thomas, Michael Brandon, Wendell Burton, Charles Aidman, Warren Berlinger, Lee DeBroux. TV remake of Stephen Crane classic, telling of the youth who runs away from his first Civil War battle but returns to be a soldier. Thomas is fine in the lead. Above average.

Red Ball Express (1952) 83m. *** D: Budd Boetticher. Jeff Chandler, Alex Nicol, Judith Braun, Hugh O'Brian, Jack Kelly, Sidney Poitier, Jack Warden. Energetic cast and fast-paced action blend well in this account of supply unit working behind the German lines.

Red Beret SEE: **Paratrooper**

Red Canyon (1949) C-82m. ** D: George Sherman. Ann Blyth, Howard Duff, George Brent, Edgar Buchanan, Chill Wills, Jane Darwell, Lloyd Bridges. Routine Zane Grey Western of wild horses being tamed.

Red Circle, The (1960-German) 94m. **½ D: Jurgen Roland. Fritz Rasp, Karl Saebisch, Renate Ewert, Klausjurgen Wussow. Scotland Yard investigates series of murders, with each victim having telltale circle mark on his neck; slickly paced.

Red Dance, The (1928) 103m. **½ D: Raoul Walsh. Charles Farrell, Dolores Del Rio, Ivan Linow, Boris Charsky, Dorothy Revier. Opulent production makes up for silly story of romance and intrigue during the Russian revolution.

Red Danube, The (1949) 119m. **½ D: George Sidney. Walter Pidgeon, Ethel Barrymore, Peter Lawford, Angela Lansbury, Janet Leigh, Louis Calhern, Francis L. Sullivan. Meandering drama of ballerina Leigh pursued by Russian agents, aided by amorous Lawford; heavy-handed at times.

Red Dragon, The (1945) 64m. D: Phil Rosen. Sidney Toler, Fortunio Bonanova, Benson Fong, Robert Emmett Keane, Willie Best, Carol Hughes. SEE: **Charlie Chan** series.

Red Dragon (1967-German) C-88m. **½ D: Ernest Hofbauer. Stewart Granger, Rosanna Schiaffino, Horst Frank, Suzanne Roquette. Granger is F.B.I. agent in Hong Kong chasing smuggling gang, Schiaffino another agent. Well paced, but predictable script.

Red Dust (1932) 83m. ***½ D: Victor Fleming. Clark Gable, Jean Harlow, Mary Astor, Donald Crisp, Gene Raymond, Tully Marshall, Willie Fung. Robust romance of Indochina rubber worker Gable, his floozie gal Harlow, and visiting Astor, who is married to Raymond, but falls for Gable. Harlow has fine comic touch. Remade as CONGO MAISIE and MOGAMBO.

Red Garters (1954) C-91m. **½ D: George Marshall. Rosemary Clooney, Jack Carson, Guy Mitchell, Pat Crowley, Gene Barry. Musical western spoof gets A for effort—with strikingly stylized color sets, offbeat casting—but falls short of target.

Red Headed Woman (1932) 74m. *** D: Jack Conway. Jean Harlow, Chester Morris, Una Merkel, Lewis Stone, May Robson, Leila Hyams, Charles Boyer. Harlow has never been sexier than in this precensorship story (by Anita Loos) of a gold-digging secretary who sets out to corral her married boss (Morris).

Red, Hot and Blue (1949) 84m. **½ D: John Farrow. Betty Hutton, Victor Mature, William Demarest, June Havoc, Frank Loesser, Raymond Walburn. Noisy Hutton vehicle of ambitious girl trying to make it big in show biz, mixed up with gangsters.

Red House, The (1947) 100m. *** D: Delmer Daves. Edward G. Robinson, Lon McCallister, Allene Roberts, Judith Anderson, Rory Calhoun, Julie London, Ona Munson. Title refers to strange old house containing many mysteries, providing constant fear for farmer Robinson. Exciting melodrama with fine cast.

Red Inn, The (1954-French) 100m. **½ D: Claude Autant-Lara. Fernandel, Francoise Rosay, Carette, Marie-Claire Olivia, Lud Germain. Bizarre account of wayside inn run by woman who robs and murders guests.

Red Light (1949) 83m. ** D: Roy Del Ruth. George Raft, Virginia Mayo, Gene Lockhart, Barton MacLane, Harry Morgan, Raymond Burr. Turgid drama of innocent Raft seeking revenge when freed from prison, hunting brother's killer.

Red Line 7000 (1965) **C-110m.** **½
D: Howard Hawks. James Caan, Laura Devon, Gail Hire, Charlene Holt, John Robert Crawford, Marianna Hill, James Ward. Attempt by director Hawks to do same kind of expert adventure pic he's done for 40 years is sabotaged by bad acting, but is a faster and less pretentious racing-car drama than GRAND PRIX.

Red Mountain (1951) **C-84m.** **½
D: William Dieterle. Alan Ladd, Lizabeth Scott, John Ireland, Arthur Kennedy. Generally actionful Western dealing with the career of Quantrill, Yankee renegade officer during Civil War.

Red Planet Mars (1952) **87m.** **½
D: Harry Horner. Peter Graves, Andrea King, Marvin Miller, Herbert Berghof, House Peters, Vince Barnett. Interesting sci-fi of scientist deciphering messages from Mars. Cast is made up of faces you remember but can't name.

Red Pony, The (1949) **C-89m.** *** D: Lewis Milestone. Myrna Loy, Robert Mitchum, Peter Miles, Louis Calhern, Shepperd Strudwick, Margaret Hamilton. Tasteful version of John Steinbeck book about boy attached to horse, seeking escape from bickering family; leisurely pacing.

Red River (1948) **125m.** **** D: Howard Hawks. John Wayne, Montgomery Clift, Joanne Dru, Walter Brennan, Coleen Gray, John Ireland, Harry Carey, Jr., Noah Beery, Jr. One of the all-time great Westerns, with young Clift rebelling against his foster-father, cattle baron Wayne, during important roundup; beautifully filmed. Clift's film debut.

Red Salute (1935) **78m.** **½ D: Sidney Lanfield. Barbara Stanwyck, Robert Young, Hardie Albright, Cliff Edwards, Ruth Donnelly, Gordon Jones. Runaway screwball Stanwyck meets no-nonsense soldier Young in this imitation IT HAPPENED ONE NIGHT with wild sociopolitical wrinkle: Barbara's boyfriend (Albright) is a student radical who makes Communist speeches! A real oddity. Also known as HER ENLISTED MAN and RUNAWAY DAUGHTER.

Red Shoes, The (1948-British) **C-133m.** **** D: Michael Powell, Emeric Pressburger. Moira Shearer,

Anton Walbrook, Marius Goring, Robert Helpmann, Albert Bassermann. Beautiful, perceptive story of young ballerina (Shearer) and neophyte composer (Goring) being taken under the wing of impresario Walbrook. Title ballet is stunning, especially in color. Sensitive, beautiful film is a genuinely moving experience.

Red Skies of Montana (1952) **C-89m.** **½ D: Joseph M. Newman. Richard Widmark, Jeffrey Hunter, Constance Smith, Richard Boone, Richard Crenna. Trite account of forest-fire fighters, salvaged by spectacular fire sequences.

Red Sky at Morning (1970) **C-112m.** *** D: James Goldstone. Richard Thomas, Catherine Burns, Desi Arnaz, Jr., Richard Crenna, Claire Bloom, John Colicos, Harry Guardino, Strother Martin, Nehemiah Persoff. Unspectacular but pleasing adaptation of Richard Bradford's novel about adolescence during WW2. Comparable to SUMMER OF '42 and in many ways better; Thomas is superb.

Red Stallion, The (1947) **C-82m.** *½ D: Lesley Selander. Robert Paige, Noreen Nash, Ted Donaldson, Jane Darwell, Daisy. Weak little film of ranch boy and his pet horse.

Red Stallion in the Rockies (1949) **C-85m.** ** D: Ralph Murphy. Arthur Franz, Wallace Ford, Ray Collins, Jean Heather, Leatrice Joy. OK outdoor drama of two men rounding up herd of wild horses.

Red Sun (1972-Italian-French-Spanish) **C-112m.** ** D: Terence Young. Charles Bronson, Ursula Andress, Toshiro Mifune, Alain Delon, Capucine. East meets West in this odd story of Samurai warrior pursuing valuable Japanese sword stolen from train crossing American West. Intriguing elements, but a misfire.

Red Sundown (1956) **C-81m.** **½ D: Jack Arnold. Rory Calhoun, Martha Hyer, Dean Jagger, Robert Middleton, James Millican. Virile cast adds zest to standard yarn of bad-guy-gone-good (Calhoun), squeezing out the criminal elements in town.

Red Tent, The (1971-Italian-Russian) **C-121m.** *** D: Mikhail K. Kalatozov. Sean Connery, Claudia Cardinale, Hardy Kruger, Peter Finch, Massimo Girotti. Top-notch adventure saga for kids and adults alike, based on true story of explorer General Nobile (Finch) whose 1928 Arctic expedition turns into disaster. Exciting scenes of survival against elements, dramatic rescue, marred by awkward flashback framework.

Red Tomahawk (1967) C-82m. *½ D: R. G. Springsteen. Howard Keel, Joan Caulfield, Broderick Crawford, Scott Brady, Wendell Corey, Richard Arlen, Tom Drake, Ben Cooper, Donald Barry. Captain Keel saves town from Sioux in routine Western with many of likable performers in the cast.

Redhead and the Cowboy, The (1950) 82m. **½ D: Leslie Fenton. Glenn Ford, Rhonda Fleming, Edmond O'Brien, Morris Ankrum. Effective Western set in Civil War times, with Fleming a Reb spy trying to get message across Union lines.

Redhead From Wyoming, The (1952) C-80m. **½ D: Lee Sholem. Maureen O'Hara, Alexander Scourby, Alex Nicol, Jack Kelly, William Bishop, Dennis Weaver. Saucy Western pepped up by exuberant O'Hara as girl who falls in love with sheriff while protecting local cattle rustler.

Redneck (1972-Italian-British) C-89m. BOMB D: Silvio Narizzano. Franco Nero, Telly Savalas, Mark Lester, Ely Galleani, Duilio Del Prete, Maria Michi. Tawdry, sadistic crime drama about two inept (and unappealing) robbers on the lam who inadvertently "kidnap" a young boy. Unpleasant and unbelievable.

Reefer Madness (1938) 71m. **½ D: Louis Gasnier. Dave O'Brien, Lillian Miles, Warren McCollum, Dorothy Short, Carleton Young, Thelma White. Low-budget exploitation film which purported to depict the evils of marijuana smoking to 1930s audiences. Today it's a camp classic, stupefyingly silly no matter what your point of view. Original titles were THE BURNING QUESTION and TELL YOUR CHILDREN.

Reflection of Fear, A (1973) C-102m. **½ D: William A. Fraker. Robert Shaw, Mary Ure, Sally Kellerman, Sondra Locke, Signe Hasso. Muddled story of beautiful girl who becomes the crucial link in chain of violence and murder.

Reflections in a Golden Eye (1967) C-108m. **½ D: John Huston. Elizabeth Taylor, Marlon Brando, Brian Keith, Julie Harris, Robert Forster, Zorro David. Kinky version of Carson McCullers' novel about homosexual army officer in the South. Not really very good, but cast, subject matter, and Huston's pretentious handling make it fascinating on a minor level. Pretty rough for TV, though.

Reflections of Murder (1974) C-100m. TVM D: John Badham. Tuesday Weld, Joan Hackett, Sam Waterston, Lucille Benson, Michael Lerner, R. G. Armstrong, Lance Kerwin. Wife and mistress conspire to kill a tyrannical schoolteacher who then returns to haunt them. First-class performances make this new version of French classic DIABOLIQUE a superior thriller. Above average.

Reform School Girl (1957) 71m. BOMB D: Edward Bernds. Gloria Castillo, Ross Ford, Edward Byrnes, Ralph Reed, Jack Kruschen, Sally Kellerman. Cheapie production about girl involved with hit-and-run murder.

Reformer and the Redhead, The (1950) 90m. **½ D: Norman Panama, Melvin Frank. June Allyson, Dick Powell, David Wayne, Cecil Kellaway, Ray Collins. Sassy shenanigans with Allyson, a zoo-keeper's daughter, courted by lawyer Powell.

Reign of Terror (1949) 89m. *** D: Anthony Mann. Robert Cummings, Arlene Dahl, Richard Hart, Richard Basehart, Arnold Moss, Beulah Bondi. Vivid costume drama set during French Revolution, with valuable diary eluding both sides of battle; Retitled: BLACK BOOK.

Reincarnation of Peter Proud, The (1975) C-104m. **½ D: J. Lee Thompson. Michael Sarrazin, Jennifer O'Neill, Margot Kidder, Cornelia Sharpe, Paul Hecht, Tony Stephano. The body of a man murdered years before roosts inside Sarrazin, in moderately gripping version of Max Erlich's book. Kidder plays the fiftyish murderess.

Reivers, The (1969) C-107m. ***½ D: Mark Rydell. Steve McQueen, Sharon Farrell, Will Geer, Michael Constantine, Rupert Crosse, Mitch Vogel, Lonny Chapman, Juano Hernandez. Picaresque film from Faulkner novel about young boy (Vogel) in 1905 Mississippi who takes off for adventurous automobile trip with devil-may-care McQueen and buddy

Crosse. Completely winning Americana, full of colorful episodes, equally colorful characters.

Relentless (1948) C-93m. **½ D: George Sherman. Robert Young, Marguerite Chapman, Willard Parker, Akim Tamiroff. Satisfactory Western about cowpoke and his gal trying to prove him innocent of murder charge.

Relentless (1977) C-100m. TVM D: Lee H. Katzin. Will Sampson, Monte Markham, John Hillerman, Marianna Hill, Larry Wilcox, John Lawlor. Stark chase movie that has American Indian state trooper pursuing a band of bank robbers and their hostage through the Arizona mountains. Sampson makes an imposing if offbeat hero. Average.

Reluctant Astronaut, The (1967) C-101m. ** D: Edward Montagne. Don Knotts, Leslie Nielsen, Joan Freeman, Arthur O'Connell, Jesse White. Featherweight comedy dealing with hicksville alumnus Knotts becoming title figure; predictable and often not even childishly humorous. For kids only.

Reluctant Debutante, The (1958) C-94m. **½ D: Vincente Minnelli. Rex Harrison, Kay Kendall, John Saxon, Sandra Dee, Angela Lansbury. Bright drawing-room comedy which Harrison, Kendall, and Lansbury make worthwhile: British parents must present their Americanized daughter to society.

Reluctant Heroes, The (1971) C-73m. TVM D: Robert Day. Ken Berry, Jim Hutton, Trini Lopez, Don Marshall, Ralph Meeker, Cameron Mitchell, Warren Oates. Odd assortment of soldiers collected to take pivotal Hill 656 under command of Army historian with no combat experience. Excellent performances work well with dialogue which would've been ruined in other hands. Above average.

Reluctant Spy, The (1963-French) 93m. **½ D: Jean-Charles Dudrumet. Jean Marais, Genevieve Page, Maurice Teynac, Jean Gallar. Marais properly spoofs James Bond spy thrillers as secret agent chasing around the Continent.

Reluctant Widow, The (1951-British) 86m. *½ D: Bernard Knowles. Jean Kent, Guy Rolfe, Kathleen Byron, Paul Dupuis. Mild drama set in late 18th century, of governess Kent marrying rogue Rolfe.

Remains to be Seen (1953) 89m. *** D: Don Weis. Van Johnson, June Allyson, Angela Lansbury, Louis Calhern, Dorothy Dandridge. Disarming comedy based on Howard Lindsay-Russel Crouse play, with Allyson a singer and Johnson the apartment-house manager involved in swank East Side N.Y.C. murder.

Remarkable Andrew, The (1942) 80m. **½ D: Stuart Heisler. William Holden, Ellen Drew, Brian Donlevy, Rod Cameron, Porter Hall, Nydia Westman, Montagu Love, Jimmy Conlin. Donlevy is the ghost of Andrew Jackson, who comes back to help crusading Holden in small town. Farfetched fantasy, well played.

Remarkable Mr. Pennypacker, The (1959) C-87m. **½ D: Henry Levin. Clifton Webb, Dorothy McGuire, Charles Coburn, Ray Stricklyn, Jill St. John, Ron Ely, David Nelson. Prodded along by Webb's brittle manner, period tale unfolds of Pennsylvania businessman who leads dual life, with two families (17 kids in all).

Rembrandt (1936-British) 84m. ***½ D: Alexander Korda. Charles Laughton, Elsa Lanchester, Gertrude Lawrence, Marius Goring, Abraham Sofaer. Handsome Korda bio of Dutch painter, full of visual tableaux and sparked by Laughton's excellent performance.

Remedy for Riches (1940) 60m. ** D: Erle C. Kenton. Jean Hersholt, Dorothy Lovett, Edgar Kennedy, Jed Prouty, Walter Catlett. Hersholt is kindly Dr. Christian in minor account of coping with patient obsessed by money.

Remember? (1939) 83m. ** D: Norman Z. McLeod. Robert Taylor, Greer Garson, Lew Ayres, Billie Burke, Reginald Owen, Laura Hope Crews, Sig Ruman. Unbelievable tale of man romancing pal's bride-to-be; pleasant but muddled.

Remember My Name (1978) C-96m. *** D: Alan Rudolph. Geraldine Chaplin, Anthony Perkins, Moses Gunn, Berry Berenson, Jeff Goldblum, Timothy Thomerson. Dreamlike film presents fragmented story of woman returning from prison, determined to disrupt her ex-husband's new life. Moody, provocative film definitely not for all tastes; striking blues vocals on soundtrack by Alberta Hunter.

Remember the Day (1941) 85m. ***

D: Henry King. Claudette Colbert, John Payne, John Shepperd (Shepperd Strudwick), Ann B. Todd, Douglas Croft, Jane Seymour, Anne Revere. Sentimental flashback story of pre-WW1 America, with fine performances by Colbert and Payne as schoolteachers who fall in love.

Remember the Night (1940) 86m. *** D: Mitchell Leisen. Barbara Stanwyck, Fred MacMurray, Beulah Bondi, Elizabeth Patterson, Sterling Holloway. Beautifully made, sentimental story of prosecutor MacMurray falling in love with shoplifter Stanwyck during Christmas court recess; builds masterfully as it creates a very special mood. Script by Preston Sturges.

Remember When (1974) C-100m. TVM D: Buzz Kulik. Jack Warden, Robby Benson, Jamie Smith-Jackson, William Schallert, Tim Matheson, Nan Martin, Robert Middleton. Nostalgic drama centering around a suburban family with four boys in combat in WW2. Warden is tops as the live-in uncle filled with memories. Written by Herman Raucher, author of SUMMER OF '42. Above average.

Rendezvous (1935) 91m. ** D: William K. Howard. William Powell, Rosalind Russell, Binnie Barnes, Lionel Atwill, Cesar Romero. OK WW1 intrigue, with Powell assigned to office work instead of combat during war, running into notorious spy ring. Russell's "comedy" character is only obtrusive here.

Rendezvous At Midnight (1935) 64m. ** D: Christy Cabanne. Ralph Bellamy, Valerie Hobson, Catherine Doucet, Irene Ware, Helen Jerome Eddy. OK whodunit of city commissioner being murdered just as his replacement (Bellamy) begins to investigate his corrupt administration.

Rendezvous Hotel (1979) C-100m. TVM D: Peter Hunt. Bill Daily, Jeff Redford, Teddy Wilson, Edward Winter, Bruce French, Sean Garrison, Jeff Donnell. Formula smile-inducer about life in a breezy California resort hotel. A beached version of LOVE BOAT is what this prospective series pilot adds up to. Average.

Renegades (1930) 84m. ** D: Victor Fleming. Warner Baxter, Myrna Loy, Noah Beery, Gregory Gaye, George Cooper, C. Henry Gordon, Bela Lugosi. Stodgy story of renegades from Foreign Legion outpost

in Morocco, one of whom (Baxter) has been betrayed by seductive spy Loy. Complex story builds to offbeat, and downbeat, ending.

Repeat Performance (1947) 93m. *** D: Alfred L. Werker. Louis Hayward, Joan Leslie, Tom Conway, Benay Venuta, Richard Basehart, Virginia Field. Woman gets chance to relive the past year, leading up to the moment she murdered her husband. Fine premise smoothly executed in this B production.

Report to the Commissioner (1975) C-112m. **½ D: Milton Katselas. Michael Moriarty, Yaphet Kotto, Susan Blakely, Hector Elizondo, Tony King, Michael McGuire. Rookie cop Moriarty accidentally kills undercover cop Blakely and becomes embroiled in department-wide cover-up. Brutal melodrama ranges from realistic to overblown; taut but not always convincing.

Reprieve SEE: **Convicts Four**

Reprisal! (1956) C-74m. **½ D: George Sherman. Guy Madison, Felicia Farr, Kathryn Grant, Michael Pate, Edward Platt. Pleasing cast enhances this tale of Madison blamed for death of rancher baron, with Grant and Farr the gals in love with him.

Reptile, The (1966-British) C-90m. *** D: John Gilling. Noel Willman, Jennifer Daniels, Ray Barrett, Jacqueline Pearce. Average film story of girl with strange power to change into snake receives excellent direction and sympathetic characterizations.

Reptilicus (1962) C-90m. ** D: Sidney Pink. Carl Ottosen, Ann Smyrner, Mimi Heinrich, Asbjorn Andersen, Marla Behrens. The tail of a prehistoric monster—recently discovered—spawns the full-sized beast. Good for laughs as script hits every conceivable monster-movie cliché, right to the final shot. Filmed in Denmark.

Repulsion (1965-British) 105m. **** D: Roman Polanski. Catherine Deneuve, Ian Hendry, John Fraser, Patrick Wymark, Yvonne Furneaux. Excellent psychological horror film of mental deterioration of secluded girl. Not for children.

Requiem for a Gunfighter (1965) C-91m. *½ D: Spencer G. Bennet. Rod Cameron, Stephen McNally, Mike Mazurki, Olive Sturgess, Tim McCoy, John Mack Brown, Bob Steele, Lane Chandler, Raymond Hatton.

Veteran cast is sole virtue of low-budget Western. Cameron impersonates a judge to insure that justice is done at murder trial.

Requiem for a Heavyweight (1962) 100m. *** D: Ralph Nelson. Anthony Quinn, Jackie Gleason, Mickey Rooney, Julie Harris, Nancy Cushman, Madame Spivy, Cassius Clay (Muhammad Ali). Grim account of fighter whose ring career is over, forcing him into corruption and degradation. Rooney as pathetic cohort and Harris as unrealistic social worker are fine. Based on Rod Serling's great teleplay; footage added to 87m. theatrical release for television.

Requiem for a Secret Agent (1965-Italian) C-105m. *½ D: Sergio Sollima. Stewart Granger, Daniela Bianchi, Giorgia Moll, Peter Van Eyck, English adventurer called upon by U.S. secret service to fight enemy spy network. Requiescat in pace.

Rest Is Silence, The (1960-German) 106m. *** D: Helmut Kautner. Hardy Kruger, Peter Van Eyck, Ingrid Andree, Adelheid Seeck, Rudolf Forster, Boy Gobert. Updating of Hamlet, with young man trying to prove uncle killed his father.

Restless Breed, The (1957) C-81m. ** D: Allan Dwan. Scott Brady, Anne Bancroft, Jim Davis, Scott Marlowe, Evelyn Rudie. Usual Western fare of Brady out to get his father's killer.

Restless Years, The (1958) 86m. **½ D: Helmut Kautner. John Saxon, Sandra Dee, Margaret Lindsay, Teresa Wright, James Whitmore. Capable cast in overblown melodramatics involving small-town life, the generation gap, skeletons in family closets, etc.

Resurrection of Zachary Wheeler, The (1971) C-100m. *** D: Bob Wynn. Angie Dickinson, Bradford Dillman, James Daly, Leslie Neilsen, Jack Carter. Offbeat mixture of sci-fi and action narrative. U.S. Senator brought to mysterious clinic in Alamogordo, New Mexico after car crash, is accidentally recognized by TV reporter. Only unconvincing aspect: fadeout explanation by clinic director.

Retik, the Moon Menace (1952) 100m. *½ D: Fred C. Brannon. George Wallace, Aline Towne, Roy Barcroft, William Bakewell, Clayton Moore. Ludicrous low-grade cliffer from Republic, involving Commando Cody, who zooms through space with his jet pack, combating alien lunar powers trying to conquer earth. Reedited movie serial: RADAR MEN FROM THE MOON.

Retreat, Hell! (1952) 95m. **½ D: Joseph H. Lewis. Frank Lovejoy, Richard Carlson, Russ Tamblyn, Anita Louise. Occasional grim action enlivens this Korean War tale.

Return from the Ashes (1965-British) 105m. *** D: J. Lee Thompson. Maximilian Schell, Samantha Eggar, Ingrid Thulin, Herbert Lom, Talitha Pol. Engrossing melodrama of a philandering husband taking up with his stepdaughter when his wife is supposedly killed. Trio of stars lend credibility to the far-fetched proceedings.

Return from the Past (1967) C-84m. BOMB D: David L. Hewitt. Lon Chaney, John Carradine, Rochelle Hudson, Roger Gentry. Veteran stars wasted in utter monstrosity; five tales of supernatural told here are five too many. Original titles: DR. TERROR'S GALLERY OF HORRORS, THE BLOOD SUCKERS.

Return from the Sea (1954) 80m. ** D: Lesley Selander. Jan Sterling, Neville Brand, John Doucette, Paul Langton, John Pickard. Tepid story of Brand-Sterling romance, set in San Diego.

Return from Witch Mountain (1978) C-95m. *** D: John Hough. Bette Davis, Christopher Lee, Kim Richards, Ike Eisenman, Denver Pyle, Dick Bakalyan. Sequel to Disney's ESCAPE FROM WITCH MOUNTAIN has Davis and Lee kidnapping Eisenman, hoping to put his special powers to evil use. Good fun from Disney.

Return of a Man Called Horse (1976) C-129m. *** D: Irvin Kershner. Richard Harris, Gale Sondergaard, Geoffrey Lewis, Bill Lucking, Jorge Luke, Enrique Lucero. Excellent sequel to A MAN CALLED HORSE with Harris returning from England to right wrongs done the Yellow Hand Sioux. by whites. Sun Vow ceremony now performed by dozen braves. Magnificent score by Laurence Rosenthal.

Return of a Stranger (1961-British) 63m. **½ D: Max Varnel. John Ireland, Susan Stephen, Cyril Shaps, Timothy Beaton. Taut thriller of psychopath Shaps released from prison, terrorizing former victim Stephen and husband Ireland.

Return of Charlie Chan, The (1971) C-97m. TVM D: Leslie Martinson. Ross Martin, Leslie Nielsen, Louise Sorel, Richard Haydn, Don Gordon. Stale attempt at camping up the venerable detective series, with Charlie brought out of retirement to solve murders aboard a luxury yacht. Understandably, this sat on the studio shelf until 1979. Filmed as HAPPINESS IS A WARM CLUE. Below average.

Return of Count Yorga (1971) C-97m. **½ D: Bob Kelljan. Robert Quarry, Mariette Hartley, Roger Perry, Yvonne Wilder. The Count goes out for more blood, wreaking havoc on neighboring orphanage.

Return of Dr. X, The (1939) 62m. ** D: Vincent Sherman. Humphrey Bogart, Rosemary Lane, Dennis Morgan, John Litel, Huntz Hall, Wayne Morris. Only Bogart as a zombie makes this low-grade sci-fi yarn worth viewing.

Return of Don Camillo, The (1965, Italian) 115m. **½ D: Julien Duvivier. Fernandel, Gino Cervi, Charles Vissieres, Edouard Delmont. Fernandel is again the irresponsible smalltown Italian priest involved in more projects of goodwill.

Return of Dracula, The (1958) 77m. ** D: Paul Landres. Francis Lederer, Norma Eberhardt, Ray Stricklyn, Jimmie Baird. Low-budget flick about the Count (Lederer) killing a man, taking his papers, and coming to U.S. Lederer thwarted by medium script.

Return of Frank James, The (1940) C-92m. *** D: Fritz Lang. Henry Fonda, Gene Tierney, Jackie Cooper, Henry Hull, John Carradine, J. Edward Bromberg, Donald Meek. Fonda reprises role from 1939 JESSE JAMES in story of attempt to avenge his brother's death; colorful production was Tierney's film debut.

Return of Jack Slade, The (1955) 79m. ** D: Harold Schuster. John Ericson, Mari Blanchard, Neville Brand, Angie Dickinson. To redeem his father's wrongdoings, Ericson joins the law to fight outlaws; adequate Western.

Return of Jesse James, The (1950) 75m. **½ D: Arthur Hilton. John Ireland, Ann Dvorak, Henry Hull, Hugh O'Brian, Reed Hadley. Compact budget Western dealing with rumors that lookalike for outlaw is notorious gunslinger.

Return of Joe Forrester, The SEE: **Cop on the Beat**

Return of Mr. Moto, The (1965-British) 71m. D: Ernest Morris. Henry Silva, Terence Longdon, Suzanne Lloyd, Marne Maitland, Martin Wyldeck. SEE: **Mr. Moto** series.

Return of Mod Squad, The (1979) C-100m. TVM D: George McGowan. Michael Cole, Clarence Williams III, Peggy Lipton, Tige Andrews, Tom Bosley, Ross Martin, Victor Buono, Tom Ewell. The three former cops of the "flower child" generation come out of TV-rerun retirement, looking decidedly long of tooth, in search of new adventure and a possible new series to equal the success of their 1968-73 hit. Average.

Return of Monte Cristo, The (1946) 91m. ** D: Henry Levin. Louis Hayward, Barbara Britton, George Macready, Una O'Connor, Henry Stephenson. Rather ordinary swashbuckler of original count's young descendant, thwarted in attempt to claim inheritance by dastardly villain.

Return of October, The (1948) C-98m. ** D: Joseph H. Lewis. Glenn Ford, Terry Moore, Albert Sharpe, James Gleason, Steve Dunne. Moore is wholesome gal who is strongly attached to her horse (October), much to her relatives' consternation.

Return of Peter Grimm, The (1935) 83m. **½ D: George Nicholls, Jr. Lionel Barrymore, Helen Mack, Edward Ellis, Donald Meek, George Breakston, Allen Vincent. Wellmeaning but meddlesome man returns after death to straighten out the mess he left behind; revival of hoary old stage play, done to the hilt, comes off fairly well but never captures whimsical spirit it so badly needs.

Return of Sabata (1972-Italian-Spanish) C-106m. *½ D: Frank Kramer. Lee Van Cleef, Reiner Schone, Annabella Incontrera, Jacqueline Alexandre, Pedro Sanchez. Below-average spaghetti Western has Van Cleef going after some swindlers who owe him $5000; only for diehard fans of both the star and this kind of film.

Return of Sophie Lang, The (1936) 65m. **½ D: George Archainbaud. Gertrude Michael, Sir Guy Standing,

Ray Milland, Elizabeth Patterson, Colin Tapley, Paul Harvey. Jewel-thief-gone-straight Michael seeks Milland's help in staying out of public eye. OK low-budgeter.

Return of the Ape Man (1944) 60m. ** D: Philip Rosen. Bela Lugosi, John Carradine, Judith Gibson, Michael Ames (Tod Andrews), Frank Moran, Mary Currier. Scientist Lugosi transplants Carradine's brain into body of recently discovered Missing Link. Typical fare; no relation to THE APE MAN.

Return of the Bad Men (1948) 90m. **½ D: Ray Enright. Randolph Scott, Robert Ryan, Anne Jeffreys, George "Gabby" Hayes, Jacqueline White, Steve Brodie, Jason Robards. OK Western, with romance, outlaws, and early Western land rush combining; Ryan is despicable villain.

Return of the Fly, The (1959) 80m. **½ D: Edward L. Bernds. Vincent Price, Brett Halsey, David Frankham, John Sutton, Dan Seymour, Danielle De Metz. Adequate sequel to THE FLY proves "like father like son." Youth attempts to reconstruct his late father's disintegrator machine and is likewise transformed into an insect.

Return of the Frontiersman (1950) C-74m. ** D: Richard Bare. Gordon MacRae, Rory Calhoun, Julie London, Jack Holt, Fred Clark. Easygoing yarn of sheriff's son falsely accused of murder.

Return of the Gunfighter (1967) C-100m. TVM D: James Nielson. Robert Taylor, Chad Everett, Ana Martin, Mort Mills, Lyle Bettger. Likeable Western, thanks mainly to excellent Taylor performance, as he comes to aid of accused killer and Mexican girl avenging death of her parents. Above average.

Return of the Hulk, The (1977) C-100m. TVM D: Alan Levi. Bill Bixby, Laurie Prange, Dorothy Tristan, William Daniels, Jack Colvin, Lou Ferrigno. Further adventures of the Marvel Comics favorite with Banner still searching for a cure for his growth affliction that uncontrollably transforms him into a raging beast. Average.

Return of the Pink Panther, The (1975-British) C-113m. **½ D: Blake Edwards. Peter Sellers, Christopher Plummer, Catherine Schell, Herbert Lom, Bert Kwouk, Peter Arne, Gregoire Aslan. Sellers' Inspector

Clouseau is a superb comedy character, but director-writer Edwards thinks big, violent gags are funny. Best part of this diamond-heist farce is the opening title, animated by Richard Williams and Ken Harris. Immediate sequel was much better.

Return of the Scarlet Pimpernel, The (1938-British) 80m. ** D: Hans Schwartz. Barry K. Barnes, Sophie Stewart, Margaretta Scott, James Mason, Francis Lister, Anthony Bushell. Far below stunning original, with lower production values and less-than-stellar cast in costumer set in 1790s London and Paris.

Return of the Seven (1966) C-96m. ** D: Burt Kennedy. Yul Brynner, Robert Fuller, Warren Oates, Jordan Christopher, Claude Akins. Nothing like the original. The gang has reformed for more protection in this drab Western, but it was a lot more fun when Eli Wallach was the heavy.

Return of the Texan (1952) 88m. ** D: Delmer Daves. Dale Robertson, Joanne Dru, Walter Brennan, Richard Boone, Robert Horton. Flabby Western about Robertson et al fighting to save his ranch.

Return of the Vampire, The (1943) 69m. ** D: Lew Landers, Kurt Neumann. Bela Lugosi, Frieda Inescort, Nina Foch, Roland Varno, Miles Mander, Matt Willis. Lugosi returns in limp attempt to capitalize on previous success as Dracula. Final scene is memorable, though.

Return of the Whistler, The (1948) 63m. D: D. Ross Lederman. Michael Duane, Lenore Aubert, Richard Lane, James Cardwell, Ann Doran. SEE: Whistler series.

Return of the World's Greatest Detective, The (1976) C-78m. TVM D: Dean Hargrove. Larry Hagman, Jenny O'Hara, Nicholas Colasanto, Woodrow Parfey, Helen Verbit, Ivor Francis. Bumbling motorcycle cop believes he actually is Sherlock Holmes and is aided in this delusion by psychiatric social worker named Doc Watson. Enjoyable comedy/drama, mixing slapstick with elements of THEY MIGHT BE GIANTS. Average.

Return to Earth (1976) C-78m. TVM D: Jud Taylor. Cliff Robertson, Ralph Bellamy, Shirley Knight, Charles Cioffi, Stefanie Powers. Robertson is A-OK in real-life drama of the breakdown of astronaut Buzz Aldrin after his 1969

moon walk. Adapted from the book Aldrin wrote with Wayne Warga. Above average.

Return to Fantasy Island (1977) C-100m. TVM D: George McGowan. Ricardo Montalban, Adrienne Barbeau, Joseph Campanella, Joseph Cotten, Laraine Day, Cameron Mitchell, Herve Villechaize. Dapper Mr. Roarke and his diminutive pal Tattoo host the regular complement of guest stars seeking dream fulfillment in this second pilot to the hit series. Average.

Return to Macon County (1975) C-90m. *½ D: Richard Compton. Don Johnson, Nick Nolte, Robin Mattson, Robert Viharo, Eugene Daniels, Matt Greene. Unworthy follow-up to MACON COUNTY LINE, as youngsters get mixed up in drag races, sex, the law, violence and murder, in about that order.

Return to Paradise (1953) C-100m. ** D: Mark Robson. Gary Cooper, Roberta Haynes, Barry Jones, Moira MacDonald. Lackluster South Sea tale of beach bum Cooper in love with native girl; loosely based on James Michener's story. Filmed in Samoa.

Return to Peyton Place (1961) C-122m. ** D: Jose Ferrer. Jeff Chandler, Eleanor Parker, Carol Lynley, Mary Astor, Tuesday Weld, Robert Sterling. Muddled follow-up to PEYTON PLACE suffers from faulty direction, poor production, and, save for stalwarts Astor and Parker, bad casting.

Return to Sender (1963-British) 63m. ** D: Gordon Hales. Nigel Davenport, Yvonne Romain, Geoffrey Keen, William Russell, John Horsley. Programmer action tale of revenge, based on Edgar Wallace yarn of industrialist's plot to ruin career and life of a D.A.

Return to Treasure Island (1954) C-75m. *½ D: E. A. Dupont. Tab Hunter, Dawn Addams, Porter Hall, James Seay, Harry Lauter. Poor updating of Stevenson novel, with student Hunter vying with crooks for buried treasure.

Return to Warbow (1958) C-67m. *½ D: Ray Nazarro. Phil Carey, Catherine McLeod, Andrew Duggan, William Leslie. Pedestrian narrative of outlaws backtracking to site of crime to collect loot left behind.

Returning Home (1975) C-78m. TVM D: Daniel Petrie. Dabney Coleman, Tom Selleck, James R. Miller,

Whitney Blake, Joan Goodfellow, Sherry Jackson. Drama based on the 1946 classic THE BEST YEARS OF OUR LIVES, with three returning WW2 vets facing the challenge of adjusting to civilian life. Or the pitfalls of telescoping a memorable flick to 78 minutes. Average.

Reunion in France (1942) 104m. ** D: Jules Dassin. Joan Crawford, John Wayne, Philip Dorn, Reginald Owen, Albert Bassermann, John Carradine, Henry Daniell. Glossy romance, with Crawford and Wayne trying to flee Nazi-occupied France; propaganda elements date badly.

Reunion in Reno (1951) 79m. **½ D: Kurt Neumann. Mark Stevens, Peggy Dow, Gigi Perreau, Frances Dee, Leif Erickson. Diverting comedy of Perreau deciding to divorce her parents so she won't be in the way.

Reunion in Vienna (1933) 100m. *** D: Sidney Franklin. John Barrymore, Diana Wynyard, Frank Morgan, May Robson, Eduardo Ciannelli, Una Merkel. Too-literal adaptation of Robert Sherwood's dated stage play depends on its stars' considerable charm to come across. Barrymore is exiled nobleman who returns to Vienna, tries to rekindle romance with Wynyard under the nose of her tolerant husband (Morgan).

Reveille With Beverly (1943) 78m. ** D: Charles Barton. Ann Miller, William Wright, Dick Purcell, Franklin Pangborn, Larry Parks. Columbia Pictures mini-musical, with Miller a versatile disk jockey throwing "big show" for servicemen. Guest stars include Frank Sinatra, Mills Brothers, Bob Crosby, Count Basie, Duke Ellington.

Revenge (1971) C-73m. TVM D: Jud Taylor. Shelley Winters, Stuart Whitman, Bradford Dillman, Carol Rossen, Roger Perry, Leslie Charleson. Crazed Mrs. Hilton (Winters) wants satisfaction for death of daughter, cages suspected businessman in basement; distraught wife eventually resorts to ESP in frantic search through San Francisco. Average.

Revenge for a Rape (1976) C-100m. TVM D: Timothy Galfas. Mike Connors, Tracy Brooks Swope, Robert Reed, Deanna Lund, Larry Watson. Predictable drama of a lone vigilante (Connors) who relentlessly tracks the three men who raped his wife. Average.

Revenge Is My Destiny (1971) C-

95m. *½ D: Joseph Adler. Sidney Blackmer, Chris Robinson, Elisa Ingram, Joe E. Ross. Vietnam vet (Robinson) returns to Miami only to find wife missing and stumbles upon sordid maze of events that lead to her death. Script has too many loopholes and does not use locations effectively.

Revenge of Frankenstein (1958-British) C-91m. *** D: Terence Fisher. Peter Cushing, Francis Matthews, Eunice Gayson, Michael Gwynn, Lionel Jeffries, John Welsh. Sequel to THE CURSE OF FRANKENSTEIN is quite effective with the good doctor still making a new body from others, ably assisted by hunchback dwarf and young medical student. Thought-provoking script has fine atmosphere, especially in color.

Revenge of the Creature (1955) 82m. ** D: Jack Arnold. John Agar, Lori Nelson, John Bromfield, Nestor Paiva, Robert B. Williams. OK sequel to CREATURE FROM THE BLACK LAGOON destroys much of that film's mystery and terror by removing gill-man from Amazonian home and placing him in Florida aquarium. Originally filmed in 3D. Look fast for Clint Eastwood in his first screen role as lab technician.

Revenge of the Gladiators (1965-Italian) C-100m. *½ D: Michele Lupo. Roger Browne, Scilla Gabel, Giacomo Rossi Stuart, Daniele Vargas, Gordon Mitchell. Badly directed story of gladiator rescuing princess from barbarians.

Revenge of the Pink Panther (1978) C-99m. ** D: Blake Edwards. Peter Sellers, Herbert Lom, Robert Webber, Dyan Cannon, Burt Kwouk. Sellers' fifth go-round as bumbling Inspector Clouseau is by far the dullest, until a bright wrap-up in Hong Kong with some good sight gags and plenty of spark from Cannon. The "plot" has Clouseau supposedly murdered, allowing him to find "killer" incognito.

Revenge of the Pirates (1951-Italian) 95m. ** D: Primo Zeglio. Maria Montez, Milly Vitale, Jean-Pierre Aumont, Saro Urzi, Paul Muller, Roberto Risso. Aumont and Montez try to spark this trite swashbuckler of wicked governor hoarding stolen gold, with Robin Hood of the seas coming to rescue.

Revenge of the Zombies (1943) 61m. *½ D: Steve Sekely. John Carradine, Robert Lowery, Gale Storm, Veda Ann Borg, Mantan Moreland, Mauritz Hugo. Low-budget mad doctor saga, with Carradine experimenting on human guinea pigs.

Revengers, The (1972) C-112m. BOMB D: Daniel Mann. William Holden, Ernest Borgnine, Susan Hayward, Woody Strode, Roger Hanin, Rene Koldehoff. Rancher goes after those who massacred his family. Holden and Borgnine are reunited, but WILD BUNCH magic isn't there; welcome screen return of Hayward is only good thing about terrible Western.

Revolt at Fort Laramie (1957) C-73m. ** D: Lesley Selander. John Dehner, Frances Helm, Gregg Palmer, Don Gordon, Robert Keys. Grade-B Western of internal rivalries of North-South soldiers at government fort during Civil War.

Revolt in the Big House (1958) 79m. **½ D: R. G. Springsteen. Gene Evans, Robert Blake, Timothy Carey, John Qualen. Taut little programmer about convict life.

Revolt of Mamie Stover, The (1956) C-92m. **½ D: Raoul Walsh. Jane Russell, Richard Egan, Joan Leslie, Agnes Moorehead, Jorja Curtright, Jean Willes, Michael Pate. Gorgeous Jane, in Technicolor, is Honolulu-based "saloon singer" in 1941. Weak plot; Jane sings "Keep Your Eyes On The Hands."

Revolt of the Zombies (1936) 65m. *½ D: Victor Halperin. Dorothy Stone, Dean Jagger, Roy D'Arcy, Robert Noland, George Cleveland. Jagger brings dead Cambodian soldiers back to life to do his evil bidding. Should have stayed dead.

Revolution (1969) C-90m. **½ D: Jack O'Connell, Today Malone. Documentary of late-60s hippie life, mostly in San Francisco, has some interesting footage, but directorial technique is sometimes too flashy. Lots of nudity that will probably be cut for TV. Music by Country Joe & the Fish, Quicksilver Messenger Service, Steve Miller Band, Mother Earth.

Revolutionary, The (1970) C-100m. *** D: Paul Williams. Jon Voight, Jennifer Salt, Seymour Cassel, Robert Duvall. Tight, well-written study of a college youth who slowly gets drawn into role of political revolutionary.

Reward, The (1965) C-92m. **½ D:

Serge Bourguignon. Max von Sydow, Yvette Mimieux, Efrem Zimbalist, Jr., Gilbert Roland, Emilio Fernandez, Henry Silva, Rodolfo Acosta. Promising premise and good cast led astray in static Western: group of bounty hunters turn on each other, as greed for larger share of reward money goads them into conflict.

Rhapsody (1954) C-115m. **½ D: Charles Vidor. Elizabeth Taylor, Vittorio Gassman, John Ericson, Louis Calhern, Michael Chekhov. Three-cornered romance among rich Taylor, violinist Gassman, and pianist Ericson: melodic interludes bolster soaper.

Rhapsody in Blue (1945) 139m. *** D: Irving Rapper. Robert Alda, Joan Leslie, Alexis Smith, Oscar Levant, Charles Coburn, Julie Bishop, Albert Bassermann, Morris Carnovsky, Rosemary DeCamp, Paul Whiteman, Hazel Scott. Hollywood biography of George Gershwin is largely pulp fiction, but comes off more credibly and interestingly than most other composer biopics, capturing Gershwin's enthusiasm for his work, and some of the inner conflicts he faced. Highlight is complete performance of title work.

Rhino! (1964) C-91m. **½ D: Ivan Tors. Robert Culp, Harry Guardino, Shirley Eaton, Harry Mekela. Diverting African game-hunting nonsense, with an enthusiastic cast, good action scenes.

Rhinoceros (1974) C-101m. BOMB D: Tom O'Horgan. Zero Mostel, Gene Wilder, Karen Black, Robert Weil, Joe Silver, Marilyn Chris, Robert Fields. Eugene Ionesco entry in "Theater of the Absurd" makes sorry transition from stage to screen as clerk Wilder refuses to conform by turning into a pachyderm. The performers try. An American Film Theater Production.

Rhubarb (1951) 95m. *** D: Arthur Lubin. Ray Milland, Jan Sterling, Gene Lockhart, Elsie Holmes. Frisky comedy of baseball team owned by a cat, from famous story by H. Allen Smith.

Rhythm on the Range (1936) 85m. **½ D: Norman Taurog. Bing Crosby, Frances Farmer, Bob Burns, Martha Raye, Lucile Gleason, Samuel S. Hinds. Film noteworthy as Raye's feature-film debut and pleasant excuse for musical nonsense. Remade as PARDNERS.

Rhythm on the River (1940) 92m. ***

D: Victor Schertzinger. Bing Crosby, Mary Martin, Basil Rathbone, Oscar Levant, Oscar Shaw. Lots of fun, with Crosby and Martin ghost-writing songs for phony Rathbone, trying to break loose on their own.

Rhythm Romance SEE: Some Like It Hot

Rice Girl (1963-Italian) C-90m. **½ D: Raffaello Matarazzo. Elsa Martinelli, Folco Lulli, Michel Auclair, Rik Battaglia, Susanne Levesy, Liliana Gerace. Atmospheric account of seamy rice workers and Martinelli's past life catching up with her.

Rich Are Always With Us, The (1932) 73m. ** D: Alfred E. Green. Ruth Chatterton, Adrienne Dore, George Brent, Bette Davis, John Miljan, Robert Warwick, Berton Churchill. Wealthy woman (Chatterton) cannot fall out of love with irresponsible husband (Miljan), even after bitter divorce and new romance with Brent. Silly script.

Rich Kids (1979) C-101m. *** D: Robert M. Young. Trini Alvarado, Jeremy Levy, John Lithgow, Kathryn Walker, Terry Kiser, Paul Dooley. Alvarado and Levy are upper class New York kids who become best friends as her parents are dissolving their marriage. Effect of divorce is focal point for this fine acting showcase, which also makes good use of N.Y. locations. Produced by Robert Altman.

Rich Man, Poor Girl (1938) 65m. ** D: Reinhold Schunzel. Robert Young, Lew Ayres, Ruth Hussey, Lana Turner, Rita Johnson, Don Castle, Guy Kibbee. Good cast, fair film. Title tells story; only noteworthy item is radiant young Turner.

Rich, Young, and Pretty (1951) C-95m. **½ D: Norman Taurog. Jane Powell, Danielle Darrieux, Wendell Corey, Vic Damone, Fernando Lamas. Frivolous MGM musical with Powell in Paris, sightseeing and romancing, meeting mother Darrieux.

Richard III (1956-British) C-158m. ***½ D: Laurence Olivier. Laurence Olivier, John Gielgud, Ralph Richardson, Claire Bloom, Alec Clunes, Cedric Hardwicke. Elaborate if stagy version of Shakespeare's chronicle of insane 15th-century British king and his court intrigues.

Richest Girl in the World, The (1934) 76m. *** D: William A. Seiter. Miriam Hopkins, Joel McCrea, Fay Wray, Reginald Denny,

Henry Stephenson. Entertaining romantic comedy by Norman Krasna about millionairess wanting to make sure her next boyfriend loves her for herself, not for her money.

Richest Girl in the World, The (1960-Danish) C-78m. *½ D: Lau Lauritzen. Nina, Frederik, Poul Reichhardt, Birgitte Bruun. Syrupy musical fluff with Nina out to marry singer Frederik; overly cute.

Richie Brockelman: Missing 24 Hours (1976) C-78m. TVM D: Hy Averback. Dennis Dugan, Suzanne Pleshette, Norman Fell, Lloyd Bochner, William Windom, Sharon Gless. Private eye caper involving a neophyte gumshoe and his amnesiac client. Plodding series pilot with a cast desperately trying to inject the needed spark. Below average.

Ricochet Romance (1954) 80m. **½ D: Charles Lamont. Marjorie Main, Chill Wills, Pedro Gonzalez-Gonzalez, Rudy Vallee, Ruth Hampton. Another Main frolic, with the rambunctious gal hired as ranch cook but putting her two cents' worth into everything.

Ride a Crooked Trail (1958) C-87m. **½ D: Jesse Hibbs. Audie Murphy, Gia Scala, Walter Matthau, Henry Silva. Trim Western with Murphy involved in bank robbery.

Ride a Violent Mile (1957) 80m. *½ D: Charles Marquis Warren. John Agar, Penny Edwards, John Pickard, Sheb Wooley, Eva Novak. Trivial Western set in Civil War times about Southern blockade runners.

Ride a Wild Pony (1976) C-91m. *** D: Don Chaffey. Michael Craig, John Meillon, Robert Bettles, Eva Griffith, Graham Rouse. Genial, atmospheric Disney story about an irresistible pony and the two children—son of poor Australian farm family and crippled rich girl—who vie for its love and ownership. Sentimental tale adapted from James Aldridge's A SPORTING PROPOSITION.

Ride Back, The (1957) 79m. *** D: Allen H. Miner. Anthony Quinn, Lita Milan, William Conrad, Ellen Hope Monroe, Louis Towers. Well-handled account of sheriff and prisoner who find they need each other's help to survive elements and Indian attacks.

Ride Beyond Vengeance (1966) C-100m. **½ D: Bernard McEveety. Chuck Connors, Michael Rennie, Kathryn Hays, Joan Blondell, Gloria

Grahame, Gary Merrill, Bill Bixby, James MacArthur. Good supporting cast makes the most of stereotyped roles in flashback account of Connors' sundry encounters with outlaws.

Ride Clear of Diablo (1954) C-80m. **½ D: Jesse Hibbs. Audie Murphy, Dan Duryea, Susan Cabot, Abbe Lane, Russell Johnson. Above-par Murphy oater, with Audie swearing revenge for family's murder.

Ride 'Em Cowboy (1942) 86m. **½ D: Arthur Lubin. Bud Abbott, Lou Costello, Dick Foran, Anne Gwynne, Johnny Mack Brown, Ella Fitzgerald, Douglass Dumbrille. Good combination of Western, comedy, and musical in A&C vehicle, with Ella and the Merry Macs singing tunes including "A Tisket A Tasket."

Ride in the Whirlwind (1966) C-82m. ** D: Monte Hellman. Cameron Mitchell, Jack Nicholson, Tom Filer, Millie Perkins, Rupert Crosse. Mild Western about three innocent cowboys forced to become fugitives when they're mistaken for stagecoach robbers. Of interest to buffs because Nicholson wrote the screenplay and Hellman (TWO-LANE BLACKTOP) directed.

Ride Lonesome (1959) C-73m. *** D: Budd Boetticher. Randolph Scott, Karen Steele, Pernell Roberts, James Best, Lee Van Cleef, James Coburn. Tightly woven script has Scott bringing in wanted outlaw, but sidetracked when he and others at stagecoach stop are threatened by impending Indian attack.

Ride Out for Revenge (1957) 79m. *½ D: Bernard Girard. Rory Calhoun, Gloria Grahame, Lloyd Bridges, Vince Edwards. Tiresome account of gold-hungry men trying to dispossess Indians from their lands.

Ride the High Country (1962) C-94m. ***½ D: Sam Peckinpah. Randolph Scott, Joel McCrea, Mariette Hartley, Ronald Starr, Warren Oates, Edgar Buchanan. Memorable Western of two aging gunfighters reunited after twenty years to deliver a gold shipment. Scott and McCrea have never been better; direction, action and scenery are first-rate. Buchanan unforgettable as drunken judge.

Ride the High Iron (1956) 74m. *½ D: Don Weis. Don Taylor, Sally Forrest, Raymond Burr, Lisa Golm, Otto Waldis, Nestor Paiva, Mae Clarke. Korean veteran Taylor works for slick P.R. man Burr who makes his living keeping people's indiscretions out of the paper. Taylor tries to latch on to rich girl whose family Burr works for. Originally made for TV but shown theatrically.

Ride the Man Down (1952) **C-90m.** ** D: Joseph Kane. Brian Donlevy, Rod Cameron, Ella Raines, Barbara Britton, Chill Wills, Jack LaRue. Lumbering account of ranchland feuding in old West.

Ride the Pink Horse (1947) **101m.** ***½ D: Robert Montgomery. Robert Montgomery, Wanda Hendrix, Rita Conde, Andrea King, Fred Clark, Iris Flores, Grandon Rhodes. Top-notch melodrama, with bad-guy Montgomery changing his outlook when he meets Hendrix; further complications draw him into suspense. Remade as THE HANGED MAN.

Ride the Wild Surf (1964) **C-101m.** **½ D: Don Taylor. Fabian, Tab Hunter, Barbara Eden, Anthony Hayes, James Mitchum, Shelley Fabares. Formula beach boys tale.

Ride to Hangman's Tree, The (1967) **C-90m.** **½ D: Al Rafkin. Jack Lord, James Farentino, Don Galloway, Melodie Johnson, Richard Anderson, Robert Yuro. Formula Universal backlot Western, of outlaws in old West.

Ride, Vaquero (1953) **C-90m.** **½ D: John Farrow. Robert Taylor, Ava Gardner, Howard Keel, Anthony Quinn, Charlita. Oddball casting perks brooding Western set on Mexican border, with sultry Gardner responsible for most of the action.

Rider on a Dead Horse (1962) **72m.** *½ D: Herbert L. Strock. John Vivyan, Bruce Gordon, Kevin Hagen, Lisa Lu, Charles Lampkin. Seedy account of trio of gold prospectors trying to do each other in.

Rider on the Rain (1970-French) **C-115m.** ***½ D: René Clement. Charles Bronson, Marlene Jobert, Jill Ireland, Annie Cordy. Chilling suspense piece about mysterious man who winds up using Jobert as accomplice when she discovers what he is up to. Best sequence: long, rainy prologue.

Riders of the Purple Sage (1925) **56m.** *** D: Lynn Reynolds. Tom Mix, Beatrice Burnham, Arthur Morrison, Warner Oland, Fred Kohler, Harold Goodwin, Marion Nixon. Engrossing Zane Grey story filmed on beautiful locations, with Mix a Texas Ranger seeking scoundrel (Oland) who abducted his sister (Burnham). Fascinating twists in this tale, first filmed in 1918, again in 1931, 1941. Mix also filmed sequel, THE RAINBOW TRAIL, as done in 1918 and 1932.

Riders of Vengeance SEE: **Raiders, The**

Riders to the Stars (1954) **C-81m.** **½ D: Richard Carlson. William Lundigan, Herbert Marshall, Richard Carlson, Martha Hyer. Labored programmer about early days of space missiles, quite outdated now.

Riding High (1943) **C-89m.** *½ D: George Marshall. Dorothy Lamour, Dick Powell, Victor Moore, Gil Lamb, Cass Daley, Milt Britton and Band, Rod Cameron. Unmemorable songs, flat script, fair performances add up to dubious entertainment; Powell is obsessed with silver mine, while wooing Lamour.

Riding High (1950) **112m.** **½ D: Frank Capra. Bing Crosby, Coleen Gray, Charles Bickford, Margaret Hamilton, Frances Gifford, James Gleason, Raymond Walburn. Musical remake of BROADWAY BILL follows it so closely that stock footage is included from 1934 film. Crosby is racehorse owner whose nag has yet to come through. OK songs, Capra touch make this pleasing if unmemorable entertainment. Oliver Hardy is fun in rare solo appearance.

Riding Shotgun (1954) **C-74m.** ** D: Andre de Toth. Randolph Scott, Wayne Morris, Joan Weldon, Joe Sawyer, James Millican. Typical, undemanding Scott Western of man seeking to clear his reputation.

Riff Raff Girls (1962-French) **97m.** **½ D: Alex Joffe. Nadja Tiller, Robert Hossein, Silvia Monfort, Roger Hanin, Pierre Blanchar. Tiller is quite convincing as club owner whose aim is to be self-sufficient; set on Brussels waterfront.

Riffraff (1935) **89m.** **½ D: J. Walter Ruben. Jean Harlow, Spencer Tracy, Una Merkel, Joseph Calleia, Victor Kilian, Mickey Rooney. Comedy-drama doesn't always work, but worth viewing for stars playing married couple in fishing business who end up on wrong side of law.

Riffraff (1947) **80m.** *** D: Ted Tetzlaff. Pat O'Brien, Anne Jeffreys, Walter Slezak, Percy Kilbride, Jerome Cowan, George Givot, Jason Robards. Fast-paced story of O'Brien foiling villains' attempts to take over oilfield in Panama.

Rififi (1954-French) 115m. **** D: Jules Dassin. Jean Servais, Carl Mohner, Magali Noel, Robert Manuel, Perlo Vita (Jules Dassin). The granddaddy of all caper/heist movies, centering on quartet of French jewel thieves who find each other more dangerous than the cops.

Rififi in Tokyo (1963-French) 89m. ** D: Jacques Deray. Karl Boehm, Michel Vitold, Charles Vanel, Eiji Okada, Keiko Kishi, Barbara Lass, Yanagi. Aging European gangster recruits men for bank heist. Cast is so-so; strictly standard plot line.

Right Approach, The (1961) 92m. **½ D: David Butler. Frankie Vaughan, Martha Hyer, Juliet Prowse, Gary Crosby, Jane Withers. Plucky minor film of Vaughan, a good-for-nothing who uses anyone to get ahead.

Right Cross (1950) 90m. **½ D: John Sturges. June Allyson, Dick Powell, Lionel Barrymore, Ricardo Montalban. Fairly compact account of boxing world, with sports-writer Powell and fighter Montalban in love with Allyson. One of Marilyn Monroe's early films.

Ring, The (1952) 79m. ** D: Kurt Neumann. Gerald Mohr, Rita Moreno, Lalo Rios, Robert Arthur. Typical boxing yarn with racial angle; Rios is determined to succeed to raise prestige of Mexican-Americans.

Ring of Bright Water (1969-British) C-107m. *** D: Jack Couffer. Bill Travers, Virginia McKenna, Peter Jeffrey, Jameson Clark, Helena Gloag. One of the best recent children's films should be a treat for adults, too; modest story of man's love for his pet otter is intelligently and believably told. Nice acting and photography.

Ring of Fear (1954) C-93m. ** D: James Grant. Clyde Beatty, Pat O'Brien, Mickey Spillane, Sean McClory, Marian Carr, John Bromfield. Agreeable blend of Mickey Spillane and life under the big top.

Ring of Fire (1961) C-91m. **½ D: Andrew L. Stone. David Janssen, Joyce Taylor, Frank Gorshin, Joel Marston, Doodles Weaver. Assistant sheriff is held hostage by trio of escaping gangsters. Highlight of film is climactic forest holocaust.

Ring of Passion (1978) C-100m. TVM D: Robert Michael Lewis. Bernie Casey, Stephen Macht, Britt Ekland, Denise Nicholas, Allen Garfield, Joseph Campanella, Beah Richards. Fact-based drama about the two Louis-Schmeling heavyweight fights, set against the politics of the pre-WW2 era. Long on ideology, short on fisticuffs, and decidedly offbeat. Average.

Ring of Terror (1962) 72m. BOMB D: Clark Paylow. George Mather, Esther Furst, Austin Green, Joseph Conway. A medical student must confront a corpse as a fraternity initiation prank in this low-budget loser.

Ring of Treason (1964-British) 90m. *** D: Robert Tronson. Bernard Lee, William Sylvester, Margaret Tyzack, David Kossoff. Solid spy thriller based on true story of ex-Navy man Lee blackmailed into helping Russian agents. Builds truly exciting atmosphere.

Rings Around the World (1967) C-98m. **½ D: Gil Cates. Don Ameche. Interesting anthology of world-renowned circus acts.

Rings on Her Fingers (1942) 85m. **½ D: Rouben Mamoulian. Henry Fonda, Gene Tierney, Laird Cregar, Spring Byington, Marjorie Gateson, Iris Adrian, Clara Blandick, Mary Treen. Con-artist Tierney falls for Fonda instead of fleecing him; standard romance with good cast.

Ringside Maisie (1941) 96m. D: Edwin L. Marin. Ann Sothern, George Murphy, Robert Sterling, Virginia O'Brien, Natalie Thompson. SEE: Maisie series.

Rio (1939) 75m. ** D: John Brahm. Basil Rathbone, Victor McLaglen, Sigrid Gurie, Robert Cummings, Leo Carrillo, Billy Gilbert. Rathbone, serving ten-year prison term, suspects his wife (Gurie) is being unfaithful. His performance is sole virtue of this slick potboiler.

Rio Bravo (1959) C-141m. ***½ D: Howard Hawks. John Wayne, Dean Martin, Ricky Nelson, Angie Dickinson, Walter Brennan, Ward Bond, John Russell, Claude Akins, Bob Steele. Sheriff Wayne tries to prevent a killer with connections from escaping from the town jail, with only a drunk Dino, leggy Angie, gimpy Brennan and lockjawed Ricky to help him. Quintessential Hawks Western, patronized by reviewers at the time of its release, is now regarded as an American classic; overlong, but great fun.

Rio Conchos (1964) C-107m. *** D: Gordon Douglas. Richard Boone, Stuart Whitman, Tony Franciosa, Edmond O'Brien. Post-Civil War Texas is setting for masculine adult Western, with Boone vs. Franciosa, and zesty characterization by O'-Brien.

Rio Grande (1950) 105m. *** D: John Ford. John Wayne, Maureen O'Hara, Ben Johnson, Harry Carey, Jr., Victor McLaglen, Claude Jarman, Jr. Post-Civil War friction between cavalry and Apaches is focal point of rugged, taut Western, featuring Wayne as tough cavalry commander.

Rio Lobo (1970) C-114m. *** D: Howard Hawks. John Wayne, Jorge Rivero, Jennifer O'Neill, Jack Elam, Victor French, Chris Mitchum, Bill Williams, Jim Davis. Attempt of Wayne and Hawks to redo RIO BRAVO and EL DORADO doesn't quite work, but film buffs will want to see it anyway. Rivero has trouble with English and O'Neill's beauty doesn't make her an actress, but Western has action, good humor.

Rio Rita (1942) 91m. **½ D: S. Sylvan Simon. Bud Abbott, Lou Costello, Kathryn Grayson, John Carroll, Tom Conway, Barry Nelson. Vintage Broadway musical brought up to date, with Nazis invading Western ranch where Bud and Lou work; some good music helps this one.

Riot (1969) C-97m. **½ D: Buzz Kulik. Jim Brown, Gene Hackman, Ben Carruthers, Mike Kellin, Gerald O'Loughlin. Unsurprising but extremely violent prison film; Hackman in stereotyped characterization. Sure to be cut for TV.

Riot in Cell Block 11 (1954) 80m. *** D: Don Siegel. Neville Brand, Emile Meyer, Frank Faylen, Leo Gordon, Robert Osterloh. Realistic, powerful prison drama still packs a punch. Among the contemporary themes in this 1954 film is "media manipulation," with prisoners trying to use press for leverage.

Riot in Juvenile Prison (1959) 71m. BOMB D: Edward L. Cahn. Jerome Thor, Marcia Henderson, Scott Marlowe, John Hoyt, Dick Tyler, Dorothy Provine, Ann Doran. Programmer fully explained by title.

Riot on Sunset Strip (1967) C-85m. *½ D: Arthur Dreifuss. Aldo Ray, Mimsy Farmer, Michael Evans, Laurie Mock, Tim Rooney, Bill Baldwin. Weak exploitation of real-life mid-60s riots on the Strip concerns cop Ray's enraged response when his daughter gets involved with drugs and hippies.

Ripped Off (1971) C-83m. **½ D: Franco Prosperi. Robert Blake, Ernest Borgnine, Gabriele Ferzetti, Catherine Spaak, Tomas Milian. Italian-made action drama, filmed in Chicago, about a boxer (Blake) who is framed for the murder of his corrupt manager, hounded by detective Borgnine, and protected by the victim's daughter (Spaak) while trying to clear himself. Also known as THE BOXER.

Riptide (1934) 90m. *** D: Edmund Goulding. Norma Shearer, Herbert Marshall, Robert Montgomery, Lilyan Tashman, Mrs. Patrick Campbell, Skeets Gallagher, Ralph Forbes. Silly but entertaining story of vivacious Shearer marrying stodgy British Lord (Marshall), then becoming involved in scandal with Montgomery. Don't miss opening scene where stars are dressed as giant insects for costume party!

Rise and Fall of Legs Diamond, The (1960) 101m. *** D: Budd Boetticher. Ray Danton, Karen Steele, Elaine Stewart, Jesse White, Simon Oakland, Robert Lowery. Snappy chronicle of Depression-days gangster, well balanced between action gun battles and Danton's romancing flashy dolls (like young Dyan Cannon).

Rise and Shine (1941) 93m. **½ D: Allan Dwan. Jack Oakie, Linda Darnell, George Murphy, Walter Brennan, Sheldon Leonard, Donald Meek, Ruth Donnelly. Oakie has field day as dumb football player abducted by crooks so team won't win big game. Film is often unconsciously funny.

Rise of Catherine the Great, The SEE: Catherine the Great

Rise of Louis XIV, The (1970-Italian) C-100m. *** D: Roberto Rossellini. Jean-Marie Patte, Raymond Jourdan, Silvagni, Katharina Renn, Dominique Vincent, Pierre Barrat. Attractive, but somewhat pedantic effort to show color-filled court of not-quite straitlaced Louis XIV. Very objective, almost documentary-like, but final effect is noninvolving.

Rising of the Moon, The (1957-Irish) 81m. **½ D: John Ford. Introduced by Tyrone Power; Cyril Cusack, Maureen Connell, Noel Purcell, Frank Lawton, Jimmy O'Dea. Trio of flavorful stories about Irish life; "Majesty of the Law," "A Minute's Wait," "1921."

Risk, The (1961-British) 81m. *** D: Roy and John Boulting. Tony Britton, Peter Cushing, Ian Bannen, Virginia Maskell, Donald Pleasence. Tense drama of spies chasing scientist who has secret formula to combat plague. Good direction and cast.

Ritual of Evil (1969) C-100m. TVM D: Robert Day. Louis Jourdan, Anne Baxter, Diana Hyland, John McMartin, Wilfrid Hyde-White, Belinda Montgomery. Curious mixture of wide-eyed paranoia and serious black magic explorations as psychiatrist Sorrell (Jourdan) investigates contributing factors of patient's suicide. Desperately in need of polished dialogue, film succeeds in spite of itself. Average.

Rituals (1978-Canadian) C-100m. *½ D: Peter Carter. Hal Holbrook, Lawrence Dane, Robin Gammell, Ken James, Gary Reineke. Ripoff of DELIVERANCE with Holbrook and four fellow M.D.s being terrorized during wilderness vacation. Unpleasant, to say the least.

Ritz, The (1976) C-91m. **½ D: Richard Lester. Jack Weston, Rita Moreno, Jerry Stiller, Kaye Ballard, F. Murray Abraham. Brisk filming of Terence McNally's play about a man fleeing his murderous brother-in-law by hiding in gay baths suffers from feeling that it's all a photographed stage performance. Moreno is memorable as no-talent entertainer Googie Gomez. Filmed in England.

Rivals (1972) C-103m. **½ D: Krishna Shah. Robert Klein, Joan Hackett, Scott Jacoby. A remarriage forces young child to try and murder the new rival for his mother's affections. Offbeat, to say the least.

River, The (1951-Indian) C-99m. **** D: Jean Renoir. Patricia Walters, Nora Swinburne, Arthur Shields, Radha, Adrienne Corri, Esmond Knight. Immensely moving, lyrical adaptation of Rumer Godden novel about English children growing up in Bengal. One of the great color films, a total triumph for cinematographer Claude and director Jean Renoir.

River Lady (1948) C-78m. ** D: George Sherman. Yvonne De Carlo, Dan Duryea, Rod Cameron, Helena Carter, Lloyd Gough, Florence Bates. Typical De Carlo vehicle about riverboat queen trying to buy her man when she can't win him with love; colorful and empty.

River Niger, The (1976) C-105m. *** D: Krishna Shah. James Earl Jones, Cicely Tyson, Glynn Turman, Lou Gossett, Roger E. Mosley, Jonelle Allen. Intelligent, moving story (based on 1972 Tony Award-winning play) of black family trying to come to terms with the world and themselves. Principals touching and convincing.

River of Gold, The (1970) C-72m. TVM D: David Friedkin. Dack Rambo, Roger Davis, Ray Milland, Suzanne Pleshette, Melissa Newman. Various groups wheel and deal, threaten each other in search for key to sunken treasure off Mexican coast. Fair attempt at giving subordinate characters some depth, but resolution strictly for laughs. Average.

River of Mystery (1969) C-96m. TVM D: Paul Stanley. Vic Morrow, Claude Akins, Niall MacGinnis, Louise Sorel, Nico Minardos, Edmond O'Brien. Two explosives experts find themselves sought after by diamond hunter and revolutionary leader in South America. Fair location work, lame script. Morrow and Akins perform well together but deserve far better material. Below average.

River of No Return (1954) C-91m. **½ D: Otto Preminger. Robert Mitchum, Marilyn Monroe, Rory Calhoun, Tommy Rettig, Murvyn Vye. Monroe hires Mitchum to catch up to would-be husband who deserted her; well-matched stars, handsome production outshine script.

River's Edge, The (1957) C-87m. *** D: Allan Dwan. Ray Milland, Anthony Quinn, Debra Paget, Byron Foulger. Melodrama about heel (Milland), his ex-girlfriend (Paget), and her husband (Quinn) trying to cross Mexican border with suitcase of money. Ray has never been nastier.

Riverrun (1970) C-87m. ** D: John Korty. John McLiam, Louise Ober, Mark Jenkins, Josephine Nichols. Unmarried couple expecting a baby has its happiness intruded upon by disagreeable visit from her sea-captain father. Mild drama has lovely photography (by Korty), but the leads are bland, story not that interesting.

[642]

Road House (1948) 95m. *** D: Jean Negulesco. Ida Lupino, Cornel Wilde, Celeste Holm, Richard Widmark, O. Z. Whitehead. Lupino comes between bitter enemies, roadhouse owner Widmark and parolee Wilde; Ida even sings in this engrossing melodrama.

Road Show (1941) 87m. **½ D: Hal Roach, Gordon Douglas, Hal Roach Jr. Adolphe Menjou, Carole Landis, John Hubbard, Charles Butterworth, Patsy Kelly, George E. Stone. Offbeat comedy of young man escaped from insane asylum arriving at traveling carnival; some bright moments in inconsequential film.

Road to Bali, The (1952) C-90m. *** D: Hal Walker. Bob Hope, Dorothy Lamour, Bing Crosby, Murvyn Vye, Ralph Moody. Only color ROAD film has lush trappings, many guest stars, as Bob and Bing save Dorothy from evil princess and jungle perils. More laughs than usual.

Road to Denver, The (1955) C-90m. **½ D: Joseph Kane. John Payne, Lee J. Cobb, Skip Homeier, Mona Freeman, Ray Middleton, Lee Van Cleef, Andy Clyde, Glenn Strange. Fast pacing aids this narrative of Payne and brother Homeier on opposite sides of the law, involved in shoot-out.

Road to Glory, The (1936) 95m. *** D: Howard Hawks. Fredric March, Warner Baxter, Lionel Barrymore, June Lang, Gregory Ratoff, Victor Kilian. Solid production, direction, and acting make more of script than is really there. Hardened officer Baxter finds his father (Barrymore) serving in his unit in WW1 France. Romantic subplot involves officer March and nurse Lang.

Road to Hong Kong, The (1962) 91m. **½ Norman Panama. Bob Hope, Bing Crosby, Joan Collins, Dorothy Lamour, Robert Morley, Walter Gotell, Peter Sellers. Final ROAD picture was the first in a decade, and while it's fun it lacks the carefree spirit of its predecessors; Bob and Bing are con men who become involved in international intrigue—and space travel! Sellers does a hilarious cameo. Filmed in England.

Road to Morocco, The (1942) 83m. *** D: David Butler. Bing Crosby, Dorothy Lamour, Bob Hope, Anthony Quinn, Vladimir Sokoloff, Monte Blue, Yvonne De Carlo, Dona Drake.

Typically funny ROAD picture, with Bing selling Bob to slave-trader in mysterious Morocco, both going after princess Lamour. Songs include: "Moonlight Becomes You."

Road to Nashville (1967) C-110m. *½ D: Robert Patrick. Marty Robbins, Doodles Weaver, Connie Smith, Richard Arlen. Inept promoter tries to line up talent for Country-Western jamboree. The music's not bad when the plot gets out of the way.

Road to Rio, The (1947) 100m. *** D: Norman Z. McLeod. Bing Crosby, Bob Hope, Dorothy Lamour, Gale Sondergaard, Frank Faylen, The Wiere Brothers. Bob and Bing are musicians trying to wrest Dorothy from sinister aunt Sondergaard. Songs: "But Beautiful," "You Don't Have To Know The Language," sung with guests, Andrews Sisters.

Road to Salina (1971-French-Italian) C-96m. **½ D: George Lautner. Mimsy Farmer, Robert Walker, Rita Hayworth, Ed Begley, Bruce Pecheur. If this film makes it to TV at all, lots of nudity will go in enjoyably trashy tale about wanderer who constantly makes love with a girl who's supposed to be his sister. Rita does the frug with Ed Begley, which is the only kinky thing the editors might leave in.

Road To Singapore, The (1940) 84m. **½ D: Victor Schertzinger. Bing Crosby, Dorothy Lamour, Bob Hope, Charles Coburn, Judith Barrett, Anthony Quinn. Bing and Bob swear off women, hiding out in Singapore; then they meet saronged Lamour. First ROAD film is not the best, but still fun.

Road to Utopia, The (1945) 90m. *** D: Hal Walker. Bing Crosby, Bob Hope, Dorothy Lamour, Hillary Brooke, Douglass Dumbrille, Jack LaRue. Bob and Bing in the Klondike with usual quota of gags, supplemented by talking animals, Dorothy's song "Personality," Robert Benchley's dry commentary.

Road to Yesterday, The (1925) 110m. *** D: Cecil B. DeMille. Joseph Schildkraut, Jetta Goudal, Vera Reynolds, William Boyd, Julia Faye. Criss-crossed couples in romantic tangle are contrasted with 17th century ancestors, who play out similar story against colorful period setting. DeMille at his best: lavish, hokey, always entertaining.

Road to Zanzibar, The (1941) 92m.

**½ D: Victor Schertzinger. Bing Crosby, Bob Hope, Dorothy Lamour, Una Merkel, Eric Blore. Weaker ROAD series entry, still amusing, with Bob and Bing circus performers traveling through jungle with Lamour and Merkel, looking for diamond mine.

Roar of the Crowd (1953) C-71m. *½ D: William Beaudine. Howard Duff, Helene Stanley, Louise Arthur, Harry Shannon, Minor Watson, Don Haggerty. Hackneyed auto-racing tale done on low budget.

Roaring Twenties, The (1939) 104m. *** D: Raoul Walsh. James Cagney, Priscilla Lane, Humphrey Bogart, Gladys George, Jeffrey Lynn, Frank McHugh, Joe Sawyer. Army buddies Cagney, Bogart, and Lynn find their lives intertwining dramatically after WW1 ends. Cagney becomes bigtime prohibition racketeer in largely hackneyed script punched across by fine cast, vivid direction.

Rob Roy, the Highland Rogue (1954) C-85m. *½ D: Harold French. Richard Todd, Glynis Johns, James Robertson Justice, Michael Gough, Finlay Currie, Jean Taylor-Smith. Disney's dreariest British film casts Todd as leader of Scottish clan planning uprising against England's King George in 18th century. Turgid and unrewarding.

Robber's Roost (1955) C-82m. ** D: Sidney Salkow. George Montgomery, Richard Boone, Bruce Bennett, Warren Stevens, Peter Graves, Sylvia Findley. Rugged cast gives zip to this Western of outlaw gangs fighting for control of ranchland.

Robbery (1967-British) C-114m. *** D: Peter Yates. Stanley Baker, Joanna Pettet, James Booth, Frank Finlay, Barry Foster, William Marlowe. Another study of the British Royal Mail robbery; few surprises, but generally exciting, well-handled.

Robbery Under Arms (1957-British) C-83m. ** D: Jack Lee. Peter Finch, Ronald Lewis, Laurence Naismith, Maureen Swanson, David McCallum. Quiet account of romance and robbery set in 19th-century Australia.

Robe, The (1953) C-135m. *** D: Henry Koster. Richard Burton, Jean Simmons, Victor Mature, Michael Rennie, Richard Boone, Dawn Addams, Dean Jagger. Episodic spectacle taken from Lloyd C. Douglas novel features Burton in Award-nominated portrayal of Gallio, Roman put in charge of execution of Christ. Big cast does well with uneven script; first Cinemascope feature.

Roberta (1935) 105m. *** D: William A. Seiter. Irene Dunne, Fred Astaire, Ginger Rogers, Randolph Scott, Helen Westley, Claire Dodd, Victor Varconi. The story of this famous Jerome Kern-Otto Harbach musical creaks and groans, but "supporting" characters Astaire and Rogers make up for it in their exuberant dance numbers. You can try counting how many times Scott says "swell," or try to spot young Lucille Ball in fashion-show sequence to get through the rest. Remade as LOVELY TO LOOK AT.

Robin and Marian (1976-British) C-112m. **½ D: Richard Lester. Sean Connery, Audrey Hepburn, Robert Shaw, Richard Harris, Nicol Williamson, Denholm Elliott, Kenneth Haigh, Ronnie Barker. Middle-aged Robin Hood returns to Sherwood Forest after years in exile, rekindles romance with Maid Marian and faces final challenge against archenemy Sheriff of Nottingham. Arid, uninvolving film strips beloved characters of all their magic. "Revisionist" script by James Goldman.

Robin and the Seven Hoods (1964) C-103m. **½ D: Gordon Douglas. Frank Sinatra, Dean Martin, Sammy Davis, Jr., Peter Falk, Barbara Rush, Bing Crosby, Victor Buono. The Rat Pack goes Chicago in musical gangster spoof that's no great shakes, but entertaining. Crosby has thankless character role. Good song, "My Kind Of Town."

Robin Hood of El Dorado, The (1936) 86m. **½ D: William Wellman. Warner Baxter, Ann Loring, Margo, Bruce Cabot, J. Carrol Naish. Pseudobiography of Mexican bandit Joaquin Murietta, who turns to crime to avenge his sister's murder. Well made, on beautiful locations, but fools around too much for its dramatic moments to be truly effective.

Robinson Crusoe of Clipper Island SEE: **Robinson Crusoe of Mystery Island**

Robinson Crusoe of Mystery Island (1936) 100m. ** D: Mack V. Wright, Ray Taylor. Mala, Rex, Buck, Mamo Clark, Herbert Rawlinson. Overly simple plot is salvaged by spotty action in this cliff-hanger set on a South Sea island; federal agents hunt down foreign powers causing chaos. Reedited movie serial: ROBINSON CRUSOE OF CLIPPER ISLAND.

Robinson Crusoe on Mars (1964) C-109m. **½ D: Byron Haskin. Paul Mantee, Vic Lundin, Adam West. Adventure film pegged on Daniel Defoe theme, with astronaut and monkey stranded on Mars, trying to eke out existence.

Robot Monster (1953) C-63m. BOMB D: Phil Tucker. George Nader, Claudia Barrett, Selena Royle, Gregory Moffett, John Mylong. One of the All-Time Worst. Bubble-blowing gorillas in space helmets destroy everyone on Earth except a boy (Moffett) and his family. So bad you might enjoy it. Originally shown in 3-D.

Rocambole (1962-French) C-106m. **½ D: Bernard Borderie. Channing Pollock, Hedy Vessel, Nadia Gray, Guy Delorme, Lilla Brignone. Further adventures of Ponson du Terrail's carefree rogue, played tongue-in-cheek by Pollock, involved in Parisian nightlife.

Rocco and His Brothers (1960-Italian) 155m. ***½ D: Lucino Visconti. Alain Delon, Renato Salvatori, Annie Girardot, Katina Paxinou, Claudia Cardinale, Roger Hanin. Long, absorbing study of poor farm woman who moves to Milan with her four sons in search of better life; Visconti's powerful emotional landscape makes this a modern classic. Beware 95m. edited version.

Rock-A-Bye-Baby (1958) C-103m. *** D: Frank Tashlin. Jerry Lewis, Marilyn Maxwell, Connie Stevens, Baccaloni, Reginald Gardiner. Movie siren Maxwell leaves her triplets with Jerry. Well-paced comedy, with Baccaloni a great comedy foil as Connie's father. Good spoofing of Hollywood religious epics included in this fine Lewis vehicle (based on THE MIRACLE OF MORGAN'S CREEK).

Rock Around the Clock (1956) 77m. ** D: Fred F. Sears. Bill Haley and His Comets, The Platters, Tony Martinez and His Band, Freddie Bell and His Bellboys, Alan Freed, Johnny Johnston. Premise is slim (unknown band brought to N.Y.C. where they become famous) but picture is good social history of phase of American culture fast disappearing.

Rock Around the World (1957-British) 71m. *½ D: Gerard Bryant.

Tommy Steele, Patrick Westwood, Dennis Price, Tom Littlewood. Humdrum account of Tommy Steele's rise in the singing profession. Originally titled THE TOMMY STEELE STORY.

Rock 'n' Roll High School (1979) C-93m. *** D: Allan Arkush. P. J. Soles, Vincent Van Patten, Clint Howard, The Ramones, Mary Woronov, Paul Bartel, Alix Elias. A 1950s movie gone berserk, with all the clichés of those high school-based rock 'n' roll sagas turned upside down in irresistible comic fashion; set to a nonstop soundtrack of golden oldies, of course.

Rock, Pretty Baby (1956) 89m. ** D: Richard Bartlett. Sal Mineo, John Saxon, Luana Patten, Edward C. Platt, Fay Wray, Rod McKuen. Prototype of rock 'n' roll entries of 1950s revolving around high school rock group's effort to win big-time musical contest.

Rocket Man, The (1954) 79m. ** D: Oscar Rudolph. Charles Coburn, Spring Byington, Anne Francis, John Agar, George Winslow. OK fantasy of Winslow possessing a space gun that turns crooked people honest.

Rocket Ship X-M (1950) 77m. **½ D: Kurt Neumann. Lloyd Bridges, Osa Massen, Hugh O'Brian, John Emery. Slightly better than average production of spaceship to moon that is blown off-course to Mars. Nice photography, good acting.

Rocket to the Moon SEE: Cat Women of the Moon

Rockford Files, The (1974) C-78m. TVM D: Richard T. Heffron. James Garner, Lindsay Wagner, William Smith, Nita Talbot, Joe Santos, Stuart Margolin. Ex-con private eye looks into a skid row bum's murder at the urging of the dead man's daughter. Garner, the reluctant hero, at what he does best. The hit series followed. Above average.

Rocking Horse Winner, The (1950-British) 91m. ***½ D: Anthony Pelissier. Valerie Hobson, John Howard Davies, John Mills, Ronald Squire. Truly unique, fascinating drama based on D. H. Lawrence story; small boy has knack for picking racetrack winners, but complications set in before long. Beautifully done.

Rocky (1976) C-119m. ***½ D: John G. Avildsen. Sylvester Stallone, Talia Shire, Burt Young, Carl Weathers, Burgess Meredith, Thayer David.

This story of a two-bit fighter who gets his "million-to-one shot" for fame, and self-respect, in a championship bout is impossible to dislike, even though it's just an old B-movie brought up to date. Knowing that the film was a similar do-or-die project for writer-star Stallone adds to its good vibes. Oscar winner as Best Picture, Best Director, Best Editing (Richard Halsey).

Rocky Horror Picture Show, The (1975-British) C-100m. *** D: Jim Sharman. Tim Curry, Susan Sarandon, Barry Bostwick, Richard O'Brien, Jonathan Adams, Meat Loaf. Outrageously kinky horror-movie spoof, spiced with sex, transvestism, and rock music, about a "straight" couple stranded in old dark house full of weirdos from planet Transylvania. The ultimate cult movie—a turn-off for some, a film that improves on repeated viewings for others.

Rocky Mountain (1950) 83m. **½ D: William Keighley. Errol Flynn, Patrice Wymore, Scott Forbes, Slim Pickens, Sheb Wooley, Yakima Canutt. Lumbering Flynn vehicle set in Civil War times, with Rebs and Yankees fighting off an Indian attack.

Rocky II (1979) C-119m. *** D: Sylvester Stallone. Sylvester Stallone, Talia Shire, Burt Young, Carl Weathers, Burgess Meredith. Officially a sequel, this slightly silly film is more of a rehash, but the climactic bout (and buildup to it) hit home.

Rodan (1957-Japanese) C-70m. ** D: Inoshiro Honda. Kenji Sawara, Yumi Shirakawa, Akihiko Hirato, Ako Kobori. Special effects star in sci-fi of prehistoric flying monster and his efforts to destroy civilization.

Rodeo (1952) C-70m. *½ D: William Beaudine. Jane Nigh, John Archer, Wallace Ford, Frances Rafferty. Tame little account of girl managing a roping show.

Roger & Harry: The Mitera Target (1977) C-78m. TVM D: Jack Starrett. John Davidson, Barry Primus, Carole Wagner Mallory, Anne Randall, Richard Lynch, Susan Sullivan, Harris Yulin, Biff McGuire. Contemporary swashbuckler featuring a pair of professional retrievers of people and jewelry, attempting to recover a kidnapped heiress. A live-action cartoon. Below average. Retitled LOVE FOR RANSOM.

Roger Touhy, Gangster (1944) 65m.

**½ D: Robert Florey. Preston Foster, Victor McLaglen, Lois Andrews, Anthony Quinn, Kent Taylor, Trudy Marshall, Kane Richmond. Supposed biographical film of famous murderer is just another gangster film.

Rogue Cop (1954) 92m. *** D: Roy Rowland. Robert Taylor, Janet Leigh, George Raft, Steve Forrest, Anne Francis, Vince Edwards. Dynamic account of policeman Taylor on the underworld payroll, tracking down his brother's killer.

Rogue Male (1976-British) C-100m. TVM D: Clive Donner. Peter O'Toole, John Standing, Alastair Sim, Cyd Hayman, Harold Pinter, Hugh Manning. Remake of MAN HUNT with O'Toole as British aristocrat who tries to assassinate Hitler in the 1930s, and then is hounded by the Gestapo. First-class BBC production with Frederic Raphael script. Above average.

Rogue River (1950) C-81m. ** D: John Rawlins. Rory Calhoun, Peter Graves, Frank Fenton, Ralph Sanford. Talky study of family relationships; not much on Western action.

Rogues' Gallery (1968) C-88m. ** D: Leonard Horn. Roger Smith, Greta Baldwin, Dennis Morgan, Farley Granger, Edgar Bergen, Brian Donlevy, Mala Powers. Private eye comes to aid of beautiful woman attempting suicide, eventually seduced into frameup scheme. Forgettable mystery drama with uneven performances, unbelievable dialogue. (Intended for theaters but never released.)

Rogue's March (1952) 84m. ** D: Allan Davis. Peter Lawford, Richard Greene, Janice Rule, Leo G. Carroll. Programmer-costumer set in India (via stock footage and rear projection scenes), with Lawford trying to redeem himself with regiment.

Rogues of Sherwood Forest (1950) C-80m. ** D: Gordon Douglas. John Derek, Diana Lynn, George Macready, Alan Hale. Despite good production and fair cast, pretty limp rejuvenation of Robin Hood.

Rogue's Regiment (1948) 86m. ** D: Robert Florey. Dick Powell, Marta Toren, Vincent Price, Stephen McNally. Powell's in the foreign legion to track down a Nazi officer in hiding; ordinary drama.

Roll, Freddy, Roll (1974) C-78m. TVM D: Bill Persky. Tim Conway, Jan Murray, Scott Brady, Henry

Jones, Ruta Lee, Moosie Drier, Robert Hogan. Overblown TV sitcom has divorced computer programmer Conway, desperate to compete for his son's attention by outdoing the boy's flamboyant new stepdad, determined to win a place in the Guinness Book of World Records as a nonstop rollerskater. Average.

Roller Boogie (1979) C-103m. BOMB D: Mark L. Lester. Linda Blair, Jim Bray, Beverly Garland, Roger Perry, Mark Goddard, Sean McClory. Blair, Bray, and friends join forces to thwart evil Goddard from closing local roller skating rink. Made to cash in on roller-disco fad, but amateurish script and performances should roll this into oblivion.

Rollerball (1975) C-128m. **½ D: Norman Jewison. James Caan, John Houseman, Maud Adams, John Beck, Moses Gunn, Ralph Richardson. Disappointing drama of the 21st Century; Caan is the champ at a violent sport in a society where violence has been outlawed. Filmed in Munich and London, based on William Harrison's story *Roller Ball Murders*.

Rollercoaster (1977) C-119m. ** D: James Goldstone. George Segal, Richard Widmark, Timothy Bottoms, Henry Fonda, Harry Guardino, Susan Strasberg. Silly disaster-type film almost redeemed by Segal's winning performance as civic inspector who tries to nail extortionist (Bottoms) before he sabotages another amusement park. Overlong, but at least TV audiences won't have to watch it in "Sensurround."

Rolling Man (1972) C-73m. TVM D: Peter Hyams. Dennis Weaver, Don Stroud, Donna Mills, Slim Pickens, Jimmy Dean, Agnes Moorehead, Sheree North. Vivid atmosphere of small-town existence excellent counterpoint to saga of Lonnie McAfee (Weaver) barely making headway through one raw deal after another: wife's desertion, murder, prison term, searching for children . . . Some characters verge on stereotypes but film's point of view, direction, and plot line make up for it. Above average.

Rolling Thunder (1977) C-99m. ** D: John Flynn. William Devane, Tommy Lee Jones, Linda Haynes, James Best, Dabney Coleman, Lisa Richards, Luke Askew. Devane comes home after eight years as Vietnamese P.O.W., sees his family murdered, and cold-bloodedly goes for revenge. Intriguing aspects of story (by Paul Schrader) and main characters thrown off-course by graphic violence and vigilante melodramatics.

Roman Holiday (1953) 119m. ***½ D: William Wyler. Audrey Hepburn, Gregory Peck, Eddie Albert, Tullio Carminati. Hepburn got first break and an Oscar as princess yearning for normal life; runs away from palace, has romance with reporter Peck.

Roman Scandals (1933) 85m. *** D: Frank Tuttle. Eddie Cantor, Ruth Etting, Gloria Stuart, David Manners, Verree Teasdale, Alan Mowbray, Edward Arnold. Old-fashioned, enjoyable musical vehicle for Cantor to romp through as dreamer who is transported back to ancient Rome. Big Busby Berkeley production numbers include young Lucille Ball.

Roman Spring of Mrs. Stone, The (1961) C-104m. *** D: Jose Quintero. Vivien Leigh, Warren Beatty, Lotte Lenya, Jill St. John, Jeremy Spenser. Middle-aged actress retreats to Rome, buying a fling at romance from gigolo Beatty. Lenya, as Leigh's waspish friend, comes off best. Adapted from Tennessee Williams novella.

Romance in Manhattan (1934) 78m. *** D: Stephen Roberts. Ginger Rogers, Francis Lederer, J. Farrell MacDonald, Arthur Hohl, Sidney Toler. Chorus girl Rogers helps illegal alien Lederer, and romance blossoms, in this most enjoyable Capraesque comedy.

Romance of a Horsethief (1971-U.S.-Yugoslav) C-100m. *½ D: Abraham Polonsky. Yul Brynner, Eli Wallach, Jane Birkin, Oliver Tobias, Lainie Kazan, David Opatoshu. Wily Jewish horsetraders scheme to outwit Cossack captain Brynner and his men, in a Polish village circa 1904. A heartfelt endeavor for director Polonsky and actor-screenwriter Opatoshu that just doesn't come off.

Romance of Rosy Ridge, The (1947) 105m. *** D: Roy Rowland. Van Johnson, Thomas Mitchell, Janet Leigh, Marshall Thompson, Selena Royle. Set in post-Civil War days, Missouri farmer Mitchell casts suspicious eye on young Johnson, who is courting his daughter, Leigh (in her film debut).

Romance on the High Seas (1948) C-99m. *** D: Michael Curtiz. Jack

Carson, Janis Paige, Don DeFore, Doris Day, Oscar Levant, S. Z. Sakall, Fortunio Bonanova, Eric Blore, Franklin Pangborn. Sparkling, trivial romantic musical on an ocean voyage, with Doris' film debut, singing "It's Magic."

Romanoff and Juliet (1961) C-103m. *** D: Peter Ustinov. Peter Ustinov, Sandra Dee, John Gavin, Akim Tamiroff, Rik Von Nutter. Ustinov wrote, directed and starred in this cold war satire with offspring of U.S. and Russian ambassadors falling in love. Italian locations substitute for mythical country which Ustinov rules.

Romantic Englishwoman, The (1975-British) C-115m. ***½ D: Joseph Losey. Michael Caine, Glenda Jackson, Helmut Berger, Beatrice Romand, Nathalie Delon, Michel Lonsdale. Caine, a successful novelist married to Jackson, invites Berger into their home to generate material for a screenplay he's writing. Underrated comedy-drama, stylish and believable.

Rome Adventure (1962) C-119m. *** D: Delmer Daves. Troy Donahue, Angie Dickinson, Rossano Brazzi, Suzanne Pleshette, Constance Ford, Al Hirt, Hampton Fancher. Plush soaper with Pleshette as schoolteacher on Roman fling to find romance, torn between roué (Brazzi) and architect (Donahue). As Troy's mistress, Dickinson has some rare repartee. Lush Max Steiner score.

Romeo and Juliet (1936) 126m. ***½ D: George Cukor. Norma Shearer, Leslie Howard, John Barrymore, Edna May Oliver, Basil Rathbone, C. Aubrey Smith, Andy Devine, Ralph Forbes. Well-acted, lavish production of Shakespeare's play about ill-fated lovers. Howard and Shearer are so good that one can forget they are too old for the roles. Not the great film it might have been, but a very good one.

Romeo and Juliet (1954-British) C-140m. *** D: Renato Castellani. Laurence Harvey, Susan Shentall, Flora Robson, Mervyn Johns, Bill Travers. Sumptuously photographed in Italy, this pleasing version of Shakespeare's tragedy has the virtue of good casting.

Romeo and Juliet (1966-British) C-126m. **½ D: Paul Czinner. Margot Fonteyn, Rudolf Nureyev, David Blair, Desmond Doyle, Julia Farron,

Michael Somes. Anyone interested in dance will want to see this filmed record of the Royal Ballet production, but actually, it doesn't adapt very well to film; zoom lens is poor substitute for immediacy of live performance.

Romeo and Juliet (1968-British-Italian) C-138m. ***½ D: Franco Zeffirelli. Leonard Whiting, Olivia Hussey, Milo O'Shea, Michael York, John McEnery, Pat Heywood, Robert Stephens. One of the best cinematic versions of Shakespeare's immortal tale of two young lovers kept apart by their families. Unique for its casting leads who were only 17 and 15, respectively, this exquisitely photographed film had a hauntingly beautiful musical score by Nino Rota.

Roof, The (1956-Italian) 98m. **½ D: Vittorio De Sica. Gabriella Pallotta, Giorgio Listuzzi, Gastone Renzelli, Maria Di Rollo. Realistic if unexciting account of young couple trying to find a home in crowded postwar Rome; they find technicality in law to solve their problem.

Rookie, The (1959) 86m. BOMB D: George O'Hanlon. Tommy Noonan, Pete Marshall, Julie Newmar, Jerry Lester, Joe Besser, Vince Barnett, Peter Leeds. Feeble Army comedy of draftee, tough sergeant, movie starlet, and other stereotypes set during 1940s.

Rookies, The (1971) C-73m. TVM D: Jud Taylor, Darren McGavin, Paul Burke, Cameron Mitchell, Robert F. Lyons, Georg Stanford Brown, Sam Melville. Rigorous training period, indoctrination, and first weeks of active duty in lives of several specially recruited young men of L.A. police force. Lots of action, but film tries to bite off more than it can chew. Average; pilot for TV series, but better than subsequent episodes.

Room at the Top (1959-British) 115m. **** D: Jack Clayton. Laurence Harvey, Simone Signoret, Heather Sears, Hermione Baddeley, Donald Wolfit, Ambrosine Philpotts, Donald Houston. Brilliant drama of Harvey sacrificing Signoret's love to get ahead by marrying factory boss' daughter. Trenchant and powerful adaptation of John Braine novel won Oscars for Signoret and screenwriter Neil Paterson. Followed by sequels LIFE AT THE TOP and MAN AT THE TOP.

Room for One More (1952) 98m. ***
D: Norman Taurog. Cary Grant,
Betsy Drake, Lurene Tuttle, George
Winslow, John Ridgely. Grant and
Drake are softhearted couple who
can't resist adopting needy kids.
Sentimental comedy retitled THE
EASY WAY, basis for later TV
show.

Room Service (1938) 78m. *** D:
William A. Seiter. Groucho, Chico
and Harpo Marx, Lucille Ball, Ann
Miller, Frank Albertson, Donald
MacBride, Cliff Dunstan. The Brothers actually have a plot in this
one, from a Broadway play about
penniless producers doing their best
to keep from being evicted from hotel
room. Not as wacky as usual, but
fun. Remade as STEP LIVELY.

Rooney (1958-British) 88m. *** D:
George Pollock. John Gregson,
Muriel Pavlow, Barry Fitzgerald,
June Thorburn. Sprightly tale of Irish
sanitation worker Gregson with an
eye for the girls, trying to avoid
marriage; Fitzgerald is bedridden
geezer whom Rooney helps.

Rooster Cogburn (1975) C-107m. **
D: Stuart Millar. John Wayne,
Katharine Hepburn, Anthony Zerbe,
Strother Martin, Richard Jordan,
John McIntire. Reprising Wayne's
character from TRUE GRIT and
teaming him with Hepburn was an
obvious attempt to spark an AFRI-
CAN QUEEN-type hit, but star-
power is all this film has going for
it. Dull story of unlikely duo going
after men who murdered her father
may play better on TV.

Roots of Heaven, The (1958) C-131m.
**½ D: John Huston. Errol Flynn,
Juliette Greco, Trevor Howard, Eddie Albert, Orson Welles, Paul
Lukas. Turgid melodramatics set in
Africa, with conglomerate cast phi-
osophizing over sanctity of elephants;
loosely based on Romain Gary novel.

Rope (1948) C-80m. *** D: Alfred
Hitchcock. James Stewart, John
Dall, Farley Granger, Cedric Hardwicke, Joan Chandler, Constance
Collier. Two young men kill college
friend as experiment in thrill-seeking,
and divulge clues to crime at dinner
party afterwards. Hitchcock's first
color film was shot in ten-minute
"takes" to provide a seamless flow
of movement. Story derived from
Leopold-Loeb murder case.

Rope of Sand (1949) 104m. *** D:
William Dieterle. Burt Lancaster,
Paul Henreid, Corinne Calvet, Claude
Rains, Peter Lorre, Sam Jaffe, John
Bromfield, Mike Mazurki. Sturdy cast
in adventure tale of smooth thief try-
ing to regain treasure he hid away,
with various parties interfering.

Rosalie (1937) 122m. ** D: W. S.
Van Dyke. Eleanor Powell, Nelson
Eddy, Frank Morgan, Edna May
Oliver, Ray Bolger, Ilona Massey,
Billy Gilbert. Elephantine MGM
musical about romance between
West Point cadet and mythical-
kingdom princess. Living proof that
money alone can't make a good
movie. Cole Porter score includes
"In the Still of the Night."

Rose, The (1979) C-125m. ** D:
Mark Rydell. Bette Midler, Alan
Bates, Frederic Forrest, Harry Dean
Stanton, Barry Primus, David Keith.
Spin-off of the Janis Joplin saga
equates show biz with hell, then
concentrates on giving the audience
too much of the latter. Midler (in
her starring debut) and Forrest deliver dynamic performances, but
film leaves a lot to be desired.

Rose Bowl Story, The (1952) C-73m.
** D: William Beaudine. Marshall
Thompson, Vera Miles, Natalie
Wood, Ann Doran, Jim Backus.
Clichéd hogwash about football play-
ers, their work and home life.

Rose for Everyone, A (1965-Italian)
C-107m. ** D: Franco Rossi. Claudia
Cardinale, Nino Manfredi, Mario
Adorf, Akim Tamiroff. Brazilian locale with NEVER ON SUNDAY
plot. Girl brings happiness to many
men and takes active interest in
their private lives as well as their
sexual lives. Nice locales, banal
story.

Rose Marie (1936) 110m. *** D:
W. S. Van Dyke II. Jeanette Mac-
Donald, Nelson Eddy, Reginald
Owen, Allan Jones, James Stewart,
Alan Mowbray, Gilda Gray. Don't
expect the original operetta: story
has opera star Jeanette searching for
fugitive brother Stewart, as mountie
Nelson pursues the same man. The
two fall in love, sing "Indian Love
Call," among others. David Niven
appears briefly as Jeanette's unsuc-
cessful suitor. Retitled INDIAN
LOVE CALL.

Rose Marie (1954) C-115m. **½ D:
Mervyn LeRoy. Ann Blyth, Howard
Keel, Fernando Lamas, Bert Lahr,
Marjorie Main, Joan Taylor, Ray
Collins. More faithful to original
operetta than 1936 version, but not

as much fun. Mountie Keel tries to "civilize" tomboy Blyth, but falls in love with her instead. Adventurer Lamas completes the triangle. Lahr sings "I'm the Mountie Who Never Got His Man" in comic highlight.

Rose of Washington Square (1939) 86m. **½ D: Gregory Ratoff. Tyrone Power, Alice Faye, Al Jolson, William Frawley, Horace McMahon, Moroni Olsen. Pleasant musical of thinly disguised Fanny Brice, with Alice singing her heart out as heel-husband Power hits the skids.

Rose Tattoo, The (1955) 117m. ***½ D: Daniel Mann. Anna Magnani, Burt Lancaster, Marisa Pavan, Ben Cooper, Virginia Grey, Jo Van Fleet. Magnani shines (she won an Oscar) as earthy widow in Gulf Coast city who puts aside her husband's memory when rambunctious truck driver Lancaster romances her. Flavorful adaptation of Tennessee Williams play.

Roseanna McCoy (1949) 100m. ** D: Irving Reis. Farley Granger, Joan Evans, Charles Bickford, Raymond Massey, Richard Basehart, Aline MacMahon. Witless drama of Hatfield-McCoy feud, with young lovers from opposite sides of the fence rekindling old wounds.

Rosebud (1975) C-126m. BOMB D: Otto Preminger. Peter O'Toole, Richard Attenborough, Cliff Gorman, Claude Dauphin, John V. Lindsay, Peter Lawford. Nadir for director Preminger and usually competent performers. Arab terrorists kill crew of yacht "Rosebud" and kidnap five wealthy young ladies aboard. O'Toole and Attenborough (to say nothing of former NY Mayor Lindsay) embarrassingly bad.

Roseland (1977) C-103m. *** D: James Ivory. Teresa Wright, Lou Jacobi, Geraldine Chaplin, Helen Gallagher, Joan Copeland, Christopher Walken, Lilia Skala, David Thomas. Trilogy set in New York's venerable Roseland Ballroom examines bittersweet lives of people who gravitate there. First story is weakest, but other two are absorbing and beautifully performed, with Copeland and Skala as standouts.

Rosemary (1958-German) 99m. **½ D: Rolf Thiele. Nadja Tiller, Peter Van Eyck, Gert Frobe, Mario Adorf, Carl Raddatz. Convincing study of famed post-WW2 Frankfurt prostitute (Tiller) who blackmailed industrialist; satirically sensational.

Rosemary's Baby (1968) C-136m. **** D: Roman Polanski. Mia Farrow, John Cassavetes, Ruth Gordon, Sidney Blackmer, Maurice Evans, Ralph Bellamy, Elisha Cook Jr., Patsy Kelly. Classic modern-day thriller by Ira Levin, perfectly realized by Polanski: Farrow is unsuspecting young wife whose husband becomes involved with witches' coven and their diabological plans, Gordon won Best Supporting Actress Oscar.

Rosetti and Ryan: Men Who Love Women (1977) C-100m. TVM D: John Astin. Tony Roberts, Squire Fridell, Patty Duke Astin, Jane Elliot, Susan Anspach, Dick O'Neill, Bill Dana, William Marshall. Freewheeling criminal lawyers with a way with women vs. hardnosed judge at the trial of their client Duke, charged with slaying her husband. Pilot for the TV series. Average.

Rosie! (1968) C-98m. *** D: David Lowell Rich. Rosalind Russell, Sandra Dee, Brian Aherne, Audrey Meadows, James Farentino, Vanessa Brown. One of Russell's best recent performances as madcap grandmother, whose children want her money now. Veteran supporting cast outshine "young" leads.

Rotten to the Core (1965-British) 90m. *** D: John Boulting. Anton Rodgers, Eric Sykes, Charlotte Rampling, Ian Bannen, Avis Bunnage, Victor Maddern. Well-handled caper of ex-con trio joining forces with crook to carry off large-scale robbery.

Rouge et Noir (1958-French) C-145m. *** D: Claude Autant-Lara. Gerard Philippe, Danielle Darrieux, Antonella Lualdi, Jean Martinelli. Flavorful handling of Stendhal novel of 1810 France, with Philippe and Darrieux a sparkling love team.

Rough Night in Jericho (1967) C-104m. ** D: Arnold Laven. Dean Martin, George Peppard, Jean Simmons, John McIntire, Slim Pickens, Don Galloway. Gory Western casts Martin as total villain who owns the town. Attractive cast can't fight clichés; some violence may be cut.

Rough Shoot SEE: **Shoot First**

Roughly Speaking (1945) 117m. *** D: Michael Curtiz. Rosalind Russell, Jack Carson, Robert Hutton, Jean Sullivan, Alan Hale, Donald Woods. Generally good but long comedy-drama of Russell raising a family while hubby Carson embarks on wild moneymaking schemes; two stars are tops.

Roughshod (1949) 88m. **½ D: Mark Robson. Robert Sterling, Claude Jarman, Jr., Gloria Grahame, Jeff Donnell, John Ireland, Myrna Dell, Martha Hyer. Intriguing drama of three fugitives out West and the disturbed farmer who fears they are seeking revenge against him.

Rounders, The (1965) C-85m. **½ D: Burt Kennedy. Glenn Ford, Henry Fonda, Sue Ane Langdon, Hope Holiday, Chill Wills, Edgar Buchanan, Kathleen Freeman. Agreeable Western about two cowboys and an ornery horse was one of the sleepers of its year; nothing much happens, but cast and scenery make it a pleasant way to kill an hour-and-a-half.

Roustabout (1964) C-101m. **½ D: John Rich. Elvis Presley, Barbara Stanwyck, Leif Erickson, Joan Freeman, Sue Ane Langdon. Elvis is a free-wheeling singer who joins Stanwyck's carnival, learns the meaning of hard work and true love. Stanwyck and supporting cast make this a pleasing Presley songer.

Rover, The (1967) C-103m. *½ D: Terence Young. Anthony Quinn, Rosanna Schiaffino, Rita Hayworth, Richard Johnson, Ivo Garrani, Mino Doro. Quinn stars as 18th-century pirate whose escape from French authorities is sidetracked by relationship with innocent, feeble-minded girl (Schiaffino). Plodding film from Joseph Conrad story; made in Italy, barely released here.

Roxie Hart (1942) 75m. **½ D: William Wellman. Ginger Rogers, Adolphe Menjou, George Montgomery, Lynne Overman, Nigel Bruce, Phil Silvers, Spring Byington, Iris Adrian. Fast-moving spoof of Roaring 20s, with Ginger as publicity-seeking gal on trial for murder, Menjou her overdramatic lawyer. Hilarious antics make up for dry spells.

Royal Affairs in Versailles (1957-French) C-152m. **½ D: Sacha Guitry. Claudette Colbert, Orson Welles, Jean-Pierre Aumont, Edith Piaf, Gerard Philippe, Jean Marais, Sacha Guitry. Overambitious, episodic approach to French history, with varying performances by host of guest stars. Retitled: AFFAIRS IN VERSAILLES.

Royal African Rifles, The (1953) C-75m. ** D: Lesley Selander. Louis Hayward, Veronica Hurst, Michael Pate, Angela Greene. Adequate actioner set in Africa in 1910, with Hayward the British officer leading mission to recover cache of arms.

Royal Family of Broadway, The (1930) 82m. ***½ D: George Cukor and Cyril Gardner. Fredric March, Ina Claire, Mary Brian, Henrietta Crosman, Charles Starrett, Arnold Korff, Frank Conroy. Delightful screen version of Edna Ferber-George S. Kaufman play about Barrymore-like theatrical family torn by conflict of show business tradition vs. "normal" private life. March is wickedly funny in his John Barrymore portrayal.

Royal Flash (1975-British) C-98m. *** D: Richard Lester. Malcolm McDowall, Alan Bates, Florinda Bolkan, Oliver Reed, Britt Ekland, Lionel Jeffries, Alastair Sim, Michael Hordern. Comic swashbuckler with McDowall forced to impersonate a Prussian nobleman and marry Ekland. Zippy Lester entry with a fine cast.

Royal Hunt of the Sun (1969-British) C-118m. *** D: Irving Lerner. Robert Shaw, Christopher Plummer, Nigel Davenport, Michael Craig, Leonard Whiting, James Donald. Colorful tale of Spanish explorer Pizzaro and his quest for gold in South America, from acclaimed stage play.

Royal Scandal, A (1945) 94m. **½ D: Ernst Lubitsch, Otto Preminger. Tallulah Bankhead, Charles Coburn, Anne Baxter, William Eythe, Vincent Price, Mischa Auer. Comedy of manners about Catherine the Great of Russia promoting favored soldier Eythe to high rank; started by Lubitsch, "finished" by Preminger.

Royal Wedding (1951) C-93m. *** D: Stanley Donen. Fred Astaire, Jane Powell, Sarah Churchill, Keenan Wynn. Astaire's dancing overcomes bland plot line of he and sister Powell performing in London at time of Queen Elizabeth II's marriage; each finds true love.

Ruby and Oswald (1978) C-133m. TVM D: Mel Stuart. Michael Lerner, Frederic Forrest, Doris Roberts, Lou Frizzell, Lanna Saunders, Brian Dennehy. Dramatic recreation of the days just preceding and following the Kennedy assassination unfortunately pales beside the real events so graphically covered live in those days. Average.

Ruby Gentry (1952) 82m. **½ D:

King Vidor. Jennifer Jones, Charlton Heston, Karl Malden, Josephine Hutchinson. Turgid, meandering account of easy-virtue Jones marrying wealthy Malden to spite Heston, the man she loves.

Ruggles of Red Gap (1935) 92m. ******** D: Leo McCarey. Charles Laughton, Mary Boland, Charlie Ruggles, ZaSu Pitts, Roland Young, Leila Hyams. Laughton is marvelous as butler won in poker game by uncouth Westerner Ruggles and socially ambitious wife Boland; Pitts is spinister he falls in love with. A completely winning movie. Remade as FANCY PANTS.

Rulers of the Sea (1939) 96m. ****½** D: Frank Lloyd. Douglas Fairbanks, Jr., Will Fyffe, Margaret Lockwood, George Bancroft, Montagu Love, Alan Ladd, Mary Gordon, Neil Fitzgerald. Well-made drama of problems surrounding first steamship voyage across Atlantic.

Rules of the Game (1939-French) 110m. ******** D: Jean Renoir. Marcel Dalio, Nora Gregor, Mila Parely, Jean Renoir. Sublime comedy-drama contrasting affairs d'amour of aristocrats and working class on weekend outing. Poignant, funny, perhaps Renoir's best film.

Ruling Class, The (1972-British) C-154m. ******** D: Peter Medak. Peter O'Toole, Alastair Sim, Arthur Lowe, Harry Andrews, Carol Browne, Michael Bryant, Carolyn Seymour. Hilarious, irreverent comedy about heir to British Lordship (O'Toole) who thinks he's Jesus Christ. No way this far-out comedy will make it to TV intact; overflowing with crazy ideas, people bursting into song, boisterously funny characterizations, and one-and-only Sim as befuddled bishop.

Rumba (1935) 77m. ****** D: Marion Gering. George Raft, Carole Lombard, Margo, Lynne Overman, Gail Patrick, Akim Tamiroff, Iris Adrian. Weak follow-up to BOLERO, with Raft and Lombard in and out of love in silly, contrived story; most of their "dancing" actually done by Veloz and Yolanda.

Rumble on the Docks (1956) 82m. ****** D: Fred F. Sears. James Darren, Laurie Carroll, Michael Granger, Jerry Janger, Robert Blake, Edgar Barrier. Low-key waterfront corruption tale, with Darren the street-gang leader aiding racketeers.

Run A Crooked Mile (1969) C-100m.

TVM D: Gene Levitt. Louis Jourdan, Mary Tyler Moore, Alexander Knox, Wilfrid Hyde-White, Laurence Naismith, Terence Alexander. Highway mishap precipitates math teacher's involvement in plot to change European gold standard. Good, intricate amnesia-gimmicked plot and fine British cast on hand in serviceable suspenser. Above average.

Run for Cover (1955) C-93m. ****½** D: Nicholas Ray. James Cagney, Viveca Lindfors, John Derek, Jean Hersholt, Ernest Borgnine. Offbeat Western has ex-con Cagney becoming sheriff, while his embittered young companion (Derek) grows restive and antagonistic. Interesting touches cannot overcome familiar storyline.

Run for the Roses (1978) C-93m. ****** D: Henry Levin. Vera Miles, Stuart Whitman, Sam Groom, Panchito Gomez, Theodore Wilson, Lisa Eilbacher. Formula family film about Puerto Rican boy living with his stepfather in Kentucky, raising a lame colt to run in the Kentucky Derby. Uninspired stuff for undemanding audiences.

Run for the Sun (1956) C-99m. ****** D: Roy Boulting. Richard Widmark, Jane Greer, Trevor Howard, Peter Van Eyck, Carlos Henning. Updating of THE MOST DANGEROUS GAME has author Widmark and magazine writer Greer stumbling onto strange plantation run by mysterious Howard and Van Eyck. Engrossing, extremely well-made film.

Run for Your Money (1949-British) 83m. ******* D: Charles Frend. Donald Houston, Meredith Edwards, Moira Lister, Alec Guinness, Hugh Griffith, Joyce Grenfell. Way-above-par comic study of two Welsh miners having a spree in London.

Run Like A Thief (1967-Spanish) C-92m. ****** D: Harry Spalding. Kieron Moore, Ina Balin, Keenan Wynn, Fernando Rey. Soldier of fortune goes after diamond hijackers with a mobster chief who foils him every step of the way.

Run of the Arrow (1957) C-86m. ****½** D: Samuel Fuller. Rod Steiger, Brian Keith, Sarita Montiel, Ralph Meeker, Charles Bronson, Tim McCoy. Unusual Western dealing with cowpoke who discovers that despite gruesome Civil War, he belongs among white men, and not warring Indians.

Run Silent, Run Deep (1958) 93m. *** D: Robert Wise. Clark Gable, Burt Lancaster, Jack Warden, Brad Dexter, Don Rickles. Battle of wits between officers Gable and Lancaster on WW2 submarine is basis for interesting drama; little action, though.

Run, Simon, Run (1970) C-73m. TVM D: George McCowan. Burt Reynolds, Inger Stevens, Royal Dano, James Best, Rodolfo Acosta, Don Dubbins, Ken Lynch. Unpretentious, straightforward tale of Papago Indian returning to tribe after prison term, swearing tribal vengeance on man who really murdered his brother. Excellent, tense atmosphere; great use of locations; convincing performances (including Stevens' last). Above average.

Run, Stranger, Run SEE: Happy Mother's Day, Love, George

Run Wild, Run Free (1969-British) C-100m. **½ D: Richard C. Sarafian. John Mills, Mark Lester, Sylvia Syms, Gordon Jackson, Bernard Miles, Fiona Fullerton. Good cast helps leisurely, but better-than-usual children's film about young mute and his love for a white colt; nice subdued photography.

Runaround, The (1946) 86m. ** D: Charles Lamont. Rod Cameron, Broderick Crawford, Ella Raines, Samuel S. Hinds. Raines is heiress whom detectives Cameron and Crawford must return to Gotham; tepid programmer.

Runaway! (1973) C-73m. TVM D: David Lowell Rich. Ben Johnson, Ben Murphy, Vera Miles, Ed Nelson, Darleen Carr, Martin Milner, Lee H. Montgomery, Ray Danton. Train careening down mountain passage without brakes, the lives of various stereotyped characters sway with Fate's whim. Some moments of good suspense, but overall, film reeks of formula. Average.

Runaway Barge, The (1975) C-78m. TVM D: Boris Sagal. Bo Hopkins, Tim Matheson, Jim Davis, Nick Nolte, Devon Ericson, Christina Hart, James Best. Adventures of three men trying to earn a living on a modern day riverboat. Typical TV action movie including a trio of two-fisted scalawags. Average.

Runaways, The (1975) C-78m. TVM D: Harry Harris. Dorothy McGuire, Van Williams, John Randolph, Neva Patterson, Josh Albee, Lenka Peterson. Poignant family drama about unhappy teenaged orphan and an escaped leopard from wild-animal compound. Well-acted filming of Victor Canning's sentimental novel. Above average.

Runner Stumbles, The (1979) C-99m. *½ D: Stanley Kramer. Dick Van Dyke, Kathleen Quinlan, Maureen Stapleton, Ray Bolger, Tammy Grimes, Beau Bridges. Sober adaptation of Milan Stitt's Broadway play, based on true story of small-town priest accused of murdering young nun for whom he'd shown unusual affection. Aloof and unconvincing, with Van Dyke unbearably stiff as the clergyman.

Running (1979-Canadian) C-103m. *½ D: Steven Hilliard Stern. Michael Douglas, Susan Anspach, Lawrence Dane, Eugene Levy, Charles Shamata. Despite the no doubt lousy retirement plan, Douglas—32, out of work and father of two daughters—wants to run for a living. A few yocks in this absurdly melodramatic jock drama, but not enough of them.

Running Man, The (1963-British) C-103m. *** D: Carol Reed. Laurence Harvey, Lee Remick, Alan Bates, Felix Aylmer, Eleanor Summerfield, Allan Cuthbertson. Harvey fakes his death to collect insurance money, but pursuing insurance investigator Bates forces him and wife Remick to go on the lam in Spain. Entertaining but not suspenseful enough.

Running Target (1956) C-83m. ** D: Marvin Weinstein. Doris Dowling, Arthur Franz, Richard Reeves, Myron Healey, James Parnell. Minor film of modern-day sheriff leading chase for escaped convicts.

Running Wild (1955) 81m. **½ D: Abner Biberman. William Campbell, Mamie Van Doren, Keenan Wynn, Walter Coy, Tawdry, actionful account of young police officer getting the goods on car thief gangs.

Running Wild (1973) C-103m. *** D: Robert McCahon. Lloyd Bridges, Dina Merrill, Pat Hingle, Morgan Woodward, Gilbert Roland, Lonny Chapman, R. G. Armstrong. Good family-oriented drama about a news photographer (Merrill) who protests treatment of wild horses while doing a story in Colorado. Beautiful scenery complements solid script.

Russians Are Coming, the Russians Are Coming, The (1966) C-120m. **½ D: Norman Jewison. Carl Reiner, Eva Marie Saint, Alan Arkin, Brian Keith, Jonathan Winters, Theodore Bikel, Paul Ford,

John Phillip Law. Popular comedy about Russian submarine that lands off New England coast was incredibly overrated in 1966; now it's merely a TV sit-com saved by pretty photography and good comic bits by Arkin and Winters.

Russian Roulette (1975) C-93m. **½ D: Lou Lombardo. George Segal, Cristina Raines, Bo Brundin, Denholm Elliott, Gordon Jackson, Peter Donat, Louise Fletcher, Val Avery. Assassins threaten to kill Soviet premier Kosygin during his trip to Vancouver; Segal is assigned to capture elusive troublemaker thought to be the hit-man in this violent, unsatisfying thriller. Filmed in Canada.

Rust Never Sleeps (1979) C-103m. *** D: Bernard Shakey (Neil Young). Ragged but rousing record of Neil Young's bizarre 1978 concert, with 16 well performed tunes by rockdom's most lovable downer. My My, Hey, Hey.

Ruthless (1948) 104m. *** D: Edgar G. Ulmer. Zachary Scott, Louis Hayward, Diana Lynn, Sydney Greenstreet, Lucille Bremer, Martha Vickers, Raymond Burr. Scott steps on everyone to become big shot in this engrossing drama. Greenstreet is especially good as Southern tycoon.

Ryan's Daughter (1970-British) C-176m. **½ D: David Lean. Robert Mitchum, Trevor Howard, Sarah Miles, Christopher Jones, John Mills, Leo McKern. Simple love story blown up to gargantuan proportions in Northern Ireland, where young girl (Miles) marries simple, plodding schoolteacher (Mitchum) and has affair with British soldier (Jones) stationed in town. Elephantine production overpowers thin story, admittedly beautiful scenes dwarfing what plot there is. Still, story moves along briskly, maintains interest, but never becomes classic film its creators were attempting. Mills won Oscar in supporting role as hunchback.

S.O.S. Pacific (1960-British) 92m. **½ D: Guy Green. Eddie Constantine, Pier Angeli, Richard Attenborough, John Gregson, Eva Bartok, Jean Anderson. Middling study of human nature when passengers on plane crash-land on nuclear-test island.

S.O.S. Titanic (1979) C-150m. TVM D: William Hale. David Janssen, Cloris Leachman, Susan St. James, David Warner, Ian Holm, Helen Mirren, Harry Andrews. Stylish docudrama about the oft-told sea disaster, mirroring the fictional elements of the 1953 movie TITANIC and the meticulously detailed facts of the 1958 A NIGHT TO REMEMBER, faithfully recreated here through James Costigan's multicharactered teleplay. Above average.

Saadia (1953) C-82m. *½ D: Albert Lewin. Cornel Wilde, Mel Ferrer, Rita Gam, Cyril Cusack, Richard Johnson. Misfire; intellectual story of modernistic Moroccan ruler and doctor vying for love of superstitious native dancing girl.

Sabaka (1955) C-81m. ** D: Frank Ferrin. Boris Karloff, Reginald Denny, Victor Jory, Lisa Howard, Jeanne Bates, Jay Novello, June Foray. Splashy trivia enhanced by veteran cast, about spooky religious cult in exotic India.

Sabotage (1936-British) 76m. *** D: Alfred Hitchcock. Sylvia Sidney, Oscar Homolka, John Loder, Desmond Tester, Joyce Barbour. Elaborately detailed thriller about woman who suspects that her kindly husband (Homolka), a movie theater manager, is keeping something from her. Full of intriguing Hitchcock touches. Based on Joseph Conrad's *Secret Agent*, originally retitled A WOMAN ALONE in this country.

Saboteur (1942) 108m. **½ D: Alfred Hitchcock. Robert Cummings, Priscilla Lane, Norman Lloyd, Otto Kruger, Murray Alper, Alma Kruger, Dorothy Peterson. Disappointing Hitchcock with intriguing Statue of Liberty climax, pegged on innocent Cummings accused of sabotage in munitions factory during WW2.

Saboteur, Code Name Morituri, The (1965) 123m. **½ D: Bernhard Wicki. Marlon Brando, Yul Brynner, Janet Margolin, Trevor Howard, Wally Cox, William Redfield, Carl Esmond. Brando highlights great cast in study of anti-Nazi German who helps British capture cargo ship. Cast is only asset; script degenerates. Also known as MORITURI.

Sabre Jet (1953) C-96m. **½ D: Louis King. Robert Stack, Coleen Gray, Richard Arlen, Julie Bishop. Routine Korean War story of lonely wives and fighting husbands.

Sabrina (1954) 113m. ***½ D: Billy

Wilder. Humphrey Bogart, Audrey Hepburn, William Holden, John Williams, Francis X. Bushman, Martha Hyer. Samuel Taylor play is good vehicle for Hepburn as chauffeur's daughter romanced by aging tycoon Bogart to keep her from playboy Holden. Offbeat casting works in this fun film.

Sabu and the Magic Ring (1957) C-61m. *½ D: George Blair. Sabu, Daria Massey, Vladimir Sokoloff, Robin Moore. Low-budget backlot Arabian Nights nonsense, with Sabu chasing thieves to regain stolen girl and priceless gem.

Sacco and Vanzetti (1971-French-Italian) C-120m. *½ D: Giuliano Montaldo. Gian Maria Volonte, Riccardo Cucciolla, Milo O'Shea, Cyril Cusack, Rosanna Fratello, Geoffrey Keen. Classic tale of American miscarriage of justice cries for cinematic treatment, but this version makes South Braintree, Massachusetts look like a town in a Clint Eastwood spaghetti Western. Joan Baez sings title song.

Sacketts, The (1979) C-200m. TVM D: Robert Totten. Sam Elliott, Tom Sellack, Jeff Osterhage, Glenn Ford, Ben Johnson, Gilbert Roland, Ruth Roman, Jack Elam, Mercedes McCambridge. Rambling sagebrush saga taken from two Louis L'Amour novels following the fortunes of the three Sackett Brothers in the post-Civil War west. Average.

Sad Horse, The (1959) C-78m. ** D: James B. Clark. David Ladd, Chill Wills, Rex Reason, Patrice Wymore. Tender, undemanding tale of a race-horse and a lonely boy (Ladd).

Sad Sack, The (1957) 98m. ** D: George Marshall. Jerry Lewis, Phyllis Kirk, David Wayne, Peter Lorre, Gene Evans, Mary Treen. Disjointed comedy vaguely based on George Baker comic strip of Army misfit. Not enough funny sequences to succeed. Lorre appears as Arab in last part of film.

Sadie McKee (1934) 90m. *** D: Clarence Brown. Joan Crawford, Franchot Tone, Gene Raymond, Edward Arnold, Esther Ralston, Leo G. Carroll, Akim Tamiroff, Gene Austin. Solidly entertaining film follows serpentine story of working-girl Crawford and the three men in her life: smooth-talking Raymond, tipsy millionaire Arnold, earnest employer Tone. Beautifully paced, handsomely filmed. Song: "All I

Do Is Dream of You," plus amusing rendition of "After You've Gone" by Austin, Candy Candido.

Saddle the Wind (1958) C-84m. *** D: Robert Parrish. Robert Taylor, Julie London, John Cassavetes, Donald Crisp. Finely acted Western of turned-good rancher (Taylor) fated to shoot it out with brother (Cassavetes).

Saddle Tramp (1950) C-77m. **½ D: Hugo Fregonese. Joel McCrea, Wanda Hendrix, John McIntire, John Russell, Ed Begley, Jeanette Nolan, Antonio Moreno. Homey Western with McCrea in title role "adopting" four kids and fighting the good cause.

Safari (1940) 80m. ** D: Edward H. Griffith. Douglas Fairbanks, Jr., Madeleine Carroll, Tullio Carminati, Lynne Overman, Muriel Angelus, Billy Gilbert. Standard jungle expedition story, with attractive stars.

Safari (1956-British) C-91m. **½ D: Terence Young. Victor Mature, Janet Leigh, John Justin, Roland Culver, Liam Redmond. Fierce jungle drama has Mature leading expedition against Mau Maus. Cast gives good performance.

Safari Drums (1953) 71m. D: Ford Beebe. Johnny Sheffield, Douglas Kennedy, Barbara Bestar, Emory Parnell, Smoki Whitfield. SEE: **Bomba, the Jungle Boy** series.

Safe at Home! (1962) 83m. ** D: Walter Doniger. Mickey Mantle, Roger Maris, William Frawley, Patricia Barry, Don Collier, Bryan Russell. Kid promises to produce Mantle and Maris for a Little League dinner: that's it.

Safe Place, A (1971) C-94m. ** D: Henry Jaglom. Tuesday Weld, Jack Nicholson, Orson Welles, Philip Proctor, Gwen Welles. Spaced-out, water-logged fantasy of weird girl who lives in dream world where she can never grow up.

Safecracker, The (1958-British) 96m. ** D: Ray Milland. Ray Milland, Barry Jones, Jeannette Sterke, Ernest Clark, Melissa Stribling, Victor Maddern. Contrived, OK story of burglar who almost goes straight, later forced to use his talents for war effort.

Safety Last (1923) 78m. (includes excerpt from HOT WATER) *** D: Fred Newmeyer, Sam Taylor. Harold Lloyd, Mildred Davis, Bill Strothers, Noah Young. Crackerjack silent comedy about go-getter Harold determined to make good in the big city includes his justly famous building-climbing sequence—still hair-raising after all these years. Edited for TV and paired with hilarious excerpt from 1924 feature HOT WATER.

Saga of Hemp Brown, The (1958) C-80m. ** D: Richard Carlson. Rory Calhoun, Beverly Garland, John Larch, Russell Johnson. Calhoun is bounced from Army, and seeks to find real crooks in just another Western.

Sahara (1943) 97m. ***½ D: Zoltan Korda. Humphrey Bogart, Bruce Bennett, Lloyd Bridges, Rex Ingram, J. Carrol Naish, Dan Duryea. Excellent actioner of British-American unit stranded in Sahara desert; Bogie's the chief, of course, with fine support by Naish and Ingram. Remade as Western LAST OF THE COMANCHES.

Saigon (1948) 94m. ** D: Leslie Fenton. Alan Ladd, Veronica Lake, Luther Adler, Douglas Dick, Wally Cassell, Morris Carnovsky. Glossy Paramount Pictures' espionage drama set in Saigon is only fair.

Sail a Crooked Ship (1961) 88m. **½ D: Irving S. Brecher. Robert Wagner, Ernie Kovacs, Dolores Hart, Carolyn Jones, Frankie Avalon, Harvey Lembeck. Bungled crime-caper comedy has hilarious moments, but not enough to make it a winner.

Sail into Danger (1957-British) 72m. ** D: Kenneth Hume. Dennis O'Keefe, Kathleen Ryan, James Hayter, Pedro de Cordoba, John Bull, Felix de Pommes. O'Keefe is ensnared into helping Ryan in smuggling plot; set in Barcelona. Meek actioner.

Sailor Beware (1951) 108m. *** D: Hal Walker. Dean Martin, Jerry Lewis, Corinne Calvet, Marion Marshall, Robert Strauss; guest, Betty Hutton. Hilarious adventures of Martin & Lewis in the Navy. Induction scenes, boxing sequence are highlights in one of the team's funniest outings.

Sailor Beware! SEE: Panic in the Parlor

Sailor of the King (1953-U.S.-British) 83m. *** D: Roy Boulting. Jeffrey Hunter, Michael Rennie, Wendy Hiller, Bernard Lee, Peter Van Eyck. Solid WW2 naval action story, based on C. S. Forester novel *Brown on Restitution*, with Hunter

rising to challenge when opportunity arises to attack German raider. British title: SINGLE HANDED. Filmed before in 1935.

Sailor Takes a Wife, The (1945) 91m. ** D: Richard Whorf. Robert Walker, June Allyson, Hume Cronyn, Audrey Totter, Eddie "Rochester" Anderson, Reginald Owen. Mild little comedy is summed up by title.

Sailor Who Fell From Grace With the Sea, The (1976-British) C-104m. *** D: Lewis John Carlino. Sarah Miles, Kris Kristofferson, Jonathan Kahn, Margo Cunningham, Earl Rhodes. A troubled, impressionable boy tries to deal with his widowed mother's love affair with an amiable sailor, and falls under the influence of a morbid young friend. Passionate love scenes, and a bizarre ending, highlight this unusual film, beautifully shot on English seacoast locations. Based on a Japanese story.

Sailor's Lady (1940) 66m. ** D: Allan Dwan. Nancy Kelly, Jon Hall, Joan Davis, Dana Andrews, Mary Nash, Larry "Buster" Crabbe, Katherine (Kay) Aldridge. Witless comedy of Kelly pretending to have baby to see if sailor-fiancee Hall will still mary her.

Sailor's Luck (1933) 78m. *** D: Raoul Walsh. James Dunn, Sally Eilers, Sammy Cohen, Victor Jory, Frank Moran, Esther Muir. Funny, offbeat film of sailors on leave; Dunn and Eilers carry boy-meets-girl plot while crazy comedy touches surround them, including Jory as oily Baron DeBartolo, landlord who runs dance marathon!

Saint, The Leslie Charteris' literate, debonair detective has been the subject of an extremely popular British television show in recent years. But he never quite made it in the movies. From 1938 to 1942, RKO tried no less than three actors in the leading role, finding moderate success but nothing earth-shaking. Louis Hayward seemed at home in the role in THE SAINT IN NEW YORK, a smooth underworld saga with a bland leading lady (Kay Sutton) and a fine supporting cast (Sig Ruman as a ganglord, Jack Carson as a thug, etc.). Nevertheless, he didn't repeat the role; it went instead to suave George Sanders, who portrayed the Saint, usually with Wendy Barrie as leading lady, in four quickly made, entertaining mysteries taking him from

Palm Springs to London. The scripts were competent, but it was Sanders' usual offhand manner that kept them alive. In 1942 stage star Hugh Sinclair took a fling in THE SAINT MEETS THE TIGER but gave up after a second effort. Sanders left the series only to begin another, The Falcon, at the same studio, although without the main titles to inform viewers which series it was, one could hardly have told the difference. The Falcon continued through the 1940s, while the Saint came to a premature end in 1942. There was one revival attempt with Louis Hayward made in England in 1953, THE SAINT'S GIRL FRIDAY, which was average but no improvement over the original series. It took British television and an actor named Roger Moore to give life to The Saint at last in the 1960s.

St. Benny the Dip (1951) 80m. **½ D: Edgar G. Ulmer. Dick Haymes, Nina Foch, Roland Young, Lionel Stander, Freddie Bartholomew. Offbeat account of con-men posing as clergymen who predictably become reformed; filmed in N.Y.C.

Saint in London, The (1939-British) 72m. D: John Paddy Carstairs. George Sanders, David Burns, Sally Gray, Henry Oscar, Ralph Truman, Norah Howard, Carl Jaffe. SEE: **The Saint** series.

Saint in New York, The (1938) 71m. D: Ben Holmes. Louis Hayward, Kay Sutton, Sig Ruman, Jonathan Hale, Frederick Burton, Jack Carson. SEE: **The Saint** series.

Saint in Palm Springs, The (1941) 65m. D: Jack Hively. George Sanders, Wendy Barrie, Paul Guilfoyle, Jonathan Hale, Linda Hayes, Ferris Taylor. SEE **The Saint** series.

St. Ives (1976) C-93m. ** D: J. Lee Thompson. Charles Bronson, John Houseman, Jacqueline Bisset, Harry Guardino, Maximilian Schell, Harris Yulin, Dana Elcar. Muddled yarn about would-be writer Bronson who becomes a pawn for wealthy conniver Houseman and his beautiful associate (Bisset) and finds himself involved in murder. Glossy but stupid.

Saint Jack (1979) C-112m. *** D: Peter Bogdanovich. Ben Gazzara, Denholm Elliott, James Villiers, Joss Ackland, Rodney Bewes, Lisa Lu, Peter Bogdanovich. Absorbing character study of an amiable, ambitious pimp who thrives in Singa-pore during early 1970s. Fine performances from Gazzara and Elliott, excellent use of location milieu.

Saint Joan (1957) 110m. ** D: Otto Preminger. Jean Seberg, Richard Widmark, Richard Todd, Anton Walbrook, John Gielgud, Felix Aylmer. Big-scale filming of Shaw's play sounded large thud when released; some good acting, but Seberg, not suited to film's tempo, throws production askew.

St. Louis Blues (1958) 93m. **½ D: Allen Reisner. Nat "King" Cole, Eartha Kitt, Ruby Dee, Pearl Bailey, Cab Calloway. Rags-to-modest-acclaim biography of blues musician W. C. Handy, with personality cast interpreting many of his well-known tunes.

St. Louis Kid (1934) 67m. **½ D: Ray Enright. James Cagney, Patricia Ellis, Allen Jenkins, Robert Barrat, Addison Richards. Cagney is dynamic self as truck driver battling crooked officials in dairy business, to protect local farmers.

Saint Meets the Tiger, The (1943-British) 70m. D: Paul Stein. Hugh Sinclair, Jean Gillie, Clifford Evans, Wylie Watson, Dennis Arundell. SEE: **The Saint** series.

Saint Strikes Back, The (1939) 67m. D: John Farrow. George Sanders, Wendy Barrie, Jonathan Hale, Jerome Cowan, Neil Hamilton, Barry Fitzgerald, Edward Gargan, Robert Strange. SEE: **The Saint** series.

Saint Takes Over, The (1940) 69m. D: Jack Hively. George Sanders, Jonathan Hale, Wendy Barrie, Paul Guilfoyle, Morgan Conway, Robert Emmett Keane, Cyrus W. Kendall. SEE: **The Saint** series.

St. Valentine's Day Massacre, The (1967) C-100m. **½ D: Roger Corman. Jason Robards, Jr., George Segal, Ralph Meeker, Jean Hale, Clint Ritchie, Frank Silvera, Joseph Campanella. This had the makings of a good film, but they blew it, with Robards (as Al Capone) and Segal (doing a Jimmy Cagney imitation) overacting as they've never done before. So much shooting throughout film that final massacre seems tame by comparison. Many familiar faces appear throughout, like Harold Stone, Kurt Kreuger, Milton Frome, Mickey Deems, John Agar, Alex D'Arcy, Reed Hadley, etc.

Sainted Sisters, The (1948) 89m.
**½ D: William Russell. Veronica Lake, Joan Caulfield, Barry Fitzgerald, William Demarest, George Reeves, Beulah Bondi. Fitzgerald's blarney is a bit overdone in this tale of two bad girls who go straight under his guidance.

Saint's Double Trouble, The (1940) 68m. D: Jack Hively. George Sanders, Helene Whitney, Jonathan Hale, Bela Lugosi, Donald MacBride, John F. Hamilton. SEE: The Saint series.

Saint's Girl Friday, The (1954-British) 68m. D: Seymour Friedman. Louis Hayward, Naomi Chance, Sydney Tafler, Charles Victor. SEE: The Saint series.

Saint's Vacation, The (1941-British) 60m. D: Leslie Fenton. Hugh Sinclair, Sally Gray, Arthur Macrae, Cecil Parker, Leueen McGrath, Gordon McLeod. SEE: The Saint series.

Sakima and the Masked Marvel (1943) 100m. **½ D: Spencer Bennet. William Forrest, Louise Currie, Johnny Arthur, Rod Bacon, Richard Clarke. Above-par Republic actioner set during WW2, with Japanese espionage in the U.S. combatted by heroic mysterious Masked Marvel. Reedited movie serial: THE MASKED MARVEL.

Salem's Lot (1979) C-200m. TVM D: Tobe Hooper. David Soul, James Mason, Lance Kerwin, Bonnie Bedelia, Lew Ayres, Elisha Cook, Ed Flanders, Marie Windsor, Clarissa Kaye. Vampires are running rampant in modern-day New England. A well-made hair-raiser whose curse is its length. Mason's great as a sinister antique dealer; Soul's so-so as the successful writer returning home to the strange goings-on. Based on Stephen King's bestselling novel. Above average.

Sally and Saint Anne (1952) 90m.
**½ D: Rudolph Maté. Ann Blyth, Edmund Gwenn, Hugh O'Brian, Jack Kelly, King Donovan. Cutesy and a bit tasteless; Blyth is daughter in screwball family who believes St. Anne will help them in times of need.

Sally, Irene and Mary (1938) 72m.
**½ D: William A. Seiter. Alice Faye, Tony Martin, Fred Allen, Joan Davis, Marjorie Weaver, Gregory Ratoff, Jimmy Durante, Louise Hovick (Gypsy Rose Lee). Predictable story of three stagestruck girls trying to break into show business, with good comedy spots by Davis, pleasant songs from Faye and Martin: "I Could Use a Dream," "This Is Where I Came In."

Sally of the Sawdust (1925) 91m.
**½ D: D. W. Griffith. W. C. Fields, Carol Dempster, Alfred Lunt, Erville Alderson, Effie Shannon. Pleasant part of sideshow con-man Fields who tries to restore his ward (Dempster) to her rightful place in society, knowing identity of her wealthy grandparents. Interesting to see W. C. in a silent film, particularly since one can compare this to its remake, POPPY.

Sally's Irish Rogue SEE: **Poacher's Daughter, The**

Salome (1953) C-103m. **½ D: William Dieterle. Rita Hayworth, Stewart Granger, Charles Laughton, Judith Anderson, Cedric Hardwicke, Maurice Schwartz. Great cast struggles with unintentionally funny script in biblical drama of illustrious dancer who offers herself to spare John the Baptist.

Salome, Where She Danced (1945) C-90m. BOMB D: Charles Lamont. Yvonne De Carlo, Rod Cameron, David Bruce, Walter Slezak, Albert Dekker, Marjorie Rambeau, J. Edward Bromberg. Ludicrous film provides some laughs while trying to spin tale of exotic dancer becoming Mata Hari-type spy.

Salt and Pepper (1968-British) C-101m. **½ D: Richard Donner. Sammy Davis, Jr., Peter Lawford, Michael Bates, Ilona Rodgers, John LeMesurier. Soho nightclub owners find trouble when two baddies turn up at their club. Contrived, broad comedy. Sequel: ONE MORE TIME.

Salty (1973) C-92m. ** D: Ricou Browning. Mark Slade, Clint Howard, Nina Foch, Julius W. Harris, Linda Scruggs. Two orphaned brothers adopt a mischievous sea lion in this predictable kiddie film made in Florida.

Salty O'Rourke (1945) 97m. *** D: Raoul Walsh. Alan Ladd, Gail Russell, William Demarest, Stanley Clements, Bruce Cabot, Spring Byington. Lively tale of smooth con-man Ladd aiming to clean up with jockey Clements, who turns out to be a large headache. Schoolteacher Russell steps in to foil Ladd's plans.

Salute to the Marines (1943) C-101m. **½ D: S. Sylvan Simon.

Wallace Beery, Fay Bainter, Reginald Owen, Keye Luke, Ray Collins, Marilyn Maxwell. OK Beery vehicle of Army veteran who reluctantly retires, finds himself caught in surprise attack on Philippines.

Salvage (1979) **C-100m. TVM D:** Lee Philips. Andy Griffith, Joel Higgins, Trish Stewart, J. Jay Saunders, Richard Jaeckel. Amiable pilot to the short-lived series in which a hotshot junkman goes into the moonshot business for himself with two young companions to recover a fortune in space junk. Average.

Salzburg Connection, The (1972) **C-92m.** *½ **D:** Lee H. Katzin. Barry Newman, Anna Karina, Klaus-Maria Brandauer, Karen Jensen, Joe Maross, Wolfgang Preiss. Terrible film version of Helen MacInnes' best-seller about American lawyer on vacation in Salzburg who gets mixed up with spies; irritating use of slow-motion and freeze-frame gimmicks.

Sam Hill: Who Killed Mr. Foster? (1971) **C-100m. TVM D:** Fielder Cook. Ernest Borgnine, Sam Jaffe, J. D. Cannon, Judy Geeson, Will Geer, John McGiver, Jay C. Flippen. Pending town election jeopardizes security of cynical Western marshal. Uneventful situations, boring dialogue; even somewhat unusual casting doesn't enliven proceedings. Below average. Also known as WHO KILLED THE MYSTERIOUS MR. FOSTER?

Sam Whiskey (1969) **C-96m.** ** **D:** Arnold Laven. Burt Reynolds, Clint Walker, Ossie Davis, Angie Dickinson, Rick Davis, William Schallert, Woodrow Parfrey. Modestly mounted, uninteresting Western wasting talents of good cast. Schemer Whiskey coerced into organizing heist of golden bell. For Western aficionados and Reynolds addicts only.

Sam's Song (1969) **C-92m.** *½ **D:** Jordan Leondopoulos. Robert De Niro, Jennifer Warren, Jered Mickey, Martin Kelley, Viva. Dreary film about film editor's weekend with friends on Long Island, interesting only for early DeNiro performance. Reissued as THE SWAP.

Samar (1962) **C-89m.** ** **D:** George Montgomery. George Montgomery, Gilbert Roland, Ziva Rodann, Joan O'Brien, Nico Minardos, Mario Barri. Average actioner has Montgomery as head of prison compound on a Philippine island who rejects

inhumane treatment of prisoners and leads them on escape route.

Same Time, Next Year (1978) **C-117m.** *** **D:** Robert Mulligan. Ellen Burstyn, Alan Alda. Bernard Slade's two-character Broadway play makes pleasing film, with Alda and Burstyn as adulterous couple who share one weekend a year for 26 years; warm, human comedy-drama reflects changes in American life and attitudes since early '50s in likable fashion.

Sammy Going South SEE: **Boy Ten Feet Tall, A**

Sammy Stops the World (1979) **C-104m.** BOMB **D:** Mel Shapiro. Sammy Davis Jr., Marian Mercer, Dennis Daniels, Donna Lowe. Pathetic update of STOP THE WORLD, I WANT TO GET OFF combines nail-your-camera-to-the-ground direction with a stage production that couldn't get by at Three Mile Island Dinner Theatre.

Samson and Delilah (1949) **C-128m.** *** **D:** Cecil B. DeMille. Victor Mature, Hedy Lamarr, George Sanders, Angela Lansbury, Henry Wilcoxon, Olive Deering, Fay Holden. With expected DeMille touches, this remains a tremendously entertaining film. Mature is surprisingly good as Samson, though his famous fight with lion is hopelessly phony; also difficult to swallow idea of Lansbury being Lamarr's *older* sister. Sanders supplies biggest surprise by underplaying his role as the Saran.

Samson and the Slave Queen (1963-Italian) **C-92m.** *½ **D:** Umberto Lenzi. Pierre Brice, Alan Steel, Moira Orfei, Maria Grazia Spina. Juvenile muscleman epic that is ludicrous in its approach to adventure.

Samurai (1979) **C-78m. TVM D:** Lee H. Katzin. Joe Penny, Dana Elcar, Beulah Quo, James Shigeta, Charles Cioffi, Geoffrey Lewis. Incredible series hopeful about an eager beaver Frisco assistant DA who moonlights as a samurai swordsman to uphold justice! Must be seen to be disbelieved, or better yet, forget it. Below average.

San Antone (1953) **90m.** **½ **D:** George Sherman. Rod Cameron, Arleen Whelan, Forrest Tucker, Katy Jurado, Rodolfo Acosta, Bob Steele, Harry Carey, Jr. Offbeat Western tends to ramble, but story of Cameron and friends being victimized by despicable Tucker and bitchy Southern belle Whelan is intriguing.

[659]

San Antonio (1945) **C-111m.** ******* D: David Butler. Errol Flynn, Alexis Smith, S. Z. Sakall, Victor Francen, Florence Bates, John Litel, Paul Kelly. Elaborate Western; predictable plot but good production as dance-hall girl Smith, working for villain Francen, falls for good-guy Flynn.

San Diego, I Love You (1944) **83m.** ******* D: Reginald Le Borg. Jon Hall, Louise Allbritton, Edward Everett Horton, Eric Blore, Buster Keaton, Irene Ryan. Whimsical comedy of unconventional family trying to promote father Horton's inventions in San Diego. Allbritton is perky, Keaton memorable in delightful sequence as bored bus driver.

San Francisco (1936) **115m.** *****½** D: W. S. Van Dyke II. Clark Gable, Jeanette MacDonald, Spencer Tracy, Jack Holt, Jessie Ralph, Ted Healy, Shirley Ross. Top-grade entertainment with extremely lavish production. Jeanette overdoes it a bit as the belle of San Francisco, but the music, Tracy's performance, and earthquake climax are still fine.

San Francisco International Airport (1970) **C-100m. TVM** D: John Llewellyn Moxey. Van Johnson, Pernell Roberts, Clu Gulager, Beth Brickell, Tab Hunter, Nancy Malone, David Hartman, Jill Donahue. Fair suspense in otherwise typical day-in-the-life portrayal of major transportation center, centering around manager and security chief. Uneven characterizations and dialogue, but pace holds interest. Average.

San Francisco Story, The (1952) **80m.** ****** D: Robert Parrish. Joel McCrea, Yvonne De Carlo, Sidney Blackmer, Florence Bates. Tame Western actioner set in gold-rush days, with cleanup of city's criminal elements.

San Pedro Bums, The (1977) **C-78. TVM** D: Barry Shear. Christopher Murney, Jeff Druce, John Mark Robinson, Stuart Pankin, Darryl McCullough, Bill Lucking. Comedy adventure of five knockabouts, living on an old fishing boat, who try to collar a gang of waterfront toughs. A real bummer that somehow became a series. Below average.

San Quentin (1937) **70m.** ****½** D: Lloyd Bacon. Pat O'Brien, Humphrey Bogart, Ann Sheridan, Veda Ann Borg, Barton MacLane. Warner Bros. formula prison film; convict Bogart's sister (Sheridan) loves warden O'Brien. MacLane is memorable as tough prison guard.

San Quentin (1946) **66m.** ****½** D: Gordon Douglas. Lawrence Tierney, Barton MacLane, Marian Carr, Harry Shannon, Carol Forman, Richard Powers (Tom Keene). Prison drama with different plot for a change, of organization for ex-cons not having intended results.

Sanctuary (1961) **100m.** ****** D: Tony Richardson. Lee Remick, Yves Montand, Bradford Dillman, Odetta, Reta - Shaw. Faulkner's novel of Southern degradation, rape, and murder, filmed before as STORY OF TEMPLE DRAKE; much more explicit here.

Sanctuary of Fear (1979) **C-100m. TVM** D: John Llewellyn Moxey. Barnard Hughes, Kay Lenz, Michael McGuire, Fred Gwynne, Elizabeth Wilson, George Hearn. Disappointing pilot to a proposed series based on G. K. Chesterton's "Father Brown," the English parish priest (here transplanted to New York) and amateur sleuth, played so wonderfully by Alec Guinness in 1954. Average. Retitled THE GIRL IN THE PARK.

Sand (1949) **C-78m.** ****** D: Louis King. Mark Stevens, Rory Calhoun, Coleen Gray, Charley Grapewin. Visually picturesque but dull account of show horse who turns wild. Retitled: WILL JAMES' SAND.

Sand Castle, The (1960) **C-67m.** ****½** D: Jerome Hill. Barry Cardwell, Laurie Cardwell, George Dunham, Alec Wilder. Imaginative little film of small boy building mud castles on the beach, dreaming of people living in his creation.

Sand Castles (1972) **C-74m. TVM** D: Ted Post. Herschel Bernardi, Jan-Michael Vincent, Bonnie Bedelia, Mariette Hartley, Gary Crosby. Love story of young female musician and spirit of young man returning to clear his name. Thanks to somber mood and offbeat point of view, not as unbearable as expected. Taped movie, not filmed. Average.

Sand Pebbles, The (1966) **C-179m.** ******* D: Robert Wise. Steve McQueen, Richard Attenborough, Richard Crenna, Candice Bergen, Simon Oakland. Often compelling drama of U.S. ship anchored off China. McQueen's performance is exceptional.

Sanders of the River (1935-British)

98m. *** D: Zoltan Korda. Paul Robeson, Leslie Banks, Nina Mae McKinney, Robert Cochran, Martin Walker. Dated adventure story (by Edgar Wallace) maintains interest today, particularly for Robeson's strong presence, and African location shooting. A fascinating relic of the sun-never-sets school of British imperialism. Remade as COAST OF SKELETONS.

Sandokan Against the Leopard of Sarawak (1964-Italian) **C-94m. **** D: Luigi Capuano. Ray Danton, Guy Madison, Franca Bettoja, Mario Petri. Danton vs. Madison in this papier mâché, run-of-the-mill epic.

Sandokan Fights Back (1964-Italian) **C-96m. **** D: Luigi Capuano. Ray Danton, Guy Madison, Franca Bettoja, Mino Doro. Unconvincing, juvenile narrative of princely ruler fighting to regain his throne.

Sandokan the Great (1965-Italian) **C-105m. **** D: Umberto Lenzi. Steve Reeves, Genevieve Grad, Rik Battaglia, Maurice Poli. Reeves is put through his gymnastic paces in this juvenile sword-and-cloak entry.

Sandpiper, The (1965) **C-116m. **½** D: Vincente Minnelli. Elizabeth Taylor, Richard Burton, Eva Marie Saint, Charles Bronson, Robert Webber, Torin Thatcher. Ordinary triangle love affair. Beatnik Taylor in love with Burton, who is married to Saint. Nothing new, but beautiful California Big Sur settings help; so does theme, "Shadow Of Your Smile."

Sandpit Generals, The SEE: **Wild Pack, The**

Sands of Beersheba (1966) **90m. **½** D: Alexander Ramati. Diane Baker, David Opatoshu, Tom Bell, Paul Stassino. Pretentious retelling of Absalom (Bell) and David (Opatoshu) conflict, filmed in Israel, dabbling in philosophy on the Arab-vs.-Jew animosity.

Sands of Iwo Jima (1949) **110m. ***½** D: Allan Dwan. John Wayne, John Agar, Adele Mara, Forrest Tucker, Arthur Franz, Julie Bishop, Richard Jaeckel. Rousing war story of cocky young man straightened out by military life, with Wayne in peak form as tough sergeant; superb battle scenes.

Sands of the Desert (1960-British) **C-92m. **** D: John Paddy Carstairs. Charlie Drake, Peter Arne, Sarah Branch, Rebecca Dignam. Heavy-handed comedy set in Arabia, with

Drake trying to uncover sabotage attempts at holiday camp.

Sands of the Kalahari (1965-British) **C-119m. ***** D: Cy Endfield. Stuart Whitman, Stanley Baker, Susannah York, Harry Andrews, Theodore Bikel, Nigel Davenport. Well-done story of plane crash survivors struggling through desert and battling simian inhabitants.

Sandy Gets Her Man (1940) **74m. *½** D: Otis Garrett, Paul Smith. Stuart Erwin, Una Merkel, Baby Sandy, Edgar Kennedy, William Frawley. Precocious Baby Sandy is final arbiter of mama's courters; naive little film kept alive by character actors in cast.

Sandy Is a Lady (1940) **65m. *½** D: Charles Lamont. Nan Grey, Baby Sandy, Eugene Pallette, Tom Brown, Mischa Auer, Billy Gilbert, Edgar Kennedy, Anne Gwynne. Simplicity-saturated comedy as precocious child helps her family get ahead.

Sangaree (1953) **C-94m. **½** D: Edward Ludwig. Fernando Lamas, Arlene Dahl, Patricia Medina, Francis L. Sullivan. Frank Slaughter's historical novel set in 1780s becomes an empty, handsome costumer.

Santa Claus Conquers the Martians (1964) **C-80m. **** D: Nicholas Webster. John Call, Leonard Hicks, Vincent Beck, Donna Conforti. Absurd fantasy; low-budget film. Santa and two earth children abducted by Martians to solve home problems.

Santa Fe (1951) **C-89m. **** D: Irving Pichel. Randolph Scott, Janis Carter, Jerome Courtland, Peter Thompson. Routine account of brothers in post-Civil War days, on opposite sides of the law.

Santa Fe Passage (1955) **C-70m. **** D: William Witney. John Payne, Faith Domergue, Rod Cameron, Slim Pickens. Routine wagon train westward; Indian attacks, love among the pioneers, etc.

Santa Fe Trail (1940) **110m. **** D: Michael Curtiz. Errol Flynn, Olivia de Havilland, Raymond Massey, Ronald Reagan, Van Heflin, Gene Reynolds. Lopsided picture can't make up its mind about anything: what side it's taking, what it wants to focus on, etc. Amid the rubble are some good action scenes as Jeb Stuart (Flynn) and cohorts go after John Brown (Massey).

Santiago (1956) **C-93m. **½** D: Gordon Douglas. Alan Ladd, Rossana Podesta, Lloyd Nolan, Chill Wills, Paul Fix. Ladd and Nolan are involved in gun-running to Cuba during fight with Spain. Ladd becomes humane when he encounters partisan Podesta.

Sapphire (1958-British) C-92m. *** D: Basil Dearden. Nigel Patrick, Yvonne Mitchell, Michael Craig, Paul Massie, Harry Baird, Bernard Miles. Unusual Scotland Yard solving-the-murder yarn, with the murdered girl being Negro, passing for white; zesty characterizations.

Saps At Sea (1940) 57m. *** D: Gordon Douglas. Stan Laurel, Oliver Hardy, James Finlayson, Ben Turpin, Rychard Cramer, Harry Bernard. L&H comedy is short and sweet: Ollie has breakdown working in horn factory, tries to relax on a small boat with Stan . . . and that's impossible. Cramer is a memorable heavy.

Saraband (1948-British) C-95m. *** D: Basil Dearden. Stewart Granger, Joan Greenwood, Flora Robson, Françoise Rosay, Peter Bull, Anthony Quayle, Michael Gough. Lavish, tearful romance with Greenwood torn between royal responsibility and love for young rogue. Originally titled SARABAND FOR DEAD LOVERS.

Saracen Blade, The (1954) C-76m. *½ D: William Castle. Ricardo Montalban, Betta St. John, Rick Jason, Carolyn Jones, Whitfield Connor. Pretty bad 13th-century stuff, of young man avenging death of father. Unbelievable script traps cast.

Sarah and Son (1930) 76m. ** D: Dorothy Arzner. Ruth Chatterton, Fredric March, Doris Lloyd, Philippe de Lacy. Chatterton, obsessed with finding the son taken from her years ago, enlists aid of lawyer March.

Sarah T.—Portrait of a Teenage Alcoholic (1975) C-100m. TVM D: Richard Donner. Linda Blair, Verna Bloom, Larry Hagman, William Daniels, Mark Hamill, Laurette Spang. Young girl turns to liquor to escape family problems; Blair shows competence with another meaty role that made her the most put-upon screen teenager of the 1970s. Average.

Saratoga (1937) 94m. **½ D: Jack Conway. Clark Gable, Jean Harlow, Lionel Barrymore, Frank Morgan, Walter Pidgeon, Una Merkel. Harlow's last film has stand-in Mary Dees doing many scenes, but comes off pretty well, with Jean as daughter of horse-breeder Barrymore, Gable an influential bookie.

Saratoga Trunk (1945) 135m. *½ D: Sam Wood. Gary Cooper, Ingrid Bergman, Flora Robson, Jerry Austin, John Warburton, Florence Bates. Elaborate but miscast, overlong version of Edna Ferber's novel of New Orleans vixen Bergman, and cowboy Cooper. Unbearable at times.

Sarge (1970) C-100m. TVM D: Richard Colla. George Kennedy, Diane Baker, Ricardo Montalban, Nico Minardos. Detective on police department decides he can do more as priest, works same district as he did as cop. Melodramatic to the hilt, Kennedy saves film with excellent performance. Average; pilot for TV series. Alternate title: SARGE: THE BADGE OR THE CROSS.

Saskatchewan (1954) C-87m. **½ D: Raoul Walsh. Alan Ladd, Shelley Winters, J. Carrol Naish, Hugh O'Brian, Robert Douglas. Cotton-candy Western about Ladd and fellow Canadian mounties trying to prevent Indian uprisings.

Sasquatch (1978) C-102m. *½ D: Ed Ragozzini. George Lauris, Steve Boergadine, Jim Bradford, Ken Kenzie. Semidocumentary about expedition that goes in search of Bigfoot, including "authentic" if blurry footage of the monster.

Satan Bug, The (1965) C-114m. *** D: John Sturges. George Maharis, Richard Basehart, Anne Francis, Dana Andrews, Edward Asner, Frank Sutton, John Larkin. Good Sturges direction in sci-fi adventure of disappearance of vial containing deadly virus and search for it.

Satan Met a Lady (1936) 75m. ** D: William Dieterle. Bette Davis, Warren William, Alison Skipworth, Arthur Treacher, Winifred Shaw, Marie Wilson, Porter Hall. Dashiell Hammett's MALTESE FALCON incognito; far below 1941 remake. William is private eye, Davis the mysterious client, Skipworth the strange woman searching for priceless artifact (ram's horn).

Satan Never Sleeps (1962) C-126m. ** D: Leo McCarey. William Holden, Clifton Webb, France Nuyen, Athene Seyler, Martin Benson, Edith Sharpe. Dreary goings-on of two priests holding fast when Communist China invades their territory.

Satan's Harvest (1970) C-104m. **
D: George Montgomery (credited on TV to Douglas K. Stone). George Montgomery, Tippi Hedren, Matt Monro, Davy Kaye, Brian O'Shaughnessy, Tromp Terreblanche, Melody O'Brian. American detective Montgomery inherits South African ranch and discovers it to be headquarters for a drug smuggling operation. Colorful scenery, tepid story.

Satan's Sadists (1970) C-88m. BOMB D: Al Adamson. Russ Tamblyn, Scott Brady, Kent Taylor, John Cardos. Renegade cyclists on the loose down the highway. Change the channel.

Satan's Satellites (1958) 70m. *½ D: Fred Brannon. Judd Holdren, Aline Towne, Wilson Wood, Lane Bradford. Condensation of serial ZOMBIES OF THE STRATOSPHERE is pretty juvenile sci-fi, but has added trivia interest today since Leonard Nimoy plays a martian who saves the earth from destruction!

Satan's School for Girls (1973) C-74m. TVM D: David Lowell Rich. Pamela Franklin, Kate Jackson, Jo Van Fleet, Roy Thinnes, Jamie Smith Jackson, Lloyd Bochner, Cheryl Jean Stoppelmoor (Ladd). What's behind spate of suicides at fashionable girls' school? Hard-nosed but vulnerable young woman (Franklin) passes herself off as student to get answer in this wide-eyed, inconsequential thriller. Below average.

Satan's Triangle (1974) C-78m. TVM D: Sutton Rolley. Kim Novak, Doug McClure, Alejandro Rey, Jim Davis, Ed Lauter, Michael Conrad. Novak, lone survivor of a shipwreck, and her two would-be survivors have a devilish time after trespassing in the Bermuda Triangle. Below average.

Satanik (1969-Spanish-Italian) C-85m. BOMB D: Piero Vivarelli. Magda Konopka, Julio Pena, Armando Calva, Umi Raho, Luigi Montini. A stolen elixir turns an ugly old woman into a young beauty, but propels her into a life of terror, and forces her to star in this awful movie.

Satellite in the Sky (1956-British) C-85m. **½ D: Paul Dickson. Kieron Moore, Lois Maxwell, Donald Wolfit, Bryan Forbes, Jimmy Hanley. Good English cast gives typical sympathetic performances in story of first satellite launching.

Saturday Morning (1971) C-82m. **½ D: Kent Mackenzie. Cinema-verité documentary chronicling the gripes of contemporary adolescents may interest those teen-agers who don't mind an hour and a half of young people saying "ya know" at least once in every sentence.

Saturday Night and Sunday Morning (1960-British) 90m. ***½ D: Karel Reisz. Albert Finney, Shirley Anne Field, Rachel Roberts, Norman Rossington. Grim yet refreshing look at angry young man, who in a burst of nonconformity alters the lives of girlfriends Field and Roberts. Superbly enacted.

Saturday Night Fever (1977) C-119m. *** D: John Badham. John Travolta, Karen Lynn Gorney, Barry Miller, Joseph Cali, Paul Pape, Donna Pescow. Travolta's first starring film is thoughtful study of Brooklyn youth who finds only meaning in his life when dancing at local disco. Film pulses to dynamic Bee Gees music score. Plethora of "street language" may offend some, but not in "alternate" 108m PG-rated version, where dialogue and certain scenes have been changed or dropped entirely.

Saturday's Children (1940) 101m. **½ D: Vincent Sherman. John Garfield, Anne Shirley, Claude Rains, Lee Patrick, George Tobias. N.Y.C. based story of poor, hardworking young lovers. Rains steals film as Shirley's sacrificing father. Based on Maxwell Anderson play.

Saturday's Hero (1951) 111m. **½ D: David Miller. John Derek, Donna Reed, Sidney Blackmer, Alexander Knox. Nicely handled account of football player Derek trying to make meaningful life at college; Reed is fine as love interest. One of Aldo Ray's first films.

Saturday's Island SEE: Island of Desire.

Saturn 3 (1980-British) C-88m. ** D: Stanley Donen. Farrah Fawcett, Kirk Douglas, Harvey Keitel, Douglas Lambert. Flashy but empty-headed outer-space opus, with Douglas and Fawcett menaced by Keitel and his sex-starved robot Hector; good-looking package with nothing inside.

Savage, The (1952) C-95m. **½ D: George Marshall. Charlton Heston, Susan Morrow, Peter Hanson, Joan Taylor, Ted de Corsia. Heston is sincere and energetic as white man raised by the Indians and forced to

[663]

choose sides when skirmishes break out.

Savage Bees, The (1976) C-99m. TVM D: Bruce Geller. Ben Johnson, Michael Parks, Horst Buchholz, Gretchen Corbett, Paul Hecht, James Best. Thriller involving a plague of African killer bees descending on New Orleans at Mardi Gras. Neat little neo-cultist chiller. Above average.

Savage Drums (1951) 73m. ** D: William Berke. Sabu, Lita Baron, H. B. Warner, Sid Melton, Steve Geray. U. S.-educated Sabu returns to the islands to put down local warfare; fair low-budgeter.

Savage Eye, The (1960) 68m. *** D: Ben Maddow, Sidney Meyers, Joseph Strick. Barbara Baxley, Herschel Bernardi, Gary Merrill, Jean Hidey. Documentary-style drama of divorcee Baxley trying to start life anew in L.A.; contrived but intriguing.

Savage Hordes, The (1961-Italian) C-82m. ** D: Remigio Del Grosso. Ettore Manni, Yoko, Akim Tamiroff, Joe Robinson, Roland Lesaffre. Routine adventure yarn set in 17th-century Poland under siege by Tartars.

Savage Innocents, The (1959-Italian-French-British) C-110m. **½ D: Nicholas Ray. Anthony Quinn, Yoko Tani, Peter O'Toole, Marie Yang. Striking but uneven film about conflict of civilization vs. simple ways of Eskimo people. Quinn gives remarkable performance as native Eskimo; beautiful documentary-type location photography combined with studio work.

Savage Is Loose, The (1974) C-114m. BOMB D: George C. Scott. George C. Scott, Trish Van Devere, John David Carson, Lee H. Montgomery. Scott produced, directed, starred in and distributed this farrago about the eventual incest between mother and son after they, along with dad, have been stranded on an island for years. Not very stimulating.

Savage Mutiny (1953) 73m. D: Spencer Bennet. Johnny Weissmuller, Angela Stevens, Lester Matthews, Paul Marion. SEE: **Jungle Jim** series.

Savage Pampas (1966-Spanish) C-100m. ** D: Hugo Fregonese. Robert Taylor, Ron Randell, Ty Hardin, Rosenda Monteros. Remake of 1946 Argentinian film PAMPA BARBARA. Taylor is rugged army captain combating outlaw Randell whose gang is made up of army deserters. Adequate actioner.

Savage Sam (1963) C-103m. **½ D: Norman Tokar. Brian Keith, Tommy Kirk, Kevin Corcoran, Dewey Martin, Jeff York, Royal Dano, Marta Kristen. Sequel to Disney's OLD YELLER has Keith and country neighbors trying to rescue children who've been kidnapped by Indians. Colorful but uneven.

Savage Seven, The (1968) C-96m. *½ D: Richard Rush. Robert Walker, Larry Bishop, Adam Roarke, Max Julien, Duane Eddy. Below-par motorcycle melodrama that lives up to its title but nothing else.

Savage Wilderness SEE: **Last Frontier, The**

Savages (1974) C-78m. TVM D: Lee H. Katzin. Andy Griffith, Sam Bottoms, Noah Beery, James Best, Randy Boone, Jim Antonio. Cat-and-mouse thriller with Griffith as sadistic hunter relentlessly pursuing his defenseless young guide in the desert. "The Most Dangerous Game" played out among the cacti, but still intriguing. Above average.

Save the Children (1973) 123m. ***½ D: Stan Lathan. Isaac Hayes, Jackson Five, Sammy Davis, Jr., Nancy Wilson, Roberta Flack, Wilson Pickett, Marvin Gaye, many others. All-star music documentary filmed at 1972 exposition in Chicago held by operation PUSH.

Save the Tiger (1973) C-101m. ** D: John G. Avildsen. Jack Lemmon, Jack Gilford, Laurie Heineman, Norman Burton, Patricia Smith, Thayer David. Pretentious script about dress manufacturer trying to reconcile hero-worship of his childhood with degradations he submits himself to in business world. Film purports to be totally honest, but phoniness comes through; David has best scenes as professional arsonist. Lemmon won "Best Actor" Oscar.

Sawdust and Tinsel (1953-Swedish) 95m. **** D: Ingmar Bergman. Harriet Andersson, Ake Gronberg, Anders Ek, Gudrun Brost. Beautiful film about human relationships set as an allegory in a small-time circus. Also known as THE NAKED NIGHT.

Saxon Charm, The (1948) 88m. *** D: Claude Binyon. Robert Montgomery, Susan Hayward, John

Payne, Audrey Totter, Harry Morgan, Cara Williams, Harry Von Zell, Heather Angel. Well-acted but unconvincing study of ruthless producer, with Montgomery miscast in lead role. Still interesting, with fine work from playwright Payne, wife Hayward, and chanteuse Totter.

Say Goodbye, Maggie Cole (1972) C-73m. TVM D: Jud Taylor. Susan Hayward, Darren McGavin, Michael Constantine, Nichelle Nichols, Dane Clark, Beverly Garland. After husband's death, research doctor returns to general practice in Chicago slum area. Impressive performances by Hayward and McGavin in touching, realistic drama. Above average.

Say Hello to Yesterday (1971-British) C-91m. *½ D: Alvin Rakoff. Jean Simmons, Leonard Whiting, Evelyn Laye, John Lee, Jack Woolgar, Constance Chapman. Ridiculous plot concerning 40-year-old Simmons' affair with 22-year-old Whiting. Symbolic touches by director Rakoff further shroud purpose of film.

Say It in French (1938) 70m. ** D: Andrew L. Stone. Ray Milland, Olympe Bradna, Irene Hervey, Janet Beecher, Mary Carlisle, Holmes Herbert, Walter Kingsford. Milland goes to great extremes with wife Bradna and ex-fiancee Hervey to pull father out of the red.

Say One for Me (1959) C-119m. *½ D: Frank Tashlin. Debbie Reynolds, Bing Crosby, Robert Wagner, Ray Walston, Les Tremayne, Connie Gilchrist, Stella Stevens, Frank McHugh, Joe Besser, Sebastian Cabot. Bing plays a Broadway priest who gets mixed up with a chorus girl (Debbie) and a TV charity show. Terribly contrived; no memorable music.

Sayonara (1957) C-147m. ***½ D: Joshua Logan. Marlon Brando, Ricardo Montalban, Miiko Taka, Miyoshi Umeki, Red Buttons, Martha Scott, James Garner. Romantic James Michener tale of Korean War pilot Brando falling in love with Japanese entertainer Taka, extremely well acted, with Oscar-winning support from Buttons and Umeki. Theme song by Irving Berlin.

Scalawag (1973) C-93m. *½ D: Kirk Douglas. Kirk Douglas, Mark Lester, Don Stroud, Neville Brand, Lesley-Anne Down. TREASURE ISLAND goes West in this weak adaptation, with a hammy Kirk as

one-legged cutthroat; songs turn up when you least expect them. Filmed in Yugoslavia.

Scalpel (1976) C-96m. *½ D: John Grissmer. Robert Lansing, Judith Chapman, Arlen Dean Snyder, David Scarroll, Sandy Martin. Plastic surgeon transforms young woman into image of his long-missing daughter, in order to dupe family out of large inheritance. Lurid, violent drama.

Scalphunters, The (1968) C-102m. **½ D: Sydney Pollack. Burt Lancaster, Shelley Winters, Ossie Davis, Telly Savalas, Armando Silvestre, Dabney Coleman. Western comedy about a fur trapper and his highly educated slave has its moments, but isn't funny enough, nor exciting enough, nor pointed enough to qualify as all-out success. Cast helps.

Scalplock (1966) C-100m. TVM D: James Goldstone. Dale Robertson, Diana Hyland, Lloyd Bochner, Robert Random, Sandra Smith. Tired Western features Robertson as gambler who wins ownership of railroad. Usual complications, stereotyped characters; even production looks rushed. Below average. Pilot for IRON HORSE TV series.

Scandal at Scourie (1953) C-90m. **½ D: Jean Negulesco. Greer Garson, Walter Pidgeon, Donna Corcoran, Agnes Moorehead, Arthur Shields. Tepid Garson-Pidgeon entry set in Canada, involving Protestant couple who shock community when they plan to adopt a Catholic child.

Scandal in Paris SEE: Thieves' Holiday

Scandal in Sorrento (1957-Italian) C-92m. *½ D: Dino Risi. Vittorio De Sica, Sophia Loren, Antonio Cifariello, Tina Pica. Listless sex romp of Loren romancing De Sica to make lover jealous.

Scandal, Inc. (1956) 79m. *½ D: Edward Mann. Robert Hutton, Patricia Wright, Paul Richards, Robert Knapp. Low-grade sensational-style account of scandal magazines.

Scandal Sheet (1931) 77m. **½ D: John Cromwell. George Bancroft, Kay Francis, Clive Brook, Lucien Littlefield, Jackie Searl. Usual triangle with good twist. Editor Bancroft has goods on Brook, the man his wife Francis plans to run off with.

Scandal Sheet (1952) 82m. **½ D: Phil Karlson. Broderick Crawford, Donna Reed, John Derek, Rosemary DeCamp, Henry O'Neill. OK melodrama of gruff newspaper editor who kills his wife and then finds his ace reporters are hot on his trail.

Scapegoat, The (1959-British) 92m. **½ D: Robert Hamer. Alec Guinness, Bette Davis, Nicole Maurey, Irene Worth, Peter Bull, Pamela Brown, Geoffrey Keen. Decent acting rescues a fuzzy script. French gentleman who murders his wife, tries to involve his British lookalike in scheme. Davis has small but impressive role as the guilty Guinness' dope-ridden mother.

Scar, The SEE: **Hollow Triumph**

Scaramouche (1952) C-118m. ***½ D: George Sidney. Stewart Granger, Eleanor Parker, Janet Leigh, Mel Ferrer, Henry Wilcoxon, Lewis Stone, Nina Foch. Excellent cast in roaring adaptation of Sabatini novel of illustrious cynic who sets out to avenge brother's death, set in 18th-century France. Impeccably done.

Scarecrow (1973) C-115m. *** D: Jerry Schatzberg. Gene Hackman, Al Pacino, Dorothy Tristan, Eileen Brennan, Ann Wedgeworth, Richard Lynch. Drifter Hackman, who wants to start car-wash business, meets drifter Pacino, who has abandoned his wife. Moody, not altogether successful tale benefits from top performances and photography, plus good use of locations.

Scared Stiff (1953) 108m. **½ D: George Marshall. Dean Martin, Jerry Lewis, Lizabeth Scott, Carmen Miranda, Dorothy Malone. Usual Martin and Lewis hijinks with duo on spooky island; Jerry and Carmen make a wild team. Remake of Bob Hope's THE GHOST BREAKERS.

Scared to Death (1947) C-65m. *½ D: Christy Cabanne. Bela Lugosi, Douglas Fowley, Joyce Compton, George Zucco, Nat Pendleton, Molly Lamont. Cheaply made chiller, loosely revolving around effects of those who confront a murderess with her crime.

Scarf, The (1951) 93m. **½ D: E. A. Dupont. John Ireland, Mercedes McCambridge, Emlyn Williams, James Barton. Capably handled drama of Ireland trying to prove his innocence of murder charge.

Scarface (1932) 90m. ***½ D: Howard Hawks. Paul Muni, Ann Dvorak, George Raft, Boris Karloff, Karen Morley, Vince Barnett. Powerful gangster film is the most potent of the 1930s, with Muni delivering emotionally charged performance as Capone-like mobster with more than just a soft spot for his sister (Dvorak). Raw, harsh, and brimming with unsubtle symbolism.

Scarface Mob, The (1962) 90m. **½ D: Phil Karlson. Robert Stack, Keenan Wynn, Barbara Nichols, Pat Crowley, Neville Brand. Two-part segment from THE UNTOUCHABLES TV series forms this film, with Eliot Ness closing in on Chicago's Al Capone mob. Narrated by Walter Winchell.

Scarlet Angel (1952) C-80m. **½ D: Sidney Salkow. Yvonne De Carlo, Rock Hudson, Richard Denning, Amanda Blake. Neat little drama set in 1860 New Orleans, with De Carlo the dance-hall girl who assumes a dead woman's identity and goes West to stay with wealthy in-laws.

Scarlet Blade, The SEE: **Crimson Blade, The**

Scarlet Claw, The (1944) 74m. D: Roy William Neill. Basil Rathbone, Nigel Bruce, Gerald Hamer, Arthur Hohl, Miles Mander, Ian Wolfe, Paul Cavanagh, Kay Harding. SEE: **Sherlock Holmes** series.

Scarlet Clue, The (1945) 65m. D: Phil Rosen. Sidney Toler, Mantan Moreland, Ben Carter, Benson Fong, Virginia Brissac, Robert Homans, Jack Norton, Janet Shaw. SEE: **Charlie Chan** series.

Scarlet Coat, The (1955) C-101m. **½ D: John Sturges. Cornel Wilde, Michael Wilding, George Sanders, Anne Francis, Bobby Driscoll. Plucky costumer livened by cast and bright photography; set in colonial America, dealing with Benedict Arnold spy caper.

Scarlet Empress, The (1934) 110m. **½ D: Josef von Sternberg. Marlene Dietrich, John Lodge, Louise Dresser, Sam Jaffe, C. Aubrey Smith, Edward Van Sloan, Ruthelma Stevens, Jane Darwell. Dietrich is exotic as Catherine the Great; lush settings are marred by misguided script and ludicrous handling of Jaffe as halfwitted Grand Duke Peter.

Scarlet Hour, The (1956) 95m. ** D: Michael Curtiz. Carol Ohmart, Tom Tryon, Jody Lawrance, James Gregory, Elaine Stritch, E. G. Marshall, Edward Binns. Sluggish study of marital discord.

Scarlet Letter, The (1926) 80m. ***

D: Victor Seastrom. Lillian Gish, Lars Hanson, Henry B. Walthall, Karl Dane, William H. Tooker, Marcelle Corday. Excellent, straightforward adaptation of Hawthorne classic about Hester Prynne (Gish) who bears scar of adultery in Salem, having had clandestine affair with minister Hanson.

Scarlet Pimpernel, The (1934-British) 95m. ***½ **D:** Harold Young. Leslie Howard, Merle Oberon, Joan Gardner, Raymond Massey, Nigel Bruce, Anthony Bushell. Excellent costumer with Howard leading double life, aiding innocent victims of French revolution while posing as foppish member of British society.

Scarlet Spear, The (1954) C-78m. BOMB **D:** George Breakston, Ray Stahl. John Bentley, Martha Hyer, Morasi. Programmer nonsense of African tribe with sacrifice ceremony.

Scarlet Street (1945) 103m. *** **D:** Fritz Lang. Edward G. Robinson, Joan Bennett, Dan Duryea, Margaret Lindsay, Rosalind Ivan. Meek, henpecked Robinson is pulled into world of crime and deception by seductive Bennett and her manipulative boyfriend Duryea. Stars and director of WOMAN IN THE WINDOW keep it interesting, but don't match earlier film. Story filmed before by Jean Renoir as LA CHIENNE.

Scars of Dracula (1971-British) C-94m. *** **D:** Roy Ward Baker. Christopher Lee, Dennis Waterman, Jenny Hanley, Christopher Matthews, Wendy Hamilton. Good fang work as young couple tangles with Dracula in search of the young man's missing brother. A doozy of a demise, we might add.

Scavenger Hunt (1979) C-117m. BOMB **D:** Michael Schultz. Richard Benjamin, James Coco, Scatman Crothers, Ruth Gordon, Cloris Leachman, Cleavon Little, Roddy McDowall, Robert Morley, Richard Mulligan, Tony Randall, Dirk Benedict, Willie Aames. Vincent Price dies, and his relatives are practically forced to kill each other for his inheritance by collecting commodes, wild animals, etc. in an allotted time. Director Schultz deserves credit for coming up with another movie as bad as SERGEANT PEPPER.

Scene of the Crime (1949) 94m. ** **D:** Roy Rowland. Van Johnson, Arlene Dahl, Gloria DeHaven, Tom Drake, Leon Ames. Bland detective whodunit, with Johnson a cop trying to solve police murder.

Scenes from a Marriage (1973-Swedish) C-168m. **** **D:** Ingmar Bergman. Liv Ullmann, Erland Josephson, Bibi Andersson, Jan Malmsjo, Anita Wall. Passionate, probing and honest look at a marriage, its disintegration, and the relationship that follows. Ullmann and Jacobson are remarkable throughout this intimate and often painful portrait, originally made as six TV episodes and edited into feature-length by writer-director Bergman.

Scenes from a Murder (1972-Italian) C-90m. ** **D:** Alberto DeMartino. Telly Savalas, Anne Heywood, Giorgio Piazza, Osvaldo Ruggeri, Rossella Falk. Murder and mayhem in the theater world with Savalas stalking an actress (Heywood) whose lover he has killed. Limp thriller.

School for Love (1955-French) 72m. ** **D:** Yves Allegret. Jean Marais, Brigitte Bardot, Isabelle Pia. Occasionally sensual flick with Bardot and Pia competing for Marais' affection. Retitled: JOY OF LOVING.

School for Scoundrels (1960-British) 94m. *** **D:** Robert Hamer. Alastair Sim, Terry-Thomas, Ian Carmichael. Entertaining comedy barb about training school for one-upmanship, giving the viewer complete course in coming out tops in any situation.

Scorchy (1976) C-99m. *½ **D:** Hikmet Avedis. Connie Stevens, Cesare Danova, William Smith, Marlene Schmidt, Normann Burton, Joyce Jameson. Tawdry action film with Stevens as undercover cop in Seattle who sets out to bust high-level drug ring. Plenty of action and gore.

Scorpio (1973) C-114m. **½ **D:** Michael Winner. Burt Lancaster, Alain Delon, Gayle Hunnicutt, Paul Scofield, John Colicos, J. D. Cannon. Tough espionage film of CIA agent in trouble, and hired killer who wants to go straight but finds himself caught in the system. Good action, dialogue, amid familiar trappings.

Scorpio Letters, The (1967) C-98m. TVM **D:** Richard Thorpe. Alex Cord, Shirley Eaton, Laurence Naismith, Oscar Beregi, Lester Matthews. American hired by British government and beautiful spy work together to track down mysterious head of blackmail ring, known only by code name. Excellent suspense in above-average spy-thriller.

Scotland Yard Inspector (1952-British) 73m. ** D: Sam Newfield. Cesar Romero, Lois Maxwell, Bernadette O'Farrell, Geoffrey Keen, Alistair Hunter, Peter Swanwick. Run-of-the-mill actioner with Romero assisting Maxwell in capturing her brother's killer.

Scotland Yard Investigator (1945) 68m. ** D: George Blair. C. Aubrey Smith, Erich von Stroheim, Stephanie Bachelor, Forrester Harvey, Doris Lloyd, Eva Moore. Low-budget mystery wastes two leading players in routine art-theft tale.

Scott Free (1976) C-78m. TVM D: William Wiard. Michael Brandon, Susan Saint James, Stephen Nathan, Robert Loggia, Ken Swofford, Michael Lerner. Glib hustler Brandon gets involved with Indians, the Mafia and the Feds over a piece of land he won in a poker game. Offbeat pilot for a series that never was. Average.

Scott Joplin (1977) C-96m. **½ D: Jeremy Kagan. Billy Dee Williams, Clifton Davis, Godfrey Cambridge, Art Carney, Seymour Cassel, Eubie Blake, Margaret Avery. Well-made, colorful but down-beat life story of famed ragtime composer. Made for TV, then given fitful theatrical release. Best sequence: the barrelhouse piano "duel."

Scott of the Antarctic (1948-British) C-110m. **½ D: Charles Frend. John Mills, Derek Bond, James Robertson Justice, Kenneth More, Christopher Lee. Unrelenting drama of dynamic British 20th-century explorer who led expedition to frigid subcontinent.

Scream and Scream Again (1970-British) C-95m. **½ D: Gordon Hessler. Vincent Price, Christopher Lee, Peter Cushing, Judy Huxtable, Alfred Marks, Peter Sallis. Distinguished cast does their darnedest to enliven (no pun intended) tired, confusing plot concerning mad scientist's organ/limbs experiments and race of emotionless beings he creates.

Scream Blacula Scream (1973) C-95m. ** D: Bob Kelljan. William Marshall, Don Mitchell, Pam Grier, Michael Conrad, Richard Lawson. Poor sequel to BLACULA finds black vampire recalled from eternal rest and forced to go out and nib-

ble again in contemporary black U.S.

Scream of Fear (1961-British) 81m. *** D: Seth Holt. Susan Strasberg, Christopher Lee, Ann Todd, Ronald Lewis. Good thriller about girl who thinks people are deliberately driving her insane.

Scream of the Wolf (1974) C-78m. TVM D: Dan Curtis. Peter Graves, Clint Walker, Jo Ann Pflug, Philip Carey, Don Megowan, Brian Richards. Predictable exercise in terror that has adventure writer Graves stalking a creature that has killed four people. Average.

Scream, Pretty Peggy (1973) C-78m. TVM D: Gordon Hessler. Bette Davis, Ted Bessell, Sian Barbara Allen, Charles Drake, Allan Arbus, Tovah Feldshuh, Jessica Rains. Thriller about a college coed who takes a housekeeper job in the mansion a deranged sculptor and his strange mother supposedly share with his insane sister. Horror tale with a touch or two of "Psycho" and Bette having a fine old time. Average.

Screaming Eagles (1956) 81m. ** D: Charles Haas. Tom Tryon, Jan Merlin, Alvy Moore, Martin Milner, Jacqueline Beer. Routine WW2 film focusing on D-Day.

Screaming Mimi (1958) 79m. ** D: Gerd Oswald. Anita Ekberg, Phil Carey, Gypsy Rose Lee, Harry Townes. Lurid caper in which energetic dancer Ekberg is convinced she's a murderess; Lee hasn't enough to do in proceedings.

Screaming Woman, The (1972) C-73m. TVM D: Jack Smight. Olivia de Havilland, Ed Nelson, Joseph Cotten, Walter Pidgeon, Laraine Stephens, Alexandra Hay. Wide-eyed thriller has recently institutionalized woman trying to convince family and neighbors that she hears voice coming from the ground. Script can't maintain credibility. Below average.

Scrooge (1970-British) C-115m. **½ D: Ronald Neame. Albert Finney, Alec Guinness, Edith Evans, Kenneth More, Michael Medwin, Laurence Naismith, David Collings. Several instantly forgettable songs mar otherwise acceptable if unexceptional musical version of Dickens' A CHRISTMAS CAROL. Finney has fun in title role.

Scudda Hoo! Scudda Hay! (1948) C-95m. ** D: F. Hugh Herbert. June

Haver, Lon McCallister, Walter Brennan, Anne Revere, Natalie Wood. Any film with a title like that can't be all good, and it isn't; McCallister's life is devoted to two mules.

Sea Around Us, The (1953) C-61m. *** Produced by: Irwin Allen. Narrated by: Don Forbes. Academy Award-winning documentary based on Rachel Carson's study of the history of the ocean, its fauna and life.

Sea Chase, The (1955) C-117m. **½ D: John Farrow. John Wayne, Lana Turner, Tab Hunter, David Farrar, Lyle Bettger, James Arness, Claude Akins. Strange WW2 film, with Wayne as German captain of fugitive ship with unusual cargo, assorted crew, plus passenger/girlfriend Turner.

Sea Devils (1953-British) C-91m. **½ D: Raoul Walsh. Yvonne De Carlo, Rock Hudson, Maxwell Reed, Denis O'Dea. Handsome pairing of De Carlo-Hudson elevates this standard sea yarn of smugglers.

Sea Gull, The (1968-British) C-141m. **½ D: Sidney Lumet. James Mason, Vanessa Redgrave, Simone Signoret, David Warner, Harry Andrews, Eileen Herlie, Denholm Elliott. Tasteful but reverentially slow-moving transcription of Chekhov play. Signoret's accent becomes rather disconcerting among British players, all trying to be 19th-century Russians.

Sea Gypsies, The (1978) C-101m. *** D: Stewart Raffill. Robert Logan, Heather Rattray, Mikki Jamison-Olsen, Shannon Saylor, Cjon Damitri Patterson. Nice family adventure has Logan sailing round the world with daughters, journalist Jamison-Olsen, and little stowaway Patterson, learning to survive when shipwrecked in Alaska. Fine location filming.

Sea Hawk, The (1940) 127m. **** D: Michael Curtiz. Errol Flynn, Brenda Marshall, Claude Rains, Donald Crisp, Flora Robson, Alan Hale, Henry Daniell. Top-notch combination of classy Warner Bros. costumer and Flynn at his dashing best in adventure on the high seas; lively balance of piracy, romance, and swordplay, handsomely photographed and staged, with rousing Korngold score.

Sea Hornet, The (1951) 84m. *½ D: Joseph Kane. Rod Cameron, Adele Mara, Adrian Booth, Chill Wills. Lowjinks about deep-water divers and their gals.

Sea of Grass, The (1947) 131m. **½ D: Elia Kazan. Katharine Hepburn, Spencer Tracy, Melvyn Douglas, Phyllis Thaxter, Robert Walker, Edgar Buchanan, Harry Carey. Plodding drama from Conrad Richter story of farmer-rancher feud over New Mexico grasslands. Walker stands out in hardworking but unsuccessful cast.

Sea of Lost Ships (1953) 85m. ** D: Joseph Kane. John Derek, Wanda Hendrix, Walter Brennan, Richard Jaeckel. Standard fare of two Coast Guard men fighting over Hendrix.

Sea of Sand SEE: **Desert Patrol**

Sea Pirate, The (1967-Italian) C-85m. **½ D: Roy Rowland. Gerald Barray, Antonella Lualdi, Genevieve Casile, Terence Morgan. Not-bad pirate tale with Barray setting off to amass a fortune so he can marry Lualdi. Colorful escapism.

Sea Shall Not Have Them, The (1954-British) 91m. ** D: Lewis Gilbert. Michael Redgrave, Dirk Bogarde, Anthony Steel, Nigel Patrick, Nigel Green, Michael Kempson. British bomber plane is forced down in the ocean during WW2; a rescue attempt is made.

Sea Tiger (1952) 75m. *½ D: Frank McDonald. John Archer, Mara Corday, Marguerite Chapman, Lyle Talbot. Heavy-handed mini-actioner, with Archer entangled with homicide; set in New Guinea.

Sea Wall, The SEE: **This Angry Age**

Sea Wife (1957-British) C-82m. *** D: Bob McNaught. Richard Burton, Joan Collins, Basil Sydney, Ronald Squire, Cy Grant. Disarming yarn of Burton and Collins surviving from a torpedoed ship. He falls in love with her, not knowing she's a nun. Set in WW2.

Sea Wolf, The (1941) 90m. ***½ D: Michael Curtiz. Edward G. Robinson, John Garfield, Ida Lupino, Alexander Knox, Gene Lockhart, Barry Fitzgerald, Stanley Ridges. Bristling Jack London tale of brutal but educated sea captain (Robinson) battling wits with accidental passenger Knox, as brash seaman Garfield and fugitive Lupino try to escape. Originally released at 100m. Remade many times (BARRICADE, WOLF LARSEN, etc.).

Sealed Cargo (1951) 90m. **½ D: Alfred L. Werker. Dana Andrews, Carla Balenda, Claude Rains, Philip

[669]

Dorn. Taut melodrama of Nazi submarines in coastal waters off Newfoundland.

Sealed Verdict (1948) 83m. ** D: Lewis Allen. Ray Milland, Florence Marly, Broderick Crawford, John Hoyt, John Ridgely. Far-fetched drama of army lawyer who falls in love with traitorous woman he is supposed to prosecute in court; pretty dismal.

Séance on a Wet Afternoon (1964-British) 115m. **** D: Bryan Forbes. Kim Stanley, Richard Attenborough, Patrick Magee, Nanette Newman, Maria Kazan, Margaret Lacey. Gripping drama of crazed medium Stanley involving husband Attenborough in shady project. Brilliant acting, direction in this must-see film.

Search (1972) SEE: Probe

Search, The (1948) 105m. **** D: Fred Zinnemann. Montgomery Clift, Ivan Jandl, Aline MacMahon, Jarmila Novotna, Wendell Corey. Poignant drama of American soldier Clift caring for concentration camp survivor Jandl in postwar Berlin, while the boy's mother desperately searches all Displaced Person's Camps for him. Beautifully acted and directed.

Search for Bridey Murphy, The (1956) 84m. **½ D: Noel Langley. Teresa Wright, Louis Hayward, Nancy Gates, Kenneth Tobey, Richard Anderson. Strange account of woman under hypnosis with recollection of prior life; low-key telling to obtain realism makes it sluggish going.

Search for Danger (1949) 62m. D: Jack Bernhard. John Calvert, Albert Dekker, Myrna Dell, Douglas Fowley, Ben Welden. SEE: The Falcon series.

Search for the Gods (1975) C-100m. TVM D: Jud Taylor. Kurt Russell, Stephen McHattie, Ralph Bellamy, Victoria Racimo, Raymond St. Jacques. Adventure drama involving an archeological dig in Pueblo territory and the discovery of a priceless medallion. Standard TV fare. Average.

Searchers, The (1956) C-119m. **** D: John Ford. John Wayne, Jeffrey Hunter, Vera Miles, Ward Bond, Natalie Wood, John Qualen, Harry Carey, Jr., Olive Carey, Antonio Moreno, Dorothy Jordan. Superb Western saga of Wayne's relentless search for niece (Wood) kidnapped by Indians, spanning many years.

Color, scenery, photography all tops, with moving, insightful script to match.

Searching Wind, The (1946) 108m. **½ D: William Dieterle. Robert Young, Sylvia Sidney, Ann Richards, Dudley Digges, Douglas Dick, Albert Basserman. Lillian Hellman's play about overdiplomatic diplomat Young about to forsake family when tragedy makes him realize mistake; talky drama.

Seaside Swingers (1965-British) C-94m. *½ D: James Hill. John Leyton, Mike Sarne, Freddie and the Dreamers, Ron Moody, Liz Fraser. Group of teen-agers working at seaside resort prepare for major talent contest which is to be the highlight of the summer season. Should have given them all the hook.

Season of Passion (1961-Australian) 93m. **½ D: Leslie Norman. Anne Baxter, John Mills, Angela Lansbury, Ernest Borgnine, Janette Craig. Tasteful study of human relationships; Mills and Borgnine are country workers who each year come to the city for their fling with Baxter and Lansbury. Based on play SUMMER OF THE 17TH DOLL by Ray Lawler.

Sebastian (1968-British) C-100m. **½ D: David Greene. Dirk Bogarde, Susannah York, Lilli Palmer, John Gielgud, Margaret Johnston, Nigel Davenport. Flashy but cluttered espionage film of counterintelligence agent Bogarde, who deciphers codes for England, becoming enmeshed in international battle of wits. Intriguing, colorful, but a bit trying.

Second Best Secret Agent in the Whole Wide World (1966-British) C-96m. **½ D: Lindsay Shonteff. Tom Adams, Peter Bull, Karel Stepanek, John Arnatt. Snappy James Bondish entry, with virtue of satirical performance by Adams and good supporting cast.

Second Chance (1953) C-81m. **½ D: Rudolph Maté. Robert Mitchum, Linda Darnell, Jack Palance, Reginald Sheffield. Two runaways—gambler's girlfriend Darnell and tainted prizefighter Mitchum—fall in love in Mexico. Complications arise when Palance arrives with orders to kill Darnell. OK melodrama, originally made in 3D.

Second Chance (1971) C-74m. TVM D: Peter Tewksbury. Brian Keith, Elizabeth Ashley, Juliet Prowse, Roosevelt Grier, Pat Carroll, William

Windom. Stockbroker drops out, buys ghost town in Nevada, converts it into haven for people who never had chance in life. Passable mixture of comedy and drama; cast far better than material. Average.

Second Chorus (1940) 83m. ** D: H. C. Potter. Fred Astaire, Paulette Goddard, Artie Shaw and Orchestra, Charles Butterworth, Burgess Meredith. Routine musical of Astaire and Meredith, members of Shaw's band, both with designs on Goddard. Easy to take, but nothing special.

Second Face, The (1950) 77m. **½ D: Jack Bernhard. Ella Raines, Bruce Bennett, Rita Johnson, Jane Darwell, John Sutton. Concise study of the effects of plastic surgery on Raines, whose face has been scarred.

Second Fiddle (1939) 86m. **½ D: Sidney Lanfield. Sonja Henie, Tyrone Power, Rudy Vallee, Edna May Oliver, Lyle Talbot, Brian Sisters. Contrived Henie musical of Power promoting Hollywood romance for Henie, falling in love himself. Irving Berlin score.

Second Greatest Sex, The (1955) C-87m. *½ D: George Marshall. Jeanne Crain, George Nader, Bert Lahr, Mamie Van Doren, Kitty Kallen, Keith Andes, Tommy Rall, Paul Gilbert, Jimmy Boyd. Second-rate updating of LYSISTRATA, about women protesting men's violence by going on sex strike.

Second Honeymoon (1937) 79m. **½ D: Walter Lang. Tyrone Power, Loretta Young, Stuart Erwin, Claire Trevor, Lyle Talbot. Power tries to win back ex-wife Young in pat marital farce with attractive cast.

Second Time Around, The (1961) C-99m. **½ D: Vincent Sherman. Debbie Reynolds, Andy Griffith, Steve Forrest, Juliet Prowse, Thelma Ritter, Isobel Elsom. Mild comic Western with widow Debbie moving to Arizona, becoming sheriff, tangling with suitors Griffith and Forrest.

Second Woman, The (1951) 91m. **½ D: James V. Kern. Robert Young, Betsy Drake, John Sutton, Henry O'Neill, Florence Bates. Brooding drama of architect Young who feels responsible for girlfriend's accidental death.

Seconds (1966) 106m. ***½ D: John Frankenheimer. Rock Hudson, Salome Jens, John Randolph, Will Geer, Jeff Corey. Frustrated middle-aged businessman is transformed into new identity (Hudson) but finds himself at odds with old and new life conflicts. Fascinating from start to finish, with good performances, striking camerawork by James Wong Howe.

Secret Agent, The (1936-British) 93m. **½ D: Alfred Hitchcock. John Gielgud, Madeleine Carroll, Robert Young, Peter Lorre, Percy Marmont, Lilli Palmer. Strange blend of comedy and thriller elements which don't quite mesh; Carroll and Gielgud are secret agents who pose as man and wife while on assignment to kill enemy spy. One of Hitchcock's oddest films.

Secret Agent Fireball (1966-Italian) C-89m. ** D: Martin Donan. Richard Harrison, Dominique Boschero, Wandisa Guida. Harrison is American superspy substituted for U.S. scientist in gambit to protect coalition between U.S.-Germany-Russia on new petroleum mechanism project; standard treatment. Retitled: KILLERS ARE CHALLENGED.

Secret Agent of Japan (1942) 72m. ** D: Irving Pichel. Preston Foster, Lynn Bari, Noel Madison, Janis Carter, Sen Yung, Addison Richards, Frank Puglia, Ian Wolfe. Dated espionage film of soldier-of-fortune Foster working in the Pacific for England before Pearl Harbor.

Secret Agent Super Dragon (1966) C-95m. *½ D: Calvin Padgett. Ray Danton, Marisa Mell, Margaret Lee, Jess Hahn. Sloppy foreign spy meller has fair cast but sometimes silly script and atrocious dubbing. Danton repeats role from CODE NAME: JAGUAR.

Secret Beyond the Door (1948) 98m. ** D: Fritz Lang. Joan Bennett, Michael Redgrave, Anne Revere, Barbara O'Neil, Natalie Schafer. Tedious Lang misfire along lines of Hitchcock's SUSPICION, with Bennett believing her husband is a demented murderer.

Secret Bride (1935) 76m. **½ D: William Dieterle. Barbara Stanwyck, Warren William, Glenda Farrell, Grant Mitchell, Arthur Byron. D.A. William is trying to expose governor Mitchell while he's secretly married to his daughter Stanwyck.

Secret Ceremony (1968-British) C-109m. ***½ D: Joseph Losey. Elizabeth Taylor, Mia Farrow, Robert Mitchum, Pamela Brown, Peggy Ashcroft. Farrow resembles Taylor's dead daughter, Taylor resembles

Farrow's death mother, and their meeting has strange results. Originally an excellent psychological drama, but then Universal cut footage and shot extra scenes to make film more "acceptable" for TV, at 101m. This rating applies only to original version.

Secret Command (1944) 82m. ★★★ D: A. Edward Sutherland. Pat O'Brien, Carole Landis, Chester Morris, Ruth Warrick, Wallace Ford. No-nonsense O'Brien tries to find source of sabotage in California shipyard during WW2. Good, fast moving espionage story. O'Brien also produced this film.

Secret Door, The (1964-British) 72m. ★½ D: Gilbert Kay. Robert Hutton, Sandra Dorne, Peter Illing, George Pastell. Uneven direction mars otherwise OK plot of U.S. safecrackers out to steal Japanese code secrets in Lisbon.

Secret Fury, The (1950) 86m. ★★★ D: Mel Ferrer. Claudette Colbert, Robert Ryan, Jane Cowl, Paul Kelly, Vivian Vance, Philip Ober. Unknown person tries to drive Claudette crazy to prevent her marriage to Ryan. Exciting whodunit with twist ending.

Secret Garden, The (1949) 92m. ★★★ D: Fred M. Wilcox. Margaret O'Brien, Herbert Marshall, Dean Stockwell, Gladys Cooper, Elsa Lanchester. Young girl who comes to live at run-down Victorian estate, finds abandoned garden, devotes herself to it and eventually changes the lives of everyone living there. Vividly atmospheric film; last reel in color.

Secret Heart, The (1946) 97m. ★★½ D: Robert Z. Leonard. Claudette Colbert, Walter Pidgeon, June Allyson, Lionel Barrymore, Robert Sterling, Patricia Medina, Marshall Thompson. This is Allyson's film, as young girl obsessed with dead father, unable to accept stepmother Colbert. Film creates eerie mood, and acting is good, but it's offbeat and not for all tastes.

Secret Invasion, The (1964) C-95m. ★★★ D: Roger Corman. Stewart Granger, Mickey Rooney, Raf Vallone, Henry Silva, Edd Byrnes, Mia Massini. Good action, location photography, and direction in story of British Intelligence using criminals to work behind enemy lines in WW2 Yugoslavia.

Secret Land, The (1948) C-71m. ★★★ Produced by: Orville O. Dull. Narrated by: Van Heflin, Robert Montgomery, Robert Taylor. Glossy but penetrating documentary study of Admiral Richard Byrd's exploratory missions to Antarctic.

Secret Life of an American Wife, The (1968) C-92m. ★★ D: George Axelrod. Walter Matthau, Anne Jackson, Patrick O'Neal, Edy Williams, Richard Bull, Paul Napier. Talky, generally unfunny Axelrod farce about neglected wife who decides to pose as a call girl with one of her husband's clients—a screen lover (Matthau). Poor follow-up to LORD LOVE A DUCK.

Secret Life of John Chapman, The (1976) C-78m. TVM D: David Lowell Rich. Ralph Waite, Susan Anspach, Pat Hingle, Elaine Heilveil, Brad Davis, Maury Cooper. Contemporary drama of college president who takes a sabbatical to become a ditch-digger and short-order cook. Earnest adaptation of John Chapman's book, *Blue Collar Journal*, with Waite wonderful as Chapman. Above average.

Secret Life of Walter Mitty, The (1947) C-105m. ★★ D: Norman Z. McLeod. Danny Kaye, Virginia Mayo, Boris Karloff, Fay Bainter, Ann Rutherford. Disappointing formula comedy casts Danny as milquetoast who dreams of manly glory; not much Thurber here, but Kaye does perform his famous "Anatole of Paris."

Secret Mark of D'Artagnan, The (1962-Italian) C-91m. ★★½ D: Siro Marcellini. George Nader, Mario Petri, Magali Noel, Georges Marchal. Loosely based on Dumas' characters, Nader is D'Artagnan fighting for Louis XIII and Richelieu; plot is silly but moves along.

Secret Mission (1942-British) 82m. ★★½ D: Harold French. Hugh Williams, James Mason, Roland Culver, Carla Lehmann, Michael Wilding, Herbert Lom, Stewart Granger. Well-paced WW2 actioner of Anglo mission in occupied France.

Secret Night Caller, The (1975) C-78m. TVM D: Jerry Jameson. Robert Reed, Hope Lange, Sylvia Sidney, Michael Constantine, Robin Mattson, Elaine Giftos. Reed is an IRS agent with a compulsion to make obscene phone calls, to the distress of his wife and family. Competent actors trapped in tawdry drama. Below average.

Secret of Blood Island, The (1965-British) C-84m. ★★½ D: Quentin

Lawrence. Barbara Shelley, Jack Hedley, Charles Tingwell, Patrick Wymark. Woman agent parachutes into Malayan prison behind enemy lines.

Secret of Convict Lake, The (1951) 83m. **½ D: Michael Gordon. Glenn Ford, Gene Tierney, Ethel Barrymore, Zachary Scott, Ann Dvorak. Set in 1870s California, escaped prisoners hide out at settlement comprised largely of women; fine cast makes the most of script.

Secret of Dr. Kildare (1939) 84m. D: Harold S. Bucquet. Lew Ayres, Lionel Barrymore, Lionel Atwill, Helen Gilbert, Laraine Day, Sara Haden, Samuel S. Hinds, Emma Dunn, Grant Mitchell, Martha O'Driscoll, Alma Kruger. SEE: **Dr. Kildare** series.

Secret of Dr. Mabuse, The (1961-German) 90m. **½ D: Fritz Lang. Peter Van Eyck. Dawn Addams, Gert Frobe. Well-paced yarn bringing back famed arch-criminal of 1920s, with Lang again directing. Mabuse still trying to rule the world, with police inspector Frobe intervening. Retitled: THE DIABOLICAL DOCTOR MABUSE.

Secret of My Success, The (1965-British) C-112m. *½ D: Andrew L. Stone. Shirley Jones, Stella Stevens, Honor Blackman, James Booth, Lionel Jeffries. Film certainly doesn't succeed. Naive boy is taken in by several crafty females on his road to maturity. Picturesque settings, variety of characterizations by Jeffries.

Secret of Santa Vittoria, The (1969) C-140m. **½ D: Stanley Kramer. Anthony Quinn, Anna Magnani, Virna Lisi, Hardy Kruger, Sergio Franchi, Renato Rascel, Eduardo Ciannelli. Entertaining story from Robert Crichton's book of Italian town which hides a million bottles of wine from occupying Germans in WW2. Story wanders, however, with needless subplots that make it over-long. Kruger excellent as civilized German officer.

Secret of the Black Trunk, The (1962-German) 96m. **½ D: Werner Klingler. Joachim Hansen, Senta Berger, Hans Reiser, Leonard Steckel, Peter Carsten. Filmed in England, this Edgar Wallace-esque yarn involves a series of murders at a famed hotel; predictable but engaging.

Secret of the Blue Room (1933) 66m. **½ D: Kurt Neumann. Lionel Atwill, Gloria Stuart, Paul Lukas, Edward Arnold, Onslow Stevens, William Janney. Atmospheric whodunit set in eerie European castle where girl's three suitors are asked to sleep in room where murder once took place. Good cast makes this one worthwhile; remade as THE MISSING GUEST and MURDER IN THE BLUE ROOM.

Secret of the Incas (1954) C-101m. **½ D: Jerry Hopper. Charlton Heston, Robert Young, Nicole Maurey, Thomas Mitchell, Glenda Farrell, Yma Sumac. Good adventure of explorer searching for location of fabled treasure. Adequate direction, good performances.

Secret of the Purple Reef, The (1960) C-80m. ** D: William Witney. Jeff Richards, Margia Dean, Peter Falk, Richard Chamberlain, Robert Earle, Terence DeMarney. Programmer whose capable cast bounces the story along; brothers seek clues to their father's killing in the Caribbean.

Secret of the Red Orchid, The SEE: **Puzzle of the Red Orchid, The**

Secret of the Whistler (1946) 65m. D: George Sherman. Richard Dix, Leslie Brooks, Mary Currier, Michael Duane, Mona Barrie, Ray Walker. SEE **Whistler** series.

Secret of Treasure Mountain (1956) 68m. *½ D: Seymour Friedman. Valerie French, Raymond Burr, William Prince, Lance Fuller, Susan Cummings. Junky trivia about hunt for buried wealth in Indian country.

Secret Partner, The (1961-British) 91m. *** D: Basil Dearden. Stewart Granger, Haya Harareet, Bernard Lee, Conrad Phillips. Fast-paced, atmospheric mystery about man trying to pull off ingenious scheme whereby he is accused of robbery.

Secret People, The (1951-British) 87m. ** D: Thorold Dickinson. Valentina Cortese, Serge Reggiani, Audrey Hepburn, Megs Jenkins, Irene Worth, Sydney Tafler. Capable cast invigorates this standard tale of intrigue set in pre-WW2 London.

Secret Service in Darkest Africa SEE: **Baron's African War, The**

Secret Seven, The (1966-Italian) C-94m. BOMB D: Alberto de Martino. Tony Russel, Helga Line, Massimo Serato, Gerard Tichy. Adventurer enlists aid of six illustrious heroes to restore rightful queen to throne. Typically poor Italian "spectacle."

[673]

Secret Six, The (1931) 83m. **½
D: George Hill. Wallace Beery,
Lewis Stone, Clark Gable, Jean Harlow, Johnny Mack Brown, Ralph
Bellamy, Marjorie Rambeau, John
Miljan. Admirably hard-boiled gangster saga with powerhouse cast;
sluggish at times, but worth seeing
for milk-drinking racketeer Beery,
aristocratic crime-lord Stone, moll-
with-a-heart-of-gold Harlow, et al.

Secret War of Harry Frigg, The
(1968) C-110m. ** D: Jack Smight.
Paul Newman, Sylva Koscina, Andrew Duggan, Tom Bosley, John
Williams. Noncom soldier selected to
free five generals held captive during
WW2 in this slick but inane comedy,
one of Newman's few real losers.

Secret Ways, The (1961) 112m. **½
D: Phil Karlson. Richard Widmark,
Sonja Ziemann, Senta Berger, Charles
Regnier. Much on-location shooting
helps strengthen caper with Widmark
as grim American sent into Communist Hungary to plan escape of
pro-West refugee.

Secret Weapon SEE: **Sherlock
Holmes and The Secret Weapon**

Secret World (1969-French) C-94m.
** D: Robert Freeman. Jacqueline
Bisset, Giselle Pascal, Pierre Zimmer, Marc Porel, Jean-Francois
Maurin. Bisset's presence gives slight
boost to pretentiously directed film
about young boy's infatuation with
his uncle's mistress.

Secrets (1971) C-86m. *½ D: Philip
Saville. Jacqueline Bisset, Per Oscarsson, Shirley Knight Hopkins,
Robert Powell, Tarka Kings, Martin
C. Thurley. A husband, wife, and
daughter all have sexual experiences
during the course of a day, which
must remain secrets. Dull, somewhat
pretentious film notable only for
nude Bisset in passionate lovemaking scene. Released in 1978.

Secrets (1977) C-100m. TVM D:
Paul Wendkos. Susan Blakely, Roy
Thinnes, Joanne Linville, John Randolph, Melody Thomas, Anthony
Eisley. Silly drama about unhappily
married young woman who, following the death of her repressive
mother, becomes a nymphomaniac
while looking for the bluebird of
happiness. Below average.

Secrets of a Secretary (1931) 71m.
** D: George Abbott. Claudette Colbert, Herbert Marshall, George Me-
taxa, Mary Boland, Berton Churchill.
Stiff drawing-room stuff, with Colbert

finding ex-hubby Marshall blackmailing her new boss.

Secrets of an Actress (1938) 71m.
**½ D: William Keighley. Kay Fran-
cis, George Brent, Ian Hunter, Gloria
Dickson, Isabel Jeans. Chic woman's
picture: Francis is glamorous actress
who attracts distraught Brent, an unhappily married architect.

Secrets of Life (1956) C-75m. ***
D: James Algar. Narrated by Winston Hibler. Disney True-Life Adventure features closeup looks at
plant life, insect life, sea creatures,
and natural wonders like volcanoes.
Wonderful footage includes time-
lapse photography of plants set to
a rousing bolero on the soundtrack.

Secrets of the Lone Wolf (1941)
67m. D: Edward Dmytryk. Warren
William, Ruth Ford, Roger Clark,
Victor Jory, Eric Blore, Thurston
Hall, Fred Kelsey. SEE: **Lone Wolf**
series.

Secrets of Three Hungry Wives
(1978) C-100m. TVM D: Gordon
Hessler. Jessica Walter, Gretchen
Corbett, Eve Plumb, Heather Mac-
Rae, James Franciscus, Craig Stevens. Sleazy melodrama that asks
the nagging question: Who killed
handsome zillionaire Franciscus
(who's been having affairs with three
bored socialites)? Who cares? Below
average.

Security Risk (1954) 69m. ** D:
Harold Schuster. John Ireland, Dorothy Malone, Keith Larsen, John
Craven, Joe Bassett. Routine F.B.I.-
vs.-Communist-agent; even Malone
isn't diverting in this "B" film.

Seduced and Abandoned (1964-Ital-
ian) 118m. ***½ D: Pietro Germi.
Stefania Sandrelli, Saro Urzi, Lando Buzzanca, Leopoldo Trieste.
Richly flavorful bed-room romp involving a sex-loving man who plays
and runs, till his activities catch up
with him.

Seduction of Joe Tynan, The (1979)
C-107m. **½ D: Jerry Schatzberg.
Alan Alda, Barbara Harris, Meryl
Streep, Rip Torn, Charles Kimbrough, Melvyn Douglas. Earnest
but shallow drama (written by Alda)
about young senator who faces moral
dilemmas while climbing political
ladder in Washington. Ludicrous
resolution really hurts film as a
whole.

Seduction of Mimi, The (1974-
Italian) C-89m. *** D: Lina Wertmuller. Giancarlo Giannini, Mariangela Melato, Agostina Belli, Elena

Fiore. Mimi is actually a man (Giannini) whose stubbornness and stupidity get him into trouble politically and sexually. Climactic scene where he tries to make love to an impossibly obese woman is unforgettable. Entertaining film was later Americanized as WHICH WAY IS UP?

See Here, Private Hargrove (1944) *** D: Wesley Ruggles. Robert Walker, Donna Reed, Keenan Wynn, Robert Benchley, Bob Crosby, Grant Mitchell. Marion Hargrove's anecdotes of army life make an amusing, episodic film; Benchley hilarious as Reed's garrulous dad. Sequel: WHAT NEXT CORPORAL HARGROVE?

See How She Runs (1978) C-100m. TVM D: Richard T. Heffron. Joanne Woodward, John Considine, Lissy Newman, Mary Beth Manning, Barnard Hughes. Breath-of-fresh-air drama about a middle-aged housewife's decision to express herself by entering the grueling 26-mile Boston Marathon. Woodward won an Emmy for her performance (and her run). One of her fictional daughters here is played by a real-life daughter, Lissy Newman, in her acting debut. Above average.

See How They Run (1965) C-100m. TVM D: David Lowell Rich. John Forsythe, Senta Berger, Jane Wyatt, Franchot Tone, Leslie Nielsen, Pamela Franklin. Pretty fair chase-drama involving three orphans journeying to America, not knowing they carry crucial evidence exposing international organization and that murderers of their father pursue them. Good performances and action, obscuring inadequate motivation and believability. Average.

See No Evil (1971-British) C-89m. *** D: Richard Fleischer. Mia Farrow, Dorothy Allison, Robin Bailey, Diane Grayson. One of the more terrifying films you can see on TV. Blind girl discovers that her uncle's entire family has been murdered and that the killer is silently stalking her. Watch out for the boots.

See the Man Run (1971) C-73m. TVM D: Corey Allen. Robert Culp, Angie Dickinson, Eddie Albert, June Allyson, Charles Cioffi, Robert Lipton. Down-and-out actor and wife devise foolproof extortion scheme, instead find themselves in middle of two-way chase. Fair performances, but

dialogue reeks and direction far too sloppy. Average.

Seeding of Sarah Burns, The (1979) C-100m. TVM D: Sandor Stern. Kay Lenz, Martin Balsam, Cliff De-Young, Cassie Yates, Charles Siebert. So-so drama of a young woman who acts as a baby factory and then has second thoughts about giving up the child to the couple who paid her. Average.

Seekers, The (1954-British) C-90m. **½ D: Ken Annakin. Jack Hawkins, Glynis Johns, Noel Purcell, Laya Raki, Tony Erstich. Sincere but clichéd account of British colonization of New Zealand in 1820s, with Hawkins and Johns a married couple emigrating there. Originally released in U.S. as LAND OF FURY.

Seizure: The Story of Kathy Morris (1980) 100m. TVM D: Gerald I. Isenberg. Leonard Nimoy, Penelope Milford, Christopher Allport, Fredric Lehne, Linda G. Miller. Pedestrian dramatic recounting of real-life singer's struggle to recover from a coma after undergoing brain surgery. Average.

Sellout, The (1952) 83m. **½ D: Gerald Mayer. Walter Pidgeon, John Hodiak, Audrey Totter, Paula Raymond, Cameron Mitchell, Karl Malden, Everett Sloane, Thomas Gomez. Small town newspaper editor Pidgeon finds himself in over his head when he tries to get the goods on corrupt sheriff Gomez. OK exposé drama.

Semi-Tough (1977) C-108m. *** D: Michael Ritchie. Burt Reynolds, Kris Kristofferson, Jill Clayburgh, Robert Preston, Bert Convy, Lotte Lenya. Easygoing comedy about two football stars and their mutual girlfriend wanders too much to hit any major targets but has some funny moments. Reynolds' charm makes up for film's other deficiencies.

Seminole (1953) C-87m. **½ D: Budd Boetticher. Rock Hudson, Barbara Hale, Anthony Quinn, Richard Carlson, Hugh O'Brian. Capable cast improves this account of the Indian tribe's effort to remain free of white man law.

Seminole Uprising (1955) C-74m. *½ D: Earl Bellamy. George Montgomery, Karin Booth, John Pickard, Ed Hinton. Trite handling of Indians vs. cavalry; too little action.

Senator Was Indiscreet, The (1947) 81m. ***½ D: George S. Kaufman. William Powell, Ella Raines, Peter

Lind Hayes, Arleen Whelan. Wit-playwright Kaufman's only directorial fling turns out quite well, with Powell as Senator whose diary causes embarrassment. Hilarious.

Send Me No Flowers (1964) C-100m. *** D: Norman Jewison. Rock Hudson, Doris Day, Tony Randall, Clint Walker, Paul Lynde. One of the top Day-Hudson comedies. Rock, convinced he has a short time to live, has Randall find new husband for wife Doris.

Senechal the Magnificent (1958-French) 78m. **½ D: Jacques Boyer. Fernandel, Nadia Gray, Georges Chamarat, Jeanne Aubert, Armontel, Robert Pizani. Fernandel is well cast as buffoon actor who, through mistaken identities and an ability to mimic, becomes a Parisian hit.

Senior Prom (1959) 82m. *½ D: David Lowell Rich. Jill Corey, Paul Hampton, Tom Laughlin, Barbara Bostock. Flimsy excuse for low-grade musical with procession of "guest stars" such as Louis Prima, Keely Smith, Mitch Miller, etc.

Senior Year (1974) C-78m. TVM D: Richard Donner. Gary Frank, Glynnis O'Connor, Barry Livingston, Debralee Scott, Scott Colomby, Lionel Johnston, Dana Elcar. Blend of nostalgia and drama, tracing lives of several high school seniors in the Fifties. A straight version of "Happy Days," earnestly acted. Became short-lived series "Sons and Daughters." Average.

Sensations (1944) 86m. **½ D: Andrew L. Stone. Eleanor Powell, Dennis O'Keefe, C. Aubrey Smith, Eugene Pallette, W. C. Fields, Cab Calloway, Sophie Tucker. Publicity-wise Powell shows press-agent O'Keefe how to attract attention in this campy musical; one incredible number has her tap-dancing inside giant pinball machine! Fields' skit is only fair, other specialty numbers are fun. Originally titled SENSATIONS OF 1945.

Sensitive, Passionate Man, A (1977) C-100m. TVM D: John Newland. Angie Dickinson, David Janssen, Mariclare Costello, Richard Venture, Rhodes Reason. Sacked aerospace engineer turns into psychotic self-destructive drunk. Pretentious weeper in which the stars try valiantly to make something out of dumb dialogue. Below average.

Senso (1954-Italian) C-90m. **½ D: Luchino Visconti. Alida Valli, Farley Granger, Massimo Girotti, Heinz Moog. Carefully paced study of human emotions, lingering on each twisted impact in relationship between aristocrat Valli and earthy, materialistic Granger. Retitled: WANTON CONTESSA: WANTON COUNTESS.

Sensualita (1954-Italian) 72m. ** D: Clemente Fracassi. Eleonora Rossi-Drago, Amadeo Nazzari, Marcello Mastroianni, Francesco Liddi, Corrado Nardi. At-times spicy account of two men fighting over sensual Rossi-Drago. Retitled: BAREFOOT SAVAGE.

Sentimental Journey (1946) 94m. ** D: Walter Lang. John Payne, Maureen O'Hara, William Bendix, Cedric Hardwicke, Glenn Langan, Mischa Auer, Connie Marshall. Maudlin yarn of dying actress O'Hara adopting little girl to give husband Payne a companion when she is gone; no holds barred here. Remade as GIFT OF LOVE.

Sentinel, The (1977) C-93m. ** D: Michael Winner. Christina Raines, Ava Gardner, Chris Sarandon, Burgess Meredith, Sylvia Miles, Jose Ferrer, Arthur Kennedy, John Carradine. Slick but empty-headed shocker about N.Y. fashion model who rents Brooklyn Heights brownstone, finds it's full of demons and she's to be the next sentinel guarding the gateway to Hell. Good cast makes it somewhat endurable.

Separate Peace, A (1972) C-104m. BOMB D: Larry Peerce. John Heyl, Parker Stevenson, William Roerick, Peter Brush, Victor Bevine, Scott Bradbury. Supposedly sensitive story of two roommates in a 1940s prep school, taken from John Knowles' overrated novel, is enough to make anyone gag. Story is morbid, the acting incredibly amateurish, and the direction has no feeling at all for the period. A total bummer.

Separate Tables (1958) 98m. **** D: Delbert Mann. Rita Hayworth, Deborah Kerr, David Niven, Wendy Hiller, Burt Lancaster. Latter-day GRAND HOTEL, from Terence Rattigan play, with Oscar-winners Niven, as seemingly debonair colonel, and Hiller, as Lancaster's timid mistress. Hayworth effective as Lancaster's ex-wife begging him for another chance.

September Affair (1950) 104m. **½ D: William Dieterle. Joseph Cotten, Joan Fontaine, Francoise Rosay, Jessica Tandy. Trim romance tale of married man Cotten and pianist Fontaine who find that they're listed as dead in plane crash and now have chance to continue their affair.

September Storm (1960) 99m. BOMB D: Byron Haskin. Joanne Dru, Mark Stevens, Robert Strauss, Asher Dann, M. Jean-Pierre Kerien, Vera Valmont. Scheming fashion model joins a group of adventurers searching for buried treasure off the coast of Majorca. Film's only novelty is lost: It was shot in 3-D Cinemascope.

September 30, 1955 (1978) C-101m. **½ D: James Bridges. Richard Thomas, Susan Tyrrell, Deborah Benson, Lisa Blount, Thomas Hulce, Dennis Quaid. Arkansas undergrad, well played by Thomas, goes off his nut when James Dean dies, with tragic results for a girl . friend. Original, if excessively uneven drama, is worth consideration for being one of the few films to deal at all seriously with the movie star mystique. Also called "9/30/55."

Serena (1962-British) 62m. **½ D: Peter Maxwell. Patrick Holt, Emrys Jones, Honor Blackman, Bruce Beeby. Neat mystery programmer with Holt the detective inspector ferreting out the killer of artist Jones' wife.

Serenade (1956) C-121m. **½ D: Anthony Mann. Mario Lanza, Joan Fontaine, Sarita Montiel, Vincent Price, Joseph Calleia, Vince Edwards. James M. Cain novel becomes surface soaper of Lanza, the protégé of swank Fontaine, manipulated by manager Price and loved by earthy Montiel; spotty musical interludes.

Sergeant, The (1968) C-107m. ** D: John Flynn. Rod Steiger, John Phillip Law, Ludmila Mikael, Frank Latimore, Elliott Sullivan. Predictable drama, set in France, about homosexual Army sergeant Steiger and his desire for handsome private Law. Director Flynn has nice eye for detail, but film doesn't make much of an impression.

Sergeant Deadhead (1965) C-89m. *½ D: Norman Taurog. Frankie Avalon, Deborah Walley, Eve Arden, Cesar Romero, Fred Clark, Buster Keaton. Bungling Army sergeant goes into space with a chimpanzee and undergoes personality change. Oh, that poor monkey. Also known as SERGEANT DEADHEAD, THE ASTRONUT.

Sergeant Madden (1939) 82m. ** D:

Josef von Sternberg. Wallace Beery, Tom Brown, Alan Curtis, Laraine Day, Fay Holden, David Gorcey, Etta McDaniel, Horace McMahon. Director Sternberg out of his element with standard Beery vehicle of policeman whose son alienates him, marries orphan girl he raised.

Sergeant Matlovich Vs. the U.S. Air Force (1978) C-100m. TVM D: Paul Leaf. Brad Dourif, Marc Singer, Frank Converse, William Daniels, Stephen Elliott, David Spielberg, Rue McClanahan. Fact-based drama about homosexual serviceman's battle to stay in uniform. Strong, adult stuff. Above average.

Sgt. Pepper's Lonely Hearts Club Band (1978) C-111m. *½ D: Michael Schultz. Peter Frampton, The Bee Gees, George Burns, Frankie Howerd, Donald Pleasence, Sandy Farina, Dianne Steinberg, Billy Preston, Steve Martin, Earth Wind & Fire. Attempt to link songs from The Beatles' classic album into some sort of storyline just doesn't work; sequences range from tolerable to embarrassing. As to The Bee Gees' acting talent, if you can't say something nice . . .

Sergeant Rutledge (1960) C-118m. *** D: John Ford. Jeffrey Hunter, Constance Towers, Billie Burke, Woody Strode, Juano Hernandez, Willis Bouchey, Mae Marsh. Unusual story of black cavalry officer (Strode) on trial for rape and murder; during court-martial his story is recounted in flashback. Interesting material in the hands of a master, John Ford.

Sergeant Ryker (1968) C-85m. **½ D: Buzz Kulik. Lee Marvin, Bradford Dillman, Vera Miles, Peter Graves, Lloyd Nolan, Murray Hamilton. Adapted from TV film THE CASE AGAINST SERGEANT RYKER, story concerns court-martial of Marvin in title role, an Army sergeant during Korean War suspected of being a traitor; Miles is his wife and Dillman the dynamic defense attorney.

Sergeant York (1941) 134m. ***½ D: Howard Hawks. Gary Cooper, Walter Brennan, Joan Leslie, George Tobias, Stanley Ridges, Margaret Wycherly, Ward Bond, Noah Beery, Jr., June Lockhart. Excellent story of pacifist York (Cooper) drafted during WW1, realizing purpose of fighting and becoming hero. Oscarwinning performance by Cooper in fine, intelligent film, balancing segments of rural America with battle scenes.

Sergeants 3 (1962) C-112m. **½ D: John Sturges. Frank Sinatra, Dean Martin, Sammy Davis, Jr., Peter Lawford, Joey Bishop. Second reworking of GUNGA DIN is amusing, but not up to 1939 original. This time it's out West with the Rat Pack as cavalry sergeants. Davis can't eclipse Sam Jaffe as Gunga Din.

Serpent of the Nile (1953) C-81m. *½ D: William Castle. Rhonda Fleming, William Lundigan, Ray-Mond Burr, Michael Ansara, Julie Newmar. Antony and Cleopatra, B-movie style; good for a few laughs, anyway. Producer Sam Katzman used all the sets left over from Rita Hayworth's SALOME.

Serpent's Egg, The (1978-German-U.S.) C-120m. *½ D: Ingmar Bergman. Liv Ullmann, David Carradine, Gert Frobe, Heinz Benent, Glynn Turman, James Whitmore. Smorgasbord of depravities makes story of Jewish trapeze artist in post-WW1 Germany an overwhelmingly unpleasant movie experience. Sven Nykvist's camerawork is brilliant as usual, but Carradine is fatally miscast.

Serpico (1973) C-129m. ***½ D: Sidney Lumet. Al Pacino, John Randolph, Jack Kehoe, Biff McGuire, Barbara Eda-Young, Cornelia Sharpe, Tony Roberts. Tough, exciting filmization of Peter Maas book based on true-life acounts of N.Y. undercover cop whose non-conformism—and exposure of department corruption—isolate him from the force.

Serpico: The Deadly Game (1976) C-100m. TVM D: Robert Collins. David Birney, Allen Garfield, Burt Young, Lane Bradbury, Walter McGinn, Tom Atkins. Birney takes over Al Pacino's role for this TV movie about New York undercover cop Frank Serpico, and his battle against corruption in and out of the department. Subsequent series also starred Birney. Average.

Servant, The (1963-British) 115m. ***½ D: Joseph Losey. Dirk Bogarde, James Fox, Sarah Miles, Wendy Craig, Catherine Lacey, Patrick Magee. Insidious study of moral degradation as corrupt manservant Bogarde becomes master of employer Fox; superb study of brooding decadence.

Session with the Committee, A (1969) C-90m. ** D: Del Jack. Peter Bonerz, Barbara Bosson, Garry Goodrow, Carl Gottlieb, Jessica Myerson, Christopher Ross, Melvin Stewart, Don Sturdy. Filmed collection of live skits by L.A. comic troupe isn't exactly "pure" cinema, but has the same appeal as a good comedy record album. Plenty of laughs.

Set This Town on Fire (1969) C-100m. TVM D: David Lowell Rich. Carl Betz, Chuck Connors, Charles Robinson, Lynda Day, James Westerfield, Jeff Corey, Paul Fix. Connors has served time on manslaughter conviction—but now he's back in town running for mayor, as local drunk has confessed to original crime. Good drama with nice small-town atmosphere, interesting subplots. Above average. Retitled THE PROFANE COMEDY.

Set-Up, The (1949) 72m. ***½ D: Robert Wise. Robert Ryan, Audrey Totter, George Tobias, Alan Baxter, James Edwards, Wallace Ford. Gutsy account of washed-up fighter refusing to give up or go crooked; Ryan has never been better.

Seven (1979) C-100m. ** D: Andy Sidaris. William Smith, Barbara Leigh, Guich Koock, Art Metrano, Martin Kove, Richard Le Pore, Susan Kiger. Brawny Smith is hired by U.S. intelligence to destroy Hawaiian crime syndicate, which he does, with enthusiastic team of "specialists." Violent, sexy, tongue-in-cheek action yarn.

Seven Alone (1975) C-96m. **½ D: Earl Bellamy. Dewey Martin, Aldo Ray, Anne Collins, Dean Smith, Stewart Peterson. OK family-wilderness picture will entertain youngsters; based on true story of seven children who make perilous 2,000 mile trek West during the 1800s after their parents die en route.

Seven Angry Men (1955) 90m. *** D: Charles Marquis Warren. Raymond Massey, Debra Paget, Jeffrey Hunter, James Best, Dennis Weaver, Dabbs Greer, Ann Tyrrell. Good historical drama of John Brown (Massey) and family fighting to free slaves during 1800s. Massey is fine in lead role.

Seven Beauties (1976-Italian) C-115m. **** D: Lina Wertmuller. Giancarlo Giannini, Fernando Rey, Shirley Stoler, Elena Fiore, Enzo Vitale. Director-writer Wertmuller's masterpiece follows a small-time casanova through the horrors of WW2 battle and imprisonment in a concentration camp, where he learns to survive—at any cost. Giannini is superb in this harrowing, unforgettable film.

Seven Brides for Seven Brothers (1954) C-103m. **** D: Stanley Donen. Howard Keel, Jane Powell, Jeff Richards, Russ Tamblyn, Tommy Rall, Virginia Gibson, Julie Newmeyer (Newmar), Ruta Kilmonis (Lee), Matt Mattox. Rollicking musical perfectly integrates song, dance, and story: Keel's decision to get himself a wife (Powell) inspires his rowdy brothers to follow suit. Tuneful Johnny Mercer-Saul Chaplin score, but it's Michael Kidd's energetic dance numbers that really stand out, with rare screen work by dancers Jacques D'Amboise and Marc Platt. The barn-raising sequence is an absolute knockout.

7 Capital Sins (1961-French) 113m. ** D: Jean-Luc Godard, Roger Vadim, Sylvaine Dhomme, Edouard Molinaro, Philippe De Broca, Claude Chabrol, Jacques Demy. Marie-Jose Nat, Dominique Paturel, Jean-Marc Tennberg, Perrette Pradier. Potpourri of directors and talents play out modern parables concerning anger, envy, gluttony, greed, laziness, lust, and pride.

Seven Cities of Gold (1955) C-103m. **½ D: Robert D. Webb. Richard Egan, Anthony Quinn, Jeffrey Hunter, Rita Moreno, Michael Rennie. Average spectacle, adventure from 50s has good cast and fair direction. "Roughneck" learns ways of God in search for fabled Indian treasure in Western U.S.

Seven Daring Girls (1960-German) 62m. *½ D: Otto Meyer. Jan Hendriks, Adrian Hoven, Ann Smyrner, Dorothee Glocklen. Poorly executed yarn of seven girls from Swiss finishing school marooned on isle inhabited by crooks seeking gold there.

Seven Days in May (1964) 118m. *** D: John Frankenheimer. Burt Lancaster, Kirk Douglas, Fredric March, Ava Gardner, Edmond O'Brien, Martin Balsam, George Macready, John Houseman. Absorbing story of military scheme to overthrow the government. Fine cast includes Lancaster and Douglas as military officials, March as U.S. President; intelligent suspense in Rod Serling screenplay.

Seven Days' Leave (1942) 87m. **½ D: Tim Whelan. Lucille Ball, Victor Mature, Harold Peary, Ginny Simms,

Peter Lind Hayes, Arnold Stang, Ralph Edwards. Two sailors ashore is basis for sprightly musicomedy with Freddy Martin and Les Brown's bands; songs include: "Can't Get Out Of This Mood."

Seven Days to Noon (1950-British) 93m. **** D: John and Roy Boulting. Barry Jones, Olive Sloane, Andre Morell, Sheila Manahan. Excellently paced thriller about scientist threatening to explode bomb in London if his demands are not met.

Seven Deadly Sins (1952) 120m. **½ D: Eduardo De Filippo, Jean Dreville, Yves Allegret, Roberto Rossellini, Carlo Rim, Claude Autant-Lara. Michele Morgan, Françoise Rosay, Gerard Philippe, Isabelle Miranda, Eduardo De Filippo. Episodic potpourri illustrating seven major vices; lack of internal continuity mars total effort.

Seven Different Ways SEE: **Quick, Let's Get Married**

711 Ocean Drive (1950) 102m. **½ D: Joseph M. Newman. Edmond O'Brien, Joanne Dru, Otto Kruger, Bert Freed. Tidy racketeer yarn of the bookie syndicate in the U.S.

Seven Faces of Dr. Lao, The (1964) C-100m. *** D: George Pal. Tony Randall, Barbara Eden, Arthur O'Connell, John Ericson, Argentina Brunetti, Noah Beery. Engaging tale of Western town brought to its senses by parables performed by Dr. Lao's traveling circus; tour de force for Randall. William Tuttle won special Oscar for makeup creations.

Seven Golden Men (1965-Italian) C-87m. **½ D: Marco Vicario. Philippe Leroy, Rossana Podesta, Gastone Moschin, Gabriele Tinti, Jose Suarez. Standard but diverting heist film, with Leroy as mastermind who plans to steal seven tons of gold from Swiss bank. Clumsy dubbing, brassy music tract. Released here in 1969.

Seven Golden Men Strike Again (1966-Italian) C-102m. ** D: Marco Vicario. Philippe Leroy, Rossana Podesta, Gastone Moschin, Giampiero Albertini, Gabriele Tinti, Maurice Poli. Espionage expert Leroy is hired under pressure from American agents to spy on Latin American general, but he and Podesta have their eye on gold instead. Complicated cat-and-mouse plot.

Seven Guns for the MacGregors (1968-Italian-Spanish) C-97m. *½ D: Frank Garfield. Robert Wood,

Manny Zarzo, Nick Anderson, Paul Carter. Standard spaghetti Western about seven brothers unjustly put in jail who escape and go after the crooked sheriff.

Seven in Darkness (1969) C-75m. TVM D: Michael Caffey. Dina Merrill, Barry Nelson, Sean Garrison, Milton Berle, Arthur O'Connell, Alejandro Rey, Lesley Ann Warren. Commercial flight carrying group on way to convention crashes on mountain; they must find their way down to nearest village. Standard melodrama with barely interesting assortment of stereotyped characters, adequate performances, dull direction. Average.

Seven Keys to Baldpate (1947) 66m. **½ D: Lew Landers. Philip Terry, Jacqueline White, Eduardo Ciannelli, Margaret Lindsay, Arthur Shields. Oft-filmed tale of mystery writer involved in murder himself is pretty good.

Seven Little Foys, The (1955) C-95m. *** D: Melville Shavelson. Bob Hope, Milly Vitale, George Tobias, Billy Gray, James Cagney. Pleasant biography of vaudevillian Eddie Foy and his performing family. Hope lively in lead role, Cagney guests as George M. Cohan; both men's footwork is admirable.

Seven Men From Now (1956) C-78m. *** D: Budd Boetticher. Randolph Scott, Gail Russell, Lee Marvin, Walter Reed, John Larch, Donald Barry. Scott tracks seven men who held up Wells Fargo station and killed his wife. Solid western from Scott-Boetticher team, with script by later director Burt Kennedy.

Seven Minutes, The (1971) C-116m. **½ D: Russ Meyer. Wayne Maunder, Marianne McAndrew, Philip Carey, Yvonne De Carlo, Jay C. Flippen, Edy Williams, John Carradine, Harold J. Stone. Host of fine character actors fail to save laughable adaptation of Irving Wallace's best-seller about pornography trial.

Seven Percent Solution, The (1976) C-113m. *** D: Herbert Ross. Nicol Williamson, Alan Arkin, Vanessa Redgrave, Robert Duvall, Laurence Olivier, Joel Grey, Samantha Eggar, Jeremy Kemp. Sherlock Holmes meets Sigmund Freud in this handsome, entertaining film from novel by Nicholas Meyer. Shifts gears from serious drama to tongue-in-cheek adventure, stays on target all the way.

Seven Samurai (1954-Japanese) 141m. **** D: Akira Kurosawa. Toshiro Mifune, Takashi Shimura, Yoshio Inaba, Isao Kimura, Seiji Miyaguchi, Minoru Chiaki. Classic film about 16th-century Japanese village which hires professional warriors to fend off bandits. Kurosawa's "eastern western" has served as model for many films since, including American remake THE MAGNIFICENT SEVEN, a title once given this film for U.S. release.

Seven Seas to Calais (1962-Italian) C-102m. **½ D: Rudolph Maté, Primo Zeglio. Rod Taylor, Keith Michell, Irene Worth, Anthony Dawson, Basil Dignam. Minor but entertaining swashbuckler with Taylor as Sir Francis Drake.

Seven Sinners (1940) 87m. *** D: Tay Garnett. Marlene Dietrich, John Wayne, Albert Dekker, Broderick Crawford, Anna Lee, Mischa Auer, Billy Gilbert. Alluring Dietrich makes Wayne forget about the Navy for a while in this engaging action-love story with excellent supporting cast. Remade as SOUTH SEA SINNER.

Seven Slaves Against the World (1965-Italian) C-96m. BOMB D: Michele Lupo. Roger Browne, Gordon Mitchell, Scilla Gabel, Germano Longo, Alfredo Rizzo. Terrible spectacle with nonexistent plot of swordsman freeing ancient city from tyrant.

Seven Surprizes (1963-Canadian) C-77m. *** Unusual program of shorts from National Film Board of Canada including delightful animated work by Norman McLaren and Evelyn Lambart. Offbeat, entertaining.

Seven Sweethearts (1942) 98m. **½ D: Frank Borzage. Kathryn Grayson, Van Heflin, Marsha Hunt, S. Z. Sakall, Cecilia Parker, Peggy Moran, Diana Lewis, Isobel Elsom, Donald Meek, Louise Beavers. Schmaltz about Sakall's brood of daughters, none of whom can marry until the eldest does. Song: "You and the Waltz and I."

Seven Thieves (1960) 102m. ***½ D: Henry Hathaway. Edward G. Robinson, Rod Steiger, Joan Collins, Eli Wallach, Alexander Scourby, Michael Dante, Berry Kroeger, Sebastian Cabot. Taut caper of well-planned Monte Carlo heist, with excellent cast giving credibility to far-fetched premise.

Seven Times Seven (1969-Italian) C-92m. ** D: Michele Lupo. Terry-Thomas, Lionel Stander, Gaston

Moschin, Gordon Mitchell, Adolfo Celi. Middling cops & robbers farce that has a gang of convicts go over the wall, rob the Royal Mint, and then break back into prison.

Seven-Ups, The (1973) C-103m. **½ D: Philip D'Antoni. Roy Scheider, Tony LoBianco, Bill Hickman, Richard Lynch, Victor Arnold. THE FRENCH CONNECTION producer directs unofficial sequel, with Scheider scoring as a tough cop. Action outweighs plot and a car chase is one of the best yet filmed. Shot in New York.

Seven Waves Away SEE: **Abandon Ship!.**

Seven Ways From Sundown (1960) C-87m. **½ D: Harry Keller. Audie Murphy, Barry Sullivan, Venetia Stevenson, John McIntire, Kenneth Tobey, Mary Field. Murphy is Texas ranger assigned to bring in seasoned killer Sullivan, with usual results.

Seven Women (1965) C-93m. ** D: John Ford. Anne Bancroft, Sue Lyon, Margaret Leighton, Flora Robson, Mildred Dunnock, Anna Lee, Betty Field, Eddie Albert, Mike Mazurki, Woody Strode. Flat soaper of dedicated missionaries in China in 1935, menaced by warrior cutthroats. Despite cast and director, a dull film.

Seven Women From Hell (1961) 88m. ** D: Robert D. Webb. Patricia Owens, Denise Darcel, Cesar Romero, John Kerr, Yvonne Craig. Able cast wasted on trite account of female prisoners in Japanese prison, set in WW2 New Guinea.

Seven Year Itch, The (1955) C-105m. *** D: Billy Wilder. Marilyn Monroe, Tom Ewell, Evelyn Keyes, Sonny Tufts, Victor Moore, Oscar Homolka, Carolyn Jones, Doro Merande. Ewell's wife summer vacations, Marilyn moves in upstairs, in this George Axelrod comedy set in N.Y.C. MM delightful as dumb blonde with more obvious assets than brains.

Seventeen (1940) 78m. **½ D: Louis King. Jackie Cooper, Betty Field, Otto Kruger, Richard Denning, Peter Lind Hayes, Betty Moran, Ann Shoemaker, Norma Nelson. Cooper is delightful as teen-ager facing adolescent problems, in adaptation of Booth Tarkington story.

1776 (1972) C-141m. *** D: Peter H. Hunt. William Daniels, David Ford, Howard da Silva, Donald Madden, Ron Holgate, Blythe Danner, Virginia Vestoff. America's first congress in struggle for independence from Britain provides framework for this Pulitzer Prize-winning musical. Almost all of the original Broadway cast remain, with Daniels as John Adams and Da Silva's Benjamin Franklin leading the pack. Witty book by Peter Stone.

Seventh Cavalry (1956) C-75m. **½ D: Joseph H. Lewis. Randolph Scott, Barbara Hale, Jay C. Flippen, Jeanette Nolan, Frank Faylen. Scott plays an officer who must prove that he didn't desert Custer at the Little Big Horn.

Seventh Cross, The (1944) 110m. *** D: Fred Zinnemann. Spencer Tracy, Signe Hasso, Hume Cronyn, Agnes Moorehead, Jessica Tandy, George Macready, Kaaren Verne, George Zucco, Felix Bressart. Seven men escape from Nazi concentration camp and are pursued by the Gestapo. Exciting film makes strong statement about a cynic who regains hope when others risk their lives to save him.

7th Dawn, The (1964-British) C-123m. *½ D: Lewis Gilbert. William Holden, Susannah York, Capucine, Tetsuro Tamba, Michael Goodliffe. Dreary tale of personal and political conflict among WW2 allies—now adversaries—in postwar Malaya.

Seventh Heaven (1927) 119m. **½ D: Frank Borzage. Janet Gaynor, Charles Farrell, Ben Bard, David Butler, Marie Mosquini, Albert Gran. One of the most famous screen romances of all time does not hold up as perfectly as one would like; Gaynor won first Academy Award as Diane, mistreated Paris waif redeemed and revived by cocky sewerworker Chico (Farrell). His performance weakens film, as does terrible war subplot and finale. Still interesting, though; beautifully filmed, with lovely theme music "Diane." Remade in 1937.

Seventh Heaven (1937) 102m. ** D: Henry King. Simone Simon, James Stewart, Jean Hersholt, Gregory Ratoff, Gale Sondergaard, J. Edward Bromberg, John Qualen. Classic silent film of poignant lovers in France doesn't do as well this time, with Gallic Stewart and soggy script.

Seventh Seal, The (1956-Sweden) 96m. **** D. Ingmar Bergman. Max von Sydow, Gunnar Bjornstrand, Nils Poppe, Bibi Andersson, Bengt Ekerot.

Sydow, a disillusioned knight on his way back from the Crusades, tries to solve the mysteries of life while playing chess game with Death, who has offered him a short reprieve. Spellbinding, one-of-a-kind masterpiece which helped gain Bergman his international acclaim.

Seventh Sin, The (1957) 94m. **½ D: Ronald Neame. Eleanor Parker, Bill Travers, Françoise Rosay, George Sanders, Jean-Pierre Aumont, Ellen Corby. Remake of Maugham's THE PAINTED VEIL has virtue of Parker's earnest performance as adulterous wife of a doctor who redeems herself during an epidemic; set in Hong Kong and inner China.

Seventh Sword (1962-Italian) C-84m. ** D: Riccardo Freda. Brett Halsey, Beatrice Altariba, Giulio Bosetti, Gabriele Antonini. Wooden costumer with Halsey trying to stamp out plot to overthrow Philip III of Spain.

Seventh Veil, The (1945-British) 95m. ***½ D: Compton Bennett. James Mason, Ann Todd, Herbert Lom, Hugh McDermott, Albert Lieven. Excellent drama of harried Todd running away from family to become pianist, sharing life with many men. Mason's bravura performance is well worth seeing.

Seventh Victim, The (1943) 71m. *** D: Mark Robson. Tom Conway, Kim Hunter, Jean Brooks, Evelyn Brent, Elizabeth Russell, Hugh Beaumont, Erford Gage, Isabel Jewell, Barbara Hale. Offbeat Val Lewton horror chiller of innocent Hunter stumbling onto N.Y.C. group of devil-worshippers. Genuinely eerie.

Seventh Voyage of Sinbad, The (1958) C-87m. ***½ D: Nathan Juran. Kerwin Mathews, Kathryn Grant, Torin Thatcher. Top-notch adventure/fantasy pits hero Sinbad against unscrupulous magician (Thatcher) who has reduced Princess Grant to miniature size. Good pacing, eye-popping special effects by Ray Harryhausen, music score by Bernard Herrmann make this a winner all the way.

Severed Head, A (1971-British) C-96m. **½ D: Dick Clement. Lee Remick, Richard Attenborough, Ian Holm, Claire Bloom, Jennie Linden, Clive Revill. Excellent cast and talented screenwriter Frederic Raphael (DARLING, TWO FOR THE ROAD) come a cropper in generally witless

adaptation of Iris Murdoch novel about assorted adulteries.

Sex and the Married Woman (1977) C-100m. TVM D: Jack Arnold. Barry Newman, Joanna Pettet, Keenan Wynn, Dick Gautier, Jayne Meadows, Nita Talbot, Chuck McCann, F. Murray Abraham. Listless comedy of how success can ruin a good marriage, with a free-spirited husband becoming jealous of his wife's sudden fame after she writes a book on the sex habits of her friends. Kooky cameos spark it minimally. Below average.

Sex and the Single Girl (1964) C-114m. **½ D: Richard Quine. Natalie Wood, Tony Curtis, Lauren Bacall, Henry Fonda, Mel Ferrer, Fran Jeffries, Edward Everett Horton, Larry Storch, Stubby Kaye, Count Basie and Orchestra. Helen Gurley Brown's book shoved aside, title used to exploit fairly amusing tale of smut-magazine editor Curtis wooing notorious female psychologist Wood. Bacall and Fonda wrap it up as a battling married couple.

Sex and the Single Parent (1979) C-100m. TVM D: Jackie Cooper. Susan St. James, Mike Farrell, Dori Brenner, Warren Berlinger, Julie Sommars, Barbara Rhoades. Sitcom approach to the plight of two divorcees whose newly realized independence and burgeoning social life is complicated by their respective children. Average.

Sex Kittens Go to College (1960) 94m. *½ D: Albert Zugsmith. Mamie Van Doren, Tuesday Weld, Mijanou Bardot, Mickey Shaughnessy, Louis Nye, Pamela Mason. Tasteless satire filled with innuendoes and pat situations. Van Doren is stripper accidentally put in charge of campus science department.

Sex Shop, Le (1973-French) C-92m. *** D: Claude Berri. Claude Berri, Juliet Berto, Nathalie Delon, Jean-Pierre Marielle, Beatrice Romand, Catherine Allegret. Amiable spoof of current preoccupation with sex; failing bookstore owner starts selling porno material, becomes increasingly fascinated by it. Clever idea well done; Rated X because of candid (yet unsensational) scenes.

Sex With a Smile (1976-Italian) C-100m. *½ Five different directors. Marty Feldman, Edwige Fenech, Tomas, Alex Marino, Enrico Monterrano, Giovanni Ralli. Five episodes that promise a lot in terms of sex and laughter, then (outside of Feldman segment) fail to deliver. Heavy on slapstick, and heavy reliance on knowledge of Italian affairs.

Shack Out on 101 (1955) 80m. **½ D: Edward Dein. Terry Moore, Frank Lovejoy, Lee Marvin, Keenan Wynn, Whit Bissell. Minor low-budget classic with capable cast sparking tale of espionage agent working at seaside hash-joint near scientific lab; very low-key production.

Shadow in the Sky (1951) 78m. **½ D: Fred M. Wilcox. Ralph Meeker, Nancy Davis, James Whitmore, Jean Hagen, Gladys Hurlbut. Meeker is quite believable as shellshocked ex-G.I. trying to regain his sanity.

Shadow in the Streets, A (1975) C-78m. TVM D: Richard D. Donner. Tony LoBianco, Sheree North, Dana Andrews, Ed Lauter, Jesse Welles, Dick Balduzzi. Paroled ex-con becomes a parole officer in attempt at rehabilitation. LoBianco's gutsy acting style and offbeat premise make this one. Above average.

Shadow Man, The (1953-British) 75m. ** D: Richard Vernon. Cesar Romero, Kay Kendall, Victor Maddern. Standard action-programmer with Romero a casino owner in love with Kendall, involved with homicide.

Shadow of a Doubt (1943) 108m. ***½ D: Alfred Hitchcock. Teresa Wright, Joseph Cotten, Macdonald Carey, Patricia Collinge, Henry Travers, Wallace Ford, Hume Cronyn. Perceptive Americana intertwined with homicidal story of Merry Widow murderer; Cronyn steals film as nosy pulp-story fan. Remade as STEP DOWN TO TERROR.

Shadow of Evil (1966) C-92m. *½ D: Andre Hunebelle. Kerwin Mathews, Pier Angeli, Robert Hossein, Stuart Nesbitt. Evil doctor plans control of the world by unleashing a virus to contaminate the inferior inhabitants. Too bad they don't have the serum perfected for movies yet.

Shadow of Fear (1956-British) 76m. ** D: Albert S. Rogell. Mona Freeman, Jean Kent, Maxwell Reed, Hugh Miller, Gretchen Franklin. Flabby suspenser of Freeman realizing that her stepmother is planning to murder her as she did hubby; set in England. Original title: BEFORE I WAKE.

Shadow of the Cat (1961-British) 79m. ** D: John Gilling. Barbara

Shelley, Andre Morell, William Lucas, Richard Warner, Freda Jackson. Engaging horror yarn about feline who avenges her mistress's murder.

Shadow of the Hawk (1976-Canadian) C-92m. *½ D: George McCowan. Jan-Michael Vincent, Marilyn Hassett, Chief Dan George, Pea Shandel, Marianne Jones. Formula action meller has Vincent battling supernatural Indian spirits.

Shadow of the Thin Man (1941) 97m. D: W. S. Van Dyke II. William Powell, Myrna Loy, Barry Nelson, Donna Reed, Sam Levene, Alan Baxter. SEE: Thin Man series.

Shadow of Zorro, The (1962-Italian) C-84m. *½ D: Joaquin Romero Marchent. Frank Latimore, Maria Luz Galicia, Mario Felciani, Marco Tulli. Clumsy film unaided by Latimore in title role of Don Jose who combats outlaws masked as Zorro.

Shadow on the Land (1968) C-100m. TVM D: Richard Sarafian. Jackie Cooper, John Forsythe, Carol Lynley, Gene Hackman. America run by totalitarian government; two men out to lead revolution. Unconvincing situations, poor dialogue, messy direction, forgettable action. Below average.

Shadow on the Wall (1950) 84m. *** D: Patrick Jackson. Ann Sothern, Zachary Scott, Nancy Davis, Gigi Perreau, Barbara Billingsley, Kristine Miller. Slick mystery of Perreau going into shock when she sees mother murdered, and the eventual trapping of killer.

Shadow on the Window (1957) 73m. ** D: William Asher. Phil Carey, Betty Garrett, John Barrymore, Jr., Corey Allen, Jerry Mathers. Fair programmer; Garrett is held hostage by robber-killers.

Shadow Over Elveron (1968) C-100m. TVM D: James Goldstone. James Franciscus, Shirley Knight, Leslie Nielsen, Franchot Tone, James Dunn, Don Ameche. Small-town corruption disgusts young physician who wants to set up practice there; whitewash murder trial becomes final straw. Most of dialogue and situations OK, performances ditto, but film as whole too insistent. Above average.

Shadows in the Night (1944) 67m. D: Eugene Forde. Warner Baxter, Nina Foch, George Zucco, Minor Watson, Ben Welden, Edward Norris, Charles Halton, Jeanne Bates. SEE: **Crime Doctor** series.

Shadows Over Chinatown (1946) 61m. D: Terry Morse. Sidney Toler, Mantan Moreland, Victor Sen Yung, Tanis Chandler, Bruce Kellogg, John Gallaudet. SEE: **Charlie Chan** series.

Shady Lady (1945) 94m. ** D: George Waggner. Charles Coburn, Robert Paige, Ginny Simms, Alan Curtis, Martha O'Driscoll, Kathleen Howard. Shaky mixture of music and drama in crime tale with genial Coburn saving the day for all in the end.

Shaft (1971) C-100m. *** D: Gordon Parks. Richard Roundtree, Moses Gunn, Charles Cioffi, Christopher St. John, Gwenn Mitchell. Slick, upbeat entertainment with black private-eye Shaft hired to find kidnapped daughter of black ganglord. Heavy doses of sex and violence. (certain to be cut for TV) professionally packaged by director Parks. Isaac Hayes' theme won Oscar.

Shaft in Africa (1973) C-112m. *** D: John Guillermin. Richard Roundtree, Frank Finlay, Vonetta McGee, Neda Arneric, Cy Grant, Jacques Marin. Strong action vehicle for Roundtree finds detective Shaft forced into helping African nation stop latter-day slave trading. Extremely tough and violent; sure to be well-edited for TV.

Shaft's Big Score! (1972) C-104m. *** D: Gordon Parks. Richard Roundtree, Moses Gunn, Drew Bundini Brown, Joseph Mascolo, Kathy Imrie, Wally Taylor, Joe Santos. Dynamic sequel to SHAFT (reteaming director Parks and writer Ernest Tidyman) has private eye Roundtree running afoul of the underworld as he investigates a friend's murder. Sexy, violent, with hair-raising chase finale.

Shaggy D.A., The (1976) C-91m. *** D: Robert Stevenson. Dean Jones, Suzanne Pleshette, Tim Conway, Keenan Wynn, Jo Anne Worley, Dick Van Patten. Sequel to Disney's SHAGGY DOG is winning slapstick romp, with Jones as helpless victim of transformations. Cast is peppered with a score of movie veterans in supporting and bit parts.

Shaggy Dog, The (1959) 104M. **½ D: Charles Barton. Fred MacMurray, Jean Hagen, Tommy Kirk, Annette Funicello, Tim Considine, Kevin

Corcoran, Cecil Kellaway, Alexander Scourby. Disney's first slapstick comedy has fine fantasy premise (a boy who turns into a sheepdog through ancient spell) but sluggish script. Some good gags, but not up to later Disney standard. Jack Albertson has bit part as reporter.

Shake Hands with the Devil (1959) 110m. ***½ D: Michael Anderson. James Cagney, Don Murray, Dana Wynter, Glynis Johns, Michael Redgrave, Cyril Cusack, Sybil Thorndike, Richard Harris. Gripping drama of war-torn Ireland in 1920s, with American student trying to stay aloof, but, drawn by circumstances, he joins rebel army lead by iron-willed Cagney. Strikingly filmed on location.

Shake, Rattle and Rock (1956) 72m. *½ D: Edward L. Cahn. Lisa Gaye, Touch (Mike) Connors, Sterling Holloway, Fats Domino, Joe Turner. Sub-par 1950s rock film with standard plot about adults trying to put the lid on kids' music. See it only to complete your Fats Domino filmography.

Shakedown (1950) 80m. **½ D: Joseph Pevney. Howard Duff, Peggy Dow, Brian Donlevy, Bruce Bennett, Peggie Castle, Anne Vernon, Lawrence Tierney. Story of photographer involved with racketeers to get ahead at any price; moves at fast clip. Look for Rock Hudson in a bit part.

Shakedown, The (1959-British) 92m. *½ D: John Lemont. Terence Morgan, Hazel Court, Donald Pleasence, Bill Owen. Lackluster account of shakedown racket involving a photography school of nudes; good cast but no script.

Shakiest Gun in the West, The (1968) C-101m. **½ D: Alan Rafkin. Don Knotts, Barbara Rhoades, Jackie Coogan, Donald Barry, Ruth McDevitt, Frank McGrath. This remake of Bob Hope's PALEFACE provides Knotts with one of his better vehicles, as a Philadelphia dentist who finds himself out West, tangled up with gunslingers and beautiful Rhoades.

Shalako (1968-British) C-113m. *½ D: Edward Dmytryk. Sean Connery, Brigitte Bardot, Stephen Boyd, Jack Hawkins, Peter Van Eyck, Honor Blackman, Woody Strode, Alexander Knox. European aristocrats on hunting tour of New Mexico during 1880s, are menaced by Apaches. Supposed potent casting of Connery and

Bardot can't revive slow-moving Western.

Shall We Dance (1937) 116m. ***½ D: Mark Sandrich. Fred Astaire, Ginger Rogers, Eric Blore, Edward Everett Horton, Ann Shoemaker. Lesser Astaire-Rogers is still top musical, with Gershwin's "Let's Call The Whole Thing Off," "They All Laughed," "They Can't Take That Away From Me" holding together flimsy plot about dance team pretending to be wed.

Shameless Old Lady, The (1965-French) 94m. *** D: Rene Allio, Sylvie, Malka Ribovska, Victor Lanoux, Etienne Bierry. Bertolt Brecht story charmingly brought to the screen. Sylvie is terrific as old woman who lives alone and follows a drab and uneventful routine until there is a strange turnabout in her relationships with others.

Shampoo (1975) C-109m. **½ D: Hal Ashby. Warren Beatty, Julie Christie, Goldie Hawn, Lee Grant, Jack Warden, Tony Bill, Carrie Fisher. Muddy satire of morals and mores in Southern California, centered around restless hairdresser and his demanding female customers. Some bright moments lost in dreary comedy-drama. Grant won Best Supporting Oscar.

Shamus (1973) C-106m. *** D: Buzz Kulik. Burt Reynolds, Dyan Cannon, Giorgio Tozzi, John Ryan, Joe Santos. Exciting but mindless story of offbeat private-eye trying to crack bizarre case while recovering from numerous beatings, jumpings, and other heroic exploits.

Shane (1953) C-118m. **** D: George Stevens. Alan Ladd, Jean Arthur, Van Heflin, Jack Palance, Brandon de Wilde, Edgar Buchanan, Elisha Cook, Jr. Former gunfighter comes to defense of homesteaders and is idolized by their son. Classic Western is splendid in every way. Breathtaking cinematography won Oscar.

Shanghai (1935) 75m. *½ D: James Flood. Loretta Young, Charles Boyer, Warner Oland, Fred Keating, Charles Grapewin, Alison Skipworth. Dreary drama of American girl falling in love with mysterious Boyer, who turns out to be (gasp!) Eurasian. Two good stars can't save this turgid outing.

Shanghai Chest, The (1948) 56m. D: William Beaudine. Roland Winters, Mantan Moreland, Deannie Best, John Alvin, Victor Sen Yung. SEE Charlie Chan series.

Shanghai Cobra, The (1945) 64m. D: Phil Karlson. Sidney Toler, Benson Fong, Mantan Moreland, Joan Barclay, James Flavin, Addison Richards. SEE: **Charlie Chan** series.

Shanghai Express (1932) 80m. *** D: Josef von Sternberg. Marlene Dietrich, Anna May Wong, Warner Oland, Clive Brook, Eugene Pallette, Louise Closser Hale. Dated but prime Dietrich vehicle, grandly photographed. Marlene is Shanghai Lily, Brook her old flame, Oland a cruel war lord, Wong a spunky partisan, in yarn of train ride through China during civil warfare. Remade as PEKING EXPRESS.

Shanghai Gesture, The (1941) 106m. ** D: Josef von Sternberg. Gene Tierney, Walter Huston, Victor Mature, Ona Munson, Maria Ouspenskaya, Phyllis Brooks, Albert Bassermann. Slow, overblown drama of Huston discovering daughter Tierney in Oriental gambling setup. Intriguing direction somehow never makes it.

Shanghai Story, The (1954) 99m. ** D: Frank Lloyd. Ruth Roman, Edmond O'Brien, Richard Jaeckel, Barry Kelley, Whit Bissell. Tawdry yet intriguing little film about Americans trapped by Red Chinese.

Shanks (1974) C-93m. ** D: William Castle. Marcel Marceau, Tsilla Chelton, Philippe Clay, Cindy Elbacher, Helena Kalliantiotes, Larry Bishop. Offbeat but unsuccessful fantasy about deaf mute puppeteer who revives and controls the dead. Marceau and fellow mime artists Chelton and Clay provide a few good moments.

Shape of Things to Come, The (1979-Canadian) C-95m. *½ D: George McCowan. Jack Palance, Carol Lynley, John Ireland, Barry Morse, Nicholas Campbell, Eddie Benton. Lackluster, low-budget remake of H. G. Wells classic, with few survivors of earth's destruction now living in peril on the moon. Diehard sci-fi fans may want to take a look, but it's hardly worth the trouble.

Sharad of Atlantis (1936) 100m. *½ D: B. Reeves Eason, Joseph Kane. Ray "Crash" Corrigan, Lois Wilde, Monte Blue, William Farnum, Boothe Howard, Lon Chaney, Jr. Mediocre actioner involving finding of underwater kingdom; uninspired special effects don't help. Reedited movie serial: UNDERSEA KINGDOM.

Share Out, The (1962-British) 62m. **½ D: Gerard Glaister. Bernard Lee, Patrick Cargill, Alexander Knox, Moira Redmond. Another Edgar Wallace actioner with Lee the Scotland Yard investigator determined to crack a blackmail ring.

Shark! (1970) C-92m. ** D: Samuel Fuller. Burt Reynolds, Barry Sullivan, Arthur Kennedy, Silvia Pinal, Enrique Lucero, Charles Berriochoa. Group of adventurers dive for sunken treasure, with sharks the main obstacle. Interesting underwater photography, but even vet action director Fuller can't save tired production.

Shark Kill (1976) C-78m. TVM D: William A. Graham. Richard Yniguez, Phillip Clark, David Huddleston, Jennifer Warren, Elizabeth Gill, Victor Campos. Thriller in the JAWS school pits two men, motivated by vengeance and a $10,000 bounty, against a great white shark. Great underwater but not-so-hot on land. Average.

Sharkfighters, The (1956) C-73m. *½ D: Jerry Hopper. Victor Mature, Karen Steele, James Olson, Philip Coolidge, Claude Akins. Bland account of Mature et al seeking some way to repel the man-killing fish.

Sharks' Treasure (1975) C-95m. ** D: Cornel Wilde. Cornel Wilde, Yaphet Kotto, John Neilson, Cliff Osmond, David Canary, David Gilliam. Old-fashioned adventure yarn about diving for sunken treasure in the Caribbean is peppered with physical-fitness messages from director-writer-star Wilde.

Sharon: Portrait of a Mistress (1977) C-100m. TVM D: Robert Greenwald. Trish Van Devere, Patrick O'Neal, Janet Margolin, Gloria De Haven, Mel Ferrer, Sam Groom, Salome Jens. Drama of a woman's series of affairs with married men. Boring soap opera, though earnestly performed. Average.

She (1935) 95m. *** D: Irving Pichel and Lansing C. Holden. Helen Gahagan, Randolph Scott, Helen Mack, Nigel Bruce, Gustav von Seyffertitz. Escapist adventure on a grand scale, from H. Rider Haggard's story of expedition seeking Flame of Eternal Life, which has been given to one all-powerful woman. Gahagan's cold personality

is major drawback, but film is still fun, with outstanding Max Steiner score.

She (1965-British) C-106m. **½ D: Robert Day. Ursula Andress, John Richardson, Peter Cushing, Bernard Cribbins, Christopher Lee, Andre Morell. Effective refilming of H. Rider Haggard's fantasy of love-starved eternal queen, seeking the reincarnation of her long-dead lover. There's Andress for the men, Richardson for the women.

She-Beast, The (1966-Italian-Yugoslavian) C-74m. *½ D: Mike Reeves. Barbara Steele, John Karlsen, Ian Ogilvy, Mel Welles, Jay Riley, Richard Watson. A witch killed by Transylvanian villagers in 18th century comes back to life as modern, attractive English girl on her honeymoon. Really tacky.

She Couldn't Say No (1954) 89m. **½ D: Lloyd Bacon. Robert Mitchum, Jean Simmons, Arthur Hunnicutt, Edgar Buchanan, Wallace Ford, Raymond Walburn. Simmons is appealing as wealthy gal who gives money away to all the folks in her town with backfiring results.

She Cried Murder (1973) C-73m. TVM D: Bernard Kowalski. Telly Savalas, Lynda Day George, Mike Farrell, Kate Reid, Jeff Toner, Stu Gillard. Young model witnesses subway murder, finds herself in a bind when she recognizes one of two police inspectors answering her phone call as the murderer. Nonexistent as psychological drama; forgettable as a chase thriller. Below average.

She Demons (1958) 80m. BOMB D: Richard E. Cunha. Irish McCalla, Tod Griffin, Victor Sen Yung, Rudolph Anders, Gene Roth. Dull cheapie about four people stranded on Pacific isle, involved with Fascist agents.

She Devil (1957) 77m. BOMB D: Kurt Neumann. Mari Blanchard, Jack Kelly, Albert Dekker, John Archer. Low-grade melodrama about homicidal girl immune to death.

She Done Him Wrong (1933) 66m. **** D: Lowell Sherman. Mae West, Cary Grant, Gilbert Roland, Noah Beery, Rochelle Hudson, Rafaela Ottiano, Louise Beavers. West repeats her stage role of Diamond Lil in Gay 90s spoof. Grant is invited by Mae to come up and see her sometime—he does, fireworks result.

She Gets Her Man (1945) 65m. ***
D: Erle C. Kenton. Joan Davis,
Leon Errol, William Gargan, Vivian
Austin, Russell Hicks, Donald Mac-
Bride. Hilarious slapstick whodunit
with daughter of legendary female
police chief hired to stop crime wave
in city. Davis and Errol make
marvelous duo in this fast-moving
farce.

She Learned About Sailors (1934)
76m. *½ D: George Marshall. Lew
Ayres, Alice Faye, Harry Green,
Frank Mitchell, Jack Durant. Silly
romantic comedy with complications
delaying inevitable final clinch between sailor Ayres and cabaret
singer Faye. Much footage devoted
to the violent comedy of Mitchell
and Durant.

She Lives! (1973) C-74m. TVM D:
Stuart Hagmann. Desi Arnaz Jr.,
Season Hubley, Anthony Zerbe,
Michael Margotta, Jack Soo. Young
college couple coping with news
that she's contracted terminal dis-
ease; inspirational love affair ensues.
Too-obvious spinoff of LOVE
STORY. Average.

She Loves Me Not (1934) 83m. ***
D: Elliott Nugent. Bing Crosby,
Miriam Hopkins, Kitty Carlisle,
Henry Stephenson, George Barbier,
Warren Hymer, Matt McHugh. Fine
Crosby musicomedy with collegiate
Bing hiding murder-witness Hopkins
in his room. Songs: "Straight From
The Shoulder," "Love In Bloom."
Remade as HOW TO BE VERY,
VERY POPULAR.

She Married Her Boss (1935) 90m.
**½ D: Gregory La Cava. Claudette
Colbert, Melvyn Douglas, Edith Fellows, Michael Bartlett, Raymond
Walburn, Jean Dixon. That's what
she did, and nothing much happens
until tipsy butler Walburn staggers
in. Good stars with fair script.

She Played With Fire (1958-British)
95m. ** D: Sidney Gilliat. Jack
Hawkins, Arlene Dahl, Dennis Price,
Violet Farebrother, Ian Hunter. OK
drama of Hawkins, insurance investigator, becoming involved with
Dahl, an arsonist.

She Waits (1971) C-74m. TVM D:
Delbert Mann. Patty Duke, David
McCallum, Lew Ayres, Beulah
Bondi, James Callahan, Nelson
Olmstead. Straightforward but ultimately boring thriller featuring Duke
as unbalanced young bride possessed by spirit of husband's first
wife. Game attempt at hypo-ing
story via direction, but you've seen
this one before. Average.

She Went to the Races (1945) 86m.
** D: Willis Goldbeck. James Craig,
Frances Gifford, Ava Gardner, Edmund Gwenn, Sig Ruman, Reginald
Owen. Gifford has developed scientific system for beating the horses,
but falls in love with horsetrainer;
mild comedy.

She-Wolf of London (1946) 61m. **
D: Jean Yarbrough. Don Porter,
June Lockhart, Sara Haden, Jan
Wiley, Lloyd Corrigan. Low-grade
thriller with Lockhart in title role.

She Wore a Yellow Ribbon (1949)
C-103m. ***½ D: John Ford. John
Wayne, Joanne Dru, John Agar,
Ben Johnson, Harry Carey Jr., Victor McLaglen, Mildred Natwick,
George O'Brien. Director Ford's
stock company in fine form. Wayne
excellent as cavalry officer about
to retire, unwilling to walk out on
impending war with Indians. Beautifully filmed in color, but a bit top-
heavy with climaxes.

She Wouldn't Say Yes (1945) 87m.
**½ D: Alexander Hall. Rosalind
Russell, Lee Bowman, Adele Jergens, Charles Winninger, Harry
Davenport, Sara Haden, Percy Kilbride. Psychiatrist Russell tests
theories on Bowman but finds herself involved with him romantically,
too; predictable but amusing comedy.

She Wrote the Book (1946) 72m. **
D: Charles Lamont. Joan Davis,
Jack Oakie, Mischa Auer, Kirby
Grant, John Litel, Jacqueline de Wit.
OK comedy about prim professor
Davis posing as author of torrid
best-seller. Fun for Davis fans, but
not one of her best vehicles.

She'll Be Sweet SEE: **Magee and
the Lady**

She'll Have to Go (1962-British)
90m. **½ D: Robert Asher. Bob
Monkhouse, Alfred Marks, Hattie
Jacques, Anna Karina, Dennis Lotus.
Broad farce about two brothers who
compete to win the family inheritance left to attractive Corsican
cousin (Karina).

She's a Soldier Too (1944) 67m **
D: William Castle. Beulah Bondi,
Lloyd Bridges, Nina Foch, Percy
Kilbride, Shelley Winters, Ida
Moore. OK little "B" film with
cab-driver Bondi helping out soldier
Bridges.

She's a Sweetheart (1944) 69m. *½

D: Del Lord. Larry Parks, Jane Frazee, Jane Darwell, Nina Foch, Ross Hunter, Carole Mathews. Musical programmer with G.I. Parks doubting the quality of vocalist Frazee's affection for him.

She's Back on Broadway (1953) C-95m. **½ D: Gordon Douglas. Virginia Mayo, Steve Cochran, Gene Nelson, Frank Lovejoy, Patrice Wymore. Fading Hollywood star returns to Broadway, finds dealing with director Cochran her biggest challenge. Good cast in slick but predictable musical drama.

She's Dressed to Kill (1979) C-100m. TVM D: Gus Trikonis. Eleanor Parker, Jessica Walter, John Rubinstein, Connie Sellecca, Jim McMullen, Clive Revill, Corinne Calvet. Who's bumping off the high-fashion models who've gathered to help a once-renowned designer stage a gala comeback in her isolated mountaintop retreat? Notable, if at all, for the wonderfully outré Parker send-up of Tallulah Bankhead. Average.

She's Working Her Way Through College (1952) C-101m. **½ D: H. Bruce Humberstone. Virginia Mayo, Ronald Reagan, Gene Nelson, Phyllis Thaxter, Roland Winters. OK musical remake of THE MALE ANIMAL, with Mayo the burlesque queen with a yen for a collegiate education.

Sheba Baby (1975) C-90m. ** D: William Girdler. Pam Grier, Austin Stoker, D'Urville Martin, Rudy Challenger, Dick Merrifield. Fair-to-middling black action-melodrama with Grier as female private eye trying to help father and friend save their loan business. Less sex and violence than usual but weak script and amateurish acting.

Sheep Has Five Legs, The (1954-French) 95m. *** D: Henri Verneuil. Fernandel, Delmont, Françoise Arnoul, Paulette Dubost. Fernandel's tour de force, playing an old wine-grower and each of his five sons who have gathered together for a family reunion.

Sheepman, The (1958) C-85m. *** D: George Marshall. Glenn Ford, Shirley MacLaine, Leslie Nielsen, Mickey Shaughnessy, Edgar Buchanan. Modest, entertaining comedy-Western with Ford battling Nielsen for sheep herds and MacLaine, though not always in that order. Shaughnessy is typically amusing.

Sheila Levine Is Dead and Living in New York (1975) C-113m. BOMB D: Sidney J. Furie. Jeannie Berlin, Roy Scheider, Rebecca Dianna Smith, Janet Brandt, Sid Melton. Dead is right. Gail Parent's sardonically funny novel about a Jewish American Princess trying to make good in New York becomes an unbelievably bad movie, that just goes on and on.

Shell Game (1975) C-78m. TVM D: Glenn Jordan. John Davidson, Tommy Atkins, Marie O'Brien, Robert Sampson, Signe Hasso, Jack Kehoe. Cross breed the old Robin Hood story with "The Sting" and you get this one about a resourceful ex-con out to fleece the crooked head of a charity fund. Below average.

Shenandoah (1965) C-105m. *** D: Andrew V. McLaglen. James Stewart, Doug McClure, Genn Corbett, Patrick Wayne, Rosemary Forsyth, Katharine Ross, George Kennedy. Rousing, well-acted saga of Virginia widower indifferent to Civil War until his family is involved. Sentimental drama captures heartbreak of America's Civil War. Basis for later Broadway musical.

Shepherd of the Hills (1941) C-98m. **½ D: Henry Hathaway. John Wayne, Betty Field, Harry Carey, Beulah Bondi, James Barton, Samuel S. Hinds. Uneven film adaptation of Wright story of emotional flare-up between Ozark natives and outsiders trying to buy land. Good performances, beautifully filmed in color.

Sheriff, The (1971) C-73m. TVM D: David Lowell Rich. Ossie Davis, Kaz Garas, Kyle Johnson, Ruby Dee, Moses Gunn, Brenda Sykes, Lynda Day, John Marley. Unimaginative title obscures solid drama dealing with controversial rape case that tears California town apart. Strong performances, uneven script; story's resolution only major liability. Above average.

Sheriff of Fractured Jaw, The (1959-British) C-103m. **½ D: Raoul Walsh. Kenneth More, Jayne Mansfield, Henry Hull, William Campbell, Bruce Cabot, Robert Morley. Innocuous Western spoof with Englishman More handed job of sheriff in war-torn town, which he handles surprisingly well.

Sherlock Holmes In 1939, by some genius of casting, Basil Rathbone and Nigel Bruce were signed to play

Sherlock Holmes and Dr. Watson in an adaptation of Sir Arthur Conan Doyle's HOUND OF THE BASKERVILLES; its immediate success prompted a follow-up, THE ADVENTURES OF SHERLOCK HOLMES, that same year. These were beautiful, atmospheric productions, faithful to Doyle's stories. Three years later, the series resumed with SHERLOCK HOLMES AND THE VOICE OF TERROR, updating the Doyle tales to have Holmes battling the Nazis. The twelve "modern" films never captured the flavor of the initial two (THE SCARLET CLAW came closest), but they were always worth seeing for the performances of the two stars: Rathbone—smooth, cunning, seldom caught by surprise; and Bruce—talkative, bumbling, never close to understanding the situation at hand. Mary Gordon made token appearances as Holmes' landlady Mrs. Hudson, and Dennis Hoey appeared in several films as Scotland Yard Inspector Lestrade, who always managed to get in the way. Holmes was at his best battling wits with Professor Moriarty, played in various episodes by George Zucco and Henry Daniell. Every episode ended with a stirring ode by Holmes to the glory of England, America, Canada, or some comparable topic, in keeping with the wartime flag-waving nature of Hollywood films. Seldom faithful to Doyle, later episodes like DRESSED TO KILL wearing thin, dialogue often awkward (S. H. IN WASHINGTON, for example), the Sherlock Holmes series relied on Rathbone and Bruce for enjoyment, and they never failed. Since that time there have been numerous Sherlock Holmes films—a plethora of them in recent years—but no attempts to launch another continuing series. The one earlier series, in 1930s England with Arthur Wontner, was never widely seen in the U.S.

Sherlock Holmes (1932) 68m. **½ D: William K. Howard. Clive Brook, Ernest Torrence, Miriam Jordan, Alan Mowbray, Reginald Owen. Genteel, stylish approach to Holmes, set in modern-day London. Yields pleasing but subdued results. Torrence is a most enjoyable Moriarty.

Sherlock Holmes and the Secret Weapon (1942) 68m. D: Roy William Neill. Basil Rathbone, Nigel

Bruce, Lionel Atwill, Kaaren Verne, William Post, Jr., Dennis Hoey, Mary Gordon, Holmes Herbert.

Sherlock Holmes and the Spider Woman (1944) 62m. D: Roy William Neill. Basil Rathbone, Nigel Bruce, Gale Sondergaard, Dennis Hoey, Mary Gordon, Arthur Hohl, Alec Craig.

Sherlock Holmes and the Voice of Terror (1942) 65m. D: John Rawlins. Basil Rathbone, Nigel Bruce, Evelyn Ankers, Reginald Denny, Thomas Gomez, Henry Daniell, Montagu Love.

Sherlock Holmes Faces Death (1943) 68m. D: Roy William Neill. Basil Rathbone, Nigel Bruce, Hillary Brooke, Milburn Stone, Arthur Margetson.

Sherlock Holmes in New York (1976) C-100m. TVM D: Boris Sagal. Roger Moore, John Huston, Patrick Macnee, Gig Young, Charlotte Rampling, David Huddleston, Signe Hasso, Leon Ames, Jackie Coogan. Stylish Holmes original that has the sleuth rushing to America after learning that Moriarty has imperiled the world's gold supply and is threatening Holmes' long-time love, Irene Adler. Period valentine for the Baker Street Irregulars and others who seek just plain entertainment. Above average.

Sherlock Holmes in Washington (1943) 71m. D: Roy William Neill. Basil Rathbone, Nigel Bruce, Marjorie Lord, Henry Daniell, George Zucco, John Archer, Gavin Muir.

Shield for Murder (1954) 80m. **½ D: Edmond O'Brien, Howard Koch. Edmond O'Brien, John Agar, Mara English, Carolyn Jones. Tidy, tough yarn of crooked detective involved in theft-murder, trying to keep his loot and avoid capture.

Shimmering Light (1978-Australian) C-85m. TVM D: Don Chaffey. Beau Bridges, Lloyd Bridges, Victoria Shaw, John Meillon, Ingrid Mason, Wendy Playfair. American dropout chucks a job with his business tycoon father to pursue his passion for surfing and find the perfect wave Down Under. Average.

Shinbone Alley (1971) C-86m. **½ D: John D. Wilson, David Detiege. Voices of Eddie Bracken, Carol Channing, John Carradine, Alan Reed Sr. Animated tale of archy and mehitabel is second-rate but tuneful, from Joe Darion musical based on Don Marquis characters.

Shine on Harvest Moon (1944) 112m. **½ D: David Butler. Ann Sheridan, Jack Carson, Dennis Morgan, Irene Manning, S. Z. Sakall, Marie Wilson, Step Brothers. Lives of great entertainers Nora Bayes and Jack Norworth merely provide starting point for fairly entertaining musical. Finale filmed in color.

Shining Hour, The (1938) 80m. **½ D: Frank Borzage. Joan Crawford, Margaret Sullavan, Robert Young, Melvyn Douglas, Fay Bainter, Allyn Joslyn. Raging fire burns out all hatred and problems from tangled family in intelligent soap opera. Crawford and Sullavan a most interesting contrast.

Shining Season, A (1979) C-100m. TVM D: Stuart Margolin. Timothy Bottoms, Allyn Ann McLerie, Rip Torn, Connie Forslund, Mason Adams. Inspired stricken-athlete story based on that of college track star John Baker who, despite a terminal illness, devoted his final year of life leading an underdog girls' track team to the championship. Above average.

Shining Star (1975) C-100m. *½ D: Sig Shore. Harvey Keitel, Ed Nelson, Cynthia Bostick, Bert Parks, Jimmy Boyd, Michael Dante. Low key yarn about mob-dominated recording company. Poor sound and photography. Saved—barely—by intriguing look behind the scenes of music business. Music by Earth, Wind and Fire. Formerly titled THAT'S THE WAY OF THE WORLD.

Shining Victory (1941) 80m. ***½ D: Irving Rapper. James Stephenson, Geraldine Fitzgerald, Donald Crisp, Barbara O'Neil, Montagu Love, Sig Ruman. Thoughtful drama of psychiatrist who falls in love with assistant. Plot may be clichéd, but production overcomes all.

Ship Ahoy (1942) 95m. **½ D: Edward Buzzell. Eleanor Powell, Red Skelton, Virginia O'Brien, Bert Lahr, John Emery, Tommy Dorsey Orch. with Frank Sinatra and Jo Stafford. Nonsensical plot of Skelton thinking U.S. agent is working for Axis; shipboard yarn has some salty dancing and singing.

Ship of Fools (1965) 149m. **** D: Stanley Kramer. Vivien Leigh, Oskar Werner, Simone Signoret, Jose Ferrer, Lee Marvin, Jose Greco, George Segal, Elizabeth Ashley, Michael Dunn, Charles Korvin, Lilia Skala. GRAND HOTEL at sea in pre-WW2 days. Superb cast including Leigh as disillusioned divorcée, Werner and Signoret as illicit lovers, Marvin as punchy baseball player. Penetrating drama, when not a soaper.

Ship That Died of Shame, The (1955-British) 91m. *** D: Basil Dearden. Richard Attenborough, George Baker, Bill Owen, Virginia McKenna, Roland Culver, Bernard Lee, Ralph Truman. Crew of British gunboat reteam after WW2 and use the same vessel for smuggling purposes, until "it" begins to rebel at their increasingly grimy exploits. Fine cast in offbeat drama.

Ship Was Loaded, The (1957-British) 81m. ** D: Val Guest. David Tomlinson, Peggy Cummins, Alfie Bass, Ronald Shiner. Inconsequential zaniness involving impersonations and shenanigans in Her Majesty's Navy. Retitled: CARRY ON ADMIRAL.

Shipmates Forever (1935) 108m. **½ D: Frank Borzage. Dick Powell, Ruby Keeler, Ross Alexander, Eddie Acuff, Dick Foran, John Arledge. Cocky Powell takes navy lightly until pressed into action. Usual plot, with songs and dances with Keeler.

Ships With Wings (1942-British) 89m. *** D: Sergei Nolbandov. John Clements, Ann Todd, Leslie Banks, Hugh Williams, Michael Wilding, Michael Rennie, Cecil Parker. Sterling, patriotic WW2 movie showing British soldiers at their finest, despite momentary lapses of discipline.

Shiralee, The (1957-British) 99m. **½ D: Leslie Norman. Peter Finch, Elizabeth Sellars, Dana Wilson, Rosemary Harrys, Tessie O'Shea, Sidney James, George Rose. Roughhewn Australian swagman takes daughter away from unfaithful wife, to accompany him on his wanderings. Moving portrayal of their relationship compensates for diffuse, episodic nature of film. On-location scenery helps, too.

Shirts/Skins (1973) C-74m. TVM D: William Graham. Bill Bixby, Doug McClure, Leonard Frey, Rene Auberjonois, McLean Stevenson, Robert Walden, Loretta Swit, Audrey Christie. Six young professionals cook up contest to settle basketball argument which snowballs, due to day-to-day pressure and group's own inter-rivalries, into near-tragic situation. Excellent performances by well-picked cast make film believable. Above average.

Shlock (1975) C-80m. **½ D: John Landis. Saul Kahan, Joseph Piantadosi, Eliza Garrett, John Landis. First film from director of ANIMAL HOUSE is enjoyable spoof of B-horror flicks; Landis (in gorilla suit by Rick Baker) plays missing link on the loose in small town. Many in-jokes for film buffs.

Shock (1946) 70m. *½ D: Alfred L. Werker. Vincent Price, Lynn Bari, Frank Latimore, Anabel Shaw, Michael Dunne, Reed Hadley. Trash, for staunch fans and no one else.

Shock Corridor (1963) 101m. *** D: Samuel Fuller. Peter Breck, Constance Towers, Gene Evans, James Best, Hari Rhodes. Journalist Breck gets admitted to mental institution to unmask murderer, but soon goes crazy himself. Powerful melodrama with raw, emotional impact. Script by director Fuller.

Shock Treatment (1964) 94m. ** D: Denis Sanders. Lauren Bacall, Stuart Whitman, Carol Lynley, Roddy McDowall, Ossie Davis, Douglass Dumbrille. Contrived thriller located at mental institution. Stereotyped performances.

Shocking Miss Pilgrim, The (1947) C-85m. ** D: George Seaton. Betty Grable, Dick Haymes, Anne Revere, Allyn Joslyn, Gene Lockhart, Elizabeth Patterson. Labored story of pioneer woman in business world. Fair Gershwin score includes "For You, For Me, For Evermore."

Shockproof (1949) 79m. *** D: Douglas Sirk. Cornel Wilde, Patricia Knight, John Baragrey, Esther Minciotti, Howard St. John. Parole officer Wilde is lured into love affair with parolee Knight which threatens to destroy him. Stylish film noir which unfortunately cops out at the end.

Shoe Shine (1946-Italian) 93m. **** D: Vittorio De Sica. Rinaldo Smerdoni, Franco Interlenghi, Annielo Mele, Bruno Ortensi, Pacifico Astrologo. Excellent postwar Italian film of two youngsters who become involved in sordid life and reform school.

Shoes of the Fisherman, The (1968) C-157m. ** D: Michael Anderson. Anthony Quinn, Laurence Olivier, Oskar Werner, David Janssen, Vittorio De Sica, Leo McKern, John Gielgud, Barbara Jefford. Pope Quinn tries to fend off atomic war plus starvation in Red China for half a film while correspondent Janssen tries to patch up his petty marital problems rest of the time. Fine cast is wasted in slapdash film version of Morris L. West's bestseller, dully directed by Anderson.

Shoot (1976-Canadian) C-98m. BOMB D: Harvey Hart. Cliff Robertson, Ernest Borgnine, Henry Silva, James Blendick, Larry Reynolds, Les Carlson, Kate Reid, Helen Shaver. There's a faint echo of DELIVERANCE in this ludicrous tale of gun-happy pals who allow the shooting of one hunter to escalate into warfare. Supposedly anti-gun, the film is also apparently anti-entertainment.

Shoot First (1953-British) 88m. **½ D: Robert Parrish, Joel McCrea, Evelyn Keyes, Herbert Lom, Marius Goring. Capable cast helps this routine espionage tale. Originally titled ROUGH SHOOT.

Shoot Loud, Louder . . . I Don't Understand (1966-Italian) C-100m. ** D: Eduardo De Filippo. Marcello Mastroianni, Raquel Welch, Guido Alberti, Leopoldo Trieste. Surrealistic but flat film in which Mastroianni plays antique dealer whose life suddenly becomes very complex.

Shoot Out at Medicine Bend (1957) 87m. ** D: Richard L. Bare. Randolph Scott, James Craig, Angie Dickinson, Dani Crayne, James Garner, Gordon Jones. Fair studio Western features Scott as leader of group avenging death of brother at hands of Sioux Indians and men who supplied faulty guns and ammunition.

Shoot the Piano Player (1962-French) 85m. **** D: François Truffaut. Charles Aznavour, Marie Dubois, Nicole Berger, Michele Mercier. Aznavour is marvelous as antihero playing away in rundown Parisian cafe, pushed by ambitious girlfriend to resume once-prominent concert career.

Shooting, The (1967) C-82m. *** D: Monte Hellman. Millie Perkins, Jack Nicholson, Will Hutchins, Warren Oates. Cryptic, unconventional Western with deceptively familiar revenge "story." Ultimately powerful film, with offbeat performance by Nicholson as a hired gun . . . and an incredible, unexpected finale.

Shooting High (1940) 65m. *½ D: Alfred E. Green. Jane Withers,

Gene Autry, Marjorie Weaver, Robert Lowery, Jack Carson. Overhelpful Withers, aided by cowboy Autry tries to restore peaceful times to her rambunctious family.

Shootist, The (1976) C-99m. ***½ D: Don Siegel. John Wayne, Lauren Bacall, Ron Howard, James Stewart, Richard Boone, Hugh O'Brien, Harry Morgan, John Carradine, Sheree North, Scatman Crothers. Intelligent story about a legendary gunfighter who learns he has cancer and tries to die in peace, but cannot escape his reputation. A fitting (and poignant) finale to Wayne's career; this was his valedictory film.

Shoot-out (1971) C-95m. ** D: Henry Hathaway. Gregory Peck, Pat Quinn, Robert F. Lyons, Susan Tyrell, Jeff Corey, James Gregory, Rita Gam, Dawn Lyn. Same producer, director and screenwriter of TRUE GRIT in another Western about cowboy and little girl. Formula doesn't work; in spite of title, film has too much talk and not enough action.

Shootout in a One-Dog Town (1974) C-78m. TVM D: Burt Kennedy. Richard Crenna, Richard Egan, Stefanie Powers, Jack Elam, Arthur O'Connell, Michael Ansara, Michael Anderson Jr., Dub Taylor. Frontier banker Crenna is pitted against gangleader Egan and his boys out to steal $200,000 in the vault. Standard hoss-opera. Average.

Shop Around the Corner, The (1940) 97m. ***½ D: Ernst Lubitsch. Margaret Sullavan, James Stewart, Frank Morgan, Joseph Schildkraut, Sara Haden. Lubitsch touch brightens story of budding romance in turn-of-the-century Vienna notions shop; Sullavan and Stewart are perfect team. Remade as IN THE GOOD OLD SUMMERTIME, then musicalized as SHE LOVES ME.

Shop on Main Street, The (1966-Czech) 128m. **** D: Jan Kadar, Elmar Klos. Josef Kroner, Ida Kaminska, Hans Slivkova, Frantisek Holly, Martin Gregor. Potent, poignant drama set in WW2 Czechoslovakia, where an old Jewish woman loses her small button shop, and depends on man who takes it over to shield her from further persecution. Oscar winner as Best Foreign Film.

Shopworn (1932) 72m. ** D: Nick Grinde. Barbara Stanwyck, Regis Toomey, ZaSu Pitts, Lucien Littlefield, Clara Blandick. Standard De-

pression soaper with Toomey's rich family rejecting working girl Stanwyck, who shows 'em all and becomes famous star.

Shopworn Angel, The (1938) 85m. *** D: H. C. Potter. Margaret Sullavan, James Stewart, Walter Pidgeon, Hattie McDaniel, Sam Levene, Nat Pendleton. Stewart and Sullavan are always a fine pair, even in this fairly routine soaper. Naive soldier falls in love with loose-moraled actress, who gradually softens under his influence. Beautifully done, including Slavko Vorkapich's masterful opening WW1 montage. Remake of 1929 film with Gary Cooper and Nancy Carroll.

Short Cut to Hell (1957) 87m. **½ D: James Cagney. Robert Ivers, Georgann Johnson, William Bishop, Murvyn Vye, Yvette Vickers, Roscoe Ates. Generally taut, if uninspired remake of Graham Greene's THIS GUN FOR HIRE, about killer reevaluating his situation. Unusual fling at directing by Cagney.

Short Eyes (1977) C-104m. ***½ D: Robert M. Young. Bruce Davison, Jose Perez, Nathan George, Don Blakely, Shawn Elliott, Miguel Pinero, Curtis Mayfield. Raw, uncompromisingly powerful story of men in prison, from Miguel Pinero's highly acclaimed play. Utterly realistic film was shot at N.Y.C.'s now-shuttered Men's House of Detention, known as The Tombs.

Short Walk to Daylight (1972) C-73m. TVM D: Barry Shear. James Brolin, Don Mitchell, James McEachin, Abbey Lincoln, Brooke Bundy, Lazaro Perez. Violent earthquake derails early morning subway in Manhattan; passengers must grope their way to safety, experience every conceivable hardship. Script piles situation upon situation, strives too hard for documentary effects; otherwise, performances OK. Average.

Shot in the Dark, A (1964) C-101m. *** D: Blake Edwards. Peter Sellers, Elke Sommer, George Sanders, Herbert Lom, Tracy Reed. Hilarious comedy tops PINK PANTHER with Sellers bumbling again as Inspector Clouseau on the loose in Paris with Elke Sommer. Scene in nudist colony is a gem.

Shotgun (1955) C-81m. ** D: Lesley Selander. Sterling Hayden, Zachary Scott, Yvonne De Carlo, Guy Prescott, Angela Greene. Unremarkable Western with sheriff Hayden vs.

culprit Scott; De Carlo is the half-breed girl they love.

Shout, The (1979-British) C-87m. **½ D: Jerzy Skolimowsky. Alan Bates, Susannah York, John Hurt, Robert Stephens, Tim Curry. Well filmed but obscure yarn about an off-his-nut wanderer who dominates the household of a young married couple. Worth a look on a slow evening.

Shout at the Devil (1976-British) C-126m. **½ D: Peter Hunt. Lee Marvin, Roger Moore, Barbara Parkins, Ian Holm, Rene Kolldehoff. Plot-heavy action nonsense, set in Mozambique, about a poacher, his daughter and an expatriate Englishman who eventually set out to blow up a German battle cruiser at the outset of WW1. Occasionally fun but overlong.

Show Boat (1936) 113m. *** D: James Whale. Irene Dunne, Allan Jones, Helen Morgan, Paul Robeson, Charles Winninger, Hattie McDaniel. Entertaining treatment of Jerome Kern-Oscar Hammerstein musical (filmed before in 1929) mixes music, sentiment, and melodrama, with enough great moments to make up for the rest: Robeson doing "Old Man River," Morgan singing her unforgettable "Bill," etc.

Show Boat (1951) C-107m. **½ D: George Sidney. Kathryn Grayson, Ava Gardner, Howard Keel, Joe E. Brown, Marge and Gower Champion, Agnes Moorehead, Robert Sterling, William Warfield. Colorful but empty musical version of Edna Ferber novel of life on the Mississippi in 1900s. Songs: "My Bill," "Can't Help Loving That Man," "Old Man River," "Make Believe."

Show Business (1944) 92m. **½ D: Edwin L. Marin. Eddie Cantor, Joan Davis, George Murphy, Nancy Kelly, Constance Moore. If you like Cantor or Davis you'll enjoy this vaudeville musical entirely supported by them; songs include "It Had To Be You."

Showdown (1963) 79m. ** D: R. G. Springsteen. Audie Murphy, Kathleen Crowley, Charles Drake, Harold Stone. Unremarkable Western with Murphy and Drake escaped convicts involved in a holdup.

Showdown (1973) C-99m. **½ D: George Seaton. Rock Hudson, Dean Martin, Susan Clark, Donald Moffat, John McLiam. Two friends in love with the same woman go their separate ways, until Hudson (now a

sheriff) is forced to hunt down Martin (now a robber). Agreeable but unexceptional Western yarn.

Showdown at Abilene (1956) C-80m. ** D: Charles Haas. Jock Mahoney, Martha Hyer, Lyle Bettger, David Janssen, Grant Williams. Standard Western fare. Mahoney as sheriff returns from Civil War sick of bloodshed.

Showdown at Boot Hill (1958) 72m. ** D: Gene Fowler, Jr. Charles Bronson, Fintan Meyler, Robert Hutton, John Carradine, Carole Mathews. Unpretentious Western of bounty killer Bronson trying to collect reward money.

Shriek of the Mutilated (1974) C-92m. BOMB D: Michael Findlay. Alan Brock, Jennifer Stock, Michael Harris, Tawn Ellis, Darcy Brown. Students hunt abominable snowman, but so-called monster turns out to be a decoy, covering up more grisly activities on remote island. Low-budget junk.

Shrike, The (1955) 88m. **½ D: Jose Ferrer. June Allyson, Jose Ferrer, Joy Page, Ed Platt, Mary Bell. Allyson almost succeeds in change of pace title role, playing ultranag who has driven her theater director husband (Ferrer) into a nervous breakdown. Based on Joseph Kramm play.

Shut My Big Mouth (1942) 71m. ** D: Charles Barton. Joe E. Brown, Adele Mara, Victor Jory, Fritz Feld, Lloyd Bridges, Forrest Tucker, Pedro de Cordoba. Meek Joe goes West and innocently gets mixed up with gang of outlaws.

Shuttered Room, The (1966-British) C-99m. **½ D: David Greene. Gig Young, Carol Lynley, Oliver Reed, Flora Robson. Young couple inherit old house in New England, threatened by local toughs and unseen presence. Good cast deserves better material; even revelation is tame. Beware cuts.

Sicilian Clan, The (1970-French) C-121m. *** D: Henri Verneuil. Jean Gabin, Alain Delon, Lino Ventura, Irina Demick, Amedeo Nazzari, Sydney Chaplin. Gangland family's plans for major jewel heist grow increasingly complex; crime caper on grandiose scale, totally implausible but great fun. Gabin is smooth head of clan, Delon a young ambitious thief hired for the occasion.

Siddhartha (1973) **C-95m.** **½ D: Conrad Rooks. Shashi Kapoor, Simi Garewal, Romesh Shama, Pinchoo Kapoor, Zul Vellani, Amrik Singh. Uneven version of famous Hermann Hesse novel follows Indian as he leaves family to find more exciting life. Too arty, but on-location photography by Sven Nykvist (Ingmar Bergman's cinematographer) is often dazzling; some lovemaking scenes may be cut for TV.

Sidekicks (1974) **C-78m. TVM** D: Burt Kennedy. Larry Hagman, Lou Gossett, Blythe Danner, Jack Elam, Harry Morgan, Gene Evans, Noah Beery, Denver Pyle. Western satire about two inept con men on the sagebrush trial trying to collect an outlaw bounty. Loosely adapted from "The Skin Game" with Gossett reprising his role of college graduate posing as a Civil War slave and Hagman as the pal continually trying to "sell" him. Average.

Sidelong Glances of a Pigeon-Kicker SEE: Pigeons

Side Street (1949) 83m. *** D: Anthony Mann. Farley Granger, Cathy O'Donnell, James Craig, Paul Kelly, Jean Hagen, Paul Harvey. Grim drama of poor clerk Granger whose minor theft snowballs, affecting his whole life.

Sidewalks of London (1938-British) 84m. *** D: Tim Whelan. Charles Laughton, Vivien Leigh, Rex Harrison, Larry Adler, Tyrone Guthrie. Atmospheric froth of street entertainer Laughton, losing protegee Leigh to aristocratic songwriter Harrison. Stars are wonderful. Original title: ST. MARTIN'S LANE.

Sidewalks of New York (1931) 70m. ** D: Jules White, Zion Myers. Buster Keaton, Anita Page, Cliff Edwards, Frank Rowan, Norman Phillips Jr. Nowhere near Keaton's silent-film classics, but this talkie vehicle has some funny moments as witless young millionaire tries to reform tough street gang.

Sidewinder 1 (1977) **C-97m.** *½ D: Earl Bellamy. Marjoe Gortner, Michael Parks, Susan Howard, Alex Cord, Charlotte Rae, Bill Vint. Lowgrade actioner about motocross (motorcycle) racing; some exciting scenes, lots of nonacting.

Sidney Sheldon's Bloodline SEE: Bloodline

Siege (1978) **C-100m. TVM** D: Richard Pearce. Martin Balsam, Sylvia Sidney, Dorian Harewood, James Sutorius. Tough senior citizen takes a stand against the gang that's been terrorizing the community. Balsam towers as the one-man vigilante army in this well-written drama. Above average.

Siege at Red River, The (1954) **C-81m.** **½ D: Rudolph Mate. Van Johnson, Joanne Dru, Richard Boone, Milburn Stone, Jeff Morrow. Predictable Western set during Civil War days with an Indian attack finale.

Siege of Pinchgut SEE: Four Desperate Men

Siege of Sidney Street, The (1960-British) 94m. ** D: Robert Baker, Monty Berman. Donald Sinden, Nicole Berger, Kieron Moore, Peter Wyngarde. Based on real incident, this film traces account of anarchists in 1910 London, with climactic confrontation between hundreds of cops and battling criminals.

Siege of Syracuse (1962-Italian) **C-97m.** *½ D: Pietro Francisci. Rossano Brazzi, Tina Louise, Enrico Maria Salerno, Gino Cervi. Another costumer more notable for what it promises than delivers.

Siege of the Saxons (1963-British) **C-85m.** **½ D: Nathan Juran. Janette Scott, Ronald Lewis, Ronald Howard, John Laurie, Mark Dignam. Colorful escapism about King Arthur's daughter trying to protect her kingdom, and her right to marry the knight she chooses, from takeover by nefarious Edmund of Cornwall.

Sierra (1950) **C-83m.** **½ D: Alfred E. Green. Audie Murphy, Wanda Hendrix, Dean Jagger, Burl Ives, Sara Allgood, James Arness. Capable cast elevates story of son and father on the lam from the law, trying to prove dad's innocence of crime. Remake of 1938 film FORBIDDEN VALLEY.

Sierra Baron (1958) **C-80m.** ** D: James B. Clark. Brian Keith, Rick Jason, Rita Gam, Mala Powers, Steve Brodie. Western set in 19thcentury California and Mexico has virtue of pleasing scenery, marred by usual land-grabbing shoot-out plot.

Sierra Passage (1951) 81m. *½ D: Frank McDonald. Wayne Morris, Lola Albright, Alan Hale, Jr., Roland Winters. Quickie oater with Morris on manhunt for father's murderer.

Sierra Stranger (1957) 74m. *½ D: Lee Sholem. Howard Duff, Dick Foran, Barton MacLane, Gloria McGhee. Tame dust-raiser of Duff intervening in a lynching, romancing McGhee.

Sign of the Cross, The (1932) 120m. **½ D: Cecil B. DeMille. Fredric March, Elissa Landi, Charles Laughton, Claudette Colbert, Ian Keith, Vivian Tobin, Nat Pendleton, Joe Bonomo. Well-meaning but heavy-handed account of Christians seeking religious freedom in Rome under Emperor Nero. Very slow going, despite fine work by March as Marcus Superbus, Laughton as Nero, and especially Colbert as alluring Poppaea. Prologue added in 1944 is no help.

Sign of the Gladiator (1959-Italian) C-84m. *½ D: Vittorio Musy Glori. Anita Ekberg, Georges Marchal, Folco Lulli, Chelo Alonso, Jacques Sernas. Gladiator allows himself to be captured by queen of Syria so he can win her confidence.

Sign of the Pagan (1954) C-92m. **½ D: Douglas Sirk. Jeff Chandler, Jack Palance, Ludmilla Tcherina, Rita Gam, Jeff Morrow, Alexander Scourby. Uneven script hampers story of Attila the Hun threatening Rome, but Sirk's tylish direction helps somewhat. Originally made in 3D.

Sign of the Ram (1948) 84m. **½ D: John Sturges. Susan Peters, Alexander Knox, Peggy Ann Garner, Dame May Whitty, Phyllis Thaxter, Ron Randell. Well-wrought drama of crippled wife using ailment to hamstring husband and children.

Sign of Zorro, The (1960) 91m. *½ D: Norman Foster, Lewis R. Foster. Guy Williams, Henry Calvin, Gene Sheldon, Britt Lomond, George J. Lewis, Lisa Gaye. Several episodes of Disney's "Zorro" TV show pasted together; clumsy continuity undermines what charm the series had to offer.

Signpost to Murder (1965) 74m. **½ D: George Englund. Stuart Whitman, Joanne Woodward, Edward Mulhare, Alan Napier, Joyce Worsley, Murray Matheson. Escapee from prison for criminally insane seeks shelter in home of woman whose husband is away. Contrived plot mars thriller but strong performances help.

Silence (1974) C-88m. **½ D: John Korty. Will Geer, Ellen Geer, Richard Kelton, Ian Geer Flanders, Craig Kelly. Outdoor drama of autistic boy Flanders lost in the wilderness is a Geer family affair, interestingly done. Aka CRAZY JACK AND THE BOY.

Silence, The (1963-Swedish) 95m. ***½ D: Ingmar Bergman. Ingrid Thulin, Gunnel Lindblom, Hakan Jahnberg, Birger Malmsten. Stark, forceful symbolic narrative of two sisters who stop at a hotel in a North European city. One sister (Thulin) is a frustrated lesbian with no future, the other (Lindblom) a free-loving mother of a 10-year-old boy.

Silence, The (1975) C-78m. TVM D: Joseph Hardy. Richard Thomas, Cliff Gorman, George Hern, Percy Granger, James Mitchell, John Kellogg. West Point cadet James Pelosi (Thomas) relives for writer Stanley Greenberg (Gorman) his true-life experiences of being subjected to total exile when accused of cheating. Mechanical performances by Thomas and Gorman (everyone else is reduced to a walk-on) make this one a bore. Average.

Silencers, The (1966) C-102m. **½ D: Phil Karlson. Dean Martin, Stella Stevens, Daliah Lavi, Victor Buono, Arthur O'Connell, Cyd Charisse, Robert Webber, James Gregory. First of Matt Helm secret agent series, also the best, faint praise though that is. However, Dino's problems with scatterbrained Stevens do generate some laughs.

Silent Call, The (1961) 63m. BOMB D: John Bushelman. Gail Russell, Roger Mobley. Very mild yarn of a dog traveling cross-country to find his master in L.A.

Silent Enemy, The (1958-British) 92m. **½ D: William Fairchild. Laurence Harvey, Dawn Addams, John Clements, Michael Craig. British Naval frogmen, headed by Harvey, are assigned to combat enemy counterpart during WW2; underwater sequences well handled, with some pre-THUNDERBALL gimmicks.

Silent Gun, The (1969) C-75m. TVM D: Michael Caffey. Lloyd Bridges, John Beck, Ed Begley, Edd Byrnes, Pernell Roberts, Susan Howard. After vowing never to use gun again, famed shooter puts himself to test and rides into town war between Boss Banner (Roberts) and pioneer settler Cole (Begley). Sad waste of talent via ludicrous script, boring direction. Average.

Silent Movie (1976) C-86m. **½ D: Mel Brooks. Mel Brooks, Marty Feldman, Dom DeLuise, Bernadette Peters, Sid Caesar; guests Burt Reynolds, James Caan, Liza Minnelli, Paul Newman, Anne Bancroft, Marcel Marceau, Harry Ritz. Disappointing attempt to revive silent comedy with Brooks as movie producer hoping for comeback. Blackout gags range from very funny to misfire. Results are only mild instead of the knockout they should have been.

Silent Night, Bloody Night (1973) C-87m. ** D: Theodore Gershuny. Patrick O'Neal, James Patterson, Mary Woronov, Astrid Heeren, John Carradine, Walter Abel. Uneven low-budgeter about escaped killer from insane asylum terrorizing small New England town, and inhabitants of mysterious old mansion that's up for sale.

Silent Night, Evil Night SEE: **Black Christmas**

Silent Night, Lonely Night (1969) C-98m. TVM D: Daniel Petrie. Lloyd Bridges, Shirley Jones, Carrie Snodgress, Robert Lipton, Lynn Carlin, Cloris Leachman. New England resort setting for chance meeting that turns to romance for two tired, lonely middle-agers (Bridges and Jones). Script—not so-so direction—culprit here in that melodrama stops far short of credibility. Average.

Silent Partner, The (1978-Canadian) C-103m. *** D: Daryl Duke. Susannah York, Christopher Plummer, Elliott Gould, Celina Lopez, Michael Kirby, Ken Pogue, John Candy. Offbeat film about dull bank teller (Gould) who inadvertently becomes involved with psychotic robber (Plummer). Well directed, with fine eye for detail, but bursts of graphic violence are jarring.

Silent Running (1972) C-89m. *** D: Douglas Trumbull. Bruce Dern, Cliff Potts, Ron Rifkin, Jesse Vint. Space-age ecology tale of botanists' fight on space station to keep Earth's final vegetation samples from being destroyed. Interesting story marked directional debut of special-effects whiz Trumbull (2001, CLOSE ENCOUNTERS).

Silent Victory: The Kitty O'Neil Story (1979) C-100m. TVM D: Lou

Antonio. Stockard Channing, James Farentino, Colleen Dewhurst, Edward Albert, Brian Dennehy. The real-life account of a deaf girl's victory over her handicap to become a top stuntwoman in Hollywood. Above average.

Silent Witness (1932) 73m. ** D: Marcel Varnel, R. L. Hough. Lionel Atwill, Greta Nissen, Weldon Heyburn, Helen Mack, Bramwell Fletcher. Stagy but pretty interesting courtroom drama with Atwill trying to protect his son from murder charge by taking blame himself.

Silent World, The (1956-French) C-86m. *** D: Jacques-Yves Cousteau. Frederic Duman, Albert Falco, Jacques-Yves Cousteau. Award-winning documentary of ocean exploration of fauna and flora of the deep.

Silk Stockings (1957) C-117m. *** D: Rouben Mamoulian. Fred Astaire, Cyd Charisse, Janis Paige, Peter Lorre, George Tobias. Words, music, dance blend perfectly in stylish remake of Garbo's NINOTCHKA. This time Charisse is cold Russian on Paris mission, Astaire the movie director man-about-town who warms her up.

Silken Affair, The (1957-British) 96m. **½ D: Roy Kellino. David Niven, Genevieve Page, Ronald Squire, Wilfrid Hyde-White. Droll little comedy of meek accountant Niven sparked by saucy Page into some fast bookkeeping manipulations.

Silver Bears (1978) C-113m. *** D: Ivan Passer. Michael Caine, Cybill Shepherd, Louis Jourdan, Martin Balsam, Stephane Audran, Tommy Smothers, David Warner, Jay Leno. Entertaining comedy better suited to TV than theater screens; fine cast in story of high-level chicanery in the world's silver market. Adapted from Paul Erdman's novel by Peter Stone; filmed in Switzerland and Morocco.

Silver Chalice, The (1954) C-144m. ** D: Victor Saville. Virginia Mayo, Pier Angeli, Jack Palance, Paul Newman, Walter Hampden, Joseph Wiseman, Alexander Scourby, Lorne Greene, E. G. Marshall, Natalie Wood. Newman's screen debut is undistinguished in story of Greek who designs framework for cup used at Last Supper. From Costain novel.

Silver City (1951) C-90m. ** D: Byron Haskin. Edmond O'Brien, Yvonne De Carlo, Richard Arlen,

Silver Dollar (1932) 84m. **½ D: Alfred E. Green. Edward G. Robinson, Bebe Daniels, Aline MacMahon, Robert Warwick, Jobyna Howland. True story (though names are changed) of self-made silver tycoon H. A. W. Tabor, who helped build Denver from mining camp to a thriving city. One of America's great sagas, hampered by unimaginative presentation.

Silver Lode (1954) C-80m. **½ D: Allan Dwan. John Payne, Lizabeth Scott, Dan Duryea, Dolores Moran. Dynamic cast boosts this story of man trying to clear himself of murder charge.

Silver Queen (1942) 80m. ** D: Lloyd Bacon. George Brent, Priscilla Lane, Bruce Cabot, Lynne Overman, Eugene Pallette, Guinn Williams. Post-Civil War tinsel of devoted girl raising money for father; hubby throws it away on "worthless" silver mine.

Silver River (1948) 110m. *½ D: Raoul Walsh. Errol Flynn, Ann Sheridan, Thomas Mitchell, Bruce Bennett, Tom D'Andrea. Mediocre Flynn vehicle: Ann and Errol marry out West, he becomes corrupt.

Silver Streak (1976) C-113m. *** D: Arthur Hiller. Gene Wilder, Jill Clayburgh, Richard Pryor, Patrick McGoohan, Ned Beatty, Ray Walston, Scatman Crothers. Nutty blend of comedy, romance, action and suspense as mild mannered editor Wilder becomes involved in murder plot on cross-country train ride. Switch from comedy to violence is sometimes jarring, but on the whole a highly entertaining picture.

Silver Whip, The (1953) 73m. **½ D: Harmon Jones. Dale Robertson, Rory Calhoun, Robert Wagner, Kathleen Crowley, Lola Albright. Occasionally actionful Western of outlaws vs. stage line.

Simba (1955-British) C-99m. ***½ D: Brian Desmond Hurst. Dirk Bogarde, Virginia McKenna, Basil Sydney, Donald Sinden. Fine cast in story of young man arriving in Kenya only to find brother killed by Mau Maus. Some grisly scenes.

Simon (1980) C-97m. **½ D: Marshall Brickman. Alan Arkin, Madeline Kahn, Austin Pendleton, Judy Graubart, William Finley, Fred Gwynne, Adolph Green. Uneven comedy about psychology professor (Arkin) who's brainwashed by group of think-tank weirdos to believe he's come from another planet. There's a cruel edge to the humor, and signs of a serious film trying to break out, in screenwriter Brickman's directorial debut.

Simon and Laura (1956-British) C-91m. **½ D: Muriel Box. Peter Finch, Kay Kendall, Muriel Pavlow, Ian Carmichael, Maurice Denham. Spunky farce involving Finch and Kendall, a married acting couple whose TV image contradicts their violent offscreen battles.

Sin of Harold Diddlebock, The (1947) 90m. **½ D: Preston Sturges. Harold Lloyd, Frances Ramsden, Jimmy Conlin, Raymond Walburn, Edgar Kennedy, Arline Judge, Lionel Stander, Rudy Vallee. Fascinating idea of updating Lloyd's 1920s character to show what's happened to that go-getter doesn't fulfill its promise. Aimless comedy can't top opening sequence from THE FRESHMAN (1925), despite enthusiasm of fine cast. Reedited to 79m. and reissued in 1950 as MAD WEDNESDAY.

Sin Town (1942) 75m. **½ D: Ray Enright. Constance Bennett, Broderick Crawford, Anne Gwynne, Ward Bond, Andy Devine, Leo Carrillo, Patric Knowles, Hobart Bosworth. Fast-moving actioner of town in uproar after newspaper editor is killed; good cast in above-average film.

Sinbad and the Eye of the Tiger (1977-British) C-113m. *½ D: Sam Wanamaker. Patrick Wayne, Jane Seymour, Taryn Power, Margaret Whiting, Patrick Troughton. Dreary followup to GOLDEN VOYAGE OF SINBAD has unusually hackneyed script (even for this kind of film), disappointing Ray Harryhausen effects, and goes on forever. For patient kids only. Taryn is Tyrone Power's daughter.

Sinbad the Sailor (1947) C-117m. *** D: Richard Wallace. Douglas Fairbanks, Jr., Maureen O'Hara, Anthony Quinn, Walter Slezak, George Tobias, Jane Greer. Tongue-in-cheek swashbuckler, with lavish color production. Great fun.

Since You Went Away (1944) 172m. ***½ D: John Cromwell. Claudette Colbert, Jennifer Jones, Joseph Cotten, Shirley Temple, Monty Woolley, Hattie McDaniel, Nazimova, Robert

Walker, Lionel Barrymore. Tearjerker-supreme with Colbert at her valiant best. Story of family suffering through WW2 with many tragedies and complications dates a bit, but still is very smooth film.

Sincerely Yours (1955) **C-115m.** BOMB D: Gordon Douglas. Liberace, Joanne Dru, Dorothy Malone, William Demarest, Richard Eyer, Lurene Tuttle. Remake of George Arliss' MAN WHO PLAYED GOD becomes a tinny vehicle for Liberace.

Sinful Davey (1969-British) **C-95m.** **½ D: John Huston. John Hurt, Pamela Franklin, Nigel Davenport, Ronald Fraser, Robert Morley, Fidelma Murphy, Maxine Audley. Tale of 19th-century Scottish highwayman and his love for a "nice" girl is rather ordinary, but does have pleasant performance by Franklin.

Sing and Swing (1963-British) **75m.** ** D: Lance Comfort. David Hemmings, Veronica Hurst, Jennifer Moss, John Pike. Virtue of modest musical is Hemmings in lead role of messenger boy who joins pals in combo; they record a song, and find their musical career in full sway. Originally titled LIVE IT UP.

Sing, Baby, Sing (1936) **87m.** *** D: Sidney Lanfield. Alice Faye, Adolphe Menjou, Gregory Ratoff, Ted Healy, Patsy Kelly, Tony Martin. Pleasant musicomedy stolen by Menjou as John Barrymore prototype involved with publicity-seeking Faye. Songs: "When Did You Leave Heaven?" "You Turned The Tables On Me," title tune. Ritz Brothers are quite good in their feature-film debut.

Sing, Boy, Sing (1958) **90m.** ** D: Henry Ephron. Tommy Sands, Lili Gentle, Edmond O'Brien, John McIntire. Expanded TV drama of the trials and tribulations of rock 'n' roll star; energetically played by cast.

Sing You Sinners (1938) **88m.** *** D: Wesley Ruggles. Bing Crosby, Fred MacMurray, Donald O'Connor, Elizabeth Patterson, Ellen Drew, John Gallaudet. Gambling gay-blade Crosby can't face responsibility, despite prodding of brother MacMurray. Fine film with "I've Got A Pocketful Of Dreams" and memorable "Small Fry" number featuring young O'Connor.

Sing Your Way Home (1945) **72m.** *½ D: Anthony Mann. Jack Haley, Anne Jeffreys, Marcy McGuire, Glenn Vernon. RKO Pictures mini-

musical set on the high seas with youthful entertainers providing modicum of singing talent.

Sing Your Worries Away (1942) **71m.** ** D: A. Edward Sutherland. June Havoc, Bert Lahr, Buddy Ebsen, Patsy Kelly, Sam Levene, Margaret Dumont, King Sisters, Alvino Rey. Mild musical comedy as the theatrical world and racketeers clash.

Singapore (1947) **79m.** ** D: John Brahm. Fred MacMurray, Ava Gardner, Roland Culver, Richard Haydn, Spring Byington. Weak drama of amnesiac Gardner forgetting her true love MacMurray. Remade as ISTANBUL.

Singapore Woman (1941) **64m.** ** D: Jean Negulesco. Brenda Marshall, David Bruce, Virginia Field, Jerome Cowan, Rose Hobart, Heather Angel. Sluggish account of young rubber planter set upon helping to remove oriental curse from Marshall. Remake of DANGEROUS.

Singer Not the Song, The (1961-British) **C-129m.** **½ D: Roy Baker. Dirk Bogarde, John Mills, Mylene Demongeot, Eric Pohlmann. Offbeat, sluggish yarn set in Mexico involving conflict of Catholic priest and local bandit to control the town, with Demongeot in love with the clergyman.

Singin' in the Rain (1952) **C-103m.** **** D: Gene Kelly, Stanley Donen. Gene Kelly, Debbie Reynolds, Donald O'Connor, Jean Hagen, Cyd Charisse, Madge Blake, Millard Mitchell. Great musical spoofing Hollywood at time of early talking pictures. O'Connor at his peak doing "Make 'em Laugh," Hagen marvelous as squeaky-voiced romantic star. Songs: title tune, "My Lucky Star," "Broadway Melody," "Good Morning."

Singing Guns (1950) **C-91m.** *½ D: R. G. Springsteen. Vaughn Monroe, Ella Raines, Walter Brennan, Ward Bond, Billy Gray. Minor happenings in the old West with singer Monroe in straight role.

Singing Kid, The (1936) **85m.** ** D: William Keighley. Al Jolson, Sybil Jason, Edward Everett Horton, Lyle Talbot, Allen Jenkins, Beverly Roberts, Claire Dodd. Formula musical with E. Y. Harburg-Harold Arlen score is for Jolson fans only, as he plays himself (more or less) in silly plot about thickwitted star's romances. Musical appearances by Cab

Calloway, Wini Shaw, The Yacht Club Boys; blackface finale.

Singing Nun, The (1966) **C-98m.** ** D: Henry Koster. Debbie Reynolds, Ricardo Montalban, Greer Garson, Agnes Moorehead, Chad Everett, Katharine Ross, Ed Sullivan. Syrupy comic-book stuff about Belgian nun whose devotion is split between religious work and making records.

Single Handed SEE: **Sailor of the King**

Sink the Bismarck! (1960-British) **97m.** *** D: Lewis Gilbert. Kenneth More, Dana Wynter, Carl Mohner, Laurence Naismith, Geoffrey Keen, Karel Stepanek, Michael Hordern. Good war film based on fact. Exciting sea battles as British navy starts deadly hunt for famed German war vessel.

Sinner, The SEE: **Desert Desperadoes**

Sinner's Holiday (1930) **60m.** **½ D: John G. Adolfi. Grant Withers, Evalyn Knapp, James Cagney, Joan Blondell, Lucille LaVerne, Noel Madison. Predictable melodrama is interesting to watch, as period piece (with good Coney Island atmosphere) and as film debuts for Cagney and Blondell, recreating stage roles in support of stars Withers and Knapp. Story involves romance, murder, and overprotective mother who runs penny arcade.

Sinners in the Sun (1932) **70m.** ** D: Alexander Hall. Carole Lombard, Chester Morris, Adrienne Ames, Cary Grant, Walter Byron, Alison Skipworth, Rita La Roy, Ida Lewis. Lovely Lombard learns that money isn't all in this slick, typical triangle; Grant has a bit role.

Sins of Jezebel (1953) **C-74m.** *½ D: Reginald Le Borg. Paulette Goddard, George Nader, John Hoyt, Eduard Franz. Embarrassing low-budget costumer with Goddard miscast in title role.

Sins of Rachel Cade, The (1961) **C-124m.** **½ D: Gordon Douglas. Angie Dickinson, Peter Finch, Roger Moore, Woody Strode, Rafer Johnson, Juano Hernandez. Turgid melodrama set in Belgian Congo with Dickinson a missionary nurse involved in romance and native conflicts.

Sins of Rome (1954-Italian) **75m.** ** D: Riccardo Freda. Ludmilla Tcherina, Massimo Girotti, Gianna Maria Canale, Yves Vincent. Rebel slave Spartacus incites fellow prisoners to fight Roman republic. Early Italian spectacle doesn't have cheaper look of later grinds.

Siren of Atlantis (1948) **75m.** BOMB D: Gregg Tallas. Maria Montez, Jean-Pierre Aumont, Dennis O'Keefe, Henry Daniell, Morris Carnovsky. Ridiculous hokum of soldiers Aumont and O'Keefe stumbling upon famed Lost Continent; Montez is the sultry queen.

Siren of Bagdad (1953) **C-77m.** **½ D: Richard Quine. Paul Henreid, Patricia Medina, Hans Conried, Charlie Lung. Comedy-adventure of magician and friend trying to save dancing girls in slave market. Conried provides film's best moments.

Sirocco (1951) **98m.** **½ D: Curtis Bernhardt. Humphrey Bogart, Marta Toren, Lee J. Cobb, Everett Sloane, Zero Mostel. Rugged Bogart perks this yarn of gunrunning set in 1920s Syria.

Sis Hopkins (1941) **98m.** **½ D: Joseph Santley. Judy Canova, Bob Crosby, Charles Butterworth, Jerry Colonna, Susan Hayward, Katharine Alexander. Fairly amusing comedy of country girl who comes to live with social uncle and attends girls' school. Even Canova is restrained!

Sisters (1973) **C-93m.** *** D: Brian DePalma. Margot Kidder, Jennifer Salt, Charles Durning, Barnard Hughes, Lisle Wilson, Bill Finley. Gory tale will certainly be cut for TV, but film in its original form generates tremendous suspense, thanks to eerie plot about reporter Salt witnessing a murder from her apartment; taut direction and great music score by Bernard Herrmann.

Sisters, The (1938) **98m.** *** D: Anatole Litvak. Errol Flynn, Bette Davis, Anita Louise, Ian Hunter, Donald Crisp, Beulah Bondi, Jane Bryan, Lee Patrick, Mayo Methot, Laura Hope Crews, Alan Hale. Davis, Louise, and Bryan are sisters whose marital problems are traced in this lavish film; Bette's got the most trouble, of course, with unreliable husband Flynn in San Francisco, 1905.

Sitting Bull (1954) **C-105m.** ** D: Sidney Salkow. Dale Robertson, Mary Murphy, J. Carrol Naish, Iron Eyes Cody, John Litel. Sluggish nonsense about army officer Robertson's efforts to prove he wasn't being overly helpful to the Indians.

Sitting Pretty (1933) **85m.** **½ D:

Harry Joe Brown. Ginger Rogers, Jack Oakie, Jack Haley, Thelma Todd, Gregory Ratoff, Lew Cody. First half is bouncy yarn of songwriters Oakie and Haley going Hollywood, meeting homespun Rogers, vamp Todd; remainder bogs down, rescued by finale "Did You Ever See a Dream Walking."

Sitting Pretty (1948) 84m. ***½ D: Walter Lang. Robert Young, Maureen O'Hara, Clifton Webb, Richard Haydn, Louise Allbritton, Ed Begley. Webb is perfect as self-centered genius who accepts job as full-time babysitter in gossip-laden suburban town. Highly entertaining comedy.

Sitting Target (1972-British) C-93m. *½ D: Douglas Hickox. Oliver Reed, Jill St. John, Ian McShane, Edward Woodward, Frank Finlay, Freddie Jones. Reed breaks out of prison to settle two scores—one of them with his cheating wife (St. John). Violent, generally unpleasant film.

Situation Hopeless—But Not Serious (1965) 97m. ** D: Gottfried Reinhardt. Alec Guinness, Michael Connors, Robert Redford, Anita Hoefer, Mady Rahl, Paul Dahlke. Odd little comedy about German clerk Guinness holding two American (Redford, Connors) prisoners for years after WW2 has ended. Interesting characterization by Guinness, but a flat film.

Six Black Horses (1962) C-80m. ** D: Harry Keller. Audie Murphy, Dan Duryea, Joan O'Brien, George Wallace. O'Brien pays two men to take her across Indian lands, intending to murder gunman of duo who killed her husband.

Six Bridges to Cross (1955) 96m. **½ D: Joseph Pevney. Tony Curtis, Julia Adams, George Nader, Sal Mineo, Jay C. Flippen. Entertaining account of Brinks robbery, tracing events leading up to famous heist; on-location filming in Boston.

Six Day Bike Rider (1934) 69m. **½ D: Lloyd Bacon. Joe E. Brown, Maxine Doyle, Frank McHugh, Lottie Williams. Intriguing gimmick has Brown trying to impress girlfriend by entering marathon race; good little comedy.

Six Hours to Live (1932) 78m. ** D: William Dieterle. Warner Baxter, Miriam Jordan, John Boles, George Marion, Beryl Mercer, Irene Ware. Unusual story of diplomat Baxter whose stubbornness at international trade conference leads to his murder; scientist brings him back to life for six hours. Stodgy production spoils interesting idea.

Six Lessons from Madame La Zonga (1941) 62m. ** D: John Rawlins. Lupe Velez, Leon Errol, Helen Parrish, Charles Lang, William Frawley, Eddie Quillan, Shemp Howard. Good cast of professional laughgetters in typical, silly outing; Leon goes Latin, and Lupe goes gold-digging after him in shipboard comedy. Title derived from popular song of the day.

Six Million Dollar Man, The (1973) C-73m. TVM D: Richard Irving. Lee Majors, Darren McGavin, Martin Balsam, Barbara Anderson, Charles Knox Robinson. Test pilot crash-lands, government steps in and has him confined to hospital where new techniques enable body to be rebuilt. Result: superhuman strength, whereupon government convinces pilot to undertake secret mission. Pilot for successful TV series. Average.

Six of a Kind (1934) 62m. *** D: Leo McCarey. W. C. Fields, George Burns, Gracie Allen, Charlie Ruggles, Mary Boland, Alison Skipworth. George and Gracie drive Mary and Charlie crazy traveling westward on vacation; Fields as pool-playing sheriff adds to confusion. Zany, wonderful nonsense.

633 Squadron (1964-British) C-101m. **½ D: Walter Grauman. Cliff Robertson, George Chakiris, Maria Perschy, Harry Andrews. Pretentious WW2 aviation film about the group's air mission to bomb German-run factory in Norway. Robertson and Chakiris are stiff-lipped throughout.

Sixty Glorious Years (1938-British) 90m. *** D: Herbert Wilcox. Anna Neagle, Anton Walbrook, C. Aubrey Smith, Walter Rilla, Charles Carson. Neagle's follow-up to VICTORIA THE GREAT is a repeat of her fine performance as England's legendary queen; good production values.

Skag (1980) C-150m. TVM D: Frank Perry. Karl Malden, Piper Laurie, Craig Wasson, Peter Gallagher, Leslie Ackerman, Kathryn Holcomb, George Voskovec. Malden's powerhouse performance as a veteran steelworker felled by a serious stroke carries this blue-collar drama (written by Abby Mann) that spun off to a series. Above average.

Skateboard (1977) C-97m. ** D:

George Gage. Allen Garfield, Kathleen Lloyd, Leif Garrett, Richard Van Der Wyk, Tony Alva, Antony Carbone. In trouble with his bookie, Garfield organizes local skateboarders into moneymaking team. Good premise given lackluster treatment.

Skatetown, U.S.A. (1979) **C-98m.** *½ D: William A. Levey. Scott Baio, Flip Wilson, Ron Palillo, Ruth Buzzi, Dave Mason, Greg Bradford, Kelly Lang, Billy Barty. Comedy fantasy for the light of heart and slow of brain, with occasionally amusing comedy bits spicing plotless look at the ultimate roller-disco palace. Film's only real distinction is that it's better than ROLLER BOOGIE.

Ski Bum, The (1971) **C-136m.** BOMB D: Bruce Clark. Zalman King, Charlotte Ramping, Joseph Mell, Dimitra Arliss, Anna Karen, Tedd King. Deservedly obscure film version of Romain Gary's novel about a ski bum who goes establishment, and winds up a pawn in a shady business deal.

Ski Fever (1969) **C-98m.** *½ D: Curt Siodmak. Martin Milner, Claudia Martin, Vivi Bach, Dietmar Schoenherr, Toni Sailor, Dorit Dom. American ski instructor giving lessons in Austria to finance his education is unpleasantly surprised to learn his duties include entertaining guests after hours. Why complain when most of them are good-looking girls? Female lead is Dean Martin's daughter.

Ski Lift to Death (1978) **C-100m.** TVM D: William Wiard. Deborah Raffin, Charles Frank, Howard Duff, Don Galloway, Don Johnson, Clu Gulager, Gail Strickland. Formula suspense thriller set in a ski resort—and even skiing star Suzy Chaffee is dragged in to give it some dazzle. Average.

Ski Party (1965) **C-90m.** ** D: Alan Rafkin. Frankie Avalon, Dwayne Hickman, Deborah Walley, Yvonne Craig, Robert Q. Lewis, Bobbi Shaw, Aron Kincaid. Beach party gang puts on some clothes in this one, but the shenanigans are the same.

Skidoo (1969) **C-98m.** **½ D: Otto Preminger. Jackie Gleason, Carol Channing, Frankie Avalon, Fred Clark, Michael Constantine, Frank Gorshin, John Phillip Law, Peter Lawford, Burgess Meredith, George Raft, Cesar Romero, Mickey Rooney, Groucho Marx, Austin Pendleton.

Avalon plays an up-and-coming gangster, Groucho a mob kingpin named "God," and every single credit to the film is sung. Consequently, about one in a thousand will have the temperament to like this; everyone else will sit there dumbstruck.

Skin Game (1971) **C-102m.** ***½ D: Paul Bogart. James Garner, Louis Gossett, Susan Clark, Brenda Sykes, Edward Asner, Andrew Duggan. Exceptional comedy about Garner and Gossett running con-game posing as master and slave in post-Civil War era. Serious undertones enhance this offbeat, entertaining film. Clark delightful as female con-artist who joins duo.

Skipper Surprised His Wife, The (1950) 85m. *½ D: Elliott Nugent. Robert Walker, Joan Leslie, Edward Arnold, Spring Byington, Jan Sterling. Unsurprising comedy; weak material about sailor Walker running home like ship. Good cast wasted.

Skirts Ahoy! (1952) **C-109m.** **½ D: Sidney Lanfield. Esther Williams, Joan Evans, Vivian Blaine, Barry Sullivan, Keefe Brasselle. Chipper cast can't buoy this worn-out story of three WAVES and their boyfriends.

Skull, The (1965-British) **C-83m.** **½ D: Freddie Francis. Peter Cushing, Patrick Wymark, Christopher Lee, Nigel Green, Jill Bennett, Michael Gough, George Coulouris, Patrick Magee. Good cast lends needed support to questionable script of skull of Marquis de Sade that has mysterious powers.

Skullduggery (1970) **C-105m.** BOMB D: Gordon Douglas. Burt Reynolds, Susan Clark, Roger C. Carmel, Chips Rafferty. Ridiculous search for the missing link; search for another movie instead.

Sky Above, The Mud Below, The (1961-French) **C-90m.** *** D: Pierre-Dominique Gaisseau. Narrated by William Peacock. Academy Award-winning documentary showing variety of primitive life found within confines of Dutch New Guinea.

Sky Commando (1953) 69m. *½ D: Fred F. Sears. Dan Duryea, Frances Gifford, Michael Connors, Michael Fox. Limping account of the responsibilities of being an Air Force officer, with usual rash of hackneyed situations.

Sky Devils (1932) 89m. ** D: A.

Edward Sutherland. Spencer Tracy, William "Stage" Boyd, Ann Dvorak, George Cooper, Billy Bevan, Yola D'Avril. Two dumbbells try to avoid WW1 service in this disjointed, low-grade comedy; Dvorak is beautiful, leftover flying scenes from HELL'S ANGELS are impressive, but stupidity reigns overall.

Sky Dragon (1949) 64m. D: Lesley Selander. Roland Winters, Keye Luke, Mantan Moreland, Tim Ryan, Milburn Stone, Joel Marston, Noel Neill, Iris Adrian, Elena Verdugo, Lyle Talbot. SEE: **Charlie Chan** series.

Sky Full of Moon (1952) 73m. ** D: Norman Foster. Carleton Carpenter, Jan Sterling, Keenan Wynn, Elaine Stewart. Unassuming comedy of naive cowpoke falling in love with a not-so-innocent in Las Vegas.

Sky Heist (1975) C-100m. TVM D: Lee H. Katzin. Don Meredith, Joseph Campanella, Stefanie Powers, Frank Gorshin, Shelley Fabares, Larry Wilcox. Police helicopter is hijacked as part of a scheme to make off with $10-million in gold bullion. Meredith heads team of airborne cops in pursuit of the perpetrators. Average.

Sky High (1922) 51m. *** D: Lynn Reynolds. Tom Mix, J. Farrell MacDonald, Eva Novak, Sid Jordan, William Buckley. Tom Mix eschews cowboy garb to play immigration officer out to crack alien-smuggling ring on Mexican border; action packed entertainment.

Sky Murder (1940) 72m. ** D: George B. Seitz. Walter Pidgeon, Donald Meek, Kaaren Verne, Edward Ashley, Joyce Compton, Tom Conway. Pidgeon as detective Nick Carter decides to help refugee Verne in above-average private-eye yarn.

Sky Riders (1976) C-93m. *** D: Douglas Hickox. James Coburn, Susannah York, Robert Culp, Charles Aznavour, Harry Andrews, John Beck. Lively thriller about a political kidnapping, highlighted by spectacular sequences of hanggliding. The aerial derring-do and the magnificent Greek scenery make this one worth sitting through.

Sky's the Limit, The (1943) 89m. *** D: Edward H. Griffith. Fred Astaire, Joan Leslie, Robert Benchley, Robert Ryan, Elizabeth Patterson, Marjorie Gateson. Fred's a flier on leave who meets photographer Leslie; Benchley's dinner speech,

Astaire's "One For My Baby" and "My Shining Hour" make this worthwhile.

Skyjacked (1972) C-100m. **½ D: John Guillermin. Charlton Heston, Yvette Mimieux, James Brolin, Claude Akins, Jeanne Crain, Susan Dey, Roosevelt Grier, Mariette Hartley, Walter Pidgeon. Commercial flight hijacked to Russia. Entertaining for first half, even exciting; second half deteriorates. Good cast will distract some from tedium elsewhere.

Skylark (1941) 94m. ***½ D: Mark Sandrich. Claudette Colbert, Ray Milland, Brian Aherne, Binnie Barnes, Walter Abel, Ernest Cossart, Grant Mitchell. Sophisticated romance with Aherne trying to take Claudette away from business-minded husband Milland. Stars are at their peak.

Skyscraper Wilderness SEE: **Big City, The**

Skyway to Death (1974) C-78m. TVM D: Gordon Hessler. Ross Martin, Stefanie Powers, Bobby Sherman, Nancy Malone, John Astin, Joseph Campanella, Tige Andrews. Group of vacationers trapped in a cable car 8000 feet up between mountain peaks; rescue attempt is hindered by an approaching windstorm. Written to formula, and acted that way as well. Average.

Slams, The (1973) C-97m. ** D: Jonathan Kaplan. Jim Brown, Judy Pace, Roland "Bob" Harris, Frank de Kova, Ted Cassidy. Mindless actioner has Brown in L.A. prison after stashing away a heroin cache and $1.5 million. Halfway through, comedy takes over for a fast pickup.

Slander (1956) 81m. **½ D: Roy Rowland. Van Johnson, Ann Blyth, Steve Cochran, Marjorie Rambeau, Richard Eyer. Slick, superficial "inside study" of the smut magazines, focusing on their exclusive on a TV personality.

Slap Shot (1977) C-122m. *** D: George Roy Hill. Paul Newman, Michael Ontkean, Lindsay Crouse, Jennifer Warren, Melinda Dillon, Strother Martin, Jerry Houser. Newman is star of bush-league hockey team that's going nowhere until they decide to play dirty. Uneven but raucously funny at times, with very satisfying wrapup. Andrew Duncan is hilarious as local sports broadcaster. If they cut the four-letter words for TV the running time should be about 17m.

Slattery's Hurricane (1949) **83m.** **½ D: Andre de Toth. Richard Widmark, Linda Darnell, Veronica Lake, John Russell, Gary Merrill. Weather-pilot Widmark, in midst of storm, thinks back on his life; Darnell and Lake are his two loves. Interesting idea; script by Herman Wouk.

Slaughter (1972) C-92m. ** D: Jack Starrett. Jim Brown, Stella Stevens, Rip Torn, Don Gordon, Cameron Mitchell, Marlene Clark, Robert Phillips. Stevens and Torn are far too good for this violent tripe about ex-Green Beret Brown who goes after syndicate when it kills his parents.

Slaughter on Tenth Avenue (1957) 103m. *** D: Arnold Laven. Richard Egan, Jan Sterling, Dan Duryea, Julie Adams, Walter Matthau, Sam Levene. Well-handled waterfront racketeer exposé, set in N.Y.C. with good supporting cast.

Slaughter Trail (1951) C-78m. ** D: Irving Allen. Brian Donlevy, Gig Young, Virginia Grey, Andy Devine. Routine narrative of outlaws killing Indians and cavalry men to get what they want.

Slaughterhouse Five (1972) C-104m. *** D: George Roy Hill. Michael Sacks, Ron Leibman, Eugene Roche, Sharon Gans, Valerie Perrine, John Dehner. Sometimes draggy, sometimes on-target, sprawling view of life through eyes of one Billy Pilgrim, professional nobody. Big-budget adaptation of Kurt Vonnegut's bizarre fantasy novel of same name, hard going for those unfamiliar with author's point of view, gains through repeat viewings. Beware cuts.

Slave, The (1963-Italian) C-102m. *½ D: Sergio Corbucci. Steve Reeves, Jacques Sernas, Gianna Maria Canale, Claudio Gora. Interminable Italian spectacle. Son of Spartacus learns story of father, vows vengeance. Good photography only asset. Also titled SON OF SPARTACUS.

Slave Girl (1947) C-80m. **½ D: Charles Lamont. Yvonne De Carlo, George Brent, Broderick Crawford, Albert Dekker, Lois Collier, Andy Devine. Tale of adventure with evil potentate holding Americans prisoner; not to be taken seriously, enjoyable on that scale.

Slave Ship (1937) 92m. *** D: Tay Garnett. Warner Baxter, Wallace Beery, Elizabeth Allan, Mickey Rooney, George Sanders, Jane Darwell, Joseph Schildkraut. Rousing drama of slave ship with fine atmosphere, good Beery-Rooney teaming, plenty of action.

Slaves (1969) C-110m. *½ D: Herbert J. Biberman. Ossie Davis, Stephen Boyd, Gale Sondergaard, Dionne Warwick, Oscar Paul Jones. Sets race relations back at least 100 years. Davis is treasured slave in white household, then changes start to come. Boyd lacks much in his Simon Legree-type role.

Slaves of Babylon (1953) C-82m. ** D: William Castle. Richard Conte, Linda Christian, Maurice Schwartz, Michael Ansara, Julie Newmar. Jumbled biblical adventure mixed with romance. Nebuchadnezzar faces army of Israelites led by shepherd. Good cast struggles with uneven script.

Slaves of the Invisible Monster (1950) 100m. BOMB D: Fred Brannon. Richard Webb, Aline Towne, Lane Bradford, Stanley Price, John Crawford, George Meeker. With the aid of secret formula arch-criminal makes himself transparent and carries out master plan; blah actioner. Reedited movie serial: THE INVISIBLE MONSTER.

Sleep My Love (1948) 97m. *** D: Douglas Sirk. Claudette Colbert, Robert Cummings, Don Ameche, Hazel Brooks, Rita Johnson, Raymond Burr, Ralph Morgan. Familiar territory covered by excellent cast as Ameche tries to drive wife Claudette crazy; Cummings saves her.

Sleeper (1973) C-88m. *** D: Woody Allen. Woody Allen, Diane Keaton, John Beck, Mary Gregory, Don Keefer, John McLiam. Woody turns to slapstick in this engagingly silly tale of a man who's frozen in 1973 and awakened 200 years later. Typical Allen combination of great jokes and duds, with more sight-gags than usual and energetic score by the Preservation Hall Jazz Band.

Sleeping Car Murders, The (1966-French) 90m. *** D: Costa-Gavras. Simone Signoret, Yves Montand, Pierre Mondy, Jean-Louis Trintinnant, Jacques Perrin, Catherine Allegret. Quick-paced, atmospheric police-chasing-mad-killer movie. Nice photography; original action good but dubbing hurts.

Sleeping Car to Trieste (1948-British) 95m. *** D: John Paddy Carstairs. Jean Kent, Albert Lieven, Derrick de Marney, Paul Dupuis, Rona Anderson, David Tomlinson. The Orient Express is the setting for fine cat-and-mouse story of espionage agents competing for possession of "hot" political diary.

Sleeping City, The (1950) 85m. **½ D: George Sherman. Richard Conte, Coleen Gray, Alex Nicol, Peggy Dow. OK mystery of private eye who seeks to uncover clues to homicide and dope smuggling at a large hospital.

Sleeping Tiger, The (1954-British) 89m. *** D: Joseph Losey. Alexis Smith, Alexander Knox, Dirk Bogarde, Hugh Griffith, Patricia McCarron. Tense triangular love tale of Smith, her psychiatrist husband Knox, and Bogarde, a crook on parole to Knox.

Slender Thread, The (1965) 98m. **½ D: Sydney Pollack. Sidney Poitier, Anne Bancroft, Telly Savalas, Steve Hill, Edward Asner. Interchange between stars is the whole film in an interesting idea that doesn't fulfill potential. Bancroft takes overdose of sleeping pills, calls L. A. suicide clinic for help; Poitier tries to keep her on phone while rescue is organized.

Sleuth (1972) C-138m. **** D: Joseph L. Mankiewicz. Laurence Olivier, Michael Caine. Lighthearted mystery tour de force for two stars, from Anthony Shaffer's play about games-playing mystery writer Olivier leading his wife's lover (Caine) into diabolical trap. But who gets the last laugh on whom? Delicious from start to finish.

Slight Case of Larceny, A (1953) 71m. ** D: Don Weis. Mickey Rooney, Eddie Bracken, Elaine Stewart, Marilyn Erskine. Low hijinks from Rooney and Bracken as two buddies who open a gas station, siphoning supplies from oil company's pipelines.

Slight Case of Murder, A (1938) 85m. ***½ D: Lloyd Bacon. Edward G. Robinson, Jane Bryan, Allen Jenkins, Ruth Donnelly, Willard Parker, John Litel, Edward Brophy, Harold Huber. Robinson's in peak comedy form as gangster who goes straight when Prohibition ends. This hilarious Damon Runyon story has

brewer Robinson going bankrupt in a rented summer house filled with characters and corpses. Remade as STOP, YOU'RE KILLING ME.

Slightly Dangerous (1943) 94m. ** D: Wesley Ruggles. Lana Turner, Robert Young, Walter Brennan, Dame May Whitty, Eugene Pallette, Florence Bates, Alan Mowbray, Bobby Blake. Slightly ridiculous comedy of waitress Turner who claims to be daughter of wealthy industrialist. Good cast in trivial piece of fluff.

Slightly French (1949) 81m. **½ D: Douglas Sirk. Dorothy Lamour, Don Ameche, Janis Carter, Willard Parker, Adele Jergens. Sassy musical of con-artist director Ameche passing off Lamour as French star.

Slightly Honorable (1940) 83m. *** D: Tay Garnett. Pat O'Brien, Edward Arnold, Broderick Crawford, Ruth Terry, Alan Dinehart, Eve Arden, Claire Dodd, Evelyn Keyes, Phyllis Brooks, Janet Beecher. Fastpaced mystery with snappy detective O'Brien involved in strange murders with corrupt politician Arnold.

Slightly Scarlet (1956) C-99m. **½ D: Allan Dwan. John Payne, Arlene Dahl, Rhonda Fleming, Kent Taylor, Ted de Corsia, Lance Fuller. Effective study of corruption within city officialdom; Payne involved with dynamic sister duo (Fleming, Dahl). Arlene steals the show as tipsy excon sister.

Slightly Terrific (1944) 61m. ** D: Edward F. Cline. Leon Errol, Anne Rooney, Eddie Quillan, Betty Kean, Lorraine Kreuger, Richard Lane. Errol fans may enjoy his antics as twin brothers involved in backing Broadway musical, but between his comic scenes you've got to endure a parade of variety acts ranging from Donald Novis to the Maritza Dancers.

Slim (1937) 80m. **½ D: Ray Enright. Pat O'Brien, Henry Fonda, Stuart Erwin, Margaret Lindsay, Dick Purcell, John Litel. Interesting little story of telephone linemen with novice Fonda admiring veteran O'Brien; danger and romance combine, with good performances.

Slim Carter (1957) C-82m. ** D: Richard Bartlett. Jock Mahoney, Julie Adams, Tim Hovey, William Hopper, Barbara Hale. Mild goings-on of Mahoney becoming popular Western star, aided by Adams, who loves him, and Hovey, an orphan who enters their lives.

Slime People, The (1962) 76m. BOMB D: Robert Hutton. Robert Hutton, Les Tremayne, Susan Hart, Robert Burton. Silly chiller of grimy blob monsters seeking to take over the earth.

Slipper and the Rose, The (1976-British) C-128m. *** D: Bryan Forbes. Richard Chamberlain, Gemma Craven, Annette Crosbie, Michael Hordern, Margaret Lockwood, Christopher Gable, Kenneth More, Edith Evans. Bright musical version of Cinderella in which everyone (including veteran British actors) sings and dances; Craven is delightful as Cindy. Songs by the Sherman Brothers. Good fun.

Slither (1973) C-97m. *** D: Howard Zieff. James Caan, Peter Boyle, Sally Kellerman, Louise Lasser, Allen Garfield, Richard B. Shull. Engaging film is essentially a massive shaggy dog joke; colorful gallery of characters engaged in hunt for elusive cache of money. Perhaps a bit too airy, but perfect TV fare.

Slow Dancing in the Big City (1978) C-101m. *½ D: John G. Avildsen. Paul Sorvino, Anne Ditchburn, Nicolas Coster, Anita Dangler, Hector Jaime Mercado. Straight-faced romantic absurdity about Jimmy Breslin-like columnist who falls for ballerina who can no longer dance. Shameless climax will fry your brain cells with its bathos.

Small Back Room, The (1949-British) 106m. ***½ D: Michael Powell, Emeric Pressburger. David Farrar, Jack Hawkins, Kathleen Byron, Anthony Bushell, Michael Gough. Mature, powerful story of munitions expert injured during WW2 who has lost his self-esteem. Beware of edited version. Retitled: HOUR OF GLORY.

Small Change (1976-French) C-104m. **** D: Francois Truffaut. Geory Desmouceaux, Philippe Goldman, Claudio Deluca, Frank Deluca, Richard Golfier, Laurent Devlaeminck. Thoroughly charming, intelligent film examines the lives of young children—their joys, sorows, frustrations, adventures—in a small French village. Wise, perceptive, and witty.

Small Miracle, The (1973) C-74m. TVM D: Jeannot Szwarc. Vittorio De Sica, Raf Vallone, Marco Della Cava, Guidarini Guidi, Jan Larsson. Moving story of young boy who believes St. Francis of Assisi will cure his lame donkey; shot in Assisi and Rome. Paul Gallico's story was filmed before, in 1952, as NEVER TAKE NO FOR AN ANSWER. Average.

Small Town Girl (1936) 90m. *** D: William Wellman. Janet Gaynor, Robert Taylor, Binnie Barnes, Lewis Stone, Andy Devine, Elizabeth Patterson, Isabel Jewell, James Stewart. Breezy romance of Gaynor trapping Taylor into marriage while he's drunk, then working to win him over sober. Musicalized in 1953 with Jane Powell. Retitled: ONE HORSE TOWN.

Small Town Girl (1953) C-93m. **½ D: Leslie Kardos. Jane Powell, Farley Granger, Ann Miller, S. Z. Sakall, Billie Burke, Bobby Van, Nat King Cole. Bland musical remake of 1936 film with Powell setting her sights on Granger, who's passing through town. Miller does eye-popping "I've Gotta Hear that Beat," staged by Busby Berkeley.

Smallest Show on Earth, The (1957-British) 80m. *** D: Basil Dearden. Bill Travers, Virginia McKenna, Margaret Rutherford, Peter Sellers, Stringer Davis. Droll comedy about young couple inheriting archaic movie house and several strange attendants as well (Sellers, Rutherford).

Smart Alecks (1942) 88m. D: Wallace Fox. Leo Gorcey, Huntz Hall, Bobby Jordan, Gabriel Dell, Maxie Rosenbloom, Gale Storm, Walter Woolf King, David Gorcey, Sunshine Sammy Morrison, Roger Pryor. SEE: Bowery Boys series.

Smart Girls Don't Talk (1948) 81m. ** D: Richard Bare. Virginia Mayo, Bruce Bennett, Helen Westcott, Robert Hutton, Tom D'Andrea. Dull drama of socialite Mayo forced to join up with racketeer.

Smart Money (1931) 90m. **½ D: Alfred E. Green. Edward G. Robinson, James Cagney, Margaret Livingston, Evalyn Knapp, Noel Francis. Known as Cagney-Robinson co-starring film, Robinson really stars, as lucky barber who becomes big-time gambler. Cagney is fine in supporting role; Boris Karloff has small part.

Smart Woman (1948) 93m. *** D: Edward A. Blatt. Brian Aherne, Constance Bennett, Barry Sullivan, Michael O'Shea, James Gleason,

Otto Kruger, Iris Adrian, Isobel Elsom, Selena Royle. Lawyer Bennett doesn't let love interfere with her determined attempt to prosecute crooked D.A. and other officials.

Smashing Time (1967-British) 96m. **½ D: Desmond Davis. Rita Tushingham, Lynn Redgrave, Michael York, Anna Quayle, Ian Carmichael. Two girls come to London to crash big-time. Spoof of trendy fashion/ show biz world tries to turn Redgrave and Tushingham into Laurel and Hardy, with middling results. Slapstick scenes only mildly funny.

Smash-Up on Interstate 5 (1976) C-100m. TVM D: John Llewellyn Moxey. Robert Conrad, Sian Barbara Allen, Buddy Ebsen, David Groh, Scott Jacoby, Sue Lyon, Vera Miles, Donna Mills, Terry Moore, Harriet Nelson, David Nelson. Familiar multi-character drama with a twist: they're involved in spectacular 39-car crash on a California freeway. Performances understandably pale beside graphic smash-up scenes which—surprise!—turn up at the beginning of the movie. Average.

Smash-Up, the Story of a Woman (1947) 103m. *** D: Stuart Heisler. Susan Hayward, Lee Bowman, Marsha Hunt, Eddie Albert, Carl Esmond, Carleton Young. One of Hayward's best performances in showy role of alcoholic wife of songwriter Bowman.

Smile (1975) C-113m. **½ D: Michael Ritchie. Bruce Dern, Barbara Feldon, Michael Kidd, Geoffrey Lewis, Nicholas Pryor, Colleen Camp, Joan Prather, Melanie Griffith. Satire on a California beauty contest is alternately hilarious and cheap. Wavers uncomfortably between comedy and drama, but Kidd is terrific as pageant's career-slumped choreographer.

Smile, Jenny, You're Dead (1974) C-100m. TVM D: Jerry Thorpe. David Janssen, John Anderson, Howard da Silva, Martin Gabel, Clu Gulager, Zalman King, Jodie Foster, Andrea Marcovicci. Well-plotted mystery in which private eye Janssen looks into the murder of a friend's son-in-law and gets emotionally involved with his daughter, the prime suspect. Pilot for Janssen's "Harry O" series. Above average.

Smile When You Say "I Do" (1973) C-74m. TVM D: Allen Funt. Extension of CANDID CAMERA

series, with creator Funt examining battle of the sexes. Average.

Smiles of a Summer Night (1955-Swedish) 108m. **** D: Ingmar Bergman. Ulla Jacobsson, Eva Dahlbeck, Margit Carlquist, Harriet Andersson, Gunnar Bjornstrand, Jarl Kulle. One of the finest romantic comedies ever made, a witty treatise on manners, mores, and sex during a weekend at a country estate in the late 19th century. This film inspired the Broadway show and subsequent film A LITTLE NIGHT MUSIC.

Smiley (1957-Australian) C-97m. **½ D: Anthony Kimmins. Ralph Richardson, John McCallum, Chips Rafferty, Reg Lye. Soft-treading narrative of young boy who wants a bicycle, becoming entangled with drug-smugglers.

Smiley Gets a Gun (1959-Australian) C-89m. ** D: Anthony Kimmins. Sybil Thorndike, Keith Calvert, Bruce Archer, Chips Rafferty, Margaret Christensen. Easy-going account of young boy trying to win the right to have a gun.

Smilin' Through (1941) C-100m. **½ D: Frank Borzage. Jeanette MacDonald, Gene Raymond, Brian Aherne, Ian Hunter, Frances Robinson, Patrick O'Moore. Overly sentimental tale of orphaned MacDonald falling in love with the son of a murderer. Filmed in 1922 with Norma Talmadge, in 1932 with Norma Shearer.

Smith! (1969) C-112m. *** D: Michael O'Herlihy. Glenn Ford, Nancy Olson, Dean Jagger, Keenan Wynn, Warren Oates, Chief Dan George. Offbeat Disney drama of stubborn, pro-Indian farmer Ford who steps forward to help Indian accused of murder. Well done, with good characterizations, but low-key qualities soften impact.

Smoke Signal (1955) C-88m. **½ D: Jerry Hopper. Dana Andrews, Piper Laurie, Rex Reason, Milburn Stone, William Talman. At-times zesty Western involving Indian massacre and survivors' trek downstream to escape.

Smokey and the Bandit (1977) C-96m. *** D: Hal Needham. Burt Reynolds, Sally Field, Jackie Gleason, Jerry Reed, Mike Henry, Paul Williams, Pat McCormick. Box-office smash is one long comedy chase, as bootlegger Reynolds outraces Sheriff Gleason for the entire film. Directorial debut of ace stuntman Needham is (expectedly) brimming with stunts. About as subtle as The 3 Stooges, but a classic compared to countless rip-offs which have followed.

Smoky (1946) **C-87m.** ******* D: Louis King. Fred MacMurray, Anne Baxter, Burl Ives, Bruce Cabot, Esther Dale, Roy Roberts. First-rate family film from famous story of man's devotion to his horse.

Smoky (1966) **C-103m.** ****** D: George Sherman. Fess Parker, Diana Hyland, Katy Jurado, Hoyt Axton, Chuck Roberson. Horse opera about especially independent horse named Smoky who knows what he wants.

Smugglers, The (1968) **C-97m. TVM** D: Norman Lloyd. Shirley Booth, Carol Lynley, Gayle Hunnicutt, Michael J. Pollard, Kurt Kasznar, David Opatoshu. Uneven mixture of wry humor and suspense in prettily packaged story of American tourists used in smuggling scheme. Entertaining cast, good location work, but abrupt resolution hurts film. Average.

Smuggler's Cove (1948) 66m. D: William Beaudine. Leo Gorcey, Huntz Hall, Gabriel Dell, Billy Benedict, David Gorcey, Martin Kosleck, Paul Harvey, Amelita Ward. SEE: Bowery Boys series.

Smuggler's Gold (1951) 64m. ****** D: William Berke. Cameron Mitchell, Amanda Blake, Carl Benton Reid, Peter Thompson. Adequate drama about deep-sea diver Mitchell coping with girlfriend's (Blake's) father who's in the smuggling game.

Smuggler's Island (1951) **C-75m.** ****** D: Edward Ludwig. Jeff Chandler, Evelyn Keyes, Philip Friend, Marvin Miller. Undemanding adventure story of diver Chandler involved with Keyes and search for sunken gold.

Snafu (1945) 82m. ****** D: Jack Moss. Robert Benchley, Vera Vague, Conrad Janis, Nanette Parks, Janis Wilson, Marcia Mae Jones, Kathleen Howard, Jimmy Lloyd, Enid Markey, Eva Puig. Young C. Janis is sent home by army because of his age, but he can't get used to civilian life again; mild comedy with fine Benchley as perplexed father.

Snake People (1968-Mexican-U.S.) C-90m. BOMB D: Enrique Vergara, Jack Hill. Boris Karloff, Julissa, Charles East. Police captain tries to investigate an island where voodoo, LSD, and snake-worshipers run rampant; ludicrous horror film wastes Karloff once again. Original title: ISLE OF THE SNAKE PEOPLE.

Snake Pit, The (1948) 108m. *******½ D: Anatole Litvak. Olivia de Havilland, Mark Stevens, Leo Genn, Celeste Holm, Glenn Langan, Helen Craig, Leif Erickson, Beulah Bondi, Lee Patrick, Isabel Jewell, Ruth Donnelly. One of the first films to deal intelligently with mental breakdowns and the painstakingly slow recovery process. Gripping film set in mental institution lacks original shock value but still packs a good punch, with de Havilland superb.

Snatched (1973) C-73m. TVM D: Sutton Roley. Howard Duff, Leslie Nielsen, Sheree North, Barbara Parkins, Robert Reed, John Saxon, Tisha Sterling. Usual kidnapping plot complicated by one of three husbands refusing to pay ransom and race against time to resupply one wife with insulin. Good cast walks through threadbare characters effortlessly; otherwise stale action. Average.

Sniper, The (1952) 87m. ******* D: Edward Dmytryk. Adolphe Menjou, Arthur Franz, Marie Windsor, Richard Kiley, Mabel Paige. Excellent, realistically filmed drama of mentally deranged sniper (Franz) who can't help himself from killing unsuspecting women. Fine performances by all.

Sniper's Ridge (1961) 61m. ****** D: John Bushelman. Jack Ging, Stanley Clements, John Goddard, Douglas Henderson. Standard Korean War battle actioner.

Snoop Sisters, The (1972) C-100m. TVM D: Leonard Stern. Helen Hayes, Mildred Natwick, Charlie Callas, Jill Clayburgh, Art Carney, Paulette Goddard. Good comedy features two mystery writers turned private eyes investigating murder of movie star (Goddard), foiling nephew's attempts to retire them. Enjoyable pilot for later series. Above average. Retitled FEMALE INSTINCT.

Snoopy, Come Home (1972) C-70m. ******* D: Bill Melendez. Voices of Chad Webber, David Carey, Stephen Shea, Bill Melendez. Charming PEANUTS feature centering around Snoopy, the world's most independent pooch.

Snorkel, The (1958-British) 74m. ******½ D: Guy Green. Peter Van Eyck, Betta St. John, Mandy Miller, Gregoire Aslan. Van Eyck ingeniously murders wife and plots to do away with stepdaughter, when she discovers his gimmick.

Snow Creature, The (1954) 70m. *½ D: W. Lee Wilder. Paul Langton, Leslie Denison, Teru Shimada, Rollin Moriyana. Often ludicrous sci-fi about abominable monster who's on the loose in the U.S.

Snow Demons (1965-Italian) C-92m. BOMB D: Anthony Dawson (Antonio Margheriti). Jack Stuart (Giacomo Rossi-Stuarti), Amber Collins (Ombretta Colli), Peter Martell, Halina Zalewska. International expedition discovers snowmen who are really aliens with sinister motives. Incredibly dull, sloppily made film. Also known as SNOW DEVILS.

Snow Devils SEE: **Snow Demons**

Snow Job (1972) C-90m. *½ D: George Englund. Jean-Claude Killy, Danielle Gaubert, Cliff Potts, Vittorio De Sica. Heist film involving the taking of $250,000 in loot. Although Killy is appropriate star for film set against the Alps, he can't act; neither can the beautiful Gaubert.

Snow Queen, The (1959) C-70m. ** D: Phil Patton. Art Linkletter, Tammy Marihugh, Jennie Lynn. Voices of Sandra Dee, Tommy Kirk, Patty McCormack, Paul Frees, June Foray. Animated cartoon with live prologue featuring Linkletter is aimed at younger set.

Snow White and the Three Stooges (1961) C-107m. BOMB D: Walter Lang. Three Stooges, Patricia Medina, Carol Heiss, Buddy Baer, Edgar Barrier. Big mistake with skating star Heiss as Snow White, Three Stooges as . . . the Three Stooges. Comics aren't given much to do, despite title; rest of film is rather stodgy. Even kids won't be thrilled with it.

Snowball (1960-British) 69m. ** D: Pat Jackson. Gordon Jackson, Zena Walker, Kenneth Griffith, Daphne Anderson. At times intriguing "B" film involving small boy's lie which led to the death of a villager.

Snowball Express (1972) C-99m. ** D: Norman Tokar. Dean Jones, Nancy Olson, Harry Morgan, Keenan Wynn, Johnny Whitaker, Michael McGreevey. Jones plays N.Y. accountant who inherits battered hotel in Rockies and tries to convert it into ski lodge. Slapstick ski chase

is highlight of formula Disney comedy.

Snowbeast (1977) C-100m. TVM D: Herb Wallerstein. Bo Svenson, Yvette Mimieux, Robert Logan, Clint Walker, Sylvia Sidney. Killer beast terrorizes ski resort during winter carnival. Dumb mystery with slaloming creature and several straight-faced actors. Below average.

Snows of Kilimanjaro, The (1952) C-117m. *** D: Henry King. Gregory Peck, Susan Hayward, Ava Gardner, Hildegarde Neff, Leo G. Carroll. Peck finds his forte as renowned writer coming to the end of his life in Africa, trying to decide if he found any meaning to his past; based on Hemingway story.

So Big (1953) 101m. *** D: Robert Wise. Jane Wyman, Sterling Hayden, Nancy Olson, Steve Forrest, Martha Hyer, Tommy Rettig. Superficial but engrossing Edna Ferber soaper about Wyman who brings up son to be self-sufficient. Filmed before in 1932.

So Dark the Night (1946) 71m. *** D: Joseph H. Lewis. Steven Geray, Micheline Cheirel, Eugene Borden, Ann Codee, Egon Brecher, Helen Freeman. Uniquely somber, fascinating story of renowned detective's search for unknown murderer in French village. A real "sleeper."

So Dear to My Heart (1948) C-84m. ***½ D: Harold Schuster. Burl Ives, Beulah Bondi, Bobby Driscoll, Luana Patten, Harry Carey. Warm, nostalgic Disney film about young boy's determination to tame a black sheep and bring him to State Fair competition. Brimming with period charm and atmosphere; several animated sequences too.

So Ends Our Night (1941) 117m. ***½ D: John Cromwell. Fredric March, Margaret Sullavan, Frances Dee, Glenn Ford, Anna Sten, Erich von Stroheim, Allan Brett. Superior filmization of Erich Maria Remarque novel of German (March) rejecting Nazi reign, fleeing his country with hot pursuit by Axis agents.

So Evil My Love (1948-British) 109m. *** D: Lewis Allen. Ray Milland, Ann Todd, Geraldine Fitzgerald, Leo G. Carroll, Raymond Huntley. Excellent study of corruption; scoundrel Milland drags innocent Todd into larceny at expense of Fitzgerald.

So Goes My Love (1946) 88m. **½ D: Frank Ryan. Myrna Loy, Don Ameche, Rhys Williams, Bobby Driscoll, Richard Gaines, Molly Lamont. Amusing period comedy of fortune-hunting Loy marrying oddball inventor Ameche.

So Long at the Fair (1950-British) 90m. *** D: Terence Fisher, Anthony Darnborough. Jean Simmons, Dirk Bogarde, David Tomlinson, Honor Blackman. Atmospheric drama set during 1889 Paris Exposition with English woman searching for brother who's mysteriously vanished. Well done.

So Proudly We Hail! (1943) 126m. *** D: Mark Sandrich. Claudette Colbert, Paulette Goddard, Veronica Lake, George Reeves, Sonny Tufts, Barbara Britton, Walter Abel. Flagwaving soaper of nurses in WW2 Pacific, headed by Colbert. Versatile cast, action scenes and teary romancing, combine well in this woman's service story. Not as stirring now as it was in 1943, when Paulette Goddard copped an Academy Award nomination.

So Red the Rose (1935) 82m. **½ D: King Vidor. Margaret Sullavan, Walter Connolly, Randolph Scott, Elizabeth Patterson, Janet Beecher, Robert Cummings, Dickie Moore. Story of Sullavan patiently waiting for Scott to return from Civil War battlefield lacks punch, but is well acted and generally enjoyable.

So This Is Love (1953) C-101m. ** D: Gordon Douglas. Kathryn Grayson, Merv Griffin, Walter Abel, Rosemary DeCamp, Jeff Donnell. Glossy, empty biography of opera star Grace Moore, antiseptically played by Kathryn Grayson.

So This Is New York (1948) 79m. *** D: Richard Fleischer. Henry Morgan, Rudy Vallee, Bill Goodwin, Hugh Herbert, Leo Gorcey, Virginia Grey, Dona Drake. Cheaply filmed but hilarious adaptation of Ring Lardner's *The Big Town*, with smalltowner Morgan inheriting money and encountering strange ways of New York City. Ingenious, offbeat script; radio/TV star Morgan fares well in screen debut, helped by top supporting cast.

So This Is Paris (1954) C-96m. **½ D: Richard Quine. Tony Curtis, Gloria DeHaven, Gene Nelson, Corinne Calvet, Paul Gilbert, Mara Corday. Perky stars enliven this unmemorable musical of gobs on leave in France.

So Well Remembered (1947-British) 114m. *** D: Edward Dmytryk. John

Mills, Martha Scott, Trevor Howard, Patricia Roc, Richard Carlson, Ivor Barnard. Author James Hilton narrates saga of earnest newspaper editor (Mills) determined to improve living conditions in factory town, sidetracked by marriage to blindly ambitious woman (Scott). Very young Juliet Mills has bit part.

So You Won't Talk (1940) 69m. ** D: Edward Sedgwick. Joe E. Brown, Frances Robinson, Vivienne Osborne, Bernard Nedell, Tom Dugan. Good, typical mistaken identity comedy with bookworm Brown, a dead ringer for notorious mobster.

So Young, So Bad (1950) 91m. ** D: Bernard Vorhaus. Paul Henreid, Anne Francis, Rita Moreno, Anne Jackson, Enid Pulver, Catherine McLeod. Inexpensively filmed in N.Y.C. but still an effective study of female juvenile delinquents.

Sodom and Gomorrah (1963-Italian) C-154m. **½ D: Robert Aldrich. Stewart Granger, Pier Angeli, Stanley Baker, Anouk Aimee, Rossana Podesta. Lavish retelling of life in biblical tin cities of sin. Strong cast, vivid scenes of vice, gore, and God's wrath, make this overly long tale of ancient Hebrews fairly entertaining.

Sofia (1948) C-82m. ** D: John Reinhardt. Gene Raymond, Sigrid Gurie, Patricia Morison, Mischa Auer. Acceptable programmer with Raymond helping nuclear scientists escape grip of Russians in Turkey.

Soft Boiled (1923) 78m. **½ D: J. G. Blystone. Tom Mix, Joseph Girard, Billie Dove, L. D. Shumway, Tom Wilson, Frank Beal. Tom Mix tries comedy, as young man with challenge to spend 30 days without losing his temper; enjoyable fluff, with typical Mix action finale.

Soft Skin, The (1964-French) 120m. *** D: François Truffaut. Françoise Dorleac, Jean Desailly, Nelly Benedetti. Moody tale of married businessman drawn into tragic affair with beautiful airline stewardess Dorleac; smooth direction uplifts basic plot.

Sol Madrid (1968) C-90m. **½ D: Brian G. Hutton. David McCallum, Stella Stevens, Telly Savalas, Ricardo Montalban, Rip Torn, Pat Hingle, Paul Lukas. Old-fashioned but solid plot about police, Mafia, and running heroin from Mexico.

Soldier Blue (1970) C-112m. ** D: Ralph Nelson. Candice Bergen, Peter

Strauss, Donald Pleasence, John Anderson, Jorge Rivero, Dana Elcar. Inevitable TV cutting of extremely violent climactic Cavalry attack will no doubt lessen effect of this film about our mistreatment of the Indians. Even so, similar theme has been handled much better elsewhere.

Soldier in Skirts SEE: **Triple Echo**

Soldier in the Rain (1963) 88m. *** D: Ralph Nelson. Jackie Gleason, Steve McQueen, Tuesday Weld, Tony Bill, Tom Poston. Strange film wavers from sentimental drama to high comedy. Gleason is swinging sergeant, McQueen his fervent admirer.

Soldier of Fortune (1955) C-96m. *** D: Edward Dmytryk. Clark Gable, Susan Hayward, Michael Rennie, Gene Barry, Tom Tully. Gable is hired to find Susan's husband (Barry) held captive in Hong Kong. Rennie is good as police chief.

Soldier of Love SEE: **Fan Fan the Tulip**

Soldiers Three (1951) 87m. *** D: Tay Garnett. Stewart Granger, Walter Pidgeon, David Niven, Cyril Cusack, Greta Gynt. Boisterous action-adventure with light touch; an unofficial remake of GUNGA DIN with three soldiering comrades in and out of spats with each other as they battle in 19th-century India.

Sole Survivor (1969) C-100m. TVM D: Paul Stanley. Vince Edwards, Richard Basehart, William Shatner, Lou Antonio, Larry Casey, Patrick Wayne, Brad Davis, Dennis Cooney, Alan Caillou, Timur Bashtu. Title refers to central character, only person to walk away from suddenly discovered B-25 crash in Libyan desert. Odd drama with Edwards' performance hands-down winner. Above average.

Solid Gold Cadillac, The (1956) 99m. *** D: Richard Quine. Judy Holliday, Paul Douglas, Fred Clark, John Williams, Arthur O'Connell. Narrated by George Burns. Dazzling Judy in entertaining comedy of small stockholder in large company becoming corporate heroine by trying to oust crooked board of directors. George S. Kaufman-Howard Teichman play adapted by Abe Burrows. Last scene originally filmed in color.

Solitary Man, The (1979) C-100m. TVM D: John Llewellyn Moxey. Earl Holliman, Carrie Snodgress, Nicolas Coster, Lara Parker, Dorrie Kavanaugh. Well-intentioned but

somber study of the breakup of a family—from the man's point of view. Predated by several months the more solid KRAMER VS. KRAMER. Average.

Solomon and Sheba (1959) C-139m. *** D: King Vidor. Yul Brynner, Gina Lollobrigida, George Sanders, Marisa Pavan, John Crawford, Alejandro Rey, Harry Andrews. Splashy spectacle with alluring Gina and stoic Brynner frolicking in biblical days. Tyrone Power died during filming in Spain, was replaced by Brynner who refilmed his early scenes.

Sombra, the Spider Woman (1947) 100m. ** D: Spencer Bennet, Fred Brannon. Bruce Edwards, Virginia Lindley, Carol Forman, Anthony Warde, Ramsay Ames. Unremarkable cliff-hanger turned feature, with title figure, daughter of Oriental archfiend, seeking to conquer the world. Reedited movie serial: THE BLACK WIDOW.

Sombrero (1953) C-103m. *½ D: Norman Foster. Ricardo Montalban, Pier Angeli, Vittorio Gassman, Yvonne De Carlo, Nina Foch, Cyd Charisse. Mishmash of three intertwining love tales set in Mexico.

Some Came Running (1958) C-127m. *** D: Vincente Minnelli. Frank Sinatra, Dean Martin, Shirley MacLaine, Martha Hyer, Arthur Kennedy. James Jones novel of disillusionment in a small Southern town post-WW2 is well done, with good performances, especially by MacLaine. Fine Elmer Bernstein score. Both MacLaine and Hyer won Oscar nominations.

Some Girls Do (1969-British) C-93m. **½ D: Ralph Thomas. Richard Johnson, Dahliah Lavi, Bebe Loncar, Robert Morley, Sydne Rome, James Villiers. Brisk thriller involving Bulldog Drummond (played with a lack of dash by Johnson) vs. longtime arch enemy Carl Peterson (Villiers) who is trying to sabotage Britain's supersonic plane plans. Morley's a particular delight in a cameo as an eccentric teacher of high cuisine.

Some Kind of a Nut (1969) C-89m. BOMB D: Garson Kanin. Dick Van Dyke, Angie Dickinson, Rosemary Forsyth, Zohra Lampert, Elliott Reid, Pippa Scott. Banker Van Dyke grows a beard and loses his job. Pathetic comedy dates more after four years than some of Kanin's earlier films do after 34.

Some Kind of Miracle (1979) C-100m. TVM D: Jerrold Freedman. David Dukes, Andrea Marcovicci, Michael C. Gynne, Art Hindle, Dick Anthony Williams, Nancy Marchand, Stephen Elliott. The trials and tribulations (mostly sexual) of a happy couple after one is permanently paralyzed in a surfing accident. Average.

Some Like It Hot (1939) 64m. **½ D: George Archainbaud. Bob Hope, Shirley Ross, Una Merkel, Gene Krupa, Richard Denning. Sideshow owner Hope takes advantage of Ross to raise money for show. Airy comedy includes song "The Lady's In Love With You." Retitled RHYTHM ROMANCE.

Some Like It Hot (1959) 120m. **** D: Billy Wilder. Marilyn Monroe, Tony Curtis, Jack Lemmon, George Raft, Pat O'Brien, Joe E. Brown, Nehemiah Persoff, Joan Shawlee, Mike Mazurki. Terrific Billy Wilder comedy. Two musicians fleeing gangsters join all-girl band heading for Miami in 1920s. Monroe croons "Running Wild" and courts Curtis, who is in rare form. Brown has film's now-classic closing line.

Some May Live (1967) 105m. ** D: Vernon Sewell. Joseph Cotten, Martha Hyer, Peter Cushing, John Ronane. Unexciting suspenser made for TV set in contemporary Saigon with Cotten a U.S. Intelligence officer setting a trap for the espionage agent within his department. Retitled: IN SAIGON, SOME MAY LIVE.

Somebody Killed Her Husband (1978) C-97m. *½ D: Lamont Johnson. Farrah Fawcett-Majors, Jeff Bridges, John Wood, Tammy Grimes, John Glover, Patricia Elliott. First starring feature for the ex-Charlie's Angel was redubbed "Somebody Killed Her Career" by industry wags, but in any case, this tepid mystery romance has little to recommend it.

Somebody Loves Me (1952) C-97m. ** D: Irving S. Brecher. Betty Hutton, Ralph Meeker, Adele Jergens, Robert Keith. Schmaltzy vaudeville biography of troupers Blossom Seeley and Benny Fields with no originality and not much entertainment either.

Somebody Up There Likes Me (1956) 113m. ***½ D: Robert Wise. Paul Newman, Pier Angeli, Everett Sloane, Eileen Heckart, Sal Mineo, Steve McQueen. Top biography of Rocky Graziano's rise from N.Y.C. sidewalks to arena success with fine Newman performance.

Someone at the Top of the Stairs (1973-British) C-74m. TVM D: John Sichel. Donna Mills, Judy Carne, Francis Wallis, Alethea Charlton, Scott Forbes. Two American girls (played by Britishers Mills and Carne) get the creeps when they move into strange Victorian boarding house in London. Familiar stuff, passably done. Average.

Someone Behind the Door (1971-French) C-97m. ** D: Nicolas Gessner. Charles Bronson, Anthony Perkins, Jill Ireland, Henri Garcin, Adriano Magestretti. Neuropsychiatrist (Perkins) turns an amnesiac murderer (Bronson) into his tool for revenge on his philandering wife; farfetched melodrama.

Someone I Touched (1975) C-78m. TVM D: Lou Antonio. Cloris Leachman, James Olson, Glynnis O'Connor, Andy Robinson, Allyn Ann McLerie, Kenneth Mars. Unbelievable melodrama about an architect, his pregnant wife, and a nubile young teen-ager who learn they have VD and try to figure out who gave it to whom. Cloris even sings the romantic title song! Below average.

Someone Is Watching Me! (1978) C-100m. TVM D: John Carpenter. Lauren Hutton, David Birney, Adrienne Barbeau, Charles Cyphers. Dandy thriller about a career woman who takes things into her own hands after being rebuffed by the police when someone begins stalking her. Above average.

Something Big (1972) C-108m. *½ D: Andrew V. McLaglen. Dean Martin, Brian Keith, Honor Blackman, Carol White, Ben Johnson. Bandits rob bandits in all-out Mexican war. "Something Big" has to be the Gatling gun, because it sure isn't the movie.

Something Evil (1970) C-73m. TVM D: Steven Spielberg. Sandy Dennis, Darren McGavin, Ralph Bellamy, Jeff Corey, Johnnie Whitaker, John Rubinstein. Worden family buys old house in Pennsylvania, unaware of lurking evil presence. Horror aspect handled matter-of-factly, combines in offbeat way with film's flippant, swaggering feel. Excellent performances. Above average.

Something for a Lonely Man (1968) C-98m. TVM D: Don Taylor. Dan Blocker, Susan Clark, John Dehner,

Warren Oates, Paul Peterson, Don Stroud. Blacksmith outcast of Arcana (Blocker) believes he finally has opportunity to bring industry to town when locomotive derails nearby, is aided by one woman who believes in him. Good character study - salvages backlot Western. Above average.

Something for Everyone (1970) C-112m. **½ D: Harold Prince. Angela Lansbury, Michael York, Anthony Corlan, Heidelinde Weis, Eva-Maria Meineke, Jane Carr. Very black comedy about amoral, bisexual young man who manipulates staff and family of impoverished Countess (Lansbury) to his advantage. Intriguing but needlessly protracted story; Broadway director Prince's first film, shot on location in Bavaria.

Something for Joey (1977) C-100m. TVM D: Lou Antonio. Geraldine Page, Gerald S. O'Loughlin, Marc Singer, Jeff Lynas, Linda Kelsey, Paul Picerni. True-life story of the relationship between Heisman Trophy winner John Cappelletti and his younger brother, Joey, stricken with leukemia. Sensitive tearjerker that never gets maudlin. Above average.

Something for the Birds (1952) 81m. **½ D: Robert Wise. Patricia Neal, Victor Mature, Edmund Gwenn, Larry Keating. Mild romantic froth, with Mature and Neal on opposite sides of issue in lobbying for bird sanctuary protection.

Something for the Boys (1944) C-83m. **½ D: Lewis Seiler. Perry Como, Carmen Miranda, Vivian Blaine, Michael O'Shea, Phil Silvers, Cara Williams, Sheila Ryan. Pleasant, slick 20th Century-Fox musical with diverting Cole Porter score, set in Southern plantation recruited as home for soldiers' wives.

Something in the Wind (1947) 89m. **½ D: Irving Pichel. Deanna Durbin, Donald O'Connor, Charles Winninger, Helena Carter. Mild comedy of errors with Durbin as female disk jockey who sings too. Easy to take, amusing.

Something of Value (1957) 113m. *** D: Richard Brooks. Rock Hudson, Dana Wynter, Sidney Poitier, Wendy Hiller, Frederick O'Neal. Robert Ruark's novel transformed to screen, sharply details brutal Mau Mau warfare in Kenya. Hudson and Poitier are fine as British colonial

farmer and his childhood friend; Hiller memorable as widow struggling to retain dignity and spirit.

Something Short of Paradise (1979) C-91m. ** D: David Helpern Jr. Susan Sarandon, David Steinberg, Jean-Pierre Aumont, Marilyn Sokol, Joe Grifasi, Robert Hitt. Aptly titled romantic comedy pairs movie-theater manager Steinberg and magazine writer Sarandon, but offers little except their likable personalities. Film buffs will enjoy main-title sequence comprised of old movie ads.

Something to Live For (1952) 89m. **½ D: George Stevens. Joan Fontaine, Ray Milland, Teresa Wright, Douglas Dick, Rudy Lee. Turgid melodrama trying to be another LOST WEEKEND. Fontaine is alcoholic in love with Milland, but he's married.

Something to Shout About (1943) 93m. ** D: Gregory Ratoff. Don Ameche, Janet Blair, Jack Oakie, Hazel Scott, William Gaxton, Veda Ann Borg, Cobina Wright Jr. Another Broadway backstage show biz tale, a wispy excuse for soft-pedaled ensemble and solo numbers.

Something to Sing About (1937) 84m. ** D: Victor Schertzinger. James Cagney, Evelyn Daw, William Frawley, Mona Barrie, Gene Lockhart. Low-budget musical doesn't live up to its title, with Cagney the only real asset in this lightweight story of a N.Y. bandleader who goes to Hollywood. Also known as BATTLING HOOFER.

Something Wild (1961) 112m. **½ D: Jack Garfein. Carroll Baker, Ralph Meeker, Mildred Dunnock, Martin Kosleck. Bizarre study of rape-victim Baker falling in love with would-be attacker Meeker, coming to rational understanding with mother Dunnock. N.Y.C. location scenes perk melodramatic soaper.

Sometimes a Great Notion (1971) C-114m. ** D: Paul Newman. Paul Newman, Henry Fonda, Lee Remick, Michael Sarrazin, Richard Jaeckel, Linda Lawson. Disappointing film version of Ken Kesey's mammoth novel about modern-day loggers in Oregon. Jaeckel's performance is outstanding and movie has one great scene involving a drowning, but otherwise film is a letdown. Retitled NEVER GIVE AN INCH for TV.

Somewhere I'll Find You (1942)

108m. **½ D: Wesley Ruggles. Lana Turner, Clark Gable, Robert Sterling, Reginald Owen, Lee Patrick, Rags Ragland, Patricia Dane. Turner and Gable are improbable as WW2 war correspondents, but their love scenes between battles are most convincing.

Somewhere in the Night (1946) 100m. **½ D: Joseph L. Mankiewicz. John Hodiak, Nancy Guild, Lloyd Nolan, Richard Conte, Josephine Hutchinson, Fritz Kortner, Sheldon Leonard. Satisfactory drama of amnesiac Hodiak trying to discover his true identity; not up to later Mankiewicz efforts.

Son-Daughter, The (1932) 79m. **½ D: Clarence Brown. Ramon Novarro, Helen Hayes, Warner Oland, Lewis Stone, Ralph Morgan. Dated drama of pre-WW1 Chinatown, notable mainly for Hayes' performance as Chinese girl sold as slave. Difficult to take bogus Chinese cast seriously.

Son of a Gunfighter (1966-Spanish) C-92m. *½ D: Paul Landres. Russ Tamblyn, Kieron Moore, James Philbrook, Fernando Rey. Title tells all in oater peppered with Anglo-Saxon actors and bits of the Old West.

Son of a Sailor (1933) 73m. *** D: Lloyd Bacon. Joe E. Brown, Jean Muir, Thelma Todd, Frank McHugh, Johnny Mack Brown, Sheila Terry. Joe blunders into espionage and recovers stolen Navy plans; always-vivacious Todd lends fine support in this entertaining comedy.

Son of Ali Baba (1952) C-75m. ** D: Kurt Neumann. Tony Curtis, Piper Laurie, Susan Cabot, Victor Jory, Hugh O'Brian. Caliph uses princess Laurie to obtain treasure of Ali Baba. After father is captured, son appears and wins hand of princess. Good sets, fair acting.

Son of Belle Starr (1953) C-70m. ** D: Frank McDonald. Keith Larsen, Dona Drake, Peggie Castle, Regis Toomey. Fictional Western history is excuse for another shootout tale.

Son of Blob SEE: Beware! The Blob

Son of Captain Blood, The (1962-Italian) C-90m. **½ D: Tullio Demichelli. Sean Flynn, Ann Todd, Alessandra Panaro, Jose Nieto. Flynn (Errol's son) is not quite at ease in title role, but film is rousing account of Blood's old crew helping

to combat the evil governor of Port Royal.

Son of Dr. Jekyll, The (1951) 77m. *½ D: Seymour Friedman. Louis Hayward, Jody Lawrance, Alexander Knox, Lester Matthews. Son discovers formula father used to become Hyde. Poorly scripted, produced. Cast manages to save film from complete ruin.

Son of Dracula (1943) 78m. **½ D: Robert Siodmak. Robert Paige, Louise Allbritton, Lon Chaney, Evelyn Ankers, Frank Craven, J. Edward Bromberg. Following in the old man's footsteps, Count Alucard (spell backwards) terrorizes a community, mostly the female population. Above-average horror.

Son of Dracula (1974-British) C-90m. *½ D: Freddie Francis. Harry Nilsson, Ringo Starr, Rosanna Lee, Freddie Jones, Dennis Price, Skip Martin. Offbeat but uninspired rock horror pic with seven tunes by Nilsson, who plays the title character. Ringo produced.

Son of Flubber (1963) 100m. **½ D: Robert Stevenson. Fred MacMurray, Nancy Olson, Keenan Wynn, Tommy Kirk, Elliott Reid, Joanna Moore, Leon Ames, Ed Wynn, Charlie Ruggles. Silly, disjointed sequel to THE ABSENT MINDED PROFESSOR has new inventions—flubbergas, dry rain—and appropriate slapstick highlights, to compensate for uneven script. Helped, too, by cast full of old pros.

Son of Frankenstein (1939) 95m. *** D: Rowland V. Lee. Basil Rathbone, Boris Karloff, Bela Lugosi, Lionel Atwill, Emma Dunn, Josephine Hutchinson, Edgar Norton. Rathbone follows in father's footsteps, revives monster (Karloff) with help of gruesome Ygor (Lugosi). Elaborate, talky production, but first-rate horror vehicle.

Son of Fury (1942) 98m. *** D: John Cromwell. Tyrone Power, Gene Tierney, George Sanders, Frances Farmer, Roddy McDowall, Kay Johnson, John Carradine, Elsa Lanchester, Harry Davenport, Dudley Digges, Ethel Griffies. Good costumer about aristocratic Sanders shunning nephew Power, who flees to desert isle to plan revenge; Tierney's on the island, too. Remade as TREASURE OF THE GOLDEN CONDOR.

Son of Godzilla (1969-Japanese) C-86m. *½ D: Jun Fukuda. Tadao

Takashima, Akira Kubo, Bibari Maeda, Akihiko Hirata, Kenji Sahara. Godzilla and son are threatened by giant mantises and a huge spider in this sci-fi story that emphasizes humor. Sequel to GODZILLA, KING OF THE MONSTERS.

Son of Kong (1933) 70m. **½ D: Ernest B. Schoedsack. Robert Armstrong, Helen Mack, Victor Wong, John Marston, Lee Kohlmar. Disappointing sequel to KING KONG. Special effects and variations on the giant ape scenes are interesting, though.

Son of Lassie (1945) C-102m. **½ D: S. Sylvan Simon. Peter Lawford, Donald Crisp, June Lockhart, Nigel Bruce, William Severn, Leon Ames, Fay Helm, Donald Curtis, Nils Asther, Helen Koford (Terry Moore). Fairly good follow-up to LASSIE COME HOME unfortunately gets the collie mixed up in war episodes.

Son of Monte Cristo, The (1940) 102m. *** D: Rowland V. Lee. Louis Hayward, Joan Bennett, George Sanders, Florence Bates, Lionel Royce, Montagu Love. Nothing new in big-scale swashbuckler, but very well done with Hayward battling Sanders and vying for Bennett's hand.

Son of Paleface (1952) C-95m. *** D: Frank Tashlin. Bob Hope, Jane Russell, Roy Rogers, Bill Williams, Harry Von Zell, Iron Eyes Cody. Slapstick follow-up to PALEFACE, with Hope playing title role in Western spoof; he gets to sally with shapely Russell again.

Son of Robin Hood, The (1959-British) C-81m. ** D: George Sherman. David Hedison, June Laverick, David Farrar, Marius Goring, George Coulouris. Bland forest tale continuing the legend of merry men led by Robin's descendant.

Son of Sinbad (1955) C-88m. *½ D: Ted Tetzlaff. Dale Robertson, Sally Forrest, Lili St. Cyr, Vincent Price. Limp Arabian Nights adventure. Sinbad, captured by caliph, forced to perform wonders to win freedom and save Baghdad from evil Tamerlane.

Son of Spartacus SEE: Slave, The.

Son of the Gods (1930) 82m. ** D: Frank Lloyd. Richard Barthelemess, Constance Bennett, Dorothy Matthews, Dickie Moore. Harmless drama. Barthelmess journeys to

Europe for college education but finds it no better than home. Fair cast trapped in hokey material.

Son of the Sheik (1926) 72m. *** D: George Fitzmaurice. Rudolph Valentino, Vilma Banky, Agnes Ayres, Karl Dane, Bull Montana. Sequel to THE SHEIK contains flavorful account of desert leader who falls in love with dancing-girl Banky. Handsomely mounted silent film is first-rate adventure/romance, with tongue slightly in cheek.

Son-Rise: A Miracle of Love (1979) C-96m. TVM D: Glenn Jordan. James Farentino, Kathryn Harrold, Stephen Elliott, Henry Olek, Michael & Casey Adams. Poignant true story of a couple who refuse to believe gloomy prognoses about their autistic son and devote their lives to treating him. The boy is played, quite remarkably, by veteran director King Vidor's 3½-year-old twin great grandsons. Above average.

Song for Miss Julie, A (1945) 69m. *½ D: William Rowland. Shirley Ross, Barton Hepburn, Jane Farrar, Roger Clark, Cheryl Walker, Elisabeth Risdon. Low-budget tale of woman who exposes family's past, then tries to cover it up again.

Song Is Born, A (1948) C-113m. **½ D: Howard Hawks. Danny Kaye, Virginia Mayo, Steve Cochran, Benny Goodman, Louis Armstrong, Charlie Barnet, Lionel Hampton. Below par musical remake of BALL OF FIRE has Kaye and Mayo supported by jazz greats.

Song of Bernadette, The (1943) 156m. **** D: Henry King. Jennifer Jones, William Eythe, Charles Bickford, Vincent Price, Lee J. Cobb, Anne Revere, Gladys Cooper. Overlong but excellent story of religious French girl in 1800s who sees great vision, incurs local wrath because of it. Winner of many Oscars including Best Actress for Jones in lead role.

Song of Freedom (1936-British) 80m. **½ D: J. Elder Wills. Paul Robeson, Elizabeth Welch, George Mozart, Esme Percy, Arthur Williams, Robert Adams. Robeson plays stevedore-turned-concert-singer who journeys to Africa in search of his roots. Promising idea doesn't quite work, but Robeson is well worth watching, as always.

Song of India (1949) 77m. ** D: Albert S. Rogell. Sabu, Gail Russell, Turhan Bey, Anthony Caruso, Aminta Dyne. Well-meaning Sabu releases jungle animals callously trapped by royal family; typical jungle escapist adventure.

Song of Love (1947) 119m. **½ D: Clarence Brown. Katharine Hepburn, Paul Henreid, Robert Walker, Henry Daniell, Leo G. Carroll, Gigi Perreau, Tala Birell, Henry Stephenson, Else Janssen. Classy production but slow-moving story of Clara Schuman (Hepburn), her composer husband (Henreid) and good friend Brahms (Walker).

Song of Norway (1970) C-142m. BOMB D: Andrew L. Stone. Florence Henderson, Toralv Maurstad, Christina Schollin, Frank Porretta, Edward G. Robinson, Harry Secombe, Robert Morley, Oscar Homolka. Horrible film. Biographical portions about Edvard Grieg are poor, not to mention weak and abridged versions of his best music. Beautiful to look at in Super Panavision, but not likely to impress on TV.

Song of Russia (1943) 107m. **½ D: Gregory Ratoff. Robert Taylor, Susan Peters, John Hodiak, Robert Benchley, Felix Bressart, Joan Lorring, Darryl Hickman. MGM's wartime attempt to do for Russia what MRS. MINIVER did for England; hokey but effective story of American conductor Taylor falling in love with Russian musician Peters. Thentopical attitude toward U.S.S.R. makes this an interesting period piece.

Song of Scheherazade (1947) C-106m. ** D: Walter Reisch. Yvonne De Carlo, Brian Donlevy, Jean-Pierre Aumont, Eve Arden, Philip Reed. Colorful tripe about Rimsky-Korsakov's true inspiration, a dancing girl (De Carlo).

Song of Songs (1933) 90m. *** D: Rouben Mamoulian. Marlene Dietrich, Brian Aherne, Lionel Atwill, Alison Skipworth, Hardie Albright, Helen Freeman. Set in 19th-century Germany, improbable romance tells of country maid Dietrich falling in love with sculptor Aherne, but marrying villainous Count Atwill. Dietrich is all, whether sulking or singing: "Johnny," "You Are My Song Of Songs."

Song of Surrender (1949) 93m. ** D: Mitchell Leisen. Wanda Hendrix, Claude Rains, Macdonald Carey, Andrea King, Henry O'Neill, Elizabeth Patterson. Mild turn-of-the-

century tale of young woman (Hendrix) and older husband Rains.

Song of the Islands (1942) C-75m. **½ D: Walter Lang. Betty Grable, Victor Mature, Jack Oakie, Thomas Mitchell, Billy Gilbert. Mature is new arrival to Pacific isle, Grable local girl he feuds with and romances. Slick musical fluff.

Song of the Open Road (1944) 93m. **½ D: S. Sylvan Simon. Edgar Bergen, W. C. Fields, Jane Powell, Bonita Granville, Reginald Denny, Rose Hobart, Sammy Kaye Orchestra. Young Powell's film debut and showcase for her vocal talents is fairly good, with token appearances by Fields and nemesis Charlie McCarthy (Bergen).

Song of the Sarong (1945) 65m. ** D: Harold Young. William Gargan, Nancy Kelly, Eddie Quillan. Gargan is involved in pearl-snatching from island natives; moderate production values.

Song of the Thin Man (1947) 86m. D: Edward Buzzell. William Powell, Myrna Loy, Keenan Wynn, Dean Stockwell, Gloria Grahame, Patricia Morison. SEE: Thin Man series

Song Remains the Same, The (1976) C-136m. ** D: Peter Clifton, Joe Massot. Amateurish mixture of fantasy sequences and documentary footage from Led Zeppelin's 1973 tour is for fans only. Even without the stereo sound, film will still clean out all eight sinus cavities.

Song to Remember, A (1945) C-113m. **½ D: Charles Vidor. Paul Muni, Merle Oberon, Cornel Wilde, Stephen Bekassy, Nina Foch, George Coulouris, Sig Arno. Colorful but superficial biography of Chopin with exaggerated Muni as his mentor, lovely Oberon as Georges Sand; good music, frail plot. Wilde was nominated for an Oscar, though.

Song Without End (1960) C-141m. **½ D: Charles Vidor, George Cukor. Dirk Bogarde, Capucine, Genevieve Page, Patricia Morison, Ivan Desny, Martita Hunt, Lou Jacobi. Beautiful music (scoring won an Oscar) submerged by dramatics of composer Franz Liszt's life. Bogarde tries; settings are lavish. Vidor died during filming, Cukor completed film.

Sonny and Jed (1973-Italian) C-98m. ** D: Sergio Corbucci. Tomas Milian, Telly Savalas, Susan George, Rosanna Janni, Laura Betti. Lighthearted spaghetti Western that teams escaped convict, pillaging his way across Mexico, with free-spirited gal who wants to become an outlaw, while shiny-domed Telly is determined lawman dogging their every move.

Sons and Lovers (1960-British) 103m. ***½ D: Jack Cardiff. Trevor Howard, Dean Stockwell, Wendy Hiller, Mary Ure, Heather Sears, William Lucas. Grim D. H. Lawrence story of sensitive youth Stockwell egged on by mother to make something of his life, away from coal-mining town and drunken father Howard. Both the film and Miss Ure were nominated for Oscars.

Sons O' Guns (1936) 82m. ** D: Lloyd Bacon. Joe E. Brown, Joan Blondell, Eric Blore, Winifred Shaw, Robert Barrat, Beverly Roberts, Craig Reynolds. Stars spark strained comedy of Brown joining the Army, sent to France where Blondell saves him from being shot as spy.

Sons of Katie Elder, The (1965) C-112m. *** D: Henry Hathaway. John Wayne, Dean Martin, Martha Hyer, Michael Anderson, Jr., Earl Holliman, Jeremy Slate, James Gregory, George Kennedy. Typical John Wayne action Western with Duke, Holliman, Anderson, and Martin the rowdy sons of frontier woman Katie Elder, who set out to avenge her death. Lively fun.

Sons of the Desert (1933) 69m. *** D: William A. Seiter. Stan Laurel, Oliver Hardy, Charley Chase, Mae Busch, Dorothy Christy, Lucien Littlefield. L&H's best feature film; duo sneaks up to fraternal convention without telling the wives; then the fun begins, with Chase as hilariously obnoxious conventioneer.

Sooky (1931) 85m. **½ D: Norman Taurog. Jackie Cooper, Jackie Coogan, Jackie Searl, Enid Bennett, Helen Jerome Eddy, Oscar Apfel. Entertaining but dated film of two young boys who become fast friends and engage in various escapades. Cooper is delightful as always.

Sooner or Later (1978) C-100m. TVM D: Bruce Hart. Denise Miller, Rex Smith, Barbara Feldon, Judd Hirsch, Lilia Skala, Morey Amsterdam, Vivian Blaine, Lynn Redgrave. Teenybopper falls for rock idol and tries to decide whether or not to "go all the way." Below average.

Sorcerer (1977) C-122m. **½ D: William Friedkin. Roy Scheider, Bruno Cremer, Francisco Rabal, Amidou, Ramon Bieri, Peter Capell.

Four fugitives in seedy Latin American town try to buy freedom by driving trucks of nitroglycerine over bumpy roads to help put out oil fire. Expensive remake of THE WAGES OF FEAR never really catches hold in spite of a few astounding scenes.

Sorcerers, The (1967-British) C-87m. **½ D: Michael Reeves. Boris Karloff, Catherine Lacey, Ian Ogilvy, Elizabeth Ercy, Susan George. Interesting but flawed low-budgetter. Husband-and-wife scientist team attempt to perfect domination-of-will techniques, persuade young man (Ogilvy) to join experiments. Downhill from there.

Sorceress, The (1955-French) 97m. **½ D: Andre Michel. Maurice Ronet, Marina Vlady, Nicole Courcel, Michel Etcheverry. Bizarre yarn of femme fatale Vlady and her beguiling alliance with Ronet.

Sorority Girl (1957) 60m. *½ D: Roger Corman. Susan Cabot, Dick Miller, Barbara Crane, Fay Baker. Tawdry account of college gal involved in absurd shenanigans on the campus.

Sorrow and the Pity, The (1972) 260m. **** D: Marcel Ophuls. Incredibly ambitious documentary about France's performance during WW2 is a total success. Film never becomes dull, in spite of four-and-a-half-hour length, even though bulk of footage is devoted to interviews with those who lived through the Nazi threat. A truly great film.

Sorrowful Jones (1949) 88m. **½ D: Sidney Lanfield. Bob Hope, Lucille Ball, William Demarest, Mary Jane Saunders, Bruce Cabot, Thomas Gomez. Average racetrack comedy, actually a remake of 1934 LITTLE MISS MARKER and hardly as good.

Sorry, Wrong Number (1948) 89m. *** D: Anatole Litvak. Barbara Stanwyck, Burt Lancaster, Ann Richards, Wendell Corey, Ed Begley, Leif Erickson. Not up to original radio thriller, movie adaptation is still tense study of woman overhearing murder plan on telephone, discovering she's to be the victim. Stanwyck won an Oscar nomination for her bravura performance.

Soul of a Monster, The (1944) 61m. BOMB D: Will Jason. Rose Hobart, George Macready, Jim Bannon, Jeanne Bates. Other-worldly Hobart has strange control over doctor Macready.

Soul of Nigger Charley, The (1973) C-104m. *½ D: Larry Spangler. Fred Williamson, D'Urville Martin, Denise Nicholas, Pedro Armendariz, Jr. Weak sequel to LEGEND OF NIGGER CHARLEY finds Charley trying to free slaves held captive by former Confederate Army officer in Mexico.

Soul Soldier (1972) 84m. BOMB D: John Cardos. Rafer Johnson, Robert DoQui, Lincoln Kilpatrick, Issac Fields, Janee Michelle, Cesar Romero. Awful movie about black troops of the 10th Cavalry and soldier who seduces the wife of his buddy.

Soul to Soul (1971) C-95m. *** D: Denis Sanders. Wilson Pickett, Ike and Tina Turner, Santana, The Isley Brothers. Good rockumentary filmed in Ghana during Independence Day celebration.

Souls at Sea (1937) 92m. *** D: Henry Hathaway. Gary Cooper, George Raft, Frances Dee, Olympe Bradna, Henry Wilcoxon, Harry Carey, Robert Cummings, Joseph Schildkraut, George Zucco. Fine actioner with Cooper and Raft struggling to save lives during ship tragedy; Cooper wrongly accused of irresponsibility. The stars make good team in entertaining tale.

Sound and the Fury, The (1959) C-115m. **½ D: Martin Ritt. Yul Brynner, Joanne Woodward, Margaret Leighton, Stuart Whitman, Ethel Waters, Jack Warden, Albert Dekker. Strange adaptation of William Faulkner novel becomes plodding tale of girl seeking independence from strict family rule in the South.

Sound of Anger, The (1968) C-100m. TVM D: Michael Ritchie. James Farentino, Guy Stockwell, Burl Ives, David Macklin, Lynda Day, Charles Aidman, Collin Wilcox. Brother lawyers drawn into murder case; sister of one of accused reveals that high-priced lawyer Nichols (Ives) hired to defend only one defendant. Uneven performances, lame script; only interesting character is Ives. Below average.

Sound of Fury, The (1951) 85m. **½ D: Cyril Endfield. Frank Lovejoy, Lloyd Bridges, Richard Carlson, Katherine Locke, Adele Jergens, Irene Vernon. Taut suspenser as manhunt closes in on kidnapper who killed his victim. Retitled: TRY AND GET ME.

Sound of Horror, The (1964-Spanish) 89m. *½ D: Jose Antonio Nieves Conde. Arturo Fernandez, Soledad Miranda, Antonio Casas, James Philbrook, Ingrid Pitt, Jose Badalo. Archeological expedition is terrorized by recently hatched prehistoric creatures; they're invisible but noisy. Pretty punk.

Sound of Music, The (1965) C-185m. ***½ D: Robert Wise. Julie Andrews, Christopher Plummer, Eleanor Parker, Peggy Wood, Richard Haydn. Call it corn if you like, but blockbuster Rodgers-Hammerstein musical based on life of Von Trapp family pleased more people than practically any other film in history. Fine music, beautiful scenery help offset coy aspects of script as singing family comes under fire in war-torn Austria. Won Academy Award as Best Picture.

Sound Off (1952) C-83m. ** D: Richard Quine. Mickey Rooney, Anne James, John Archer, Sammy White. Too-often unimaginative Army comedy with Rooney as a performer who's drafted and can't stop showing off.

Sounder (1972) C-105m. **** D: Martin Ritt. Cicely Tyson, Paul Winfield, Kevin Hooks, Carmen Mathews, Taj Mahal, James Best, Janet MacLachlan. Beautiful film, romanticizing in a positive sense experiences of black sharecropper family in 1930s, and the maturation of young Hooks. Full of fine performances that make characters utterly real.

Sounder, Part Two SEE: **Part 2, Sounder**

South of Pago Pago (1940) 98m. ** D: Alfred E. Green. Victor McLaglen, Jon Hall, Frances Farmer, Olympe Bradna, Gene Lockhart. Juvenile actioner of pirates stealing natives' supply of pearls, encountering local hostility; Farmer is properly sultry.

South of St. Louis (1949) C-88m. **½ D: Ray Enright. Joel McCrea, Alexis Smith, Zachary Scott, Dorothy Malone, Douglas Kennedy, Alan Hale, Victor Jory. Three ranching partners (McCrea, Scott, Kennedy) fall into dispute over land, money, Civil War gun-running, and women. Unmemorable Western has good cast, fast pacing, and Technicolor on its side.

South Pacific (1958) C-171m. **½ D: Joshua Logan. Rossano Brazzi,

Mitzi Gaynor, John Kerr, Ray Walston, Juanita Hall, France Nuyen. Disappointing filmization of Rodgers & Hammerstein show; adaptation of James Michener's moving vignettes about WW2 life on Pacific island needs dynamic personalities to make it catch fire, and they aren't here. Even location filming is lackluster. Adequate but hardly memorable; songs include "Bali H'ai," "There Is Nothing Like a Dame," "Happy Talk," "You've Got to be Taught," etc.

South Sea Sinner (1950) 88m. ** D: H. Bruce Humberstone. Macdonald Carey, Shelley Winters, Luther Adler, Frank Lovejoy, Liberace. Muddled melodrama involving fugitive from justice being intimidated by those on island who knew his past; Winters is blowsy cafe singer. Remake of 1940 SEVEN SINNERS.

South Sea Woman (1953) 99m. **½ D: Arthur Lubin. Burt Lancaster, Virginia Mayo, Chuck Connors, Arthur Shields, Paul Burke. Murky tropical isle story of love and deceit with soldier Lancaster sparking with Mayo.

Southern Star, The (1969-British-French-U.S.) C-102m. **½ D: Sidney Hayers. George Segal, Ursula Andress, Orson Welles, Ian Hendry, Harry Andrews, Michel Constantin. Uneven combination comedy-adventure detailing multiparty chase for possession of unusually large diamond boasts beautiful locations in Senegal, Africa, but not much else.

Southern Yankee, A (1948) 90m. *** D: Edward Sedgwick. Red Skelton, Brian Donlevy, Arlene Dahl, George Coulouris, Lloyd Gough, John Ireland, Charles Dingle, Joyce Compton. Hilarious Skelton comedy set during Civil War with Red a bumbling Yankee spy down South. Reminiscent of silent comedies, since Buster Keaton devised many of the film's gags.

Southerner, The (1945) 91m. **** D: Jean Renoir. Zachary Scott, Betty Field, Beulah Bondi, Bunny Sunshine, Jay Gilpin, Estelle Taylor, Percy Kilbride, Blanche Yurka. Superb drama of family struggling to make farmland self-supporting against serious odds.

Southside 1-1000 (1950) 73m. **½ D: Boris Ingster. Don DeFore, Andrea King, George Tobias, Barry Kelley. Straightforward narrative of

federal agent capturing counterfeiters.

Southwest Passage (1954) C-82m. ** D: Ray Nazarro. Joanne Dru, Rod Cameron, John Ireland, John Dehner, Guinn Williams, Mark Hanna. Familiar tale of bank robber and gal joining up with settlers heading West, staving off Indian attack.

Soylent Green (1973) C-100m. ** D: Richard Fleischer. Charlton Heston, Leigh Taylor-Young, Chuck Connors, Joseph Cotten, Brock Peters, Paula Kelly, Edward G. Robinson. Cardboard sci-fi film has New York a hopeless mess in year 2022, due to pollution, overcrowding; hardnosed cop Heston accidentally stumbles onto explosive government secret. Heavy-handed film too concerned with its "important message." Sci-fi was better when entertainment was foremost. Robinson's last film.

Space Children, The (1958) 69m. *½ D: Jack Arnold. Michel Ray, Adam Williams, Peggy Webber, Johnny Washbrook, Jackie Coogan. Pacifist-oriented sci-fi located at missile test center on Pacific Island; badly done.

Space Master X-7 (1958) 70m. ** D: Edward Bernds. Bill Williams, Lyn Thomas, Robert Ellis, Paul Frees. OK sci-fi: space missile returning to earth carries hidden fungus cargo, which could destroy civilization.

Spaceflight IC-1 (1965-British) 65m. **½ D: Bernard Knowles. Bill Williams, Norma West, John Cairney, Linda Marlowe, Jeremy Longhurst. Fair sci-fi has a few imaginative touches.

Spaceship to the Unknown (1936) 97m. **½ D: Frederick Stephani. Buster Crabbe, Jean Rogers, Frank Shannon, Charles Middleton, Priscilla Lawson, John Lipson. Newly edited version of FLASH GORDON serial covering first half of original story. With planet Mongo heading toward collision with Earth, Flash, Dale Arden, and Dr. Zarkov fly rocket ship to remedy impending disaster. Uninspired handling of footage from this famous serial.

Spaceways (1953-British) 76m. *½ D: Terence Fisher. Howard Duff, Eva Bartok, Andrew Osborn, Alan Wheatley. Cheapie sci-fi about space missile and man's flight into outer stratosphere.

Spanish Affair (1958-Spanish) C-95m. ** D: Don Siegel. Richard Kiley, Carmen Sevilla, Jose Guardiola, Jesus Tordesillas. Virtually a travelogue pegged on slight plot of Kiley, American architect, traveling in Iberia, falling in love with local gal; nice scenery.

Spanish Gardener, The (1956-British) **C-95m.** ******* D: Philip Leacock. Dirk Bogarde, Maureen Swanson, Jon Whiteley, Cyril Cusack, Bernard Lee, Michael Hordern. When gardener befriends employer's young son, diplomat father becomes jealous of their relationship. Intelligent and beautifully filmed adaptation of A. J. Cronin novel.

Spanish Main, The (1945) **C-100m.** ****½** D: Frank Borzage. Paul Henreid, Maureen O'Hara, Walter Slezak, Binnie Barnes, John Emery, Barton MacLane. Colorful escapism with swashbuckling pirate Henreid foiling villain Slezak, winning fair maiden O'Hara.

Spare The Rod (1961-British) **93m.** ****½** D: Leslie Norman. Max Bygraves, Donald Pleasence, Jean Anderson, Betty McDowall, Peter Reynolds, Geoffrey Keen. Bygraves is idealistic teacher in tough London school trying to communicate with pupils and cope with the system; OK drama.

Sparkle (1976) **C-100m.** ****½** D: Sam O'Steen. Philip M. Thomas, Irene Cara, Lonette McKee, Dwan Smith, Mary Alice, Dorian Harewood, Tony King. Rise of singing group not unlike The Supremes suffers from cliché overdose, but benefits from slick filmmaking, good musical numbers (by Curtis Mayfield), vivid performance by McKee.

Sparrows (1926) **84m.** ******* D: William Beaudine. Mary Pickford, Gustav von Seyffertitz, Roy Stewart, Mary Louise Miller, Charlotte Mineau, Spec O'Donnell. One of Mary's best silent pictures is a full-blooded melodrama about intrepid girl who struggles to protect band of younger orphans from their wicked captor.

Spartacus (1960) **C-196m.** *****½** D: Stanley Kubrick. Kirk Douglas, Laurence Olivier, Jean Simmons, Tony Curtis, Charles Laughton, Peter Ustinov, John Gavin, Nina Foch, Herbert Lom, John Ireland, Charles McGraw, Woody Strode. Great spectacle based on historical fact. Douglas heads huge cast as leader of slaves rebelling against Republican Rome. Beautiful Alex North score.

Spawn of the North (1938) **110m.**

*** D: Henry Hathaway. George Raft, Henry Fonda, Dorothy Lamour, Louise Platt, John Barrymore, Akim Tamiroff, Lynne Overman. Action-packed film of Canadian fisheries with good cast; Lamour surprisingly good, Barrymore amusing as talky newspaperman. Remade as ALASKA SEAS.

Speak Easily (1932) **82m.** ******* D: Edward Sedgwick. Buster Keaton, Jimmy Durante, Ruth Selwyn, Thelma Todd, Hedda Hopper, Sidney Toler. Dimwitted professor Keaton gets involved with show troupe en route to Broadway. One of Keaton's best talkies, with Durante in good form, Todd a wonderful vamp, Toler an amusing stage manager.

Speaking of Murder (1959-French) **80m.** ****½** D: Gilles Grangier. Jean Gabin, Annie Girardot, Paul Frankeur, Lino Ventura. Sensibly handled drama of brothers involved with life of crime.

Special Agent (1935) **78m.** ****½** D: William Keighley. Bette Davis, George Brent, Ricardo Cortez, Jack LaRue, Henry O'Neill. Programmer about Brent using Davis to get lowdown on racketeer Cortez.

Special Day, A (1977-Italian-Canadian) **C-106m.** ****½** D: Ettore Scola. Sophia Loren, Marcello Mastroianni, John Vernon, Françoise Berd, Nicole Magny. Two lonely people chance to meet on an eventful day in 1938; Loren is frumpy housewife, Mastroianni a troubled homosexual. Fine performances bolster this pleasant but trifling film.

Special Delivery (1955) **86m.** ****** D: John Brahm. Joseph Cotten, Eva Bartok, Niall MacGinnis, Rene Deltgen. Mild froth with Cotten on U.S. diplomatic staff posted in Iron Curtain country, dealing with an abandoned baby and curvaceous refugee Bartok.

Special Delivery (1976) **C-99m.** ******* D: Paul Wendkos. Bo Svenson, Cybill Shepherd, Michael Gwynne, Tom Atkins, Sorrell Booke. Diverting comedy-action caper has Vietnam vets led by Svenson robbing a bank. When only Svenson escapes, he has to contend with nutty artist Shepherd and killers after he stuffs the loot into a mailbox.

Special Olympics (1978) **C-100m.** TVM D: Lee Philips. Charles Durning, Philip Brown, George Parry, Irene Tedrow, Mare Winningham, Herb Edelman. Heartwarmer about

a widower's struggle to hold together his family of three teenagers,
one mentally retarded, finding self-
fulfillment in his love of sports.
Above average.

Special Section (1975-French) C-
110m. ** D: Costa-Gavras. Louis
Seigner, Michel Lonsdale, Jacques
Perrin, Bruno Cremer, Pierre Dux,
Henri Serre. Overlong, excessively
wordy drama of true happening in
occupied Paris in 1941. Four ex-
pendables are tried and ceremonially
condemned for the murder of a
young German naval cadet. Some
interest.

Specialists, The (1975) C-78m. TVM
D: Richard Quine. Robert York,
Maureen Reagan, Jack Hogan, Jed
Allen, Alfred Ryder, Harry Townes.
Drama based on the doings of the
U.S. Public Health Department, with
two dogged dog-and-cat-team doctors
trying to thwart possible epidemics.
Familiar hospital-style plot complica-
tions in this pilot for unsold series
called "Vector." Average.

Specter of the Rose (1946) 90m. ***
D: Ben Hecht. Judith Anderson,
Michael Chekhov, Ivan Kirov, Viola
Essen, Lionel Stander, Charles
"Red" Marshall. Stagey but truly
unusual Hecht film of insane ballet
dancer (Kirov) accused of murder,
and woman (Essen) who loves him
nevertheless.

Spectre (1977) C-100m. TVM D:
Clive Donner. Robert Culp, Gig
Young, John Hurt, Gordon Jackson,
Ann Bell, James Villiers, Marjel
Bennett. Classy demonology exercise
involving flamboyant criminologist
and his associate, an alcoholic doctor, who investigate devilish doings
in Playboy-type English abbey. Unusually lavish production helps
hurdle the foolishness. Average.

Speed Crazy (1959) 75m. BOMB D:
William Hole, Jr. Brett Halsey,
Yvonne Lime, Charles Wilcox, Slick
Slavin. Programmer sports car rac-
ing yarn, tied in with homicide and
police hunt for killer.

Speedtrap (1977) C-98m. ** D: Earl
Bellamy. Joe Don Baker, Tyne Daly,
Richard Jaeckel, Robert Loggia,
Morgan Woodward, Timothy Carey.
Private eye Baker is called in by the
cops to trap an elusive car thief, and
teamed with policewoman Daly.
Predictable screeching tires can't
save muddled script.

Speedway (1968) C-94m. ** D: Norman Taurog. Elvis Presley, Nancy

Sinatra, Bill Bixby, Gale Gordon.
Routine Presley tuner about big-
hearted stock car racer.

Speedy (1928) 71m. *** D: Ted
Wilde. Harold Lloyd, Ann Christy,
Bert Woodruff, Brooks Benedict,
Babe Ruth. Contrived but enjoyable
comedy has Harold trying to save
New York's last horse-drawn trolley,
run by his girlfriend's father, from
extinction. Vivid N.Y. location work
includes hair-raising chase scene,
and appealing cameo by Babe Ruth.
Edited for TV.

Spell, The (1977) C-78m. TVM D:
Lee Philips. Lee Grant, James Olson,
Susan Myers, Lelia Goldoni, Helen
Hunt, Jack Colvin, Barbara Bostock.
Occult thriller has an unloved teen-
ager turning her supernatural powers
on her tormentors. Merely a sani-
tized-for-TV CARRIE and a poor
substitute. Below average.

Spellbound (1945) 111m. ***½ D:
Alfred Hitchcock. Ingrid Bergman,
Gregory Peck, Leo G. Carroll, John
Emery, Michael Chekhov, Wallace
Ford, Rhonda Fleming, Bill Goodwin, Regis Toomey. Absorbing tale
of psychiatrist Bergman trying to
uncover Peck's hangups; Dali dream
sequences, innovative Miklos Rosza
score help Hitchcock create another
unique film.

Spencer's Mountain (1963) C-119m.
** D: Delmer Daves. Henry Fonda,
Maureen O'Hara, James MacArthur,
Donald Crisp, Wally Cox. Mawkish
sudser about Wyoming landowner
Fonda who keeps promising to build
another family house. Good cast
stuck with inferior script.

Spider, The (1945) 62m. ** D: Robert D. Webb. Richard Conte, Faye
Marlowe, Kurt Kreuger, John
Harvey, Ann Savage, Cara Williams,
Martin Kosleck. Programmer mystery yarn from 20th Century-Fox,
not allowing Conte to be his violent
best.

Spider and the Fly, The (1951-Brit-
ish) 87m. **½ D: Robert Hamer.
Guy Rolfe, Nadia Gray, Eric Portman, Maurice Denham, James Hayter, Arthur Lowe. Effective drama
of Gallic law enforcer and British
crook teaming up to retrieve government document; good interplay between cast members.

Spider-Man (1977) C-78m. TVM D:
E. W. Swackhamer. Nicholas Hammond, David White, Michael Pataki,
Hilly Hicks, Jeff Donnell, Lisa Eilbacher, Thayer David. Comic book

superhero pursues evil extortionist whose mind-control plot threatens the world. Played straight with special effects that aren't half bad. Average.

Spider Woman SEE: **Sherlock Holmes and the Spider Woman**

Spider Woman Strikes Back, The (1946) 59m. BOMB D: Arthur Lubin. Brenda Joyce, Gale Sondergaard, Kirby Grant, Rondo Hatton, Milburn Stone, Hobart Cavanaugh. Pitiful waste of fine actress Sondergaard in nonsense about evil Spider Woman; very campy.

Spies (1928-German) 90m. ***½ D: Fritz Lang. Rudolph Klein-Rogge, Gerda Maurus, Willy Fritsch, Lupu Pick, Fritz Rasp. Silent spy-thriller still packs a wallop as government agent Fritsch determines to capture master-fiend Haighi, who runs international organization of spies. One of Lang's early masterpieces.

Spies A Go Go SEE: **Nasty Rabbit, The**

Spikes Gang, The (1974) C-96m. BOMB D: Richard Fleischer. Lee Marvin, Ron Howard, Charlie Martin Smith, Arthur Hunnicutt, Noah Beery. Veteran gunfighter turns a trio of runaway boys into bank robbers; old-hat storyline in one of its least distinguished tellings.

Spin A Dark Web (1956-British) 76m. *½ D: Vernon Sewell. Faith Domergue, Lee Patterson, Rona Anderson, Martin Benson. Feeble sensationalism with Domergue queen of the racketeers.

Spinout (1966) C-90m. **½ D: Norman Taurog. Elvis Presley, Shelley Fabares, Diane McBain, Deborah Walley, Cecil Kellaway, Una Merkel. Typical Presley vehicle finds the singer racing autos and wooing the girls.

Spiral Road, The (1962) C-145m. *** D: Robert Mulligan. Rock Hudson, Burl Ives, Gena Rowlands, Geoffrey Keen. Overlong but interesting story of dedicated jungle doctor Hudson curing leprosy outbreak in Batavia.

Spiral Staircase, The (1946) 83m. ***½ D: Robert Siodmak. Dorothy McGuire, George Brent, Ethel Barrymore, Kent Smith, Rhonda Fleming, Gordon Oliver, Elsa Lanchester, Sara Allgood. Superb Hitchcock-like thriller with unforgettable performance by McGuire as mute servant

in eerie household which is harboring a killer.

Spirit Is Willing, The (1967) C-100m. *½ D: William Castle. Sid Caesar, Vera Miles, Barry Gordon, John McGiver, Cass Daley, Mary Wickes, Jesse White, Harvey Lembeck, Jay C. Flippen, Jill Townsend, John Astin, Doodles Weaver. Some good comedy performers are thrown away in stupid comedy about Caesar and family's summer house that happens to be haunted.

Spirit of Culver (1939) 89m. ** D: Joseph Santley. Jackie Cooper, Freddie Bartholomew, Tim Holt, Andy Devine, Gene Reynolds, Jackie Moran. All the usual prep-academy clichés adapted for military school setting with Cooper and Bartholomew predictable. Remake of 1932 film TOM BROWN OF CULVER.

Spirit of St. Louis, The (1957) C-138m. **** D: Billy Wilder. James Stewart, Patricia Smith, Murray Hamilton, Marc Connelly. Long but inventive presentation of Lindbergh's flight across the Atlantic is mainly a tour de force by Stewart, backed by good Franz Waxman music score.

Spirit of West Point, The (1947) 77m. **½ D: Ralph Murphy. Felix "Doc" Blanchard, Glenn Davis, Tom Harmon, Robert Shayne, Anne Nagel, Alan Hale, Jr. Good saga of West Point's football heroes, played by themselves; realistically done.

Spirits of the Dead (1969-French-Italian) C-117m. ***½ D: Roger Vadim, Louis Malle, Federico Fellini. Brigitte Bardot, Alain Delon, Jane Fonda, Terence Stamp, Peter Fonda, James Robertson Justice. Three separate horror tales, impossible to describe, delightful to watch, done with skill and flair by three top directors (in order as listed).

Spiritualist, The SEE: **Amazing Mr. X, The**

Spitfire (1934) 88m. *** D: John Cromwell. Katharine Hepburn, Robert Young, Ralph Bellamy, Martha Sleeper, Sara Haden, Sidney Toler. Hepburn as backwoods girl in love with married Young is effective. Bellamy in the background again.

Spitfire (1942-British) 90m. *** D: Leslie Howard. Leslie Howard, David Niven, Rosamund John, Roland Culver, Anne Firth, David Horne, J. H. Roberts. Howard is man who developed the ace fighting-plane Spitfire and saw it become one of the Allies' most valuable

[721]

WW2 assets. Good biographical drama. Original title: FIRST OF THE FEW.

Splendor (1935) 77m. **½ D: Elliott Nugent. Miriam Hopkins, Joel McCrea, Paul Cavanagh, Helen Westley, Billie Burke, Katharine Alexander, David Niven. Familiar story of McCrea's family upset when he loves poor-girl Hopkins instead of upper-class young lady; based on Rachel Crothers' story.

Splendor in the Grass (1961) C-124m. *** D: Elia Kazan. Natalie Wood, Warren Beatty, Pat Hingle, Audrey Christie, Sean Garrison, Sandy Dennis, Phyllis Diller, Barbara Loden, Zohra Lampert. Sentimental sudser by William Inge about emotionally broken girl (Wood) rebuilding her life; set in late 1920s Midwest.

Split, The (1968) C-91m. *½ D: Gordon Flemyng. Jim Brown, Diahann Carroll, Julie Harris, Ernest Borgnine, Gene Hackman, Jack Klugman, Warren Oates, James Whitmore, Donald Sutherland. Cast is good, but it's no match for routine, clichéd story of plot to rob L.A. Coliseum during a Rams game. Only for those who love caper movies.

Split Second (1953) 85m. **½ D: Dick Powell. Stephen McNally, Alexis Smith, Jan Sterling, Paul Kelly, Richard Egan. Most capable cast elevates contrived story of escaped convict McNally holding several people hostage at a bomb-testing site.

Spoilers, The (1942) 87m. **½ D: Ray Enright. Marlene Dietrich, Randolph Scott, John Wayne, Margaret Lindsay, Harry Carey, Richard Barthelmess. Retelling of famous Yukon tale has good cast but thuds out as average Western, with Dietrich as stereotyped saloon gal.

Spoilers, The (1955) C-84m. **½ D: Jesse Hibbs. Anne Baxter, Jeff Chandler, Rory Calhoun, Barbara Britton, Raymond Walburn. Fifth filming of Rex Beach's Klondike actioner; elaborate fight scene intact.

Spoilers of the Forest (1957) C-68m. ** D: Joseph Kane. Rod Cameron, Vera Ralston, Ray Collins, Hillary Brooke, Edgar Buchanan. Another timberland Western, with Cameron a tree-cutting foreman, romancing Ralston.

Spook Busters (1946) 68m. D: William Beaudine. Leo Gorcey, Huntz Hall, Douglass Dumbrille, Tanis Chandler, Bobby Jordan, Gabriel Dell, Billy Benedict. SEE: **Bowery Boys** series.

Spook Chasers (1957) 62m. D: George Blair. Huntz Hall, Stanley Clements, Percy Helton, Darlene Fields, Bill Henry, Pierre Watkin. SEE: **Bowery Boys** series.

Spook Who Sat By the Door, The (1973) C-102m. *½ D: Ivan Dixon. Lawrence Cook, Paula Lawrence, Janet League, J. A. Preston, Paul Butler. Cook, token black in the CIA, uses his knowledge to organize bands of teenaged guerrillas to bring whitey to his knees. Offbeat but offensive, and way too talky for cheap action fare.

Spooks Run Wild (1941) 69m. D: Phil Rosen. Béla Lugosi, Huntz Hall, Leo Gorcey, Bobby Jordan, Sunshine Sammy Morrison, Davd O'Brien, Dennis Moore. SEE: **Bowery Boys** series.

Sporting Club, The (1971) C-105m. BOMB D: Larry Peerce. Robert Fields, Nicolas Coster, Maggie Blye, Jack Warden, Richard Dysart, William Roerick. Badly directed dud about violence and promiscuity among some beautiful people in Northern Michigan has enough ineptitude to offend everyone. Lots of gore will be cut.

Spree (1967) C-84m. *½ D: Mitchell Leisen, Walon Green. Vic Damone, Julliet Prowse, Jayne Mansfield, Mickey Hargitay. Dull documentary on Las Vegas cabaret acts.

Spring and Port Wine (1970-British) C-101m. *** D: Peter Hammond. James Mason, Susan George, Diana Coupland, Marjorie Rhodes, Arthur Lowe. Unpretentious little gem about the generation gap in a lower-middle-class English family. Mason has one of his better later roles as the strict patriarch.

Spring in Park Lane (1947-British) 100m. **½ D: Herbert Wilcox. Anna Neagle, Michael Wilding, Tom Wallis, Marjorie Fielding, Nicholas Phipps, Josephine Fitzgerald. Stylish romance story of Wilding courting Neagle, his employer's niece.

Spring Madness (1938) 80m. **½ D: S. Sylvan Simon. Maureen O'Sullivan, Lew Ayres, Ruth Hussey, Burgess Meredith, Ann Morriss, Joyce Compton, Jacqueline Wells (Julie Bishop), Frank Albertson. Collegiate romance between O'Sullivan and brainy Ayres, elevated by strong cast. Enjoyable fluff.

Spring Parade (1940) 89m. ******* D: Henry Koster. Deanna Durbin, Robert Cummings, Mischa Auer, Henry Stephenson, Butch and Buddy, Anne Gwynne. Delightful Austrian fluff with Durbin romancing Cummings, working for baker S. Z. Sakall, dancing with wacky Auer, and singing, of course.

Spring Reunion (1957) 79m. ****** D: Robert Pirosh. Betty Hutton, Dana Andrews, Jean Hagen, James Gleason, Laura LaPlante, George Chandler. Potentially good soaper marred by low-budget production; Andrews and Hutton revive old memories at high school reunion and try to plan new future together; Hagen has some fine comic moments. Silent star LaPlante plays Hutton's mother.

Springfield Rifle (1952) C-93m. ****½** D: Andre de Toth. Gary Cooper, Phyllis Thaxter, David Brian, Lon Chaney, Paul Kelly. Unmemorable Cooper fare, with Gary joining up with outlaws to determine who's stealing government arms.

Springtime in the Rockies (1942) C-91m. ****½** D: Irving Cummings. Betty Grable, Carmen Miranda, Cesar Romero, Charlotte Greenwood, Edward Everett Horton, Jackie Gleason. Attractive cast in show biz musical; Harry James and band provide music, including "I Had The Craziest Dream."

Sputnik (1958-French) 85m. ****** D: Jean Dreville. Noel-Noel, Denise Gray, Noel Roquevert, Mischa Auer. Mild Cold War spoof involving Russian missile experiment which has backfired and naive Frenchman caught in the Red trap. Retitled: A DOG, A MOUSE AND A SPUTNIK.

Spy Chasers (1955) 61m. D: Edward Bernds. Leo Gorcey, Huntz Hall, Bernard Gorcey, Leon Askin, Sig Ruman, Veola Vonn, Bennie Bartlett, Richard Benedict. SEE: Bowery Boys series.

Spy Hunt (1950) 75m. ****½** D: George Sherman. Howard Duff, Marta Toren, Robert Douglas, Philip Dorn, Walter Slezak. Diverting yarn of espionage agent planting microfilmed secrets in panthers' collars; when they escape captivity various sides of the law seek the animals.

Spy in Black, The (1939-British) 82m. ******* D: Michael Powell. Conrad Veidt, Sebastian Shaw, Valerie Hobson, Marius Goring, June Duprez. Intriguing espionage melodrama set in WW1 Scotland with Veidt as German naval officer/spy and Hobson a charming double agent. Nice surprise twists in story, and bittersweet romance worked in.

Spy in Your Eye (1966-Italian) C-88m. ****** D: Vittorio Sala. Brett Halsey, Dana Andrews, Pier Angeli, Gaston Moschin. Hokum has Andrews as scientist with tele-camera implanted in eye, Halsey as U.S. agent trying to rescue Andrews' daughter (Angeli) captured by the Russians.

Spy Killer, The (1969) C-74m. TVM D: Roy Baker. Robert Horton, Sebastian Cabot, Jill St. John, Barbara Shelley, Lee Montague, Kenneth Warren. Former wife of spy-turned-private-eye part of plan to force agent back into service. His objective: little black book with list of agents. Overly confused drama, seemingly cynical of government secret services, but overall point of view hazy and dialogue sometimes awful. British-made. Average.

Spy Smasher SEE: Spy Smasher Returns

Spy Smasher Returns (1942) 100m. ****½** D: William Witney. Kane Richmond, Sam Flint, Marguerite Chapman, Hans Schumm, Tristram Coffin. Above par actioner from Republic Pictures dealing with famed crusader for good causes fighting for Allies in France during WW2, aided by twin brother. Reedited movie serial: SPY SMASHER.

Spy Who Came In from the Cold, The (1965) 112m. *****½** D: Martin Ritt. Richard Burton, Claire Bloom, Oskar Werner, Peter Van Eyck, George Voskovec, Sam Wanamaker, Cyril Cusack. John LeCarre's potent account of a Cold War spy's existence—minus glamorous trappings of movie cliché. Burton is excellent as embittered agent at the end of his career.

Spy Who Loved Me, The (1977) C-125m. *****½** D: Lewis Gilbert. Roger Moore, Barbara Bach, Curt Jurgens, Richard Kiel, Caroline Munro, Bernard Lee. Rousing, lavishly produced James Bond adventure (Moore's third), with wily .007 joining forces with a seductive Russian agent to quash arch-villian Stromberg's (Jurgens) plans for world destruction. At his best doing battle with a persistent steel-toothed goon,

menacingly played by seven-foot-two-inch giant Kiel. Grand fun for one and all.

Spy with a Cold Nose, The (1966-British) **C-93m.** ** D: Daniel Petrie. Laurence Harvey, Daliah Lavi, Lionel Jeffries, Eric Portman, Denholm Elliott. Tame spoof on secret agent movies. British agents plant bug in bulldog Disraeli, gift to Russian ambassador. Cast tries to keep story afloat.

Spy With My Face, The (1966) **C-88m.** **½ D: John Newland. Robert Vaughn, Senta Berger, David McCallum, Leo G. Carroll. Another expanded MAN FROM U.N.C.L.E. TV series entry, with Vaughn matching wits with his double (working for foreign powers); Berger the enemy femme fatale.

S*P*Y*S (1974) **C-87m. BOMB** D: Irvin Kershner. Donald Sutherland, Elliott Gould, Zouzou, Joss Ackland, Shane Rimmer, Vladek Sheybal. Sutherland-Gould teaming fails to regenerate M*A*S*H electricity in a good director's worst film. Laughless CIA spoof about the defection of a Russian dancer is unworthy of anyone's time.

Squad Car (1960) **60m. BOMB** D: Ed Leftwich. Vici Raaf, Paul Bryar, Don Marlowe, Lyn Moore. Grade-C narrative of police investigating homicide and counterfeiting.

Square Jungle, The (1955) **86m.** **½ D: Jerry Hopper. Tony Curtis, Pat Crowley, Ernest Borgnine, Paul Kelly, Jim Backus. Overly-familiar boxing yarn with Curtis the fighter on the way up—Crowley his girl.

Square Ring, The (1955-British) **73m.** ** D: Michael Relph. Basil Dearden, Jack Warner, Kay Kendall, Joan Collins, Robert Beatty, Bill Owen, Maxwell Reed. Uninspired intertwining of events in lives of people involved in the fight game.

Squeaker, The (1965-German) **95m.** **½ D: Alfred Vohrer. Heinz Drache, Eddie Arent, Klaus Kinski, Barbara Rutting. Over complex actioner with a variety of plots spinning from action of underworld selling off proceeds of diamond robbery.

Squirm (1976) **C-92m.** *** D: Jeff Lieberman. Don Scardino, Patricia Pearcy, R. A. Dow, Jean Sullivan, Peter MacLean, Fran Higgins. Above-average horror outing builds to good shock sequences: when power line falls to the ground on rainy Georgia night, it drives large, slimy sandworms from the ground, which terrorize small town.

Sssssss (1973) **C-99m.** *** D: Bernard L. Kowalski. Strother Martin, Dirk Benedict, Heather Menzies, Richard B. Shull, Tim O'Connor, Jack Ging. Well-done horror tale of doctor who finds a way of transforming man into King Cobra. Exceptional job done by the makeup department.

SST—Death Flight (1977) **C-100m. TVM** D: David Lowell Rich. Barbara Anderson, Bert Convy, Peter Graves, Lorne Greene, Season Hubley, Tina Louise, George Maharis, Burgess Meredith, Doug McClure, Martin Milner, Brock Peters, Robert Reed, Susan Strasberg. Terror aloft with traditional celebrity-studded passenger list. Sabotage aboard the inaugural flight of America's first SST turns it into a nightmare. Sounds familiar—and looks it. Average. Title changed to SST—DISASTER IN THE SKY.

Stablemates (1938) **89m.** ** D: Sam Wood. Wallace Beery, Mickey Rooney, Arthur Hohl, Margaret Hamilton, Minor Watson, Marjorie Gateson. Sticky story of jockey Rooney and racetrack mentor Beery. All the stops out during the syrupy scenes.

Stage Door (1937) **92m.** **** D: Gregory La Cava. Katharine Hepburn, Ginger Rogers, Adolphe Menjou, Andrea Leeds, Gail Patrick, Constance Collier, Lucille Ball, Eve Arden, Ann Miller, Ralph Forbes, Franklin Pangborn. Theatrical boarding house is setting for superb film of Edna Ferber-George S. Kaufman play with fine acting by Hepburn as rich girl trying to succeed on her own, Menjou as propositioning producer, Leeds as hypersensitive actress.

Stage Door Canteen (1943) **132m.** **½ D: Frank Borzage. Cheryl Walker, William Terry, Marjorie Riordan, Lon McCallister, Margaret Early, Michael Harrison (Sunset Carson). Soldier falls in love with canteen hostess. Plot abetted by cameo bits by Tallulah Bankhead, Katharine Hepburn, Harpo Marx, George Raft, Paul Muni, Merle Oberon, Helen Hayes, Ed Wynn, many others.

Stage Fright (1950) **110m.** **½ D: Alfred Hitchcock. Marlene Dietrich, Jane Wyman, Michael Wilding, Richard Todd, Kay Walsh, Alastair

Sim, Joyce Grenfell, Sybil Thorndike. Drama student is suspected when actress' husband is murdered; some exciting moments, but the Master misses on this one. Filmed in London with delightful British cast; Marlene sings "The Laziest Gal in Town."

Stage Struck (1936) 86m. **½ D: Busby Berkeley. Dick Powell, Joan Blondell, Warren William, Frank McHugh, Jeanne Madden. Throwaway film with stale plot kept barely alive by energetic cast; backstage musical has no real production numbers. Highlight is The Yacht Club Boys' insane "The Body Beautiful." Leading lady Madden remained obscure after this one.

Stage Struck (1958) C-95m. **½ D: Sidney Lumet. Henry Fonda, Susan Strasberg, Joan Greenwood, Christopher Plummer, Herbert Marshall. Faded remake of MORNING GLORY retelling the ascent of Broadway-bound actress. Supporting cast hampered by unconvincing Strasberg in lead role and by unreal theater world atmosphere.

Stagecoach (1939) 99m. ***½ D: John Ford. John Wayne, Claire Trevor, Thomas Mitchell, Louise Platt, Andy Devine, George Bancroft, John Carradine, Berton Churchill, Donald Meek. Classic Western focusing on relationships between assorted stagecoach passengers, under pressure from Indian attack. Fine acting by all; Mitchell as drunken doctor won Oscar. Pictorially beautiful, ineptly remade in 1966.

Stagecoach (1966) C-115m. **½ D: Gordon Douglas. Ann-Margret, Alex Cord, Red Buttons, Michael Connors, Bing Crosby, Bob Cummings, Van Heflin, Slim Pickens, Stefanie Powers, Keenan Wynn. Colorful, star-studded Western is OK, but can't hold a candle to the 1939 masterpiece. Overlong, with only occasional action scenes to liven it up.

Stagecoach to Dancers' Rock (1962) 72m. ** D: Earl Bellamy. Warren Stevens, Martin Landau, Jody Lawrance, Judy Dan. Modest production involves stage passengers left stranded in wastelands when driver discovers one of them has smallpox.

Stagecoach to Fury (1956) 76m. *½ D: William Claxton. Forrest Tucker, Mari Blanchard, Wallace Ford,

Margia Dean. Flat outlaw holdup oater.

Staircase (1969-British) C-100m. ** D: Stanley Donen. Richard Burton, Rex Harrison, Cathleen Nesbitt, Beatrix Lehmann. Shock value of Burton and Harrison as a gay couple was all this film had going for it in 1969, and nothing has changed since then, except heightened sophistication of audiences. A curio, to be sure.

Stairway to Heaven (1945-British) C-104m. ***½ D: Michael Powell, Emeric Pressburger. David Niven, Kim Hunter, Raymond Massey, Robert Coote, Roger Livesey, Richard Attenborough. HERE COMES MR. JORDAN on a more elaborate scale. A gem about pilot Niven accidentally taken to Heaven where he must plead for return to life. Original title: A MATTER OF LIFE AND DEATH.

Stakeout on Dope Street (1958) 83m. *½ D: Irvin Kershner. Yale Wexler, Jonathan Haze, Morris Miller, Abby Dalton, Herschel Bernardi. Trio of youths discover cache of heroin, believing their futures will now be uncomplicated; good premise poorly executed.

Stalag 17 (1953) 120m. **** D: Billy Wilder. William Holden, Don Taylor, Otto Preminger, Robert Strauss, Harvey Lembeck, Sig Ruman. Granddaddy of all WW2 POW films. Holden (in Oscar-winning performance) is pessimistic sergeant suspected of being German spy. Wilder brilliantly blends drama with comedy to show monotonous, anxiety-ridden life of POWs. Wonderful comic relief by Strauss and Lembeck.

Stalking Moon, The (1969) C-109m. ** D: Robert Mulligan. Gregory Peck, Eva Marie Saint, Robert Forster, Noland Clay, Russell Thorson, Frank Silvera. Army scout helps white woman who has lived with the Apaches to escape with her young half-breed son, while boy's father comes after them. Potentially interesting Western is both slick and dull; nice photography.

Stalk the Wild Child (1976) C-78m. TVM D: William Hale. David Janssen, Trish Van Devere, Benjamin Bottoms, Joseph Bottoms, Jamie Smith Jackson, Allan Arbus. Behavioral psychologist Janssen attempts to civilize a youth raised by wild dogs. Well-intentioned but plodding. Below average.

Stallion Road (1947) 91m. *½ D: James V. Kern. Ronald Reagan, Alexis Smith, Zachary Scott, Peggy Knudsen, Patti Brady, Harry Davenport. Dedicated veterinarian Reagan and novelist friend Scott vie for the affection of horse rancher Smith; second-string cast in formula script.

Stamboul Quest (1934) 88m. **½ D: Sam Wood. Myrna Loy, George Brent, Lionel Atwill, C. Henry Gordon, Mischa Auer. Exotic combination of romance and intrigue with German spy Loy falling in love with American student Brent in WW1 Turkey.

Stampede (1949) 78m. **½ D: Lesley Selander. Rod Cameron, Gale Storm, Johnny Mack Brown, Don Castle, John Miljan. Good Western of range war between cattle ranchers.

Stand at Apache River, The (1953) C-77m. ** D: Lee Sholem. Stephen McNally, Julia Adams, Hugh Marlowe, Jack Kelly, Hugh O'Brian. Title tells all.

Stand by for Action (1942) 109m. **½ D: Robert Z. Leonard. Robert Taylor, Brian Donlevy, Charles Laughton, Walter Brennan, Marilyn Maxwell, Henry O'Neill. We're still waiting. Good cast in standard WW2 Navy saga.

Stand-In (1937) 91m. *** D: Tay Garnett. Leslie Howard, Humphrey Bogart, Joan Blondell, Alan Mowbray, Marla Shelton, C. Henry Gordon, Jack Carson. Enjoyable spoof of Hollywood, with stuffy banker Howard sent to assess dwindling fortunes of Colossal Pictures, becoming involved with perky stand-in Blondell and mercurial producer Bogart to save company from ruin.

Stand Up and Be Counted (1972) C-99m. *½ D: Jackie Cooper. Jacqueline Bisset, Stella Stevens, Steve Lawrence, Gary Lockwood, Lee Purcell, Loretta Swit, Hector Elizondo. Touted as first film about Women's Lib; writer Bisset returns to home town, first becomes aware of abuses women must endure. Cardboard all the way; only standout is Stevens' comic performance.

Stand Up and Cheer (1934) 80m. *** D: Hamilton MacFadden. Warner Baxter, Madge Evans, James Dunn, John Boles, Shirley Temple. Enjoyable Depression film about presidential commission to lighten coun-

try's spirits; Shirley steals show singing "Baby Take A Bow."

Stand Up and Fight (1939) 105m. ** D: W. S. Van Dyke II. Wallace Beery, Robert Taylor, Florence Rice, Charles Bickford, Charles Grapewin, Selmer Jackson. OK Western with railroading pioneer Taylor meeting crisis after crisis, battling stubborn stage-rider Beery.

Standing Room Only (1944) 83m. *½ D: Sidney Lanfield. Fred MacMurray, Paulette Goddard, Edward Arnold, Hillary Brooke, Roland Young, Anne Revere. Topical wartime comedy is now dated. MacMurray and Goddard can't find rooms, so they work as servants.

Standing Tall (1978) C-100m. TVM D: Harvey Hart. Robert Forster, Linda Evans, Will Sampson, L. Q. Jones, Chuck Connors, Robert Donner. Depression-era western pitting a small-time half-breed cattle rancher against a ruthless land baron. The time period might change, but the formula remains the same. Average.

Stanley & Livingstone (1939) 101m. *** D: Henry King. Spencer Tracy, Cedric Hardwicke, Richard Greene, Nancy Kelly, Walter Brennan, Charles Coburn. Elaborate production with Tracy as determined reporter who searches Africa for missing missionary (Hardwicke) at turn of century. Entertaining drama with beautifully understated performance by Tracy.

Star! (1968) C-175m. **½ D: Robert Wise. Julie Andrews, Richard Crenna, Michael Craig, Daniel Massey, Robert Reed, Bruce Forsyth, Beryl Reid. Razzle-dazzle biography of stage star Gertrude Lawrence never rings true, but does have mammoth production numbers worth seeing (especially in color). Julie tries, but never comes across; Massey is amusing if affected as Noel Coward. After box office flop, film was trimmed to 120 minutes and retitled THOSE WERE THE HAPPY TIMES.

Star, The (1953) 89m. ***½ D: Stuart Heisler. Bette Davis, Sterling Hayden, Natalie Wood, Warner Anderson. Incisive study of Oscar-winning actress (Davis) trying to make a comeback, but finding love instead; film is filled with many true Hollywoodisms.

Star Dust (1940) 85m. **½ D: Walter Lang. Linda Darnell, John

Payne, Roland Young, Charlotte Greenwood, William Gargan, Mary Beth Hughes, Mary Healy, Donald Meek. Hokey, entertaining yarn about talent scout Young (from Amalgamated Studios) discovering star-struck Darnell and football player Payne, bringing them to Hollywood.

Star in the Dust (1956) €-80m. **
D: Charles Haas. John Agar, Mamie Van Doren, Richard Boone, Leif Erickson, Coleen Gray, James Gleason. Intriguing cast put through tame paces of sheriff Agar forced to fight his townsfolk to retain law and order.

Star Is Born, A (1937) C-111m. ***½ D: William Wellman. Fredric March, Janet Gaynor, Adolphe Menjou, May Robson, Andy Devine, Lionel Stander. Two remakes haven't dimmed the glow of this drama about a self-destructive actor and the young movie hopeful he marries. March and Gaynor are at their best and 1930s flavor (captured in early Technicolor) is a plus; screenplay by Dorothy Parker, Alan Campbell, and Robert Carson was inspired in part by 1932 film WHAT PRICE HOLLYWOOD. Oscar-winner for original story.

Star Is Born, A (1954) €-154m. ***½ D: George Cukor. Judy Garland, James Mason, Jack Carson, Charles Bickford, Tom Noonan. Lengthy but well-acted musical remake of 1937 film of girl's overnight Hollywood success and decline of star-husband. Judy at pinnacle singing "The Man That Got Away."

Star Is Born, A (1976) €-140m. **½ D: Frank Pierson. Barbra Streisand, Kris Kristofferson, Gary Busey, Oliver Clark, Paul Mazursky. Bynow familiar story is given an unconvincing treatment, with change of setting to the world of rock music. Only comes to life during Streisand's vibrant song numbers, which transcend script and surrounding drama.

Star Maker, The (1939) 94m. **½ D: Roy Del Ruth. Bing Crosby, Louise Campbell, Laura Hope Crews, Ned Sparks, Ethel Griffies, Billy Gilbert. Crosby plays Gus Edwards, vaudeville impresario who turned talented youngsters into stars. Pleasant musical doesn't always stick to facts.

Star of India (1954-British) C-84m. **½ D: Arthur Lubin. Cornel Wilde,

Jean Wallace, Herbert Lom. So-so costumer, overly earnest. Wilde is Gallic nobleman trying to reestablish his rightful inheritance.

Star Spangled Girl (1971) C-92m. *½ D: Jerry Paris. Sandy Duncan, Tony Roberts, Todd Susman, Elizabeth Allen. Very unfunny Neil Simon comedy about the saccharine-sweet girl-next-door who falls in with two ultraradical campus newspaper editors.

Star Spangled Rhythm (1942) 99m. *** D: George Marshall. Bing Crosby, Ray Milland, Bob Hope, Veronica Lake, Dorothy Lamour, Susan Hayward, Dick Powell, Alan Ladd, Paulette Goddard, Cecil B. DeMille, Arthur Treacher, Eddie Anderson, William Bendix. Paramount's star-packed WW2 extravaganza, filled with songs and sketches, no plot. Better numbers include: "That Old Black Magic," "Time To Hit The Road To Dreamland."

Star Trek—The Movie (1979) C-132m. *½ D: Robert Wise. William Shatner, Leonard Nimoy, DeForest Kelley, Stephen Collins, Persis Khambatta, George Takei, Nichelle Nichols. The first $40 million TV show is for Trekkies only, with Shatner's performance one of the worst ever seen in a film of this magnitude. Too bad the money couldn't have been spent on something truly substantial—like a theatrical version of GILLIGAN'S ISLAND.

Star Wars (1977) C-121m. ***½ D: George Lucas. Mark Hamill, Harrison Ford, Carrie Fisher, Peter Cushing, Alec Guinness, Anthony Daniels, Kenny Baker. Elaborate, imaginative update of Flash Gordon incredibly became one of the most popular films of all time. It's a hip homage to B-movie ethics and heroism in the space age, as a callow youth (Hamill) becomes an interplanetary hero with the help of some human and robot friends. R2D2 and C-3PO steal the show. Oscars for various technical achievements and John Williams' rousing score. Followed by sequel THE EMPIRE STRIKES BACK.

Starcrash (1979) C-92m. *½ D: Lewis Coates. Marjoe Gortner, Caroline Munro, Christopher Plummer, David Hasselhoff, Robert Tessier, Joe Spinell. Grinning Gortner and sexy Munro are recruited to save the universe from destruction by bad-guy Spinell. Moronic sci-fi movie with clumsy special effects; good for a few laughs, nothing more.

Stardust (1975-British) C-97m. ***½ D: Michael Apted. David Essex, Adam Faith, Larry Hagman, Keith Moon, Dave Edmunds, Ines Des Longchamps, Edd Byrnes. Powerful sequel to THAT'LL BE THE DAY follows amazing rise and fall of Beatles-like rock group and its lead singer (Essex). Candid, provocative, and utterly believable.

Starlift (1951) 103m. ** D: Roy Del Ruth. Janice Rule, Dick Wesson, Ron Hagerthy, Richard Webb. Flimsy account of GI romancing an actress, allowing for scenes of movie stars entertaining troops. Cameos by Warner Bros. people like Cagney, Virginia Mayo, Ruth Roman, Doris Day, Gordon MacRae, etc.

Stars and Stripes Forever (1952) C-89m. **½ D: Henry Koster. Clifton Webb, Robert Wagner, Ruth Hussey, Debra Paget, Finlay Currie. Diverting, fictionalized biography of John Philip Sousa, well-played by Webb, with standard march tunes worked into plot nicely.

Stars Are Singing, The (1953) C-99m. **½ D: Norman Taurog. Rosemary Clooney, Anna Maria Alberghetti, Lauritz Melchoir, Fred Clark. Frothy musical with ridiculous plot-line of immigration authorities tracking down Alberghetti as contestant on TV talent show.

Stars in My Crown (1950) 89m. ***½ D: Jacques Tourneur. Joel McCrea, Ellen Drew, Dean Stockwell, Alan Hale, Lewis Stone, Ed Begley, Amanda Blake, James Arness. Gentle, moving story of a quiet but persuasive minister in rural 19th-century America; episodic film creates warm feeling for characters and setting. Prime Americana from Joe David Brown's popular book.

Stars Look Down, The (1939-British) 110m. **** D: Carol Reed. Michael Redgrave, Margaret Lockwood, Emlyn Williams, Nancy Price, Edward Rigby, Cecil Parker. Absorbing classic about Welsh miners trying to work despite unsafe mining conditions; most realistic atmosphere.

Starsky and Hutch (1974) C-78m. TVM D: Barry Shear. David Soul, Paul Michael Glaser, Antonio Fargas, Michael Lerner, Richard Ward, Gilbert Green. Tough pair of undercover cops investigate a double homicide and discover they are the intended victims. OK pilot to hit TV series. Average.

Start Cheering (1938) 78m. *** D: Albert S. Rogell. Jimmy Durante, Walter Connolly, Joan Perry, Charles Starrett, Gertrude Niesen, Hal LeRoy, The 3 Stooges, Broderick Crawford, Louis Prima. Snappy collegiate musical about rugged movie-star Starrett going back to school, with cohorts Connolly and Durante tagging along. Modest, enjoyable film with plenty of specialty numbers, guest stars, songs.

Start the Revolution Without Me (1970) C-98m. *** D: Bud Yorkin. Gene Wilder, Donald Sutherland, Hugh Griffith, Jack MacGowran, Billie Whitelaw, Victor Spinetti, Orson Welles. Madcap comedy involving two sets of twins who meet just before French Revolution. Somewhat ignored in 1970, film now has a deserved cult following; the cast, especially Wilder, is hilarious.

Starting Over (1979) C-106m. *** D: Alan J. Pakula. Burt Reynolds, Jill Clayburgh, Candice Bergen, Charles Durning, Frances Sternhagen, Austin Pendleton, Mary Kay Place. Likeable comedy about divorced man who falls in love but can't erase feelings for his ex-wife; top performances, but unfortunately, story goes awry toward conclusion for a lackluster turn of events and denouement.

State Department—File 649 (1948) C-87m. ** D: Peter Stewart (Sam Newfield). Virginia Bruce, William Lundigan, Raymond Bond, Nana Bryant. Minor espionage story of American agent involved in Oriental intrigue with a demonic warlord.

State Fair (1933) 80m. *** D: Henry King. Janet Gaynor, Will Rogers, Lew Ayres, Sally Eilers, Norman Foster, Louise Dresser, Victor Jory, Frank Craven. Not just a Rogers vehicle, but slice of life 30s-style as country farm family gets ready for annual outing to state fair: Mom's entering baking contest, Dad the pig contest, son and daughter looking for first love. Great atmosphere, good performances.

State Fair (1945) C-100m. *** D: Walter Lang. Jeanne Crain, Dana Andrews, Dick Haymes, Vivian Blaine, Charles Winninger, Fay Bainter, Donald Meek, Frank McHugh. Bright, engaging musical of family's adventures at Iowa State Fair; colorful with fine songs:

"Grand Night For Singing," "It Might As Well Be Spring." Retitled: IT HAPPENED ONE SUMMER.

State Fair (1962) C-118m. BOMB D: Jose Ferrer. Pat Boone, Bobby Darin, Pamela Tiffin, Ann-Margret, Alice Faye, Tom Ewell. Remake of sprightly 1945 musical is pretty bad. Faye came out of retirement to play Tiffin's mother—bad mistake. Ewell even sings to a cow!

State of Siege (1973-French) C-120m. *** D: Costa-Gavras. Yves Montand, Renato Salvatori, O. E. Hasse, Jacques Weber, Jean-Luc Bideau, Evangeline Peterson. Highly controversial film, based on fact, about political assassination in Uruguay caused a hubbub when it was yanked for political reasons from the opening of Washington's American Film Institute Theater. Film is interesting, but way too one-sided to be truly effective.

State of the Union (1948) 124m. ***½ D: Frank Capra. Spencer Tracy, Katharine Hepburn, Angela Lansbury, Van Johnson, Adolphe Menjou, Lewis Stone. Howard Lindsay-Russel Crouse play becomes smooth film with Presidential candidate (Tracy) battling for integrity with his wife (Hepburn); good support from Lansbury as millionairess backing campaign, Johnson as campaign manager.

State Penitentiary (1950) 66m. ** D: Lew Landers. Warner Baxter, Karin Booth, Robert Shayne, Richard Benedict. Programmer with Baxter a prisoner seeking to escape.

State Secret SEE: **Great Manhunt, The**

State's Attorney (1932) 79m. *** D: George Archainbaud. John Barrymore, Helen Twelvetrees, William "Stage" Boyd, Ralph Ince, Jill Esmond. Good Barrymore vehicle casts him as flamboyant courtroom attorney with higher ambitions; barely credible but great fun to watch. Co-scripted by Gene Fowler.

Station Six-Sahara (1964-British) 99m. *½ D: Seth Holt. Carroll Baker, Peter Van Eyck, Ian Bannen, Denholm Elliott, Biff McGuire. Dreary yarn of five love-starved men who find something new to fight over when sexpot Baker and her estranged husband crash land at their desert oasis.

Station West (1948) 92m. *** D: Sidney Lanfield. Dick Powell, Jane Greer, Tom Powers, Steve Brodie,

Gordon Oliver, Raymond Burr, Agnes Moorehead, Burl Ives. Entertaining adaptation of Luke Short story about undercover military Intelligence officer Powell stirring up trouble in Western town to find who's behind series of gold robberies. Sharp dialogue throughout.

Statue, The (1971-British) C-84m. BOMB D: Rod Amateau. David Niven, Virna Lisi, Robert Vaughn, Ann Bell, John Cleese, David Mills. Poor comedy concerning 20-foot statue (replica of Niven) with enormous male organ. Sure to be edited for TV, but no great loss.

Stavisky (1974-French) C-117m. ***½ D: Alain Resnais. Jean-Paul Belmondo, Anny Duperey, Charles Boyer, Francois Perier, Roberto Biasco. Stylish bio of the French swindler of the early 1930s; pleasant cast, lavish photography, fine Stephen Sondheim score.

Stay Away, Joe (1968) C-102m. *½ D: Peter Tewksbury. Elvis Presley, Burgess Meredith, Joan Blondell, Katy Jurado, Thomas Gomez, Henry Jones, L. Q. Jones. Bad film, even for Presley, about contemporary Indians. In addition to reinforcing stereotypes, movie fails as entertainment.

Stay Hungry (1976) C-103m. *** D: Bob Rafelson. Jeff Bridges, Sally Field, Arnold Schwarzenegger, R. G. Armstrong, Helena Kallianiotes, Roger E. Mosley. Charles Gaines novel about body-building in the "New South" is eccentric mixture of comedy and drama, but many fine scenes, happy performances from Field and Schwarzenegger make it worthwhile.

Steagle, The (1971) C-90m. ** D: Paul Sylbert. Richard Benjamin, Chill Wills, Cloris Leachman, Jean Allison, Susan Tyrrell. Missile crisis causes professor to go berserk and try living in lifestyles that previously were mental fantasies. Far-fetched.

Steamboat Bill, Jr. (1928) 71m. **½ D: Charles F. Riesner. Buster Keaton, Ernest Torrence, Marion Byron, Tom Lewis, Tom McGuire. Buster plays a milquetoast who must prove his manhood to steamboat captain father (Torrence). Not one of Keaton's best silents, but there are great moments, and the classic, eye-popping cyclone finale.

Steamboat 'Round the Bend (1935) 96m. **½ D: John Ford. Will Rogers, Anne Shirley, Irvin S. Cobb, Eugene Pallette, John McGuire,

Stepin Fetchit. Enjoyable period-piece, but Rogers' usual witticisms are sorely missed. Shirley is particularly good as swamp-girl taken in by steamboat captain Rogers.

Steel Against the Sky (1941) 68m. ** D: A. Edward Sutherland. Lloyd Nolan, Alexis Smith, Craig Stevens, Gene Lockhart, Edward Ellis. Routine tale of brothers Nolan and Stevens, steel workers, both interested in Smith.

Steel Bayonet (1958-British) 84m. ** D: Michael Carreras. Leo Genn, Kieron Moore, Michael Medwin, Robert Brown. Military unit is ordered to defend deserted farmhouse/lookout base at all costs; tame WW2 film set in Africa.

Steel Cage, The (1954) 80m. ** D: Walter Doniger. Paul Kelly, Maureen O'Sullivan, Walter Slezak, John Ireland, Lawrence Tierney, Alan Mowbray, George E. Stone, Lyle Talbot. Pedestrian telling of life at San Quentin, despite good cast. Sequel to DUFFY OF SAN QUENTIN.

Steel Claw, The (1961) C-96m. **½ D: George Montgomery. George Montgomery, Charito Luna, Mario Barri, Paul Sorensen. Montgomery turns partisan leader when he loses hand in WW2, forcing his marine discharge; on-location filming in Philippines and sufficient combat action spark story along.

Steel Cowboy (1978) C-100m. TVM D: Harvey Laidman. James Brolin, Rip Torn, Strother Martin, Jennifer Warren, Melanie Griffith, Julie Cobb. Good-old-buddy adventure flick about an independent trucker who puts his marriage on the line to save his rig by hauling stolen cattle. Average.

Steel Fist, The (1952) 73m. *½ D: Wesley Barry. Roddy McDowall, Kristine Miller, Harry Lauter, Rand Brooks. Quickie flick with McDowall involved in escape from Iron Curtain country; low production values.

Steel Helmet, The (1951) 84m. ***½ D: Samuel Fuller. Gene Evans, Robert Hutton, Steve Brodie, James Edwards, Richard Loo, Sid Melton. Evans is a gutsy American sergeant caught in dizzying turn of events in early days of Korean war; solid melodrama written and directed by Fuller, with surprisingly contemporary view of war itself.

Steel Jungle, The (1956) 86m. *½ D: Walter Doniger. Perry Lopez, Beverly Garland, Allison Hayes,

Walter Abel, Ted de Corsia, Kenneth Tobey. Lukewarm account of prison life.

Steel Key, The (1953-British) 74m. **½ D: Robert Baker. Terence Morgan, Joan Rice, Raymond Lovell, Dianne Foster, Esmond Knight. Espionage and homicide abound in this fast-clipping caper about stolen formulas for processing hardened steel.

Steel Lady, The (1953) 84m. **½ D: E. A. Dupont. Rod Cameron, Tab Hunter, John Dehner, Anthony Caruso. Fair adventure of four trapped men in desert who find old German tank.

Steel Town (1952) C-85m. ** D: George Sherman. Ann Sheridan, John Lund, Howard Duff, James Best, Nancy Kulp. Uninspired story of steelmaking and the personal problems of nephew of steel plant owner; Sheridan tries, but can't perk up this programmer.

Steel Trap, The (1952) 85m. **½ D: Andrew L. Stone. Joseph Cotten, Teresa Wright, Jonathan Hale, Walter Sande. Trim caper of Cotten who steals money from his bank and over the weekend decides to replace it.

Steelyard Blues (1973) C-93m. *** D: Alan Myerson. Jane Fonda, Donald Sutherland, Peter Boyle, Garry Goodrow, Howard Hesseman, John Savage. Entertaining comic concoction about band of misfits who become involved in nutty project of rejuvenating abandoned airplane. Amiably antiestablishment film highlights Boyle as an ingenious fantasist named Eagle. Retitled THE FINAL CRASH.

Stella (1950) 83m. **½ D: Claude Binyon. Ann Sheridan, Victor Mature, David Wayne, Frank Fontaine. Screwball comedy and murder doesn't blend well in tale of nutty family that tries to hide a most persistently visible corpse.

Stella Dallas (1937) 111m. *** D: King Vidor. Barbara Stanwyck, John Boles, Anne Shirley, Barbara O'Neil, Alan Hale, Tim Holt, Marjorie Main. Definitive soap opera of woman who sacrifices everything for her daughter; Stanwyck was nominated for an Oscar. Filmed before in 1925.

Step by Step (1946) 62m. ** D: Phil Rosen. Lawrence Tierney, Anne Jeffreys, Lowell Gilmore, George Cleveland. Patriotic programmer with Tierney a WW2 veteran uncovering Fascist agents in America.

Step Down to Terror (1958) 75m. ** D: Harry Keller. Colleen Miller, Charles Drake, Rod Taylor, Josephine Hutchinson. Washed-out remake of Hitchcock's SHADOW OF A DOUBT, retells account of psychomurderer returning to home town after long absence.

Step Lively (1944) 88m. *** D: Tim Whelan. Frank Sinatra, George Murphy, Adolphe Menjou, Gloria DeHaven, Eugene Pallette, Anne Jeffreys, Walter Slezak. Brisk musical remake of ROOM SERVICE with producer Murphy wheeling and dealing to get his show produced. Engagingly frantic, with sharp dialogue, funny contribution by Slezak.

Step Out of Line (1970) C-100m. TVM D: Bernard McEveety. Vic Morrow, Peter Falk, Peter Lawford, Jo Ann Pflug. Korean War vets, all in financial straits, decide at reunion party to pull bank robbery. Good performances enliven otherwise standard script, predictable outcome. Average.

Stepford Wives, The (1975) C-115m. *** D: Bryan Forbes. Katharine Ross, Paula Prentiss, Nanette Newman, Patrick O'Neal, Tina Louise, Peter Masterson. Effective chiller finds suburban housewives Ross and Prentiss trying to understand perpetually blissful state of the women of Stepford, Connecticut. From Ira Levin's best-seller.

Steppenwolf (1974) C-105m. **½ D: Fred Haines. Max von Sydow, Dominique Sanda, Pierre Clementi, Carla Romanelli, Alfred Bailloux. Literal adaptation of Herman Hesse's unfilmable novel about a misanthropic writer and an enigmatic young woman. Visually jazzy, rarely boring, but a dead end.

Steppin' In Society (1945) 72m. *½ D: Alexander Esway. Edward Everett Horton, Ruth Terry, Gladys George, Jack LaRue, Lola Lane, Iris Adrian, Isabel Jewell. Minor flick with vacationing judge Horton involved with rehabilitating jailbirds.

Sterile Cuckoo, The (1969) C-107m. *** D: Alan J. Pakula. Liza Minnelli, Wendell Burton, Tim McIntire. Lonely Pookie Adams (Minnelli) forces herself on shy freshman Burton, who's impelled to pay attention. Winning look at young love and sensitive feelings gives Liza a standout role, with Burton equally fine as naive boy who eventually outgrows Pookie.

Stevie (1978-British) C-102m. *** D: Robert Enders. Glenda Jackson, Mona Washbourne, Alec McCowen, Trevor Howard. Film version of Hugh Whitemore's London stage play about British poetess Stevie Smith (Jackson), who lives with her maiden aunt (Washbourne). A finely wrought character study, with excellent performances all around.

Stickin' Together (1978) C-78m. TVM D: Jerry Thorpe. Clu Gulager, Sean Roche, Sean Marshall, Lori Walsh, Randi Kiger, Keith Mitchell. Cutesy family tale of a bunch of orphans who find a surrogate uncle in a Hawaiian beach bum. This was the pilot to the short-run series THE MACKENZIES OF PARADISE COVE. Average.

Stigma (1972) C-93m. BOMB D: David E. Durston. Philip M. Thomas, Harlan Cary Poe, Josie Johnson, Peter H. Clune, William Magerman, Connie Van Ess. Title refers to venereal disease; assorted orgies catch up with some young people in absurd melodrama. Some scenes may be cut.

Stiletto (1969) C-98m. *½ D: Bernard Kowalski. Alex Cord, Britt Ekland, Patrick O'Neal, Joseph Wiseman, Barbara McNair, Roy Scheider. Weak Mafia melodrama about handsome killer who lives like a playboy, kills for money. Repercussions abound when he decides to quit his job.

Sting, The (1973) C-129m. ***½ D: George Roy Hill. Paul Newman, Robert Redford, Robert Shaw, Charles Durning, Ray Walston, Eileen Brennan, Harold Gould. Two small-time Chicago con-men try to put "the sting" on a bigwig from New York (Shaw). This long but entertaining film won seven Oscars, including Best Picture, and sparked national revival of Scott Joplin's ragtime music.

Stingray (1978) C-100m. *½ D: Richard Taylor. Sherry Jackson, Christopher Mitchum, Bill Watson, Les Lannom, Sondra Theodore, Bert Hinchman. Low-grade mix of action, blood, and comedy as Mitchum and Lannom buy a Stingray, unaware that it's filled with stolen loot and dope, prompting pursuit by murderous Jackson. Filmed in and around St. Louis.

Stolen Face, A (1952-British) 72m. **½ D: Terence Fisher. Lizabeth Scott, Paul Henreid, Andre Morell, Susan Stephen, Mary Mackenzie,

John Wood. Interesting but far-fetched drama of plastic surgeon Henreid trying to transform female convict into replica of the woman he loves but cannot have.

Stolen Heaven (1938) 88m. **½ D: Andrew L. Stone. Gene Raymond, Olympe Bradna, Glenda Farrell, Lewis Stone, Porter Hall, Douglass Dumbrille, Joe Sawyer. Offbeat story of jewel thieves posing as musicians, on the lam but having change of heart when they meet kindly maestro Stone.

Stolen Hours, The (1963) C-100m. **½ D: Daniel Petrie. Susan Hayward, Michael Craig, Diane Baker, Edward Judd, Paul Rogers. Hayward takes Bette Davis' DARK VICTORY, transplants it to contemporary England, in tale of woman with fatal illness trying to get as much out of life as she can. Original is far superior in all departments.

Stolen Kisses (1968-French) C-90m. **** D: François Truffaut. Jean-Pierre Leaud, Delphine Seyrig, Michel Lonsdale, Claude Jade, Harry Max, Daniel Ceccaldi. Already regarded as a classic, this alternately touching and hilarious film about an inept but likable jerk-of-all-trades is possibly Truffaut's best movie and one of the best treatments of young love ever put on the screen.

Stolen Life, A (1946) 107m. **½ D: Curtis Bernhardt. Bette Davis, Glenn Ford, Dane Clark, Walter Brennan, Charlie Ruggles, Bruce Bennett, Peggy Knudsen. A twin takes her sister's place as wife of the man they both love in this slick but far-fetched soaper with Bette in dual role; remake of 1939 film with Elisabeth Bergner.

Stone (1979) C-100m. TVM D: Corey Allen. Dennis Weaver, Pat Hingle, Roy Thinnes, Vic Morrow, Mariette Hartley, Joby Baker, Joey Forman, Kim Hamilton, Steve Allen. Literate cop show pitting a veteran detective-moonlighting-as-novelist (a thinly disguised Joseph Wambaugh) against his hard-nosed superior who's trying to get him off the force. Pilot to Weaver's newest series. Above average.

Stone Killer, The (1973) C-95m. **½ D: Michael Winner. Charles Bronson, Martin Balsam, David Sheiner, Norman Fell, Ralph Waite. Incredibly bloody film about hard-headed cop trying to unravel chain of mys-

tery that leads to elaborate plan, using Vietnam vets to stage underworld massacre. Well-made but incessantly bloody.

Stonestreet: Who Killed the Centerfold Model? (1977) C-78m. TVM D: Russ Mayberry. Barbara Eden, Joseph Mascolo, Joan Hackett, Richard Basehart, Louise Latham, Sally Kirkland. Private eye Eden on a missing-person case that involves blackmail, homicide and the porno rackets. Competent pilot movie for a "Police Woman"-style series. Average.

Stooge, The (1952) 100m. **½ D: Norman Taurog. Dean Martin, Jerry Lewis, Polly Bergen, Eddie Mayehoff, Marion Marshall. Egocentric singer (Martin) learns the hard way just how important his stooge (Lewis) is to his success. Martin & Lewis go dramatic with middling results.

Stoolie, The (1974) C-90m. **½ D: John G. Avildsen. Jackie Mason, Dan Frazer, Marcia Jean Kurtz, Anne Marie. A slice of low life is portrayed in this flawed but interesting little film, with Mason as a paid police informer who absconds to Miami with $7,500 in a misguided attempt to "retire."

Stop! Look! and Laugh! (1960) 78m. **½ D: Jules White. The Three Stooges, Paul Winchell, Jerry Mahoney, Knucklehead Smiff, The Marquis Chimps, Officer Joe Bolton. Original 3 Stooges' funniest sequences strung together by Paul Winchell and dummies is aimed at children. Much of it is familiar, but still amusing.

Stop Me Before I Kill! (1961-British) 109m. ** D: Val Guest. Claude Dauphin, Diane Cilento, Roland Lewis, Françoise Rosay. Turgid dramatics: mentally unhinged man's new marriage is threatened by his illness and his psychiatrist's yen for his wife. Originally titled THE FULL TREATMENT.

Stop the World, I Want to Get Off (1966-British) C-98m. **½ D: Philip Saville. Tony Tanner, Millicent Martin, Leila Croft, Valerie Croft. Only the music by Tony Newley and Leslie Bricusse still remains charming in this allegory of opportunity set in a circus. Heavy-handed.

Stop Train 349 (1964-German-French) 95m. ** D: Rolf Haedrich. Jose Ferrer, Sean Flynn, Nicole Courcel, Jess Hahn. Average thriller of Communist manhunt for East

German refugee hidden aboard U.S. military train heading from Berlin to west zone.

Stop, You're Killing Me (1952) C-86m. ** D: Roy Del Ruth. Broderick Crawford, Claire Trevor, Virginia Gibson, Sheldon Leonard, Margaret Dumont. Mild froth based on Damon Runyon story of racketeer Crawford going legitimate. Remake of A SLIGHT CASE OF MURDER.

Stopover Tokyo (1957) C-100m. **½ D: Richard L. Breen. Robert Wagner, Joan Collins, Edmond O'Brien, Ken Scott. Lumbering spy tale, loosely based on John P. Marquand novel. On location filming in Japan makes a pretty background, but flat characters remain.

Stork Club, The (1945) 98m. **½ D: Hal Walker. Betty Hutton, Barry Fitzgerald, Don DeFore, Andy Russell, Iris Adrian, Robert Benchley. Hat-check girl Hutton mysteriously becomes wealthy in fanciful musicomedy, mainly for Betty's fans. She sings "Doctor, Lawyer, Indian Chief."

Stork Talk (1961-British) 97m. ** D: Michael Forlong. Tony Britton, Anne Heywood, John Turner, Nicole Perroult. Harmless sex comedy involving married couples' indiscretions and the pat resolution of their problems.

Storm, The (1938) 75m. **½ D: Harold Young. Charles Bickford, Barton MacLane, Preston Foster, Tom Brown, Nan Grey, Andy Devine. Not-bad yarn of brothers Bickford and MacLane constantly arguing, mostly over women, reconciled during climactic storm.

Storm at Daybreak (1933) 80m. **½ D: Richard Boleslawski. Kay Francis, Nils Asther, Jean Parker, Walter Huston, Phillips Holmes, Eugene Pallette. Lavishly mounted soaper set in Serbia. Francis is wife of mayor Huston, and having affair with convalescing soldier Asther.

Storm Center (1956) 85m. *½ D: Daniel Taradash. Bette Davis, Brian Keith, Kim Hunter, Paul Kelly. Librarian becomes center of controversy over censorship and communism. Not even Davis can uplift clichés.

Storm Fear (1955) 88m. ** D: Cornel Wilde. Cornel Wilde, Jean Wallace, Dan Duryea, Lee Grant. Good cast elevates this yarn of wounded bank robber hiding out at brother's home, intimidating everyone.

Storm in a Teacup (1937-British) 87m. *** D: Victor Saville, Ian Dalrymple. Vivien Leigh, Rex Harrison, Cecil Parker, Sara Allgood, Arthur Wontner, Ivor Barnard. Witty social comedy barbing over words, loves and politics.

Storm Over Lisbon (1944) 86m. ** D: George Sherman. Vera Ralston, Richard Arlen, Erich von Stroheim, Otto Kruger, Eduardo Ciannelli, Mona Barrie. WW2 intrigue in Lisbon with nightclub performer Ralston siding with Von Stroheim to get goods on American Arlen; low-grade rehash of typical WW2 material.

Storm Over the Nile (1956-British) C-113m. **½ D: Zoltan Korda, Terence Young. Anthony Steel, Laurence Harvey, James Robertson Justice, Mary Ure. Remake of THE FOUR FEATHERS lacks class and flair, but story is still good.

Storm Rider, The (1957) 70m. *½ D: Edward Bernds. Scott Brady, Mala Powers, Bill Williams, John Goddard. Sagebrush lowjinks of cattle owners vs. ranchers.

Storm Warning (1950) 93m. ** D: Stuart Heisler. Ginger Rogers, Ronald Reagan, Doris Day, Steve Cochran. Rogers inadvertently witnesses a Ku Klux Klan murder in this overheated melodrama, with Day turning in her first dramatic performance as Ginger's younger married sister.

Stormy Weather (1943) 77m. **½ D: Andrew L. Stone. Lena Horne, Bill Robinson, Cab Calloway and his Band, Katherine Dunham, Fats Waller, Dooley Wilson, Nicholas Brothers. Delightful musical numbers strung together by silly show biz script which tries to pair Bojangles and Horne as romantic duo. Waller does "Ain't Misbehavin'," Lena sings title number.

Story of a Three Day Pass, The (1967-French) 87m. *** D: Melvin Van Peebles. Harry Baird, Nicole Berger, Christian Marin, Pierre Doris. Flawed but impressive film about affair between black American soldier and white French girl.

Story of a Woman (1970) C-90m. *½ D: Leonardo Bercovici. Bibi Andersson, Robert Stack, James Farentino, Annie Girardot, Didi Perego, Mario Nascimbene. Turgid tale of pianist who tries to remain faithful to her husband, even though she's still hung up on old flame; Bibi is wasted.

Story of Adele H, The (1975-French) C-97m. **½ D: Francois Truffaut. Isabelle Adjani, Bruce Robinson, Sylvia Marriott, Reubin Dorey, Joseph Blatchley, M. White. Understated drama of young woman's obsession with a soldier who does not return her love. Adjani's performance is excellent, but film is curiously unmoving.

Story of Alexander Graham Bell, The (1939) 97m. *** D: Irving Cummings. Don Ameche, Loretta Young, Henry Fonda, Charles Coburn, Spring Byington, Gene Lockhart, Polly Ann Young. Ameche overacts at times in title role, but entertaining version of inventor is given plush 20th Century-Fox presentation.

Story of David, The (1976) C-250m. TVM D: Alex Segal, David Lowell Rich. Timothy Bottoms, Anthony Quayle, Keith Michell, Jane Seymour, Susan Hampshire. Vivid Biblical drama with two hours devoted to the Old Testament shepherd boy who slew Goliath, and two given over to the now-King David's involvement with Bathsheba. Told with reverence, acted with sincerity, produced with authenticity. Above average.

Story of Dr. Wassell, The (1944) C-140m. **½ D: Cecil B. DeMille. Gary Cooper, Laraine Day, Signe Hasso, Dennis O'Keefe, Paul Kelly, Philip Ahn, Barbara Britton. Far from top-grade Cooper or DeMille is this story of dedicated Navy doctor who saved fighting men in Japan during WW2; slow-moving account.

Story of Esther Costello, The (1957-British) 103m. **½ D: David Miller. Joan Crawford, Rossano Brazzi, Heather Sears, Lee Patterson, Fay Compton, Bessie Love, Ron Randell. Socialite rehabilitates impoverished blind and deaf girl and promotes charity fund in her name. Interesting look at charity huckstering but melodrama is overwrought and often unintentionally funny.

Story of G.I. Joe, The (1945) 109m. ***½ D: William Wellman. Burgess Meredith, Robert Mitchum, Freddie Steele, Wally Cassell, Jimmy Lloyd. Meredith is superb as war correspondent Ernie Pyle living with Yank soldiers on front lines to report their stories; Mitchum's first outstanding film role as soldier.

Story of Jacob and Joseph, The (1974) C-100m. TVM D: Michael Cacoyannis. Keith Michell, Tony LoBianco, Colleen Dewhurst, Herschel Bernardi, Harry Andrews, Julian Glover. Two-part Biblical movie. First, the tale of Jacob (Michell) and Esau (Glover) and the fight over their birthright. Second, adventures of Joseph (LoBianco) and his brothers who sold him into slavery. Alan Bates narrates these impressively acted stories, written by Ernest Kinoy and reverently approached by director Cacoyannis. Above average.

Story of Louis Pasteur, The (1936) 85m. ***½ D: William Dieterle. Paul Muni, Josephine Hutchinson, Anita Louise, Donald Woods, Fritz Leiber. The achievements of the famous French scientist are chronicled in this engrossing film. Muni gives Oscar-winning performance.

Story of Mankind, The (1957) C-100m. ** D: Irwin Allen. Ronald Colman, Hedy Lamarr, Groucho, Harpo, Chico Marx, Virginia Mayo, Agnes Moorehead, Vincent Price, Francis X. Bushman, Charles Coburn, Marie Windsor, John Carradine. Ambitious in concept, laughable in juvenile results. Hendrik Van Loon book of highlights of man's history becomes string of clichéd costume episodes, badly cast and poorly handled.

Story of Molly X, The (1949) 82m. **½ D: Crane Wilbur. June Havoc, John Russell, Dorothy Hart, Charles McGraw. Havoc is most earnest as gangster's widow who goes out to find her husband's killer.

Story of Pretty Boy Floyd, The (1974) C-78m. TVM D: Clyde Ware. Martin Sheen, Kim Darby, Michael Parks, Ellen Corby, Joseph Estevez, Bill Vint, Abe Vigoda, Steven Keats, Ford Rainey. Sheen gives nicely-shaded portrait of the Depression-era farmboy who became infamous bank robber and killer. Picturesque, violent, and surprisingly literate. Above average.

Story of Robin Hood, The (1952) C-83m. *** D: Ken Annakin. Richard Todd, Joan Rice, Peter Finch, James Hayter, James Robertson Justice, Martita Hunt, Hubert Gregg. Zesty, colorful retelling of the familiar story, filmed in England by Walt Disney with excellent cast. Not as personality-oriented as other versions, but just as good in its own way.

Story of Ruth, The (1960) C-132m. **½ D: Henry Koster. Stuart Whitman, Tom Tryon, Peggy Wood, Viveca Lindfors, Jeff Morrow, Elana Eden. Static biblical nonepic retelling story of woman renouncing her "gods" when she discovers true faith.

Story of Seabiscuit, The (1949) C-93m. **½ D: David Butler. Shirley Temple, Barry Fitzgerald, Lon McCallister, Rosemary DeCamp. Standard horseracing saga with Fitzgerald supporting most of the film as a dedicated trainer.

Story of the Count of Monte Cristo, The SEE: **Count of Monte Cristo**

Story of Three Loves, The (1953) C-122m. *** D: Vincente Minnelli. Pier Angeli, Ethel Barrymore, Kirk Douglas, Farley Granger, Leslie Caron, James Mason, Agnes Moorehead, Zsa Zsa Gabor. Excellent cast in three varying stories of human relationships.

Story of Vernon & Irene Castle, The (1939) 93m. *** D: H. C. Potter. Fred Astaire, Ginger Rogers, Edna May Oliver, Walter Brennan, Lew Fields. Usual Astaire-Rogers breeziness suffers from slow handling of events in lives of famous early 20th-century dancing duo. Still good, with many fine period dance and song numbers.

Story of Will Rogers, The (1952) C-109m. *** D: Michael Curtiz. Will Rogers, Jr., Jane Wyman, Carl Benton Reid, James Gleason, Mary Wickes, Eddie Cantor. One of few show biz biographies that rings true, with Rogers Jr. faithfully portraying his father, rodeo star turned humorist; Wyman as his loving wife.

Story on Page One, The (1959) 123m. *** D: Clifford Odets. Rita Hayworth, Anthony Franciosa, Gig Young, Mildred Dunnock, Hugh Griffith, Sanford Meisner, Robert Burton. Lovers Hayworth and Young dispose of Rita's husband, hire Franciosa to represent them in court. Odets' stark film has high tension and sincere performances. Dunnock's Mama portrayal is a bit much.

Storyteller, The (1977) C-100m. TVM D: Robert Markowitz. Martin Balsam, Patty Duke Astin, James Daly, Doris Roberts, David Spielberg, Rose Gregorio. Veteran writer is troubled by charges his TV play motivated a teen-ager to set his school on fire and die in the blaze.

Balsam's fine performance fails to save this disappointing study of the effect of TV violence on children. Average.

Stowaway (1936) 86m. **½ D: William A. Seiter. Robert Young, Alice Faye, Shirley Temple, Eugene Pallette, Helen Westley, Arthur Treacher. Predictable yet engaging shipboard story with Faye and Young romancing, Temple the incurably curious child.

Stowaway Girl (1957-British) 87m. **½ D: Guy Hamilton. Trevor Howard, Elsa Martinelli, Pedro Armendariz, Donald Pleasence, Warren Mitchell. Trim, sensible romancer of middle-aged captain Howard's infatuation with Martinelli, who hid aboard his ship. Originally titled MANUELA.

Stowaway to the Moon (1975) C-100m. TVM D: Andrew V. McLaglen. Lloyd Bridges, Michael Link, Jeremy Slate, Morgan Paull, James McMullan, John Carradine, Keene Curtis. Delightful family-oriented tale about an 11-year-old rocket enthusiast (Link) who fulfills his life's dream by sneaking aboard a space capsule about to blast off. Above average.

Straight Time (1978) C-114m. *** D: Ulu Grosbard. Dustin Hoffman, Theresa Russell, Gary Busey, Harry Dean Stanton, M. Emmet Walsh, Rita Taggart. Hoffman knocks heads with slimy parole officer Walsh following his release from prison and begins a downward slide. Engrossing if not particularly distinguished melodrama gets a real shot in the arm from terrific supporting performances.

Strait-Jacket (1964) 89m. **½ D: William Castle. Joan Crawford, Diane Baker, Leif Erickson, Anthony Hayes, John Howard St. John, Rochelle Hudson. Crawford served twenty years for axe murders; now, living peacefully with daughter Baker, murders start again and she's suspect. Crawford's strong portrayal makes this one of best in horror-star entries.

Stranded (1935) 76m. ** D: Frank Borzage. Kay Francis, George Brent, Patricia Ellis, Donald Woods, Robert Barrat, Barton MacLane. Francis is a travelers' aid worker solving everybody's problems, tangling with band of racketeers.

Strange Adventure, A (1956) *½ D: William Witney. Joan Evans, Ben

Cooper, Marla English, Jan Merlin, Nick Adams. Murky little drama of speed-demon youths involved in hold-up.

Strange Affair, The (1968-British) C-106m. **½ D: David Greene. Michael York, Jeremy Kemp, Susan George, Jack Watson, Nigel Davenport, George A. Cooper, Barry Fantoni. Pretty good police melodrama about young recruit York's dallying with sexy hippie and superior Kemp's failure to get needed conviction; George steals the show in one of her first film appearances.

Strange Affair of Uncle Harry, The (1945) 80m. *** D: Robert Siodmak. George Sanders, Geraldine Fitzgerald, Ella Raines, Sara Allgood, Moyna MacGill, Samuel S. Hinds. Engrossing melodrama about mild-mannered Sanders falling in love, but unable to break from grip of domineering sister (Fitzgerald). Vivid, if not always believable, with unfortunate ending demanded by 1940s censorship. Originally titled UNCLE HARRY.

Strange Affection (1957-British) 84m. ** D: Wolf Rilla. Richard Attenborough, Colin Petersen, Jill Adams, Terence Morgan. OK drama involving conflict between son and father, climaxing when former is arrested for latter's crime. Original title: THE SCAMP.

Strange and Deadly Occurrence, The (1974) C-78m. TVM D: John Llewellyn Moxey. Robert Stack, Vera Miles, L. Q. Jones, Herb Edelman, Dena Dietrich, Margaret Willock. Family is terrorized by mysterious force in their newly purchased country home. Occult tale with standard thrills at predictable intervals. Average.

Strange Awakening (1958-British) 75m. *½ D: Montgomery Tully. Lex Barker, Carole Mathews, Nora Swinburne, Richard Molinos, Peter Dyneley. Barker is tourist in France involved in snowballing case of fraud; muddled drama.

Strange Bargain (1949) 68m. ** D: Will Price. Martha Scott, Jeffrey Lynn, Harry Morgan, Katherine Emery, Henry O'Neill. Routine story of innocent young man who gets mixed up in underworld activities.

Strange Bedfellows (1964) C-98m. **½ D: Melvin Frank. Rock Hudson, Gina Lollobrigida, Gig Young, Terry-Thomas, Nancy Kulp. Hudson ambles through another marital mix-

up comedy, this one with fiery Gina and lots of slapstick. Mild entertainment.

Strange Cargo (1940) 105m. *** D: Frank Borzage. Joan Crawford, Clark Gable, Ian Hunter, Peter Lorre, Albert Dekker, Paul Lukas, Eduardo Ciannelli. Intriguing allegorical film of prisoners escaping from Devils Island with Christ-like presence of Hunter. Not for all tastes, but there are fine, realistic performances by Crawford, Gable, and supporting cast.

Strange Case of Madeleine SEE: Madeleine

Strange Confession SEE: Imposter, The

Strange Conquest (1946) 64m. ** D: John Rawlins. Jane Wyatt, Lowell Gilmore, Julie Bishop, Samuel S. Hinds, Abner Biberman. Inauspicious programmer from Universal Pictures set in the deep jungles where dedicated men try to conquer native diseases. Remake of THE CRIME OF DR. HALLET.

Strange Countess, The (1961-German) 96m. ** D: Josef Von Baky. Joachim Fuchsberger, Lil Dagover, Marianne Hoppe, Brigitte Grothum. Dagover is in title role, involved with fortune-hunting killers; from Edgar Wallace yarn.

Strange Death of Adolf Hitler, The (1943) 72m. ** D: James Hogan. Ludwig Donath, Fritz Kortner, Gale Sondergaard, George Dolenz, Fred Giermann, William Trenk, Merrill Rodin. Interesting story of Hitler's double helping to set trap for Fuehrer's death.

Strange Door, The (1951) 81m. *½ D: Joseph Pevney. Charles Laughton, Boris Karloff, Sally Forrest, Richard Stapley. Pretty bad adaptation of Stevenson story. Laughton overacts as cruel tyrant who gets back at dead sweetheart by imprisoning members of family. Intended horror film may seem comic.

Strange Fascination (1952) 80m. BOMB D: Hugo Haas. Cleo Moore, Hugo Haas, Mona Barrie, Karen Sharpe. Lurid nonsense with pianist Haas ensnared by vixen Moore.

Strange Holiday (1942) 62m. ** D: Arch Oboler. Claude Rains, Bobbie Stebbins, Barbara Bates, Paul Hilton, Tommy Cook, Martin Kosleck. Adaptation of Oboler's radio play about businessman who returns from vacation to find U.S. democracy overthrown. Unreleased until 1946.

Strange Homecoming (1974) **C-78m.** TVM D: Lee H. Katzin. Robert Culp, Glen Campbell, Barbara Anderson, Whitney Blake, John Crawford, Leif Garret, Tara Talboy, Gerrit Graham. Murderer-on-the-lam Culp returns home after 18 years and moves in with family of his small-town sheriff brother. Culp injects what life he can into limp story. Below average.

Strange Illusion (1945) **80m.** ** D: Edgar G. Ulmer. James Lydon, Sally Eilers, Warren William, Regis Toomey. Intriguing but unconvincing melodrama, sort of a poor man's SUSPICION, with teenaged Lydon having doubts about smooth-talker (William) who's wooing his widowed mother (Eilers). Surprisingly bizarre touches for a low-budget quickie.

Strange Interlude (1932) **110m.** *** D: Robert Z. Leonard. Norma Shearer, Clark Gable, May Robson, Maureen O'Sullivan, Robert Young, Ralph Morgan, Henry B. Walthall, Mary Alden. Eugene O'Neill talky play becomes marathon of inner thoughts revealed only to audience in chronicle of Gable, Shearer, et al growing old without resolving their problems. Engrossing film, with Shearer at her radiant best.

Strange Intruder (1956) **82m.** ** D: Irving Rapper. Edmund Purdom, Ida Lupino, Ann Harding, Jacques Bergerac. Peculiar tale of Purdom promising dying Korean War buddy that he'll visit the man's family; he does, with strange results.

Strange Journey (1946) **65m.** *½ D: James Tinling. Paul Kelly, Osa Massen, Hillary Brooke, Bruce Lester. Low-budget adventure story with group of people on desert isle fighting over treasure map.

Strange Lady in Town (1955) **C-112m.** **½ D: Mervyn LeRoy. Greer Garson, Dana Andrews, Cameron Mitchell, Lois Smith, Walter Hampden. Unsuccessful grand-scale soaper-Western. Set in 1880s Texas, Garson is the doctor coming to Santa Fe, involved with Andrews, perplexed by outlaw brother Mitchell.

Strange Love of Martha Ivers, The (1946) **117m.** *** D: Lewis Milestone. Barbara Stanwyck, Kirk Douglas, Lizabeth Scott, Van Heflin, Judith Anderson, Darryl Hickman. Gripping melodrama, with Stanwyck bound to her husband by crime she committed long ago.

Strange Mr. Gregory, The (1946)

63m. ** D: Phil Rosen. Edmund Lowe, Jean Rogers, Don Douglas, Marjorie Hoshelle, Robert Emmett Keane. Low-budget drama of magician who goes to any length to win love of married woman.

Strange New World (1975) **C-100m.** TVM D: Robert Butler. John Saxon, Kathleen Miller, Keene Curtis, Martine Beswick, James Olson, Ford Rainey. Sci-fi adventure with three astronauts returning to Earth after 180 years in suspended animation and finding that scientists have developed eternal life by cloning. Below par for the genre, helped only slightly by subsequent editing to 78 minutes. Below average.

Strange One, The (1957) **100m.** *** D: Jack Garfein. Ben Gazzara, George Peppard, Pat Hingle, Mark Richman, Geoffrey Horne. Bizarre military school account of far-out Gazzara's peculiar hold over various underclassmen. Remarkably frank version of Calder Willingham's END AS A MAN.

Strange Possession of Mrs. Oliver, The (1977) **C-78m.** TVM D: Gordon Hessler. Karen Black, George Hamilton, Robert F. Lyons, Lucille Benson, Jean Allison, Gloria LeRoy. Pretentious split-personality study of a bored housewife who assumes a seductive blonde's identity, unaware that the girl she pretends to be really exists. Black chews the scenery, all kept in dreamy soft focus by director Hessler. Below average.

Strange Shadows in An Empty Room (1977) **C-99m.** *½ D: Martin Herbert. Stuart Whitman, John Saxon, Martin Landau, Tisa Farrow, Gayle Hunnicutt, Carole Laure. Far-fetched, violent film has police detective Whitman searching for his sister's murderer. Tawdry stuff; filmed in Montreal.

Strange Triangle (1946) **65m.** ** D: Ray McCarey. Preston Foster, Signe Hasso, John Shepperd (Shepperd Strudwick), Roy Roberts. OK drama with Hasso the maneuvering dame who inspires murder and robbery.

Strange Vengeance of Rosalie, The (1972) **C-107m.** ** D: Jack Starrett. Bonnie Bedelia, Ken Howard, Anthony Zerbe. Offbeat story of girl who holds man captive in rambling house. Far-fetched tale goes way off-base.

Strange Woman, The (1946) **100m.** ** D: Edgar G. Ulmer. Hedy Lamarr, George Sanders, Louis Hayward,

Gene Lockhart, Hillary Brooke, June Storey. Lamarr's a legendary man-killer in this tedious costumer.

Stranger, The (1946) 95m. *** D: Orson Welles. Orson Welles, Loretta Young, Edward G. Robinson, Richard Long, Martha Wentworth. Fine study of escaped Nazi war criminal Welles sedately living in small town, about to marry unsuspecting Young. Robinson nicely understates role as federal agent out to get him.

Stranger, The (1967-Italian-French) C-105m. ***½ D: Luchino Visconti. Marcello Mastroianni, Anna Karina, Bernard Blier, Georges Wilson, Bruno Cremer. Fine adaptation of Albert Camus' existential novel about a man who feels completely isolated from society. Mastroianni is perfectly cast in lead.

Stranger and the Gunfighter, The (1976) C-107m. ** D: Anthony Dawson (Antonio Margheriti). Lee Van Cleef, Lo Lieh, Patty Shepard, Julian Ugarte, Karen Yeh. Lively, low-grade tongue-in-cheek Western has hard-drinking cowboy joining forces with kung-fu expert to recover missing fortune. Made in Europe.

Stranger at My Door (1956) 85m. **½ D: William Witney. Macdonald Carey, Patricia Medina, Skip Homeier, Stephen Wootton, Slim Pickens. Offbeat Western about clergyman jeopardizing his family's safety when he tries to reform an outlaw.

Stranger Came Home, A SEE: Unholy Four

Stranger in Between, The (1952-British) 84m. *** D: Charles Crichton. Dirk Bogarde, Elizabeth Sellars, Kay Walsh, Jon Whiteley, Geoffrey Keen. Odd but very entertaining film about orphan boy who grows to understand murderer as both flee police in England. Warm, compasionate performances. Originally titled HUNTED.

Stranger in My Arms (1959) 88m. **½ D: Helmut Kautner. June Allyson, Jeff Chandler, Sandra Dee, Charles Coburn, Mary Astor, Peter Graves, Conrad Nagel. Undemanding old-fashioned weeper, with a high-breed soaper cast, based on Robert Wilder novel. Allyson falls in love with Chandler, army buddy of her late husband. Astor is the domineering mother-in-law.

Stranger in Our House (1978) C-100m. TVM D: Wes Craven. Linda Blair, Lee Purcell, Jeremy Slate, Carol Lawrence, Macdonald Carey, Jeff McCracken, Jeff East. Teenage witchcraft thriller with always put-upon Linda Blair in constant peril. Based on Lois Duncan's novel SUMMER OF FEAR. Average.

Stranger in the House SEE: Black Christmas

Stranger in Town (1966-Italian-U.S.) C-86m. *½ D: Vance Lewis. Tony Anthony, Frank Wolff, Yolanda Modio, Gia Sandri. Poor imitation of Sergio Leone Western finds Anthony blood-bathing a murderous bandit into submission.

Stranger on Horseback (1955) C-66m. ** D: Jacques Tourneur. Joel McCrea, Kevin McCarthy, Jaclynne Greene, Miroslava, Nancy Gates, John Carradine. McCrea is tight-lipped judge who's forced to kill in order to set justice straight and bring a murderer to trial.

Stranger on the Prowl (1953-Italian) 82m. **½ D: Joseph Losey. Paul Muni, Vittorio Manunta, Joan Lorring, Aldo Silvani. Murky drama of Muni a fugitive on the run who tries to set a young would-be-crook straight.

Stranger on the Run (1967) C-97m. TVM D: Don Siegel. Henry Fonda, Michael Parks, Anne Baxter, Dan Duryea, Sal Mineo, Lloyd Bochner, Michael Burns, Tom Reese, Bernie Hamilton, Zalman King. Solidly conceived, well-executed chase thriller features Fonda as drifter in Banner, New Mexico, trying to deliver message to sister of prison friend, accused of murder, chased by railroad police into desert. Great entertainment with something to say. Above average.

Stranger on the Third Floor, The (1940) 64m. *** D: Boris Ingster. Peter Lorre, John McGuire, Margaret Tallichet, Charles Waldron, Elisha Cook Jr. Reporter's testimony has convicted Cook in brutal murder case, but the newspaperman has second thoughts. Excellent little "sleeper" with one nightmare montage that's a knockout.

Stranger Returns, The (1968-U.S.-Italy) C-90m. BOMB D: Vance Lewis. Tony Anthony, Dan Vadis, Daniele Vargas, Marco Gugielmi, Jill Banner. Sequel to A STRANGER IN TOWN has Anthony chasing solid gold stagecoach full of thieves.

Western is worthless, even if TV stations don't cut the gore.

Stranger Who Looks Like Me, The (1974) C-78m. TVM D: Larry Peerce. Beau Bridges, Meredith Baxter, Whitney Blake, Walter Brooke, Neva Patterson, Mary Murphy, Ford Rainey. Adoptees Bridges and Baxter pursue frustrating searches for their natural parents. OK examination of a growing contemporary phenomenon. Baxter and real mother Blake have a few nice scenes together. Above average.

Stranger Within, The (1974) C-78m. TVM D: Lee Philips. Barbara Eden, George Grizzard, Joyce Van Patten, David Doyle, Nehemiah Persoff. Melodrama about a woman whose unborn baby begins to control her mind and body. Suspiciously reminiscent of ROSEMARY'S BABY with offbeat touches added by occult/suspense writer Richard Matheson. Average.

Stranger Wore a Gun, The (1953) C-83m. ** D: Andre de Toth. Randolph Scott, Claire Trevor, Joan Weldon, George Macready, Lee Marvin. Oddball plot in this Scott Western; Randy is befriended by bandit and becomes involved in a holdup before he can return to normal living.

Strangers (1953-Italian) 97m. *½ D: Roberto Rossellini. Ingrid Bergman, George Sanders, Paul Muller, Maria Mauban, Natalia Ray. Tedious hokum of married couple Bergman and Sanders trying to reconcile their faltering relationship while on Italian holiday.

Strangers at Sunrise (1969) C-99m. **½ D: Percival Rubens. George Montgomery, Deana Martin, Brian O'Shaughnessy, Tromp Terreblanche. Turn of the century South African western with American mining engineer (Montgomery), attracted by the gold rush, trying to clear his name when the British accuse him of spying for the Boers.

Stranger's Hand, The (1954-Italian) 86m. *** D: Mario Soldati. Richard Basehart, Trevor Howard, Alida Valli, Eduardo Ciannelli. Brooding suspenser involving British espionage officer who disappears on his trip to Venice to see his young son. Based on Graham Greene story.

Strangers in Love (1932) 76m. ** D: Lothar Mendes. Kay Francis, Fredric March, Stuart Erwin, Juliette Compton, Sidney Toler, George Bar-

bier, Lucien Littlefield. Mild comedy; Francis is secretary who loves March, weakling playboy forced to impersonate twin brother to expose family fraud.

Strangers in 7A (1972) C-73m. TVM D: Paul Wendkos. Andy Griffith, Ida Lupino, Michael Brandon, James Watson Jr., Suzanne Hildur, Tim McIntire. Bar-girl deliberate lure to get use of middle-aged superintendent's apartment for robbery. Good tension toward end, plus unusual script sympathetic to victim's point of view. Above average.

Strangers May Kiss (1931) 85m. ** D: George Fitzmaurice. Norma Shearer, Robert Montgomery, Neil Hamilton, Marjorie Rambeau, Jed Prouty, Henry Armetta, Irene Rich. Polished but ridiculous soaper of Shearer in love with unreliable Hamilton. Film's conclusion is not to be believed. Montgomery contributes fine performance, and Ray Milland appears unbilled in one scene.

Strangers on a Train (1951) 101m. **** D: Alfred Hitchcock. Farley Granger, Robert Walker, Ruth Roman, Leo G. Carroll, Patricia Hitchcock, Marion Lorne. Walker gives his finest performance as psychopath involved with tennis star Granger in "exchange murders." Lorne is unforgettable as doting mother. First-class Hitchcock. Remade as ONCE YOU KISS A STRANGER.

Strangers: The Story of a Mother and Daughter (1979) C-100m. TVM D: Milton Katselas. Bette Davis, Gena Rowlands, Ford Rainey, Donald Moffat, Royal Dano. Davis at her latter-day best (winning an Emmy Award) and matched scene for scene by Rowlands in this drama about a lonely widow's resentment over her estranged daughter's unexpected homecoming after twenty years. Above average.

Strangers When We Meet (1960) C-117m. **½ D: Richard Quine. Kirk Douglas, Kim Novak, Ernie Kovacs, Barbara Rush, Walter Matthau, Virginia Bruce, Kent Smith. Expensive soaper with attractive stars; both are married, but fall in love with each other. Based on Evan Hunter novel.

Strangler, The (1964) 89m. *** D: Burt Topper. Victor Buono, David McLean, Ellen Corby, Jeanne Bates, Wally Campo. Buono gives fine performance as mad killer who strangles women and pitches Boston into frenzy.

Stranglers of Bombay, The (1960-British) 81m. **½ D: Terence Fisher. Andrew Cruickshank, Marne Maitland, Guy Rolfe, Paul Stassino, Jan Holden, Tutte Lemkow. Grisly story of fanatical Indian cult attempting to drive British from trading station. Good cast helped by tense direction.

Strategic Air Command (1955) C-114m. **½ D: Anthony Mann. June Allyson, James Stewart, Frank Lovejoy, Barry Sullivan, Bruce Bennett, Rosemary DeCamp. Film only gets off the ground when Stewart does, as baseball player recalled to air force duty; Allyson is his sugary wife.

Stratton Story, The (1949) 106m. ***½ D: Sam Wood. James Stewart, June Allyson, Frank Morgan, Agnes Moorehead, Bill Williams. Stewart is fine as Monty Stratton, baseball player whose loss of one leg did not mark an end to his career; well-played by good cast.

Straw Dogs (1971) C-116m. ***½ D: Sam Peckinpah. Dustin Hoffman, Susan George, Peter Vaughan, T. P. McKenna, Peter Arne. One of the most controversial violence-theme films in recent memory. Hoffman portrays American mathematician whose pacifism is put to supremely violent test when he and British wife move to isolated village. Filmed in England.

Strawberry Blonde, The (1941) 97m. *** D: Raoul Walsh. James Cagney, Olivia de Havilland, Rita Hayworth, Alan Hale, Jack Carson, George Tobias, Una O'Connor, George Reeves. Cagney's dynamic in 1890s story of dentist infatuated with gold-digger Hayworth, and his subsequent marriage to De Havilland. Remade as ONE SUNDAY AFTERNOON, the title of the early Gary Cooper film of which this is a remake.

Strawberry Statement, The (1970) C-103m. ** D: Stuart Hagmann. Bruce Davison, Kim Darby, Bob Balaban, James Kunen, Jeannie Berlin. Cluttered adaptation of James Kunen's book about Columbia University's riots tries to be too many things at once—comedy, social commentary, musical. Good performances.

Street Angel (1928) 102m. *** D: Frank Borzage. Janet Gaynor, Charles Farrell, Alberto Rabagliati, Gino Conti, Guido Trento, Henry Armetta. Italian girl fleeing from police joins traveling circus, meets and falls in love with young painter who finds her an inspiration. Followup to success of SEVENTH HEAVEN is actually much better, a delicate, beautifully photographed romance.

Street Killing (1976) C-78m. TVM D: Harvey Hart. Andy Griffith, Bradford Dillman, Harry Guardino, Robert Loggia, Don Gordon, Adam Wade. Crime drama has Griffith as N.Y. prosecuting attorney seeking to prove that a mugging-murder was ordered by the Mafia. Run-of-the-mill pilot for possible series for Griffith, cast against type. Average.

Street of Chance (1942) 74m. **½ D: Jack Hively. Burgess Meredith, Claire Trevor, Sheldon Leonard, Frieda Inescort. Effective Paramount "B" flick with Meredith an amnesia victim seeking clues to his past.

Street People (1976-Italian) C-92m. *½ D: Maurice Lucidi. Roger Moore, Stacy Keach, Ivo Garrani, Fausto Tozzi, Ettore Manni. Insipid though energetic gangster flick punctuated by several car chases. San Francisco mafioso dispatches nephew Moore (would you believe him as a Sicilian?) and the latter's Grand-Prix driving buddy Keach to find out which rival Don hid a million-dollar cache of pure heroin in the cross he imported from Italy as a gift for his church.

Street Scene (1931) 80m. ***½ D: King Vidor. Sylvia Sidney, William Collier Jr., David Landau, Estelle Taylor, Walter Miller, Beulah Bondi. Heartbreakingly realistic account of life in N.Y. tenements, and younger generation's desperation to get out. Elmer Rice's Pulitzer Prize-winning play enhanced by fine performances, striking camerawork, Alfred Newman's classic music score.

Street With No Name, The (1948) 91m. *** D: William Keighley. Mark Stevens, Richard Widmark, Lloyd Nolan, Barbara Lawrence, Ed Begley, Donald Buka. Fine movie based on actual F.B.I. case of agent uncovering head of city mob. Suspense well handled.

Streetcar Named Desire, A (1951)

122m. **** D: Elia Kazan. Marlon Brando, Vivien Leigh, Kim Hunter, Karl Malden. Multi-Oscar-winning film from Tennessee Williams play. Brando superb as animalistic human interacting with wistful, neurotic Leigh. Brooding production set in grim New Orleans tenement district.

Streets of L.A., The (1979) C-100m. TVM D: Jerrold Freedman. Joanne Woodward, Robert Webber, Michael C. Gwynne, Fernando Allende, Isela Vega. The strength is Joanne Woodward in this contemporary drama about a tenacious woman who goes alone into the Los Angeles barrio in pursuit of teenaged hoods who slashed her tires. Without her, the whole idea would be just plain silly. Average.

Streets of Laredo (1949) C-92m. **½ D: Leslie Fenton. Macdonald Carey, William Holden, William Bendix, Mona Freeman. Standard Western, remake of THE TEXAS RANGERS, but not as good. Three pals out West split when two turn to law and another becomes lawbreaker.

Streets of San Francisco, The (1972) C-98m. TVM D: Walter Grauman. Karl Malden, Michael Douglas, Robert Wagner, Kim Darby, Andrew Duggan, John Rubinstein. Moody atmosphere reminiscent of "Peter Gunn" in sinister police whodunit as Detectives Stone and Keller (Malden & Douglas) piece together last days in life of young woman. Explanation, both devious and acceptable, real tour de force. Above average; pilot for TV series.

Strictly Dishonorable (1951) 86m. ** D: Melvin Frank, Norman Panama. Ezio Pinza, Janet Leigh, Millard Mitchell, Gale Robbins. Tame shenanigans of opera star Pinza marrying Leigh to save her reputation.

Strike Force (1975) C-78m. TVM D: Barry Shear. Cliff Gorman, Joey Gentry, Donald Blakely, Richard Gere, Walter Spenser, Edward Griver. N.Y.C. detective Gorman teams with a Federal agent and a state trooper to crack a narcotics case. Just another cop show. Average.

Strike Me Pink (1936) 100m. *½ D: Norman Taurog. Eddie Cantor, Ethel Merman, Sally Eilers, Parkyakarkus, William Frawley, Brian Donlevy. One of Cantor's worst films, built around his run-in with racketeers at amusement park which

he manages. Good slapstick chase finale, forgettable music numbers.

Strike Up the Band (1940) 120m. **½ D: Busby Berkeley. Mickey Rooney, Judy Garland, Paul Whiteman, June Preisser, William Tracy, Larry Nunn. Rooney is leader of high school band competing in Whiteman's nationwide radio contest. Garland sings "Our Love Affair," performs "Nell of New Rochelle," "Do The Conga."

Strip, The (1951) 85m. ** D: Leslie Kardos. Mickey Rooney, Sally Forrest, William Demarest, James Craig. Rooney gives sincere, energetic performance as former drummer involved with gangsters, trying to help Forrest get a movie break. Routine film enlivened by great music of Louis Armstrong, Jack Teagarden and all-star group.

Stripper, The (1963) 95m. **½ D: Franklin Schaffner. Joanne Woodward, Richard Beymer, Claire Trevor, Carol Lynley, Robert Webber, Gypsy Rose Lee. Aging stripper falls in love with teen-age boy in this OK filmization of William Inge's play "A Loss of Roses." Director Schaffner's first movie.

Stromboli (1950-Italian) 81m. *½ D: Roberto Rossellini. Ingrid Bergman, Mario Vitale, Renzo Cesana, Mario Sponza. Rambling dreariness with Bergman marrying a fisherman; even erupting volcano doesn't jar this plodding film, which reportedly looks better in original Italian 107m. version.

Strongest Man in the World, The (1975) C-92m. ** D: Vincent McEveety. Kurt Russell, Joe Flynn, Eve Arden, Cesar Romero, Phil Silvers, Dick Van Patten. Formula Disney comedy about students' discovery of formula which, when mixed with breakfast cereal, produces super-strength. Fine opening and closing, with comic special effects, but draggy "plotting" in between as crooks try to steal formula.

Stronghold (1951) 82m. *½ D: Steve Sekely. Veronica Lake, Zachary Scott, Arturo de Cordova, Rita Macedo. Pedestrian costumer set in 1860s, with Lake fleeing U.S. and becoming embroiled in Mexican revolution.

Stud, The (1978-British) C-95m. BOMB D: Quentin Masters. Joan Collins, Oliver Tobias, Sue Lloyd, Mark Burns, Walter Gotell, Emma Jacobs. A waiter works his way up in the world (so to speak) by sleeping with the boss' wife. Idiotic softcore porn written by Jackie Collins (Joan's sister).

Student Connection, The (1975-Spanish) **C-92m.** *½ D: Rafael Romero Merchent. Ray Milland, Sylva Koscina, Ramon Oliveros, Maria Silva, Franco Ciacobini. Flat melodrama about a headmaster at a boys' school whose initial crime of passion (killing his mistress' husband) leads to a succession of murders when he learns that one of his students caught him in the original act.

Student Prince, The (1954) **C-107m.** ** D: Richard Thorpe. Ann Blyth, Edmund Purdom, John Ericson, Louis Calhern, Edmund Gwenn. Romberg music, dubbed voice of Mario Lanza chief assets in venerable operetta about heir to throne sent to Heidelberg for one last fling, where he falls in love with barmaid Blyth. Filmed in 1927 with Ramon Novarro and Norma Shearer.

Study in Terror, A (1965-British) **C-94m.** *** D: James Hill. John Neville, Donald Houston, Georgia Brown, John Fraser, Anthony Quayle, Barbara Windsor. Compact little British thriller pits Sherlock Holmes against Jack the Ripper; violent, well-paced, and well cast.

Stunt Seven (1979) **C-100m. TVM** D: John Peyser. Christopher Connelly, Christopher Lloyd, Bill Macy, Peter Haskell, Elke Sommer, Patrick Macnee. Pilot film to a never-made-it series about an intrepid team of stunt experts who battle for law and order. Average.

Stunts (1977) **C-89m.** **½ D: Mark L. Lester. Robert Forster, Fiona Lewis, Joanna Cassidy, Darrell Fetty, Bruce Glover, James Luisi. When a stunt man dies while making a film, his brother (Forster) takes his place in order to probe the "accident." Engaging B movie with terrific action scenes and a wild helicopter-and-car finale. Retitled WHO IS KILLING THE STUNTMEN?

Stunts Unlimited (1980) **C-78m. TVM** D: Hal Needham. Glenn Corbett, Susanna Dalton, Sam Jones, Chip Mayer, Alejandro Rey. Former US intelligence agent Corbett recruits three Hollywood stunt performers to help recover a stolen laser gun in this formula pilot to a prospective series. Skimpy storyline provides padding between stuntman-turned-director Needham's bag of tricks. Average.

Subject Was Roses, The (1968) **C-107m.** *** D: Ulu Grosbard. Patricia Neal, Jack Albertson, Martin Sheen, Don Saxon, Elaine Williams, Grant Gordon. Frank D. Gilroy's Pulitzer Prize-winning play about young veteran's strained relationship with his parents makes a generally good film. Neal's first film after her near-fatal stroke and Albertson's Oscar-winning performance.

Submarine Command (1951) **87m.** **½ D: John Farrow. William Holden, Nancy Olson, William Bendix, Don Taylor. Predictable but acceptable post-WW2 account of naval military life; Olson is wholesome love interest.

Submarine X-1 (1968-British) **C-89m.** **½ D: William Graham. James Caan, Rupert Davies, David Sumner, William Dysart, Norman Bowler. After losing submarine in battle with German ship, naval officer Caan gets second chance in daring raid with midget subs. Standard WW2 fare.

Subterfuge (1969-British) **C-92m.** ** D: Peter Graham Scott. Gene Barry, Joan Collins, Richard Todd, Suzanna Leigh, Michael Rennie. American agent Barry is forced into helping British Intelligence in this routine espionage drama.

Subterraneans, The (1960) **C-89m.** **½ D: Ranald MacDougall. Leslie Caron, George Peppard, Janice Rule, Roddy McDowall, Anne Seymour, Jim Hutton, Scott Marlowe. Glossy, superficial study of life and love among the beatniks, with pure cornball stereotype performances.

Subway in the Sky (1959-German) **85m.** *½ D: Muriel Box. Van Johnson, Hildegarde Neff, Katherine Kath, Cec Linder, Albert Lieven, Edward Judd. Flabby caper of soldier Johnson in post-WW2 Berlin, involved in the black market; terrible waste of Neff's talents.

Success, The (1963-Italian) **103m.** *** D: Dino Risi. Vittorio Gassman, Anouk Aimee, Jean-Louis Trintignant. Intelligent delineation by Gassman as businessman overwhelmed by success urge makes this drama worthy.

Such a Gorgeous Kid Like Me (1973-French) **C-98m.** ***½ D: François Truffaut. Bernadette Lafont, Claude Brasseur, Charles Denner, Guy Marchand, Philippe Leotard. Delightful comedy of female prisoner who relates her sordid past to criminology student, gradually entices him just as she did her former "victims." Lafont ideal in leading role.

Such Good Friends (1971) C-100m. *** D: Otto Preminger. Dyan Cannon, James Coco, Jennifer O'Neill, Ken Howard, Nina Foch, Laurence Luckinbill, Louise Lasser, Burgess Meredith, Sam Levene. Tart black comedy about man going to hospital, prompting wife (Cannon) to reexamine their relationship and learn about his romantic sideline activities. Fine ensemble acting buoys acidly funny script (by Elaine May, who used a pseudonym).

Sudan (1945) C-76m. ** D: John Rawlins. Maria Montez, Jon Hall, Turhan Bey, Andy Devine, George Zucco, Robert Warwick. Queen Montez escapes evil prime minister Zucco with help of Hall and Bey in colorful but empty adventure-romance.

Sudden Danger (1955) 85m. *½ D: Hubert Cornfield. Bill Elliott, Tom Drake, Beverly Garland, Lucien Littlefield, Minerva Urecal, Lyle Talbot, Frank Jenks. Bland hunt-the-murderer-tale.

Sudden Fear (1952) 110m. ***½ D: David Miller. Joan Crawford, Jack Palance, Gloria Grahame, Bruce Bennett, Touch (Mike) Connors. Excellent murder yarn with Crawford a famous playwright who marries Palance, then discovers he's trying to kill her.

Sudden Terror (1970-British) C-95m. ** D: John Hough. Mark Lester, Lionel Jeffries, Susan George, Tony Bonner, Jeremy Kemp. Adequate variation on boy-who-cried-wolf theme: prankish youngster (Lester) witnesses murder of visiting black dignitary, but can't convince others. Almost ruined by self-conscious direction. Good cast, though. Originally titled EYEWITNESS.

Suddenly (1954) 77m. ***½ D: Lewis Allen. Frank Sinatra, Sterling Hayden, James Gleason, Nancy Gates. Tense Presidential assassination story, with Sinatra a hired killer. Fine performance by Mr. S.

Suddenly, It's Spring (1947) 87m. ** D: Mitchell Leisen. Paulette Goddard, Fred MacMurray, Macdonald Carey, Arleen Whelan, Lillian Fontaine. Strained comedy about married couple Goddard and MacMurray refusing to divorce each other.

Suddenly, Last Summer (1959) 114m. ***½ D: Joseph L. Mankiewicz. Elizabeth Taylor, Katharine Hepburn, Montgomery Clift, Mercedes McCambridge, Albert Dekker. Fascinating if talky Tennessee Williams yarn about wealthy Southern matriarch (Hepburn), her supposedly mad daughter-in-law (Taylor) and a neurosurgeon (Clift); grandly acted.

Suddenly, Love (1978) C-100m. TVM D: Stuart Margolin. Cindy Williams, Paul Shenar, Linwood Boomer, Eileen Heckart, Joan Bennett, Lew Ayres, Kurt Kasznar. Glossy Ross Hunter-produced soap opera involving the unlikely relationship of a plain girl from the ghetto and a socially prominent attorney. It's all updated "Helen Trent." Average.

Suddenly Single (1971) C-73m. TVM D: Jud Taylor. Hal Holbrook, Barbara Rush, Margot Kidder, Agnes Moorehead, Michael Constantine, Harvey Korman, Cloris Leachman. Fair mix of comedy and drama. Young-ish pharmacist divorced by wife, tries to make it in singles world. Only questionable aspect film's ending. Above average.

Suez (1938) 104m. *** D: Allan Dwan. Tyrone Power, Loretta Young, Annabella, Henry Stephenson, Maurice Moscovich, Joseph Schildkraut, Sidney Blackmer. Power is French architect sent to build Suez Canal; his real problem is choosing between aristocratic Loretta and down-to-earth Annabella. Elaborate Darryl Zanuck production surrounds good cast of 1850s France-Egypt.

Sugarfoot (1951) C-80m. **½ D: Edwin L. Marin. Randolph Scott, Adele Jergens, Raymond Massey, S. Z. Sakall. Above-par Scott Western. Randy is ex-Rebel officer who encounters his old adversary in Arizona. Retitled: SWIRL OF GLORY.

Sugarland Express, The (1974) C-109m. ***½ D: Steven Spielberg. Goldie Hawn, Ben Johnson, Michael Sacks, William Atherton. Perfect entertainment, based on fact, about two fugitive parents pursued by every cop in Texas in an attempt to reclaim their baby. Spielberg's first feature; his second was JAWS.

Suicide Battalion (1958) 79m. BOMB D: Edward L. Cahn. Michael Connors, John Ashley, Jewell Lain, Russ Bender. Static WW2 non-actioner. Army duo goes on mission to destroy government records hidden in building basement at Pearl Harbor.

Suicide Commando (1969-Italian) C-94m. *½ D: Camillo Bazzoni. Aldo Ray, Pamela Tudor, Gaetano Cimarosa, Luis Davila, Manuel Zarzo. Familiar war heroics with beefy Ray leading five man team in reeking wholesale havoc on German airfield, paving way for D-Day landing.

Suicide Mission (1956-Norwegian) 70m. ** D: Michael Forlong. Leif Larsen, Michael Aldridge, Atle Larsen, Per Christensen. Standard WW2 actioner, set in Norway.

Suicide Run SEE: **Too Late the Hero**

Suicide Squadron SEE: **Dangerous Moonlight**

Suicide's Wife, The (1979) C-100m. TVM D: John Newland. Angie Dickinson, Gordon Pinsent, Zohra Lampert, Todd Lookinland, Peter Donat. Undemanding drama about a woman's struggle to rebuild her life after her professor husband takes his. Average.

Sullivans, The (1944) 111m. *** D: Lloyd Bacon. Anne Baxter, Thomas Mitchell, Selena Royle, Ward Bond, Bobby Driscoll, Addison Richards. Patriotic drama from true story of five brothers during WW2 whose devotion for each other took precedence over everything else. They are played by Edward Ryan, John Campbell, James Cardwell, John Alvin, and George Offerman Jr.

Sullivan's Empire (1967) C-91m. **½ D: Harvey Hart, Thomas Carr. Martin Milner, Clu Gulager, Karen Jensen, Linden Chiles, Don Quine, Arch Johnson. Unconvincing adventure yarn of rich landowner's trio of sons searching for father, whose plane crashed in South American jungle.

Sullivan's Travels (1941) 91m. ***½ D: Preston Sturges. Joel McCrea, Veronica Lake, Robert Warwick, William Demarest, Franklin Pangborn, Porter Hall. Movie director McCrea is tired of making trivial films, sets out to bum around country to capture flavor for a meaningful movie project. Satirical comedy hits bullseye, punctuated by fine dramatic episodes.

Summer and Smoke (1961) C-118m. ***½ D: Peter Glenville. Laurence Harvey, Geraldine Page, Rita Moreno, Una Merkel, Earl Holliman, Pamela Tiffin. Vivid performance by Page as Southern spinster yearning for love of young doctor Harvey;

he ignores her, and both their lives are ruined. Sober Tennessee Williams play remains stagy.

Summer Holiday (1948) C-92m. **½ D: Rouben Mamoulian. Mickey Rooney, Gloria De Haven, Walter Huston, Frank Morgan, Butch Jenkins, Marilyn Maxwell, Anne Francis. Average musical adaptation of O'Neill play AH, WILDERNESS, about sensitive young boy who falls in love. Use of color is film's greatest asset.

Summer Interlude SEE: **Illicit Interlude**

Summer Love (1958) 85m. ** D: Charles Haas. John Saxon, Molly Bee, Rod McKuen, Judi Meredith, Jill St. John. Sequel to ROCK, PRETTY BABY has Saxon et al hired to perform at summer resort camp; perky performances.

Summer Magic (1963) C-100m. **½ D: James Neilson. Hayley Mills, Burl Ives, Dorothy McGuire, Deborah Walley, Eddie Hodges, Una Merkel. Disney's rehash of MOTHER CAREY'S CHICKENS has McGuire as widow who raises family on a shoestring in rambling Maine house. Pleasant but forgettable.

Summer of '42 (1971) C-102m. *** D: Robert Mulligan. Jennifer O'Neill, Gary Grimes, Jerry Houser, Oliver Conant, Katherine Allentuck, Christopher Norris. Enticing if unprofound nostalgia by Herman Raucher about teenager Grimes with crush on young war-bride O'Neill. Captures 1940s flavor, adolescent boyhood, quite nicely. Followed by sequel, CLASS OF '44.

Summer of My German Soldier (1978) C-100m. TVM D: Michael Tuchner. Kristy McNichol, Bruce Davison, Esther Rolle, Michael Constantine, Barbara Barrie. Bittersweet romance of a Jewish teenager and an escaped Nazi POW in a small Georgia town during WW2. Loving if occasionally oversentimental, with an Emmy Award-winning performance by Esther Rolle as the family housekeeper. Above average.

Summer Place, A (1959) C-130m. *** D: Delmer Daves. Richard Egan, Dorothy McGuire, Sandra Dee, Arthur Kennedy, Troy Donahue, Constance Ford, Beulah Bondi. Lushly photographed soaper of adultery and teenage love at resort house on Maine coast. Excellent Max Steiner score.

Summer Stock (1950) C-100m. ***
D: Charles Walters. Judy Garland,
Gene Kelly, Eddie Bracken, Marjorie
Main, Gloria De Haven, Phil Silvers,
Hans Conried. Kelly's theater troupe
take over Judy's farm, she gets show
biz bug. Thin plot, breezy Judy, fran-
tic Silvers, chipper De Haven.

Summer Storm (1944) 106m. *** D:
Douglas Sirk. George Sanders, Linda
Darnell, Edward Everett Horton, Sig
Ruman, Anna Lee, Sarah Padden,
Frank Orth. Darnell has one of her
best roles as beautiful woman who
brings tragedy to all involved with
her, including herself; from Chekhov's story.

Summer Wishes, Winter Dreams
(1973) C-93m. *** D: Gilbert Cates.
Joanne Woodward, Martin Balsam,
Sylvia Sidney, Dori Brenner, Ron
Rickards. Sensitive character study
of frigid woman (Woodward) obsessed by her childhood, upset by
her own aloofness towards others;
Balsam equally good as understanding husband.

Summer Without Boys, A (1973) C-
74m. TVM D: Jeannot Szwarc. Barbara Bain, Kay Lenz, Michael Moriarty. Entertaining melodrama about
WW2 era triangle affair, from
daughter's (Lenz) point of view;
she and her mother are competing
for same young man. Good performances, average script.

Summertime (1955) C-99m. ***½ D:
David Lean. Katharine Hepburn,
Rossano Brazzi, Isa Miranda, Darren McGavin. Lilting film of
spinster vacationing in Venice, falling in love with married man. Hepburn's sensitive portrayal is one of
her best. Based on Arthur Laurents'
THE TIME OF THE CUCKOO.
Beautifully filmed on location.

Summertime Killer (1973-French-
Italian-Spanish) C-109m. ** D: Antonio Isasi. Karl Malden, Christopher Mitchum, Raf Vallone,
Claudine Auger, Olivia Hussey.
Varied cast in OK revenge meller
about a man pursuing his father's
murderers. Lots of action, if not
much continuity.

Summertree (1971) C-88m. ** D:
Anthony Newley. Michael Douglas,
Jack Warden, Brenda Vaccaro, Barbara Bel Geddes, Kirk Callaway,
Bill Vint. Highly acclaimed (if overrated) off-Broadway play by Ron
Cowen fails as a film; Douglas plays
a young music student who clashes
with parents over Vietnam War.

Sun Also Rises, The (1957) C-129m.
*** D: Henry King. Tyrone Power,
Ava Gardner, Errol Flynn, Mel Ferrer, Gregory Ratoff, Robert Evans,
Juliette Greco, Eddie Albert. Hemingway story of expatriates in Parisian 1920s has slow stretches;
worthwhile for outstanding cast,
especially Flynn as a souse. Mexico
City locations add flavor to tale of
search for self-identity.

Sun Comes Up, The (1949) C-93m.
** D: Richard Thorpe. Jeannette
MacDonald, Lloyd Nolan, Claude
Jarman, Jr., Lewis Stone, Dwayne
Hickman. Colorful but overly senti-
mental story of young orphan and
embittered widow who blames her
son's dog, Lassie, for his death.
MacDonald's last film.

Sun Never Sets, The (1939) 98m.
**½ D: Rowland V. Lee. Douglas
Fairbanks, Jr., Basil Rathbone, Barbara O'Neil, Lionel Atwill, Virginia
Field, C. Aubrey Smith. Enjoyable
patriotic drama of British brothers
trying to prevent outbreak of war in
Africa. Well done with top-notch
cast.

Sun Shines Bright, The (1953) 92m.
*** D: John Ford. Charles Winninger, Arleen Whelan, John Russell,
Stepin Fetchit, Russell Simpson. This
is director Ford's favorite film;
charmingly picaresque remake of
JUDGE PRIEST with Winninger
involved in political contest in small
Southern town. Fine array of Ford
regulars in character roles.

Sun Valley Serenade (1941) 86m. ***
D: H. Bruce Humberstone. Sonja
Henie, John Payne, Glenn Miller,
Milton Berle, Lynn Bari, Joan Davis.
Light musicomedy with Henie a war
refugee, Payne her foster parent,
traveling with the Miller band and
manager Berle to Sun Valley. Songs:
"It Happened in Sun Valley," "Chat-
tanooga Choo-Choo."

Sunbonnet Sue (1945) 89m. ** D:
Ralph Murphy. Gale Storm, Phil Regan, George Cleveland, Minna Gombell, Edna Holland, Raymond Hatton. Programmer musical of the Gay
90s enhanced by bouncy Storm in
title role, as songstress in father's
lower N.Y.C. saloon.

Sunburn (1979) C-94m. **½ D: Richard C. Sarafian. Farrah Fawcett-
Majors, Charles Grodin, Art Carney,
Joan Collins, Alejandro Rey, William Daniels. Insurance investigator
Grodin has Farrah pose as his wife
in order to crack a murder/suicide

[745]

case in Acapulco. Sloppily made film benefits from appealing performances. Eleanor Parker, Keenan Wynn, and John Hillerman get co-starring billing but barely appear at all.

Sunday, Bloody Sunday (1971-British) C-110m. *** D: John Schlesinger. Glenda Jackson, Peter Finch, Murray Head, Peggy Ashcroft, Tony Britton, Maurice Denham, Bessie Love. Glenda loves Murray, but Peter loves Murray, too. Murray loves both, in very good, adult script by Penelope Gilliatt. Schlesinger's direction less forceful than usual, also less effective. Head's bland portrayal offsets brilliant work by Jackson and Finch. A mixed bag, not an early candidate for TV.

Sunday Dinner for a Soldier (1944) 86m. *** D: Lloyd Bacon. Anne Baxter, John Hodiak, Charles Winninger, Anne Revere, Chill Wills, Bobby Driscoll, Jane Darwell. Winning film of family that invites soldier to dinner; they are repaid for their kindness; enjoyable comedy-drama.

Sunday in New York (1963) C-105m. *** D: Peter Tewksbury. Cliff Robertson, Jane Fonda, Rod Taylor, Robert Culp, Jim Backus. Entire cast bubbles in this sex romp of virginal Fonda discovering New York and love. Peter Nero's score is perky.

Sunday Woman, The (1976-Italian) C-110m. *** D: Luigi Comencini. Marcello Mastroianni, Jacqueline Bisset, Jean-Louis Trintignant, Aldo Reggiani, Pino Caruso. Detective Mastroianni investigates murder among idle rich in Torino, falls in love with wealthy Bisset. Good whodunit makes interesting observations about social structure.

Sundays and Cybele (1962-French) 110m. ***½ D: Serge Bourguignon. Hardy Kruger, Nicole Courcel, Patricia Gozzi, Daniel Ivernel. Intelligently told account of shell-shocked Kruger finding source of communication with the world via orphaned waif Gozzi, with tragic results. Splendidly realized film.

Sundown (1941) 90m. **½ D: Henry Hathaway. Gene Tierney, Bruce Cabot, George Sanders, Harry Carey, Joseph Calleia, Dorothy Dandridge, Reginald Gardiner. Tierney is surprisingly cast as native girl who assists British troops in Africa dur-

ing WW2; fairly interesting, lushly photographed, but never scores.

Sundowners, The (1950) C-83m. **½ D: George Templeton. Robert Preston, Cathy Downs, Robert Sterling, John Barrymore, Jr., Jack Elam. Tightly edited Western about brothers fighting on opposite sides of the law.

Sundowners, The (1960) C-113m. **** D: Fred Zinnemann. Deborah Kerr, Robert Mitchum, Peter Ustinov, Glynis Johns, Dina Merrill, Chips Rafferty. First-rate film of Australian family whose lives are devoted to sheepherding. Entire cast excellent, Kerr especially fine. Wonderfully filmed on location.

Sunflower (1970-Italian) C-101m. ** D: Vittorio De Sica. Sophia Loren, Marcello Mastroianni, Ludmilla Savelyeva, Anna Carena. Weak love story of woman who searches for her lost lover. Sophia is wasted in this soppy tale.

Sunny (1941) 98m. **½ D: Herbert Wilcox. Anna Neagle, Ray Bolger, John Carroll, Edward Everett Horton, Grace Hartman, Paul Hartman. Wealthy Carroll loves show-girl Neagle in pleasant musicomedy with she and Bolger dancing in film's most enjoyable sequence.

Sunny Side of the Street (1951) C-71m. *½ D: Richard Quine. Frankie Laine, Terry Moore, Jerome Courtland, Audrey Long. Moore has fickle notions over aspiring Laine in this low-grade musical, with guest stars such as Billy Daniels, Toni Arden.

Sunny Side Up (1929) 115m. *** D: David Butler. Janet Gaynor, Charles Farrell, El Brendel, Marjorie White, Joe Brown, Frank Richardson, Jackie Cooper. Charming antique, quite impressive for early-talkie musical. Fluffy story of tenement girl falling in love with wealthy Farrell sufficient excuse for DeSylva-Brown-Henderson songs: "I'm a Dreamer," "If I Had a Talking Picture of You," title tune, and bizarre production number to "Turn on the Heat."

Sunnyside (1979) C-100m. ½ D: Timothy Galfas. Joey Travolta, John Lansing, Stacey Pickren, Andrew Rubin, Michael Tucci, Talia Balsam, Joan Darling. John Travolta's brother made bid for stardom in this cliché-ridden picture about a street kid who wants to end local gang warfare and leave that life behind. Sorry, Joey.

Sunrise (1927) 110m. **** D: F. W. Murnau. George O'Brien, Janet Gaynor, Bodil Rosing, Margaret Livingston, J. Farrell MacDonald. Exquisite silent film is just as powerful today as when it was made, telling simple story of farmer who plans to murder his wife, led on by another woman. Triumph of direction, camerawork, art direction, and performances, all hauntingly beautiful.

Sunrise at Campobello (1960) C-143m. *** D: Vincent J. Donehue. Ralph Bellamy, Greer Garson, Hume Cronyn, Jean Hagen, Ann Shoemaker, Alan Bunce, Tim Considine, Zina Bethune, Frank Ferguson, Lyle Talbot. Sincere story of President Franklin Delano Roosevelt, his battle in politics and valiant struggle against polio. Well acted; Bellamy and Garson ARE Mr. and Mrs. Roosevelt.

Sunset Boulevard (1950) 110m. **** D: Billy Wilder. Gloria Swanson, William Holden, Erich von Stroheim, Fred Clark, Jack Webb, Hedda Hopper, Buster Keaton, Cecil B. DeMille, Anna Q. Nilsson, Nancy Olson. Faded silent-film star Norma Desmond (Swanson), living in the past with butler (Von Stroheim) shelters hack screen writer (Holden) as boyfriend. Bitter, funny, fascinating; Gloria's tour de force.

Sunshine (1973) C-130m. TVM D: Joseph Sargent. Cristina Raines, Cliff DeYoung, Brenda Vaccaro, Meg Foster, Bill Mumy, Lindsay Green Bush. Penetrating character studies of non-Establishment couple and the woman's doctor in story of terminal cancer case. Deliberately slow pacing, flashback approach hampers lead performances. Songs by John Denver.

Sunshine Boys, The (1975) C-111m. *** D: Herbert Ross. Walter Matthau, George Burns, Richard Benjamin, Lee Meredith, Carol Arthur. Two cranky ex-vaudevillians are persuaded to reteam for a TV special in this popular Neil Simon comedy. Some of the "humor" is abrasive, but Matthau and Oscar-winner Burns are masters at work.

Sunshine Christmas (1977) C-100m. TVM D: Glenn Jordan. Cliff DeYoung, Barbara Hershey, Pat Hingle, Eileen Heckart, Elizabeth Cheshire, Meg Foster. Well-made sequel to SUNSHINE (1973) and the subsequent short-lived TV series. Charming, sincerely acted tale of how long-widowed DeYoung takes his adopted daughter Cheshire to meet his parents for Christmas and then falls in love with his childhood sweetheart. Above average.

Sunshine Patriot, The (1968) C-98m. TVM D: Joseph Sargent. Cliff Robertson, Dina Merrill, Luther Adler, Wilfrid Hyde-White, Antoinette Bower, Lilia Skala. Identity switch only way master spy can get out of sticky situation behind Iron Curtain and bring crucial microfilm to superiors. Fair suspense in gimmicky spy tale, but film doesn't take advantage of basic premise. Average.

Super Cops, The (1974) C-94m. ***½ D: Gordon Parks. Ron Leibman, David Selby, Sheila Frazier, Pat Hingle, Dan Frazer. Fast, funny, tough telling of the exploits of the Batman and Robin team of David Greenberg (Leibman) and Robert Hantz (Selby), who used unorthodox methods to stop the drug market in Brooklyn's black Bedford-Stuyvesant area. Filmed on location, with Greenberg and Hantz in bits.

Super Dude SEE: **Hangup**

Superdad (1974) C-96m. BOMB D: Vincent McEveety. Bob Crane, Kurt Russell, Barbara Rush, Joe Flynn, Kathleen Cody, Dick Van Patten. Disney generation gap comedy is superbad. Crane competes with daughter's fiancé in effort to prove future son-in-law worthy.

Superdome (1978) C-100m. TVM D: Jerry Jameson. David Janssen, Edie Adams, Ken Howard, Van Johnson, Donna Mills, Jane Wyatt, Peter Haskell, Clifton Davis. Flyweight thriller that looks like a road-company TWO-MINUTE WARNING as a silent killer stalks New Orleans at Super Bowl time, terrifying a stellar TV roster. Average.

Superfly (1972) C-96m. *** D: Gordon Parks Jr. Ron O'Neal, Carl Lee, Sheila Frazier, Julius W. Harris, Charles McGregor. Morally dubious but undeniably exciting tale of Harlem drug dealer out for one last killing before he quits the business. Film was accused of glorifying drug pushers, a stigma that may keep it off TV. Benefits from excellent Curtis Mayfield score.

Superfly T.N.T. (1973) C-87m. BOMB D: Ron O'Neal. Ron O'Neal, Roscoe Lee Browne, Sheila Frazier, Jacques Sernas, William Berger, Roy Bosier. Confused, sloppily constructed and executed "B" film about black ex-drug pusher, dissatisfied with idyllic existence in Europe, deciding to aid official from African country (Browne).

Superman (1978) C-143m. ***½ D: Richard Donner. Christopher Reeve, Margot Kidder, Marlon Brando, Gene Hackman, Ned Beatty, Jackie Cooper, Glenn Ford, Valerie Perrine. Dynamic, grandly entertaining saga of the Man of Steel, tracing his life from Krypton to Smallville to Metropolis, mixing equal parts sincerity, special effects, and send-up. Great fun.

Supernatural (1933) 60m. **½ D: Victor Halperin. Carole Lombard, Randolph Scott, Vivienne Osborne, H. B. Warner, Beryl Mercer, William Farnum. Eerie tale of spirits taking over innocent people is far-fetched; Lombard is film's highlight.

Support Your Local Gunfighter (1971) C-92m. *½ D: Burt Kennedy. James Garner, Suzanne Pleshette, Jack Elam, Joan Blondell, Harry Morgan, Marie Windsor, Henry Jones, Chuck Connors, Grady Sutton. Weak follow-up to SHERIFF. This time, Garner escapes from his wedding and becomes a gunfighter, due to mistaken identity.

Support Your Local Sheriff! (1969) C-92m. *** D: Burt Kennedy. James Garner, Joan Hackett, Walter Brennan, Harry Morgan, Henry Jones, Jack Elam, Bruce Dern. Broad Western spoof with laconic Garner outwitting bad guys by sheer brainpower, romancing scatterbrained Hackett. Never as funny as it might be, but amusing and enjoyable.

Suppose They Gave a War and Nobody Came? (1970) C-113m. *½ D: Hy Averback. Tony Curtis, Brian Keith, Ernest Borgnine, Suzanne Pleshette, Ivan Dixon, Tom Ewell, Bradford Dillman, Arthur O'Connell, Don Ameche. Con game in the military, pretty poor at that. Suppose they show this film and nobody watches it? (Retitled WAR GAMES for TV)

Surgeon's Knife, The (1957-British) 75m. ** D: Gordon Parry. Donald Houston, Adrienne Corri, Lyndon Brook. Tepid drama of doctor Houston implicated in criminal negligence, becoming involved in murder.

Surprise Package (1960-British) 100m. **½ D: Stanley Donen. Yul Brynner, Mitzi Gaynor, Barry Foster, Eric Pohlmann, Noel Coward, George Coulouris. Versatile Brynner tries screwball comedy, not doing too badly as devil-may-care gambler planning big-time robbery; Gaynor is sprightly leading lady.

Surrender (1950) 90m. **½ D: Allan Dwan. Vera Ralston, John Carroll, Walter Brennan, Francis Lederer, Jane Darwell, Jeff York. Ralston is exotic if overdramatic gal playing everyone against each other; Republic Pictures' nicely mounted costumer.

Surrender—Hell! (1959) 85m. ** D: John Barnwell. Keith Andes, Susan Cabot, Paraluman, Nestor de Villa. Predictable account of Andes rallying partisan forces to combat Jap control of Philippines.

Survival (1976) C-85m. ** D: Michael Campus. Barry Sullivan, Anne Francis, Sheree North, Chuck McCann, Otis Young. Intriguing psychodrama that talks itself to death. Elaborate dinner party evolves into parlor games where each guest must justify his existence, and all but two will be permanently eliminated by the vote of the others.

Survival of Dana (1979) C-100m. TVM D: Jack Starrett. Melissa Sue Anderson, Robert Carradine, Marion Ross, Talia Balsam. Pretty high school coed moves to new town, falls in with wrong crowd; you've seen it all before. Average.

Susan and God (1940) 115m. **½ D: George Cukor. Joan Crawford, Fredric March, Ruth Hussey, John Carroll, Rita Hayworth, Nigel Bruce, Bruce Cabot, Rose Hobart, Rita Quigley, Marjorie Main, Gloria De Haven. Crawford is satisfying as woman whose religious devotion loses her the love of her family. Gertrude Lawrence fared better on stage.

Susan Slade (1961) C-116m. **½ D: Delmer Daves. Troy Donahue, Dorothy McGuire, Connie Stevens, Lloyd Nolan, Brian Aherne, Kent Smith. Slick soaper beautifully photographed. McGuire pretends to be mother of daughter's (Stevens) illegitimate child. Donahue is Connie's true love.

Susan Slept Here (1954) C-98m. **½ D: Frank Tashlin. Dick Powell, Debbie Reynolds, Anne Francis, Glenda Farrell, Alvy Moore. Cutesy sex comedy filled with innuendoes, but little action.

Susannah of the Mounties (1939) 78m. **½ D: William A. Seiter. Shirley Temple, Randolph Scott,

Margaret Lockwood, J. Farrell Mac-Donald, Moroni Olsen, Victor Jory. Mountie Scott raises orphan Shirley in this predictable but entertaining Temple vehicle.

Suspect, The (1944) 85m. ***½ D: Robert Siodmak. Charles Laughton, Ella Raines, Dean Harens, Molly Lamont, Henry Daniell, Rosalind Ivan. Superb, Hitchcock-like thriller of henpecked Laughton planning to get his wife out of the way so he can pursue lovely Raines.

Suspected Alibi SEE: **Suspended Alibi**

Suspended Alibi (1956-British) 64m. *½ D: Alfred Shaughnessy. Patrick Holt, Honor Blackman, Andrew Keir, Valentine Dyall. Holt becomes involved in homicide via circumstantial evidence in this coincidence-laden drama. Retitled: SUSPECTED ALIBI.

Suspense (1946) 101m. ** D: Frank Tuttle. Barry Sullivan, Belita, Bonita Granville, Albert Dekker. Cheapie mystery caper with flavorful unraveling of homicide at an ice show.

Suspicion (1941) 99m. ***½ D: Alfred Hitchcock. Cary Grant, Joan Fontaine, Cedric Hardwicke, Nigel Bruce, Dame May Whitty, Isabel Jeans, Heather Angel. Fontaine won Oscar for portraying wife who believes husband Grant is trying to kill her. Suspenser is helped by Bruce as Cary's pal, but leaves viewer flat with finale.

Sutter's Gold (1936) 94m. **½ D: James Cruze. Edward Arnold, Lee Tracy, Binnie Barnes, Katharine Alexander, Addison Richards, Montagu Love, Harry Carey. Biography of Johan Sutter starts off well, bogs down midway through story. Arnold is always good, but he's fighting a mediocre script here. Look for Billy Gilbert as a Spanish general taken hostage.

Suzy (1936) 99m. ** D: George Fitzmaurice. Jean Harlow, Franchot Tone, Cary Grant, Lewis Stone, Benita Hume. Fine cast sinks in romantic WW1 spy drama with Cary as a French flyer, Tone as Harlow's husband. Intended as semi-tragedy.

Svengali (1931) 76m. *** D: Archie Mayo. John Barrymore, Marian Marsh, Donald Crisp, Carmel Myers, Bramwell Fletcher, Luis Alberni. Absorbing tale of artist's obsession with young girl, Trilby, who becomes singing artist under his hypnotic spell. Prime Barrymore in interesting

production with bizarre sets by Anton Grot, memorable visual effects.

Svengali (1955-British) C-82. **½ D: Noel Langley. Hildegarde Neff, Donald Wolfit, Terence Morgan, Noel Purcell, Alfie Bass. Lacks flair of earlier version of du Maurier's novel about mesmerizing teacher and his beautiful actress-pupil Trilby.

Swamp Diamonds SEE: **Swamp Women**

Swamp Fire (1946) 69m. ** D: William Pine. Johnny Weissmuller, Virginia Grey, Buster Crabbe, Carol Thurston, Pedro DeCordoba, Marcelle Corday. Ex-navy man Weissmuller has lost his nerve; friends try to help him out.

Swamp Water (1941) 90m. **½ D: Jean Renoir. Walter Brennan, Walter Huston, Anne Baxter, Dana Andrews, Virginia Gilmore, John Carradine. Atmospheric tale of fugitive Brennan hiding out in Georgia swamp, how other characters are drawn into resulting conflict. Doesn't really hit bull's-eye, but well-done. Remade as LURE OF THE WILDERNESS.

Swamp Women (1955) C-73m. *½ D: Roger Corman. Michael Connors, Marie Windsor, Beverly Garland, Carole Mathews, Susan Cummings. Heavy-handed nonsense of four female convicts escaping jail, chasing after buried loot. Retitled: SWAMP DIAMONDS; CRUEL SWAMP.

Swan, The (1956) C-112m. *** D: Charles Vidor. Grace Kelly, Alec Guinness, Louis Jourdan, Agnes Moorehead, Jessie Royce Landis, Brian Aherne. Mild Molnar comedy of manners, attractive cast but not much sparkle. Jourdan good as Kelly's suitor, but she's promised to prince Guinness. Filmed before in 1925 and 1930.

Swanee River (1939) C-84m. **½ D: Sidney Lanfield. Don Ameche, Al Jolson, Andrea Leeds, Felix Bressart, Russell Hicks. Bio of Stephen Foster where every song he writes is cued by a line of dialogue; clichés fill the movie, but it's fun on that level. Jolson is terrific as E.P. Christy, and the minstrel numbers are exceptionally well done.

Swap, The SEE: **Sam's Song**

Swarm, The (1978) C-116m. BOMB D: Irwin Allen. Michael Caine, Katharine Ross, Richard Widmark, Henry Fonda, Richard Chamberlain, Olivia de Havilland, Fred MacMurray, Ben Johnson, Lee Grant, Jose Ferrer. This formula disaster film from Irwin Allen has no sting at all, succeeds only in wasting a lot of talented actors.

Swashbuckler (1976) C-101m. BOMB D: James Goldstone. Robert Shaw, James Earl Jones, Peter Boyle, Genevieve Bujold, Beau Bridges, Geoffrey Holder, Avery Schreiber. Poorly constructed, bubble-headed picture—laced with kinky sex scenes —would make Errol Flynn turn over in his grave. Incredible waste of talent.

Sweepings (1933) 80m. ***½ D: John Cromwell. Lionel Barrymore, William Gargan, Gloria Stuart, George Meeker, Eric Linden, Gregory Ratoff. Compelling Edna Ferber-ish saga of self-made man who devotes his life to building giant department store, hoping that his four children will carry on his work. Fine acting, inventive direction and camerawork—plus montages by Slavko Vorkapich—make this something special. Remade as THREE SONS in 1939.

Sweet Adeline (1935) 87m. **½ D: Mervyn LeRoy. Irene Dunne, Donald Woods, Hugh Herbert, Ned Sparks, Joseph Cawthorn, Louis Calhern, Winifred Shaw. Combination of spy chase and operetta isn't always smooth, but songs like "Why Was I Born" and Dunne's know-how make this enjoyable.

Sweet and Lowdown (1944) 75m. ** D: Archie Mayo. Linda Darnell, Jack Oakie, Lynn Bari, James Cardwell, Allyn Joslyn, Dickie Moore. Thin story-line of Benny Goodman giving poor musician the big break, causing a rift with girlfriend Darnell.

Sweet Bird of Youth (1962) C-120m. ***½ D: Richard Brooks. Paul Newman, Geraldine Page, Shirley Knight, Ed Begley, Madeleine Sherwood, Mildred Dunnock. Tennessee Williams' play, cleaned up for the movies, still is powerful drama. Newman returns to Southern town in entourage of dissipated movie queen Page, causing corrupt town "boss" Begley (who won an Oscar) to have him fixed proper. Glossy production with cast on top of material.

Sweet Body of Deborah, The (1969-Italian-French) C-105m. BOMB D: Romolo Guerrieri. Carroll Baker, Jean Sorel, Evelyn Stewart, Luigi Pistilli, Michel Bardinet. Not much

of Deborah's body will be left after TV cuts, but it didn't help film originally, anyway; terrible junk about scheme to get some insurance money.

Sweet Charity (1969) C-133m. *** D: Bob Fosse. Shirley MacLaine, John McMartin, Ricardo Montalban, Sammy Davis, Jr., Chita Rivera, Paula Kelly, Stubby Kaye. Fine, overlooked filmusical from Neil Simon play based on Fellini's NIGHTS OF CABIRIA, about prostitute-with-heart-of-gold who falls in love with naive young man who doesn't know about her "work." Cy Coleman-Dorothy Fields score includes "Big Spender," "If They Could See Me Now," rousing "Rhythm of Life." Fosse's debut as film director.

Sweet Hostage (1975) C-100m. TVM D: Lee Philips. Linda Blair, Martin Sheen, Jeanne Cooper, Lee DeBroux, Dehl Berti, Bert Remsen. Drama about an escaped psychopath and illiterate farm girl he drags to a deserted cabin to become his teacher, friend and lover. Performances of Sheen and Blair almost make this talky adaptation of Nathaniel Benchley's *Welcome to Xanadu* worthwhile. Average.

Sweet Love, Bitter (1967) 92m. *** D: Herbert Danska. Dick Gregory, Don Murray, Diane Varsi, Robert Hooks. Loosely based on Charlie "Bird" Parker, the jazz musician. Film is sometimes-touching story of men on the skids.

Sweet November (1968) C-114m. **½ D: Robert Ellis Miller. Sandy Dennis, Anthony Newley, Theodore Bikel, Burr DeBenning, Sandy Baron, Marj Dusay, Martin West. Kooky Dennis takes a new lover every month, helping insecure men find confidence, then sending them away; her plans go awry when one of them (Newley) insists on marrying her. Some touching moments in this likable (if implausible) comedy-drama.

Sweet Revenge (1977) C-90m. BOMB D: Jerry Schatzberg. Stockard Channing, Sam Waterston, Franklin Ajaye, Richard Doughty. Public defender Waterston falls in love with a car thief (Channing) in this turkey, originally called DANDY, THE ALL-AMERICAN GIRL.

Sweet Ride, The (1968) C-110m. *½ D: Harvey Hart. Tony Franciosa, Michael Sarrazin, Jacqueline Bisset, Bob Denver, Michael Wilding, Michele Carey, Warren Stevens. Absurd claptrap about a tennis bum, a surfer and a beautiful girl; some of the Malibu scenery is nice.

Sweet Rosie O'Grady (1943) C-74m. **½ D: Irving Cummings. Betty Grable, Robert Young, Adolphe Menjou, Reginald Gardiner, Virginia Grey, Phil Regan. Pleasant musical of ex-burlesque star and exposé reporter. Menjou steals film as editor of Police Gazette.

Sweet Smell of Success (1957) 96m. ***½ D: Alexander Mackendrick. Burt Lancaster, Tony Curtis, Marty Milner, Sam Levene, Barbara Nichols, Susan Harrison. Brittle Clifford Odets-Ernest Lehman script of vicious N.Y.C. columnist (Lancaster) and scheming press agent (Curtis) pulls no punches. Vivid performances and fine jazz score.

Sweet, Sweet Rachel (1971) C-73m. TVM D: Sutton Roley. Alex Dreier, Stefanie Powers, Pat Hingle, Louise Latham, Brenda Scott, Steve Ihnat. Wide-eyed, out-of-breath "thriller" pits ESP expert against unseen presence trying to drive beautiful woman crazy. Sloppy direction all but ruins fascinating premise. Average.

Sweethearts (1938) C-120m. **½ D: W. S. Van Dyke II. Jeanette MacDonald, Nelson Eddy, Frank Morgan, Florence Rice, Ray Bolger, Mischa Auer. Enjoyable but overlong; Nelson and Jeanette are stage stars of Victor Herbert operetta who are manipulated by their producer (Morgan) into having a marital spat. Handsome color production filled with Herbert melodies.

Swept Away . . . by an unusual destiny in the blue sea of August (1975-Italian) C-116m. **** D: Lina Wertmuller. Giancarlo Giannini, Mariangela Melato. A slovenly sailor is cast adrift on an island with his employer, a rich, selfish woman. Cut off from society, he reverses their roles, stripping her of pride and vanity, and controlling her completely. This fascinating and provocative adult film put writer-director Wertmuller on the map in this country.

Swimmer, The (1968) C-94m. ***½ D: Frank Perry. Burt Lancaster, Janet Landgard, Janice Rule, Tony Bickley, Marge Champion, Bill Fiore, Kim Hunter, Joan Rivers. Middle-aged man swims from pool to pool on journey home during hot afternoon; each pool evokes past moments and events. Fascinating, vastly underrated film adapted from John Cheever short story; Lancaster is superb, and location filming in Connecticut perfectly captures mood.

Swindle, The (1962-Italian) 92m. ** D: Federico Fellini. Broderick Crawford, Giulietta Masina, Richard Basehart, Franco Fabrizi. Cast is better than story: trio of crooks fleece people in Rome, each planning rich future life.

Swing Fever (1944) 80m. *½ D: Tim Whelan. Kay Kyser, Marilyn Maxwell, William Gargan, Lena Horne. Most uneven blend of music, boxing, and romance pegged on personality of Kyser.

Swing High, Swing Low (1937) 95m. ** D: Mitchell Leisen. Carole Lombard, Fred MacMurray, Charles Butterworth, Jean Dixon, Dorothy Lamour, Harvey Stephens, Anthony Quinn. Musical drama with cornball plot of musician MacMurray's rise and fall. Redeemed somewhat by good cast, glossy production. From the stage play *Burlesque*, made before as THE DANCE OF LIFE and remade as WHEN MY BABY SMILES AT ME.

Swing Shift Maisie (1943) 87m. D: Norman Z. McLeod. Ann Sothern, James Craig, Jean Rogers, Connie Gilchrist, John Qualen, Kay Medford. SEE: Maisie series.

Swing Time (1936) 105m. **** D: George Stevens. Fred Astaire, Ginger Rogers, Victor Moore, Helen Broderick, Eric Blore, Betty Furness. One of the best Astaire-Rogers films, with stars as dance team whose romance is hampered by Fred's engagement to girl back home (Furness). Fine support by Moore and Broderick, unforgettable Jerome Kern-Dorothy Fields songs "A Fine Romance," "Pick Yourself Up." Oscar-winning "The Way You Look Tonight." Astaire's Bojangles production number is a screen classic.

Swinger, The (1966) C-81m. ** D: George Sidney. Ann-Margret, Tony Franciosa, Robert Coote, Horace McMahon, Nydia Westman. Brassy, artificial yarn of good-girl Ann-Margret posing as swinger to impress girlie magazine editor Franciosa.

Swingtime Johnny (1944) 61m. *½ D: Edward Cline. Andrews Sisters, Harriet Hilliard, Peter Cookson, Tim Ryan. Show biz performers desert the theater for work in munitions factory; lowbrow entertainment.

Swirl of Glory SEE: **Sugarfoot**

Swiss Conspiracy, The (1975-U.S.-German) C-88m. ** D: Jack Arnold. David Janssen, Senta Berger, John Ireland, John Saxon, Elke Sommer, Ray Milland, Anton Diffring. Confusing cat-and-mouse intrigue set in Switzerland, where Janssen is hired to protect valued bank customers with large secret accounts.

Swiss Family Robinson (1940) 93m. *** D: Edward Ludwig. Thomas Mitchell, Edna Best, Freddie Bartholomew, Tim Holt, Terry Kilburn. Mitchell leads family to remote island where they live idyllic existence. Fine adaptation of Johann Wyss book.

Swiss Family Robinson (1960) C-128m. ***½ D: Ken Annakin. John Mills, Dorothy McGuire, James MacArthur, Janet Munro, Sessue Hayakawa, Tommy Kirk, Kevin Corcoran. Rollicking entertainment Disney-style, with shipwrecked family building island paradise, neatly dispatching Hayakawa and his pirate band. Pure escapism, larger than life.

Swiss Family Robinson, The (1975) C-100m. TVM D: Harry Harris. Martin Milner, Pat Delany, Cameron Mitchell, Michael-James Wixted, Eric Olson, John Vernon. Adventure classic distilled by Irwin Allen, the disaster master of the movies. It's still worthy of family viewing and somehow had enough thrills to spare for a brief subsequent series. Average.

Swiss Miss (1938) 72m. ** D: John Blystone. Stan Laurel, Oliver Hardy, Della Lind, Walter Woolf King, Eric Blore, Adia Kuznetzof, Charles Judels. Contrived romantic story with music tries hard to submerge L&H, but Stan and Ollie's scenes save film, especially when Ollie serenades his true love with Stan playing tuba.

Switch (1975) C-78m. TVM D: Robert Day. Robert Wagner, Eddie Albert, Charles Durning, Sharon Gless, Ken Swofford, Charlie Callas, Jaclyn Smith. Ex-con man Wagner teams up with ex-cop Albert in private eye agency to prove that a cop rather than a con pulled off a diamond heist. TV's best STING rip-off, owing much to the charm of its two leads, went on to become the hit series. Above average.

Sword and the Rose, The (1953)

C-93m. ***½ D: Ken Annakin. Richard Todd, Glynis Johns, James Robertson Justice, Michael Gough, Jane Barrett. Colorful filming of *When Knighthood was in Flower*, with Johns as Mary Tudor, who uses wiles and power to kindle romance with Todd—but runs afoul of villainous Duke (Michael Gough). Rich period flavor, fine performance by Justice as King Henry VIII. Filmed in England by Walt Disney.

Sword in the Desert (1949) 100m. **½ D: George Sherman. Dana Andrews, Marta Toren, Stephen McNally, Jeff Chandler, Philip Friend. Interesting account of underground trail of European refugees during WW2; fairly good suspenser.

Sword of Ali Baba, The (1965) C-81m. ** D: Virgil Vogel. Peter Mann, Jocelyn Lane, Peter Whitney, Gavin MacLeod, Frank Puglia. Outrageous remake of Jon Hall Ali Baba film of 1940s, using much footage from original. Puglia repeats role from original film.

Sword of El Cid, The (1962-Spanish) C-85m. ** D: Miguel Iglesias. Roland Carey, Sandro Moretti, Chantal Deberg, Daniela Bianchi. Sparse plot ruins this potentially good costumer with Moretti et al battling corrupt ruler of Catalonia.

Sword of Lancelot (1963-British) C-116m. **½ D: Cornel Wilde. Cornel Wilde, Jean Wallace, Brian Aherne, George Baker. Camelot comes alive, minus music, with profuse action and splendid scenery. Some may find Wilde's approach too juvenile, overly sincere, and Aherne a bit too cavalier. Originally titled LANCELOT AND GUINEVERE.

Sword of Monte Cristo, The (1951) C-80m. ** D: Maurice Geraghty. George Montgomery, Paula Corday, Berry Kroeger, William Conrad, Steve Brodie. Uninspired adventure of woman who finds legendary sword of Count with key to treasure inscribed on it. Army officer joins her in fight against evil prime minister.

Sword of Sherwood Forest (1961-British) C-80m. **½ D: Terence Fisher. Richard Greene, Niall MacGinnis, Peter Cushing, Nigel Green. Fair British continuation of Robin Hood saga as Earl of Newark plots murder of Archbishop of Canterbury.

Sword of the Conqueror (1961-Italian) C-85m. *½ D: Carlo Campogalliani. Jack Palance, Eleonora Rossi-Drago, Guy Madison, Carlo D'Angelo. Flabby epic not livened by cast or sets; set in 6th-century Byzantine empire days.

Swordsman, The (1948) C-81m. ** D: Joseph H. Lewis. Larry Parks, Ellen Drew, George Macready, Edgar Buchanan. Parks and Drew have Romeo-Juliet relationship in 18th-century Scotland; OK costumer.

Swordsman of Siena, The (1961-Italian) C-97m. ** D: Gus Agosta. Stewart Granger, Sylva Koscina, Christine Kaufmann, Tullio Carminati, Gabriele Ferzetti. Predictable, swashbuckler about 16th-century adventurer with mixed loyalties who becomes involved in Spanish underground movement. Good cast saddled with tired script.

Sybil (1976) C-198m TVM D: Daniel Petrie. Joanne Woodward, Sally Field, Brad Davis, Martine Bartlett, Jane Hoffman, William Prince. Emmy-winning psychological study of a young woman who, disturbed by childhood experiences, has developed sixteen separate personalities. Field is remarkable in title role and Woodward brings special glow to the role of psychiatrist. Fascinating but deeply disturbing drama. Above average.

Sylvia (1965) 115m. **½ D: Gordon Douglas. Carroll Baker, George Maharis, Joanne Dru, Peter Lawford, Viveca Lindfors, Edmond O'Brien, Aldo Ray, Ann Sothern. Baker's prelude to HARLOW is much better, despite overuse of flashbacks and rambling episodes. Baker plays a bad girl turned good; melodrama unfolds as detective Maharis investigates her life. Good cameos.

Sylvia Scarlett (1935) 97m. *** D: George Cukor. Katharine Hepburn, Cary Grant, Brian Aherne, Edmund Gwenn, Natalie Paley, Dennie Moore. Offbeat, charming comedydrama; Hepburn and ne'er-do-well father Gwenn take to the road when he gets in trouble. She disguises as a boy as they travel with cockney Grant in touring show. Most unusual film made interesting by performances of Hepburn and Grant.

Sympathy for the Devil (1970-French) C-92m. ** D: Jean-Luc Godard. Muddled documentary which utilizes the Rolling Stones as a catchall for interspersed study of revolution.

Symphony of Six Million (1932) 94m. **½ D: Gregory LaCava. Irene Dunne, Ricardo Cortez, Anna Appel, Gregory Ratoff, Lita Chevret. Predictable but well-made Fannie Hurst soap opera has young doctor Cortez abandoning his Jewish-ghetto neighborhood, family, friends—and crippled sweetheart Dunne—to join Park Avenue set and make big money.

Synanon (1965) 107m. **½ D: Richard Quine. Chuck Connors, Stella Stevens, Alex Cord, Richard Conte, Eartha Kitt, Edmond O'Brien, Chanin Hale, Alejandro Rey. Potentially powerful study of dope-addiction treatment via the Synanon House methods bogs down in pat romantic tale with stereotyped performances.

Syncopation (1942) 88m. ** D: William Dieterle. Adolphe Menjou, Jackie Cooper, Bonita Granville, Todd Duncan, Connee Boswell, Hall Johnson Choir. Uneven story traces history of Jazz from 1906, with Cooper as young struggling trumpeter (dubbed by Bunny Berigan). Film redeemed somewhat by terrific jam session featuring Benny Goodman, Harry James, Charlie Barnet, Gene Krupa, and other musical greats.

System, The (1953) 90m. ** D: Lewis Seiler. Frank Lovejoy, Joan Weldon, Bob Arthur, Jerome Cowan. Uneven scripting spoils this potentially good study of gambling syndicate in large metropolitan city.

System, The (1966) SEE: **Girl-Getters, The**

T-Men (1947) 96m. *** D: Anthony Mann. Dennis O'Keefe, June Lockhart, Alfred Ryder, Charles McGraw, Wallace Ford, Mary Meade. Semidocumentary-style story of undercover treasury agents trying to get to the bottom of counterfeit ring. Vividly exciting; director Mann and cameraman John Alton went out of their way to use unusual, effective lighting and compositions in this A-1 film.

T. R. Baskin (1971) C-90m. **½ D: Herbert Ross. Candice Bergen, Peter Boyle, James Caan, Marcia Rodd, Erin O'Reilly, Howard Platt. Beautiful young small-town girl tries to make it in Chicago, finds problems in the big city. Wildly uneven comedy drama has a few good scenes, good acting by Caan in small role.

Taffy and the Jungle Hunter (1965) C-87m. ** D: Terry O. Morse. Jacques Bergerac, Manuel Padilla, Shary Marshall, Hari Rhodes. Unassuming tale of son of big game hunter who takes off for jungle adventures with pet elephant and chimp.

Taggart (1964) C-85m. **½ D: R. G. Springsteen. Tony Young, Dan Duryea, Peter Duryea, David Carradine, Jean Hale, Harry Carey, Jr., Bob Steele. Neat little action Western with Young on a revenge hunt, pursued by gunslingers in Indian territory.

Tail Gunner Joe (1977) C-144m. TVM D: Jud Taylor. Peter Boyle, John Forsythe, Heather Menzies, Burgess Meredith, Patricia Neal, Jean Stapleton, Ned Beatty, John Carradine. The rise and fall of Senator Joseph McCarthy, with a stunning performance by Boyle. Gripping drama woven with the author's bias. Above average.

Tail Spin (1939) 84m. ** D: Roy Del Ruth. Alice Faye, Constance Bennett, Nancy Kelly, Joan Davis, Charles Farrell, Jane Wyman. Hackneyed saga of female flyers, with nonsinging Faye in charge, worrier Kelly, funny-girl Davis, etc.

Tailor's Maid, The (1959-Italian) C-92m. **½ D: Mario Monicelli. Vittorio De Sica, Marcello Mastroianni, Marisa Merlini, Fiorella Mari, Memmo Carotenuto, Raffaele Pisu. Saucy, inconsequential comedy about an amorous tailor.

Take, The (1974) C-93m. **D: Robert Hartford-Davis. Billy Dee Williams, Eddie Albert, Vic Morrow, Frankie Avalon, Albert Salmi. Tepid action pic concerns police Lt. Williams' efforts to stop syndicate chief Morrow while accepting bribe money on the side. Surprisingly neat cameo by Avalon as a cheap crook.

Take a Chance (1933) 84M. *½ D: Laurence Schwab, Monte Brice. James Dunn, Cliff Edwards, June Knight, Charles "Buddy" Rogers, Lillian Roth, Dorothy Lee. Awful adaptation of Broadway musical about carnival hucksters aiming for the big time, redeemed somewhat by fine score and campy number with "Ukulele Ike" Edwards.

Take a Hard Ride (1975) C-109m. ** D: Anthony Dawson. Jim Brown, Lee Van Cleef, Fred Williamson, Catherine Spaak, Jim Kelly, Dana Andrews, Barry Sullivan, Harry Carey Jr. Oddball Western filmed in Canary Islands. Brown must carry large bankroll across Mexican bor-

der, attracts a colorful band of "comrades" for his journey, runs afoul of bandit Van Cleef. Good personalities wasted in blah script.

Take a Letter, Darling (1942) 93m. *** D: Mitchell Leisen. Rosalind Russell, Fred MacMurray, Constance Moore, Robert Benchley, Macdonald Carey, Dooley Wilson, Cecil Kellaway. Witty repartee as advertising exec Roz hires MacMurray as secretary; but relationship doesn't end there. Benchley is wry as Russell's game-playing business partner.

Take Care of my Little Girl (1951) C-93m. ** D: Jean Negulesco. Jeanne Crain, Dale Robertson, Mitzi Gaynor, Jean Peters, Jeffrey Hunter, George Nader, Helen Westcott. Overdramatic story of sorority life at college.

Take Down (1978) C-107m. *** D: Kieth Merrill. Edward Herrmann, Kathleen Lloyd, Lorenzo Lamas, Maureen McCormick, Nick Beauvy, Kevin Hooks, Stephen Furst. Seriocomic look at high school wrestling, focusing on rebellious student Lamas and reluctant coach Herrmann. Well done.

Take Her, She's Mine (1963) C-98m. ** D: Henry Koster. James Stewart, Sandra Dee, Audrey Meadows, Robert Morley, Philippe Forquet, John McGiver. Obvious family comedy with Stewart the harried father of wild teen-age daughter Dee. Predictable gags don't help.

Take It or Leave It (1944) 70m. *½ D: Benjamin Stoloff. Phil Baker, Edward Ryan, Marjorie Massow, Stanley Prager, Roy Gordon. Claptrap hinged on lives of contestants on popular quiz show; film uses clips from older pictures to liven proceedings.

Take Me Out to the Ball Game (1949) C-93m. *** D: Busby Berkeley. Frank Sinatra, Esther Williams, Gene Kelly, Betty Garrett, Edward Arnold, Jules Munshin, Richard Lane, Tom Dugan. Contrived but colorful turn-of-the-century musical, with Sinatra and Kelly joining Williams' baseball team. "O'Brien to Ryan to Goldberg" and Kelly's "The Hat My Father Wore on St. Patrick's Day" are musical highlights.

Take Me to Town (1953) C-81m. **½ D: Douglas Sirk. Ann Sheridan, Sterling Hayden, Philip Reed, Lee Patrick, Lane Chandler. Unpretentious Americana of saloon singer Sheridan on the lam, finding love with widowed preacher Hayden and his three children.

Take One False Step (1949) 94m. **½ D: Chester Erskine. William Powell, Shelley Winters, James Gleason, Marsha Hunt, Dorothy Hart, Sheldon Leonard. OK mystery-drama with innocent Powell hunted by police as he tries to clear himself of murder charge.

Take the High Ground (1953) C-101m. *** D: Richard Brooks. Richard Widmark, Karl Malden, Elaine Stewart, Steve Forrest, Carleton Carpenter. Taut account of infantry basic training with on-location filming at Fort Bliss, Texas helping.

Take the Money and Run (1969) C-85m. *** D: Woody Allen. Woody Allen, Janet Margolin, Marcel Hillaire, Jacquelyn Hyde; narrator, Jackson Beck. Woody's first film as director/writer/star is full of funny ideas, telling documentary-style, life story of compulsive thief. Nonstop parade of jokes; some work, some don't. Louise Lasser seen briefly.

Taking of Pelham One Two Three, The (1974) C-102m. ***½ D: Joseph Sargent. Walter Matthau, Robert Shaw, Martin Balsam, Hector Elizondo, Tony Roberts, James Broderick. Ruthless criminal and three cohorts take over N.Y. subway train and hold passengers hostage for one million dollars. First-rate crime thriller from John Godey's bestseller is bursting with heart-stopping excitement and powerful performances.

Taking Off (1971) C-93m. ***½ D: Milos Forman. Lynn Carlin, Buck Henry, Linnea Heacock, Audra Lindley, Paul Benedict, Georgia Engel. Beguilingly funny look at American life-styles from two generations' point of view, centering on runaway girl (Heacock) who drives parents (Carlin, Henry) into new experiences of their own. Carly Simon seen as one of auditioning singers.

Tale of Two Cities, A (1917) 70m. *** D: Frank Lloyd. William Farnum, Jewel Carmen, Joseph Swickard, Herschell Mayall, Rosita Marstini. Ambitious silent-film version of Dickens story was a big hit in 1917, and it's easy to see why: Farnum is an appealing hero, production is first-rate, and battle scenes are reminiscent of Griffith's INTOLERANCE.

Tale of Two Cities, A (1935) 128m.

**** D: Jack Conway. Ronald Colman, Elizabeth Allan, Edna May Oliver, Reginald Owen, Basil Rathbone, Blanche Yurka, Isabel Jewell. Dickens' panorama of the 1790s French Revolution becomes an MGM blockbuster, with Colman as carefree lawyer awakened to responsibility, aiding victims of the Reign of Terror. Tremendous cast in a truly lavish production.

Tale of Two Cities, A (1958-British) 117m. *** D: Ralph Thomas. Dirk Bogarde, Dorothy Tutin, Cecil Parker, Stephen Murray, Athene Seyler, Christopher Lee. Faithful retelling of Dickens story in this well-made British production, with Bogarde a good Sydney Carton.

Talent for Loving, A (1969) C-110m. ** D: Richard Quine. Richard Widmark, Topol, Cesar Romero, Genevieve Page, Judd Hamilton, Caroline Munro. Rambunctious Western concerning a professional gambler trapped into marrying within rich Mexican family cursed by the Aztecs with a talent for loving. From Richard Condon's novel.

Tales from the Crypt (1972-British) C-92m. **½ D: Freddie Francis. Ralph Richardson, Peter Cushing, Joan Collins, Richard Greene, Patrick Magee, Ian Hendry, Nigel Patrick. Five stories of terror involving deceit, mayhem, and a few well-timed laughs. Nothing extraordinary, however.

Tales of Adventure SEE: **Jack London's Tales of Adventure**

Tales of Hoffman (1951-British) C-118m. **½ D: Michael Powell, Emeric Pressburger. Moira Shearer, Robert Rounseville, Leonide Massine, Robert Helpmann, Pamela Brown. Jacques Offenbach's fantasy opera of student who engages in bizarre dreams, revealing three states of his life. Striking and offbeat film, not for all tastes. Cut from original 138m. release.

Tales of Manhattan (1942) 118m. *** D: Julien Duvivier. Henry Fonda, Rita Hayworth, Ginger Rogers, Charles Boyer, Edward G. Robinson, Charles Laughton, Ethel Waters, Eddie Anderson, Thomas Mitchell, Gail Patrick, Roland Young. Episodic film about a tailcoat passed from hand to hand is extremely variable, but stars make it worthwhile.

Tales of Robin Hood (1951) 60m. *½ D: James Tinling. Robert Clarke,

Mary Hatcher, Paul Cavanagh, Wade Crosby. Minor account of folklore hero.

Tales of Terror (1962) **C-90m.** ******* D: Roger Corman. Vincent Price, Peter Lorre, Basil Rathbone, Debra Paget, Maggie Pierce, Leona Gage. Four Edgar Allan Poe stories distilled into three-part film with Lorre's performance—as vengeful husband walling up adulterous wife—the standout. Odd color effects will suffer on small screen.

Tales That Witness Madness (1973-British) **C-90m.** ***½** D: Freddie Francis. Kim Novak, Georgia Brown, Joan Collins, Jack Hawkins, Donald Houston, Suzy Kendall, Donald Pleasence. Absurd collection of four TWILIGHT ZONE-ish stories. A waste of time and talent.

Talk About a Stranger (1952) 65m. ****** D: David Bradley. George Murphy, Nancy Davis, Billy Gray, Kurt Kasznar, Lewis Stone. Boy tries to find out more about a mysterious neighbor in OK programmer.

Talk of the Town, The (1942) 118m. ******** D: George Stevens. Jean Arthur, Ronald Colman, Cary Grant, Glenda Farrell, Edgar Buchanan, Charles Dingle, Rex Ingram. Intelligent comedy with brilliant cast; fugitive Grant hides out with unsuspecting professor Colman and landlady Arthur, and tries to convince legal-minded Colman there's a human side to all laws. Splendid.

Tall Blond Man With One Black Shoe, The (1972-French) **C-90m.** ******* D: Yves Robert. Pierre Richard, Bernard Blier, Jean Rochefort, Mireille Darc, Jean Carmet. Engaging French farce with rival secret agents making life a shambles for the Tall Blond Man (Richard) who's been innocently pegged a spy. Followed by RETURN OF . . . sequel in 1974.

Tall, Dark and Handsome (1941) 78m. ****½** D: H. Bruce Humberstone. Cesar Romero, Virginia Gilmore, Charlotte Greenwood, Milton Berle, Sheldon Leonard. Amusing Runyonesque gangster comedy about an underworld bigwig who's really a softie. Remade as LOVE THAT BRUTE.

Tall in the Saddle (1944) 87m. ******* Edwin L. Marin. John Wayne, Ella Raines, Ward Bond, Gabby Hayes, Elisabeth Risdon, Raymond Hatton. Cowboy Wayne avoids women until

he goes to work at Raines' ranch; good, enjoyable Western.

Tall Lie, The SEE: **For Men Only**

Tall Man Riding (1955) **C-83m.** ****½** D: Lesley Selander. Randolph Scott, Dorothy Malone, Peggie Castle, John Dehner, Lane Chandler. Sturdy Western with Scott involved in outmaneuvering greedy ranchers during territorial land granting in Montana.

Tall Men, The (1955) **C-122m.** BOMB D: Raoul Walsh. Clark Gable, Jane Russell, Robert Ryan, Cameron Mitchell, Mae Marsh. Dismal oater unsaved by Jane in bloomers. Gable and Mitchell as brothers fight snowstorm and Indians. Blah.

Tall Story (1960) 91m. ****½** D: Joshua Logan. Anthony Perkins, Jane Fonda, Ray Walston, Marc Connelly, Anne Jackson, Murray Hamilton, Bob Wright, Bart Burns. Fast-moving froth about man-hungry coed Fonda (in film debut) falling in love with college basketball star Perkins. Based on Howard Lindsay-Russell Crouse play.

Tall Stranger, The (1957) **C-81m.** ****** D: Thomas Carr. Joel McCrea, Virginia Mayo, Michael Ansara, Michael Pate. Standard fare of McCrea helping wagon convoy cross Colorado territory.

Tall T, The (1957) **C-78m.** ******* D: Budd Boetticher. Randolph Scott, Richard Boone, Maureen O'Sullivan, Henry Silva, Skip Homeier, Arthur Hunnicutt. Scott becomes involved with kidnapped O'Sullivan, and tries to undermine unity of outlaw gang holding her prisoner. Solid Western all the way.

Tall Target, The (1951) 78m. ******* D: Anthony Mann. Dick Powell, Paula Raymond, Adolphe Menjou, Marshall Thompson, Ruby Dee, Will Geer. Gripping suspense as detective Powell follows tip that Abraham Lincoln is going to be assassinated during 1861 train ride.

Tall Women, The (1966-Spanish) **C-101m.** ****** D: Sidney Pink. Anne Baxter, Maria Perschy, Rosella Como, John Clarke. Western about seven women making their way through Indian country. Foreign-made movie suffers from dubbing and mediocre acting.

Tamango (1957-French) **C-98m.** ****** D: John Berry. Dorothy Dandridge, Curt Jurgens, Jean Servais, Roger Hanin, Guy Mairesse. Offbeat misfire about Dutch captain Jurgens involved with slave trader, romancing native Dandridge and trying to quell slave mutiny aboard.

Tamarind Seed, The (1974) C-123m. *** D: Blake Edwards. Julie Andrews, Omar Sharif, Anthony Quayle, Daniel O'Herlihy, Sylvia Sims, Oscar Homolka. Well-mounted espionage/romance set in London, Paris and Barbados; shows what a capable director can do with sappy material.

Taming of the Shrew, The (1967-U.S.-Italian) C-126m. ***½ D: Franco Zeffirelli. Elizabeth Taylor, Richard Burton, Vernon Dobtcheff, Michael Hordern, Natasha Pyne, Michael York, Cyril Cusack. Colorful version of Shakespeare's romp is well served by Richard and Elizabeth, good supporting cast, lovely photography, and good musical score by Nino Rota. Shakespeare purists may object, but Zeffirelli has succeeded in making a film, instead of a photographed stage play.

Taming Sutton's Gal (1957) 71m. *½ D: Lesley Selander. John Lupton, Gloria Talbott, Jack Kelly, May Wynn, Verna Felton. Tedious hokum involving moonshiner's amorous wife.

Tam-Lin SEE: **Devil's Widow, The**

Tammy and the Bachelor (1957) C-89m. *** D: Joseph Pevney. Debbie Reynolds, Walter Brennan, Leslie Nielsen, Mala Powers, Fay Wray, Sidney Blackmer, Louise Beavers. Unpretentious if cutesy romantic corn of country gal Reynolds falling in love with pilot Nielsen whom she's nursed back to health after plane crash.

Tammy and the Doctor (1963) C-88m. **½ D: Harry Keller. Sandra Dee, Peter Fonda, Macdonald Carey, Beulah Bondi, Margaret Lindsay, Reginald Owen. Sugary fluff involving homespun Tammy (Dee) courted by doctor Fonda; supporting cast adds touching cameos.

Tammy and the Millionaire (1967) C-87m. ** D: Sidney Miller, Ezra Stone, Leslie Goodwins. Debbie Watson, Frank McGrath, Denver Pyle, George Furth, Donald Woods, Dorothy Green. Low-grade TV pilot expanded to feature, diluting the fuzzy folksy charm of backwoods girl trying to better the world.

Tammy Tell Me True (1961) C-97m. ** D: Harry Keller. Sandra Dee, John Gavin, Virginia Grey, Beulah Bondi, Cecil Kellaway. Tired romance of girl coming to college for first time, makes name for herself

by helping dean of women. Script and acting very uneven.

Tampico (1944) 75m. ** D: Lothar Mendes. Edward G. Robinson, Lynn Bari, Victor McLaglen, Marc Lawrence, Mona Maris. Merchantmarine skipper Robinson senses espionage on his boat, but suspects wrong party. Routine WW2 intrigue, partially salvaged by stars.

Tanganyika (1954) C-81m. ** D: Andre de Toth. Van Heflin, Ruth Roman, Howard Duff, Jeff Morrow. OK adventure of explorer attempting land claim in East Africa with numerous perils along the way.

Tangier (1946) 76m. **½ D: George Waggner. Maria Montez, Preston Foster, Robert Paige, Louise Allbritton, Kent Taylor, Sabu, J. Edward Bromberg, Reginald Denny. Limp intrigue in Tangier with vengeful dancer Montez, isn't even in color.

Tangier Incident (1953) 77m. *½ D: Lew Landers. George Brent, Mari Aldon, Dorothy Patrick, Bert Freed. Tame actioner with Brent a federal agent hunting an espionage ring.

Tank Force (1958-British) C-81m. *½ D: Terence Young. Victor Mature, Leo Genn, Anthony Newley, Luciana Paluzzi. Clichéd dud of WW2 with assorted British prisoners escaping across Libyan desert. Originally titled NO TIME TO DIE.

Tanks Are Coming, The (1951) 90m. ** D: Lewis Seiler. Steve Cochran, Philip Carey, James Dobson, Mari Aldon, Paul Picerni. Moderate WW2 actioner set during Allied capture of Berlin.

Tap Roots (1948) C-109m. **½ D: George Marshall. Van Heflin, Susan Hayward, Boris Karloff, Julie London. Average historical drama about two lovers in secessionist Mississippi. Uneven script and standard acting.

Tarantula (1955) 80m. **½ D: Jack Arnold. John Agar, Mara Corday, Leo G. Carroll, Nestor Paiva, Ross Elliott. Above average horror film. Laboratory freak breaks loose and runs rampant; frightening special effects.

Tarantulas: The Deadly Cargo (1977) C-100m. TVM D: Stuart Hagmann. Claude Akins, Charles Frank, Deborah Winters, Pat Hingle, Sandy McPeak. Horde of deadly tarantulas spread terror through small town. Would-be thriller commits the unpardonable sin of being dull. Below average.

Taras Bulba (1962) C-122m. **½
D: J. Lee Thompson. Tony Curtis,
Yul Brynner, Christine Kaufmann,
Sam Wanamaker. Cardboard cos-
tumer of 16th-century Ukraine, cen-
tering on Cossack life and fighting.
Nice photography (on location in
Argentina) and fine musical score.

Tarawa Beachhead (1958) 77m. **½
D: Paul Wendkos. Kerwin Mathews,
Julie Adams, Ray Danton, Karen
Sharpe. Standard account of WW2
military assault with usual focus on
problems of troops.

Target Earth (1954) 75m. **½ D:
Sherman Rose. Richard Denning,
Virginia Grey, Kathleen Crowley,
Richard Reeves, Robert Ruark, Steve
Pendleton. People in deserted city
trapped by invading robot force.
Competently acted movie starts off
beautifully but bogs down too soon.

Target for an Assassin (1976-South
African) C-102m. *½ D: Peter Collinson. Anthony Quinn, John Phillip
Law, Simon Sabela, Marius Weyers,
Sandra Prinsloo. Unbelievable story
about two men who conspire against
black African leader—one, a paid
assassin, the other a desperate
down-and-outer who kidnaps him for
ransom. Original title: TIGERS
DON'T CRY.

Target Risk (1975) C-78m. TVM D:
Robert Scheerer. Bo Svenson, Meredith Baxter, Robert Coote, Keenan
Wynn, John P. Ryan, Philip Bruns.
Gem courier Svenson is pressed into
pulling off jewel heist to ransom his
kidnapped girlfriend. Pilot for projected series that never materialized.
Average.

Target, Sea of China (1954) 100m.
*½ D: Franklin Adreon. Harry
Lauter, Aline Towne, Lyle Talbot,
Robert Shayne, Fred Graham. Sloppy cliff-hanger nonsense of conspirators from unnamed foreign power
aiding the rebellious natives. Reedited movie serial: TRADER TOM
OF THE CHINA SEAS.

Target Unknown (1951) 90m. **½
D: George Sherman. Mark Stevens,
Alex Nicol, Joyce Holden, Robert
Douglas, Don Taylor, Gig Young.
Imaginative handling of worn-out
premise of group of Allied soldiers
caught in Nazi-occupied France.

Target Zero (1955) 92m. ** D: Harmon Jones. Richard Conte, Charles
Bronson, Chuck Connors, Peggie
Castle. Unrewarding Korean War
film.

Targets (1968) C-92m. *** D: Peter
Bogdanovich. Boris Karloff, Tim O'-
Kelly, Nancy Hseuh, James Brown,
Sandy Baron, Peter Bogdanovich.
Bogdanovich's first film is exciting
tale of sniper who kills wife and
family, then starts taking shots at
drive-in movie patrons. Lacks motivation, but makes up for that flaw
with lots of thrills.

Tarnished Angels, The (1958) 91m.
***½ D: Douglas Sirk. Rock Hud-
son, Dorothy Malone, Robert Stack,
Jack Carson, Robert Middleton.
Compelling adaptation of William
Faulkner's fatalistic drama *Pylon*,
set in 1930s, with Hudson as newspaperman drawn to barnstorming
pilot Stack—his curious life-style
and ethics, his put-upon wife, and
his frustrated mechanic.

Tarnished Lady (1931) 83m. **½ D:
George Cukor. Tallulah Bankhead,
Clive Brook, Phoebe Foster, Osgood
Perkins, Elizabeth Patterson. Bankhead marries Brook for his money
but falls in love with him almost too
late. Ornate triangle has good performances.

Tartars, The (1962-Italian) C-83m.
** D: Richard Thorpe, Orson
Welles, Victor Mature, Folco Lulli,
Liana Orfei. Welles' performance of
Burundai, head of Tartar invasion of
Volga River, plus appearance of
Mature, are only distinguishing fea-
tures of otherwise routine spectacle.

Tartu SEE: **Adventures of Tartu**

Tarzan Although Edgar Rice Burroughs' king of the jungle has been
played by some fourteen people from
1918 to the present, most aficionados
agree that Johnny Weissmuller, who
essayed the role from 1932 to 1948,
was the one and only Tarzan. His
early MGM efforts such as TAR-
ZAN THE APE MAN and TAR-
ZAN AND HIS MATE, co-starring
lovely Maureen O'Sullivan as Jane,
were "class" films with fine production values, plenty of action, and
excitement. Later entries at MGM
like TARZAN'S NEW YORK AD-
VENTURE became more standard-
ized, like other series films, with
comedy relief supplied by Cheetah
the chimp, and family interest
sparked by Johnny Sheffield as Boy.
On the whole, however, the six
Weissmuller-O'Sullivan efforts were
quite enjoyable. In 1942, Maureen
left the series, but Weissmuller continued in lesser but still entertaining
episodes produced for RKO release.
Lex Barker took over the role in

1949, and continued through 1955; these films lost much of the original sparkle as budgets and inventiveness diminished. Various people (Denny Miller, Gordon Scott, Mike Henry, Ron Ely) have played Tarzan since, with Scott faring best in his late 1950s-early 60s entries, one of which, TARZAN'S GREATEST ADVENTURE, is an excellent jungle-adventure film shot in color with the added curio interest of pre-James Bond Sean Connery in the cast. Other recent Tarzan films have been sloppily thrown together; the 1959 "remake" of Weissmuller's 1932 TARZAN THE APE MAN was comprised mostly of stock footage from other films and tinted scenes from the original, with expected low-grade results. Other Tarzans, from Buster Crabbe to Bruce Bennett, have popped up from time to time in various competent vehicles, but none of them have ever come up to the plateau of the handsomely mounted MGM efforts of the 1930s. The latest Tarzan features with Ron Ely (TARZAN'S JUNGLE REBELLION, TARZAN'S DEADLY SILENCE) have actually been episodes of the recent TV series strung together, adequate small-screen entertainment but hardly comparable to the actionful efforts of Johnny Weissmuller, whose early films retain much of their excitement for a new generation of fans through TV screenings.

Tarzan and His Mate (1934) 105m. D: Cedric Gibbons, Jack Conway. Johnny Weissmuller, Maureen O'-Sullivan, Neil Hamilton, Paul Cavanagh, Forrester Harvey.

Tarzan and the Amazons (1945) 76m. D: Kurt Neumann. Johnny Weissmuller, Brenda Joyce, Johnny Sheffield, Henry Stephenson, Maria Ouspenskaya, Barton MacLane.

Tarzan and the Great River (1967) C-99m. D: Robert Day. Mike Henry, Jan Murray, Manuel Padilla Jr., Diana Millay, Rafer Johnson.

Tarzan and the Green Goddess (1938) 72m. D: Edward Kull. Herman Brix (Bruce Bennett), Ula Holt, Frank Baker, Don Castello, Lewis Sargent. (adapted from 1935 serial)

Tarzan and the Huntress (1947) 72m. D: Kurt Neumann. Johnny Weissmuller, Brenda Joyce, Johnny Sheffield, Patricia Morison, Barton MacLane.

Tarzan and the Jungle Boy (1968) C-99m. D: Robert Day. Mike Henry,

Alizia Gur, Ronald Gans, Rafer Johnson, Ed Johnson, Steven Bond.

Tarzan and the Leopard Woman (1946) 72m. D: Kurt Neumann. Johnny Weissmuller, Brenda Joyce, Johnny Sheffield, Acquanetta, Edgar Barrier, Tommy Cook.

Tarzan and the Lost Safari (1957-British) C-84m. D: H. Bruce Humberstone. Gordon Scott, Yolande Donlan, Betta St. John, Wilfrid Hyde-White, George Coulouris.

Tarzan and the Mermaids (1948) 68m. D: Robert Florey. Johnny Weissmuller, Brenda Joyce, Linda Christian, John Laurenz, Fernando Wagner.

Tarzan and the She-Devil (1953) 76m. D: Kurt Neumann. Lex Barker, Joyce McKenzie, Raymond Burr, Monique Van Vooren, Tom Conway.

Tarzan and the Slave Girl (1950) 74m. D: Lee Sholem. Lex Barker, Vanessa Brown, Robert Alda, Denise Darcel, Hurd Hatfield.

Tarzan and the Trappers (1958) 74m. D: H. Bruce Humberstone. Gordon Scott, Eve Brent, Rickie Sorenson, Leslie Bradley, Maurice Marsac.

Tarzan and the Valley of Gold (1966) C-90m. D: Robert Day. Mike Henry, David Opatoshu, Manuel Padilla Jr., Nancy Kovack, Don Megowan.

Tarzan Escapes (1936) 95m. D: Richard Thorpe. Johnny Weissmuller, Maureen O'Sullivan, John Buckler, Benita Hume, William Henry.

Tarzan Finds a Son (1939) 90m. D: Richard Thorpe. Johnny Weissmuller, Maureen O'Sullivan, Johnny Sheffield, Ian Hunter, Frieda Inescort, Laraine Day, Henry Wilcoxon.

Tarzan Goes to India (1962-British) C-86m. D: John Guillermin. Jock Mahoney, Mark Dana, Simi, Leo Gordon.

Tarzan, The Ape Man (1932) 99m. D: W. S. Van Dyke. Johnny Weissmuller, Maureen O'Sullivan, C. Aubrey Smith, Neil Hamilton, Doris Lloyd.

Tarzan, The Ape Man (1959) C-82m. D: Joseph M. Newman. Dennis Miller, Joanna Barnes, Cesare Danova, Robert Douglas, Thomas Yangha.

Tarzan the Fearless (1933) 85m. D: Robert Hill. Buster Crabbe, Jacqueline Wells (Julie Bishop), E. Alyn Warren, Edward Woods, Philo McCullough, Mathew Betz, Frank Lackteen, Mischa Auer. (adapted from serial)

Tarzan the Magnificent (1960-British) C-88m. D: Robert Day. Gordon

Scott, Jock Mahoney, Betta St. John, John Carradine, Alexandra Stewart, Lionel Jeffries, Earl Cameron.

Tarzan Triumphs (1943) 78m. D: William Thiele. Johnny Weissmuller, Frances Gifford, Johnny Sheffield, Stanley Ridges, Sig Ruman.

Tarzan's Deadly Silence (1970) C-99m. D: Robert L. Friend. Ron Ely, Manuel Padilla Jr., Jock Mahoney, Woody Strode, Gregorio Acosta, Nichelle Nichols.

Tarzan's Desert Mystery (1943) 70m. D: William Thiele. Johnny Weissmuller, Nancy Kelly, Johnny Sheffield, Otto Kruger, Joseph Sawyer, Lloyd Corrigan, Robert Lowery.

Tarzan's Fight for Life (1958) C-86m. D: H. Bruce Humberstone. Gordon Scott, Eve Brent, Rickie Sorensen, Jil Jarmyn.

Tarzan's Greatest Adventure (1959-British) C-88m. D: John Guillermin. Gordon Scott, Anthony Quayle, Sara Shane, Niall MacGinnis, Scilla Gabel, Sean Connery.

Tarzan's Hidden Jungle (1955) 73m. D: Harold Schuster. Gordon Scott, Vera Miles, Peter Van Eyck, Jack Elam, Rex Ingram.

Tarzan's Jungle Rebellion (1970) C-92m. D: William Witney. Ron Ely, Manuel Padilla Jr., Ulla Stromsted, Sam Jaffe, William Marshall, Lloyd Haynes.

Tarzan's Magic Fountain (1949) 73m. D: Lee Sholem. Lex Barker, Brenda Joyce, Evelyn Ankers, Albert Dekker, Alan Napier, Charles Drake, Henry Brandon.

Tarzan's New York Adventure (1942) 71m. D: Richard Thorpe. Johnny Weissmuller, Maureen O'Sullivan, Johnny Sheffield, Virginia Grey, Charles Bickford, Paul Kelly, Russell Hicks, Miles Mander.

Tarzan's Peril (1951) 79m. D: Byron Haskin. Lex Barker, Virginia Huston, George Macready, Douglas Fowley.

Tarzan's Revenge (1938) 70m. D: Ross Lederman. Glenn Morris, Eleanor Holm, George Barbier, C. Henry Gordon, Hedda Hopper, George Meeker.

Tarzan's Savage Fury (1952) 80m. D: Cyril Endfield. Lex Barker, Dorothy Hart, Patric Knowles, Charles Korvin.

Tarzan's Secret Treasure (1941) 81m. D: Richard Thorpe. Johnny Weissmuller, Maureen O'Sullivan, Johnny Sheffield, Reginald Owen, Barry Fitzgerald, Tom Conway.

Tarzan's Three Challenges (1963) C-92m. D: Robert Day. Jock Mahoney, Woody Strode, Ricky Der, Tsuruko Kobayashi.

Task Force (1949) 116m. **½ D: Delmer Daves. Gary Cooper, Jane Wyatt, Wayne Morris, Walter Brennan, Julie London. Well-made but unremarkable story of a Naval officer's career, tracing aircraft carrier development.

Taste of Evil, A (1971) C-73m. TVM D: John Llewellyn Moxey. Barbara Parkins, Barbara Stanwyck, Roddy McDowall, William Windom, Arthur O'Connell, Bing Russell. Susan Jenning's return from mental institution after traumatic rape incident predictably slides into near-total relapse: is it her imagination? Mechanical plot line should have been far, far better. Average.

Taste of Honey, A (1961-British) 100m. ***½ D: Tony Richardson. Rita Tushingham, Robert Stephens, Dora Bryan, Murray Melvin, Paul Danquah. Homely young girl who has affair with black sailor and becomes pregnant, is cared for by homosexual friend. Shelagh Delaney's London and Broadway stage hit is poignant and uncompromising film with fine, sensitive performances.

Taste the Blood of Dracula (1970-British) C-95m. **½ D: Peter Sasdy. Christopher Lee, Geoffrey Keen, Gwen Watford, Linda Hayden, Roy Kinnear, Ralph Bates. Fourth in Hammer series (and direct sequel to DRACULA HAS RISEN FROM THE GRAVE) with Lee as famed but uninteresting vampire out to avenge death of Black Magic wizard by affluent thrill seekers in Victorian England. Direction, acting, production not bad, but what was point of having Dracula in film? Beginning and end best parts.

Tattered Dress, The (1957) 93m. **½ D: Jack Arnold. Jeff Chandler, Jeanne Crain, Jack Carson, Gail Russell, George Tobias. Slowly paced but engaging account of lawyer Chandler defending society couple accused of murder; Crain is his sympathetic wife.

Tattered Web, The (1971) C-73m. TVM D: Paul Wendkos. Lloyd Bridges, Frank Converse, Broderick Crawford, Murray Hamilton, Sallie Shockley, Ann Helm. Good supporting cast bolsters so-so morality play of police detective trying to restore his dignity. Average.

Taxi (1932) 70m. **½ D: Roy Del Ruth. James Cagney, Loretta Young, George E. Stone, Dorothy Burgess, Guy Kibbee, Nat Pendleton. Cagney is fine in actionful vehicle about war among cab drivers, but nothing can top his Yiddish opening.

Taxi (1953) 77m. ** D: Gregory Ratoff. Dan Dailey, Constance Smith, Neva Patterson, Blanche Yurka, Stubby Kaye. Mild little comedy of N.Y.C. cab driver Dailey trying to help an Irish girl find her hubby.

Taxi Driver (1976) C-113m. ** D: Martin Scorsese. Robert DeNiro, Cybill Shepherd, Peter Boyle, Jodie Foster, Albert Brooks, Leonard Harris, Harvey Keitel. To some, Scorsese and writer Paul Schrader's perception of hell—as a crazed taxi driver's vision of N.Y.C.—was brilliant. To us, this gory, cold-blooded story of sick man's supposed catharsis through violence is ugly and unredeeming. Judge for yourself. Bernard Herrmann's final music score is one of film's few virtues.

Taxi For Tobruk (1965-French) 90m. **½ D: Denys De La Patelliere. Lino Ventura, Hardy Kruger, Charles Aznavour, German Cobos. Engaging study of French soldiers and their German prisoner crossing the desert during WW2.

Taza, Son of Cochise (1954) C-79m. ** D: Douglas Sirk. Rock Hudson, Barbara Rush, Gregg Palmer, Bart Roberts (Rex Reason), Morris Ankrum. Production cannot help clichéd story of Indians fighting among themselves and against settlers.

Tea and Sympathy (1956) C-122m. *** D: Vincente Minnelli. Deborah Kerr, John Kerr, Leif Erickson, Edward Andrews, Darryl Hickman, Dean Jones, Norma Crane. Glossy but well-acted version of Robert Anderson play about prep school boy's affair with a teacher's wife, skirting homosexual issues. Both Kerrs give sensitive portrayals.

Tea for Two (1950) C-98m. **½ D: David Butler. Doris Day, Gordon MacRae, Gene Nelson, Eve Arden, Billy DeWolfe. One of Day's better Warner Bros. musicals, with socialite Doris catching the show biz bug.

Teacher and the Miracle, The (1961-Italian) 88m. **½ D: Aldo Fabrizi. Eduardo Nevola, Marco Paolette, Mary Lamar, Jose Calvo. Good tearjerker of man broken by death of son who had inspired him to start art school. Cast gives adequate performance.

Teacher's Pet (1958) 120m. *** D: George Seaton. Clark Gable, Doris Day, Gig Young, Mamie Van Doren, Nick Adams, Charles Lane. City editor Gable accidentally enrolls in Doris' journalism course, tries to pursue her after class. Airy, amusing, with Young memorable as Doris' intellectual boyfriend.

Teahouse of the August Moon, The (1956) C-123m. ***½ D: Daniel Mann. Marlon Brando, Glenn Ford, Machiko Kyo, Eddie Albert, Paul Ford. Outstanding comedy based on John Patrick play of army officers involved with Americanization of post-WW2 Okinawa. A warm and memorable film.

Techman Mystery, The (1954-British) 89m. ** D: Wendy Toye. Margaret Leighton, John Justin, Meier Tzelniker, Roland Culver, George Coulouris, Michael Medwin. Justin is writer commissioned to do a biography of Medwin, presumably dead war hero, with surprising results. Capably acted.

Teenage Bad Girl SEE: Bad Girl

Teenage Doll (1957) 68m. BOMB D: Roger Corman. June Kenney, Fay Spain, Richard Devon, Dorothy Neumann. Sloppy juvenile delinquency street gang narrative.

Teen-age Millionaire (1961) 84m. BOMB D: Lawrence Doheny. Jimmy Clanton, ZaSu Pitts, Rocky Graziano, Diane Jergens, Chubby Checker. Virtually witless musical of teen-ager with huge inheritance becoming recording star.

Teen-age Rebel (1956) 94m. **½ D: Edmund Goulding. Ginger Rogers, Michael Rennie, Betty Lou Keim, Mildred Natwick, Rusty Swope, Warren Berlinger, Lilli Gentle, Louise Beavers, Irene Hervey. Pat yet provocative film of divorcee Rogers, now remarried, trying to reestablish understanding with her daughter.

Teen-agers From Outer Space (1959) 86m. BOMB D: Tom Graeff. David Love, Dawn Anderson, Harvey B. Dunn, Bryant Grant, Tom Lockyear. Ridiculous sci-fi about alien youths who bring monster to earth.

Telefon (1977) C-102m. *** D: Don Siegel. Charles Bronson, Lee Remick, Donald Pleasence, Tyne Daly, Patrick Magee, Alan Badel. Slick espionage thriller from Walter Wager's ingenious novel; Bronson is Russian agent sent to stop crazy defector from triggering hypnotized spies to commit sabotage throughout U.S.

Tell It to the Judge (1949) 87m. **½ D: Norman Foster. Rosalind Russell, Robert Cummings, Gig Young, Marie McDonald, Harry Davenport, Douglass Dumbrille. Flyweight marital farce with Russell and Cummings in and out of love every ten minutes; enjoyable if you like the stars.

Tell Me Lies (1968-British) C-118m. ** D: Peter Brook. Glenda Jackson, The Royal Shakespeare Company, Kingsley Amis, Stokely Carmichael, Paul Scofield. Strange, unsuccessful combination of songs, skits, and newsreel footage attacking U.S. involvement in Vietnam wasn't even liked by doves. Interesting now merely as historical document.

Tell Me My Name (1977) C-80m. TVM D: Delbert Mann. Arthur Hill, Barbara Barrie, Barnard Hughes, Valerie Mahaffey. Weeper about mother forced to reveal her past after being confronted by illegitimate 19-year-old daughter. Formula soap opera for which even the fine performers cannot work up much enthusiasm. Below average.

Tell Me That You Love Me, Junie Moon (1970) C-112m. ***½ D: Otto Preminger. Liza Minnelli, Ken Howard, Robert Moore, James Coco, Kay Thompson, Fred Williamson. Moving story of three misfits who decide to live together: facially scarred Minnelli, epileptic Howard, wheelchair-bound homosexual Moore. Moments of comedy, melodrama, compassion expertly blended by Preminger in one of his best films.

Tell Them Willie Boy Is Here (1969) C-96m. *** D: Abraham Polonsky. Robert Redford, Katharine Ross, Robert Blake, Susan Clark, Barry Sullivan. Massive manhunt for Indian who killed in self-defense pretends to be more important than it is, but is so well-crafted the preaching can be overlooked.

Tell-Tale Heart, The (1963-British) 81m. ** D: Ernest Morris. Laurence Payne, Adrienne Corri, Dermot Walsh, Selma Vaz Dias. Edgar Allan Poe yarn elaborated into tale of jealous love murder; not sufficiently atmospheric.

Tempest (1928) 102m. *** D: Sam Taylor. John Barrymore, Camilla Horn, Louis Wolheim, George Fawcett, Ullrich Haupt, Michael Visaroff. Lushly filmed tale of Russian Revolution, with peasant Barrymore rising to rank of sergeant, controlling fate of Princess (Horn) who had previously scorned him.

Tempest (1959-Italian) C-125m. **½ D: Alberto Lattuada. Silvana Mangano, Van Heflin, Viveca Lindfors, Geoffrey Horne, Oscar Homolka, Robert Keith, Agnes Moorehead, Finlay Currie, Vittorio Gassman, Helmut Dantine. Turgid, disjointed costumer set in 18th-century Russia, loosely based on Pushkin novel about peasant uprising to dethrone Catherine the Great (Lindfors).

Temptation (1946) 92m. **½ D: Irving Pichel. Merle Oberon, George Brent, Paul Lukas, Charles Korvin, Lenore Ulric, Ludwig Stossel. Woman-with-a-past Oberon marries archeologist Brent, then falls in love with unscrupulous Korvin. Nothing new, but smoothly done.

Tempter, The (1974-Italian) C-96m. BOMB D: Alberto de Martino. Carla Gravina, Mel Ferrer, Arthur Kennedy, George Coulouris, Alida Valli, Umberto Orsini. Frenzied but pointless rip-off of THE EXORCIST with Gravina as Ferrer's demonized daughter. Bleahh.

Temptress, The (1926) 117m. **½ D: Fred Niblo. Greta Garbo, Antonio Moreno, Roy D'Arcy, Marc MacDermott, Lionel Barrymore, Virginia Brown Faire. Garbo's second American film is dated curio about wicked woman who drives men to death and destruction, only to have her own life ruined by falling in love with Moreno.

10 (1979) C-122m. ** D: Blake Edwards. Dudley Moore, Julie Andrews, Bo Derek, Robert Webber, Dee Wallace, Sam Jones, Brian Dennehy, Max Showalter. Middle-aged songwriter finds himself hung up on sex, especially when he sets eyes on beautiful Derek. Blake Edwards' idea of a real sophisticated movie; sporadically funny but tiresome, glib, and pompous.

Ten Commandments, The (1956) C-220m. **** D: Cecil B. DeMille. Charlton Heston, Yul Brynner, Anne Baxter, Edward G. Robinson, Yvonne De Carlo, Debra Paget, John Derek, Cedric Hardwicke, Nina Foch, Martha Scott, Judith Anderson, Vincent Price, John Carradine. Vivid storytelling at its best. Biblical epic follows Moses' life from birth and abandonment through manhood, slavery, and trials in leading the Jews out of Egypt. Few subtleties in DeMille's second handling of this tale (first filmed in 1923) but few lulls either. Parting of the Red Sea, writing of the tablets are unforgettable highlights.

Ten Days to Tulara (1958) 77m. BOMB D: George Sherman. Sterling Hayden, Grace Raynor, Rodolfo Hoyos, Carlos Muzquiz. Dud adventure account of Hayden et al pursued across Mexico by police for the gold they carry.

Ten Days Wonder (1972-French) C-101m. **½ D: Claude Chabrol. Orson Welles, Anthony Perkins, Marlene Jobert, Michel Piccoli, Guido Alberti, Ermano Casanova. Ellery Queen meets Claude Chabrol in erratic but moody mystery concerning Perkins' love affair with stepmother Jobert. Film doesn't work, but is often fascinating to watch.

Ten from Your Show of Shows (1973) 92m. **** D: Max Liebman. Sid Caesar, Imogene Coca, Carl Reiner, Howard Morris. Incomparable collection from early 50s TV show displaying comic genius of four stars, working with classic material by Mel Brooks, among others. Ten skits include FROM HERE TO ETERNITY spoof, silent-movie send-up, Swiss clock, and final, unbearably funny takeoff on THIS IS YOUR LIFE. A must.

Ten Gentlemen From West Point (1942) 102m. *** D: Henry Hathaway. George Montgomery, Maureen O'Hara, John Sutton, Laird Cregar, Victor Francen, Harry Davenport, Ward Bond, Tom Neal. Early years of West Point, with focus on vicious commander Cregar and other assorted military film clichés; somehow it's still entertaining.

Ten Little Indians (1965) 92m. **½ D: George Pollock. Hugh O'Brian, Shirley Eaton, Fabian, Leo Genn, Stanley Holloway, Wilfrid Hyde-White, Daliah Lavi. Fair remake of Agatha Christie's whodunit AND THEN THERE WERE NONE, with suspects trapped in remote Alpine village. Gimmick of murder-minute for audience to guess killer.

Ten Little Indians (1975-British) C-98m. *½ D: Peter Collinson. Oliver Reed, Elke Sommer, Herbert Lom, Richard Attenborough, Charles Aznavour, Stephane Audran, Gert Frobe, Adolfo Celi, voice of Orson Welles. Third and weakest rendering of Agatha Christie whodunit,

set this time in Iran. Great plot cannot survive such tired telling.

Ten North Frederick (1958) 102m. *** D: Philip Dunne. Gary Cooper, Diane Varsi, Suzy Parker, Geraldine Fitzgerald, Tom Tully, Stuart Whitman. Grasping wife (Fitzgerald) prods her husband (Cooper) into big-time politics, with disastrous results. He finds personal solace in love affair with much younger woman (Parker). Good performances in somewhat soapy adaptation of John O'Hara novel.

Ten Rillington Place (1971-British) C-111m. *** D: Richard Fleischer. Richard Attenborough, Judy Geeson, John Hurt, Gabrielle Daye, Andre Morell. Low-key presentation of famous John Christie-Timothy Evans murder case of England which ended death penalty in that country. No overt editorializing but psychological undertone exists; outstanding performances by entire cast and location filming inseparable with film's total effect.

Ten Seconds to Hell (1959) 93m. **½ D: Robert Aldrich. Jeff Chandler, Jack Palance, Martine Carol, Robert Cornthwaite, Dave Willock, Wesley Addy. Chandler and Palance are almost believable as Germans involved in defusing mobs in Berlin, while competing for Carol's affection. \

Ten Tall Men (1951) C-97m. **½ D: Willis Goldbeck. Burt Lancaster, Jody Lawrance, Gilbert Roland, Kieron Moore. Tongue-in-cheek Foreign Legion tale, with dynamic Lancaster pushing the action along.

Ten Thousand Bedrooms (1957) C-114m. ** D: Richard Thorpe. Dean Martin, Anna Maria Alberghetti, Eva Bartok, Walter Slezak, Paul Henreid. Martin's first effort without Jerry is pretty tired: he's a playboy loose in Rome who finds love.

Ten Wanted Men (1955) C-80m. ** D: H. Bruce Humberstone. Randolph Scott, Jocelyn Brando, Richard Boone, Minor Watson. Soaper set on the sagebrush, with Scott a cattle rancher involved in gun battle to protect his nephew's right to marry his true love.

Ten Who Dared (1960) C-92m. BOMB D: William Beaudine. Brian Keith, John Beal, James Drury, R. G. Armstrong, Ben Johnson, L. Q. Jones. Dreadful Disney film based on true story of Major John Wesley Powell's exploration of Colorado

River in 1869; cast is drowned in cliches, while action is sparse. Forget it.

Tenafly (1972) **C-100m. TVM** D: Richard Colla. James McEachin, Mel Ferrer, Ed Nelson, John Ericson, Lillian Lebman. Unusual mixture of whodunit suspense narrative and slice-of-life comedy as black private-eye investigates death of talkshow host's wife. Average.

Tenant, The (1976-French-American) **C-125m. ***½** D: Roman Polanski. Roman Polanski, Isabelle Adjani, Melvyn Douglas, Jo Van Fleet, Shelley Winters, Bernard Fresson, Claude Dauphin. Unique, bizarrely cast horror film about a timid clerk who rents an apartment whose previous inhabitant attempted suicide. Critically drubbed upon release, but a sure bet to become cult item over the years.

Tender Comrade (1943) **102m. **** D: Edward Dmytryk. Ginger Rogers, Robert Ryan, Ruth Hussey, Patricia Collinge, Mady Christians, Kim Hunter, Jane Darwell. Saga of girls who worked in factories while husbands and sweethearts were at war. Too syrupy at times.

Tender Is the Night (1962) **C-146m. **½** D: Henry King. Jennifer Jones, Jason Robards, Jr., Joan Fontaine, Tom Ewell, Jill St. John. Sluggish, unflavorful version of F. Scott Fitzgerald novel with Jones unsatisfactory as mentally unstable wife of psychiatrist Robards; Fontaine is her chic sister; set in 1920s Europe.

Tender Scoundrel (1966-French-Italian) **C-94m. *½** D: Jean Becker. Jean-Paul Belmondo, Nadja Tiller, Robert Morley, Genevieve Page. Dumb story of delightful rogue and ladies' man who is constantly on the hustle.

Tender Trap, The (1955) **C-111m. ***½** D: Charles Walters. Frank Sinatra, Debbie Reynolds, Celeste Holm, David Wayne, Carolyn Jones, Lola Albright, Tom Helmore. Delightful romp of swinging bachelor Sinatra who stumbles into marriage with determined Debbie in N.Y.C.; impeccable support from Holm and Wayne, plus a fine title tune help out.

Tender Years, The (1947) **81m. **** D: Harold Schuster. Joe E. Brown, Richard Lyon, Noreen Nash, Charles Drake, Josephine Hutchinson. Warm drama of minister trying to protect dog his son is attached to; notable

mainly for rare dramatic performance by Brown.

Tenderfoot, The (1932) **70m. **½** D: Ray Enright. Joe E. Brown, Ginger Rogers, Lew Cody, George Chandler, Allan Lane, Vivien Oakland. Brown's a naive cowboy who wants to back a Broadway show in the worst way—and does.

Tennessee Champ (1954) **C-73m. **½** D: Fred M. Wilcox. Shelley Winters, Keenan Wynn, Dewey Martin, Earl Holliman, Dave O'Brien. Good performances highlight average story of boxer who reforms crooked employer.

Tennessee Johnson (1942) **103m. **½** D: William Dieterle. Van Heflin, Lionel Barrymore, Ruth Hussey, Marjorie Main, Charles Dingle, Regis Toomey, Grant Withers, Lynne Carver, Noah Beery, Sr., Morris Ankrum. Sincere historical drama of President Andrew Johnson's rise and subsequent conflicts with Congress, given a glossy MGM production.

Tennessee's Partner (1955) **C-87m. **½** D: Allan Dwan. John Payne, Rhonda Fleming, Ronald Reagan, Coleen Gray, Morris Ankrum. Offbeat little Western with Payne excellent in an unusual "heel" characterization, Reagan accidentally becoming his pal.

Tension (1949) **95m. **½** D: John Berry. Richard Basehart, Audrey Totter, Cyd Charisse, Barry Sullivan, Tom D'Andrea. Timid Basehart methodically seeks revenge on his conniving wife who walked out on him; quiet melodrama.

Tension at Table Rock (1956) **C-93m. **** D: Charles Marquis Warren. Richard Egan, Dorothy Malone, Cameron Mitchell, Billy Chapin, Angie Dickinson. Soaper Western with Egan on the lam for a murder committed in self-defense.

Tentacles (1977-Italian) **C-90m. *½** D: Oliver Hellman. John Huston, Shelley Winters, Henry Fonda, Bo Hopkins, Delia Boccardo, Cesare Danova. Giant octopus threatens a seaside community in this rip-off of JAWS. Some unexpected casting and the spectacle of having killer whales emerge the heroes save the picture from total decay.

Tenth Avenue Angel (1948) **74m. BOMB** D: Roy Rowland. Margaret O'Brien, Angela Lansbury, George Murphy, Phyllis Thaxter, Warner Anderson. Capable cast lost in terrible script about street urchin who prevents young man from becoming gangster.

Tenth Month, The (1979) **C-130m.** TVM D: Joan Tewksbury. Carol Burnett, Keith Michell, Dina Merrill, Melissa Converse, Cristina Raines, Richard Venture. Overlong drama that addresses the question: should a middle-aged divorcee who has an affair with a married man and becomes pregnant keep and raise the child alone? Based on Laura Z. Hobson's novel about single parenthood. Average.

Tenth Victim, The (1965-Italian) **C-92m.** *** D: Elio Petri. Marcello Mastroianni, Ursula Andress, Elsa Martinelli, Salvo Randone, Massimo Serato. Sci-fi of futuristic society where violence is channeled into legalized murder hunts. Here, Ursula hunts Marcello. Intriguing idea, well done.

Teresa (1951) **102m.** ** D: Fred Zinnemann. John Ericson, Pier Angeli, Patricia Collinge, Richard Bishop, Peggy Ann Garner. Intriguing, but superficially told story of WW2 veteran Ericson who returns to U.S. with his Italian bride, encountering home-town prejudice. Rod Steiger plays psychiatrist in film debut.

Term of Trial (1963-British) **113m.** **½ D: Peter Glenville. Laurence Olivier, Simone Signoret, Sarah Miles, Terence Stamp, Roland Culver, Hugh Griffith. Talky story of schoolmaster charged with assault by young Miles, and subsequent trial's effect on Olivier's wife, Signoret. Despite fine cast, a wearisome film.

Terminal Man, The (1974) **C-107m.** *** D: Mike Hodges. George Segal, Joan Hackett, Richard A. Dysart, Jill Clayburgh, Donald Moffat, Matt Clark. Cold but engrossing thriller has computer scientist Segal coming under influence of computers in his brain which cause violence. Well-acted.

Terraces (1977) **C-78m.** TVM D: Lila Garrett. Lloyd Bochner, Jane Dulo, Arny Freeman, Eliza Garrett, Bill Gerber, Kit McDonough, Julie Newmar, Lola Albright. Soap opera dealing with various people sharing adjoining terraces in an expensive high-rise. Below average.

Terrible Beauty, A SEE: **Night Fighters**

Terrible People, The (1960-German) **95m.** ** D: Harold Reinl. Eddi Arent, Karin Dor, Elizabeth Flick-

enschildt, Fritz Rasp, Joachim Fuchsberger. Fair action story of condemned bank crook vowing to return from dead to punish those who prosecuted him. Retitled: HAND OF THE GALLOWS.

Terror, The (1963) **C-81m.** **½ D: Roger Corman. Boris Karloff, Jack Nicholson, Sandra Knight, Richard Miller. Engaging chiller nonsense with Karloff the mysterious owner of a castle where eerie deeds occur; set on Baltic coast in 1800s. This is the legendary Corman "quickie" that was shot in less than three days!

Terror at Midnight (1956) **70m.** ** D: Franklin Adreon. Scott Brady, Joan Vohs, Frank Faylen, John Dehner. Undynamic telling of Vohs being blackmailed and her law-enforcer boyfriend (Brady) helping out.

Terror by Night (1946) **60m.** D: Roy William Neill. Basil Rathbone, Nigel Bruce, Alan Mowbray, Dennis Hoey, Renee Godfrey, Mary Forbes. SEE: **Sherlock Holmes** series.

Terror Castle SEE: **Horror Castle**

Terror House SEE: **Folks at Red Wolf Inn, The**

Terror in a Texas Town (1958) **80m.** **½ D: Joseph H. Lewis. Sterling Hayden, Sebastian Cabot, Carol Kelly, Eugene Martin, Ned Young, Victor Millan. Offbeat western drama about Scandinavian sailor (Hayden) who comes to his father's farm in Texas, finds town terrorized by Cabot, who's forcing everyone to sell their oil-rich land. Incredible final shootout.

Terror in the Sky (1971) **C-72m.** TVM D: Bernard Kowalski. Leif Ericson, Doug McClure, Roddy McDowall, Keenan Wynn, Lois Nettleton. Pilot, co-pilot, and several passengers on commercial flight develop food poisoning (during flight of course), must turn to ex-combat helicopter pilot (McClure) to land plane. Neglible suspense, despite good performances. Average.

Terror in the Wax Museum (1973) **C-93m.** *½ D: Georg Fenady. Ray Milland, Broderick Crawford, Elsa Lanchester, Maurice Evans, Shani Wallis, John Carradine, Louis Hayward, Patric Knowles, Mark Edwards. Low-budget and low-grade murder mystery takes little advantage of wax museum horror potential; a good cast wasted. If you look closely you can see the "wax figures" moving.

Terror of Frankenstein (1975-Swedish-Irish) **C-91m.** ******* D: Calvin Floyd. Leon Vitali, Per Oscarsson, Nicholas Clay, Stacey Dorning, Jan Ohlsson. Literate, well-made adaptation of the classic story, definitely worth a look for horror buffs.

Terror Is a Man (1959) **89m.** ****** D: Gerry DeLeon. Francis Lederer, Greta Thyssen, Richard Derr, Oscar Keesee. On Blood Island, doctor experiments with panther to turn him into a human. Filmed in the Philippines, this sci-fi horror story comes to life in last third of picture. Also known as BLOOD CREATURE.

Terror of the Red Mask (1960-Italian) **C-90m.** ****** D: Piero Pierotti. Lex Barker, Chelo Alonso, Massimo Serato. Costumer strains to have air of a chiller as hero Barker swordfights his way through castle of horror.

Terror of the Tongs (1961-British) **C-90m.** ****½** D: Anthony Bushell. Geoffrey Toone, Bert Kwouk, Brian Worth, Christopher Lee, Richard Leech. Atmospheric British thriller of captain searching for killers of daughter; eventually breaks entire Tong society in Hong Kong. Good acting but may be a little gruesome for some viewers. Released theatrically in b&w.

Terror on a Train (1953-British) **72m.** ****½** D: Ted Tetzlaff. Glenn Ford, Anne Vernon, Maurice Denham, Victor Maddern. Tense little film of Ford defusing time bomb placed aboard train full of high explosives.

Terror on the Beach (1973) **C-74m.** TVM D: Paul Wendkos. Dennis Weaver, Estelle Parsons, Scott Hylands, Kristoffer Tabori, Susan Dey, Michael Christian, Henry Olek. Middle-class family harassed for no apparent reason during seaside vacation. Plot's resolution weakest point of otherwise interestingly directed thriller. Above average.

Terror on the 40th Floor (1974) **C-100m.** TVM D: Jerry Jameson. John Forsythe, Anjanette Comer, Joseph Campanella, Lynn Carlin, Don Meredith, Laurie Heineman, Kelly Jean Peters, Pippa Scott. Road company TOWERING INFERNO has fire engulfing a skyscraper, trapping a group of people in a penthouse. Average.

Terror Out of the Sky (1978) **C-100m.** TVM D: Lee H. Katzin. Efrem Zimbalist, Jr., Tovah Feldshuh, Dan Haggerty, Bruce French, Lonny Chapman, Ike Eisenmann. Those savage bees return in this sequel to THE SAVAGE BEES, with the little stingers threatening a new invasion and two bee specialists and a free-lance pilot determined to thwart it. Several notches below its predecessor. Average.

Terrorists, The (1975-British) **C-97m.** ***½** D: Casper Wrede. Sean Connery, Ian McShane, Jeffrey Wickham, Isabel Dean, John Quentin. Muddled thriller about political terrorism and airline hijacking is indifferently acted by Connery and McShane, amateurishly directed, and tediously unspooled. Pity, because premise is sound and photography (by Ingmar Bergman's right hand, Sven Nykvist) is smashing. Filmed in Norway.

Terrornauts, The (1967-British) **C-75m.** ***½** D: Montgomery Tully. Simon Oates, Zena Marshall, Charles Hawtrey, Patricia Hayes, Stanley Meadows, Max Adrian. Alien forces kidnap an entire building on Earth, people and all. Based on Murray Leinster's novel *The Wailing Asteroid*, this sci-fi flick is hampered by low budget.

Tess of the Storm Country (1960) **C-84m.** ****½** D: Paul Guilfoyle. Diane Baker, Jack Ging, Lee Philips, Wallace Ford, Robert F. Simon, Bert Remsen. Grace White's period novel of Scottish girl and uncle coming to America and adjusting to life in Pennsylvania Dutch country; leisurely paced, nicely done.

Test Pilot (1938) **118m.** ******* D: Victor Fleming. Clark Gable, Myrna Loy, Spencer Tracy, Lionel Barrymore, Samuel S. Hinds, Marjorie Main, Louis Jean Heydt. Blend of romantic comedy and drama doesn't always work; Tracy steals film as Gable's pal in story of daredevils who try out new aircraft.

Testament of Dr. Mabuse, The (1961-German) **87m.** ****½** D: Werner Klinger. Gert Frobe, Senta Berger, Walter Rilla, Helmut Schmid, Charles Regnier. Engaging continuation of arch-criminal series with infamous Dr. M masterminding his schemes from within his mental institution cell; actionful drama.

Texan Meets Calamity Jane, The (1950) **C-71m.** BOMB D: Ande Lamb. Evelyn Ankers, James Ellison, Jack Ingram, Lee "Lasses" White. Ankers is too subdued as famed cowgirl of yesteryear, involved in fight to prove claim to prosperous saloon.

Texans, The (1938) 92m. **½ D: James Hogan. Randolph Scott, Joan Bennett, May Robson, Walter Brennan, Robert Cummings, Robert Barrat. Post-Civil War Texas is setting for average Western with good cast.

Texas (1941) 93m. *** D: George Marshall. William Holden, Glenn Ford, Claire Trevor, George Bancroft, Edgar Buchanan. High-level Western of two friends, one a rustler, the other a cattleman, competing for Trevor's affection.

Texas Across the River (1966) C-101m. *** D: Michael Gordon. Dean Martin, Alain Delon, Joey Bishop, Rosemary Forsyth, Peter Graves, Tina Marquand (Aumont). Diverting takeoff on cowboy-and-Indian films, with Bishop hilarious as a deadpan Indian and Marquand cute as a young squaw.

Texas, Brooklyn and Heaven (1948) 76m. ** D: William Castle. Guy Madison, Diana Lynn, James Dunn, Lionel Stander, Florence Bates, Roscoe Karns. Stale "comedy" of cowboy who falls in love with city girl who loves horses. B-cast.

Texas Carnival (1951) C-77m. ** D: Charles Walters. Esther Williams, Red Skelton, Ann Miller, Keenan Wynn, Howard Keel. Emptier than usual, this flabby MGM vehicle with Williams, Skelton, and Keel leaves them high and dry with no fresh material.

Texas Lady (1955) C-86m. ** D: Tim Whelan. Claudette Colbert, Barry Sullivan, Greg Walcott, Horace McMahon, John Litel. Genteel oater; Colbert lovely as crusading newspaper editor in old West. Mediocre script.

Texas Rangers, The (1936) 95m. *** D: King Vidor. Fred MacMurray, Jack Oakie, Jean Parker, Lloyd Nolan, Edward Ellis. Fine, elaborate Western of three comrades who split up; MacMurray and Oakie become rangers, Nolan an outlaw. Remade as STREETS OF LAREDO.

Texas Rangers, The (1951) C-68m. *½ D: Phil Karlson. George Montgomery, Gale Storm, Jerome Courtland, Noah Beery, Jr. Aimless Western involving Texas law enforcers against gang of outlaws.

Texas Rangers Ride Again (1940) 68m. ** D: James Hogan. John Howard, Akim Tamiroff, Ellen Drew, May Robson. Standard Western fare

of lawmen involved with cow rustlers in the modern-day West.

Texican, The (1966) C-91m. ** D: Lesley Selander. Audie Murphy, Broderick Crawford, Diana Lorys, Luz Marquez, Antonio Casas, Antonio Perel. Routine Spanish-made Western pits ex-lawman Murphy against ruthless frontier town boss Crawford, trying to clear his name.

Thaddeus Rose and Eddie (1978) C-100m. TVM D: Jack Starrett. Johnny Cash, Diane Ladd, Bo Hopkins, June Carter Cash, James Hampton, Noble Willingham. Two irresponsible good old boys from Texas, and the gals they love. Marks the TV acting debuts of country singers Johnny and June Carter Cash. Average.

Thank God, It's Friday (1978) C-90m. BOMB D: Robert Klane. Donna Summer, Valerie Landsburg, Terri Nunn, Chick Vennera, Ray Vitte, Jeff Goldblum, Paul Jabara. Perhaps the worst film ever to have won some kind of Oscar (for Summer's hit song, "Last Dance"), this one-night-in-the-life-of-a-disco comedy is about as monotonous and uninventive as disco music itself. A must-see for morons.

Thank You All Very Much (1969-British) C-105m. *** D: Waris Hussein. Sandy Dennis, Ian McKellen, Eleanor Bron, John Standing. Absorbing study of unwed mother who decides to have her baby. Realistic and touching.

Thank You, Aunt (1967-Italian) 93m. ** D: Salvatore Samperi. Lisa Gastoni, Lou Castel, Gabriele Ferzetti. Utterly perverse tale of psychopathic young man (Castel) who comes to live with attractive young aunt (Gastoni) whom he torments with sex-games and rituals. Ugh. Released here as GRAZIE, ZIA in 1969.

Thank You Jeeves (1936) 68m. ** D: Arthur Collins. Arthur Treacher, Virginia Field, David Niven, Lester Matthews. Treacher is at peak form playing impeccable butler whose love of decorum leads him, on merry chase. Retitled: THANK YOU MR. JEEVES.

Thank You Mr. Jeeves SEE: **Thank You Jeeves**

Thank You, Mr. Moto (1937) 67m. D: Norman Foster. Peter Lorre, Pauline Frederick, Sidney Blackmer, Sig Ruman, John Carradine, Nedda Harrigan, Philip Ahn. SEE: **Mr. Moto** series.

Thank Your Lucky Stars (1943)

127m. *** D: David Butler. Eddie Cantor, Humphrey Bogart, Bette Davis, Olivia de Havilland, Errol Flynn, John Garfield, Joan Leslie, Ida Lupino, Dennis Morgan, Ann Sheridan. Very lame plot frames all-star Warner Bros. show, with Davis singing "They're Either Too Young Or Too Old," other staid stars breaking loose.

Thanks a Million (1935) 87m. ******* D: Roy Del Ruth. Dick Powell, Ann Dvorak, Fred Allen, Patsy Kelly, Alan Dinehart, Margaret Irving, Paul Whiteman and Orchestra, Yacht Club Boys. Very entertaining musical of crooner Powell running for governor, with help of wisecracking manager Allen, sweetheart Dvorak, and blustery politician Raymond Walburn. Good fun, with several breezy tunes and specialties by Whiteman and Yacht Club Boys. Remade as IF I'M LUCKY.

That Certain Age (1938) 95m. ****½** D: Edward Ludwig. Deanna Durbin, Melvyn Douglas, Jackie Cooper, Irene Rich, Nancy Carroll, John Halliday, Jack Searl. Deanna develops crush on her parents' houseguest, sophisticated Douglas, leaving boyfriend Cooper out in the cold—and saddled with responsibility for putting on amateur show. Silly script made bearable by smooth jabs.

That Certain Feeling (1956) C-103m. BOMB D: Norman Panama, Melvin Frank. Bob Hope, Eva Marie Saint, George Sanders, Pearl Bailey. Incredibly bad Hope comedy with Bob as neurotic cartoonist; Sanders gives only life to stale film. Pearl sings title song.

That Certain Summer (1972) C-74m. TVM D: Lamont Johnson. Hal Holbrook, Hope Lange, Martin Sheen, Joe Don Baker, Scott Jacoby, Marlyn Mason, James McEachin. Divorcé Doug Salter (Holbrook) must find way to discuss homosexuality with son during one of their usual reunions in San Francisco. Outstanding performances by entire cast in sensibly scripted, carefully crafted film, well done by any medium's standards. Above average.

That Certain Woman (1937) 93m. ****½** D: Edmund Goulding. Bette Davis, Henry Fonda, Donald Crisp, Ian Hunter, Minor Watson, Sidney Toler, Anita Louise. Remake of Gloria Swanson's early talkie THE TRESPASSER features Bette as a gangster's widow who's trying to

start life fresh, falling in love for real with Fonda. Well-acted soaper.

That Cold Day in the Park (1969) C-113m. *½ D: Robert Altman. Sandy Dennis, Michael Burns, Susanne Benton, John Garfield Jr., Luana Anders, Michael Murphy. Strange, plodding film with frustrated spinster taking in young man she sees in the park. What follows is bizarre and unmoving; a far cry from Altman's later work. Filmed in Canada. TV print cut to 92m.

That Darn Cat (1965) C-116m. ******* D: Robert Stevenson. Hayley Mills, Dean Jones, Dorothy Provine, Roddy McDowall, Neville Brand, Elsa Lanchester, William Demarest, Frank Gorshin, Ed Wynn. Long but entertaining suspense comedy from Disney, about a cat that leads FBI man Jones on trail of kidnapped woman. Slapstick scenes and character vignettes highlight this colorful film.

That Forsyte Woman (1949) C-114m. ****½** D: Compton Bennett. Errol Flynn, Greer Garson, Walter Pidgeon, Robert Young, Janet Leigh, Harry Davenport. Rather superficial adaptation of John Galsworthy novel of a faithless woman (Garson) who finds herself attracted by her niece's fiancee; Good-looking, but no match for the later BBC-TV series.

That Funny Feeling (1965) C-93m. ****½** D: Richard Thorpe. Sandra Dee, Bobby Darin, Donald O'Connor, Nita Talbot, Larry Storch, Leo G. Carroll, Robert Strauss. Funny only if you adore Darin and Dee, and even then story of footloose playboys wears thin.

That Gang of Mine (1940) 62m. D: Joseph H. Lewis. Bobby Jordan, Leo Gorcey, Clarence Muse, Dave O'Brien, Joyce Bryant, Donald Haines, David Gorcey. SEE: Bowery Boys series.

That Girl from Paris (1936) 105m. ****½** D: Leigh Jason. Lily Pons, Jack Oakie, Gene Raymond, Herman Bing, Mischa Auer, Frank Jenks, Lucille Ball. Breezy Pons vehicle. She flees Continental wedding and runs to America. Tuneful songs, fine supporting cast.

That Hagen Girl (1947) 83m. BOMB D: Peter Godfrey. Shirley Temple, Ronald Reagan, Dorothy Peterson, Charles Kemper, Rory Calhoun. Atrocious "comedy" of Temple convinced she's Reagan's illegitimate daughter.

That Hamilton Woman (1941) 128m.
*** D: Alexander Korda. Vivien
Leigh, Laurence Olivier, Alan Mowbray, Sara Allgood, Gladys Cooper,
Henry Wilcoxon, Heather Angel.
Olivier and Leigh—both breathtak-
ingly beautiful—enact ill-fated historical romance of Lord Admiral
Nelson and Lady Emma Hamilton
in American-made film intended to
spur pro-British feelings. P.S. It
was Winston Churchill's favorite
movie. Also known as LADY
HAMILTON.

That Kind of Woman (1959) 92m.
** D: Sidney Lumet. Sophia Loren,
Tab Hunter, George Sanders, Jack
Warden, Barbara Nichols, Keenan
Wynn. Flat attempt to recreate WW2
romantic comedy with Loren and
Hunter not a very dynamic combina-
tion.

That Lady (1955) C-100m. **½ D:
Terence Young. Olivia de Havilland,
Gilbert Roland, Paul Scofield, Dennis
Price, Christopher Lee. Unemotional
costumer set in 16th-century Spain,
with De Havilland a widowed noblewoman involved in court intrigue.

That Lady in Ermine (1948) C-89m.
*** D: Ernst Lubitsch, Otto Premin-
ger. Betty Grable, Douglas Fairbanks, Jr., Cesar Romero, Walter
Abel, Reginald Gardiner, Harry
Davenport. Entertaining if overblown
musical of mythical kingdom where
ancestors magically return.

That Man Bolt (1973) C-105m. **
D: Henry Levin, David Lowell Rich.
Fred Williamson, Byron Webster,
Teresa Graves, Jack Ging, Miko
Mayama. Scenic actioner, filmed in
Hong Kong, Las Vegas and L.A.,
mixes kung fu, some comedy and
two songs by Graves. Plot has Wil-
liamson as international courier of
syndicate money.

That Man from Rio (1964-French)
C-114m. *** D: Philippe De Broca.
Jean-Paul Belmondo. Françoise Dorleac, Jean Servais, Adolfo Celi, Simone Renant. Engaging spoof of
Bond-type movies features Belmondo
as hero, chasing double-crosser and
thief in search for Brazilian treasure.
Nice color photography complements fast-moving script.

That Man George (1966-French-Span-
ish-Italian) C-90m. ** D: Jacques
Deray. George Hamilton, Claudine
Auger, Alberto De Mendoza, Daniel
Ivernel. Routine tale of robbery of
armored van transporting bullion
from gold mine.

That Man in Istanbul (1966) C-117m.
**½ D: Anthony Isasi. Horst Buch-
holz, Sylva Koscina, Mario Adorf,
Klaus Kinski. Fairly engaging spy
romp featuring Koscina as FBI agent
with Buchholz as playboy in search
for missing scientist.

That Midnight Kiss (1949) C-96m.
**½ D: Norman Taurog. Kathryn
Grayson, Mario Lanza, Jose Iturbi,
Ethel Barrymore, Keenan Wynn, J.
Carrol Naish, Jules Munshin. Flimsy
musical romance between Lanza and
Grayson salvaged by pleasant musi-
cal interludes and glossy production.

That Night (1957) 88m. **½ D: John
Newland. John Beal, Augusta Dabney, Malcolm Brodrick, Shepperd
Strudwick, Rosemary Murphy.
Straightforward account of man suffering a heart attack, and the effect
it has on his family.

That Night in Rio (1941) C-90m.
**½ D: Irving Cummings. Alice
Faye, Don Ameche, Carmen Miranda, S. Z. Sakall, J. Carrol Naish,
Curt Bois, Leonid Kinsky, Frank
Puglia. Standard 20th Century-Fox
musical of mistaken identities, uses
Miranda to best advantage. Filmed
before as FOLIES BERGERE, and
again as ON THE RIVIERA.

That Night with You (1945) 84m. **
D: William A. Seiter. Franchot
Tone, Susanna Foster, David Bruce,
Louise Allbritton, Jacqueline de Wit,
Buster Keaton. OK vehicle for so-
prano Foster who connives her way
to a show biz break via producer
Tone.

That Touch of Mink (1962) C-99m.
**½ D: Delbert Mann. Cary Grant,
Doris Day, Gig Young, Audrey
Meadows, John Astin. Attractive cast
in silly piece of fluff with Grant vs.
Day. Amusing at times, but wears
thin. Astin is memorable as a creep
with designs on poor Doris.

That Uncertain Feeling (1941) 84m.
*** D: Ernst Lubitsch. Merle Obe-
ron, Melvyn Douglas, Burgess Meredith, Alan Mowbray, Olive Blakeney,
Harry Davenport, Eve Arden. Chic
little Lubitsch comedy about married
couple with problems, and their absurd pianist friend. Stolen hands-
down by Meredith as the musical
malcontent.

That Way with Women (1947) 84m.
** D: Frederick de Cordova. Dane
Clark, Martha Vickers, Sydney
Greenstreet, Alan Hale, Craig Stev-
ens. Tired reworking of George Ar-
liss' MILLIONAIRE, with Green-

street as wealthy man who plays Cupid for Clark and Vickers.

That Woman Opposite SEE: City After Midnight

That Wonderful Urge (1948) 82m. **½ D: Robert B. Sinclair. Tyrone Power, Gene Tierney, Arleen Whelan, Reginald Gardiner, Lucile Watson, Gene Lockhart, Gertrude Michael, Porter Hall. Fairly entertaining remake of LOVE IS NEWS about heiress getting back at nasty reporter. Good cast.

That'll Be the Day (1974-British) C-90m. *** D: Claude Whatham. David Essex, Ringo Starr, Rosemary Leach, James Booth, Billy Fury, Keith Moon. Compelling story traces British working-class youth (Essex) from adolescence to early adulthood, as his growing frustrations find their eventual outlet in rock music. First half of dynamic story, continued in STARDUST, where character's resemblance to John Lennon crystallizes.

That's Entertainment! (1974) C-132m. **** D: Jack Haley, Jr. Fred Astaire, Bing Crosby, Gene Kelly, Peter Lawford, Liza Minnelli, Donald O'Connor, Debbie Reynolds, Mickey Rooney, Frank Sinatra, James Stewart, Elizabeth Taylor. Stars host nostalgia bash with scenes from nearly 100 MGM musicals. There are many cherished moments with the above-named stars plus unexpectedly delightful numbers with Esther Williams, Clark Gable (singing and dancing!), Jimmy Durante, and Eleanor Powell, whose challenge dance with Astaire is unforgettable. Only complaint: why cut the final AMERICAN IN PARIS ballet?

That's Entertainment, Part 2 (1976) C-133m. ***½ D: Gene Kelly. Fred Astaire and Gene Kelly host this inevitable sequel and do some engaging song-and-dance work. Film hasn't cohesion or momentum of its predecessor, but the material is irresistible. This time, comedy and drama are included along with musical numbers—Tracy and Hepburn, Marx Brothers, etc. Most imaginative segment of all is title sequence by Saul Bass.

That's My Boy (1951) 98m. ** D: Hal Walker. Dean Martin, Jerry Lewis, Marion Marshall, Eddie Mayehoff, Ruth Hussey, Polly Bergen. Ex-football star Mayehoff wants klutzy son Lewis to follow in his footsteps, induces Martin to coach him. Supposed comic idea is played

straight, with very few laughs, maudlin situations . . . yet it was considered quite funny in 1951 when M&L were in their heyday.

That's the Spirit (1945) 93m. ** D: Charles Lamont. Peggy Ryan, Jack Oakie, June Vincent, Gene Lockhart, Johnny Coy, Andy Devine, Arthur Treacher, Irene Ryan, Buster Keaton. Whimsy is too studied in this syrupy fantasy of Oakie returning from heaven to make explanations to wife on earth.

That's The Way of the World SEE: Shining Star

Theatre of Blood (1973-British) C-104m. **½ D: Douglas Hickox. Vincent Price, Diana Rigg, Robert Morley, Ian Hendry, Harry Andrews, Coral Browne, Robert Coote, Michael Hordern, Jack Hawkins, Diana Dors, Dennis Price, Milo O'Shea. A one-joke film, albeit a great joke: hammy Shakespearean actor Price vows revenge on critics who've blasted him, murders them one by one. Somewhat spoiled by incredibly gory killings; great cast has fun with it, though.

Theatre of Death (1967-British) C-90m. **½ D: Samuel Gallu. Christopher Lee, Julian Glover, Lelia Goldoni, Jenny Till, Evelyn Laye, Ivor Dean. Vampire-like murders revolving around Paris' Grand Guignol stage sensation and its beautiful young starlet under sinister hypnotic trance. Solid, low-budget mystery-thriller benefits from believable performances.

Thelma Jordan SEE: File on Thelma Jordan

Them (1954) 94m. ***½ D: Gordon Douglas. James Whitmore, Edmund Gwenn, Joan Weldon, James Arness, Onslow Stevens. Good cast gives added boost to nail-biting story of giant ant mutations running wild in the Southwest. Very good direction and intelligent script with some truly memorable scenes.

Then Came Bronson (1969) C-100m. TVM D: William Graham. Michael Parks, Bonnie Bedelia, Akim Tamiroff, Martin Sheen, Sheree North, Gary Merrill. Young newspaper reporter (Parks) shook up after suicide of friend, buys friend's motorcycle and sets out on shore road journey, meeting runaway bride (Bedelia), befriending her. Soft, somber film, with a couple of OK episodes, fair performances. Above average; pilot for TV series.

Then There Were Three (1961-Italian) 82m. ** D: Alex Nicol. Frank Latimore, Alex Nicol, Barry Cahill, Sid Clute. Routine WW2 actioner concerning Nazi officer going behind Allied lines to hunt down Italian partisans.

Theodora Goes Wild (1936) 94m. ***½ D: Richard Boleslawski. Irene Dunne, Melvyn Douglas, Thomas Mitchell, Thurston Hall, Rosalind Keith, Spring Byington. Dunne's first starring comedy is a delightful story about small-town woman who writes scandalous best-seller and falls in love with sophisticated New Yorker who illustrated the book. Lots of funny twists in this engaging farce.

Theodora, Slave Empress (1954-Italian) 88m. ** D: Riccardo Freda. Gianna Maria Canale, Georges Marchal, Renato Baldini, Henri Guisol, Irene . Papas. Better-than-average production values are only asset in standard plot of hero thwarting plan of Roman generals to overthrow empress.

There Goes My Heart (1938) 84m. *** D: Norman Z. McLeod. Fredric March, Virginia Bruce, Patsy Kelly, Alan Mowbray, Nancy Carroll, Eugene Pallette, Claude Gillingwater, Arthur Lake. Typical 30s fluff about runaway heiress Bruce spotted by reporter March; good cast makes one forget trite story-line.

There Was A. Crooked Man . . . (1970) C-125m. *** D: Joseph L. Mankiewicz. Kirk Douglas, Henry Fonda, Hume Cronyn, Warren Oates, Burgess Meredith, Arthur O'Connell, Martin Gabel, John Randolph, Lee Grant. Bawdy, entertaining Western/comedy/prison-film with Douglas as cocky inmate at territorial prison circa 1883 who matches wits with progressive warden Fonda towards one goal: escape. Powerhouse cast, handsome production.

There's A Girl In My Soup (1970-British) C-95m. *½ D: Roy Boulting. Goldie Hawn, Peter Sellers, Tony Britton, Nicky Henson, Diana Dors. Middle-aged Sellers groping for youth, finds kook. Silly story, just a few real laughs.

There's Always a Price Tag (1958-French) 102m. **½ D: Denys de la Patelliere. Michele Morgan, Daniel Gelin, Peter Van Eyck, Bernard Blier. Morgan is excellent in DOUBLE INDEMNITY-type plot about wife who conspires to murder her

husband, but film drags and loses credibility after promising start.

There's Always a Woman (1938) 82m. *** D: Alexander Hall. Joan Blondell, Melvyn Douglas, Mary Astor, Frances Drake, Jerome Cowan, Robert Paige, Thurston Hall. Fine blend of mystery and comedy as D.A. Douglas and detective-wife Blondell try to solve same crime.

There's Always Tomorrow (1956) 84m. **½ D: Douglas Sirk. Barbara Stanwyck, Fred MacMurray, Joan Bennett, Pat Crowley, William Reynolds. MacMurray is in a rut, at work and at home, making him particularly susceptible to old-flame Stanwyck, who comes back into his life. Sudsy but well-acted soap opera, filmed before in 1934.

There's No Business Like Show Business (1954) C-117m. *½ D: Walter Lang. Ethel Merman, Donald O'Connor, Marilyn Monroe, Dan Dailey, Johnny Ray, Mitzi Gaynor. Gaudy musicomedy of show biz family spawned by vaudevillians Merman and Dailey; loud and obnoxious, with Marilyn's moments the only good ones in the film.

There's One Born Every Minute (1942) 59m. ** D: Harold Young. Hugh Herbert, Tom Brown, Peggy Moran, Guy Kibbee, Gus Schilling, Edgar Kennedy, Carl "Alfalfa" Switzer, Elizabeth Taylor. Contrived comedy of nutty family whose erstwhile head (Herbert) runs a pudding company. Notable as screen debut of young Elizabeth Taylor as junior member of the clan.

These Are the Damned (1962-British) 77m. **½ D: Joseph Losey. Macdonald Carey, Shirley Anne Field, Viveca Lindfors, Alexander Knox, Oliver Reed, James Villiers. Film begins as unusual love story set against background of violent "Teddy boys" in England, then halfway through, switches to TWILIGHT ZONE-ish sci-fi. Abrupt continuity not helped by fact that about 10 minutes are missing from original British running time. Original title: THE DAMNED.

These Glamour Girls (1939) 80m. **½ D: S. Sylvan Simon. Lew Ayres, Lana Turner, Richard Carlson, Anita Louise, Marsha Hunt, Ann Rutherford, Mary Beth Hughes, Jane Bryan, Tom Brown. Turner is effective as nonsocialite who turns the tables on sneering gals at swank college weekend; naive but polished gloss.

These Thousand Hills (1959) C-96m. *** D: Richard Fleischer. Don Murray, Richard Egan, Lee Remick, Patricia Owens, Stuart Whitman, Albert Dekker, Harold J. Stone. Adult Western with Murray a rancher who learns to accept responsibility and maintain loyalty to dependent friends; sturdy cast.

These Three (1936) 93m. **** D: William Wyler. Miriam Hopkins, Merle Oberon, Joel McCrea, Catherine Doucet, Alma Kruger, Bonita Granville, Marcia Mae Jones. Penetrating drama of two young women (Oberon, Hopkins) running school, ruined by lies of malicious student Granville; loosely based on Lillian Hellman's CHILDREN'S HOUR. Superb acting by all, with Granville especially impressive. Remade in 1961 as THE CHILDREN'S HOUR.

These Wilder Years (1956) 91m. **½ D: Roy Rowland. James Cagney, Barbara Stanwyck, Walter Pidgeon, Betty Lou Keim, Don Dubbins. Unusual to see Cagney in this kind of soap opera, about a man who wants to find his illegitimate son, and becomes involved with teenage unwed mother (Keim) through intervention of foundling home director Stanwyck.

They All Kissed the Bride (1942) 85m. **½ D: Alexander Hall. Joan Crawford, Melvyn Douglas, Roland Young, Billie Burke, Allen Jenkins. Good stars in fairly amusing film of man being arrested for kissing bride at wedding.

They Call It Murder (1971) C-100m. TVM D: Walter Grauman. Jim Hutton, Lloyd Bochner, Jessica Walter, Carmen Mathews, Leslie Nielsen, Jo Ann Pflug. Miscasting and unimaginative dialogue abounds in adaptation of Erle Stanley Gardner novel with D.A. Doug Selby hard pressed to link swimming pool murder, car crash fatality, and large insurance claim. Average.

They Call It Sin (1932) 75m. ** D: Thornton Freeland. Loretta Young, David Manners, George Brent, Louis Calhern, Una Merkel, Elizabeth Patterson. Typical, standard soaper of Young's unhappy love affair while silent suitor stands by.

They Call Me Mister Tibbs (1970) C-108m. ** D: Gordon Douglas, Sidney Poitier, Barbara McNair, Martin Landau, David Sheiner. Weak sequel to IN THE HEAT OF THE NIGHT finds black detective Virgil Tibbs investigating murder of girl, with priest-friend Landau implicated.

They Call Me Trinity (1972-Italian) C-110m. *½ D: E. B. Clucher (Enzo Barboni). Terence Hill, Bud Spencer, Farley Granger, Steffen Zacharias, Dan Sturkie, Gisela Hahn. Labored Italian "comedy" Western features two drifters leading underdog Mormon farmers in fight against outlaws, then turn sides at film's fade out and ride off with defeated gang. Forgettable.

They Came from Beyond Space (1967-British) C-85m. BOMB D: Freddie Francis. Robert Hutton, Jennifer Jayne, Zia Mohyeddin, Bernard Kay, Michael Gough. Hutton is free to combat spacemen because the silver plate he carries inside his skull makes him immune to their powers.

They Came to Blow Up America (1943) 73m. ** D: Edward Ludwig. George Sanders, Anna Sten, Ward Bond, Dennis Hoey, Sig Ruman, Ludwig Stossel, Robert Barrat. Overzealous espionage yarn designed for WW2 audiences, dated now. Good cast is only virtue.

They Came to Cordura (1959) C-123m. **½ D: Robert Rossen. Gary Cooper, Rita Hayworth, Van Heflin, Tab Hunter, Richard Conte, Michael Callan, Dick York. Soapy oater set in 1916 Mexico. Cooper is Army officer accused of cowardice, sent to find five men worthy of Medal of Honor. Hayworth is shady lady he meets on the way.

They Came to Rob Las Vegas (1968-Spanish-French-Italian) C-128m. ** D: Antonio Isasi. Gary Lockwood, Elke Sommer, Lee J. Cobb, Jack Palance. Big heist is small potatoes as armed robbers plot to intercept Vegas gambling money.

They Dare Not Love (1941) 76m. *½ D: James Whale. George Brent, Martha Scott, Paul Lukas, Egon Brecher, Roman Bohnen, Edgar Barrier. Good story idea submerged by silly script and Brent's miscasting as dashing Austrian prince, who tries to bargain with Gestapo officer Lukas on behalf of his country. Lloyd Bridges has small role as Nazi seaman.

They Died with Their Boots On (1941) 138m. *** D: Raoul Walsh. Errol Flynn, Olivia de Havilland, Arthur Kennedy, Charley Grapewin,

Gene Lockhart, Anthony Quinn, Stanley Ridges, Sydney Greenstreet. Sweeping Hollywood version of Little Big Horn with Flynn flamboyant as Custer. Fine vignettes amidst episodic buildup to lavish massacre scene.

They Drive By Night (1940) 93m. ***½ D: Raoul Walsh. George Raft, Ann Sheridan, Ida Lupino, Humphrey Bogart, Gale Page, Alan Hale, Roscoe Karns. Marvelous melodrama of truck-driving brothers battling crooked bosses, with appealing Sheridan and bravura Lupino sparking cast. Unforgettable dialogue. Partial reworking of BORDERTOWN.

They Gave Him a Gun (1937) 94m. ** D: W. S. Van Dyke II. Spencer Tracy, Gladys George, Franchot Tone, Edgar Dearing, Charles Trowbridge. Fine cast does more than justice to weak psychological story of war-hardened Tone turning to crime, Tracy trying to stop him.

They Got Me Covered (1943) 95m. ** D: David Butler. Bob Hope, Dorothy Lamour, Lenore Aubert, Otto Preminger, Eduardo Ciannelli, Marion Martin, Donald Meek. Spy yarn set in Washington was topical at the time, awkward now; not up to Hope standards.

They Knew What They Wanted (1940) 96m. *** D: Garson Kanin. Carole Lombard, Charles Laughton, William Gargan, Harry Carey, Frank Fay. Laughton and Lombard are excellent in this flawed adaptation of Sidney Howard's play (filmed twice before). He's an Italian grapegrower in California who conducts correspondence with waitress and asks her to marry him. Fay is too sanctimonious for words as local priest.

They Live by Night (1949) 95m. ***½ D: Nicholas Ray. Farley Granger, Cathy O'Donnell, Howard da Silva, Jay C. Flippen, Helen Craig. Director Ray's first film is sensitive, well-made story of young lovers who are fugitives from the law. Set in 1930s, it avoids clichés and builds considerable impact instead. Based on Edward Anderson's THIEVES LIKE US, remade in 1974 under that name.

They Loved Life SEE: Kanal

They Made Me a Criminal (1939) 92m. **½ D: Busby Berkeley. John Garfield, Claude Rains, Gloria Dickson, May Robson, Billy Halop, Huntz Hall, Barbara Pepper, Ward Bond, Ann Sheridan. Garfield takes it on the lam when he thinks he's killed a boxing opponent, stays out West with Robson and Dead End Kids. Enjoyable, with Rains miscast as a Dick Tracy type. Remake of THE LIFE OF JIMMY DOLAN.

They Made Me a Criminal (1948-British) SEE: I Became a Criminal

They Met In Argentina (1941) 77m. *½ D: Leslie Goodwins, Jack Hively. Maureen O'Hara, James Ellison, Alberto Vila, Buddy Ebsen. Limp musical of O'Hara, a Latin heiress caught between U. S. engineer and local sportsman. Skip it.

They Met In Bombay (1941) 86m. **½ D: Clarence Brown. Clark Gable, Rosalind Russell, Peter Lorre, Jessie Ralph, Reginald Owen. Two jewel thieves team up in ordinary romantic comedy-actioner, spiced by Lorre as money-hungry cargo-ship captain.

They Might Be Giants (1971) C-98m. *** D: Anthony Harvey. Joanne Woodward, George C. Scott, Jack Gilford, Lester Rawlins. Fun yarn of slightly daffy gentleman who believes he is Sherlock Holmes, and his psychiatrist tagalong whose real name is Dr. Watson. Theatrical version of film ran only 88m.

They Only Come Out at Night (1975) C-78m. TVM D: Daryl Duke. Jack Warden, Charles Ynfante, Madeline Thornton-Sherwood, Tim O'Connor, Joe Mantell, Lili Valenty, Barbara Luna. Veteran detective Warden investigates slayings of several elderly women. Standard whodunit served as tv pilot to Warden's "Jigsaw John." Average.

They Only Kill Their Masters (1972) C-97m. **½ D: James Goldstone. James Garner, Katharine Ross, Hal Holbrook, Harry Guardino, June Allyson, Christopher Connelly, Tom Ewell, Peter Lawford, Edmond O'Brien, Arthur O'Connell, Ann Rutherford. Complicated modern-day whodunit set in coastal California town tries for Dashiell Hammett feeling, doesn't quite make it. Policeman Garner tries to solve murder of pregnant woman, with formidable Doberman pinscher figuring prominently. Not bad, but a letdown.

They Ran for Their Lives (1969) C-92m. ** D: Oliver Drake (John Payne). John Payne, Jim Davis, Luana Patten, John Carradine. Fair drama featuring Payne as nobody coming to aid of young woman who's being pursued by thugs after classified documents which once belonged to her father.

They Rode West (1954) C-84m. **½ D: Phil Karlson. Robert Francis, Donna Reed, May Wynn, Phil Carey, Onslow Stevens. Camp commander prevents army surgeon from attempting to treat Indian epidemic. Good cast highlights better than average Western.

They Shall Have Music (1939) 101m. *** D: Archie Mayo. Jascha Heifetz, Joel McCrea, Andrea Leeds, Walter Brennan, Gene Reynolds, Marjorie Main, Terry Kilburn. Cornerstone of Samuel Goldwyn's efforts to bring classical music to the masses, and make a movie star out of Heifetz. Plot involves disadvantaged kids who help Brennan save his settlement music school by convincing Heifetz to give a benefit.

They Shoot Horses, Don't They? (1969) C-121m. ***½ D: Sydney Pollack. Jane Fonda, Michael Sarrazin, Susannah York, Gig Young, Red Buttons, Bonnie Bedelia, Bruce Dern, Allyn Ann McLerie. 1930s marathon dance becomes microcosm of life, with myriad of subplots, characters' lives intertwining. Fonda is self-destructive girl who attracts aimless Sarrazin with tragic results; Young won Oscar as oily promoter of grueling "contest." Fascinating.

They Went That-A-Way and That-A-Way (1978) C-95m. *½ D: Edward Montagne, Stuart E. McGowan. Tim Conway, Chuck McCann, Richard Kiel, Dub Taylor, Reni Santoni, Lenny Montana. Lame prison comedy (with script by Conway) puts Conway and McCann through lackluster routines as a road-company Laurel and Hardy.

They Were Expendable (1945) 135m. ***½ D: John Ford. Robert Montgomery, John Wayne, Donna Reed, Jack Holt, Ward Bond, Louis Jean Heydt, Marshall Thompson. Grade A WW2 action film of PT boat combat in the Pacific, well handled by fine cast and director Ford.

They Were Sisters (1945-British) 110m. **½ D: Arthur Crabtree. Phyllis Calvert, James Mason, Hugh Sinclair, Dulcie Gray, Pamela Kellino (Mason). Fresh approach to stock drama of trio of sisters with contrasting marriages and lives.

They Were So Young (1955-German) 80m. *** D: Kurt Neumann. Scott Brady, Raymond Burr, Johanna Matz, Ingrid Stenn. Nicely produced, grim melodrama of girls sent to South America to be used by crooks. Even without "names" in cast, film would be good.

They Who Dare (1953-British) C-101m. **½ D: Lewis Milestone. Dirk Bogarde, Denholm Elliott, Akim Tamiroff, Eric Pohlmann, David Peel. Effective WW2 actioner with good character delineation, tracing commando raid on German-controlled Aegean air fields.

They Won't Believe Me (1947) 95m. ***½ D: Irving Pichel. Robert Young, Susan Hayward, Jane Greer, Rita Johnson, Tom Powers, Don Beddoe. Fine melodrama inspired by James Cain influence. Philandering Young gets involved with three different women, leading to tragedy and fine twist ending. Young excels in unsympathetic role; Johnson does wonders with her scenes as his wife.

They Won't Forget (1937) 95m. **** D: Mervyn LeRoy. Claude Rains, Gloria Dickson, Otto Kruger, Allyn Joslyn, Elisha Cook Jr., Edward Norris. Electrifying drama begins when pretty high school student is murdered in Southern town. A man is arrested, and a big-time Northern lawyer takes the case, but everyone seems more interested in exploiting personal interests than in seeing justice triumph. No punches are pulled in this still-powerful film. Lana Turner plays the unfortunate girl, in her first important role.

They've Kidnapped Anne Benedict SEE: **Abduction of Saint Anne**

Thief, The (1952) 85m. **½ D: Russell Rouse. Ray Milland, Rita Gam, Martin Gabel, Harry Bronson. Spy yarn set in N.Y.C. with a difference: no dialogue. Gimmick grows wearisome, script is tame.

Thief, The (1971) C-74m. TVM D: William Graham. Richard Crenna, Angie Dickinson, Cameron Mitchell. Ex-con finds himself unable to repay debt, must obtain sum of money very quickly. Uneven performances in formula drama, enlivened by crisp direction. Average.

Thief of Bagdad, The (1924) 140m. *** D: Raoul Walsh. Douglas Fairbanks, Julanne Johnston, Anna May Wong, Sojin, Snitz Edwards, Charles Belcher, Brandon Hurst. Dashing Fairbanks is sent on magic quest in Arabian Nights-type fantasy/adventure with lovely Johnston the princess who rides off with Doug on his magic carpet. Quite long, but never dull; one of the most imaginative of all silent films.

Thief of Bagdad, The (1940-British) C-106m. **** D: Ludwig Berger, Tim Whelan, Michael Powell. Sabu, John Justin, June Duprez, Conrad Veidt, Rex Ingram, Miles Malleson, Mary Morris. Remarkable fantasy of native boy, Sabu outdoing evil magician Veidt in Arabian Nights fable with incredible Technicolor special effects. Ingram gives splendid performance as a genie.

Thief of Baghdad (1961-Italian) C-90m. ** D: Arthur Lubin. Steve Reeves, Giorgia Moll, Arturo Dominici, Edy Vessel. Reeves searches for enchanted blue rose so he can marry Sultan's daughter. Nothing like Sabu version but occasionally atmospheric.

Thief of Baghdad, The (1978-British-French) C-100m. TVM D: Clive Donner. Roddy McDowall, Peter Ustinov, Kabir Bedi, Frank Finlay, Marina Vlady, Terence Stamp, Pavla Ustinov. More flying carpet and genie-in-the-magic-lamp fantasy in this fourth filming of the Arabian Nights adventure that's handsome enough but nowhere near the definitive 1940 version. Average.

Thief of Damascus (1952) C-78m. ** D: Will Jason. Paul Henreid, John Sutton, Jeff Donnell, Lon Chaney, Elena Verdugo. Jumbled costume spectacle featuring Aladdin, Sinbad and Ali Baba out to rescue princess.

Thief of Paris, The (1967) C-119m. *** D: Louis Malle. Jean-Paul Belmondo, Genevieve Bujold, Marie Dubois, Francoise Fabian, Julien Guiomar. Solid comedy-drama with personal setbacks turning Belmondo to thievery for revenge on society; soon he finds that robbery has become his whole life.

Thief Who Came to Dinner, The (1973) C-105m. ** D: Bud Yorkin. Ryan O'Neal, Jacqueline Bisset, Warren Oates, Jill Clayburgh, Charles Cioffi, Ned Beatty, Austin Pendleton, Gregory Sierra, Michael Murphy, John Hillerman. Disappointing caper comedy (considering cast and director) about a computer expert who becomes a jewel thief in Houston's top social circles. Clayburgh (pre-stardom) has small but telling role as O'Neal's ex-wife.

Thieves (1977) C-92m. BOMB D: John Berry. Marlo Thomas, Charles Grodin, Irwin Corey, Hector Elizondo, Mercedes McCambridge, John McMartin, Gary Merrill, Ann Wedgeworth. Pretentious, boring adaptation of Herb Gardner's play about crazy couple trying to recapture their innocence in a corrupt N.Y.C. Corey adds only life to so-called comedy.

Thieves Fall Out (1941) 72m. ** D: Ray Enright. Eddie Albert, Joan Leslie, Alan Hale, William T. Orr, John Litel, Anthony Quinn, Edward Brophy. Innocuous drama of rival mattress factory families and their problems. Good cast working with limited material.

Thieves' Highway (1949) 94m. *** D: Jules Dassin. Richard Conte, Valentina Cortese, Lee J. Cobb, Barbara Lawrence, Jack Oakie, Millard Mitchell. Exciting drama of underworld mobsters moving in on the California trucking business; fast-moving film has Cortese's American debut.

Thieves' Holiday (1946) 100m. *** D: Douglas Sirk. George Sanders, Signe Hasso, Carole Landis, Akim Tamiroff, Gene Lockhart. Famous French thief and rogue, beautifully played by Sanders, works his way into position as prefect of police. Delightful romantic adventure. Originally titled SCANDAL IN PARIS.

Thieves Like Us (1974) C-123m. ***½ D: Robert Altman. Keith Carradine, Shelley Duvall, John Schuck, Bert Remsen, Louise Fletcher, Ann Latham, Tom Skerritt. Three misfits escape from prison camp in 1930s Midwest, go on a crime spree; the youngest (Carradine) falls in love with a simple, uneducated girl (Duvall). Despite familiar trappings, Altman digs deep into period atmosphere and strong characterizations; this film gets better every time you look at it. Remake of THEY LIVE BY NIGHT.

Thin Air (1969-British) C-91m. *½ D: Gerry Levy. George Sanders, Maurice Evans, Patrick Allen, Neil Connery, Hilary Dwyer, Robert Flemyng. Parachutists keep disappearing, due to unseen forces; routine sci-fi with little to recommend it. Originally titled THE BODY STEALERS (INVASION OF THE BODY STEALERS).

Thin Ice (1937) 78m. *** D: Sidney Lanfield. Sonja Henie, Tyrone Power, Arthur Treacher, Joan Davis, Alan Hale. Early Sonja Henie, and very good, with dashing prince Power in love with commoner Henie.

Thin Man, The One series stands apart from the others: its episodes were filmed two and three years apart, its stars were those of the major rank, and the films were not looked down at as Grade-B efforts. This was **The Thin Man**, a highly successful series launched quite unexpectedly in 1934 with a delightfully unpretentious blend of screwball comedy and murder mystery, from a story by Dashiell Hammett. William Powell and Myrna Loy starred as Nick and Nora Charles, a perfectly happy, sophisticated couple whose marriage never stood in the way of their having fun and going off on detective capers. This blithe, carefree portrayal of a modern American couple was beautifully handled by Loy and Powell, and audiences loved it. Five Thin Man films followed, from 1936 to 1947. None of them fully captured the essence of the original, although they retained much of the charm and had the infallible byplay of the two stars, aided by their dog Asta, who soon became a star in his own right. AFTER THE THIN MAN featured an upcoming actor named James Stewart as a suspect, and Sam Levene in the detective role played in the original by Nat Pendleton (and repeated in ANOTHER THIN MAN). ANOTHER THIN MAN also introduced Nick Charles, Jr. as a baby, who grew up in each successive film. THE THIN MAN GOES HOME presented Nick's parents (Harry Davenport and Lucile Watson), who never wanted him to be a detective in the first place. The final film, SONG OF THE THIN MAN, had Nick and Nora frequenting many jazz hangouts (à la PETER GUNN) for some offbeat sequences. While the original THIN MAN rated above its follow-ups, even the weakest entries in the series were fresh and enjoyable, thanks mainly to the two stars. By the way, the name "Thin Man" did not refer to William Powell; it was a character in the original film played by Edward Ellis.

Thin Man, The (1934) 93m. D: W. S. Van Dyke II. William Powell, Myrna Loy, Maureen O'Sullivan, Nat Pendleton, Minna Gombell, Cesar Romero, Natalie Moorhead, Edward Ellis, Porter Hall.

Thin Man Goes Home, The (1944) 100m. D: Richard Thorpe. William Powell, Myrna Loy, Lucile Watson, Gloria De Haven, Anne Revere, Helen Vinson, Harry Davenport, Leon Ames, Donald Meek, Edward Brophy.

Thin Red Line, The (1964) 99m. **½ D: Andrew Marton. Keir Dullea, Jack Warden, James Philbrook, Kieron Moore. James Jones' novel about relationship between sergeant Warden and private Dullea, who cannot come to terms, is focus of WW2 tale, set in Guadalcanal.

Thing (From Another World), The (1951) 87m. ***½ D: Christian Nyby. Margaret Sheridan, Kenneth Tobey, Robert Cornthwaite, Douglas Spencer, James Arness. Top sci-fi flick. Scientists in Arctic station stumble upon humanoid creature from space. Tense direction (often credited to producer Howard Hawks); good acting. Young Arness plays the monster.

Thing That Couldn't Die, The (1958) 69m. ** D: Will Cowan. Andra Martin, William Reynolds, Carolyn Kearney, Jeffrey Stone. Title monster is a century-old head seeking the rest of itself; fair.

Thing with Two Heads, The (1972) C-93m. ** D: Lee Frost. Ray Milland, Rosie Grier, Don Marshall, Roger Perry, Chelsea Brown. Fantastic tale of bigot who finds his head transplanted onto black man's body. You've been warned.

Things to Come (1936-British) 92m. *** D: William Cameron Menzies. Raymond Massey, Cedric Hardwicke, Ralph Richardson, Maurice Braddell, Edward Chapman, Ann Todd. Stunning visualization of H. G. Wells' depiction of the future. Massey portrays new world leader, Richardson the despotic ruler during wartime. Aloof but always interesting, enhanced by Menzies' sets, vibrant music. Cut from 113m. original release.

Think Fast, Mr. Moto (1937) 66m. D: Norman Foster. Peter Lorre, Virginia Field, Sig Ruman, Murray Kinnell, Lotus Long, J. Carrol Naish, Fredrick Vogeding, George Cooper SEE: **Mr. Moto** series.

Third Day, The (1965) C-119m. **½ D: Jack Smight. George Peppard, Elizabeth Ashley, Roddy McDowall, Arthur O'Connell, Mona Washbourne, Herbert Marshall, Robert Webber, Charles Drake, Sally Kellerman, Arte Johnson. Capable cast helps standard amnesia tale about Peppard's inability to remember events that have caused him to be accused of murder.

Third Finger, Left Hand (1940) 96m. ** D: Robert Z. Leonard. Myrna Loy, Melvyn Douglas, Raymond Walburn, Lee Bowman, Bonita Granville. Mediocre comedy with attractive stars swallowed up. Loy loves Douglas but gives him a hard time in his pursuit.

Third Girl from the Left, The (1973) C-74m. TVM D: Peter Medak. Kim Novak, Tony Curtis, Michael Brandon, George Furth, Barbi Benton, Louis Guss. Embarrassing, clichéd dialogue all but spoils old-fashioned melodrama featuring Novak as "the last of the chorus girl troupers," experiencing second thoughts over impending marriage to singer Jordon (Curtis). Average.

Third Key, The (1956-British) 96m. *** D: Charles Frend. Jack Hawkins, John Stratton, Dorothy Alison, Geoffrey Keen, Ursula Howells. Exciting story of Scotland Yard investigation, as Inspector Hawkins and rookie sergeant (Stratton) diligently pursue safecracking incident to its surprising conclusion. Retitled THE LONG ARM.

Third Man, The (1949-British) 104m. **** D: Carol Reed. Orson Welles, Joseph Cotten, Valli, Trevor Howard, Wilfrid Hyde-White. Graham Greene's account of mysterious Harry Lime (Welles) in post-WW2 Vienna becomes screen classic, with pulp-writer Cotten on manhunt for Harry. "Third Man Theme" à la zither adds just the right touch.

Third Man on the Mountain (1959) C-105m. *** D: Ken Annakin. James MacArthur, Michael Rennie, Janet Munro, James Donald, Herbert Lom, Laurence Naismith. Fine Disney adventure about Swiss boy (MacArthur) determined to climb the Matterhorn (here called the Citadel) who learns more than just mountain-climbing in his dogged pursuit. Look quickly to spot MacArthur's mother Helen Hayes in a cameo as tourist.

Third Secret, The (1964-British) 103m. **½ D: Charles Crichton. Stephen Boyd, Jack Hawkins, Richard Attenborough, Diane Cilento, Pamela Franklin, Paul Rogers, Alan Webb. OK whodunit with Boyd tracking down the murderer of his psychoanalyst; no real surprises here.

3rd Voice, The (1960) 79m. *** D:

Hubert Cornfield. Edmond O'Brien, Laraine Day, Julie London, Ralph Brooks, Roque Ybarra, Henry Delgado. Neat suspense film involving murder, impersonation and double-crossing.

13 Fighting Men (1960) 69m. *½ D: Harry Gerstad. Grant Williams, Brad Dexter, Carole Mathews, Robert Dix, Richard Garland, Rayford Barnes, John Erwin. Minor film about Union soldiers fighting off Rebel troops to protect gold shipment.

13 Frightened Girls (1963) C-89m. ** D: William Castle. Murray Hamilton, Joyce Taylor, Hugh Marlowe, Khigh Dhiegh. Mishmash of espionage intrigue with Taylor a double agent using a string of associates to penetrate diplomatic secrets.

13 Ghosts (1960) 88m. ** D: William Castle. Charles Herbert, Jo Morrow, Martin Milner, Rosemary DeCamp, Donald Woods, Margaret Hamilton, John Van Dreelen. Medium thriller loses main attraction on TV; device enabling viewers to see or screen out ghosts in certain scenes. Fairly interesting, but nothing special.

Thirteen Hours By Air (1936) 80m. **½ D: Mitchell Leisen. Fred MacMurray, Joan Bennett, ZaSu Pitts, John Howard, Bennie Bartlett, Grace Bradley, Alan Baxter. Dated but diverting tale of transcontinental flight, with romance, murder, and intrigue surrounding mysterious passengers.

13 Rue Madeleine (1946) 95m. **½ D: Henry Hathaway. James Cagney, Annabella, Richard Conte, Frank Latimore, Walter Abel, Melville Cooper, Sam Jaffe. OK documentary-style story of O.S.S. agents' attempt to locate German missile site in France during WW2. Good cast also includes young E. G. Marshall, Karl Malden, Red Buttons.

13 West Street (1962) 80m. **½ D: Philip Leacock. Alan Ladd, Rod Steiger, Jeanne Cooper, Michael Callan, Dolores Dorn. Taut actioner with Ladd out to get gang of hoodlums; most capable cast.

Thirteen Women (1932) 73m. ** D: George Archainbaud. Irene Dunne, Ricardo Cortez, Myrna Loy, Jill Esmond, Florence Eldredge, Kay Johnson. Silly tripe with Loy as a half-caste with hypnotic powers who has sworn revenge on sorority sisters who rejected her years ago in school.

13th Hour, The (1947) 65m. D: William Clemens. Richard Dix, Karen Morley, Mark Dennis, John Kellogg,

Bernadene Hayes, Jim Bannon, Regis Toomey. SEE: The Whistler series.
13th Letter, The (1951) 85m. **½ D: Otto Preminger. Linda Darnell, Charles Boyer, Michael Rennie, Constance Smith, Judith Evelyn. Interesting account of effect of series of poison pen letters on townsfolk, set in Canada. Remake of H. G. Clouzot's LE CORBEAU.

---30--- (1959) 96m. *½ D: Jack Webb. Jack Webb, William Conrad, David Nelson, Whitney Blake, Louise Lorimer, Joe Flynn, James Bell. Hackneyed, over-written tale of a typical night on a big-city newspaper. Conrad chews the scenery as city editor, but the script's main villain, abetted by atrocious music score.

Thirty Day Princess (1934) 75m. **½ D: Marion Gering. Sylvia Sidney, Cary Grant, Edward Arnold, Lucien Littlefield. Pleasant minor account of Sidney substituting for an ill princess who must make a goodwill tour in U. S., with expected results.

30 Foot Bride of Candy Rock, The (1959) 75m. ** D: Sidney Miller. Lou Costello, Dorothy Provine, Gale Gordon, Charles Lane, Jimmy Conlin, Peter Leeds. Lou Costello's only starring film without Bud Abbott is nothing much, mildly entertaining, with Miss Provine enlarged to gigantic proportions.

30 Is a Dangerous Age, Cynthia (1968-British) C-98m. **½ D: Joseph McGrath. Dudley Moore, Eddie Foy, Jr., Suzy Kendall, John Bird. Man who has frittered away his life decides that within 6 weeks he wants to be married and famous. Funny, but sometimes falls flat.

39 Steps, The (1935-British) 87m. **** D: Alfred Hitchcock. Robert Donat, Madeleine Carroll, Lucie Mannheim, Godfrey Tearle, Peggy Ashcroft. Classic Hitchcock mystery with overtones of light comedy and romance, as innocent Donat is pulled into spy-ring activities. Memorable banter between Donat and Carroll, who thinks he's a criminal, set style for sophisticated dialogue for years. Remade twice.

39 Steps, The (1978-British) C-102m. **½ D: Don Sharp. Robert Powell, David Warner, Eric Porter, Karen Dotrice, John Mills, George Baker. Based more on John Buchan's book than Hitchcock adaptation, remake isn't bad but lacks panache; Powell

plays innocent man pursued by villains who believe he's obtained details of their plot to hatch WW1.

Thirty Seconds Over Tokyo (1944) 138m. *** D: Mervyn LeRoy. Van Johnson, Robert Walker, Spencer Tracy, Phyllis Thaxter, Scott McKay, Robert Mitchum, Stephen McNally, Louis Jean Heydt, Leon Ames, Paul Langton. Exciting WW2 actioner of first American attack on Japan with sturdy cast, guest appearance by Tracy as General Doolittle.

36 Hours (1964) 115m. **½ D: George Seaton. James Garner, Eva Marie Saint, Rod Taylor, Werner Peters, Celia Lovsky, Alan Napier. Intriguing WW2 yarn with Garner as captured spy begins well, but peters out fast. Taylor as German officer is interesting casting.

30 Years of Fun (1963) 85m. **** Compiled by Robert Youngson. Charlie Chaplin, Buster Keaton, Laurel and Hardy, Harry Langdon, Sydney Chaplin, Charley Chase, etc. Without repeating from previous films, Youngson presents hilarious silent comedy footage. Included is rare sequence of Laurel and Hardy performing together for the first time in 1917.

This Above All (1942) 110m. *** D: Anatole Litvak. Tyrone Power, Joan Fontaine, Thomas Mitchell, Nigel Bruce, Gladys Cooper, Sara Allgood, Philip Merivale. Timely WW2 film shows its age; still good with strong cast in Eric Knight tale of embittered soldier Power finding courage and love with patriotic Britisher Fontaine.

This Angry Age (1958-Italian-U.S.) C-111m. ** D: Rene Clement. Silvana Mangano, Anthony Perkins, Alida Valli, Richard Conte, Jo Van Fleet, Nehemiah Persoff. Ludicrous mishmash set in Indo-China with Van Fleet a stereotyped, dominating mother who's convinced that her children (Perkins and Mangano) can make their rice fields a going proposition. Originally titled THE SEA WALL.

This Could Be the Night (1957) 103m. **½ D: Robert Wise. Jean Simmons, Paul Douglas, Anthony Franciosa, Joan Blondell, Neile Adams, ZaSu Pitts, J. Carrol Naish. Forced, frantic comedy of prim teacher Simmons working as secretary to gangster Douglas who runs a nightclub; Franciosa is the young associate who romances her.

This Day and Age (1933) 85m. ***
D: Cecil B. DeMille. Charles Bickford, Judith Allen, Richard Cromwell, Harry Green, Eddie Nugent, Ben Alexander, Bradley Page. Fascinating story of high-schoolers taking law into their own hands to pin mobster Bickford for murder of tailor Green. Anything but subtle, yet powerfully effective.

This Earth Is Mine (1959) C-125m. **½ D: Henry King. Rock Hudson, Jean Simmons, Dorothy McGuire, Claude Rains, Kent Smith, Anna Lee, Ken Scott. Disjointed soaper set in 1930s California vineyards about intertwining family romances, with Hudson-Simmons love story the focal point.

This Gun for Hire (1942) 80m. ***
D: Frank Tuttle. Alan Ladd, Veronica Lake, Robert Preston, Laird Cregar, Tully Marshall, Pamela Blake. Ladd came into his own as paid gunman seeking revenge on man who double-crossed him, with Lake as a fetching vis à vis. Remade as SHORT CUT TO HELL.

This Happy Breed (1944-British) C-114m. ***½ D: David Lean. Robert Newton, Celia Johnson, John Mills, Kay Walsh, Stanley Holloway. Splendidly acted saga follows British family from 1919 to 1939 in this adaptation of Noel Coward play.

This Happy Feeling (1958) C-92m. *** D: Blake Edwards. Debbie Reynolds, Curt Jurgens, John Saxon, Alexis Smith, Estelle Winwood, Mary Astor. Most engaging cast gives zip to simple yarn of Reynolds enthralled by actor Jurgens, but sparked by suitor Saxon; Winwood fine as eccentric housekeeper.

This Is My Affair (1937) 99m. ***
D: William A. Seiter. Barbara Stanwyck, Robert Taylor, Victor McLaglen, Brian Donlevy, Sidney Blackmer, John Carradine, Sig Ruman. Exciting film of Taylor joining gang of bank robbers on orders from President McKinley to expose powerful mob; Stanwyck is saloon singer who loves Taylor.

This Is My Love (1954) C-91m. ** D: Stuart Heisler. Linda Darnell, Rick Jason, Dan Duryea, Faith Domergue, Hal Baylor, Jerry Mathers. Darnell and her sister Domergue (who's married to invalid Duryea) compete for affections of Jason in this murky soap-drama.

This Is the Army (1943) C-121m. ***
D: Michael Curtiz. George Murphy, Joan Leslie, George Tobias, Alan Hale, Ronald Reagan, Joe Louis, Kate Smith, Irving Berlin. Soldiers who staged Irving Berlin's WW1 musical "Yip Yip Yaphank" reunite to help mount similar WW2 effort; corny but enjoyable framework (with Warner Bros. cast) for filmed record of legendary 1940s show, a topical melange of songs and skits. P.S. This is the film where George Murphy plays Ronald Reagan's father!

This Is the Life (1944) 87m. ** D: Felix E. Feist. Donald O'Connor, Peggy Ryan, Susanna Foster, Patric Knowles. Spunky cast of versatile performers with Foster torn between swank Knowles and performer O'Connor.

This Is the Night (1932) 78m. **½ D: Frank Tuttle. Lily Damita, Charles Ruggles, Roland Young, Thelma Todd, Cary Grant. Grant's feature film debut isn't bad, with Young hiring Damita to pose as his wife so he can pursue Todd. Grant is Todd's husband.

This Is the West That Was (1974) C-78m. TVM D: Fielder Cook. Ben Murphy, Kim Darby, Jane Alexander, Matt Clark, Tony Franciosa, Stuart Margolin, Stefan Gierasch, Luke Askew. Light-hearted look at the Wild Bill Hickok-Calamity Jane-Buffalo Bill Cody legend. Western spoof that never gets going, despite game cast. Average.

This Island Earth (1955) C-87m. **½ D: Joseph M. Newman. Jeff Morrow, Faith Domergue, Rex Reason, Lance Fuller. Imaginative photography highlights average story of scientist shanghaied by aliens to help their war-torn planet.

This Land Is Mine (1943) 103m. ** D: Jean Renoir. Charles Laughton, Maureen O'Hara, George Sanders, Walter Slezak, Kent Smih, Una O'Connor, Philip Merivale. Meek French teacher Laughton, aroused by Nazi occupation, becomes hero. Patriotic wartime film is dated and disappointing today.

This Love of Ours (1945) 90m. **½ D: William Dieterle. Merle Oberon, Charles Korvin, Claude Rains, Carl Esmond, Sue England, Jess Barker, Harry Davenport, Ralph Morgan. Sudsy soaper of Korvin leaving wife Oberon, meeting twelve years later, falling in love again. Rains steals show in supporting role. Remade as NEVER SAY GOODBYE.

This Man Must Die (1970-French) C-115m. ***½ D: Claude Chabrol. Michel Duchaussoy, Jean Yanne, Caroline Cellier, Lorraine Rainer, Marc DiNapoli, Guy Marly. Outstanding film about man who sets out to find the person who killed his young son in hit-and-run accident and the complications which ensue. This may be the best of many fine Chabrol dramas; Yanne and Cellier are unforgettable, the photography beautiful.

This Man Stands Alone (1979) C-100m. TVM D: Jerrold Freedman. Louis Gossett, Jr., Clu Gulager, Mary Alice, Barry Brown, James McEachin, Lonny Chapman. Based on true story of a black civil rights activist who runs for sheriff in a southern town and beats a popular segregationist. Compromised by cardboard characterizations, despite the earnest efforts of the always-fine Gossett. Average.

This Man's Navy (1945) 100m. *** D: William Wellman. Wallace Beery, Tom Drake, James Gleason, Jan Clayton, Selena Royle, Noah Beery, Sr., Henry O'Neill, Steve Brodie. Usual Beery service-story nicely rehashed; Beery treats Drake as a son, gets vicarious pleasure out of his navy career.

This Modern Age (1931) 76m. ** D: Nick Grinde. Joan Crawford, Neil Hamilton, Marjorie Rambeau, Hobart Bosworth, Emma Dunn. Upper-class Hamilton loves Crawford, but his family doesn't take to the poor working-girl. Standard predictable plot.

This Property Is Condemned (1966) C-110m. ** D: Sydney Pollack. Natalie Wood, Robert Redford, Charles Bronson, Kate Reid, Mary Badham, Robert Blake. Often absurd film version of Tennessee Williams one-acter has doe-eyed Wood falling for Redford, the out-of-towner staying in her mama's boarding house. Except for James Wong Howe's photography, this is trash without the style that often makes trash enjoyable.

This Rebel Age SEE: **Beat Generation, The**

This Rebel Breed (1960) 90m. ** D: Richard L. Bare. Rita Moreno, Mark Damon, Dyan Cannon, Gerald Mohr, Jay Novello, Eugene Martin, Tom Gilson, Richard Rust. Above-average tale detailing the apprehension of teen-age gangs. Retitled: THREE SHADES OF LOVE.

This Savage Land (1968) C-98m. TVM D: Vincent McEveety. Barry Sullivan, Glenn Corbett, Kathryn Hays, Andrew Prine, George C. Scott, John Drew Barrymore. Widower and family sell Ohio spread, head West for new start, ride into town embroiled in vigilante dispute. Excellent performances (especially Scott) in surprisingly believable script. Above average.

This Side of the Law (1950) 74m. ** D: Richard L. Bare. Viveca Lindfors, Kent Smith, Janis Paige, Monte Blue. Hokey script has Smith hired by crooked lawyer to impersonate missing wealthy man.

This Sporting Life (1963-British) 129m. ***½ D: Lindsay Anderson. Richard Harris, Rachel Roberts, Alan Badel, William Hartnell. Grim, adult story of rugby star Harris having an affair with landlady Roberts, leading to his overwhelming disillusionment with success and life.

This Thing Called Love (1941) 98m. *** D: Alexander Hall. Rosalind Russell, Melvyn Douglas, Binnie Barnes, Allyn Joslyn, Gloria Dickson, Lee J. Cobb. Adult comedy of newlyweds who set up three-month trial run for their marriage. Stars' expertise puts it over.

This Time for Keeps (1947) C-105m. **½ D: Richard Thorpe. Esther Williams, Lauritz Melchior, Jimmy Durante, Johnnie Johnston, Xavier Cugat. Empty-headed, enjoyable Williams bathing-suit musical with Durante around to relieve tedium.

This Woman Is Dangerous (1952) 100m. **½ D: Felix E. Feist. Joan Crawford, Dennis Morgan, David Brian, Robert Webb, Sherry Jackson. In typical tough-girl role, Crawford finds true love after countless mishaps, including an eye operation.

This Woman Is Mine (1941) 91m. ** D: Frank Lloyd. Franchot Tone, John Carroll, Walter Brennan, Carol Bruce, Nigel Bruce, Leo G. Carroll. Standard love triangle on merchant boat in northern waters plying the fur trade.

Thomas Crown Affair, The (1968) C-102m. *** D: Norman Jewison. Steve McQueen, Faye Dunaway, Paul Burke, Jack Weston, Biff McGuire, Yaphet Kotto. Glittery production complements story of supercool millionaire McQueen who plots perfect bank robbery, as insurance investigator Dunaway coldly determines to nab the gentleman-thief.

Perfect nonthink entertainment; Jewison's use of multi-image screens may suffer on TV.

Thomasine & Bushrod (1974) C-95m. *** D: Gordon Parks, Jr. Max Julien, Vonetta McGee, George Murdock, Glynn Turman, Juanita Moore. OK mixture of black exploitation and Western action with comedy, as a black BONNIE AND CLYDE team operate in 1911 Texas. Julien scripted and co-produced, along with the classy-looking McGee. Shot in New Mexico.

Thoroughbreds Don't Cry (1937) 80m. **½ D: Alfred E. Green. Judy Garland, Mickey Rooney, Sophie Tucker, C. Aubrey Smith, Frankie Darro, Henry Kolker, Helen Troy. Fairly good racetrack story with jockey Rooney involved in crooked deals, young Garland adding some songs.

Thoroughly Modern Millie (1967) C-138m. **½ D: George Roy Hill. Julie Andrews, Mary Tyler Moore, Carol Channing, James Fox, John Gavin, Beatrice Lillie. Up to a point this Ross Hunter attempt to recapture some of Andrews' BOY FRIEND magic is successful, but after nearly two and a half hours, one begins to yawn. 1920s farce has a fatal case of the cutes.

Those Calloways (1965) C-131m. *** D: Norman Tokar. Brian Keith, Vera Miles, Brandon de Wilde, Walter Brennan, Ed Wynn, Linda Evans, Philip Abbott. Long, episodic but rewarding Disney film about an eccentric New England man (Keith) and his family, focusing on his determined efforts to use nearby lake for bird sanctuary before it's bought up by business interests.

Those Daring Young Men in Their Jaunty Jalopies (1969-British-U.S.) C-93m. **½ D: Ken Annakin. Tony Curtis, Susan Hampshire, Terry-Thomas, Eric Sykes, Gert Frobe, Peter Cook, Dudley Moore, Jack Hawkins. Slapstick adventures of participants in 1500 mile car race to Monte Carlo. Despite funny routines, 1920s period-piece backfires a bit too much.

Those Fantastic Flying Fools (1967) C-95m. **½ D: Don Sharp. Burl Ives, Troy Donahue, Gert Frobe, Terry-Thomas, Hermione Gingold, Daliah Lavi, Lionel Jeffries. Lightweight tale of Victorian England moon race adapted from Jules Verne story. Originally titled BLAST-OFF.

Those Magnificent Men In Their

Flying Machines (1965) C-132m. *** D: Ken Annakin. Stuart Whitman, Sarah Miles, James Fox, Alberto Sordi, Robert Morley, Gert Frobe, Jean-Pierre Cassel, Terry-Thomas, Irina Demick, Flora Robson, Red Skelton. Long but enjoyable film of great airplane race involving international conflicts, cheating, and romance. Skelton does funny cameo in amusing prologue, tracing history of aviation.

Those Redheads from Seattle (1953) C-90m. ** D: Lewis R. Foster. Rhonda Fleming, Gene Barry, Agnes Moorehead, Teresa Brewer, Guy Mitchell. Modestly produced musical nonsense set in gold-rush era with Moorehead the mother of four gals who takes her brood to Alaska.

Those Were the Days (1940) 76m. ** D: Jay Reed. William Holden, Bonita Granville, Ezra Stone, Judith Barrett, Alan Ladd. Pat college campus yarn, making the most of wholesome romance among naive students.

Thou Shalt Not Commit Adultery (1978) C-100m. TVM D: Delbert Mann. Louise Fletcher, Wayne Rogers, Bert Convy, Robert Reed. Tepid contemporary interpretation of one of the Ten Commandments, sudsed-up by having a paralytic's wife having extramarital affairs with his permission. Below average.

Thou Shalt Not Kill (1961-Italian) 129m. **½ D: Claude Autant-Lara. Laurent Terzieff, Horst Frank, Suzanne Flon, Mica Orlovic. Too-often sterile narrative dealing with trial of French conscientious objector, with side-plot of German priest facing penalty for having killed Frenchman during WW2.

Thousand and One Nights, A (1945) C-93m. *** D: Alfred E. Green. Cornel Wilde, Evelyn Keyes, Phil Silvers, Adele Jergens, Dusty Anderson, Dennis Hoey, Rex Ingram. Good escapism based on Arabian Nights fables; colorful production with serviceable cast including Ingram repeating genie-ish role from THIEF OF BAGDAD.

Thousand Clowns, A (1965) 118m. ***½ D: Fred Coe. Jason Robards, Barbara Harris, Martin Balsam, Barry Gordon, Gene Saks, William Daniels. Faithful adaptation of Herb Gardner's Broadway comedy about society dropout who's being pressured to drop in again for the sake of young nephew who lives with him. Perfectly cast, filmed in N.Y., with Balsam's Oscar-winning performance as Robards' brother.

Thousand Eyes of Dr. Mabuse, The (1960-German) 103m. **½ D: Fritz Lang. Dawn Addams, Peter Van Eyck, Gert Frobe, Wolfgang Preiss. Fast-moving if unconvincing revival of arch-villain of 1920s, with Frobe the police agent tracking down the reincarnated Mabuse in Berlin; gimmicky, complex plot line.

Thousand Plane Raid, The (1969) C-94m. *½ D: Boris Sagal. Christopher George, Laraine Stephens, J. D. Cannon, Gary Marshall, Michael Evans. Thoroughly routine suspenser about plot to bomb German aircraft factory near end of WW2.

Thousands Cheer (1943) C-126m. *** D: George Sidney. Mickey Rooney, Judy Garland, Gene Kelly, Red Skelton, Eleanor Powell, Ann Sothern, Lucille Ball, Virginia O'Brien, Frank Morgan, Kathryn Grayson, Lena Horne. Grayson lives with officer-father John Boles at army base, decides to prepare all-star show for soldiers. Filmy plot, great entertainment.

Threat, The (1960) 66m. ** D: Charles R. Rondeau. Robert Knapp, Linda Lawson, Lisabeth Hush, James Seay, Mary Castle, Barney Phillips. Standard find-the-real-murderer yarn.

Three Avengers, The (1964-Italian) C-97m. *½ D: Gianfranco Parolini. Alan Steel, Mimmo Palmara, Lisa Gastoni, Rosalba Neri. Below par Ursus (Steel) adventure tale, dealing with evil ruler of Atra.

Three Bad Men (1926) 92m. ***½ D: John Ford. George O'Brien, Lou Tellegen, J. Farrell MacDonald, Tom Santschi, Frank Campeau. Three gruff outlaws become benevolent protectors of young girl whose father is killed during Western settlement period. Beautiful mixture of action, drama, comedy, and sentiment in one of Ford's best silents.

Three Bad Sisters (1956) 76m. *½ D: Gilbert L. Kay. Marla English, Kathleen Hughes, Sara Shane, John Bromfield, Jess Barker, Madge Kennedy. Aimless account of title figures fighting among themselves to outdo the others, fighting over their father's estate.

Three Bites of the Apple (1967) C-105m. *½ D: Alvin Ganzer. David McCallum, Sylva Koscina, Tammy Grimes, Harvey Korman, Domenico Modugno, Aldo Fabrizi. Good scenery is only plus of flimsy comedy

about McCallum's attempts to avoid heavy taxation of money he's won in a casino on the Riviera.

Three Blind Mice (1938) 75m. **½ D: William A. Seiter. Loretta Young, Joel McCrea, David Niven, Stuart Erwin, Marjorie Weaver, Pauline Moore, Binnie Barnes. Familiar idea of three fortune-hunting girls going after well-heeled male prospects; slickly done. Remade, reworked many times.

Three Blondes In His Life (1960) 81m. ** D: Leon Chooluck. Jock Mahoney, Greta Thyssen, Anthony Dexter, Jesse White. Occasionally tangy rehash of romances and misconduct of now-deceased insurance investigator.

Three Brave Men (1957) 88m. **½ D: Philip Dunne. Ray Milland, Frank Lovejoy, Ernest Borgnine, Nina Foch, Andrew Duggan. Veteran navy employee (Borgnine) is accused of Communist affiliations. Film is well intentioned, but has too many clichés to be effective. From Pulitzer Prize-winning story.

Three Broadway Girls SEE: **Greeks Had a Word for Them, The**

Three Came Home (1950) 106m. ***½ D: Jean Negulesco. Claudette Colbert, Patric Knowles, Florence Desmond, Sessue Hayakawa, Helen Westcott. Stunning performances by Colbert and Hayakawa make this a must. British families living on Borneo during WW2 are sent to prison camps by Japanese, but cultured officer Hayakawa takes an interest in authoress Colbert.

Three Cases of Murder (1954-British) 99m. *** D: David Eady, Wendy Toye, George More O'Ferrall. Alan Badel, Hugh Pryse, John Gregson, Elizabeth Sellars, Emrys Jones; Orson Welles. Three offbeat murder stories; opener "In the Picture" is genuinely eerie, closer "Lord Mountdrago" (from Somerset Maugham story) has Welles in absorbing tale of a government official haunted by rival.

Three Cheers for the Irish (1940) 100m. **½ D: Lloyd Bacon. Thomas Mitchell, Dennis Morgan, Priscilla Lane, Alan Hale, Virginia Grey, Irene Hervey. Breezy little comedy of family feud when Irish Mitchell's daughter Lane falls for Scottish Morgan.

Three Coins in the Fountain (1954) C-102m. *** D: Jean Negulesco. Clifton Webb, Dorothy McGuire, Jean Peters, Louis Jourdan, Maggie Mc-

[782]

Namara, Rossano Brazzi. Splashy romance yarn made ultra-pleasing by Rome locations. Three women make wishes for romance at Fountain of Trevi, spurring several amorous adventures. Remade as THE PLEASURE SEEKERS.

Three Comrades (1938) 100m. ***½ D: Frank Borzage. Robert Taylor, Margaret Sullavan, Franchot Tone, Robert Young, Guy Kibbee, Lionel Atwill. Beautifully poignant film of Erich Maria Remarque's tale of post-WW1 Germany, and three life-long friends who share a love for Margaret Sullavan. Excellent performances all around.

Three-Cornered Moon (1933) 77m. *** D: Elliott Nugent. Claudette Colbert, Richard Arlen, Mary Boland, Wallace Ford, Hardie Albright, Lyda Roberti. Predates golden age of screwball comedies, but tops many of them; Boland is head of wacky family combating Depression.

Three Daring Daughters (1948) C-115m. **½ D: Fred M. Wilcox. Jeanette MacDonald, Jose Iturbi, Elinor Donahue, Ann B. Todd, Jane Powell, Edward Arnold, Harry Davenport. Woman magazine editor tells her daughters that she's remarrying. Despite predictable results, well-acted MGM comedy succeeds.

Three Days of the Condor (1975) C-117m. *** D: Sydney Pollack. Robert Redford, Faye Dunaway, Cliff Robertson, Max von Sydow, John Houseman. Redford, a reader for U.S. intelligence office, learns more than he should, and suddenly finds himself a hunted man. Dunaway is excellent as innocent woman who shelters him. Good suspense yarn.

Three Desperate Men (1951) 71m. *½ D: Sam Newfield. Preston Foster, Virginia Grey, Jim Davis, Ross Latimer. Flabby little oater about three brothers who become outlaws.

Three Faces of Eve, The (1957) 91m. ***½ D: Nunnally Johnson. Joanne Woodward, David Wayne, Lee J. Cobb, Nancy Kulp, Vince Edwards. Narration: Alistair Cooke. Academy Award tour de force by Woodward as schizophrenic with three contrasting personalities and three separate lives. Cobb is psychiatrist who tries to cure her.

Three Faces West (1940) 79m. **½ D: Bernard Vorhaus. John Wayne, Charles Coburn, Sigrid Gurie, Spencer Charters. Unusual group traveling West includes Westerner Wayne, refugee Gurie. Above-average Western with offbeat romantic duo.

Three for Bedroom C (1952) C-74m. ** D: Milton Bren. Gloria Swanson, Fred Clark, James Warren, Steve Brodie, Hans Conried, Margaret Dumont. Sadly uneven comedy of romance between movie star and scientist aboard transcontinental train heading to L.A. A derailment for Swanson after her triumph in SUNSET BOULEVARD.

Three for Jamie Dawn (1956) 81m. ** D: Thomas Carr. Laraine Day, Ricardo Montalban, Richard Carlson, June Havoc. Diverting story poorly executed, about jury members being pressured to swing a not-guilty verdict for the defendant.

Three for the Show (1955) C-93m. ** D: H. C. Potter. Betty Grable, Marge and Gower Champion, Jack Lemmon, Myron McCormick. Music is only thing that holds slight plot together in this dud remake of TOO MANY HUSBANDS.

Three Girls About Town (1941) 73m. **½ D: Leigh Jason. Joan Blondell, Binnie Barnes, Janet Blair, John Howard, Robert Benchley, Eric Blore, Hugh O'Connell, Una O'Connor. Wacky but amusing comedy of three sisters encountering a corpse in N.Y.C. hotel and the frantic consequences.

Three Godfathers (1948) C-105m. *** D: John Ford. John Wayne, Pedro Armendariz, Harry Carey Jr., Ward Bond, Mae Marsh, Jane Darwell, Ben Johnson, Mildred Natwick. Sturdy, sentimental, sometimes beautiful rendition of Peter B. Kyne's oft-filmed saga of three bandits who "adopt" a baby born in the desert. Final scene doesn't ring true, but director Ford makes up for it in balance of film. Remade for TV as THE GODCHILD.

Three Guns for Texas (1968) C-99m. TVM D: David Lowell Rich, Paul Stanley, Earl Bellamy. Neville Brand, Peter Brown, Martin Milner, William Smith. Boring exploits of three Texas Rangers, strung together from three episodes of LAREDO TV series. Forgettable action, fair repartee between leads. Average.

Three Guys Named Mike (1951) 90m. **½ D: Charles Walters. Jane Wyman, Van Johnson, Barry Sullivan, Howard Keel, Phyllis Kirk. Pleasant, undemanding fluff of Wyman being courted by three suitors.

Three Hearts for Julia (1943) 89m. ** D: Richard Thorpe. Ann Sothern, Melvyn Douglas, Lee Bowman, Richard Ainley, Felix Bressart, Marta Linden, Reginald Owen. Only debonair Douglas could seem right as husband romancing his wife (Sothern) who is divorcing him, but he can't support whole film.

Three Hours to Kill (1954) C-77m. *** D: Alfred L. Werker. Dana Andrews, Donna Reed, Dianne Foster, Stephen Elliott. Andrews plays stagecoach driver unjustly accused of killing fiancé's brother; he returns to find real killer. Tight, well-done movie.

300 Spartans, The (1962) C-114m. *½ D: Rudolph Maté. Richard Egan, Ralph Richardson, Diane Baker, Barry Coe. Events leading up to heroic Greek stand against Persians at Thermopylae; strictly cardboard, except for location filming.

300 Year Weekend, The (1977) C-123m. *½ D: Victor Stoloff. William Devane, Michael Tolan, Sharon Laughlin, Roy Cooper, Gabriel Dell, M'el Dowd. Dreary drama about a marathon group-encounter session *does* seem to go on for 300 years.

Three Husbands (1950) 78m. **½ D: Irving Reis. Eve Arden, Ruth Warrick, Vanessa Brown, Shepperd Strudwick, Billie Burke, Emlyn Williams, Jane Darwell. Pleasing comedy of three husbands trying to find out whether or not deceased playboy spent time with their wives.

Three in the Attic (1968) C-92m. **½ D: Richard Wilson. Christopher Jones, Judy Pace, Yvette Mimieux, Maggie Thrett. Silly tale of youth with so much style that he works three girls at once until they get wise and decide to lock him in and drain him of his potency.

Three Into Two Won't Go (1969-British) C-93m. ** D: Peter Hall. Rod Steiger, Claire Bloom, Judy Geeson, Peggy Ashcroft, Paul Rogers. Marriage of Steiger and Bloom breaks up when he becomes infatuated with sexy hitchhiker Geeson. Originally an OK drama, but Universal shot extra footage and reedited original film to 100m. for television.

Three Is a Family (1944) 81m. **½ D: Edward Ludwig. Fay Bainter, Marjorie Reynolds, Charlie Ruggles, Helen Broderick, Arthur Lake, Hattie McDaniel, Jeff Donnell, Walter Catlett, Cheryl Walker. Above-par fluff

of hectic homelife in apartment filled with family, friends, and new babies.

Three Little Girls in Blue (1946) C-90m. *** D: H. Bruce Humberstone. June Haver, George Montgomery, Vivian Blaine, Celeste Holm, Vera-Ellen. Colorful tale of three sisters out to trap wealthy husbands; familiar plot with good tunes like "You Make Me Feel So Young."

Three Little Words (1950) C-102m. *** D: Richard Thorpe. Fred Astaire, Vera-Ellen, Red Skelton, Arlene Dahl, Keenan Wynn, Gloria De Haven, Debbie Reynolds, Carleton Carpenter. Standard MGM musical about famous songwriters Kalmar and Ruby and their climb to fame; bouncy cast, fine tunes.

Three Lives of Thomasina, The (1964) C-97m. *** D: Don Chaffey. Patrick McGoohan, Susan Hampshire, Karen Dotrice, Vincent Winter, Denis Gilmore, Laurence Naismith, Finlay Currie. Charming Disney film made in England from Paul Gallico's story about a heartless veterinarian, his daughter's devotion to her pet cat, and a mystical young woman with life-giving "powers." A winner.

Three Loves Has Nancy (1938) 69m. **½ D: Richard Thorpe. Janet Gaynor, Robert Montgomery, Franchot Tone, Guy Kibbee, Claire Dodd, Reginald Owen. Breezy little romantic triangle with stood-up bride Gaynor playing the field for a while.

Three Men in a Boat (1956-British) C-84m. ** D: Ken Annakin. Laurence Harvey, Jimmy Edwards, David Tomlinson, Shirley Eaton, Jill Ireland, Martita Hunt, Adrienne Corri. Diverting minor comedy about trio of fun-loving men who take a boat trip up the Thames and find romantic adventures.

Three Men in White (1944) 85m. D: Willis Goldbeck. Lionel Barrymore, Van Johnson, Marilyn Maxwell, Keye Luke, Ava Gardner, Alma Kruger, Rags Ragland. SEE: **Dr. Kildare** series.

Three Men On a Horse (1936) 88m. *** D: Mervyn LeRoy. Frank McHugh, Sam Levene, Joan Blondell, Teddy Hart, Guy Kibbee, Carol Hughes, Allen Jenkins, Edgar Kennedy. First-rate comedy of timid McHugh who always picks winning race-horses; stagy but funny. Blondell's fun as Levene's Brooklynese girlfriend. Adapted from Broadway play by George Abbott and John Cecil Holm.

3 Murderesses (1960-French) C-96m. **½ D: Michel Boisrond. Alain Delon, Mylene Demongeot, Pascale Petit, Jacqueline Sassard, Anita Ruf, Simone Renant. Most diverting cast in standard playboy yarn with Delon romancing trio of contrasting females. Originally titled WOMEN ARE WEAK.

Three Musketeers, The (1935) 90m. ** D: Rowland V. Lee. Walter Abel, Paul Lukas, Ian Keith, Onslow Stevens, Ralph Forbes, Margot Grahame, Heather Angel. Dullest version of Dumas' story, with Abel miscast as D'Artagnan.

Three Musketeers, The (1939) 73m. *** D: Allan Dwan. Don Ameche, Ritz Brothers, Lionel Atwill, Binnie Barnes, Gloria Stuart, Pauline Moore, John Carradine, Joseph Schildkraut. Spirited musical, generally faithful to Dumas story; Ameche flavorful as D'Artagnan, Barnes lovely as Lady DeWinter, Ritz Brothers funny substitutes for unsuspecting musketeers.

Three Musketeers, The (1948) C-125m. **½ D: George Sidney. Lana Turner, Gene Kelly, June Allyson, Van Heflin, Angela Lansbury, Robert Coote, Frank Morgan, Vincent Price, Keenan Wynn, Gig Young. Oddball, lavish production of Dumas tale with Kelly as D'Artagnan. Occasional bright moments, but continual change of tone, and Heflin's drowsy characterization, bog down the action. Lana makes a stunning Lady DeWinter.

Three Musketeers, The (1974-British) C-105m. ***½ D: Richard Lester. Oliver Reed, Raquel Welch, Richard Chamberlain, Michael York, Frank Finlay, Christopher Lee, Geraldine Chaplin, Faye Dunaway, Charlton Heston. Delightful tongue-in-cheek version of Dumas classic, artfully mixing swashbuckling adventure and romance with broad slapstick. Raquel Welch's finest hour. Followed by sequel (which was actually filmed simultaneously) THE FOUR MUSKETEERS.

Three on a Couch (1966) C-109m. *½ D: Jerry Lewis. Jerry Lewis, Janet Leigh, Mary Ann Mobley, Gila Golan, Leslie Parrish, James Best, Kathleen Freeman. For psychiatrist Leigh to marry him, Lewis has to play five roles; one of them is "straight" but unintentionally funny, the other four zany, but unintentionally unfunny. The women are attractive.

Three on a Date (1978) C-100m. TVM D: Bill Bixby. June Allyson, Ray Bolger, Loni Anderson, John Byner, Gary Crosby, Carol Lawrence, Rick Nelson, Patrick Wayne, Didi Conn. TV game show winners, plus chaperone, on a Hawaiian holiday in this LOVE BOAT variation that's equally as inspired in concept an execution. Average.

Three on a Match (1932) 64m. *** D: Mervyn LeRoy. Warren William, Joan Blondell, Bette Davis, Ann Dvorak, Humphrey Bogart, Lyle Talbot, Glenda Farrell, Anne Shirley, Edward Arnold. Fine, fast-moving melodrama of three girls who renew childhood friendship, only to find suspense and tragedy. Dvorak is simply marvelous. Remade as BROADWAY MUSKETEERS.

Three on a Spree (1961-British) 83m. *½ D: Sidney J. Furie. Jack Watling, Carole Lesley, Renee Houston, John Slater. Disconcerting, poorly directed comedy of man forced to spend a million pounds in sixty days to inherit eight million, à la Brewster's Millions.

Three Ring Circus (1954) C-103m. ** D: Joseph Pevney. Dean Martin, Jerry Lewis, Joanne Dru, Zsa Zsa Gabor, Wallace Ford, Elsa Lanchester. So-so Martin and Lewis comedy has them as discharged servicemen up to trouble in a circus.

Three Sailors and a Girl (1953) C-95m. ** D: Roy Del Ruth. Jane Powell, Gordon MacRae, Gene Nelson, Sam Levene, Jack E. Leonard. Bland musical of three gobs who invest ship's surplus funds in a musical show, starring Powell.

Three Secrets (1950) 98m. *** D: Robert Wise. Eleanor Parker, Patricia Neal, Ruth Roman, Frank Lovejoy, Leif Erikson. Sturdy melodrama; three women wait anxiously for word of which one's child survived plane crash.

Three Shades of Love SEE: **This Rebel Breed**

Three Sisters, The (1966) 168m. **½ D: Paul Bogart. Kim Stanley, Geraldine Page, Shelley Winters, Kevin McCarthy, Sandy Dennis. Taped recreation of Actors Studio Broadway production of Chekhov's play about 19th-century Russia and relationships amidst a most unhappy family.

Three Sisters (1970-British) C-165m.

[785]

**** D: Laurence Olivier, John Sichel. Laurence Olivier, Joan Plowright, Alan Bates, Jeanne Watts, Louise Purnell, Derek Jacobi. Brilliant rendering of Chekhov play about three daughters of deceased Russian colonel living in provinces, circa 1900. Olivier's vibrant production is definitive screen version of this classic. Released here in 1974 by American Film Theater.

Three Smart Girls (1937) 84m. ***½ D: Henry Koster. Deanna Durbin, Binnie Barnes, Alice Brady, Ray Milland, Barbara Read, Mischa Auer, Nan Grey, Charles Winninger. Delightful musicomedy with Deanna's debut as matchmaking young girl who brings parents back together. Songs: "Someone To Care For Me," "My Heart Is Singing."

Three Smart Girls Grow Up (1939) 90m. *** D: Henry Koster. Deanna Durbin, Charles Winninger, Nan Grey, Helen Parrish, Robert Cummings, William Lundigan. Little Deanna is still matchmaking for sisters, warming up stern father, singing "Because" and winning over everyone in sight.

Three Stooges Go Around the World in a Daze, The (1963) 94m. **½ D: Norman Maurer. Three Stooges, Jay Sheffield, Joan Freeman, Walter Burke, Peter Forster. Even those who dislike the Stooges may enjoy this funny updating of Jules Verne's tale, replete with sight gags and world travel.

Three Stooges in Orbit, The (1962) 87m. ** D: Edward Bernds. The Three Stooges, Carol Christensen, Edson Stroll, Emil Sitka. Nutty scientist Sitka invents contraption that flies and floats. The Stooges accidentally launch it and run headlong into the Army, with usual slapstick results for younger audiences.

Three Stooges Meet Hercules, The (1962) 89m. ** D: Edward Bernds. The Three Stooges, Vicki Trickett, Quinn Redeker, George N. Neise. Time machine takes the Stooges back to era of Roman legions; they are trapped on galley ship, battle cyclops, and wind up with chariot chase. Good slapstick for kids.

Three Strangers (1946) 92m. ***½ D: Jean Negulesco. Sydney Greenstreet, Geraldine Fitzgerald, Peter Lorre, Joan Lorring, Robert Shayne, Marjorie Riordan. Greenstreet and Lorre team up with Fitzgerald as partners holding winning sweepstakes

ticket under unusual circumstances. Bizarre John Huston script makes fascinating viewing.

Three Stripes in the Sun (1955) 93m. **½ D: Richard Murphy. Aldo Ray, Phil Carey, Dick York, Chuck Connors, Mitsuko Kimura. Good film of American GI falling in love with Japanese orphanage worker after years of hating enemy.

Three the Hard Way (1974) C-93m. **½ D: Gordon Parks, Jr. Jim Brown, Fred Williamson, Jim Kelly, Sheila Frazier, Jay Robinson, Alex Rocco. Top black action cast in nonstop but nearly bloodless thriller of white supremist Robinson's insane plot to eliminate blacks by a serum in the water supply.

3:10 to Yuma (1957) ***½ D: Delmer Daves. Glenn Ford, Van Heflin, Leora Dana, Felicia Farr, Henry Jones, Richard Jaeckel. Outstanding Western of farmer Heflin bringing in killer Ford to claim reward; suspenseful, well-handled oater.

3,000 Mile Chase, The (1977) C-100m. TVM D: Russ Mayberry. Cliff DeYoung, Glenn Ford, Blair Brown, David Spielberg, Priscilla Pointer, Brendan Dillon. Professional courier's efforts to deliver the key witness in narcotics czar's trial come under attack by latter's hit men. DeYoung is earnest; Ford's along for the ride in familiar chase plot. Average.

Three Tough Guys (1974) C-92m. **½ D: Duccio Tessari. Lino Ventura, Fred Williamson, Isaac Hayes, Paula Kelly. Oddball but fast-moving actioner, an Italian-U. S. production made in Chicago and Rome. Tough priest Ventura and ex-cop Hayes solve million-dollar bank robbery. Hayes, who also did the music, is nicely subdued as an actor.

Three Violent People (1956) C-100m. **½ D: Rudolph Maté. Charlton Heston, Anne Baxter, Gilbert Roland, Tom Tryon, Forrest Tucker, Elaine Stritch, Barton MacLane. Adequately paced Western set in post-Civil War Texas; Heston, returning home with bride Baxter, is forced to fight carpetbaggers and deal with wife's shady past.

Three Wise Fools (1946) 90m. ** D: Edward Buzzell. Margaret O'Brien, Lionel Barrymore, Lewis Stone, Edward Arnold, Thomas Mitchell, Cyd Charisse. Intended as fanciful, this turns out mawkish with adorable

O'Brien winning over three crusty old men.

3 Women (1977) C-125m. ***½ D: Robert Altman. Sissy Spacek, Shelley Duvall, Janice Rule, Robert Fortier, Ruth Nelson, John Cromwell. Brilliant, moody, thought-provoking film about a strange young girl (Spacek) who gets a job in an old-age convalescent home and attaches herself to coworker Duvall, who fancies herself a social butterfly. Their interrelationship, and involvement with a quiet, embittered woman (Rule) forms the "plot." Hypnotic film for Altman fans, heavy going for others; a completely unconventional movie.

Three Worlds of Gulliver, The (1960-British) C-100m. *** D: Jack Sher. Kerwin Mathews, Jo Morrow, June Thorburn, Lee Patterson, Gregoire Aslan, Basil Sydney. Hero is washed overboard and finds himself in the Land of Lilliputs . . . but that's just the beginning. Well-made adventure/fantasy designed for kids, fun for older viewers too. Fine special effects by Ray Harryhausen.

Three Young Texans (1954) C-78m. ** D: Henry Levin. Mitzi Gaynor, Keefe Brasselle, Jeffrey Hunter, Harvey Stephens, Dan Riss. Standard Western movie has Hunter pulling railroad robbery to prevent crooks from forcing his father to do same job, expected complications.

Three's a Crowd (1969) C-75m. TVM D: Harry Falk. Larry Hagman, Jessica Walter, E. J. Peaker, Harvey Korman, Michael Lerner, Norman Fell. After pilot Carson (Hagman) remarries following plane crash death of wife Ann, first wife discovered in desert. Formula complications abound in spirited comedy with resolution taking place in hotel. Average.

Threepenny Opera (1963) C-83m. **½ D: Wolfgang Staudte. Curt Jurgens, Hildegarde Neff, Sammy Davis, Jr., Gert Frobe. Stylized rendition of Kurt Weill-Bertolt Brecht version of THE BEGGAR'S OPERA, set in London's Soho District, following exploits of Mack The Knife (Jurgens).

Thrill of a Romance (1945) C-105m. ** D: Richard Thorpe. Van Johnson, Esther Williams, Frances Gifford, Henry Travers, Spring Byington, Lauritz Melchior. Typical Williams swim-romance vehicle with one good song, "I Should Care."

Thrill of Brazil, The (1946) 91m. **½ D: S. Sylvan Simon. Evelyn Keyes, Keenan Wynn, Ann Miller, Allyn Joslyn, Tito Guizar. Pleasant South-of-the-border romance with music and spirited cast giving life to ordinary script.

Thrill of It All, The (1963) C-108m. *** D: Norman Jewison. Doris Day, James Garner, Arlene Francis, Edward Andrews, Reginald Owen, ZaSu Pitts. Enjoyable spoof of TV and commercials by Carl Reiner; good vehicle for Day as housewife-turned-TV spokeswoman. Reiner has a particularly funny series of cameos.

Through a Glass Darkly (1962-Swedish) 91m. ***½ D: Ingmar Bergman. Harriet Andersson, Gunnar Bjornstrand, Max von Sydow, Lars Passgard. Four-character drama about just-released mental patient, her husband, her father and her younger brother who spend summer together on secluded island. Moody, evocative story of insanity—well-deserved Oscar winner, one of Bergman's best.

Thumb Tripping (1972) C-94m. **½ D: Quentin Masters. Michael Burns, Meg Foster, Marianna Hill, Bruce Dern, Mike Conrad, Joyce Van Patten. Amusing as a period piece on the hippie era, with Burns and Foster as hitchhikers who decide to travel together and share experiences.

Thunder Afloat (1939) 94m. **½ D: George B. Seitz. Wallace Beery, Chester Morris, Virginia Grey, Clem Bevans, John Qualen, Regis Toomey. Above-average Beery vehicle of old salt pitted against rival (Morris) when he joins the Navy.

Thunder Alley (1967) C-90m. *½ D: Richard Rush. Annette Funicello, Fabian, Diane McBain, Warren Berlinger, Jan Murray, Maureen Arthur. Fabian's inept stock-car driving gets him suspended from racing, but unfortunately, the acting profession doesn't have the same rules.

Thunder and Lightning (1977) C-95m. **½ D: Corey Allen. David Carradine, Kate Jackson, Roger C. Carmel, Sterling Holloway, Ed Barth, Ron Feinberg. Amiable moonshine picture with attractive pairing of Carradine and Jackson and lots of expected car smash-ups.

Thunder Bay (1953) C-102m. *** D: Anthony Mann. James Stewart, Joanne Dru, Gilbert Roland, Dan Duryea, Jay C. Flippen. Action-packed account of oil-drillers vs. Louisiana shrimp fishermen, with a peppery cast.

Thunder Below (1932) 67m. **½ D: Richard Wallace. Tallulah Bankhead, Charles Bickford, Paul Lukas, Eugene Pallette, James Finlayson, Edward Van Sloan. Tallulah loves Lukas, but when husband Bickford goes blind, she can't bear to leave him. Melodramatic triangle story, well-acted by all.

Thunder Birds (1942) C-78m. ** D: William Wellman. Gene Tierney, Preston Foster, John Sutton, Dame May Whitty, Reginald Denny, Iris Adrian. Tame adventure as two rival fliers romance Tierney between air exploits.

Thunder in Carolina (1960) C-92m. ** D: Paul Helmick. Rory Calhoun, Alan Hale, Connie Hines, John Gentry, Ed McGrath, Troyanne Ross. Programmer account of stockcar racing in the South.

Thunder in the East (1953) 98m. **½ D: Charles Vidor. Alan Ladd, Deborah Kerr, Charles Boyer, Corinne Calvet, Cecil Kellaway. Melodramatic hodgepodge with Ladd a gunrunner mercenary involved in India with local political upheavals.

Thunder in the Sun (1959) C-81m. **½ D: Russell Rouse. Susan Hayward, Jeff Chandler, Jacques Bergerac, Blanche Yurka, Carl Esmond, Fortunio Bonanova. Hayward is romanced by wagon train scout Chandler and Bergerac, head of French Basque immigrants on way to California.

Thunder in the Valley (1947) C-103m. **½ D: Louis King. Lon McCallister, Peggy Ann Garner, Edmund Gwenn, Reginald Owen. Usual tale of boy in love with his dog, cruel father who doesn't share his feelings; colorful but standard.

Thunder of Drums, A (1961) C-97m. **½ D: Joseph M. Newman. George Hamilton, Luana Patten, Richard Boone, Charles Bronson, Richard Chamberlain, Slim Pickens. Better than average cast saves average story of new lieutenant having rough time in cavalry.

Thunder on the Hill (1951) 84m. *** D: Douglas Sirk. Claudette Colbert, Ann Blyth, Robert Douglas, Anne Crawford, Gladys Cooper. Nun Colbert can't believe visitor Blyth, about to be hanged, is murderess, sets out to prove her innocent; Cooper fine as Mother Superior. Sincere, interesting drama.

Thunder Over Arizona (1956) C-75m. ** D: Joseph Kane. Skip Homeier, Kristine Miller, George Macready, Wallace Ford. Undemanding minor Western showing the corruption and greed of people incited by a rich silver ore discovery.

Thunder Over Hawaii SEE: **Naked Paradise**

Thunder Over Tangier (1957-British) 66m. *½ D: Lance Comfort. Robert Hutton, Martin Benson, Derek Sydney, Lisa Gastoni. Flabby account of refugees being conned with phony passports.

Thunder Over the Plains (1953) C-82m. ** D: Andre de Toth. Randolph Scott, Lex Barker, Phyllis Kirk, Henry Hull, Elisha Cook, Jr. Routine Western set in post-Civil War Texas, with Scott as army officer sent to prevent carpetbaggers from harassing all.

Thunder Pass (1954) 76m. ** D: Frank McDonald. Dane Clark, Andy Devine, Dorothy Patrick, Raymond Burr. Usual story of resolute army officer (Clark) pushing settlers onward in face of Indian attack.

Thunder Road (1958) 92m. **½ D: Arthur Ripley. Robert Mitchum, Gene Barry, Jacques Aubuchon, Keely Smith. Fast-paced account of Mitchum returning home down South after Korean War, becoming involved in bootleg liquor running; minor slice of Americana. Star's son Jim Mitchum makes film debut as Robert's *brother*.

Thunder Rock (1942-British) 95m. *** D: John and Roy Boulting. James Mason, Michael Redgrave, Barbara Mullen, Lilli Palmer. Allegorical fable of discouraged newspaperman given renewed faith by visions of various drowned people. Excellent cast makes this most enjoyable.

Thunderball (1965-British) C-120m. **½ D: Terence Young. Sean Connery, Claudine Auger, Adolfo Celi, Luciana Paluzzi, Rik Van Nutter, Bernard Lee, Roland Culver. Fourth James Bond film isn't as lively as the others. Plenty of gimmicks, as Miami, Florida is threatened with destruction, but film tends to bog down—especially underwater. Celi makes a formidable Bond villain.

Thunderbirds (1952) 98m. **½ D: John H. Auer. John Derek, John Barrymore, Jr., Mona Freeman, Gene Evans. Standard tale of training aviators for WW2, with typical romantic interludes.

Thunderbolt and Lightfoot (1974) C-114m. *** D: Michael Cimino. Clint Eastwood, Jeff Bridges, George Kennedy, Geoffrey Lewis, Catherine Bach, Gary Busey. Long but colorful, tough melodrama in the famaliar Eastwood mold. Good characterizations as bitter ex-pals Eastwood and Kennedy reteam to retrieve armored car loot . . . but Bridges steals the picture.

Thundercloud SEE: Colt .45

Thunderhead—Son of Flicka (1945) C-78m. **½ D: Louis King. Roddy McDowall, Preston Foster, Rita Johnson, James Bell, Diana Hale, Carleton Young. Good, colorful attempt to repeat MY FRIEND FLICKA's success; doesn't match original, but it's enjoyable.

Thundering Jets (1958) 73m. *½ D: Helmut Dantine. Rex Reason, Dick Foran, Audrey Dalton, Robert Dix. Still another account of flight officer trying to reevaluate his handling of servicemen.

Thunderstorm (1956-Spanish) 81m. BOMB D: John Guillermin. Carlos Thompson, Linda Christian, Charles Korvin, Gary Thorne. Warmed-over trivia concerning Christian's provocative arrival in a small fishing village on the Spanish coast.

Thursday's Game (1974) C-100m. TVM D: Robert Moore. Gene Wilder, Bob Newhart, Ellen Burstyn, Cloris Leachman, Martha Scott, Nancy Walker, Valerie Harper, Rob Reiner, Norman Fell, Richard Schaal, Dick Gautier, John Archer. Sparkling adult comedy about poker-playing buddies Wilder and Newhart and their marital and business problems. Absolutely tops with dandy cast and a gloriously intelligent often hilarious script. Filmed in 1971, sat on shelf for several years. Above average.

THX-1138 (1971) C-88m. **½ D: George Lucas. Robert Duvall, Donald Pleasence, Maggie McOmie, Don Pedro Colley. Feature version of prize-winning short Lucas made in college is a futuristic tale in the 1984 vein about robotlike society where sex is forbidden and everyone looks the same. Dull script, but visually impressive; by the director who was to later make STAR WARS.

Tiara Tahiti (1962-British) C-100m. ** D: William (Ted) Kotcheff. James Mason, John Mills, Claude Dauphin, Herbert Lom. Mild happenings involving Mason and Mills as two former Army officers who have an old grudge to settle; establishment of a resort hotel on Tahiti sets the wheels in motion.

. . . tick . . . tick . . . tick . . . (1970) C-100m. ** D: Ralph Nelson. Jim Brown, George Kennedy, Fredric March, Lynn Carlin, Don Stroud, Janet MacLachlan. Poor man's IN THE HEAT OF THE NIGHT with black man (Brown) replacing white sheriff (Kennedy) in Southern town, flaring local hostilities. March adds film's only spice as aging, cantankerous mayor.

Ticket to Tomahawk, A (1950) C-90m. **½ D: Richard Sale. Dan Dailey, Anne Baxter, Rory Calhoun, Walter Brennan, Marilyn Monroe, Chief Yowlachie. Good musical Western spoof. Drummer in theatrical troupe involves himself in railroad fight; Monroe has bit part.

Tickle Me (1965) C-90m. **½ D: Norman Taurog. Elvis Presley, Jocelyn Lane, Julie Adams, Jack Mullaney, Merry Anders, Connie Gilchrist. That's the only way to get any laughs out of this one: Elvis works at all-girl dude ranch singing his usual quota of songs.

Ticklish Affair, A (1963) C-89m. ** D: George Sidney. Shirley Jones, Gig Young, Red Buttons, Carolyn Jones, Edgar Buchanan. Amiable film of Navy commander Young falling in love with widow Jones; all it lacks is wit, sparkle and a fresh script.

Tidal Wave (1975) C-90m. *½ D: Shiro Moriana, Andrew Meyer. Lorne Greene, Kiliu Kobayashi, Rhonda Leigh Hopkins, Hiroshi Fujioka. Laughable Americanization of big-budget Japanese film; epic special effects dwarfed by idiotic new footage with Greene, and horrible dubbing. For diehard disaster buffs only.

Tiger and the Pussycat, The (1967-Italian-U.S.) C-105m. **½ D: Dino Risi. Ann-Margret, Vittorio Gassman, Eleanor Parker, Antonella Stani, Fiorenzo Fiorentini. Innocuous sex-comedy of middle-aged businessman Gassman unintentionally getting involved with promiscuous young Ann-Margret. Italian and American players work well together.

Tiger Bay (1959-British) 105m. *** D: J. Lee Thompson. Hayley Mills, Horst Buchholz, Yvonne Mitchell,

John Mills. Film debut of Hayley Mills as youth who witnesses Buchholz killing his girlfriend; sensitive study of truth triumphing.

Tiger By the Tail (1968) C-99m. ** D: R. G. Springsteen. Christopher George, Tippi Hedren, Dean Jagger, Charo, Glenda Farrell, Lloyd Bochner, Alan Hale, Skip Homeier, R. G. Armstrong. Vietnam war hero is accused of murdering his brother and recruits his socialite girlfriend in hunt for the real killer. Overly talkative thriller.

Tiger Makes Out, The (1967) C-94m. **½ D: Arthur Hiller. Eli Wallach, Anne Jackson, Bob Dishy, John Harkins, Ruth White, Rae Allen, Charles Nelson Reilly. One-man crusader against society (Wallach) symbolically kidnaps suburban housewife (Jackson). Originally a one-act play by Murray Schisgal, expanded screenplay loses focus, relies on vivid N.Y. locations and funny cameos by character actors. Dustin Hoffman's film debut.

Tiger of the Seven Seas (1962-Italian) C-90m. ** D: Luigi Capuano. Gianna Maria Canale, Anthony Steel, Grazia Maria Spina, Ernesto Calindri. Follow-up to QUEEN OF THE PIRATES, with Canale the center of romance and swordfighting in this OK pirate yarn.

Tiger Shark (1932) 80m. *** D: Howard Hawks. Edward G. Robinson, Richard Arlen, Zita Johann, J. Carrol Naish, Vince Barnett. Robinson gives rich, colorful performance as Portugese tuna fisherman who marries wayward girl out of pity, then sees her fall in love with his best friend. Authentically filmed amid fisheries on Monterey coast.

Tiger Walks, A (1964) C-91m. **½ D: Norman Tokar. Brian Keith, Vera Miles, Pamela Franklin, Sabu, Kevin Corcoran, Peter Brown, Edward Andrews. Oddball Disney film about young girl (Franklin) whose compassion for tiger which has broken away from zoo stirs controversy and political wheeling-and-dealing. Surprisingly bitter portrait of small-town America.

Tiger Woman, The SEE: **Jungle Gold**

Tight Little Island (1948-British) 81m. **** D: Alexander Mackendrick. Basil Radford, Catherine Lacey, Bruce Seton, Joan Greenwood, Wylie Watson. Hilarious British comedy of sinking ship loaded with liquor providing problems for Scottish island thirsting for the cargo.

Tight Shoes (1941) 68m. ** D: Albert S. Rogell. Broderick Crawford, Binnie Barnes, John Howard, Anne Gwynne. Cast pushes hard to make this Damon Runyon yarn amusing at times: Crawford is big-shot crook who has big feet.

Tight Spot (1955) 97m. ***½ D: Phil Karlson. Ginger Rogers, Edward G. Robinson, Brian Keith, Lorne Greene, Katherine Anderson. Solid little film, with Rogers in one of her best performances as a former gangster's moll who's on the spot because she has agreed to testify against him.

Tijuana Story, The (1957) 72m. BOMB D: Leslie Kardos. James Darren, Jean Willes, Robert McQueeney, Rodolfo Acosta, Robert Blake. Juvenile melodrama of Darren a victim of narcotic addiction, set in Mexico.

Till the Clouds Roll By (1946) C-137m. **½ D: Richard Whorf. Van Johnson, June Allyson, Lucille Bremer, Judy Garland, Kathryn Grayson, Van Heflin, Lena Horne, Tony Martin, Angela Lansbury, Dinah Shore, Frank Sinatra. Glossy biography of songwriter Jerome Kern (Robert Walker) has often unbearable plot interspersed with good numbers by guest stars.

Till the End of Time (1946) 105m. *** D: Edward Dmytryk. Dorothy McGuire, Guy Madison, Robert Mitchum, Bill Williams, Tom Tully, William Gargan, Jean Porter. Story similar to BEST YEARS OF OUR LIVES, of three returning WW2 veterans; married McGuire, disillusioned, engages in romance. Good drama.

'Til We Meet Again (1940) 99m. **½ D: Edmund Goulding. Merle Oberon, George Brent, Pat O'Brien, Geraldine Fitzgerald, Binnie Barnes, Frank McHugh. Overblown remake of ONE WAY PASSAGE recounts romance between suave crook Brent and fatally ill Oberon; McHugh repeats comedy-relief role from 1932 original.

Till We Meet Again (1944) 88m. ** D: Frank Borzage. Ray Milland, Barbara Britton, Walter Slezak, Lucile Watson, Mona Freeman. Fair wartime drama of nun Britton helping pilot Milland return to Allied lines; elements don't always click in this one.

Tillie and Gus (1933) 58m. ***½ D: Francis Martin. W. C. Fields, Alison Skipworth, Baby LeRoy, Edgar Kennedy. Fields vs. Baby LeRoy, plus riverboat race, spark this W. C. romp, with comedian croaking "Bringing In The Sheaves" after each poker game.

Tillie's Punctured Romance (1914) 73m. **½ D: Mack Sennett. Charlie Chaplin, Marie Dressler, Mabel Normand, Mack Swain, Charles Bennett, Chester Conklin, Keystone Kops. A comic curio, the first full-length comedy feature film, with Dressler repeating stage role as farm girl fleeced by city-slicker Chaplin (appearing out of his usual character). Not terribly funny, or coherent, but there are good moments; mainly interesting for historical purposes.

Timber Queen (1943) 66m. *½ D: Frank McDonald. Richard Arlen, Mary Beth Hughes, June Havoc, Sheldon Leonard. Static programmer with pilot Arlen helping Hughes solve her business problems and romancing her.

Timberjack (1955) C-94m. ** D: Joseph Kane. Vera Ralston, Sterling Hayden, David Brian, Adolphe Menjou, Hoagy Carmichael. Young man fights crooks taking over lumber mill who also killed his father. Harmless potboiler.

Timbuktu (1959) 91m. ** D: Jacques Tourneur. Victor Mature, Yvonne De Carlo, George Dolenz, John Dehner, Marcia Henderson, James Foxx. Mature plays adventurer involved in African story of plot to overthrow government. Script is below average; cast is uneven.

Time After Time (1979) C-112m. **½ D: Nicholas Meyer. Malcolm McDowell, David Warner, Mary Steenburgen, Charles Cioffi, Kent Williams. Fanciful tale of H. G. Wells following Jack the Ripper from Victorian England to 1979 America in his time machine. Engaging premise eroded by story loopholes, and halfhearted attempts at social comment. Best is Steenburgen in an appealing, star-making performance as Wells' modern American girlfriend.

Time Bomb (1961-French) 92m. ** D: Yves Ciampi. Curt Jurgens, Mylene Demongeot, Alain Saury, Robert Porte, Jean Durand. So-so story of captain plotting to collect insurance by planting bomb on ship. Fair cast.

Time for Killing, A (1967) C-88m. ** D: Phil Karlson. Glenn Ford, Inger Stevens, George Hamilton, Paul Petersen, Timothy Carey, Kenneth Tobey. Fair Civil War drama pits Union Captain Ford against Confederate Major Hamilton, when the latter kidnaps Ford's bride-to-be. Director Karlson has done some good minor films in the past, but this isn't one of them; also known as THE LONG RIDE HOME.

Time for Love, A (1973) C-100m. TVM D: George Schaefer, Joseph Sargent. Jack Cassidy, John Davidson, Lauren Hutton, Christopher Mitchum, Bonnie Bedelia, Jo Anna K. Cameron. Two stories: meeting uninhibited girl at business convention, junior executive decides to dump plans of marrying wealthy socialite; pop star can't take crazy professional pressures, hitchhikes to small coastal town, meets simple teacher of deaf children. Not as bad as it sounds, with occasionally good dialogue, no-nonsense direction. Above average.

Time for Loving (1971-British) C-104m. **½ D: Christopher Miles. Mel Ferrer, Joanna Shimkus, Britt Ekland, Philippe Noiret, Susan Hampshire, Mark Burns, Lila Kedrova, Robert Dhery, Michel Legrand. Sophisticated Jean Anouilh liaison trilogy in the LA RONDE style. Sometimes it's called PARIS WAS MADE FOR LOVERS.

Time Limit (1957) 96m. *** D: Karl Malden. Richard Widmark, Richard Basehart, June Lockhart, Rip Torn, James Douglas. Imaginative direction and acting spark this courtroomer concerning the trial of American military officer suspected of collaborating with enemy while P.O.W. in North Korea.

Time Lost and Time Remembered (1966-British) 91m. *** D: Desmond Davis. Sarah Miles, Cyril Cusack, Julian Glover, Sean Caffrey. Thoughtful study of Miles' unhappy marriage to older man, emphasized by visit home where she discovers new set of values.

Time Machine, The (1960) C-103m. *** D: George Pal. Rod Taylor, Alan Young, Yvette Mimieux, Sebastian Cabot, Tom Helmore, Whit Bissell, Doris Lloyd. H. G. Wells' fantasy reduced to comic book level, but still entertaining, with Taylor as single-minded scientist who invents time-travel device and has vivid, frustrating experiences in the past and future.

Time Machine, The (1978) C-100m. TVM D: Henning Schellerup. John Beck, Priscilla Barnes, Andrew Duggan, Rosemary DeCamp, Jack Kruschen. Updated version of the H. G. Wells classic, given a "Classics Illustrated" treatment. Average.

Time of Indifference (1964-Italian) 84m. ** D: Francesco Maselli. Rod Steiger, Shelley Winters, Claudia Cardinale, Paulette Goddard, Tomas Milian. Turgid melodrama of moral and social decay in Italy during late 1920s, focusing on one nouveau-poor family; from novel by Alberto Moravia.

Time of Their Lives, The (1946) 82m. *** D: Charles Barton. Bud Abbott, Lou Costello, Marjorie Reynolds, Binnie Barnes, John Shelton, Gale Sondergaard, Jess Barker. Most unusual film for A&C, and one of their best. Costello and Reynolds are killed during Revolutionary times, and their ghosts haunt a country estate where Abbott and friends come to live. Imaginative, funny, and well done.

Time of Your Life, The (1948) 109m. **** D: H. C. Potter. James Cagney, William Bendix, Wayne Morris, Jeanne Cagney, Broderick Crawford, Ward Bond, James Barton. Thoughtful film based on William Saroyan play about assorted customers of small saloon in Big City; superb performances.

Time Out for Love (1961-French) 91m. **½ D: Phillipe De Broca. Jean Seberg, Maurice Ronet, Micheline Presle, Françoise Prevost. Amusing adult study of Yank Seberg engulfed by seemingly immoral world of new acquaintances, with their own code of standards. Retitled: FIVE DAY LOVER.

Time Out of Mind (1947) 88m. ** D: Robert Siodmak. Phyllis Calvert, Robert Hutton, Ella Raines, Eddie Albert, Leo G. Carroll. Plodding period-piece of girl in love above her station, seeing her lover live unhappy life.

Time, the Place and the Girl, The (1946) C-105m. **½ D: David Butler. Dennis Morgan, Martha Vickers, Jack Carson, Janis Paige, S. Z. Sakall, Alan Hale, Donald Woods. Flimsy story of two go-getters trying to operate nightclub; lively cast and OK songs.

Time to Live and a Time to Die, A (1958) C-132m. *** D: Douglas Sirk.

John Gavin, Lilo Pulver, Jock Mahoney, Don DeFore, Keenan Wynn. Intensely dramatic love story set against background of WW2. German soldier on furlough from battle falls in love, inevitably must return to the trenches. Well-directed version of Erich Maria Remarque novel.

Time To Sing, A (1968) C-92m. *½ D: Arthur Dreifuss. Hank Williams Jr., Ed Begley, Shelley Fabares, Charles Robinson, D'Urville Martin, Donald Woods, Clara Ward. Downhome tale of Williams suppressing love for singing to please uncle-guardian (Begley). Script aimed at 10-year-old mentality, matched by Williams' wooden performance.

Time Travelers (1976) C-78m. TVM D: Alexander Singer. Sam Groom, Tom Hallick, Richard Basehart, Trish Stewart, Francine York, Booth Coleman. Producer Irwin Allen's attempt to resurrect his previous cult series, "Time Tunnel," has two scientists searching for cure to a mysterious epidemic and finding themselves in Chicago of 1871 on the eve of the great fire. Footage from "In Old Chicago" is better than any of the new stuff. Taken from an original, unpublished short story by Rod Serling. Average.

Time Travelers, The (1964) C-82m. **½ D: Ib Melchior. Preston Foster, Philip Carey, Merry Anders, John Hoyt. Spirited flashes of imagination heighten this ordinary sci-fi story of predestined journey into past and future.

Time Without Pity (1956-British) 88m. **½ D: Joseph Losey. Michael Redgrave, Ann Todd, Peter Cushing, Leo McKern. Tense little film of father's effort to prove son's innocence of murder charge; occasionally overly talky.

Timetable (1956) 79m. ** D: Mark Stevens. Mark Stevens, King Calder, Felicia Farr, Marianne Stewart. Small-scale account of insurance detective involved in investigation of robbery he engineered.

Tin Pan Alley (1940) 94m. *** D: Walter Lang. Alice Faye, Betty Grable, Jack Oakie, John Payne, Esther Ralston, Allen Jenkins, Nicholas Brothers, John Loder. Predictable plot of struggling pre-WW1 songwriters enlivened by colorful numbers including "Sheik of Araby" production with Billy Gilbert as sultan. Oakie is in top form.

Tin Star, The (1957) 93m. *** D: Anthony Mann. Henry Fonda, Anthony Perkins, Betsy Palmer, Neville Brand, Lee Van Cleef, Michael Ray. Fledgling sheriff Perkins turns to bounty hunter Fonda to help combat outlaws preying on his town; solid, well-acted Western.

Tingler, The (1959) 82m. **½ D: William Castle. Vincent Price, Judith Evelyn, Darryl Hickman, Patricia Cutts, Philip Coolidge. Juvenile horror-fantasy is fun on its own terms as Price discovers nerve in spine that controls fright emotion. Gimmicked up for theaters, but special shock sequences still come across on TV.

Tip on a Dead Jockey (1957) 99m. *** D: Richard Thorpe. Dorothy Malone, Robert Taylor, Martin Gabel, Jack Lord. Neat account of Taylor tied in with smuggling syndicate in Madrid, romancing Malone. Good adaptation of Irwin Shaw story.

Titanic (1953) 98m. *** D: Jean Negulesco. Clifton Webb, Barbara Stanwyck, Robert Wagner, Richard Basehart, Audrey Dalton, Thelma Ritter, Brian Aherne. Hollywoodized version of sea tragedy centers on shipboard story. Not bad, but events better told in A NIGHT TO REMEMBER.

Titfield Thunderbolt, The (1953-British) C-84m. *** D: Charles Crichton. Stanley Holloway, George Relph, Naunton Wayne, Godfrey Tearle. Boisterous comedy about villagers who are attached to their antiquated railway line and run it themselves in competition with the local bus line.

To All My Friends On Shore (1971) C-74m. TVM D: Gilbert Cates. Bill Cosby, Gloria Foster, Dennis Hines, Ray Mason, Dennis Pate. Problems confronted in father-son relationship when they get word that child has incurable disease. Uneven performances, but film's conception and point of view exceptionally strong, refreshing. Above average.

To Be or Not To Be (1942) 99m. ***½ D: Ernst Lubitsch. Jack Benny, Carole Lombard, Robert Stack, Lionel Atwill, Felix Bressart, Sig Ruman, Helmut Dantine, Stanley Ridges. Excellent black comedy of wartime Poland about acting troupe which becomes involved in international affairs; Lombard's last film,

Benny's best. His scene playing Hamlet is standout.

To Bed . . . Or Not To Bed (1963-Italian) 103m. **½ D: Gian Luigi Polidoro. Alberto Sordi, Bernard Tarschys, Inger Sjostrand, Ulf Palms. Saucy sex romp with Sordi expecting to find free love on business trip to Stockholm, discovering home sweet home is best. Retitled: THE DEVIL.

To Catch a Thief (1955) C-106m. *** D: Alfred Hitchcock. Grace Kelly, Cary Grant, Jessie Royce Landis, John Williams, Charles Vanel. The French Riviera serves as picturesque backdrop for this entertaining (if fluffy) Hitchcock caper with Grant as reformed cat burglar suspected in new wave of jewel robberies. Chic and elegant in every way—and Kelly never looked more ravishing.

To Commit a Murder (1970-French) C-91m. *½ D: Edouard Molinaro. Louis Jourdan, Senta Berger, Edmond O'Brien, Bernard Blier, Fabrizzio Capucci. Playboy/writer Jourdan gets involved with a plot to abduct French nuclear scientist; interesting idea poorly handled.

To Die in Madrid (1965-French) 87m. **** D: Frederic Rossif. Narrated by John Gielgud and Irene Worth. Masterpiece in documentary filmmaking dealing with bloody civil war in Spain in which more than a million people died.

To Die in Paris (1968) C-100m. TVM D: Charles Dubin, Allen Reisner. Louis Jourdan, Kurt Krueger, Robert Ellenstein, John Marley, Ludwig Donath, Letitia Roman. Exploits of head of resistance in Paris during WW2. Bertine, imprisoned during ordinary round up of suspicious characters, must, prevent captors from realizing who he is, be on lookout for assassin sent by underground who can't risk situation. Good tension, uneven production values, adequate performances. Above average.

To Die of Love (1972-French) C-110m. **½ D: Andre Cayatte. Annie Girardot, Bruno Pradal, Francois Simon, Monique Melinand, Nathalie Neil, Nicolas Dumayet. Girardot's superb performance carries true story about French schoolteacher who was driven to suicide after she was forced to abandon 16-year-old student she loved. More interesting for subject matter than for actual execution.

To Each His Own (1946) 122m. *** D: Mitchell Leisen. Olivia de Havilland, John Lund, Mary Anderson, Roland Culver, Philip Terry, Griff Barnett. Well-turned soaper of unwed mother giving up baby, lavishing love on him as his "aunt" without revealing truth. Fine support by Culver as aging Olivia's beau. De Havilland won Best Actress Oscar.

To Find a Man (1972) C-90m. *** D: Buzz Kulik. Pamela Martin, Darren O'Connor, Lloyd Bridges, Phyllis Newman, Tom Ewell, Tom Bosley. Solid comedy-drama about two high-schoolers' attempts to find an abortionist. Study of friendships is good, and exceedingly fine acting of youthful leads is a definite plus.

To Have and Have Not (1944) 100m. ***½ D: Howard Hawks. Humphrey Bogart, Lauren Bacall, Walter Brennan, Dolores Moran, Hoagy Carmichael, Sheldon Leonard. Loosely based on Hemingway story of skipper-for-hire Bogart tangled up in WW2 intrigue; very good, but really comes to life in love scenes between Bogart and Bacall (their first film together and her screen debut). Yes, it's true: Andy Williams dubbed Bacall's singing voice. Remade as THE BREAKING POINT and THE GUN RUNNERS.

To Hell and Back (1955) C-106m. *** D: Jesse Hibbs. Audie Murphy, Marshall Thompson, Susan Kohner, Charles Drake, Gregg Palmer, Jack Kelly, David Janssen. Very good war film based on Audie Murphy's autobiography, with excellent battle sequences making up for uneven script.

To Kill a Clown (1972) C-104m. ** D: George Bloomfield. Alan Alda, Blythe Danner, Heath Lamberts, Eric Clavering. Couple whose marriage is on the rocks get trapped on island off New England coast by crippled, deranged Vietnam veteran. Weird mixture of traditional chiller film elements and topical considerations.

To Kill a Cop (1978) C-200m. TVM D: Gary Nelson. Joe Don Baker, Louis Gossett, Jr., Patrick O'Neal, Desi Arnaz, Jr., Christine Belford, Eartha Kitt, Rosey Greer. Police action drama about a maverick chief of detectives, a string of cop killings, and a black revolutionary leader plotting a police massacre. Based on the best-seller by Robert Daley, it became the pilot to the EISCHIED TV series. Average.

To Kill a Mockingbird (1962) 129m. ***½ D: Robert Mulligan. Gregory Peck, Mary Badham, Philip Alford, John Megna, Brock Peters. Leisurely-paced, flavorful filming of Harper Lee novel. Peck won Oscar as lawyer who defends Negro accused of rape. Badham, Alford, and Megna superb as youngsters trying to understand life in their small Southern town.

To Mary—With Love (1936) 87m. **½ D: John Cromwell. Warner Baxter, Myrna Loy, Ian Hunter, Claire Trevor, Jean Dixon, Pat Somerset. Dated but good drama of Baxter and Loy having stormy period of marriage but ending up loving each other more than ever.

To Paris with Love (1955-British) C-78m. **½ D: Robert Hamer. Alec Guinness, Austin Trevor, Odile Versois, Vernon Gray. Fair comedy of rich father taking son to Paris to learn facts of life. Guinness stands out in average British cast.

To Please a Lady (1950) 91m. **½ D: Clarence Brown. Clark Gable, Barbara Stanwyck, Adolphe Menjou, Roland Winters. Unremarkable love story of reporter Stanwyck and race-car driver-heel Gable.

To Sir with Love (1967-British) C-105m. ***½ D: James Clavell. Sidney Poitier, Judy Geeson, Christian Roberts, Suzy Kendall, Lulu, Faith Brook, Patricia Routledge. Excellent film of novice Poitier assigned to roughhouse London school, gradually earning respect from his students. Well acted, with nice work by young British newcomers.

To the Devil a Daughter (1976-British-German) C-93m. **½ D: Peter Sykes. Richard Widmark, Christopher Lee, Honor Blackman, Denholm Elliott, Natassja Kinski, Michael Goodliffe. Occult novelist Widmark is enlisted to help young girl who's being pursued by defrocked priest (Lee) for Satanic ritual. Hammer Films adaptation of Dennis Wheatley book is well made but lacks punch.

To the Ends of the Earth (1948) 109m. ***½ D: Robert Stevenson. Dick Powell, Signe Hasso, Ludwig Donath, Vladimir Sokoloff, Edgar Barrier. Fast-moving thriller of government agent tracking down narcotics smuggling ring has good acting and ironic ending.

To the Shores of Tripoli (1942) C-86m. **½ D: H. Bruce Humberstone. John Payne, Maureen O'Hara, Randolph Scott, Nancy Kelly, William Tracy, Maxie Rosenbloom, Iris

Adrian. Spoiled rich-boy Payne joins Marines with off-handed attitude, doesn't wake up until film's end. Routine material.

To the Victor (1948) 100m. **½ D: Delmer Daves. Dennis Morgan, Viveca Lindfors, Victor Francen, Bruce Bennett, Dorothy Malone. Story of collaborators standing trial in France for war crimes sadly could have been much better.

To Trap a Spy (1966) C-90m. **½ D: Don Medford. Robert Vaughn, David McCallum, Luciana Paluzzi, Patricia Crowley. Expanded from initial segment of MAN FROM U.N.C.L.E. TV series, reflects small budget and cast's newness at formula action-espionage type plot.

Toast of New Orleans, The (1950) C-97m. **½ D: Norman Taurog. Kathryn Grayson, Mario Lanza, David Niven, Rita Moreno, J. Carrol Naish. Lanza plays fisherman transformed into operatic star. Rest of cast good, and Lanza sings "Be My Love."

Toast of New York, The (1937) 109m. *** D: Rowland V. Lee. Edward Arnold, Cary Grant, Frances Farmer, Jack Oakie, Donald Meek, Clarence Kolb, Billy Gilbert, Stanley Fields. Arnold is in fine form as rags-to-riches businessman Jim Fiske in late 19th century. Grant is his partner in good biographical drama, well staged.

Tobacco Road (1941) 84m. **½ D: John Ford. Charley Grapewin, Marjorie Rambeau, Gene Tierney, William Tracy, Elizabeth Patterson, Dana Andrews. Southern degradation is theme of filmization of Erskine Caldwell hit play, well directed by Ford with good cast; punch isn't always there though.

Tobor the Great (1954) 77m. *½ D: Lee Sholem. Charles Drake, Karin Booth, Billy Chapin, Taylor Holmes, Steven Geray. Weak sci-fi adventure of enemy agents plotting to capture secret robot plans; terrible acting and dialogue.

Tobruk (1967) C-110m. **½ D: Arthur Hiller. Rock Hudson, George Peppard, Nigel Green, Guy Stockwell, Jack Watson, Norman Rossington, Percy Herbert, Liam Redmond. WW2 actioner of Allies trying to destroy Rommel's fuel supply in the Sahara, bogs down in pretentiousness, much social comment, etc.

Toby Tyler, or Ten Weeks with a Circus (1960) C-96m. **½ D: Charles

Barton. Kevin Corcoran, Henry Calvin, Gene Sheldon, Bob Sweeney, Richard Eastham, James Drury. Likable Disney fare about a young boy who runs away to join the circus at the turn of the century.

Today We Live (1933) 113m. ** D: Howard Hawks. Joan Crawford, Gary Cooper, Robert Young, Franchot Tone, Roscoe Karns. Stilted Faulkner story of WW1 heroism, despite star-studded cast.

Todd Killings, The (1971) C-93m. ** D: Barry Shear. Robert F. Lyons, Richard Thomas, Barbara Bel Geddes, Sherry Miles, Gloria Grahame, Edward Asner, Belinda Montgomery. Good cast in sleazy story of hip girl-getter Lyons actually involved in series of murders. Retitled A DANGEROUS FRIEND.

Together Again (1944) 93m. *** D: Charles Vidor. Irene Dunne, Charles Boyer, Charles Coburn, Mona Freeman, Elizabeth Patterson. Little bit of nothing carried off beautifully by Dunne, lady mayor of small town, and Boyer, suave New Yorker; charming comedy.

Together Brothers (1974) C-94m. **½ D: William A. Graham. Anthony Wilson, Ahmad Nurradin, Glynn Turman, Richard Yniguez, Lincoln Kilpatrick, Owen Pace. Suspense thriller with five young blacks scouring ghetto for the killer of their policeman friend. Violent treatment balanced by sensitive character studies.

Togetherness (1970) C-103m. ** D: Arthur Marks. George Hamilton, Peter Lawford, John Banner, Olinka Berova, Jesse White. American playboy Hamilton woos Communist athlete Berova in this dated comedy filmed in Greece.

Tokyo After Dark (1959) 80m. ** D: Norman Herman. Michi Kobi, Richard Long, Lawrence Dobkin, Paul Dubov, Butch Yamaoto. Uninspired account of military cop Long on the lam in Tokyo from unintentional homicide.

Tokyo Joe (1949) 88m. **½ D: Stuart Heisler. Humphrey Bogart, Florence Marly, Sessue Hayakawa, Alexander Knox, Jerome Courtland. Lesser Bogart film about American in post-war Tokyo pulled into smuggling and blackmail for the sake of his ex-wife and child.

Tokyo Olympiad (1966) C-93m. **½ D: Kon Ichikawa. If you're lucky enough to see superb original version of this documentary about 1964

Olympics, shoot this rating to ***½, but the U.S. version was cut from 132 minutes, and virtually destroyed by insipid narration.

Tokyo Rose (1945) 69m. ** D: Lew Landers. Byron Barr, Osa Massen, Don Douglas, Richard Loo, Keye Luke, Grace Lem, Leslie Fong, H. T. Tsiang. Timid drama of slinky female propagandist for Axis during WW2.

Toll Gate, The (1920) 59m. *** D: Lambert Hillyer. William S. Hart, Anna Q. Nilsson, Jack Richardson, Joseph Singleton, Richard Headrick. One of Hart's best films, casting him as fleeing outlaw who stops to save young boy's life, becomes involved with the child's widowed mother.

Tom Brown's School Days (1940) 86m. **½ D: Robert Stevenson. Cedric Hardwicke, Freddie Bartholomew, Gale Storm, Jimmy Lydon, Josephine Hutchinson, Billy Halop, Polly Moran. Nostalgic account of life at Victorian boys' school. Although most of cast is American, British flavor seeps thru. Retitled: ADVENTURE AT RUGBY.

Tom Brown's Schooldays (1951-British) 93m. ***½ D: Gordon Parry. John Howard Davies, Robert Newton, James Hayter, John Charlesworth. Well-acted film of Victorian England school life with exceptional British cast and good direction.

Tom, Dick and Harry (1941) 86m. ***½ D: Garson Kanin. Ginger Rogers, George Murphy, Alan Marshal, Burgess Meredith, Joe Cunningham, Jane Seymour, Phil Silvers. Spirited comic dilemma as wide-eyed Ginger chooses among three anxious suitors: sincere Murphy, wealthy Marshal, nonconformist Meredith. Silvers has hilarious role as obnoxious ice-cream man. Remade as THE GIRL MOST LIKELY.

Tom Jones (1963-British) C-131m. **** D: Tony Richardson. Albert Finney, Susannah York, Hugh Griffith, Joyce Redman, Edith Evans, Diane Cilento, Joan Greenwood, Peter Bull, David Warner. Oscar-winning adaptation of Henry Fielding novel about wild exploits of rustic playboy in 18th-century England. Beautiful cast and direction. Bawdy humor is not really for the kids in vivid period piece. Academy Awards for Best Picture, Best Director, Best Screenplay (John Osborne), and Best Scoring (John Barry). Great fun!

Tom Sawyer (1973) C-104m. *** D: Don Taylor. Johnnie Whitaker, Celeste Holm, Warren Oates, Jeff East, Jodie Foster. Well-crafted remake of Tom Sawyer, the boy wonder of Hannibal, Mo., and his friends Huckleberry Finn and Becky Thatcher. A musical with charm.

tom thumb (1958) C-98m. ***½ D: George Pal. Russ Tamblyn, June Thorburn, Peter Sellers, Terry-Thomas, Alan Young, Jessie Matthews, Bernard Miles. Excellent children's picture with Tamblyn as tiny Tom Thumb, taken in by kindly couple but exploited by villainous Terry-Thomas and henchman Sellers. Charming Puppetoons sequences, Oscar-winning special effects, and perfect Peggy Lee-Sonny Burke score.

Toma (1973) C-74m. TVM D: Richard Heffron. Tony Musante, Simon Oakland, Susan Strasberg, Nicholas Colasanto, Robert Yuro, Dave Toma. Leader of Syndicate numbers racket stalked by disguise-master undercover policeman. Excellent lead performance by Musante in challenging role, as he pleads with superiors for less interference and sweats it out when his family becomes Syndicate hostages. Above average; pilot for TV series.

Tomahawk (1951) C-82m. **½ D: George Sherman. Yvonne De Carlo, Van Heflin, Preston Foster, Jack Oakie, Alex Nicol. Colorful Western spiked with sufficient action to overcome bland account of friction between redskins and the army.

Tomb of Ligeia (1965-British) C-81m. *** D: Roger Corman. Vincent Price, Elizabeth Shepherd, John Westbrook, Derek Francis. Horrifying story of life after death, and the effect it has on the dead woman's husband (Price). Based on the Poe story.

Tomboy and the Champ (1961) C-92m. ** D: Francis D. Lyon. Candy Moore, Ben Johnson, Jesse White, Jess Kirkpatrick, Rex Allen. Mild "B" film about a young girl and her prize cow; strictly for children, who will probably enjoy it, despite standard plot devices.

Tommy (1975-British) C-111m. *** D: Ken Russell. Ann-Margret, Oliver Reed, Roger Daltrey, Elton John, Eric Clapton, Keith Moon, Robert Powell, Tina Turner, The Who, Jack Nicholson. Energetic rendering of The Who's best-selling rock opera, with standout musical performances by Clapton, John and Turner. Loss of stereophonic sound on TV may diminish film's effectiveness.

Tommy Steele Story, The SEE: Rock Around the World

Tomorrow (1972) 103m. ***½ D: Joseph Anthony. Robert Duvall, Olga Bellin, Sudie Bond, Richard McConnell, Peter Masterson, William Hawley. Overlooked Faulkner story about a handyman who cares for and eventually falls in love with an abandoned pregnant woman. Bellin is excellent, Duvall astonishingly good in best-ever screen presentation of the author's work.

Tomorrow at Ten (1964-British) 80m. **½ D: Lance Comfort. John Gregson, Robert Shaw, Alec Clunes, Alan Wheatley. Taut drama involving kidnapper of youth who dies leaving boy in house with time bomb set to explode.

Tomorrow Is Another Day (1951) 90m. **½ D: Felix E. Feist. Ruth Roman, Steve Cochran, Lurene Tuttle, Ray Teal, Morris Ankrum. Frank little film of ex-con Cochran marrying dime-a-dance girl Roman, heading for California, thinking he's killed her old boyfriend.

Tomorrow Is Forever (1946) 105m. *** D: Irving Pichel. Claudette Colbert, Orson Welles, George Brent, Lucile Watson, Richard Long, Natalie Wood. Weepy yarn of man (Welles) listed dead in war, returning with new face to find wife Colbert remarried to Brent. Bravura work by Welles with good support by Wood as his adopted daughter.

Tomorrow Never Comes (1977-Canadian-British) C-109m. ** D: Peter Collinson. Oliver Reed, Susan George, Raymond Burr, John Ireland, Stephen McHattie, Donald Pleasence. Young man goes bananas when he learns his girlfriend has been unfaithful, leading to violent standoff with police in busy resort town. Uninvolving melodrama.

Tomorrow the World (1944) 86m. ***½ D: Leslie Fenton. Fredric March, Betty Field, Agnes Moorehead, Skippy Homeier, Joan Carroll, Boots Brown. Thoughtful drama of American couple adopting German boy, trying to undo rigid Nazi influence in him.

Tonight and Every Night (1945) C-92m. *** D: Victor Saville. Rita Hayworth, Janet Blair, Lee Bowman, Marc Platt, Leslie Brooks, Professor Lamberti, Florence Bates. Entertaining wartime musical of British theater that never misses a performance, despite bombings and personal hardships. Try spotting Shelley Winters as one of the chorines.

Tonight at 8:30 (1952-British) C-81m. ***½ D: Anthony Pelissier. Valerie Hobson, Stanley Holloway, Nigel Patrick. Three Noel Coward playlets comprise this satirical study of English life. Retitled: MEET ME TONIGHT.

Tonight We Raid Calais (1943) 70m. **½ D: John Brahm. Annabella, John Sutton, Lee J. Cobb, Beulah Bondi, Blanche Yurka, Howard da Silva, Marcel Dalio. Fast-paced if undistinguished WW2 tale of sabotage mission in France with good performances by entire cast.

Tonight We Sing (1953) C-109m. **½ D: Mitchell Leisen. David Wayne, Ezio Pinza, Roberta Peters, Anne Bancroft. Hodgepodge supposedly based on impresario Sol Hurok's life, allowing for disjointed string of operatic/musical interludes.

Tonight's the Night (1954) C-88m. *** D: Mario Zampi. David Niven, Yvonne De Carlo, Barry Fitzgerald, George Cole, Robert Urquhart. Good British cast bolsters appealing comedy about house in Ireland which natives claim is haunted.

Tonka (1958) C-97m. **½ D: Lewis R. Foster. Sal Mineo, Philip Carey, Jerome Courtland, Rafael Campos, H. M. Wynant, Joy Page. Mineo stands out in this modest Disney film about an Indian brave's attachment to a wild horse, which he captures and tames. Weak resolution, and cut-rate version of Custer's Last Stand detract from promising story.

Tony Draws a Horse (1951-British) 90m. **½ D: John Paddy Carstairs. Cecil Parker, Anne Crawford, Derek Bond, Barbara Murray. Witty little film about parents bickering over proper psychology in dealing with their undisciplined child.

Tony Rome (1967) C-110m. **½ D: Gordon Douglas. Frank Sinatra, Jill St. John, Richard Conte, Sue Lyon, Gena Rowlands, Simon Oakland, Jeffrey Lynn, Lloyd Bochner, Lloyd Gough. Good cast in moderately diverting detective caper. Private-eye Rome (Sinatra) hired by millionaire (Oakland) to find out why his daughter would wind up drunk and unconscious in low-class Miami hotel. Beware cuts.

Too Bad She's Bad (1955-Italian) 95m. ** D: Alessandro Blasetti. Sophia Loren, Vittorio De Sica, Marcello Mastroianni, Lina Furia. Unremarkable little comedy about life and love among happy-go-lucky crooks, set in Rome.

Too Far to Go (1979) C-100m. TVM D: Fielder Cook. Michael Moriarty, Blythe Danner, Kathryn Walker, Ken Kercheval, Josef Sommer, Glenn Close. Moriarty and Danner bring distinction to this middling study of the dissolution of a marriage. Taken from 17 short stories by John Updike. Average.

Too Hot to Handle (1938) 105m. *** D: Jack Conway. Clark Gable, Myrna Loy, Walter Pidgeon, Leo Carrillo, Johnny Hines, Virginia Weidler. Gable & Pidgeon are rival newsreel photographers vying for aviatrix Loy in this fast-paced action-comedy; Gable's scene faking enemy attack on China is a gem.

Too Hot to Handle (1959-British) C-92m. ** D: Terence Young. Jayne Mansfield, Leo Genn, Carl Boehm. Seamy study of chanteuse Mansfield involved with one man too many in the nightclub circuit.

Too Late Blues (1962) 100m. ** D: John Cassavetes. Bobby Darin, Stella Stevens, Cliff Carnell, Seymour Cassel. Pretentious nonsense about jazz musician Darin involved with selfish dame Stevens.

Too Late for Tears (1949) 99m. **½ D: Byron Haskin. Lizabeth Scott, Don Defore, Dan Duryea, Arthur Kennedy, Kristine Miller. Scott goes after big money, but gets tangled with gangsters and murder; sturdy melodrama.

Too Late the Hero (1970) C-133m. *** D: Robert Aldrich. Michael Caine, Cliff Robertson, Henry Fonda, Ian Bannen, Harry Andrews, Denholm Elliott, Ronald Fraser. Two reluctant soldiers (Robertson, Caine) sent on suicide mission on Pacific island during WW2; turns into battle of wits between them and Japanese officer. Action-packed film builds to pulsating finale. Retitled SUICIDE RUN.

Too Many Crooks (1958-British) 85m. **½ D: Mario Zampi. Terry-Thomas, George Cole, Brenda De Banzie, Sydney Tafler. OK satire on racketeer films buoyed by Terry-Thomas' presence.

Too Many Girls (1940) 85m. *** D: George Abbott. Lucille Ball, Richard Carlson, Eddie Bracken, Ann Miller, Hal LeRoy, Desi Arnaz, Frances Langford. Engaging Rodgers-Hart musical comedy with winning cast, sharp dialogue. Four boys are hired to keep an eye on footloose Lucy at Pottawatomie College in Stopgap, New Mexico. Stagey presentation of musical numbers seems to work fine here; Van Johnson very noticeable as one of the chorus boys.

Too Many Husbands (1940) 84m. *** D: Wesley Ruggles. Jean Arthur, Fred MacMurray, Melvyn Douglas, Harry Davenport, Dorothy Peterson. Jean's about to marry Douglas when husband MacMurray, thought dead, turns up. Excellent comedy from Maugham's play HOME AND BEAUTY. Remade as THREE FOR THE SHOW.

Too Much Harmony (1933) 76m. **½ D: A. Edward Sutherland. Bing Crosby, Jack Oakie, Grace Bradley, Judith Allen, Lilyan Tashman, Ned Sparks. Pleasant, if plotty, backstage musical with some good song numbers, including "Thanks," "The Day You Came Along."

Too Much, Too Soon (1958) 121m. ** D: Art Napoleon. Dorothy Malone, Errol Flynn, Efrem Zimbalist, Jr., Ray Danton. But not enough, in sensationalistic tale of Diana Barrymore's decline. Flynn steals the show as John Barrymore.

Too Young to Kiss (1951) 91m. **½ D: Robert Z. Leonard. June Allyson, Van Johnson, Gig Young, Paula Corday. Allyson is fetching as pianist posing as child prodigy to get her big break falling in love with Johnson.

Too Young to Know (1945) 86m. ** D: Frederick de Cordova. Joan Leslie, Robert Hutton, Rosemary DeCamp, Dolores Moran. Slick, empty drama of career gal Leslie torn between husband and job.

Top Banana (1954) C-100m. *** D: Alfred E. Green. Phil Silvers, Rose Marie, Danny Scholl, Judy Lynn, Jack Albertson. Very funny comedy has Silvers as TV comic about to lose sponsor, his girl and peace of mind. Adapted from Broadway show.

Top Gun (1955) 73m. **½ D: Ray Nazarro. Sterling Hayden, William Bishop, Karin Booth, Regis Toomey, Rod Taylor, Denver Pyle. Fair movie with adequate-to-good cast of man cleared of murder and elected marshal.

Top Hat (1935) 105m. **** D: Mark Sandrich. Fred Astaire, Ginger Rogers, Edward Everett Horton, Helen Broderick, Eric Blore, Erik Rhodes. What can we say? Merely a knockout of a musical with Astaire and Rogers at their brightest doing "Cheek to Cheek," "Isn't This a Lovely Day to be Caught in the Rain," "Top Hat, White Tie, and Tails," other Irving Berlin songs, as the duo goes through typical mistaken-identity plot.

Top Man (1943) 74m. ** D: Charles Lamont. Donald O'Connor, Susanna Foster, Peggy Ryan, Richard Dix, Lillian Gish, Noah Beery Jr. Youthful O'Connor heads the family when Dad goes off to war; typical assembly-line musical comedy from Universal, with guest spots by Count Bassie, Borrah Minnevitch's Harmonica Rascals.

Top O' the Morning (1949) 100m. **½ D: David Miller. Bing Crosby, Barry Fitzgerald, Ann Blyth, Hume Cronyn, Eileen Crowe. Crosby-Fitzgerald malarkey is wearing thin in this fanciful musical of Bing searching for thief hiding the blarney stone.

Top of the World (1955) 90m. ** D: Lewis R. Foster. Dale Robertson, Evelyn Keyes, Frank Lovejoy, Nancy Gates. Set in Alaska, movie revolves around jet pilot Robertson, his ex-wife Keyes and her new boyfriend Lovejoy.

Top Secret (1978) C-100m. TVM D: Paul Leaf. Bill Cosby, Tracy Reed, Gloria Foster, Sheldon Leonard. Dated spy caper that even Cosby, as a hip American agent on the trail of stolen plutonium in Italy, cannot pump life into. Below average.

Top Secret Affair (1957) 100m. **½ D: H. C. Potter. Susan Hayward, Kirk Douglas, Paul Stewart, Jim Backus, John Cromwell. John P. Marquand's MELVILLE GOODWIN, U.S.A. becomes fair comedy, with most credit going to Hayward as fiery publisher who knows all about Senate appointee's (Douglas) past.

Topaz (1969) C-127m. *** D: Alfred Hitchcock. John Forsythe, Frederick Stafford, Dany Robin, John Vernon, Karin Dor, Michel Piccoli, Philippe Noiret, Claude Jade, Roscoe Lee Browne. French Intelligence agent Stafford works with American official Forsythe to dig out info on Russia's involvement in Cuba. Whirlwind plot circles globe, maintains intrigue level; good, not great Hitchcock, from Leon Uris' book.

Topaze (1933) 78m. *** D: Harry D'Arrast. John Barrymore, Myrna Loy, Albert Conti, Luis Alberni, Reginald Mason, Jobyna Howland. Delightful film adapted by Ben Hecht from Marcel Pagnol's play about an impeccably honest but naive schoolteacher in France who unwittingly becomes a dupe for wealthy Baron's business scheme. Barrymore is perfect in lead. Remade as I LIKE MONEY.

Topkapi (1964) C-120m. **** D: Jules Dassin. Melina Mercouri, Peter Ustinov, Maximilian Schell, Robert Morley, Akim Tamiroff, Despo Diamantidou. First-rate entertainment of would-be thieves who plan perfect crime in Constantinople museum; inspired, lighthearted caper has inspired many imitations. Filmed in Istanbul, with Ustinov's performance copping an Academy Award.

Topper (1937) 97m. ***½ D: Norman Z. McLeod. Constance Bennett, Cary Grant, Roland Young, Billie Burke, Alan Mowbray, Hedda Hopper, Eugene Pallette. Delightful gimmick comedy with ghosts Grant and Bennett dominating life of meek Young; sparkling cast in adaptation of Thorne Smith novel.

Topper (1979) C-100m. TVM D: Charles S. Dubin. Kate Jackson, Andrew Stevens, Jack Warden, Rue McClanahan, James Karen, Charles Siebert. Breezy updating of the 1937 classic. The two leads also produced this one, aiming for a new TOPPER TV series. Average.

Topper Returns (1941) 85m. *** D: Roy Del Ruth. Joan Blondell, Roland Young, Carole Landis, Billie Burke, Dennis O'Keefe, Patsy Kelly, Eddie "Rochester" Anderson. Topper becomes involved with a murder in the last of this series, with hilarious results; Blondell is his ghostly companion.

Topper Takes a Trip (1939) 85m. *** D: Norman Z. McLeod. Constance Bennett, Roland Young, Billie Burke, Alan Mowbray, Verree Teasdale, Franklin Pangborn. Cary Grant is missing, but TOPPER cast returns for repeat success as Young is frustrated on Riviera vacation by ghostess Bennett.

Tops Is the Limit SEE: **Anything Goes** (1936)

Tora! Tora! Tora! (1970-U.S.-Japanese) C-143m. *** D: Richard Fleischer, Toshio Masuda, Kinji Fukasaku. Martin Balsam, Soh Yamamura, Jason Robards, Joseph Cotten, Tatsuya Mihashi, E. G. Marshall, James Whitmore, Wesley Addy. Events leading up to Pearl Harbor attack, from American and Japanese points of view. Well-documented screenplay shows major and minor blundering on both sides, then recreates attack with frightening realism. Well-made film creates incredible tension.

Torch, The (1950-Mexican) 90m. ** D: Emilio Fernandez. Paulette Goddard, Pedro Armendariz, Gilbert Roland, Walter Reed. Mexican revolutionary captures town and falls for daughter of nobility. Script very uneven; fine photography.

Torch Song (1953) C-90m. *** D: Charles Walters. Joan Crawford, Michael Wilding, Marjorie Rambeau, Gig Young. Save for Wilding's poorly-conceived role as blind pianist, an untarnished account of Broadway musical star Crawford clawing to stay on top; beautiful acting by Rambeau as Joan's salty mother.

Tormented (1960) 75m. BOMB D: Bert I. Gordon. Richard Carlson, Juli Reding, Susan Gordon, Lugene Sanders, Joe Turkel, Lillian Adams. Low-budget hog-wash of guilt-ridden pianist dubious over his forthcoming marriage to society gal.

Torn Between Two Lovers (1979) C-100m. TVM D: Delbert Mann. Lee Remick, Joseph Bologna, George Peppard, Giorgio Tozzi, Molly Cheek. Romantic drama graced by ever-lovely Remick playing a married socialite who has an affair with a dashing architect she meets on a trip. Title comes from the hit song of the late '70s. Average.

Torn Curtain (1966) C-128m. **½ D: Alfred Hitchcock. Paul Newman, Julie Andrews, Lila Kedrova, David Opatoshu, Ludwig Donath. Oddly unmoving Hitchcock thriller about American scientist pretending to be defector. Slick but empty film. TV prints are cut to 121m., excising violent scenes—including an oven murder.

Torpedo Alley (1953) 84m. ** D: Lew Landers. Dorothy Malone, Mark Stevens, Charles Winninger, Bill Williams. Typical Korean War actioner involving U.S. submarine offensives.

Torpedo Bay (1964-Italian-French) 91m. **½ D: Charles Frend. James Mason, Lilli Palmer, Gabriele Ferzeti, Alberto Lupo, Geoffrey Keen. British and Italian naval crews meet each other on neutral territory during WW2; modest but fairly interesting drama.

Torpedo of Doom, The (1938) 100m. *** D: William Witney, John English. Lee Powell, Herman Brix (Bruce Bennett), Eleanor Stewart, Montagu Love, Hugh Sothern. Superior cliff-hanger from Republic's golden age of serials, involving dynamic duo of Marines undergoing innumerable obstacles to subdue a world-hungry scientist; quite actionful. Reedited movie serial: FIGHTING DEVIL DOGS.

Torpedo Run (1958) C-98m. **½ D: Joseph Pevney. Glenn Ford, Ernest Borgnine, Diane Brewster, Dean Jones. Sluggish WW2 revenge narrative of sub-commander Ford whose family was aboard Jap prison ship he had to blow up.

Torrid Zone (1940) 88m. ***½ D: William Keighley. James Cagney, Ann Sheridan, Pat O'Brien, Andy Devine, Helen Vinson, Jerome Cowan, George Tobias. South-of-the-border action and romance with nightclub star Sheridan coming between rivals O'Brien and Cagney. Zesty dialogue in this one is memorable.

Tortilla Flat (1942) 105m. *** D: Victor Fleming. Spencer Tracy, Hedy Lamarr, John Garfield, Frank Morgan, Akim Tamiroff, Donald Meek, John Qualen, Allen Jenkins. Steinbeck's salty novel of California fishing community vividly portrayed by three top stars, stolen by Morgan as devoted dog-lover.

Torture Chamber of Dr. Sadism, The (1967-German) C-90m. **½ D: Harald Reinl. Christopher Lee, Lex Barker, Karin Dor, Carl Lange, Vladimir Medar. A resurrected Lee seeks revenge on Barker and Dor; after luring them to his castle they are mentally and physically tortured. Based on Poe's PIT AND THE PENDULUM. Atmospheric, but not for the squeamish. Also known as THE BLOOD DEMON.

Torture Garden (1968-British) C-93m. **½ D: Freddie Francis. Jack Palance, Burgess Meredith, Beverly Adams, Peter Cushing, Barbara Ewing, Michael Bryant, Maurice Denham. Anthology horror film revolving around sideshow weirdie Dr. Diabolo (Meredith) with power to let curious visitors see and experience their near-future; each experience becomes film in itself. Good cast and production, but stories uneven; first and last tales best.

Touch, The (1971-U.S.-Swedish) C-112m. *½ D: Ingmar Bergman. Elliott Gould, Bibi Andersson, Max von Sydow, Sheila Reid. Bergman's first English-language film should be called THE TETCHED, in view of the fact that Andersson leaves doctor-husband Von Sydow for boorish Gould. The two Bergman regulars are fine, but Gould is miscast and dialogue embarrassingly awkward.

Touch and Go (1955-British) C-85m. **½ D: Michael Truman. Jack Hawkins, Margaret Johnston, Roland Culver, June Thorburn. Wry study of sturdy English family trying to overcome obstacles upsetting their planned emigration to Australia.

Touch of Class, A (1973) C-105m. ** D: Melvin Frank. George Segal, Glenda Jackson, Paul Sorvino, Hildegard Neil, Cec Linder, K. Callan, Mary Barclay. Undeniable chemistry of Segal and Jackson can only occasionally breathe life into this stale comedy about married man who intends nothing more than having a carefree affair, only to fall genuinely in love. Jackson won Best Actress Oscar.

Touch of Evil (1958) 93m. *** D: Orson Welles. Charlton Heston, Janet Leigh, Orson Welles, Joseph Calleia, Akim Tamiroff, Marlene Dietrich, Mercedes McCambridge, Zsa Zsa Gabor. Intriguing, if too slowly paced account of Mexican police official Heston and new wife Leigh involved in murder frameup; Dietrich most effective as fortune-telling cafe hostess. Welles' original 108m. version has recently been discovered, may turn up on TV.

Touch of Larceny, A (1959-British) 93m. *** D: Guy Hamilton. James Mason, George Sanders, Vera Miles, Oliver Johnston, William Kendall, Duncan Lamont. Ingenious comedy of officer who uses availability of military secrets to his advantage in off-beat plan.

Touchables, The (1968-British) C-97m. BOMB D: Robert Freeman. Judy Huxtable, Esther Anderson, Marilyn Richard, Kathy Simmonds. Dreary tale of four girls and a guy who try to kidnap pop singing idol. Terrible.

Tougher They Come, The (1950)

69m. *½ D: Ray Nazarro. Wayne Morris, Preston Foster, William Bishop, Kay Buckley. Trivial study of ruthless operators trying to take over lumber camp.

Toughest Gun in Tombstone (1958) 72m. *½ D: Earl Bellamy. George Montgomery, Beverly Tyler, Don Beddoe, Jim Davis. Weak shoot-out tale with Montgomery in the title role.

Toughest Man Alive, The (1955) 72m. ** D: Sidney Salkow. Dane Clark, Lita Milan, Ross Elliott, Myrna Dell, Syd Saylor, Anthony Caruso. Mild caper of tracking down gun-smuggling in South America.

Toughest Man in Arizona, The (1952) C-90m. **½ D: R. G. Springsteen. Vaughn Monroe, Joan Leslie, Edgar Buchanan, Victor Jory. While waging war on crime marshal Monroe falls for girl with expected results. Fairly well produced and acted.

Tourist Trap, The (1979) C-85m. BOMB D: David Schmoeller. Chuck Connors, Jon Van Ness, Jocelyn Jones, Robin Sherwood, Tanya Roberts, Keith McDermott. Shades of Roger Corman's BUCKET OF BLOOD: those life-size dummies in Connors' "museum" are strangely lifelike, aren't they? Not so much that the idiots he lures there ever catch on. Worthless thriller.

Tovarich (1937) 98m. *** D: Anatole Litvak. Claudette Colbert, Charles Boyer, Basil Rathbone, Anita Louise, Isabel Jeans, Morris Carnovsky. Boyer and Colbert, royal Russians, flee the Revolution with court treasury but nothing for themselves. Enjoyable but dated romantic comedy set in Paris.

Toward the Unknown (1956) C-115m. *** D: Mervyn LeRoy. William Holden, Lloyd Nolan, Virginia Leith, Charles McGraw. Intelligent narrative involving test pilots, focusing on air officer Holden eager to make his men respect him.

Tower of Evil SEE: **Horror on Snape Island**

Tower of London (1939) 92m. **½ D: Rowland V. Lee. Basil Rathbone, Boris Karloff, Barbara O'Neil, Ian Hunter, Vincent Price, Nan Grey, Leo G. Carroll. Muddled historical melodrama (not a horror film, as many believe), with Rathbone as unscrupulous, power-hungry Richard III and Karloff as his dutiful executioner Mord. Court intrigue leads to uninspired battle scenes.

Tower of London (1962) 79m. *½
D: Roger Corman. Vincent Price,
Michael Pate, Joan Freeman, Robert
Brown. Remake of 1939 film has
Price, who played Duke of Clarence
first time around, tackling role of
Richard III in a flat, papier-mâché
production.

Towering Inferno, The (1974) C-
165m. **½ D: John Guillermin and
Irwin Allen. Steve McQueen, Paul
Newman, William Holden, Faye
Dunaway, Fred Astaire, Susan Blakely, Richard Chamberlain, Jennifer
Jones, O. J. Simpson, Robert
Vaughn, Robert Wagner. All-star
idiocy about a burning building.
Purports to pay tribute to firemen
but spends most of its time devising
grisly ways for people to die. The
pyrotechnics are gripping, but the
movie is just another cold-blooded
Hollywood "product."

Town Like Alice, A (1956-British)
107m. **½ D: Jack Lee. Virginia
McKenna, Peter Finch, Maureen
Swanson, Vincent Ball. Taut WW2
tale, well acted, about Japanese oppression of stranded group of British
females. Retitled: RAPE OF MA-
LAYA.

Town on Trial (1956-British) 95m.
*½ D: John Guillermin. John Mills,
Charles Coburn, Barbara Bates, Elizabeth Seal. Restrained murder-hunt
story raking up the coals of a small
British town, as the police hunt the
girl's killer.

Town Tamer (1965) C-89m. ** D:
Lesley Selander. Dana Andrews,
Terry Moore, Pat O'Brien, Lon
Chaney, Bruce Cabot, Lyle Bettger,
Coleen Gray, Barton MacLane, Richard Arlen, Sonny Tufts. As title indicates, Andrews cleans up community, and among the rubble are some
veteran actors. Routine Western has
minor nostalgia value, in light of the
cast.

Town That Dreaded Sundown, The
(1977) C-90m. **½ D: Charles B.
Pierce. Ben Johnson, Andrew Prine,
Dawn Wells, Christine Ellsworth,
Charles B. Pierce. OK thriller made
from true story of a hooded killer
who terrorized town of Texarkana
in the mid-40s. Ben Johnson's presence gives it some stature.

Town Without Pity (1961) 105m. **½
D: Gottfried Reinhardt. Kirk Douglas, E. G. Marshall, Christine Kaufmann, Robert Blake, Richard Jaeckel,
Frank Sutton, Barbara Rutting.
Courtroom drama of G.I.s accused
of raping German girl. Decent cast,
but could have been better handled.

Toy Tiger (1956) C-88m. **½ D:
Jerry Hopper. Jeff Chandler, Laraine
Day, Tim Hovey, Cecil Kellaway.
Pleasant remake of MAD ABOUT
MUSIC with Hovey "adopting"
Chandler as his father to back up
tales to school chums about a real
dad. Day is Hovey's mother.

Toy Wife, The (1938) 95m. ** D:
Richard Thorpe. Luise Rainer, Melvyn Douglas, Robert Young, Barbara
O'Neil, H. B. Warner, Alma Kruger,
Libby Taylor. Southern belle Rainer
is pursued by Young and Douglas,
can't decide which one to marry; inconsequential confection.

Toys in the Attic (1963) 90m. **½
D: George Roy Hill. Dean Martin,
Geraldine Page, Yvette Mimieux,
Wendy Hiller, Gene Tierney, Nan
Martin. Timid adaptation of Hellman
play about man returning home with
childlike bride; Page and Hiller are
Martin's overprotective sisters.

Track of the Cat (1954) C-102m. **
D: William Wellman. Robert Mitchum, Teresa Wright, Tab Hunter,
Diana Lynn, Beulah Bondi. Slow-
moving film of cougar hunt and family difficulties. Photography is main
asset.

Track of the Moon Beast (1976) C-
90m. BOMB D: Richard Ashe.
Chase Cordell, Donna Leigh Drake,
Gregorio Sala, Patrick Wright.
Young man becomes a hideous monster because of meteor fragment
lodged in his body. Good horror
makeup, but lousy film.

Track of Thunder (1968) C-83m. **
D: Joseph Kane. Tom Kirk, Ray
Stricklyn, H. M. Wynant. Average
melodrama of feuding small-time
stock car racers.

Track the Man Down (1955-British)
75m. ** D: R. G. Springsteen. Kent
Taylor, Petula Clark, Renee Houston, George Rose. Dog-tracking
background makes this standard
Scotland Yard murder hunt above
par.

Trackdown (1976) C-98m. **½ D:
Richard T. Heffron. Jim Mitchum,
Karen Lamm, Anne Archer, Erik
Estrada, Cathy Lee Crosby, Vince
Cannon. Montana rancher Mitchum
comes to L.A. in search of his runaway sister, who's fallen into seamy
street life. Not much depth but lots
of action.

Trackers, The (1971) C-73m. TVM

D: Earl Bellamy. Sammy Davis, Jr., Ernest Borgnine, Julie Adams, Connie Kreski, Jim Davis. Fair chase drama sprinkled with character portraits: Borgnine as vengeful rancher, out to get men who killed son and kidnapped daughter, scornful of black professional tracker who doesn't mind telling employer what he thinks about him. Otherwise, resolution unsatisfying. Average.

Trade Winds (1938) 90m. *** D: Tay Garnett. Fredric March, Joan Bennett, Ralph Bellamy, Ann Sothern, Sidney Blackmer, Thomas Mitchell. Debonair detective March goes after murder-suspect Bennett; by the end of the around-the-world chase, they fall in love and solve mystery.

Trader Horn (1931) 120m. *** D: W. S. Van Dyke II. Harry Carey, Edwina Booth, Duncan Renaldo, Olive Golden (Carey), Mutia Omoolu, C. Aubrey Smith. Early talkie classic filmed largely in African jungles still retains plenty of excitement in tale of veteran native dealer Carey encountering tribal hostility.

Trader Horn (1973) C-105m. *½ D: Reza S. Badiyi. Rod Taylor, Anne Heywood, Jean Sorel, Don Knight, Ed Bernard, Stack Pierce. Laughable remake of 1931 version has Taylor famed explorer and trader of African interior, accompanied by young widow. Obvious use of stock footage and the fact that cast never leaves backlot ruins all notion of believability.

Trader Tom of the China Seas SEE: Target, Sea of China

Traffic (1972-French) C-89m. ** D: Jacques Tati. Jacques Tati, Maria Kimberly, Marcel Fraval, H. Bostel, Tony Kneppers. Initially enjoyable outing with M. Hulot (Tati) trying to transport car from France to Dutch auto show bogs down in aimless side trips. Bright spots overwhelmed by general lethargy.

Trail of the Lonesome Pine (1936) C-102m. *** D: Henry Hathaway. Sylvia Sidney, Henry Fonda, Fred MacMurray, Fred Stone, Fuzzy Knight, Beulah Bondi, Spanky MacFarland, Nigel Bruce. Classic story of feuding families and changes that come about when railroad is built on their land. Still remarkably strong today, with fine performances. Touted as first outdoor film in full Technicolor.

Trail of the Vigilantes (1940) 78m.

**½ D: Allan Dwan. Franchot Tone, Broderick Crawford, Peggy Moran, Andy Devine. Tone is Eastern law enforcer out West to hunt down outlaw gang; lively comedy-Western.

Trail Street (1947) 84m. ** D: Ray Enright. Randolph Scott, Robert Ryan, Anne Jeffreys, George "Gabby" Hayes, Madge Meredith, Steve Brodie. Scott stars as Bat Masterson, saving local townspeople from corrupt rule; standard oater, nothing more.

Train, The (1965) 113m. **** D: John Frankenheimer. Burt Lancaster, Paul Scofield, Michel Simon, Jeanne Moreau, Albert Remy, Wolfgang Preiss. Gripping WW2 actioner of French Resistance trying to waylay train carting French art treasures to Germany. High-powered excitement all the way.

Train Robbers, The (1973) C-92m. *½ D: Burt Kennedy. John Wayne, Ann-Margret, Rod Taylor, Ben Johnson, Christopher George, Ricardo Montalban. Title pretty much explains this poor Wayne Western that looks as if it were shot in three days for some quick cash; Ann-Margret comes off best.

Train Robbery Confidential (1962-Brazilian) 102m. **½ D: Roberto Farias. Eliezer Gomes, Reginaldo Farias, Grande Otelo, Atila Iorio. Labored account of six men involved in railroad heist, with disintegration of friendship due to greed.

Trained to Kill (1975) C-91m. *½ D: Daniel J. Vance. Stephen Sandor, Rockne Tarkington, Richard X. Slattery, Heidi Vaughn, Michael Lane. A Vietnam vet is forced to confront a sadistic gang in his home town; low-grade, graphically violent drama, made in 1973 as THE NO MERCY MAN.

Traitors, The (1963-British) 71m. **½ D: Robert Tronson. Patrick Allen, James Maxwell, Zena Walker, Harold Goodwin, Sean Lynch. Fair spy meller of U.S. and British agent assigned to catch source of security leak in NATO.

Traitor's Gate (1955-British) 80m. **½ D: Freddie Francis. Gary Raymond, Albert Lieven, Margot Trooger, Catherina Von Schell. Two brothers are involved at sea in plot to steal crown jewels. Based on Edgar Wallace novel, film has fair acting, good direction.

Tramp, Tramp, Tramp (1942) 70m.

**½ D: Charles Barton. Jackie Gleason, Florence Rice, Jack Durant, Bruce Bennett. Meager comedy as Gleason and Durant, 4-F rejects, protect the homefront, becoming involved in murder caper.

Tramplers, The (1966-Italian) **C-105m. ** D:** Albert Band. Joseph Cotten, Gordon Scott, James Mitchum, Ilaria Occhini. Foreign-made Western in post-Civil War South, with Cotten the domineering father; all just an excuse for gun-play.

Transatlantic Merry-Go-Round (1934) **92m. ** D:** Ben Stoloff. Jack Benny, Nancy Carroll, Gene Raymond, Sidney Blackmer, Patsy Kelly, Mitzi Green, Boswell Sisters. Whodunit set against musical story of oceangoing radio troupe led by Benny. Just fair, with some odd production numbers, and a plot resolution that's for the birds.

Transatlantic Tunnel (1935-British) **94m. **½ D:** Maurice Elvey. Richard Dix, Leslie Banks, Madge Evans, Helen Vinson, C. Aubrey Smith, George Arliss, Walter Huston. Disappointing story about building of transatlantic tunnel bogs down in two-dimensional character conflicts. Futuristic sets are main distinction. Originally titled THE TUNNEL.

Transplant (1979) **C-100m. TVM D:** William A. Graham. Kevin Dobson, Melinda Dillon, Granville Van Dusen, Ronny Cox, Bibi Besch. Hard-driving young executive with weak heart agonizes over whether to undergo a transplant. Average.

Trap, The (1947) **68m. D:** Howard Bretherton. Sidney Toler, Mantan Moreland, Victor Sen Yung, Tanis Chandler, Larry Blake, Kirk Alyn, Rita Quigley, Anne Nagel. SEE: Charlie Chan series.

Trap, The (1959) **C-84m. **½ D:** Norman Panama. Richard Widmark, Lee J. Cobb, Tina Louise, Earl Holliman, Carl Benton Reid, Lorne Greene. Turgid drama set in Southwest desert town, with gangsters on the lam intimidating the few townspeople.

Trap, The (1966-British) **C-106m. *** D:** Sidney Hayers. Rita Tushingham, Oliver Reed, Rex Sevenoaks, Barbara Chilcott, Linda Goranson. Fur trapper Reed, having missed annual wife auction after three winters in the snow, settles for orphaned mute Rita. Vivid 1890s tale, well photographed by Robert Krasker.

Trapeze (1956) **C-105m. *** D:** Carol Reed. Burt Lancaster, Tony Curtis, Gina Lollobrigida, Katy Jurado. Moody love triangle with a European circus background; aerialist Lancaster and Curtis vie in the air and on the ground for Gina's attention.

Trapped (1949) **78m. **½ D:** Richard Fleischer. Lloyd Bridges, Barbara Payton, John Hoyt, James Todd. Narrative-style of federal agent manhunt against counterfeit gang; tightly edited.

Trapped (1973) **C-74m. TVM D:** Frank De Filittia. James Brolin, Susan Clark, Earl Holliman, Tammy Harrington, Robert Hooks, Ivy Jones, Bob Hastings. Man mugged in department store bathroom awakens to find he's been locked in overnight, attacked by security dogs. Good premise gone awry, thanks to faulty script and subplot. Average.

Trapped Beneath the Sea (1974) **C-100m. TVM D:** William A. Graham. Lee J. Cobb, Martin Balsam, Paul Michael Glaser, Cliff Potts, Laurie Prange, Joshua Bryant. Drama about efforts to rescue crew of four stranded in a mini-sub off Florida coast. Based on an actual event of June 17, 1973, and tautly told. Above average.

Trapped by Boston Blackie (1948) **67m. D:** Seymour Friedman. Chester Morris, June Vincent, Richard Lane, Patricia White (Barry), Edward Norris, George E. Stone. SEE: **Boston Blackie** series.

Trapped in Tangiers (1960-Italian) **74m. BOMB D:** Antonio Cervi. Edmund Purdom, Genevieve Page, Gino Cervi, Jose Guadiola, Felix Bafauce, Antonio Molino. Dubbed dialog kills otherwise unsophisticated actioner of American uncovering dope ring in Tangiers.

Trauma (1962) **92m. ** D:** Robert Malcolm Young. John Conte, Lynn Bari, Lorre Richards, David Garner, Warren Kemmerling, William Bissell. Heavy-handed chiller involving Richards' attempt to recover lost memory of past horrors in spooky mansion.

Traveling Executioner, The (1970) **C-95m. *½ D:** Jack Smight. Stacy Keach, Marianna Hill, Bud Cort, Graham Jarvis, James J. Sloyan. Story of a man's love for an electric chair (spiritual) and love for a woman prisoner (sexual) may or may not be intended for laughs; either way, film is dull and the usually fine Keach gives hammy performance.

Traveling Saleswoman (1950) 75m. ** D: Charles F. Riesner. Joan Davis, Andy Devine, Adele Jergens, Chief Thundercloud. Davis and Devine mug it up as soap saleswoman and fiancé in stale Western comedy.

Travels with My Aunt (1972) C-109m. **½ D: George Cukor. Maggie Smith, Alec McCowen, Lou Gossett, Robert Stephens, Cindy Williams. Stylish adaptation of Graham Greene book about straitlaced McCowen being swept into crazy world of his aunt (Smith) who takes him all over Europe on what turns out to be shady scheme. Deliberately paced film never really gets going, leaves viewer in midair like final tossed coin.

Travis Logan, D.A. (1970) C-100m. TVM D: Paul Wendkos. Vic Morrow, Hal Holbrook, Brenda Vaccaro, George Grizzard, Scott Marlowe. Barely clever attempt by man to plan perfect murder thwarted by central character Logan (Morrow), enlivened by somewhat offbeat direction. Average.

Treasure Island (1934) 105m. ***½ D: Victor Fleming. Wallace Beery, Jackie Cooper, Lewis Stone, Lionel Barrymore, Otto Kruger, Nigel Bruce, Douglass Dumbrille. Stirring adaptation of Robert Louis Stevenson pirate yarn of 18th-century England and journey to isle of hidden bounty; Beery is a boisterous Long John Silver in fine film with top production values. Only flaw is a stiff young Cooper as Jim Hawkins.

Treasure Island (1950) C-96m. ***½ D: Byron Haskin. Bobby Driscoll, Robert Newton, Basil Sydney, Walter Fitzgerald, Denis O'Dea, Ralph Truman, Finlay Currie. Vivid Disney version of Robert Louis Stevenson's classic, filmed in England, with Driscoll a fine Jim Hawkins and Newton the definitive Long John Silver. Changes the novel's original ending, but who's quibbling?

Treasure Island (1972-British) C-94m. ** D: John Hough. Orson Welles, Kim Burfield, Walter Slezak, Lionel Stander. Weak retelling of classic tale finds very hammy Welles in the role of Long John Silver.

Treasure of Lost Canyon, The (1952) C-82m. ** D: Ted Tetzlaff. William Powell, Julia Adams, Rosemary DeCamp, Charles Drake, Tommy Ivo. Mild Western uplifted by Powell as old prospector. Youth uncovers treasure which causes unhappiness to all.

Treasure of Matecumbe (1976) C-117m. **½ D: Vincent McEveety. Robert Foxworth, Joan Hackett, Peter Ustinov, Vic Morrow, Johnny Doran, Billy "Pop" Attmore. Two boys with treasure map are aided in their quest by Foxworth, Hackett, and Ustinov . . . and pursued by bad-guy Morrow. Ustinov adds life to Disney film, but the "quest" seems endless.

Treasure of Monte Cristo, The (1960-British) C-95m. ** D: Robert S. Baker, Monty Berman. Rory Calhoun, Patricia Bredin, Peter Arne, Gianna Maria Canale. Uninspired variation on Dumas tale, with Calhoun aiding Bredin unearth buried treasure; slow-moving yarn.

Treasure of Pancho Villa, The (1955) C-96m. *½ D: George Sherman. Rory Calhoun, Shelley Winters, Gilbert Roland, Joseph Calleia. Good cast wasted in plodding account of famed 1910s Mexican bandit.

Treasure of Ruby Hills (1955) 71m. *½ D: Frank McDonald. Zachary Scott, Carole Mathews, Barton MacLane, Dick Foran, Lola Albright. Uninspired Western of land-grabbing ranchers.

Treasure of San Gennaro, The (1966-Italian-German-French) C-102m. ** D: Dino Risi. Nino Manfredi, Senta Berger, Harry Guardino, Claudine Auger, Toto, Mario Adorf. American Guardino and girlfriend Berger plan to rob the treasure of Naples' patron saint, San Gennaro, in typical caper film occasionally redeemed by good comic bits. Poorly dubbed.

Treasure of Silver Lake, The (1965-German) C-88m. ** D: Harald Reinl. Lex Barker, Gotz George, Pierre Brice, Herbert Lom, Karin Dor, Marianne Hoppe. Dubbed dialogue almost ruins average Western based on Karl May novels with familiar characters Shatterhand and Winnetou.

Treasure of the Golden Condor (1953) C-93m. **½ D: Delmer Daves. Cornel Wilde, Constance Smith, Fay Wray, Anne Bancroft, Leo G. Carroll, Bobby Blake. Predictable costumer set in 18th-century Latin America, with noble-born Wilde out to claim his fortune. Remake of SON OF FURY.

Treasure of the Sierra Madre, The (1948) 124m. **** D: John Huston.

Humphrey Bogart, Walter Huston, Tim Holt, Bruce Bennett, Barton MacLane, Alfonso Bedoya. Excellent story of gold-prospecting greed, and human nature at its worst, with Bogart, Huston, and Holt as unlikely trio of prospectors. John Huston won Oscars for Best Direction and Screenplay, and his father Walter won as Best Supporting Actor. (That's John as an American tourist near the beginning, and young Robert Blake as a beggar.)

Tree Grows in Brooklyn, A (1945) 128m. ***½ D: Elia Kazan. Dorothy McGuire, Joan Blondell, James Dunn, Lloyd Nolan, Peggy Ann Garner, Ted Donaldson, James Gleason, Ruth Nelson, John Alexander. Sensitive film of Betty Smith's novel of young girl Garner struggling in unhappy family atmosphere; Dunn won Oscar for performance as alcoholic father, Garner received a special Oscar for hers.

Tree Grows in Brooklyn, A (1974) C-78m. TVM D: Joseph Hardy. Cliff Robertson, Diane Baker, James Olson, Pamelyn Ferdin, Nancy Malone, Allyn Ann McLerie, Michael-James Wixted. Lovingly made remake of the 1945 classic with a sterling performance by Robertson and fine work by the others. Above average.

Trent's Last Case (1952-British) 90m. **½ D: Herbert Wilcox. Michael Wilding, Margaret Lockwood, Orson Welles, Hugh McDermott. Superior cast in lukewarm tale of the investigation of businessman's suicide.

Trial (1955) 105m. *** D: Mark Robson. Glenn Ford, Dorothy McGuire, John Hodiak, Arthur Kennedy, Katy Jurado, Rafael Campos. Intelligent filming of Don Mankiewicz novel. Courtroomer involves Mexican boy accused of murder, but actually tied in with pro- vs. anti-communist politics.

Trial, The (1963-French-Italian-German) 118m. ***½ D: Orson Welles. Anthony Perkins, Jeanne Moreau, Romy Schneider, Elsa Martinelli, Orson Welles, Akim Tamiroff. Gripping, if somewhat muddled, adaptation of Kafka novel of man in nameless country arrested for crime that is never explained to him. Not for all tastes.

Trial by Combat SEE: **Dirty Knight's Work**

Trial of Billy Jack, The (1974) C-175m. *½ D: Frank Laughlin. Tom Laughlin, Delores Taylor, Victor

Izay, Teresa Laughlin, William Wellman, Jr., Sacheen Littlefeather. Further adventures of Mr. Peace-through-Violence prove that Laughlin is the only actor intense enough to risk a hernia from reading lines.

Trial of Chaplain Jensen, The (1975) C-78m. TVM D: Robert Day. James Franciscus, Joanna Miles, Lynda Day George, Dorothy Tristan, Charles Durning, Harris Yulin. Franciscus is the only U.S. Navy officer ever court-martialed for adultery. True but trite. Average.

Trial of Lee Harvey Oswald, The (1977) C-210m. TVM D: David Greene. Ben Gazzara, Lorne Greene, John Pleshette, Mo Malone, Frances Lee McCain, Lawrence Pressman, Marisa Pavan. Intriguing courtroom drama from the "what if?" school of story-telling. Pleshette is quite good as Oswald, who may or may not have been involved in any of the Kennedy assassination conspiracy theories (including several that are quite bizarre), which are explored here. Above average.

Trial Run (1969) C-98m. TVM D: William Graham. James Franciscus, Leslie Nielsen, Diane Baker, Janice Rule, John Vernon, David Sheiner, Fred Beir. Cynical, near-brilliant look at high-priced modern-day lawyers. Louis Coleman (Franciscus) will stop at nothing for status in Forbes & Harkness firm. Some overly flashy direction, one lop-sided sequence, but strong drama nonetheless. Above average.

Triangle Factory Fire, The (1979) C-100m. TVM D: Mel Stuart. Tom Bosley, David Dukes, Tovah Feldshuh, Janet Margolin, Stephanie Zimbalist, Lauren Front. How to turn a real-life catastrophe (the turn-of-the-century fire that revolutionized working conditions and fire regulations) into a perfectly dull soap opera. Average.

Tribe, The (1974) C-78m. TVM D: Richard A. Colla. Victor French, Warren Vanders, Henry Wilcoxon, Adriana Shaw, Stewart Moss, Sam Gilman, Meg Wylie. Offbeat drama about cave men, with group of Cro-Magnons battling vicious Neanderthals at the dawn of history. Beside ONE MILLION B.C. these folks are Rhodes scholars. Below average.

Tribes (1970) C-74m. TVM D: Joseph Sargent. Darren McGavin, Jan-Michael Vincent, Earl Holliman, John Gruber. Marine drill instructor has tough time dealing with long-hair (Vincent). Weird mix of social commentary, comedy, drama with McGavin miscast as instructor. Above average.

Tribute to a Bad Man (1956) C-95m. *** D: Robert Wise. James Cagney, Don Dubbins, Stephen McNally, Irene Papas. Cagney is the whole show in this Western about a resourceful, ruthless land baron using any means possible to retain his vast possessions.

Trick Baby (1973) C-89m. ** D: Larry Yust. Kiel Martin, Mel Stewart, Dallas Edwards Hayes, Beverly Ballard. Con-man who passes for white uses trickery to cash in on society. Usual black exploitation film.

Trilogy of Terror (1975) C-78m. TVM D: Dan Curtis. Karen Black, Robert Burton, John Karlen, George Gaynes, James Storm, Gregory Harrison, Kathryn Reynolds. Karen plays four tormented women in three exercises in the bizarre by writer Richard Matheson. Best: the third, "Prey,"—has devil doll hounding her to death. This segment alone is worth your time. Above average.

Trio (1950-British) 91m. ***½ D: Ken Annakin, Herbert French. Nigel Patrick, Jean Simmons, Wilfrid Hyde-White, Roland Culver, Michael Rennie, Felix Aylmer. Absorbing adaptation of three Somerset Maugham stories. Acting very fine throughout; last story weakest of three.

Trip, The (1967) C-85m. ** D: Roger Corman. Peter Fonda, Susan Strasberg, Bruce Dern, Dennis Hopper. Spaced-out tale of one man's hallucinations while under the influence of L.S.D. Colorful but meaningless.

Triple Cross (1967-French-British) C-126m. ** D: Terence Young. Christopher Plummer, Yul Brynner, Romy Schneider, Trevor Howard, Gert Frobe, Claudine Auger. Adequate WW2 spy yarn features Plummer as British safecracker who works both sides of fence. A bit too long.

Triple Deception (1956-British) C-85m. ** D: Guy Green. Michael Craig, Julia Arnall, Brenda De Banzie, Geoffrey Keen, Eric Pohlmann, Patrick Westwood. On-location filming in France enhances murder tale with Craig the wily imposter caught in his own web.

Triple Echo (1973-British) C-90m. *** D: Michael Apted. Glenda Jackson, Oliver Reed, Brian Deacon, Jenny Lee Wright. High-powered

talent in sensitive story of transvestite in English countryside of WW2. Young Deacon, an army deserter, is persuaded by lonely farm woman Jackson to pose as her sister, then tough tank Sgt. Reed becomes involved. Retitled SOLDIER IN SKIRTS.

Triple Trouble (1950) 66m. D: Jean Yarbrough. Leo Gorcey, Huntz Hall, Gabriel Dell, Lyn Thomas, George Chandler, Bernard Gorcey. SEE: Bowery Boys series.

Tripoli (1950) C-95m. ** D: Will Price. John Payne, Maureen O'Hara, Howard da Silva, Connie Gilchrist. Good cast cannot save average script of U.S. marines battling Barbary pirates in 1805; sole standout is Howard da Silva.

Triumph of Hercules, The (1964-Italian) C-90m. ** D: Alberto De Martino. Dan Vadis, Moira Orfei, Pierre Cressoy, Marilu Tolo, Piero Lupi. Average gymnastic run-through with Vadis more resourceful than most Hercules.

Triumph of the Ten Gladiators (1964-Italian) C-94m. ** D: Nick Nostro. Dan Vadis, Helga Line, Stanley Kent, Gianni Rizzo, Halina Zalewska, John Heston. If not strong on plot, film allows for exuberances of swordplay and knockout brawls; set in ancient Rome.

Triumph of the Will (1935-German) 110m. **** D: Leni Riefenstahl. Riefenstahl's infamous documentary on Hitler's 1934 Nuremberg rallies is rightly regarded as the greatest propaganda film of all time. Fascinating and (of course) frightening to see.

Trog (1970-British) C-91m. BOMB D: Freddie Francis. Joan Crawford, Michael Gough, Kim Braden, David Griffin, John Hamill. Missing Link discovered by anthropologist Crawford naturally gets loose and does its thing. Do yours—don't watch it. This was Crawford's last film.

Trojan Horse, The (1962-Italian) C-105m. **½ D: Giorgio Ferroni. Steve Reeves, John Drew Barrymore, Hedy Vessel, Juliette Mayniel. Above-average production values and Barrymore's presence in role of Ulysses inflates stale tale of otherwise stale version of Homer's epic.

Trojan Women, The (1972-Greek-U.S.) C-105m. BOMB D: Michael Cacoyannis. Katharine Hepburn, Irene Papas, Vanessa Redgrave, Genevieve Bujold, Patrick Magee.

Euripides tragedy of women of Troy and their plight when Trojan army was defeated is so mangled that even the presence of four brilliant actresses can't untangle the mess.

Trooper Hook (1957) 81m. **½ D: Charles Marquis Warren. Joel McCrea, Barbara Stanwyck, Earl Holliman, Susan Kohner, Sheb Wooley, Celia Lovsky. Woman scorned by whites for having lived with Indians and having child by the chief, begins anew with cavalry officer.

Tropic Holiday (1938) 78m. **½ D: Theodore Reed. Dorothy Lamour, Ray Milland, Martha Raye, Bob Burns, Tito Guizar. Non-message fun musical set in Mexico, with perky performances by all.

Tropic of Cancer (1970) C-87m. **** D: Joseph Strick. Rip Torn, James Callahan, Ellen Burstyn, David Bauer, Laurence Ligneres, Phil Brown. Unlikely candidate for TV; X-rated, flavorful adaptation of Henry Miller's diary of survival in Paris. Successfully captures Miller's lusty point of view, and seamy portrait of Parisian life. Also, quite funny.

Tropic Zone (1953) C-94m. *½ D: Lewis R. Foster. Ronald Reagan, Rhonda Fleming, Estelita, Noah Beery. Blah actioner set in South America with Reagan fighting the good cause to save a banana plantation from outlaws.

Trottie True SEE: Gay Lady, The

Trouble Along the Way (1953) 110m. **½ D: Michael Curtiz. John Wayne, Donna Reed, Charles Coburn, Sherry Jackson, Marie Windsor. Unusually sentimental Wayne vehicle casts him as divorced man trying to maintain custody of his daughter (Jackson), who earns back self-respect by coaching football team for small Catholic school.

Trouble at 16 SEE: Platinum High School

Trouble Comes to Town (1972) C-74m. TVM D: Daniel Petrie. Lloyd Bridges, Pat Hingle, Hari Rhodes, Janet MacLachlan, Sheree North, Thomas Evans, Joe Bottoms. Southern Sheriff (Bridges), against protests of blacks and whites, takes in son of man who saved his life in Korea, eventually leading to strained situation. Better-than-average script by David Westheimer, good casting of important role, intelligent resolution. Above average.

Trouble for Two (1936) 75m. *** D:

J. Walter Ruben. Robert Montgomery, Rosalind Russell, Frank Morgan, Reginald Owen, Louis Hayward. Unique, offbeat film of Montgomery and Russell joining London Suicide Club; based on chilling Robert Louis Stevenson story.

Trouble in Paradise (1932) 83m. **** D: Ernst Lubitsch. Kay Francis, Miriam Hopkins, Herbert Marshall, Charles Ruggles, Edward Everett Horton, C. Aubrey Smith. Sparkling Lubitsch froth about chic Francis mixed up with con-artist couple (Marshall and Hopkins) in Paris. A witty, delightful classic.

Trouble in Store (1953-British) 85m. **½ D: John Paddy Carstairs. Margaret Rutherford, Norman Wisdom, Moira Lister, Megs Jenkins. Full of fun sight gags and good character actors, film traces ups-and-downs of naive department store worker.

Trouble in the Glen (1953-British) C-91m. ** D: Herbert Wilcox. Margaret Lockwood, Orson Welles, Forrest Tucker, Victor McLaglen. Scottish-based drama of feud over closing of road that has been used for a long time. Average-to-poor script benefits from Welles.

Trouble Makers (1948) 69m. D: Reginald LeBorg. Leo Gorcey, Huntz Hall, Gabriel Dell, Helen Parrish, Lionel Stander, Frankie Darro. SEE: Bowery Boys series.

Trouble Man (1972) C-99m. ** D: Ivan Dixon. Robert Hooks, Paul Winfield, Ralph Waite, William Smithers, Paula Kelly, Julius W. Harris. Hooks is superslick black troubleshooter caught in gang warfare. Cliché-ridden script includes about four hundred killings, glorifying underworld life. Well-made but tasteless.

Trouble With Angels, The (1966) C-112m. **½ D: Ida Lupino. Rosalind Russell, Hayley Mills, June Harding, Binnie Barnes, Mary Wickes, Gypsy Rose Lee. Cutesy study of Pennsylvania convent school, with students Mills and Harding driving mother superior Russell to distraction. Episodic, occasionally touching comedy. Followed by sequel WHERE ANGELS GO . . . TROUBLE FOLLOWS.

Trouble with Girls, The (1969) C-104m. **½ D: Peter Tewksbury. Elvis Presley, Marlyn Mason, Nicole Jaffe, Sheree North, Edward Andrews, John Carradine, Vincent Price. One of the better Presley ve-

hicles has Elvis as manager of a Chautauqua company in the 1920s; film has nice feeling for the period.
Trouble with Harry, The (1955) C-99m. *** D: Alfred Hitchcock. Shirley MacLaine, John Forsythe, Edmund Gwenn, Mildred Natwick, Mildred Dunnock. Offbeat, often hilarious black comedy courtesy Mr. Hitchcock about murdered man causing all sorts of problems for peaceful neighbors in New England community. Gwenn is fine as usual, MacLaine appealing in her first film.
Trouble with Women, The (1947) 80m. ** D: Sidney Lanfield. Ray Milland, Teresa Wright, Brian Donlevy, Rose Hobart, Charles Smith, Lewis Russell. Professor Milland announces that women like to be treated rough; you can guess the rest of this tame comedy.
Troublemaker, The (1964) 80m. ***½ D: Theodore Flicker. Tom Aldredge, Joan Darling, Theodore Flicker, Buck Henry, Godfrey Cambridge, Al Freeman, Jr. Hilarious offbeat story of country boy trying to set up coffee house in Greenwich Village. Very fine performances, great direction. Catch this one.
Truck Turner (1974) C-91m. *½ D: Jonathan Kaplan. Isaac Hayes, Yaphet Kotto, Alan Weeks, Annazette Chase, Sam Laws, Nichelle Nichols. Extremely violent black exploiter, with Hayes only distinguishing feature as a skip-tracer (a detective who hunts bail jumpers). His original score is familiar.
True Confession (1937) 85m. *½ D: Wesley Ruggles. Carole Lombard, Fred MacMurray, John Barrymore, Una Merkel, Porter Hall, Edgar Kennedy, Lynne Overman. Alarmingly unfunny "comedy" about pathological liar Lombard and the trouble she causes for herself and good-natured husband MacMurray. Remade with Betty Hutton as CROSS MY HEART.
True Grit (1969) C-128m. *** D: Henry Hathaway. John Wayne, Glen Campbell, Kim Darby, Jeremy Slate, Robert Duvall, Strother Martin, Dennis Hopper, Jeff Corey. Film version of Charles Portis's wonderful novel about an over-the-hill marshal who helps 14-year-old track down her father's killer. Not as good as the book, but Wayne's Oscar-winning performance and rousing last half-hour make it fine screen entertainment.

True Grit (1978) C-100m. TVM D: Richard T. Heffron. Warren Oates, Lisa Pelikan, Lee Meriwether, James Stephens, Jeff Osterhage, Lee H. Montgomery, Ramon Bieri. The further adventures of Rooster Cogburn put Oates in the unfortunate position of trying to fill the Duke's boots in this busted series pilot. Average.
True Story of Jesse James, The (1957) C-92m. **½ D: Nicholas Ray. Robert Wagner, Jeffrey Hunter, Hope Lange, Agnes Moorehead, John Carradine, Frank Gorshin. Offbeat version of traditional story, with Wagner as Jesse and Hunter as Frank James; highlighted by sequence of Great Northfield Minnesota Raid.
True Story of Lynn Stuart, The (1958) 78m. **½ D: Lewis Seiler. Betsy Palmer, Jack Lord, Barry Atwater, Kim Spaulding. Modest, straightforward account of housewife Palmer posing as gun moll to trap gang.
True to Life (1943) 94m. *** D: George Marshall. Mary Martin, Franchot Tone, Dick Powell, Victor Moore, Mabel Paige. Engaging comedy of radio writer Powell going to live with "typical" American family to get material for his soap opera.
True to the Army (1942) 76m. ** D: Albert S. Rogell. Allan Jones, Ann Miller, Judy Canova, Jerry Colonna. Zany nonsense erupts when military life and romance clash; loud WW2 escapism.
True to the Navy (1930) 71m. **½ D: Frank Tuttle. Clara Bow, Fredric March, Sam Hardy, Eddie Featherstone, Jed Prouty. Enjoyable early-talkie with aggressive young sailor March wooing soda-fountain waitress Bow; the two make a good team.
Trunk, The (1960-British) 72m. *½ D: Donovan Winter. Phil Carey, Julia Arnall, Dermot Walsh, Vera Day. Programmer involving trumped-up murder charge and usual dose of red herrings; ill-conceived tale.
Trunk to Cairo (1966-Israeli) C-80m. *½ D: Menahem Golan. Audie Murphy, George Sanders, Marianne Koch, Hans Von Borsodi, Joseph Yadin. Murphy, in rare non-Western role, plays still another secret agent in Cairo to investigate Sanders' attempt to build a rocket bound for the moon.
Truth about Spring, The (1965-British) C-102m. *** D: Richard

Thorpe. Hayley Mills, John Mills, James MacArthur, Lionel Jeffries, Harry Andrews, Niall MacGinnis, David Tomlinson. Skipper Mills introduces daughter Hayley to first boyfriend, MacArthur, in enjoyable film geared for young viewers.

Truth about Women, The (1958-British) C-98m. **½ D: Muriel Box. Laurence Harvey, Julie Harris, Diane Cilento, Mai Zetterling, Eva Gabor. Multi-episode tale about playboy Harvey's flirtations; well mounted and cast, but slow-going.

Try and Get Me SEE: **Sound of Fury, The**

Trygon Factor, The (1967-British) C-87m. *½ D: Cyril Frankel. Stewart Granger, Susan Hampshire, Robert Morley, Cathleen Nesbitt. Impossible-to-follow Scotland Yard whodunit. Centers around bizarre old English family and series of interesting murders.

Tugboat Annie (1933) 87m. **½ D: Mervyn LeRoy. Marie Dressler, Wallace Beery, Robert Young, Maureen O'Sullivan, Willard Robertson, Frankie Darro. Marie is skipper of the tugboat *Narcissus*, Beery her ne'er-do-well husband in this rambling, episodic comedy drama; inimitable stars far outclass their wobbly material.

Tugboat Annie Sails Again (1940) 77m. ** D: Lewis Seiler. Marjorie Rambeau, Alan Hale, Jane Wyman, Ronald Reagan, Clarence Kolb, Charles Halton. Airy comedy with predictable plot about Annie's job in jeopardy. Rambeau takes up where Marie Dressler left off; Reagan saves the day for her.

Tulsa (1949) C-90m. *** D: Stuart Heisler. Susan Hayward, Robert Preston, Pedro Armendariz, Lloyd Gough, Chill Wills, Ed Begley. Bouncy drama of oil-woman Hayward fighting for her property, forgetting about human values while involved in wildcat drilling.

Tumbleweed (1953) C-79m. ** D: Nathan Juran. Audie Murphy, Lori Nelson, Chill Wills, Lee Van Cleef. Bland oater with Murphy trying to prove he didn't desert wagon train under Indian attack.

Tumbleweeds (1925) 81m. ***½ D: King Baggot. William S. Hart, Barbara Bedford, Lucien Littlefield, J. Gordon Russell, Richard R. Neill. One of the all-time great Westerns, with Hart deciding to get in on the opening of the Cherokee Strip in 1889, particularly if pretty Bedford is willing to marry him and settle there. Land-rush scene is one of the great spectacles in silent films. Above running time does not include a short, poignant introduction Hart made to accompany 1939 reissue of this classic, which may be shown along with TV print.

Tuna Clipper (1949) 79m. *½ D: William Beaudine. Roddy McDowall, Elena Verdugo, Roland Winters, Rick Vallin, Dickie Moore. Flabby tale of youth (McDowall) who pushes himself into rugged fishing life to prove his worth.

Tunes of Glory (1960-British) C-106m. **** D: Ronald Neame. Alec Guinness, John Mills, Susannah York, Kay Walsh, Dennis Price, John Fraser, Allan Cuthbertson. Superbly acted character drama of conflict between callous colonel and younger replacement; set in Scotland.

Tunnel, The SEE: **Transatlantic Tunnel**

Tunnel of Love, The (1958) 98m. *** D: Gene Kelly. Doris Day, Richard Widmark, Gig Young, Gia Scala. Bright comedy of married couple Widmark and Day enduring endless red tape to adopt a child. Good cast spices adaptation of Joseph Fields-Peter de Vries play.

Turn the Key Softly (1953-British) 83m. ** D: Jack Lee. Yvonne Mitchell, Terence Morgan, Joan Collins, Kathleen Harrison, Thora Hird, Geoffrey Keen. Film recounts incidents in lives of three women exconvicts upon leaving prison; contrived dramatics.

Turnabout (1940) 83m. ** D: Hal Roach. John Hubbard, Carole Landis, Adolphe Menjou, Mary Astor, William Gargan, Joyce Compton, Verree Teasdale. Certainly unique, but incredibly bad comedy, risque in its day, about husband and wife switching personalities thanks to magic Buddha; story by Thorne Smith, later a short-lived TV series in the 1970s.

Turning Point, The (1952) 85m. **½ D: William Dieterle. William Holden, Alexis Smith, Edmond O'Brien, Ed Begley, Don Porter. Love and intrigue with Holden investigating internal corruption within crime-investigation committee.

Turning Point, The (1977) C-119m. **½ D: Herbert Ross. Anne Bancroft, Shirley MacLaine, Mikhail

[810]

Baryshnikov, Leslie Browne, Tom Skerritt, Martha Scott. Two friends who started in ballet are reunited after many years; Bancroft is now a star ballerina, MacLaine a Midwestern housewife/dance teacher whose daughter (Browne) is embarking on her own ballet career. Promising idea bogs down in clichés, with supposedly liberated treatment of women's relationships exemplified by wild catfight. Those few dance sequences presented intact give film its only value.

Turning Point of Jim Malloy, The (1975) C-78m. TVM D: Frank D. Gilroy. John Savage, Biff McGuire, Peggy McKay, Gig Young, Kathleen Quinlan, Janis Paige. Nostalgic drama based on John O'Hara's youth in a small Pennsylvania town and his first exposure to the world of journalism under the tutelage of an alcoholic reporter. Atmospheric, lovingly filmed version of O'Hara's "Gibbsville" from his collection *The Doctor's Son*. Also called JOHN O'HARA'S GIBBSVILLE, it later spun off to a brief series. Above average.

Tutiles of Tahiti, The (1942) 91m. *** D: Charles Vidor. Charles Laughton, Jon Hall, Peggy Drake, Florence Bates, Mala, Alma Ross, Victor Francen. Laughton and family lead leisurely life on South Seas island, avoiding any sort of hard labor. That's it . . . but it's good.

12 Angry Men (1957) 95m. **** D: Sidney Lumet. Henry Fonda, Lee J. Cobb, Ed Begley, E. G. Marshall, Jack Klugman, Jack Warden, Martin Balsam. Brilliant courtroom film; Fonda does his best to convince 11 other jurors that their hasty conviction of boy on trial should be reconsidered.

Twelve Chairs, The (1970) C-94m. *** D: Mel Brooks. Ron Moody, Frank Langella, Dom DeLuise, Mel Brooks, Bridget Brice, Robert Bernal. Impoverished Russian nobleman Moody seeks one of 12 dining chairs, now scattered, with jewels sewn into seat. DeLuise hilarious as his chief rival. Unsympathetic characters hamper film's success, though mastermind Brooks still provides many laughs; filmed in Yugoslavia.

Twelve Hours to Kill (1960) 83m. *½ D: Edward L. Cahn. Nico Minardos, Barbara Eden, Grant Richards, Russ Conway, Art Baker, Gavin MacLeod. Poor crime melodrama of gangland

murder witnessed by Greek immigrant in New York.

Twelve O'Clock High (1949) 132m. **** D: Henry King. Gregory Peck, Hugh Marlowe, Gary Merrill, Millard Mitchell, Dean Jagger. Taut WW2 story of U.S. flyers in England, an officer replaced for getting too involved with his men (Merrill) and his successor who has same problem (Peck). Jagger won Oscar in supporting role; Peck has never been better.

12 to the Moon (1960) 74m. BOMB D: David Bradley. Ken Clark, Michi Kobi, Tom Conway, Tony Dexter, John Wengraf, Anna-Lisa. Aimless account about international exploration of moon.

Twentieth Century (1934) 91m. **** D: Howard Hawks. John Barrymore, Carole Lombard, Walter Connolly, Roscoe Karns, Ralph Forbes, Edgar Kennedy. Super screwball comedy based on Ben Hecht-Charles MacArthur play. Producer Barrymore makes Lombard a star, then tries to woo her back aboard cross-country train trip. Connolly and Karns add fine support as Barrymore's cronies.

Twenty-Four Hours to Kill (1965-British) C-92m. **½ D: Peter Bezencenet. Mickey Rooney, Lex Barker, Walter Slezak, Michael Medwin, Helga Somerfeld, Wolfgang Lukschy. OK suspenser with Rooney marked for execution by Slezak's smuggling ring when his plane is forced to land in Beirut for 24 hours.

25th Hour, The (1967-French-Italian-Yugoslavian) C-119m. ** D: Henri Verneuil. Anthony Quinn, Virna Lisi, Michael Redgrave, Gregoire Aslan, Marcel Dalio, Serge Reggiani. Story of Rumanian peasant's Nazi-enforced eight-year separation from his beautiful wife is indifferently done, in spite of capable acting by Quinn and Lisi.

20 Million Miles to Earth (1957) 82m. **½ D: Nathan Juran. William Hopper, Joan Taylor, Frank Puglia, Thomas B. Henry. Monster runs wild in Italy; intelligent script with good special effects by Ray Harryhausen.

Twenty Million Sweethearts (1934) 89m. **½ D: Ray Enright. Dick Powell, Ginger Rogers, Pat O'Brien, Allen Jenkins, Grant Mitchell, The Mills Brothers. Contrived musical about unscrupulous promoter O'Brien building Powell into radio star, career coming between him and happy marriage to Ginger. Plot soon wears thin, as does constant repetition of Powell's "I'll String Along with You," but bright cast helps out. Two good songs by the Mills Bros.

20 Mule Team (1940) 84m. ** D: Richard Thorpe. Wallace Beery, Leo Carrillo, Marjorie Rambeau, Anne Baxter, Douglas Fowley. Minor Western of borax-miners in Arizona with usual Beery mugging and standard plot. Baxter's first film.

21 Days Together (1938-British) 72m. **½ D: Basil Dean. Vivien Leigh, Laurence Olivier, Hay Petrie, Leslie Banks, Francis L. Sullivan. Galsworthy's play of lovers with three weeks together before man goes on trial for murder; Olivier and Leigh are fine in worthwhile, but not outstanding, film. Original title: 21 DAYS.

Twenty-One Hours at Munich (1976) C-100m. TVM D: William A. Graham. William Holden, Shirley Knight, Franco Nero, Anthony Quayle, Noel Willman. Well-done re-creation of the events surrounding 1972 Munich Olympics massacre, despite Holden's being miscast as the Munich police chief. Above average.

Twenty Plus Two (1961) 102m. ** D: Joseph M. Newman. David Janssen, Jeanne Crain, Dina Merrill, Agnes Moorehead, Brad Dexter. Poor production values detract from potential of yarn with private eye Janssen investigating a murder, encountering a neat assortment of people.

27th Day, The (1957) 75m. **½ D: William Asher. Gene Barry, Valerie French, Arnold Moss, George Voskovec. Imaginative sci-fi study of human nature with five people given pellets capable of destroying the world.

20,000 Eyes (1961) 60m. *½ D: Jack Leewood. Gene Nelson, Merry Anders, John Banner, James Brown. Flabby robbery caper done on shoestring budget.

20,000 Leagues Under the Sea (1954) C-127m. **** D: Richard Fleischer. Kirk Douglas, James Mason, Paul Lukas, Peter Lorre, Robert J. Wilke, Carleton Young. Superb Disney fantasy-adventure on grand scale, from Jules Verne's novel. Scientist Lukas and sailor Douglas get involved with power-hungry Captain Nemo (Mason) who operates futuristic submarine. Memorable action sequences, fine cast make this a winner.

20,000 Pound Kiss, The (1963-British) 57m. **½ D: John Moxey. Dawn Addams, Michael Goodliffe, Richard Thorp, Anthony Newlands. Edgar Wallace tale of blackmail, with a most intricate plot.

20,000 Years in Sing Sing (1933) 81m. *** D: Michael Curtiz. Spencer Tracy, Bette Davis, Lyle Talbot, Sheila Terry, Warren Hymer, Louis Calhern, Grant Mitchell. Still-powerful prison drama has only teaming of Tracy and Davis. He's a hardened criminal, she's his girl. Remade as CASTLE ON THE HUDSON.

23 Paces to Baker Street (1956) C-103m. *** D: Henry Hathaway. Van Johnson, Vera Miles, Cecil Parker, Patricia Laffan, Maurice Denham, Estelle Winwood. Absorbing suspenser filmed in London has blind playwright Johnson determined to thwart crime plans he has overheard.

Twice in a Lifetime (1974) C-78m. TVM D: Herschel Daugherty. Ernest Borgnine, Della Reese, Eric Laneuville, Slim Pickens, Herb Jeffries, Arte Johnson. Scruffy old salt operating a salvage tug clashes with unscrupulous yard foreman determined to retain control of the docks. Borgnine at his most bombastic is nicely balanced by Ms. Reese from her waterfront cafe. Another pilot film that never earned series status. Below average.

Twice Round the Daffodils (1962-British) 89m. ** D: Gerald Thomas. Juliet Mills, Donald Sinden, Donald Houston, Kenneth Williams. Mills is charming nurse in a male TB ward, trying to avoid romantic inclinations of her patients; expected sex jokes abound.

Twice-Told Tales (1963) C-119m. *** D: Sidney Salkow. Vincent Price, Sebastian Cabot, Mari Blanchard, Brett Halsey, Richard Denning. Episodic adaptation of Hawthorne stories has good cast, imaginative direction, and sufficient atmosphere to keep one's interest.

Twilight for the Gods (1958) C-120m. **½ D: Joseph Pevney. Rock Hudson, Cyd Charisse, Arthur Kennedy, Leif Erickson. Ernest K. Gann book becomes turgid soaper of people on run-down vessel heading for Mexico, their trials and tribulations to survive when ship goes down.

Twilight of Honor (1963) 115m. **½ D: Boris Sagal. Richard Chamberlain, Nick Adams, Joan Blackman, Claude Rains, Joey Heatherton,

James Gregory. Average drama of struggling lawyer Chamberlain who wins murder case with assistance of older expert Rains.

Twilight's Last Gleaming (1977-U.S.-German) C-146m. **½ D: Robert Aldrich. Burt Lancaster, Richard Widmark, Charles Durning, Melvyn Douglas, Paul Winfield, Burt Young, Joseph Cotten, Roscoe Lee Browne, Richard Jaeckel. Unstable Air Force officer seizes missile installation, threatens to start World War III unless U.S. comes clean on its former Vietnam policy. OK if overlong programmer from Walter Wager's novel *Viper Three*.

Twin Beds (1942) 85m. ** D: Tim Whelan. Joan Bennett, George Brent, Mischa Auer, Una Merkel, Glenda Farrell. Life of married couple Bennett and Brent is constantly interrupted by wacky neighbor Auer; and it's his film too.

Twin Detectives (1976) C-78m. TVM D: Robert Day. Jim Hager, Jon Hager, Lillian Gish, Patrick O'Neal, Michael Constantine, Otis Young, Lynda Day George. Comedy-mystery involving identical twin private eyes, a spunky old lady, a psychic con group, and a murdered medium. The Hager Brothers are country singers/comics from "Hee Haw," and should have stayed there. And whatever possessed dear Miss Gish to make her TV movie debut in this bit of fluff! Below average.

Twinkle in God's Eye, The (1955) 73m. ** D: George Blair. Mickey Rooney, Coleen Gray, Hugh O'Brian, Joey Forman, Michael Connors. Simple yarn of clergyman Rooney trying to convert wrongdoers in Western town to God's faith via good humor.

Twins of Evil (1972-British) C-85m. **½ D: John Hough. Peter Cushing, Madeline Collinson, Mary Collinson, Luan Peters, Harvey Hall. Twins' evil affects neighbors. Silly, racy, with just one plus: two girls (real twins) who are absolutely stunning.

Twist of Fate (1954-British) 89m. ** D: David Miller. Ginger Rogers, Herbert Lom, Stanley Baker, Jacques Bergerac, Margaret Rawlings. Lukewarm script benefits from good performances in story of Riviera-based actress who discovers that fiancé is dangerous criminal. Original title: THE BEAUTIFUL STRANGER.

Twist of Sand, A (1968-British) C-90m. ** D: Don Chaffey. Richard Johnson, Honor Blackman, Jeremy Kemp, Peter Vaughan, Roy Dotrice. Ex-submarine commander Johnson leads crew of smugglers on expedition for diamonds in ordinary programmer.

Two Against the World (1936) 64m. ** D: William McGann. Humphrey Bogart, Beverly Roberts, Linda Perry, Carlyle Moore, Jr., Henry O'Neill, Helen MacKellar, Claire Dodd. Remake of FIVE STAR FINAL set in radio station is more contrived, not as effective. Retitled: ONE FATAL HOUR.

Two and Two Make Six (1961-British) 89m. ** D: Freddie Francis. George Chakiris, Janette Scott, Alfred Lynch, Jackie Lane. Mild romantic yarn of A.W.O.L. soldier Chakiris falling in love with Scott.

Two Dollar Bettor (1951) 73m. ** D: Edward L. Cahn. John Litel, Marie Windsor, Steve Brodie, Barbara Logan. Nifty little programmer showing the snowballing of businessman Litel's problems, once he gets racetrack fever.

Two English Girls (1972-French) C-108m. ***½ D: François Truffaut. Jean-Pierre Leaud, Kika Markham, Stacey Tendeter, Sylvia Marriott, Marie Mansart. Potentially sappy film about young writer's lengthy love affair with two sisters makes beautiful film, thanks to fine performances and superb photography; directed with great feeling by Truffaut.

Two-Faced Woman (1941) 94m. **½ D: George Cukor. Greta Garbo, Melvyn Douglas, Constance Bennett, Roland Young, Robert Sterling, Ruth Gordon, Frances Carson. Garbo's last film to date, in which MGM tried unsuccessfully to Americanize her personality. Attempted chic comedy of errors is OK, but not what viewer expects from the divine Garbo. Constance Bennett is much more at home in proceedings, stealing the film with her hilarious performance.

Two Faces of Dr. Jekyll, The (1961) C-88m. ** D: Terence Fisher. Paul Massie, Dawn Addams, Christopher Lee, David Kossoff, Francis De Wolff, Norma Maria. Uneven, sometimes unintentionally funny low-key psychological reworking of Stevenson story stresses Mr. and Mrs. relationship, plus fact that doctor himself is a weakling. Unfortunately, dialogue and situations are boring. Formerly known as HOUSE OF FRIGHT.

Two Flags West (1950) 92m. ** D: Robert Wise. Joseph Cotten, Linda Darnell, Jeff Chandler, Cornel Wilde, Dale Robertson. Very uneven Civil War Western. Battle scenes of good quality mixed with unappealing script and weak performances.

Two for the Money C-73m. TVM D: Bernard Kowalski. Robert Hooks, Stephen Brooks, Neville Brand, Walter Brennan, Catherine Burns, Mercedes McCambridge, Richard Dreyfuss. Two cops leave the department to track down a mass murderer who's been loose for twelve years. Well done. Average.

Two for the Road (1967-British) C-112m. *** D: Stanley Donen. Audrey Hepburn, Albert Finney, Eleanor Bron, William Daniels, Claude Dauphin, Nadia Gray. Beautifully acted film of bickering couple Hepburn and Finney stopping to reminisce about their twelve years of marriage, trying to work to save their happiness. Perceptive, winning film, well directed by Donen.

Two for the Seesaw (1962) 120m. *** D: Robert Wise. Robert Mitchum, Shirley MacLaine, Edmond Ryan, Elisabeth Fraser. Intelligent handling of William Gibson play. Mitchum is Midwest lawyer trying to rebuild life in N.Y.C., involved with eccentric gal MacLaine.

Two for Tonight (1935) 61m. **½ D: Frank Tuttle. Bing Crosby, Joan Bennett, Mary Boland, Lynne Overman, Thelma Todd, James Blakeley. Songwriter Crosby is forced to write musical play in one week. Entertaining slapstick musical with Boland as his mother, Bennett his girl.

Two Gals and a Guy (1951) 71m. ** D: Alfred E. Green. Janis Paige, Robert Alda, James Gleason, Lionel Stander. Trials and tribulations of married vocal duo, caught up in the early days of TV performing; standard production.

Two Gentlemen Sharing (1969-British) C-92m. ** D: Ted Kotcheff. Robin Phillips, Judy Geeson, Hal Frederick, Esther Anderson, Norman Rossington. Unusual story of mixed racial couples is done more with the sensational in mind than honest portrayal.

Two Girls and a Sailor (1944) 124m. *** D: Richard Thorpe. Van Johnson, June Allyson, Gloria DeHaven, Jose Iturbi, Jimmy Durante, Lena Horne, Donald Meek, Virginia O'Brien, Harry James, Xavier Cugat

orchestras. Weak plot of Allyson-Johnson-DeHaven triangle doesn't interfere with large cast and many fine musical numbers; breezy entertainment.

Two Girls on Broadway (1940) 71m. ** D: S. Sylvan Simon. Lana Turner, George Murphy, Joan Blondell, Kent Taylor, Wallace Ford. Sisters love same man (Murphy) but everything works out in this routine musical, sparked by snappy Blondell. Remake of THE BROADWAY MELODY (1929).

Two Gun Lady (1956) 75m. ** D: Richard Bartlett. Peggie Castle, Marie Windsor, William Talman. Simple oater of sure-shot gal and law enforcer tracking down her father's murderer.

Two Guns and a Badge (1954) 69m. *½ D: Lewis D. Collins. Wayne Morris, Morris Ankrum, Beverly Garland, Roy Barcroft. Poor script uplifted by competent cast in story of ex-convict who is mistakenly hired as deputy sheriff.

Two Guys from Milwaukee (1946) 90m. **½ D: David Butler. Dennis Morgan, Jack Carson, Joan Leslie, Janis Paige, S. Z. Sakall, Patti Brady. Silly story of European prince Morgan Americanized by cabdriver Carson; cast is so engaging it doesn't matter.

Two Guys from Texas (1948) C-86m. **½ D: David Butler. Dennis Morgan, Jack Carson, Dorothy Malone, Penny Edwards, Forrest Tucker. Average musical about two stranded vaudevillians who get involved with crooks and gals. Good cast succeeds. Remake of THE COWBOY FROM BROOKLYN.

Two-Headed Spy, The (1958-British) 93m. *** D: Andre de Toth. Jack Hawkins, Gia Scala, Alexander Knox, Felix Aylmer, Donald Pleasence, Michael Caine, Laurence Naismith. Exciting true story of British spy (Hawkins) who operated in Berlin during WW2 is loaded with heart-stopping tension and suspense. Fine performances all around; one of Caine's earliest roles.

Two Hundred Motels (1971) C-98m. **½ D: Frank Zappa, Tony Palmer. Frank Zappa, Mothers of Invention, Theodore Bikel, Ringo Starr, Keith Moon. Visual, aural assault disguised as movie; completely berserk, freeform film (shot on videotape in England) featuring bizarre humor of Zappa and the Mothers. Some of it ingenious, some funny, but not spellbinding enough to maintain entire film. Funny X-rated animation sequence.

Two-Lane Blacktop (1971) **C-101m.** ***½ D: Monte Hellman. James Taylor, Warren Oates, Laurie Bird, Dennis Wilson, David Drake, Richard Ruth. Cult film about race across the Southwest between a '55 Chevy and a new GTO has intense direction to compensate for low-key script; Oates' performance is about as good as you'll ever see and should have had the Oscar.

Two Little Bears, The (1961) **81m.** ** D: Randall Hood. Eddie Albert, Jane Wyatt, Soupy Sales, Nancy Kulp, Brenda Lee. Harmless fable-comedy of Albert confused to discover that his two children turn into bears at night, cavorting around the house.

Two Lost Worlds (1950) **61m.** *½ D: Norman Dawn. Laura Elliot, James Arness, Bill Kennedy, Gloria Petroff. Draggy story of shipwreck on unchartered island with prehistoric monsters; stock footage courtesy of ONE MILLION B.C. Cast doesn't reach island until last twenty minutes; you may not wait that long.

Two Loves (1961) **C-100m.** ** D: Charles Walters. Shirley MacLaine, Laurence Harvey, Jack Hawkins, Juano Hernandez, Nobu McCarthy. Plodding sudser set in New Zealand with spinster teacher MacLaine trying to decide between suitors Harvey and Hawkins.

Two Minute Warning (1976) **C-115m.** *½ D: Larry Peerce. Charlton Heston, John Cassavetes, Martin Balsam, Beau Bridges, David Janssen, Jack Klugman, Gena Rowlands. Pointless story of attempt to catch sniper in packed football stadium. Usual melange of hackneyed characters in this contrived Hollywood product. Merv Griffin sings the national anthem! (Film heavily doctored for network showing, with nearly one hour added including new cast and subplot; this review applies to original theatrical version)

Two Mrs. Carrolls, The (1947) **99m.** **½ D: Peter Godfrey. Humphrey Bogart, Barbara Stanwyck, Alexis Smith, Nigel Bruce, Isobel Elsom. Shrill murder drama with Bogie as psychopathic artist who paints wives as Angels of Death, then kills them; Stanwyck registers all degrees of panic as the next marital victim.

Two Mules for Sister Sara (1970) **C-105m.** *** D: Don Siegel. Clint Eastwood, Shirley MacLaine, Manolo Fabregas, Alberto Morin, Armando Silvestre. Engaging story of drifter Eastwood helping nun MacLaine across Mexican desert, becoming wary of her un-pious nature. Beautifully shot, well-acted, good fun, marred by needlessly violent massacre climax.

Two of a Kind (1951) **75m.** **½ D: Henry Levin. Edmond O'Brien, Lizabeth Scott, Terry Moore, Alexander Knox. Uninspired suspenser about con-artists plotting to dupe an elderly couple out of their inheritance fund.

Two of Us, The (1968-French) **C-86m.** ***½ D: Claude Berri. Michel Simon, Alain Cohen, Luce Fabiole, Roger Carel, Paul Preboist, Charles Denner. Charming film of growing relationship between young Jewish boy sent away from WW2 Paris and blustery, anti-Semitic guardian who lives in the country. Warm, funny, beautifully acted.

Two on a Bench (1971) **C-73m.** TVM D: Jerry Paris. Patty Duke, Ted Bessell, Andrew Duggan, John Astin, Alice Ghostley. Dull comedy throws Duke and Bessell at each other, hired to find out which one is working for spy. Boston locations only asset in listless, unimaginatively written and conceived comedy of errors. Below average.

Two on a Guillotine (1965) **107m.** **½ D: William Conrad. Connie Stevens, Dean Jones, Cesar Romero, Parley Baer, Virginia Gregg, Connie Gilchrist. To receive inheritance from late father (Romero), Connie must spend night in haunted house. Familiar plot with some visual scares.

Two People (1973) **C-100m.** **½ D: Robert Wise. Peter Fonda, Lindsay Wagner, Estelle Parsons, Alan Fudge, Geoffrey Horne, Frances Sternhagen. Soapy, but oddly affecting drama about Army deserter returning home to face the consequences and fashion model with whom he falls in love. Beautiful photography and likable performance by Wagner.

Two Rode Together (1961) **C-109m.** **½ D: John Ford. James Stewart, Richard Widmark, Linda Cristal, Shirley Jones, Andy Devine, Mae Marsh, Henry Brandon, Anna Lee. Fair Western with Stewart as cynical marshal hired to rescue pioneers captured by the Comanches years ago; Widmark is cavalry officer who accompanies him.

Two Seconds (1932) 68m. **½ D: Mervyn LeRoy. Edward G. Robinson, Vivienne Osborne, Preston Foster, J. Carrol Naish, Guy Kibbee, Berton Churchill. Offbeat and engrossing, if not entirely successful, melodrama tells Robinson's life as he sees it in two seconds it takes for him to die in electric chair. Often overplayed, sometimes unusually effective; a most interesting curio.

Two Sisters from Boston (1946) 112m. *** D: Henry Koster. Kathryn Grayson, June Allyson, Lauritz Melchior, Jimmy Durante, Peter Lawford, Ben Blue. Grayson and Allyson go to work in Durante's Bowery saloon in this entertaining turn-of-the-century musical; bright score helps.

Two Smart People (1946) 93m. ** D: Jules Dassin. Lucille Ball, John Hodiak, Lloyd Nolan, Hugo Haas, Lenore Ulric, Elisha Cook, Jr. Conniving couple involved in art forgery; laughs don't come very often.

2001: A Space Odyssey (1968-British) C-139m. **** D: Stanley Kubrick. Keir Dullea, William Sylvester, Gary Lockwood, Daniel Richter; voice of HAL, Douglas Rain. A milestone film: Space travel is placed into context of man's history, from first confrontation with a Greater Power to future time warp where life cycle has no meaning. For now, it's man vs. machinery of his own making in an unforgettable space journey with computer H.A.L. in control. A visual feast, film also boasts distinction of having put Richard Strauss into the Top 40 with "Also Spake Zarasthrustra." Cut by 17 minutes after premiere, by Kubrick himself, to present length.

2000 Years Later (1969) C-80m. ** D: Bert Tenzer. Terry-Thomas, Edward Everett Horton, Pat Harrington, Lisa Seagram. Amusing story of 20th-century man exploiting a Roman soldier who comes back to life after 2000 years.

Two Tickets to Broadway (1951) C-106m. **½ D: James V. Kern. Tony Martin, Janet Leigh, Gloria De-Haven, Eddie Bracken, Ann Miller, Smith and Dale, Barbara Lawrence. Modest musical involving Martin et al trying to get on Bob Crosby's TV show; some bright moments.

Two Tickets to London (1943) 79m.

** D: Edwin L. Marin. Michele Morgan, Alan Curtis, Barry Fitzgerald, C. Aubrey Smith. Passable drama of Curtis helped by Morgan in hunting down espionage agents.

Two Way Stretch (1960-British) 78m. *** D: Robert Day. Peter Sellers, Wilfrid Hyde-White, Lionel Jeffries, Liz Fraser, Maurice Denham. Wry shenanigans of Sellers et al as prisoners who devise a means of escaping to commit a robbery and then return to safety of their cells.

Two Weeks in Another Town (1962) C-107m. *** D: Vincente Minnelli. Kirk Douglas, Edward G. Robinson, Cyd Charisse, George Hamilton, Claire Trevor, Daliah Lavi, Rossana Schiaffino, Constance Ford. Overly ambitious attempt to intellectualize Irwin Shaw novel, revolving around problems of people involved in movie-making in Rome.

Two Weeks in September (1967-French) C-96m. **½ D: Serge Bourguignon. Brigitte Bardot, Laurent Terzieff, Michael Sarne, James Robertson Justice. Bardot, mistress to older man, has fling with younger lover, can't decide between the two. Location shooting in London and Scotland enhances OK story.

Two Weeks With Love (1950) C-92m. **½ D: Roy Rowland. Jane Powell, Ricardo Montalban, Louis Calhern, Ann Harding, Debbie Reynolds, Carleton Carpenter. Reynolds fans will enjoy her role as daughter vacationing in Catskills proving to her parents that she's grown up, and singing "Abba Dabba Honeymoon."

Two Wives at One Wedding (1960-British) 66m. *½ D: Montgomery Tully. Gordon Jackson, Christina Gregg, Lisa Daniely, Andre Maranne. Trite minor film involving Jackson confronted by extortion gang charging him with bigamy.

Two Women (1961-Italian) 99m. **** D: Vittorio De Sica. Sophia Loren, Raf Vallone, Eleanora Brown, Jean-Paul Belmondo. Loren deservedly won Oscar for heart-wrenching portrayal of Italian mother who, along with young daughter, is raped by Allied Moroccan soldiers during WW2. How they survive is an intensely moving story, based on an Alberto Moravia novel.

Two Worlds of Jennie Logan, The (1979) C-100m. TVM D: Frank DeFelitta. Lindsay Wagner, Marc Singer, Alan Feinstein, Linda Gray, Henry Wilcoxon, Joan Darling.

Stylish murder mystery/romantic drama taking place simultaneously in two centuries. Based on David Williams' *Second Sight*. Above average.

Two Yanks in Trinidad (1942) 88m. ** D: Gregory Ratoff. Brian Donlevy, Pat O'Brien, Janet Blair, Donald MacBride. Donlevy and O'Brien are hoods who join the army, turning their talents to fighting the enemy; flat patriotism.

Two Years Before the Mast (1946) 98m. *½ D: John Farrow. Alan Ladd, Brian Donlevy, William Bendix, Esther Fernandez, Howard da Silva, Barry Fitzgerald. Badly scripted story of Richard Henry Dana's (Donlevy) crusade to expose mistreatment of men at sea. Da Silva is standout as tyrannical captain.

Two-Five, The (1978) C-74m. TVM D: Bruce Kessler. Don Johnson, Joe Bennett, Michael Durrell, George Murdock, John Crawford. Predictable cop show pilot has a couple of eager-beaver rookies out to save their harassed commander's hide by nabbing a drug kingpin in their own unorthodox ways. Average.

Twonky, The (1953) 72m. *½ D. Arch Oboler. Hans Conried, Gloria Blondell, Trilby Conried, Billy Lynn. Satirical sci-fi is misfire entertainment, when Conried's TV set actually takes charge of his life, possessed by a spirit from the future.

Tycoon (1947) C-128m. **½ D: Richard Wallace. John Wayne, Laraine Day, Cedric Hardwicke, Judith Anderson, James Gleason, Anthony Quinn, Grant Withers. Wayne plays determined young railroad pioneer in this overlong, but well-acted drama with fine cast; better than usual Wayne vehicles.

Typhoon (1940) C-70m. **½ D: Louis King. Dorothy Lamour, Robert Preston, Lynne Overman, J. Carrol Naish, Chief Thundercloud, Jack Carson. Another Lamour sarong epic, typically romantic; Overman provides good comedy support.

Tyrant of the Sea (1950) 70m. ** D: Lew Landers. Rhys Williams, Ron Randell, Valentine Perkins, Doris Lloyd, Lester Matthews, Terry Kilburn, William Fawcett. Undistinguished melodrama set in 1803. Napoleon is ready to invade England, and only retired tough sea captain (Williams) can destroy French landing barges and save the country. Meanwhile, romance blossoms between young Lt. Randell and captain's daughter Perkins.

UFO (Unidentified Flying Objects) (1956) 92m. ** D: Winston Jones. Documentary-style account of unknown missiles, detailing various reports of unidentified flying objects being spotted. Film lacks excitement.

UFO Incident, The (1975) C-100m. TVM D: Richard A. Colla. James Earl Jones, Estelle Parsons, Barnard Hughes, Dick O'Neill, Beeson Carroll, Terrence O'Connor. Absorbing, fact-based, semi-sci-fi drama tracing story of New England couple who claim to have been taken aboard a UFO and examined medically. Long on monologues, skimpy in action, it's kept afloat by two leads and Hughes, the doctor who probes their memories. Above average.

U.M.C. (1969) C-100m. TVM D: Boris Sagal. James Daly, Richard Bradford, Maurice Evans, Kevin McCarthy, Shelley Fabares, William Windom, J. D. Cannon, Edward G. Robinson. Excellent cast in moderately effective behind-the-scenes drama of university medical center; script and subplots strictly formula. Pilot for TV series; average. Retitled OPERATION HEARTBEAT.

U-238 and the Witch Doctor (1953) 100m. *½ D: Fred C. Brannon. Clayton Moore, Phyllis Coates, Johnny Spencer (Sands), Roy Glenn, John Cason. Tedious cliff-hanger utilizing an abundance of stock footage and minimum of action in tame account of uranium hunt in Africa, involving battles with natives and animals. Re-edited movie serial: JUNGLE DRUMS OF AFRICA.

Ugetsu (1953-Japanese) 96m. ***½ D: Kenji Mizoguchi. Machiko Kyo, Masayuki Mori, Kinyo Tanaka, Sakae Ozawa. Eerie ghost story set in 16th-century Japan tells of two peasants who leave their families; one seeks wealth in the city and the other wishes to become a samurai warrior. This superbly photographed film was a Venice Film Festival prize winner.

Ugly American, The (1963) C-120m. **½ D: George H. Englund. Marlon Brando, Sandra Church, Pat Hingle, Eiji Okada, Arthur Hill, Jocelyn Brando. Brando is American ambassador to Asian country; his arrival stirs up pro-communist elements, leading to havoc. Political revelations of U.S. power struggle isn't meat for exciting film. Based on Burdick-Lederer book.

Ugly Dachshund, The (1966) C-93m. ** D: Norman Tokar. Dean Jones, Suzanne Pleshette, Charlie Ruggles, Kelly Thordsen, Parley Baer. Silly, featherweight Disney comedy about husband and wife who train their respective dogs for competition at dog show. Fun for kids, but too contrived and silly for anyone else to enjoy.

Ultimate Chase, The SEE: **Ultimate Thrill, The**

Ultimate Imposter, The (1979) C-100m. TVM D: Paul Stanley. Joseph Hacker, Keith Andes, Erin Gray, Tracy Brooks Swope, Bobby Riggs. Computer-age secret agent, using the latest gadgetry, sets out to help a Russian submarine commander defect. Silly premise that ended up as a busted series pilot. Below average.

Ultimate Thrill, The (1974) C-110m. ** D: Robert Butler. Eric Braeden, Britt Ekland, Barry Brown, Michael Blodgett, John Davis Chandler. Executive is drawn into murder by his paranoiac fears; undistinguished programmer retitled THE ULTIMATE CHASE for network showing.

Ultimate Warrior, The (1975) C-94m. **½ D: Robert Clouse. Yul Brynner, Max von Sydow, Joanna Miles, William Smith, Stephen McHattie, Lane Bradbury. Routine acting and directing spoil potentially intriguing futuristic fantasy. In the 21st century, Brynner and Von Sydow each control a decreasing band of people fighting for whatever is left in N.Y.C. following ecological disasters.

Ulysses (1955-Italian) C-104m. *** D: Mario Camerini. Kirk Douglas, Silvana Mangano, Anthony Quinn, Sylvie, Rossana Podesta. Ambitious filming of Homerian epic of post-Trojan war adventures; done on a lavish scale, but starts to bog down after a while.

Ulysses (1967) 140m. **½ D: Joseph Strick. Barbara Jefford, Milo O'Shea, Maurice Roeves, T. P. McKenna, Martin Dempsey, Sheila O'Sullivan. Idea of putting Joyce's massive novel on the screen seemed daring in 1967, but now seems like a stupid stunt. Lots of good prose makes it to the screen, but end result is interesting curio, not a film.

Ulysses Against Hercules (1961-Italian) C-99m. *½ D: Mario Caiano.

Georges Marchal, Michael Lane, Alessandra Panaro, Gianni Santuccio. Childish blend of myth and muscleman antics with Hercules (Lane) sent to punish Ulysses (Marchal); special effects of bird-men not up to snuff.

Ulzana's Raid (1972) C-103m. ***½ D: Robert Aldrich. Burt Lancaster, Bruce Davison, Jorge Luke, Richard Jaeckel, Joaquin Martinez, Lloyd Bochner, Karl Swenson. Cavalry-and-Indians tale was well received by some of the more perceptive critics, but lots and lots of violent footage will be cut for TV. One of Burt's best recent performances.

Umberto D (1955-Italian) 89m. ***½ D: Vittorio De Sica. Carlo Battisti, Maria Pia Casilio, Lina Gennari. Remarkably realistic study of elderly man living alone on meager pension, determined to retain his dignity to the end.

Umbrellas of Cherbourg, The (1964-French) C-91m. ***½ D: Jacques Demy. Catherine Deneuve, Nino Castelnuovo, Anne Vernon, Marc Michel, Ellen Farnen. Haunting music (score by Michel Legrand, lyrics by Demy) and gorgeous photography make this an outstanding romantic drama. Dubbing hurts original effect.

Uncanny, The (1977-British-Canadian) C-85m. ** D: Denis Heroux. Peter Cushing, Ray Milland, Susan Penhaligon, Joan Greenwood, Alexandra Stewart, Chloe Franks, Donald Pleasence, Samantha Eggar, John Vernon. Lackluster trilogy of "supernatural" tales built around author Cushing's assertion that cats are conspiring against mankind.

Uncertain Glory (1944) 102m. ** D: Raoul Walsh. Errol Flynn, Jean Sullivan, Paul Lukas, Lucile Watson, Faye Emerson, Douglass Dumbrille, Dennis Hoey, Sheldon Leonard. Wavering script about French philanderer Flynn deciding to give his life for his country.

Unchained (1955) 75m. ** D: Hall Bartlett. Elroy Hirsch, Barbara Hale, Chester Morris, Johnny Johnston, Peggy Knudsen, Jerry Paris. Fair drama of life at prison farm at Chino, California; highlighted by theme song: "Unchained Melody."

Uncle Harry SEE: **Strange Affair of Uncle Harry, The**

Uncle Joe Shannon (1978) C-115m. BOMB D: Joseph C. Hanwright. Burt Young, Doug McKeon, Madge

Sinclair, Jason Bernard, Bert Remsen, Allan Rich. Slobbering, self-indulgent film (written by Young) about down-and-out trumpet player and young boy who tries to resist his charm. Several hands from ROCKY—including Young—were hoping to duplicate that film's success. Maynard Ferguson dubbed Young's trumpet licks.

Unconquered (1947) C-146m. **½ D: Cecil B. DeMille. Gary Cooper, Paulette Goddard, Howard da Silva, Boris Karloff, Cecil Kellaway, Ward Bond, Katherine de Mille. Gargantuan DeMille colonists-vs.-Indians nonsense, one of his most ludicrous films but still fun.

Undefeated, The (1969) C-119m. ** D: Andrew V. McLaglen. John Wayne, Rock Hudson, Tony Aguilar, Roman Gabriel, Bruce Cabot, Lee Meriwether, Ben Johnson, Merlin Olsen. Aside from interesting Wayne-Hudson teaming and the presence of football stars Gabriel and Olsen, this routine Western has little to offer. Post-Civil War tale casts two stars as Union and Confederate colonels.

Under Capricorn (1949-British) C-117m. ** D: Alfred Hitchcock. Ingrid Bergman, Joseph Cotten, Michael Wilding, Margaret Leighton, Cecil Parker. Stuffy costumer set in 19th-century Australia; Bergman is frail wife of hardened husband Cotten; Wilding comes to visit, upsetting everything. Leighton excellent in supporting role.

Under Fire (1957) 78m. ** D: James B. Clark. Rex Reason, Steve Brodie, Jon Locke, Harry Morgan. Bland war tale about soldiers alleged to have deserted under enemy fire.

Under Milk Wood (1973-British) C-90m. ** D: Andrew Sinclair. Richard Burton, Elizabeth Taylor, Peter O'Toole, Glynis Johns, Sian Phillips, Vivien Merchant. Rather obscure Dylan Thomas, not in terms of his work but in the vehicle's ambitions. Beautiful pictures, but rather overbearing technique weighs down the acting.

Under My Skin (1950) 86m. **½ D: George Blair. John Garfield, Micheline Prelle, Luther Adler, Steven Geray. Pensive study of once-crooked jockey, trying to reform for his son's sake. Based on Ernest Hemingway's MY OLD MAN.

Under Ten Flags (1960-U.S.-Italian) 92m. **½ D: Duilio Coletti. Van Heflin, Charles Laughton, Mylene Demongeot, John Ericson, Liam Redmond, Alex Nicol. German attack-ship during WW2 uses a variety of dodges to elude British pursuers, in naval cat-and-mouse game, told from Axis point of view. Filmed in Italy.

Under the Gun (1950) 83m. **½ D: Ted Tetzlaff. Richard Conte, Audrey Totter, Sam Jaffe, Royal Dano. Effective study of gangsters behind bars, played by competent cast.

Under the Red Robe (1937-British) 82m. **½ D: Victor Seastrom. Conrad Veidt, Raymond Massey, Annabella, Romney Brent, Sophie Stewart. Offbeat costumer with Veidt as hero, Annabella lovely heroine, and Massey the cruel villain in story of French Cardinal Richelieu's oppression of the Huguenots. Offbeat sense of humor adds to film's enjoyment.

Under the Yum Yum Tree (1963) C-110m. **½ D: David Swift. Jack Lemmon, Carol Lynley, Dean Jones, Edie Adams, Imogene Coca, Paul Lynde, Robert Lansing. Obvious sex comedy owes most of its enjoyment to Lemmon as love-hungry landlord trying to romance tenant Lynley who's living with her fiancé (Jones).

Under Two Flags (1936) 96m. *** D: Frank Lloyd. Ronald Colman, Claudette Colbert, Victor McLaglen, Rosalind Russell, Gregory Ratoff, Nigel Bruce. Debonair Colman is caught between two women (aristocratic Russell and camp follower Colbert) and the envy of jealous commandant McLaglen in this unbelievable but entertaining Foreign Legion story, from the book by Ouida (filmed before in 1916 and 1922). Originally released at 110m.

Under Western Skies (1945) 83m. *½ D: Jean Yarbrough. Martha O'Driscoll, Noah Beery, Jr., Leon Errol. Uninspired blend of shoot-em-up and musical, with scatterbrained jokes tossed in.

Undercover Girl (1950) 83m. ** D: Joseph Pevney. Alexis Smith, Scott Brady, Richard Egan, Gladys George, Regis Toomey. Smith in title role joins police to locate her father's killer; George in cameo is outstanding.

Undercover Maisie (1947) 90m. D: Harry Beaumont. Ann Sothern, Barry Nelson, Mark Daniels, Leon Ames, Clinton Sundberg. SEE: Maisie series.

Under-Cover Man (1932) 70m. ** D: James Flood. George Raft, Nancy

Carroll, Roscoe Karns, Gregory Ratoff, Lew Cody. Good but familiar tale of Raft devoting his life to finding father's killer. Well acted.

Undercover Man, The (1949) 85m. *** D: Joseph H. Lewis. Glenn Ford, Nina Foch, James Whitmore, Barry Kelley, Howard St. John. Realistic drama of mob-leader being hunted down by secret service men who hope to nail him on tax-evasion charge.

Undercover with the KKK (1979) C-100m. TVM D: Barry Shear. Don Meredith, James Wainwright, Ed Lauter, Albert Salmi, Maggie Blye, Slim Pickens, Michele Carey. Story of Gary Thomas Rowe, recruited by the FBI to infiltrate the KKK around the time of Martin Luther King's march on Montgomery. Between completion of this film and its first showing, Rowe was indicted for murder of one of the Freedom Riders, forcing some re-editing, new prologue, and epilogue spoken by Robert Stack. Retitled THE FREEDOM RIDERS.

Undercovers Hero (1975-British) C-95m. BOMB D: Roy Boulting. Peter Sellers, Lila Kedrova, Curt Jurgens, Beatrice Romand, Jenny Hanley, Rex Stallings. Inept WW2 "comedy," with Sellers in six roles, including Hitler; a total dud. Made in 1973, barely released here.

Undercurrent (1946) 116m. **½ D: Vincente Minnelli. Katharine Hepburn, Robert Taylor, Robert Mitchum, Edmund Gwenn, Marjorie Main, Jayne Meadows. Stale melodramatics of woman realizing her husband is wicked, saved only by fine cast and usual high MGM production quality.

Underground (1941) 95m. *** D: Vincent Sherman. Jeffrey Lynn, Philip Dorn, Kaaren Verne, Mona Maris, Frank Reicher, Martin Kosleck. Gripping story of German underground movement, with Dorn shielding his activities from loyal soldier-brother Lynn. Kosleck is definitive Nazi swine.

Underground Man, The (1974) C-100m. TVM D: Paul Wendkos. Peter Graves, Jack Klugman, Judith Anderson, Celeste Holm, Jo Ann Pflug, Vera Miles, Kay Lenz, Jim Hutton, Sharon Farrell. Standard mystery-drama, with Graves as Ross MacDonald's private eye Lew Archer, searching for kidnapped son of an old girlfriend, and finding tangled web of infidelity, long-hidden mur-

der, and other standard elements. Below average.

Undersea Girl (1957) 75m. BOMB D: John Peyser. Mara Corday, Pat Conway, Dan Seymour, Florence Marly, Myron Healey. Flabby murder yarn with all sides of law hunting for loot buried on ocean bottom.

Undersea Kingdom SEE: **Sharad of Atlantis**

Undersea Odyssey, An SEE: **Neptune Factor, The**

Undertow (1949) 71m. **½ D: William Castle. Scott Brady, John Russell, Dorothy Hart, Peggy Dow, Bruce Bennett, Rock Hudson. Well done story of man accused of murder he didn't commit, trying to bail himself out without being caught first.

Underwater! (1955) C-99m. ** D: John Sturges. Jane Russell, Gilbert Roland, Richard Egan, Lori Nelson. Standard skin-diving fare devised to show off Russell in bathing suit.

Underwater City, The (1962) C-78m. ** D: Frank McDonald. William Lundigan, Julie Adams, Roy Roberts, Carl Benton Reid, Chet Douglas, Paul Dubov. Mildly diverting sci-fi about engineer who builds experimental underwater city. Released theatrically in b&w.

Underwater Warrior (1958) 90m. **½ D: Andrew Marton. Dan Dailey, Claire Kelly, James Gregory, Ross Martin. On-location filming in the Philippines adds zest to narrative-style account of frogmen in action during closing days of WW2.

Underworld After Dark SEE: **Big Town After Dark**

Underworld Informers (1965-British) 105m. *** D: Ken Annakin. Nigel Patrick, Catherine Woodville, Margaret Whiting, Colin Blakely, Harry Andrews, Frank Finlay. Tight, taut crime tale as Scotland Yard inspector Patrick must clear his name by bringing in notorious gangland leaders. Vivid atmosphere, fine acting by all.

Underworld Story, The (1950) 90m. *** D: Cy Endfield. Gale Storm, Dan Duryea, Herbert Marshall, Mary Anderson, Michael O'Shea. Surprisingly effective gangster yarn of reporter joining small town newspaper and uncovering corruption; cast is uniformly good.

Underworld, U.S.A. (1961) 99m. **½ D: Samuel Fuller. Cliff Robertson, Dolores Dorn, Beatrice Kay, Robert Emhardt, Larry Gates. Robertson sees his father murdered and develops lifetime obsession to get even with the mob responsible. One of director Fuller's most visually striking films; unfortunately, script goes astray and doesn't fulfill intial promise.

Undying Monster, The (1942) 60m. ** D: John Brahm. James Ellison, John Howard, Heather Angel, Bramwell Fletcher. London is setting for OK chiller of a werewolf on the prowl; nothing new.

Unearthly, The (1957) 73m. *½ D: Brooke L. Peters. John Carradine, Allison Hayes, Myron Healey, Sally Todd. Unconvincing sci-fi about scientific experiments on human guinea pigs.

Unfaithful, The (1947) 109m. **½ D: Vincent Sherman. Ann Sheridan, Lew Ayres, Zachary Scott, Eve Arden, Steven Geray, John Hoyt. Title refers to Sheridan who gets tangled in murder while husband is out of town; good cast in fairly interesting drama. Remake of THE LETTER.

Unfaithfully Yours (1948) 105m. **** D: Preston Sturges. Rex Harrison, Linda Darnell, Barbara Lawrence, Rudy Vallee, Kurt Kreuger, Lionel Stander, Edgar Kennedy. Brilliant Sturges comedy of symphony conductor Harrison who suspects his wife of infidelity, plans her demise during concert. Great moments from Vallee, Kennedy; often side-splittingly funny.

Unfaithfuls, The (1960-Italian) 89m. **½ D: Stefano Steno. Mai Britt, Gina Lollobrigida, Pierre Cressoy, Marina Vlady, Anna Maria Ferrero, Tina Lattanzi, Carlo Romano. Multi-faceted film of life among rich, corrupt society of Rome.

Unfinished Business (1941) 96m. ** D: Gregory LaCava. Irene Dunne, Robert Montgomery, Preston Foster, Eugene Pallette, Dick Foran, Esther Dale, Walter Catlett. Ordinary romance between aristocratic Montgomery and ambitious singer Dunne.

Unfinished Dance, The (1947) C-101m. **½ D: Henry Koster. Margaret O'Brien, Cyd Charisse, Karin Booth, Danny Thomas, Esther Dale. Sugar-sweet story of young dancer O'Brien whose idol is ballerina Charisse. Remake of French Film BALLERINA.

Unfinished Journey of Robert Kennedy, The (1969) C-75m. TVM D: Mel Stuart. Excellent Wolper documentary narrated by John Huston mixes survey of political career and interviews on private life. Above average.

Unforgiven, The (1960) C-125m. *** D: John Huston. Burt Lancaster, Audrey Hepburn, Audie Murphy, John Saxon, Charles Bickford, Lillian Gish. Western set in 1850s Texas tells of two families at odds with Indians over Hepburn, whom the savages claim as one of theirs. Gish and Bickford are outstanding in stellar-cast story, with rousing Indian attack climax.

Unguarded Moment, The (1956) C-95m. **½ D: Harry Keller. Esther Williams, George Nader, John Saxon, Edward Andrews, Les Tremayne, Jack Albertson. Mild drama of school teacher whose emotional stability is endangered by lusting pupil. Film noteworthy only for Williams' non-aquatic role; co-scripted by Rosalind Russell.

Unholy Four, The (1953-British) 80m. *½ D: Terence Fisher. Paulette Goddard, William Sylvester, Patrick Holt, Paul Carpenter, Jeremy Hawk. Muddled drama of amnesiac Sylvester caught up in a murder plot. Retitled: A STRANGER CAME HOME.

Unholy Garden, The (1931) 85m. **½ D: George Fitzmaurice. Ronald Colman, Fay Wray, Estelle Taylor, Tully Marshall, Warren Hymer. Forgettable but very entertaining fluff with Colman an adventurer/thief in desert setting; murder, action, romance neatly blended, carried by Colman's effortless charm.

Unholy Night, The (1929) 94m. ** D: Lionel Barrymore. Ernest Torrence, Dorothy Sebastian, Roland Young, Natalie Moorhead, Sidney Jarvis, Polly Moran. With the murder of several members of their regiment, veterans from the Indian war gather at Young's London home to ferret out the murderer. Stagy melodrama, much hamming, especially by Boris Karloff as Indian mystic.

Unholy Partners (1941) 94m. *** D: Mervyn LeRoy. Edward G. Robinson, Edward Arnold, Laraine Day, Marsha Hunt, William T. Orr, Don Beddoe, Walter Kingsford. Intriguing premise: Robinson starts sensationalistic newspaper after WW1, is forced to bargain with underworld king Arnold. Day gives fine performance as E.G.'s girl Friday; Hunt sings "After You've Gone."

Unholy Rollers (1972) C-88m. **½ D: Vernon Zimmerman. Claudia Jennings, Louis Quinn, Betty Anne Rees, Robert Collins. Behind-the-scenes life on roller derby circuit, Roger Corman-style; raunchy low-budgeter offers some fun.

Unholy Three, The (1925) 86m. **½ D: Tod Browning. Lon Chaney, Mae Busch, Matt Moore, Victor McLaglen, Harry Earles. In departure from horrific roles, Chaney plays sideshow ventriloquist who teams with strongman and midget to form underworld trio. Corny aspects of story can't mar fascination with basic idea, or Chaney's performance. Remade in 1930.

Unholy Three, The (1930) 68m. **½ D: Jack Conway. Lon Chaney, Lila Lee, Elliott Nugent, Harry Earles, John Miljan, Ivan Linow. Almost scene-for-scene remake of 1925 film was Chaney's only talkie; he's terrific, other players less so. Denouement rewritten for this remake to take advantage of sound. Midget Earles is largely incoherent.

Unholy Wife, The (1957) C-94m. *½ D: John Farrow. Rod Steiger, Diana Dors, Tom Tryon, Beulah Bondi, Marie Windsor. Muddled melodrama about farmer's wife attempting to kill husband.

Unidentified Flying Objects SEE: UFO

Unidentified Flying Oddball (1979) C-93m. **½ D: Russ Mayberry. Dennis Dugan, Jim Dale, Ron Moody, Kenneth More, John Le Mesurier, Rodney Bewes, Sheila White. Innocuous Disney update of Mark Twain's *Connecticut Yankee in King Arthur's Court*, with young Dugan (and a lookalike robot) catapulted back to medieval times.

Uninvited, The (1944) 98m. ***½ D: Lewis Allen. Ray Milland, Ruth Hussey, Donald Crisp, Cornelia Otis Skinner, Alan Napier, Gail Russell. Ghost suspenser about Russell haunted by dead mother's spectre; Milland and Hussey try to solve mystery. No trick ending in this ingenious film.

Union Depot (1932) 75m. **½ D: Alfred E. Green. Joan Blondell. Douglas Fairbanks, Jr., Guy Kibbee, Alan Hale, Dickie Moore, Junior Coghlan, Dorothy Christy. GRAND HOTEL at train station: Tramp

finds money, young lovers meet, etc. Fast-paced and diverting film.

Union Pacific (1939) 135m. *** D: Cecil B. DeMille. Barbara Stanwyck, Joel McCrea, Robert Preston, Brian Donlevy, Anthony Quinn, Lynne Overman, Evelyn Keyes, Fuzzy Knight, J. M. Kerrigan, Akim Tamiroff. Brawling DeMille saga of nationwide railroad building with McCrea the hero, Preston the villain, Stanwyck (with Irish brogue!) in between. Action scenes, including spectacular train wreck, are highlights.

Union Station (1950) 80m. **½ D: Rudolph Maté. William Holden, Nancy Olson, Barry Fitzgerald, Jan Sterling, Allene Roberts, Lyle Bettger. Dated police techniques, plus general implausibility, detract from well-made film about manhunt for kidnapper of young blind woman (Roberts).

Unknown, The (1946) 70m. ** D: Henry Levin. Jim Bannon, Barton Yarborough, Karen Morley, Jeff Donnell, Robert Scott, Robert Wilcox. So-so entry in brief I LOVE A MYSTERY series with Bannon as Jack Packard, Yarborough as Doc Young. This one involves oddball family, with daughter Donnell coming home to see her deranged mother (Morley) after twenty years.

Unknown Guest, The (1943) 64m. **½ D: Kurt Neumann. Victor Jory, Pamela Blake, Veda Ann Borg, Harry Hayden, Emory Parnell. Murder whodunit manages to create suspense and perk interest, largely due to Jory's performance in this programmer.

Unknown Island (1948) C-76m. *½ D: Jack Bernhard. Virginia Grey, Philip Reed, Richard Denning, Barton MacLane. Boring story of scientists searching for prehistoric monsters on strange island has unimaginative special effects, little else.

Unknown Man, The (1951) 86m. **½ D: Richard Thorpe. Walter Pidgeon, Ann Harding, Barry Sullivan, Keefe Brasselle. Most capable cast enhances this yarn of lawyer discovering client in murder trial was guilty, and the strange triumph of justice he plots.

Unknown Terror, The (1957) 77m. ** D: Charles Marquis Warren. John Howard, Paul Richards, May Wynn, Mala Powers, Sir Lancelot. Unremarkable chiller supposedly set in South America, involving uncontrollable fungus.

Unmarried Woman, An (1978) C-124m. **** D: Paul Mazursky. Jill Clayburgh, Alan Bates, Michael Murphy, Cliff Gorman, Pat Quinn, Kelly Bishop, Lisa Lucas. Intelligent, compassionate look at how a woman copes when her husband walks out on her. Mazursky (who also wrote script) pulls no punches and makes no compromises—his characters are living, breathing people and his film is a gem. Clayburgh is magnificent in title role.

Unseen, The (1945) 81m. ** D: Lewis Allen. Joel McCrea, Gail Russell, Herbert Marshall, Phyllis Brooks, Isobel Elsom, Norman Lloyd. Man who made THE UNINVITED tries similar venture but doesn't succeed, with governess Russell haunted again by strange mystery; very weak ending.

Unsinkable Molly Brown, The (1964) C-128m. *** D: Charles Walters. Debbie Reynolds, Harve Presnell, Ed Begley, Jack Kruschen, Hermione Baddeley. Big, splashy, tuneful musical. Debbie is energetically entertaining as backwoods girl who knows what she wants, eventually gets to be wealthiest woman in Denver in the late 1800s. Meredith Willson score.

Unsuspected, The (1947) 103m. **½ D: Michael Curtiz. Claude Rains, Joan Caulfield, Audrey Totter, Constance Bennett, Hurd Hatfield. Predictable melodrama with good cast; superficially charming. Radio star Rains has murder on his mind, with niece Caulfield the victim.

Untamed (1955) C-111m. *** D: Henry King. Tyrone Power, Susan Hayward, Agnes Moorehead, Richard Egan, Rita Moreno, John Justin. Quite vivid account of Boer trek through hostile South African country, with Power romancing Hayward.

Untamed Breed, The (1948) C-79m. ** D: Charles Lamont. Sonny Tufts, Barbara Britton, William Bishop, Edgar Buchanan. Routine trials and tribulations of breeding cattle in old Texas, amid romance and gunplay.

Untamed Frontier (1952) C-75m. **½ D: Hugo Fregonese. Joseph Cotten, Shelley Winters, Scott Brady, Suzan Ball, Antonio Moreno. Range war between Texan cattle owners is basis for this Western improved by good cast.

Untamed Heiress (1954) 70m. *½ D: Charles Lamont. Judy Canova, Donald Barry, Taylor Holmes, George Cleveland. Slight Canova shenanigans involving the search for daughter of woman who financed a now-wealthy man.

Untamed Women (1952) 70m. *½ D: W. Merle Connell. Mikel Conrad, Doris Merrick, Richard Monahan, Mark Lowell, Midge Ware, Carol Brewster. Campy nonsense about Air Force flyers stranded on Pacific island ruled by strange women, last descendants of the Druids. Caveat emptor!

Untamed Youth (1957) 80m. *½ D: Howard W. Koch. Mamie Van Doren, Lori Nelson, John Russell, Lurene Tuttle. Mishmash of dramatics, sensationalism and music set on a reform school farm.

Until Hell Is Frozen (1960-German) 87m. ** D: Leopold Lahola. Charles Millot, Gotz George, Anna Smolik, Pierre Parel. Rambling account of P.O.W.'s in Russian prison camp in 1950, detailing their vain efforts to escape; muddled drama.

Until They Sail (1957) 95m. **½ D: Robert Wise. Paul Newman, Joan Fontaine, Jean Simmons, Sandra Dee, Piper Laurie. Soaper courtroom story set in WW2 New Zealand with sisters (Fontaine, Simmons, Laurie and Dee) involved in love, misery and murder. From James Michener story.

Unwed Father (1974) C-78m. TVM D: Jeremy Kagan. Joseph Bottoms, Kay Lenz, Joseph Campanella, Kim Hunter, Beverly Garland, William H. Bassett. Bottoms is a high-schooler battling to gain custody of his illegitimate baby. Unconvincing social drama additionally crippled by weak performances. Below average.

Unwed Mother (1958) 74m. *½ D: Walter Doniger. Norma Moore, Robert Vaughn, Diana Darrin, Billie Bird. Title tells all in this unsensational programmer.

Up from the Beach (1965) 99m. **½ D: Robert Parrish. Cliff Robertson, Red Buttons, Irina Demick, Marius Goring, Slim Pickens, James Robertson Justice, Broderick Crawford. Static film of American sergeant Robertson involved with French civilians in love and war during Normandy invasion.

Up Front (1951) 92m. **½ D: Alexander Hall. David Wayne, Tom Ewell, Marina Berti, Jeffrey Lynn, Richard Egan. Sometimes amusing

WW2 comedy based on Bill Mauldin's cartoon characters Willie and Joe, and their military shenanigans. Sequel: BACK AT THE FRONT.

Up Goes Maisie (1946) 89m. D: Harry Beaumont. Ann Sothern, George Murphy, Hillary Brooke, Stephen McNally, Ray Collins, Jeff York, Gloria Grafton. SEE: Maisie series.

Up in Arms (1944) C-106m. **½ D: Elliott Nugent. Danny Kaye, Dana Andrews, Constance Dowling, Dinah Shore, Louis Calhern, Lyle Talbot, Margaret Dumont, Elisha Cook, Jr. Danny's first feature film doesn't wear well, biggest asset being vivacious Dinah Shore; Virginia Mayo is one of chorus girls. Only those great patter songs hold up.

Up in Central Park (1948) 88m. ** D: William A. Seiter. Deanna Durbin, Dick Haymes, Vincent Price, Albert Sharpe, Tom Powers. Nothing-special musical features Durbin as Irish colleen in turn-of-century New York as she and reporter uncover "Boss Tweed."

Up in Mabel's Room (1944) 76m. *** D: Allan Dwan. Marjorie Reynolds, Dennis O'Keefe, Gail Patrick, Mischa Auer, Charlotte Greenwood, Lee Bowman. Engaging comedy of innocent O'Keefe embarrassed by presence of old flame Patrick in front of wife Reynolds.

Up in Smoke (1957) 64m. D: William Beaudine. Huntz Hall, Stanley Clements, Benny Rubin, Jack Mulhall, Judy Bamber. SEE: Bowery Boys series.

Up in Smoke (1978) C-86m. *** D: Lou Adler. Cheech Marin, Tommy Chong, Stacy Keach, Tom Skerritt, Edie Adams, Strother Martin. This silly pothead comedy breaks down all resistance with its cheerful vignettes about two dummies in search of "good grass." Nothing great, but undeniably funny; Cheech and Chong's first movie.

Up in the Cellar (1970) C-92m. *** D: Theodore J. Flicker. Wes Stern, Joan Collins, Larry Hagman, Judy Pace. Above-average story of alluring youth who knows how to turn women on. Flicker's screenplay is exceptionally sharp, which is why the film works.

Up Periscope (1959) C-111m. **½ D: Gordon Douglas. James Garner, Edmond O'Brien, Andra Martin, Alan Hale, Carleton Carpenter, Frank Gifford. Garner is Navy Lieutenant transferred to submarine during WW2, with usual interaction among crew as they reconnoiter Jap-held island.

Up the Creek (1958-British) 83m. **½ D: Val Guest. David Tomlinson, Wilfrid Hyde-White, Peter Sellers, Vera Day, Michael Goodliffe. Broad naval spoof à la MR. ROBERTS, which leans too much on slap-stick rather than barbs; Hyde-White is best as nonplussed admiral.

Up the Down Staircase (1967) C-124m. *** D: Robert Mulligan. Sandy Dennis, Patrick Bedford, Eileen Heckart, Ruth White, Jean Stapleton, Sorrell Booke, Ellen O'Mara. Film version of Bel Kaufman's bestseller about New York City public schools is too slickly handled to be taken seriously, but generally entertaining. Good acting, especially by O'Mara as pathetic student.

Up the MacGregors (1967-Italian-Spanish) C-93m. *½ D. Frank Garfield. David Bailey, Agata Flori, Leo Anchoriz, Roberto Camardiel. Sequel to SEVEN GUNS FOR THE MACGREGORS (but released here earlier) is distinguished from a million other Italian Westerns only by its relatively restrained use of violence.

Up the Sandbox (1972) C-97m. **½ D: Irvin Kershner. Barbra Streisand, David Selby, Jane Hoffman, John C. Becher, Jacobo Morales. Uneasy mixture of naturalism and fantasy somewhat redeemed by Streisand's performance, some funny sequences, and genuine feeling for plight of neglected young mother in New York City.

Up to His Ears (1965-French-Italian) C-94m. *** D: Philippe De Broca. Jean-Paul Belmondo, Ursula Andress, Maria Pacome, Valerie Lagrange, Jess Hahn. Wealthy young man decides to end his troubles by hiring a killer to do him in, then changes his mind. Energetic comedy runs hot and cold, but has many delicious moments.

Upper Hand, The (1967-French) C-86m. **½ D: Denys de la Patelliere. Jean Gabin, George Raft, Gert Frobe, Nadja Tiller. Labored international underworld yarn, with wooden performances by cast involved in gold smuggling.

Upstairs and Downstairs (1961-British) C-100m. *** D: Ralph Thomas.

[824]

Mylene Demongeot, Michael Craig, Anne Heywood, James Robertson Justice. Witty study of human nature: Craig married boss' daughter (Heywood) and they must entertain firm's clients. Film traces chaos of party-giving, and odd assortment of servants who come and go.

Uptight (1968) C-104m. *** D: Jules Dassin. Raymond St. Jacques, Ruby Dee, Frank Silvera, Julian Mayfield, Roscoe Lee Browne, Max Julien. Tough remake of THE INFORMER, ghetto-style. Black revolutionaries betrayed by one of their own.

Uptown Saturday Night (1974) C-104m. **½ D: Sidney Poitier. Sidney Poitier, Bill Cosby, Harry Belafonte, Calvin Lockhart, Flip Wilson, Richard Pryor, Rosalind Cash, Roscoe Lee Browne, Paula Kelly. Undeniably entertaining, this film still looks like an "Amos 'n Andy" script dusted off. Broad, silly comedy about two pals (Poitier, Cosby) who try to retrieve some stolen money and get involved with an underworld kingpin (Belafonte, in an uproarious Godfather parody). Followed by two sequels, LET'S DO IT AGAIN and A PIECE OF THE ACTION.

Uranium Boom (1956) 67m. *½ D: William Castle. Dennis Morgan, Patricia Medina, William Talman, Tina Carver. Dull account of two ore prospectors striking it rich, but more concerned with who will win Medina's love.

Ursus in the Land of Fire (1963-Italian) C-87m. *½ D: Giorgio Simonelli. Ed Fury, Claudia Mori, Adriano Micantoni, Luciana Gilli. Stupid muscleman mini-film, with Fury battling all odds to help Gilli regain her throne.

Ursus in the Valley of the Lions (1961-Italian) C-82m. ** D: Carlo Ludovico Bragaglia. Ed Fury, Moira Orfei, Mary Marlon, Alberto Lupo, Gerard Herter. Routine costumer with Fury teaming with friendly lions to overcome the barbarians.

Us SEE: **Benefit of the Doubt, The**

Users, The (1978) C-125m. TVM D: Joseph Hardy. Jaclyn Smith, Tony Curtis, Joan Fontaine, Red Buttons, George Hamilton, John Forsythe, Darren McGavin. Smalltown gal with dark past masterminds a fading film star's comeback. It's Hollywood at its most deliciously decadent in this lavishly appointed adap-

tation of Joyce Haber's thinly veiled roman à clef. Average.

Utah Blaine (1957) 75m. *½ D: Fred F. Sears. Rory Calhoun, Angela Stevens, Max Baer, Paul Langton. Undistinguished Western about Calhoun helping to overcome landgrabbing outlaws.

Utopia (1950-French) 80m. *½ D: Leo Joannon. Stan Laurel, Oliver Hardy, Suzy Delair, Max Elloy. L&H's final film saddles the great comics with poor script and production, despite decent premise of the duo inheriting a uranium-rich island. Also known as ATOLL K.

V. I. P.S, The (1963-British) C-119m. **½ D: Anthony Asquith. Elizabeth Taylor, Richard Burton, Louis Jourdan, Margaret Rutherford, Rod Taylor, Maggie Smith, Orson Welles, Linda Christian, Elsa Martinelli. Glossy Grand Hotel plot, set in London airport. Everyone is terribly rich and beautiful; if you like watching rich, beautiful people, fine. If not, it's all meaningless. Rutherford (who won an Oscar for this) is excellent.

Vacation from Marriage (1945-British) 92m. *** D: Alexander Korda. Robert Donat, Deborah Kerr, Glynis Johns, Ann Todd, Roland Culver, Elliot Mason. Donat and Kerr sparkle in story of dull couple separated by WW2, each rejuvenated by wartime romance. Johns is perky as Kerr's military friend. British version, titled PERFECT STRANGERS, ran 102m.

Vacation in Hell, A (1979) C-100m. TVM D: David Greene. Priscilla Barnes, Barbara Feldon, Andrea Marcovicci, Maureen McCormick, Michael Brandon. Vacationers at a posh island resort wander into the jungle and face terror. Average.

Vagabond King, The (1956) C-86m. ** D: Michael Curtiz. Kathryn Grayson, Oreste, Rita Moreno, Cedric Hardwicke, Walter Hampden, Leslie Nielsen. Bland remake of Rudolph Friml's operetta (filmed before in 1930), about poet-scoundrel Francois Villon. Oreste was touted as new musical star in 1956, but didn't quite make it.

Valachi Papers, The (1972-Italian) C-125m. **½ D: Terence Young. Charles Bronson, Lino Ventura, Jill Ireland, Joseph Wiseman, Walter Chiari, Amedeo Nazzari. Sloppy but engrossing account of Mafia life as seen through eyes of famed informer Joseph Valachi (Bronson). Lots of blood will go for TV screening, but gangland flavor will remain.

Valdez is Coming (1971) **C-90m.** **½ D: Edwin Sherin. Burt Lancaster, Susan Clark, Jon Cypher, Barton Heyman, Hector Elizondo. OK Western for undemanding viewers, with Lancaster a Mexican-American deputy sheriff forced to confront ruthless land baron after triggering local hostilities. Filmed in Spain.

Valentine (1979) **C-100m. TVM** D: Lee Philips. Mary Martin, Jack Albertson, Loretta Swit, Danny De-Vito, Lloyd Nolan, Judy Norton-Taylor. Two young-at-heart senior citizens fall in love in this poignant drama that marked Mary Martin's TV-movie debut. Average.

Valentino (1951) **C-102m.** *½ D: Lewis Allen. Anthony Dexter, Eleanor Parker, Richard Carlson, Patricia Medina. Undistinguished, superficial biography of famed star of American silent films.

Valentino (1977) **C-127m.** *½ D: Ken Russell. Rudolf Nureyev, Leslie Caron, Michelle Phillips, Carol Kane, Felicity Kendal, Seymour Cassel, Peter Vaughan. Typically excessive, visually flamboyant Ken Russell "biography" offers little insight on great screen lover, and suffers further from Nureyev's awkward performance. But any film that casts Huntz Hall as movie mogul Jesse Lasky can't be *all* bad.

Valerie (1957) **84m.** *½ D: Gerd Oswald. Sterling Hayden, Anita Ekberg, Anthony Steel, Malcolm Atterbury. Unmemorable account (via flashbacks) of facts leading up to the wounding of Hayden's wife, and death of her parents.

Valiant Is the Word for Carrie (1936) **110m.** **½ D: Wesley Ruggles. Gladys George, Arline Judge, John Howard, Dudley Digges, Harry Carey, Isabel Jewell, Jackie Moran. Get out your handkerchief for this one, the epitome of 1930s soapers as selfless Gladys George devotes herself to orphan children. She won an Oscar nomination for her performance.

Valley of Decision, The (1945) **111m.** *** D: Tay Garnett. Greer Garson, Gregory Peck, Donald Crisp, Lionel Barrymore, Preston Foster, Marsha Hunt. Not overpowering, as intended, but good film of housemaid Garson marrying master's son Peck, continuing life in same household; set in Pittsburgh.

Valley of Eagles (1951-British) **85m.** **½ D: Terence Young. Jack Warner, Nadia Gray, Christopher Lee, Anthony Dawson. Above-par chase tale of scientist tracking down his wife and assistant who stole his research data and headed for the north country.

Valley of Gwangi (1969) **C-95m.** **½ D: James O'Connolly. James Franciscus, Gila Golan, Richard Carlson, Laurence Naismith, Dennis Kilbane. Standard reworking of King Kong theme: adventurers in Mexico stumble upon prehistoric monster, hit on idea to display their find in zoo-type situation, make money. Script and production have holes, but film is sparked by Ray Harryhausen special effects.

Valley of Mystery (1967) **C-90m.** ** D: Joseph Leytes. Richard Egan, Peter Graves, Joby Baker, Lois Nettleton, Harry Guardino, Julie Adams, Fernando Lamas. Lackluster drama pitting plane passengers and crew against jungle perils, personal conflict when flight crash lands. Made for TV but released to theaters first.

Valley of the Dolls (1967) **C-123m.** BOMB D: Mark Robson. Barbara Parkins, Patty Duke, Sharon Tate, Susan Hayward, Paul Burke, Tony Scotti, Martin Milner. Scattered unintentional laughs do not compensate for terribly written, acted, and directed adaptation of Jacqueline Susann novel about three young women in show biz.

Valley of the Dragons (1961) **79m.** *½ D: Edward Bernds. Cesare Danova, Sean McClory, Joan Staley, Danielle De Metz, Roger Til. Sloppy low-budget sci-fi about two men's adventures on a prehistoric planet.

Valley of the Giants (1938) **C-79m.** ** D: William Keighley. Wayne Morris, Claire Trevor, Frank McHugh, Alan Hale, Donald Crisp, Charles Bickford. Color is only asset of juvenile film about man whose love of redwoods surpasses everything else. Remade as THE BIG TREES.

Valley of the Headhunters (1953) **67m.** D: William Berke. Johnny Weissmuller, Christine Larson, Nelson Leigh, Vince Townsend, Steven Ritch. SEE: **Jungle Jim** series.

Valley of the Kings (1954) C-86m. ** D: Robert Pirosh. Robert Taylor, Eleanor Parker, Kurt Kasznar, Carlos Thompson. Despite stars, a meandering adventure yarn of excavations in Egypt for tombs of ancient pharaohs.

Valley of the Redwoods (1960) 63m. *½ D: William Witney. John Hudson, Lynn Bernay, Ed Nelson, Michael Forest, Robert Shayne, John Brinkley. Programmer involving payroll theft and escape of robbers to Canada.

Valley of the Sun (1942) 84m. *** D: George Marshall. Lucille Ball, Cedric Hardwicke, Dean Jagger, James Craig, Billy Gilbert, Antonio Moreno, Tom Tyler. Intrigue of the old West with crooked white man provoking Indian uprising as he is being hunted by colonial agent.

Valley of the Zombies (1946) 56m. *½ D: Philip Ford. Robert Livingston, Adrian Booth, Ian Keith, Thomas Jackson, LeRoy Mason. Witless horror epic of man-returned-from-dead bent on revenge.

Value for Money (1955-British) C-89m. *** D: Ken Annakin. John Gregson, Diana Dors, Derek Farr, Donald Pleasence, Cyril Smith. Funny little comedy about young man inheriting father's money and his enjoyment of same.

Vampire (1979) C-100m. TVM D: E. W. Swackhamer. Jason Miller, E. G. Marshall, Richard Lynch, Jessica Walter, Kathryn Harrold, Barrie Youngfellow, Jonelle Allen. Brooding architect and retired cop join forces to destroy a modern-day vampire who's stalking San Francisco taking vengeance on those who despoiled his resting place. Campy, and a pleasant surprise. Above average.

Vampire, The (1957) 74m. *½ D: Paul Landres. John Beal, Coleen Gray, Dabbs Greer, Raymond Greenleaf. Minor chiller with scientist turned into blood-seeker. Retitled: MARK OF THE VAMPIRE.

Vampire Bat, The (1933) 63m. **½ D: Frank Strayer. Lionel Atwill, Melvyn Douglas, Fay Wray, Dwight Frye, Lionel Belmore. Good cast helps average story along. Atwill stars as mad doctor forced to kill townsfolk in search of "blood substitute."

Vampire Circus (1972-British) C-87m. *½ D: Robert Young. Laurence Payne, Thorley Walters, John Moulder-Brown, Lynne Frederick. Vampire kills young girl; villagers kill vampire, who pronounces curse on the unsuspecting hamlet, which has its effects some years later. Muddled Hammer horror film.

Vampire Lovers, The (1971-British) C-88m. **½ D: Roy Ward Baker. Ingrid Pitt, Pippa Steele, Madeleine Smith, Peter Cushing, George Cole, Dawn Addams, Kate O'Mara. Rather erotic chiller about lesbian vampires will probably be cut for TV; story filmed previously by Roger Vadim as BLOOD AND ROSES.

Vampire Men of the Lost Planet (1970) C-85m. BOMB D: Al Adamson. John Carradine, Robert Dix, Vicki Volanti, Joey Benson, Jennifer Bishop. Scientist traces epidemic of vampire attacks on earth to strange, distant planet, with the aid of stock footage from other movies. A real mishmosh, released theatrically as HORROR OF THE BLOOD MONSTER, CREATURES OF THE PREHISTORIC PLANET, and HORROR CREATURES OF THE PREHISTORIC PLANET.

Vanessa, Her Love Story (1935) 74m. ** D: William K. Howard. Helen Hayes, Robert Montgomery, Otto Kruger, May Robson, Lewis Stone. Soapy story of gypsy love with Hayes attracted to roguish Montgomery. Dated romance doesn't come off too well today.

Vanished (1971) C-200m. TVM D: Buzz Kulik. Richard Widmark, Skye Aubrey, James Farentino, Arthur Hill, Robert Hooks, E. G. Marshall, Eleanor Parker. Presidential advisor disappears mysteriously; F.B.I. advises they've information that man in question was homosexual; why won't President make statement? Interesting resolution, but film's point of view seems like standard mystery drama. From Fletcher Knebel's best-seller. Good cast, though. Average.

Vanishing American, The (1955) 90m. ** D: Joseph Kane. Scott Brady, Audrey Totter, Forrest Tucker, Gene Lockhart, Jim Davis, Jay Silverheels. Mild, minor film about landgrabbers trying to take Navajo territory.

Vanishing Point (1971) C-107m. ** D: Richard C. Sarafian. Barry Newman, Cleavon Little, Dean Jagger, Victoria Medlin. Initially intriguing story of sprawling car chase with disc jockey helping driver elude police, eventually disappoints. Exceptional rock score.

Vanishing Prairie, The (1954) C-75m. *** D: James Algar. Narrated by Winston Hibler. Disney's second True-Life Adventure feature provides astonishing footage of animal life in the great plains, including the birth of a buffalo calf. Fine presentation with little Disney gimmickry; Academy Award winner.

Vanishing Virginian, The (1942) 97m. *½ D: Frank Borzage. Kathryn Grayson, Frank Morgan, Spring Byington, Natalie Thompson. Tepid drama about suffragette movement down South.

Vanishing Wilderness (1974) C-93m. *** D: Arthur Dubs, Heinz Seilmann. Cowboy actor Rex Allen narrates this stunningly photographed wildlife documentary which covers virtually all of North America—from the alligators of the Everglades to the polar bears of the Arctic. Topnotch but for excessive narration and heavenly choirs punctuating each scene.

Vanquished, The (1953) C-84m. *½ D: Edward Ludwig. John Payne, Jan Sterling, Coleen Gray, Lyle Bettger, Ellen Corby. Bland little Western about corruption within a town's administration.

Variety Girl (1947) 83m. **½ D: George Marshall. Mary Hatcher, Olga San Juan, De Forest Kelley, William Demarest, Frank Faylen, Frank Ferguson. Hatcher and San Juan head for Hollywood with hopes of stardom; flimsy excuse for Paramount guest stars Bob Hope, Bing Crosby, Gary Cooper, Ray Milland, etc. Hope and Crosby come off best in amusing golfing scene. Puppetoon segment in color.

Varsity Show (1937) 81m. *** D: William Keighley. Dick Powell, Priscilla Lane, Fred Waring, Walter Catlett, Ted Healy, Rosemary Lane. Powell is Broadway producer who agrees to stage a show at his alma mater; result is a parade of musical numbers, including fine specialties by Buck and Bubbles, and rousing finale staged by Busby Berkeley. Originally released at 121m.

Vatican Affair, The (1969-Italian) C-94m. ** D: Emilio Miraglia. Walter Pidgeon, Ira Furstenberg, Klaus Kinski, Tino Carraro. Pidgeon masterminds Vatican robbery in routine heist film.

Vault of Horror (1973-British) C-

93m. **½ D: Roy Ward Baker. Daniel Massey, Anna Massey, Terry-Thomas, Glynis Johns, Curt Jurgens, Dawn Addams, Tom Baker, Denholm Elliott, Michael Craig, Edward Judd. Five horror tales interwoven by thin connecting thread, dealing with murder, torture, bloodthirsty vampires, voodoo, adapted from old E. C. Comics. Fine cast with so-so material.

Vega$ (1978) C-74m. TVM D: Richard Lang. Robert Urich, Tony Curtis, Red Buttons, Will Sampson, June Allyson, Edd Byrnes, Jack Kelly, Greg Morris. The pilot to the hit series about a flashy private eye who makes the Strip his beat and has scantily clad pretties in constant pursuit. Average.

Veils of Bagdad (1953) C-82m. **½ D: George Sherman. Victor Mature, Virginia Field, James Arness, Nick Cravat. Standard Arabian nights costumer, with Mature zestier than most such cardboard heroes.

Velvet Touch, The (1948) 97m. **½ D: John Gage. Rosalind Russell, Leo Genn, Claire Trevor, Sydney Greenstreet, Leon Ames, Frank McHugh. Satisfying murder mystery features Russell as stage actress who commits perfect crime, with a nifty ending.

Vendetta (1950) 84m. ** D: Mel Ferrer. Faith Domergue, George Dolenz, Hillary Brooke, Nigel Bruce, Joseph Calleia, Hugo Haas. Florid but uneven costume melodrama about a woman who must avenge her family's honor when her father is murdered. Howard Hughes' expensive showcase for beautiful but untalented Domergue.

Venetian Affair (1967) C-92m. ** D: Jerry Thorpe. Robert Vaughn, Elke Sommer, Felicia Farr, Karl Boehm, Luciana Paluzzi, Boris Karloff. Limp spy vehicle not far removed from Vaughn's "Man from UNCLE" TV series. International intrigue isn't too intriguing in this one; Karloff is good in a supporting role.

Vengeance of Fu Manchu, The (1968-British) C-91m. ** D: Jeremy Summers. Christopher Lee, Douglas Wilmer, Tsai Chin, Horst Frank, Maria Rohm, Howard Marion Crawford. Third entry in low-budget series that keeps Sax Rohmer stories in period. Lee again stars as evil genius this time out to destroy world police organization, and discredit arch-nemesis Nayland Smith

(Wilmer). Good cast working below capabilities; lousy script.

Vengeance of She, The (1968-British) C-101m. ** D: Cliff Owen. John Richardson, Olinka Berova, Edward Judd, Colin Blakely. Woman mistaken for reincarnated she-goddess in weak sequel to Haggard's original.

Vengeance Valley (1951) C-83m. ** D: Richard Thorpe. Burt Lancaster, Robert Walker, Joanne Dru, Sally Forrest, John Ireland, Carleton Carpenter. Hugh O'Brian. Sex in the West with Lancaster and Walker as battling brothers, Dru and Forrest their women. Walker plays slimy villain with gusto.

Venus in Furs (1970-British-Italian-German) 86m. *½ D: Jess Franco. James Darren, Barbara McNair, Maria Rohm, Klaus Kinski, Dennis Price, Margaret Lee. Musician is baffled to see a woman who had previously washed ashore in a mutilated state; poor mystery, bound to be cut for TV.

Vera Cruz (1954) C-94m. *** D: Robert Aldrich. Gary Cooper, Burt Lancaster, Denise Darcel, Cesar Romero. Lumbering yet exciting Western set in 1860s Mexico with Cooper and Lancaster involved in plot to overthrow Emperor Maximilian.

Verboten! (1959) 93m. **½ D: Samuel Fuller. James Best, Susan Cummings, Tom Pittman, Paul Dubov, Dick Kallman, Steven Geray. American soldier falls in love with embittered German girl in occupied Berlin after WW2. High-pitched drama, flamboyantly directed by Fuller.

Verdict, The (1946) 86m. **½ D: Don Siegel. Peter Lorre, Sydney Greenstreet, Joan Lorring, George Coulouris, Arthur Shields, Rosalind Ivan, Holmes Herbert. Greenstreet and Lorre make the most of this "perfect crime" yarn, with Greenstreet as Scotland Yard inspector who's "retired" when his methods are thought to be outmoded.

Vertigo (1958) C-120m. ***½ D: Alfred Hitchcock. James Stewart, Kim Novak, Barbara Bel Geddes, Tom Helmore. Fascinating Hitchcock tale set in Frisco that defies rational description. Stewart is police detective with fear of heights who finds himself in a baffling situation involving an unusual girl (Novak). To reveal many more details would spoil a great film. Fine musical score by Bernard Herrmann adds to atmosphere.

Very Honorable Guy, A (1934) 62m. *½ D: Lloyd Bacon. Joe E. Brown, Alice White, Alan Dinehart, Hobart Cavanaugh, Al Dubin. Flat comedy from Damon Runyon story about gambler who sells his body to science—ahead of time—in order to pay off debt. Change of pace for Brown doesn't work at all.

Very Important Person SEE: Coming-Out Party

Very Missing Person, A (1972) C-73m. TVM D: Russ Mayberry. Eve Arden, Julie Newmar, James Gregory, Skye Aubrey. Arden recreates Hildegarde Withers character first played in 1930s by Edna May Oliver in standard detective thriller in which woman's disappearance leads to murder. Average.

Very Special Favor, A (1965) C-104m. **½ D: Michael Gordon. Rock Hudson, Leslie Caron, Charles Boyer, Walter Slezak, Dick Shawn, Larry Storch, Nita Talbot, Jay Novello. Too-often blah, forced comedy of Boyer asking Hudson to romance daughter Caron.

Very Thought of You, The (1944) 99m. ** D: Delmer Daves. Eleanor Parker, Dennis Morgan, Dane Clark, Faye Emerson, Beulah Bondi. Flat romance of couple marrying during WW2, encountering family wrath when they returned home; unusual Daves backfire.

Vice Squad (1931) 80m. ** D: John Cromwell. Paul Lukas, Kay Francis, Helen Johnson (Judith Wood), Esther Howard, William B. Davidson. Lukas is excellent in tale of corrupt vice squad, but production needs a shot of adrenalin. Good potential dissipated by slow presentation.

Vice Squad (1953) 87m. **½ D: Arnold Laven. Edward G. Robinson, Paulette Goddard, K. T. Stevens, Lee Van Cleef. Well-paced account of events in typical day of police detective department.

Vicious Circle, The SEE: The Circle

Vicki (1953) 85m. **½ D: Harry Horner. Jeanne Crain, Jean Peters, Elliott Reid, Casey Adams, Richard Boone, Carl Betz, Aaron Spelling. Remake of I WAKE UP SCREAMING, with Boone the resolute cop convinced agent Reid killed chanteuse girlfriend Peters. Dramatic flair isn't always evident.

Victim (1961-British) 100m. ***½ D:

Basil Dearden. Dirk Bogarde, Sylvia Sims, Dennis Price, Peter McEnery, Donald Churchill. Fine thriller with lawyer Bogarde risking reputation by trying to confront gang of blackmailers who murdered his one-time male lover. Considered daring at the time for treatment of homosexuality.

Victim, The (1972) C-73m. TVM D: Herschel Daugherty. Elizabeth Montgomery, George Maharis, Eileen Heckart, Sue Ane Langdon, Jess Walton, Ross Elliott. Unaware that after telephone conversation sister was murdered, wealthy Katherine Wainwright travels through rainstorm to be at her side. Slowly, she realizes something is definitely wrong. OK performances, but crazy direction ruins intended suspense. Average.

Victors, The (1963) 175m. *** D: Carl Foreman. George Hamilton, George Peppard, Vince Edwards, Eli Wallach, Melina Mercouri, Romy Schneider, Jeanne Moreau, Peter Fonda, Senta Berger, Elke Sommer, Albert Finney. Sprawling WW2 drama of Allied soldiers on the march through Europe, focusing on their loving and fighting. Good cast and direction overcomes ambling script.

Victory (1940) 78m. *** D: John Cromwell. Fredric March, Betty Field, Cedric Hardwicke, Jerome Cowan, Rafaela Ottiano, Sig Ruman. March is authentic in tale of loner whose idyllic island life is disrupted by band of cutthroats; flavorful adaptation of Joseph Conrad novel sags at the end. Filmed before as DANGEROUS PARADISE (1929).

Victory at Entebbe (1976) C-150m. TVM D: Marvin J. Chomsky. Kirk Douglas, Elizabeth Taylor, Burt Lancaster, Linda Blair, Helen Hayes, Anthony Hopkins, Helmut Berger, David Groh, Theodore Bikel, Richard Dreyfuss, Jessica Walter, Julius Harris, Harris Yulin. Cliché-ridden recreation of lightning raid by Israeli commandos to free Jewish hostages imprisoned by Arab terrorists in Uganda. Only Lancaster and Hopkins, as Israeli defense minister Shimon Peres and Prime Minister Yitzhak Rabin, manage anything like thoughtful impersonations, while Harris does Idi Amin like a vaudeville turn (as written). Originally taped for topicality, later committed to film. See RAID ON ENTEBBE

or OPERATION THUNDERBOLT for better treatment of the subject. Average.

Victory at Sea (1954) 108m. *** Produced by: Henry Salomon. Narrated by: Alexander Scourby. Briskly edited version of popular TV documentary series, highlighting Allied fight during WW2. Excellent photography, rousing Richard Rodgers score.

View from Pompey's Head, The (1955) C-97m. **½ D: Philip Dunne. Richard Egan, Dana Wynter, Cameron Mitchell, Marjorie Rambeau, Sidney Blackmer, Bess Flowers. Superficial gloss from Hamilton Basso novel about social and racial prejudice in small Southern town; Blackmer as aging novelist and Rambeau his wife come off best.

View from the Bridge, A (1962) 110m. *** D: Sidney Lumet. Raf Vallone, Maureen Stapleton, Carol Lawrence, Jean Sorel. Effective adaptation of Arthur Miller drama set near Brooklyn waterfront, involving dock worker Vallone's rejection of wife Stapleton and suppressed love of niece Lawrence; Sorel is smuggled-in immigrant Lawrence loves.

Vigil in the Night (1940) 96m. *** D: George Stevens. Carole Lombard, Brian Aherne, Anne Shirley, Rhys Williams, Peter Cushing, Rafaela Ottiano, Ethel Griffies. Compelling drama of provincial hospital life in England, with outstanding work by Lombard as dedicated nurse, Shirley as her flighty sister, Aherne as doctor. Potentially corny script made credible and exciting by good cast, fine direction pulling viewer into the story.

Vigilantes Return, The (1947) C-67m. ** D: Ray Taylor. Margaret Lindsay, Jon Hall, Paula Drew, Andy Devine, Robert Wilcox, Jack Lambert. Standard Western with marshal Hall sent to bring law and order to untamed town.

Viking Queen, The (1967-British) C-91m. ** D: Don Chaffey. Don Murray, Carita, Donald Houston, Andrew Keir, Adrienne Corri, Niall MacGinnis, Wilfrid Lawson. Empty-headed costumer of early England under Roman rule, with plenty of gore as anarchists incite a violent uprising among the people. Murray and fine British actors are lost.

Vikings, The (1958) C-114m. **½ D: Richard Fleischer. Kirk Douglas, Tony Curtis, Ernest Borgnine, Janet

Leigh. Big-name cast and on-location photography in Norway and Brittany are only standouts in routine Viking adventure.

Villa! (1958) C-72m. *½ D: James B. Clark. Brian Keith, Cesar Romero, Margia Dean, Rodolfo Hoyos. Dull recreation of events in life of Mexican bandit.

Villa Rides (1968) C-125m. ** D: Buzz Kulik. Yul Brynner, Robert Mitchum, Charles Bronson, Herbert Lom, Jill Ireland. Witless retelling of Villa's Mexican campaign, with broadened focus on cohort Bronson, captured pilot Mitchum.

Village of the Damned (1960-British) 78m. *** D: Wolf Rilla. George Sanders, Barbara Shelley, Michael Gwynne, Laurence Naismith, John Phillips, Richard Vernon. Fine adaptation of John Wyndham novel about mishap in English village followed by birth of strange, emotionless children. Well-made chiller, followed by sequel CHILDREN OF THE DAMNED.

Village of the Giants (1965) C-80m. BOMB D: Bert I. Gordon. Tommy Kirk, Johnny Crawford, Beau Bridges, Ronny Howard, Tisha Sterling, Tim Rooney. Poor special effects are just one problem with this silly film about teenagers growing to tremendous heights. Based on H. G. Wells story, refilmed by Gordon in 1976 as FOOD FOR THE GODS.

Villain (1971-British) C-98m. *½ D: Michael Tuchner. Richard Burton, Ian McShane, Nigel Davenport, Fiona Lewis, Donald Sinden, Cathleen Nesbitt. Nasty stomach-churning melodrama about British underworld, taken from James Barlow's novel *The Burden of Proof*. Burton plays vicious homosexual thug only a mother (Nesbitt) could love.

Villain, The (1979) C-89m. ** D: Hal Needham. Kirk Douglas, Ann-Margret, Arnold Schwarzenegger, Paul Lynde, Foster Brooks, Ruth Buzzi, Jack Elam. Lynde plays an Indian chief named Nervous Elk, and so it goes. Combination Western spoof/Road Runner cartoon makes CAT BALLOU look subtle, but may make you laugh if it hits you in a silly frame of mind.

Villain Still Pursued Her, The (1940) 66m. ** D: Edward F. Cline. Anita Louise, Richard Cromwell, Hugh Herbert, Alan Mowbray, Buster Keaton, Billy Gilbert, Margaret Hamilton. Laughs are few and far between in this full-length spoof of old-time melodramas in which boos and hisses are encouraged. Even pie-throwing sequence is dull. Keaton adds brightest moments.

Vintage, The (1957) C-92m. ** D: Jeffrey Hayden. Pier Angeli, Michele Morgan, John Kerr, Mel Ferrer, Theodore Bikel, Leif Erickson. Strangely cast melodrama set in vineyard of France involving two brothers on the lam.

Violent City SEE: The Family

Violent Enemy, The (1968-British) C-94m. *** D: Don Sharp. Tom Bell, Susan Hampshire, Ed Begley, Jon Laurimore, Michael Standing, Noel Purcell. Intense drama of IRA plot to blow up British power plant, and various motives involved.

Violent Four, The (1968-Italian) C-98m. ** D: Carlo Lizzani. Gian Maria Volonte, Thomas Milian, Margaret Lee, Carla Gravina, Don Backy. Unexceptional tale of notorious Italian robbery gang which stages massive bank holdup schemes, becoming police's number-one target.

Violent Men, The (1955) C-96m. **½ D: Rudolph Maté, Barbara Stanwyck, Glenn Ford, Edward G. Robinson, Dianne Foster, Brian Keith, Richard Jaeckel. Robinson is unscrupulous, wealthy rancher in conflict with good folk of the valley, Stanwyck his wife. Some good action sequences.

Violent Ones, The (1967) C-84m. *½ D: Fernando Lamas. Fernando Lamas, Aldo Ray, Tommy Sands, David Carradine, Lisa Gaye, Melinda Marx. Junk about lawman Lamas' problems in getting Mexican community to refrain from lynching his prisoners when they are suspected of raping and murdering Marx.

Violent Professionals, The (1973-Italian) C-92m. ** D: Sergio Martino. Richard Conte, Luc Merenda, Silvana Tranquilli, Steffan Zaccharias. Mezza-mezza Italian action flick about a suspended cop who infiltrates the mob to get the goods on a notorious gang boss. Violent indeed.

Violent Road (1958) 86m. **½ D: Howard W. Koch. Brian Keith, Dick Foran, Efrem Zimbalist, Jr., Merry Anders. Well-done programmer involving men driving explosives over bumpy road, allowing for each to reexamine his way of life.

Violent Saturday (1955) C-91m. ***

D: Richard Fleischer. Victor Mature, Richard Egan, Lee Marvin, Sylvia Sidney, Ernest Borgnine, Tommy Noonan. Effective study of repercussion on small town when bank robbers carry out a bloody holdup.

Violent Summer (1961-French) 85m. ** D: Michel Boisrond. Martine Carol, Jean Desailly, Dahlia Lavi, Henri-Jacques Huet. Unconvincing tale of murder of a halfwit girl, with most of the guests at a Riviera resort home prime suspects; too many loose threads.

Virgin and the Gypsy, The (1970-British) C-92m. **½ D: Christopher Miles. Joanna Shimkus, Franco Nero, Honor Blackman, Mark Burns, Maurice Denham, Fay Compton, Kay Walsh. D. H. Lawrence's novella comes to screen as interesting, atmospheric, but unbelievable love story. Girl falls for vagabond gypsy and suffers consequences.

Virgin Island (1959-British) C-84m. **½ D: Pat Jackson. John Cassavetes, Virginia Maskell, Sidney Poitier, Colin Gordon. Leisurely study of author Cassavetes and bride Maskell moving to Caribbean isle; film lightly touches on racial issue.

Virgin of Nuremburg, The SEE: **Horror Castle**

Virgin Queen, The (1955) C-92m. *** D: Henry Koster. Bette Davis, Richard Todd, Joan Collins, Herbert Marshall, Dan O'Herlihy, Rod Taylor. Davis is in full authority in her second portrayal of Queen Elizabeth I, and her conflicts with Walter Raleigh.

Virgin Soldiers, The (1970-British) C-96m. *** D: John Dexter. Lynn Redgrave, Hywel Bennett, Nigel Davenport, Nigel Patrick, Tsai Chin, Jack Shepherd, Rachel Kempson. Solid, unpretentious adaptation of successful play by newcomer director. Two kinds of army virginity examined: Hywel Bennett, one of many raw British recruits in Malaysia, unexposed to sex or to combat. Great cast, excellent production.

Virgin Spring, The (1960-Swedish) 88m. *** D: Ingmar Bergman. Max von Sydow, Brigitta Valberg, Gunnel Lindblom, Brigitta Pattersson, Axel Duberg. Brooding dramatic fable involving farmer's daughter raped and murdered by lusting visitors, with a magical spring bursting forth from her death spot.

Virginia (1941) C-110m. ** D: Edward H. Griffith. Madeleine Carroll, Fred MacMurray, Sterling Hayden, Helen Broderick, Marie Wilson, Carolyn Lee. Well-mounted but tedious film of Southern woman (Carroll) who must sacrifice her property and herself in order to raise money to live.

Virginia City (1940) 121m. **½ D: Michael Curtiz. Errol Flynn, Miriam Hopkins, Randolph Scott, Humphrey Bogart, Frank McHugh, Alan Hale. Big cast in lush Civil War Western, doesn't live up to expectations; Bogart cast as slimy Mexican bandido.

Virginia Hill Story, The (1974) C-78m. TVM D: Joel Schumacher. Dyan Cannon, Harvey Keitel, Allen Garfield, John Vernon, Herbert Anderson, Bobby Benson, John Quade, Conrad Janis. Dramatized biography tracing life and loves of gangster Bugsy Siegel's moll and the testimony about organized crime she gave before the Kefauver committee. Cannon gives a florid portrayal in the title role, Keitel is properly sinister as Siegel, and Anderson is stentorian as Kefauver. Above average.

Virginian, The (1929) 90m. **½ D: Victor Fleming. Gary Cooper, Richard Arlen, Walter Huston, Mary Brian, Chester Conklin, Eugene Pallette. Owen Wister's novel becomes stiff but interesting Western, salvaged by good climactic shoot-out; Huston is slimy villain, and Cooper has one of his better early roles.

Virginian, The (1946) C-90m. **½ D: Stuart Gilmore. Joel McCrea, Brian Donlevy, Sonny Tufts, Barbara Britton, Fay Bainter, Henry O'Neill, William Frawley, Vince Barnett, Paul Guilfoyle. Remake of '29 classic Western follows story closely. Good, not great, results due to story showing its age. McCrea is hero, Donlevy the villain. Tufts a good-guy-turned-bad.

Virtuous Sin, The (1930) 82m. BOMB D: George Cukor, Louis Gasnier. Walter Huston, Kay Francis, Kenneth MacKenna, Jobyna Howland, Paul Cavanagh. Laughably bad production with alluring Francis giving herself to Russian general Huston so he will exempt her husband from death sentence. A real turkey.

Viscount, The (1967-French-Italian-Spanish) C-98m. BOMB D: Maurice Cloche, Kerwin Mathews, Edmond

O'Brien, Jane Fleming, Yvelle Lebon, Jean Yanne, Fernando Rey. In spite of the presence of such well-known European actors as Yanne and Rey, grade-D spy film is a waste of time.

Visions . . . (1972) C-73m. TVM D: Lee Katzin. Monte Markham, Telly Savalas, Barbara Anderson, Lonny Chapman, Tim O'Connor, Richard Erdman. College professor flashes on visions of someone planting explosives in buildings, relates experience to Denver police who keep surveillance on him for fear he may be mad bomber. Fairly tense situations, but film's pacing too hurried and sloppy. Average. Alternate title: VISIONS OF DEATH.

Visions of Eight (1973) C-110m. ** D: Juri Ozerov, Mai Zetterling, Arthur Penn, Michael Phleghar, Kon Ichikawa, Milos Forman, Claude Lelouch, John Schlesinger. Seemingly good idea of having eight different directors give eight different views of 1972 Olympics results in strangely disappointing film, considering all the talent involved; with possible exception of Schlesinger's final chapter on marathon run, none of the episodes stay in the memory.

Visit, The (1964) 100m. **½ D: Bernhard Wicki. Ingrid Bergman, Anthony Quinn, Irina Demick, Paolo Stoppa, Hans-Christian Blech, Romolo Valli, Valentina Cortesa, Eduardo Ciannelli. Intriguing but uneven film parable of greed and evil; wealthy Bergman returns to European home town, offering a fantastic sum to the people there if they will legitimately kill her first seducer (Quinn). Actors struggle with melodramatic script; results are interesting if not always successful.

Visit to a Chief's Son (1974) C-92m. **½ D: Lamont Johnson. Richard Mulligan, Johnny Sekka, John Philip Hogdon, Jesse Kinaru, Chief Lomoiro, Jock Anderson. OK family drama about a self-centered father and son who become humanized on an African safari.

Visit to a Small Planet (1960) 85m. **½ D: Norman Taurog. Jerry Lewis, Joan Blackman, Earl Holliman, Fred Clark, Lee Patrick, Gale Gordon. Gore Vidal satire becomes talky Lewis vehicle with Jerry the alien landed on earth to observe man's strange ways.

Visitors, The (1972) C-88m. BOMB D: Elia Kazan. Patrick McVey, Patricia Joyce, James Woods, Chico Martinez. Deplorable story of two Vietnam vets who, upon release from prison for sex crime, invade the house of third vet who testified at their trial. Unlikely for TV showing.

Viva Knievel! (1977) C-106m. BOMB D: Gordon Douglas. Evel Knievel, Gene Kelly, Lauren Hutton, Red Buttons, Leslie Nielsen, Frank Gifford, Cameron Mitchell. Hopeless "tribute" to the kiddie/yahoo idol, released just before he got six months in the pokey for assaulting a writer with a baseball bat. Only for collectors of the bizarre.

Viva Las Vegas (1964) C-86m. **½ D: George Sidney. Elvis Presley, Ann-Margret, Cesare Danova, William Demarest. Perky cast and colorful gambling city locale elevate this Presley vehicle, with Elvis a sports car racer.

Viva Maria! (1965-French) C-119m. ***½ D: Louis Malle. Brigitte Bardot, Jeanne Moreau, George Hamilton, Gregor Von Rezzori, Paulette Dubost. Rollicking tale of two beautiful entertainers/revolutionaries in Mexico has inconsistent first half, then takes off for hilarious finish. Lots of fun.

Viva Max! (1969) C-92m. **½ D: Jerry Paris. Peter Ustinov, Pamela Tiffin, Jonathan Winters, John Astin, Keenan Wynn, Harry Morgan, Alice Ghostley, Kenneth Mars. Mildly amusing yarn of eccentric Mexican general recapturing Alamo, sending equally inept American militia to rout him out. Forced humor doesn't always work.

Viva Villa! (1934) 115m. ***½ D: Jack Conway. Wallace Beery, Leo Carrillo, Fay Wray, Donald Cook, Stuart Erwin, Joseph Schildkraut, Katherine DeMille. Viva Beery, in one of his best films as the rowdy Mexican rebel who led the fight for Madera's Mexican Republic. Film plays with facts, but is entertaining.

Viva Zapata! (1952) 113m. **** D: Elia Kazan. Marlon Brando, Jean Peters, Anthony Quinn, Joseph Wiseman, Margo, Mildred Dunnock. Vibrant film about Mexican peasant's rise to power and eventual Presidency. Brando is perfect in title role, Quinn equally fine in Oscar-winning performance as his brother. Script by John Steinbeck.

Vivacious Lady (1938) 90m. *** D: George Stevens. James Stewart, Ginger Rogers, James Ellison, Beulah

Bondi, Charles Coburn, Frances Mercer, Grady Sutton, Franklin Pangborn. Overlong but entertaining comedy of professor Stewart marrying nightclub singer Rogers, trying to break the news to his conservative family and fiancé back home. Bondi is fun in amusing variation on usual motherly role.

Vogues (1937) C-108m. ** D: Irving Cummings. Warner Baxter, Joan Bennett, Helen Vinson, Mischa Auer, Alan Mowbray, Jerome Cowan, Marjorie Gateson, Polly Rowles, Hedda Hopper. Minor musical with wealthy Bennett deciding to work as fashion model to chagrin of fiancé Baxter. One good song, "That Old Feeling." Original title: VOGUES OF 1938.

Voice in the Mirror (1958) 102m. **½ D: Harry Keller. Richard Egan, Julie London, Arthur O'Connell, Walter Matthau, Troy Donahue. Effective, unpretentious account of Egan trying to combat alcoholism, with help of wife London.

Voice in the Wind (1944) 85m. *** D: Arthur Ripley. Francis Lederer, Sigrid Gurie, J. Edward Bromberg, J. Carrol Naish. Low-key drama of pianist Lederer haunted by Nazi oppression, later rekindling old love affair; unusual film, well acted.

Voice of Bugle Ann, The (1936) 70m. **½ D: Richard Thorpe. Lionel Barrymore, Maureen O'Sullivan, Eric Linden, Dudley Digges, Spring Byington, Charles Grapewin. Sentimental tale of remarkable dog's owner taking revenge on person who kills the animal; not always convincing.

Voice of Merrill, The SEE: **Murder Will Out**

Voice of Terror SEE: **Sherlock Holmes & the Voice of Terror**

Voice of the Turtle (1947) 103m. ***½ D: Irving Rapper. Eleanor Parker, Ronald Reagan, Eve Arden, Kent Smith, Wayne Morris. Delightful comedy of wide-eyed Parker letting soldier Reagan share apartment with her; from Broadway hit play. Retitled: ONE FOR THE BOOK.

Voice of the Whistler (1946) 60m. D: William Castle. Richard Dix, Lynn Merrick, Rhys Williams, James Cardwell, Donald Woods, Gigi Perreau. SEE: **Whistler** series.

Voices (1979) C-107m. ** D: Robert Markowitz. Michael Ontkeon, Amy Irving, Alex Rocco, Barry Miller, Herbert Berghof, Viveca Lindfors. Aspiring rock singer falls for deaf woman (well played by Irving) who, never having heard him sing, is able to return his love. Sincerely intentioned drama is ultimately compromised by Hollywood formulas.

Volcano (1953-Italian) 106m. ** D: William Dieterle. Anna Magnani, Rossano Brazzi, Geraldine Brooks, Eduardo Ciannelli. Slowly paced dramatics about two sisters involved with unprincipled diver.

Volcano (1969) SEE: **Krakatoa, East of Java**

Voltaire (1933) 72m. *** D: John G. Adolfi. George Arliss, Margaret Lindsay, Doris Kenyon, Reginald Owen, Alan Mowbray. Excellent if stagy recreation of life and wit of famous 18th-century French writer.

Von Richthofen and Brown (1971) C-97m. ** D: Roger Corman. John Phillip Law, Barry Primus, Peter Masterson, Robert La Tourneaux. Weak historical drama of WW1 pilots and aerial dogfights. Aerial work is excellent; it's the ground work which crashes.

Von Ryan's Express (1965) C-117m. *** D: Mark Robson. Frank Sinatra, Trevor Howard, Raffaella Carra, Brad Dexter, Sergio Fantoni, Edward Mulhare, James Brolin, John Leyton, Vito Scotti. Exciting WW2 saga with Sinatra a POW colonel who leads daring escape by taking over freight train. Strong supporting cast.

Voodoo Island (1957) 76m. ** D: Reginald Le Borg. Boris Karloff, Beverly Tyler, Murvyn Vye, Elisha Cook. Boring horror-thriller has Karloff asked by businessmen to investigate strange doings on potential motel-island resort.

Voodoo Man (1944) 62m. ** D: William Beaudine. Bela Lugosi, John Carradine, George Zucco, Michael Ames (Tod Andrews), Henry Hall, Wanda McKay, Louise Currie. With touching devotion to zombie-wife, Lugosi performs harrowing experiments with unsuspecting girls to cure her. Campy B film.

Voodoo Tiger (1952) 67m. D: Spencer Bennet. Johnny Weissmuller, Jean Byron, Jeanne Dean, Robert Bray, Tamba. SEE: **Jungle Jim** series.

Voodoo Woman (1957) 77m. *½ D: Edward L. Cahn. Marla English, Tom Conway, Michael Connors, Lance Fuller. Cheater-chiller with few scares in lowjinks about deranged scientist changing English into a zombie-ite.

Voyage, The (1973-Italian) **C-95m.** ** D: Vittorio De Sica. Sophia Loren, Richard Burton, Ian Bannen, Barbara Pilavin, Annabella Incontrera, Paolo Lena. Listless adaptation of Pirandello story about star-crossed lovers Burton and Loren, forbidden to marry and shadowed by tragedy. Attractive stars and surroundings, but a draggy film.

Voyage of the Damned (1976-British-Spanish) **C-134m.** *** D: Sam Wanamaker. Faye Dunaway, Oskar Werner, Max von Sydow, Orson Welles, Malcolm McDowell, James Mason, Lee Grant, Wendy Hiller, Jose Ferrer, Luther Adler, Julie Harris, Maria Schell, Ben Gazzara. Absorbing drama based on fact: in 1939 a boatload of Jewish refugees from Germany bound for Havana was denied permission to land anywhere and forced to return to Germany. Picture almost dissolves into its separate stories, but von Sydow as ship's captain holds it together. Originally released at 158m.

Voyage of the Yes, The (1972) **C-73m.** TVM D: Lee Katzin. Desi Arnaz, Jr., Mike Evans, Beverly Garland, Skip Homeier, Della Reese, Scoey Mitchell, Two teenagers in small sailboat battle elements and their own prejudices. OK once they get into the boat; marginal material a waste. Average.

Voyage to the Bottom of the Sea (1961) **C-105m.** *** D: Irwin Allen. Walter Pidgeon, Joan Fontaine, Robert Sterling, Barbara Eden, Michael Ansara, Peter Lorre, Frankie Avalon. Entertaining, colorful nonsense of conflicts aboard massive submarine, with Pidgeon the domineering captain. No deep thinking, just fun.

Vulture, The (1967-British-Canadian) **C-91m.** *½ D: Lawrence Huntington. Robert Hutton, Akim Tamiroff, Broderick Crawford, Diane Clark, Phillip Friend, Patrick Holt. Disappointing, unsatisfying sci-fi horror film with laughable mad scientist (Tamiroff) who becomes half-man, half-bird, and avenges death of his ancestor. Released theatrically in b&w.

W (1974) **C-95m.** *½ D: Richard Quine. Twiggy, Michael Witney, Dirk Benedict, John Vernon, Alfred Ryder. Ex-model Twiggy struggles through story in which sadistic Benedict, her ex-husband convicted of her supposed murder, menaces her and new husband Witney. Flamboyant but unsuccessful thriller, retitled I WANT HER DEAD.

W. C. Fields and Me (1976) **C-111m.** *** D: Arthur Hiller. Rod Steiger, Valerie Perrine, John Marley, Jack Cassidy, Bernadette Peters, Billy Barty. Story of comedian's romance with Carlotta Monti is a cut above most Hollywood bios, thanks to Steiger's excellent performance, authentic atmosphere, good cast. Has little relation to the truth, but still entertaining.

W.W. and the Dixie Dancekings (1975) **C-91m.** **½ D: John G. Avildsen. Burt Reynolds, Art Carney, Conny Van Dyke, Jerry Reed, James Hampton, Ned Beatty. Lightly likable film about a con-man who hooks up with struggling country-western group and stops at nothing to promote their success. Lacks substance and believability.

Wabash Avenue (1950) **C-92m.** *** D: Henry Koster. Betty Grable, Victor Mature, Phil Harris, Reginald Gardiner, James Barton, Margaret Hamilton. Bright, colorful period piece with scoundrel Mature trying to break up romance between saloon-owner Harris and his musical star, Grable. Done with conviction and enthusiasm; enjoyable remake of CONEY ISLAND.

WAC from Walla Walla, The (1952) **83m.** *½ D: William Witney. Judy Canova, Stephen Dunne, Allen Jenkins, Irene Ryan, George Cleveland. Lame-brained service adventure of perennial yokel Canova.

Wackiest Ship in the Army, The (1960) **C-99m.** *** D: Richard Murphy. Jack Lemmon, Ricky Nelson, John Lund, Chips Rafferty, Tom Tully, Joby Baker. Comedy-drama sometimes has you wondering if it's serious or not; it succeeds most of the time. Offbeat WW2 story doesn't make fun of the war, for a change, and is entertaining.

Waco (1966) **C-85m.** *½ D: R. G. Springsteen. Howard Keel, Jane Russell, Brian Donlevy, Wendell Corey, Terry Moore, John Smith, John Agar, Gene Evans, Richard Arlen, Ben Cooper, Jeff Richards. Gunfighter Keel comes to clean up town, but former girl friend Russell is now married to Reverend Corey. Nice veteran cast, but film is only for Western addicts.

Wages of Fear, The (1955-French) **105m.** ***½ D: H. G. Clouzot. Yves

Montand, Charles Vanel, Peter Van Eyck, Vera Clouzot. Marvelous, taut suspenser set in South America of men driving trucks filled with high explosives over bumpy roads. Remade as SORCERER.

Wagonmaster (1950) 86m. *** D: John Ford. Ben Johnson, Joanne Dru, Ward Bond, Alan Mowbray, Jane Darwell, James Arness. Good Ford Western about two roaming cowhands who join a Mormon wagontrain heading for Utah frontier. Dru is love interest.

Wagons Roll at Night, The (1941) 84m. **½ D: Ray Enright. Humphrey Bogart, Sylvia Sidney, Eddie Albert, Joan Leslie, Sig Ruman, Cliff Clark, Charley Foy, Frank Wilcox. KID GALAHAD in circus trappings is OK, thanks to cast: Bogie's the circus manager, Sidney his star, Albert the hayseed turned lion-tamer.

Waikiki Wedding (1937) 89m. *** D: Frank Tuttle. Bing Crosby, Martha Raye, Shirley Ross, Bob Burns, Leif Erickson, Grady Sutton, Anthony Quinn. Press-agent Crosby promotes Ross as Pineapple Queen, sings "Blue Hawaii" and "Sweet Leilani" in this above-average musicomedy.

Wait 'Til the Sun Shines, Nellie (1952) C-108m. *** D: Henry King. Jean Peters, David Wayne, Hugh Marlowe, Albert Dekker, Warren Stevens. Nostalgic film of the hopes and disappointments of small town barber Wayne in the early 1900s.

Wait Until Dark (1967) C-108m. *** D: Terence Young. Audrey Hepburn, Alan Arkin, Richard Crenna, Efrem Zimbalist, Jr., Jack Weston, Samantha Jones. Solid shocker with Hepburn as blind woman left alone in apartment, terrorized by psychotic Arkin and henchmen looking for heroin they think is planted there. Memorable nail-biter, with flashy role for Arkin.

Wake Island (1942) 87m. *** D: John Farrow. Brian Donlevy, Robert Preston, Macdonald Carey, Albert Dekker, Walter Abel, Barbara Britton, William Bendix. Stirring war film of U.S.'s fight to hold Pacific island at outbreak of WW2. True facts realistically filmed make the movie worthwhile.

Wake Me When It's Over (1960) C-126m. *** D: Mervyn LeRoy. Dick Shawn, Ernie Kovacs, Margo Moore, Jack Warden. Entertaining

comedy of hustling Shawn making the most of his army station in the Far East by building a fancy hotel with army supplies. Kovacs lends good support.

Wake Me When the War is Over (1969) C-73m. TVM D: Gene Nelson. Ken Berry, Eva Gabor, Werner Klemperer, Danielle DeMetz, Jim Backus, Hans Conried, Parley Baer. Bumbling American officer (Berry) thinks WW2 is still on, thanks to efforts of odd German baroness (Gabor) and her friends. Fair comedy but for Berry. Average.

Wake of the Red Witch (1948) 106m. **½ D: Edward Ludwig. John Wayne, Gail Russell, Luther Adler, Gig Young. Rivalry between East Indies magnate and adventuresome ship's captain over pearls and women. Film is a bit confused, but nicely photographed.

Wake Up and Dream (1946) C-92m. ** D: Lloyd Bacon. June Haver, John Payne, Charlotte Greenwood, Connie Marshall, John Ireland, Clem Bevans, Lee Patrick. Moody film from Robert Nathan's story about girl determined to find brother missing from WW2.

Wake Up and Live (1937) 91m. *** D: Sidney Lanfield. Alice Faye, Walter Winchell, Ben Bernie, Jack Haley, Patsy Kelly, Joan Davis, Grace Bradley, Warren Hymer. Fast-moving spoof of radio with battling Winchell and Bernie, mike-frightened singer Haley, and Faye singing "There's A Lull In My Life."

Walk a Crooked Mile (1948) 91m. **½ D: Gordon Douglas. Louis Hayward, Dennis O'Keefe, Louise Allbritton, Carl Esmond, Onslow Stevens, Raymond Burr. Average melodrama about secret service agent who breaks up mob with help of Scotland Yard.

Walk, Don't Run (1966) C-114m. *** D: Charles Walters. Cary Grant, Samantha Eggar, Jim Hutton, John Standing, Miiko Taka, Ted Hartley. Enjoyable fluff about Eggar unwittingly agreeing to share her apartment with businessman Grant and athlete Hutton during the Tokyo Olympics. Stars are most agreeable in this remake of THE MORE THE MERRIER.

Walk East on Beacon (1952) 98m. **½ D: Alfred L. Werker. George Murphy, Finlay Currie, Virginia Gilmore, George Roy Hill. Good documentary-style drama of FBI investigation of espionage; on-location filming in Boston.

Walk in the Shadow (1966-British) 93m. *** D: Basil Dearden. Patrick McGoohan, Janet Munro, Paul Rogers, Megs Jenkins. Fine courtroom melodrama, as emotions flare after a girl's drowning.

Walk in the Spring Rain (1970) C-100m. **½ D: Guy Green. Anthony Quinn, Ingrid Bergman, Fritz Weaver, Katherine Crawford. Happily married Bergman has extramarital affair in this low-key romantic drama. One expects more from such a cast.

Walk in the Sun, A (1945) 117m. ***½ D: Lewis Milestone. Dana Andrews, Richard Conte, Sterling Holloway. George Tyne, John Ireland, Herbert Rudley, Lloyd Bridges, Huntz Hall. Human aspect of war explored as American battalion attacks German hideout in Italy; good character studies of men in war.

Walk into Hell (1957-Australian) C-93m. *½ D: Lee Robinson. Chips Rafferty, Francoise Christophe, Reginald Lye, Pierre Cressoy. Lumbering account of civilized Australians vs. native customs, filmed on location in New Guinea.

Walk Like a Dragon (1960) 95m. **½ D: James Clavell. Jack Lord, Nobu McCarthy, James Shigeta, Mel Torme, Josephine Hutchinson, Rodolfo Acosta. Offbeat Western drama of Lord saving McCarthy from life of prostitution, taking her to his home town, overcoming expected obstacles.

Walk on the Wild Side (1962) 114m. **½ D: Edward Dmytryk. Laurence Harvey, Capucine, Jane Fonda, Anne Baxter, Barbara Stanwyck. Lurid hodgepodge set in 1930's New Orleans, loosely based on Nelson Algren novel of Harvey seeking lost love Capucine, now a member of bordello run by lesbian Stanwyck.

Walk Proud (1979) C-102m. ** D: Robert Collins. Robbie Benson, Sarah Holcomb, Domingo Ambriz, Pepe Serna, Trinidad Silva. Sincerely intentioned but not very forceful gang picture about a Chicano (Benson) who falls for a WASP beauty who goes to his high school. Looks like a made-for-TV.

Walk Softly, Stranger (1950) 81m. *** D: Robert Stevenson. Joseph Cotten, Valli, Spring Byington, Paul Stewart, Jack Paar. Small-time crook Cotten reforms because of the love and faith of crippled girl Valli.

Walk Tall (1960) C-60m. *½ D: Maury Dexter. Willard Parker, Joyce Meadows, Kent Taylor. Flabby oater about capture of outlaws who killed Indian squaws.

Walk the Dark Street (1956) 74m. *½ D: Wyott Ordung. Chuck Connors, Don Ross, Regina Gleason, Eddie Kafafian. Uninspired revenge hunt, set in a metropolitan city, of two men stalking each other with rifles.

Walk the Proud Land (1956) C-88m. *** D: Jesse Hibbs. Audie Murphy, Anne Bancroft, Pat Crowley, Charles Drake. Sturdy scripting makes this oater attractive; Murphy is Indian agent trying to quell strife between redskins and settlers, with the capture of Geronimo his major feat.

Walk With Love and Death, A (1969) C-90m. ** D: John Huston. Anjelica Huston, Assaf Dayan, Anthony Corlan, John Hallam, Robert Lang, Michael Gough. Fine period flavor but little else of note in story of young love set against turmoil of 14th-century France. Director Huston's daughter plays lead, Huston himself does small role.

Walkabout (1971-Australian) C-95m. *** D: Nicolas Roeg. Jenny Agutter, Lucien John, David Gumpilil, John Meillon. Lost in wilderness of Australia, two children rely on young aborigine in order to survive. Beautifully filmed story.

Walking Dead, The (1936) 66m. *** D: Michael Curtiz. Boris Karloff, Edmund Gwen, Marguerite Churchill, Ricardo Cortez, Barton MacLane, Warren Hull, Joe Sawyer. Karloff is framed and executed, but professor brings him back to life. As he regains his memory, he seeks out those who framed him. Good horror tale.

Walking Hills, The (1949) 78m. *** D: John Sturges. Randolph Scott, Ella Raines, William Bishop, Edgar Buchanan, Arthur Kennedy. Well-acted oater of Westerners searching for abandoned gold mine.

Walking My Baby Back Home (1953) C-95m. **½ D: Lloyd Bacon. Donald O'Connor, Buddy Hackett, Janet Leigh, Lori Nelson. Confused musical comedy redeemed by Buddy Hackett's wacky humor.

Walking Stick, The (1970-British) C-101m. **½ D: Eric Till. Samantha Eggar, David Hemmings, Emlyn

Williams, Phyllis Calvert, Ferdy Mayne, Francesca Annis. Potentially interesting story of beautiful crippled woman coerced into assisting her worthless lover in a robbery is just too low-key to be consistently absorbing. Eggar's performance helps.

Walking Tall (1973) C-125m. **½ D: Phil Karlson. Joe Don Baker, Elizabeth Hartman, Gene Evans, Rosemary Murphy, Noah Beery, Felton Perry. Violent action drama about determined Southern sheriff's one-man war against local corruption. Huge theatrical success, and the first of three movies based on the exploits of real-life, baseball-bat-wielding Buford Pusser, with a muscular performance by Baker. Considerably toned down for TV.

Walking Tall, Part Two SEE: **Part 2, Walking Tall**

Walking Through the Fire (1979) C-100m. TVM D: Robert Day. Bess Armstrong, Tom Mason, Richard Masur, Swoozie Kurtz, Bonnie Bedelia, June Lockhart, J. D. Cannon. Affecting dramatization of Laura Lee's personal chronicle of her struggle with Hodgkin's disease and its effect on her unborn child. Above average.

Wall of Noise (1963) 112m. **½ D: Richard Wilson. Suzanne Pleshette, Ty Hardin, Dorothy Provine, Ralph Meeker. Turgid racetrack drama with adultery, and not horses, the focal point.

Wallflower (1948) 77m. *** D: Frederick de Cordova. Joyce Reynolds, Robert Hutton, Janis Paige, Edward Arnold, Barbara Brown. Amusing comedy based on Broadway success; two stepsisters (Reynolds and Paige) vie for the same love.

Walls Came Tumbling Down, The (1946) 82m. *** D: Lothar Mendes. Lee Bowman, Marguerite Chapman, Edgar Buchanan, Lee Patrick, J. Edward Bromberg. Detective Bowman goes to work when priest is murdered, in fast-moving private eye film.

Walls of Gold (1933) 74m. *½ D: Kenneth MacKenna. Sally Eilers, Norman Foster, Ralph Morgan, Rosita Moreno, Rochelle Hudson, Frederic Santley, Mary Mason. Terrible soaper about love conflicts among the well-to-do; Eilers does something to ruffle fiancé Foster, so to spite her he marries her sister, and she marries his uncle. Forget it.

Walls of Hell, The (1964) 88m. ** D: Gerardo De Leon. Jock Mahoney, Fernando Poe, Jr., Mike Parsons, Paul Edwards, Jr. WW2 actioner set in Manila. Filmed in the Philippines, suffers from amateurish native casting.

Walls of Jericho, The (1948) 106m. ** D: John M. Stahl. Cornel Wilde, Linda Darnell, Anne Baxter, Kirk Douglas, Ann Dvorak, Marjorie Rambeau, Henry Hull, Colleen Townsend, Barton MacLane. Good cast tries to perk up story of ambitious lawyer in Jericho, Kansas, whose marital problems stand in the way of success; pretty dreary going most of the way.

Waltz of the Toreadors (1962-British) C-105m. *** D: John Guillermin. Peter Sellers, Dany Robin, Margaret Leighton, John Fraser. Jean Anouilh's saucy sex romp gets top notch handling with Sellers the retired military officer who still can't keep his eye off the girls.

Wanda Nevada (1979) C-105m. *½ D: Peter Fonda. Peter Fonda, Brooke Shields, Fiona Lewis, Luke Askew, Ted Markland, Severn Darden, Paul Fix, Henry Fonda. Fonda wins Shields in a poker game, and they set out together to prospect for gold in the Grand Canyon. If this film were any more "laid-back" it would be nonexistent.

Wanderers, The (1979) C-113m. ***½ D: Philip Kaufman. Ken Wahl, John Friedrich, Karen Allen, Toni Kalem, Alan Rosenberg, Linda Manz. Impressionistic look at Bronx-Italian high school life in 1963 isn't always consistent in tone, but there are dozens of privileged moments. A good bet for future cult status.

Wanted for Murder (1946-British) 95m. **½ D: Lawrence Huntington. Eric Portman, Dulcie Gray, Derek Farr, Roland Culver, Stanley Holloway. Engaging whodunit yarn, effectively underplayed by the cast.

Wanted: The Sundance Woman (1976) C-100m. TVM D: Lee Philips. Katharine Ross, Steve Forrest, Stella Stevens, Hector Elizondo, Michael Constantine, Katherine Helmond. Ross again is Etta Place in sequel to BUTCH CASSIDY AND THE SUNDANCE KID—or, what happened to Etta following their deaths—she's running guns for Pancho Villa. Sparkling humor of the original has fizzled. Average. Retitled MRS. SUNDANCE RIDES AGAIN.

Wanton Contessa SEE: **Senso**

War Against Mrs. Hadley, The (1942) 86m. ** D: Harold Bucquet. Edward Arnold, Fay Bainter, Richard Ney, Sara Allgood, Spring Byington, Jean Rogers, Frances Rafferty, Dorothy Morris, Rags Ragland, Isobel Elsom, Van Johnson. Mild WW2 human-interest tale about matron Bainter who refuses to participate in war support.

War and Peace (1956) C-208m. **½ D: King Vidor. Audrey Hepburn, Henry Fonda, Mel Ferrer, Vittorio Gassman, John Mills, Herbert Lom, Oscar Homolka, Anita Ekberg, Mai Britt. Tolstoy's sprawling novel fails to come alive in this overlong, over-simplified adaptation. Star-studded cast and spectacular battle scenes cannot compensate for clumsy script and some profound miscasting. Filmed in Italy.

War and Peace (1968-Russian) C-373m. **** D: Sergei Bondarchuk. Ludmila Savelyeva, Vyacheslav Tihonov, Hira Ivanov-Golovko, Irina Gubanova, Antonia Shuranova, Sergei Bondarchuk. Even in theaters, poor English dubbing hurt this definitive film version of Tolstoy's novel, and on TV, the commercials and multiple-night showings may damage it more. Even so, it should be seen for production values alone; a dazzling film.

War Arrow (1953) C-78m. ** D: George Sherman. Maureen O'Hara, Jeff Chandler, Suzan Ball, Charles Drake, Jay Silverheels. Western story of U.S. Cavalry man Chandler coming to Texas to train Seminole Indians to subdue a Kiowa uprising. O'Hara is object of his love.

War Between Men and Women, The (1972) C-110m. **½ D: Melville Shavelson. Jack Lemmon, Barbara Harris, Jason Robards, Herb Edelman, Lisa Gerritsen, Severn Darden. Fans of James Thurber won't think much of this on-and-off mixture of famed writer-cartoonist's material and Hollywood schmaltz, but film occasionally makes for pleasant comedy-romance. Barbara Harris comes off best in likable cast.

War Between the Planets (1965-Italian) C-80m. BOMB D: Anthony Dawson (Antonio Margheriti). Jack Stuart (Giacomo Rossi-Stuarti), Amber Collins (Ombretta Colli), Peter Martell, Halina Zalewska. Alien planet is on collision course with earth, but valiant efforts by scientific

forces snatch victory from the jaws of boredom. Fun only if you like spaghetti sci-fi. Made at same time as other losers such as WAR OF THE PLANETS, WILD WILD PLANET, etc. Also known as PLANET ON THE PROWL.

War Between the Tates, The (1977) C-100m. TVM D: Lee Philips. Elizabeth Ashley, Richard Crenna, Ann Wedgeworth, Annette O'Toole, Granville Van Dusen. Domestic drama has small-town professor trying to resolve crisis when his wife learns of his affair with one of his students. This adaptation of Alison Lurie's best-seller has lost some of its bite, but Ashley's rich portrait compensates. Average.

War Drums (1957) C-75m. **½ D: Reginald LeBorg. Lex Barker, Joan Taylor, Ben Johnson, Stuart Whitman. Sufficiently bloody Western set in Civil War days of Indian uprisings against onslaught of gold miners.

War Game, The (1967-British) 47m. **½ D: Peter Watkins. Originally intended as a straight BBC documentary, this filmed projection of nuclear holocaust's aftermath was more than the network bargained for; effective as propaganda and not bad as film.

War Games SEE: **Suppose They Gave a War and Nobody Came?**

War Gods of the Deep (1965-British) C-85m. **½ D: Jacques Tourneur. Vincent Price, Tab Hunter, David Tomlinson, Susan Hart, John Le-Mesurier. Gill-men invade remote seacoast town. Actually, two films in one: establishing menace, first half has odd, almost poetic feel to it, but second half deteriorates, with shoddy underwater city. Originally titled THE CITY UNDER THE SEA.

War Hunt (1962) 81m. **½ D: Denis Sanders. John Saxon, Robert Redford, Charles Aidman, Sydney Pollack. Well-done Korean War story focusing on kill-happy soldier Saxon who tries to help an orphan boy. Redford's film debut.

War Is Hell (1964) 81m. ** D: Burt Topper. Tony Russell, Baynes Barron, Tony Rich, Burt Topper. Korean War actioner with no new ideas to offer. Introduced by Audie Murphy.

War Italian Style (1967-Italian) C-84m. ** D: Luigi Scattini. Buster Keaton, Franco and Ciccio, Martha Hyer, Fred Clark. Sloppy meandering spy satire set in WW2 Italy, redeemed barely by Keaton's appearance.

War Lord, The (1965) C-123m. *** D: Franklin Schaffner. Charlton Heston, Richard Boone, Rosemary Forsyth, Maurice Evans, Guy Stockwell, Niall MacGinnis, Henry Wilcoxon. Overambitious to be intelligent, would-be epic lacks scope and sweep needed for spectacle. Medieval tale of knight Heston demanding his feudal tribute, another man's bride Forsyth. Based on Leslie Stevens play THE LOVERS.

War Lover, The (1962-British) 105m. **½ D: Philip Leacock. Steve McQueen, Robert Wagner, Shirley Ann Field, Gary Cockrell. John Hersey's thoughtful novel becomes superficial account of McQueen and Wagner, two WW2 pilots in England, both in love with Field; aerial photography is above par.

War of Children, A (1972) C-73m. TVM D: George Schaefer. Jenny Agutter, Vivien Merchant, John Ronane, Danny Figgis, Anthony Andrews, Aideen O'Kelly. Solid James Costigan-written script about mad warfare in modern-day Northern Ireland, centering around single family. Good cast, totally location-shot. Above average.

War of the Planets (1965-Italian) C-99m. BOMB D: Anthony Dawson. Tony Russel, Lisa Gastoni, Massimo Serato, Franco Nero, Carlo Giustini. Light creatures attack earth but are repelled. Cheap sets and plodding script make this a loser.

War of the Satellites (1958) 66m. *½ D: Roger Corman. Dick Miller, Susan Cabot, Richard Devon, Eric Sinclair. Tedious sci-fi about missile expert whose mind is controlled by alien forces.

War of the Wildcats, The (1943) 102m. **½ D: Albert S. Rogell. John Wayne, Martha Scott, Albert Dekker, Gabby Hayes, Marjorie Rambeau, Sidney Blackmer, Dale Evans. Slugger Wayne brooks no nonsense in this oil-drilling yarn; good action, obligatory romance. Originally titled IN OLD OKLAHOMA.

War of the Worlds (1953) C-85m. ***½ D: Byron Haskin. Gene Barry, Les Tremayne, Ann Robinson, Henry Brandon, Jack Kruschen. Vivid, frightening adaptation of H. G. Wells' story about a Martian invasion. Dramatically sound and filled

with dazzling special effects; superior sci-fi, produced by George Pal.

War of the Zombies (1965-Italian) C-85m. ** D: Giuseppe Vari. John Drew Barrymore, Susi Andersen, Ettore Manni, Ida Galli. Standard European spectacle plot: Rome sends best legionnaire to quell disturbance in Eastern province in clutches of mad priest (Barrymore). Production values somewhat better than usual.

War Paint (1953) C-89m. **½ D: Lesley Selander. Robert Stack, Joan Taylor, Charles McGraw, Peter Graves. Action-packed film of U. S. cavalry detachment overcoming danger and villainous attempts to prevent delivery of peace treaty to an Indian Chief.

War Wagon, The (1967) C-101m. ** D: Burt Kennedy. John Wayne, Kirk Douglas, Howard Keel, Robert Walker, Keenan Wynn, Bruce Cabot, Joanna Barnes. Sluggish Western actioner about theft and recovery of Brink's-like wagon hauling a half-million dollars in gold. Fine cast saddled with ponderous script.

Warlock (1959) C-121m. *** D: Edward Dmytryk. Richard Widmark, Henry Fonda, Anthony Quinn, Dorothy Malone, Dolores Michaels, Wallace Ford, Tom Drake, Richard Arlen, Regis Toomey. Intelligent, well-paced Western giving new depth to usual cowboys-vs.-outlaws shootout.

Warlords of Atlantis (1978-British) C-96m. **½ D: Kevin Connor. Doug McClure, Peter Gilmore, Shane Rimmer, Lea Brodie, Cyd Charisse, Daniel Massey. Monsters and mayhem abound in this palatable Saturday matinee item with McClure joining British scientists in search for underwater city.

Warm December, A (1973) C-100m. ** D: Sidney Poitier. Sidney Poitier, Esther Anderson, Yvette Curtis, George Baker, Earl Cameron. Story of Poitier's love for Anderson, who is dying of sickle cell anemia, isn't as sappy as it might be, but isn't particularly good, either. Anderson is attractive. Made in England.

Warning Shot (1967) C-100m. ***½ D: Buzz Kulik. David Janssen, Ed Begley, Keenan Wynn, Lillian Gish, Eleanor Parker, Stefanie Powers, George Sanders, Steve Allen, Carroll O'Connor, Joan Collins, Walter Pidgeon. Exciting action-filled melodrama about cop's attempt to clear his name after killing a supposedly innocent doctor. TV-vet Kulik made this one exciting for theaters, and it's even better on TV.

Warpath (1951) **C-95m.** **½ D: Byron Haskin. Edmond O'Brien, Dean Jagger, Forrest Tucker, Polly Bergen. Nifty action Western with O'Brien hunting down outlaws who killed his girlfriend; an Indian attack is thrown in for good measure.

Warrior and the Slave Girl, The (1958-Italian) **C-84m.** ** D: Vittorio Cottafavi. Ettore Manni, Georges Marchal, Gianna Maria Canale, Rafael Calvo. Unsubtle costumer set in ancient Armenia, with Canale the evil princess, subdued by Roman Manni; usual amount of swordplay.

Warrior Empress, The (1960-Italian) **C-87m.** ** D: Pietro Francisci. Kerwin Mathews, Tina Louise, Riccardo Garrone, Antonio Batistella, Enrico Maria Salerno. Senseless mixture of fantasy and adventure with Phaon (Mathews) falling in love with Sappho (Louise), overcoming treacherous Salerno.

Warriors, The (1955-British) **C-85m.** **½ D: Henry Levin. Errol Flynn, Joanne Dru, Peter Finch, Patrick Holt, Yvonne Furneaux, Michael Hordern. Flynn's final swashbuckler casts him as British prince protecting French conquests (and lovely Dru) from attacks by Finch and his supporters. Well-made but awfully familiar. British title: THE DARK AVENGER.

Warriors, The (1979) **C-90m.** *** D: Walter Hill. Michael Beck, James Remar, Thomas Waites, Dorsey Wright, Brian Tyler, Deborah Van Valkenburgh. Comic book plot about NYC gang violence is redeemed by lightning pace, tough action sequences, creative use of color. Notorious for the number of violent incidents it allegedly instigated, but worthy of some respect.

Warriors Five (1962-Italian) **84m.** **½ D: Leopoldo Savona. Jack Palance, Giovanna Ralli, Serge Reggiani, Folco Lulli. Moderate actioner set in WW2 Italy with Palance behind enemy lines trying to combat the Germans.

Washington Story (1952) **81m.** ** D: Robert Pirosh. Van Johnson, Patricia Neal, Louis Calhern, Sidney Blackmer, Elizabeth Patterson. Newspaperwoman Neal assigned to harass Congress and selects young Congressman Johnson as her target; just fair.

Watch It, Sailor! (1961-British) **81m.** ** D: Wolf Rilla. Dennis Price, Liz Fraser, Irene Handl, Graham Stark, Marjorie Rhodes. Mildly amusing stage farce adapted to screen, with Price managing to outdo Fraser's mother (Rhodes), getting to the church on time.

Watch on the Rhine (1943) **114m.** ***½ D: Herman Shumlin. Bette Davis, Paul Lukas, Geraldine Fitzgerald, Lucile Watson, Beulah Bondi, George Coulouris, Donald Woods. Fine filmization of Lillian Hellman's timely WW2 play of German Lukas and wife Davis pursued and harried by Nazi agents in Washington. Lukas gives the performance of his career, which won him Academy Award; Bette somewhat overshadowed.

Watch the Birdie (1950) **70m.** **½ D: Jack Donahue. Red Skelton, Arlene Dahl, Ann Miller, Leon Ames, Pamela Britton, Richard Rober, Mike Mazurki. Average Skelton comedy features him as photographer, silly father and grandfather. Rest of cast is also good with routine material, reworking of Buster Keaton's CAMERAMAN.

Watch Your Stern (1960-British) **88m.** ** D: Gerald Thomas. Kenneth Connor, Eric Barker, Leslie Phillips, Joan Sims, Hattie Jacques. Amusing, obvious shenanigans on the seas, with Connor impersonating a scientist sent to perfect a Naval torpedo weapon.

Waterhole # 3 (1967) **C-95m.** **½ D: William Graham. James Coburn, Carroll O'Connor, Claude Akins, Bruce Dern, Joan Blondell, James Whitmore. Amusing Western comedy of three confederates who rob Army of a fortune in gold and bury it in desert waterhole.

Waterloo (1971-Italian-Russian) **C-123m.** ** D: Sergei Bondarchuk. Rod Steiger, Christopher Plummer, Orson Welles, Jack Hawkins, Virginia McKenna, Michael Wilding. Cumbersome historical film centering around Napoleon's defeat at Waterloo. Tremendous action but muddled plot.

Waterloo Bridge (1940) **103m.** ***½ D: Mervyn LeRoy. Vivien Leigh, Robert Taylor, Lucile Watson, Virginia Field, Maria Ouspenskaya, C. Aubrey Smith. Sentimental love story, well-acted, of soldier and ballet dancer meeting during air raid, falling in love instantly. Beautiful performance by lovely Leigh. First made in 1931, remade as GABY.

Waterloo Road (1944-British) **76m.** ***½ D: Sidney Gilliat. John Mills,

Stewart Granger, Alastair Sim, Joy Shelton, Beatrice Varley, Alison Leggatt, Jean Kent. Excellent wartime drama about soldier who goes AWOL when he learns his wife has been seeing another man. Evocative of its period, film also benefits from spry touches of humor.

Watermelon Man (1970) C-97m. **½ D: Melvin Van Peebles. Godfrey Cambridge, Estelle Parsons, Howard Caine, D'Urville Martin, Kay Kimberly. Provocative serio-comedy about bigoted white man who suddenly turns black and sees his life go upside down. Worth seeing, although Herman Raucher's one-joke script makes its point and then has nowhere to go. TV print edited to 91m.

Watership Down (1978-British) C-92m. *** D: Martin Rosen. Voices of John Hurt, Richard Briers, Sir Ralph Richardson, Denholm Elliott, Harry Andrews, Joss Ackland; narrated by Michael Hordern. Stylish animated-cartoon from Richard Adams' best-selling book about a family of rabbits seeking a safe place to live, encountering many perils along the way; not a kiddie film by any means. Bird character voiced by Zero Mostel provides only comic relief.

Wattstax (1973) C-98m. ***½ D: Mel Stuart. Isaac Hayes, The Staple Singers, Luther Ingram, Rev. Jesse Jackson, Richard Pryor, Rufus Thomas, Carla Thomas, Bar-Kays, Kim Weston, The Emotions, Johnnie Taylor. Exciting, vibrant documentary with music, centering around L.A. community of Watts, and the black experience. Pryor's monologues are exceptionally good.

Watusi (1959) C-85m. **½ D: Kurt Neumann. George Montgomery, Taina Elg, David Farrar, Rex Ingram, Dan Seymour. MGM fabricated a plot similar to KING SOLOMON'S MINES to utilize leftover footage from its 1950 version of H. Rider Haggard yarn.

Way Ahead, The SEE: **Immortal Battalion, The**

Way Down East (1920) 119m. **½ D: D. W. Griffith. Lillian Gish, Richard Barthelmess, Lowell Sherman, Mary Hay. Heavy-handed melodrama which became silent classic, noted for Gish's performance as wronged waif, and dramatic climax on ice-flow; set in New England.

Way Down East (1935) 80m. *½ D: Henry King. Rochelle Hudson, Henry Fonda, Russell Simpson, Slim Summerville, Spring Byington, Edward Trevor. Romantic melodrama set in New England was hokey as a 1920 silent; the remake hasn't improved with age. Ridiculous script conquers all.

Way for a Sailor (1930) 83m. ** D: Sam Wood. John Gilbert, Wallace Beery, Leila Hyams, Jim Tully, Polly Moran. Early talkie with silent-star Gilbert as devoted sailor who loses girl for the sea. Mostly a curio for film buffs.

Way of a Gaucho (1952) C-91m. ** D: Jacques Tourneur. Gene Tierney, Rory Calhoun, Richard Boone, Everett Sloane. Soaper set in 1870's Argentina of Tierney and Calhoun trying to make a go of life on the Pampas.

Way of All Flesh, The (1940) 86m. ** D: Louis King. Akim Tamiroff, Gladys George, William Henry, Muriel Angelus, Berton Churchill, Roger Imhof. Overly sentimental tale of poor immigrant who is "taken" and must pay for his error; George is superlative as always. Remake of Emil Jannings silent film.

Way of Youth, The (1959-French) 81m. ** D: Michel Boisrond. Francoise Arnoul, Lino Ventura, Bourvil, Alain Delon. Obvious sensuality fails to arouse sufficient interest in contrived story of adultery and ill-gotten gains.

Way Out, The (1956-British) 90m. ** D: Montgomery Tully. Gene Nelson, Mona Freeman, John Bentley, Michael Goodliffe, Sydney Tafler. Lumbering story of husband who committed a crime going on the lam with wife.

Way Out West (1936) 65m. ***½ D: James W. Horne. Stan Laurel, Oliver Hardy, Sharon Lynn, James Finlayson, Rosina Lawrence, Stanley Fields, Vivien Oakland. Stan and Ollie are sent to deliver mine deed to daughter of late prospector, but crooked Finlayson leads them to wrong girl. One of their best features; moves well without resorting to needless romantic subplot. Another bonus: some charming musical interludes.

Way to Love, The (1933) 80m. *** D: Norman Taurog. Maurice Chevalier, Ann Dvorak, Edward Everett Horton, Minna Gombell, Nydia Westman, Douglass Dumbrille, John Miljan. Chevalier falls in love with lady knife-thrower (Dvorak) in bouncy musicomedy; songs include title tune, "I'm A Lover Of Paris."

Way to the Gold, The (1957) 94m. ** D: Robert D. Webb. Jeffrey Hunter, Sheree North, Barry Sullivan, Neville Brand, Walter Brennan. Meandering buried-loot-hunt story.

Way Way Out (1966) C-106m. BOMB D: Gordon Douglas. Jerry Lewis, Connie Stevens, Robert Morley, Dennis Weaver, Howard Morris, Brian Keith, Dick Shawn, Anita Ekberg. Out of many contenders, this is possibly the worst Jerry Lewis comedy of them all. Plot concerns comedian's trip to the moon with sexy astronaut Stevens; hopefully they took the film's negative along.

Way We Were, The (1973) C-118m. *** D: Sydney Pollack. Barbra Streisand, Robert Redford, Bradford Dillman, Murray Hamilton, Viveca Lindfors, Lois Chiles. First-class love story about political activist Streisand and her complete opposite, Waspish Joe College-type Redford, from late 30s to early 50s. Prerelease cutting excised meatiest sequences on blacklist era in Hollywood, alas, leaving Hamilton and Lindfors with bit parts, and some confusion in following last portion of plot. Still quite good, with literate Arthur Laurents script from his own novel.

Way West, The (1967) C-122m. *½ D: Andrew V. McLaglen. Kirk Douglas, Robert Mitchum, Richard Widmark, Lola Albright, Michael Witney, Stubby Kaye, Sally Field. Despite cast, this version of A. B. Guthrie, Jr.'s, epic novel fails completely. McLaglen's lackluster direction partially to blame, but big problem is script, which may hold all-time record for undeveloped subplots. Mitchum is good, through it all.

Wayward Bus, The (1957) 89m. ** D: Victor Vicas. Joan Collins, Jayne Mansfield, Dan Dailey, Rick Jason. Low-brow version of John Steinbeck novel about passengers on bus in California, with trite interpretation of their interaction.

Wayward Girl, The (1957) 71m. *½ D: Lesley Selander. Marcia Henderson, Peter Walker, Whit Bissell, Ray Teal. Turgid nonsense about mother and stepdaughter vying for same lover, leading to murder.

Wayward Girl, The (1959-Norwegian) 91m. **½ D: Edith Carlmar. Liv Ullmann, Atle Merton, Rolf Soder,

Tore Foss, Nana Stenersen. Moralistic romance tale of young lovers who seek refuge on a deserted farm, becoming involved with the returning owner.

Wayward Wife, The (1955-Italian) 91m. ** D: Mario Soldati. Gina Lollobrigida, Gabriele Ferzetti, Franco Interlenghi, Renato Baldini. Unimaginative, predictable film of blackmail. Lollobrigida, girl with a past, finds her marriage threatened.

We Are All Murderers (1957-French) 113m. *** D: André Cayatte. Marcel Mouloudji, Raymond Pellegrin, Louis Seigner, Antoine Balpetre. Most effective social plea against capital punishment, focusing on youth bred to kill in war involved in murder after the armistice.

We Are in the Navy Now (1962-British) C-102m. ** D: Wendy Toye. Kenneth More, Lloyd Nolan, Joan O'Brien, Mischa Auer. Farcical service comedy without wit or slapstick to see it through. Original title: WE JOINED THE NAVY.

We Are Not Alone (1939) 112m. ***½ D: Edmund Goulding. Paul Muni, Jane Bryan, Flora Robson, Una O'Connor, Henry Daniell, Cecil Kellaway, Alan Napier. Superb acting and overall production make tale of man in love with governess (Bryan), accused of murdering his wife (Robson) a must. From novel by James Hilton.

We Joined the Navy SEE: We Are in the Navy Now

We Live Again (1934) 82m. ** D: Rouben Mamoulian. Fredric March, Anna Sten, Sam Jaffe, C. Aubrey Smith, Jane Baxter, Ethel Griffies. Cumbersome costumer with March the Russian nobleman in love with peasant girl Sten. Based on Leo Tolstoy's *Resurrection*, filmed several times before.

We Still Kill the Old Way (1967-Italian) C-92m. ** D: Elio Petri. Irene Papas, Gian Maria Volonte, Luigi Pistilli. Crimes of honor in old Sicily purport to show old-world Mafia methods; actually nothing more than a small revenge film.

We Were Dancing (1942) 94m. ** D: Robert Z. Leonard. Norma Shearer, Melvyn Douglas, Gail Patrick, Marjorie Main, Reginald Owen, Connie Gilchrist, Sig Ruman. Hokey story of princess running off with another man at her engagement party. Shearer et al. try, but material defeats them.

We Were Strangers (1949) 106m.
**½ D: John Huston. Jennifer Jones,
John Garfield, Pedro Armendariz,
Gilbert Roland, Ramon Novarro.
Slow-moving story of romance set
against a Cuban intrigue background,
with promising cast and director but
disappointing results.

We Who Are Young (1940) 79m. **
D: Harold S. Bucquet. Lana Turner,
John Shelton, Gene Lockhart, Grant
Mitchell, Henry Armetta, Jonathan
Hale, Clarence Wilson. Turner mar-
ries Shelton though his company's
policy forbids it; aimless comedy-
drama.

We're Going to Be Rich (1938-
British) 78m. **½ D: Monty Banks.
Gracie Fields, Victor McLaglen,
Brian Donlevy, Coral Browne, Ted
Smith, Gus McNaughton. Entertainer
Fields finds herself in the midst of
an African oil-boom in this OK
story with musical numbers; Donlevy
and McLaglen in contrived rivalry
supply much of the plot.

We're No Angels (1955) C-106m.
**½ D: Michael Curtiz. Humphrey
Bogart, Aldo Ray, Joan Bennett,
Peter Ustinov, Basil Rathbone, Leo
G. Carroll. Mild entertainment as
three escapees from Devils Island
find refuge with French family and
extricate them from predicament.

We're Not Dressing (1934) 63m. ***
D: Norman Taurog. Bing Crosby,
Carole Lombard, George Burns,
Gracie Allen, Ethel Merman, Leon
Errol, Ray Milland. Musical "Admi-
rable Crichton" with rich-girl Lom-
bard falling in love with sailor
Crosby when entourage is ship-
wrecked on desert isle. Merman is
man-chasing second fiddle, with
Burns and Allen on tap as local
expeditionists. Great fun; Bing sings
"Love Thy Neighbor."

We're Not Married (1952) 85m. ***
D: Edmund Goulding. Ginger Rogers,
Fred Allen, Victor Moore, Marilyn
Monroe, Paul Douglas, David Wayne,
Eddie Bracken, Mitzi Gaynor. Fine
froth served up in several episodes
as married couples discover their
weddings weren't legalized; segments
vary in quality but the top-notch cast
generally delivers the goods.

We've Never Been Licked (1943)
103m. ** D: John Rawlins. Richard
Quine, Noah Beery, Jr., Robert
Mitchum, Anne Gwynne, Martha
O'Driscoll. Overly patriotic and melo-
dramatic account of American youth

brought up in Japan, and his involvement in WW2.

Weak and the Wicked, The (1953-
British) 81m. **½ D: J. Lee Thompson. Glynis Johns, John Gregson,
Diana Dors, Jane Hylton. Frank
study of women's prison life, focusing on their rehabilitation.

Weaker Sex, The (1945-British) 89m.
** D: Roy Baker. Ursula Jeans,
Cecil Parker, Joan Hopkins, Derek
Bond, Thora Hird, Bill Owen. Jeans
is staunch English housewife showing her patriotic zest during WW2;
small-scale drama.

Weapon, The (1956-British) 80m.
**½ D: Hal E. Chester. Steve Coch-
ran, Lizabeth Scott, Herbert Marshall, Nicole Maurey. Minor, trim
account of youngster who accidentally
shoots his pal.

Web, The (1947) 87m. *** D:
Michael Gordon. Ella Raines, Edmond O'Brien, William Bendix, Vincent Price, Maria Palmer. Tough
bodyguard engages in murder, then
finds himself a patsy for boss'
schemes. Exciting melodrama, one of
O'Brien's best early roles.

Web of Evidence (1959-British) 88m.
**½ D: Jack Cardiff. Van Johnson,
Vera Miles, Emlyn Williams, Bernard Lee, Jean Kent, Ralph Truman, Leo McKern. Sincere drama of
Johnson in England finding clues to
prove his father innocent of long-
standing murder sentence. Original
title: BEYOND THIS PLACE.

Web of Fear (1963-French) 92m.
**½ D: Francois Villiers. Michele
Morgan, Dany Saval, Claude Rich,
George Rigaud. Morgan is music
teacher set up as patsy by Saval
and Rich in this moody drama of
passion and murder.

Web of Passion (1959-French) C-
101m. **½ D: Claude Chabrol.
Madeleine Robinson, Antonella
Lualdi, Jean Paul Belmondo, Jacques
Dacqmine. Non-conformist Belmondo
insinuates himself into a family's
graces, delighting in breaking down
their standards, with murders resulting. Talky but intriguing drama. Retitled: LEDA.

Web of the Spider (1970-Italian) C-
94m. ** D: Anthony Dawson. Anthony Franciosa, Michele Mercier,
Peter Carsten, Karen Field, Silvano
Tranquilli. Overly familiar thriller
about the skeptic who accepts a
wager that he cannot survive the
night alone in a haunted house.
Franciosa and associates try vainly

to give it a fresh twist but are upstaged by shrieking spirits, howling winds, and assorted creepy crawlies.

Wedding, A (1978) **C-125m.** **½ D: Robert Altman. Carol Burnett, Desi Arnaz Jr., Amy Stryker, Vittorio Gassman, Geraldine Chaplin, Mia Farrow, Paul Dooley, Lillian Gish, John Cromwell, Pat McCormick, Howard Duff, Pam Dawber. Uneven, unfocused look at family intrigues surrounding a nouveau riche wedding; some amusing moments and pointed characterizations, but picture doesn't quite gel.

Wedding in White (1972-Canadian) **C-106m.** *** D: William Fruet. Donald Pleasence, Carol Kane, Doris Petrie, Doug McGrath, Leo Phillips. Fine performances in sad tale of girl impregnated by brother's drunken pal during WW2 and her father's efforts to save the family's honor. Best Picture at Canadian Film Festival.

Wedding Night, The (1935) **84m.** **½ D: King Vidor. Gary Cooper, Anna Sten, Ralph Bellamy, Walter Brennan, Helen Vinson, Sig Ruman. Study of romance and idealism; unbelievable love yarn but entertaining. Another attempt to make Anna Sten a new Garbo.

Weddings and Babies (1960) **81m.** **½ D: Morris Engel. Viveca Lindfors, John Myhers. Charming love story between photographer and model, shot on-location in New York; modest but engaging production.

Wee Geordie (1956-British) **C-93m.** ***½ D: Frank Launder. Bill Travers, Alastair Sim, Norah Gorsen, Molly Urquhart, Francis De Wolff. Flavorful romp with Travers a Scottish shotputter who goes to the Olympics. Despite predictable sight gags and romance, film makes one relish each situation.

Wee Willie Winkle (1937) **74m.** *** D: John Ford. Shirley Temple, Victor McLaglen, C. Aubrey Smith, Cesar Romero, Constance Collier, Mary Forbes, June Lang. Kipling tale adapted for Temple as heroine of British regiment in India. Good action scenes, and Shirley and McLaglen make a fine team. Originally released at 99m.

Week-end In Havana (1941) **C-80m.** **½ D: Walter Lang. Alice Faye, Carmen Miranda, John Payne, Cesar Romero, Cobina Wright, Jr., George Barbier, Leonid Kinskey, Sheldon Leonard, Billy Gilbert. Colorful musical has Faye landing in Havana, torn between Payne and Romero; Miranda lends peppery support.

Week-end Marriage (1932) **66m.** ** D: Thornton Freeland. Loretta Young, Norman Foster, Aline MacMahon, George Brent, Vivienne Osborne, Roscoe Karns. Comedy courtship leads to drama of money-hungry husband after marriage; nothing special.

Weekend at Dunkirk (1965-France-Italy) **C-101m.** ** D: Henri Verneuil. Jean-Paul Belmondo, Catherine Spaak, Georges Geret, Jean-Pierre Marielle, Pierre Mondy. Dull war film, based on well-known French novel, about four French soldiers on the Dunkirk Beach around evacuation time early in WW2.

Weekend at the Waldorf (1945) **130m.** *** D: Robert Z. Leonard. Ginger Rogers, Lana Turner, Walter Pidgeon, Van Johnson, Edward Arnold, Phyllis Thaxter, Keenan Wynn, Robert Benchley. Glossy remake of GRAND HOTEL with Rogers and Pidgeon outshining others; very superficial but entertaining.

Weekend for Three (1941) **61m.** ** D: Irving Reis. Dennis O'Keefe, Jane Wyatt, Philip Reed, ZaSu Pitts. Conventional marital comedy too domesticated for zesty tastes.

Weekend Nun, The (1972) **C-78m.** TVM D: Jeannot Szwarc. Joanna Pettet, Vic Morrow, Ann Sothern, James Gregory, Beverly Garland, Barbara Werle, Kay Lenz. Sister Damian (Pettet) innocently assumes she can work as probation officer and remain true to her vows, but experiences on job and with realistic partner Jardine (Morrow), culminating in tragic accident, make her realize she must make major vocational decision. Well-conceived, smoothly executed morality play, complete with fine performance by entire cast. Above average.

Weekend of Terror (1970) **C-73m.** TVM D: Jud Taylor. Robert Conrad, Lee Majors, Lois Nettleton, Carol Lynley, Jane Wyatt, Kevin Hagen. Three nuns taken hostage by kidnappers searching for girl who resembles original hostage killed accidentally. If you can get by embarassing dialogue, fair suspense with predictable resolution. Average.

Weekend with Father (1951) **83m.** **½ D: Douglas Sirk. Van Heflin, Patricia Neal, Virginia Field, Gigi

[845]

Perreau, Richard Denning. Pleasant frou-frou of widow and widower courting despite their childrens' interference.

Weird Woman (1944) 64m. **½ D: Reginald LeBorg. Lon Chaney, Jr., Anne Gwynne, Evelyn Ankers, Ralph Morgan, Lois Collier. Chaney's exgirlfriend objects to his Tropic-Isle bride, connives to get even. Way-out chiller is good fun. Remade as BURN, WITCH, BURN.

Welcome Home, Johnny Bristol (1971) C-100m. TVM D: George McCowan. Martin Landau, Jane Alexander, Brock Peters, Forrest Tucker, Martin Sheen, Pat O'Brien. Returning Vietnam vet in flashback-ridden thriller dealing with bizarre reactions to Vermont home town and ways in which it has changed. Unconvincing characters in forgettable drama. Below average.

Welcome Home, Soldier Boys (1972) C-91m. ** D: Richard Compton. Joe Don Baker, Paul Koslo, Alan Vint, Elliott Street, Jennifer Billingsley, Billy "Green" Bush, Geoffrey Lewis, Francine York. Sensationalistic melodrama about four ex-Green Berets who adjust to civilian life by gang-raping a girl and burning down a town. Topical, but that's all.

Welcome Stranger (1947) 107m. *** D: Elliott Nugent. Bing Crosby, Barry Fitzgerald, Joan Caulfield, Wanda Hendrix, Frank Faylen, Elizabeth Patterson. Entertaining film of Crosby filling in for vacationing doctor in small community, getting involved with local girl and lovely little town.

Welcome to Hard Times (1967) C-105m. *** D: Burt Kennedy. Henry Fonda, Janice Rule, Keenan Wynn, Janis Paige, John Anderson, Aldo Ray. Intriguing, if not fast-moving account of run-down town plagued by destructive outlaws, with Fonda finally forced to shoot it out to save what's left.

Welcome to L.A. (1977) C-106m. ***½ D: Alan Rudolph. Keith Carradine, Sally Kellerman, Geraldine Chaplin, Harvey Keitel, Lauren Hutton, Viveca Lindfors, Sissy Spacek, Denver Pyle, John Considine, Richard Baskin. Promising directorial debut from Rudolph in visually stunning story of assorted Southern California wackos and their sorry love lives. Not for every taste, but it will probably become a cult film. Produced by Robert Altman.

Welcome to the Club (1971) C-88m. ** D: Walter Shenson. The Warblers, Jack Warden, Brian Foley, Andy Jarell. Japanese setting for discrimination in military as morale officer in the Navy tries to find quarters for USO entertainers.

Well, The (1951) 85m. *** D: Leo Popkin, Russell Rouse. Richard Rober, Harry Morgan, Barry Kelley, Christine Larson, Maidie Norman, Ernest Anderson. Incisive study of crowd psychology, focusing on effects of townfolk when Negro child becomes lodged in deep well.

Well-Groomed Bride, The (1946) 75m. ** D: Sidney Lanfield. Olivia de Havilland, Ray Milland, Sonny Tufts, James Gleason, Percy Kilbride. Two Oscar-winners suffer with ridiculous comedy of stubborn girl insisting on champagne for her wedding.

Wells Fargo (1937) 115m. *** D: Frank Lloyd. Joel McCrea, Frances Dee, Ralph Morgan, Johnny Mack Brown, Porter Hall, Robert Cummings, Harry Davenport. McCrea, struggling to build famous express service, loses love of his wife (Dee) in process. Large-scale Western is long, but filled with action.

Werewolf, The (1956) 83m. *½ D: Fred F. Sears. Steven Ritch, Don Megowan, Joyce Holden, Eleanore Tanin, Harry Lauter. Yet another telling of the half-man, half-wolf breed. Scientists, seeking cure for radiation poisoning, inject man with serum and he becomes a werewolf. Loses a lot in the retelling.

Werewolf in a Girl's Dormitory (1963-Italian) 84m. BOMB D: Richard Benson. Carl Schell, Barbara Lass, Curt Lowens, Maurice Marsac. Title tells all in generally witless, plotless story of killer-beast on the loose.

Werewolf of London (1935) 75m. **½ D: Stuart Walker. Henry Hull, Warner Oland, Valerie Hobson, Lester Matthews, Spring Byington. Dated but still effective thriller of scientist Hull, who stumbles onto curse of lycanthropy and terrorizes London as a mad killer. Oland is fun as mysterious man who warns Hull of impending doom.

Werewolf of Washington (1973) C-90m. *½ D: Milton Moses Ginsberg. Dean Stockwell, Biff McGuire, Clifton James, Beeson Carroll, Jane House, Michael Dunn. Juvenile attempt to mix Watergate horrors with the more traditional kind. For the curious only.

West 11 (1963-British) 93m. *½ D: Michael Winner. Alfred Lynch, Kathleen Breck, Eric Portman, Diana Dors, Kathleen Harrison. Lumbering account of out-of-work Lynch agreeing to murder Portman's aunt, with the crime bringing about a reformation of his character.

West of Suez SEE: **Fighting Wildcats**

West of Zanzibar (1928) 77m. *** D: Tod Browning. Lon Chaney, Lionel Barrymore, Mary Nolan, Warner Baxter, Jacqueline Gadsdon. Seamy story of crippled Chaney ruling jungle monarchy, swearing revenge on man who ruined his life, by despoiling man's daughter (Nolan). Hokey ending mars bizarre tale; remade as KONGO.

West of Zanzibar (1954-British) C-84m. ** D: Harry Watt. Anthony Steel, Sheila Sim, Edric Connor, Orlando Martins. Ivory hunters meet up with jungle obstacles and native tribes; Steel and Sim share the adventures.

West Point of the Air (1935) 100m. **½ D: Richard Rosson. Wallace Beery, Robert Young, Maureen O'Sullivan, Lewis Stone, James Gleason, Rosalind Russell, Robert Taylor. Commander Beery pushes reluctant son Young through army air-training for his own satisfaction. Good cast enlivens standard drama.

West Point Story, The (1950) 107m. **½ D: Roy Del Ruth. James Cagney, Virginia Mayo, Doris Day, Gordon MacRae, Gene Nelson. Pat musical about Broadway director and hoofer Cagney staging a spectacular revue at West Point.

West Side Story (1961) C-155m. **** D: Robert Wise, Jerome Robbins. Natalie Wood, Richard Beymer, George Chakiris, Rita Moreno, Russ Tamblyn. Vivid film adaptation of the landmark Broadway musical, updating Romeo and Juliet story to youth-gang atmosphere of late 1950s New York. Wood and Beymer lack charisma, but everything surrounding them is great: Robbins' choreography, Leonard Bernstein-Stephen Sondheim score. Winner of 10 Academy Awards including Best Picture, Director, Supporting Actor and Actress (Chakiris, Moreno).

Westbound (1959) C-72m. **½ D: Budd Boetticher. Randolph Scott,

Virginia Mayo, Karen Steele, Michael Dante, Andrew Duggan, Michael Pate. Trim sagebrush tale of Yankee officer Scott organizing a stage coach line to bring in gold from California.

Western Union (1941) C-94m. *** D: Fritz Lang. Robert Young, Randolph Scott, Dean Jagger, Virginia Gilmore, John Carradine, Slim Summerville, Chill Wills, Barton MacLane. Elaborate Western of cross-country cables being established amid various conflicts. Standard plot devices don't spoil big-scale excitement.

Westerner, The (1940) 100m. ***½ D: William Wyler. Gary Cooper, Walter Brennan, Fred Stone, Doris Davenport, Forrest Tucker, Lillian Bond. Excellent tale of land disputes getting out of hand in the old West, with Brennan's Judge Bean winning him an Oscar.

Westward Ho, The Wagons (1956) C-90m. ** D: William Beaudine. Fess Parker, Kathleen Crowley, Jeff York, David Stollery, Sebastian Cabot, George Reeves. Lackluster pioneer saga has Disney polish but no excitement as wagon train travels West. Four Mouseketeers from the "Mickey Mouse Club" appear—Karen, Cubby, Tommy, and Doreen.

Westward Passage (1932) 75m. ** D: Robert Milton. Ann Harding, Laurence Olivier, Irving Pichel, ZaSu Pitts, Irene Purchell, Bonita Granville, Ethel Griffies. Acting uplifts clichéd tale of girl who divorces to marry for true love, despite sacrifices.

Westward the Women (1951) 118m. *** D: William Wellman. Robert Taylor, Denise Darcel, Beverly Dennis, John McIntire, Hope Emerson, Lenore Lonergan, Julie Bishop, Marilyn Erskine. Intriguing Western with Taylor heading wagon train full of females bound for California to meet mail-order husbands.

Westworld (1973) C-88m. *** D: Michael Crichton. Richard Benjamin, Yul Brynner, James Brolin, Norman Bartold, Alan Oppenheimer, Victoria Shaw. Adult vacation resort of the future offers opportunity to live in various fantasy worlds serviced by robots. Benjamin chooses old-time Western town, but begins to fear when one of the robots malfunctions. Engaging story by Crichton; followed by sequel FUTUREWORLD.

Wetbacks (1956) C-89m. *½ D: Hank McCune. Lloyd Bridges, Nancy Gates, John Hoyt, Barton MacLane.

Tawdry study of smuggling Mexicans across Texas border.

What a Life (1939) **75m.** D: Jay Theodore Reed. Jackie Cooper, Betty Field, John Howard, Janice Logan, Vaughan Glaser, Lionel Stander, Hedda Hopper. See: **Henry Aldrich** series.

What a Way to Go! (1964) **C-124m.** **½ D: J. Lee Thompson. Shirley MacLaine, Paul Newman, Dean Martin, Robert Mitchum, Gene Kelly, Bob Cummings, Dick Van Dyke, Reginald Gardiner, Margaret Dumont, Fifi D'Orsay. Elaborate comedy of perennial widow MacLaine has few bright spots. Authors Comden and Green use gimmick of spoofing various movie-period styles, but it fails to utilize the talent-loaded cast. Kelly stars in the funniest sequence.

What a Woman! (1943) **94m.** **½ D: Irving Cummings. Rosalind Russell, Brian Aherne, Willard Parker, Alan Dinehart, Ann Savage. Literary agent Russell sells film rights to spicy novel, and unwillingly becomes involved with its bookish author (Parker) in this lightweight comedy vehicle.

What Are Best Friends For? (1973) **C-78m.** **TVM** D: Jay Sandrich. Ted Bessell, Lee Grant, Larry Hagman, Barbara Feldon, Nina Talbot, George Furth, Corinne Camacho. Bouncy comedy about the efforts of a married couple to find companionship for their recently divorced friend. Sparkling performances make something out of almost nothing. Average.

What Became of Jack and Jill? (1972-British) **C-93m.** **½ D: Bill Bain. Vanessa Howard, Paul Nicholas, Mona Washbourne, Peter Copley, Peter Jeffrey. Game attempt at detailing modern day, no-holds-barred love affair twisted by intrusion of grandmother; defeated by smug script, odd point of view.

What Did You Do in the War, Daddy? (1966) **C-119m.** *** D: Blake Edwards. James Coburn, Dick Shawn, Sergio Fantoni, Aldo Ray, Harry Morgan, Carroll O'Connor, Giovanna Ralli. A not too funny but quite pleasant film about group of misfit American soldiers trying to tame wacky Italian town into surrender.

What Do You Say to a Naked Lady? (1970) **C-90m.** *** D: Allen Funt. Amusing X-rated CANDID CAMERA effort will have to be edited

for TV. Accent is on sex, and some of the reactions to stunts, and queries, are hilarious.

What Ever Happened to Baby Jane? (1962) **132m.** ***½ D: Robert Aldrich. Bette Davis, Joan Crawford, Victor Buono, Marjorie Bennett, Anna Lee. Far-fetched, thoroughly engaging black comedy of two former movie stars; Joan's a cripple at the mercy of demented sister Baby Jane Hudson (Davis). Bette has a field day in her macabre characterization, with Buono a perfect match.

What Every Woman Knows (1934) **92m.** ***½ D: Gregory LaCava. Helen Hayes, Brian Aherne, Madge Evans, Lucile Watson, Dudley Digges, Donald Crisp. Charming, funny adaptation of James Barrie's play about a woman who is "the brains" behind her well-meaning but none-too-bright politician husband. Beautifully acted and surprisingly contemporary.

What Every Woman Wants (1962-British) **69m.** *½ D: Ernest Morris. William (James) Fox, Hy Hazell, Dennis Lotis, Elizabeth Shepherd. Dull marital comedy of wives trying to reform husbands.

What Next, Corporal Hargrove? (1945) **95m.** **½ D: Richard Thorpe. Robert Walker, Keenan Wynn, Jean Porter, Chill Wills, Hugo Haas, William Phillips, Fred Essler, Cameron Mitchell. Hargrove (Walker) is in France with con-man buddy (Wynn) in OK sequel to SEE HERE, PRIVATE HARGROVE; trivial and episodic.

What! No Beer? (1933) **66m.** ** D: Edward Sedgwick. Buster Keaton, Jimmy Durante, Roscoe Ates, Phyllis Barry, John Miljan, Edward Brophy, Henry Armetta. Mediocre prohibition comedy about dimwitted bootleggers Keaton and Durante; plot makes no sense, Durante is incredibly overbearing. Best scenes involve Buster and leading-lady Barry.

What Price Glory? (1926) **120m.** *** D: Raoul Walsh. Victor McLaglen, Edmund Lowe, Dolores Del Rio, William V. Mong, Phyllis Haver, Leslie Fenton, Barry Norton. Boisterous rivalry between Capt. Flagg (McLaglen) and Sgt. Quirt (Lowe) centers on lovely Charmaine (Del Rio) when they go to France during WW1. Zesty comedy, with plenty of fireworks for lip-readers, abruptly turns grim as focus shifts to horrors of war, only to return to Flagg-Quirt hijinks for finale. Fine entertainment, from Laurence Stallings-Maxwell Anderson play; two main characters reappeared in a handful of sequels, none of them as good as this. Remade in 1952.

What Price Glory (1952) C-111m. **½ D: John Ford. James Cagney, Corinne Calvet, Dan Dailey, Robert Wagner, Marisa Pavan. Classic silent film becomes shallow Cagney-Dailey vehicle of battling Army men Flagg and Quirt in WW1 France.

What Price Hollywood? (1932) 88m. *** D: George Cukor. Constance Bennett, Lowell Sherman, Neil Hamilton, Gregory Ratoff, Brooks Benedict. Soused movie director Sherman helps waitress Bennett fulfill her ambition to become a movie star—while he sinks into alcoholic ruin. Surprisingly sharp-eyed look at Hollywood—both comic and dramatic—that served as inspiration for later A STAR IS BORN.

What Price Murder (1958-French) 105m. **½ D: Henri Verneuil. Henri Vidal, Mylene Demongeot, Isa Miranda, Alfred Adam. Well-turned murder mystery of hubby and secretary planning to do away with wife.

What's a Nice Girl Like You . . . ? (1971) C-73m. TVM D: Jerry Paris. Brenda Vaccaro, Jack Warden, Vincent Price, Roddy McDowall, Edmond O'Brien, Jo Anne Worley. Entertaining comedy about Bronx ugly-duckling drawn into elaborate extortion plot which calls for her to impersonate rich socialite. Some good bits, but film lags in wrong places. Average.

What's Good for the Goose (1969-British) C-105m. BOMB D: Menahem Golan. Norman Wisdom, Sally Geeson, Sally Bazely, Sarah Atkinson, Terence Alexander. Weak, unfunny, uninteresting sex romp wherein the object is to score as often as possible. Skip it.

What's New, Pussycat? (1965) C-108m. ** D: Clive Donner. Peter Sellers, Peter O'Toole, Romy Schneider, Capucine, Paula Prentiss, Woody Allen, Ursula Andress. Disturbed fashion editor O'Toole goes to psychiatrist Sellers for help with his romantic problems, but Sellers is even crazier than he. Scripted by Woody Allen (who also makes his acting debut) and like many of his later comedies, one sits through a lot of misfired gags to get to a few undeniable gems.

What's So Bad About Feeling Good? (1968) C-94m. **½ D: George Seaton. George Peppard, Mary Tyler Moore, Dom DeLuise, John McMartin, Don Stroud, Nathaniel Frey. Amiable attempt at old-fashioned Capraesque comedy, with pixillated toucan spreading good feelings throughout N.Y.C. Doesn't hit bullseye, but has its moments.

What's the Matter with Helen? (1971) C-101m. *** D: Curtis Harrington. Debbie Reynolds, Shelley Winters, Dennis Weaver, Agnes Moorehead, Michael MacLiammoir. Campy murder tale set in 1930s. Reynolds and Winters try to erase their sordid past, start anew in Hollywood with school for talented kids. Good fun; Debbie ideal in period setting.

What's Up, Doc? (1972) C-94m. *** D: Peter Bogdanovich. Barbra Streisand, Ryan O'Neal, Kenneth Mars, Austin Pendleton, Madeline Kahn, Sorrell Booke, Michael Murphy. Modern-day screwball comedy with impish Streisand making life miserable for stuffy musicologist O'Neal and his fiancée (Kahn), becoming involved in mixup over stolen jewels. Great comic chase scenes highlight overpowering farce, Bogdanovich's bouquet to 1930s Hollywood.

What's Up, Tiger Lily? (1966) C-80m. *** Compiled by Woody Allen. Slick Japanese imitation-James-Bond movie is re-edited by Allen turning the whole thing into one long, very funny joke, where the object of international intrigue is a valued eggsalad recipe. Unnecessary musical interludes by The Lovin' Spoonful.

Whatever Happened to Aunt Alice? (1969) C-101m. *** D: Lee H. Katzin. Geraldine Page, Ruth Gordon, Rosemary Forsyth, Robert Fuller, Mildred Dunnock. Eccentric Page stays wealthy by murdering her housekeepers, stealing their savings. Gordon hires on as next "victim," trying to solve missing-persons mystery. Played to the hilt; most enjoyable.

Wheel of Fortune SEE: **Man Betrayed, A**

Wheeler Dealers, The (1963) C-106m. *** D: Arthur Hiller. Lee Remick, James Garner, Jim Backus, Phil Harris, Shelley Berman, Louis Nye. Funny, fast-moving spoof of Texas millionaires who play with investments just for fun. Garner also catches Lee Remick along the way.

When a Stranger Calls (1979) C-97m. *½ D: Fred Walton. Carol Kane, Charles Durning, Colleen Dewhurst, Tony Beckley, Rachel Roberts, Ron O'Neal. Psycho murders two children after terrorizing their baby sitter, returns seven years later to extend his crime. Unpleasant, improbable melodrama falls apart after OK opening 20 minutes.

When a Woman Loves (1959-Japanese) C-97m. **½ D: Heinosuke Gosho. Ineko Arima, Shin Saburi, Yatsuko Tan-ami, Nobuko Otowa. Utilizing flashbacks, film recalls love affair between Saburi and older man Arima, a war correspondent; sentimental weeper with almost enough class.

When Comedy Was King (1960) 81m. **** Compiled by Robert Youngson. Charlie Chaplin, Buster Keaton, Laurel and Hardy, Ben Turpin, Fatty Arbuckle, Wallace Beery, Gloria Swanson. Second Youngson compilation of silent comedy clips has many old favorites in classic scenes. Chaplin, Keaton, Laurel & Hardy, Keystone Kops, Charley Chase and others shine in this outstanding film.

When Dinosaurs Ruled the Earth (1970-British) C-96m. *** D: Val Guest. Victoria Vetri, Robin Hawdon, Patrick Allen, Drewe Henley, Magda Konopka, Patrick Holt. Fast-paced, enjoyable prehistoric actioner with Vetri and Hawdon lovers ostracized by respective tribes. Beautiful locations, very good special effects, and honorable attempt to simulate period.

When Eight Bells Toll (1971-British) C-94m. ** D: Etienne Perier. Anthony Hopkins, Robert Morley, Nathalie Delon, Jack Hawkins, Corin Redgrave, Derek Bond. Alistair MacLean story of gold piracy at sea lacks flash and finesse.

When Every Day Was the Fourth of July (1978) C-100m. TVM D: Dan Curtis. Dean Jones, Louise Sorel, Harris Yulin, Geoffrey Lewis, Henry Wilcoxon, Scott Brady, Katy Kurtzman. Heart-touching period piece, fictionalized from events in director-writer Curtis' boyhood, about a young girl who talks her lawyer father into defending the town weirdo, a mute handyman, on homicide charges and incurring the scorn of the community. Above average.

When Gangland Strikes (1956) 70m. ** D: R. G. Springsteen. Raymond Greenleaf, Marjie Millar, John Hudson, Anthony Caruso. Blasé handling of law enforcer's dilemma between duty and protecting family when he's blackmailed. Remake of 1939 film MAIN STREET LAWYER.

When Hell Broke Loose (1958) 78m. ** D: Kenneth Crane. Charles Bronson, Violet Rensing, Richard Jaeckel, Arvid Nelson. Low-keyed trim episode involving assassination attempt on General Eisenhower, set in WW2 Europe.

When Hell Was in Session (1979) C-100m. TVM D: Paul Krasny. Hal Holbrook, Eva Marie Saint, Mako, Ronny Cox, Renne Jarrett, Richard Evans, William Kirby Cullen. Holbrook gives a harrowing portrayal of Navy Commander Jeremiah Denton in this dramatization of the officer's experience as a Vietnam POW for seven-and-a-half years. Not for the squeamish. Above average.

When I Grow Up (1951) 80m. *** D: Michael Kanin. Bobby Driscoll, Robert Preston, Martha Scott, Sherry Jackson. Effective low-key study of the generation gap, with Driscoll most appealing as the child who runs away from home.

When in Rome (1952) 78m. **½ D: Clarence Brown. Van Johnson, Paul Douglas, Joseph Calleia, Mimi Aguglia, Tudor Owen. Tasteful yet unrestrained tale of con-artist Douglas disguising himself as priest attending Holy Year pilgrimage in Italy; through American priest Johnson et al. he finds new faith.

When Ladies Meet (1941) 108m. ** D: Robert Z. Leonard. Joan Crawford, Robert Taylor, Greer Garson, Herbert Marshall, Spring Byington. Attractive performers in plodding remake of '33 Ann Harding-Myrna Loy vehicle of Rachel Crothers' play. Authoress Crawford loves Marshall, who's married to Garson; Taylor loves Joan. Talk marathon on woman's rights is vastly outdated. Taylor and Garson try to bring life to film, but can't.

When Lovers Meet SEE: **Lover Come Back** (1946)

When Michael Calls (1971) C-73m. TVM D: Philip Leacock. Elizabeth Ashley, Ben Gazzara, Michael Douglas, Karen Pearson. Thriller-mystery of mother receiving strange phone calls from voice sounding like dead son, with subplot about divorce. Tame, predictable resolution in film that can't even build tension convincingly. Below average.

When My Baby Smiles at Me (1948) C-98m. **½ D: Walter Lang. Betty Grable, Dan Dailey, Jack Oakie, June Havoc, James Gleason, Richard Arlen. Strictly routine musical about burlesque team that breaks up when one member gets job on Broadway. Eventually they're reteamed, of course. Based on famous play *Burlesque.* Filmed before as DANCE OF LIFE and SWING HIGH, SWING LOW.

When She Was Bad . . . (1979) C-100m. TVM D: Peter Hunt. Cheryl Ladd, Robert Urich, Eileen Brennan, Dabney Coleman, Marcia Lewis, Ramon Bieri, Nicole Eggert. Pretty young housewife and mother, unable to cope with marriage, becomes a child beater. Title refers not to the youngster but to the mother. Below average.

When Strangers Marry (1944) 67m. ** D: William Castle. Robert Mitchum, Kim Hunter, Dean Jagger, Neil Hamilton. Hunter is caught in midst of murder plot involving husband and old boyfriend; programmer mystery flick. Retitled: BETRAYED.

When the Boys Meet the Girls (1965) C-110m. ** D: Alvin Ganzer. Connie Francis, Harve Presnell, Herman's Hermits, Louis Armstrong, Liberace, Sue Ane Langdon, Fred Clark, Frank Faylen, Sam the Sham. Rehash of GIRL CRAZY, turned into a dull guest-star showcase.

When the Daltons Rode (1940) 80m. *** D: George Marshall. Randolph Scott, Kay Francis, Brian Donlevy, George Bancroft, Andy Devine, Broderick Crawford, Stuart Erwin. Fine Western actioner with good cast, typical plot; Francis and Scott provide romantic relief.

When the Legends Die (1972) C-105m. *** D: Stuart Millar. Richard Widmark, Frederic Forrest, Luana Anders, Vito Scotti, Herbert Nelson. Offbeat story of aging rodeo cowboy who cannot accept fact that years are creeping up on him, and young Indian he befriends.

When the Redskins Rode (1951) C-78m. *½ D: Lew Landers. Jon Hall, Mary Castle, James Seay, John Ridgley. Lame-brained Western set during French and Indian War of 1750s.

When Time Ran Out . . . (1980) C-121m. BOMB D: James Goldstone. Paul Newman, Jacqueline Bisset, William Holden, James Franciscus, Edward Albert, Red Buttons, Ernest Borgnine, Burgess Meredith, Barbara Carrera. WHEN IDEAS RAN OUT, or, THE BLUBBERING INFERNO: Irwin Allen's shameless rehash of all his disaster-movie clichés is a monumental bore that even a volcanic eruption cannot save.

When Tomorrow Comes (1939) 90m. **½ D: John M. Stahl. Irene Dunne, Charles Boyer, Barbara O'Neil, Nydia Westman, Onslow Stevens. Standard soapy story enhanced by leading players; Boyer loves Dunne, although he's already married. Remade as INTERLUDE.

When Willie Comes Marching Home (1950) 82m. **½ D: John Ford. Dan Dailey, Corinne Calvet, Colleen Townsend, William Demarest, Mae Marsh. Schmaltzy WW2 adventures of West Virginia youth Dailey, including interlude with French underground leader Calvet.

When Worlds Collide (1951) C-81m. **½ D: Rudolph Maté. Richard Derr, Barbara Rush, Peter Hanson, Larry Keating, John Hoyt. Cardboard characters and corny dialogue detract from story of scientists preparing for the end of the world. Special effects won Oscar for this George Pal production.

When You Comin' Back, Red Ryder? (1979) C-118m. *½ D: Milton Katselas. Marjoe Gortner, Hal Linden, Lee Grant, Peter Firth, Candy Clark, Pat Hingle, Stephanie Faracy, Audra Lindley, Bill McKinney. Stagy, unpleasant film of Mark Medoff's play about a psycho terrorizing a disparate group of people in roadside diner. Has its moments, but not enough to justify nearly two hours of viewing.

When You're In Love (1937) 104m. **½ D: Robert Riskin. Grace Moore, Cary Grant, Aline MacMahon, Thomas Mitchell, Emma Dunn. Overlong but enjoyable vehicle for opera star Moore who "hires" Grant as her husband. Most 98m. TV prints are missing film's highlight, where star sings "Minnie the Moocher."

When's Your Birthday? (1937) 77m. **½ D: Harry Beaumont. Joe E. Brown, Marian Marsh, Edgar Kennedy, Margaret Hamilton, Frank Jenks. Entertaining Brown vehicle of timid boxer whose prowess depends on position of stars; good supporting cast.

Where Angels Go, Trouble Follows

(1968) **C-95m.** **½ D: James Neilson. Rosalind Russell, Stella Stevens, Binnie Barnes, Mary Wickes, Dolores Sutton, Susan Saint James, Barbara Hunter; guest stars Milton Berle, Arthur Godfrey, Van Johnson, William Lundigan, Robert Taylor. For "Flying Nun" fans only; contrived comedy follow-up to TROUBLE WITH ANGELS with Mother Superior Russell pitted against young, progressive nun Stevens.

Where Are Your Children? (1943) **73m.** *½ D: William Nigh. Jackie Cooper, Patricia Morison, Gale Storm, Gertrude Michael, John Litel, Evelynne Eaton. Thoughtless study of juvenile delinquency.

Where Danger Lives (1950) **84m.** ** D: John Farrow. Robert Mitchum, Faith Domergue, Claude Rains, Maureen O'Sullivan. Young physician Mitchum becomes involved with woman (Domergue) who is bordering on insanity.

Where Do We Go From Here? (1945) **C-77m.** **½ D: Gregory Ratoff. Fred MacMurray, June Haver, Joan Leslie, Gene Sheldon, Anthony Quinn, Carlos Ramirez, Otto Preminger. Engaging but ultimately silly musical comedy about genie enabling MacMurray to travel backwards into American history. Ira Gershwin-Kurt Weill score includes wonderful mini-opera involving Christopher Columbus.

Where Does It Hurt? (1972) **C-90m.** BOMB D: Rod Amateau. Peter Sellers, Jo Ann Pflug, Rick Lenz, Harold Gould, Hope Summers, Eve Bruce, Kathleen Freeman. Abysmal, tasteless "comedy" about hospital run by corrupt Sellers, staffed by money-hungry incompetents. If offensive dialogue is cut for TV, running time will be 10 minutes. Good cast wasted.

Where Eagles Dare (1969) **C-158m.** ***½ D: Brian G. Hutton. Richard Burton, Clint Eastwood, Mary Ure, Michael Hordern, Patrick Wymark, Robert Beatty, Anton Diffring, Donald Houston, Ingrid Pitt. Modern-day version of Republic serial, with slam-bang cliff-hanger action that never lets up. Burton and company assigned to free American officer held captive in German mountain castle during WW2. Terrific.

Where Have All the People Gone? (1974) **C-78m.** TVM D: John Llewellyn Moxey. Peter Graves, Verna Bloom, George O'Hanlon, Jr., Kath-

leen Quinlan, Michael-James Wixted. Graves and his family are among survivors of a radiation explosion. "End of the world" tale unevenly spun, indifferently acted. Average.

Where It's At (1969) **C-104m.** **½ D: Garson Kanin. David Janssen, Robert Drivas, Rosemary Forsyth, Brenda Vacarro, Don Rickles, Edy Williams. Pleasant but undistinguished comedy about strained relationship between Las Vegas casino owner Janssen and Princeton-graduate son Drivas. Some of film's funniest bits involve nudity, so they may not make it to TV.

Where Love Has Gone (1964) **C-114m.** **½ D: Edward Dmytryk. Bette Davis, Susan Hayward, Michael Connors, Jane Greer, Joey Heatherton, George Macready. Glossy drama of Heatherton killing her mother's (Hayward) lover; Davis is the domineering grandmother. Greer is a sympathetic probation officer. Based on Harold Robbins' novel.

Where the Boys Are (1960) **C-99m.** **½ D: Henry Levin. Dolores Hart, George Hamilton, Yvette Mimieux, Jim Hutton, Barbara Nichols, Paula Prentiss, Connie Francis. Not-bad film about teenagers during Easter Vacation in Ft. Lauderdale. Connie Francis, in her first film, is pretty good; other young players seen to good advantage. Nichols is hilarious as usual as a flashy blonde.

Where the Bullets Fly (1966-British) **C-88m.** **½ D: John Gilling. Tom Adams, Dawn Addams, Tim Barrett, Michael Ripper. Well-paced super spy satire involving Adams tracking down special fuel formula.

Where the Hot Wind Blows (1960-Italian) **120m.** ** D: Jules Dassin. Gina Lollobrigida, Pierre Brasseur, Marcello Mastroianni, Melina Mercouri, Yves Montand, Paola Stoppa. Artsy film that meanders around subject of legalized immorality in small Italian village. Retitled: THE LAW.

Where the Red Fern Grows (1974) **C-90m.** *** D: Norman Tokar. James Whitmore, Beverly Garland, Jack Ging, Lonny Chapman, Stewart Peterson. Appealing family drama about a boy's devotion to two hunting dogs, and how his experiences teach him about responsibility and growing up. Set in 1930's in Oklahoma.

Where the Sidewalk Ends (1950) **95m.** *** D: Otto Preminger. Dana Andrews, Gene Tierney, Gary Merrill, Karl Malden, Ruth Donnelly, Craig Stevens. While investigating a murder, brutal cop (Andrews) inadvertently kills a man, then tries to conceal his own guilt while continuing his search for murderer. Moody crime melodrama with excellent characterizations.

Where the Spies Are (1965-British) C-110m. *** D: Val Guest. David Niven, Françoise Dorleac, John Le Mesurier, Cyril Cusack, Eric Pohlmann, Reginald Beckwith. Well made mixture of dry comedy and suspense in tale of doctor forced into spying. Good cast names enhance already fine movie.

Where There's Life (1947) 75m. *** D: Sidney Lanfield. Bob Hope, Signe Hasso, William Bendix, George Coulouris. Wacky comedy with radio star Hope earmarked as new king of mythical European country, trying to elude the menacing "messengers" who have come for him.

Where Were You When the Lights Went Out? (1968) C-94m. *½ D: Hy Averback. Doris Day, Robert Morse, Terry-Thomas, Steve Allen, Jim Backus, Patrick O'Neal, Pat Paulsen, Ben Blue, Earl Wilson. Below average Doris Day comedy centering around the massive N.Y.C. blackout on November 9, 1965.

Where's Charley? (1952) C-97m. *** D: David Butler. Ray Bolger, Allyn McLerie, Robert Shackleton, Mary Germaine, Horace Cooper, Margaretta Scott. Bolger recreates Broadway role in musical adaptation of CHARLEY'S AUNT, as Oxford student whose face-saving impersonation of dowdy dowager leads to endless complications. Frank Loesser score includes "Once in Love with Amy." Filmed in England.

Where's Jack? (1969-British) C-119m. **½ D: James Clavell. Tommy Steele, Stanley Baker, Fiona Lewis, Alan Badel, Dudley Foster, Noel Purcell. Despite great cast and production values, surprisingly unengrossing historical adventure tale of Britain's most celebrated thief and escape artist, Jack Sheppard (Steele) wanted by British government and notorious mercenary (Baker).

Where's Poppa? (1970) C-87m. **½ D: Carl Reiner. George Segal, Ruth Gordon, Trish Van Devere, Ron Leibman, Rae Allen, Vincent Gardenia, Barnard Hughes. Absurdist comedy has cult following, but grisly subject matter makes it an acquired taste; Segal plays a repressed N.Y. lawyer whose senile mother dominates his life. Outlandish gags involve mugging, rape, nursing homes and other ills. Original ending was *too* potent, and changed. Reissued as GOING APE.

Which Way to the Front? (1970) C-96m. *½ D: Jerry Lewis. Jerry Lewis, John Wood, Jan Murray, Kaye Ballard, Robert Middleton, Paul Winchell, Sidney Miller, Gary Crosby. One of Jerry's worst has him a 4-F millionaire playboy who enlists other 4-Fs to fight Hitler.

Whiffs (1975) C-91m. *½ D: Ted Post. Elliott Gould, Eddie Albert, Harry Guardino, Godfrey Cambridge, Jennifer O'Neill, Alan Manson. Gould is guinea pig for Army Chemical Corps who has outlived his usefulness . . . but the military isn't rid of him so easily. Another sorry attempt to recapture the lunacy of M*A*S*H.

While the City Sleeps (1956) 100m. *** D: Fritz Lang. Dana Andrews, Ida Lupino, Rhonda Fleming, George Sanders, Vincent Price, Thomas Mitchell, Sally Forrest, Howard Duff. Veteran cast and intertwining storylines keep interest in account of newspaper reporters and police on the track of a berserk killer.

Whiplash (1948) 91m. ** D: Lewis Seiler. Dane Clark, Alexis Smith, Zachary Scott, Eve Arden, Jeffrey Lynn. Unmoving melodrama about artist turning into grim prizefighter. Script is main defect; acting OK.

Whipsaw (1935) 83m. **½ D: Sam Wood. Myrna Loy, Spencer Tracy, Harvey Stephens, William Harrigan, Clay Clement. Tracy uses bad-girl Loy to lead him to band of thieves; predictable complications follow in familiar but well-done crime drama.

Whirlpool (1949) 97m. *** D: Otto Preminger. Gene Tierney, Richard Conte, Jose Ferrer, Charles Bickford, Eduard Franz, Fortunio Bonanova, Constance Collier. Tense melodrama of nefarious hypnotist Ferrer using innocent Tierney to carry out his evil schemes.

Whispering Ghosts (1942) 75m. ** D: Alfred L. Werker. Brenda Joyce, Milton Berle, John Shelton, John Carradine. Berle is effective as bumbling performer trying to live up to radio role as crackerjack detective.

Whispering Smith (1948) C-88m. *** D: Leslie Fenton. Alan Ladd, Brenda

Marshall, Robert Preston, Donald Crisp, William Demarest. Well-acted Western about soft-spoken special agent investigating robberies who finds friend involved with crooks.

Whispering Smith Vs. Scotland Yard (1952-British) 77m. ** D: Francis Searle. Richard Carlson, Greta Gynt, Rona Anderson, Herbert Lom, Dora Bryan. Famed detective proves conclusively that suicide was actually well-staged murder. Good cast in below-average mystery.

Whistle at Eaton Falls, The (1951) 96m. **½ D: Robert Siodmak. Lloyd Bridges, Dorothy Gish, Carleton Carpenter, Murray Hamilton, Anne Francis, Ernest Borgnine, Doro Merande, Arthur O'Connell. Set in New Hampshire, this documentary-style film deals with labor relation problems in a small town when new plant manager has to lay off workers. Gish is factory owner in interesting supporting role.

Whistle Down the Wind (1962-British) 98m. *** D: Bryan Forbes. Hayley Mills, Bernard Lee, Alan Bates, Norman Bird, Diane Clare. Poignant, if artificial, drama of murderer on the run (Bates) seeking refuge in a barn, with three country children thinking him to be Christ.

Whistle Stop (1946) 85m. ** D: Leonide Moguy. George Raft, Ava Gardner, Victor McLaglen, Tom Conway, Jorja Curtright, Florence Bates, Charles Drake. Minor drama of nice-girl Gardner caught between no-account playboy Raft and uncouth nightclub owner McLaglen.

Whistler, The One of the most unusual—and one of the best—mystery series of the 30s and 40s was based on a popular radio show called "The Whistler." The premise of the show, and at least one of the films, was a mysterious figure who walked along whistling a haunting tune. "I am the Whistler," he would say. "And I know many things." He would introduce the current mystery and reappear from time to time to bridge gaps from one setting to another. Veteran Richard Dix starred in all but one of the eight Whistler films, but in keeping with the series' flexibility in presenting a new story every time, he alternated from hero to villain in various entries in the series. In the initial film, THE WHISTLER, Dix was a victim of circumstances about to be killed; in THE POWER OF THE WHISTLER he was an amnesiac murderer; in THE MYSTERIOUS INTRUDER he was a private eye; and in THE 13TH HOUR an innocent man framed for a murder he didn't commit. The one non-Dix film, RETURN OF THE WHISTLER, followed the radio format of the mysterious narrator with excellent results. That entry, and several others, had stories written by Cornell Woolrich, while others were written by Eric Taylor; they were all tightly knit, engrossing little mysteries, competently acted by contract players and directed in several cases by William Castle. One of the few series to gain acceptance with the public and critics alike, the Whistler films hold up quite well today as examples of the kind of mystery film "they just don't make any more."

Whistler, The (1944) 59m. D: William Castle. Richard Dix, Gloria Stuart, Alan Dinehart, Joan Woodbury, J. Carrol Naish, Byron Foulger, Trevor Bardette.

Whistling in Brooklyn (1943) 87m. **½ D: S. Sylvan Simon. Red Skelton, Ann Rutherford, Jean Rogers, "Rags" Ragland, Ray Collins, Henry O'Neill, William Frawley, Sam Levene. Skelton again, as radio sleuth "The Fox," mixed up in murder and pretending to be a member of the Dodgers ball team.

Whistling in Dixie (1942) 74m. *** D: S. Sylvan Simon. Red Skelton, Ann Rutherford, George Bancroft, Guy Kibbee. Red, as radio's "Fox" marries Ann, but their Southern honeymoon is interrupted by murder and mystery. Funny Skelton vehicle.

Whistling in the Dark (1941) 77m. *** D: S. Sylvan Simon. Red Skelton, Ann Rutherford, Virginia Grey, Conrad Veidt, "Rags" Ragland, Eve Arden. Faithful remake of 1933 film isn't as wacky as subsequent outings with Skelton as radio sleuth "The Fox," but still enjoyable; Red is held by fiendish Veidt and forced to spell out plans for "perfect murder."

White Angel, The (1936) 75m. ** D: William Dieterle. Kay Francis, Ian Hunter, Donald Woods, Nigel Bruce, Donald Crisp, Henry O'Neill, Billy Mauch. Lavish but unsuccessful biography of Florence Nightingale with Francis miscast in reworked history of 19th-century British nursing pioneer.

White Banners (1938) 88m. *** D: Edmund Goulding. Claude Rains,

Fay Bainter, Jackie Cooper, Bonita Granville, Henry O'Neill, Kay Johnson. Bainter moves in with troubled family, tries to solve their problems; moralistic filming of Lloyd C. Douglas novel is noteworthy for Bainter's fine performance.

White Buffalo, The (1977) C-97m. *½ D: J. Lee Thompson. Charles Bronson, Jack Warden, Will Sampson, Kim Novak, Clint Walker, Stuart Whitman, Slim Pickens, John Carradine. Wild Bill Hickok is haunted by the image of a buffalo that symbolizes his fear of death; strange, murky film, with atypical Bronson role, good support from Warden and Novak.

White Cargo (1942) 90m. ** D: Richard Thorpe. Hedy Lamarr, Walter Pidgeon, Frank Morgan, Richard Carlson, Reginald Owen. Lamarr is the seductive Tondelayo who entrances all at British plantation post in Africa, Pidgeon the expeditionist who really falls for her. Exotic love scenes, corny plot.

White Christmas (1954) C-120m. ** D: Michael Curtiz. Bing Crosby, Danny Kaye, Rosemary Clooney, Vera-Ellen, Dean Jagger. Nice Irving Berlin score is unfortunately interrupted by limp plot of army buddies Crosby and Kaye boosting popularity of winter resort run by their ex-officer Jagger. "What Can You Do With A General" stands out as Berlin's least memorable tune. Partial re-working of HOLIDAY INN, not half as good.

White Cliffs of Dover, The (1944) 126m. *** D: Clarence Brown. Irene Dunne, Alan Marshal, Van Johnson, C. Aubrey Smith, Dame May Whitty, Roddy McDowall, Peter Lawford. American Dunne marries Britisher Marshal in patriotic WW1 romancer. Slick but shallow.

White Comanche (1968-U.S.-Spanish) C-90m. *½ D: Gilbert Lee Kay (Jose Briz). William Shatner, Joseph Cotten, Rossana Yani, Perla Cristal, Vidal Molina. Strictly humdrum tortilla western.

White Cradle Inn SEE: High Fury
White Dawn, The (1974) C-109m. **½ D: Philip Kaufman. Warren Oates, Timothy Bottoms, Lou Gossett, Simonie Kopapik, Joanasie Salomonie. OK adventure about three whalers in 1896 who become lost in the Arctic and their subsequent exploitation of the Eskimos who save them. Brilliant location photography partially compensates for rambling narrative.

White Fang (1972-Italian) C-97m. *** D: Lucio Fulci. Franco Nero, Virna Lisi, Fernando Rey, Rik Battaglia. Unexpectedly rewarding version of Jack London's tale of a dog in the wilds of Alaska, made with an international cast.

White Feather (1955) C-102m. **½ D: Robert D. Webb. Robert Wagner, Jeffrey Hunter, Debra Paget, John Lund, Eduard Franz, Hugh O'Brian. Pat Western film with some good action scenes of government agent Wagner attempting to convince Indian tribe to move to reservation; Paget and Hunter are members of Cheyenne tribe who resist.

White Heat (1949) 114m. ***½ D: Raoul Walsh. James Cagney, Virginia Mayo, Edmond O'Brien, Margaret Wycherly, Steve Cochran. Cagney returned to gangster films, older but forceful as ever, as psychopathic hood with mother obsession; Mayo is his neglected wife, O'Brien the cop out to get him. "Top of the World" finale is now movie legend.

White Lightning (1973) C-101m. **½ D: Joseph Sargent. Burt Reynolds, Jennifer Billingsley, Ned Beatty, Bo Hopkins, Matt Clark, Louise Latham, Diane Ladd. Formula melodrama with moonshiner Burt going after crooked sheriff who drowned his brother; pleasant cast helps this OK action pic. Sequel: GATOR.

White Line Fever (1975) C-92m. *** D: Jonathan Kaplan. Jan-Michael Vincent, Kay Lenz, Slim Pickens, L. Q. Jones, Leigh French, Don Porter. A B-picture that hits bull's-eye. Vincent is a young trucker who battles corruption on the road and off, with a diesel truck as his "good buddy."

White Nights (1957-Italian) 94m. *** D: Luchino Visconti. Maria Schell, Jean Marais, Marcello Mastroianni. Elaborately interwoven love tale arising from casual meeting; based on Dostoyevsky story.

White Savage (1943) C-75m. **½ D: Arthur Lubin. Jon Hall, Maria Montez, Sabu, Don Terry, Turhan Bey, Thomas Gomez, Sidney Toler. Standard escapist fare, in glorious color, with island princess Montez trying to remove obstacles that bar marriage to shark-hunter Hall.

White Sister (1973-Italian) C-104m. **½ D: Alberto Lattuada. Sophia

Loren, Adriano Celentano, Fernando Rey. Strange love story of hospital Mother Superior and self-professed young Communist who helps run the wards.

White Sister, The (1933) 110m. **½ D: Victor Fleming. Helen Hayes, Clark Gable, Lewis Stone, Louise Closser Hale, May Robson, Edward Arnold. Dated but interesting remake of 1923 silent with Lillian Gish and Ronald Colman; this time Hayes is woman who enters convent when she thinks her lover (Gable) has been killed in the war. Fine performances provide major interest today, not the predictable story line.

White Slave Ship (1962-Italian) C-92m. *½ D: Silvio Amadio. Pier Angeli, Edmund Purdom, Armand Mestral, Ivan Desny. Childish hokum, set in 18th century, of rebellion aboard vessel carrying women to the colonies.

White Squaw, The (1956) 75m. *½ D: Ray Nazarro. David Brian, May Wynn, William Bishop, Nancy Hale. Tedious narrative and a reverse situation; government taking away land from white rancher to give back to the Indians.

White Tie and Tails (1946) 81m. **½ D: Charles Barton. Dan Duryea, William Bendix, Ella Raines, Clarence Kolb, Frank Jenks, John Miljan, Scotty Beckett. Breezy film with usual-villain Duryea in good comedy form as butler who pretends to be master of house while boss is away.

White Tower, The (1950) C-98m. *** D: Ted Tetzlaff. Glenn Ford, Claude Rains, Valli, Oscar Homolka, Cedric Hardwicke, Lloyd Bridges. Mountain-climbing drama about people risking their lives to climb the Swiss Alps.

White Voices (1965-Italian) C-93m. *** D: Pasquale Festa Campanile, Massimo Franciosa. Paolo Ferrari, Sandra Milo, Anouk Aimee, Graziella Granata, Barbara Steele, Jeanne Valerie. Good lusty adventure à la Tom Jones concerns exploits of castrati-singers who have retained high singing voices by means of operation.

White Warrior, The (1961-Italian) C-86m. *½ D: Riccardo Freda. Steve Reeves, Giorgia Moll, Renato Baldini, Gerard Herter. Tiring spectacle about tribal chieftain leading rebellion against advancing troops of Czar, set in 19th century.

White Wilderness (1958) C-73m. *** D: James Algar. Narrated by Winston Hibler. Typically good Disney True-Life feature takes a look at the Arctic region, its flora and fauna; highlight is extended sequence on lemmings and their yearly suicide ritual.

White Witch Doctor (1953) C-96m. **½ D: Henry Hathaway. Susan Hayward, Robert Mitchum, Walter Slezak, Timothy Carey. Bakuba territory is scene of diverse interests of nurse Hayward who wants to bring modern medicine to natives and adventurers Mitchum and Slezak bent on finding hidden treasure.

White Zombie (1932) 73m. *** D: Victor Halperin. Bela Lugosi, Madge Bellamy, Robert Frazer, Brandon Hurst. Eerily made film about army of zombies at sugar mill working for white leader; unique chiller.

Who? (1974-British) C-93m. **½ D: Jack Gold. Elliott Gould, Trevor Howard, Joseph Bova, Ed Grover, James Noble, John Lehne. Gould plays FBI agent investigating American scientist's car crash in Russia, and subsequent reappearance with a strangely restructured face. Intriguing if not completely satisfying spy/sci-fi mix.

Who Done It? (1942) 75m. **½ D: Erle C. Kenton. Bud Abbott, Lou Costello, Louise Allbritton, Mary Wickes, William Gargan, William Bendix. Murder at a radio station is setting for better than usual A&C horseplay, with Bendix a flustered detective.

Who Goes There? SEE: Passionate Sentry, The.

Who Is Harry Kellerman and Why Is He Saying Those Terrible Things About Me? (1971) C-108m. ** D: Ulu Grosbard. Dustin Hoffman, Barbara Harris, Jack Warden, David Burns, Dom DeLuise, Betty Walker. Muddled comedy-drama casts Dustin as successful rock composer-singer who finds money doesn't answer all of life's questions. Harris comes along late in film to save this debacle with an outstanding performance.

Who is Killing the Great Chefs of Europe? (1978) C-112m. *** D: Ted Kotcheff. George Segal, Jacqueline Bisset, Robert Morley, Jean-Pierre Cassel, Philippe Noiret, Jean Rochefort, Madge Ryan. Slick comedy whodunit with self-explanatory title has luscious views of European scenery and food, plus a magnificently funny role for Morley as the world's premier gourmet.

Who Is Killing the Stuntmen? SEE: Stunts

Who Is the Black Dahlia? (1975) C-100m. TVM D: Joseph Pevney. Efrem Zimbalist, Jr., Ronny Cox, Macdonald Carey, Lucie Arnaz, Tom Bosley, Gloria DeHaven, Rick Jason, June Lockhart, Mercedes McCambridge, Donna Mills. Veteran L. A. detective Zimbalist attempts to piece together clues in the murder of a woman in 1947. Based on a true unsolved murder case, this atmospheric crime drama is intriguingly written and well cast down to the cameos. Above average.

Who Killed Gail Preston? (1938) 60m. **½ D: Leon Barsha. Don Terry, Rita Hayworth, Robert Paige, Wyn Cahoon, Gene Morgan, Marc Lawrence, Arthur Loft. Minor whodunit fairly well played; murder in a nightclub is the premise.

Who Killed Mary What's'ername? (1971) C-90m. **½ D: Ernie Pintoff. Red Buttons, Alice Playten, Sylvia Miles, Sam Waterston, Dick Williams, Conrad Bain. Diabetic ex-boxer sets out to find a prostitute's murderer when he becomes angered at everyone's indifference. Whodunit isn't bad, but nothing special; acting is generally good.

Who Killed Teddy Bear? (1965) 91m. *½ D: Joseph Cates. Juliet Prowse, Sal Mineo, Jan Murray, Elaine Stritch. Sleazy, leering low-budgeter about a psychopath (Mineo) who preys on a dicotheque hostess (Prowse).

Who Killed the Mysterious Mr. Foster? SEE: Sam Hill: Who Killed Mr. Foster?

Who Says I Can't Ride a Rainbow! (1971) C-85m. **½ D: Edward Mann. Jack Klugman, Norma French, Reuben Figueroa, David Mann. Offbeat story of man who feels it is the children of the world who will determine its future.

Who Slew Auntie Roo? (1971) C-89m. ** D: Curtis Harrington. Shelley Winters, Mark Lester, Chloe Franks, Ralph Richardson, Lionel Jeffries, Hugh Griffith. Sickie about daffy old lady who steers unwitting children into her lair. Made in England.

Who Stole the Body? (1962-French) 92m. ** D: Jean Girault. Francis Blanche, Darry Cowl, Clement Harari, Daniel Ceccaldi, Mario David. Weak farce on horror films, with Blanche and Cowl two dimwits trying to solve a crime.

Who Was That Lady? (1960) 115m. *** D: George Sidney. Tony Curtis, Dean Martin, Janet Leigh, James Whitmore, John McIntire, Barbara Nichols, Joi Lansing. Spicy shenanigans move along at lively pace as Curtis and Martin pretend to be secret agents to confuse Tony's jealous wife Leigh; based on Norman Krasna play.

Who'll Save Our Children? (1978) C-100m. TVM D: George Schaefer. Shirley Jones, Len Cariou, Cassie Yates, Conchata Farrell, Frances Sternhagen. Well-acted drama about foster parents who battle to keep the youngsters they have raised when the natural parents, who deserted the children years earlier, sue to reclaim them. Above average.

Who'll Stop the Rain (1978) C-126m. *** D: Karel Reisz. Nick Nolte, Tuesday Weld, Michael Moriarty, Anthony Zerbe, Richard Masur, Ray Sharkey. Robert Stone's National Book Award-winning *Dog Soldiers* suffers from excessively genteel treatment in telling its truly mean story about the smuggling of heroin from Vietnam to California. Strong performances in virtually every role.

Who's Afraid of Virginia Woolf? (1966) 129m. ***½ D: Mike Nichols. Elizabeth Taylor, Richard Burton, George Segal, Sandy Dennis. Two couples get together for an evening of bitter conversation; Burton and Taylor's finest hour (together) in searing Edward Albee drama. Taylor and Dennis won acting Oscars, as did Haskell Wexler's incisive b&w photography. Film broke Hollywood taboos for adult material, would cause lesser furor today, though some language still won't be heard on TV.

Who's Been Sleeping in My Bed? (1963) C-103m. **½ D: Daniel Mann. Dean Martin, Elizabeth Montgomery, Carol Burnett, Martin Balsam, Jill St. John. Undemanding fluff of TV star Martin being urged altar-wise by fianceé Montgomery; Burnett is his psychiatrist's nurse.

Who's Got the Action? (1962) C-93m. **½ D: Daniel Mann. Dean Martin, Lana Turner, Eddie Albert, Nita Talbot, Walter Matthau. Strained froth of Turner combatting hubby Martin's horse-racing fever by turning bookie.

Who's Minding the Mint? (1967) C-97m. ***½ D: Howard Morris. Jim

Hutton, Dorothy Provine, Milton Berle, Joey Bishop, Bob Denver, Walter Brennan, Victor Buono, Jack Gilford, Jamie Farr, Jackie Joseph. Hilarious comedy, neglected at time of release, is tremendous fun in the classic comedy tradition, with motley gang of thieves helping U.S. Mint worker Hutton recover money he accidentally destroyed. Buono is especially funny as pompous ex-skipper.

Who's Minding the Store? (1963) C-90m. **½ D: Frank Tashlin. Jerry Lewis, Agnes Moorehead, Jill St. John, John McGiver, Ray Walston, Francesca Bellini. Jerry Lewis vehicle with bumbling idiot (guess who?) set loose in department store. Great supporting cast in stereotyped comic foil roles, plus one good inventive bit; the rest, familiar reworking of standard comedy themes.

Whole Town's Talking, The (1935) 95m. *** D: John Ford. Edward G. Robinson, Jean Arthur, Wallace Ford, Arthur Byron, Donald Meek. Entertaining comedy with meek Robinson a lookalike for notorious gangster; fine performances by E. G. and Arthur.

Whole Truth, The (1958-British) 84m. **½ D: John Guillermin. Stewart Granger, Donna Reed, George Sanders, Gianna Maria Canale. Good cast lends strength to fair plot of almost perfect attempt to pin murder of movie starlet on producer Granger.

Whole World Is Watching, The (1969) C-97m. TVM D: Richard Colla. Joseph Campanella, James Farentino, Burl Ives, Hal Holbrook, Steve Ihnat, Rick Ely, Stephen McNally. Young lawyer brothers defend student radical accused of murdering policeman during campus riot. OK tension during trial, but major characters come across as stereotypes. Average.

Whoopee (1930) C-93m. *** D: Thornton Freeland. Eddie Cantor, Eleanor Hunt, Paul Gregory, John Rutherford, Ethel Shutta, Spencer Charters. Antique movie musical sparked by Cantor's performance as a hyper-hypochondriac, and Busby Berkeley's wonderful production numbers. Cantor sings "Making Whoopee" and "My Baby Just Cares for Me"; the girl who sings the first chorus of the opening song is very young Betty Grable.

Why Bother to Knock (1964-British) 88m. *½ D: Cyril Frankel. Elke

Sommer, Richard Todd, Nicole Maurey, Scot Fitch. Trashy smut about Todd traipsing around Europe giving out keys to his pals, with the girls all turning up unexpectedly.

Why Must I Die? (1960) 86m. ** D: Roy Del Ruth. Terry Moore, Debra Paget, Bert Freed, Julie Reding. Similar to I WANT TO LIVE except in quality. Moore is singer falsely convicted of murder, with expected histrionics.

Why Worry? (1923) 77m. (includes excerpt from short-subject NEVER WEAKEN) ***½ D: Fred Newmeyer, Sam Taylor. Harold Lloyd, Jobyna Ralston, John Aasen, Leo White, James Mason. Hilarious story of millionaire playboy Lloyd who stumbles into revolution-ridden country and inadvertently becomes involved. Packed with belly-laugh sight-gags. Edited for TV and paired with excerpt from 1921 daredevil short NEVER WEAKEN.

Why Would Anyone Want to Kill a Nice Girl Like You? (1969-British) C-99m. ** D: Don Sharp. Eva Renzi, David Buck, Peter Vaughan, Paul Hubschmid, Sophie Hardy, Kay Walsh. A young tourist on the French Riviera thinks someone is trying to kill her, but none of the local officials will believe her. Familiar storyline handled in routine fashion.

Wichita (1955) C-81m. **½ D: Jacques Tourneur. Joel McCrea, Vera Miles, Lloyd Bridges, Wallace Ford, Peter Graves. Action-filled Western; good cast helps Wyatt Earp (McCrea) restore order to Western town overrun with outlaws.

Wicked as They Come (1957-British) 94m. ** D: Ken Hughes. Arlene Dahl, Phil Carey, Herbert Marshall, David Kossoff. Dahl cavorts nicely in this minor story of a girl from the poor part of town involved with the wrong people.

Wicked City, The (1950-French) 76m. *½ D: Francois Villiers. Maria Montez, Jean-Pierre Aumont, Lilli Palmer, Marcel Dalio. Even exotic Montez can't spice lazy telling of unscrupulous gal and the gob she involves in her sordid life.

Wicked Dreams of Paula Schultz, The (1968) C-113m. BOMB D: George Marshall. Elke Sommer, Bob Crane, Werner Klemperer, Joey Forman, John Banner, Maureen Arthur. Laughless dud about beautiful East German Olympic hopeful who pole-vaults over Berlin Wall to freedom; unlike many stupid comedies, this one doesn't even have a particularly engaging cast.

Wicked Lady, The (1945-British) 104m. **½ D: Leslie Arliss. Margaret Lockwood, James Mason, Patricia Roc, Michael Rennie, Martita Hunt, Felix Aylmer. Title refers to Lockwood, in this unconvincing costumer of female outlaw who teams with robber Mason in evil doings.

Wicked, Wicked (1973) C-95m. BOMB D: Richard L. Bare. Tiffany Bolling, Scott Brady, David Bailey, Edd Byrnes. Disastrous mystery-thriller centering around series of hotel murders. Film was released in Duo-vision split-screen process with two things happening at once. Pity there was not enough material for even one.

Wicked Woman (1954) 77m. *½ D: Russell Rouse. Richard Egan, Beverly Michaels, Percy Helton, Evelyn Scott. Lumbering drama about no-good waitress leading assorted men astray.

Wicker Man, The (1973-British) 87m. ***½ D: Robin Hardy. Edward Woodward, Christopher Lee, Diane Cilento, Britt Ekland, Ingrid Pitt, Lindsay Kemp. Little seen in this country, horror thriller is short on shocks but long on eroticism; it has been hailed as a classic. Unfortunately, it's cut from original 102m. and will be cut further on TV. Story follows Scottish police sergeant investigating disappearance of young girl on Summerisle, run by Lord Lee and peopled with villagers who observe pagan customs for the sake of their crops. Completely absorbing.

Wide Blue Road, The (1956-Italian) 100m. **½ D: Gillo Pontecorvo. Yves Montand, Alida Valli, Francisco Rabal, Peter Carsten, Ronaldino. Montand is non-plussed playboy taking pleasure where he finds it until Valli comes into picture. Performers outshine dialogue.

Wide Open Faces (1938) 67m. **½ D: Kurt Neumann. Joe E. Brown, Jane Wyman, Alison Skipworth, Lyda Roberti, Alan Baxter, Lucien Littlefield, Sidney Toler. Enjoyable Brown vehicle with top-notch supporting cast; innocent soda jerk mixed up with gangster.

Widow (1976) C-100m. TVM D: J. Lee Thompson. Michael Learned, Bradford Dillman, Farley Granger, Louise Sorel, Robert Lansing, Carol Rossen, Eric Olson. Dreary soap

opera about a woman with two children trying to adjust emotionally after her husband's death, taken from Lynn Caine's best-seller. Below average.

Widow, The (1955-Italian) ** D: Lewis Milestone. Patricia Roc, Anna Maria Ferrero, Massimo Serrato, Akim Tamiroff. Uneven soaper with Roc involved with lover Serrato, a sports car racer, who falls for Ferrero; film meanders.

Wife, Doctor and Nurse (1937) 85m. **½ D: Walter Lang. Loretta Young, Warner Baxter, Virginia Bruce, Jane Darwell, Sidney Blackmer, Minna Gombell. Baxter is caught between two women, but seems disinterested in both. Bright comedy with expert cast.

Wife, Husband and Friend (1939) 80m. *** D: Gregory Ratoff. Loretta Young, Warner Baxter, Binnie Barnes, George Barbier, Cesar Romero, Renie Riano. Entertaining comedy about aspiring singer Young whose husband Baxter tries to show her up; fun, but better as EVERYBODY DOES IT.

Wife of Monte Cristo, The (1946) 80m. ** D: Edgar G. Ulmer. John Loder, Lenore Aubert, Charles Dingle, Eduardo Ciannelli, Eva Gabor, Martin Kosleck. Corruption in the medical profession proves a formidable match for the Count; standard low-budget swashbuckler.

Wife Takes a Flyer, The (1942) 86m. ** D: Richard Wallace. Joan Bennett, Franchot Tone, Allyn Joslyn, Cecil Cunningham, Chester Clute. Weak WW2 espionage of Tone pretending to be Bennett's husband to escape from Holland.

Wife vs. Secretary (1936) 88m. **½ D: Clarence Brown. Clark Gable, Jean Harlow, Myrna Loy, May Robson, George Barbier, James Stewart, Hobart Cavanaugh. Perfect example of Hollywood gloss, with three top-notch stars towering over inferior material. Harlow is particularly good in tale of secretary who becomes invaluable to her boss (Gable), causing complications in both of their lives.

Wife Wanted (1946) 73m. ** D: Phil Karlson. Kay Francis, Paul Cavanagh, Robert Shayne, Veda Ann Borg. In her last film, Francis is film star innocently hooked up with lonely-heart crooks; low production values.

Wilby Conspiracy, The (1975) C-

[859]

101m. ******* D: Ralph Nelson. Sidney Poitier, Michael Caine, Nicol Williamson, Prunella Gee, Persis Khambatta, Saeed Jaffrey. Slick chase movie about black African political activist and the reluctant white companion he drags with him on cross-country flight from the law. Memories of Poitier's earlier THE DEFIANT ONES keep focusing throughout, but the two stars maintain a light touch. Sinister Williamson steals it from them both.

Wild and the Innocent, The (1959) C-84m. ****½** D: Jack Sher. Audie Murphy, Joanne Dru, Gilbert Roland, Jim Backus, Sandra Dee, George Mitchell, Peter Breck. Murphy and Dee make an engaging duo as trapper and untamed country girl involved in gunplay in town during July 4th holiday.

Wild and the Willing, The (1962-British) 112m. ****** D: Ralph Thomas. Virginia Maskell, Paul Rogers, Samantha Eggar, Ian McShane, Richard Warner. Life and love at a provincial university, with over-earnest attempt to be realistic and daring.

Wild and Wonderful (1964) C-88m. ****½** D: Michael Anderson. Tony Curtis, Christine Kaufmann, Larry Storch, Marty Ingels. Empty slapstick froth involving canine movie star with Curtis and Kaufmann romancing.

Wild and Wooly (1978) C-100m. TVM D: Philip Leacock. Chris DeLisle, Susan Bigelow, Jessica Walters, Doug McClure, David Doyle, Ross Martin, Vic Morrow. It's CHARLIE'S ANGELS in the Old West, with three gals breaking out of prison to try to thwart the assassination of Teddy Roosevelt. A pilot that led nowhere. Average.

Wild Angels, The (1966) C-93m. ***½** D: Roger Corman. Peter Fonda, Nancy Sinatra, Bruce Dern, Lou Procopio, Coby Denton, Marc Cavell. Predecessor of EASY RIDER without that film's class; story of destructive motorcycle gang is OK after about 24 beers.

Wild Blue Yonder, The (1951) 98m. ****½** D: Allan Dwan. Wendell Corey, Vera Ralston, Forrest Tucker, Phil Harris, Walter Brennan. Standard WW2 aviation yarn, saluting the B-29 bomber, detailing friendship of Corey and Tucker, rivalry for nurse Ralston, etc. Just for change of pace, Harris sings "The Thing."

Wild Bunch, The (1969) C-134m.

***½ D: Sam Peckinpah. William Holden, Ernest Borgnine, Robert Ryan, Edmond O'Brien, Ben Johnson, Warren Oates, Jaime Sanchez, Strother Martin, L. Q. Jones. Controversial landmark Western is a masterpiece to some, a mindless exercise in violence to others; in either event, TV is no place to judge since Peckinpah's poetic bloodbaths are all but gone. Story has outlaw gang, circa 1913, going for one last outing, hired by Mexican renegade general.

Wild Cats on the Beach (1959-Italian) C-96m. ****½** D: Vittorio Sala. Elsa Martinelli, Alberto Sordi, Georges Marchal, Antonio Cifariello. Quartet of love tales set at resort area of Cote D'Azur; varying in quality.

Wild Child, The (1970-French) 85m. ******* D: Francois Truffaut. Francois Truffaut, Jean-Pierre Cargol, Jean Daste, Paul Ville. Initially absorbing true story of wild boy raised alone in French woods and the doctor who tries to civilize him. Simply told, deliberately old-fashioned in technique; film loses steam halfway through. Truffaut is ideal as the doctor. Set in 1700s.

Wild Company (1930) 73m. ***½** D: Leo McCarey. H. B. Warner, Frank Albertson, Sharon Lynn, Joyce Compton, Claire McDowell, Bela Lugosi. Badly dated melodrama of flaming youth and generation-gap; devil-may-care Albertson ignores parents' warnings about company he keeps, gets into trouble over underworld murder. Lugosi plays nightclub owner.

Wild Country, The (1971) C-100m. ****½** D: Robert Totten. Steve Forrest, Vera Miles, Ronny Howard, Jack Elam, Frank deKova, Morgan Woodward, Clint Howard. Standard Disney fare, adapted from Ralph Moody's *Little Britches*, about joys and hardships faced by family which moves from Pittsburgh to Wyoming in 1880s. Magnificent scenery.

Wild Drifter SEE: **Cockfighter**

Wild for Kicks (1962-British) 92m. ****** D: Edmond T. Greville. David Farrar, Noelle Adam, Christopher Lee, Gillian Hills, Shirley Ann Field, Oliver Reed. Strange little drama of rebellious teenager involved in murder. Retitled: BEAT GIRL.

Wild Geese, The (1978-British) C-132m. ****½** D: Andrew V. McLaglen. Richard Burton, Roger Moore, Richard Harris, Hardy Kruger, Stewart Granger, Jack Watson, Frank Finlay, Winston Ntshona. Silly but entertaining action yarn with Burton miscast as leader of mercenaries who rescue kidnapped African leader. Better (and shorter) script would have helped.

Wild Geese Calling (1941) 77m. ** D: John Brahm. Henry Fonda, Joan Bennett, Warren William, Ona Munson, Barton MacLane, Russell Simpson. Action and romance in 1890s Oregon and Alaska, but not enough of either to push this one over the hump.

Wild Gold (1934) 75m. ** D: George Marshall. John Boles, Claire Trevor, Harry Green, Roger Imhof, Monroe Owsley, Ruth Gillette. Strange blend of comedy, melodrama, romance, and music in hodgepodge story of miner Boles infatuated with singer Trevor, facing irate husband, unexpected disaster in remote forest cabin. Uses stock footage from silent film THE JOHNSTOWN FLOOD.

Wild Harvest (1947) 92m. *½ D: Tay Garnett. Alan Ladd, Dorothy Lamour, Robert Preston, Lloyd Nolan, Richard Erdman, Allen Jenkins. Pretty dismal film of traveling grain-harvesters with Preston and Ladd rivaling for Lamour's love.

Wild Heart, The (1952-British) C-82m. ** D: Michael Powell, Emeric Pressburger. Jennifer Jones, David Farrar, Cyril Cusack, Sybil Thorndike, Edward Chapman, Esmond Knight. Muddled tale of strange Welsh girl in late 19th century whose life is dominated by superstitions; she marries minister but is stirred by lusty squire. Beautiful color location photography. Cut and reedited from 1950 British release called GONE TO EARTH.

Wild Heritage (1958) C-78m. **½ D: Charles Haas. Will Rogers, Jr., Maureen O'Sullivan, Rod McKuen, Casey Tibbs. Soaper involving events in the intertwining lives of two westward-bound pioneer families.

Wild in the Country (1961) C-114m. **½ D: Philip Dunne. Elvis Presley, Hope Lange, John Ireland, Tuesday Weld, Gary Lockwood. Literate Presley vehicle with Elvis a back-country youth with potential writing talents; film is earnest but clichéd.

Wild in the Sky (1972) C-87m. **½ D: William T. Naud. George Stanford Brown, Brandon de Wilde, Keenan Wynn, Tim O'Connor, Dick Gautier, Robert Lansing. Zany idea doesn't quite come off, in story of three prisoners who hijack a plane. Retitled BLACK JACK.

Wild in the Streets (1968) C-97m. **½ D: Barry Shear. Shelley Winters, Christopher Jones, Diane Varsi, Hal Holbrook, Millie Perkins, Ed Begley, Richard Pryor, Bert Freed. Millionaire singing idol/drug pusher runs for President after voting age is lowered to 14. Wildly overrated by some critics, film is nonetheless enjoyable on a nonthink level.

Wild Is the Wind (1957) 114m. **½ D: George Cukor. Anna Magnani, Anthony Quinn, Anthony Franciosa, Dolores Hart. Turgid soaper set in the West, with Quinn marrying the sister of his dead wife, not able to separate the two. Good acting helps script along; both leads won Oscar nominations.

Wild Man of Borneo, The (1941) 78m. ** D: Robert B. Sinclair. Frank Morgan, Mary Howard, Billie Burke, Donald Meek, Marjorie Main, Connie Gilchrist, Bonita Granville, Dan Dailey. Good cast in weak sideshow comedy; Morgan masquerades as title character in one of his less memorable roles.

Wild McCullochs, The (1975) C-93m. ** D: Max Baer. Forrest Tucker, Max Baer, Julie Adams, Janice Heiden, Dennis Redfield, Don Grady, William Demarest. Oddly old-fashioned film—set in 1949—has Tucker as self-made Texas millionaire who tries to raise his sons in his two-fisted image, with tragic results.

Wild North, The (1952) C-97m. ** D: Andrew Marton. Stewart Granger, Cyd Charisse, Wendell Corey, J. M. Kerrigan, Ray Teal. Undazzling account of accused murderer hunted by Mountie, with the expected proving of innocence before finale; Charisse is love interest.

Wild One, The (1954) 79m. ***½ D: Laslo Benedek. Marlon Brando, Mary Murphy, Robert Keith, Lee Marvin. Original motorcycle film with Brando's renowned performance as gangleader terrorizing small town; dated, but worth viewing for acting.

Wild Pack, The (1971) C-102m. **½ D: Hall Bartlett. Kent Lane, Tisha Sterling, John Rubinstein, Butch Patrick, Mark de Vries, Peter Nielsen. Fairly interesting drama, set in Brazil, about day-to-day life of a group of black and white orphans who steal food; film won grand prize at Moscow Film Festival. Also known as THE SANDPIT GENERALS.

Wild Party, The (1956) 81m. *½ D: Harry Horner. Anthony Quinn, Carol Ohmart, Arthur Franz, Jay Robinson, Kathryn Grant. Blah attempt at naturalistic drama with Quinn the has-been football star going mildly berserk at a sleazy roadside dance hall.

Wild Party, The (1975) C-95m. ** D: James Ivory. James Coco, Raquel Welch, Perry King, Tiffany Bolling, David Dukes. Uneven evocation of 1920s Hollywood with Coco as a Fatty Arbuckle-type comedian who throws a lavish party to try and save his failing career. Film has definite assets but just doesn't come off.

Wild Racers, The (1968) C-79m. *½ D: Daniel Haller. Fabian, Mimsy Farmer, Judy Cornwall, David Landers. Dumb racer Fabian loves his work and one-night stands; Farmer is his latest challenge.

Wild River (1960) C-110m. ***½ D: Elia Kazan. Montgomery Clift, Lee Remick, Jo Van Fleet, Albert Salmi, Jay C. Flippen, James Westerfield. Clift plays Tennessee Valley Authority official trying to convince elderly Van Fleet to sell her property for new projects. Kazan's exquisite evocation of 1950s Tennessee—and moving romance between Clift and Remick—give this film its strength.

Wild Rovers (1971) C-109m. ***½ D: Blake Edwards. William Holden, Ryan O'Neal, Karl Malden, Lynn Carlin, Tom Skerritt, Joe Don Baker, Rachel Roberts. Underrated Western about two cowpokes who become fugitives after they rob a bank on whim. Choppy script seems unimportant in light of Holden's performance, incredibly lyrical scenes. Some violence may be cut for TV.

Wild Seed, The (1965) 99m. *** D: Brian Hutton. Michael Parks, Celia Kaye, Ross Elliott, Woodrow Chambliss, Eva Novak. Arty yet gripping story of runaway Kaye traveling to California, guided by road bum Parks.

Wild Stallion (1952) C-72m. *½ D: Lewis D. Collins. Martha Hyer, Edgar Buchanan, Hugh Beaumont, Ben Johnson. Shoddy military academy

saga interlaced with soapish romance, told via flashbacks.

Wild Strawberries (1957-Sweden) 90m. **** D: Ingmar Bergman. Victor Sjostrom, Ingrid Thulin, Bibi Andersson, Gunnar Bjornstrand, Folke Sundquist, Bjorn Bjelvenstam. Elderly Stockholm professor reviews the disappointments of his life, while traveling by car to receive an honorary degree. Superb use of flashbacks and brilliant performance by Sjostrom make this Bergman classic an emotional powerhouse. A staple of any serious filmgoer's education.

Wild Westerners, The (1962) C-70m. *½ D: Oscar Rudolph. James Philbrook, Nancy Kovack, Duane Eddy, Guy Mitchell. Humdrum account of marshal and new wife overcoming obstacles to bring gold east for Yankee cause.

Wild, Wild Planet (1965-Italian) C-93m. *½ D: Anthony Dawson. Tony Russel, Lisa Gastoni, Massimo Serato, Franco Nero, Carlo Giustini. Female alien uses robots to gain control of earth scientists by shrinking them. Fairly good ending does not redeem lackluster film. Made at same time as WAR OF THE PLANETS and other losers.

Wild Wild West Revisited, The (1979) C-100m. TVM D: Burt Kennedy. Robert Conrad, Ross Martin, Paul Williams, Harry Morgan, Rene Auberjonois, Robert Shields, Lorene Yarnell. The resourceful duo of the old-time series (1965-69) come out of retirement in this proposed series pilot to hunt down the baddy who has been cloning world leaders in his scheme to dominate the planet. Average.

Wild Wild Winter (1966) C-80m. ** D: Lennie Weinrib. Gary Clarke, Chris Noel, Steve Franken, Don Edmonds. Light-headed ski-slope musical froth, for and by the teenage set.

Wild Women (1970) C-73m. TVM D: Don Taylor. Hugh O'Brian, Anne Francis, Marilyn Maxwell, Marie Windsor, Sherry Jackson, Cynthia Hull. Army engineering company mapping crucial Texas trails in 1840s disguised as wagon train; "wives" are recruited from Federal prisons. Tame mixture of comedy and adventure which refuses to label women prostitutes.

Will James' Sand SEE: **Sand**

Will Penny (1968) C-108m. ***½ D: Tom Gries. Charlton Heston, Joan Hackett, Donald Pleasence, Lee

Majors, Bruce Dern, Ben Johnson, Slim Pickens, Clifton James. One of the best films on the cowboy/ loner ever to come out of Hollywood. Heston's character is one of great strength; supporting actors are exceptional. Memorable score by David Raksin.

Will Success Spoil Rock Hunter? (1957) C-94m. ***½ D: Frank Tashlin. Tony Randall, Jayne Mansfield, Betsy Drake, Joan Blondell, John Williams, Henry Jones. Guest star, Groucho Marx. Clever satire uses George Axelrod play about ad man who tries to persuade glamorous star to endorse his product as springboard for scattershot satire on 1950s morals, television, sex, business, et al. Director-writer Tashlin in peak form.

Willa (1979) C-100m. TVM D: Joan Darling and Claudio Guzman. Deborah Raffin, Clu Gulager, Cloris Leachman, Diane Ladd, John Amos, Nancy Marchand, Mary Wickes. Hash-slinging waitress embarks on a new career as a lady trucker after being abandoned by her husband. Average.

Willard (1971) C-95m. ** D: Daniel Mann. Bruce Davison, Elsa Lanchester, Ernest Borgnine, Sondra Locke, Michael Dante, Jody Gilbert, Joan Shawlee. Touching story of a boy and his rat captured public's fancy at the box office, but film's lack of style prevents it from being anything more than a second-rate thriller. Sequel: BEN.

Willie and Joe Back at the Front SEE: Back at the Front

Willie Dynamite (1973) C-102m. *** D: Gilbert Moses. Roscoe Orman, Diana Sands, Thalmus Rasulala, Roger Robinson, George Murdock. Multi-ingredients mix well in a good black actioner, with Orman as a pimp to topple big-shot Robinson, an outrageous homosexual. Sands is fine in her last film.

Willy McBean and his Magic Machine (1965-Japanese) C-94m. **½ D: Arthur Rankin Jr. Voices of Larry Mann, Billie Richards, Alfie Scopp, Paul Ligman, Bunny Cowan, Paul Soles. Puppet novelty item about mad professor and his time machine; OK for kids.

Willy Wonka and the Chocolate Factory (1971) C-94m. **½ D: Mel Stuart. Gene Wilder, Jack Albertson, Peter Ostrum, Michael Bollner, Ursula Reit. Adaptation of Roald Dahl's book has all the ingredients for classic fantasy, as enigmatic Wilder gives kids a tour of his mystery-shrouded chocolate factory, but cruel edge taints film's enjoyment. Anthony Newley-Leslie Bricusse score includes "Candy Man."

Wilma (1977) C-100m. TVM D: Bud Greenspan. Cicely Tyson, Shirley Jo Finney, Jason Bernard, Joe Seneca, Denzel Washington Jr. Uninspired drama about the early years of Wilma Rudolph (Finney) who beat polio to become the gold medal-winning Olympics track star. Lackluster performances generated by so-so script. Below average.

Wilson (1944) C-154m. ***½ D: Henry King. Alexander Knox, Charles Coburn, Geraldine Fitzgerald, Thomas Mitchell, Cedric Hardwicke, Vincent Price, Mary Anderson, Francis X. Bushman. Superb biography of WW1-era President whose League of Nations idea became an obsession; one of Hollywood's solid films . . . but beware of cutting.

Win, Place or Steal (1975) C-81m. ** D: Richard Bailey. Dean Stockwell, Russ Tamblyn, Alex Karras, McLean Stevenson, Alan Oppenheimer, Kristina Holland. OK racetrack caper comedy, with Tamblyn and Karras doing a Laurel and Hardy.

Winchester '73 (1950) 92m. ***½ D: Anthony Mann. James Stewart, Shelley Winters, Dan Duryea, Stephen McNally, Charles Drake, Millard Mitchell, Rock Hudson, Tony Curtis. Exceptional Western story of Stewart tracking down a man—and his stolen gun—through series of interrelated episodes, leading to memorable shootout among rock-strewn hills. First-rate in every way, this landmark film was largely responsible for renewed popularity of Westerns in the 1950s.

Winchester '73 (1967) C-97m. TVM D: Herschel Daugherty. Tom Tryon, John Saxon, Dan Duryea, Joan Blondell, John Drew Barrymore, Ned Romero. OK remake of 1950 version with Saxon returning home from prison seething hate, eventually stealing priceless rifle from brother sheriff Tryon. Action mostly good; only resolution seems poorly handled. Average.

Wind Across the Everglades (1958) C-93m. **½ D: Nicholas Ray. Burl Ives, Christopher Plummer, Gypsy Rose Lee, George Voskoyec, Tony Galento. Oddball film, strangely cast, of life in 1900s Florida, with focus on natural beauty preservation attempt by Plummer.

Wind and the Lion, The (1975) C-119m. **½ D: John Milius. Sean Connery, Candice Bergen, Brian Keith, John Huston, Geoffrey Lewis, Steve Kanaly. Milius brings modern sensibilities to an old-fashioned adventure-romance, with uneven results. Connery is Moroccan sheik who kidnaps American woman and her son, sparking international incident in which Teddy Roosevelt (Keith) becomes involved.

Wind Cannot Read, The (1958-British) C-110m. **½ D: Ralph Thomas, Dirk Bogarde, Yoko Tani, Ronald Lewis, John Fraser, Anthony Bushell, Michael Medwin. Tidy tale of Bogarde escaping from Japanese prison camp during WW2 to find his ailing wife Tani.

Winds of Kitty Hawk, The (1978) C-100m. D: E. W. Swackhamer. Michael Moriarty, David Huffman, Tom Bower, Eugene Roche, Scott Hylands, John Randolph, Kathryn Walker. Stunningly photographed but tediously talky dramatization about the Wright Brothers, their efforts to fly, and their feud with Glenn Curtiss and his patron, Alexander Graham Bell. Stacy and James Keach covered much of the same ground in half the time some years earlier in their production on public television. Off the ground, there's magic. Above average.

Windom's Way (1957-British) C-108m. *** D: Ronald Neame. Peter Finch, Mary Ure, Natasha Parry, Robert Flemyng, Michael Hordern, Gregoire Aslan. Dedicated doctor (Finch) working in Malayan village tries to encourage resistance to Communist takeover. Strong performances in this intelligent film.

Window, The (1949) 73m. *** D: Ted Tetzlaff. Bobby Driscoll, Barbara Hale, Arthur Kennedy, Paul Stewart, Ruth Roman. "Sleeper" film less impressive now than in 1949; still good, with young Driscoll witnessing murder, unable to convince parents he's not lying. Parents' dialogue weakens credibility, but suspense still mounts; extremely well photographed and staged.

Window in London, A SEE: Lady in Distress

Windows (1980) C-96m. BOMB. D: Gordon Willis. Elizabeth Ashley, Talia Shire, Joseph Cortese. Homicidal lesbian Ashley in love with mousy neighbor Shire, who is in turn in love with bland detective Cortese. Reactionary, offensive thriller whose only element of mystery is why it was ever filmed. Heavy-handed directorial debut by gifted cinematographer Willis.

Wing and a Prayer (1944) 97m. *** D: Henry Hathaway. Don Ameche, Dana Andrews, Charles Bickford, Cedric Hardwicke, Richard Jaeckel, Harry Morgan. Fine WW2 actioner of brave pilots aboard aircraft carrier. Excellent cast does well in exciting story.

Winged Victory (1944) 130m. **½ D: George Cukor. Lon McCallister, Jeanne Crain, Edmond O'Brien, Don Taylor, Judy Holliday, Lee J. Cobb, Peter Lind Hayes, Red Buttons, Barry Nelson, Gary Merrill, Martin Ritt. WW2 saga is less stirring today than in 1944, but graphic depiction of young men's training for pilot duty is still quite interesting. So is the opportunity of seeing future stars early in their careers. Story by Moss Hart.

Wings for the Eagle (1942) 85m. ** D: Lloyd Bacon. Ann Sheridan, Dennis Morgan, Jack Carson, George Tobias, Don DeFore. Sincere tribute to aircraft workers during WW2 has little meaning today, but Sheridan et al give good performances.

Wings in the Dark (1935) 75m. **½ D: James Flood. Myrna Loy, Cary Grant, Hobart Cavanaugh, Roscoe Karns, Dean Jagger. Strange film of two flyers, Loy and Grant, in love. She does stunts, he wants to fly Atlantic, but goes blind.

Wings of Chance (1961-Canadian) C-76m. *½ D: Edward Dew. Frances Rafferty, Jim Brown, Richard Tretter, Patrick Whyte. Tame tale of plane crash in the northern woods and rescue attempts.

Wings of Eagles, The (1957) C-110m. **½ D: John Ford. John Wayne, Maureen O'Hara, Dan Dailey, Ward Bond, Ken Curtis, Edmund Lowe, Kenneth Tobey. Biography of Frank "Spig" Wead, pioneer WW1 aviator who later turns to screenwriting; first half is slapstick comedy, with no sense of period detail, then abruptly changes to drama for balance of film. Very mixed bag; film buffs will have fun watching Bond play "John Dodge," spoofing director Ford.

Wings of Fire (1967) C-100m. TVM

D: David Lowell Rich. Suzanne Pleshette, James Farentino, Ralph Bellamy, Juliet Mills, Jeremy Slate, Lloyd Nolan. Headstrong flier Pleshette enters air race to save floundering freight service run by father and associate. Hokey melodrama has climax and resolution unusually contrived. Below average.

Wings of the Hawk (1953) **C-80m.** ** **D:** Budd Boetticher. Van Heflin, Julia Adams, Abbe Lane, Antonio Moreno, Noah Beery. Heflin is hero of thwarted attempt of renegades to overthrow Mexican government; Adams and Lane help him.

Wings of the Morning (1937-British) **C-89m.** **½ **D:** Harold Schuster. Annabella, Henry Fonda, John McCormack, Irene Vanbrugh, Philip Frost, Sam Livesey. Trifling story of gypsies, crucial horserace, blossoming love between Fonda and Annabella, initially disguised as a boy. Much ado about nothing. England's first Technicolor film still boasts beautiful pastel hues as major attraction, along with sequence of famed tenor McCormack doing several songs.

Winner Take All (1932) **68m.** **½ **D:** Roy Del Ruth. James Cagney, Virginia Bruce, Marion Nixon, Guy Kibbee, Alan Mowbray, Dickie Moore. Minor but engaging Cagney vehicle with Jimmy as a thick-witted, cocky prizefighter torn between goodgirl Nixon and fickle society-girl Bruce.

Winner Take All (1975) **C-100m. TVM D:** Paul Bogart. Shirley Jones, Laurence Luckinbill, Sam Groom, Joan Blondell, Sylvia Sidney, Joyce Van Patten. Drama about a compulsive woman gambler. The cast doesn't cut it, but then the script didn't offer much. Below average.

Winning (1969) **C-123m.** *** **D:** James Goldstone. Paul Newman, Joanne Woodward, Richard Thomas, Robert Wagner, David Sheiner. Above average racing story of man who will let nothing stand in the way of track victory.

Winning Team, The (1952) **98m.** **½ **D:** Lewis Seiler. Doris Day, Ronald Reagan, Frank Lovejoy, Russ Tamblyn, Tom Brown. Pleasant Americana about career of baseball player Grover Cleveland Alexander.

Winslow Boy, The (1950-British) **117m.** ***½ **D:** Anthony Asquith. Robert Donat, Margaret Leighton, Cedric Hardwicke, Francis L. Sullivan. Superior courtroom melodrama from Terence Rattigan's play, headed by Donat as barrister defending innocent boy (Neil North) accused of school theft.

Winter à Go-Go (1965) **C-88m.** ** **D:** Richard Benedict. James Stacy, William Wellman, Jr., Beverly Adams, Jill Donohue, Julie Parrish. Lowbrow shenanigans at a ski resort run by Stacy for the young, affluent set.

Winter Carnival (1939) **105m.** **½ **D:** Charles F. Riesner. Richard Carlson, Ann Sheridan, Helen Parrish, James Corner, Virginia Gilmore, Robert Walker, Joan Leslie, Peggy Moran. Contrived romance flick set at Dartmouth College during festive weekend; Sheridan is divorcée in love with professor Carlson.

Winter Kill (1974) **C-100m. TVM D:** Jud Taylor. Andy Griffith, John Larch, Tim O'Connor, Sheree North, Nick Nolte, Elayne Heilviel, Charles Tyner, Louise Latham. Resort-town sheriff Griffith tracks murderer, who leaves spray-painted messages at the scene. Another Griffith pilot that failed to catch on. Average.

Winter Kills (1979) **C-96m.** *½ **D:** William Richert. Jeff Bridges, John Huston, Anthony Perkins, Sterling Hayden, Eli Wallach, Belinda Baur, Richard Boone, Ralph Meeker, Dorothy Malone, Toshiro Mifune, Elizabeth Taylor. Younger brother of an assassinated U.S. president tries to solve the case, opens up several cans of political worms. The only fun in this glossy trash comes from trying to decide which member of the supporting cast looks most embarrassed.

Winter Light (1962-Swedish) **80m.** ***½ **D:** Ingmar Bergman. Ingrid Thulin, Gunnar Bjornstrand, Max von Sydow, Gunnel Lindblom, Allan Edwall. A difficult film for non-Bergman buffs, this look at a disillusioned priest in a small village is the second of Bergman's trilogy on faith (the first, THROUGH A GLASS DARKLY; the third, THE SILENCE). Powerful, penetrating drama.

Winter Meeting (1948) **104m.** **½ **D:** Brentaigne Windust. Bette Davis, Janis Paige, James Davis, John Hoyt, Florence Bates. Sluggish script of disillusioned poetess who loves embittered war hero, prevents well-acted film from achieving greater heights.

Winter Rates SEE: Out of Season.

Winter's Tale, The (1968-British) **C-**

151m. ** D: Frank Dunlop. Laurence Harvey, Jane Asher, Diana Churchill, Moira Redmond, Jim Dale. Filmed record of 1966 Edinburgh Festival presentation of Shakespeare's play is as static as a photographed stage play can be; may play better on TV.

Winterhawk (1976) C-98m. ** D: Charles B. Pierce. Michael Dante, Leif Erickson, Woody Strode, Denver Pyle, Elisha Cook Jr., L. Q. Jones, Arthur Hunnicutt, Dawn Wells. Well-meaning but overly melodramatic story of Blackfoot Indian brave (Dante) who comes to white man for smallpox serum, is attacked instead, and gets revenge by kidnapping two white youngsters. Quite violent at times.

Winterset (1936) 78m. ** D: Alfred Santell. Burgess Meredith, Margo, Eduardo Ciannelli, John Carradine, Edward Ellis, Mischa Auer. Meredith plays young man determined to find the man responsible for crime his father paid for with his life. Once-powerful film (with stars of Maxwell Anderson's Broadway play recreating their stage roles) seems artificial and pretentious today.

Wintertime (1943) 82m. ** D: John Brahm. Sonja Henie, Jack Oakie, Cesar Romero, Carole Landis, Cornel Wilde. Henie gives her all to save uncle's hotel from bankruptcy. Innocuous, below par for her vehicles.

Wipeout! (1972-Italian) C-100m. *½ D: Fernando Di Leo. Henry Silva, Richard Conte, Vittorio Caprioli, Gianni Garko, Howard Ross, Marino Mase. Predictably violent Italian-made Mafia movie. Conte is a capo who hires hit-man Silva to wipe out his rivals, then plans to turn him over to the law.

Wiretappers (1956) 80m. BOMB D: Dick Ross. Bill Williams, Georgia Lee, Douglas Kennedy, Phil Tead. Obnoxious little film blending crime and religion. Williams is seedy character working for two rival syndicates.

Wise Blood (1979) C-108m. ***½ D: John Huston. Brad Dourif, Daniel Shor, Amy Wright, Harry Dean Stanton, Ned Beatty, Mary Nell Santacroce. Brilliant translation of Flannery O'Connor's peculiar hell-and-salvation tale. Flawless cast, led by Dourif as obsessed preacher of The Church Without Christ, inhabits Georgia Gothic world as though born in it. A great, off-beat return for Huston.

Wise Girl (1937) 70m. **½ D: Leigh Jason. Miriam Hopkins, Ray Milland, Walter Abel, Guinn Williams, Henry Stephenson. Pleasant screwball comedy about rich-girl Hopkins pretending to be poor in order to track down her late sister's kids, who are living with starving Greenwich Village artist Milland.

Wistful Widow of Wagon Gap, The (1947) 78m. ** D: Charles Barton. Bud Abbott, Lou Costello, Marjorie Main, George Cleveland, Gordon Jones, William Ching, Peter Thompson. Raucous widow Main and A&C have to carry this one without much material. Best sequence comes when Lou becomes sheriff.

Witch Doctor SEE: **Men of Two Worlds**

Witch Without A Broom, A (1968-Spanish) C-78m. *½ D: Joe Lacy. (Jose Maria Elorrita). Jeffrey Hunter, Maria Perschy, Perla Cristal, Gustavo Rojo. Jeff finds himself bewitched by a 15th-century apprentice sorceress who takes him on an odyssey from the Stone Age to a futuristic Martian jaunt. Pointless fantasy.

Witchcraft (1964-British) 79m. ** D: Don Sharp. Lon Chaney, Jack Hedley, Jill Dixon, Viola Keats. Standard plot of witch cult happenings in English village after grave of 300-year-old witch is unearthed.

Witchmaker, The (1969) C-99m. BOMB D: William O. Brown. John Lodge, Alvy Moore, Thordis Brandt, Anthony Eisley, Shelby Grant. Satanism and supernatural elements are behind a series of grisly murders of young women in Louisiana swamp; bloody, and bloody awful.

With a Song in My Heart (1952) C-117m. *** D: Walter Lang. Susan Hayward, Rory Calhoun, David Wayne, Thelma Ritter, Robert Wagner, Una Merkel. Well-intentioned schmaltz based loosely on events in life of singer Jane Froman with Hayward most earnest as the spunky songstress.

With Fire and Sword (1961-Italian) C-96m. *½ D: Fernando Cerchio. Jeanne Crain, John Drew Barrymore, Pierre Brice, Akim Tamiroff. Costume spaghetti about Cossacks vs. Poles; embarrassing minor epic. Retitled: DAGGERS OF BLOOD.

With Six You Get Eggroll (1968) C-95m. ** D: Howard Morris. Doris

[866]

Day, Brian Keith, Pat Carroll, Barbara Hershey, George Carlin, Alice Ghostley. Oft-told tale of a widow and widower who try to move their children under the same roof. Slow on laughs.

With This Ring (1978) C-100m. TVM D: James Sheldon. Tony Bill, Tom Bosley, Diana Canova, John Forsythe, Scott Hylands, Donny Most, Dick Van Patten, Betty White. Formula sitcom approach to the wedding game, with all the predictability of a "Love Boat" episode. Mary Francis Crosby, Bing's daughter, made her TV acting debut in this one. Average.

Within These Walls (1945) 71m. ** D: H. Bruce Humberstone. Thomas Mitchell, Mary Anderson, Edward Ryan, Mark Stevens, B. S. Pully, Roy Kelly, Harry Shannon. Fairly good but predictable prison drama with warden Mitchell faced with his own son as a prisoner.

Without Apparent Motive (1972-French) C-102m. ** D: Philippe Labro. Jean-Louis Trintignant, Dominique Sanda, Sacha Distel, Carla Gravina, Paul Crauchet, Laura Antonelli, Jean-Pierre Marielle. Powerhouse European cast can't do much for Ed McBain tale about detective Trintignant's attempts to solve series of unpredictable killings; Erich Segal plays an astrologer.

Without Honor (1949) 69m. ** D: Irving Pichel. Laraine Day, Dane Clark, Franchot Tone, Agnes Moorehead, Bruce Bennett. Good cast talks endlessly in melodrama of woman who thinks she's killed a man.

Without Love (1945) 111m. *** D: Harold S. Bucquet. Spencer Tracy, Katharine Hepburn, Lucille Ball, Keenan Wynn, Carl Esmond, Patricia Morison. Tracy and Hepburn have never been livelier, but script lets them down in story of inventor and widow who marry for convenience, later fall in love. Wynn and Ball are excellent second leads.

Without Reservations (1946) 107m. *** D: Mervyn LeRoy. Claudette Colbert, John Wayne, Don DeFore, Anne Triola, Phil Brown, Thurston Hall, Louella Parsons. Authoress Colbert meets perfect man to play hero in movie version of her new book: soldier Wayne. Engaging comedy-romance, with some amusing swipes at Hollywood and several surprise guest stars.

Witness Chair, The (1936) 64m. *½

D: George Nicholls. Ann Harding, Walter Abel, Douglass Dumbrille, Frances Sage, Moroni Olsen. Faithful secretary tries to take the rap for the boss she's secretly in love with in this unbelievable courtroom/whodunit; polished but dull.

Witness for the Prosecution (1957) 114m. **** D: Billy Wilder. Marlene Dietrich, Tyrone Power, Charles Laughton, Elsa Lanchester, John Williams, Henry Daniell, Una O'Connor. Fantastically effective London courtroom suspenser from Agatha Christie story. Dietrich is peerless as wife of alleged killer (Power), Laughton at his best as defense attorney, and Lanchester delightful as his long-suffering nurse.

Witness in the Dark (1959-British) 62m. *½ D: Wolf Rilla. Patricia Dainton, Conrad Phillips, Madge Ryan, Nigel Green, Enid Lorimer. Uncommonly obvious suspenser with murderer seeking to kill blind girl who was present when crime was committed.

Witness to Murder (1954) 83m. *** D: Roy Rowland. Barbara Stanwyck, George Sanders, Gary Merrill, Jesse White. Shrill suspenser of Stanwyck witnessing act of murder and trying to convince police of what she saw.

Wives and Lovers (1963) 103m. **½ D: John Rich. Janet Leigh, Van Johnson, Shelley Winters, Martha Hyer, Ray Walston. Surface, slick entertainment; newly famous writer Johnson, wife Leigh and child move to surburia. Literary agent Hyer on the make almost causes divorce; Winters is wise-cracking neighbor.

Wives Never Know (1936) 75m. **½ D: Elliott Nugent. Charlie Ruggles, Mary Boland, Adolphe Menjou, Vivienne Osborne, Claude Gillingwater, Fay Holden, Louise Beavers. Flimsy tale of couple trying to awaken each other's love; Ruggles and Boland are always worth watching, and Menjou adds dash.

Wives Under Suspicion (1938) 75m. **½ D: James Whale. Warren William, Gail Patrick, Constance Moore, William Lundigan, Ralph Morgan. Minor but interesting drama of callous D.A. William waking up to love when he thinks his wife (Patrick) is seeing another man. Remake of THE KISS BEFORE THE MIRROR.

Wiz, The (1978) C-133m. ** D: Sidney Lumet. Diana Ross, Michael Jackson, Nipsey Russell, Ted Ross, Mabel King, Theresa Merritt,

Thelma Carpenter, Lena Horne, Richard Pryor. Diana Ross weeps and whines her way through modern black variation on THE WIZARD OF OZ, from the Broadway show by William F. Brown and Charlie Smalls. Some good musical numbers, fine supporting cast, but dreary finale—and drearier performance by Ross—really weigh it down.

Wizard of Baghdad, The (1960) C-92m. ** D: George Sherman. Dick Shawn, Diane Baker, Barry Coe, John Van Dreelen, Robert F. Simon, Vaughn Taylor. Blah satire on costumers, with Shawn a lazy genie.

Wizard of Oz, The (1939) C-101m. **** D: Victor Fleming. Judy Garland, Frank Morgan, Bert Lahr, Jack Haley, Ray Bolger, Billie Burke, Margaret Hamilton, Charley Grapewin, Clara Blandick, Singer Midgets. American classic from Frank Baum tale of Kansas girl sailing "Over The Rainbow" to land of Oz with assorted unusual friends. Fine Harold Arlen-E. Y. Harburg songs. Just as good the fifth time as it is the first.

Wizards (1977) C-80m. BOMB D: Ralph Bakshi. Animated sci-fi tale of future world after devastation, with warring factions that conjure up Hitler's armies. Turgid, unappealing film for adults or children.

Wolf Dog (1958-Canadian) 61m. *½ D: Sam Newfield. Jim Davis, Allison Hayes, Tony Brown, Austin Willis. Low-jinks about farm life in the north country involving land-hungry ranchers.

Wolf Larsen (1958) 83m. **½ D: Harmon Jones. Barry Sullivan, Peter Graves, Gita Hall, Thayer David. Nicely done version of Jack London's THE SEA WOLF with Sullivan effective as the tyrannical captain of the eerie ship.

Wolf Larsen (1975-Italian) C-92m. ** D. Giuseppi Vari. Chuck Connors, Barbara Bach, Giuseppi Pambieri. Tired new version of Jack London's SEA WOLF with Connors chewing up scenery as the sadistic sea captain. Retitled LEGEND OF THE SEA WOLF.

Wolf Man, The (1941) 71m. ***½ D: George Waggner. Claude Rains, Ralph Bellamy, Warren William, Patric Knowles, Bela Lugosi, Lon Chaney, Jr., Evelyn Ankers. One of the finest horror films ever made, with sturdy cast; Chaney is Larry Talbot, cursed by lycanthropy, Rains his unknowing father, Lugosi and Ouspen-

skaya local gypsies who foretell his doom, Bellamy and William helpless inspectors. Literate, very engrossing.

Woman and the Hunter, The (1957) 79m. *½ D: George Breakston. Ann Sheridan, David Farrar, John Loder. Tedious love triangle set in the jungles of Kenya; Sheridan tries hard but material defeats all.

Woman-Bait SEE: Inspector Maigret

Woman Called Moses, A (1978) C-200m. TVM D: Paul Wendkos. Cicely Tyson, Will Geer, Robert Hooks, James Wainwright, Dick Anthony Williams, Jason Bernard, Harry Rhodes. Dramatization of the life of Harriet Tubman, who founded the underground railway that helped fellow former slaves to freedom in the antebellum South. There's the expected exceptional performance by Tyson and the last work of Will Geer, but the whole project nearly goes down the tube because of an irrelevant narration provided by Orson Welles at his most imperious. Average.

Woman Chases Man (1937) 71m. **½ D: John G. Blystone. Miriam Hopkins, Joel McCrea, Charles Winninger, Ella Logan, Broderick Crawford. Sometime hilarious, often strained screwball comedy of architect Hopkins going after her boss, McCrea.

Woman Eater (1959-British) 70m. *½ D: Charles Saunders. George Coulouris, Robert MacKenzie, Norman Claridge, Marpessa Dawn, Jimmy Vaughan. Hokey chiller about flesh-eating tree with preference for females.

Woman Hater (1949-British) 70m. ** D: Terence Young. Stewart Granger, Edwige Feuillere, Ronald Squire, Mary Jerrold. Contrived battle of wits between confirmed bachelor and single girl leads to predictable romance.

Woman Hunter, The (1972) C-73m. TVM D: Bernard Kowalski. Barbara Eden, Robert Vaughn, Stuart Whitman, Sydney Chaplin, Larry Storch, Enrique Lucero. Wealthy, unstable Dina Hunter (Eden) on Mexican holiday, fearful that murderer is stalking her and jewels. Unconvincing climax in suspense film that seems excuse for Eden to show off fashions. Average.

Woman in a Dressing Gown (1957-British) 93m. *** D: J. Lee Thompson. Yvonne Mitchell, Anthony Quayle, Sylvia Syms, Andrew Ray,

Carole Lesley. Excellent British drama about middle-aged man lured away from his unkempt wife by an attractive young woman at his office. Mature, intelligent, and moving.

Women in Bondage (1943) 70m. ** D: Steve Sekely. Gail Patrick, Nancy Kelly, Gertrude Michael, Anne Nagel, Tala Birell, Alan Baxter, H. B. Warner. Exploitation patriotism hammering away at Nazi maltreatment of conquered people. Dates badly.

Woman in Green, The (1945) 68m. D: Roy William Neill. Basil Rathbone, Nigel Bruce, Hillary Brooke, Henry Daniell, Paul Cavanagh, Matthew Boulton, Eve Amber. SEE: Sherlock Holmes series.

Woman in Hiding (1949) 92m. ** D: Michael Gordon. Ida Lupino, Howard Duff, Stephen McNally, Peggy Dow, John Litel. Overdone dramatics of wife discovering husband is killer, fleeing before it's too late; some restraint would have been most helpful.

Woman in Question (1952-British) 82m. *** D: Anthony Asquith. Dirk Bogarde, Jean Kent, Susan Shaw, Hermione Baddeley. Police inspector, investigating murder of a fortune teller, turns up with questions of character and mystery surrounding her life. Retitled: FIVE ANGLES ON MURDER.

Woman in Red (1935) 68m. ** D: Robert Florey. Barbara Stanwyck, Gene Raymond, Genevieve Tobin, John Eldredge, Philip Reed, Dorothy Tree. Routine courtroom drama of Stanwyck and Raymond marriage interrupted by charge that she's been seeing Eldredge.

Woman in the Window, The (1944) 99m. ***½ D: Fritz Lang. Joan Bennett, Edward G. Robinson, Dan Duryea, Raymond Massey, Bobby Blake, Dorothy Peterson. High-grade melodrama about Robinson meeting subject of alluring painting (Bennett), becoming involved in murder and witnessing his own investigation. Surprise ending tops exciting film.

Woman in White, The (1948) 109m. *** D: Peter Godfrey. Eleanor Parker, Alexis Smith, Sydney Greenstreet, Gig Young, Agnes Moorehead. Florid gothic thriller from Wilkie Collins book about strange household and tormented Parker. Greenstreet has villainous role.

Woman Obsessed (1959) C-102m. **½ D: Henry Hathaway. Susan Hay-

ward, Stephen Boyd, Barbara Nichols, Dennis Holmes, Theodore Bikel, Ken Scott. Energetic stars try hard in Canadian ranch-life soaper of widow Hayward who marries Boyd, with predictable clashing and making up.

Woman of Affairs, A (1928) 108m. *** D: Clarence Brown. Greta Garbo, John Gilbert, Lewis Stone, John Mack Brown, Douglas Fairbanks Jr., Hobart Bosworth, Dorothy Sebastian. Smooth, entertaining late-silent with Garbo as reckless socialite who undertakes serious burden of making good her late husband's thefts. Fine cast; story is diluted from Michael Arlen's THE GREEN HAT.

Woman of Distinction, A (1950) 85m. *** D: Edward Buzzell. Rosalind Russell, Ray Milland, Edmund Gwenn, Janis Carter, Francis Lederer. Minor but very enjoyable slackstick, as visiting professor Milland causes scandal involving college dean Russell. Energetic cast puts this over; brief guest appearance by Lucille Ball.

Woman of Dolwyn, The SEE: Dolwyn.

Woman of Rome (1956-Italian) 93m. ** D: Luigi Zampa. Gina Lollobrigida, Daniel Gelin, Franco Fabrizi, Raymond Pellegrin. Old stuff of girl of easy virtue with Lollobrigida for scenery.

Woman of Straw (1964-British) C-117m. **½ D: Basil Dearden. Sean Connery, Gina Lollobrigida, Ralph Richardson, Alexander Knox. Muddled suspenser of Connery and Lollobrigida plotting the "perfect murder" of old Richardson with ironic results.

Woman of the North Country (1952) C-90m. ** D: Joseph Kane. Gale Storm, Ruth Hussey, Rod Cameron, John Agar, J. Carrol Naish. Predictable love and fight tale set in the mining lands; Storm's last film to date.

Woman of the River (1957-Italian) C-92m. ** D: Mario Soldati. Sophia Loren, Gerard Oury, Lise Bourdin, Rik Battaglia. Seamy, gloomy account of Loren involved with passion and criminals.

Woman of the Town, The (1943) 90m. *** D: George Archainbaud. Claire Trevor, Albert Dekker, Barry Sullivan, Henry Hull, Marion Martin. First-class Western with Dekker as Bat Masterson who must choose between love for dance-hall girl Trevor or law and order.

Woman of the Year (1942) 112m. ***½ D: George Stevens. Spencer Tracy, Katharine Hepburn, Fay Bainter, Reginald Owen, Roscoe Karns, William Bendix. First teaming of Tracy and Hepburn is a joy. He's a sports reporter, she's a world-famed political commentator brought down to earth by Tracy. Unforgettable scene of Hepburn trying to understand her first baseball game.

Woman of the Year (1976) C-100m. TVM D: Jud Taylor. Renee Taylor, Joseph Bologna, Dick O'Neill, Anthony Holland, Dick Bakalyan, Virginia Christine. Breezy comedy about the improbable marriage of an easy-going sports columnist and a celebrated society reporter. Taylor and Bologna are surprisingly comfortable in the shoes of Hepburn and Tracy. Above average.

Woman on Pier 13 SEE: I Married a Communist

Woman on the Beach, The (1947) 71m. *** D: Jean Renoir. Joan Bennett, Robert Ryan, Charles Bickford, Nan Leslie, Walter Sande. Ryan falls in love with Bennett but becomes wary of her blind husband Bickford; taut melodrama with fine performances all around.

Woman on the Run (1950) 77m. *** D: Norman Foster. Ann Sheridan, Dennis O'Keefe, Robert Keith, Frank Jenks. Sheridan is most convincing as wife trying to find her husband, witness to gangland murder, before the underworld does.

Woman Rebels, A (1936) 88m. *** D: Mark Sandrich. Katharine Hepburn, Herbert Marshall, Elizabeth Allan, Donald Crisp, Doris Dudley, Van Heflin, David Manners. Hepburn is marvelous as young girl whose experiences in Victorian England lead to her crusading for Women's Rights. Well-mounted soap opera is surprisingly timely.

Woman They Almost Lynched (1953) 90m. ** D: Allan Dwan. John Lund, Joan Leslie, Audrey Totter, Brian Donlevy, Ellen Corby, Minerva Urecal, Jim Davis. Civil War period film about refined young woman Leslie who comes to Western town and learns to tote gun.

Woman Times Seven (1967) C-99m. *** D: Vittorio De Sica. Shirley MacLaine, Peter Sellers, Rossano Brazzi, Vittorio Gassman, Lex Barker, Elsa Martinelli, Robert Morley,

Patrick Wymark, Adrienne Corri, Alan Arkin, Michael Caine, Anita Ekberg, Philippe Noiret. A seven-episode film with MacLaine showing seven types of women; some funny moments, some perceptive comments, but with that cast and director, it should have been much better.

Woman Under the Influence, A (1974) C-155m. ** D: John Cassavetes. Peter Falk, Gena Rowlands, Katherine Cassavetes, Lady Rowlands, Fred Draper. Typically overlong, overindulgent Cassavetes film, vaguely delineating relationship of woman who's cracking up and her hardhat husband who can't handle it. Strong performances by Rowlands and Falk are chief virtue of this one.

Woman Who Came Back, The (1945) 68m. ** D: Walter Colmes. John Loder, Nancy Kelly, Otto Kruger, Ruth Ford, Harry Tyler. Fair yarn of woman (Kelly) who is convinced she has received witches' curse from ancient descendant.

Woman Who Cried Murder, The SEE: **Death Scream**

Woman's Devotion, A (1956) C-88m. ** D: Paul Henreid. Ralph Meeker, Janice Rule, Paul Henreid, Rosenda Monteros. Choppy mystery of artist Meeker and wife Rule, involved in a murder while in Mexico.

Woman's Face, A (1941) 105m. *** D: George Cukor. Joan Crawford, Melvyn Douglas, Conrad Veidt, Osa Massen, Reginald Owen, Albert Basserman, Marjorie Main. One of Crawford's most substantial roles in exciting yarn of low-living girl whose life changes when she undergoes plastic surgery. Taut climax spotlights villain Veidt.

Woman's Secret, A (1949) 85m. *** D: Nicholas Ray. Maureen O'Hara, Melvyn Douglas, Gloria Grahame, Bill Williams, Victor Jory. Intriguing flashback drama of woman killing singer she built up to success; good performances by two female stars.

Woman's Vengeance, A (1947) 96m. ***½ D: Zoltan Korda. Charles Boyer, Ann Blyth, Jessica Tandy, Cedric Hardwicke, Mildred Natwick. Outstanding drama of philandering Boyer put on trial when his wife is found dead; brilliant cast gives vivid realistic performances. Based on an Aldous Huxley story.

Woman's World (1954) C-94m. *** D: Jean Negulesco. Clifton Webb, June Allyson, Van Heflin, Arlene Dahl, Lauren Bacall, Fred MacMurray. Sophisticated look at big business, the men and women involved, with arch Webb the corporation boss choosing a new successor.

Women, The (1939) 132m. ***½ D: George Cukor. Joan Crawford, Norma Shearer, Paulette Goddard, Rosalind Russell, Joan Fontaine, Hedda Hopper, Marjorie Main, Virginia Weidler, Mary Boland, Ruth Hussey, Mary Beth Hughes, Virginia Grey. All-star feminist cast shines in this adaptation (by Anita Loos) of Clare Boothe Luce's dated play about divorce, cattiness, and competition in circle of "friends." Crawford has one of her best roles as bitchy Crystal Allen. Fashion show was originally in color; remade as THE OPPOSITE SEX.

Women Are Like That (1938) 78m. **½ D: Stanley Logan. Kay Francis, Pat O'Brien, Ralph Forbes, Melville Cooper. Smooth fluff: Francis is daughter of ad executive in love with copywriter O'Brien.

Women Are Weak SEE: 3 Murderesses.

Women at West Point (1979) C-100m. TVM D: Vincent Sherman. Linda Purl, Leslie Ackerman, Jameson Parker, Andrew Stevens, Edward Edwards, Jack Blessing. Fictionalized drama about the first women to enter the U.S. Military Academy in 1976 emerges, unfortunately, as "Gidget Becomes a Plebe." Below average.

Women in Chains (1971) C-73m. TVM D: Bernard Kowalski. Ida Lupino, Lois Nettleton, Jessica Walter, Belinda Montgomery, John Larch, Penny Fuller. Probation officer wants to see prison system first hand, arranges fake identity, finds herself in tough situation when only person aware of situation dies. Good production tries hard, but unbelievable script and uneven performances render film merely average.

Women in Love (1970-British) 129m. ***½ D: Ken Russell. Alan Bates, Oliver Reed, Glenda Jackson, Eleanor Bron, Jennie Linden, Alan Webb. Fine adaptation of D. H. Lawrence novel about two interesting love affairs. Tends to bog down toward the end, but acting and direction are really impressive. Jackson won her first Oscar for this performance.

Women of Devils Island (1961-Italian) C-95m. *½ D: Domenesco Paolella. Guy Madison, Michele

Mercier, Frederica Ranchi. Humdrum mini-epic with Madison helping aristocratic woman held prisoner on swamp-surrounded island.

Women of Pitcairn Island, The (1956) 72m. *½ D: Jean Yarbrough. James Craig, Lynn Bari, John Smith, Arleen Whelan, Sue England, Carol Thurston, Charlita. Low-budget garbage about families developing from people who remained on island after MUTINY ON THE BOUNTY.

Women's Prison (1955) 80m. ** D: Lewis Seiler. Ida Lupino, Jan Sterling, Audrey Totter, Phyllis Thaxter, Howard Duff, Mae Clarke, Gertrude Michael, Juanita Moore. Film depicts deplorable prison conditions, and cruelty of superintendent Lupino. Totter and Thaxter are the victims whom Duff tries to help.

Won Ton Ton, the Dog Who Saved Hollywood (1976) C-92m. ** D: Michael Winner. Bruce Dern, Madeline Kahn, Art Carney, Phil Silvers, Teri Garr, Ron Leibman. Fine cast struggles through inept comedy set in 1920s Hollywood. Dog comes off better than many veteran stars who make pointless cameo appearances (from Rhonda Fleming to the Ritz Brothers).

Wonder Bar (1934) 84m. **½ D: Lloyd Bacon. Al Jolson, Kay Francis, Dolores Del Rio, Dick Powell, Ricardo Cortez, Louise Fazenda, Hal LeRoy, Guy Kibbee. Very strange, often tasteless musical drama set in Paris nightclub with murder, romance, and the incredible "Goin' to Heaven on a Mule" production number, sure to be cut by most TV stations.

Wonder Man (1945) C-98m. *** D: H. Bruce Humberstone. Danny Kaye, Virginia Mayo, Vera-Ellen, Donald Woods, S. Z. Sakall, Allen Jenkins, Ed Brophy, Steve Cochran, Otto Kruger. Kaye's fun as twins, the serious one forced to take the place of his brash entertainer brother when the latter is killed. Big, colorful production.

Wonder Woman (1974) C-78m. TVM D: Vincent McEveety. Cathy Lee Crosby, Kaz Garas, Richardo Montalban, Andrew Prine, Charlene Holt, Richard X. Slattery. Live-action cartoon—the one that didn't make it—about a superhuman female who uses her powers to stalk an elusive espionage agent. Below average.

Wonderful Country, The (1959) C-

96m. **½ D: Robert Parrish. Robert Mitchum, Julie London, Gary Merrill, Pedro Armendariz, Jack Oakie, Albert Dekker. Brooding Western involving Mitchum running guns along Mexico-Texas line, romancing London.

Wonderful World of the Brothers Grimm, The (1962) C-129m. *** D: Henry Levin, George Pal. Laurence Harvey, Claire Bloom, Karl Boehm, Yvette Mimieux, Barbara Eden, Walter Slezak, Russ Tamblyn, Buddy Hackett, Terry-Thomas. Fanciful adaptations of Grimm tales offset by OK look at famed brothers' lives. Best of all are Puppetoons sequences in toy shop, Hackett battling fire-breathing dragon. Colorful entertainment.

Wonders of Aladdin, The (1961) C-93m. ** D: Henry Levin. Donald O'Connor, Noelle Adam, Vittorio De Sica, Aldo Fabrizi. Few wonders to behold in this mild Italian-made children's fantasy which the kids might enjoy.

Wooden Horse, The (1950-British) 101m. *** D: Jack Lee. Leo Genn, David Tomlinson, Anthony Steel, Peter Burton, Anthony Dawson, Bryan Forbes, Peter Finch. Sturdy, exciting P.O.W. drama of men who determine to tunnel their way out of Nazi prison camp.

Woodstock (1970) C-184m. **** D: Michael Wadleigh. Joan Baez, Richie Havens, Crosby Stills and Nash, Jefferson Airplane, Joe Cocker, Sly and the Family Stone, Ten Years After, Santana, Country Joe and the Fish, John Sebastian, The Who. 1970 Oscar-winner as Best Documentary, film brilliantly captures unique communal experience of outdoor rock festival, along with great performances which highlighted unusual weekend bash. Among highlights: Cocker, Sly Stone, The Who. Unfortunately, certain scenes will be cut for TV, and effect of multiscreen images, stereophonic sound will be lost.

Words and Music (1948) C-119m. **½ D: Norman Taurog. Mickey Rooney, Tom Drake, June Allyson, Ann Sothern, Judy Garland, Gene Kelly, Lena Horne, Cyd Charisse, Betty Garrett, Perry Como, Janet Leigh. Sappy biography of songwriters Rodgers (Drake) and Hart (Rooney) is salvaged somewhat by their wonderful music, including Kelly's dance to "Slaughter on Tenth Avenue."

Work Is a 4-Letter Word (1967-British) C-93m. **½ D: Peter Hall. David Warner, Cilla Black, Elizabeth Spriggs, Zia Mohyeddin, Joe Gladwyn. Zany, but hit-and-miss comedy based on the play EH? about young man who raises giant mushrooms that produce euphoria when eaten. Warner is well cast.

Working Man, The (1933) 75m. **½ D: John G. Adolfi. George Arliss, Bette Davis, Hardie Albright, Theodore Newton, Gordon Westcott. Charming story of ambitious businessman Arliss becoming interested in the children of his long-time rival.

World and the Flesh (1932) 75m. ** D: John Cromwell. George Bancroft, Miriam Hopkins, Alan Mowbray, George E. Stone. Labored drama of soldier-of-fortune Bancroft asking price of Hopkins to save her wealthy friends from Russian Revolution; moves very slowly.

World Changes, The (1933) 90m. **½ D: Mervyn LeRoy. Paul Muni, Mary Astor, Aline MacMahon, Donald Cook, Guy Kibbee, Margaret Lindsay, Anna Q. Nilsson, Patricia Ellis. Tale of ambitious farm-boy Muni whose life falls apart as he becomes wealthy businessman. Astor is excellent as crazed wife.

World for Ransom (1954) 80m. **½ D: Robert Aldrich. Dan Duryea, Gene Lockhart, Patric Knowles, Reginald Denny, Nigel Bruce, Marian Carr. Duryea has his hands full when he pokes his nose into high-tension scheme to kidnap nuclear scientist in Singapore. Offbeat programmer traded on popularity of Duryea's CHINA SMITH TV series.

World in His Arms, The (1952) C-104m. *** D: Raoul Walsh. Gregory Peck, Ann Blyth, Anthony Quinn, Andrea King, Eugenie Leontovich, Sig Ruman. Unlikely but entertaining tale of skipper Peck romancing Russian Blyth, set in 1850s San Francisco.

World in My Corner (1956) 82m. **½ D: Jesse Hibbs. Audie Murphy, Barbara Rush, Jeff Morrow, John McIntire, Tommy Rall. Murphy is poor boy who rises to fame via boxing, almost ruined by rich life with Rush standing by.

World Moves On, The (1934) 90m. **½ D: John Ford. Madeleine Carroll, Franchot Tone, Reginald Denny, Stepin Fetchit, Lumsden Hare, Raul

Roulien, Louise Dresser, Sig Ruman. Long but interesting family saga covering 100 years as Louisiana family is split, three sons heading business operations in England, France, Germany, experiencing tremendous changes from peaceful 19th century through WW1.

World of Abbott and Costello, The (1965) 75m. ** Narrated by Jack E. Leonard. Bud Abbott, Lou Costello, Marjorie Main, Bela Lugosi, Tom Ewell, others. Inept compilation of A&C footage, with curious selection of scenes, senseless narration. Still, there's "Who's on First" and other fine routines that survive even this lackluster treatment.

World of Henry Orient, The (1964) C-106m. ***½ D: George Roy Hill. Peter Sellers, Paula Prentiss, Angela Lansbury, Phyllis Thaxter, Tom Bosley, Tippy Walker, Merrie Spaeth. Marvelous comedy of two teenage girls who idolize eccentric pianist (Sellers) and follow him around NY. Bosley and Lansbury are superb as Walker's parents, with Thaxter appealing as Spaeth's understanding mother.

World of Suzie Wong, The (1960) C-129m. **½ D: Richard Quine. William Holden, Nancy Kwan, Sylvia Syms, Michael Wilding, Laurence Naismith. Holden's sluggish performance as American artist in love with prostitute Kwan doesn't help this soaper, lavishly filmed in Hong Kong.

World Premiere (1941) 70m. *½ D: Ted Tetzlaff. John Barrymore, Frances Farmer, Eugene Pallette, Virginia Dale, Ricardo Cortez, Sig Ruman. Poor excuse for comedy involves idiotic producer Barrymore, jealous movie stars, publicity stunts, and Nazi saboteurs. A real waste.

World, the Flesh, and the Devil, The (1959) 95m. **½ D: Ranald MacDougall. Harry Belafonte, Inger Stevens, Mel Ferrer. Belafonte and Stevens are only survivors of worldwide nuclear explosion; their uneasy relationship is jarred by arrival of Ferrer. Intriguing film starts well, bogs down halfway through, and presents ridiculous conclusion.

World Was His Jury, The (1958) 82m. *½ D: Fred F. Sears. Edmond O'Brien, Mona Freeman, Karin Booth, Robert McQueeney. Routine account of ship's captain proven innocent of negligence in sea disaster.

World Without End (1956) C-80m.

**½ D: Edward Bernds. Hugh Marlowe, Nancy Gates, Nelson Leigh, Rod Taylor. Space flight headed for Mars breaks the time barrier and ends up on Earth in the 26th century. Pretty good sci-fi.

World Without Sun (1964) C-93m. **** D: Jacques Cousteau. Excellent, Oscar-winning documentary of Cousteau and his oceanauts, creating an underwater adventure that challenges any fiction.

World's Greatest Athlete, The (1973) C-93m. ***½ D: Robert Scheerer. John Amos, Jan-Michael Vincent, Tim Conway, Roscoe Lee Browne, Dayle Haddon, Howard Cosell. Hard-luck coach Amos returns to his roots in Africa and discovers superathlete Vincent; vibrant Disney comedy with excellent special effects. Conway particularly funny in sequence in which he shrinks to Tom Thumb size.

World's Greatest Lover, The (1977) C-89m. **½ D: Gene Wilder. Gene Wilder, Carol Kane, Dom DeLuise, Fritz Feld, Carl Ballantine, Michael Huddleston, Matt Collins. Sporadically funny comedy set in 1920s Hollywood, with Wilder screen-testing as new movie sheik and wife Kane deserting him for real-life Valentino. Wild slapstick combines with occasional vulgarities and moments of poignancy in this uneven film.

Worst Secret Agents SEE: Oh! Those Most Secret Agents.

Worst Woman in Paris?, The (1933) 78m. **½ D: Monta Bell. Benita Hume, Adolphe Menjou, Harvey Stephens, Helen Chandler, Margaret Seddon. Glossy Lubitsch-like comedy of chic Hume walking out on wealthy husband Menjou, returning to America, falling in love with naive young Stephens.

Wrath of God, The (1972) C-111m. ** D: Ralph Nelson. Robert Mitchum, Rita Hayworth, Frank Langella, John Colicos, Victor Buono. If you take this film—about a defrocked priest in a revolution-ridden country south of the border—seriously, it's an OK action yarn. If you accept it as tongue-in-cheek, it may yield greater enjoyment.

Wreck of the Hesperus, The (1948) 70m. ** D: John Hoffman. Willard Parker, Edgar Buchanan, Patricia White (Barry). Loosely based on Longfellow poem, this low-budget flick suffers from lack of production values to enhance special effects of storms at sea.

Wreck of the Mary Deare, The (1959-U.S.-British) C-105m. **½ D: Michael Anderson. Gary Cooper, Charlton Heston, Michael Redgrave, Emlyn Williams, Cecil Parker, Alexander Knox, Virginia McKenna, Richard Harris. Sticky going: Skipper of sunken ship accused of negligence, cleared at inquest by testimony of salvage boat captain. Special effects are real star.

Wrecking Crew, The (1969) C-105m. *½ D: Phil Karlson. Dean Martin, Elke Sommer, Sharon Tate, Nancy Kwan, Nigel Green, Tina Louise. Most recent and hopefully the last Matt Helm caper is this childish leering about a crime ring that hijacks a billion dollars in gold; a very funny performance by the late Sharon Tate is only redeeming feature.

Written on the Wind (1956) C-99m. *** D: Douglas Sirk. Rock Hudson, Lauren Bacall, Robert Stack, Dorothy Malone, Robert Keith, Grant Williams. Florid melodrama of irresponsible playboy-millionaire Stack, his nymphomaniac sister Malone, and how they destroy themselves and others around them. Irresistible kitsch. Malone won Oscar for her performance.

Wrong Arm of the Law, The (1963-British) 91m. *** D: Cliff Owen. Peter Sellers, Lionel Jeffries, Bernard Cribbins, Irene Browne. Nifty hi-jinks; cockney trio have police and crooks after them because they've been dressing as cops and confiscating loot from apprehended robbers.

Wrong Box, The (1966-British) C-105m. ***½ D: Bryan Forbes. John Mills, Ralph Richardson, Michael Caine, Peter Cook, Dudley Moore, Nanette Newman, Peter Sellers. Scramble for inheritance is basis for wacky black comedy set in Victorian England; aging brothers Mills and Richardson are trying to do each other in (with help from family cohorts) in order to be sole survivor. Sellers hilarious as oddball doctor.

Wrong Kind of Girl SEE: Bus Stop

Wrong Man, The (1956) 105m. *** D: Alfred Hitchcock. Henry Fonda, Vera Miles, Anthony Quayle, Nehemiah Persoff. Unusual Hitchcock film done as semidocumentary, using true story of NY musician (Fonda) falsely accused of robbery. Miles is

excellent as wife who cracks under strain; offbeat and compelling.

WUSA (1970) C-115m. ** D: Stuart Rosenberg. Paul Newman, Joanne Woodward, Anthony Perkins, Laurence Harvey, Pat Hingle, Cloris Leachman, Don Gordon, Leigh French. If John Wayne can make bad right-wing movies, the Newmans are certainly entitled to make bad left-wing ones. Premise is sound enough, but it doesn't make the film any better; tale of superpatriotic radio station and the people it affects sounds like some underground newspapers' editorials.

Wuthering Heights (1939) 103m. **** D: William Wyler. Merle Oberon, Laurence Olivier, David Niven, Flora Robson, Donald Crisp, Geraldine Fitzgerald, Leo G. Carroll, Cecil Kellaway, Hugh Williams. Stirring adaptation of Emily Brontë's novel stops at chapter 17, but viewers won't argue: sensitive direction with sweeping performances of downbeat story of strange love in pre-Victorian England. Haunting, a must-see film.

Wuthering Heights (1971-British) C-105m. *** D: Robert Fuest. Anna Calder-Marshall, Timothy Dalton, Harry Andrews, Pamela Browne, Judy Cornwell, Ian Ogilvy. Good, realistic treatment of Brontë's novel with authentic locations and atmosphere, Dalton and Calder-Marshall believable looking as Heathcliff and Cathy, but film's point of view indistinct and pace too fast.

Wyoming (1940) 89m. ** D: Richard Thorpe. Wallace Beery, Leo Carrillo, Ann Rutherford, Lee Bowman, Joseph Calleia, Bobs Watson. OK oater with Beery and Carrillo fun as on-again, off-again comrades.

Wyoming (1947) 84m. **½ D: Joseph Kane. William Elliott, Vera Ralston, John Carroll, "Gabby" Hayes, Albert Dekker, Virginia Grey. Not-bad Wild Bill Elliott Western of ranchers vs. homesteaders in Wyoming territory.

Wyoming Kid, The SEE: Cheyenne

Wyoming Mail (1950) C-87m. **½ D: Reginald LeBorg. Stephen McNally, Alexis Smith, Ed Begley, Richard Egan, James Arness, Frankie Darro. Postal robbery in old West, with capable cast shining up script's dull spots.

Wyoming Renegades (1955) C-73m. *½ D: Fred F. Sears. Phil Carey, Gene Evans, Martha Hyer, William Bishop, Aaron Spelling. Confused

Western portraying the story of ex-bandit Carey who wants to go straight. Hyer helps him.

X-15 (1961) C-106m. ** D: Richard Donner. David McLean, Charles Bronson, Ralph Taeger, Brad Dexter, Mary Tyler Moore, Patricia Owens. Narrated by James Stewart. Mild narrative about life and loves of re-searchers at a California missile base.

X—the Man with the X-Ray Eyes (1963) C-80m. **½ D: Roger Corman. Ray Milland, Diana Van Der Vlis, Harold J. Stone, John Hoyt, Don Rickles. Not-bad little film about mad scientist Milland developing serum that enables him to see through things.

X The Unknown (1956-British) 80m. **½ D: Leslie Norman. Dean Jagger, Leo McKern, William Lucas, Edward Chapman, Anthony Newley, Peter Hammond. Well-thought-out sci-fi production set in Scotland. Radioactive mud from the earth's center grows and absorbs anything in its path. Effective chiller.

X, Y and Zee (1972-British) C-110m. ** D: Brian Hutton. Elizabeth Taylor, Michael Caine, Susannah York, Margaret Leighton, John Standing. Contrived, often perverse tale of woman, her husband, another woman and the way the three are inter-changeable in relationships. Taylor-York love scene ranks high in the annals of poor taste. Sure to be cut on TV. Originally titled ZEE AND COMPANY.

Yakuza, The (1975) C-112m. *** D: Sydney Pollack. Robert Mitchum, Takakura Ken, Brian Keith, Herb Edelman, Richard Jordan, Kishi Keiko. Mitchum tries to aid pal Keith by returning to Japan after several years, gets more than he bargains for from title organization, a kind of Oriental Mafia. Mitchum and Ken are fine in suspenseful action pic. Retitled: BROTHERHOOD OF THE YAKUZA.

Yank at Eton, A (1942) 88m. ** D: Norman Taurog. Mickey Rooney, Freddie Bartholomew, Tina Thayer, Ian Hunter, Edmund Gwenn, Alan Mowbray, Peter Lawford, Terry Kil-burn. Rooney goes to school in En-gland and it's a wonder he's not ejected immediately.

Yank at Oxford, A (1938-U.S.-British) 100m. *** D: Jack Conway. Robert Taylor, Lionel Barrymore, Maureen O'Sullivan, Vivien Leigh, Edmund Gwenn. Attractive cast, in-cluding young Leigh, in familiar story of cocky American trying to adjust to Oxford, and vice versa.

Yank in Indo-China, A (1952) 67m. *½ D: Wallace Grissell. John Ar-cher, Douglas Dick, Jean Willes, Don Harvey. Just adequate yarn of Amer-ican pilots involved in guerilla war-fare.

Yank in Korea, A (1951) 73m. *½ D: Lew Landers. Lon McCallister, William Phillips, Brett King, Larry Stewart. Corny war actioner.

Yank in the RAF, A (1941) 98m. *** D: Henry King. Tyrone Power, Betty Grable, John Sutton, Reginald Gar-diner, Donald Stuart, Richard Fraser. Power's only there so he can see London-based chorine Grable; they make a nice team. Songs: "Another Little Dream Won't Do Us Any Harm," "Hi-Ya Love."

Yank in Viet-Nam, A (1964) 80m. ** D: Marshall Thompson. Marshall Thompson, Enrique Magalona, Mario Barri, Urban Drew. Low-budget topi-cal actioner set in Saigon, with ma-rine Thompson attempting to help the South Vietnamese. Retitled: YEAR OF THE TIGER.

Yankee Buccaneer (1952) C-86m. **½ D: Frederick de Cordova. Jeff Chandler, Scott Brady, Suzan Ball, David Janssen. Standard pirate tale, invigorated by healthy cast.

Yankee Doodle Dandy (1942) 126m. ***½ D: Michael Curtiz. James Cagney, Joan Leslie, Walter Huston, Irene Manning, Rosemary DeCamp, Jeanne Cagney, S. Z. Sakall, Walter Catlett, Frances Langford, George Tobias. Cagney wraps up film in neat little package all his own with dy-namic recreation of George M. Co-han's life and times; he deservedly won Oscar for rare song-and-dance performance.

Yankee Pasha (1954) C-84m. **½ D: Joseph Pevney. Jeff Chandler, Rhonda Fleming, Mamie Van Doren, Bart Roberts (Rex Reason). Nicely paced costumer set in 1800's with Chandler crossing the ocean to France and beyond to find his true love, captured by pirates.

Yanks (1979) C-139m. **½ D: John Schlesinger. Richard Gere, Lisa Eichhorn, Vanessa Redgrave, William Devane, Chick Vannera, Wendy Morgan, Rachel Roberts. Lavish production about WW2 romances between U.S. soldiers and British women doesn't really deliver the goods, due to choppy structure and flabby direction. Gere's so-called star power seems to be a casualty of energy crisis cutbacks.

Yaqui Drums (1956) 71m. *½ D: Jean Yarbrough. Rod Cameron, J. Carrol Naish, Mary Castle, Robert Hutton. Soggy account of rancher vs. criminal saloon owner in old West.

Year of the Tiger SEE: Yank in Viet-Nam, A

Yearling, The (1946) C-134m. ***½ D: Clarence Brown. Gregory Peck, Jane Wyman, Claude Jarman Jr., Chill Wills, Margaret Wycherly, Henry Travers, Jeff York, June Lockhart. Marjorie Kinnan Rawlings' sensitive tale of a boy attached to a young deer was exquisitely filmed on location in Technicolor, with memorable performances. Beware 94m. reissue print.

Years Between, The (1946-British) 88m. **½ D: Compton Bennett. Michael Redgrave, Valerie Hobson, Flora Robson, James McKechnie. Sensitively handled story of oft-told tale of man returning from war to discover wife thought him dead and is now about to remarry.

Yellow Balloon, The (1952-British) 80m. **½ D: J. Lee Thompson. Andrew Ray, Kenneth More, Veronica Hurst, William Sylvester, Bernard Lee. Sensible suspenser of small boy who witnesses chum's murder and is exploited by cheap crook.

Yellow Cab Man, The (1950) 85m. *** D: Jack Donahue. Red Skelton, Gloria De Haven, Walter Slezak, Edward Arnold, Polly Moran. Fine Skelton romp with Red as would be inventor of unbreakable glass, involved with gangsters and crooked businessman; Slezak is perfect as bad-guy.

Yellow Canary, The (1943-British) 84m. **½ D: Herbert Wilcox. Anna Neagle, Richard Greene, Albert Lieven, Margaret Rutherford, Valentine Dyall. Above average WW2 spy drama with Neagle feigning Nazi loyalty to obtain secrets for the Allies.

Yellow Jack (1938) 83m. ***½ D: George B. Seitz. Robert Montgomery, Virginia Bruce, Lewis Stone, Stanley Ridges, Henry Hull, Andy De-

vine. Stirring tribute to dedicated man searching for yellow fever cure in 1890s Cuba, from Sidney Howard play.

Yellow Mountain, The (1954) C-78m. *½ D: Jesse Hibbs. Lex Barker, Mala Powers, Howard Duff, William Demarest. Unremarkable tale of Barker rivaling Duff for gold and love of Powers.

Yellow Rolls-Royce, The (1965-British) C-122m. *** D: Anthony Asquith. Rex Harrison, Shirley MacLaine, Ingrid Bergman, Jeanne Moreau, Edmund Purdom, George C. Scott, Omar Sharif, Art Carney, Alain Delon, Roland Culver, Wally Cox. Slick drama involving trio of owners of title car, focusing on how romance plays a part in each of their lives; contrived but ever-so-smoothly handled.

Yellow Sky (1948) 98m. *** D: William Wellman. Gregory Peck, Anne Baxter, Richard Widmark, Robert Arthur, John Russell, Harry Morgan, James Barton. Exciting Western with exceptional cast in story of confrontation in Arizona ghost town.

Yellow Submarine (1968-British) C-85m. **** D: George Dunning. The Beatles. Pure delight, a phantasmagorical animated feature with as much to hear as there is to see: Beatles songs, puns, non sequitur jokes combined with surreal pop-art visions in story of Beatles trying to save Pepperland from the Blue Meanies. Unique, refreshing.

Yellow Ticket (1931) 81m. *** D: Raoul Walsh. Elissa Landi, Laurence Olivier, Lionel Barrymore, Walter Byron, Sarah Padden, Mischa Auer, Boris Karloff. Colorful melodrama set in czarist Russia, with peasant girl Landi coming under lecherous eye of officer Barrymore. Handsome production, lusty storytelling add up nicely; Karloff has good bit part.

Yellow Tomahawk, The (1954) C-82m. ** D: Lesley Selander. Rory Calhoun, Peggie Castle, Noah Beery, Warner Anderson. Calhoun is Indian guide who goes to any length to prevent redskin attack on settlers.

Yellowstone Kelly (1959) C-91m. **½ D: Gordon Douglas. Clint Walker, Edward Byrnes, John Russell, Ray Danton, Claude Akins, Rhodes Reason, Warren Oates. Rugged Western involving Indian uprising, with Walker the burly hero.

Yes, My Darling Daughter (1939)

86m. **½ D: William Keighley. Priscilla Lane, Fay Bainter, Roland Young, May Robson, Jeffrey Lynn, Ian Hunter. Everybody is enthused about young lovers running off together except young man in question (Lynn). Mildly amusing comedy.

Yes, Sir, That's My Baby (1949) C-82m. **½ D: George Sherman. Donald O'Connor, Charles Coburn, Gloria De Haven, Joshua Shelley, Barbara Brown. Flimsy musical of football-crazy O'Connor on college campus, rescued by spirit and verve of cast.

Yesterday, Today and Tomorrow (1964-Italian) C-119m. **** D: Vittorio de Sica. Sophia Loren, Marcello Mastroianni, Tina Pica, Giovanni Ridolfi. Spicy trio of tales giving insight into Italian morals; flavorfully acted by all.

Yesterday's Child (1977) C-78m. TVM D: Corey Allen, Bob Rosenbaum. Shirley Jones, Ross Martin, Claude Akins, Geraldine Fitzgerald, Stephanie Zimbalist, Patrick Wayne. Wealthy family is stunned when teen-aged girl turns up claiming to be their child kidnapped 14 years earlier. Melodramatic nonsense adapted from Doris Miles Disney's fine mystery novel *Night of Clear Choice.* And two directors were needed to put this one together! Below average.

Yesterday's Enemy (1959-British) 95m. *½ D: Val Guest. Stanley Baker, Guy Rolfe, Leo McKern, Gordon Jackson, David Oxley, Philip Ahn. Mild WW2 actioner set in Burma.

Yojimbo (1961-Japanese) 110m. **** D: Akira Kurosawa. Toshiro Mifune, Eijiro Tono, Seizaburo Kawazu, Isuzu Yamada. Shattering samurai picture whose plot resembles Western; Samuari up for hire in town with two warring factions. Beautiful on all accounts.

Yokel Boy (1942) 69m. *½ D: Joseph Santley. Albert Dekker, Joan Davis, Eddie Foy, Jr., Alan Mowbray. Silly slapstick satire on gangster movies.

Yolanda and the Thief (1945) C-108m. **½ D: Vincente Minnelli. Fred Astaire, Lucille Bremer, Frank Morgan, Mildred Natwick, Mary Nash. Opulent musical fantasy about a con-man (Astaire) who tries to convince rich convent-bred girl (Bremer) that he's her guardian angel. Unusual film that you'll either

love or hate. Best musical number: "Coffee Time."

You and Me (1938) 90m. *** D: Fritz Lang. Sylvia Sidney, George Raft, Robert Cummings, Roscoe Karns, Barton MacLane, Harry Carey, George E. Stone. Fine film of girl with a past (Sidney) marrying ex-con Raft, facing various problems together. Perceptive social commentary, well-played. Also has songs by Kurt Weill.

You Are What You Eat (1968) C-75m. ** D: Barry Feinstein. Tiny Tim, Peter Yarrow, Paul Butterfield, Barry McGuire, Father Malcom Boyd, The Electric Flag, Harper's Bizarre, Super Spade. Documentary of the mid-60s does, by the mere appearance of some of the era's luminaries, carry one back a few years; however, film is ill-conceived, haphazardly put together. Not much compared to some later social documents.

You Belong to Me (1941) 94m. **½ D: Wesley Ruggles. Barbara Stanwyck, Henry Fonda, Edgar Buchanan, Roger Clark, Ruth Donnelly, Melville Cooper. Brisk yarn of doctor Stanwyck and hubby Fonda who's wary of her male patients. Remade as EMERGENCY WEDDING.

You Came Along (1945) 103m. **½ D: John Farrow. Robert Cummings, Lizabeth Scott, Don DeFore, Charles Drake, Kim Hunter, Julie Bishop. Effective drama of three army buddies on bond-selling tours, their romantic involvements.

You Can't Cheat an Honest Man (1939) 76m. ***½ D: George Marshall. W. C. Fields, Edgar Bergen, Constance Moore, James Bush, Mary Forbes, Thurston Hall. Fields (as Larson E. Whipsnade) runs circus, with interference from Bergen and Charlie McCarthy in frantic nonsense comedy, notch below other Fields romps but still hilarious.

You Can't Get Away With Murder (1939) 78m. **½ D: Lewis Seiler. Humphrey Bogart, Billy Halop, Gale Page, John Litel, Henry Travers, Joe Sawyer. Average but well-acted crime tale of young Halop teaming with gangster Bogart, taking rap with him in Sing Sing.

You Can't Go Home Again (1979) C-100m. TVM D: Ralph Nelson. Lee Grant, Chris Sarandon, Hurd Hatfield, Tammy Grimes, Roland Winter, Malachy McCourt. Mediocre adaptation of the Thomas Wolfe classic about the struggles of a young writer in the 20s and the affair he has with an older married woman. Average.

You Can't Have Everything (1937) 99m. *** D: Norman Taurog. Alice Faye, Ritz Bros., Don Ameche, Charles Winninger, Tony Martin, Louise Hovick (Gypsy Rose Lee). Good show-biz musical as Faye writes drama which only succeeds as musical. Ritz Bros. have good material, Louis Prima adds music.

You Can't Run Away from It (1956) C-95m. ** D: Dick Powell. June Allyson, Jack Lemmon, Charles Bickford, Paul Gilbert, Jim Backus, Stubby Kaye, Henny Youngman. Slight musical remake of IT HAPPENED ONE NIGHT. Lemmon as reporter, Allyson a madcap heiress.

You Can't Steal Love SEE: **Live a Little, Steal a Lot**

You Can't Take It With You (1938) 127m. ***½ D: Frank Capra. Jean Arthur, Lionel Barrymore, James Stewart, Edward Arnold, Mischa Auer, Ann Miller, Spring Byington. George S. Kaufman-Moss Hart play about eccentric but blissfully happy household becomes prime Capracorn, not quite as compelling today as MR. DEEDS or MR. SMITH, but still highly entertaining. Oscar winner for Best Picture, Best Director.

You for Me (1952) 71m. **½ D: Don Weis. Peter Lawford, Jane Greer, Gig Young, Paula Corday, Elaine Stewart. Unpretentious romantic comedy with Greer as the well-intentioned nurse involved with a variety of suitors.

You Gotta Stay Happy (1948) 100m. **½ D: H. C. Potter. Joan Fontaine, James Stewart, Eddie Albert, Roland Young, Willard Parker. OK comedy about millionairess who runs off on wedding night to find new marriage. Could have been much better.

You Know What Sailors Are (1954-British) C-89m. ** D: Ken Annakin. Akim Tamiroff, Donald Sinden, Sarah Lawson, Naunton Wayne. Attempted cold-war spoof of British navy officer, jokingly telling cohorts that salvaged scrap is a new secret weapon.

You Lie So Deep, My Love (1975) C-78m. TVM D: David Lowell Rich. Don Galloway, Barbara Anderson, Angel Tompkins, Walter Pidgeon, Anne Shedeen, Russell Johnson.

Wealthy woman tries to save her failing marriage while philandering husband is willing to murder to get out of it (with her money). Standard drama packed with unpleasant characters. Below average.

You Light Up My Life (1977) C-90m. ** D: Joseph Brooks. Didi Conn, Joe Silver, Michael Zaslow, Stephen Nathan, Melanie Mayron. Title song may be most memorable thing about this film, but Conn and Silver are worth watching in loosely structured story of show-business-oriented girl trying to break loose and establish herself while putting her life in order. Produced, directed, written, and musically supervised by Brooks.

You Must Be Joking! (1965-British) C-100m. *** D: Michael Winner. Michael Callan, Lionel Jeffries, Denholm Elliott, Wilfrid Hyde-White, Bernard Cribbins, Gabriella Licudi. Engaging poke at British army as zany psychologist (Jeffries) rounds up five weirdos to establish, via special testing, the "complete, quick thinking" exemplary British soldier.

You Never Can Tell (1951) 78m. **½ D: Lou Breslow. Dick Powell, Peggy Dow, Charles Drake, Joyce Holden. Sometimes amusing fantasy of a murdered dog returning to earth in form of a human (Powell) to find his killer.

You Only Live Once (1937) 86m. *** D: Fritz Lang. Sylvia Sidney, Henry Fonda, William Gargan, Barton MacLane, Jean Dixon, Jerome Cowan, Margaret Hamilton, Ward Bond, Guinn Williams. Dated, but beautiful, sensitive film of escaped convict Fonda and devoted girl Sidney fleeing from police; superb direction and acting.

You Only Live Twice (1967-British) C-116m. **½ D: Lewis Gilbert. Sean Connery, Akiko Wakabayashi, Tetsuro Tamba, Mie Hama, Karin Dor, Bernard Lee, Donald Pleasence. Big James Bond production with first look at arch-nemesis Blofeld (Pleasence), Japanese locales, but plot (SPECTRE out to cause major powers to declare war on each other) and lack of convincing, clever crisis situations are liabilities film can't shake off.

You Said a Mouthful (1932) 75m. *** D: Lloyd Bacon. Joe E. Brown, Ginger Rogers, Preston Foster, Guinn Williams, Sheila Terry, Selmer Jackson. One of Brown's best vehicles, about inventor of unsinkable bathing suit; Rogers is his vivacious leading lady.

You Were Meant for Me (1948) 92m. *** D: Lloyd Bacon. Jeanne Crain, Dan Dailey, Oscar Levant, Barbara Lawrence, Selena Royle. Nice combination of musical score and script of girl who marries band leader; their experiences in Depression are basis of film.

You Were Never Lovelier (1942) 97m. ***½ D: William A. Seiter. Fred Astaire, Rita Hayworth, Adolphe Menjou, Leslie Brooks, Adele Mara, Xavier Cugat. Astaire pursuing Hayworth via matchmaking father Menjou becomes lilting musical with such songs as title tune, "Dearly Beloved," "I'm Old-Fashioned."

You'll Like My Mother (1972) C-92m. **½ D: Lamont Johnson. Patty Duke, Rosemary Murphy, Sian Barbara Allen, Richard Thomas, Dennis Rucker. Offbeat thriller with psychological undertones. Duke plays pregnant widow journeying to visit mother of husband whom she's never met. Some good moments, but doesn't add up.

You'll Never Get Rich (1941) 88m. ***½ D: Sidney Lanfield. Fred Astaire, Rita Hayworth, John Hubbard, Robert Benchley, Osa Massen, Frieda Inescort, Guinn Williams. Delicious musicomedy has Astaire drafted at inconvenient time, but show he's doing still goes on, and he manages to get Hayworth too. Cole Porter score includes "So Near And Yet So Far."

You'll Never See Me Again (1973) C-73m. TVM D: Jeannot Szwarc. David Hartman, Joseph Campanella, Jane Wyatt, Ralph Meeker, Jess Walton, Colby Chester, Bill Zuckert. Marital quarrel results in chance nosebleed, angry exit by wife. Husband follows to in-laws' house, discovers wife never arrived, eventually arrested by police. Straightforward suspense film with few novel ingredients, adequate performances, predictable resolution. Average.

You're a Big Boy Now (1966) C-96m. ***½ D: Francis Ford Coppola. Elizabeth Hartman, Peter Kastner, Geraldine Page, Julie Harris, Rip Torn, Michael Dunn, Tony Bill, Karen Black. Beguiling, way-out film of young man with over-protective parents learning about life from callous young actress Hartman. Far-out film will not appeal to everyone, but

acting is marvelous with Dolph Sweet hilarious as tough cop. Location filming in NY adds to film too.

You're a Sweetheart (1937) 96m. ** D: David Butler. Alice Faye, George Murphy, Ken Murray, Andy Devine, Charles Winninger, Donald Meek, Bobby Watson. Routine musical with go-getter Murphy dreaming up publicity stunt for show which stars Faye. Title song became a standard.

You're in the Army Now (1941) 79m. ** D: Lewis Seiler. Jimmy Durante, Phil Silvers, Jane Wyman, Regis Toomey, Joe Sawyer. Rather obvious service comedy with Durante and Silvers trying hard to rise above their material. Some funny scenes, with finale lifted from Chaplin's THE GOLD RUSH.

You're in the Navy Now (1951) 93m. ** D: Henry Hathaway. Gary Cooper, Jane Greer, Millard Mitchell, Eddie Albert, Lee Marvin, Jack Webb. Flat naval comedy set in WW2 with Cooper commanding a dumb crew on the U.S.S. *Teakettle* (the ship is outfitted with a steam engine).

You're My Everything (1949) C-94m. *** D: Walter Lang. Dan Dailey, Anne Baxter, Anne Revere, Stanley Ridges, Buster Keaton, Alan Mowbray, Selena Royle. Musical runs hot and cold, spoofing Hollywood of the 20s and 30s, but bogging down in slurpy romance; worthwhile for first half.

You're Never Too Young (1955) C-102m. *** D: Norman Taurog. Dean Martin, Jerry Lewis, Diana Lynn, Raymond Burr, Nina Foch, Veda Ann Borg. Fast, funny remake of MAJOR & THE MINOR with Jerry disguised as 12-year old, involved in jewel robbery.

You're Not So Tough (1940) 71m. D: Joe May. Nan Grey, Henry Armetta, Rosina Galli, Billy Halop, Huntz Hall, Gabriel Dell. SEE: **Bowery Boys** series.

You're Only Young Once (1938) 78m. D: George B. Seitz. Lewis Stone, Cecilia Parker, Mickey Rooney, Fay Holden, Frank Craven, Ann Rutherford, Eleanor Lynn See: **Andy Hardy** series.

You're Telling Me (1934) 67m. ***½ D: Erle C. Kenton. W. C. Fields, Joan Marsh, Larry "Buster" Crabbe, Louise Carter, Kathleen Howard, Adrienne Ames. Hilarious remake of Fields' silent film SO'S YOUR OLD MAN, with thin storyline (about a friendly foreign Princess giving lowly, browbeaten Fields respectability in his home town) a perfect excuse for some of his funniest routines—including classic golf game.

You're Telling Me (1942) 60m. *½ D: Charles Lamont. Hugh Herbert, Jane Frazee, Robert Paige, Richard Davies, Anne Gwynne, Mischa Auer, Ernest Truex. Tired comedy vehicle for Hugh as bumbler given job with radio advertising agency, involved with matchmaking on the side.

You've Got To Walk It Like You Talk It Or You'll Lose That Beat (1971) C-85m. **½ D: Peter Locke. Zalman King, Richard Pryor, Bob Downey, Liz Torres, Roz Kelly. Uneven satire on today's youth movements. Tries to cover too much ground.

Young Americans (1967) C-104m. ** D: Alex Grasshoff. Although this documentary about the "Young Americans" singing group won an Academy Award (which it was forced to relinquish when it was discovered that it had played theatrically before the year of its contention), not everyone will be able to take it; production is smooth, but the kids sell America like those guys on TV sell machines that slice carrots 144 different ways.

Young and Dangerous (1957) 78m. ** D: William Claxton. Mark Damon, Edward Binns, Lili Gentle, Ann Doran, Connie Stevens. Damon, a footloose youth, turns respectable for love of a nice girl. The usual.

Young and Innocent (1937-British) 80m. *** D: Alfred Hitchcock. Derrick de Marney, Nova Pilbeam, Percy Marmont, Edward Rigby, Mary Clare, Basil Radford. A Hitchcock thriller with charm and humor; young girl helps runaway man innocently accused of murder to find the real culprit. Pleasant echoes of 39 STEPS; nightclub revelation scene is especially memorable. First shown in U.S. as THE GIRL WAS YOUNG.

Young and the Damned, The SEE Los Olvidados

Young and Wild (1958) 69m. *½ D: William Witney. Gene Evans, Scott Marlowe, Carolyn Kearney, Robert Arthur. Trashy account of thrill-seeking teenagers on the loose with a stolen car.

Young and Willing (1943) 82m. **½ D: Edward H. Griffith. William Holden, Eddie Bracken, Barbara Britton, James Brown, Martha O'Driscoll, Robert Benchley, Susan Hayward. Perennial summer-stock comedy OUT OF THE FRYING PAN becomes naive but zany comedy of show biz hopefuls trying to make good.

Young at Heart (1954) C-117m. *** D: Gordon Douglas. Doris Day, Frank Sinatra, Gig Young, Ethel Barrymore, Dorothy Malone. Musical remake of FOUR DAUGHTERS with Sinatra romancing Day amid much tear-shedding. Slickly done.

Young Bess (1953) C-112m. *** D: George Sidney. Jean Simmons, Charles Laughton, Deborah Kerr, Stewart Granger, Cecil Kellaway, Leo G. Carroll. Splashy costumer with Simmons as Elizabeth I; Laughton repeating role of Henry VIII. Fine cast does quite well in historical setting.

Young Billy Young (1969) C-89m. **½ D: Burt Kennedy. Robert Mitchum, Angie Dickinson, Robert Walker, David Carradine. Typical oater of youth in New Mexico town and the corrupt people that have to be eliminated before the last reel.

Young Captives, The (1959) 61m. ** D: Irvin Kershner. Steven Marlo, Tom Selden, Luana Patten, Ed Nelson, Joan Granville. Lurid melodrama of newly-weds involved with psychopathic killer.

Young Cassidy (1965-British) C-110m. *** D: Jack Cardiff, John Ford. Rod Taylor, Julie Christie, Maggie Smith, Flora Robson, Michael Redgrave, Edith Evans, Jack MacGowran. Taylor's best role to date as the earthy intellect Sean O'Casey, set in 1910 Dublin, filled with atmosphere and fine supporting players.

Young Country, The (1970) C-73m. TVM D: Roy Huggins. Roger Davis, Joan Hackett, Walter Brennan, Wally Cox, Skip Young, Pete Duel, Barbara Gates. Offbeat casting in comedy Western about likable gambler Moody (Davis) hard pressed to track down money once belonging to mysterious gunman (Cox). Granted film's unconvincing transitions, characters are given decent dialogue and resolution actually acceptable. Above average.

Young Daniel Boone (1950) C-71m. *½ D: Reginald LeBorg. David Bruce, Kristine Miller, Mary Treen, Don Beddoe. Programmer adventure involving historical figure in conflict with Indians and settlers.

Young Dillinger (1965) 102m. **½ D: Terry O. Morse. Nick Adams, Mary Ann Mobley, Robert Conrad, John Ashley, Victor Buono, John Hoyt, Reed Hadley. Adams gives force to chronicle of gangster John Dillinger, his rise and seemingly inevitable fall; sufficient gunplay.

Young Dr. Kildare (1938) 81m. D: Harold S. Bucquet. Lew Ayres, Lionel Barrymore, Lynne Carver, Nat Pendleton, Jo Ann Sayers, Samuel S. Hinds. SEE: **Dr. Kildare** series.

Young Doctors, The (1961) 100m. *** D: Phil Karlson. Fredric March, Ben Gazzara, Dick Clark, Eddie Albert, Ina Balin, Aline MacMahon. Sturdy cast uplifts soaper set in large city hospital.

Young Don't Cry, The (1957) 89m. ** D: Alfred L. Werker. Sal Mineo, James Whitmore, J. Carrol Naish, Paul Carr. OK drama of loner youth Mineo who takes pity on an escaped murderer.

Young Frankenstein (1974) 108m. ***½ D: Mel Brooks. Gene Wilder, Peter Boyle, Marty Feldman, Madeline Kahn, Cloris Leachman, Teri Garr. Finely tuned parody of old FRANKENSTEIN pictures, with appropriate music (by John Morris), sets, laboratory equipment (some of it from the 1930s), and b&w camerawork. Plus vivid characterizations by mad doctor Wilder, monster Boyle, hunchback assistant Feldman, et al. Spoof of blind-man sequence from BRIDE OF FRANKENSTEIN with Gene Hackman is uproarious.

Young Fury (1965) C-80m. **½ D: Christian Nyby. Rory Calhoun, Virginia Mayo, Lon Chaney, John Agar, Richard Arlen, Linda Foster. Tired gunslinger returns home to discover son leading gang of young hellions terrorizing countryside. Standard formula plot highlighted by cast chock-full of old stars.

Young Girls of Rochefort, The (1968-French) C-124m. ***½ D: Jacques Demy. Catherine Deneuve, Françoise Dorleac, Gene Kelly, George Chakiris, Danielle Darrieux, Grover Dale, Michel Piccoli. Director Demy's follow-up to THE UMBRELLAS OF CHERBOURG is an homage to the Hollywood musical, but what it has in style it lacks in substance; contrived story and repetitive Michel Legrand sure wear thin, and even Gene Kelly can't save it.

Young Guns, The (1956) 84m. ** D: Albert Band. Russ Tamblyn, Gloria Talbott, Perry Lopez, Scott Marlowe. Routine account of Tamblyn trying to erase everyone's memory of gunslinger father so he can live peaceful life.

Young Guns of Texas (1962) C-78m. **½ D: Maury Dexter. James Mitchum, Alana Ladd, Jody McCrea, Chill Wills. Second generation of movie stars perform satisfactorily in account of gold and girl hunt in old West, tied in with Indian raid.

Young Hellions SEE: **High School Confidential.**

Young Ideas (1943) 77m. *½ D: Jules Dassin. Susan Peters, Herbert Marshall, Mary Astor, Elliott Reid, Richard Carlson. Dismal comedy about writer who disappears and shows up later at resort spot, married to man her family considers unsuitable.

Young in Heart, The (1938) 90m. ***½ D: Richard Wallace. Janet Gaynor, Douglas Fairbanks, Jr., Paulette Goddard, Roland Young, Billie Burke, Minnie Dupree, Richard Carlson. Refreshing comedy about wacky family of con-artists going straight under influence of unsuspecting Dupree.

Young Jesse James (1960) 73m. *½ D: William Claxton. Ray Stricklyn, Willard Parker, Merry Anders, Robert Dix, Emile Meyer, Jacklyn O'Donnell. Title tells all in this routine oater.

Young Joe, The Forgotten Kennedy (1977) C-100m. TVM D: Richard T. Heffron. Peter Strauss, Barbara Parkins, Stephen Elliott, Darleen Carr, Simon Oakland, Lance Kerwin. Strauss gives sincere performance in tear-stained drama that strives to fulfill the public's never-ending fascination with the legendary Kennedy family. Average.

Young Land, The (1959) C-89m. **½ D: Ted Tetzlaff. Pat Wayne, Yvonne Craig, Dennis Hopper, Dan O'Herlihy, Cliff Ketchum. Sincere Western of pre-Mexican war Texas.

Young Lawyers, The (1969) C-75m. TVM D: Harvey Hart. Jason Evers, Judy Pace, Zalman King, Tom Fielding, Anjanette Comer, Keenan Wynn, James Shigeta, Richard Pryor. Three law students, working for famous Boston attorney who gave up practice to direct neighborhood law office, defend two musicians charged with robbing and beating cab driver. Extensive location work and script which tackles legal problems squarely are film's major assets, but watch out for resolution. Above average.

Young Lions, The (1958) **167m.** *****½** D: Edward Dmytryk. Marlon Brando, Montgomery Clift, Dean Martin, Hope Lange, Barbara Rush, Maximilian Schell, Mai Britt. One of all-time best WW2 studies, based on Irvin Shaw novel. Martin and Clift, U.S. soldiers, Brando a confused Nazi officer; effectively photographed, with Hugo Friedhofer's fine score.

Young Love, First Love (1979) **C-100m. TVM** D: Steven Hilliard Stern. Valerie Bertinelli, Timothy Hutton, Arlen Dean Snyder, Fionnuala Flanagan, Leslie Ackerman. Title tells all in this routine story that asks the nagging question: Should Valerie go "all the way"? Average.

Young Lovers, The (1964) **105m. **** D: Samuel Goldwyn, Jr. Peter Fonda, Nick Adams, Sharon Hugueny, Deborah Walley, Kent Smith. Amateurish, meandering drama of college youths involved in romance.

Young Man with a Horn (1950) **112m. ***** D: Michael Curtiz. Kirk Douglas, Lauren Bacall, Doris Day, Juano Hernandez, Hoagy Carmichael, Mary Beth Hughes. Effective drama of trumpet-player Douglas compulsively drawn to music, with Bacall the bad girl, Day the wholesome one. Based on Bix Beiderbecke's life.

Young Man with Ideas (1952) **84m. **½** D: Mitchell Leisen. Glenn Ford, Ruth Roman, Denise Darcel, Nina Foch, Mary Wickes. Idealistic lawyer Ford overcomes all temptations in quest to move his family to California.

Young Mr. Lincoln (1939) **100m. ***½** D: John Ford. Henry Fonda, Alice Brady, Marjorie Weaver, Donald Meek, Richard Cromwell, Eddie Quillan, Milburn Stone, Ward Bond, Francis Ford. Fine Ford Americana with Abraham Lincoln (Fonda) facing years of struggle as a beginning lawyer in the 1800s. Brady lends fine support.

Young Mr. Pitt, The (1942-British) **118m. **½** D: Carol Reed. Robert Donat, Robert Morley, Phyllis Calvert, John Mills, Max Adrian. Long, only occasionally moving historical drama of young British prime min-

ister during Napoleonic era; thinly veiled WW2 morale-booster.

Young One, The (1960-Mexican) **96m.** ***½** D: Luis Bunuel. Zachary Scott, Bernie Hamilton, Key Meersman, Crahan Denton. Turgid melodramatics with Scott keeping Meersman, conflicting with a black musician on the run who comes to their deserted island.

Young People (1940) **78m. **** D: Allan Dwan. Shirley Temple, Jack Oakie, Charlotte Greenwood, Arleen Whelan, George Montgomery, Kathleen Howard. Show-biz team Oakie and Greenwood raise orphaned Shirley in this weak musical, a later and lesser Temple vehicle. Songs: "Fifth Avenue."

Young Philadelphians, The (1959) **136m. ***** D: Vincent Sherman. Paul Newman, Barbara Rush, Alexis Smith, Brian Keith, Diane Brewster, Billie Burke, John Williams, Robert Vaughn, Otto Kruger, Adam West. Newman and Rush have memorable roles as poor lawyer who schemes to the top, and society girl he hopes to win; Vaughn is army buddy Newman defends on murder charge, Smith quite good as frustrated wife of attorney Kruger.

Young Pioneers (1976) **C-100m. TVM** D: Michael O'Herlihy. Roger Kern, Linda Purl, Robert Hays, Shelly Juttner, Robert Donner, Frank Marth. Homesteading adventures of newlyweds in Dakota wilderness of the 1870s. Uncluttered, occasionally interesting family-style Western. Average.

Young Pioneers' Christmas (1976) **C-100m. TVM** D: Michael O'Herlihy. Roger Kern, Linda Purl, Robert Hays, Kay Kimler, Robert Donner, Britt Leach. Further adventures of those pioneering young folks in poignant sequel to YOUNG PIONEERS. More of the same—with tinsel added. Average.

Young Racers, The (1963) **C-87m. **** D: Roger Corman. Mark Damon, William Campbell, Patrick Magee, Luana Anders, Robert Campbell. Juvenile nonsense about sports car racing involving ex-racer turned exposé writer, trying to do a book on the sport.

Young Rebel (1969-French-Italian-Spanish) **C-111m. **** D: Vincent Sherman. Horst Buchholz, Gina Lollobrigida, Jose Ferrer, Louis Jourdan, Francisco Rabal. Despite cast, ordinary historical claptrap about Buchholz being sent to Spain by Pope Pius V to obtain help in fighting the Moors. Also known as CERVANTES.

Young Runaways, The (1968) C-91m. ** D: Arthur Dreifuss. Brooke Bundy, Kevin Coughlin, Lloyd Bochner, Patty McCormack, Lynn Bari, Norman Fell. Silly B-picture about restless teen-agers and how they are swept up into sordid lifestyles. Interesting mainly for early look at Richard Dreyfuss as cocky car thief.

Young Savages, The (1961) 110m. *** D: John Frankenheimer. Burt Lancaster, Dina Merrill, Shelley Winters, Telly Savalas, Chris Robinson, Pilar Seurat, Milton Selzer. Lancaster is idealistic D.A. battling all odds to see justice done in streetgang slaying; at times brutal, too often pat. Based on Evan Hunter novel A MATTER OF CONVICTION.

Young Stranger, The (1957) 84m. *** D: John Frankenheimer. James MacArthur, James Daly, Kim Hunter, James Gregory, Marian Seldes, White Bissell. Excellent drama about a teenage boy's brush with delinquency and strained relationship with his wealthy, neglectful father. Surprisingly undated, sincere little film; MacArthur's impressive screen debut (and director Frankenheimer's, too).

Young, the Evil, and the Savage, The (1968-Italian) C-82m. *½ D: Antonio Margheriti. Michael Rennie, Mark Damon, Eleanor Brown, Sally Smith, Pat Valturri, Ludmilla Lvova. Standard story of strangler on the loose at fashionable girls college with Rennie wooden as police inspector assigned to case.

Young Tom Edison (1940) 82m. *** D: Norman Taurog. Mickey Rooney, Fay Bainter, George Bancroft, Virginia Weidler, Eugene Pallette, Victor Kilian. Inventor's early life depicted with flair by effective Rooney, who could tone down when he had to; followed by Spencer Tracy's EDISON THE MAN.

Young Warriors, The (1967) C-93m. ** D: John Peyser. James Drury, Steve Carlson, Jonathan Daly, Robert Pine, Michael Stanwood. Clichéd WW2 yarn filled with Universal Pictures contract players; loosely derived from Richard Matheson novel.

Young Widow (1946) 100m. ** D: Edwin L. Marin. Jane Russell, Marie

Wilson, Louis Hayward, Faith Domergue, Kent Taylor, Penny Singleton, Cora Witherspoon. Soap-opera is not Russell's forte and she can't support teary WW2 tale of woman who can't forget her late husband.

Young Winston (1972-English) 145m. *** D: Richard Attenborough. Simon Ward, Anne Bancroft, Robert Shaw, John Mills, Jack Hawkins, Patrick Magee, Robert Flemyng, Laurence Naismith. Entertaining account of Winston Churchill's early life, from school days to journalistic experience in Africa, up to first election to Parliament. Handsome production, good performances, and rousing battle scenes.

Young Wives' Tale (1951-British) 78m. **½ D: Henry Cass. Joan Greenwood, Nigel Patrick, Audrey Hepburn, Derek Farr. Comedy of situations deriving from post-war housing shortage and fabricated mistaken relationships.

Youngblood Hawke (1964) 137m. **½ D: Delmer Daves. James Franciscus, Suzanne Pleshette, Mary Astor, Eva Gabor, Genevieve Page, Kent Smith, Mildred Dunnock, Lee Bowman. Trivial but somehow engrossing account of southern writer who becomes N.Y.C. success, confronted by a myriad of loves; Astor comes off well as the Broadway star. Edward Andrews has fine role as acid literary critic.

Younger Brothers, The (1949) C-77m. **½ D: Edwin L. Marin. Wayne Morris, Janis Paige, Bruce Bennett, Geraldine Brooks, Robert Hutton, Alan Hale, Fred Clark. OK Western of notorious Younger brothers and the incident that drives them to renewed violence and terror.

Youngest Profession, The (1943) 82m. **½ D: Edward Buzzell. Lana Turner, Greer Garson, Walter Pidgeon, Robert Taylor, William Powell, Virginia Weidler, Edward Arnold, Jean Porter. Weidler and Porter are incurable autograph hounds in innocent little film with many MGM guest stars puffing up slight vehicle.

Youngest Spy, The SEE: **My Name Is Ivan.**

Your Cheatin' Heart (1964) 99m. *** D: Gene Nelson. George Hamilton, Susan Oliver, Red Buttons, Arthur O'Connell, Rex Ingram. Hamilton's best role to date, as the country-western singer Hank Williams who couldn't cope with fame on the ole opry circuit; songs dubbed by

Hank Williams, Jr. Oliver most effective as Hank's wife.

Your Money or Your Wife (1972) **C-73m. TVM** D: Allen Reisner. Ted Bessell, Elizabeth Ashley, Jack Cassidy, Betsy von Furstenberg. Good premise gone awry in novel-based story of two scriptwriters cooking up imaginary kidnap plot, then putting it to work. Unconvincing character development, sloppy direction, passable performances. Average.

Your Past Is Showing (1957-British) **92m.** *** D: Mario Zampi. Terry-Thomas, Peter Sellers, Peggy Mount, Shirley Eaton. Droll hi-jinks of a strange grouping of folks brought together to rid themselves of the editor of a smut-exposé magazine. Originally titled THE NAKED TRUTH.

Your Three Minutes Are Up (1973) **C-92m.** ***½ D: Douglas N. Schwartz. Beau Bridges, Ron Leibman, Janet Margolin, Kathleen Freeman, David Ketchum, Stu Nisbet, Read Morgan. Overlooked comedy with serious undertones vividly captures two American lifestyles in story of ultra-straight Bridges hanging out with swinging buddy Leibman, who's out to beat the system. Unpretentious film says more about our society than many more "important" movies of recent vintage; solid performances.

Your Turn, Darling (1963-French) **93m.** ** D: Bernard Borderie. Eddie Constantine, Henri Cogan, Gaia Germani, Elga Andersen. Constantine is Lemmy Caution, U.S. secret agent involved with gang of spies; lumbering account.

Yours, Mine and Ours (1968) **C-111m.** *** D: Melville Shavelson. Lucille Ball, Henry Fonda, Van Johnson, Tom Bosley. For once, a wholesome "family" picture with some intelligent scripting. Based on real situation of widowed mother of eight marrying widower with ten more children. Lucy's drunk scene is a delight in warm, well-made comedy.

Yuma (1970) **C-73m. TVM** D: Ted Post. Clint Walker, Barry Sullivan, Edgar Buchanan, Kathryn Hays, Peter Mark Richman, Morgan Woodward. Marshal of frontier town center of plot to discredit him, stalked by brother of prisoner, must unravel chain of events to unmask plan's creator. Old-fashioned Western lacks script with punch, but fair direction

and actionful resolution make up for lulls. Average.

Z (1969-French) **C-127.** *** D: Costa-Gavras. Yves Montand, Irene Papas, Jean-Louis Trintignant, Charles Denner, Georges Geret, Jacques Perrin, Francois Perier. Oscar-winning foreign film, based on true-life incident, concerns political assassination of Montand and chilling aftermath. Talky film praised more for its topicality than cinematics is nonetheless gripping; good acting.

Z.P.G. (1972-British) **C-95m.** ** D: Michael Campus. Oliver Reed, Geraldine Chaplin, Don Gordon, Diane Cilento. Sci-fi tale with style but no class. Reproduction becomes crime punishable by death in the future, but some people try to defy the law.

Zabriskie Point (1970) **C-112m.** **½ D: Michelangelo Antonioni. Mark Frechette, Daria Halprin, Rod Taylor, Paul Fix. Rambling study by a foreigner of the aggressive, materialistic, unflinching American lifestyle. Worth watching but difficult to stay with, though there's a real eye-opening finale.

Zachariah (1971) **C-93m.** **½ D: George Englund. John Rubinstein, Pat Quinn, Don Johnson, Country Joe and the Fish, Elvin Jones, Doug York Rock Ensemble, Dick Van Patten. Audacious rock Western with elements of a morality play and moments of sharp satire; co-scripted by members of Firesign Theater. Certainly offbeat, but how much you like it is strictly personal taste.

Zamba (1949) **75m.** *½ D: William Berke. Jon Hall, June Vincent, George Cooper, Jane Nigh, George O'Hanlon. Juvenile adventure story of boy raised by gorillas; rough going.

Zandy's Bride (1974) **C-116m.** *½ D: Jan Troell. Gene Hackman, Liv Ullmann, Eileen Heckart, Susan Tyrrell, Sam Bottoms, Joe Santos. Two frequently wasted stars in tepid romance of a mail-order bride and her pioneer husband; no one needs *these* scenes from a marriage.

Zarak (1957-British) **C-99m.** **½ D: Terence Young. Victor Mature, Michael Wilding, Anita Ekberg, Bernard Miles, Finlay Currie. Hokum set in India with Mature the head of native outlaws, Wilding the British officer sent to get him.

Zardoz (1974-British) **C-105m.** **½

D: John Boorman. Sean Connery, Charlotte Rampling, Sara Kestelman, Sally Anne Newton, John Alderton, Niall Buggy. Weird sci-fi entry, set in 2293, about technology gone wild in society run by group of eternally young intellectuals. Visually striking cult film will leave most viewers dissatisfied.

Zebra in the Kitchen (1965) C-93m. **½ D: Ivan Tors. Jay North, Martin Milner, Andy Devine, Joyce Meadows, Jim Davis, Dorothy Green. Wholesome family fare of young North involved with wild pets and the city zoo's attempt to keep its inmates locked up.

Zeppelin (1971-British) C-101m. *** D: Etienne Perrier. Michael York, Elke Sommer, Peter Carsten, Marius Goring, Anton Diffring, Andrew Keir. Colorful cast and atmosphere (including interesting special effects) click in entertaining story of German-born British aviator emotionally torn by duty and homeland during World War I.

Zero Hour! (1957) 81m. **½ D: Hall Bartlett. Dana Andrews, Linda Darnell, Sterling Hayden, Elroy Hirsch. Effective suspenser of passenger plane and effect of potential disaster when pilots are felled by ptomaine poisoning.

Ziegfeld Follies (1946) C-110m. **½ D: Vincente Minnelli. William Powell, Judy Garland, Lucille Ball, Fred Astaire, Fanny Brice, Lena Horne, Red Skelton, Victor Moore, Virginia O'Brien, Cyd Charisse, Gene Kelly, Edward Arnold, Esther Williams. Variable all-star film introduced by Powell as Ziegfeld in heaven. Highlights are Brice-Hume Cronyn sketch, Astaire-Kelly dance, Moore-Arnold comedy routine, Skelton and Horne's solos, Garland's "The Interview."

Ziegfeld Girl (1941) 131m. *** D: Robert Z. Leonard. James Stewart, Lana Turner, Judy Garland, Hedy Lamarr, Tony Martin, Jackie Cooper, Ian Hunter, Philip Dorn, Charles Winninger. Large-scale musical drama opens brightly, bogs down into melodrama and preposterous subplot resolutions, as the lives of three girls (Turner, Garland, Lamarr) are changed by being recruited as Ziegfeld Follies girls. Busby Berkeley's "You Stepped Out of a Dream" is most famous number, but somewhat overshadowed by Judy "I'm Always Chasing Rainbows," "Minnie from Trinidad."

Ziegfeld: The Man and His Women (1978) C-150m. TVM D: Buzz Kulik. Paul Shenar, Samantha Eggar, Barbara Parkins, Pamela Peadon, Valerie Perrine, Inga Swenson, Ron Hussman, Nehemiah Persoff, David Opatoshu. Flashy, sumptuously mounted account of the life and times of Flo Ziegfeld, as told by the women in his life: Billie Burke (Eggar), Anna Held (Parkins), Marilyn Miller (Peadon) and Lillian Lorraine (Perrine). Shenar, who played Orson Wells in THE NIGHT THAT PANICKED AMERICA, is miscast in the pivotal title role. Average.

Zigzag (1970) 105m. **½ D: Richard A. Colla. George Kennedy, Anne Jackson, Eli Wallach, Steve Ihnat, William Marshall, Joe Maross. Dying man (Kennedy) plots his own murder so family can collect insurance money, but plans go awry. Good performances in moderately interesting drama.

Zita (1968-French) C-91m. *** D: Robert Enrico. Joanna Shimkus, Katina Paxinou, Suzanne Flon, Jose Marie Flotats, Paul Crauchet. Delicate story of young girl who learns about life as her beloved aunt is dying; love blossoms, as she breaks away from mother-figure to become an adult herself. Charming.

Zombies of Mora Tau (1957) 70m. *½ D: Edward L. Cahn. Gregg Palmer, Allison Hayes, Autumn Russell, Joel Ashley. Juvenile hodgepodge about zombies guarding diamonds hidden in a sunken ship.

Zombies on Broadway (1945) 68m. ** D: Gordon Douglas. Wally Brown, Alan Carney, Bela Lugosi, Anne Jeffreys, Sheldon Leonard, Frank Jenks. Press agents Brown and Carney (cut-rate version of Abbott and Costello) search for zombie to use in nightclub stunt. Lugosi adds only spice as zombie expert.

Zoo in Budapest (1933) 85m. ***½ D: Rowland V. Lee. Gene Raymond, Loretta Young, O. P. Heggie, Paul Fix, Wally Albright. Wonderfully whimsical love story set in famous Budapest zoo where Raymond, who has spent his life there, falls in love with runaway Young, who's hiding inside zoo grounds. Beautifully filmed.

Zorba the Greek (1964) 146m. ***½ D: Michael Cacoyannis. Anthony Quinn, Alan Bates, Irene Papas, Lila Kedrova, George Foundas.

Brooding, flavorful rendering of Kazantzakis novel. Quinn is zesty in title role of earthy peasant, Bates his intellectual British cohort. Kedrova won Oscar as dying prostitute.

Zorro (1961-Spanish) **C-90m.** **½ D: Joaquin Luis Romero Marchent. Frank Latimore, Mary Anderson, Ralph Marsch, Howard Vernon. Foreign-made Western with salty flavor of old California; Latimore is appropriately zealous as Zorro.

Zorro (1975-Italian-French) **C-100m.** *** D: Duccio Tessari. Alain Delon, Stanley Baker, Ottavia Piccolo, Moustache, Enzo Cerusico, Adriana Asti. Zesty retelling of saga of legendary masked rider and hero of the oppressed, not as distinctive as earlier versions but fun on its own terms.

Zorro Rides Again (1937) **68m.** ** D: William Witney, John English. John Carroll, Helen Christian, Reed Howes, Duncan Renaldo, Noah Beery. Edited from vintage Republic serial, recounting adventures of Carroll in old West to help railroad; just so-so.

Zotz! (1962) **87m.** ** D: William Castle. Tom Poston, Julia Meade, Jim Backus, Fred Clark. Goofy attempt at humorous chiller with Poston a teacher who gains mystical power over others.

Zulu (1964-British) **C-138m.** *** D: Cy Endfield. Stanley Baker, Jack Hawkins, Ulla Jacobsson, Michael Caine, Nigel Green, James Booth. Based on fact, story of handful of British soldiers fighting thousands of African warriors. Good stiff upper-lip adventure.

Zuma Beach (1978) **C-100m.** TVM D: Lee H. Katzin. Suzanne Somers, Steven Keats, Michael Biehn, Mark Wheeler, Kimberly Beck, Perry Lang. Fading rock star becomes involved with high schoolers at a beach party. OK if watching lithesome Suzanne in a bathing suit is enough to keep you interested for 100m. Average.

Recommended Reading from SIGNET and MENTOR

☐ **GUIDE TO FILMMAKING by Edward Pincus.** From choosing the camera to screening the movie—a complete and practical production manual for the student, teacher, and independent filmmaker. (#E9089—$2.50)

☐ **THE LIVELIEST ART by Arthur Knight.** From the nickelodeon to the wide screen, here is a fascinating appraisal of a unique art and the heroes, villains, hits and flops that have shaped its first half century. With 31 illustrations.
(#ME1743—$2.50)

☐ **AN INTRODUCTION TO AMERICAN MOVIES by Steven C. Earley.** The most comprehensive history of the movie industry, this excellent guide analyzes every major film genre for plot, acting, directing, and cinematic techniques. "Immensely readable, handsomely illustrated and excellently written, it's an important addition to the film library. . . ."—*Variety* Glossary, Index, and eight pages of photos.
(#ME1638—$2.25)

☐ **CBS: REFLECTIONS IN A BLOODSHOT EYE by Robert Metz.** The anecdote-packed, uncensored inside story of America's greatest entertainment factory and communications empire by veteran *New York Times* Columnist Robert Metz . . . "Lays it all bare!"—*San Francisco Chronicler* (#E7115—$2.25)

☐ **THE TODAY SHOW by Robert Metz.** An entertaining behind-the-screen look at one of America's most significant long-running television shows, from its roots in the earliest days of television, through the rise of Barbara Walters in the Sixties, up to the present day. . . . "A superb behind-the-scenes look!"—*Publishers Weekly* With 8 pages of stirring photos.
(#E8214—$2.25)

Buy them at your local

bookstore or use coupon

on next page for ordering.

SIGNET Books of Special Interest

☐ **THE SIGNET BOOK OF MOVIE LISTS by Jeff Rovin.** The most spectacular collection of fascinating facts about films, stars, money, gossip, winners and flops—everything on the screen and behind-the-scenes! With 8 pages of star-studded photos.   (#E8929—$1.75)*

☐ **SINATRA: An Unauthorized Biography by Earl Wilson.** Sinatra the swinger . . . the singer . . . the legend . . . the man. The nationally syndicated columnist and bestselling author reveals all in this sensational biography. With eight pages of candid photos.   (#E7487—$2.25)

☐ **THE MAKING OF KUBRICK'S 2001 edited by Jerome Agel.** Here is the full inside story, the germination, production, execution, response, the experiences of creating this profound, expensive—and controversial motion picture.
(#J7139—$1.95)

☐ **THE OFFICIAL MOVIE TRIVIA QUIZ BOOK #2 by Martin A. Gross.** Here's a great new book jampacked with all sorts of quizzes to test your movie memories. Flicks from past to present, from Charlie Chaplin to Sylvester Stallone. With 8 pages of nostalgic photos.   (#W7898—$1.50)

☐ **BOGIE: The Biography of Humphrey Bogart by Joe Hyams; with an Introduction by Lauren Bacall.** BOGIE does more than report events. It relives a life. The brawls, the sprees, the razor-edged wisecracks: Hyams describes them all. He recaptures the deep friendships—with Spencer Tracy, Judy Garland, Katharine Hepburn. He probes Bogart's stormy youth; his stubborn climb to stardom; his three rocky marital adventures and his last happy marriage to Lauren Bacall.
(#E9189—$1.75)

* Price slightly higher in Canada

Quality Plume Books You'll Want to Read

☐ **OF MICE AND MAGIC: A History of American Animated Cartoons by Leonard Maltin.** With a lively text that draws on interviews with many of the people involved, a wonderful profusion of illustrations, and a detailed filmography, this book by a noted film historian brings together all the personalities, artistry, technology, economics, and sheer pleasure that have made the animated cartoon play so fascinating a part in the story of cinema. (#Z5240—$9.95)

☐ **AMERICAN FILM NOW: The People, The Power, The Money, The Movies by James Monaco.** Hollywood movies today are bigger—but are they better than ever? In this major examination of modern American cinema, one of our leading film critics ponders this question in a sweeping study of Hollywood today. With over 200 movie stills. (#Z5212—$7.95)

☐ **CAMERADO: Hollywood and the American Man by Donald Spoto.** A study of mens' changing cultural images as reflected by the male stars (Astaire, Peck, Cagney, Brando, Stallone) against whom other men often judge themselves . . . "A pleasure to read!"—*Publishers Weekly* (#Z5186—$4.95)

☐ **TV GUIDE®: THE FIRST 25 YEARS compiled and edited by Jay S. Harris in association with the editors of TV GUIDE® Magazine.** A quarter century of TV passes before your eyes exactly as it was recorded by the most successful magazine ever published. With a treasury of vivid photos, including full-color reproduction of *TV Guide's* most memorable covers, and more than 25 years of prime-time schedule listings, this book is a rich feast of nostalgia. (#Z5225—$8.95)

In Canada, please add $1.00 to the price of each book.

Buy them at your local
bookstore or use coupon
on next page for ordering.

Quality PLUME and MERIDIAN Books
of Special Interest